American Constitutionalism

Powers, Rights, and Liberties

American Constitutionalism

Powers, Rights, and Liberties

Howard Gillman
University of California, Irvine

Mark A. Graber
University of Maryland

Keith E. Whittington
Princeton University

New York Oxford
Oxford University Press

Oxford University Press is a department of the University of Oxford.
It furthers the University's objective of excellence in research, scholarship, and education by publishing worldwide.

Oxford New York
Auckland Cape Town Dar es Salaam Hong Kong Karachi
Kuala Lumpur Madrid Melbourne Mexico City Nairobi
New Delhi Shanghai Taipei Toronto

With offices in
Argentina Austria Brazil Chile Czech Republic France Greece
Guatemala Hungary Italy Japan Poland Portugal Singapore
South Korea Switzerland Thailand Turkey Ukraine Vietnam

For titles covered by Section 112 of the US Higher Education Opportunity Act, please visit www.oup.com/us/he for the latest information about pricing and alternate formats.

Published in the United States of America by
Oxford University Press
198 Madison Avenue, New York, NY 10016
http://www.oup.com

Library of Congress Cataloging-in-Publication Data
Gillman, Howard, author.
American constitutionalism: powers, rights, and liberties / Howard Gillman, University of California, Irvine; Mark A. Graber, University of Maryland; Keith E. Whittington, Princeton University.
pages cm
ISBN 978-0-19-934338-6
1. Constitutional history--United States. I. Graber, Mark A., author. II. Whittington, Keith E., author. III. Title.
KF4541.G553 2015
342.7302'9--dc23 2014012434

Printing number: 9 8 7 6 5 4 3 2 1

Printed in the United States of America
on acid-free paper

Brief Contents

Topical Outline xv

Tables, Figures, and Illustrations xix

Preface xxiii

Part 1 **Themes**

1 **Introduction to American Constitutionalism 3**

Part 2 **Development**

2 **The Colonial Era: Before 1776 31**

3 **The Founding Era: 1776–1791 71**

4 **The Early National Era: 1791–1828 133**

5 **The Jacksonian Era: 1829–1860 217**

6 **Secession, Civil War, and Reconstruction: 1861–1876 291**

7 **The Republican Era: 1877–1932 369**

8 **The New Deal and Great Society Era: 1933–1968 477**

9 **Liberalism Divided: 1969–1980 617**

Part 3 **Contemporary Issues**

10 **The Reagan Era: 1981–1993 711**

11 **The Contemporary Era: 1994–Present 833**

Appendices 983

Glossary 1011

Index 1017

Cases 1047

Contents

Topical Outline xv

Tables, Figures, and Illustrations xix

Preface xxiii

Part 1 **Themes**

1 **Introduction to American Constitutionalism 3**

I. **What Is a Constitution? 4**

II. **Constitutional Purposes 6**

III. **Constitutional Interpretation and Decision Making 9**

A. **Constitutional Arguments 10**

B. **Sources of Constitutional Argument 13**

C. **The Politics of Constitutional Argument 13**

IV. **Constitutional Authority 17**

V. **Constitutional Change 22**

VI. **Constitutional Politics and Law 24**

Suggested Readings 25

Part 2 **Development**

2 **The Colonial Era: Before 1776 31**

I. **Introduction 31**

II. **Foundations 34**

A. **Sources 35**

B. **Principles 36**

C. **Scope 36**

III. **Judicial Power and Constitutional Authority 37**

William Blackstone, Commentaries on the Laws of England 38

Massachusetts Assembly Memorial 41

John Dickinson, Letters from a Farmer in Pennsylvania 42

IV. **Powers of the National Government 43**

V. **Separation of Powers 43**

VI. **Individual Rights 44**

A. **Property 44**

B. **Religion 45**

William Blackstone, Of Offences Against God and Religion 46

John Locke, A Letter Concerning Toleration 48

Roger Williams, The Bloudy Tenent 50

C. **Guns 51**

D. **Personal Freedom and Public Morality 52**

VII. **Democratic Rights 53**

A. **Free Speech 53**

The Zenger Trial 54

B. **Voting 57**

VIII. **Equality 58**

A. **Equality Under Law 58**

B. **Race 59**

Somerset v. Stewart 60

C. **Gender 61**

IX. **Criminal Justice 62**

A. **Due Process and Habeas Corpus 63**

B. **Search and Seizure 65**

Entick v. Carrington 65

C. **Interrogations 67**

D. **Juries and Lawyers 69**

E. **Punishments 69**

Suggested Readings 70

3 **The Founding Era: 1776–1791 71**

I. **Introduction 71**

II. **Foundations 77**
A. **Sources 77**
The Ratification Debates over the National Bill of Rights 77
B. **Principles 83**
Thomas Jefferson, Declaration of Independence 84
James Madison, Federalist 10 85
C. **Scope 87**

III. **Judicial Power and Constitutional Authority 88**
A. **Judicial Review 88**
Robert Yates, Brutus Essays 88
Alexander Hamilton, Federalist 78 90

IV. **Powers of the National Government 93**
Articles of Confederation 93
The Virginia Plan 95
The New Jersey Plan 96
Article I, Section 8 of the Constitution of the United States 98

V. **Federalism 99**
Debate in the Constitutional Convention 99

VI. **Separation of Powers 101**
Debate in the Constitutional Convention 102
Federalist 51, 70, and 71 106
"Centinel," Letter No. 1 108

VII. **Individual Rights 109**
A. **Property 110**
B. **Religion 111**
The Virginia Debate over Religious Assessments 113
House Debate over Conscientious Objectors 116
C. **Guns 117**
D. **Personal Freedom and Public Morality 117**

VIII. **Democratic Rights 117**
A. **Free Speech 118**
B. **Voting 119**
John Adams and Benjamin Franklin on Universal Male Suffrage 119

IX. **Equality 121**
A. **Equality Under Law 122**
B. **Race 122**
Commonwealth v. Jennison 123
Thomas Jefferson, Notes on the State of Virginia 124
C. **Gender 125**
John Adams and Abigail Adams, Correspondence on Women's Rights 126

X. **Criminal Justice 127**
A. **Due Process and Habeas Corpus 128**
B. **Search and Seizure 128**
C. **Interrogations 128**
D. **Juries and Lawyers 128**
E. **Punishments 129**
Benjamin Rush, On Punishing Murder by Death 129

Suggested Readings 130

4 **The Early National Era: 1791–1828 133**

I. **Introduction 133**

II. **Foundations 138**
A. **Sources 139**
Calder v. Bull 139
B. **Principles 141**
C. **Scope 142**

III. **Judicial Power and Constitutional Authority 142**
Marbury v. Madison 145
Thomas Jefferson on Departmentalism 151
Martin v. Hunter's Lessee 152

IV. **Powers of the National Government 155**
Debate on the Bank of the United States 159
McCulloch v. Maryland 164
Spencer Roane and John Marshall on McCulloch v. Maryland 169
Gibbons v. Ogden 172
House Report on Internal Improvements 176
James Monroe, Views of the President of the United States on the Subject of Internal Improvements 177

V. **Federalism 178**
Chisholm v. Georgia 180
Virginia and Kentucky Resolutions of 1798 183

VI. **Separation of Powers 185**
House Debate on Removal of Executive Officers 187

VII. **Individual Rights 190**
A. **Property 190**
Fletcher v. Peck 193
B. **Religion 195**
Thomas Jefferson, Letter to the Danbury Baptists 196

C. **Guns 196**
Bliss v. Commonwealth 197
D. **Personal Freedom and Public Morality 198**
VIII. **Democratic Rights 198**
A. **Free Speech 198**
Debate over the Sedition Act 199
B. **Voting 202**
Massachusetts Debates Property Qualifications 203
IX. **Equality 204**
A. **Equality Under Law 205**
Holden v. James 205
B. **Race 206**
Congressional Debate over the Missouri Compromise 207
C. **Gender 208**
X. **Criminal Justice 209**
A. **Due Process and Habeas Corpus 209**
B. **Search and Seizure 210**
Mayo v. Wilson 210
C. **Interrogations 212**
D. **Juries and Lawyers 212**
United States v. Callender 213
E. **Punishments 214**
Suggested Readings 215

5 **The Jacksonian Era: 1829–1860 217**

I. **Introduction 217**
II. **Foundations 222**
A. **Sources 222**
B. **Principles 223**
C. **Scope 223**
Barron v. Baltimore 224
III. **Judicial Power and Constitutional Authority 225**
Debate on the Electoral Accountability of the Judiciary, Ohio Constitutional Convention 226
Luther v. Borden 229
IV. **Powers of the National Government 231**
Andrew Jackson, Veto Message Regarding the Bank of the United States 233
Prigg v. Pennsylvania 236
Dred Scott v. Sandford 240
Abraham Lincoln, Speech on Slavery in the Territories 243
V. **Federalism 244**
Cooley v. Board of Wardens of the Port of Philadelphia 246
John C. Calhoun, "Fort Hill Address" 248
VI. **Separation of Powers 249**
The Debate over the Removal of the Deposits 250
House Debate on the Veto Power 255
VII. **Individual Rights 258**
A. **Property 258**
Proprietors of the Charles River Bridge v. Proprietors of the Warren Bridge 258
Wynehamer v. People 260
B. **Religion 264**
C. **Guns 264**
D. **Personal Freedom and Public Morality 265**
VIII. **Democratic Rights 265**
A. **Free Speech 266**
Congress Debates Incendiary Publications in the Mail 266
B. **Voting 271**
IX. **Equality 271**
A. **Equality Under Law 271**
B. **Race 272**
Dred Scott v. Sandford 273
Roberts v. City of Boston 279
C. **Gender 281**
Elizabeth Cady Stanton, Keynote Address, Seneca Falls Convention 282
X. **Criminal Justice 283**
A. **Due Process and Habeas Corpus 283**
The Booth Cases 284
B. **Search and Seizure 287**
C. **Interrogations 287**
D. **Juries and Lawyers 288**
E. **Punishments 288**
Suggested Readings 288

6 **Secession, Civil War, and Reconstruction: 1861–1876 291**

I. **Introduction 291**
II. **Foundations 295**
A. **Sources 296**
Debates over the Thirteenth Amendment 296
Debates over the Fourteenth Amendment 299

B. **Principles 304**
C. **Scope 305**
Slaughter-House Cases 306

III. **Judicial Power and Constitutional Authority 310**
Ex parte McCardle 311

IV. **Powers of the National Government 313**
Hepburn v. Griswold 314
Legal Tender Cases 317
Senate Debate over the Civil Rights Act of 1866 320

V. **Federalism 323**
South Carolina Ordinance of Secession 324
Jeremiah Black, Opinion on the Power of the President in Executing the Laws 326
Abraham Lincoln, First Inaugural Address 327
Texas v. White 329

VI. **Separation of Powers 333**
Abraham Lincoln, Emancipation Proclamation 333
Benjamin Curtis, Executive Power 334
Prize Cases 337

VII. **Individual Rights 340**
A. **Property 341**
B. **Religion 341**
C. **Guns 341**
D. **Personal Freedom and Public Morality 341**

VIII. **Democratic Rights 342**
A. **Free Speech 342**
The Trial of Clement Vallandigham 342
B. **Voting 345**

IX. **Equality 346**
A. **Equality Under Law 346**
Thomas Cooley, A Treatise on the Constitutional Limitations Which Rest upon the Legislative Power of the States of the American Union 346
B. **Race 349**
Congressional Debates over the Second Freedmen's Bureau Act 350
C. **Gender 354**
The Senate Debates Women's Suffrage 354

X. **Criminal Justice 357**
A. **Due Process and Habeas Corpus 357**
Ex parte Merryman 358
Edward Bates, Opinion on the Suspension of the Privilege of the Writ of Habeas Corpus 359
Ex parte Milligan 361
B. **Search and Seizure 366**
C. **Interrogations 366**
D. **Juries and Lawyers 367**
E. **Punishments 367**

Suggested Readings 367

7 **The Republican Era: 1877–1932 369**

I. **Introduction 369**

II. **Foundations 376**
A. **Sources 377**
Congressional Debate over Prohibition 377
B. **Principles 379**
C. **Scope 379**
Balzac v. Porto Rico 380
Civil Rights Cases 382

III. **Judicial Power and Constitutional Authority 386**
Theodore Roosevelt, A Charter of Democracy 387
William Howard Taft, Veto of Arizona Statehood 388

IV. **Powers of the National Government 390**
Congressional Debate over Lynching 393
Senate Debate on the Sherman Anti-Trust Act 395
United States v. E. C. Knight Company 397
Hammer v. Dagenhart 400
Missouri v. Holland 403

V. **Federalism 405**
Wabash, St. Louis and Pacific Railway Company v. Illinois 406
Munn v. State of Illinois 409

VI. **Separation of Powers 413**
Myers v. United States 414
Presidents on Presidential Power 418

VII. **Individual Rights 420**
A. **Property 421**
Pennsylvania Coal Co. v. Mahon 424
In re Jacobs 426
Lochner v. New York 428
Muller v. Oregon 432
B. **Religion 434**
Reynolds v. United States 436
C. **Guns 438**
D. **Personal Freedom and Public Morality 438**
Meyer v. Nebraska 438
Buck v. Bell 440

VIII. **Democratic Rights 441**
A. **Free Speech 441**
Schenck v. United States 444
Whitney v. California 446
Near v. Minnesota 449
B. **Voting 451**
IX. **Equality 453**
A. **Equality Under Law 453**
B. **Race 454**
Plessy v. Ferguson 455
John B. Knox, Address to the Alabama Constitutional Convention 459
C. **Gender 461**
Debates over the Blanket Amendment 461
X. **Criminal Justice 464**
A. **Due Process and Habeas Corpus 464**
B. **Search and Seizure 464**
Weeks v. United States 465
People v. Defore 466
Olmstead v. United States 467
C. **Interrogations 470**
D. **Juries and Lawyers 470**
Powell v. Alabama 471
E. **Punishments 473**
Suggested Readings 474

8 **The New Deal and Great Society Era: 1933–1968 477**

I. **Introduction 477**
II. **Foundations 486**
A. **Sources 486**
B. **Principles 486**
United States v. Carolene Products Co. 487
C. **Scope 488**
Duncan v. Louisiana 490
Shelley v. Kraemer 494
III. **Judicial Power and Constitutional Authority 496**
Franklin D. Roosevelt, Undelivered Speech on the Gold Clause Cases 498
Franklin D. Roosevelt, Fireside Chat on Court-Packing Plan 500
Senate Judiciary Committee Report on President Roosevelt's Court-Packing Plan 504
The Southern Manifesto 505
Dwight Eisenhower, Address to the Nation on the Introduction of Troops in Little Rock 506
Cooper v. Aaron 507
Baker v. Carr 509
IV. **Powers of the National Government 516**
Schechter Poultry Corp. v. United States 518
National Labor Relations Board v. Jones & Laughlin Steel Corp. 520
Wickard v. Filburn 524
Congressional Debate over the Civil Rights Act of 1964 526
Heart of Atlanta Motel, Inc. v. United States 528
V. **Federalism 531**
VI. **Separation of Powers 533**
Youngstown Sheet & Tube Co. v. Sawyer (Steel Seizure Case) 534
United States v. Curtiss-Wright Export Corporation 543
VII. **Individual Rights 545**
A. **Property 545**
Home Building & Loan Association v. Blaisdell 545
West Coast Hotel Co. v. Parrish 549
Williamson v. Lee Optical, Inc. 551
B. **Religion 552**
Engel v. Vitale 553
C. **Guns 556**
D. **Personal Freedom and Public Morality 556**
Griswold v. Connecticut 557
VIII. **Democratic Rights 561**
A. **Free Speech 562**
West Virginia State Board of Education v. Barnette 563
Dennis v. United States 566
New York Times Co. v. Sullivan 570
Brandenburg v. Ohio 573
B. **Voting 574**
Congressional Reports on the Voting Rights Act of 1965 575
Katzenbach v. Morgan 578
Reynolds v. Sims 581
IX. **Equality 586**
A. **Equality Under Law 586**
B. **Race 589**
Korematsu v. United States 590
Civil Rights Advocates Debate Strategy 594
Brown v. Board of Education of Topeka (Brown I) 597
Green v. County School Board of New Kent County 600
C. **Gender 603**

X. **Criminal Justice 603**
A. **Due Process and Habeas Corpus 603**
B. **Search and Seizure 604**
Mapp v. Ohio 605
C. **Interrogations 607**
Miranda v. Arizona 608
D. **Juries and Lawyers 612**
Gideon v. Wainwright 612
E. **Punishments 613**
Suggested Readings 614

9 **Liberalism Divided: 1969–1980 617**

I. **Introduction 617**
II. **Foundations 623**
A. **Sources 624**
B. **Principles 624**
C. **Scope 626**
Moose Lodge No. 107 v. Irvis 626
III. **Judicial Power and Constitutional Authority 628**
IV. **Powers of the National Government 629**
V. **Federalism 630**
VI. **Separation of Powers 631**
Leonard C. Meeker, Memorandum on the Legality of the United States Participation in the Defense of Vietnam 632
J. William Fulbright, Congress and Foreign Policy 633
The War Powers Act of 1973 634
Richard Nixon, Veto of the War Powers Resolution 636
United States v. United States District Court (the "Keith Case") 637
United States v. Nixon 639
VII. **Individual Rights 643**
A. **Property 643**
B. **Religion 644**
Wisconsin v. Yoder 645
C. **Guns 647**
D. **Personal Freedom and Public Morality 648**
Roe v. Wade 650
Debate over the Human Life Amendment 655
VIII. **Democratic Rights 657**
A. **Free Speech 658**
New York Times Co. v. United States 658
Buckley v. Valeo 663
B. **Voting 667**
Congressional Debate on the Voting Rights Act of 1970 668
Richardson v. Ramirez 672
IX. **Equality 673**
A. **Equality Under Law 674**
San Antonio Independent School District v. Rodriguez 674
B. **Race 677**
Swann v. Charlotte-Mecklenburg Board of Education 679
Executive and Legislative Attacks on Busing 681
Regents of the University of California v. Bakke 683
Washington v. Davis 688
C. **Gender 689**
Debate over the Equal Rights Amendment 691
Frontiero v. Richardson 693
X. **Criminal Justice 695**
A. **Due Process and Habeas Corpus 696**
In re Winship 697
B. **Search and Seizure 699**
C. **Interrogations 699**
Harris v. New York 700
D. **Juries and Lawyers 701**
E. **Punishments 702**
Gregg v. Georgia 704
Suggested Readings 707

Part 3 **Contemporary Issues**

10 **The Reagan Era: 1981–1993 711**

I. **Introduction 711**
II. **Foundations 718**
A. **Sources 718**
B. **Principles 720**
Office of Legal Policy, Guidelines on Constitutional Litigation 720
C. **Scope 722**
III. **Judicial Power and Constitutional Authority 722**
William H. Rehnquist, The Notion of a Living Constitution 723
William J. Brennan, The Constitution of the United States: Contemporary Ratification 725
The Nomination of Robert H. Bork to the U.S. Supreme Court 727

IV. **Powers of the National Government 732**
South Dakota v. Dole 733

V. **Federalism 735**
Garcia v. San Antonio Metropolitan Transit Authority 736

VI. **Separation of Powers 740**
Immigration and Naturalization Service v. Chadha 742
Morrison v. Olson 747

VII. **Individual Rights 754**
A. **Property 754**
Lucas v. South Carolina Coastal Council 756
B. **Religion 758**
Lee v. Weisman 759
Employment Division v. Smith 763
House Committee on the Judiciary, Report on the Religious Freedom Restoration Act 767
C. **Guns 768**
D. **Personal Freedom and Public Morality 769**
Planned Parenthood of Southeastern Pennsylvania v. Casey 770
Bowers v. Hardwick 778

VIII. **Democratic Rights 780**
A. **Free Speech 781**
Texas v. Johnson 783
Doe v. University of Michigan 786
B. **Voting 787**
Senate Committee on the Judiciary, Senate Report on the Voting Rights Act Amendments of 1982 790
Shaw v. Reno 793

IX. **Equality 796**
A. **Equality Under Law 797**
Plyler v. Doe 798
B. **Race 801**
City of Richmond v. J. A. Croson Co. 803
C. **Gender 807**
Johnson v. Transportation Agency, Santa Clara County 808

X. **Criminal Justice 811**
A. **Due Process and Habeas Corpus 812**
Herrera v. Collins 812
B. **Search and Seizure 816**
United States v. Leon 816
C. **Interrogations 820**
D. **Juries and Lawyers 821**
Batson v. Kentucky 822
E. **Punishments 826**
McCleskey v. Kemp 827

Suggested Readings 831

11 **The Contemporary Era: 1994–Present 833**

I. **Introduction 833**

II. **Foundations 839**
A. **Sources 839**
B. **Principles 840**
C. **Scope 840**
Boumediene v. Bush 841

III. **Judicial Power and Constitutional Authority 846**
City of Boerne v. Flores 850
The Nomination of Samuel Alito to the U.S. Supreme Court 853

IV. **Powers of the National Government 855**
United States v. Lopez 857
National Federation of Independent Business v. Sebelius 864

V. **Federalism 877**
Printz v. United States 879

VI. **Separation of Powers 884**
Walter Dellinger, Presidential Authority to Decline to Execute Unconstitutional Statutes 887
John Yoo, The President's Constitutional Authority to Conduct Military Operations 890
Memoranda on Standards of Conduct of Interrogation ("Torture Memos") 893
Caroline D. Krass, Memorandum Opinion on the Authority to Use Military Force in Libya 899

VII. **Individual Rights 901**
A. **Property 902**
Kelo v. City of New London 903
B. **Religion 907**
C. **Guns 909**
District of Columbia v. Heller 910
D. **Personal Freedom and Public Morality 915**
Lawrence v. Texas 918
The Defense of Marriage Act 922

VIII. **Democratic Rights 925**
A. **Free Speech 926**
Citizens United v. Federal Election Commission 931

B. **Voting 935**
Bush v. Gore 937
Shelby County v. Holder 941

IX. **Equality 945**
A. **Equality Under Law 947**
B. **Race 948**
Grutter v. Bollinger 950
C. **Gender 954**
United States v. Virginia 955

X. **Criminal Justice 959**
A. **Due Process and Habeas Corpus 960**
B. **Search and Seizure 961**
C. **Interrogations 962**
Dickerson v. United States 963
D. **Juries and Lawyers 966**
E. **Punishments 966**
F. **Infamous Crimes and Criminals 968**
The USA Patriot Act 970
Hamdi v. Rumsfeld 973
House Hearings on Disclosure of NSA Intelligence Gathering 977

Suggested Readings 981

Appendices

1 **Constitution of the United States of America 983**

2 **Researching and Reading Government Documents 997**

3 **Chronological Table of Presidents, Congress, and the Supreme Court 1007**

Glossary 1011

Index 1017

Cases 1047

Topical Outline

I. **Introduction**

II. **Foundations**

A. **Sources**

The Ratification Debates over the National Bill of Rights 77
Calder v. Bull 139
Debates over the Thirteenth Amendment 296
Debates over the Fourteenth Amendment 299
Congressional Debate over Prohibition 377

B. **Principles**

Thomas Jefferson, Declaration of Independence 84
James Madison, Federalist 10 85
United States v. Carolene Products Co. 487
Office of Legal Policy, Guidelines on Constitutional Litigation 720

C. **Scope**

Barron v. Baltimore 224
Slaughter-House Cases 306
Balzac v. Porto Rico 380
Civil Rights Cases 382
Duncan v. Louisiana 490
Shelley v. Kraemer 494
Moose Lodge No. 107 v. Irvis 626
Boumediene v. Bush 841

III. **Judicial Power and Constitutional Authority**

William Blackstone, Commentaries on the Laws of England 38
Massachusetts Assembly Memorial 41
John Dickinson, Letters from a Farmer in Pennsylvania 42
Marbury v. Madison 145
Thomas Jefferson on Departmentalism 151
Martin v. Hunter's Lessee 152
Debate on the Electoral Accountability of the Judiciary, Ohio Constitutional Convention 226
Luther v. Borden 229
Ex parte McCardle 311
Theodore Roosevelt, A Charter of Democracy 387
William Howard Taft, Veto of Arizona Statehood 388
Franklin D. Roosevelt, Undelivered Speech on the Gold Clause Cases 498
Franklin D. Roosevelt, Fireside Chat on Court-Packing Plan 500
Senate Judiciary Committee Report on President Roosevelt's Court-Packing Plan 504
The Southern Manifesto 505
Dwight Eisenhower, Address to the Nation on the Introduction of Troops in Little Rock 506
Cooper v. Aaron 507
Baker v. Carr 509
William H. Rehnquist, The Notion of a Living Constitution 723
William J. Brennan, The Constitution of the United States: Contemporary Ratification 725
The Nomination of Robert H. Bork to the U.S. Supreme Court 727
City of Boerne v. Flores 850
The Nomination of Samuel Alito to the U.S. Supreme Court 853

A. **Judicial Review**

Robert Yates, Brutus Essays 88
Alexander Hamilton, Federalist 78 90

IV. **Powers of the National Government**

Articles of Confederation 93
The Virginia Plan 95
The New Jersey Plan 96
Article I, Section 8 of the Constitution of the United States 98

Debate on the Bank of the United States 159
McCulloch v. Maryland 164
Spencer Roane and John Marshall on McCulloch v. Maryland 169
Gibbons v. Ogden 172
House Report on Internal Improvements 176
James Monroe, Views of the President of the United States on the Subject of Internal Improvements 177
Andrew Jackson, Veto Message Regarding the Bank of the United States 233
Prigg v. Pennsylvania 236
Dred Scott v. Sandford 240
Abraham Lincoln, Speech on Slavery in the Territories 243
Hepburn v. Griswold 314
Legal Tender Cases 317
Senate Debate over the Civil Rights Act of 1866 320
Congressional Debate over Lynching 393
Senate Debate on the Sherman Anti-Trust Act 395
United States v. E. C. Knight Company 397
Hammer v. Dagenhart 400
Missouri v. Holland 403
Schechter Poultry Corp. v. United States 518
National Labor Relations Board v. Jones & Laughlin Steel Corp. 520
Wickard v. Filburn 524
Congressional Debate over the Civil Rights Act of 1964 526
Heart of Atlanta Motel, Inc. v. United States 528
South Dakota v. Dole 733
United States v. Lopez 857
National Federation of Independent Business v. Sebelius 864

V. **Federalism**

Debate in the Constitutional Convention 99
Chisholm v. Georgia 180
Virginia and Kentucky Resolutions of 1798 183
Cooley v. Board of Wardens of the Port of Philadelphia 246
John C. Calhoun, "Fort Hill Address" 248
South Carolina Ordinance of Secession 324
Jeremiah Black, Opinion on the Power of the President in Executing the Laws 326
Abraham Lincoln, First Inaugural Address 327
Texas v. White 329
Wabash, St. Louis and Pacific Railway Company v. Illinois 406
Munn v. State of Illinois 409
Garcia v. San Antonio Metropolitan Transit Authority 736
Printz v. United States 879

VI. **Separation of Powers**

Debate in the Constitutional Convention 102
Federalist 51, 70, and 71 106
"Centinel," Letter No. 1 108
House Debate on Removal of Executive Officers 187
The Debate over the Removal of the Deposits 250
House Debate on the Veto Power 255
Abraham Lincoln, Emancipation Proclamation 333
Benjamin Curtis, Executive Power 334
Prize Cases 337
Myers v. United States 414
Presidents on Presidential Power 418
Youngstown Sheet & Tube Co. v. Sawyer (Steel Seizure Case) 534
United States v. Curtiss-Wright Export Corporation 543
Leonard C. Meeker, Memorandum on the Legality of the United States Participation in the Defense of Vietnam 632
J. William Fulbright, Congress and Foreign Policy 633
The War Powers Act of 1973 634
Richard Nixon, Veto of the War Powers Resolution 636
United States v. United States District Court (the "Keith Case") 637
United States v. Nixon 639
Immigration and Naturalization Service v. Chadha 742
Morrison v. Olson 747
Walter Dellinger, Presidential Authority to Decline to Execute Unconstitutional Statutes 887
John Yoo, The President's Constitutional Authority to Conduct Military Operations 890
Memoranda on Standards of Conduct of Interrogation ("Torture Memos") 893
Caroline D. Krass, Memorandum Opinion on the Authority to Use Military Force in Libya 899

VII. **Individual Rights**

A. **Property**

Fletcher v. Peck 193
Proprietors of the Charles River Bridge v. Proprietors of the Warren Bridge 258
Wynehamer v. People 260
Pennsylvania Coal Co. v. Mahon 424
In re Jacobs 426
Lochner v. New York 428
Muller v. Oregon 432
Home Building & Loan Association v. Blaisdell 545
West Coast Hotel Co. v. Parrish 549
Williamson v. Lee Optical, Inc. 551
Lucas v. South Carolina Coastal Council 756
Kelo v. City of New London 903

B. **Religion**

William Blackstone, Of Offences Against God and Religion 46
John Locke, A Letter Concerning Toleration 48
Roger Williams, The Bloudy Tenent 50
The Virginia Debate over Religious Assessments 113
House Debate over Conscientious Objectors 116
Thomas Jefferson, Letter to the Danbury Baptists 196
Reynolds v. United States 436
Engel v. Vitale 553
Wisconsin v. Yoder 645
Lee v. Weisman 759
Employment Division v. Smith 763
House Committee on the Judiciary, Report on the Religious Freedom Restoration Act 767

C. **Guns**

Bliss v. Commonwealth 197
District of Columbia v. Heller 910

D. **Personal Freedom and Public Morality**

Meyer v. Nebraska 438
Buck v. Bell 440
Griswold v. Connecticut 557
Roe v. Wade 650
Debate over the Human Life Amendment 655
Planned Parenthood of Southeastern Pennsylvania v. Casey 770
Bowers v. Hardwick 778
Lawrence v. Texas 918
The Defense of Marriage Act 922

VIII. **Democratic Rights**

A. **Free Speech**

The Zenger Trial 54
Debate over the Sedition Act 199
Congress Debates Incendiary Publications in the Mail 266
The Trial of Clement Vallandigham 342
Schenck v. United States 444
Whitney v. California 446
Near v. Minnesota 449
West Virginia State Board of Education v. Barnette 563
Dennis v. United States 566
New York Times Co. v. Sullivan 570
Brandenburg v. Ohio 573
New York Times Co. v. United States 658
Buckley v. Valeo 663
Texas v. Johnson 783
Doe v. University of Michigan 786
Citizens United v. Federal Election Commission 931

B. **Voting**

John Adams and Benjamin Franklin on Universal Male Suffrage 119
Massachusetts Debates Property Qualifications 203
Congressional Reports on the Voting Rights Act of 1965 575
Katzenbach v. Morgan 578
Reynolds v. Sims 581
Congressional Debate on the Voting Rights Act of 1970 668
Richardson v. Ramirez 672
Senate Committee on the Judiciary, Senate Report on the Voting Rights Act Amendments of 1982 790
Shaw v. Reno 793
Bush v. Gore 937
Shelby County v. Holder 941

IX. **Equality**

A. **Equality Under Law**

Holden v. James 205
Thomas Cooley, A Treatise on the Constitutional Limitations Which Rest upon the Legislative Power of the States of the American Union 346
San Antonio Independent School District v. Rodriguez 674
Plyler v. Doe 798

B. **Race**
Somerset v. Stewart 60
Commonwealth v. Jennison 123
Thomas Jefferson, Notes on the State of Virginia 124
Congressional Debate over the Missouri Compromise 207
Dred Scott v. Sandford 273
Roberts v. City of Boston 279
Congressional Debates over the Second Freedmen's Bureau Act 350
Plessy v. Ferguson 455
John B. Knox, Address to the Alabama Constitutional Convention 459
Korematsu v. United States 590
Civil Rights Advocates Debate Strategy 594
Brown v. Board of Education of Topeka (Brown I) 597
Green v. County School Board of New Kent County 600
Swann v. Charlotte-Mecklenburg Board of Education 679
Executive and Legislative Attacks on Busing 681
Regents of the University of California v. Bakke 683
Washington v. Davis 688
City of Richmond v. J. A. Croson Co. 803
Grutter v. Bollinger 950

C. **Gender**
John Adams and Abigail Adams, Correspondence on Women's Rights 126
Elizabeth Cady Stanton, Keynote Address, Seneca Falls Convention 282
The Senate Debates Women's Suffrage 354
Debates over the Blanket Amendment 461
Debate over the Equal Rights Amendment 691
Frontiero v. Richardson 693
Johnson v. Transportation Agency, Santa Clara County 808
United States v. Virginia 955

X. **Criminal Justice**

A. **Due Process and Habeas Corpus**
The Booth Cases 284
Ex parte Merryman 358
Edward Bates, Opinion on the Suspension of the Privilege of the Writ of Habeas Corpus 359
Ex parte Milligan 361
In re Winship 697
Herrera v. Collins 812

B. **Search and Seizure**
Entick v. Carrington 65
Mayo v. Wilson 210
Weeks v. United States 465
People v. Defore 466
Olmstead v. United States 467
Mapp v. Ohio 605
United States v. Leon 816

C. **Interrogations**
Miranda v. Arizona 608
Harris v. New York 700
Dickerson v. United States 963

D. **Juries and Lawyers**
United States v. Callender 213
Powell v. Alabama 471
Gideon v. Wainwright 612
Batson v. Kentucky 822

E. **Punishments**
Benjamin Rush, On Punishing Murder by Death 129
Gregg v. Georgia 704
McCleskey v. Kemp 827

F. **Infamous Crimes and Criminals: The War on Terror**
The USA Patriot Act 970
Hamdi v. Rumsfeld 973
House Hearings on Disclosure of NSA Intelligence Gathering 977

Tables, Figures, and Illustrations

Figure 1-1 Left-Right Distribution of Justices, Congress, and President in 1974 14

Figure 1-2 The Supreme Court and Public Opinion, 1957–1997 20

Box 2-1 A Partial Cast of Characters of the Colonial Era 32

Table 2-1 Major Constitutional Issues and Statements of the Colonial Era 34

Illustration 2-1 Sir William Blackstone 39

Illustration 2-2 Andrew Hamilton Defending John Peter Zenger in Court 55

Illustration 2-3 A Slave Auction in Virginia 60

Illustration 2-4 Governor John Winthrop 68

Box 3-1 A Partial Cast of Characters of the Founding Era 72

Table 3-1 Ratification of the U.S. Constitution by State 74

Table 3-2 Selected State Constitutional Provisions Regarding Religion, 1800 112

Illustration 3-1 Behold! A Fabric Now to Freedom Rear'd 75

Illustration 3-2 A Society of the Patriotic Ladies at Edenton in North Carolina 125

Box 4-1 A Partial Cast of Characters of the Early National Era 136

Table 4-1 Major Issues and Decisions of the Early National Era 134

Table 4-2 Some Early Cases of Judicial Review in American Courts 144

Table 4-3 Selection of U.S. Supreme Court Cases Reviewing Federal Laws Under the Necessary and Proper Clause 157

Table 4-4 Selection of U.S. Supreme Court Cases Reviewing State Laws Under the Contracts Clause 191

Figure 4-1 Partisan Control of the U.S. Government, 1789–1828 135

Figure 4-2a Property Qualifications for Suffrage, 1820 202

Figure 4-2b Property Qualifications for Suffrage, 1850 203

Figure 4-3 Missouri Compromise: Slave States, Free States, and Territories 206

Box 5-1 A Partial Cast of Characters of the Jacksonian Era 220

Table 5-1 Major Issues and Decisions of the Jacksonian Era 218

Table 5-2 Supreme Court Justices and Federal Judicial Circuits, 1842–1860 226

Table 5-3 Major State Statutes in First Wave of Alcohol Prohibition 261

Figure 5-1 Partisan Control of the U.S. Government, 1829–1860 219

Figure 5-2 Map of Federal Judicial Circuits, 1837 227

Illustration 5-1 General Jackson Slaying the Monster Bank 233

Illustration 5-2 New Method of Assorting the Mail, as Practised by Southern Slave-Holders 267

Box 6-1 A Partial Cast of Characters of the Civil War and Reconstruction 294

Table 6-1 Major Issues and Decisions of the Civil War and Reconstruction 292

Table 6-2a Passage and Ratification of the Fourteenth Amendment, U.S. Senate Vote (June 8, 1866) 301

Table 6-2b Passage and Ratification of the Fourteenth Amendment, U.S. House of Representatives Vote (June 13, 1866) 301

Table 6-2c Passage and Ratification of the Fourteenth Amendment, State Ratification (28 of 37 Needed) 302

Table 6-3 Selection of U.S. Supreme Court Cases Reviewing Presidential Powers as Commander in Chief 338

Illustration 6-1 The First Vote 300

Illustration 6-2 Milk Tickets for Babies, In Place of Milk 315

Illustration 6-3a U.S. Associate Justice Stephen Field 347

Illustration 6-3b Michigan Chief Justice Thomas Cooley 347

Illustration 6-4 Lambdin P. Milligan 362

Box 7-1 A Partial Cast of Characters of the Republican Era 375

Table 7-1 Percentage of Popular Vote in Presidential Election by Political Party, 1876–1932 372

Table 7-2 Major Issues and Decisions of the Republican Era 374

Table 7-3 Selection of U.S. Supreme Court Cases Reviewing Federal Laws Under the Interstate Commerce Clause 391

Table 7-4 Selection of U.S. Supreme Court Cases Reviewing State Laws Under Due Process Clause 422

Table 7-5 Selection of Legal Interest Groups and Their Signature Victories 432

Table 7-6 Selection of U.S. Supreme Court Cases Reviewing State and Federal Laws Restricting Dangerous Speech 442

Table 7-7 Selection of U.S. Supreme Court Cases Reviewing State and Federal Laws Regulating Elections 451

Figure 7-1 Partisan Control of the U.S. Government, 1861–1932 370

Figure 7-2 (A) Average Republican Party Vote, 1876–1892; (B) Average Republican Party Vote, 1896–1928 371

Figure 7-3 Supreme Court Invalidation of State and Federal Laws, 1850–1950 386

Illustration 7-1 "The Constitution Follows the Flag" Song Sheet 381

Illustration 7-2 What It Is Bound To Come To 435

Illustration 7-3 You and I Cannot Live in the Same Land 445

Box 8-1 A Partial Cast of Characters of the New Deal/Great Society Era 484

Table 8-1 Major Issues and Decisions of the New Deal and Great Society Era 480

Table 8-2 Tiers of Scrutiny of Legislative Classifications 487

Table 8-3 U.S. Supreme Court Cases Applying the Federal Bill of Rights to the States 490

Table 8-4 Selection of U.S. Supreme Court Cases Reviewing State Laws Under the Interstate Commerce Clause 531

Table 8-5 Public School Teacher Attitudes on Prayer in the Classroom, 1965 553

Table 8-6 Selection of State and Lower Federal Court Applications of *Engel v. Vitale* 555

Table 8-7 Selection of U.S. Supreme Court Cases Reviewing State Apportionment of Legislative Districts 582

Table 8-8 Selection of U.S. Supreme Court Cases Reviewing State Laws Under Equal Protection Clause 587

Figure 8-1 Partisan Control of the U.S. Government, 1933–1980 477

Figure 8-2 Agenda Change of the U.S. Supreme Court, 1933–1988 482

Figure 8-3 Precedents Overruled by the U.S. Supreme Court, 1790–2004 497

Figure 8-4 U.S. Supreme Court Invalidation of State and Federal Laws, 1930-1980 497

Figure 8-5 Difference between White and Black Southern Registration and Voting Rates, 1964–2008 574

Figure 8-6 Percentage of All Black Southern Schoolchildren Attending School with Whites 602

Figure 8-7 Individual Justice Support for Claimants in Criminal Procedure and Civil Liberties Cases on the Vinson and Warren Courts 604

Illustration 8-1 Good Morning, Judge! 478

Illustration 8-2 "Three's a Crowd!" 501

Illustration 8-3 Justice Robert H. Jackson 524

Illustration 8-4 Her Legal Status 557

Illustration 8-5 Elementary School Children Saluting the Flag, March 1943 564

Illustration 8-6 Thurgood Marshall and Spottswood W. Robinson III 596

Illustration 8-7 Elementary School Desegregation Protest in New Orleans, November 1960 601

Box 9-1 A Partial Cast of Characters of the Era of Liberalism Divided 622

Table 9-1 Major Issues and Decisions of the Era of Liberalism Divided 621

Figure 9-1 Partisan Identification of Southerners and Non-Southerners Since 1950 618

Figure 9-2 Left-Right Location of Supreme Court Relative to Other Branches, 1950–2002 628

Figure 9-3 Public Support for Abortion Rights, 1972–2008 649

Figure 9-4 Partisan Divergence in Public Support for Abortion Rights, 1972–2008 654

Figure 9-5 Percentage of Victories in U.S. Supreme Court by Claimants in Criminal Justice Cases, 1950–1990 696

Figure 9-6 Executions in the United States, 1930–2010 703

Illustration 9-1 President Richard Nixon Presents William Rehnquist with His Commission to Be Associate Justice 630

Illustration 9-2 "He Says He's From the Phone Company" 640

Illustration 9-3 "Alternative to *Roe v. Wade*" 651

Illustration 9-4a Chief Justice Warren Burger 659

Illustration 9-4b Associate Justice William Brennan 659

Illustration 9-5 Equal Rights Amendment Rally with Eleanor Smeall, Betty Ford, and Lady Bird Johnson 692

Illustration 9-6 Troy Leon Gregg 704

Box 10-1 A Partial Cast of Characters of the Reagan Era 716

Table 10-1 Major Issues and Decisions of the Reagan Era 714

Figure 10-1 Partisan Control of the U.S. Government, 1981–2012 712

Figure 10-2 Trust in Government Index, 1958–2004 712

Figure 10-3 Individual Justice Support for Claimants in Religious Liberty Cases on Burger and Rehnquist Courts 763

Figure 10-4 North Carolina Congressional District 12, 1992 793

Figure 10-5 Public Support for the Death Penalty, 1953–2011 827

Illustration 10-1 "You Were Expecting Maybe Edward M. Kennedy?" 728

Illustration 10-2 Jagdish Rai Chadha, the respondent in *Immigration and Naturalization Service v. Chadha* 745

Illustration 10-3 Race and Jury Selection 822

Box 11-1 A Partial Cast of Characters of the Contemporary Era 837

Table 11-1 Major Issues and Decisions of the Contemporary Era 834

Figure 11-1 Supreme Court Invalidation of State and Federal Laws, 1970–2012 847

Figure 11-2 Percentage of Federal Circuit Court Nominations Not Confirmed, 1945–2012 849

Figure 11-3 Federalism References in Party Platforms, 1960–1996 856

Figure 11-4 Individual Justice Support for Claimants in Criminal Procedure Cases Before the Roberts Court 961

Illustration 11-1 Judicial Nominations 848

Illustration 11-2 The National Security State 885

Illustration 11-3 War Powers 889

Illustration 11-4 Life, Liberty, and the Pursuit of Tax Revenue 903

Illustration 11-5 Massachusetts Chief Justice Margaret Marshall 917

Illustration 11-6 Westboro Baptist Church Demonstration at Military Funeral, December 2005 928

Illustration 11-7 Diversity and College Admissions 949

Illustration 11-8 Juveniles and the Death Penalty 967

Figure A-1 Getting to the U.S. Supreme Court 999

Figure A-2 Number of Supreme Court Cases with Separate Opinions 1000

Appendix 3 Chronological Table of Presidents, Congress, and the Supreme Court 1007

Preface

This textbook pioneers a new approach to American constitutionalism. Our target audience consists of professors, students, and readers interested in researching, teaching, and learning about constitutional politics in the United States. This preface explains four crucial features of the material that follows.

- We discuss *all important debates* in American constitutional history.
- We include readings from *all prominent participants* in these constitutional debates.
- We organize these constitutional debates by *historical era.*
- Chapter introductions clearly lay out the *political and legal contexts.*

Our goal is to familiarize readers with the central constitutional issues that have excited Americans over the years—and that are still vigorously debated in our time. We hope to break the habit of equating American constitutionalism with the decisions of the Supreme Court of the United States. Constitutionalism in the United States covers more topics, is more complex, and is more interesting than one would gather from merely reading essays by judges in law reports.

American Constitutionalism is directed at all persons who hope to become sophisticated observers and informed participants in a constitutional regime, not just the very few who make arguments before federal judges or the extraordinary few who become federal judges. Our text provides readers with the materials they need to form educated opinions on the fundamental questions of American constitutionalism.

Constitutional norms pervade all of American politics, and all of us participate in constitutional politics. The very vocabulary that ordinary Americans use when talking about politics reflects the language chosen by long-dead framers. When we think that government is treating us unfairly, we complain that we have been denied "the equal protection of the laws." We insist or deny that national health care is a legitimate exercise of the congressional power under Article I "to regulate commerce among the several states." We debate whether the individual mandate in the Affordable Care Act of 2010 is a "necessary and proper" exercise of the constitutional power "to lay and collect Taxes and provide for the general welfare of the United States."

Sophisticated observers and informed participants need a different introduction to American constitutionalism than lawyers practicing before the Supreme Court. Both should be exposed to such judicial landmarks as *McCulloch v. Maryland* (1819), the decision that defined the scope of national powers, and *Brown v. Board of Education* (1954), the decision that declared unconstitutional the laws that mandated racial segregation in public schools. For this reason, *American Constitutionalism* includes generous selections from the most important cases decided by the Supreme Court of the United States.

Participants in constitutional politics should be familiar with important constitutional issues that are *not* being litigated, and may never have been litigated, before the Supreme Court. They should know the basic arguments for and against presidential power to initiate military action in foreign countries, even if that constitutional question has not been decided by the Supreme Court. Sophisticated observers should be aware of the ways in which Supreme Court rulings may be consequences of previous constitutional choices made by other constitutional authorities. *Brown*, for example, occurred only after Presidents Roosevelt, Truman, and Eisenhower had packed the federal courts with racial liberals who believed Jim Crow unconstitutional.

American Constitutionalism provides the tools and resources for readers to develop this more comprehensive perspective on American constitutional politics. If our goal is to understand American constitutionalism, then we should be open to the full range of the American constitutional experience. If our goal is to engage the fundamental questions that have roiled American politics and understand the dynamics of constitutional development, then we must widen our point of view. We must incorporate the constitutional politics underlying landmark Supreme Court decisions, and we must include landmark constitutional decisions made by elected officials and state courts. *American Constitutionalism* offers these materials.

Constitutional arguments are as much the stuff of politics as the pork barrel and the logroll. The interplay of legal principles, moral values, partisan interests, and historical developments is a central feature of our constitutional system. Basic constitutional institutions provide normative and procedural frameworks that allow political debate and decision making to move forward in ways that political winners and losers alike usually consider legitimate. At the same time, preexisting constitutional commitments confer advantages on some political movements and partisan coalitions relative to others.

With the materials that follow we hope to provide an understanding of how constitutionalism actually works in the United States. We reject the simple view that constitutionalism has nothing to do with politics—and the equally simple view that constitutionalism is nothing more than a dressed-up version of ordinary politics. American constitutionalism is a distinctive form of politics with distinctive goals and modes of justification. Understanding the interplay between all the different elements of constitutional law and politics is a precondition for any realistic assessment of how American constitutionalism actually works, how that system of governance should work, and how our political order might work better.

All Important Constitutional Debates

American Constitutionalism covers the major constitutional controversies that have excited Americans from the Colonial Era to the present. Readings range from protests that the Stamp Act violated the unwritten English Constitution to the arguments made in the contemporary controversy over "enhanced" methods of interrogating suspected terrorists. Along the way, we include the constitutional debates over the Bill of Rights, the Louisiana Purchase, slavery in the territories, Prohibition, women's suffrage, the New Deal, and presidential power to order troops into foreign countries.

When determining what materials to include, we looked to the impact of the controversy on American constitutional development. We devote space to the constitutional disputes over the Emancipation Proclamation and the proposed Human Life Amendment. Both debates were central to the constitutional politics of the time and provide foundations for contemporary constitutional politics. We spend less time on technical legal questions primarily of interest to lawyers with a federal courts practice. We believe that scarce space in a textbook aimed at providing a deeper understanding of the workings of our constitutional system is better spent covering such issues as the constitutional debates during the 1920s over federal anti-lynching laws than the precise details of the state market exception to the dormant commerce clause. The former tell us more than the latter about the politics and principles of American constitutionalism.

All Important Constitutional Participants

American Constitutionalism examines the contributions of all Americans to important constitutional debates. These contributions include Supreme Court opinions, the arguments that lawyers made before the Supreme Court, the judicial opinions and legal arguments in lower federal court and state court cases, presidential speeches, opinions of the attorney general, congressional debates and legislative reports, party manifestos, pamphlets produced by interest groups, and scholarly commentaries. A comprehensive education in American constitutionalism should include Salmon Chase's argument that Congress had no constitutional power to pass a fugitive slave act, the prominent state court decisions interpreting provisions in state bills of rights, President Nixon's veto of the War Powers Resolution, the congressional debates over the ratification of the post–Civil War Amendments, and the Margold Report outlining the

NAACP's strategy during the 1930s and 1940s for securing a Supreme Court decision that ended the policy of "separate but equal."

We include these materials because we recognize that American constitutionalism takes shape in the legislative and executive branches of government as well as in the judiciary. Constitutional provisions and principles are elaborated within the national government, by state and local officials, and on the streets and in meeting places throughout the United States. Constitutional meaning is determined by government officials, party platforms, campaign speeches, legal treatises, and newspaper articles.

Our emphasis on all participants is closely related to our concern with presenting all major constitutional debates. Consider the constitutional issues raised by national expansion and presidential war-making powers. These matters were debated and settled by elected officials. We would only skim the surface of the constitutional controversies raised during the contemporary War on Terror if we limited materials to Supreme Court rulings. Even when courts make constitutional rulings, those rulings are typically preceded and structured by constitutional politics outside the judiciary. The Supreme Court in *Planned Parenthood v. Casey* (1992) refrained from overruling *Roe v. Wade* in part because pro-choice Democrats in 1986 were able to prevent President Reagan from appointing Robert Bork, a vigorous critic of *Roe*, to the Supreme Court. The Supreme Court in *McCulloch v. Maryland* declared that congressional decisions made during the preceding decade had partly settled questions about the constitutionality of a national bank. Elected officials often decide the fate of judicial decisions once they are handed down. If we pay too much attention to *Brown v. Board of Education* (1954), we will overlook the crucial role that the Civil Rights Act of 1964 played in ending school segregation. If we concentrate too narrowly on the words of the Court in *Brown*, we miss the equally significant and diverse words of Harry Truman, Dwight Eisenhower, the Southern Manifesto, and Martin Luther King, Jr.

Historical Organization

American Constitutionalism is organized historically. This text combines materials on the structures and powers of government with those focusing on rights and liberties in a single volume. This connects the several facets of constitutionalism in a natural way that is consistent with the development of law and politics. The single-volume format also facilitates one-semester classes. We divide American constitutional development into ten relatively distinct and stable political regimes: Colonial (before 1776), Founding (1776–1791), Early National (1791–1828), Jacksonian (1829–1860), Civil War/Reconstruction (1861–1876), Republican (1877–1932), New Deal/Great Society (1933–1968), Liberalism Divided (1969–1980), Reagan (1981–1993), and Contemporary (1994–present). These ten eras are characterized by important constitutional stabilities that mark each period off from previous and later eras.

Constitutional questions about secession and slavery were settled by the Civil War. Americans during the Jacksonian Era bitterly debated the constitutional issues associated with territorial expansion, banking, and internal improvements. Americans after Reconstruction were far more concerned with national power to regulate railroads and drinking. New Dealers temporarily settled the constitutional questions over national power to regulate the economy that divided Americans from 1876 to 1932. Many of these issues reemerged in new forms during the Contemporary Era. *Brown v. Board of Education* was hotly contested during the New Deal and Great Society Era. Americans after 1968 celebrated *Brown* and debated whether that decision supported or undermined affirmative action.

A historical approach to American constitutionalism provides a sound framework for understanding crucial episodes in American constitutional politics. Consider struggles over constitutional authority. Thomas Jefferson, Andrew Jackson, Abraham Lincoln, and Franklin Roosevelt maintained that the president, when making constitutional decisions, should not always be bound by past Supreme Court decisions. Other presidents have accepted judicial rulings as authoritative. Our period divisions enable readers to see patterns in this cycle of presidential assertion and deference.

The historical approach also enables students to see vital connections between different constitutional issues. Debates over slavery ranged from arguments about the scope of the federal power to regulate the interstate slave trade under the interstate commerce clause to conflicts over whether the Sixth Amendment gave alleged fugitive slaves the right to a jury trial. The movement for racial equality during the 1950s and 1960s challenged existing constitutional understandings of the First Amendment, constitutional criminal procedure, cruel and unusual punishment, equal protection, the scope of federal power over interstate commerce, and state power to regulate interstate commerce in the absence of federal power. We risk losing these connections between constitutional provisions when we cabin American constitutionalism into artificial doctrinal categories and treat them as timeless abstractions.

The Political and Legal Contexts

American Constitutionalism provides readers with information about the political and legal contexts in which constitutional controversies arise, are debated, and are settled. A concise introduction to each chapter identifies the central features of American constitutional politics during a particular era. These crucial elements are both political and legal.

The *political elements* include the most important partisan coalitions that fought for electoral supremacy, the main interests that supported those coalitions, the positions that those coalitions took on the most important issues that divided Americans during the time, and the extent to which one coalition was more successful than others at gaining control of the national government. The *Dred Scott* decision (1857), which declared that Congress could not ban slavery in American territories, articulated the constitutional commitments of Jacksonian Democrats, who largely controlled the national government from 1828 to 1860.

The *legal elements* include the most important schools of constitutional and legal thought in a particular era, the general principles that most people believed best justified the constitutional order, what governing authorities thought were the best methods for interpreting the Constitution, and the available precedents that could be invoked to justify future constitutional developments. New Deal liberals, when justifying extensive government regulation of the national economy, relied heavily on notions of a "living Constitution" that had become increasingly prominent in legal thought during the early twentieth century.

Pedagogical Framework

The context presented in chapter introductions is part of a consistent pedagogical framework:

- An opening chapter lays out the nature of American constitutionalism, starting with the five basic questions that underpin constitutional debates. We believe that this chapter is an essential introduction for students unfamiliar with the nature of a constitution, constitutional interpretation, constitutional authority, and constitutional change.
- Each historical chapter is divided into a consistent set of topical sections.
- After the period introduction, sections within each subsequent chapter summarize the major issues of the time. Each section begins with a bulleted list of major developments, for ease of reference and to facilitate understanding.
- All readings are prefaced with explanatory headnotes, and all headnotes to court cases end with questions. We believe that this design more effectively creates engaged readers and engaged citizens.
- Period images, such as political cartoons, illustrate controversies and contexts.
- Tables throughout the volume summarize key issues and court cases.
- All chapters end with suggested readings.

We hope that the materials provided here allow readers to think not only about questions of constitutional interpretation and what the various texts mean, but also about questions of constitutional design and practice. If resolving fundamental disputes were merely a matter of consulting a neutral referee whose authority was acknowledged by all players, such as the Supreme Court, then constitutional politics would be a simple matter of appeals, decisions, and essays in law books. Because our system does not work in this way, we have written this book.

For ease of use, the readings in the text are modernized, and we generally use modern terminology to refer to political and constitutional concepts. Since U.S. Supreme Court cases can now be easily found, we have generally cited them only by party names and decision date. We provide footnote citations to state cases only when they are not otherwise identified in excerpts. To help readers distinguish references to U.S. Supreme Court cases and state cases, we have added state identifiers to the decision dates when we mention state cases—for example, *Smith v. Jones* (MD 1823). All excerpts from presidential speeches and party platforms are taken from the terrific American Presidency Project at the University of California, Santa Barbara. These materials can be found at http://www.presidency.ucsb.edu/index.php. All quotations from *The Federalist Papers* are taken from *The Federalist: A Collection of Essays, Written in Favour of the New Constitution, as Agreed Upon by the Federal Convention, September 17, 1787, in Two Volumes* (New York: J. and A. McLean, 1788).

Supplements

A single volume (or even two volumes) alone could not have space to include all the participants in all the debates without growing so large as to be both costly and intimidating. While we have kept chapters flexible so that instructors can skip around, we nonetheless took a further step: we have made many more readings available on the Web as part of the extensive supplements available with this book.

We also make available correlation guides to match our coverage to more traditional sequences. We wish to make our unusual range of coverage suitable to *any* class. Yet we also hope in this way to make the transition to a new approach easier. We believe that a historical organization best reflects the lived experience of the political actors who challenged existing constitutional practices and the constitutional authorities who determined the validity of those challenges.

Acknowledgments

American Constitutionalism was inspired by and is for our teachers and our students. Walter Murphy, Sanford Levinson, Mark Tushnet, Stephen Elkins, Lou Fisher, Bruce Ackerman, Martin Shapiro, and Rogers Smith are foremost among our many teachers. From them and others we learned that American constitutionalism was about the construction of a political regime and not limited to close analysis of a few Supreme Court opinions. Leslie Goldstein, Judith Baer, Gary Jacobsohn, H. W. Perry, Gordon Silverstein, Paul Frymer, Julie Novkov, George Lovell, Daniel Carpenter, Cornell Clayton, Michael McCann, Barry Friedman, Jack Balkin, Randy Barnett, Douglas Reed, Steve Griffin, Karen Orren, Pamela Brandwein, Kevin McMahon, Tom Keck, Keith Bybee, Shep Melnick, Ken Kersch, Ron Kahn, Stephen Skowronek, and many others have simultaneously been our teachers and our students. For the past quarter-century we have participated in a common project devoted to elaborating new constitutional histories, new constitutional theories, and new constitutional visions all aimed at exploring the ways in which the study of American constitutional politics might differ from the study of constitutional law. We are particularly grateful for the opportunities granted us to teach with and learn from Kim Scheppele, Ran Hirschl, Gary Jacobsohn, Leslie Goldstein, and Thomas Ginsburg, who have consistently reminded us that we can understand American constitutionalism only by understanding constitutionalism outside of the United States. Over the past decade, we have welcomed Mariah Zeisberg, Tom Clark, Bradley Hays, Steve Simon, Beau Breslin, Doug Edlin, Helen Knowles, David Erdos, Justin Crowe, John Compton, David Glick, and Emily Zackin to this constitutionalist fellowship. Each of these talented scholars has been tolerant of our foibles while diligently pointing out the many mistakes made in the initial elaboration of this new American constitutionalism. Finally, we should acknowledge the debt we owe to our students at Princeton University, the University of Southern California, and the University of Maryland. They will inherit American constitutionalism, if not *American Constitutionalism*. From them, we have learned that less is often more. We have experienced firsthand the hunger in younger Americans for ways to better understand and reform the American constitutional order.

The three of us owe a special debt of gratitude to the many persons who directly assisted in the actual writing of *American Constitutionalism*. The list of friends and colleagues who responded promptly when we asked for advice about such matters as executive privilege in the Jacksonian Era or Sunday laws in the 1920s is probably longer than this volume, if that can be imagined. Nevertheless, we ought to single out Rogers Smith and Sandy Levinson for being particularly helpful with their comments and assistance. A legion of research assistants worked diligently to find cases, make tables, correct typos, and insert periods. They include Deborah Beim, David Bridge, Benjamin Bruins, Jonathan Cheng, Colleen Clary, Ina Cox, Danny Frost, Wandaly Fernandez, David Glick, Abigail Graber, Ayana Mayberry, April Morton, David Myers, Herschel Nachlis, Benjamin Newton, David Nohe, Ryan Palmer, Amanda Radke, Jennifer Ratcliff, Jessica Rebarber, Edward Reilly, Clara Shaw, Michael Sullivan, Thaila Sundaresan, Jeff Tessin, and Katie Zuber.

Many friends and colleagues helped us test earlier iterations of *American Constitutionalism*. Each of them not only provided vital encouragement to us at initial stages of the project, but also gave us plain, hard truths about the difficult choices we needed to make in order to bring this book to market. We thank them profusely for their counsel, as well as their students, whose comments on earlier editions we did our best to incorporate in the later volumes.

This project would not exist if not for Jennifer Carpenter and John Haber, our editors at Oxford University Press. They combined consistent encouragement, meticulous editing, and the patience of Job. Most important, they kept the faith that what we had to say mattered if said right and clearly. Other members of Oxford University Press, most notably Pamela Hanley, Diane Kohnen, and Maegan Sherlock, demonstrated the same standard of exemplary professionalism and friendship. Sarah Vogelsong was a fabulous copyeditor. Sue McCarty provided first-rate help on the references.

We would like to thank the reviewers whose perceptive comments and suggestions helped contribute to the creation of *American Constitutionalism: Powers, Rights, and Liberties*: Emily Bentley, Savannah State University; John Brigham, University of Massachusetts, Amherst; Jennifer Denbow, University of New England; Joseph F. Kobylka, Southern Methodist University; Kim Seckler, New Mexico State University; Mihaela Serban, Ramapo College of New Jersey; and Seana Sugrue, Ave Maria University.

We must also thank the many reviewers who closely examined each chapter of volumes I and II of *American Constitutionalism* to ensure its scholarly integrity and suitability to their course in constitutional law: Christopher W. Bonneau, University of Pittsburgh; Jennifer Bowie, George Mason University; Daniel Breen, Brandeis University; Rose Corrigan, Drexel University; McKinzie Craig, Texas A&M University; John P. Feldmeier, Wright State University; Michael P. Fix, Georgia State University; Louis Gordon, California State University, San Bernardino; Hans J. Hacker, Arkansas State University; Charles Hersch, Cleveland State University; Jeffrey D. Hockett, University of Tulsa; Melvin C. Laracey, University of Texas at San Antonio; Mark C. Miller, Clark University; Wayne D. Moore, Virginia Polytechnic Institute and State University; Paul Nolette, Marquette University; Adam W. Nye, Pennsylvania State University; Rogers M. Smith, University of Pennsylvania; Isaac Unah, University of North Carolina at Chapel Hill; Teena Wilhelm, University of Georgia; and Martha T. Zingo, Oakland University. Still others have class-tested drafts of this text with their students: Helen Knowles, Whitman College; and Emily Zackin, Hunter College.

Before, during, and after writing this book, we drew inspiration from our families, who seem appropriately amused with our fascination for American constitutional development. Mark Graber wishes to extend his love and appreciation to his mother, Anita Wine Graber, his spouse, Julia Bess Frank, and children—Naomi, Abigail, and Rebecca. Keith Whittington thanks Tracey and Taylor for their great patience and love. Howard Gillman thanks Ellen, Arielle, and Danny. The good news for our families is that if they are reading this, the volume is finally done. The bad news is that we are probably still down in the basement, obsessed by some other project on which we have already missed a deadline.

American Constitutionalism

Powers, Rights, and Liberties

Part 1 **Themes**

Chapter 1

Introduction to American Constitutionalism

On May 10, 1776, the Second Continental Congress passed what John Adams called "the most important resolution that was ever taken in America."[1] The resolution recommended that each colony draft and ratify a state constitution. Citizens were requested to "adopt such government as shall, in the opinions of the representatives of the people, best conduce to the happiness and safety of their constituents in particular, and America in general."[2] The reaction was overwhelming. Americans paraded in joy on the streets of Philadelphia, eager to get on with the work of self-government. Within a year, every colony but Rhode Island and Connecticut had established a new constitution.

These celebrations highlight the American commitment to constitutionalism. Government in the United States is constitutional government. A written constitution, citizens of all political persuasions agree, is fundamental law. Constitutional law is higher than ordinary law made by legislatures or common law announced by justices. Federal, state, and local authorities exercise power legitimately only when the written constitution authorizes their actions and decisions. America's commitment to constitutionalism extends far beyond traditional governing institutions. Student governments, the Parent-Teacher Association (PTA), such civic organizations as the Knights of Columbus, and even many chess clubs have constitutions that create, empower, and limit their leaders and members.

Five Basic Questions. This shared American commitment to constitutionalism masks disputes over what that commitment to constitutionalism entails. Consider the controversy over *Roe v. Wade* (1973), the Supreme Court decision that held that the Constitution protects abortion rights. We might initially see that dispute as limited to the proper interpretation of such constitutional provisions as the due process clause of the Fourteenth Amendment. On closer inspection, the debate over *Roe* is rooted in more basic debates over the nature of constitutionalism. Persons who support that decision often speak of "a living constitution" that incorporates social and political changes. Opponents of *Roe* often champion "strict construction," which insists that constitutions limit government only when constitutional provisions are interpreted in a manner consistent with their original meaning.

Five basic questions lie beneath most constitutional disputes.

1. What is a constitution?
2. What purposes should constitutions serve?
3. How should constitutions be interpreted?
4. How should constitutional disputes be resolved?
5. How are constitutions ratified, changed, and repudiated?

American constitutional history and the experience of other constitutional democracies demonstrate that many practices that Americans now take for granted are not necessary elements of constitutional government. Federal courts presently enjoy a near monopoly on constitutional decision making, but that preeminence is the product of a long historical struggle. Most constitutional decision makers in the United States think the notion of an "unconstitutional constitutional amendment" is legal nonsense. Courts in India and Germany, by comparison, have declared some constitutional amendments unconstitutional. Most troubling perhaps, the conventional view that the Constitution is

1. David McCullough, *John Adams* (New York: Simon & Schuster, 2001), 109.

2. *Journal of the Second Continental Congress*, vol. 5 (1776), 342.

responsible for what is good about the United States may be wrong. Leading scholars have recently asserted that the Constitution of the United States is responsible for many of the ills of American society.[3] Constitutional defects may even have caused the Civil War.[4]

Constitutionalism as Governance. The basic questions of constitutionalism are difficult, because constitutionalism is more than textual interpretation. Constitutionalism is a distinctive form of politics and governance. Constitutions structure ordinary politics, and politics structure how constitutional systems operate. Consider contemporary campaigns for the White House. Candidates for the presidency spend huge amounts of money and time in a few swing states because Article II of the Constitution requires the winning candidate to receive a majority of electoral votes rather than a majority of popular votes. Change the constitutional rules for electing the president and the politics of presidential elections will change. Presidential candidates would spend more time in New York and Los Angeles if the Constitution required them to gain a majority of the popular vote. The constitutional rules for making laws structure politics by encouraging legislative compromises and privileging the status quo. Articles I and II require policy proposals to run a difficult obstacle course before becoming settled law. Divided government, threats of presidential veto, and judicial review may slow the policy-making process and moderate policy swings. At the same time, the Constitution gives great power to a few political actors. The difficulty of passing legislation often vests presidents and justices with the practical power to resolve constitutional controversies. For the past forty years, neither pro-life nor pro-choice advocates in the elected branches of government have gained the political power necessary to reverse any Supreme Court decision on abortion.

How the Constitution is interpreted at any time is influenced significantly by ordinary politics. Since the beginning of the republic, arguments about the meaning and purpose of the Constitution have reflected the partisan divisions of their time period. The Constitution declares that government institutions may not lawfully impose "cruel and unusual punishments," but liberals and conservatives have different views on whether the death penalty constitutes cruel treatment. Political processes determine how those disputes get resolved. Presidents and senators use mostly partisan criteria when considering appointments to the Supreme Court, precisely so that justices will advance their distinctive understanding of how the Constitution should be interpreted. The Supreme Court has become more conservative in recent years because political conservatives have appointed a majority of its justices. Elections have had an extraordinary influence on constitutional development. Abraham Lincoln had very different understandings about the constitutionality of secession and slavery than the other three candidates for president in 1860. Change the result of the national election that year and American constitutional history would likely have taken a very different path.

Students of constitutional systems must accept as natural these relationships between constitutional politics and ordinary politics. Constitutional study should illuminate these relationships, not disguise them by focusing solely on how to find right answers to disputes over the meaning of particular constitutional words. Rather than obsess about whether constitutionalism is pure law or pure politics, we should study the distinctive ways American constitutionalism blends legal and political considerations.

I. What Is a Constitution?

Although constitutionalism has a long tradition in politics and political theory, substantial disagreement exists over the history and substance of that tradition. Many commentators believe the constitutional tradition began in ancient Greece. They see Aristotle's *Politics* as the first great work of constitutionalism and identify constitutionalism with the study of political regimes. Others find the first seeds of constitutionalism in ancient Rome and the Middle Ages. Constitutional regimes developed as rulers became committed to governing in a manner consistent with certain fundamental legal principles and the rule of law. A third understanding of constitutionalism developed in England and the United States during the seventeenth and eighteenth centuries. The liberal constitutionalism of the Enlightenment was committed to limited government and individual liberty, expressed in the notion that governing institutions could not pass certain kinds of laws.

3. See Sanford Levinson, *Our Undemocratic Constitution: Where the Constitution Goes Wrong (and How We the People Can Correct It)* (New York: Oxford University Press, 2006).

4. See Mark A. Graber, *Dred Scott and the Problem of Constitutional Evil* (New York: Cambridge University Press, 2006).

Contemporary constitutionalism is committed to law and legality. The constitutional commitment to the rule of law requires that governing officials be chosen on the basis of preexisting legal standards and that government officials may act only when their conduct is sanctioned by preexisting legal standards. Consider what Mary Jones must demonstrate in order to veto a bill passed by both houses of Congress requiring states to recognize same-sex marriages.

- Ms. Jones must demonstrate that she is president of the United States according to the qualifications for the presidency set out in Article II.
- Ms. Jones must demonstrate that Article II vests her with the power to veto bills passed by Congress.
- Ms. Jones must demonstrate that the veto does not violate any other rule laid down in the Constitution.

Political actors have no legal authority when they take actions that are inconsistent with constitutional standards. You have a right to disobey all unconstitutional laws passed by your state legislature (although you take the risk that the law will not be declared unconstitutional).

Ancient Constitutionalism. Political thinkers in ancient Greece and Rome used the terms *politeia* and *constitutio* to refer to "the total composition, the shape or form of the state."[5] Ancient constitutionalism focused on the *telos* of a polity, or the particular goods and vision of the good life that the polity sought to promote. The first sentence of Aristotle's *Politics* declares, "Every state is a community of some kind, and every community is established with a view to some good."[6] Ancient constitutionalists studied how social institutions were internally organized and interacted with other social institutions to generate a good society. They were particularly interested in political socialization, the practices by which citizens developed political identities, interests, and values.

American constitutionalism, in this view, is characterized by a two-party system and consumerism, as well as by the institutions explicitly laid out in Articles I, II, and III. Constitutional analysis, from an Aristotelian perspective, must take as a given both the Bill of Rights and the Super Bowl. Aristotelians further contend that American constitutional institutions and practices must be rooted in the broader political culture of the United States and not be designed for some mythical people who live a life of unadulterated virtue. Steven Elkin points out that while "a commercial republican regime" may not be "the best regime," such a society may be "the best regime for the kind of people we are with our history and capacities."[7] An ideal people might be less concerned with material prosperity than Americans, but any political coalition that fails to "grow the economy" is unlikely to survive in the United States.

Constitutions as Fundamental Law. Constitutions are commonly regarded as higher or fundamental law. Constitutions authorize the making of ordinary law and provide the foundations for ordinary lawmaking by establishing the rules for determining who makes the law. They set out the processes by which governing officials may make laws, and they limit the laws those governing officials may enact. Article I provides for a House of Representatives that is elected every two years, requires all bills to pass the House (and Senate) by a majority vote, and forbids the House from creating titles of nobility. These constitutional principles and rules are legally binding. No person has a legal obligation to obey an official decree not sanctioned by the Constitution. Charles McIlwain observes that in constitutional government, "any exercise of authority beyond these limits by any government is an exercise of 'power without right.'"[8]

The constitutional commitment to fundamental law entails a commitment to the rule of law. Rule following, Frederick Schauer points out, fosters

> the interrelated virtues of reliance, predictability, and certainty.... [D]ecision-makers who follow rules even when other results appear preferable enable those affected to predict in advance what the decisions are likely to be. Consequently, those affected by the decisions of others can plan their activities more successfully under a regime of rules than under more particularistic decision-making.[9]

---

5. Graham Maddox, "A Note on the Meaning of 'Constitution,'" *American Political Science Review* 76 (1982): 806.

6. Aristotle, *The Politics and the Constitution of Athens* (New York: Cambridge University Press, 1996), 11.

7. Stephen L. Elkin, *Reconstructing the Commercial Republic* (Chicago: University of Chicago Press, 2006), 10.

8. Charles Howard McIlwain, *Constitutionalism* (Ithaca, NY: Cornell University Press, 1947), 11.

9. Frederick Schauer, *Playing by the Rules* (New York: Oxford University Press, 1991), 254.

Persons in regimes that respect the rule of law at all times know the legal consequences of contemplated actions. All citizens are capable of learning in advance what conduct government permits, what conduct government sanctions, and how severely government sanctions such conduct. This legal regularity enables people to preserve their liberty by acting in a manner consistent with known laws.

Liberal Constitutionalism. Liberal constitutionalists identify constitutionalism with a system of "protected freedom for the individual." Constitutions protect rights. Giovanni Sartori regards a constitution as "a fundamental law, or a fundamental set of principles, and a correlative institutional arrangement, which would restrict arbitrary power and ensure a 'limited government.'"[10] Prominent contemporary thinkers reject claims that just *any* plan of government amounts to a constitution. Constitutions establish textual and practical protections for certain liberties. "For a constitutionalist," Walter Murphy and his co-authors insist, "a law enacted by a Congress chosen after open public debate and free elections and signed by a President similarly chosen would still be illegitimate if it violated a fundamental guarantee, such as the right to free exercise of religion."[11]

Liberal constitutions protect two kinds of rights. The first are *fundamental or natural rights.* These rights exist apart from the constitution. Political liberalism is committed to some version of universal rights, the claim that persons have some rights simply by virtue of being persons. These rights may be "endowed by their Creator," as Thomas Jefferson maintained, or inherent in some aspect of the human condition, as many philosophers believe. Liberal constitutions recognize and guarantee these fundamental rights but do not "create" them.

The second kind of rights are *positive rights*. These are rights created by the constitution or laws passed under the constitution. Positive rights are contingent, rather than essential, features of a liberal constitutional scheme. State legislatures routinely establish new positive rights such as the right to swim in a public pool or the right to deduct charitable contributions when paying income taxes. Unlike fundamental rights, no constitutional problem exists when positive rights are repealed by statutory revision or constitutional amendment. Rights created by government may be abolished by government.

10. Giovanni Sartori, "Constitutionalism: A Preliminary Discussion," *American Political Science Review* 56 (1962): 855.

11. Walter F. Murphy, James E. Fleming, Sotirios A. Barber, and Stephen Macedo, *American Constitutional Interpretation*, 3rd ed. (New York: Foundation Press, 2003), 48–49.

II. Constitutional Purposes

Fundamental laws that limit government serve many purposes. Good constitutions provide governing officials with necessary power and organize politics. They enable governments to make credible commitments to investors and foreign powers, prevent governing officials from enriching and entrenching themselves, promote deliberation on the public interest, enable a society to realize national aspirations, and facilitate compromises among persons who disagree on national aspirations.

Constitutionalism also entails some rule by the dead, not normally considered a virtue in a democracy.[12] Americans are not constitutionally free to decide whether an established state religion, all things considered, promotes the public good. We must instead determine whether that policy is consistent with words ratified more than two hundred years ago by men who owned slaves and wore wigs. New Yorkers may blame the constitutional requirement of equal state representation in the U.S. Senate for inefficient and unjust allocations of federal funds.[13] Nevertheless, New Yorkers are not free to secure alternative arrangements by ordinary democratic means. If we want to change those rules, we have to change the Constitution.

Empowering Officials and Organizing Politics. Constitutions both limit and empower government. Constitutions empower government by establishing the background rules that enable ordinary politics to take place. Stephen Holmes points out that "constitutions

12. The U.S. Constitution was mostly written in 1789, but it would pose the same obstacle of dead political majorities obstructing present ones if it had been written in 1989. For a provocative discussion, see Andrei Marmor, "Are Constitutions Legitimate?" *Canadian Journal of Law and Jurisprudence* 20 (2007): 69.

13. Frances E. Lee and Bruce I. Oppenheimer, *Sizing Up the Senate: The Unequal Consequences of Equal Representation* (Chicago: University of Chicago Press, 1999).

may be usefully compared to the rules of a game."[14] Just as the rules of baseball enable persons to play that game and the rules of grammar enable persons to speak English, so constitutional rules enable persons to engage in democratic politics. Constitutional rules help us determine when someone's idea becomes a statute with the force of law and whether a government official has lost his or her right to rule. We know who the president is because Article II provides the rules that enable us to identify the winner of a presidential election.

Constitutions empower government by resolving background issues in ways that facilitate debate on more important matters. If every political question were open at all times, little could be accomplished. Before having a vote on whether to raise taxes, we might have to vote on whether majorities should have the power to raise taxes. Nothing would ever be settled. By settling such questions as how to elect a president, whether to have a state religion, or whose orders army officers must follow, the Constitution enables our politics to revolve around such substantive issues as health care and the proper level of taxation. The absence of constitutional rules would not result in unlimited legal power, but anarchy.

Securing Rights. Constitutional rights and liberties can be divided into four rough categories. *Individual rights* limit the extent to which national and state officials may regulate personal behavior. *Political rights* grant persons powers to influence state and national policy making. *Equality rights* guarantee all persons the same government benefits and burdens that are provided to other similarly situated persons. *Procedural rights* ensure that persons are given a fair hearing before the state is permitted to take away any of the previous rights. These individual, political, equality, and procedural rights are usually understood as *limits* on government power. The most important constitutional provisions on civil liberties are phrased in the negative.

The Constitution of the United States is increasingly distinctive in its emphasis on negative liberties, or freedoms from government. Many new constitutions in other countries require that the government provide specific goods or services for all citizens. The constitution of South Africa declares that "everyone has the right to have access to adequate housing" and that "the state must take reasonable legislative and other measures, within its available resources, to achieve the progressive realisation of this right." Some commentators think that American constitutional provisions, when properly interpreted, also protect what are called *positive rights*.[15]

Constitutional rights are connected in at least three ways. Some rights help secure other rights, providing functional connections. Procedural rights enable persons to better secure other freedoms. American colonists believed that the right to trial by jury helped guarantee free speech and property rights. Different rights are connected by politics. Political parties, political movements, and interest groups typically pursue a variety of rights policies. Rights are connected by their broader underlying principles. Justice James McReynolds in *Meyer v. Nebraska* (1923) maintained that this general principle encompassed "the right of the individual to contract, to engage in any of the common occupations of life, to acquire useful knowledge, to marry, establish a home and bring up children, to worship God according to the dictates of his own conscience, and generally to enjoy those privileges long recognized as common law as essential to the orderly pursuit of happiness by free men."

Rule of Law and Credible Commitments. The rule of law facilitates prosperity, international relations, and peaceful cooperation. Political regimes need to secure cooperation from many parties, ranging from ordinary citizens to private investors to foreign officials. Governments can always promise that they will respect rights, repay loans, and honor treaties. Constitutional institutions that respect the rule of law make those promises more credible. Credible commitments are particularly important for nations with market economies. Governments must make the constitutional guarantees necessary to entice private investors and lay the foundations for commercial development. When constitutional commitments are credible, skeptics buy into a new political system and a society may achieve gains in overall welfare.

14. Stephen Holmes, *Passions and Constraints* (Chicago: University of Chicago Press, 1995), 163.

15. See Sotirios A. Barber, *Welfare and the Constitution* (Princeton, NJ: Princeton University Press, 2005). For a classic statement of the alternative position, see *Jackson v. City of Joliet*, 715 F.2d 1200, 1203 (7th Cir. 1983), specifically, "The Constitution is a charter of negative rather than positive liberties."

Many constitutional provisions seek to reassure various constituencies. The supremacy clause of the Constitution of the United States reassures foreign governments that treaty obligations will be enforced in federal courts. The Bill of Rights reassured some anxious anti-Federalists that the national government would respect fundamental rights. The proposed apportionment of the seats in the Senate and the House of Representatives convinced representatives of small states and slave states that their interests would be protected in the powerful national government created by the Constitution.

Preventing Self-Dealing by Governing Officials. Many constitutional rules and practices are designed to prevent government officials from *self-dealing*, or engaging in efforts to either enrich themselves or entrench their power. Robert Michels's famous "iron law of oligarchy" postulated that official self-dealing is likely because all political leaders have different interests than their constituents.[16] The average member of Congress, for example, has far more money invested in the stock market than the average American. For this reason, we have good reason to fear that majorities in Congress may adopt securities regulations that promote the interests of the wealthy few at the expense of popular majorities.

Well-designed constitutions help guarantee that when conflicts arise between the rulers and the ruled, they are resolved in the public interest. Fixed constitutional rules prevent incumbents from unfairly entrenching themselves in office by manipulating electoral arrangements. The First Amendment recognizes that elected officials may not be the best judges of whether speech criticizing their performance should be prohibited.

Some constitutional rules and practices prevent self-dealing by popular majorities. Constitutional guarantees of equality require that popular and legislative majorities govern by general rules that apply to majorities and minorities alike. Majorities determine whether abortion should be banned or whether troops should be sent into combat, but they may not prohibit only Baptists from terminating pregnancies or draft only poor persons to fight a war. "There is no more effective practical guarantee against arbitrary and unreasonable government," Justice Robert Jackson declared, "than to require that the principles of law which government impose upon a minority must be imposed generally."[17]

Promoting the Public Interest. All constitutions seek to facilitate intelligent policy through a political structure that encourages deliberation. Americans want a government that respects rights and promotes general prosperity. We want an economic system that provides jobs for college graduates, but we recognize that we cannot simply mandate by constitutional law that the gross domestic product grow by 4 percent every year. Instead, the constitutional rules for staffing the government and making laws must establish the sort of political process that fosters consistent economic growth.

The constitutional system for selecting governing officials is the first means by which the Constitution of the United States promotes deliberation and intelligent policy. The framers thought that particularly capable rulers would most likely gain office under Articles I and II. "The aim of every political constitution," James Madison wrote, is "first to obtain for rulers men who possess most wisdom to discern, and most virtue to pursue, the common good of the society."[18] Madison defended large legislative districts because he thought that they increased the number of worthy candidates. Large electoral districts also forced voters to transcend narrow concerns. More cosmopolitan representatives, in turn, would make better laws.

The division of power among the national executive, legislature, and judiciary is the second means for promoting intelligent legislation in the public interest. If two, three, and four heads are better than one, then requiring legislation to be approved by the Senate, House of Representatives, president, and Supreme Court is likely to yield particularly intelligent laws. "The separation of powers," Elkin writes, "sets up an institutional structure in which national lawmaking must revolve around the efforts of the branches to convince one another of the merits of its views."[19]

Federalism is the third constitutional means for promoting intelligent decision making. The division of

16. Robert Michels, *Political Parties* (New York: Free Press, 1968).

17. *Railway Express Agency, Inc. v. New York*, 336 U.S. 106, 112–13 (1949) (Jackson, J., concurring).

18. James Madison, "No. 57," in *The Federalist Papers*, ed. Clinton Rossiter (New York: Mentor, 1961), 350.

19. Elkin, *Reconstructing the Commercial Republic*, 35.

power between the federal government and the states ideally enables policy to be made by those legislators most familiar with the relevant issues and with the incentives to act on them in the public interest. National issues are resolved by national officials who have developed expertise in national problems. Local issues are resolved by local officials who have developed expertise in local problems. Federalism allows for policy experimentation and diversity as local officials respond to local conditions, pressures, and sentiments.

National Aspirations. Constitutions embody national aspirations. We may aspire to be the sort of people who protect fundamental rights, have a vigorous economy, or rule the world. Our constitution should remind us of those aspirations, declare these aspirations to the world, and provide a framework for achieving those aspirations. Consider the First Amendment, which protects the right to free speech. That provision promotes democratic aspirations in several ways. Political leaders must explain why their actions do not violate that cherished liberty. The more citizens who exercise free speech rights, the more likely public debate will be intelligent and diverse.

Constitutions may also serve as a bulwark against temptations to act in ways inconsistent with our notions of the best life. Just as students aspiring to law school have been known to miss class or skimp on their readings, so nations have been known to adopt policies that, on reflection, do not seem consistent with their notions of justice. Few Americans today think that interning Japanese Americans during World War II reflected the best American values. A constitution, by reminding us of our values as a nation, may help return us to those values. Just as a New Year's resolution written on the wall of a dorm may remind students that they must somehow finish their assignment to read this chapter, so the equal protection clause may remind Americans and their governors that we must treat people of all races and ethnicities equally.

Constitutions as Compromises. Successful constitutions are compromises between people and political movements with very different aspirations and very different interests. The price of national unity or peaceful coexistence is often a less coherent constitution. We may have to make concessions to those we regard as less virtuous than ourselves in order to achieve more common goals, such as a government strong enough to prevent foreign invasion. Article IV, Section 2, of the Constitution required citizens of a free state to return fugitive slaves to their southern owners. The "federal ratio" compromised both slave-state and free-state interests by allowing slaves to count as three-fifths of a person when apportioning House seats and Electoral College votes.[20] Northern opponents of slavery accepted such injustices to build support for a constitution that would be broadly acceptable. They believed the benefits of union outweighed the costs of slavery. Whether they were right is a bitterly disputed question.

III. Constitutional Interpretation and Decision Making

Americans engage in two distinctive debates over constitutional interpretation. *Normative* controversies concern the best way to ascertain what the Constitution of the United States means. Law professors, justices, and others debate whether constitutional provisions mean what they meant when ratified, how one determines that meaning, and how decisions about constitutional issues ought to be made. The second debate is over whether any of these normative theories actually explains constitutional decision making. Prominent political scientists insist that constitutional decision makers are interested only in making good policy. Their constitutional arguments merely mask conclusions reached on other grounds.

The stakes in these debates are the influence of constitutionalism on politics. At one extreme is the view that legal and policy arguments are completely distinct. Proponents of this position think notions of good policy should and do play no role in constitutional analysis. At the other extreme is the view that no practical difference exists between legal and policy arguments. Proponents of this position think people can use common methods of constitutional interpretation to support whatever policies they believe best. We believe that the relationship between law and politics is more complex than either of these positions suggests. Constitutional arguments are

20. In the apportionment of seats to the House of Representatives, states received a number of seats based on their population, calculating their free inhabitants as one person each and their enslaved inhabitants as three-fifths of a person each. States receive a number of votes in the Electoral College equal to their number of seats in the House and the Senate.

best understood as practices that constrain and structure the influence of policy preferences on legal decisions, but they are not devices that assure a complete separation of law and politics.

A. Constitutional Arguments

The constitutional text plainly resolves some matters while leaving others open for debate and investigation. The president, Article II plainly states, must be at least thirty-five years old. No one seriously claims that the best high school newspaper editor in the nation is constitutionally eligible to be the next president of the United States. The constitutional status of federal laws imposing capital punishment is harder to discern. The Eighth Amendment forbids "cruel and unusual punishments" without specifying what punishments are cruel and unusual. The amendment also fails to elaborate any elements of a cruel and unusual punishment. Constitutional decision makers and commentators have developed six approaches to interpreting such constitutional provisions.[21]

Originalism. Historical or originalist arguments maintain that constitutional provisions mean what they meant when they were ratified. Thomas Jefferson advised Supreme Court Justice William Johnson, "On every question of construction, carry ourselves back to the time when the Constitution was adopted, recollect the spirit manifested in the debates and, instead of trying what meaning may be squeezed out of the text or invented against it, conform to the probable one in which it was passed."[22]

Proponents of originalism sometimes refer to the original *intentions* underlying constitutional provisions, but most now emphasize original *meanings*. As Randy Barnett describes the original-meaning approach, "Each word must be interpreted the way a normal speaker of English would have read it when it was enacted."[23] What matters is the public meaning of the constitutional text at the time the provision was ratified—not private understandings between particular framers, specific goals or applications the framers had in mind, or what that constitutional language might mean in the present. That most framers expected George Washington to be the first president has no bearing on the proper interpretation of the provisions in Article II discussing the constitutional qualifications for that office.

Originalists dispute how to interpret more abstract clauses in the Constitution, such as the declaration that "Congress shall make no law . . . abridging the freedom of speech." Some insist that this provision should be interpreted as protecting only those free speech rights that persons in 1791 believed were constitutionally protected. Others believe that such provisions should be interpreted as stating a general principle, but not any specific application of that principle. According to Jack Balkin, a leading advocate of the latter approach, "the task of interpretation is to look to original meaning and underlying principle and decide how best to apply them in current circumstances."[24] Consider abortion rights. Some originalists consider only whether the framers of any constitutional provision believed that provision protected abortion rights. Balkin considers what the framers of the Fourteenth Amendment meant by the principle of equal protection. He would have us make an independent judgment as to how that principle applies to abortion.

Textualism. Textualist arguments emphasize the specific language of the Constitution. These arguments consider the relationship among the terms used, as well as the common meaning of those terms. Justice Joseph Story was a leading nineteenth-century champion of textualism. In Story's view, interpreters should look only to "what is written," not to "scattered documents" and "probable guesses" about what those who adopted the Constitution meant. "It is obvious, that there can be no security to the people in any constitution of government," he wrote, "if they are not to judge of it by the fair meaning of the words of the text."[25] Leslie Goldstein,

21. There is no single typology of methods of constitutional interpretation, but a useful discussion of some common forms of constitutional argument can be found in Philip Bobbitt, *Constitutional Fate* (New York: Oxford University Press, 1982), 3–119.

22. Thomas Jefferson, "To William Johnson, Jun 12, 1823," in *The Writings of Thomas Jefferson*, ed. Paul Leicester Ford (New York: G. P. Putnam's Sons, 1899), 10:231.

23. Randy E. Barnett, *Restoring the Lost Constitution* (Princeton, NJ: Princeton University Press, 2004), xiii.

24. Jack M. Balkin, "Original Meaning and Abortion," *Constitutional Commentary* 24 (2007): 293. Note that, like many recent scholars, Balkin attempts to ground a right to abortion, in part, in an equality argument rather than the right to privacy argument used by the Court in *Roe v. Wade* (1973). See also Mark A. Graber, *Rethinking Abortion* (Princeton, NJ: Princeton University Press, 1996).

25. Joseph Story, *Commentaries on the Constitution of the United States* (Boston: Hillard, Gray, 1833), 1:391.

a leading contemporary textualist, adopts a similar position. She "believes it is inappropriate for judges to strike down statutes on the basis of anything other than a principle fairly inferable from the constitutional text (although such principle need not have been present in the conscious minds of the framers)."[26]

Textualists dispute the best ways of reading the Constitution. Some textualists place constitutional language in a historical context, looking to usages at the time constitutional words were ratified. They make use of eighteenth-century dictionaries when interpreting the meaning of "commerce" in the interstate commerce clause.[27] Other textualists focus on the language without regard to any particular historical context. They are willing to use modern dictionaries. When determining whether secularism is a religion for First Amendment purposes, these textualists look to the contemporary meaning of "religion," without worrying whether people in 1791 relied on similar definitions.

The most famous textual argument in American constitutional history is probably Justice Hugo Black's claim that the First Amendment prohibits *all* regulations of speech, no matter how dangerous it may be. The relevant text reads, "Congress shall make no law . . . abridging the freedom of speech." "No law," Black bluntly stated, "means no law."[28] Black did not do extensive historical research on free speech practices in 1791 or on the framers' general principles. That the text said "no law" was good enough for him.

Doctrinalism. Doctrinal arguments resolve contemporary controversies by interpreting past precedents. Rather than focus on the constitutional text or on what various provisions meant when adopted, doctrinalism emphasizes what government officials, particularly judges, have said about the Constitution over time. The Constitution is interpreted in light of previous constitutional decisions or precedents.

Doctrinal arguments often rely on analogies to previous constitutional decisions. If the justices have declared that the Constitution protects the right to burn the flag of the United States, then the justices should declare that the Constitution protects the right to burn a map of the United States or the Texas state flag. All three cases treat burning certain objects as a form of political speech.

Extending principles articulated in one case to analogous cases characterizes the *common law* method of reasoning, which the United States inherited from England. Common law practice allows the law to develop over time as new cases arise. Common law justices apply inherited principles to new facts, sometimes subtly altering those principles in light of social developments. Justice Oliver Wendell Holmes stated, "When we are dealing with words that are also a constituent act, like the Constitution of the United States, we must realize that they have called into life a being the development of which could not have been foreseen completely by the most gifted of its begetters."[29] The framers said nothing explicitly about state and federal power to regulate trains. The Supreme Court in the late nineteenth century determined that train lines were subject only to federal regulation after a series of precedents clarified state and federal power over interstate commerce.

Doctrinalists often debate what constitutional principles were established in past decisions. Consider the present controversies over the meaning of *Brown v. Board of Education* (1954). Chief Justice John Roberts in 2007 insisted that that past precedent forbade local officials from using race when assigning children to various high schools. In "*Brown v. Board of Education* . . . ," he argued, "we held . . . government classification and separation on grounds of race themselves denoted inferiority." Justice Breyer responded with a contrary doctrinal argument. He declared that race-conscious assignments "represent local efforts to bring about the kind of racially integrated education that *Brown v. Board of Education* . . . long ago promised."[30] Both justices relied on *Brown* but disputed the best interpretation of that precedent.

26. Leslie Friedman Goldstein, *In Defense of the Text* (Savage, MD: Rowman & Littlefield, 1991), 3.

27. For historically oriented textualist approaches, see Antonin Scalia, *A Matter of Interpretation* (Princeton, NJ: Princeton University Press, 1997); Akhil Reed Amar, *The Bill of Rights* (New Haven, CT: Yale University Press, 1998).

28. Edmund Cahn, "Justice Black and First Amendment 'Absolutes': A Public Interview," *New York University Law Review* 37 (1962): 549, 553–54.

29. *Missouri v. Holland*, 252 U.S. 416, 433 (1920). See also David A. Strauss, "Common Law Constitutional Interpretation," *University of Chicago Law Review* 63 (1996): 877; Stephen M. Griffin, "Rebooting Originalism," *University of Illinois Law Review* 2008 (2008): 1185.

30. *Parents Involved in Community Schools v. Seattle School District*, 127 S. Ct. 2738, 2767, 2800 (2007).

Doctrinal arguments may also cite past legislative and executive decisions. The justices in *Youngstown Sheet & Tube Company v. Sawyer* (1952) did so after President Harry Truman seized steel mills without congressional authorization. Several judicial opinions analyzed at great length past presidential decisions to act without congressional authorization. The majority of justices concluded that the few instances in which presidents seized property on their own initiative did not provide sufficient precedential support for Truman's decision to take possession of the steel mines.

Precedents do not have the same binding force as text. The doctrine of *stare decisis* states that courts should generally adhere to the principles laid down in previous rulings, but *stare decisis* is not absolute. Constitutional decision makers may overrule precedents they believe wrongly decided. The Supreme Court during the New Deal overruled several past decisions limiting congressional power to regulate the economy. In *Lawrence v. Texas* (2003), the Court overruled *Bowers v. Hardwick* (1986), which had decided that states had the power to prohibit sexual relations between adults of the same gender.

Structuralism. Structural arguments rely on the general principles that best explain the structure of and relationships between governing institutions. Structural arguments, Charles Black notes, provide an "inference from the structures and relationships created by the constitution in all its parts or in some principal part."[31] Such basic principles as the "separation of powers," "democracy," and "federalism" are not stated explicitly in the constitutional text. Nevertheless, those principles help us understand the constitutional institutions established by Articles I, II, and III. When determining whether the president should have a line item veto, a structuralist will look at the general principles underlying the separation of powers. Structuralists will decide whether states may constitutionally regulate interstate commerce on the basis of their understanding of the constitutional commitment to federalism.

Justice Scalia's opinion in *Printz v. United States* (1997) is a good example of a structural argument. *Printz* struck down a federal requirement that local officials implement a federal gun control regulation. Scalia acknowledged that "there is no constitutional text speaking to this precise question," but he insisted that Congress could not mandate that state officials enforce federal laws. He began with a general principle. Scalia declared that the Constitution "contemplates that a State's government will represent and remain accountable to its own citizens." He then applied that principle to the issue before the court. Preventing the federal government from "impress[ing] into its service—at no cost to itself" the police officers to which local citizens have assigned other tasks, Scalia concluded, is essential to maintaining a "healthy balance of power between the States and the Federal Government."

Prudentialism. Prudential arguments examine the costs and benefits of different constitutional policies. Justice Robert Jackson made a prudential argument in a dissent in *Terminiello v. City of Chicago* (1949) when he criticized a decision protecting speakers who directed abusive language at their audience. "If the Court does not temper its doctrinaire logic with a little practical wisdom," Jackson warned, "it will convert the constitutional Bill of Rights into a suicide pact." Given several plausible interpretations of the Constitution, prudentialists claim that decision makers should choose the interpretation with the best consequences.

Prudential arguments are often employed when constitutional decision makers believe that their decisions are likely to be disobeyed. Legal scholar Alexander Bickel, a leading proponent of prudentialism, called on justices to avoid hot-button constitutional issues by employing various legal technicalities either to dismiss cases or to decide cases on much narrower grounds.[32] Justice Jackson made this kind of prudential argument in *Korematsu v. United States* (1944) when urging his colleagues, unsuccessfully, to avoid determining the constitutionality of the executive decision to detain Japanese Americans during World War II. "If we cannot confine military expedients by the Constitution," he wrote, "neither would I distort the Constitution to approve all that the military may deem expedient." The Court was under great pressure to uphold the government's actions. The question for Jackson was how to allow the government to act without creating damaging constitutional precedents.

---

31. Charles L. Black, Jr., *Structure and Relationship in Constitutional Law* (Baton Rouge: Louisiana State University, 1969), 7.

32. Alexander M. Bickel, *The Least Dangerous Branch* (Indianapolis: Bobbs-Merrill, 1962), 111–98.

Aspirationalism. Aspirational arguments interpret constitutional provisions in light of the fundamental principles of justice underlying the Constitution. Ronald Dworkin, the leading proponent of aspirationalism, insists that constitutional decision makers have an obligation to make the Constitution "the best it can be."[33] They do so, he believes, by discerning what general principles best justify American constitutional practice and then determining whether particular governmental practices are consistent with that normative commitment. Justice William Brennan, a longtime leader of the liberal wing of the Court, was a vocal advocate of the aspirationalist approach. In his view, the "Constitution is a sublime oration on the dignity of man, a bold commitment by the people to the ideal of libertarian dignity protected through law." Constitutional interpreters, Brennan believed, should interpret constitutional provisions in light of these aspirations.[34]

Justice Anthony Kennedy's opinion in *Lawrence v. Texas* (2003) provides a good example of an aspirationalist argument. As Scalia did in *Printz*, Kennedy began with a general principle. "In our tradition the State is not omnipresent in the home," he wrote. From these principles, Kennedy deduced that government could not prohibit consenting adults from engaging in private homosexual acts.

B. Sources of Constitutional Argument

The laws applied by judges derive from a variety of sources. Some of those sources are more controversial than others, and they do not all stand on an equal footing. Constitutional law is higher than statutory law. Statutory law is higher than all forms of judge-made common law. All federal laws possess a higher legal authority than state constitutions or state law. No lower legal authority may pass a law that contradicts a higher legal authority. If the Constitution of the United States grants women the right to terminate a pregnancy, then Congress cannot constitutionally pass a federal law declaring that unborn children have an absolute right to life. No state may ban abortion by constitutional decree or legislative edict. Similarly, if Congress passes a law forbidding race discrimination in employment, then no state may ratify a state constitutional provision or pass a state law that permits employers to hire only white workers. The place of natural law and the law of nations in the American constitutional hierarchy is less clear. General agreement presently exists that constitutional provisions are a higher legal authority than natural law or the law of nations. Some commentators insist that ambiguous constitutional provisions should be interpreted in a manner consistent with natural law or the law of nations, but others vigorously reject such claims, insisting that ambiguous constitutional provisions should be interpreted in light of established practices in the United States.

C. The Politics of Constitutional Argument

Scholars debate whether any theory of constitutional decision making actually influences constitutional practice. Two reasons exist for doubting whether constitutional forms actually constrain constitutional arguments. Legitimate constitutional arguments may exist for practically any policy. Two prominent law professors claim, "The range of permissible constitutional arguments now extends so far that a few workable ones are always available in a pinch."[35] Both proponents and opponents of abortion, a federal health care system, or federal aid to cities, in this view, can make intellectually respectable constitutional arguments for their preferred policy. Political actors may not make good-faith efforts to interpret the Constitution when they know the best interpretation is inconsistent with their policy preferences. Conservatives charge liberal pro-choice advocates with manufacturing a right to abortion out of thin jurisprudential air. Liberals charge conservatives with grossly distorting precedent in *Bush v. Gore* (2000) in order to hand George W. Bush the 2000 presidential election.

Lawyers and political scientists have developed four different models for thinking about the way judges and other constitutional authorities reach decisions. The attitudinal and strategic models claim that justices are far more concerned with policy than law. The legal model claims that constitutional decision

33. Ronald Dworkin, *Law's Empire* (Cambridge, MA: Harvard University Press, 1986), 53.

34. William J. Brennan, "The Constitution of the United States: Contemporary Ratification," *South Texas Law Review* 27 (1986): 438.

35. Pamela S. Karlan and Daniel R. Ortiz, "Constitutional Farce," in *Constitutional Stupidities, Constitutional Tragedies*, ed. William N. Eskridge, Jr., and Sanford Levinson (New York: New York University Press, 1998), 180.

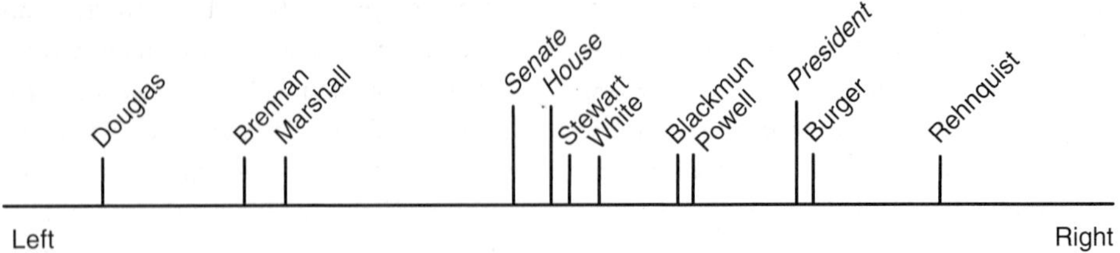

Figure 1-1 Left-Right Distribution of Justices, Congress, and President in 1974

Sources: Lee Epstein, Andrew D. Martin, Jeffrey A. Segal, and Chad Westerland, "Judicial Common Space", http://epstein.law.northwestern.edu/research/JCS.html; Keith T. Poole, "Common Space Scores, Congress 75–108," http://voteview.com/basic.htm.

Note: House and Senate reflect the median members of the chamber.

makers place greater emphasis on legal criteria than proponents of the attitudinal or strategic model recognize. Finally, the historical institutionalist model seeks to combine the best insights of the attitudinal, strategic, and legal models of constitutional decision making.

The Attitudinal Model. Many prominent political scientists point to evidence that constitutional arguments do not constrain constitutional decision makers. Jeffrey Segal and Harold Spaeth are the two leading proponents of the attitudinal model of judicial decision making. They insist that Supreme Court decisions are based almost entirely on policy preferences. "Justices," they write, "make decisions by considering the facts of the case in light of their ideological attitudes and values."[36] Supreme Court justices, in this view, are particularly well positioned to act on their ideology and values. Unlike legislators, they cannot easily be held accountable for their decisions by voters or other political actors. Unlike lower court judges, their decisions are not reviewed by other courts and cannot be easily overturned. The cases that reach the Supreme Court are precisely those in which the law is unclear and political values might matter. As a result, justices are likely to decide cases in a manner consistent with their political values.

Proponents of the attitudinal model point out that justices routinely form conservative and liberal voting blocs. These blocs hold together across a range of issues and legal contexts. The same justices who consistently cast liberal votes in free speech cases also cast liberal votes in cases concerning federalism and the meaning of the commerce clause. If they know that the Roberts Court voted 5–4 on some case and that Justice Ruth Bader Ginsburg was in the majority and Justice Clarence Thomas was in the minority, court watchers (and students taking constitutional law classes) can normally predict with a high degree of accuracy how the other seven justices voted.

The Supreme Court makes decisions by majority rule, which magnifies the power of the justice occupying the ideological center.

Figure 1-1 places the nine justices along a spectrum, with the most liberal on the left and the most conservative on the right, based on their voting behavior during the 1974 Court term. The justices on what was then the Burger Court formed three distinctly visible blocs. Justices William O. Douglas, William Brennan, and Thurgood Marshall occupied the liberal wing. At the other end of the spectrum, Chief Justice Warren Burger and Justice William Rehnquist formed a looser conservative bloc. In the center, Justices Harry Blackmun and Lewis Powell formed a more conservative pairing, and Justices Potter Stewart and Byron White shared space at the median. This alignment was typical. We can see who the swing voters on the Court were and which justices tended to vote together. Equally as important, we can see whose votes were necessary to form a majority. Centrist justices control judicial decision making, because the more ideologically extreme justices must appeal to the more moderate justices in order to get the five votes necessary to decide a case. In recent terms, Justice Anthony Kennedy has been in the majority on almost all 5–4 votes because he has occupied the center of the Roberts Court on almost all major constitutional issues. This has given Kennedy the power to make his particular constitutional vision the law of the land.

36. Jeffrey A. Segal and Harold J. Spaeth, *The Supreme Court and the Attitudinal Model Revisited* (New York: Cambridge University Press, 2002), 110.

Figure 1-1 also helps us see the potential importance of changing a justice and how policy attitudes influence the judicial selection process. In 1975, Justice Douglas was replaced by John Paul Stevens. Stevens voted just to the left of Stewart. The replacement of Douglas with Stevens meant the Court traded a strong liberal for a centrist liberal. On those issues in which Stevens was the median justice, his appointment meant the Court would hand down more conservative decisions after 1975 than it had before. That the Republican president Ford and the Democratic Senate in 1975 would agree on a justice more like Stevens than Douglas is not surprising. Stevens had policy views far closer to those of President Ford and the Senate majority in 1975 than had Douglas, who had been appointed by Franklin Roosevelt during the New Deal in 1939.[37]

Changing the composition of the Court has major consequences only when replacements have different values than their predecessors. William Brennan and Thurgood Marshall voted in favor of civil liberty claims more than three-quarters of the time. They consistently supported expanded rights for criminal defendants, a broad right to privacy, robust protections for free speech, and a sharp separation of church and state. When Brennan and Marshall left the bench in the early 1990s, the Court lost major voices (and votes) for constitutional liberalism. Supreme Court decisions moved rightward when Brennan was replaced by the less liberal David Souter and Marshall was replaced by the very conservative Clarence Thomas. The departure of Chief Justice William Rehnquist in 2005 had less of an influence on the Supreme Court. Rehnquist voted in favor of liberal rights claims less than a quarter of the time.[38] His replacement, John Roberts, was just as conservative of a constitutional decision maker.

37. By the time of Douglas's departure from the Court in 1975, the Senate had shifted to the left and Gerald Ford had replaced Richard Nixon in the White House. After Watergate, the president was not well positioned to push for a justice closer to his preferences than to the Senate's.

38. Jeffrey A. Segal, Lee Epstein, Harold J. Spaeth, and Thomas G. Walker, *The Supreme Court Compendium*, 4th ed. (Washington, DC: CQ Press, 2006), 534–35. For details on Rehnquist and Brennan, see Keith E. Whittington, "William H. Rehnquist: Nixon's Strict Constructionist, Reagan's Chief Justice," in *Rehnquist Justice*, ed. Earl M. Maltz (Lawrence: University Press of Kansas, 2003); Frank I. Michelman, *Brennan and Democracy* (Princeton, NJ: Princeton University Press, 2005).

The Strategic Model. The strategic model suggests that justices seek to achieve their policy preferences by adjusting their behavior to take into account the behavior of other actors. Constitutional decision makers vote and write strategically, rather than sincerely. Persons engage in sincere voting when they vote solely on the basis of their personal preferences. An opponent of the death penalty votes sincerely when he or she votes to declare all death sentences unconstitutional. Persons engage in sophisticated voting or vote strategically when they vote in the way they believe will achieve the best feasible policy under the circumstances. An opponent of the death penalty might sign an opinion holding that capital punishment may be constitutionally imposed, but only when the condemned person was represented at trial by a criminal defense specialist, if this was the practical alternative the justice believed would result in the fewest executions.

Majority opinions are often the subject of negotiation among the justices. Justices compromise their best interpretation of the Constitution in order to unite on a view of the law that a majority will find acceptable. Justice Brennan famously joked that with five votes he could do anything. Brennan was not satisfied with voicing his vision of the law in dissent if he could make a majority that would implement a slightly less ideal doctrine. In 1974, Brennan could easily write an opinion that would win the support of Thurgood Marshall. The question was how many compromises Brennan would make to win the support of Stewart and White—or even Blackmun or Powell. For example, Brennan believed that laws discriminating on the basis of gender should be evaluated using the same strict standard as laws discriminating on the basis of race. Nevertheless, he signed an opinion in *Craig v. Boren* (1976) declaring that gender discriminations would be evaluated using a slightly less strict standard. Brennan did so because he knew the Court could use *Craig* precedent to strike down most (if not all) gender discriminations he thought unconstitutional. Three-quarters of a loaf, he decided, was better than none.

Justices need the cooperation of colleagues on the bench, lower court judges, legislators, executive branch officials, and ultimately the citizenry to achieve policy and legal goals. Governing officials implement judicial decisions, appoint likeminded justices to the bench, and preserve the constitutional and statutory foundations of judicial independence. Justices interested in making good policy must make accommodations to win that cooperation. As Lee Epstein and Jack Knight observe:

> If their objective is to see their favored policies become the law of the land, they must take into account the preferences of other actors and the actions they expect them to take. Failing to do so may have undesirable consequences: Congress could replace their most preferred position with their least, or the public may refuse to comply with a ruling, in which case their policy fails to take on the force of law.[39]

When justices act too far outside the political mainstream, they invite backlash. After the justices in *Furman v. Georgia* (1972) declared all laws imposing the death penalty unconstitutional, two-thirds of the states passed new death penalty statutes. As a result, more people were executed during the 1980s than during the 1960s. Perhaps a more strategically minded justice should have made a narrower ruling in the *Furman* case. Such a ruling might have prohibited William Furman from being executed but might not have declared all death penalty laws unconstitutional.[40]

Considerable evidence exists that justices engage in strategic decision making. The Supreme Court refrained from deciding whether Lincoln's use of martial law during the Civil War was constitutional until after General Lee surrendered. John Marshall refused to issue a writ of mandamus in *Marbury v. Madison* (1803) because he believed that such an order would not be obeyed. Marshall explicitly engaged in strategic behavior when, as a circuit justice, he refused to discuss the constitutionality of a Virginia law forbidding black seamen from entering the state. "I am not fond of butting against a wall in sport," he informed Justice Joseph Story.[41]

The Legal Model. Proponents of the legal model believe that history, text, and precedent influence constitutional decision makers, even when they do not provide answers to all constitutional questions.[42] Legalists ask whether and how legal materials shape and influence judicial outcomes. If Justice Scalia says that judges should be guided by the original meaning of the Constitution, legalists are interested in determining whether he is willing to follow the line suggested by historical evidence that privileges liberal results. To the extent that Scalia remains an originalist when history supports liberal causes, law is influencing his constitutional decisions. In fact, Scalia has shown a real liberal streak in criminal justice cases, sometimes emphasizing historical arguments on behalf of defendant rights. Nevertheless, he has also been criticized for ignoring historical evidence, as in the case determining the constitutionality of affirmative action under the Fourteenth Amendment.

American constitutional history is littered with instances in which law influenced constitutional decisions. Felix Frankfurter, before joining the Court, was a prominent proponent of free speech rights. Frankfurter was also committed to judicial restraint. When on the Court, he often voted to sustain what he thought were unwise legislative decisions regulating speech. Abraham Lincoln believed that slavery was an atrocious evil, but he also thought that the Constitution did not allow Congress to interfere with slavery in the states. Lincoln similarly recognized the constitutional authority of the fugitive slave clause. Free-state citizens, he claimed throughout his career, were constitutionally obliged to return fugitive slaves to their masters.

Historical Institutionalism. The historical institutionalist school of political science insists that these three models take too narrow a perspective on constitutional decision making.[43] Constitutional authorities are neither automatons who leave all personal considerations

39. Lee Epstein and Jack Knight, *The Choices Justices Make* (Washington, DC: CQ Press, 1998), 15.

40. Edward Keynes, with Randall K. Miller, *The Court vs. Congress* (Durham, NC: Duke University Press, 1989); Donald Grier Stephenson, Jr., *Campaigns and the Court* (New York: Columbia University Press, 1999), 163–89; Gerald N. Rosenberg, "Judicial Independence and the Reality of Political Power," *Review of Politics* 54 (1992): 369; Lee Epstein and Joseph F. Kobylka, *The Supreme Court and Legal Change* (Chapel Hill: University of North Carolina Press, 1992).

41. John Marshall, quoted in Charles Warren, *The Supreme Court in United States History* (Boston: Little, Brown, 1922), 1:86.

42. For an extended discussion of this position, see Lief Carter and Thomas Burke, *Reason in Law*, 8th ed. (New York: Longman, 2009); Howard Gillman, "What's Law Got to Do with It? Judicial Behavioralists Test the 'Legal Model' of Judicial Decision Making," *Law and Social Inquiry* 26 (2001): 465.

43. For an extended discussion, see Rogers M. Smith, "Historical Institutionalism and the Study of Law," in *The Oxford Handbook of Law and Politics*, ed. Keith E. Whittington, R. Daniel Kelemen, and Gregory A. Caldeira (New York: Oxford University Press, 2008); Ronald Kahn and Ken I. Kersch, *The Supreme Court and American Political Development* (Lawrence: University Press of Kansas, 2006).

out of decisions or single-minded policy entrepreneurs. Rather, historical institutionalists think that judges and others try to make the best decision from a value or policy perspective that is permitted by legal text, history, and precedent.

Most constitutional decisions are based on a complex mix of attitudinal, strategic, and legal factors. These factors cannot be neatly isolated. Some constitutional rules permit strategic voting. The justices may deny for any reason a writ of certiorari, the writ needed to have the Supreme Court decide a case. When justices refuse to hear a case they think too politically explosive, they are acting both legally (the law permits them to deny certiorari) and strategically (they are trying to avoid antagonizing elected officials). Many commentators insist that decision makers have a *legal* obligation to act on their best understanding of abstract principles. Justice Thurgood Marshall's insistence that the death penalty is cruel and unusual punishment was simultaneously legal (the law required him to act on his best understanding of "cruel") and attitudinal (Justice Marshall believed capital punishment was unjust).

Historical institutionalists are interested in why people with particular policy preferences and constitutional visions had constitutional authority at a particular time. Rather than ask what particular Supreme Court justices thought about pornography or originalism, they ask why obscenity issues arose during the time period when those particular justices were on the Court. This approach explains constitutional decisions as consequences of their political, historical, ideological, and institutional contexts. The liberalism of the Warren Court, for instance, was deeply rooted in the liberalism of the New Deal and Great Society coalition that dominated American politics from 1932 to 1968. Liberals staffed the Supreme Court because liberals controlled the branches of the national government that appointed and confirmed Supreme Court justices. Constitutional decisions in the nineteenth century were equally as rooted in political and social contexts. Justice Brown, when sustaining laws mandating racial segregation in *Plessy v. Ferguson* (1897), wrote that "legislation is powerless to eradicate racial instincts, or to abolish distinctions based upon physical differences." His decision was rooted in the common assumption of the time that "stateways cannot change folkways."

Both historical and institutional factors influence constitutional practice. History creates some constitutional options while foreclosing others. Consider the reason why states at present may not violate free speech rights. An initial reading of the Constitution might suggest that the provision in the Fourteenth Amendment prohibiting states from abridging the "privileges and immunities" of American citizens provides the best grounds for declaring unconstitutional state restrictions on free speech. A series of precedents dating from the *Slaughter-House Cases* (1873) foreclosed that constitutional basis for protecting political dissent. During the early twentieth century, a different line of precedents interpreted the due process clause of the Fourteenth Amendment as protecting fundamental rights. For this reason, free speech advocates at present speak of "due process" rather than "privileges and immunities" when challenging the constitutionality of state measures that restrict expression. Institutional positions similarly influence constitutional perspectives. Justices are more familiar with the criminal process than other governing officials. Perhaps for this reason, judges have historically cared more about the rights of criminal suspects than have elected officials. Judges are also, unsurprisingly, more committed to preserving the constitutional powers of the federal courts than are legislators or members of the executive branch.

IV. Constitutional Authority

Throughout this book, you will see constitutional disputes arise and be settled. One such dispute is whether the Constitution permitted a person to be executed. Another dispute was whether President Jefferson had the constitutional authority to purchase Louisiana from France. In each case, some governing official, governing institution, or governing officials had to determine authoritatively whether a proposed action was constitutional. Such a decision need not establish a principle that binds all constitutional actors for all time. Sometimes there is a virtue in "leaving things undecided."[44] Nevertheless, what to do in the immediate present must always be resolved. Some decisions cannot be reversed. Whether a condemned prisoner may be executed without delay cannot be left unsettled, even if future controversies over capital punishment

44. See Cass R. Sunstein, *One Case at a Time* (Cambridge, MA: Harvard University Press, 1999).

.e decided differently. Americans who believe that President Jefferson acted unconstitutionally when purchasing Louisiana cannot easily declare that the regions west of the Mississippi River are no longer a part of the United States.

Everyone interprets the Constitution, but not everyone has the authority to settle constitutional disputes. In principle, any of the three branches of government could be the ultimate interpreter of the Constitution.[45] Prominent Americans before the Civil War insisted that individual states had the power to determine whether national legislation was constitutional. After the Civil War, most persons abandoned claims that states, the national executive, or the national legislature had the power to settle constitutional disputes. Judicial review, the judicial power to declare laws unconstitutional, is now entrenched. How that power can be justified and how courts should exercise that power remains unsettled.

For the past 150 years, debates about constitutional authority have been between proponents of two doctrines—*judicial supremacy* and *departmentalism*. Proponents of each view offer competing understandings of democracy and constitutionalism. Proponents of judicial supremacy emphasize the fundamental constitutional commitment to limited government. Proponents of departmentalism emphasize the fundamental democratic commitment to majority rule.

Judicial Supremacy. Most Americans support judicial supremacy, the view that the Supreme Court is the institution authorized to resolve disputes over the Constitution. With few exceptions, Supreme Court justices have aggressively asserted that their institution has the final authority to determine what the Constitution means. Judicial supremacy includes the judicial power to ignore unconstitutional acts when resolving specific cases and to establish principles that bind all other actors. When state officials in Arkansas questioned the correctness of *Brown v. Board of Education* (1954), Chief Justice Earl Warren treated them to a stern civics lecture. "The federal judiciary is supreme in the exposition of the law of the Constitution," he stated, "and that principle has . . . been respected by this Court and the Country as a permanent and indispensable feature of our constitutional system."[46]

Proponents of this view claim that judicial supremacy is a necessary ingredient of constitutionalism. If the Constitution is fundamental law, they believe, then the primary responsibility for interpreting the Constitution should be vested in the institution responsible for interpreting the law—the judiciary. As Justice Kennedy recently asserted, "If Congress could define its own powers by altering the Fourteenth Amendment's meaning, no longer would the Constitution be 'superior paramount law, unchangeable by ordinary means.'"[47]

Departmentalism. Departmentalists believe that all institutions have an equal right to interpret the Constitution. Most accept judicial review, the judicial power to make constitutional decisions that bind the particular parties before the court. However, proponents of departmentalism reject the position that elected officials must always adhere to the principles justices announce in those decisions. They maintain that this judicial supremacy subverts constitutionalism by inviting politicians to ignore their constitutional responsibilities and allowing unchecked judges to warp constitutional principles through abuse and misinterpretation.

Throughout American history, prominent political leaders have asserted an equal right to constitutional authority. James Madison explained, "As the legislative, executive, and judicial departments are co-ordinate, and each equally bound to support the Constitution, it follows that each must, in the exercise of its functions, be guided by the text of the Constitution according to its own interpretation of it."[48] President Lincoln vigorously denied that his administration had a constitutional obligation to respect *Dred Scott v. Sandford* (1857), which ruled that the federal government could not ban slavery in the territories. "The candid citizen must confess that if the policy of the government . . . is to be irrevocably fixed by decisions of the Supreme Court,"

45. Mechanisms, such as constitutional amendments or referenda, that would put this role outside the three branches of government are also possible.

46. *Cooper v. Aaron*, 358 U.S. 1, 18 (1958).

47. *City of Boerne v. Flores*, 521 U.S. 507, 529 (1997). For a leading scholarly defense of judicial supremacy, see Larry Alexander and Frederick Schauer, "On Extrajudicial Constitutional Interpretation," *Harvard Law Review* 110 (1997): 1359.

48. James Madison, "To Mr. __, 1834," in *Letters and Other Writings of James Madison* (Philadelphia: J. B. Lippincott, 1867), 4:349.

he contended in his first inaugural, "the people will have ceased to be their own rulers." Lincoln thought that his administration was bound by the legal decision in the court case between Dred Scott and John Sanford. Lincoln admitted that his government could not forcibly free Dred Scott if the courts held that he was legally bound. But the government did not have to accept the "political rule" that the Supreme Court had laid down in the case. When in power, Republicans did not hesitate to ban slavery in the federal territories and the District of Columbia.

The Countermajoritarian Difficulty. Debates over constitutional authority for the last fifty years have been shaped by a concern with what has become known as "the countermajoritarian difficulty." Alexander Bickel introduced this problem to American constitutionalism when he declared, "When the Supreme Court declares unconstitutional a legislative act or the action of an elected executive, it thwarts the will of representatives of the actual people of the here and now; it exercises control, not in behalf of the prevailing majority, but against it."[49] Bickel and others regard judicial review as antidemocratic because the practice empowers a small, elite body of electorally unaccountable individuals to undo the policies that have emerged from the democratic process. Judicial review is also undemocratic, they think, because the justices often assume that they should resist democratic majorities and their policy preferences.

Proponents of judicial power offer several responses to the countermajoritarian difficulty. One approach provides a democratic foundation for judicial review. Arguments in this vein contend that the courts should use the power of judicial review only to enforce principles that the people have clearly endorsed.[50] A second approach claims judicial review makes democracy work better. Judges act democratically, in this view, when they prevent politicians from silencing critics. Chief Justice Harlan Fiske Stone argued that "legislation which restricts those political processes which can ordinarily be expected to bring about repeal of undesirable legislation" should "be subjected to more exacting judicial scrutiny" than other types of legislation.[51] A third approach embraces the antidemocratic character of courts. In this view, majority rule is not the only political value that our society should protect and uphold. Judges should stand up for substantively important rights and values, even when those values are not popular.[52]

Critics of judicial power are more skeptical of these efforts to reconcile democracy and judicial review. Some argue that the courts should exercise "judicial restraint" and use the power of judicial review only when the political branches have made a clear constitutional mistake.[53] Others argue that "the people" should play a more active role in constitutional interpretation and in checking judges.[54] A few voices contend that judicial review cannot be squared with democracy. Jeremy Waldron concludes, "When citizens or their representatives disagree about what rights we have or what those rights entail, it seems something of an insult to say that this is not something they are to be permitted to sort out by majoritarian processes, but that the issue is to be assigned instead for final determination to a small group of judges."[55]

Countermajoritarian, Majoritarian, or Nonmajoritarian. Many political scientists question whether the countermajoritarian difficulty provides the right framework for thinking about constitutional authority and judicial power. They think judicial decisions are (almost) as consistent with majoritarian sentiments as decisions made by other governing officials. A half-century ago Robert Dahl observed that "it would appear . . . somewhat unrealistic to suppose that a Court whose members are recruited in the fashion of Supreme Court Justices would long hold to norms of Right or Justice substantially at odds with the rest

49. Bickel, *Least Dangerous Branch*, 17.

50. This was Bickel's own solution to the difficulty. For some recent efforts of this sort, see Bruce Ackerman, *We the People* (Cambridge, MA: Harvard University Press, 1991); Keith E. Whittington, *Constitutional Interpretation* (Lawrence: University Press of Kansas, 1999).

51. *United States v. Carolene Products Co.*, 304 U.S. 144, 152n4 (1938). The classic scholarly elaboration of this argument is John Hart Ely, *Democracy and Distrust* (Cambridge, MA: Harvard University Press, 1980).

52. See Ronald Dworkin, *A Matter of Principle* (Cambridge, MA: Harvard University Press, 1985).

53. A modern version of this view can be found in Robert H. Bork, *The Tempting of America* (New York: Free Press, 1990).

54. See Larry D. Kramer, *The People Themselves* (New York: Oxford University Press, 2004).

55. Jeremy Waldron, *Law and Disagreement* (New York: Oxford University Press, 1999), 15.

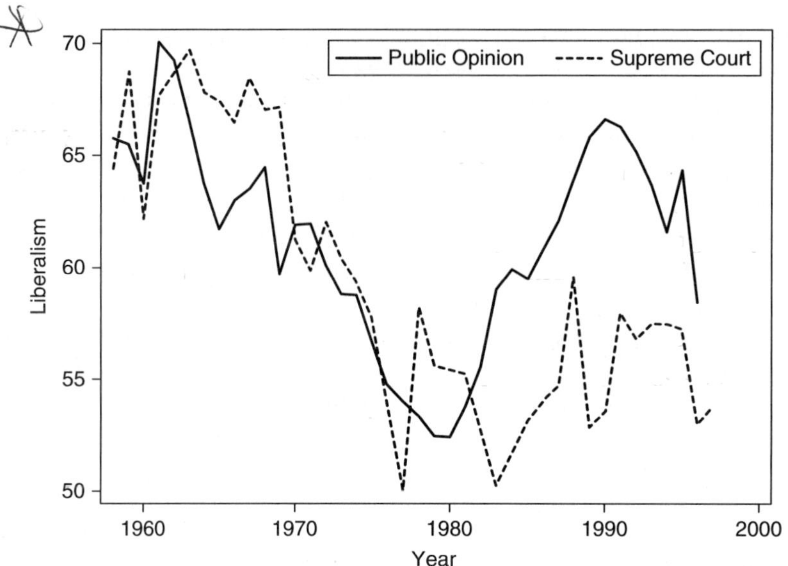

Figure 1-2 The Supreme Court and Public Opinion, 1957–1997

Source: Kevin T. McGuire, "The Least Dangerous Branch Revisited," Replication Data, http://www.unc.edu/~kmcguire/data.opinion.zip. Copyright © Cambridge University Press 2011.

Note: The two series are a public mood score and percentage of Supreme Court decisions in a liberal direction in cases reversing lower courts across three issue domains. The two series are scaled to public mood for presentation.

of the political elite."[56] Both political and sociological factors explain the judicial tendency to remain in the mainstream of American politics. Federal judges are nominated and confirmed through a political process. Presidents are unlikely to select individuals for the bench whose constitutional philosophies are at odds with their own. When liberals control the White House and Senate, as they did in the 1930s and 1960s, they appoint liberals to the Supreme Court. When conservatives hold greater sway, as they did in the 1920s and 1980s, they appoint conservatives to the Court. With some lag, the center of the Court tends to sit in the political mainstream of the particular historical era. The *Dred Scott* case reflected the pro-slavery and racist views of the reigning Jacksonian majority. Moreover, the sitting justices tend to share the common prejudices and values of their time. As Justice Benjamin Cardozo observed, the "great tides and currents which engulf the rest of men do not turn aside in their course and pass the judges by."[57] The Supreme Court became more liberal on race at approximately the same time most American elites became more liberal on race.

The Court does not simply stand outside or against political movements. The same events that move electoral politics often move the courts, though often at different speeds and times. Figure 1-2 maps the overall liberal tendency of public opinion and the liberalism of Supreme Court decisions in the latter half of the twentieth century.[58] The Court followed the public's more conservative mood in the 1970s, although judicial decisions did not turn in a more liberal direction as sharply as public opinion did in the late 1980s and early 1990s.

When justices declare laws unconstitutional, they are often acting in a manner consistent with the values

56. Robert A. Dahl, "Decision Making in a Democracy: The Supreme Court as a National Policy Maker," *Journal of Public Law* 6 (1957): 291.

57. Benjamin N. Cardozo, *The Nature of the Judicial Process* (New Haven, CT: Yale University Press, 1921), 168.

58. See also Kevin T. McGuire and James A. Stimson, "The Least Dangerous Branch Revisited: New Evidence on Supreme Court Responsiveness to Public Preferences," *Journal of Politics* 66 (2004): 1018.

shared by members of the dominant political coalition. Elected officials frequently encourage the Court to exercise the power of judicial review and to take the lead in interpreting the Constitution. Congress during the 1850s passed legislation facilitating a judicial decision on the constitutional status of slavery in the territories. Political leaders lay the groundwork for the justices to develop particular lines of doctrine. Archibald Cox, the solicitor general for the Kennedy administration, developed the arguments used by the Supreme Court in *Baker v. Carr* (1962) to support giving courts the power to determine whether malapportioned state legislatures violated the equal protection clause. The Court often acts when there are divisions among political leaders over the policy at issue or relatively little political support for the policy that is being struck down. The judicial majority in *Lawrence v. Texas* (2003), when ruling that consenting adults had a right to participate in same-sex intimate behavior, pointed out that the vast majority of states had already repealed prohibitions on gay and lesbian behavior. Judicial review still raises important and difficult questions, but the politics of judicial review is more complicated than the countermajoritarian image of an isolated Court standing up against a united political majority.[59]

The Politics of Constitutional Authority. For more than two hundred years, Americans have witnessed contests for constitutional authority. Sometimes these struggles pit judges against elected officials. More often, elected officials empower the courts to interpret the Constitution. They staff courts with justices willing to declare limits on government power. They pass laws making constitutional challenges to federal and state laws easier. They pass vague legislation that may force courts to make policy in the guise of statutory or constitutional interpretation. Presidents do not nominate individuals to the Supreme Court who are pledged to uphold all laws against constitutional challenge.

Elected officials have various reasons for supporting judicial power. National government officials may want to keep local political majorities in line. Political moderates may want to avoid difficult decisions that might divide their political coalitions. Party leaders with a tenuous hold on elected office may want to ensure that courts will protect their interests when they are out of power. As you read later chapters, you should consider whose interests are being served by appeals to the courts. You should also consider the implications of the judiciary's actions for other political actors.

Struggles for constitutional authority do not end when the judiciary speaks. Justices do not enforce their decrees. Elected officials often do not comply with constitutional orders in cases they believe wrongly decided. "Where there is local hostility to change," Gerald Rosenberg concludes, "court orders will be ignored." In his view, "community pressure, violence, or threats of violence, and lack of market response all serve to curtail actions to implement court decisions."[60] Many famous judicial decisions declaring laws unconstitutional had almost no immediate consequence. Ten years after *Brown v. Board of Education* was decided, less than 2 percent of African American children in the Deep South were attending integrated schools.[61] Judicial decisions prohibiting state organized prayer in public schools had little immediate effect on that religious practice in schools across the United States.[62]

Judicial decisions shape, but do not end, political struggles over constitutional meaning. Political movements hardly ever fold their tents after judicial defeats. The Republican Party after *Dred Scott* remained committed to prohibiting slavery in the territories. Contemporary pro-life forces remain committed to reversing Supreme Court decisions prohibiting bans on abortion. Contemporary pro-choice forces remain committed to reversing Supreme Court decisions sustaining regulations on abortion. Constitutional conflicts are settled politically, not legally. Constitutional politics come to an end only when the forces backing the losing issue concede defeat and lose political interest in the issue.

---

59. See, for example, Mark A. Graber, "The Non-Majoritarian Difficulty: Legislative Deference to the Judiciary," *Studies in American Political Development* 7 (1993): 35; Howard Gillman, "How Parties Can Use the Courts to Advance Their Agendas: Federal Courts in the United States, 1875–1891," *American Political Science Review* 96 (2002): 511; Keith E. Whittington, "'Interpose Your Friendly Hand': Political Foundations of Judicial Review by the United States Supreme Court," *American Political Science Review* 99 (2005): 583.

60. Gerald N. Rosenberg, *The Hollow Hope* (Chicago: University of Chicago Press, 1991), 337.

61. Ibid., 50.

62. Kenneth M. Dolbeare and Phillip E. Hammond, *The School Prayer Decisions* (Chicago: University of Chicago Press, 1971).

V. Constitutional Change

Problems of constitutional change seem simpler than problems of constitutional interpretation and authority. "The Ratification of the Conventions of Nine States," Article VII plainly declares, "shall be sufficient for the Establishment of this Constitution between the States so ratifying the Same." Article V declares that when two-thirds of both houses propose a constitutional amendment, that amendment becomes constitutional law if ratified by three-fourths of all state legislatures or by conventions in three-fourths of all states, with Congress choosing the mode of state ratification. Two-thirds of the states may call a convention to propose amendments that, again, must be ratified by three-quarters of all states. These apparently plain requirements for ratification and amendment, however, mask difficult issues.

Creating Constitutions. Constitutions do not become authoritative sources of fundamental law merely because their stated conditions for ratification are satisfied. Otherwise, the authors of this book could write a new Constitution of the United States and condition legitimacy on our approval plus the approval of our five best friends. Federalists in 1787 acknowledged that their proposal to require ratification by nine states was quite different from the unanimous state approval for constitutional change set out in the Articles of Confederation. James Madison in *Federalist* 40 maintained that popular ratification compensated for any legal irregularities in the drafting process. The persons who framed the Constitution of the United States, he wrote,

> must have reflected, that . . . since it is impossible for the people spontaneously and universally to move in concert towards their object; and it is therefore essential that such changes be instituted by some INFORMAL AND UNAUTHORIZED PROPOSITIONS, made by some patriotic and respectable citizen or number of citizens. . . . They must have borne in mind, that as the plan to be framed and proposed was to be submitted TO THE PEOPLE THEMSELVES, the disapprobation of this supreme authority would destroy it forever; its approbation blot out antecedent errors and irregularities.[63]

63. Madison, "No. 40," in *Federalist Papers* (see note 18), 253.

Akhil Amar has suggested that a new constitution would be legitimate today if a bare majority of American voters signed a petition for a national constitutional convention, a majority of the delegates at that convention approved the constitution, and that constitution was then approved by a national electoral majority.[64] Amar and Madison recognize that constitutions take hold and are considered legitimate because they are embraced by the people and accepted as legitimate, not because constitutional founders follow preexisting rules for constitutional change.

Limits on Constitutional Change. Conventional wisdom in the United States insists that Americans are free to adopt any constitutional amendment that does not abolish state equality in the Senate. Justice Frank Murphy in *Schneiderman v. United States* (1943) insisted that the constitutional amendment process allows citizens to fundamentally alter the constitutional regime, even including transforming the United States into a communist dictatorship. "Article V," he wrote, "contains procedural provisions for constitutional change by amendment without any present limitation whatsoever except that no State may be deprived of equal representation in the Senate without its consent."[65] On this view, Americans could amend the constitution to establish a state religion or a monarchy.

Walter Murphy disagrees. He points out that the "word *amend* comes from the Latin *emendere*, to correct." For this reason, Murphy maintains, "abolishing constitutional democracy and substituting a different system would not be an amendment at all, but a re-creation, a re-forming, not simply of political structures but also of the people themselves."[66] On this view, not even a supermajority could constitutionally repeal the free speech clause or the Thirteenth Amendment's prohibition of slavery.

This possibility of unconstitutional constitutional amendments is not hypothetical outside of the United States. Constitutional courts elsewhere have declared constitutional amendments void on the ground that they are inconsistent with fundamental constitutional principles. Some Americans have sought to persuade the

64. Akhil Reed Amar, "Amending the Constitution Outside Article V," *University of Chicago Law Review* 55 (1988): 1064–65.

65. *Schneiderman v. United States*, 320 U.S. 118, 137 (1943).

66. Walter F. Murphy, *Constitutional Democracy* (Baltimore: Johns Hopkins University Press, 2007), 506.

Supreme Court to make similar decisions. Opponents of the Nineteenth Amendment, which gave women the right to vote, asserted that principles of federalism implied that a majority of states could not change the voting requirements in states that did not ratify that amendment. The Supreme Court rebuffed this claim in *Leser v. Garnett* (1922).

Amending the Constitution Outside of Article V. Whether Article V provides the only procedures for constitutional amendment is controversial. Bruce Ackerman maintains that a combination of political mobilization, elections, judicial decisions, and "super-statutes" should be treated as valid constitutional amendments. The Jeffersonian victory in 1800, the success of the New Deal in the 1930s, and the victory of the civil rights movement in the 1960s are all examples of "constitutional moments." The policies adopted during these periods of sweeping political change, Ackerman thinks, should trump the constitutional text. Future judges should take their guidance from these policies as if they were written into the Constitution.[67]

Ackerman's critics insist that Article V sets out the exclusive processes for constitutional amendment. As David Dow argues, the constitutional provisions for amendment are "an example of yet another text the meaning of which is essentially clear." Permitting committed popular majorities to amend the Constitution without going through the Article V process might weaken the constitutional commitment to liberty. "If the Constitution is to continue to be the ultimate source that protects individual rights against encroachment by government power and political majorities," Dow contends, "then the affirmative words in Article V must be understood to negative other conceivable modes of amendment."[68]

Constitutional Change Without Constitutional Amendments. Constitutional changes do not always require constitutional amendment. The framers recognized that time would clarify some constitutional meanings. "All new laws, though penned with the greatest technical skill, and passed on the fullest and most mature deliberation," Madison wrote in *Federalist* 37, "are considered as more or less obscure and equivocal, until their meaning be liquidated and ascertained by a series of particular discussions and adjudications." The Constitution left undefined how executive branch officials were to be removed from office. Presidential power to cashier an executive branch employee was debated by the First Congress and not clearly settled until the twentieth century. The understanding that federal judges should not engage in partisan politics dates from the failed impeachment of Justice Samuel Chase in 1805, not the drafting of Article III of the Constitution in 1787. New practices and principles may take on constitutional significance, such as the tradition that presidents should serve no more than two terms of office. When Franklin Roosevelt violated that tradition, Americans quickly formalized the prohibition by ratifying the Twenty-Second Amendment.

The status of state-mandated segregation in the United States provides a good example for thinking about the nature of constitutional change. In 1900, all but a few well-trained lawyers thought that state-mandated racial segregation was an acceptable practice under the equal protection clause of the Fourteenth Amendment. Within two decades after *Brown v. Board of Education* (1954), every well-trained lawyer recognized that government-sponsored racial segregation was hardly ever constitutionally valid. Effective constitutional requirements had radically changed, but no new constitutional text had been adopted.

Consider the different ways of describing this change in constitutional practice. Some would argue that "the Constitution" had not changed, but that earlier judges, government officials, and lawyers had simply misinterpreted the equal protection clause. Others would argue that the underlying constitutional principles stayed the same, but that the implications of those constitutional principles changed over time given new circumstances or even new thinking. The Constitution does not change, in this view, but doctrines applying the Constitution do. Americans learned that separate was not equal. Still others would argue that the Court and other constitutional decision makers simply changed the constitutional rules. Perhaps the segregation question was like the question of executive removal, a matter to be "liquidated and ascertained" after a series of adjudications such as *Brown*. Perhaps segregation was acceptable under the original Fourteenth Amendment and *Brown* was part of a process of altering the meaning of that amendment.

67. Ackerman, *We the People*.

68. David R. Dow, "The Plain Meaning of Article V," in *Responding to Imperfection*, ed. Sanford Levinson (Princeton, NJ: Princeton University Press, 1995), 127.

The Merits of Constitutional Change. The framers debated the virtues of frequent constitutional change. Most believed fundamental constitutional change should be difficult. Prominent founders declared that constitutional change should take place only when society agreed on the constitutional flaw to be repaired. James Madison worried that frequent constitutional changes or constitutional conventions would "deprive the government of that veneration which time bestows on every thing."[69] His friend Thomas Jefferson thought constitutional change should take place more often. Jefferson declared, "Laws and institutions must go hand in hand with the progress of the human mind." In Jefferson's view, "as new discoveries are made, new truths disclosed, and manners and opinions change with the change of circumstances, institutions must advance also, and keep pace with the times."[70]

These debates over the merits of frequent constitutional change remain vibrant. Contemporary Madisonians insist that experience demonstrates why constitutions should be difficult to amend. Kathleen Sullivan writes,

> It is a bad idea to politicize the Constitution. The very idea of a constitution turns on the separation of the legal and political realms. The Constitution sets up the framework of government. It also sets forth a few fundamental political ideas (equality, representation, individual liberties) that place limits on how far any temporary majority may go. This is our higher law. All the rest is left to politics. Losers in the short run yield to the winners out of respect for the constitutional framework set up for the long run. This makes the peaceful conduction of ordinary politics possible. Without such respect for the constitutional framework, politics would degenerate into fractious war. But the more a constitution is politicized, the less it operates as a fundamental charter of government. The more a constitution is amended, the more it seems like ordinary legislation.[71]

Contemporary Jeffersonians insist on a more majoritarian process for constitutional change. Sanford Levinson condemns "the ability of thirteen houses in as many states to block constitutional amendments desired by the overwhelming majority of Americans as well as, possibly, eighty-six out of the ninety-nine legislative houses in the American states. . . . [N]o other country—nor, for that matter, any of the fifty American states," he observes, "makes it so difficult to amend its constitution."[72] Both Sullivan and Levinson agree that the Constitution of the United States is presently one of the most difficult and most rarely amended constitutions still in use.[73] They dispute whether this longevity is a virtue.

VI. Constitutional Politics and Law

Constitutions work (when they work) not by announcing clear rules that people can simply obey, but by constraining, constructing, and constituting politics. Constitutions *constrain* politics when citizens and governing officials subordinate their policy preferences to constitutional norms. Constitutions *construct* politics when citizens and governing officials follow the rules that determine whose policy preferences and constitutional understandings are the official law of the land. Constitutions *constitute* politics when citizens and elected officials internalize constitutional values so that they regard constitutional processes as the only legitimate means for resolving legal and policy disputes.

In healthy constitutional regimes, the constructive and constitutive functions play a far greater role than the constraining function. The Constitution shapes politics by creating a language for talking and thinking about such issues as abortion. Instead of discussing "Should abortion be legal?" we discuss "Should *Roe* be overruled?" or "Does the due process clause of the Fourteenth Amendment encompass the right to terminate a pregnancy?" or "Do women need a right to abortion to enjoy the equal protection of those laws?" These questions are answered by governing officials selected according to constitutional rules. The Supreme Court established by Article III decides whether to overrule *Roe*. The president established by Article II nominates Supreme Court justices. The Senate established by Article I confirms those nominations. Candidates for those offices articulate very

69. Madison, "No. 49," in *Federalist Papers* (see note 18), 314.

70. Jefferson, "To Samuel Kercheval, July 12, 1816," in *Writings* (see note 22), 10:43.

71. Kathleen Sullivan, "What's Wrong with Constitutional Amendments?" in *The New Federalist Papers* (New York: W. W. Norton, 1997), 63–64.

72. Levinson, *Our Undemocratic Constitution*, 7, 160.

73. Donald S. Lutz, "Toward a Theory of Constitutional Amendment," *American Political Science Review* 88 (1994): 355.

different constitutional visions on the campaign trail. These visions include beliefs about whether *Roe* and other cases were rightly decided, as well as beliefs about legitimate methods of constitutional decision making, what institutions have the right to make authoritative constitutional decisions, and the legitimate forms of constitutional change. Who decides whether *Roe* should be overruled depends both on ordinary partisan processes and on the rules laid out by the Constitution. A Senate whose members were elected in particular states might have very different views about abortion than a Senate whose members were elected by a national majority.

In the past fifty years, countries as diverse as Nepal, South Africa, Hungary, and Israel have ratified new constitutions and established institutions for implementing them. Most have adopted such features as a Bill of Rights and judicial review.[74] Few countries have as strict a separation of powers as the United States or as difficult an amendment process. Whether these constitutions will endure is an open question. In sharp contrast to the Constitution of the United States, which is over two hundred years old, the average national constitution lasts only seventeen years.[75]

These developments abroad cast light on American constitutionalism. By comparison with other nations, we can become more aware of our own assumptions. Often in this book, you will encounter assertions that some distinctive American practice is necessary for human flourishing, the rule of law, or preventing tyranny. That may not always be true. Constitutional democracies that do without judicial supremacy or federalism do not routinely send dissenters to the gulag or execute more innocent people than the United States. Constitutional practices in the United States may nevertheless fit Americans best, even if they are not rooted in universal norms. Comparative analysis may shed light on the political and social factors that explain why practices that are good for Americans may nevertheless not be easy to export to other countries. We may also learn that some foreign constitutional practices may thrive on American soil.

Veneration must be earned. Whether we should venerate the Constitution of the United States depends on the results of a close encounter with the American constitutional experience. The first step is to know how the American constitutional system has operated over time, what purposes and interests that system has served, how that system has been maintained, and how that system has been reformed. This is what we hope to illuminate in the chapters to come.

74. The specific form of constitutional review adopted in most other countries differs from the American form of judicial review, however. Most nations have created a specific constitutional court separate from their regular judicial system, operating under different rules, and usually staffed with more politically accountable officials.

75. Zachary Elkins, Thomas Ginsburg, and James Melton, *The Endurance of National Constitutions* (New York: Cambridge University Press, 2009).

Suggested Readings

Ackerman, Bruce A. 1991. *We the People: Foundations.* Cambridge, MA: Harvard University Press.

———. 2007. "The Living Constitution." *Harvard Law Review* 120:1737–1812.

Amar, Akhil Reed. 1998. *The Bill of Rights: Creation and Reconstruction.* New Haven, CT: Yale University Press.

———. 2005. *America's Constitution: A Biography.* New York: Random House.

Baer, Judith A., and Leslie Friedman Goldstein. 2006. *The Constitutional and Legal Rights of Women: Cases in Law and Social Change*, 3rd ed. New York: Oxford University Press.

Balkin, Jack M. 2011. *Living Originalism.* Cambridge, MA: Harvard University Press.

Barber, Sotorios A. 1983. *On What the Constitution Means.* Baltimore, MD: Johns Hopkins University Press.

Barnett, Randy. 2004. *Restoring the Lost Constitution: The Presumption of Liberty.* Princeton, NJ: Princeton University Press.

Bedau, Hugo Adam. 1982. *The Death Penalty in America*, 3rd ed. New York: Oxford University Press.

Bickel, Alexander M. 1962. *The Least Dangerous Branch: The Supreme Court at the Bar of Politics.* Indianapolis: Bobbs-Merrill.

Bobbitt, Philip. 1982. *Constitutional Fate: Theory of the Constitution.* New York: Oxford University Press.

Bodenhamer, David J. 1992. *Fair Trial: Rights of the Accused in American History.* New York: Oxford University Press.

Brandwein, Pamela. 1999. *Reconstructing Reconstruction: The Supreme Court and the Production of Historical Truth.* Durham, NC: Duke University Press.

Clayton, Cornell W., and Howard Gillman, eds. 1999. *Supreme Court Decision Making: New Institutionalist Approaches.* Chicago: University of Chicago Press.

Cornell, Saul. 2006. *A Well-Regulated Militia: The Founding Fathers and the Origins of Gun Control in America.* New York: Oxford University Press.

Curtis, Michael Kent. 2000. *Free Speech, "The People's Darling Privilege": Struggles for Freedom of Expression in American History.* Durham, NC: Duke University Press.

Dahl, Robert A. 1957. "Decision Making in a Democracy: The Supreme Court as a National Policymaker." *Journal of Public Law* 6:279–95.

Devins, Neal, and Louis Fisher. 2004. *The Democratic Constitution*. New York: Oxford University Press.

Dinan. John J. 2006. *The American State Constitutional Tradition*. Lawrence: University Press of Kansas.

Dworkin, Ronald. 1977. *Taking Rights Seriously*. Cambridge, MA: Harvard University Press.

Ely, James W., Jr. 2008. *The Guardian of Every Other Right: A Constitutional History of Property Rights*, 3rd ed. New York: Oxford University Press.

Ely, John Hart. 1980. *Democracy and Distrust: A Theory of Judicial Review*. Cambridge, MA: Harvard University Press.

Epp, Charles. 1998. *The Rights Revolution: Lawyers, Activists, and Supreme Courts in Comparative Perspectives*. Chicago: University of Chicago Press.

Epstein, Lee, and Jack Knight. 1998. *The Choices Justices Make*. Washington, DC: CQ Press.

Fisher, Louis. 2002. *Religious Liberty in America: Political Safeguards*. Lawrence: University Press of Kansas.

Fleming, James E. 2006. *Securing Constitutional Democracy: The Case of Autonomy*. Chicago: University of Chicago Press.

Friedman, Barry. 2009. *The Will of the People: How Public Opinion Has Influenced the Supreme Court and Shaped the Meaning of the Constitution*. New York: Farrar, Straus and Giroux.

Gillman, Howard. 2002. "How Political Parties Can Use the Courts to Advance Their Agendas: Federal Courts in the United States, 1875–1891." *American Political Science Review* 96:511–524.

Graber, Mark A. 1993. "The Non-Majoritarian Problem: Legislative Deference to the Judiciary." *Studies in American Political Development* 7:35–73.

Griffin, Stephen. 1996. *American Constitutionalism: From Theory to Politics*. Princeton, NJ: Princeton University Press.

Helmholz, R. M., Charles M. Gray, John H. Langbein, and Eben Moglen. 1997. *The Privilege Against Self-Incrimination: Its Origins and Development*. Chicago: University of Chicago Press.

Kahn, Ronald, and Ken I. Kersch, eds. 2006. *The Supreme Court and American Political Development*. Lawrence: University Press of Kansas.

Keck, Thomas M. 2007. "Party, Policy or Duty: Why Does the Supreme Court Invalidate Federal Statues?" *American Political Science Review* 101:321–38.

Kersch, Ken I. 2004. *Constructing Civil Liberties: Discontinuities in the Development of American Constitutional Law*. New York: Cambridge University Press.

Kettner, James H. 1978. *The Development of American Citizenship, 1608–1870*. Chapel Hill: University of North Carolina Press.

Keyssar, Alexander. 2000. *The Right to Vote: The Contested History of Democracy in the United States*. New York: Basic.

Klarman, Michael J. 2004. *From Jim Crow to Civil Rights: The Supreme Court and the Struggle for Civil Rights*. New York: Oxford University Press.

Klinkner, Philip A., and Rogers M. Smith. 1999. *The Unsteady March: The Rise and Decline of Racial Equality in America*. Chicago: University of Chicago Press.

Kramer, Larry D. 2004. *The People Themselves: Popular Constitutionalism and Judicial Review*. New York: Oxford University Press.

Kyvig, David E. 1996. *Explicit and Authentic Acts: Amending the U.S. Constitution, 1776–1995*. Lawrence: University Press of Kansas.

Levinson, Sanford. 2006. *Our Undemocratic Constitution: Where the Constitution Goes Wrong (and How the People Can Correct It)*. New York: Oxford University Press.

McIlwain, Charles Howard. 1947. *Constitutionalism: Ancient and Modern*, rev. ed. Ithaca, NY: Cornell University Press.

McMahon, Kevin. 2003. *Reconsidering Roosevelt on Race: How the Presidency Paved the Road to* Brown. Chicago: University of Chicago Press.

Moore, Wayne D. 1996. *Constitutional Rights and Powers of the People*. Princeton, NJ: Princeton University Press.

Nieman, Donald G. 1991. *Promises to Keep: African-Americans and the Constitutional Order, 1776 to the Present*. New York: Oxford University Press.

Neuman, Gerald L. 1996. *Strangers to the Constitution: Immigrants, Borders, and Fundamental Law*. Princeton, NJ: Princeton University Press.

Peretti, Terri Jennings. 2001. *In Defense of a Political Court*. Princeton, NJ: Princeton University Press.

Powe, Lucas A., Jr. 2009. *The Supreme Court and the American Elite*. Cambridge, MA: Harvard University Press.

Rosenberg, Gerald N. 2008. *The Hollow Hope: Can Courts Bring about Social Change?*, 2nd ed. Chicago: University of Chicago Press.

Scalia, Antonin. 1997. *A Matter of Interpretation: Federal Courts and the Law*. Princeton, NJ: Princeton University Press.

Segal, Jeffrey A., and Harold J. Spaeth. 2002. *The Supreme Court and the Attitudinal Model Revisited*. New York: Cambridge University Press.

Silverstein, Gordon. 2009. *Law's Allure: How Law Shapes, Constrains, Saves, and Kills Politics*. New York: Cambridge University Press.

Smith, Rogers M. 1997. *Civic Ideals: Conflicting Visions of Citizenship in U.S. History*. New Haven, CT: Yale University Press.

Sunstein, Cass A. 1999. *One Case at a Time: Judicial Minimalism on the Supreme Court*. Cambridge, MA: Harvard University Press.

Tushnet, Mark. 1999. *Taking the Constitution Away from the Courts*. Princeton, NJ: Princeton University Press.

———. 2010. *Why the Constitution Matters*. New Haven, CT: Yale University Press.

VanBurkelo, Sandra F. 2001. *"Belonging to the World": Women's Rights and American Constitutional Culture*. New York: Oxford University Press.

Waldron, Jeremy. 1999. *Law and Disagreement*. New York: Oxford University Press.

Wert, Justin J. 2011. *Habeas Corpus in America: The Politics of Individual Rights*. Lawrence: University Press of Kansas.

Whittington, Keith E. 1999a. *Constitutional Construction: Divided Powers and Constitutional Meaning*. Cambridge, MA: Harvard University Press.

———. 1999b. *Constitutional Interpretation: Textual Meaning, Original Intent, and Judicial Review*. Lawrence: University Press of Kansas.

———. 2007. *Political Foundations of Judicial Supremacy: The President, the Supreme Court, and Constitutional Leadership in U.S. History*. Princeton, NJ: Princeton University Press.

Wunder, John R. 1994. *"Retained by the People": A History of American Indians and the Bill of Rights*. New York: Oxford University Press.

Yalof, David. 1999. *Pursuit of Justices: Presidential Politics and the Pursuit of Supreme Court Nominations*. Chicago: University of Chicago Press.

Zietlow, Rebecca E. 2006. *Enforcing Equality: Congress, the Constitution and the Protection of Individual Rights*. New York: New York University Press.

Part 2 **Development**

Chapter 2

The Colonial Era: Before 1776

I. Introduction

The American revolutionaries marched backward into the American Revolution.[1] When justifying their complaints against England and the British Parliament, such colonial leaders as Patrick Henry and Samuel Adams demanded that Americans have ancient rights restored, not new rights granted. The pamphlets American revolutionaries wrote, the resolutions they made, and the speeches they gave vigorously maintained that they were being denied the hard-won, well-established liberties of native-born Englishmen. James Otis of Massachusetts in 1764 spoke of "our rights as men and freeborn British subjects."[2] Benjamin Franklin and John Adams insisted that "the Colonists do not deserve to be deprived of the native right of Britons, the right of being taxed only by representatives chosen by themselves."[3] When the colonies urged residents of Quebec to send representatives to the Continental Congress, they presented themselves as the defenders of the longstanding English Constitution. Their "Appeal to the Inhabitants of Quebec" declared that existing constitutional protections for rights were sufficient to "defy time, tyranny, treachery, internal, and foreign wars."[4]

The first constitutional debates in America were debates about the British constitution. The Declaration of Independence was the last move in an extended dialogue between partisans of the colonies in North America and the partisans of the English authorities in London. The colonists and imperial officials offered competing interpretations of the British constitution to justify their actions, both to one another and to interested observers in North America and in the British Isles. As that dialogue progressed, the two sides found themselves drifting further apart. Their disagreements over taxes and trade soon exposed deeper constitutional disagreements. The Americans came to think that the English government had violated the British constitution—and that that constitution no longer suited their needs. They would have to adopt a new one.

Developments. Colonial Era constitutional debates built on and altered inherited English traditions. In doing so, they divided Patriot from Loyalist, American from English. What Otis, Franklin, Adams, and other colonists described as well-established liberties were consequences of recent political struggles. During the almost 160 years between the first settlement of the Jamestown Colony (1607) and the Declaration of Independence (1766), both Great Britain and the colonies experienced violent contests over what constituted the rights of Englishmen.

Political relationships were likewise revolutionized. While each of the colonies was tied to Britain, there were no formal connections among them. Proposals to organize the colonies as a collective hardly got off the ground until the eve of the American Revolution. The most notable plan emerged from a 1754 conference in Albany, New York. Largely the brainchild of Benjamin Franklin, it would have created a continental government to conduct war and trade, with the power to raise its own taxes and army. Despite the threat of war with

1. Quentin Skinner, *Visions of Politics: Regarding Method* (New York: Cambridge University Press, 2002), 149–50.

2. James Otis, *The Rights of the British Colonies Asserted and Proved*, in *Tracts of the American Revolution*, ed. Merrill Jensen (Indianapolis: Bobbs-Merrill, 1978), 24.

3. Daniel Leonard and John Adams, *Massachusettensis and Novanglus*, in *Tracts of the American Revolution* (see note 2), 307.

4. *Journals of the American Congress: From 1774 to 1788* (Washington, DC: Way and Gideon), 1:41.

Box 2-1 A Partial Cast of Characters of the Colonial Era

John Adams	■ Patriot ■ Author of important works on parliamentary authority over the colonies and constitutional government in the new republic ■ Influential member of the Continental Congress ■ First vice president under Federalist George Washington (1789–1801) ■ Last Federalist president of the United States (1797–1801) ■ Only president to be defeated for reelection until John Quincy Adams (1828)
Samuel Adams	■ Patriot ■ Newspaper writer critical of Parliament ■ Popular leader of protests against parliamentary taxes in the colonies ■ Member of Massachusetts' colonial assembly ■ Governor of Massachusetts (1793–1797) ■ Opposed ratification of the U.S. Constitution
William Penn	■ Converted to Quakerism ■ Became the most prominent writer defending the Quaker faith ■ Arrested for violating laws against Quaker meetings and publishing without a license ■ Founded Pennsylvania as a Quaker haven in 1683 ■ Drafted the Frame of Government of Pennsylvania, which included guarantees for religious liberty
James Otis	■ Patriot ■ Lawyer who argued against the legality of general writs of assistance before Massachusetts colonial court ■ Wrote prominent pamphlets on limits of parliamentary authority over colonies ■ Early proponent of judicial review
Roger Williams	■ Puritan ■ Separationist who favored complete separation of church and state ■ Fled England in 1630 ■ Convicted of sedition for questioning legitimacy of colonial charter ■ Exiled from Massachusetts Bay Colony in 1636 ■ Founded Rhode Island Colony on separationist principles in 1643

the French and their Native American allies, jealousies among the colonies and nervousness in Britain doomed the planned union. "Everybody cries, a Union is absolutely necessary," Franklin complained, "but when they come to the Manner and Form of the Union, their weak Noodles are perfectly distracted." The next year he proposed that the British *impose* a union on the colonies; otherwise they could "never expect to see an American War carried on as it ought to be." London declined.[5] Two decades passed before the colonists found a common enemy that pulled them together.

Factions (Parties and Interest Groups). Constitutional politics during the Colonial Era was structured by competition among factions. Political alliances in

5. Benjamin Franklin, *The Writings of Benjamin Franklin*, ed. Albert H. Smyth (New York: Macmillan, 1905), 3:242, 267.

England at the time the colonies were settled were based largely on relationships between powerful families and individuals. Colonial politics during most of the sixteenth and seventeenth centuries similarly consisted of struggles for power between families, rather than contests over political principles. Parties united by policy commitments first developed in England. By the seventeenth century, clear differences had emerged between Whigs, who favored greater parliamentary power, and Tories, who favored preserving more royal power. Members of these parties began coordinating their political actions and distributing the rewards of political success to fellow partisans.

The English Civil War, when Parliament rebelled against the king, and subsequent factional struggles in England shaped colonial understandings of fundamental rights and liberties. Americans were aware of the political upheavals taking place in England during the seventeenth century. They assumed that the liberties asserted in the 1689 English Bill of Rights belonged to them as English colonists. The more English politics became a struggle between Whigs and Tories for control of the government, the more Americans became convinced that governing officials in Great Britain no longer had the republican independence necessary for good governance.

Courts. Colonists looked more to juries than judges to protect their fundamental rights. The colonists regarded royally appointed judges as instruments of royal power. Juries were the bulwark of individual freedom. The colonists celebrated such English decisions as *Bushell's Case* (1670), which held that a judge could not imprison juries for declaring a defendant not guilty. A New York jury in *Zenger's Case* (1735) ignored the charge given by a royally appointed judge and protected the right of a printer to publish criticisms of the royal governor.

Judicial review was at most a gleam in the eye of a few justices and political activists. Lord Edward Coke asserted in *Dr. Bonham's Case* (1610), "The common law will control acts of parliament, and sometimes adjudge them to be utterly void."[6] Some colonists insisted that *Bonham's Case* established the precedential foundations for English courts to declare unconstitutional parliamentary edicts mandating the use of general warrants and other actions thought to violate what colonists believed were their constitutional rights as Englishmen. These pleas to the judiciary fell on deaf ears. No British or colonial court ever declared unconstitutional a law the colonists claimed violated their constitutional rights. William Blackstone expressed conventional English wisdom when he rejected judicial power to overturn legislation. His *Commentaries on the Laws of England* declared, "If the parliament will positively enact a thing to be done which is unreasonable, I know of no power in the ordinary forms of the constitution, that is vested with authority to control it."[7]

Constitutional Thought. American colonists were influenced by developments in English political thought during the seventeenth and eighteenth centuries. The English Civil War and the Glorious Revolution inspired two novel perspectives on the purpose of constitutional government. Liberalism was the first. John Locke and other liberal thinkers claimed that society was based on a social contract between free persons in a state of nature. The purpose of the government created by this contract was to protect certain natural rights, most notably life, liberty, and property. Republicanism was the second. James Harrington and other seventeenth-century republican thinkers understood freedom as self-government. Constitutions guaranteed that all citizens had the opportunity to participate in the political processes that determined what liberties were protected.

Most fundamental controversies in the Colonial Era were over which institution had the power to pass legislation regulating behavior. The English Bill of Rights limited only royal power to abridge rights. English liberty was protected as long as Parliament determined whether the public good required increased taxation or restrictions on free speech rights. Many Americans insisted that the principles underlying the English Bill of Rights supported their position that the rights of Englishmen in the colonies could be restricted only by institutions in which the colonists were represented. This is the meaning of the slogan, "No Taxation Without Representation." Other colonists advanced the more novel (for the time) position that no government official could violate certain natural rights. Such leading proponents of religious freedom as Roger Williams, the

6. *Dr. Bonham's Case*, 77 Eng. Rep. 646 (K.B.) 652; 8 Co. Rep. 107 a, 118 a (1610).

7. William Blackstone, *Blackstone's Commentaries on the Laws of England*, ed. St. George Tucker (Philadelphia: William Young Birch and Abraham Small, 1803), 1:90–91.

Table 2-1 Major Constitutional Issues and Statements of the Colonial Era

Major Political Issues	Major Constitutional Issues
English Civil War and Glorious Revolution	Magna Carta (1215)
Foundation of Plymouth Colony	English Bill of Rights (1689)
Foundation of Virginia Colony	Relationship between church and state
Growth of religious diversity	Prior restraint of publications
Maryland Toleration Act of 1649	Seditious libel
English restrictions on Quakers	Military exemptions for Quakers
Rise of slavery	*Somerset v. Stewart* (1773)
Liberal and republican political thought	Closer union of colonies
Rights of representation	Parliamentary taxation power in colonies
French and Indian War	Parliamentary trade regulation power in colonies
Closer union of colonies	Privy Council view of colonial laws
Sugar Act of 1764	Martial law
Stamp Act of 1768	Criticism of general search warrants
Quartering Act of 1768	Debate over confessions extracted through coercion
Townshend Revenue Act of 1767	Juries decide facts and law
Boston Port Act of 1774	New conception of constitutionalism
Massachusetts Government Act of 1774	
Independence of colonies	

founder of Rhode Island Colony, insisted, "All Civil States with their Officers of justice" are "not Judges, Governours or *Defenders* of the Spiritual or Christian state and Worship."[8]

Legacies. The central political debate of the era was over limits on the authority of Parliament in the colonies. On that issue, constitutional interpretation eventually gave way to revolution. The Americans stopped trying to live within the British constitution. Instead, in 1776, they drew on the British constitutional tradition to explain why they could no longer accept being bound by its terms. The Declaration of Independence gave the final American position: Parliament could have no authority in the thirteen colonies. From that point on, the constitutional debate would be exclusively American. It would focus on why revolution was justified and what a constitution drafted in America should look like.

8. Roger Williams, *The Bloudy Tenent* (London: n.p., 1644), 3.

The long political struggle with Britain before 1776 deepened American constitutional thought and practice. Americans developed their ideas about democracy and representation, federalism (the division of power between a central authority and regional or local governments), separation of powers (the division of responsibilities among the executive, legislative, and judicial branches), rights and liberties, and the nature of constitutionalism. The rights and liberties enumerated in the constitutions Americans ratified after the Revolution were those rights and liberties that had been contested in England and the colonies immediately prior to the Revolution.

II. Foundations

MAJOR DEVELOPMENTS

- First statutory declarations of fundamental rights
- Rise of liberal and republican political thought
- Debates over rights of representation

The American revolutionaries who demanded their rights engaged in practices that were both centuries old and novel. From at least 1215, the year the Magna Carta was written and signed, Englishmen had demanded that their king respect their rights. Over the years these rights became embodied in such parliamentary enactments as the English Bill of Rights (1689) and such common law judicial decisions as *Wilkes v. Wood* (1763). What changed was who demanded rights. Throughout much of English history, kings, aristocrats, and religious elites were the only persons who insisted that they had fundamental rights and liberties. The Magna Carta was a peace treaty between King John I and rebellious English barons. No prominent person at Runnymede, where that enactment was sealed, thought that the Magna Carta limited aristocrats' power to rule over ordinary people. Over time, more and more English subjects insisted that they also had fundamental rights, and by the time the colonies were settled, legal authorities recognized that the principles of the Magna Carta limited royal power over all persons, not just persons with a title. Over the next 150 years, liberal and republican political thinkers popularized claims that government was the product of a social contract in which all rulers promised to protect the fundamental rights of all people.

English authorities and prominent colonists disputed the parties to that social contract. Most English political thinkers regarded the social contract as being between the king and the people. Rights were limits on royal power, not limits on the power of the people's representatives in Parliament. The king could not censor speech, but Parliament could pass laws punishing those who advocated what the majority believed to be bad ideas. American political thinkers challenged two elements of English constitutional thought. First, they insisted that a Parliament in which the American colonies were not represented could not make binding law for American colonists. Second, they began to think of the social contract as binding popular majorities as well as the king. All citizens, in this view, were parties to the social contract. This meant that all governing institutions had to protect fundamental rights.

A. Sources

The English Constitution to which American colonists appealed in the eighteenth century was different from the Constitution to which Americans appeal in the twenty-first century. The English Constitution was (and still is) unwritten. That constitution consists of the statutes, judicial decisions, and customary practices that make up the fundamental laws of England. The English Bill of Rights is part of the English Constitution even though that enactment was passed by normal parliamentary procedures. Eighteenth-century English judges did not believe that they could determine whether parliamentary laws were inconsistent with their nation's constitution. Judges might strain to interpret laws as being consistent with what they believed to be fundamental constitutional principles, but the English Constitution was and is not judicially enforceable. English judges did not and do not declare laws unconstitutional.

American colonists looked to three particular sources for their constitutional rights and liberties. The first was English decrees, most notably the Magna Carta (1215), the Petition of Right (1628), and the English Bill of Rights (1689). These enactments established due process rights and the right not to be taxed without consent. The second source was common law decisions handed down during the late seventeenth and eighteenth centuries. Such decisions as *Ex parte Bushell* (1670) and *Wilkes v. Wood* (1763) established the right to trial by jury and forbade general warrants. The third source of rights was colonial charters and laws. The Connecticut Charter (1662), for example asserted, "That all, and every the Subjects of Us, . . . shall have and enjoy all Liberties and Immunities . . . as if they . . . were born within the realm of England." The Charter of Rhode Island and Providence Plantations (1663) guaranteed religious freedom. The Massachusetts Body of Liberties (1641) forbade "cruel and unusual punishments."

American colonists believed that the rights declared by various English decrees, common law decisions, and colonial charters were *constitutional* rights, even if they were not judicially enforceable or written down in a distinctive constitutional text. When colonists complained that Parliament was violating their rights, they typically complained that Parliament was violating their *constitutional* rights. "If she would strip us of all the advantages derived to us from the English constitution," one colonist declared, "why should we desire to continue our connection?"[9] James Otis

9. William Goddard (?), *The Constitutional Courant*, in *Tracts of the American Revolution* (see note 2), 91.

insisted that the basic rights of the American colonists were "founded on the principles of liberty and the British constitution." Furthermore, he claimed, "by this constitution, every man in the dominion is a free man," and "no parts of his Majesty's dominion can be taxed without their consent."[10]

B. Principles

Political liberals in the seventeenth and eighteenth centuries believed that government existed to protect individual rights. Thomas Hobbes and other English liberal philosophers maintained that government was a social contract between all inhabitants of a community. People agreed to a common ruler, usually a king, on the condition that the ruler protected their life, liberty, and property. Government officials who failed to protect life, liberty, and property forfeited their right to rule. Those they offended need not wait for God's justice in the afterlife. Citizens had the right to rebel against any monarch or governor who consistently refused to respect their liberties. Locke, the most influential political liberal of the seventeenth century, claimed in his *Second Treatise on Government* that these rights were derived from natural law. He stated, "MEN being, as has been said, by nature, all free, equal, and independent, no one can be put out of this estate, and subjected to the political power of another, without his own consent."[11] More commonly, English liberals assumed that government was obligated to respect certain time-honored rights set out in the Magna Carta and the English Bill of Rights.

Republican thinkers in the seventeenth and eighteenth centuries emphasized the importance of political participation and civic virtue. Such thinkers as James Harrington and Jean-Jacques Rousseau asserted that people were free to the extent that they were self-governing. Republicans believed that the most fundamental liberty people enjoyed was the right to participate in the political process. Maximilian Petty, a seventeenth-century English radical, declared, "We judge that all inhabitants that have not lost their birthright should have an equal voice in elections."[12] Consider the famous expression, "No Taxation Without Representation." The colonists who made this assertion were not objecting to exorbitant taxation. That would be a liberal claim. Rather, they insisted that people could be taxed only with the permission of their elected representatives. Republican political thought is more concerned with the processes by which political decisions are made than with the substance of those decisions. Classical republicans are also more concerned with promoting the public good than with individual rights. Gordon Wood notes, "Liberty was realized when the citizens were virtuous—that is, willing to sacrifice their private interests for the sake of the community, including serving in public office without pecuniary rewards."[13]

The leading liberal and republican thinkers during the seventeenth and eighteenth centuries agreed that rights holders could be limited by nationality, religion, race, gender, class, and other characteristics. The English Bill of Rights discusses the rights of Englishmen. Whether colonists enjoyed those rights was contested. Frenchmen and Spaniards had to look elsewhere for their liberties. John Locke's influential *Letter Concerning Toleration* limited religious freedom to members of Protestant sects. Most classical liberal and republican thinkers believed that women and persons of color were incapable of exercising certain fundamental rights. Many believed that only property holders could exercise certain rights.

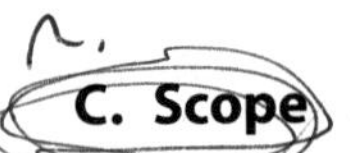

C. Scope

American colonists enjoyed the rights of Englishmen. The common law was clear on this point. Chief Justice Edward Coke stated in *Calvin's Case* (1608) that English subjects who moved to English territory retained the same rights they had enjoyed in England. He wrote, "In the case of . . . conquest, . . . the King's subjects . . . are capable of lands in the kingdom or country conquered, and may maintain any real action, and have the like privileges and benefits there, as they may have in England."[14] Most English authorities agreed that Englishmen who moved to England's colonies in the Americas did not surrender their rights as Englishmen.

10. James Otis, *The Rights of the British Colonies Asserted and Proved*, in *Tracts of the American Revolution* (see note 2), 22, 39.

11. John Locke, *Two Treatises on Government* (London: R. Butler, 1821), 269.

12. Newton Key and Robert Bucholz, eds., *Sources and Debates in English History, 1485–1715*, 2nd ed. (San Francisco: Wiley-Blackwell, 2009), 189.

13. Gordon Wood, *The Radicalism of the American Revolution* (Knopf: New York, 1991), 104.

14. *Calvin's Case*, 77 Eng. Rep. 377, 398 (K.B.); 7 Co. Rep. 1 a, 17 b (1608).

Immigrants enjoyed the same rights and privileges. When the colonies naturalized settlers from France, Germany, and other European countries, those persons gained the same rights they would have obtained had they been naturalized in England.

English legal authorities maintained that people in both London and Boston had to pay whatever taxes Parliament thought appropriate. That no colonist could vote for any representative in Parliament was of no legal or constitutional significance. Very few English subjects who resided in England during the eighteenth century voted in parliamentary elections. Parliament was expected to represent the interests of all English subjects, whether or not they voted, and no matter where they resided. The political theory of the time regarded American colonists, as well as Englishmen without the vote, as virtually represented in Parliament. People are virtually represented in a legislature when governing officials can be trusted to consider their interests fairly. Thomas Whatley, the member of Parliament most responsible for the Stamp Act of 1765, relied on the principle of virtual representation when defending the right of Parliament to tax the colonies. He asserted,

> The fact is, that the inhabitants of the colonies are represented in Parliament; they do not indeed choose the members of that assembly; neither are nine tenths of the people of *Britain* electors; for the right of election is annexed to certain species of property, to peculiar franchises, and to inhabitancy in some particular places; but these descriptions comprehend only a very small part of the land, the property, and the people of this island. . . . All British Subjects are really in the same; none are actually, all are virtually represented in Parliament; for every Member of Parliament sits in the House not as a representative of his own constituents, but as one of that august Assembly by which all the commons of *Great Britain* are represented.[15]

By the 1750s and 1760s, many prominent colonists were no longer satisfied with being virtually represented in Parliament. Such revolutionaries as Patrick Henry in Virginia and Samuel Adams in Massachusetts insisted that the right of Englishmen to be taxed only with their consent meant that the colonies either had to be represented in Parliament or could be taxed only by the local colonial legislature. In 1768 Adams drafted a protest on behalf of the colonial legislature in Massachusetts explicitly asserting that the Stamp Act and other taxes imposed by Parliament violated the right of English subjects in the colonies to be taxed only with the consent of their representatives. The Massachusetts Circular Letter of February 11, 1768, declared,

> It is moreover their humble opinion, which they express with the greatest deference to the wisdom of the Parliament that the acts made there imposing duties of the people of this province with the sole & express purpose of raising a revenue, are infringements of their natural & constitutional rights because as they are not represented in the British Parliament, His Majesty's Commons in Britain, by those acts, grant their property without their consent.
>
> The House further are of the opinion that their constituents considering their local circumstances cannot by any possibility be represented in the Parliament, & that it will forever be impracticable that they should be equally represented there & consequently not at all; being separated by an ocean of a thousand leagues: and that his Majesty's royal predecessors for this reason were graciously pleased to form a subordinate legislature here that their subjects might enjoy the unalienable right of a representation.[16]

III. Judicial Power and Constitutional Authority

MAJOR DEVELOPMENTS

- Debate over the supreme legal authority of Parliament
- Suggestion that courts have the right to declare statutes unconstitutional

Everyone recognized that it was possible to debate whether Parliament had violated the British constitution. What was not generally recognized in Britain in the mid-eighteenth century were legal limits on

15. Thomas Whately, *The Regulations Lately Made Concerning the Colonies, and the Taxes Imposed upon Them, Considered*, 3rd ed. (London: J. Wilkie, 1775), 101–10.

16. Harry Alonzo Cushing, ed., *The Writings of Samuel Adams* (New York: G. P. Putnam's Sons, 1904), 1:184–88.

Parliament that could be judicially enforced. There was no *judicial review*. There were things that Parliament *should* not do, but there was nothing that Parliament *could* not do.

The colonists challenged that basic assumption. Many argued that colonial and British courts could refuse to enforce an act of Parliament that they thought violated the Constitution. This suggestion was not universally accepted even in the colonies, but it was at least taken seriously. If judicial review is one of the great innovations of American constitutionalism, it was contemplated more than a decade before the Revolution.

Some form of judicial review felt natural—in part because the colonists had already experienced it. Colonial charters routinely guaranteed the liberties that the settlers would have enjoyed in England. The charters also prohibited the colonial assembly from making policies that were contrary to the laws of England and allowed appeals in legal cases from colonial courts to the Privy Council, a precursor to the modern British cabinet. This group of advisors to the monarch served as a kind of supreme court. More important, colonial assemblies were required to send a copy of their laws to the Privy Council for its approval. The Privy Council was concerned with ensuring the supremacy of English law across the empire, along with a reasonable uniformity. It wished to prevent the colonies from making policies that would undercut the policies being pursued by England.

In addition to looking out for English interests, the Privy Council was also active in blocking the colonial assemblies from violating traditional English liberties. Criminalizing "Devilish practices," for example, was too vague to satisfy the requirements of due process. The Privy Council agreed with Quaker complaints when Connecticut required that they be taxed to support Puritan ministers; this violated the charter's protection of liberty of conscience. The Council slapped down assemblies that tried to impose outcomes in legal cases or to issue bills of attainder, which impose criminal punishments on individuals without trials.[17]

To bolster their view that Parliament was hedged in by legal boundaries, the colonists reached back into English legal history. Pride of place was given to a controversial 1610 judicial opinion by Lord Edward Coke in *Dr. Bonham's Case*. Coke argued that "it appears in our books, that in many cases, the common law will control acts of parliament, and sometimes adjudge them to be utterly void: for when an act of parliament is against common right and reason, or repugnant, or impossible to be performed, the common law will control it, and adjudge such act to be void."[18] Yet by the end of the seventeenth century—after the Glorious Revolution in which Parliament won its supremacy over the king—there was still no notion of constitutional review of Parliament. At least from the perspective of Chief Justice John Holt, sitting on the King's Bench in 1702, "an act of Parliament can do no wrong, though it may do several things that look pretty odd."[19] The law professor William Blackstone captured the consensus in England at the time of the American Revolution: the authority of Parliament was absolute and could not be questioned in any court.

To stop what they saw as parliamentary abuses, the colonists took the first tentative steps toward inventing judicial review. Full realization of that power would have to await independence, when legal charters could not be set aside at the whim of a foreign sovereign. But it was a powerful idea about what the role of a judge in a constitutional system might be. The colonists urged colonial judges not to enforce laws that were inconsistent with the constitution. Coke at least hinted that "acts of parliament" could be judged "void" in a court of law. The Massachusetts lawyer James Otis invoked *Bonham's Case* when arguing that the colonial courts should intervene when English officials acted illegally.

William Blackstone, Commentaries on the Laws of England (1765)[20]

William Blackstone was a professor of law at Oxford University, and his lectures there became the basis of the Commentaries. *The* Commentaries *aimed to synthesize the English laws. Though it attracted some critics, the treatise was quickly taken as authoritative throughout the British Empire. The* Commentaries *became the cornerstone of American understanding of the British common law that they had in-*

17. Elmer Beecher Russell, *The Review of American Colonial Legislation by the King in Council* (New York: Columbia University Press, 1915), 141–52.

18. *Dr. Bonham's Case*, 8 Co. Rep. 107a, 118a (1610).

19. *City of London v. Wood*, 12 Mod. 669, 688 (1702).

20. Excerpt taken from St. George Tucker, ed., *Blackstone's Commentaries* (Philadelphia: William Young Birch and Abraham Small, 1803), 1:108–10, 2:160–62.

Illustration 2-1 Sir William Blackstone

Source: Samuel Bellin, engraver (1799–1893), *Sir William Blackstone*. Emmet Collection, Miriam and Ira D. Wallach Division of Art, Prints and Photographs, The New York Public Library, Astor, Lenox and Tilden Foundations.

herited and incorporated into their own legal and constitutional system, but Blackstone's conception of legislative authority was not so easily accepted in America.

St. George Tucker was variously a state and federal judge in Virginia after independence, a professor of law at the College of William and Mary, and a states' rights Jeffersonian. Tucker published a popular American edition of Blackstone's commentaries in 1803 that included his extended commentary on the U.S. Constitution, along with critical notes on Blackstone. We include some of Tucker's footnotes here, along with Blackstone's text. Blackstone argued that there were no legal limits on the power of the English Parliament of the late eighteenth century. Parliamentary power was absolute. The colonists struggled with Blackstone's claim during the Revolutionary Era, but after the Revolution, they were free to take a different path. In a footnote to Blackstone, St. George Tucker argues that the American constitutions can be distinguished from the British one by being "acts of the people, and not of government." Is this difference enough to support judicial review? Is Tucker successful in his effort to separate American constitutionalism from these parts of Blackstone?

I know it is generally laid down more largely, that acts of parliament contrary to reason are void.[21] But if the parliament will positively enact a thing to be done which is

21. One would imagine that it could not be deemed any great stretch of the freedom of opinion, to pronounce that any legislative act which prescribes a thing contrary to reason, is void; yet the caution of the learned commentator [Blackstone] on this occasion is certainly conformable to the principles of the British government; in which, it seems to be agreed by all their Jurists, the authority of parliament is absolute and uncontrollable; insomuch that it may alter or change the constitution itself. But, in America, the constitutions, both of the individual states, and of the federal government, being the acts of the people, and not of the government . . . the legislature can possess, no power, or obligation over the other branches of government, in any case, where the principles of the Constitution, may be in any degree infringed by an acquiescence under the authority of the legislative department. . . . [Footnote by Tucker]

unreasonable, I know of no power in the ordinary forms of the constitution, that is vested with authority to control it; and the examples usually alleged in support of this sense of the rule do none of them prove, that, where the main object of a statute is unreasonable, the judges are at liberty to reject it; for that were to set the judicial power above that of the legislature, which would be subversive of all government. But where some collateral matter arises out of the general words, and happens to be unreasonable; there the judges are in decency to conclude that this consequence was not foreseen by the parliament, and therefore they are at liberty to expound the statute by equity, and only *quoad hoc* [to this extent] disregard it. . . . [T]here is no court that has power to defeat the intent of the legislature, when couched in such evident and express words, as leave no doubt whether it was the intent of the legislature or no.

. . .

. . . [O]ur more distant plantations [colonies] in America, and elsewhere, are also in some respect subject to English laws. . . . But this must be understood with very many and very great restrictions. Such colonists carry with them only so much of the English law, as is applicable to their own situation and the condition of an infant colony; such, for instance, as the general rules of inheritance, and of protection from personal injuries. . . . The artificial refinements and distinctions incident to the property of a great and commercial people, the laws of police and revenue, (such especially as are enforced by penalties) . . . are neither necessary nor convenient for them, and therefore are not in force. What shall be admitted and what rejected, at what times, and under what restrictions, must, in case of dispute, be decided in the first instance by their own provincial judicature, subject to the revision and control of the king in council: the whole of their constitution being also liable to be new-modeled and reformed by the general superintending power of the legislature in the mother country. . . .

. . .

The power and jurisdiction of parliament, says Sir Edward Coke, is so transcendent and absolute, that it cannot be confined, either for causes or persons, within any bounds. . . It hath sovereign and uncontrollable authority in the making, confirming, enlarging, restraining, abrogating, repealing, reviving and expounding of laws, concerning matters of all possible denominations, ecclesiastical, or temporal, civil, military, maritime, or criminal; this being the place where that absolute despotic power, which must, in all governments,[22] reside somewhere, is entrusted by the constitution of these kingdoms. All mischiefs and grievances, operations and remedies, that transcend the ordinary course of the laws, are within the reach of this extraordinary tribunal. It can regulate or new model the succession to the crown. . . . It can alter the established religion of the land. . . . It can change and create afresh even the constitution of the kingdom and of parliaments themselves; as was done by the act of union, and the several statutes for triennial and septennial elections. It can, in short, do everything that is not naturally impossible; and, therefore, some have not scrupled to call its power, by a figure rather too bold, the omnipotence of parliament.[23] True it is, that what the parliament doth, no authority upon earth can undo. So that it is a matter most essential to the liberties of this kingdom, that such members be delegated to this important trust, as are most eminent for their probity, their fortitude, and their knowledge. . . .

It must be owned that Mr. Locke, and other theoretical writers, have held that "there remains still inherent in the people a supreme power to remove or alter the legislative, when they find the legislative act contrary to the trust reposed in them: for, when such trust is abused, it is thereby forfeited, and devolves to those who gave it."[24] But, however, just this conclusion may be, in theory, we cannot practically adopt it, nor take any *legal* steps for carrying it into execution, under any dispensation of government at present actually existing. For this devolution of power, to the people at large, includes in it a dissolution of the whole

---

22. In the United States this absolute power is not delegated to the government: it remains with the people, whose safety requires that the government which they have themselves established, should be limited. "The powers not delegated to the United States by the constitution, nor prohibited by it to the states, are reserved to the states respectively, or to the people." Amendments to the C. U.S. Art. 12 [now the 10th Amendment]. [Footnote by Tucker]

23. Since, according to the fundamental principles of both the Federal and State Constitution, and Government, the supreme power . . . resides in the people, it follows that it is the right of the people to make laws. But as the exercise of that Right by the people at large would be equally inconvenient and impracticable, the constitution of the State has vested that power in the General Assembly of the Commonwealth. . . . It is from these express provisions both in the State, and Federal Constitutions, and not from metaphysical deduction, that the State, and Federal Legislatures derive the power of making Laws. . . . [Footnote by Tucker]

24. This principle is expressly recognized in our government. Amendments to C. U.S. Art. 11, 12. See Declaration of Independence, and Virginia Bill of Rights, Art. 3. [Footnote by Tucker]

form of government established by the people. . . . So long, therefore, as the English constitution lasts, we may venture to affirm, that the power of parliament is absolute and without control.

Massachusetts Assembly Memorial (1764)[25]

Samuel Adams in 1764 drafted instructions for the Boston delegates to the Massachusetts House of Representatives calling on them to work for the immediate repeal of the Sugar Act. The instructions expressed particular concern with the precedent that the Sugar Act was setting: "If our trade may be taxed, why not our lands? . . . This we apprehend annihilates our charter right to govern and tax ourselves."[26] James Otis was one of those delegates, and he in turn drafted the Memorial, which was passed by the House and sent to London. The Memorial includes the development of a theory of judicial review that did not depend on the existence of a written constitution.

James Otis had been the advocate general for the vice-admiralty court in the Massachusetts Colony, whose jurisdiction included enforcing the Navigation Acts that regulated colonial overseas trade. Otis deplored broke with the administration over the use of writs of assistance, which authorized customs agents looking for smugglers to conduct forcible searches on their own initiative of private property throughout the Boston area. In 1761, Otis appealed to the Superior Court, asking it to refuse to issue such writs on the grounds that they were unconstitutional. Otis's argument stood out for its reference to Dr. Bonham's Case *as an English precedent for the power of judicial review. Chief Judge Thomas Hutchinson rejected that power. He later recounted,*

> *The Stamp duty, although I always feared the consequence of it would be bad, both to the nation & colonies, and privately & publicly declared my thoughts upon it, yet after the passing the act I could not avoid considering it legally right, the Parliament being beyond dispute the supreme legislature of the British dominions; but our friends to liberty take advantage of a maxim they find in Lord Coke that an act of Parliament against Magna Charta or the peculiar rights of Englishmen is ipso facto void. This, taken in the latitude the people are often disposed to take it, must be fatal to all Government & it seems to have determined great part of the colonies to oppose the execution of the act with force & to show their resentment against all in authority who will not join with them.*[27]

Why did both Blackstone and Thomas Hutchinson think that the doctrine that "an act of Parliament against Magna Charta or the peculiar right of Englishmen is ipso facto void" would be "fatal to all government"? What are the dangers of such a doctrine? Within the British constitutional system, who would have the right to say that an act of Parliament was unconstitutional?

. . .

The absolute rights of Englishmen, as frequently declared in Parliament, from Magna Charta to this time, are the rights of *personal security, personal liberty,* and of *private property.*

. . .

It is presumed, that upon these principles, the colonists have been by their several charters declared natural subjects, and entrusted with the power of making *their own local laws,* not repugnant to the laws of England, and with *the power of taxing themselves.*

This legislative power is subject by the same charter to the King's negative, as in Ireland. This effectually secures the *dependence* of the colonies on Great-Britain. . . .

. . .

. . . The common law is received and practiced upon here, and in the rest of the colonies; and all ancient and modern acts of Parliament that can be considered as part of, or in amendment of the common law, together with all such acts of Parliament as expressly name the plantations; so that the power of the British Parliament is held as sacred and as uncontrollable in the colonies as in England. The question is not upon the general power or right of the Parliament, but whether right it is not circumscribed within some equitable and reasonable bounds? It is hoped it will not be considered a new doctrine, that even the authority of the Parliament of *Great-Britain* is circumscribed by certain bounds, which if exceeded, their acts become

25. Excerpt taken from the appendix to James Otis, *The Rights of the British Colonies Asserted and Proved* (Boston: Edes and Gill, 1764), 70–80.

26. John Adams, in Charles Francis Adams, ed., *The Works of John Adams* (Boston: Little, Brown and Company, 1856), 10:294.

27. Quoted in Horace Gray, "Appendix," in Josiah Quincy, ed., *Reports of Cases* (Boston: Little, Brown and Co., 1865), 415, 441.

those of mere *power* without *right*, and consequently void. The judges of England have declared in favor of these sentiments when they expressly declare, that *acts of Parliament against natural equity are void*. That *acts against the fundamental principles of the British constitution are void*.[28] This doctrine is agreeable to the law of nature and nations, and to the divine dictates of natural and revealed religion. It is contrary to reason that the supreme power should have right to alter the constitution. This would imply that those who are entrusted with sovereignty by the people have a right to do as they please. In other words, that those who are invested with power to protect the people, and support their rights and liberties, have a right to make slaves of them. This is not very remote from a flat contradiction. . . .

It is now near three hundred years since the continent of North America was first discovered, and that by British subjects. Ten generations have passed away through infinite toils and bloody conflicts in settling this country. None of those ever dreamed but that they were entitled at least to equal privileges with those of the same rank born within the realm.

John Dickinson, Letters from a Farmer in Pennsylvania (1768)[29]

John Dickinson was a philosophically attuned lawyer and politician in Philadelphia. Though a defender of the proprietary government of Pennsylvania against critics such as Benjamin Franklin, he opposed parliamentary taxation of the colonies. Dickinson was slow to embrace the call for American independence, but he became a key drafter of the first federal constitution after independence, the Articles of Confederation. These newspaper articles, published pseudonymously as Letters from a Farmer, *were particularly concerned with the Townshend Act. In this letter, Dickinson addresses the issue of whether the taxes were too small to justify the level of protest that was building in the colonies. When can constitutional violations be overlooked? What are the consequences of accepting a constitutional violation? Should we be as concerned about constitutionally questionable legislation that is of little or no practical consequence? Is Dickinson right to think that how power is "checked and controlled" is more important than how it is actually "exercised"?*

Letter VII

. . .

. . . [I]n truth, all men are subject to frailties of nature; and therefore whatever regard we entertain for *persons* of those who govern us, we should always remember that their conduct as *rulers*, may be influenced by human infirmities.

. . . Where these laws are to bind *themselves*, it may be expected, that the House of Commons will very carefully consider them: But when they are making laws that are not designed to bind *themselves*, we cannot imagine that their deliberations will be as cautious and scrupulous, as in their own case.

. . .

Some persons may think this act of no consequence, because the duties are so *small*. A fatal error. *That* is the very circumstance most alarming to me. For I am convinced, that the authors of this law would never have obtained an act to raise so trifling a sum as it must do, had they not intended by *it* to establish a *precedent* for future use. To console ourselves with the *smallness* of the duties, is to walk deliberately into the snare that is set for us, praising the *neatness* of the workmanship. Suppose the duties imposed by the late act could be paid by these distressed colonies with the utmost ease, and that the purposes to which they are to be applied, were the most reasonable and equitable that can be conceived . . . yet even in such a supposed case, these colonies ought to regard the act with abhorrence. For WHO ARE A FREE PEOPLE? Not *those*, over whom government is reasonably and equitably exercised, but those, who live under a government so *constitutionally checked and controlled*, that proper provision is made against its being otherwise exercised.

The late act is founded on the destruction of this constitutional security. If the Parliament has a right to lay a duty of four shillings and eight-pence on a hundred weight of glass, or a ream of paper, they have a right to lay a duty of any other sum on either. . . . In short, if they have a right *to* levy a tax of *one penny* upon us, they have a right to levy a *million* upon us: For where does their right stop? . . .

28. Here Otis inserted a long footnote citing *Dr. Bonham's Case* and other authorities.

29. Excerpt taken from John Dickinson, *Letters from a Farmer in Pennsylvania, to the Inhabitants of the British Colonies* (Philadelphia: David Hall and William Sellers, 1768), 33–38.

IV. Powers of the National Government

MAJOR DEVELOPMENTS

- The debate over the scope of English authority over the internal policy of the colonies
- The struggle over Parliament's right to represent the colonists and impose internal taxes
- The question of whether the colonies should be independent of England

The primary constitutional debate of the Colonial Era—the one that drove all others and eventually led to the Declaration of Independence—was over the extent of Parliament's policy-making authority over the colonies. In this, there were two closely intertwined issues.

The first issue was the precursor to the federalism debate that has echoed down through all of American history. How much power does and should the central government have? In the imperial context prior to 1776, this meant how much control the British government should have over public policy in the North American colonies. Was British authority absolute? Could the Parliament or the monarch dictate any policy in the colonies, or were there constitutional limits on their authority in North America? Were there areas of public policy or particular governmental powers that were under the exclusive control of local colonial governments? Was drawing a line between the scope of British authority and the scope of colonial authority possible? Or would any attempt to do so give way in one direction or the other—either to absolute British domination or to colonial independence? Could there be federalism within the constitution of the British Empire?

The second issue arose from the first. This was essentially a debate about the nature and meaning of representative government. Were the colonies adequately represented in Parliament, and did that make a difference in how much policy-making authority Parliament had over colonial affairs? This is what the cry of "No Taxation Without Representation" was about. If the colonists were not represented in Parliament, then the principles of the British Constitution dictated that Parliament did not have the right to tax the colonists. Since the colonists did not elect any members of Parliament, the challenge for the defenders of parliamentary authority was to show that the British legislature adequately represented their interests anyway. Taxation was the flashpoint for the debate, but the colonists had already begun to question whether their interests were represented in more than just local assemblies. Once they did, they soon began asking whether Parliament should have any say in North American affairs. If Parliament did not represent American interests, then Parliament should not tax Americans. If that was true, then should Parliament make trade, military, or social policy for Americans?

Colonial thinking evolved over the course of the 1760s and 1770s. It went from emphasizing that certain kinds of taxes imposed by the British Parliament were unconstitutional to arguing that Parliament had no authority in the colonies. It went from arguing that the colonists were subject only to the king to concluding that the Americans owed no allegiance to England at all. Samuel Adams in Massachusetts helped push the line, later joined by such young lawyers as John Adams and Thomas Jefferson. As early as 1768, Samuel Adams helped pen a public letter protesting the Townshend Act, arguing that the colonists' "local circumstances cannot by any possibility be represented in the Parliament."[30] As tensions mounted and London declared martial law in Boston to enforce English taxes, the possibility and legitimacy of English rule in the American colonies was increasingly put into question. A debate over centralization gave way to a debate over independence.

V. Separation of Powers

MAJOR DEVELOPMENTS

- Use of the power of the purse by the legislature to check colonial governors

British authorities generally exercised their influence over the colonies most directly through the governor, the personal representative of the crown (in the royal colonies), or the proprietor (in the proprietary colonies). The governor was usually advised by a council, or upper legislative chamber, and had the power to appoint judges and executive officers within the colony.

The colonists were generally represented in a lower legislative chamber, the members of which were locally elected. Laws, taxes, and appropriations from the colonial treasury had to pass through the legislature but were subject to an absolute gubernatorial veto, which could not be overridden by a subsequent legislative vote.

30. Samuel Adams, "Massachusetts Circular Letter, February 11, 1768," in *Writings of Samuel Adams* (see note 16), 1:188.

The popular assembly held the power of the purse in the colonial government, but the governor held the power of appointment and veto. Colonial governors not only needed to run the government, but also hoped to be compensated generously for their public service. The assemblies' jealously controlled the purse strings and used their authority, modeled on Parliament's, to keep the governor in check. The governors sometimes called on English authorities to grant them fiscal independence from the assembly. London declined to do so until the colonies were nearly in open revolt against the crown in the 1770s. As resistance to the enforcement of the Townshend Act and the collection of its taxes grew, Massachusetts governor Thomas Hutchinson, on the basis of royal instructions, suspended the state's General Assembly. In the summer of 1772, he announced that the assembly would no longer control his salary and that the colonial government would now be funded by a parliamentary tax. Under pressure from the tax crisis, the English authorities finally made the governor financially independent of the colonial legislature. Within two years, Parliament had suspended the Massachusetts Colony's charter and replaced Hutchinson with a military governor.

VI. Individual Rights

MAJOR DEVELOPMENTS

- Establishment of the principle that government cannot take private property without compensation
- Increased recognition of the freedom of religion
- Development of the right to bear arms
- Substantial morals regulation

Englishmen and American colonists believed that government should protect individual rights. The persons who instigated the English Civil War and the American Revolution insisted that rebellion was justified because governing authorities had violated fundamental liberties. Nevertheless, individual rights claims in the seventeenth and eighteenth centuries differed from many rights claims at the turn of the twenty-first century. Contemporary Americans tend to conceive of rights as limits on all government officials. No government official may violate our freedom of speech or interfere with our intimate affairs. By contrast, the English Bill of Rights conceptualized rights as limits only against *executive* action or abuse. The king could not levy taxes, disarm good citizens, or interfere with debate in Parliament, but Parliament could tax citizens as representatives saw fit. Elected officials could adopt other restrictions on individual action that the people's representatives thought contributed to the public good.

Colonial Americans and their British counterparts believed that government in a free society should provide substantial protection for property rights. English political theorists and the American colonists maintained that property guaranteed independence. Persons who owned land or freeholds were self-sustaining, able to earn a living without relying on other persons. "Liberty," Americans proclaimed, "consists in an independency upon the will of another," and a slave was a person "who depends upon the will of another for the enjoyment of his life and property."[31] Confident that only property holders were truly free, American colonies restricted the franchise to persons who owned property—often, considerable property. Few explicit protections for property rights were thought necessary when colonial legislatures tended to be composed of those local notables who owned the most property.

A. Property

Englishmen and American colonists on the eve of the American Revolution believed that persons had three fundamental property rights:

1. Government could not confiscate property.
2. Government could take property for a public purpose only when government paid the fair value of that property to the original property holder.
3. Government could not tax a person without the consent of that person as manifested by the people's representatives.

William Blackstone elaborated on these property rights in his *Commentaries on the Laws of England*. The section on property states,

> The third absolute right, inherent in every Englishman, is that of property: which consists in the free use, enjoyment, and disposal of all his acquisitions, without any control or diminution, save only by the laws of the land.... Upon this principle the great charter [Magna Carta] has declared that no freeman

31. Wood, *Radicalism*, 179.

shall be disseised, or divested, of his freehold, or of his liberties, or free customs, but by the judgment of his peers, or by the law of the land. . . . So great moreover is the regard of the law for private property, that it will not authorize the least violation of it; no, not even for the general good of the whole community. If a new road, for instance, were to be made through the grounds of a private person, it might perhaps be extensively beneficial to the public; but the law permits no man, or set of men, to do this without consent of the owner of the land. In vain may it be urged, that the good of the individual ought to yield to that of the community; for it would be dangerous to allow any private man, or even any public tribunal, to be the judge of this common good, and to decide whether it be expedient or no. Besides, the public good is in nothing more essentially interested, than in the protection of every individual's private rights, as modeled by the municipal law. In this and similar cases the legislature alone can, and indeed frequently does, interpose, and compel the individual to acquiesce. But how does it interpose and compel? Not by absolutely stripping the subject of his property in an arbitrary manner; but by giving him a full indemnification and equivalent for the injury thereby sustained. The public is now considered as an individual, treating with an individual for an exchange. All that the legislature does is to oblige the owner to alienate his possessions for a reasonable price; and even this is an exertion of power, which the legislature indulges with caution, and which nothing but the legislature can perform. Nor is this the only instance in which the law of the land has postponed even public necessity to the sacred and inviolable rights of private property. For no subject of England can be constrained to pay any aids or taxes, even for the defence of the realm or the support of government, but such as are imposed by his own consent, or that of his representatives in parliament.[32]

B. Religion

Both England and the colonies were wracked by religious disputes during the seventeenth century and the first part of the eighteenth century. Conventional wisdom in 1600 maintained that government should advance the one true religion. In England this meant the Anglican, or Episcopalian, Church. Government officials appointed Anglican ministers, paid their salaries, sponsored Anglican religious ceremonies, and required all subjects to worship God in a manner consistent with Anglican doctrines. Blackstone's *Commentaries* detailed the numerous offenses against religion that proponents of the union between the English state and the Anglican Church demanded government officials punish. Over the next 150 years, prominent voices challenged this union. Some, like the Puritans who founded the Massachusetts Bay Colony, believed wholeheartedly in the union of church and state but thought that England had established the wrong church. They left England because they were convinced that their version of Protestantism was the one true religion that ought to be established. Other religious dissenters accepted establishment but called for some tolerance for religious dissenters in order to preserve the peace. The Maryland Toleration Act declared that government should not "molest" any form of private Christian worship. John Locke, Roger Williams, William Penn, and their followers went further. They insisted that government and government officials had no business advancing the one true religion. Religion, in their view, was a private matter between God and an individual's conscience.

These struggles were eventually settled in favor of an increased commitment to greater religious freedom in both England and the American colonies:

- The colonies on the eve of the American Revolution provided far less support for religion and mandated far less religious observance than had been the case during the years when those colonies were established.
- American colonists were increasingly likely to tolerate all major Protestant sects, although many colonies still imposed significant disabilities on Catholics and Jews.
- A few colonies, most notably Rhode Island, recognized the right to free exercise of religion.
- American colonists debated whether the freedom of conscience required that government give special exemptions to members of such sects as the Quakers, who had religious objections to taking certain oaths and bearing arms.

These developments reflected the increased influence of liberal ideas on colonial politics, changes in Protestant

32. Blackstone, *Commentaries*, 2:138–39.

religious commitments, and the brute fact of religious diversity in the colonies. Such political liberals as John Locke insisted that religion was a private affair. Locke's *Letter on Toleration* maintained that government ought to be concerned with protecting rights, not promoting religious observance. Roger Williams, a devout Protestant, reached the same conclusion for more sectarian reasons. His 1644 book *The Bloudy Tenent* asserted that religious coercion was inconsistent with religious obligations. Religious diversity made establishments difficult. In sharp contrast to England in 1600, most American colonies by 1750 lacked a religious majority capable of maintaining a strong union between a particular religious sect and the state. Tolerance was as much a pragmatic political necessity as a deeply felt commitment. Many arguments for religious toleration, in both England and the colonies, emphasized the costs of religious warfare.

Proponents of the traditional union between church and state maintained that government should promote religious belief and that widespread religious faith was necessary to ensure a virtuous citizenry. Government and church cooperated to maintain and spread the one true religion. "Christianity," William Blackstone claimed, "is a part of the laws of England."[33] The Virginia Colony required that all ministers preach in a manner consistent with the "doctrines, rights, and religion now professed and established within the realme of England." Massachusetts in the seventeenth century was governed by a religious theocracy, whose members punished all conduct inconsistent with their conception of Christianity. Government in the seventeenth century had two means for enforcing religious conformity. First, the law compelled persons to attend specific religious services and prohibited the religious practices of rival sects. Virginia in 1611 passed laws requiring all persons to attend church. Massachusetts in the seventeenth century executed alleged witches and confessed Quakers. Second, the colonies imposed secular burdens on members of disfavored religions. Many colonies compelled voters or officeholders to take an oath that they believed in the divinity of Jesus Christ. Some colonies insisted that officeholders swear that they rejected elements of the Catholic faith. One common oath required public officials to declare, "I do believe that there is not any transubstantiation in the Sacrament of the Lord's Supper, or in the Elements of Bread and Wine, at or after the Consecration thereof, by any person whatever."

Proponents of religious toleration criticized these restrictions. The most common attack on religious conformity in the seventeenth century was rooted in religious belief. Roger Williams and John Locke believed that true Christianity was inconsistent with both state support for religion and religious coercion. William Penn, the Quaker who founded the Pennsylvania Colony, maintained that laws requiring religious conformity violated God's law. Penn's essay "The Great Case of Liberty of Conscience" asserted, "The Imposition, Restraint, and Persecution, for Matters relating to Conscience, directly invade the Divine Prerogative, and Divest the Almighty of a Due, proper to none besides himself."[34]

The most important political controversy that tested the meaning of religious toleration in colonial America was over whether Quakers and other religious pacifists should be required to perform military service. Many colonies and towns passed laws requiring all men (or all white men) to serve in the local militia. These measures promoted self-defense, a secular governmental purpose. Relationships with Native American tribes in many colonies were tense. A French invasion was possible. Quakers and other religious pacifists claimed exemptions from these laws because they believed that God forbade all military action. Laws requiring religious believers to behave in ways they believed forbidden by divine sanction, Quakers and their supporters maintained, violated the freedom of conscience.

William Blackstone, Of Offences Against God and Religion (1773)[35]

William Blackstone championed the traditional union of church and state. Government, he insisted, had the obligation to teach religious doctrine and punish religious dissenters. What reasons does Blackstone give for maintaining the union between church and state? What policies does he believe necessary to maintain that union? Blackstone emphasizes the suppression of Catholics (papists)—a hostility shared by many American Protestants of the period. What, from Blackstone's perspective, is the main threat that Catholicism presents to the political regime? Blackstone notes a "difference between

33. Blackstone, *Commentaries*, 5:59.

34. William Penn, *The Select Works of William Penn*, 3rd ed. (London: James Phillips, 1782), 12.

35. Excerpt taken from Blackstone, *Commentaries*, 4:42–43.

tolerance and establishment." What is that difference? Why does he think that this difference is important?

First then, such crimes and misdemeanors, as more immediately offend Almighty God, by openly transgressing the precepts of religion either natural or revealed. . . .

. . . [T]he first is that of apostacy, or a total renunciation of christianity, by embracing either a false religion, or no religion at all. . . . Doubtless the preservation of christianity, as a national religion, is, abstracted from its own intrinsic truth, of the utmost consequence to the civil state. . . . The belief of a future state of rewards and punishments, the entertaining just ideas of the moral attributes of the supreme being, and a firm persuasion that he superintends and will finally compensate every action in human life . . . these are the grand foundation of all judicial oaths; . . . all moral evidence therefore, all confidence in human veracity, must be weakened by irreligion, and overthrown by infidelity. Wherefore all affronts to christianity, or endeavors to depreciate it's efficacy, are highly deserving of human punishment. . . .

. . .

Another species of offences against religion are those which affect the established church. . . .

. . . [F]irst, of the offence of reviling the ordinances of the church. This is a crime of a much grosser nature than the other of mere non-conformity: since it carries with it the utmost indecency, arrogance, and ingratitude: indecency, by setting up private judgment in opposition to public; arrogance, by treating with contempt and rudeness what has at least a better chance to be right, than the singular notions of any particular man; and ingratitude, by denying that indulgence and liberty of conscience to the members of the national church. . . . Nor can their continuance to this time be thought too severe and intolerant; when we consider, that they are leveled at an offence, to which men cannot now be prompted by any laudable motive; not even by a mistaken zeal for reformation: since from political reasons . . . [it] would now be extremely unadvisable to make any alterations in the service of the church. . . . And therefore the virulent declamations of peevish or opinionated men on topics so often refuted, and of which the preface to the liturgy is itself a perpetual refutation, can be calculated for no other purpose, than merely to disturb the consciences, and poison the minds of the people.

Non-conformity to the worship of the church is the other, or negative branch of this offence. . . . [U]ndoubtedly all persecution and oppression of weak consciences, on the score of religious persuasions, are highly unjustifiable upon every principle of natural reason, civil liberty, or found religion. But care must be taken not to carry this indulgence into such extremes, as may endanger the national church: there is always a difference to be made between toleration and establishment.

Non-conformists are of two sorts: first, such as absent themselves from the divine worship in the established church . . . and attend the service of no other persuasion. These . . . forfeit one shilling to the poor every lord's day they so absent themselves, and . . . to the king if they continue such default for a month together. . . .

The second species of non-conformists are those who offend through a mistaken or perverse zeal. Such were esteemed by our laws, enacted since the time of the reformation, to be papists and protestant dissenters. . . . [T]he laws against the former are much more severe. . . . [T]he principles of the papists being deservedly looked upon to be subversive of the civil government, but not those of the protestant dissenters. As to the papists, their tenets are undoubtedly calculated for the introduction of all slavery, both civil and religious. . . . He is bound indeed to protect the established church, by admitting none but it's genuine members to offices of trust and emolument: for, if every sect was to be indulged in a free communion of civil employments, the idea of a national establishment would at once be destroyed, and the Episcopal church would be no longer the church of England. . . .

As to papists, . . . [i]f once they could be brought to renounce the supremacy of the pope, they might quietly enjoy their seven sacraments, their purgatory, and auricular confession; their worship of relics and images; nay even their transubstantiation. But while they acknowledge a foreign power, superior to the sovereignty of the kingdom, they cannot complain if the laws of that kingdom will not treat them upon the footing of good subjects. . . .

In order the better to secure the established church against perils from non-conformists of all denominations . . . there are . . . two bulwarks erected; called the corporation and test acts. By the former . . . no person can be legally elected to any office relating to the government . . . unless, within a twelve month before, he has received the sacrament of the lord's supper according to the rites of the church of England: and he is also enjoined to take the oaths of allegiance and supremacy at the same time that he takes the oath of office. . . . The other, called the test act, directs all officers civil and military to take the oaths and make the declaration against transubstantiation . . . , and also within the same time to receive the sacrament of the lord's supper. . . .

The fourth species of offences therefore, more immediately against God and religion, is that of blasphemy against the Almighty, by denying his being or providence; or by contumelious reproaches of our Saviour Christ. Whither also may be referred all profane scoffing at the holy scripture, or exposing it to contempt and ridicule. These are offences punishable at common law by fine and imprisonment, or other infamous corporal punishment: christianity is part of the laws of England.

Somewhat allied to this, though in an inferior degree, is the offence of profane and common swearing and cursing. . . .

A sixth species of offences against God and religion . . . is . . . the offence of witchcraft. . . . To deny the possibility, nay, actual existence, of witchcraft and sorcery, is at once flatly to contradict the revealed word of God. . . . But all executions for this dubious crime are now at an end. . . . And accordingly it is with us enacted by statute . . . that no prosecution shall for the future be carried on against any person for conjuration, witchcraft, sorcery, or enchantment. . . .

Profanation of the lord's day, or sabbath-breaking, is a ninth offence against God and religion, punished by the municipal laws of England. For, besides the notorious indecency and scandal, of permitting any secular business to be publicly transacted on that day, in a country professing christianity, and the corruption of morals which usually follows it's profanation, the keeping one day in seven holy, as a time of relaxation and refreshment as well as for public worship, is of admirable service to a state, considered merely as a civil institution. It humanizes by the help of conversation and society the manners of the lower classes; which would otherwise degenerate into a sordid ferocity. . . ; it enables the industrious workman to pursue his occupation in the ensuing week with health and cheerfulness: it imprints on the minds of the people that sense of their duty to God, so necessary to make them good citizens. . . .

John Locke, A Letter Concerning Toleration (1689)[36]

John Locke was a leading proponent of disestablishment, the view that government should not support religion. His influential Letter Concerning Toleration *gave both religious and nonreligious reasons for separating church and state. Locke insisted that Jesus Christ rejected the union of church and state. He also maintained that state support for religion and religious coercion are inconsistent with liberal political principles. What are those liberal political principles? Why does Locke think these principles justify the separation of church and state? Locke insists that some religious doctrines should not be tolerated. Is this lack of toleration consistent with his liberal perspective? Does Locke maintain that Catholics, who believe in papal authority, should not be tolerated? Locke argues that religious persons have an obligation to obey all laws that have secular purposes, even if those laws burden religious practice. How does he justify that conclusion?*

. . .

I esteem that toleration to be the chief characteristic mark of the true Church. . . .

. . . The business of true religion is . . . not instituted in order to the erecting of an external pomp, nor to the obtaining of ecclesiastical dominion, nor to the exercising of compulsive force, but to the regulating of men's lives, according to the rules of virtue and piety. . . . For it is impossible that those should sincerely and heartily apply themselves to make other people Christians, who have not really embraced the Christian religion in their own hearts. If the Gospel and the apostles may be credited, no man can be a Christian without charity and without that faith which works, not by force, but by love. Now, I appeal to the consciences of those that persecute, torment, destroy, and kill other men upon pretence of religion, whether they do it out of friendship and kindness towards them or no? . . .

. . .

The toleration of those that differ from others in matters of religion is so agreeable to the Gospel of Jesus Christ, and to the genuine reason of mankind, that it seems monstrous for men to be so blind as not to perceive the necessity and advantage of it in so clear a light. . . . [T]hat none may impose either upon himself

36. Excerpt taken from John Locke, *A Letter Concerning Toleration* (n.p.: J. Brook, 1796).

or others, by the pretences of loyalty and obedience to the prince, or of tenderness and sincerity in the worship of God; I esteem it above all things necessary to distinguish exactly the business of civil government from that of religion and to settle the just bounds that lie between the one and the other. . . .

The commonwealth seems to me to be a society of men constituted only for the procuring, preserving, and advancing their own civil interests.

Civil interests I call life, liberty, health, and indolence of body; and the possession of outward things, such as money, lands, houses, furniture, and the like.

It is the duty of the civil magistrate, by the impartial execution of equal laws, to secure unto all the people in general and to every one of his subjects in particular the just possession of these things belonging to this life. . . .

Now that the whole jurisdiction of the magistrate reaches only to these civil concernments, and that all civil power, right and dominion, is bounded and confined to the only care of promoting these things; and that it neither can nor ought in any manner to be extended to the salvation of souls, these following considerations seem unto me abundantly to demonstrate.

First, because the care of souls is not committed to the civil magistrate, any more than to other men. It is not committed unto him, I say, by God; because it appears not that God has ever given any such authority to one man over another as to compel anyone to his religion. Nor can any such power be vested in the magistrate by the consent of the people, because no man can so far abandon the care of his own salvation as blindly to leave to the choice of any other, whether prince or subject, to prescribe to him what faith or worship he shall embrace. For no man can, if he would, conform his faith to the dictates of another. All the life and power of true religion consist in the inward and full persuasion of the mind; and faith is not faith without believing. . . .

In the second place, the care of souls cannot belong to the civil magistrate, because his power consists only in outward force; but true and saving religion consists in the inward persuasion of the mind, without which nothing can be acceptable to God. . . .

. . . Magistracy does not oblige him to put off either humanity or Christianity; but it is one thing to persuade, another to command; one thing to press with arguments, another with penalties. . . . Every man has commission to admonish, exhort, convince another of error, and, by reasoning, to draw him into truth; but to give laws, receive obedience, and compel with the sword, belongs to none but the magistrate. And, upon this ground, I affirm that the magistrate's power extends not to the establishing of any articles of faith, or forms of worship, by the force of his laws. For laws are of no force at all without penalties, and penalties in this case are absolutely impertinent, because they are not proper to convince the mind. . . .

. . .

. . . [N]o private person has any right in any manner to prejudice another person in his civil enjoyments because he is of another church or religion. All the rights and franchises that belong to him as a man, or as a denizen, are inviolably to be preserved to him. These are not the business of religion. No violence nor injury is to be offered him, whether he be Christian or Pagan. . . . If any man err from the right way, it is his own misfortune, no injury to thee; nor therefore art thou to punish him in the things of this life because thou supposest he will be miserable in that which is to come.

. . . [T]he civil government can give no new right to the church, nor the church to the civil government. So that, whether the magistrate join himself to any church, or separate from it, the church remains always as it was before—a free and voluntary society. It neither requires the power of the sword by the magistrate's coming to it, nor does it lose the right of instruction and excommunication by his going from it. . . .

. . .

You will say . . . if some congregations should have a mind to sacrifice infants, or (as the primitive Christians were falsely accused) lustfully pollute themselves in promiscuous uncleanness, or practice any other such heinous enormities, is the magistrate obliged to tolerate them, because they are committed in a religious assembly? I answer: No. These things are not lawful in the ordinary course of life, nor in any private house; and therefore neither are they so in the worship of God, or in any religious meeting. But, indeed, if any people congregated upon account of religion should be desirous to sacrifice a calf, I deny that that ought to be prohibited by a law. Meliboeus, whose calf it is, may lawfully kill his calf at home, and burn any part of it that he thinks fit. For no injury is thereby done to any one, no prejudice to another man's goods. And for the same reason he may kill his calf also in a religious meeting. . . . But if peradventure such were the state of things that the interest of the commonwealth required all slaughter of beasts should be forborne for some while, in order to the increasing of the stock of cattle that had been destroyed by some extraordinary murrain, who sees not that the magistrate, in such a case, may forbid all his subjects to kill any calves for any use whatsoever? Only it is to be observed that, in this case, the law is not made about a religious, but a political matter; nor is the sacrifice, but the slaughter of calves, thereby prohibited.

By this we see what difference there is between the Church and the Commonwealth. Whatsoever is lawful in the Commonwealth cannot be prohibited by the magistrate in the Church. Whatsoever is permitted unto any of his subjects for their ordinary use, neither can nor ought to be forbidden by him to any sect of people for their religious uses. . . .

. . .

. . . [T]here is absolutely no such thing under the Gospel as a Christian commonwealth. There are, indeed, many cities and kingdoms that have embraced the faith of Christ, but they have retained their ancient form of government, with which the law of Christ hath not at all meddled. He, indeed, hath taught men how, by faith and good works, they may obtain eternal life; but He instituted no commonwealth. He prescribed unto His followers no new and peculiar form of government, nor put He the sword into any magistrate's hand, with commission to make use of it in forcing men to forsake their former religion and receive His.

. . .

. . . [T]he magistrate ought not to forbid the preaching or professing of any speculative opinions in any Church because they have no manner of relation to the civil rights of the subjects. If a Roman Catholic believe that to be really the body of Christ which another man calls bread, he does no injury thereby to his neighbor. If a Jew do not believe the New Testament to be the Word of God, he does not thereby alter anything in men's civil rights. If a heathen doubt of both Testaments, he is not therefore to be punished as a pernicious citizen. The power of the magistrate and the estates of the people may be equally secure whether any man believe these things or no. I readily grant that these opinions are false and absurd. But the business of laws is not to provide for the truth of opinions, but for the safety and security of the commonwealth and of every particular man's goods and person. And so it ought to be. For the truth certainly would do well enough if she were once left to shift for herself. She seldom has received and, I fear, never will receive much assistance from the power of great men, to whom she is but rarely known and more rarely welcome. . . .

. . .

. . . [N]o opinions contrary to human society, or to those moral rules which are necessary to the preservation of civil society, are to be tolerated by the magistrate. . . .

Another more secret evil, but more dangerous to the commonwealth, is when men arrogate to themselves, and to those of their own sect, some peculiar prerogative covered over with a specious show of deceitful words, but in effect opposite to the civil right of the community. . . . These, therefore, and the like, who attribute unto the faithful, religious, and orthodox, that is, in plain terms, unto themselves, any peculiar privilege or power above other mortals, in civil concernments; or who upon pretence of religion do challenge any manner of authority over such as are not associated with them in their ecclesiastical communion, I say these have no right to be tolerated by the magistrate; as neither those that will not own and teach the duty of tolerating all men in matters of mere religion. . . .

Again: That Church can have no right to be tolerated by the magistrate which is constituted upon such a bottom that all those who enter into it do thereby ipso facto deliver themselves up to the protection and service of another prince. . . .

Lastly, those are not at all to be tolerated who deny the being of a God. Promises, covenants, and oaths, which are the bonds of human society, can have no hold upon an atheist. The taking away of God, though but even in thought, dissolves all; besides also, those that by their atheism undermine and destroy all religion, can have no pretence of religion whereupon to challenge the privilege of a toleration. As for other practical opinions, though not absolutely free from all error, if they do not tend to establish domination over others, or civil impunity to the Church in which they are taught, there can be no reason why they should not be tolerated. . . .

Roger Williams, **The Bloudy Tenent** (1644)[37]

Roger Williams is considered the founder of religious freedom in the United States. Shortly after his 1631 arrival in the Massachusetts Bay Colony, Williams sided with those

37. Excerpt taken from Roger Williams, *The Bloudy Tenent* (London: n.p., 1644).

Puritans who insisted on a complete separation with the Anglican Church. Unlike other separationists who favored the union of a more purified church and state, Williams concluded that any union of church and state was inconsistent with Christian doctrine. Exiled from Massachusetts in 1635, Williams settled in what is now Providence, Rhode Island. Eventually he founded the Rhode Island Colony, which was committed to a complete separation of church and state. The 1663 Charter of Rhode Island declared,

> *No person within the said colony, at any time hereafter, shall be any ways molested, punished, disquieted, or called in question, for any differences in opinion in matters of religion, and do not actually disturb the civil peace of our said colony; but that all and every person and persons may, from time to time, and at all times hereafter, freely and fully have and enjoy his and their own judgments and consciences, in matters of religious concernments.*

The Bloudy Tenent *was published in London while Williams was trying to convince English authorities to grant Rhode Island a charter. The book was considered so radical that Parliament ordered every copy burned. Nevertheless,* The Bloudy Tenent *had substantial influence throughout the colonies. Consider when you read the introduction whether Williams is best conceptualized as a political liberal or a liberal Protestant. Which of his arguments might appeal to a contemporary secular citizen? Which are based entirely on religious doctrine?*

First, That the blood of so many hundred thousand souls of *Protestants* and *Papists,* spilt in the *Wars* of *present* and *former Ages,* for their respective *Consciences,* is not *required* nor *accepted* by *Jesus Christ* the *Prince* of *Peace.*

Secondly, Pregnant *Scriptures* and *Arguments* are throughout the Work proposed against the *Doctrine* of *persecution* for *cause* of *Conscience.*

...

Fourthly, The *Doctrine of persecution* for cause of *Conscience,* is proved guilty of all the *blood* of the *Souls* crying for *vengeance* under the *Altar.*

Fifthly, All *Civil States* with their *Officers* of *justice* in their respective *constitutions* and *administrations* are proved *essentially Civil,* and therefore not *Judges, Governours* or *Defenders* of the *Spiritual or Christian state* and *Worship.*

Sixly, It is the will and command of *God,* that (since the coming of his Son the *Lord Jesus)* a *permission* of the most *Paganish, Jewish, Turkish,* or *Antichristian consciences* and *worships,* be granted to *all* men in all *Nations* and *Countries:* and they are only to *be fought* against with that *Sword* which is only (in *Soul matters) able* to *conquer,* to wit, the *Sword of Gods Spirit,* the *Word* of *God.*

...

Eightly, *God* requires not a *uniformity* of *Religion* to be *enacted* and *enforced* in any *civil state;* which enforced uniformity (sooner or later) is the greatest occasion of *civil War, ravishing* of *conscience, persecution* of *Christ Jesus* in his servants, and of the *hypocrisy* and *destruction* of *millions* of *souls.*

Ninthly, In holding an enforced *uniformity* of *Religion* in a *civil state,* we must necessarily *disclaim* our desires and hopes of the *Jews conversion* to *Christ.*

Tenthly, An enforced *uniformity* of *Religion* throughout a *Nation* or *civil state,* confounds the *Civil* and *Religious,* denies the principles of Christianity and civility, and that *Jesus Christ* is come in the Flesh.

Eleventhly, The permission of other *consciences* and *worships* then a state professes, only can (according to God) procure a firm and lasting *peace* (good *assurance* being taken according to the *wisdom* of the *civil state* for *uniformity* of *civil obedience* from all sorts).

Twelfthly, lastly, true *civility* and *Christianity* may both flourish in a *state* or *Kingdom,* notwithstanding the *permission* of diverse and contrary *consciences,* either of *Jew* or *Gentile.*

C. Guns

English subjects and American colonists believed that they had a right to be armed. The English Bill of Rights asserted, "The subjects which are Protestants may have arms for their defence suitable to their conditions and as allowed by law." Blackstone claimed that the right of self-defense entailed the right to bear arms. His *Commentaries* declared that Englishmen had the right "of having arms for their defense, suitable to their condition and degree, and such as are allowed by law." This liberty, Blackstone continued, "under due restrictions," was derived from "the natural right of resistance and self-preservation, when the sanctions of society and laws are found insufficient to restrain the violence of oppression."[38] John Adams, when defending the soldiers accused of the Boston

38. Blackstone, *Commentaries,* 1:139.

Massacre, stated, "The inhabitants had a right to arm themselves at that time, for their defence."[39]

This right to bear arms was often derived from a civic obligation to serve in the local militia. Most Americans on the eve of the Revolution believed that the community was best defended by an armed citizenry, not a professional army. Pennsylvania was one of many jurisdictions that linked gun rights and opposition to a standing army. The state's first constitution stated, "The people have a right to bear arms for the defense of themselves and the state; and as standing armies in the time of peace are dangerous to liberty, they ought not be kept up." Consistent with this obligation, some communities required men of a certain age to maintain weapons in good condition and prohibited persons not eligible for militia service, such as free persons of color, from bearing arms.

Both English and colonial practice suggest that the right to bear arms served three other important purposes besides militia service. The first was protection against private violence. Life on the American frontier was dangerous. Colonists believed that arms were needed to thwart attacks from Native Americans and common criminals. Thomas Jefferson anticipated claims made by many contemporary proponents of gun rights when he asserted, "Laws forbidding people to bear arms are of this nature; they only disarm those who are neither inclined nor determined to commit crimes and political tyrants."[40] Second, colonists wanted protection against vicious rulers. "It is a natural right which the people have reserved to themselves, confirmed by the [English] Bill of Rights," the *New York Journal* stated in 1769, "to keep arms for their own defense."[41] Third, some colonists considered weapons as necessary means for hunting, a vital source of food in early America. Joyce Lee Malcolm notes that riots took place in seventeenth-century England when laws aimed at preventing the killing of too many wild animals disarmed English citizens.[42]

39. Frederic Kidder and John Adams, *History of the Boston Massacre, March 5, 1770* (Albany, NY: Joel Munsell, 1870), 237.

40. Thomas Jefferson, in Gilbert Chinard, ed., *The Commonplace Book of Thomas Jefferson* (Baltimore, MD: Johns Hopkins University Press, 1926), 314.

41. *New York Journal*, April 13, 1769, 1, col. 3.

42. Joyce Lee Malcolm, *To Keep and Bear Arms: The Origins of an Anglo-American Right* (Cambridge, MA: Harvard University Press, 1994), 11–15.

D. Personal Freedom and Public Morality

Governing authorities during the colonial era believed that the state should regulate morality. "Adultery, fornication, uncleanliness, lasciviousness, idolatry, and such-like things" were among the "immoralities" that John Locke in his *Letter Concerning Toleration* urged government to "root out."[43] Blackstone maintained that government should prosecute "open and notorious lewdness: either by frequenting houses of ill fame, . . . or by some grossly scandalous and public indecency," as well as drunkenness. These were offenses against "religion and morality." The *Commentaries* also stated that abortion performed after quickening was a crime. "Life is the immediate gift of God," Blackstone wrote,

> a right inherent by nature in every individual; and it begins in contemplation of law as soon as an infant is able to stir in the mother's womb. For if a woman is quick with child, and by a potion, or otherwise, kills it in her womb; or if any one beat her, whereby the child dies in her body, and she is delivered of a dead child; this, though not murder, was by the ancient law homicide or manslaughter. But at present it is not looked upon in quite so atrocious a light, though it remains a very heinous misdemeanor.[44]

Two hundred years later, pro-choice activists noted that Blackstone said nothing about abortion before quickening. This is correct, but neither Blackstone nor any other common law authority maintained that persons had a right to terminate a pregnancy at any time. Blackstone did recognize a right to marry if at the time when the marriage contract was made the persons involved were willing to contract, able to contract, and did contract to marry according to existing legal rules.[45]

Political and legal commentary in the Colonial Era planted some seeds for the development of greater individual choice on moral matters. Locke and Blackstone emphasized that government could regulate individual behavior only when doing so advanced the public good. Locke suggested that individuals might have quite broad privacy rights on matters that Blackstone described as "matters of mere indifference." Locke's *Letter*

43. Locke, *Letter Concerning Toleration*, 8.

44. Blackstone, *Commentaries*, 1:125–26.

45. Blackstone, *Commentaries*, 1:421.

Concerning Toleration argued that government should not prohibit self-regarding acts, or acts that have no consequences to other people.[46] Both Blackstone and Locke were firmly convinced that gambling, promiscuity, and similar acts harmed the public. When, however, some Americans came to the conclusion that these were actually "matters of mere indifference," they could point to seventeenth- and eighteenth-century legal sources for arguments that these morality laws violated individual rights.

VII. Democratic Rights

MAJOR DEVELOPMENTS

- No prior restraints on free speech
- Debate over seditious libel, the crime of criticizing the government
- Property restrictions on voting and officeholding
- Citizenship and allegiance determined by place of birth

The American regime during the Colonial Era began making the transition from a monarchy to a republic. In a monarchy, kings and nobles rule over their subjects. Power is inherited and often rooted in divine sanction. King George III was entitled to rule England because he was the eldest son of King George II and because God authorized his family, the Hanovers, to rule the land. Subjects who criticized the king or his chosen ministers undermined the public peace and challenged divine authority. In a republic, representatives govern citizens. Power is gained through election and rooted in the consent of the people. Patrick Henry had the right to cast a vote in the Virginia House of Burgesses because he was elected as a representative by his fellow citizens. Citizens who criticized their representatives were simply engaging in self-government.

None of the colonies were pure republican regimes on the eve of the American Revolution. Until the Declaration of Independence, Americans acknowledged the authority of the king of England. Voting and speech rights were limited. No colony met contemporary democratic standards, even when considering only the status of white men. Instead, the leading champions of republican government during the mid-eighteenth century hoped to establish a more natural aristocracy. This natural aristocracy would foster government by the most virtuous citizens rather than government by people who happened to be born into noble families. Prominent American elites regarded free speech and voting rights as means for helping society identify those persons who could best govern. This desire to create a "republic of virtue" justified limiting participation rights. All colonies restricted voting to property holders on the ground that poorer citizens lacked the independence and capacities necessary to identify and select the best rulers. In colonial America, the liberty to speak did not include a license to say anything about any topic. Persons had to prove they spoke the truth with good motives. Unsurprisingly, Americans who criticized the distant English Parliament found this standard easier to meet than Americans who criticized members of the local legislature.

A. Free Speech

The Colonial Era witnessed frequent controversies over free speech in both Great Britain and the Americas. The most important disputes were over who determined what speech could be restricted. During the seventeenth century English legal authorities debated whether persons should be permitted to publish books or pamphlets freely, or if they should be required to first obtain a license from the king or a representative of the throne. During the eighteenth century American colonists debated whether a judge or a jury should determine whether an author was guilty of criminal libel.

Free speech disputes concerned the opinions persons could express as well as which governing officials could limit speech. English common law recognized the crime of seditious libel, or speaking ill of the king, the government, or government officials. Truth was not a defense against this charge. Eighteenth-century proponents of free speech in both England and the colonies sought greater protection for expression rights. In their view, persons had the right to criticize government officials as long as they spoke truthfully and with good motives.

Blackstone and most eighteenth-century English lawyers believed that government had the power to punish any speech that had a "pernicious tendency." They had no doubt that government could punish seditious libel. Such criticisms, whether true or false,

46. Locke, *Letter Concerning Toleration*, 28.

were thought to threaten the public peace and undermine the political order. Blackstone wrote,

> [L]ibels . . . are malicious defamations of any person, and especially a magistrate, [that] provoke him to wrath, or expose him to public hatred, contempt, and ridicule. The direct tendency of these libels is the breach of the public peace, by stirring up the objects of them to revenge, and perhaps to bloodshed. . . . [I]t is immaterial with respect to the essence of a libel, whether the matter of it be true or false; since the provocation, and not the falsity, is the thing to be punished criminally. . . . [I]n a criminal prosecution, the tendency which all libels have to create animosities, and to disturb the public peace, is the sole consideration of the law. And therefore, in such prosecutions, the only facts to be considered are, first, the making or publishing of the book or writing; and secondly, whether the matter be criminal: and, if both these points are against the defendant, the offence against the public is complete.[47]

Seditious libel had two crucial elements. First, truth was not a defense against the charge. A prosecutor who demonstrated that a printer had published an essay that was critical of the government had proved seditious libel. Second, the jury decided only whether the defendant had published the offending work. Judges determined whether the work was defamatory, a criticism of the government or a government official.

Prominent English dissenters and many American colonists criticized the criminalization of seditious libel, with John Trenchard and Thomas Gordon being the most notable critics. Writing under the pseudonym "Cato," they published more than one hundred essays between 1720 and 1723 attacking what they perceived to be the increasing corruption of English politics. Their most influential essay, "Of Freedom of Speech," contended that seditious libel was inconsistent with English freedom.

> Without freedom of thought, there can be no such thing as wisdom; and no such thing as public liberty, without freedom of speech: Which is the right of every man, as far as by it he does not hurt and control the right of another; and this is the only check which it ought to suffer, the only bounds which it ought to know.
>
> . . .
>
> That men ought to speak well of their governors, is true, while their governors deserve to be well spoken of; but to do public mischief, without hearing of it, is only the prerogative and felicity of tyranny: A free people will be showing that they are so, by their freedom of speech.
>
> The administration of government is nothing else, but the attendance of the trustees of the people upon the interest and affairs of the people. And as it is the part and business of the people, for whose sake alone all public matters are, or ought to be, transacted, to see whether they be well or ill transacted; so it is the interest, and ought to be the ambition, of all honest magistrates, to have their deeds openly examined, and publicly scanned.[48]

Trenchard and Gordon had more influence in the colonies than in England. Many colonists regarded their essays as documenting disturbing political trends in Great Britain that threatened American liberties. The essay on freedom of speech was particularly influential. Magistrates who punished good-faith criticisms, colonists thought, were more interested in holding power than in governing for the republican good.

The *Zenger* Trial (1733–1734)[49]

John Peter Zenger was the publisher of the New York Weekly Journal. *From 1733 to 1734 the* Weekly Journal *published articles criticizing William Crosby, the royal governor of New York. One essay complained that the people of New York "think, as matters now stand, that their liberties and properties are precarious, and that slavery is likely to be entailed on them and their posterity if some past things be not amended, and this they collect from many past proceedings." That essay was most likely penned by James Alexander, a prominent opponent of the royal government and a patron of the* Weekly Journal. *Unable to prove that Alexander wrote the offending articles, Governor Crosby had Zenger arrested and charged with seditious libel.*

Crosby's actions were consistent with early eighteenth-century legal practice. Seditious libel was the common law crime of bringing the government into contempt. The

47. Blackstone, *Commentaries*, 5:149–50.

48. John Trenchard and Thomas Gordon, *Cato's Letters* (London: W. Wilkins, 1723), 1:98.

49. Excerpt taken from John Peter Zenger, *A Brief Narrative of the Case and Trial of John Peter Zenger* (London: n.p., 1738).

Illustration 2-2 Andrew Hamilton Defending John Peter Zenger in Court
Source: Library of Congress, Prints and Photographs Division, Washington, DC 20540 USA.

prosecution had to prove only that the defendant had published material that defamed or criticized a public official. Truth was not a defense. "The greater the truth, the greater the libel," lawyers believed. The trial judge determined whether the publication was defamatory; the jury decided only whether the defendant had published the offending matter. For these reasons, Zenger had every reason to believe he would be imprisoned. He published the Weekly Journal. *The essays he published were defamatory.*

Zenger's champions insisted that the concept of seditious libel was inconsistent with the freedom of speech. Benjamin Franklin, then publisher of a newspaper in Philadelphia, arranged for Zenger to be defended by Andrew Hamilton, a prominent colonial lawyer. At trial, Hamilton urged the jury to find Zenger not guilty if they believed that the Weekly Journal *had published true criticisms of the royal governor. Persons, Hamilton claimed, were free to speak the truth about government as long as they had good motives for raising their concerns. The trial judge, James Delancy, rejected this interpretation of the common law and frequently informed the jury that they were only to determine publication. These instructions seemed to seal Zenger's fate. Nevertheless, the jury came back almost immediately with a verdict of not guilty.*

The Zenger trial was the most important free speech dispute in colonial America. After the verdict was handed down, James Alexander published a widely circulated account of the trial. Many colonial Americans agreed with Hamilton that truth for good motives could not be prosecuted. Nevertheless, official law continued to maintain that publication was the only element of libel. Political dissenters before the Revolution criticized government at their risk.

The Zenger trial highlighted the close connection between the right to a jury and free speech during the eighteenth century. When local juries rather than royally appointed judges determined law, all persons who obtained a jury trial were in practice free to make popular criticisms of governing officials. Not surprisingly, colonists who criticized locally elected officials were less likely to regard the jury as a bulwark of freedom.

When you read the following excerpts, compare how the prosecution and defense define free speech. What reasons does each give for its broader and narrower conceptions of that right? Who should decide the meaning of free speech? What are the advantages and disadvantages of having juries determine that law?

Case for the Prosecution (RICHARD BRADLEY)

. . . [L]ibeling has always been discouraged as a thing that tends to create differences among men, ill blood among the people, and oftentimes great bloodshed between the party libeling and the party libeled.

. . .

. . . [A]s Mr. Hamilton has confessed the printing and publishing of these libels, I think the jury must find a verdict for the king. For supposing they were true, the law says that they are not the less libelous for that. Nay, indeed the law says their being true is an aggravation of the crime.

. . .

. . . That by government we were protected in our lives, religion, and properties; and for these reasons great care had always been taken to prevent everything that might tend to scandalize magistrates and others concerned in the administration of the government, especially the supreme magistrate. And that there were many instances of very severe judgments, and of punishments, inflicted upon such as had attempted to bring the government into contempt by publishing false and scurrilous libels against it, or by speaking evil and scandalous words of men in authority, to the great disturbance of the public peace. . . .

. . . [L]ibel [is] a malicious defamation of any person, expressed either in printing or writing, signs or pictures, to asperse the reputation of one that is alive, or the memory of one that is dead. If he is a private man, the libeler deserves a severe punishment, but if it is against a magistrate or other public person, it is a greater offense. For this concerns not only the breach of the peace but the scandal of the government. What greater scandal of government can there be than to have corrupt or wicked magistrates appointed by the king to govern his subjects? A greater imputation to the state there cannot be than to suffer such corrupt men to sit in the sacred seat of justice, or to have any meddling in or concerning the administration of justice. . . .

. . .

Mr. HAMILTON: Summation for Zenger

. . .

. . . [I]t is natural, it is a privilege, I will go farther, it is a right, which all free men claim, that they are entitled to complain when they are hurt. They have a right publicly to remonstrate against the abuses of power in the strongest terms, to put their neighbors upon their guard against the craft or open violence of men in authority, and to assert with courage the sense they have of the blessings of liberty, the value they put upon it, and their resolution at all hazards to preserve it as one of the greatest blessings heaven can bestow.

. . .

But to proceed. I beg leave to insist that the right of complaining or remonstrating is natural; that the restraint upon this natural right is the law only; and that those restraints can only extend to what is false. For as it is truth alone that can excuse or justify any man for complaining of a bad administration, I as frankly agree that nothing ought to excuse a man who raises a false charge or accusation even against a private person, and that no manner of allowance ought to be made to him who does so against a public magistrate.

Truth ought to govern the whole affair of libels. And yet the party accused runs risk enough even then; for if he fails in proving every title of what he has written, and to the satisfaction of the court and jury too, he may find to his cost that when the prosecution is set on foot by men in power it seldom wants friends to favor it.

. . .

There is heresy in law as well as in religion, and both have changed very much. We well know that it is not two centuries ago that a man would have been burned as a heretic for owning such opinions in matters of religion as are publicly written and printed at this day. They were fallible men, it seems, and we take the liberty not only to differ from them in religious opinions, but to condemn them and their opinions too. I must presume that in taking these freedoms in thinking and speaking about matters of faith or religion, we are in the right; for although it is said that there are very great liberties of this kind taken in New York, yet I have heard of no information preferred by Mr. Attorney for any offenses of this sort. From which I think it is pretty clear that in New York a man may make very free with his God, but he must take a special care what he says of his governor.

It is agreed upon by all men that this is a reign of liberty. While men keep within the bounds of truth I hope they may with safety both speak and write their sentiments of the conduct of men in power, I mean of that part of their conduct only which affects the liberty or property of the people under their administration. Were this to be denied, then the next step may make them slaves; for what notions can be entertained of slavery beyond that of suffering the greatest injuries and oppressions without the liberty of complaining, or if they do, to be destroyed, body and estate, for so doing?

It is said and insisted on by Mr. Attorney that government is a sacred thing; that it is to be supported and reverenced; that it is government that protects our persons and estates, prevents treasons, murders, robberies, riots, and all the train of evils that overturns kingdoms and states and ruins particular persons. And if those in the administration, especially the supreme magistrate, must have all their conduct censured by private men, government cannot subsist. This is called a licentiousness not to be tolerated. It is said that it brings the rulers of the people into contempt, and their authority not to be regarded, and so in the end the laws cannot be put into execution.

These, I say, and such as these, are the general topics insisted upon by men in power and their advocates. But I wish it might be considered at the same time how often it has happened that the abuse of power has been the primary cause of these evils, and that it was the injustice and oppression of these great men that has commonly brought them into contempt with the people. The craft and art of such men is great, and who that is the least acquainted with history or law can be ignorant of the specious pretenses that have often been made use of by men in power to introduce arbitrary rule, and to destroy the liberties of a free people?

. . .

Gentlemen: The danger is great in proportion to the mischief that may happen through our too great credulity. A proper confidence in a court is commendable, but as the verdict, whatever it is, will be yours, you ought to refer no part of your duty to the discretion of other persons. If you should be of the opinion that there is no falsehood in Mr. Zenger's papers, you will, nay pardon me for the expression, you ought, to say so—because you do not know whether others—I mean the Court—may be of that opinion. It is your right to do so, and there is much depending upon your resolution as well as upon your integrity.

But to conclude: the question before the Court and you, Gentlemen of the jury, is not of small or private concern. It is not the cause of one poor printer, nor of New York alone, which you are now trying. No! It may in its consequence affect every free man that lives under a British government on the main of America. It is the best cause. It is the cause of liberty. And I make no doubt but your upright conduct this day will not only entitle you to the love and esteem of your fellow citizens, but every man who prefers freedom to a life of slavery will bless and honor you as men who have baffled the attempt of tyranny, and by an impartial and uncorrupt verdict have laid a noble foundation for securing to ourselves, our posterity, and our neighbors, that to which nature and the laws of our country have given us a right—the liberty both of exposing and opposing arbitrary power (in these parts of the world at least) by speaking and writing truth.

B. Voting

Property requirements were common in both England and the colonies. Persons without property were thought to lack the necessary independence and virtues for exercising the suffrage. Blackstone asserted,

> The true reason of requiring any qualification, with regard to property, in voters, is to exclude such persons as are in so mean a situation that they are esteemed to have no will of their own. If these persons had votes, they would be tempted to dispose of them under some undue influence or other. This would give a great, an artful, or a wealthy man, a larger share in elections than is consistent with general liberty. If it were probable that every man would give his vote freely and without influence of any kind, then, upon the true theory and genuine principles of liberty, every member of the community, however poor, should have a vote in electing those delegates, to whose charge is committed the disposal of his property, his liberty, and his life. But, since that can hardly be expected in persons of indigent fortunes, or such as are under the immediate dominion of others, all popular states have been obliged to establish certain qualifications; whereby some, who are suspected to have no will of their own, are excluded from voting, in order to set other individuals, whose wills may be supposed independent, more thoroughly upon a level with each other.[50]

---

50. Blackstone, *Commentaries*, 2:169–70.

Property qualifications determined those persons who were eligible to be elected to the colonial legislature. Many colonies enacted onerous property qualifications for membership in the upper house of the local legislature and somewhat less restrictive property qualifications for membership in the lower house.

Colonists were often disenfranchised on the basis of gender, race, and religion. Most colonies disenfranchised women, although women did vote in some elections. Most, but not all, southern colonies limited the ballot to white persons. Religious restrictions were common. Catholics were deprived of the vote in five colonies. Jews were disenfranchised in four. Some colonies required officeholders to swear a religious oath that effectively barred most non-Protestants from sitting in the legislature.

VIII. Equality

MAJOR DEVELOPMENTS

- Increased demands for equality under the law
- The establishment of slavery in the colonies and the principle *"in favorem libertatis"* in the common law
- Traditional gender roles maintained

American colonists took for granted some longstanding inequalities, rejected others, and added some new forms of status hierarchy. Every colony maintained traditional gender roles. Many, but not all, gave Protestants far more rights than they did Catholics and Jews. The colonists, however, rejected the traditional English aristocracy. When colonial Americans demanded equality before the law, they meant that no person should have special legal rights because he or she was born to a noble family.

The colonists were less egalitarian than the English when making racial distinctions. English law in the seventeenth and eighteenth centuries did not sharply discriminate against persons of color, in large part because hardly any Africans (or Asians) resided in England. Efforts to establish slavery in England failed, partly because of an important legal decision, *Somerset v. Stewart* (1773), which denied any common law right to hold a person as a slave. The American colonists established slavery by statutory decree during the seventeenth century. By 1750 most Africans residing in the colonies were enslaved. Those who were not enslaved suffered heavy legal disabilities. Prominent Englishmen regarded this combination of anti-aristocratic sentiment and slaveholding as hypocritical. "How is it that we hear the loudest yelps for liberty among the drivers of negroes?" a leading English essayist complained in 1775.[51]

A. Equality Under Law

Colonial Americans understood equality to mean that (1) they should have the same rights as British subjects who resided in England, (2) government should not establish an aristocracy in which nobles acquired special political and legal rights at birth, and (3) government officials should not give special favors to privileged citizens. This "rage for equality" was not universal. Colonial American law governing race, gender, and Native American issues was inegalitarian, to say the least. The initial American demands for equality are best characterized as the demands of the local propertied elite for the same status as the native propertied elite in England. Still, egalitarian rhetoric proved hard to restrain. The egalitarian claims made by colonial notables were soon put forth by ordinary Americans demanding the same rights and privileges as these notables.

The principle of "equality to other British subjects" meant that the king should not discriminate between residents of Great Britain and Englishmen who resided in the Americas. Thomas Jefferson began *A Summary View of the Rights of British America* (1774) by "reminding" King George III "that our ancestors, before their emigration to America, were the free inhabitants of the British dominions in Europe." Instead of being governed by "equal and impartial legislation," Jefferson complained, the colonists were the victims of "arbitrary acts." Parliamentary edicts repeatedly denied the colonists rights and privileges possessed by persons residing in England. *A Summary View* insisted that such policies violated the equal rights of American colonists in one of two ways: "Either . . . justice is not the same in America as in Britain," Jefferson stated, "or else . . . the British parliament pays less regard to it here than there." Jefferson concluded the pamphlet by insisting that all American grievances could be resolved if Parliament recognized that English residents of the colonies had the same rights as English residents of Great Britain: "The whole art of government consists in the art of being honest. Only aim to do your duty, and

51. James Boswell, *Life of Johnson* (London: Henry Frowde, 1904), 2:154.

mankind will give you credit where you fail. No longer persevere in sacrificing the rights of one part of the empire to the inordinate desires of another; but deal out to all equal and impartial right."[52]

Opposition to an entitled nobility was another central component of the colonial culture of equality. Most foreign observers regarded the colonies as unparalleled egalitarian societies in large part because no American aristocracy ever developed. All eighteenth-century European countries had persons of various noble ranks. These were the barons, dukes, and earls that one encounters in old movies and romance novels. Nobles enjoyed special political and legal privileges. In Great Britain, certain nobles had the right to sit in the House of Lords. Criminal procedure was often different when a lord was on trial. Analogous practices either never existed in the colonies or were soon abandoned. No one had a right to sit in a colonial legislature because of his birth (or because he purchased a title). No one gained any special legal privileges because he was the oldest son of a person with special privileges. The colonial principle of equality under law entitled persons to be judged by their individual characteristics, not by their birth status. Americans on the eve of the Revolution took pride in their commitment to "a natural aristocracy." In the New World, fame and power reflected virtue, not birth. American colonists condemned a regime in which "all power might center on one family," and in which public office "like a precious jewel will be handed down from father to son."[53] The Virginia Declaration of Rights declared: "No Man or set of Men are entitled to exclusive or separate Emoluments or Privileges from the Community, but in Consideration of public Services; which not being descendible, or hereditary, the Ideal of man born a Magistrate, a Legislator, or a Judge is unnatural and absurd." Equality under law meant equality of opportunity. People were judged by their public service, not by titles gained by distant ancestors.

Americans deplored "class legislation." The constitutional commitment to equality before the law required that legislation have a public purpose and not, as the hated English laws did, be motivated by the desire to benefit one class of persons (English supporters of George III) at the expense of another (American colonists).

52. Thomas Jefferson, *A Summary View of the Rights of British America*, in *Tracts of the American Revolution* (see note 2), 256–76.

53. Wood, *Radicalism*, 181.

B. Race

Human bondage flourished in the American colonies. Virginians by 1619 were purchasing Africans to work their lands. Whether these workers were initially slaves is not entirely clear. Some historical evidence indicates that the first blacks in the colonies were treated similarly to white indentured servants. By the 1660s colonial law clearly sanctioned slavery. By 1700 every colony had laws mandating permanent enslavement.

The increased colonial commitment to liberal political thought threatened slavery. During the seventeenth and early eighteenth centuries few persons questioned the morality of human bondage. The colonial tendency to rely on liberal notions of natural rights when protesting against various parliamentary edicts, however, inspired some persons to view domestic practices in light of those values. If all persons had a natural right to life, liberty, and property, then slavery was a worse violation of natural law than taxation without representation. Such arguments were more frequently heard in the northern colonies, whose economies depended less on slavery. Many Quakers in the middle South were also influenced by the belief that liberalism and slavery were inconsistent.

The growing anti-slavery movement in England and the colonies received a dramatic boost in 1773 when Lord Mansfield decided *Somerset v. Stewart*. During the seventeenth and eighteenth centuries some merchants imported into England slaves they had purchased in the West Indies or in the American colonies. By the 1760s England had a significant black population whose legal status was unclear. *Somerset v. Stewart* resolved that uncertainty. Lord Mansfield insisted that slavery was so odious to basic natural law principles that property in human beings could exist legally only in places where statutory law explicitly stated that one human being could own another. A person claiming a right to hold a slave had to point to an explicit law that legalized slavery. He could not rely on the common law of property or any other common law doctrine. Because Parliament had never passed a law making slavery legal in England, this decision meant that no person could be legally held as a slave in that country.

Somerset had no direct effect on enslaved persons of color in the New World. In 1773 statutes existed in all colonies (and the West Indies) legalizing human bondage. Masters could point to specific rules that entitled them to possess other human beings.

The status of free blacks in colonial America was ambiguous and varied by colony. Most southern colonies enacted regulations sharply restricting the rights of freed slaves or persons of color who were born free. In 1668 Virginia passed laws mandating that free blacks "ought not in all respects . . . be admitted to a full fruition of the exemptions and immunities of the English."[54] Nevertheless, some blacks voted and were considered citizens in some states. Northern colonies placed fewer restrictions on free blacks. Whether this practice reflected a genuine commitment to racial equality or was simply the consequence of blacks being too few in number to attract much legislative concern was for the future to determine.

Somerset v. Stewart, 20 Howell's 1 (1772)

Charles Stewart brought his slave, James Somerset, to England in 1769. Two years later Stewart attempted to ship Somerset back to the West Indies. English abolitionists thwarted this effort by obtaining a writ of habeas corpus on Somerset's behalf. Somerset was being illegally detained, they declared, because slavery did not exist in England.[55]

Illustration 2-3 A Slave Auction in Virginia

Source: Illustrated London News, February 16, 1861, Valentine Richmond History Center.

54. Rogers Smith, *Civic Ideals: Contested Visions of Citizenship in U.S. History* (New Haven, CT: Yale University Press, 1999), 65.

55. For a good discussion of *Somerset*, see George Van Cleve, "Forum: Somerset's Case Revisited: Somerset's Case and Its Antecedents in Imperial Perspective," *Law and History Review* 24 601 (2006).

Lord Mansfield's decision freeing Somerset is one of the most important rulings in Anglo-American judicial history. Abolitionists were thrilled that Mansfield insisted that slavery could exist only by positive law. Somerset *seems to hold that a court must declare an alleged slave free unless a statute clearly mandates enslavement. American abolitionists soon declared that* "In favorem libertatis" *was both a common law and a constitutional principle.*

Consider the following questions as you read the short paragraph that follows and later discussions of slavery. What exactly did Somerset *hold? Was the decision the great triumph for freedom that abolitionists proclaimed, or was the ruling narrower? What impact did* Somerset *have on American constitutional law? Is* "In favorem libertatis" *a constitutional principle? Did that principle survive the abolition of slavery?*

Transcript of LORD MANSFIELD'S Judgment

The cause returned is, the slave absented himself, and departed from his master's service, and refused to return and serve him during his stay in England; whereupon, by his master's orders, he was put on board the ship by force, and there detained in secure custody, to be carried out of the kingdom and sold. So high an act of dominion must derive its authority, if any such it has, from the law of the kingdom where executed. A foreigner cannot be imprisoned here on the authority of any law existing in his own country: the power of a master over his servant is different in all countries, more or less limited or extensive; the exercise of it therefore must always be regulated by the laws of the place where exercised. The state of slavery is of such a nature, that it is incapable of now being introduced by Courts of Justice upon mere reasoning or inferences from any principles, natural or political; it must take its rise from positive law; the origin of it can in no country or age be traced back to any other source: immemorial usage preserves the memory of positive law long after all traces of the occasion; reason, authority, and time of its introduction are lost; and in a case so odious as the condition of slaves must be taken strictly, the power claimed by this return was never in use here; no master ever was allowed here to take a slave by force to be sold abroad because he had deserted from his service, or for any other reason whatever; we cannot say the cause set forth by this return is allowed or approved of by the laws of this kingdom, therefore the man must be discharged.

C. Gender

Men and women had very different legal rights and duties in colonial America. Women in most colonies could not vote, hold public office, engage in most professions, or serve on juries. Women who attempted to engage in traditional male activities were often severely sanctioned. The most fundamental right of women in colonial America was to decide on a marriage partner. Once that choice was made, the married woman was subordinated to her husband. John Winthrop, the first leader of the Massachusetts Bay Colony, asserted, "The woman's own choice . . . makes . . . a man her husband; yet being so chosen, he is her lord."[56] A husband controlled virtually all of his wife's legal affairs. The common law considered a married woman to be a "feme covert." Blackstone offered the conventional description of this term and the rights of women under common law in his *Commentaries*:

> By marriage, the husband and wife are one person in law: that is, the very being or legal existence of the woman is suspended during the marriage, or at least is incorporated and consolidated into that of the husband: under whose wing, protection, and cover, she performs every thing; and is therefore called in our law-french a feme-covert; is said to be covert-baron, or under the protection and influence of her husband, her baron, or lord; and her condition during her marriage is called her coverture. Upon this principle, of a union of person in husband and wife, depend almost all the legal rights, duties, and disabilities, that either of them acquire by the marriage. . . . For this reason, a man cannot grant any thing to his wife, or enter into covenant with her: for the grant would be to suppose her separate existence: . . . and therefore it is also generally true, that all compacts made between husband and wife, when single, are voided by the intermarriage. . . . The husband is bound to provide his wife with necessaries by law, as much as himself; and if she contracts debts for them, he is obliged to pay them. . . . If the wife be indebted before marriage, the husband is bound afterwards to pay the debt; for he has adopted her and her circumstances

56. John Winthrop, "A Little Speech on Liberty," in *From Many, One: Readings in American Political and Social Thought* (edited by Richard C. Sinopoli) (Georgetown University Press: Washington, DC, 1997), 334.

together. If the wife be injured in her person or her property, she can bring no action for redress without her husband's concurrence, and in his name, as well as her own: neither can she be sued, without making the husband a defendant. There is indeed one case where the wife shall sue and be sued as a feme sole, viz. where the husband has abjured the realm, or is banished: for then he is dead in law. . . .

. . .

The husband also (by the old law) might give his wife moderate correction. For, as he is to answer for her misbehaviour, the law thought it reasonable to entrust him with this power of restraining her, by domestic chastisement, in the same moderation that a man is allowed to correct his servants or children. . . . But this power of correction was confined within reasonable bounds; and the husband was prohibited to use any violence to his wife. . . .

But, with us, . . . this power of correction began to be doubted: and a wife may now have security of the peace against her husband; or, in return, a husband against his wife. Yet the lower rank of people, who were always fond of the old common law, still claim and exert their ancient privilege: and the courts of law will still permit a husband to restrain a wife of her liberty, in case of any gross misbehavior.

These are the chief legal effects of marriage during the coverture; upon which we may observe, that even the disabilities, which the wife lies under, are for the most part intended for her protection and benefit. So great a favourite is the female sex of the laws of England.[57]

IX. Criminal Justice

MAJOR DEVELOPMENTS

- Development of due process and habeas corpus
- Strict limits on general warrants
- Development of the right coercive interrogations
- Emphasis on the right to trial by jury and jury nullification
- Beginnings of the right to counsel

The rights of persons accused of a crime have an ancient lineage in the common law. The most famous sentence in the Magna Carta (1215) asserts, "No free man shall be seized or imprisoned, or stripped of his rights or possessions, or outlawed or exiled, or deprived of his standing in any other way, nor will we proceed with force against him, or send others to do so, except by the lawful judgment of his equals or by the law of the land." By the Colonial Era these words were understood as requiring *due process* of law in criminal cases. Persons accused of crimes could be convicted and sentenced only if the government followed certain rules during the investigation and prosecution of the offense. One study of colonial laws and practices found a general consensus that criminal defendants enjoyed the following:

1. No search or seizure without warrant
2. Right to reasonable bail
3. Confessions out of court invalid
4. Right to have cause determined with reasonable speed
5. Grand jury indictment in capital cases
6. Right to know the charges
7. Straightforward pleading with double jeopardy barred
8. Right to challenge the jurors
9. Process to compel witnesses for the defense
10. Right to confront accusers
11. Trial by jury
12. Limitation of punishment to the convict: no corruption of blood or forfeiture
13. No cruel or unusual punishment
14. Equal protection of the law: dependent classes—women, children, and servants—have access to the courts
15. Equal execution of the law: no capricious mitigation or application of penalties
16. Limited right of appeal[58]

By the time the *Mayflower* landed on Plymouth Rock in 1620, a general consensus existed that prosecutors had to prove that a criminal defendant was guilty of the charged offense. As early as the 1400s the chief justice of England asserted, "One would much rather that twenty guilty persons should escape the punishment of death, than that one innocent person should be condemned, and suffer capitally."[59]

57. Blackstone, *Commentaries*, 1:430–33.

58. David J. Bodenhamer, *Fair Trial: Rights of the Accused in American History* (New York: Oxford University Press, 1992), 19.

59. Ibid., 13.

This long list of rights better describes colonial theory than the actual processes that were followed when persons were suspected or accused of criminal offenses. Investigations and trials during the seventeenth and eighteenth centuries were rarely conducted according to legal formalities. Colonial America had fewer public prosecutors, fewer police officers, and far fewer defense attorneys than the United States did during the nineteenth century. Most criminal trials consisted of the accused being hauled up in front of the judge, a quick judicial survey of the evidence, a conviction, and the sentence. Few defendants knew or exercised their rights, and few judges were interested in protecting defendants' rights. The point of the criminal process was to identify and punish guilty people. Criminal trials took place only when a person of significant political interest was charged with violating the law. John Peter Zenger had a jury trial, complete with all legal formalities, when he was accused of seditious libel by the royal governor, because his trial was of great political interest to local political elites. Very few thieves in New York had a similar legal experience.

The jury trial was the most important procedural right that protected substantive liberties. Juries in the seventeenth and eighteenth centuries often determined both the facts and the law of a case. Some judges instructed juries that they could decide what conduct was legal. More often, juries disregarded judicial instructions when acquitting defendants who had violated the letter of an unpopular law. Colonial juries, by deciding the law and facts of a case, prevented government officials appointed by English authorities from passing and enforcing onerous measures. Many colonial juries refused to convict smugglers, for example, because most colonists enjoyed illegally imported goods. This practice, known as jury nullification, provided persons with a practical right to perform any action that their neighbors believed should be lawful.

A. Due Process and Habeas Corpus

Most American colonists and English legal authorities regarded the Magna Carta as the foundation of their liberty. During the last part of the twelfth and the first part of the thirteenth centuries, English monarchs raised taxes considerably to finance crusades, other military adventures, and an increasingly lavish royal court. Prominent English barons objected to these financial sacrifices. In 1215 King John I forestalled a full-scale revolt by making a series of commitments to the nobility that became known as the Magna Carta. Section 39 of this document would become the most influential concession. That provision asserted, "No free man shall be seized or imprisoned, or stripped of his rights or possessions, or outlawed or exiled, or deprived of his standing in any other way, nor will we proceed with force against him, or send others to do so, except by the lawful judgment of his equals or by the law of the land." As originally understood, the Magna Carta only limited royal power over the English aristocracy. Over time, the charter became the foundation for the rights of all English citizens. Section 39 came to stand for the principle that persons could be punished only if a jury determined that they had violated some preexisting law.

By the sixteenth century the Magna Carta's phrase "by law of the land" was equated with the concept of "due process of law." The leading treatise on the common law at the time the colonies were first settled, Edward Coke's *Institutes of the Laws of England*, made that link explicit when asserting that due process was a fundamental right of all English subjects. Coke declared, "The true sense and exposition of ['by the law of the land' was] . . . without due process of law; . . . it be contained in the great charter, that no man be taken, imprisoned, or put out of his free-hold without process of the law; that is, by indictment or presentment of good and lawful men."[60] Persons could be imprisoned in a manner consistent with due process, the *Institutes* maintained, only if they had violated "the common law, statute law, or the customs of England." Persons could be prosecuted only for violating a preexisting law. Coke insisted that due process also required that the indictment or presentment be sufficiently clear to enable the accused person to know the charges against him and give that person a chance to make a defense. He declared, "No man ought to be put from his livelihood without answer." Finally, due process entailed the right to a jury trial. A person could be deprived of his property or liberty, Coke wrote, only by "the lawful judgment [or] verdict of his equals."[61]

The writ of *habeas corpus* dates from the late twelfth century.[62] Habeas corpus was initially an instrument

60. Edward Coke, *The Second Part of the Institutes of the Laws of England* (London: W. Clarke and Sons, 1809), 2:50.

61. Ibid., 2:46–47.

62. Justin J. Wert, *Habeas Corpus in America: The Politics of Individual Rights* (Lawrence: University Press of Kansas, 2011).

of royal power. Royal justices used the writ to take cases from local courts to ensure that local aristocrats were behaving in a manner consistent with royal edicts and royal concerns. A king might use a writ of habeas corpus to make sure that his rules determined who hunted in the local forest. The persons most often protected by habeas corpus were royal officials and royal favorites, who sought the writ after being charged with offenses in local courts by local nobles.

The modern writ of habeas corpus took shape in the early seventeenth century. During the mid-1620s King Charles I raised revenues without consulting Parliament. Persons who refused to pay his unpopular duties and taxes were imprisoned. Habeas corpus was initially ineffective. Royal justices in *Darnel's Case* (1627–1628) refused to grant a writ of habeas corpus to persons languishing in jail for refusing to make forced loans to the king. Parliament, frustrated with the king, reacted vigorously. In 1628 that legislative body passed the Petition of Right. This measure declared that the king could not raise revenues without the consent of Parliament. Any person imprisoned for failing to pay an illegal tax, the Petition of Right provided, had the right to habeas corpus.

Fifty years later Parliament expanded the writ of habeas corpus. The Habeas Corpus Act of 1679 prevented executive officials from using various subterfuges to prevent persons from seeking that writ. The measure required governing officials to produce the body of any person seeking a writ of habeas corpus before a judge within three days. Such tactics as removing a prisoner from the country were forbidden. If the jailer could not demonstrate that the person was being detained because he had violated or was suspected of violating the laws of the land, then the judge was authorized to free the detainee. The Habeas Corpus Act of 1679 asserted,

> Whereas great delays have been used by . . . Officers to whose Custody any of the Kings Subjects have been committed for criminal or supposed criminal matters in making returns of Writs of Habeas Corpus to them . . . contrary to their duty and the known laws of the land whereby many of the Kings Subjects have been and hereafter may be long detained in prison in such cases where by law they are bailable to their great charge and vexation. For the prevention whereof and the more speedy relief of all persons imprisoned for any such criminal or supposed criminal matters be it enacted . . . that whensoever any person or persons shall bring any Habeas Corpus directed unto any Sheriff . . . or other Person . . . for any person in his or their custody said officer . . . shall within three days . . . bring or cause to be brought the body of the party so committed or restrained unto or before the Lord Chancellor or . . . the Judges or Barons of the said Court from whence the said Writ shall issue or unto and before such other . . . persons before whom the said Writ is made returnable . . . , and shall certify the true causes of his Detainer or Imprisonment unless the commitment of the said party be in any place beyond the distance of twenty miles from the place or places where such Court or Person is or shall be residing and if beyond the distance of twenty miles and not above one hundred miles then within the space of ten days and if beyond the distance of one hundred miles then within the space of twenty days.
>
> And if any person or persons shall be or stand committed or detained as aforesaid for any Crime unless for Treason or Felony plainly expressed in the Warrant of Commitment, it shall and may be lawful to and for the person or persons so committed or detained by legal Process or any one his or their behalf to appeal or complain to . . . any one of His Majesties Justices . . . and the said . . . Justices . . . are hereby authorized. . . to award and grant an Habeas Corpus.

Blackstone described the Habeas Corpus Act of 1679 as "another Magna Carta." His *Commentaries* asserted,

> The glory of the English law consist[s] in clearly defining the times, the causes, and the extent, when, wherefore, and to what degree, the imprisonment of the subject may be lawful. This induces an absolute necessity of expressing upon every commitment the reason for which it is made; that the court upon an habeas corpus may examine into it's validity; and according to the circumstances of the case may discharge, admit to bail, or remand the prisoner.[63]

The extent to which American colonists enjoyed habeas corpus is unclear.[64] Colonial courts in the

---

63. Blackstone, *Commentaries*, 4:133.

64. This paragraph relies on Michael O'Neill, "On Reforming the Federal Writ of Habeas Corpus," *Seton Hall Law Review* 26 (1996): 1493.

eighteenth century sometimes issued the writ. Judges based these decisions on the common law right of habeas corpus or claims that Englishmen living in the colonies enjoyed the benefits of the Habeas Corpus Act. Nevertheless, when colonial legislatures passed laws explicitly authorizing courts to issue writs of habeas corpus, those measures were disallowed by the Privy Council in England. Such decisions angered colonists. When the royal governor of Massachusetts refused to authorize habeas corpus, Cotton Mather, the leading intellectual in New England at the turn of the eighteenth century, declared, "We are slaves."

B. Search and Seizure

The common law sharply limited official power to search private residences. William Pitt, a prominent English politician and prime minister, poetically expressed this right to privacy when he stated, "The poorest man may, in his cottage, bid defiance to all the forces of the Crown. It may be frail; its roof may shake; the wind may blow through it; the storm may enter; the rain may enter; but the King of England may not enter; all his forces dare not cross the threshold of the ruined tenement."[65] Both public officials and private persons who conducted searches without warrants took grave risks. If they found evidence of a crime, the evidence would be admitted at the resulting criminal trial. If a public official or private person failed to find incriminating evidence, he or she could be sued for trespass. The reasonableness of the search was not a legal defense. If every person living in your apartment complex swore that you had illegal drugs in your room and a police officer conducted a warrantless search on that basis, eighteenth-century law permitted you to sue the police officer for trespass if no illegal goods were discovered. Damages could be significant.

Governing officials could claim immunity from lawsuits only if they first obtained a search warrant from a local magistrate. The common law rules that governed search warrants were strict and celebrated by American colonists. *Wilkes v. Wood* (1763) ruled that general search warrants were invalid. *Entick v. Carrington* (1765) ruled that a warrant to search for private papers was invalid. Government could search only for illegal, usually stolen, goods. Warrants were valid only if they specified what illegal goods were being searched for and where those illegal goods were located.

65. Henry Brougham, *The Critical and Miscellaneous Writings of Henry Lord Brougham* (Philadelphia: Lea & Blanchard, 1841), 1:264.

Entick v. Carrington, 19 Howell's State Trials 1029 (1765)

John Entick was the author of several pamphlets criticizing the English government. Under English law at the time, any writing that defamed a government official was considered criminal libel, and persons who penned such works could be criminally punished. Lord Halifax, the secretary of state, issued a warrant in 1762 authorizing his agents to seize all of Entick's writings. Led by Nathan Carrington, the agents searched Entick's house for four hours and carried away more than one hundred pamphlets. Entick responded by suing Carrington for trespass. Carrington claimed that a person with a valid warrant could not be sued for trespass. Entick replied that Lord Halifax had no power to issue a general warrant that authorized persons to search homes for evidence of criminal libel. The jury delivered a special verdict, deciding that if the warrant were invalid, Carrington should be required to pay three hundred pounds in damages. Lord Chief Judge Camden was asked to determine whether the warrant was valid.

Chief Judge Camden ruled that the warrant was illegal. Entick, he declared, was entitled to damages. Pay careful attention to two features of this opinion. First, Camden distinguishes between searches for papers and searches for stolen goods. What is that distinction? Why the different rules? Do you agree? Second, Camden condemns the crime of seditious libel while seemingly preventing that crime from being prosecuted. During the eighteenth century most political essays were anonymous or written under pseudonyms. If, after Entick v. Carrington, *the government could not search private homes for papers, how could officials prove that private persons who used pseudonyms were guilty of seditious libel?*

LORD CHIEF JUDGE CAMDEN'S Judgment

[T]he defendants . . . are under a necessity to maintain the legality of the warrants, under which they have acted, and to shew that the secretary of state in the instance now before us, had a jurisdiction to seize the defendants' papers. If he had no such jurisdiction, the law is clear, that the officers are as much responsible for the trespass as their superior.

This, though it is not the most difficult, is the most interesting question in the cause; because if this point should be determined in favor of the jurisdiction, the secret cabinets and bureaus of every subject in this kingdom will be thrown open to the search and inspection of a messenger, whenever the secretary of state shall think fit to charge, or even to suspect, a person to be the author, printer, or publisher of a seditious libel.

. . .

This power, so claimed by the secretary of state, is not supported by one single citation from any law book extant. . . .

If honestly exerted, it is a power to seize that man's papers, who is charged upon oath to be the author or publisher of a seditious libel; if oppressively, it acts against every man, who is so described in the warrant, though he be innocent.

It is executed against the party, before he is heard or even summoned; and the information, as well as the informers, is unknown.

. . .

If this injury falls upon an innocent person, he is as destitute of remedy as the guilty: and the whole transaction is so guarded against discovery, that if the officer should be disposed to carry off a bank bill he may do it with impunity, since there is no man capable of proving either the taker or the thing taken.

. . .

The great end, for which men entered into society, was to secure their property. That right is preserved sacred and incommunicable in all instances, where it has not been taken away or abridged by some public law for the good of the whole. The cases where this right of property is set aside by private law, are various. Distresses, executions, forfeitures, taxes, etc., are all of this description; wherein every man by common consent gives up that right, for the sake of justice and the general good. By the laws of England, every invasion of private property, be it ever so minute, is a trespass. No man can set his foot upon my ground without my license, but he is liable to an action, though the damage be nothing; which is proved by every declaration in trespass, where the defendant is called upon to answer for bruising the grass and even treading upon the soil. If he admits the fact, he is bound to show by way of justification, that some positive law has empowered or excused him. The justification is submitted to the judges, who are to look into the books; and if such a justification can be maintained by the text of the statute law, or by the principles of common law. If no excuse can be found or produced, the silence of the books is an authority against the defendant, and the plaintiff must have judgment.

According to this reasoning, it is now incumbent upon the defendants to show the law by which this seizure is warranted. If that cannot be done, it is a trespass.

Papers are the owner's goods and chattels: they are his dearest property; and are so far from enduring a seizure, that they will hardly bear an inspection; and though the eye cannot by the laws of England be guilty of a trespass, yet where private papers are removed and carried away, the secret nature of those goods will be an aggravation of the trespass, and demand more considerable damages in that respect. Where is the written law that gives any magistrate such a power? I can safely answer, there is none; and therefore it is too much for us without such authority to pronounce a practice legal, which would be subversive of all the comforts of society.

But though it cannot be maintained by any direct law, yet it bears a resemblance, as was urged, to the known case of search and seizure for stolen goods.

I answer that the difference is apparent. In the one, I am permitted to seize my own goods, which are placed in the hands of a public officer, till the felon's conviction shall entitle me to restitution. In the other, the party's own property is seized before and without conviction, and he has no power to reclaim his goods, even after his innocence is cleared by acquittal.

. . .

Observe too the caution with which the law proceeds in this singular case. There must be a full charge upon oath of a theft committed. The owner must swear that the goods are lodged in such place. He must attend at the execution of the warrant to shew them to the officer, who must see that they answer the description. And, lastly, the owner must abide the event at his peril; for if the goods are not found, he is a trespasser; and the officer being an innocent person, will be always a ready and convenient witness against him.

. . .

On the contrary, in the case before us nothing is described, nor distinguished. No charge is requisite to prove that the party has any criminal papers in his custody; no person present to separate or select; no person to prove in the owner's behalf the officer's misbehavior. . . .

. . .

To search, seize, and carry away all the papers of the subject upon the first warrant; that such a right should have existed from the time whereof the memory of man runneth not to the contrary, and never yet have found a place in any book of law is incredible. But if so strange a thing could be supposed, I do not see, how we could declare the law upon such evidence.

. . .

If the power of search is to follow the right of seizure, every body sees the consequence. He that has it or has had it in his custody; he that has published, copied or maliciously reported it, may fairly be under a reasonable suspicion of having the thing in his custody, and consequently become the object of the search warrant. If libels may be seized it ought to be laid down with precision, when, where, upon what charge, against whom, by what magistrate, and in what stage of the prosecution. All these particulars must be explained and proved to be law, before this general proposition can be established.

As therefore no authority in our book can be produced to support such a doctrine, . . . I cannot be persuaded that such a power can be justified by the common law.

. . .

It is then said, that it is necessary for the ends of government to lodge such a power with a state officer; and that it is better to prevent the publication before than to punish the offender afterwards. I answer, if the legislature be of that opinion, they will revive the Licensing Act. But if they have not done that I conceive they are not of that opinion. And with respect to the argument of state necessity, or a distinction that has been aimed at between state offenses and others, the common law does not understand that kind of reasoning, nor do our books take notice of any such distinctions.

. . .

It is very certain that the law obligeth no man to accuse himself; because the necessary means of compelling self-accusation, falling upon the innocent as well as the guilty, would be both cruel and unjust; and it should seem, that search for evidence is disallowed upon the same principle. There too the innocent would be confounded with the guilty.

. . .

I have now taken notice of every thing that has been urged upon the present point; and upon the whole we are all of opinion, that the warrant to seize and carry away the party's papers in the case of a seditious libel, is illegal and void. . . .

C. Interrogations

General agreement existed among English and colonial legal authorities that persons could not be compelled to testify against themselves. At a minimum this meant that governing authorities could not torture persons to gain confessions. Common law practice suggested that the right against compelled testimony had three other functions. First, persons had a right not to answer inappropriate questions, even when their questioning did not involve torture or compulsion. Second, requiring persons to confess their crimes under oath or in public violated their right to conscience. Third, prosecutors in an adversary system of criminal justice had an obligation to make their case for conviction without relying on the defendant for incriminating evidence.[66]

The controversy over the "oath ex officio" highlights the connection that Anglo-American legal authorities made between the right not to testify against oneself and privacy. This oath was used by religious authorities in England during the sixteenth and seventeenth centuries. Members of the Star Chamber, a special tribunal established by Queen Elizabeth I to root out heresy, made extensive use of sworn testimony. Members of the Star Chamber made persons swear they would tell the truth when interrogated. This was the oath ex officio. The person was then asked various questions, often about their religious or political beliefs. Punishment followed if what he or she expressed was heretical or seditious. Opponents of the oath ex officio and the Star Chamber raised several objections to this practice. Many common people did not understand the intricacies of religious doctrine. Under oath they might unknowingly confess to holding beliefs that governing officials thought heretical (imagine trying to state every tenet of your religious faith, knowing that you will be tortured if you make a mistake). Prominent legal authorities questioned whether persons should be punished for their private beliefs. Edward Coke contended, "No free man should be compelled to answer for his secret thoughts and opinions."[67] No good reason existed for punishing a person

66. This section relies heavily on R. H. Helmholz, Charles M. Gray, John H. Langbein, Eben Moglen, Henry E. Smith, and Albert W. Alschuler, *The Privilege Against Self-Incrimination: Its Origins and Development* (Chicago: University of Chicago Press, 1997).

67. William J. Stuntz, "The Substantive Origins of Criminal Procedure," 105 *Yale L. J.* 393, 141 (1995).

Illustration 2-4 Governor John Winthrop

Source: Charles W. Sharpe, engraver, *Jo. Winthrop, Governor of Massachusetts, 1630–49.* Emmet Collection, Miriam and Ira D. Wallach Division of Art, Prints and Photographs, The New York Public Library, Astor, Lenox and Tilden Foundations.

who had never publicly expressed or acted on privately held unorthodox beliefs about Jesus Christ. In 1641 Parliament abolished the Star Chamber. By the late seventeenth century, the oath ex officio had been abandoned.[68]

The right to remain silent may have been an element of the adversary system of criminal justice that was emerging in the eighteenth century. As criminal trials became contests between prosecutors and defense attorneys, legal authorities insisted that the government prove guilt without any help from the defendant. The defendant's right to remain silent was a right not to provide the prosecution with any evidence that might point toward conviction. Some sources suggest that colonists opposed using confessions as the primary evidence of guilt. John Winthrop and other governing officials in the seventeenth century did not believe that persons could be questioned about crimes unless extrinsic evidence pointed to their culpability. The rule that a person could be questioned only after other evidence pointed to his or her guilt meant that the prosecution could not rely solely on confessions to secure criminal convictions.

Stronger claims about the relationship between the right against self-incrimination and the adversary system are anachronistic. Until the turn of the eighteenth century criminal defendants were required to represent themselves at trial. Very few had defense lawyers on the eve of the Revolution. A criminal defendant who lacked a defense attorney could not remain silent. To do so would forfeit his right to make a defense.

68. See John H. Wigmore, "The Privilege Against Self-Crimination: Its History," *Harvard Law Review* 15 (1902): 1610.

D. Juries and Lawyers

The right to trial by jury and the right to an attorney were well established in both English and American law on the eve of the American Revolution. By 1776 the right to a jury trial had assumed contemporary form. Persons accused of serious crimes could be punished only if a jury voted to convict him or her. The right to an attorney in the Colonial Era was quite different from contemporary practice. Americans at the turn of the twenty-first century recognize the right of a person accused of a crime to be defended by a court-appointed attorney paid for by the government. The colonists recognized only the right of a person accused of a crime to hire a defense attorney.

The jury trial was a staple of common law justice. That procedure dates from the Assize of Clarendon (1166), which established the manner in which the king's ministers brought the king's justice to the entire realm. When the royal officials or "court" entered a township, they assembled twenty-four men thought to be trustworthy. Those men were asked who had broken the king's law. The practice gradually evolved into what we call the *grand jury*, the institution that indicts persons suspected of committing crimes. Over time, English kings also made use of a petit jury. This group of twelve persons determines whether persons charged with crimes by the grand jury are guilty.

Both Englishmen and colonial Americans regarded the jury as the leading bulwark of rights. In a series of important cases, most notably the trial of William Penn in England and the trial of John Peter Zenger in the colonies, juries thwarted unpopular prosecutions. In the Penn trial, a jury refused to convict William Penn of unlawful assembly for preaching Quaker gospel in public. The trial judge imprisoned the jury for refusing to convict, but the jurors in *Bushell's Case* (1670) were freed on a writ of habeas corpus. *Bushell's Case* immediately came to stand for the principle that judges could not interfere with a jury verdict. If a jury declared a person not guilty, neither the jury nor the defendant could be punished.

Juries in the Colonial Era often judged both fact and law. Juries were expected to find such facts as whether a defendant had published an offending criticism of a government official, whether a killing was done in self-defense, or whether goods had been illegally smuggled. Many prominent lawyers insisted that juries also had the right to determine the relevant law. In this view, a jury could determine both whether the defendant had published a criticism of a public official and whether that criticism was protected by the common law. Most judges in both England and the colonies opposed this claimed jury power to determine the law. Nevertheless, jury nullification was quite common. When popular defendants were charged with violating unpopular laws, many juries simply refused to convict. This capacity for nullifying unpopular laws explains why American colonists far preferred rule by local juries to decisions made by royally appointed judges.

The right to counsel developed more slowly in colonial America than the right to a jury trial. English law until the late seventeenth century required persons to defend themselves. Conventional wisdom maintained that innocent persons did not need assistance at trial. Reform was slow. The Treason Act of 1695 gave accused traitors the right "to make . . . full Defense, by Counsel learned in the Law." Gradually, a series of decisions and statutes permitted defense counsel to play a more active role in all felony cases. Defense counsel did not become a regular participant in English criminal trials until the nineteenth century.

The American colonies retained the traditional suspicion of lawyers but were more liberal than the English on the right to retain counsel. Massachusetts in the seventeenth century gave persons a right to employ counsel as long as counsel was not paid. By the eve of the American Revolution the law in most colonies permitted most criminal defendants to be represented by an attorney if they could afford such representation. This right to counsel was nevertheless the least important right associated with the criminal defense process. Americans celebrated such decisions as *Entick v. Carrington*, *Wilkes v. Wood*, and *Bushell's Case*. No similar canonical ruling on the right to counsel was handed down by an English or colonial judge during the seventeenth and eighteenth centuries.

E. Punishments

Crime and punishment repulsed and fascinated people living in the seventeenth and eighteenth centuries. Numerous crimes were punishable by death. Relying heavily on biblical command, the Massachusetts Body of Liberties declared the following to be capital offenses.

If any man after legal conviction shall have or worship any other god, but the lord god, he shall be put to death.

If any man or woman be a witch, (that is hath or consulted with a familiar spirit,) They shall be put to death.

If any person shall Blaspheme the name of god, the father, Son or Holy Ghost, with direct, express, presumptuous or high handed blasphemy, or shall curse god in the like manner, he shall be put to death.

If any person commit any willful murder, which is manslaughter, committed upon premeditated malice, hatred, or Cruelty, . . . he shall be put to death.

If any person slay an other suddenly in his anger or Cruelty of passion, he shall be put to death.

If any person shall slay an other through guile, either by poisoning or other such devilish practice, he shall be put to death.

If any man or woman shall lye with any beast or brute creature by Carnal Copulation, They shall surely be put to death. And the beast shall be slain, and buried and not eaten.

If any man lies with [a man] as he lies with a woman, both of them have committed abomination, they both shall surely be put to death.

If any person commit Adultery with a married or [engaged] wife, the Adulterer and Adulteress shall surely be put to death.

If any man steals a man . . . , he shall surely be put to death.

If any man rise up by false witness, wittingly and of purpose to take away any man's life, he shall be put to death.

This list was humane by English standards. English law punished more than one hundred crimes by death.

Suggested Readings

Bailyn, Bernard. 1967. *The Ideological Origins of the American Republic.* Cambridge, MA: Harvard University Press.

Bilder, Mary Sarah. 2004. *The Transatlantic Constitution: Colonial Legal Culture and the Empire.* Cambridge, MA: Harvard University Press.

Bodenhamer, David J. 1992. *Fair Trial: Rights of the Accused in American History.* New York: Oxford University Press.

Breen, T. H. 2010. *American Insurgents, American Patriots: The Revolution of the People.* New York: Hill and Wang.

Brewer, John. 1990. *The Sinews of Power: War, Money, and the English State, 1688–1783.* Cambridge, MA: Harvard University Press.

Greene, Jack P. 1986. *Peripheries and Center: Constitutional Development in the Extended Polities of the British Empire and the United States, 1607–1788.* Athens: University of Georgia Press.

Hamburger, Philip. 2008. *Law and Judicial Duty.* Cambridge, MA: Harvard University Press.

Hatfield, April Lee. 2007. *Atlantic Virginia: Intercolonial Relations in the Seventeenth Century.* Philadelphia: University of Pennsylvania Press.

Helmholz, R. H., Charles M. Gray, John H. Langbein, Eben Moglen, Henry E. Smith, and Albert W. Alschuler. 1997. *The Privilege Against Self-Incrimination: Its Origins and Development.* Chicago: University of Chicago Press.

Hulsebosch, Daniel J. 2005. *Constituting Empire: New York and the Transformation of Constitutionalism in the Atlantic World, 1664–1830.* Chapel Hill: University of North Carolina Press.

Kammen, Michael G. 1986. *Spheres of Liberty: Changing Perceptions of Liberty in American Culture.* Madison: University of Wisconsin Press.

LaCroix, Alison L. 2010. *The Ideological Origins of American Federalism.* Cambridge, MA: Harvard University Press.

Lutz, Donald S. 1988. *The Origins of American Constitutionalism.* Baton Rouge: Louisiana State University Press.

Maier, Pauline. 1997. *American Scripture: Making the Declaration of Independence.* New York: Vintage.

McIlwain, Charles Howard. 1923. *The American Revolution: A Constitutional Interpretation.* New York: Macmillan.

McLaughlin, Andrew C. 1932. *The Foundations of American Constitutionalism.* New York: New York University Press.

Morgan, Edmund. 1956. *The Birth of the Republic, 1763–89.* Chicago: University of Chicago Press.

Pocock, J. G. A., ed. 1980. *Three British Revolutions: 1641, 1688, 1776.* Princeton, NJ: Princeton University Press.

Reid, Thomas Phillip. 1986–1993. *The Constitutional History of the American Revolution*, 4 vols. Madison: University of Wisconsin Press.

Russell, Elmer Beecher. 1915. *The Review of American Colonial Legislation by the King in Council.* New York: Columbia University Press.

Smith, Joseph Henry. 1950. *Appeals to the Privy Council from the American Plantations.* New York: Columbia University Press.

Stoner, James R. 1992. *The Common Law and Liberal Theory: Coke, Hobbes, and the Origins of American Constitutionalism.* Lawrence: University Press of Kansas.

Chapter 3

The Founding Era: 1776–1791

I. Introduction

Once the "thirteen united States of America" declared their independence from Great Britain in 1776, the authority to govern within those states shifted. Now Parliament, the states claimed, had no authority at all—not over taxes, not over trade, not over anything. With no more allegiance to the king, there was no need for American laws to be consistent with English law or English liberties. If "absolute despotic power" (as the English jurist William Blackstone had called the sovereign power) over the Americans was going to reside somewhere, it was now going to reside in America.

The task of governing the former colonies could not be put off, but the effort at constitution-making stretched across more than a decade. From its beginning, however, this effort proceeded on two tracks. One track played out in the individual states, as the Americans shook off their colonial governments. After 1776—and, if the Revolution were a success, long into the future—new republican governments would provide for law and order in the states. Even as the military struggle for independence continued, individuals continued to get married, make contracts, commit crimes, and die and pass their property on to their heirs. Even during war, the Americans needed law and government. The state governments also played an important part in fighting the war, and they needed to organize themselves to play that part well.

Developments. This first decade of American constitutionalism was a time of experimentation. In several states, the first revolutionary constitutions were soon judged inadequate, and new constitutions were written to replace them. The first state constitutions often did not distinguish very clearly between the state legislature and the Constitutional Convention. Often, in fact, one elected assembly both wrote the constitution and governed under it. It is no surprise that these constitutions emphasized the power of the legislature. The powerful governors of the Colonial Era were swept away, and the new state governors were weak and highly constrained. The executives had few powers of their own. In many states, the executive could be appointed and removed by the legislative branch. Governors were hemmed in by executive councils, which were themselves appointed by the legislature and acted as a further check on the governor's decisions.

Founding Era Americans contested the value of enumerating rights in a constitution. Some state constitutions contained a bill of rights. Others did not. Often, the rights enumerated were haphazard.[1] Some state constitutions included a right to free speech; others did not. No evidence suggests that the presence or absence of particular rights in state constitutions reflected carefully considered views about the importance of the right in question. A second wave of constitutions emphasized checks and balances. State constitutional revision was a first step toward reining in state legislatures, but for reformers like James Madison state-level revision was not enough. National constitutional reform would be needed as well.

The first federal constitution, the Articles of Confederation, had been cobbled together during the Revolution. Benjamin Franklin, an advocate of union since the Albany Congress of 1754, had proposed a set of articles to the Continental Congress in 1775. John Dickinson introduced a draft of the Articles of

1. Leonard W. Levy, *Origins of the Bill of Rights* (New Haven, CT: Yale University Press, 1999), 186.

Box 3-1 A Partial Cast of Characters of the Founding Era

George Mason	■ Virginia anti-Federalist ■ Virginia revolutionary active in protesting parliamentary violations of the British constitution ■ Drafted Virginia Declaration of Rights and state constitution in 1776 ■ Member of Philadelphia convention that drafted U.S. Constitution ■ Opposed ratification of U.S. Constitution in Virginia convention because of absence of a bill of rights ■ Helped draft amendment proposals in Virginia convention that became basis for the Bill of Rights
James Madison	■ Virginia Federalist ■ Managed the passage of the Virginia Statute for Religious Freedom ■ Leading figure in the Philadelphia Constitutional Convention ■ An author of the *Federalist* essays supporting ratification ■ Authored the Bill of Rights ■ Advocated a moderate form of strict constructionism in constitutional interpretation ■ Secretly authored the Virginia Resolutions of 1798 ■ Helped create the Jeffersonian Republican Party ■ Secretary of state for Republican Thomas Jefferson (1801–1809) ■ President of the United States (1809–1817)
James Wilson	■ Federalist ■ Author of important revolutionary pamphlet on legal authority of Parliament over the colonies ■ Signer of the Declaration of Independence ■ Pennsylvania delegate to the Philadelphia Constitutional Convention ■ Appointed by Federalist George Washington to be one of the first members of the U.S. Supreme Court (1789–1798) ■ Delivered founding lectures on law at the University of Pennsylvania
Benjamin Rush	■ Pennsylvania Federalist ■ Signer of the Declaration of Independence ■ Member of the Pennsylvania state ratification convention for U.S. Constitution ■ Founder of Dickinson College ■ Advocate of government support for the distribution and reading of the Bible ■ Anti-slavery advocate ■ Prison reformer and opponent of capital punishment
Robert Yates	■ Anti-Federalist ■ Chief judge of New York Supreme Court (1790–1798) ■ Delegate to Philadelphia Constitutional Convention but left early out of opposition to the powerful national government ■ Likely authored the "Brutus" essays criticizing the Constitution

Confederation to the Congress on July 12, 1776. With more urgent matters on the agenda, the Articles were not approved by Congress until 1777 and not ratified in the last state until 1781. The first constitution was immediately problematic, and James Madison, among others, began to lobby for reform before the ink was even dry on the Articles. Like many of the revolutionary state constitutions, the Articles reflected the Americans' extreme distrust of governors and kings. It provided for no national executive or judicial branches. All national powers were held by the Confederation Congress, to be delegated out to appointed committees, commissions, or individuals as the legislature saw fit. Congress's authority was limited, and it had little muscle to put behind its decisions. Each state held an equal number of seats in Congress, and most important decisions required a supermajority or unanimous vote. Its enforcement powers, short of mustering the Continental Army, were limited. Its revenues were dependent on loans and requisitions from the states, and by the end of its life the Confederation had exhausted its credit and no state was willing to send it money. The national government, James Madison later observed, had sunk into a "state of imbecility" and "impotency."

James Madison took the initiative, drafting what became known as the Virginia Plan, the framework for a completely restructured and more powerful national government. The delegates generally agreed about the goal—that was, after all, why they were there—so they quickly sat down to serious negotiation over the details of what the government would look like. They faced two critical and related issues: Who would dominate the new national government, and what powers would it exercise? If they knew who could be expected to control the government, they would also know what powers they could safely entrust to it. Those who could expect to be well endowed with seats in the House of Representatives, seats in the Senate, and electoral votes for the president could afford to be generous with national power. Those who could foresee themselves as being part of the national minority were likely to be more cautious. Across multiple policy issues of tax, trade, foreign policy, and slavery and the design of the several branches of government, the necessary compromises and adjustments could be made to satisfy almost everyone in attendance.

2. *Annals of Congress*, 1st Cong., 1st Sess., April 9, 1789, 1:107.

The original U.S. Constitution did not include a bill of rights, although the text did enumerate some liberties. Federalists claimed that such an enumeration was unnecessary. Prominent advocates of ratification insisted that the federal government lacked the powers necessary to violate fundamental rights and that a well-designed government could be trusted to protect fundamental rights, even when those rights were not explicitly enumerated.

Concerned with popular support for the Constitution, James Madison and other Federalists promised to pass a bill of rights during the First Congress. Madison honored that commitment, proposing an early version in late spring 1789. That proposal, in substantially revised form, was ratified in 1791. Few Americans in the Founding Era celebrated the significance of those constitutional amendments. The Federalists remained more concerned with the structure of the national government than with the precise enumeration of constitutional liberties.

Factions (Parties and Interest Groups). National constitutional politics were shaped by the debate between Federalists and anti-Federalists. Federalists favored a strong national government with sufficient powers to promote national interests. Anti-Federalists favored a more limited government that lacked the power to oppress ordinary citizens. Federalists tended to be more affluent than anti-Federalists and more involved in commercial activities. The precise composition of each faction varied from state to state.

The Federalists and anti-Federalists who debated whether to ratify the Constitution were not parties in a modern sense. Neither faction had an organizational structure. Neither existed before the ratification debates, and the alliances formed during those debates quickly disintegrated. By the end of the Founding Era, James Madison and Alexander Hamilton, two of the authors of *The Federalist Papers*, were the leaders of rival factions in the national government.

Courts. Some Americans in the Founding Era suggested that courts might limit the incidence of minority or majority tyranny. Alexander Hamilton in *Federalist* 78 claimed that a federal judiciary would provide additional protection for individual rights. Nevertheless, in 1787 the framers focused on the structure of governing institutions as the primary device for limiting government and protecting individual rights.

Table 3-1 Ratification of the U.S. Constitution by State

State	Convention Majority	Ratification Date	Final Vote
Delaware	Federalist	Dec. 7, 1787	100%
Pennsylvania	Federalist	Dec. 12, 1787	67%
New Jersey	Federalist	Dec. 19, 1787	100%
Georgia	Federalist	Jan. 2, 1788	100%
Connecticut	Federalist	Jan. 9, 1788	76%
Massachusetts	Anti-Federalist	Feb. 6, 1788	53%
Maryland	Federalist	April 28, 1788	85%
South Carolina	Federalist	May 23, 1788	67%
New Hampshire	Anti-Federalist	June 21, 1788	55%
Constitution meets Article VII requirement for ratification			
Virginia	Evenly split	June 25, 1788	53%
New York	Anti-Federalist	July 26, 1788	53%
George Washington inaugurated as first president April 30, 1789			
Bill of Rights passed by Congress Sept. 25, 1789			
North Carolina	Federalist	Nov. 21, 1789	71%
Rhode Island	Anti-Federalist	May 29, 1790	52%

The possibility of judicial review played a greater role during the debates over the Bill of Rights. During the Virginia ratification convention, George Mason and Patrick Henry promoted the potential of judicial power to declare laws unconstitutional in speeches criticizing the lack of textual protections for individual liberties in the original Constitution.[3] "In the arguments in favor of a declaration of rights you omit one which has a great weight with me," Jefferson wrote Madison, "the legal check which it puts into the hands of the judiciary." Madison, when introducing the Bill of Rights in Congress, asserted, "If they are incorporated into the constitution, independent tribunals of justice will consider themselves in a peculiar manner the guardians of those rights." Proponents of a bill of rights also emphasized how enumerating liberties would provide civic education in fundamental principles. Constitutions taught people about their rights. The anti-Federalist Brutus stated that "a full declaration of rights" should have been included in the original version of the Constitution because "the principles . . . upon which the social compact is founded, ought to have been clearly and precisely stated."[4]

Constitutional Thought. The most important constitutional debates between 1776 and 1791 were over the balance of power between the central government and the state governments, the allocation of power between the legislative and executive branches, and what government institutions best protected individual rights. With respect to the protection of rights, many Americans initially believed that regular elections and fair criminal trials sufficed to secure a free regime. Local majority rule guaranteed the selection of governing officials who

3. Merrill Jensen, ed., *The Documentary History of the Ratification of the Constitution* (Madison: State Historical Society of Wisconsin, 1978), 10:1219, 1361.

4. Brutus, "Essays of Brutus," in *The Anti-Federalist: Writings by the Opponents of the Constitution*, ed. Herbert Storing (Chicago: University of Chicago Press, 1981), 117.

SACRED TO LIBERTY JUSTICE AND PEACE
Behold! a Fabric now to Freedom rear'd,
Approv'd by Friends, and ev'n by Foes rever'd;
Where Justice, too, and Peace, by us ador'd,
Shall heal each Wrong, and keep ensheath'd the Sword.
Approach then, Concord, fair Columbia's Son;
And, faithful Clio, write that 'WE ARE ONE'.

Illustration 3-1 Behold! A Fabric Now to Freedom Rear'd
Allegorical James Trenchard engraving celebrating the ratification of the U.S. Constitution and the union of the thirteen states.
Source: Trenchard, James, b. 1747, engraver. Library of Congress Prints and Photographs Division Washington, DC 20540, USA.

would govern consistently and share broad understandings of justice. Trial by jury enabled local citizens to check the rare elected official bent on restricting popular rights. Majority rule was also consistent with the common understanding that rights could be limited when doing so was in the public interest. Americans in the late eighteenth century believed that restrictions on liberties that served the public good did not violate fundamental rights. No one had a right to use property in ways that harmed others. Most framers thought that government authorities could restrict speech and limit voting rights when such measures served common social interests.

What kind of constitution had the Federalists made? The anti-Federalists argued that it was a "consolidated" and "aristocratic" constitution that would restrict rather than enhance liberty. It created a government that allocated extraordinary powers to itself and yet was distant from the people. Progressive scholars at the turn of the twentieth century became newly fascinated by the anti-Federalist concerns. Most prominently, the historian Charles Beard argued that the creation of the Constitution was one battle in the long-running war between commercial and agricultural interests in the United States. The personal economic interests of the Convention delegates, he claimed, motivated reform and decisions over the details of the proposed Constitution. Those who supported the Constitution were creditors and represented business interests, he argued, and those opposed to it were debtors and heavily invested in land. The details of Beard's argument have not held up, but other scholars have also emphasized the importance of real interests, whether economic or political, in shaping the constitutional politics of the Founding Era.[5]

Over the past few decades, scholars have also emphasized the importance of ideas to the constitutional debates. A central theme is the tension between liberal and republican ideas in the Founding Era. Liberalism, in the tradition of English philosophers John Locke and later John Stuart Mill, emphasizes individualism and rights against government power. Republicanism, in the tradition of the Italian writer Niccolo Machiavelli and the English writer James Harrington, emphasizes civic virtue, political community, and skepticism of government corruption. These traditions can be mutually reinforcing: both value democracy and limited government. But the constitutional reforms of the 1780s can be seen as a shift in emphasis toward liberalism and away from the more republican constitutions of the Revolutionary Era. The Constitution created a more distant, less accountable, and more complex machinery of government. It would refine the sentiments of the people rather than mirror them and provide more institutional protections of rights, especially the rights of property.[6]

Legacies. The founding generation bequeathed to their descendants a remarkably enduring constitutional structure, a set of enumerated rights, and a set of institutions designed to protect those rights. They did not bequeath an end to debates over the nature of federal-state relations, the precise boundaries of the separation of powers, or the best understanding of American rights and liberties. Rather, those debates were mostly subsumed into debates about the meaning of the Constitution. Future generations of Americans determined what rights state and federal governments protected by interpreting the constitutional provisions ratified during the 1780s. When controversies broke out in 1798, 1917, and 1969 over government power to regulate political dissent, all parties turned to the protections for free speech that the founders had placed in the state and federal constitutions. The constitutional politics responsible for protecting these rights and liberties were also established by the founders. Supreme Court justices from 1789 to the present have been appointed according to the rules laid out in Article III of the U.S. Constitution. Presidential candidates who promise to ban abortion or support gun control must gain office according to the rules laid down in Article II, as modified by the Twelfth Amendment.

Throughout history many constitutional commentators have insisted that constitutional provisions be interpreted in a manner consistent with their original meaning. Critics claim that no clear agreement existed on the meaning of crucial constitutional provisions or on more general constitutional principles.[7] This chapter discusses how the meaning of the constitutional text was understood during the Founding Era, as well as disagreements over what it meant and even whether it was desirable. Later chapters illuminate the debates that have emerged or continued over time about the meaning of the Constitution.

5. Charles A. Beard, *An Economic Interpretation of the Constitution of the United States* (New York: Free Press, 1986); Forrest McDonald, *We the People* (Chicago: University of Chicago Press, 1958); John Patrick Diggins, "Power and Authority in American History: The Case of Charles Beard and His Critics," *American Historical Review* 86 (1981): 701–730; Robert A. McGuire, *To Form a More Perfect Union* (New York: Oxford University Press, 2003).

6. Gordon S. Wood, *The Creation of the American Republic, 1776–1787* (New York: Norton, 1972); Forrest McDonald, *Novus Ordo Seclorum* (Lawrence: University Press of Kansas, 1985).

7. On the originalism debate, see Keith E. Whittington, *Constitutional Interpretation* (Lawrence: University Press of Kansas, 1999); Jack N. Rakove, ed., *Interpreting the Constitution* (Boston: Northeastern University Press, 1990).

II. Foundations

MAJOR DEVELOPMENTS

- Debates over the value of enumerating rights in a constitution
- Ratification of bills of rights in state constitutions
- Ratification of the Bill of Rights in the federal Constitution

Americans believed that a written constitution was superior to the unwritten English Constitution. Written constitutions were clearer. By writing down their fundamental laws, the founders believed that they had established firm limitations on government power. A "written constitution," St. George Tucker declared in *Kamper v. Hawkins*, is "not an 'ideal thing, but a real existence: it can be produced in a visible form': its principles can be ascertained from the living letter, not from obscure reasoning or deductions only."[8] English authorities questioned whether past practice supported an absolute prohibition on general warrants. Americans could point to the language in the Fourth Amendment that states, "No Warrants shall issue, but upon probable cause, . . . and particularly describing the place to be searched, and the persons or things to be seized." Written constitutions were less subject to alteration by ordinary politics than unwritten constitutions. By establishing a written constitution with specific rules for amendment, Americans believed that they had prevented elected officials from changing fundamental laws without approval from the people. Parliament claimed the authority to determine what speech was constitutionally protected. Congress had no similar power to alter unilaterally the First Amendment to the Constitution.

A. Sources

Americans established numerous new constitutional protections for rights. State constitutions included either a bill of rights or various provisions protecting fundamental rights. The Bill of Rights was added to the national Constitution in 1791. Section 14 of the Northwest Ordinance guaranteed the fundamental liberties of persons living in the Northwest Territories. These documents, combined with the post–Civil War amendments to the federal Constitution, provide the legal foundations for fundamental rights in the United States.

Bills of rights and related enactments in the late eighteenth century were outcomes of political struggles over how consensual rights were best protected. Most Americans agreed that government should protect property rights, free speech, the right to a jury trial, and habeas corpus. With the important exceptions of religious freedom and slavery, few substantial disputes broke out between 1776 and 1791 over the substance of these rights. Federalists and anti-Federalists debated the institutional practices that best secured rights against oppressive government actions, but they did not dramatically disagree about what rights needed protecting.

Constitutions were not the only source of fundamental rights during the Founding Era. Many political activists insisted that government officials had obligations to protect natural rights, regardless of whether those rights were specifically enumerated in the relevant constitutional text. James Varnum in *Trevett v. Weeden* (RI 1786) maintained, "The Judges, and all others, are bound by the laws of nature in preference to any human laws, because they were ordained by God himself anterior to any civil or political institutions."[9] Several judges claimed that the law of nations bound state governments. Judge James Duane in *Rutgers v. Waddington* (NY 1784) asserted, "By our excellent constitution, the common law is declared to be part of the law of the land; and the *jus gentium* [law of nations] is a branch of the common law."

The Ratification Debates over the National Bill of Rights

Participants in the debates over whether to ratify the Constitution expressed more concern with the omission of a bill of rights than did the persons who framed the Constitution. The most important anti-Federalist writings condemned the drafting convention's failure to provide explicit constitutional protections for such liberties as the freedom of speech and the freedom of religion. Such leading Federalists as James Wilson and Alexander Hamilton defended this

8. *Kamper v. Hawkins*, 3 Va. 20, 78–79 (VA 1793).

9. Bernard Schwartz, ed., *The Bill of Rights: A Documentary History* (New York: Chelsea House, 1971), 424.

omission. They insisted that a bill of rights was unnecessary in a popular government with strictly enumerated powers.

Debate was particularly intense in Pennsylvania, where James Wilson and John Smilie engaged in an early and influential exchange over whether the Constitution should provide specific guarantees for fundamental rights. Wilson and his Federalist allies gained a majority for ratification at the state convention. Smilie and other Pennsylvania allies then issued a public dissent that attacked the absence of a constitutional bill of rights. Confronted with these anti-Federalist criticisms in the closely contested New York ratifying convention, Alexander Hamilton in Federalist *84 penned the classic Federalist defense for the constitutional failure to include a bill of rights.*

As the debates wore on, some Federalists moved toward a compromise position. James Madison in his correspondence with Thomas Jefferson indicated that he was not opposed to a bill of rights, even though he did not think such provisions particularly important. Many state ratification conventions approved the Constitution with the understanding that amendments protecting fundamental rights would swiftly be added. Virginia, New York, Massachusetts, South Carolina, New Hampshire, and North Carolina proposed amendments when voting to ratify the Constitution.

As you read the subsequent materials, consider the following questions. To what extent was the debate over the Bill of Rights a debate over what rights the Constitution should protect, and to what extent was it a debate over how the Constitution should protect rights? How did the different participants in the debate believe a bill of rights would function? Did the Federalists have an effective answer to anti-Federalist concerns that the federal government could exercise Article I powers to curtail rights? Did Hamilton and Wilson believe that the federal government would never censor the press, or that any censorship would be for a legitimate government purpose (and hence not violate the freedom of the press)? To what extent were anti-Federalists concerned with individual rights or government powers? To what extent would that distinction make little sense to the participants in the ratification debates over the Bill of Rights?

The Pennsylvania Ratification Debates (October 28, 1787)[10]

JAMES WILSON

I cannot say, Mr. President, what were the reasons of every member of that Convention for not adding a bill of rights. I believe the truth is, that such an idea never entered the mind of many of them. . . . A proposition to adopt a measure that would have supposed that we were throwing into the general government every power not expressly reserved by the people, would have been spurned at, in that house, with the greatest indignation. Even in a single government, if the powers of the people rest on the same establishment as is expressed in this Constitution, a bill of rights is by no means a necessary measure. In a government possessed of enumerated powers, such a measure would be not only unnecessary, but preposterous and dangerous. Whence comes this notion that in the United States there is no security without a bill of rights? Have the citizens of South Carolina no security for their liberties? They have no bill of rights. Are the citizens on the eastern side of the Delaware less free, or less secured in their liberties, than those on the western side? The state of New Jersey has no bill of rights. The state of New York has no bill of rights. The states of Connecticut and Rhode Island have no bill of rights. I know not whether I have exactly enumerated the states who have not thought it necessary to add *a bill of rights* to their constitutions; but this enumeration, sir, will serve to show by experience, as well as principle, that, even in single governments, a bill of rights is not an essential or necessary measure. But in a government consisting of enumerated powers, such as is proposed for the United States, a bill of rights would not only be unnecessary, but, in my humble judgment, highly imprudent. In all societies, there are many powers and rights which cannot be particularly enumerated. A bill of rights annexed to a constitution is *an enumeration of the powers* reserved. If we attempt an enumeration, every thing that is not enumerated is presumed to be given. The consequence is, that an imperfect enumeration would throw all implied power into the scale of the government, and the rights of the people would be rendered incomplete. On the other hand, an imperfect enumeration of the powers of government reserves all implied power to the people; and by that means the constitution becomes incomplete. But of the two, it is much safer to run the risk on the side of the constitution; for an omission in the

10. Excerpt taken from Jonathan Elliot, ed., *The Debates in the Several State Conventions on the Adoption of the Federal Constitution as Recommended by the General Convention at Philadelphia in 1787*, 2nd ed. (Washington, DC: Jonathan Elliot, 1836), 2:408–09.

enumeration of the powers of government is neither so dangerous nor important as an omission in the enumeration of the rights of the people. . . .

November 28, 1787[11]

John Smilie

The arguments which have been urged, Mr. President, have not, in my opinion, satisfactorily shown that a bill of rights would have been an improper, nay, that it is not a necessary appendage to the proposed system. . . . [T]he members of the federal convention were themselves convinced, in some degree, of the expediency and propriety of a bill of rights, for we find them expressly declaring that the writ of habeas corpus and the trial by jury of criminal cases shall not be suspended or infringed. How does this indeed agree with the maxim that whatever is not given is reserved? Does it not rather appear from the reservation of these two articles that everything else, which is not specified, is included in the powers delegated to the government? This, Sir, must prove the necessity of a full and explicit declaration of rights; and when we further consider the extensive, and undefined powers vested in the administrators of this system, when we consider the system itself as a great political compact between the governors and the governed, a plain, strong, and accurate criterion by which the people might at once determine when, and in what instance their rights were violated, is a preliminary, without which, this plan ought not to be adopted. So loosely, so inaccurately are the powers which are enumerated in this constitution defined, that it will be impossible, without a test of that kind, to ascertain the limits of authority, and to declare when government has degenerated into oppression. In that event the contest will arise between the people and the rulers: "You have exceeded the powers of your office, you have oppressed us," will be the language of the suffering citizen. The answer of the government will be short—"We have not exceeded our power; you have no test by which you can prove it." Hence, Sir, it will be impracticable to stop the progress of tyranny, for there will be no check but the people and their exertions must be futile and uncertain; since it will be difficult, indeed, to communicate to them the violation that has been committed, and their proceedings will be neither systematical nor unanimous. It is said, however, that the difficulty of framing a bill of rights was insurmountable; but, Mr. President, I cannot agree in this opinion. Our experience, and the numerous precedents before us, would have furnished a very sufficient guide. At present there is no security even for the rights of conscience, and under the sweeping force of the sixth article, every principle of a bill of rights, every stipulation for the most sacred and invaluable privileges of man, are left at the mercy of government.

The Address and Reasons of Dissent of the Minority of the Convention of Pennsylvania to Their Constituents (1787)[12]

. . . We offered our objections to the convention, and opposed those parts of the plan, which, in our opinion, would be injurious to you, in the best manner we were able; and closed our arguments by offering the following propositions to the convention.

1. The right of conscience shall be held inviolable, and neither the legislative, executive nor judicial powers of the United States shall have authority to alter, abrogate, or infringe any part of the constitution of the several states, which provide for the preservation of liberty in matters of religion.
2. That in controversies respecting property, and in suits between man and man, trial by jury shall remain as heretofore, as well in the federal courts, as in those of the several states.
3. That in all capital and criminal prosecutions, a man has a right to demand the cause and nature of his accusation, as well in the federal courts, as in those of the several states; to be heard by himself and his counsel, to be confronted with the accusers and witnesses; to call for evidence in his favor, and a speedy trial by an impartial jury of his vicinage, without whose unanimous consent, he cannot be found guilty, nor can he be compelled to give evidence against himself; and that no man be deprived of his liberty, except by the law of the land or the judgment of his peers.

11. Excerpt taken from John Bach McMaster and Frederick D. Stone, eds., *Pennsylvania and the Federal Constitution, 1787–1788* (Lancaster: Historical Society of Pennsylvania, 1888), 1:254–56.

12. Excerpt taken from McMaster and Stone, *Pennsylvania and the Federal Constitution*, 2:461–82.

4. That excessive bail ought not to be required, nor excessive fines imposed, nor cruel nor unusual punishments inflicted.
5. That warrants unsupported by evidence, whereby any officer or messenger may be commanded or required to search suspected places, or to seize any person or persons, his or their property, not particularly described, are grievous and oppressive, and shall not be granted either by the magistrates of the federal government or others.
6. That the people have a right to the freedom of speech, of writing and publishing their sentiments, therefore, the freedom of the press shall not be restrained by any law of the United States.
7. That the people have a right to bear arms for the defence of themselves and their own state, or the United States, or for the purpose of killing game; and no law shall be passed for disarming the people or any of them, unless for crimes committed, or real danger of public injury from individuals; and as standing armies in the time of peace are dangerous to liberty, they ought not to be kept up: and that the military shall be kept under strict subordination to and be governed by the civil powers.
8. The inhabitants of the several states shall have liberty to fowl and hunt in seasonable times, on the lands they hold, and on all other lands in the United States not inclosed, and in like manner to fish in all navigable waters, and others not private property, without being restrained therein by any laws to be passed by the legislature of the United States.
9. That no law shall be passed to restrain the legislatures of the several states from enacting laws for imposing taxes, except imposts and duties upon goods imported or exported, and postage on letters shall be levied by the authority of Congress.
10. That the house of representatives be properly increased in number; that elections shall remain free; that the several states shall have power to regulate the elections for senators and representatives, without being controled either directly or indirectly by any interference on the part of the Congress, and that elections of representatives be annual.
11. That the power of organizing, arming and disciplining the militia (the manner of disciplining the militia to be prescribed by Congress) remain with the individual states, and that Congress shall not have authority to call or march any of the militia out of their own state, without the consent of such state, and for such length of time only as such state shall agree.

That the sovereignty, freedom and independency of the several states shall be retained, and every power, jurisdiction and right which is not by this constitution expressly delegated to the United States in Congress assembled.

. . .

The first consideration that this review suggests, is the omission of a *BILL* of *RIGHTS*, ascertaining and fundamentally establishing those unalienable and personal rights of men, without the full, free, and secure enjoyment of which there can be no liberty, and over which it is not necessary for a good government to have the control. The principal of which are the rights of conscience, personal liberty by the clear and unequivocal establishment of the writ of habeas *corpus*, jury trial in criminal and civil cases, by an impartial jury of the vicinage or county, with the common law proceedings, for the safety of the accused in criminal prosecutions, and the liberty of the press, that scourge of tyrants, and the grand bulwark of every other liberty and privilege; the stipulations heretofore made in favor of them in the state constitutions, are entirely superceded by this constitution. . . .

Alexander Hamilton, Federalist 84[13]

. . .

The most considerable of the remaining objections is that the plan of the convention contains no bill of rights. . . .

. . . The Constitution proposed by the convention contains . . . a number of such provisions.

. . .

The establishment of the writ of habeas corpus, the prohibition of ex-post-facto laws, and of TITLES OF NOBILITY . . . are perhaps greater securities to liberty

13. Excerpt taken from *The Federalist: A Collection of Essays, Written in Favour of the New Constitution, as Agreed Upon by the Federal Convention, September 17, 1787, in two volumes* (New York: J. and A. McLean, 1788).

and republicanism than [the Constitution of New York] contains. The creation of crimes after the commission of the fact, or, in other words, the subjecting of men to punishment for things which, when they were done, were breaches of no law, and the practice of arbitrary imprisonments, have been, in all ages, the favorite and most formidable instruments of tyranny. . . .

Nothing need be said to illustrate the importance of the prohibition of titles of nobility. This may truly be denominated the corner-stone of republican government; for so long as they are excluded, there can never be serious danger that the government will be any other than that of the people.

. . .

It has been several times truly remarked that bills of rights are, in their origin, stipulations between kings and their subjects, abridgements of prerogative in favor of privilege, reservations of rights not surrendered to the prince. Such was MAGNA CHARTA . . . , the PETITION OF RIGHT . . . (and) the Declaration of Right . . . in 1688, (which was) . . . afterwards thrown into the form of an act of parliament called the Bill of Rights. It is evident, therefore, that, according to their primitive signification, they have no application to constitutions professedly founded upon the power of the people, and executed by their immediate representatives and servants. Here, in strictness, the people surrender nothing; and as they retain every thing they have no need of particular reservations. "WE, THE PEOPLE of the United States, to secure the blessings of liberty to ourselves and our posterity, do ORDAIN and ESTABLISH this Constitution for the United States of America." Here is a better recognition of popular rights, than volumes of those aphorisms which make the principal figure in several of our State bills of rights, and which would sound much better in a treatise of ethics than in a constitution of government.

. . .

I go further, and affirm that bills of rights, in the sense and to the extent in which they are contended for, are not only unnecessary in the proposed Constitution, but would even be dangerous. They would contain various exceptions to powers not granted; and, on this very account, would afford a colorable pretext to claim more than were granted. For why declare that things shall not be done which there is no power to do? Why, for instance, should it be said that the liberty of the press shall not be restrained, when no power is given by which restrictions may be imposed? I will not contend that such a provision would confer a regulating power; but it is evident that it would furnish, to men disposed to usurp, a plausible pretense for claiming that power. They might urge with a semblance of reason, that the Constitution ought not to be charged with the absurdity of providing against the abuse of an authority which was not given, and that the provision against restraining the liberty of the press afforded a clear implication, that a power to prescribe proper regulations concerning it was intended to be vested in the national government. This may serve as a specimen of the numerous handles which would be given to the doctrine of constructive powers, by the indulgence of an injudicious zeal for bills of rights.

On the subject of the liberty of the press, . . . I contend, that whatever has been said about it in that of any other State, amounts to nothing. What signifies a declaration, that "the liberty of the press shall be inviolably preserved"? What is the liberty of the press? Who can give it any definition which would not leave the utmost latitude for evasion? I hold it to be impracticable; and from this I infer, that its security, whatever fine declarations may be inserted in any constitution respecting it, must altogether depend on public opinion, and on the general spirit of the people and of the government. And here, after all, as is intimated upon another occasion, must we seek for the only solid basis of all our rights.

. . . The truth is, after all the declamations we have heard, that the Constitution is itself, in every rational sense, and to every useful purpose, A BILL OF RIGHTS. The several bills of rights in Great Britain form its Constitution, and conversely the constitution of each State is its bill of rights. And the proposed Constitution, if adopted, will be the bill of rights of the Union. Is it one object of a bill of rights to declare and specify the political privileges of the citizens in the structure and administration of the government? This is done in the most ample and precise manner in the plan of the convention. . . . Is another object of a bill of rights to define certain immunities and modes of proceeding, which are relative to personal and private concerns? This we have seen has also been attended to, in a variety of cases, in the same plan. . . .

Thomas Jefferson and James Madison, Correspondence (1787–1789)[14]

Thomas Jefferson to James Madison, December 20, 1787

. . . I will now add what I do not like. First the omission of a bill of rights providing clearly & without the aid of sophisms for freedom of religion, freedom of the press, protection against standing armies, restriction against monopolies, the eternal & unremitting force of the habeas corpus laws, and trials by jury in all matters of fact triable by the laws of the land & not by the law of nations. To say, as Mr. Wilson does, that a bill of rights was not necessary because all is reserved in the case of the general government which is not given, while in the particular ones all is given which is not reserved, might do for the audience to whom it was addressed, but is surely . . . opposed by strong inferences from the body of the instrument, as well as from the omission of the clause of our present confederation which had declared that in express terms. . . . Let me add that a bill of rights is what the people are entitled to against every government on earth, general or particular, & what no just government should refuse, or rest on inferences.

James Madison to Thomas Jefferson, October 17, 1788

. . .

My own opinion has always been in favor of a bill of rights; provided that it be so framed as not to imply powers not meant to be included in the enumeration. At the same time I have never thought the omission a material defect, nor been anxious to supply it even by subsequent amendment, for any other reason than that it is anxiously desired by others. I have favored it because I suppose it might be of use, and if properly executed could not be of disservice.

I have not viewed it in an important light—

1. because I conceive that in a certain degree . . . the rights in question are reserved by the manner in which the federal powers are granted.
2. because there is great reason to fear that a positive declaration of some of the most essential rights could not be obtained in the requisite latitude. I am sure that the rights of conscience in particular, if submitted to public definition would be narrowed much more than they are ever likely to be by an assumed power.
3. because the limited powers of the federal Government and the jealousy of the subordinate Governments, afford a security which has not existed in the case of the State Governments, and exists in no other.
4. because experience proves the inefficiency of a bill of rights on those occasions when its controul is most needed. Repeated violations of these parchment barriers have been committed by overbearing majorities in every State. In Virginia I have seen the bill of rights violated in every instance where it has been opposed to a popular current. Notwithstanding the explicit provision contained in that instrument for the rights of Conscience, it is well known that a religious establishment would have taken place in that State, if the Legislative majority had found as they expected, a majority of the people in favor of the measure; and I am persuaded that if a majority of the people were now of one sect, the measure would still take place. . . .

Wherever the real power in a government lies, there is the danger of oppression. In our Governments the real power lies in the majority of the Community, and the invasion of private rights is chiefly to be apprehended, not from acts of Government contrary to the sense of its constituents, but from acts in which the Government is the mere instrument of the major number of the Constituents. The difference so far as it relates to the point in question—the efficacy of a bill of rights in controlling abuses of power—lies in this: that in a monarchy the latent force of the nation is superior to that of the Sovereign, and a solemn charter of popular rights must have a great effect, as a standard for trying the validity of public acts, and a signal for rousing & uniting the superior force of the community; whereas in a popular Government, the political and physical power may be considered as vested in the same hands, that is in a majority of the people, and, consequently the tyrannical will of the Sovereign is not [to] be controlled by the dread of an appeal to any other force within the community. What use then it may be asked can a bill of rights serve in popular Governments? I answer the two following which, though less essential than in other Governments, sufficiently recommend the precaution: 1. The political

14. Excerpt taken from James Morton Smith, ed., *The Republic of Letters: The Correspondence Between Thomas Jefferson and James Madison, 1776–1826* (New York: W. W. Norton, 1995) 1:512, 564–65, 587–88.

truths declared in that solemn manner acquire by degrees the character of fundamental maxims of free Government, and as they become incorporated with the national sentiment, counteract the impulses of interest and passion. 2. Although it be generally true as above stated that the danger of oppression lies in the interested majorities of the people rather than in usurped acts of the Government, yet there may be occasions on which the evil may spring from the latter source; and on such, a bill of rights will be good ground for an appeal to the sense of the community. . . .

Supposing a bill of rights to be proper. . . . I am inclined to think that absolute restrictions in cases that are doubtful, or where emergencies may overrule them, ought to be avoided. The restrictions however strongly marked on paper will never be regarded when opposed to the decided sense of the public, and after repeated violations in extraordinary cases they will lose even their ordinary efficacy. Should a Rebellion or insurrection alarm the people as well as the Government, and a suspension of the Habeas Corpus be dictated by the alarm, no written prohibitions on earth would prevent the measure. . . .

Thomas Jefferson to James Madison, March 15, 1789

. . .

[Y]our thoughts on the subject of the Declaration of rights in the letter of Oct. 17. I have weighted with great satisfaction. . . . [I]n the arguments in favor of a declaration of rights you omit one which has a great weight with me, the legal check which it puts into the hands of the judiciary. This is a body, which if rendered independent, & kept strictly to their own department merits great confidence for their learning & integrity. . . .

I cannot refrain from making short answers to the objections which your letter states to have been missed.

1. That the rights in question are reserved by the manner in which the federal powers are granted. Answer. . . . [A] constitutive act which leaves some precious article unnoticed, and raises implications against others, a declaration of rights becomes necessary by way of supplement. This is the case of our new federal constitution. This instrument forms us into one state as to certain objects, and gives us a legislative & executive body for these objects. It should therefore guard us against their abuses of power within the field submitted to them.
2. A positive declaration of some essential rights could not be obtained in the requisite latitude. Answer. Half a loaf is better than no bread. If we cannot secure all our rights, let us secure what we can.
3. The limited powers of the federal government & jealousy of the subordinate governments afford a security which exists in no other instance. Answer. The first member of this seems resolvable into the 1st. objection before stated. The jealousy of the subordinate governments is a precious reliance. But observe that those governments are only agents. They must have principles furnished them whereon to found their opposition. The declaration of rights will be the text whereby they will try all the acts of the federal government. In this view it is necessary to the federal government also: as by the same text they may try the opposition of the subordinate governments.
4. Experience proves the inefficacy of a bill of rights. True. But though it is not absolutely efficacious under all circumstances, it is of great potency always, and rarely inefficacious. A brace the more will often keep up the building which would have fallen with that brace the less. There is a remarkable difference between the characters of the inconveniencies which attend a Declaration of rights, & those which attend the want of it. The inconveniences of the Declaration are that it may cramp government in it's useful exertions. But the evil of this is shortlived, moderate, & reparable. The inconveniencies of the want of a Declaration are permanent, afflicting & irreparable: they are in constant progression from bad to worse. The executive in our governments is not the sole, it is scarcely the principal object of my jealousy. The tyranny of the legislatures is the most formidable dread at present, and will be for long years. . . .

B. Principles

Political elites in the Founding Era favored republican government. They believed that republics were committed to the following principles:

1. The people are the source of all political authority.
2. The purpose of government is to protect natural rights and advance the public good.

3. All government officials, not just the king (or chief executive), must respect natural rights.
4. The most important rights that government protects are life, liberty, and property.
5. Government may regulate behavior when doing so promotes the public good. No one may harm others or act contrary to the public good.
6. All political decisions are made by the people's elected representatives or by persons appointed by the people's elected representatives.
7. A well-designed republic follows procedures for staffing the government that privilege the selection of particularly virtuous persons with the probity to protect private rights and the wisdom to identify the public good.
8. A well-designed republic follows procedures for making laws that limit temptations for self-seeking behavior and provide incentives for representatives to protect private rights and seek the common good.

These principles differ from contemporary notions of democratic government. Most of the framers believed in the existence of a common good that was not simply an aggregation of individual interests. Numerous constitutional provisions were designed to prevent legislation that advanced the interests of one social group at the expense of another. Most of the framers believed that some people had more capacity to govern than others and that constitutions should be designed to ensure the election of the best-qualified governors, as opposed to the most popular citizens. The persons responsible for the Constitution had no conception of electoral competition between political parties as being central to a democracy or vital for maintaining governmental accountability.

Thomas Jefferson, Declaration of Independence (1776)

The Declaration of Independence provided the theoretical justification for the American Revolution. King George III, Thomas Jefferson declared, had violated the fundamental rights of American colonists. The English people had done nothing to prevent those rights violations. This combination of tyranny and indifference provided legitimate grounds for the colonial decision to declare independence.

Jefferson's claim that "all men are created equal" echoes arguments made in John Locke's Second Treatise on Government. *What similarities do you detect in the reasoning? Do you detect important differences as well? Jefferson's complaints against King George III also echo seventeenth- and eighteenth-century English complaints against Charles I and other monarchs. Compare the Declaration of Independence to the English Bill of Rights (1689). To what extent did Jefferson accuse George III of repeating the crimes of Charles I? What new offenses did the Declaration include? What is the relationship between the Declaration and the American Bill of Rights? To what extent were Americans in 1776 and Americans in 1791 concerned with the same rights and the same threats to rights?*

. . .

We hold these truths to be self-evident, that all men are created equal, that they are endowed by their Creator with certain unalienable rights, that among these are life, liberty and the pursuit of happiness. That to secure these rights, governments are instituted among men, deriving their just powers from the consent of the governed. That whenever any form of government becomes destructive to these ends, it is the right of the people to alter or to abolish it, and to institute new government, laying its foundation on such principles and organizing its powers in such form, as to them shall seem most likely to effect their safety and happiness. . . . The history of the present King of Great Britain is a history of repeated injuries and usurpations, all having in direct object the establishment of an absolute tyranny over these states. To prove this, let facts be submitted to a candid world.

. . .

He has dissolved representative houses repeatedly, for opposing with manly firmness his invasions on the rights of the people.

. . .

He has made judges dependent on his will alone, for the tenure of their offices, and the amount and payment of their salaries.

He has erected a multitude of new offices, and sent hither swarms of officers to harass our people, and eat out their substance.

He has kept among us, in times of peace, standing armies without the consent of our legislature.

. . .

He has combined with others [Parliament] to subject us to a jurisdiction foreign to our constitution, and unacknowledged by our laws; giving his assent to their acts of pretended legislation:

For quartering large bodies of armed troops among us:

. . .

For imposing taxes on us without our consent:

For depriving us in many cases, of the benefits of trial by jury:

. . .

For suspending our own legislatures, and declaring themselves invested with power to legislate for us in all cases whatsoever.

. . . He has excited domestic insurrections amongst us, and has endeavored to bring on the inhabitants of our frontiers, the merciless Indian savages, whose known rule of warfare, is undistinguished destruction of all ages, sexes and conditions.[15]

. . .

Nor have we been wanting in attention to our British brethren. We have warned them from time to time of attempts by their legislature to extend an unwarrantable jurisdiction over us. We have reminded them of the circumstances of our emigration and settlement here. We have appealed to their native justice and magnanimity, and we have conjured them by the ties of our common kindred to disavow these usurpations, which, would inevitably interrupt our connections and correspondence. They too have been deaf to the voice of justice and of consanguinity. We must, therefore, acquiesce in the necessity, which denounces our separation, and hold them, as we hold the rest of mankind, enemies in war, in peace friends.

We, therefore, the representatives of the United States of America, in General Congress, assembled, appealing to the Supreme Judge of the world for the rectitude of our intentions, do, in the name, and by the authority of the good people of these colonies, solemnly publish and declare, that these united colonies are, and of right ought to be free and independent states; that they are absolved from all allegiance to the British Crown, and that all political connection between them and the state of Great Britain, is and ought to be totally dissolved. . . .

James Madison, ***Federalist*** **10**

Federalist *10 is presently considered the most important analysis of the Founding Era concerning how republican governments protect rights. In it, Madison distinguishes republics from democracies, elaborates the purposes of republic government, and explains why the institutions set out in the proposed Constitution will promote republican commitments to private rights and the common good. Few framers agreed with Madison's claim that larger polities were more likely than smaller polities to protect rights.*[16] *Nevertheless,* Federalist *10 articulates the broad Federalist consensus that republican ends are better secured by constitutional design than by textual guarantees. Extended republics with religious diversity, Madison contends, are more likely than small, religiously homogenous republics to protect religious freedoms, no matter what language they use in their respective constitutional texts.*

When reading the next selection, consider the following questions. How does Madison think a well-designed republic protects private rights and promotes the public interest? Is his republican scheme sound? Do Madisonian institutions remain good means for protecting private rights and promoting the public interest? What sort of office seekers are privileged by the constitutional rules for staffing the national government? What sorts of policies are privileged by the constitutional rules for making laws? If you wanted a better class of officeholders, how might you change the constitutional rules?

15. At this point, Jefferson penned an attack on the international slave trade:

> [H]e has waged cruel war against human nature itself, violating it's most sacred rights of life & liberty in the persons of a distant people who never offended him, captivating & carrying them to slavery in another hemisphere, or to incur miserable death in their transportations thither. This piratical warfare, the opprobrium of infidel powers, is the warfare of the Christian king of Great Britain. determined to keep open a market where MEN should be bought & sold, he has prostituted his negative for suppressing every legislative attempt to prohibit or to restrain this execrable commerce and that this assemblage of horrors might want no fact of distinguished die, he is now exciting those very people to rise in arms against us, and to purchase that liberty of which he has deprived them, by murdering the people upon whom he also obtruded them; thus paying off former crimes which he urges them to commit against the lives of another.

Congress voted to delete this passage.

16. Larry D. Kramer, "Madison's Audience," *Harvard Law Review* 112 (1999): 611.

AMONG the numerous advantages promised by a well constructed Union, none deserves to be more accurately developed than its tendency to break and control the violence of faction. . . . Complaints are everywhere heard from our most considerate and virtuous citizens . . . that our governments are too unstable, that the public good is disregarded in the conflicts of rival parties, and that measures are too often decided, not according to the rules of justice and the rights of the minor party, but by the superior force of an interested and overbearing majority. However anxiously we may wish that these complaints had no foundation, the evidence, of known facts will not permit us to deny that they are in some degree true. . . .

By a faction, I understand a number of citizens, whether amounting to a majority or a minority of the whole, who are united and actuated by some common impulse of passion, or of interest, adverse to the rights of other citizens, or to the permanent and aggregate interests of the community.

. . .

There are . . . two methods of removing the causes of faction: the one, by destroying the liberty which is essential to its existence; the other, by giving to every citizen the same opinions, the same passions, and the same interests.

It could never be more truly said than of the first remedy, that it was worse than the disease. Liberty is to faction what air is to fire, an aliment without which it instantly expires. But it could not be less folly to abolish liberty, which is essential to political life, because it nourishes faction, than it would be to wish the annihilation of air, which is essential to animal life, because it imparts to fire its destructive agency.

The second expedient is as impracticable as the first would be unwise. As long as the reason of man continues fallible, and he is at liberty to exercise it, different opinions will be formed. . . . The diversity in the faculties of men, from which the rights of property originate, is not less an insuperable obstacle to a uniformity of interests. The protection of these faculties is the first object of government. From the protection of different and unequal faculties of acquiring property, the possession of different degrees and kinds of property immediately results; and from the influence of these on the sentiments and views of the respective proprietors, ensures a division of the society into different interests and parties.

The latent causes of faction are thus sown in the nature of man. . . . [T]he most common and durable source of factions has been the various and unequal distribution of property. Those who hold and those who are without property have ever formed distinct interests in society. Those who are creditors, and those who are debtors, fall under a like discrimination. A landed interest, a manufacturing interest, a mercantile interest, a moneyed interest, with many lesser interests, grow up of necessity in civilized nations, and divide them into different classes, actuated by different sentiments and views. The regulation of these various and interfering interests forms the principal task of modern legislation, and involves the spirit of party and faction in the necessary and ordinary operations of the government.

. . .

It is in vain to say that enlightened statesmen will be able to adjust these clashing interests, and render them all subservient to the public good. Enlightened statesmen will not always be at the helm. . . .

. . .

If a faction consists of less than a majority, relief is supplied by the republican principle, which enables the majority to defeat its sinister views by regular vote. . . . When a majority is included in a faction, the form of popular government, on the other hand, enables it to sacrifice to its ruling passion or interest both the public good and the rights of other citizens. To secure the public good and private rights against the danger of such a faction, and at the same time to preserve the spirit and the form of popular government, is then the great object to which our inquiries are directed. . . .

. . .

. . . [A] pure democracy, by which I mean a society consisting of a small number of citizens, who assemble and administer the government in person, can admit of no cure for the mischiefs of faction. A common passion or interest will, in almost every case, be felt by a majority of the whole; a communication and concert result from the form of government itself; and there is nothing to check the inducements to sacrifice the weaker party or an obnoxious individual. Hence it is that such democracies have ever been spectacles of turbulence and contention; have ever been found incompatible with personal security or the rights of property; and have in general been as short in their lives as they have been violent in their deaths. . . .

A republic, by which I mean a government in which the scheme of representation takes place, opens a different prospect, and promises the cure for which we are seeking. . . .

The two great points of difference between a democracy and a republic are: first, the delegation of the government, in the latter, to a small number of citizens elected by the rest; secondly, the greater number of citizens, and greater sphere of country, over which the latter may be extended.

The effect of the first difference is, on the one hand, to refine and enlarge the public views, by passing them through the medium of a chosen body of citizens, whose wisdom may best discern the true interest of their country, and whose patriotism and love of justice will be least likely to sacrifice it to temporary or partial considerations. Under such a regulation, it may well happen that the public voice, pronounced by the representatives of the people, will be more consonant to the public good than if pronounced by the people themselves, convened for the purpose. . . .

. . . [A]s each representative will be chosen by a greater number of citizens in the large than in the small republic, it will be more difficult for unworthy candidates to practice with success the vicious arts by which elections are too often carried; and the suffrages of the people being more free, will be more likely to centre in men who possess the most attractive merit and the most diffusive and established characters.

. . .

The other point of difference is, the greater number of citizens and extent of territory which may be brought within the compass of republican than of democratic government; and it is this circumstance principally which renders factious combinations less to be dreaded in the former than in the latter. The smaller the society, the fewer probably will be the distinct parties and interests composing it; the fewer the distinct parties and interests, the more frequently will a majority be found of the same party; and the smaller the number of individuals composing a majority, and the smaller the compass within which they are placed, the more easily will they concert and execute their plans of oppression. Extend the sphere, and you take in a greater variety of parties and interests; you make it less probable that a majority of the whole will have a common motive to invade the rights of other citizens; or if such a common motive exists, it will be more difficult for all who feel it to discover their own strength, and to act in unison with each other. . . .

. . .

The influence of factious leaders may kindle a flame within their particular States, but will be unable to spread a general conflagration through the other States. A religious sect may degenerate into a political faction in a part of the Confederacy; but the variety of sects dispersed over the entire face of it must secure the national councils against any danger from that source. A rage for paper money, for an abolition of debts, for an equal division of property, or for any other improper or wicked project, will be less apt to pervade the whole body of the Union than a particular member of it; in the same proportion as such a malady is more likely to taint a particular county or district, than an entire State. . . .

C. Scope

The founders did not clarify three questions about which governing officials were limited by the Bill of Rights and when those governing officials were limited:

1. Were state governments limited by the provisions in the Bill of Rights?
2. Was the federal government limited by the provisions in the Bill of Rights when making laws for American territories?
3. Were federal officials limited by the provisions in the Bill of Rights when they acted in foreign territory?

Madison's original Bill of Rights included a provision declaring "No state shall violate the equal rights of conscience, or the freedom of the press, or the trial by jury in criminal cases." The congressional decision to reject that provision suggests a general understanding that the first ten amendments limited only federal power. No one suggested otherwise during the framing debates. No prominent framer discussed whether the Bill of Rights limited federal power in American territories or federal power overseas. These issues, ignored in the 1790s, became important during the early nineteenth century.

III. Judicial Power and Constitutional Authority

MAJOR DEVELOPMENTS

- Establishment of an independent federal judiciary
- Development of judicial review in the state courts
- Debate over the value of constitutional interpretation by federal judges

Judicial power was not quite an afterthought in the decade after the Declaration of Independence, but it was close. No one questioned the importance of the courts to maintaining law and order and to keeping society running smoothly. Judges had important work to perform in the United States, just as they had in the colonies. It was, however, thought to be pretty much the *same* work as they had performed in the colonies. The basic transition from empire to independence, from monarchy to republic, required a transformation in constitutional forms and a transformation in the laws, but the courts seemed little affected by those transformations. The founding generation did not think very much about the courts. They thought that the role of these courts was fairly uncontroversial.

A. Judicial Review

The courts were charged with adhering to the Constitution when its requirements became relevant to the performance of their duties. Pennsylvania had experimented, less than satisfactorily, with a council of censors to "enquire whether the constitution has been preserved inviolate" in its state constitution of 1776. James Madison had unsuccessfully urged the federal Constitutional Convention to make all state laws subject to something like Privy Council review in Congress. The Convention responded instead with the supremacy clause, which specified that the Constitution and federal law had legal priority over state law. State and federal courts were both expected to recognize that priority when deciding whether and how to apply state laws in the cases that came before them. There was general agreement that judges would have the power to declare state laws void if they violated the U.S. Constitution. Meanwhile, some argued that *all* constitutions were legally superior to *all* statutes and that judges were obliged to ignore laws that violated constitutional requirements. Legislators did not always accept the idea that judges were entitled to look behind the law and determine whether the legislature was authorized to pass particular laws in the first place. In the absence of a special institution like a council of censors, perhaps it was up to the conscience of the legislators, or to the people themselves, to measure the consistency of the law with the Constitution and to determine what action, if any, might be needed. This was a judicial power that would become of greater interest over time.

Robert Yates, **Brutus Essays** (1787)[17]

Robert Yates was a judge on the New York Supreme Court who later served as its chief justice. He had been a delegate to the federal Constitutional Convention but left when it became obvious that the Convention would not limit itself to minor revisions of the Articles of Confederation. He became a prominent and influential anti-Federalist in New York.

Yates was likely the author of the "Brutus" essays published in the New York newspapers during the ratification debates. The quality of the Brutus essays helped spur Alexander Hamilton to mount a response with the Federalist *essays. Several of the Brutus essays focused on the proposed federal judiciary. Among the author's criticisms was a concern with how the federal courts might interpret the Constitution. Brutus was convinced that federal judges would find it in their interest to interpret the terms of the Constitution broadly so as to expand their own jurisdiction and influence, and that Congress would be supportive of such loose interpretations because they would ultimately expand federal legislative power as well. Judicial interpretation would become the vehicle for expanding federal power. Was Brutus worried about the antidemocractic or "countermajoritarian" nature of judicial review, or did he have other concerns about judicial interpretation of the Constitution?*

No. 11

. . .

The judicial are not only to decide questions arising upon the meaning of the constitution in law, but also in equity.

---

17. Excerpt taken from *New York Journal,* January 31–February 7, 1788.

By this they are empowered, to explain the constitution according to the reasoning spirit of it, without being confined to the words or letter.

. . .

They will give the sense of every article of the constitution, that may from time to time come before them. And in their decisions they will not confine themselves to any fixed or established rules, but will determine, according to what appears to them, the reason and spirit of the constitution. The opinions of the supreme court, whatever they may be, will have the force of law; because there is no power provided in the constitution, that can correct their errors, or control their adjudications. From this court there is no appeal. And I conceive the legislature themselves, cannot set aside a judgment of this court, because they are authorized by the constitution to decide in the last resort. The legislature must be controlled by the constitution, and not the constitution by them. They have therefore no more right to set aside any judgment pronounced upon the construction of the constitution, than they have to take from the president, the chief command of the army and navy, and commit it to some other person. The reason is plain; the judicial and executive derive their authority from the same source, that the legislature do theirs; and therefore in all cases, where the constitution does not make the one responsible to, or controllable by the other, they are altogether independent of each other.

The judicial power will operate to effect, in the most certain, but yet silent and imperceptible manner, what is evidently the tendency of the constitution:—I mean, an entire subversion of the legislative, executive and judicial powers of the individual states. Every adjudication of the supreme court, on any question that may arise upon the nature and extent of the general government, will affect the limits of the state jurisdiction. In proportion as the former enlarge the exercise of their powers, will that of the latter be restricted.

That the judicial power of the United States, will lean strongly in favor of the general government, and will give such an explanation to the constitution, as will favor an extension of its jurisdiction, is very evident from a variety of considerations.

1st. The constitution itself strongly countenances such a mode of construction. Most of the articles in this system, which convey powers of any considerable importance, are conceived in general and indefinite terms, which are either equivocal, ambiguous, or which require long definitions to unfold the extent of their meaning. . . .

This constitution gives sufficient color for adopting an equitable construction, if we consider the great end and design it professedly has in view—these appear from its preamble to be, "to form a more perfect union, establish justice, insure domestic tranquility, provide for the common defense, promote the general welfare, and secure the blessings of liberty to ourselves and posterity." The design of this system is here expressed, and it is proper to give such a meaning to the various parts, as will best promote the accomplishment of the end; this idea suggests itself naturally upon reading the preamble, and will countenance the court in giving the several articles such a sense, as will the most effectually promote the ends the constitution had in view—how this manner of explaining the constitution will operate in practice, shall be the subject of future enquiry.

2d. Not only will the constitution justify the courts in inclining to this mode of explaining it, but they will be interested in using this latitude of interpretation. Every body of men invested with office are tenacious of power; they feel interested, and hence it has become a kind of maxim, to hand down their offices, with all its rights and privileges, unimpaired to their successors; the same principle will influence them to extend their power, and increase their rights; this of itself will operate strongly upon the courts to give such a meaning to the constitution in all cases where it can possibly be done, as will enlarge the sphere of their own authority. Every extension of the power of the general legislature, as well as of the judicial powers, will increase the powers of the courts; and the dignity and importance of the judges, will be in proportion to the extent and magnitude of the powers they exercise. . . . From these considerations the judges will be interested to extend the powers of the courts, and to construe the constitution as much as possible, in such a way as to favor it; and that they will do it, appears probable.

. . .

No. 12

. . .

First. Let us enquire how the judicial power will effect an extension of the legislative authority.

Perhaps the judicial power will not be able, by direct and positive decrees, ever to direct the legislature, because it is not easy to conceive how a question can be brought before them in a course of legal discussion, in which they can give a decision, declaring, that the legislature have certain powers which they have not exercised, and which, in consequence of the determination of the judges, they will be bound to exercise. But it is easy to see, that in their adjudications they may establish certain principles, which being received by the legislature, will enlarge the sphere of their power beyond all bounds.

It is to be observed, that the supreme court has the power, in the last resort, to determine all questions that may arise in the course of legal discussion, on the meaning and construction of the constitution. This power they will hold under the constitution, and independent of the legislature. The latter can no more deprive the former of this right, than either of them, or both of them together, can take from the president, with the advice of the senate, the power of making treaties, or appointing ambassadors.

In determining these questions, the court must and will assume certain principles, from which they will reason, in forming their decisions. These principles, whatever they may be, when they become fixed, by a course of decisions, will be adopted by the legislature, and will be the rule by which they will explain their own powers. This appears evident from this consideration, that if the legislature pass laws, which, in the judgment of the court, they are not authorized to do by the constitution, the court will not take notice of them; for it will not be denied, that the constitution is the highest or supreme law. And the courts are vested with the supreme and uncontrollable power, to determine, in all cases that come before them, what the constitution means; they cannot, therefore, execute a law, which, in their judgment, opposes the constitution, unless we can suppose they can make a superior law give way to an inferior. The legislature, therefore, will not go over the limits by which the courts may adjudge they are confined. And there is little room to doubt but that they will come up to those bounds, as often as occasion and opportunity may offer, and they may judge it proper to do it. For as on the one hand, they will not readily pass laws which they know the courts will not execute, so on the other, we may be sure they will not scruple to pass such as they know they will give effect, as often as they may judge it proper.

From these observations it appears, that the judgment of the judicial, on the constitution, will become the rule to guide the legislature in their construction of their powers.

What the principles are, which the courts will adopt, it is impossible for us to say; but taking up the powers as I have explained them in my last number, which they will possess under this clause, it is not difficult to see, that they may, and probably will, be very liberal ones.

. . .

Alexander Hamilton, ***Federalist*** **78**

The Federalist Papers *were originally written as a series of essays under the pen name of "Publius" for the New York newspapers during the New York ratification debates. They were later collected and published in book form, originally in two volumes, for wider distribution. Within a decade, the authors of the collection, but not the authors of the individual essays, were publicly identified as Alexander Hamilton, James Madison, and John Jay. The* Federalist *was immediately recognized as a great and influential commentary on the meaning of the Constitution, and it has long been used as a prominent statement of the promises made about and the public understandings of the Constitution at the time of its ratification.*

The essays were organized by Alexander Hamilton, who was fighting an uphill battle for ratification in New York. Secretary of Foreign Affairs John Jay was to be the other major contributor, but illness prevented him from writing. Hamilton turned to James Madison as a replacement. As a leading Federalist politician in New York, Jay was a natural contributor to the project. Madison, who was bogged down in his own closely fought ratification battle in his home state of Virginia, was in some ways a less obvious choice. But Madison was a fast and effective writer and had been orchestrating the national Federalist ratification campaign for some time, and Hamilton knew that he could be persuasive to moderates on the merits of the proposed Constitution.

Hamilton specifically responded to the Brutus essays on the judiciary in a group of late essays that were only included in the book form of The Federalist. *The first of these, No. 78, is among the most influential of all the* Federalist *essays. Here Hamilton tries to reassure the anti-Federalists that the federal courts will not be oppressive. What is more, Hamilton discusses how the courts will interpret the Constitution. In doing so, he, like Brutus, anticipates the power of judicial review and offers a justification for it. How effective is this as a response to Brutus? Hamilton argues that the judiciary is the "least dangerous branch." Why does he think that is true, and how persuasive is he?*

. . . The standard of good behavior for the continuance in office of the judicial magistracy, is certainly one of the most valuable of the modern improvements in the practice of government. In a monarchy it is an excellent barrier to the despotism of the prince; in a republic it is a no less excellent barrier to the encroachments and oppressions of the representative body. And it is the best expedient which can be devised in any government, to secure a steady, upright, and impartial administration of the laws.

Whoever attentively considers the different departments of power must perceive, that, in a government in which they are separated from each other, the judiciary, from the nature of its functions, will always be the least dangerous to the political rights of the Constitution; because it will be least in a capacity to annoy or injure them. The Executive not only dispenses the honors, but holds the sword of the community. The legislature not only commands the purse, but prescribes the rules by which the duties and rights of every citizen are to be regulated. The judiciary, on the contrary, has no influence over either the sword or the purse; no direction either of the strength or of the wealth of the society; and can take no active resolution whatever. It may truly be said to have neither FORCE nor WILL, but merely judgment; and must ultimately depend upon the aid of the executive arm even for the efficacy of its judgments.

. . . [T]he judiciary is beyond comparison the weakest of the three departments of power; . . . it can never attack with success either of the other two; and . . . all possible care is requisite to enable it to defend itself against their attacks. . . . [T]hough individual oppression may now and then proceed from the courts of justice, the general liberty of the people can never be endangered from that quarter; I mean so long as the judiciary remains truly distinct from both the legislature and the Executive. For I agree, that "there is no liberty, if the power of judging be not separated from the legislative and executive powers." . . . [A]s liberty can have nothing to fear from the judiciary alone, but would have every thing to fear from its union with either of the other departments; that as all the effects of such a union must ensue from a dependence of the former on the latter, notwithstanding a nominal and apparent separation; that as, from the natural feebleness of the judiciary, it is in continual jeopardy of being overpowered, awed, or influenced by its coordinate branches; and that as nothing can contribute so much to its firmness and independence as permanency in office, this quality may therefore be justly regarded as an indispensable ingredient in its constitution, and, in a great measure, as the citadel of the public justice and the public security.

The complete independence of the courts of justice is peculiarly essential in a limited Constitution. By a limited Constitution, I understand one which contains certain specified exceptions to the legislative authority; such, for instance, as that it shall pass no bills of attainder, no ex-post-facto laws, and the like. Limitations of this kind can be preserved in practice no other way than through the medium of courts of justice, whose duty it must be to declare all acts contrary to the manifest tenor of the Constitution void. Without this, all the reservations of particular rights or privileges would amount to nothing.

Some perplexity respecting the rights of the courts to pronounce legislative acts void, because contrary to the Constitution, has arisen from an imagination that the doctrine would imply a superiority of the judiciary to the legislative power. It is urged that the authority which can declare the acts of another void, must necessarily be superior to the one whose acts may be declared void. As this doctrine is of great importance in all the American constitutions, a brief discussion of the ground on which it rests cannot be unacceptable.

There is no position which depends on clearer principles, than that every act of a delegated authority, contrary to the tenor of the commission under which it is exercised, is void. No legislative act, therefore, contrary to the Constitution, can be valid. To deny this, would be to affirm, that the deputy is greater than his principal; that the servant is above his master; that the representatives of the people are superior to the people themselves; that men acting by virtue of powers, may do not only what their powers do not authorize, but what they forbid.

If it be said that the legislative body are themselves the constitutional judges of their own powers, and that the construction they put upon them is conclusive upon the other departments, it may be answered, that this cannot be the natural presumption, where it is not to be collected from any particular provisions in the Constitution. It is not otherwise to be supposed, that the Constitution could intend to enable the representatives of the people to substitute their WILL to that of their constituents. It is far more rational to suppose, that the courts were designed to be an intermediate body between the people and the legislature, in order, among other things, to keep the latter within the limits assigned to their authority. The interpretation of the laws is the proper and peculiar province of the courts. A constitution is, in fact, and must be regarded by the judges, as a fundamental law. It therefore belongs to them to ascertain its meaning, as well as the meaning of any particular act proceeding from the legislative body. If there should happen to be an irreconcilable variance between the two, that which has the superior obligation and validity ought, of course, to be preferred; or, in other words, the Constitution ought to be preferred to the statute, the intention of the people to the intention of their agents.

Nor does this conclusion by any means suppose a superiority of the judicial to the legislative power. It only supposes that the power of the people is superior to both; and that where the will of the legislature, declared in its statutes, stands in opposition to that of the people, declared in the Constitution, the judges ought to be governed by the latter rather than the former. They ought to regulate their decisions by the fundamental laws, rather than by those which are not fundamental.

. . . It not uncommonly happens, that there are two statutes existing at one time, clashing in whole or in part with each other, and neither of them containing any repealing clause or expression. . . . So far as they can, by any fair construction, be reconciled to each other, reason and law conspire to dictate that this should be done; where this is impracticable, it becomes a matter of necessity to give effect to one, in exclusion of the other. The rule which has obtained in the courts for determining their relative validity is, that the last in order of time shall be preferred to the first. . . .

But in regard to the interfering acts of a superior and subordinate authority, of an original and derivative power, the nature and reason of the thing indicate the converse of that rule as proper to be followed. They teach us that the prior act of a superior ought to be preferred to the subsequent act of an inferior and subordinate authority; and that accordingly, whenever a particular statute contravenes the Constitution, it will be the duty of the judicial tribunals to adhere to the latter and disregard the former.

It can be of no weight to say that the courts, on the pretense of a repugnancy, may substitute their own pleasure to the constitutional intentions of the legislature. This might as well happen in the case of two contradictory statutes; or it might as well happen in every adjudication upon any single statute. The courts must declare the sense of the law; and if they should be disposed to exercise WILL instead of JUDGMENT, the consequence would equally be the substitution of their pleasure to that of the legislative body. The observation, if it prove any thing, would prove that there ought to be no judges distinct from that body.

. . . If, then, the courts of justice are to be considered as the bulwarks of a limited Constitution against legislative encroachments, this consideration will afford a strong argument for the permanent tenure of judicial offices, since nothing will contribute so much as this to that independent spirit in the judges which must be essential to the faithful performance of so arduous a duty.

This independence of the judges is equally requisite to guard the Constitution and the rights of individuals from the effects of those ill humors, which the arts of designing men, or the influence of particular conjunctures, sometimes disseminate among the people themselves, and which, though they speedily give place to better information, and more deliberate reflection, have a tendency, in the meantime, to occasion dangerous innovations in the government, and serious oppressions of the minor party in the community. Though I trust the friends of the proposed Constitution will never concur with its enemies, in questioning that fundamental principle of republican government, which admits the right of the people to alter or abolish the established Constitution, whenever they find it inconsistent with their happiness, yet it is not to be inferred from this principle, that the representatives of the people, whenever a momentary inclination happens to lay hold of a majority of their constituents, incompatible with the provisions in the existing Constitution, would, on that account, be justifiable in a violation of those provisions; or that the courts would be under a greater obligation to connive at infractions in this shape, than when they had proceeded wholly from the cabals of the representative body. Until the people have, by some solemn and authoritative act, annulled or changed the established form, it is binding upon themselves collectively, as well as individually; and no presumption, or even knowledge, of their sentiments, can warrant their representatives in a departure from it, prior to such an act. But it is easy to see, that it would require an uncommon portion of fortitude in the judges to do their duty as faithful guardians of the Constitution, where legislative invasions of it had been instigated by the major voice of the community.

There is yet a further and a weightier reason for the permanency of the judicial offices, which is deducible from the nature of the qualifications they require. It has been frequently remarked, with great propriety, that a voluminous code of laws is one of the inconveniences necessarily connected with the advantages of a free government. To avoid an arbitrary discretion in the courts, it is indispensable that they should be bound down by strict rules and precedents, which serve to define and point out their duty in every particular case that comes before them; . . . and must demand long and laborious study to acquire a competent knowledge of them. Hence it is, that there can be but few men in the society who will have sufficient skill in the laws to qualify them for the stations of judges. . . . [A] temporary duration in office, which would naturally discourage such characters from quitting a lucrative line of practice to accept a seat on the bench, would have a tendency to throw the administration of justice into hands less able, and less well qualified, to conduct it with utility and dignity. . . .

IV. Powers of the National Government

MAJOR DEVELOPMENTS

- The compromise over the basis of representation in the national government
- The decision to give the national government taxing and regulatory authority
- The debate over how extensive the powers delegated to the national government should be

This section includes some of the key documents of the debate surrounding the creation of the Constitution that address the powers of the national government. The Articles of Confederation created a weak national government with few powers and equal representation for the states. The Philadelphia Convention in 1787 revolved around two competing plans to change the Articles: the Virginia Plan introduced by Edmund Randolph at the beginning of the Convention and the New Jersey Plan introduced by William Paterson as a response to it. The Virginia Plan proposed scrapping the Articles of Confederation and creating a more powerful national government with democratic representation. The New Jersey Plan proposed making more modest changes to the Confederation, adding some important powers to the national government but keeping equal state representation. The Philadelphia Convention came to a compromise between the two plans, but the Virginia Plan set the agenda. Nationalists like Alexander Hamilton, James Madison, and James Wilson would strongly defend bold constitutional change both inside the Convention and during the ratification debates in the states. Some "small-state" Federalists like Roger Sherman looked for compromise inside the Convention but defended the Constitution during ratification. Anti-Federalists like Patrick Henry became strong opponents of the Constitution during the ratification debates.

Articles of Confederation (1777)

The Articles of Confederation were the first federal constitution of the United States. They were largely drafted by Delaware's John Dickinson and Virginia's Richard Henry Lee and, after substantial negotiation, unanimously passed by the Continental Congress in 1777. The document was then sent to the state legislatures for ratification and was formally ratified by the last of the thirteen legislatures (Maryland) in 1781. Between 1776 and 1781 the Continental Congress operated without the benefit of a formal constitution, though the government largely acted as if the terms of the Articles applied. Compared to the later U.S. Constitution, the structure of the Articles of Confederation created a weak central government and emphasized legislative supremacy. The Confederation Congress had responsibility for national security and foreign affairs but had no power to raise taxes, raise an army, or punish those who violated its decisions.

. . .

II. Each state retains its sovereignty, freedom, and independence, and every power, jurisdiction, and right, which is not by this Confederation expressly delegated to the United States, in Congress assembled.

III. The said States hereby severally enter into a firm league of friendship with each other, for their common defense, the security of their liberties, and their mutual and general welfare, binding themselves to assist each other, against all force offered to, or attacks made upon them, or any of them, on account of religion, sovereignty, trade, or any other pretense whatever.

. . .

V. For the most convenient management of the general interests of the United States, delegates shall be annually appointed in such manner as the legislatures of each State shall direct, to meet in Congress on the first Monday in November, in every year, with a power reserved to each State to recall its delegates, or any of them, at any time within the year, and to send others in their stead for the remainder of the year.

. . .

Each State shall maintain its own delegates in a meeting of the States, and while they act as members of the committee of the States.

In determining questions in the United States in Congress assembled, each State shall have one vote.

. . .

VII. When land forces are raised by any State for the common defense, all officers of or under the rank of colonel, shall be appointed by the legislature of each State respectively, by whom such forces shall be raised, or in such manner as such State shall direct, and all vacancies shall be filled up by the State which first made the appointment.

VIII. All charges of war, and all other expenses that shall be incurred for the common defense or general welfare, and allowed by the United States in Congress assembled, shall be defrayed out of a common treasury, which shall be supplied by the several States in proportion to the value of all land within each State. . . .

The taxes for paying that proportion shall be laid and levied by the authority and direction of the legislatures of the several States within the time agreed upon by the United States in Congress assembled.

IX. The United States in Congress assembled, shall have the sole and exclusive right and power of determining on peace and war . . . —of sending and receiving ambassadors—entering into treaties and alliances, provided that no treaty of commerce shall be made whereby the legislative power of the respective States shall be restrained from imposing such imposts and duties on foreigners, as their own people are subjected to, or from prohibiting the exportation or importation of any species of goods or commodities whatsoever—of establishing rules for deciding in all cases, what captures on land or water shall be legal, and in what manner prizes taken by land or naval forces in the service of the United States shall be divided or appropriated—of granting letters of marque and reprisal in times of peace—appointing courts for the trial of piracies and felonies committed on the high seas and establishing courts for receiving and determining finally appeals in all cases of captures, provided that no member of Congress shall be appointed a judge of any of the said courts.

The United States in Congress assembled shall also be the last resort on appeal in all disputes and differences now subsisting or that hereafter may arise between two or more States concerning boundary, jurisdiction or any other causes whatever. . . .

. . .

The United States in Congress assembled shall also have the sole and exclusive right and power of regulating the alloy and value of coin struck by their own authority, or by that of the respective States—fixing the standards of weights and measures throughout the United States—regulating the trade and managing all affairs with the Indians, not members of any of the States, provided that the legislative right of any State within its own limits be not infringed or violated—establishing or regulating post offices from one State to another, throughout all the United States, and exacting such postage on the papers passing through the same as may be requisite to defray the expenses of the said office—appointing all officers of the land forces, in the service of the United States, excepting regimental officers—appointing all the officers of the naval forces, and commissioning all officers whatever in the service of the United States—making rules for the government and regulation of the said land and naval forces, and directing their operations.

. . .

The United States in Congress assembled shall never engage in a war, nor grant letters of marque or reprisal in time of peace, nor enter into any treaties or alliances, nor coin money, nor regulate the value thereof, nor ascertain the sums and expenses necessary for the defense and welfare of the United States, or any of them, nor emit bills, nor borrow money on the credit of the United States, nor appropriate money, nor agree upon the number of vessels of war, to be built or purchased, or the number of land or sea forces to be raised, nor appoint a commander in chief of the army or navy, unless nine States assent to the same: nor shall a question on any other point, except for adjourning from day to day be determined, unless by the votes of the majority of the United States in Congress assembled.

. . .

XIII. Every State shall abide by the determination of the United States in Congress assembled, on all questions which by this confederation are submitted to them. And the Articles of this Confederation shall be inviolably observed by every State, and the Union shall be perpetual; nor shall any alteration at any time hereafter be made in any of them; unless such alteration be agreed to in a Congress of the United States, and be afterwards confirmed by the legislatures of every State.

The Virginia Plan (1787)[18]

The Virginia Plan was presented by eminent Virginia delegate Edmund Randolph in the opening days of the Philadelphia Convention and set the agenda for the rest of the Convention's work. It immediately dispensed with the auspices under which the Convention had been assembled—to propose amendments to the existing Articles of Confederation—and instead outlined a completely new constitution for the United States. Although presented by Randolph, the plan was prepared by the young James Madison. Madison had insisted to Randolph that constitutional reform could not be contemplated in a piecemeal fashion. Only a negotiated package would win national support and solve the problems of the Confederation.

Madison anticipated that Randolph and others would "think this project, if not extravagant, absolutely unattainable and unworthy of being attempted." In particular Madison proposed to shift the United States from a confederated basis of equal state representation to a "republican" basis of representation by population, a federal government empowered to legislate on all national issues, and a national veto over state laws. But he expected that the

> *northern States will be reconciled to it [the principle of proportional representation] by the actual superiority of their populousness; the Southern by their expected superiority on this point. This principle established, the repugnance of the large States to part with power will in a great degree subside, and the smaller States must ultimately yield to the predominant will. It is also already seen by many, and must by degrees be seen by all, that, unless the Union be organized efficiently on republican principles, innovations of a much more objectionable form may be obtruded, or, in the most favorable event, the partition of the Empire, into rival and hostile confederacies will ensue.*[19]

1. Resolved that the Articles of Confederation ought to be so corrected and enlarged, as to accomplish the objects proposed by their institution, namely common Defense Security of Liberty and general welfare.

2. Resolved therefore that the right of Suffrage in the National Legislature ought to be, proportioned to the quotas of Contribution, or to the number of free inhabitants, as the one or the other, may serve best in different cases.

3. Resolved that the National Legislature ought to consist of two branches.

4. Resolved that the Members of the first Branch of the National Legislature ought to be elected by the people of the several States every—for the term of three years, to be of the age of—at least. To receive liberal stipends, by which they may be compensated for the devotion of their time to public service—to be ineligible to any office established by a particular State, or under the authority of the United States, (except those peculiarly belonging to the functions of the first Branch) during the term of service, and for the space of one—after the expiration; to be incapable of re-election for the space of—after the expiration of their term of service, and to be subject to recall.

5. Resolved that the members of the second Branch of the Legislature, ought to be elected by the individual Legislatures: to be of the age of — years at least; to hold their Offices for a term sufficient to ensure their independency. . . .

6. Resolved that each Branch ought to possess the right of originating acts, that the National Legislature ought to be empowered to enjoy, the Legislative rights vested in Congress by the Confederation, and moreover to Legislate all cases to which the Separate States are incompetent; or in which the harmony of the United States may be interrupted, by the exercise of individual Legislation—to negative all Laws passed by the several States, contravening, in the opinion of

18. Excerpt taken from *The Documentary History of the Constitution of the United States of America* (Washington, DC: Department of State, 1894), 1:332–35.

19. James Madison, "To Edmund Randolph, April 8, 1787," in *The Writings of James Madison*, ed. Gaillard Hunt (New York: G. P. Putnam's Sons, 1904), 2:340.

the National Legislature, The articles of Union; or any Treaty subsisting under the Authority of the Union—and to call forth the force of the Union, against any Member of the Union, failing to fulfill its duties under the articles thereof.

7. Resolved that a national Executive be instituted to consist of a single person, with powers to carry into execution the National Laws, and to appoint to Offices, in cases not otherwise provided for, to be chosen by the National Legislature, for the term of seven years—to receive punctually at stated times a fixed compensation, for the services rendered, in which no increase or diminution shall be made, so as to affect the Magistracy existing at the time of such increase or diminution, and to be ineligible a second time.

8. Resolved that the Executive and a convenient number of the National Judiciary ought to compose a Council of revision, with authority to examine every act of the National Legislature, before it shall operate, and every act of a particular Legislature before a negative thereon shall be final; and that the dissent of the said council shall amount to a rejection, unless the act of the National Legislature, be again passed, or that of a particular Legislature be again negatived by—of the Members of each Branch.

9. Resolved that a National Judiciary be established to Consist of one Supreme Tribunal, to hold their Offices during good behavior, and to receive punctually at stated times fixed compensation for their services, in which no increase or diminution shall be made, so as to affect the persons actually in office at the time of such increase or diminution.

That the jurisdiction of the inferior Tribunals, shall be to hear and determine in the first instance, and of the Supreme Tribunal to hear and determine in the dernier resort; all piracies and felonies on the high Seas, Captures from an Enemy; cases in which Foreigners, or Citizens of other States applying to such jurisdictions, may be interested, or which respect the collection of the national Revenue, Impeachment of any national officer and questions which may involve, the National peace and harmony.

10. Resolved that provision ought to be made for the admission of States lawfully arising within the limits of the United States whether from a voluntary junction of Government and Territory or otherwise, with the Consent of a number of Voices in the National Legislatures less than the whole.

11. Resolved that a republican Government of each State (except in the Voluntary junction of Government and Territory) ought to be guaranteed by the United States to each State.

. . .

12. That provision ought to be made for the amendment of the Articles of the Union, whensoever it shall seem necessary (and that the assent of the National Legislature, ought to be required).

13. Resolved that the Legislative, Executive and judicial powers of the several States, ought to be bound by oath to support the Articles of Union.

14. Resolved that the amendments which shall be offered to the Confederation, by the Convention, ought at a proper time, or times, after the approbation of Congress, to be submitted to an assembly or assemblies of representatives, recommended by the several Legislatures, to be expressly chosen by the people to consider and decide thereon.

The New Jersey Plan (1787)[20]

The New Jersey Plan was presented to the Philadelphia Convention by William Paterson of New Jersey on behalf of the "small," or less populous, states. It was a hastily drafted alternative to the Virginia Plan, which had dominated the Convention's initial deliberations. The New Jersey Plan challenged Madison's basic assumption that the governance of the United States should be shifted to a "republican" basis, with representation determined by population. Instead, it proposed to keep the basic plan of the Confederation and represent each state equally in Congress. The New Jersey Plan proposed relatively modest revisions of the existing Articles of Confederation, addressing some longstanding problems of concern to the Federalists but leaving many of the basic structural assumptions of the Confederation in place. The conflict between the two plans eventually led to a compromise (called the " Connecticut Compromise") in the creation of the U.S. Senate as a second congressional chamber in which each state would have equal representation. What other differences are there between these two plans?

1. Resolved that the articles of Confederation ought to be so revised, corrected & enlarged, as to render the federal Constitution adequate to the exigencies of Government, & the preservation of the Union.

2. Resolved that in addition to the powers vested in the United States in Congress, by the present existing

20. Excerpt taken from *Documentary History of the Constitution of the United States*, 322–26.

articles of Confederation, they be authorized to pass acts for raising a revenue, by levying a duty or duties on all goods or merchandizes of foreign growth or manufacture, imported into any part of the United States, by Stamps on paper, vellum or parchment, and by a postage on all letters or packages passing through the general post-Office, to be applied to such federal purposes as they shall deem proper & expedient; to make rules & regulations for the collection thereof; and the same from time to time, to alter & amend in such manner as they shall think proper: to pass Acts for the regulation of trade & commerce as well with foreign nations as with each other: provided that all punishments, fines, forfeitures & penalties to be incurred for contravening such acts rules and regulations shall be adjudged by the Common law Judiciaries of the State in which any offence contrary to the true intent & meaning of such Acts rules & regulations shall have been committed or perpetrated, with liberty of commencing in the first instance all suits & prosecutions for that purpose in the superior Common law Judiciary in such State, subject nevertheless, for the correction of all errors, both in law & fact in rendering judgment, to an appeal to the Judiciary of the United States.

3. Resolved that whenever requisitions shall be necessary, instead of the rule for making requisitions mentioned in the articles of Confederation, the United States in Congress be authorized to make such requisitions in proportion to the whole number of white & other free citizens & inhabitants of every age sex and condition including those bound to servitude for a term of years & three fifths of all other persons not comprehended in the foregoing description, except Indians not paying taxes; that if such requisitions be not complied with, in the time specified therein, to direct the collection thereof in the noncomplying States & for that purpose to devise and pass acts directing & authorizing the same; provided that none of the powers hereby vested in the United States in Congress shall be exercised without the consent of at least — States, and in that proportion if the number of Confederated States should hereafter be increased or diminished.

4. Resolved that the United States in Congress be authorized to elect a federal Executive to consist of persons, to continue in office for the term of years, to receive punctually at stated times a fixed compensation for their services, in which no increase or diminution shall be made so as to affect the persons composing the Executive at the time of such increase or diminution, to be paid out of the federal treasury; to be incapable of holding any other office or appointment during their time of service and for years thereafter; to be ineligible a second time, & removable by Congress on application by a majority of the Executives of the several States; that the Executives besides their general authority to execute the federal acts ought to appoint all federal officers not otherwise provided for, & to direct all military operations; provided that none of the persons composing the federal Executive shall on any occasion take command of any troops, so as personally to conduct any enterprise as General, or in other capacity.

5. Resolved that a federal Judiciary be established to consist of a supreme Tribunal the Judges of which to be appointed by the Executive, & to hold their offices during good behavior, to receive punctually at stated times a fixed compensation for their services in which no increase or diminution shall be made, so as to affect the persons actually in office at the time of such increase or diminution; that the Judiciary so established shall have authority to hear & determine in the first instance on all impeachments of federal officers, & by way of appeal in the dernier resort in all cases touching the rights of Ambassadors, in all cases of captures from an enemy, in all cases of piracies & felonies on the high seas, in all cases in which foreigners may be interested, in the construction of any treaty or treaties, or which may arise on any of the Acts for regulation of trade, or the collection of the federal Revenue: that none of the Judiciary shall during the time they remain in Office be capable of receiving or holding any other office or appointment during their time of service, or for thereafter.

6. Resolved that all Acts of the United States in Congress made by virtue & in pursuance of the powers hereby & by the articles of confederation vested in them, and all Treaties made & ratified under the authority of the United States shall be the supreme law of the respective States so far forth as those Acts or Treaties shall relate to the said States or their Citizens, and that the Judiciary of the several States shall be bound thereby in their decisions, any thing in the respective laws of the Individual States to the contrary notwithstanding; and that if any State, or any body of men in any State shall oppose or prevent the carrying into execution such acts or treaties, the federal Executive shall be authorized to call forth the power of the

Confederated States, or so much thereof as may be necessary to enforce and compel an obedience to such Acts, or an Observance of such Treaties.

7. Resolved that provision be made for the admission of new States into the Union.

8. Resolved the rule for naturalization ought to be the same in every State.

9. Resolved that a Citizen of one State committing an offence in another State of the Union, shall be deemed guilty of the same offence as if it had been committed by a Citizen of the State in which the Offence was committed.

Article I, Section 8 of the Constitution of the United States (1787)

The Virginia Plan simply said that Congress should have the power to act when the several states were "incompetent." Like the Articles of Confederation, the New Jersey Plan gave Congress a specific but limited list of powers. The U.S. Constitution adopted the strategy of the New Jersey Plan, but the powers granted to the new national government were more extensive than what Paterson had proposed. This "enumeration of powers" was contained in Section 8 of Article I of the Constitution. During the ratification debates, Federalists like James Madison and James Wilson emphasized this comprehensive list of powers given to the national government not just as a significant expansion of national power, but also as a limit on the power of government. They saw it as an alternative to a bill of rights.

Section 8 included provisions that would soon become especially controversial, the so-called "sweeping" clauses that had the potential to sweep in more, not yet clearly known, powers that the federal government could exercise. The "necessary and proper" provision at the end of Section 8 dropped the word "expressly" from a similar provision in the Articles of Confederation (and from the proposed amendments that emerged out of many state ratifying conventions), which some would argue was a signal that the clause should be read broadly as a grant of "implied" powers. Some saw the "general welfare" clause at the beginning of Section 8 as an echo of the Virginia Plan, empowering Congress to take whatever actions might be in the national interest. The significance of the list of powers in Section 8 is still up for debate. Some argue that it imposes important limits on national powers, while others contend that it does not significantly constrain Congress from acting in the national interest.

The Congress shall have Power To lay and collect Taxes, Duties, Imposts and Excises, to pay the Debts and provide for the common Defence and general Welfare of the United States; but all Duties, Imposts and Excises shall be uniform throughout the United States;

To borrow Money on the credit of the United States;

To regulate Commerce with foreign Nations, and among the several States, and with the Indian Tribes;

To establish an uniform Rule of Naturalization, and uniform Laws on the subject of Bankruptcies throughout the United States;

To coin Money, regulate the Value thereof, and of foreign Coin, and fix the Standard of Weights and Measures;

To provide for the Punishment of counterfeiting the Securities and current Coin of the United States;

To establish Post Offices and post Roads;

To promote the Progress of Science and useful Arts, by securing for limited Times to Authors and Inventors the exclusive Right to their respective Writings and Discoveries;

To constitute Tribunals inferior to the supreme Court;

To define and punish Piracies and Felonies committed on the high Seas, and Offences against the Law of Nations;

To declare War, grant Letters of Marque and Reprisal, and make Rules concerning Captures on Land and Water;

To raise and support Armies, but no Appropriation of Money to that Use shall be for a longer Term than two Years;

To provide and maintain a Navy;

To make Rules for the Government and Regulation of the land and naval Forces;

To provide for calling forth the Militia to execute the Laws of the Union, suppress Insurrections and repel Invasions;

To provide for organizing, arming, and disciplining, the Militia, and for governing such Part of them as may be employed in the Service of the United States, reserving to the States respectively, the Appointment of the Officers, and the Authority of training the Militia according to the discipline prescribed by Congress;

To exercise exclusive Legislation in all Cases whatsoever, over such District (not exceeding ten Miles square) as may, by Cession of particular States, and the Acceptance of Congress, become the Seat of the Government of the United States, and to exercise like

Authority over all Places purchased by the Consent of the Legislature of the State in which the Same shall be, for the Erection of Forts, Magazines, Arsenals, dock-Yards, and other needful Buildings;—And

To make all Laws which shall be necessary and proper for carrying into Execution the foregoing Powers, and all other Powers vested by this Constitution in the Government of the United States, or in any Department or Officer thereof.

V. Federalism

MAJOR DEVELOPMENTS

- The decision not to include a congressional veto over state legislation in the Constitution
- The inclusion of a supremacy clause in the Constitution and judicial review of state legislation that conflicts with the terms of the Constitution
- The adoption of six-year terms for U.S. senators without possibility of recall between elections

The Articles of Confederation tried to establish a fairly loose union. Under them, the national government had little independent existence. The legislators who ran the national government were chosen by, and paid by, the state governments for short terms and could be recalled at any time if they strayed too far. The national government was dependent on the states for the money and enforcement powers required to implement any decisions that it might make. The restrictions on the states were the bare essentials needed to make the union meaningful (e.g., states were not supposed to conduct their own foreign policy), but the central government could only try to mediate conflicts when they arose.

The Constitution sought to create a tighter, "more perfect" union. The national government was given more autonomy from the states, both in making and in implementing its policy decisions. The state governments were to be represented in only one chamber of the legislature, and those legislators (known as senators) were to have the longest of any elected term of office and could not be recalled. The U.S. senators were to be as independent as possible from their state governments. The states were guaranteed no role in financing or implementing national policy and thus were given less opportunity to obstruct or ignore national policy. The central government was now to be responsive to and act directly on the will of individual citizens, not that of the states, as the Confederation government did. At the same time, more restrictions were placed on the states, and those restrictions were made legally binding, that is, enforceable in court.

A key issue in the creation of a federal constitution was how best to represent the interests of the states. This issue was particularly pressing for the United States, where the union of states was itself somewhat fragile and the existing federal constitution (the Articles of Confederation) gave the states a great deal of power. The states expected their social and political interests to be taken into account in any new federal arrangement. At the same time, those various interests could easily conflict, and the federal government needed to be able to act in the collective interests of the whole. Finding the right balance of securing the self-interest of the individual states and creating a workable union was a primary challenge of the Philadelphia Convention. The problem of representing state interests within the new federal government appeared at various points over the course of the Convention debates. In the end, neither side was completely happy with the results.

Debate in the Constitutional Convention (1787)[21]

The Virginia Plan included a provision for a congressional veto of state laws, which James Madison regarded as essential to the success of any federal system. The congressional veto over state laws would both protect national interests from local interference and protect individual and local minorities from abuses by state governments. At the end of this debate, the provision was deleted by a vote of seven states to three.

Madison thought this was one of the great failures of the Convention. The proposal for a congressional veto was replaced with the supremacy clause in Article VI of the Constitution, which made the federal Constitution, federal treaties, and federal statutes legally superior to conflicting state constitutions and laws and ensured that this supremacy would be enforceable in state and federal court. The supremacy clause largely borrows from the New Jersey Plan and relies on the courts, rather than Congress, to monitor

21. Excerpt taken from *The Papers of James Madison* (Washington, DC: Langtree & O'Sullivan, 1840).

the states for compliance with the Constitution. Madison's proposed veto would have also given Congress a wide-ranging authority to veto state laws for any reason that it wanted. The supremacy clause narrows the federal veto to those instances in which the states run afoul of federal authority.

How did Madison's proposed national veto on state laws differ from the power of judicial review that we know today? Why would its proponents view it as the cornerstone of a national government? Were they right?

June 8th

Mr. CHARLES PINCKNEY (South Carolina) moved "that the National Legislature should have authority to negative all laws which they should judge to be improper." He urged that such a universality of the power was indispensably necessary to render it effectual; that the States must be kept in due subordination to the nation; that if the States were left to act of themselves in any case, it would be impossible to defend the national prerogatives, however extensive they might be on paper; that the acts of Congress had been defeated by this means; nor had foreign treaties escaped repeated violations; that this universal negative was in fact the corner stone of an efficient national Government; that under the British Government the negative of the Crown had been found beneficial, and the States are more one nation now, than the *Colonies* were then.

Mr. JAMES MADISON (Virginia) seconded the motion. He could not but regard an indefinite power to negative legislative acts of the States as absolutely necessary to a perfect system. Experience had evinced a constant tendency in the States to encroach on the federal authority; to violate national Treaties; to infringe the rights & interests of each other; to oppress the weaker party within their respective jurisdictions. A negative was the mildest expedient that could be devised for preventing these mischiefs. The existence of such a check would prevent attempts to commit them. Should no such precaution be engrafted, the only remedy would lie in an appeal to coercion. Was such a remedy eligible? Was it practicable? Could the national resources, if exerted to the utmost enforce a national decree against Massachusetts abetted perhaps by several of her neighbors? It would not be possible. A small proportion of the Community, in a compact situation, acting on the defensive, and at one of its extremities might at any time bid defiance to the National authority. Any Government for the United States formed on the supposed practicability of using force against the unconstitutional proceedings of the States, would prove as visionary & fallacious as the Government of Congress. The negative would render the use of force unnecessary. The States could of themselves then pass no operative act, any more than one branch of a Legislature where there are two branches, can proceed without the other. But in order to give the negative this efficacy, it must extend to all cases. A discrimination would only be a fresh source of contention between the two authorities. In a word, to recur to the illustrations borrowed from the planetary system. This prerogative of the General Government is the great pervading principle that must control the centrifugal tendency of the States; which, without it, will continually fly out of their proper orbits and destroy the order & harmony of the political System.

Mr. HUGH WILLIAMSON (North Carolina) was against giving a power that might restrain the States from regulating their internal police.

Mr. ELBRIDGE GERRY (Massachusetts) could not see the extent of such a power, and was against every power that was not necessary. He thought a remonstrance against unreasonable acts of the States would reclaim them. If it should not force might be resorted to. He had no objection to authorize a negative to paper money and similar measures. When the confederation was depending before Congress, Massachusetts was then for inserting the power of emitting paper money among the exclusive powers of Congress. He observed that the proposed negative would extend to the regulations of the Militia, a matter on which the existence of a State might depend. The National Legislature with such a power may enslave the States. Such an idea as this will never be acceded to. It has never been suggested or conceived among the people. . . . The States too have different interests and are ignorant of each other's interests. The negative therefore will be abused. . . .

Mr. ROGER SHERMAN (Connecticut) thought the cases in which the negative ought to be exercised, might be defined. He wished the point might not be decided till a trial at least should be made for that purpose.

Mr. JAMES WILSON (Pennsylvania) . . . We are now one nation of brethren. We must bury all local interests & distinctions. . . . [But] [n]o sooner were the State Governments formed than their jealousy and ambition began to display themselves. Each endeavored to cut a slice from the common loaf, to add to its own morsel, till at length the confederation became frittered down to the impotent condition in which it now stands. . . . To correct its vices is the business of this convention. One of its vices is the want of an effectual control in the whole over its parts. What danger is there that the whole will unnecessarily sacrifice a part? But reverse the case, and leave the whole at the mercy of each part, and will not the general interest be continually sacrificed to local interests?

. . .

Mr. GUNNING BEDFORD (Delaware). In answer to his colleague's question where would be the danger to the States from this power, would refer him to the smallness of his own State which may be injured at pleasure without redress. It was meant he found to strip the small States of their equal right of suffrage. In this case Delaware would have about 1/90 for its share in the General Councils, whilst Pennsylvania and Virginia would possess 1/3 of the whole. Is there no difference of interests, no rivalry of commerce, of manufactures? Will not these large States crush the small ones whenever they stand in the way of their ambitious or interested views? This shows the impossibility of adopting such a system as that on the table, or any other founded on a change in the principle of representation. And after all, if a State does not obey the law of the new System, must not force be resorted to as the only ultimate remedy, in this as in any other system. . . . Besides, how can it be thought that the proposed negative can be exercised? Are the laws of the States to be suspended in the most urgent cases until they can be sent seven or eight hundred miles, and undergo the deliberations of a body who may be incapable of Judging of them? Is the National Legislature too to sit continually in order to revise the laws of the States?

Mr. MADISON observed that the difficulties which had been started were worthy of attention and ought to be answered before the question was put. The case of laws of urgent necessity must be provided for by some emanation of the power from the National Government into each State so far as to give a temporary assent at least. This was the practice in Royal Colonies before the Revolution and would not have been inconvenient, if the supreme power of negativing had been faithful to the American interest, and had possessed the necessary information. He supposed that the negative might be very properly lodged in the Senate alone, and that the more numerous & expensive branch therefore might not be obliged to sit constantly.—He asked Mr. Bedford what would be the consequence to the small States of a dissolution of the Union which seemed likely to happen if no effectual substitute was made for the defective System existing, and he did not conceive any effectual system could be substituted on any other basis than that of a proportional suffrage? If the large States possessed the avarice & ambition with which they were charged, would the small ones in their neighborhood, be more secure when all control of a General Government was withdrawn?

VI. Separation of Powers

MAJOR DEVELOPMENTS

- Establishment of a unitary executive with a single president
- Establishment of an independently elected president who is not accountable to the legislature
- Emphasis on checks and balances in the constitutional scheme

Both the idea and the practice of the separation of powers were in their infancy during the Founding Era. For many, the British example echoed the classical idea that good government was characterized by a "balance of powers." In this conception, the powers that had to be balanced were social interests, particularly those of the wealthy and those of the poor. A balanced or mixed constitution was one that incorporated each of these constituencies into the political system, most commonly by representing them in different institutions. Thus, a three-part balance of powers might include the king (representing himself or perhaps the nation as a collective), the House of Lords (representing the aristocracy), and the House of Commons (representing "the people"). For some, this was the ideal to be reconstituted in America, although perhaps in a more republican form.

What Montesquieu and some other political thinkers of the seventeenth and eighteenth centuries introduced to address this issue was a modern separation of functional powers. Within this theory, there were three basic types of functions that governmental officials might perform, and those functions should and could be entrusted to different officials. Traditionally, the king made, applied, and enforced the law. It was only with the creation of representative assemblies or autonomous councils of advisors, like the Parliament, that it was possible to begin to think of *setting* policy (the job of the legislature) as distinct from *implementing* that policy (the job of the executive). The two tasks could then be performed by different institutions—or "branches" of government. A strict separation of powers would insist that different powers or functions of government should be carefully classified and placed in different hands. Safety for liberty came from preventing the executive from having any share of the legislative power, and vice versa. There would be a rule of law and not of men only if the same person did not both make and apply the law. The separation of powers also built a fail-safe into the government. The abuse of government power would require the cooperation of all the branches of government. The legislature could do nothing without the executive, and the executive could do nothing without the prior authorization of the legislature.

Checks and balances modified the strict separation of powers. The argument for a strict separation of powers held that no person should ever perform more than one type of function. The executive could not "share" in the legislative power if the system was to be stable and if the separation of powers was to do its work of preventing the abuse of power. A concern soon developed, however, that one branch could pull additional powers under its purview if the other branches were not empowered to resist that encroachment. The legislature might entice or coerce the executive into going along with its plans, unless the executive was both rendered sufficiently independent of the legislature and armed with weapons to resist the legislature. Care had to be taken not only to separate the powers but also to ensure that they stayed separated. Ironically, the solution to this problem was the careful mixing of powers, the creation of checks and balances that regulated how one branch might interfere with another. Thus, the executive might be given a share of the "legislative" power in the form of a veto on proposed laws, and the legislature might be given a share of the "executive" power in the form of a veto over the appointment of executive officers. Powers would no longer be strictly separated by function, but the branches of government would be counterbalanced. The creation of checks and balances required forgetting some of the lessons that the theory of separation of powers had taught.

There was room for disagreement about the details, but the founding generation believed that a true government had three branches exercising distinct powers. The Confederation was, in this sense, not a true government, since it only possessed a legislative branch. It was consequently extremely weak. The national government could only be strengthened if it were given additional powers and the appropriate institutions to exercise them and exercise them well. The government could only be strengthened *safely* if those powers were carefully distributed and counterbalanced. The state governments had always been committed to the ideal of separation of powers, but they had begun with relatively strong legislatures. As time went on, the writers of state constitutions also looked to strengthen the relative power and capacities of the other institutions of government.[22]

In the Philadelphia Convention, the delegates disagreed among themselves over how best to structure the executive branch. Crucial issues to be decided included whether there would be one president or a plural executive, whether the president should be accountable to the legislature or only to the people, and how long the president should serve in office. During the ratification debates, James Madison defended the principle of checks and balances while Alexander Hamilton advocated an "energetic" executive. Anti-Federalists such as "Centinel" were more critical of constitutional checks and balances and instead argued that the Constitution should have emphasized term limits and frequent elections to keep government officials under control.

Debate in the Constitutional Convention (1787)[23]

The delegates to the Philadelphia Convention had very vague ideas of how the executive branch should be organized. They were convinced that the national government needed an executive branch—even the New Jersey Plan

22. For more on the separation of powers in the Founding Era, see Keith E. Whittington, "The Separation of Powers at the Founding," in *Separation of Powers*, ed. Katy J. Harriger (Washington, DC: CQ Press, 2003), 15–38; M. J. C. Vile, *Constitutionalism and the Separation of Powers*, 2nd ed. (Indianapolis: Liberty Fund, 1998).

23. Excerpt taken from *Papers of James Madison*.

included executive officers. But that left open the question of what kind of executive branch should be established. Some believed that the federal constitution should follow the example of the states, with their weak governors, multiple executive officeholders, and close accountability of the executive to the legislature. Others thought that this model was something to be avoided and that a more powerful, independent executive would be more likely to provide an effective check on the legislature and good administration for the government. Delegates also grappled with additional questions about the nature of the executive. Should there be one chief executive, or should there be an executive council with no one at the top? Should the executive be independent of the legislature, or should the executive be a tool of the legislature? Alexander Hamilton shook up the Convention by proposing the creation of a monarchy, in which the ruler would be elected for life, which he thought would be no more powerful than the president already being contemplated by the Convention but would spare the nation the "tumults" of the frequent competition for high office. The Convention eventually favored a strong, unified executive, but even within that agreement there were details to be settled, such as whether and under what conditions the president could be removed from office and whether the president should have a veto power.

June 2nd

Mr. JOHN DICKINSON (Delaware) . . . A limited Monarchy he considered as one of the best Governments in the world. It was not certain that the same blessings were derivable from any other form. It was certain that equal blessings had never yet been derived from any of the republican form. A limited Monarchy however was out of the question. The spirit of the times—the state of our affairs, forbade the experiment, if it were desirable. Was it possible moreover in the nature of things to introduce it even if these obstacles were less insuperable? A House of Nobles was essential to such a Government could these be created by a breath, or by a stroke of the pen? No. They were the growth of ages, and could only arise under a complication of circumstances none of which existed in this Country. But though a form the most perfect perhaps in itself be unattainable, we must not despair. If ancient republics have been found to flourish for a moment only & then vanish for ever, it only proves that they were badly constituted; and that we ought to seek for every remedy for their diseases. One of these remedies he conceived to be the accidental lucky division of this Country into distinct States; a division which some seemed desirous to abolish altogether. . . .

Mr. EDMUND RANDOLPH (Virginia) opposed it with great earnestness, declaring that he should not do justice to the Country which sent him if he were silently to suffer the establishment of a Unity in the Executive department. He felt an opposition to it which he believed he should continue to feel as long as he lived. He urged 1. that the permanent temper of the people was adverse to the very semblance of Monarchy. 2. that a unity was unnecessary a plurality being equally competent to all the objects of the department. 3. that the necessary confidence would never be reposed in a single Magistrate. 4. that the appointments would generally be in favor of some inhabitant near the center of the Community, and consequently the remote parts would not be on an equal footing. He was in favor of three members of the Executive to be drawn from different portions of the Country.

Mr. PIERCE BUTLER (South Carolina) contended strongly for a single magistrate as most likely to answer the purpose of the remote parts. If one man should be appointed he would be responsible to the whole, and would be impartial to its interests. If three or more should be taken from as many districts, there would be a constant struggle for local advantages. In Military matters this would be particularly mischievous. . . .

June 4th

DOC. BENJAMIN FRANKLIN (Pennsylvania), said he . . . had some experience of this check in the Executive on the Legislature, under the proprietary Government of Pennsylvania. The negative [veto] of the Governor was constantly made use of to extort money. No good law whatever could be passed without a private bargain with him. An increase of his salary, or some donation, was always made a condition; till at last it became the regular practice, to have orders in his favor on the Treasury, presented along with the bills to be signed, so that he might actually receive the former before he should sign the latter. . . . This was a mischievous sort of check. . . . He was afraid, if a negative should be given as proposed, that more power and money would be demanded, till at last enough would be gotten to influence and bribe the Legislature into a complete subjection to the will of the Executive.

Mr. ROGER SHERMAN (Connecticut) was against enabling any one man to stop the will of the whole. No one man could be found so far above all the rest in wisdom. He thought we ought to avail ourselves of his wisdom in revising the laws, but not permit him to overrule the decided and cool opinions of the Legislature.

Mr. JAMES MADISON (Virginia) supposed that if a proper proportion of each branch should be required to overrule the objections of the Executive, it would answer the same purpose as an absolute negative. It would rarely if ever happen that the Executive constituted as ours is proposed to be would, have firmness enough to resist the legislature, unless backed by a certain part of the body itself. . . .

Mr. JAMES WILSON (Pennsylvania) believed as others did that this power would seldom be used. The Legislature would know that such a power existed, and would refrain from such laws, as it would be sure to defeat. Its silent operation would therefore preserve harmony and prevent mischief. The case of Pennsylvania formerly was very different from its present case. The Executive was not then as now to be appointed by the people. It will not in this case as in the one cited be supported by the head of a Great Empire, actuated by a different & sometimes opposite interest. . . . The requiring a large proportion of each House to overrule the Executive check might do in peaceable times; but there might be tempestuous moments in which animosities may run high between the Executive and Legislative branches, and in which the former ought to be able to defend itself.

Mr. GUNNING BEDFORD (Delaware) was opposed to every check on the Legislative. . . . He thought it would be sufficient to mark out in the Constitution the boundaries to the Legislative Authority, which would give all the requisite security to the rights of the other departments. The Representatives of the people were the best Judges of what was for their interest, and ought to be under no external control whatever. The two branches would produce a sufficient control within the Legislature itself.

June 18th

Mr. HAMILTON (New York) . . . In his private opinion he had no scruple in declaring, supported as he was by the opinions of so many of the wise and good, that the British Government was the best in the world: and that he doubted much whether any thing short of it would do in America. He hoped Gentlemen of different opinions would bear with him in this, and begged them to recollect the change of opinion on this subject which had taken place and was still going on. It was once thought that the power of Congress was amply sufficient to secure the end of their institution. The error was now seen by everyone. The members most tenacious of republicanism, he observed, were as loud as any in declaiming against the vices of democracy. This progress of the public mind led him to anticipate the time, when others as well as himself would . . . praise . . . it [as] the only Government in the world "which unites public strength with individual security."—In every community where industry is encouraged, there will be a division of it into the few & the many. Hence separate interests will arise. There will be debtors, and creditors, etc. Give all power to the many, they will oppress the few. Give all power to the few, they will oppress the many. Both therefore ought to have power, that each may defend itself against the other. To the want of this check we owe our paper money, installment laws, etc. To the proper adjustment of it the British owe the excellence of their Constitution. Their house of Lords is a most noble institution. Having nothing to hope for by a change, and a sufficient interest by means of their property, in being faithful to the national interest, they form a permanent barrier against every pernicious innovation, whether attempted on the part of the Crown or of the Commons. No temporary Senate will have firmness enough to answer the purpose. . . . Gentlemen differ in their opinions concerning the necessary checks, from the different estimates they form of the human passions. They suppose seven years a sufficient period to give the senate an adequate firmness, from not duly considering the amazing violence & turbulence of the democratic spirit. When a great object of Government is pursued, which seizes the popular passions, they spread like wild fire, and become irresistible. He appealed to the gentlemen from the New England States whether experience had not there verified the remark.—As to the Executive, it seemed to be admitted that no good one could be established on Republican principles. Was not this giving up the merits of the question: for can there be a good Government without a good Executive? The English model was the only good one on this subject. The Hereditary interest of the King was so interwoven with that of the Nation, and his personal emoluments so great, that he was placed above the danger of being corrupted from abroad—and at the same time was both sufficiently independent and sufficiently controlled, to answer the purpose of the institution at home. One of the weak sides of Republics was their being liable to foreign influence and corruption. Men of little character, acquiring great power become easily the tools of intermeddling Neighbors. . . . What is the inference from all these observations? That we ought to go as far in order to attain stability and permanency, as republican principles will admit. Let one branch of the Legislature hold their places for life or at least during good behavior. Let the Executive also be for life. . . . But is this a Republican Government, it will be asked? Yes if all the Magistrates are appointed, and vacancies are filled, by the people, or a process of election originating with the people. . . . An Executive for life has not this motive for forgetting his fidelity, and will therefore be a safer depository of power. It will be objected probably, that such an Executive will be an elective Monarch, and will give birth to the tumults which characterize that form of Government. He would reply that Monarch is an indefinite term. It marks not either the degree or duration of power. If this Executive Magistrate would be a monarch for life—the other proposed by the Report from the Committee of the whole, would be a monarch for seven years. The circumstance of being elective was also applicable to both. It had been observed by judicious writers that elective monarchies would be the best if they could be guarded against the tumults excited by the ambition and intrigues of competitors. He was not sure that tumults were an inseparable evil. . . . But will such a plan be adopted out of doors? In return he would ask will the people adopt the other plan? At present they will adopt neither. But he sees the Union dissolving or already dissolved—he sees evils operating in the States which must soon cure the people of their fondness for democracies—he sees that a great progress has been already made & is still going on in the public mind. He thinks therefore that the people will in time be unshackled from their prejudices. . . .

June 20th

Mr. MADISON thought it indispensable that some provision should be made for defending the Community against the incapacity, negligence or perfidy of the chief Magistrate. The limitation of the period of his service, was not a sufficient security. He might lose his capacity after his appointment. He might pervert his administration into a scheme of peculation or oppression. He might betray his trust to foreign powers. The case of the Executive Magistracy was very distinguishable, from that of the Legislature or of any other public body, holding offices of limited duration. It could not be presumed that all or even a majority of the members of an Assembly would either lose their capacity for discharging, or be bribed to betray, their trust. Besides the restraints of their personal integrity and honor, the difficulty of acting in concert for purposes of corruption was a security to the public. And if one or a few members only should be seduced, the soundness of the remaining members, would maintain the integrity and fidelity of the body. In the case of the Executive Magistracy which was to be administered by a single man, loss of capacity or corruption was more within the compass of probable events, and either of them might be fatal to the Republic.

Mr. CHARLES PINCKNEY (South Carolina) did not see the necessity of impeachments. He was sure they ought not to issue from the Legislature who would in that case hold them as a rod over the Executive and by that means effectually destroy his independence. His revisionary power in particular would be rendered altogether insignificant.

Mr. ELBRIDGE GERRY (Massachusetts) urged the necessity of impeachments. A good magistrate will not fear them. A bad one ought to be kept in fear of them. He hoped the maxim would never be adopted here that the chief magistrate could do no wrong.

Mr. RUFUS KING (Massachusetts) expressed his apprehensions that an extreme caution in favor of liberty might enervate the Government we were forming. He wished the House to recur to the primitive axiom that the three great departments of Governments should be separate and independent. . . . Would this be the case, if the Executive should be impeachable? . . . The Executive was to hold his place for a limited term like the members of the Legislature: Like them . . . he would periodically be tried for his behavior by his electors, who would continue or discontinue him in trust according to the manner in which he had discharged it. Like them therefore, he ought to be subject to no intermediate trial, by impeachment. . . . But under no circumstances ought he to be impeachable by the Legislature. This would be destructive of his independence and of the principles of the Constitution. He relied on the vigor of the Executive as a great security for the public liberties.

Mr. RANDOLPH. The propriety of impeachments was a favorite principle with him. Guilt wherever found ought to be punished. The Executive will have great opportunities of abusing his power; particularly in time of war when the military force, and in some respects the public money will be in his hands. Should no regular punishment be provided, it will be irregularly inflicted by tumults and insurrections. He is aware of the necessity of proceeding with a cautious hand, and of excluding as much as possible the influence of the Legislature from the business. He suggested for consideration an idea which had fallen [from Col. Hamilton] of composing a forum out of the Judges belonging to the States: and even of requiring some preliminary inquest whether just grounds of impeachment existed.

Federalist 51, 70, and 71

As The Federalist *explained it, the Constitution created a system of checks and balances among multiple institutions while also placing different powers where they could be best used in the new government. They authors used the essays to justify the organization and details of each component of the proposed government. Often these justifications provided rationales for what Hamilton and Madison knew had been ad hoc compromises in the Convention itself, but in hindsight and in public they argued that the design of the Constitution was not merely acceptable but desirable. These essays include some of the most sophisticated discussions of the idea of checks and balances ever written, but they are also trying to imagine how the system will operate once put into motion. As you read, you should consider how well these expectations conform to our experience. The founders did not anticipate highly organized, mass political parties, but they were familiar with and critical of short-lived or personality-based factions that operated inside and outside of legislative assemblies. Do party ties fulfill, subvert, or work alongside the constitutional separation of powers that the founding generation put in place?*

No. 51 (James Madison)

TO WHAT expedient, then, shall we finally resort, for maintaining in practice the necessary partition of power among the several departments, as laid down in the Constitution? The only answer that can be given is, that . . . the defect must be supplied, by so contriving the interior structure of the government as that its several constituent parts may, by their mutual relations, be the means of keeping each other in their proper places. . . .

In order to lay a due foundation for that separate and distinct exercise of the different powers of government, which to a certain extent is admitted on all hands to be essential to the preservation of liberty, it is evident that each department should have a will of its own; and consequently should be so constituted that the members of each should have as little agency as possible in the appointment of the members of the others. Were this principle rigorously adhered to, it would require that all the appointments for the supreme executive, legislative, and judiciary magistracies should be drawn from the same fountain of authority, the people, through channels having no communication whatever with one another. Perhaps such a plan of constructing the several departments would be less difficult in practice than it may in contemplation appear. Some difficulties, however, and some additional expense would attend the execution of it. Some deviations, therefore, from the principle must be admitted. In the constitution of the judiciary department in particular, it might be inexpedient to insist rigorously on the principle: first, because peculiar qualifications being essential in the members, the primary consideration ought to be to select that mode of choice which best secures these qualifications; secondly, because the permanent tenure by which the appointments are held in that department, must soon destroy all sense of dependence on the authority conferring them.

It is equally evident, that the members of each department should be as little dependent as possible on those of the others, for the emoluments annexed to their offices. Were the executive magistrate, or the judges, not independent of the legislature in this particular, their independence in every other would be merely nominal.

But the great security against a gradual concentration of the several powers in the same department, consists in giving to those who administer each department the necessary constitutional means and personal motives to resist encroachments of the others. The provision for defense must in this, as in all other cases, be made commensurate to the danger of attack. Ambition must be made to counteract ambition. The interest of the man must be connected with the constitutional rights of the place. It may be a reflection on human nature, that such devices should be necessary to control the abuses of government. But what is government itself, but the greatest of all reflections on human nature? If men were angels, no government would be necessary. If angels were to govern men, neither external nor internal controls on government would be necessary. In framing a government which is to be administered by men over men, the great difficulty lies in this: you must first enable the government to control the governed; and in the next place oblige it to control itself. A dependence on the people is, no doubt, the primary control on the government; but experience has taught mankind the necessity of auxiliary precautions.

But it is not possible to give to each department an equal power of self-defense. In republican government, the legislative authority necessarily predominates. The remedy for this inconveniency is to divide the legislature into different branches; and to render them, by different modes of election and different principles of action, as little connected with each other as the nature of their common functions and their common dependence on the society will admit. It may even be necessary to guard against dangerous encroachments by still further precautions. As the weight of the legislative authority requires that it should be thus divided, the weakness of the executive may require, on the other hand, that it should be fortified. An absolute negative on the legislature appears, at first view, to be the natural defense with which the executive magistrate should be armed. But perhaps it would be neither altogether safe nor alone sufficient. . . . May not this defect of an absolute negative be supplied by some qualified connection between this weaker department and the weaker branch of the stronger department, by which the latter may be led to support the constitutional rights of the former, without being too much detached from the rights of its own department?

. . .

. . . In a single republic, all the power surrendered by the people is submitted to the administration of a single government; and the usurpations are guarded against by a division of the government into distinct and separate departments. In the compound republic of America, the power surrendered by the people is first divided between two distinct governments, and then the portion allotted to each subdivided among distinct and separate departments. Hence a double security arises to the rights of the people. The different governments will control each other, at the same time that each will be controlled by itself. . . .

No. 70 (Alexander Hamilton)

. . . Energy in the Executive is a leading character in the definition of good government. It is essential to the protection of the community against foreign attacks; it is not less essential to the steady administration of the laws; to the protection of property against those irregular and high-handed combinations which sometimes interrupt the ordinary course of justice; to the security of liberty against the enterprises and assaults of ambition, of faction, and of anarchy. . . .

. . . A feeble Executive implies a feeble execution of the government. A feeble execution is but another phrase for a bad execution; and a government ill executed, whatever it may be in theory, must be, in practice, a bad government.

. . .

The circumstances which constitute safety in the republican sense are, 1st. a due dependence on the people, secondly a due responsibility.

. . .

. . . Decision, activity, secrecy, and dispatch will generally characterize the proceedings of one man, in a much more eminent degree, than the proceedings of any greater number, and in proportion as the number is increased, these qualities will be diminished.

. . .

No. 71 (Alexander Hamilton)

. . .

There are some who would be inclined to regard the servile pliancy of the Executive to a prevailing current, either in the community or in the legislature, as its best recommendation. But such men entertain very crude notions, as well of the purposes for which government was instituted, as of the true means by which the public happiness may be promoted. The republican principle demands that the deliberate sense of the community should govern the conduct of those to whom they entrust the management of their affairs; but it does not require an unqualified complaisance to every sudden breeze of passion, or to every transient impulse which the people may receive from the arts of men, who flatter their prejudices to betray their interests. It is a just observation, that the people commonly INTEND the PUBLIC GOOD. This often applies to their very errors. But their good sense would despise the adulator who should pretend that they always

REASON RIGHT about the MEANS of promoting it. . . . When occasions present themselves, in which the interests of the people are at variance with their inclinations, it is the duty of the persons whom they have appointed to be the guardians of those interests, to withstand the temporary delusion, in order to give them time and opportunity for more cool and sedate reflection. Instances might be cited in which a conduct of this kind has saved the people from very fatal consequences of their own mistakes, and has procured lasting monuments of their gratitude to the men who had courage and magnanimity enough to serve them at the peril of their displeasure.

But however inclined we might be to insist upon an unbounded complaisance in the Executive to the inclinations of the people, we can with no propriety contend for a like complaisance to the humors of the legislature. The latter may sometimes stand in opposition to the former, and at other times the people may be entirely neutral. In either supposition, it is certainly desirable that the Executive should be in a situation to dare to act his own opinion with vigor and decision.

The same rule which teaches the propriety of a partition between the various branches of power, teaches us likewise that this partition ought to be so contrived as to render the one independent of the other. To what purpose separate the executive or the judiciary from the legislative, if both the executive and the judiciary are so constituted as to be at the absolute devotion of the legislative? Such a separation must be merely nominal, and incapable of producing the ends for which it was established. It is one thing to be subordinate to the laws, and another to be dependent on the legislative body. The first comports with, the last violates, the fundamental principles of good government; and, whatever may be the forms of the Constitution, unites all power in the same hands. . . . The representatives of the people, in a popular assembly, seem sometimes to fancy that they are the people themselves, and betray strong symptoms of impatience and disgust at the least sign of opposition from any other quarter; as if the exercise of its rights, by either the executive or judiciary, were a breach of their privilege and an outrage to their dignity. They often appear disposed to exert an imperious control over the other departments; and as they commonly have the people on their side, they always act with such momentum as to make it very difficult for the other members of the government to maintain the balance of the Constitution.

. . .

"Centinel," **Letter No. 1** (1787)[24]

Centinel was the pen name for one of the most significant anti-Federalist writers during the ratification debates. His letters were first published in the Philadelphia newspapers during the weeks leading up to the ratification vote in Pennsylvania, but they were widely circulated across the state and the country. The Centinel letters may not have all been written by the same person, but the first letter is now commonly attributed to Samuel Bryan, an up-and-coming state government official. Bryan was also a primary force behind a minority report of the Pennsylvania anti-Federalists at the state ratification convention. The Centinel essays were particularly class-conscious, critical of the "wealthy and ambitious, who in every community think they have a right to lord it over their fellow creatures" and who now hoped that the people could be led to adopt "any extreme of government."[25] Rather than a complicated scheme of checks and balances, Centinel emphasized the importance of clear lines of accountability between the governors and the governed, with term limits ("rotation"), a free press, and frequent elections as the keys to maintaining liberty.

. . .

. . . I believe it will be found that the form of government, which holds those entrusted with power, in the greatest responsibility to their constituents, the best calculated for freemen. A republican, or free government, can only exist where the body of the people are virtuous, and where property is pretty equally divided; in such a government the people are the sovereign and their sense or opinion is the criterion of every public measure; for when this ceases to be the case, the nature of the government is changed, and an aristocracy, monarchy or despotism will rise on its ruin. The highest responsibility is to be attained, in a simple structure of government, for the great body of the people never steadily attend to the operations of government, and for want of due information are liable

24. Excerpt taken from Centinel, *To the People of Pennsylvania* (Philadelphia: Eleazer Oswald, 1787).

25. Ibid.

to be imposed on—If you complicate the plan by various orders, the people will be perplexed and divided in their sentiments about the sources of abuses or misconduct, some will impute it to the senate, others to the house of representatives, and so on, that the interposition of the people may be rendered imperfect or perhaps wholly abortive. But if, imitating the constitution of Pennsylvania, you vest all the legislative power in one body of men (separating the executive and the judicial) elected for a short period, and necessarily excluded by rotation from permanency, and guarded from precipitancy and surprise by delays imposed on its proceedings, you will create the most perfect responsibility for then, whenever the people feel a grievance they cannot mistake the authors, and will apply the remedy with certainty and effect, discarding them at the next election. This tie of responsibility will obviate all the dangers apprehended from a single legislature, and will the best secure the rights of the people.

...

... [I]f the United States are to be melted down into one empire, it becomes you to consider, whether such a government, however constructed, would be eligible in so extended a territory; and whether it would be practicable, consistent with freedom? It is the opinion of the greatest writers, that a very extensive country cannot be governed on democratical principles, on any other plan, than a confederation of a number of small republics, possessing all the powers of internal government, but united in the management of their foreign and general concerns.

It would not be difficult to prove, that any thing short of despotism, could not bind so great a country under one government; and that whatever plan you might, at first setting out, establish, it would issue in a despotism.

...

... [W]e see, the house of representatives, are on the part of the people to balance the senate, who I suppose will be composed of the *better sort*, the *well born*, etc. The number of the representatives (being only one for every 30,000 inhabitants) appears to be too few, either to communicate the requisite information, of the wants, local circumstances and sentiments of so extensive an empire, or to prevent corruption and undue influence, in the exercise of such great powers; the term for which they are to be chosen, too long to preserve a due dependence and accountability to their constituents; and the mode and places of their election not sufficiently ascertained, for as Congress have the control over both, they may govern the choice, by ordering the *representatives* of a *whole* state, to be *elected* in *one* place, and that too may be the most *inconvenient*.

The senate, the great efficient body in this plan of government is constituted on the most unequal principles. The smallest state in the union has equal weight with the great states of Virginia, Massachusetts, or Pennsylvania—The Senate, besides its legislative functions, has a very considerable share in the Executive; none of the principal appointments to office can be made without its advice and consent. The term and mode of its appointment, will lead to permanency; the members are chosen for six years, the mode is under the control of Congress, and as there is no exclusion by rotation, they may be continued for life, which, from their extensive means of influence, would follow of course. The President, who would be a mere pageant of state, unless he coincides with the views of the Senate, would either become the head of the aristocratic junto in that body, or its minion; besides, their influences being the most predominant, could the best secure his re-election to office. And from his power of granting pardons, he might screen from punishment the most treasonable attempts on the liberties of the people, when instigated by the Senate.

From this investigation into the organization of this government, it appears that it is devoid of all responsibility or accountability to the great body of the people, and that so far from being a regular balanced government, it would be in practice a *permanent* ARISTOCRACY.

VII. Individual Rights

MAJOR DEVELOPMENTS

- State courts declare legislative takings unconstitutional
- First constitutional protections for contract rights
- Greater emphasis on religious freedom

The Preface to the Constitution of the United States promises that Americans will enjoy the "blessings of liberty." These blessings include various property rights, the freedom of religion, the right to bear arms, and free speech. During the Founding Era, general agreement existed on paradigmatic rights violations. Government could not confiscate property, execute Baptists, or disarm the local militia. Nevertheless, Americans from 1776 to 1791 did little to spell out the precise contours of most individual rights. Members of the First Congress did not discuss at length the meaning of various provisions in the Bill of Rights. As a result, the rights controversies of the 1780s were not settled. Some representatives in the First Congress asked whether the free exercise clause gave religious pacifists a right to avoid military service, but neither the brief debate that followed nor the text of the First Amendment clearly answered their question.

Americans in the Founding Era agreed that "the blessings of liberty" could be restricted when the common good justified regulation. Legal authorities commonly distinguished between liberty and license, acts inconsistent with the public welfare, safety, health, or morality. No person in the late eighteenth century had a right to harm himself, other people, or the community. "Every one," a New England minister declared, "must be required to do all he can that tends to the highest good of the state."[26] During the Revolution, many communities confiscated privately owned horses and weapons in order to provide the Continental Army with necessary supplies. Compensation for these confiscations was almost always inadequate and sometimes not paid at all.

A. Property

The U.S. Constitution provided three direct protections for property rights:

1. The Fifth Amendment states, "No person shall . . . be deprived of life, liberty, or property, without due process of law."
2. The Fifth Amendment also states, "Nor shall private property be taken for public use, without just compensation."
3. Article I, Section 10 states, "No State shall . . . make any Thing but gold and silver Coin a Tender in Payment of Debts" or "pass any . . . Law impairing the Obligation of Contracts."

Many state constitutions included a due process clause, a takings clause, or clauses aimed at protecting similar rights. Some state constitutions prohibited entails, legal devices that allowed aristocrats to ensure that their large holdings could not be broken up into smaller estates. By forbidding entails and related common law practices, Founding Era constitutionalists thought they were enabling more citizens to acquire property and preventing a permanent class of large landholders from forming.

Property qualifications for voting were an important indirect constitutional protection for property rights. All states in 1790 required that persons own some property in order to vote. The Constitution of the United States incorporates these requirements by making the right to vote for a member of the House of Representatives conditional on the right to vote in certain state elections. If a person did not meet the property requirements to vote for a member of the lower house of the Maryland legislature, then that person had no constitutional right to vote in a federal election. Federalists were confident that a legislature composed of representatives elected by property holders did not need further written limitations on their power to regulate property. Such officials could be trusted to regulate property only when the regulation was consistent with the interests of most property holders.

Contracts and commercial paper played an increasingly prominent role in economic life during the late eighteenth century. The commercial revolution that was underway in England and the United States created a new class of entrepreneurs whose wealth lay in stocks, bonds, and debts. These holdings needed constitutional protection. When Madison in *Federalist* No. 10 described the "improper and wicked project[s]" that threatened new forms of property, he was referring to the "rage for paper money, for an abolition of debts." Paper money and an abolition of debts, Federalists agreed, transferred property (the debt) from A (the creditor) to B (the debtor) without due process of law.

Article I, Section 10 provides two constitutional protections for creditors. First, by preventing states from printing paper money (which causes inflation), the Constitution requires borrowers to pay their debts in currency worth approximately what the currency was worth when the loan was made. Second, the contracts clause, which forbids states from passing legislation that "impair(s) the obligation of contract," prevents

26. Willi Paul Adams, *The First American Constitutions: Republican Ideology and the Making of the State Constitutions in the Revolutionary Era* (Lanham, MD: Rowman & Littlefield, 2001), 217.

local governments from freeing borrowers from their legal obligation to pay their debts.

Leading Federalists expected the contracts clause to provide crucial protections for property. Madison asserted that the provision was a "bulwark in favor of personal security and private rights." Charles Pinckney of South Carolina declared that the contracts clause was "the soul of the Constitution." "No more shall paper money, no more shall tender-laws, drive their commerce from our shores," he stated, "and darken the American name in every country where it is known." Anti-Federalists feared that the contracts clause was one of many constitutional provisions that favored the formation of a wealthy aristocracy. Luther Martin of Maryland complained that states would not long be able "to prevent the *wealthy creditor* and the *monied man* from *totally* destroying the *poor* though even *industrious debtor*."[27]

The most common constitutional dispute in the Founding Era was over what constituted taking from A and giving to B. Suppose both A and B claimed a valid title to the Blackacre Estate. Could a legislature resolve that dispute in favor of A? Several state courts rejected that legislative power. *Bayard v. Singleton* (NC 1787) and *Bowman v. Middleton* (SC 1792) held that juries were the appropriate constitutional institution for resolving disputes over property. Legislation resolving land disputes unconstitutionally took property without due process of law because persons had a constitutional right to have a jury determine whether their title to the property was valid. The South Carolina Court of Common Pleas in *Bowman* declared, "It was against common right, as well as against Magna Charta, to take away the freehold of one man, and vest it in another; and that too, to the prejudice of third persons, without any compensation, or even a trial by a jury of the country, to determine the right in question."[28]

B. Religion

Most Americans were committed to protecting some religious freedoms. The First Amendment declares, "Congress shall make no law . . . prohibiting the free exercise" of religion. Many state constitutions included similar provisions protecting religious belief. Such clauses were no longer controversial by 1790. Americans in the Founding Era agreed that persons ought to be free to act according to their religious convictions in private.

The First Amendment also declares, "Congress shall make no law respecting an establishment of religion." Establishment clauses were more controversial. Many states in 1790 had established churches, even though popular support for establishment was weakening. A number of states constitutionally prohibited religious establishments. Some commentators today maintain that the establishment clause of the U.S. Constitution was intended to protect federalism, not individual rights. The establishment clause, in this view, protects state religious establishments and state decisions to forego a religious establishment from federal interference. Congress left Massachusetts free to establish the Congregational Church, Virginia free to establish the Anglican Church, and Pennsylvania free to have no establishment.[29]

The difference between Article VI of the U.S. Constitution and many state constitutions demonstrates the clear influence that federalism exerted on the idea of religious freedom. Persons of all religious faiths are eligible to hold all federal offices. Article VI asserts, "No religious Test shall ever be required as a Qualification to any Office or public Trust under the United States." This provision was controversial. Anti-Federalists feared that a "godless" Constitution lacked the moral foundations necessary to maintain republican government. In contrast, many state constitutions imposed religious tests. The Delaware Constitution required all officeholders to take the following oath: "I, [name], do profess faith in God the Father, and in Jesus Christ His only Son, and in the Holy Ghost, one God, blessed for evermore; and I do acknowledge the holy scriptures of the Old and New Testament to be given by divine inspiration." The constitution of South Carolina declared that all executive branch officials in the state must be of "the Protestant religion" and required all voters to "acknowledge . . . the being of a God." Some state constitutions forbade members of the clergy from holding public office. The constitution

27. James W. Ely, Jr., *The Guardian of Every Other Right*, 3rd ed. (New York: Oxford University Press, 2007), 50–51.

28. *Bowman v. Middleton*, 1 Bay 252 (SC 1792).

29. Akhil Reed Amar, *The Bill of Rights: Creation and Reconstruction* (New Haven, CT: Yale University Press, 1998), 32–33.

Table 3-2 Selected State Constitutional Provisions Regarding Religion, 1800

State	Established Church	Religious Test for Legislators
Vermont	Prohibited	Prohibited
New Hampshire	Yes	Protestant
Massachusetts	Yes	Protestant
Connecticut	Yes	None
Rhode Island	Prohibited	None
New York	Prohibited	Protestant
New Jersey	Prohibited	Protestant
Pennsylvania	Prohibited	Christian/Jewish
Delaware	Prohibited	Prohibited
Maryland	None	Christian
Virginia	None	None
North Carolina	Prohibited	Protestant
South Carolina	Prohibited	Protestant
Georgia	Prohibited	None
Tennessee	Prohibited	Prohibited
Kentucky	Prohibited	Prohibited

Source: John K. Wilson, "Religion Under the State Constitutions, 1776–1800," *Journal of Church and State* 4 (1990): 753.

of New York stated, "And whereas the ministers of the gospel are, by their profession, dedicated to the service of God and the care of souls, and ought not to be diverted from the great duties of their function; therefore, no minister of the gospel, or priest of any denomination whatsoever, shall, at any time hereafter, under any presence or description whatever, be eligible to, or capable of holding, any civil or military office or place within this State."

Proponents of religious freedom in the Founding Era relied heavily on religious arguments to support disestablishment and the freedom of conscience. James Madison claimed that state support for religion was "adverse to the diffusion of the light of Christianity."[30] Many Baptists insisted that God had ordained the separation of church and state.

No consensus formed on the precise meaning of free exercise or establishment. Congress did not debate the particulars of any provision in the Bill of Rights at length. No one answered when Representative Egbert Benson of New York asked whether the free exercise clause required Congress to grant exemptions to persons with religious scruples about military service. We know that the precise wording of the religion clauses changed during congressional debate, but we do not know why the final language was accepted and other phrases rejected.

State constitutions were often sectarian. Eleven of the thirteen states had some form of establishment when the Constitution was ratified, and most required religious tests for office. Virginians abandoned an official state religion only after a bitter debate. During the 1780s James Madison and Thomas Jefferson engaged in a lengthy campaign for religious freedom in the state. Their opponents included Patrick Henry and other Virginia elites who favored maintaining the official status of the Anglican Church. That struggle ended with the passage of the Virginia Act for Religious Freedom, the law that disestablished the Anglican Church.

30. Madison, *Writings*, 2:189.

The Virginia Debate over Religious Assessments

The Virginia debate over religious assessments was the most important controversy concerning religious establishment that took place in the United States between the Revolution and the ratification of the Bill of Rights. The controversy began in 1784 when Patrick Henry proposed that all citizens be taxed to support Christian instruction. Henry's bill sought a multiple establishment, similar to that instituted in South Carolina, under which taxpayers could designate which Christian church they wished to support. Quakers and Mennonites could make other religious uses of the assessment. James Madison and Thomas Jefferson vigorously opposed state support for religious instruction. In 1785 Madison drafted the "Memorial and Remonstrance Against Religious Assessments." That pamphlet was widely circulated and is generally credited with being responsible for the defeat of Henry's proposal. In 1786 the Virginia legislature passed the Act for Establishing Religious Freedom. Thomas Jefferson, who drafted that bill, insisted that his tombstone mention only that he was the author of the Declaration of Independence, the founder of the University of Virginia, and the person responsible for the bill establishing religious freedom in Virginia.

Consider the following when reading the subsequent materials. Do Madison and Jefferson reject Henry's claim that religious belief is vital to a republican state? Are their arguments for religious freedom more secular or as religious as the arguments that Roger Williams and William Penn made for religious freedom in the seventeenth century? To what extent is the dispute between Madison/Jefferson and Henry over the proper place of religion in a liberal state? To what extent is their dispute over the best means for promoting Christianity? Suppose that Henry had proposed the following. "All persons shall be taxed $5 to pay for after-school activities. All persons may designate which after-school activities they support." If some Virginians decided their taxes should go toward religious instruction, would Madison and Jefferson have opposed that proposed bill?

A Bill Establishing a Provision for Teachers of the Christian Religion (1784)[31]

Whereas the general diffusion of Christian knowledge hath a natural tendency to correct the morals of men, restrain their vices, and preserve the peace of society; which cannot be effected without a competent provision for learned teachers, who may be thereby enabled to devote their time and attention to the duty of instructing such citizens, as from their circumstances and want of education, cannot otherwise attain such knowledge; and it is judged that such provision may be made by the Legislature, without counteracting the liberal principle heretofore adopted and intended to be preserved by abolishing all distinctions of pre-eminence amongst the different societies or communities of Christians;

Be it therefore enacted by the General Assembly, That for the support of Christian teachers, _____ per centum on the amount, or _____ in the pound on the sum payable for tax on the property within this Commonwealth, is hereby assessed, and shall be paid by every person chargeable with the said tax at the time the same shall become due. . . .

And be it enacted, That for every sum so paid, the Sheriff or Collector shall give a receipt, expressing therein to what society of Christians the person from whom he may receive the same shall direct the money to be paid. . . .

And be it further enacted, That the money to be raised by virtue of this Act, shall be by the Vestries, Elders, or Directors of each religious society, appropriated to a provision for a Minister or Teacher of the Gospel of their denomination, or the providing places of divine worship, and to none other use whatsoever, except in the denominations of Quakers and Menonists, who may receive what is collected from their members, and place it in their general fund, to be disposed of in a manner which they shall think best calculated to promote their particular mode of worship.

James Madison, "Memorial and Remonstrance Against Religious Assessments" (1785)[32]

. . .

. . . [W]e hold it for a fundamental and undeniable truth, "that religion or the duty which we owe to our Creator and the manner of discharging it, can be directed only by reason and conviction, not by force or violence." The Religion then of every man must be left to the conviction and conscience of every man; and it is the right of every man to exercise it as these may

31. Excerpt taken from *A Bill Establishing a Provision for Teachers of the Christian Religion* (Richmond, VA: n.p., 1784).

32. Excerpt taken from Madison, *Writings*, 2:183.

dictate. This right is in its nature an unalienable right. It is unalienable, because the opinions of men, depending only on the evidence contemplated by their own minds cannot follow the dictates of other men: It is unalienable also, because what is here a right towards men, is a duty towards the Creator. It is the duty of every man to render to the Creator such homage and such only as he believes to be acceptable to him. This duty is precedent, both in order of time and in degree of obligation, to the claims of Civil Society. Before any man can be considered as a member of Civil Society, he must be considered as a subject of the Governor of the Universe: And if a member of Civil Society, do it with a saving of his allegiance to the Universal Sovereign. We maintain therefore that in matters of Religion, no man's right is abridged by the institution of Civil Society and that Religion is wholly exempt from its cognizance. True it is, that no other rule exists, by which any question which may divide a Society, can be ultimately determined, but the will of the majority; but it is also true that the majority may trespass on the rights of the minority.

. . .

. . . Who does not see that the same authority which can establish Christianity, in exclusion of all other Religions, may establish with the same ease any particular sect of Christians, in exclusion of all other Sects? That the same authority which can force a citizen to contribute three pence only of his property for the support of any one establishment, may force him to conform to any other establishment in all cases whatsoever?

. . . [T]he Bill violates the equality which ought to be the basis of every law, and which is more indispensible, in proportion as the validity or expediency of any law is more liable to be impeached. If "all men are by nature equally free and independent," all men are to be considered as entering into Society on equal conditions; as relinquishing no more, and therefore retaining no less, one than another, of their natural rights. Above all are they to be considered as retaining an "equal title to the free exercise of Religion according to the dictates of Conscience." Whilst we assert for ourselves a freedom to embrace, to profess and to observe the Religion which we believe to be of divine origin, we cannot deny an equal freedom to those whose minds have not yet yielded to the evidence which has convinced us. If this freedom be abused, it is an offence against God, not against man: To God, therefore, not to man, must an account of it be rendered. . . .

. . . [T]he Bill implies either that the Civil Magistrate is a competent Judge of Religious Truth; or that he may employ Religion as an engine of Civil policy. The first is an arrogant pretension falsified by the contradictory opinions of Rulers in all ages, and throughout the world: the second an unhallowed perversion of the means of salvation.

. . . [T]he establishment proposed by the Bill is not requisite for the support of the Christian Religion. To say that it is, is a contradiction to the Christian Religion itself, for every page of it disavows a dependence on the powers of this world: it is a contradiction to fact; for it is known that this Religion both existed and flourished, not only without the support of human laws, but in spite of every opposition from them, and not only during the period of miraculous aid, but long after it had been left to its own evidence and the ordinary care of Providence. . . .

. . . [E]xperience witnessed that ecclesiastical establishments, instead of maintaining the purity and efficacy of Religion, have had a contrary operation. During almost fifteen centuries has the legal establishment of Christianity been on trial. What have been its fruits? More or less in all places, pride and indolence in the Clergy, ignorance and servility in the laity, in both, superstition, bigotry and persecution. . . .

. . . [T]he establishment in question is not necessary for the support of Civil Government. If it be urged as necessary for the support of Civil Government only as it is a means of supporting Religion, and it be not necessary for the latter purpose, it cannot be necessary for the former. If Religion be not within the cognizance of Civil Government how can its legal establishment be necessary to Civil Government? What influence in fact have ecclesiastical establishments had on Civil Society? In some instances they have been seen to erect a spiritual tyranny on the ruins of the Civil authority; in many instances they have been seen upholding the thrones of political tyranny: in no instance have they been seen the guardians of the liberties of the people. . . .

. . . [T]he proposed establishment is a departure from the generous policy, which, offering an Asylum to the persecuted and oppressed of every Nation and Religion, promised a lustre to our country, and an accession to the number of its citizens. . . .

. . .

... [I]t will destroy that moderation and harmony which the forbearance of our laws to intermeddle with Religion has produced among its several sects. Torrents of blood have been spilt in the old world, by vain attempts of the secular arm, to extinguish Religious discord, by proscribing all difference in Religious opinion. Time has at length revealed the true remedy. Every relaxation of narrow and rigorous policy, wherever it has been tried, has been found to assuage the disease. . . .

... [T]he policy of the Bill is adverse to the diffusion of the light of Christianity. . . . Instead of Levelling as far as possible, every obstacle to the victorious progress of Truth, the Bill with an ignoble and unchristian timidity would circumscribe it with a wall of defence against the encroachments of error.

...

... [F]inally, "the equal right of every citizen to the free exercise of his Religion according to the dictates of conscience" is held by the same tenure with all our other rights. If we recur to its origin, it is equally the gift of nature; if we weigh its importance, it cannot be less dear to us; if we consult the "Declaration of those rights which pertain to the good people of Virginia, as the basis and foundation of Government," it is enumerated with equal solemnity, or rather studied emphasis. Either the, we must say, that the Will of the Legislature is the only measure of their authority; and that in the plenitude of this authority, they may sweep away all our fundamental rights; or, that they are bound to leave this particular right untouched and sacred: Either we must say, that they may control the freedom of the press, may abolish the Trial by Jury, may swallow up the Executive and Judiciary Powers of the State; nay that they may despoil us of our very right of suffrage, and erect themselves into an independent and hereditary Assembly or, we must say, that they have no authority to enact into the law the Bill under consideration.

An Act for Establishing Religious Freedom (1786)[33]

Whereas, Almighty God hath created the mind free; that all attempts to influence it by temporal punishments or burdens, or by civil incapacitations tend only to beget habits of hypocrisy and meanness, and are a departure from the plan of the holy author of our religion, who being Lord, both of body and mind yet chose not to propagate it by coercions on either, ... that the impious presumption of legislators and rulers, ... who, being themselves but fallible and uninspired men have assumed dominion over the faith of others, setting up their own opinions and modes of thinking as the only true and infallible, and as such endeavoring to impose them on others, hath established and maintained false religions over the greatest part of the world and through all time; that to compel a man to furnish contributions of money for the propagation of opinions which he disbelieves is sinful and tyrannical; that even the forcing him to support this or that teacher of his own religious persuasion is depriving him of the comfortable liberty of giving his contributions to the particular pastor, whose morals he would make his pattern, and whose powers he feels most persuasive to righteousness ... ; that our civil rights have no dependence on our religious opinions any more than our opinions in physics or geometry, that therefore the proscribing any citizen as unworthy the public confidence, by laying upon him an incapacity of being called to offices of trust and emolument, unless he profess or renounce this or that religious opinion, is depriving him injuriously of those privileges and advantages, to which, in common with his fellow citizens, he has a natural right, that it tends only to corrupt the principles of that very Religion it is meant to encourage, by bribing with a monopoly of worldly honours and emoluments those who will externally profess and conform to it; . . . that to suffer the civil magistrate to intrude his powers into the field of opinion and to restrain the profession or propagation of principles on supposition of their ill tendency is a dangerous fallacy which at once destroys all religious liberty because he being of course judge of that tendency will make his opinions the rule of judgment and approve or condemn the sentiments of others only as they shall square with or differ from his own; that it is time enough for the rightful purposes of civil government, for its officers to interfere when principles break out into overt acts against peace and good order; and finally, that Truth is great, and will prevail if left to herself, that she is the proper and sufficient antagonist to error, and has nothing to fear from the conflict, unless by human interposition disarmed of her

33. B. L. Rayner, *Sketches of the Life, Writings, and Opinions of Thomas Jefferson* (New York: A. Francis and W. Boardman, 1832), 159–60.

natural weapons free argument and debate, errors ceasing to be dangerous when it is permitted freely to contradict them: Be it enacted by General Assembly that no man shall be compelled to frequent or support any religious worship, place, or ministry whatsoever, nor shall be enforced, restrained, molested, or burdened in his body or goods, nor shall otherwise suffer on account of his religious opinions or belief, but that all men shall be free to profess, and by argument to maintain, their opinions in matters of Religion, and that the same shall in no wise diminish, enlarge or affect their civil capacities. And though we well know that this Assembly elected by the people for the ordinary purposes of Legislation only, have no power to restrain the acts of succeeding Assemblies constituted with powers equal to our own, and that therefore to declare this act irrevocable would be of no effect in law; yet we are free to declare, and do declare that the rights hereby asserted, are of the natural rights of mankind, and that if any act shall be hereafter passed to repeal the present or to narrow its operation, such act will be an infringement of natural right.

House Debate over Conscientious Objectors (1789)[34]

Madison's proposed bill of rights included the following clause: "No person religiously scrupulous of bearing arms, shall be compelled to render military service in person." This provision was one of the few debated in the First Congress. Many representatives favored granting religious pacifists exemptions from military service. Nevertheless, Madison's proposal was rejected. Consider the significance of this deletion when reading the following excerpts from that debate. Was the clause dropped because representatives rejected the right to an exemption or because the clause was thought unnecessary? How should this debate over military exemptions for religious pacifists influence current controversies over whether religious believers have rights to exemptions from other general laws that burden their religious practices?

REPRESENTATIVE JAMES JACKSON (Georgia)

[He] did not expect that all the people of the United States would turn Quaker or Moravians [religious sects that had conscientious objection to military service]; consequently one part would have to defend the other in case of invasion. Now this, in his opinion, was unjust, unless the constitution secured an equivalent: for this reason he moved to amend the clause, by inserting at the end of it, "upon paying an equivalent, to be established by law."

REPRESENTATIVE ROGER SHERMAN (Connecticut)

[H]e did not see an absolute necessity for a clause of this kind. We do not live under an arbitrary Government, said he, and the States, respectively, will have the government of the militia, unless when called into actual service.

REPRESENTATIVE EGBERT BENSON (New York)

No man can claim this indulgence of right. It may be a religious persuasion, but it is no natural right, and therefore ought to be left to the discretion of the Government. If this stands part of the constitution, it will be a question before the Judiciary on every regulation you make with respect to the organization of the militia, . . . whether it comports with this declaration or not.

REPRESENTATIVE THOMAS SCOTT (Pennsylvania)

[He] objected to the clause in the sixth amendment, "No person religiously scrupulous shall be compelled to bear arms." He observed that if this becomes part of the constitution, such persons can neither be called upon for their services, nor can an equivalent be demanded. . . . I conceive it, said he, to be a legislative right altogether. There are many sects I know, who are religiously scrupulous in this respect; I do not mean to deprive them of any indulgence the law affords; my design is to guard against those who are of no religion. It has been urged that religion is on the decline; if so, the argument is more strong in my favor, for when the time comes that religion shall be discarded, the generality of persons will have recourse to these pretexts to get excused from bearing arms.

REPRESENTATIVE ELIAS BOUDINOT (New Jersey)

Can any dependence, said he, be placed in men who are conscientious in this respect? Or what justice can there be in compelling them to bear arms, when, according to their religious principles, they would rather die than use them. . . . I hope that in establishing this Government, we may show the world that proper care is taken that the Government may not interfere with the religious sentiments of any person.

34. *Annals of Congress*, 1st Cong., 1st Sess. (1789), 750–51, 766–67.

C. Guns

The Second Amendment to the U.S. Constitution declares, "A well regulated Militia, being necessary to the security of a free State, the right of the people to keep and bear Arms, shall not be infringed." This amendment explicitly connects the right to bear arms with militia service. During the ratification debates, anti-Federalists insisted that the Constitution gave Congress the power to disband all state militias. The national legislature, they feared, was empowered to raise a large professional army capable of violating fundamental rights. George Mason, the leading opponent of ratification in Virginia, expressed these concerns when he declared,

> There are various ways of destroying the militia. A standing army may be perpetually established in their stead. I abominate and detest the idea of a government, where there is a standing army. The militia may be here destroyed by that method which has been practiced in other parts of the world before; that is, by rendering useless—by disarming them. . . .
>
> No man has a greater regard for the military gentlemen than I have. . . . But when once a standing army is established in any country, the people lose their liberty. When, against a regular and disciplined army, yeomanry are the only defence,—yeomanry, unskilled and unarmed,—what chance is there for preserving freedom.[35]

The Second Amendment places the institution of state militia on a constitutional foundation. By preventing national officials from disarming the local citizens who might constitute the local militia, the Constitution maintains state militia as a vital protection for local liberties. Or so most Americans in 1791 believed.

The Bill of Rights does not explicitly connect the right to bear arms with three other important eighteenth-century concerns: protection against criminals, protection against oppressive government officials, and hunting. Many state constitutions recognized a right to use weapons in self-defense. Article XIII of the Virginia Declaration of Rights asserts, "The people have a right to bear arms for the defence of themselves and the state." Some anti-Federalists wanted state constitutions and the federal Constitution to include specific protections for hunting. The dissenting minority in Pennsylvania proposed a constitutional amendment stating, "That the people have a right to bear arms for the defence of themselves and their own state, or the United States, or for the purpose of killing game and no law shall be passed for disarming the people or any of them, unless for crimes committed, or real danger of public injury from individuals."

35. David E. Young, ed., *The Origin of the Second Amendment: A Documentary History of the Bill of Rights 1787–1792*, 2nd ed. (Ontonagon, MI: Golden Oak, 1995), 400.

D. Personal Freedom and Public Morality

The Ninth Amendment declares, "The enumeration in the Constitution, of certain rights, shall not be construed to deny or disparage others retained by the people." During the ratification debates, Federalists claimed that a complete enumeration of rights was impossible. James Iredell informed the North Carolina ratifying convention, "Let any one make what collection or enumeration of rights he pleases, I will immediately mention twenty or thirty more rights not contained in it."[36] Iredell and others correctly observed that no one can list every possible fundamental right and attempting to do so would make the Constitution unwieldy. The Ninth Amendment alleviated this fear of an incomplete enumeration.

VIII. Democratic Rights

MAJOR DEVELOPMENTS

- Debates over whether free speech rights are limited to prior restraints
- Property qualifications for voting and officeholding

The American founders intended to establish a constitutional republic. In *Federalist* 10 James Madison emphasized that republican government "promise[d] the cure" for faction, the disease that proved fatal for all democratic governments. Republican institutions, he believed, encouraged the selection of virtuous rulers who would protect individual rights and pursue the common good. In a democracy, which Madison defined as a regime in which people met as a whole to

36. Elliot, *Debates*, 4:167.

determine laws and policies, policy reflected only what a majority of ordinary people thought good at a particular time.

Most Federalists shared Madison's analysis of the best form of popular government, even though many more often used *republic* and *democracy* as synonyms. The persons responsible for the Constitution were inclined to view elections more as a means for empowering a natural aristocracy who would govern wisely than as a means for facilitating government by popular opinion. Committed to popular government, the framers recognized the value of free speech, voting rights, and citizenship. Nevertheless, proponents of a constitutional republic in the late eighteenth century were more inclined than contemporary democrats to limit expression, suffrage, and citizenship when they thought that restrictions on these liberties promoted the public good.

A. Free Speech

Americans in the Founding Era were constitutionally committed to free speech. The First Amendment to the Constitution of the United States declares, "Congress shall make no law . . . abridging the freedom of speech, or of the press; or the right of the people peaceably to assemble, and to petition the Government for a redress of grievances." State constitutions contained similar provisions. The constitution of Massachusetts asserted, "The liberty of the press is essential to the security of freedom in a State; it ought not, therefore, to be restricted in this commonwealth." Some states had no explicit constitutional protection for free speech. This absence seems better explained by the Federalist belief that enumerated rights served little purpose than by any hostility to free speech.

Americans in the late eighteenth century disputed what speech merited constitutional protection. In 1788 James Wilson informed the Pennsylvania ratification convention that "what is meant by the liberty of the press is, that there should be no antecedent restraint upon it; but that every author is responsible when he attacks the security or welfare of the government, or the safety, character and property of the individual."[37] Three years later, Wilson gave a broader definition of free speech, claiming that the "citizen under a free government has a right to think, to speak, to write, to print, and to publish freely, but with decency and truth, concerning public men, public bodies, and public measures."[38] Americans championed more libertarian understandings of free speech rights when they wished to speak than when they wished to prevent others from speaking. The same advocates of revolution in Boston who condemned English authorities for prosecuting the radical *Boston Gazette* later attempted to silence "the scandalous license of the tory presses."[39]

Most Americans in the Founding Era rejected Blackstone's claim that government could punish seditious libel, defined as criticism, true or false, of government officials. Consider the 1789 correspondence between John Adams and William Cushing, the chief justice of the Massachusetts Supreme Judicial Court. Cushing was concerned with the proper interpretation of the free speech clause in the Massachusetts Constitution. His letter maintained that republican governments provided constitutional protection for true comments about government.

> Judge Blackstone says . . . the liberty of the press consists in laying no *previous* restraints upon publication, and not in freedom from censure for criminal matter, when published. . . .
>
> But the words of our article understood according to plain English, make no such distinction, and must exclude *subsequent* restraints, as much as *previous* restraints. In other words, if all men are restrained by the fear of jails, scourges and loss of ears from examining the conduct of persons in administration and where their conduct is illegal, tyrannical and tending to overthrow the Constitution and introduce slavery, are so restrained from declaring it to the public *that* will be as effectual a restraint as any *previous* restraint whatever.
>
> . . . This liberty of publishing truth can never effectually injure a good government, or honest administrators; but it may save a state from the necessity of a revolution, as well as bring one about, when it is necessary.

37. Elliot, *Debates*, 2:420.

38. James DeWitt Andrews, ed., *The Works of James Wilson* (Chicago: Callaghan and Co., 1896), 2:287.

39. Stephen M. Feldman, *Free Expression and Democracy in America* (Chicago: University of Chicago Press, 2008), 50–51.

B. Voting

The American Revolution inspired ordinary citizens to fight more vigorously for voting rights. Poorer citizens, who had been barred from voting during the Colonial Era, claimed that the principles that justified separation from England should be more rigorously applied in domestic politics. If a Parliament in which no Americans were represented had no authority outside of England, they reminded political leaders in the states, what right did a legislature chosen only by large property holders have to make laws for citizens denied the ballot? Persons seeking an expanded suffrage declared, "No man can be bound by a law that he has not given his consent to, either by his person, or legal representative."[40] Many Revolutionary War veterans insisted that they had earned the right to vote by their service to the country. One newspaper editorial demanded the ballot be given to "every man who pays his shot and bears his lot."[41]

Federalists repudiated these democratic challenges to their republican commitments. They defended the traditional view that persons who lacked sufficient property lacked the capacities necessary to vote. John Adams stated, "Men in general in every Society, who are wholly destitute of Property, are also too little acquainted with public Affairs to form a Right Judgment, and too dependent upon other Men to have a Will of their own."[42] James Madison agreed. He informed the Constitutional Convention in Philadelphia,

> The freeholders of the Country would be the safest depositories of Republican liberty. In future times a great majority of the people will not only be without landed, but any other sort of, property. These will either combine under the influence of their common situation; in which case, the rights of property & the public liberty will not be secure in their hands; or which is more probable, they will become tools of opulence & ambition, in which case there will be equal danger on another side.[43]

Proponents of voting rights enjoyed limited success during the Founding Era. Most states reduced property qualifications, and Vermont abandoned wealth qualifications completely. Most states limited the ballot to free white men, but women were allowed to vote in New Jersey, and free African Americans voted in some states. The U.S. Constitution incorporated these state legal developments. Article I, Section 4 entitles any person to vote in a federal election who, by state law, may vote for a member of the house in the state legislature with the most members (states tended to have higher property qualifications for the upper, smaller house of the state legislature). State laws extending or narrowing the suffrage would have the same consequences for state and federal elections.

John Adams and Benjamin Franklin on Universal Male Suffrage

The vast majority of the Revolutionary War leadership believed that the establishment of some property qualifications was a vital means for preserving property rights. John Adams was a particularly vigorous defender of this inherited wisdom. Adams insisted that suffrage restrictions ensured that voters had the interests, capacities, and independence necessary to choose the most qualified representatives. Benjamin Franklin was one of the few well-known political actors who favored giving most men the right to vote. He criticized proposals for a freehold requirement in Pennsylvania. In sharp contrast to Adams, Franklin questioned whether property holders had any more capacity to govern than less economically fortunate citizens.

As you read these excerpts, consider how Franklin responds to Adams's argument. Is Adams correct to think that a regime that values property must impose some property qualifications on voters? Is Franklin committed to republican notions of private right and the common good, or are his values more democratic? What are those values? Keep these excerpts in mind when you read the section on gender equality. Does Franklin give any reasons for denying the ballot to women?

40. Ronald M. Peters, Jr., *The Massachusetts Constitution of 1780: A Social Compact* (Amherst: University of Massachusetts Press, 1974), 131.

41. This paragraph and the next borrow heavily from Alexander Keyssar, *The Right to Vote: The Contested History of Democracy in the United States* (New York: Basic, 2000), 3–25.

42. John Adams to James Sullivan, May 26, 1776, in *Papers of John Adams*, ed. Robert J. Taylor, Mary-Jo Kline, Gregg L. Lint, and Celeste Walker (Cambridge, MA: Belknap Press of Harvard University Press, 1977), 1:395.

43. Max Farrand, *Records of the Federal Convention of 1787* (New Haven: Yale University Press, 1911), 2:203–04.

John Adams, Letter to James Sullivan (May 26, 1776)[44]

. . .

It is certain in Theory, that the only moral Foundation of Government is the Consent of the People. But to what an Extent Shall We carry this Principle? Shall We Say, that every Individual of the Community, old and young, male and female, as well as rich and poor, must consent, expressly to every Act of Legislation? No, you will Say. This is impossible. How then does the Right arise in the Majority to govern the Minority, against their Will? Whence arises the Right of the Men to govern Women, without their Consent? Whence the Right of the old to bind the Young, without theirs.

But let us first Suppose, that the whole Community of every Age, Rank, Sex, and Condition, has a Right to vote. This Community, is assembled—a Motion is made and carried by a Majority of one Voice. The Minority will not agree to this. Whence arises the Right of the Majority to govern, and the Obligation of the Minority to obey? from Necessity, you will Say, because there can be no other Rule. But why exclude Women? You will Say, because their Delicacy renders them unfit for Practice and Experience, in the great Business of Life, and the hardy Enterprises of War, as well as the arduous Cares of State. Besides, their attention is so much engaged with the necessary Nurture of their Children, that Nature has made them fittest for domestic Cares. And Children have not Judgment or Will of their own. True. But will not these Reasons apply to others? Is it not equally true, that Men in general in every Society, who are wholly destitute of Property, are also too little acquainted with public Affairs to form a Right Judgment, and too dependent upon other Men to have a Will of their own? If this is a Fact, if you give to every Man, who has no Property, a Vote, will you not make a fine encouraging Provision for Corruption by your fundamental Law? Such is the Frailty of the human Heart, that very few Men, who have no Property, have any Judgment of their own. They talk and vote as they are directed by Some Man of Property, who has attached their Minds to his Interest.

. . .

. . . Power always follows Property. . . . We may advance one Step farther and affirm that the Balance of Power in a Society, accompanies the Balance of Property in Land. The only possible Way then of preserving the Balance of Power on the side of equal Liberty and public Virtue, is to make the Acquisition of Land easy to every Member of Society: to make a Division of the Land into Small Quantities, So that the Multitude may be possessed of landed Estates. If the Multitude is possessed of the Balance of real Estate, the Multitude will have the Balance of Power, and in that Case the Multitude will take Care of the Liberty, Virtue, and Interest of the Multitude in all Acts of Government.

. . .

The Same Reasoning, which will induce you to admit all Men, who have no Property, to vote, with those who have, for those Laws, which affect the Person will prove that you ought to admit Women and Children: for generally Speaking, Women and Children, have as good Judgment, and as independent Minds as those Men who are wholly destitute of Property: these last being to all Intents and Purposes as much dependent upon others, who will please to feed, cloth, and employ them, as Women are upon their Husbands, or Children on their Parents.

. . .

Depend upon it, sir, it is dangerous to open So fruitful a Source of Controversy and Altercation, as would be opened by attempting to alter the Qualifications of Voters. There will be no End of it. New Claims will arise. Women will demand a Vote. Lads from 12 to 21 will think their Rights not enough attended to, and every Man, who has not a Farthing, will demand an equal Voice with any other in all Acts of State. It tends to confound and destroy all Distinctions, and prostrate all Ranks, to one common Level.

Benjamin Franklin, Queries and Remarks Respecting Alterations in the Constitution of Pennsylvania (1789)[45]

. . . What is the Proportion of Freemen possessing Lands and Houses of one thousand Pounds Value compared to that of Freemen whose Possessions are inferior? Are they as one to ten? Are they even as one

44. Excerpt taken from John Adams, *The Works of John Adams*, ed. Charles Francis Adams, vol. 9 (Boston: Little, Brown and Company, 1854), 375.

45. Excerpt taken from Jared Sparks, ed., *Works of Benjamin Franklin* (Boston: Hillard, Gray and Company, 1840), 5:167.

to twenty? I should doubt whether they are as one to fifty. If this Minority is to choose a Body expressly to control that which is to be chosen by the great Majority of the Freemen, what have this great Majority done to forfeit so great a Portion of their Right in Elections? Why is this Power of Control, contrary to the Spirit of all Democracies, to be vested in a Minority, instead of a Majority? Then is it intended or is it not that the Rich should have a Vote in the Choice of Members for the lower House, while those of inferior Property are deprived of the Right of voting for Members of the upper House? And why should the upper House, chosen by a Minority have equal Power with the lower, chosen by a Majority? Is it supposed that Wisdom is the necessary Concomitant of Riches, and that one Man worth a thousand Pound must have as much Wisdom as twenty, who have each only 999? And why is Property to be represented at all? . . . Private Property . . . is a Creature of Society and is subject to the Calls of that Society whenever its Necessities shall require it, even to its last Farthing; its Contributions therefore to the public Exigencies are not to be considered as conferring a Benefit on the Public, entitling the Contributors to the Distinctions of Honor and Power; but as the Return of an Obligation previously received or the Payment of a just Debt. The Combinations of Civil Society are not like those of a Set of Merchants who club their Property in different Proportions for Building and Freighting a Ship, and may therefore have some Right to vote in the Disposition of the Voyage in a greater or less Degree according to their respective Contributions; but the important Ends of Civil Society are the personal Securities of Life and Liberty; these remain the same in every Member of the Society, and the poorest continues to have an equal Claim to them with the most opulent, whatever Difference Time, Chance or Industry may occasion in their Circumstances. On these Considerations I am sorry to see the Signs this Paper I have been considering affords of a Disposition among some of our People to commence an Aristocracy, by giving the Rich a Predominancy in Government, a Choice peculiar to themselves in one half the Legislature, to be proudly called the UPPER House, and the other Branch chosen by the Majority of the People degraded by the Denomination of the LOWER, and giving to this *upper House* a Permanency of four Years, and but two to the *lower*. . .

IX. Equality

MAJOR DEVELOPMENTS

- Rejection of aristocracy
- The federal Constitution protects slavery, but Massachusetts declares human bondage unconstitutional
- Consensus that gender distinctions are based on real differences between men and women

Americans are born equal. The Declaration of Independence proclaims, "All men are created equal," and many state constitutions repeat this language. The Virginia Declaration of Rights asserts:

> That all men are by nature equally free and independent, and have certain inherent rights, of which, when they enter into a state of society, they cannot, by any compact, deprive or divest their posterity; namely, the enjoyment of life and liberty, with the means of acquiring and possessing property, and pursuing and obtaining happiness and safety.

Neither the Constitution of the United States nor the Bill of Rights includes a similar clause. Nevertheless, in 1789 all prominent framers believed that Americans were constitutionally committed to republican equality. "Equality," a national consensus maintained, "ought to be the basis of every law."[46]

This professed commitment to equality coexisted with the preservation of remarkable inequalities. The U.S. Constitution rejects a hereditary aristocracy. Article I, Section 9 asserts, "No Title of Nobility shall be granted by the United States." In every state, however, men had different rights than women, white persons had different rights than persons of color, persons with more property had different rights than persons with less property, and so on. Americans maintained that such legal distinctions were justified because they reflected "real differences" between people. Seventeenth-century laws that permitted only nobles to hunt in the forest violated egalitarian norms, because every good republican knew that no real difference existed between nobles and ordinary citizens. Laws that limited militia service to white men were justified, however, because most prominent Americans

46. James Madison, in *The Mind of the Founder: Sources of the Political Thought of James Madison*, ed. Marvin Meyers (Indianapolis: Bobbs-Merrill, 1973), 10–11.

were certain that the distinctive characteristics of white men made them more qualified for militia service than women or persons of color.

A. Equality Under Law

Americans maintained that regimes committed to equality under law respect three principles[47]:

1. No one has a legal right *solely* because of his or her status.
2. Government has a right to regulate whenever doing so promotes the common good.
3. Laws that treat persons differently must be based on real distinctions between the groups involved and cannot be efforts to favor one group at the expense of another.

Federalists sought to realize these ideals by designing constitutional institutions that could not be captured by interest groups. Madison articulated this commitment to a faction-free society when he told Jefferson that the U.S. Constitution fashioned a government that "may be sufficiently neutral between different parts of the Society to control one part from invading the rights of another, and at the same time sufficiently controlled itself, from setting up an interest adverse to that of the entire society."[48] Madison also thought that representation would promote equality by connecting the interests of government officials with the interests of their constituents. In *Federalist* 57, he asserted, "I will add, as a fifth circumstance in the situation of the House of Representatives, restraining them from oppressive measures, that they can make no law which will not have its full operation on themselves and their friends, as well as on the great mass of the society."

State constitutions provided more explicit protections for equality under the law. Many prohibited laws granting special rights to specific citizens. The Massachusetts Constitution of 1780 declared, "No man, nor corporation, or association of men, have any other title to obtain advantages, or particular and exclusive privileges, distinct from those of the community, than what arises from the consideration of services rendered to the public." The Maryland and North Carolina constitutions explicitly forbade the state legislature from granting monopolies.

47. For more elaboration on the themes in this brief subsection, see Howard Gillman, *The Constitution Besieged: The Rise and Demise of Lochner Era Police Powers Jurisprudence* (Durham, NC: Duke University Press, 1993).

48. Madison to Jefferson, October 24, 1787, in *Republic of Letters* (see note 13), 1:502.

B. Race

Heated debates over slavery occurred in the Constitutional Convention. Some northerners, inspired by revolutionary rhetoric, maintained that slavery was an evil that ought to be abolished as soon as possible. Gouverneur Morris described human bondage as "a nefarious practice, . . . the curse of heaven on the States where it prevailed."[49] Slaveholders from South Carolina and Georgia aggressively defended the practice. Charles Pinckney informed the convention, "If slavery be wrong, it is justified by the example of all the world."[50] Many delegates insisted that slavery was wrong but maintained that anti-slavery constitutional provisions were unnecessary or unwise. They thought that human bondage was likely to die a natural death or that compromise was necessary to achieve a national union. "Let us not intermeddle," Oliver Ellsworth of Connected advised. He thought that "poor laborers [would] soon be so plenty as to render slavery useless."[51]

The resulting bargaining over human bondage provided slaveholders with important constitutional protections. Some guarantees were substantive. Article I, Section 2 declares that slaves count as three-fifths of a person when determining how seats are allocated in the House of Representatives. If South Carolina had 1 million citizens and 1 million slaves, then the state had 1.6 million persons for apportionment purposes. Article I, Section 9 forbade Congress from banning the international slave trade until 1808. Article IV, Section 2 requires all states to return fugitive slaves to their owners. Other constitutional protections were institutional. The framers designed every government institution with the balance of power between the slave and (soon-to-be) free states in mind. Because of the common assumption that southern states would grow faster than northern states, most political elites believed that Articles I, II, and III guaranteed that the slave states would have the power to prevent any anti-slavery measure from becoming law.

49. Farrand, *Records*, 2:221.

50. Ibid., 2:371.

51. Ibid.

Americans made some racial progress during the Founding Era. Some northern states freed slaves. *Commonwealth v. Jennison* (MA 1783) effectively ended slavery in Massachusetts. Other states adopted measures that gradually abolished slavery. Pennsylvania passed a post-nati ("born after") law that freed all children of slaves once they reached a certain age. Several southern states eased burdens on manumission. Some slave-state citizens thought that such laws, which enabled slaveholders to voluntarily free their slaves, were the first step toward a more general abolition.

These trends toward emancipation and liberal manumission were not accompanied by any tendency to increase the rights of free blacks. At the time the Constitution was ratified, free blacks were permitted to vote in some states. Nevertheless, all states discriminated on the basis of race. White Americans were confident that such discriminations were based on real differences between the races. Thomas Jefferson insisted that the phrase "all men are created equal" encompassed persons of color. Nevertheless, his *Notes on Virginia* expressed the conventional wisdom that whites and blacks were too different to share the same civic space.

Commonwealth v. Jennison (1783)[52]

After Nathaniel Jennison beat Quock Walker, Walker sued Jennison for battery. Jennison moved to dismiss the suit because Walker was his slave. Under common law, masters had the right to beat their slaves and apprentices, but not their servants or employees. A jury found that Walker was free and awarded him fifty pounds in damages. Shortly thereafter, Jennison was indicted for assaulting Walker. Jennison again claimed that he had the right to discipline his slave. The prosecution responded that slavery no longer existed in Massachusetts, because the "free and equal" clause of the 1780 Massachusetts Constitution had legally emancipated slaves in the state.

Chief Justice William Cushing accepted the prosecution's arguments when rejecting Jennison's defense that he had a right to beat his slave. He contended that Jennison had beaten a free man because all slaves in Massachusetts were emancipated by the constitution of 1780. Compare Commonwealth v. Jennison *to* Somerset v. Stewart *(1773). What are the main similarities and differences in the opinions? Would Lord Mansfield have endorsed Justice Cushing's opinion?*

The impact of Jennison *is controversial. A general consensus exists that the opinion dealt a mortal blow to slavery in Massachusetts. Some commentators think that Justice Cushing's decision played an important role in the emancipation process. Others claim that slavery was for all practical purposes moribund in Massachusetts when* Jennison *was decided. Similar questions about the impact of judicial decisions recur throughout this text. When thinking about* Jennison, *consider whether judicial decisions are capable of playing major roles in fights for civil liberties, or whether they are effective only when most influential persons have abandoned the practice under constitutional attack.*

Chief Justice William Cushing declared that "every subject is entitled to liberty." After Jennison, was Walker a citizen of Massachusetts?

. . .

. . . It is true, without investigating the rights of Christians to hold Africans in perpetual servitude, that they had been considered by some of the Province laws as actually existing among us; but nowhere do we find it expressly established. . . . But whatever sentiments have formerly prevailed or slid in upon us by the example of others on the subject, they can no longer exist. Sentiments more favorable to the natural rights of mankind, and to that innate desire of liberty, which heaven, without regard to complexion or shape, has planted in the human breast—have prevailed since the glorious struggle for our rights began. And these sentiments led the framers of our constitution of government—by which the people of this Commonwealth have solemnly bound themselves to each other—to declare—that all men are born free and equal; and that every subject is entitled to liberty, and to have it guarded by the laws, as well as his life and property. In short, without resorting to implication in constructing the constitution, slavery is in my judgment effectively abolished as it can be by the granting of rights and privileges wholly incompatible and repugnant to its existence. The court are therefore fully of opinion that perpetual servitude can no longer be tolerated in our government, and that liberty can only be forfeited by some criminal conduct or relinquished by personal consent or contract.

52. Excerpt taken from *Proceedings of the Massachusetts Historical Society* (Boston: Massachusetts Historical Society, 1875), 292.

Thomas Jefferson, Notes on the State of Virginia (1787)[53]

Thomas Jefferson embodied the American ambivalence toward slavery. A slaveholder who had several children with his slave mistress, Jefferson also penned a series of powerful anti-slavery appeals. Most Americans in the late eighteenth century shared Jefferson's abstract anti-slavery sentiments and his commitment to white supremacy. Prominent framers who lived north of South Carolina frequently asserted that slavery was evil. Slaveholders in Virginia confessed that they hated the practice. "There is not a man living who wishes more sincerely than I do," said George Washington, "to see a plan adopted for the abolition of [slavery]."[54] Most Americans were also unprepared to live in a multiracial society. One delegate to a southern ratification convention maintained, "It is impossible for us to be happy if, after manumission, they are to stay among us."[55]

Jefferson's Notes on the State of Virginia *reflects both these anti-slavery and racist themes. Jefferson condemned both human bondage and a multiracial society. Herbert Storing claims that although Jefferson acknowledged that all persons had a fundamental right to be free, he contended that no one has a fundamental right to be an American citizen.[56] Does this explain Jefferson's beliefs? What other reasons might explain Jefferson's combination of anti-slavery convictions and racism?*

. . . Why [after emancipating all slaves] not retain and incorporate the blacks into the state. . . . Deep rooted prejudices entertained by the whites; ten thousand recollections, by the blacks, of the injuries they have sustained; new provocations; the real distinctions which nature has made; and many other circumstances, will divide us into parties, and produce convulsions which will probably never end but in the extermination of the one or the other race.—To these objections, which are political, may be added others, which are physical and moral. The first difference which strikes us is that of color. . . . And is this difference of no importance? Is it not the foundation of a greater or less share of beauty in the two races? Are not the fine mixtures of red and white, the expressions of every passion by greater or less suffusions of color in the one, preferable to that eternal monotony, which reigns in the countenances, that immoveable veil of black which covers all the emotions of the other race? . . . They seem to require less sleep. A black, after hard labor through the day, will be induced by the slightest amusements to sit up till midnight, or later, though knowing he must be out with the first dawn of the morning. They are at least as brave, and more adventuresome. . . . Comparing them by their faculties of memory, reason, and imagination, it appears to me, that in memory they are equal to the whites; in reason much inferior, as I think one could scarcely be found capable of tracing and comprehending the investigations of Euclid; and that in imagination they are dull, tasteless, and anomalous. . . . [N]ever yet could I find that a black had uttered a thought above the level of plain narration; never see even an elementary trait of painting or sculpture. In music they are more generally gifted than the whites with accurate ears for tune and time. . . .

. . . Notwithstanding these considerations which must weaken their respect for the laws of property, we find among them numerous instances of the most rigid integrity, and as many as among their better instructed masters, of benevolence, gratitude, and unshaken fidelity. . . . This unfortunate difference of colour, and perhaps of faculty, is a powerful obstacle to the emancipation of these people. Many of their advocates, while they wish to vindicate the liberty of human nature, are anxious also to preserve its dignity and beauty. Some of these, embarrassed by the question "What further is to be done with them?" join themselves in opposition with those who are actuated by sordid avarice only. Among the Romans emancipation required but one effort. The slave, when made free, might mix with, without staining the blood of his master. But with us a second is necessary, unknown to history. When freed, he is to be removed beyond the reach of mixture.

. . .

. . . There must doubtless be an unhappy influence on the manners of our people produced by the existence of slavery among us. The whole commerce between master and slave is a perpetual exercise of the

53. Excerpt taken from Paul Leicester Ford, ed., *The Writings of Thomas Jefferson* (New York: G. P. Putnam's Sons, 1894), 3:244–46, 250, 267–68.

54. George Washington to Robert Morris, April 12, 1786, in *The Writings of George Washington*, ed. Jared Sparks (Boston: Russell, Odiorne, and Metcalf & Hilliard, Gray & Co., 1835), 9:159.

55. Elliot, *Debates*, 4:101.

56. Herbert J. Storing, "Slavery and the Moral Foundations of the American Republic," *in Slavery and Its Consequences*, ed. Robert A. Goldwin and Art Kaufman (Washington, DC: American Enterprise Institute, 1988), 59.

most boisterous passions, the most unremitting despotism on the one part, and degrading submissions on the other.... And can the liberties of a nation be thought secure when we have removed their only firm basis, a conviction in the minds of the people that these liberties are of the gift of God? That they are not to be violated but with his wrath? Indeed I tremble for my country when I reflect that God is just: that his justice cannot sleep for ever: that considering numbers, nature and natural means only, a revolution of the wheel of fortune, an exchange of situation, is among possible events: that it may become probable by supernatural interference! The Almighty has no attribute which can take side with us in such a contest.— But it is impossible to be temperate and to pursue this subject through the various considerations of policy, of morals, of history natural and civil. We must be contented to hope they will force their way into every one's mind. I think a change already perceptible, since the origin of the present revolution. The spirit of the master is abating, that of the slave rising from the dust, his condition mollifying, the way I hope preparing, under the auspices of heaven, for a total emancipation, and that this is disposed, in the order of events, to be with the consent of the masters, rather than by their extirpation.

C. Gender

The egalitarian principles that inspired the American Revolution had little practical influence on gender equality. "American judges and lawyers sometimes gave thought to the implications of republicanism for women," one study points out, "but . . . they ultimately

Illustration 3-2 A Society of the Patriotic Ladies at Edenton in North Carolina

This satirical British cartoon depicts the launch of a boycott of English tea and clothing organized by the women of Edenton, North Carolina, in 1774.

Source: Robert Sayer and John Bennett (Firm), publisher; Dawe, Philip, artist. Library of Congress Prints and Photographs Division Washington, DC 20540, USA.

refused to meddle with tradition."[57] The Revolutionary War created opportunities for women to become more involved in political and economic life than had previously been possible. Sandra VanBurkleo notes, "Women joined in processions, circulated petitions, supplied troops with food 'liberated' from shops, cooked and sewed, harassed Loyalist women, made ammunition, boycotted tea and other British goods, donned homespun, published inspirational poetry, occasionally took men's places on the front lines, spied, and eagerly talked politics at the dinner table."[58] Inspired by these efforts, Samuel Adams informed his spouse that he saw "no Reason why a Man may not communicate his political opinions to his wife, if he pleases."[59] Nevertheless, prominent men resisted efforts to obliterate what they thought were natural gender differences. Consider Isaac Backus, a leader in the struggle for religious freedom in Massachusetts. His Christian principles required the female members of his congregation "to keep silent in the church." Natural rights were for one sex only. The Creator gave "liberty to all men . . . opposing women to men, sex to sex."[60] The U.S. Constitution made no mention of gender, and state constitutions framed in the Founding Era limited the vote to male inhabitants who met other qualifications. New Jersey was the only state in 1791 that permitted women tovote.

John Adams and Abigail Adams, **Correspondence on Women's Rights** (1776)[61]

The following correspondence between John and Abigail Adams demonstrates how the egalitarian rhetoric of the American Revolution was invoked to support women's rights, as well as the practical limits on such advocacy. Unlike many men of the Founding Era, John Adams regarded his wife as a valued political advisor. When John was in Philadelphia representing Massachusetts in the Continental Congress, he relied on Abigail to provide him with intelligence on local events. Much of their correspondence dealt with important questions of war and politics. In early spring 1776, Abigail turned her attention to gender. She suggested that the principles underlying the American Revolution supported greater rights for women. John refused to take these claims seriously.

Abigail Adams employs standard liberal justifications when asserting women's rights. What was Abigail asking for when she told John he should "remember the ladies"? Was John's response consistent with the liberal commitments of the late eighteenth century? Could he have defended existing restrictions on woman's rights?

Abigail Adams to John Adams, March 31, 1776

. . .

I have sometimes been ready to think that the passion for Liberty cannot be Equally Strong in the Breasts of those who have been accustomed to deprive their fellow Creatures of theirs. Of this I am certain that it is not founded upon that generous and christian principal of doing to others as we would that others should do unto us.

. . .

. . . I long to hear that you have declared an independancy—and by the way in the new Code of Laws which I suppose it will be necessary for you to make I desire you would Remember the Ladies, and be more generous and favorable to them than your ancestors. Do not put such unlimited power into the hands of the Husbands. Remember all Men would be tyrants if they could. If particular care and attention is not paid to the Ladies we are determined to foment a Rebellion, and will not hold ourselves bound by any Laws in which we have no voice, or Representation.

That your Sex are Naturally Tyrannical is a Truth so thoroughly established as to admit of no dispute, but such of you as wish to be happy willingly give up the harsh title of Master for the more tender and endearing one of Friend. Why then, not put it out of the power of the vicious and the Lawless to use us with cruelty and indignity with impunity. Men of Sense in all Ages abhor those customs which treat us only as the vassals of your Sex. Regard us then as Beings placed by providence under your protection and in imitation of the Supreme Being make use of that power only for our happiness.

---

57. Sandra F. VanBurkleo, *"Belonging to the World": Women's Rights and American Constitutional Culture* (New York: Oxford University Press, 2001), 37.

58. Ibid., 47.

59. Ibid.

60. Ibid., 37, 39, 47.

61. Excerpts taken from Charles Francis Adams, ed., *Familiar Letters of John Adams, and His Wife Abigail Adams* (New York: Hurd and Houghton, 1876), 150, 155.

John Adams to Abigail Adams, April 14, 1776

. . .

As to your extraordinary Code of Laws, I cannot but laugh. We have been told that our Struggle has loosened the bands of Government every where. That Children and Apprentices were disobedient—that schools and Colleges were grown turbulent—that Indians slighted their Guardians and Negroes grew insolent to their Masters. But your Letter was the first Intimation that another Tribe more numerous and powerful than all the rest were grown discontented.—This is rather too coarse a Compliment but you are so saucy, I wont blot it out.

Depend upon it, We know full better than to repeal our Masculine systems. Although they are in full Force, you know they are little more than Theory. We dare not exert our Power in its full Latitude. We are obliged to go fair, and softly, and in Practice you know. We are the subjects. We have only the Name of Masters, and rather than give up this, which would completely subject us to the Despotism of the Petticoat, I hope General Washington, and all our brave Heroes would fight. I am sure every good Politician would plot, as long as he would against Despotism, Empire, Monarchy, Aristocracy, Oligarchy, or Ochlocracy.—A fine Story indeed. I begin to think the Ministry as deep as they are wicked. After stirring up Tories, Landjobbers, Trimmers, Bigots, Canadians, Indians, Negroes, Hanoverians, Hessians, Russians, Irish Roman Catholics, Scotch Renegades, at last they have stimulated the [ladies] to demand new Privileges and threaten to rebel.

Abigail Adams to John Adams, May 7, 1776

. . .

I cannot say that I think you very generous to the Ladies, for whilst you are proclaiming peace and good will to Men, Emancipating all nations, you insist upon retaining an absolute power over Wives. But you must remember that arbitrary power is like most other things which are very hard, very liable to be broken—and not withstanding all your wise Laws and Maxims we have it in our power not only to free ourselves but to subdue our Masters, and without violence throw both your natural and legal authority at our feet.

X. Criminal Justice

MAJOR DEVELOPMENTS

- New constitutional protections for habeas corpus, due process, and other rights
- More emphasis on the right to a jury trial than on the right to an attorney
- The birth of the movement to abolish capital punishment

Americans established written constitutional protections for persons suspected or convicted of criminal offenses. Article I, Section 9 of the U.S. Constitution declares, "The privilege of the Writ of Habeas Corpus shall not be suspended, unless when in Cases of Rebellion or Invasion the public Safety may require it." Article III, Section 2 guarantees jury trials in federal courts for persons accused of crimes. The Bill of Rights offers protections against unreasonable searches and seizures, forbids general warrants, prohibits the practices of compelling persons to testify against themselves and trying a person twice for the same offense, requires grand juries, mandates due process of law, demands speedy and public trials before an impartial jury, insists that criminal defendants be informed of the charges against them, provides persons accused of crimes with the opportunity to confront their accusers and subpoena witnesses to testify on their behalf, grants criminal defendants the right to have a lawyer, and bans barbaric punishments. State constitutions provided similar guarantees for persons suspected or convicted of crimes. The precise rights protected and the precise language used to protect those rights varied from state to state. This variation more often reflected local idiosyncrasies than it did fundamental differences over what constituted fair criminal procedure.

A few controversies took place between 1776 and 1791 over constitutional criminal procedure. State courts debated when persons had the right to a jury trial, and state legislatures considered reducing the number of crimes punishable by death. With those exceptions, judges did not issue major decisions on state criminal procedure during this period, and elected officials did not issue new edicts on what constituted a fair trial. Participants in constitutional conventions rarely discussed at any length the precise meaning of such phrases as "cruel and unusual punishment" or "due process of law."

A. Due Process and Habeas Corpus

Americans inherited from Great Britain a constitutional commitment to due process of law and habeas corpus. General agreement existed on what constituted due process. Criminal defendants had a right to notice of the charges against them and the opportunity to respond to those charges. Americans also agreed on the basic contours of habeas corpus. Persons detained by a government official had the right to a judicial proceeding that determined whether they were being lawfully confined.

B. Search and Seizure

The Fourth Amendment to the U.S. Constitution of declares, "The right of the people to be secure in their persons, houses, papers, and effects, against unreasonable searches and seizures, shall not be violated, and no Warrants shall issue, but upon probable cause, supported by Oath or affirmation, and particularly describing the place to be searched, and the persons or things to be seized." Most state constitutions contained similar provisions. The 1786 constitution of Vermont states,

> That the people have a right to hold themselves, their houses, papers and possessions, free from search or seizure: and therefore warrants, without oaths or affirmations first made, affording sufficient foundation for them, and whereby any officer or messenger may be commanded or required to search suspected places, or to seize any person or persons, his, her or their property not particularly described, are contrary to that right, and ought not to be granted.

Americans believed that constitutional prohibitions on unreasonable searches and general warrants incorporated the principles asserted in *Wilkes v. Wood* (1763) and *Entick v. Carrington* (1765). General warrants that granted the warrant holder discretion to determine where the search would take place and what goods could be searched for were invalid. Victims had the right to receive monetary damages in a trespass suit against those who had engaged in illegal searches. The exclusionary rule was a nineteenth-century innovation, unknown to the framers.

C. Interrogations

The Fifth Amendment declares, "No person . . . shall be compelled in any criminal case to be a witness against himself." Several state constitutions contain similar provisions. The constitution of Pennsylvania asserts, "Nor can [the defendant in a criminal prosecution] be compelled to give evidence against himself." General agreement existed that persons suspected of crimes could not be required to testify under oath. Historians debate whether the Fifth Amendment was thought to provide criminal suspects with other constitutional protections.

Commentators offer two distinctive analyses of Founding Era thought on the Fifth Amendment. Some insist that constitutional provisions prohibiting compelled testimony restricted only improper questioning. Confessions could not be forced by torture or the threat of divine punishment (the oath), but a magistrate could interrogate criminal suspects when evidence pointed to their guilt. Others insist that constitutional provisions prohibiting compelled testimony protected a right to remain silent. This constitutional commitment to an adversarial system gave defendants an absolute right to not cooperate with prosecutors and others who were seeking to prove them guilty of criminal offenses.

D. Juries and Lawyers

Americans agreed that persons suspected of a crime had a right to a jury trial but disputed whether access to defense counsel merited constitutional protection. The U.S. Constitution recognizes both the right to a jury trial and the right to an attorney. The Sixth Amendment declares, "In all criminal prosecutions, the accused shall enjoy the right to a speedy and public trial, by an impartial jury of the State and district wherein the crime shall have been committed, . . . and to have the Assistance of Counsel for his defence." Every state constitution that includes a declaration of rights guarantees the right to a jury trial. The constitution of New Jersey states, "The inestimable right of trial by jury shall remain confirmed as a part of the law of this Colony, without repeal, forever." Very few state constitutions at the time protected the right to be represented by counsel. Defense counsel was a relatively new phenomenon in the eighteenth century. Many Americans believed that innocent persons suspected of a crime should defend themselves.

Judicial decisions protecting the right to a jury trial facilitated jury review of the substantive criminal law for violations of fundamental rights. Juries decided both the facts and the law of the case. Members of a jury were empowered to determine whether a person accused of being a public drunk was actually drunk in public, as well as whether the law against public drunkenness was consistent with community norms. The highest court in Connecticut ruled that a jury verdict could not be overturned for "mistak[ing] the law or the evidence, for by the practice of this state, they are judges of both." In 1791 Justice James Wilson of the U.S. Supreme Court declared, "Verdicts in criminal cases, generally determine the question of law, as well as the question of fact."[62] Juries often decided cases on legal grounds, even when instructed to give a verdict on the facts. Zenger was found not guilty, even though the judge informed the jury that they were to determine only publication and not whether the publication was libelous.

E. Punishments

The American founders placed constitutional restrictions on the punishments that legislatures and judges could impose on persons found guilty of criminal offenses. The Eighth Amendment to the U.S. Constitution declares, "Nor [shall] cruel and unusual punishments [be] inflicted." Many, but not all, state constitutions included similar provisions. The Delaware Declaration of Rights and Fundamental Rules states, "Nor [shall] cruel *or* unusual punishments [be] inflicted." The principles underlying these provisions were uncontroversial. No record exists of them being debated either during a state constitutional convention or during discussions over the Bill of Rights.

What constituted a cruel and unusual punishment was controversial. Many late eighteenth-century political thinkers championed liberal theories of crime and punishment. Inspired by such works as Cesar Beccaria's *Of Crimes and Punishment* (1764), prominent Americans advocated penal reform. Two reforms in particular were popular. First, public officials sought to make punishments better fit offenses. The Pennsylvania Constitution of 1776 called on the state legislature to pass laws making "punishments . . . in general more proportionate to the crimes." Second, Americans emphasized the rehabilitation of criminal offenders. Robert Turnbull declared, "We know that there are in every man . . . some few sparks of honor, a certain consciousness of the intrinsic nature of moral goodness, which though they be latent and apparently extinguished, yet may at any time be kindled and roused into action by the application of proper stimulus."[63] Jefferson spoke of "so many who, if reformed, might be restored sound members to society."[64] Reformers thought that both proportionality and rehabilitation could be best achieved by a relatively new institution: the penitentiary. Criminals no longer needed to be executed, some proponents of liberal theories of criminal justice proclaimed. They could be retrained.

Americans began debating the death penalty late in the Founding Era. Capital punishment had long been imposed for many crimes. The Puritan settlers in Massachusetts relied heavily on the Bible when determining appropriate sanctions, and the Bible demands the death sentence for both violent and nonviolent crimes. The common law imposed capital punishment for crimes ranging from murder to ordinary theft. Inspired by liberal thinking, some legislatures and prominent elites sought to reduce the incidence of capital punishment. Pennsylvania limited capital punishment to treason, murder, rape, and arson.[65] Thomas Jefferson proposed imposing capital punishment only for murder. Benjamin Rush and Benjamin Franklin urged fellow citizens to abolish executions.

Benjamin Rush, On Punishing Murder by Death (1792)[66]

Benjamin Rush was a signer of the Declaration of Independence. He was a leading political activist, a prominent physician, and a close friend of many of the founding fathers. He was also one of the first prominent Americans to call for the abolition of capital punishment. The following excerpt outlines his reasons for thinking that a liberal republic should not punish murder by death.

62. *Witter v. Brewster,* Kirby 422, 423 (CT 1788); Bird Wilson, ed., *Works of James Wilson* (Philadelphia: Bronson and Chauncey, 1804), 2:387.

63. David J. Bodenhamer, *Fair Trial: Rights of the Accused in American History* (New York: Oxford University Press, 1992), 58.

64. Thomas Jefferson, "A Bill for Proportioning Crimes and Punishments in Cases Heretofore Capital," in *The Papers of Thomas Jefferson,* ed. Julian P. Boyd (Princeton, NJ: Princeton University Press), 2:492.

65. Bodenhamer, *Fair Trial,* 57.

66. Excerpt taken from Dagobert D. Runes, ed., *The Selected Writings of Benjamin Rush* (New York: Philosophical Library, 1947).

When reading this essay, think about possible connections between liberal theories of government and liberal theories of punishment. To what extent is Rush a classical liberal, influenced by such liberal thinkers as John Locke? To what extent is he better described as a religious liberal similar to Roger Williams? Rush claims that "capital punishments are the natural offspring of monarchical governments." Why does he make this claim? Is he correct that republicans are committed to milder forms of punishment?

The punishment of murder by death, is contrary to reason, and to the order and happiness of society.

It lessens the horror of taking away human life, and thereby tends to multiply murders.

It produces murder, by its influence upon people who are tired of life, and who, from a supposition, that murder is a less crime than suicide, destroy a life (and often that of a near connexion) and afterwards deliver themselves up to justice, that they may escape from their misery by means of a halter.

The punishment of murder by death, multiplies murders, from the difficulty it creates of convicting persons who are guilty of it. Humanity, revolting at the idea of the severity and certainty of a capital punishment, often steps in, and collects such evidence in favour of a murderer, as screens him from justice altogether, or palliates his crime into manslaughter. If the punishment of murder consisted in long confinement, and hard labor, it would be proportioned by the measure of our feelings of justice, and every member of society would be a watchman or a magistrate, to apprehend a destroyer of human life, and to bring him to punishment.

. . .

III. The punishment of murder by death, is contrary to divine revelation. . . .

. . .

I cannot take leave of this subject without remarking that capital punishments are the natural offspring of monarchical governments. Kings believe that they possess their crowns by a *divine* right: no wonder, therefore, they assume the divine power of taking away human life. Kings consider their subjects as their property: no wonder, therefore, they shed their blood with as little emotion as men shed the blood of their sheep or cattle. But the principles of republican governments speak a very different language. They teach us the absurdity of the divine origin of kingly power. They approximate the extreme ranks of men to each other. They restore man to his God—to society—and to himself. They revive and establish the relations of fellow-citizen, friend, and brother. They appreciate human life, and increase public and private obligations to preserve it. They consider human sacrifices as no less offensive to the sovereignty of the people, than they are to the majesty of heaven. They view the attributes of government, like the attributes of the Deity, as infinitely more honoured by destroying evil by means of *merciful* than by exterminating punishments. The United States have adopted these peaceful and benevolent forms of government. It becomes them therefore to adopt their mild and benevolent principles. An execution in a republic is like a human sacrifice in religion. It is an offering to monarchy, and to that malignant being, who has been styled a murderer from the beginning, and who delights equally in murder, whether it be perpetrated by the cold, but vindictive arm of the law, or by the angry hand of private revenge.

Suggested Readings

Adams, Willi Paul. 1980. *The First American Constitutions: Republican Ideology and the Making of the State Constitutions in the Revolutionary Era*. Chapel Hill: University of North Carolina Press.

Amar, Akhil Reed. 2005. *America's Constitution: A Biography*. New York: Random House.

Beard, Charles A. 1935. *An Economic Interpretation of the Constitution of the United States*. New York: Free Press.

Bowen, Catherine Drinker. 1966. *Miracle at Philadelphia: The Story of the Constitutional Convention, May to September 1787*. Boston: Little, Brown and Company.

Cornell, Saul. 1999. *The Other Founders: Anti-Federalism and the Dissenting Tradition in America, 1788–1828*. Chapel Hill: University of North Carolina Press.

Edling, Max M. 2003. *A Revolution in Favor of Government: Origins of the U.S. Constitution and the Making of the American State*. New York: Oxford University Press.

Gibson, Alan Ray. 2007. *Understanding the Founding: The Crucial Questions*. Lawrence: University Press of Kansas.

Hendrickson, David C. 2006. *Peace Pact: The Lost World of the American Founding*. Lawrence: University Press of Kansas.

Holton, Woody. 2007. *Unruly Americans and the Origins of the Constitution*. New York: Hill and Wang.

Jillson, Calvin C. 1988. *Constitution Making: Conflict and Consensus in the Federal Convention of 1787*. New York: Agathon.

Kramer, Larry D. 2004. *The People Themselves: Popular Constitutionalism and Judicial Review*. New York: Oxford University Press.

Kramick, Isaac, and R. Laurence Moore. 1996. *The Godless Constitution: The Case Against Religious Correctness*. New York: W. W. Norton & Company.

Kruman, Marc. 1997. *Between Liberty and Authority: State Constitution Making in Revolutionary America*. Chapel Hill: University of North Carolina Press.

Lutz, Donald S. 1980. *Popular Consent and Popular Control: Whig Political Theory in the Early State Constitution*. Baton Rouge: Louisiana State University Press.

Maier, Paul. 2010. *Ratification: The People Debate the Constitution, 1787–1788*. New York: Simon and Schuster.

McDonald, Forrest. 1958. *We the People: The Economic Origins of the Constitution*. Chicago: University of Chicago Press.

———. 1985. *Novus Ordo Sectorum: The Intellectual Origins of the Constitution*. Lawrence: University Press of Kansas.

Morgan, Edmund S. 1988. *Inventing the People: The Rise of Popular Sovereignty in America*. New York: W. W. Norton.

Nedelsky, Jennifer. 1994. *Private Property and the Limits of American Constitutionalism: The Madisonian Framework and Its Legacy*. Chicago: University of Chicago Press.

Rakove, Jack N. 1979. *The Beginnings of National Politics: An Interpretive History of the Continental Congress*. New York: Knopf.

———. 1996. *Original Meanings: Politics and Ideas in the Making of the Constitution*. New York: Knopf.

Robertson, David Brian. 2005. *The Constitution and America's Destiny*. New York: Cambridge University Press.

Tsesis, Alexander. 2012. *For Liberty and Equality: The Life and Times of the Declaration of Independence*. New York: Oxford University Press.

Wood, Gordon S. 1969. *The Creation of the American Republic, 1776–1787*. Chapel Hill: University of North Carolina Press.

Chapter 4

The Early National Era: 1791–1828

I. Introduction

The Constitution of the United States that took effect on March 4, 1789 was a stunning success. Significant opposition ceased almost immediately. Former Federalists and anti-Federalists alike welcomed clear constitutional rules—and dutifully followed them. National elections were held every two years in the manner prescribed. Elected officials from all regions of the United States agreed that Congress could regulate interstate commerce and that no state could establish titles of nobility. Few forms of government can claim the institutional stability of the United States. Fewer still have experienced the almost complete disappearance of criticism of their constitution shortly after its ratification.

The Constitution, it was widely agreed, contained the right answer to all vital political questions. But this consensus came at a price: vigorous disagreement over *what the right answer was*. Controversies broke out under the first president, George Washington, over the powers of the national government, the status of states in the union, the powers of the national executive, and judicial authority to declare laws unconstitutional. Most of these controversies were not fully resolved by the end of the Early National Era. Many remain unsettled today, but the Constitution's achievement was nevertheless real. Americans from 1789 to 1829 established the terms on which these questions were debated. How that first generation of Americans thought about these basic constitutional problems remains central, even if they did not settle how to frame the issues once and for all. They launched debates that have often been transformed by events and by new ways of thinking about the Constitution.

Constitutional disagreements were fueled by the constitutional text and the rise of partisan coalitions. The Constitution provided an outline of the national government, but the framers did not specify every detail. No provision explicitly determines whether Congress may grant corporate charters, whether the president may claim executive privilege when Congress requests certain documents, or whether the Supreme Court may declare laws unconstitutional. When disputes over these issues arose, political leaders often disagreed. The founding generation believed that political parties (or "factions") were dangerous in a republic, but their dream of nonpartisan politics lasted longer than the reality. National political leaders almost immediately began to form political parties, starting in the late 1790s with Federalists and Republicans. When controversies arose, these parties looked to both constitutional principle and concrete political interest. Federalists generally construed national powers more broadly than Republicans, but not always. When debating the Louisiana Purchase in 1803, Republicans were far more likely than Federalists to claim a constitutional power to acquire new territory, in part because most people believed the new territories would increase the strength of the Republican coalition.

Developments. The federal government was successfully launched under the new U.S. Constitution during this period, but the process was not an easy one. After the constitutional ratification debates of 1787 and 1788, the country mostly rallied around the election of George Washington to the presidency in 1789.[1]

1. The lingering holdouts of North Carolina and Rhode Island from the union were the notable exceptions.

Table 4-1 Major Issues and Decisions of the Early National Era

Major Political Issues	Major Constitutional Issues	Major Court Decisions
Incorporation of Bank of the United States	Scope of necessary and proper clause	*Chisholm v. Georgia* (1793)
Imposition of federal taxes	Presidential removal power	*Hylton v. United States* (1796)
Relations with England and France	Treaty powers	*Calder v. Bull* (1798)
Judiciary Act of 1801 and its repeal	Executive privilege	*Marbury v. Madison* (1803)
Embargo	Free speech	*Stuart v. Laird* (1803)
Louisiana Purchase	Adoption of Bill of Rights	*Fletcher v. Peck* (1810)
Yazoo land scandal	Judicial independence	*Martin v. Hunter's Lessee* (1816)
Democratization	Regulation of commerce	*Dartmouth College v. Woodward* (1819)
War of 1812	Spending power	*McCulloch v. Maryland* (1819)
Internal improvements	Contracts clause	*Cohens v. Virginia* (1821)
Missouri Compromise	Judicial review	*Gibbons v. Ogden* (1824)

The outlines of the federal government were established. A system of taxes was put in place, although internal taxes were so controversial that they gave rise to violent tax protests and one of the first exercises of judicial review in *Hylton v. United States* (1796). Amidst great protest, the Bank of the United States was chartered to help finance the federal government and spur the economy. A modest military was built, and diplomatic issues with Britain were settled. But as the government built new institutions and made new policy, Americans divided over what direction the government should take. Debate turned into protest, which turned into the formation of an opposition party. For a founding generation that regarded protests and parties as dangerous to the health of a republic, these developments were an ominous sign, and the government took steps to crush the opposition by force in the late 1790s.

When Jeffersonians won both houses of Congress and the presidency in the 1800 elections, many Federalists feared that constitutional government would not survive. Jeffersonians cut taxes and spending, shrank the military, and engaged in a brief struggle with the courts. Federalists had tried to pack the courts with their allies before leaving office, but Jeffersonians responded by undoing what Federalists had done and impeaching two federal judges, including a Supreme Court justice. On the whole, however, Jeffersonians built on Federalist accomplishments. They added huge swaths of new territory with the Louisiana Purchase. They accepted the first Bank of the United States and eventually chartered a second bank in 1816. They opened the door to protectionist tariffs and federal support for "internal improvements" and transportation projects, though they disagreed among themselves about how far those policies could go. Especially after the War of 1812 with Britain, many Jeffersonian leaders accepted that the federal government would need to be active and strong enough to protect the nation. Congress occupied the center of government, and the Senate was just emerging from the shadow of the House of Representatives as an important political force. By the end of the Early National Era, the foundations of government were secure, the size and circumstances of the nation had significantly changed, and the terms of constitutional debate had become familiar.

Parties. Party competition between Federalists and Jeffersonians existed only from 1791 to 1808; from 1808 until 1828 political competition occurred between two different Jeffersonian factions, National Republicans and Old Republicans. During the 1790s Federalists were the stronger of the two coalitions, in no small part because they enjoyed the support of President Washington. Led by Treasury Secretary Alexander Hamilton, Federalists favored a broad, or expansive,

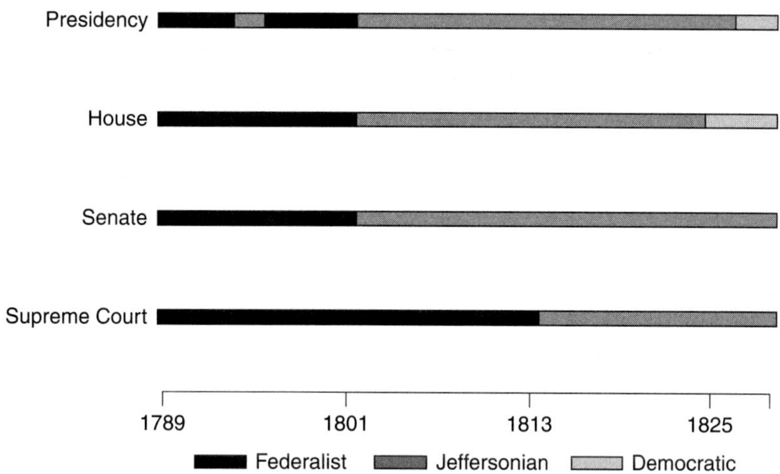

Figure 4-1 Partisan Control of the U.S. Government, 1789–1828

construction of national powers. They insisted that the Constitution was an agreement among the people of the United States, not a compact between formerly sovereign states. Federalists supported giving the president independent powers to conduct foreign policy. After some initial hesitation, they became strong supporters of a powerful judiciary with the power to declare federal laws unconstitutional. Federalists acted on these constitutional commitments when they controlled the national government from 1789 to 1800. They promoted economic development, a posture of national strength, a relatively friendly attitude toward Britain, limits on political participation, the promotion of religious establishments, and maintaining vested property rights. Congress passed legislation incorporating a national bank, assumed outstanding state debts from the American Revolution, imposed tariffs on imported goods, and created an extensive federal judiciary. President Washington acted independently of Congress when he issued the Neutrality Proclamation, which announced that the United States would not take sides in the ongoing war between England and France.

Jeffersonians, often known as Republicans or Democratic-Republicans, opposed Federalist constitutional visions and Federalist policies. Led by Secretary of State Thomas Jefferson and James Madison, Republicans favored a strict, or narrow, construction of the powers of the new national government in the 1790s. They believed that the separate states, and not the people, were the crucial parties to the Constitution. Jefferson and his political allies favored a weaker president than did the Federalists. After some initial hesitation, they also favored a weaker federal judiciary. They favored a more agrarian, laissez-faire economic policy, smaller government, and friendlier relations with France.

The Early National Era witnessed a dramatic change in partisan control of the government. From 1789 until 1801 Federalists controlled all three branches of the national government. From 1801 until 1828 Jeffersonians controlled all elected branches of the national government. By 1812 Jeffersonian appointees also held a majority on the Supreme Court. This change in partisan control explains why many studies of American politics refer to the "Federalist Era" and the "Jeffersonian Era," rather than the "Early National Era."

The transition from Federalist to Jeffersonian rule had far fewer consequences for constitutional rights than either Federalists or Jeffersonians had anticipated. Most rights issues in the Early National Era were local and influenced by the distinctive structures of local politics. The most important national rights debates after 1801 were over slavery. That matter divided Americans by section, not by partisanship. The National Republican wing of the Jeffersonian coalition, which included James Madison and John Quincy Adams, held views on property rights and related issues that were quite similar to earlier Federalist positions.

The Jeffersonians proclaimed that the "Revolution of 1800" would return government to its true principles. No sooner had Jeffersonians gained unified control of the national government, however, than the coalition splintered. Almost immediately after Jefferson's inauguration, some doctrinaire Republicans complained that the administration made too many compromises with federal power. Led by John Randolph in Congress, Chief Justice Spencer Roane of the Virginia Court of Appeals, the Virginia writer and politician John Taylor of Caroline, and Thomas Ritchie, editor of the influential *Richmond Enquirer,* these Old Republicans insisted on a sharper narrowing of federal power. Often encouraged by Jefferson once he left the White House, they opposed most federal efforts to develop the national economy and challenged federal judicial authority over the states.

Box 4-1 A Partial Cast of Characters of the Early National Era

Thomas Jefferson	▪ Republican ▪ Author of the Declaration of Independence ▪ Secretary of state to Federalist George Washington (1790–1793) ▪ Vice president to Federalist John Adams (1797–1801) ▪ President of the United States (1801–1809) ▪ Founder of the Jeffersonian Republican Party ▪ Secret author of the Kentucky Resolution of 1798 ▪ Leading political proponent of "strict constructionism" in constitutional interpretation
John Marshall	▪ Moderate Federalist ▪ Secretary of state to Federalist John Adams (1800–1801) ▪ Chief justice of the U.S. Supreme Court (1801–1835), appointed to the Supreme Court by John Adams after the election of 1800 ▪ Leading judicial proponent of broad, nationalist interpretation of the Constitution ▪ Author of most of the Court's important constitutional opinions in the early republic
Joseph Story	▪ National Republican ▪ Massachusetts Speaker of the House (1811) ▪ Associate justice of the U.S. Supreme Court (1812–1845) ▪ Harvard law professor ▪ Madison's fourth choice to fill a vacancy on the Supreme Court, opposed by Jefferson, who regarded Story as being too much of a Federalist ▪ Close ally of John Marshall and a leading treatise writer in the early republic
Spencer Roane	▪ Republican ▪ Chief judge of the Virginia Court of Appeals (1794–1822) ▪ Leading states' rights activist in the state courts during the early republic ▪ Part of the "Richmond Junto" that surrounded the influential *Richmond Enquirer* newspaper and criticized any deviations from strict constructionist philosophy
James Monroe	▪ Republican ▪ Anti-Federalist in the Virginia ratification convention ▪ Favored as an alternative candidate for president to James Madison by strict constructionist Republicans in 1808 ▪ Secretary of state to Republican James Madison (1811–1817) ▪ Last president of the United States in the "Virginia Dynasty" and last president of the revolutionary generation (1817–1825) ▪ Presided over the "Era of Good Feelings" and the final collapse of the Federalist Party

Other Jeffersonians became more comfortable with national power. This faction, which became known as National Republicans, included Henry Clay of Kentucky, John C. Calhoun of South Carolina, and Daniel Webster of Massachusetts. This younger generation of political leaders was dismayed by the weaknesses in the national government exposed by the War of 1812. They sponsored aggressive federal efforts to develop the nation's economic infrastructure. By 1820, National Republicans were enthusiastic proponents of a more powerful national state and federal judicial authority.

Interest Groups. Neither permanent nor national interest groups formed during the Early National Era. Various social and economic interests—slaveowners, large landowners, farmers, wage-earners, mercantilists, bankers, traders, and so on—were part of the central dynamics of constitutional politics, but during this era those interests did not transform into the kind of formally organized activity that contemporary Americans associate with interest groups. People often responded to particular grievances by forming a committee in a particular town or community. Most rights and liberties issues interested political activists in only a few states. These associations rarely survived the particular incident that initially gave them life.

Courts. The federal judiciary went through a difficult period of transition in the early years under the Constitution. The Judiciary Act of 1789, which created the federal judiciary, was a compromise measure: it limited judicial power and forced the Supreme Court justices to spend time "riding circuit," or hearing cases while sitting as members of federal trial courts throughout the country. When the Federalists lost the election of 1800, they immediately passed the Judiciary Act of 1801, expanding the size and power of the federal courts. These judges became known as the "midnight appointments," because the Federalists worked until the very last minute of their term of office to leave no vacancies on the bench when Jefferson assumed the presidency. When they assumed power, Jeffersonians repealed the entire Judiciary Act of 1801 and pursued impeachment charges against two federal judges, including Justice Samuel Chase.

The Supreme Court in the Early National Era was dominated by John Marshall, a Federalist judicial appointee who served as chief justice from 1801 until 1835. Although Republicans gained control of the national government in 1801, most Republican judicial appointees identified with the more nationalist wing of the Jeffersonian coalition. The result was an enduring majority coalition of Federalists and National Republicans that was committed to extending national power and protecting vested property rights.

The differences between the federal courts and the elected branches of the government resulted in two parallel constitutional tracks by the 1820s. The first track was official constitutional law as found in Supreme Court decisions. This track, as articulated in *Marbury v. Madison*, *McCulloch v. Maryland*, and *Gibbons v. Ogden*, vested the national government with broad powers. It rejected claims that states retained any independent sovereignty and claimed that the federal judiciary was the institution responsible for determining the meaning of ambiguous constitutional provisions. The second track was the dominant constitutional understandings of elected officials. This track, as articulated by Presidents Jefferson, Madison, and Monroe, suggested sharp constitutional limits on federal power. It insisted that states retained vital constitutional roles, and claimed that elected officials had independent power to interpret the Constitution. The clash between these two constitutional tracks intensified during the Jacksonian Era, as the Old Republicans became Democrats and the National Republicans became the Whigs.

Constitutional Thought. The central jurisprudential debates of the Early National Era were over the authority of the national government over the states and the role of natural law in constitutional decision making. Even at a time when the federal government was establishing its position in the new constitutional system, the passage of the Virginia and Kentucky Resolutions of 1798 revealed a willingness on the part of some determined state leaders to assert the sovereign right of states to resist some exercises of national power. With respect to the protection of rights and liberties, many constitutional decision makers during this era were willing to rely heavily on broad principles rather than on mere textual guarantees. Justice Samuel Chase in *Calder v. Bull* (1798) claimed, "An ACT of the Legislature (for I cannot call it a law) contrary to the great first principles of the social compact, cannot be considered a rightful exercise of legislative authority." Other constitutional decision makers insisted that interpretation be confined to the words of the constitutional text. Justice James Iredell in the same case insisted, "The Court cannot pronounce [a law] to be void, merely because it is, in their judgment, contrary to the principles of natural justice."

Legacies. The Early National Era marked the beginning of constitutional politics in the United States. During the 1790s both Federalists and Jeffersonians perceived their rivals as betraying the original Constitution. Federalists insisted that politics was not the proper forum for determining the constitutional meaning of free speech or what constituted "impairing the obligation of contract." Jeffersonians saw a return to monarchy behind every Federalist pronouncement. While the rhetoric of constitutional betrayal remains a staple of American political discourse, ordinary constitutional politics became less heated over time. Many political elites recognized, often grudgingly, that persons could in good faith dispute the meaning of particular constitutional provisions. Constitutional disagreement became a legitimate subject for ordinary politics rather than an automatic threat to regime stability. The Missouri Compromise demonstrated that when the constitutional disagreement was significant, the foundations of the national polity shook. Nevertheless, Americans by 1828 disagreed peacefully about the constitutional rights of religious dissenters, gun holders, and criminal suspects.

The practice of constitutional interpretation was the most important legacy that Americans of the Early National Era left to their descendants. Constitutional decision makers initially resolved disputes by referring to natural law, without focusing on specific constitutional provisions. Justice William Johnson in *Fletcher v. Peck* (1810) asserted that he would base his decision on "general principle, on the reason and nature of things." Supreme Court Justice Joseph Story referred to natural law at great length when discussing the legal status of the international slave trade. By the beginning of the Jacksonian Era, such expressions were appearing less frequently in mainstream American constitutional discourse. Rather than pointing to natural law, constitutional decision makers spoke of precedent or common understandings at the time constitutional provisions were ratified. Why this transformation took place is not clear. The increased role of courts in constitutional decision making may explain the growing American tendency to make legal arguments for rights rather than rely on natural law. Americans may also have relied more on legal discourse after discovering that they did not agree on how to apply natural law to specific circumstances. Finally, the turn from natural law to constitutional law may have been rhetorical. Constitutional opinions that refer to precedent and history may mask decisions based on contested judgments about natural law and good policy.

Many precedents established during the Early National period are now considered authoritative. Two are particularly important: *Marbury v. Madison* (1803) and *McCulloch v. Maryland* (1819). *Marbury* is commonly said to have established judicial review. *McCulloch*, most would agree, gives the federal government the power to respond to all national crises. (Whether *Marbury* and *McCulloch* had the same meaning and authority in the Early National period is less clear.) Other precedents were set outside the Court. The First Congress has been referred to as a "continuing constitutional convention." An extraordinary number of constitutional questions, big and small, transformed the constitutional text into a working government.[2]

II. Foundations

MAJOR DEVELOPMENTS

- Decline of reasoning based on natural law in constitutional decision making
- Greater influence of courts in constitutional decision making
- Debate over the status of the slave trade in customary international law

After the Constitution was ratified, governing authorities were immediately confronted with basic questions about the sources, principles, and scope of constitutional rights and liberties. Americans did not settle any of these matters. Constitutional decision makers eventually subordinated natural law and the law of nations to written constitutional provisions. Justices gained increased authority to settle constitutional disputes. Prominent officials insisted that Congress did not have unlimited power when governing American territories. All these resolutions were tentative. All were challenged during the Early National Era and remained contested afterwards.

2. David P. Currie, *The Constitution in Congress: The Federalist Period* (Chicago: University of Chicago Press, 1997), 3.

A. Sources

Americans became increasingly committed to establishing positive law protections for fundamental rights. Founding Era state constitutions often either lacked a bill of rights or included a haphazard listing of liberties. In contrast, every state admitted to the Union between 1791 and 1828 placed a bill of rights in the state constitution. The number of rights enumerated increased. The Alabama Declaration of Rights (1819) contained twice as many provisions as the Virginia Declaration of Rights (1776). Little was left to the imagination.

This increased tendency to enumerate rights in state constitutions coincided with a decreased tendency for legal authorities to rely primarily on natural law or the law of nations when imposing limits on government power. Many constitutional decisions and arguments in the Founding Era relied exclusively on natural law. Constitutional decisions and arguments in the Early National Era more frequently pointed to specific constitutional language, such as "due process of law." References to natural law decreased, while references to past legal precedents and practices at the time of ratification increased.

Justices from 1789 to 1829 did not initially agree on whether constitutional provisions provided the only legal grounds for striking down federal and state laws. Several decisions that were handed down suggest that natural law was considered an independent basis for judicial action. The South Carolina Court of Common Pleas made no mention of a specific constitutional provision when striking down a state law in *Bowman v. Middleton* (SC 1792). Justice William Johnson's concurring opinion in *Fletcher v. Peck* (1810) relied on "general principle, on the reason and nature of things." Justice Samuel Chase in *Calder v. Bull* (1798) declared, "I cannot subscribe to the omnipotence of a State Legislature, or that it is absolute and without control; although its authority should not be expressly restrained by the Constitution, or fundamental law, of the State." Other justices questioned references to natural law. "It is true, that some speculative jurists have held, that a legislative act against natural justice must, in itself, be void," Justice James Iredell claimed in *Calder*, "but I cannot think that, under such a government, any Court of Justice would possess a power to declare it so."

These references to natural law became fewer and fewer as the Early National Era progressed. Several explanations exist for the increased judicial tendency to rely on the constitutional text. The justices may have found little need to make independent references to natural law. In most cases, they could reach a desired result by citing constitutional language and interpreting that language in a manner consistent with natural law principles. The specter of slavery hovered over early efforts to rely on natural law, because most Americans of the period believed that slavery was inconsistent with natural law. If natural law was a legitimate independent source for judicial decisions, judicial recourse to it might compel justices to make a politically charged ruling that federal courts were not prepared to make during the period from 1789 to 1829.

The law of nations was also considered an important source of constitutional meaning. Constitutional authorities in the new republic thought that all sovereign nations were obligated to respect international law. Justice James Wilson in *Ware v. Hylton* (1796) proclaimed, "When the United States declared their independence they were bound to receive the law of nations, in its modern state of purity and refinement." John Jay agreed, arguing that the law of nations was "part of the laws of this, and of every civilized nation."[3] The precise contours of this obligation were unclear. Justices on the early Supreme Court believed that they should enforce international law when state and federal law were silent. No judge during this period determined whether international law provided sufficient grounds for voiding an inconsistent federal or state law.

Calder v. Bull, 3 U.S. 386 (1798)

Norman Morrison wrote a will that left his estate to his grandson, Caleb Bull. In 1793 the Court of Probate for Hartford, Connecticut, concluded that the will was void. The Connecticut legislature two years later passed a law setting aside that decree and granting a new hearing. At this second hearing, the court approved Morrison's will. The Calder family, who stood to inherit under the first probate decision, appealed that decision to the Supreme Court of the United States. The Calders maintained that the state decree setting aside the first probate ruling was an ex post facto law, prohibited by the constitution of Connecticut and the Constitution of the United States.

3. John Jay, "Charge to the Grand Jury for the District of New York," *New Hampshire Gazette*, April 4, 1790.

The Supreme Court unanimously rejected that claim. All four justices who heard the case agreed that the ex post facto clause banned only retrospective criminal laws and not laws adjusting property rights. Justices Samuel Chase and James Iredell engaged in an important debate over the role of natural law in constitutional decision making. Iredell asserted that courts had no business striking down laws solely on the ground that the legislation was inconsistent with natural justice. Chase asserted that no people empowered a legislature to violate certain fundamental rights. Chase did not state clearly whether he believed that fundamental law provided a standard that justices should use when interpreting the Constitution (i.e., a presumption against interpreting constitutional provisions as inconsistent with fundamental rights) or whether he believed that fundamental law provided an independent ground for judicial decisions to void legislation (i.e., that courts should void laws that violate fundamental rights, even when the Constitution explicitly sanctions that violation). Which interpretation do you believe is correct? Should judicial power include the power to set aside clearly unjust laws?[4]

JUSTICE CHASE delivered the opinion of the Court.

. . . I cannot subscribe to the omnipotence of a State Legislature, or that it is absolute and without control; although its authority should not be expressly restrained by the Constitution, or fundamental law, of the State. The people of the United States erected their Constitutions, or forms of government, to establish justice, to promote the general welfare, to secure the blessings of liberty; and to protect their persons and property from violence. The purposes for which men enter into society will determine the nature and terms of the social compact; and as they are the foundation of the legislative power, they will decide what are the proper objects of it: The nature, and ends of legislative power will limit the exercise of it. This fundamental principle flows from the very nature of our free Republican governments, that no man should be compelled to do what the laws do not require; nor to refrain from acts which the laws permit. There are acts which the Federal, or State, Legislature cannot do, without exceeding their authority. There are certain vital principles in our free Republicans governments, which will determine and over-rule an apparent and flagrant abuse of legislative power; as to authorize manifest injustice by positive law; or to take away that security for personal liberty, or private property, for the protection whereof the government was established. An ACT of the Legislature (for I cannot call it a law) contrary to the great first principles of the social compact, cannot be considered a rightful exercise of legislative authority. The obligation of a law in governments established on express compact, and on republican principles, must be determined by the nature of the power, on which it is founded. A few instances will suffice to explain what I mean. A law that punished a citizen for an innocent action, or, in other words, for an act, which, when done, was in violation of no existing law; a law that destroys, or impairs, the lawful private contracts of citizens; a law that makes a man a Judge in his own cause; or a law that takes property from A. and gives it to B: It is against all reason and justice, for a people to entrust a Legislature with SUCH powers; and, therefore, it cannot be presumed that they have done it. The genius, the nature, and the spirit, of our State Governments, amount to a prohibition of such acts of legislation; and the general principles of law and reason forbid them. The Legislature may enjoin, permit, forbid, and punish; they may declare new crimes; and establish rules of conduct for all its citizens in future cases; they may command what is right, and prohibit what is wrong; but they cannot change innocence into guilt; or punish innocence as a crime; or violate the right of an antecedent lawful private contract; or the right of private property. To maintain that our Federal, or State, Legislature possesses such powers, if they had not been expressly restrained; would, in my opinion, be a political heresy, altogether inadmissible in our free republican governments. . . .

JUSTICE IREDELL, concurring in part.

. . . It is true, that some speculative jurists have held, that a legislative act against natural justice must, in itself, be void; but I cannot think that, under such a government, any Court of Justice would possess a power to declare it so. . . .

. . . [I]t has been the policy of all the American states, which have, individually, framed their state

4. See Douglas E. Edlin, *Judges and Unjust Laws: Common Law Constitutionalism and the Foundations of Judicial Review* (Ann Arbor: University of Michigan Press, 2008).

constitutions since the revolution, and of the people of the United States, when they framed the Federal Constitution, to define with precision the objects of the legislative power, and to restrain its exercise within marked and settled boundaries. If any act of Congress, or of the Legislature of a state, violates those constitutional provisions, it is unquestionably void; though, I admit, that as the authority to declare it void is of a delicate and awful nature, the Court will never resort to that authority, but in a clear and urgent case. If, on the other hand, the Legislature of the Union, or the Legislature of any member of the Union, shall pass a law, within the general scope of their constitutional power, the Court cannot pronounce it to be void, merely because it is, in their judgment, contrary to the principles of natural justice. The ideas of natural justice are regulated by no fixed standard: the ablest and the purest men have differed upon the subject; and all that the Court could properly say, in such an event, would be, that the Legislature (possessed of an equal right of opinion) had passed an act which, in the opinion of the judges, was inconsistent with the abstract principles of natural justice. There are then but two lights, in which the subject can be viewed: 1st. If the Legislature pursue the authority delegated to them, their acts are valid. 2d. If they transgress the boundaries of that authority, their acts are invalid. In the former case, they exercise the discretion vested in them by the people, to whom alone they are responsible for the faithful discharge of their trust: but in the latter case, they violate a fundamental law, which must be our guide, whenever we are called upon as judges to determine the validity of a legislative act.

B. Principles

Rights in the American constitutional republic differed from rights in the English constitutional monarchy. Rights in a constitutional monarchy limited only the power of the king. Rights in a constitutional republic limited all governing officials. This difference created an enforcement problem. Parliament was responsible for ensuring that English monarchs respected the constitutional limits on their power. If, however, rights limited all governing officials, including the national legislature, what institution ensured that Congress respected constitutional limits?

Over time, more and more political actors claimed that the federal judiciary was the proper forum for resolving disputes over constitutional rights and liberties. Thomas Jefferson in the Kentucky Resolutions insisted that states retained the authority to determine the meaning of constitutional provisions. "As in all other cases of compact among powers having no common judge," he wrote, "each party has an equal right to judge for itself."[5] The Massachusetts legislature responded by insisting on judicial supremacy. The state legislature was "persuaded that the decision of all cases in law and equity arising under the Constitution of the United States, and the construction of all laws made in pursuance thereof, are exclusively vested by the people in the judicial courts of the United States."[6] Shortly thereafter, the Supreme Court in *Marbury v. Madison* (1803) asserted the judicial power to declare laws unconstitutional. "It is emphatically the province and duty of the judicial department to say what the law is," John Marshall's unanimous opinion decreed.

As time passed, state courts became more effective participants in constitutional politics. Increasingly, officials and citizens looked to judicial doctrine when determining state and federal constitutional standards. Local judges routinely resolved disputes over constitutional rights. By the end of the Early National Era, most of the original states had begun to develop lines of precedents on the meaning of state constitutional protections for property rights and persons suspected of criminal offenses.

Judicial review was not a firmly established principle at the end of the Early National Era. Most major national controversies over civil liberties were settled outside of the federal courts. States often ignored federal court rulings, and state judiciaries struggled to exercise independent constitutional authority. When the Supreme Court of Kentucky challenged the state legislature too aggressively, elected officials in that state established a new judicial system. Nevertheless, by 1828, the courts had partly

5. Paul Leicester Ford, ed., *The Writings of Thomas Jefferson* (New York: G. P. Putnam's Sons, 1896), 7:292.

6. "Response of the Senate of the Commonwealth of Massachusetts to the Virginia Legislature's Resolution Condemning the Alien and Sedition Laws," *Niles' Weekly Register*, February 9, 1799, 43 (suppl.): 3.

remade republican constitutionalism. Constitutional rights and liberties were increasingly understood as legal limitations on official power that were enforceable in courts of law.

C. Scope

Americans considered but failed to resolve permanently three important questions about the scope of the Bill of Rights:

1. Did the Bill of Rights limit state power?
2. Did the Bill of Rights limit federal power in the territories?
3. Did the Bill of Rights protect aliens?

A few state courts briefly considered the first question, dividing on whether the Bill of Rights limited state power. Congress briefly considered but did not decide whether the Bill of Rights limited federal power to govern American territories acquired by the Louisiana Purchase.[7] More extensive debates over the constitutional rights of aliens were also inconclusive.

III. Judicial Power and Constitutional Authority

MAJOR DEVELOPMENTS

- Creation of the federal judicial system
- Federal courts staffed largely by justices committed to broad interpretation of the Constitution
- Courts assert right to declare statutes unconstitutional
- U.S. Supreme Court affirms its right to review state court rulings on federal law

The process of adding flesh to the bones of Article III of the U.S. Constitution began with the Judiciary Act of 1789, which launched the federal court system. The Judiciary Act ensured that there would be a federal court system and that federal judges would have a chance to interpret the U.S. Constitution, implement treaties, and apply federal law. Drafted largely by future Chief Justice Oliver Ellsworth, the Judiciary Act of 1789 was the first major piece of legislation passed by Congress and signed into law by President Washington. It provided for a Supreme Court with one chief justice and five associate justices; three circuit courts of appeals presided over by two justices from the Supreme Court and one district judge; and thirteen district courts, one in each state, each with a single presiding judge. Supreme Court justices would spend most of their time "riding circuit," or acting as circuit court judges. That left them relatively little time for sitting with their fellow justices to hear cases as the Supreme Court.

Both Article III of the Constitution and the Judiciary Act of 1789 detail the types of cases over which the federal judicial power "shall extend." These texts define the *jurisdiction* of the federal courts—the cases that those courts have the legal power to hear and resolve. Federal jurisdiction is established either by the type of party involved (e.g., "cases affecting ambassadors" or cases "between citizens of different states") or by the type of law involved (e.g., "cases . . . arising under this Constitution [or] the laws of the United States"). Article III specifies that the U.S. Supreme Court has original jurisdiction in a small number of cases. Those cases begin in the Supreme Court. In all other cases, the Supreme Court only has appellate jurisdiction. Those cases reach the Supreme Court after they have been initiated in some other court.

The limits Congress placed on the federal court system in 1789 began a controversy over federal jurisdiction that has never been settled. Article III, Section 1 declares, "The judicial Power of the United States, shall be vested in one supreme Court, and in such inferior Courts as the Congress may from time to time ordain and establish." Proponents of mandatory federal jurisdiction emphasize the word "shall." They insist that Congress must enable some federal court to hear all cases involving federal law or what is known as diversity of citizenship. Proponents of discretionary federal jurisdiction disagree. They note Article III, Section 2 states: "In all Cases affecting Ambassadors, other public Ministers and Consuls, and those in which a State shall be Party, the supreme Court shall have original Jurisdiction. In all . . . other Cases . . ., the supreme Court shall have

7. See Sarah H. Cleveland, "Powers Inherent in Sovereignty: Indians, Aliens, Territories and the Nineteenth Century Origins of Plenary Power of Foreign Affairs," *Texas Law Review* 81 (2002): 171–81.

appellate Jurisdiction, . . . with such Exceptions, . . . as the Congress shall make." In their view, Congress may make exceptions to the Court's appellate jurisdiction by permitting some cases involving federal law or diversity of citizenship to be resolved entirely by state courts.

Unfortunately, we do not have detailed records of the debate over the Judiciary Act. For this reason, we do not know whether members of Congress in 1789 thought that they could deprive federal courts of jurisdiction over most questions of federal constitutional law. Perhaps they thought that Section 25 of the Judiciary Act, which provided for a limited set of appeals to the U.S. Supreme Court, provided sufficient protection for federal interests. As it stood, however, Section 25 became an important vehicle for bringing constitutional cases before the Supreme Court through much of the nineteenth century.

The power of judicial review was anticipated at the time of the founding but was not well understood. No American constitution granted such a power explicitly, though provisions such as the supremacy clause of Article VI of the federal Constitution seemed to imply a form of it: "The Constitution . . . shall be the supreme Law of the Land; and the Judges of every State shall be bound thereby, any Thing in the Constitution or Laws of any State to the Contrary notwithstanding." Controversy surrounded some early exercises of judicial review. Still, by the 1790s courts were widely regarded as useful for interpreting constitutions and remedying some constitutional violations. As Table 4-2 indicates, many courts struggled with and asserted the power of judicial review in the first years of the republic.

In *Marbury v. Madison* (1803), Chief Justice John Marshall provided a detailed justification for the power of judicial review. Marshall's opinion declared that Jefferson had acted illegally when his administration refused to deliver a judicial commission to William Marbury. Marshall also maintained that federal courts could order the Jefferson administration to deliver the commission. Finally, he stated that the Supreme Court had the power to declare federal laws unconstitutional. His lengthy defense of judicial authority seemed a powerful rebuke to the Jefferson administration. The force of *Marbury*, however, was substantially muted. Marshall had declared unconstitutional only an obscure provision in the Judiciary Act of 1789. This provision gave the Supreme Court jurisdiction to issue the writ ordering the Jefferson administration to deliver the commission. Lacking jurisdiction, Marshall concluded that the Court could issue no order in *Marbury*. Soon after *Marbury*, the arshall Court had another opportunity to consider the constitutionality of Jeffersonian policies toward the courts. In *Stuart v. Laird* (1803), the Court heard a challenge to the repeal of the Judiciary Act of 1801 and the dismissal of numerous Federalist judges. The stakes were much higher in *Stuart* than in *Marbury*, and in that case the Court simply issued a brief opinion upholding the repeal. In short, the Marshall Court was more willing in *Marbury* than in *Stuart* to deliver a lecture on Federalist constitutional principles. Yet in both cases the justices avoided directly challenging Jefferson or the Republican Congress.

The rise of partisanship raised doubts about the constitutional commitment to a judiciary above politics. Jeffersonians did not generally disagree with Marshall's reasoning on the power of judicial review. Where they and the Federalists split was over the importance of constitutional interpretation by judges. Federalists insisted that constitutional controversies were best resolved in the courts. Jeffersonians frequently questioned whether judges should have the final word on constitutional meaning. Jefferson believed that each department of government should have the same authority to interpret the Constitution. His "departmentalist" view contrasted sharply with a conception of "judicial supremacy" that presumed courts had the final say and that other institutions of government were obligated to defer to judicial understandings.

While federal judicial review of congressional statutes was a source of some theoretical debate, federal judicial review of state law was taken for granted during most of the Early National Era. Controversies over the judicial power to strike down state laws first broke out during the 1810s. Proponents of state sovereignty raised two objections to Section 25 of the Judiciary Act. The first was rooted in the more radical interpretation of the Virginia and Kentucky Resolutions. If the Constitution was a compact between otherwise sovereign states, then the state courts were the proper authorities for determining whether state laws were consistent with the federal Constitution. Second, and representing a more technical point, even if federal courts had the right to declare state

Table 4-2 Some Early Cases of Judicial Review in American Courts

Case	Court	Decision
Ten-Pound Act Cases (1786)	New Hampshire Inferior Court	Struck down state statute expanding the set of civil suits that could be tried without a jury as violating state constitution
Bayard v. Singleton, 1 N.C. 5 (1787)	North Carolina Supreme Court	Struck down state statute denying British loyalists the right to challenge state seizure of property as violating state constitution
Cases of the Judges, 8 Va. 135 (1788)	Virginia Court of Appeals	Declaration that state law requiring court of appeals judges to also sit on district courts violated the state constitution
Bowman v. Middleton, 1 S.C.L. 252 (1792)	South Carolina Supreme Court	Struck down an act transferring a land title without trial by jury as "against common right . . . [and] the Magna Carta"
Hayburn's Case, 2 U.S. 408 (1792)	U.S. Federal Circuit Court of Pennsylvania	First instance in which a law of Congress was declared unconstitutional; struck down a federal statute requiring judges to review pension applications as violating the federal Constitution
Kamper v. Hawkins, 3 Va. 20 (1793)	Virginia General Court	Struck down state statute transferring some powers of chancery courts to district courts as violating state constitution
Vanhorne's Lessee v. Dorrance, 2 U.S. 297 (1795)	U.S. Circuit Court	Articulated argument for judicial review; struck down a state statute regarding property claims as violating state constitution and upheld two others as not violating federal Constitution
Hylton v. United States, 3 U.S. 171 (1796)	U.S. Supreme Court	First instance of Supreme Court review of a federal statute; upheld a federally imposed tax as not violating federal Constitution
United States v. La Vengeance, 3 U.S. 297 (1796)	U.S. Supreme Court	Upheld use of admiralty courts for enforcing embargo statutes as not violating federal right to trial by jury
Calder v. Bull, 3 U.S. 386 (1798)	U.S. Supreme Court	Upheld state statute altering probate rules as not violating federal Constitution
Cooper v. Telfair, 4 U.S. 14 (1800)	U.S. Supreme Court	Upheld a state statute regarding penalties and property confiscation for persons convicted of treason as not violating state constitution
Mossman v. Higginson, 4 U.S. 12 (1800)	U.S. Supreme Court	Struck down a section of the Judiciary Act of 1789 for being in conflict as applied with the federal Constitution
Stidger v. Rogers, 2 Ky. 52 (1801)	Kentucky Supreme Court	Struck down an act of assembly allowing the court, rather than juries only, to ascertain the value of property as violating the state constitution
Marbury v. Madison, 5 U.S. 137 (1803)	U.S. Supreme Court	Struck down a section of the Judiciary Act of 1789 that expanded original jurisdiction as violating the federal Constitution
Stuart v. Laird, 5 U.S. 299 (1803)	U.S. Supreme Court	Upheld the Judiciary Act of 1802 as not in conflict with the federal Constitution

laws unconstitutional, federal courts had no right to review the rulings of state supreme courts and overrule them. If Congress permitted state supreme courts to resolve constitutional issues, then Congress had to allow those state courts to have the final word on the cases that they heard. In this view, Congress could empower the federal courts to strike down state laws, but not by accepting those cases on appeal from the state courts.

The U.S. Supreme Court in *Martin v. Hunter's Lessee* (1816) ruled that federal courts could declare state laws unconstitutional and that Congress could give federal courts the power to reverse state court decisions. The *Martin* decision emphasized the importance of uniformity. If each state could determine the meaning of the federal Constitution, Justice Story reasoned, the result would be constitutional chaos. Virginia might pass laws taxing the national bank that Massachusetts thought unconstitutional.

The position of the courts was generally considered to be stronger at the end of the Early National Era than at the beginning. The role and membership of the state and federal courts had stabilized. They routinely interpreted state and federal constitutions, and sometimes declared statutes unconstitutional. The U.S. Supreme Court under Chief Justice John Marshall frequently provoked controversy, but it steered a relatively moderate path. The Court avoided issuing decisions that would be ignored or opposed by major Jeffersonian leaders.

Marbury v. Madison, 5 U.S. 137 (1803)

The lame-duck Federalist Congress was busy after the election of 1800. In addition to passing the Judiciary Act of 1801, it also passed a law organizing the District of Columbia. Section 11 of that statute authorized the president to appoint an unspecified number of justices of the peace. John Adams nominated William Marbury to one of those new justiceships. The Senate confirmed his appointment the day before Jeffersonians took control of the national government.

Marbury's commission was signed and sealed but not delivered during the haste and confusion that marked the last hours of the Adams administration. Such tasks fell to Adams's secretary of state, John Marshall, who in turn employed his brother James to make the deliveries. Thomas Jefferson, outraged by these last-minute appointments, ordered that the leftover commissions remain undelivered. Determined to hold office, Marbury in December 1801 asked the Supreme Court for a writ of mandamus ordering Jefferson's secretary of state, James Madison, to deliver his commission. The administration refused to recognize the Court's jurisdiction in the matter. In fact, it declined to send an attorney to argue the case or to even admit that a commission for Marbury had ever existed.

The central issue of the Marbury *litigation was thought to be whether the justices could order the executive to deliver the commission. Whether the justices had the power to declare laws unconstitutional was not as clearly at issue. To most people, a more pressing test of that power involved the law repealing the Judiciary Act of 1801. The Court heard a challenge to that repeal at about the same time in* Stuart v. Laird *(1803).*

Federalists failed on all fronts. They did not preserve their circuit court justiceships or secure Marbury his office. They neither persuaded elected officials to restore the Judiciary Act of 1801 nor convinced the Supreme Court to declare the repeal unconstitutional. Marbury never obtained his commission.

Marshall organized his Marbury opinion in what might seem an unorthodox fashion. Justices typically first consider whether they have jurisdiction to hear a case. Only after determining that they have the power to adjudicate do they turn to the substantive dispute. Marbury *has a different structure. The first sections of John Marshall's opinion decided that Marbury had a right to the commission and that a writ of mandamus was the appropriate remedy. Only after deciding the substantive issue did Marshall turn to the jurisdictional issue, which had not been argued at any length before the justices. Marshall determined that Section 13 of the Judiciary Act of 1789 was unconstitutional. This section was interpreted as giving the Court the power to issue a writ of mandamus in a case of original jurisdiction, that is, a case originating in the Supreme Court itself. If Section 13 was unconstitutional, then the Court did not have the legal power to issue the order to the executive branch to force the delivery of the commission in this case.*

Last, Marshall turned to whether justices should nevertheless be guided by an unconstitutional law. Here he made his argument for judicial review of federal law. Many commentators think that Marshall had strategic reasons for structuring the Marbury *opinion in this way. He was able both to declare that the Jefferson administration's actions were illegal and to defend the power of judicial review. Yet he could still avoid having to issue a judicial order that the president would almost certainly have ignored.*

Marshall's argument in Marbury *became the canonical defense of judicial review in the United States. The argument in defense of the power of judicial review was neither surprising nor original by 1803. Nevertheless,* Marbury *was the first time the U.S. Supreme Court had fully defended the right to declare federal laws unconstitutional. As you read, consider how persuasive Marshall's argument is. How else might judicial review be defended? What exactly is the power that Marshall is defending? Is the power outlined in* Marbury *limited to laws that are clearly unconstitutional? Is it limited to laws affecting the judiciary, or can the Court strike down any type of law? Are the other branches of government obliged to follow the conclusions about constitutional meaning that the Court reaches, or do those conclusions only guide the actions of the judges?*

CHIEF JUSTICE MARSHALL delivered the opinion of the Court.

. . .

In the order in which the court has viewed this subject, the following questions have been considered and decided.

1st. Has the applicant a right to the commission he demands?

2d. If he has a right, and that right has been violated, do the laws of this country afford him a remedy?

3d. If they do afford him a remedy, is it a mandamus issuing from this court?

. . .

1st. Has the applicant a right to the commission he demands?

. . .

In order to determine whether he is entitled to this commission, it becomes necessary to inquire whether he has been appointed to this office. For if he has been appointed, the law continues him in office for five years, and he is entitled to the possession of those evidences of office, which, being completed, became his property.

. . .

. . .[T]he clauses of the constitution and laws of the United States, which affect this part of the case . . . seem to contemplate three distinct operations.

1st. The nomination. This is the sole act of the president, and is completely voluntary.

2d. The appointment. This is also the act of the president, and is also a voluntary act, though it can only be performed by and with the advice and consent of the senate.

3d. The commission. To grant a commission to a person appointed, might, perhaps, be deemed a duty enjoined by the constitution. "He shall," says that instrument, "commission all the officers of the United States."

. . .

The last act to be done by the president is the signature of the commission. He has then acted on the advice and consent of the senate to his own nomination. The time for deliberation has then passed. He has decided. His judgment, on the advice and consent of the senate concurring with his nomination, has been made, and the officer is appointed. . . .

Some point of time must be taken when the power of the executive over an officer, not removable at his will, must cease. The point of time must be when the constitutional power of appointment has been exercised. And the power has been exercised when the last act, required from the person possessing the power, has been performed. This last act is the signature of the commission. . . .

. . .

The commission being signed, the subsequent duty of the secretary of state is prescribed by law and not to be guided by the will of the president. He is to affix the seal of the United States to the commission, and is to record it.

This is not a proceeding which may be varied, if the judgment of the executive shall suggest one more eligible; but is a precise course accurately marked out by law, and is to be strictly pursued. It is the duty of the secretary of state to conform to the law, and in this he is an officer of the United States, bound to obey the laws. He acts, in this respect . . . under the authority of the law, and not by the instructions of the president. It is a ministerial act which the law enjoins on a particular officer for a particular purpose.

If it should be supposed, that the solemnity of affixing the seal is necessary not only to the validity of the commission, but even to the completion of an appointment, still when the seal is affixed the appointment is made, and the commission is valid. No other solemnity is required by law; no other act is to be performed on the part of the government. All that the executive can do to invest the person with his office is done. . . .

. . .

Mr. Marbury, then, since his commission was signed by the President and sealed by the Secretary of State, was appointed, and as the law creating the office gave the officer a right to hold for five years independent of the Executive, the appointment was not revocable, but vested in the officer legal rights which are protected by the laws of his country.

To withhold the commission, therefore, is an act deemed by the Court not warranted by law, but violative of a vested legal right.

This brings us to the second inquiry, which is:

2d. If he has a right, and that right has been violated, do the laws of this country afford him a remedy?

The very essence of civil liberty certainly consists in the right of every individual to claim the protection of the laws whenever he receives an injury. One of the first duties of government is to afford that protection. In Great Britain, the King himself is sued in the respectful form of a petition, and he never fails to comply with the judgment of his court.

. . .

The Government of the United States has been emphatically termed a government of laws, and not of men. It will certainly cease to deserve this high appellation if the laws furnish no remedy for the violation of a vested legal right.

If this obloquy is to be cast on the jurisprudence of our country, it must arise from the peculiar character of the case.

It behooves us, then, to inquire whether there be in its composition any ingredient which shall exempt from legal investigation or exclude the injured party from legal redress. . . .

. . .

By the Constitution of the United States, the President is invested with certain important political powers, in the exercise of which he is to use his own discretion, and is accountable only to his country in his political character and to his own conscience. To aid him in the performance of these duties, he is authorized to appoint certain officers, who act by his authority and in conformity with his orders.

In such cases, their acts are his acts; and whatever opinion may be entertained of the manner in which executive discretion may be used, still there exists, and can exist, no power to control that discretion. The subjects are political. They respect the nation, not individual rights, and, being entrusted to the Executive, the decision of the Executive is conclusive. The application of this remark will be perceived by adverting to the act of Congress for establishing the Department of Foreign Affairs. This officer, as his duties were prescribed by that act, is to conform precisely to the will of the President. He is the mere organ by whom that will is communicated. The acts of such an officer, as an officer, can never be examinable by the Courts.

But when the Legislature proceeds to impose on that officer other duties; when he is directed peremptorily to perform certain acts; when the rights of individuals are dependent on the performance of those acts; he is so far the officer of the law, is amenable to the laws for his conduct, and cannot at his discretion, sport away the vested rights of others.

The conclusion from this reasoning is that, where the heads of departments are the political or confidential agents of the Executive, merely to execute the will of the President, or rather to act in cases in which the Executive possesses a constitutional or legal discretion, nothing can be more perfectly clear than that their acts are only politically examinable. But where a specific duty is assigned by law, and individual rights depend upon the performance of that duty, it seems equally clear that the individual who considers himself injured has a right to resort to the laws of his country for a remedy.

. . .

It is then the opinion of the Court:

1st. That, by signing the commission of Mr. Marbury, the President of the United States appointed him a justice of peace for the County of Washington in the District of Columbia, and that the seal of the United States, affixed thereto by the Secretary of State, is conclusive testimony of the verity of the signature, and of the completion of the appointment, and that the appointment conferred on him a legal right to the office for the space of five years.

2d. That, having this legal title to the office, he has a consequent right to the commission, a refusal to deliver which is a plain violation of that right, for which the laws of his country afford him a remedy.

It remains to be inquired whether,

3d. He is entitled to the remedy for which applies. This depends on,

1st. The nature of the writ applied for; and,

2d. The power of this court.

. . .

. . . [T]o render the mandamus a proper remedy, the officer to whom it is to be directed, must be one to whom, on legal principles, such a writ may be directed; and the person applying for it must be without any other specific and legal remedy.

1st. With respect to the officer to whom it would be directed. The intimate political relation, subsisting between the President of the United States and the heads of departments, necessarily renders any legal investigation of the acts of one of those high officers peculiarly irksome, as well as delicate, and excites some hesitation with respect to the propriety of entering into such investigation. Impressions are often received without much reflection or examination, and it is not wonderful that, in such a case as this, the assertion by an individual of his legal claims in a court of justice, to which claims it is the duty of that court to attend, should, at first view, be considered by some as an attempt to intrude into the cabinet and to intermeddle with the prerogatives of the Executive.

It is scarcely necessary for the Court to disclaim all pretensions to such a jurisdiction. An extravagance so absurd and excessive could not have been entertained for a moment. The province of the Court is solely to decide on the rights of individuals, not to inquire how the Executive or Executive officers perform duties in which they have a discretion. Questions, in their nature political or which are, by the Constitution and laws, submitted to the Executive, can never be made in this court.

But, if this be not such a question; if, so far from being an intrusion into the secrets of the cabinet, it respects a paper which, according to the law, is upon record, and to a copy of which the law gives a right . . . ?

. . .

It is not by the office of the person to whom the writ is directed, but the nature of the thing to be done, that the propriety or impropriety of issuing a mandamus is to be determined. Where the head of a department acts in a case in which Executive discretion is to be exercised, in which he is the mere organ of Executive will, it is again repeated, that any application to a court to control, in any respect, his conduct, would be rejected without hesitation.

But where he is directed by law to do a certain act affecting the absolute rights of individuals, in the performance of which he is not placed under the particular direction of the President, and the performance of which the President cannot lawfully forbid, and therefore is never presumed to have forbidden—as for example, to record a commission, or a patent for land, which has received all the legal solemnities; or to give a copy of such record—in such cases, it is not perceived on what ground the Courts of the country are further excused from the duty of giving judgment that right to be done to an injured individual than if the same services were to be performed by a person not the head of a department.

. . .

This, then, is a plain case of a mandamus, either to deliver the commission or a copy of it from the record, and it only remains to be inquired:

Whether it can issue from this Court.

The act to establish the judicial courts of the United States authorizes the Supreme Court "to issue writs of mandamus, in cases warranted by the principles and usages of law, to any courts appointed, or persons holding office, under the authority of the United States."

The Secretary of State, being a person, holding an office under the authority of the United States, is precisely within the letter of the description, and if this Court is not authorized to issue a writ of mandamus to such an officer, it must be because the law is unconstitutional, and therefore absolutely incapable of conferring the authority and assigning the duties which its words purport to confer and assign.

The Constitution vests the whole judicial power of the United States in one Supreme Court, and such inferior courts as Congress shall, from time to time, ordain and establish. This power is expressly extended to all cases arising under the laws of the United States. . . .

In the distribution of this power it is declared that "The Supreme Court shall have original jurisdiction in all cases affecting ambassadors, other public ministers and consuls, and those in which a state shall be a party. In all other cases, the Supreme Court shall have appellate jurisdiction."

. . .

If it had been intended to leave it in the discretion of the Legislature to apportion the judicial power between the Supreme and inferior courts according to the will of that body, it would certainly have been useless to have proceeded further than to have defined the judicial power and the tribunals in which it should be vested. The subsequent part of the section is mere surplusage—is entirely without meaning—if such is to be the construction. If Congress remains at liberty to give this court appellate jurisdiction where the Constitution has declared their jurisdiction shall be original, and original jurisdiction where the

Constitution has declared it shall be appellate, the distribution of jurisdiction made in the Constitution, is form without substance.

Affirmative words are often, in their operation, negative of other objects than those affirmed, and, in this case, a negative or exclusive sense must be given to them or they have no operation at all.

It cannot be presumed that any clause in the Constitution is intended to be without effect, and therefore such construction is inadmissible unless the words require it.

. . .

When an instrument organizing fundamentally a judicial system, divides it into one supreme, and so many inferior courts as the legislature may ordain and establish; then enumerates its powers, and proceeds so far to distribute them, as to define the jurisdiction of the supreme court by declaring the cases in which it shall take original jurisdiction, and that in others it shall take appellate jurisdiction; the plain import of the words seems to be, that in one class of cases its jurisdiction is original and not appellate; in the other it is appellate, and not original. . . .

To enable this court then to issue a mandamus, it must be shown to be an exercise of appellate jurisdiction, or to be necessary to enable them to exercise appellate jurisdiction.

. . .

It is the essential criterion of appellate jurisdiction that it revises and corrects the proceedings in a cause already instituted, and does not create that case. Although, therefore, a mandamus may be directed to courts, yet to issue such a writ to an officer for the delivery of a paper is, in effect, the same as to sustain an original action for that paper, and therefore seems not to belong to appellate, but to original jurisdiction. . . .

The authority, therefore, given to the Supreme Court by the act establishing the judicial courts of the United States to issue writs of mandamus to public officers appears not to be warranted by the Constitution, and it becomes necessary to inquire whether a jurisdiction so conferred can be exercised.

The question, whether an act, repugnant to the constitution, can become the law of the land, is a question deeply interesting to the United States; but, happily, not of an intricacy proportioned to its interest. It seems only necessary to recognize certain principles, supposed to have been long and well established, to decide it.

That the people have an original right to establish, for their future government, such principles as, in their opinion, shall most conduce to their own happiness, is the basis, on which the whole American fabric has been erected. The exercise of this original right is a very great exertion; nor can it, nor ought it to be frequently repeated. The principles, therefore, so established, are deemed fundamental. And as the authority, from which they proceed, is supreme, and can seldom act, they are designed to be permanent.

This original and supreme will organizes the government, and assigns, to different departments, their respective powers. It may either stop here; or establish certain limits not to be transcended by those departments.

The government of the United States is of the latter description. The powers of the legislature are defined, and limited; and that those limits may not be mistaken, or forgotten, the constitution is written. To what purpose are powers limited, and to what purpose is that limitation committed to writing, if these limits may, at any time, be passed by those intended to be restrained? The distinction, between a government with limited and unlimited powers, is abolished, if those limits do not confine the persons on whom they are imposed, and if acts prohibited and acts allowed, are of equal obligation. It is a proposition too plain to be contested, that the constitution controls any legislative act repugnant to it; or, that the legislature may alter the constitution by an ordinary act.

Between these alternatives there is no middle ground. The constitution is either a superior, paramount law, unchangeable by ordinary means, or it is on a level with ordinary legislative acts, and like other acts, is alterable when the legislature shall please to alter it.

If the former part of the alternative be true, then a legislative act contrary to the constitution is not law: if the latter part be true, then written constitutions are absurd attempts, on the part of the people, to limit a power, in its own nature illimitable.

Certainly all those who have framed written constitutions contemplate them as forming the fundamental and paramount law of the nation, and consequently the theory of every such government must be, that an act of the legislature, repugnant to the constitution, is void.

This theory is essentially attached to a written constitution, and is consequently to be considered, by this court, as one of the fundamental principles of our society. It is not therefore to be lost sight of in the further consideration of this subject.

If an act of the legislature, repugnant to the constitution, is void, does it, notwithstanding its invalidity, bind the courts, and oblige them to give it effect? Or, in other words, though it be not law, does it constitute a rule as operative as if it was a law? This would be to overthrow in fact what was established in theory; and would seem, at first view, an absurdity too gross to be insisted on. It shall, however, receive a more attentive consideration.

It is emphatically the province and duty of the judicial department to say what the law is. Those who apply the rule to particular cases, must of necessity expound and interpret that rule. If two laws conflict with each other, the courts must decide on the operation of each.

So if a law be in opposition to the constitution; if both the law and the constitution apply to a particular case, so that the court must either decide that case conformably to the law, disregarding the constitution; or conformably to the constitution, disregarding the law; the court must determine which of these conflicting rules governs the case. This is of the very essence of judicial duty.

If then the courts are to regard the constitution; and the constitution is superior to any ordinary act of the legislature; the constitution, and not such ordinary act, must govern the case to which they both apply.

Those then who controvert the principle that the constitution is to be considered, in court, as a paramount law, are reduced to the necessity of maintaining that courts must close their eyes on the constitution, and see only the law.

This doctrine would subvert the very foundation of all written constitutions. It would declare that an act, which, according to the principles and theory of our government, is entirely void; is yet, in practice, completely obligatory. It would declare, that if the legislature shall do what is expressly forbidden, such act, notwithstanding the express prohibition, is in reality effectual. It would be giving to the legislature a practical and real omnipotence, with the same breath which professes to restrict their powers within narrow limits. It is prescribing limits, and declaring that those limits may be passed at pleasure.

That it thus reduces to nothing what we have deemed the greatest improvement on political institutions—a written constitution—would of itself be sufficient, in America, where written constitutions have been viewed with so much reverence, for rejecting the construction. But the peculiar expressions of the constitution of the United States furnish additional arguments in favor of its rejection.

The judicial power of the United States is extended to all cases arising under the constitution.

Could it be the intention of those who gave this power, to say that, in using it, the constitution should not be looked into? That a case arising under the constitution should be decided without examining the instrument under which it arises?

This is too extravagant to be maintained.

In some cases then, the constitution must be looked into by the judges. And if they can open it at all, what part of it are they forbidden to read, or to obey?

There are many other parts of the constitution which serve to illustrate this subject.

It is declared that "no tax or duty shall be laid on articles exported from any state."

Suppose a duty on the export of cotton, of tobacco, or of flour; and a suit instituted to recover it. Ought judgment to be rendered in such a case? Ought the judges to close their eyes on the constitution, and only see the law?

The constitution declares that "no bill of attainder or ex post facto law shall be passed."

If, however, such a bill should be passed and a person should be prosecuted under it; must the court condemn to death those victims whom the constitution endeavors to preserve?

"No person," says the constitution, "shall be convicted of treason unless on the testimony of two witnesses to the same overt act, or on confession in open court."

Here the language of the constitution is addressed especially to the courts. It prescribes, directly for them, a rule of evidence not to be departed from. If the legislature should change that rule, and declare one witness, or a confession out of court, sufficient for conviction, must the constitutional principle yield to the legislative act?

From these, and many other selections which might be made, it is apparent, that the framers of the constitution contemplated that instrument, as a rule for the government of courts, as well as of the legislature.

Why otherwise does it direct the judges to take an oath to support it? This oath certainly applies, in an especial manner, to their conduct in their official character. How immoral to impose it on them, if they were to be used as the instruments, and the knowing instruments, for violating what they swear to support!

The oath of office, too, imposed by the legislature, is completely demonstrative of the legislative opinion on the subject. It is in these words, "I do solemnly swear that I will administer justice without respect to persons, and do equal right to the poor and to the rich; and that I will faithfully and impartially discharge all the duties incumbent on me as according to the best of my abilities and understanding, agreeably to the constitution, and laws of the United States."

Why does a judge swear to discharge his duties agreeably to the constitution of the United States, if that constitution forms no rule for his government? If it is closed upon him, and cannot be inspected by him?

If such be the real state of things, this is worse than solemn mockery. To prescribe, or to take this oath, becomes equally a crime.

It is also not entirely unworthy of observation, that in declaring what shall be the supreme law of the land, the constitution itself is first mentioned; and not the laws of the United States generally, but those only which shall be made in pursuance of the constitution, have that rank.

Thus, the particular phraseology of the constitution of the United States confirms and strengthens the principle, supposed to be essential to all written constitutions, that a law repugnant to the constitution is void; and that courts, as well as other departments, are bound by that instrument.

The rule must be discharged.

Thomas Jefferson on Departmentalism[8]

The Virginia and Kentucky Resolutions of 1798 claimed that states were authorized to interpret the U.S. Constitution and evaluate the constitutionality of federal statutes, while leaving unclear what the consequences would be if a federal law were found unconstitutional by one or more states. In Marbury, *Chief Justice John Marshall argued that an unconstitutional law is necessarily null and void. An invalid law cannot be binding on the courts, for the "courts, as well as other departments, are bound by" the Constitution. The Constitution is, said Marshall, "a rule for the government of courts, as well as of the legislature."*

Thomas Jefferson developed a different approach, sometimes called the departmentalist *(or coordinate) view of constitutional interpretation. He maintained each branch (or department) of government has equal authority to interpret the Constitution for itself when performing its duties. The courts must be guided by their own best understandings of constitutional requirements when meeting their responsibilities. Nonetheless, judicial interpretations of the Constitution are not necessarily supreme over the competing interpretations offered by Congress or the president.*

Jefferson articulated this principle on various occasions. Three are excerpted here. The first two excerpts are from letters President Jefferson sent to former first lady Abigail Adams. In these letters, the president explained his policy of pardoning everyone who had been convicted under the Sedition Act of 1798. The later letter to Judge Spencer Roane of the Virginia Supreme Court of Appeals contains Jefferson's reaction to Roane's Hampden essays criticizing John Marshall's opinion in McCulloch v. Maryland. *Although Roane was concerned with the relationship between the U.S. Supreme Court and the states, Jefferson thought the Virginia judge had not been careful enough to recognize the limited authority that the Supreme Court had to dictate constitutional meaning to the other branches of the federal government and to the states.*

To Abigail Adams, July 22, 1804

. . . [You wrote] that I "liberated a wretch who was suffering for a libel against Mr. Adams." I do not know who was the particular wretch alluded to; but I discharged every person under punishment or prosecution under the sedition law, because I considered, and now consider, that law to be a nullity, as absolute and as palpable as if Congress had ordered us to fall down and worship a golden image; and that it was as much my duty to arrest its execution in every stage, as it would have been to have rescued from the fiery furnace those who should have been cast into it for refusing to worship their image. It was accordingly done in every instance, without asking what the offenders had done, or against whom they had offended, but whether the pains they were suffering were inflicted under the pretended sedition law. . . .

To Abigail Adams, September 11, 1804

. . . You seem to think it devolved on the judges to decide on the validity of the sedition law. But nothing in the Constitution has given them a right to decide for the Executive, more than to the Executive to decide

8. Excerpt taken from Ford, *Writings of Thomas Jefferson*, 10:86, 88; 12:135.

to them. The judges, believing the law constitutional, had a right to pass a sentence of fine and imprisonment; because the power was placed in their hands by the Constitution. But the Executive, believing the law to be unconstitutional, was bound to remit the execution of it; because that power has been confided to him by the Constitution. That instrument meant that its co-ordinate branches should be checks on each other. But the opinion which gives to the judges the right to decide what laws are constitutional, and what not, not only for themselves in their own sphere of action, but for the Legislative and Executive also, in their spheres, would make the judiciary a despotic branch. Nor does the opinion of unconstitutionality, and consequent nullity of that law, remove all restraint for the overwhelming torrent of slander, which is confounding all vice and virtue, all truth and falsehood, in the U.S. The power to do that is fully possessed by the several State Legislatures. It was reserved to them, and was denied to the General Government, by the Constitution, according to our construction of it.

To Spencer Roane, September 6, 1819

. . . In denying the right they [the federal judiciary] usurp of exclusively explaining the constitution, I go further than you do, if I understand rightly your quotation from the Federalist, of an opinion that "the judiciary is the last resort in relation *to the other departments* of the government, but not in relation to the rights of the parties to the compact under which the judiciary is derived." If this opinion be sound, then indeed is our constitution a complete *felo de se* [suicide]. For intending to establish three departments, co-ordinate and independent, that they might check and balance one another, it has given, according to this opinion, to one of them alone, the right to prescribe rules for the government of the others, and to that one too, which is unelected by, and independent of the nation. For experience has already shown that the impeachment it has provided is not even a scare-crow. . . . The constitution, on this hypothesis, is a mere thing of wax in the hands of the judiciary, which they may twist and shape into any form they please. It should be remembered, as an axiom of eternal truth in politics, that whatever power in any government is independent, is absolute also; in theory only, at first, while the spirit of the people is up, but in practice, as fast as that relaxes. Independence can be trusted nowhere but with the people in mass. They are inherently independent of all but moral law. My construction of the constitution is very different from that you quote. It is that each department is truly independent of the others, and has an equal right to decide for itself what is the meaning of the constitution in the cases submitted to its action; and especially, where it is to act ultimately and without appeal. . . .

. . .

Martin v. Hunter's Lessee, 14 U.S. 304 (1816)

In 1781, Denny Martin inherited Lord Thomas Fairfax's property in Virginia. During the Revolution, Virginia had confiscated those lands after Fairfax fled to England. The state had then sold the land to David Hunter. Martin claimed that the original confiscation was invalid under the peace treaties the United States had signed with Great Britain. After a long delay, the Virginia Court of Appeals finally ruled in favor of Hunter in 1810, but in 1813 the U.S. Supreme Court overruled the Virginia court. The U.S. Supreme Court held that Fairfax's American property was protected under the Jay Treaty of 1794. In a strongly worded opinion by Justice Story (John Marshall, who had purchased some of the land from Martin, did not participate in the litigation), the Supreme Court sent a writ of mandamus to the Virginia court, directing it to issue a new decision favoring Martin.

The Virginia Court of Appeals responded by declaring Section 25 of the Judiciary Act of 1789 an unconstitutional infringement on states' rights. Section 25 empowered the U.S. Supreme Court to hear appeals from the state supreme courts when federal treaties or constitutional rights were questioned. The Virginia court found particularly objectionable the Supreme Court's assumption that it could issue a writ of mandamus to the Virginia court. (Thomas Jefferson had earlier objected to the assertion that the Supreme Court could issue such writs to cabinet officials.) The court contended that the two judicial systems were completely independent of one another, and hence the Supreme Court had no authority to supervise or direct the Virginia judges as the mandamus writ implied. More generally, it argued that the Virginia Court of Appeals was not an "inferior court" over which the U.S. Supreme Court could exercise appellate jurisdiction.

The case then came back to the U.S. Supreme Court to determine the constitutionality of Section 25 of the Judiciary Act. This time, Justice Story wrote a sweeping nationalist vision of the Constitution that anticipated John Marshall's similar effort in McCulloch.

At stake was the critical issue of whether the federal government could exercise any control over state courts. At a time when the federal court system was very small, and the federal government often relied on the state courts to enforce federal statutes, this issue had significant implications for how much control the federal government would have over how federal policy was implemented. As Martin *indicated, the decision also had significant implications for how effectively the federal government could enforce international treaties and ensure that the states met their constitutional obligations.*

Although Judge Spencer Roane on the Virginia court was influential in Jeffersonian circles for his doctrinaire constitutional philosophy, national Republican leaders had little interest in repealing Section 25. Repeal was sometimes discussed during the Jeffersonian period, but Congress took no action to support the Virginia court and overturn Martin. *As you read* Martin, *consider whether Congress could, according to Story, constitutionally repeal Section 25 of the Judiciary Act of 1789. Compare Justice Story's opinion in* Martin *to Chief Justice Marshall's opinion in* Marbury. *How do they differ in their discussions of judicial review? One hundred years later, Justice Holmes asserted, "I do not think the United States would come to an end if we lost our power to declare an Act of Congress void. I do think the Union would be imperiled if we could not make that declaration as to the laws of the several States."[9] Do you agree?*

JUSTICE STORY delivered the opinion of the Court.

. . .

The constitution of the United States was ordained and established, not by the states in their sovereign capacities, but emphatically, as the preamble of the constitution declares, by "the people of the United States." There can be no doubt that it was competent to the people to invest the general government with all the powers which they might deem proper and necessary; to extend or restrain these powers according to their own good pleasure, and to give them a paramount and supreme authority. As little doubt can there be, that the people had a right to prohibit to the states the exercise of any powers which were, in their judgment, incompatible with the objects of the general compact; to make the powers of the state governments, in given cases, subordinate to those of the nation, or to reserve to themselves those sovereign authorities which they might not choose to delegate to either. The constitution was not, therefore, necessarily carved out of existing state sovereignties, nor a surrender of powers already existing in state institutions, for the powers of the states depend upon their own constitutions; and the people of every state had the right to modify and restrain them, according to their own views of policy or principle. On the other hand, it is perfectly clear that the sovereign powers vested in the state governments, by their respective constitutions, remained unaltered and unimpaired, except so far as they were granted to the government of the United States.

These deductions do not rest upon general reasoning, plain and obvious as they seem to be. They have been positively recognized by one of the articles in amendment of the constitution, which declares, that "the powers not delegated to the United States by the constitution, nor prohibited by it to the states, are reserved to the states respectively, or to the people."

The government, then, of the United States, can claim no powers which are not granted to it by the constitution, and the powers actually granted, must be such as are expressly given, or given by necessary implication. On the other hand, this instrument, like every other grant, is to have a reasonable construction, according to the import of its terms; and where a power is expressly given in general terms, it is not to be restrained to particular cases, unless that construction grow out of the context expressly, or by necessary implication. The words are to be taken in their natural and obvious sense, and not in a sense unreasonably restricted or enlarged.

The constitution unavoidably deals in general language. It did not suit the purposes of the people, in framing this great charter of our liberties, to provide for minute specifications of its powers, or to declare the means by which those powers should be carried into execution. It was foreseen that this would be a perilous and difficult, if not an impracticable, task. The instrument was not intended to provide merely for the exigencies of a few years, but was to endure through a long lapse of ages, the events of which were locked up in the inscrutable purposes of Providence. It could not be foreseen what new changes and modifications of power might be indispensable to effectuate the general objects of the charter; and restrictions and specifications, which, at the present, might seem salutary, might, in the end, prove the overthrow of the

9. Oliver Wendell Holmes, Jr., "Law and the Court, Speech at a Dinner of the Harvard Law School Association of New York on February 13, 1913," in *Collected Legal Papers*, ed. Learned Hand (New York: Harcourt, Brace, and Company, 1921), 295–296.

system itself. Hence its powers are expressed in general terms, leaving to the legislature, from time to time, to adopt its own means to effectuate legitimate objects, and to mould and model the exercise of its powers, as its own wisdom, and the public interests, should require.

. . .

But, even admitting that the language of the constitution is not mandatory, and that congress may constitutionally omit to vest the judicial power in courts of the United States, it cannot be denied that when it is vested, it may be exercised to the utmost constitutional extent. . . .

As, then, by the terms of the constitution, the appellate jurisdiction is not limited as to the supreme court, and as to this court it may be exercised in all other cases than those of which it has original cognizance, what is there to restrain its exercise over state tribunals in the enumerated cases? The appellate power is not limited by the terms of the third article to any particular courts. The words are, "the judicial power (which includes appellate power) shall extend to all cases," etc., and "in all other cases before mentioned the supreme court shall have appellate jurisdiction." It is the case, then, and not the court, that gives the jurisdiction. If the judicial power extends to the case, it will be in vain to search in the letter of the constitution for any qualification as to the tribunal where it depends. . . .

. . . If state tribunals might exercise concurrent jurisdiction over all or some of the other classes of cases in the constitution without control, then the appellate jurisdiction of the United States might, as to such cases, have no real existence, contrary to the manifest intent of the constitution. . . .

. . .

A moment's consideration will show us the necessity and propriety of this provision in cases where the jurisdiction of the state courts is unquestionable. . . . Suppose an indictment for a crime in a state court, and the defendant should allege in his defense that the crime was created by an ex post facto act of the state, must not the state court, in the exercise of a jurisdiction which has already rightfully attached, have a right to pronounce on the validity and sufficiency of the defense? It would be extremely difficult, upon any legal principles, to give a negative answer to these inquiries. . . .

It must, therefore, be conceded that the constitution not only contemplated, but meant to provide for cases within the scope of the judicial power of the United States, which might yet depend before state tribunals. It was foreseen that in the exercise of their ordinary jurisdiction, state courts would incidentally take cognizance of cases arising under the constitution, the laws, and treaties of the United States. . . .

. . .

It is a mistake that the constitution was not designed to operate upon states, in their corporate capacities. It is crowded with provisions which restrain or annul the sovereignty of the states in some of the highest branches of their prerogatives. . . . The courts of the United States can, without question, revise the proceedings of the executive and legislative authorities of the states, and if they are found to be contrary to the constitution, may declare them to be of no legal validity. Surely the exercise of the same right over judicial tribunals is not a higher or more dangerous act of sovereign power. . . .

. . .

It is further argued, that no great public mischief can result from a construction which shall limit the appellate power of the United States to cases in their own courts: . . . because state judges are bound by an oath to support the constitution of the United States, and must be presumed to be men of learning and integrity. . . . The constitution has presumed (whether rightly or wrongly we do not inquire) that state attachments, state prejudices, state jealousies, and state interests, might sometimes obstruct, or control, or be supposed to obstruct or control, the regular administration of justice. Hence, in controversies between states; between citizens of different states; between citizens claiming grants under different states; between a state and its citizens, or foreigners, and between citizens and foreigners, it enables the parties, under the authority of congress, to have the controversies heard, tried, and determined before the national tribunals. . . .

This is not all. A motive of another kind, perfectly compatible with the most sincere respect for state tribunals, might induce the grant of appellate power over their decisions. That motive is the importance, and even necessity of uniformity of decisions throughout the whole United States, upon all subjects within the purview of the constitution. Judges of equal learning and integrity, in different states, might differently interpret a statute, or a treaty of the United States, or even the constitution itself. . . .

There is an additional consideration, which is entitled to great weight. The constitution of the

United States was designed for the common and equal benefit of all the people of the United States. The judicial power was granted for the same benign and salutary purposes. It was not to be exercised exclusively for the benefit of parties who might be plaintiffs, and would elect the national forum, but also for the protection of defendants who might be entitled to try their rights, or assert their privileges, before the same forum. Yet, if the construction contended for be correct, it will follow, that as the plaintiff may always elect the state court, the defendant may be deprived of all the security which the constitution intended in aid of his rights. Such a state of things can, in no respect, be considered as giving equal rights. . . .

On the whole, the court are of opinion, that the appellate power of the United States does extend to cases pending in the state courts; and that the 25th section of the judiciary act, which authorizes the exercise of this jurisdiction in the specified cases, by a writ of error, is supported by the letter and spirit of the constitution. We find no clause in that instrument which limits this power; and we dare not interpose a limitation where the people have not been disposed to create one.

Strong as this conclusion stands upon the general language of the constitution, it may still derive support from other sources. It is an historical fact, that this exposition of the constitution, extending its appellate power to state courts, was, previous to its adoption, uniformly and publicly avowed by its friends, and admitted by its enemies, as the basis of their respective reasonings, both in and out of the state conventions. It is an historical fact, that at the time when the judiciary act was submitted to the deliberations of the first congress, composed, as it was, not only of men of great learning and ability, but of men who had acted a principal part in framing, supporting, or opposing that constitution, the same exposition was explicitly declared and admitted by the friends and by the opponents of that system. It is an historical fact . . . that no state tribunal has ever breathed a judicial doubt on the subject, or declined to obey the mandate of the supreme court, until the present occasion. This weight of contemporaneous exposition by all parties, this acquiescence of enlightened state courts, and these judicial decisions of the supreme court through so long a period, do, as we think, place the doctrine upon a foundation of authority which cannot be shaken, without delivering over the subject to perpetual and irremediable doubts.

. . .

It is the opinion of the whole court, that the judgment of the court of appeals of Virginia, rendered on the mandate in this case, be reversed, and the judgment of the district court, held at Winchester be, and the same is hereby affirmed.

JUSTICE JOHNSON, concurring.

. . .

IV. Powers of the National Government

MAJOR DEVELOPMENTS

- The struggle between broad and strict constructions of national powers
- The establishment of a national power to acquire and govern new territories
- Interstate commerce defined as including navigation and all forms of commercial intercourse that concern more than one state

Constitutional disputes over the powers of the national government divided Americans during the Early National period. Everyone recognized that the federal government established by the Constitution was far more powerful than the one established by the Articles of Confederation. Article I vested Congress with the power to raise revenues by taxation, the power to regulate interstate commerce, the power to raise armies, and other powers that the national government had previously lacked. However, Americans who agreed that the Constitution established a more powerful government still disagreed over just how powerful that government could be. Members of the First Congress debated when and whether Congress could pass laws that promoted the abolition of slavery. Members of the Second Congress debated whether Congress had the power to incorporate a national bank. Over the next forty years, debates broke out over whether Congress had the power to impose a military draft, acquire new territories, attach conditions to the admission of a new state, forbid speech criticizing the national government, build roads and canals within a state, and forbid exports to foreign countries.

The central issue in each of these debates was how liberally or strictly constitutional powers should be construed. This concern with liberal or strict construction in turn had three aspects. The first was the proper definition of a constitutional power. Article I permitted Congress to regulate "interstate commerce." Read very broadly, the clause permitted the federal government to regulate any activity that affected commerce in more than one state. Read very narrowly, that clause permitted the federal government to regulate only the actual act of transporting commercial goods across state lines. The second source of controversy was whether the federal government had *implied* powers. The Constitution nowhere stated that the federal government could build canals. Interpreted broadly, the Constitution nevertheless permitted the federal government to build canals whenever doing so was a means to promote interstate commerce or some other explicit constitutional power. Interpreted narrowly, the Constitution did not permit Congress to exercise any power not explicitly enumerated in Article I, Section 8. The third source of controversy was over the provision in Article I, Section 8 gave the national legislature the power to pass all laws that were "necessary and proper" to carrying out the powers vested in the federal government. Was the necessary and proper clause a substantive grant of its own, a "sweeping clause" that gave Congress an expansive set of additional powers? Or did it just state the obvious, that Congress could pass laws to carry out its responsibilities?

Republicans thought the Tenth Amendment reinforced their view that the powers of the national government had to be strictly construed so that it did not encroach on the proper, reserved powers of the states. Federalists thought significant that the Tenth Amendment did not refer to powers *"expressly* delegated" to the national government, which was how a similar provision in the Articles of Confederation was formulated. Federalists took that change of language to imply that the powers of the national government should be read as expansively as necessary to realize the aspirations and goals of the new nation.

As Federalists gradually disappeared as a significant political force and Republicans coped with the demands of governing, new debates arose. New circumstances and new policy proposals expanded the range of important debates over national power. Many of these new debates did not pit the Republicans against the Federalists. Instead, these debates occurred among the Republicans themselves. Each faction claimed its own commitment to Jeffersonian orthodoxy, but what did Republican principles require?

Federalists and, later, National Republicans insisted that the powers granted to the new government should be interpreted liberally, with a broad construction. Jeffersonians insisted that national powers be read strictly, in accord with the constitutional enumeration of powers. This meant that many new policies raised constitutional questions that had to be overcome, and not all were easily answered. Some of the most intense debates revolved around the necessary and proper clause and the notion of implied powers. The basic tension between implied powers and the idea of enumerated powers arose in such varied contexts as the debate over the creation of the Bank of the United States, the passage of the Sedition Act of 1798, and the proposal for a military draft during the War of 1812.

At the center of many of these debates was the necessary and proper clause, located at the end of Article I, Section 8. In the debate in the House of Representatives over the creation of the Bank of the United States, James Madison offered a strict constructionist view. He argued that the interpreter should be careful not to find implied powers that would alter the basic character of the government. These powers, he said, must not go against the understanding of those who adopted the Constitution. Treasury Secretary Alexander Hamilton countered that the national government should be able to take all reasonable actions to meet its responsibilities that are not specifically prohibited. Two decades later, Chief Justice Marshall would largely endorse Hamilton's views in *McCulloch v. Maryland,* which provoked a public rebuke from the Jeffersonian Judge Spencer Roane of the Virginia Court of Appeals The bank debate was perhaps the most important and long-lasting of the disagreements over the necessary and proper clause in the early republic, but it was not the only one. The clause was also central to efforts to criticize and defend the Sedition Act of 1798. It was also used to justify and denounce President James Monroe's proposal for a military draft during the War of 1812.

The necessary and proper clause was not the only constitutional provision contested by adversaries over federal power. Section 8 of Article I of the U.S. Constitution gives Congress the power to "regulate Commerce with foreign Nations, and among the several States, and with the Indian Tribes." Many thought that the inability of Congress to regulate commerce effectively was one of the flaws of the Articles of Confederation that needed to be remedied with the drafting of a new constitution. The power to regulate commerce included the power to regulate both international and interstate trade. But what did the power

Table 4-3 Selection of U.S. Supreme Court Cases Reviewing Federal Laws Under the Necessary and Proper Clause

Case	Vote	Outcome	Decision
United States v. Fisher, 6 U.S. (2 Cranch) 358 (1805)	5–0	Upheld	Federal law prioritizing the United States in the payment of all insolvent debtors or estates is a valid means of paying government debt
McCulloch v. Maryland, 17 U.S. (14 Wheat) 316 (1819)	7–0	Upheld	Federal law establishing a bank of the United States is legitimately grounded in the government's power to tax and spend
United States v. Coombs, 37 U.S. (12 Pet.) 72 (1838)	9–0	Upheld	Federal statute punishing looting from ships stranded on shore is a valid extension of the power to regulate interstate commerce
Legal Tender Cases, 79 U.S. 457 (1871)	5–4 (1 concurrence)	Upheld	Federal law declaring paper notes to be legal tender in payment of debts is a valid extension of the power to coin money and regulate currency
United States v. Fox, 95 U.S. 670 (1877)	9–0	Struck down	Federal law criminalizing past fraudulent acts of those who file bankruptcy petitions is not a valid use of the bankruptcy power
Ex parte Yarbrough, 110 U.S. 651 (1884)	9–0	Upheld	Federal law punishing those who conspire to intimidate voters in federal elections is a valid means to regulate elections
United States v. Gettysburg Electric Railroad Co., 160 U.S. 668 (1896)	9–0	Upheld	Federal law condemning land in order to create Gettysburg memorial is a valid means of exercising the war power
Selective Draft Law Cases, 245 U.S. 366 (1918)	9–0	Upheld	Federal law compelling military service is a valid means of raising an army
Lambert v. Yellowley, 272 U.S. 581 (1926)	5–4	Upheld	Federal law restricting the use of medically prescribed liquor is a valid use of power to prohibit alcohol under the Eighteenth Amendment
Schechter Poultry Corp. v. United States, 295 U.S. 495 (1935)	9–0 (1 concurrence)	Struck down	Federal law empowering the president to develop industrial codes of fair competition is not a valid means of exercising the legislative power
Carter v. Carter Coal Company, 298 U.S. 238 (1936)	5–4	Struck down	Federal law regulating employee wages and hours in the coal industry is not a valid means of regulating interstate commerce
United States v. Classic, 313 U.S. 299 (1941)	4–3	Upheld	Federal law regulating state primaries for national office is a valid means of regulating elections
Lichter v. United States, 334 U.S. 742 (1948)	8–1	Upheld	Federal law regulating excessive profits on the production of war goods is a valid means of raising armies

(*Continued*)

Table 4-3 (*Continued*)

Case	Vote	Outcome	Decision
United States ex rel. Toth v. Quarles, 350 U.S. 11 (1955)	6–3	Struck down	Federal law allowing for the prosecution of discharged servicemen in military courts martial is not a valid means of regulating the military
Katzenbach v. McClung, 379 U.S. 294 (1964)	9–0	Upheld	Federal law prohibiting discrimination in public restaurants is a valid means of regulating interstate commerce
Oregon v. Mitchell, 400 U.S. 112 (1970)	5–4 (4 concurring in part and dissenting in part)	Upheld/struck down	Federal law fixing the voting age at eighteen is a valid means of regulating elections when applied to federal elections but not when applied to state and local elections
Printz v. United States, 521 U.S. 898 (1997)	5–4 (2 concurrences)	Struck down	Federal law requiring state officials to perform background checks of prospective handgun purchasers is not a proper exercise of a federal power
Gonzales v. Raich, 545 U.S. 1 (2005)	6–3 (1 concurrence)	Upheld	Federal law regulating the manufacture or use of marijuana within a state that overrides conflicting local regulation is a valid means of regulating interstate commerce
United States v. Comstock, 130 S. Ct. 1949 (2010)	7–2 (2 concurrences)	Upheld	Federal law allowing civil commitment of dangerously mentally ill federal prisoners beyond their sentences is a valid means of caring for federal prisoners

to regulate include? What was part of commerce? What was commerce "with foreign nations" and "among the several states"?

Marshall did not have to wrestle with the question of what was included in the power to "regulate" in *Gibbons v. Ogden*. Other early debates did raise that question. In the winter of 1807–1808, Congress passed, at the urging of President Jefferson, the Embargo Act, which barred all foreign trade. Jeffersonians hoped that the embargo would keep the United States out of the ongoing war between England and France. First, it would put economic pressure on the European powers. Second, it would prevent a diplomatic crisis if an American trading ship were to be seized at sea. The embargo put a severe strain on the domestic economy, particularly in New England and parts of the South that were heavily involved in the international trade. Many New Englanders insisted that an absolute prohibition on commerce did not qualify as a "regulation"? Whether the United States could sponsor internal improvements was another of the sustained constitutional debates of the Early National period. This debate did not truly begin until the Federalists had largely passed from the national political scene and Jeffersonians were competing among themselves for control over the government. During this period Congress considered numerous proposals for federally sponsored lighthouses, roads, and canals. Many Americans were particularly enthusiastic about the National or Cumberland Road, a turnpike connecting the Potomac and Mississippi rivers that began to be constructed in 1811. Demands for federally sponsored improvements increased after the War of 1812, with young nationalists like Henry Clay and

John C. Calhoun leading the charge. Old Republicans were less enthusiastic. Days before the Court handed down its decision in *Gibbons*, Jeffersonian congressman John Randolph complained in the House that bills to provide for roads and canals required an excessively "*liberal* construction" of the power "to regulate" commerce. If Congress were to adopt such an approach, then "they may not only enact a sedition law, . . . but they may emancipate every slave in the United States."[10]

The constitutional debates over internal improvements that took place in the early nineteenth century were similar to the constitutional debate over the national bank. National Republicans argued for a broad construction of constitutional provisions that could give Congress the power to build roads and canals in existing states. Old Republicans argued for a strict construction of the enumerated powers, which would make many internal improvement projects difficult to justify. There was no explicit federal power to build roads outlined in the Constitution. Anticipating the logic of *McCulloch v. Maryland*, advocates of construction projects argued that federally funded internal improvements were an implied power. They were necessary and proper means for exercising one of the enumerated powers, whether delivering the mails or regulating interstate commerce.

No major internal improvements bills became law during this period after 1810. Advocates of internal improvements thought that President James Madison's approval of the Second Bank of the United States meant that he would also accept other parts of the National Republican program. They were taken by surprise when Madison reaffirmed his strict constructionist views and vetoed a major internal improvements bill on his last day in office:

> To refer the power in question to the clause "to provide for the common defense and general welfare" would be contrary to the established and consistent rules of interpretation, as rendering the special and careful enumeration of powers which follow the clause nugatory and improper. Such a view of the Constitution would have the effect of giving to Congress a general power of legislation instead of the defined and limited one hitherto understood to belong to them, the terms "common defense and general welfare" embracing every object and act within the purview of a legislative trust.[11]

President James Monroe, Madison's successor, took much the same view and was willing to use his veto pen to back it up.

Debate on the Bank of the United States

The debate over whether Congress could incorporate a national bank was the most important and sustained constitutional controversy in the early republic over how strictly constitutional powers should be construed. Secretary of the Treasury Alexander Hamilton initiated the controversy at the end of 1790 when he proposed that Congress create a national bank. In a cash-poor country with no national currency, Hamilton hoped that the bank would provide a common means of exchange and would pull together the wealth needed to finance the growth of a private manufacturing sector in the economy, as well as the needs of the federal government.

The constitutional debate was initially taken up in Congress. The resulting controversy helped solidify a partisan split between the loyal friends of the Washington administration, who believed the bank was wise policy and a legitimate exercise of constitutional power, and representatives such as James Madison, who had grown increasingly suspicious of Hamilton's economic program. Federalists won the first round when Congress passed a bill to incorporate a national bank by a nearly two-to-one margin.

President George Washington took the constitutional objections raised in Congress seriously. He requested opinions from the members of his cabinet on the constitutional question. Alexander Hamilton prepared an efficient defense of the measure. Thomas Jefferson, serving as secretary of state, and Attorney General Edmund Randolph argued against it. Washington was persuaded by Hamilton and his supporters and signed the bill into law, launching the first Bank of the United States with a twenty-year charter.

The constitutional controversy over the national bank remained vibrant after the bank bill became law. When he became president, Jefferson directed his reluctant treasury secretary, Albert Gallatin, to provide no special assistance to the bank:

> *This institution is one of the most deadly hostility existing, against the principles and form of our Constitution. . . . An institution like this, penetrating by*

10. *Annals of Congress*, 18th Cong., 1st Sess. (1824), 1306, 1308.

11. House of Representatives Report No. 11, 15th Cong., 1st Sess., 1817.

> *its branches every part of the Union, acting by command and in phalanx, may, in a critical moment, upset the government. I deem no government safe which is under the vassalage of any self-constituted authorities, or any other authority than that of the nation, or its regular functionaries. What an obstruction could not this bank of the United States, with all its branch banks, be in time of war! It might dictate to us the peace we should accept, or withdraw its aids. Ought we then to give further growth to an institution so powerful, so hostile?*[12]

A Republican-dominated Congress initially refused to renew the bank's charter when the first charter expired in 1811. The War of 1812, however, convinced many more Republicans that a national bank was more vital to national security and commercial prosperity than Jefferson had once thought. President Madison vetoed a bill incorporating a Second Bank of the United States, but his message indicated that his objections were no longer constitutional. Madison's veto message "[w]aiv[ed] the question of the constitutional authority of the Legislature to establish an incorporated bank as being precluded in [his] judgment by repeated recognitions under varied circumstances of the validity of such an institution in acts of the legislative, executive, and judicial branches of the Government, accompanied by indications, in different modes, of a concurrence of the general will of the nation."[13] *For mainstream national Republicans, the question of the constitutionality of the bank was settled by precedent and popular acquiescence. The country had lived with the bank for two decades. The people had accepted that exercise of federal power. When Congress passed a modified bill incorporating a national bank in 1816, Madison signed the measure into law.*

The constitutional controversy shifted to the federal courts after Madison signed the bill incorporating the Second Bank of the United States. Many Old Republicans felt betrayed. They charged that mere precedent could not overturn the constitutional principles that had helped launch the Republican movement in the 1790s. Local officials, tied politically and economically to state-chartered banks that competed with the national bank, joined their campaign. In the midst of a recession that had thrown many states into a fiscal crisis, several states adopted laws either prohibiting or heavily taxing any bank other than a state-operated one.

The Marshall Court, to the delight of many National Republicans, ruled these measures unconstitutional, with strong support from the executive and legislative branches of the national government. In McCulloch v. Maryland *(1819), the justices unanimously declared that Congress was constitutionally authorized to incorporate a national bank and that no state could pass any law that interfered with the exercise of that power. Opposition to the national bank remained intense in many local communities during the 1820s. Nevertheless, National Republicans on the Supreme Court and in Congress through the rest of the Early National period had the power to prevent any serious attack on the Second Bank of the United States.*

Whether constitutional powers should be liberally or narrowly construed was the central question in the bank debate. Federalists and Republicans recognized that no constitutional provision explicitly declared that Congress had the power to incorporate a national bank—or, for that matter, to grant corporate charters. Proponents of the national bank did not find this omission constitutionally troublesome. Hamilton and Marshall regarded the bank as a useful means to implementing an enumerated power, particularly the power to borrow money. Madison and Jefferson insisted that the doctrine of implied powers called into question the very idea of a government of enumerated powers. The bank was a major exercise of national power. Yet creating a bank and chartering corporations were not among the enumerated powers of the federal government.

When reading the constitutional debates over the Bank of the United States, keep these considerations in mind. Proponents of the bank insisted that Congress had implied as well as explicit powers. How did they justify those implied powers? How far could such implied powers extend without subverting the constitutional scheme? The bank debate raised basic questions about how to interpret the Constitution. How do various participants in the debate treat the significance of the document's drafting history? Did the ratification debates and the recently proposed Ninth and Tenth Amendments affect how participants thought the Constitution should be interpreted? The bank debate took place in Congress, in the president's cabinet, in the Supreme Court, and in the newspapers. Do you detect any differences in the constitutional arguments that were made in different settings? To what extent were participants in the debate over the bank in one institution willing to defer to a constitutional decision reached by persons in another governing institution?

---

12. Thomas Jefferson, "To Albert Gallatin, December 13, 1803," in *Writings of Thomas Jefferson* (see note 5), 8:285.

13. James Madison, "Veto Message, January 30, 1815," in *A Compilation of the Messages and Papers of the Presidents*, ed. James D. Richardson (New York: Bureau of National Literature, 1897), 2:540.

House Debate on the Bank (1791)[14]

MR. JAMES MADISON (Republican, Virginia) . . .

. . .

In making these remarks on the merits of the bill, he had reserved to himself the right to deny the authority of Congress to pass it. He had entertained this opinion from the date of the Constitution. His impression might, perhaps, be the stronger, because he well recollected that a power to grant charters of incorporation had been proposed in the General Convention and rejected.

. . .

As preliminaries to a right interpretation, he laid down the following rules:

An interpretation that destroys the very characteristics of the Government cannot be just.

Where a meaning is clear, the consequences, whatever they may be, are to be admitted—where doubtful, it is fairly triable by its consequences.

In controverted cases, the meaning of the parties to the instrument, if to be collected by reasonable evidence, is a proper guide.

Contemporary and concurrent expositions are a reasonable evidence of the meaning of the parties.

In admitting or rejecting a constructive authority, not only the degree of its incidentality to an express authority is to be regarded, but the degree of its importance also; since on this will depend the probability or improbability of its being left to construction.

Reviewing the Constitution with an eye to these positions, it was not possible to discover in it the power to incorporate a Bank. . . .

. . .

From the view of the power of incorporation exercised in the bill, it could never be deemed an accessory or subaltern power to be deduced by implication, as a means of executing another power; it was in its nature a distinct, an independent and substantive prerogative, which not being enumerated in the Constitution, could never have been meant to be included in it, and not being included, could never be rightfully exercised.

. . .

But the proposed Bank could not even be called necessary to the Government; at most it could be but convenient. Its uses to the Government could be supplied by keeping taxes a little in advance; by loans from individuals; by other Banks. . . .

He proceeded next to the contemporary expositions given to the Constitution.

The defense against the charge founded on the want of a bill of rights pre-supposed, he said, that the powers not given were retained; and that those given were not to be extended by remote implications. On any other supposition, the power of Congress to abridge the freedom of the press, or the rights of conscience, etc. could not have been disproved.

The explanations in the State Conventions all turned on the same fundamental principle, and on the principle that the terms necessary and proper gave no additional powers to those enumerated.

. . .

The explanatory amendments proposed by Congress themselves, at least, would be good authority with them; all these renunciations of power proceeded on a rule of construction, excluding the latitude now contended for. These explanations were the more to be respected, as they had not only been proposed by Congress, but ratified by nearly three-fourths of the States. He read several of the articles proposed, remarking particularly on the [Ninth] and [Tenth]; the former, as guarding against a latitude of interpretation; the latter, as excluding every source of power not within the Constitution itself.

. . .

MR. THEODORE SEDGWICK (Federalist, Massachusetts) said . . .

He would only observe, in answer to everything which has been said of the danger of extending construction and implication, that the whole business of Legislation was a practical construction of the powers of the Legislature; and that probably no instrument for the delegation of power could be drawn with such precision and accuracy as to leave nothing to necessary implication. That all the different Legislatures in the United States had, and this, in his opinion, indispensably must construe the powers which had been granted to them, and they must assume such auxiliary powers as are necessarily implied in those which are expressly granted. In doing which, it was no doubt their duty to be careful not to exceed those limits to which it was intended they should be restricted. By any other limitation the Government

14. Excerpt taken from *Annals of the Debates in Congress*, 1st Cong., 3rd Sess., February 2, 4, 1791, 1944–51, 1960–62.

would be so shackled that it would be incapable of producing any of the effects which were intended by its institutions.

Thomas Jefferson, Opinion on the Constitutionality of the Bill for Establishing a National Bank (1791)[15]

. . .

I consider the foundation of the Constitution as laid on this ground that "all powers not delegated to the U.S. by the Constitution, not prohibited by it to the states, are reserved to the states or to the people" [Tenth Amendment]. To take a single step beyond the boundaries thus specially drawn around the powers of Congress, is to take possession of a boundless field of power, no longer susceptible of any definition.

The incorporation of a bank, and other powers assumed by this bill have not, in my opinion, been delegated to the U.S. by the Constitution.

I. They are not among the powers specially enumerated, for these are

1. A power to lay taxes for the purpose of paying the debts of the U.S. But no debt is paid by this bill, nor any tax laid. . . .
2. "to borrow money." But this bill neither borrows money, nor ensures the borrowing it. The proprietors of the bank will be just as free as any other money holders, to lend or not to lend their money to the public. . . .
3. "to regulate commerce with foreign nations, and among the states, and with the Indian tribes." To erect a bank, and to regulate commerce, are very different acts. He who erects a bank creates a subject of commerce in its bills: so does he who makes a bushel of wheat, or digs a dollar out of the mines. Yet neither of these persons regulates commerce thereby. To erect a thing which may be bought and sold, is not to prescribe regulations for buying and selling. Besides; if this was an exercise of the power of regulating commerce, it would be void, as extending as much to the internal commerce of every state, as to its external. . . .

15. Excerpt taken from Thomas Jefferson, "Opinion on the Constitutionality of a National Bank," in *Writings of Thomas Jefferson* (see note 5), 5:284.

Still less are these powers covered by any other of the special enumerations.

II. Nor are they within either of the general phrases, which are the two following.

1. "To lay taxes to provide for the general welfare of the U.S." that is to say "to lay taxes for the purpose of providing for the general welfare." For the laying of taxes is the power and the general welfare the purpose for which the power is to be exercised. They are not to lay taxes ad libitum for any purpose they please; but only to pay the debts or provide for the welfare of the Union. In like manner they are not to do anything they please to provide for the general welfare, but only to lay taxes for that purpose. To consider the latter phrase, not as describing the purpose of the first, but as giving a distinct and independent power to do any act they please, which might be for the good of the Union, would render all the preceding and subsequent enumerations of power completely useless. . . .
2. The second general phrase is "to make all laws necessary and proper for carrying into execution the enumerated powers." But they can all be carried into execution without a bank. A bank therefore is not necessary, and consequently not authorized by this phrase.

It has been much urged that a bank will give great facility, or convenience in the collection of taxes. Suppose this were true: yet the constitution allows only the means which are "necessary" not those which are merely "convenient" for effecting the enumerated powers. If such a latitude of construction be allowed to this phrase as to give any non-enumerated power, it will go to everyone, for [there] is no one which ingenuity may not torture into a convenience, in some way or other, to some one of so long a list of enumerated powers. It would swallow up all the delegated powers, and reduce the whole to one phrase as before observed. Therefore it was that the constitution restrained them to the necessary means, that is to say, to those means without which the grant of the power would be nugatory.

. . .

The Negative of the President is the shield provided by the constitution to protect against the invasions of the legislature 1. the rights of the Executive 2. of the Judiciary 3. of the states and state legislatures. The present is the case of a right remaining exclusively with the states and is consequently one of those intended by the constitution to be placed under his protection.

It must be added however, that unless the President's mind on a view of everything which is urged for and against this bill, is tolerably clear that it is unauthorized by the constitution, if the pro and the con hang so even as to balance his judgment, a just respect for the wisdom of the legislature would naturally decide the balance in favor of their opinion. It is chiefly for cases where they are clearly misled by error, ambition, or interest, that the constitution has placed a check in the negative of the President.

Alexander Hamilton, Opinion as to the Constitutionality of the Bank of the United States (1791)[16]

. . .

. . . [P]rinciples of construction like those espoused by the Secretary of State and Attorney General, would be fatal to the just and indispensable authority of the United States.

. . .

Now it appears to the Secretary of the Treasury that this general principle is inherent in the very definition of government, and essential to every step of progress to be made by that of the United States, namely: That every power vested in a government is in its nature sovereign, and includes, by force of the term, a right to employ all the means requisite and fairly applicable to the attainment of the ends of such power, and which are not precluded by restrictions and exceptions specified in the Constitution, or not immoral, or not contrary to the essential ends of political society.

. . .

The circumstance that the powers of sovereignty are in this country divided between the National and State governments, does not afford the distinction required. It does not follow from this, that each of the portion of powers delegated to the one or to the other, is not sovereign with regard to its proper objects. It will only follow from it, that each has sovereign power as to certain things, and not as to other things. To deny that the government of the United States has sovereign power, as to its declared purposes and trusts, because its power does not extend to all cases would be equally to deny that the State governments have sovereign power in any case, because their power does not extend to every case. . . .

. . .

This general and indisputable principle puts at once an end to the abstract question, whether the United States have power to erect a corporation. . . . For it is unquestionably incident to sovereign power to erect corporations. . . .

. . .

. . . It is conceded that implied powers are to be considered as delegated equally with express ones. Then it follows, that as a power of erecting a corporation may as well be implied as any other thing, it may as well be employed as an instrument or mean of carrying into execution any of the specified powers, as any other instrument or mean whatever. The only question must be in this, as in every other case, whether the mean to be employed or in this instance, the corporation to be erected, has a natural relation to any of the acknowledged objects or lawful ends of the government. . . .

. . .

It is certain that neither the grammatical nor popular sense of the term [*necessary*] requires that construction [offered by Jefferson and Randolph]. According to both, necessary often means no more than needful, requisite, incidental, useful, or conducive to. It is a common mode of expression to say, that it is necessary for a government or a person to do this or that thing, when nothing more is intended or understood, than that the interests of the government or person require, or will be promoted by, the doing of this or that thing. The imagination can be at no loss for exemplifications of the use of the word in this sense. And it is the true one in which it is to be understood as used in the Constitution. The whole turn of the clause containing it indicates, that it was the intent of the Convention, by that clause, to give a liberal latitude to the exercise of the specified powers. The expressions have peculiar comprehensiveness. They are "to make all laws necessary and proper for carrying into execution the foregoing powers, and all other powers vested by the Constitution in the government of the United States, or in any department or officer thereof."

To understand the word as the Secretary of State does, would be to depart from its obvious and popular sense, and to give it a restrictive operation, an idea

---

16. Excerpt taken from Paul Leicester Ford, *The Federalist* (New York: Henry Holt and Co., 1898), 655.

never before entertained. It would be to give it the same force as if the word absolutely or indispensably had been prefixed to it.

Such a construction would beget endless uncertainty and embarrassment. The cases must be palpable and extreme, in which it could be pronounced, with certainty, that a measure was absolutely necessary, or one, without which, the exercise of a given power would be nugatory. There are few measures of any government which would stand so severe a test. To insist upon it, would be to make the criterion of the exercise of any implied power, a case of extreme necessity; which is rather a rule to justify the overleaping of the bounds of constitutional authority, than to govern the ordinary exercise of it.

. . .

This restrictive interpretation of the word necessary is also contrary to this sound maxim of construction, namely, that the powers contained in a constitution of government, especially those which concern the general administration of the affairs of a country, its finances, trade, defense, etc., ought to be construed liberally in advancement of the public good. This rule does not depend on the particular form of a government, or on the particular demarcation of the boundaries of its powers, but on the nature and object of government itself. The means by which national exigencies are to be provided for, national inconveniences obviated, national prosperity promoted, are of such infinite variety, extent, and complexity, that there must of necessity be great latitude of discretion in the selection and application of those means. Hence, consequently, the necessity and propriety of exercising the authorities entrusted to a government on principles of liberal construction.

. . .

[The doctrine which is contended for] leaves . . . a criterion of what is constitutional, and of what is not so. This criterion is the end, to which the measure relates as a mean. If the end be clearly comprehended within any of the specified powers, and if the measure have an obvious relation to that end, and is not forbidden by any particular provision of the Constitution, it may safely be deemed to come within the compass of the national authority. There is also this further criterion, which may materially assist the decision: Does the proposed measure abridge a pre-existing right of any State or of any individual? If it does not, there is a strong presumption in favor of its constitutionality, and slighter relations to any declared object of the Constitution may be permitted to turn the scale.

. . .

McCulloch v. Maryland, 17 U.S. 316 (1819)

James McCulloch was the cashier of the Baltimore branch of the Bank of the United States. The Maryland state legislature imposed a tax on the notes of any bank not incorporated by the state of Maryland. When McCulloch refused to pay, Maryland brought suit in state court to collect the unpaid taxes. The Maryland government won at trial, and the ruling was affirmed by the Maryland Supreme Court. McCulloch appealed to the U.S. Supreme Court.

The case received extensive newspaper coverage, and the courtroom was jammed. The bank's legal team was led by Daniel Webster. A member of the House of Representatives, Webster was a rising star among the lawyers who regularly argued cases before the U.S. Supreme Court. The U.S. attorney general, William Wirt, also argued on behalf of the bank. Both Webster and Wirt contended that Maryland's tax was an unconstitutional interference with the policies of the federal government. Maryland's legal team included Luther Martin, the elderly state attorney general and a delegate to the Philadelphia Constitutional Convention. They argued that the bank was unconstitutional and that the states had full authority to tax any business operating within their borders. The federal bank could hardly expect to compete with state banks while contributing nothing to state coffers.

Oral argument lasted for days. There was little doubt, however, about how the Court would rule. Chief Justice John Marshall's views on the subject were well known, and there was no reason to believe that a majority of his brethren on the Court disagreed with him. Opponents of the national bank therefore looked to open other fronts in their war against the bank. They convinced the U.S. House of Representatives to investigate charges that the directors of the bank and its branches (including McCulloch himself) had manipulated bank operations to enrich themselves and damage the state banks. The investigating committee (which included future president John Tyler) found that the charges were largely accurate. While the Supreme Court was hearing oral arguments in the McCulloch *case, the Republican House overwhelmingly voted down resolutions to revoke the bank's charter. Congress would not take action against the bank. Shortly thereafter, the Supreme Court unanimously upheld the constitutionality of the bank charter and struck down the state tax as unconstitutional.*

The opinion that Marshall wrote for the Court was more surprising. Marshall was not content to declare that the bank was constitutional. His unanimous opinion asserted that the necessary and proper clause permitted the national government to pass any *legislation that was considered a reasonable means to secure a legitimate constitutional end. Marshall also indicated that any state effort to interfere with the national bank would be unconstitutional. "The power to tax," he declared, "involves the power to destroy." Under this ruling, even a tax aimed at all banks might be unconstitutional as applied to the national bank. Former President Madison complained that this broad interpretation of the necessary and proper clause and the implied powers of Congress obliterated "the landmarks intended by a specification of the powers of Congress." He hoped that "sound arguments & conciliatory expostulations addressed both to Congress & to their Constituents" might yet keep Congress within its original constitutional bound. Such arguments might cause it to "abstain" from the powers that the Court was attempting to give it.*[17]

Some states initially remained resistant to the bank and to the Court's decision. Ohio, for example, forcibly entered the bank's vaults and seized the money owed for taxes of the same sort that the Court had struck down in McCulloch. The bank sued, and the Ohio legislature eventually backed down, appropriating money to repay the bank for what the state government had confiscated.[18]

McCulloch v. Maryland *is one of the most important constitutional decisions in American history. Marshall's analysis of implied powers and the meaning of the necessary and proper clause have had enormous influence. How does Marshall understand the constitutional meaning of "necessary and proper"? What is the constitutional foundation for that understanding? Is he correct that a "stricter" construction would make government in the United States unworkable? The law incorporating the national bank did not forbid (or sanction) state taxes on that institution. Marshall nevertheless declared the Maryland tax unconstitutional. On what basis did he do so? Why did he assert that a state tax on a national bank is particularly constitutionally problematic?*

17. Quoted in Keith E. Whittington, "The Road Not Taken: *Dred Scott*, Judicial Authority, and Political Questions," *Journal of Politics* 63 (2001): 373.

18. On the background and aftermath of *McCulloch*, see Mark R. Killenbeck, *M'Culloch v. Maryland* (Lawrence: University Press of Kansas, 2006); Richard E. Ellis, *Aggressive Nationalism* (New York: Oxford University Press, 2007).

CHIEF JUSTICE MARSHALL delivered the opinion of the Court.

In the case now to be determined, the defendant, a sovereign state, denies the obligation of a law enacted by the legislature of the Union, and the plaintiff, on his part, contests the validity of an act which has been passed by the legislature of that state. The constitution of our country, in its most interesting and vital parts, is to be considered; the conflicting powers of the government of the Union and of its members, as marked in that constitution, are to be discussed; and an opinion given, which may essentially influence the great operations of the government. No tribunal can approach such a question without a deep sense of its importance, and of the awful responsibility involved in its decision. But it must be decided peacefully, or remain a source of hostile legislation, perhaps, of hostility of a still more serious nature; and if it is to be so decided, by this tribunal alone can the decision be made. On the supreme court of the United States has the constitution of our country devolved this important duty.

The first question made in the cause is, has Congress power to incorporate a bank? It has been truly said, that this can scarcely be considered as an open question, entirely unprejudiced by the former proceedings of the nation respecting it. . . .

. . . An exposition of the constitution, deliberately established by legislative acts, on the faith of which an immense property has been advanced, ought not to be lightly disregarded.

The power now contested was exercised by the first Congress elected under the present constitution. The bill for incorporating the bank of the United States did not steal upon an unsuspecting legislature, and pass unobserved. Its principle was completely understood, and was opposed with equal zeal and ability. After being resisted, first in the fair and open field of debate, and afterwards in the executive cabinet, with as much persevering talent as any measure has ever experienced, and being supported by arguments which convinced minds as pure and as intelligent as this country can boast, it became a law. The original act was permitted to expire; but a short experience of the embarrassments to which the refusal to revive it exposed the government, convinced those who were most prejudiced against the measure of its necessity, and induced the passage of the present law. It would require no ordinary share of intrepidity to assert that a measure adopted under these circumstances was a bold and plain usurpation, to which the constitution gave no countenance.

These observations belong to the cause; but they are not made under the impression that, were the question entirely new, the law would be found irreconcilable with the constitution.

. . .

This government is acknowledged by all to be one of enumerated powers. The principle, that it can exercise only the powers granted to it, would seem too apparent to have required to be enforced by all those arguments which its enlightened friends, while it was depending before the people, found it necessary to urge. That principle is now universally admitted. But the question respecting the extent of the powers actually granted, is perpetually arising, and will probably continue to arise, as long as our system shall exist.

. . .

Among the enumerated powers, we do not find that of establishing a bank or creating a corporation. But there is no phrase in the instrument which, like the Articles of Confederation, excludes incidental or implied powers; and which requires that every thing granted shall be expressly and minutely described. Even the 10th amendment, which was framed for the purpose of quieting the excessive jealousies which had been excited, omits the word "expressly." . . . The men who drew and adopted this amendment had experienced the embarrassments resulting from the insertion of this word in the articles of confederation, and probably omitted it to avoid those embarrassments. A constitution, to contain an accurate detail of all the subdivisions of which its great powers will admit, and of all the means by which they may be carried into execution, would partake of the prolixity of a legal code, and could scarcely be embraced by the human mind. It would probably never be understood by the public. Its nature, therefore, requires, that only its great outlines should be marked, its important objects designated, and the minor ingredients which compose those objects be deduced from the nature of the objects themselves. . . . In considering this question, then, we must never forget, that it is a constitution we are expounding.

Although, among the enumerated powers of government, we do not find the word "bank" or "incorporation," we find the great powers to lay and collect taxes; to borrow money; to regulate commerce; to declare and conduct a war; and to raise and support armies and navies. The sword and the purse, all the external relations, and no inconsiderable portion of the industry of the nation, are entrusted to its government. It can never be pretended that these vast powers draw after them others of inferior importance, merely because they are inferior. Such an idea can never be advanced. But it may with great reason be contended, that a government, entrusted with such ample powers, on the due execution of which the happiness and prosperity of the nation so vitally depends, must also be entrusted with ample means for their execution. The power being given, it is the interest of the nation to facilitate its execution. . . .

. . .

. . . Congress is not empowered by it to make all laws, which may have relation to the powers conferred on the government, but such only as may be "necessary and proper" for carrying them into execution. The word "necessary," is considered as controlling the whole sentence, and as limiting the right to pass laws for the execution of the granted powers, to such as are indispensable, and without which the power would be nugatory. That it excludes the choice of means, and leaves to Congress, in each case, that only which is most direct and simple.

Is it true, that this is the sense in which the word "necessary" is always used? Does it always import an absolute physical necessity, so strong, that one thing, to which another may be termed necessary, cannot exist without that other? We think it does not. If reference be had to its use, in the common affairs of the world, or in approved authors, we find that it frequently imports no more than that one thing is convenient, or useful, or essential to another. To employ the means necessary to an end, is generally understood as employing any means calculated to produce the end. . . . The word "necessary" . . . has not a fixed character peculiar to itself. It admits of all degrees of comparison; and is often connected with other words, which increase or diminish the impression the mind receives of the urgency it imports. A thing may be necessary, very necessary, absolutely or indispensably necessary. . . . This comment on the word is well illustrated, by the passage cited at the bar, from the 10th section of the 1st article of the constitution. It is, we think, impossible to compare the sentence which prohibits a State from laying "imposts, or duties on imports or exports, except what may be absolutely necessary for executing its inspection laws," with that which authorizes Congress "to make all laws which shall be necessary and proper for carrying into execution" the powers of the general government, without feeling a conviction that the convention understood itself to change materially the meaning of the word "necessary," by prefixing the word "absolutely." This word, then, like others, is used in various senses; and, in its construction, the subject, the context, the intention of the person using them, are all to be taken into view.

Let this be done in the case under consideration. The subject is the execution of those great powers on which the welfare of a nation essentially depends. It must have been the intention of those who gave these powers, to insure, as far as human prudence could insure, their beneficial execution. This could not be done by confining the choice of means to such narrow limits as not to leave it in the power of Congress to adopt any which might be appropriate, and which were conducive to the end. This provision is made in a constitution intended to endure for ages to come, and, consequently, to be adapted to the various crises of human affairs. To have prescribed the means by which government should, in all future time, execute its powers, would have been to change, entirely, the character of the instrument, and give it the properties of a legal code. It would have been an unwise attempt to provide, by immutable rules, for exigencies which, if foreseen at all, must have been seen dimly, and which can be best provided for as they occur. To have declared that the best means shall not be used, but those alone without which the power given would be nugatory, would have been to deprive the legislature of the capacity to avail itself of experience, to exercise its reason, and to accommodate its legislation to circumstances. . . .

. . .

We admit, as all must admit, that the powers of the government are limited, and that its limits are not to be transcended. But we think the sound construction of the constitution must allow to the national legislature that discretion, with respect to the means by which the powers it confers are to be carried into execution, which will enable that body to perform the high duties assigned to it, in the manner most beneficial to the people. Let the end be legitimate, let it be within the scope of the constitution, and all means which are appropriate, which are plainly adapted to that end, which are not prohibited, but consist with the letter and spirit of the constitution, are constitutional.

. . .

. . . Should Congress, in the execution of its powers, adopt measures which are prohibited by the constitution; or should Congress, under the pretext of executing its powers, pass laws for the accomplishment of objects not entrusted to the government; it would become the painful duty of this tribunal, should a case requiring such a decision come before it, to say that such an act was not the law of the land. But where the law is not prohibited, and is really calculated to effect any of the objects entrusted to the government, to undertake here to inquire into the degree of its necessity, would be to pass the line which circumscribes the judicial department, and to tread on legislative ground. This court disclaims all pretensions to such a power.

. . .

It being the opinion of the Court, that the act incorporating the bank is constitutional; and that the power of establishing a branch in the State of Maryland might be properly exercised by the bank itself, we proceed to inquire —

2. Whether the State of Maryland may, without violating the constitution, tax that branch?

. . .

. . . [T]he constitution and the laws made in pursuance thereof are supreme; . . . they control the constitution and laws of the respective States, and cannot be controlled by them. From this, which may be almost termed an axiom, other propositions are deduced as corollaries. . . . These are, 1st. that a power to create implies a power to preserve. 2nd. That a power to destroy, if wielded by a different hand, is hostile to, and incompatible with these powers to create and to preserve. 3d. That where this repugnancy exists, that authority which is supreme must control, not yield to that over which it is supreme.

. . .

. . . It is admitted that the power of taxing the people and their property is essential to the very existence of government, and may be legitimately exercised on the objects to which it is applicable, to the utmost extent to which the government may choose to carry it. The only security against the abuse of this power, is found in the structure of the government itself. In imposing a tax the legislature acts upon its constituents. This is in general a sufficient security against erroneous and oppressive taxation.

The people of a State, therefore, give to their government a right of taxing themselves and their property, and as the exigencies of government cannot be limited, they prescribe no limits to the exercise of this right, resting confidently on the interest of the legislator, and on the influence of the constituents over their representative, to guard them against its abuse. But the means employed by the government of the Union have no such security, nor is the right of a State to tax them sustained by the same theory. . . .

. . .

If we measure the power of taxation residing in a State, by the extent of sovereignty which the people of a single State possess, and can confer on its government, we have an intelligible standard, applicable to every case to which the power may be applied. We have a principle which leaves the power of taxing the people and property of a State unimpaired; which leaves to a State the command of all its resources, and which places beyond its reach, all those powers which are conferred by the people of the United States on the government of the Union, and all those means which are given for the purpose of carrying those powers into execution. We have a principle which is safe for the States, and safe for the Union. . . .

We find, then, on just theory, a total failure of this original right to tax the means employed by the government of the Union, for the execution of its powers. The right never existed, and the question whether it has been surrendered, cannot arise.

. . .

That the power to tax involves the power to destroy; that the power to destroy may defeat and render useless the power to create; that there is a plain repugnance, in conferring on one government a power to control the constitutional measures of another, which other, with respect to those very measures, is declared to be supreme over that which exerts the control, are propositions not to be denied. But all inconsistencies are to be reconciled by the magic of the word CONFIDENCE. Taxation, it is said, does not necessarily and unavoidably destroy. To carry it to the excess of destruction would be an abuse, to presume which, would banish that confidence which is essential to all government.

But is this a case of confidence? Would the people of any one State trust those of another with a power to control the most insignificant operations of their State government? We know they would not. Why, then, should we suppose that the people of any one State should be willing to trust those of another with a power to control the operations of a government to which they have confided their most important and most valuable interests? In the legislature of the Union alone, are all represented. The legislature of the Union alone, therefore, can be trusted by the people with the power of controlling measures which concern all, in the confidence that it will not be abused. This, then, is not a case of confidence, and we must consider it as it really is.

. . .

It has also been insisted, that, as the power of taxation in the general and State governments is acknowledged to be concurrent, every argument which would sustain the right of the general government to tax banks chartered by the States, will equally sustain the right of the States to tax banks chartered by the general government.

But the two cases are not on the same reason. The people of all the States have created the general government, and have conferred upon it the general power of taxation. The people of all the States, and the States themselves, are represented in Congress, and, by their representatives, exercise this power. When they tax the chartered institutions of the States, they tax their constituents; and these taxes must be uniform. But, when a State taxes the operations of the government of the United States, it acts upon institutions created, not by their own constituents, but by people over whom they claim no control. It acts upon the measures of a government created by others as well as themselves, for the benefit of others in common with themselves. The difference is that which always exists, and always must exist, between the action of the whole on a part, and the action of a part on the whole—between the laws of a government declared to be supreme, and those of a government which, when in opposition to those laws, is not supreme.

. . .

We are unanimously of opinion, that the law passed by the legislature of Maryland, imposing a tax on the Bank of the United States, is unconstitutional and void.

This opinion does not deprive the States of any resources which they originally possessed. It does not extend to a tax paid by the real property of the bank, in common with the other real property within the State, nor to a tax imposed on the interest which the citizens of Maryland may hold in this institution, in common with other property of the same description throughout the State. But this is a tax on the operations of the bank, and is, consequently, a tax on the operation of an instrument employed by the government of the Union to carry its powers into execution. Such a tax must be unconstitutional.

Spencer Roane and John Marshall on McCulloch v. Maryland[19]

John Marshall's opinion in McCulloch v. Maryland *was immediately recognized as having historic significance, and orthodox Republicans, including Thomas Jefferson and James Madison, did not like it. Neither Jefferson nor Madison doubted that the Bank of the United States had to be accepted. Madison had signed the Second Bank of the United States into law. Yet they recognized that* McCulloch *was not just about the bank. It was about the shape of the union and the basic nature of the federal Constitution.*

Marshall had already, anonymously, defended the McCulloch *opinion in the newspapers. In the spring of 1819, a "furious hurricane" broke out in the form of the "Hampden essays," a series of essays anonymously authored by Virginia Chief Judge Spencer Roane and printed in the influential* Richmond Enquirer. *Marshall and Roane had fought a lengthy battle over the supremacy of the Supreme Court over state courts in interpreting the Constitution in the* Martin *case (discussed in Section III of this chapter), and Marshall easily recognized the author of the Hampden essays. Roane's essays challenged the liberal construction of federal power. He was particularly concerned with language in* McCulloch *that he believed would enable the federal government to deprive state governments of their traditional functions. Eager to blunt the force of Roane's arguments, Marshall hurriedly prepared a response under the pen name "A Friend of the Constitution."*

In the end, the controversy over the McCulloch *decision passed without the serious attacks on the Court that Marshall feared, and Marshall and Roane moved on to disagreeing over other cases. The Hampden essay may be read as a missing Jeffersonian dissent from the* McCulloch *decision. How much did Roane and Marshall disagree?*

Spencer Roane, "Hampden" (1819)

. . .

. . . *They* have not dared to break down the barriers of the constitution, by a *general* act declaratory of their power. That measure would be too bold for these ephemeral deputies of the people.—That people hold them in check, by a short rein, and would consign them to merited infamy, at the next election. . . . They have adopted a safer course. . . . [T]hey have succeeded in seeing the constitution expounded, not by what it actually contains, but by the *abuses* committed under it. A new mode of amending the constitution has been added to the ample ones provided in that instrument, and the strongest checks established in it, have been made to yield to the force of precedents! The time will soon arrive, if it is not already at hand, when the constitution may be expounded without ever looking into it!—by merely reading the acts of a renegade congress. . . .

The warfare waged by the judicial body has been of a bolder tone and character. . . . They resolved . . . to put down all discussions of the kind, in future, by a judicial *coup de main*: to give a *general* letter of attorney to the future legislators of the union: and to tread under foot all those parts and articles of the constitution which had been, heretofore, deemed to set limits to the power of the federal legislature. That man must be a deplorable idiot who does not see that there is no earthly difference between an *unlimited* grant of power, and a grant limited in its terms, but accompanied with *unlimited* means of carrying it into execution.

. . . It was only necessary, in that case, to decide whether or not the bank law was "necessary and proper," within the meaning of the constitution, for carrying into effect some of the granted powers; but the court have, in effect, expunged those words from the constitution. . . .

. . .

If, in relation to the powers of the general government, the express grants . . . do not confer on the government power sufficiently ample, let those powers be extended by amendment to the constitution. Let us now do what our convention did in 1789, in relation to the articles of confederation. Let us extend their powers, but let this be the act of the people, and not that of subordinate agents. But let us see how far the amendments are to extend, and not, by opening wide the door of implied or constructive powers, grant we know not how much, nor enter into a field of indeterminable limits. Let us . . . extend the powers of the general government, if it be necessary; but until they are extended, let us only exercise such powers as are clear and undoubted. . . .

. . .

The principle of the common law, is, that when any one grants a thing he grants also that *without*

19. Excerpts taken from *John P. Branch Historical Papers of Randolph-Macon College* 4 (1904): 357–63.

which the grant cannot have its effect; as, if I grant you my trees in a wood, you may come with carts over my land to carry the wood off. So a right of way arises on the same principle of necessity, by operation of the law. . . . [W]hen the law giveth any thing to any one, it impliedly giveth whatever is necessary for taking or enjoying the same: it giveth "what is convenient, vis. entry, egress and regress as much as is necessary." The term "convenient" is here used in a sense convertible with the term "necessary," and is not allowed the latitude of meaning given to it by the supreme court. It is so restricted in tenderness to the rights of the other party. The right of way, passing in the case above mentioned, is also that, merely, of a private way, and does not give a high road, or avenue, through another's land, though such might be most convenient to the purposes of the grantee. It is also a principle of the common law that the incident is to be taken according to "a reasonable and easy sense," and not strained to comprehend things remote, "unlikely or unusual." The connection between the grant and the incident must be easy and clear: the grant does not carry with it as incidents things which are remote or doubtful.

. . .

The court is pleased to remind us . . . that it is a *constitution* that we are expounding. That constitution, however, conveys only *limited* and specified powers to the government, the extent of which must be traced in the instrument itself. The residuary powers abide in the state governments, and the people. If it is a constitution, it is also a *compact* and a limited and defined compact. The states have also constitutions, and their people rights, which ought also to be respected. It is on behalf of these constitutions, and these rights, that the enlarged and boundless power of the general government is objected to. . . .

. . .

The supreme court seems to consider it as quite unimportant, so long as the great principles involving human liberty are not invaded, by which set of the representatives of the people, the powers of government are to be exercised. I beg leave to say, on the other hand, that the adjustment of those powers made by the constitution, between the general and state governments, is beyond their power, and ought not to be set aside. That adjustment has been made by the *people* themselves, and they only are competent to change it. . . . [F]or the powers of the general government are few and defined, and relate chiefly to external objects, while the states retain a residuary and inviolable sovereignty over all other subjects; over all those great subjects which immediately concern the prosperity of the people. Are these last powers of so trivial a character that it is entirely unimportant which of the governments act upon them? Are the representatives of Connecticut in congress, best qualified to make laws, on the subject of our negro population? Or ought the South Carolina nabobs to regulate *their* steady habits? Is it the wish of any state, or at least of any of the larger states, that the whole circle of legislative powers should be confined to a body in which, in one branch at least, the small state of Delaware has as much weight as the great state of New York; having fourteen times its population? . . .

. . . [T]he great fault of the present times is, in considering the constitution as perfect. It is considered as a nose of wax, and is stretched and contradicted at the arbitrary will and pleasure of those who are entrusted to administer it. It is considered as *perfect*, in contravention of the opinion of those who formed it. Their opinion is greatly manifested, in the ample provisions it contains for its amendment. It is so considered in contravention of everything that is human: for nothing made by man is perfect. It is construed to this effect, by the *in's*, to the prejudice of the *out's*, by the agents of one government in prejudice of the rights of another; and by those who, possessing power, will not fail to "feel it, and forget right."

. . .

How . . . in this contest between the head and one of the members of our confederacy, in this vital contest for power, between them, can the supreme court assert its *exclusive* right to determine the controversy. It is not denied but that the judiciary of this country is in the daily habit of far outgoing that of any other. It often puts its veto upon the acts of the immediate representatives of the people. . . . [In the present case] it claims the right, in effect, to change the government: to convert a federal into a consolidated government. The supreme court is also pleased to say, that this important right and duty has been devolved upon it by the *constitution*.

If there is a clause to that effect in the constitution, I wish the supreme court had placed their finger upon it. . . .

John Marshall, "A Friend of the Constitution" (1819)

. . .

The zealous and persevering hostility with which the constitution was originally opposed, cannot be forgotten. The deep rooted and vindictive hate, which grew out of unfounded jealousies, and was aggravated by defeat, though suspended for a time, seems never to have been appeased. The desire to strip the government of those effective powers, which enable it to accomplish the objects for which it was created; and, by construction, essentially to reinstate that miserable confederation, whose incompetency to the preservation of our union, the short interval between the treaty of Paris and the meeting of the general convention at Philadelphia, was sufficient to demonstrate, seems to have recovered all its activities. The leaders of this plan, like skillful engineers, batter the weakest part of the citadel. . . . The judicial department, being without power, without patronage, without the legitimate means of ingratiating itself with the people, forms the weakest part; and is, at the same time, necessary to the very existence of the government and to the effectual execution of its laws. . . .

. . .

. . . The constitution has defined the powers of the government, and has established that division of power which its framers, and the American people, believed to be most conducive to the public happiness and to public liberty. The equipoise thus established is as much disturbed by taking weights out of the scale containing the powers of the government, as by putting weights into it. His hand is unfit to hold the state balance who occupies himself entirely in giving a preponderance to one of the scales.

. . .

The object of language is to communicate the intention of him who speaks, and the great duty of a judge who construes an instrument, is to find the intention of its makers. There is no technical rule applicable to every case, which enjoins us to interpret arguments in a more restricted sense than their words import. The nature of the instrument, the words that are employed, the object to be effected, are all to be taken into consideration, and to have their due weight.

. . .

It can scarcely be necessary to say, that no one of the circumstances which might seem to justify rather a strict construction in the particular cases quoted by Hampden, apply to a constitution. It is not a contract between enemies seeking each other's destruction, and anxious to insert every particular, lest a watchful adversary should take advantage of the omission.—Nor is it a case where implications in favor of one man impair the vested rights of another. Nor is it a contract for a single object, every thing relating to which, might be recollected and inserted. It is the act of a people, creating a government, without which they cannot exist as a people. The powers of this government are conferred for their own benefit, are essential to their own prosperity, by persons chosen for that purpose by themselves. The object of the instrument is not a single one which can be minutely described, with all its circumstances. The attempt to do so, would totally change its nature, and defeat its purposes. It is intended to be a general system for all future times, to be adapted by those who administer it, to all future occasions that may come within its own view. . . . The legislature is an emanation from the people themselves. It is a part chosen to represent the whole, and to mark, according to the judgment of the nation, its course, within those great outlines which are given in the constitution. It is impossible to construe such an instrument rightly, without adverting to its nature, and marking the points of difference which distinguish it from ordinary contracts.

. . .

If we were now making, instead of a controversy, a constitution, where else could this important duty of deciding questions which grow out of the constitution, and the laws of the union, be safely or wisely placed? Would any sane mind prefer to the peaceful and quiet mode of carrying the laws of the union into execution by the judicial arm, that they should be trampled under foot, or enforced by the sword? . . .

. . .

To whom more safely than to the judges are judicial questions to be referred? . . . Their paramount interest is the public prosperity, in which is involved their own and that of their families.—*No* tribunal can be less liable to be swayed by unworthy motives from a conscientious performance of duty. It is not then the party sitting in his own cause. It is the application of individuals by one department to the acts of another department of the government. The people are the authors of all; the departments are their agents; and if the judge be personally disinterested, he is as exempt from any political interest that might influence his opinion, as imperfect human institutions can make him. . . .

Gibbons v. Ogden, 22 U.S. 1 (1824)

New York required that steamships operating in its waters hold a license to do so, and a monopoly on issuing such licenses was awarded to Robert Livingston and Robert Fulton in reward for their innovations in developing the steam engine. Aaron Ogden, the outgoing governor of New Jersey, persuaded the New Jersey legislature to grant him a similar "monopoly;" his aim was to cut into Livingston's steamer business between New York City and New Jersey. When Ogden's political opponents succeeded in repealing his New Jersey monopoly, he jumped across the border. He managed to convince the heirs of the recently deceased Fulton and Livingston to grant him a New York license to run ships between New York City and New Jersey. Meanwhile, Thomas Gibbons, Ogden's former business partner, had started up a competing ferry business, running two steamships on an unannounced schedule between Elizabethtown, New Jersey, and New York City. Seeking to keep the case in the friendly New York courts, Ogden sought an injunction against Gibbons and won on the basis of his New York state steamship license. Gibbons responded that he had been licensed by the federal government to operate in coastal waters. He appealed the case to the U.S. Supreme Court.

Gibbons *raised two basic issues. First, did the Constitution implicitly prohibit or exclude the states from passing laws of this sort? Did the states have a concurrent power to regulate interstate commerce, or was this an exclusive power of the federal government? Even if the states could not "regulate interstate commerce," could they pass laws for other purposes that affected interstate commerce? Second, did the Constitution authorize Congress to preempt state laws of this sort with regulations of its own, and had Congress done so in this case? New York's laws granting a steamboat monopoly were adopted soon after the Constitution and were approved by Governor John Jay, among others. The state had long sought to exploit its position as the leading hub of imports into the United States. Tensions had built between New York and neighboring states over the taxation and regulation of commerce passing through the New York ports, fueling the movement to alter the Articles of Confederation.*

The steamboat license was seen as a new variation on that old problem, but it was less clear whether it was a variation that the Constitution covered. Ogden relied on the services of two former New York state attorneys general to argue his case; Gibbons turned to Daniel Webster. Although the dispute was a private suit, the U.S. attorney general was also given time to present arguments in the case, intervening on behalf of Gibbons and urging the Supreme Court to "interpose [its] friendly hand" to end New York's obstruction of interstate commerce.

The Supreme Court unanimously declared that Gibbons had a right to operate a ferry between New Jersey and New York. Chief Justice Marshall's majority opinion ruled that the commerce clause gave the federal government the power to license ships operating in coastal waters and that New York could not prohibit a ship with a federal license from operating in state waters. Justice Johnson's concurring opinion declared unconstitutional the New York law granting Ogden a monopoly on a second ground. Johnson asserted that the commerce power granted to the federal government was exclusive. In his view, states could not pass laws regulating interstate commerce, even when the state law was not inconsistent with an existing federal law. Marshall maintained this position had "great force" but was content to rest his decision on his finding that the New York law authorizing the monopoly was inconsistent with federal law.

The result in Gibbons *was highly popular, but Marshall's opinion was more controversial. Few were sorry that the Supreme Court had declared unconstitutional New York's effort to monopolize the interstate steamship trade. But in doing so, Marshall took time to give a relatively broad reading to the interstate commerce clause. How far does Marshall's reading of the interstate commerce clause extend? What might the implications for contemporary debates over internal improvements or slavery have been? How much support does* Gibbons *provide for modern regulatory policy?*

CHIEF JUSTICE MARSHALL delivered the opinion of the Court.

. . .

This [Constitution] contains an enumeration of powers expressly granted by the people to their government. It has been said, that these powers ought to be construed strictly. But why ought they to be so construed? Is there one sentence in the constitution which gives countenance to this rule? In the last of the enumerated powers, that which grants, expressly, the means for carrying all others into execution, Congress is authorized "to make all laws which shall be necessary and proper" for the purpose. But this limitation on the means which may be used, is not extended to the powers which are conferred; nor is there one sentence in the constitution, which has been pointed out by the gentlemen of the bar, or which we have been able to discern, that prescribes this rule. We do not, therefore, think ourselves justified in adopting it. What do gentlemen mean, by a strict construction? If they contend only against that enlarged construction, which would extend words beyond their natural and obvious import, we might question the application of the term, but should not controvert the principle. If they contend for that narrow construction which, in support of some theory not to be found in the constitution, would deny to the government those powers which the words of the grant, as usually understood, import, and which are consistent with the general views and objects of the instrument; for that narrow construction, which would cripple the government, and render it unequal to the object, for which it is declared to be instituted, and to which the powers given, as fairly understood, render it competent; then we cannot perceive the propriety of this strict construction, nor adopt it as the rule by which the constitution is to be expounded. As men, whose intentions require no concealment, generally employ the words which most directly and aptly express the ideas they intend to convey, the enlightened patriots who framed our constitution, and the people who adopted it, must be understood to have employed words in their natural sense, and to have intended what they have said. If, from the imperfection of human language, there should be serious doubts respecting the extent of any given power, it is a well settled rule, that the objects for which it was given, especially when those objects are expressed in the instrument itself, should have great influence in the construction. We know of no reason for excluding this rule from the present case. . . .

The words are, "Congress shall have power to regulate commerce with foreign nations, and among the several States, and with the Indian tribes."

The subject to be regulated is commerce; and . . . it becomes necessary to settle the meaning of the word. The counsel for the appellee would limit it to traffic, to buying and selling, or the interchange of commodities, and do not admit that it comprehends navigation. . . . Commerce, undoubtedly, is traffic, but it is something more: it is intercourse. It describes the commercial intercourse between nations, and parts of nations, in all its branches, and is regulated by prescribing rules for carrying on that intercourse. The mind can scarcely conceive a system for regulating commerce between nations, which shall exclude all laws concerning navigation, which shall be silent on the admission of the vessels of the one nation into the ports of the other, and be confined to prescribing rules for the conduct of individuals, in the actual employment of buying and selling, or of barter.

If commerce does not include navigation, the government of the Union has no direct power over that subject, and can make no law prescribing what shall constitute American vessels, or requiring that they shall be navigated by American seamen. Yet this power has been exercised from the commencement of the government, has been exercised with the consent of all, and has been understood by all to be a commercial regulation. All America understands, and has uniformly understood, the word "commerce," to comprehend navigation. It was so understood, and must have been so understood, when the constitution was framed. The power over commerce, including navigation, was one of the primary objects for which the people of America adopted their government, and must have been contemplated in forming it. The convention must have used the word in that sense, because all have understood it in that sense; and the attempt to restrict it comes too late.

. . .

The subject to which the power is next applied, is to commerce "among the several States." The word "among" means intermingled with. A thing which is among others, is intermingled with them. Commerce among the States, cannot stop at the external boundary line of each State, but may be introduced into the interior.

It is not intended to say that these words comprehend that commerce, which is completely internal, which is carried on between man and man in a State, or between different parts of the same State, and which does not extend to or affect other States. Such a power would be inconvenient, and is certainly unnecessary.

Comprehensive as the word "among" is, it may very properly be restricted to that commerce which concerns more States than one. The phrase is not one which would probably have been selected to indicate the completely interior traffic of a State, because it is not an apt phrase for that purpose; and the enumeration of the particular classes of commerce, to which the power was to be extended, would not have been made, had the intention been to extend the power to every description. . . . The genius and character of the whole government seem to be, that its action is to be applied to all the external concerns of the nation, and to those internal concerns which affect the States generally; but not to those which are completely within a particular State, which do not affect other States, and with which it is not necessary to interfere, for the purpose of executing some of the general powers of the government. The completely internal commerce of a State, then, may be considered as reserved for the State itself.

. . .

We are now arrived at the inquiry—What is this power?

It is the power to regulate; that is, to prescribe the rule by which commerce is to be governed. This power, like all others vested in Congress, is complete in itself, may be exercised to its utmost extent, and acknowledges no limitations, other than are prescribed in the constitution. . . . The wisdom and the discretion of Congress, their identity with the people, and the influence which their constituents possess at elections, are, in this, as in many other instances, as that, for example, of declaring war, the sole restraints on which they have relied, to secure them from its abuse. They are the restraints on which the people must often rely solely, in all representative governments.

. . .

The grant of the power to lay and collect taxes is, like the power to regulate commerce, made in general terms, and has never been understood to interfere with the exercise of the same power by the States; and hence has been drawn an argument which has been applied to the question under consideration. But the two grants are not, it is conceived, similar in their terms or their nature. Although many of the powers formerly exercised by the States, are transferred to the government of the Union, yet the State governments remain, and constitute a most important part of our system. The power of taxation is indispensable to their existence, and is a power which, in its own nature, is capable of residing in, and being exercised by, different authorities at the same time. We are accustomed to see it placed, for different purposes, in different hands. . . . When, then, each government exercises the power of taxation, neither is exercising the power of the other. But, when a State proceeds to regulate commerce with foreign nations, or among the several States, it is exercising the very power that is granted to Congress, and is doing the very thing which Congress is authorized to do. There is no analogy, then, between the power of taxation and the power of regulating commerce.

In discussing the question, whether this power is still in the States, in the case under consideration, we may dismiss from it the inquiry, whether it is surrendered by the mere grant to Congress, or is retained until Congress shall exercise the power. We may dismiss that inquiry, because it has been exercised, and the regulations which Congress deemed it proper to make, are now in full operation. The sole question is, can a State regulate commerce with foreign nations and among the States, while Congress is regulating it?

. . .

. . . [T]he inspection laws are said to be regulations of commerce, and are certainly recognized in the constitution, as being passed in the exercise of a power remaining with the States.

That inspection laws may have a remote and considerable influence on commerce, will not be denied; but that a power to regulate commerce is the source from which the right to pass them is derived, cannot be admitted. The object of inspection laws, is to improve the quality of articles produced by the labor of a country. . . . They act upon the subject before it becomes an article of foreign commerce, or of commerce among the States, and prepare it for that purpose. They form a portion of that immense mass of legislation, which embraces every thing within the territory of a State, not surrendered to the general government. . . . Inspection laws, quarantine laws, health laws of every description, as well as laws for regulating the internal commerce of a State, and those which respect turnpike roads, ferries, etc. are component parts of this mass.

No direct general power over these objects is granted to Congress; and, consequently, they remain subject to State legislation. . . .

. . .

It has been contended by the counsel for the appellant, that, as the word "to regulate" implies in its nature, full power over the thing to be regulated, it excludes, necessarily, the action of all others that would perform the same operation on the same thing. . . . It produces a uniform whole, which is as much disturbed and deranged by changing what the regulating power designs to leave untouched, as that on which it has operated.

There is great force in this argument, and the Court is not satisfied that it has been refuted.

Since, however, in exercising the power of regulating their own purely internal affairs, whether of trading or police, the States may sometimes enact laws, the validity of which depends on their interfering with, and being contrary to, an act of Congress passed in pursuance of the constitution, the Court will enter upon the inquiry, whether the laws of New York, as expounded by the highest tribunal of that State, have, in their application to this case, come into collision with an act of Congress, and deprived a citizen of a right to which that act entitles him. Should this collision exist, it will be immaterial whether those laws were passed in virtue of a concurrent power "to regulate commerce with foreign nations and among the several States," or, in virtue of a power to regulate their domestic trade and police. In one case and the other, the acts of New York must yield to the law of Congress; and the decision sustaining the privilege they confer, against a right given by a law of the Union, must be erroneous.

. . .

This section [of the act of Congress] seems to the Court to contain a positive enactment, that the vessels it describes shall be entitled to the privileges of ships or vessels employed in the coasting trade. These privileges cannot be separated from the trade, and cannot be enjoyed, unless the trade may be prosecuted. The grant of the privilege is an idle, empty form, conveying nothing, unless it convey the right to which the privilege is attached, and in the exercise of which its whole value consists. To construe these words otherwise than as entitling the ships or vessels described, to carry on the coasting trade, would be, we think, to disregard the apparent intent of the act.

. . .

JUSTICE JOHNSON, concurring.

In attempts to construe the constitution, I have never found much benefit resulting from the inquiry, whether the whole, or any part of it, is to be construed strictly, or literally. The simple, classical, precise, yet comprehensive language, in which it is couched, leaves, at most, but very little latitude for construction; and when its intent and meaning is discovered, nothing remains but to execute the will of those who made it, in the best manner to effect the purposes intended. . . .

. . .

For a century the States had submitted, with murmurs, to the commercial restrictions imposed by the parent State [Britain]; and now [after the Revolution], finding themselves in the unlimited possession of those powers over their own commerce, which they had so long been deprived of, and so earnestly coveted, that selfish principle which, well controlled, is so salutary, and which, unrestricted, is so unjust and tyrannical, guided by inexperience and jealousy, began to show itself in iniquitous laws and impolitic measures, from which grew up a conflict of commercial regulations, destructive to the harmony of the States, and fatal to their commercial interests abroad.

This was the immediate cause, that led to the forming of a convention [to draft the Constitution and grant a power over commerce for "the purpose of remedying those evils"].

. . .

The "power to regulate commerce," here meant to be granted, was that power to regulate commerce which previously existed in the States. . . . And since the power to prescribe the limits to its freedom, necessarily implies the power to determine what shall remain unrestrained, it follows, that the power must be exclusive; it can reside but in one potentate; and hence, the grant of this power carries with it the whole subject, leaving nothing for the State to act upon.

. . .

But, it is almost laboring to prove a self-evident proposition, since the sense of mankind, the practice of the world, the contemporaneous assumption, and continued exercise of the power, and universal acquiescence, have so clearly established the right of Congress over navigation, and the transportation of both men and their goods, as not only incidental to, but actually of the essence of, the power to regulate commerce. . . .

It is impossible, with the views which I entertain of the principle on which the commercial privileges of the people of the United States, among themselves, rests, to concur in the view which this Court takes of the effect of the coasting license in this cause. I do not regard it as the foundation of the right set up in behalf of the appellant. If there was any one object riding over every other in the adoption of the constitution, it was to keep the commercial intercourse among the States free from all invidious and partial restraints. And I cannot overcome the conviction, that if the licensing act was repealed to-morrow, the rights of the appellant to a reversal of the decision complained of, would be as strong as it is under this license. . . .

. . . [T]his Court doth further DIRECT, ORDER, and DECREE, that the bill of the said Aaron Ogden be dismissed, and this same is hereby dismissed accordingly.

House Report on Internal Improvements (1817)[20]

The House of Representatives appointed a committee to respond to Madison's veto of an internal improvements bill. The committee was led by Henry St. George Tucker, a Republican from an influential Virginia family of judges and politicians. Tucker, a veteran of the War of 1812 and serving only his second term of office in the House, allied himself with other young insurgents such as Henry Clay and John Calhoun who were willing to take a more vigorous view of federal power and what was necessary to avoid a repeat of the indignities that had befallen the United States in that war. Proponents of broad interpretations of federal power insisted that, particularly with state approval, such policies were necessary given the congressional power to raise armies and regulate interstate commerce.

In the extended debate that followed the committee's report, Tucker expressed exasperation with the charge that he and his allies

> *are deserting the great principles of the Republicans of 1798, and subverting the acknowledged rights of the States, by a construction too latitudinous. . . . In the construction of this Constitution, there is not, there cannot be, a system of orthodoxy. Agreeing, as we do, in principle, there must always be a variety of application. The instrument, conferring upon us incidental, as well as express powers, there must always be great differences of opinion, as to the "direct relationship," and "real necessity" of the accessory powers. Sir, with these things before your eyes, who shall pretend to say what is orthodoxy—what is heterodoxy? It is impossible. It remains to us to act according to our consciences, without attempting a conformity to any particular sect or persuasion.*[21]

. . .

It is true that the wants of the Union cannot confer power under the Constitution; but they may justly be touched upon as affording aid in its construction. They must have clearly foreseen, and must have been supposed to be provided for. If the power to carry on war implies "the necessary and proper" means of conducting it to a safe and proper issue, and if, without the use of these means, the burdens, and the privations, and the miseries of war, are to be infinitely increased, and its issue (always doubtful) rendered yet more precarious and unprosperous, are we not justified in presuming those means to have been contemplated as being vested in the General Government? Are we not justified in asserting that "necessary" power—the power of constructing roads and canals—at least with the assent of the States?

If your committee have not erred in attributing to Congress a Constitutional power to make roads and canals, either as an original or accessory power, it would seem that no doubt could remain of the right of applying our revenues to these purposes. If, indeed, the power was denied to the General Government of constructing roads and canals themselves, a question might still arise, whether it had not power to appropriate part of the revenue "to aid in the construction of roads and canals by the States."

There is perhaps no part of the Constitution more unlimited than that which relates to the application of the revenues which are to be raised under its authority. That power is given to "lay and collect taxes to pay the debts and provide for the common defense and general welfare of the United States;" and though it be really admitted, that, as this clause is only intended to designate the objects for which revenue is to be raised, it cannot be construed to extend the specified powers of Congress, yet it would be difficult to reconcile either the generality of the expression or the course of administration under it, with the idea that Congress has not a discretionary power over its expenditures, limited by their application "to the common defense and general welfare."

. . .

Nor, is there any danger that such power will be abused, while the vigor of representative responsibility remains unimpaired. It is on this principle that the framers of the Constitution mainly relied for protection of the public purse. It was a safe reliance. It was manifest that there was no other subject on which representative responsibility would be so great. On the other hand, while this principle is calculated to prevent abuses in the appropriation of public money, it was equally necessary to get an extensive discretion to the legislative body in the disposition of the revenues; since no human foresight could discern, nor human industry enumerate, the infinite variety of purposes to which the public money might advantageously and legitimately be applied. The attempt would have been to *legislate*, not

20. Excerpt taken from *Annals of Congress*, 15th Cong., 1st Sess., December 15, 1817, 453–60.

21. *Annals of Congress*, 15th Cong., 1st Sess., March 13, 1818, 1323.

frame a *Constitution*; to foresee and provide specifically for the wants of future generations, not to frame a rule of conduct for the legislative body. . . .

James Monroe, Views of the President of the United States on the Subject of Internal Improvements (1822)[22]

President James Monroe continued Madison's opposition to federally sponsored internal improvements. After he vetoed legislation that would have expanded the national road, Monroe wrote a long state paper detailing why he regarded internal improvements to be unconstitutional. Monroe believed the national government could fund state government projects when those internal improvements had national significance. He emphatically rejected claims that various enumerated powers sanctioned federal control of the internal transportation system or federal power to build its system.

Monroe made sure that a copy of his essay was delivered to the justices of the Supreme Court. Justice William Johnson informed the president that the McCulloch *opinion had already settled the issue—in favor of congressional power. The news had no influence on Monroe.*

It may be presumed that the proposition relating to internal improvements by roads and canals, which has been several times before Congress, will be taken into consideration again. . . . It seems to be the prevailing opinion that great advantage would be derived from the exercise of such a power by Congress. Respecting the right [of Congress to do so] there is much diversity of sentiment. It is of the highest importance that this question should be settled. If the right exists, it ought forthwith to be exercised. If it does not exist, surely those who are friends to the power ought to unite in recommending an amendment to the Constitution to obtain it. I propose to examine this question.

. . .

If the United States possesses this power, it must be either because it has been specifically granted or that it is incidental and necessary to carry into effect some specific grant. . . .

The first of these grants is in the following words: "Congress shall have the power to establish post-offices and post-roads." What is the just import of these words and the extent of the grant? . . . If we were to ask any number of our most enlightened citizens, who had no connection with public affairs and whose minds were unprejudiced, what was the import of the word "establish" and the extent of the grant which it controls, we do not think there would be any difference of opinion among them. . . . The use of the existing road . . . in passing it as others do is all that would be thought of, the jurisdiction and soil remaining to the State, with a right in the State or those authorized by its legislature to change the road at pleasure.

. . .

The next object of inquiry is whether the right to declare war includes the right to adopt and execute this system of improvement. . . .

. . .

. . . [N]o war with any great power can be prosecuted with success without the command of the resources of the Union in all these respects. . . . But these powers have all been granted specifically with many others, in great detail, which experience has shown were necessary for the purposes of war. By specifically granting, then, these powers it is manifest that every power was thus granted which it was intended to grant for military purposes, and that it was also intended that no important power should be included in this grant by way of incident, however useful it might be for some of the purposes of the grant.

. . .

I come next to the right to regulate commerce, the third source from whence the right to make internal improvement is claimed. . . . Commerce between independent powers or communities is universally regulated by duties and imposts. It was so regulated by the states before the adoption of this Constitution equally in respect to each other and to foreign powers. The goods and vessels employed in the trade are the only subjects of regulation. It can act on none other. A power, then, to impose such duties and imposts in regard to foreign nations and to prevent any on the trade between the States was the only power granted.

. . .

The fourth claim is founded on the right of Congress to "pay the debts and provide for the common defense and general welfare" of the United States. . . .

. . .

22. Excerpt taken from James Monroe, "Views of the President of the United States on the Subject of Internal Improvements," in *A Compilation of the Messages and Papers of the Presidents*, ed. James D. Richardson (New York: Bureau of National Literature, 1897), 2:713.

. . . Have Congress a right to raise and appropriate the money to any and to every purpose according to their will and pleasure? They certainly have not. The Government of the United States is a limited Government, instituted for great national purposes, and for those only. Other interests are committed to the States, whose duty it is to provide for them. Each government should look to the great and essential purposes for which it was instituted, and confine itself to those purposes. A State government will rarely if ever apply money to national purposes without making it a charge to the nation. The people of the state would not permit it. Nor will Congress be apt to apply money in aid of the State administrations for purposes strictly local in which the nation at large has no interest, although the state should desire it. The people of the other states would condemn it. They would declare that Congress has no right to tax them for such a purpose, and would dismiss at the next election such of their representatives as had voted for that measure, especially if it should be severely felt. . . .

. . .

The right of appropriation is nothing more than a right to apply the public money to this or that purpose. It has no incidental power, nor does it draw after it any consequences of that kind. All that Congress could do under it in the case of internal improvements would be to appropriate the money necessary to make them. For every act requiring legislative sanction or support the State authority must be relied on. The condemnation of the land, if the proprietors should refuse to sell it, the establishment of turnpikes and tolls, and the protection of the work when finished must be done by the State. To these purposes the powers of the General Government are believed to be utterly incompetent.

. . .

V. Federalism

MAJOR DEVELOPMENTS

- The Eleventh Amendment prohibits federal courts from adjudicating lawsuits against a state brought by a citizen of another state or country
- The compact theory of the relationship between the states and national government

Ratification left open many important constitutional questions about the place of states in the national union. General agreement existed that all states had surrendered certain vital powers. Article I clearly forbade New Jersey from declaring war on France, or North Carolina from granting titles of nobility. Other constitutional questions were less clear. In particular, Americans disputed whether the states or the people of the United States were the parties to the Constitution. The answer to that question influenced how constitution decision makers understood the proper balance of power between state governments and the national government, what governing institutions were authorized to resolve constitutional disputes between the states and the national government, and whether states could be sued in federal court.

State governments were clearly not fully sovereign after the ratification of the U.S. Constitution. There was less certainty over whether they possessed some measure of sovereignty. Even if they were not fully sovereign, they seemed to possess important legal and political characteristics of sovereignty. Many were surprised when the U.S. Supreme Court ruled in *Chisholm v. Georgia* (1793) that a citizen of South Carolina could sue the state of Georgia in federal court. Bipartisan majorities in Congress proposed the Eleventh Amendment in response, and the states quickly ratified it. The amendment gave constitutional recognition to some degree of state sovereign immunity by prohibiting federal courts from hearing suits against a state filed by a citizen of some other state or country.

Many Jeffersonians believed that the Constitution formed a "compact" between sovereign states. Jefferson maintained, "the constitution of the United States is a compact of independent nations subject to the rules acknowledged in similar cases, as well that of amendment provided within itself, as, in case of abuse, justly dreaded but unavoidable *ultimo ratio gentium* [the last argument of nations]."[23] The compact theory of union implied a strict construction of national powers. The sovereign states that formed the union should not easily be understood to have given up powers to the general government. To Jefferson and many of his allies, the states were also necessarily the ultimate interpreters of the Constitution. (Madison was more ambivalent on this point.) Since these parties constituted the union and delegated powers to the national government, they must be able to interpret the terms of that grant of power.

23. Thomas Jefferson, "To Edward Everett, April 8, 1826," in *Writings of Thomas Jefferson* (see note 5), 10:385.

Federalists and National Republicans rejected the compact theory of the Constitution. In their view, the Constitution was an agreement among the people of the United States. Chief Justice John Marshall went out of his way in *McCulloch v. Maryland* (1819) to reject the compact theory. He declared, "The government of the Union, then (whatever may be the influence of this fact on the case), is, emphatically and truly, a government of the people. In form, and in substance, it emanates from them. Its powers are granted by them, and are to be exercised directly on them, and for their benefit." Justice Joseph Story agreed. His opinion in *Martin v. Hunter's Lessee* (1816) asserted, "The constitution of the United States was ordained and established, not by the states in their sovereign capacities, but emphatically, as the preamble of the constitution declares, by 'the people of the United States.'" Officials who rejected compact theory interpreted congressional powers broadly. If the Constitution was made by and for the people of the nation as a whole, they claimed, then the best repository of their power and guardian of their interest was the Congress made up of their elected representatives.

The Articles of Confederation declared that each state retained its "sovereignty, freedom, and independence." The U.S. Constitution did not. The Constitution imposed new obligations and restrictions on the states, and directed state and federal judges to enforce those constitutional requirements. The states under the Articles of Confederation, like all governments, had traditionally enjoyed "sovereign immunity." They could not be subjected against their will to court proceedings that could result in financial losses. The state governments could be sued in state courts, and their treasuries imperiled, only if they chose to waive that immunity.

The Constitution of the United States complicated traditional notions of sovereign immunity. All agreed the federal government enjoyed sovereign immunity. No one can sue the United States unless a federal statute permits that lawsuit. Whether state governments could be sued in federal courts raised more difficult issues. Sovereign governments cannot be sued without their permission in their courts or foreign courts. Federal courts are neither state courts nor foreign courts. Did immunity principles apply there as well?

Both the federal government and the states during the late eighteenth century had financial reasons for being concerned with the status of sovereign immunity. During the Revolutionary War, states borrowed money freely from citizens of other states and other countries. Most Federalists wanted to ensure that creditors were paid back. Repayment would demonstrate that the United States was a trustworthy economic partner and would ease tensions between the United States and foreign countries. States, many of which had limited capacity to repay debts, wanted to keep the option to repudiate those obligations. Needless to say, federal courts were more likely than state courts to issue orders on behalf of creditors against the debtor states.

The issue of state sovereign immunity was controversial from the moment that the Constitution was proposed. During the ratification debates, Federalists such as Alexander Hamilton reassured skeptics that nothing in the Constitution altered state sovereign immunity. Creditors quickly tested these assurances. In an early important decision, the U.S. Supreme Court ruled in *Chisholm v. Georgia* (1793) that the states did not enjoy sovereign immunity in federal court. Chief Justice Jay observed simply, "The people are the sovereign of this country." In a republican government, he wrote, "justice is the same whether due from one man or a million."

Chisholm did not resolve the nature of our federal system. A day after the decision was announced, a proposal to amend the Constitution was introduced into the House of Representatives. Congress finally proposed a constitutional amendment on March 4, 1794: "The Judicial power of the United States shall not be construed to extend to any suit in law or equity, commenced or prosecuted against one of the United States by Citizens of another State, or by Citizens or Subjects of any Foreign State." This amendment was ratified by the required three-fourths of state legislatures by February 7, 1795, almost exactly two years after the *Chisholm* decision was handed down. It became the Eleventh Amendment to the Constitution—the first amendment to be passed after the ratification of the promised Bill of Rights.

Chisholm v. Georgia was the first U.S. Supreme Court decision reversed through the amendment process. Given that this was the Court's first important opinion, this was not an auspicious beginning. The Eleventh Amendment represented a clear, decisive, and across-the-board rebuke of the Court's understanding of the Constitution. On the other hand, that opposition to the decision took the form of a constitutional amendment rather than a denial of the Court's authority to interpret the Constitution is noteworthy. As Hamilton suggested, enforcing judicial decisions was not going to be easy. Neither state nor federal politicians were eager to see repeated showdowns either. Would states like Georgia carry out their threat to execute anyone attempting to make good on a federal court order to collect a debt against a state? Better to make such lawsuits go away. By changing the Constitution, rather than declaring the Court's opinion to be irrelevant, the opponents of *Chisholm* helped to establish a precedent: justices had the final say over the meaning of the document.

The Alien and Sedition Acts of 1798 further explored problems of federalism and constitutional authority in the new nation. The Alien Act expanded presidential power to detain and deport aliens and increased the residency requirements for citizenship. The Sedition Act prohibited speech and writings that brought the government into contempt. Once these measures became law, the Adams administration launched a series of prosecutions that shut down many Jeffersonian newspapers. One congressman was jailed. Jeffersonians responded with a public campaign against the acts.

The Jeffersonians' most visible and significant protest came in the form of the Virginia and Kentucky Resolutions of 1798. The Virginia Resolutions were secretly drafted by Congressman James Madison and adopted by the Virginia state legislature. The Kentucky Resolutions were secretly drafted by Vice President Thomas Jefferson and adopted by the Kentucky state legislature. The Virginia and Kentucky bodies were the only two state legislatures firmly in Republican control in 1798. Several states responded, particularly in New England, by criticizing Virginia and Kentucky for claiming the right to judge the constitutionality of acts of Congress. Congress responded with a report of defending the Alien and Sedition Acts. James Madison left the U.S. House of Representatives in order to win a seat in the Virginia legislature. Once there, he authored a 1799 report for that body that defended and elaborated on the 1798 resolutions.

Chisholm v. Georgia, 2 U.S. 419 (1793)

Chisholm v. Georgia was the first important decision of the U.S. Supreme Court and the first example of how judicial opinions do not always settle constitutional disputes. Alexander Chisholm was a citizen of South Carolina and the executor of the estate of a South Carolina merchant. He believed the state of Georgia owed the merchant's estate some money, arising out of a contract to supply Georgia with clothing during the Revolutionary War. Chisholm sued the state in federal court, relying on the language in Article III, Section 2 of the Constitution, which declared that the jurisdiction of federal courts extended to controversies between "a State and Citizens of another State." The state of Georgia refused to appear in court, claiming that it was a sovereign state and thus (by definition) immune from the legal processes of another government. Georgia interpreted the language in Article III as intended to give states recourse as plaintiffs in federal courts against citizens in other states. It was not, the state believed, intended to force states to act as defendants in federal courts against creditors from other states.

The attorney general of the United States urged the Supreme Court to assert jurisdiction over Georgia, and the Court was accommodating. The five-member Court ruled 4 to 1 against the state's assertion of sovereign immunity. James Wilson and John Jay wrote in strong, nationalist terms that sovereignty resided only in the people of the United States. Justice Iredell was the only dissenting vote, but even he did not assert a theory of state sovereignty. He merely emphasized the absence of a congressional statute authorizing this kind of lawsuit.

Before John Marshall became chief justice in 1801, the justices each wrote opinions in every case, a practice known as "seriatim" opinions. These opinions are presented here after the argument made by the attorney general. Consider whether the justices were basing their arguments on a literal reading of the text, structural considerations, or general principles of the constitutional system. Possessing sovereign immunity being a government means. What role does such a legal background play in constitutional interpretation? Can it be assumed that the Constitution overturned such a basic principle by mere implication? What are possible justifications for sovereign immunity? Is it consistent with a democratic government?

Mr. RANDOLPH [Attorney General of the United States], for the plaintiff. . . .

1st. The Constitution vests a jurisdiction in the Supreme Court over a State, as a defendant, at the suit of a private citizen of another State. Consult the letter of the Constitution, or rather the influential words of the cause in question. The judicial power is extended to controversies between a State and citizens of another State. . . . Human genius might be challenged to restrict these words to a plaintiff state alone. . . .

With the advantage of the letter on our side, let us now advert to the spirit of the Constitution, or rather its genuine and necessary interpretation. . . .

Are States . . . to enjoy the high privilege of acting . . . eminently wrong, without control; or does a remedy exist? The love of morality would lead us to wish that some check should be found; if the evil, which flows from it, be not too great for the good contemplated. . . . Government itself would be useless, if a pleasure to obey or transgress with impunity should be substituted in the place of a sanction to its laws. . . . What is to be done, if in consequence of a bill of attainder, or an ex post facto law, the estate of a citizen shall be confiscated, and deposited in the treasury of a State? What, if a State should adulterate or coin money below the Congressional standard, emit bills of credit, or enact unconstitutional tenders, for the purpose of extinguishing its own debts? What if a State should impair her own contracts? These evils, and others which might be enumerated like them, cannot be corrected without a suit against the State. . . .

. . .

With this discussion, though purely legal, it will be impossible to prevent the world from blending political considerations. Some may call this an attempt to consolidate. But before such an imputation shall be pronounced, let them examine well, if the fair interpretation of the Constitution does not vindicate my opinions. Above all, let me personally assure them, that the prostration of State-rights is no object with me; but that I remain in perfect confidence, that with the power, which the people and the Legislatures of the States indirectly hold over almost every movement of the National Government, the States need not fear an assault from bold ambition, or any approaches of covered stratagem. . . .

JUSTICE IREDELL, dissenting.

This is the first instance wherein the important question involved in this cause has come regularly before the Court. . . . What controversy of a civil nature can be maintained against a State by an individual? . . .

. . .

. . . So much, however, has been said on the Constitution, that it may not be improper to intimate that my present opinion is strongly against any construction of it, which will admit, under any circumstances, a compulsive suit against a State for the recovery of money. I think every word in the Constitution may have its full effect without involving this consequence, and that nothing but express words, or an insurmountable implication (neither of which I consider, can be found in this case) would authorize the deduction of so high a power. This opinion I hold, however, with all the reserve proper for one, which, according to my sentiments in this case, may be deemed in some measure extra-judicial. With regard to the policy of maintaining such suits, that is not for this Court to consider, unless the point in all other respects was very doubtful. Policy might then be argued from with a view to preponderate the judgment. Upon the question before us, I have no doubt. I have therefore nothing to do with the policy. But I confess, if I was at liberty to speak on that subject, my opinion on the policy of the case would also differ from that of the Attorney General. It is, however, a delicate topic. . . .

JUSTICE BLAIR, concurring.

. . .

JUSTICE WILSON, concurring.

. . .

To the Constitution of the United States the term SOVEREIGN, is totally unknown. There is but one place where it could have been used with propriety. But, even in that place it would not, perhaps, have comported with the delicacy of those, who ordained and established that Constitution. They might have announced themselves "SOVEREIGN" people of the United States: But serenely conscious of the fact, they avoided the ostentatious declaration. . . .

. . . [A State] is an artificial person. It has its affairs and its interests: It has its rules: It has its rights: And it has its obligations. It may acquire property distinct from that of its members: It may incur debts to be discharged out of the public flock, not out of the private fortunes of individuals. It may be bound by contracts; and for damages arising from the breach of those contracts. . . . A State, like a merchant, makes a contract. A dishonest State, like a dishonest merchant, willfully refuses to discharge it: The latter is amenable to a Court of Justice: Upon general principles of right, shall the former when summoned to answer the fair demands of its creditor, be permitted, proteus-like, to assume a new appearance, and to insult him and justice, by declaring I am a SOVEREIGN State? Surely not. . . .

. . .

But, in my opinion, this doctrine rests not upon the legitimate result of fair and conclusive deduction from the Constitution: It is confirmed, beyond all doubt, by the direct and explicit declaration of the Constitution itself. "The judicial power of the United States shall extend, to controversies between two States." . . . Can the most consummate degree of professional ingenuity devise a mode by which this "controversy between two States" can be brought before a Court of law; and yet neither of those States be a Defendant? "The judicial power of the United States shall extend to controversies, between a State and citizens of another State." Could the strictest legal language; could even that language, which is peculiarly appropriated to an art, deemed, by a great master, to be one of the most honorable, laudable, and profitable things in our law; could this strict and appropriated language, describe, with more precise accuracy, the cause now depending before the tribunal? Causes, and not parties to causes, are weighed by justice, in her equal scales: On the former solely, her attention is fixed: To the latter, she is, as she is painted, blind. . . .

JUSTICE CUSHING, concurring.

. . .

CHIEF JUSTICE JAY, concurring.

In determining the sense in which Georgia is a sovereign State, it may be useful to turn our attention to the political situation we were in, prior to the Revolution, and to the political rights which emerged from the Revolution. . . .

The Revolution, or rather the Declaration of Independence, found the people already united for general purposes, and at the same time providing for their more domestic concerns by State conventions, and other temporary arrangements. From the crown of Great Britain, the sovereignty of their country passed to the people of it. . . . "We the people of the United States, do ordain and establish this Constitution." Here we see the people acting as sovereigns of the whole country; and in the language of sovereignty, establishing a Constitution by which it was their will, that the State Governments should be bound, and to which the State Constitutions should be made to conform. . . .

Let us now proceed to enquire whether Georgia has not, by being a party to the national compact, consented to be suable by individual citizens of another State. This enquiry naturally leads our attention, 1st. To the design of the Constitution. 2d. To the letter and express declaration in it.

Prior to the date of the Constitution, the people had not any national tribunal to which they could resort for justice; the distribution of justice was then confined to State judicatories, in whose institution and organization the people of the other States had no participation, and over whom they had not the least control. . . . There was danger that from this source animosities would in time result; and as the transition from animosities to hostilities was frequent in the history of independent States, a common tribunal for the termination of controversies became desirable, from motives both of justice and of policy.

Prior also to that period, the United States had, by taking a place among the nations of the earth, become amenable to the laws of nations; and it was their interest as well as their duty to provide, that those laws should be respected and obeyed; in their national character and capacity, the United States were responsible to foreign nations for the conduct of each State, relative to the laws of nations, and the performance of treaties; and there the inexpediency of referring all such questions to State Courts, and particularly to the Courts of delinquent States became apparent. . . .

These were among the evils against which it was proper for the nation, that is, the people of all the United States, to provide by a national judiciary, to be instituted by the whole nation, and to be responsible to the whole nation.

Let us now turn to the Constitution. . . .

The question now before us renders it necessary to pay particular attention to that part of the 2d section, which extends the judicial power "to controversies between a State and citizens of another State." It is contended, that this ought to be construed to reach none of these controversies, excepting those in which a State may be Plaintiff. The ordinary rules for construction will easily decide whether those words are to be understood in that limited sense.

This extension of power is remedial, because it is to settle controversies. It is therefore, to be construed liberally. It is politic, wise, and good that, not only the controversies, in which a State is Plaintiff, but also those in which a State is Defendant, should be settled; both cases, therefore, are within the reason of the remedy; and ought to be so adjudged, unless the obvious, plain, and literal sense of the words forbid it. If we attend to the words, we find them to be express, positive, free from ambiguity, and without room for such implied expressions. . . . If the Constitution really meant to extend these powers only to those controversies in which a State might be Plaintiff, to the exclusion of those in which citizens had demands against a State, it is inconceivable that it should have attempted to convey that meaning in words, not only so incompetent, but also repugnant to it; if it meant to exclude a certain class of these controversies, why were they not expressly excepted; on the contrary, not even an intimation of such intention appears in any part of the Constitution. . . .

. . .

For my own part, I am convinced that the sense in which I understand and have explained the words "controversies between States and citizens of another State," is the true sense. The extension of the judiciary power of the United States to such controversies, appears to me to be wise, because it is honest, and because it is useful. It is honest, because it provides for doing justice without respect of persons, and by securing individual citizens as well as States, in their respective rights, performs the promise which every free Government makes to every free citizen, of equal justice and protection. It is useful, because it is honest, because it leaves not even the most obscure and friendless citizen without means of obtaining justice from a neighboring State; because it obviates occasions of quarrels between States on account of the claims of their respective citizens; because it recognizes and strongly rests on this great moral truth, that justice is the same whether due from one man or a million, or from a million to one man; because it teaches and greatly appreciates the value of our free republican national Government, which places all our citizens on an equal footing, and enables each and every of them to obtain justice without any danger of being overborne by the weight and number of their opponents; and, because it brings into action, and enforces this great and glorious principle, that the people are the sovereign of this country, and consequently that fellow citizens and joint sovereigns cannot be degraded by appearing with each other in their own Courts to have their controversies determined. The people have reason to prize and rejoice in such valuable privileges; and they ought not to forget, that nothing but the free course of Constitutional law and Government can ensure the continuance and enjoyment of them. . . .

Virginia and Kentucky Resolutions of 1798[24]

Resolutions of the Virginia Legislature (1798)

1. Resolved, That the General Assembly of Virginia doth unequivocally express a firm resolution to maintain and defend the Constitution of the United States, and the Constitution of this State, against every aggression, either foreign or domestic, and that it will support the government of the United States in all measures warranted by the former.

2. That this Assembly most solemnly declares a warm attachment to the union of the States, to maintain which, it pledges all its powers; and that for this end it is its duty to watch over and oppose every infraction of those principles, which constitute the only basis of that union, because a faithful observance of them can alone secure its existence, and the public happiness.

3. That this Assembly doth explicitly and peremptorily declare that it views the powers of the Federal Government as resulting from the compact, to which the States are parties, as limited by the plain sense and intention of the instrument constituting that compact; as no further valid than they are authorized by the grants enumerated in that compact, and that in case of a deliberate, palpable, and dangerous exercise of other powers not granted by the said compact, the States, who are the parties thereto, have the right, and are in duty bound, to interpose for arresting the progress of the evil, and for maintaining within their respective limits, the authorities, rights, and liberties appertaining to them.

4. That the General Assembly doth also express its deep regret that a spirit has in sundry instances been manifested by the Federal Government, to enlarge its powers by forced constructions of the constitutional charter which defines them; and that indications have appeared of a design to expound certain general phrases (which, having been copied from the very limited grant of powers in the former articles of confederation, were the less liable to be misconstrued), so as to destroy the meaning and effect of the particular enumeration, which necessarily explains and limits the

24. Excerpt taken from Herman V. Ames, ed., *State Documents on Federal Relations* (Philadelphia: Department of History at the University of Pennsylvania, 1900–1906).

general phrases, and so as to consolidate the States by degrees into one sovereignty, the obvious tendency and inevitable result of which would be to transform the present republican system of the United States into an absolute, or at best, a mixed monarchy.

5. That the General Assembly doth particularly protest against the palpable and alarming infractions of the Constitution, in the two late cases of the "alien and sedition acts," . . . [which] exercises in like manner a power not delegated by the Constitution, but on the contrary expressly and positively forbidden by one of the amendments thereto; a power which more than any other ought to produce universal alarm, because it is leveled against that right of freely examining public characters and measures, and of free communication among the people thereon, which has ever been justly deemed the only effectual guardian of every other right.

6. That this State having by its convention which ratified the federal Constitution, expressly declared, "that among other essential rights, the liberty of conscience and of the press cannot be cancelled, abridged, restrained, or modified by any authority of the United States," and from its extreme anxiety to guard these rights from every possible attack of sophistry or ambition, having with other States recommended an amendment for that purpose, which amendment was in due time annexed to the Constitution, it would mark a reproachful inconsistency and criminal degeneracy, if an indifference were now shown to the most palpable violation of one of the rights thus declared and secured, and to the establishment of a precedent which may be fatal to the other.

7. That the good people of this commonwealth having ever felt, and continuing to feel the most sincere affection to their brethren of the other States, the truest anxiety for establishing and perpetuating the union of all, and the most scrupulous fidelity to that Constitution which is the pledge of mutual friendship, and the instrument of mutual happiness, the General Assembly doth solemnly appeal to the like dispositions of the other States, in confidence that they will concur with this commonwealth in declaring, as it does hereby declare, that the acts aforesaid are unconstitutional, and that the necessary and proper measure will be taken by each, for co-operating with this State in maintaining unimpaired the authorities, rights, and liberties reserved to the States respectively, or to the people.

. . .

Resolutions of the Kentucky Legislature (1798)

1. Resolved, That the several states composing the United States of America, are not united on the principle of unlimited submission to their general government; but that by compact, under the style and title of a Constitution for the United States, and of amendments thereto, they constituted a general government for special purposes, delegated to that government certain definite powers, reserving, each state to itself the residuary mass of right to their own self-government; and that whensoever the general government assumes undelegated powers, its acts are unauthoritative, void, and of no force: That to this compact each state acceded as a state, and is an integral party, its co-states forming as to itself, the other party: That the government created by this compact was not made the exclusive or final judge of the extent of the powers delegated to itself; since that would have made its discretion, and not the Constitution, the measure of its powers; but that, as in all other cases of compact among parties having no common judge, each party has an equal right to judge for itself, as well of infractions, as of the mode and measure of redress.

. . .

3. Resolved, That it is true as a general principle, and is also expressly declared by one of the amendments to the Constitution, that "the powers not delegated to the United States by the Constitution, nor prohibited by it to the states, are reserved to the states respectively, or to the people;" and that no power over the freedom of religion, freedom of speech, or freedom of the press, being delegated to the United States by the Constitution, nor prohibited by it to the states, all lawful powers respecting the same did of right remain, and were reserved to the states, or to the people; that thus was manifested their determination to retain to themselves the right of judging how far the licentiousness of speech and of the press may be abridged without lessening their useful freedom, and how far those abuses which cannot be separated from their use, should be tolerated rather than the use be destroyed; . . . and that in addition to this general principle and express declaration, another and more special provision has been made by one of the amendments to the Constitution, which expressly declares, that "Congress shall make no law respecting an establishment of religion, or prohibiting the free exercise

thereof, or abridging the freedom of speech, or of the press," . . . therefore the act of the Congress of the United States, passed on the 14th day of July, 1798, entitled, "an act in addition to the act for the punishment of certain crimes against the United States," which does abridge the freedom of the press, is not law, but is altogether void and of no effect.

. . .

9. Resolved, lastly, That the Governor of this commonwealth be, and is hereby authorized and requested to communicate the preceding resolutions to the legislatures of the several states, to assure them that this commonwealth considers union for specified national purposes, and particularly for those specified in their late federal compact, to be friendly to the peace, happiness, and prosperity of all the states: that, faithful to that compact, according to the plain intent and meaning in which it was understood and acceded to by the several parties, it is sincerely anxious for its preservation: that it does also believe, that to take from the states all the powers of self-government, and transfer them to a general and consolidated government, without regard to the special obligations and reservations solemnly agreed to in that compact, is not for the peace, happiness or prosperity of these states: and that therefore, this commonwealth is determined, as it doubts not its co-states are, tamely to submit to undelegated and consequently unlimited powers in no man or body of men on earth: . . . that these and successive acts of the same character, unless arrested on the threshold, may tend to drive these states into revolution and blood, and will furnish new calumnies against republican governments, and new pretexts for those who wish it to be believed, that man cannot be governed but by a rod of iron: . . . In questions of power, then, let no more be heard of confidence in man, but bind him down from mischief, by the chains of the Constitution. That this commonwealth does, therefore, call on its co-states for an expression of their sentiments on the acts concerning aliens, and for the punishment of certain crimes herein before specified, plainly declaring whether these acts are or are not authorized by the Federal compact. And it doubts not that their sense will be so announced, as to prove their attachment unaltered to limited government, whether general or particular, and that the rights and liberties of their co-states, will be exposed to no dangers by remaining embarked on a common bottom with their own: That they will concur with this commonwealth in considering the said acts as so palpably against the Constitution, as to amount to an undisguised declaration, that the compact is not meant to be the measure of the powers of the general government, but that it will proceed in the exercise over these states of all powers whatsoever: That they will view this as seizing the rights of the states, and consolidating them in the hands of the general government with a power assumed to bind the states, (not merely in cases made federal,) but in all cases whatsoever, by laws made, not with their consent, but by others against their consent: That this would be to surrender the form of government we have chosen, and to live under one deriving its powers from its own will, and not from our authority; and that the co-states, recurring to their natural right in cases not made federal, will concur in declaring these acts void and of no force and will each unite with this commonwealth, in requesting their repeal at the next session of Congress.

VI. Separation of Powers

MAJOR DEVELOPMENTS

- Creation of the executive branch of the national government
- First debates over the power of the president to act independently in foreign and domestic affairs
- First assertions of executive privilege

The constitutional provisions of Article II could be interpreted broadly or narrowly, just like the provisions of Article I. A broad interpretation of the provisions of Article II tended to favor implied presidential powers. A narrow interpretation tended to restrict presidential power. The debate over separation of powers was not usually framed as a debate between the strict and broad construction of constitutional powers, but the effects were similar. At least initially, the participants were similar as well. Such Federalists as Alexander Hamilton advocated a broad interpretation of presidential powers. Some Jeffersonians were more critical.

Constitutional ambiguities, institutional affiliations, and partisan politics all influenced early debates over the separation of powers. Americans quickly discovered that the constitutional text did not provide as detailed instructions for constructing the executive branch of the government as it did for constructing the national legislature. Under what conditions, for example, could a president remove a cabinet officer? No explicit constitutional text guided the members of the First Congress.

When debating the scope of independent presidential power, presidents unsurprisingly tended to take a broader view of executive authority than did many members of Congress. President Washington did not wait for Congress to weigh in before declaring American neutrality in the war between France and England. The framers did not anticipate, however, how partisan considerations influenced constitutional debates over the separation of powers. *Federalist* 51 predicted that elected officials would consistently side with their home institutions when conflict occurred between the branches of the national government. Presidents would seek to augment executive power. Senators would promote the powers of the Senate. Once the questions of institutional authority and power were tangled up in questions of substantive public policy and partisan loyalties, constitutional deliberations and outcomes were necessarily affected. Federalist members of the House of Representatives during the debate over the Jay Treaty, for example, supported the prerogatives of the Federalist Washington administration rather than the powers of the House of Representatives to derail the treaty.

Many basic issues of separation of powers arose during the early republic. Some were rather decisively resolved, such as the question of what to call the president in official documents. (A simple "President of the United States" was deemed adequate.) So was whether the president should treat the Senate like an executive council and consult with it in person on such matters as treaty negotiations. (After a brief, unhappy experiment, President Washington vowed not to return to the Senate chamber—ratification of completed treaties would be sufficient.) Others were less firmly settled. Thomas Jefferson, for example, decided to deliver the State of the Union address to Congress in writing rather than in person (a practice that endured for a century).

Debates over executive power require attention to whether the president is ever authorized to act beyond the Constitution. The U.S. Constitution does not make explicit provision for its suspension during times of emergency or in circumstances in which its requirements no longer seem to serve the public good.[25] But the problem was well understood by the founders. *Federalist* 41 pointed out, "It is in vain to oppose constitutional barriers to the impulse of self-preservation" while warning that "it is worse than vain; because it plants in the Constitution itself necessary usurpations of power, every precedent of which is a germ of unnecessary and multiplied repetitions."

There have been two basic models for addressing this problem within American constitutionalism.[26] The first model is associated most closely with Thomas Jefferson. His strict construction of the Constitution implied that government officials should be acutely aware of the proper limits on their power. The best response when constitutional norms conflict with the public good is to seek a constitutional amendment. Jefferson contemplated this course of action as president, faced with his own doubts about the constitutionality of the Louisiana Purchase. As Jefferson explained to one of his political lieutenants before the Louisiana Purchase:

> When an instrument admits two constructions, the one safe, the other dangerous, the one precise, the other indefinite, I prefer that which is safe & precise. I had rather risk an enlargement of powers from the nation [by constitutional amendment], where it is found necessary, than to assume it by construction that would make our powers boundless. Our peculiar security is in possession of a written Constitution. Let us not make it a blank paper by construction.[27]

Jefferson recognized that constitutional amendments are not always feasible. In such circumstances, the

---

25. The Constitution does make reference to a power to suspend the writ of habeas corpus (Art. I, sec. 9). Habeas corpus allows judges to question the circumstances of and justification for holding a prisoner.

26. For background, see Clement Fatovic, "Constitutionalism and Presidential Prerogative: Jeffersonian and Hamiltonian Perspectives," *American Journal of Political Science* 48 (2004): 429. Also useful are George Thomas, "As Far as Republican Principles Will Admit: Presidential Prerogative and Constitutional Government," *Presidential Studies Quarterly* 30 (2000): 534; Jeremy D. Bailey, *Thomas Jefferson and Executive Power* (New York: Cambridge University Press, 2007); Harvey C. Mansfield, Jr., *Taming the Prince* (Baltimore, MD: Johns Hopkins University Press, 1993).

27. Thomas Jefferson, "To Wilson C. Nicholas, September 7, 1803," in *Writings of Thomas Jefferson (see note 5)*, 8:247.

president must maintain a strict construction of the Constitution but, if necessary, frankly act "beyond the constitution." The president can then only "rely on the nation to sanction an act done for its great good, without its previous authority."[28]

The other model for addressing this problem is most closely associated with Alexander Hamilton. Hamilton was no friend to the strict constructionists. He was quite comfortable with broad and flexible interpretations of government power. He thus did not have to face the intellectual difficulty that confronted the Jeffersonians as they attempted to govern. Moreover, Hamilton was acutely aware of the need to meet crises as and when they develop. He saw them as routine features of human society, the norm rather than the exception. It was the day-to-day challenge of government to deal with the unexpected and restore order in a chaotic world. This combination of broad constructionism and crisis government implied a quite different understanding of the prerogative power. In writings ranging from his contributions to the *Federalist Papers* to his Pacificus essays, Hamilton defended the need for "energy" in the executive branch. The executive need not ever turn to extraconstitutional powers, because the prerogative power was built into the Hamiltonian Constitution. There was no need for special justifications or absolutions. The president could simply *act*.

In the early republic, presidents took a relatively narrow view of the circumstances in which they could veto legislation. By contrast, modern presidents feel free to exercise this influence over the lawmaking process whenever they have a policy disagreement with Congress. During the Early National period, most believed that presidents should veto bills that they considered to be *unconstitutional* or otherwise clearly improper; they should not veto a bill merely because they considered it unwise. The reasoning had to do with separation of powers: Congress was considered the policy-making branch, and it was assumed that presidents should defer to their policy judgments except in the most extraordinary cases. George Washington vetoed only two bills in eight years. The first was a bill apportioning congressional seats that he believed failed to meet constitutional requirements. The second veto rejected a bill reducing the size of the army, a reduction that the president thought was "injurious to the public."[29] The army bill particularly affected the president's ability to carry out the duties of his own office, but Washington made no constitutional arguments in vetoing it. His successors, John Adams and Thomas Jefferson, vetoed no bills. The next president, James Madison, used the regular veto just five times: four for constitutional reasons (involving the separation of church and state, the scope of Congress' power to promote internal improvements, and the president's appointment powers) and another because he considered the bill so poorly crafted as to be fatally flawed.

28. Thomas Jefferson, "To John Dickinson, August 9, 1803," in *Writings of Thomas Jefferson* (see note 5), 8:262.

House Debate on Removal of Executive Officers (1789)[30]

The first important concrete constitutional debate in American history was over whether the president could remove a cabinet official, such as the secretary of state, without Senate approval. James Madison initiated the first debate over the removal power when he drafted the bills establishing what became the State, Treasury, and War Departments. His legislative proposal declared that these three departments should each be headed by a secretary, "who shall be appointed by the President, by and with the advice of the Senate; and to be removable by the President." Some argued that this language in the statute did not add to or change the powers that the president already had. They insisted that a unilateral presidential removal power was implicit in the presidential office. Other supporters of the provision contended that Congress had discretionary authority when legislatively creating an office to specify the procedure by which an officeholder might be removed. On this reading, the president could remove lower-level executive officers if and only if Congress empowered him to do so through statute. Some opponents of the provision argued that impeachment was the only constitutional option for removing officials. More commonly, opponents reasoned that executive officers could be removed only by the bodies that had appointed them. Given the constitutional requirement that the Senate

29. George Washington, "Veto Message of February 28, 1797," in *A Compilation of the Messages and Papers of the Presidents*, ed. James D. Richardson (New York: Bureau of National Literature, 1897), 1:211.

30. Excerpt taken from *Annals of Congress*, 1st Cong., 1st Sess., May 19, June 17, 1789, 393–95, 521–25.

approve cabinet officials, this meant that both the president and the Senate must concur to remove an official. The "executive power" of appointment was shared by the president and Senate, and by implication the executive power of removal was also shared.

A congressional majority supported Madison's proposal, but the significance of that decision was unclear. Even representatives who supported unilateral presidential removal power did not agree on why such a power could be wielded. Were they delegating that power or merely recognizing that the Constitution authorized it?

MR. JAMES MADISON (Republican, Virginia)

I look upon every constitutional question, whatever its nature may be, as of great importance. I look upon the present to be doubly so, because its nature is of the highest moment to the well-being of the Government. I have listened with attention to the objections which have been stated, and to the replies that have been made, and I think the investigation of the meaning of the constitution has supported the doctrine I brought forward. If you consult the expediency, it will be greatly against the doctrine advanced by gentlemen on the other side of the question. . . . It has been said, we may guard against the inconveniency of that construction, by limiting the duration of the office to a term of years; but, during that term, there is no way of getting rid of a bad officer but by impeachment. During the time this is depending, the person may continue to commit those crimes for which he is impeached, because if his construction of the constitution is right, the President can have no more power to suspend than he has to remove.

. . .

It is said, that it comports with the nature of things, that those who appoint should have the power of removal; but I cannot conceive that this sentiment is warranted by the constitution; I believe it would be found very inconvenient in practice. It is one of the most prominent features of the constitution, a principle that pervades the whole system, that there should be the highest degree of responsibility in all the executive officers thereof; any thing, therefore, which tends to lessen this responsibility, is contrary to its spirit and intention, and, unless it is saddled upon us expressly by the letter of that work, I shall oppose the admission of it into any act of the Legislature. Now, if the heads of the executive departments are subjected to removal by the President alone, we have in him security for the good behavior of the officer. If he does not conform to the judgment of the President in doing the executive duties of his office, he can be displaced. This makes him responsible to the great executive power, and makes the President responsible to the public for the conduct of the person he has nominated and appointed to aid him in the administration of his department. But if the President shall join in a collusion with the officer, and continue the bad man in office, the case of impeachment will reach the culprit, and drag him forth to punishment. But if you take the other construction, and say he shall not be displaced by and with the advice and consent of the Senate, the President is no longer answerable for the conduct of the officer; all will depend on the Senate. You here destroy a real responsibility without obtaining even the shadow; for no gentleman will pretend to say the responsibility of the Senate can be of such a nature as to afford substantial security. But why, it may be asked, was the Senate joined with the President in appointment to office, if they have responsibility? I answer, merely for the sake of advising, being supposed, from their nature, better acquainted with the characters of the candidates than an individual; yet even here the President is held to the responsibility he nominates, and, with their consent, appoints. No person can be forced upon him as an assistant by any other branch of the Government.

. . .

MR. ELBRIDGE GERRY (Republican, Massachusetts)

I wish, sir, to consider this question so far, as to ascertain whether it is, or is not, unconstitutional. I have listened with attention to the arguments which have been urged on both sides; and it does appear to me, that the clause [the statutory provision specifying presidential removal] is as inconsistent with the constitution as any set of words which could possibly be inserted in the bill.

. . . The gentlemen will agree, that this House has not the power of removal; they will also agree that it does not vest in the Judiciary; then it must vest in the President, or the President by and with the advice and consent of the Senate; in either of these cases, the clause is altogether useless and nugatory. It is useless if the power vests in the President; because, when the question comes before him, he will decide upon the provision made in the constitution, and not on what is contained in this clause. If the power vests in the President and Senate, the Senate will not consent to pass the bill with this clause in it; therefore the attempt is nugatory. But if the Senate will assent to the exercise of the power of removal by the President alone, whenever he thinks proper to use it so, then in that case the clause is, as I said before, both useless and nugatory.

... The gentlemen in favor of this clause have not shown that, if the construction that the power vests in the President and Senate is admitted, it will be an improper construction. I call on gentlemen to point out the impropriety, if they discover any. To me, it appears to preserve the unity of the several clauses of the constitution; while their construction produces a clashing of powers, and renders of none effect some powers the Senate by express grants possess. What becomes of their power of appointing, when the President can remove at discretion? . . .

It is said, that the President shall be subject to an impeachment for dismissing a good man. This in my mind involves an absurdity. How can the House impeach the President for doing an act which the Legislature has submitted to his discretion?

But what consequence may result from giving the President an absolute control over all officers? Among the rest, I presume he is to have an unlimited control over the officers of the Treasury. I think if this is the case, you may as well give him at once the appropriation of the revenue; for of what use is it to make laws on this head, when the President, by looking at the officer, can make it his interest to break him? We may expect to see institutions arising under the control of the revenue, and not of the law.[31]

...

But if we give the President the power to remove, (though I contend if the constitution has not given it him, there is no power on earth that can except the people, by an alteration of the constitution, though I will suppose it for argument's sake,) you virtually give him a considerable power over the appointment, independent of the Senate; for if the Senate should reject his first nomination, which will probably be his favorite, he must continue to nominate until the Senate concur; then immediately after the recess of the Senate, he may remove the officer, and introduce his own creature, as he has this power expressly by the constitution. The influence created by this circumstance, would prevent his removal from an office which he held by a temporary appointment from his patron.

This has been supposed by some gentlemen to be an omitted case, and that Congress have the power of supplying the defect. Let gentlemen consider the ground on which they tread. If it is an omitted case, an attempt in the Legislature to supply the defect, will be in fact an attempt to amend the constitution. But this can only be done in the way pointed out by the fifth article of that instrument, and an attempt to amend it in any other way may be a high crime or misdemeanor, or perhaps something worse. . . .

...

The system, it cannot be denied, is in many parts obscure; if Congress are to explain and declare what it shall be, they certainly will have it in their power to make it what they please. It has been a strong objection to the constitution, that it was remarkably obscure; nay, some have gone so far as to assert that it was studiously obscure, that it might be applied to every purpose by Congress. By this very act the House are assuming a power to alter the constitution. The people of America can never be safe, if Congress have a right to exercise the power of giving constructions to the constitution different from the original instrument. Such a power would render the most important clause in the constitution nugatory, and one without which, I will be bold to say, this system of Government would never have been ratified. If the people were to find that Congress meant to alter it in this way, they would revolt at the idea; it would be repugnant to the principles of the revolution, and to the feelings of every freeman in the United States.

It is said, that the power to advise the President in appointing officers, is an exception to a general rule. To what general rule? That the President, being an executive officer, has the right of appointment. From whence is this general rule drawn? Not from the constitution, nor from custom, because the State Governments are generally against it. . . .

It is said to be the duty of the President to see the laws faithfully executed, and he could not discharge this trust without the power of removal. I ask the gentleman, if the power of suspension, which we are willing to give, is not sufficient for that purpose? In case the Senate should not be sitting, the officer could be suspended, and at their next session the causes which require his removal might be inquired into.

...

The dangers which lie against investing this power jointly in the Senate and President have been pointed out; but I think them more than counterbalanced by the dangers arising from investing it in the President alone. . . . It is said, that if the Senate should have this power, the Government would contain a two-headed monster; but it appears to me, that if it consists in blending the power of making treaties and appointing officers, as executive

31. In this connection, consider the debate over Jackson's removal of the deposits in Chapter 5.

powers, with their legislative powers, the Senate is already a two-headed monster; if it is a two-headed monster, let us preserve it as a consistent one; for surely it will be a very inconsistent monster, while it has the power of appointment, if you deprive it of the power of removing. It was said, that the judges could not have the power of deciding on this subject, because the constitution is silent; but I ask, if the judges are not *ex officio* judges of the law; and whether they would not be bound to declare the law a nullity, if this clause is continued in it and is inconsistent with the constitution? There is a clause in this system of government that makes it their duty. I allude to that which authorizes the President to obtain the opinions of the heads of departments in writing; so the President and Senate may require the opinion of the judges respecting this power, if they have any doubts concerning it.

. . .

VII. Individual Rights

MAJOR DEVELOPMENTS

- Use of due process and takings clauses to protect property rights
- Debates over whether the United States is a Christian country
- First decisions on the constitutional meaning of the right to bear arms

Government was a regular presence in the lives of most Americans during the Early National Era. State and local officials built roads, regulated the numerous mills springing up along the rivers, punished drunkenness, and forbade people from carrying concealed weapons. Proponents of these measures insisted that they advanced the common good. Opponents insisted that government officials were violating constitutional rights to property, religion, personal choice, and gun ownership. Many persons affected by state regulations brought lawsuits against the government. For the first time, courts were asked to determine the proper balance between individual rights and the common good.

A. Property

Americans during the Early National Era struggled to determine which government regulations unconstitutionally took property from A and gave it to B. All constitutional decision makers agreed that government could not play favorites. Unlike the king of England, the governor of Tennessee was constitutionally prohibited from giving an estate to his mistress or raising taxes on towns suspected of being loyal to a different political faction. As government regulations became routine and commercial practices changed, controversies arose over whether new forms of regulation were legitimate efforts to secure the common good or unconstitutional attempts to enrich some citizens at the expense of others. By the 1820s, courts had become the forum for settling many constitutional controversies over property rights. Justice Story in *Wilkinson v. Leland* (1829) declared, "Government can scarcely be deemed to be free, where the rights of property are left solely dependent upon the will of a legislative body, without any restraint. The fundamental maxims of a free government seem to require that the rights of personal liberty and private property should be held sacred." Most early nineteenth-century judges claimed that courts should prevent government from redistributing property and ensure that all government regulations promoted the public good. When you read the materials in this section, consider whether that is a fair characterization of judicial behavior. How did justices characterize the public interest and private rights when disputes over property arose?

Disputes over the meaning of the contracts clause were the most enduring constitutional debates of the Early National Era and reflected the deep concern over the stability of property that animated many Americans who pushed for the formation of a stronger national government during the 1780s. Americans in the Founding Era expected that the contracts clause would prevent states from passing debtor relief laws or legislation requiring creditors to forgive past debts. They were not disappointed. Bankruptcy issues came before the Marshall Court in *Sturges v. Crowninshield* (1819) and *Ogden v. Saunders* (1827). The justices in those cases ruled that states could pass bankruptcy laws that regulated only those contracts made after the statute was enacted. If you declared bankruptcy in 2010 and the bankruptcy law in your state was passed in 2005, then that statute determined whether you had to pay debts you contracted in 2007 (*Ogden*), but not whether you had to pay debts you contracted in 2003 (*Sturges*).

The Supreme Court supported private investors in two important decisions. *Fletcher v. Peck* (1810) ruled that state land grants were contracts subject to contracts clause strictures. *Dartmouth College v. Woodward* (1819) determined that corporate charters were contracts for constitutional purposes. In the latter case, the Marshall Court held that nonprofit corporate charters had the same constitutional status as for-profit corporate charters. Both *Fletcher* and *Dartmouth*, if broadly interpreted, provide powerful limitations on state capacity to redistribute land and regulate business enterprises.

The first Marshall Court cases on property rights suggest a certain ambiguity in the source of the limits on government power. Chief Justice Marshall concluded his *Fletcher* opinion by declaring that "the state of Georgia was restrained, either by general principles which are common to our free institutions, or by the particular provisions of the constitution of the United States." This claim is similar to Justice Chase's assertion in *Calder v. Bull* (1798) that certain natural rights are judicially enforceable, even in the absence of a specific constitutional provision. Justice Johnson's concurrence in *Fletcher* invoked "a general principle, on the reason and nature of things; a principle which will impose laws even on the Deity."

Cases decided in the Marshall Court over time placed more emphasis on constitutional provisions and less emphasis on natural law. The *Dartmouth* case and other decisions handed down during the 1820s relied exclusively on the contracts clause. Constitutional authorities nevertheless regarded the obligation of contracts as rooted in natural justice, even if judicial power was increasingly seen as grounded in the constitutional text.

An investor-friendly contracts clause jurisprudence developed during the first third of the nineteenth century. These decisions help explain why many business elites became firm supporters of judicial power. Federal courts, Daniel Webster and his business-friendly allies were convinced, could be trusted to protect property rights against democratic legislatures. Courts, in their view, were the national institution that had the special capacity to secure the liberties of affluent Americans, a minority that elites thought needed special judicial protection from popular majorities. Table 4-4 illustrates how contracts clause cases were an important part of the early Supreme Court's work but later declined in frequency as the justices limited the scope of that constitutional provision.

Table 4-4 Selection of U.S. Supreme Court Cases Reviewing State Laws Under the Contracts Clause

Case	Vote	Outcome	Decision
Fletcher v. Peck, 10 U.S. (6 Cranch) 187 (1810)	4–1	Struck down	Legislature cannot rescind grants once the rights have been vested
New Jersey v. Wilson, 11 U.S. (7 Cranch) 164 (1812)	7–0	Struck down	Legislature cannot revoke tax immunity that was part of a land grant to a Native American tribe
Dartmouth College v. Woodward, 17 U.S. (4 Wheat.) 518 (1819)	6–1	Struck down	A corporate charter is a contract that cannot be altered by the state
Sturges v. Crowninshield, 17 U.S. (4 Wheat.) 122 (1819)	7–0	Struck down	States cannot adopt a bankruptcy law that retroactively applies to preexisting contracts
Green v. Biddle, 21 U.S. (8 Wheat.) 1 (1823)	6–1	Struck down	States cannot violate an interstate compact regarding land titles
Ogden v. Saunders, 25 U.S. (12 Wheat.) 213 (1827)	4–3	Upheld	States may adopt a bankruptcy law that prospectively applies to new contracts
Mason v. Haile, 25 U.S. (12 Wheat.) 370 (1827)	6–1	Upheld	States may alter remedies for enforcing contracts by discharging individuals from debtors' prison
Charles River Bridge v. Warren Bridge, 36 U.S. (11 Pet.) 420 (1837)	5–2	Upheld	Charters and grants should be construed strictly so as not to impair future legislative discretion
Bronson v. Kinzie, et al., 42 U.S. (1 How.) 311 (1843)	6–1	Struck down	State law that substantially alters available remedies impairs the obligation of contracts

(Continued)

Table 4-4 *(Continued)*

Case	Vote	Outcome	Decision
Gelpcke v. City of Dubuque, 68 U.S. (1 Wall.) 175 (1863)	9–1	Struck down	Municipal bonds are valid contracts even if a state court later determines that the city did not have legal authority to issue the bonds
Von Hoffman v. City of Quincy, 71 U.S. (4 Wall.) 535 (1866)	9–0	Struck down	A state cannot withdraw from a city the taxation power necessary to repay bonds
Pennsylvania College Cases, 80 U.S. (13 Wall.) 190 (1871)	9–0	Upheld	A state may amend, alter, or repeal any corporate charters granted after the adoption of a general reservation statute
Beer Company v. Massachusetts, 97 U.S. 25 (1877)	9–0	Upheld	Legislature has no power to contract away its police powers, and so alcohol prohibition is a valid regulation of a corporation chartered to manufacture alcohol
Stone v. Mississippi, 101 U.S. 814 (1880)	9–0	Upheld	The granting of a twenty-five-year charter to a lottery company does not preclude a state from subsequently banning the sale of lottery tickets through either legislation or constitutional amendment
City of Cleveland v. Cleveland City Railway Company, 194 U.S. 517 (1904)	8–0	Struck down	A city ordinance lowering streetcar fares violates a corporate charter that specified a five-cent fare
Home Building & Loan Association v. Blaisdell, 290 U.S. 398 (1934)	5–4	Upheld	States can exercise police powers to modify mortgage remedies in an economic emergency
W. B. Worthen Co. v. Thomas, 292 U.S. 426 (1934)	9–0	Struck down	State law protecting insurance benefits from debt collectors cannot be justified as an emergency measure
United States Trust Co. v. New Jersey, 431 U.S. 1 (1977)	4–3	Struck down	The repeal of a bi-state agreement that blocked the ability of a rail line to subsidize passengers by spending bond reserves is invalid
Allied Structural Steel Co. v. Spannaus, 438 U.S. 234 (1978)	5–3	Struck down	A state statute requiring companies to pay pensions to all long-term employees if a plant closes or a pension plan is terminated, regardless of the terms of the employment contract, is invalid
Exxon Corp. v. Eagerton, 462 U.S. 176 (1983)	9–0	Upheld	A statutory provision that oil and gas severance tax cannot be passed on to consumers, regardless of existing contracts allowing pass-throughs, is valid as a generally applicable statute
Energy Reserves Group v. Kansas Power & Light, 459 U.S. 400 (1983)	9–0	Upheld	A state may alter contracts to set price levels on natural gas if doing so serves a significant public purpose and is a reasonable means for accomplishing that goal
Keystone Bituminous Coal Association v. DeBenedictis, 480 U.S. 470 (1987)	5–4	Upheld	A state may alter land titles on mining rights if doing so serves a substantial public interest and the state itself is not a contracting party

Fletcher v. Peck, 10 U.S. 87 (1810)

John Peck of Massachusetts sold fifteen thousand acres of land along the Yazoo River to Robert Fletcher of New Hampshire. Fletcher immediately sued Peck in federal court, claiming that the title to the land Peck sold was defective. Georgia owned the disputed lands when the Constitution was ratified. In 1795 the Georgia legislature granted some 35 million acres of Yazoo lands, making up most of what is now Alabama and Mississippi, to four companies for little more than a penny per acre. Evidence soon emerged that the entire legislature had been bribed, and most members were turned out in the next election. The new Georgia legislature repealed the land grant in 1796. Fletcher claimed that the repeal divested Peck of his title, since by law the title had reverted back to Georgia. Peck claimed that he had good title to the Yazoo property because he had purchased the lands unaware of the original corrupt bargain. Under the common law, Peck asserted, buyers acquire good title when they are not aware that the seller gained the property fraudulently (this is called being a "holder in due course").

The Yazoo affair sparked a national controversy. Many "innocent" land purchasers, rebuffed by the Georgia legislature, turned to Congress with requests for reimbursement. When Thomas Jefferson assumed the presidency, he appointed a commission to investigate the scandal. Jefferson and his political ally James Madison hoped to encourage persons to settle the western frontier by establishing the principle that democratic governments respected vested property rights. More radical Jeffersonians opposed any government assistance for land speculators who were benefiting from a corrupt bargain.

Many investors thought that the courts provided a better forum than Congress for resolving their rights to the Yazoo lands. Fletcher v. Peck *was a collusive suit. Peck and Fletcher structured their transaction to maximize the chance of getting the Supreme Court to decide whether Georgia could constitutionally repeal the land grant. The case quickly attracted top legal and political talent. Future justice Joseph Story, future president John Quincy Adams, federal Constitutional Convention delegate Luther Martin, and Congressman Robert Harper participated. Peck won at trial, and the verdict was appealed to the Supreme Court of the United States.*

The Marshall Court unanimously held that the Georgia law rescinding the land grant unconstitutionally deprived the third-party purchasers of their property. Chief Justice Marshall's opinion declared that land grants were contracts. Therefore, laws rescinding land grants impaired the obligation of contracts. When reading this case, consider the following questions. On what basis does Chief Justice Marshall find that a state grant of land is a contract? What theory of constitutional interpretation does he employ? Is his execution of that theory sound? Consider the references to general principles discussed in the introduction to the section on the contracts clause. Is Fletcher v. Peck *an appropriate instance of natural justice? Would your opinion be different if there had been no fraud or bribery in the original transaction?*

The Supreme Court's decision in Fletcher *did not end the controversy. Resolution did not come until 1814, when Congress paid $5 million to acquire the disputed territory and settle all the private legal claims.*

CHIEF JUSTICE MARSHALL, delivered the opinion of the court as follows:

. . .

The lands in controversy vested absolutely in James Gunn and others, the original grantees, by the conveyance of the governor, made in pursuance of an act of assembly to which the legislature was fully competent. Being thus in full possession of the legal estate, they, for a valuable consideration, conveyed portions of the land to those who were willing to purchase. If the original transaction was infected with fraud, these purchasers did not participate in it, and had no notice of it. They were innocent. Yet the legislature of Georgia has involved them in the fate of the first parties to the transaction, and, if the act be valid, has annihilated their rights also.

. . .

It is not intended to speak with disrespect of the legislature of Georgia, or of its acts. Far from it. The question is a general question, and is treated as one. For although such powerful objections to a legislative grant, as are alleged against this, may not again exist, yet the principle, on which alone this rescinding act is to be supported, may be applied to every case to which it shall be the will of any legislature to apply it. The principle is this; that a legislature may, by its own act, divest the vested estate of any man whatever, for reasons which shall, by itself, be deemed sufficient. . . . [T]hose who purchased parts of [the granted land] were not stained by that guilt which infected the original transaction. Their case is not distinguishable from the ordinary case of purchasers of a legal estate without knowledge of any secret fraud which might have led to the emanation of the original grant. According to the well known course of equity, their rights could not be affected by such fraud. Their situation was the same, their title was the same, with that of every other member of the community who holds land by regular conveyances from the original patentee.

Is the power of the legislature competent to the annihilation of such title, and to a resumption of the property thus held?

The principle asserted is, that one legislature is competent to repeal any act which a former legislature was competent to pass; and that one legislature cannot abridge the powers of a succeeding legislature.

The correctness of this principle, so far as respects general legislation, can never be controverted. But, if an act be done under a law, a succeeding legislature cannot undo it. The past cannot be recalled by the most absolute power. Conveyances have been made, those conveyances have vested legal estates, and, if those estates may be seized by the sovereign authority, still, that they originally vested is a fact, and cannot cease to be a fact.

When, then, a law is in its nature a contract, when absolute rights have vested under that contract, a repeal of the law cannot divest those rights; and the act of annulling them, if legitimate, is rendered so by a power applicable to the case of every individual in the community.

It may well be doubted whether the nature of society and of government does not prescribe some limits to the legislative power; and, if any be prescribed, where are they to be found, if the property of an individual, fairly and honestly acquired, may be seized without compensation. . . .

The validity of this rescinding act, then, might well be doubted, were Georgia a single sovereign power. But Georgia cannot be viewed as a single, unconnected, sovereign power, on whose legislature no other restrictions are imposed than may be found in its own constitution. She is a part of a large empire; she is a member of the American union; and that union has a constitution the supremacy of which all acknowledge, and which imposes limits to the legislatures of the several states, which none claim a right to pass. The constitution of the United States declares that no state shall pass any bill of attainder, ex post facto law, or law impairing the obligation of contracts.

Does the case now under consideration come within this prohibitory section of the constitution?

In considering this very interesting question, we immediately ask ourselves what is a contract? Is a grant a contract? . . .

If, under a fair construction of the constitution, grants are comprehended under the term contracts, is a grant from the state excluded from the operation of the provision? Is the clause to be considered as inhibiting the state from impairing the obligation of contracts between two individuals, but as excluding from that inhibition contracts made with itself?

The words themselves contain no such distinction. They are general, and are applicable to contracts of every description. If contracts made with the state are to be exempted from their operation, the exception must arise from the character of the contracting party, not from the words which are employed.

Whatever respect might have been felt for the state sovereignties, it is not to be disguised that the framers of the constitution viewed, with some apprehension, the violent acts which might grow out of the feelings of the moment; and that the people of the United States, in adopting that instrument, have manifested a determination to shield themselves and their property from the effects of those sudden and strong passions to which men are exposed. The restrictions on the legislative power of the states are obviously founded in this sentiment; and the constitution of the United States contains what may be deemed a bill of rights for the people of each state.

No state shall pass any bill of attainder, ex post facto law, or law impairing the obligation of contracts.

A bill of attainder may affect the life of an individual, or may confiscate his property, or may do both. In this form the power of the legislature over the lives and fortunes of individuals is expressly restrained. What motive, then, for implying, in words which import a general prohibition to impair the obligation of contracts, an exception in favour of the right to impair the obligation of those contracts into which the state may enter?

The state legislatures can pass no ex post facto law. An ex post facto law is one which renders an act punishable in a manner in which it was not punishable when it was committed. Such a law may inflict penalties on the person, or may inflict pecuniary penalties which swell the public treasury. The legislature is then prohibited from passing a law by which a man's estate, or any part of it, shall be seized for a crime which was not declared, by some previous law, to render him liable to that punishment. Why, then, should violence be done to the natural meaning of words for the purpose of leaving to the legislature the power of seizing, for public use, the estate of an individual in the form of a law annulling the title by which he holds that estate? The court can perceive no sufficient grounds for making this distinction. . . .

JUSTICE JOHNSON, concurring.

In this case I entertain, on two points, an opinion different from that which has been delivered by the court.

I do not hesitate to declare that a state does not possess the power of revoking its own grants. But I do it on a general principle, on the reason and nature of things: a principle which will impose laws even on the deity.

A contrary opinion can only be maintained upon the ground that no existing legislature can abridge the powers of those which will succeed it. To a certain extent this is certainly correct; but the distinction lies between power and interest, the right of jurisdiction and the right of soil.

. . . When the legislature have once conveyed their interest or property in any subject to the individual, they have lost all control over it; have nothing to act upon; it has passed from them; is vested in the individual; becomes intimately blended with his existence, as essentially so as the blood that circulates through his system. The government may indeed demand of him the one or the other, not because they are not his, but because whatever is his is his country's. . . .

B. Religion

Constitutional debates over religion changed subtly after federal and state constitutions were ratified. Americans during the Colonial and Founding Eras debated the place of religion in a Christian commonwealth. Roger Williams, James Madison, and other proponents of religious freedom provided Christian justifications for disestablishment and the liberty of conscience. Americans during the Early National Era debated the place of religion in a constitutional republic where the vast majority of citizens were Christians. Proponents of religious freedom gave secular justifications for their preferred practices. Many proponents of test oaths and laws banning blasphemy provided more secular reasons for maintaining what had formerly been viewed as laws protecting and promoting Christianity. Americans in 1829 were still living in a Christian society. Whether American culture or American law could be described as Christian, however, was controversial, and would become even more controversial during the Second Great Awakening, the religious revival that took place in Jacksonian America.

By the early nineteenth century, a national consensus had formed that government should permit people to worship (or not worship) God in private according to their personal religious beliefs. George Washington's "Letter to the Jews of Newport" asserted that "all possess alike liberty of conscience" in the United States.[32] Proponents of religious establishments agreed that government should not regulate private religious life. One champion of test oaths in the Massachusetts Constitutional Convention maintained, "He would have no sect preferred, no restraint upon the consciences, opinions, or even caprices of men."[33]

The same consensus did not exist on rights to exemptions from otherwise valid laws. The majority of state court decisions concluded that the principle of freedom of conscience did not entitle persons to violate state laws that interfered with cherished religious practices. *Commonwealth v. Wolf* (PA 1817) is a typical instance in which state courts rejected claims that religious minorities had rights to exemptions from state laws aimed at secular goods.[34] *People v. Phillips* (NY 1813) is an important exception to the general tendency of courts to reject claims for religious exemptions.[35] In that case, a New York court declared that priests had a right not to reveal confessions. The relatively small number of cases that considered whether religious believers had constitutional rights to exemptions do not permit clear conclusions on whether *Phillips* represents a strong strand of Early National Era thinking or is best understood as an aberrant decision.

Americans debated whether to retain any religious establishments. Some constitutional decision makers insisted that "Christianity . . . is the law of our land."[36] They believed that Christian religious establishments

32. *The Papers of George Washington, Presidential Series* (edited by W. W. Abbott and Dorothy Twohig) (Charlottesville, VA: University Press of Virginia, 1987), 6: 284-86.

33. *Journal of Debates and Proceedings in the Convention of Delegates Chosen to Revise the Constitution of Massachusetts* (Boston: Office of the Daily Advertiser), 93.

34. *Commonwealth v. Wolf*, 3 Serg. & R. 48 (Sup. Ct. Penn. 1817).

35. *People v. Phillips*, Court of General Sessions, City of New York (June 14, 1813).

36. *Updegraph v. Commonwealth*, 11 Serg. & Rawle 394, 409 (Pa. 1824).

were necessary means for fostering a virtuous republican citizenry. Other Americans sought to build a "wall of separation" between church and state. Led by Thomas Jefferson, they maintained that combining government and religion corrupted both.

Proponents of religious disestablishment gained strength after the Constitution was ratified. Most states repealed constitutional provisions requiring that officeholders be devout Christians. Several abjured financial support for religious institutions. Successful champions of these reforms increasingly relied on secular arguments. Opponents of test oaths in the Massachusetts Constitutional Convention insisted, "It was an established principle that acts, not opinions, were the subject of laws."[37] Thomas Jefferson's famous "Letter to the Danbury Baptists" placed more emphasis on the liberal principle that government should regulate only action than on the Christian principle that expressions of faith should be sincere.

Thomas Jefferson, **Letter to the Danbury Baptists** (1802)[38]

Thomas Jefferson fought to limit the influence of politics on religious affairs. In contrast to Federalists, who believed state support for religion to be crucial for maintaining public morality, Jefferson and his supporters worried that state establishments fostered European-style religious persecutions. Chapter 3 discusses his responsibility for the bill that established religious freedom in Virginia. During the election of 1800, Jefferson wrote a letter to his friend Benjamin Rush asserting, "The Congregationalist and Episcopalian clergy in the United States entertained a very favorable hope of obtaining an establishment of a particular form of Christianity thro' the US." Jefferson promised to defeat such schemes. He informed Rush that he had "sworn upon the altar of god, eternal hostility against every form of tyranny over the mind of man."[39]

Jefferson expressed similar commitments to religious liberty when serving as president. Responding to a congratulatory letter from members of the Baptist Church in Connecticut, he penned the famous phrase "a wall of separation between Church and State." This phrase is often repeated in debates over the meaning of the establishment clause. Consider these words in the broader context of the letter to the Danbury Baptists. What did Jefferson mean by "a wall of separation between Church and State"? Was he merely making a literary allusion? Does that phrase or his letter provide any clear principles that might help resolve contemporary debates over prayer at school graduations or school choice programs?

Believing with you that religion is a matter which lies solely between Man & his God, that he owes account to none other for his faith or his worship, that the legitimate powers of government reach actions only, & not opinions, I contemplate with sovereign reverence that act of the whole American people which declared that their legislature should "make no law respecting an establishment of religion, or prohibiting the free exercise thereof," thus building a wall of separation between Church & State. Adhering to this expression of the supreme will of the nation in behalf of the rights of conscience, I shall see with sincere satisfaction the progress of those sentiments which tend to restore to man all his natural rights, convinced he has no natural right in opposition to his social duties. . . .

C. Guns

Many early nineteenth-century Americans revered guns. Men commonly carried guns for self-defense and as part of their obligation to serve in the militia. Proponents of states' rights celebrated the Second Amendment for ensuring the integrity of a state militia capable of defending against a potentially oppressive national government. St. George Tucker, the most important Jeffersonian constitutional treatise writer, described the "right to bear arms" protected by the Second Amendment as "the true palladium of liberty." He continued:

> The right of self defence is the first law of nature: in most governments it has been the study of rulers to confine this right within the narrowest limits possible. Wherever standing armies are kept up, and the right of the people to keep and bear arms is, under any colour or pretext whatsoever, prohibited, liberty, if not already annihilated, is on the brink of destruction.[40]

37. *Journal of Debates and Proceedings*, 88.

38. Excerpt from H. A. Washington, ed., *The Writings of Thomas Jefferson*, (Washington, DC: Taylor & Maury, 1854), 8:133.

39. Thomas Jefferson to Benjamin Rush, September 23, 1800, in *The Papers of Thomas Jefferson*, ed. Barbara Oberg (Princeton, NJ: Princeton University Press, 2005), 32:166–68.

40. St. George Tucker, *Blackstone's Commentaries: With Notes of Reference* (Union, NJ: Lawbook Exchange, 1996), 1:300.

Many elected officials feared guns. Private violence plagued towns and cities. As a result, states and localities, concerned with crime rates, passed bans on concealed weapons. The preface to a Louisiana concealed weapons law worried about "assassinations and attempts to commit the same" that "have of late been of such frequent occurrences as to become a subject of serious alarm to the peaceable and well disposed inhabitants of the state."[41] Gun owners challenged these measures as violating their constitutional right to bear arms.

The first major constitutional decision in American history on the right to bear arms protected the rights of gun owners. In *Bliss v. Commonwealth* (KY 1822), the Supreme Court of Kentucky declared a concealed weapons ban unconstitutional. "Whatever restrains the full and complete exercise of that right," the justices declared, "is forbidden by the explicit language in the constitution."

Bliss v. Commonwealth, 2 Litt. 90 (KY 1822)

Bliss appeared in public with a ceremonial sword sheathed in his cane. He was arrested and indicted under a Kentucky law that forbade persons from carrying concealed weapons. At trial, Bliss was found guilty and fined $100. He appealed to the Court of Appeals of Kentucky on the ground that the state law violated the state constitutional right to bear arms.

The court of appeals agreed with Bliss that the law was unconstitutional. The justices ruled that the state constitution forbade any legislation regulating the right to bear arms. On what basis does the court reach this conclusion? The Kentucky Constitution in 1822 granted persons the right to "bear arms in defense of themselves and the state." This language differs from that of the Second Amendment to the U.S. Constitution, which is prefaced by a reference to state militias. Does the decision by the Court of Appeals of Kentucky provide any hint about whether the precise wording of the constitutional right to bear arms influenced the judicial decision in Bliss?

[The Constitution of Kentucky] provides, "that the right of the citizens to bear arms in defense of themselves and the state, shall not be questioned."

41. Saul Cornell, *The Other Founders: Anti-Federalism and the Dissenting Tradition in America, 1788–1828* (Chapel Hill: University of North Carolina Press, 1999), 141.

The provision contained in this section, perhaps, is as well calculated to secure to the citizens the right to bear arms in defense of themselves and the state, as any that could have been adopted by the makers of the constitution. If the right be assailed, immaterial through what medium, whether by an act of the legislature or in any other form, it is equally opposed to the comprehensive import of the section. The legislature is nowhere expressly mentioned in the section; but the language employed is general, without containing any expression restricting its import to any particular department of government; and in the twenty-eighth section of the same article of the constitution, it is expressly declared, "that every thing in that article is excepted out of the general powers of government, and shall forever remain inviolate; and that all laws contrary thereto, or contrary to the constitution, shall be void."

. . .

That the provisions of the act in question do not import an entire destruction of the right of the citizens to bear arms in defense of themselves and the state, will not be controverted by the court; for though the citizens are forbid wearing weapons concealed in the manner described in the act, they may, nevertheless, bear arms in any other admissible form. But to be in conflict with the constitution, it is not essential that the act should contain a prohibition against bearing arms in every possible form—it is the right to bear arms in defense of the citizens and the state, that is secured by the constitution, and whatever restrains the full and complete exercise of that right, though not an entire destruction of it, is forbidden by the explicit language of the constitution.

Not merely all legislative acts, which purport to take it away; but all which diminish or impair it as it existed when the constitution was formed, are void.

If, therefore, the act in question imposes any restraint on the right, immaterial what appellation may be given to the act, whether it be an act regulating the manner of bearing arms or any other, the consequence, in reference to the constitution, is precisely the same, and its collision with that instrument equally obvious.

And can there be entertained a reasonable doubt but the provisions of the act import a restraint on the right of the citizens to bear arms? The court apprehends not. The right existed at the adoption of the constitution; it had then no limits short of the moral power of the citizens to exercise it, and it in fact consisted in nothing else but in the liberty of the citizens to bear arms. Diminish that liberty, therefore, and you necessarily restrain the right; and such is the diminution and restraint, which the act in question most indisputably imports, by prohibiting the citizens wearing weapons in a manner which was lawful to wear them when the constitution was adopted. In truth, the right of the citizens to bear arms, has been as directly assailed by the provisions of the act, as though they were forbid carrying guns on their shoulders, swords in scabbards, or when in conflict with an enemy, were not allowed the use of bayonets; and if the act be consistent with the constitution, it can not be incompatible with that instrument for the legislature, by successive enactments, to entirely cut off the exercise of the right of the citizens to bear arms. For, in principle, there is no difference between a law prohibiting the wearing concealed arms, and a law forbidding the wearing such as are exposed; and if the former be unconstitutional, the latter must be so likewise. . . .

D. Personal Freedom and Public Morality

Family and morals laws were not constitutionalized during the Early National Era. No significant constitutional debates took place over whether persons had a right to marry, use birth control, terminate pregnancies, or have sexual relationships outside of marriage. Few major federal or state constitutional decisions or debates seem to have taken place over whether government could regulate such personal habits as drinking or gambling. Legislation dictating who could marry whom, for example, was not subject to constitutional challenge before 1829. Courts had little difficulty sustaining statutes banning obscenity as legitimate means for ensuring a decent moral climate.

VIII. Democratic Rights

MAJOR DEVELOPMENTS

- Federalists pass, but Jeffersonians fail to renew, the Alien and Sedition Acts
- States weaken property qualifications for voting

Intense partisan conflicts broke out during the Early National Era over democratic rights. Federalists and their successors believed that constitutional politics in the United States should be modeled on English constitutional politics, abandoning only a hereditary monarch and aristocracy. They proposed national sedition laws, sought to maintain a restricted suffrage, and maintained that a person's political allegiance was determined by birth. Jeffersonians championed a more inclusive constitutional politics. They sought to expand free speech rights, reduce qualifications for voting, and provide greater opportunities for people to choose their political allegiance.

Jeffersonians enjoyed varying degrees of success in implementing their more democratic agenda. Voting became more egalitarian between 1789 and 1829. Property qualifications were replaced with less onerous taxpaying requirements or else were abandoned completely. The national government abandoned speech restrictions after 1801. Jeffersonians refused to renew the Sedition Act of 1798, Jefferson pardoned all persons convicted under that Federalist measure, and Madison resisted temptations during the War of 1812 to pass a new sedition law. State constitutional law rarely reflected the libertarian sentiments that Jeffersonians articulated when discussing national constitutional standards. Local constitutional authorities frequently punished libel, blasphemy, and obscenity. Few constitutional questions about citizenship were firmly resolved. Jeffersonians criticized Federalist judicial decisions claiming that persons had no right to expatriation, but the extent to which citizens of the United States had a constitutional right to emigrate remained unsettled.

A. Free Speech

The Early National Era witnessed bitter national and state controversies over free speech. Political leaders routinely perceived what we might think of as normal political criticism as attempts to undermine government. Federalists who controlled the national government from 1789 to 1801 were particularly prone to interpret political dissent as sedition. Most Federalists believed that ordinary persons should limit their political participation to electing virtuous people to run the government. Private political organizations and commentary were considered illegitimate attempts to interfere with the people's elected representatives. Many Jeffersonian state officials were equally sensitive to political criticism. Just as Federalists saw Jacobins (the most extreme faction of the French Revolution) behind every criticism of the Washington and Adams administrations, so to many Jeffersonians were sure that adverse commentary on Thomas Jefferson or James Madison was rooted in a secret desire to restore monarchy to the United States.

National controversies over free speech were more partisan than local controversies. Federalists believed that sedition laws were a vital means for ensuring respect for the national government. Jeffersonians insisted that the national government had no power to pass a sedition law and that sedition laws violated the First Amendment. After Jefferson took office, Federalists proposed and Jeffersonians rejected a measure that would have extended the Sedition Act of 1798. Federalists and Jeffersonians in the states were less principled. Local elected officials of all persuasions restricted political criticism.

Most governing authorities believed that persons had a constitutional right to make true criticisms of government for good reasons. The Sedition Act of 1798 considered truth a valid defense in sedition prosecutions. Such influential state court decisions as *People v. Croswell* (NY 1804)[42] endorsed the truth defense. Some commentators went further. James Madison insisted that political opinions were constitutionally protected. Tunis Wortman, the author of the first book-length study on free speech published in the United States, condemned any restriction on free speech.[43]

Madison was guided by these libertarian sentiments when he refused to call for a sedition law during the War of 1812. State judges were less libertarian. Local officials punished political commentators after juries determined that they had not published the truth for good reasons. States also prohibited obscenity. In *Commonwealth v. Sharpless* (PA 1815), the Supreme Court of Pennsylvania stated, "Actions of *public indecency* [are] always indictable, as tending to corrupt the public morals."[44]

Debate over the Sedition Act (1798–1799)

Political tensions increased during the 1790s. Newspapers were filled with scandalous, often anonymous, gossip and opinion about political leaders. Few commentators practiced any restraint when commenting on political opponents. The president of Yale asserted that Thomas Jefferson would have "the bible cast into a bonfire, . . . our wives and daughters the victims of legal prostitution."[45] Jefferson described Washington and Adams as "apostates who have gone over to [English] heresies, men who were Samsons in the field and Solomons in the council, but who have had their heads shorn by that harlot England."[46] New forms of political organization further heated up the political environment. Thomas Jefferson and James Madison organized an anti-administration faction in both Congress and the states. George Washington denounced Democratic-Republican clubs for their scrutiny and often-harsh criticism of government officials. War with France became increasingly likely. Americans were outraged when the French foreign minister demanded bribes before meeting with an American delegation sent to negotiate a new peace treaty (the XYZ Affair). With anti-French passions peaking, Federalists in Congress and the Adams administration hoped to put an end to the "factions" dividing the nation and encouraging foreign enemies.

These tensions culminated in the Sedition Act of 1798, which cracked down on speech and writings that brought the government into contempt. In keeping with Colonial and Founding Era practice, Federalists permitted truth as a defense. The Sedition Act also required that a jury determine whether a piece of writing was seditious. Federalists claimed that the law was a constitutional means for maintaining support for the government. Harrison Otis stated, "Every independent Government has a right to preserve and defend itself against injuries and outrages which endanger its existence."[47]

Adams administration officials implemented the Sedition Act immediately. The resulting prosecutions and convictions shut down several prominent Jeffersonian newspapers. Matthew Lyon of Vermont, a Jeffersonian representative in Congress, was one victim of the legislation. Sentenced to prison for criticizing the Adams administration, he became a popular hero and easily won reelection.

Jeffersonians conducted a public campaign against the Sedition Act, with the Virginia and Kentucky Resolutions of 1798 being the most visible and significant protests. These resolutions, secretly penned by James Madison and Thomas Jefferson, condemned both the Sedition Act and other

42. *People v. Croswell*, 3 Johns. Cas, 337 (N.Y. Sup. 1804).

43. Tunis Wortman, *A Treatise Concerning Political Enquiry and the Liberty of the Press* (New York: George Forman, 1800), 121.

44. *Commonwealth v. Sharpless*, 2 Serg. & Rawle 91 (Pa. 1815).

45. Stephen M. Feldman, *Free Expression and Democracy in America: A History* (Chicago: University of Chicago Press, 2008), 78.

46. *Writings of Thomas Jefferson* (see note 5), 7:76.

47. *Annals of Congress*, 5th Cong., 2nd Sess., 1798, 2:2145–48.

Federalist measures. One year later, James Madison submitted a report to the Virginia legislature that elaborated both federalism and free speech criticisms of Federalist policy. States, he insisted, had reserved the power to determine when seditious speech should be punished. Going beyond the reigning free speech orthodoxy, Madison declared that constitutional republicans must protect opinion, as well as true criticisms of public officials.

The Virginia and Kentucky Resolutions and Madison's report became celebrated touchstones of Jeffersonian political ideology and constitutional thought. Their immediate influence on free speech practice is less certain. When Jefferson assumed the presidency, he and his political allies in Congress refused to extend the Sedition Act after its expiration in 1800. This refusal suggests a commitment to free speech principles. Nevertheless, many Jeffersonians in the states, often with Jefferson's permission, prosecuted Federalists who made what they believed were unfair criticisms of Republican politicians and policies. This suggests that the principles of federalism were the more practical grounds for criticizing the Sedition Act.

When reading the following materials, think about the following interpretation of how Federalists understood popular government:

> *Federalists claimed the people "deliberated" only via their representatives in the legislature and therefore that only the legislature could authoritatively declare what public opinion was or fully participate in the political deliberations of the polity. The "representative" quality of political debate justified Federalist repression. The modern system of political deliberation, in which the people "discuss" politics via the mass media and political organizations, the Federalists argued, only empowers nonrepresentative minorities. Instead, if popular participation is restricted to the right of petition and election, methods that inform and motivate representatives without intruding directly into political deliberations, the whole people can participate equally in debate via their representatives.*[48]

Does this passage explain why Federalists supported the Sedition Act (and condemned private political clubs), even when Thomas Jefferson was president? How did Federalists understand political participation in a constitutional republic? How did opponents of the Sedition Act understand the role of political participation in a constitutional republic?

The Report of a Select Committee on the Petitions Praying for a Repeal of the Alien and Sedition Laws (1799)[49]

. . .

. . . [A] law to punish false, scandalous, and malicious writings against the Government, with the intent to stir up sedition, is a law necessary for carrying into effect the power vested by the Constitution in the Government of the United States, and in the departments and officers thereof, and, consequently, such a law as Congress may pass; because the direct tendency of such writings is to obstruct the acts of the Government by exciting opposition to them, to endanger its existence by rendering it odious and contemptible in the eyes of the people, and to produce seditious combinations against the laws, the power to punish which has never been questioned; because it would be manifestly absurd to suppose that a Government might punish sedition, and yet be void of power to prevent it by punishing those acts which plainly and necessarily lead to it; and, because, under the general power to make all laws proper and necessary for carrying into effect the powers vested by the Constitution in the Government of the United States, Congress has passed many laws for which no express provision can be found in the Constitution, and the constitutionality of which has never been questioned, such as the first section of the act now under consideration for punishing seditious combinations. . . .

. . . [T]he liberty of the press consists not in a license for every man to publish what he pleases without being liable for punishment, if he should abuse this license to the injury of others, but in a permission to publish, without previous restraint, whatever he may think proper, being answerable to the public and individuals, for any abuse of this permission to their prejudice. In like manner, as the liberty speech does not authorize a man to speak malicious slanders

48. James P. Martin, "When Repression Is Democratic and Constitutional: The Federalist Theory of Representation and the Sedition Act of 1798," *University of Chicago Law Review* 66 (1999): 117.

49. Excerpt taken from *Annals of Congress*, 5th Cong., 3rd Sess., 1799, 2986–90.

against his neighbor, nor the liberty of action justify him in going, by violence, into another man's house, or in assaulting any person whom he may meet in the streets. In the several States the liberty of the press has always been understood in this manner, and no other. . . .

. . .

. . . [H]ad the Constitution intended to prohibit Congress from legislating at all on the subject of the press, which is the construction whereon the objections to this law are founded, it would have used the same expressions as in that part of the clause which relates to religion and religious laws; whereas, the words are wholly different: "Congress," says the Constitution, . . . "shall make no law respecting the establishment of religion, or prohibiting the free exercise thereof, or abridging the freedom of speech or the press." Here it is manifest that the Constitution intended to prohibit Congress from legislating on all the subjects of religious establishments, and the prohibition is made in the most express terms. Had the same intention prevailed respecting the press, the same expressions would have been used, and Congress would have been "prohibited from passing a law respecting the press." They are not, however, "prohibited" from legislating at all on the subject, but merely from abridging the liberty of the press. . . . Its liberty, according to the well known and universally admitted definition, consists in permission to publish, without previous restraint upon the press, but subject to punishment afterwards for improper publications. A law, therefore, to impose previous restraint upon the press, and not one to inflict punishment on wicked and malicious publications, would be a law to abridge the liberty of the press, and, as such, unconstitutional.

James Madison, Virginia Report of 1799[50]

. . .

The freedom of the press under the common law; is, in the defences of the sedition-act, made to consist in an exemption from all *previous* restraint on printed publications, by persons authorized to inspect and prohibit them. It appears to the committee, that this idea of the freedom of the press, can never be admitted to be the American idea of it: since a law inflicting penalties on printed publications, would have a similar effect with a law authorizing a previous restraint on them. . . .

In the British government, the danger of encroachments on the rights of the people, is understood to be confined to the executive magistrate. . . . Hence . . . all the ramparts for protecting the rights of the people, such as the magna charta, their bill of rights, etc., are not reared against the parliament, but against the royal prerogative. . . . Under such a government as this, an exemption of the press from previous restraint by licensers appointed by the king, is all the freedom that can be secured to it.

In the United States, the case is altogether different. The people, not the government, possess the absolute sovereignty. The legislature, no less than the executive, is under limitations of power. Encroachments are regarded as possible from the one, as well as from the other. Hence, in the United States, the great and essential rights of the people are secured against legislative, as well as against executive ambition. . . .

The state of the press, therefore, under the common law, cannot, in this point of view, be the standard of its freedom in the United States.

. . .

The nature of governments elective, limited, and responsible, in all their branches, may well be supposed to require a greater freedom of animadversion than might be tolerated by the genius of such a government as that of Great Britain. In the latter, it is a maxim, that the king . . . can do no wrong. . . . In the United States, the executive magistrates are not held to be infallible, nor the legislatures to be omnipotent; and both being elective, are both responsible. Is it not natural and necessary, under such different circumstances, that a different degree of freedom, in the use of the press, should be contemplated?

. . .

The practice of America must be entitled to much more respect. In every state, probably, in the Union, the press has exerted a freedom in canvassing the merits and measures of public men, of every description, which has not been confined to the strict limits of the common law. On this footing, the freedom of the press has stood; on this footing it yet stands. . . .

. . .

50. Excerpt taken from *The Virginia Report of 1799–1800, Touching the Alien and Sedition Laws* (Richmond, VA: J. W. Randolph, 1850), 210–27.

Is then the federal government, it will be asked, destitute of every authority for restraining the licentiousness of the press, and for shielding itself against the libelous attacks which may be made on those who administer it?

The Constitution alone can answer the question. If no such power be expressly delegated, and it be not both necessary and proper to carry into execution an express power; above all, if it be expressly forbidden by a declaratory amendment to the Constitution, the answer must be, that the federal government is destitute of all such authority.

. . .

Let it be recollected, lastly, that the right of electing members of the government, constitutes more particularly the essence of a free and responsible government. The value and efficacy of this right, depends on the knowledge of the comparative merits and demerits of the candidates for public trust; and on the equal freedom, consequently, of examining and discussing these merits and demerits of the candidates respectively. It has been seen, that a number of important elections will take place whilst the act is in force. . . . Should there happen, then, as is extremely probable in relation to some or other of the branches of the government, to be competitions between those who are and those who are not, members of the government, what will be the situations of the competitors? Not equal; because the characters of the former will be covered by the "sedition-act" from animadversions exposing them to disrepute among the people; whilst the latter may be exposed to contempt and hatred of the people, without violation of the act. What will be the situation of the people? Not free; because they will be compelled to make their election between competitors, whose pretensions they are not permitted, by the act, equally to examine, to discuss, and to ascertain. And from both situations, will not those in power derive an undue advantage for continuing themselves in it; which by impairing the right of election, endangers the blessings of the government founded on it?

B. Voting

Between 1789 and 1828, Americans moved toward universal white male suffrage. As Figures 4-2a and 4-2b illustrate, property qualifications were abandoned as the Early National Era progressed. Congress in 1811 permitted all taxpayers who lived in the Northwest Territories to vote in territorial elections. Many states similarly reformed their suffrage laws. A growing consensus emerged that productive persons who paid taxes were as good republican citizens as persons who owned land. Some states eliminated property qualifications entirely.

Numerous partisan struggles took place over voting rights. Federalists and their successors insisted that property qualifications and a restricted suffrage were vital means for protecting property rights and promoting the public good. One representative to the Massachusetts Constitutional Convention declared,

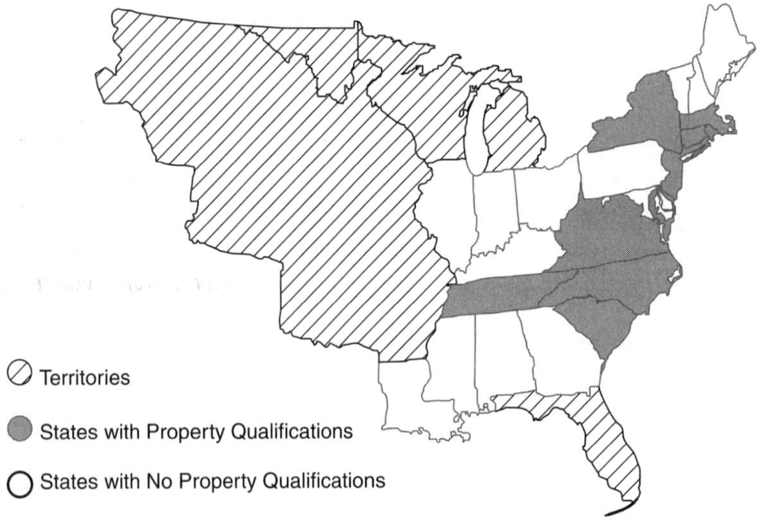

Figure 4-2a Property Qualifications for Suffrage, 1820

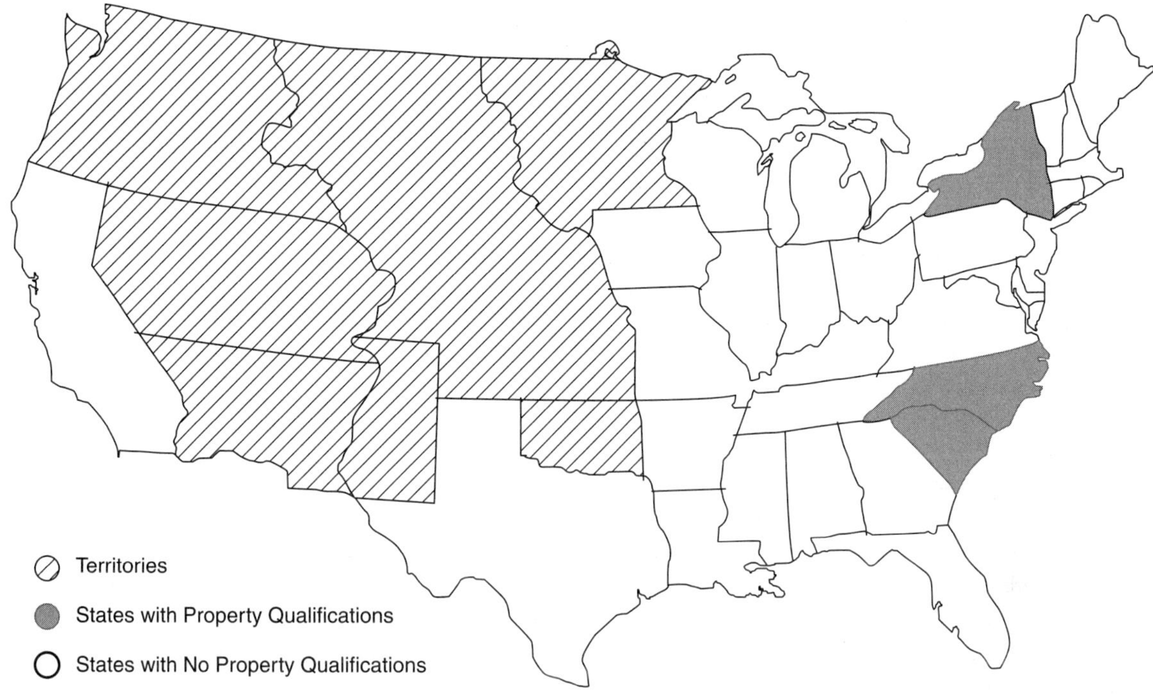

Figure 4-2b Property Qualifications for Suffrage, 1850

"It was . . . wholly inequitable in its nature, that men without a dollar should, in any way, determine the rights of property."[51] Jeffersonians responded that men who fought in the Revolution and against the British during the War of 1812 ought to have access to the ballot. Many linked taxation to representation. "[T]here ought to be a representation on the foundation of equality," another representative responded. "This could not be, so long as any people, who are taxed, do not vote."[52]

Massachusetts Debates Property Qualifications (1820)[53]

In 1820 Massachusetts held a convention to revise the state constitution. Such constitutional conventions were common in the early nineteenth century and throughout American history. State constitutions in the United States are regularly amended, revised, and replaced. Many constitutional conventions in the Early National Era considered suffrage reform. Debates were particularly lively in Massachusetts. The Massachusetts Constitution of 1780 limited voting in state senate elections to persons with a freehold worth £60 and required that voters in elections for the lower house be property holders. Many delegates believed those qualifications too restrictive. They preferred either a taxpayer qualification or no economic qualification. The convention eventually substituted a taxpayer qualification for the property qualification.

Many participants in the debate over voting qualifications relied heavily on arguments drawn from republican principles. Why do proponents of property qualifications think restrictions on the suffrage consistent with republicanism? Why do opponents of restrictions disagree? Imagine that you are engaged in an argument about property qualifications. Would you rely on similar or different arguments than those voiced in 1820?

REVEREND EDMUND FOSTER (Littleton)

. . . Men in this Commonwealth become freemen when they arrive at twenty-one years of age; and why oblige them to buy their freedom? They perform militia duty—they pay a tax for all they possess, that is, their polls. . . . Men who have no property are put in

51. *Journal of Debates and Proceedings in the Convention of Delegates Chosen to Revise the Constitution of Massachusetts* (Boston: Boston Daily Advertiser), 247.

52. Ibid., 124.

53. Excerpt taken from ibid., 247–57.

the situation of the slaves of Virginia; they ought to be saved from the degrading feelings.

WARREN DUTTON (Boston)

... He thought it expedient to retain the [freehold] qualification in the constitution. It was in the nature of a privilege, and, as such, it was connected with many virtues, which conduced to the good order of society. It was a distinction to be sought for; it was the reward of good conduct. It encouraged industry, economy and prudence; it elevated the standard of all our civil institutions, and gave dignity and importance to those who chose, and those who were chosen. It acted as a stimulus to exertion to acquire what it was a distinction to possess. He maintained that in this country, where the means of subsistence were so abundant, and the demand for labor so great, every man of sound body could acquire the necessary qualification. If he failed to do this, it must be, ordinarily, because he was indolent or vicious.... He also considered it as unreasonable, that a man who had no property should act indirectly upon the property of others. If gentlemen would look to the statute book, to the business of the Legislature, or to the courts of law, how much of all that was done, would be found to relate to the rights of property. It lay at the foundation of the social state, it was the spring of all action and all employment. It was therefore... wholly inequitable in its nature, that men without a dollar should, in any way, determine the rights of property, or have any concern in its appropriation. He also contended, that the principle of the resolution was anti-republican. It greatly increased the number of voters and those of a character most liable to be improperly influenced or corrupted....

GEORGE BLAKE (Boston)

... Life was as dear to a poor man as to a rich man; so was liberty. Every subject therefore, involving only life and liberty, could be acted upon, with as good authority, by the poor as by the rich....

JOSIAH QUINCY (Boston)

... [Mr. Blake's] principle was this.... "Every man, whose life and liberty is made liable to the laws, ought therefore to have a voice, in the choice of his legislators." Grant this argument to be just. Is it not equally applicable to women and to minors? ... The denial of this right to them shows, that the principle is not just....

... The theory of our constitution is, that extreme poverty ... is inconsistent with independence. It therefore assumes a qualification of a very low amount, which, according to its theory, is the lowest consistent with independence....

... Everything indicates that the destinies of the country will eventuate in the establishment of a great manufacturing interest in the Commonwealth. There is nothing in the condition of our country, to prevent manufacturers from being absolutely dependent upon their employers, here as they are everywhere else. The whole body of every manufacturing establishment, therefore, are dead votes, counted by the head, by their employer. Let the gentlemen from the country consider, how it may affect their rights, liberties and properties, if in every county of this Commonwealth there should arise... one, two, or three manufacturing establishments, each sending... from one to eight hundred votes to the polls depending on the will of one employer.

HOLDER SLOCUM (Dartmouth)

... Taxation and representation should go hand and hand. Take this text and apply it to the men who are excluded by this qualification from the rights of voting. Who are they? The laboring parts of society? How long have they been fettered? Forty years? Who achieved our independence? This class of men. And shall we then disenfranchise them? I hope not.... If a man was a Newton or a Locke, if he is poor, he may stand by and see his liberties voted away. Suppose an invasion should happen—these men would be obliged to come forward in defense of their country. He felt conscientiously bound to give them the right of voting....

IX. Equality

MAJOR DEVELOPMENTS

- Strong animus against class legislation
- State courts rule that free African Americans are not citizens of the United States

Americans during the Early National Era faced the challenge of implementing constitutional commitments to the proposition that "all men are created equal" in a society marked by substantial inequalities. Many Americans invoked egalitarian values when challenging legal practices they believed gave special privileges to some citizens or imposed special burdens on others. Jeffersonians made egalitarian claims when weakening religious establishments and undermining property qualifications for voting. State courts invoked constitutional commitments to equality when striking down local regulations that judges believed unfairly provided special advantages to some citizens or unique disabilities to others. Radicals suggested that these constitutional commitments to equality justified emancipating slaves, giving women political rights, and improving the status of Native Americans. Most Americans were more complacent. They thought that laws treating people differently on the basis of race, gender, or ethnicity were justified by real differences between white men, on the one hand, and women, blacks, and Native Americans on the other. Many liberalizing trends from the Founding Era slowed, stalled, or were reversed during the early years of the American republic.

A. Equality Under Law

Jeffersonian Republicans celebrated a constitutional commitment to equality under law. They believed that such Federalist proposals as the national bank were inconsistent with constitutional requirements that government not give special privileges to any class of citizens. Thomas Jefferson's first inaugural address declared that government should entertain "a due sense of our equal right to the use of our own faculties, to the acquisitions of our own industry, to honor and confidence from our fellow-citizens, resulting not from birth, but from our actions and their sense of them." Jefferson called on his fellow citizens to support "equal and exact justice to all men, of whatever state or persuasion, religious or political."

Jeffersonian decision makers developed constitutional doctrines that facilitated this commitment to "equal and exact justice to all men." Several state courts declared unconstitutional legislation that judges believed arbitrarily distinguished between equal citizens. *Holden v. James* (MA 1814) voided a Massachusetts law that granted specific persons exemptions from state laws. "An act conferring upon any one citizen, privileges to the prejudice of another, and which is not applicable to others, in like circumstances," the Supreme Court of Vermont in *Ward v. Bernard* (VT 1815) agreed, "does not enter into the idea of municipal law, having no relation to the community in general."[54]

54. *Ward v. Bernard*, 1 Aik. 121 (VT 1815).

Holden v. James, 11 Mass. 396 (1814)

Moses Holden believed that he was entitled to some money from the estate of Amos Ranger. Eleazer James, the administrator of that estate, disagreed. Massachusetts law permitted lawsuits against an administrator of an estate only within four years of the person taking that office. Such a restriction is called a statute of limitations and remains quite common. The purpose of such statutes is to prevent people from bringing lawsuits long after the details of events are forgotten. James became the administrator of the Ranger estate in December 1806. In 1813, the Massachusetts legislature passed a law that suspended the statute of limitations only with respect to the claim Holden had against James. James insisted that the legislature had no power to pass that law. In his view, the Massachusetts Constitution permitted elected officials to repeal the statute of limitations but not to pass a law granting a specific person an exemption from an otherwise general law.

The Supreme Judicial Court of Massachusetts declared unconstitutional Holden's exemption from the statute of limitations. Justice Jackson ruled that legislation exempting one person from a legal requirement unconstitutionally gave "special privileges" to a particular individual. His opinion emphasizes the differences between the American and English forms of government. What are those differences? How did Jackson's conception of those differences influence his opinion?

JUSTICE JACKSON, delivered the opinion of the Court.

. . .

The principles of our government are widely different [from England] in this particular. Here the sovereign and absolute power resides in the people; and the legislature can only exercise what is delegated to them according to the constitution. It is obvious that the exercise of the power in question would be equally oppressive to the subject, and subversive of his right to protection, "according to standing laws," whether exercised by one man or by a number of men. It cannot be supposed that the people, when adopting this general principle from the *English* bill of rights, and inserting it in our constitution, intended to bestow, by implication, on the General Court one of the most odious and oppressive prerogatives of the ancient kings of *England*. It is manifestly contrary to the first principles of civil liberty and natural justice, and to the spirit of our constitution and laws, that any one citizen should enjoy privileges and advantages which are denied to all others under like circumstances; or that any one should be subjected to losses, damages, suits, or actions, from which all others, under like circumstances, are exempted.

There is no doubt that the legislature may suspend a law, or the execution or operation of a law, whenever they shall think it expedient. But in such case, the law thus suspended will have no effect or operation whatever during the time for which it is so suspended.... So the privilege and benefit of the writ of *habeas corpus* may be suspended by the legislature, under the circumstances mentioned in the constitution. But it was never supposed that it could be suspended as to certain individuals by name, and left to be enjoyed by all the other citizens....

B. Race

The United States became a more racially stratified society during the Early National Era. When the Constitution was ratified, most political elites believed that slavery was a necessary evil and hoped that human bondage would eventually disappear. Few thought seriously about the legal and constitutional status of free blacks. Some Americans in the following years insisted that governing authorities promote emancipation and treat free blacks as equal citizens. Far more political elites articulated explicit constitutional commitments to white supremacy. Constitutional decision makers maintained that real racial differences justified keeping blacks in bondage, required that any program for emancipation be combined with measures for returning freed slaves to Africa, and supported laws denying fundamental rights to free persons of color. The Jeffersonians who were most likely to invoke egalitarian norms in debates between different groups of white persons were, if anything, more racist than more elitist Federalists.

Federal laws encapsulate the legal and constitutional status of free blacks during this period. The First Congress in 1790 indicated that black citizens were undesirable by limiting naturalization to "free white person[s]." The Fugitive Slave Act of 1793 permitted slaveholders to recover alleged runaways merely by obtaining a certificate from a local magistrate. Congress refused to provide blacks alleged to be slaves with any procedural protections. White persons' property rights trumped black persons' rights to due process and freedom. The Missouri Compromise in 1820 recognized that slavery was likely to be an enduring institution. Congress sought to maintain a permanent balance between the slave and free states by permitting slavery in territories south of the 36°30′ parallel line (the southern border of Missouri) and banning slavery in the territories north of that line. Slaveholders in 1820 insisted they had a constitutional right to bring slaves into American territories. Many

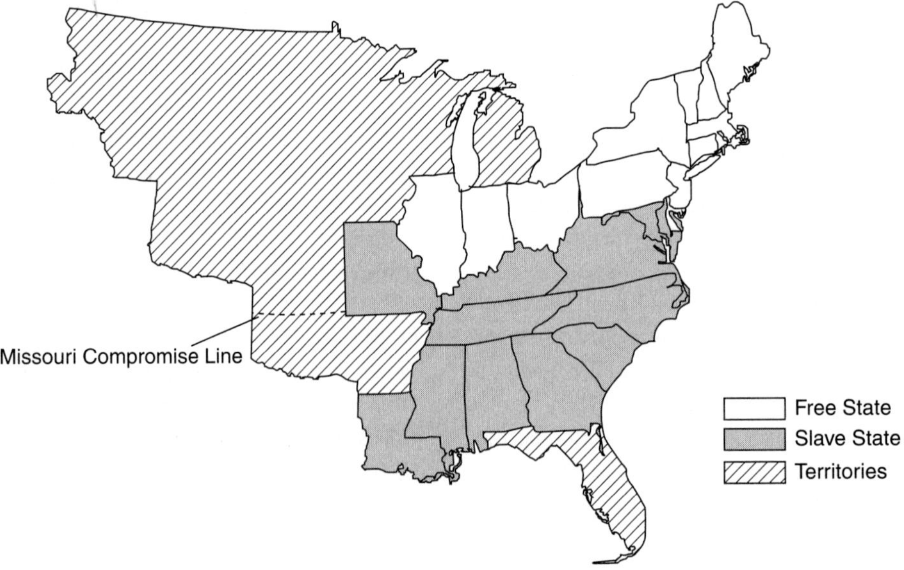

Figure 4-3 Missouri Compromise: Slave States, Free States, and Territories

supported the final compromise only because they believed the northern regions of the Louisiana Purchase unlikely to be settled for the foreseeable future.

Congressional Debate over the Missouri Compromise (1818–1821)[55]

Sectional tensions intensified in 1818 when the people of the Missouri Territory petitioned Congress for admission into the Union. Representative James Tallmadge of New York proposed that Missouri be admitted only if the state agreed to pass laws mandating the gradual emancipation of slavery. Several days later, Representative John Taylor of New York proposed banning slavery in the Arkansas Territory. In the days and months that followed, many Americans feared that the quarrels over these proposals would destroy the national union.

Congress eventually reached a series of compromises. Both Missouri and Maine were admitted to the Union at the same time. Their joint admission maintained the balance in the Senate between the free and slave states. Many people perceived this equality to be a vital procedural guarantee for slavery, since slaveholders, by voting as a bloc, could prevent any perceived anti-slavery measure from becoming law. Free- and slave-state representatives also agreed to divide the remaining territories. The Missouri Compromise prohibited slavery in the Louisiana Territory north of latitude 36°30′, the southern border of Missouri. Slavery remained legal in territories below that line.

Participants in the Missouri controversy bitterly disputed whether persons had a constitutional right to bring slaves into the territories. Representatives from the free states pointed to Article IV, Section 3 of the Constitution, which states, "The Congress shall have Power to dispose of and make all needful Rules and Regulations respecting the Territory . . . belonging to the United States." They interpreted this clause as empowering the national legislature to ban slavery in American territories. Thomas Morril of New Hampshire stated, "Congress have a right and power to prohibit slavery in every territory within its dominion."[56] Southern representatives claimed that the Constitution recognized the right to bring slaves into territories. "I have an equal right with my worthy friend from Pennsylvania," Richard Johnson of Kentucky declared, "to remove with my property (slaves and all) to Missouri, a common property, purchased with the money of the whole people."[57]

The following are two brief excerpts from the debate over the Missouri Compromise. What arguments did Alexander Smyth of Virginia make in favor of the right to bring slaves into the territories? What is the relationship between those arguments and various arguments made about property and equality during the Early National Era? Why did Timothy Fuller of Massachusetts insist that Congress had the power to ban slavery in the territories? Whose definition of "republicanism" is most consistent with American constitutional understandings in 1820?

Many Americans soon regarded the Missouri Compromise as sacred legislation. What is the significance of the Missouri Compromise? Does the Compromise establish the principle that Congress may abolish slavery in all territories or only in some territories? Most southerners voted for the compromise only because they believed the northern territories unlikely to be settled in the foreseeable future. That assumption was mistaken. Does this indicate only that southern representatives made a bargain that turned out badly? Might the Missouri Compromise stand for the principle that slavery could be prohibited in territories only when southerners agreed to waive perceived constitutional rights to settle those regions?

REPRESENTATIVE ALEXANDER SMYTH (Virginia, Republican)

. . .

Has the power to legislate over slavery been delegated to the United States? It has not. Has it been prohibited to the States? It has not. Then it is reserved to the States, respectively, or to the people. . . . And any attempt by Congress to deprive them of this reserved power, will be unjust, tyrannical, unconstitutional, and void.

The only condition that may constitutionally be annexed to the admission of a new State is, that its constitution shall be republican. . . .

. . .

The people of each of the States who adopted the Constitution, except Massachusetts, owned slaves, yet they certainly considered their own constitutions to be republican. . . .

55. Excerpt taken from *Annals of Congress*, 16th Cong., 1st Sess., 1820, 35:993–98, 36:1467–70.

56. *Annals of Congress*, 16th Cong., 1st Sess., 1820, 35:137–38.

57. *Annals of Congress*, 16th Cong., 1st Sess., 1820, 35:351–52.

The Constitution recognizes the right to the slave property, and it thereby appears that it was intended, by the Convention and by the people, that that property should be secure.

. . .

. . . [T]he adoption of the proposition on your table[58] . . . would be a direct violation of the Constitution, which provides that "no person shall be deprived of property without due process of law; nor shall private property be taken for public use without just compensation." If you cannot take property even for public use, without just compensation, you certainly have not power to take it away for the purpose of annihilation, without compensation. . . . You cannot force the people to give up their property. You cannot force a portion of the people to emancipate their slaves.

. . .

. . . It is a principle of the Constitution that no advantage shall be given to some of the States over others. . . . It is a sacred duty of Congress to do equal and impartial justice to every part of the Union.

. . . If $15,000,000 of the money raised by taxes paid by the whole people, are appropriated to purchase a territory, is it just to exclude therefrom the inhabitants of a part of the States? The inhabitants of the slave-holding States being slaveholders, you exclude them, if you exclude their slaves, as effectually as you would exclude married men by a law that children and married women should not come into the territory. . . .

Shall the slaveholders be declared incapable of holding any share of the territory purchased with the money of the whole people? Have they not contributed their full proportion of the money paid for the territory? . . .

REPRESENTATIVE TIMOTHY FULLER (Massachusetts, Republican)

. . .

. . . If we proclaim the glorious truth, that "all men are born free and equal" in our constitutions, and, while acting under them, forge the chains of millions of our unoffending species, can we expect to escape derision and contempt? . . .

. . .

. . . [N]othing is more easily demonstrated, than that the establishment of slavery is a direct violation of the very first principle of republican government—political equality. . . . While they remain territories, . . . we may prohibit slavery by an act of legislation; our power being equivalent by the third section, fourth article, to that of the State Legislature. . . .

. . .

The authority of the General Government over the Territories, while they remain such, is very extensive; "to make all needful rules and regulations respecting them," comprehending legislative and executive jurisdiction. . . .

. . .

[Fuller then emphasized the provision in the Northwest Ordinance prohibiting slavery in the Northwest Territories as proof that Congress had the power to ban slavery in the territories acquired by the Louisiana Purchase.]

C. Gender

Americans during the Early National Era became committed to "separate spheres" for men and women. Proponents of "separate spheres" insisted that men and women were equal republican citizens but that perceived natural differences between the sexes justified giving each different rights and responsibilities. Men were responsible for public affairs; women were responsible for private affairs. Supreme Court Justice James Wilson expressed the emerging conventional wisdom when he declared:

> You have, indeed, heard much of public government and public law: but these things were not made for themselves: they were made for something better; and of that something better, you form the better part—I mean society—I mean particularly domestic society: there the lovely and accomplished woman shines with superior luster.[59]

Married women remained *femes covert*, women whose legal status was determined entirely by their spouse's status. *Martin v. Commonwealth* (MA 1805) held that married men could suffer legal consequences for fleeing the United States during the American Revolution, but married women, who had an obligation to follow their husbands, could not.[60]

---

58. Smyth is referring to the proposed emancipation of slaves in Missouri. Other slaveholders made the same argument with respect to the emancipation of slaves in the territories.

59. James Wilson, *The Works of James Wilson*, ed. James DeWitt Andrews (Chicago: Callaghan and Co., 1896), 1:30–31.

60. *Martin v. Commonwealth*, 1 Mass 347 (1805).

Voices for greater gender equality could be heard. In 1792 Mary Wollstonecraft published *A Vindication of the Rights of Women*, which many feminists consider the first important defense of women's rights. Wollstonecraft was English, but her arguments circulated in the United States. American proponents of greater gender equality often championed increased educational opportunities for women. Some educated women demanded political rights. Priscilla Mason, one of the first graduates of the Young Ladies Academy in Philadelphia, called for "equal participation in honor and office." Mason believed that women and men were different, but that gender differences supported greater female participation in public life:

> But supposing now that we possessed all the talents of the orator, in the highest perfection; where shall we find a theater for the display of them? The Church, the Bar, and the Senate are shut against us. Who shut them? Man; despotic man, first made us incapable of the duty, and then forbid us the exercise. Let us by suitable education, qualify ourselves for those high departments—they will open before us.[61]

X. Criminal Justice

MAJOR DEVELOPMENTS

- The Supreme Court narrowly defines treason
- State courts permit constables and private persons to make warrantless arrests and search private places for illegal goods on the condition that they may be sued for false imprisonment and trespass if the victim of their search is innocent
- Judges and juries dispute whether juries in criminal trials may determine the law as well as the facts

Americans in the Early National Era were determined to establish a republican system of criminal justice. The national and state bills of rights promised a criminal process structured by formal procedures and respect for individual rights. Keeping these promises proved more difficult than placing good language in constitutional texts. Due process was difficult to achieve in a society with few professional police officers, fewer prosecutors, and even fewer defense attorneys. Most criminal defendants were tried almost immediately after arrest in proceedings that lacked most constitutional formalities.

Questions about constitutional criminal justice occupied the national stage only during two major political trials. The first were the trials of persons accused of violating the Sedition Act of 1798. During these trials Jeffersonians accused Federalists of violating the constitutional rights of criminal defendants in order to imprison critics of Federalist officeholders. The second trials were of persons accused of being members of the Burr conspiracy, a plot allegedly aimed at securing the independence of the western states under the leadership of former vice president Burr. During these trials Federalists regularly accused President Thomas Jefferson of violating the constitutional rights of criminal defendants in order to imprison his political rivals.

A. Due Process and Habeas Corpus

The Supreme Court in *Ex parte Bollman* (1807) forged a subtle link between habeas corpus and due process. Chief Justice John Marshall freed two alleged participants in the Burr conspiracy because he determined that Jefferson did not have sufficient evidence to prove that the two had committed treason. *Bollman* held that government officials cannot imprison or detain people on the ground that they have committed a crime when no evidence exists that they have actually committed the crime in question. The due process clause does not permit people to be tried or convicted of crimes in the absence of sufficient evidence. If a person is imprisoned for a crime for which the government does not have sufficient evidence, then that person can obtain a writ of habeas corpus to vindicate his or her due process right. Future generations debated what other due process rights could be vindicated by habeas corpus appeals.

Criminal trials in the early nineteenth century were similar in theory and practice to criminal trials during the Colonial and Founding Eras. In theory, all parties were committed to due process of law. All criminal defendants had a constitutional right to notice of the charges against them and an opportunity to rebut those charges. *United States v. Gooding* (1827) suggested that the prosecution in a criminal trial bears

61. Priscilla Mason, "Salutatory Oration," in *The Rise and Progress of the Young Ladies Academy of Philadelphia* (Philadelphia: Stewart and Cochran, 1794), 90–93.

the burden of proof. In rendering an opinion in this case, Justice Joseph Story wrote, "The general rule of our jurisprudence is, that the party accused need not establish his innocence; but it is for the government itself to prove his guilt, before it is entitled to a verdict or conviction." In practice, most criminal trials remained brief and informal. Some evidence suggests that many trial judges made sincere efforts to enforce constitutional norms. Still, with rare exceptions, persons suspected of crimes did not have the knowledge or resources necessary to assert or realize their right to due process.

B. Search and Seizure

Early search and seizure cases explored the conditions under which any person could search and arrest persons suspected of crimes. Very few communities had professional police forces. Town constables had no more privileges than ordinary citizens. *Mayo v. Wilson* (1817) treated as reasonable any search that successfully identified a criminal. Persons who made false arrests were subject to lawsuits. Under this rule, you are free to physically detain a movie star whom you see shoplifting. If, however, he or she was given the merchandise by management, you can be sued. As the Supreme Court of New Hampshire said in *Mayo*, "He who arrests upon suspicion must take care that his cause of suspicion be such, as will bear the test, for otherwise he may be punishable for false imprisonment."

Mayo v. Wilson, 1 N.H. 53 (1817)

James Wilson and Simeon Dodge were constables in Francestown, New Hampshire. On Sunday, March 3, 1816, they stopped Solomon Mayo, who was travelling in a sleigh loaded with commercial goods. Mayo sued Wilson and Dodge for trespass and false arrest because they did not have an arrest warrant. He insistrf that the state constitution permitted arrests only when persons had a warrant from a magistrate. Wilson and Dodge claimed they did not need a warrant because New Hampshire law permitted them to arrest any person suspected of traveling unnecessarily on Sunday.

Chief Justice Richardson claimed that the search was constitutional. His opinion ruled that the New Hampshire Constitution should be interpreted according to the common law, which permitted persons to make arrests without warrants under certain conditions. What were those conditions? Chief Justice Richardson declares that any person may arrest a person he or she sees engaging in a crime. May private persons make arrests in other circumstances? What did the New Hampshire court consider the point of the warrant requirement to be?

CHIEF JUSTICE RICHARDSON delivered the opinion of the Court.

. . .

By the 15th article of the bill of rights prefixed to the constitution of this state, it is declared that "no subject shall be arrested, imprisoned, despoiled or deprived of his property, immunities or privileges, put out of the protection of the law, exiled, or deprived of his life, liberty or estate, but by the judgment of his peers, or the law of the land." By the 19th article of the same bill of rights, it is declared "that every subject hath a right to be secure from all unreasonable searches and seizures of his person, his house, his papers and all his possessions. Therefore all warrants to search suspected places, or arrest a person for examination or trial in prosecutions, for criminal matters are contrary to this right, if the cause or foundation of them be not previously supported by oath or affirmation." . . . And we have no doubt that the phrase *by the law of the land* in our constitution, means the same thing as *by due process of law.*

. . .

There is a sound and safe rule for the construction of statutes, which it is believed will enable us to determine with great certainty, the true meaning of these clauses in the constitution, and that is, if a statute make use of a word, the meaning of which is well known at common law, the word shall be understood in the statute, in the same sense it was understood at common law. . . . The clause in our constitution now under consideration happens to be a literal translation from *Magna Carta*. . . . The phrase "per legem terræ" [by the law of the land] in Magna Carta, has a meaning as fixed and as well determined as any phrase known in the common law. The makers of the constitution having adopted a phrase from Magna Carta, the meaning of which in that instrument was so well known must be intended to have used it in the same sense in which it has always been understood to have been used there. . . . [P]rocess of law for the purpose of an arrest is two fold, either by the king's writ, or by what is called a warrant in law. . . . [A] warrant in law is again two fold, *viz.* 1. a warrant in deed by authority of a legal magistrate, or 2. that which each private person is invested with and may exercise. [The following are] the cases where the law warrants a private person to arrest and imprison another. 1. If a man is present when another commits treason, felony or notorious breach of the peace, he has a right instantly to arrest and commit him, lest he should escape. 2. If an affray be made to the breach of the peace, any present may during the continuance of the affray by warrant in law restrain any of the offenders, but if the affray be over there must be an express warrant. 3. If one man dangerously wound another, any person may arrest him, that he be safely kept, till it be known whether the person shall die or not. 4. Suspicion also, when it is violent and strong is in many cases a good cause of imprisonment, but he who arrests upon suspicion must take care that his cause of suspicion be such, as will bear the test, for otherwise he may be punishable for false imprisonment. 5. A watchman may arrest a night walker at unseasonable hours by the common law. But with respect to persons arrested by private authority, there must be an information on oath before a magistrate, and a commitment thereon in a reasonable time, which is esteemed twenty-four hours, otherwise the person is to be no longer detained.... It seems clear that an arrest if authorized by the statute or common law, though without writ or warrant in deed, has always been considered in *England* as warranted *per legem terræ*, by due process of law, within the meaning of *magna carta*, and we have no doubt, that any arrest here authorized by our common or statute law must be considered an arrest by the law of the land, by due process, within the meaning of our constitution. We think that the 15th article in our bill of rights, was not intended to abridge the power of the legislature, but to assert the right of every citizen to be secure from all arrests not warranted by law.

...

The second article of the bill of rights declares, that all men have certain natural, essential, inherent rights, among which are the enjoying and defending life and liberty, and acquiring, possessing and defending property; but the third article declares, that, when men enter into a state of society, they surrender up some of their natural rights to that society. All society is founded upon the principle, that each individual shall submit to the will of the whole. When we become members of society, then, we surrender our natural right, to be governed by our own wills in every case, where our own wills would lead us counter to the general will. We agree to conform our actions to the rules prescribed by the whole, and we agree to pay the forfeiture, which the general will may impose upon the violation of those rules, whether it be the loss of property, of liberty, or of life. Upon this agreement rests all legitimate government, and the general will duly expressed is alone law. The people of this state have formed a constitution in which they have agreed upon the manner in which the public will shall be expressed, and upon the extent, to which individuals shall surrender their natural rights: and the people being the fountain of all power, and the constitution their will duly expressed, it is clear that the constitution is a part of the law of the land paramount to all other laws.

By the constitution, the power to declare the general will is confided to a general court. "Full power and authority are hereby given and granted to said general court from time to time to make, ordain and establish all manner of wholesome and reasonable laws, statutes, ordinances, directions and instructions, either with penalties or without, so as the same be not repugnant or contrary to this constitution." The people of this state seem to have been extremely anxious that their natural rights should be surrendered only to the will of the whole, or in other words, to the law. It is therefore declared in the 12th article of the bill of rights that the inhabitants of this state are not controlable by any other laws than those to which they or their representative body have given their assent. The constitution is a part of the law of the land, made by the people themselves, and the constitution having declared that all laws which had been adopted and approved, and usually practised on in the courts of law should remain and be in force until altered by the legislature, the common and statute law in force before the adoption of the constitution may be considered as adopted and made by the people themselves. It is clear then that the people of this state are controlable only by the constitution, by the common and statute law adopted by the constitution and not altered, and by laws made by the general court in pursuance of the constitution. The last clause in the 15th article of the bill of rights only asserts the same thing. No subject shall be arrested, &c. but by the judgment of his peers or the law of the land. This clause may be thus analized. 1. No subject shall be arrested but by the law of the land: that is, by due process of law warranted by the constitution, by the common law adopted by the constitution and not altered, or by statutes made in pursuance of the constitution. Thus if the house of representatives were to commit or arrest a person for a contempt in their presence, it would be by process of law, expressly warranted by the constitution. If this court were to arrest a person for a contempt in its presence, it would be by process of law warranted by the common law adopted by the constitution. When an individual is arrested for travelling on Sunday, it is by process warranted by a statute made in pursuance of the constitution.

...

In giving a construction to the 19th article of the bill of rights it must be recollected that by the common law, which the constitution adopts, in certain cases of open and manifest guilt, and in some cases of strong suspicion an arrest might be made without a warrant, but in all other cases, a warrant founded upon a complaint under oath was required. In the cases where an arrest was permitted without a warrant, such an arrest was no more unreasonable and no more dangerous to personal liberty, than an arrest by a warrant, because it was not permitted but in cases where there was strong evidence of guilt.

The 19th article of the bill of rights does not seem intended to restrain the legislature from authorizing arrests without warrant, but to guard against the abuse of warrants issued by magistrates.

On the whole we are clearly of opinion that the act in question is not unconstitutional and that the plea is good.

C. Interrogations

Americans conducted criminal investigations and interrogations during the Early National Era much as they had done in the Founding and Colonial Eras. Criminal investigation remained largely informal and often private. A general consensus existed that persons could not be forced to answer under oath any questions that might incriminate or embarrass them. Supreme Court Justice James Iredell spoke for most Americans when in *United States v. Gooseley* (n.d.) he asserted that a witness under oath was "not bound to tell anything that might tend to criminate himself."[62] Confessions gained without oaths were admitted when judges determined that they were probably true. The Supreme Court of Pennsylvania in *State v. Guild* (PA 1828) maintained, "The question must turn, not on the possibility, but the presence of influence; not whether influence once existed, but, whether it continued to exert its force."[63]

D. Juries and Lawyers

Americans in the Early National Era loved juries a bit less than they had during the Colonial and Founding Eras. Most Americans who lived between 1789 and 1829 considered the jury trial the most important bulwark against tyranny. *Zylstra v. Corporation of City of Charleston* (SC 1794) gave the right to a jury trial "a rank among the first of those which belong to us as freemen."[64] Some elites were less certain. Prominent Federalist judges proposed limiting the traditional role of the jury. Justice Samuel Chase in *United States v. Callender* (1800) opposed attempts to have the jury determine the constitutionality of the Sedition Act. Rejecting Andrew Hamilton's argument in the *Zenger* trial, Chase asserted, "The petit jury have no right to decide on the constitutionality of the statute on which the [defendant] is indicted."

Few Americans waxed as eloquent on lawyers as they did on juries. Still, the right to counsel gained ground during this period. Political elites concluded that the rare criminal defendant who could afford an attorney had a right to hire that attorney. Zephaniah Swift, the leading constitutional commentator in Connecticut, regarded the right to counsel as a modern, liberal innovation. He asserted,

> Our ancestors, when they first enacted their laws respecting crimes, influenced by the illiberal principles which they had imbibed in their native country, denied counsel to prisoners to plead for them to anything but points of law. It is manifest that there is as much necessity for counsel to investigate matters of fact, as points of law, if truth is to be discovered.
>
> The legislature has become so thoroughly convinced of the impropriety and injustice of shackling and restricting a prisoner with respect to his defence, that they have abolished all those odious

62. *United States v. Gooseley*, 25 F. Cas. 1363, 1364 (C.C.D. Va.).

63. *State v. Guild*, 10 N.J.L. 163 (Sup. Ct. 1828).

64. *Zylstra v. Corporation of City of Charleston*, 1 S.C.L. (1 Bay), 382, 391–92 (S. C. Ct. Com. Pl. 1794).

laws, and every person when he is accused of a crime, is entitled to every possible privilege in making his defence, and manifesting his innocence, by the instrumentality of counsel, and the testimony of witnesses.[65]

Swift in this passage was discussing the right to hire an attorney. Legal aid for persons who could not afford a lawyer was almost unheard of and not considered a constitutional right.

United States v. Callender, 25 F. Cas. 239 (C.C.D. Va. 1800)

James Callender was charged with violating the Sedition Act after he made such claims as: "The reign of Mr. Adams has been one continued tempest of malignant passions." During the course of his trial, his counsel asserted that the Sedition Act was unconstitutional and that juries had the right to determine the constitutionality of federal laws. Justice Samuel Chase immediately interrupted. Chase ruled that juries were not empowered to decide the constitutionality of legislation. That task was reserved for judicial determination.

The colloquy between Callender's defense attorneys and the judges highlights increasing controversy over the role of the jury in a criminal trial. During the eighteenth century, most Americans celebrated the right of juries to determine both law and fact. Federalists questioned whether juries should retain this power. In their view, professional judges were better suited to determine the law of a case than were amateur juries. Professional judges might also be more committed to upholding national laws than local juries. Jeffersonians disagreed. They regarded the jury as the best protection against federal oppression.

Compare how Callender's lawyers and Justice Chase understand the respective roles of judge and jury in a criminal trial. What do each see as the virtues of judges and juries? How do those virtues influence their understanding of the proper roles of each in a criminal trial? What are the vices and virtues of having juries determine the constitutionality of federal statutes?

Argument of GEORGE NICHOLAS:

First, that a law contrary to the constitution is void; and, secondly, that the jury have a right to consider the law and the fact. First, it seems to be admitted on all hands, that, when the legislature exercise a power not given them by the constitution, the judiciary will disregard their acts. The second point, that the jury have a right to decide the law and the fact, appears to me equally clear. In the exercise of the power of determining law and fact, a jury cannot be controlled by the court. . . .

. . . [I]f an act of congress contravene the constitution of the United States, a jury have a right to say that it is null, and that they will not give the efficacy of a law to an act which is void in itself; believing it to be contrary to the constitution, they will not convict any man of a violation of it; if this jury believed that the sedition act is not a law of the land, they cannot find the defendant guilty. The constitution secures to every man a fair and impartial trial by jury, in the district where the fact shall have been committed: and to preserve this sacred right unimpaired, it should never be interfered with. If ever a precedent is established, that the court can control the jury so as to prevent them from finding a general verdict, their important right, without which every other right is of no value, will be impaired, if not absolutely destroyed. Juries are to decide according to the dictates of conscience and the laws of the country, and to control them would endanger the right of this most invaluable mode of trial.

Opinion of JUSTICE CHASE:

. . .

. . . The petit jury, to discharge their duty, must first inquire, whether the traverser committed all or any of the facts alleged in the indictment to have been done by him, some time before the indictment. If they find that he did commit all or any of the said facts, their next inquiry is, whether the doing such facts have been made criminal and punishable by the statute of the United States, on which the traverser is indicted. . . . By this provision, I understand that a right is given to the jury to determine what the law is in the case before them; and not to decide whether a statute of the United States produced to them, is a law or not, or whether it is void, under an opinion that it is unconstitutional, that is, contrary to the constitution of the United States. . . . It is one thing to decide what the law is, on the facts proved, and another and a very different thing, to determine that the statute produced is no law. . . .

65. Zephaniah Swift, *A System of Laws of the State of Connecticut* (Windham, CT: John Byrne, 1796), 2:398–99.

... Was it ever intended, by the framers of the constitution, or by the people of America, that it should ever be submitted to the examination of a jury, to decide what restrictions are expressly or impliedly imposed by it on the national legislature? I cannot possibly believe that congress intended, by the statute, to grant a right to a petit jury to declare a statute void. . . .

... If a petit jury can rightfully exercise this power over one statute of congress, they must have an equal right and power over any other statute, and indeed over all the statutes; for no line can be drawn, no restriction imposed on the exercise of such power; it must rest in discretion only. If this power be once admitted, petit jurors will be superior to the national legislature, and its laws will be subject to their control. The power to abrogate or to make laws nugatory, is equal to the authority of making them. The evident consequences of this right in juries will be, that a law of congress will be in operation in one state and not in another. A law to impose taxes will be obeyed in one state, and not in another, unless force be employed to compel submission. The doing certain acts will be held criminal, and punished in one state, and similar acts may be held innocent, and even approved and applauded in another. The effects of the exercise of this power by petit jurors may be readily conceived. It appears to me that the right now claimed has a direct tendency to dissolve the union of the United States, on which, under Divine Providence, our political safety, happiness, and prosperity depend.

...

... [T]he judicial power of the United States is the only proper and competent authority to decide whether any statute made by congress (or any of the state legislatures) is contrary to, or in violation of, the federal constitution. . . . No position can be more clear than that all the federal judges are bound by the solemn obligation of religion, to regulate their decisions agreeably to the constitution of the United States, and that it is the standard of their determination in all cases that come before them. I believe that it has been the general and prevailing opinion in all the Union, that the power now wished to be exercised by a jury, properly belonged to the federal courts. . . . It is now contended, that the constitutionality of the laws of congress should be submitted to the decision of a petit jury. May I ask, whence this change of opinion? I declare that the doctrine is entirely novel to me, and that I never heard of it before my arrival in this city. It appears to me to be not only new, but very absurd and dangerous, in direct opposition to, and a breach of the constitution. . . . It must be evident, that decisions in the district or circuit courts of the United States will be uniform, or they will become so by the revision and correction of the supreme court; and thereby the same principles will pervade all the Union; but the opinions of petit juries will very probably be different in different states.

The decision of courts of justice will not be influenced by political and local principles, and prejudices. If inferior courts commit error, it may be rectified; but if juries make mistakes, there can be no revision or control over their verdicts, and therefore, there can be no mode to obtain uniformity in their decisions. Besides, petit juries are under no obligation by the terms of their oath, to decide the constitutionality of any law; their determination, therefore, will be extra judicial. . . .

E. Punishments

Constitutional authorities interpreted "cruel and unusual punishment" provisions in state constitutions by looking at common law practice. Controversies broke out over how to determine the common law. Some constitutional decision makers interpreted both the common and constitutional law to be relatively unchanging. The Supreme Court of Virginia in *Commonwealth v. Wyatt* (VA 1828) permitted a convicted person to be repeatedly whipped on the ground that whipping was not unknown to the common law. "The punishment of offences by stripes is certainly odious," the justices decreed, "but cannot be said to be *unusual*."[66] Other constitutional decision makers interpreted the common and constitutional law to be more capable of growth. In *James v. Commonwealth* (PA 1825), the Supreme Court of Pennsylvania looked to more recent common law developments when determining that ducking women in the river was an unconstitutional punishment. "[T]his customary ancient punishment for ducking scolds," the justices stated, "was never adopted, and therefore, is not the common law of Pennsylvania."[67]

66. *Commonwealth v. Wyatt*, 6 Rand. 694 (VA 1828).

67. *James v. Commonwealth*, 12 Serg. & Rawle 220 (PA 1825).

Suggested Readings

Ackerman, Bruce A. 2005. *The Failure of the Founding Fathers: Jefferson, Marshall, and the Rise of Presidential Democracy.* Cambridge, MA: Harvard University Press.

Banning, Lance. 1995. *The Sacred Fire of Liberty: James Madison and the Founding of the American Republic.* Ithaca, NY: Cornell University Press.

Brown, Everett S. 1920. *The Constitutional History of the Louisiana Purchase, 1803–1812.* Berkeley: University of California Press.

Brown, Roger H. 2000. *Redeeming the Republic: Federalists, Taxation, and the Origins of the Constitution.* Baltimore, MD: Johns Hopkins University Press.

Cornell, Saul. 1999. *The Other Founders: Anti-Federalism and the Dissenting Tradition in America, 1788–1828.* Chapel Hill: University of North Carolina Press.

Currie, David P. 2001a. *The Constitution in Congress: The Federalist Period, 1789–1801.* Chicago: University of Chicago Press.

———. 2001b. *The Constitution in Congress: The Jeffersonians.* Chicago: University of Chicago Press.

Elkins, Stanley, and Eric McKitrick. 2001. *The Age of Federalism: The Early American Republic, 1788–1800.* New York: Oxford University Press.

Graber, Mark. A. 1998. "Federalist or Friends of Adams: The Marshall Court and Party Politics." *Studies in American Political Development* 12: 229–66.

Killenbeck, Mark R. 2006. M'Culloch v. Maryland: *Securing a Nation.* Lawrence: University Press of Kansas.

Larson, John Lauritz. 2000. *Internal Improvements: National Public Works and the Promise of Popular Government in the Early United States.* Chapel Hill: University of North Carolina.

Levy, Leonard W. 1985. *Emergence of a Free Press.* New York: Oxford University Press.

Magrath, C. Peter. 1967. *Yazoo: Law and Politics in the New Republic: The Case of* Fletcher v. Peck. New York: W. W. Norton & Company.

Mayer, David N. 1994. *The Constitutional Thought of Thomas Jefferson.* Charlottesville: University of Virginia Press.

Newmyer, R. Kent. 2002. *John Marshall and the Heroic Age of the Supreme Court.* Baton Rouge: Louisiana State University Press.

Rosen, Gary. 1999. *American Compact: James Madison and the Problem of Founding.* Lawrence: University Press of Kansas.

Scalia, Laura J. 1999. *America's Jeffersonian Experiment: Remaking State Constitutions, 1820–1850.* De Kalb: Northern Illinois University Press.

Van Cleve, George. 2010. *A Slaveholder's Union: Slavery, Politics, and the Constitution in the Early American Republic.* Chicago: University of Chicago Press.

White, G. Edward. 1988. *The Marshall Court and Cultural Change, 1815–1835.* New York: Oxford University Press.

Chapter 5

The Jacksonian Era: 1829–1860

I. Introduction

Andrew Jackson's inauguration in 1829 turned into a drunken revelry. Twenty thousand admirers stormed the White House, destroying furniture and carpets in a desperate effort to greet the new president. Order was restored only when an intrepid member of Jackson's coterie arranged for free whiskey to be distributed on the White House lawn. Traditional Washingtonians were horrified by what they saw. Margaret Bayard Smith, a prominent Washington socialite, complained that "the Majesty of the People had disappeared," replaced by "a rabble, a mob, of boys, negros, women, children, scrambling, fighting, romping."[1] Looking at the debris and carnage, Supreme Court Justice Joseph Story and Senator Daniel Webster of Massachusetts concluded that the old order was dead. "The reign of King Mob," Story wrote, "seemed triumphant."[2]

Webster and Story were right to note that Jackson's inaugural marked the coming to power of a new generation of constitutional politicians. The first five presidents played prominent roles in either the American Revolution or the Constitutional Convention. John Quincy Adams, the sixth president, was both by blood and temperament allied with the framing generation. Andrew Jackson and his successors came of age during the Early National Era. Jackson lacked personal or familial relationships with any founders. He was from the West, calling home a state that did not exist at the time of the Revolution. The persons responsible for the Constitution of 1787 who witnessed the Jackson phenomenon were appalled by the state of American constitutional politics. James Madison in 1834 fervently hoped that "the danger and even existence of the parties which have grown up under the auspices of [Jackson's] name will expire with his natural or official life."[3]

Different beliefs about the constitutional status of democracy were at the heart of the generation gap between Jacksonians and the framers. Jacksonians proclaimed that the Constitution of the United States was committed to democracy and equality. The 1844 Democratic Party platform spoke of such "cardinal principles in the democratic faith" as "a clear reliance upon the intelligence, patriotism, and the discriminating justice of the American masses." In his 1832 Bank veto message, President Jackson declared, "If [government] would confine itself to equal protection, and, as Heaven does its rains, shower its favors alike on the high and the low, the rich and the poor, it would be an unqualified blessing."

Middle- and lower-middle-class white men were the primary beneficiaries of the Jacksonian constitutional commitments to democracy and equality. Most states adopted (near) universal male suffrage. State courts declared laws that gave special privileges to some men unconstitutional. The same constitutional decision makers often informed women, free persons of color, Native Americans, and (sometimes) aliens that real differences between them and white Americans justified the imposition of distinct liabilities on the basis of gender, race, and ethnicity. Many of the constitutional

1. Margaret Bayard Smith, *First Forty Years of Washington Society*, ed. Gaillard Hunt (New York: C. Scribner's Sons, 1906), 295.

2. Joseph Story, "To Mrs. Joseph Story, March 3, 1829," in *The Life and Letters of Joseph Story*, ed. William W. Story (Boston: Little and Brown, 1851), 1:563.

3. James Madison, "To Edward Coles, August 29, 1834," in *The Letters and Other Writings of James Madison* (Philadelphia: Lippincott, 1865), 4:357.

Table 5-1 Major Issues and Decisions of the Jacksonian Era

Major Political Issues	**Major Constitutional Issues**	**Major Court Decisions**
Continuance of the Second Bank of the United States	Admission of new states	*Worcester v. Georgia* (1832)
Internal improvements	Territorial governance	*Mayor of New York v. Miln* (1837)
Protective tariffs	Religious liberty	*Proprietors of the Charles River Bridge v. Proprietors of the Warren Bridge* (1837)
Slavery	Regulation of commerce	*Prigg v. Pennsylvania* (1842)
Mexican War	Due process protections for property rights	*Luther v. Borden* (1849)
Nullification	Fugitive slave clause	*Cooley v. Board of Wardens* (1852)
Native American removal	Nullification	*Wynehamer v. People* (NY 1856)
Rise of mass political parties	Presidential veto power	*Dred Scott v. Sandford* (1857)
Temperance	Suffrage	*Ableman v. Booth* (1859)

controversies in Jacksonian America ultimately turned on the question of what constitutional commitments to democracy and equality meant in practice.

Developments. The Jacksonian democratizing imperative influenced every governing institution in the United States. The deferential politics of congressional elections in Jeffersonian America was replaced by a partisan free-for-all in which elections were typically won by the candidate who secured the most alcohol and voters (the number of which sometimes exceeded the number of persons actually eligible to vote).[4] The Senate, originally conceived of as a republican aristocracy that would advise the president, increasingly behaved as the second house of the national legislature.[5] Jacksonian presidents such as Martin Van Buren and James Polk claimed to be the best representatives of the people and refrained from adopting the Washingtonian pose of leaders above the political fray. Their cabinets consisted of presidential loyalists who implemented presidential policy and mobilized support for the president. An increasing number of states opted for elected judiciaries. Federal courts were the only governing institution not fundamentally transformed by the democratic spirit.

Parties. The first mass political parties in American history were organized during the Jacksonian Era. By 1838 two political parties, the Whigs and the Democrats, were competing throughout the country. Democrats and Whigs battled as equals in state and congressional elections, but Democrats won six of the eight presidential elections held between 1828 and 1856. Democrats then used their control over the White House to gain control of the federal judiciary. Roger Taney, chief justice of the United States from 1836 to 1864, was a member of Andrew Jackson's cabinet before being appointed to the Court. A majority of the justices on the Supreme Court from 1835 until the 1860s were Democratic appointees with substantial experience in electoral politics. But this was the first era of frequent divided government. More often than not, each party controlled at least one of the three elected bodies of the national government.

In national elections, Democrats and Whigs emphasized issues of government power. Whigs favored a national bank, high tariffs, and internal improvements, known collectively as the "American System." Many Whigs were former National Republicans committed to a broader interpretation of federal powers.

4. Richard Franklin Bensel, *The American Ballot Box in the Mid-Nineteenth Century* (New York: Cambridge University Press, 2004).

5. Elaine K. Swift, *The Making of an American Senate* (Ann Arbor: University of Michigan Press, 2002).

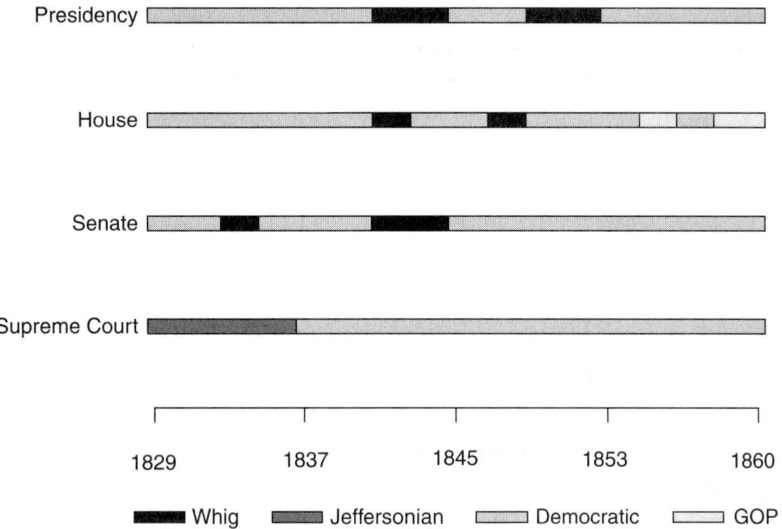

Figure 5-1 Partisan Control of the U.S. Government, 1829–1860

Jacksonians maintained that all these policies were either unconstitutional or unsound. They inherited a version of the strict constructionist constitutional philosophy that had guided the Jeffersonian Republicans. The parties also disputed some national rights and liberties issues. Democrat demands that Native American tribes be removed to regions west of the Mississippi triumphed over Whig opposition. Northern Whigs were more anti-slavery than northern Jacksonians. When slavery was debated during the 1840s and 1850s, however, section was more important than partisan identities.

During the 1850s the Whigs collapsed and the Republican Party was organized. Unlike either Democrats or Whigs, Republicans took a firm anti-slavery stand. Policies such as banning slavery in the territories, Abraham Lincoln and his political allies insisted, placed slavery "on a course of ultimate extinction."[6] The Republicans inherited many of the Whig constituencies and concerns, at least in the North, but downplayed many of the social issues other than slavery that had roiled antebellum politics. State and local politics often saw conflicts over social reform measures aimed at tempering alcohol consumption and restricting gambling and prostitution. The same Protestant religious revival that fed temperance and nativism early in the Jacksonian Era helped fuel anti-slavery and feminist movements in the later antebellum period.

Interest Groups. Jacksonian democracy spawned numerous political movements. Americans organized to abolish slavery, emancipate women, prohibit drinking, limit immigration, and advance numerous other causes. Such public interest groups as the American Temperance Society and the American Anti-Slavery Society established chapters in many states. Women played a major role in many political movements. Social reform movements such as the temperance crusade, which sought to reform American drinking habits, were deeply religious in nature.

These political movements were distinct from the major national political parties of Jacksonian America. Prominent members of both major parties served on the national board of the American Temperance Society. The American Anti-Slavery Society remained suspicious of the Republican Party, a coalition that many abolitionists regarded as far too moderate. Frequently, members of political movements formed third parties, which sometimes siphoned crucial votes away from Democrats and Whigs. The Free Soil and Liberty parties were anti-slavery. The American Party was anti-immigrant.

6. Abraham Lincoln, *Political Debates Between Abraham Lincoln and Stephen A. Douglas in the Celebrated Campaign of 1858 in Illinois* (Cleveland, OH: O. S. Hubbell and Co., 1895), 2.

Box 5-1 A Partial Cast of Characters of the Jacksonian Era

Andrew Jackson	▪ Democrat ▪ Brief political career in Tennessee ▪ Popular military leader in War of 1812 and in Indian wars in Georgia and Spanish Florida ▪ Lost controversial presidential election of 1824 that was settled in the House of Representatives ▪ President of the United States (1829–1837) ▪ Founder of the Democratic Party ▪ Advocate of presidential power, nationalism, popular democracy, and strict constructionism
Roger Taney	▪ Democrat ▪ Entered politics as a Maryland Federalist ▪ U.S. attorney general under Democrat Andrew Jackson (1831–1833) ▪ Authored important presidential papers, including bank veto message ▪ U.S. secretary of treasury under Jackson (1833–1834); removed federal funds from Bank of the United States ▪ Nomination as associate justice, defeated by Whig Senate, confirmed as chief justice by Democratic Senate to succeed John Marshall (1836–1864) ▪ Advocate of states' rights and strict constructionism, defender of slave interests, and the author of *Dred Scott* decision
Daniel Webster	▪ Whig ▪ Began career as Massachusetts Federalist ▪ Member of the U.S. House of Representatives (1813–1817, 1823–1827) ▪ Member of U.S. Senate (1827–1841, 1845–1850) ▪ Whig candidate for president in 1836 ▪ U.S. secretary of state under several Whig presidents (1841–1843, 1850–1852) ▪ Leading Supreme Court litigator and advocate of property rights, national union, and broad construction of congressional powers
Benjamin R. Curtis	▪ Whig ▪ Student of Justice Joseph Story and protégé of Daniel Webster ▪ Argued a prominent anti-slavery case in the Supreme Judicial Court of Massachusetts ▪ Member of Massachusetts state legislature (1849–1851) ▪ Associate justice of U.S. Supreme Court (1851–1857) ▪ Authored key dissent in *Dred Scott* case ▪ Critic of presidential power during Lincoln administration ▪ Served as chief counsel to President Andrew Johnson during his impeachment
John C. Calhoun	▪ Democrat ▪ Began career as South Carolina "war hawk" and National Republican ▪ Member of U.S. House of Representatives (1811–1817) ▪ Member of U.S. Senate (1832–1843, 1845–1850) ▪ U.S. secretary of war under Republican James Monroe (1817–1825) ▪ U.S. vice president under Republican John Quincy Adams and Democrat Andrew Jackson (1825–1832) ▪ U.S. secretary of state under Whig John Tyler (1844–1845) ▪ Broke with Jackson and flirted with Whig and local states' rights parties ▪ Advocate of states' rights and Southern sectional interests, known as leading theorist of state nullification

(Continued)

Box 5-1 *(Continued)*

Elizabeth Cady Stanton	■ Social activist ■ Organizer of Seneca Falls Conference of 1848 ■ Author of Declaration of Sentiments urging women's rights ■ Founder of Women's State Temperance Society in 1852 ■ Advocate of universal suffrage after the Civil War ■ Founder of National Woman Suffrage Association in 1869

Courts. One consequence of the repeated Whig failure to pass their legislative program was that the Supreme Court of the United States rarely spoke on the constitutional issues that divided Democrats and Whigs. This silence surprised some observers who expected a reconstituted bench to overturn such landmark decisions of the Early National period as *McCulloch v. Maryland* (1819). By the end of the 1830s, the federal judiciary had passed into Democratic hands. The new judicial majority was composed of men who had previously championed strict construction in Congress or in Jackson's cabinet. Roger Taney, Andrew Jackson's close political advisor, replaced John Marshall as chief justice. Taney and his judicial allies nevertheless had no opportunity to revisit *McCulloch,* because Jackson and President Tyler vetoed Whig bills rechartering the national bank. Had Jackson or Tyler signed those bills, most politically astute commentators believed the Taney Court would have declared that Congress had no power to incorporate a national bank. The Supreme Court did not consider whether the internal improvements bill passed by Congress in 1846 was constitutional for the same reason. President Polk vetoed the bill, preventing the passage of a law the justices might have declared unconstitutional. Slavery was something of an exception to this general pattern of staying in the background of notable political disputes, with the Supreme Court issuing important decisions upholding the Fugitive Slave Act and striking down laws prohibiting slavery in the territories.

State courts played a more important role in resolving rights and liberties questions. During the early Jacksonian Era, many states adopted constitutional reforms creating elected judiciaries and imposing new limitations on state legislatures. These measures were expected to make the courts more independent of elected politicians, and the newly elected judges rewarded that expectation by striking down more state laws. After state legislatures passed measures limiting religious freedom, curbing antislavery advocacy, prohibiting concealed weapons, or mandating prayer in school, opponents often turned to local courts for redress. Both Democrats and Whigs could become judicial activists, depending on the issue before the court.

Constitutional Thought. Democrats and Whigs refined a distinctive nineteenth-century framework for thinking about constitutional rights and liberties. Americans from the Founding Era until the New Deal treated what contemporary Americans consider constitutional rights claims as issues of government powers. Constitutional decision makers considering official actions restricting religious liberty or property rights assessed whether the contested regulation (a) served some legitimate government purpose to promote the health, safety, and morality of the community as a whole (the definition of the states' inherent "police powers") and (b) was not merely an arbitrary (unjustifiable) attempt to bestow special burdens or benefits on particular groups. If they concluded that a law limiting drinking protected the public health, the legislation was declared constitutional. If they determined that state officials had acted with the purpose of restricting liberty or sought to benefit one class at the expense of another, the law was declared unconstitutional. This practice was not uniform. Nevertheless, constitutional decision makers were far more likely to understand rights as the residuum of legitimate government power than as a trump against otherwise legitimate government power. The exercise of government power, in turn, always needed to be justified as contributing to the common good. Officials who exercised government power to benefit a favored faction and not to enhance the public welfare necessarily violated the rights of the citizenry to be free from such illegitimate intrusions into their private affairs and such abuses of the public purse.[7]

Legacies. Mass political parties were the most important Jacksonian contribution to American constitutionalism. The framers had sought to prevent parties from arising. Jeffersonians had regarded parties as a necessary evil. Americans during the Jacksonian Era, in contrast, celebrated parties as the best vehicle for ensuring mass participation in politics and guaranteeing that political decisions would reflect popular opinions. An influential Jacksonian journal spoke for both Democrats and, eventually, Whigs when declaring, "When men are governed by a common principle, which is fully indulged and equally operative in all parts of the country, the agency of party conduces to the public good."[8]

While many social movements and public interest groups that flourished before the Civil War have not survived, their influence on the constitutional politics of rights and liberties has become an enduring feature of the American constitutional order. From the Jacksonian Era to the present, social movements and public interest groups have had substantial influence on constitutional debates over most rights and liberties. National elections are usually fought over the economy or foreign policy. Social movements championing abolitionism, prohibition, women's suffrage, the freedom of the press, and the right to bear arms ensure that controversies over rights and liberties are always on the national and local agendas.

The modern presidency is rooted in Jacksonian practice. During the Early National period, Americans debated whether cabinet officials had obligations to be loyal to the president and whether presidents could use the veto to influence policy making in Congress. These issues were largely, but not completely, settled by 1860. President Andrew Jackson established durable precedents when he made routine use of the veto and insisted that his cabinet officials either carry out his orders or be removed from office. Abraham Lincoln, a Whig in the 1840s, adopted the Jacksonian conception of the presidency upon taking office in 1861.

7. See Howard Gillman, *The Constitution Besieged: The Rise and Demise of Lochner Era Police Powers Jurisprudence* (Durham, NC: Duke University Press, 1993).

8. Albany Argus, quoted in Michael Wallace, "Changing Concepts of Party in the United States: New York, 1815–1828," *American Historical Review* 74 (1968): 490.

II. Foundations

MAJOR DEVELOPMENTS

- Broad celebration of constitutional liberties
- Disputes over the constitutional status of slavery
- Bill of Rights limits only the federal government

Americans in the Jacksonian Era regarded the Constitution framed and ratified by the previous generation as binding, but they did not agree on why the U.S. Constitution should be venerated. All parties to constitutional debates highlighted certain features of the constitutional past while downplaying, if not ignoring, others. Prominent Democrats emphasized the more democratic elements of American constitutionalism. Prominent Whigs stressed the republican commitments to a virtuous citizenry. Republicans highlighted the more anti-slavery strands of American constitutionalism. Pro-slavery advocates pointed to such provisions as the fugitive slave clause, which they claimed demonstrated a special constitutional commitment to human bondage.

A. Sources

Americans in the Jacksonian Era inherited from the Early National Era a commitment to constitutional foundations for the authority and limits of government. Constitutional decision makers pointed to specific provisions in federal and state constitutions when justifying their rulings. References to natural law or fundamental principles as independent sources of rights and liberties largely, although not completely, disappeared from legal discourse.

Some northern abolitionists challenged this consensus. To them, Americans were too complacent in accepting slavery as a necessary constitutional evil. William Lloyd Garrison condemned the Constitution as committing the country to preserving injustice. In 1843 he successfully persuaded the American Anti-Slavery Society to pass a resolution stating, "The compact which exists between the North and the South is a covenant with death and an agreement with hell; involving both parties in atrocious criminality, and should be immediately annulled."[9] On July 4, 1854, Garrison publicly burned a copy of the Constitution.[10] Wendell Phillips detailed the abolitionist critique of the Constitution in *The Constitution, a Pro-Slavery Compact*. That work asserted that the framers committed the United States to protecting slavery for as long as slaveholders sought constitutional protection. A higher moral law stood superior to constitutional law. Other anti-slavery advocates celebrated a Constitution they interpreted as either outlawing slavery or placing slavery on "a course of ultimate extinction." Many argued that federal statutes protecting slavery were unconstitutional. Frederick Douglass was a leading champion of this view. His works "denied that the Constitution guarantees the right to hold property in man."[11]

B. Principles

The Democrats and the Whigs were the two major national parties during most of the Jacksonian Era. The national party platforms of each coalition focused on national powers. Democrats opposed the national bank, federally funded internal improvements, and protective tariffs. Whigs favored these measures. Democrats and Whigs in the states more often disputed rights and liberties. Whigs favored using government power to improve citizens and foster a uniform Protestant culture; Democrats opposed such Whig initiatives as common (public) schools and temperance laws. Whigs supported nativism and limiting voting rights; Democrats championed the rights of (white) immigrants and an expanded suffrage. Northern Whigs were far more inclined than northern Democrats to support the rights of women, blacks, and Native Americans.

During the 1850s party competition between Democrats and Republicans replaced party competition between Democrats and Whigs. Most Republicans, including Abraham Lincoln, were former Whigs. Nevertheless, the political realignment of the 1850s was based on a change in the basis of partisan competition, not a change in party labels. Democrats and Republicans primarily fought over slavery, and former southern Whigs like Alexander Stephens (the future vice president of the Confederacy) became Democrats as the Republican Party grew. Republicans insisted that slavery be prohibited in all American territories, blamed slaveholders for civil rights violations in the Territory of Kansas, and demanded that Kansas enter the Union as a free state. Democrats maintained that the Constitution gave slaveholders the right to bring their slaves into American territories and blamed abolitionists for the violence that took place in Kansas during the 1850s. Most Democrats, although not all, believed that Kansas should enter the Union as a slave state.

C. Scope

Americans in the Jacksonian Era disputed the scope of the first ten amendments to the U.S. Constitution. The best-known controversy was over whether the federal Bill of Rights limited the power of state governments. The more important controversy was over whether the Bill of Rights limited congressional power in the territories. By 1860 a consensus had been reached. The Supreme Court in *Barron v. Baltimore* (1833) ruled that states had no constitutional obligation to respect the liberties set out in the first ten amendments to the Constitution. The Supreme Court in *Dred Scott v. Sandford* (1857) ruled that when governing territories, Congress had to respect the liberties set out in the first ten amendments. This consensus about the scope of the Bill of Rights in the states (no) and territories (yes) was not universal. Several state supreme courts suggested that states should respect the liberties set out in the Bill of Rights, either because these liberties were fundamental or because the federal Constitution bound both the states and Congress. Chief Justice Joseph Henry Lumpkin of the Supreme Court of Georgia asserted in *Campbell v. State* (GA 1852), "The rights which the [first ten amendments to the Constitution of the United States] were designed to protect, were too sacred to be violated by any republican tribunal, legislative or judicial."[12] Anti-slavery advocates complained that *Barron* left local officials in the South free to muzzle anti-slavery speech. These antebellum concerns resurfaced after the Civil War when Americans revisited the status of the Bill of Rights in the states and territories.

---

9. Wendell Phillips Garrison and Francis Jackson Garrison, *William Lloyd Garrison, 1805–1879, The Story of His Life Told by His Children* (New York: Century Co., 1889), 3:88.

10. Henry Mayer, *All on Fire: William Lloyd Garrison and the Abolition of Slavery* (New York: St. Martin's Griffin, 1998), 444–45.

11. Frederick Douglass, *Selected Speeches and Writings*, ed. Philip S. Foner (Chicago: Chicago Review Press, 2000), 380.

12. *Campbell v. State*, 11 Ga. 353 (1852).

Barron v. Baltimore, 32 U.S. 243 (1833)

John Barron and John Craig owned a wharf in the Baltimore Harbor. Baltimore adopted a commercial development plan that required officials to divert several local streams. These internal improvements lowered the water level on the Barron and Craig property. When their wharf became useless, Barron sued for damages. He claimed that the city had taken property from him in violation of the due process clause of the Fifth Amendment. The city responded that localities had the right to divert streams as part of general police powers and that the Fifth Amendment of the federal Constitution limited only national power. Barron was awarded compensation at trial, but the state court of appeals reversed the ruling. Barron appealed this decision to the Supreme Court of the United States, claiming that both the national government and local authorities were limited by the Fifth Amendment.

The Supreme Court unanimously rejected Barron's *appeal. Chief Justice Marshall's opinion held that the Bill of Rights limited only federal power, and that local governments only had to respect whatever rights were found in the relevant state constitution. If the constitution of Maryland did not have a due process clause or Maryland courts did not interpret the due process clause of the state constitution as protecting Barron or a similarly situated person, then the local action was constitutional. What reasons does Marshall give for this ruling? Do you believe the ruling sound? When thinking about this decision, you might consider that after Andrew Jackson was elected president in 1828, the Supreme Court consistently found state actions to be constitutional. Compare* Barron *to such cases as* Fletcher v. Peck *(1810), in which the Supreme Court declared a state law unconstitutional. How do you explain the different result in* Barron? *Does* Barron *present a different legal issue, one that merits a different legal result? Was the Marshall Court far more deferential to states after 1828 because the judges feared political backlash in the wake of the Jacksonian states' rights revolution?*

CHIEF JUSTICE MARSHALL delivered the opinion of the Court.

. . .

The constitution was ordained and established by the people of the United States for themselves, for their own government, and not for the government of the individual states. Each state established a constitution for itself, and, in that constitution, provided such limitations and restrictions on the powers of its particular government as its judgment dictated. The people of the United States framed such a government for the United States as they supposed best adapted to their situation, and best calculated to promote their interests. The powers they conferred on this government were to be exercised by itself; and the limitations on power, if expressed in general terms, are naturally, and, we think, necessarily applicable to the government created by the instrument. They are limitations of power granted in the instrument itself; not of distinct governments, framed by different persons and for different purposes.

If these propositions be correct, the fifth amendment must be understood as restraining the power of the general government, not as applicable to the states. In their several constitutions they have imposed such restrictions on their respective governments as their own wisdom suggested; such as they deemed most proper for themselves. It is a subject on which they judge exclusively, and with which others interfere no farther than they are supposed to have a common interest.

. . .

The ninth section having enumerated, in the nature of a bill of rights, the limitations intended to be imposed on the powers of the general government, the tenth proceeds to enumerate those which were to operate on the state legislatures. These restrictions are brought together in the same section, and are by express words applied to the states. "No state shall enter into any treaty," etc. Perceiving that in a constitution framed by the people of the United States for the government of all, no limitation of the action of government on the people would apply to the state government, unless expressed in terms; the restrictions contained in the tenth section are in direct words so applied to the states.

. . .

Had the people of the several states, or any of them, required changes in their constitutions; had they required additional safeguards to liberty from the apprehended encroachments of their particular governments: the remedy was in their own hands, and would have been applied by themselves. A convention would have been assembled by the discontented state, and the required improvements would have been made by itself. The unwieldy and cumbrous machinery of procuring a recommendation from two-thirds of congress, and the assent of three-fourths of their sister states, could never have occurred to any human being as a mode of doing that which might be effected by the state itself. Had the framers of these amendments intended them to be limitations on the powers of the state governments, they would have imitated the framers of the original constitution, and have expressed that intention. Had congress engaged in the extraordinary occupation of improving the constitutions of the several states by affording the people additional protection from the exercise of power by their own governments in matters which concerned themselves alone, they would have declared this purpose in plain and intelligible language.

. . .

We are of opinion that the provision in the fifth amendment to the constitution, declaring that private property shall not be taken for public use without just compensation, is intended solely as a limitation on the exercise of power by the government of the United States, and is not applicable to the legislation of the states. . . .

III. Judicial Power and Constitutional Authority

MAJOR DEVELOPMENTS

- Most elected officials support the judicial power to declare laws unconstitutional
- Jacksonians reorganize the federal judicial system in ways that guarantee a slave-state majority on the Supreme Court
- Most states adopt constitutional provisions requiring state judges to be elected

The constitutional authority of state and federal courts was well established by the end of the Jacksonian Era. The Supreme Court of the United States in *Ableman v. Booth* (1858) strongly reasserted the judicial power to declare federal and state laws unconstitutional, bluntly stated that state courts were bound by federal judicial interpretations of the Constitution, and indicated that elected officials in the national government were similarly bound to obey federal judicial rulings. Most state courts before the Civil War successfully asserted the power to declare that state laws violated the state constitution. These assertions of judicial authority enjoyed bipartisan support. Whigs historically favored strong courts. Democrats became more partial to federal courts as those courts became staffed with justices appointed by Democrats.

Occasional flare-ups of court-curbing occurred, but federal and state courts survived them largely unscathed. In 1824, the Kentucky legislature disbanded the state supreme court after the justices struck down a popular mortgage relief law. Over the next two elections, supporters of the courts and judicial review won decisive victories at the polls. The state judiciary was reinstated, much to the satisfaction of watchful national leaders.[13] Judge William Gibson of the Pennsylvania Supreme Court sharply criticized *Marbury v. Madison* (1803) when dissenting in *Eakin v. Raub* (1825). President Jackson pointedly passed over Gibson when later considering appointments to the Supreme Court of the United States. Southern Jacksonians in 1831 sought to repeal Section 25 of the Judiciary Act of 1789, the provision that gave the Supreme Court the power to review constitutional decisions made by state courts. A coalition of Whigs and northern Democrats defeated that proposal by a 3–1 margin. When anti-slavery advocates during the 1840s and 1850s bitterly condemned the pro-southern bias of federal judicial decisions in fugitive slave cases, Democrats in all three branches of the national government reiterated commitments to judicial power.

The more important debates over constitutional authority in Jacksonian America were over who would control the courts and how judges should use the power of judicial review. Jacksonians inherited a federal court system with seven circuits. The first three circuits were entirely within free states, the next three were entirely within slave states, and the mixed Seventh Circuit contained Ohio (free), Kentucky (slave), and Tennessee (slave). Many new western states were not included. Congress repeatedly failed during the 1820s and early 1830s to expand the federal judicial system. Divided government ensured that members of one party did not provide the president of another party with the opportunity to make additional

13. See, generally, Theodore W. Ruger, "'A Question Which Convulses a Nation': The Early Republic's Greatest Debate About the Judicial Review Power," *Harvard Law Review* 117 (2004): 826.

Table 5-2 Supreme Court Justices and Federal Judicial Circuits, 1842–1860

Federal Judicial Circuits	Supreme Court Justices
Free-State Circuits	
First Circuit ME, MA, NH RI	Joseph Story (MA) (1812–1845) Levi Woodbury (NH) (1845–1851) Benjamin Curtis (MA) (1851–1857) Nathan Clifford (ME) (1858–1881)
Second Circuit CT, NY, VT	Smith Thompson (NY) (1823–1843) Samuel Nelson (NY) (1845–1872)
Third Circuit NJ, PA	Henry Baldwin (PA) (1830–1844) Robert Grier (PA) (1846–1870)
Seventh Circuit IL, IN, MI, OH	John McLean (OH) (1829–1861)
Slave-State Circuits	
Fourth Circuit DE, MD	Roger B. Taney (MD) (1836–1864)
Fifth Circuit NC, VA	Peter Daniel (VA) (1842–1860)
Sixth Circuit GA, SC	James Wayne (GA) (1835–1867)
Eighth Circuit MO, KY, TN	John Catron (TN) (1837–1865)
Ninth Circuit AL, AR, LA, MS	John McKinley (AL) (1838–1852) John Campbell (AL) (1853–1861)

judicial appointments. Representatives from the free and slave states were also concerned with the balance of sectional power in the federal judiciary.

This impasse was broken after the national elections of 1834 and 1836 left Democrats in control of both houses of Congress and the White House. The Judiciary Act of 1837 expanded the membership of the Supreme Court by two justices. This measure enabled Democrats to secure a majority on the Court for the next thirty years. The Judiciary Act of 1837 also reorganized the federal judiciary so that the majority of justices on the Supreme Court resided in the slaveholding states. In 1855, a Tenth Circuit was created for California, but for the first time no Supreme Court seat was associated with that circuit. With these reforms in place, the slave states were assured a 5–4 advantage on the Supreme Court for the rest of the antebellum period.

Debate on the Electoral Accountability of the Judiciary, Ohio Constitutional Convention (1850)[14]

By the end of the Jacksonian Era, almost three-quarters of the states chose judges by popular election. Nineteen of the twenty-one state constitutional conventions held between 1846 and 1850 adopted elected judiciaries. Other states shifted to elected judiciaries by specific constitutional amendment, rather than as part of a larger constitutional reform. In most states, the adoption of elected judiciaries was bipartisan and relatively uncontroversial. Most

14. Excerpt taken from *Report of the Debates and Proceedings of the Convention for the Revision of the Constitution of the State of Ohio, 1850–51* (Columbus: S. Medary, 1851), 1:681–91.

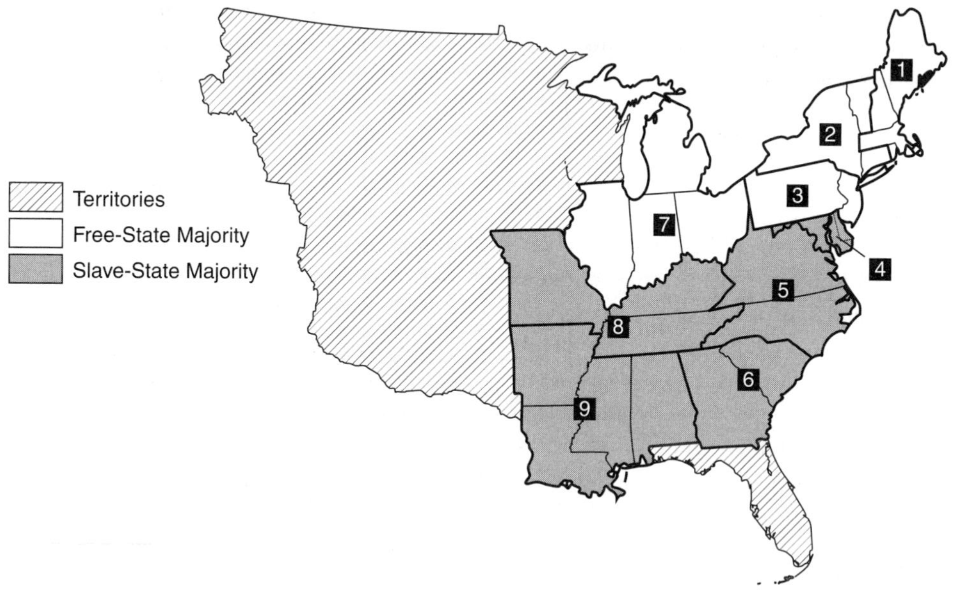

Figure 5-2 Map of Federal Judicial Circuits, 1837

Democrats and some Whigs regarded appointed judiciaries as instruments of partisan mobilization rather than as instruments of justice. Judicial offices were awarded as the political spoils of electoral victory. Appointment fights were bruising and often left judicial seats vacant. Justice in court was neither reliable nor fast. Making judges electorally accountable to the people, proponents of elected judiciaries hoped, would promote courts that served the public's interest.[15]

Ohio was among the states that adopted an elected judiciary. The 1850 state constitution, which remains in effect today, provided for five-year terms for the judges of the state supreme court. The debate in the Ohio convention was not over whether judges should be elected. All sides admitted that there was no other politically realistic option. The delegates instead debated how long the judicial term of office should be. Democrats, the majority party in Ohio, favored shorter terms of office than Whigs. Who had the better argument? Should judges face the voters frequently or infrequently? Which better advances the will of the people?

15. On elected judiciaries, see Kermit L. Hall, "The Judiciary on Trial: State Constitutional Reform and the Rise of an Elected Judiciary, 1846–1860," *Historian* 45 (1983): 337; F. Andrew Hanssen, "Learning About Judicial Independence: Institutional Change in the State Courts," *Journal of Legal Studies* 33 (2004): 431; Jed Shugerman, "Economic Crisis and the Rise of Judicial Elections and Judicial Review," *Harvard Law Review* 123 (2010): 1061.

Mr. M. H. MITCHELL (Democrat) . . . As to how far I would have the popular sentiment, or impulse, as some have expressed it, to operate on the court, I beg leave to say, that I have such confidence in the great mass of mankind, as to believe that they will come to right conclusions at last; and that the settled opinions of the popular mind may be always safely trusted. But I also know that the masses of mankind, like the waves of the ocean, are subject to fluctuation; and if you could find the true criterion by which to judge of what really is the popular sentiment, you must take more than a mere period—you must take a reasonable, perhaps I might say considerable period together, so as to get their settled opinion. . . .

This is the proper process of reasoning to follow, when inquiring as to what is really the character and feeling of the community at large. And this is what the judge should have always in his mind. Acting upon this rule, he would ever be preserved from the influence of the sudden emotions and impulses and excitement of the day or any short period of time. He would always take a survey of the popular feeling for an extended period of time. . . . Neither should a judge forget that it is his great duty to discharge with fidelity every trust which is committed to him by the community. So, then, he should hold himself accountable, not that he should obey the impulses of their excited minds, or the ebullitions of their passions, but that he should always be obedient to their sober judgment, and with studied reference to that he should always act. It is in this manner that the impulses and sentiments of mankind should always act upon a judicial tribunal. . . .

. . .

Mr. CHARLES REEMELIN (Democrat) . . . I [am] in favor of impartial courts, at the same time that I said I was opposed to independent courts. Impartial between man and man, and not independent of public opinion, popular feeling, and even, if you please, popular impulses. I want no balance wheel in our government, but the balance wheel of public opinion. I have confidence in the public opinion; I want it to have its due, frequent, and unbiased influence on every part of our government. I do not want a judge to go out into the streets, and ask himself whether the man whose case he is adjudicating upon is a whig, or a democrat, but I want a judge above him, to whom he must soon render an account, and that judge is the people of Ohio.

. . .

Mr. REUBEN HITCHCOCK (Whig) . . . [W]e have been informed . . . as to what the object is. It is to make a political court, to decide the causes according to the political dogmas of the day. The gentleman says, to be sure, we would not have the principle prevail where individuals are before the court as suitors, but where the public is concerned, or where a corporation is concerned, the court is to carry out, not the law but the political opinions of those who appointed them. That I understand to be the object of the gentlemen, and now I ask, is it the desire of this body to have the court so constituted, that it shall not in all cases be controlled by the law of the land but shall be controlled by the political dogmas of any political party? What does the gentleman desire? A political court not to be controlled by law—not to decide cases according to the constitution and the law but to decide cases as shall be dictated them by those who appointed them. Is that the object? . . .

. . .

Why Mr. Chairman, if such is to be the case, it may operate upon us all. This popular prejudice at one time may be running in one direction; and thus those who to-day gain their rights, or succeed in that which they pretend to be right, through popular prejudice, may to-morrow, by a change of parties, be placed in a situation to lose as much or still more than they have gained. Now it seems to me, Mr. Chairman, this is worthy of the utmost consideration. We should reflect upon this subject before we act.

. . .

Mr. HENRY STANBERY (Whig) . . . I did not know that our judges performed their duties more faithfully than in other countries. The judges of England, though appointed by the Crown, had been faithful and impartial in discharging the duties of their high station. None more so. The judges, in many of the States of the Union, appointed by the Executive, and holding by a life tenure, are equally faithful and honest.

Mr. DANIEL ROBERTSON (Democrat). Then the gentleman is in favor of the appointment of judges by the Executive, is he not?

Mr. STANBERY. Not at all. I am in favor of their election by the people. But that is not the point. I was answering the assertion that frequent elections of the judges, and short terms of office, would insure more capable and impartial officers. That is what I very much doubt. I may say, it is what I do not expect. I fear the contrary.

. . . In the history of the world, not an instance can be found, in which the liberties of the people have been taken away by the judiciary. It holds neither the sword nor the purse. It wields no patronage. We must protect it, rather than guard against it. It is our safeguard, when properly constituted, against political power, wherever that power may be lodged. We must make it independent, to secure impartiality and honesty. From the earliest times—from the times when man first conceived a right idea of the judicial character, independence and impartiality have been deemed its essential attributes. In the early ages, when the virtues were deified, justice was well personified, a bandage was drawn over her eyes, and even balances put into her hands, to indicate perfect impartiality—complete independence of all extraneous influences.

I never want to see a judge upon the bench, who must look to the people before he can decide a case—who must constantly consult and be governed by popular impulses—who shall be always under a fear of accountability to those who make and unmake him. How can such a judge take a solemn oath to discharge his high office without fear, favor or affection; he who is constantly in dread—who is trembling at every step, lest his decisions may not be acceptable to a popular majority.

. . .

Mr. BENJAMIN STANTON (Whig). I will trust to the influence of reason and authority upon an upright and intelligent judge. If I differ with him upon a constitutional question; if he holds that the constitution means one thing and I hold that it means or ought to mean another, I will seek to change it by amendment, and not by judicial construction. When a constitution, or law has received a settled judicial construction I will abide by it, until it is changed by the proper authority and not seek to work a revolution by an appeal from the court to the ballot box upon the construction of a law. I will never consent that the independence of the judiciary shall be destroyed, and the constitution changed by construction of an appeal to the people in the election of judges—*never*, NEVER! . . .

. . . [I]f I had the making of the constitution, I would elect the judges of the court of last resort for a long term, and make them ineligible for a re-election.

It seems to be imagined by some gentlemen that the majority, which is the governing power, should be at all times absolutely omnipotent. That there should be no obstacles or restraints to prevent them from sacrificing the most sacred rights of individuals at pleasure. That the life, liberty, reputation and property of every individual in community should at all times be at the mercy of the governing power.

An upright and independent judiciary would be an effectual protection to the inalienable rights of individuals, and hence it must be got rid of. There must be an appeal from the court to the ballot box. Everything must be sacrificed to a domineering partisan majority. Sir, I demure most earnestly to any such doctrine. I ought not to hold my life, liberty, and property at the mercy of the majority. . . .

. . .

Mr. JOSEPH McCORMICK (Democrat) . . .

I hold, sir, that democracy looks to a pure and disinterested judiciary; that democracy seeks for the sacrifice of no right; that it seeks for the promotion of law and order, and for a proper and consistent state of things; that it asks not for the government of lynch law; that it asks not to make the judiciary subservient in the wishes and caprices of individuals or cliques—all these things I openly disclaim as constituting any part of my democracy; yet I am in favor of the election of judges by the people, and not only so, but I am in favor of a short term of office.

Luther v. Borden, 48 U.S. 1 (1849)

The state of Rhode Island in 1841 was governed by the same charter granted to the Rhode Island Colony in 1663. That charter extended suffrage to landholders and heavily favored the rural areas of the state in the apportionment of legislative seats. As the state urbanized, many citizens demanded that the state adopt a new constitution that expanded the suffrage. The state legislature resisted calls for reform, and the royal charter included no provisions for amendment. Frustrated, reformers sponsored a popular convention that drafted a new constitution. That constitution was promulgated and "ratified" in town meetings across the state. A government, led by Thomas Dorr, was elected by universal white male suffrage under the new radical constitution. The charter government refused to recognize the new constitution. Members of the established government of Rhode Island in 1842 sponsored a separate constitutional convention that adopted a modestly reformed constitution. The old charter government, led by Samuel King, was reelected under that new reformed constitution. This left Rhode Island with two separate groups of elected officials claiming to be the legitimate government of the state under two different constitutions.

The King government triumphed by declaring martial law and successfully disbursing the Dorr government. While Rhode Island was under martial law, official government troops led by Luther Borden raided the house of Martin Luther, a shoemaker and bit player in the Dorr reform movement. Luther sued Borden for trespass in federal court. He claimed that the King government was not the lawful authority in 1842. The federal circuit court rejected Luther's argument, and he appealed to the U.S. Supreme Court.

The Supreme Court ruled that federal courts could not determine the lawful government of Rhode Island. Chief Justice Taney maintained that the question of which government was the lawful government of a state was a political question entrusted to elected officials. The judicial majority in Luther v. Borden *then determined that Governor King was constitutionally authorized to declare martial law. Justice Woodbury dissented on that issue only.*

This case is commonly regarded as the starting point for the "political question" doctrine. This doctrine does not prohibit justices from deciding cases that are controversial or involve matters of public policy, but it does state that political questions have some characteristics or element that makes their solution best suited for elected officials. Such questions are considered non-justiciable by proponents of this doctrine because they had been specifically delegated to a different institution, were intrinsically mixed up with policy judgments, or lacked an adequate standard that could guide judges. Specifically, Taney concluded that the courts were not the proper body for determining whether the government exercising power within a state met the requirements of a republican government, as guaranteed in Article IV of the U.S. Constitution.

You might consider the following questions when reading Taney's opinion. Are there constitutional questions that cannot be answered by the courts? What considerations might lead the courts to stay out of a constitutional controversy? What practical considerations might explain why the Taney Court was reluctant to intervene in the Dorr War?

CHIEF JUSTICE TANEY delivered the opinion of the Court.

. . .

. . . [T]he question presented is certainly a very serious one: For, if this court is authorized to enter upon this inquiry as proposed by the plaintiff, and it should be decided that the charter government had no legal existence during the period of time above mentioned,—if it had been annulled by the adoption of the opposing government,—then the laws passed by its legislature during that time were nullities; its taxes wrongfully collected; its salaries and compensation to its officers illegally paid; its public accounts improperly settled; and the judgments and sentences of its courts in civil and criminal cases null and void, and the officers who carried their decisions into operation answerable as trespassers, if not in some cases as criminals.

When the decision of this court might lead to such results, it becomes its duty to examine very carefully its own powers before it undertakes to exercise jurisdiction.

Certainly, the question which the plaintiff proposed to raise by the testimony he offered has not heretofore been recognized as a judicial one in any of the State courts. In forming the constitutions of the different States, after the Declaration of Independence, and in the various changes and alterations which have since been made, the political department has always determined whether the proposed constitution or amendment was ratified or not by the people of the State, and the judicial power has followed its decision. In Rhode Island, the question has been directly decided. . . .

. . .

. . . [T]he Constitution of the United States, as far as it has provided for an emergency of this kind, and authorized the general government to interfere in the domestic concerns of a State, has treated the subject as political in its nature, and placed the power in the hands of that department.

The fourth section of the fourth article of the Constitution of the United States provides that the United States shall guarantee to every State in the Union a republican form of government, and shall protect each of them against invasion; and on the application of the legislature or of the executive (when the legislature cannot be convened) against domestic violence.

Under this article of the Constitution it rests with Congress to decide what government is the established one in a State. For as the United States guarantee to each State a republican government, Congress must necessarily decide what government is established in the State before it can determine whether it is republican or not. And when the senators and representatives of a State are admitted into the councils of the Union, the authority of the government under which they are appointed, as well as its republican character, is recognized by the proper constitutional authority. And its decision is binding on every other department of the government, and could not be questioned in a judicial tribunal. . . .

. . .

By this act [of Congress of February 28, 1795, for calling out the militia], the power of deciding whether the exigency had arisen upon which the government of the United States is bound to interfere, is given to the President. He is to act upon the application of the legislature or of the executive, and consequently he must determine what body of men constitute the legislature, and who is the governor, before he can act. . . . And the President must, of necessity, decide which is the government, and which party is unlawfully arrayed against it, before he can perform the duty imposed upon him by the act of Congress.

After the President has acted and called out the militia, is a Circuit Court of the United States authorized to inquire whether his decision was right? Could the court, while the parties were actually contending in arms for the possession of the government, call witnesses before it and inquire which party represented a majority of the people? If it could, then it would become the duty of the court (provided it came to the conclusion that the President had decided incorrectly) to discharge those who were arrested or detained by the troops in the service of the United States or the government which the President was endeavoring to maintain. If the judicial power extends so far, the guarantee contained in the Constitution of the United States is a guarantee of anarchy, and not of order. . . .

. . .

It is said that this power in the President is dangerous to liberty, and may be abused. All power may be abused if placed in unworthy hands. But it would be difficult, we think, to point out any other hands in which this power would be more safe, and at the same time equally effectual. When citizens of the same State are in arms against each other, and the constituted authorities unable to execute the laws, the interposition of the United States must be prompt, or it is of little value. The ordinary course of proceedings in courts of justice would be utterly unfit for the crisis. And the elevated office of the President, chosen as he is by the people of the United States, and the high responsibility he could not fail to feel when acting in a case of so much moment, appear to furnish as strong safeguards against a willful abuse of power as human prudence and foresight could well provide. At all events, it is conferred upon him by the Constitution and laws of the United States, and must therefore be respected and enforced in its judicial tribunals.

. . .

Much of the argument on the part of the plaintiff turned upon political rights and political questions, upon which the court has been urged to express an opinion. We decline doing so. The high power has been conferred on this court of passing judgment upon the acts of the State sovereignties, and of the legislative and executive branches of the federal government, and of determining whether they are beyond the limits of power marked out for them respectively by the Constitution of the United States. This tribunal, therefore, should be the last to overstep the boundaries which limit its own jurisdiction. And while it should always be ready to meet any question confided to it by the Constitution, it is equally its duty not to pass beyond its appropriate sphere of action, and to take care not to involve itself in discussions which properly belong to other forums. No one, we believe, has ever doubted the proposition, that, according to the institutions of this country, the sovereignty in every State resides in the people of the State, and that they may alter and change their form of government at their own pleasure. But whether they have changed it or not by abolishing an old government, and establishing a new one in its place, is a question to be settled by the political power. And when that power has decided, the courts are bound to take notice of its decision, and to follow it.

The judgment of the Circuit Court must therefore be affirmed.

JUSTICE WOODBURY, dissenting.

. . .

IV. Powers of the National Government

MAJOR DEVELOPMENTS

- Jackson and his successors veto on constitutional grounds bills incorporating a national bank and providing federal funding for internal improvements
- Congress annexes Texas by joint resolution
- The Supreme Court sustains federal fugitive slave acts but rules that Congress has no power to ban slavery in the western territories

The scope of congressional authority to promote commercial prosperity, acquire new territories, and protect slavery remained the most important constitutional controversies over the powers of the national government during the Jacksonian Era. Debates over congressional power to promote commercial prosperity focused on the constitutionality of the national bank, federally funded internal improvements, and protective tariffs. Whether Congress could annex, by a joint resolution, the Republic of Texas was the primary constitutional debate over national expansion. Slaveholders and anti-slavery activists disputed whether Congress could prohibit slavery in American territories and whether Congress could pass a fugitive slave law.

Most prominent political actors championed broad national powers during some of these debates and rejected national power in others. Democrats opposed and Whigs favored broad national power to promote commercial prosperity. The parties reversed their positions on national expansion. Most Democrats thought Texas could be annexed by a joint resolution passed by majorities in both the Senate and the House. Most Whigs insisted that Texas could be annexed only by a treaty ratified by a two-thirds majority of the

Senate. Many anti-slavery activists maintained that Congress could ban slavery in the territories but could not pass a fugitive slave law. Many slaveholders maintained that Congress could not ban slavery in the territories but could pass a fugitive slave law.

Southern Democrats triumphed during most of these constitutional debates. President Jackson and his successors vetoed bills incorporating the national bank and providing federal funds for internal improvements. Congress reduced tariffs. Texas was admitted to the Union by a joint resolution of both houses of Congress. The Supreme Court in *Prigg v. Pennsylvania* (1842) ruled that Congress could pass fugitive slave laws. Congress passed a controversial fugitive slave law in 1850. Congress in 1854 repealed the provision in the Missouri Compromise prohibiting slavery in all territories above the 36°30′ parallel line. The Supreme Court in *Dred Scott v. Sandford* (1857) declared that this provision had always been unconstitutional because Congress had no power to ban slavery in the territories.

The presidential veto power proved to be a critical tool for enforcing the Democratic view of the scope of congressional power. Jackson and his successors in the White House successfully prevented Whigs from implementing their vision of national power, and Democratic vetoes repeatedly emphasized a strict construction of national authority. Sophisticated politicians understood that *McCulloch v. Maryland* (1819) was no longer a vital precedent. Jackson's bank veto message, not Marshall's *McCulloch* opinion, was the canonical document of the Jacksonian Era on the scope of the necessary and proper clause.

But Democrats sometimes pressed for the use of national power. Article IV, Section 2 of the U.S. Constitution requires states to return escaped slaves. That provision declares, "No Person held to Service or Labour in one State, under the Laws thereof, escaping into another, shall, in Consequence of any Law or Regulation therein, be discharged from such Service or Labour, But shall be delivered up on Claim of the Party to whom such Service or Labour may be due." Among the questions this provision left open was the extent of congressional power over the rendition process, the process by which fugitive slaves were identified, captured, and returned. Anti-slavery advocates insisted that free states retained the power to require that masters rely on free-state government officials to apprehend a fugitive and to hold a hearing to determine whether an alleged fugitive was actually an escaped slave. They sought to enforce that understanding with state-level "personal liberty" laws that obstructed the recovery of alleged fugitive slaves. Slave-state representatives claimed that the fugitive slave clause prohibited any state law that might interfere in any way with the rendition process determined by Congress. They sought to implement national rules of rendition that favored slavemasters. Democrats generally lent their support to slavery advocates. They were often joined by so-called "Cotton" Whigs, who tried to emphasize the need for national unity and to deemphasize slavery issues. The growing influence of a faction of "Conscience" Whigs, who favored stronger measures to oppose slavery, within the party made that stance increasingly difficult and fed the development of new anti-slavery parties, from the Free Soil Party of the late 1840s to the more durable Republican Party in the mid-1850s.

Whether Congress could prohibit slavery in the territories was the most explosive constitutional question of Jacksonian politics. The stakes were both political and economic. Conventional wisdom maintained that the congressional decision to ban or permit human bondage in the territories determined the balance of power in Congress between the free and slave states. Most slaveholders and abolitionists agreed that slave territories invariably became slave states and free territories invariably became free states. Conventional wisdom also maintained that slavery could survive economically only by expanding into new territories. Slaveholders and abolitionists agreed that slavery would eventually wither away if the practice were confined to the original slave states and slave territories. Here slaveholders contended that Congress could not constitutionally prohibit slavery in American territories. The territories were to be held as common property of all the states, and Congress could not discriminate against citizens from the slave states nor ban the entrance of the property that they lawfully possessed when they migrated from the slave states to the western territories. Their opponents contended that Congress held plenary power over the territories and was free to ban slavery within any federally controlled territory. Such a power was implicit, they thought, in prior congressional actions, including the Northwest Ordinance of 1787 and the Missouri Compromise of 1820, which prohibited slavery in specific northern territories.

Illustration 5-1 General Jackson Slaying the Monster Bank

Source: Division of Home and Community Life, National Museum of American History, Smithsonian Institution. Harry T. Peters, "America on Stone" Lithography Collection.

Andrew Jackson, Veto Message Regarding the Bank of the United States (1832)[16]

The Second Bank of the United States was given a twenty-year charter in 1816. Jackson's political opponents decided they could embarrass the president by seeking an early re-charter of that institution before the 1832 election. President Jackson surprised many by vetoing the bill and offering powerful constitutional arguments against the bank. Jackson was far more astute than his opponents, who thought the bank veto would destroy Jackson politically. Jacksonians trumpeted their opposition to the bank in the 1832 presidential election and won a landslide victory.

Jackson's veto message established that McCulloch v. Maryland *(1819) did not settle the constitutionality of the national bank. The first part argued that the constitutionality of the bank was still a live issue that could be determined only by elected officials. Jackson then argued that the bank was not necessary and proper to the exercise of federal powers. The president concluded his message by denouncing the bank bill as factional legislation that aimed to create a monopoly to benefit the rich.*

Whigs made an effort to charter a third national bank of the United States after gaining control of all three branches of the national government in 1840. Unfortunately, President Harrison died before legislation was passed. His successor, Vice President John Tyler, had a more narrow understanding of federal power than Jackson did. When Congress presented Tyler with a bank bill, he rejected the measure on the ground that the bank would have the power

16. Excerpt taken from Andrew Jackson, "Veto Message Regarding the Bank of the United States (July 10, 1832)," in *A Compilation of the Messages and Papers of the President 1789–1897,* ed. James D. Richardson (Washington, DC: Government Printing Office, 1896), 2:576.

to establish branches in the states without state approval. When Congress passed a national bank bill that confined the offices of that bank to the District of Columbia, President Tyler vetoed the measure on the ground that the measure unconstitutionally "invested" a "local bank" with "general powers to operate over the Union."[17] *Whigs never again made a serious effort to charter a national bank.*

How do these events help you understand the constitutional status of McCulloch after the bank veto? What did the necessary and proper clause "mean" in the late 1830s? What would have been the best "authority" to cite when fashioning a constitutional argument for a lawyer in the 1840s?

. . .

A bank of the United States is in many respects convenient for the Government and useful to the people. Entertaining this opinion, and deeply impressed with the belief that some of the powers and privileges possessed by the existing bank are unauthorized by the Constitution, subversive of the rights of the States, and dangerous to the liberties of the people, I felt it my duty at an early period of my Administration to call the attention of Congress to the practicability of organizing an institution combining all its advantages and obviating these objections. I sincerely regret that in the act before me I can perceive none of those modifications of the bank charter which are necessary, in my opinion, to make it compatible with justice, with sound policy, or with the Constitution of our country.

. . .

It is maintained by the advocates of the bank that its constitutionality in all its features ought to be considered as settled by precedent and by the decision of the Supreme Court. To this conclusion I can not assent. Mere precedent is a dangerous source of authority, and should not be regarded as deciding questions of constitutional power except where the acquiescence of the people and the States can be considered as well settled. So far from this being the case on this subject, an argument against the bank might be based on precedent. One Congress, in 1791, decided in favor of a bank; another, in 1811, decided against it. One Congress, in 1815, decided against a bank; another, in 1816, decided in its favor. Prior to the present Congress, therefore, the precedents drawn from that source were equal. If we resort to the States, the expressions of legislative, judicial, and executive opinions against the bank have been probably to those in its favor as 4 to 1. There is nothing in precedent, therefore, which, if its authority were admitted, ought to weigh in favor of the act before me.

If the opinion of the Supreme Court covered the whole ground of this act, it ought not to control the coordinate authorities of this Government. The Congress, the Executive, and the Court must each for itself be guided by its own opinion of the Constitution. Each public officer who takes an oath to support the Constitution swears that he will support it as he understands it, and not as it is understood by others. It is as much the duty of the House of Representatives, of the Senate, and of the President to decide upon the constitutionality of any bill or resolution which may be presented to them for passage or approval as it is of the supreme judges when it may be brought before them for judicial decision. The opinion of the judges has no more authority over Congress than the opinion of Congress has over the judges, and on that point the President is independent of both. The authority of the Supreme Court must not, therefore, be permitted to control the Congress or the Executive when acting in their legislative capacities, but to have only such influence as the force of their reasoning may deserve.

But in the case relied upon the Supreme Court have not decided that all the features of this corporation are compatible with the Constitution. It is true that the court have said that the law incorporating the bank is a constitutional exercise of power by Congress. . . .

. . . [But] the principle here affirmed is that the "degree of its necessity," involving all the details of a banking institution, is a question exclusively for legislative consideration. A bank is constitutional, but it is the province of the Legislature to determine whether this or that particular power, privilege, or exemption is "necessary and proper" to enable the bank to discharge its duties to the Government, and from their decision there is no appeal to the courts of justice. Under the decision of the Supreme Court, therefore, it is the exclusive province of Congress and the President to decide whether the particular features of this act are *necessary* and *proper* in order to enable the bank to perform conveniently and efficiently the public duties assigned to it as a fiscal agent, and therefore constitutional, or *unnecessary* and *improper*, and therefore unconstitutional.

17. John Tyler, "Veto Messages," in *Compilation of the Messages* (see note 16), 4:70.

Without commenting on the general principle affirmed by the Supreme Court, let us examine the details of this act in accordance with the rule of legislative action which they have laid down. It will be found that many of the powers and privileges conferred on it can not be supposed necessary for the purpose for which it is proposed to be created, and are not, therefore, means necessary to attain the end in view, and consequently not justified by the Constitution.

The original act of incorporation . . . enacts "that no other bank shall be established by any future law of the United States during the continuance of the corporation hereby created, for which the faith of the United States is hereby pledged. . . ."

If Congress possessed the power to establish one bank, they had power to establish more than one if in their opinion two or more banks had been "necessary" to facilitate the execution of the powers delegated to them in the Constitution. . . . It was possessed by one Congress as well as another, and by all Congresses alike. . . . But the Congress of 1816 have taken it away from their successors. . . . It can not be *"necessary"* or *"proper"* for Congress to barter away or divest themselves of any of the powers vested in them by the Constitution to be exercised for the public good. . . . This restriction on themselves and grant of a monopoly to the bank is therefore unconstitutional.

. . .

This act authorizes and encourages transfers of its stock to foreigners and grants them an exemption from all State and national taxation. So far from being *"necessary and proper"* that the bank should possess this power to make it a safe and efficient agent of the Government in its fiscal operations, it is calculated to convert the Bank of the United States into a foreign bank, to impoverish our people in time of peace, to disseminate a foreign influence through every section of the Republic, and in war to endanger our independence.

. . .

The Government of the United States have no constitutional power to purchase lands within the States except "for the erection of forts, magazines, arsenals, dockyards, and other needful buildings," and even for these objects only "by the consent of the legislature of the State in which the same shall be." By making themselves stockholders in the bank and granting to the corporation the power to purchase lands for other purposes they assume a power not granted in the Constitution and grant to others what they do not themselves possess. It is not *necessary* to the receiving, safe-keeping, or transmission of the funds of the Government that the bank should possess this power, and it is not *proper* that Congress should thus enlarge the powers delegated to them in the Constitution.

. . .

By its silence, considered in connection with the decision of the Supreme Court in the case of McCulloch against the State of Maryland, this act takes from the States the power to tax a portion of the banking business carried on within their limits, in subversion of one of the strongest barriers which secured them against Federal encroachments. . . .

Upon the formation of the Constitution the States guarded their taxing power with peculiar jealousy. They surrendered it only as it regards imports and exports. In relation to every other object within their jurisdiction, whether persons, property, business, or professions, it was secured in as ample a manner as it was before possessed. . . . Every private business, whether carried on by an officer of the General Government or not, whether it be mixed with public concerns or not, even if it be carried on by the Government of the United States itself, separately or in partnership, falls within the scope of the taxing power of the State. . . . Over this whole subject-matter it is just as absolute, unlimited, and uncontrollable as if the Constitution had never been adopted, because in the formation of that instrument it was reserved without qualification.

The principle is conceded that the States can not rightfully tax the operations of the General Government. They can not tax the money of the Government deposited in the State banks, nor the agency of those banks in remitting it; but will any man maintain that their mere selection to perform this public service for the General Government would exempt the State banks and their ordinary business from State taxation? Had the United States, instead of establishing a bank at Philadelphia, employed a private banker to keep and transmit their funds, would it have deprived Pennsylvania of the right to tax his bank and his usual banking operations? It will not be pretended. Upon what principal, then, are the banking establishments of the Bank of the United States and their usual banking operations to be exempted from taxation? . . .

It can not be *necessary* to the character of the bank as a fiscal agent of the Government that its private business should be exempted from that taxation to which all the State banks are liable, nor can I conceive it *"proper"* that the substantive and most essential powers reserved by the States shall be thus attacked and annihilated as a means of executing the powers delegated to the General Government. . . .

If our power over means is so absolute that the Supreme Court will not call in question the constitutionality of an act of Congress . . . it becomes us to proceed in our legislation with the utmost caution. . . .

. . .

It is to be regretted that the rich and powerful too often bend the acts of government to their selfish purposes. Distinctions in society will always exist under every just government. Equality of talents, of education, or of wealth can not be produced by human institutions. In the full enjoyment of the gifts of Heaven and the fruits of superior industry, economy, and virtue, every man is equally entitled to protection by law; but when the laws undertake to add to these natural and just advantages artificial distinctions, to grant titles, gratuities, and exclusive privileges, to make the rich richer and the potent more powerful, the humble members of society—the farmers, mechanics, and laborers—who have neither the time nor the means of securing like favors to themselves, have a right to complain of the injustice of their Government. There are no necessary evils in government. Its evils exist only in its abuses. If it would confine itself to equal protection, and, as Heaven does its rains, shower its favors alike on the high and the low, the rich and the poor, it would be an unqualified blessing. In the act before me there seems to be a wide and unnecessary departure from these just principles.

Nor is our Government to be maintained or our Union preserved by invasions of the rights and powers of the several States. In thus attempting to make our General Government strong we make it weak. Its true strength consists in leaving individuals and States as much as possible to themselves—in making itself felt, not in its power, but in its beneficence; not in its control, but in its protection; not in binding the States more closely to the center, but leaving each to move unobstructed in its proper orbit.

Experience should teach us wisdom. Most of the difficulties our Government now encounters and most of the dangers which impend over our Union have sprung from an abandonment of the legitimate objects of Government by our national legislation, and the adoption of such principles as are embodied in this act. Many of our rich men have not been content with equal protection and equal benefits, but have besought us to make them richer by act of Congress. By attempting to gratify their desires we have in the results of our legislation arrayed section against section, interest against interest, and man against man, in a fearful commotion which threatens to shake the foundations of our Union. It is time to pause in our career to review our principles, and if possible revive that devoted patriotism and spirit of compromise which distinguished the sages of the Revolution and the fathers of our Union. If we can not at once, in justice to interests vested under improvident legislation, make our Government what it ought to be, we can at least take a stand against all new grants of monopolies and exclusive privileges, against any prostitution of our Government to the advancement of the few at the expense of the many, and in favor of compromise and gradual reform in our code of laws and system of political economy.

Prigg v. Pennsylvania, 41 U.S. 539 (1842)

Edward Prigg was a professional slavecatcher hired to find and capture Margaret Morgan, who had allegedly fled to Pennsylvania from slavery in Maryland. After local officials refused his requests for help, Prigg and his associates abducted Morgan and her family. Pennsylvania charged Prigg with a felony for forcibly removing a black person from the state to be kept as a slave. Prigg was convicted by a state jury and his conviction was upheld by the Pennsylvania Supreme Court. He appealed that decision to the U.S. Supreme Court. Prigg claimed that the Pennsylvania law violated the U.S. Constitution. Both Pennsylvania and Maryland officials cooperated in order to make sure the Supreme Court adjudicated this test case.

The Supreme Court reversed Prigg's conviction. Justice Joseph Story's opinion for the Court held that owners were free to engage in self-help when capturing escaped slaves, that the Fugitive Slave Act of 1793 was constitutional, and that federal power over the rendition process was exclusive. States, Story maintained, could not pass any laws regulating the rendition of fugitive slaves. Chief Justice Roger Taney, Justice Peter Daniel, and Justice Smith Thompson rejected Story's claim that the federal power over fugitive slaves was exclusive. They believed that states were empowered to pass laws that assisted masters seeking to recover fugitive slaves. Justice John McLean's dissent rejected claims that owners could rely on self-help when capturing fugitive slaves.[18]

As you read, consider what a strict constructionist reading of the fugitive slave clause might be. How would a person read provisions relating to slavery narrowly? Note the similarities between Justice Story's broad construction of federal power over fugitive slaves and John Marshall's broad interpretation in McCulloch v. Maryland *(1819) of the necessary and proper clause. Do these similarities demonstrate principled jurisprudence or a failure to recognize important distinctions between the two constitutional issues? Justice Story maintained that his opinion in Prigg was actually a "triumph of freedom." Why might he have thought that? Was he correct?*

JUSTICE STORY delivered the opinion of the Court.

. . .

. . . Historically, it is well known, that the object of [the Fugitive Slave Clause] was to secure to the citizens of the slaveholding states the complete right and title of ownership in their slaves, as property, in every state in the Union into which they might escape from the state where they were held in servitude. The full recognition of this right and title was indispensable to the security of this species of property in all the slaveholding states; and, indeed, was so vital to the preservation of their domestic interests and institutions, that it cannot be doubted that it constituted a fundamental article, without the adoption of which the Union could not have been formed. Its true design was to guard against the doctrines and principles prevalent in the non-slaveholding states, by preventing them from intermeddling with, or obstructing, or abolishing the rights of the owners of slaves.

By the general law of nations, no nation is bound to recognize the state of slavery, as to foreign slaves found within its territorial dominions, when it is in opposition to its own policy and institutions, in favor of the subjects of other nations where slavery is recognized. If it does it, it is as a matter of comity, and not as a matter of international right. The state of slavery is deemed to be a mere municipal regulation, founded upon and limited to the range of the territorial laws. . . . It is manifest from this consideration, that if the Constitution had not contained this clause, every non-slave-holding state in the Union would have been at liberty to have declared free all runaway slaves coming within its limits, and to have given them entire immunity and protection against the claims of their masters; a course which would have created the most bitter animosities, and engendered perpetual strife between the different states. The clause was, therefore, of the last importance to the safety and security of the southern states; and could not have been surrendered by them without endangering their whole property in slaves. The clause was accordingly adopted into the Constitution by the unanimous consent of the framers of it; a proof at once of its intrinsic and practical necessity.

. . .

The clause manifestly contemplates the existence of a positive, unqualified right on the part of the owner of the slave, which no state law or regulation can in any way qualify, regulate, control, or restrain. . . . Now, certainly, without indulging in any nicety of criticism upon words, it may fairly and reasonably be said, that any state law or state regulation, which interrupts, limits, delays, or postpones the right of the owner to the immediate possession of the slave, and the immediate command of his service and labor, operates, pro-tanto, a discharge of the slave therefrom. . . .

. . . [U]nder and in virtue of the Constitution, the owner of a slave is clothed with entire authority, in every state in the Union, to seize and recapture his slave, whenever he can do it without any breach of the peace, or any illegal violence. In this sense, and to this extent this clause of the Constitution may properly be said to execute itself; and to require no aid from legislation, state or national.

. . .

And this leads us to the consideration of the other part of the clause, which implies at once a guaranty and duty. It says, "But he (the slave) shall be delivered up on claim of the party to whom such service or labor may be due." Now, we think it exceedingly difficult, if not impracticable, to read this language and not to feel that it contemplated some further remedial redress than that which might be administered at the hands of the owner himself. . . . The slave is to be delivered up on the claim. By whom to be delivered up? In what mode to be delivered up? How, if a refusal takes place, is the right of delivery to be enforced? Upon what proofs? . . .

18. On the background to *Prigg,* see also Paul Finkelman, "Story Telling on the Court: *Prigg v. Pennsylvania* and Justice Joseph Story's Judicial Nationalism," *Supreme Court Review 1994* (1995): 247.

These, and many other questions, will readily occur upon the slightest attention to the clause; and it is obvious that they can receive but one satisfactory answer. They require the aid of legislation to protect the right, to enforce the delivery, and to secure the subsequent possession of the slave. If, indeed, the Constitution guarantees the right, and if it requires the delivery upon the claim of the owner, (as cannot well be doubted) the natural inference certainly is, that the national government is clothed with the appropriate authority and functions to enforce it.... The states cannot ... be compelled to enforce them; and it might well be deemed an unconstitutional exercise of the power of interpretation, to insist that the states are bound to provide means to carry into effect the duties of the national government, nowhere delegated or entrusted to them by the Constitution. On the contrary, the natural, if not the necessary conclusion is, that the national government, in the absence of all positive provisions to the contrary, is bound, through its own proper departments, legislative, judicial, or executive, as the case may require, to carry into effect all the rights and duties imposed upon it by the Constitution....

...

Congress has taken this very view of the power and duty of the national government. As early as the year 1791, the attention of Congress was drawn to it.... The result of their deliberations was the passage of the [Fugitive Slave Act of 1793].

... [T]his act may be truly said to cover the whole ground of the Constitution.... If this be so, then it would seem, upon just principles of construction, that the legislation of Congress, if constitutional, must supersede all state legislation upon the same subject; and by necessary implication prohibit it.... [T]he legislation of Congress, in what it does prescribe, manifestly indicates that it does not intend that there shall be any further legislation to act upon the subject-matter....

But it has been argued, that the act of Congress is unconstitutional, because it does not fall within the scope of any of the enumerated powers of legislation confided to that body; and therefore it is void.... No one has ever supposed that Congress could, constitutionally, by its legislation, exercise powers, or enact laws beyond the powers delegated to it by the Constitution; but it has, on various occasions, exercised powers which were necessary and proper as means to carry into effect rights expressly given, and duties expressly enjoined thereby. The end being required, it has been deemed a just and necessary implication, that the means to accomplish it are given also; or, in other words, that the power flows as a necessary means to accomplish the end.

...

The remaining question is, whether the power of legislation upon this subject is exclusive in the national government, or concurrent in the states, until it is exercised by Congress. In our opinion it is exclusive....

...

It is scarcely conceivable that the slaveholding states would have been satisfied with leaving to the legislation of the non-slaveholding states, a power of regulation, in the absence of that of Congress, which would or might practically amount to a power to destroy the rights of the owner.... [C]onstrue the right of legislation as exclusive in Congress, and every evil, and every danger vanishes.... But, upon the other supposition, the moment he passes the state line, he becomes amenable to the laws of another sovereignty, whose regulations may greatly embarrass or delay the exercise of his rights; and even be repugnant to those of the state where he first arrested the fugitive. Consequences like these show that the nature and objects of the provision imperiously require, that, to make it effectual, it should be construed to be exclusive of state authority....

...

JUSTICE WAYNE, concurring.

...

My object, and the only object which I have in view, in what I am about to say, is, to establish the position that Congress has the exclusive right to legislate upon this provision of the Constitution....

...

It is admitted, that the provision raises what is properly termed a perfect obligation upon all of the states to abstain from doing any thing which may interfere with the rights secured. Will this be so, if any part of what may be necessary to discharge the obligation is reserved by each state, to be done as each may think proper? ... That was not anticipated by the representatives of the slaveholding states in the convention, nor could it have been intended by the framers of the Constitution.

Is it not more reasonable to infer, as the states were forming a government for themselves, to the extent of the powers conceded in the Constitution, to which legislative power was given to make all laws necessary and proper to carry into execution all powers vested in it—that they meant that the right for which some of the states stipulated, and to which all acceded, should, from the peculiar nature of the property in which only some of the states were interested—be carried into execution by that department of the general government in which they were all to be represented, the Congress of the United States.

. . . But it is said, all that is contended for, is, that the states may legislate to aid the object, and that such legislation will be constitutional if it does not conflict with the remedies which Congress may enact. This is a cautious way of asserting the right in the states, and it seems to impose a limitation which makes it unobjectionable. But the reply to it is, that the right to legislate a remedy, implies so much indefinite power over the subject, and such protracted continuance, as to the mode of finally determining whether a fugitive owes service and labor, that the requirements of the remedy, without being actually in conflict with the provision or the enactments of Congress might be oppressive to those most interested in the provision, by interposing delays and expenses more costly than the value of the fugitive sought to be reclaimed.

. . .

CHIEF JUSTICE TANEY, concurring.

. . . I think the states are not prohibited; and that, on the contrary, it is enjoined upon them as a duty to protect and support the owner when he is endeavoring to obtain possession of his property found within their respective territories.

. . . [T]he laws of the different states, in all other cases, constantly protect the citizens of other states in their rights of property, when it is found within their respective territories; and no one doubts their power to do so. And in the absence of any express prohibition, I perceive no reason for establishing, by implication, a different rule in this instance; where, by the national compact, this right of property is recognized as an existing right in every state of the Union.

. . .

. . . There are other clauses in the Constitution in which other individual rights are provided for and secured in like manner; and it never has been suggested that the states could not uphold and maintain them, because they were guarantied by the Constitution of the United States. On the contrary, it has always been held to be the duty of the states to enforce them; and the action of the general government has never been deemed necessary except to resist and prevent their violation.

. . .

JUSTICE THOMPSON, concurring.

. . .

. . . The provision in the Constitution under consideration, is one under which such conflicting legislation may arise; and harmony is produced by making the state law yield to that of the United States. But to assert that the states cannot legislate on the subject at all, in the absence of all legislation by Congress, is, in my judgment, not warranted by any fair and reasonable construction of the provision. . . . [W]hat becomes of the right where there is no law on the subject? Should Congress repeal the law of 1793, and pass no other law on the subject, I can entertain no doubt that state legislation, for the purpose of restoring the slave to his master, and faithfully to carry into execution the provision of the Constitution, would be valid.

JUSTICE DANIEL, concurring.

. . .

. . . I cannot regard the third clause of the fourth article as falling either within the definition or meaning of an exclusive power. . . .

. . .

If there is a power in the states to authorize and order their arrest and detention for delivery to their owners, not only will the probabilities of recovery be increased by the performance of duties enjoined by law upon the citizens of those states, as well private persons as those who are officers of the law; but the incitements of interest, under the hope of reward, will in a certain class of persons powerfully co-operate to the same ends. . . . But those who argue from such possible or probable abuses against all regulations by the states touching this matter, should dismiss their apprehensions, under the recollection that should those abuses be attempted, the corrective may be found, as it is now about to be applied to some extent, in the controlling constitutional authority of this Court.

. . .

JUSTICE McLEAN, dissenting.

. . .

. . . That the Constitution was adopted in a spirit of compromise, is matter of history. And all experience shows that to attain the great objects of this fundamental law, it must be construed and enforced in a spirit of enlightened forbearance and justice. . . .

. . .

The nature of the power shows that it must be exclusive.

. . .

The necessity for this provision was found in the views and feelings of the people of the states opposed to slavery; and who, under such an influence, could not be expected favorably to regard the rights of the master. Now, by whom is this paramount law to be executed?

It is contended that the power to execute it rests with the states. The law was designed to protect the rights of the slaveholder against the states opposed to those rights; and yet, by this argument, the effective power is in the hands of those on whom it is to operate.

This would produce a strange anomaly in the history of legislation. It would show an inexperience and folly in the venerable framers of the Constitution, from which, of all public bodies that ever assembled, they were, perhaps, most exempt.

. . .

It is contended, that the power to legislate on this subject is concurrently in the states and federal government. That the acts of the latter are paramount, but that the acts of the former must be regarded as of authority, until abrogated by the federal power. How a power exercised by one sovereignty can be called concurrent, which may be abrogated by another, I cannot comprehend. . . .

. . .

Dred Scott v. Sandford, 60 U.S. 394 (1857)

Dred Scott was the slave of John Emerson, an army doctor. Emerson took Scott to military forts in the free state of Illinois and in the Wisconsin Territory (where slavery was barred by the Missouri Compromise) before returning to St. Louis, Missouri (where slavery was legal). Some time after Emerson's death, Scott sued Emerson's widow and her brother, John Sanford,[19] *for his freedom. Scott claimed he had been freed by his travels in free territory. Sanford claimed that slavery reattached once Scott returned to Missouri. A trial court declared Scott free, but the Missouri Supreme Court reversed that decision. Scott then filed a similar lawsuit in federal court. That federal lawsuit raised two new constitution questions. The first was whether Scott, if free, was a citizen of the United States entitled to sue another citizen of the United States in federal court. The second was whether Congress had the power to ban slavery in the territories. After the federal district court rejected Scott's freedom suit, he appealed to the U.S. Supreme Court.*

The Supreme Court held that former slaves could not become American citizens and that Congress could not prohibit slavery in American territories acquired after the Constitution was ratified. Chief Justice Taney's opinion for the Court insisted that Article IV either was limited to the territory the United States possessed in 1787 or merely vested Congress with the power to hold and sell public lands. The concurring opinions in Dred Scott *maintained that bans on slavery in the territories unconstitutionally discriminated against slaveholders and the slaveholding states. The dissenting opinions in* Dred Scott *asserted that Article IV vested Congress with the same power to govern the territories as the national legislature had to govern the District of Columbia or as state governments had to govern their states.*

As you read, consider how these arguments over the power to regulate slavery in the territories compare with arguments over the necessary and proper clause. Many commentators contend that Dred Scott *was the worst decision ever made by the Supreme Court. Was Justice Taney guilty of poor legal reasoning, or is the main flaw with* Dred Scott *the judicial decision to protect slavery and racism? (Other aspects of the case are excerpted and discussed later in this chapter in Section IX.)*

CHIEF JUSTICE TANEY delivered the opinion of the court.

. . .

The counsel for the plaintiff has laid much stress upon that article of the Constitution which confers on Congress the power "to dispose and make all needful rules and regulations respecting the territory or other property belonging to the United States;" but, in the judgment of the court, that provision has no bearing on the present controversy, and the power there given, whatever it may be, is confined, and was intended to be confined, to the territory which at that time belonged to, or was claimed by, the United States. . . . It was a special provision for a known and particular territory, and to meet a present emergency, and nothing more.

. . .

The language used in this clause, the arrangement and combination of the powers, and the somewhat unusual phraseology it uses . . . all indicate the design and meaning of the clause to be such as we have mentioned. It does not speak of *any* territory, nor of

19. The Court reporter misspelled Sanford's name.

Territories, but uses language which, according to its legitimate meaning, points to a particular thing. The power is given in relation only to *the* territory of the United States. . . . It begins its enumeration of powers by that of disposing, in other words, making sale of the lands, or raising money from them, which, as we have already said, was the main object of the cession and which is accordingly the first thing provided for in the article. It then gives the power which was necessarily associated with the disposition and sale of the lands—that is, the power of making needful rules and regulations respecting the territory. . . .

. . .

The words "needful rules and regulations" would seem, also, to have been cautiously used for some definite object. They are not the words usually employed by statesmen, when they mean to give the powers of sovereignty, or to establish a Government, or to authorize its establishment. . . .

. . .

There is certainly no power given by the Constitution to the Federal Government to establish or maintain colonies bordering the United States or at a distance, to be ruled and governed at its pleasure; nor to enlarge its territorial limits in any way, except by admission of new States. . . .

. . .

Taking this rule to guide us, it may be safely assumed that citizens of the United States who migrate to a Territory belonging to the people of the United States, cannot be ruled as mere colonists, dependent upon the will of the General Government, and to be governed by any laws it may think proper to impose. . . . Whatever it acquires, it acquires for the benefit of the people of the several States who created it. It is their trustee acting for them, and charged with the duty of promoting the interests of the whole people of the Union in the exercise of the powers specifically granted.

. . .

Upon these considerations, it is the opinion of this court that the act of Congress which prohibited a citizen from holding and owning property of this kind in the territory of the United States north of the line therein mentioned, is not warranted by the Constitution, and is therefore void; and that neither Dred Scott himself, nor any his family, were made free by being carried into this territory; even if they had been carried there by the owner, with the intention of becoming a permanent resident.

. . .

JUSTICE WAYNE . . .

JUSTICE NELSON . . .

JUSTICE GRIER . . .

JUSTICE DANIEL

. . .

But whatever power vested in Congress, and whatever the precise subject to which that power extended, it is clear that the power related to a subject appertaining to the *United States*, and one to be disposed of and regulated for the benefit and under the authority of the *United States*. Congress was made simply the agent or *trustee* for the United States, and could not, without a breach of trust and a fraud, appropriate the subject of the trust to any other beneficiary . . . than the United States, or to the people of the United States, upon equal grounds, legal or equitable. Congress could not appropriate that subject to any one class or portion of the people, to the exclusion of others, politically and constitutionally equals; but every citizen would, if any *one* could claim it, have the like rights of purchase, settlement, occupation, or any other right, in the national territory.

Nothing can be more conclusive to show the equality of this with every other right in all the citizens of the United States, and the iniquity and absurdity of the pretension to exclude or to disenfranchise a portion of them because they are the owners of slaves, than the fact that the same instrument, which imparts to Congress its very existence and its every function, guarantees to every slaveholder the title to his property, and gives him the right to its reclamation throughout the entire extent of the nation; and, further, that the only private property which the Constitution has *specifically recognized*, and has imposed it as a direct obligation both on the States and the Federal Government to protect and enforce, is the property of the master in his slave. . . .

. . .

JUSTICE CAMPBELL

. . .

Whatever these [state] Constitutions and laws validly determine to be property, it is the duty of the Federal Government, through the domain of jurisdiction merely Federal, to recognize to be property.

And this principle follows from the structure of the respective Governments, State and Federals, and their reciprocal relations. . . . A proscription, therefore, of the Constitution and the laws of one or more States, determining property, on the part of the Federal Government, by which the stability of its social system may be endangered, is plainly repugnant to the conditions on which the Federal Constitution was adopted, or which the Government was designed to accomplish. . . . Wherever a master is entitled to go within the United States, his slave may accompany him, without any impediment from, or fear of, Congressional legislation or interference. . . .

. . .

JUSTICE CATRON . . .

JUSTICE McLEAN [dissenting]

. . . The power to make all needful rules and regulations is a power to legislate. This no one will controvert, as Congress cannot make "rules and regulations," except by legislation. But it is argued that the word "territory" is used as synonymous with the word "land." . . . That this is not the true construction of the section appears from the fact that in the first line of the section "the power to dispose of the public lands" is given expressly, and, in addition, to make all needful rules and regulations. The power to dispose of is complete in itself, and requires nothing more. . . .

. . .

But, if it be admitted that the word "territory" as used means land, and nothing but land, the power of Congress to organize a temporary Government is clear. It has power to make all needful regulations respecting the public lands, and the extent of those "needful regulations" depends upon the direction of Congress, where the means are appropriate to the end, and do not conflict with any of the prohibitions of the Constitution. If a temporary Government be deemed needful, necessary, requisite, or is wanted, Congress has the power to establish it. . . .

If Congress should deem slaves or free colored persons injurious to the population of a free Territory, as conducing to lessen the value of the public lands, or on any other ground connected with the public interest, they have the power to prohibit them from becoming settlers in it. This can be sustained on the ground of a sound national policy. . . . [I]t is only necessary to say that . . . the repugnancy to slavery would probably prevent fifty or a hundred freemen from settling in a slave Territory, where one slaveholder would be prevented from settling in a free Territory.

. . .

JUSTICE CURTIS [dissenting]

. . .

No reason has been suggested why any reluctance should have been felt, by the framers of the Constitution, to apply this ["needful rules and regulations"] provision to all the territory which might belong to the United States, or why any distinction should have been made, founded on the accidental circumstances of the dates of the cessions; a circumstance in no way material as respects the necessity for rules and regulations, or the propriety of conferring on the Congress power to make them. And if we look at the course of the debates in the Convention on this article, we shall find that the then unceded lands [belonging to North Carolina and Georgia], so far from having been left out of view in adopting this article, constituted, in the minds of members, a subject of paramount importance.

. . .

If, then, this clause does contain a power to legislate respecting the territory, what are the limits of that power?

To this I answer, that, in common with all the other legislative powers of Congress, it finds limits in the express prohibitions on Congress not to do certain things; that, in the exercise of the legislative power, Congress cannot pass an ex post facto law or bill of attainder, and so in respect to each of the other prohibitions contained in the Constitution.

Besides this, the rules and regulations must be needful. But undoubtedly the question whether a particular rule or regulation be needful, must be finally determined by Congress itself. Whether a law be needful, is a legislative or political, not a judicial, question. Whatever Congress deems needful is so, under the grant of power.

. . .

The Constitution declares that Congress shall have power to make "*all* needful rules and regulations" respecting the territory belonging to the United States.

The assertion is, though the Constitution says all, it does not mean all—though it says all, without qualification, it means all except such as allow or prohibit slavery. It cannot be doubted that it is incumbent on those who would introduce an exception not found in the language of the instrument, to exhibit some solid and satisfactory reason, drawn from the subject-matter or the purposes and objects of the clause, the context, or from other provisions of the Constitution, showing that the words employed in this clause are not to be understood according to their clear, plain, and natural signification.

The subject-matter is the territory of the United States out of the limits of every State, and consequently under the exclusive power of the people of the United States. Their will respecting it, manifested in the Constitution, can be subject to no restriction. . . .

A practical construction, nearly contemporaneous with the adoption of the Constitution, and continued by repeated instances through a long series of years, may always influence, and in doubtful cases should determine, the judicial mind, on a question of the interpretation of the Constitution.

. . .

I consider the passage of this law [the law confirming the Northwest Ordinance] to have been an assertion by the first Congress of the power of the United States to prohibit slavery within this part of the territory of the United States. . . .

. . .

With the weight of . . . considerations [of natural right or the political equality of the sections of the nation], when presented to Congress to influence its action, this court has no concern. One or the other may be justly entitled to guide or control the legislative judgment upon what is a needful regulation. The question here is, whether they are sufficient to authorize this court to insert into the clause of the Constitution an exception of the exclusion or allowance of slavery, not found therein, nor in any other part of that instrument. To engraft on any instrument a substantive exception not found in it, must be admitted to be a matter attended with great difficulty. . . . To allow this to be done with the Constitution, upon reasons purely political, renders its judicial interpretation impossible—because judicial tribunals, as such, cannot decide upon political considerations. Political reasons have not the requisite certainty to afford rules of judicial interpretation. They are different in different men. They are different in the same men at different times. And when a strict interpretation of the Constitution, according to the fixed rules which govern the interpretation of law, is abandoned, and the theoretical opinions of individuals are allowed to control its meaning, we have no longer a Constitution; we are under the government of individual men, who for the time being have power to declare what the Constitution is, according to their own views of what it ought to mean. When such a method of interpretation of the Constitution obtains, in place of a republican Government, with limited and defined powers, we have a Government which is merely an exponent of the will of Congress; or what, in my opinion, would not be preferable, an exponent of the individual political opinions of the members of this court.

. . .

Abraham Lincoln, Speech on Slavery in the Territories (1860)[20]

Abraham Lincoln emerged after the passage of the Kansas-Nebraska Act of 1854 as a prominent organizer of the Republican Party in Illinois and a popular speaker for the anti-slavery cause. Lincoln made opposition to both the Kansas-Nebraska Act and the Dred Scott *decision the centerpiece of his 1858 campaign to unseat Democratic senator Stephen A. Douglas. For Lincoln, Congress had both the constitutional authority and the moral obligation to exclude slavery from the territories. He lost the Senate election in 1858. Nevertheless, the national prominence Lincoln achieved during his famous debates with Douglas made him a frontrunner for the Republican presidential nomination.*

The following excerpt is taken from a speech Lincoln gave on February 27, 1860, at the Cooper Institute in New York. Lincoln was not an official candidate for the presidency at this time. Nineteenth-century politicians did not publicly seek the White House. That was considered bad form. Nevertheless, the Cooper Institute address was part of a series of speeches that Lincoln and his political advisors thought would foster eastern Republican support for his nomination in the summer party convention.

. . .

Does the proper division of local from federal authority, or anything in the Constitution, forbid *our Federal Government* to control as to slavery in *our Federal Territories?*

. . .

In 1789, by the first Congress which sat under the Constitution, an act was passed to enforce the Ordinance of '87, including the prohibition of slavery in the Northwestern Territory. . . . It went through all its stages without a word of opposition, and finally passed both branches without yeas and nays, which is

20. Excerpt taken from Abraham Lincoln, "Address at Cooper Institute, New York City," in *The Collected Works of Abraham Lincoln,* ed. Roy P. Basler (New Brunswick, NJ: Rutgers University Press, 1953), 3:522–50.

equivalent to a unanimous passage. In this Congress there were sixteen of the thirty-nine fathers who framed the original Constitution. . . .

This shows that, in their understanding, no line dividing local from federal authority, nor anything in the Constitution, properly forbade Congress to prohibit slavery in the federal territory; else both their fidelity to correct principle, and their oath to support the Constitution, would have constrained them to oppose the prohibition.

. . .

[*Lincoln then offered a survey of congressional votes on slavery in the territories between 1784 and the Missouri Compromise in 1820.*]

. . . Here, then, we have twenty-three out of our thirty-nine fathers "who framed the Government under which we live," . . . and twenty-one of them—a clear majority of the whole "thirty-nine"—so acting upon it as to make them guilty of gross political impropriety and willful perjury, if, in their understanding, any proper division between local and federal authority, or anything in the Constitution they had made themselves, and sworn to support, forbade the Federal Government to control as to slavery in the federal territories. Thus the twenty-one acted; and, as actions speak louder than words, so actions, under such responsibility, speak still louder.

. . .

Now, and here, let me guard a little against being misunderstood. I do not mean to say we are bound to follow implicitly in whatever our fathers did. To do so, would be to discard all the lights of current experience—to reject all progress—all improvement. What I do say is, that if we would supplant the opinions and policy of our fathers in any case, we should do so upon evidence so conclusive, and argument so clear, that even their great authority, fairly considered and weighed, cannot stand; and most surely not in a case whereof we ourselves declare they understood the question better than we.

But enough! Let all who believe that "our fathers, who framed the Government under which we live, understood this question just as well, and even better, than we do now," speak as they spoke, and act as they acted upon it. This is all Republicans ask—all Republicans desire—in relation to slavery. As those fathers marked it, so let it be again marked, as an evil not to be extended, but to be tolerated and protected only because of and so far as its actual presence among us makes that toleration and protection a necessity. Let all the guaranties those fathers gave it, be, not grudgingly, but fully and fairly maintained. For this Republicans contend, and with this, so far as I know or believe, they will be content.

. . .

Will they be satisfied if the Territories be unconditionally surrendered to them? We know they will not. In all their present complaints against us, the Territories are scarcely mentioned. Invasions and insurrections are the rage now. Will it satisfy them, if, in the future, we have nothing to do with invasions and insurrections? We know it will not. We so know, because we know we never had anything to do with invasions and insurrections; and yet this total abstaining does not exempt us from the charge and the denunciation.

. . .

. . . [W]hat will convince them? This, and this only: cease to call slavery *wrong*, and join them in calling it *right*. . . . Wrong as we think slavery is, we can yet afford to let it alone where it is, because that much is due to the necessity arising from its actual presence in the nation; but can we, while our votes will prevent it, allow it to spread into the National Territories, and to overrun us here in these Free States? . . .

. . .

V. Federalism

MAJOR DEVELOPMENTS

- The Supreme Court permits states to regulate local incidents of interstate commerce
- President Jackson vigorously opposes nullification
- Georgia ignores a Supreme Court decision declaring that states may not exercise sovereignty over Native American lands

Disagreements over the place of states in the national union roiled American politics from the beginning of the Jacksonian Era on. In January of 1830, Daniel Webster concluded a strongly nationalist speech by linking union to the most fundamental American value. He declared on the floor of the Senate, "Liberty and Union, Now and Forever, One and Inseparable." Webster's gambit bore fruit when the Democratic Party elite gathered at a Jefferson Day dinner later that year. The "states' rights" faction of the Democratic

Party hoped to pull President Jackson into its orbit. The president had resolved to side with Webster, on this issue at least. After an evening filled with toasts to the memory of Jefferson and Virginia's resistance to the federal sedition laws, President Jackson pointedly offered a toast to "our Union: It must be preserved." No one was more surprised than Jackson's vice president, John C. Calhoun, whose own political future depended on holding the support of the states' rights faction within his home state of South Carolina and in the national Democratic Party. Visibly disturbed, Calhoun countered: "The Union, next to our liberty, most dear. May we all remember that it can be preserved by respecting the rights of the States and by distributing equally the benefits and burdens of Union." South Carolina senator Robert Hayne quickly persuaded the president to amend his toast to "our *Federal* Union—It must be preserved." The amendment gave the southerners something they could spin in their favor, but no one mistook the president's sentiment. Secretary of State Martin Van Buren, who had helped set the president's strategy for the dinner, offered a more conciliatory toast emphasizing the virtues of "mutual forbearance and reciprocal concessions" and the "patriotic spirit" that would allow them to preserve the Union.[21]

Most Jacksonians sought to toe the fine line President Jackson walked between nationalism and states' rights. Jackson repeatedly insisted that federal power was supreme and that federal authorities determined the balance of power between the federal government and the states. He rejected claims by more extreme states' rights proponents that the Constitution was a compact with the states that permitted each state to nullify perceived unconstitutional laws. Nevertheless, when questions about state control over Native Americans and commercial enterprise arose, Jackson, his Democratic Party successors, and the Democratic majority on the Taney Court consistently declared that the Constitution vested far more power in state governments than the Marshall Court had been willing to recognize.

The regulation of interstate commerce was one key point of contention. The Marshall Court interpreted federal commercial power broadly. *Gibbons v. Ogden* (1824) and *Brown v. Maryland* (1827) established that, as the justices stated in the latter case, federal power over interstate commerce "cannot be stopped at the external boundary of a State, but must enter its interior." Congress from 1825 to 1860 rarely tested the limits of this power. The issue that occupied the late Marshall and Taney Courts was the extent to which states could regulate interstate commerce in the absence of any conflicting federal law.

During the Jacksonian Era, much of this debate focused on what has become known as the negative, or dormant, commerce clause. To what extent did the constitutional grant of power to Congress to regulate commerce among the several states implicitly restrict the authority of the state governments to regulate commerce crossing state borders? Justice Joseph Story and many Whigs claimed that the federal power over interstate commerce was exclusive. They interpreted the commerce clause as declaring that Congress and only Congress could regulate interstate commerce. State laws that affected interstate commerce were unconstitutional, even when no federal law regulated the matter. Chief Justice Roger Taney and many Democrats maintained that the federal government and state governments had concurrent power over commercial activity. They interpreted the commerce clause as permitting the states to regulate at will, unless state law conflicted with a valid federal law. Still others suggested that state police powers might trump federal authority to regulate interstate commerce when the two came into conflict. Moderates strove to find a middle ground between the exclusive and concurrent interpretations of the commerce power. They claimed that in the absence of federal regulation, the constitutionality of state laws that affected interstate commerce depended on particular circumstances.

The Supreme Court during the 1830s and 1840s was usually sharply divided when adjudicating dormant commerce clause cases, in part because many of these cases raised explosive political issues. In *Groves v. Slaughter* (1841), the justices inconclusively sparred over federal and state power to regulate the interstate slave trade. In *The License Cases* (1847), the Court produced six separate opinions while sustaining a new state licensing system for alcoholic beverages. In *The Passenger Cases* (1849), the justices generated a welter of opinions while striking down state taxes on ships entering their ports carrying indigent alien passengers. The Court finally gave some coherence to commerce clause doctrine in *Cooley v. Board of Wardens of the Port*

21. Martin Van Buren, *The Autobiography of Martin Van Buren* (Washington, DC: Government Printing Office, 1920), 2:415–16.

of Philadelphia (1852), emphasizing that the boundary between the spheres of state and federal regulation should turn on the pragmatic issue of regulatory effectiveness. Congress should predominate in situations in which the objects of regulation were "in their nature national" and required nationally uniform rules; states should predominate in situations in which policy decisions would benefit from "local knowledge and experience." The federal government had exclusive power over all commercial matters of national importance. States retained concurrent power to regulate local aspects of interstate commerce in the absence of federal law.

The Jacksonian Era also saw renewed conflict over state authority to interpret the Constitution, as well as a temporary settlement of the issue. Compact theory was an article of faith for many southerners and some northerners during the Jacksonian Era. Proponents of this theory maintained that the Constitution was a compact or treaty between otherwise independent states. Among the attributes of sovereignty retained by the states, according to this theory, was the power to determine whether a federal law was unconstitutional. Thomas Jefferson had suggested as much in his Kentucky Resolution of 1798, and nullification was a means by which a state could exercise the sovereign power to "judge for itself" whether the federal government was acting constitutionally and thus declare federal laws to be void within the borders of the state when those laws were judged to be unconstitutional. South Carolina's John C. Calhoun became the leading theoretician of the nullification argument, rushing to stay ahead of his state's political leaders who were looking to denounce the protectionist tariffs that were seen as damaging the cotton trade. When the state issued an ordinance of nullification in 1832, President Jackson threatened to send in federal troops and hang the nullifiers as traitors. In his annual message to Congress, Jackson first offered a carrot calling for an end to the protectionist tariff. A few weeks later Jackson showed the stick in a special proclamation that declared that the doctrine of nullification was "incompatible with the existence of the Union" and the practical equivalent of secession. A congressional compromise phased out the protectionist tariff and ended the crisis. Nullification did not look like the same kind of peaceful constitutional check as judicial review or the presidential veto that its proponents had promised.

Cooley v. Board of Wardens of the Port of Philadelphia, 53 U.S. 299 (1852)

In 1789 Congress passed a statute adopting state laws then in force regarding the use of pilots to assist in navigating ships through local rivers and ports. In 1803 Pennsylvania passed a law requiring that foreign or large coastal ships arriving or departing from Philadelphia employ a local pilot. The board of wardens for the port of Philadelphia brought action in state court to collect pilot fees from Aaron Cooley, who had failed to employ a pilot for two ships making use of the port. After losing in state court, Cooley appealed to the U.S. Supreme Court. He argued that the Pennsylvania pilot law was either an unconstitutional regulation of interstate commerce or in conflict with the 1789 federal statute. Pennsylvania responded that the pilot law was a constitutional exercise of a concurrent power to regulate commerce that did not conflict with any existing federal regulation.

The Supreme Court ruled that Pennsylvania could constitutionally require that ships hire local pilots. Justice Benjamin Curtis's majority opinion distinguished between situations requiring a national, uniform regulation and situations better addressed by divergent local regulations. Pilotage, he concluded, was a matter best addressed by local law. The distinction drawn in Cooley *between national and local concerns became the leading approach to dormant commerce clause issues during the rest of the nineteenth century. How useful does this formulation seem for resolving commerce clause disputes?*

JUSTICE CURTIS delivered the opinion of the Court.

. . .

That the power to regulate commerce includes the regulation of navigation, we consider settled. And when we look to the nature of the service performed by pilots, to the relations which that service and its compensations bear to navigation between the several States, and between the ports of the United States and foreign countries, we are brought to the conclusion, that [such regulations] do constitute regulations of navigation, and consequently of commerce, within the just meaning of this clause of the Constitution.

. . .

If the law of Pennsylvania, now in question, had been in existence at the date of this act of Congress [leaving in place state laws regarding pilots], we might hold it to have been adopted by Congress, and thus made a law of the United States, and so valid. . . .

But the law on which these actions are founded was not enacted till 1803. What effect then can be attributed to so much of the act of 1789, as declares, that pilots shall continue to be regulated in conformity, "with such laws as the States may respectively hereafter enact for the purpose, until further legislative provision shall be made by Congress"?

If the States were divested of the power to legislate on this subject by the grant of the commercial power to Congress, it is plain this act could not confer upon them power thus to legislate. If the Constitution excluded the States from making any law regulating commerce, certainly Congress cannot regrant, or in any manner reconvey to the States that power. And yet this act of 1789 gives its sanction only to laws enacted by the States. This necessarily implies a constitutional power to legislate. . . . Entertaining these views we are brought directly and unavoidably to the consideration of the question, whether the grant of the commercial power to Congress, did per se deprive the States of all power to regulate pilots. . . . If they are excluded it must be because the nature of the power, thus granted to Congress, requires that a similar authority should not exist in the States. . . .

The diversities of opinion . . . which have existed on this subject, have arisen from the different views taken of the nature of this power. But when the nature of a power like this is spoken of, when it is said that the nature of the power requires that it should be exercised exclusively by Congress, it must be intended to refer to the subjects of that power, and to say they are of such a nature as to require exclusive legislation by Congress. Now the power to regulate commerce, embraces a vast field, containing not only many, but exceedingly various subjects, quite unlike in their nature; some imperatively demanding a single uniform rule, operating equally on the commerce of the United States in every port; and some, like the subject now in question, as imperatively demanding that diversity, which alone can meet the local necessities of navigation.

Either absolutely to affirm, or deny that the nature of this power requires exclusive legislation by Congress, is to lose sight of the nature of the subjects of this power, and to assert concerning all of them, what is really applicable but to a part. Whatever subjects of this power are in their nature national, or admit only of one uniform system, or plan of regulation, may justly be said to be of such a nature as to require exclusive legislation by Congress. That this cannot be affirmed of laws for the regulation of pilots and pilotage is plain. The act of 1789 contains a clear and authoritative declaration by the first Congress, that the nature of this subject is such, that until Congress should find it necessary to exert its power, it should be left to the legislation of the States; that it is local and not national; that it is likely to be the best provided for, not by one system, or plan of regulations, but by as many as the legislative discretion of the several States should deem applicable to the local peculiarities of the ports within their limits.

. . .

JUSTICE McLEAN, dissenting.

. . .

That a State may regulate foreign commerce, or commerce among the States, is a doctrine which has been advanced by individual judges of this court; but never before, I believe, has such a power been sanctioned by the decision of this court. In this case, the power to regulate pilots is admitted to belong to the commercial power of Congress; and yet it is held, that a State, by virtue of its inherent power, may regulate the subject, until such regulation shall be annulled by Congress. This is the principle established by this decision. Its language is guarded, in order to apply the decision only to the case before the court. But such restrictions can never operate, so as to render the principle inapplicable to other cases. And it is in this light that the decision is chiefly to be regretted. The power is recognized in the State, because the subject is more appropriate for State than Federal action; and consequently, it must be presumed the Constitution cannot have intended to inhibit State action. This is not a rule by which the Constitution is to be construed. It can receive but little support from the discussions which took place on the adoption of the Constitution, and none at all from the earlier decisions of this court.

. . .

I think the charge of half-pilotage is correct under the circumstances, and I only object to the power of the State to pass the law. Congress, to whom the subject peculiarly belongs, should have been applied to, and no doubt it would have adopted the act of the State.

JUSTICE DANIEL, concurring.

. . . The power delegated to Congress by the Constitution relates properly to the terms on which commercial engagements may be prosecuted; the character of the articles which they may embrace; the permission or terms according to which they may be introduced; and do not necessarily nor even naturally extend to the means of precaution and safety adopted within the waters or limits of the States by the authority of the latter for the preservation of vessels and cargoes, and the lives of navigators or passengers. These last subjects are essentially local—they must depend upon local necessities which call them into existence, must differ according to the degrees of that necessity. It is admitted, on all hands, that they cannot be uniform or even general, but must vary so as to meet the purposes to be accomplished. They have no connection with contract, or traffic, or with the permission to trade in any subject, or upon any conditions. . . . This is a power which is deemed indispensable to the safety and existence of every community. It may well be made a question, therefore, whether it could, under any circumstances, be surrendered; but certainly it is one which cannot be supposed to have been given by mere implication, and as incidental to another, to the exercise of which it is not indispensable. It is not just nor philosophical to argue from the possibility of abuse against the rightful existence of this power in the States; such an argument would, if permitted, go to the overthrow of all power in either the States or in the federal government, since there is no power which may not be abused. . . . I am forced to conclude that this is an original and inherent power in the States, and not one to be merely tolerated, or held subject to the sanction of the federal government.

John C. Calhoun, **"Fort Hill Address"** (1831)[22]

John C. Calhoun of South Carolina started his career as a "war hawk" during the War of 1812. He made common cause with other young nationalists such as Henry Clay and Daniel Webster. The three supported federal policies such as protective tariffs and internal improvements aimed at building national strength. By the 1820s, tariff rates had been raised to unprecedented levels. They were no longer justified as short-term measures to nurture "infant industries" but as permanent features of American political economy. South Carolina turned hostile to federal economic policies that subsidized northern manufacturing interests. Calhoun turned hostile as well. He became the leading spokesman and theorist of conservative southern constitutionalism and compact theory.

The Fort Hill Address was Calhoun's first public statement on nullification. He presented nullification as the natural extension of the Virginia and Kentucky Resolutions of 1798. In contrast to Jefferson's philosophy, Calhoun's theory required a special popular state convention (rather than the state legislature) to determine whether the federal law in question was unconstitutional and to determine the appropriate action that the state could take. Is nullification a natural extension of the Virginia and Kentucky Resolutions of 1798? Is state nullification a less reasonable inference to be drawn from the constitutional scheme than the power of judicial review?

. . .

The great and leading principle is, that the General Government emanated from the people of the several States, forming distinct political communities, and acting in their separate and sovereign capacity, and not from all of the people forming one aggregate political community; that the Constitution of the United States is, in fact, a compact, to which each State is a party, in the character already described; and that the several States, or parties, have a right to judge of its infractions; and in case of a deliberate, palpable, and dangerous exercise of power not delegated, they have the right, in the last resort, to use the language of the Virginia Resolutions, "to interpose for arresting the progress of the evil, and for maintaining, within their respective limits, the authorities, rights, and liberties appertaining to them." This right of interposition, thus solemnly asserted by the State of Virginia, be it called what it may—State-right, veto, nullification, or by any other name—I conceive to be the fundamental principle of our system, resting on facts historically as certain as our revolution itself, and deductions as simple and demonstrative as that of any political, or moral truth whatever; and I firmly believe that on its recognition depend the stability and safety of our political institutions.

. . .

It has been well said by one of the most sagacious men of antiquity, that the object of a constitution is, to *restrain the government, as that of laws* is to restrain *individuals.* The remark is correct; nor is it less true, where the government is vested in a majority, than where it is in a single or a few individuals—in a republic, than a monarchy or aristocracy. No one can have a higher respect for the maxim that the majority ought to govern than I have, taken in its proper sense,

22. Excerpt taken from John C. Calhoun, "Address on the Relation Which the States and the Federal Government Bear to Each Other (26 July 1831)," in *Works of John C. Calhoun*, ed. Richard C. Cralle (New York: D. Appleton and Company, 1855), 6:59.

subject to the restrictions imposed by the Constitution, and confined to objects in which every portion of the community have similar interests; but it is a great error to suppose, as many do, that the right of a majority to govern is a natural and not a conventional right; and, therefore absolute and unlimited. By nature, every individual has the right to govern himself; and governments, whether founded on majorities or minorities, must derive their right from the assent, expressed or implied, of the governed, and be subject to such limitations as they may impose. Where the interests are the same, that is, where the laws that may benefit one, will benefit all, or the reverse, it is just and proper to place them under the control of the majority; but where they are dissimilar, so that the law that may benefit one portion may be ruinous to another, it would be, on the contrary, unjust and absurd to subject them to its will; and such, I conceive to be the theory on which our Constitution rests.

. . .

Should the General Government and a State come into conflict, we have a higher remedy: the power which called the General Government into existence, which gave it all of its authority, and can enlarge, contract, or abolish its powers at its pleasure, may be invoked. The States themselves may be appealed to—three-fourths of which, in fact, form a power, whose decrees are the Constitution itself, and whose voice can silence all discontent [by amending the Constitution]. . . . [T]o avoid the supposed dangers of [appealing to the states], it is proposed to resort to the novel, the hazardous, and, I must add, fatal project of giving to the General Government the sole and final right of interpreting the Constitution—thereby reversing the whole system, making that instrument the creature of its will, instead of a rule of action impressed on it at its creation, and annihilating, in fact, the authority which imposed it, and from which the Government itself derives its existence.

. . .

In examining this point, we ought not to forget that the Government, through all its departments, judicial as well as others, is administered by delegated and responsible agents; and that *the power which really controls, ultimately, all the movements is not in the agents, but those who elect or appoint them.* To understand, then, its real character, and what would be the action of the system in any supposable case, we must raise our view from the mere agents to this high controlling power, which finally impels every movement of the machine. . . . The judges are, in fact, as truly the judicial representatives of this united majority, as the majority of Congress itself, or the President, is its legislative or executive representative; and to confide the power to the Judiciary to determine finally and conclusively, what powers are delegated, and what reserved, would be, in reality, to confide it to the majority, whose agents they are, and by whom they can be controlled in various ways; and, of course, to subject (against the fundamental principle of our system and all sound political reasoning) the reserved powers of the States, with all of the local and peculiar interests they were intended to protect, to the will of the very majority against which the protection was intended. Nor will the tenure by which the judges hold their office, however valuable the provision in many other respects, materially vary the case. Its highest possible effect would be to *retard,* and not *finally* to *resist,* the will of a dominant majority.

. . .

. . . Stripped of all its covering, the naked question is, whether ours is a federal or a consolidated government; a constitutional or absolute one; a government resting ultimately on the solid basis of the sovereignty of the States, or on the unrestrained will of a majority; a form of government, as in all other unlimited ones, in which injustice, and violence, and force must finally prevail. *Let it never be forgotten that, where the majority rules, the minority is the subject;* and that, if we should absurdly attribute to the former, the exclusive right of construing the Constitution, there would be, in fact, between the sovereign and subject, under such a government, no Constitution; or, at least, nothing deserving the name, or serving the legitimate object of so sacred an instrument.

. . .

VI. Separation of Powers

MAJOR DEVELOPMENTS

- President Jackson claims the right to remove cabinet officials at will
- The Senate censures President Jackson
- Democrats and Whigs debate the constitutional powers of the president during wartime
- Americans debate the proper use of the veto power

The Democratic and Whig parties had sharp differences over the proper constitutional balance of power between the president and Congress. These differences were partly rooted in politics. During the early years of the Jacksonian Era, Andrew Jackson occupied the White House, and his opponents controlled or significantly influenced at least one chamber of Congress. Perhaps as an accident of these circumstances, the Democratic Party became ideologically committed to a strong presidency, and the Whigs became equally committed to a weak presidency.[23] Long after Jackson left office, Democrats continued to believe in a strong presidency that could take independent action when warranted. Whigs continued to complain about the strong presidency and to press their presidential candidates to pledge to be more deferential to Congress should they occupy the Oval Office.

Disputes over executive powers stretched across a multitude of issues. Most famously, Jackson and his successors made aggressive use of the presidential veto to block the policies of their legislative opponents. They exercised a broad authority to determine how federal policy was implemented. President Jackson claimed constitutional authority to remove federal deposits from the national bank and fire cabinet officials who refused to carry out his orders. President James Polk claimed constitutional authority to move U.S. troops into territories whose ownership was disputed by Mexico. Whigs rejected these claims and developed contrasting theories of limited executive power. As the minority party in the national government, Whigs could rarely do little more than complain, but they did complain very loudly. Senate Whigs censured Jackson after he removed the deposits from the banks. Whigs in the House of Representatives sought to impeach President Tyler for an improper use of the veto power. Abraham Lincoln first attracted national attention when he claimed that Polk unconstitutionally provoked the Mexican War.

Whigs were more successful when disputes over the separation of powers broke out in the states. Jacksonians in the national government established the principle that cabinet officers were subordinate to the president. Whigs in many states successfully vested such officers as the secretary of state with terms of office and powers independent from those of the governor. Both national and state practices established in the Jacksonian Era were enduring. Twenty-first-century presidents may remove cabinet officials at will. Some members of the executive branch of most state governments are elected by the general public, have independent powers, and may not be removed by the governor.

23. The Whigs took their party name from the English opponents of executive power during the reign of King James II of England (1685–1688).

The Debate over the Removal of the Deposits

President Jackson's decision to remove federal deposits from the Bank of the United States triggered vigorous and wide-ranging constitutional disputes over the separation of powers. After vetoing the recharter of the national bank in 1832 and being resoundingly vindicated for that decision during the 1832 national election, Jackson determined to drive a stake through the heart of the "Monster Bank." He was convinced that the bank's director, Nicholas Biddle, was using his position of power to corrupt politics. Although the charter granted to the bank in 1816 did not expire until 1836, Jackson realized that Biddle would be crippled if all of the federal government's money was withdrawn from the bank. His decision to remove the deposits triggered three distinct constitutional debates:

- *Could the president without congressional authorization remove the deposits?*
- *Could the president without congressional authorization remove the secretary of the treasury after he refused to remove the deposits?*
- *Could the Senate censure the president for these actions?*

The initial constitutional debates over the removal of the deposits took place within Jackson's cabinet. Jackson first urged the secretary of the treasury, William Duane, to remove the deposits from the national bank. Duane refused. He maintained that Congress had conferred on the secretary of the treasury alone the power to move government deposits. Jackson then ordered Duane to remove the deposits. He insisted that cabinet officials had a duty to implement presidential decrees. Jackson bluntly informed Duane, "A secretary, sir, is merely an executive agent, a subordinate" to the president. Congress, Jackson continued, required no further explanation than that the removal was done at the direction of the president. When Duane again refused to act, the president informed him that his "services as Secretary of the

Treasury [we]re no longer required."[24] *Attorney General Roger Taney, the only cabinet member who supported removal, was appointed acting secretary of the treasury. Taney promptly carried out the president's will.*

The congressional reaction to the removal order was immediate and furious. Such strict constructionists as John C. Calhoun and John Tyler joined forces with such nationalists as Henry Clay and Daniel Webster to denounce what they took to be a lawless abuse of presidential power. Clay, recognizing that the Democratic majority in the House of Representatives would not impeach President Jackson, introduced a formal resolution of censure in the Senate. Clay's speech defending the censure resolution condemned Jackson for removing the deposits and for treating the secretary of the treasury as a mere subordinate with no responsibility to Congress. His censure resolution passed 26–20 on a largely party-line vote. The Whig-controlled Senate then refused to confirm Taney as secretary of the treasury, the first time the Senate had refused to confirm a cabinet nominee. A few months later, the Senate refused to confirm Taney when Jackson nominated him to be an associate justice on the Supreme Court.

Jackson and his allies had the last laugh. Jackson's "Protest of the Censure Resolution" provided a strong defense of presidential power and a sharp criticism of the constitutionality of the censure resolution. Democrats won control of the Senate in the 1834 midterm elections. The newly elected Senate confirmed Jackson's choice of Roger Taney to serve as chief justice and voted to expunge the censure resolution from the journal of the Senate just before Martin Van Buren was inaugurated as Jackson's successor as president.

Andrew Jackson, Paper on the Removal of the Deposits (1833)[25]

. . .

Can it now be said that the question of a recharter of the bank was not decided at the election which ensued? Had the veto been equivocal, or had it not covered the whole ground; if it had merely taken exceptions to the details of the bill or the time of its passage; if it had not met the whole ground of constitutionality and expediency, then there might have been some plausibility for the allegation that the question was not decided by the people. It was to compel the President to take his stand that the question was brought forward into which his adversaries sought to force him, and frankly declared his unalterable opposition to the bank as being both unconstitutional and inexpedient. On that ground the case was argued to the people; and now that the people have sustained the President, notwithstanding the array of influence and power which was brought to bear upon him, it is too late, he confidently thinks, to say that the question has not been decided. Whatever may be the opinions of others, the President considers his reelection as a decision of the people against the bank. . . .

. . .

It is for the wisdom of Congress to decide upon the best substitute to be adopted in the place of the Bank of the United States, and the President would have felt himself relieved from a heavy and painful responsibility if in the charter to the bank Congress had reserved to itself the power of directing at its pleasure the public money to be elsewhere deposited, and had not devolved that power exclusively on one of the Executive Departments. It is useless now to inquire why this high and important power was surrendered by those who are peculiarly and appropriately the guardians of the public money. Perhaps it was an oversight. But as the President presumes that the charter to the bank is to be considered a contract on the part of the Government, it is now not in the power of Congress to disregard its stipulations; and by the terms of that contract the public money is to be deposited in the bank during the continuance of its charter unless the Secretary of the Treasury shall otherwise direct. Unless, therefore, the Secretary of the Treasury first acts, Congress have no power over the subject, for they can not add a new clause to the charter or strike one out of it without the consent of the bank, and consequently the public money must remain in that institution until the last hour of its existence unless the Secretary of the Treasury shall remove it at an earlier day. The responsibility is thus thrown upon the executive branch of the Government of deciding how long before the expiration of the charter the public interest will require the deposits to be placed elsewhere; and although according to the frame and principle of our Government this decision would seem more properly to belong to the legislative power, yet as the law has imposed it upon the executive department the duty ought to be

24. Quoted in Robert V. Remini, *Andrew Jackson and the Bank War* (New York: W.W. Norton, 1967), 123, 124.

25. Excerpt taken from Andrew Jackson, "Removal of the Public Deposits, September 18, 1833," in *Compilation of the Messages* (see note 16), 3:1224.

faithfully and firmly met, and the decision made and executed upon the best lights that can be obtained and the best judgment that can be formed. . . . And while the President anxiously wishes to abstain from the exercise of doubtful powers and to avoid all interference with the rights and duties of others, he must yet with unshaken constancy discharge his own obligations, and can not allow himself to turn aside in order to avoid any responsibility which the high trust with which he has been honored requires him to encounter; and it being the duty of one of the Executive Departments to decide in the first instance . . . the President has felt himself bound to examine the question carefully and deliberately in order to make up his judgment on the subject, and in his opinion the near approach of the termination of the charter and the public considerations heretofore mentioned are of themselves amply sufficient to justify the removal of the deposits, without reference to the conduct of the bank or their safety in its keeping.

. . .

In conclusion, the President must be permitted to remark that he looks upon the pending question as of higher consideration than the mere transfer of a sum of money from one bank to another. Its decision may affect the character of our Government for ages to come. Should the bank be suffered longer to use the public moneys in the accomplishment of its purposes, with the proofs of its faithlessness and corruption before our eyes, the patriotic among our citizens will despair of success in struggling against its power, and we shall be responsible for entailing it upon our country forever. Viewing it as a question of transcendent importance, both in the principles and consequences it involved, the President could not, in justice to the responsibility which he owes the country, refrain from pressing upon the Secretary of the Treasury his view of the considerations which impel to immediate action. Upon him has been devolved by the Constitution and the suffrages of the American people the duty of superintending the operations of the Executive Departments of the Government and seeing that the laws are faithfully executed. In the performance of this high trust it is his undoubted right to express to those whom the laws and his own choice have made his associates in the administration of the Government his opinion of their duties under circumstances as they arise. It is this right which he now exercises. Far be it from him to expect or require that any member of the Cabinet should at his request, order, or dictation do any act which he believes unlawful or in his conscience condemn. From them and from his fellow-citizens in general he desires only that aid and support which their reason approves and their conscience sanctions.

. . .

Henry Clay, Speech on the Removal of the Deposits (1833)[26]

1. *Resolved*, That, by dismissing the late Secretary of the Treasury because he would not, contrary to his sense of his own duty, remove the money of the United States in deposit with the Bank of the United State and its branches, in conformity with the President's opinion; and by appointing his successor to effect such removal, which has been done, the President has assumed the exercise of a power over the treasury of the United States, not granted to him by the constitution and laws, and dangerous to the liberties of the people.

. . .

. . . We are . . . in the midst of a revolution, hitherto bloodless, but rapidly tending towards a total change of the pure republican character of the Government, and to the concentration of all power in the hands of one man. The powers of Congress are paralyzed, except when exerted in conformity with his will, by frequent and an extraordinary exercise of the executive veto, not anticipated by the founders of the constitution, and not practiced by any of the predecessors of the present Chief Magistrate. . . . The constitutional participation of the Senate in the appointing power is virtually abolished, by the constant use of the power of removal from office without any known cause, and by the appointment of the same individual to the same office, after his rejection by the Senate. . . .

. . .

Up to the period of the termination of the last session of Congress, the exclusive constitutional power of Congress over the treasury of the United States had never been contested. Among its earliest acts was one to establish the Treasury Department, which provided

26. Excerpt taken from Henry Clay, *Speech of the Honorable Henry Clay on the Subject of the Removal of the Deposits* (Washington, DC: Duff Green, 1834).

for the appointment of a Treasurer. . . . When the existing bank was established, it was provided that the public moneys should be deposited with it, and consequently that bank became the treasury of the United States. . . .

. . .

. . . Th[e] [Constitution] confers on the President the right to require the opinion, in writing, of the principal officers of the executive departments, separately, on subjects appertaining to their respective offices. Instead of conforming to this provision, the President reads to those officers, collectively, his opinion and decision, in writing, upon an important matter which related only to one of them, and to him exclusively. This paper is afterwards formally promulgated to the world, with the President's authority. And why? Can it be doubted that it was done under the vain expectation that *a name* would quash all inquiry, and secure the general approbation of the people? Those who now exercise power in this country appear to regard all the practices and usages of their predecessors as wrong. They look upon all precedents with contempt, and, casting them scornfully aside, appear to be resolved upon a new era of administration. . . .

. . .

. . . What power has the President over the public treasury? Is it in the bank charter? . . . The Secretary of the Treasury alone is designated. The President is not, by the remotest allusion, referred to. And, to put the matter beyond all controversy, whenever the Secretary gives an order or direction for the removal, he is to report his reasons—to whom? To the President? No! directly to Congress. . . . The constitution had ordained that no money should be drawn from the treasury but in consequence of appropriations made by law. It remained for Congress to provide *how* it should be drawn. And that duty is performed by the act constituting the Treasury Department. According to that act, the Secretary of the Treasury is to prepare and sign, the Comptroller to countersign, the Register to record, and, finally, the Treasurer to pay a warrant issued, *and only issued*, in virtue of a prior act of appropriation. Each is referred to the law as the guide of his duty; each acts on his own separate responsibility; each is a check upon every other; and all are placed under the control of Congress. The Secretary is to report to Congress, and to each branch of Congress. The great principle of division of duty, and of control and responsibility—that principle which lies at the bottom of all free government—that principle, without which there can be no free government—is upheld throughout. . . .

Thus is it evident that the President, neither by the act creating the Treasury Department, nor by the bank charter, has any power over the public treasury. Has he any by the constitution? None, none. We have already seen that the constitution positively forbids any money from being drawn from the treasury but in virtue of a previous act of appropriation. But the President himself says that "upon him has been devolved, by the constitution, and the suffrages of the American people, the duty of superintending the operation of the executive departments of the Government, and seeing that the laws are faithfully executed." If there existed any such double source of executive power, it has been seen that the Treasury Department is not an executive department; but that, in all that concerns the public treasury, the Secretary is the agent or representative of Congress, acting in obedience to their will, and maintaining a direct intercourse with them. By what authority does the President derive power from the mere result of an election? In another part of the same cabinet paper he refers to the suffrages of the people as a source of power independent of the constitution, if not overruling it. At all events, he seems to regard the issue of the election as an approbation of all constitutional opinions previously expressed by him, no matter in what ambiguous language. I differ, sir, entirely from the President. No such conclusions can be legitimately drawn from his re-election. He was re-elected from his presumed merits generally, and from the attachment and confidence of the people, and also from the unworthiness of his competitor. The people had no idea, by that exercise of their suffrage, of expressing their approbation of all the opinions which the President held. . . .

. . .

. . . [H]e is charged by the constitution to "take care that the laws be faithfully executed." And the question is, what does this injunction really import? . . . [The] enormous pretension of the Executive claims that if a treaty or law exists, contrary to the constitution, in the President's opinion; or if a judicial opinion be pronounced, in his opinion repugnant to the constitution, to a treaty, or to a law, he is not bound to afford the executive aid in the execution of any such treaty, law, or decision. If his be sound doctrine, it is evident that every thing resolves itself into the President's opinion.

There is an end to all constitutional government, and a sole functionary engrosses the whole power supposed hitherto to have been assigned to various responsible officers, checking and checked by each other. Can this be true? Is it possible that there is any one so insensible to the guaranties of civil liberty as to subscribe to this monstrous pretension? . . .

. . .

Andrew Jackson, Protest of the Censure Resolution (1834)[27]

. . .

The whole executive power being vested in the President, who is responsible for its exercise, it is a necessary consequence that he should have a right to employ agents of his own choice to aid him in the performance of his duties, and to discharge them when he is no longer willing to be responsible for their acts. In strict accordance with this principle, the power of removal, which, like that of appointment, is an original executive power, is left unchecked by the Constitution in relation to all executive officers, for whose conduct the President is responsible while it is taken from him in relation to judicial officers, for whose acts he is not responsible. . . .

But if there were any just ground for doubt on the face of the Constitution whether all executive officers are removable at the will of the President, it is obviated by the cotemporaneous construction of the instrument and the uniform practice under it.

The power of removal was a topic of solemn debate in the Congress of 1789 while organizing the administrative departments of the Government, and it was finally decided that the President derived from the Constitution the power of removal so far as it regards that department for whose acts he is responsible. Here, then, we have the concurrent authority of President Washington, the Senate, and the House of Representatives, members of whom had taken an active part in the convention which framed the Constitution and in the State conventions which adopted it, that the President derived an unqualified power of removal from that instrument itself, which is "beyond the reach of legislative authority." Upon this principle the Government has now been steadily administered for about forty-five years, during which there have been numerous removals made by the President, or by his direction, embracing every grade of executive officers from the heads of Departments to the messengers of bureaus.

The Treasury Department in the discussions of 1789 was considered on the same footing as the other Executive Departments, and in the act establishing it were incorporated the precise words indicative of the sense of Congress that the President derives his power to remove the Secretary from the Constitution, which appear in the act establishing the Department of Foreign Affairs. . . .

The custody of public property, under such regulations as may be prescribed by legislative authority, has always been considered an appropriate function of the executive department in this and all other Governments. . . .

Public money is but a species of public property. It can not be raised by taxation or customs, nor brought into the Treasury in any other way except by law; but whenever or howsoever obtained, its custody always has been and always must be, unless the Constitution be changed, entrusted to the executive department. No officer can be created by Congress for the purpose of taking charge of it whose appointment would not by the Constitution at once devolve on the President and who would not be responsible to him for the faithful performance of his duties. The legislative power may undoubtedly bind him and the President by any laws they may think proper to enact; they may prescribe in what place particular portions of the public property shall be kept and for what reason it shall be removed, as they may direct that supplies for the Army or Navy shall be kept in particular stores, and it will be the duty of the President to see that the law is faithfully executed; yet will the custody remain in the executive department of the Government. Were the Congress to assume, with or without a legislative act, the power of appointing officers, independently of the President, to take the charge and custody of the public property contained in the military and naval arsenals, magazines, and storehouses, it is believed that such an act would be regarded by all as a palpable usurpation of executive power, subversive of the form as well as the fundamental principles of our Government. But where is the difference in principle whether the public property be in the form of arms,

27. Excerpt taken from Andrew Jackson, "Protest, April 15, 1834," in *Compilation of the Messages* (see note 16), 3:1288–1312.

munitions or war, and supplies or in gold and silver or bank notes? None can be perceived; none is believed to exist. Congress can not, therefore, take out of the hands of the executive department the custody of the public property or money without an assumption of executive power and a subversion of the first principles of the Constitution.

. . .

It can not be doubted that it was the legal duty of the Secretary of the Treasury to order and direct the deposits of the public money to be made elsewhere than in the Bank of the United States *whenever sufficient reasons existed for making the change.* If in such a case he neglected or refused to act, he would neglect or refuse to execute the law. What would be the sworn duty of the President? Could he say that the Constitution did not bind him to see the law faithfully executed because it was one of his Secretaries and not himself upon whom the service was specially imposed? Might he not be asked whether there was any such limitation to his obligations prescribed in the Constitution? Whether he is not equally bound to take care that the laws be faithfully executed, whether they impose duties on the highest officer of State or the lowest subordinate in any of the Departments? Might not he be told that it was for the sole purpose of causing all executive officers, from the highest to the lowest, faithfully to perform the services required of them by law that the people of the United States have made him their Chief Magistrate and the Constitution has clothed him with the entire executive power of this Government? The principles implied in these questions appear too plain to need elucidation.

. . .

Thus was it settled by the Constitution, the laws, and the whole practice of the Government that the entire executive power is vested in the President of the United States; that as incident to that power the right of appointing and removing those officers who are to aid him in the execution of the laws, with such restrictions only as the Constitution prescribes, is vested in the President; that the Secretary of the Treasury is one of those officers; that the custody of the public property and money is an Executive function which, in relation to the money, has always been exercised through the Secretary of the Treasury and his subordinates; that in the performance of these duties he is subject to the supervision and control of the President, and in all important measures having relation to them consults the Chief Magistrate and obtains his approval and sanction; that the law establishing the bank did not, as it could not, change the relation between the President and the Secretary—did not release the former from his obligation to see the law faithfully executed nor the latter from the President's supervision and control; that afterwards and before the Secretary did in fact consult and obtain the sanction of the President to transfers and removals of the public deposits, and that all the departments of the Government, and the nation itself, approved or acquiesced in these acts and principles as in strict conformity with our Constitution and laws.

House Debate on the Veto Power (1842)[28]

After William Henry Harrison died, Vice President John Tyler ascended to the presidency. Tyler was a Jeffersonian Old Republican who had broken with Jackson over the administration's handling of nullification and the removal of the deposits from the Bank of the United States. Regarding the "exercise of some independence of judgment" as the responsibility of holding office, Tyler resolved as president to carry out the duties of his office as he understood them.[29] *He vetoed bills that would revive the Bank of the United States, impose protective tariffs, and provide federal funding for internal improvements. Although Whigs held majorities in both chambers of Congress when Tyler first took office, they did not have the votes needed to override those vetoes.*

After Tyler vetoed a second tariff bill, former president John Quincy Adams, now serving in the House of Representatives, moved that the veto be referred to a select committee chaired by Adams. The House complied. Adams produced a report denouncing Tyler's use of the veto power and reaffirming Whig commitments to legislative supremacy in policy making. The report called for Tyler's impeachment and for a constitutional amendment allowing a simple majority in both houses of Congress to override a presidential veto. Both recommendations failed. Are there circumstances under which the use of the presidential veto would be inappropriate? Does the president ever have an obligation to defer to the legislative majority?

28. Excerpt taken from *Report on Veto of New Tariff of Duties*, 27th Cong., 2nd Sess., August 16, 1842, H.R. Report 998.

29. John Tyler, "Veto Message, August 9, 1842," in *Compilation of the Messages* (see note 16), 5:2037.

Majority Report delivered by JOHN QUINCY ADAMS (Whig, Massachusetts)

. . .

. . . In the spirit of the Constitution of the United States, the executive is not only separated from the legislative power, but made dependent upon, and responsible to it. Until a very recent period of our history, all reference, in either house of Congress, to the opinions or wishes of the President, relating to any subject in deliberation before them, was regarded as an outrage upon the rights of the deliberative body, among the first of whose duties it is to spurn the influence of the dispenser of patronage and power. Until very recently, it was sufficient greatly to impair the influence of any member to be suspected of personal subserviency to the Executive; and any allusion to his wishes, in debate, was deemed a departure not less from decency than from order. . . .

. . . [T]he measure first among those deemed by the Legislature of the Union indispensably necessary for the salvation of its highest interests, and for the restoration of its credit, its honor, its prosperity, was prostrated, defeated, annulled, by the weak and wavering obstinacy of one man, accidentally, and not by the will of the people, invested with that terrible power—as if prophetically described by one of his own chosen ministers, at this day, as "the right to deprive the people of self-government."

. . .

They perceive that the whole legislative power of the Union has been, for the last fifteen months, with regard to the action of Congress upon measures of vital importance, in a state of suspended animation, strangled by the *five* times repeated stricture of the executive cord. They observe that, under these unexampled obstructions to the exercise of their high and legitimate duties, they have hitherto preserved the most respectful forbearance towards the executive chief; that while he has, time after time, annulled, by the mere act of his will, their commission from the people to enact laws for the common welfare, they have forborne even the expression of their resentment for these multiplied insults and injuries. They believed they have a high destiny to fulfill, by administering to the people, in the form of law, remedies for the suffering which they had too long endured. The will of one man had frustrated all their labors, and prostrated all their powers. The majority of the committee believed that the case has occurred, in the annals of our Union, contemplated by the founders of the Constitution by the grant to the House of Representatives of the power to impeach the President of the United States; but they are aware that the resort to that expedient might, in the present condition of public affairs, prove abortive. They see that the irreconcilable difference of opinion and of action between the legislative and executive department of the Government is but sympathetic with the same discordant views and feelings among the people. To them alone the final issue of the struggle must be left. . . .

. . . [T]he abusive exercise of the constitutional power of the president to arrest the action of Congress upon measures vital to the welfare of the people, has wrought conviction upon the minds of the majority of the committee, that the veto power in itself must be restrained and modified by an amendment of the Constitution itself: a resolution for which they accordingly herewith respectfully report.

. . .

Instead of the words "two-thirds," twice repeated in the second paragraph of the said seventh section [of Article I], substitute, in both cases, the words "a majority of the whole number."

Protest and Counter Report of THOMAS W. GILMER (Whig, Virginia)

. . .

. . . Under the specious pretext of defending Congress from what is imagined to be an attack on their constitutional right, it is sought to strip the other departments of Government of powers which the Constitution has confided to them; to remove every constitutional obstruction to the arbitrary will of Congress; to destroy the equilibrium of our well-considered system of government; and to assume unlimited jurisdiction, not only over the co-ordinate branches, but over the States and the people. Encouraged by the present embarrassed condition of the country and our public affairs, deriving fresh political hopes from the general gloom and despondency which their own proceedings have cast over the union, it is attempted to extort from the sufferings of the people some sanction for principles of government which their judgment has never failed to repudiate. The history of our Government abounds in examples of conflicts between the several departments. It has sometimes happened that all the departments combined to overthrow the Constitution, and, but for the intelligence of the people, and the controlling power of the suffrage, in restoring the supremacy of the Constitution over the

Legislature, the Executive, and the Judiciary, such combinations must have been fatal to our institutions. While it is the privilege and the duty of every citizen to arraign either department of the government, or any public officer, for infidelity to the Constitution and the laws, it is neither wise, just, nor patriotic, for one of those departments to impair the confidence or the harmony which should subsist between the separate branches of the public service, by fomenting prejudices and discord. They are all agents of the people. Their duties are prescribed by a law which all acknowledge as supreme.

. . . Zeal in the pursuit of some cherished object of interest or ambition induces some men not only to complain when they are thwarted by what they easily believe to be an improper exercise of power, but to make war on the established forms of government, and to seek, by revolution or radical change, what they cannot lawfully obtain. The disposition, which has been recently manifested to some extent, to disturb the well-adjusted checks of the Constitution, by claiming powers for Congress which that instrument does not confer, or by denying to a co-ordinate branch of Government powers which it does confer, in order to establish a particular system of party policy, or to carry an election, must be regarded with deep regret and serious apprehension by the people—those whose province it is to judge, and who, free from the bias of mere party politics, can think and feel and act under the superior influences of patriotism. Our government has survived the shock of many severe political contests, because hitherto these contests have involved only a difference of opinion as to the principle and policy of the Government, as organized. It has been deemed unwise, as well as dangerous, to exasperate local or general prejudices against the acknowledged forms of Government, and to enlist the spirit of revolution as an auxiliary to the spirit of party.

. . .

Has the president either assumed a power which does not belong to his office, or has he abused a power which does belong to it? It has not been denied that the power in question exists under the Constitution. Indeed, it has been proposed to abolish it by amendment. If it has been abused, it was done either corruptly and wantonly, or under an error of Executive judgment. If there is evidence of the least corruption in the President's conduct, he should be impeached. The power of impeachment has been confided to the House of Representatives. It is the duty, therefore, of the majority, who accuse the president, to arraign him under the articles of impeachment before the Senate, if they believe him to be guilty of any impeachable offense. If he has neither assumed power, nor abused it corruptly, then the issue dwindles to a mere question—who is right as to a measure of policy? . . . If the charge preferred by this majority is understood, it involves no breach of the Constitution, or of any law on the part of the President; but they accuse him of obstructing *their* will. The accusation implies either a general infallibility on the part of the accusers, or a particular exemption from error on this occasion; or it denies the President the right and the responsibility of judging on a subject which Congress submitted to his judgment. They will find that there are two sides to this question. The Executive is a co-ordinate department of the Government. The President is under no obligation implicitly to approve every bill which the Legislature may pass. He is commanded either to approve, or, if he cannot approve, to return, with objections, *all bills* sent to him; and Congress are required to send to him *all bills* which they pass. . . .

. . .

Minority Report of Mr. INGERSOLL (Democrat, Pennsylvania) and Mr. ROOSEVELT (Democrat, New York)

Free government depends on constitutional checks; otherwise, democracy is despotism. Each house of Congress has an absolute negative upon the other. The American Judiciary exercise the power to annul laws. The Union and the States, respectively, in some instances, nullify each other's legislation; the sovereign arbiter, being the people, never yet, in more than fifty years of prosperous experience, failing to interpose their political omnipotence, peacefully, intelligently, and for the general welfare. In addition to these fundamental principles, which are the conservative bases of our free institutions, the Constitution of the United States required the Executive Magistrate, if he disapproves an act of Congress, to return it, with his objections, to its authors, and call upon them to reconsider, before it can become a law. . . . What has been passionately stigmatized as the one-man power in this country, is, in principle, the same thing as the separation of Congress into two bodies, to correct the errors of each other; though much less powerful, because the power of the majority, by a single vote in either House, is absolute, while that of the Executive is merely suspensive and subordinate. Had all the members of the

House of Representatives voted on the tariff bill, it would have either been carried or lost by one vote—and that, the casting vote of the Speaker. There is much of one-man power in all free government.

. . .

VII. Individual Rights

MAJOR DEVELOPMENTS

- Decline of contracts clause and rise of due process protections for property rights
- Struggles between Protestants and Catholics over religious freedom
- Debate over whether the right to bear arms is limited to militia service
- Debate over whether temperance laws violate individual rights

Jacksonian Era Americans applied an inherited framework for thinking about individual constitutional rights to a bewildering array of new circumstances. Founding and Early National Era precedents established that government officials could regulate individuals whenever restraints promoted the common good and did not benefit one class of persons at the expense of another. Technological, cultural, and political developments exerted pressure on this understanding of individual rights. The transportation revolution created demands for new regulations on property that accommodated perceived needs for trains and canals. Moral crusaders inspired by the Second Great Awakening passed laws regulating drinking, gambling, and such hotbeds of sin as bowling alleys. Many Protestants insisted that state support for Christianity was necessary to maintain the private virtues essential for republican government. Government officials responded to urban crime waves with gun control laws. Opponents challenged the constitutionality of all these laws. The resulting debates raised constitutional questions about what constituted the public good and the relationships between the public good and new regulations.

A. Property

The constitutional politics and laws of property rights were altered subtly during the Jacksonian Era. During the Early National Era federal courts relying on the contracts clause of the national Constitution provided the most important protections for economic freedom. *Proprietors of the Charles River Bridge v. Proprietors of the Warren Bridge* (1837) weakened contracts clause protections for property holders. That decision held that courts should construe contractual ambiguities in bargains between state officials and private parties in favor of state power. State courts, by comparison, protected property rights more aggressively during the Jacksonian Era than they had during the Early National Era. State judges, relying on the takings and due process clauses of state constitutions, restricted state power to pass internal improvements, build roads, and adjust property rights. The vast majority of cases protecting property rights before 1828 prohibited government from passing laws that divested people of their entire right to a particular piece of property. During the Jacksonian Era, some state courts interpreted state constitutional provisions as limiting state regulations of property and economic freedom, even when those regulations left persons with nominal title to their land or possessions.

Proprietors of the Charles River Bridge v. Proprietors of the Warren Bridge, 36 U.S. 420 (1837)

In 1785 the Massachusetts legislature granted a charter to the proprietors of the Charles River Bridge Company. That corporate charter authorized the company to build a bridge over the Charles River and collect tolls for forty years. In 1792 a new charter was issued to the Charles River Bridge Company extending the right to collect tolls until 1856. In 1828 the Massachusetts legislature, responding to increased transportation needs, authorized the Warren Bridge Company to build a second bridge across the Charles River. The proprietors of the Warren Bridge were permitted to collect tolls for no more than six years before turning the bridge over to the state. The proprietors of the Charles River Bridge sued to block the opening of the Warren Bridge. They claimed that the charter that Massachusetts gave to the Warren Bridge Company deprived them of the promised benefits of collecting tolls for forty years and thus impaired the state obligations outlined in their corporate charter. After a divided state court ruled in favor of the Warren Bridge Company, the proprietors of the Charles River Bridge appealed that decision to the Supreme Court of the United States.

The Supreme Court by a 5–2 vote sustained the Massachusetts law incorporating the Warren Bridge Company. Chief Justice Taney's opinion held that the contracts clause protected exclusive privileges only when those exclusive privileges were explicitly written in the corporate charter. His conclusion articulates the Jacksonian antipathy to private privilege and monopoly. Why did Chief Justice Taney reach this conclusion? Why did Justice Story disagree? Both Taney and Story insisted that their interpretation of the contracts clause promoted economic growth. Who is right? Should such considerations influence the proper interpretation of the contracts clause?

CHIEF JUSTICE TANEY delivered the opinion of the Court.

. . .

. . . It is well settled by the decisions of this Court, that a state law may be retrospective in its character, and may divest vested rights; and yet not violate the constitution of the United States, unless it also impairs the obligation of a contract. . . .

. . . [The plaintiff] must show that the state had entered into a contract with them, or those under whom they claim, not to establish a free bridge at the place where the Warren Bridge is erected. Such, and such only, are the principles upon which the plaintiffs in error can claim relief in this case.

. . .

. . . The act of incorporation is silent in relation to the contested power. . . .

. . . [T]he object and end of all government is to promote the happiness and prosperity of the community by which it is established; and it can never be assumed, that the government intended to diminish its power of accomplishing the end for which it was created. And in a country like ours, free, active, and enterprising, continually advancing in numbers and wealth; new channels of communication are daily found necessary, both for travel and trade; and are essential to the comfort, convenience, and prosperity of the people. A state ought never to be presumed to surrender this power, because, like the taxing power, the whole community have an interest in preserving it undiminished. And when a corporation alleges, that a state has surrendered for seventy years, its power of improvement and public accommodation, in a great and important line of travel, along which a vast number of its citizens must daily pass; the community have a right to insist . . . "that its abandonment ought not to be presumed, in a case, in which the deliberate purpose of the state to abandon it does not appear." The continued existence of a government would be of no great value, if by implications and presumptions, it was disarmed of the powers necessary to accomplish the ends of its creation; and the functions it was designed to perform, transferred to the hands of privileged corporations. . . .

. . .

Indeed, the practice and usage of almost every state in the Union, old enough to have commenced the work of internal improvement, is opposed to the doctrine contended for on the part of the plaintiffs in error. Turnpike roads have been made in succession, on the same line of travel; the later ones interfering materially with the profits of the first. These corporations have, in some instances, been utterly ruined by the introduction of newer and better modes of transportation, and travelling. In some cases, rail roads have rendered the turnpike roads on the same line of travel so entirely useless, that the franchise of the turnpike corporation is not worth preserving. Yet in none of these cases have the corporations supposed that their privileges were invaded, or any contract violated on the part of the state. . . .

. . . How far must the new improvement be distant from the old one? How near may you approach without invading its rights in the privileged line? If this Court should establish the principles now contended for, what is to become of the numerous rail roads established on the same line of travel with turnpike companies; and which have rendered the franchises of the turnpike corporations of no value? Let it once be understood that such charters carry with them these implied contracts, and give this unknown and undefined property in a line of travelling; and you will soon find the old turnpike corporations awakening from their sleep, and calling upon this Court to put down the improvements which have taken their place. The millions of property which have been invested in rail roads and canals, upon lines of travel which had been before occupied by turnpike corporations, will be put in jeopardy. We shall be thrown back to the improvements of the last century, and obliged to stand still, until the claims of the old turnpike corporations shall be satisfied; and they shall consent to permit these states to avail themselves of the lights of modern science, and to partake of the benefit of those improvements which are now adding to the wealth and prosperity, and the convenience and comfort, of every other part of the civilized world. . . .

. . .

JUSTICE McLEAN, concurring. . . .

JUSTICE STORY, dissenting.

. . .

. . . [I]t has been argued, and the argument has been pressed in every form which ingenuity could suggest, that if grants of this nature are to be construed liberally, as conferring any exclusive rights on the grantees, it will interpose an effectual barrier against all general improvements of the country. For myself, I profess not to feel the cogency of this argument; either in its general application to the grant of franchises, or in its special application to the present grant. . . . For my own part, I can conceive of no surer plan to arrest all public improvements, founded on private capital and enterprise, than to make the outlay of that capital uncertain, and questionable both as to security, and as to productiveness. No man will hazard his capital in any enterprise, in which, if there be a loss, it must be borne exclusively by himself; and if there be success, he has not the slightest security of enjoying the rewards of that success for a single moment. . . .

. . . The prohibition [against a new bridge] arises by natural, if not by necessary implication. It would be against the first principles of justice to presume that the legislature reserved a right to destroy its own grant. That was the doctrine in *Fletcher v. Peck* [1810] . . . in this Court: and in other cases turning upon the same great principle of political and constitutional duty and right. Can the legislature have power to do that indirectly, which it cannot do directly? If it cannot take away, or resume the franchise itself, can it take away its whole substance and value? If the law will create an implication that the legislature shall not resume its own grant, is it not equally as natural and as necessary an implication, that the legislature shall not do any act directly to prejudice its own grant, or to destroy its value?

. . .

To sum up, then, the whole argument on this head; I maintain, that, upon the principles of common reason and legal interpretation, the present grant carries with it a necessary implication that the legislature shall do no act to destroy or essentially to impair the franchise; that . . . there is an implied agreement that the state will not grant another bridge between Boston and Charlestown, so near as to draw away the custom from the old one; and . . . that there is an implied agreement of the state to grant the undisturbed use of the bridge and its tolls, so far as respects any acts of its own, or of any persons acting under its authority. In other words, the state, impliedly, contracts not to resume its grant, or to do any act to the prejudice or destruction of its grant. . . . I maintain, that under the principles of the common law, there exists no more right in the legislature of Massachusetts, to erect the Warren Bridge, to the ruin of the franchise of the Charles River Bridge, than exists to transfer the latter to the former, or to authorize the former to demolish the latter. If the legislature does not mean in its grant to give any exclusive rights, let it say so, expressly; directly; and in terms admitting of no misconstruction. The grantees will then take at their peril, and must abide the results of their overweening confidence, indiscretion, and zeal. . . .

Wynehamer v. People, 2 Parker Crim. Rep. 490 (NY 1856)

Thomas Toynbee was arrested for selling a glass of brandy to a customer. This act violated a New York law that declared, "Intoxicating liquor, except as hereinafter provided, shall not be sold, or kept for sale, or with intent to be sold, by any person, for himself or any other person." Toynbee was convicted and required to pay a $50 fine. Toynbee's sentence was reversed by the Supreme Court of New York, which declared the ban on the sale of intoxicating beverages unconstitutional. The state appealed that decision to the New York Court of Appeals. The court of appeals combined Toynbee's case with that of James Wynehamer, whose conviction for selling intoxicating liquors had been affirmed by a different lower state court.

The New York Court of Appeals confirmed the state supreme court's ruling in Wynehamer's case and declared unconstitutional the legislative ban on selling intoxicating liquors. Justice Comstock insisted that the New York law violated property rights protected by the due process clause of the state constitution. What were those property rights? How do the judges distinguish between laws that regulate property and laws that confiscate property? Do you find that distinction convincing? Suppose evidence came to light in 1850 that intoxicating beverages caused heart disease. Would the New York law then be constitutional?

Table 5-3 Major State Statutes in First Wave of Alcohol Prohibition

State	Adoption	Type	Fate
Massachusetts	1838	No liquor sales in quantities smaller than 15 gallons	Repealed, 1840
Rhode Island	1838	Local-option licensing law	Replaced, 1853
Mississippi	1839	No liquor sales in quantities smaller than 1 gallon	Repealed, 1842
Vermont	1844	Local option for prohibition	Replaced, 1850
Pennsylvania	1846	Local option for prohibition	Struck down, 1847
Delaware	1847	Local option for prohibition	Struck down, 1847
Maine	1851	Statutory prohibition	Repealed, 1856
Massachusetts	1852	Statutory prohibition	Repealed, 1868
Rhode Island	1853	Statutory prohibition	Struck down and modified, 1854; replaced, 1863
Michigan	1853	Statutory prohibition	Struck down, 1854
Indiana	1853	Statutory prohibition	Struck down, 1855
Connecticut	1854	Statutory prohibition	Replaced, 1872
Minnesota	1854	Statutory prohibition for Sioux Indian territory	Replaced, 1887
Delaware	1855	Statutory prohibition	Replaced, 1857
Iowa	1855	Statutory prohibition	Struck down and modified, 1857; replaced, 1858
Indiana	1855	Statutory prohibition	Repealed, 1857
Nebraska	1855	Statutory prohibition	Repealed, 1858
Michigan	1855	No liquor sales in quantities smaller than 5 gallons	Repealed, 1875
New York	1855	Statutory prohibition	Replaced, 1857
New Hampshire	1855	Alcohol can only be kept and sold by town liquor agents	Repealed, 1903

Source: Ernest Hurst Cherrington, *Standard Encyclopedia of the Alcohol Problem*, 6 vols. (Westerville, OH: American Issue Publishing Co., 1925).

JUSTICE COMSTOCK delivered the opinion of the Court.

. . .

. . . It is . . . universally admitted that when this law was passed, intoxicating liquors, to be used as a beverage, were *property* in the most absolute and unqualified sense of the term; and as such, as much entitled to the protection of the constitution as lands, houses, or chattels of any description. From the earliest ages they have been produced and consumed as a beverage, and have constituted an article of great importance in the commerce of the world. In this country, the right of property in them was never, so far as I know, for an instant questioned. In this state, they were bought and sold like other property; they were seized and sold upon legal process for the payment of debts; they were, like other goods, the subject of actions at law, and, when the owner died, their value constituted a fund for the benefit of his creditors, or went to his children and kindred, according to law or the will of the deceased. . . .

It may be said, it is true, that intoxicating drinks are a species of property which performs no beneficent part in the political, moral, or social economy of the world. It may even be urged, and I will admit, demonstrated with reasonable certainty, that the abuses to which it is liable are so great that the people of this state can dispense with its very existence, not only without injury to their aggregate interests, but with absolute benefit. The same can be said, although, perhaps, upon less palpable grounds, of other descriptions of property. Intoxicating beverages are by no means the only article of admitted property and of lawful commerce in this state, against which arguments of this sort may be directed. But if such arguments can be allowed to subvert the fundamental idea of property, then there is no private right entirely safe, because there is no limitation upon the absolute discretion of the legislature, and the guarantees of the constitution are a mere waste of words.

. . .

These observations appear to me quite elementary, yet they seem to be necessary in order to exclude the discussion of extraneous topics. They lead us directly to the conclusion that all property is alike in the characteristic of inviolability. If the legislature has no power to confiscate and destroy property in general, it has no such power over any particular species. There may be, and there doubtless are, reasons of great urgency for regulating the trade in intoxicating drinks, as well as in other articles of commerce. In establishing such regulations merely, the legislature may proceed upon such views of policy, of economy, or morals, as may be addressed to its discretion. The whole field of discussion is open, when the legislature, keeping within its acknowledged powers, seeks to regulate and restrain a traffic, the general lawfulness of which is admitted; but when the simplest question is propounded, whether it can confiscate and *destroy* property lawfully acquired by the citizen in intoxicating liquors, then we are to remember that all property is equally sacred in the view of the constitution, and therefore that speculations as to its chemical or scientific qualities, or the mischief engendered by its abuse, have very little to do with the inquiry. Property, if protected by the constitution from such legislation as that we are now considering, is protected because *it is property* innocently acquired under existing laws, and not upon any theory which even so much as opens the question of its utility. If intoxicating liquors are property, the constitution does not permit a legislative estimate to be made of its usefulness with a view to its destruction. In a word, that which belongs to the citizen in the sense of property, and as such has to him a commercial value, cannot be pronounced worthless or pernicious, and so destroyed or deprived of its essential attributes.

. . .

I am brought, therefore, to a more particular consideration of the limitations of power contained in the fundamental law: "No member of this state shall be disfranchised or deprived of any of the rights or privileges secured to any citizen thereof, unless by the law of the land, or the judgment of his peers. No person shall be deprived of life, liberty or property, without due process of law; nor shall private property be taken for public use without just compensation." . . .

No doubt, it seems to me, can be admitted of the meaning of these provisions. To say, as has been suggested, that the law of the land, or "due process of law," may mean the very act of legislation which deprives the citizen of his rights, privileges, or property, leads to a simple absurdity. The constitution would then mean, that no person shall be deprived of his property or rights, unless the legislature shall pass a law to effectuate the wrong, and this would be throwing the restraint entirely away.

The true interpretation of these constitutional phrases is, that where rights are acquired by the citizen under the existing law, there is no power in any branch of the government to take them away; but where they are held contrary to the existing law, or are forfeited by its violation, then they may be taken from him—not by an act of the legislature, but in the due administration of the law itself, before the judicial tribunals of the state. The cause or occasion for depriving the citizen of his supposed rights must be found in the law as it is, or, at least, it cannot be *created* by a legislative act which aims at their destruction. Where rights of property are admitted to exist, the legislature cannot say they shall exist no longer; nor will it make any difference although a process and a tribunal are appointed to execute the sentence. If this is the "law of the land," and "due process of law," within the meaning of the constitution, then the legislature is omnipotent. It may, under the same interpretation pass a law to take away the liberty or life without a pre-existing cause, appointing judicial and executive agencies to execute its will. Property is placed, by the constitution, in the same category with liberty and life.

. . .

Material objects . . . are property, in the true sense, because they are impressed by the laws and usages of society with certain qualities, among which are, fundamentally, the right of the occupant or owner to use and enjoy them exclusively, and his absolute power to sell and dispose of them; and as property consists in the artificial impression of these qualities upon material things, so, whatever removes the impression destroys the notion of property, although the things themselves may remain physically untouched.

. . .

Unless, therefore, the right of property in liquor is denied altogether, and this has never been done, or unless they can be distinguished from every other species of property, and this has not been attempted, the act cannot stand consistently with the constitution. The provisions of the constitution should receive a beneficent and liberal interpretation, where the fundamental rights of the citizen are concerned. . . .

. . .

JUSTICE T. A. JOHNSON, dissenting:

. . .

That intemperance, pauperism and crime are evils, with which the government is necessarily compelled to deal, none will deny. In the judgment of the legislative bodies, by which this statute was enacted, one great source of all these great, oppressive and dangerous evils was the traffic in intoxicating liquors. So injurious, in their opinion, has this traffic become under existing restrictions, in its consequences upon the community, that it ought to be subjected to still more rigorous and extensive restrictions and prohibitions, and impressed with additional features of criminality. If the legislature had the power to enact a law to accomplish this end, the right to choose the means best calculated to effect it was necessarily vested in it; unless, indeed, the use of such means is forbidden by the constitution. . . . The argument is, that the value of property as an article of trade is an essential element of it as property, and that to the extent to which the restriction or prohibition diminishes its value for such purposes, to the same extent the owner is deprived of his property, although neither the title nor the possession of such owner is in any respect interfered with; and that this is accomplished by the operation of the act, independent of any trial or judgment, in other words, without due process of law. Is not this a strained and unwarrantable construction and application of this provision of the constitution? Clearly it is. This provision has no application whatever to a case where the market value of property is incidentally diminished by the operation of a statute passed for an entirely different object, and a purpose in itself legitimate, and which in no respect affects the title, possession, personal use or enjoyment of the owner. Such a construction would prohibit all regulations by the legislature, and all restrictions upon the internal trade and commerce of the state; it would place the right of traffic above every other right, and render it independent of the power of the government. "Deprived" is there used in its ordinary and popular sense, and relates simply to divesting of, forfeiting, alienating, taking away property. It applies to property in the same sense that it does to life and liberty, and no other. . . .

. . .

A distinction has been attempted to be drawn between the power to restrict, by way of regulation, and the power to prohibit. But this distinction, if there be one, is altogether too narrow and uncertain to serve as the test of the rightful exercise of a power like that of making laws for the government of a state. The right to restrict and regulate includes that of prohibition. . . .

This whole controversy, so far as it involves any question of principle, is narrowed down to a struggle for the right of the individual to traffic, in whatever the law adjudges to be property, at his discretion, irrespective of consequences, over the right of government to control and restrict it within limits compatible with the public welfare and security. Everything beyond this is merged in considerations of expediency. This right of the owner to traffic in his property never was, since the institution of society, a right independent of the control of government. It is a right surrendered necessarily to the government, by every one when he enters into society and becomes one of its members. A government which does not possess the power to make all needful regulations in respect to its internal trade and commerce, to impose such restrictions upon it as may be deemed necessary for the good of all, and even to prohibit and suppress entirely any particular traffic which is found to be injurious and demoralizing in its tendencies and consequences, is no government. It must lack that essential element of sovereignty, indispensably necessary to render it capable of accomplishing the primary object for which governments are instituted, that of affording security, protection and redress to all interests and all classes and conditions of persons within their limits. . . .

B. Religion

Increased religious diversity altered American constitutional politics, and religious fervor gave rise to various moral reform movements. Religious Americans formed associations dedicated to Sabbath-keeping, temperance, the suppression of gambling and prostitution, prison and asylum reform, the destruction of slavery, and women's rights. Proponents of nativism and school reform often allied closely with moral reform movements. National political parties kept their distance, but both major political parties relied heavily on ethnic and religious groups in many localities to build their organizations and voting base. Whigs absorbed many evangelical Protestants. Most Catholics became Democrats. Whigs became the party of moral reform, whereas Democrats often campaigned on the freedom of religion.

Catholics were the focus of many important constitutional debates over religion. Many nativists questioned whether Catholics could be good republican citizens. Samuel Morse declared, "Popery is also a political, a despotic system, which we must repel as altogether incompatible with the existence of freedom."[30] Proponents of religious diversity regarded these anti-Catholic polemics as "a direct attack upon the Constitution itself" and "beneath criticism."[31] Catholics objected to the widespread practice of reading from the King James Bible in public schools. Protestants objected to Catholic calls for states to fund parochial schools.

C. Guns

Jacksonians closely tied the right to bear arms to citizenship. In *Dred Scott v. Sandford* (1857), Chief Justice Roger Taney insisted that state laws in the eighteenth century prohibiting persons of color from serving in the militia or bearing arms demonstrated that the framers believed that free persons of color were not American citizens. Constitutional commentators linked gun rights with a citizen's obligation to serve in the militia. Supreme Court Justice Joseph Story declared that "the importance" of the Second Amendment "will scarcely be doubted." He added:

> The militia is the natural defence of a free country against sudden foreign invasions, domestic insurrections, and domestic usurpations of power by rulers. It is against sound policy for a free people to keep up large military establishments and standing armies in time of peace, both from the enormous expenses, with which they are attended, and the facile means, which they afford to ambitious and unprincipled rulers, to subvert the government, or trample upon the rights of the people. The right of the citizens to keep, and bear arms has justly been considered, as the palladium of the liberties of a republic; since it offers a strong moral check against the usurpation and arbitrary power of rulers.[32]

Other commentators insisted that citizens enjoyed a fundamental right to self-defense. American abolitionists maintained that persons of color were citizens who had the right to use weapons to protect themselves and their families. Joel Tiffany declared, "The right to keep and bear arms also implies the right to use them if necessary in self defense."[33]

Americans did not agree on the relationship between the right to bear arms, militia service, and self-defense. The Supreme Court of Arkansas in *State v. Buzzard* (AR 1842) limited the bearing of arms to militia service. Other state courts connected the bearing of arms with self-defense. *Nunn v. State* (GA 1846) spoke of a citizen's "natural right of self-defense, or of his constitutional right to keep and bear arms."[34] Race also

30. Samuel F. B. Morse, *Foreign Conspiracy Against the Liberties of the United States*, 7th ed. (New York: American and Foreign Christian Union, 1855), 112.

31. Philip Phillips, "On the Religious Proscription of Catholics, July 4, 1855," reprinted in *American Jewish Archives* October (1959): 182.

32. Joseph Story, *Commentaries on the Constitution of the United States*, abridged ed. (Boston: Hilliary, Gray and Company, 1833), 708.

33. Joel Tiffany, *A Treatise on the Unconstitutionality of American Slavery* (Miami: Mnemosyne, [1849] 1969), 117–18.

34. *Nunn v. State*, 1 Kelley 243 (GA 1846).

influenced gun rights. State constitutions and statutes limited militia service and the bearing of arms to free white citizens. *State v. Newsom* (NC 1844) held that free persons of color were not among the "people" whom the constitution of North Carolina declared "have a right to bear arms for the defense of the State."[35]

D. Personal Freedom and Public Morality

Drinking raised bitterly contested issues of public morality during the mid-eighteenth century. Temperance brought together a broad coalition of supporters. Women were concerned about the sobriety of their husbands; native Protestants were concerned about the sobriety of Catholic immigrants; businessmen were concerned about the sobriety of their workers. Temperance societies first relied on moral suasion and community pressure. When those seemed inadequate, reformers turned to legal regulation and eventually prohibition. As detailed in Table 5-2, the American Temperance Society persuaded many state legislatures, particularly in the Northeast, to pass laws restricting or prohibiting the sale of alcohol. Other Americans who resented these intrusions on both their businesses and their private lives insisted that these laws violated numerous constitutional rights.[36]

Most direct constitutional attacks on temperance laws failed. *People v. Gallagher* (MI 1856) is one prominent example of a state court decision sustaining state power to restrict alcoholic beverages. Judge Johnson insisted that courts must defer to the legislative judgment that "intemperance was an evil, . . . very much aggravated by the unrestricted traffic of intoxicating liquors."[37] The Supreme Court of Delaware reached the same conclusion. If owners had a constitutional right to sell alcoholic beverages, the justices concluded,

> the sovereignty of the State would be robbed of nearly all its police power, and the individual right to dispose of his property would be above the right of the public to be protected in their morals, health, peace or safety. Poisonous drugs; unwholesome food; infected goods; demoralizing books or prints; combustible and explosive substances; dangerous animals; and every species of property could be held and transferred at the will of the owner. . . . The right to sell it is conferred by law and may be taken away by law, or its use prohibited in any specified form which is deemed to be injurious or demoralizing.[38]

VIII. Democratic Rights

MAJOR DEVELOPMENTS

- Debate over anti-slavery petitions and speech
- Near-universal white male suffrage
- Greater recognition of expatriation rights

Jacksonians revered democracy. Members of the dominant coalition enthusiastically called themselves "Democrats" or "the Democracy"—a label that has stuck for almost two hundred years. The *Democratic Review* was a leading journal of the period. John L. O'Sullivan, the owner of that periodical, declared that "the first principle of democracy" was "an abiding confidence in the virtue, intelligence, and full capacity for self-government, of the great mass of our people, our industrious, honest, manly, intelligent millions of freemen."[39]

These democratic sentiments inaugurated a new era of constitutional politics. Political elites of the Founding and Early National Eras maintained that governing should be done by a "natural aristocracy" chosen by a voting system designed to privilege the "best persons." Jacksonians rejected this elitist politics. Their constitution was unashamedly "democratic." Andrew Jackson expressed this sensibility when he declared in his First Annual Message to Congress that the "duties of all public offices are, or at least admit of being made, so plain and simple that men of intelligence may readily qualify themselves for their performance."

Jacksonians fell far short of their democratic ideals. Most Americans favored silencing anti-slavery advocates by legal or extralegal means. States removed

35. *State v. Newsom*, 27 N.C. (5 Ired.) 250 (1844).

36. John Compton has recently argued that property rights may have trumped the public good in morals cases more often than conventional wisdom suggests. See John W. Compton, "A Moral Revolution: Evangelical Reform and the Transformation of American Constitutionalism, 1830–1937" (Ph.D. diss., University of California, Los Angeles, 2011).

37. *People v. Gallagher*, 4 Mich. 244 (1856).

38. *State v. Allmond*, 7 Del. 612 (1858).

39. John L. O'Sullivan, "An Introductory Statement of the Democratic Principle," in *Social Theories of Jacksonian Democracy: Representative Writings of the Period 1825–1850*, ed. Joseph L. Blau (New York: Liberal Arts Press, 1954), 22.

economic qualifications for voting but often added new restrictions aimed at limiting the political power of new immigrants. Nonwhites were routinely denied citizenship and the rights associated with citizenship. Whether the United States would have scored higher on a contemporary democratic index in 1860 than in 1828 is doubtful. Certainly the improvement would not be substantial.

Americans both expanded and narrowed understandings of popular government during this era. From the perspective of native white men uninterested in slavery, the Jacksonian Era fulfilled the democratic promise of the Constitution. By the 1850s, most states had instituted near-universal white male suffrage, vigorous political debate was taking place on the issues dividing Jacksonians from Whigs, and white men enjoyed a broad set of rights associated with citizenship. Jacksonian democracy was largely confined to these white men. Jackson and his successors built on past precedents that understood the United States as a white man's country, rather than on those that emphasized a constitutional commitment to the rights of all persons.

A. Free Speech

Free speech rights in Jacksonian America varied according to the subject. Persons spoke freely on matters that divided Democrats from Whigs. Americans vigorously debated the merits of the national bank and internal improvements. Americans opposed to the Mexican War suffered no legal consequences when they called President Polk a liar and the military conflict a "senseless quest for more room."[40] Anti-slavery advocacy, however, bore the brunt of censorship. Prominent abolitionists after 1830 insisted on the immediate emancipation of all slaves. Slaveholders decried such advocacy as inciting slave rebellions. Political moderates decried such advocacy as threatening the union.

Slaveholders and their political (usually Democratic Party) allies had various means for silencing anti-slavery speech.

- Anti-abolitionist mobs in the North destroyed abolitionist presses and murdered one abolitionist editor.
- Anti-abolitionist post officers refused to deliver anti-slavery pamphlets.
- Anti-abolitionist members of Congress refused to consider anti-slavery petitions.
- Anti-abolitionist state legislators proposed criminalizing anti-slavery advocacy.

These efforts enjoyed mixed success. Mob violence failed to suppress abolitionist journals. Congress passed vague legislation regulating the post office that some presidents interpreted as prohibiting postmasters from delivering anti-slavery materials. From 1836 until 1844 Congress tabled all anti-slavery petitions. Southern states criminalized anti-slavery advocacy, and *State v. Worth* (NC 1860) held that one such statute was constitutional.[41] Northern states refused to censor abolitionists.

Efforts to silence abolitionists often backfired. Many northerners who were not particularly concerned with the plight of African American slaves were distressed when their white neighbors were arrested or attacked for speaking out against slavery. Anti-slavery advocates in the North found that they could organize mass support for their cause by placing greater emphasis on how slaveowner demands for national censorship violated the rights of white citizens. The motto of the anti-slavery Free Soil Party was "Free Soil, Free Speech, Free Labor and Free Men." The Republican Party's 1856 platform complained that "the freedom of speech and of the press has been abridged."

Congress Debates Incendiary Publications in the Mail (1836)

The first constitutional controversy over abolitionist speech arose when the American Anti-Slavery Society in 1835 mailed abolitionist pamphlets to prominent southern citizens. Amos Kendall, the U.S. postmaster general, informed local postmasters that they had no obligation to deliver abolitionist literature, even though no law existed on the subject. "Without claiming for the General Government the power to pass laws prohibiting the discussions of any sort, as a means of protecting States from domestic violence," he wrote, "it may be safely assumed, that the United States have no right through their officers or departments, knowingly to be instrumental in producing, within the several

40. Frederick Merk, "Dissent in the Mexican War," *Proceedings of the Massachusetts Historical Society* 81 (1969): 48–50.

41. *State v. Worth*, 52 N.C. 488 (1860).

Illustration 5-2 New Method of Assorting the Mail, as Practised by Southern Slave-Holders
Depiction of an 1835 mob entering a post office and burning abolitionist literature in Charleston, South Carolina. The mob was led by former governor Robert Y. Hayne. No arrests were made. Virginia responded the next year by passing a state law requiring federal postmasters to report the arrival of any abolitionist literature to the local justice of the peace, who was charged with the duty of immediately burning any materials that he deemed to be dangerous.

Source: [Boston?], 1835. Library of Congress, Prints and Photographs Division, Washington, DC 20540, USA.

States, the very mischief which the Constitution commands them to repress."[42] *Both Kendall and President Jackson immediately urged Congress to pass a law legally banning anti-slavery literature from the mails.*

Two controversies erupted when Jackson made this proposal. One controversy was over federalism. Senator John C. Calhoun of South Carolina insisted that the federal government had no power to determine what literature could be mailed. He thought the federal government should prohibit only material that was banned in the recipient state. The other controversy was over free speech. Representative Hiland Hall claimed that Congress could not constitutionally exclude anti-slavery speech from the mails. These legislative divisions prevented Congress from taking a clear stand on the controversy over abolitionist pamphlets. The Post Office Act of 1836 asserted that postmasters could not "unlawfully" refuse to deliver the mail but did not specify what constituted an unlawful refusal. Many Jacksonian postmaster generals interpreted that law as prohibiting postmasters from delivering anti-slavery literature in states where that literature was prohibited.

Consider the relationship between the postal power and free speech when reading the following materials. How do the participants in this debate conceptualize that relationship? Is the debate over whether the post office may refuse to deliver literature that is not protected by the First Amendment? Does the post office have to mail literature that is protected by the First Amendment? How do the various participants in the debate conceptualize the First Amendment?

42. "Report of the Postmaster General," H. Doc. 2, 24th Cong., 1st Sess., 1835, Appendix 9.

John Calhoun, Report from the Select Committee on the Circulation of Incendiary Publications[43]

. . .

The Select Committee fully concur with the President . . . as to the character and tendency of the papers, which have been attempted to be circulated in the South, through the mail, and participate with him in the indignant regret, which he expresses at conduct so destructive of the peace and harmony of the country, and repugnant to the Constitution, and the dictates of humanity and religion. They also concur in the hope that, if the strong tone of disapprobation which these unconstitutional and wicked attempts have called forth, does not arrest them, the non-slaveholding States will be prompt to exercise their power to suppress them, as far as their authority extends. But while they agree with the President as to the evil and its highly dangerous tendency, and the necessity of arresting it, they have not been able to assent to the measure of redress which he recommends; that Congress should pass a law prohibiting under severe penalty the transmission of incendiary publications, though the mail, intended to instigate the slaves to insurrection.

After the most careful and deliberate investigation, they have been constrained to adopt the conclusion that Congress has not the power to pass such a law: that it would be a violation of one of the most sacred provisions of the Constitution, and subversive of reserved powers essential to the preservation of the domestic institutions of the slaveholding states. . . .

. . . [The Committee] refer to the amended Article of the Constitution which . . . provides that Congress shall pass no law, which shall abridge the liberty of the press, a provision, which interposes . . . an insuperable objection to the measure recommended by the President. . . .

. . . Madison, in his celebrated report to the Virginia Legislature in 1799, against the Alien and Sedition Law, . . . conclusively settled the principle that Congress has no right, in any form, or in any manner, to interfere with the freedom of the press. . . .

. . . Assuming [the Sedition Act] to be unconstitutional . . . which no one now doubts, it will not be difficult to show that if, instead of inflicting punishment for publishing, the act had inflicted punishment for circulating through the mail, for the same offense, it would have been equally unconstitutional. The one would have abridged the freedom of the press as effectually as the other. The object of publishing is circulation, and to prohibit circulation is, in effect, to prohibit publication. They have both a common object. The communication of sentiments and opinions to the public, and the prohibition of one may as effectually suppress such communication, as the prohibition of the other, and, of course, would as effectually interfere with the freedom of the press, and be equally unconstitutional.

. . . [I]f it be admitted, that Congress has the right to discriminate in reference to their character, what papers shall, or what shall not be transmitted by the mail, [that] would subject the freedom of the press, on all subjects, political, moral, and religious, completely to its will and pleasure. . . .

. . .

. . . Nothing is more clear, than that the admission of the right on the part of Congress to determine what papers are incendiary, and as such to prohibit their circulation through the mail, necessarily involves the right to determine, what are not incendiary and to enforce their circulation. Nor is it less certain, that to admit such a right would be virtually to clothe Congress with the power to abolish slavery, by giving it the means of breaking down all the barriers which the slave holding States have erected for the protection of their lives and property. It would give Congress without regard to the prohibitory laws of the States the authority to open the gates to the flood of incendiary publications, which are ready to break into those States, and to punish all, who dare resist, as criminals. Fortunately, Congress has no such right. The internal peace and security of the States are under the protection of the States themselves, to the entire exclusion of all authority and control on the part of Congress. It belongs to them, and not to Congress, to determine what is, or is not, calculated to disturb their peace and security, and of course in the case under consideration, it belongs to the Slave holding States to determine, what is incendiary and intended to incite to insurrection, and to adopt such defensive measures, as may be necessary for their security, with unlimited means of carrying them into effect, except such as may be expressly inhibited to the States by the Constitution.

---

43. Sen. Doc. 118, 24th Cong., 1st Sess., 1836, reprinted in Clyde N. Wilson, ed., *The Papers of John C. Calhoun* (Columbia: University of South Carolina Press, 1980), 13:53–60.

. . .

If, consequently, the right to protect her internal peace and security belongs to a State, the general Government is bound to respect the measures adopted by her for that purpose, and to cooperate in their execution, as far as its delegated powers may admit, or the measure may require. Thus, in the present case, the slave-holding States having the unquestionable right to pass all such laws as may be necessary to maintain the existing relation between master and slave, in those States, their right, of course, to prohibit the circulation of any publication, or any intercourse, calculated to disturb or destroy that relation is incontrovertible. In the execution of the measures, which may be adopted by the States for this purpose, the powers of Congress over the mail, and of regulating commerce with foreign nations and between the States, may require co-operation on the part of the general Government; and it is bound, in conformity with the principle established, to respect the laws of the State in their exercise, and so to modify its acts, as not only not to violate those of the States, but, as far as practicable, to cooperate in their execution.

. . .

Regarding [the above principle] as established . . . the Committee . . . have prepared a Bill . . . prohibiting under penalty of fine and dismissal from office, any Deputy Postmaster, in any State, Territory or District, from knowingly receiving and putting into the mail, any letter, packet, pamphlet, paper, or pictorial representation, directed to any Post office or person in a State, Territory or District, by the laws of which the circulation is forbidden. . . .

Report of the Minority of the Committee on Post Offices and Post Roads on the President's Message[44]

. . .

. . . [T]he establishment of a censorship over all publications . . . must necessarily operate with extreme harshness. . . . In order to make the law effectual, a censor must be appointed in the vicinity of every printing press, whose duty it would be to examine every number of every periodical, and every edition of all other publications, for which a mail circulation was sought, and certify their fitness for such circulation to the postmasters. . . . One of the obvious legal effects of this mode of legislation would be to transfer the power of determining a publisher's right to circulate, and also his right of property in the publications, from a jury of his peers to the summary discretion of any one of many thousand individuals. The medium of mail circulation has become so useful and important to the press of the country, and would be so trammeled and obstructed by the previous submission of all matters to be transmitted to the tribunal of a licenser, that this species of censorship could be scarcely less exceptionable and oppressive than a censorship that should extend to the restraint of the actual printing of publications. On the whole, a law of this description would be in such direct opposition to all the preconceived opinions of the People of this country, so abhorrent to their notions of the principles of civil liberty, and so utterly destructive of the freedom of the press, that the undersigned will not permit themselves seriously to apprehend that, under any possible circumstances, such a law can ever find a place on our statute book. . . .

The second mode of legislation [is] prohibiting the circulation by mail of such publications as the States shall prohibit. . . . If one State has a right to call on Congress to enact laws to prevent the effect of a mail circulation of publications within its limits, any other State has the same right; and if the judgment of one State is to be received as evidence of the evil tendency of particular publications, the judgment of every other State must have the same force, and impose the same obligation on Congress. A statute, therefore, founded on this principle, would provide that it should be an offense against the United States for any person to send through the mail into any State any publication the circulation of which might be prohibited by the laws of such State. A statute of this description would not only punish the citizen of Massachusetts before the federal court in his State for sending publications by mail on the subject of slavery into Georgia, but would also punish the citizen of Georgia, before the federal court in his State, for sending a publication on any subject into Massachusetts, that subject, whatever it might be, having previously come under the interdict of the law of Massachusetts. . . . One State might prohibit the dissemination of the Catholic doctrine;

44. *Register of the Debates in Congress*, 24th Cong., 1st Sess., 1836, 2944; also appears as "Proposed Report by Mr. Hall (of Vt.) on Incendiary Publications," *National Intelligencer*, April 8, 1836, 2. See Richard John, "Hiland Hall's 'Report on Incendiary Publications,' A Forgotten Nineteenth-Century Defense of the Freedom of the Press," *American Journal of Legal History* 41 (1997): 94.

another, that of the Protestant; one that of one political sentiment, and another that of its opposite. . . .

. . .

We are then thrown back on the question of what authority Congress possesses over "incendiary publications," by the grants of power contained in the Constitution, under the restrictions on the exercise of those powers found in that instrument? . . . The mode which this species of legislation provides, for executing the judgment which the Government forms of the character of publications, is most exceptionable and alarming. It does not, like other statutes, provide for the trial and punishment of the actual offender, but for the manual seizure and destruction of the article which it judges to be offensive. It deprives the citizen of his right of trial by jury to determine the fact of the unlawfulness of the publication, and takes from him his property without any "process of law" whatever. In this respect it is a direct violation of the fifth article of the amendment to the constitution. It is a censorship of the Press, committed to this summary discretion of any single Post Master—a censorship exercised in secret and upon evidence which can only be reached by an inquisitorial scrutiny into the contents of the mails, which must at once destroy all confidence in this security for any purpose. It is believed that a law with such odious features could not long be tolerated by any free people.

. . . The minority have not been able to come to the conclusion that Congress possesses the constitutional power to restrain the mail circulation of the publications specified in the message. On the contrary, they believe that any legislation for that purpose would come in direct conflict with that clause in the Constitution which prohibits Congress from making any law "abridging the freedom of speech or of the press." . . . The meaning of the term abridge is not qualified in the Constitution by the specification of any particular degree beyond which the liberty of the press is not permitted to be diminished. The slightest contraction or lessening of that liberty is forbidden. Nor does the Constitution point out any particular mode by which the freedom of the press may not be abridged. All modes of abridgment whatever are excluded, whether by the establishment of a censorship, the imposition of punishments, a tax on the promulgation of obnoxious opinions, or by any other means which can be devised to give a legislative preference, either in publication or circulation, to one sentiment emanating from the press, over that of another. Otherwise, the clause, by being susceptible of evasion, would be nugatory and useless. It was not against particular forms of legislation but to secure the substance of the freedom of the press, that the clause was made a part of the Constitution. The object of publication is circulation. The mere power to print, without the liberty to circulate, would be utterly valueless. The Post Office power, which belongs to the General Government, is an exclusive power. Under that power Congress has the entire control of the whole regular circulation of the country. Neither a State nor individuals, in opposition to the will of Congress, can establish or carry on the business of such circulation. A power, therefore, in Congress to judge of the moral, religious, political, or physical tendency of publications, and to deny the medium of mail circulation to those it deemed of an obnoxious character, would not only enable Congress to abridge the freedom of the press, but absolutely and completely to destroy it. . . .

. . .

. . . The prohibition of "incendiary publications" from mail circulation is not within the legitimate scope of the post office power; the power of proscribing them not being at all necessary to the safe, convenient, or expeditious transportation of the mail. . . . A law to prevent their circulation would be founded in erroneous and unconstitutional principles. Under cover of providing for the convenient transportation of the mail, and of preventing its use for evil purposes, it would assume a power in Congress to judge of the tendency of opinions emanating from the press; a power to discriminate between packages, not in reference to their bulk or form, but in relation to the sentiments they might be designed to inculcate. One class of opinions, meeting the approbation of Congress, is permitted a free circulation; another class of opinions, which Congress denominate "dangerous, seditious, and incendiary," is prohibited. . . . The People of the United States never intended that the Government of the Union should exercise over the press the power of discriminating between true and erroneous opinions, of determining that this sentiment was patriotic, that seditious and incendiary, and therefore wisely prohibited Congress all power over the subject. The minority of the committee respectfully submit to the House that Congress does not possess the constitutional power to distinguish from other publications, of like size and form, the "incendiary publications" specified in the Message of the President, or in any way to restrain their mail circulation.

B. Voting

Democrats and Whigs vigorously disputed voting rights. Many Democrats insisted that all free white male inhabitants should have the right to vote. A "democrat," they believed, was "one who favors universal suffrage."[45] Many Whigs insisted that only citizens who owned property should cast ballots, or that government should be structured in ways that gave property holders extra representatives. Judge Abel P. Upshur of Virginia maintained, "If men enter into the social compact upon unequal terms; if one man brings into the partnership, his rights of person alone, and another brings into it, equal rights of person and all the rights of property beside, can they be said to have an equal interest in the common stock?"[46]

Democrats won struggles over voting rights when the focus of the debate was the rights of native-born Americans. Whigs and nativists were more successful when attempting to restrict the rights of noncitizens and immigrants. Most states abandoned both property and taxpaying requirements for voting. Most, but not all, states limited voting to citizens. Many adopted voting registration statutes to prevent fraud (and possibly limit immigrant voting). State courts declared these laws constitutional. Chief Justice Shaw in *Capen v. Foster* (MA 1832) declared registration laws "a reasonable and convenient regulation of the mode of exercising the right of voting."[47]

Legislators apportioned legislatures by both geography and population. As the population moved west and new towns sprang up, legislators were not always quick to change electoral boundaries to recognize these communities. Battles over how to conduct elections were often heated, partisan, and sometimes played out in state constitutional conventions called to restructure the legislature. Disputes over how the Rhode Island legislature was elected led to armed clashes in 1842 between the incumbent government and reformers. In most states, the move toward more fair apportionment of legislatures was less violent. Until the twentieth century, the courts stayed on the sidelines while such political battles played themselves out.

IX. Equality

MAJOR DEVELOPMENTS

- Courts restrict "class legislation"
- Constitutional decision makers reject African American citizenship
- The movement for women's rights is organized

Jacksonians held a powerful but restrictive conception of equality. Constitutional decision makers often scrutinized very strictly legislation and legislative proposals that they believed treated one class of persons differently from another class of persons. *Wally's Heirs v. Kennedy* (TN 1831) insisted, "The rights of every individual must stand or fall by the same rule or *law* that governs every other member of the body politic."[48] This equality was confined to white men. A few radicals aside, most Democrats and Whigs endorsed rules or laws for women, persons of color, and Native Americans that differed from those that governed every other member of the body politic. Persons of color, in particular, were regarded as legally inferior to whites. Roger Taney's opinion in *Dred Scott v. Sandford* (1857) infamously asserted that African Americans, free or enslaved, "had no rights which the white man was bound to respect."

A. Equality Under Law

Jacksonians hated class legislation, which, they insisted, unjustifiably provided special benefits to or imposed distinctive burdens on only one group of citizens. President Andrew Jackson's Farewell Address attacked the "spirit of monopoly and thirst for exclusive privileges." Jackson had earlier condemned the Bank of the United States for "enabl[ing] one class of society . . . to act injuriously upon the interests of all the others and to exercise more that its just proportion of influence in political affairs. . . . Men who love liberty desire nothing but equal rights and equal laws." The *Evening Post*, an important Jacksonian periodical,

---

45. Alexander Keyssar, *The Right to Vote: The Contested History of Democracy in the United States* (New York: Basic Books, 2001), 27.

46. Abel P. Upshur, "Speech Before the Convention, 27 October 1829," quoted in Erik S. Root, *All Honor to Jefferson? The Virginia Slavery Debates and the Positive Good Thesis* (Lanham: Lexington Books, 2008), 85.

47. *Capen v. Foster*, 12 Pick. 485 (MA 1832).

proclaimed that "the functions of Government . . . are . . . restricted to the making of *general laws*, uniform and universal in their operation."[49] The Supreme Court of Tennessee in *Wally's Heirs v. Kennedy* (TN 1831) declared:

> The clause, "law of the land," means a general public law, equally binding upon every member of the community. The rights of every individual must stand or fall by the same rule or law, that governs every other member of the body politic, or land, under similar circumstances; and every partial, or private law, which directly proposes to destroy or affect individual rights, or does the same thing by affording remedies leading to similar consequences, is unconstitutional and void.[50]

B. Race

Four developments structured the constitutional politics of slavery. The first was the dramatic increase in free-state populations. Contrary to original expectations, the population of the northwestern states grew substantially more rapidly than the population of the southwestern states. One immediate consequence of this demographic development was that both houses of Congress had free-state majorities after 1850. Many southerners had good reason for fearing that the free states would soon have permanent control over all national institutions. The second development was the continued entrenchment of slavery in most slave states. Such border states as Delaware aside, no southern state seemed likely to emancipate slaves in the foreseeable future. George Washington and the founding generation of Virginians often asserted that slavery was a necessary evil that they hoped would someday disappear. Southern Jacksonians more often asserted that slavery was a positive good that promoted white civilization. Third, a growing anti-slavery movement demanded that the national government pass legislation promoting emancipation. More radical abolitionists, led by William Lloyd Garrison, insisted that slavery be abolished immediately. More moderate anti-slavery advocates, led first by William Seward and later by Abraham Lincoln, insisted that slavery be abolished in all territories. Federal measures that confined slavery to existing states, they believed, fostered the eventual emancipation of all slaves. The fourth development that structured the constitutional politics of slavery was westward expansion. More territory gained by the Louisiana Purchase was settled, and the United States acquired new southwestern territories after the Mexican War. The free and slave states competed vigorously, and often violently, for control over these territories. All parties knew that extra slave or free states would alter political power in Congress.

Americans before the Civil War debated the constitutional status of free blacks as well as the constitutional status of slavery. Constitutional decision makers usually concluded that free blacks were not citizens under the national and state constitutions. Some western states prohibited free blacks from becoming residents. States such as Massachusetts that did not attach racial conditions to citizenship were nevertheless ambivalent on whether race provided legitimate grounds for distinguishing between state citizens. In *Roberts v. City of Boston* (MA 1849), the Supreme Judicial Court of Massachusetts ruled that Boston could constitutionally segregate city schools. The segregation ordinance was almost immediately repealed, in large part because many local officials believed the measure unconstitutional.

Dred Scott v. Sandford (1857) sought to resolve questions about the status of free blacks and the status of slavery in the territories. Chief Justice Taney ruled that former slaves could not become national citizens and that Congress had no power to ban slavery in the territories. Hopes that a judicial ruling would settle these controversies were soon dashed. The controversy over Kansas statehood aggravated latent tensions between northern and southern Democrats. On the eve of the 1860 presidential election, southern Democrats demanded that Congress enact a slave code for the territories. Northern Democrats offered as a compromise a proposal to have the matter adjudicated by the Supreme Court. When that compromise was rejected, the Democratic Party divided—a division that ensured that Abraham Lincoln won the 1860 presidential election. Shortly after Lincoln gained the White House, six slave states seceded from the Union.

---

48. *Wally's Heirs*, 2 Yerg. 554 (TN 1831).
49. "True Functions of Government," *Evening Post*, November 21, 1834.
50. *Wally's Heirs v. Kennedy*, 2 Yerg. 544 (TN 1831).

Dred Scott v. Sandford, 60 U.S. 393 (1857)

John Emerson's hypochondria was responsible for the most infamous case in American judicial history. Emerson was an army surgeon who complained of health problems wherever he was posted. He could not stomach Rock Island, Illinois, nor a stint in Louisiana, nor, finally, a posting at Fort Snelling in Minnesota Territory. Emerson was accompanied on his travels by Dred Scott, his slave. While Emerson served at Fort Snelling, Dred Scott married Harriet Robinson, another slave.[51] *In 1838 Emerson returned to Missouri with both Dred and Harriet Scott as slaves. When Emerson died, Irene and John Sanford (misspelled in the case name) inherited the Scotts.*

During the late 1840s the Scotts sued Sanford in state court, claiming that their previous residence in a free state and a free territory had emancipated them. The case initially presented fairly simple state law issues. Both free and slave states during the early nineteenth century made a distinction between residence and sojourning. Slaves who resided in free states with their masters were emancipated. Slaves who traveled through free states with their masters remained slaves. Had Missouri applied these conventional rules, the Scotts would have won their freedom suit, because Emerson had resided in both a free state and a free territory. State constitutional law, however, was in flux. Several northern state courts had abandoned the residence/sojourning distinction. In Commonwealth v. Aves (MA 1836), *Chief Justice Lemuel Shaw of the Supreme Judicial Court of Massachusetts ruled that slaves traveling with their masters were free the instant they entered the state. In response the Missouri Supreme Court in Dred Scott's case ruled that slavery reattached whenever a slaveholder returned with his slaves from a free state or territory, no matter how long the northern stay.*

The Scotts re-filed their freedom lawsuit in federal court, hoping that a federal judge might treat their claims under federal common law rather than state law.[52] *This move changed the legal claims open to both parties. Sanford claimed that Dred Scott could not sue in federal court because Dred Scott was not a citizen under Article III of the U.S. Constitution. If a slave or a former slave could not be an American citizen, then Scott and Sanford did not meet the diversity of citizenship requirement for federal jurisdiction. The federal district court did not rule on this matter, claiming that the issue of citizenship had been waived. The trial court instead supported the state court ruling that slavery had reattached when the Scotts returned to Missouri.*[53] *When Scott appealed that decision, Sanford added as alternative ground for judgment the claim that Scott did not become free in Minnesota because the congressional ban on slavery in that territory was unconstitutional.*

The Supreme Court by a 7–2 vote ruled that Scott was a slave. Chief Justice Taney's opinion for the Court declared that former slaves could not constitutionally become American citizens and that Congress could not ban slavery in American territories. Almost every facet of the Dred Scott *decision was and continues to be controversial. Consider Justice Taney's decision to rule on the constitutionality of the Missouri Compromise after he declared that former slaves, because they were not citizens of the United States, could not bring lawsuits in federal court. Was this, as many northerners charged, a judicially inappropriate effort to discuss the merits of a case in which the Court had declined jurisdiction? Or, as Taney insisted, was the discussion of the Missouri Compromise an alternative ground for rejecting jurisdiction? Virtually all commentators agree that the* Dred Scott *ruling is wrong as a matter of constitutional law.*[54] *Do you agree with this assessment? To what extent is what is wrong with* Dred Scott *only what is wrong with slavery and racism? Could a person who believed in slavery and racism find Chief Justice Taney's arguments constitutionally plausible? If Taney was wrong, was he wrong because he used the wrong method of constitutional interpretation or because he misapplied the right method of constitutional interpretation? What method did Taney use? Was he an originalist, or did he implicitly reject originalism? What methods did the dissents use? Was the argument between the dissenting and majority opinions an argument about method or application of method?*

Justice Benjamin Curtis's dissent is considered a masterpiece of legal writing. Curtis concluded that Congress could decide whether to ban slavery in the territories.

51. Lea VanderVelde, *Mrs. Dred Scott: A Life on Slavery's Frontier* (New York: Oxford University Press, 2009).

52. This argument relied heavily on *Tyson v. Swift*, 41 U.S. 1 (1842). In *Tyson*, the justices ruled that when resolving diversity cases, federal courts need not rely on the law of the state in which the contested action took place.

53. Several justices in *Dred Scott* refused to consider the citizenship issue on that grounds.

54. The seminal expression of the scholarly consensus is Don E. Fehrenbacher, *The* Dred Scott *Case: Its Significance in American Law and Politics* (New York: Oxford University Press, 1978). But also see Mark A. Graber, Dred Scott *and the Problem of Constitutional Evil* (New York: Cambridge University Press, 2006).

He asserted that free blacks were American citizens only if the state in which they were born treated free blacks as citizens. Very few states did so in 1856. Justice John McLean's dissent maintained that Congress was constitutionally obligated to ban slavery in the territories and that all free persons of color born in the United States were American citizens. What explains why Curtis took the more narrow position? Which position is constitutionally correct? If you were on the Taney Court, would you write a narrower or a broader dissent?

Most legal commentators believe that Dred Scott *helped cause the Civil War. Robert McCloskey declared that the Taney Court tragically "imagined that a flaming political issue could be quenched by calling it a 'legal' issue and deciding it judicially."*[55] *Both northern and southern Democrats, however, rallied around the* Dred Scott *decision in the spring and summer of 1857. Democrats gained votes at the expense of Republicans in every northern election held between March and September of that year. They fractured in the late fall over Kansas statehood. Did* Dred Scott *nevertheless aggravate sectional tensions by increasing Republican militancy and providing another barrier between northern and southern Democrats when the controversy over Kansas statehood emerged? Is the real lesson of the 1850s that no American institution was able to fashion a successful compromise over slavery?*

CHIEF JUSTICE TANEY delivered the opinion of the court.

. . .

The words "people of the United States" and "citizens" are synonymous terms, and mean the same thing. They both describe the political body who . . . form the sovereignty, and who hold the power and conduct the Government through their representatives. . . . The question before us is, whether [former slaves and their descendants] compose a portion of this people, and are constituent members of this sovereignty? We think they are not, and that they are not included, and were not intended to be included, under the word "citizens" in the Constitution, and can therefore claim none of the rights and privileges which that instrument provides for and secures to citizens of the United States. On the contrary, they were at that time considered as a subordinate and inferior class of beings, who had been subjugated by the dominant race, and, whether emancipated or not, yet remained subject to their authority, and had no rights or privileges but such as those who held the power and the Government might choose to grant them.

. . .

In discussing this question, we must not confound the rights of citizenship which a State may confer within its own limits, and the rights of citizenship as a member of the Union. It does not by any means follow, because he has all the rights and privileges of a citizen of a State, that he must be a citizen of the United States. . . . For, previous to the adoption of the Constitution of the United States, every State had the undoubted right to confer on whomsoever it pleased the character of citizen, and to endow him with all its rights. But this character of course was confined to the boundaries of the State, and gave him no rights or privileges in other States beyond those secured to him by the laws of nations and the comity of States. . . . Each State may still confer them upon an alien, or any one it thinks proper, or upon any class or description of persons; yet he would not be a citizen in the sense in which that word is used in the Constitution of the United States, nor entitled to sue as such in one of its courts, nor to the privileges and immunities of a citizen in the other States. . . . The Constitution has conferred on Congress the right to establish a uniform rule of naturalization, and this right is evidently exclusive. . . . Consequently, no State, since the adoption of the Constitution, can by naturalizing an alien invest him with the rights and privileges secured to a citizen of a State under the Federal Government. . . .

. . .

It is true, every person, and every class and description of persons, who were at the time of the adoption of the Constitution recognized as citizens in the several States, became also citizens of this new political body; but none other; it was formed by them, and for them and their posterity, but for no one else. . . .

. . .

In the opinion of the court, the legislation and histories of the times, and the language used in the Declaration of Independence, show, that neither the class of persons who had been imported as slaves, nor their descendants, whether they had become free or not, were then acknowledged as a part of the people, nor intended to be included in the general words used in that memorable instrument.

. . .

55. Robert McCloskey, *The American Supreme Court*, 4th ed., rev. Sanford Levinson (Chicago: University of Chicago Press, 2005), 62.

They had for more than a century before been regarded as beings of an inferior order, and altogether unfit to associate with the white race, either in social or political relations; and so far inferior, that they had no rights which the white man was bound to respect; and that the negro might justly and lawfully be reduced to slavery for his benefit. . . .

. . .

The language of the Declaration of Independence is equally conclusive:

. . .

It . . . say[s]: "We hold these truths to be self-evident: that all men are created equal; that they are endowed by their Creator with certain unalienable rights; that among them is life, liberty, and the pursuit of happiness; that to secure these rights, Governments are instituted, deriving their just powers from the consent of the governed."

The general words above quoted would seem to embrace the whole human family, and if they were used in a similar instrument at this day would be so understood. But it is too clear for dispute, that the enslaved African race were not intended to be included, and formed no part of the people who framed and adopted this declaration; for if the language, as understood in that day, would embrace them, the conduct of the distinguished men who framed the Declaration of Independence would have been utterly and flagrantly inconsistent with the principles they asserted; and instead of the sympathy of mankind, to which they so confidently appealed, they would have deserved and received universal rebuke and reprobation.

. . .

. . . [W]hen we look to the condition of this race in the several States at the time, it is impossible to believe that these rights and privileges were intended to be extended to them. . . .

By the laws of New Hampshire, collected and finally passed in 1815, no one was permitted to be enrolled in the militia of the State, but free white citizens; and the same provision is found in a subsequent collection of the laws, made in 1855. Nothing could more strongly mark the entire repudiation of the African race. The alien is excluded, because, being born in a foreign country, he cannot be a member of the community until he is naturalized. But why are the African race, born in the State, not permitted to share in one of the highest duties of the citizen? The answer is obvious; he is not, by the institutions and laws of the State, numbered among its people. He forms no part of the sovereignty of the State, and is not therefore called on to uphold and defend it.

. . .

Undoubtedly, a person may be a citizen, that is, a member of the community who form the sovereignty, although he exercises no share of the political power, and is incapacitated from holding particular offices.

Women and minors, who form a part of the political family, cannot vote; and when a property qualification is required to vote or hold a particular office, those who have not the necessary qualification cannot vote or hold the office, yet they are citizens.

So, too, a person may be entitled to vote by the law of the State, who is not a citizen even of the State itself. And in some of the States of the Union foreigners not naturalized are allowed to vote. And the State may give the right to free negroes and mulattoes, but that does not make them citizens of the State, and still less of the United States. And the provision in the Constitution giving privileges and immunities in other States, does not apply to them.

. . .

No one, we presume, supposes that any change in public opinion or feeling, in relation to this unfortunate race, in the civilized nations of Europe or in this country, should induce the court to give to the words of the Constitution a more liberal construction in their favor than they were intended to bear when the instrument was framed and adopted. Such an argument would be altogether inadmissible in any tribunal called on to interpret it. If any of its provisions are deemed unjust, there is a mode prescribed in the instrument itself by which it may be amended; but while it remains unaltered, it must be construed now as it was understood at the time of its adoption. It is not only the same in words, but the same in meaning, and delegates the same powers to the Government, and reserves and secures the same rights and privileges to the citizen; and as long as it continues to exist in its present form, it speaks not only in the same words, but with the same meaning and intent with which it spoke when it came from the hands of its framers, and was voted on and adopted by the people of the United States. Any other rule of construction would abrogate the judicial character of this court, and make it the mere reflex of the popular opinion or passion of the day. This court was not created by the Constitution for such purposes. Higher and graver trusts have been confided to it, and it must not falter in the path of duty.

. . .

The act of Congress, upon which the plaintiff relies [as the basis of his freedom claim], declares that slavery and involuntary servitude, except as a punishment for crime, shall be forever prohibited in all that part of the territory ceded by France . . . which lies north of thirty-six degrees thirty minutes north latitude, and not included within the limits of Missouri. . . .

The counsel for the plaintiff has laid much stress upon that article in the Constitution which confers on Congress the power "to dispose of and make all needful rules and regulations respecting the territory or other property belonging to the United States"; but, in the judgment of the court, that provision has no bearing on the present controversy, and the power there given, whatever it may be, is confined, and was intended to be confined, to the territory which at that time belonged to, or was claimed by, the United States, and was within their boundaries as settled by the treaty with Great Britain, and can have no influence upon a territory afterwards acquired from a foreign Government. . . .

. . .

. . . [T]he power of Congress over the person or property of a citizen can never be a mere discretionary power under our Constitution and form of Government. The powers of the Government and the rights and privileges of the citizen are regulated and plainly defined by the Constitution itself. And when the Territory becomes a part of the United States, the Federal Government enters into possession in the character impressed upon it by those who created it. It enters upon it with its powers over the citizen strictly defined, and limited by the Constitution, from which it derives its own existence, and by virtue of which alone it continues to exist and act as a Government and sovereignty. . . .

. . .

For example, no one, we presume, will contend that Congress can make any law in a Territory respecting the establishment of religion, or the free exercise thereof, or abridging the freedom of speech or of the press, or the right of the people of the Territory peaceably to assemble, and to petition the Government for the redress of grievances.

. . .

. . . [T]he rights of property are united with the rights of person, and placed on the same ground by the fifth amendment to the Constitution, which provides that no person shall be deprived of life, liberty, and property, without due process of law. And an act of Congress which deprives a citizen of the United States of his liberty or property, merely because he came himself or brought his property into a particular Territory of the United States, and who had committed no offence against the laws, could hardly be dignified with the name of due process of law.

. . .

It seems, however, to be supposed, that there is a difference between property in a slave and other property, and that different rules may be applied to it in expounding the Constitution of the United States. . . .

. . . [N]o laws or usages of other nations, or reasoning of statesmen or jurists upon the relations of master and slave, can enlarge the powers of the Government, or take from the citizens the rights they have reserved. And if the Constitution recognizes the right of property of the master in a slave, and makes no distinction between that description of property and other property owned by a citizen, no tribunal, acting under the authority of the United States, whether it be legislative, executive, or judicial, has a right to draw such a distinction, or deny to it the benefit of the provisions and guarantees which have been provided for the protection of private property against the encroachments of the Government.

. . . [T]he right of property in a slave is distinctly and expressly affirmed in the Constitution. . . . [N]o word can be found in the Constitution which gives Congress a greater power over slave property, or which entitles property of that kind to less protection than property of any other description. The only power conferred is the power coupled with the duty of guarding and protecting the owner in his rights.

Upon these considerations, it is the opinion of the court that the act of Congress which prohibited a citizen from holding and owning property of this kind in the territory of the United States north of the line therein mentioned, is not warranted by the Constitution, and is therefore void; and that neither Dred Scott himself, nor any of his family, were made free by being carried into this territory; even if they had been carried there by the owner, with the intention of becoming a permanent resident. . . .

JUSTICE WAYNE, concurring. . . .
JUSTICE NELSON, concurring. . . .
JUSTICE DANIEL, concurring. . . .

JUSTICE CAMPBELL, concurring. . . .
JUSTICE CATRON, concurring. . . .
JUSTICE McLEAN, dissenting. . . .
JUSTICE GRIER, concurring. . . .

JUSTICE CURTIS, dissenting. . . .

. . .

To determine whether any free persons, descended from Africans held in slavery, were citizens of the United States under the Confederation, and consequently at the time of the adoption of the Constitution of the United States, it is only necessary to know whether any such persons were citizens of either of the States under the Confederation, at the time of the adoption of the Constitution.

Of this there can be no doubt. At the time of the ratification of the Articles of Confederation, all free native-born inhabitants of the States of New Hampshire, Massachusetts, New York, New Jersey, and North Carolina, though descended from African slaves, were not only citizens of those States, but such of them as had the other necessary qualifications possessed the franchise of electors, on equal terms with other citizens.

. . .

. . . I shall not enter into an examination of the existing opinions of that period respecting the African race, nor into any discussion concerning the meaning of those who asserted, in the Declaration of Independence, that all men are created equal; that they are endowed by their Creator with certain inalienable rights; that among these are life, liberty, and the pursuit of happiness. My own opinion is, that a calm comparison of these assertions of universal abstract truths, and of their own individual opinions and acts, would not leave these men under any reproach of inconsistency; that the great truths they asserted on that solemn occasion, they were ready and anxious to make effectual, wherever a necessary regard to circumstances, which no statesman can disregard without producing more evil than good, would allow; and that it would not be just to them, nor true in itself, to allege that they intended to say that the Creator of all men had endowed the white race, exclusively, with the great natural rights which the Declaration of Independence asserts. . . .

. . .

. . . [M]y opinion is, that, under the Constitution of the United States, every free person born on the soil of a State, who is a citizen of that State by force of its Constitution or laws, is also a citizen of the United States.

. . .

It has been often asserted that the Constitution was made exclusively by and for the white race. It has already been shown that in five of the thirteen original States, colored persons then possessed the elective franchise, and were among those by whom the Constitution was ordained and established. If so, it is not true, in point of fact, that the Constitution was made exclusively by the white race. And that it was made exclusively for the white race is, in my opinion, not only an assumption not warranted by anything in the Constitution, but contradicted by its opening declaration, that it was ordained and established by the people of the United States, for themselves and their posterity. And as free colored persons were then citizens of at least five States, and so in every sense part of the people of the United States, they were among those for whom and whose posterity the Constitution was ordained and established.

. . . [C]itizenship, under the Constitution of the United States, is not dependent on the possession of any particular political or even of all civil rights; and any attempt so to define it must lead to error. To what citizens the elective franchise shall be confided, is a question to be determined by each State, in accordance with its own views of the necessities or expediencies of its condition. What civil rights shall be enjoyed by its citizens, and whether all shall enjoy the same, or how they may be gained or lost, are to be determined in the same way.

. . .

It has been urged that the words "rules and regulations" are not appropriate terms in which to convey authority to make laws for the government of the territory.

But it must be remembered that this is a grant of power to the Congress—that it is therefore necessarily a grant of power to legislate—and, certainly, rules and regulations respecting a particular subject, made by the legislative power of a country, can be nothing but laws. Nor do the particular terms employed, in my judgment, tend in any degree to restrict this legislative power. . . .

. . .

If, then, this clause does contain a power to legislate respecting the territory, what are the limits of that power?

To this I answer, that, in common with all the other legislative powers of Congress, it finds limits in the express prohibitions on Congress not to do certain things; that, in the exercise of the legislative power, Congress cannot pass an ex post facto law or bill of attainder; and so in respect to each of the other prohibitions contained in the Constitution.

Besides this, the rules and regulations must be needful. But undoubtedly the question whether a particular rule or regulation be needful, must be finally determined by Congress itself. Whether a law be needful, is a legislative or political, not a judicial, question. Whatever Congress deems needful is so, under the grant of power.

. . .

But it is insisted, that whatever other powers Congress may have respecting the territory of the United States, the subject of negro slavery forms an exception.

The Constitution declares that Congress shall have power to make "*all* needful rules and regulations" respecting the territory belonging to the United States.

There is nothing in the context which qualifies the grant of power. The regulations must be "respecting the territory." An enactment that slavery may or may not exist there, is a regulation respecting the territory. Regulations must be needful; but it is necessarily left to the legislative discretion to determine whether a law be needful. No other clause of the Constitution has been referred to at the bar, or has been seen by me, which imposes any restriction or makes any exception concerning the power of Congress to allow or prohibit slavery in the territory belonging to the United States.

. . .

This provision [in the Northwest Ordinance banning slavery] shows that it was then understood Congress might make a regulation prohibiting slavery, and that Congress might also allow it to continue to exist in the Territory; and accordingly, when, a few days later, Congress passed the act of May 20th, 1790 [which permitted slavery in the southwest territories].

. . .

[With respect to policy arguments for permitting slavery in the territory], this court has no concern. One or the other may be justly entitled to guide or control the legislative judgment upon what is a needful regulation. The question here is, whether they are sufficient to authorize this court to insert into this clause of the Constitution an exception of the exclusion or allowance of slavery, not found therein, nor in any other part of that instrument. To engraft on any instrument a substantive exception not found in it, must be admitted to be a matter attended with great difficulty. And the difficulty increases with the importance of the instrument, and the magnitude and complexity of the interests involved in its construction. To allow this to be done with the Constitution, upon reasons purely political, renders its judicial interpretation impossible—because judicial tribunals, as such, cannot decide upon political considerations. Political reasons have not the requisite certainty to afford rules of juridical interpretation. They are different in different men. They are different in the same men at different times. And when a strict interpretation of the Constitution, according to the fixed rules which govern the interpretation of laws, is abandoned, and the theoretical opinions of individuals are allowed to control its meaning, we have no longer a Constitution; we are under the government of individual men, who for the time being have power to declare what the Constitution is, according to their own views of what it ought to mean. When such a method of interpretation of the Constitution obtains, in place of a republican Government, with limited and defined powers, we have a Government which is merely an exponent of the will of Congress; or what, in my opinion, would not be preferable, an exponent of the individual political opinions of the members of this court.

. . .

I confess myself unable to perceive any difference whatever between my own opinion of the general extent of the power of Congress and the opinion of the majority of the court, save that I consider it derivable from the express language of the Constitution, while they hold it to be silently implied from the power to acquire territory. Looking at the power of Congress over the Territories as of the extent just described, what positive prohibition exists in the Constitution, which restrained Congress from enacting a law in 1820 to prohibit slavery north of thirty-six degrees thirty minutes north latitude?

The only one suggested is that clause in the fifth article of the amendments of the Constitution which declares that no person shall be deprived of his life, liberty, or property, without due process of law. . . .

Slavery, being contrary to natural right, is created only by municipal law.

. . .

. . . [T]hey who framed and adopted the constitution were aware that persons held to service under the laws of a State are property only to the extent and under the conditions fixed by those laws; that they must cease to be available as property, when their owners voluntarily place them permanently within another jurisdiction, where no municipal laws on the subject of slavery exist; and that, being aware of these principles, and having said nothing to interfere with or displace them, or to compel Congress to legislate in any particular manner on the subject, and having empowered Congress to make all needful rules and regulations respecting the territory of the United States, it was their intention to leave to the discretion of Congress what regulations, if any, should be made concerning slavery therein. Moreover, if the right exists, what are its limits, and what are its conditions? If citizens of the United States have the right to take their slaves to a Territory, and hold them there as slaves, without regard to the laws of the Territory, I suppose this right is not to be restricted to the citizens of slaveholding States. A citizen of a State which does not tolerate slavery can hardly be denied the power of doing the same thing.

Nor, in my judgment, will the position, that a prohibition to bring slaves into a Territory deprives any one of his property without due process of law, bear examination.

. . .

And if a prohibition of slavery in a Territory in 1820 violated this principle, . . . the ordinance of 1787 also violated it; and what power had, I do not say the Congress of the Confederation alone, but the Legislature of Virginia, or the Legislature of any or all the States of the Confederacy, to consent to such a violation? . . . It was certainly understood by the Convention which framed the Constitution, and has been so understood ever since, that, under the power to regulate commerce, Congress could prohibit the importation of slaves; and the exercise of the power was restrained till 1808. A citizen of the United States owns slaves in Cuba, and brings them to the United States, where they are set free by the legislation of Congress. Does this legislation deprive him of his property without due process of law? If so, what becomes of the laws prohibiting the slave trade? If not, how can similar regulation respecting a Territory violate the fifth amendment of the Constitution? . . .

Roberts v. City of Boston, 59 Mass. 198 (1849)

Sarah Roberts, a five-year-old African-American, applied to attend the Boston primary school nearest her place of residence. Her application was rejected. The school committee insisted that Roberts attend one of the two schools that Boston maintained for children of color. After negotiations between the free black community of Boston and the school board failed, Benjamin Roberts, Sarah's father, filed a lawsuit claiming that racially separate schools violated the state constitutional commitment to equality. The school committee asserted by resolution that "the continuance of the separate schools for colored children, and the regular attendance of all such children upon the schools, is not only legal and just, but is best adapted to promote the education of that class of our population." After the trial court rejected his contention, Roberts appealed to the Supreme Judicial Court of Massachusetts. Charles Sumner, a leading abolitionist and later a senator from Massachusetts, argued the case for the Roberts family.

The African American community proved more successful in legislative and electoral politics than in judicial politics. The Supreme Judicial Court of Massachusetts rejected the Roberts lawsuit. Chief Justice Lemuel Shaw agreed that free blacks had a constitutional right to equal treatment but nevertheless insisted that the school committee made a reasonable decision when mandating racial segregation in the Boston public schools. Proponents of school desegregation in Massachusetts did not abandon their cause after that judicial defeat. In 1854 the Free Soil Party won a dramatic victory in the state election. The next year Free Soil majorities in the Massachusetts legislature passed a law outlawing racial segregation in public schools.[56]

When reading the excerpts from the Sumner argument and the Shaw opinion, keep in mind that Massachusetts was one of the few states in Jacksonian America in which free blacks were state citizens. For this reason many persons after the Civil War insisted that Roberts *was a precedent that cast light on the citizenship rights guaranteed by the Fourteenth Amendment. Should the Fourteenth Amendment be read in*

56. For the full details of the struggle for desegregated schools in Jacksonian Massachusetts, see J. Morgan Kousser, "'The Supremacy of Equal Rights': The Struggle Against Racial Discrimination in Antebellum Massachusetts and the Foundations of the Fourteenth Amendment," *Northwestern Law Review* 82 (1988): 941.

light of Chief Justice Shaw's claim that segregated schools are consistent with constitutional equality? Or should it be read in light of the subsequent decision of the Massachusetts legislature that segregated education violated the Massachusetts Constitution?

Mr. SUMNER argued as follows:—

1. According to the spirit of American institutions, and especially of the constitution of Massachusetts . . . all men, without distinction of color or race, are equal before the law.

. . .

4. The exclusion of colored children from the public schools, which are open to white children, is a source of practical inconvenience to them and their parents, to which white persons are not exposed, and is, therefore, a violation of equality.

5. The separation of children in the public schools of Boston, on account of color or race, is in the nature of caste, and is a violation of equality.

6. . . . The regulations and by-laws of municipal corporations must be reasonable, or they are inoperative and void. . . . So, the regulations and by-laws of the school committee must be reasonable; and their discretion must be exercised in a reasonable manner. The discrimination made by the school committee of Boston, on account of color, is not legally reasonable. A colored person may occupy any office connected with the public schools, from that of governor, or secretary of the board of education, to that of member of a school committee, or teacher in any public school, and as a voter he may vote for members of the school committee. It is clear, that the committee may classify scholars, according to age and sex, for these distinctions are inoffensive, and recognized as legal or according to their moral and intellectual qualifications, because such a power is necessary to the government of schools. But the committee cannot assume, without individual examination, that an entire race possess certain moral or intellectual qualities, which render it proper to place them all in a class by themselves.

But it is said, that the committee, in thus classifying the children, have not violated any principle of equality, inasmuch as they have provided a school with competent instructors for the colored children, where they enjoy equal advantages of instruction with those enjoyed by the white children. To this there are several answers: 1st, The separate school for colored children is not one of the schools established by the law relating to public schools, and having no legal existence, cannot be a legal equivalent. 2d. It is not in fact an equivalent. It is the occasion of inconveniences to the colored children, to which they would not be exposed if they had access to the nearest public schools; it inflicts upon them the stigma of caste; and although the matters taught in the two schools may be precisely the same, a school exclusively devoted to one class must differ essentially, in its spirit and character, from that public school known to the law, where all classes meet together in equality. 3d. Admitting that it is an equivalent, still the colored children cannot be compelled to take it. They have an equal right with the white children to the general public schools.

7. . . . Slavery was abolished in Massachusetts, by virtue of the declaration of rights in our constitution, without any specific words of abolition in that instrument, or in any subsequent legislation. . . . The same words, which are potent to destroy slavery, must be equally potent against any institution founded on caste. . . . If there should be any doubt in this case, the court should incline in favor of equality; as every interpretation is always made in favor of life and liberty. . . .

The fact, that the separation of the schools was originally made at the request of the colored parents, cannot affect the rights of the colored people, or the powers of the school committee. The separation of the schools, so far from being for the benefit of both races, is an injury to both. It tends to create a feeling of degradation in the blacks, and of prejudice and uncharitableness in the whites.

CHIEF JUSTICE SHAW delivered the opinion of the Court.

. . .

The great principle, advanced by the learned and eloquent advocate of the plaintiff, is, that by the constitution and laws of Massachusetts, all persons without distinction of age or sex, birth or color, origin or condition, are equal before the law. This, as a broad general principle, such as ought to appear in a declaration of rights, is perfectly sound; it is not only expressed in terms, but pervades and animates the whole spirit of our constitution of free government. But, when this great principle comes to be applied to the actual and various conditions of persons in society, it will not warrant the assertion, that men and women are legally clothed with the same civil and political powers, and that children and adults are legally to have the same functions and be subject to the same treatment; but only that the rights of all, as they are settled and regulated by law, are equally entitled to the paternal consideration and protection of the law, for their maintenance and security. What those rights are, to which individuals, in the infinite variety of circumstances by which they are surrounded in society, are entitled, must depend on laws adapted to their respective relations and conditions.

Conceding, therefore, in the fullest manner, that colored persons, the descendants of Africans, are entitled by law, in this commonwealth, to equal rights, constitutional and political, civil and social, the question then arises, whether the regulation in question, which provides separate schools for colored children, is a violation of any of these rights.

. . .

The power of general superintendence vests a plenary authority in the [school] committee to arrange, classify, and distribute pupils, in such a manner as they think best adapted to their general proficiency and welfare. If it is thought expedient to provide for very young children, it may be, that such schools may be kept exclusively by female teachers, quite adequate to their instruction, and yet whose services may be obtained at a cost much lower than that of more highly-qualified male instructors. So if they should judge it expedient to have a grade of schools for children from seven to ten, and another for those from ten to fourteen, it would seem to be within their authority to establish such schools. So to separate male and female pupils into different schools, it has been found necessary, that is to say, highly expedient, at times, to establish special schools for poor and neglected children, who have passed the age of seven, and have become too old to attend the primary school, and yet have not acquired the rudiments of learning, to enable them to enter the ordinary schools. If a class of youth, of one or both sexes, is found in that condition, and it is expedient to organize them into a separate school, to receive the special training, adapted to their condition, it seems to be within the power of the superintending committee, to provide for the organization of such special school.

. . .

In the absence of special legislation on this subject, the law has vested the power in the committee to regulate the system of distribution and classification; and when this power is reasonably exercised, without being abused or perverted by colorable pretences, the decision of the committee must be deemed conclusive. The committee, apparently upon great deliberation, have come to the conclusion, that the good of both classes of schools will be best promoted, by maintaining the separate primary schools for colored and for white children, and we can perceive no ground to doubt, that this is the honest result of their experience and judgment.

It is urged, that this maintenance of separate schools tends to deepen and perpetuate the odious distinction of caste, founded in a deep-rooted prejudice in public opinion. This prejudice, if it exists, is not created by law, and probably cannot be changed by law. Whether this distinction and prejudice, existing in the opinion and feelings of the community, would not be as effectually fostered by compelling colored and white children to associate together in the same schools, may well be doubted; at all events, it is a fair and proper question for the committee to consider and decide upon, having in view the best interests of both classes of children placed under their superintendence, and we cannot say, that their decision upon it is not founded on just grounds of reason and experience, and in the results of a discriminating and honest judgment. . . .

C. Gender

Women more vociferously demanded equal rights during the later part of the Jacksonian Era. If, as the Supreme Court of Tennessee insisted in *Wally's Heirs v. Kennedy* (TN 1831), "the rights of every individual must stand or fall by the same rule or law that governs every other member of the body politic," then, many early feminists claimed, women ought to be governed by the same rule or law that governed men. The first major women's rights convention was held at Seneca Falls, New York, in 1848. That convention adopted a Declaration of Sentiments that demanded that women be granted "immediate admission to all the rights and privileges which belong to them as citizens of the United States."[57] The Seneca Falls Convention was immediately followed by other women's rights conventions. Participants in these conventions called for the right to vote, the right to economic equality, and the right to more equitable treatment in marriage.

57. Rogers M. Smith, *Civic Ideals: Conflicting Visions of Citizenship in U.S. History* (New Haven, CT: Yale University Press, 1999), 232.

The early women's rights movement enjoyed more success in legislative settings than in courtrooms. Many state legislatures liberalized previous restrictions on married women owning property. Some states passed laws granting women more rights to the custody of their children after divorce. Judges were less moved by pleas for gender equality. In *White v. White* (NY 1849), New York judges declared that a married women's property act could not be applied retroactively. In *Shanks v. DuPont* (1830), the Supreme Court upheld the traditional position that a woman's citizenship followed her husband's citizenship.

Men were particularly illiberal when women demanded greater political rights. Elizabeth Cady Stanton, Lucretia Mott, and other feminist leaders successfully placed gender issues on the agendas of state constitutional conventions. Nevertheless, suffrage rights were at most briefly debated before being resoundingly rejected. Few women voted before the Civil War. Communities that permitted women to vote typically restricted the ballot to local matters. Members of the Kansas Constitutional Convention of 1859 expressed the consensus view when concluding, "The [political] rights of women are safe in present hands."[58]

Elizabeth Cady Stanton, Keynote Address, Seneca Falls Convention (July 19, 1848)[59]

The Seneca Falls Convention was the first important gathering for women's rights held in the United States. Individual women had demanded political equality before 1848. Abigail Adams was among the many women who criticized the male monopoly on political power. Women did not organize to demand rights, however, during the Founding and Early National Eras. Gender politics in the United States changed after an international anti-slavery conference in London refused to seat a delegation of abolitionist women from the United States. Outraged, Elizabeth Cady Stanton and Lucretia Mott resolved to create a women's movement. Their goal was to obtain for women the same equal political and economic rights that radical abolitionists demanded for persons of color.

Compare Elizabeth Cady Stanton's "Keynote Address" to the other Jacksonian readings in this chapter. To what extent might all the following arguments be described as conventional Jacksonian demands for equality, with the only difference being that the equality demanded is between men and women rather than between different classes of men? To what extent did Stanton and her political supporters make different kinds of equality arguments to justify gender equality?

. . .

. . . [W]e are assembled to protest against a form of government existing without the consent of the governed—to declare our right to be free as man is free, to be represented in the government which we are taxed to support, to have such disgraceful laws as give man the power to chastise and imprison his wife, to take the wages which she earns, the property which she inherits, and, in case of separation, the children of her love; laws which make her the mere dependent on his bounty. It is to protest against such unjust laws as these that we are assembled today, and to have them, if possible, forever erased from our statute books, deeming them a shame and a disgrace to a Christian republic in the nineteenth century. We have met to uplift woman's fallen divinity upon an even pedestal with man's. And, strange as it may seem to many, we now demand our right to vote according to the declaration of the government under which we live.

This right no one pretends to deny. We need not prove ourselves equal to Daniel Webster to enjoy this privilege, for the ignorant Irishman in the ditch has all the civil rights he has. We need not prove our muscular power equal to this same Irishman to enjoy this privilege, for the most tiny, weak, ill-shaped stripling of twenty-one has all the civil rights of the Irishman. We have no objection to discuss the question of equality, for we feel that the weight of argument lies wholly with us, but we wish the question of equality kept distinct from the question of rights, for the proof of the one does not determine the truth of the other. All white men in this country have the same rights, however they may differ in mind, body, or estate.

The right is ours. The question now is: how shall we get possession of what rightfully belongs to us? We should not feel so sorely grieved if no man who had not attained the full stature of a Webster, Clay, Van Buren, or Gerrit Smith [a noted abolitionist] could claim the right of the elective franchise. But to

58. *Kansas Constitutional Convention, a Reprint of the Proceedings and Debates of the Convention Which Framed the Constitution of Kansas at Wyandotte in July* (Topeka: Kansas State Printing Plant, 1920), 169.

59. Excerpt taken from *Address of Mrs. Elizabeth Cady Stanton: Delivered at Seneca Falls and Rochester, NY, July 19th and August 2d, 1848* (New York: R. J. Johnston, 1870).

have drunkards, idiots, horse-racing, rum-selling rowdies, ignorant foreigners, and silly boys fully recognized, while we ourselves are thrust out from all the rights that belong to citizens, it is too grossly insulting to the dignity of woman to be longer quietly submitted to.

. . .

Verily, the world waits the coming of some new element, some purifying power, some spirit of mercy and love. The voice of woman has been silenced in the state, the church, and the home, but man cannot fulfill his destiny alone, he cannot redeem his race unaided. There are deep and tender chords of sympathy and love in the hearts of the downfallen and oppressed that woman can touch more skillfully than man.

The world has never yet seen a truly great and virtuous nation, because in the degradation of woman the very fountains of life are poisoned at their source. It is vain to look for silver and gold from mines of copper and lead.

. . .

We do not expect our path will be strewn with the flowers of popular applause, but over the thorns of bigotry and prejudice will be our way, and on our banners will beat the dark storm clouds of opposition from those who have entrenched themselves behind the stormy bulwarks of custom and authority, and who have fortified their position by every means, holy and unholy. But we will steadfastly abide the result. Unmoved we will bear it aloft. Undauntedly we will unfurl it to the gale, for we know that the storm cannot rend from it a shred, that the electric flash will but more clearly show to us the glorious words inscribed upon it, "Equality of Rights."

X. Criminal Justice

MAJOR DEVELOPMENTS

- Alleged fugitive slaves denied jury trials
- Judges wrest power to determine the law from juries
- First decisions on right to counsel

Americans in the Jacksonian Era faced conflicting pressures when considering the rights of persons suspected and convicted of criminal offenses. Most persons wanted a criminal justice system that punished persons who had committed what all agreed were moral wrongs. The law of self-incrimination emphasized the likelihood of a confession being true or false. Professional police officers and urban residents put pressure on courts to reduce due process protections for persons accused of ordinary crimes. Controversies over constitutional criminal procedure also erupted as part of more fundamental controversies over substantive criminal offenses. Free- and slave-state citizens disagreed vehemently over whether alleged fugitive slaves and those who assisted fugitive slaves were entitled to jury trials and habeas corpus. Justices hostile to temperance laws often protected the rights of persons accused of possessing, selling, or drinking liquor or other intoxicating beverages. Such decisions as *Fisher v. McGirr* (MA 1854), which protected persons suspected of storing alcoholic beverages from intrusive searches, enabled Jacksonians to protect the right to drink without overturning temperance laws.

A. Due Process and Habeas Corpus

During the Jacksonian Era Americans debated whether fugitive slaves and persons who assisted fugitive slaves merited strong due process and habeas corpus protections, while agreeing that ordinary criminals enjoyed only a bare procedural minimum of these protections at their trials. Bitter sectional debates broke out over whether the Fugitive Slave Acts of 1793 and 1850 provided sufficient constitutional protections to alleged fugitive slaves. Equally bitter sectional debates broke out over whether state courts could issue writs of habeas corpus to federal officials on behalf of alleged fugitive slaves and those accused of helping them escape north. No analogous debates broke out over whether persons accused of ordinary crimes merited the same substantial constitutional protections. Sherman Booth became a household name after he helped spirit Joshua Glover, an alleged fugitive slave, from a Wisconsin prison to Canada. Booth aggressively pushed the limits of judicial procedures. However, whether the mayor of Hagerstown, Maryland, remembered Eliza Shafer the day after fining her for "lewd" behavior is doubtful. Shafer was denied even a trial, with the state supreme court observing that cities could only expect to preserve public order if individuals accused of committing common but relatively small infractions could be "summarily punished." Such ordinary criminals were below the notice of the Constitution.

The *Booth* Cases (1854–1858)

Sherman Booth was an anti-slavery journalist who lived in Milwaukee, Wisconsin. In March 1854 Booth helped a fugitive slave, Joshua Glover, break out of prison and escape to Canada. On May 26 Booth was arrested by a federal commissioner for violating the Fugitive Slave Act of 1850. Booth immediately asked the Supreme Court of Wisconsin for a writ of habeas corpus. Booth's petition asserted that he was being illegally detained by federal officials, because the Fugitive Slave Act was unconstitutional. Justice Abram Smith granted the writ, and his decision was later affirmed by the Supreme Court of Wisconsin (Booth I). *The justices in* Booth I *ruled that state courts could issue writs of habeas corpus to persons being detained by a federal commissioner because federal commissioners had no authority to determine whether a federal law was constitutional. The state court justices then determined that the Fugitive Slave Act of 1850 was unconstitutional and issued the writ. On July 8 a federal grand jury indicted Booth for aiding and abetting the escape of Joshua Glover. Two days later a federal district judge issued an arrest warrant. Booth again asked the Supreme Court of Wisconsin for a writ of habeas corpus. This time the Wisconsin Supreme Court* (Booth II) *unanimously rejected his petition. Unlike federal commissioners, the state justices reasoned, federal courts were authorized by the Constitution of the United States to make an independent determination of whether the Fugitive Slave Act of 1850 was unconstitutional. At his federal court trial Booth was found guilty of helping Joshua Glover escape from federal marshals but was not found guilty of violating the Fugitive Slave Act of 1850. Once more Booth appealed to the Wisconsin Supreme Court for a writ of habeas corpus. This time, the court* (Booth III) *unanimously granted the writ. All three judges insisted that federal courts had jurisdiction only over federal crimes. Helping someone escape from a federal marshal was not a federal crime, they noted, in the crucial absence of evidence that Booth had helped a runaway slave escape from a federal marshal. Federal authorities in Wisconsin appealed this decision to the Supreme Court of the United States.*

Roger Taney, writing for a unanimous Court in Ableman v. Booth, *reversed the Supreme Court of Wisconsin's decision. State courts, he declared, had no power to issue a writ of habeas corpus to a person in federal custody on the ground that federal courts had misinterpreted federal law or the federal Constitution.*

The Taney Court decision did not bring the Booth affair to a halt. The Wisconsin Supreme Court refused to retract the writ of habeas corpus. The Wisconsin legislature passed a resolution nullifying Ableman v. Booth. *Nevertheless, Booth was re-arrested. He remained in prison long after his thirty-day sentence ended because he refused to pay the $1,000 fine. President James Buchanan pardoned Booth on his last day in office. Litigation over the escape of Joshua Glover did not end until the closing days of the Civil War.*[60]

The follow pages excerpt Justice Smith's initial decision to grant the writ of habeas corpus and the opinion of the Supreme Court of the United States in Ableman v. Booth. *Consider first the questions that these materials raise about habeas corpus. The Wisconsin Supreme Court claimed a right to issue writs of habeas corpus to persons imprisoned by a federal commissioner. Why did they make that claim? Did the Taney Court in* Ableman *dispute that claim, or was* Ableman *directed only at the authority of state courts to question persons detained by federal judges? Consider the Fugitive Slave Act of 1850. Why did Justices Smith and Whiton consider that law unconstitutional?*

In re Booth [Booth I], 3 Wis. 1 *(1854)*

JUSTICE SMITH

. . .

. . . [T]he States will never submit to the assumption, that United States commissioners have the power to hear and determine upon the rights and liberties of their citizens, and issue process to enforce their adjudications, which is beyond the examination or review of the state judiciary. They will cheerfully submit to the exercise of all power and authority by the federal judiciary, which is delegated to that department by the federal constitution; but they have a right to insist, and they will insist that the state judiciary shall be and remain supreme in all else, and that the functions of the federal judiciary within the territory of the states shall be exercised by the officers designated or provided for by the constitution of the United States, and that they shall not be transferred to subordinate and irresponsible functionaries, holding their office at the will of the federal courts, doing their duty and obeying their mandates, for which neither the one nor the other is responsible.

---

60. Readers interested in all the bloody details should consult H. Robert Baker, *The Rescue of Joshua Glover: A Fugitive Slave, the Constitution, and the Coming of the Civil War* (Athens: Ohio University Press, 2006).

. . .

. . . [T]he *status* of the fugitive is essentially different in this state, from his *status* or condition in the state from whence he fled. In the latter, he remained subject to all the disabilities of his class, though he may have escaped from the domicil or premises of his master. Here, he is entitled to the full and complete protection of our laws; as much so as any other human being, so long as he is unclaimed. He may sue and be sued; he may acquire and hold property; he is, to all intents and purposes, a free man, until a lawful claim is made for him; and this claim must be made by the person to whom his service or labor is due, under the laws of the state from which he escaped. No one else can interfere with him. If no *claim* is set up to his service or labor by the person to whom his service or labor is due, there is no power or authority, or person on earth, that can derive any advantage from his former condition, or assert it, to his prejudice. So long as the owner does not choose to assert his *claim*, the cottage of the fugitive in Wisconsin is as much his castle—his property, liberty and person are as much the subject of legal protection, as those of any other person. Our legal tribunals are as open to his complaint or appeal, as to that of any other man. He *may* never be claimed; and if not, he would remain forever free, and transmit freedom to his posterity born on our soil.

. . .

We have seen how the power of legislation was granted to congress in respect to public records, etc. We have seen that no such power is granted in respect to the surrender of fugitives from labor, and that it was not even asked for; and from the known temper and scruples of the national convention, we may safely affirm, that had it been asked it would not have been granted, and had it been granted, no union could have been formed upon such a basis. The history of the times fully justifies this conclusion. Can it be supposed for a moment, that had the framers of the constitution imagined, that under this provision the federal government would assume to override the state authorities, appoint subordinate tribunals in every county in every state, invested with jurisdiction beyond the reach or inquiry of the state judiciary, to multiply executive and judicial officers *ad infinitum*, wholly independent of, and irresponsible to the police regulations of the state, and that the whole army and navy of the union could be sent into a state, without the request, and against the remonstrance of the legislature thereof; nay, even that under its operation, the efficacy of the writ of habeas corpus could be destroyed, if the privileges thereof were not wholly suspended; if the members of the convention had dreamed that they were incorporating such a power into the constitution, does any one believe, that it would have been adopted without opposition and without debate? And if these results had suggested themselves to the states on its adoption, would it have been passed by them, *sub silentio*, jealous as they were of state rights and state sovereignty? The idea is preposterous. The union would never have been formed upon such a basis. It is an impeachment of historic truth, to assert it.

. . .

. . . But it may be asked, how are the rights here stipulated and guaranteed, to be enforced? I answer, that every state officer, executive, legislative and judicial, who takes an oath to support the constitution of the United States, is bound to provide for, and aid in their enforcement, according to the true intent and meaning of the constitution. . . .

. . .

To my mind, therefore, it is apparent that congress has no constitutional power to legislate on this subject. It is equally apparent, that the several states can pass no laws, nor adopt any regulations, by which the fugitive may be discharged from service. . . .

. . .

The clause as finally adopted reads, "but shall be delivered up on claim of the party *to whom such service or labor is* DUE." Here is a fact to be ascertained, before the fugitive can be legally delivered up, viz: that his service or labor is really due to the party who claims him. How is the fact to be ascertained? . . . What authority shall determine it? Clearly the authority of the state whose duty it is to deliver up the fugitive when the fact is determined. Until the issue which the constitution itself creates, is decided, the *person* is entitled to the protection of the laws of the state. When the issue is determined against the fugitive, then the constitutional compact rises above the laws and regulations of the state, and to the former the latter must yield.

. . . The law of 1850, by providing for a trial of the constitutional issue, between the *parties* designated thereby, by officers not recognized by any constitution, state or national, is unconstitutional and void.

It has been already said, that until the claim of the owner be interposed, the fugitive in this state is, to all intents and purposes, a free man.

. . . Therefore the trial thereof must not only be had before a judicial tribunal, but whether proceedings be commenced by the fugitive to resist the claimant, or by the claimant to enforce, and establish his claim, it would seem that either party would be entitled to a jury. . . .

. . .

Again, the constitution provides that no person shall be deprived of life, liberty or property, without *due process of law.* This last phrase has a distinct technical meaning, viz: regular judicial proceedings, according to the course of the common law, or by a regular suit commenced and prosecuted according to the forms of law. An essential requisite is due process to bring the party into court. It is in accordance with the first principles of natural law. Every person is entitled to his "day in court," to be legally notified of the proceedings taken against him, and duly summoned to defend. The passing of judgment upon any person without his "day in court"; without due process, or its equivalent, is contrary to the law of nature, and of the civilized world, and without the express guaranty of the constitution, it would be implied as a fundamental condition of all civil governments. But the tenth section of the act of 1850, expressly nullifies this provision of the constitution. It provides that the claimant may go before any court of record, or judge, in vacation, and without process, make proof of the escape, and the owing of service or labor; whereupon a record is made of the matters proved, and a general description of the person alleged to have escaped; a transcript of such record made out and attested by the clerk with the seal of the court, being exhibited to the judge or commissioner, must be taken and held to be conclusive evidence of the fact of escape, and that service or labor is due to the party mentioned in the record, and *may* be held sufficient evidence of the identity of the person escaping.

Here is a palpable violation of the constitution. Can that be said to be by due *process* of law which is without process altogether? Here the *status* or condition of the person is instantly changed in his absence, without process, without notice, without opportunity, to meet or examine the witnesses against him, or rebut their testimony. A record is made, which is conclusive against him, "in any state or territory in which he may be found." It is not a process to bring the person before the court in which the record is made up, but it is to all intents and purposes, a judgment of the court or judge, which commits the person absolutely to the control and possession of the claimant, to be taken whithersoever he pleases, to be dragged from a state where the legal presumption is in favor of his freedom, to any state or territory where the legal presumption is against his freedom. . . .

Ableman v. Booth, 62 U.S. 506 (1858)

CHIEF JUSTICE TANEY delivered the opinion of the court.

. . .

. . . [N]o one will suppose that a Government which has now lasted nearly seventy years, enforcing its laws by its own tribunals, and preserving the union of the States, could have lasted a single year, or fulfilled the high trusts committed to it, if offences against its laws could not have been punished without the consent of the State in which the culprit was found.

. . . [N]o State can authorize one of its judges or courts to exercise judicial power, by *habeas corpus* or otherwise, within the jurisdiction of another and independent Government. And although the State of Wisconsin is sovereign within its territorial limits to a certain extent, yet that sovereignty is limited and restricted by the Constitution of the United States. And the powers of the General Government, and of the State, although both exist and are exercised within the same territorial limits, are yet separate and distinct sovereignties, acting separately and independently of each other, within their respective spheres. And the sphere of action appropriated to the United States is as far beyond the reach of the judicial process issued by a State judge or a State court, as if the line of division was traced by landmarks and monuments visible to the eye. . . .

. . . The Constitution was not formed merely to guard the States against danger from foreign nations, but mainly to secure union and harmony at home; for if this object could be attained, there would be but little danger from abroad; and to accomplish this purpose, it was felt by the statesmen who framed the Constitution, and by the people who adopted it, that it was necessary that many of the rights of sovereignty which the States then possessed should be ceded to the General Government; and that, in the sphere of action assigned to it, it should be supreme, and strong enough to execute its own laws by its own tribunals, without interruption from a State or from State authorities. And it was evident that anything short of this would be inadequate to the main objects for which the Government was established; and that local interests, local passions or prejudices, incited and fostered by individuals for sinister purposes, would lead to acts of aggression and injustice by one State upon the rights of another, which would ultimately terminate in violence and force, unless there was a common arbiter between them, armed with power enough to protect and guard the rights of all, by appropriate laws, to be carried into execution peacefully by its judicial tribunals.

...

We do not question the authority of State court, or judge, who is authorized by the laws of the State to issue the writ of *habeas corpus*, to issue it in any case where the party is imprisoned within its territorial limits, provided it does not appear, when the application is made, that the person imprisoned is in custody under the authority of the United States. The court or judge has a right to inquire, in this mode of proceeding, for what cause and by what authority the prisoner is confined within the territorial limits of the State sovereignty. And it is the duty of the marshal, or other person having the custody of the prisoner, to make known to the judge or court, by a proper return, the authority by which he holds him in custody. This right to inquire by process of *habeas corpus*, and the duty of the officer to make a return, grows, necessarily, out of the complex character of our Government, and the existence of two distinct and separate sovereignties within the same territorial space, each of them restricted in its powers, and each within its sphere of action, prescribed by the Constitution of the United States, independent of the other. But, after the return is made, and the State judge or court judicially apprized that the party is in custody under the authority of the United States, they can proceed no further. They then know that the prisoner is within the dominion and jurisdiction of another Government, and that neither the writ of *habeas corpus*, nor any other process issued under State authority, can pass over the line of division between the two sovereignties. He is then within the dominion and exclusive jurisdiction of the United States. If he has committed an offence against their laws, their tribunals alone can punish him. If he is wrongfully imprisoned, their judicial tribunals can release him and afford him redress. . . . No State judge or court, after they are judicially informed that the party is imprisoned under the authority of the United States, has any right to interfere with him, or to require him to be brought before them. . . .

B. Search and Seizure

The constitutional law of search and seizure in Jacksonian America depended partly on the crime being investigated. Many cities and towns established professional police forces. The expansion of the criminal law and the rise of professional police forces during the Jacksonian Era initiated a lengthy process of working out detailed constitutional rules for how searches could be conducted. Police officers sought to relax previous constitutional understandings that permitted constables to be sued for trespass whenever a warrantless search failed to generate evidence of criminal conduct. State courts proved sympathetic to these claims. In *Rohan v. Sawin* (MA 1850), the Supreme Judicial Court of Massachusetts declared that innocent persons subject to warrantless arrests could not sue police officers for damages if the police officer had probable cause for making the arrest. The Supreme Judicial Court in *Commonwealth v. Dana* (MA 1841) provided another boon to law enforcement professionals when permitting prosecutors to introduce in criminal trials evidence that had been unconstitutionally obtained by government officials. Massachusetts justices were more sympathetic to defendants' rights when cases involving state bans on intoxicating liquors came before the court. In *Fisher v. McGirr* (MA 1854), the justices declared unconstitutional a Massachusetts law that authorized government officials to search private residences for illegal alcoholic beverages.

C. Interrogations

The Jacksonian conception of an involuntary confession was both more and less protective of criminal defendants than are contemporary conceptions. Confessions were inadmissible only if unreliable. If a reliable confession were extracted by some means other than torture, most courts permitted the admission to be used as evidence against the criminal defendant. *Miranda* warnings were more than one hundred years in the future. Nevertheless, Jacksonians found some confessions that are admissible at present to be unreliable. Plea bargaining—when persons plead guilty to a lesser charge in return for not being prosecuted for a more serious crime—is routine in the United States today. Antebellum constitutional decision makers were more suspicious of this process. *People v. McMahon* (NY 1857) expressed the conventional understanding that confessions were unreliable if induced by promises of leniency or a lesser sentence. Justice Selden declared: "However slight the threat or small the inducement thus held out, the statement will be excluded as not voluntary. It is plain therefore that, in such cases at least, by voluntary is meant, proceeding from the spontaneous suggestion of the party's own mind, free from the influence of any extraneous disturbing cause."[61]

D. Juries and Lawyers

The increased professionalization of the criminal justice process influenced the right to a jury and the right to an attorney. Judges, more confident of their legal knowledge, wrested control over the law from juries. Most states adopted the rule of *Commonwealth v. Anthes* (MA 1855), which held that the jury in a criminal trial should determine only the facts. The law was for judges to pronounce. State appellate courts during the mid-nineteenth century placed more emphasis on the right to an attorney. As more states and localities employed professional prosecutors, more jurisdictions insisted that criminal defendants be represented by attorneys. *State v. Cummings* (LA 1850) noted how "often the greatest injustice and oppression occurred" when persons accused of crime defended themselves in court.[62]

E. Punishments

Persons convicted of crimes were often punished severely. *State v. McCauley* (CA 1860) articulated the conventional judicial view that punishments were cruel and unusual only if they were "of a barbarous character, and unknown to the common law."[63] *McCauley* sustained a state law mandating convict labor. Other cases sustained flogging and banishment. Judges typically discussed only the method of punishment, not whether the punishment was excessive. The Supreme Judicial Court of Massachusetts in *Commonwealth v. Hutchings* (MA 1855) asserted, "The question whether the punishment is too severe, and disproportionate to the offence, is for the legislature to determine."[64]

Some state legislatures were more lenient than state courts. Michigan (1846), Rhode Island (1852), and Wisconsin (1853) abolished capital punishment. During the Michigan legislative debates on this issue, opponents of state executions maintained that the death penalty violated the fundamental right to life. Legislators in all three states were influenced by recent executions of possibly innocent persons. States that did not abolish the death penalty often reduced the number of crimes punishable by death. Many adopted a distinction between first- and second-degree murder primarily for the purpose of enabling juries to convict guilty persons without fear of sending them to be executed.

Suggested Readings

Allen, Austin. 2006. *Origins of the* Dred Scott *Case: Jacksonian Jurisprudence and the Supreme Court, 1837–1857.* Athens: University of Georgia Press.

Baker, H. Robert. 2006. *The Rescue of Joshua Glover: A Fugitive Slave, the Constitution, and the Coming of the Civil War.* Athens: Ohio University Press.

Bestor, Arthur. 1961. "State Sovereignty and Slavery: A Reinterpretation of Proslavery Constitutional Doctrine, 1846–1860." *Journal of the Illinois State Historical Society* 54:117–180.

Carpenter, Jesse T. 1930. *The South as a Conscious Minority, 1789–1861: A Study in Political Thought.* New York: New York University Press.

Currie, David P. 2005a. *The Constitution in Congress: Democrats and Whigs, 1829–1861.* Chicago: University of Chicago Press.

———. 2005b. *The Constitution in Congress: Descent into the Maelstrom, 1829–1861.* Chicago: University of Chicago Press.

Ellis, Richard E. 1987. *The Union at Risk: Jacksonian Democracy, States' Rights, and the Nullification Crisis.* New York: Oxford University Press.

Fehrenbacher, Don E. 1978. *The* Dred Scott *Case: Its Significance in American Law and Politics.* New York: Oxford University Press.

61. *People v. McMahon*, 15 N.Y. 384 (1857).

62. *State v. Cummings*, 5 La. Ann. 330 (1850).

63. *State v. McCauley*, 15 Cal. 429 (1860).

64. *Commonwealth v. Hutchings*, 5 Gray 482 (Mass. 1855).

Graber, Mark A. 2004. "Resolving Political Questions into Judicial Questions: Tocqueville's Thesis Revisited." *Constitutional Commentary* 16:485–545.

———. 2006. Dred Scott *and the Problem of Constitutional Evil*. New York: Cambridge University Press.

Howe, Daniel Walker. 1979. *The Political Culture of the American Whigs*. Chicago: University of Chicago Press.

Hyman, Harold M, and William M. Wiecek. 1982. *Equal Justice Under Law: Constitutional Development, 1835–1876*. New York: Harper & Row.

Kutler, Stanley I. 1989. *Privilege and Creative Destruction: The* Charles River Bridge *Case*. Baltimore, MD: Johns Hopkins University Press.

Magliocca, Gerald N. 2007. *Andrew Jackson and the Constitution: The Rise and Fall of Generational Regimes*. Lawrence: University Press of Kansas.

Newmyer, R. Kent. 1968. *The Supreme Court Under Marshall and Taney*. New York: Thomas Y. Crowell Company.

Norgren, Jill. 1996. *The Cherokee Cases: The Confrontation of Law and Politics*. New York: McGraw-Hill.

Novak, William J. 1996. *The People's Welfare: Law and Regulation in Nineteenth-Century America*. Chapel Hill: University of North Carolina Press.

Peterson, Merrill D. 1987. *The Great Triumvirate: Webster, Clay, and Calhoun*. New York: Oxford University Press.

Richards, Leonard I. 2000. *The Slave Power: The Free North and Southern Domination, 1780–1860*. Baton Rouge: Louisiana State University Press.

Scalia, Laura J. 1999. *America's Jeffersonian Experiment: Remaking State Constitutions, 1820–1850*. De Kalb: Northern Illinois University Press.

Swisher, Carl B. 1936. *Roger B. Taney*. New York: Macmillan.

———. 1974. *The Taney Period*. New York: Macmillan.

Whittington, Keith E. 2001. "The Road Not Taken: *Dred Scott*, Constitutional Law, and Political Questions." *Journal of Politics* 63:365–91.

Wiecek, William M. *The Sources of Antislavery Constitutionalism in America, 1760–1848*. Ithaca, NY: Cornell University Press, 1977.

Chapter 6

Secession, Civil War, and Reconstruction: 1861–1876

I. Introduction

The Civil War was the greatest constitutional crisis in the history of the United States. The crisis was constitutional in that the survival of the constitutional order established in 1789 was at stake. The crisis was also constitutional in that each section of the country advanced very different interpretations of the Constitution. The sectional differences over the constitutional status of slavery are discussed in the previous chapter on Jacksonian constitutional politics. The debate over secession presented in this chapter highlights a second major difference between northern and southern constitutional understandings. Abraham Lincoln and his political allies insisted that secession was unconstitutional because "we, the people" formed the United States in 1776 and no state was constitutionally authorized to destroy the resulting nation. Jefferson Davis and his political allies insisted that the Constitution was an agreement between the states, all of which retained the sovereign power to determine whether that agreement had been violated.

Lincoln's decision to resupply Fort Sumter in the Charleston Harbor and the subsequent beginning of the Civil War ended constitutional debates over secession and slavery while beginning new ones over war powers and individual liberties. During the Civil War, martial law was declared in many northern communities, habeas corpus was frequently suspended, southern ports were blockaded, southern property was confiscated, the federal government printed paper money, a draft was instituted, and most slaves were declared free. Robert E. Lee's surrender at Appomattox helped transform the constitutional politics of the Civil War into the constitutional politics of Reconstruction. Reconstruction witnessed military rule throughout the South; frequent exercises of congressional power under the post–Civil War Amendments to prohibit slavery, protect certain fundamental rights, and prevent racial discrimination in voting; and the first impeachment trial of a sitting president in American history. The result of these events were intense struggles over the constitutional meaning of the Civil War, over the meaning of the post–Civil War Amendments, and over which government institution was constitutionally authorized to decide these contested issues.

Developments. During the Civil War, Congress passed and Lincoln signed constitutionally controversial legislation mandating a military draft and making paper money legal tender. Congress retroactively ratified Lincoln's decision to blockade southern ports, only slightly modified his decisions to suspend habeas corpus and impose martial law, and tacitly approved the Emancipation Proclamation. Republicans divided over whether the party should transform the constitutional order or seek only to prohibit slavery. More radical Republicans proposed confiscating Confederate property with a minimum of judicial procedure. Abraham Lincoln and more conservative Republicans rejected these proposals. Many Republicans, including members of Lincoln's cabinet, opposed suspending habeas corpus and declaring martial law during the Civil War. Lincoln thought such measures were constitutional means for ensuring national security. War Democrats supported some restrictions on civil liberties. Peace Democrats maintained that Lincoln was a tyrant bent on subverting longstanding constitutional freedoms.

Table 6-1 Major Issues and Decisions of the Civil War and Reconstruction

Major Political Issues	Major Constitutional Issues	Major Court Decisions
Secession	Secession	*Ex parte Merryman* (1861)
Slavery	Suspension of habeas corpus	*Prize Cases* (1863)
Taxation	Confiscation	*Ex parte Milligan* (1866)
Military draft	Emancipation	*Mississippi v. Johnson* (1867)
Western settlement	Civil rights	*Ex parte McCardle* (1868)
War	Legal tender	*Texas v. White* (1869)
Black civil rights	Martial law	*In re Tarble* (1871)
Martial law	Reconstruction of the South	*Legal Tender Cases* (1871)
Black suffrage	Test oaths	*Slaughter-House Cases* (1872)
	Black suffrage	*United States v. Cruikshank* (1875)
		Tennessee v. Davis (1880)

During the first years of Reconstruction, Republican congressional understandings of the constitutional order generally prevailed over the Democratic understandings championed by President Andrew Johnson, a former Jacksonian senator from Tennessee who became Lincoln's running mate in 1864 as part of a Republican/Unionist effort to broaden the ticket's appeal. Congress proposed and states quickly ratified the Thirteenth, Fourteenth, and Fifteenth Amendments. The first of these amendments abolished slavery. The second asserted that states could not deny persons of color (and others) certain fundamental rights. The third forbade voters from being discriminated against for racial reasons. Each amendment declared, "Congress shall have power to enforce, by appropriate legislation, the provisions of this article." Congressional majorities construed those powers broadly when passing such measures as the Civil Rights Act of 1866, which prohibited racial discrimination in contract, property, and criminal law; and the Civil Rights Act of 1875, which guaranteed individuals equal access regardless of race to all inns, theaters, and public transportation. When other branches interfered with Reconstruction, Congress cleared out those obstructions. When doubts were raised about the constitutionality of martial law in the South, Congress voted to strip the Supreme Court's jurisdiction to hear a case raising the issue. When President Johnson repeatedly vetoed Reconstruction measures and hampered enforcement efforts, the House of Representatives impeached him in 1868.

President Johnson, by slowing the pace of Reconstruction, successfully limited what Republicans achieved in the decade after the Civil War. The Republican effort to remake the South did not last long. Republicans suffered severe political losses in the 1867 state elections and the 1874 national elections, reversing the gains they had made in 1866. The more radical Republicans lacked the votes to convict President Johnson at his impeachment trial before the Senate and faced increasing difficulty passing and implementing their racially egalitarian program. As time went on, more and more Republicans asserted that their party would be better off emphasizing economic policy rather than the rights of former slaves. After barely hanging on to the presidency in the disputed election of 1876, Republicans ended Reconstruction. Significant voices were still heard calling for federal efforts on behalf of blacks after 1876, but federal power would not be exercised on their behalf for almost a century.

Parties. Republicans won every national election held between 1860 and 1872. Abraham Lincoln was elected in 1860 and 1864. Ulysses Grant won the 1868 and 1872 presidential elections. Republicans gained majorities in both houses of Congress in 1860, when the vast majority of southern representatives resigned their seats. They maintained their majorities until 1874, when Democrats gained control of the House of Representatives. Republican majorities in Congress were augmented after the Civil War when Congress refused to seat Democrats representing southern states who could not take an oath that they had been loyal to the Union. The loyalty oath, in conjunction with other Reconstruction measures, left such states as South Carolina either unrepresented in Congress or represented by Republicans appointed by local military authorities.

The dominant Republican Party was united only on a commitment to fight the Civil War to the finish and to achieve at least formal racial equality during Reconstruction. Party members were internally divided between radicals and moderates, with the radicals often willing to push more aggressively for legislation and constitutional amendments that expanded national and congressional power to fight slavery, promote racial equality in practice, and otherwise reconstruct the South. These divisions created opportunities for Democrats committed to retaining "the Constitution as it was," including President Johnson, to slow the pace of reform or win compromises.

Interest Groups. With one important and controversial exception, interest groups played little role in the constitutional politics of the Civil War and Reconstruction. The Republican Party was the major vehicle for securing emancipation and the rights of former slaves. Slaveholders in the South worked through conventional politics to secure their ends. The most important nongovernmental organization during Reconstruction was the Ku Klux Klan, which sought to restore white supremacy through terror and violence rather than litigation or political mobilization. The constitutional politics of the 1870s often centered on the extent to which the federal government had the power to suppress Klan violence. Federal attorneys relying on the Enforcement Acts of 1870 and 1871 were able to win prosecutions that severely weakened the Klan in South Carolina. Nevertheless, the Supreme Court in later cases, most notably *United States v. Cruikshank* (1876), ruled that the federal government could not normally prosecute Klan vigilantes and other violent white supremacists unless it proved specific intent to interfere with a narrow set of federal rights.

Courts. The Supreme Court remained passive during the Civil War but provided some support for conservative constitutional visions during Reconstruction. Federal constitutional questions about rights and liberties raised between 1861 and 1865 were resolved by Congress and the president, not federal courts. The justices intervened only to declare the Union blockade of southern ports constitutional in *The Prize Cases* (1863). The Supreme Court became more active after Robert E. Lee surrendered at Appomattox and the Confederacy collapsed. In *Ex parte Milligan* (1865) the justices declared that President Lincoln had unconstitutionally declared martial law during the Civil War. Over the next several years the justices declared several minor Reconstruction laws unconstitutional. They did not issue any ruling directly addressing the constitutionality of military rule in the South. During the 1870s the Supreme Court handed down several decisions that narrowed the scope of the post–Civil War Amendments and congressional power to enforce those amendments. The *Slaughter-House Cases* (1873) held that the basic liberties set out in the Bill of Rights were not among the privileges and immunities of U.S. citizens that the Fourteenth Amendment declared states could no longer abridge. In *United States v. Cruikshank* (1876) the justices overturned a jury verdict against the perpetrators of a massacre of former slaves on the ground that the indictment for murder did not accuse the white supremacists of violating a specific federal right.

History and politics help explain why a court whose majority was appointed by Republicans was conservative on racial issues. The Jacksonian holdovers from the Taney Court consistently supported Democratic opposition to Reconstruction whenever doing so was politically feasible. They were often joined by such War Democrats as Stephen Field, whom Lincoln appointed to the bench in an effort to promote national unity. Furthermore, prominent northern elites quickly tired of Reconstruction. During the 1870s many preferred reconciliation with the South and the promotion of business enterprise to racial equality. The elite Republicans on the federal bench shared the northern elite's weariness with Civil War issues. Chief Justice Salmon Chase, appointed in 1864, was the only Lincoln appointee to the Supreme Court affiliated with the most anti-slavery wing of the Republican Party. When Chase died in 1873 and was replaced by Chief Justice Morrison Waite, a railroad lawyer, no powerful voice for racial equality remained on the nation's highest bench.

Constitutional Thought. The Civil War was the first sustained occasion Americans had for considering constitutional questions about rights and liberties during wartime. Justice David Davis in *Ex parte Milligan* (1866) eloquently stated that Americans retain their liberties in full when the United States is involved in military hostilities. His opinion asserted,

> The Constitution of the United States is a law for rulers and people, equally in war and in peace, and covers with the shield of its protection all classes of men, at all times, and under all circumstances. No doctrine, involving more pernicious consequences, was ever invented by the wit of man than that any of its provisions can be suspended during any of the great exigencies of government.

Box 6-1 A Partial Cast of Characters of the Civil War and Reconstruction

Abraham Lincoln	■ Whig and Republican ■ Representative from Illinois (1847–1849) ■ President of the United States (1861–1865), assassinated 1865 ■ Known for his dedication to preserving the Union and his success in leading the North to victory in the Civil War ■ Believed secession was unconstitutional and, despite his Whig background, defended executive power during his administration
Jefferson Davis	■ Democrat ■ President of the Confederacy (1861–1865) ■ Representative (1845–1846) and senator (1847–1851, 1857–1861) from Mississippi ■ Secretary of war under President Pierce (1853–1857) ■ Known as a states' rights strict constructionist
Salmon Chase	■ Free Soiler and Republican ■ Senator from Ohio (1849–1855) ■ Rival for leadership of Republican Party ■ Secretary of the treasury under Lincoln (1861–1864) ■ Appointed by Lincoln to be chief justice of the United States (1864–1873) ■ Oversaw key wartime policies as both treasury secretary and justice; sometimes skeptical of the scope of national power
Charles Sumner	■ Free Soiler and Republican ■ Radical abolitionist senator from Massachusetts (1851–1874) ■ Opposed secession and remained in the Senate when Tennessee left the union ■ Helped galvanize northern public opinion against the expansion of slavery in the antebellum period and led efforts to take a hard-line view against the South during the war and Reconstruction
Andrew Johnson	■ Democrat and Unionist ■ Representative (1843–1853) and senator (1857–1862; 1875) from Tennessee ■ Governor of Tennessee (1853–1857) ■ Opposed secession and remained in the Senate when Tennessee left the Union ■ Appointed by Lincoln to be military governor of Tennessee after Union troops recaptured the state (1862–1865) ■ Vice president during Lincoln's second term on "Union Party" ticket (1865) ■ President of the United States upon Lincoln's assassination (1865–1869) ■ Opposed congressional Reconstruction; impeached by the House in 1868

While Abraham Lincoln never acknowledged that he had violated constitutional rights, he insisted that such violations were justified in wartime. His message to Congress on July 4, 1861, claimed,

> The whole of the laws which were required to be faithfully executed were being resisted and failing of execution in nearly one-third of the States. Must they be allowed to finally fail of execution, even had it been perfectly clear that by the use of the means necessary to their execution some single law, made in such extreme tenderness of the citizen's liberty that practically it relieves more of the guilty than of the innocent, should to a very limited extent be violated? To state the question more directly, are all the laws but one to go unexecuted, and the Government itself go to pieces lest that one be violated? Even in such a case, would not the official oath be broken if the Government should be overthrown when it was believed that disregarding the single law would tend to preserve it?[1]

Legacies. The Civil War and Reconstruction made permanent changes in the American constitutional order. Secession and compact theory as practical alternatives did not survive the Confederate military defeat. No major political movement after 1865 endorsed the right to secede. Compact theory remained moribund until revived only very briefly by southern segregationists in the wake of the Supreme Court's decision in *Brown v. Board of Education* (1954).

The Thirteenth, Fourteenth, and Fifteenth Amendments are the most important constitutional legacies of the Civil War. Before the Civil War slavery was legal in many states; overt racial discrimination was rampant; and, following the Supreme Court's ruling in *Barron v. Baltimore* (1833), states were constitutionally responsible for protecting fundamental freedoms. The Reconstruction Amendments abolished slavery, forbade overt racial discrimination, and prohibited states from violating certain fundamental freedoms. Some commentators think that these amendments perfected the Constitution of 1789, because the Reconstruction Congress made constitutionally explicit what Abraham Lincoln insisted were the original anti-slavery commitments of the constitutional order. Other commentators regard the Reconstruction Amendments as fashioning an entirely different constitutional regime. In this transformed constitutional order Americans gained new fundamental rights and new institutional means for protecting those fundamental rights.

Americans then and now dispute the nature of the constitutional commitments made from 1861 to 1876. President Johnson and Republicans in Congress fought over whether the Thirteenth Amendment permitted Congress to establish relief agencies for newly freed slaves. Contemporary debates over affirmative action, guns, gay marriage, and other liberties require Americans to ask such questions as, "What was the Civil War about?" "To what extent did the Reconstruction Amendments alter fundamental constitutional commitments?" and "What is entailed by the constitutional commitment to abolishing slavery and securing racial equality?"

II. Foundations

MAJOR DEVELOPMENTS

- Debate over the constitutional amendments necessary to realize the fruits of the Civil War
- Debate over the meaning of racial equality
- The Supreme Court rules that the new amendments do not require states to respect the liberties enumerated in the Bill of Rights

The Thirteenth, Fourteenth, and Fifteenth Amendments were the first significant textual changes to the Constitution of the United States. Americans transformed a Constitution that had been designed to accommodate slavery and was arguably for white persons only into one that prohibited slavery and mandated some form of racial equality. The precise transformation was controversial in 1865 and remains controversial today. Consider the Thirteenth Amendment. Americans during the Civil War and Reconstruction did not agree on what the Constitution should say about slavery. The Crittenden Commission in 1860 recommended amendments that entrenched slavery. Americans in 1865, after an intense political struggle, adopted a constitutional amendment prohibiting slavery. No agreement exists, then or now, on the precise meaning of that amendment or the extent to which emancipating

1. Abraham Lincoln, "Special Session Message," in *A Compilation of the Messages and Papers of the Presidents*, ed. James D. Richardson (Washington, DC: Government Printing Office, 1897), 6:25.

all slaves fundamentally changed the nature of the American constitutional regime.

A. Sources

Americans during the Civil War and Reconstruction Era ratified a new pro-slavery Constitution of the Confederacy, rejected proposed amendments that would have entrenched slavery in the Constitution of the United States, and adopted three new amendments to that Constitution. These amendments abolished slavery, committed the United States to racial equality and equality under law, protected certain fundamental rights, and outlawed racial discrimination in voting. No other era in American history has witnessed such important proposals for change and actual changes to the constitutional text.

Debates over the Thirteenth Amendment (1864–1865)[2]

The Thirteenth Amendment to the Constitution of the United States prohibits slavery and gives Congress the power to implement this constitutional commitment to freedom. The text declares,

1. *Neither slavery nor involuntary servitude, except as a punishment for crime whereof the party shall have been duly convicted, shall exist within the United States, or any place subject to their jurisdiction.*
2. *Congress shall have power to enforce this article by appropriate legislation.*

The Thirteenth Amendment passed both houses of Congress in late January 1865 and was ratified by a sufficient number of states before the end of that year.

Anti-slavery advocates overcame numerous political difficulties when framing and ratifying the Thirteenth Amendment. Whether Americans would write a constitutional amendment abolishing slavery was not a foregone conclusion at the end of the Civil War. Democrats were leery. How southern states could be induced to ratify was uncertain. The House of Representatives in 1864 failed to give a proposed Thirteenth Amendment the necessary two-thirds majority. The Lincoln administration made substantial use of patronage when securing a successful vote in 1865. New Jersey, Kentucky, and Delaware voted to reject the Thirteenth Amendment. Rumors persist that the final votes for the amendment were procured by bribery. Many southern states ratified on the condition that the amendment be narrowly interpreted.

Two distinctive debates took place when Americans considered a constitutional amendment prohibiting slavery. Republicans debated the scope of the proposed Thirteenth Amendment. Charles Sumner, Frederick Douglass, and other radical Republicans sought to include guarantees for specific rights, most notably equality under law. Sumner proposed a constitutional amendment that stated, "Everywhere within the limits of the United States, and of each State or Territory thereof, all persons are equal before the law, so that no person can hold another as a slave." Republican moderates rejected this language. Some insisted that Congress had the power to guarantee newly freed slaves equality under the law. Others preferred leaving the amendment ambiguous. Democrats debated whether to support the Thirteenth Amendment. Proponents insisted that the Democratic Party would not be viable in the North until the party took a strong anti-slavery stand. Montgomery Blair, a former Democrat and member of Lincoln's cabinet, advised party leaders that "by giving up the past, [and] considering slavery extinct," they could "make an issue upon which not only the Democracy of the North and South may unite against the abolitionists, but on which the larger portion of the Republicans will join us in sustaining the exclusive right of Gov[ernment] of the white race." Opponents believed that the amendment promoted a racial amalgamation inconsistent with what they perceived to be the original constitutional commitment to white supremacy. Celebrating "the Constitution as it is," pro-slavery Democrats declared that persons of color were incapable of living as free persons in a republican society. Joel Barlow, a prominent journalist, asserted that "to free" slaves "would be an act of cruelty."[3]

Consider this mixture of principle and politics when reading the following excerpts. What principles best explain ratification? What did different proponents of the Thirteenth Amendment think the abolition of slavery entailed? To what extent did Republicans dispute basic principles, and to what extent did party disputes concern the language that best expressed those principles? How did politics influence the language and ratification of the

2. *Congressional Globe*, 38th Cong., 1st Sess., 1864, 1439–90.

3. Michael Vorenberg, *Final Freedom: The Civil War, the Abolition of Slavery and the Thirteenth Amendment* (New York: Cambridge University Press, 2001), 78–79. The discussion in the introduction to this reading relies heavily on Vorenberg's work.

Thirteenth Amendment? Would you have insisted on a more strongly worded amendment or settled for the language most likely to be ratified?

SENATOR JAMES HARLAN (Republican, Iowa)

. . .

. . . I ask whence the origin of the title to the services of the adult offspring of the slave mother? Or is it not manifest that there is no just title? Is it not a mere usurpation without any known mode of justification, under any existing code of laws, human or divine?

If it cannot be thus justified, is it a desirable institution? If the supposed owner had no title, is it the duty of the nation to maintain the usurped claim of the master to the services of his slaves? Are the incidents of slavery sufficiently desirable to justify such policy? Some of the incidents of slavery may be stated as follows: it necessarily abolishes the conjugal relation. . . . [T]he prohibition of the conjugal relation is a necessary incident of slavery, and that slavery cannot or would not be maintained in the absence of such a regulation.

The existence of this institution therefore requires the existence of a law that annuls the law of God establishing the relation of man and wife, which is taught by the churches to be a sacrament as holy in its nature and its design as the eucharist itself. If informed that in these Christian States of the Union men were prohibited by positive statute law from partaking of the emblems of the broken body and shed blood of the Saviour, what Senator could hesitate to vote for their repeal and future inhibition? And yet here one of these holy sacraments that we are taught to regard with the most sacred feelings, equally holy, instituted by the Author of our being, deemed to be necessary for the preservation of virtue in civil society, is absolutely inhibited by the statute laws of the States where slavery exists. The conjugal relation is abrogated among four million human beings, who are thus driven to heterogeneous intercourse like the beasts of the field, the most of whom are natives of these Christian States. If you continue slavery you must continue this necessary incident of its existence.

Another incident is the abolition practically of the parental relation, robbing the offspring of the care and attention of his parents, severing a relation which is universally cited as the emblem of the relation sustained by the Creator to the human family. And yet, according to the matured judgment of the slave States, this guardianship of the parent over his own children must be abrogated to secure the perpetuity of slavery.

But again, it abolishes necessarily the relation of person to property. It declares the slave to be incapable of acquiring and holding property, and that this disability shall extend to his offspring from generation to generation throughout the coming age. We sometimes shed tears over the misfortunes of men, and when by flood or storm or fire they are robbed of their earthly possessions contributions are made to enable them to start again in their accustomed business pursuits; but the Senator who votes to perpetuate slavery votes not only to sweep away every shred of property that four million people can possibly hold, but he votes to destroy their capacity to acquire and hold it and to impose this disability on their posterity forever. . . .

But it also necessarily, as an incident of its continuance, deprives all those held to be slaves of a status in court. Having no rights to maintain and no legal wrongs to redress, they are held to be incapable of bringing a suit in the courts of the United States; a disability as it seems to me that ought to shock the sensibilities of any Christian statesman. Robbed of all their rights, and then robbed of their capacity to complain of wrongs; robbed of the power to appear before impartial tribunals for the redress of any grievances, however severe!

As an incident of this condition, they are robbed of the right to testify; and, as if to put the cap on this climax of gigantic iniquity, they are denied the right to human sympathy. . . .

. . .

And then another incident of this institution is the suppression of the freedom of speech and of the press, not only among those down-trodden people themselves but among the white race. Slavery cannot exist where its merits can be freely discussed; hence in the slave States it becomes a crime to discuss its claims for protection or the wisdom of its continuance. Its continuance also requires perpetuity of the ignorance of its victims. It is therefore made a felony to teach slaves to read and write.

It also precludes the practical possibility of maintaining schools for the education of those of the white race who have not the means to provide for their own mental culture. It consequently degrades the white as well as African race. It also impoverishes the State, as is manifest by a comparison of the relative wealth, population, and prosperity of the free and slave States of the Union.

. . .

If I am right in my conclusions that slavery as it exists in this country cannot be justified by human reason, has no foundation at common law, and is not supported by the positive municipal laws of the States, nor by the divine law, and that none of its incidents are desirable, and that its abolition would injure no one, and will do no wrong, but will secure unity of purpose, unity of action, and military strength here at home, and the support of the strong nations of the world, as it seems to me, the Senate of the United States ought not to hesitate to take the action necessary to enable the people of the States to terminate its existence forever. . . .

SENATOR CHARLES SUMNER (Republican, Massachusetts)

. . .

There is nothing in the Constitution on which slavery can rest, or find any the least support. Even on the face of that instrument, it is an outlaw; but if we look further at its provisions we find at least four distinct sources of power, which, if executed, must render slavery impossible, while the preamble makes them all vital for freedom: first, the power to provide for the common defense and welfare; secondly, the power to raise armies and maintain navies; thirdly, the power to guaranty to every State a republican form of government; and fourthly, the power to secure liberty to every person restrained without due process of law. But all these provisions are something more than powers; they are duties also. And yet we are constantly and painfully reminded in this Chamber that pending measures against slavery are unconstitutional. Sir, this is an immense mistake. Nothing against slavery can be unconstitutional. It is only hesitation which is unconstitutional.

And yet slavery still exists—in defiance of all these requirements of the Constitution; nay, more, in defiance of reason and justice, which can never be disobeyed with impunity—it exists, the perpetual spoiler of human rights and disturber of the public peace, degrading master as well as slave, corrupting society, weakening government, impoverishing the very soil itself, and impairing the natural resources of the country. Such an outrage, so offensive in every respect, not only to the Constitution, but also to the whole system of order by which the universe is governed, is plainly a national nuisance, which, for the general welfare and in the name of justice, ought to be abated. But at this moment, when it menaces the national life, it will not be enough to treat slavery merely as a nuisance; for it is much more. It is a public enemy and traitor wherever it shows itself, to be subdued, in the discharge of solemn guaranties of Government and of personal rights, and in the exercise of unquestionable and indefeasible rights of self-defence. . . . But whether regarded as national nuisance or as public enemy and traitor, it is obnoxious to the same judgment, and must be abolished.

If, in abolishing slavery, any injury were done to the just interests of any human being or to any rights of any kind, there might be something "to give us pause," even against these irresistible requirements. But nothing of the kind can ensue. No just interests and no rights can suffer. It is the rare felicity of such an act, as well outside as inside the rebel States, that, while striking a blow at the rebellion, and assuring future tranquillity, so that the Republic shall no longer be a house divided against itself, it will add at once to the value of the whole fee simple wherever slavery exists, will secure individual rights, and will advance civilization itself.

. . .

Again, we are brought by learned Senators to the Constitution, which requires that there shall be "just compensation" where "private property" is taken for public use. But plainly on the present occasion the requirement of the Constitution is absolutely inapplicable, for there is no "private property" to take. Slavery is but a bundle of barbarous pretensions, from which certain persons are to be released. . . .

. . .

. . . The people must be summoned to confirm the whole work. It is for them to put the cap-stone upon the sublime structure. An amendment of the Constitution may do what courts and Congress decline to do, or, even should they act, it may cover their action with its panoply. Such an amendment in any event will give completeness and permanence to emancipation, and bring the Constitution into avowed harmony with the Declaration of Independence. Happy day, long wished for, destined to gladden those beatified spirits who have labored on earth to this end, but died without the sight.

. . .

Let me say frankly that I should prefer a form of expression different from that which has the sanction of the committee. . . . I know nothing better than these words:

> All persons are equal before the law, so that no person can hold another as a slave; and the Congress shall have power to make all laws necessary and proper to carry this declaration into effect everywhere within the United States and the jurisdiction thereof.

The words in the latter part supersede all questions as to the applicability of the declaration to States. But the distinctive words in this clause assert the equality of all persons before the law. . . .

. . .

It will be felt at once that this expression, "equality before the law," gives precision to that idea of human rights which is enunciated in our Declaration of Independence. The sophistries of [John C.] Calhoun . . . are all overthrown by this simple statement. . . .

SENATOR LAZARUS POWELL (Democrat, Kentucky)

. . .

I do not believe it was ever designed by the founders of our Government that the Constitution of the United States should be so amended as to destroy property. I do not believe it is the province of the Federal Government to say what is or what is not property. Its province is to guard, protect, and secure, rather than to destroy. If you admit the principle contended for by the gentlemen who urge this amendment, logic would lead them to the conclusion that the General Government could, by an amendment to its Constitution, regulate every domestic matter in the States. If it, by constitutional amendment, can regulate the relation of master and servant, it certainly can, on the same principle, make regulations concerning the relation of parent and child, husband and wife, and guardian and ward. If it has the right to strike down property in slaves, it certainly would have a right to strike down property in horses, to make a partition of the land, and to say that none shall hold land in any State in the Union in fee simple. . . .

. . .

But it is said slavery is the cause of the war, and because it is the cause of the war it must die. If that is the kind of logic on which honorable Senators act they could destroy almost everything that is pure, good, and holy in the world. The blessed religion of our Saviour has been the pretext of more wars perhaps than any other subject. Why not strike down the Christian religion because it has been the subject-matter about which throats have been cut, cities sacked, and empires overthrown? There have been furious wars about territory and territorial boundaries, and there will continue to be such wars as long as the cupidity of man prompts him to make conquests. Why not destroy all tenure in land? Ferocious wars have been waged about women. In Homeric verse we have the historical record of a ten years' contest for frail Helen. Why not destroy the loveliest of God's handiwork. . . .

. . . I desire the Union to be restored, restored as it was with the Constitution as it is; and I verily believe that if you pass this amendment to the Constitution it will be the most effective disunion measure that could be passed by Congress. . . .

. . .

. . . You seem to care for nothing but the negro. That seems to be your sole desire. You seem to be inspired by no other wish than to elevate the negro to equality and give him liberty. . . . I believe this government was made by white men and for white men; and if it is ever preserved it must be preserved by white men. . . . I would ask the Senators who are so zealous for the negro to point me to a place on the earth where he has been so civilized, so humanized, so christianized, so well cared for as he is in a state of slavery in the United States of America. He has existed, I suppose, as long as the other peoples of the earth; but if you were today to strike from existence everything that the woolly-headed negro has given to art, to science, to the mechanic arts, to literature, or to any of the industrial pursuits, the world would not miss it. He is an inferior man in his capacity, and no fanaticism can raise him to the talent of the Caucasian race. The white man is his superior, and will be so whether you call him a slave or an equal. It has ever been so, and I can see no reason why the history of all the past should be reversed. . . .

Debates over the Fourteenth Amendment (1866)[4]

The bipartisan coalition that secured the Thirteenth Amendment fractured when considering the Fourteenth Amendment. Republicans were outraged by southern behavior immediately

4. *Congressional Globe*, 39th Cong., 1st Sess., 1866, 2538, 1088–91, 2768–69, 3148.

Illustration 6-1 The First Vote

Source: Waud, Alfred R. (Alfred Rudolph), 1828–1891, artist, 1867 November 16. Library of Congress, Prints and Photographs Division, Washington, DC 20540, USA.

after the Civil War. Most former slave states passed Black Codes. These laws prohibited persons of color from engaging in many occupations and exercising such political rights as serving on juries and voting. Southern Unionists were also persecuted and denied fundamental rights. While most Republicans believed that the Thirteenth Amendment gave Congress the power to outlaw these rights violations, party members agreed that a more specific constitutional amendment was necessary to secure greater racial equality. Democrats aggressively challenged Republican efforts to reconstruct the South. Party members, even those who supported the Thirteenth Amendment, insisted on retaining what they believed was a constitutional commitment to white supremacy.

Politics and principle freely mixed during the debates over the Fourteenth Amendment. Republicans feared that a reconstructed South might provide the Democratic Party with the votes necessary to return that coalition to national power. Such an outcome was likely if former slaves, who were being denied the ballot, counted as full persons for purposes of apportioning representatives in Congress. Many Democrats believed that their party could make substantial inroads in the North by running as the party committed to rule by white men.

The Republican Party internally divided over the text and scope of an appropriate constitutional amendment. After the elections of 1864 and 1866, party members enjoyed the majorities necessary to ratify the constitutional amendment of their choice but could not agree on principles or language. Such radical Republicans as Thaddeus Stevens and Charles Sumner favored a package of constitutional amendments and statutes that would grant persons of color the same political, civil, and economic rights as white persons enjoyed. They championed a Fourteenth Amendment that declared: "Congress shall have power to make all laws necessary and proper to secure all citizens of the United States, in every State, the same political rights and privileges; and to all persons in every State equal protection in the enjoyment of life, liberty and property." More conservative Republicans insisted that the federal Constitution and federal law not undermine the economic status quo in the South. They favored constitutional amendments and federal statutes that were limited to guaranteeing former slaves (and southern Unionists) formal legal equality.

The resulting Fourteenth Amendment was a compromise between more radical and more conservative Republican factions. The crucial provisions of that text declare:

> 1. *All persons born or naturalized in the United States, and subject to the jurisdiction thereof, are citizens of the United States and of the State wherein they reside. No State shall make or enforce any law which shall abridge the privileges or immunities of citizens of the United States; nor shall any State deprive any person of life, liberty, or property, without due process of law; nor deny to any person within its jurisdiction the equal protection of the laws.*
>
> . . .
>
> 5. *The Congress shall have power to enforce, by appropriate legislation, the provisions of this article.*

Section 2 of the Fourteenth Amendment penalizes states that deprive male citizens of the right to vote in a federal election for reasons other than participation in the rebellion or criminal offenses by reducing the offending state's representation in Congress in proportion to the percentage of men disenfranchised. Section 3 declares former state and federal officials who sided with the Confederacy ineligible to hold political office. Section 4 states that the United States is not liable for debts incurred by the Confederate government or states that joined the Confederacy.

The Fourteenth Amendment was proposed by Congress in June 1866, but the state ratification process was not completed until July 1868. Congress refused to acknowledge efforts by several states to rescind ratification, while accepting ratification votes from states that had previously voted down the amendment. Some southern legislatures were not allowed representation in Congress until the state legislature approved the Fourteenth Amendment.[5]

When reading the following excerpts, consider the relationship between the constitutional amendment proposed by the more radical Republicans and the final version of the Fourteenth Amendment. What rights did the most radical faction of the Republican Party seek to protect? What rights did the most conservative faction of the Republican Party seek to protect? To what extent did the persons who proposed different Fourteenth Amendments believe they were using different words to protect the same constitutional rights? To what extent do you believe the final language of the Fourteenth Amendment reflects a self-conscious decision to reject more radical Republican claims? To what extent does the final language of the Fourteenth Amendment reflect a self-conscious decision to not decide either the precise constitutional status of persons of color or what constituted the fundamental rights of American citizens? Do you believe that the original and final versions of the Fourteenth Amendment are substantially different? Compare the final version of the Fourteenth Amendment with the most radical interpretation of the Thirteenth Amendment. Do any significant differences exist between the Thirteenth Amendment as interpreted by Charles Sumner and the Fourteenth Amendment? Did the Fourteenth Amendment narrow or broaden the more radical version of the Thirteenth Amendment?

The Thirteenth, Fourteenth, and Fifteenth Amendments include provisions that declare, "The Congress shall have power to enforce, by appropriate legislation, the provisions of this article." Future generations debated whether that language gives Congress the authority to interpret the meaning of the post–Civil War Amendments. Do the following excerpts cast any light on how the framers of those amendments understood constitutional authority? Such Democrats as Andrew Rogers insisted that the Fourteenth Amendment radically altered the Constitution. Did Republicans agree?

Table 6-2a Passage and Ratification of the Fourteenth Amendment, U.S. Senate Vote (June 8, 1866)

Party	Ayes	Nays
Republican	32	3
Democratic	0	7
Union	1	1
Total	33	11

Table 6-2b Passage and Ratification of the Fourteenth Amendment, U.S. House of Representatives Vote (June 13, 1866)

Party	Ayes	Nays	No Vote
Republican	130	0	6
Democratic	0	36	3
Union	8	0	1
Total	138	36	10

5. John William Burgess, *Reconstruction and the Constitution, 1866–1876* (New York: Charles Scribner's Sons, 1905), 198–99.

Table 6-2c Passage and Ratification of the Fourteenth Amendment, State Ratification (28 of 37 Needed)

Year	Ratify	Reject	Rescind
1866	6	4	
1867	16	4	
1868	6	0	2

REPRESENTATIVE JOHN BINGHAM (Republican, Ohio)

. . .

. . . I repel the suggestion made here in the heat of debate, that the committee or any of its members who favor the proposition seek in any form to mar the Constitution of the country or take away from any State any right that belongs to it, or from any citizen of any State any right that belongs to him under that Constitution. The proposition pending before the House is simply a proposition to arm the Congress of the United States, by consent of the people of the United States, with the power to enforce the bill of rights as it stands in the Constitution today. . . .

. . .

Gentlemen admit the force of the provisions in the bill of rights, that the citizens of the United States shall be entitled to all the privileges and immunities of citizens of the United States in the several States, and that no person shall be deprived of life, liberty, or property without due process of law; but they say, "We are opposed to its enforcement by act of Congress under an amended Constitution, as proposed." That is the sum and substance of all the argument that we have heard on this subject. Why are gentlemen opposed to the enforcement of the bill of rights, as proposed? Because they aver it would interfere with the reserved rights of the States! Who ever before heard that any State had reserved to itself the right, under the Constitution of the United States, to withhold from any citizen within its limits, under any pretext whatever, any of the privileges of a citizen of the United States, or to impose upon him, no matter from what State he may have come, any burden contrary to that provision of the Constitution which declares that the citizen shall be entitled in the several States to all the immunities of a citizen of the United States?

What does the word immunity in your Constitution mean? Exemption from unequal burdens. Ah! say the gentlemen who oppose this amendment, we are not opposed to equal rights; we are not opposed to the bill of rights that all shall be protected alike in life, liberty, and property; we are only opposed to enforcing it by national authority, even by the consent of the loyal people of all the States.

REPRESENTATIVE ANDREW J. ROGERS (Democrat, New Jersey)

. . .

. . . [T]he first section of this program of disunion is the most dangerous to liberty. It saps the foundation of the Government; it destroys the elementary principles of the States; it consolidates everything into one imperial despotism; it annihilates all the rights which lie at the foundation of the Union of the States, and which have characterized this Government and made it prosperous and great during the long period of its existence.

This section of the joint resolution is no more nor less than an attempt to embody in the Constitution of the United States that outrageous and miserable civil rights bill which passed both Houses of Congress and was vetoed by the President of the United States upon the ground that it was a direct attempt to consolidate the power of the States and to take away from them the elementary principles which lie at their foundation. It is only an attempt to ingraft upon the Constitution of the United States one of the most dangerous, most wicked, most intolerant, and most odious propositions ever introduced into this House or attempted to be ingrafted upon the fundamental law of the Federal Union.

. . . What are privileges and immunities? Why, sir, all the rights we have under the laws of the country are embraced under the definition of privileges and immunities. The right to marry is a privilege. The right to contract is a privilege. The right to be a juror is a privilege. The right to be a judge or President of the United States is a privilege. I hold if that ever becomes a part of the fundamental law of the land it will prevent any State from refusing to allow anything to anybody embraced under the term of privileges and immunities. If a negro is refused the right to be a juror, that will take away from him his privileges and immunities as a citizen of the United States, and the Federal Government will step in and interfere, and the result will be a contest between the powers of the Federal Government and the powers of the States. It will rock the earth like the throes of an earthquake until its tragedy will summon the inhabitants of the world to witness its dreadful shock.

. . .

Yes, gentlemen, it is but the negro again appearing in the background. The only object of the constitutional amendment is to drive the people of the South, ay, and even the people of the North, wherever there is much of a negro population, to allow that population not qualified but universal suffrage, without regard to intelligence or character, to allow them to come to the ballot-box and cast their votes equally with white men.

. . .

Sir, I want it distinctly understood that the American people believe that this Government was made for white men and white women. They do not believe, nor can you make them believe—the edict of God Almighty is stamped against it—that there is a social equality between the black race and the white.

I have no fault to find with the colored race. I have not the slightest antipathy to them. I wish them well, and if I were in a State where they exist in large numbers I would vote to give them every right enjoyed by the white people except the right of a negro man to marry a white woman and the right to vote. But, sir, this proposition goes further than any that has ever been attempted to be carried into effect. Why, sir, even in Rhode Island today there is a property qualification in regard to the white man's voting as well as the negro. And yet Representatives of the eastern, middle, western, and some of the border States come here and attempt in this indirect way to inflict upon the people of the South negro suffrage. God deliver this people from such a wicked, odious, pestilent despotism! God save the people of the South from the degradation by which they would be obliged to go to the polls and vote side by side with the negro!

. . .

REPRESENTATIVE ROGERS

. . . I only wish to know what you mean by "due process of law."

REPRESENTATIVE BINGHAM

I reply to the gentleman, the courts have settled that long ago, and the gentleman can go and read their decisions.

. . .

The question is, simply, whether you will give by this amendment to the people of the United States the power, by legislative enactment, to punish officials of the States for violation of the oaths enjoined upon them by their Constitution? That is the question, and the whole question. The adoption of the proposed amendment will take from the States no rights that belong to the States. They elect their Legislatures; they enact their laws for the punishment of crimes against life, liberty, or property; but in the event of the adoption of this amendment, if they conspire together to enact laws refusing the equal protection to life, liberty, or property, the Congress is thereby vested with power to hold them to answer before the bar of the national courts for the violation of their oaths and of the rights of their fellow-men. Why should it not be so? That is the question. Why should it not be so? Is the bill of rights to stand in our Constitution hereafter, as in the past five years within eleven States, a mere dead letter? It is absolutely essential to the safety of the people that it should be enforced. . . .

SENATOR BENJAMIN WADE (Republican, Ohio)

I move to amend the joint resolution by . . . substituting the proposition which I send to the Chair to be read.

. . .

> SEC. 2. No class of persons as to the right of any of whom to suffrage discrimination shall be made, by any State, shall be included in the basis of representation, unless such discrimination be in virtue of impartial qualifications founded on intelligence or property or because of alienage, or for participation in rebellion or other crime. . . .

. . . There are some reasons, and many believe there are good reasons, for restricting universal suffrage, and upon such principles as not to justify the inflicting of a punishment or penalty upon a State which adopts restricted suffrage. It is already done in some of the New England States. . . . I believe the constitution of [Massachusetts] restricts the right of suffrage to persons who can read the Constitution of the United States and write their names. I am not prepared to say that that is not a wise restriction. At all events, a State has the right to try that experiment; but if she tries it, under the report of the committee she must lose, in the proportion that she has such persons among her inhabitants, her representatives in Congress. I do not think that ought to be so. . . .

Under [my proposed] amendment you ascertain the classes of the population, and when any discrimination shall be made upon any of these subjects the whole of that particular class will be excluded. There is only one question to be determined. If the exclusion is because of race or color, the question is what amount of colored population is there in the State, and in exactly that proportion she is to lose representation. . . .

. . .

I have seen other suggested amendments which I would like to have prevail. . . . I am for the suffrage to our friends in the South, the men who have stood by us in this rebellion, the men who have hazarded their lives and all that they hold dear to defend our country. I think our friends, the colored people of the South, should not be excluded from the right of voting, and they shall not be if my vote with the votes of a sufficient number who agree with me in Congress shall be able to carry it. . . . My own opinion is that if you go down to the very foundation of justice, so far from weakening yourself with the people, you will strengthen yourself immensely by it; but I know that it is not the opinion of many here, and I suppose we must accommodate ourselves to the will of majorities, and if we cannot do all we would, do all we can. . . .

REPRESENTATIVE THADDEUS STEVENS (Republican, Pennsylvania)

. . .

In my youth, in my manhood, in my old age, I fondly dreamed that when any fortunate chance should have broken up for awhile the foundation of our institutions, and released us from obligations the most tyrannical that ever man imposed in the name of freedom, that the intelligent, pure and just men of this Republic, true to their professions and their consciences, would have so remodeled all our institutions as to have freed them from every vestige of human oppression, of inequality of rights, of the recognized degradation of the poor, and the superior caste of the rich. In short, that no distinction would be tolerated in this purified Republic but what arose from merit and conduct. This bright dream has vanished "like the baseless fabric of a vision." I find that we shall be obliged to be content with patching up the worst portions of the ancient edifice, and leaving it, in many of its parts, to be swept through by the tempests, the frosts, and the storms of despotism.

Do you inquire why, holding these views and possessing some will of my own, I accept so imperfect a proposition? I answer, because I live among men and not among angels; among men as intelligent, as determined, and as independent as myself, who, not agreeing with me, do not choose to yield, their opinions to mine. Mutual concession, therefore, is our only resort, or mutual hostilities.

. . .

The first section [of the proposed Fourteenth Amendment] is altered by defining who are citizens of the United States and of the States. This is an excellent amendment, long needed to settle conflicting decisions between the several States and the United States. It declares this great privilege to belong to every person born or naturalized in the United States.

The second section has received but slight alteration. I wish it had received more. It contains much less power than I could wish; it has not half the vigor of the amendment which was lost in the Senate. It . . . would have worked the enfranchisement of the colored man in half the time.

The third section has been wholly changed by substituting the ineligibility of certain high offenders for the disfranchisement of all rebels until 1870.

This I cannot look upon as an improvement. It opens the elective franchise to such as the States choose to admit. In my judgment, it endangers the Government of the country, both State and national; and may give the next Congress and President to the reconstructed rebels. With their enlarged basis of representation, and exclusion of the loyal men of color from the ballot-box, I see no hope of safety unless in the prescription of proper enabling acts, which shall do justice to the freedmen and enjoin enfranchisement as a condition precedent.

. . .

. . . [L]et us no longer delay; take what we can get now, and hope for better things in further legislation; in enabling acts or other provisions. . . .

B. Principles

The debates underlying secession and the Civil War were about slavery. Differences existed between more northern and more southern states over such questions as federal power to sponsor internal improvements, but the existence of slavery made those differences irreconcilable. Abraham Lincoln on the campaign trail repeatedly spoke of an original constitutional understanding that slavery was "in a course of ultimate extinction." His Gettysburg Address maintained that the United States was constitutionally "dedicated to the proposition that all men are created equal." Southerners offered an alternative to Lincoln's anti-slavery constitutional vision. Confederate vice president Alexander Stephens declared that the fundamental constitutional principle of the Confederate Constitution was "that the negro is not equal to the white man; that slavery—subordination to the superior race—is his natural and normal condition."[6]

The Thirteenth Amendment transformed constitutional debates over the place of slavery in the constitutional regime into constitutional controversies over the significance of emancipation. African American leaders and more radical Republicans believed that the post–Civil War constitutional order fundamentally altered previous constitutional commitments. Frederick Douglass spoke for this constitutional vision when he declared, "No war but an Abolition war; no peace but an Abolition peace; liberty for all, chains for none; the black man a soldier in war, a laborer in peace; a voter at the South as well as at the North; America his permanent home, and all Americans his fellow countrymen."[7] Democrats, more conservative Republicans, and white southerners minimized the significance of the three new constitutional amendments. President Andrew Johnson and his political allies interpreted the post–Civil War Constitution only as abolishing slavery and granting free blacks formal equality. Johnson's veto of the Civil Rights Act of 1866 maintained,

> The white race and the black race of the South have hitherto lived together under the relation of master and slave—capital owning labor. Now, suddenly, that relation is changed, and as to ownership capital and labor are divorced. They stand now each master of itself. In this new relation, one being necessary to the other, there will be a new adjustment, which both are deeply interested in making harmonious. Each has equal power in settling the terms, and if left to the laws that regulate capital and labor it is confidently believed that they will satisfactorily work out the problem. Capital, it is true, has more intelligence, but labor is never so ignorant as not to understand its own interests, not to know its own value, and not to see that capital must pay that value.[8]

C. Scope

Americans have debated for more than 150 years whether the persons responsible for the Fourteenth Amendment intended to incorporate the Bill of Rights. The most recent commentary concludes that Reconstruction Republicans did intend to nationalize the Bill of Rights.[9] Conventional wisdom fifty years ago supported the opposite conclusion.[10] Both Representative John Bingham and Senator Jacob Howard, the legislators who led the floor fights for the Fourteenth Amendment, made speeches interpreting the Fourteenth Amendment as incorporating the Bill of Rights. How widely their interpretation was shared or known is not entirely clear.

The Supreme Court of the United States firmly rejected contentions that the Fourteenth Amendment nationalized the Bill of Rights. Justice Samuel Miller's majority opinion in the *Slaughter-House Cases* (1873) emphatically challenged assertions that "by the simple declaration that no State should make or enforce any law which shall abridge the privileges and immunities of citizens of the United States," the Fourteenth Amendment "transfer[red] the security and protection of all the civil rights . . . from the States to the Federal government." *United States v. Cruikshank* (1876) more explicitly stated that *Barron v. Baltimore* (1833) remained the constitutional law of the land. The First Amendment, Chief Justice Waite's opinion stated, "like the other amendments proposed and adopted at the same time, was not intended to limit the powers of the State governments in respect to their own citizens, but to operate upon the National government alone."

---

6. Alexander H. Stephens, *A Constitutional View of the Late War Between the States* (Philadelphia: National Publishing Co., 1870), 2:705.

7. Frederick Douglass, *Frederick Douglass: Selected Speeches and Writings*, ed. Philip S. Foner (Chicago: Chicago Review Press, 1999), 566.

8. Andrew Johnson, "Veto Messages," in *Compilation of the Messages* (see note 1), 6:412.

9. The most influential recent works on this subject are Michael Kent Curtis, *No State Shall Abridge: The Fourteenth Amendment and the Bill of Rights* (Durham, NC: Duke University Press, 1987); and Akhil Reed Amar, *The Bill of Rights: Creation and Reconstruction* (New Haven, CT: Yale University Press, 2000).

10. See especially Charles Fairman, "Does the Fourteenth Amendment Incorporate the Bill of Rights? The Original Understanding," *Stanford Law Review* 2 (1949): 5.

Slaughter-House Cases, 83 U.S. 36 (1873)

The Republican-controlled state legislature of Louisiana in 1869 passed a law incorporating the Crescent City Live-Stock Landing and Slaughtering Company. The legislation required all butchers in New Orleans to use the "grand slaughterhouse" controlled by the Crescent City Company. The state legislature claimed that moving animal slaughtering operations into one central, regulated location was a justifiable exercise of the state's "police power," which is the traditional legislative authority to pass laws that promote public health, safety, or morality. Dispossessed butchers disagreed. They believed that the Crescent City monopoly unconstitutionally deprived them of their right to make a living. That the Crescent City Company was controlled by a group of seventeen wealthy and politically influential individuals fed public antipathy. Southern Democrats charged that the "carpet bagging" Republican legislature responsible for the monopoly was more interested in conferring illegitimate special privileges on favored groups than in promoting the general interest.

The disgruntled butchers, acting as the Butchers' Benevolent Association of New Orleans, brought suit against the Crescent City Company and the state of Louisiana. John Campbell, a former associate justice of the Supreme Court,[11] *represented the dispossessed butchers. His brief claimed that the Louisiana monopoly violated the Thirteenth Amendment and three provisions of the Fourteenth Amendment. Campbell placed special emphasis on the provision in the Fourteenth Amendment that prohibited states from enforcing "any law which shall abridge the privileges and immunities of citizens of the United States." He argued that one of the privileges and immunities of U.S. citizens was the right to labor freely in an honest vocation. Campbell also noted that the Fourteenth Amendment prohibits states from denying any person "equal protection of the law." In his view, this monopoly unequally bestowed artificial privileges on some butchers at the expense of others. Finally, Campbell pointed out that the Fourteenth Amendment declares that states shall not "deprive any person of life, liberty, or property, without due process of law." He argued that the legislature's interference with the ability of butchers to pursue an honest living deprived them of both their liberty to work and the value of their property. For good measure, this son of the Confederacy added that the Thirteenth Amendment prohibits the sort of "involuntary servitude" that would be created when butchers had to pay monopolists a set fee for the privilege of conducting their business. When the Supreme Court of Louisiana rejected these arguments, Campbell and the Butchers' Benevolent Association appealed to the Supreme Court of the United States.*

The Supreme Court of the United States by a 5–4 vote ruled that state-granted monopolies did not violate the Thirteenth or Fourteenth Amendments. Justice Samuel Miller's majority opinion insisted that states remained responsible for protecting the fundamental rights of citizens. Miller's controversial opinion sharply distinguished between the "privileges and immunities" of state citizens and the "privileges and immunities" of citizens of the United States. He narrowly interpreted the due process and equal protection clauses.

Slaughter-House *is one of the most important and contested decisions ever made by the Supreme Court of the United States. When reading the case, consider how Justice Miller interprets the privileges and immunities clause, the due process clause, and the equal protection clause of the Fourteenth Amendment. On what points did he and the dissenting opinion disagree? Why did Justice Miller insist that the post–Civil War Amendments do not create a substantial change in the institutions responsible for protecting fundamental freedoms? Why did Justice Field disagree? Who has the better argument?*

Slaughter-House *was the first case in which the Supreme Court discussed the meaning of the post–Civil War Amendments. This may seem surprising, given that the issues before the court directly concerned the rights of butchers, not the rights of former slaves. Nevertheless,* Slaughter-House *is often regarded as sharply curtailing the constitutional rights of persons of color. To what extent do you believe that John Campbell, who as a justice supported the* Dred Scott *decision, might have seen* Slaughter-House *as a vehicle for cabining the post–Civil War Amendments? Justice Miller's decision asserted that the primary purpose of these amendments was the protection of the freedmen. How, if at all, did his opinion nevertheless narrow constitutional protections for persons of color?*

JUSTICE MILLER delivered the opinion of the court.

. . .

The power here exercised by the legislature of Louisiana is, in its essential nature, one which has been, up to the present period in the constitutional history of this country, always conceded to belong to the States. . . .

11. Campbell resigned from the Court in 1861 after Alabama seceded from the Union.

This [police] power is, and must be from its very nature, incapable of any very exact definition or limitation. Upon it depends the security of social order, the life and health of the citizen, the comfort of an existence in a thickly populated community, the enjoyment of private and social life, and the beneficial use of property. . . . The regulation of the place and manner of conducting the slaughtering of animals, and the business of butchering within a city, and the inspection of the animals to be killed for meat, and of the meat afterwards, are among the most necessary and frequent exercises of this power. . . .

It cannot be denied that the statute under consideration is aptly framed to remove from the more densely populated part of the city, the noxious slaughter-houses, and large and offensive collections of animals necessarily incident to the slaughtering business of a large city, and to locate them where the convenience, health, and comfort of the people require they shall be located. And it must be conceded that the means adopted by the act for this purpose are appropriate, are stringent, and effectual. . . .

. . .

It may, therefore, be considered as established, that the authority of the legislature of Louisiana to pass the present statute is ample, unless some restraint in the exercise of that power be found in the constitution of that State or in the amendments to the Constitution of the United States, adopted since the date of the decisions we have already cited. . . .

. . .

The most cursory glance at [the Thirteenth and Fourteenth Amendments] discloses a unity of purpose, when taken in connection with the history of the times, which cannot fail to have an important bearing on any question of doubt concerning their true meaning. . . .

The institution of African slavery, as it existed in about half the States of the Union, and the contests pervading the public mind for many years, between those who desired its curtailment and ultimate extinction and those who desired additional safeguards for its security and perpetuation, culminated in the effort, on the part of most of the States in which slavery existed, to separate from the Federal government, and to resist its authority. This constituted the war of the rebellion, and whatever auxiliary causes may have contributed to bring about this war, undoubtedly the overshadowing and efficient cause was African slavery. . . .

. . .

We repeat, then, in the light of this recapitulation of events, almost too recent to be called history, but which are familiar to us all; and on the most casual examination of the language of these amendments, no one can fail to be impressed with the one pervading purpose found in them all, lying at the foundation of each, and without which none of them would have been even suggested; we mean the freedom of the slave race, the security and firm establishment of that freedom, and the protection of the newly-made freeman and citizen from the oppressions of those who had formerly exercised unlimited dominion over him. . . .

We do not say that no one else but the negro can share in this protection. Both the language and spirit of these articles are to have their fair and just weight in any question of construction. Undoubtedly while negro slavery alone was in the mind of the Congress which proposed the thirteenth article, it forbids any other kind of slavery, now or hereafter. If Mexican peonage or the Chinese coolie labor system shall develop slavery of the Mexican or Chinese race within our territory, this amendment may safely be trusted to make it void. And so if other rights are assailed by the States which properly and necessarily fall within the protection of these articles, that protection will apply, though the party interested may not be of African descent. . . .

. . . [T]he distinction between citizenship of the United States and citizenship of a State is clearly recognized and established [by the Fourteenth Amendment]. . . .

We think this distinction and its explicit recognition in this amendment of great weight in this argument, because the next paragraph of this same section, which is the one mainly relied on by the plaintiffs in error, speaks only of privileges and immunities of citizens of the United States, and does not speak of those of citizens of the several States.

The language is, "No State shall make or enforce any law which shall abridge the privileges or immunities of citizens of the United States." It is a little remarkable, if this clause was intended as a protection to the citizen of a State against the legislative power of his own State, that the word citizen of the State should be left out when it is so carefully used, and used in contradistinction to citizens of the United States, in the very sentence which precedes it. It is too clear for argument that the change in phraseology was adopted understandingly and with a purpose. . . .

Fortunately we are not without judicial construction of this clause of the Constitution. The first and the leading case on the subject is that of *Corfield v. Coryell*, decided by Mr. Justice Washington in the Circuit Court for the District of Pennsylvania in 1823. "The inquiry," he says, "is, what are the privileges and immunities of citizens of the several States? We feel no hesitation in confining these expressions to those privileges and immunities which are fundamental; which belong of right to the citizens of all free governments, and which have at all times been enjoyed by citizens of the several States which compose this Union, from the time of their becoming free, independent, and sovereign. What these fundamental principles are, it would be more tedious than difficult to enumerate. They may all, however, be comprehended under the following general heads: protection by the government, with the right to acquire and possess property of every kind, and to pursue and obtain happiness and safety, subject, nevertheless, to such restraints as the government may prescribe for the general good of the whole." . . .

. . . Was it the purpose of the fourteenth amendment, by the simple declaration that no State should make or enforce any law which shall abridge the privileges and immunities of citizens of the United States, to transfer the security and protection of all the civil rights which we have mentioned, from the States to the Federal government? And where it is declared that Congress shall have the power to enforce that article, was it intended to bring within the power of Congress the entire domain of civil rights heretofore belonging exclusively to the States?

All this and more must follow, if the proposition of the plaintiffs in error be sound. For not only are these rights subject to the control of Congress whenever in its discretion any of them are supposed to be abridged by State legislation, but that body may also pass laws in advance, limiting and restricting the exercise of legislative power by the States, in their most ordinary and usual functions, as in its judgment it may think proper on all such subjects. . . . The argument we admit is not always the most conclusive which is drawn from the consequences urged against the adoption of a particular construction of an instrument. But when, as in the case before us, these consequences are so serious, so far-reaching and pervading, so great a departure from the structure and spirit of our institutions; when the effect is to fetter and degrade the State governments by subjecting them to the control of Congress, in the exercise of powers heretofore universally conceded to them of the most ordinary and fundamental character; when in fact it radically changes the whole theory of the relations of the State and Federal governments to each other and of both these governments to the people; the argument has a force that is irresistible, in the absence of language which expresses such a purpose too clearly to admit of doubt.

We are convinced that no such results were intended by the Congress which proposed these amendments, nor by the legislatures of the States which ratified them.

. . .

The argument has not been much pressed in these cases that the defendant's charter deprives the plaintiffs of their property without due process of law, or that it denies to them the equal protection of the law. . . .

We are not without judicial interpretation, . . . both State and National, of the meaning of [the due process] clause. And it is sufficient to say that under no construction of that provision that we have ever seen, or any that we deem admissible, can the restraint imposed by the State of Louisiana upon the exercise of their trade by the butchers of New Orleans be held to be a deprivation of property within the meaning of that provision.

"Nor shall any State deny to any person within its jurisdiction the equal protection of the laws."

In the light of the history of these amendments, and the pervading purpose of them, which we have already discussed, it is not difficult to give a meaning to this clause. The existence of laws in the States where the newly emancipated negroes resided, which discriminated with gross injustice and hardship against them as a class, was the evil to be remedied by this clause, and by it such laws are forbidden.

. . . We doubt very much whether any action of a State not directed by way of discrimination against the negroes as a class, or on account of their race, will ever be held to come within the purview of this provision. It is so clearly a provision for that race and that emergency, that a strong case would be necessary for its application to any other. . . .

. . .

JUSTICE FIELD, dissenting:

. . .

The act of Louisiana presents the naked case, unaccompanied by any public considerations, where a right to pursue a lawful and necessary calling, previously enjoyed by every citizen, and in connection with which a thousand persons were daily employed, is taken away and vested exclusively for twenty-five years, for an extensive district and a large population, in a single corporation, or its exercise is for that period restricted to the establishments of the corporation, and there allowed only upon onerous conditions. . . .

The question presented is, therefore, one of the gravest importance, not merely to the parties here, but to the whole country. It is nothing less than the question whether the recent amendments to the Federal Constitution protect the citizens of the United States against the deprivation of their common rights by State legislation. In my judgment the fourteenth amendment does afford such protection, and was so intended by the Congress which framed and the States which adopted it. . . .

The amendment does not attempt to confer any new privileges or immunities upon citizens, or to enumerate or define those already existing. It assumes that there are such privileges and immunities which belong of right to citizens as such, and ordains that they shall not be abridged by State legislation. If this inhibition has no reference to privileges and immunities of this character, but only refers, as held by the majority of the court in their opinion, to such privileges and immunities as were before its adoption specially designated in the Constitution or necessarily implied as belonging to citizens of the United States, it was a vain and idle enactment, which accomplished nothing, and most unnecessarily excited Congress and the people on its passage. With privileges and immunities thus designated or implied no State could ever have interfered by its laws, and no new constitutional provision was required to inhibit such interference. The supremacy of the Constitution and the laws of the United States always controlled any State legislation of that character. But if the amendment refers to the natural and inalienable rights which belong to all citizens, the inhibition has a profound significance and consequence.

What, then, are the privileges and immunities which are secured against abridgment by State legislation? . . .

The terms, privileges and immunities, are not new in the amendment; they were in the Constitution before the amendment was adopted. They are found in the second section of the fourth article, which declares that "the citizens of each State shall be entitled to all privileges and immunities of citizens in the several States," and they have been the subject of frequent consideration in judicial decisions. [*Justice Field then quoted the same passage from* Corfield v. Coryell *that Justice Miller had quoted*.] This appears to me to be a sound construction of the clause in question. The privileges and immunities designated are those which of right belong to the citizens of all free governments. Clearly among these must be placed the right to pursue a lawful employment in a lawful manner, without other restraint than such as equally affects all persons. . . .

. . . The privileges and immunities of citizens of the United States, of every one of them, is secured against abridgment in any form by any State. The fourteenth amendment places them under the guardianship of the National authority. All monopolies in any known trade or manufacture are an invasion of these privileges, for they encroach upon the liberty of citizens to acquire property and pursue happiness. . . .

. . .

This equality of right, with exemption from all disparaging and partial enactments, in the lawful pursuits of life, throughout the whole country, is the distinguishing privilege of citizens of the United States. To them, everywhere, all pursuits, all professions, all avocations are open without other restrictions than such as are imposed equally upon all others of the same age, sex, and condition. The State may prescribe such regulations for every pursuit and calling of life as will promote the public health, secure the good order and advance the general prosperity of society, but when once prescribed, the pursuit or calling must be free to be followed by every citizen who is within the conditions designated, and will conform to the regulations. This is the fundamental idea upon which our institutions rest, and unless adhered to in the legislation of the country our government will be a republic only in name. The fourteenth amendment, in my judgment, makes it essential to the validity of the legislation of every State that this equality of right should be respected. . . . That only is a free government, in the American sense of the term, under which the inalienable right of every citizen to pursue his happiness is unrestrained, except by just, equal, and impartial laws.

JUSTICE BRADLEY, dissenting. . . .

JUSTICE SWAYNE, dissenting. . . .

III. Judicial Power and Constitutional Authority

MAJOR DEVELOPMENTS

- Republicans restructure the federal judiciary
- Lincoln challenges judicial authority
- The Supreme Court finds jurisdictional reasons not to rule on whether crucial Reconstruction Acts are constitutional

The Republican Party that controlled the national government during the Civil War and Reconstruction had a love-hate relationship with the federal judiciary. Most Republicans began their careers as Whigs, and most Whigs before the Civil War were strong supporters of federal judicial power. The U.S. Supreme Court earned the wrath of Republicans throughout the nation, however, by holding in *Dred Scott v. Sandford* (1856) that slavery could not be banned in American territories. While many Republicans were content to attack particular Supreme Court decisions, some began questioning past commitments to judicial power. Lincoln, his political allies, and his political successors adopted various strategies to prevent judges appointed by Jacksonian presidents from interfering with Republican policies. Republican officials sometimes ignored judicial decrees. Republicans in Congress manipulated federal jurisdiction to keep risky cases away from the Court. When vacancies arose, Lincoln placed reliable allies on the federal bench. The Judiciary Act of 1862 reorganized the federal judiciary to guarantee a free-state majority on the Supreme Court. Republicans from 1863 to 1871 alternately added and subtracted seats on the Supreme Court to gain and maintain a friendly tribunal.

Abraham Lincoln rose to fame attacking the *Dred Scott* decision. During the Lincoln–Douglas debates (1858) he repeatedly asserted that *Dred Scott* was part of a Democratic conspiracy to make slavery a national institution. Lincoln distinguished between judicial review, which is the judicial power to interpret the Constitution when deciding the legal rights of the parties before the Court, and judicial supremacy, which is the judicial power to determine official constitutional meanings. When taking the presidential oath in 1861, Lincoln reiterated his commitment to reversing the result of *Dred Scott* and his opposition to judicial supremacy.

> I do not forget the position assumed by some that constitutional questions are to be decided by the Supreme Court, nor do I deny that such decisions must be binding in any case upon the parties to a suit as to the object of that suit. . . . At the same time, the candid citizen must confess that if the policy of the Government upon vital questions affecting the whole people is to be irrevocably fixed by decisions of the Supreme Court, the instant they are made, in ordinary litigation between parties, in personal actions, the people will have ceased to be their own rulers, having to that extent practically resigned their Government into the hands of that eminent tribunal. Nor is there in this view any assault upon the court or the judges. It is a duty from which they may not shrink to decide cases properly brought before them, and it is no fault of theirs if others seek to turn their decisions to political purposes.[12]

Republican attitudes toward the federal judiciary fluctuated during the decade after the Civil War. Republicans in Congress initially regarded federal courts staffed increasingly by Lincoln appointees as allies in their effort to reconstruct the South. The Civil Rights Act of 1866 and the Habeas Corpus Act of 1867 enabled former slaves and southern Unionists to litigate in federal courts their new statutory and constitutional rights. Republican confidence in the federal judiciary soon faded. Justice David Davis's majority opinion in *Ex parte Milligan* cast considerable doubt on whether the Supreme Court would support crucial Reconstruction measures, most notably the imposition of martial law in the South. Republicans were outraged. Many questioned their initial support for empowering federal courts.

Buoyed by *Milligan* and rumors that several justices were prepared to declare crucial Reconstruction measures unconstitutional, prominent Democrats looked for a test case to bring before what they perceived to be a sympathetic judiciary. Their initial efforts failed on jurisdictional grounds. In *Mississippi v. Johnson* (1867), the Supreme Court ruled that judges could not issue an injunction prohibiting a president from enforcing

12. Abraham Lincoln, "First Inaugural Address," in *Compilation of the Messages* (see note 1), 6:9.

federal law. In *Georgia v. Stanton* (1867), the Court ruled that a state lacked standing to make a general attack on Reconstruction measures. Democrats finally appeared to hit pay dirt when the justices scheduled arguments to determine whether William McCardle, a racist newspaper editor from Mississippi, could be constitutionally tried by a military commission for encouraging resistance to Reconstruction.

Faced with the possibility that military rule in the South might be declared unconstitutional, Republicans in Congress took several steps to protect their legislative handiwork. First, they passed legislation shrinking the size of the court from ten to eight justices. This measure prevented President Andrew Johnson from filling any vacancies with a nominee hostile to Reconstruction. Second, Congress, over a presidential veto, repealed the Habeas Corpus Act of 1867. That repeal stripped the Court of the jurisdiction necessary to decide McCardle's case. The repeal was passed after the Supreme Court had already heard arguments in *Ex parte McCardle* (1869). Nevertheless, the justices delayed their decision until what became known as Repealer Act became law. The justices then sustained the Repealer Act and dismissed McCardle's case for want of jurisdiction. The Supreme Court never determined whether Congress could impose martial law in the Reconstruction South.

These tensions between the Court and Congress did not simmer long. Shortly after President Grant took office, Congress voted to increase the number of Supreme Court justices to nine. Although this broke with the practice of having one justice for every circuit, the extra appointment combined with the resignation of Justice Grier in 1870 enabled President Grant to appoint two orthodox Republicans to the bench. Within a year, the justices had overruled *Hepburn v. Griswold* (1870) and sustained Republican legislation passed during the Civil War that required creditors to accept paper money. As a federal bench augmented by Republican appointments became more sympathetic to Congress (and Congress became less enthusiastic about racial equality), Republicans in Congress again became more interested in expanding than in contracting judicial power. The Judiciary Act of 1875, passed by a lame-duck Republican Congress, was the first federal law since the repealed Federalist Judiciary Act of 1801 that gave federal courts the jurisdiction necessary to resolve virtually all federal questions.

Ex parte McCardle, 74 U.S. 506 (1868)[13]

The Union Army in 1867 arrested William McCardle, a newspaper editor in Vicksburg, Mississippi. McCardle was charged with inciting insurrection by writing inflammatory editorials about Reconstruction. While awaiting trial by a military tribunal, McCardle filed for a writ of habeas corpus under the terms of the Habeas Corpus Act of 1867. That statute empowered federal courts to issue the writ in "all cases where any person may be restrained of his or her liberty in violation of the constitution, or of any treaty or law of the United States." Congress intended the Habeas Corpus Act to extend federal court protection to former slaves and southern Unionists, but opponents of Reconstruction quickly recognized that the text also authorized federal courts to adjudicate cases challenging the constitutionality of martial law in the South. The district judge who upheld McCardle's detention expressed gratitude that the Supreme Court would review the case "where any error I may have committed may be corrected."

The Supreme Court placed McCardle on the docket at the same time that the Senate was considering whether to impeach President Johnson. Immediately before and during oral arguments, Republicans became concerned that the Supreme Court might declare the Reconstruction Acts unconstitutional. Acting quickly, Congress repealed that part of the Habeas Corpus Act of 1867 on which McCardle relied for jurisdiction and applied the repeal to pending cases (like McCardle's). In other words, in order to prevent the Supreme Court from striking down Reconstruction, Republicans in Congress took away the Court's authority to hear McCardle's case.

President Johnson vetoed the Repealer Act. His veto message argued:

> *The legislation proposed in the second section, it seems to me, is not in harmony with the spirit and intention of the Constitution. It cannot fail to affect most injuriously the just equipoise of our system of government; for it establishes a precedent which, if followed, may eventually sweep away every check on arbitrary and unconstitutional legislation. Thus far,*

13. *Ex parte McCardle* was actually handed down on April 12, 1869. Supreme Court practice during the mid-nineteenth century was to cite cases by the beginning date of the Supreme Court term—in this case, December 1868—rather than the date the decision was announced.

> *during the existence of the government, the Supreme Court of the United States has been viewed by the people as the true expounder of their Constitution, and in the most violent party conflicts its judgments and decrees have always been sought and deferred to with confidence and respect. . . . [This bill] will be justly held by a large portion of the people as an admission of the unconstitutionality of the act on which its judgment may be forbidden or forestalled, and may interfere with that willing acquiescence in its provisions which is necessary for the harmonious and efficient execution of any law.*[14]

Both the House and the Senate overrode the veto. The Supreme Court delayed making a decision on the merits in McCardle *until the Repealer Act became law and then unanimously denied jurisdiction. Chief Justice Salmon Chase's opinion ruled that the congressional power to determine the appellate jurisdiction of the Supreme Court included the power to strip the court of jurisdiction over cases pending before that tribunal. Some commentators suggest that the justices behaved strategically in* McCardle, *using the jurisdictional excuse to avoid having to rule on the merits of the case and inviting congressional reprisal. Others argue that Congress took advantage of existing rules governing the Court's appellate jurisdiction to prevent a direct confrontation between the two branches over the constitutionality of martial law in the South. Most commentators agree that the judicial majority would have declared crucial Reconstruction measures unconstitutional had Congress not repealed the offending provisions of the Habeas Corpus Act of 1867. Chief Justice Chase informally reported to the district judge in the case that "the Court would doubtless have held that [McCardle's] imprisonment for trial before a military commission was illegal" had the justices decided on the constitutional of Reconstruction.*[15] *But what is the significance of the last paragraph in the opinion?*

Consider the interplay of law and politics when reading McCardle. *To what extent do you believe existing law compelled the Supreme Court not to discuss the constitutionality of martial law in any of these cases? To what extent to you believe the justices made a purely strategic decision not to challenge Congress? To what extent do the decisions presented here integrate legal and political considerations?*

---

14. Andrew Johnson, "Veto Messages" in *Compilation of the Messages* (see note 1), 6:648.

15. Quoted in Charles Fairman, *Reconstruction and Reunion, 1864–88* (New York: Macmillan, 1971), 494.

CHIEF JUSTICE CHASE delivered the opinion of the Court.

The first question necessarily is that of jurisdiction; for, if the act of March, 1868, takes away the jurisdiction defined by the act of February, 1867, it is useless, if not improper, to enter into any discussion of other questions.

It is quite true, as was argued by the counsel for the petitioner, that the appellate jurisdiction of this court is not derived from acts of Congress. It is, strictly speaking, conferred by the Constitution. But it is conferred "with such exceptions and under such regulations as Congress shall make."

. . .

. . . In the case of *Durousseau v. The United States* (1810) . . . the court held, that while "the appellate powers of this court are not given by the [Judiciary Act of 1789], but are given by the Constitution," they are, nevertheless, "limited and regulated by that act, and by such other acts as have been passed on the subject." The court said, further, that the judicial act was an exercise of the power given by the Constitution to Congress "of making exceptions to the appellate jurisdiction of the Supreme Court." "They have described affirmatively," said the court, "its jurisdiction, and this affirmative description has been understood to imply a negation of the exercise of such appellate power as is not comprehended within it."

. . .

The exception to appellate jurisdiction in the case before us, however, is not an inference from the affirmation of other appellate jurisdiction. It is made in terms. The provision of the act of 1867, affirming the appellate jurisdiction of this court in cases of habeas corpus is expressly repealed. It is hardly possible to imagine a plainer instance of positive exception.

We are not at liberty to inquire into the motives of the legislature. We can only examine into its power under the Constitution; and the power to make exceptions to the appellate jurisdiction of this court is given by express words.

What, then, is the effect of the repealing act upon the case before us? We cannot doubt as to this. Without jurisdiction the court cannot proceed at all in any cause. Jurisdiction is power to declare the law, and when it ceases to exist, the only function remaining to the court is that of announcing the fact and dismissing the cause. And this is not less clear upon authority than upon principle.

...

... [T]he effect of repealing acts upon suits under acts repealed, has been determined by the adjudications of this court. In [two previous cases] it was held that no judgment could be rendered in a suit after the repeal of the act under which it was brought and prosecuted.

It is quite clear, therefore, that this court cannot proceed to pronounce judgment in this case, for it has no longer jurisdiction of the appeal; and judicial duty is not less fitly performed by declining ungranted jurisdiction than in exercising firmly that which the Constitution and the laws confer.

Counsel seem to have supposed, if effect be given to the repealing act in question, that the whole appellate power of the court, in cases of habeas corpus, is denied. But this is an error. The act of 1868 does not except from that jurisdiction any cases but appeals from Circuit Courts under the act of 1867. It does not affect the jurisdiction which was previously exercised.

The appeal of the petitioner in this case must be DISMISSED FOR WANT OF JURISDICTION.

IV. Powers of the National Government

MAJOR DEVELOPMENTS

- Congress enacts the first national military draft
- Congress finances the Civil War by printing paper money and making that currency legal tender for all public and private debts
- The post–Civil War Amendments provide Congress with increased, but vague, powers to protect civil rights
- Americans debate whether the Constitution provides the national government with adequate powers

The national government exercised unprecedented powers during the Civil War and Reconstruction. Congress during the Civil War passed legislation making paper money legal tender for existing debts, confiscating Confederate property, and conscripting northerners for the Union Army. These measures tested the limits of congressional power under Article I, Section 8 to make laws "necessary and proper" for fulfilling national responsibilities. Congress during Reconstruction passed legislation providing freedmen with land and educational opportunities; prohibiting racial discrimination in state contract, property, and criminal laws; and mandating severe sentences for private persons who denied or conspired with others to deny "the privileges and immunities of citizens of the United States." These measures tested the limits of the congressional power to "enforce" the Thirteenth, Fourteenth, and Fifteenth Amendments "by appropriate legislation." Republicans who supported these policies insisted that the Constitution empowered the national government to take all steps necessary to win the Civil War, abolish slavery, and secure racial justice. Democrats claimed that these policies violated a Constitution that granted very limited powers to the national government.

The Republican decision to finance the Civil War by printing paper money generated the most important controversy over Article I powers. The Legal Tender Act of 1862 authorized the government to issue up to $50 million in Treasury notes and made those notes legal tender for all private and public debts. This proposal was extremely controversial. Republican leaders in Congress insisted that making paper money legal tender was a necessary and proper means for exercising the constitutional power "to borrow money." Democrats claimed that no enumerated power authorized Congress to make paper money legal tender and that the Legal Tender Act unconstitutionally interfered with existing contractual obligations. Republicans suffered some defections in the Senate, but not enough to jeopardize passage of the bill.

Political and constitutional controversies over the Legal Tender Act intensified after the Civil War. The Supreme Court in *Hepburn v. Griswold* (1870) surprised many observers by declaring the Legal Tender Act unconstitutional. That decision was a judicial move to defend hard money and contract rights. President Grant made two nominations to the Supreme Court on the same day *Hepburn* was announced. William Strong filled the seat of Justice Robert Grier, a member of the *Hepburn* majority who had resigned. Joseph Bradley filled a new ninth seat on the Court, the seat that had been temporarily eliminated during the Johnson presidency. This gave the Republican Party six justices on a nine-member bench (Justice Field was a War Democrat). With a full complement of nine justices, the Court first ordered a new hearing on the legal tender laws and then, in the *Legal Tender Cases*, overruled *Hepburn v. Griswold*. Chief Justice Chase and the other three remaining members of the *Hepburn* majority publicly dissented from the order to rehear the case and the final decision. The narrow 5–4 decision in the *Legal Tender*

Cases nevertheless endured. Opponents raised constitutional objections to making paper money legal tender throughout the late nineteenth century, but this critique gradually disappeared. Few Americans at present are aware that many distinguished constitutional decision makers in the nineteenth century thought unconstitutional the notation on the contemporary dollar bill, "This Note is Legal Tender for all Debts, Public and Private."

The national government gained important new constitutional powers immediately after the Civil War. The last sections of the Thirteenth, Fourteenth, and Fifteenth Amendments declare, "Congress shall have power to enforce this article by appropriate legislation." Congress immediately exercised that authority in the following acts:

- The Freedmen's Bureau Act of 1866 provided former slaves and other refugees with land and educational opportunities.
- The Civil Rights Act of 1866 forbade states from engaging in race discrimination when passing or enforcing contract, property, or criminal laws.
- The Enforcement Act of 1870 prohibited private conspiracies to deny persons the right to vote and other privileges and immunities of U.S. citizenship.
- The Ku Klux Klan Act of 1871 provided both criminal and civil sanctions for private persons who deprived other persons of their constitutional rights.
- The Civil Rights Act of 1875 prohibited inns, public conveyances, and places of public amusement from engaging in racial discrimination.

Controversies over the congressional power to enforce the post–Civil War Amendments broke out immediately after these amendments were ratified. Republican political leaders insisted that each of the previously listed statutes was a legitimate exercise of national power under the post–Civil War Amendments. Democrats claimed that each bill went far beyond enforcing the rights protected by the Thirteenth, Fourteenth, and Fifteenth Amendments. Over time, more Republicans became sympathetic to narrower interpretations of the congressional power granted by the Thirteenth, Fourteenth, and Fifteenth Amendments. Senator Lyman Trumbull of Illinois was the leading sponsor of the Civil Rights Act of 1866 and a leading opponent of the Enforcement Act of 1870. Republican opposition doomed efforts to place a ban on school segregation in the Civil Rights Act of 1875.

The Supreme Court at the end of Reconstruction imposed limits on congressional power to enforce the post–Civil War Amendments. In *United States v. Reese* (1875), the Supreme Court quashed an indictment against several election judges in Kentucky who refused to allow an African American to cast a ballot. Chief Justice Morrison Waite's majority opinion declared unconstitutional the provision in the Enforcement Act of 1870 authorizing punishments for "any person who shall . . . hinder, delay, prevent, or obstruct, any citizen . . . from voting at any election." This was not "appropriate legislation" under the Fifteenth Amendment, he declared, because "it is only when the wrongful refusal at such an election is because of race, color, or previous condition of servitude that Congress can interfere and provide for its punishment."

Hepburn v. Griswold, 75 U.S. 603 (1870)

Mrs. Hepburn in 1860 made a promissory note to Henry Griswold to pay over eleven thousand "dollars." When the contract was made, the parties understood that "dollars" meant gold and silver coins. Days after the note came due, Congress passed the Legal Tender Act. That bill required that creditors take the paper money printed by the United States as payment for all debts. Griswold in 1864 filed suit to collect the unpaid debt. Hepburn immediately tendered U.S. notes in payment of the debt. Griswold refused to receive that paper currency. The Louisville trial court accepted the notes as satisfying the debt and closed the case. Griswold appealed that verdict to the Kentucky Court of Errors. Two months after Lee's surrender, the Kentucky court ruled the Legal Tender Act could not be constitutionally enforced for contracts made before that measure became law. Hepburn appealed that decision to the U.S. Supreme Court.

The Supreme Court, by a 5–3 majority, declared the Legal Tender Act unconstitutional. Chief Justice Salmon Chase's majority opinion ruled that requiring creditors to accept paper money for payment of debts was neither constitutionally necessary nor constitutionally proper. Chase was the only Republican in the majority in the Hepburn *decision. He was joined by all four of the Democrats on the Court, including the only War Democrat that Lincoln appointed to the Court, Stephen Field. Lincoln's other three appointees dissented. One of the justices in the majority, Robert Grier, was senile and may not have understood the significance of his vote.*

Illustration 6-2 Milk Tickets for Babies, In Place of Milk

Sources: David A. Wells, *Robinson Crusoe's Money,* with illustrations by Thomas Nast (New York: Harper & Brothers, 1876), 97.

The Hepburn *case revived* McCulloch v. Maryland *(1819). The Taney Court studiously ignored John Marshall's opinion in the bank case. Most Jacksonians regarded as a dead letter both the judicial decision that Congress had the power to incorporate a national bank and Chief Justice John Marshall's broad interpretation of the necessary and proper clause. The opinions in* Hepburn v. Griswold *include the first judicial discussions in over fifty years of the passages in the* McCulloch *opinion examining national power. How did Chief Justice Chase interpret* McCulloch? *Compare his interpretation to Justice Strong's interpretation in the* Legal Tender Cases. *Do they both capture aspects of John Marshall's legacy?*

CHIEF JUSTICE CHASE delivered the opinion of the Court.

. . .

We must inquire then whether [requiring that government notes be accepted as legal tender in payment of debts] can be done in the exercise of an implied power.

The rule for determining whether a legislative enactment can be supported as an exercise of an implied power was stated by Chief Justice Marshall, speaking for the whole court, in the case of *McCullough v. The State of Maryland*; and the statement then made has ever since been accepted as a correct exposition of the Constitution. His words were these: "Let the end be legitimate, let it be within the scope of the Constitution, and all means which are appropriate, which are plainly adapted to that end, which are not prohibited, but consistent with the letter and spirit of the Constitution, are constitutional."...

...

It is said that this is not a question for the court deciding a cause, but for Congress exercising the power. But the decisive answer to this is that the admission of a legislative power to determine finally what powers have the described relation as means to the execution of other powers plainly granted, and, then, to exercise absolutely and without liability to question, in cases involving private rights, the powers thus determined to have that relation, would completely change the nature of American government....

Undoubtedly among means appropriate, plainly adapted, really calculated, the legislature has unrestricted choice. But there can be no implied power to use means not within the description.

...

We are unable to persuade ourselves that an expedient of this sort is an appropriate and plainly adapted means for the execution of the power to declare and carry on war....

But there is another view, which seems to us decisive, to whatever express power the supposed implied power in question may be referred. In the rule stated by Chief Justice Marshall, the words appropriate, plainly adapted, really calculated, are qualified by the limitation that the means must be not prohibited, but consistent with the letter and spirit of the Constitution. Nothing so prohibited or inconsistent can be regarded as appropriate, or plainly adapted, or really calculated means to any end.

Let us inquire, then, first whether making bills of credit a legal tender, to the extent indicated, is consistent with the spirit of the Constitution.

Among the great cardinal principles of that instrument, no one is more conspicuous or more venerable than the establishment of justice. And what was intended by the establishment of justice in the minds of the people who ordained it is, happily, not a matter of disputation....

...

But we think it clear that those who framed and those who adopted the Constitution, intended that the spirit of this prohibition should pervade the entire body of legislation, and that the justice which the Constitution was ordained to establish was not thought by them to be compatible with legislation of an opposite tendency. In other words, we cannot doubt that a law not made in pursuance of an express power, which necessarily and in its direct operation impairs the obligation of contracts, is inconsistent with the spirit of the Constitution.

...

But there is another provision in the same amendment, which, in our judgment, cannot have its full and intended effect unless construed as a direct prohibition of the legislation which we have been considering. It is that which declares that "no person shall be deprived of life, liberty, or property, without due process of law."

...

We confess ourselves unable to perceive any solid distinction between such an act and an act compelling all citizens to accept, in satisfaction of all contracts for money, half or three-quarters or any other proportion less than the whole of the value actually due, according to their terms. It is difficult to conceive what act would take private property without process of law if such an act would not.

We are obliged to conclude that an act making mere promises to pay dollars a legal tender in payment of debts previously contracted, is not a means appropriate, plainly adapted, really calculated to carry into effect any express power vested in Congress; that such an act is inconsistent with the spirit of the Constitution; and that it is prohibited by the Constitution.

It is not surprising that amid the tumult of the late civil war, and under the influence of apprehensions for the safety of the Republic almost universal, different views, never before entertained by American statesmen or jurists, were adopted by many. The time was not favorable to considerate reflection upon the constitutional limits of legislative or executive authority. If power was assumed from patriotic motives, the assumption found ready justification in patriotic hearts. Many who doubted yielded their doubts; many who did not doubt were silent. Some who were strongly averse to making government notes a legal tender felt themselves constrained to acquiesce in the views of the advocates of the measure. Not a few who then insisted upon its necessity, or acquiesced in that view, have, since the return of peace, and under the influence of the calmer time, reconsidered their conclusions, and now concur in those which we have just announced. These conclusions seem to us to be fully sanctioned by the letter and spirit of the Constitution.

We are obliged, therefore, to hold that the defendant in error was not bound to receive from the plaintiffs the currency tendered to him in payment of their note, made before the passage of the act of February 25th, 1862.

JUSTICE MILLER (with SWAYNE and DAVIS), dissenting.

. . .

Legal Tender Cases, 79 U.S. 457 (1871)

Mrs. Lee in 1861 was a loyal citizen of Pennsylvania who owned sheep in Texas. The Confederate government in 1863 confiscated the sheep and sold them to Knox. After the Civil War, Lee sued Knox for the purchase price of the sheep. When the trial court ruled that Knox was liable, he offered to pay his debt in paper currency. Lee insisted that the debt be paid in gold and silver coin, which after the Civil War were worth far more than the face value of the greenbacks the United States had printed. The trial court rejected her claim and permitted Knox to pay his debt in paper notes. Both Knox and Lee appealed to the Supreme Court. Knox insisted he should not be held responsible for the Confederate decision to confiscate the sheep. Lee maintained that she should be paid either in gold and silver or in the actual dollars equal to the value of the sheep in gold and silver.

The Supreme Court in the Legal Tender Cases *overruled* Hepburn v. Griswold *(1870). Justice William Strong's opinion declared that persons gained no legally enforceable property rights when they purchased the goods of loyal citizens that were confiscated by the Confederacy and that the government could require creditors to take paper currency, even an inflated paper currency, as payment for debts. The* Legal Tender Cases *were decided by a narrow 5–4 majority. That majority was soon augmented by additional Republican appointees to the Supreme Court. Justice Field's retirement in 1897 ended for all practical purposes the constitutional attack on making paper money legal tender.*

JUSTICE STRONG delivered the opinion of the Court.

. . .

It would be difficult to overestimate the consequences which must follow our decision. They will affect the entire business of the country, and take hold of the possible continued existence of the government. If it be held by this court that Congress has no constitutional power, under any circumstances, or in any emergency, to make treasury notes a legal tender for the payment of all debts (a power confessedly possessed by every independent sovereignty other than the United States), the government is without those means of self-preservation which, all must admit, may, in certain contingencies, become indispensable, even if they were not when the acts of Congress now called in question were enacted. It is also clear that if we hold the acts invalid as applicable to debts incurred, or transactions which have taken place since their enactment, our decision must cause, throughout the country, great business derangement, widespread distress, and the rankest injustice. . . .

The consequences of which we have spoken, serious as they are, must be accepted, if there is a clear incompatibility between the Constitution and the legal tender acts. But we are unwilling to precipitate them upon the country unless such an incompatibility plainly appears. A decent respect for a coordinate branch of the government demands that the judiciary should presume, until the contrary is clearly shown, that there has been no transgression of power by Congress. . . . Such has always been the rule. . . .

Nor can it be questioned that, when investigating the nature and extent of the powers, conferred by the Constitution upon Congress, it is indispensable to keep in view the objects for which those powers were granted. . . . In no other way can the intent of the framers of the instrument be discovered. . . .

. . .

And here it is to be observed it is not indispensable to the existence of any power claimed for the Federal government that it can be found specified in the words of the Constitution, or clearly and directly traceable to some one of the specified powers. Its existence may be deduced fairly from more than one of the substantive powers expressly defined, or from them all combined. It is allowable to group together any number of them and infer from them all that the power claimed has been conferred. . . .

. . .

. . . [T]he whole history of the government and of congressional legislation has exhibited the use of a very wide discretion, even in times of peace and in the absence of any trying emergency, in the selection of the necessary and proper means to carry into effect the great objects for which the government was framed, and this discretion has generally been unquestioned, or, if questioned, sanctioned by this court. This is true not only when an attempt has been made to execute a single power specifically given, but equally true when the means adopted have been appropriate to the execution, not of a single authority, but of all the powers created by the Constitution. Under the power to establish post-offices and post-roads Congress has provided for carrying the mails, punishing theft of letters and mail robberies, and even for transporting the mails to foreign countries. Under the power to regulate commerce, provision has been made by law for the improvement of harbors, the establishment of observatories, the erection of lighthouses, break-waters, and buoys, the registry, enrolment, and construction of ships, and a code has been enacted for the government of seamen. . . .

. . .

It was . . . in *McCulloch v. Maryland* (1819) that the fullest consideration was given to this clause of the Constitution granting auxiliary powers, and a construction adopted that has ever since been accepted as determining its true meaning. . . . [T]his court then held that the sound construction of the Constitution must allow to the national legislature that discretion with respect to the means by which the powers it confers are to be carried into execution, which will enable that body to perform the high duties assigned to it in the manner most beneficial to the people. . . .

With these rules of constitutional construction before us, settled at an early period in the history of the government, hitherto universally accepted, and not even now doubted, we have a safe guide to a right decision of the questions before us. Before we can hold the legal tender acts unconstitutional, we must be convinced they were not appropriate means, or means conducive to the execution of any or all of the powers of Congress, or of the government, not appropriate in any degree (for we are not judges of the degree of appropriateness), or we must hold that they were prohibited. . . .

. . .

It may be conceded that Congress is not authorized to enact laws in furtherance even of a legitimate end, merely because they are useful, or because they make the government stronger. There must be some relation between the means and the end; some adaptedness or appropriateness of the laws to carry into execution the powers created by the Constitution. But when a statute has proved effective in the execution of powers confessedly existing, it is not too much to say that it must have had some appropriateness to the execution of those powers. . . .

. . . [W]e proceed to inquire whether it was forbidden by the letter or spirit of the Constitution. . . . To assert . . . that the clause enabling Congress to coin money and regulate its value tacitly implies a denial of all other power over the currency of the nation, is an attempt to introduce a new rule of construction against the solemn decisions of this court. So far from its containing a lurking prohibition, many have thought it was intended to confer upon Congress that general power over the currency which has always been an acknowledged attribute of sovereignty in every other civilized nation than our own, especially when considered in connection with the other clause which denies to the States the power to coin money, emit bills of credit, or make anything but gold and silver coin a tender in payment of debts. . . .

. . .

We come next to the argument much used, and, indeed, the main reliance of those who assert the unconstitutionality of the legal tender acts. It is that they are prohibited by the spirit of the Constitution because they indirectly impair the obligation of contracts. . . . The argument assumes two things,—first, that the acts do, in effect, impair the obligation of contracts, and second, that Congress is prohibited from taking any action which may indirectly have that effect. . . . We have been asked whether Congress can declare that a contract to deliver a quantity of grain may be satisfied by the tender of a less quantity. Undoubtedly not. But this is a false analogy. There is a wide distinction between a tender of quantities, or of specific articles, and a tender of legal values. Contracts for the delivery of specific articles belong exclusively to the domain of State legislation, while contracts for the payment of money are subject to the authority of Congress, at least so far as relates to the means of payment. They are engagements to pay with lawful money of the United

States, and Congress is empowered to regulate that money. It cannot, therefore, be maintained that the legal tender acts impaired the obligation of contracts.

. . .

Closely allied to the objection we have just been considering is the argument pressed upon us that the legal tender acts were prohibited by the spirit of the Fifth Amendment, which forbids taking private property for public use without just compensation or due process of law. That provision has always been understood as referring only to a direct appropriation, and not to consequential injuries resulting from the exercise of lawful power. It has never been supposed to have any bearing upon, or to inhibit laws that indirectly work harm and loss to individuals. A new tariff, an embargo, a draft, or a war may inevitably bring upon individuals great losses; may, indeed, render valuable property almost valueless. They may destroy the worth of contracts. . . .

. . .

But, without extending our remarks further, it will be seen that we hold the acts of Congress constitutional as applied to contracts made either before or after their passage. In so holding, we overrule so much of what was decided in *Hepburn v. Griswold*, as ruled the acts unwarranted by the Constitution so far as they apply to contracts made before their enactment. That case was decided by a divided court, and by a court having a less number of judges than the law then in existence provided this court shall have. These cases have been heard before a full court, and they have received our most careful consideration. The questions involved are constitutional questions of the most vital importance to the government and to the public at large. We have been in the habit of treating cases involving a consideration of constitutional power differently from those which concern merely private right. We are not accustomed to hear them in the absence of a full court, if it can be avoided. Even in cases involving only private rights, if convinced we had made a mistake, we would hear another argument and correct our error. And it is no unprecedented thing in courts of last resort, both in this country and in England, to overrule decisions previously made. We agree this should not be done inconsiderately, but in a case of such far-reaching consequences as the present, thoroughly convinced as we are that Congress has not transgressed its powers, we regard it as our duty so to decide and to affirm both these judgments.

. . .

JUSTICE BRADLEY, concurring.

. . .

The doctrine so long contended for, that the Federal Union was a mere compact of States, and that the States, if they chose, might annul or disregard the acts of the National legislature, or might secede from the Union at their pleasure, and that the General government had no power to coerce them into submission to the Constitution, should be regarded as definitely and forever overthrown. This has been finally effected by the National power, as it had often been before, by overwhelming argument.

. . .

Such being the character of the General government, it seems to be a self-evident proposition that it is invested with all those inherent and implied powers which, at the time of adopting the Constitution, were generally considered to belong to every government as such, and as being essential to the exercise of its functions. . . .

. . .

. . . [T]he historical fact [is] that when the Constitution was adopted, the employment of bills of credit was deemed a legitimate means of meeting the exigencies of a regularly constituted government, and that the affixing to them of the quality of a legal tender was regarded as entirely discretionary with the legislature. . . .

. . .

This power is entirely distinct from that of coining money and regulating the value thereof. It is not only embraced in the power to make all necessary auxiliary laws, but it is incidental to the power of borrowing money. It is often a necessary means of anticipating and realizing promptly the national resources, when, perhaps, promptness is necessary to the national existence. . . .

. . .

No one supposes that these government certificates are never to be paid—that the day of specie payments is never to return. And it matters not in what form they are issued. . . . But it is the prerogative of the legislative department to determine when the fit time for payment has come. It may be long delayed, perhaps many may think it too long after the exigency has passed. But the abuse of a power, if proven, is no argument against its existence. And the courts are not responsible therefore. Questions of political expediency belong to the legislative halls, not to the judicial forum. . . .

. . .

It is absolutely essential to independent national existence that government should have a firm hold on the two great sovereign instrumentalities of the sword and the purse, and the right to wield them without restriction on occasions of national peril. In certain emergencies government must have at its command, not only the personal services—the bodies and lives—of its citizens, but the lesser, though not less essential, power of absolute control over the resources of the country. . . .

. . .

But the creditor interest will lose some of its gold! Is gold the one thing needful? Is it worse for the creditor to lose a little by depreciation than everything by the bankruptcy of his debtor? Nay, is it worse than to lose everything by the subversion of the government? What is it that protects him in the accumulation and possession of his wealth? Is it not the government and its laws? And can he not consent to trust that government for a brief period until it shall have vindicated its right to exist? All property and all rights, even those of liberty and life, are held subject to the fundamental condition of being liable to be impaired by providential calamities and national vicissitudes. . . . There are times when the exigencies of the state rightly absorb all subordinate considerations of private interest, convenience, or feeling. . . .

. . .

I do not say that it is a war power, or that it is only to be called into exercise in time of war; for other public exigencies may arise in the history of a nation which may make it expedient and imperative to exercise it. But of the occasions when, and of the times how long, it shall be exercised and in force, it is for the legislative department of the government to judge. Feeling sensibly the judgments and wishes of the people, that department cannot long (if it is proper to suppose that within its sphere it ever can) misunderstand the business interests and just rights of the community.

. . .

Regarding the question of power as so important to the stability of the government, I cannot acquiesce in the decision of *Hepburn v. Griswold*. I cannot consent that the government should be deprived of one of its just powers by a decision made at the time, and under the circumstances, in which that decision was made. . . . Where the decision is recent, and is only made by a bare majority of the court, and during a time of public excitement on the subject, when the question has largely entered into the political discussions of the day, I consider it our right and duty to subject it to a further examination, if a majority of the court are dissatisfied with the former decision. . . .

CHIEF JUSTICE SALMON CHASE, dissenting

. . .

JUSTICE STEPHEN FIELD, dissenting

. . .

Senate Debate over the Civil Rights Act of 1866[16]

The Civil Rights Act of 1866 was designed to outlaw the Black Codes passed by southern legislatures in the wake of the Thirteenth Amendment and to guarantee civic equality to persons of color. The crucial provision of the measure required that persons of color enjoy the same rights and liberties "for the security of persons and property as is enjoyed by white citizens." This guarantee nullified laws enacted by southern legislatures immediately after the Civil War that limited African American employment and housing opportunities, restricted these individuals' rights to testify in courts, and provided special punishments when they were convicted of criminal offenses. Persons of color who claimed that their rights were violated could remove lawsuits from state to federal courts, where they were more likely to gain a sympathetic hearing. The Civil Rights Act of 1866 did not outlaw all forms of racial discrimination. Such radical Republicans as Charles Sumner failed to convince fellow partisans to include voting rights in the Civil Rights Act or pass additional legislation enfranchising free persons of color. Most Republicans agreed that the measure did not prohibit laws banning interracial marriages.

Republicans and Democrats engaged in a lengthy partisan dispute over whether the Civil Rights Act of 1866 was constitutional. President Johnson, when vetoing the measure on March 27, 1866, complained that the bill was "an absorption and assumption of power by the General Government which, if acquiesced in, must sap and destroy our federative system of limited powers, and break down the barriers which preserve the rights of the States." He continued:

> *Hitherto every subject embraced in the enumeration of rights contained in this bill has been considered as exclusively belonging to the States. They all relate*

16. Excerpt taken from *Congressional Globe*, 39th Cong., 1st Sess., 1866, 474–75, 684, 1783–84.

to the internal police and economy of the respective States. They are matters which in each State concern the domestic condition of its people, varying in each according to its own peculiar circumstances and the safety and well-being of its own citizens. I do not mean to say that upon all these subjects there are not federal restraints—as, for instance, in the State power of legislation over contracts. . . . If it be granted that Congress can repeal all State laws discriminating between whites and blacks in the subjects covered by this bill, why, it may be asked, may not Congress repeal, in the same way, all State laws discriminating between the two races on the subject of suffrage and office? . . .

. . .

. . . It cannot . . . be justly claimed that, with a view to the enforcement of this article of the Constitution [the Thirteenth Amendment], there is at present any necessity for the exercise of all the powers which this bill confers. Slavery has been abolished, and at present nowhere exists within the jurisdiction of the United States; nor has there been, nor is likely there will be, any attempt to revive it by the people or the States. If, however, any such attempt shall be made, it will then become the duty of the General Government to exercise any and all incidental powers necessary and proper to maintain inviolate this great constitutional law of freedom.[17]

Several weeks later, Senator Lyman Trumbull responded that the Civil Rights Act was well within the powers granted to Congress by the Thirteenth Amendment.

Whatever may have been the opinion of the President at one time as to "good faith requiring the security of the freedmen in their liberty and their property" it is now manifest from the character of his objections to this bill that he will approve no measure that will accomplish the object. That the second clause of the [Thirteenth] Amendment gives this power there can be no question. Some have contended that it gives the power even to confer the right of suffrage. I have not thought so, because I have never thought suffrage any more necessary to the liberty of a freedman than of a non-voting white, whether child or female. But his liberty under the Constitution he is entitled to, and whatever is necessary to secure it to him he is entitled to have, be it the ballot or the bayonet. If the bill now before us, and which goes no further than to secure civil rights to the freedman, cannot be passed, then the constitutional amendment proclaiming freedom to all the inhabitants of the land is a cheat and a delusion.[18]

A two-thirds majority in both the House of Representatives and the Senate almost immediately overrode Johnson's veto. This was the first veto override of an important piece of legislation in American history.

The Civil Rights Act of 1866 sought to protect the rights of free persons of color by intertwining those rights with the rights of white persons. Rather than declare that persons of color have certain substantive rights, the law declares that persons of color will enjoy the same rights as white persons. This was thought to guarantee a robust set of rights and liberties, because white voters could restrict the liberty of persons of color only by restricting their liberty to the same degree. What do you think of this strategy for using equal protection to protect substantive rights? Is this strategy likely to be an effective means for protecting the rights of persons who cannot vote? If you were in Congress in 1866, would you have reluctantly settled for "half a loaf," or would you have insisted that the Civil Rights Act include voting rights?

SENATOR LYMAN TRUMBULL (Republican, Illinois)

. . .

Mr. President, I regard the bill to which the attention of the Senate is now called as the most important measure that has been under its consideration since the adoption of the constitutional amendment abolishing slavery. That amendment declared that all persons in the United States should be free. This measure is intended to give effect to that declaration and secure to all persons within the United States practical freedom. There is very little importance in the general declaration of abstract truths and principles unless they can be carried into effect, unless the persons who are to be affected by them have some means of availing themselves of their benefits. . . . [O]f what avail will it now be that the Constitution of the United States has declared that slavery shall not exist, if in the late slaveholding States laws are to be enacted and enforced depriving persons of African descent of privileges which are essential to freemen?

17. Andrew Johnson, "Veto Messages" in *Compilation of the Messages* (see note 1), 6:405.

18. *Congressional Globe*, 39th Cong., 1st Sess., 1866, 1761.

. . .

. . . [T]he question will arise, has Congress authority to pass such a bill? Has Congress authority to give practical effect to the great declaration that slavery shall not exist in the United States? If it has not, then nothing has been accomplished by the adoption of the constitutional amendment. . . .

. . .

. . . [U]nder the constitutional amendment which we have now adopted, and which declares that slavery shall no longer exist, and which authorizes Congress by appropriate legislation to carry this provision into effect, I hold that we have a right to pass any law which, in our judgment, is deemed appropriate, and which will accomplish the end in view, secure freedom to all people in the United States. The various State laws to which I have referred—and there are many others—although they do not make a man an absolute slave, yet deprive him of the rights of a freeman; and it is perhaps difficult to draw the precise line, to say where freedom ceases and slavery begins, but a law that does not allow a colored person to go from one county to another is certainly a law in derogation of the rights of a freeman. A law that does not allow a colored person to hold property, does not allow him to teach, does not allow him to preach, is certainly a law in violation of the rights of a freeman, and being so may properly be declared void.

. . .

Senator CHARLES SUMNER (Republican, Massachusetts)

. . . Whatever legislation seems "appropriate" to "enforce" the abolition of Slavery, whatever means seem proper to this end, must be within the powers of Congress under the Constitutional Amendment. You cannot deny this principle without setting aside those most remarkable judgments which stand as landmarks of constitutional history. But who can doubt that the abolition of the whole Black Code, in all its oligarchical pretensions, civil and political, is "appropriate" to "enforce" the abolition of Slavery? Mark the language of the grant. Congress may "enforce" abolition, and nobody can question the "means" it thinks best to employ. Let it not hesitate to adopt the "means" that promise to be most effective. As the occasion is extraordinary, so the "means" employed must be extraordinary.

But the Senate has already by solemn vote affirmed this very jurisdiction. You have, Sir, decreed that blacks shall enjoy the same civil rights as whites,—in other words, that with regard to civil rights there shall be no oligarchy, aristocracy, caste, or monopoly, but that all shall be equal before the law, without distinction of color. And this great decree you have made, as "appropriate legislation" under the Constitutional Amendment, to "enforce" the abolition of Slavery. Surely you have not erred. Beyond all question, the protection of the colored race in civil rights is essential to complete the abolition of Slavery; but the protection of the colored race in political rights is not less essential, and the power is as ample in one case as in the other. In each you legislate for the maintenance of that Liberty so tardily accorded, and the legislation is just as "appropriate" in one case as in the other. Protection in civil rights by Act of Congress will be a great event. It will be great in itself. It will be greater still, because it establishes the power of Congress, without further amendment of the National Constitution, to protect every citizen in all his rights, including of course the elective franchise. . . .

. . .

Senator EDGAR COWAN (Republican, Pennsylvania)

. . . Where do we get the power to pass this bill? From what clause of the Constitution is it extracted? Where is it? Has anybody satisfied this Senator, or that one, or all of them, that there is such a power in the Constitution?

What is the fair construction of that amendment of the Constitution abolishing slavery? That amendment declares that "neither slavery nor involuntary servitude, except as a punishment for crime whereof the party shall have been duly convicted . . . shall exist within the United States or any place subject to its jurisdiction." What was the slavery mentioned there? What was the involuntary servitude mentioned there? Was it the service that was due from the minor to his parent? Was it the right the husband had to the services of his wife? Nobody can pretend that those things were within the purview of that amendment; nobody believes it. . . . The true meaning and intent of that amendment was simply to abolish negro slavery. That was the whole of it. What did it give to the negro? It abolished his slavery. Wherein did his slavery consist? It consisted in the restraint that another man had over his liberty, and the right that that other had to take the proceeds of his labor. This amendment deprived the master of that right, and conferred it upon the negro. What more did it do? Nothing, by the terms of it, and nobody can construe its terms to extend it beyond that. It gave to the negro that which is described in the elementary books as the right of personal liberty. What is that right of personal liberty? The right to go wherever one pleases without restraint or hindrance on the part of any other person.

That is followed by a subsequent clause, in which, it is stated that Congress shall have a right to enforce this provision by "appropriate legislation." What is the appropriate legislation? The appropriate legislation is that legislation which allows a personal liberty to the negro and prevents anybody from restraining him in that liberty. . . .

. . .

. . . I suppose it will not be pretended by any lawyer in the world that the subject-matter of that amendment extended to anybody but slaves. We have seen that it did not extend to minors, it did not extend to apprentices, it did not extend to married women. We know that it did not extend to anybody who before that time was free. Did anybody ever suppose that it had any operation whatever upon the *status* of the free negro, a negro who was born free or who had been emancipated ten years before it was passed? Certainly not. Nobody ever dreamed of such a thing. Its operation was wholly confined to the slave; it made the slave free; it did not affect anybody else except the master by depriving him of his slave.

Now what does this bill do? This bill, pretending to be based upon the amendment of the Constitution, whose subject-matter was slaves, and which cannot be extended beyond that, proposes to legislate for a very large number of persons who were not slaves, and who were not within its purview or its operation. I mean this bill purports to give power to Congress to legislate in regard to free negroes and mulattoes. To my mind that is as clear and conclusive an objection to it upon the score of constitutionality as ever was made to a bill in the world. However constitutional it might be with regard to the emancipated slave, clearly it is as unconstitutional to all other people not embraced within that amendment.

Civil Rights Act of 1866[19]

An Act to Protect All Persons in the United States in their Civil Rights, and Furnish the Means for the Vindication

Be it Enacted . . . That all persons born in the United States and not subject to any foreign power, excluding Indians, not taxed, are hereby declared to be citizens of the United States; and such citizens of every race and color, without regard to any previous condition of slavery or involuntary servitude, except as a punishment for crime whereof the party shall have been duly convicted, shall have the same right in every State and Territory in the United States to make and enforce contracts; to sue, be parties, and give evidence; to inherit, purchase, lease, sell, hold, and convey real and personal property; and to full and equal benefit of all laws and proceedings for the security of persons and property as is enjoyed by white citizens, and shall be subject to like punishment, pains, and penalties, and to none other, any law, statute, ordinance, regulation, or custom, to the contrary notwithstanding.

. . .

SEC. 3. That the district courts of the United States, within their respective districts, shall have, exclusively of the courts of the several States, cognizance of all crimes and offenses committed against the provisions of this act, and also, concurrently with the circuit courts of the United States, of all causes, civil and criminal, affecting persons who are denied or cannot enforce in the courts or judicial tribunals of the State or locality where they may be any of the rights secured to them by the first section of this act; and if any suit or prosecution, civil or criminal, has been or shall be commenced in any State court against any such person, for any cause whatsoever, or against any officer, civil or military, or other person, for any arrest or imprisonment, trespasses, or wrongs done or committed by virtue or under color of authority derived from this act . . . such defendant shall have the right to remove such cases for trial to the proper district or circuit court. . . .

V. Federalism

MAJOR DEVELOPMENTS

- Americans debate the constitutionality of secession
- Americans debate the constitutional status of those states that seceded from the Union
- The Supreme Court declares that the United States is an "indestructible Union, composed of indestructible States"

Both the Civil War and Reconstruction raised fundamental questions about the relationship between the states and the federal government. The central question

19. Excerpt taken from Civil Rights Act of 1866, 14 Stat. 27 (1866).

at the heart of the Civil War was whether secession was constitutional. The central question at the heart of Reconstruction was the extent to which the Civil War changed the relationship between the states and the federal government. While political actors made references to high political principles, they always kept in mind the perceived beneficiaries of increased national or state power. Southerners became more committed and northerners less committed to federalism when control of national institutions shifted from the slave to the free states.

Abraham Lincoln's election to the presidency in 1860 made the prospect of disunion immediate and real. The election of a Republican president dedicated to the anti-slavery cause was of immediate concern to southern slave states. More broadly, the election of 1860 indicated that the era of national coalitions committed to satisfying the demands of slaveholding interests was over. The price of union for slaveholders seemed too high if they were consigned to being a permanent minority. Secession was justified, South Carolinians insisted, because free states had violated basic constitutional commitments. Lincoln in response insisted that the Constitution contemplated a perpetual union.

The status of the states that passed secession ordinances in 1860 and 1861 created constitutional problems during the Civil War. The Confederate government contended that these states had formed an independent nation. The North rejected this theory. Lincoln justified the use of military force on the grounds that secession was unconstitutional and illegitimate. If southern secession ordinances were null and void and the southern states were still in the Union after 1861, however, then the constitutional basis on which the North waged a "war" against them was not clear. If the slave states were still members of the Union, were they entitled to representation in Congress?

President Andrew Johnson and the Reconstruction Congress bitterly contested basic questions about the constitutional status of former Confederate states after the Civil War. Johnson believed that the aim of the war was to restore as soon as possible the southern states as loyal and equal members of the United States. He and his supporters insisted that the southern states should be immediately represented in Congress and that local authorities should be trusted to administer the law in the former Confederate states. Proponents of congressional Reconstruction maintained that the southern states had forfeited crucial constitutional powers and privileges when they had attempted to secede. On this ground, the Republican majority voted to deny the southern states representation in Congress and placed them under military government.

The participants in these debates offered numerous theories about the constitutional status of the southern states. The competing theories all justified some federal intervention in the South, but they differed in their implications for the scope, pace, and administration of that intervention. Each had conceptual difficulties. The main theories were:

- Secession had no effect on the constitutional status of any state because secession was null and void.
- Secession suspended normal government operations, but only until the federal government reestablished loyal governments in the former Confederate states.
- States forfeited their political rights by attempting to secede, but not their territorial integrity.
- States that attempted to secede reverted to territorial status.
- The former Confederate states were conquered provinces with no constitutional status, rights, or powers.

The Supreme Court in *Texas v. White* (1869) adopted a version of the third option. Chief Justice Chase's majority opinion asserted that while state rights were "suspended" during the Civil War, "the Constitution, in all its provisions, looks to an indestructible Union, composed of indestructible States."

South Carolina Ordinance of Secession (1860)[20]

South Carolina seceded from the Union almost immediately after Abraham Lincoln won the 1860 presidential election. Secession ordinances were soon adopted in Florida, Mississippi, Georgia, Alabama, Louisiana, and Texas. Virginia, North Carolina, Arkansas, and Tennessee adopted secession ordinances after the military action at Fort Sumter. Substantial

20. Excerpt taken from *Declaration of the Immediate Causes Which Induce and Justify the Secession of South Carolina from the Federal Union and the Ordinance of Secession* (Charleston, SC: Evans & Cogswell, 1860).

secession sentiment existed in Maryland, Kentucky, and Missouri, but through a combination of political and military maneuvering, Unionist forces maintained control in those states. "I want God on my side," Lincoln declared before the Civil War, "but I must have Kentucky."[21]

That South Carolina was the first state to secede is not surprising. Politically and economically dominated by large plantation owners, South Carolina had the highest ratio of slaves to citizens of any state in the Union. South Carolina politicians and activists had long been the leading voices of dis-Unionist and pro-slavery sentiment. John C. Calhoun, Robert Barnwell Rhett, George McDuffie, James Henry Hammond, and other South Carolinians instigated many antebellum controversies between the North and the South.

The South Carolina Secession Ordinance relied on both appeals to natural law and appeals to constitutional right. The argument from natural law relied on the natural right of revolution articulated in the Declaration of Independence. The argument from the Constitution built on the Jeffersonian commitment to the compact theory of the federal government. South Carolinians who relied on compact theory emphasized the "secession" of the states in 1787 from the union created by the Articles of Confederation and the unenumerated, reserved powers of the states recognized in the Tenth Amendment.

Declaration of the Immediate Causes Which Induce and Justify the Secession of South Carolina from the Federal Union

. . .

In the year 1765, that portion of the British Empire embracing Great Britain, undertook to make laws for the government of that portion composed of the thirteen American Colonies. A struggle for the right of self-government ensued, which resulted, on the 4th of July, 1776, in a Declaration, by the Colonies, "that they are, and of right ought to be, FREE AND INDEPENDENT STATES; and that, as free and independent States, they have full power to levy war, conclude peace, contract alliances, establish commerce, and to do all other acts and things which independent States may of right do."

They further solemnly declared that whenever any "form of government becomes destructive of the ends for which it was established, it is the right of the people to alter or abolish it, and to institute a new government." . . .

In pursuance of this Declaration of Independence, each of the thirteen States proceeded to exercise its separate sovereignty. . . . For purposes of defense, they united their arms and their counsels; and, in 1778, they entered into a League known as the Articles of Confederation, whereby they agreed to entrust the administration of their external relations to a common agent, known as the Congress of the United States, expressly declaring, in the first Article "that each State retains its sovereignty, freedom and independence, and every power, jurisdiction and right which is not, by this Confederation, expressly delegated to the United States in Congress assembled."

. . .

The parties to whom th[e] Constitution was submitted, were the several sovereign States; they were to agree or disagree, and when nine of them agreed the compact was to take effect among those concurring; and the General Government, as the common agent, was then invested with their authority.

If only nine of the thirteen States had concurred, the other four would have remained as they then were—separate, sovereign States, independent of any of the provisions of the Constitution. . . .

By this Constitution, certain duties were imposed upon the several States, and the exercise of certain of their powers was restrained, which necessarily implied their continued existence as sovereign States. But to remove all doubt, an amendment was added, which declared that the powers not delegated to the United States by the Constitution, nor prohibited by it to the States, are reserved to the States, respectively, or to the people. . . .

. . .

We hold that the Government thus established is subject to the two great principles asserted in the Declaration of Independence; and we hold further, that the mode of its formation subjects it to a third fundamental principle, namely: the law of compact. We maintain that in every compact between two or more parties, the obligation is mutual; that the failure of one of the contracting parties to perform a material part of the agreement, entirely releases the obligation of the other; and that where no arbiter is provided, each party is remitted to his own judgment to determine the fact of failure, with all its consequences.

---

21. Eric Foner, *The Fiery Trial: Abraham Lincoln and American Slavery* (New York: W. W. Norton & Company, Inc., 2010), 169.

In the present case, that fact is established with certainty. We assert that fourteen of the States have deliberately refused, for years past, to fulfill their constitutional obligations, and we refer to their own Statutes for the proof.

The Constitution of the United States, in its fourth Article, provides as follows: "No person held to service or labor in one State, under the laws thereof, escaping into another, shall, in consequence of any law or regulation therein, be discharged from such service or labor, but shall be delivered up, on claim of the party to whom such service or labor may be due."

This stipulation was so material to the compact, that without it that compact would not have been made. . . .

. . .

. . . For many years these laws were executed. But an increasing hostility on the part of the non-slaveholding States to the institution of slavery, has led to a disregard of their obligations, and the laws of the General Government have ceased to effect the objects of the Constitution. . . . Thus the constituted compact has been deliberately broken and disregarded by the non-slaveholding States, and the consequence follows that South Carolina is released from her obligation.

. . .

For twenty-five years this agitation has been steadily increasing, until it has now secured to its aid the power of the common Government. Observing the forms of the Constitution, a sectional party has found within that Article establishing the Executive Department, the means of subverting the Constitution itself. A geographical line has been drawn across the Union, and all the States north of that line have united in the election of a man to the high office of President of the United States, whose opinions and purposes are hostile to slavery. He is to be entrusted with the administration of the common Government, because he has declared that that "Government cannot endure permanently half slave, half free," and that the public mind must rest in the belief that slavery is in the course of ultimate extinction.

. . .

On the 4th day of March next, this party will take possession of the Government. It has announced that the South shall be excluded from the common territory, that the judicial tribunals shall be made sectional, and that a war must be waged against slavery until it shall cease throughout the United States.

The guaranties of the Constitution will then no longer exist; the equal rights of the States will be lost. The slaveholding States will no longer have the power of self-government, or self-protection, and the Federal Government will have become their enemy.

. . .

We, therefore, the People of South Carolina, by our delegates in Convention assembled, appealing to the Supreme Judge of the world for the rectitude of our intentions, have solemnly declared that the Union heretofore existing between this State and the other States of North America, is dissolved, and that the State of South Carolina has resumed her position among the nations of the world, as a separate and independent State; with full power to levy war, conclude peace, contract alliances, establish commerce, and to do all other acts and things which independent States may of right do.

Jeremiah Black, Opinion on the Power of the President in Executing the Laws (1860)[22]

James Buchanan was the first president who confronted secession. Seven southern states withdrew from the Union after Lincoln's election but before his inauguration. Previous Jacksonian Democrats had been both pro-slavery and pro-Union. President Andrew Jackson urged Congress to prohibit persons from sending abolitionist materials in the mail but threatened to use military force when faced with South Carolina's nullification movement. Buchanan amply demonstrated his commitment to the pro-slavery cause during his administration, most notably by vigorously championing a disputed pro-slavery constitution in the Territory of Kansas. Buchanan's response to the secession crisis of 1860 was much more tepid. In sharp contrast to Jackson's behavior in the nullification crisis, Buchanan during the secession crisis emphasized that the president should not predetermine how events play out before Congress takes a stand on the issue. His main goal was to prevent a civil war from breaking out during the last weeks of his presidency. Buchanan explained in his final state of the union address,

> *The Executive has no authority to decide what shall be the relations between the Federal Government and South Carolina. He has been invested with no such discretion. He possesses no power to change the*

22. Excerpt taken from 9 Op. Atty. Gen. 516 (November 20, 1860).

relations heretofore existing between them, much less to acknowledge the independence of that State. This would be to invest a mere executive officer with the power of recognizing the dissolution of the Confederacy among our thirty-three sovereign States. It bears no resemblance to the recognition of a foreign de facto government—involving no such responsibility. Any attempt to do this would, on his part, be a naked act of usurpation. It is therefore my duty to submit to Congress the whole question in all its bearings.[23]

Several weeks before giving that address, Buchanan delivered a message to Congress expressing his official opinion of the president's constitutional role in the crisis. That message was actually written by Attorney General Jeremiah Black, who had emerged as a powerful anti-secessionist voice within Buchanan's cabinet. Buchanan and Black opposed secession. Nevertheless, both were convinced that the president could not launch an offensive war against the seceding states.

. . .

The existing laws put and keep the Federal Government strictly on the defensive. You can use force only to repel an assault on the public property, and aid the courts in the performance of their duty. . . .

If one of the States should declare her independence, your action cannot depend upon the rightfulness of the cause upon which such declaration is based. Whether the retirement of a State from the Union be the exercise of a right reserved in the Constitution, or a revolutionary movement, it is certain that you have not in either case the authority to recognize the independence or to absolve her from her federal obligations. Congress, or the other States in convention assembled, must take such measures as may be necessary and proper. . . .

Whether Congress has the constitutional right to make war against one or more States, and require the Executive of the Federal Government to carry it on by means of force to be drawn from the other States, is a question for Congress itself to consider. It must be admitted that no such power is expressly given, nor are there any words in the Constitution which imply it. . . . Our forefathers do not seem to have thought that war was calculated "to form a more perfect union, establish justice, insure domestic tranquility, provide for the common defense, promote the general welfare, and secure the blessings of liberty to ourselves and our posterity." There was undoubtedly a strong and universal conviction among the men who framed and ratified the Constitution, that military force would not only be useless, but pernicious, as a means of holding the States together.

If it be true that war cannot be declared, nor a system of general hostilities carried on by the Central Government against a State, then it seems to follow that an attempt to do so would be *ipso facto* an expulsion of such State from the Union. Being treated as an alien and an enemy, she would be compelled to act accordingly. . . .

The right of the General Government to preserve itself in its whole constitutional vigor, by repelling a direct and positive aggression upon its property or its officers, cannot be denied. But this is a totally different thing from an offensive war, to punish the people for the political misdeeds of their State Government, or to prevent a threatened violation of the Constitution, or to enforce an acknowledgement that the Government of the United States is supreme. The States are colleagues of one another, and if some of them shall conquer the rest and hold them as subjugated provinces, it would totally destroy the whole theory upon which they are now connected.

If this view of the subject be correct, as I think it is, then the Union must utterly perish at the moment when Congress shall arm one part of the people against another for any purpose beyond that of merely protecting the General Government in the exercise of its proper constitutional function.

Abraham Lincoln, First Inaugural Address (1861)[24]

President Abraham Lincoln agreed with Buchanan that secession was not constitutional, but they sharply disagreed on whether and how the president should respond in the absence of congressional instruction. Lincoln in his first inaugural address asserted that secession had no constitutional foundation. In sharp contrast to Buchanan, who believed that the Republican Party had unconstitutionally provoked secession,

23. James Buchanan, "Fourth Annual Message" in *Compilation of the Messages* (see note 1), 5:635.

24. Excerpt taken from Abraham Lincoln, "First Inaugural Address," in *Compilation of the Messages* (see note 1), 6:5–12.

Lincoln insisted that no legitimate excuse existed for secession. Lincoln maintained that the government had the power to meet secession with military force. Although for political reasons, Lincoln sought to provoke the South into firing the first shots at Fort Sumter, he had no constitutional qualms about treating secession as inaugurating a civil war.

Lincoln elaborated on the unconstitutionality of secession in his July 4, 1861, address to Congress. That speech declared,

> *Much is said about the "sovereignty" of the States; but the word, even, is not in the national Constitution; nor, as is believed, in any of the State constitutions. What is a "sovereignty," in the political sense of the term? Would it be far wrong to define it "A political community, without a political superior"? Tested by this, no one of our States, except Texas, ever was a sovereignty. And even Texas gave up the character on coming into the Union; by which act, she acknowledged the Constitution of the United States, and the laws and treaties of the United States made in pursuance of the Constitution, to be, for her, the supreme law of the land. The States have their status IN the Union, and they have no other legal status. If they break from this, they can only do so against law, and by revolution. The Union, and not themselves separately, procured their independence, and their liberty. By conquest, or purchase, the Union gave each of them, whatever of independence, and liberty, it has. The Union is older than any of the States; and, in fact, it created them as States. Originally, some dependent colonies made the Union; and, in turn, the Union threw off their old dependence, for them, and made them States, such as they are. Not one of them ever had a State constitution, independent of the Union. Of course, it is not forgotten that all the new States framed their constitutions, before they entered the Union; nevertheless, dependent upon, and preparatory to, coming into the Union.*[25]

Fellow-Citizens of the United States:

. . .

Apprehension seems to exist among the people of the Southern States that by the accession of a Republican Administration their property and their peace and personal security are to be endangered. There has never been any reasonable cause for such apprehension. Indeed, the most ample evidence to the contrary has all the while existed and been open to their inspection. It is found in nearly all the published speeches of him who now addresses you. I do but quote from one of those speeches when I declare that—"I have no purpose, directly or indirectly, to interfere with the institution of slavery in the States where it exists. I believe I have no lawful right to do so, and I have no inclination to do so."

. . .

I hold that in contemplation of universal law and of the Constitution the Union of these States is perpetual. Perpetuity is implied, if not expressed, in the fundamental law of all national governments. It is safe to assert that no government proper ever had a provision in its organic law for its own termination. Continue to execute all the express provisions of our National Constitution, and the Union will endure forever, it being impossible to destroy it except by some action not provided for in the instrument itself.

. . .

Descending from these general principles, we find the proposition that in legal contemplation the Union is perpetual confirmed by the history of the Union itself. The Union is much older than the Constitution. It was formed, in fact, by the Articles of Association in 1774. It was matured and continued by the Declaration of Independence in 1776. It was further matured, and the faith of all the then thirteen States expressly plighted and engaged that it should be perpetual, by the Articles of Confederation in 1778. And finally, in 1787, one of the declared objects for ordaining and establishing the Constitution was "to form a more perfect Union."

But if destruction of the Union by one or by a part only of the States be lawfully possible, the Union is less perfect than before the Constitution, having lost the vital element of perpetuity.

It follows from these views that no State upon its own mere motion can lawfully get out of the Union; that resolves and ordinances to that effect are legally void, and that acts of violence within any State or States against the authority of the United States are insurrectionary or revolutionary, according to circumstances.

. . .

All profess to be content in the Union if all constitutional rights can be maintained. Is it true, then, that any right plainly written in the Constitution has been denied? I think not. Happily, the human mind is so

25. Abraham Lincoln, "Special Session Message" in *Compilation of the Messages* (see note 1), 6:27.

constituted that no party can reach to the audacity of doing this. Think, if you can, of a single instance in which a plainly written provision of the Constitution has ever been denied. If by the mere force of numbers a majority should deprive a minority of any clearly written constitutional right, it might in a moral point of view justify revolution; certainly would if such right were a vital one. But such is not our case. All the vital rights of minorities and of individuals are so plainly assured to them by affirmations and negations, guaranties and prohibitions, in the Constitution that controversies never arise concerning them. But no organic law can ever be framed with a provision specifically applicable to every question which may occur in practical administration. No foresight can anticipate nor any document of reasonable length contain express provisions for all possible questions. Shall fugitives from labor be surrendered by national or by State authority? The Constitution does not expressly say. May Congress prohibit slavery in the Territories? The Constitution does not expressly say. Must Congress protect slavery in the Territories? The Constitution does not expressly say.

From questions of this class spring all our constitutional controversies, and we divide upon them into majorities and minorities. If the minority will not acquiesce, the majority must, or the Government must cease. There is no other alternative, for continuing the Government is acquiescence on one side or the other. If a minority in such case will secede rather than acquiesce, they make a precedent which in turn will divide and ruin them, for a minority of their own will secede from them whenever a majority refuses to be controlled by such minority. For instance, why may not any portion of a new confederacy a year or two hence arbitrarily secede again, precisely as portions of the present Union now claim to secede from it? All who cherish disunion sentiments are now being educated to the exact temper of doing this.

. . .

Plainly the central idea of secession is the essence of anarchy. A majority held in restraint by constitutional checks and limitations, and always changing easily with deliberate changes of popular opinions and sentiments, is the only true sovereign of a free people. Whoever rejects it does of necessity fly to anarchy or to despotism. Unanimity is impossible. The rule of a minority, as a permanent arrangement, is wholly inadmissible; so that, rejecting the majority principle, anarchy or despotism in some form is all that is left.

. . .

I am loath to close. We are not enemies, but friends. We must not be enemies. Though passion may have strained it must not break our bonds of affection. The mystic chords of memory, stretching from every battlefield and patriot grave to every living heart and hearthstone all over this broad land, will yet swell the chorus of the Union, when again touched, as surely they will be, by the better angels of our nature.

Texas v. White, 74 U.S. 700 (1869)

The federal government in 1851, as part of a settlement over state boundaries, issued to Texas $5 million in government bonds. The bonds paid 5 percent interest and could be redeemed for their face value after December 31, 1864. In an effort to raise revenue during the Civil War, the Texas legislature in 1862 directed that all the remaining bonds be sold. George White in 1865 purchased $210,000 worth of bonds from the Confederate state of Texas. After the war, the provisional and Reconstruction governments of Texas renounced the bond sale as part of an illegal conspiracy to overthrow the federal government. In February 1867 Texas asked the U.S. Supreme Court for an injunction prohibiting the United States from redeeming or paying interest on the Texas indemnity bonds sold by the Texas legislature during the Civil War. Texas argued that as secession was null and void, all acts performed by the Confederate state of Texas, including the bond sales, were also null and void.

Texas v. White *presented several difficulties for the Supreme Court. The first was jurisdictional. The parties disputed whether the Reconstruction government in Texas was a "state" that could initiate a lawsuit directly in the Supreme Court. Simply deciding whether the Supreme Court could hear the case seemingly required the justices to rule on the legal status and constitutionality of the Reconstruction governments. With congressional Reconstruction already well under way and the impeachment of Andrew Johnson still a fresh memory, the Court was ill positioned to regard the legitimacy of the Reconstruction governments as an open question. Nevertheless, how to explain their status under the Constitution was hardly clear.*

The merits of the case were no easier than the jurisdictional issue. Texas v. White *raised the classic legal problem of regime change: What was the status of actions previously taken by the* ancien regime *after the revolution? What was the legal status of the secessionist governments during the Civil War itself? Were any of their actions valid? If the old government had disposed of public property, whether for good, bad, or corrupt reasons, did the new government have to respect those arrangements?*

On the one hand, something was wrong with the idea that the U.S. government was obliged to pay those who had financed the southern "rebellion." On the other hand, there was long-term value in stabilizing property rights and not subjecting the legitimacy of a government to judicial scrutiny. If the bond sales of the "illegal" government were open to question, what about other routine acts of that government, such as granting marriage licenses or executing wills?

The Supreme Court in Texas v. White *granted the injunction prohibiting the federal government from paying bondholders who had purchased bonds from Texas during the Civil War. Chief Justice Salmon Chase's majority opinion declared that Texas was a state entitled to bring a lawsuit in federal courts and that all state legislative actions from 1861 to 1865 intended to facilitate secession and the war effort were void. All the justices were clear that in 1869 there was only one right answer to the question of the legitimacy of secession: the Union was "indissoluble" and "perpetual." Chase wrote that the United States was an "indestructible Union, composed of indestructible States." The court was otherwise divided 5–3, even on issues of style. Polk's appointee Justice Robert Grier, writing in dissent, kept the old habits. He referred to the "United States" as a plural noun. Lincoln's appointee, Chief Justice Salmon Chase, adopted the new style. His nation was no longer "these United States," but "the United States."*

CHIEF JUSTICE CHASE delivered the opinion of the Court.

. . .

In the Constitution the term state most frequently expresses the combined idea . . . of people, territory, and government. A state, in the ordinary sense of the Constitution, is a political community of free citizens, occupying a territory of defined boundaries, and organized under a government sanctioned and limited by a written constitution, and established by the consent of the governed. It is the union of such states, under a common constitution, which forms the distinct and greater political unit, which that Constitution designates as the United States, and makes of the people and states which compose it one people and one country.

. . .

It is needless to discuss, at length, the question whether the right of a State to withdraw from the Union for any cause, regarded by herself as sufficient, is consistent with the Constitution of the United States.

The Union of the States never was a purely artificial and arbitrary relation. It began among the Colonies, and grew out of common origin, mutual sympathies, kindred principles, similar interests, and geographical relations. It was confirmed and strengthened by the necessities of war, and received definite form, and character, and sanction from the Articles of Confederation. By these the Union was solemnly declared to "be perpetual." And when these Articles were found to be inadequate to the exigencies of the country, the Constitution was ordained "to form a more perfect Union." It is difficult to convey the idea of indissoluble unity more clearly than by these words. What can be indissoluble if a perpetual Union, made more perfect, is not?

But the perpetuity and indissolubility of the Union, by no means implies the loss of distinct and individual existence, or of the right of self-government by the States. Under the Articles of Confederation each State retained its sovereignty, freedom, and independence, and every power, jurisdiction, and right not expressly delegated to the United States. Under the Constitution, though the powers of the States were much restricted, still, all powers not delegated to the United States, nor prohibited to the States, are reserved to the States respectively, or to the people. . . . [I]t may be not unreasonably said that the preservation of the States, and the maintenance of their governments, are as much within the design and care of the Constitution as the preservation of the Union and the maintenance of the National government. The Constitution, in all its provisions, looks to an indestructible Union, composed of indestructible States.

When, therefore, Texas became one of the United States, she entered into an indissoluble relation. All the obligations of perpetual union, and all the guaranties of republican government in the Union, attached at once to the State. The act which consummated her admission into the Union was something more than a compact; it was the incorporation of a new member into the political body. And it was final. . . .

Considered therefore as transactions under the Constitution, the ordinance of secession, adopted by the convention and ratified by a majority of the citizens of Texas, and all the acts of her legislature intended to give effect to that ordinance, were absolutely null. . . . If this were otherwise, the State must have become foreign, and her citizens foreigners. The war must have ceased to be a war for the suppression of rebellion, and must have become a war for conquest and subjugation.

. . .

But in order to the exercise, by a State, of the right to sue in this court, there needs to be a State government, competent to represent the State in its relations with the National government, so far at least as the institution and prosecution of a suit is concerned.

And it is by no means a logical conclusion, from the premises which we have endeavored to establish, that the governmental relations of Texas to the Union remained unaltered. . . . All admit that, during this condition of civil war, the rights of the State as a member, and of her people as citizens of the Union, were suspended. The government and the citizens of the State, refusing to recognize their constitutional obligations, assumed the character of enemies, and incurred the consequences of rebellion.

These new relations imposed new duties upon the United States. The first was that of suppressing the rebellion. The next was that of re-establishing the broken relations of the State with the Union. The first of these duties having been performed, the next necessarily engaged the attention of the National government.

The authority for the performance of the first had been found in the power to suppress insurrection and carry on war; for the performance of the second, authority was derived from the obligation of the United States to guarantee to every State in the Union a republican form of government. The latter, indeed, in the case of a rebellion which involves the government of a State, and for the time excludes the National authority from its limits, seems to be a necessary complement to the former.

. . .

In the exercise of the power conferred by the guaranty clause, as in the exercise of every other constitutional power, a discretion in the choice of means is necessarily allowed. It is essential only that the means must be necessary and proper for carrying into execution the power conferred, through the restoration of the State to its constitutional relations, under a republican form of government, and that no acts be done, and no authority exerted, which is either prohibited or unsanctioned by the Constitution.

. . .

Whether the action then taken was, in all respects, warranted by the Constitution, it is not now necessary to determine. The power exercised by the President was supposed, doubtless, to be derived from his constitutional functions, as commander-in-chief; and, so long as the war continued, it cannot be denied that he might institute temporary government within insurgent districts, occupied by the National forces, or take measures, in any State, for the restoration of State government faithful to the Union, employing, however, in such efforts, only such means and agents as were authorized by constitutional laws.

But, the power to carry into effect the clause of guaranty is primarily a legislative power, and resides in Congress. . . .

. . .

The action of the President must, therefore, be considered as provisional, and, in that light, it seems to have been regarded by Congress. . . .

. . .

. . . The necessary conclusion is that the suit was instituted and is prosecuted by competent authority.

The question of jurisdiction being thus disposed of, we proceed to the consideration of the merits as presented by the pleadings and the evidence.

. . .

The legislature of Texas, at the time of the [sale of the bonds], constituted one of the departments of a State government, established in hostility to the Constitution of the United States. It cannot be regarded, therefore, in the courts of the United States, as a lawful legislature, or its acts as lawful acts. And, yet, it is an historical fact that the government of Texas, then in full control of the State, was its only actual government; and certainly if Texas had been a separate State, and not one of the United States, the new government, having displaced the regular authority, and having established itself in the customary seats of power, and in the exercise of the ordinary functions of administration, would have constituted, in the strictest sense of the words, a de facto government, and its acts, during the period of its existence as such, would be effectual, and, in almost all respects, valid. And, to some extent, this is true of the actual government of Texas, though unlawful and revolutionary, as to the United States.

It is not necessary to attempt any exact definitions, within which the acts of such a State government must be treated as valid, or invalid. It may be said, perhaps with sufficient accuracy, that acts necessary to peace and good order among citizens, such for example, as acts sanctioning and protecting marriage and the domestic relations, governing the course of descents, regulating the conveyance and transfer of property, real and personal, and providing remedies for injuries to person and estate, and other similar acts, which would be valid if emanating from a lawful government, must be regarded in general as valid when proceeding from an actual, though unlawful government; and that acts in furtherance or support of rebellion against the United States, or intended to defeat the just rights of citizens, and other acts of like nature, must, in general, be regarded as invalid and void.

. . .

[The agency that sold the bonds to White] was organized not for the defence of the State against a foreign invasion or for its protection against domestic violence, within the meaning of these words as used in the National Constitution, but for the purpose, under the name of defence, of levying war against the United States. This purpose was undoubtedly unlawful, for the acts which it contemplated are, within the express definition of the Constitution, treasonable.

. . .

It follows that the title of the State was not divested by the act of the insurgent government in entering into this contract.

. . .

On the whole case, therefore, our conclusion is that the State of Texas is entitled to the relief sought by her bill, and a decree must be made accordingly.

JUSTICE GRIER, dissenting.

. . .

The original jurisdiction of this court can be invoked only by one of the United States. The Territories have no such right conferred on them by the Constitution, nor have the Indian tribes who are under the protection of the military authorities of the government.

Is Texas one of these United States? Or was she such at the time this bill was filed, or since?

This is to be decided as a political fact, not as a legal fiction. This court is bound to know and notice the public history of the nation.

If I regard the truth of history for the last eight years, I cannot discover the State of Texas as one of these United States. . . .

. . .

Is Texas a State, now represented by members chosen by the people of that State and received on the floor of Congress? Has she two senators to represent her as a State in the Senate of the United States? Has her voice been heard in the late election of President? Is she not now held and governed as a conquered province by military force? The act of Congress of March 2d, 1867, declares Texas to be a "rebel State," and provides for its government until a legal and republican State government could be legally established. It constituted Louisiana and Texas the fifth military district, and made it subject, not to the civil authority, but to the "military authorities of the United States."

It is true that no organized rebellion now exists there, and the courts of the United States now exercise jurisdiction over the people of that province. But this is no test of the State's being in the Union; Dakota is no State, and yet the courts of the United States administer justice there as they do in Texas. The Indian tribes, who are governed by military force, cannot claim to be States of the Union. Wherein does the condition of Texas differ from theirs?

. . . I do not consider myself bound to express any opinion judicially as to the constitutional right of Texas to exercise the rights and privileges of a State of this Union, or the power of Congress to govern her as a conquered province, to subject her to military domination, and keep her in pupilage. I can only submit to the fact as decided by the political position of the government; and I am not disposed to join in any essay to prove Texas to be a State of the Union, when Congress have decided that she is not. It is a question of fact, I repeat, and of fact only. Politically, Texas is not a State in this Union. Whether rightfully out of it or not is a question not before the court.

. . .

. . . The contest now is between the State of Texas and her own citizens. She seeks to annul a contract with the respondents, based on the allegation that there was no authority in Texas competent to enter into an agreement during the rebellion. . . . She now sets up the plea of insanity, and asks the court to treat all her acts made during the disease as void.

. . .

. . . She cannot, like the chameleon, assume the color of the object to which she adheres, and ask this court to involve itself in the contradictory positions, that she is a State in the Union and was never out of it, and yet not a State at all for four years, during which she acted and claims to be "an organized political body," exercising all the powers and functions of an independent sovereign State. . . .

. . .

JUSTICE SWAYNE, with whom JUSTICE MILLER joins, dissenting.

I concur with my brother Grier as to the incapacity of the State of Texas, in her present condition, to maintain an original suit in this court. The question, in my judgment, is one in relation to which this court is bound by the action of the legislative department of the government.

Upon the merits of the case, I agree with the majority of my brethren.

. . .

VI. Separation of Powers

MAJOR DEVELOPMENTS

- President Lincoln unilaterally orders a blockade of southern ports, suspends habeas corpus, imposes martial law, and issues the Emancipation Proclamation
- Congress ratifies the blockade and empowers the president to suspend habeas corpus but limits presidential power to impose martial law
- The Supreme Court sustains President Lincoln's decision to order a blockade but declares unconstitutional his decision to impose martial law in places where federal courts are open
- The Senate fails by one vote to impeach President Johnson after Johnson violates the Tenure of Office Act by unilaterally removing a cabinet official from office

As president, Lincoln frequently acted unilaterally. He insisted that as commander in chief he had power to raise troops, blockade southern ports, declare martial law, suspend habeas corpus, and issue the Emancipation Proclamation. Sometimes he maintained that presidential powers were necessary because Congress was not in session. Other times, as was the case with the Emancipation Proclamation, Lincoln declared that his actions did not require subsequent legislative ratification. While most Democrats and some Republicans carped at Lincoln's tendency to act unilaterally, legislative majorities during the Civil War usually either supported or did not aggressively challenge Lincoln's actions.

President Lincoln in his first eighteen months in office repeatedly insisted that the Civil War was being fought solely to preserve national union and not to emancipate slaves. Nevertheless, by 1862, Lincoln was planning on issuing a presidential proclamation emancipating slaves. He refrained from making his intentions public until after the Union Army at the Battle of Antietam successfully prevented a Confederate invasion of the North.

On September 22, 1862, Lincoln declared that "all persons held as slaves within any State . . . in rebellion against the United States shall be . . . forever free" as of January 1, 1863. The Emancipation Proclamation redefined the northern war effort as directed at securing freedom as well as maintaining union. The proclamation had an important foreign policy aim. By converting a war for union into a war for human freedom, Lincoln put public pressure on European powers not to recognize or aid the Confederacy. Former justice Benjamin Curtis and many Democrats denounced the Emancipation Proclamation, but Republican majorities in Congress, if anything, sought to prod Lincoln into freeing more slaves.

Separation of powers questions intensified during Reconstruction. The national legislature and national executive from 1865 to 1868 bitterly disputed the constitutionality of military Reconstruction and federal legislation protecting persons of color. Johnson was a Jacksonian Democrat from Tennessee who, while a firm Union supporter during the Civil War, believed that Reconstruction should be largely limited to the abolition of slavery. The Republicans who controlled Congress insisted that persons of color be treated as political equals. While much of the struggle between the president and Congress was over national powers, separation of powers issues arose when Johnson refused to obey a federal law prohibiting the president from removing cabinet officials without congressional approval. Johnson was impeached by the House of Representatives. The Senate failed to remove him from office by one vote.

Abraham Lincoln, Emancipation Proclamation (1862)[26]

The Emancipation Proclamation freed only those slaves in areas not under Union military control on January 1, 1863. A broader emancipation act might have caused political and

26. Excerpt taken from Abraham Lincoln, "Emancipation Proclamation," in *Compilation of the Messages* (see note 1), 6:157–59.

legal problems. Politically, the act would have created problems in the border states of Maryland, Delaware, Missouri, and Kentucky, where slavery remained legal until the passage of the Thirteenth Amendment. Moreover, Lincoln did not believe a general emancipation order was constitutional. Lincoln and most Republicans believed that Congress had no power to emancipate slaves in existing states. This limit on congressional power explains why Lincoln turned to his Article II power as commander in chief to justify depriving the Confederacy of a vital labor force. This presidential power extended only over the seceding states. Slaves in such states as Maryland and Kentucky were not contributing to the Confederate war effort. Hence, Lincoln could not have issued an order as commander in chief freeing all slaves in those states.

The Emancipation Proclamation enjoyed a mixed reception in the North. African Americans were overjoyed. Black abolitionists in Boston spontaneously began singing "Blow Ye the Trumpet Blow" when the proclamation was promulgated.[27] *Lincoln's critics were less exuberant. Former Supreme Court justice Benjamin Curtis spoke of "military despotism." Many Democrats complained that uncompensated emancipation deprived loyal southerners of their property without due process of law.*

The Emancipation Proclamation is presently one of the most celebrated documents in American constitutional history. Consider when reading the following materials the reason for the celebration. Should we celebrate Lincoln's constitutional reasoning? Should we care whether an order freeing slaves is constitutional?

Whereas, on the twenty-second day of September, in the year of our Lord one thousand eight hundred and sixty-two, a proclamation was issued by the President of the United States, containing, among other things, the following, to wit:

> "That on the first day of January, in the year of our Lord one thousand eight hundred and sixty-three, all persons held as slaves within any State or designated part of a State, the people whereof shall then be in rebellion against the United States, shall be then, thenceforward, and forever free; and the Executive Government of the United States, including the military and naval authority thereof, will recognize and maintain the freedom of such persons, and will do no act or acts to repress such persons, or any of them, in any efforts they may make for their actual freedom.
>
> "That the Executive will, on the first day of January aforesaid, by proclamation, designate the States and parts of States, if any, in which the people thereof, respectively, shall then be in rebellion against the United States. . . . "

Now, therefore I, Abraham Lincoln, President of the United States, by virtue of the power in me vested as Commander-in-Chief, of the Army and Navy of the United States in time of actual armed rebellion against the authority and government of the United States, and as a fit and necessary war measure for suppressing said rebellion, do . . . designate as the States and parts of States wherein the people thereof respectively, are this day in rebellion against the United States, the following [at this point Lincoln listed all areas not under Union control]. And by virtue of the power, and for the purpose aforesaid, I do order and declare that all persons held as slaves within said designated States, and parts of States, are, and hence forward shall be free; and that the Executive government of the United States, including the military and naval authorities thereof, will recognize and maintain the freedom of said persons.

. . .

And upon this act, sincerely believed to be an act of justice, warranted by the Constitution, upon military necessity, I invoke the considerate judgment of mankind, and the gracious favor of Almighty God.

Benjamin Curtis, Executive Power (1862)[28]

Benjamin Curtis was a leading northern critic of the Emancipation Proclamation. When on the Supreme Court, Curtis wrote a powerful dissent in Dred Scott *that temporarily made him a hero to the anti-slavery movement. Curtis resigned from the Court the next year to return to private legal practice. During the Civil War, the former Whig became a vocal opponent of expanded presidential power. Curtis targeted the Emancipation Proclamation as one of Lincoln's worse abuses of power. He paired that proclamation with Lincoln's proclamations suspending habeas corpus and setting up trials by military commissions in the*

27. See Ronald Garet, "'Proclaim Liberty,'" *Southern California Law Review* 74 (2000): 158.

28. Excerpt taken from Benjamin Curtis, *Executive Power* (Boston: Little, Brown, 1862), 14–17, 19, 21, 24–29.

North. These proclamations, Curtis believed, could not be constitutionally justified by the president's power as commander in chief.

. . .

This [emancipation] proclamation . . . proposes to repeal and annul valid State laws which regulate the domestic relations of their people.

. . . [T]his executive decree holds out this proposed repeal of State laws as a threatened penalty for the continuance of a governing majority of the people of each State, or part of a State, in rebellion against the United States. So that the President hereby assumes to himself the power to denounce it as a punishment against the entire people of a State, that the valid laws of that State which regulate the domestic condition of its inhabitants shall become null and void, at a certain future date, by reason of the criminal conduct of a governing majority of its people.

This penalty, however . . . is not to be inflicted on those persons who have been guilty of treason. The freedom of their slaves was already provided for by the act of Congress, recited in a subsequent part of the Proclamation. It is upon the slaves of loyal persons, or of those who, from their tender years, or other disability, cannot be either disloyal or otherwise, that the proclamation is to operate, if at all; and it is to operate to set them free, in spite of the valid laws of their States. . . .

. . .

The only supposed source or measure of these vast powers appears to have been designated by the President, in his reply to the address of the Chicago clergymen, in the following words: "Understand, I raise no objection against it on legal or constitutional grounds; for, as commander-in-chief of the army and navy, in time of war, I suppose I have a right to take any measure which may best subdue the enemy."

. . . [I]f the President of the United States has an implied constitutional right, as commander-in-chief of the army and navy in time of war, to disregard any one positive prohibition of the Constitution, or to exercise any one power not delegated to the United States by the Constitution, because, in his judgment, he may thereby "best subdue the enemy," he has the same right, for the same reason, to disregard each and every provision of the Constitution, to exercise all power needful, in his opinion, to enable him "best to subdue the enemy."

. . .

The necessary result of this interpretation of the Constitution is that, in time of war, the President has any and all power which he may deem it necessary to exercise, to subdue the enemy; and that every private and personal right of individual security against mere executive control, and every right reserved to the States or the people, rests merely upon executive discretion.

. . .

He is general-in-chief; but can a general-in-chief disobey any law of his own country? When he can, he superadds to his rights as commander the powers of a usurper; and that is military despotism. . . . And that, under the Constitution and laws of the United States, no more than under the government of Great Britain, or under any free or any settled government, the mere authority to command an army is not an authority to disobey the laws of the country.

. . . [A]ll the powers of the President are executive merely. He cannot make a law. He cannot repeal one. He can only execute of the laws. He can neither make nor suspend nor alter them. . . .

. . .

In time of war, a military commander, whether he be the commander-in-chief or one of his subordinates, must possess and exercise powers both over the persons and the property of citizens which do not exist in time of peace. But he possesses and exercises such powers, not in spite of the Constitution and laws of the United States, or in derogation from their authority, but in virtue thereof and in strict subordination thereto. The general who moves his army over private property in the course of his operations in the field, or who impresses into the public service means of transportation or subsistence, to enable him to act against the enemy, or who seizes persons within his lines as spies, or destroys supplies in immediate danger of falling into the hands of the enemy, uses authority unknown to the Constitution and laws of the United States in time of peace, but not unknown to that Constitution and those laws in time of war. The power to declare war includes the power to use the customary and necessary means effectually to carry it on. . . . And, in time of war without any special legislation, not the commander-in-chief only, but every commander of an expedition or of a military post is lawfully empowered by the Constitution and laws of the United States to do whatever is necessary, and is sanctioned by the laws of war to accomplish the lawful objects of his command. But it is obvious that this implied authority must find early limits somewhere. If it were admitted that a commanding general in the field might do whatever in his discretion might be necessary to subdue the enemy, he could levy contributions to pay his soldiers; he could force conscripts in to his service; he could drive out of the entire country all persons not desirous to aid him: in short, he would be the absolute master of the country for the time being.

No one has ever supposed—no one will now undertake to maintain—that the commander-in-chief, in time of war, has any such lawful authority as this.

What, then, is his authority over the persons and property of citizens? I answer, that . . . over all persons and property within the sphere of his actual operations in the field, he may lawfully exercise such restraint and control as the successful prosecution of his particular military enterprise may, in his honest judgment, absolutely require. . . . And there his lawful authority ends.

But when the military commander controls the persons or property of citizens who are beyond the sphere of his actual operation in the field, when he makes laws to govern their conduct, he becomes a legislator. . . .

It is manifest that, in proclaiming these edicts, the President is not acting under the authority of military law: first, because military law extends only over the persons actually enlisted in the military service; and, second, because these persons are governed by laws enacted by the legislative power. It is equally manifest that he is not acting under that implied authority which grows out of particular actual military operations; for these executive decrees do not spring from the special emergencies of any particular military operations, and are not limited to any field in which any such operations are carried on.

. . .

These conclusions concerning the powers of the President cannot be shaken by the assertion that "rebels have no rights."

It is not true of those States; for the Government of the United States has never admitted, and cannot admit, that as States, they are in rebellion. . . .

Nor is the assertion that "rebels have no rights" applicable to the people of those States. . . . When many millions of people are involved in civil war, humanity, and that public law which in modern times is humane, forbid their treatment as outlaws. And if public law and the Constitution and laws of the United States are now their rules of duty towards us, on what ground shall we deny that public law and the Constitution, and the laws made under it, are also our rules of duty towards them?

But, if it were conceded that "rebels have no rights," there would still be matter demanding the gravest consideration. For the inquiry which I have invited is not what are their rights, but what are our rights.

Whatever may be thought of the wisdom of the proclamation of the President, concerning the emancipation of slaves, no one can doubt its practical importance, if it is to take effect. To set free about four millions of slaves, at an early fixed day, with absolutely no preparation for their future, and with no preparation for our future, in their relations with us, and to do this by force, must be admitted to be a matter of vast concern, not only to them and to their masters, but to the whole continent on which they must live. There may be great diversities of opinion concerning the effects of such an act. But that its effects must be of stupendous importance, extending not only into the border loyal States, but into all the States, North as well as South. . . . It is among the rights of all of us that the powers of each State to govern its own internal affairs should not be trespassed on by any department of the Federal power; and it is a right essential to the maintenance of our system of government. It is among the rights of all of us that the executive power should be kept within its prescribed constitutional limits, and should not legislate, but its decrees, upon subjects of transcendent importance to the whole people.

A leading and influential newspaper, while expressing entire devotion to the President, and approbation of his proclamation of emancipation, says: "The Democrats talk about 'unconstitutional acts.' Nobody pretends that this act is constitutional, and nobody cares whether it is or not."

Among all the causes of alarm which now distress the public mind, there are few more terrible to reflecting men, than the tendency to lawlessness which is manifesting itself in so many directions. No stronger evidence of this could be afforded than the open declaration of a respectable and widely circulated journal, that "nobody cares" whether a great public act of the President of the United States is in conformity with or is subversive of the supreme law of the land. . . .

. . .

Prize Cases, 67 U.S. 635 (1863)

President Lincoln responded to the attack on Fort Sumter by ordering a blockade of southern ports and calling for military volunteers. The blockade was particularly crucial to Union military success. The states that seceded had little industrial capacity and were dependent on foreign trade for the supplies necessary to fight a war. Confederate leaders were convinced that European demand for cotton would eventually lead to European support for and recognition of southern independence. Thus, the blockade was both a military and a political necessity. If successful, the Union blockade would isolate the South economically and diplomatically, helping to starve the Confederacy into submission.

On July 10, 1861, the Quaker City *captured the* Amy Warwick. *The* Quaker City *was a Union ship enforcing the blockade against the South. The* Amy Warwick *was owned by several merchants who lived in Richmond, Virginia. The captain and crew of the* Quaker City *claimed the cargo of the* Amy Warwick. *This was consistent with the traditional right of a captain and crew to claim as a prize any ship they captured attempting to run a lawful blockade. The owners of the* Amy Warwick *insisted the blockade was unlawful. They pointed out that Lincoln initially acted without congressional approval, ordering the blockade before Congress was in session. Although Congress ratified the blockade in July, the owners questioned whether that ratification could be retroactively applied to ships captured before the ratifying legislation was passed. Lincoln and the Republican Congress insisted that the national government could blockade the South because blockades were legitimate under international law. Opponents of the blockade rejected assertions that the Constitution incorporated international law. They also contested claims that international law authorized blockades during a civil war.*

The judicial majority in the Prize Cases affirmed both presidential authority and national power. Justice Robert Grier ruled that the president had the power under both the Constitution and international law to order a blockade in response to an insurrection, although his majority opinion did not make clear what the constitutional consequences would be had Congress not affirmed presidential policy. The newly constituted nine-member Court was closely divided, voting 5–4 on the case. Judicial appointments proved decisive. The surviving members of the Taney Court voted 4–2 against the constitutionality of the blockade. The three Lincoln appointees supported the blockade.

JUSTICE GRIER delivered the opinion of the Court.

. . .

Had the President a right to institute a blockade of ports in possession of persons in armed rebellion against the Government, on the principles of international law, as known and acknowledged among civilized States?

. . .

By the Constitution, Congress alone has the power to declare a national or foreign war. It cannot declare war against a State, or any number of States, by virtue of any clause in the Constitution. The Constitution confers on the President the whole Executive power. He is bound to take care that the laws be faithfully executed. He is Commander-in-chief. . . . He has no power to initiate or declare a war either against a foreign nation or a domestic State. But by the Acts of Congress of February 28th, 1795, and 3d of March, 1807, he is authorized to call out the militia and use the military and naval forces of the United States in case of invasion by foreign nations, and to suppress insurrection against the government of a State or of the United States.

If a war be made by invasion of a foreign nation, the President is not only authorized but bound to resist force by force. He does not initiate the war, but is bound to accept the challenge without waiting for any special legislative authority. And whether the hostile party be a foreign invader, or States organized in rebellion, it is none the less a war, although the declaration of it be "unilateral." . . .

. . .

It is not the less a civil war, with belligerent parties in hostile array, because it may be called an "insurrection" by one side, and the insurgents be considered as rebels or traitors. It is not necessary that the independence of the revolted province or State be acknowledged in order to constitute it a party belligerent in a war according to the law of nations. Foreign nations acknowledge it as war by a declaration of neutrality. The condition of neutrality cannot exist unless there be two belligerent parties. . . .

. . .

Whether the President in fulfilling his duties, as Commander-in-chief, in suppressing an insurrection, has met with such armed hostile resistance, and a civil war of such alarming proportions as will compel him to accord to them the character of belligerents, is a question to be decided by him, and this Court must be

Table 6-3 Selection of U.S. Supreme Court Cases Reviewing Presidential Powers as Commander in Chief

Case	Vote	Outcome	Decision
Brown v. United States, 12 U.S. 110 (1814)	5–2	Struck down	President has no independent authority to seize alien enemies or their property within the United States
Cross, Hobson & Co. v. Harrison, 57 U.S. 164 (1854)	9–0	Upheld	President has independent authority to form a civil government and collect taxes in a conquered territory
Prize Cases, 67 U.S. 635 (1863)	5–4	Upheld	President "bound to accept the challenge" of a de facto war and exercise war powers on his own authority
Ex parte Milligan, 71 U.S. 2 (1866)	9–0	Struck down	President cannot declare martial law where civilian courts are operating
The Grapeshot, 76 U.S. 129 (1869)	8–0	Upheld	President has independent authority to establish civil courts in a conquered territory
Totten v. United States, 92 U.S. 105 (1875)	9–0	Upheld	President has independent authority to employ covert operatives
Swaim v. United States, 165 U.S. 553 (1897)	9–0	Upheld	Statutes supplement president's own power to convene a court martial
Dooley v. United States, 182 U.S. 222 (1901)	5–4	Struck down	Power of president to set tariff rates in conquered territory ends with ratification of peace treaty
Santiago v. Nogueras, 214 U.S. 260 (1909)	9–0	Upheld	Power of president to maintain civilian courts in conquered territory continues after ratification of peace treaty
Ex parte Quirin, 317 U.S. 1 (1942)	9–0	Upheld	President has power to try war saboteurs by military commission
Youngstown Sheet & Tube Co. v. Sawyer, 343 U.S. 579 (1952)	6–3	Struck down	President does not have power to seize industrial plants to support war effort
Orloff v. Willoughby, 345 U.S. 83 (1953)	6–3	Upheld	President has discretion over commissioning military officers
United States ex rel. Toth v. Quarles, 350 U.S. 11 (1955)	6–3	Struck down	Neither president nor Congress can extend jurisdiction of courts martial to include veterans
Cafeteria & Restaurant Workers Unions v. McElroy, 367 U.S. 886 (1961)	5–4	Upheld	President has power to regulate and control access to military bases
Department of the Navy v. Egan, 484 U.S. 518 (1988)	5–3	Upheld	President can control identification of and access to classified materials
Hamdan v. Rumsfeld, 548 U.S. 557 (2006)	5–3	Struck down	President cannot create tribunals for trial and punishment of war criminals except in necessity

governed by the decisions and acts of the political department of the Government to which this power was entrusted. . . . The proclamation of blockade is itself official and conclusive evidence to the Court that a state of war existed. . . .

. . .

If it were necessary to the technical existence of a war, that it should have a legislative sanction, we find it in almost every act passed at the extraordinary session of the Legislature of 1861, which was wholly employed in enacting laws to enable the Government to prosecute the war with vigor and efficiency. And finally, in 1861, we find Congress . . . in anticipation of such astute objections, passing an act "approving, legalizing, and making valid all the acts, proclamations, and orders of the President, etc., as if they had been issued and done under the previous express authority and direction of the Congress of the United States."

Without admitting that such an act was necessary under the circumstances, it is plain that if the President had in any manner assumed powers which it was necessary should have the authority or sanction of Congress, . . . this ratification has operated to perfectly cure the defect. . . .

. . .

On this first question therefore we are of the opinion that the President had a right, jure belli, to institute a blockade of ports in possession of the States in rebellion, which neutrals are bound to regard.

. . .

JUSTICE NELSON, with whom CHIEF JUSTICE TANEY, JUSTICE CATRON and JUSTICE CLIFFORD join, dissenting.

. . .

By our constitution . . . Congress shall have power "to declare war, grant letters of marque and reprisal, and make rules concerning captures on land and water."

. . .

In the case of a rebellion or resistance of a portion of the people of a country against the established government, there is no doubt, if in its progress and enlargement the government thus sought to be overthrown sees fit, it may by the competent power recognize, or declare the existence of a state of civil war, which will draw after it all the consequences and rights of war between the contending parties as in the case of a public war. . . . But before this insurrection against the established Government can be dealt with on the footing of a civil war, within the meaning of the law of nations and the Constitution of the United States, and which will draw after it belligerent rights, it must be recognized or declared by the war-making power of the Government. No power short of this can change the legal status of the Government or the relations of its citizens from that of peace to a state of war, or bring into existence all those duties and obligations to neutral third parties growing out of a state of war. The war power of the Government must be exercised before this changed condition of the Government and people and of neutral third parties can be admitted. There is no difference in this respect between a civil or a public war.

. . .

An idea seemed to be entertained that all that was necessary to constitute a war was organized hostility in the district of country in a state of rebellion—that conflicts on land and on sea—the taking of towns and capture of fleets—in fine, the magnitude and dimensions of the resistance against the Government—constituted war with all the belligerent rights belonging to civil war. . . .

Now, in one sense, no doubt this is war, and may be a war of the most extensive and threatening dimensions and effects, but it is a statement simply of its existence in a material sense, and has no relevancy or weight when the question is what constitutes war in a legal sense, in the sense of the law of nations, and of the Constitution of the United States. For it must be a war in this sense to attach to it all the consequences that belong to belligerent rights. Instead, therefore, of inquiring after armies and navies, and victories lost and won, or organized rebellion against the general Government, the inquiry should be into the law of nations and into the municipal fundamental laws of the Government. For we find there that to constitute a civil war in the sense in which we are speaking, before it can exist, in contemplation of law, it must be recognized or declared by the sovereign power of the State, and which sovereign power by our Constitution is lodged in the Congress of the United States—civil war, therefore, under our system of government, can exist only by an act of Congress, which requires the assent of two of the great departments of the Government, the Executive and Legislative.

We have thus far been speaking of the war power under the Constitution of the United States, and as known and recognized by the law of nations. But we are asked, what would become of the peace and integrity of the Union in case of an insurrection at home or invasion from abroad if this power could not be exercised by the President in the recess of Congress, and until that body could be assembled?

The framers of the Constitution fully comprehended this question, and provided for the contingency. . . .

. . .

. . . The whole military and naval power of the country is put under the control of the President to meet the emergency. He may call out a force in proportion to its necessities, one regiment or fifty, one ship-of-war or any number at his discretion. . . . But whatever its numbers, whether great or small, that may be required, ample provision is here made; and whether great or small, the nature of the power is the same. It is the exercise of a power under the municipal laws of the country and not under the law of nations; and, as we see, furnishes the most ample means of repelling attacks from abroad or suppressing disturbances at home until the assembling of Congress, who can, if it be deemed necessary, bring into operation the war power, and thus change the nature and character of the contest. Then, instead of being carried on under the municipal [militia] law of 1795, it would be under the law of nations, and the Acts of Congress as war measures with all the rights of war.

. . .

The Acts of 1795 and 1807 did not, and could not under the Constitution, confer on the President the power of declaring war against a State of this Union, or of deciding that war existed, and upon that ground authorize the capture and confiscation of the property of every citizen of the State whenever it was found on the waters. . . . This great power over the business and property of the citizen is reserved to the legislative department by the express words of the Constitution. It cannot be delegated or surrendered to the Executive. Congress alone can determine whether war exists or should be declared; and until they have acted, no citizen of the State can be punished in his person or property, unless he had committed some offence against a law of Congress passed before the act was committed, which made it a crime, and defined the punishment. The penalty of confiscation for the acts of others with which he had no concern cannot lawfully be inflicted.

. . .

Congress on the 6th of August, 1862, passed an Act confirming all acts, proclamations, and orders of the President, after the 4th of March, 1861, respecting the army and navy, and legalizing them, so far as was competent for that body. . . . An ex post facto law is defined, when, after an action, indifferent in itself, or lawful, is committed, the Legislature then, for the first time, declares it to have been a crime and inflicts punishment upon the person who committed it. The principle is sought to be applied in this case. Property of the citizen or foreign subject engaged in lawful trade at the time, and illegally captured . . . may be held and confiscated by subsequent legislation. . . .

. . . Here the captures were without any Constitutional authority, and void; and, on principle, no subsequent ratification could make them valid.

Upon the whole . . . I am compelled to the conclusion that . . . the President had no power to set on foot a blockade under the law of nations, and that the capture of the vessel and cargo in this case, and in all cases before us in which the capture occurred before the 13th of July, 1861 [when Congress first authorized a blockade], for breach of blockade, or as enemies' property, are illegal and void, and that the decrees of condemnation should be reversed and the vessel and cargo restored.

VII. Individual Rights

MAJOR DEVELOPMENTS

- Some confiscation of property in both North and South
- Congress grants exemptions from the draft to religious pacifists
- National debates over the right to bear arms

The status of individual rights during the Civil War and Reconstruction confounds common claims that personal liberties are the first casualty of war. The American experience was far more complex. Both the Union and the Confederacy passed unprecedented measures to confiscate property. The Union measure, however, was scaled down considerably and only sporadically enforced. Americans also gained religious freedoms during the Civil War. For the first time, persons other than Protestants served as military chaplains, and Congress granted religious pacifists exemptions from military service. The Civil War had little influence on other rights. While the conflict raged, Americans rarely considered the right to bear arms or the right to marry. Little debate took place on the constitutionality of morals laws.

A. Property

Many important Civil War and Reconstruction measures raised questions about constitutional property rights. Critics claimed that the First and Second Confiscation Acts, the Emancipation Proclamation, the Legal Tender Act, and the Ironclad Oath violated the due process and takings clauses of the Fifth Amendment. Former Justice John Campbell urged the Supreme Court in the *Slaughter-House Cases* (1873) to declare that state-chartered monopolies violated the constitutional right to pursue an ordinary calling protected by the Thirteenth Amendment and various clauses of the Fourteenth Amendment. Proponents of these federal and state regulations claimed that each was a legitimate exercise of federal war powers or state police powers.

The constitutional status of many property rights was less settled politically than legally at the end of Reconstruction. Slavery was dead. Professionals had a constitutional right to not be forced to swear to their past loyalty. The Supreme Court ruled that government could print paper money and that state monopolies did not violate constitutional rights to practice a common calling. Nevertheless, *Knox v. Lee* (1871) and the *Slaughter-House Cases* (1873) were decided by narrow judicial majorities. Moreover, property claims during the Civil War and Reconstruction were asserted by Democrats or persons identified with Democratic causes. No one knew whether the Republican majority on the Supreme Court and in the national legislature would be more sympathetic when, in the future, Republicans or persons identified with Republican causes claimed that their constitutional property rights had been violated.

B. Religion

Americans became more tolerant of religious diversity during the Civil War and Reconstruction Era. Religious (and racial) prejudices weakened in the North when men of different religious faiths (and races) fought together in the Union Army. The federal government made two landmark decisions recognizing the rights of religious minorities. For the first time in history, Congress permitted non-Protestants to become military chaplains. For the first time, Congress granted religious pacifists exemptions from compulsory military service. The Supreme Court struck a blow for religious freedom when the judicial majority in *Cummings v. Missouri* (1867) ruled that ministers could not be required to swear that they had always been loyal to the United States.

C. Guns

Republicans aggressively championed the right of persons of color to bear arms. Anti-slavery advocates were outraged when un-reconstructed southern legislatures forbade former slaves from joining the state militia or bearing arms. Some Republicans identified the right to bear arms with a right to self-defense. Senator Samuel Pomeroy of Kansas asserted, "Every man . . . should have the right to bear arms for the defense of himself and family and his homestead."[29]

Most legal scholars in the Reconstruction Era more narrowly interpreted the right to bear arms. John Norton Pomeroy's *An Introduction to the Constitutional Law of the United States* declared, "The object of this clause is to secure a well-armed militia."[30]

D. Personal Freedom and Public Morality

Anti-slavery advocates advanced three constitutional arguments that had enduring significance for government power to regulate individual behavior. First, abolitionists consistently asserted that the Declaration of Independence provided the foundational principles of American constitutionalism. To the extent that the post–Civil War Constitution incorporated the Declaration of Independence, that Constitution aimed to protect what Jefferson described as "unalienable rights" to "life, liberty, and the pursuit of happiness." That "pursuit" might justify constitutional rights to drink, bowl, and enjoy various intimate relationships. Second, the persons responsible for the Thirteenth Amendment defined the badges and incidents of slavery broadly. Senator James Harlan's speech defending the proposed Thirteenth Amendment stated that among the "incidents of slavery" were "abolit[ion] of the conjugal relationship," "annul[ment] [of] the law of God establishing the relation of man and wife," and

29. *Congressional Globe*, 39th Cong., 1st Sess., 1866, 1182.

30. John Norton Pomeroy, *An Introduction to the Constitutional Law of the United States* (New York: Hurd and Houghton, 1868), 152–53.

"the abolition practically of the parental relation."[31] So viewed, the constitutional prohibition on involuntary servitude could be interpreted as guaranteeing family rights, as well as rights to property and free labor. Third, prominent Supreme Court justices interpreted the Fourteenth Amendment as protecting fundamental rights. Justice Field's dissent in the *Slaughter-House Cases* (1873) insisted that the privileges and immunities clause "refer[red] to the natural and inalienable rights which belong to all citizens" and emphasized "the right to pursue a lawful employment in a lawful manner." His opinion created an opening for advocates for a more libertarian perspective on government regulation to argue that a wide variety of personal choices were among "the natural and inalienable rights" protected by the Fourteenth Amendment.

VIII. Democratic Rights

MAJOR DEVELOPMENTS

- Lincoln administration restricts criticism of war policies
- Many states require voters to take loyalty oaths

The Civil War was the first military conflict in American history in which the federal government restricted basic democratic rights. The Lincoln administration arrested prominent war critics and temporarily shut down newspapers hostile to the war effort. The Union Army interfered with voting in crucial border states. After the Civil War Republicans in Congress required all national representatives to swear that they had never been disloyal to the United States. Many states insisted that voters take similar oaths. Union military officials in the South interfered with elections and suppressed anti-Reconstruction speech.

A. Free Speech

Abraham Lincoln had a narrow conception of free speech rights in wartime. As president, he ordered subordinates to arrest persons whose speech he believed interfered with the war effort. Lincoln claimed that these restrictions on free speech were necessary to maintain the morale of the army. In 1863, he wrote, "Must I shoot a simple-minded soldier boy who deserts, while I must not touch a hair of a wiley agitator who induces him to desert?"[32] Both Democrats and Republicans sharply condemned administration efforts to restrict political dissent. Many of Lincoln's otherwise strongest political supporters shared this commitment to protecting First Amendment rights in wartime. Senator Lyman Trumbull of Illinois, a Republican supporter of other Lincoln wartime policies, told a Chicago crowd that Republicans "have been the advocate of free speech for the last forty years, and should not allow the party which during the whole time has been using the gag to usurp our place."[33]

The Trial of Clement Vallandigham (1863)[34]

Clement Vallandigham was a three-term member of the House of Representatives (1856–1862) and the most prominent northern defender of secession. His speeches caustically denounced Lincoln, Lincoln's war policies, and all policies aimed at freeing slaves. On April 13, 1863, General Ambrose Burnside, the Union commander in the Ohio region, issued a general order decreeing that all persons "declaring sympathies for the enemy" be tried as "spies or traitors" by a military court. Undeterred, Vallandigham on May 1 gave a public speech that depicted the Civil War as "a war for the purpose of crushing out liberty and erecting a despotism" and "a war for the freedom of the blacks and the enslavement of the whites." Four days later Vallandigham was arrested. A military court found him guilty. Abraham Lincoln ordered that he be exiled to the Confederacy. Vallandigham sought a writ of habeas corpus. His claim was rejected by the local circuit court of the United States. In 1864 the Supreme Court claimed not to have jurisdiction to hear an appeal of that decision. Vallandigham escaped to Canada. While he was abroad, Ohio Democrats nominated him to be the party candidate for governor.

The following excerpts are from Vallandigham's military trial and his habeas corpus appeal. Consider the following questions when reading these materials. Was Vallandigham arrested because his speech was disloyal, or because his

31. See "Debates over the Thirteenth Amendment," in Section II of this chapter.

32. Abraham Lincoln, "To Erastus Corning and Others," *Collected Works of Abraham Lincoln* (edited by Roy P. Basler) (New Brunswick, NJ: Rutgers University Press, 1953), 6:266.

33. Curtis, *No State Shall Abridge*, 329.

34. Excerpt taken from *The Trial of Hon. Clement Vallandigham* (Cincinnati, OH: Bickey and Carroll, 1863).

speech had a tendency to depress northern morale? Suppose Vallandigham had claimed that many northern generals were incompetent (many were). Would he have been arrested? Does George Pugh's argument for Vallandigham accept any government power to restrict speech in wartime? Few people have heard of Pugh's constitutional defense of free speech. Is that obscurity best explained by Pugh's client or by the quality of Pugh's defense?

Application for Habeas Corpus: Statement of Major General Burnside

. . .

If I were to indulge in wholesale criticisms of the policy of the Government, it would demoralize the army under my command, and every friend of his country would call me a traitor. If the officers or soldiers were to indulge in such criticisms, it would weaken the army to the extent of their influence; and if this criticism were universal in the army, it would cause it to be broken to pieces, the Government to be divided, our homes to be invaded, and anarchy to reign. My duty to my Government forbids me to indulge in such criticisms; officers and soldiers are not allowed so to indulge, and this course will be sustained by all honest men.

. . . If it is my duty and the duty of the troops to avoid saying anything that would weaken the army, by preventing a single recruit from joining the ranks, by bringing the laws of Congress into disrepute, or by causing dissatisfaction in the ranks, it is equally the duty of every citizen in the Department to avoid the same evil. If it is my duty to prevent the propagation of this evil in the army, or in a portion of my Department, it is equally my duty in all portions of it; and it is my duty to use all the force in my power to stop it.

If I were to find a man from the enemy's country distributing in my camps speeches of their public men that tended to demoralize the troops or to destroy their confidence in the constituted authorities of the Government, I would have him tried, and hung if found guilty, and all the rules of modern warfare would sustain me. Why should such speeches from our own public men be allowed?

The press and public men, in a great emergency like the present, should avoid the use of party epithets and bitter invectives, and discourage the organization of secret political societies, which are always undignified and disgraceful to a free people, but now they are absolutely wrong and injurious; they create dissensions and discord, which just now amount to treason. The simple names "Patriot" and "Traitor" are comprehensive enough.

. . .

It is said that the speeches which are condemned have been made in the presence of large bodies of citizens, who, if they thought them wrong, would have then and there condemned them. That is no argument. These citizens do not realize the effect upon the army of our country, who are its defenders. They have never been in the field; never faced the enemies of their country; never undergone the privations of our soldiers in the field; and, besides, they have been in the habit of hearing their public men speak, and, as a general thing, of approving of what they say; therefore, the greater responsibility rests upon the public men and upon the public press, and it behooves them to be careful as to what they say. They must not use license and plead that they are exercising liberty. In this Department it cannot be done. I shall use all the power I have to break down such license, and I am sure I will be sustained in this course by all honest men. At all events, I will have the consciousness, before God, of having done my duty to my country, and when I am swerved from the performance of that duty by any pressure, public or private, or by any prejudice, I will no longer be a man or a patriot.

. . . If the people do not approve th[e] [policy of the Lincoln administration], they can change the constitutional authorities of that Government, at the proper time and by the proper method. Let them freely discuss the policy in a proper tone; but my duty requires me to stop license and intemperate discussion, which tends to weaken the authority of the Government and army: whilst the latter is in the presence of the enemy, it is cowardly so to weaken it. This license could not be used in our camps—the man would be torn in pieces who would attempt it. There is no fear of the people losing their liberties; we all know that to be the cry of demagogues, and none but the ignorant will listen to it; all intelligent men know that our people are too far advanced in the scale of religion, civilization, education, and freedom, to allow any power on earth to interfere with their liberties; but this same advancement in these great characteristics of our people teaches them to make all necessary sacrifices for their country when an emergency requires. They will support the constituted authorities of the Government, whether they agree with them or not. Indeed, the army itself is a part of the people, and is so thoroughly educated in the love of civil liberty, which is the best guarantee for the permanence of our republican institutions, that it would itself be the first to oppose any attempt to continue the exercise of military authority after the establishment of peace by the overthrow of the rebellion. No man on earth can lead our citizen soldiery to the establishment of a military despotism, and no man living would have the folly to attempt it. To do so would be to seal his own doom. On this point there can be no ground for apprehension on the part of the people. . . .

Opening Argument of the Honorable George E. Pugh

. . .

. . . [T]he right of the American people to deliberate upon and freely to speak of what General Burnside calls the "Policy of the Government" at all times—whether of peace or of war, of safety or of peril, of ease or of difficulty—is a right supreme, and absolute, and unquestionable. They can exhort each other to impeach the President or any executive officer; to impeach any magistrate of judicial authority; to condemn Congressmen and legislators of every description. They can, at pleasure, indulge in criticism, by "wholesale" or otherwise, not only upon "the policy" adopted or proposed by their servants, military as well as civil, but upon the conduct of those servants in each and every particular, upon their actions, their words, their probable motives, their public characters. And, in speaking of such subjects, any citizen addressing his fellow-citizens, by their consent, in a peaceable assembly, may use invective, or sarcasm, or ridicule, or passionate apostrophe or appeal, or—what is, ordinarily, much better—plain, solid, unostentatious argument. There is no style of rhetoric to be prescribed for the people. They are the masters of every style, and of every art and form of utterance. General Burnside suggests that "the press and public men, in a great emergency like the present, should avoid the use of party epithets and bitter invectives." I esteem that as excellent advice on all occasions; but, unfortunately, the General and I must both succumb, with what grace we can, to the choice or fancy of the people. They will render his advice or my advice effectual, if they approve it, by not reading such papers and not listening to such orators as habitually violate or trifle with decorum. There is no other way; there can be no censorship, civil or military, in this regard. That would inevitably, and at once, destroy the liberty of speech and of the press: that presupposes an incapacity of the people to distinguish right from wrong, truth from falsehood, reason from intemperance, or decency from outrage. And, if we cannot confide in the good sense of the people as to these things, how can we confide in them at all?

I know that much is written and spoken every day, and in the most public manner, at which honorable men feel indignant, or, at least, annoyed. But does it really affect the people at large? Does it alienate them from the Government under which they live? Does it induce them to think less dearly of their kinsmen, their friends, their neighbors, in military service; or to be unmindful of the toils of any soldier in camp, or on the march, or of his sufferings in the awful day of battle? Does it palsy the ministering hand? Does it prevent the sympathizing tear? . . . General Burnside errs, and errs greatly, in supposing that our people are often excited by some false or foul word; but, by and by, assertion meets contradiction, violence encounters violence; and so, at length, slowly perhaps, but certainly, will justice achieve her victory, and conclude the contest.

. . .

. . . [B]ut the effect on the soldiers. Well, sir, let us inquire into that. The soldiers have been citizens; they have been in the habit of attending public meetings, and of listening to public speakers. They are not children, but grown men—stalwart, sensible, and gallant men—with their hearts in the right place, and with arms ready to strike whenever and wherever the cause of their country demands. The General assures us of more, even, than this: "No man on earth," he says, "can lead our citizen-soldiery to the establishment of a military despotism." And are these the men to be discouraged, and, especially, to feel weary in heart or limb—unable to cope with an enemy in the field—because Mr. Vallandigham, or any other public speaker, may have said something, at Mount Vernon or elsewhere, with which they do not agree? The soldiers have not chosen me for their eulogist; but I will say, of my own accord, that they are no such tender plants as General Burnside imagines. They know, exactly, for what they went into the field; they are not alarmed, nor dissatisfied, nor discouraged, because their fellow citizens, at home, attend public meetings, and listen to public speeches, as heretofore; they have no serious misgiving as to the estimation in which they are holden by the people of the Northern and Northwestern States, without any distinction of sects, parties, or factions.

. . .

Mr. Vallandigham said, furthermore, as the Judge-Advocate assures us, "that, if the Administration had so wished, the war could have been honorably terminated months ago." That allegation may be true; I have no means, except from what is alleged subsequently, of deciding whether it be true or false. Nor do I find myself much enlightened by the next sentence imputed to Mr. Vallandigham: that "peace might have been honorably obtained by listening to the proposed intermediation of France." I do not know what terms, if any, the Emperor of the French suggested; but they would have to be very advantageous, as well as unmistakably honorable, before I would consent to his interference, or the interference of any other monarch, with the affairs of our distracted republic. And yet, if Mr. Vallandigham thinks otherwise, he has the same right to declare and to maintain his opinion as I have to maintain or to declare mine. But he made another accusation, and of much more serious importance: he said "that propositions by which the Southern States could be won back, and the South be guaranteed their rights under the Constitution, had been rejected, the day before the late battle at Fredericksburg, by Lincoln and his minions"—"meaning thereby," as the Judge-Advocate kindly informs us, "the President of the United States and those under him in authority." I never heard that it was actionable, at common law, to say of one man, orally, that he was the minion of another; and, far less, that it could be a matter of State prosecution. As to the rest, the accusation is one of fact—positive, distinct, with addition of time and circumstances. Is it true, or is it false? Sir, I do not know; but I do know that *that* is a vital question to the American people. Was it for making such an accusation that Mr. Vallandigham has been arrested; and is it by imprisoning him, or otherwise stopping his mouth, that Mr. Lincoln would answer to such an accusation in the face of his countrymen, of the civilized world, of the tribunal of God and of history? As to General Burnside, whose personal sincerity in these proceedings, as well as at the battle of Fredericksburg, I do not intend to question, what living man is more interested to have the truth, or the falsehood, of that accusation publicly ascertained?

. . .

These are obviously conclusions of the speaker—correctly or incorrectly drawn—from premises of which little, very little indeed, is narrated by the specification. I do not undertake to say, and I cannot say, at present, whether such conclusions are correct or incorrect; but what are they—and, in asking this question, I would lay my hand, if possible, upon the heart of every freeman—what are they but the impassioned appeals of a sincere, conscientious, honorable, and, if you please, over-vigilant citizen? Granted—if you will have it so—that he is in error, and greatly in error: I do not ask you to approve his conclusions, or in any manner to accept his opinions; but I do ask you, in all truthfulness, whether these words bear any taint of treason or disloyalty? They were intended, most evidently, to arouse the people to a sense of the vast peril in which all of us now stand; and, although they are startling, and seem very bitter, should we not err upon the side of jealousy rather than upon the side of laxity and too much confidence in our rulers, at a time when, month by month, day by day, the Union of our fathers, the Constitution by which that Union was ordained, and the Liberty of which the Constitution and the Union were intended as perpetual guarantees, are fading into a dim, a broken, and a most sorrowful vision?

. . .

Since, what time, I would inquire, has it become an offense of such magnitude for any citizen to propose the cessation of a war which he believes to be unnecessary and injudicious. . . .

B. Voting

Americans eliminated some restrictions on voting rights while imposing new qualifications. The Fifteenth Amendment forbade states from making racial discriminations when determining who was eligible to vote. During the Civil War soldiers were permitted to vote by absentee ballot. Republicans were unwilling to abolish other restrictions on voting. Congress during the debate over the Fifteenth Amendment rejected language that would forbid states from imposing property or literacy qualifications. National legislators also repeatedly rejected calls for constitutional amendments or federal laws granting women the right to vote. The U.S. Supreme Court in *Minor v. Happersett* (1874) held that the post–Civil War Amendments did not give women the right to vote.

IX. Equality

MAJOR DEVELOPMENTS

- Continued animus against class legislation
- Persons of color declared equal before the law
- Congress debates what legislation enforces the constitutional rights of persons of color
- Federal officials reject claims that new constitutional amendments give women the right to vote

Americans from 1861 to 1876 transformed some inherited understandings of constitutional equality while preserving others. The Fourteenth Amendment made explicit that all persons had a *federal* constitutional right to equality under the law. Section 1 declared, "No state . . . shall deny to any person within its jurisdiction the equal protection of the law." Section 5 gave Congress the power to enforce that guarantee. While the Fourteenth Amendment did not explicitly mention race, Americans understood that some previously accepted racial discriminations were now unconstitutional. Nevertheless, most constitutional authorities did not believe that they were making fundamental changes to longstanding constitutional practices. Legislatures could make distinctions when "real differences" existed between different persons. Gender discriminations survived intact, as did the constitutional status of Native Americans. Many Americans believed that some racial distinctions remained constitutional after the Fourteenth Amendment was ratified.

A. Equality Under Law

Republicans deliberately drafted constitutional provisions that spoke of general rights to equality rather than a specific right against racial discrimination. During the debates over the Fourteenth Amendment, congressmen rejected proposed versions that forbade "discrimination . . . as to the civil rights of persons because of race, color, or previous condition of servitude" in favor of language forbidding states to "deny to any person . . . the equal protection of the laws." Republicans favored the broader language partly because they were committed to a broader principle of equality. Senator Charles Sumner of Massachusetts insisted, "Equality [is] the master principle of our system, and the very frontispiece of our constitution."[35] Republicans were also concerned with the equality rights of specific white persons. Southern states before the Civil War repressed anti-slavery advocacy, and many southern Unionists feared reprisals from former Confederates. Union military commanders warned Congress that southern Republicans of all races were not "secure in the enjoyment of their rights . . . and could not rely upon the State Courts for justice."[36] Constitutional amendments couched in general language promised to secure the rights of white southern Unionists as well as free blacks.

Thomas Cooley, A Treatise on the Constitutional Limitations Which Rest upon the Legislative Power of the States of the American Union (1868)[37]

Thomas McIntyre Cooley was the chief justice of the Michigan Supreme Court, a professor of law at the University of Michigan School of Law, the first chairperson of the Interstate Commerce Commission, and the leading legal treatise writer of the post–Civil War period. His most important work, Constitutional Limitations, *was "written in full sympathy with all those restraints which the caution of the fathers has imposed upon the exercise of the powers of government" and is the most cited constitutional treatise of the era. Courts after the Civil War quoted extensively from Cooley when adjudicating various state constitutional questions on issues ranging from the power of municipal corporations to the constitutional meaning of free speech.*

Cooley's analysis of "unequal and partial legislation" was particularly influential. The first edition of Constitutional Limitations *was published in 1868, the year the Fourteenth Amendment was ratified. In this work, Cooley emphasizes equality as a master principle of American constitutional law. His treatise focuses as much on general constitutional commitments as on specific constitutional provisions.*

35. Charles Sumner, *The Works of Charles Sumner* (Boston: Lee and Shepard, 1875), 9:477.

36. William E. Nelson, *The Fourteenth Amendment: From Political Principle to Judicial Doctrine* (Cambridge, MA: Harvard University Press, 1988), 42.

37. Excerpt taken from Thomas M. Cooley, *A Treatise on the Constitutional Limitations Which Rest upon the Legislation Power of the States of the American Union* (Boston: Little, Brown, and Company, 1874), 389–96.

Illustration 6-3a U.S. Associate Justice Stephen Field

Illustration 6-3b Michigan Chief Justice Thomas Cooley

Stephen Field (6-3a) and Thomas M. Cooley (6-3b) were among the most influential jurists in post-Civil War America. Ironically, neither was partisan Republican. Stephen Field of California was an anti-slavery Democrat and Abraham Lincoln's only Democratic appointee to the U.S. Supreme Court. Thomas Cooley had been a Democrat in Michigan before joining the Free Soil movement but became a more independent "Liberal Republican" during Reconstruction. From his dissent in the *Slaughter-House Cases* (1873) through his concurrence in the *Income Tax Cases* (1895), Field vigorously defended property rights. Thomas Cooley had a more varied career, serving as chief justice of the Michigan Supreme Court, founding commissioner of the Interstate Commerce Commission, and professor at the University of Michigan law school, where he became a leading treatise writer. His views on the limited powers of the state and the expansive rights of individuals were highly influential with judges and lawyers across the country.

Sources: Library of Congress, Prints and Photographs Division, Washington, DC 20540, USA; Bentley Image Bank, Bentley Historical Library.

Cooley and other constitutional commentators insisted that partial legislation was unconstitutional. On what basis did Cooley make that constitutional claim? How did he determine the constitutional status of special legislation? Notice how little attention Cooley paid to the equal protection rights of persons of color. Did he believe that the equal protection clause had any impact on free-state policies?

. . .

Laws public in their objects may be general or local in their application; they may embrace many subjects or one, and they may extend to all the citizens or be confined to particular classes, as minors, or married women, bankers or traders, and the like. The power that legislates for the State at large must determine whether particular rules shall extend to the whole State and all its citizens, or to a part of the State or a class of its citizens only. The circumstances of a particular locality, or the prevailing public opinion in that section of the State, may require or make acceptable different police regulations from those demanded in another, or call for different taxation, and a different application of the public moneys. The legislature may, therefore, prescribe or authorize different laws of police, allow the right of eminent domain to be exercised in different cases and through different modes, and prescribe peculiar restrictions upon taxation in each distinct municipality, provided the State constitution does not forbid. This is done constantly, and the fact that the laws are local in their operation is not supposed to render them objectionable in principle. The legislature may also deem it desirable to establish peculiar rules for the several occupations, and distinctions in the rights, obligations, and legal capacities of different classes of citizens. The business of common carriers, for instance, or of bankers, may require special statutory regulations for the general benefit, and it may be desirable to give one class of laborers a special lien for their wages, while it would be impracticable or impolitic to do the same by persons engaged in some other employments. If otherwise unobjectionable, all that can be required in these cases is, that they be general in their application to the class or the locality to which they apply, and they are then *general laws* in the constitutional sense.

But a statute would not be constitutional which should proscribe a class or a party for opinion's sake, or which should select particular individuals from a class or locality, and subject them to peculiar rules, or impose upon them special obligations or burdens, from which others in the same locality or class are exempt.

The legislature may suspend the operation of the general laws of the State; but when it does so, the suspension must be general, and cannot be made in individual cases, or for particular localities. Privileges may be granted to individuals, when by so doing the rights of other persons are not injuriously affected; disabilities may be removed; the legislature as *parens patrim* may grant authority to the guardians of incompetent persons to exercise a statutory authority over their estate for their assistance, comfort, or support, and for the discharge of legal or equitable liens upon it; but every one has a right to demand that he be governed by general rules, and a special statute that singles his case out as one to be regulated by a different law from that which is applied in all similar cases would not be legitimate legislation, but an arbitrary mandate, unrecognized in free government. Mr. Locke has said of those who make the laws: "They are to govern by promulgated, established laws, not to be varied in particular cases, but to have one rule for rich and poor, for the favorite at court and the countryman at plough"; and this may be justly said to have become a maxim in the law, by which may be tested the authority and binding force of legislative enactments.

Special courts could not be created for the trial of the rights and obligations of particular individuals; and those cases in which legislative acts granting new trials or other special relief in judicial proceedings, while they have been regarded as usurpations of judicial authority, have also been considered obnoxious to the objection that they undertook to suspend general laws in special cases. The doubt might also arise whether a regulation made for any one class of citizens, entirely arbitrary in its character, and restricting their rights, privileges, or legal capacities in a manner before unknown to the law, could be sustained, notwithstanding its generality. Distinctions in these respects should be based upon some reason which renders them important,—like the want of capacity in infants, and insane persons; but if the legislature should undertake to provide that persons following some specified lawful trade or employment should not have capacity to make contracts, or to receive conveyances, or to build such houses as others were allowed to erect, or in any other way to make such use of their property as was permissible to others, it can scarcely be doubted that the act would transcend the due bounds of legislative power, even if it did not come in conflict with express constitutional provisions. The man or the class forbidden the acquisition or enjoyment of property in the manner permitted to the community at large would be deprived of *liberty* in particulars of primary importance to his or their "pursuit of happiness."

Equality of rights, privileges, and capacities unquestionably should be the aim of the law; and if special privileges are granted, or special burdens or restrictions imposed in any case, it must be presumed that the legislature designed to depart as little as possible from this fundamental maxim of government. The State, it is to be presumed, has no favors to bestow, and designs to inflict no arbitrary deprivation of rights. Special privileges are obnoxious, and discriminations against persons or classes are still more so, and as a rule of construction are always to be leaned against as probably not contemplated or designed. It has been held that a statute requiring attorneys to render services in suits for poor persons without fee or reward was to be confined strictly to the cases therein prescribed; and if by its terms it expressly covered civil cases only, it could not be extended to embrace defences of criminal prosecutions. So where a constitutional provision confined the elective franchise to "*white* male citizens," and it appeared that the legislation of the State had always treated of negroes, mulattoes, and *other colored persons*, in contradistinction to white, it was held that although quadroons, being a recognized class of colored persons, must be excluded, yet that the rule of exclusion would not be carried further. . . .

There are unquestionably cases in which the State may grant privileges to specified individuals without violating any constitutional principle, because, from the nature of the case, it is impossible they should be possessed and enjoyed by all; and if it is important that they should exist, the proper State authority must be left to select the grantees. Of this class are grants of the franchise to be a corporation. Such grants, however, which confer upon a few persons what cannot be shared by the many, and which, though supposed to be made on public grounds, are nevertheless frequently of great value to the corporators and therefore sought with avidity, are never to be extended by construction beyond the plain terms in which they are conferred. No rule is better settled than that charters of incorporation are to be construed strictly against the corporators. . . .

. . .

[*The third edition of* Constitutional Limitations, *published in 1874, added the following commentary on the equal protection clause to this section.*[38]]

. . . It was not within the power of the States before the adoption of the fourteenth amendment, to deprive citizens of the equal protection of the laws; but there were servile classes not thus shielded, and when these were made freemen, there were some who disputed their claim to citizenship, and some State laws were in force which established discriminations against them. To settle doubts and preclude all such laws, the fourteenth amendment was adopted; and the same securities which one citizen may demand, all others are now entitled to.

B. Race

The Civil War witnessed an unprecedented surge in the American constitutional commitment to racial equality. Slavery and white supremacy were central to the Jacksonian constitutional order and the early Civil War regime. Congress in 1861 proposed an amendment that forbade the federal government from emancipating slaves. Federal troops in 1863 were called into New York City to quell a riot by angry white citizens who did not want to fight in a war that they perceived as a fight for African American rights. Constitutional commitments changed dramatically during and immediately after the Lincoln presidency. At the end of the Civil War Americans passed a constitutional amendment abolishing slavery. Within three years they ratified a constitutional amendment guaranteeing freed slaves "the equal protection of the laws." In 1872 Americans ratified the Fifteenth Amendment, which forbade states from making racial discriminations in voting laws.

Republicans after the Civil War disputed the best means for promoting racial equality. Moderate Republicans insisted that strong prohibitions on discrimination in property, contract, and criminal law were constitutionally sufficient. Some radicals, led by Representative Thaddeus Stevens of Pennsylvania, insisted that economic equality was a prerequisite to all other equalities. Stevens proposed laws that would require the federal government to confiscate the plantations of former slaveholders and provide all families of freedmen with forty acres.[39] Other radicals insisted that Congress first enfranchise persons of color. Representative James Ashley of Ohio declared, "If I were a black man, with the chains just stricken from my limbs . . . and you should offer me the ballot, or a cabin and forty acres of cotton land, I would take the ballot."[40]

The racial practices that Americans abandoned were far clearer than the racial practices they adopted. General agreement existed that the post–Civil War Constitution prohibited slavery and made persons of color American citizens. Controversies quickly developed, however, over what the abolition of slavery and equal citizenship meant in constitutional practice. One view, championed in such cases as *In re Turner* (1867) and by such congressional radicals as Charles Sumner, maintained that the new racial regime required both courts and elected officials to guarantee persons of color a wide array of political, economic,

---

38. Thomas M. Cooley, *A Treatise on the Constitutional Limitations Which Rest upon the Legislative Power of the States of the American Union*, 3rd ed. (Boston: Little, Brown, and Company, 1874), 466.

39. *Congressional Globe*, 40th Cong., 1st Sess., 1867, 205.

40. Eric Foner, *Reconstruction: America's Unfinished Revolution, 1863–1877* (New York: Harper & Row, 1988), 236.

and civil rights. According to another view, championed by President Andrew Johnson and most northern Democrats, the abolition of slavery meant that persons of color were free to forge their own lives under whatever laws and discriminations localities believed promoted the public welfare. The Supreme Court in such cases as *United States v. Cruikshank* (1876) articulated a constitutional vision closer to—although not identical with—the northern Democratic interpretation of the post–Civil War Amendments.

Congressional Debates over the Second Freedmen's Bureau Act (1866)

The Second Freedmen's Bureau Act was a Republican effort to extend the life and expand the duties of the Freedmen's Bureau established by law in March 1865. Republicans hoped to provide persons of color with the economic and educational opportunities they thought necessary for equal citizenship. The constitutional debate over the measure was partisan. Republicans insisted that the Second Freedmen's Bureau Act was a legitimate exercise of both the war power and Section 2 of the Thirteenth Amendment. Democrats rejected both claims. President Andrew Johnson and other Democrats further insisted that the provisions in the bill authorizing the federal government to obtain land and use military commissions violated the due process clause of the Fifth Amendment and the right to a jury trial guaranteed by the Sixth Amendment. The Second Freedman's Bureau Act easily passed both houses of Congress but was vetoed by President Johnson on February 19, 1866. Congress failed to override that veto. Within six months Republicans passed a slightly revised version of the Second Freedmen's Bureau Act and successfully overrode President Johnson's veto.

The following excerpts focus on congressional power under Section 2 of the Thirteenth Amendment. Note that the Second Freedmen's Bureau Act refers to "refugees and freedmen." Eric Schnapper, a prominent contemporary proponent of affirmative action, maintains that these references demonstrate that Reconstruction Republicans approved of those racial classifications that they believed promoted racial equality. He writes,

> *From the closing days of the Civil War until the end of civilian Reconstruction some five years later, Congress adopted a series of social welfare programs whose benefits were expressly limited to blacks. These programs were generally open to all blacks, not only to recently freed slaves, and were adopted over repeatedly expressed objections that such racially exclusive measures were unfair to whites. The race-conscious Reconstruction programs were enacted concurrently with the fourteenth amendment and were supported by the same legislators who favored the constitutional guarantee of equal protection. This history strongly suggests that the framers of the amendment could not have intended it generally to prohibit affirmative action for blacks or other disadvantaged groups.*[41]

Schnapper correctly claims that opponents of the Freedmen's Bureau bill repeatedly condemned that proposal for unconstitutionally giving special treatment to persons of color. Does he also correctly characterize proponents of the measure as championing race-conscious measures? Does the text of the Second Freedmen's Bureau Act rely on racial classifications? To what extent did Senator Trumbull interpret the bill as providing benefits to all persons of color, as opposed to all former slaves?

The Proposed Second Freedmen's Act

. . .

Sec. 3. *And be it further enacted,* That the Secretary of War may direct such issues of provisions, clothing, fuel, and other supplies, including medical stores and transportation, and afford such aid, medical or otherwise, as he may deem needful for the immediate and temporary shelter and supply of destitute and suffering refugees and freedmen, their wives and children, under such rules and regulations as he may direct: *Provided,* That no person shall be deemed "destitute," "suffering," or "dependent upon the government for support," within the meaning of this act, who, being able to find employment, could by proper industry and exertion avoid such destitution, suffering, or dependence.

Sec. 4. *And be it further enacted,* That the President is hereby authorized to reserve from sale or from settlement, under the homestead or pre-emption laws, and to set apart for the use of freedmen and loyal refugees, male or female, unoccupied public lands in Florida, Mississippi, Alabama, Louisiana, and Arkansas, not exceeding in all three millions of acres of good land; and the Commissioner, under the direction of the

41. Eric Schnapper, "Affirmative Action and the Legislative History of the Fourteenth Amendment," *Virginia Law Review* 71 (1985): 753.

President, shall cause the same from time to time to be allotted and assigned, in parcels not exceeding forty acres each, to the loyal refugees and freedmen, who shall be protected in the use and enjoyment thereof for such term of time and at such annual rent as may be agreed on between the Commissioner and such refugees or freedmen. . . .

Sec. 6. *And be it further enacted*, That the Commissioner shall, under the direction of the President, procure in the name of the United States, by grant or purchase, such lands within the districts aforesaid as may be required for refugees and freedmen dependent on the government for support; and he shall provide or cause to be erected suitable buildings for asylums and schools. . . .

Sec. 7. *And be it further enacted*, That whenever in any State or district in which the ordinary course of judicial proceedings has been interrupted by the rebellion, and wherein, in consequence of any State or local law, ordinance, police or other regulation, custom, or prejudice, any of the civil rights or immunities belonging to white persons, including the right to make and enforce contracts, to sue, be parties, and give evidence, to inherit, purchase, lease, sell, hold and convey real and personal property, and to have full and equal benefit of all laws and proceedings for the security of person and estate, including the constitutional right of bearing arms, are refused or denied to negroes, mulattoes, freedmen, refugees, or any other persons, on account of race, color, or any previous condition of slavery or involuntary servitude, or wherein they or any of them are subjected to any other or different punishment, pains, or penalties, for the commission of any act or offence, than are prescribed for white persons committing like acts or offences, it shall be the duty of the President of the United States, through the Commissioner, to extend military protection and jurisdiction over all cases affecting such persons so discriminated against.

The Senate Debate[42]

SENATOR THOMAS HENDRICKS (Democrat, Indiana)

. . .

. . . If they have been made free and brought into the class of citizens, upon what principle can you authorize the Government of the United States to buy homes for them? Upon what principle can you authorize the Government of the United States to buy lands for the poor people in any State in the Union? They may be very meritorious; their cases may appeal with great force to our sympathies; it may almost appear necessary to prevent suffering that we should buy a home for each poor person in the country; but where is the power of the General Government to do this thing? Is it true that by this revolution the persons and property of the people have been brought within the jurisdiction of Congress and taken from without the control and jurisdiction of the States? I have understood heretofore that it has never been disputed that the duty to provide for the poor, the insane, the blind, and all who are dependent upon society, rests upon the States, and that the power does not belong to the General Government. What has occurred, then, in this war that has changed the relation of the people to the General Government to so great an extent that Congress may become the purchaser of homes for them? If we can go so far, I know of no limit to the powers of Congress. . . .

. . .

It is claimed that under this second section Congress may do anything necessary, in its judgment, not only to secure the freedom of the negro, but to secure him all civil rights that are secured to white people. I deny that construction, and it will be a very dangerous construction to adopt. The first section abolishes slavery. The second section proves that Congress may enforce the abolition of slavery "by appropriate legislation." What is slavery? It is not a relation between the slave and the State; it is not a public relation; it is a relation between two persons whereby the conduct of the one is placed under the will of the other. It is purely and entirely a domestic relation, and is so classed by all law writers; the law regulates that relation as it regulates other domestic relations. This constitutional amendment broke asunder this private relation between the master and his slave, and the slave then, so far as the right of the master was concerned, became free; but did the slave, under that amendment, acquire any other right than to be free from the control of his master? The law of the State which authorized this relation is abrogated and annulled by this provision of the Federal Constitution, but no new rights are conferred upon the freedman.

Then, sir, to make a contract is a civil right which has ordinarily been regulated by the States. The form of that contract and the ceremonies that shall attend it

42. *Congressional Globe*, 39th Cong., 1st Sess., 1866, 317–22.

are not to be regulated by Congress, but by the States. Suppose that it becomes the judgment of the State that a contract between a colored man and a white man shall be evidenced by other solemnities and instruments than are required between two white men, shall not the State be allowed to make such a provision? Is it a civil right to give evidence in courts? Is it a civil right to sit upon a jury? If it be a civil right to sit upon a jury, this bill will require that if any negro is refused the privilege of sitting upon a jury, he shall be taken under the military protection of the Government. Is the right to marry according to a man's choice a civil right? Marriage is a civil contract, and to marry according to one's choice is a civil right. Suppose a State shall deny the right of amalgamation, the right of a negro man to intermarry with a white woman, then that negro may be taken under the military protection of the Government; and what does that mean? . . .

. . .

My judgment is that under the second section of the [Thirteenth] amendment we may pass such a law as will secure the freedom declared in the first section, but that we cannot go beyond that limitation. If a man has been, by this provision of the Constitution, made free from his master, and that master undertakes to make him a slave again, we may pass such laws as are sufficient in our judgment to prevent that act; but if the Legislature of the State denies to the citizen as he is now called, the freedom, equal privileges with the white man, I want to know if that Legislature, and each member of that Legislature, is responsible to the penalties prescribed in this bill? It is not an act of the old master; it is an act of the State government, which defines and regulates the civil rights of the people.

. . .

SENATOR LYMAN TRUMBULL (Republican, Illinois)

. . .

. . . [W]hat was the object of the Freedmen's Bureau, and why was it established? It was established to look after a large class of people who, as the results of the war, had been thrown upon the hands of the Government, and must have perished but for its fostering care and protection. Does the Senator mean to deny the power of this Government to protect people under such circumstances? . . .

. . . [W]e have thrown upon us four million people who have toiled all their lives for others; who, unlike the Indians, had no property at the beginning of the rebellion; who were never permitted to own anything, never permitted to eat the bread their own hands had earned; many of whom are without any means of support, in the midst of a prejudiced and hostile population who have been struggling to overthrow the Government. These four million people, made free by the acts of war and the constitutional amendment, have been, wherever they could, loyal and true to the Union; and the Senator seriously asks, what authority have we to appropriate money to take care of them? What would he do with them? Would he allow them to starve and die? Would he turn them over to the mercy of the men who, through their whole lives, have had their earnings, to be enslaved again? It is not the first time that money has been appropriated to take care of the destitute African. For years it has been the law that whenever persons of African descent were brought to our shores with the intention of reducing them to slavery, the Government should, if possible, rescue and restore them to their native land; and we have appropriated hundreds of thousands of dollars for this object. . . .

. . .

. . . [T]he Senator from Indiana says it extends all over the United States. Well, by its terms it does, though practically it can have little if any operation outside of the late slaveholding States. If freedmen should congregate in large numbers at Cairo, Illinois or at Evansville, Indiana, and become a charge upon the people of those States, the Freedmen's Bureau would have a right to extend its jurisdiction over them, provide for their wants, secure for them employment, and place them in situations where they could provide for themselves. . . .

. . .

. . . The cheapest way by which you can save this race from starvation and destruction is to educate them. They will soon become self-sustaining. The report of the Freedmen's Bureau shows that today more than seventy thousand black children are being taught in the schools which have been established in the South. We shall not long have to support any of these blacks out of the public Treasury if we educate and furnish them land upon which they can make a living for themselves.

. . .

. . . I think [the Thirteenth] amendment does confer authority to enact these provisions into law and execute them. . . . What was the object of the constitutional amendment abolishing slavery? It was not, as the Senator says, simply to take away the power of the master over the slave. Did we not mean something more than that? Did we mean that hereafter slavery should not exist, no matter whether the servitude was claimed as due to an individual or the State? The constitutional amendment abolishes just as absolutely all provisions of State or local law which make a man a slave as it takes away the power of his former master to control him.

If the construction put by the Senator from Indiana upon the amendment be the true one, and we have merely taken from the master the power to control the slave and left him at the mercy of the State to be deprived of his civil rights, the trumpet of freedom that we have been blowing throughout the land has given an "uncertain sound," and the promised freedom is a delusion. Such was not the intention of Congress, which proposed the constitutional amendment, nor is such the fair meaning of the amendment itself. With the destruction of slavery necessarily follows the destruction of the incidents to slavery. When slavery was abolished, slave codes in its support were abolished also.

Those laws that prevented the colored man going from home, that did not allow him to buy or to sell, or to make contracts; that did not allow him to own property; that did not allow him to enforce rights; that did not allow him to be educated, were all badges of servitude made in the interest of slavery and as a part of slavery. They never would have been thought of or enacted anywhere but for slavery, and when slavery falls they fall also. The policy of the States where slavery has existed has been to legislate in its interest; and out of deference to slavery, which was tolerated by the Constitution of the United States, even some of the non-slaveholding States passed laws abridging the rights of the colored man which were restraints upon liberty. When slavery goes, all this system of legislation, devised in the interests of slavery and for the purpose of degrading the colored race, of keeping the negro in ignorance, of blotting out from his very soul the light of reason, if that were possible, that he might not think, but know only, like the ox, to labor, go with it.

Now, when slavery no longer exists, the policy of the Government is to legislate in the interest of freedom. Now, our laws are to be enacted with a view to educate, improve, enlighten, and Christianize the negro; to make him an independent man; to teach him to think and to reason; to improve that principle which the great Author of all has implanted in every human breast, which is susceptible of the highest cultivation, and destined to go on enlarging and expanding through the endless ages of eternity.

I have no doubt that under this provision of the Constitution we may destroy all these discriminations in civil rights against the black man; and if we cannot, our constitutional amendments amount to nothing. It was for that purpose that the second clause of that amendment was adopted, which says that Congress shall have authority, by appropriate legislation, to carry into effect the article prohibiting slavery. Who is to decide what that appropriate legislation is to be? The Congress of the United States; and it is for Congress to adopt such appropriate legislation as it may think proper, so that it be a means to accomplish the end. If we believe a Freedmen's Bureau necessary, if we believe an act punishing any man who deprives a colored person of any civil rights on account of his color necessary—if that is one means to secure his freedom, we have the constitutional right to adopt it. If in order to prevent slavery Congress deem it necessary to declare null and void all laws which will not permit the colored man to contract, which will not permit him to testify, which will not permit him to buy and sell, and to go where he pleases, it has the power to do so, and not only the power, but the duty to do so. . . .

But, says the Senator from Indiana, we have laws in Indiana prohibiting black people from marrying whites, and are you going to disregard these laws? Are our laws enacted for the purpose of preventing amalgamation to be disregarded, and is a man to be punished because he undertakes to enforce them? I beg the Senator from Indiana to read the bill. One of its objects is to secure the same civil rights and subject to the same punishments persons of all races and colors. How does this interfere with the law of Indiana preventing marriages between whites and blacks? Are not both races treated alike by the law of Indiana? Does not the law make it just as much a crime for a white man to marry a black woman as for a black woman to marry a white man, and *vice versa*?

C. Gender

The women's rights movement was greatly disappointed in the course of American constitutionalism from 1861 to 1876. Proponents of women's suffrage before the Civil War often played important roles in the abolitionist movement. Many established cordial relationships with prominent anti-slavery Republicans. When the Civil War ended, such activists as Elizabeth Cady Stanton and Susan B. Anthony called for constitutional amendments establishing gender as well as racial equality. They were quickly disenchanted. Republicans during Reconstruction declared, "This was the negro's hour." During the decade after the Civil War, Congress repeatedly defeated or tabled proposals for women's suffrage. Worse, from the perspective of the women's movement, Americans inserted the word "male" into the Constitution. Section 2 of the Fourteenth Amendment deprives states of representation only to the extent that the state deprives male citizens of voting rights.

Federal courts were no more sympathetic to women's claims. In *Bradwell v. State* (1873) and *Minor v. Happersett* (1874) the Supreme Court of the United States ruled that the privileges and immunities clause of the Fourteenth Amendment gave neither women nor anyone else the constitutional right to be an attorney or to vote. Justice Joseph Bradley, who thought that the privileges and immunities clause protected the right of men to become lawyers, claimed that woman were not constitutionally suited for the legal profession.

The Senate Debates Women's Suffrage (1866)[43]

Senator Edgar Cowan of Pennsylvania sparked a vigorous legislative debate over women's rights when he proposed that a bill granting men of color the right to vote in the District of Columbia should also grant women the ballot. Cowan was one of the most conservative Republicans in the Senate. He hoped that his amendment might divide moderate and radical Republicans in ways that prevented any change in the voting laws. Some Republicans took Cowan's bait, insisting that women had the same right to vote as did persons of color. Other Republicans, after announcing that they agreed with the principle of female suffrage, insisted that this was not the proper occasion for granting women the ballot. Still other Republicans insisted that the reasons for granting persons of color the ballot did not justify granting women the ballot. After three days of debate, Senator Cowan's amendment was voted down by a 37–9 vote.

Consider both the general principles and strategies adopted in the discussion of Senator Cowan's proposed amendment. What reasons did pro-suffrage Republicans give for granting women the right to vote? To what extent did they claim that the same principle justified granting the ballot to persons of color and granting the ballot to women? On what grounds did other Republicans claim that differences exist between men of color and women that justified giving the ballot only to the former?

One hundred years later white supremacists repeated the Cowan gambit. During the debates over the Civil Rights Act of 1964, opponents of African American rights supported a statutory amendment forbidding gender as well as race discrimination. They miscalculated. Racial liberals during the Great Society had the votes necessary to accept the clause prohibiting gender discrimination as well as the votes necessary to pass a bill outlawing both racial and gender discrimination. Pro-suffrage advocates were not as fortunate in 1866. Most Republicans, even those who supported women's rights, refused to support the statutory amendment enfranchising women. Might women have been granted the right to vote if proponents of women's suffrage had held firm? What would you have done if you were a senator in 1866?

SENATOR EDGAR COWAN (Republican, Pennsylvania)

. . .

. . . I should like to hear even the most astute and learned Senator upon this floor give any better reason for the exclusion of females from the right of suffrage than there is for the exclusion of negroes. . . .

Now, for my part, I very much prefer, if the franchise is to be widened, if more people are to be admitted to the exercise of it, to allow females to participate than I would negroes; but certainly I shall never give my consent to the disfranchisement of females who live in society, who pay taxes, who are governed by the laws, and who have a right, I think, even in that respect, at times to throw their weight in the balance for the purpose of correcting the corruptions and the viciousness to which the male portions of the family

43. *Congressional Globe*, 39th Cong., 2nd Sess., 1866, 46–47, 55–66, 77–84, 107.

tend. I think they have a right to throw their influence into the scale; and I should like to hear any reason to be offered why this should not be so.

Taxation and representation ought to go hand in hand. That we have heard here until all ears have been wearied with it. If taxation and representation are to go hand in hand, why should they not go hand in hand with regard to the female as well as the male? Is there any reason why Mrs. Smith should be governed by a goatherd of a mayor any more than John Smith, if he could correct it?He is paid by taxes levied and assessed on her property just in the same way as he is paid out of taxes levied on the property of John. If she commits an offense she is subjected to be tried, convicted, and punished by the other sex alone; and she has no protection whatever in any way either as to her property, her person, or to her liberty very often.

. . .

Mr. President, if we are to adventure ourselves upon this wide sea of universal suffrage, I object to manhood suffrage. I do not know anything specially about manhood which dedicates it to this purpose more than exists about womanhood. Womanhood to me is rather the more exalted of the two. It is purer; it is higher; it is holier; and it is not purchasable at the same price that the other is, in my judgment. If you want to widen the franchise so as to purify your ballot-box, throw the virtue of the country into it; throw the temperance of the country into it; throw the angel element, if I may so express myself, into it. Let there be as little diabolism as possible, but as much of the divinity as you can get. . . .

SENATOR BENJAMIN WADE (Republican, Ohio)

. . . I have always been of the opinion that in a republican Government the right of voting ought to be limited only by the years of discretion. . . .

. . .

. . . I think it will puzzle any gentleman to draw a line of demarcation between the right of the male and the female on this subject. Both are liable to all the laws you pass; their property, their persons, and their lives are affected by the laws. Why, then, should not the females have a right to participate in their construction as well as the male part of the community? There is no argument that I can conceive of or that I have yet heard that makes any discrimination between the two on the question of right.

Why should there be any restriction? Is it because gentleman apprehend that the female portion of the community are not as virtuous, that they are not as well calculated to consider what laws and principles of the government will conduce to their welfare as men are? The great mass of our educated females understand all these great concerns of Government infinitely better than that great mass of ignorant population from other countries which you admit to the polls without hesitation.

But, sir, the right of suffrage in my judgment has bearings altogether beyond any rights of persons or property that are to be vindicated by it. I lay it down that in any free community, if any particular class of that community are excluded from this right they cannot maintain their dignity. . . . My judgment is that if this right is accorded to females you would find that they would be elevated in their minds and in their intellects. The best discipline you can offer them would be to permit and to require them to participate in these great concerns of Government, so that their rights and the rights of their children should depend in a manner upon the way in which they understand these great things.

. . .

I do not believe that it will have any unfavorable effect upon the female character if women are permitted to come up to the polls and vote. I believe it would exercise a most humane and civilizing influence upon the roughness and rudeness with which men meet on those occasions if the polished ladies of the land would come up to the ballot-box clothed with these rights and participate in the exercise of the franchise. It has not been found that association with ladies is apt to make men rude and uncivilized and I do not think the reflex of it prevents that lady-like character which we all prize so highly. I do not think it has that effect. On the other hand, in my judgment, if it was popular to-day for ladies to go to the polls, no man would regret their presence there, and the districts where their ballots were given would be harmonized, civilized, and rendered more gentlemanly, if I may say so, on the one side and on the other, and it would prevent the rude collisions that are apt to occur at these places, while it would reflect back no uncivilizing or unladylike influence upon the female part of the community. That is the way I judge it. Of course, as it has never been tried in this country, it is more or less of an experiment; but here in this District is the very place to try your experiment.

I know that the same things were said about the abolition of slavery. I was here. . . . I agree, however, that there is not the same pressing necessity for allowing females as there is for allowing the colored people to vote; because the ladies of the land are not under the ban of a hostile race grinding them to powder. They are in high fellowship with those that do govern, who, to a great extent, act as their agents, their friends, promoting their interests in every vote they give, and therefore communities get along very well without conferring this right upon the female. But when you speak of it as a right and as a great educational power in the hands of females, and I am called on to vote on the subject, I will vote that which I think under all circumstances is right, just, and proper. I shrink not from the question because I am told by gentlemen that it is unpopular. The question with me is, is it right? Show me that it is wrong, and then I will withhold my vote; but I have heard no argument that convinces me that the thing is not right.

. . . It seems to me there is a wrong done to those who are shut out from any participation in the Government, and that it is a violation of their rights; and what odds does it make whether you call it a natural or conventional or artificial right? I contend that when you set up a Government you shall call every man who has arrived at the years of discretion who has committed no crime, into your community and ask him to participate in setting up that Government; and if you shut him out without any reason, you do him a wrong, one of the greatest wrongs that you can inflict upon a man. . . .

SENATOR HENRY WILSON (Republican, Massachusetts)

. . .

. . . [W]hile I will vote now or at any time for woman suffrage . . . as a distinct separate measure, I am unalterably opposed to connecting that question with the pending question of negro suffrage. The question of negro suffrage is now an imperative necessity; a necessity that the negro should possess it for his own protection; a necessity that he should possess it that the nation may preserve its power, its strength, and its utility. . . .

. . .

. . . This bill, embodying pure manhood suffrage, is destined to become the law in spite of all opposition and all lamentations. I am opposed, therefore, to associating with this achieved measure the question of suffrage for women.

. . .

. . . I am for securing the needed suffrage for the colored race. I am for enfranchising the black man, and then if this other question shall come up in due time and I have a vote to give I shall be ready to give my vote for it. But to vote for it now is to couple it with the great measure now pressing upon us, to weaken that measure and to endanger its immediate triumph, and therefore I shall vote against the amendment proposed by the Senator from Pennsylvania, made, it is too apparent, not for the enfranchisement of woman, but against the enfranchisement of the black man.

SENATOR REVERDY JOHNSON (Democrat, Maryland)

. . .

Ladies have duties peculiar to themselves which cannot be discharged by anybody else; the nurture and education of the children; the demands upon them consequent upon the preservation of their household; and they are supposed to be more or less in their proper vocation when they are attending to those particular duties. But independent of that, I think that if it was submitted to the ladies—I mean the ladies in the true acceptation of the term—of the United States, the privilege would not only not be asked for, but would be rejected. I do not think the ladies of the United States would agree to enter into a canvass and to undergo what is often the degradation of seeking to vote, particularly in the cities, getting up to the polls, crowded out and crowded in. I rather think they would feel it, instead of a privilege, a dishonor.

There is another reason why the right should not be extended to them, unless it is the purpose of the honorable member and of the Senate to go a step further. The reason why the males are acceded the privilege, and why it was almost universal in the United States with reference to those of a certain age, is that they may be called upon to defend the country in time of war or in time of insurrection. I do not suppose it is pretended that the ladies should be included in the militia organization or be compelled to take up arms to defend the country. That must be done by the male sex, I hope.

. . .

The honorable member from Ohio seems to suppose that the right should be given as a means, if I understand him, of protecting themselves and as a means of elevating them intellectually. I had supposed the theory was that the woman was protected by the man. If she is insulted she is not expected to knock the man who insults her down, or, during the days of the duello to send him a challenge. She goes to her male friend, her husband or brother or acquaintance. Nature has not made her for the rough and tumble, so to speak, of life. She is intended to be delicate. She is intended to soften the asperities and roughness of the male sex. She is intended to comfort him in the days of his trial, not to participate herself actively in the contest either in the forum, in the council chamber, or on the battlefield. As to her not being protected, what lady has ever said that her rights were not protected because she had not the right of suffrage? There are women, respectable I have no doubt in point of character, moral and virtuous women no doubt, but they are called, and properly called, the "strong-minded": they are in the public estimation contradistinguished from the delicate; they are men in women's garb.

. . .

. . . I have seen elections in Baltimore, where they are just as orderly as they are in other cities; but we all know that in times of high party excitement it is impossible to preserve that order which would be sufficient to protect a delicate female from insult, and no lady would venture to run the hazard of being subjected to the insults that she would be almost certain to receive.

They do not want this privilege. As to protecting themselves, as to taking a part in the Government in order to protect themselves, if they govern those who govern, is not that protection enough? And who does not know that they govern us? Thank God they do. . . .

X. Criminal Justice

MAJOR DEVELOPMENTS

- Supreme Court declares that martial law cannot be imposed when civilian courts are open
- Police and judges battle over confessions
- Greater emphasis on right to counsel than trial by jury

The constitutional politics of criminal justice was structured by two different wars. The first was the Civil War and the aftermath of the Union victory. From 1861 to 1865 the Lincoln administration suspended habeas corpus, declared martial law, and arrested without first obtaining warrants numerous persons suspected of interfering with the Union military effort. Congress in 1867 declared martial law throughout much of the South. The second war was the municipal war against crime fought by urban politicians and increasingly professionalized police forces.

Courts during the war against secession and the war against crime often rejected executive demands for greater power. The Supreme Court in *Ex parte Milligan* (1866) ruled that citizens could not be tried by military commissions in places where courts were open. Many state judges exhibited a traditional antipathy to confessions. Courts were nevertheless largely ineffective in their struggle to curb executive behavior in either the war against secession or the war against crime. Shortly after *Milligan* was handed down, Congress passed the First Reconstruction Act, which imposed martial law throughout the South. Policemen continued to seek confessions, confident that in most cases the confessed criminal would not litigate the constitutionality of the means by which the confession was obtained.

A. Due Process and Habeas Corpus

Federal and military officials frequently suspended habeas corpus and declared martial law. Less than two months after taking the oath of office, President Lincoln ordered that habeas corpus be suspended in Maryland to secure the safe transportation of troops from the northern states to the nation's capital. On September 24, 1862, Lincoln suspended habeas corpus and imposed martial law throughout the United States. Congress later authorized these presidential suspensions by passing the Habeas Corpus Act of 1863. The Republican majority in Congress sanctioned the use of military tribunals when passing the Conscription Act of 1863. Four years later Congress passed the First Reconstruction Act, which permitted Union military commanders in the South to use military commissions to try civilians.

Many prominent Americans challenged the constitutionality of official decisions to suspend habeas corpus and declare martial law. Some constitutional objections were based on the separation of powers. Chief Justice Roger Taney in *Ex parte Merryman* (1861) held that President Lincoln acted unconstitutionally when he suspended habeas corpus and declared martial law without congressional authorization. During the debate over the Habeas Corpus Act of 1863, Democrats asserted that only Congress could suspend habeas corpus and that Congress could not delegate to the president the power to determine when suspending habeas corpus or declaring martial law was appropriate. Other constitutional objections were based on individual rights. Lincoln's critics as well as opponents of Reconstruction maintained that federal laws imposing martial law in places where the courts were open violated the right to trial by jury.

The constitutional debates over habeas corpus and martial law were bipartisan during the Civil War. Leading Republicans opposed the Lincoln administration's efforts to restrict civil liberties during wartime. Senator Lyman Trumbull of Illinois, the main sponsor of the Habeas Corpus Act of 1863, was a moderate Republican and a vigorous critic of the Lincoln administration's attempts to suspend habeas corpus and impose martial law without congressional authorization. All five justices Lincoln appointed to the Supreme Court joined the decision in *Ex parte Milligan* (1865) that held that the president had no power to declare martial law where courts were open. Democrats also opposed Lincoln administration restrictions. Governor Horatio Seymour of New York and his political allies were particularly vigorous critics.

Ex parte Merryman, 17 F. Cas. 144 (1861)

John Merryman was a prominent Marylander and a proponent of secession. Republicans believed he was secretly conspiring with other secessionists to prevent northern state militias from coming to Washington, DC. Worried about the safety of the nation's capital, Abraham Lincoln on April 27, 1861, suspended habeas corpus in Baltimore. That suspension enabled the Union Army to detain persons suspected of aiding the Confederacy for any period of time without charging them with a crime. Merryman was one of the first persons arrested under this order. He was held at Fort McHenry, outside of Baltimore. Merryman's friends asked Chief Justice Roger Taney, who was also the local federal circuit court judge, for a writ of habeas corpus/ Such a writ required the federal government to produce Merryman in an open courtroom and either charge him with a crime or release him. When the Lincoln administration refused to produce Merryman after Taney issued the writ, Taney wrote an opinion declaring unconstitutional the presidential suspension of habeas corpus. After delivering his opinion, the chief justice of the United States told friends that he expected that to be arrested and imprisoned by the army. Taney was never arrested, but Merryman remained in prison until July 12, 1861. He was subsequently indicted for treason but never tried.

Why did Chief Justice Taney reject presidential power to suspend habeas corpus? Was he too quick to reject emergency powers?

CHIEF JUSTICE TANEY delivered the opinion for the Court.

. . .

As the case comes before me, therefore, I understand that the president not only claims the right to suspend the writ of habeas corpus himself, at his discretion, but to delegate that discretionary power to a military officer, and to leave it to him to determine whether he will or will not obey judicial process that may be served upon him. No official notice has been given to the courts of justice, or to the public, by proclamation or otherwise, that the president claimed this power, and had exercised it in the manner stated in the return. And I certainly listened to it with some surprise, for I had supposed it to be one of those points of constitutional law upon which there was no difference of opinion, and that it was admitted on all hands, that the privilege of the writ could not be suspended, except by act of congress.

. . .

The clause of the constitution, which authorizes the suspension of the privilege of the writ of habeas corpus, is in the 9th section of the first article. This article is devoted to the legislative department of the United States, and has not the slightest reference to the executive department. . . .

. . .

It is the second article of the constitution that provides for the organization of the executive department, enumerates the powers conferred on it, and prescribes its duties. And if the high power over the liberty of the citizen now claimed, was intended to be conferred on the president, it would undoubtedly be found in plain words in this article; but there is not a word in it that can furnish the slightest ground to justify the exercise of the power.

. . . The short term for which [the president] is elected, and the narrow limits to which his power is confined, show the jealousy and apprehension of future danger which the framers of the constitution felt in relation to that department of the government, and how carefully they withheld from it many of the powers belonging to the executive branch of the English government which were considered as dangerous to the liberty of the subject; and conferred (and that in clear and specific terms) those powers only which were deemed essential to secure the successful operation of the government.

. . .

Even if the privilege of the writ of habeas corpus were suspended by act of congress, and a party not subject to the rules and articles of war were afterwards arrested and imprisoned by regular judicial process, he could not be detained in prison, or brought to trial before a military tribunal, for the article in the amendments to the constitution immediately following the one above referred to (that is, the sixth article) provides, that "in all criminal prosecutions, the accused shall enjoy the right to a speedy and public trial by an impartial jury of the state and district wherein the crime shall have been committed, which district shall have been previously ascertained by law; and to be informed of the nature and cause of the accusation; to be confronted with the witnesses against him; to have compulsory process for obtaining witnesses in his favor; and to have the assistance of counsel for his defence."

. . .

With such provisions in the constitution, expressed in language too clear to be misunderstood by any one, I can see no ground whatever for supposing that the president, in any emergency, or in any state of things, can authorize the suspension of the privileges of the writ of habeas corpus, or the arrest of a citizen, except in aid of the judicial power. He certainly does not faithfully execute the laws, if he takes upon himself legislative power, by suspending the writ of habeas corpus, and the judicial power also, by arresting and imprisoning a person without due process of law.

. . .

The right of the subject to the benefit of the writ of habeas corpus, it must be recollected, was one of the great points in controversy, during the long struggle in England between arbitrary government and free institutions, and must therefore have strongly attracted the attention of the statesmen engaged in framing a new and, as they supposed, a freer government than the one which they had thrown off by the revolution. From the earliest history of the common law, if a person were imprisoned, no matter by what authority, he had a right to the writ of habeas corpus, to bring his case before the king's bench; if no specific offence were charged against him in the warrant of commitment, he was entitled to be forthwith discharged; and if an offence were charged which was bailable in its character, the court was bound to set him at liberty on bail. . . .

. . .

. . . [N]o power in England short of that of parliament can suspend or authorize the suspension of the writ of habeas corpus. I quote again from Blackstone: "But the happiness of our constitution is, that it is not left to the executive power to determine when the danger of the state is so great as to render this measure expedient. It is the parliament only or legislative power that, whenever it sees proper, can authorize the crown by suspending the habeas corpus for a short and limited time, to imprison suspected persons without giving any reason for so doing." If the president of the United States may suspend the writ, then the constitution of the United States has conferred upon him more regal and absolute power over the liberty of the citizen, than the people of England have thought it safe to entrust to the crown. . . .

. . .

Edward Bates, **Opinion on the Suspension of the Privilege of the Writ of Habeas Corpus** (1861)[44]

Abraham Lincoln's message to Congress on July 4, 1861, responded to Taney's accusation of lawlessness in Ex parte Merryman. *While defending the constitutionality of his decision to suspend habeas corpus, Lincoln indicated that he may have had supraconstitutional reasons for taking unilateral executive action:*

> *Soon after the first call for militia, it was considered a duty to authorize the Commanding General, in proper cases, according to his discretion, to suspend the privilege of the writ of habeas corpus; or, in other words, to arrest, and detain, without resort to the ordinary processes and forms of law, such individuals*

44. Excerpt taken from 10 Op. Atty Gen. 74, July 5, 1861.

as he might deem dangerous to the public safety. This authority has purposely been exercised but very sparingly. Nevertheless, the legality and propriety of what has been done under it, are questioned; and the attention of the country has been called to the proposition that one who is sworn to "take care that the laws be faithfully executed," should not himself violate them. Of course some consideration was given to the questions of power, and propriety, before this matter was acted upon. The whole of the laws which were required to be faithfully executed, were being resisted, and failing of execution, in nearly one-third of the States. Must they be allowed to finally fail of execution, even had it been perfectly clear, that by the use of the means necessary to their execution, some single law, made in such extreme tenderness of the citizen's liberty, that practically, it relieves more of the guilty, than of the innocent, should, to a very limited extent, be violated? To state the question more directly, are all the laws, but one, to go unexecuted, and the government itself go to pieces, lest that one be violated? Even in such a case, would not the official oath be broken, if the government should be overthrown, when it was believed that disregarding the single law, would tend to preserve it? But it was not believed that this question was presented. It was not believed that any law was violated.[45]

Attorney General Edward Bates followed up Lincoln's speech with an official opinion justifying the president's suspension of the writ of habeas corpus as consistent with the Constitution. Bates insisted that impeachment is the only remedy for an abusive suspension of habeas corpus. Was he correct as a constitutional matter? Was he correct as a practical matter? President Lincoln was unwilling to obey the judicial order in Merryman. *During times of national crisis, is the judiciary likely to be able to impose constitutional limitations on the president without legislative support? What are the constitutional means for challenging a president during wartime? How many of these means are politically feasible? Suppose you believed that Merryman and his allies were a serious threat to efforts to move Union troops from New York to the defense of Washington, DC. What would you have done in Lincoln's place?*

. . .

45. Abraham Lincoln, "Special Session Message," in *Compilation of the Messages* (see note 14), 6:24.

. . . I am clearly of opinion that, in a time like the present, when the very existence of the nation is assailed, by a great and dangerous insurrection, the President has the lawful discretionary power to arrest and hold in custody persons known to have criminal intercourse with the insurgents, or persons against whom there is probable cause for suspicion of such criminal complicity. . . .

The Constitution requires the President, before he enters upon the execution of his office, to take an oath that he "will faithfully execute the office of President of the United States, and will, to the best of his ability, preserve, protect and defend the Constitution of the United States."

The duties of the office comprehend all the executive power of the nation, which is expressly vested in the President by the Constitution, (Article II, Sec. 1,) and, also, all the powers which are specially delegated to the President, and yet are not, in their nature, executive powers. For example, the veto power; the treaty making power; the appointing power; the pardoning power. These belong to that class which, in England, are called prerogative powers, inherent in the crown. And yet the framers of our Constitution thought proper to preserve them, and to vest them in the President, as necessary to the good government of the country. The executive powers are granted generally, and without specification; the powers not executive are granted specially, and for purposes obvious in the context of the Constitution. And all these are embraced within the duties of the President, and are clearly within that clause of his oath which requires him to "faithfully execute the office of President."

The last clause of the oath is peculiar to the President. All the other officers of the Government are required to swear only "to support this Constitution;" while the President must swear to "preserve, protect, and defend" it, which implies the power to perform what he is required in so solemn a manner to undertake. And then follows the broad and compendious injunction to "take care that the laws be faithfully executed." And this injunction, embracing as it does all the laws—Constitution, treaties, statutes—is addressed to the President alone, and not to any other department or officer of the Government. And this constitutes him, in a peculiar manner, and above all other officers, the guardian of the Constitution—its preserver, protector, and defender.

It is the plain duty of the President (and his peculiar duty, above and beyond all other departments of the Government) to preserve the Constitution and execute the laws all over the nation; and it is plainly impossible for him to perform this duty without putting down rebellion, insurrection, and all unlawful combinations to resist the General Government. . . .

The argument may be briefly stated thus: It is the President's bounden duty to put down the insurrection, as . . . the "combinations are too powerful to be suppressed by the ordinary course of judicial proceedings, or by the powers vested in the marshals." And this duty is imposed upon the President for the very reason that the courts and the marshals are too weak to perform it. The manner in which he shall perform that duty is not prescribed by any law, but the means of performing it are given, in the plain language of the statutes, and they are all means of force—the militia, the army, and the navy. The end, the suppression of the insurrection, is required of him; the means and instruments to suppress it are lawfully in his hands; but the manner in which he shall use them is not prescribed, and could not be prescribed, without a foreknowledge of all the future changes and contingencies of the insurrection. He is, therefore, necessarily, thrown upon his discretion, as to the manner in which he will use his means to meet the varying exigencies as they rise. If the insurgents assail the nation with an army, he may find it best to meet them with an army, and suppress the insurrection in the field of battle. If they seek to prolong the rebellion, and gather strength by intercourse with foreign nations, he may choose to guard the coast and close the ports with a navy, as one of the most efficient means to suppress the insurrection. And if they employ spies and emissaries, to gather information, to forward rebellion, he may find it both prudent and humane to arrest and imprison them. And this may be done, either for the purpose of bringing them to trial and condign punishment for their crimes, or they may be held in custody for the milder end of rendering them powerless for mischief, until the exigency is past.

In such a state of things, the President must, of necessity, be the sole judge, both of the exigency which requires him to act, and of the manner in which it is most prudent for him to employ the powers entrusted to him, to enable him to discharge his constitutional and legal duty—that is, to suppress the insurrection and execute the laws. . . .

This is a great power in the hands of the chief magistrate; and because it is great, and is capable of being perverted to evil ends, its existence has been doubted and denied. It is said to be dangerous, in the hands of an ambitious and wicked President, because he may use it for the purposes of oppression and tyranny. Yes, certainly it is dangerous—all power is dangerous—and for the all-pervading reason that all power is liable to abuse; all the recipients of human power are men, not absolutely virtuous and wise. Still it is a power necessary to the peace and safety of the country, and undeniably belongs to the Government, and therefore must be exercised by some department or officer thereof.

Why should this power be denied to the President, on the ground of its liability to abuse, and not denied to the other departments on the same grounds? Are they more exempt than he is from the frailties and vices of humanity? Or are they more trusted by the law than he is trusted, in their several spheres of action? If it be said that a President may be ambitious and unscrupulous, it may be said with equal truth, that a legislature may be factious and unprincipled, and a court may be venal and corrupt. But these are crimes never to be presumed, even against a private man, and much less against any high and highly-trusted public functionary. They are crimes, however, recognized as such, and made punishable by the Constitution; and whoever is guilty of them, whether a President, a senator, or a judge, is liable to impeachment and condemnation.

Ex parte Milligan, 71 U.S. 2 (1866)

Lambdin P. Milligan, a Confederate sympathizer in Indiana, was arrested by military authorities in 1864 and accused of plotting to steal and provide weapons for the Confederate Army. The Habeas Corpus Act of 1863 required that persons denied habeas corpus be indicted by a grand jury and tried by a civilian court within a short period of time after their detention. Lincoln administration officials tried Milligan before a military tribunal, which sentenced him to death. Milligan appealed to a federal circuit court for a writ of habeas corpus on the ground that his imprisonment, trial, and sentence were unconstitutional. Although both justices on the circuit court probably agreed that Milligan was being illegally detained, they agreed to disagree, because the Supreme Court at that time was obligated to hear all cases whenever the two federal circuit justices hearing the appeal certified their disagreement on the legal issues. President Andrew Johnson assured judicial review by delaying Milligan's scheduled execution until after the Supreme Court determined whether Milligan had been legally convicted.

The Supreme Court decided Milligan *in a rapidly changing political environment. By the spring of 1865 few persons were deeply concerned with the status of persons detained for interfering with the Union war effort. Lincoln intimated that after a Confederate surrender he planned to release all detainees and pardon most people convicted of wartime offenses. Republicans in 1865 were far more concerned with how the decision in* Milligan *cast light on the constitutionality of martial law in the Reconstruction South.*

The Supreme Court unanimously declared that Milligan had been illegally convicted by a military commission. Judge David Davis's majority opinion insisted that neither Congress nor the president could impose martial law in places where the courts were open. Chief Justice Chase, in a concurring opinion, maintained that Milligan was illegally convicted because President Lincoln did not follow the procedures laid out in the Habeas Corpus Act of 1863. Unlike Justice Davis, Chief Justice Chase believed that Congress could impose martial law in places where courts were open.

Illustration 6-4 Lambdin P. Milligan

Source: Library of Congress Prints and Photographs Division Washington, D.C. 20540 USA.

The majority opinion in Milligan *was and is controversial. One Republican journal compared Justice Davis's effort to limit federal power to the* Dred Scott *decision. Republicans were particularly concerned with the broad scope of* Milligan, *because Congress was debating legislation authorizing martial law in the Reconstruction South. Davis's opinion cast doubt on whether such legislation would be constitutional when southern courts were open. Justice Davis privately indicated surprise that his opinion in* Milligan *should have so troubled Republicans in Congress. Given that Justice Davis frequently indicated in "private" that much Reconstruction legislation was unconstitutional, was this profession sincere? Could Republicans impose martial law in the South if, as* Milligan *held, martial law may never be declared when the courts are open and functioning? If the judicial majority had no intention of commenting on martial law in the South, then why did the Court not decide the case on the statutory grounds on which Chief Justice Chase's opinion relied? Lincoln's judicial appointees split 3–2 in favor of congressional power to impose martial law. The Jacksonian holdovers on the Supreme Court split 4–1 in favor of denying congressional power. What do you think explains that division?*

Milligan *has been hailed as one of the greatest opinions for individual liberty ever issued by the Supreme Court. Is this characterization correct? How much courage was needed for a judge to assert a right to a civilian trial after the war was over? Does* Milligan *better stand for the proposition that unconstitutional rights deprivations during a war are likely to be remedied only after the war?*

JUSTICE DAVIS delivered the opinion of the court.

. . .

. . . Milligan, not a resident of one of the rebellious states, or a prisoner of war, but a citizen of Indiana for twenty years past, and never in the military or naval service, is, while at his home, arrested by the military power of the United States, imprisoned, and, on certain criminal charges preferred against him, tried, convicted, and sentenced to be hanged by a military commission, organized under the direction of the military commander of the military district of Indiana. Had this tribunal the legal power and authority to try and punish this man?

No graver question was ever considered by this court, nor one which more nearly concerns the rights of the whole people; for it is the birthright of every American citizen when charged with crime, to be tried and punished according to law. The power of punishment is, alone through the means which the laws have provided for that purpose, and if they are ineffectual, there is an immunity from punishment, no matter how great an offender the individual may be, or how much his crimes may have shocked the sense of justice of the country, or endangered its safety. By the protection of the law human rights are secured; withdraw that protection, and they are at the mercy of wicked rulers, or the clamor of an excited people. If there was law to justify this military trial, it is not our province to interfere; if there was not, it is our duty to declare the nullity of the whole proceedings. . . . By th[e] Constitution and the laws authorized by it this question must be determined. The provisions of that instrument on the administration of criminal justice are too plain and direct, to leave room for misconstruction or doubt of their true meaning. Those applicable to this case are found in that clause of the original Constitution which says, "That the trial of all crimes, except in case of impeachment, shall be by jury"; and in the fourth, fifth, and sixth articles of the amendments. . . . These securities for personal liberty thus embodied, were such as wisdom and experience had demonstrated to be necessary for the protection of those accused of crime. And so strong was the sense of the country of their importance, and so jealous were the people that these rights, highly prized, might be denied them by implication, that when the original Constitution was proposed for adoption it encountered severe opposition; and but for the belief that it would be so amended as to embrace them, it would never have been ratified.

. . . The Constitution of the United States is a law for rulers and people, equally in war and in peace, and covers with the shield of its protection all classes of men, at all times, and under all circumstances. No doctrine, involving more pernicious consequences, was ever invented by the wit of man than that any of its provisions can be suspended during any of the great exigencies of government. Such a doctrine leads directly to anarchy or despotism, but the theory of necessity on which it is based is false; for the government, within the Constitution, has all the powers granted to it, which are necessary to preserve its existence; as has been happily proved by the result of the great effort to throw off its just authority.

Have any of the rights guaranteed by the Constitution been violated in the case of Milligan? and if so, what are they?

. . .

. . . [I]t is said that the jurisdiction is complete under the "laws and usages of war."

It can serve no useful purpose to inquire what those laws and usages are, whence they originated, where found, and on whom they operate; they can never be applied to citizens in states which have upheld the authority of the government, and where the courts are open and their process unobstructed. This court has judicial knowledge that in Indiana the Federal authority was always unopposed, and its courts always open to hear criminal accusations and redress grievances; and no usage of war could sanction a military trial there for any offence whatever of a citizen in civil life, in nowise connected with the military service. Congress could grant no such power; and to the honor of our national legislature be it said, it has never been provoked by the state of the country even to attempt its exercise. One of the plainest constitutional provisions was, therefore, infringed when Milligan was tried by a court not ordained and established by Congress, and not composed of judges appointed during good behavior.

. . .

Another guarantee of freedom was broken when Milligan was denied a trial by jury. The great minds of the country have differed on the correct interpretation to be given to various provisions of the Federal Constitution; and judicial decision has been often invoked to settle their true meaning; but until recently no one ever doubted that the right of trial by jury was fortified in the organic law against the power of attack. It is now assailed; but if ideas can be expressed in words, and language has any meaning, this right—one of the most valuable in a free country—is preserved to every one accused of crime who is not attached to the army, or navy, or militia in actual service. . . .

The discipline necessary to the efficiency of the army and navy, required other and swifter modes of trial than are furnished by the common law courts; and, in pursuance of the power conferred by the Constitution, Congress has declared the kinds of trial, and the manner in which they shall be conducted, for offences committed while the party is in the military or naval service. Every one connected with these branches of the public service is amenable to the jurisdiction which Congress has created for their government, and, while thus serving, surrenders his right to be tried by the civil courts. All other persons, citizens of states where the courts are open, if charged with crime, are guaranteed the inestimable privilege of trial by jury. This privilege is a vital principle, underlying the whole administration of criminal justice; it is not held by sufferance, and cannot be frittered away on any plea of state or political necessity. When peace prevails, and the authority of the government is undisputed, there is no difficulty of preserving the safeguards of liberty; for the ordinary modes of trial are never neglected, and no one wishes it otherwise; but if society is disturbed by civil commotion—if the passions of men are aroused and the restraints of law weakened, if not disregarded—these safeguards need, and should receive, the watchful care of those intrusted with the guardianship of the Constitution and laws. In no other way can we transmit to posterity unimpaired the blessings of liberty, consecrated by the sacrifices of the Revolution.

It is claimed that martial law covers with its broad mantle the proceedings of this military commission. The proposition is this: that in a time of war the commander of an armed force (if in his opinion the exigencies of the country demand it, and of which he is to judge), has the power, within the lines of his military district, to suspend all civil rights and their remedies, and subject citizens as well as soldiers to the rule of his will; and in the exercise of his lawful authority cannot be restrained, except by his superior officer or the President of the United States.

. . .

The statement of this proposition shows its importance; for, if true, republican government is a failure, and there is an end of liberty regulated by law. Martial law, established on such a basis, destroys every guarantee of the Constitution, and effectually renders the "military independent of and superior to the civil power"—the attempt to do which by the King of Great Britain was deemed by our fathers such an offence, that they assigned it to the world as one of the causes which impelled them to declare their independence. Civil liberty and this kind of martial law cannot endure together; the antagonism is irreconcilable; and, in the conflict, one or the other must perish.

. . .

It is essential to the safety of every government that, in a great crisis, like the one we have just passed through, there should be a power somewhere of suspending the writ of habeas corpus. In every war, there are men of previously good character, wicked enough to counsel their fellow-citizens to resist the measures deemed necessary by a good government to sustain its just authority and overthrow its enemies; and their influence may lead to dangerous combinations. In the emergency of the times, an immediate public investigation according to law may not be possible; and yet, the peril to the country may be too imminent to suffer such persons to go at large. Unquestionably, there is then an exigency which demands that the government, if it should see fit in the exercise of a proper discretion to make arrests, should not be required to produce the persons arrested in answer to a writ of habeas corpus. The Constitution goes no further. It does not say after a writ of habeas corpus is denied a citizen, that he shall be tried otherwise than by the course of the common law; if it had intended this result, it was easy by the use of direct words to have accomplished it. The illustrious men who framed that instrument were guarding the foundations of civil liberty against the abuses of unlimited power; they were full of wisdom, and the lessons of history informed them that a trial by an established court, assisted by an impartial jury, was the only sure way of protecting the citizen against oppression and wrong. Knowing this, they limited the suspension to one great right, and left the rest to remain forever inviolable. But, it is insisted that the safety of the country in time of war demands that this broad claim for martial law shall be sustained. If this were true, it could be well said that a country, preserved at the sacrifice of all the cardinal principles of liberty, is not worth the cost of preservation. Happily, it is not so.

. . .

It is difficult to see how the safety of the country required martial law in Indiana. If any of her citizens were plotting treason, the power of arrest could secure them, until the government was prepared for their trial, when the courts were open and ready to try them. It was as easy to protect witnesses before a civil as a military tribunal; and as there could be no wish to convict, except on sufficient legal evidence, surely an ordained and established court was better able to judge of this than a military tribunal composed of gentlemen not trained to the profession of the law.

It follows, from what has been said on this subject, that there are occasions when martial rule can be properly applied. If, in foreign invasion or civil war, the courts are actually closed, and it is impossible to administer criminal justice according to law, then, on the theatre of active military operations, where war really prevails, there is a necessity to furnish a substitute for the civil authority, thus overthrown, to preserve the safety of the army and society; and as no power is left but the military, it is allowed to govern by martial rule until the laws can have their free course. As necessity creates the rule, so it limits its duration; for, if this government is continued after the courts are reinstated, it is a gross usurpation of power. Martial rule can never exist where the courts are open, and in the proper and unobstructed exercise of their jurisdiction. It is also confined to the locality of actual war. Because, during the late Rebellion it could have been enforced in Virginia, where the national authority was overturned and the courts driven out, it does not follow that it should obtain in Indiana, where that authority was never disputed, and justice was always administered. And so in the case of a foreign invasion, martial rule may become a necessity in one state, when, in another, it would be "mere lawless violence."

The CHIEF JUSTICE (with JUSTICE SWAYNE, JUSTICE WAYNE, and JUSTICE MILLER), concurring.

. . .

The crimes with which Milligan was charged were of the gravest character, and the petition and exhibits in the record, which must here be taken as true, admit his guilt. But whatever his desert of punishment may be, it is more important to the country and to every citizen that he should not be punished under an illegal sentence, sanctioned by this court of last resort, than that he should be punished at all. The laws which protect the liberties of the whole people must not be violated or set aside in order to inflict, even upon the guilty, unauthorized though merited justice.

. . .

The holding of the Circuit and District Courts of the United States in Indiana had been uninterrupted. The administration of the laws in the Federal courts had remained unimpaired. Milligan was imprisoned under the authority of the President, and was not a prisoner of war. No list of prisoners had been furnished to the judges, either of the District or Circuit Courts, as required by the law. A grand jury had attended the Circuit Courts of the Indiana district, while Milligan was there imprisoned, and had closed its session without finding any indictment or presentment or otherwise proceeding against the prisoner.

His case was thus brought within the precise letter and intent of the act of Congress, unless it can be said that Milligan was not imprisoned by authority of the President; and nothing of this sort was claimed in argument on the part of the government.

. . .

And it is equally clear that he was entitled to the discharge prayed for.

. . .

But the opinion which has just been read goes further; and as we understand it, asserts not only that the military commission held in Indiana was not authorized by Congress, but that it was not in the power of Congress to authorize it; from which it may be thought to follow, that Congress has no power to indemnify the officers who composed the commission against liability in civil courts for acting as members of it.

We cannot agree to this.

. . .

We think that Congress had power, though not exercised, to authorize the military commission which was held in Indiana.

. . .

It is not denied that the power to make rules for the government of the army and navy is a power to provide for trial and punishment by military courts without a jury. It has been so understood and exercised from the adoption of the Constitution to the present time.

. . .

We think, therefore, that the power of Congress, in the government of the land and naval forces and of the militia, is not at all affected by the fifth or any other amendment. It is not necessary to attempt any precise definition of the boundaries of this power. But may it not be said that government includes protection and defence as well as the regulation of internal administration? And is it impossible to imagine cases in which citizens conspiring or attempting the destruction or great injury of the national forces may be subjected by Congress to military trial and punishment in the just exercise of this undoubted constitutional power? Congress is but the agent of the nation, and does not the security of individuals against the abuse of this, as of every other power, depend on the intelligence and virtue of the people, on their zeal for public and private liberty, upon official responsibility secured by law, and upon the frequency of elections, rather than upon doubtful constructions of legislative powers?

But we do not put our opinion, that Congress might authorize such a military commission as was held in

Indiana, upon the power to provide for the government of the national forces.

Congress has the power not only to raise and support and govern armies but to declare war. It has, therefore, the power to provide by law for carrying on war. This power necessarily extends to all legislation essential to the prosecution of war with vigor and success, except such as interferes with the command of the forces and the conduct of campaigns. That power and duty belong to the President as commander-in-chief. Both these powers are derived from the Constitution, but neither is defined by that instrument. Their extent must be determined by their nature, and by the principles of our institutions.

...

Where peace exists the laws of peace must prevail. What we do maintain is, that when the nation is involved in war, and some portions of the country are invaded, and all are exposed to invasion, it is within the power of Congress to determine in what states or districts such great and imminent public danger exists as justifies the authorization of military tribunals for the trial of crimes and offences against the discipline or security of the army or against the public safety.

...

We cannot doubt that, in such a time of public danger, Congress had power, under the Constitution, to provide for the organization of a military commission, and for trial by that commission of persons engaged in this conspiracy. The fact that the Federal courts were open was regarded by Congress as a sufficient reason for not exercising the power; but that fact could not deprive Congress of the right to exercise it. Those courts might be open and undisturbed in the execution of their functions, and yet wholly incompetent to avert threatened danger, or to punish, with adequate promptitude and certainty, the guilty conspirators.

In Indiana, the judges and officers of the courts were loyal to the government. But it might have been otherwise. In times of rebellion and civil war it may often happen, indeed, that judges and marshals will be in active sympathy with the rebels, and courts their most efficient allies.

We have confined ourselves to the question of power. It was for Congress to determine the question of expediency. And Congress did determine it. That body did not see fit to authorize trials by military commission in Indiana, but by the strongest implication prohibited them. With that prohibition we are satisfied, and should have remained silent if the answers to the questions certified had been put on that ground, without denial of the existence of a power which we believe to be constitutional and important to the public safety,—a denial which, as we have already suggested, seems to draw in question the power of Congress to protect from prosecution the members of military commissions who acted in obedience to their superior officers, and whose action, whether warranted by law or not, was approved by that up-right and patriotic President under whose administration the Republic was rescued from threatened destruction. . . .

B. Search and Seizure

The ordinary constitutional politics of search and seizure was influenced by the increasing perception that professional police officers needed greater leeway to fight crime than the common law provided. Many state courts, building on precedents from the Jacksonian Era, provided professional police officers with constitutional immunities from lawsuits brought by innocent victims of police mistakes. State courts permitted unconstitutionally seized goods to be admitted in a criminal trial. The Supreme Judicial Court of Maine emphatically rejected the adoption of a rule to exclude illegally seized evidence from trial in *State v. McCann* (ME 1873).

C. Interrogations

The official constitutional law of investigations and interrogations diverged sharply from unofficial constitutional practice. Official constitutional law was hostile to confessions, particularly when any suspicion existed that the confession was motivated by either coercion or the hope of leniency. *McGlothlin v. State* (TN 1865) articulated the traditional common law antipathy to confessions as the primary evidence used to convict persons suspected of crime. "A confession, to be received," the justices determined,

> must be freely and voluntarily made, and where the mind has been placed under restraints, by the flattery of hope or the terror of fear, for the purpose of forcing the accused to make a confession, it must appear that prior to the confession, it had become again free, and totally relieved from the influence

of the hopes or fears, induced by the promises or threats which had been used, else the confession will not be admissible.[46]

Constitutional practice relied more heavily on confessions than opinions such as *McGlothlin* suggest. Police officers frequently beat suspects or otherwise induced confessions to prevent crime and obtain convictions.

D. Juries and Lawyers

Criminal defendants enjoyed increased access to lawyers and decreased access to juries during the Civil War and Reconstruction. More states provided attorneys to persons accused of crime. Many constitutional authorities asserted or implied that poor persons had a right to a state-appointed attorney. Thomas Cooley in 1874 declared, "Perhaps the privilege most important to the person accused of crime . . . is that to be defended by counsel."[47] The jury came under increased attack. Presidential and congressional decisions to impose martial law denied jury trials to persons accused of supporting the Confederacy or opposing Reconstruction. In ordinary criminal trials, states began to experiment with alternatives to the jury trial.

E. Punishments

The Civil War and Reconstruction left the constitutional politics of punishment untouched. Few criminal defendants challenged the constitutionality of their sentences, and no state or federal court declared a criminal sanction unconstitutional. The Supreme Court of the Territory of New Mexico expressed the conventional wisdom of the time in *Garcia v. Territory of New Mexico* (NM 1869) when rejecting a constitutional attack on whipping. The cruel and unusual punishment clause, Chief Judge Watts asserted, "was never designed to abridge or limit the selection by the law-making power of such kind of punishment as was deemed most effective in the punishment and suppression of crime."[48]

The status of capital punishment in the United States also remained largely unchanged. Maine and Iowa abolished that sanction in the early 1870s but reinstituted the death penalty within the decade. Abraham Lincoln commuted many death sentences of soldiers who deserted during the Civil War. Nevertheless, Lincoln expressed no qualms about the constitutionality of executions. During the first year of his presidency Lincoln was asked to commute the death sentence of Nathaniel Gordon, a notorious slave trader. Many northerners urged Lincoln to halt the execution on the ground that no slave trader had ever been executed in the United States. Lincoln refused. Nathaniel Gordon was hanged on February 21, 1862.

46. *McGlothlin v. State*, 2 Coldw. 223 (TN 1865).

47. Cooley, *Constitutional Limitations*, 3rd ed., 330.

48. *Garcia v. Territory of New Mexico*, 1 N.M. 415 (1869).

Suggested Readings

Ackerman, Bruce. 1991. *We the People. Vol. 2: Transformations.* Cambridge, MA: Belknap Press of Harvard University Press.

Belz, Herman. 1976. *A New Birth of Freedom: The Republican Party and the Freedmen's Rights 1861 to 1866.* Westport, CT: Greenwood.

Benedict, Michael Les. 1974. *A Compromise of Principle: Congressional Republicans and Reconstruction, 1863–1869.* New York: Norton.

———. 2006. *Preserving the Constitution: Essays on Politics and the Constitution in the Reconstruction Era.* New York: Fordham University Press.

Berger, Raoul. 1977. *Government by Judiciary: The Transformation of the Fourteenth Amendment.* Cambridge, MA: Harvard University Press.

Brandon, Mark. 1998. *Free in the World: American Slavery and Constitutional Failure.* Princeton, NJ: Princeton University Press.

Brandwein, Pamela. 1999. *Reconstructing Reconstruction: The Supreme Court and the Production of Historical Truth.* Durham, NC: Duke University Press.

Curtis, Michael Kent. 1986. *No State Shall Abridge: The Fourteenth Amendment and the Bill of Rights.* Durham, NC: Duke University Press.

DeRosa, Marshall. 1991. *The Confederate Constitution of 1861: An Inquiry into American Constitutionalism.* Columbia: University of Missouri Press.

Fairman, Charles. 1971. *Reconstruction and Reunion, 1864–88.* New York: Macmillan.

Farber, Daniel A. 2003. *Lincoln's Constitution.* Chicago: University of Chicago Press.

Fletcher, George. 2001. *Our Secret Constitution: How Lincoln Redefined American Democracy.* New York: Oxford University Press.

Foner, Eric. 1988. *Reconstruction: America's Unfinished Revolution, 1863–1877.* New York: Harper & Row.

Graber, Mark A. 2006. Dred Scott *and the Problem of Constitutional Evil.* New York: Cambridge University Press.

Hamilton, Daniel W. 2007. *The Limits of Sovereignty: Property Confiscation in the Union and the Confederacy During the Civil War.* Chicago: University of Chicago Press.

Hyman, Harold M. 1973. *A More Perfect Union: The Impact of the Civil War and Reconstruction on the Constitution.* New York: Knopf.

Hyman, Harold M., and William M. Wiecek. 1982. *Equal Justice Under Law: Constitutional Development, 1835–1875.* New York: Harper & Row.

Kaczorowski, Robert J. 1985. *The Politics of Judicial Interpretation: The Federal Courts, Department of Justice and Civil Rights, 1866–1876.* Dobbs Ferry, NY: Oceana.

Kutler, Stanley I. 1968. *Judicial Power and Reconstruction Politics.* Chicago: University of Chicago Press.

Lane, Charles. 2008. *The Day Freedom Died: The Colfax Massacre, the Supreme Court, and the Betrayal of Reconstruction.* New York: Henry Holt and Co.

Lurie, Jonathan. 2003. *The* Slaughterhouse Cases*: Regulation, Reconstruction, and the Fourteenth Amendment.* Lawrence: University Press of Kansas.

McKitrick, Eric. 1960. *Andrew Johnson and Reconstruction.* Chicago: University of Chicago Press.

McPherson, James M. 1988. *Battle Cry of Freedom: The Civil War.* New York: Oxford University Press.

Neely, Mark E., Jr. 1991. *The Fate of Liberty: Abraham Lincoln and Civil Liberties.* New York: Oxford University Press.

Nelson, William E. 1988. *The Fourteenth Amendment: From Political Principle to Judicial Doctrine.* Cambridge, MA: Harvard University Press.

Randall, James G. 1951. *Constitutional Problems Under Lincoln.* Urbana: University of Illinois Press.

Ross, Michael A. 2003. *Justice of Shattered Dreams: Samuel Freeman Miller and the Supreme Court During the Civil War Era.* Baton Rouge: Louisiana State University Press.

Streichler, Stuart. 2005. *Justice Curtis in the Civil War Era: At the Crossroads of American Constitutionalism.* Charlottesville: University of Virginia Press.

Swisher, Carl B. 1974. *History of the Supreme Court of the United States. Volume 5: The Taney Period.* New York: Macmillan.

Tsesis, Alexander. 2004. *The Thirteenth Amendment and American Freedom: A Legal History.* New York: New York University Press.

Vorenberg, Michael. 2001. *Final Freedom: The Civil War, the Abolition of Slavery, and the Thirteenth Amendment.* New York: Cambridge University Press.

Whittington, Keith E. 1999. *Constitutional Construction: Divided Powers and Constitutional Meaning.* Cambridge, MA: Harvard University Press.

Wills, Garry. 1992. *Lincoln at Gettysburg: The Words that Remade America.* New York: Simon and Schuster.

Chapter 7

The Republican Era: 1877–1932

I. Introduction

Industrialization, immigration, and imperialism changed the face of American constitutional politics. Industrialization witnessed the emergence of large corporations that many reformers believed needed to be regulated by the national government and created a working class that many reformers believed needed far more state protection than had previously been the case. Constitutional controversies broke out over when Congress could prohibit monopolies and whether elected officials could pass laws establishing minimum wages or limiting working hours for certain vulnerable laborers. Immigration threatened to undermine the cultural, religious, and ideological homogeneity that many nineteenth-century thinkers thought essential for a constitutional republic. Nativists initiated constitutional controversies when they tightened requirements for American citizenship and passed laws suppressing such strange, dangerous, and un-American political ideas as socialism and anarchism. Imperialism forced Americans to confront whether "the Constitution followed the flag." Both Congress and the Supreme Court debated whether American officials in foreign countries had to respect the liberties enumerated in the Bill of Rights.

Developments. The turn of the twentieth century was a period of political reform. Civil service reform at the national level finally took root (but not before President James Garfield was assassinated in 1881 by a disappointed office seeker). States and localities went even further. They experimented with nonpartisan elections, initiatives, referendums, direct primaries, and recall elections, among other things. States also shifted away from the party ballot—a ballot printed and distributed by the political parties, who naturally listed only their own candidates. Under that system, voters could then simply choose a ballot and place it in the official ballot box. The party ballot was replaced by the "Australian" ballot, a ballot printed by the government that listed all qualified candidates. Now voters could secretly mark the candidates they favored. However, ballot reform was accompanied by other changes that tended to dampen voter participation. These changes included voter registration requirements and literacy tests—and, in the South, legal and extralegal means to keep blacks from the polls.[1]

The Spanish-American War in 1898 marked America's emergence as a global power and left the United States with its first overseas possessions, some temporary (such as Cuba and the Philippines) and others more permanent (such as Puerto Rico and Hawaii). World War I, the failure of the League of Nations, and debates over isolationism left Americans disillusioned and unsure about their place in the world. World War I and the Wilson administration in the 1910s opened the door to a significant increase in the regulatory power and activity of the federal government, and government only partly retreated from that high point in the 1920s.

---

1. On reforms in democratic politics during this period, see Michael E. McGerr, *The Decline of Popular Politics* (New York: Oxford University Press, 1986); Alexander Keyssar, *The Right to Vote* (New York: Basic Books, 2000); J. Morgan Kousser, *The Shaping of Southern Politics* (New Haven, CT: Yale University Press, 1974).

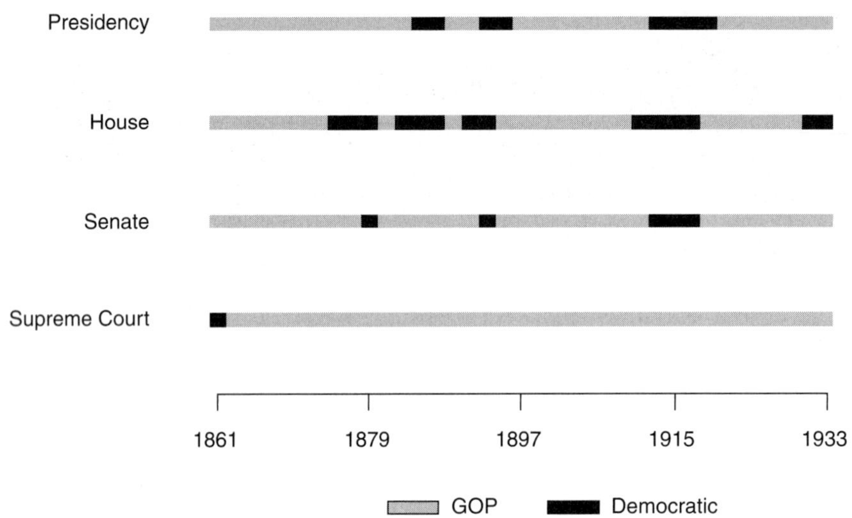

Figure 7-1 Partisan Control of the U.S. Government, 1861–1932

Demands for government regulation and national expansion reconfigured notions of rights and liberties as well as the structure and powers of governing institutions. The federal government's efforts to suppress political dissent during World War I inspired unprecedented debates over the meaning of the First Amendment. American imperialism raised questions about whether persons living in newly acquired territories had the same rights as persons living in New York City or Des Moines. Members of an emerging African American middle class developed national strategies for challenging segregation. New organizations such as the American Civil Liberties Union (ACLU) and the National Association for the Advancement of Colored People (NAACP) became permanent participants in national struggles over rights and liberties. Police efforts to fight crime led to debates over wiretapping and the exclusionary rule.

Parties. Democrats and Republicans competed as near equals during the late nineteenth century, with Republicans gaining the advantage after the elections of 1896. Elections in the late nineteenth century were volatile. Democrats and Republicans took turns occupying the White House from 1876 until 1900. One hundred–seat swings in the House of Representatives were not uncommon. Only the Senate remained a stable bulwark of Republican strength, ensuring that party's control over federal judicial appointments. Electoral politics stabilized in the first quarter of the twentieth century, with Republicans winning every presidential election held from 1896 until 1932, with the exception of the 1912 and 1916 elections. Democrat Woodrow Wilson gained office in 1912 only after a schism in the Republican Party resulted in William Howard Taft running on the Republican Party ticket and former Republican president Theodore Roosevelt campaigning on the Progressive Party ticket. Wilson was barely reelected in 1916, and Republicans easily won the next three presidential elections. Republicans also usually controlled at least one, if not both, houses of Congress. The vast majority of federal judges after 1900 were appointed by Republican presidents. As Figure 7-2 illustrates, both the Democrats and the Republicans (also known as the Grand Old Party, or GOP) solidified their hold over their core regions of support after 1896, reducing the number of closely divided states to a mere handful. Moreover, while the Democrats retained their hold on the South and reached into the rural Midwest, the Republicans kept a firm hold on the populous industrial states of the North. When the GOP was united, its advantage in the Electoral College was nearly insurmountable.

Mainstream Republicans dedicated themselves to maintaining a friendly climate for their corporate allies. Protectionist tariffs and a return to the gold standard (or "hard" money, after the wartime experiment with legal tender) were central planks in their economic platform. The postwar Republicans also sought the settlement of the West and the creation of an integrated national market. National railroads and interstate corporations knit distant communities

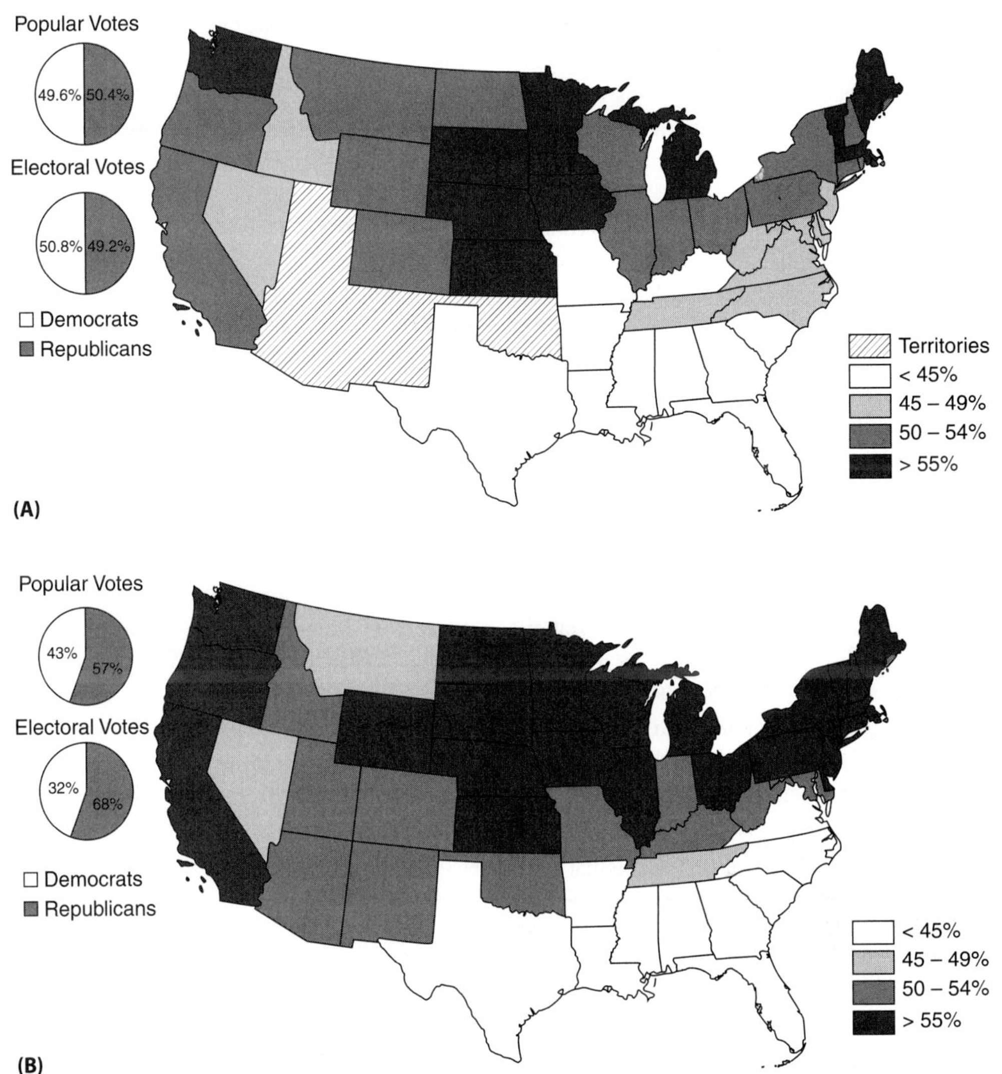

Figure 7-2 (A) Average Republican Party Vote, 1876–1892; (B) Average Republican Party Vote, 1896–1928

Note: State-by-state shading reflects average Republican Party share of the two-party vote, against next largest party in any given election in that state. Figure excludes the election of 1912.

together into a common market. Federal courts prevented states from adopting policies that hampered economic integration. More conservative Democrats shared this business orientation, even as they were more inclined to favor free trade and restricting the power of the national government in the name of states' rights.

The Civil War both structured and increasingly confused partisan alignments. Republicans in the North often "waved the bloody shirt" to maintain voting allegiances. Once Reconstruction ended the South became solidly Democratic. Western states were often up for grabs. Partisan alignments rooted in the constitutional struggles of the 1860s and 1870s, however, often had difficulty incorporating new issues. By 1900 the Republican and Democratic label mattered less than at any previous time in the past fifty years. Prominent Democrats and Republicans in the Northeast favored business interests. Western and southern Populists pushed Democrats more toward economic reform. Progressives from all regions of the country pushed Republicans in similar directions. Sectionalism often better explained constitutional positions than did partisan affiliation. Nevertheless, conservatives and liberals in both major parties were found in every region.

Third parties played a prominent role in constitutional politics. The Populist Party championed far greater regulation of business enterprise than did either Democrats or Republicans. The 1896 Populist Party platform declared, "We believe that the power of government—in other words, of the people—should be expanded . . . as rapidly and as far as the good sense of an intelligent people and the teachings of experience shall justify, to the end that oppression, injustice and poverty, shall eventually cease in the land." The Progressive Party in 1912 called for federal laws mandating an eight-hour workday and a six-day work week, requiring minimum wages, prohibiting child labor, and adopting health and safety standards for risky occupations. Neither Populists nor Progressives gained national power, but each major party had a significant faction that was committed to more moderate versions of populist or progressive reform. William Jennings Bryan, the three-time Democratic Party candidate for president, was also nominated for the presidency by the Populist Party in 1896. Herbert Hoover, the successful Republican candidate for the presidency in 1928, gained a reputation as a progressive reformer in the 1910s.

Interest Groups. The Republican Era witnessed the rise of permanent organized groups that relied on lobbying and litigation to achieve their constitutional visions. The elite lawyers who formed the American Bar Association in 1878 fought for a strong judiciary that would protect individual property rights and act as a bulwark against progressive legislation. The American Federation of Labor (AFL), founded in 1886, focused on using collective bargaining to secure higher wages, a shorter workday, and job security. The AFL also discriminated against black workers, opposed women's employment, and supported the exclusion of Chinese workers. Two women's groups, the National Woman Suffrage Association (NWSA) and the American Woman Suffrage Association, fought to secure gender equality. After the ratification of the Nineteenth Amendment the NWSA became the League of Women Voters. The NAACP, which quickly

Table 7-1 Percentage of Popular Vote in Presidential Election by Political Party, 1876–1932

Year	Republican	Democrat	Populist	Socialist	Progressive	Other
1876	**48**	51				1
1880	**48**	48				3
1884	48	**49**				3
1888	**48**	49				4
1892	43	**46**	9			2
1896	**51**	47				2
1900	**52**	46	0	1		2
1904	**56**	38	1	3		2
1908	**52**	43		3		3
1912	23	**42**		6	27	2
1916	46	**49**		3		1
1920	**60**	34		3		2
1924	**54**	29			17	1
1928	**58**	41		1		0
1932	40	**57**		2		1

Note: Winning party marked in bold.

became the most important organization committed to racial equality, was founded in 1909. The ACLU was organized after World War I. The Anti-Saloon League, the largest interest group in the United States during the Republican Era, led the fight for Prohibition.

Courts. State and federal courts were important and permanent institutional players in the constitutional politics of the Republican Era. Struggles over the proper interpretation of the post–Civil War Amendments, legislation expanding the jurisdiction of federal courts, the rise of the elite bar, and the mobilization of rights-based interest groups all empowered judges as constitutional decision makers. The Supreme Court of the United States was repeatedly called on to determine whether the federal government had the power to regulate what had previously been concerned local matters and whether various economic regulations interfered with the rights protected by the due process clauses of the Fifth and Fourteenth Amendments. *Lochner v. New York* (1905), the most famous civil liberties decision of the Republican Era, held unconstitutional a New York law that restricted bakers to a sixty-hour work week on the ground that the measure violated the freedom of workers to contract with their employers to work longer hours. In other cases, the justices ruled that states were obligated to respect only a few provisions in the Bill of Rights, that Congress was limited only by the due process clause of the Fifth Amendment when governing overseas territories, that the Fourth and Fifth Amendments restricted congressional power to investigate and prosecute businesses, and that government could regulate free speech that had a tendency to produce harmful social consequences.

In a series of important rulings decided on the eve of the 1896 national elections, Supreme Court justices supported the conservative wing of the Republican Party. *United States v. E. C. Knight* (1895) sharply limited the reach of the Sherman Anti-Trust Act. *Pollock v. Farmer's Loan & Trust Company* (1895) struck down the income tax provisions of the Tariff Act of 1894. *In re Debs* (1895) upheld a contempt citation against Eugene Debs, a prominent labor leader and socialist. These decisions inspired a strong Populist and Progressive backlash against judicial power. For the next few decades, various reformers proposed limiting or abolishing judicial power. No proposal succeeded. When Franklin Roosevelt took office, courts were still powerful participants in American constitutional politics.

Constitutional Thought. Constitutional struggles between 1877 and 1932 focused on the threats that a more activist democracy posed to state rights, individual liberty, and equality. Conservative constitutional decision makers worried that popular majorities might pass class legislation designed to benefit one group of people at the expense of another, perhaps by bestowing special privileges on workers or redistributing property. Most conservatives were committed to some version of dual federalism, the belief that some matters are exclusively subject to federal regulation and other matters exclusively subject to state regulation. Late nineteenth-century populists and early twentieth-century progressives believed that elected officials could generally be trusted to pass regulations that promoted the public good. They justified expanded government power as a strong counterweight to powerful private economic interests.

For most of the Republican Era "civil rights and liberties" was not a distinctive area of constitutional law. Constitutional thinkers incorporated speech and other rights issues into existing conceptions of legitimate government power. State legislatures possessed "the police power," which authorized elected officials to pass any law that advanced the public welfare. Legislation that clearly promoted the health or morality of the public was constitutional, no matter what burden the law placed on the individual right. Laws that did not really promote the well being of the public or, worse, provided benefits to some people at the expense of others were held to be unconstitutional. This conceptual framework helps explain why the Supreme Court in *Holden v. Hardy* (1898) declared that states could regulate the working hours of coal miners but in *Lochner v. New York* (1905) declared unconstitutional a state law regulating the hours that bakers could work. The burden such legislation placed on individual rights was the same. The difference between the cases was that the justices believed that limiting the hours that a miner could work promoted public health (because coal mining was considered dangerous and exhausting work), whereas restricting bakers served no purpose other than to enable bakers to make more favorable contracts with their employers.[2]

---

2. See Howard Gillman, *The Constitution Besieged: The Rise and Demise of Lochner Era Police Powers Jurisprudence* (Durham, NC: Duke University Press, 1993).

Table 7-2 Major Issues and Decisions of the Republican Era

Major Political Issues	Major Constitutional Issues	Major Court Decisions
Erosion of federal commitment to black civil rights	Expansion of federal judicial power	*Munn v. Illinois* (1877)
Jim Crow	Application of Fourteenth Amendment against exercises of state police powers	*Reynolds v. United States* (1878)
Industrialization	"State action" requirement	*Civil Rights Cases* (1883)
Labor unrest	Separate but equal	*In re Jacobs* (NY 1885)
Populism and Progressivism	Income tax	*Wabash, St. Louis & Pacific Railroad v. Illinois* (1886)
Social Darwinism	The "living" Constitution	*Fong Yue Ting v. United States* (1893)
Workplace regulation	Application of Constitutional protections to overseas territories	*Income Tax Cases* (1895)
Prohibition	Child labor	*Plessy v. Ferguson* (1896)
Creation of National Association for the Advancement of Colored People	Liberty of contract	*Lochner v. New York* (1905)
Founding of the American Civil Liberties Union	Free speech and advocacy of unlawful conduct	*Ex parte Young* (1908)
Immigration and nativism	Railroad regulation	*Weeks v. United States* (1914)
Spanish-American War	Prohibition Amendment	*Buchanan v. Warley* (1917)
World War I	Direct democracy	*Hammer v. Dagenhart* (1918)
Women's suffrage movement	Women's suffrage amendment	*Schenck v. United States* (1919)
Eugenics	Privacy rights	*Adkins v. Children's Hospital* (1923)
	Sterilization laws	*Meyer v. Nebraska* (1923)
	Sunday closing laws	*Whitney v. California* (1927)
	Constitutional protections for members of the Mormon Church	*Olmstead v. United States* (1928)
	Rights to citizenship	*Near v. Minnesota* (1931)
	Birth of the exclusionary rule	*Powell v. Alabama* (1932)
	Nationalization of the right to counsel	

Legacies. Judicial power was the most important legacy of the Republican Era. State and federal courts had historically not been involved in the major political fights that wracked antebellum America. Participants in debates over national expansion, the American system, and numerous other matters, made constitutional arguments, but with the exception of slavery issues, these concerns were settled in legislative and electoral arenas. By comparison, courts by the turn of the twentieth century were routinely settling disputes over the precise boundaries between federal and state powers, the meaning of racial equality, national power in American territories, and almost every other issue that politicians debated in constitutional terms. Before the Civil War, *Marbury v. Madison* (1803) was most often cited as a case on federal jurisdiction. After the Civil

Box 7-1 A Partial Cast of Characters of the Republican Era

Stephen J. Field	■ Conservative Democrat ■ Justice on California Supreme Court (1857–1863) ■ Appointed by Abraham Lincoln to the U.S. Supreme Court (1863–1897) ■ Known for his belief in a strong role for judicial review, strict limits on federal power, and broad protections for the rights of private property
William Howard Taft	■ Republican ■ Federal circuit court judge (1892–1900) ■ Civil governor of the Philippines (1901–1903) ■ Secretary of war (1904–1908) ■ President of the United States (1909–1913) ■ Appointed by Warren Harding to be chief justice of the United States (1921–1930) ■ Known as a reformer but ultimately collided with the Progressives in his own party ■ Defeated for reelection when Theodore Roosevelt ran an independent campaign for the White House in 1912; later became an influential and active chief justice
Louis Brandeis	■ Progressive Democrat ■ Successful Boston lawyer and activist in Progressive, labor, and Zionist causes ■ Leading defender of workplace regulation; developed the factually oriented "Brandeis brief" to support the constitutionality of such laws ■ Appointed by Woodrow Wilson to the U.S. Supreme Court, leading to a contentious confirmation battle ■ First Jew to serve on the U.S. Supreme Court (1916–1939) ■ Important advocate on the Court for free speech and a right to privacy
Oliver Wendell Holmes, Jr.	■ Progressive Republican ■ Influential Boston legal scholar and a precursor to the "legal realist" movement ■ Served on the Supreme Judicial Court of Massachusetts (1882–1902) ■ Appointed by Theodore Roosevelt to the U.S. Supreme Court (1902–1932) ■ Known for his view that the law evolves over time and that courts should generally be deferential to what political majorities decide
David J. Brewer	■ Conservative Republican ■ Served in a variety of judicial positions in Kansas, culminating in his election to the state supreme court (1870–1884) ■ Appointed by Chester Arthur to the U.S. Circuit Court (1884–1889) ■ Appointed by Benjamin Harrison to U.S. Supreme Court (1889–1910) ■ Popular speaker and prominent Christian author ■ Among the more conservative justices on the Court, but a frequent supporter of minority rights

(*Continued*)

Box 7-1 *(Continued)*

Theodore Roosevelt	▪ Progressive Republican ▪ Governor of New York (1889–1900) ▪ Vice president of the United States (1901) ▪ President of the United States (1901–1909) ▪ Known for his commitment to reform causes, active government, national power, and a strong executive ▪ Unsuccessfully ran an independent campaign for the White House in 1912 as a Progressive, emphasizing themes of reform and direct democracy
John Marshall Harlan	▪ Whig and Republican ▪ Slaveholding Unionist from Kentucky who joined the Union Army ▪ Kentucky attorney general (1863–1867) ▪ Appointed by Rutherford B. Hayes to the U.S. Supreme Court (1877–1911) ▪ Critic of the Court's decisions on race and congressional power

War, *Marbury* was frequently cited as establishing the judicial power to settle constitutional disputes ranging from prohibition to anti-trust.[3]

The other important legacy of the Republican Era was a negative one. For the next eighty years a broad consensus existed that the Supreme Court abused the power of judicial review when protecting the freedom of contract and other economic rights. In this view, judges across the country, spurred on by a conservative and elite bar, used the pretense of protecting individual freedom to promote conservative policy preferences for laissez-faire economics. *Lochner v. New York* (1905) became the primary example of justices substituting their personal views for constitutional law. "Lochnerizing" was the worst accusation that could be leveled against a judicial opinion or constitutional argument. Whenever justices have subsequently sought to protect constitutional rights and liberties they have had to self-consciously distinguish their decisions from Republican Era decisions protecting the freedom of contract.

The Republican Era witnessed the gradual emergence of modern civil rights and liberties. The NAACP achieved its first judicial victories during the 1910s and 1920s. Judicial liberals during the 1940s, 1950s, and 1960s relied heavily on the arguments for strong free speech protections that Justices Oliver Wendell Holmes and Louis Brandeis had pioneered in a series of dissents written during and immediately after World War I. The Supreme Court first announced the exclusionary rule in *Weeks v. United States* (1914), holding that evidence obtained in violation of the Fourth Amendment could not be used in federal criminal proceedings. Other judicial opinions supported the privilege against self-incrimination and emphasized the importance of individual privacy against the expanding powers of government. In these and other matters constitutional decision makers established foundations for rights that later constitutional decision makers built on, modified, or decisively rejected.

II. Foundations

MAJOR DEVELOPMENTS

- Women's suffrage and Prohibition amendments
- Supreme Court rules that federal officials governing overseas territories are not restricted by the Bill of Rights
- State officials required to respect certain fundamental rights but not most provisions in the Bill of Rights

Americans struggled with constitutional change during the Republican Era. The meaning of the post–Civil War Amendments was unclear. Women, prohibitionists, and others proposed additional constitutional

3. See Robert Lowry Clinton, Marbury v. Madison *and Judicial Review* (Lawrence: University of Kansas Press, 1989).

amendments. Constitutional issues arose in new circumstances. Technological changes that the framers had not foreseen raised questions about the constitutional status of wiretapping and whether noise from a new urban train line unconstitutionally took property from disturbed homeowners. The acquisition of Puerto Rico and the Philippines after the Spanish-American War raised questions about the constitutional limits on federal laws governing foreign territories. The combination of immigration, industrialization, and imperialism forced Americans to think about how a Constitution forged in the late eighteenth century should function at the turn of the twentieth century. Many commentators championed a living Constitution, with flexible standards that adjusted to changing political, economic, and social conditions.[4]

A. Sources

Americans added four new amendments to the Constitution during the Republican Era. The Sixteenth Amendment (1913) authorized a federal income tax. The Seventeenth Amendment (1913) mandated popular elections for the Senate. The Eighteenth Amendment (1919) prohibited the manufacture, sale, and transportation of intoxicating liquors. The Nineteenth Amendment (1920) prohibited states from denying individuals the right to vote on the basis of gender.

The Supreme Court at the turn of the century reaffirmed past commitments to customary international law as a source of individual rights. Justice Gray's majority opinion in *The Paquete Habana* (1900) asserted, "International law is part of our law." What that phrase means remains the subject of enduring controversy.

Congressional Debate over Prohibition (1917)[5]

Prohibition was the reform cause of the Republican Era. More Americans at the turn of the twentieth century were members of such organizations as the Women's Christian Temperance Union (WCTU) and the Anti-Saloon League than were members of any other public interest group. Prohibitionists included among their ranks suffragettes, Boston Puritans, rural sharecroppers, and the Ku Klux Klan. During the nineteenth century members of this coalition fought for state and local laws banning the manufacture, sale, and use of intoxicating liquors. Experience demonstrated that state and local laws were easily circumvented when nearby communities remained "wet." Determined to fashion a "dry" America, Prohibition forces began an aggressive push for a constitutional amendment.

Participants in the debate over the proposed Eighteenth Amendment discussed both the powers of government and individual rights. Proponents of Prohibition insisted that federal power was necessary because drinking was a national problem that state laws could not adequately address. In their view drinking was a vice and a menace to the public good. Opponents of Prohibition raised concerns about police powers that had historically been reserved to the states. Many insisted that Americans had a fundamental right to drink, beer in particular. Prohibition was more popular among the people than among elected officials. Many members of Congress voted for the Prohibition amendment, confident that the text would not be ratified by the required three-quarters of the states. They were wrong. The Senate approved the Eighteenth Amendment in August 1917. The House approved it in December 1917. Thirteenth months later two-thirds of the states had approved the amendment. That most of the nation's brewers had Germanic surnames in the wake of World War I furthered the Prohibition cause.

When reading the following excerpts of the debates, consider the place of Prohibition in the constitutional politics of the Republican Era. What were the most important differences between supporters and opponents of Prohibition? To what extent did the debates over Prohibition replay other debates over police powers and the proper balance between federal and state power that took place from 1877 to 1932?

SENATOR BOIES PENROSE (Republican, Pennsylvania)

. . .

Serious doubt may be expressed whether any amendment to the Constitution may properly be placed in that instrument which, without the consent of all the States, would deprive any one of them of one or more of the several reserved powers. . . .

. . .

The police power is the most vital of all the reserved powers in the States, but under this proposed

4. See Howard Gillman, "The Collapse of Constitutional Originalism and the Rise of the Notion of the 'Living Constitution' in the Course of American State-Building," *Studies in American Political Development* 11 (1997): 191–247.

5. *Congressional Record*, 65th Cong., 1st Sess., August 1, 1917, 5636–45.

amendment certain States in the Union which did not, in 1789, and in all likelihood now, could never be made to surrender the police power to the Federal Government, will find a large part of that power wrenched from them, not only without their consent but in defiance of their wishes.

. . .

The proposition is intrinsically and radically vicious and intolerable. Legislation of this character, in my opinion, ought to be preeminently and primarily of strictly State concern. There are many States now having prohibition laws where the people acquiesce in them more or less willingly; but if these laws had been handed to them by a mandate from a central authority in Washington, the result in many cases would have been resentment and revolution.

The only practical way to establish prohibition or any other police proposition over an area of country is through the agencies of the States. Otherwise, it would take an American army to enforce it.

. . .

It, in my opinion, will be inevitable that our system of government will break down if we continue the course which has been followed during the last few years of centralizing everything in the Congress of the United States here in Washington. I believe that the doctrine of State rights, which was once so vigorously maintained by great men in the Senate, and concerning which a great civil war was fought, is more important today than at any other time in the history of the country, in view of our tremendous growth of population and resources and wealth and diversified interests.

SENATOR WILLIAM KENYON (Republican, Iowa)

. . .

No one rises on this floor or elsewhere to defend the American saloon directly.

The American saloon has no conscience. It never did a good act or failed to do a bad one. It is a trap for the youth; a destroyer for the old; a foul spawning place for crime; a corrupter of politics; knows no party; supports those men for office whom it thinks can be easiest influenced; has no respect for law or the courts; debauches city councils, juries and everyone it can reach in power in the unity of its vote, and creates cowards in office.

It flatters, tricks, cajoles, and deceives in order to accomplish its purpose; is responsible for more ruin and death than all the wars the nation has ever engaged in; has corrupted more politics, ruined more lives, widowed more women, orphaned more children, destroyed more homes, caused more tears to flow, broken more hearts, undermined more manhood, and sent more people to an early grave than any other influence in our land.

Its day has come. No subterfuge can long save it. It will be drafted into the open, the influences behind it stripped of their masks. A mighty public conscience is aroused, moving on rapidly, confidently, undismayed, and undeceived. Behind it are the churches of the Nation—Protestant and Catholic—schools, colleges, and homes. This public conscience is not discouraged by defeat or deceived by any cunning devices, by any shams or pretenses. Its cause is the cause of humanity, of righteousness, and God Almighty fights with it.

. . .

No denunciation, no slurs, no jests on the floor of the Senate, no hurling of epithet, no cheap ribaldry in the cloakrooms will stop this fight. It is going on in Congress, and it is going on in the Nation until the tear-producing, orphan-making, home-wrecking, manhood debauching, character-destroying, hell-filling saloon is just as certainly doomed as slavery was doomed.

A saloonless Nation means an efficient Nation, better able to cope with any problem threatening it from without or within.

SENATOR HENRY MYERS (Democrat, Montana)

. . .

There are many things which are now on the statute books of our country by virtue of national legislation which in the beginning of our history were not considered proper subjects of national legislation. Pure-food control, sanitation, child-labor regulation, limitation of hours of labor for men, women, and children—all these things were attained in the face of intense opposition. It took time and toilsome effort. The people in attaining them were fettered by traditions of the dark ages of the past, but by persistent effort they emerged and came out in the bright sunlight of a better day.

I believe that the people of this country, through an enlightened conscience and a sounder public opinion, have about arrived at a point where they are ready to adopt by a national constitutional amendment national prohibition of the manufacture and use of liquor. The time has come to strike for it. The people are ready to pass on it. They want a chance. It is the sense of an enlightened public, sustained by the best professional and scientific authorities, that the use of liquor has no merit in it, neither as food nor medicine. It is a palpable evil, socially, physically, morally, politically, economically. The progress in this reform has been slow, but steady and sure, and I believe the day for marking the milepost of that achievement is finally at hand.

. . .

SENATOR JOHN WEEKS (Republican, Massachusetts)

. . .

. . . [T]here is no attempt made by the proponents of this legislation to make provision for any compensation on account of the destruction of a business which has continued to exist during the entire life of the Republic by national license. I am opposed to confiscation of property in any form at any time, whether or not I entirely approve of the individuals engaged in this business or the character of the business conducted. When we propose confiscation we are inaugurating a policy which is likely to be most far-reaching in its effect. Some one may conclude that some other form of business is not entirely for the public interest, and the fact that we have established a confiscation precedent may result in its being extended to other fields.

Finally, it seems to me that the individual has rights which should be protected. The vast majority of those who indulge in stimulants, in these days especially, do so to a very moderate degree. I am not satisfied that the multitudinous statistics which are given out about the harm coming from wines and light beers are well founded. . . .

There are innumerable things in which we indulge which are undoubtedly more or less harmful to individuals, and I think that statement would be equally true in its application to food consumed in unreasonable quantities and at unreasonable times.

B. Principles

Late nineteenth-century Americans discovered that their newly amended Constitution had an uncertain mission. Many radical Republicans during Reconstruction insisted that the Thirteenth, Fourteenth, and Fifteenth Amendments revolutionized the constitutional politics of fundamental rights. They looked forward to a new regime in which the federal government would promote political and economic equality. Conservative Republicans and Democrats, in contrast, thought those amendments did little more than end slavery. They looked forward to "the Constitution as it was," minus human bondage. Prominent constitutional elites less concerned with racial issues championed the free labor constitutional commitments of the early Republican Party. They hoped that the end of slavery meant the end of discriminatory legislation intended to benefit some people at the expense of others.

Much constitutional thinking in the Republican Era was rooted in one of two schools of political thought: social Darwinism or pragmatism. Both reflected the influence of Charles Darwin, the scientist who formulated the theory of evolution or natural selection. Social Darwinists maintained that government should avoid economic regulation and let natural selection determine wages, prices, and other business practices. Pragmatists insisted on a living Constitution, one that adjusted constitutional rules and principles in light of political and social changes.

C. Scope

Constitutional authorities rejected three distinct attempts to substantially broaden the scope of federal constitutional protections for civil rights. *Ross v. McIntyre* (1891) held that the Bill of Rights had no extraterritorial effect. American officials in foreign countries had to consult treaties, but not the Constitution, when determining whether their actions were legal. *Balzac v. Porto Rico* (1922) and other *Insular Cases*, most notably *Downes v. Bidwell* (1903) and *Hawaii v. Mankichi* (1903), concluded that Congress was limited by the Bill of Rights only when governing territories being prepared for statehood. Oklahoma residents had the right to trial by jury, but persons residing in Puerto Rico or the Philippines did not. A Supreme Court majority in *Hurtado v. California* (1884) ruled that state governments were not limited by any provision in the Bill of Rights. That position was modified after 1895. In a series of cases, judicial majorities determined that the due process clause of the Fourteenth Amendment had some overlap with the Bill of Rights. *Twining v. New Jersey* (1908) declared that the crucial due process issue was whether the right in question was "a fundamental principle of liberty and justice which inheres in the very idea of free government and is the inalienable right of a citizen of such a government." By 1932 the justices had ruled that states could not take property without compensation or to benefit private parties, could not deprive a person of the right to counsel, and could not violate free speech rights.

The state action requirement debuted in the Republican Era. The Supreme Court in the *Civil Rights Cases* (1883) held that the Fourteenth Amendment was a restriction only against the official actions of state government and thus did not prohibit purely private interference with individual rights. That ruling did not absolutely bar federal efforts to combat all private discrimination. The justices recognized that the Thirteenth Amendment has no state action requirement. Republican Era justices also recognized that private individuals could be held to constitutional standards when their discrimination had some connection to official action or law. Nevertheless, the state action requirement, combined with the continued vitality of *Barron v. Baltimore* (1833), sharply limited federal protection for individual rights in the states.

Balzac v. Porto Rico, 258 U.S. 298 (1922)

Jesus Balzac was the editor of a local paper in Puerto Rico. In 1918 he was charged with criminal libel for publishing a series of articles critical of the territorial governor. At trial Balzac claimed that his conduct was protected by the First Amendment and that the Sixth Amendment guaranteed him the right to a jury trial. Both contentions were overruled. Balzac was found guilty and sentenced to four months in prison. After the Supreme Court of Puerto Rico affirmed that decision, Balzac appealed to the Supreme Court of the United States.

The Supreme Court of the United States unanimously upheld Balzac's conviction. Chief Justice Taft's opinion declared that the Bill of Rights only limited federal power in incorporated territories being prepared for statehood. The parties to Balzac *agreed that all Puerto Rican residents were citizens of the United States under the Foraker Act of 1900. Why did Taft nevertheless conclude that Puerto Rico was an unincorporated territory? How did Taft distinguish between Puerto Rico and Texas, which was considered an incorporated territory? To what extent do you believe that the race of most inhabitants of a territory influenced judicial and legislative decisions on whether it was incorporated? Notice that Taft decided the First Amendment issue on the merits of the case rather than claiming that Congress was not bound by that provision. Does this imply that persons living in unincorporated territories have the right to free speech?*

Balzac *was decided unanimously, but the claim that the Bill of Rights limited federal power only in incorporated territories had been heatedly contested in previous cases. Consider Justice Harlan's dissent in* Hawaii v. Mankichi *(1903), which declared,*

> *In my opinion, the Constitution of the United States became the supreme law of Hawaii immediately upon the acquisition by the United States of complete sovereignty over the Hawaiian Islands, and without any act of Congress formally extending the Constitution to those islands. . . . From the moment when the government of Hawaii accepted the joint resolution of 1898 by a formal transfer of its sovereignty to the United States, . . . every human being in Hawaii charged with the commission of crime there could have rightly insisted that neither his life nor his liberty could be taken, as punishment for crime, by any process or as the result of any mode of procedure that was inconsistent with the Constitution of the United States. Can it be that the Constitution is the supreme law in the states of the Union, in the organized territories of the United States, between the Atlantic and Pacific oceans, and in the District of Columbia, and yet was not . . . the supreme law in territories and among peoples situated as were the territory and people of Hawaii, and over which the United States had acquired all rights of sovereignty of whatsoever kind? A negative answer to this question, and a recognition of the principle that such an answer involves, would place Congress above the Constitution. It would mean that the benefit of the constitutional provisions designed for the protection of life and liberty may be claimed by some of the people subject to the authority and jurisdiction of the United States, but cannot be claimed by others equally subject to its authority and jurisdiction. It would mean that the will of Congress, not the Constitution, is the supreme law of the land for certain peoples and territories under our jurisdiction. It would mean that the United States may acquire territory by cession, conquest, or treaty, and that Congress may exercise sovereign dominion over it, outside of and in violation of the Constitution and under regulations that could not be applied to the organized territories of the United States and their inhabitants. It would mean that, under the influence and guidance of commercialism and the supposed necessities of trade, this*

country had left the old ways of the fathers, as defined by a written constitution, and entered upon a new way, in following which the American people will lose sight of, or become indifferent to, principles which had been supposed to be essential to real liberty. It would mean that, if the principles now announced should become firmly established, the time may not be far distant when, under the exactions of trade and commerce, and to gratify an ambition to become the dominant political power in all the earth, the United States will acquire territories in every direction, which are inhabited by human beings, over which territories, to be called "dependencies" or "outlying possessions," we will exercise absolute dominion, and whose inhabitants will be regarded as "subjects" or "dependent peoples," to be controlled as Congress may see fit, not as the Constitution requires nor as the people governed may wish. Thus, will be engrafted upon our republican institutions, controlled by the supreme law of a written Constitution, a colonial system entirely foreign to the genius of our government and abhorrent to the principles that underlie and pervade the Constitution.

Illustration 7-1 "The Constitution Follows the Flag" Song Sheet
This 1901 patriotic song from the Spanish-American War reflected a popular phrase of the time.

Source: George Alexander and Jean Schwartz, "The Constitution Follows the Flag" [song sheet], 1901. Music Division, The New York Public Library for the Performing Arts, Astor, Lenox and Tilden Foundations.

CHIEF JUSTICE TAFT delivered the opinion of the Court.

. . .

It is well settled that these provisions for jury trial in criminal and civil cases apply to the Territories of the United States. *Webster v. Reid* (1850). But it is just as clearly settled that they do not apply to territory belonging to the United States which has not been incorporated into the Union. *Hawaii v. Mankichi* (1903). It was further settled in *Downes v. Bidwell* (1903) that neither the Philippines nor Porto Rico was territory which had been incorporated in the Union or become a part of the United States, as distinguished from merely belonging to it. . . .

. . .

. . . [T]he Porto Rican can not insist upon the right of trial by jury, except as his own representatives in his legislature shall confer it on him. The citizen of the United States living in Porto Rico cannot there enjoy a right of trial by jury under the federal Constitution, any more than the Porto Rican. It is locality that is determinative of the application of the Constitution, in such matters as judicial procedure, and not the status of the people who live in it.

. . .

The jury system needs citizens trained to the exercise of the responsibilities of jurors. In common-law countries centuries of tradition have prepared a conception of the impartial attitude jurors must assume. The jury system postulates a conscious duty of participation in the machinery of justice which it is hard for people not brought up in fundamentally popular government at once to acquire. One of its greatest benefits is in the security it gives the people that they, as jurors, actual or possible, being part of the judicial system of the country, can prevent its arbitrary use or abuse. Congress has thought that a people like the Filipinos, or the Porto Ricans, trained to a complete judicial system which knows no juries, living in compact and ancient communities, with definitely formed customs and political conceptions, should be permitted themselves to determine how far they wish to adopt this institution of Anglo-Saxon origin, and when. . . .

. . .

A second assignment of error is based on the claim that the alleged libels here did not pass the bounds of legitimate comment on the conduct of the Governor of the island, against whom they were directed, and that its prosecution is a violation of the First Amendment to the Constitution, securing free speech and a free press. A reading of the two articles removes the slightest doubt that they go far beyond the "exuberant expressions of meridional speech."... Indeed, they are so excessive and outrageous in their character that they suggest the query whether their superlative vilification has not overleaped itself and become unconsciously humorous. But this is not a defense.

JUSTICE HOLMES concurs in the result.

Civil Rights Cases, 109 U.S. 3 (1883)

Murray Stanley, Samuel Nichols, Michael Ryan, and Samuel Singleton were indicted in four separate cases for violating the Civil Rights Act of 1875, which forbade racial discrimination by "inns, public conveyances on land and water, theaters, and other places of public amusement." The local circuit courts divided evenly on whether that law was constitutional. Around the same time, Robinson brought a suit against the Memphis & Charleston Railroad for refusing to allow his wife to ride in the ladies' car. A jury found for the railway company. The Supreme Court combined these five cases when considering the constitutionality of the Civil Rights Act of 1875.

The Supreme Court by an 8–1 vote declared the crucial provision of the Civil Rights Act unconstitutional. Justice Bradley's majority opinion ruled that the Fourteenth Amendment forbade only states, and not private parties, from denying equal protection. The Fourteenth Amendment, a judicial majority held, required plaintiffs alleging rights violations to prove "state action." Private discrimination was beyond the scope of the amendment and, by extension, beyond the scope of Congress' power to enforce the provisions of the amendment. How did Justice Bradley reach that conclusion? Why did he reject the claim that Congress does not have power under the Thirteenth Amendment to forbid some private discrimination? Why did Justice Harlan disagree with that conclusion? (Justice Harlan felt so strongly that the majority had erred that he decided to write his dissent with the same pen and inkwell that Chief Justice Taney used to write the Dred Scott *opinion.) If state officials decide not to protect blacks from hostile or discriminatory behavior by other people in the state, would that be a kind of "state action" that would fall under the scope of the equal protection clause? Shortly after passing the Civil Rights Act of 1875, national party leaders struck a bargain to end Reconstruction. Did that bargain influence the justices? Would the case have been decided differently if the issues had come before the justices in 1870?*

JUSTICE BRADLEY delivered the opinion of the Court.

. . .

The first section of the fourteenth amendment... declares that "no state shall make or enforce any law which shall abridge the privileges or immunities of citizens of the United States; nor shall any state deprive any person of life, liberty, or property without due process of law; nor deny to any person within its jurisdiction the equal protection of the laws." It is state action of a particular character that is prohibited. Individual invasion of individual rights is not the subject-matter of the amendment. It has a deeper and broader scope. It nullifies and makes void all state legislation, and state action of every kind, which impairs the privileges and immunities of citizens of the United States, or which injures them in life, liberty, or property without due process of law, or which denies to any of them the equal protection of the laws. It not only does this, but... the last section of the amendment invests congress with power to enforce it by appropriate legislation. To enforce what? To enforce the prohibition. To adopt appropriate legislation for correcting the effects of such prohibited state law and state acts, and thus to render them effectually null, void, and innocuous. This is the legislative power conferred upon congress, and this is the whole of it. It does not invest congress with power to legislate upon subjects which are within the domain of state legislation; but to provide modes of relief against state legislation, or state action, of the kind referred to. It does not authorize congress to create a code of municipal law for the regulation of private rights; but to provide modes of redress against the operation of state laws, and the action of state officers, executive or judicial, when these are subversive of the fundamental rights specified in the amendment. Positive rights and privileges are undoubtedly secured by the fourteenth amendment; but they are secured by way of prohibition against state laws and state proceedings affecting those rights and privileges, and by power given to congress to legislate for the purpose of carrying such prohibition into effect; and such legislation must necessarily be predicated upon such supposed state laws or state proceedings, and be directed to the correction of their operation and effect....

. . .

And so in the present case, until some state law has been passed, or some state action through its officers or agents has been taken, adverse to the rights of citizens sought to be protected by the fourteenth amendment, no legislation of the United States under said amendment, nor any proceeding under such legislation, can be called into activity, for the prohibitions of the amendment are against state laws and acts done under state authority. . . .

An inspection of the law shows that it makes no reference whatever to any supposed or apprehended violation of the fourteenth amendment on the part of the states. It is not predicated on any such view. It proceeds *ex directo* to declare that certain acts committed by individuals shall be deemed offenses, and shall be prosecuted and punished by proceedings in the courts of the United States. It does not profess to be corrective of any constitutional wrong committed by the states; it does not make its operation to depend upon any such wrong committed. It applies equally to cases arising in states which have the justest laws respecting the personal rights of citizens, and whose authorities are ever ready to enforce such laws as to those which arise in states that may have violated the prohibition of the amendment. In other words, it steps into the domain of local jurisprudence, and lays down rules for the conduct of individuals in society towards each other, and imposes sanctions for the enforcement of those rules, without referring in any manner to any supposed action of the state or its authorities.

. . .

In this connection it is proper to state that civil rights, such as are guaranteed by the constitution against state aggression, cannot be impaired by the wrongful acts of individuals, unsupported by state authority in the shape of laws, customs, or judicial or executive proceedings. The wrongful act of an individual, unsupported by any such authority, is simply a private wrong, or a crime of that individual; an invasion of the rights of the injured party, it is true, whether they affect his person, his property, or his reputation; but if not sanctioned in some way by the state, or not done under state authority, his rights remain in full force, and may presumably be vindicated by resort to the laws of the state for redress. An individual cannot deprive a man of his right to vote, to hold property, to buy and to sell, to sue in the courts, or to be a witness or a juror; he may, by force or fraud, interfere with the enjoyment of the right in a particular case; he may commit an assault against the person, or commit murder, or use ruffian violence at the polls, or slander the good name of a fellow-citizen; but unless protected in these wrongful acts by some shield of state law or state authority, he cannot destroy or injure the right; he will only render himself amenable to satisfaction or punishment; and amenable therefore to the laws of the state where the wrongful acts are committed. Hence, in all those cases where the constitution seeks to protect the rights of the citizen against discriminative and unjust laws of the state by prohibiting such laws, it is not individual offenses, but abrogation and denial of rights, which it denounces, and for which it clothes the congress with power to provide a remedy. . . .

. . .

. . . Conceding . . . that congress has a right to enact all necessary and proper laws for the obliteration and prevention of slavery, with all its badges and incidents, is [it] also true, that the denial to any person of admission to the accommodations and privileges of an inn, a public conveyance, or a theater, does subject that person to any form of servitude, or tend to fasten upon him any badge of slavery? If it does not, then power to pass the law is not found in the thirteenth amendment.

. . .

After giving to these questions all the consideration which their importance demands, we are forced to the conclusion that such an act of refusal has nothing to do with slavery or involuntary servitude, and that if it is violative of any right of the party, his redress is to be sought under the laws of the state; or, if those laws are adverse to his rights and do not protect him, his remedy will be found in the corrective legislation which congress has adopted, or may adopt, for counteracting the effect of state laws, or state action, prohibited by the fourteenth amendment. It would be running the slavery argument into the ground to make it apply to every act of discrimination which a person may see fit to make as to the guests he will entertain, or as to the people he will take into his coach or cab or car, or admit to his concert or theater, or deal with in other matters of intercourse or business. Innkeepers and public carriers, by the laws of all the states, so far as we are aware, are bound, to the extent of their facilities, to furnish proper accommodation to all unobjectionable persons who in good faith apply for them. If the laws themselves make any unjust discrimination, amenable to the prohibitions of the fourteenth amendment, congress has full power to afford a remedy under that amendment and in accordance with it.

When a man has emerged from slavery, and by the aid of beneficent legislation has shaken off the inseparable concomitants of that state, there must be some stage in the progress of his elevation when he takes the rank of a mere citizen, and ceases to be the special favorite of the laws, and when his rights as a citizen, or a man, are to be protected in the ordinary modes by which other men's rights are protected. There were thousands of free colored people in this country before the abolition of slavery, enjoying all the essential rights of life, liberty, and property the same as white citizens; yet no one, at that time, thought that it was any invasion of their personal *status* as freemen because they were not admitted to all the privileges enjoyed by white citizens, or because they were subjected to discriminations in the enjoyment of accommodations in inns, public conveyances, and places of amusement. Mere discriminations on account of race or color were not regarded as badges of slavery. . . .

. . .

JUSTICE HARLAN, dissenting.

The opinion in these cases proceeds, as it seems to me, upon grounds entirely too narrow and artificial. The substance and spirit of the recent amendments of the constitution have been sacrificed by a subtle and ingenious verbal criticism. . . . Constitutional provisions, adopted in the interest of liberty, and for the purpose of securing, through national legislation, if need be, rights inhering in a state of freedom, and belonging to American citizenship, have been so construed as to defeat the ends the people desired to accomplish, which they attempted to accomplish, and which they supposed they had accomplished by changes in their fundamental law.

. . .

That there are burdens and disabilities which constitute badges of slavery and servitude, and that the express power delegated to congress to enforce, by appropriate legislation, the thirteenth amendment, may be exerted by legislation of a direct and primary character, for the eradication, not simply of the institution, but of its badges and incidents, are propositions which ought to be deemed indisputable. They lie at the very foundation of the civil rights act of 1866. . . . I do not contend that the thirteenth amendment invests congress with authority, by legislation, to regulate the entire body of the civil rights which citizens enjoy, or may enjoy, in the several states. But I do hold that since slavery, as the court has repeatedly declared, was the moving or principal cause of the adoption of that amendment, and since that institution rested wholly upon the inferiority, as a race, of those held in bondage, their freedom necessarily involved immunity from, and protection against, all discrimination against them, because of their race, in respect of such civil rights as belong to freemen of other races. Congress, therefore, under its express power to enforce that amendment, by appropriate legislation, may enact laws to protect that people against the deprivation, *on account of their race*, of any civil rights enjoyed by other freemen in the same state; and such legislation may be of a direct and primary character, operating upon states, their officers and agents, and also upon, at least, such individuals and corporations as exercise public functions and wield power and authority under the state.

. . .

It remains now to inquire what are the legal rights of colored persons in respect of the accommodations, privileges, and facilities of public conveyances, inns, and places of public amusement.

As to public conveyances on land and water. . . . [T]his court . . . said that a common carrier is "in the exercise of a sort of public office and has public duties to perform, from which he should not be permitted to exonerate himself without the assent of the parties concerned." To the same effect . . . , it was ruled that railroads are public highways, established, by authority of the state, for the public use; that they are none the less public highways because controlled and owned by private corporations; that it is a part of the function of government to make and maintain highways for the conveyance of the public; that no matter who is the agent, and what is the agency, the function performed is *that of the state*; that although the owners may be private companies, they may be compelled to permit the public to use these works in the manner in which they can be used. . . .

. . .

Such being the relations these corporations hold to the public, it would seem that the right of a colored person to use an improved public highway, upon the terms accorded to freemen of other races, is as fundamental in the state of freedom, established in this country, as are any of the rights which my brethren concede to be so far fundamental as to be deemed the essence of civil freedom. "Personal liberty consists," says Blackstone, "in the power of locomotion, of changing situation, or removing one's person to whatever place one's own inclination may direct, without restraint, unless by due course of law." But of what value is this right of locomotion, if it may be clogged by such burdens as congress intended by the act of 1875 to remove? . . .

. . .

. . . [A] keeper of an inn is in the exercise of a *quasi* public employment. The law gives him special privileges, and he is charged with certain duties and responsibilities to the public. The public nature of his employment forbids him from discriminating against any person asking admission as a guest on account of the race or color of that person.

As to places of public amusement. . . . [They] are established and maintained under direct license of the law. The authority to establish and maintain them comes from the public. The colored race is a part of that public. The local government granting the license represents them as well as all other races within its jurisdiction. A license from the public to establish a place of public amusement, imports, in law, equality of right, at such places, among all the members of that public. . . .

. . .

The assumption that [the fourteenth] amendment consists wholly of prohibitions upon state laws and state proceedings in hostility to its provisions, is unauthorized by its language. . . .

. . .

But what was secured to colored citizens of the United States—as between them and their respective states—by the grant to them of state citizenship? With what rights, privileges, or immunities did this grant from the nation invest them? There is one, if there be no others—exemption from race discrimination in respect of any civil right belonging to citizens of the white race in the same state. That, surely, is their constitutional privilege when within the jurisdiction of other states. And such must be their constitutional right, in their own state, unless the recent amendments be "splendid baubles," thrown out to delude those who deserved fair and generous treatment at the hands of the nation. Citizenship in this country necessarily imports equality of civil rights among citizens of every race in the same state. It is fundamental in American citizenship that, in respect of such rights, there shall be no discrimination by the state, or its officers, or by individuals, or corporations exercising public functions or authority, against any citizen because of his race or previous condition of servitude. . . .

. . .

If, then, exemption from discrimination in respect of civil rights is a new constitutional right, secured by the grant of state citizenship to colored citizens of the United States, why may not the nation, by means of its own legislation of a primary direct character, guard, protect, and enforce that right? It is a right and privilege which the nation conferred. It did not come from the states in which those colored citizens reside. It has been the established doctrine of this court during all its history, accepted as vital to the national supremacy, that congress, in the absence of a positive delegation of power to the state legislatures, may by legislation enforce and protect any right derived from or created by the national constitution.

. . .

. . . If the grant to colored citizens of the United States of citizenship in their respective states imports exemption from race discrimination, in their states, in respect of the civil rights belonging to citizenship, then, to hold that the amendment remits that right to the states for their protection, primarily, and stays the hands of the nation, until it is assailed by state laws or state proceedings, is to adjudge that the amendment, so far from enlarging the powers of congress,—as we have heretofore said it did,—not only curtails them, but reverses the policy which the general government has pursued from its very organization. Such an interpretation of the amendment is a denial to congress of the power, by appropriate legislation, to enforce one of its provisions. . . . I venture, with all respect for the opinion of others, to insist that the national legislature may, without transcending the limits of the constitution, do for human liberty and the fundamental rights of American citizenship, what it did, with the sanction of this court, for the protection of slavery and the rights of the masters of fugitive slaves. . . .

. . .

My brethren say that when a man has emerged from slavery, and by the aid of beneficient legislation has shaken off the inseparable concomitants of that state, there must be some stage in the progress of his elevation when he takes the rank of a mere citizen, and ceases to be the special favorite of the laws, and when his rights as a citizen, or a man, are to be protected in the ordinary modes by which other men's rights are protected. It is, I submit, scarcely just to say that the colored race has been the special favorite of the laws. What the nation, through congress, has sought to accomplish in reference to that race is, what had already been done in every state in the Union for the white race, to secure and protect rights belonging to them as freemen and citizens; nothing more. The one underlying purpose of congressional legislation has been to enable the black race to take the rank of mere citizens. The difficulty has been to compel a recognition of their legal right to take that rank, and to secure the enjoyment of privileges belonging, under the law, to them as a component part of the people for whose welfare and happiness government is ordained. At every step in this direction the nation has been confronted with class tyranny, which a contemporary English historian says is, of all tyrannies, the most intolerable, "for it is ubiquitous in its operation, and weighs, perhaps, most heavily on those whose obscurity or distance would withdraw them from the notice of a single despot." To-day it is the colored race which is denied, by corporations and individuals wielding public authority, rights fundamental in their freedom and citizenship. At some future time it may be some other race that will fall under the ban. If the constitutional amendments be enforced, according to the intent with which, as I conceive, they were adopted, there cannot be, in this republic, any class of human beings in practical subjection to another class, with power in the latter to dole out to the former just such privileges as they may choose to grant. . . .

III. Judicial Power and Constitutional Authority

MAJOR DEVELOPMENTS

- Expansion of federal judicial review of the states
- Growth of constitutional litigation in state and federal courts
- Debate over judicial deference to legislatures
- Proposals to recall judges and judicial decisions

The Republican Era saw a dramatic expansion of judicial review. Both state courts and federal courts became more active in exercising the power of judicial review in the years after the Civil War. The Fourteenth Amendment to the U.S. Constitution provided one important, but ill-defined, tool for lawyers to use to draw judges into political battles. This crucial Reconstruction Amendment gave the federal courts a new basis on which to judge state actions, and over time it became one of the most litigated pieces of text

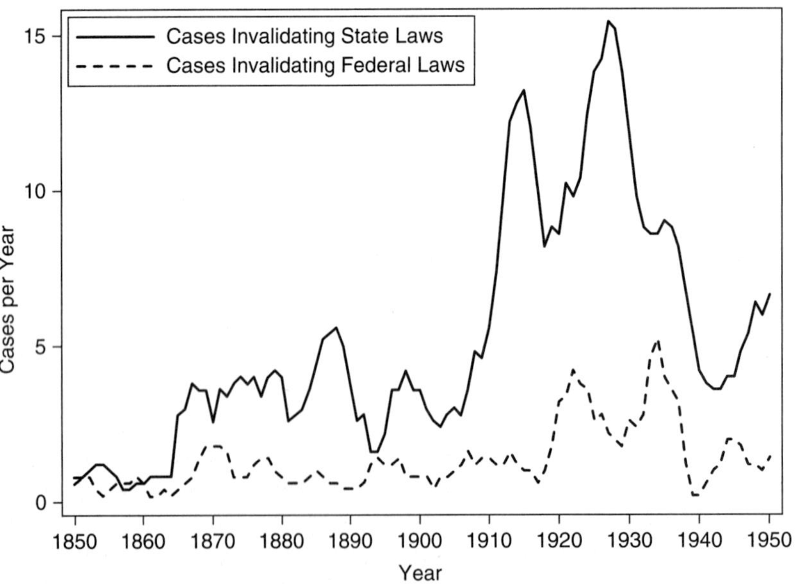

Figure 7-3 Supreme Court Invalidation of State and Federal Laws, 1850–1950

Source: Congressional Research Service, *The Constitution of the United States of America, Analysis and Interpretation* (Washington, DC: Government Printing Office, 2004); Keith E. Whittington, *The Judicial Review of Congress* [dataset].

Note: Centered, five-year moving averages.

in the U.S. Constitution. But state and federal courts also became more active in practicing horizontal judicial review and evaluating the actions of the other branches of their own government.

Along with the increase in judicial scrutiny of legislation came a growing controversy over whether and how courts used the power to interpret the Constitution and review statutes. Advocates of judicial review, who were mostly on the political right during this period, argued that independent courts were important guardians of rights and should carefully scrutinize legislation. Critics of judicial review, who were mostly on the political left, argued that the courts needed to be checked and that judges should be highly deferential to legislative decisions.

The expansion of judicial power was not just the creation of eager judges. In the wake of the midterm elections of 1874, in which Democrats regained control of the House of Representatives, the lame-duck Republican leaders in 1875 quickly introduced a bill to expand the jurisdiction of federal courts. The Judiciary and Removal Act of 1875 redirected litigation involving national commercial interests out of state courts and into the more conservative (Republican) federal judiciary. Technically, this meant granting the federal judiciary "federal questions" jurisdiction—that is, the authority to have original jurisdiction in all civil and criminal cases "arising under" the laws of the United States. It also granted "removal jurisdiction": lawsuits that began in state courts could be "removed" into federal courts if the case involved issues of federal law or parties from different states. The act attempted to prevent obstruction of removal in two ways. First, it authorized federal judges to hold plaintiffs in default if a state court blocked removal. Second, a state court clerk who refused to effectuate a removal was now guilty of a misdemeanor, punishable by a year of imprisonment and a $1,000 fine.

Theodore Roosevelt, **A Charter of Democracy** (1912)[6]

Theodore Roosevelt launched himself back into presidential politics in 1912 with an attack on judges. He had been out of the White House for four years, and during that time he had become increasingly radical. He was frustrated with the more conservative administration of his successor, William Howard Taft. As the 1912 elections approached, Roosevelt, still an extremely popular figure, decided to challenge Taft and retake command of the country. Taft refused to back down, however, and won renomination from the Republican Party. Roosevelt made an independent "Bull Moose" run with the Progressive Party and bested Taft at the polls but badly trailed Democratic nominee Woodrow Wilson, who won the presidency with less than 42 percent of the popular vote.

Roosevelt's attack on the courts instantly put him on the front pages of the papers, but it proved to be a mixed bag politically. His first political speech in 1912 was an address to the Ohio state constitutional convention as he toured through the state, where he endorsed the application of the recall to judges and elaborated at length on the need to subject judicial decisions to popular check. He developed the theme at length in the early part of his campaign but gradually pulled back from it in favor of other themes as the campaign wore on. The issue clearly separated Roosevelt from Taft, but the New York Times *reported that many Republicans thought judicial recall was "veriest nonsense" and editorialized that the recall was the "craziest of all suggestions that have come out of the bosom of Progressivism."*[7] *The Ohio convention itself voted down the judicial recall proposal.*

Mr. President and Members of the Ohio Constitutional Convention:

I believe in pure democracy. With Lincoln, I hold that "this country, with its institutions, belongs to the people who inhabit it. Whenever they shall grow weary of the existing Government, they can exercise their Constitutional right of amending it."

...

I am emphatically a believer in constitutionalism, and because of this fact I no less emphatically protest against any theory that would make of the Constitution a means of thwarting instead of securing the absolute right of the people to rule themselves and to provide for their own social and industrial well-being.

All Constitutions, that of the States no less than that of the Nation, are designed, and must be interpreted and administered so as to fit human rights.

Lincoln so interpreted and administered the National Constitution. Buchanan attempted the reverse,

6. Excerpt taken from Theodore Roosevelt, *Progressive Principles* (New York: Progressive National Service, 1913), 46–83.

7. "Taft Will Answer Roosevelt Speech," *New York Times*, February 23, 1912, 1; "The Pathology of the Progressives," *New York Times*, February 15, 1912, 10.

attempted to fit human rights to, and limit them by, the Constitution. It was Buchanan who treated the courts as a fetish, who protested against and condemned all criticism of the judges for unjust and unrighteous decisions, and upheld the Constitution as an instrument for the protection of privilege and of vested wrong. It was Lincoln who appealed to the people against the judges when the judges went wrong, who advocated and secured what was practically the recall of the *Dred Scott* decision, and who treated the Constitution as a living force for righteousness.

. . .

I therefore very earnestly ask you clearly to provide in this Constitution means which will enable the people readily to amend it if at any point it works injustice, and also means which will permit the people themselves by popular vote, after due deliberation and discussion, but finally and without appeal, to settle what the proper construction of any Constitutional point is.

. . .

There remains the question of the recall of judges. . . .

. . .

An independent and upright judiciary which fearlessly stands for the right, even against popular clamor, but which also understands and sympathizes with popular needs, is a great asset of popular government.

There is no public servant and no private man whom I place above a judge of the best type, and very few whom I rank beside him. I believe in the cumulative value of the law and in its value as an impersonal, disinterested basis of control. . . . But I agree with every great jurist, from Marshall downwards, when I say that every judge is bound to consider two separate elements in his decision of a case, one the terms of the law, and the other the conditions of actual life to which the law is applied. . . . Both the law and life are to be considered in order that the law and the Constitution shall become, in John Marshall's words, "a living instrument and not a dead letter." . . . Moreover, never forget that the judge is just as much the servant of the people as any other official. . . .

. . .

But either the recall will have to be adopted or else it will have to be made much easier than it now is to get rid, not merely of a bad judge, but of a judge who, however virtuous, has grown so out of touch with social needs and facts that he is unfit longer to render good service on the bench.

. . .

. . . [W]hen a judge decides a Constitutional question, when he decides what the people as a whole can or cannot do, the people should have the right to recall that decision if they think it wrong. We should hold the judiciary in all respect; but it is both absurd and degrading to make a fetish of a judge or of anyone else. Abraham Lincoln said in his first inaugural:

> "If the policy of the Government upon vital questions affecting the whole people is to be irrevocably fixed by decisions of the Supreme Court, . . . the people will have ceased to be their own rulers, having to that extent practically resigned their Government into the hands of that eminent tribunal. Nor is there in this view any assault upon the courts or the judges."

. . .

William Howard Taft, **Veto of Arizona Statehood** (1912)[8]

William Howard Taft's early career in public office was in and around the judiciary. He served as an Ohio Superior Court judge, as U.S. solicitor general (the deputy attorney general who represents the federal government in court), and as a U.S. circuit court judge before giving up that position to hold a series of executive offices in the federal government, culminating in his election as president in 1908. Even as president, however, he still cherished his lifelong ambition of being chief justice on the U.S. Supreme Court, an appointment that he finally won in 1921.

During Taft's political career, judges were both condemned and revered. Radicals, Populists, Progressives, labor leaders, and others harshly criticized the federal and state judiciaries, their powers, and their jurisprudence. For them, the courts were a reactionary and unaccountable force in politics in need of legislative and constitutional checks on their powers. Conservatives in the Democratic and, especially, the Republican parties replied aggressively. The defense of the judiciary was one of the few political issues that

8. Excerpt taken from William Howard Taft, "Veto Message, August 22, 1911," in *A Compilation of the Messages and Papers of the Presidents*, ed. James D. Richardson (New York: Bureau of National Literature, 1916), 17:7636–44.

truly inspired Taft, and the perceived threat to the courts was what led him to seek renomination and reelection for the presidency, an office that he found otherwise tiresome. Although the Democrat Woodrow Wilson captured the White House in 1912, Taft accomplished his major aim of keeping a more radical Theodore Roosevelt from taking back the Republican Party and returning to the presidency after a four-year absence.

The "recall" of elected officials was one of several popular institutional reforms that swept through the states during the Progressive Era. Like the initiative and referendum, the recall promised to put in the hands of the people another tool for maintaining popular control of the government. Recall provisions in state constitutions allowed voters to petition for the removal of government officials before the natural end of their term of office. If enough signatures were collected on such a petition, a special election would be held to determine whether the official in question would retain office or be immediately removed. In 1910 popular conventions were held in the territories of Arizona and New Mexico to draft proposed constitutions as part of the process of applying for statehood. The Arizona Constitution, dominated by Democrats, included many of the popular institutional features of the era, including initiative, referendum, and recall provisions. The constitution was ratified by Arizona voters and forwarded to Congress and the president for their approval and admission for statehood. In August 1911 President Taft vetoed the statehood application because the recall provision of the Arizona Constitution applied to judges as well as other elected officials. The recall provision was quickly modified, and Arizona was admitted as a state in February 1912. Later that year, the voters of the state approved a constitutional amendment to restore the judicial recall provision. When a county judge later challenged his recall, the Arizona Supreme Court upheld the recall provision of the state constitution as raising matters that "pertain to the sovereign powers of the people in their political aspect, have been unalterably settled, and may not be changed except in the manner provided by the Constitution."[9]

To the House of Representatives:

I return herewith, without my approval, House joint resolution No. 14, "To admit the Territories of New Mexico and Arizona as States into the Union on an equal footing with the original States."

. . .

. . . Under the Arizona constitution all elective officers, and this includes county and State judges, six months after their election are subject to recall. . . .

This provision of the Arizona constitution, in its application to county and State judges, seems to me so pernicious in its effect, so destructive of independence in the judiciary, so likely to subject the rights of the individual to the possible tyranny of a popular majority, and, therefore, to be so injurious to the cause of free government, that I must disapprove a constitution containing it. . . .

A government is for the benefit of all the people. . . . A popular government is not a government of a majority, by a majority, for a majority of the people. It is a government of the whole people, by a majority of the whole people under such rules and checks as will secure a wise, just, and beneficent government for all the people. . . . Constitutions are checks on the hasty action of the majority. They are self-imposed restraints of a whole people upon a majority of them to secure sober action and a respect to other individuals, and in his relation to the whole people in their character as a state or government.

. . .The executive and legislative branches are representative of the majority of the people which elected them in guiding the course of the Government within the limits of the Constitution. . . . But the judicial branch of the Government is not representative of a majority of the people in any such sense, even if the mode of selecting the judges is by popular election. . . . They are not popular representatives. On the contrary, to fill their office properly, they must be independent. . . .

. . . In order to maintain the rights of the minority and the individual and to preserve our constitutional balance we must have judges with courage to decide against the majority when justice and law require.

By the recall in the Arizona constitution it is proposed to give the majority the power to remove arbitrarily, and without delay, any judge who may have the courage to render an unpopular decision. . . . We can not be blind to the fact that often an intelligent and respectable electorate may be so roused upon an issue that it will visit with condemnation the decision of a just judge, though exactly in accord with the law governing the case, merely because it affects unfavorably their contest. . . . Supporters of such a system seem to think that it will work only in the interest of the poor, the humble, the weak and the oppressed; that it will

9. *Abbey v. Green*, 28 Ariz. 53 (1925).

strike down only the judge who is supposed to favor rich corporations and be affected by the corrupting influence of the rich. Nothing could be further from the ultimate result. The motive it would offer to unscrupulous combinations to seek to control politics in order to control judges is clear. Those would profit by the recall who have the best opportunity of rousing the majority of the people to action on a sudden impulse. Are they likely to be the wisest or the best people in a community? Do they not include those who have money enough to employ the firebrands and slanderers in a community and the stirrers-up of social hate? . . . The character of the judges would deteriorate to that of trimmers and time-servers, the independent judicial action would be a thing of the past. . . .

. . .

IV. Powers of the National Government

MAJOR DEVELOPMENTS

- Limited federal power to remedy state discrimination
- Growth of federal regulation of immigration
- Struggle over federal regulation of interstate commerce
- Struggle over federal taxing authority
- Acceptance of wartime draft
- Ambiguous status of territories

The federal government tested the limits of its constitutional powers in new ways in the Republican Era. Problems of race, industrialization, class conflict, and agricultural dislocation seemed nearly intractable and repeatedly intruded into national politics. International wars gave the United States control over foreign territory and created new pressure to mobilize resources to fight foreign powers on a global scale. Social reformers crusaded for causes ranging from alcohol and drug prohibition to the end of child labor to women's rights to the stamping out of pornography and prostitution. Independent political parties and internal factions pressured Republicans and Democrats on a national level to respond to social ills with campaign promises and new legislation regulating trusts and protecting labor.

Federal power to protect persons of color was sharply narrowed in the first years of the Republican Era. In *U.S. v. Reese* (1876) a unanimous Court declared unconstitutional Sections 3 and 4 of the Civil Rights Act of 1870 (also known as the Enforcement Act of 1870), which made it a federal offense for state election inspectors to refuse to receive or count votes or to obstruct any citizen from voting. In his opinion for the Court, Chief Justice Waite emphasized that under the Fifteenth Amendment Congress had the authority to pass a law that addressed racial discrimination in voting but not to protect voting rights more generally, as the language of the statute seemed to do. *U.S. v. Cruikshank* (1876) quashed federal indictments alleging conspiracy "to injure, oppress, threaten or intimidate any citizen, with intent to prevent or hinder his free exercise and enjoyment of any right or privilege granted or secured to him by the Constitution or laws of the United States." *Cruikshank* was sparked by an incident in which a mob of whites attacked and killed between sixty and one hundred African Americans who had taken refuge in a local courthouse. Almost one hundred whites were indicted for violating Section 6 of the Enforcement Act of 1870, but only a handful were eventually arrested and tried. In his opinion for the Court, the Chief Justice held that the rights at issue were protected against infringement by state and federal authorities, not against infringement by private individuals. Because there was no indication that the defendants were acting as agents of the state, the federal government had no authority to intervene under the Civil War Amendments. Seven years later, in the *Civil Rights Cases*, the Supreme Court declared unconstitutional crucial provisions of the Civil Rights Act of 1875. Justice Bradley's majority opinion held that Congress had no power to forbid inns, public conveyances, places, and public amusement and other private enterprises from engaging in racial discrimination. The Fourteenth Amendment, he maintained, permitted Congress to regulate only state actors.

In the late nineteenth century, Congress became more active in trying to regulate national economic actors and activity. One of the landmark regulatory acts of the period after the Civil War was the Interstate Commerce Act of 1887, which led to the creation of the Interstate Commerce Commission to regulate the routes and prices of interstate railroads. Interstate railroad regulation was a relatively clear-cut use of the interstate commerce clause, but other actions that Congress wanted to take to regulate economic and social behavior were more controversial. Intense constitutional controversies broke out when Congress considered the Sherman Anti-Trust Act, which gave

Table 7-3 Selection of U.S. Supreme Court Cases Reviewing Federal Laws Under the Interstate Commerce Clause

Case	Vote	Outcome	Decision
Gibbons v. Ogden, 22 U.S. 1 (1824)	7–0	Upheld	Federal law licensing coastal ships to transport passengers upheld
The Daniel Bell, 77 U.S. 557 (1870)	9–0	Upheld	Federal law requiring inspection of steamships in the "navigable waters of the United States" extended to local vessels carrying goods bound for interstate markets
In re Rahrer, 140 U.S. 545 (1891)	9–0	Upheld	Federal law subjecting alcohol transported through interstate commerce to local prohibition laws when it reaches its destination upheld
United States v. E. C. Knight, 156 U.S. 1 (1895)	8–1	Struck down	Federal law regulating anticompetitive behavior could not be applied to the merger of manufacturers
Champion v. Ames, 188 U.S. 321 (1903)	5–4	Upheld	Federal law prohibiting the shipment of lottery tickets across state lines upheld
Northern Securities Company v. United States, 193 U.S. 197 (1904)	5–4	Upheld	Federal law regulating anticompetitive behavior could be applied to the merger of interstate railroads
Hammer v. Dagenhart, 247 U.S. 251 (1918)	5–4	Struck down	Federal law prohibiting the shipment of goods produced by child labor across state lines struck down
Stafford v. Wallace, 258 U.S. 495 (1922)	7–1	Upheld	Federal law regulating anticompetitive behavior in stockyards upheld as part of the "stream" of interstate commerce
Brooks v. United States, 267 U.S. 432 (1925)	9–0	Upheld	Federal law punishing the movement of stolen cars across state lines upheld
Carter v. Carter Coal Co., 298 U.S. 238 (1936)	5–4	Struck down	Federal law regulating hours and wages in mining struck down
National Labor Relations Board v. Jones & Laughlin Steel Corp., 301 U.S. 1 (1937)	5–4	Upheld	Federal law regulating labor conditions of industrial plants upheld
Wickard v. Filburn, 317 U.S. 111 (1942)	8–0	Upheld	Federal law setting production quotas for wheat declared constitutional as applied to self-sustaining farms
United States v. Sullivan, 332 U.S. 689 (1948)	6–3	Upheld	Federal law punishing alteration of drug labels declared constitutional as applied to local druggist who transferred pills from a bulk bottle to a pillbox for his customers
Katzenbach v. McClung, 379 U.S. 294 (1964)	9–0	Upheld	Federal law prohibiting discrimination in public accommodations declared constitutional as applied to local restaurant
Perez v. United States, 402 U.S. 146 (1971)	8–1	Upheld	Federal law punishing loan sharking upheld

(*Continued*)

Table 7-3 (*Continued*)

Case	Vote	Outcome	Decision
Fry v. United States, 421 U.S. 542 (1975)	7–1	Upheld	Federal law imposing national wage freeze could be constitutionally applied to state employees
United States v. Lopez, 514 U.S. 549 (1995)	5–4	Struck down	Federal law punishing the possession of a firearm in a school zone struck down
Gonzales v. Raich, 545 U.S. 1 (2005)	6–3	Upheld	Federal law punishing the intrastate production and use of marijuana under state regulation declared constitutional as applied

the federal government power to regulate monopolies in "restraint of trade," even when the business in question seemed to operate entirely within a state. Other constitutional controversies arose when Congress exercised the commerce power for reasons that seemed more related to morals than commerce.

The U.S. Supreme Court struggled to develop doctrines to help make sense of this new legislative and economic landscape and to provide guidance about the limits of congressional power under the interstate commerce clause. *United States v. E. C. Knight* (1895) made a categorical distinction between commercial activities (the transport and trading of goods), which Congress could regulate, and other sorts of productive activities (such as farming, mining, or manufacturing), which Congress could not. Moreover, *E. C. Knight* distinguished between local commercial activities that had a direct effect on interstate commerce and those that had an indirect effect. The former could be regulated by Congress. The latter could not. (Congress could always regulate interstate commercial activities, such as the interstate shipment of goods on railroads.) *Swift v. United States* (1905) supplemented this doctrine by distinguishing between local activities that were inside the interstate "stream of commerce" and those that were outside it. *Champion v. Ames* (1903) indicated that Congress had a kind of police power when operating within the boundaries of the commerce clause and that it could regulate items in interstate commerce for a variety of purposes and with a variety of means. But *Hammer v. Dagenhart* (1918) suggested some limits to that doctrine—for example, that Congress could not use the power to regulate interstate commerce as a back door to regulating production.

The Supreme Court in the early twentieth century proved sympathetic to most efforts to prosecute trusts. Railroads proved to be the easy case for federal regulation (since they were in the business of moving goods across state lines), but the Court was equally willing to grant federal authority over such varied enterprises as the selling of cast iron pipes (*Addyston Pipe & Steel Co. v. United States* [1899]); the dealing of tiles and grates brought in from out of state (*W. W. Montague & Co. v. Lowry* [1904]); the buying, slaughtering, and shipping of livestock (*Swift & Co. v. United States* [1905]); and the refining, transportation, and selling of oil (*Standard Oil Company of New Jersey v. United States* [1910]). The political climate in favor of anti-trust activity also changed when the "trust-buster" Teddy Roosevelt succeeded McKinley as president in 1901.

Federal taxation power took center stage at the turn of the twentieth century. Populists demanded and Democrats in the national government in 1894 passed the first peacetime income tax in American history. That provision, which was part of the Wilson Tariff of 1894, imposed a 2 percent tax on corporate income and various sources of personal income over $4,000. Critics charged that the measure violated Article I of the Constitution, which requires that "direct" taxes be apportioned among the states by population. The Supreme Court agreed, striking down the income tax in *Pollock v. Farmers' Loan and Trust Company* (1894). That decision helped mobilize William Jennings Bryan and the Populists to take over the Democratic Party in the 1896 convention. In 1913 Congress passed and the states ratified the Sixteenth Amendment, which overturned *Pollock*. That text declares, "The Congress shall have power to lay and collect taxes on incomes, from whatever source derived, without apportionment among the several States, and without regard to any census or enumeration."

The Court was also confronted with the question of how Congress could use the taxing power. The *Child*

Labor Tax Case (1922) struck down an effort by Congress to tax goods made with child labor that crossed state borders. The Court was convinced that the tax was designed purely as a regulatory measure and not as a revenue measure and moreover that it was attempting to regulate something that was otherwise outside the scope of federal power in the early twentieth century (labor conditions in manufacturing). Congress could not do indirectly with the taxation power what it was prohibited from doing directly with the regulatory power under the interstate commerce clause.

The Supreme Court took a broader view of the treaty power in *Missouri v. Holland* (1920), a case arising out of a lengthy effort to create national hunting regulations. Traditionally, the states had presumptive constitutional authority to regulate game hunting within their borders. The Wilson administration sought a way around the states by negotiating a treaty with Canada that empowered the Department of Agriculture to regulate bird hunting. In writing the decision upholding the federal government, Justice Oliver Wendell Holmes, Jr., made a classic defense of a living Constitution that grows and adapts to the changing needs of the times.

Congressional Debate over Lynching[10]

Although lynch law had always existed in the United States, lynching became increasingly racial, sectional, and brutal after the Civil War. More than 4,000 persons were lynched between Reconstruction and World War II. The vast majority of lynching victims were persons of color, and the vast majority of lynchings took place in former slave states. In sharp contrast to pre–Civil War lynchings, which were largely summary affairs, southern lynch mobs typically devised grotesque tortures for their African American victims. One account observed:

> *The two Negroes . . . were tied to trees and while the funeral pyres were being prepared [they were to be burned alive], they were forced to hold out their hands while one finger at a time was chopped off. The fingers were distributed as souvenirs. The ears . . . were cut off. [One of the victims] was beaten severely, his skull fractured and one of his eyes, knocked out with a stick, hung by a shred from the socket.*[11]

Although lynch mobs functioned openly, participants rarely faced arrest, much less conviction. One study found that southern states were fifty times more likely to achieve convictions in ordinary homicides, in which perpetrators typically made some attempt to cover their tracks, than in lynchings, which were done in public—sometimes on courthouse lawns.[12]

Most American elites during the Progressive Era condemned any resort to extralegal punishments and barbarisms. "Lynching," a prominent politician stated, "is the darkest blot upon an otherwise splendid civilization."[13] *What could be done to remove this stain was more controversial. Several Reconstruction measures aimed at safeguarding persons of color from lynching either had been declared unconstitutional or had been repealed, and Justice Department officials thought inadequate those measures that were still on the books. Whether revised measures could pass constitutional muster was an open question. Even Moorfield Storey, the main constitutional litigator for the NAACP during the Progressive Era initially had doubts about the constitutionality of federal anti-lynching legislation.*

The movement for such legislation, however, picked up steam after World War I. Some prominent political elites were horrified by the racial violence against persons of color that broke out in the war's aftermath. The return of the Republican Party, the political coalition more sympathetic to persons of color, improved the chances of favorable legislation. The Republican Party platform in 1920 "urge[d] Congress to consider the most effective means to end lynching in this country which continues to be a terrible blot on our American civilization," and similar language was used in the Republican Party platforms in 1924 and 1928. Nevertheless, although anti-lynching bills were routinely introduced in Congress, none became law. In fact, no civil rights legislation would be passed by Congress from 1876 until 1957, which meant that a Republican-dominated Supreme Court was never asked to consider the fairly broad understanding of federal power underlying various anti-lynching measures.

10. Excerpt taken from House Committee on the Judiciary, *Constitutionality of a Federal Anti Lynching Law*, 67th Cong., 1st Sess., 1921, 16; *Congressional Record*, 67th Cong., 2nd Sess., 1922, 1290.

11. Barbara Holden-Smith, "Lynching, Federalism, and the Intersection of Race and Gender in the Progressive Era," *Yale Journal of Law & Feminism* 8 (1996): 31.

12. James Harmon Chadbourn, *Lynching and the Law* (Chapel Hill: University of North Carolina Press, 1933), 13–14.

13. Representative Burton, *Congressional Record*, 67th Cong., 2nd Sess., January 17, 1922, 1276.

The Dyer bill was the best hope proponents of federal anti-lynching legislation had for securing favorable law. Proposed by Representative Leonidas Dyer of Missouri, the measure passed the House in 1922 but was defeated by a filibuster in the Senate. Unlike previous Reconstruction measures, the Dyer bill focused on state officers who either made no effort to prevent or participated in lynchings. States were deemed to have denied persons equal protection of the law if they "fail[ed], neglect[ed], or refuse[d]" to provide and maintain protection to the life of any person within its jurisdiction against a mob or riotous assemblage. State officers who did not make "reasonable efforts" to prevent lynching or punish lynchers were subject to severe criminal sanctions. The Dyer bill also authorized federal attorneys to try as criminals any private persons who conspired with a state official during a lynching. Significantly, these offenses could be tried in federal courts when state courts refused to convict.

Proponents of the Dyer bill insisted that Section 5 of the Fourteenth Amendment permitted Congress to legislate against both state action and state inaction that violated constitutional rights. This constitutional understanding was supported by the Harding administration. Opponents of the measure insisted that Congress could constitutionally punish only positive state action that was consistent with discriminatory state law. Did Justice Bradley's opinion in the Civil Rights Cases *make clear whether the federal government could punish state actors who failed to protect fundamental rights? Can a state violate the equal protection clause not just by engaging in discriminatory conduct itself, but by virtue of a sufficient level of disregard for protecting certain classes of people? How far might that principle be extended?*

Letter of Attorney General H. M. Daugherty to Representative A. J. Volstead (Republican, Minnesota) (1921)

. . .

Considerable discussion has taken place as to the constitutionality of the proposed legislation, it being contended that the fourteenth amendment gave Congress power to legislate so as to prevent a denial of the equal protection of the laws by the States and not as to acts of individuals not clothed with State authority.

. . . It will be observed that . . . the State may act through its legislative, its judicial, or its executive authorities, and the act of any one these is the act of the State. . . .

. . .

"The constitutional provision, therefore, must mean that no agency of the State, or of the officers or agents by whom its powers are exerted, shall deny to any person within its jurisdiction the equal protection of the laws. Whoever, by virtue of public position under a State government, deprives another of property, life, or liberty without due process of law or denies or takes away the equal protection of the laws, violates the constitutional inhibition, and as he acts in the name and for the State and is clothed with the State's power his act is that of the State. This must be so or the constitutional prohibition has no meaning. Then the State has clothed one of its agents with power to annul or to evade it." *Ex parte Virginia* (1879)

. . . To my mind there can be no doubt that negativity on the part of the State may be, as well as any act of a positive nature by such State, a denial of the equal protection of the laws and thus be within the prohibition of the fourteenth amendment so as to give Congress power to act with reference to it. . . .

. . .

Section 12 and section 13 provide for the punishment of State and municipal officers who fail in their duty to prevent lynchings or who suffer persons accused of crime to be taken from their custody for the purpose of lynching. These sections seem to me to strike at the heart of the evil, namely, the failure of State officers to perform their duty in such cases. The fourteenth amendment recognizes as preexisting the right to due process of law and to the equal protection of the law and guarantees against State infringement of those rights. A State officer charged with the protection of those rights who fails or refuses to do all in his power to protect an accused person against mob action denies to such person due process of law and the equal protection of the laws in every sense of the term. . . .

. . .

Speech of Representative HARRY HAWES (Democrat, Missouri)

. . .

[The Fourteenth Amendment] relates to the laws of a State, does not relate, nor was it intended to relate, to the individual action of a citizen, nor was it directed toward the malfeasance or nonfeasance of a State officer.

. . .

Mob violence is a criminal offense in all States. Persons who form part of a mob which takes human life are guilty of murder. Penalties are provided for unlawful assemblage. Penalties are provided for interfering with an officer in the discharge of his duty or taking a prisoner from an officer. There is no State, whose laws in this respect have been questioned by a single proponent of this bill.

The fourteenth amendment does not relate to the acts of individuals or the acts of official agents of a State where the acts of such agents were outside the pale of the law and not in conformity with the law of the Commonwealth. The fourteenth amendment deals directly with the State and the agencies of the State performing certain specific acts for the State.

. . .

If the Federal Government assumes the right to punish an officer of a State for failure to prevent a crime, or a prosecuting attorney for failure to prosecute a crime, then the Federal Government can go into the business of prosecuting the chicken thief, the crap shooter, the card player, the drunkard, the wife beater, or the thief.

It was never intended that the fourteenth amendment should apply other than to the acts of States or the agents of States, in so far as they complied with the laws of the State. It is not the act of the official, or his omission to act, that is controlled by the fourteenth amendment, but it is the State law that controls the act and provides the things guaranteed in the fourteenth amendment.

. . .

Senate Debate on the Sherman Anti-Trust Act[14]

Rapid industrialization set the stage for the rise of large corporations that had the capacity to exert dominating influence over important aspects of the national economy. Of particular concern was the developing practice of the most powerful companies of creating "trust" agreements whereby they gained control over competing firms by combining them into one large firm. Critics believed that these so-called "trusts," or combinations, undermined the advantages of capitalism by establishing monopolies within particular industries. Since these trusts operated on a nationwide scale there was pressure put on Congress to devise mechanisms to break up those trusts that were designed to restrict competition. This sort of direct federal regulation of American industry was unprecedented in American history, but then again, before the late nineteenth century American industry mostly operated at the local level and thus was considered best overseen by state and local governments.

Did the congressional authority "to regulate commerce . . . among the states" include the power to regulate the business practices of companies large enough to have an impact on the operations of national markets, or was it limited to regulating the actual movement of goods across state lines? Did it cover control over "manufacturing" or "production" that took place in just one state as long as the goods were headed for a national market? Or did it only include the subsequent "transportation" or "distribution" of goods among the states? This controversy would preoccupy legislators and judges for more than forty years, culminating in a historic clash between the Supreme Court and Franklin Delano Roosevelt in the 1930s.

The discussion began in earnest during congressional debates over the passage of the Sherman Anti-Trust Act in 1890. The first federal statute of its kind, the act sought to prohibit anti-competitive, monopolistic business practices. Proponents of the bill such as Ohio Republican John Sherman pushed for an expansive reading of the Constitution that would give Congress the explicit power to regulate manufacturing, but critics such as Republican Judiciary Committee Chair George Edmunds questioned whether Congress should make promises that it could not constitutionally keep, promises that were "purely deceptive and illusory, mere dust and ashes," and worked to produce a more vaguely worded but narrower statute.[15]

SENATOR JAMES GEORGE (Democrat, Mississippi)

. . . Mr. President, I now proceed to show that the bill is utterly unconstitutional.

This task is an easy one, since the principles applicable to this examination have again and again been settled by the Supreme Court. I warn Senators now that no attempt will be made to show the bill unconstitutional upon that narrow and strict theory of State rights which they may suppose is entertained

14. Excerpt taken from *Congressional Record*, 51st Cong., 1st Sess., 1890, 1768–71, 2460–62, 3147–48.

15. *Congressional Record*, 51st Cong., 1st Sess., March 27, 1890, 2728.

by the Southern people and by them only. In all I shall say on this subject, I shall plant my argument on an exposition of the Constitution made by the tribunal which the Constitution itself appoints to perform that duty. . . .

The power to enact the bill is claimed in the bill itself under the commercial clause of the Constitution: the power "to regulate commerce with foreign nations and among the States."

. . . So far as this bill is concerned, it is needful only to specify the acts . . . which constitute interstate or foreign commerce. They embrace purchase, sale, exchange, barter, transportation, and intercourse for the purpose of trade in all its forms. . . .

. . . But, Mr. President, among these commercial acts are not manufactures or any other kind of production, nor sales, nor transportation purely within a State or wholly outside the territorial jurisdiction of the United States. The bill proceeds on the idea that as to interstate commerce the jurisdiction of Congress extends to the regulation of the production and manufacture of articles taking place in a State, if only it be intended, that, after such manufacture or production shall be complete, all or a portion of the articles shall become subjects of interstate commerce, and shall in fact be transported as such.

This basis of the bill is expressly confuted by the decisions I shall quote.

The Supreme Court in *Veazie v. Moor* (1852) speaking of the commercial clause of the Constitution, says it can not "be properly concluded that because the products of domestic enterprise in agriculture or manufactures or in the arts may ultimately become the subjects of foreign (or interstate) commerce, the control of the means or the encouragements by which enterprise is fostered and protected is legitimately within the import of the phrase 'foreign commerce,' or fairly implied by any investiture of the power to regulate such commerce. A pretension so far reaching as this would extend to contracts between citizen and citizen of the same State; would control the pursuits of the planter, the grazier, the manufacturer, the mechanic, the immense operations of the collieries and mines and furnaces of the country; for there is not one of these vocations the results of which may not become the subject of foreign (interstate) commerce."

. . . The Constitution is a reasonable instrument, designed to specify powers delegated to a general government. So far as these powers are granted expressly or by necessary implication for the execution of express powers, they are full and complete, as well as supreme; but the Constitution neither authorizes nor tolerates the absurdity of the exercise of a power as a necessary incident to and in aid of the execution of an express power when no attempt is made to execute the express power. . . .

SENATOR JOHN SHERMAN (Republican, Ohio)

. . . I respectfully submit that, in his subtle argument, [Senator George] has entirely overlooked the broad jurisdiction conferred by the Constitution upon courts of the United States in ordinary cases of law and equity between certain parties, as well as cases arising under the Constitution, laws, and treaties of the United States. . . .

. . . All the combinations at which this bill aims are combinations embracing persons and combinations of several States. Each State can deal with a combination within the State, but only the General Government can deal with combinations reaching not only the several States, but the commercial world. This bill does not include combinations within a State. . . .

. . . By the Constitution of the United States this jurisdiction of the courts of the United States extends to all cases in law and equity between certain parties. What is meant by the words of "cases in law and equity?" Does this include only cases growing out of the Constitution, statutes, and treaties of the United States? It has been held over and over again that, by these words, the Constitution has adopted as a rule of remedial justice the common law of England as administered by courts of law and equity.

. . . I submit that this bill as it stands, without any reference to specific powers granted to Congress by the Constitution, is clearly authorized under the judicial article of the Constitution. This bill declares a rule of public policy in accordance with the rule of the common law.

. . . One would think that with this conception of the evil to be dealt with he would for once turn his telescope upon the Constitution to find out power to deal with so great a wrong, and not, as usual, to reverse it, to turn the little end of the telescope to the Constitution, and then, with subtle reasoning, to dissipate the powers of the Government into thin air. . . .

. . . What is the meaning of the word "commerce?" It means the exchange of commodities between different places or communities. . . . The power of Congress extends to all this commerce, except only that limited within the bounds of a State.

. . .

. . . It is said that commerce does not commence until production ends and the voyage commences. This may be true as far as the actual ownership or sale of articles within a State is subject to State authorities. . . . This bill does not propose to deal with property within a State or with combinations within the State, but only when a combination extends to two or more States or engages in either State or foreign commerce.

. . . If their productions competed with those of similar partnerships or corporations in other States it would be all right. But to prevent such competition they unite the interests of all these partnerships and corporations into a combination, sometimes called a trust, sometimes a new corporation located in a city remote from the places of production, and then regulate and control the sale and transportation of all the products of many States. . . . Sir, the object aimed at by this bill is to secure competition of the productions of different States which necessarily enter into interstate and foreign commerce.

. . . In no respect does the work of our fathers in framing the Constitution of the United States appear more like the work of the Almighty Ruler of the Universe rather than the conception of human minds than by the gradual development and application of the powers conferred by it upon different branches of the Federal Government. Many of these powers have remained dormant, unused, but plainly there, awaiting the growth and progress of our country, and when the time comes and the occasion demands we find in that instrument . . . all the powers necessary to govern a continental empire. . . .

SENATOR GEORGE.

Mr. President, I am afraid we have got into this condition about the pending bill, that we have a disposition to do something, and that very speedily, whether that something amounts to much or not. I am afraid that there will be a great disappointment among the people of this country about the effects of this bill when it shall become a law. It covers professedly a very narrow territory, leaving a very large number of these institutions, these trusts, or whatever we may call them, entirely without the purview of the bill.

That is not the fault of the committee, Mr. President. The bill has been very ingeniously and properly drawn to cover every case which comes within what is called the commercial power of Congress. There is a great deal of this matter outside of that. This bill being of that character, it necessarily will be a disappointing measure to the people of this country.

SENATOR GEORGE EDMUNDS (Republican, Vermont).

We all felt it, and the [Judiciary] committee, I think unanimously, including my friend from Mississippi [Senator George], thought that if we were really in earnest in wishing to strike at these evils broadly, in the first instance, as a new line of legislation, we would frame a bill that should be clearly within our constitutional power, that we should make its definitions out of terms that were well known to the law already, and would leave it to the courts in the first instance to say how far they could carry it or its definitions as applicable to each particular case as it might arise.

United States v. E. C. Knight Company, 156 U.S. 1 (1895)

The American Sugar Refining Company, incorporated in New Jersey, manufactured about 65 percent of the refined sugar sold in the United States. In 1892 it acquired through an exchange of stock control over four Philadelphia-based sugar refineries, including E. C. Knight, which together accounted for another 33 percent of the national sugar market. The "sugar trust" was among the most notorious in the country at the time, and the Democratic Cleveland administration yielded to political pressure to prosecute the trust. The United States Department of Justice charged that the acquisition violated the 1890 Sherman Anti-Trust Act by creating a combination in restraint of trade and asked the federal circuit court to void the sale. The circuit court declined to do so, and the government appealed to the Supreme Court. In order to determine whether the Sherman Act could reach the sugar trust, the Court had to determine the scope of congressional authority under the commerce clause. In an 8–1 ruling, the Court held that Congress could not regulate the production of goods under the commerce clause and that the executive could not use the Sherman Act to block the operation of the sugar trust. Justice John Marshall Harlan filed the lone dissent. What work did the Court's interpretation of the commerce clause leave for Congress? Was E. C. Knight *consistent with what legislators might have expected? Was it consistent with the Marshall Court's approach to the commerce clause in* Gibbons v. Ogden *(1824)?*

CHIEF JUSTICE FULLER delivered the opinion of the Court.

. . .

The fundamental question is, whether conceding that the existence of a monopoly in manufacture is established by the evidence, that monopoly can be directly suppressed under the act of Congress in the mode attempted by this bill.

It cannot be denied that the power of a State to protect the lives, health, and property of its citizens, and to preserve good order and the public morals, "the power to govern men and things within the limits of its dominion," is a power originally and always belonging to the States, not surrendered by them to the general government, nor directly restrained by the Constitution of the United States, and essentially exclusive. The relief of the citizens of each State from the burden of monopoly and the evils resulting from the restraint of trade among such citizens was left with the States to deal with, and this court has recognized their possession of that power even to the extent of holding that an employment or business carried on by private individuals, when it becomes a matter of such public interest and importance as to create a common charge or burden upon the citizens, in other words, when it becomes a practical monopoly, to which the citizen is compelled to resort and by means of which a tribute can be exacted from the community, is subject to regulation by state legislative power. On the other hand, the power of Congress to regulate commerce among the several States is also exclusive. The Constitution does not provide that interstate commerce shall be free, but, by the grant of this exclusive power to regulate it, it was left free except as Congress might impose restraints. . . .

The argument is that the power to control the manufacture of refined sugar is a monopoly over a necessary of life, to the enjoyment of which by a large part of the population of the United States interstate commerce is indispensable, and that, therefore, the general government in the exercise of the power to regulate commerce may repress such monopoly directly and set aside the instruments which have created it. But this argument cannot be confined to the necessaries of life merely, and must include all articles of general consumption. . . .

It is vital that the independence of the commercial power and of the police power, and the delimitation between them, however sometimes perplexing, should always be recognized and observed, for while the one furnishes the strongest bond of union, the other is essential to the preservation of the autonomy of the States as required by our dual form of government, and acknowledged evils, however grave and urgent they may appear to be, had better be borne, than the risk be run, in the effort to suppress them, of more serious consequences by resort to expedients of even doubtful constitutionality.

. . . The regulation of commerce applies to the subjects of commerce and not to matters of internal police. Contracts to buy, sell, or exchange goods to be transported among the several States, the transportation and its instrumentalities, and articles bought, sold, or exchanged for the purposes of such transit among the States, or put in the way of transit, may be regulated, but this is because they form part of interstate trade or commerce. The fact that an article is manufactured for export to another State does not itself make it an article of interstate commerce, and the intent of the manufacturer does not determine the time when the article or product passes from the control of the State and belongs to commerce. . . .

. . . [I]n *Kidd v. Pearson* (1888) where the question was discussed whether the right of a State to enact a statute prohibiting within its limits the manufacture of intoxicating liquors, except for certain purposes, could be overthrown by the fact that the manufacturer intended to export the liquors when made, it was held that the intent of the manufacturer did not determine the time when the article or product passed from the control of the State and belonged to commerce, and that, therefore, the statute, in omitting to except from its operation the manufacture of intoxicating liquors within the limits of the State for export, did not constitute an unauthorized interference with the right of Congress to regulate commerce. And [Justice] Lamar remarked "No distinction is more popular to the common mind, or more clearly expressed in economic and political literature, than that between manufacture and commerce. Manufacture is transformation—the fashioning of raw materials into a change of form for use. The functions of commerce are different. The buying and selling and the transportation incidental thereto constitute commerce, and the regulation of commerce in the constitutional sense embraces the regulation at least of such transportation. If it be held that the term includes the regulation of all such manufacturers as are intended to be the subject of commercial transactions in the future, it is impossible to deny that it would also include all productive industries that contemplate the same thing. The result would be the Congress would be invested, to the exclusion of the States, with the power to regulate, not only manufactures, but also agriculture, horticulture, stock raising, domestic fisheries, mining—in short, every branch of human industry. . . . "

. . . [T]he contracts and acts of the defendants related exclusively to the acquisition of the Philadelphia refineries and the business of sugar refining in Pennsylvania, and bore no direct relationship to commerce between the States or with foreign nations. . . . [I]t does not follow that an attempt to monopolize, or the actual monopoly of, the manufacture was an attempt . . . to monopolize commerce, even though, in order to dispose of the product, the instrumentality of commerce was necessarily invoked. There was nothing in the proofs to indicate any intention to put a restraint upon trade or commerce. . . . The subject-matter of the sale was shares of manufacturing stock, . . . yet the act of Congress only authorized the Circuit Courts to proceed by way of preventing and restraining violations of the act in respect to contracts, combinations, or conspiracies in restraint of interstate or international trade or commerce. . . .

The Circuit Court declined, upon the pleadings and proofs, to grant the relief prayed, and dismissed the bill, and we are of the opinion that the Circuit Court of Appeals did not err in affirming that decree.

JUSTICE HARLAN, dissenting.

. . . If this combination, so far as its operations necessarily or directly affect interstate commerce, cannot be restrained or suppressed under some power granted to Congress, it will be cause for regret that the patriotic statesmen who framed the Constitution did not foresee the necessity of investing the national government with power to deal with gigantic monopolies holding in their grasp, and injuriously controlling for their own interest, the entire trade *among the States* in food products that are essential to the comfort of every household in the land.

The court holds it to be vital in our system of government to recognize and give effect to both the commercial power of the nation and the police powers of the States, to the end that the Union be strengthened and the autonomy of the States preserved. In this view I entirely concur. Undoubtedly, the preservation of the just authority of the States is an object of deep concern to every lover of his country. No greater calamity could befall our free institutions than the destruction of that authority, by whichever means such a result might be accomplished. . . . But it is equally true that the preservation of the just authority of the General Government is essential as well to the safety of the States as to the attainment of the important ends for which that government was ordained by the People of the United States, and the destruction of *that* authority would be fatal to the peace and well-being of the American people. The Constitution which enumerates the power committed to the nation for the objects of interest to the people of all the States should not, therefore, be subjected to an interpretation so rigid, technical, and narrow, that those objects cannot be accomplished. . . .

Congress is invested with power to regulate commerce with foreign nations and among the several States. . . .

. . .

. . . It would seem to be indisputable that no *combination* of corporations or individuals can, *of right*, impose unlawful restraints upon *interstate* trade, whether upon transportation or upon such interstate intercourse and traffic as precede transportation, any more than it can, of right, impose unreasonable restraints upon the completely internal traffic of a State. . . .

. . . The jurisdiction of the general government extends over every foot of territory within the United States. Under the power with which it is invested, Congress may remove unlawful obstructions, of whatever kind, to the free course of trade among the States. In so doing it would not interfere with the "autonomy of the States," because the power thus to protect interstate commerce is expressly given by the people of all the States. . . . Any combination, therefore, that disturbs or unreasonably obstructs freedom in buying and selling articles manufactured to be sold to persons in other States or to be carried to other States—a freedom that cannot exist if the right to buy and sell is fettered by unlawful restraints that crush out competition—affects, not incidentally, but directly, the people of all the States, and the remedy for such an evil is found only in the exercise of powers confided to a government which, this court has said, was the government of all, exercising powers delegated by all, representing all, acting for all. *McCulloch v. Maryland* (1819).

. . . There is no dispute here as to the lawfulness of the business of refining sugar, *apart from the undue restraint which the promoters of such business, who have combined to control prices, seek to put upon the freedom of interstate traffic in that article.*

It may be admitted that an act which did nothing more than forbid, and which had no other object than to forbid, the *mere* refining of sugar in any State, would be in excess of any power granted to Congress. But the act of 1890 is not of that character. It does not strike at the manufacture simply of articles that are legitimate or recognized subjects of commerce, but at *combinations* that unduly restrain, because they monopolize, *the buying and selling of articles* which are to go into interstate commerce.

. . . It is said that manufacture precedes commerce and is not a part of it. But it is equally true that when manufacture ends, that which has been manufactured becomes a subject of commerce, that buying and selling succeed manufacture, come into existence after the process of manufacture is completed, precede transportation, and are as much commercial intercourse, where articles are bought *to be* carried from one State to another, as is the manual transportation of such articles after they have been so purchased. The distinction was recognized by this court in *Gibbons v. Ogden* (1824), where the principal question was whether commerce included navigation. Both the court and counsel recognized buying and selling or barter *as included in commerce*. . . .

. . .

. . . The end proposed to be accomplished by the act of 1890 is the protection of trade and commerce among the States against unlawful restraints. Who can say that that end is not legitimate or is not within the scope of the Constitution? The means employed are the suppression, by legal proceedings, of combinations, conspiracies, and monopolies, which by their inevitable and admitted tendency, improperly restrain trade and commerce among the States. Who can say that such means are not appropriate to attain the end of freeing commercial intercourse among the States from burdens and exactions imposed upon it by combinations which, under principles long recognized in this country as well as at the common law, are illegal and dangerous to the public welfare? What clause of the Constitution can be referred to which prohibits the means thus prescribed in the act of Congress?

. . . While the opinion of the court in this case does not declare the act of 1890 to be unconstitutional, it defeats the main object for which it was passed. For it is, in effect, held that the statute would be unconstitutional if interpreted as embracing such unlawful restraints upon the purchasing of goods in one State to be carried to another State as necessarily arise from the existence of combinations formed for the purpose and with the effect, not only of monopolizing the ownership of all such goods in every part of the country, but of controlling the prices for them in all the States. . . . In my judgment, the general government is not placed by the Constitution in such a condition of helplessness that it must fold its arms and remain inactive while capital combines, under the name of a corporation, to destroy competition, not in one State only, but throughout the entire country. . . . The doctrine of the autonomy of the States cannot properly be invoked to justify a denial of power in the national government to meet such an emergency.

. . . The common government of all the people is the only one that can adequately deal with a matter which directly and injuriously affects the entire commerce of the country, which concerns equally all the people of the Union, and which, it must be confessed, cannot be adequately controlled by any one State. Its authority should not be so weakened by construction that it cannot reach and eradicate evils that, beyond all question, tend to defeat an object which that government is entitled, by the Constitution, to accomplish.

Hammer v. Dagenhart, 247 U.S. 251 (1918)

The prohibition of child labor was an international cause of Progressive reformers at the turn of the twentieth century. Most states adopted child labor laws, but the laws varied in what they prohibited, and enforcement was uneven. Established manufacturers in northern states were particularly concerned about growing competition from the economically less developed South, where child labor laws, as well as other labor regulations, were often looser. The reform campaign turned to the federal government to impose a national uniform standard. Facing a tough reelection campaign in which Progressive activists could play a pivotal role, President Woodrow Wilson swallowed his doubts about the constitutionality of the measure. He helped convince southern senators not to filibuster the measure for the good of the Democratic Party, and in 1916 he signed into law the Keating–Owen Act, banning the interstate shipment of goods produced with child labor.

The law was quickly challenged when a North Carolina father sought an injunction to allow his two minor sons to continue working in a local cotton mill. Since its decision in E. C. Knight *(1895) the Court had characterized Congress' control over the movement of goods across state lines as "plenary." It had allowed Congress to prohibit the interstate shipment of lottery tickets and the interstate transportation of women for immoral purposes. Could there be any doubt that Congress could prohibit the interstate shipment of goods made by child labor? On what grounds could such a prohibition be considered unconstitutional? A sharply divided 5–4 Court struck down the statute as inconsistent with the interstate commerce clause.*

Congress tried to get around the decision by using its taxation power to discourage goods produced with child labor, but the Court struck that down also in Bailey v. Drexel Furniture Co. *(1922). Congress passed a constitutional amendment empowering the federal government to regulate child labor in 1924, but ratification bogged down in the southern states. By the end of the 1920s child labor had dramatically declined in the United States, but it was not federally regulated until the New Deal.*

JUSTICE DAY delivered the opinion of the Court.

. . .

The controlling question for decision is: Is it within the authority of Congress in regulating commerce among the States to prohibit the transportation in interstate commerce of manufactured goods, the product of a factory in which, within thirty days prior to their removal therefrom, children under the age of fourteen have been employed or permitted to work. . . .

. . .

. . . The thing intended to be accomplished by this statute is the denial of the facilities of interstate commerce to those manufacturers in the States who employ children within the prohibited ages. The act in its effect does not regulate transportation among the States, but aims to standardize the ages at which children may be employed in mining and manufacturing within the States. The goods shipped are of themselves harmless. The act permits them to be freely shipped after thirty days from the time of their removal from the factory. When offered for shipment, and before transportation begins, the labor of their production is over, and the mere fact that they were intended for interstate commerce transportation does not make their production subject to federal control under the commerce power.

Commerce "consists of intercourse and traffic . . . and includes the transportation of persons and property, as well as the purchase, sale and exchange of commodities." The making of goods and the mining of coal are not commerce, nor does the fact that these things are to be afterwards shipped or used in interstate commerce, make their production a part thereof. . . .

Over interstate transportation, or its incidents, the regulatory power of Congress is ample, but the production of articles, intended for interstate commerce, is a matter of local regulation.

When the commerce begins is determined, not by the character of the commodity, nor by the intention of the owner to transfer it to another state for sale, nor by his preparation of it for transportation, but by its actual delivery to a common carrier for transportation, or the actual commencement of its transfer to another state. . . . If it were otherwise, all manufacture intended for interstate shipment would be brought under federal control to the practical exclusion of the authority of the States, a result certainly not contemplated by the framers of the Constitution when they vested in Congress the authority to regulate commerce among the States. . . .

It is further contended that the authority of Congress may be exerted to control interstate commerce in the shipment of child-made goods because of the effect of the circulation of such goods in other States where the evil of this class of labor has been recognized by local legislation, and the right to thus employ child labor has been more rigorously restrained than in the State of production. In other words, that the unfair competition, thus engendered, may be controlled by closing the channels of interstate commerce to manufacturers in those States where the local laws do not meet what Congress deems to be the more just standard of other States.

There is no power vested in Congress to require the States to exercise their police power so as to prevent possible unfair competition. Many causes may cooperate to give one State, by reason of local laws or conditions, an economic advantage over others. The Commerce Clause was not intended to give to Congress a general authority to equalize such conditions. . . .

The grant of power to Congress over the subject of interstate commerce was to enable it to regulate such commerce, and not to give it authority to control the States in their exercise of the police power over local trade and manufacture.

The grant of authority over a purely federal matter was not intended to destroy the local power always existing and carefully reserved to the States in the Tenth Amendment to the Constitution.

. . .

We have neither authority nor disposition to question the motives of Congress in enacting this legislation. The purposes intended must be attained consistently with constitutional limitations and not by an invasion of the powers of the States. This court has no more important function than that which devolves upon it the obligation to preserve inviolate the constitutional limitations upon the exercise of authority, federal and state, to the end that each may continue to discharge, harmoniously with the other, the duties entrusted to it by the Constitution.

In our view the necessary effect of this act is, by means of a prohibition against the movement in interstate commerce of ordinary commercial commodities, to regulate the hours of labor of children in factories and mines within the States, a purely state authority. Thus the act in a twofold sense is repugnant to the Constitution. It not only transcends the authority delegated to Congress over commerce but also exerts a power as to a purely local matter to which the federal authority does not extend. The far reaching result of upholding the act cannot be more plainly indicated than by pointing out that if Congress can thus regulate matters entrusted to local authority by prohibition of the movement of commodities in interstate commerce, all freedom of commerce will be at an end, and the power of the States over local matters may be eliminated, and thus our system of government be practically destroyed. . . .

JUSTICE HOLMES, with whom JUSTICE MCKENNA, JUSTICE BRANDEIS, and JUSTICE CLARKE join, dissenting.

. . .

The first step in my argument is to make plain what no one is likely to dispute—that the statute in question is within the power expressly given to Congress if considered only as to its immediate effects and that if invalid it is so only upon some collateral ground. The statute confines itself to prohibiting the carriage of certain goods in interstate or foreign commerce. Congress is given power to regulate such commerce in unqualified terms. It would not be argued today that the power to regulate does not include the power to prohibit. Regulation means the prohibition of something. . . .

The question then is narrowed to whether the exercise of its otherwise constitutional power by Congress can be pronounced unconstitutional because of its possible reaction upon the conduct of the States in a matter upon which I have admitted that they are free from direct control. I should have thought that that matter had been disposed of so fully as to leave no room for doubt. . . .

The manufacture of oleomargarine is as much a matter of state regulation as the manufacture of cotton cloth. Congress levied a tax upon the compound when colored so as to resemble butter that was so great as obviously to prohibit the manufacture and sale. In a very elaborate discussion the present Chief Justice excluded any inquiry into the purpose of an act which apart from that purpose was within the power of Congress. . . . Fifty years ago a tax on state banks, the obvious purpose and actual effect of which was to drive them, or at least their circulation, out of existence, was sustained, although the result was one that Congress had no constitutional power to require. The Court made short work of the argument as to the purpose of the act. . . . And to come to cases upon interstate commerce, notwithstanding *United States v. E. C. Knight Co.* (1895) . . . the Sherman Act has been made an instrument for the breaking up of combinations in restraint of trade and monopolies, using the power to regulate commerce as a foothold, but not proceeding because that commerce was the end actually in mind. The objection that the control of the States over production was interfered with was urged again and again but always in vain. . . .

. . .

The act does not meddle with anything belonging to the States. They may regulate their internal affairs and their domestic commerce as they like. But when they seek to send their products across the state line they are no longer within their rights. If there were no Constitution and no Congress their power to cross the line would depend upon their neighbors. Under the Constitution such commerce belongs not to the States but to Congress to regulate. It may carry out its views of public policy whatever indirect effect they may have upon the activities of the States. Instead of being encountered by a prohibitive tariff at her boundaries the State encounters the public policy of the United States which it is for Congress to express. The public policy of the United States is shaped with a view to the benefit of the nation as a whole. If, as has been the case within the memory of men still living, a State should take a different view of the propriety of sustaining a lottery from that which generally prevails, I cannot believe that the fact would require a different decision from that reached in *Champion v. Ames* (1903). Yet in that case it would be said with quite as much force as in this that Congress was attempting to intermeddle with the State's domestic affairs. The national welfare as understood by Congress may require a different attitude within its sphere from that of some self-seeking State. It seems to me entirely constitutional for Congress to enforce its understanding by all the means at its command.

Missouri v. Holland, 252 U.S. 416 (1920)

*Since the late nineteenth century, conservationists had lobbied the states to regulate game hunting, winning a U.S. Supreme Court case recognizing the constitutional power of the states to prohibit hunters from taking their game out of state on the theory that wild game was the common property of the citizens of the state in which they were found and could be regulated by the state government for the benefit of its own citizens (*Geer v. Connecticut *[1896]). But by the early twentieth century, conservationists had tired of wrestling with holdout states that favored hunters, and they turned to the federal government to trump them. Early bills to impose national restrictions on bird hunting went nowhere in Congress, but supporters of the regulation were able to attach such a measure as an amendment to an Agriculture Department appropriations bill in 1912. The provision was immediately challenged in court, and a federal district court judge in Arkansas held it to be an unconstitutional infringement on states' rights. Fearing that it would likely lose the case in the U.S. Supreme Court, the Woodrow Wilson administration moved to create a new constitutional basis for the rule. It approached the Canadian government about the possibility of negotiating a treaty that would empower Congress to regulate migratory birds.*

In 1916 the United States and Great Britain completed a treaty committing each nation to regulating the hunting of birds that migrated between the United States and Canada. (Great Britain still had official authority over Canada.) Congress was reluctant, but in 1918, on the basis of the treaty, it passed the Migratory Bird Treaty Act. This empowered the secretary of agriculture to create a national hunting season for such birds and made the violation of those regulations a federal crime. In most of the United States, states changed their own policies to match the new federal restrictions, and state game wardens cooperated with the relatively few federal game wardens that existed to enforce the laws. But cooperation was not universal, and many hunters flouted the federal laws in the Midwest and the South.

Missouri attorney general Frank McAllister was among those who opposed the federal limitations on hunting. When federal game warden Ray Holland received a tip that McAllister was going with friends on an out-of-season hunt, Holland was eager to set an example. He arrested McAllister (who had bagged seventy-six ducks), resulting in a fine. McAllister responded by having the state file suit in U.S. district court to prevent Holland from enforcing the federal regulations, which were in conflict with both the state's own hunting laws and the state's traditional property rights to wild game within its borders. The district court upheld the federal act, concluding that the regulation of migratory birds was not "remote" from the natural subject matter of international treaties and could be seen as benefiting "all the states." Missouri appealed to the U.S. Supreme Court.

The Supreme Court's opinion upholding the ruling of the district court and the Migratory Bird Treaty Act is famous for its broad reading of the federal treaty power as a source of congressional authority in domestic affairs that supplemented the powers enumerated in Article I, Section 8 of the Constitution. The decision came in the immediate aftermath of World War I and the debates over American involvement in the League of Nations. It was handed down just a few months before Warren G. Harding won the presidency and returned the federal government to the Republican Party, calling for a return to "normalcy," which meant in part the demobilization of the military and a withdrawal of the United States from European affairs. Others, with some success, would urge a policy of American "isolationism" from the international economic and diplomatic arena. The Supreme Court was not going to force that choice. Instead, it gave a free hand to Congress and the president to take the actions that they thought were in the national interest, even if those actions trenched on the traditional authority of the states to regulate persons and property within their borders.

The opinion by Justice Oliver Wendell Holmes, Jr., in this case is also famous for its bold declaration of the philosophy of a living Constitution, an "organism" that can grow beyond the expectations of those who drafted it. Even before joining the Court, Holmes was a leading advocate of a "realistic" view of the law. In keeping with the evolutionary theories that were prominent in his day and as likely to be applied to social phenomenon (e.g., "social Darwinism") as biological ones, Holmes argued that law does not embody timeless principles faithfully handed down from ancient sources but instead reflects the changing needs of contemporary society. As you read the following opinion consider whether he could have reached the same conclusion without relying on the metaphor of the living Constitution.

JUSTICE HOLMES delivered the opinion of the Court.

. . .

To answer this question it is not enough to refer to the Tenth Amendment, reserving the powers not delegated to the United States, because by Article II, Section 2, the power to make treaties is delegated expressly, and by Article VI treaties made under the authority of the United States, along with the Constitution and laws of the United States made in pursuance thereof, are declared the supreme law of the land. If the treaty is valid there can be no dispute about the validity of the statute under Article I, Section 8, as a necessary and proper means to execute the powers of the Government. The language of the Constitution as to the supremacy of treaties being general, the question before us is narrowed to an inquiry into the ground upon which the present supposed exception is placed.

It is said that a treaty cannot be valid if it infringes the Constitution, that there are limits, therefore, to the treaty-making power, and that one such limit is that what an act of Congress could not do unaided, in derogation of the powers reserved to the States, a treaty cannot do. An earlier act of Congress that attempted by itself and not in pursuance of a treaty to regulate the killing of migratory birds within the States had been held bad in the District Court. . . . Those decisions were supported by arguments that migratory birds were owned by the States in their sovereign capacity for the benefit of their people, and that under cases like *Geer v. Connecticut* (1896), this control was one that Congress had no power to displace. The same argument is supposed to apply now with equal force.

. . . Acts of Congress are the supreme law of the land only when made in pursuance of the Constitution, while treaties are declared to be so when made under the authority of the United States. It is open to question whether the authority of the United States means more than the formal acts prescribed to make the convention. We do not mean to imply that there are no qualifications to the treaty-making power; but they must be ascertained in a different way. It is obvious that there may be matters of the sharpest exigency for the national well being that an act of Congress could not deal with but that a treaty followed by such an act could, and it is not lightly to be assumed that, in matters requiring national action, "a power which must belong to and somewhere reside in every civilized government" is not to be found. . . . [W]hen we are dealing with words that also are a constituent act, like the Constitution of the United States, we must realize that they have called into life a being the development of which could not have been foreseen completely by the most gifted of its begetters. It was enough for them to realize or to hope that they had created an organism; it has taken a century and has cost their successors much sweat and blood to prove that they created a nation. The case before us must be considered in the light of our whole experience and not merely in that of what was said a hundred years ago. The treaty in question does not contravene any prohibitory words to be found in the Constitution. The only question is whether it is forbidden by some invisible radiation from the general terms of the Tenth Amendment. We must consider what this country has become in deciding what that Amendment has reserved.

The State as we have intimated founds its claim of exclusive authority upon an assertion of title to migratory birds, an assertion that is embodied in statute. No doubt it is true that as between a State and its inhabitants the State may regulate the killing and sale of such birds, but it does not follow that its authority is exclusive of paramount powers. To put the claim of the State upon title is to lean upon a slender reed. Wild birds are not in the possession of anyone; and possession is the beginning of ownership. The whole foundation of the State's rights is the presence within their jurisdiction of birds that yesterday had not arrived, tomorrow may be in another State and in a week a thousand miles away. If we are to be accurate we cannot put the case of the State upon higher ground than that the treaty deals with creatures that for the moment are within the state borders, that it must be carried out by officers of the United States within the same territory, and that but for the treaty the State would be free to regulate this subject itself.

As most of the laws of the United States are carried out within the States and as many of them deal with matters which in the silence of such laws the State might regulate, such general grounds are not enough to support Missouri's claim. Valid treaties of course "are as binding within the territorial limits of the States as they are elsewhere throughout the dominion of the United States." . . . No doubt the great body of private relations usually fall within the control of the State, but a treaty may override its power. We do not have to invoke the later developments of constitution law for this proposition; it was recognized as early as *Hopkirk v. Bell* (1806), with regard to statutes of limitation, and even earlier, as to confiscation, in *Ware v. Hylton* (1796). . . .

Here a national interest of very nearly the first magnitude is involved. It can be protected only by national action in concert with that of another power. The subject-matter is only transitorily within the State and has no permanent habitat therein. But for the treaty and the statute there soon might be no birds for any powers to deal with. We see nothing in the Constitution that compels the Government to sit by while a food supply is cut off and the protectors of our forests and our crops are destroyed. It is not sufficient to rely upon the States. The reliance is vain, and were it otherwise, the question is whether the United States is forbidden to act. We are of opinion that the treaty and statute must be upheld.

JUSTICE VAN DEVANTER and JUSTICE PITNEY dissent without an opinion

V. Federalism

MAJOR DEVELOPMENTS

- Rise of the dormant commerce clause
- Constitutional innovation in the states
- Development of police powers jurisprudence
- Modification of state sovereign immunity

Populist and Progressive reformers regarded states as potential sources of political power that might be used to discipline economic forces. In many places, state governments proved relatively easy for popular movements to influence or capture, and they created the first opportunity to test new policies to control corporations and redistribute wealth. Progressive justice Louis Brandeis saw states as "laboratories of democracy," where courageous citizens could "try novel social and economic experiments without risk to the rest of the country."[16] Minimum wage and maximum working hours, workplace safety regulations, consumer health protection, price controls, railroad regulation, business and occupational licensing, alcohol prohibition, and much more were pioneered in the states.

Conservatives raised the Federalist specter of excessively democratic states abusing government power at the expense of traditional legal rights and unpopular minorities (though not all minorities were of equal concern, with propertied interests taking a much higher priority than racial minorities, for example). Moreover, conservatives rejected Brandeis's premise that state experimentation posed no risk to its neighbors or to the nation at large. Political movements to protect local economic interests—whether farmers and workers or local businesses—from national competition hobbled the new interstate corporations that could realize great efficiencies and gains in production through economies of scale. These movements also threatened the creation of an integrated national market on which workers and businesses in other parts of the country depended.

Railroad regulation was a particular flashpoint for constitutional debates over state economic powers. Railroads were tying the country together, exposing local economies to national economic forces. Faced with different costs and levels of competition, railroads often charged different rates for "long-haul" freights than for "short-haul" freights. State legislatures, particularly in the Midwest, responded with various schemes to regulate railroad rates, from banning discriminatory rates to establishing regulatory commissions that set a schedule of fares. Congress faced competing pressures. Unable to balance the conflicting demands of railroads, big shippers, and small shippers, Congress remained silent on the issue of railroad rates.

---

16. *New State Ice v. Liebmann*, 285 U.S. 262, 311 (1932).

The Supreme Court responded to this congressional silence by developing judicial limits on state regulation. The justices in *Munn v. Illinois* (1877) suggested that the due process clause of the Fourteenth Amendment might protect business enterprise from some regulations and in such cases as *Chicago, Milwaukee and St. Paul Railway Company v. Minnesota* (1890) and *Smyth v. Ames* (1898) struck down state laws regulating railroad rates. Other cases created the doctrine of the "dormant commerce clause" by extending the language in *Cooley v. Board of Wardens* (1852) suggesting that some issues are best addressed by a national law. In *Wabash, St. Louis and Pacific Railway Company v. Illinois* (1886) the Court determined that it could strike down state laws that interfered with the dormant (that is, as-yet unexpressed) authority of the federal government. Consequently, when it came to the free flow of goods across a national market, the Court's presumption was that the United States would be treated internally as a free trade zone. The states could not regulate interstate commerce in a manner that would obstruct the free flow of goods without explicit congressional authorization. If Congress was frozen by competing interests, the Court would make sure that the states would be frozen also. This constitutional project was resisted by Populists and localists but was fundamental to the vision of conservative Democrats and Republicans alike. Large economic interests in the East hailed the Court's decision as "fundamental to the existence of the Union and to the existence of trade."[17]

The late Republican Era was a period of policy, institutional, and constitutional innovation in the states. Some of those innovations were later nationalized, whether in the form of statutes, judicial opinions, or constitutional amendments. Four amendments, the Sixteenth through the Nineteenth, were added to the U.S. Constitution between 1913 and 1920. They were the first constitutional amendments since Reconstruction, and they were prefigured by reforms that had been occurring in the states. Women's suffrage, alcohol prohibition, and direct election of U.S. senators had all been extensively tried at the state level before a constitutional amendment passed through Congress. The income tax amendment was different. Wisconsin was a leader in developing an income tax, but most states passed on the idea, arguing that the tax was unenforceable and would only lead wealthy taxpayers to flee to neighboring states.[18]

The states also experimented with new forms of democratic decision making. In an initiative, a statute is placed by petition on a ballot for citizens to accept or reject. In a referendum, it is the legislature that places the statute on a ballot. Both of these reforms were designed to check legislatures that were viewed as overly influenced by special interests or political parties. Populists and Progressives, especially in the young western states, embraced these mechanisms of "direct legislation" as vehicles for a politics free from corruption and partisanship. South Dakota was the first state to adopt a state-level initiative and referendum process in 1898, but other states soon followed. By 1918, when the first wave of reform stalled out, twenty-four states had adopted the mechanisms.

In a highly influential decision in *Kadderly v. Portland* (1903), the Oregon Supreme Court blessed the initiative and referendum process. In *Pacific States Telephone and Telegraph Co. v. Oregon* (1912), the U.S. Supreme Court was asked whether the "Oregon System" was consistent with the republican guarantee clause of the U.S. Constitution. The Court decided that this was a "political question" that could not be answered by the courts. In the meantime, state courts across the country followed *Kadderly*. They accepted the initiative and referendum system as consistent with a republican form of government—so long as some form of representative government and constitutional limitations on government powers remained in place.

Wabash, St. Louis and Pacific Railway Company v. Illinois, 118 U.S. 557 (1886)

In the latter half of the nineteenth century, the economics of railroads provoked bitter political struggles in the Midwest. The railroads were subject to fierce competition on long-haul

17. *The Nation*, October 28, 1886, 339.

18. Alabama's experience was typical, with the state auditor complaining in 1883, "Taxes upon salaries . . . are regarded with disfavor by almost every taxpayer. . . . They are in the very nature of things attained by processes inquisitorial in character, and therefore to most persons exceedingly obnoxious. In addition to this the law has never been and probably never will be properly executed, and consequently does not bear equally alike upon all. . . . I do not hesitate therefore to give it as my opinion that it should be repealed." Alabama dropped the income tax—a holdover from the Civil War—the next year. Edwin R. A. Segliman, *The Income Tax* (New York: Macmillan, 1914), 411.

routes across the country but frequently held monopolies on the short-haul branches that linked to these longer railways. That often meant that farmers, ranchers, and small merchants and producers in the small towns and the countryside frequently paid higher rates on a per-mile basis to ship goods than did the big economic players who operated on a national scale and shipped between the major cities. Competition on the long-haul lines could drive prices below the costs of operating the lines; the short-haul business subsidized the long-haul routes, helping the railroads maintain overall profitability. Short-haul shippers demanded an equalization of rates, ending the price discrimination between shippers, and state governments responded.

The Illinois legislature took the direct route, prohibiting rates that discriminated between short-haul and long-haul shippers. Railroads could not charge more for the transportation of any passenger or freight within the state than it charged for an equivalent shipment "over a greater distance." The Wabash, St. Louis and Pacific Railway Company was charged with violating the act for charging ten cents per hundred pounds more for shipping goods to New York City from Gilman, Illinois, than from Peoria, Illinois, even though the trip from Peoria was eighty-six miles longer within the state than was the trip from Gilman. The railway company was found guilty in state court, and the verdict was affirmed by the state supreme court. From there, the railway company appealed to the U.S. Supreme Court, arguing that the shipments from the cities in Illinois to New York City were part of interstate commerce and that the Illinois legislature could not constitutionally regulate such acts. In a 6–3 decision, the U.S. Supreme Court agreed, reversing the judgment of the state court.

JUSTICE MILLER delivered the opinion of the Court.

. . .

If the Illinois statute could be construed to apply exclusively to contracts for a carriage which begins and ends within the State, disconnected from a continuous transportation through or into other States, there does not seem to be any difficulty in holding it to be valid. For instance, a contract might be made to carry goods for a certain price from Cairo to Chicago, or from Chicago to Alton. The charges for these might be within the competency of the Illinois Legislature to regulate. The reason for this is that both the charge and the actual transportation in such cases are exclusively confined to the limits of the territory of the State, and is not commerce among the States, or interstate commerce, but is exclusively commerce within the State. So far, therefore, as this class of transportation, as an element of commerce, is affected by the statute under consideration, it is not subject to the constitutional provision concerning commerce among the States. . . .

. . .

The Supreme Court of Illinois does not place its judgment in the present case on the ground that the transportation and the charge are exclusively State commerce, but, conceding that it may be a case of commerce among the States, or interstate commerce, which Congress would have the right to regulate if it had attempted to do so, argues that this statute of Illinois belongs to that class of commercial regulations which may be established by the laws of a State until Congress shall have exercised its power on that subject. . . .

In *Munn v. Illinois* (1877), the language of this court upon that subject is as follows:

> . . . The warehouses of these plaintiffs in error are situated and their business carried on exclusively within the limits of the State of Illinois. . . . Their regulation is a thing of domestic concern, and certainly, until Congress acts in reference to their interstate relations, the State may exercise all the powers of government over them, even though in so doing it may indirectly operate upon commerce outside its immediate jurisdiction. We do not say that a case may not arise in which it will be found that a State, under the form of regulating its own affairs, has encroached upon the exclusive domain of Congress in respect to interstate commerce, but we do say that, upon the facts as they are represented to us in this record, that has not been done.

. . . [I]t must be admitted that, in a general way, the court treated the cases then before it as belonging to that class of regulations of commerce which, like pilotage, bridging navigable rivers, and many others, could be acted upon by the States in the absence of any legislation by Congress on the same subject.

By the slightest attention to the matter it will be readily seen that the circumstances under which a bridge may be authorized across a navigable stream within the limits of a State, for the use of a public highway, and the local rules which shall govern the conduct of the pilots of each of the varying harbors of the coasts of the United States, depend upon principles far more limited in their application and importance than those which should regulate the transportation of persons and property across the half or the whole of the continent, over the territories of half a dozen States, through which they are carried without change of car or breaking bulk.

. . .

It cannot be too strongly insisted upon that the right of continuous transportation from one end of the country to the other is essential in modern times to that freedom of commerce from the restraints which the State might choose to impose upon it, that the commerce clause was intended to secure. This clause, giving to Congress the power to regulate commerce among the States and with foreign nations, as this court has said before, was among the most important of the subjects which prompted the formation of the Constitution. . . . And it would be a very feeble and almost useless provision, but poorly adapted to secure the entire freedom of commerce among the States which was deemed essential to a more perfect union by the framers of the Constitution, if at every stage of the transportation of goods and chattels through the country, the State within whose limits a part of this transportation must be done could impose regulations concerning the price, compensation, or taxation, or any other restrictive regulation interfering with and seriously embarrassing this commerce.

The argument on this subject can never be better stated than it is by Chief-Justice Marshall in *Gibbons v. Ogden* (1824). He there demonstrates that commerce among the States, like commerce with foreign nations, is necessarily a commerce which crosses State lines, and extends into the States, and the power of Congress to regulate it exists wherever that commerce is found. . . .

. . .

We must, therefore, hold that it is not, and never has been, the deliberate opinion of a majority of this court that a statute of a State which attempts to regulate the fares and charges by railroad companies within its limits, for a transportation which constitutes a part of commerce among the States, is a valid law.

. . .

. . . That this species of regulation is one which must be, if established at all, of a general and national character, and cannot be safely and wisely remitted to local rules and local regulations, we think is clear from what has already been said. And if it be a regulation of commerce, as we think we have demonstrated it is, and as the Illinois court concedes it to be, it must be of that national character, and the regulation can only appropriately exist by general rules and principles, which demand that it should be done by the Congress of the United States under the commerce clause of the Constitution.

The judgment of the Supreme Court of Illinois is therefore reversed, and the case remanded to that court for further proceedings in conformity with this opinion.

JUSTICE BRADLEY, with whom THE CHIEF JUSTICE and JUSTICE GRAY join, dissenting.

. . .

The principal question in this case . . . is whether, in the absence of congressional legislation, a State legislature has the power to regulate the charges made by the railroads of the State for transporting goods and passengers to and from places within the State, when such goods or passengers are brought from, or carried to, points without the State, and are, therefore, in the course of transportation from another State, or to another State. . . . We think that the State does not lose its power to regulate the charges of its own railroads in its own territory, simply because the goods or persons transported have been brought from or are destined to a point beyond the State in another State.

. . .

. . . Does it follow . . . that because Congress has the power to regulate this matter (though it has not exercised that power), therefore the State is divested of all power of regulation? That is the question before us.

We had supposed that this question was concluded by the previous decisions of this court: that all local arrangements and regulations respecting highways, turnpikes, railroads, bridges, canals, ferries, dams, and wharves, within the State, their construction and repair, and the charges to be made for their use, though materially affecting commerce, both internal and external, and thereby incidentally operating to a certain extent as regulations of interstate commerce, were within the power and jurisdiction of the several States. That is still our opinion.

. . .

The doctrines announced in these cases apply not only to dams in, and bridges over, navigable streams, but to all structures and appliances in a state which may incidentally interfere with commerce, or which may be erected or created for the furtherance of commerce, whether by water or by land. It is matter of common knowledge that from the beginning of the government the States have exercised almost exclusive control over roads, bridges, ferries, wharves, and harbors. No one has doubted their right to do so. . . .

. . .

There is a class of subjects, it is true, pertaining to interstate and foreign commerce, which require general and uniform rules for the whole country, so as to obviate unjust discriminations against any part, and in respect of which local regulations made by the States would be repugnant to the power vested in Congress, and, therefore, unconstitutional; but there are other subjects of local character and interest which not only admit of, but are generally best regulated by, State authority. This distinction is pointed out and enforced in the case of *Cooley v. The Port Wardens of Philadelphia* (1852). . . .

. . .

Now, since every railroad may be, and generally is, a medium of transportation for interstate commerce, and affects that commerce; and since the charges of fare and freight for such transportation affect and incidentally regulate that commerce; and since the railroad could not be built, and the charges upon it could not be exacted, without authority from the State, it follows as a necessary consequence that the State, in the exercise of its undoubted functions and sovereignty, does, in the establishment and regulation of railroads, to a certain and a very material extent, not only do that which affects but incidentally regulates commerce. It does so by the very act of authorizing the construction of railroads and the collection of fares and freights thereon. No one doubts its powers to do this. The very being of the plaintiffs in error, the very existence of their railroad, the very power they exercise of charging fares and freights, are all derived from the State. And yet, according to the argument of the plaintiffs in error, pursued to its legitimate consequences, the act of the State in doing all this ought to be regarded as null and void because it operates as a regulation of commerce among the States. . . . And since its being, its franchises, its powers, its road, its right to charge, all come from the State, and are the creation of State law, how can it be contended that the State has no power of regulation over those charges, and over the conduct of the company in the transaction of its business whilst acting within the State and using its railroad lying within the bounds of the State? . . .

. . .

To sum up the matter in a word: we hold it to be a sound proposition of law, that the making of railroads and regulating the charges for their use is not such a regulation of commerce as to be in the remotest degree repugnant to any power given to Congress by the Constitution, so long as that power is dormant, and has not been exercised by Congress. . . .

. . .

The inconveniences which it has been supposed in argument would follow from the execution of the laws of Illinois, we think have been greatly exaggerated. But if it should be found to present any real difficulty in the modes of transacting business on through lines, it is always in the power of Congress to make such reasonable regulations as the interests of interstate commerce may demand, without denuding the States of their just powers over their own roads and their own corporations.

Munn v. State of Illinois, 94 U.S. 113 (1877)

In the early 1870s an agrarian political movement known as the Patrons of Husbandry, also known as "the Grange," developed in the Midwest in response to the economic power of railroads, corporations, and other property owners who were in a position to take advantage of farmers. Farmers were especially upset at the rates set by railroads for hauling crops to market and by the owners of the grain elevators for storing the waiting crops. In Illinois, Iowa, Minnesota, and Wisconsin, state legislatures responded by regulating the maximum prices that railroads and grain elevators could charge. The maximum rate law at issue in Munn *applied to grain elevators and was challenged on the ground that by preventing property owners from setting their own prices, the legislature had effectively deprived them of property without due process of law, in violation of the Fourteenth Amendment.*

The Court handed down its 7–2 decision on March 1, 1877, the day before President Rutherford B. Hayes was declared elected by the Electoral Commission that was charged with resolving the disputed 1876 presidential election. In a decision written by the chief justice, with substantial help from Bradley (a dissenter in the Slaughter-House Cases*), the Court ruled that property that is "clothed with a public interest"—in the sense that it is "used in a manner to make it of public consequence, and affect the community at large"—could be regulated* *"by the public for the common good." Field—the most stridently conservative of this generation of justices—filed a dissent for himself and Justice Strong (who voted with the majority in* Slaughter-House*). One key issue for the justices was how broadly the category of businesses "affected with a public interest" should be understood. The common law had long recognized an expanded role for state regulation of such enterprises, and the Fourteenth Amendment's due process clause might be assumed to take into account that traditional distinction. But how strictly should the category be interpreted? Did grain elevators merit that heightened level of government regulation?*

As in the Slaughter-House Cases *(1873), a majority of the justices understood the importance of property rights but felt obligated to be cautious about the reach of federal judicial power under the newly passed Fourteenth Amendment. As it turned out, by the late 1870s most of these so-called Granger laws had been removed from the books by state legislatures, without having been ordered to do so by federal judges. Nevertheless, many conservatives were extremely disappointed by the result in* Munn*. At one point Field became so frustrated with his brethren's apparent disregard for property rights that he explored a run for the presidency in 1884 as a way to "have placed on the Bench able and conservative men and thus have brought back the decisions of the Court to that line from which they should not have departed."[19] Field also arranged for well-known conservative lawyers, such as John Norton Pomeroy, to write articles for prominent legal journals criticizing decisions such as* Munn v. Illinois *for striking "at the stability of private property," a right that represented "the very foundation of modern society and civilization."[20] The conservative American Bar Association was also formed around the time of* Munn *so as to organize elite commercial bar advocacy for more sympathetic judicial decision making.*

It would take only thirteen years for the Court, led by a new chief justice, to declare in Chicago, Milwaukee & St. Paul Railway v. Minnesota*, also known as the* Minnesota Rate Case *(1890), that judges were obligated under the due process clause to protect the property rights of investors or corporations by reviewing the reasonableness of any rates set by state authorities—thus essentially overruling* Munn v. Illinois*. Chief Justice Waite ended his opinion in* Munn *by declaring, "For protection against abuses by legislatures the people must resort to the polls, not to the courts." By the turn of the century, property owners were successfully resorting to the federal courts.*

CHIEF JUSTICE WAITE delivered the opinion of the Court.

. . .

Every statute is presumed to be constitutional. The courts ought not to declare one to be unconstitutional, unless it is clearly so. If there is doubt, the expressed will of the legislature should be sustained.

The Constitution contains no definition of the word "deprive," as used in the Fourteenth Amendment['s due process clause]. To determine its signification, therefore, it is necessary to ascertain the effect which usage has given it, when employed in the same or a like connection.

While this provision of the amendment is new in the Constitution of the United States, as a limitation upon the powers of the States, it is old as a principle of civilized government. It is found in Magna Charta, and, in substance if not in form, in nearly or quite all the constitutions that have been from time to time adopted by the several States of the Union. By the Fifth Amendment, it was introduced into the Constitution of the United States as a limitation upon the powers of the national government, and by the Fourteenth, as a guaranty against any encroachment upon an acknowledged right of citizenship by the legislatures of the States. . . .

When one becomes a member of society, he necessarily parts with some rights or privileges which, as an individual not affected by his relations to others, he might retain. "A body politic," as aptly defined in the preamble of the Constitution of Massachusetts, "is a social compact by which the whole people covenants with each citizen, and each citizen with the whole people, that all shall be governed by certain laws for the common good." This does not confer power upon the whole people to control rights which are purely and exclusively private, . . . but it does authorize the establishment of laws requiring each citizen to so conduct himself, and so use his own property, as not unnecessarily to injure another. This is the very essence of government, and has found expression in the maxim sic utere tuo ut alienum non laedas ["one should use his own property in such a manner as not to injure that of another"]. From this source come the police powers, which, as was said by Chief Justice

19. Howard Jay Graham, "Four Letters of Mr. Justice Field," *Yale Law Journal* 47 (1938): 1107.

20. John Norton Pomeroy, "The Supreme Court and State Repudiation," *American Law Review* 17 (1883): 712.

Taney in the *License Cases* (1847), "are nothing more or less than the powers of government inherent in every sovereignty, . . . that is to say, . . . the power to govern men and things." Under these powers the government regulates the conduct of its citizens one towards another, and the manner in which each shall use his own property, when such regulation becomes necessary for the public good. In their exercise it has been customary in England from time immemorial, and in this country from its first colonization, to regulate ferries, common carriers, hackmen, bakers, millers, wharfingers, innkeepers, etc., and in so doing to fix a maximum of charge to be made for services rendered, accommodations furnished, and articles sold. To this day, statutes are to be found in many of the States upon some or all these subjects; and we think it has never yet been successfully contended that such legislation came within any of the constitutional prohibitions against interference with private property. . . .

From this it is apparent that, down to the time of the adoption of the Fourteenth Amendment, it was not supposed that statutes regulating the use, or even the price of the use, of private property necessarily deprived an owner of his property without due process of law. . . .

This brings us to inquire as to the principles upon which this power of regulation rests, in order that we may determine what is within and what without its operative effect. Looking, then, to the common law, from whence came the right which the Constitution protects, we find that when private property is "affected with a public interest, it ceases to be juris privati only." This was said by Lord Chief Justice Hale more than two hundred years ago . . . and has been accepted without objection as an essential element in the law of property ever since. Property does become clothed with a public interest when used in a manner to make it of public consequence, and affect the community at large. When, therefore, one devotes his property to a use in which the public has an interest, he, in effect, grants to the public an interest in that use, and must submit to be controlled by the public for the common good, to the extent of the interest he has thus created. He may withdraw his grant by discontinuing the use; but, so long as he maintains the use, he must submit to the control. . . .

. . . It remains only to ascertain whether the warehouses of these plaintiffs in error, and the business which is carried on there, come within the operation of this principle.

For this purpose we accept as true the statements of fact contained in the elaborate brief of one of the counsel of the plaintiffs in error. From these it appears that " . . . The quantity [of grain] received in Chicago has made it the greatest grain market in the world. . . . The grain warehouses or elevators in Chicago are immense structures, holding from 300,000 to 1,000,000 bushels at one time, according to size. They are divided into bins of large capacity and great strength. . . . They are located with the river harbor on one side and the railway tracks on the other; and the grain is run through them from car to vessel, or boat to car, as may be demanded in the course of business. . . . " . . .

Under such circumstances it is difficult to see why, if the common carrier, or the miller, or the ferryman, or the innkeeper, or the wharfinger, or the baker, or the cartman, or the hackney-coachman, pursues a public employment and exercises "a sort of public office," these plaintiffs in error do not. They stand, to use again the language of their counsel, in the very "gateway of commerce," and take toll from all who pass. Their business most certainly "tends to a common charge, and is become a thing of public interest and use." . . . Certainly, if any business can be clothed "with a public interest, and cease to be juris privati only," this has been. It may not be made so by the operation of the Constitution of Illinois or this statute, but it is by the facts.

We also are not permitted to overlook the fact that, for some reason, the people of Illinois, when they revised their Constitution in 1870, saw fit to make it the duty of the general assembly to pass laws "for the protection of producers, shippers, and receivers of grain and produce," art. 13, sect. 7; and by sect. 5 of the same article, to require all railroad companies receiving and transporting grain in bulk or otherwise to deliver the same at any elevator to which it might be consigned, that could be reached by any track that was or could be used by such company, and that all railroad companies should permit connections to be made with their tracks, so that any public warehouse, etc., might be reached by the cars on their railroads. This indicates very clearly that during the twenty years in which this peculiar business had been assuming its present "immense proportions," something had occurred which led the whole body of the people to suppose that remedies such as are usually employed to prevent abuses by virtual monopolies might not be inappropriate here. For our purposes we must assume that, if a state of facts could exist that would justify such legislation, it actually did exist when the statute now under consideration was passed. For us the question is one of power, not of expediency. If no state of circumstances could exist to justify such a statute, then we may declare this one void, because in excess of the legislative power of the State. But if it could, we must presume it did. Of the propriety of legislative interference within the scope of legislative power, the legislature is the exclusive judge. . . .

We know that this is a power which may be abused; but that is no argument against its existence. For protection against abuses by legislatures the people must resort to the polls, not to the courts. . . .

JUSTICE FIELD, dissenting.

I am compelled to dissent from the decision of the court in this case, and from the reasons upon which that decision is founded. The principle upon which the opinion of the majority proceeds is, in my judgment, subversive of the rights of private property, heretofore believed to be protected by constitutional guaranties against legislative interference, and is in conflict with the authorities cited in its support. . . .

The question presented . . . is one of the greatest importance,—whether it is within the competency of a State to fix the compensation which an individual may receive for the use of his own property in his private business, and for his services in connection with it.

The declaration of the [state] Constitution of 1870, that private buildings used for private purposes shall be deemed public institutions, does not make them so. The receipt and storage of grain in a building erected by private means for that purpose does not constitute the building a public warehouse. There is no magic in the language, though used by a constitutional convention, which can change a private business into a public one, or alter the character of the building in which the business is transacted. . . . One might as well attempt to change the nature of colors, by giving them a new designation. The defendants were no more public warehousemen, as justly observed by counsel, than the merchant who sells his merchandise to the public is a public merchant, or the blacksmith who shoes horses for the public is a public blacksmith; and it was a strange notion that by calling them so they would be brought under legislative control. . . .

. . . But it would seem from its opinion that the court holds that property loses something of its private character when employed in such a way as to be generally useful. The doctrine declared is that property "becomes clothed with a public interest when used in a manner to make it of public consequence, and affect the community at large;" and from such clothing the right of the legislature is deduced to control the use of the property, and to determine the compensation which the owner may receive for it. When Sir Matthew Hale, and the sages of the law in his day, spoke of property as affected by a public interest, and ceasing from that cause to be juris privati solely, that is, ceasing to be held merely in private right, they referred to property dedicated by the owner to public uses, or to property the use of which was granted by the government, or in connection with which special privileges were conferred. Unless the property was thus dedicated, or some right bestowed by the government was held with the property, either by specific grant or by prescription of so long a time as to imply a grant originally, the property was not affected by any public interest so as to be taken out of the category of property held in private right. But it is not in any such sense that the terms "clothing property with a public interest" are used in this case. From the nature of the business under consideration—the storage of grain—which, in any sense in which the words can be used, is a private business, in which the public are interested only as they are interested in the storage of other products of the soil, or in articles of manufacture, it is clear that the court intended to declare that, whenever one devotes his property to a business which is useful to the public,—"affects the community at large,"—the legislature can regulate the compensation which the owner may receive for its use, and for his own services in connection with it. . . .

If this be sound law, if there be no protection, either in the principles upon which our republican government is founded, or in the prohibitions of the Constitution against such invasion of private rights, all property and all business in the State are held at the mercy of a majority of its legislature. The public has no greater interest in the use of buildings for the storage of grain than it has in the use of buildings for the residences of families, nor, indeed, anything like so great an interest; and, according to the doctrine announced, the legislature may fix the rent of all tenements used for residences, without reference to the cost of their erection. If the owner does not like the rates prescribed, he may cease renting his houses. . . . The public is interested in the manufacture of cotton, woollen, and silken fabrics, in the construction of machinery, in the printing and publication of books and periodicals, and in the making of utensils of every variety, useful and ornamental; indeed, there is hardly an enterprise or business engaging the attention and labor of any considerable portion of the community, in which the public has not an interest in the sense in which that term is used by the court in its opinion; and the doctrine which allows the legislature to interfere with and regulate the charges which the owners of property thus employed shall make for its use, that is, the rates at which all these different kinds of business shall be carried on, has never before been asserted, so far as I am aware, by any judicial tribunal in the United States.

. . . All that is beneficial in property arises from its use, and the fruits of that use; and whatever deprives a person of them deprives him of all that is desirable or valuable in the title and possession. . . .

No State "shall deprive any person of life, liberty, or property without due process of law," says the Fourteenth Amendment to the Constitution. . . . By the term "liberty," as used in the provision, something more is meant than mere freedom from physical restraint or the bounds of a prison. It means freedom to go where one may choose, and to act in such manner, not inconsistent with the equal rights of others, as his judgment may dictate for the promotion of his happiness; that is, to pursue such callings and avocations as may be most suitable to develop his capacities, and give to them their highest enjoyment.

The same liberal construction which is required for the protection of life and liberty, in all particulars in which life and liberty are of any value, should be applied to the protection of private property. If the legislature of a State, under pretence of providing for the public good, or for any other reason, can determine, against the consent of the owner, the uses to which private property shall be devoted, or the prices which the owner shall receive for its uses, it can deprive him of the property as completely as by a special act for its confiscation or destruction. . . .

The power of the State over the property of the citizen under the constitutional guaranty is well defined. The State may take his property for public uses, upon just compensation being made therefore. It may take a portion of his property by way of taxation for the support of the government. It may control the use and possession of his property, so far as may be necessary for the protection of the rights of others, and to secure to them the equal use and enjoyment of their property. The doctrine that each one must so use his own as not to injure his neighbor—sic utere tuo ut alienum non laedas—is the rule by which every member or society must possess and enjoy his property; and all legislation essential to secure this common and equal enjoyment is a legitimate exercise of State authority. Except in cases where property may be destroyed to arrest a conflagration or the ravages of pestilence, or be taken under the pressure of an immediate and overwhelming necessity to prevent a public calamity, the power of the State over the property of the citizen does not extend beyond such limits. . . .

. . .

. . . The business of a warehouseman was, at common law, a private business, and is so in its nature. It has no special privileges connected with it, nor did the law ever extend to it any greater protection than it extended to all other private business. No reason can be assigned to justify legislation interfering with the legitimate profits of that business, that would not equally justify an intermeddling with the business of every man in the community, so soon, at least, as his business became generally useful.

JUSTICE STRONG, dissenting.

VI. Separation of Powers

MAJOR DEVELOPMENTS

- Struggle over presidential appointment and removal power
- Expanding unilateral activity by the president
- Expanded rulemaking activity by the executive branch

The late nineteenth century was an era of congressional government. The early twentieth century witnessed the birth of the modern presidency. In between was struggle.

During the Republican Era, presidents fought Congress for control of the power of executive appointment and removal. Civil service reform at the turn of the century reduced the number of offices available for political allocation and the political importance of patronage. The rise of the regulatory state and the increasing complexity of government policy even in such traditional domains as the setting of taxes meant that legislatures were no longer the only, or necessarily even the primary, site of policy making. Independent regulatory bodies and agencies within the executive branch were increasingly important players on the policy stage. Foreign affairs were becoming a routine and significant part of the federal government's agenda, and one in which the president had an outsized role. (President Theodore Roosevelt won a Nobel Peace Prize in 1906 for his role in resolving international disputes, including the concluding of a peace treaty between Russia and Japan.) The president naturally assumed a leadership role in times of crisis, and as the nineteenth century became the twentieth the opportunities for crisis management multiplied. The integrated economy gave local events new national significance.

The Supreme Court weighed in on the question of the presidential power to remove executive branch officials from office in *Myers v. United States* (1926). The First Congress had given the power to (or recognized the power of) the president to remove executive officers. Jacksonians had adopted the spoils system and the practice of mass dismissals of lower-level officials after an election. The Reconstruction Congress had sought to control President Andrew Johnson by requiring Senate approval before a cabinet officer could be removed. Civil service reform had limited the ability of presidents to remove low-level officials at their discretion. *Myers* allowed former president William Howard Taft to add the Supreme Court's voice to those debates. The statutory provision at issue in *Myers* was particularly restrictive—requiring Senate approval for the removal of a postmaster general—and it provided an opportunity for Taft to lend the Court's support to the White House in its struggles with Congress over the appointment and removal power. But in the early twentieth century, the more Progressive justices dissented and sided with Congress against the Woodrow Wilson White House on this issue, voicing their view that Congress should be able to impose the statutory controls on any lower-level government officials that it wants.

The growth of the bureaucracy and administrative agencies in the decades after the Civil War put pressure on traditional ideas about legislative delegations. According to Article I of the U.S. Constitution, "all legislative Powers herein granted shall be vested in a Congress of the United States." This vesting clause suggests that Congress alone must exercise the legislative powers of the federal government. Congress cannot delegate the federal legislative powers, or a part of them, to someone else. Statutes passed during the Republican Era, however, were often broadly worded and called on administrative agencies to engage in extensive rulemaking in order to fulfill their missions. When did permissible administrative rulemaking become impermissible lawmaking? When did permissible delegations of executive discretion become impermissible delegations of legislative authority? A particularly influential answer emerged from the Taft Court in *J. W. Hampton, Jr. & Co. v. United States* (1928), which held that so long as Congress provided an "intelligible principle" for the executive and the courts to follow, the delegation was permissible.

Myers v. United States, 272 U.S. 52 (1926)

In the midst of its battle with Andrew Johnson over the control of the policy and administration of the federal government, Congress passed the Tenure of Office Act of 1867, which barred the president from removing executive branch officials from office without the consent of the Senate. The Tenure of Office Act was later repealed, but Congress adopted new measures that imposed similar restrictions on the presidential removal power. An 1876 statute provided that postmasters could be "removed by the President by and with the advice and consent of the Senate."

Frank S. Myers had been appointed to a four-year term as postmaster at Portland, Oregon, by Woodrow Wilson in 1917. In 1920, several months before the expiration of that four-year term, Wilson ordered, without explanation, that Myers be removed from office, and failed to notify the Senate of the removal. Myers protested his removal and brought suit in the Court of Claims to recover the amount of his salary from the date of the removal order, a total of $8,838.71. Meanwhile, the president had filled Myers's office through a recess appointment. The Court of Claims dismissed the suit on the grounds that Myers did not file it sufficiently promptly. Myers appealed to the Supreme Court, which accepted his suit as timely (the government *did not contest that issue). Since Solicitor General James Beck was arguing, on behalf of the administration, that the statute was unconstitutional, the Court invited Senator George Pepper to participate in the case. Myers died during the litigation, and the suit was continued by his estate.*

Arising at the end of the Republican Era, the case pointed to a tension in Progressive sensibilities about government administration. On the one hand, by the 1920s the civil service system was well established; the Jacksonian spoils system and freewheeling executive discretion to make removals and appointments for political reasons had been firmly rejected. On the other hand, there was a heightened appreciation of the value of the power of the executive branch under unified leadership. A "chief executive officer" could marshal that power to ensure efficient and effective administration.

For both the parties before the Court and the justices, the question of whether Congress could restrict the president's removal power largely turned on the question of what practical construction had been given to the power by government action over time. The value and meaning of the House debate over the removal power in 1789 and of the Tenure of Office Act of 1867 were important points of disagreement among the justices. Was the restriction on the removal of postmasters a break from historical practice or an embodiment of it? Do restrictions on the president's ability to remove executive branch officials undercut the president's ability to meet his Article II responsibilities? Keep in mind that the majority opinion was written by William Howard Taft—the only justice who had also been president of the United States. Taft wrote for a 6–3 majority striking down the statutory restrictions on the presidential removal power. The opinion sustained Woodrow Wilson's right to fire the postmaster without seeking Senate approval.

CHIEF JUSTICE TAFT delivered the opinion of the Court.

This case presents the question whether under the Constitution the President has the exclusive power of removing executive officers of the United States whom he has appointed by and with the advice and consent of the Senate.

. . .

The question where the power of removal of executive officers appointed by the President by and with the advice and consent of the Senate was vested, was presented early in the first session of the First Congress. There is no express provision respecting removals in the Constitution, except . . . for removal from office by impeachment. . . .

. . .

[In the First Congress] the exact question which the House voted upon was whether it should recognize and declare the power of the President under the constitution to remove the Secretary of Foreign Affairs without the advice and consent of the Senate. . . . [T]he vote was, and was intended to be, a legislative declaration that the power to remove officers appointed by the President and the Senate vested in the President alone, and until the Johnson Impeachment trial in 1868, its meaning was not doubted even by those who questioned its soundness. . . .

. . .

. . . [T]he Constitution was so framed as to vest in the Congress all legislative powers therein granted, to vest in the President the executive power, and to vest in one Supreme Court and such inferior courts as Congress might establish, the judicial power. From this division on principle, the reasonable construction of the Constitution must be that the branches should be kept separate in all cases in which they were not expressly blended, and the Constitution should be expounded to blend them no more than it affirmatively requires. . . .

. . .

The vesting of the executive power in the President was essentially a grant of the power to execute the laws. But the President alone and unaided could not execute the laws. He must execute them by the assistance of subordinates. This view has since been repeatedly affirmed by this Court. . . . As he is charged specifically to take care that they be faithfully executed, the reasonable implication, even in the absence of express words, was that as part of his executive power he should select those who were to act for him under his direction in the execution of the laws. The further implication must be, in the absence of any express limitation respecting removals, that as his selection of administrative officers is essential to the execution of the laws by him, so must be his power of removing those for whom he can not continue to be responsible. . . . It was urged that the natural meaning of the term "executive power" granted the President included the appointment and removal of executive subordinates. If such appointments and removals were not an exercise of the executive power, what were they? They certainly were not the exercise of legislative or judicial power in government as usually understood.

. . .

The requirement of the second section of Article II that the Senate should advise and consent to the Presidential appointments, was to be strictly construed. . . .

. . .

A reference of the whole power of removal to general legislation by Congress is quite out of keeping with the plan of government devised by the framers of the Constitution. It could never have been intended to leave to Congress unlimited discretion to vary fundamentally the operation of the great independent executive branch of government and thus most seriously to weaken it. It would be a delegation by the Convention to Congress of the function of defining the primary boundaries of another of the three great divisions of government. The inclusion of removals of executive officers in the executive power vested in the President by Article II, according to its usual definition, and the implication of his power of removal of such officers from the provision of section 2 expressly recognizing in him the power of their appointment, are a much more natural and appropriate source of the removing power.

. . .

. . . To Congress under its legislative power is given the establishment of offices, the determination of their functions and jurisdiction, the prescribing of reasonable and relevant qualifications and rules of eligibility of appointees, and the fixing of the term for which they are to be appointed, and their compensation—all except as otherwise provided by the Constitution.

. . .

Made responsible under the Constitution for the effective enforcement of the law, the President needs as an indispensable aid to meet it the disciplinary influence upon those who act under him of a reserve power of removal. . . .

. . .

We come now to a period in the history of the Government when both Houses of Congress attempted to reverse this constitutional construction and to subject the power of removing executive officers appointed by the President and confirmed by the Senate to the control of the Senate—indeed, finally, to the assumed power in Congress to place the removal of such officers anywhere in the Government.

. . .

The extreme provisions of all this [Reconstruction Era] legislation were a full justification for the considerations so strongly advanced by Mr. Madison and his associates in the First Congress for insisting that the power of removal of executive officers by the President alone was essential in the division of powers between the executive and the legislative bodies. It exhibited in a clear degree the paralysis to which a partisan Senate and Congress could subject the executive arm and destroy the principle of executive responsibility and separation of the powers, sought for by the framers of our Government, if the President had no power of removal save by consent of the Senate. It was an attempt to re-distribute the powers and minimize those of the President.

. . .

The attitude of the Presidents on this subject has been unchanged and uniform to the present day whenever an issue has clearly been raised. . . .

. . .

An argument *ab inconvenienti* has been made against our conclusion in favor of the executive power of removal by the President, without the consent of the Senate—that it will open the door to a reintroduction of the spoils system. The evil of the spoils system aimed at in the civil service law and its amendments is in respect of inferior offices. It has never been attempted to extend that law beyond them. Indeed, Congress forbids its extension to appointments confirmed by the Senate, except with the consent of the Senate. . . .

. . .

. . . When, on the merits, we find our conclusion strongly favoring the view which prevailed in the First Congress, we have no hesitation in holding that conclusion to be correct; and it therefore follows that the Tenure of Office Act of 1867, in so far as it attempted to prevent the President from removing executive officers who had been appointed by him by and with the advice and consent of the Senate, was invalid, and that subsequent legislation of the same effect was equally so.

For the reasons given, we must therefore hold that the provision of the law of 1876, by which the unrestricted power of removal of first class postmasters is denied to the President, is in violation of the Constitution, and invalid. This leads to an affirmance of the judgment of the Court of Claims.

JUSTICE HOLMES, dissenting.

...

The arguments drawn from the executive power of the President, and from his duty to appoint officers of the United States (when Congress does not vest the appointment elsewhere), to take care that the laws be faithfully executed, and to commission all officers of the United States, seem to me spider's webs inadequate to control the dominant facts.

We have to deal with an office that owes its existence to Congress and that Congress may abolish tomorrow. Its duration and the pay attached to it while it lasts depend on Congress alone. Congress alone confers on the President the power to appoint to it and at any time may transfer the power to other hands. With such power over its own creation, I have no more trouble in believing that Congress has power to prescribe a term of life for it free from any interference than I have in accepting the undoubted power of Congress to decree its end. . . . The duty of the President to see that the laws be executed is a duty that does not go beyond the laws or require him to achieve more than Congress sees fit to leave within his power.

JUSTICE McREYNOLDS, dissenting.

...

May the President oust at will all postmasters appointed with the Senate's consent for definite terms under an Act which inhibits removal without consent of that body? May he approve a statute which creates an inferior office and prescribes restrictions on removal, appoint an incumbent, and then remove without regard to the restrictions? . . . I think there is no such power. Certainly it is not given by any plain words of the Constitution; and the argument advanced to establish it seems to me forced and unsubstantial.

A certain repugnance must attend the suggestion that the President may ignore any provision of an Act of Congress under which he has proceeded. He should promote and not subvert orderly government. The serious evils which followed the practice of dismissing civil officers as caprice or interest dictated, long permitted under congressional enactments, are known to all. It brought the public service to a low estate and caused insistent demand for reform. . . .

...

Nothing short of language clear beyond serious disputation should be held to clothe the President with authority wholly beyond congressional control arbitrarily to dismiss every officer whom he appoints except a few judges. There are no such words in the Constitution, and the asserted inference conflicts with the heretofore accepted theory that this government is one of carefully enumerated powers under an intelligible charter. . . .

If the phrase "executive power" infolds the one now claimed, many others heretofore totally unsuspected may lie there awaiting future supposed necessity; and no human intelligence can define the field of the President's permissible activities. "A masked battery of constructive powers would complete the destruction of liberty."

...

I find no suggestion of the theory that "the executive power" of Art. II, Sec. 1, includes all possible federal authority executive in nature unless definitely excluded by some constitutional provision, prior to the well-known House debate of 1789, when Mr. Madison seems to have given it support. . . .

...

JUSTICE BRANDEIS, dissenting.

In 1833 Justice Story, after discussing in §§ 1537–1543 of his *Commentaries on the Constitution* the much debated question concerning the President's power of removal, said in §1544:

> If there has been any aberration from the true constitutional exposition of the power of removal (which the reader must decide for himself), it will be difficult, and perhaps impracticable, after forty years' experience, to recall the practice to the correct theory. But, at all events, it will be a consolation to those who love the Union, and honor a devotion to the patriotic discharge of duty, that in regard to "inferior officers" (which appellation probably includes ninety-nine out of a hundred of the lucrative offices in the government), the remedy for any permanent abuse is still within the power of Congress, by the simple expedient of requiring the consent of the Senate to removals in such cases.

Postmasters are inferior officers. Congress might have vested their appointment in the head of the department. The Act of July 12, 1876, c. 176, §6, 19 Stat. 78, 80, reenacting earlier legislation, provided that "postmasters of the first, second, and third classes shall be appointed and may be removed by the President by and with the advice and consent of the Senate, and shall hold their offices for four years unless sooner removed or suspended according to law." That statute has been in force unmodified for half a century. Throughout the period, it has governed a large majority of all civil offices to which appointments are made by and with the advice and consent of the Senate. May the President, having acted under the statute in so far as it creates the office and authorizes the appointment, ignore, while the Senate is in session, the provision which prescribes the condition under which a removal may take place?

. . .

To imply a grant to the President of the uncontrollable power of removal from statutory inferior executive offices involves an unnecessary and indefensible limitation upon the constitutional power of Congress to fix the tenure of inferior statutory offices. . . .

. . .

The separation of the powers of government did not make each branch completely autonomous. It left each, in some measure, dependent upon the others, as it left to each power to exercise, in some respects, functions in their nature executive, legislative and judicial. Obviously the President cannot secure full execution of the laws, if Congress denies to him adequate means of doing so. Full execution may be defeated because Congress declines to create offices indispensable for that purpose. Or, because Congress, having created the office, declines to make the indispensable appropriation. Or, because Congress, having both created the office and made the appropriation, prevents, by restrictions which it imposes, the appointment of officials who in quality and character are indispensable to the efficient execution of the law. If, in any such way, adequate means are denied to the President, the fault will lie with Congress. The President performs his full constitutional duty, if, with the means and instruments provided by Congress and within the limitations prescribed by it, he uses his best endeavors to secure the faithful execution of the laws enacted. . . .

. . .

Presidents on Presidential Power

At the turn of the century, the president emerged from the shadow of Congress. The growing importance of foreign policy, the administrative state, interest groups, the railroads, and the radio all created opportunities for the president to influence politics. In this period, the presidents were unusually thoughtful and articulate about the powers, duties, and responsibilities of the White House. They often found that they had to justify their actions and the powers that they claimed for themselves. In the Jacksonian Era, the Democrats and Whigs had developed contrasting views on presidential power. During the Republican Era the differences were institutional rather than partisan. Presidents of both parties pushed the power of the executive forward; congressional leaders of both parties resisted. As Teddy Roosevelt explained to his supporters, "I believe in a strong executive; I believe in power."[21]

Of particular note is the so-called "stewardship theory" of presidential power. Teddy Roosevelt argued that "every executive officer, and above all every executive officer in high position, [is] a steward of the people bound actively and affirmatively to do all he couldfor the people."[22] *As you will see, the more judicially minded Taft—whose reelection campaign in 1912 was derailed by Roosevelt's decision to run as a third-party candidate—strongly disagreed with Roosevelt's views.*

Theodore Roosevelt, An Autobiography (1913)[23]

The most important factor in getting the right spirit in my Administration, next to the insistence upon courage, honesty, and a genuine democracy of desire to serve the plain people, was my insistence upon the theory that the executive power was limited only by specific restrictions and prohibitions appearing in the Constitution or imposed by the Congress under its Constitutional powers. My view was that every executive officer, and above all every executive officer in high position, was a steward of the people bound actively and affirmatively to do all he could for the people, and not to content himself with the negative merit of keeping his talents undamaged in a napkin. I declined to adopt the view that what was imperatively necessary for the Nation could not be done by the President unless he could find some specific authorization to do it. My belief was that it was

21. Theodore Roosevelt, *Theodore Roosevelt and His Time Shown in His Own Letters*, ed. Joseph Bucklin Bishop (New York: Charles Scribner's Sons, 1920), 2:94.

22. Theodore Roosevelt, *An Autobiography* (New York: Charles Scribner's Sons, 1913), 357.

23. Excerpt taken from Theodore Roosevelt, *An Autobiography* (New York: Charles Scribner's Sons, 1913), 388–89, 504, 514–16.

not only his right but his duty to do anything the needs of the Nation demanded unless such action was forbidden by the Constitution or by the laws. Under this interpretation of executive power I did and caused to be done many things not previously done by the President and the heads of the departments. I did not usurp power, but I did greatly broaden the use of executive power. In other words, I acted for the public welfare, I acted for the common well-being of all our people, whenever and in whatever manner was necessary, unless prevented by direct constitutional or legislative prohibition. . . .

. . .

. . . [O]ccasionally great national crises arise which call for immediate and vigorous executive action, and . . . in such cases it is the duty of the President to act upon the theory that he is the steward of the people, and . . . the proper attitude for him to take is that he is bound to assume that he has the legal right to do whatever the needs of the people demand, unless the Constitution or the laws expressly forbid him to do it.

. . .

So great was that public interest in the Coal Strike of 1902, so deeply and strongly did I feel the wave of indignation which swept over the whole country that had I not succeeded in my efforts to induce the operators to listen to reason, I should reluctantly but none the less decisively have taken a step which would have brought down upon my head the execrations of many of "the captains of industry," as well as of sundry "respectable" newspapers who dutifully take their cue from them. . . . The mines were in the State of Pennsylvania. There was no duty whatever laid upon me by the Constitution in the matter, and I had in theory no power to act directly unless the Governor of Pennsylvania . . . should notify me as commander-in-chief of the army of the United States to intervene to keep order.

[Roosevelt then explained that he first had tried to negotiate a settlement himself, eventually getting the agreement of the miner union and the mine operators for him to appoint an arbitration commission, which was successful in ending the strike.]

. . . The method of action upon which I had determined in the last resort was to get the Governor of Pennsylvania to ask me to keep order. Then I would put in the army under the command of some first-rate general. . . . I sent for him, telling him that if I had to make use of him it would be because the crisis was only less serious than that of the Civil War, that the action taken would be practically a war measure, and that if I sent him he must act in a purely military capacity under me as commander-in-chief, paying no heed to any authority, judicial or otherwise, except mine. . . . Although there would have been plenty of muttering, nothing would have been done to interfere with the solution of the problem which I had devised, until the solution was accomplished and the problem ceased to be a problem. Once this was done, and when people were no longer afraid of a coal famine . . . then my enemies would have plucked up heart and begun a campaign against me. I doubt if they could have accomplished much anyway, for the only effective remedy against me would have been impeachment, and that they would not have ventured to try.

William Howard Taft, Our Chief Magistrate and His Powers (1916)[24]

. . . In theory, the Executive power and the Legislative power are independent and separate, but it is not always easy to draw the line and to say where Legislative control and direction to the Executive must cease, and where his independent discretion begins. In theory, all the Executive officers appointed by the President directly or indirectly are his subordinates, and yet Congress can undoubtedly pass laws definitely limiting their discretion and commanding a certain course by them which it is not within the power of the Executive to vary. Fixing the method in which Executive power shall be exercised is perhaps one of the chief functions of Congress. . . .

. . .

Two principles, limiting Congressional interference with the Executive powers, are clear. *First*, Congress may not exercise any of the powers vested in the President, and *second*, it may not prevent or obstruct the use of means given him by the Constitution for the exercise of those powers.

. . .

The President is made Commander-in-Chief of the army and navy by the Constitution evidently for the purpose of enabling him to defend the country against invasion, to suppress insurrection and to take care

24. Excerpt taken from William Howard Taft, *Our Chief Magistrate and His Powers* (New York: Columbia University Press, 1916), 125–26, 129, 139–40, 145–46.

that the laws be faithfully executed. If Congress were to attempt to prevent his use of the army for any of these purposes, the action would be void.... Congress could not take away from him that discretion and place it beyond his control in any of his subordinates, nor could they themselves, as the people in Athens attempted to, carry on campaigns by votes in the market-place.

...

The true view of the Executive functions is, as I conceive it, that the President can exercise no power which cannot be fairly and reasonably traced to some specific grant of power or justly implied and included within such express grant as proper and necessary to its exercise. Such specific grant must be either in the Federal Constitution or in an act of Congress passed in pursuance thereof. There is no undefined residuum of power which he can exercise because it seems to him to be in the public interest, and there is nothing in the *Neagle* case and its definition of a law of the United States, or in other precedents, warranting such an inference. The grants of Executive power are necessarily in general terms in order not to embarrass the Executive within the field of action plainly marked for him, but his jurisdiction must be justified and vindicated by affirmative constitutional or statutory provision, or it does not exist. There have not been wanting, however, eminent men in high public office holding a different view and who have insisted upon the necessity for an undefined residuum of Executive power in the public interest....

...

My judgment is that the view of ... Mr. Roosevelt, ascribing an undefined residuum of power to the President is an unsafe doctrine and that it might lead under emergencies to results of an arbitrary character, doing irremediable injustice to private right. The mainspring of such a view is that the Executive is charged with responsibility for the welfare of all the people in a general way, that he is to play the part of a Universal Providence and set all things right, and that anything that in his judgment will help the people he ought to do, unless he is expressly forbidden not to do it. The wide field of action that this would give to the Executive one can hardly limit. It is enough to say that Mr. Roosevelt has expressly stated how far he thought this principle would justify him in going in respect to the coal famine and the Pennsylvania anthracite strike which he did so much useful work in settling. What was actually done was the result of his activity, his power to influence public opinion and the effect of the prestige of his great office in bringing the parties to the controversy, the mine owners and the strikers, to a legal settlement by arbitration. No one has a higher admiration for the value of what he did there than I have. But if he had failed in this, he says he intended to take action on his theory of the extent of the executive power already stated....

Now it is perfectly evident that Mr. Roosevelt thinks he was charged with the duty, not only to suppress disorder in Pennsylvania, but to furnish coal to avoid the coal famine in New York and New England, and therefore he proposed to use the army of the United States to mine the coal which should prevent or relieve the famine. It was his avowed intention to take the coal mines out of the hands of their lawful owners and to mine the coal which belonged to them and sell it in the eastern market, against their objection, without any court proceeding of any kind and without any legal obligation on their part to work the mines at all. It was an advocacy of the higher law and his obligation to execute it which is a little startling in a constitutional republic.... The benevolence of his purpose no one can deny, but no one who looks at it from the standpoint of a government of law could regard it as anything but lawless. I venture to think however, that Mr. Roosevelt is mistaken in what he thinks he would have done. Mr. Roosevelt in office was properly amenable to the earnest advice of those whom he trusted, and there were men about him who would probably have dissuaded him from such a course.

VII. Individual Rights

MAJOR DEVELOPMENTS

- Federal and state justices protect the freedom of contract
- Debates over whether the United States is a Christian country
- Judges provide due process protection to some noneconomic behaviors, including, in some states, drinking

Americans proposed numerous unprecedented regulations on individual behavior during the Republican Era. Populists insisted that government sharply limit the prices that railroads could charge farmers and riders. Progressives championed minimum wage and maximum hour laws for workers. Protestants called on government to regulate drinking and birth control. Urban reformers advocated zoning laws. Doctors asked states to ban abortion.

Proponents made two related claims when defending the constitutionality of these proposals. Reformers frequently insisted that government was merely exercising traditional police powers in light of new conditions and social science research. That government had not previously regulated behavior did not mean that government could not regulate behavior when scientific examination of novel social conditions determined that the regulation served the public good. Many progressives celebrated a "living Constitution." Under living constitutionalism some forms of behavior that had been constitutionally protected in the past became legitimate subjects for regulation in the present as social needs and practices changed. Opponents claimed that proposed reforms violated individual and property rights. Many insisted that the due process clauses of the federal and state constitutions protected the "right of the citizen to be free in the enjoyment of all his faculties."[25] This right encompassed a freedom of contract and, often, such freedoms as the right to go to private school or the right to drink. Others critics invoked an inherited constitutional animus against class legislation. The Supreme Court in *Adair v. United States* (1908) declared unconstitutional a law prohibiting "yellow dog" contracts (contracts in which employees promised not to join a union) on the ground that "the right of a person to sell his labor upon such terms as he deems proper is, in its essence, the same as the right of the purchaser of labor to prescribe the conditions upon which he will accept such labor from the person offering to sell it."

A. Property

The Republican Era was the high-water mark for constitutional protection of property rights. *Lochner v. New York* (1905), the most famous constitutional decision of the period, held that maximum hour laws for bakers violated the freedom of contract protected by the due process clause of the Fourteenth Amendment. Other federal and state court decisions struck down regulations that provided various protections for workers and consumers. Some decisions spoke of the freedom of contract. Others emphasized traditional common law protections for liberty and property.

State courts were initially more willing than federal courts to impose substantive due process limitations on laws regulating economic bargains. State judges interpreting state due process clauses during the late nineteenth century declared unconstitutional laws limiting the hours women could work (*Ritchie v. People* [IL 1895]) and laws forbidding persons from manufacturing cigars in a tenement house (*In re Jacobs* [NY 1885]). The Supreme Court of Illinois in *Ritchie v. People* set out the basic constitutional principle underlying these decisions. "Liberty," Judge Magruder wrote, "includes the right to make contracts, as well with reference to the amount and duration of labor to be performed as concerning any other lawful matter. Hence the right to make contracts is an inherent and inalienable one, and any attempt to unreasonably abridge it is opposed to the constitution."[26] The U.S. Supreme Court under Chief Justice Morrison Waite (1873–1888) was more reluctant. When sustaining laws regulating the prices that grain elevators could charge, Waite's majority opinion in *Munn v. Illinois* (1877) asserted, "When . . . one devotes his property to a use in which the public has an interest, he, in effect, grants to the public an interest in that use, and must submit to be controlled by the public for the common good." Nevertheless, while *Munn* upheld state regulatory power, the opinion hinted at greater judicial protection for property that was not "clothed with a public interest."

The U.S. Supreme Court more strictly scrutinized laws regulating the bargaining process after Grover Cleveland appointed Melville Fuller to the chief justiceship in 1888. Over the next thirty years judicial majorities struck down many state and a few federal laws that opponents claimed violated the freedom of contract or otherwise unconstitutionally interfered with private bargains. *Lochner v. New York* (1905) is the most famous of these decisions. That decision declared unconstitutional a New York law that limited bakers to

25. *Allgeyer v. Louisiana*, 165 U.S. 578 (1897).

26. *Ritchie v. People*, 40 N.E. 453 (Ill. 1895).

Table 7-4 Selection of U.S. Supreme Court Cases Reviewing State Laws Under Due Process Clause

Case	Vote	Outcome	Decision
Slaughter-House Cases, 83 U.S. 36 (1873)	5–4	Upheld	States may limit how butchers practice their profession and establish a monopoly slaughterhouse as a public health measure
Hurtado v. California, 110 U.S. 516 (1884)	8–1	Upheld	The use of a grand jury is not essential to the requirements of due process
Barbier v. Connolly, 113 U.S. 27 (1885)	9–0	Upheld	Cities may prohibit operation of commercial or public laundries at night as a public safety measure
Powell v. Pennsylvania, 127 U.S. 678 (1888)	8–1	Upheld	States may prohibit the manufacture or sale of oleomargarine as a public health measure
Smyth v. Ames, 169 U.S. 466 (1898)	9–0	Struck down	States may not impose a maximum rate on railroad charges that deprive corporations of a reasonable profit on their operations
Austin v. Tennessee, 179 U.S. 343 (1900)	5–4	Upheld	States may prohibit the sale of cigarettes as a public health measure
Lochner v. New York, 198 U.S. 45 (1905)	5–4	Struck down	States may not impose a maximum hours limitation on commercial bakers as a public health measure
Twining v. New Jersey, 211 U.S. 78 (1908)	8–1	Upheld	State criminal procedures must not violate fundamental principles of liberty and justice, but state courts may allow juries to draw conclusions about guilt from the defendant's refusal to testify
Murphy v. California, 225 U.S. 623 (1912)	9–0	Upheld	Non-useful occupations, such as operating a pool hall, that have naturally pernicious tendencies may be regulated or prohibited even in the absence of demonstrated harms
Bunting v. Oregon, 243 U.S. 426 (1917)	5–3	Upheld	State may pass a general maximum hour law as a health measure for factory employees
Meyer v. Nebraska, 262 U.S. 390 (1923)	7–2	Struck down	States may not prohibit the teaching of foreign languages
Pierce v. Society of Sisters, 268 U.S. 510 (1925)	9–0	Struck down	States may not require parents to send children to public school rather than private school
Village of Euclid v. Ambler Realty Co., 272 U.S. 365 (1926)	6–3	Upheld	Cities may adopt comprehensive zoning plans detailing permitted land use and building restrictions
New State Ice Co. v. Liebmann, 285 U.S. 262 (1932)	7–2	Struck down	States may not require licenses before a new company can enter an industry
Nebbia v. New York, 291 U.S. 502 (1934)	5–4	Upheld	States may set a minimum retail price for milk
West Coast Hotel v. Parrish, 300 U.S. 379 (1937)	5–4	Upheld	States may require employers to pay a legal minimum wage
Williamson v. Lee Optical Co., 348 U.S. 483 (1955)	8–0	Upheld	States may prohibit nonlicensed individuals from fitting lenses into eyeglasses as a public health measure

(Continued)

Table 7-4 (*Continued*)

Case	Vote	Outcome	Decision
Griswold v. Connecticut, 381 U.S. 479 (1965)	7–2	Struck down	States may not prohibit the use of contraceptives by married couples
Loving v. Virginia, 388 U.S. 1 (1967)	9–0	Struck down	Individuals have a fundamental right to marry a person of another race that states cannot restrict
Roe v. Wade, 410 U.S. 113 (1973)	7–2	Struck down	Individuals have a fundamental right to choose whether to reproduce, and states cannot impose an absolute prohibition on abortion
Moore v. City of East Cleveland, 431 U.S. 494 (1977)	5–4	Struck down	House ordinances with restrictive definition of "family" for single-family units violate basic values recognized in substantive due process
Michael H. v. Gerald D, 491 U.S. 110 (1989)	5–4	Upheld	States may presume that children born within a marriage are the result of the marriage and deny visitation rights to a natural father
Bennis v. Michigan, 516 U.S. 442 (1996)	7–2	Upheld	States may seize a car used in the act of prostitution, regardless of the innocence of the owner of the car
Washington v. Glucksberg, 521 U.S. 702 (1997)	9–0	Upheld	States may prohibit doctor-assisted suicide
Lawrence v. Texas, 539 U.S. 558 (2003)	6–3	Struck down	States may not criminalize consensual homosexual sodomy

working ten hours a day and sixty hours a week. Other famous decisions include:

- *Allgeyer v. Louisiana* (1897), which declared unconstitutional a Louisiana law limiting contracts with out-of-state insurance companies.
- *Adair v. United States* (1908), which declared unconstitutional a federal law prohibiting "yellow dog" contracts.
- *Coppage v. Kansas* (1915), which declared unconstitutional a state law prohibiting yellow dog contracts.
- *Adkins v. Children's Hospital* (1923), which declared unconstitutional a minimum wage law for women.

Courts sustained most state and federal regulations. Justice McKenna, when sustaining laws limiting the hours persons could work in factories, asserted, "In view of the well-known fact that the custom in our industries does not sanction a longer service than ten hours per day, it cannot be held, as a matter of law, that the legislative requirement is unreasonable or arbitrary as a matter of law."[27] The Supreme Court was particularly deferential to legislation restricting property rights passed during or in the wake of World War I. *Block v. Hirsh* (1921) sustained a federal law designed to prevent price gouging in the Washington, DC, housing market by permitting tenants to remain on the property after their lease expired as long as they paid rent. Justice Holmes's majority opinion stated, "Circumstances have clothed the letting of buildings in the District of Columbia with a public interest so great as to justify regulation by law."

The Supreme Court did not significantly expand previous interpretations of the takings clause. *Mugler v. Kansas* (1887) sustained a Kansas law forbidding the manufacture of alcoholic beverages as a constitutional exercise of the police power. Justice Harlan's majority opinion declared, "If such manufacture does prejudicially affect the rights and interests of the community, it follows, from the very premises stated, that society has the power to protect itself, by legislation, against the injurious consequences of that business." *Village of Euclid v. Ambler Realty Co.* (1926) upheld the creation of local zoning ordinances, with Justice Sutherland's majority opinion stating, "The exclusion of buildings devoted to business, trade, etc., from residential

27. *Bunting v. Oregon*, 243 U.S. 426 (1917).

districts, bears a rational relation to the health and safety of the community." *Miller v. Schoene* (1928) sustained a Virginia decision to cut down private cedar trees in order to prevent a fungus from infecting private apple orchards. Justice Stone's opinion for the court held that states could decide that some forms of private property were more valuable than others when deciding what property to protect. He wrote, "It would have been none the less a choice if, instead of enacting the present statute, the state, by doing nothing, had permitted serious injury to the apple orchards within its borders to go on unchecked."

Federal justices during the Republican Era limited the scope of the contracts clause. *Stone v. Mississippi* (1879) gave local government broad power to abrogate existing contracts when doing so advanced the public good. When ruling that a state could not contract away the right to ban lotteries in this case, Chief Justice Waite bluntly stated, "All agree that the legislature cannot bargain away the police power of a State." *Pennsylvania Coal Co. v. Mahon* (1922) was the most important exception to the judicial tendency in the Republican Era to reject takings clause attacks on state policies. That decision struck down a Pennsylvania law prohibiting coal companies from mining beneath homes, even after the company had explicitly reserved the right to mine beneath homes as part of their contracts giving surface rights to homeowners.

Pennsylvania Coal Co. v. Mahon, 260 U.S. 393 (1922)

H. J. Mahon owned a house in Pittston, Pennsylvania. When that property was purchased from the Pennsylvania Coal Company, the original buyer agreed that Pennsylvania Coal retained the right to mine under the surface of the land and that the company was not responsible for any damage done to the surface by those mining operations. In 1921 the Pennsylvania legislature passed the Kohler Act, which forbade companies from engaging in mining operations that might threaten the foundations of any dwelling. Mahon sought a judicial decree prohibiting Pennsylvania Coal from mining under his house. A lower Pennsylvania court rejected his claim. After that decision was reversed by the Supreme Court of Pennsylvania, Pennsylvania Coal appealed to the Supreme Court of the United States.

The Supreme Court by a 4–3 vote declared the Kohler Act unconstitutional. Justice Holmes's majority opinion insisted that government took property, even when the state did not actually take physical possession, when government regulations substantially reduced or destroyed the value of the property. Such actions became known as "regulatory takings." What is the constitutional foundation for regulatory takings? Is compensation for such takings inherent in the language of the takings clause, the original understanding of the framers, or the general principles underlying property rights? Pennsylvania Coal Company *is the only constitutional case in which Justice Holmes wrote the majority opinion and Justice Brandeis issued the dissent. In most other cases, whether the issue was the freedom of contract or the freedom of speech, the two justices voted together. Why did Holmes and Brandeis differ in this case? Why did Holmes think that the regulation went "too far"? Why did Brandeis maintain that government could prevent Pennsylvania Coal from mining under the surface of Mahon's house, even though the company had reserved that right when it first sold the land?*

JUSTICE HOLMES delivered the opinion of the Court.

. . .

Government hardly could go on if to some extent values incident to property could not be diminished without paying for every such change in the general law. As long recognized, some values are enjoyed under an implied limitation and must yield to the police power. But obviously the implied limitation must have its limits or the contract and due process clauses are gone. One fact for consideration in determining such limits is the extent of the diminution. When it reaches a certain magnitude, in most if not in all cases there must be an exercise of eminent domain and compensation to sustain the act. So the question depends upon the particular facts. The greatest weight is given to the judgment of the legislature but it always is open to interested parties to contend that the legislature has gone beyond its constitutional power.

This is the case of a single private house. No doubt there is a public interest even in this, as there is in every purchase and sale and in all that happens within the commonwealth. . . . But usually in ordinary private affairs the public interest does not warrant much of this kind of interference. A source of damage to such a house is not a public nuisance even if similar damage is inflicted on others in different places. The damage is not common or public. . . . Furthermore, it is not justified as a protection of personal safety. That could be provided for by notice. Indeed the very foundation of this bill is that the defendant gave timely notice of its intent to mine under the house. On the other hand the extent of the taking is great. It purports to abolish what is recognized in Pennsylvania as an estate in land—a very valuable estate—and what is declared by the Court below to be a contract hitherto binding the plaintiffs. If we were called upon to deal with the plaintiffs' position alone we should think it clear that the statute does not disclose a public interest sufficient to warrant so extensive a destruction of the defendant's constitutionally protected rights.

...

It is our opinion that the act cannot be sustained as an exercise of the police power, so far as it affects the mining of coal under streets or cities in places where the right to mine such coal has been reserved.... What makes the right to mine coal valuable is that it can be exercised with profit. To make it commercially impracticable to mine certain coal has very nearly the same effect for constitutional purposes as appropriating or destroying it. This we think that we are warranted in assuming that the statute does.

...

The rights of the public in a street purchased or laid out by eminent domain are those that it has paid for. If in any case its representatives have been so short sighted as to acquire only surface rights without the right of support we see no more authority for supplying the latter without compensation than there was for taking the right of way in the first place and refusing to pay for it because the public wanted it very much. The protection of private property in the Fifth Amendment presupposes that it is wanted for public use, but provides that it shall not be taken for such use without compensation.... When this seemingly absolute protection is found to be qualified by the police power, the natural tendency of human nature is to extend the qualification more and more until at last private property disappears. But that cannot be accomplished in this way under the Constitution of the United States.

The general rule at least is that while property may be regulated to a certain extent, if regulation goes too far it will be recognized as a taking.... In general it is not plain that a man's misfortunes or necessities will justify his shifting the damages to his neighbor's shoulders.... We are in danger of forgetting that a strong public desire to improve the public condition is not enough to warrant achieving the desire by a shorter cut than the constitutional way of paying for the change. As we already have said this is a question of degree—and therefore cannot be disposed of by general propositions....

... So far as private persons or communities have seen fit to take the risk of acquiring only surface rights, we cannot see that the fact that their risk has become a danger warrants the giving to them greater rights than they bought.

JUSTICE BRANDEIS dissenting.

...

Every restriction upon the use of property imposed in the exercise of the police power deprives the owner of some right theretofore enjoyed, and is, in that sense, an abridgment by the state of rights in property without making compensation. But restriction imposed to protect the public health, safety or morals from dangers threatened is not a taking. The restriction here in question is merely the prohibition of a noxious use. The property so restricted remains in the possession of its owner. The state does not appropriate it or make any use of it. The state merely prevents the owner from making a use which interferes with paramount rights of the public. Whenever the use prohibited ceases to be noxious—as it may because of further change in local or social conditions—the restriction will have to be removed and the owner will again be free to enjoy his property as heretofore.

The restriction upon the use of this property cannot, of course, be lawfully imposed, unless its purpose is to protect the public. But the purpose of a restriction does not cease to be public, because incidentally some private persons may thereby receive gratuitously valuable special benefits. Thus, owners of low buildings may obtain, through statutory restrictions upon the height of neighboring structures, benefits equivalent to an easement of light and air.... Restriction upon use does not become inappropriate as a means, merely because it deprives the owner of the only use to which the property can then be profitably put. The liquor [*Mugler v. Kansas* (1887)] case[] settled that.... Nor is a restriction imposed through exercise of the police power inappropriate as a means, merely because the same end might be effected through exercise of the power of eminent domain, or otherwise at public expense.

Every restriction upon the height of buildings might be secured through acquiring by eminent domain the right of each owner to build above the limiting height; but it is settled that the state need not resort to that power. . . . If by mining anthracite coal the owner would necessarily unloose poisonous gases, I suppose no one would doubt the power of the state to prevent the mining, without buying his coal fields. And why may not the state, likewise, without paying compensation, prohibit one from digging so deep or excavating so near the surface, as to expose the community to like dangers? In the latter case, as in the former, carrying on the business would be a public nuisance.

. . .

It is said that this is a case of a single dwelling house, that the restriction upon mining abolishes a valuable estate hitherto secured by a contract with the plaintiffs, and that the restriction upon mining cannot be justified as a protection of personal safety, since that could be provided for by notice. . . . May we say that notice would afford adequate protection of the public safety where the Legislature and the highest court of the state, with greater knowledge of local conditions, have declared, in effect, that it would not? If the public safety is imperiled, surely neither grant, nor contract, can prevail against the exercise of the police power. . . . The rule that the state's power to take appropriate measures to guard the safety of all who may be within its jurisdiction may not be bargained away was applied to compel carriers to establish grade crossings at their own expense, despite contracts to the contrary. . . .

In re Jacobs, 2 N.Y. Crim. R. 539 (1885)

Peter Jacobs made cigars in a New York tenement house. On May 14, 1884, he was arrested and charged with violating a state law that forbade "the manufacture of cigars or preparation of tobacco in any form on any floor, or in any part of any floor, in any tenement-house." Jacobs sought a petition of habeas corpus on the ground that his arrest was unconstitutional. He insisted that the New York statute violated his right to not have property or liberty taken away without due process of law. After the Supreme Court of New York rejected his claim, Jacobs appealed to the New York Court of Appeals. His case soon became a cause célèbre. William Evarts, a leading member of the bar, former secretary of state, and soon-to-be U.S. senator, represented Jacobs before the court of appeals in an effort to set an important precedent limiting legislative power.

The Court of Appeals of New York granted the writ of habeas corpus. In an influential opinion, Judge Earl asserted that the ban on manufacturing cigars in a tenement house deprived Jacobs of both liberty and property in violation of the due process clause of both the New York and the federal constitutions. How did Judge Earl define liberty and property? How did he define the police power? Why did he believe that the New York regulation was unconstitutional? Does the specter of "class legislation" play a role in his analysis? Suppose New York wanted to pass a narrower regulation. What language would you recommend that state lawmakers use?

JUDGE EARL delivered the opinion of the Court.

. . .

What does this act attempt to do? In form, it makes it a crime for a cigarmaker in New York and Brooklyn, the only cities in the State having a population exceeding 500,000, to carry on a perfectly lawful trade in his own home. Whether he owns the tenement-house or has hired a room therein for the purpose of prosecuting his trade, he cannot manufacture therein his own tobacco into cigars for his own use or for sale, and he will become a criminal for doing that which is perfectly lawful outside of the two cities named—everywhere else, so far as we are able to learn, in the whole world. He must either abandon the trade by which he earns a livelihood for himself and family, or, if able, procure a room elsewhere, or hire himself out to one who has a room upon such terms as, under the fierce competition of trade and the inexorable laws of supply and demand, he may be able to obtain from his employer. He may choose to do his work where he can have the supervision of his family and their help, and such choice is denied him. He may choose to work for himself rather than for a taskmaster, and he is left without freedom of choice. He may desire the advantage of cheap production in consequence of his cheap rent and family help, and of this he is deprived. In the unceasing struggle for success and existence which pervades all societies of men, he may be deprived of that which will enable him to maintain his hold, and to survive. . . . It is, therefore, plain that this law interferes with the profitable and free use of his property by the owner or lessee of a tenement-house who is a cigarmaker, and trammels him in the application of his industry and the disposition of his labor, and thus, in a strictly legitimate sense, it arbitrarily deprives him of his property and of some portion of his personal liberty.

The constitutional guaranty that no person shall be deprived of his property without due process of law may be violated without the physical taking of property for public or private use. Property may be destroyed, or its value may be annihilated; it is owned and kept for some useful purpose and it has no value unless it can be used. Its capability for enjoyment and adaptability to some use are essential characteristics and attributes without which property cannot be conceived; and hence any law which destroys it or its value, or takes away any of its essential attributes, deprives the owner of his property.

The constitutional guaranty would be of little worth, if the legislature could, without compensation, destroy property or its value, deprive the owner of its use, deny him the right to live in his own house, or to work at any lawful trade therein. If the legislature has the power under the Constitution to prohibit the prosecution of one lawful trade in a tenement-house, then it may prevent the prosecution of all trades therein. . . .

So, too, one may be deprived of his liberty and his constitutional rights thereto violated without the actual imprisonment or restraint of his person. Liberty, in its broad sense as understood in this country, means the right, not only of freedom from actual servitude, imprisonment or restraint, but the right of one to use his faculties in all lawful ways, to live and work where he will, to earn his livelihood in any lawful calling, and to pursue any lawful trade or avocation. All laws, therefore, which impair or trammel these rights, which limit one in his choice of a trade or profession, or confine him to work or live in a specified locality, or exclude him from his own house, or restrain his otherwise lawful movements . . . are infringements upon his fundamental rights of liberty, which are under constitutional protection. . . .

But the claim is made that the legislature could pass this act in the exercise of the police power which every sovereign State possesses. That power is very broad and comprehensive, and is exercised to promote the health, comfort, safety and welfare of society. Its exercise in extreme cases is frequently justified by the maxim *salus populi suprema lex est* ["let the welfare of the people be the supreme law"]. It is used to regulate the use of property by enforcing the maxim *sic utere tuo, ut alienum non lædas* ["so use your own so as not to harm that of another"]. Under it the conduct of an individual and the use of property may be regulated so as to interfere, to some extent, with the freedom of the one and the enjoyment of the other; and in cases of great emergency engendering overruling necessity, property may be taken or destroyed without compensation, and without what is commonly called due process of law. . . .

. . .

Generally it is for the legislature to determine what laws and regulations are needed to protect the public health and secure the public comfort and safety, and while its measures are calculated, intended, convenient and appropriate to accomplish these ends, the exercise of its discretion is not subject to review by the courts. But they must have some relation to these ends. Under the mere guise of police regulations, personal rights and private property cannot be arbitrarily invaded, and the determination of the legislature is not final or conclusive. If it passes an act ostensibly for the public health, and thereby destroys or takes away the property of a citizen, or interferes with his personal liberty, then it is for the courts to scrutinize the act and see whether it really relates to and is convenient and appropriate to promote the public health. . . .

We will now once more recur to the law under consideration. It does not deal with tenement-houses as such; it does not regulate the number of persons who may live in any one of them, or be crowded into one room, nor does it deal with the mode of their construction for the purpose of securing the health and safety of their occupants or of the public generally. It deals mainly with the preparation of tobacco and the manufacture of cigars, and its purpose obviously was to regulate them. We must take judicial notice of the nature and qualities of tobacco. It has been in general use among civilized men for more than two centuries. It is used in some form by a majority of the men in this State, by the good and bad, learned and unlearned, the rich and the poor. Its manufacture into cigars is permitted without any hindrance, except for revenue purposes, in all civilized lands. It has never been said, so far as we can learn, and it was not affirmed even on the argument before us, that its preparation and manufacture into cigars were dangerous to the public health. We are not aware, and are not able to learn, that tobacco is even injurious to the health of those who deal in it, or are engaged in its production or manufacture. We certainly know enough about it to be sure that its manipulation in one room can produce no harm to the health of the occupants of other rooms in the same house. . . . What possible relation can cigar-making in any building have to the health of the general public? . . . What possible relation to the health of the occupants of a large tenement-house could cigar-making in one of its remote rooms have? If the legislature had in mind the protection of the occupants of tenement-houses, why was the act confined in its operation to the two cities only? It is plain that this is not a health law, and that it has no relation whatever to the public health. Under the guise of promoting the public health the legislature might as well have banished cigarmaking from all the cities of the State, or confined it to a single city or town, or have placed under a similar ban the trade of a baker, of a tailor, of a shoemaker, of a woodcarver, or of any other of the innocuous trades carried on by artisans in their own homes. The power would have been the same, and its exercise, so far as it concerns fundamental, constitutional rights, could have been justified by the same arguments. Such legislation may invade one class of rights to-day and another to-morrow, and if it can be sanctioned under the Constitution, while far removed in time we will not be far away in practical statesmanship from those ages when governmental prefects supervised the building of houses, the rearing of cattle, the sowing of seed and the reaping of grain, and governmental ordinances regulated the movements and labor of artisans, the rate of wages, the price of food, the diet and clothing of the people, and a large range of other affairs long since in all civilized lands regarded as outside of governmental functions. Such governmental interferences disturb the normal adjustments of the social fabric, and usually derange the delicate and complicated machinery of industry and cause a score of ills while attempting the removal of one.

When a health law is challenged in the courts as unconstitutional on the ground that it arbitrarily interferes with personal liberty and private property without due process of law, the courts must be able to see that it has at least in fact some relation to the public health, that the public health is the end actually aimed at, and that it is appropriate and adapted to that end. This we have not been able to see in this law, and we must, therefore, pronounce it unconstitutional and void. . . .

Lochner v. New York, 198 U.S. 45 (1905)

Joseph Lochner owned the Lochner Home Bakery. In 1899 and 1901 he was fined for allowing employees to work more than ten hours a day, or sixty hours a week. This violated the New York Bakeshop Act of 1895, which limited the hours that bakers could work. Proponents of the measure maintained that bakers' exposure to flour dust for many hours in poorly ventilated bakeries was dangerous. Opponents argued that the law violated "liberty of contract," did little to protect the health of bakers, and was primarily motivated by the desire to promote the interests of organized labor at the expense of "boss bakers" who owned small shops and operated on a small margin of profit. By a closely divided vote the Court of Appeals of New York sustained Lochner's fine. Lochner appealed that decision to the Supreme Court of the United States.

The Supreme Court by a 5–4 vote declared that the Bakeshop Act violated the due process clause of the Fourteenth Amendment. Justice Peckham's majority opinion ruled that the measure was neither a valid health law nor a valid labor law. Justice Harlan's dissent insisted that the law was a valid health law, even if it was not a valid labor law. Justice Holmes's dissent maintained that the law was both a valid health law and a valid labor law. Lochner v. New York *has a special place in the canon of constitutional history as the exemplar of justices abusing their power by deciding cases on the basis of their personal views. As you read the case, consider whether this accusation is fair—or, if fair, whether* Lochner *is an especially egregious example of this phenomenon. What standard of review did the various justices apply? Did they dispute the standard of review or the application of that standard to the facts in* Lochner? *Justice Holmes's* Lochner *dissent became a rallying cry for Progressives. How consistent is that dissent with Republican Era constitutional jurisprudence? Would you be willing to apply the principles of that dissent to racial segregation or free speech? If not, why do those rights raise different issues?*

JUSTICE PECKHAM delivered the opinion of the court.

. . .

The statute necessarily interferes with the right of contract between the employer and employees concerning the number of hours in which the latter may labor in the bakery of the employer. The general right to make a contract in relation to his business is part of the liberty of the individual protected by the Fourteenth Amendment of the Federal Constitution. Under that provision, no State can deprive any person of life, liberty or property without due process of law. The right to purchase or to sell labor is part of the liberty protected by this amendment unless there are circumstances which exclude the right. There are, however, certain powers, existing in the sovereignty of each State in the Union, somewhat vaguely termed police powers, the exact description and limitation of which have not been attempted by the courts. Those powers, broadly stated and without, at present, any attempt at a more specific limitation, relate to the safety, health, morals and general welfare of the public. Both property and liberty are held on such reasonable conditions as may be imposed by the governing power of the State in the exercise of those powers, and with such conditions the Fourteenth Amendment was not designed to interfere.

. . .

It must, of course, be conceded that there is a limit to the valid exercise of the police power by the State. There is no dispute concerning this general proposition. Otherwise the Fourteenth Amendment would have no efficacy, and the legislatures of the States would have unbounded power, and it would be enough to say that any piece of legislation was enacted to conserve the morals, the health or the safety of the people; such legislation would be valid no matter how absolutely without foundation the claim might be. The claim of the police power would be a mere pretext—become another and delusive name for the supreme sovereignty of the State to be exercised free from constitutional restraint. This is not contended for. In every case that comes before this court, therefore, where legislation of this character is concerned and where the protection of the Federal Constitution is sought, the question necessarily arises: is this a fair, reasonable and appropriate exercise of the police power of the State, or is it an unreasonable, unnecessary and arbitrary interference with the right of the individual to his personal liberty or to enter into those contracts in relation to labor which may seem to him appropriate or necessary for the support of himself and his family? . . .

. . .

The question whether this act is valid as a labor law, pure and simple, may be dismissed in a few words. There is no reasonable ground for interfering with the liberty of person or the right of free contract by determining the hours of labor in the occupation of a baker. There is no contention that bakers as a class are not equal in intelligence and capacity to men in other trades or manual occupations, or that they are able to assert their rights and care for themselves without the protecting arm of the State, interfering with their independence of judgment and of action. They are in no sense wards of the State. Viewed in the light of a purely labor law, with no reference whatever to the question of health, we think that a law like the one before us involves neither the safety, the morals, nor the welfare of the public, and that the interest of the public is not in the slightest degree affected by such an act. The law must be upheld, if at all, as a law pertaining to the health of the individual engaged in the occupation of a baker. It does not affect any other portion of the public than those who are engaged in that occupation. Clean and wholesome bread does not depend upon whether the baker works but ten hours per day or only sixty hours a week. The limitation of the hours of labor does not come within the police power on that ground.

. . .

We think the limit of the police power has been reached and passed in this case. There is, in our judgment, no reasonable foundation for holding this to be necessary or appropriate as a health law to safeguard the public health or the health of the individuals who are following the trade of a baker. . . .

We think that there can be no fair doubt that the trade of a baker, in and of itself, is not an unhealthy one to that degree which would authorize the legislature to interfere with the right to labor, and with the right of free contract on the part of the individual, either as employer or employee. In looking through statistics regarding all trades and occupations, it may be true that the trade of a baker does not appear to be as healthy as some other trades, and is also vastly more healthy than still others. To the common understanding, the trade of a baker has never been regarded as an unhealthy one. . . . It is unfortunately true that labor, even in any department, may possibly carry with it the seeds of unhealthiness. But are we all, on that account, at the mercy of legislative majorities? A printer, a tinsmith, a locksmith, a carpenter, a cabinetmaker, a dry goods clerk, a bank's, a lawyer's or a physician's clerk, or a clerk in almost any kind of business, would all come under the power of the legislature on this assumption. No trade, no occupation, no mode of earning one's living could escape this all-pervading power, and the acts of the legislature in limiting the hours of labor in all employments would be valid although such limitation might seriously cripple the ability of the laborer to support himself and his family.... It might be said that it is unhealthy to work more than that number of hours in an apartment lighted by artificial light during the working hours of the day; that the occupation of the bank clerk, the lawyer's clerk, the real estate clerk, or the broker's clerk in such offices is therefore unhealthy, and the legislature, in its paternal wisdom, must therefore have the right to legislate on the subject of, and to limit the hours for, such labor, and, if it exercises that power and its validity be questioned, it is sufficient to say it has reference to the public health; it has reference to the health of the employees condemned to labor day after day in buildings where the sun never shines; it is a health law, and therefore it is valid, and cannot be questioned by the courts.

It is also urged, pursuing the same line of argument, that it is to the interest of the State that its population should be strong and robust, and therefore any legislation which may be said to tend to make people healthy must be valid as health laws, enacted under the police power. If this be a valid argument and a justification for this kind of legislation, it follows that the protection of the Federal Constitution from undue interference with liberty of person and freedom of contract is visionary wherever the law is sought to be justified as a valid exercise of the police power. Scarcely any law but might find shelter under such assumptions, and conduct, properly so called, as well as contract, would come under the restrictive sway of the legislature. Not only the hours of employees, but the hours of employers, could be regulated, and doctors, lawyers, scientists, all professional men, as well as athletes and artisans, could be forbidden to fatigue their brains and bodies by prolonged hours of exercise, lest the fighting strength of the State be impaired. We mention these extreme cases because the contention is extreme. We do not believe in the soundness of the views which uphold this law. On the contrary, we think that such a law as this, although passed in the assumed exercise of the police power, and as relating to the public health, or the health of the employees named, is not within that power, and is invalid. The act is not, within any fair meaning of the term, a health law, but is an illegal interference with the rights of individuals, both employers and employees, to make contracts regarding labor upon such terms as they may think best, or which they may agree upon with the other parties to such contracts. . . .

. . . In our judgment, it is not possible, in fact, to discover the connection between the number of hours a baker may work in the bakery and the healthful quality of the bread made by the workman. The connection, if any exists, is too shadowy and thin to build any argument for the interference of the legislature. If the man works ten hours a day, it is all right, but if ten and a half or eleven, his health is in danger and his bread may be unhealthful, and, therefore, he shall not be permitted to do it. This, we think, is unreasonable, and entirely arbitrary. When assertions such as we have adverted to become necessary in order to give, if possible, a plausible foundation for the contention that the law is a "health law," it gives rise to at least a suspicion that there was some other motive dominating the legislature than the purpose to subserve the public health or welfare.

. . .

JUSTICE HARLAN, with whom JUSTICE WHITE and JUSTICE DAY joined, dissenting.

. . .

Granting then that there is a liberty of contract which cannot be violated even under the sanction of direct legislative enactment, but assuming, as according to settled law we may assume, that such liberty of contract is subject to such regulations as the State may reasonably prescribe for the common good and the wellbeing of society, what are the conditions under which the judiciary may declare such regulations to be in excess of legislative authority and void? . . .

. . . If there be doubt as to the validity of the statute, that doubt must therefore be resolved in favor of its validity, and the courts must keep their hands off, leaving the legislature to meet the responsibility for unwise legislation. If the end which the legislature seeks to accomplish be one to which its power extends, and if the means employed to that end, although not the wisest or best, are yet not plainly and palpably unauthorized by law, then the court cannot interfere. In other words, when the validity of a statute is questioned, the burden of proof, so to speak, is upon those who assert it to be unconstitutional. . . .

. . .

It is plain that this statute was enacted in order to protect the physical wellbeing of those who work in bakery and confectionery establishments. It may be that the statute had its origin, in part, in the belief that employers and employees in such establishments were not upon an equal footing, and that the necessities of the latter often compelled them to submit to such exactions as unduly taxed their strength. Be this as it may, the statute must be taken as expressing the belief of the people of New York that, as a general rule, and in the case of the average man, labor in excess of sixty hours during a week in such establishments may endanger the health of those who thus labor. Whether or not this be wise legislation it is not the province of the court to inquire. Under our systems of government, the courts are not concerned with the wisdom or policy of legislation. So that, in determining the question of power to interfere with liberty of contract, the court may inquire whether the means devised by the State are germane to an end which may be lawfully accomplished and have a real or substantial relation to the protection of health, as involved in the daily work of the persons, male and female, engaged in bakery and confectionery establishments. But when this inquiry is entered upon, I find it impossible, in view of common experience, to say that there is here no real or substantial relation between the means employed by the State and the end sought to be accomplished by its legislation. Nor can I say that the statute has no appropriate or direct connection with that protection to health which each State owes to her citizens, or that it is not promotive of the health of the employees in question, or that the regulation prescribed by the State is utterly unreasonable and extravagant or wholly arbitrary. Still less can I say that the statute is, beyond question, a plain, palpable invasion of rights secured by the fundamental law. Therefore, I submit that this court will transcend its functions if it assumes to annul the statute of New York. It must be remembered that this statute does not apply to all kinds of business. . . .

. . .

. . . What the precise facts are it may be difficult to say. It is enough for the determination of this case, and it is enough for this court to know, that the question is one about which there is room for debate and for an honest difference of opinion. There are many reasons of a weighty, substantial character, based upon the experience of mankind, in support of the theory that, all things considered, more than ten hours' steady work each day, from week to week, in a bakery or confectionery establishment, may endanger the health, and shorten the lives of the workmen, thereby diminishing their physical and mental capacity to serve the State, and to provide for those dependent upon them.

. . .

JUSTICE HOLMES dissenting.

. . .

This case is decided upon an economic theory which a large part of the country does not entertain. If it were a question whether I agreed with that theory, I should desire to study it further and long before making up my mind. But I do not conceive that to be my duty, because I strongly believe that my agreement or disagreement has nothing to do with the right of a majority to embody their opinions in law. It is settled by various decisions of this court that state constitutions and state laws may regulate life in many ways which we, as legislators, might think as injudicious, or, if you like, as tyrannical, as this, and which, equally with this, interfere with the liberty to contract. Sunday laws and usury laws are ancient examples. A more modern one is the prohibition of lotteries. The liberty of the citizen to do as he likes so long as he does not interfere with the liberty of others to do the same, which has been a shibboleth for some well known writers, is interfered with by school laws, by the Post Office, by every state or municipal institution which takes his money for purposes thought desirable, whether he likes it or not. The Fourteenth Amendment does not enact Mr. Herbert Spencer's *Social Statics*. . . . [A] constitution is not intended to embody a particular economic theory, whether of paternalism and the organic relation of the citizen to the State or of laissez faire. It is made for people of fundamentally differing views, and the accident of our finding certain opinions natural and familiar or novel and even shocking ought not to conclude our judgment upon the question whether statutes embodying them conflict with the Constitution of the United States.

General propositions do not decide concrete cases. The decision will depend on a judgment or intuition more subtle than any articulate major premise. But I think that the proposition just stated, if it is accepted, will carry us far toward the end. Every opinion tends to become a law. I think that the word liberty in the Fourteenth Amendment is perverted when it is held to prevent the natural outcome of a dominant opinion, unless it can be said that a rational and fair man necessarily would admit that the statute proposed would infringe fundamental principles as they have been understood by the traditions of our people and our law. It does not need research to show that no such sweeping condemnation can be passed upon the statute before us. A reasonable man might think it a proper measure on the score of health. Men whom I certainly could not pronounce unreasonable would uphold it as a first installment of a general regulation of the hours of work. Whether in the latter aspect it would be open to the charge of inequality I think it unnecessary to discuss.

Muller v. Oregon, 208 U.S. 412 (1908)

Curt Muller owned the Grand Laundry in Mulnomah County, Oregon. On September 4, 1905, he required a female employee, Mrs. E. Gotcher, to work more than ten hours. This violated an Oregon statute that declared, "No female [shall] be employed in any mechanical establishment, or factory, or laundry in this state more than ten hours during any one day." Muller was arrested, tried, convicted, and fined $10. The Supreme Court of Oregon sustained his conviction. Muller appealed to the Supreme Court of the United States.

The Supreme Court unanimously upheld the conviction. Justice Brewer's opinion declared that differences between men and women justified permitting states to pass regulations limiting the hours women worked. What did Justice Brewer believe are the differences between men and women? Why did he believe these differences have constitutional significance?

Table 7-5 Selection of Legal Interest Groups and Their Signature Victories

Organization and Year of Founding	Notable U.S. Supreme Court Victories
National Consumers' League (1899)	*Muller v. Oregon* (1908) *Bunting v. Oregon* (1917)
American Jewish Congress (1918)	*McCollum v. Board of Education* (1948) *Shelley v. Kraemer* (1948)
American Civil Liberties Union (1920)	*Mapp v. Ohio* (1961) *Griswold v. Connecticut* (1965)
National Association for the Advancement of Colored People Legal Defense Fund (1939)*	*Brown v. Board of Education* (1954) *Furman v. Georgia* (1972)
Americans United for Separation of Church and State (1947)	*Flast v. Cohen* (1968) *Lemon v. Kurtzman* (1971)
National Center for Law and Economic Justice (1965)	*Goldberg v. Kelly* (1970) *Califano v. Westcott* (1979)
Lambda Legal (1973)	*Romer v. Evans* (1996) *Lawrence v. Texas* (2003)
Center for Individual Rights (1988)	*Rosenberger v. Rector and Visitors of University of Virginia* (1995) *Gratz v. Bollinger* (2003)
Institute for Justice (1991)	*Zelman v. Simmons-Harris* (2002) *Granholm v. Heald* (2005)

*The NAACP was founded in 1909. The Legal Defense Fund, which is now entirely independent of the NAACP, became a separate organization in 1939.

In 1908 Muller was considered a triumph for Progressives. The National Consumers League assisted Oregon in defending this law by securing the services of one of the leading Progressive lawyers in the country—future Supreme Court justice Louis D. Brandeis. Brandeis devised an innovative legal strategy. His brief offered only two short pages of legal argument but then included fifteen pages of excerpts from other state and foreign statutes regulating working hours for women (to establish that Oregon's judgment was supported by many other legislatures) and ninety-five pages of medical reports supporting the assertion that long working hours had a detrimental effect on women's health. As you read the opinion, consider whether the justices were more influenced by Brandeis's data or by their "general knowledge" of the role of women in society. Was Muller a liberal or conservative decision?

LOUIS D. BRANDEIS, "Brief for the State of Oregon"

The legal rules applicable to this case are few and are well established, namely:

First: The right to purchase or to sell labor is a part of the "liberty" protected by the Fourteenth Amendment of the Federal Constitution.

Second: This right to "liberty" is, however, subject to such reasonable restraint of action as the State may impose in the exercise of the police power for the protection of health, safety, morals, and the general welfare.

. . .

Fourth: Such a law will not be sustained if the Court can see that it has no real or substantial relation to public health, safety, or welfare, or that it is "an unreasonable, unnecessary and arbitrary interference with the right of the individual to his personal liberty or to enter into those contracts in relation to labor which may seem to him appropriate or necessary for the support of himself and his family."

But "If the end which the Legislature seeks to accomplish be one to which its power extends, and if the means employed to that end, although not the wisest or best, are yet not plainly and palpably unauthorized by law, then the Court cannot interfere. In other words, when the validity of a statute is questioned, the burden of proof, so to speak, is upon those who assail it.

Fifth: . . .

The facts of common knowledge of which the Court may take judicial notice . . . establish, we submit, conclusively, that there is reasonable ground for holding that to permit women in Oregon to work in a "mechanical establishment, or factory, or laundry" more than ten hours in one day is dangerous to the public health, safety, morals, or welfare.

These facts of common knowledge will be considered under the following heads:

Part I. Legislation (foreign and American), restricting the hours of labor for women.

Part II. The world's experience upon which the legislation limiting the hours of labor for women is based.

. . .

JUSTICE BREWER delivered the opinion of the Court.

. . .

. . . We held in *Lochner v. New York* (1905) that a law providing that no laborer shall be required or permitted to work in bakeries more than sixty hours in a week or ten hours in a day was not, as to men, a legitimate exercise of the police power of the State, but an unreasonable, unnecessary, and arbitrary interference with the right and liberty of the individual to contract in relation to his labor, and, as such, was in conflict with, and void under, the Federal Constitution. That decision is invoked by plaintiff in error as decisive of the question before us. But this assumes that the difference between the sexes does not justify a different rule respecting a restriction of the hours of labor.

. . .

The legislation and opinions referred to in the margin [of the Brandeis brief] may not be, technically speaking, authorities, and in them is little or no discussion of the constitutional question presented to us for determination, yet they are significant of a widespread belief that woman's physical structure, and the functions she performs in consequence thereof, justify special legislation restricting or qualifying the conditions under which she should be permitted to toil. Constitutional questions, it is true, are not settled by even a consensus of present public opinion, for it is the peculiar value of a written constitution that it places in unchanging form limitations upon legislative action, and thus gives a permanence and stability to popular government which otherwise would be lacking. At the same time, when a question of fact is debated and debatable, and the extent to which a special constitutional limitation goes is affected by the truth in respect to that fact, a widespread and long-continued belief concerning it is worthy of consideration. We take judicial cognizance of all matters of general knowledge.

. . .

That woman's physical structure and the performance of maternal functions place her at a disadvantage in the struggle for subsistence is obvious. This is especially true when the burdens of motherhood are upon her. Even when they are not, by abundant testimony of the medical fraternity, continuance for a long time on her feet at work, repeating this from day to day, tends to injurious effects upon the body, and, as healthy mothers are essential to vigorous offspring, the physical wellbeing of woman becomes an object of public interest and care in order to preserve the strength and vigor of the race.

Still again, history discloses the fact that woman has always been dependent upon man. He established his control at the outset by superior physical strength, and this control in various forms, with diminishing intensity, has continued to the present. As minors, though not to the same extent, she has been looked upon in the courts as needing especial care that her rights may be preserved. Education was long denied her, and while now the doors of the schoolroom are opened and her opportunities for acquiring knowledge are great, yet, even with that and the consequent increase of capacity for business affairs, it is still true that, in the struggle for subsistence, she is not an equal competitor with her brother. Though limitations upon personal and contractual rights may be removed by legislation, there is that in her disposition and habits of life which will operate against a full assertion of those rights. She will still be where some legislation to protect her seems necessary to secure a real equality of right. Doubtless there are individual exceptions, and there are many respects in which she has an advantage over him; but, looking at it from the viewpoint of the effort to maintain an independent position in life, she is not upon an equality. Differentiated by these matters from the other sex, she is properly placed in a class by herself, and legislation designed for her protection may be sustained even when like legislation is not necessary for men, and could not be sustained. It is impossible to close one's eyes to the fact that she still looks to her brother, and depends upon him. Even though all restrictions on political, personal, and contractual rights were taken away, and she stood, so far as statutes are concerned, upon an absolutely equal plane with him, it would still be true that she is so constituted that she will rest upon and look to him for protection; that her physical structure and a proper discharge of her maternal functions—having in view not merely her own health, but the wellbeing of the race—justify legislation to protect her from the greed, as well as the passion, of man. The limitations which this statute places upon her contractual powers, upon her right to agree with her employer as to the time she shall labor, are not imposed solely for her benefit, but also largely for the benefit of all. Many words cannot make this plainer. The two sexes differ in structure of body, in the functions to be performed by each, in the amount of physical strength, in the capacity for long-continued labor, particularly when done standing, the influence of vigorous health upon the future wellbeing of the race, the self-reliance which enables one to assert full rights, and in the capacity to maintain the struggle for subsistence. This difference justifies a difference in legislation, and upholds that which is designed to compensate for some of the burdens which rest upon her. . . .

B. Religion

Establishment clause debates became more secular during the Republican Era. Proponents of state support for religious practices and religious institutions emphasized the secular benefits of such measures. Wilbur Crafts, a Presbyterian moral reformer, claimed to have entirely secular reasons for supporting legislation that declared Sunday a day of rest. "The Sabbath laws, like the marriage laws," he wrote, "can be justified on hygienic, social and moral grounds to those who reject the religious ones." Nathaniel Nash, a leading opponent of such measures, maintained that "nothing seems clearer than that compulsory Sabbath or Lord's-day observances are *persecution*, and hence a violation of the rights of man. . . . "[28] The Supreme Court regularly sustained legislation that provided resources to religious groups on the ground that such laws served secular ends. In *Bradfield v. Roberts* (1899) Justice Peckham described as "wholly immaterial" the fact that a hospital receiving government funds was run by the Roman Catholic Church.

Few elected officials, political activists, or judges thought that unpopular religious believers enjoyed

28. Wilbur Fisk Crafts, *Addresses on the Civil Sabbath* (New York: Authors' Publishing Co., 1890), 20; Nathaniel C. Nash, *The Sunday Law, Unconstitutional and Unscriptural* (Boston: Nathaniel C. Nash, 1868), 21.

WHAT IT IS BOUND TO COME TO.

Union Soldier.—COME, COME, GET ON INTO THE DIVORCE COURT. THIS POLYGAMY BUSINESS IS PLAYED OUT. HEREAFTER YOU CHAPS CAN HAVE ONLY ONE POLLY APIECE.

Illustration 7-2 What It Is Bound To Come To
Political cartoon depicting Mormon leader Brigham Young and his wives being forced into divorce court by a U.S. soldier.

Source: Library of Congress, Prints and Photographs Division, Washington, DC 20540, USA.

much constitutional protection, particularly when their religious practices seemed inconsistent with accepted standards of morality. Constitutional decision makers in all branches of state government expressed little sympathy for demands for constitutionally based exemptions. The New York Court of Appeals in *People v. Pierson* (NY 1903) brusquely turned aside the plea of a man who sought to heal a sick child by prayer instead of seeing a doctor. "Full and free enjoyment of religious profession and worship is guarantied," the justices declared, "but acts which are not worship are not."[29]

Mormons were the main target of ostensibly neutral laws that burdened religious practices. The Republican Party repeatedly condemned that sect's commitment to plural marriage. The party's 1876 platform insisted,

> The constitution confers upon congress sovereign power over the territories of the United States for their government. And in the exercise of this power it is the right and duty of congress to prohibit and extirpate in the territories that relic of barbarism, polygamy; and we demand such legislation as will secure this end and the supremacy of American institutions in all the territories.

Congress passed numerous acts designed to achieve those goals. Some directly outlawed polygamy. Others attached civil penalties to persons who engaged in or advocated polygamy. All were sustained without dissent by the Supreme Court of the United States.

29. *People v. Pierson*, 68 N.E. 243 (N.Y. 1903).

Reynolds v. United States, 98 U.S. 145 (1878)

George Reynolds was a prominent member of the Mormon Church. Committed to following church decrees, he practiced polygamy. He first married Polly Ann Tuddenham and then Amelia Jane Schofield. The second marriage violated a federal law forbidding multiple marriages in American territories. At trial Reynolds was convicted, sentenced to two years in prison, and fined $500. He appealed to the Territorial Supreme Court. When his claims were rejected, Reynolds appealed to the Supreme Court of the United States.

Reynolds v. United States *was one episode in the lengthy conflict between the Mormon Church and the federal government over both polygamy and Mormon claims about revelations. Mainstream Christians during the late nineteenth century did not take kindly to religious leaders who claimed to be contemporary prophets. The conflict was also political. The Mormon leadership in Utah was committed to establishing a theocracy, which many Americans regarded as treasonous. Brigham Young, the spiritual leader of the Latter-Day Saints and former territorial governor, declared, "If I am controlled by the Spirit of the Most High, I am a king." Such declarations were frowned upon by national political leaders. President Rutherford Hayes declared, "The Territory [of Utah] is virtually under theocratic government of the Mormon Church. The Union of Church and State is complete. . . . Polygamy and every other evil sanctioned by the Church is safe. To destroy the temporal power of the Mormon Church is the end in view."*[30]

The Supreme Court unanimously ruled that Reynolds had been constitutionally convicted. Chief Justice Waite's opinion for the Court is best known for the sharp distinction that he drew between religious beliefs and religious actions. What is that distinction, and what is its constitutional justification? Did Waite insist that religious action may always be regulated? If so, what exactly does free exercise protect? Waite connected polygamy with "statutory despotism." Was he referring to the intrinsic qualities of multiple marriages or to the actual conflict between the Mormon Church and the United States? Might the Reynolds *opinion have been different had the Mormons merely been an obscure religious group? Do you believe that marriage laws and political institutions are politically or constitutionally connected? What is the connection? Consider the following assertion by Martha Ertman:*

> *The story of* Reynolds *demonstrates its limited relevance to same-sex marriage and gay rights. In contrast to the practice and preferences of nineteenth-century Mormons to separate, if not fully secede, from American law and culture, same-sex marriage is fundamentally an assimilationist move for gay people to further integrate into American life.*[31]

Is Ertman correct to claim that same-sex marriage and plural marriage are disanalogous? Is the analogy correct on cultural, political, or constitutional grounds? How do your beliefs about the cultural and political fights over both practices influence your thinking about the constitutionality of both practices?

Mormons eventually abandoned the fight for polygamy. In 1890 the Mormon leadership claimed to have had a revelation from God urging the sect to forswear multiple marriages. Statehood for Utah followed in 1896. George Reynolds, however, remained unrepentant. After being released from prison he married a third wife, Mary Goold, and began living underground. By the time Reynolds died in 1909 he had fathered thirty-two children.

CHIEF JUSTICE WAITE delivered the opinion of the court.

. . .

Before the adoption of the Constitution, attempts were made in some of the colonies and States to legislate not only in respect to the establishment of religion, but in respect to its doctrines and precepts as well. The people were taxed, against their will, for the support of religion, and sometimes for the support of particular sects to whose tenets they could not and did not subscribe. Punishments were prescribed for a failure to attend upon public worship, and sometimes for entertaining heretical opinions. The controversy upon this general subject was animated in many of the States, but seemed at last to culminate in Virginia. In 1784, the House of Delegates of that State having under consideration "a bill establishing provision for teachers of the Christian religion," . . . directed that . . . the people be requested "to signify their opinion respecting the adoption of such a bill at the next session of assembly."

30. Martha M. Ertman, "The Story of *Reynolds v. United States*: Federal 'Hell Hounds' Punishing Mormon Treason," in *Family Law Stories*, ed. Carol Sanger (Eagan, MN: Foundation Press, 2008), 68–69.

31. Ibid., 55.

. . . Mr. Madison prepared a "Memorial and Remonstrance," . . . in which he demonstrated "that religion, or the duty we owe the Creator," was not within the cognizance of civil government. . . . At the next session the proposed bill was not only defeated, but another, "for establishing religious freedom," drafted by Mr. Jefferson, was passed. . . . In the preamble of this act . . . after a recital "that to suffer the civil magistrate to intrude his powers into the field of opinion, and to restrain the profession or propagation of principles on supposition of their ill tendency, is a dangerous fallacy which at once destroys all religious liberty," it is declared "that it is time enough for the rightful purposes of civil government for its officers to interfere when principles break out into overt acts against peace and good order." In these two sentences is found the true distinction between what properly belongs to the church and what to the State.

. . . [A]t the first session of the first Congress the amendment now under consideration was proposed with others by Mr. Madison. It met the views of the advocates of religious freedom, and was adopted. Mr. Jefferson afterwards, in reply to an address to him by a committee of the Danbury Baptist Association . . . took occasion to say:

> Believing with you that religion is a matter which lies solely between man and his God; that he owes account to none other for his faith or his worship; that the legislative powers of the government reach actions only, and not opinions,—I contemplate with sovereign reverence that act of the whole American people which declared that their legislature should "make no law respecting an establishment of religion or prohibiting the free exercise thereof," thus building a wall of separation between church and State. Adhering to this expression of the supreme will of the nation in behalf of the rights of conscience, I shall see with sincere satisfaction the progress of those sentiments which tend to restore man to all his natural rights, convinced he has no natural right in opposition to his social duties.

Coming as this does from an acknowledged leader of the advocates of the measure, it may be accepted almost as an authoritative declaration of the scope and effect of the amendment thus secured. Congress was deprived of all legislative power over mere opinion, but was left free to reach actions which were in violation of social duties or subversive of good order.

Polygamy has always been odious among the northern and western nations of Europe, and, until the establishment of the Mormon Church, was almost exclusively a feature of the life of Asiatic and of African people. At common law, the second marriage was always void . . . and from the earliest history of England polygamy has been treated as an offence against society. . . .

. . . [W]e think it may safely be said there never has been a time in any State of the Union when polygamy has not been an offence against society, cognizable by the civil courts and punishable with more or less severity. In the face of all this evidence, it is impossible to believe that the constitutional guaranty of religious freedom was intended to prohibit legislation in respect to this most important feature of social life. Marriage, while from its very nature a sacred obligation, is nevertheless, in most civilized nations, a civil contract, and usually regulated by law. Upon it society may be said to be built, and out of its fruits spring social relations and social obligations and duties, with which government is necessarily required to deal. In fact, according as monogamous or polygamous marriages are allowed, do we find the principles on which the government of the people, to a greater or less extent, rests. Professor Lieber says, polygamy leads to the patriarchal principle, and which, when applied to large communities, fetters the people in stationary despotism, while that principle cannot long exist in connection with monogamy. . . .

. . . Laws are made for the government of actions, and while they cannot interfere with mere religious belief and opinions, they may with practices. Suppose one believed that human sacrifices were a necessary part of religious worship, would it be seriously contended that the civil government under which he lived could not interfere to prevent a sacrifice? Or if a wife religiously believed it was her duty to burn herself upon the funeral pile of her dead husband, would it be beyond the power of the civil government to prevent her carrying her belief into practice?

So here, as a law of the organization of society under the exclusive dominion of the United States, it is provided that plural marriages shall not be allowed. Can a man excuse his practices to the contrary because of his religious belief? To permit this would be to make the professed doctrines of religious belief superior to the law of the land, and in effect to permit every citizen to become a law unto himself. Government could exist only in name under such circumstances. . . .

JUSTICE FIELD, concurring

. . . .

C. Guns

The right to bear arms faded from prominence after the Civil War and Reconstruction. The Supreme Court in a series of decisions including *United States v. Cruikshank* (1876), *Presser v. Illinois* (1886), and *Miller v. Texas* (1894) ruled that state laws restricting gun rights did not violate the federal Constitution. These decisions unanimously held that the right to bear arms was not one of the fundamental rights protected by the privileges and immunities or due process clauses of the Fourteenth Amendment. "The second amendment declares that [the right to bear arms] shall not be infringed," Justice William Woods declared in *Presser*, "but this, as has been seen, means no more than that it shall not be infringed by Congress."

D. Personal Freedom and Public Morality

The turn of the twentieth century witnessed unprecedented demands for federal and state regulation of individual behavior. Americans joined crusades to restrict birth control, abortion, drinking, drug use, and, as fans of *The Music Man* may remember, pool. Some states required all persons to be vaccinated against disease. Others passed eugenic laws that ordered the sterilization of criminals and persons thought to be mentally unfit. Some laws were rooted in Protestant moral virtues. Others reflected new social science research on public health. Most Progressive reformers combined appeals to moral virtue and social science. These demands for state regulation inspired new constitutional rights claims. Novel exercises of the police power, opponents claimed, unreasonably restricted traditional individual rights.

Judges treated regulations of personal behavior in much the same way that they treated economic regulations. The vast majority of federal and state regulations passed judicial muster as legitimate exercises of the police power. The Supreme Court of Washington, when sustaining a ban on opium in *Territory v. Ah Lim* (WA 1890), asserted that "the state has an interest in the health of its citizens, and has a right to see to it that its citizens are self-supporting."[32] Justice Holmes in *Buck v. Bell* (1927) notoriously asserted, "Three generations of imbeciles are enough" when sustaining a Virginia law that permitted state officials to sterilize persons they believed to be "feebleminded."

Courts struck down some state regulations of personal behavior. These cases relied on the same rights principles the justices employed in such cases as *Lochner v. New York* (1905). The Supreme Court of the United States in *Meyer v. Nebraska* (1923) asserted that "liberty" in the Fourteenth Amendment

> denotes not merely freedom from bodily restraint, but also the right of the individual to contract, to engage in any of the common occupations of life, to acquire useful knowledge, to marry, establish a home and bring up children, to worship God according to the dictates of his own conscience, and generally to enjoy those privileges long recognized at common law as essential to the orderly pursuit of happiness by free men. (among others)

Meyer declared unconstitutional a state law forbidding persons to teach German. Several state courts found a constitutional right to drink. When striking down a state prohibition law in *Commonwealth v. Campbell* (KY 1909), the Court of Appeals of Kentucky asserted that "the question of what a man will drink, or eat, or wear, provided the others are not invaded, is one which addresses itself alone to the will of the citizen." Unlike *Lochner*, these individual rights cases were not discredited during the New Deal. Several became foundations for judicial decisions protecting the right to use birth control and obtain a legal abortion.

Meyer v. Nebraska, 262 U.S. 390 (1923)

Robert T. Meyer taught at Zion Parochial School in Hamilton County, Nebraska. The children of German immigrants who attended the school received their religious instruction in German. This practice violated a Nebraska law that declared, "No person, individually or as a teacher, shall, in any private, denominational, parochial or public school, teach any subject to any person in any language than the

32. *Territory v. Ah Lim*, 1 Wash. 156 (1890).

English language." A trial court found Meyer guilty of violating this statute and fined him $25. After the Supreme Court of Nebraska sustained this sentence, Meyer appealed to the Supreme Court of the United States.

The Supreme Court by a 7–2 vote declared the Nebraska law unconstitutional. Justice James McReynolds asserted both that teaching German was a liberty protected by the Fourteenth Amendment and that the prohibition was supported by no legitimate rationale for the promotion of public health, safety, or morality. The Nebraska law prohibiting the use of German in schools was part of a national effort to assimilate immigrants by insisting on the use of the English language. Did Justice McReynolds reject this goal or merely the law as a means to a goal? Compare Meyer *to* Lochner v. New York *(1905). Was* Meyer *a straightforward application of* Lochner, *complete with Justice Holmes's dissent? Did the justices debate the importance of protecting certain fundamental rights or dispute whether the law actually advanced public health, safety, or morality? If the same lawsuit were brought today, the decision in* Meyer *would no doubt rely heavily on the freedom of religion. Was* Meyer *really a religious freedom case brought before the incorporation of the First Amendment? What would be the result if the same case came before the contemporary Supreme Court?*

JUSTICE McREYNOLDS delivered the opinion of the Court.

. . .

While this Court has not attempted to define with exactness the liberty . . . guaranteed [by the due process clause of the Fourteenth Amendment], the term has received much consideration and some of the included things have been definitely stated. Without doubt, it denotes not merely freedom from bodily restraint, but also the right of the individual to contract, to engage in any of the common occupations of life, to acquire useful knowledge, to marry, establish a home and bring up children, to worship God according to the dictates of his own conscience, and generally to enjoy those privileges long recognized at common law as essential to the orderly pursuit of happiness by free men. . . .

The American people have always regarded education and acquisition of knowledge as matters of supreme importance which should be diligently promoted. . . . Corresponding to the right of control, it is the natural duty of the parent to give his children education suitable to their station in life, and nearly all the States, including Nebraska, enforce this obligation by compulsory laws.

Practically, education of the young is only possible in schools conducted by especially qualified persons who devote themselves thereto. The calling always has been regarded as useful and honorable, essential, indeed, to the public welfare. Mere knowledge of the German language cannot reasonably be regarded as harmful. Heretofore it has been commonly looked upon as helpful and desirable. Plaintiff in error taught this language in school as part of his occupation. His right thus to teach and the right of parents to engage him so to instruct their children, we think, are within the liberty of the Amendment.

. . .

It is said the purpose of the legislation was to promote civic development by inhibiting training and education of the immature in foreign tongues and ideals before they could learn English and acquire American ideals, and "that the English language should be and become the mother tongue of all children reared in this State." It is also affirmed that the foreign born population is very large, that certain communities commonly use foreign words, follow foreign leaders, move in a foreign atmosphere, and that the children are thereby hindered from becoming citizens of the most useful type, and the public safety is imperiled.

That the State may do much, go very far, indeed, in order to improve the quality of its citizens, physically, mentally and morally, is clear; but the individual has certain fundamental rights which must be respected. The protection of the Constitution extends to all, to those who speak other languages as well as to those born with English on the tongue. Perhaps it would be highly advantageous if all had ready understanding of our ordinary speech, but this cannot be coerced by methods which conflict with the Constitution—a desirable end cannot be promoted by prohibited means.

. . .

The desire of the legislature to foster a homogeneous people with American ideals prepared readily to understand current discussions of civic matters is easy to appreciate. Unfortunate experiences during the late war and aversion toward every characteristic of truculent adversaries were certainly enough to quicken that aspiration. But the means adopted, we think, exceed the limitations upon the power of the State and conflict with rights assured to plaintiff in error. . . .

. . . [M]ere abuse incident to an occupation ordinarily useful is not enough to justify its abolition, although regulation may be entirely proper. No emergency has arisen which renders knowledge by a child of some language other than English so clearly harmful as to justify its inhibition with the consequent infringement of rights long freely enjoyed. We are constrained to conclude that the statute as applied is arbitrary and without reasonable relation to any end within the competency of the State.

. . .

JUSTICE HOLMES, dissenting.[33]

We all agree, I take it, that it is desirable that all the citizens of the United States should speak a common tongue, and therefore that the end aimed at by the statute is a lawful and proper one. The only question is whether the means adopted deprive teachers of the liberty secured to them by the Fourteenth Amendment. It is with hesitation and unwillingness that I differ from my brethren with regard to a law like this, but I cannot bring my mind to believe that, in some circumstances, and circumstances existing, it is said, in Nebraska, the statute might not be regarded as a reasonable or even necessary method of reaching the desired result. The part of the act with which we are concerned deals with the teaching of young children. Youth is the time when familiarity with a language is established and if there are sections in the state where a child would hear only Polish or French or German spoken at home, I am not prepared to say that it is unreasonable to provide that, in his early years, he shall hear and speak only English at school. But, if it is reasonable, it is not an undue restriction of the liberty either of teacher or scholar. No one would doubt that a teacher might be forbidden to teach many things, and the only criterion of his liberty under the Constitution that I can think of is "whether, considering the end in view, the statute passes the bounds of reason and assumes the character of a merely arbitrary fiat." . . . I think I appreciate the objection to the law, but it appears to me to present a question upon which men reasonably might differ, and therefore I am unable to say that the Constitution of the United States prevents the experiment's being tried.

. . .

33. This dissent was actually issued in a companion case, *Bartels v. Iowa*, 262 U.S. 404 (1923).

JUSTICE SUTHERLAND concurs in this opinion.

Buck v. Bell, 274 U.S. 200 (1927)

Carrie Buck was a nineteen-year-old rape victim who became pregnant. The family with whom she lived had her committed to the Virginia State Colony for Epileptics and Feeble-Minded. After she gave birth to her daughter, the superintendent of the colony recommended sterilization when he discovered that a revised Binet-Simon I.Q. test revealed Carrie Buck's mental age as nine and her mother's mental age as younger than eight. Virginia law permitted forced sterilization of people considered "feebleminded." That law reflected Progressive Era enthusiasm for race improvement through eugenic sterilization. The Supreme Court of Appeals of the State of Virginia approved the sterilization order. Buck appealed to the Supreme Court of the United States.

The Supreme Court by an 8–1 vote sustained the Virginia forced sterilization law. Justice Holmes, a eugenics enthusiast, insisted that state laws mandating sterilization were reasonable exercises of the police power. How did he reach that conclusion? Read Buck *in light of Holmes's dissents in freedom of contract and freedom of speech cases. How does the opinion influence your understanding of Progressive constitutional thought before the New Deal?*

Subsequent investigations found that neither Carrie Buck nor her daughter Vivian were mentally handicapped.

JUSTICE HOLMES delivered the opinion of the Court.

. . .

. . . The judgment finds the facts that have been recited and that Carrie Buck "is the probable potential parent of socially inadequate offspring, likewise afflicted, that she may be sexually sterilized without detriment to her general health and that her welfare and that of society will be promoted by her sterilization," and thereupon makes the order. In view of the general declarations of the Legislature and the specific findings of the Court obviously we cannot say as matter of law that the grounds do not exist, and if they exist they justify the result. We have seen more than once that the public welfare may call upon the best citizens for their lives. It would be strange if it could not call upon those who already sap the strength of the State for these lesser sacrifices, often not felt to be such by those concerned, in order to prevent our being swamped with incompetence. It is better for all the world, if instead of waiting to execute degenerate offspring for crime, or to let them starve for their imbecility, society can prevent those who are manifestly unfit from continuing their kind. The principle that sustains compulsory vaccination is broad enough to cover cutting the Fallopian tubes. Three generations of imbeciles are enough. But, it is said, however it might be if this reasoning were applied generally, it fails when it is confined to the small number who are in the institutions named and is not applied to the multitudes outside. It is the usual last resort of constitutional arguments to point out shortcomings of this sort. But the answer is that the law does all that is needed when it does all that it can, indicates a policy, applies it to all within the lines, and seeks to bring within the lines all similarly situated so far and so fast as its means allow. Of course so far as the operations enable those who otherwise must be kept confined to be returned to the world, and thus open the asylum to others, the equality aimed at will be more nearly reached.

JUSTICE BUTLER dissents.

VIII. Democratic Rights

MAJOR DEVELOPMENTS

- First federal laws restricting speech since 1798
- Justice Holmes introduces the "clear and present danger" test for free speech
- Ongoing debates over universal suffrage and laws regulating elections

The Republican Era witnessed sharp disputes over democracy and pluralism. Supreme Court opinions in the late nineteenth century insisted that the United States was a constitutional *republic*. Justice Louis Brandeis, appointed by President Wilson in 1915, wrote the first opinions in Supreme Court history that referred to the United States as a constitutional *democracy*. This debate transcended party labels. Members of the Republican Party had no greater tendency to claim the United States was a republic than members of the Democratic Party. Many constitutional decision makers commonly referred to the United States as a democratic republic. Still, more than a verbal quibble was taking place. Civic republicans in the eighteenth and nineteenth centuries emphasized the importance of cultural homogeneity and consensus on basic values. In contrast, a growing number of Americans at the turn of the twentieth century celebrated pluralism. Some clashes between civic republicans and pluralists took place over such individual rights issues as prohibition and eugenics. Others concerned free speech, voting, and citizenship.

A. Free Speech

The constitutional politics of free speech was reconfigured at the turn of the twentieth century. Conservative libertarians who regarded both free speech and the freedom of contract as aspects of "the right of the citizen to be free in the enjoyment of all his faculties"[34] were the leading proponents of expression rights during the first half of the Republican Era. Progressives who linked free speech to democratic governance were the leading proponents of free speech in the second half of the Republican Era. Most Progressives, however, insisted that elected representatives had the power to regulate free speech and the liberty of contract whenever such regulation promoted the public good.

Events immediately before and during World War I transformed free speech debates in the United States.[35] Prominent Americans feared that the new wave of immigrants from eastern and southern Europe either retained loyalties to their place of birth or were committed to a Socialist revolution. These fears were heightened when individual anarchists at the turn of the century assassinated several heads of state (including President William McKinley), the Communist revolution in Russia toppled the Czar, the Socialist Party in the United States gained an increasing share of the vote in many urban communities, and militant labor leaders threatened mass strikes. Even before the United States entered World War I, many Americans were calling for legislation that would restrict "disloyal" utterances, usually associated with immigrants. These concerns inspired the passage of the Espionage Act of 1917, the Sedition Act of 1918, and many similar state statutes. More than two thousand persons were arrested for violating federal restrictions on speech. More than one thousand were convicted.

---

34. *Allgeyer*, 165 U.S. 578.

35. See Mark A. Graber, *Transforming Free Speech: The Ambiguous Legacy of Civil Libertarianism* (Berkeley: University of California Press, 1992).

Table 7-6 Selection of U.S. Supreme Court Cases Reviewing State and Federal Laws Restricting Dangerous Speech

Case	Vote	Outcome	Decision
United States ex rel. Turner v. Williams, 194 U.S. 279 (1904)	9–0	Upheld	Anarchist aliens can be denied entry into the country because of their views
Fox v. Washington, 236 U.S. 273 (1915)	9–0	Upheld	Speech that "encourages and incites" illegal behavior can be prohibited
Schenck v. United States, 249 U.S. 47 (1919)	9–0	Upheld	Writers of pamphlets can be punished if the writings present a clear and present danger that military recruitment will be disrupted
Abrams v. United States, 250 U.S. 616 (1919)	7–2	Upheld	Writers of leaflets that have a tendency to obstruct the war effort may be punished
Gilbert v. Minnesota, 254 U.S. 325 (1920)	7–2	Upheld	States may also punish speech that has the tendency to obstruct the federal war effort
Gitlow v. New York, 268 U.S. 652 (1925)	7–2	Upheld	Writers of pamphlets with a tendency to produce industrial unrest and a threat to government stability can be prosecuted for criminal anarchism
Whitney v. California, 274 U.S. 357 (1927)	9–0	Upheld	States may punish those who use speech to produce a clear and present danger to society by, for example, forming a revolutionary Communist Party
Near v. Minnesota, 283 U.S. 697 (1931)	5–4	Struck down	State efforts to block the publication of "defamatory" newspaper was an unconstitutional prior restraint
DeJonge v. Oregon, 299 U.S. 353 (1937)	9–0	Struck down	Individuals have a right of association that encompasses the right to speak at a public meeting sponsored by the Communist Party
Herndon v. Lowry, 301 U.S. 242 (1937)	5–4	Struck down	Membership in the Communist Party and solicitation of a few members fails to establish an attempt to incite others to insurrection
Chaplinsky v. New Hampshire, 315 U.S. 568 (1942)	9–0	Upheld	"Fighting words" or verbal insults are a type of speech, like libel and obscenity, with no social value that are not entitled to constitutional protection
Terminiello v. Chicago, 337 U.S. 1 (1949)	5–4	Struck down	Inflammatory speech is constitutionally protected, even if the audience reacts violently toward the speaker
Feiner v. New York, 340 U.S. 315 (1951)	6–4	Upheld	Speech that causes imminent public discord or incites a riot may be suppressed
Dennis v. United States, 341 U.S. 494 (1951)	6–2	Upheld	A leader of the revolutionary Communist Party may be charged with conspiracy that presents a clear and present danger to the government
Yates v. United States, 354 U.S. 298 (1957)	6–1	Struck down	Speech is protected if one advocates or teaches about forcible overthrow of the government as an abstract principle rather than as an incitement to concrete action

(Continued)

Table 7-6 *(Continued)*

Case	Vote	Outcome	Decision
Sweezy v. New Hampshire, 354 U.S. 234 (1957)	6–2	Struck down	Legislative investigation into a college teacher's lectures on Socialism and membership in the Progressive Party is unconstitutional
Brandenburg v. Ohio, 395 U.S. 444 (1969)	9–0	Struck down	Government may only punish speech that aims to produce imminent lawless action, not speech that merely advocates lawless action
R.A.V. v. City of St. Paul, 505 U.S. 377 (1992)	9–0	Struck down	Hate crimes ordinance held to be unconstitutional content-based restriction on speech
Virginia v. Black, 538 U.S. 343 (2003)	7–2	Struck down	Cross-burning statutes are unconstitutional to the extent that a jury may presume a threat merely from evidence of cross-burning
Holder v. Humanitarian Law Project, 130 S. Ct. 2705 (2010)	6–3	Upheld	Congress may prohibit individuals and groups from providing "material support," including "expert advice and assistance," to specified terrorist groups
Snyder v. Phelps, 131 S. Ct. 1207 (2011)	8–1	Struck down	Speech on a public sidewalk, about a public issue, cannot be liable for a tort of emotional distress, even if the speech is outside a memorial service and is found to be "outrageous"

The Supreme Court initially relied on traditional conceptions of the police powers when it unanimously sustained the convictions of persons found guilty of violating the Espionage Act or related restrictions on free speech. Judicial opinions in free speech cases emphasized that elected officials could restrict speech when reasonable persons might think the regulation served the public interest. In *Schenck v. United States* (1919), Justice Holmes asserted, "The question in every case is whether the words used are used in such circumstances and are of such a nature as to create a clear and present danger that they will bring about the substantive evils that Congress has a right to prevent." One week later, when sustaining the conviction of prominent Socialist leader Eugene V. Debs, Holmes asserted that persons could be constitutionally convicted when "the words used had as their natural tendency and reasonably probable effect to obstruct the recruiting service."[36] This formulation, different in tone from "clear and present danger," is sometimes referred to as the "bad tendency test." This test permits government to regulate all speech that may cause some harm that the government has the authority to prevent (such as draft obstruction, or even litter).

The Red Scare that took place after World War I inspired continued restrictions on political dissent, but these restrictions were no longer unanimously sustained by the Supreme Court. In *Abrams v. United States* (1919), the justices ruled by a 7–2 vote that Jacob Abrams could be sentenced to ten years in prison for urging workers to protest American involvement in the Russian Revolution by a general strike. Justice Holmes, joined by Justice Brandeis, issued a sharp dissent. The most famous passage in that dissent asserted,

> But when men have realized that time has upset many fighting faiths, they may come to believe even more than they believe the very foundations of their own conduct that the ultimate good desired is better reached by free trade in ideas—that the best test of truth is the power of the thought to get itself accepted in the competition of the market, and that truth is the only ground upon which their wishes safely can be carried out. That, at any rate, is the theory of our Constitution. It is an experiment, as all life is an experiment. Every year, if not every day, we have to wager our salvation upon some

36. *Debs v. United States*, 249 U.S. 211 (1919).

> prophecy based upon imperfect knowledge. While that experiment is part of our system, I think that we should be eternally vigilant against attempts to check the expression of opinions that we loathe and believe to be fraught with death, unless they so imminently threaten immediate interference with the lawful and pressing purposes of the law that an immediate check is required to save the country.

By the end of the Republican Era the more Progressive justices on the court were clearly imposing a higher standard in free speech cases than was called for by inherited police powers logic. Brandeis's concurring opinion in *Whitney v. California* (1927) rejected claims that elected officials could regulate speech as freely as he believed they could regulate property. He insisted that speech, unlike property, could be regulated only when persons incited imminent and serious violence. By a 5–4 vote in *Near v. Minnesota* (1931), the Supreme Court formally imposed a similarly high standard when declaring constitutional limits on legislation imposing prior restraints on speech. Chief Justice Hughes's majority opinion declared that elected officials could adopt prior restraints "only in exceptional cases."

Schenck v. United States, 249 U.S. 47 (1919)

Charles Schenck was the general secretary of the American Socialist Party. American Socialists opposed the government's decision in 1917 to declare war on Germany. During the week of August 13–20, 1917, Schenck and other Socialists distributed pamphlets to the general public and persons eligible for the draft that condemned the Wilson administration and insisted that the draft was unconstitutional. Schenck was promptly arrested, convicted, and sentenced to ten years in prison for violating the Espionage Act of 1917. He appealed to the Supreme Court of the United States.

The Supreme Court unanimously ruled that Schenck had been constitutionally convicted. Justice Holmes's majority opinion declared that government may limit speech when there is "a clear and present danger" that the speaker "will bring about the substantive evils that Congress has a right to prevent." How protective of speech was this test in Schenck? Suppose that Schenck had merely told persons eligible for the draft that they would be better off going to college and making money than volunteering for the army. Could he have been constitutionally convicted under the Espionage Act?

JUSTICE HOLMES delivered the opinion of the Court.

. . .

The document in question upon its first printed side recited the first section of the Thirteenth Amendment, said that the idea embodied in it was violated by the conscription act and that a conscript is little better than a convict. In impassioned language it intimated that conscription was despotism in its worst form and a monstrous wrong against humanity in the interest of Wall Street's chosen few. It said, "Do not submit to intimidation," but in form at least confined itself to peaceful measures such as a petition for the repeal of the act. The other and later printed side of the sheet was headed "Assert Your Rights." It stated reasons for alleging that any one violated the Constitution when he refused to recognize "your right to assert your opposition to the draft," and went on, "If you do not assert and support your rights, you are helping to deny or disparage rights which it is the solemn duty of all citizens and residents of the United States to retain." It described the arguments on the other side as coming from cunning politicians and a mercenary capitalist press, and even silent consent to the conscription law as helping to support an infamous conspiracy. It denied the power to send our citizens away to foreign shores to shoot up the people of other lands, and added that words could not express the condemnation such cold-blooded ruthlessness deserves, &c., &c., winding up, "You must do your share to maintain, support and uphold the rights of the people of this country." Of course the document would not have been sent unless it had been intended to have some effect, and we do not see what effect it could be expected to have upon persons subject to the draft except to influence them to obstruct the carrying of it out. The defendants do not deny that the jury might find against them on this point.

But it is said, suppose that that was the tendency of this circular, it is protected by the First Amendment to the Constitution. . . . It well may be that the prohibition of laws abridging the freedom of speech is not confined to previous restraints, although to prevent them may have been the main purpose. . . . We admit that in many places and in ordinary times the defendants in saying all that was said in the circular would have been within their constitutional rights. But the character of every act depends upon the circumstances in which it is done. . . The most stringent protection of free speech would not protect a man in falsely

VOL. 1 SAN FRANCISCO, JULY 1, 1916 No. 15

YOU AND I CANNOT LIVE IN THE SAME LAND

Illustration 7-3 You and I Cannot Live in the Same Land
This 1916 cover illustration from the San Francisco anarchist magazine *The Blast* reflects the sense of conflict between the government and dissident political movements in the early twentieth century, as well as the growing interest in free speech arguments on the political left during World War I.

Source: The Blast, Volume. 1, Issue 15, July 1, 1916, page 1123. Republished in Alexander Berkman, ed., *The Blast* (Oakland, CA: AK Press, 2005).

shouting fire in a theatre and causing a panic. . . . The question in every case is whether the words used are used in such circumstances and are of such a nature as to create a clear and present danger that they will bring about the substantive evils that Congress has a right to prevent. It is a question of proximity and degree. When a nation is at war many things that might be said in time of peace are such a hindrance to its effort that their utterance will not be endured so long as men fight and that no Court could regard them as protected by any constitutional right. It seems to be admitted that if an actual obstruction of the recruiting service were proved, liability for words that produced that effect might be enforced. . . . If the act, (speaking, or circulating a paper,) its tendency and the intent with which it is done are the same, we perceive no ground for saying that success alone warrants making the act a crime. . . .

Whitney v. California, 274 U.S. 357 (1927)

In 1919 Charlotte Anita Whitney helped to organize the California branch of the Communist Labor Party. The platform and declaration of principles of the national organization asserted:

> *The Communist Labor Party of the United States of America declares itself in full harmony with the revolutionary working class parties of all countries and stated by the Third International formed at Moscow.*
>
> *The most important means of capturing state power for the workers is the action of the masses, proceeding from the place where the workers are gathered together—in the shops and factories. The use of the political machinery of the capitalist state for this purpose is only secondary.*[37]

Whitney believed that the California chapter should take a more moderate position. At the state organizing convention, she proposed the following resolution:

> *The C. L. P. of California fully recognizes the value of political action as a means of spreading communist propaganda; it insists that in proportion to the development of the economic strength of the working class, it, the working class, must also develop its political power. The C. L. P. of California proclaims and insists that the capture of political power, locally or nationally by the revolutionary working class can be of tremendous assistance to the workers in their struggle of emancipation. Therefore, we again urge the workers who are possessed of the right of franchise to cast their votes for the party which represents their immediate and final interest—the C. L. P.—at all elections, being fully convinced of the utter futility of obtaining any real measure of justice or freedom under officials elected by parties owned and controlled by the capitalist class.*[38]

Whitney was subsequently arrested and tried for criminal syndicalism, understood as "advocating, teaching or aiding and abetting the commission of crime, sabotage (which word is hereby defined as meaning willful and malicious physical damage or injury to physical property), or unlawful acts of force and violence or unlawful methods of terrorism as a means of accomplishing a change in industrial ownership or control or effecting any political change." She was convicted, even though she testified at trial that she only championed legal methods for promoting social change. The Supreme Court of California sustained her conviction. Whitney appealed those rulings to the Supreme Court of the United States.

The Supreme Court had reviewed a similar challenge to a state criminal anarchy statute two years earlier in Gitlow v. New York *(1925). The justices in that case incorporated the First Amendment. Justice Sanford's majority opinion agreed with the defense that "freedom of speech and of the press . . . are among the fundamental personal rights and 'liberties' protected by the due process clause of the Fourteenth Amendment from impairment by the States." That principle, however, did Benjamin Gitlow little good. The justices by a 7–2 vote sustained his conviction for publishing "The Left-Wing Manifesto." "That a State in the exercise of its police power may punish those who abuse this freedom by utterances inimical to the public welfare, tending to corrupt public morals, incite to crime, or disturb the public peace," Justice Sanford stated, "is not open to question." Justices Holmes and Brandeis dissented.*

The Supreme Court also sustained Whitney's conviction by the same 7–2 vote. Justice Sanford's majority opinion

37. "Platform and Program of the Communist Labor Party of America, Adopted by Its Founding Convention, Sept. 5, 1919," as published in *The Ohio Socialist*, September 17, 1919, 3.

38. Haig A. Bosmajian, *Anita Whitney, Louis Brandeis, and the First Amendment* (Cranbury, NJ: Associated University Presses, 2010), 75.

claimed that courts should defer to legislative findings that certain utterances tend to present a clear and present danger. Justice Brandeis insisted that convictions for speech were constitutional only if the particular speaker was guilty of inciting an audience to imminent and serious violence. As precedential support for this claim, Brandeis cited a series of cases in which the justices protected property rights. Was this citation correct? Did the justices in Lochner v. New York *(1905) worry about whether Joseph Lochner's actions threatened public harm, or did they conclude that baking as a whole was not an unhealthy trade? Suppose that in 1925 the Supreme Court had abandoned the freedom of contract. Could Brandeis have written the* Whitney *concurrence?*

The most famous passage of the Whitney *concurrence begins by asserting, "Those who won our independence." Does Brandeis's opinion accurately describe how the American revolutionaries or constitutional framers understood free speech? Does it accurately describe their more general principles? What, in your judgment, provides the foundation for Brandeis's theory of free speech? Is that theory sound?*

JUSTICE SANFORD delivered the opinion of the Court.

...

... [T]he freedom of speech which is secured by the Constitution does not confer an absolute right to speak, without responsibility, whatever one may choose, or an unrestricted and unbridled license giving immunity for every possible use of language and preventing the punishment of those who abuse this freedom; and [that] a State in the exercise of its police power may punish those who abuse this freedom by utterances inimical to the public welfare, tending to incite to crime, disturb the public peace, or endanger the foundations of organized government and threaten its overthrow by unlawful means, is not open to question....

By enacting the provisions of the Syndicalism Act the State has declared, through its legislative body, that to knowingly be or become a member of or assist in organizing an association to advocate, teach or aid and abet the commission of crimes or unlawful acts of force, violence or terrorism as a means of accomplishing industrial or political changes, involves such danger to the public peace and the security of the State, that these acts should be penalized in the exercise of its police power. That determination must be given great weight. Every presumption is to be indulged in favor of the validity of the statute ... and it may not be declared unconstitutional unless it is an arbitrary or unreasonable attempt to exercise the authority vested in the State in the public interest....

The essence of the offense denounced by the Act is the combining with others in an association for the accomplishment of the desired ends through the advocacy and use of criminal and unlawful methods. It partakes of the nature of a criminal conspiracy.... That such united and joint action involves even greater danger to the public peace and security than the isolated utterances and acts of individuals is clear....

...

JUSTICE BRANDEIS, concurring.

...

Despite arguments to the contrary which had seemed to me persuasive, it is settled that the due process clause of the Fourteenth Amendment applies to matters of substantive law as well as to matters of procedure. Thus all fundamental rights comprised within the term liberty are protected by the federal Constitution from invasion by the states. The right of free speech, the right to teach and the right of assembly are, of course, fundamental rights.... These may not be denied or abridged. But, although the rights of free speech and assembly are fundamental, they are not in their nature absolute. Their exercise is subject to restriction, if the particular restriction proposed is required in order to protect the state from destruction or from serious injury, political, economic or moral. That the necessity which is essential to a valid restriction does not exist unless speech would produce, or is intended to produce, a clear and imminent danger of some substantive evil which the state constitutionally may seek to prevent has been settled. See *Schenck v. United States* (1918)....

... The Legislature must obviously decide, in the first instance, whether a danger exists which calls for a particular protective measure. But where a statute is valid only in case certain conditions exist, the enactment of the statute cannot alone establish the facts which are essential to its validity. Prohibitory legislation has repeatedly been held invalid, because unnecessary, where the denial of liberty involved was that of engaging in a particular business. The powers of the courts to strike down an offending law are no less when the interests involved are not property rights, but the fundamental personal rights of free speech and assembly.

. . .

Those who won our independence believed that the final end of the state was to make men free to develop their faculties, and that in its government the deliberative forces should prevail over the arbitrary. They valued liberty both as an end and as a means. They believed liberty to be the secret of happiness and courage to be the secret of liberty. They believed that freedom to think as you will and to speak as you think are means indispensable to the discovery and spread of political truth; that without free speech and assembly discussion would be futile; that with them, discussion affords ordinarily adequate protection against the dissemination of noxious doctrine; that the greatest menace to freedom is an inert people; that public discussion is a political duty; and that this should be a fundamental principle of the American government. They recognized the risks to which all human institutions are subject. But they knew that order cannot be secured merely through fear of punishment for its infraction; that it is hazardous to discourage thought, hope and imagination; that fear breeds repression; that repression breeds hate; that hate menaces stable government; that the path of safety lies in the opportunity to discuss freely supposed grievances and proposed remedies; and that the fitting remedy for evil counsels is good ones. Believing in the power of reason as applied through public discussion, they eschewed silence coerced by law—the argument of force in its worst form. Recognizing the occasional tyrannies of governing majorities, they amended the Constitution so that free speech and assembly should be guaranteed.

Fear of serious injury cannot alone justify suppression of free speech and assembly. Men feared witches and burnt women. It is the function of speech to free men from the bondage of irrational fears. To justify suppression of free speech there must be reasonable ground to fear that serious evil will result if free speech is practiced. There must be reasonable ground to believe that the danger apprehended is imminent. There must be reasonable ground to believe that the evil to be prevented is a serious one. Every denunciation of existing law tends in some measure to increase the probability that there will be violation of it. Condonation of a breach enhances the probability. Expressions of approval add to the probability. Propagation of the criminal state of mind by teaching syndicalism increases it. Advocacy of lawbreaking heightens it still further. But even advocacy of violation, however reprehensible morally, is not a justification for denying free speech where the advocacy falls short of incitement and there is nothing to indicate that the advocacy would be immediately acted on. The wide difference between advocacy and incitement, between preparation and attempt, between assembling and conspiracy, must be borne in mind. In order to support a finding of clear and present danger it must be shown either that immediate serious violence was to be expected or was advocated, or that the past conduct furnished reason to believe that such advocacy was then contemplated.

Those who won our independence by revolution were not cowards. They did not fear political change.

They did not exalt order at the cost of liberty. To courageous, self-reliant men, with confidence in the power of free and fearless reasoning applied through the processes of popular government, no danger flowing from speech can be deemed clear and present, unless the incidence of the evil apprehended is so imminent that it may befall before there is opportunity for full discussion. If there be time to expose through discussion the falsehood and fallacies, to avert the evil by the processes of education, the remedy to be applied is more speech, not enforced silence. Only an emergency can justify repression. Such must be the rule if authority is to be reconciled with freedom. Such, in my opinion, is the command of the Constitution. It is therefore always open to Americans to challenge a law abridging free speech and assembly by showing that there was no emergency justifying it.

Moreover, even imminent danger cannot justify resort to prohibition of these functions essential to effective democracy, unless the evil apprehended is relatively serious. Prohibition of free speech and assembly is a measure so stringent that it would be inappropriate as the means for averting a relatively trivial harm to society. A police measure may be unconstitutional merely because the remedy, although effective as means of protection, is unduly harsh or oppressive. Thus, a state might, in the exercise of its police power, make any trespass upon the land of another a crime, regardless of the results or of the intent or purpose of the trespasser. It might, also, punish an attempt, a conspiracy, or an incitement to commit the trespass. But it is hardly conceivable that this court would hold constitutional a statute which punished as a felony the mere voluntary assembly with a society formed to teach that pedestrians had the moral right to cross uninclosed, unposted, waste lands and to advocate their doing so, even if there was imminent danger that advocacy would lead to a trespass. The fact that speech is likely to result in some violence or in destruction of property is not enough to justify its suppression. There must be the probability of serious injury to the State. Among free men, the deterrents ordinarily to be applied to prevent crime are education and punishment for violations of the law, not abridgment of the rights of free speech and assembly.

. . .

[Brandeis concurred rather than dissented only because Whitney did not raise these issues at trial.]

Near v. Minnesota, 283 U.S. 697 (1931)

Jay Near was the owner of the Saturday Press, *a newspaper published in Minneapolis, Minnesota. In his paper, Near combined anti-Semitic diatribes with attacks on official corruption. The November 19, 1927, edition of the* Saturday Press *asserted, "There have been too many men in this city and especially those in official life, who HAVE been taking orders and suggestions from JEW GANGSTERS, therefore we HAVE Jew Gangsters, practically ruling Minneapolis." Partly in response to the* Saturday Press, *Minnesota passed a law permitting local officials to abate as a nuisance any "malicious, scandalous and defamatory newspaper, magazine or other periodical." Once a newspaper was declared a nuisance, further publication of scandalous material could be punished as contempt of court. Almost immediately after this law was passed, local officials in Minneapolis brought an action seeking to prevent further publication of the* Saturday Press. *The local trial court ruled that the* Press *was a "malicious, scandalous and defamatory newspaper" and declared the journal a public nuisance. After the Supreme Court of Minnesota sustained that verdict, Near, with the financial and legal help of the more prestigious* Chicago Tribune, *appealed to the Supreme Court of the United States.*[39]

The Supreme Court declared by a 5–4 vote that Jay Near had a constitutional right to continue to publish the Saturday Press. *Chief Justice Hughes declared that the injunction against further publication violated the longstanding First Amendment ban on prior restraints. His opinion is cited today for the proposition that prior restraints on free speech are almost never constitutional. Would Hughes have agreed with this interpretation of his opinion? Notice that he emphasized that under Minnesota law, Minnesota officials were not obligated to prove Near's publications false. Suppose, as Justice Butler claimed, that Near's statements had been proven false. Would* Near *have been decided the same way? Should* Near *have been decided the same way? What is the special harm of prior restraints? Was Hughes correct when he asserted that subsequent libel suits provide sufficient protections for public figures who are accused of misdeeds? Was Justice Butler right to distinguish this case from the censorship practices in England?*

CHIEF JUSTICE HUGHES delivered the opinion of the Court.

. . .

The question is whether a statute authorizing such proceedings in restraint of publication is consistent with the conception of the liberty of the press as historically conceived and guaranteed. In determining the extent of the constitutional protection, it has been generally, if not universally, considered that it is the chief purpose of the guaranty to prevent previous restraints upon publication. The struggle in England, directed against the legislative power of the licenser, resulted in renunciation of the censorship of the press. The liberty deemed to be established was thus described by Blackstone:

> The liberty of the press is indeed essential to the nature of a free state; but this consists in laying no *previous* restraints upon publications, and not in freedom from censure for criminal matter when published. Every freeman has an undoubted right to lay what sentiments he pleases before the public; to forbid this is to destroy the freedom of the press; but if he publishes what is improper, mischievous or illegal, he must take the consequence of his own temerity.

. . . The criticism upon Blackstone's statement has not been because immunity from previous restraint upon publication has not been regarded as deserving of special emphasis, but chiefly because that immunity cannot be deemed to exhaust the conception of the liberty guaranteed by state and federal constitutions. . . . In the present case, we have no occasion to inquire as to the permissible scope of subsequent punishment. For whatever wrong the appellant has committed or

39. For a very readable and colorful account of the times and trials of Jay Near and *Near v. Minnesota*, see Fred W. Friendly, *Minnesota Rag: Corruption, Yellow Journalism, and the Case that Saved the Freedom of the Press* (New York: Vintage Books, 1982).

may commit by his publications the State appropriately affords both public and private redress by its libel laws. . . . [T]he statute in question does not deal with punishments; it provides for no punishment, except in case of contempt for violation of the court's order, but for suppression and injunction, that is, for restraint upon publication.

The objection has also been made that the principle as to immunity from previous restraint is stated too broadly, if every such restraint is deemed to be prohibited. That is undoubtedly true; the protection even as to previous restraint is not absolutely unlimited. But the limitation has been recognized only in exceptional cases. . . . No one would question but that a government might prevent actual obstruction to its recruiting service or the publication of the sailing dates of transports or the number and location of troops. . . . These limitations are not applicable here. . . .

The exceptional nature of its limitations places in a strong light the general conception that liberty of the press, historically considered and taken up by the Federal Constitution, has meant, principally, although not exclusively, immunity from previous restraints or censorship. The conception of the liberty of the press in this country had broadened with the exigencies of the colonial period and with the efforts to secure freedom from oppressive administration. That liberty was especially cherished for the immunity it afforded from previous restraint of the publication of censure of public officers and charges of official misconduct. . . .

. . .

The fact that, for approximately one hundred and fifty years, there has been almost an entire absence of attempts to impose previous restraints upon publications relating to the malfeasance of public officers is significant of the deep-seated conviction that such restraints would violate constitutional right. Public officers, whose character and conduct remain open to debate and free discussion in the press, find their remedies for false accusations in actions under libel laws providing for redress and punishment, and not in proceedings to restrain the publication of newspapers and periodicals. The general principle that the constitutional guaranty of the liberty of the press gives immunity from previous restraints has been approved in many decisions under the provisions of state constitutions.

The importance of this immunity has not lessened. While reckless assaults upon public men, and efforts to bring obloquy upon those who are endeavoring faithfully to discharge official duties, exert a baleful influence and deserve the severest condemnation in public opinion, it cannot be said that this abuse is greater, and it is believed to be less, than that which characterized the period in which our institutions took shape. Meanwhile, the administration of government has become more complex, the opportunities for malfeasance and corruption have multiplied, crime has grown to most serious proportions, and the danger of its protection by unfaithful officials and of the impairment of the fundamental security of life and property by criminal alliances and official neglect, emphasizes the primary need of a vigilant and courageous press, especially in great cities.

The fact that the liberty of the press may be abused by miscreant purveyors of scandal does not make any the less necessary the immunity of the press from previous restraint in dealing with official misconduct. Subsequent punishment for such abuses as may exist is the appropriate remedy consistent with constitutional privilege.

. . .

JUSTICE BUTLER (with JUSTICE VAN DEVANTER, JUSTICE McREYNOLDS, and JUSTICE SUTHERLAND), dissenting.

. . .

The record shows, and it is conceded, that defendants' regular business was the publication of malicious, scandalous and defamatory articles concerning the principal public officers, leading newspapers of the city, many private persons and the Jewish race. It also shows that it was their purpose at all hazards to continue to carry on the business. In every edition, slanderous and defamatory matter predominates to the practical exclusion of all else. Many of the statements are so highly improbable as to compel a finding that they are false. The articles themselves show malice.

. . .

The Act was passed in the exertion of the State's power of police, and this court is, by well established rule, required to assume, until the contrary is clearly made to appear, that there exists in Minnesota a state of affairs that justifies this measure for the preservation of the peace and good order of the State.

. . .

The Minnesota statute does not operate as a *previous* restraint on publication within the proper meaning of that phrase. It does not authorize administrative control in advance such as was formerly exercised by the licensers and censors but prescribes a remedy to be enforced by a suit in equity. In this case, there was previous publication made in the course of the business of regularly producing malicious, scandalous and defamatory periodicals. The business and publications unquestionably constitute an abuse of the right of free press. The statute denounces the things done as a nuisance on the ground, as stated by the state supreme court, that they threaten morals, peace and good order. There is no question of the power of the State to denounce such transgressions....

There is nothing in the statute purporting to prohibit publications that have not been adjudged to constitute a nuisance. It is fanciful to suggest similarity between the granting or enforcement of the decree authorized by this statute to prevent *further* publication of malicious, scandalous and defamatory articles and the *previous* restraint upon the press by licensers as referred to by Blackstone and described in the history of the times to which he alludes....

B. Voting

Immigration fostered fierce contests over voting rights. Many prominent Americans insisted that stern measures were needed to prevent the foreign born from introducing "un-American" ideas into the polity.

Table 7-7 Selection of U.S. Supreme Court Cases Reviewing State and Federal Laws Regulating Elections

Case	Vote	Outcome	Decision
Minor v. Happersett, 88 U.S. 162 (1875)	9–0	Upheld	State restriction of suffrage to male citizens is constitutional
Ex parte Yarbrough, 110 U.S. 651 (1884)	9–0	Upheld	Congress has power to regulate fraud or violence against voters in federal elections
Davis v. Beason, 133 U.S. 333 (1890)	8–0	Upheld	Territorial regulation that bars individuals who practiced or advocated the crime of bigamy from voting is constitutional
Williams v. Mississippi, 170 U.S. 213 (1898)	8–0	Upheld	A literacy test does not on its face impose a racially discriminatory qualification for voting
Mason v. Missouri, 179 U.S. 328 (1900)	9–0	Upheld	States may change voter registration laws and adopt different voter registration laws for different parts of the state without violating equal protection requirements
Newberry v. United States, 256 U.S. 232 (1921)	8–1	Struck down	Congress has no power to regulate state primaries
Grovey v. Townsend, 295 U.S. 45 (1935)	9–0	Upheld	The federal Constitution did not prohibit the Texas Democratic Party from organizing a "whites only" primary election
Breedlove v. Suttles, 302 U.S. 277 (1937)	9–0	Upheld	Poll taxes do not interfere with any federal constitutional privilege, and reasonable exemptions from a poll tax are consistent with equal protection requirements
United States v. Classic, 313 U.S. 299 (1941)	6–3	Struck down	The right of qualified voters to vote in a primary and have their votes counted is secured by the federal Constitution when state law makes the primary election an integral part of the procedure for choosing representatives

(Continued)

Table 7-7 *(Continued)*

Case	Vote	Outcome	Decision
Smith v. Allwright, 321 U.S. 649 (1944)	9–0	Struck down	Party primaries are part of the machinery of state government, and racially exclusive "white primaries" violate equal protection requirements
Mills v. Alabama, 384 U.S. 214 (1966)	9–0	Struck down	States may not prohibit "electioneering," as applied to newspaper editorial, on Election Day
Katzenbach v. Morgan, 384 U.S. 641 (1966)	7–2	Upheld	Congress may ban the use of literacy tests as a voter qualification even though the Supreme Court had not found such tests to be a violation of equal protection requirements
Williams v. Rhodes, 393 U.S. 23 (1968)	6–3	Struck down	Complex and high hurdles for new and minor parties to be listed on the ballot violate the equal protection clause
Kramer v. Union Free School District No. 15, 395 U.S. 621 (1969)	6–3	Struck down	Restriction of eligible voters in school board elections to real property owners or parents of schoolchildren violates the equal protection clause
Oregon v. Mitchell, 400 U.S. 112 (1970)	5–4	Struck down	Congress may impose an eighteen-year minimum age requirement for federal elections but has no authority to set a minimum voting age for state and local elections
Buckley v. Valeo, 424 U.S. 1 (1976)	7–1	Struck down	Congress may restrict individual contributions to campaigns but may not limit independent expenditures
Brown v. Hartlage, 456 U.S. 45 (1982)	9–0	Struck down	States may not prohibit candidates from making campaign promises as a means of preventing electoral corruption
Federal Election Commission v. Conservative Political Action Committee, 470 U.S. 480 (1985)	7–2	Struck down	Congress may not limit the amount of expenditures by an independent political action committee (PAC) in support of candidates
Burson v. Freeman, 504 U.S. 191 (1992)	5–3	Upheld	State may create a no-campaigning buffer zone around polling places
U.S. Term Limits v. Thornton, 514 U.S. 779 (1995)	5–4	Struck down	States may not impose term limits on incumbent members of Congress
Republican Party of Minnesota v. White, 536 U.S. 765 (2002)	5–4	Struck down	States may not prohibit judicial candidates from discussing issues that might come before the court
McConnell v. Federal Election Commission, 540 U.S. 93 (2003)	5–4	Upheld	Congress may regulate donations to political parties and may regulate corporate campaign expenditures close to primary and general elections
Citizens United v. Federal Election Commission, 558 U.S. 50 (2010)	5–4	Struck down	Congress may not impose a broad ban on corporate entities spending general funds on "electioneering communications"

In an essay entitled "The Failure of Universal Suffrage," Francis Parkman asserted, "When extensive districts and, notably, large portions of populous cities are filled by masses of imported ignorance and hereditary ineptitude, the whole ferments together till the evil grows insufferable."[40] Other Americans insisted that all persons in a democracy were entitled to cast ballots. John Martin Luther Babcock declared, "The basis of the right of suffrage [is that] in the broad realm of natural rights, one man is essentially as good as another."[41] Proponents of restricted suffrage proposed voter registration laws, literacy tests, and the increased use of party primaries for fostering a more intelligent (and, in the South, a white) electorate. Many proponents of women's suffrage claimed that giving women the vote was a necessary means to counteract the influence of foreign-born voters and voters of color.

The Republican Era witnessed increased regulation of the electoral process. Legislatures required the secret ballot, imposed limits on campaign finance, and prohibited fusion (the practice of two parties nominating the same candidate in order to have that candidate mentioned twice on the ballot). Some reforms were aimed at restricting and regulating voter participation. Others reflected Progressive antipathy to political parties and political machines. Many states and communities adopted the secret, or "Australian," ballot. Reformers believed that secret ballots reduced corrupt party influence on voters and required that the individual voter demonstrate a certain degree of intelligence.

IX. Equality

MAJOR DEVELOPMENTS

- Attacks on administrative discretion that might lead to the unequal application of the laws
- The birth of Jim Crow and the NAACP
- Women gain the right to vote but dispute whether to pursue an equal rights amendment

Americans in the Republican Era tested the meaning of both the new equal protection clause in the federal Constitution and the inherited equal protection clauses in state constitutions. White southerners adopted Jim Crow policies that rigidly segregated persons by race. Women demanded the right to vote and sit on juries. Employers insisted that minimum wage laws gave their employees special advantages in the bargaining process. Other businesses complained that laws granting government bureaucrats discretion to determine whether businesses were upholding safety and other regulations denied equality under law. Native Americans explored whether various provisions in the post–Civil War Amendments changed their constitutional status.

The success of equality claims varied by forum and issue. Federal courts were generally unsympathetic to claims that persons had been denied equal protection of the laws. Justice Oliver Wendell Holmes, Jr., in *Buck v. Bell* (1927) described equal protection as the "last resort" for desperate litigators. The justices sustained racial segregation, declared that the Fourteenth Amendment did not make Native American citizens, gave no constitutional rights to women, and generally rejected equal protection claims brought by those who objected to state regulations or bureaucratic decisions. Federal courts did prove somewhat more sympathetic to African American rights toward the end of the Republican Era and were far more willing to hear due process attacks on state regulations. Other constitutional decision makers were more sympathetic to a broad array of equal protection claims. While courts in the southern states sustained Jim Crow legislation, some northern state courts ruled that school districts could not overtly segregate by race. The Nineteenth Amendment granted women the right to vote, and some state courts gave women the right to sit on juries. The Dawes Act declared that Native Americans who left their tribes were citizens of the United States. Many state court decisions found that laws granting too much bureaucratic discretion were inconsistent with state constitutional commitments to equality under law.

A. Equality Under Law

Government efforts to regulate an increasingly industrial state strained existing notions of equality under law. Opponents of labor regulations claimed

40. Francis Parkman, "The Failure of Universal Suffrage," *North American Review* 127 (July–Aug. 1888): 1–20.

41. John Martin Luther Babcock, *The Right of the Ballot: A Reply to Francis Parkman and Others Who Have Asserted "The Failure of Universal Suffrage"* (Boston: Press of John Wilson & Son, 1879), 8.

that such measures were class legislation that favored employees at the expense of employers. The legislative habit of passing special legislation that provided benefits for specific persons or businesses often violated state constitutional provisions specifically designed to limit or eradicate that practice.

Administrative discretion provided another challenge to inherited notions of equality under law. State governments at the turn of the century increased the number of civil servants and other officials with the authority to determine whether businesses were operating safely and in a manner consistent with legal standards. Many persons complained that these standards permitted arbitrary and capricious treatment in violation of constitutional commitments to equality. The Supreme Court in both *Barbier v. Connolly* (1884) and *Yick Wo v. Hopkins* (1886) insisted that bureaucratic discretion uncabined by clear legal standards was unconstitutional. Justice Matthews's opinion in *Yick Wo* asserted, "The very idea that one man may be compelled to hold his life, or the means of living, or any material right essential to the enjoyment of life, at the mere will of another, seems to be intolerable in any country where freedom prevails, as being the essence of slavery itself." State courts expressed similar concern with bureaucratic discretion. *Mayor and City Council of Baltimore v. Radecke* (MD 1878) declared unconstitutional a law that permitted the mayor to rescind at will permits for steam engines, because the local ordinance "lays down no *rules* by which its *impartial execution* can be secured or partiality and oppression prevented."[42]

B. Race

Reconstruction efforts to secure racial equality collapsed during the first half of the Republican Era. Republican administrations made some effort to secure African American voting rights in the late 1870s and 1880s. Nevertheless, voting laws were too weak and federal enforcement too sporadic to have any substantial effect on African American voting. Republicans made one last-ditch effort during 1889–1890 to pass a stronger voting rights act. That effort failed. Three years later, after the Democrats regained control of the House of Representatives, Congress repealed Reconstruction Era laws requiring federal supervision of elections.

The ongoing federal retreat on Reconstruction emboldened southern champions of white supremacy. Southern constitutional conventions in the late 1890s and early decades of the twentieth century aggressively sought to marginalize persons of color. The keynote speaker at the Alabama Constitutional Convention of 1901 bluntly declared that the purpose of the new state constitution was "within the limits imposed by the Federal Constitution, to establish white supremacy in this State."[43] Such Supreme Court decisions as *Plessy v. Ferguson* (1896) and such state court decisions as *Ratcliffe v. Beale* (MS 1896) indicated that justices had no intention of interfering with race relations in the South. The Supreme Court in *Giles v. Harris* (1903) abandoned all efforts to ensure racial equality in this region.

Defenders of Jim Crow often justified their race-based decision making by differentiating between what they claimed were natural distinctions among the races and inappropriate acts of discrimination against particular races. Constitutional decision makers insisted that racial discriminations violated the Fourteenth Amendment. When declaring unconstitutional a law prohibiting persons of color from sitting on juries, the Supreme Court in *Strauder v. West Virginia* (1879) asserted that the post–Civil War Constitution required "that the law in the States shall be the same for the black as for the white; that all persons, whether colored or white, shall stand equal before the laws of the States." Most constitutional commentators and decision makers believed, however, that laws reflecting "real" differences between the races were in the public interest.

The modern civil rights movement was born in the first decades of the twentieth century. In 1905, W. E. B. DuBois and William Monroe Trotter founded the Niagara Movement. The Niagara Declaration of Principles stated,

> Suffrage: . . . [W]e believe that this class of American citizens should protest emphatically and continually against the curtailment of their

42. *Mayor and City Council of Baltimore v. Radecke*, 49 Md. 217 (1878).

43. Julie Novkov, *Racial Union* (Ann Arbor: University of Michigan Press, 2009), 72.

political rights. We believe in manhood suffrage; we believe that no man is so good, intelligent or wealthy as to be entrusted wholly with the welfare of his neighbor.

Civil Liberty: We believe also in protest against the curtailment of our civil rights. All American citizens have the right to equal treatment in places of public entertainment according to their behavior and deserts.

Economic Opportunity: We especially complain against the denial of equal opportunities to us in economic life; in the rural districts of the South this amounts to peonage and virtual slavery; all over the South it tends to crush labor and small business enterprises; and everywhere American prejudice, helped often by iniquitous laws, is making it more difficult for Negro-Americans to earn a decent living.

Education: Common school education should be free to all American children and compulsory. High school training should be adequately provided for all, and college training should be the monopoly of no class or race in any section of our common country. We believe that, in defense of our own institutions, the United States should aid common school education, particularly in the South, and we especially recommend concerted agitation to this end. We urge an increase in public high school facilities in the South, where the Negro-Americans are almost wholly without such provisions. We favor well-equipped trade and technical schools for the training of artisans, and the need of adequate and liberal endowment for a few institutions of higher education must be patent to sincere well-wishers of the race.

Courts: We demand upright judges in courts, juries selected without discrimination on account of color and the same measure of punishment and the same efforts at reformation for black as for white offenders. We need orphanages and farm schools for dependent children, juvenile reformatories for delinquents, and the abolition of the dehumanizing convict-lease system.[44]

44. W. E. B. DuBois, "Declaration of Principles," in *African American Political Thought, 1890–1930: Washington, DuBois, Garvey, and Randolph*, ed. Cary D. Wintz (Armonk, NY: M. E. Sharpe, 1996), 103–04.

Between 1909 and 1911 the Niagara Movement was reconstituted as the NAACP. The mission statement of that group declared that the NAACP would "promote equality of rights and eradicate caste or race prejudice among the citizens of the United States; advance the interest of colored citizens; secure for them impartial suffrage; and increase their opportunities for securing justice in the courts, education for the children, employment according to their ability and complete equality before law."[45] NAACP litigation campaigns and greater elite support for pruning the excesses of Jim Crow help explain why the Supreme Court became more receptive to constitutional claims raised by African Americans in the last decades of the Republican Era. The justices from 1911 to 1932 declared unconstitutional peonage laws that essentially forced African Americans to remain with their present employers (*Bailey v. Alabama* [1911], *United States v. Reynolds* [1914]), struck down laws mandating residential segregation (*Buchanan v. Warley* [1917]), put some teeth into the concept of "separate but equal" (*McCabe v. Atchison, Topeka & Santa Fe Railway Company* [1914]), and voided some state restrictions on African American voting (*Guinn and Beal v. United States* [1915]). These decisions mostly influenced American race relations at the margins. Nevertheless, both the institutional and precedential foundations for the modern civil rights movement were in place when Franklin Delano Roosevelt became president.

Plessy v. Ferguson, 163 U.S. 537 (1896)

Homer Plessy was a person of color who on June 7, 1892, purchased a first-class ticket on the East Louisiana Railway to travel from New Orleans to Covington, Louisiana. Plessy sat down in a car reserved for white persons only. After refusing to obey the conductor's order to move, Plessy was removed from the train and arrested for violating state segregation laws. The Louisiana state legislature in 1890 had decreed "that all railway companies carrying passengers in their coaches in this state, shall provide equal but separate accommodations for the white, and colored races" and that "any passenger insisting on going into a coach or compartment to which by race he does not belong, shall be liable to a fine of twenty-five dollars, or in

45. "The N.A.A.C.P.," *Crisis* 2 (1911): 193.

lieu thereof to imprisonment for a period of not more than twenty days in the parish prison." A trial court convicted Plessy, and that conviction was sustained by the Supreme Court of Louisiana. Plessy appealed to the Supreme Court of the United States.

Plessy v. Ferguson *is an early example of a test case. Homer Plessy did not act spontaneously on June 7. The Committee of Citizens, a group of prominent African Americans in New Orleans, recruited Plessy to challenge the constitutionality of early segregation laws. Plessy was chosen because he had only one great-grandparent who was a person of color and could be identified as a person of color only by acquaintances. Given his complexion, Plessy would have been allowed to occupy the car reserved for white persons had the East Louisiana Railway not cooperated with the Committee of Citizens in bringing the test case. Eager to overturn the Louisiana law and similar ones being passed in the Jim Crow South, the Committee of Citizens recruited Albion Tourgee, a prominent Republican journalist and lawyer, to argue its case before the Supreme Court.*[46]

The Supreme Court rejected Plessy's appeal by a 7–1 vote. Justice Brown's majority opinion declared that racial segregation was a reasonable exercise of the police power. Compare the majority opinion in Plessy *to the opinions in* Lochner v. New York *(1905). Was the judicial majority in* Plessy *more deferential to the state legislature than was the judicial majority in* Lochner, *or were the same standards applied in both the race and the contract cases? Notice the majority's assumption that race is a fixed category that legislation is "powerless" to change. What was the point of that assertion? Louisiana was not attempting to force integration, but to mandate segregation.*

Justice Harlan's dissent is most noted for the claim, "There is no caste here. Our constitution is color-blind, and neither knows nor tolerates classes among citizens." Many contemporary Americans cite this claim when asserting that affirmative action programs are unconstitutional. Others insist that such assertions read Harlan out of context. Based on your reading of the dissent, which reading do you think is correct? Consider in this context two other Harlan opinions issued shortly after Plessy. *In* Cumming v. Richmond County Board of Education *(1899) a unanimous Supreme Court found no problems with a local school board that in a financial crisis chose to close the high school for students of color while keeping open the high school for white students. After noting that the plaintiffs in the case had not challenged the segregation laws but merely the allocation of funds to segregated schools, Harlan's opinion stated,*

> *The board had before it the question whether it should maintain, under its control, a high school for about 60 colored children or withhold the benefits of education in primary schools from 300 children of the same race. It was impossible, the board believed, to give educational facilities to the 300 colored children who were unprovided for, if it maintained a separate school for the 60 children who wished to have a high-school education. Its decision was in the interest of the greater number of colored children, leaving the smaller number to obtain a high-school education in existing private institutions at an expense not beyond that incurred in the high school discontinued by the board.*

In Berea College v. Commonwealth of Kentucky *(1908) a judicial majority ruled that Kentucky could prohibit any association incorporated by the state from "teach[ing] white and negro children in a private school at the same time and place." Justice Harlan was the sole dissenter. He declared,*

> *The capacity to impart instruction to others is given by the Almighty for beneficent purposes; and its use may not be forbidden or interfered with by government,—certainly not, unless such instruction is, in its nature, harmful to the public morals or imperils the public safety. The right to impart instruction, harmless in itself or beneficial to those who receive it, is a substantial right of property,—especially, where the services are rendered for compensation. But even if such right be not strictly a property right, it is, beyond question, part of one's liberty as guaranteed against hostile state action by the Constitution of the United States. . . . If pupils, of whatever race,—certainly, if they be citizens,—choose, with the consent of their parents, or voluntarily, to sit together in a private institution of learning while receiving instruction which is not in its nature harmful or dangerous to the public, no government, whether Federal or state, can legally forbid their coming together, or being together temporarily, for such an innocent purpose.*

Harlan in both Cumming *and* Berea College *asserted that the constitutionality of segregated schools was not an issue*

46. For a good case study of the *Plessy* litigation, see Charles A. Lofgren, *The* Plessy *Case: A Legal Historical Interpretation* (New York: Oxford University Press, 1987).

in these cases. Did his dissent in Plessy *commit him to declaring such measures unconstitutional in related cases? Does Harlan's refusal to commit on this issue in subsequent cases suggest that he regarded school segregation as an open question, perhaps because he may have thought the police powers case stronger?*

Many years later, at a memorial service for Justice Harlan, Justice Brown recanted his original opinion in Plessy.[47]

JUSTICE BROWN delivered the opinion of the court.

. . .

That [the Louisiana law] does not conflict with the thirteenth amendment . . . is too clear for argument. Slavery implies involuntary servitude,—a state of bondage; the ownership of mankind as a chattel, or, at least, the control of the labor and services of one man for the benefit of another, and the absence of a legal right to the disposal of his own person, property, and services. . . .

A statute which implies merely a legal distinction between the white and colored races—a distinction which is founded in the color of the two races, and which must always exist so long as white men are distinguished from the other race by color—has no tendency to destroy the legal equality of the two races, or re-establish a state of involuntary servitude. . . .

. . .

. . . The object of the [Fourteenth] amendment was undoubtedly to enforce the absolute equality of the two races before the law, but, in the nature of things, it could not have been intended to abolish distinctions based upon color, or to enforce social, as distinguished from political, equality, or a commingling of the two races upon terms unsatisfactory to either. Laws permitting, and even requiring, their separation, in places where they are liable to be brought into contact, do not necessarily imply the inferiority of either race to the other, and have been generally, if not universally, recognized as within the competency of the state legislatures in the exercise of their police power. The most common instance of this is connected with the establishment of separate schools for white and colored children, which have been held to be a valid exercise of the legislative power even by courts of states where the political rights of the colored race have been longest and most earnestly enforced.

. . .

It is claimed by the plaintiff in error that, in a mixed community, the reputation of belonging to the dominant race, in this instance the white race, is "property," in the same sense that a right of action or of inheritance is property. Conceding this to be so, for the purposes of this case, we are unable to see how this statute deprives him of, or in any way affects his right to, such property. If he be a white man, and assigned to a colored coach, he may have his action for damages against the company for being deprived of his so-called "property." Upon the other hand, if he be a colored man, and be so assigned, he has been deprived of no property, since he is not lawfully entitled to the reputation of being a white man.

In this connection, it is also suggested by the learned counsel for the plaintiff in error that the same argument that will justify the state legislature in requiring railways to provide separate accommodations for the two races will also authorize them to require separate cars to be provided for people whose hair is of a certain color, or who are aliens, or who belong to certain nationalities, or to enact laws requiring colored people to walk upon one side of the street, and white people upon the other, or requiring white men's houses to be painted white, and colored men's black, or their vehicles or business signs to be of different colors, upon the theory that one side of the street is as good as the other, or that a house or vehicle of one color is as good as one of another color. The reply to all this is that every exercise of the police power must be reasonable, and extend only to such laws as are enacted in good faith for the promotion of the public good, and not for the annoyance or oppression of a particular class. . . .

So far, then, as a conflict with the fourteenth amendment is concerned, the case reduces itself to the question whether the statute of Louisiana is a reasonable regulation, and with respect to this there must necessarily be a large discretion on the part of the legislature. In determining the question of reasonableness, it is at liberty to act with reference to the established usages, customs, and traditions of the people, and with a view to the promotion of their comfort, and the preservation of the public peace and good order. Gauged by this standard, we cannot say

47. H. B. Brown, "The Dissenting Opinions of Mr. Justice Harlan," *American Law Review* 46 (1912): 321.

that a law which authorizes or even requires the separation of the two races in public conveyances is unreasonable, or more obnoxious to the fourteenth amendment than the acts of congress requiring separate schools for colored children in the District of Columbia, the constitutionality of which does not seem to have been questioned, or the corresponding acts of state legislatures.

We consider the underlying fallacy of the plaintiff's argument to consist in the assumption that the enforced separation of the two races stamps the colored race with a badge of inferiority. If this be so, it is not by reason of anything found in the act, but solely because the colored race chooses to put that construction upon it. . . . The argument . . . assumes that social prejudices may be overcome by legislation, and that equal rights cannot be secured to the negro except by an enforced commingling of the two races. We cannot accept this proposition. If the two races are to meet upon terms of social equality, it must be the result of natural affinities, a mutual appreciation of each other's merits, and a voluntary consent of individuals. . . . Legislation is powerless to eradicate racial instincts, or to abolish distinctions based upon physical differences, and the attempt to do so can only result in accentuating the difficulties of the present situation. If the civil and political rights of both races be equal, one cannot be inferior to the other civilly or politically. If one race be inferior to the other socially, the constitution of the United States cannot put them upon the same plane.

. . .

JUSTICE BREWER did not hear the argument or participate in the decision of this case.

JUSTICE HARLAN, dissenting.

In respect of civil rights, common to all citizens, the constitution of the United States does not, I think, permit any public authority to know the race of those entitled to be protected in the enjoyment of such rights. . . . Indeed, such legislation as that here in question is inconsistent not only with that equality of rights which pertains to citizenship, national and state, but with the personal liberty enjoyed by every one within the United States.

. . .

. . . Every one knows that the statute in question had its origin in the purpose, not so much to exclude white persons from railroad cars occupied by blacks, as to exclude colored people from coaches occupied by or assigned to white persons. . . . No one would be so wanting in candor as to assert the contrary. . . .

. . . If a state can prescribe, as a rule of civil conduct, that whites and blacks shall not travel as passengers in the same railroad coach, why may it not so regulate the use of the streets of its cities and towns as to compel white citizens to keep on one side of a street, and black citizens to keep on the other? Why may it not, upon like grounds, punish whites and blacks who ride together in street cars or in open vehicles on a public road or street? Why may it not require sheriffs to assign whites to one side of a court room, and blacks to the other? And why may it not also prohibit the commingling of the two races in the galleries of legislative halls or in public assemblages convened for the consideration of the political questions of the day? Further, if this statute of Louisiana is consistent with the personal liberty of citizens, why may not the state require the separation in railroad coaches of native and naturalized citizens of the United States, or of Protestants and Roman Catholics?

. . .

The white race deems itself to be the dominant race in this country. And so it is, in prestige, in achievements, in education, in wealth, and in power. So, I doubt not, it will continue to be for all time, if it remains true to its great heritage, and holds fast to the principles of constitutional liberty. But in view of the constitution, in the eye of the law, there is in this country no superior, dominant, ruling class of citizens. There is no caste here. Our constitution is color-blind, and neither knows nor tolerates classes among citizens. In respect of civil rights, all citizens are equal before the law. The humblest is the peer of the most powerful. The law regards man as man, and takes no account of his surroundings or of his color when his civil rights as guarantied by the supreme law of the land are involved. It is therefore to be regretted that this high tribunal, the final expositor of the fundamental law of the land, has reached the conclusion that it is competent for a state to regulate the enjoyment by citizens of their civil rights solely upon the basis of race.

In my opinion, the judgment this day rendered will, in time, prove to be quite as pernicious as the decision made by this tribunal in the *Dred Scott* Case.

. . . The present decision, it may well be apprehended, will not only stimulate aggressions, more or less brutal and irritating, upon the admitted rights of colored citizens, but will encourage the belief that it is possible, by means of state enactments, to defeat the beneficent purposes which the people of the United States had in view when they adopted the recent amendments of the constitution, by one of which the blacks of this country were made citizens of the United States and of the states in which they respectively reside, and whose privileges and immunities, as citizens, the states are forbidden to abridge. Sixty millions of whites are in no danger from the presence here of eight millions of blacks. The destinies of the two races, in this country, are indissolubly linked together, and the interests of both require that the common government of all shall not permit the seeds of race hate to be planted under the sanction of law. What can more certainly arouse race hate, what more certainly create and perpetuate a feeling of distrust between these races, than state enactments which, in fact, proceed on the ground that colored citizens are so inferior and degraded that they cannot be allowed to sit in public coaches occupied by white citizens? That, as all will admit, is the real meaning of such legislation as was enacted in Louisiana.

. . .

I am of opinion that the state of Louisiana is inconsistent with the personal liberty of citizens, white and black, in that state, and hostile to both the spirit and letter of the constitution of the United States. If laws of like character should be enacted in the several states of the Union, the effect would be in the highest degree mischievous. Slavery, as an institution tolerated by law, would, it is true, have disappeared from our country; but there would remain a power in the states, by sinister legislation, to interfere with the full enjoyment of the blessings of freedom, to regulate civil rights, common to all citizens, upon the basis of race, and to place in a condition of legal inferiority a large body of American citizens, now constituting a part of the political community, called the "People of the United States," for whom, and by whom through representatives, our government is administered. Such a system is inconsistent with the guaranty given by the constitution to each state of a republican form of government, and may be stricken down by congressional action, or by the courts in the discharge of their solemn duty to maintain the supreme law of the land, anything in the constitution or laws of any state to the contrary notwithstanding. . . .

John B. Knox, Address to the Alabama Constitutional Convention (1901)[48]

The Alabama Constitutional Convention of 1901 was one of many southern constitutional conventions that took place at the turn of the twentieth century. These conventions were devoted to promoting white supremacy, although delegates also considered other issues related to representation, state debts, industrialization, and various matters of more local interest. White supremacists in the South recognized that they could not pass laws that bluntly declared that persons of color could not vote. Nevertheless, such federal court decisions as Williams v. Mississippi *(1898) gave southerners confidence that measures designed to disenfranchise persons of color would pass judicial scrutiny as long as they did not rely explicitly on racial classifications.*

John B. Knox, a local attorney, was elected to preside over the Alabama Constitutional Convention. The following excerpt is from his initial address to the delegates. Both Knox and the resulting Alabama Constitution focused primarily on laws disenfranchising persons of color. Why did white supremacists rely so heavily on disenfranchisement as opposed to other racist measures? Why were they so confident that the Alabama Constitution would survive federal judicial review?

. . .

In my judgment, the people of Alabama have been called upon to face no more important situation than now confronts us, unless it be when they, in 1861, stirred by the momentous issue of impending conflict between the North and the South, were forced to decide whether they would remain in or withdraw from the Union.

Then, as now, the negro was the prominent factor in the issue.

. . .

And what is it that we want to do? Why it is within the limits imposed by the Federal Constitution, to establish white supremacy in this State.

48. Excerpt taken from John Barnett Knox, *Address of Hon. John B. Knox* (Montgomery, AL: Brown's Printing Co., 1901).

This is our problem, and we should be permitted to deal with it, unobstructed by outside influences, with a sense of our responsibilities as citizens and our duty to posterity.

. . .

. . . [W]e may congratulate ourselves that this sectional feeling which has served to impair the harmony of our common country, and to limit the power and retard the development of the greatest government on earth, is fast yielding to reason.

. . .

The Southern man knows the negro, and the negro knows him. The only conflict which has, or is ever likely to arise, springs from the effort of ill-advised friends in the North to confer upon him, without previous training or preparation, places of power and responsibility, for which he is wholly unfitted, either by capacity or experience.

. . .

But if we would have white supremacy, we must establish it by law—not by force or fraud. If you teach your boy that it is right to buy a vote, it is an easy step for him to learn to use money to bribe or corrupt officials or trustees of any class. If you teach your boy that it is right to steal votes, it is an easy step for him to believe that it is right to steal whatever he may need or greatly desire. The results of such an influence will enter every branch of society, it will reach your bank cashiers, and affect positions of trust in every department; it will ultimately enter your courts, and affect the administrations of justice.

. . .

Mississippi is the pioneer State in this movement. In addition to the payment of a poll tax, there it is provided that only those can vote who have been duly registered, and only those can register who can read, or understand when read to them, any clause in the Constitution. The decision as to who are sufficiently intelligent to meet the requirements of the understanding clause is exclusively in the hands of the registrars.

. . .

In Louisiana and North Carolina, the methods of relief adopted are substantially the same, and require, in addition to the poll tax clause, that the voter shall register in accordance with the provisions of the Constitution, and only those are authorized to register who are able to read and write any section of the Constitution in the English language, with the further proviso, that no male person who was, on January 1st, 1867, or at any time prior thereto, entitled to vote under the laws of any State in the United States, wherein he then resided, and no lineal descendant of any such person, shall be denied the right to register and vote at any election, by reason of his failure to possess the educational qualifications prescribed, provided he registers within the time limited by the terms of the Constitution. . . .

. . .

These provisions are justified in law and in morals, because it is said that the negro is not discriminated against on account of his race, but on account of his intellectual and moral condition. There is a difference, it is claimed with great force, between the uneducated white man and the ignorant negro. There is in the white man an inherited capacity for government, which is wholly wanting in the negro. Before the art of reading and writing was known, the ancestors of the Anglo-Saxon had established an orderly system of government, the basis in fact of the one under which we now live. That the negro on the other hand, is descended from a race lowest in intelligence and moral perceptions of all the races of men. . . .

As stated by Judge [Thomas] Cooley, the right of suffrage is not a natural right, because it exists where it is allowed to be exercised only for the good of the State—to say that those whose participation in the affairs of the State would endanger and imperil the good of the State have nevertheless, the right to participate, is not only folly in itself, but it is to set the individual above the State.

The election laws in Massachusetts contain substantially the same provisions as are embodied in the Constitutions of Louisiana and North Carolina just referred to. The election law of that State, as it stands today, provides that the voter must be able to read the Constitution of the Commonwealth in the English language, and to write his name, except that "no person who is prevented from reading and writing as aforesaid, by physical disability, or who had the right to vote on the first day of May in the year 1857, shall, if otherwise qualified, be deprived of the right to vote by reason of not being able so to read or write."

. . .

The exception in the Massachusetts law was, no doubt, directed against illiterate and incompetent immigrants, whereas the provisions in the Constitutions of Louisiana and North Carolina were directed against illiterate and incompetent negroes, as well as foreigners.

But it is beyond the province of courts . . . to inquire into the motives of the law-making power; their function is confined to ascertaining the meaning and effect of the law drawn in question. . . .

. . .

It has been urged in some quarters as a reason why this movement for a new Constitution should be defeated that we propose to adopt a suffrage plan which will offer to the negro an incentive to obtain an education, while the child of the white man will be without a like stimulus, because protected in his right to vote without regard to the density of his ignorance.

I do not understand that any delegate to the Convention is pledged to any such legislation. We are pledged, "not to deprive any white man of the right to vote," but this does not extend unless this Convention chooses to extend it beyond the right of voters now living. It is a question worthy of careful consideration, whether we would be warranted in pursuing any course which would have a tendency to condemn any part of our population to a condition of perpetual illiteracy. Provisions of the Constitution prescribing educational qualifications for voters as they affect those who now have no right to vote but in the course of time will acquire the right are wisely intended to serve not as a curse, but as a noble stimulus to the acquirement of an education and to a proper preparation for meeting and discharging the duties of a citizen. . . .

C. Gender

Women debated the next steps toward gender equality. Alice Paul and other members of the National Woman's Party insisted on the Blanket Amendment, a constitutional provision that would provide the same protection against gender discrimination as the Fourteenth Amendment provided against racial discrimination. Many Progressive women opposed this amendment, believing that women needed special protections in industry that might be declared unconstitutional if the Blanket Amendment were ratified. This schism remained vibrant long after the Republican Era ended.

Debates over the Blanket Amendment (1924)[49]

Shortly after the Nineteenth Amendment was ratified, the National Woman's Party drafted and several members of Congress proposed the Blanket Amendment. The original version of this proposal, later known as the Equal Rights Amendment, declared, "Men and women shall have Equal Rights throughout the United States and every place subject to its jurisdiction." The Blanket Amendment sparked a sharp controversy among women's groups. Many women favored tearing down all laws that discriminated between men and women. Women associated with the labor movement, however, insisted that elected officials should be free to pass legislation that provided special protections to women in the work force.

The August 1924 edition of Forum *presented a debate between two prominent feminist activists. Doris Stevens was a leader in the fight for women's suffrage and a founder of the National Woman's Party. Alice Hamilton was the first female professor of medicine at Harvard Medical School. On what points did Stevens and Hamilton agree? On what points did they disagree? Did they disagree on the consequences of the Blanket Amendment or on the principles embodied in the Blanket Amendment? Whose view would you have supported in 1924? Hamilton made more generalizations about women than did Stevens. How do you think these generalizations influenced her opinions? Do you believe that Hamilton would have taken a different position today? Would you?*

Doris Stevens, "Suffrage Does Not Give Equality"

. . .

When women finally got the right to vote, after seventy-five years of agitation in the United States, many good citizens sighed with relief and said, "Now that's over. The woman problem is disposed of." But was it? Exactly what do women want now? Just this. They want the same rights, in law and in custom, with which every man is now endowed through the accident of being born a male. . . .

There is not a single State in the Union in which men and women live under equal protection of the

49. "The Blanket Amendment—A Debate," *Forum* 72 (August 1924): 148.

law. There is not a State which does not in some respects still reflect toward women the attitude of either the old English Common Law or the Napoleonic Code. Woman is still conceived to be in subjection to, and under the control of the husband, if married, or of the male members of the family, if unmarried. In most of the States the father and mother have been made equal guardians of their children, but many of these States still deny the mother equal rights to the earnings and services of the children. . . . In forty States the husband owns the services of his wife in the home. In most of these States this means that the husband recovers the damages for the loss of her services to him. More than half the States do not permit women to serve on juries. Some legislators oppose jury service for women because of "moral hazard" of deliberating in a room with men. . . . In only a third of the States is prostitution a crime for the male as well as the female.

With the removal of all legal discriminations against women solely on account of sex, women will possess with men:

- Equal control of their children
- Equal control of their property
- Equal control of their earnings
- Equal right to make contracts
- Equal citizenship rights
- Equal inheritance rights
- Equal control of national, state, and local government
- Equal opportunities in schools and universities
- Equal opportunities in government service
- Equal opportunities in professions and industries
- Equal pay for equal work

. . .

. . . The amendment under consideration will in no way affect [helpful maternal legislation], for the simple reason that it is not based on sex, but upon the special need of a given group under certain circumstances. The same is true of widows' pensions. Such pensions are written for the benefit of the child, and are being given more and more to whichever parent of the child survives, widow or widower. . . . The final objection says: Grant political, social, and civil equality to women, but do not give equality to women in industry.

Here lies the heart of the whole controversy. It is not astonishing, but very intelligent indeed, that the battle should center on the point of woman's right to sell her labor on the same terms as man. For unless she is able equally to compete, to earn, to control, and to invest her money, unless in short woman's economic position is made more secure, certainly she cannot establish equality in fact. She will have won merely the shadow of power without essential and authentic substance.

Those who would limit only women to certain occupations and to certain restricted hours of work, base their program of discrimination on two points, the "moral hazard" to women and their biological inferiority. It is a philosophy which would penalize all women because some women are morally frail and physically weak. It asks women to set their pace with the weakest members of their sex. All men are not strong. Happily it has not occurred to society to limit the development of all men because some are weak. Would these protectionists be willing to say that because some men-members of the Cabinet had been suspected of moral frailty, no men should henceforth serve as Cabinet Ministers? . . .

. . . Women will be quite as sensible and adroit at avoiding work beyond their strength as men have been, once they have a free choice. What reason is there to believe that if tomorrow the whole industrial field were opened to women on the same terms as men, women would insist on doing the most menial tasks in the world, the most difficult, the tasks for which they are least fitted? . . .

. . .

But, it is argued, women are more easily exploited in industry than men. There are reasons for that outside of sex, not the least of which is the shocking neglect by men's labor organizations to organize women in their trades. . . . Protection is a delusion. Protection, no matter how benevolent in motive, unless applied alike to both sexes, amounts to actual penalization.

The Woman's Party is not an industrial organization and therefore does not propose to say whether workers shall work eight or four hours a day, or what wages shall be paid for such work; whether more leisure for the masses shall be got by legislation or unionism. In the best interests of women, it stands against restrictions which are not alike for both sexes, and which, therefore, constantly limit the scope of women's entry into the field of more desirable and better paid work. It believes that no human being, man or woman, should be exploited by industry. As firmly it believes that just so long as sex is made the artificial barrier to labor-selling, merit can never become the criterion of an applicant for a job. . . .

Alice Hamilton, "Protection for Women Workers"

. . . I belong to the group which holds that the right method is to repeal or alter one by one the laws that now hamper women or work injustice to them, and which opposes the constitutional amendment sponsored by the Woman's Party on the ground that it is too dangerously sweeping and all-inclusive. If no legislation is to be permitted except it apply to both sexes, we shall find it impossible to regulate by law the hours of wages or conditions of work of women and that would be, in my opinion, a harm far greater than the good that might be accomplished by removing certain antiquated abuses and injustices, which, bad as they are, do not injure nearly as many women as would be affected if all protective laws for working women were rendered unconstitutional.

. . .

We are told by members of the Women's Party that if we "free" the working woman, allow her to "compete on equal terms with men," her industrial status will at once be raised. She is supposed now to be suffering from the handicap of laws regulating her working conditions and hours of labor and longing to be rid of them. . . . Will anyone say that it is better to be a woman wage earner in Indiana where hours are practically unrestricted than in Ohio where a woman is sure of a nine-hour day and a six-day week? Is the textile worker in Rhode Island freer and happier than her sister in Massachusetts because she is not handicapped by legal restrictions, except a ten-hour day, while the Massachusetts woman may work only nine hours, and that not without a break, must have time for her noon-day meal, one day of rest in seven, no night work, and is not allowed to sell her work for less than a minimum living wage? . . . I should like to ask Kansas women if they envy the freedom of the women of Missouri and if they are ready to give up the laws which provide for an eight-hour day and a six-day week and a minimum wage and no night work.

One great source of weakness in the women's labor movement is the fact that so many of them are very young. . . .

. . . [Young women are] reckless of health and strength, individualistic, lacking the desire to organize, and quite powerless, without organization, to control in any way the conditions of their work.

On the other hand, the older women are as a rule even harder to bring together and more devoid of courage. They are usually mothers of families, widows, or deserted, or with sick or incompetent husbands; they carry the double burden of housework and factory work and they are recognized by all who know the labor world as the most hopeless material for the union organizer, incapable of rebellion, capable of endless submission. It is for these women that the laws prohibiting night work are most needed. The father of a family, if he works at night, can get his sleep during the day and yet have his meals served and his children cared for; the mother of a family cannot, even if her husband is there. . . .

. . .

The advocates of the blanket amendment say that they do not oppose laws designed to protect the child, that they are ready to favor protection of "pregnant persons" and "nursing persons." . . . But the damage done by an industrial poison may antedate pregnancy. Women who have worked in a lead trade before marriage and still more women who work in lead after marriage are more likely to be sterile than women who have worked in other trades; if they conceive they are less likely to carry the child to term; and if they do they are less likely to bear a living child and their living children are less able to survive the first weeks of life.

. . .

In Holland, I am told, the two sexes have recently been put on an equality in industry, not by taking privileges away from the women, but by extending them to the men. Holland is an old country, which has long been used to labor legislation. I cannot believe that we in the United States are nearing that point very fast, though I should like to think so. Meantime, until we reach it, I must, as a practical person, familiar with the great, inarticulate body of working women, reiterate my belief that they are largely helpless, that they have very special needs which unaided they cannot attain, and that it would be a crime for the country to pass legislation which would not only make it impossible to better their lot in the near future but would even deprive them of the small measure of protection they now enjoy.

X. Criminal Justice

MAJOR DEVELOPMENTS

- Birth of the modern exclusionary rule
- Nationalization of the right to counsel
- Supreme Court adopts more progressive notions of "cruel and unusual" punishments

Criminal justice in the Republican Era varied according to the crime and the criminal. Many constitutional decision makers who championed the freedom of contract defended the right of businesses to be free from invasive investigations. Current understandings of the Fourth Amendment and the exclusionary rule date from constitutional decisions protecting business enterprises from undue government regulation. During the first quarter of the twentieth century, proponents of civil liberties became concerned with how the police and courts treated persons of color and political dissidents. The National Popular Government League, a nonpartisan organization of leading Progressive elites, complained in 1920 about "continued violation of [the] Constitution and breaking of . . . Laws by the Department of Justice." These complaints included "wholesale arrests . . . without warrant or any process of law; men and women . . . jailed and held *incomunicado* without access of friends or counsel; homes . . . entered without search-warrant . . . workingmen and workingwomen suspected of radical views shamefully abused and maltreated."[50] The foundational decisions on modern habeas corpus and right to counsel were Progressive Era responses to racism and criminal justice in the South. Prohibition also influenced constitutional criminal procedure. American courts in the 1920s were overwhelmed with the novel constitutional claims that arose when police officers used new technologies for detecting bootleggers and bootleggers used such new inventions as the car in attempting to evade capture.

A. Due Process and Habeas Corpus

The combination of race, religion, habeas corpus, and due process was combustible in the early twentieth century. Leo Frank's conviction and death sentence for murder sparked a national controversy, as northern Jews mobilized in response to the "blood libel," the claim that Leo Frank engaged in a Jewish ritual when he allegedly murdered a Christian virgin in order to use her blood to make matzah for Passover. The Supreme Court majority was unmoved by claims that Frank was a victim of mob justice. Justice Pitney's majority opinion in *Frank v. Mangum* (1915) maintained that habeas corpus relief was appropriate only when a state court lacked jurisdiction and that the Georgia trial court that had convicted Frank had jurisdiction over murder. "Mere errors in point of law," he declared, "however serious, committed by a criminal court in the exercise of its jurisdiction over a case properly subject to its cognizance, cannot be reviewed by habeas corpus." Justice Holmes, who dissented in *Frank*, was more successful eight years later in *Moore v. Dempsey* (1923), in which his majority opinion insisted that a mob-dominated trial so lacked due process that the federal courts could oust the state court from control of the case.

Several cases in the 1920s suggested a developing bipartisan consensus on minimum due process standards. *Powell v. Alabama* (1932) ruled that persons had a due process right to counsel in all cases and a right to state-appointed counsel when necessary to achieve justice. *Connally v. General Construction Co.* (1926) declared unconstitutional a state law that required employers to pay "the current rate of per diem wages in the locality" on the ground that the measure was unconstitutionally vague. Justice Sutherland's opinion for the Court stated, "A statute which either forbids or requires the doing of an act in terms so vague that men of common intelligence must necessarily guess at its meaning and differ as to its application violates the first essential of due process of law."

B. Search and Seizure

The Supreme Court provided some constitutional protection for businesses against intrusive government investigations. *Boyd v. United States* (1886) invoked both the Fourth and Fifth Amendments when declaring unconstitutional a federal attorney's effort to compel a business to turn over its records. Relying heavily on *Entick v. Carrington* (1765), Justice Bradley's majority opinion asserted, "Any compulsory discovery by extorting the party's oath, or compelling the production of his private books and papers, to convict

50. National Popular Government League, *Report upon the Illegal Practices by the United States Department of Justice* (Washington, DC: National Popular Government League, 1920), 2–3.

him of crime, or to forfeit his property, is contrary to the principles of a free government." *Gouled v. United States* (1921) articulated what became known as the "mere evidence" rule. Government may use search warrants to look for stolen property or dangerous objects, but not to recover incriminating papers.

Federal courts provided less protection to criminal suspects when considering the constitutional status of inventions or technologies unknown to the common law. In *Carroll v. United States* (1925) the Supreme Court ruled that police officers could search cars without a warrant as long as they had probable cause for thinking that the occupants were transporting illegal goods. In justifying less cumbersome access to cars, Chief Justice Taft's majority opinion pointed out that, unlike a house, a "vehicle can be quickly moved out of the locality or jurisdiction in which the warrant must be sought." A 5–4 judicial majority in *Olmstead v. United States* (1928) determined that police could wiretap a person without first obtaining a warrant. Chief Justice Taft's majority opinion asserted that the protections of the Fourth Amendment did not apply because "there was no searching. There was no seizure. The evidence was secured by the use of the sense of hearing and that only. There was no entry of the houses or offices of the defendants." Justice Brandeis's historic dissenting opinion is the first effort to apply the Fourth Amendment to the realm of electronic surveillance by equating the amendment with "the right most valued by civilized men": the "right to be let alone."

The Progressive Era witnessed the birth of the modern exclusionary rule. That rule requires courts in criminal cases to exclude any evidence that the prosecution has obtained illegally or unconstitutionally. By the beginning of the New Deal, the federal government and a significant minority of states had adopted the exclusionary rule. The Supreme Court in *Weeks v. United States* (1914) explained that the federal government should not "execute the criminal laws of the country . . . by means of unlawful seizures and enforced confessions," since the fruits of such actions would themselves be tainted by lawlessness.

Most state courts did not follow the lead of the U.S. Supreme Court when interpreting the requirements of their constitutions. "Courts in the administration of the criminal law," *Gindrat v. People* (IL 1891) stated, "are not accustomed to be over-sensitive in regard to the sources from which evidence comes, and will avail themselves of all evidence that is competent and pertinent."[51] When criticizing the exclusionary rule in *People v. Defore* (NY 1926), Judge Cardozo bluntly described the exclusionary rule as mandating "the criminal is to go free because the constable has blundered."[52]

Weeks v. United States, 232 U.S. 383 (1914)

Fremont Weeks was arrested and charged with selling lottery tickets through the mail. After he was arrested at his place of work, both local police officers and a federal marshal entered his house without a warrant, searched his rooms, and seized various incriminating papers. Before the trial Weeks demanded that the police return his property. The federal district court denied that motion and permitted the property to be introduced at the criminal trial. Weeks was convicted, fined, and sentenced to a jail term. He immediately appealed to the U.S. Supreme Court.

The Supreme Court held that Weeks had been unconstitutionally convicted. Justice Day's unanimous opinion ruled that federal prosecutors could not introduce physical evidence at trial that had been obtained by an unconstitutional search. Weeks *is the first clear instance in which federal courts applied the exclusionary rule, the rule that unconstitutionally seized evidence may not be introduced at a criminal trial. What is the justification for that rule? What was the scope of that rule in 1914? Suppose that the police officers had returned the papers to Weeks but testified about their contents at trial. Would the Supreme Court have permitted that evidence?*

Weeks *is a Fifth Amendment case that limits the use of unconstitutionally seized evidence in federal trials. Justice Day made no effort to apply the decision to state criminal trials.*

JUSTICE DAY delivered the opinion of the court:

. . .

. . . The tendency of those who execute the criminal laws of the country to obtain conviction by means of unlawful seizures and enforced confessions, the latter often obtained after subjecting accused persons to unwarranted practices destructive of rights secured by the Federal Constitution, should find no sanction in the judgments of the courts, which are charged at all

51. *Gindrat v. Illinois*, 138 Ill. 103 (1891).
52. *People v. Defore*, 242 N.Y. 13 (1926).

times with the support of the Constitution, and to which people of all conditions have a right to appeal for the maintenance of such fundamental rights.

. . .

The case in the aspect in which we are dealing with it involves the right of the court in a criminal prosecution to retain for the purposes of evidence the letters and correspondence of the accused, seized in his house in his absence and without his authority, by a United States marshal holding no warrant for his arrest and none for the search of his premises. The accused, without awaiting his trial, made timely application to the court for an order for the return of these letters, as well or other property. This application was denied, the letters retained and put in evidence, after a further application at the beginning of the trial, both applications asserting the rights of the accused under the 4th and 5th Amendments to the Constitution. If letters and private documents can thus be seized and held and used in evidence against a citizen accused of an offense, the protection of the 4th Amendment, declaring his right to be secure against such searches and seizures, is of no value, and, so far as those thus placed are concerned, might as well be stricken from the Constitution. The efforts of the courts and their officials to bring the guilty to punishment, praiseworthy as they are, are not to be aided by the sacrifice of those great principles established by years of endeavor and suffering which have resulted in their embodiment in the fundamental law of the land. The United States marshal could only have invaded the house of the accused when armed with a warrant issued as required by the Constitution, upon sworn information, and describing with reasonable particularity the thing for which the search was to be made. Instead, he acted without sanction of law, doubtless prompted by the desire to bring further proof to the aid of the government, and under color of his office undertook to make a seizure of private papers in direct violation of the constitutional prohibition against such action. Under such circumstances, without sworn information and particular description, not even an order of court would have justified such procedure; much less was it within the authority of the United States marshal to thus invade the house and privacy of the accused.... To sanction such proceedings would be to affirm by judicial decision a manifest neglect, if not an open defiance, of the prohibitions of the Constitution, intended for the protection of the people against such unauthorized action.

. . .

We therefore reach the conclusion that the letters in question were taken from the house of the accused by an official of the United States, acting under color of his office, in direct violation of the constitutional rights of the defendant; that having made a seasonable application for their return, which was heard and passed upon by the court, there was involved in the order refusing the application a denial of the constitutional rights of the accused, and that the court should have restored these letters to the accused. In holding them and permitting their use upon the trial, we think prejudicial error was committed. As to the papers and property seized by the policemen, it does not appear that they acted under any claim of Federal authority such as would make the amendment applicable to such unauthorized seizures. The record shows that what they did by way of arrest and search and seizure was done before the finding of the indictment in the Federal court; under what supposed right or authority does not appear. What remedies the defendant may have against them we need not inquire, as the 4th Amendment is not directed to individual misconduct of such officials. Its limitations reach the Federal government and its agencies....

People v. Defore, 242 N.Y. 13 (1926)

John Defore was arrested by a police officer who believed that Defore had stolen an overcoat. The officer, who lacked either an arrest or a search warrant, searched the boardinghouse where Defore resided. The search revealed a blackjack, a weapon that was illegal under New York law. Defore was arrested and tried for possessing that weapon. His motion to have the weapon excluded was rejected, and he was convicted. Defore appealed that decision to the Court of Appeals of New York.

The New York Court of Appeals rejected Defore's appeal. Judge Cardozo insisted that New York law did not require illegally obtained evidence to be excluded at a criminal trial. Benjamin Cardozo was considered one of the most Progressive justices on the state bench. Why would a Progressive judge in the 1920s reject the exclusionary rule?

JUDGE CARDOZO delivered the opinion of the Court.

. . .

We hold with the defendant that the evidence against him was the outcome of a trespass. The officer might have been resisted, or sued for damages, or even prosecuted for oppression. . . . He was subject to removal or other discipline at the hands of his superiors. These consequences are undisputed. The defendant would add another. We must determine whether evidence of criminality, procured by an act of trespass, is to be rejected as incompetent for the misconduct of the trespasser.

. . . *Weeks v. United States* (1914) held that articles wrongfully seized by agents of the federal government should have been returned to the defendant or excluded as evidence, if a timely motion to compel return had been made before the trial. . . . There has been no blinking the consequences. The criminal is to go free because the constable has blundered.

The new doctrine has already met the scrutiny of courts of sister states. The decisions have been brought together for our guidance through the industry of counsel. In 45 states (exclusive of our own) the subject has been considered. Fourteen states have adopted the rule of the *Weeks* case either as there laid down or as subsequently broadened. Thirty-one have rejected it.

. . .

The federal rule as it stands is either too strict or too lax. A federal prosecutor may take no benefit from evidence collected through the trespass of a federal officer. The thought is that, in appropriating the results, he ratifies the means. . . . He does not have to be so scrupulous about evidence brought to him by others. How finely the line is drawn is seen when we recall that marshals in the service of the nation are on one side of it, and police in the service of the states on the other. The nation may keep what the servants of the states supply. . . . We must go farther or not so far. The professed object of the trespass rather than the official character of the trespasser should test the rights of government. . . . The incongruity of other tests gains emphasis from the facts of the case before us. The complainant, the owner of the overcoat, co-operated with the officer in the arrest and the attendant search. Their powers were equal, since the charge was petit larceny, a misdemeanor. If one spoke or acted for the state, so also did the other. A government would be disingenuous, if, in determining the use that should be made of evidence drawn from such a source, it drew a line between them. This would be true whether they had acted in concert or apart. We exalt form above substance when we hold that the use is made lawful because the intruder is without a badge of office. We break with precedent altogether when we press the prohibition farther.

. . .

We are confirmed in this conclusion when we reflect how far-reaching in its effect upon society the new consequences would be. The pettiest peace officer would have it in his power, through overzeal or indiscretion, to confer immunity upon an offender for crimes the most flagitious. A room is searched against the law, and the body of a murdered man is found. If the place of discovery may not be proved, the other circumstances may be insufficient to connect the defendant with the crime. The privacy of the home has been infringed, and the murderer goes free. Another search, once more against the law, discloses counterfeit money or the implements of forgery. The absence of a warrant means the freedom of the forger. Like instances can be multiplied. We may not subject society to these dangers until the Legislature has spoken with a clearer voice. . . .

Olmstead v. United States, 277 U.S. 438 (1928)

Federal agents suspected that Roy Olmstead was the leader of a multimillion-dollar conspiracy to import and sell intoxicating liquors in violation of federal prohibition laws. In order to gain the necessary evidence to arrest and convict Olmstead, federal agents tapped his home and office phones. These wiretaps enabled the agents to overhear conversations in which Olmstead and his confederates engaged in illegal business transactions and bribed local police officers in Seattle, Washington. After five months, Olmstead was arrested, tried, and convicted of violating federal laws against "unlawfully possessing, transporting and importing intoxicating liquors." Olmstead appealed this conviction to the U.S. Supreme Court on two grounds. First, he claimed that the admission of the wiretaps at trial violated his Fourth and Fifth Amendment rights. Second, he claimed that federal agents could not use at trial evidence gathered in ways that violated local laws. Since wiretapping was illegal in Washington, evidence gained by wiretapping could not be used in federal courts in Washington.

The Supreme Court by a 5–4 vote sustained Olmstead's conviction. Chief Justice Taft's majority opinion ruled that the Fourth and Fifth Amendments prohibited only physical searches. Taft also ruled that federal courts could admit evidence obtained by means that violated local laws. Both the Taft majority opinion and the Brandeis dissent examine original understandings and recent precedents. How does each interpret these legal sources? Who had the better argument? Olmstead *was the first major case on constitutional criminal procedure in which the more liberal justices on the Supreme Court offered a more expansive reading of constitutional rights than did the more conservative justices. What might explain that change?*

CHIEF JUSTICE TAFT delivered the opinion of the Court.

. . .

The well-known historical purpose of the Fourth Amendment, directed against general warrants and writs of assistance, was to prevent the use of governmental force to search a man's house, his person, his papers, and his effects, and to prevent their seizure against his will. . . .

. . .

The amendment itself shows that the search is to be of material things—the person, the house, his papers, or his effects. The description of the warrant necessary to make the proceeding lawful is that it must specify the place to be searched and the person or things to be seized.

. . . The Fourth Amendment may have proper application to a sealed letter in the mail, because of the constitutional provision for the Postoffice Department and the relations between the government and those who pay to secure protection of their sealed letters. . . . It is plainly within the words of the amendment to say that the unlawful rifling by a government agent of a sealed letter is a search and seizure of the sender's papers or effects. The letter is a paper, an effect, and in the custody of a government that forbids carriage, except under its protection.

The United States takes no such care of telegraph or telephone messages as of mailed sealed letters. The amendment does not forbid what was done here. There was no searching. There was no seizure. The evidence was secured by the use of the sense of hearing and that only. There was no entry of the houses or offices of the defendants.

. . .

The language of the amendment cannot be extended and expanded to include telephone wires, reaching to the whole world from the defendant's house or office. The intervening wires are not part of his house or office, any more than are the highways along which they are stretched.

. . .

Neither the cases we have cited nor any of the many federal decisions brought to our attention hold the Fourth Amendment to have been violated as against a defendant, unless there has been an official search and seizure of his person or such a seizure of his papers or his tangible material effects or an actual physical invasion of his house "or curtilage" for the purpose of making a seizure.

. . .

What has been said disposes of the only question that comes within the terms of our order granting certiorari in these cases. But some of our number, departing from that order, have concluded that there is merit in the twofold objection, overruled in both courts below, that evidence obtained through intercepting of telephone messages by a government agent was inadmissible, because the mode of obtaining it was unethical and a misdemeanor under the law of Washington.

. . .

A standard which would forbid the reception of evidence, if obtained by other than nice ethical conduct by government officials, would make society suffer and give criminals greater immunity than has been known heretofore. In the absence of controlling legislation by Congress, those who realize the difficulties in bringing offenders to justice may well deem it wise that the exclusion of evidence should be confined to cases where rights under the Constitution would be violated by admitting it.

JUSTICE BRANDEIS, dissenting.

. . .

"We must never forget," said Mr. Chief Justice Marshall in *McCulloch v. Maryland* (1819) "that it is a Constitution we are expounding." Since then this court has repeatedly sustained the exercise of power by Congress, under various clauses of that instrument, over objects of which the fathers could not have dreamed. . . . We have likewise held that general limitations on the powers of government, like those embodied in the due process clauses of the Fifth and Fourteenth Amendments, do not forbid the United States or the states from meeting modern conditions by regulations which "a century ago, or even half a century ago, probably would have been rejected as arbitrary and oppressive." . . . Clauses guaranteeing to the individual protection against specific abuses of power, must have a similar capacity of adaptation to a changing world. . . .

When the Fourth and Fifth Amendments were adopted, "the form that evil had theretofore taken" had been necessarily simple. Force and violence were then the only means known to man by which a government could directly effect self-incrimination. It could compel the individual to testify—a compulsion effected, if need be, by torture. It could secure possession of his papers and other articles incident to his private life—a seizure effected, if need be, by breaking and entry. Protection against such invasion of "the sanctities of a man's home and the privacies of life" was provided in the Fourth and Fifth Amendments by specific language. . . . But "time works changes, brings into existence new conditions and purposes." Subtler and more far-reaching means of invading privacy have become available to the government. Discovery and invention have made it possible for the government, by means far more effective than stretching upon the rack, to obtain disclosure in court of what is whispered in the closet.

Moreover, "in the application of a Constitution, our contemplation cannot be only of what has been, but of what may be." The progress of science in furnishing the government with means of espionage is not likely to stop with wire tapping. Ways may some day be developed by which the government, without removing papers from secret drawers, can reproduce them in court, and by which it will be enabled to expose to a jury the most intimate occurrences of the home. Advances in the psychic and related sciences may bring means of exploring unexpressed beliefs, thoughts and emotions. . . . Can it be that the Constitution affords no protection against such invasions of individual security?

. . .

The evil incident to invasion of the privacy of the telephone is far greater than that involved in tampering with the mails. Whenever a telephone line is tapped, the privacy of the persons at both ends of the line is invaded, and all conversations between them upon any subject, and although proper, confidential, and privileged, may be overheard. Moreover, the tapping of one man's telephone line involves the tapping of the telephone of every other person whom he may call, or who may call him. As a means of espionage, writs of assistance and general warrants are but puny instruments of tyranny and oppression when compared with wire tapping.

. . .

. . . The makers of our Constitution undertook to secure conditions favorable to the pursuit of happiness. They recognized the significance of man's spiritual nature, of his feelings and of his intellect. They knew that only a part of the pain, pleasure and satisfactions of life are to be found in material things. They sought to protect Americans in their beliefs, their thoughts, their emotions and their sensations. They conferred, as against the government, the right to be let alone—the most comprehensive of rights and the right most valued by civilized men. To protect that right, every unjustifiable intrusion by the government upon the privacy of the individual, whatever the means employed, must be deemed a violation of the Fourth Amendment. And the use, as evidence in a criminal proceeding, of facts ascertained by such intrusion must be deemed a violation of the Fifth.

Applying to the Fourth and Fifth Amendments the established rule of construction, the defendants' objections to the evidence obtained by wire tapping must, in my opinion, be sustained. It is, of course, immaterial where the physical connection with the telephone wires leading into the defendants' premises was made. And it is also immaterial that the intrusion was in aid of law enforcement. Experience should teach us to be most on our guard to protect liberty when the government's purposes are beneficent. Men born to freedom are naturally alert to repel invasion of their liberty by evil-minded rulers. The greatest dangers to liberty lurk in insidious encroachment by men of zeal, well-meaning but without understanding.

. . .

Independently of the constitutional question, I am of opinion that the judgment should be reversed. By the laws of Washington, wire tapping is a crime. . . . To prove its case, the government was obliged to lay bare the crimes committed by its officers on its behalf. A federal court should not permit such a prosecution to continue.

. . .

Decency, security, and liberty alike demand that government officials shall be subjected to the same rules of conduct that are commands to the citizen. In a government of laws, existence of the government will be imperiled if it fails to observe the law scrupulously. Our government is the potent, the omnipresent teacher. For good or for ill, it teaches the whole people by its example. Crime is contagious. If the government becomes a lawbreaker, it breeds contempt for law; it invites every man to become a law unto himself; it invites anarchy. To declare that in the administration of the criminal law the end justifies the means—to declare that the government may commit crimes in order to secure the conviction of a private criminal—would bring terrible retribution. Against that pernicious doctrine this court should resolutely set its face.

JUSTICE HOLMES, dissenting.

My brother BRANDEIS has given this case so exhaustive an examination that I desire to add but a few words. While I do not deny it I am not prepared to say that the penumbra of the Fourth and Fifth Amendments covers the defendant, although I fully agree that courts are apt to err by sticking too closely to the words of a law where those words import a policy that goes beyond them. But I think . . . that apart from the Constitution the government ought not to use evidence obtained and only obtainable by a criminal act. There is no body of precedents by which we are bound, and which confines us to logical deduction from established rules. Therefore we must consider the two objects of desire, both of which we cannot have, and make up our minds which to choose. It is desirable that criminals should be detected, and to that end that all available evidence should be used. It also is desirable that the government should not itself foster and pay for other crimes, when they are the means by which the evidence is to be obtained. If it pays its officers for having got evidence by crime I do not see why it may not as well pay them for getting it in the same way, and I can attach no importance to protestations of disapproval if it knowingly accepts and pays and announces that in future it will pay for the fruits. We have to choose, and for my part I think it a less evil that some criminals should escape than that the government should play an ignoble part.

. . .

JUSTICE BUTLER, dissenting.

. . .

Telephones are used generally for transmission of messages concerning official, social, business and personal affairs including communications that are private and privileged—those between physician and patient, lawyer and client, parent and child, husband and wife. The contracts between telephone companies and users contemplate the private use of the facilities employed in the service. The communications belong to the parties between whom they pass. During their transmission the exclusive use of the wire belongs to the persons served by it. Wire tapping involves interference with the wire while being used. Tapping the wires and listening in by the officers literally constituted a search for evidence. As the communications passed, they were heard and taken down. . . .

This court has always construed the Constitution in the light of the principles upon which it was founded. The direct operation or literal meaning of the words used do not measure the purpose or scope of its provisions. Under the principles established and applied by this court, the Fourth Amendment safeguards against all evils that are like and equivalent to those embraced within the ordinary meaning of its words. . . .

JUSTICE STONE, dissenting. . . .

C. Interrogations

Plea bargaining came of age during the Republican Era. Until the early twentieth century, many judges looked askance at the practice of obtaining confessions by reducing the criminal charge. By the end of the Republican Era the vast majority of convictions were obtained through confessions induced by a plea bargain.[53] This remains a central reality of our current system of criminal justice.

D. Juries and Lawyers

The jury trial continued to decline in constitutional status. Most criminal suspects avoided a jury trial by pleading guilty to a lesser offense. More defendants chose to be tried by a single judge. The Supreme Court in *Patton v. United States* (1930) concluded that the jury trial was a right of the accused that could be waived and not a vital structure of government that ensured popular participation in the criminal process. Justice Sutherland's opinion for the Court asserted that

53. For more information, see Albert W. Alschuler, "Plea Bargaining and Its History," *Columbia Law Review* 79 (1979): 1–43.

constitutional protections for a jury trial were "meant to confer a right upon the accused which he may forego at his election."[54]

Constitutional decision makers were far more supportive of the practice of providing defendants with lawyers. Numerous state courts emphasized the central role of an attorney in the criminal process. The Supreme Court of California in *People v. Napthaly* (CA 1895) declared, "Under our law every person accused of a felony is entitled to the aid of counsel, whether imprisoned or admitted to bail; and a refusal of an opportunity to procure such counsel amounts to the deprivation of an important right, essential to his safety."[55] Many state courts ruled that in certain circumstances the right to counsel included the right of an indigent person to have a court-appointed counsel. The U.S. Supreme Court in *Powell v. Alabama* (1932) relied heavily on these state constitutional decisions when holding that the due process clause of the Fourteenth Amendment protected the right to be represented by private defense counsel and required state-appointed counsel in certain circumstances.

Powell v. Alabama, 287 U.S. 45 (1932)

Ozie Powell was one of nine African American teenagers, later known as the Scottsboro Boys, who travelled on the Southern Railroad from Chattanooga to Memphis. While the train was in Alabama, the African American teenagers fought with several white teenagers. All but one of the white teenagers were thrown off the train. The white youths immediately reported what had happened to a stationmaster, who called a posse of men to stop the train. When the train was stopped, two white women onboard, Victoria Price and Ruby Bates, claimed that they had been raped by the African American teenagers. Twelve days later all nine teenagers were put on trial for their lives. Counsel were appointed on the day of the trial and were not given any time to prepare. Eight of the nine boys were convicted and sentenced to death. The Supreme Court of Alabama affirmed that decision by a 6–1 vote (the justices did reverse one sentence). Powell appealed to the Supreme Court of the United States. The plight of the Scottsboro Boys received national attention, with both the NAACP and the American Communist Party offering to provide legal assistance. (The defendants chose the Communists.)[56]

The Supreme Court by a 7–2 vote reversed the convictions of the seven Scottsboro Boys still under a death sentence. Justice Sutherland's majority opinion ruled that the due process clause of the Fourteenth Amendment required counsel to be appointed in certain capital cases. Justice Sutherland noted that English common law did not recognize a right to counsel. Why did he nevertheless assume that due process entails the right to counsel and, in certain cases, the right to court-appointed counsel? Powell v. Alabama *is one of the most celebrated civil liberties cases in American history. The author, Justice Sutherland, was a firm proponent of the freedom of contract and other property rights. Do you see any connections between Justice Sutherland's commitment to the* Lochner *line of decisions and his support for the Scottsboro Boys?*

JUSTICE SUTHERLAND delivered the opinion of the Court.

. . .

. . . [D]uring perhaps the most critical period of the proceedings against these defendants, that is to say, from the time of their arraignment until the beginning of their trial, when consultation, thorough-going investigation and preparation were vitally important, the defendants did not have the aid of counsel in any real sense, although they were as much entitled to such aid during that period as at the trial itself.

. . . The defendants, young, ignorant, illiterate, surrounded by hostile sentiment, haled back and forth under guard of soldiers, charged with an atrocious crime regarded with especial horror in the community where they were to be tried, were thus put in peril of their lives within a few moments after counsel for the first time charged with any degree of responsibility began to represent them.

It is not enough to assume that counsel thus precipitated into the case thought there was no defense, and exercised their best judgment in proceeding to trial without preparation. Neither they nor the court

54. For a survey of the history, see Stephen A. Siegel, "The Constitution on Trial: Article III's Jury Trial Provision, Originalism, and the Problem of Motivated Reasoning," *Santa Clara Law Review* 52 (2012): 373–455.

55. *People v. Napthaly*, 105 Cal. 641 (1895).

56. The story of the Scottsboro Boys is fascinating. For a good account, see James E. Goodman, *Stories of Scottsboro* (New York: Vintage, 1995).

could say what a prompt and thorough-going investigation might disclose as to the facts. No attempt was made to investigate. No opportunity to do so was given. Defendants were immediately hurried to trial. . . . Under the circumstances disclosed, we hold that defendants were not accorded the right of counsel in any substantial sense. To decide otherwise, would simply be to ignore actualities. . . .

. . . The prompt disposition of criminal cases is to be commended and encouraged. But in reaching that result a defendant, charged with a serious crime, must not be stripped of his right to have sufficient time to advise with counsel and prepare his defense. To do that is not to proceed promptly in the calm spirit of regulated justice but to go forward with the haste of the mob.

. . .

If recognition of the right of a defendant charged with a felony to have the aid of counsel depended upon the existence of a similar right at common law as it existed in England when our Constitution was adopted, there would be great difficulty in maintaining it as necessary to due process. Originally, in England, a person charged with treason or felony was denied the aid of counsel, except in respect of legal questions which the accused himself might suggest. At the same time parties in civil cases and persons accused of misdemeanors were entitled to the full assistance of counsel. . . .

. . .

The rule was rejected by the colonies. . . .

. . .

It thus appears that in at least twelve of the thirteen colonies the rule of the English common law, in the respect now under consideration, had been definitely rejected and the right to counsel fully recognized in all criminal prosecutions, save that in one or two instances the right was limited to capital offenses or to the more serious crimes; and this court seems to have been of the opinion that this was true in all the colonies. . . .

. . .

It never has been doubted by this court, or any other so far as we know, that notice and hearing are preliminary steps essential to the passing of an enforceable judgment, and that they, together with a legally competent tribunal having jurisdiction of the case, constitute basic elements of the constitutional requirement of due process of law. . . .

What, then, does a hearing include? Historically and in practice, in our own country at least, it has always included the right to the aid of counsel when desired and provided by the party asserting the right. The right to be heard would be, in many cases, of little avail if it did not comprehend the right to be heard by counsel. Even the intelligent and educated layman has small and sometimes no skill in the science of law. If charged with crime, he is incapable, generally, of determining for himself whether the indictment is good or bad. He is unfamiliar with the rules of evidence. Left without the aid of counsel he may be put on trial without a proper charge, and convicted upon incompetent evidence, or evidence irrelevant to the issue or otherwise inadmissible. He lacks both the skill and knowledge adequately to prepare his defense, even though he have a perfect one. He requires the guiding hand of counsel at every step in the proceedings against him. Without it, though he be not guilty, he faces the danger of conviction because he does not know how to establish his innocence. If that be true of men of intelligence, how much more true is it of the ignorant and illiterate, or those of feeble intellect. If in any case, civil or criminal, a state or federal court were arbitrarily to refuse to hear a party by counsel, employed by and appearing for him, it reasonably may not be doubted that such a refusal would be a denial of a hearing, and, therefore, of due process in the constitutional sense.

. . .

In the light of the facts outlined in the forepart of this opinion—the ignorance and illiteracy of the defendants, their youth, the circumstances of public hostility, the imprisonment and the close surveillance of the defendants by the military forces, the fact that their friends and families were all in other states and communication with them necessarily difficult, and above all that they stood in deadly peril of their lives—we think the failure of the trial court to give them reasonable time and opportunity to secure counsel was a clear denial of due process.

But passing that, and assuming their inability, even if opportunity had been given, to employ counsel, as the trial court evidently did assume, we are of opinion that, under the circumstances just stated, the necessity of counsel was so vital and imperative that the failure of the trial court to make an effective appointment of counsel was likewise a denial of due process within the meaning of the Fourteenth

Amendment. Whether this would be so in other criminal prosecutions, or under other circumstances, we need not determine. All that it is necessary now to decide, as we do decide, is that in a capital case, where the defendant is unable to employ counsel, and is incapable adequately of making his own defense because of ignorance, feeble-mindedness, illiteracy, or the like, it is the duty of the court, whether requested or not, to assign counsel for him as a necessary requisite of due process of law; and that duty is not discharged by an assignment at such a time or under such circumstances as to preclude the giving of effective aid in the preparation and trial of the case. To hold otherwise would be to ignore the fundamental postulate, already adverted to, "that there are certain immutable principles of justice which inhere in the very idea of free government which no member of the Union may disregard."...

...

JUSTICE BUTLER (joined by JUSTICE McREYNOLDS), dissenting.

...

If correct, the ruling that the failure of the trial court to give petitioners time and opportunity to secure counsel was denied of due process is enough, and with this the opinion should end. But the Court goes on to declare that "the failure of the trial court to make an effective appointment of counsel was likewise a denial of due process within the meaning of the Fourteenth Amendment." This is an extension of federal authority into a field hitherto occupied exclusively by the several States. Nothing before the Court calls for a consideration of the point. It was not suggested below and petitioners do not ask for its decision here. The Court, without being called upon to consider it, adjudges without a hearing an important constitutional question concerning criminal procedure in state courts....

E. Punishments

Constitutional decision makers took one of two different general approaches when determining whether a specific punishment was cruel or unusual. The deferential approach maintained that constitutional limitations on punishment forbade only particularly barbarous punishments such as torture. This approach focused entirely on the punishment and not at all on the crime. Burning at the stake was barbaric and could not be imposed for any crime. Prison was not barbaric, so a legislature could punish any crime with as long a sentence as elected officials thought appropriate. *Hobbs v. State* (IN 1893) was a leading case for the deferential position. The Supreme Court of Indiana brushed aside a claim that two years in prison for "riotous conspiracy" was unconstitutional. Judge Hackney wrote:

> The word "cruel," when considered in relation to the time when it found place in the bill of rights, meant, not a fine or imprisonment, or both, but such as that inflicted at the whipping post, in the pillory, burning at the stake, breaking on the wheel, etc. The word, according to modern interpretation, does not affect legislation providing imprisonment for life or for years, or the death penalty by hanging or electrocution. If it did, our laws for the punishment of crime would give no security to the citizen. Neither is punishment by fine or imprisonment "unusual."[57]

An increasing minority of states adopted a more Progressive approach to constitutional limitations on punishment. Judges who adopted this approach were willing to consider whether punishments permitted at the founding could become unconstitutional, and whether the constitutionality of a punishment depended on the crime. A long prison term might be a constitutional punishment for armed robbery, but not for parking one's horse in the wrong stall. *McDonald v. Commonwealth* (MA 1899) was a leading state authority for the Progressive approach. The Supreme Judicial Court of Massachusetts sustained a state law enhancing the sentences of repeat criminals but insisted that the state constitution limited prison sentences for certain crimes. Judge Morton wrote,

> It would be going too far to say that their power is unlimited in these respects. Ordinarily, the terms "cruel and unusual" imply something inhuman and barbarous in the nature of the punishment. But it is possible that imprisonment in the state prison for a long term of years might be so disproportionate to the offense as to constitute a cruel and unusual punishment.[58]

57. *Hobbs v. State*, 32 N.E. 1019 (Ind. 1893).

58. *McDonald v. Commonwealth*, 173 Mass. 322 (1899).

The Supreme Court of the United States took a deferential approach in the late nineteenth century but moved toward a more progressive approach during the twentieth century. When sustaining firing squads (*Wilkerson v. Utah* [1878]) and the electric chair (*In re Kemmler* [1890]) as constitutional modes of execution, Supreme Court justices limited application of the cruel and unusual punishment clause to "punishments of torture . . . and all others in the same line of unnecessary cruelty." The White Court took a different approach in *Weems v. United States* (1910). The judicial majority in that case declared that a prison term in chains that lasted more than a decade was a constitutionally disproportionate punishment for a financial crime. Nevertheless, *Weems* was the only case in which the Supreme Court before the New Deal Era ruled that a punishment was cruel and unusual.

Suggested Readings

Arkes, Hadley. 1994. *The Return of George Sutherland: Restoring a Jurisprudence of Natural Rights.* Princeton, NJ: Princeton University Press.

Baer, Judith A. 1978. *The Chains of Protection: The Judicial Response to Women's Labor Legislation.* Westport, CT: Greenwood Press.

Benedict, Michael Les. 1985. "Laissez-Faire and Liberty: A Re-Evaluation of the Meaning and Origins of Laissez-Faire Constitutionalism." *Law and History* 3:293–331.

Beth, Loren P. 1971. *The Development of the American Constitution, 1877–1917.* New York: Harper & Row.

Bickel, Alexander M., and Benno C. Schmidt, Jr. 2007. *The Judiciary and Responsible Government, 1910–21.* New York: Cambridge University Press.

Brandwein, Pamela. 2011. *Rethinking the Judicial Settlement of Reconstruction.* New York: Cambridge University Press.

Cardozo, Benjamin N. 1921. *The Nature of the Judicial Process.* New Haven, CT: Yale University Press.

Carpenter, Daniel P. 2001. *The Forging of Bureaucratic Autonomy: Reputations, Networks, and Policy Innovation in Executive Agencies, 1862–1928.* Princeton, NJ: Princeton University Press.

Chafee, Zechariah. 1941. *Free Speech in the United States.* Cambridge, MA: Harvard University Press.

Clemens, Elisabeth S. 1997. *The People's Lobby: Organizational Innovation and the Rise of Interest Group Politics in the United States, 1890–1925.* Chicago: University of Chicago Press.

Cott, Nancy F. 1987. *The Grounding of Modern Feminism.* New Haven, CT: Yale University Press.

Fiss, Owen M. 1993. *The Troubled Beginnings of the Modern State.* New York: Macmillan.

Gillman, Howard. 1993. *The Constitution Besieged: The Rise and Demise of Lochner Era Police Power Jurisprudence.* Durham, NC: Duke University Press.

———. 2002. "How Political Parties Can Use the Courts to Advance Their Agendas: Federal Courts in the United States, 1875–1891." *American Political Science Review* 96:511–24.

Gordon, Sarah Barringer. 2002. *The Mormon Question: Polygamy and Constitutional Conflict in Nineteenth-Century America.* Chapel Hill: University of North Carolina Press.

Graber, Mark A. 1991. *Transforming Free Speech: The Ambiguous Legacy of Civil Libertarianism.* Berkeley: University of California Press.

Hamm, Richard F. 1995. *Shaping the Eighteenth Amendment: Temperance Reform, Legal Culture and the Polity, 1880–1920.* Chapel Hill: University of North Carolina Press.

Hirschon, Stanley P. 1962. *Farewell to the Bloody Shirt: Northern Republicans and the Southern Negro, 1877–1893.* Bloomington: Indiana University Press.

Hoffer, Williamjames Hull. 2007. *To Enlarge the Machinery of Government: Congressional Debates and the Growth of the American State, 1858–1891.* Baltimore, MD: Johns Hopkins University Press.

Hofstadter, Richard. 1955. *The Age of Reform.* New York: Random House.

James, Scott C. 2000. *Presidents, Parties, and the State: A Party System Perspective on Democratic Regulatory Choice, 1884–1936.* New York: Cambridge University Press.

Keller, Morton. 1977. *Affairs of State: Public Life in Late Nineteenth Century America.* Cambridge, MA: Harvard University Press.

———. 1990. *Regulating a New Economy: Public Policy and Economic Change in America, 1900–1933.* Cambridge, MA: Harvard University Press.

Kens, Paul. 1990. *Judicial Power and Reform Politics: The Anatomy of* Lochner v. New York. Lawrence: University Press of Kansas.

———. 1997. *Justice Stephen Field: Shaping American Liberty from the Gold Rush to the Gilded Age.* Lawrence: University Press of Kansas.

Kull, Andrew. 1992. *The Color-Blind Constitution.* Cambridge, MA: Harvard University Press.

Lane, Charles. 2008. *The Day Freedom Died: The Colfax Massacre, the Supreme Court, and the Betrayal of Reconstruction.* New York: Henry Holt and Co.

Lofgren, Charles A. 1987. *The* Plessy *Case: A Legal-Historical Interpretation.* New York: Oxford University Press.

Mason, Alpheus T. 1965. *William Howard Taft: Chief Justice.* New York: Simon and Schuster.

Milkis, Sidney M. 2009. *Theodore Roosevelt, the Progressive Party, and the Transformation of American Democracy.* Lawrence: University Press of Kansas.

Murphy, Paul L. 1979. *World War I and the Origins of Civil Liberties in the United States.* New York: Norton.

Novkov, Julie. 2008. *Racial Union: Law, Intimacy, and the White State in Alabama, 1865–1954.* Ann Arbor: University of Michigan Press.

Paul, Arnold M. 1960. *Conservative Crisis and the Rule of Law: Attitudes of Bar and Bench, 1887–1895.* Ithaca, NY: Cornell University Press.

Polenberg, Richard. 1996. *Fighting Faiths: The* Abrams *Case, the Supreme Court and Free Speech.* New York: Notable Trials Library.

Przybyszewski, Linda. 1999. *The Republic According to John Marshall Harlan.* Chapel Hill: University of North Carolina Press.

Purcell, Edward A., Jr. 2000. *Brandeis and the Progressive Constitution: Erie, the Judicial Power, and the Politics of the Federal Courts in Twentieth-Century America.* New Haven, CT: Yale University Press.

Rabban, David M. 1997. *Free Speech in Its Forgotten Years.* New York: Cambridge University Press.

Richardson, Heather Cox. 2001. *The Death of Reconstruction: Race, Labor, and Politics in the Post–Civil War North.* Cambridge, MA: Harvard University Press.

Ritter, Gretchen. 2006. *The Constitution as Social Design: Gender and Civic Membership in the American Constitutional Order.* Palo Alto, CA: Stanford University Press.

Ross, William G. 1994. *A Muted Fury: Populists, Progressives, and Labor Unions Confront the Courts, 1890–1937.* Princeton, NJ: Princeton University Press.

Siegel, Reva B. 2002. "She the People: The Nineteenth Amendment, Sex Equality, Federalism, and the Family." *Harvard Law Review* 115:947–1046.

Skowronek, Stephen. 1982. *Building a New American State: The Expansion of National Administrative Capacity, 1877–1920.* New York: Cambridge University Press.

Sparrow, Bartholomew H. 2006. *The* Insular Cases *and the Emergence of American Empire.* Lawrence: University Press of Kansas.

Strum, Philippa. 1984. *Louis D. Brandeis: Justice for the People.* Cambridge, MA: Harvard University Press.

Sullivan, Kathleen S. 2007. *Constitutional Context: Women and Rights Discourse in Nineteenth-Century America.* Baltimore, MD: Johns Hopkins University Press.

Swisher, Carl B. 1930. *Stephen Field: Craftsman of the Law.* Chicago: University of Chicago Press.

Tamanaha, Brian Z. 2010. *Beyond the Formalist-Realist Divide: The Role of Politics in Judging.* Princeton, NJ: Princeton University Press.

Urofsky, Melvin I. 2009. *Louis D. Brandeis: A Life.* New York: Pantheon.

White, G. Edward. 1993. *Justice Oliver Wendell Holmes: Law and the Inner Self.* New York: Oxford University Press.

Wiebe, Robert H. 1966. *The Search for Order, 1877–1920.* New York: Hill and Wang.

Wood, Stephen B. 1968. *Constitutional Politics in the Progressive Era: Child Labor and the Law.* Chicago: University of Chicago Press.

Woodward, C. Vann. 1966. *The Strange Career of Jim Crow,* rev. ed. New York: Oxford University Press.

Chapter 8

The New Deal and Great Society Era: 1933–1968

I. Introduction

The period from 1933 to 1968 was the heyday of political and constitutional liberalism. Franklin Roosevelt was first elected to the presidency in 1932, and he brought large Democratic majorities with him to Washington. The policies of Roosevelt and his allies were deeply controversial, but liberals won the major debates. American politics after 1940 was largely a contest between those who would expand and those who would merely maintain the liberal programs established during President Franklin Roosevelt's first two terms of office. Roosevelt's shifting bundle of proposals to get the United States out of the Great Depression in the 1930s was known as the New Deal. Subsequent Democratic presidents offered ambitious plans of their own, with the most famous being Lyndon Johnson's Great Society in the 1960s, which expanded the social safety net and launched new civil rights initiatives. Republicans such as Dwight Eisenhower and Richard Nixon promised to manage those programs better than Democrats. Liberal Democrats and liberal Republicans in Congress enthusiastically endorsed the New Deal and Great Society. Conservative Republicans and southern Democrats acted as temporary brakes, slowing and moderating liberal policies.

Developments. In the decades following the Great Depression liberals transformed the American constitutional landscape. These transformations included the complete abandonment of commerce clause, spending clause, federalism, and other limits on congressional power to regulate in the national interest; the rejection

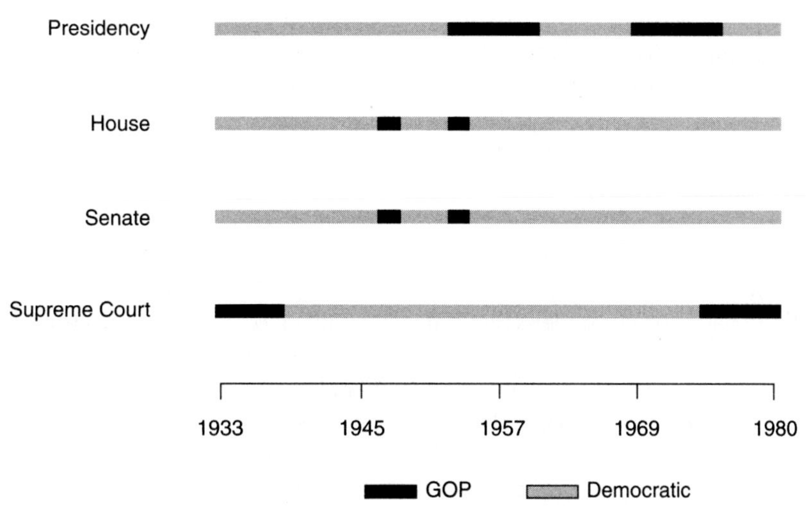

Figure 8-1 Partisan Control of the U.S. Government, 1933–1980

Illustration 8-1 Good Morning, Judge!
Source: Pittsburgh Press, January 9, 1937. Courtesy FDR Library.

of the freedom of contract; the abolition of Jim Crow; the nationalization of almost every provision in the Bill of Rights; the expansion of constitutional protections for persons accused of crime; the reapportionment of all congressional districts consistent with the principle of one person, one vote; and a dramatic expansion in free speech rights. The New Deal and Great Society Era witnessed such constitutional landmarks as *Brown v. Board of Education* (1954), the Voting Rights Act of 1965, and *Miranda* warnings. Much contemporary constitutional debate is over whether to expand, maintain, or abandon the constitutional heritage of the New Deal and Great Society Era.

During the first decade of the New Deal and Great Society Era, liberals established the principle that the national government was responsible for resolving all national problems, even if such matters had historically been regulated only by states. When Roosevelt and Congress took unprecedented steps to get the country out of the Depression, the U.S. Supreme Court reacted with alarm. During FDR's first term, the conservative Court struck down federal laws in thirteen cases and state laws in another thirty cases. After Roosevelt responded with a plan to "reorganize" the federal judiciary by adding new justices to the Supreme Court and new judges to the lower courts, the centrist justices on the Court switched sides. The Court never again struck down a New Deal statute, and President Roosevelt soon replaced the conservative judges by normal means.

Liberal rights commitments unfolded in two stages. From 1933 until 1960 liberals debated what constitutional rights and liberties were entailed by political liberalism and the institutional responsibilities for securing those rights and liberties. New Dealers in the elected branches of government agreed that traditional property rights were subject to regulation by popular majorities but debated whether the same popular majorities should be able to regulate communist speech. New Dealers on the Supreme Court debated whether justices should strike down legislation restricting political dissent. The Truman administration and the early Warren Court declared a constitutional commitment to racial equality, but the United States in 1960 remained a largely segregated polity. From 1961 to 1968 all three branches of the national government became committed to modern liberal understandings of constitutional rights and liberties. The Supreme Court nationalized the Bill of Rights, struck down school prayer, ordered states to reapportion legislative districts, mandated both the exclusionary rule and *Miranda* warnings, and provided new protections for political dissenters. Great Society liberals in Congress passed such measures as the Civil Rights Act of 1964 and the Voting Rights Act of 1965. Great Society liberals in the executive branch vigorously enforced those measures, publicly championed liberal notions of racial equality, and submitted amicus briefs to the Supreme Court urging the justices to adopt liberal understandings of constitutional rights.

Parties. Liberals exercised more influence over constitutional development during the New Deal and Great Society Era than at any other time in American history. From 1933 until 1968 liberals either controlled or exercised significant power in all three branches of the national government and in many states. The liberal spirit in the United States was bipartisan, except in the South. Political liberalism found a congenial home among Democrats, despite the ongoing presence in the party of southern white supremacists. Liberal Democrats controlled the presidency for all but eight years of the New Deal and Great Society Era and the Congress for all but four years. Many Republicans, particularly those from the Northeast and the West Coast, supported liberal Democrats. Republicans such as Thomas Dewey, the GOP nominee for president in both 1944 and 1948, Herbert Brownell, the attorney general under President Eisenhower, and Nelson Rockefeller, the long-time Republican governor of New York, were as progressive as (if not more progressive than) their Democratic rivals. The Supreme Court was a bastion of bipartisan constitutional liberalism, particularly after Republican Earl Warren was appointed chief justice in 1954 and several very liberal justices joined the bench in the early 1960s. That liberalism can be partly traced to self-conscious decisions by the national executive. Aware that the federal judiciary could be a crucial ally in administrative struggles against conservatives in Congress and the states, members of the Justice Department in the Roosevelt, Truman, Eisenhower, Kennedy, and Johnson administrations frequently vetted judicial nominees on the basis of their progressive positions and commitment to racial equality.

Divisions among New Dealers initially hampered efforts to achieve liberal constitutional visions. We presently think of liberals as being committed to economic redistribution, free speech, racial equality, and the rights of persons suspected of criminal offenses. Until the 1960s, however, few persons who thought of themselves as liberals shared all these values. Southern Democrats supported Social Security but not *Brown v. Board of Education* (1954). President Truman was a racial liberal who ordered that the military be desegregated, but he supported restricting free speech, especially for Communists. Liberals during the 1940s and 1950s disputed whether state officials ought to enjoy the same freedom from constitutional restrictions when catching criminals as they enjoyed when regulating the economy, or whether strict adherence to the rules of constitutional criminal procedure was necessary to protect the rights of African Americans and other minorities. Liberal efforts were also hampered by powerful conservatives in both Congress and the states. A conservative coalition in Congress composed of midwestern Republicans and southern Democrats stalled proposed measures on racial equality, passed laws restricting free speech rights, and threatened to restrain a federal judiciary perceived as too soft on Communism, too internationalist, and, for southerners, too sympathetic to persons of color. State judges frequently condemned judicial decisions that nationalized federal policy.

Progressives in the elected branches of government fought back, using their power to maintain and augment the influence of progressives in the judiciary. Liberals in the Eisenhower Justice Department refused to support court-curbing proposals made in Congress. Congress was largely deaf to the pleas of state justices concerned with the nationalizing tendencies of the Warren Court.

Interest Groups. Public interest groups played an important role in bringing liberal constitutional complaints to public attention. Elite advocacy organizations

Table 8-1 Major Issues and Decisions of the New Deal and Great Society Era

Major Political Issues	Major Constitutional Issues	Major Court Decisions
Great Depression	Abandonment of Article I limits on federal power	*Home Building & Loan Association v. Blaisdell* (1934)
New Deal	Growth of administrative state	*Carter v. Carter Coal Co.* (1936)
World War II	Abandonment of dual federalism	*United States v. Curtiss-Wright Export Corp.* (1936)
Cold War	Abandonment of freedom of contract	*National Labor Relations Board v. Jones & Laughlin Steel* (1937)
McCarthyism	Decline of protection for property rights	*West Coast Hotel Co. v. Parrish* (1937)
Civil rights movement	Nationalization of the Bill of Rights	*Palko v. Connecticut* (1937)
Police brutality	Enhanced judicial protections for "discrete and insular minorities"	*United States v. Carolene Products* (1938)
Little Rock crisis	Assault on "separate but equal"	*Skinner v. Oklahoma* (1942)
Civil Rights Act of 1964	Increased tendency to find state action	*Ex parte Quirin* (1942)
Voting Rights Act of 1965	Enhanced scrutiny of government	*Barnette v. West Virginia State Board of Education* (1943)
Vietnam War	Support for religion	*Smith v. Allwright* (1944)
War on poverty	New federal rights guarantees for criminal defendants	*Korematsu v. United States* (1944)
Urban rioting	One person, one vote	*Shelley v. Kraemer* (1948)
	New protections for privacy and personal liberty	*Dennis v. United States* (1951)
	Enhanced protections for free speech and press	*Youngstown Sheet & Tube Co. v. Sawyer* (1962)
		Brown v. Board of Education (1954)
		Mapp v. Ohio (1961)
		Engle v. Vitale (1962)
		Baker v. Carr (1962)
		Sherbert v. Verner (1963)
		Gideon v. Wainwright (1963)
		Reynolds v. Sims (1964)
		New York Times v. Sullivan (1964)
		Griswold v. Connecticut (1965)
		Harper v. Virginia State Board of Elections (1966)
		Katzenbach v. Morgan (1966)
		Miranda v. Arizona (1966)
		Katz v. United States (1967)
		Duncan v. Louisiana (1968)
		Brandenburg v. Ohio (1969)

such as the ACLU and the NAACP Legal Defense and Education Fund made major contributions to mid-twentieth-century constitutional liberalism. The ACLU and the NAACP provided legal support for persons claiming constitutional violations and lobbied sympathetic officials for favorable civil liberties and rights policies.[1] The Supreme Court handed down a series of decisions favoring the legal and constitutional rights of poor people only after the publicly funded Legal Services Corporation put those issues on the docket of the federal bench.[2] Liberal grassroots rights movements, most notably the Southern Christian Leadership Conference, also influenced the course of American constitutionalism. These groups achieved their goals by protest and, later, through the ballot box. President Roosevelt desegregated the federal workplace in order to prevent a mass civil rights march from taking place in Washington, DC, during World War II.[3] Martin Luther King's protests in Birmingham and Selma influenced the timing and content of the Civil Rights Act of 1964 and the Voting Rights Act of 1965.

Courts. The federal judiciary underwent a great ideological transformation during this period. The federal courts, led by the U.S. Supreme Court, had been dominated by conservatives for many decades. Many of those judges were skeptical of the constitutionality of progressive reform legislation passed in the first decades of the twentieth century, and they were likewise skeptical of the constitutionality of the New Deal in the first years of Franklin Roosevelt's administration. By the end of the Roosevelt presidency, the Supreme Court had been remade. Franklin Roosevelt made nine appointments to the Supreme Court, and the New Deal Court dramatically reshaped constitutional law in the late 1930s and 1940s. In the 1950s and 1960s, the Warren Court pushed constitutional law in new directions, generating great controversy but also setting landmarks that remain central to law and society today. During these decades, the Supreme Court was more closely allied with the political left as it has ever been.

The New Deal Court under the successive leadership of chief justices Charles Evans Hughes, Harlan Fiske Stone, and finally Fred Vinson embraced the constitutional changes that were taking place in the 1930s and 1940s. Under the commerce clause, the justices accepted that the federal government could regulate all economic activity when doing so was in the national interest. Under the spending clause, the justices accepted that the federal government could make expenditures that Congress believed served the general welfare without regard to their connection to an enumerated power or any Tenth Amendment restriction. In the name of facilitating a "workable government," the Court approved as consistent with the separation of powers legislation that made broad delegations of power to the executive branch or administrative agencies. In the interest of alleviating judicial oversight of legislative policy making, the Court adopted a deferential standard for reviewing government regulations that were said to interfere with the contracts or due process clauses of the Constitution.

Prominent liberals were initially more ambivalent about the responsibility of justices to protect fundamental rights. Alexander Bickel famously summed up what he labeled the "countermajoritarian difficulty" when he declared, "When the Supreme Court declares unconstitutional a legislative act or the action of an elected executive, it thwarts the will of the representatives of the actual people of the here and now."[4] Some judicial liberals insisted that unelected justices had special roles to play in a liberal democracy. Justice Hugo Black in *Chambers v. Florida* (1940) maintained, "Under our constitutional system, courts stand against any winds that blow as havens of refuge for those who might otherwise suffer because they are helpless, weak, outnumbered, or because they are non-conforming victims of prejudice and public excitement." Other judicial liberals insisted that the commitment to democracy entailed the constitutional right of popular majorities to adopt illiberal policies. In a famous series of lectures that criticized such instances of judicial activism as *Brown v. Board of Education*, Judge Learned Hand stated,

1. Charles R. Epp, *The Rights Revolution: Lawyers, Activists, and Supreme Courts in Comparative Perspective* (Chicago: University of Chicago Press, 1998).

2. Susan E. Lawrence, *The Poor in Court: The Legal Services Program and Supreme Court Decision Making* (Princeton, NJ: Princeton University Press, 1990).

3. Philip A. Klinkner and Rogers M. Smith, *The Rise and Decline of Racial Equality in America* (Chicago: University of Chicago Press, 1999).

4. Alexander M. Bickel, *The Least Dangerous Branch: The Supreme Court at the Bar of Politics* (New Haven, CT: Yale University Press, 1962), 16–17.

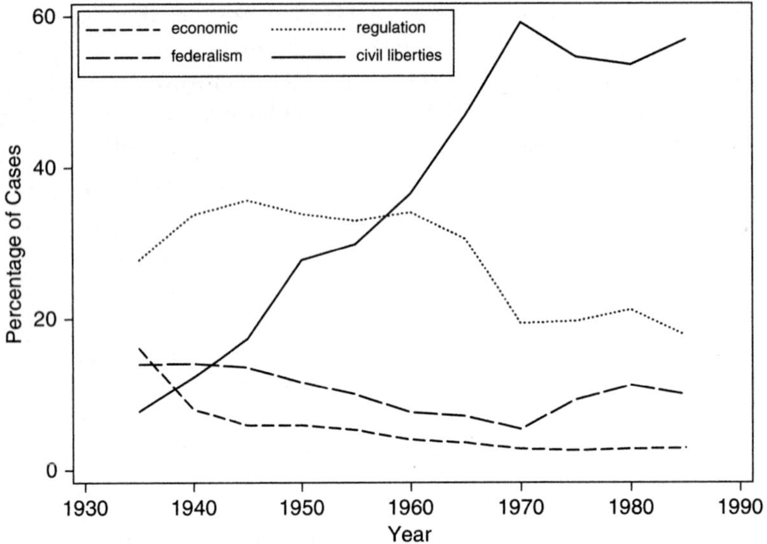

Figure 8-2 Agenda Change of the U.S. Supreme Court, 1933–1988

Source: Richard L. Pacelle, Jr., *The Transformation of the Supreme Court's Agenda* (Boulder, CO: Westview Press, 1991), Table 3.1.

Note: Five-year intervals averaged.

"It would be most irksome to be ruled by a bevy of Platonic Guardians, even if I knew how to choose them, which I assuredly do not."[5]

The Warren Court resolved this debate in favor of judicial activism. Building on some earlier cases, liberal justices launched a "rights revolution" across a wide range of issues. In numerous cases, primarily involving state law and often arising in the South, the Warren Court extended individual rights ranging from free speech to religious free exercise to constitutional criminal procedure to sexual liberty. The Court likewise embarked on new efforts to address racial civil rights and restructure legislative apportionment. The Court's work during this period was important, prominent, and controversial. During these decades, the Court addressed basic social and political questions and often issued bold decisions calling for the reform of social and political institutions. Those efforts were not always successful, but many decisions remain landmarks in constitutional law. The Court's work generated heated controversy and sometimes-successful resistance. But the Court also had numerous allies, generally including the leadership of the national government and a growing number of liberal interest groups dedicated to litigating constitutional cases.

Constitutional Thought. Two fundamental and related principles lay at the core of the New Deal/Great Society constitutional vision. The first principle was that the national government was responsible for resolving all national economic and, increasingly, all social problems. New Dealers often quoted from the Virginia Plan to the Constitutional Convention, insisting that the national government was constitutionally authorized "to legislate in all cases to which the separate States are incompetent, or in which the harmony of the United States may be interrupted by the exercise of individual Legislation."[6] The second principle was that the national government was responsible for guaranteeing to all American citizens a broad array of positive and negative freedoms. Proponents of the New Deal and Great Society argued that negative rights (protections from government) such as free speech and equal protection had not yet been given sufficient breadth. They added economic security to the positive rights (duties on government) that

5. Learned Hand, *The Bill of Rights* (New York: Atheneum, 1972), 73.

6. Max Farrand, ed., *The Records of the Federal Convention of 1787* (New Haven, CT: Yale University Press, 1966), 1:23.

they believed warranted constitutional protection. While courts played an increasing role protecting these freedoms, the Constitution vested primary responsibility in the national executive and legislature.

Constitutional liberals were committed to a living Constitution. In this view, while the Constitution remained the foundation for rights and liberties, the content of those rights and liberties evolved in response to changing sociological, economic, and political conditions. Chief Justice Earl Warren articulated this commitment to living constitutionalism when he declared, "The words of the [Eighth] Amendment are not precise, and . . . their scope is not static. The Amendment must draw its meaning from the evolving standards of decency that mark the progress of a maturing society."[7] Sometimes these evolving standards limited the scope of preexisting constitutional rights. Many progressive thinkers insisted that nineteenth-century constitutional understandings of property rights were increasingly anachronistic in light of new industrial and political conditions. More often, the idea of a living Constitution provided grounds for expanding constitutional rights and liberties. *Brown v. Board of Education* provides a good example of this constitutional logic. Chief Justice Warren's opinion in this case began by noting that the original understanding of the Fourteenth Amendment was "inconclusive," in part because "the conditions of public education did not approximate those existing today." The status of separate but equal, he declared, had to be judged in light of contemporary conditions. Warren wrote, "We must consider public education in the light of its full development and its present place in American life throughout the Nation." His unanimous opinion highlighted contemporary social science research indicating that racial segregation harmed children of color. Past decisions sustaining Jim Crow policies were determined not to be relevant to the issue before the Court, because previous generations of justices were unaware of modern research findings. "Whatever may have been the extent of psychological knowledge at the time of *Plessy v. Ferguson*," Warren wrote, "this finding is amply supported by modern authority." *Brown* did not reject the original constitutional commitment to equality. The justices, however, insisted on applying that commitment in light of modern conditions and knowledge.

7. *Trop v. Dulles*, 356 U.S. 86, 100 (1958).

Legacies. The New Deal and Great Society reshaped the constitutional landscape. Commentators at the time referred to the events of the New Deal as a constitutional revolution. The court decisions, statutes, and political mobilization of the 1950s and 1960s are often referred to as a rights revolution. Constitutional scholar Bruce Ackerman has aptly characterized the post–New Deal era as a "third republic" in American history, as distinctive and as notable as the periods after the founding and after Reconstruction.[8] Many constitutional debates that were familiar throughout American history came to an end during these revolutions. Other debates were transformed, and still other debates began. Constitutionally speaking, we live in a post–New Deal world.

The New Deal and Great Society Era exerts a powerful influence on contemporary constitutional understandings. Contemporary liberals bear a close family resemblance to the Great Society liberals of 1965 and some resemblance to the New Deal liberals of 1935 but have little more than the label "liberal" in common with persons who considered themselves liberal in 1875. Many Americans remain committed to the constitutional visions championed by Martin Luther King, Jr., Franklin Roosevelt, Earl Warren, and Lyndon Johnson. Many contemporary progressives insist that a newly empowered progressive regime need do little more than build on the legacy left by the progressive giants of the 1940s, 1950s, and 1960s. To a remarkable degree many constitutional conservatives are heirs to the tradition marked out by such liberal dissenters on the Warren Court as John Harlan and Felix Frankfurter rather than successors to the constitutional conservatism of the justices who opposed the New Deal.[9]

During the New Deal and Great Society Era liberals for the first time in American history regarded federal courts as a valued, preeminent, and often exclusive site for pursuing a progressive constitutional politics. Previously, progressives had sought to win the support of elected officials and avoid losing their legislative gains in the courtroom. Judges during and immediately after Reconstruction did more to emasculate federal legislation promoting racial equality than to overturn state legislation promoting white supremacy. Labor unions at the turn of the twentieth century regarded courts as

8. Bruce Ackerman, *We the People*, vol. 1 (Cambridge, MA: Harvard University Press, 1991).

9. See Thomas M. Keck, *The Most Activist Supreme Court in History: The Road to Modern Judicial Conservatism* (Chicago: University of Chicago Press, 2004).

Box 8-1 A Partial Cast of Characters of the New Deal/Great Society Era

Thurgood Marshall	■ Democrat ■ Lead litigator for the NAACP Legal Defense Fund ■ Appointed by Kennedy to U.S. Court of Appeals (1961–1965) ■ U.S. solicitor general (1965–1967) ■ Appointed by Johnson to U.S. Supreme Court (1967–1991) ■ Major architect of the NAACP's school desegregation campaign leading to *Brown v. Board of Education* (1954) ■ Known for his close alliance with Brennan as a defender of individual rights on the Supreme Court
Felix Frankfurter	■ Progressive who supported Teddy Roosevelt's Bull Moose Campaign but otherwise described himself as "politically homeless" ■ Helped found the American Civil Liberties Union and served as counsel for the National Consumers League ■ Professor at Harvard Law School (1914–1917, 1919–1939) ■ Like his mentor Oliver Wendell Holmes, Jr., criticized judicial review of progressive economic regulation ■ Advised Franklin Roosevelt on domestic policy ■ Appointed by Roosevelt to Supreme Court (1939–1962) ■ As a justice, known for his advocacy of judicial restraint when reviewing legislation and for his reluctance to apply the federal Constitution to the states
Franklin D. Roosevelt	■ Democrat ■ Assistant secretary of the navy (1913–1920) ■ Governor of New York (1929–1932) ■ President of the United States (1933–1945) ■ Longest-serving president in U.S. history, serving through both the Great Depression and World War II ■ Built a new Democratic coalition of labor and agriculture and launched an aggressive and controversial program of active government, expanded central power, and stronger executive power in both domestic and foreign affairs
Earl Warren	■ Republican ■ California attorney general (1939–1943) ■ California governor (1943–1953) ■ Appointed by Eisenhower to be chief justice of the United States (1953–1969) ■ An exceedingly popular California politician; was simultaneously nominated by the Republican, Democratic, and Progressive Parties for statewide office ■ Led an increasingly liberal Court that supported congressional and presidential power and carved out new civil rights and civil liberties

(Continued)

Box 8-1 *(Continued)*

Robert H. Jackson	■ Democrat ■ Successful New York lawyer who joined Franklin Roosevelt's Justice Department ■ U.S. solicitor general (1938–1940) ■ U.S. attorney general (1940–1941) ■ Appointed by Roosevelt to Supreme Court (1941–1954) ■ U.S. chief counsel for Nuremberg trials (1945) ■ Known for his pragmatic, functionalist approach to constitutional problems ■ Last person appointed to the Supreme Court who did not graduate from a law school
Hugo Black	■ Democrat ■ U.S. senator (1927–1937) ■ Appointed by Roosevelt to Supreme Court (1937–1971) ■ A liberal New Dealer, Black was a supporter of the Court-packing plan while in the Senate ■ On the Court he was known for his textualism, appeals to history, and his simultaneous emphasis on judicial restraint and firm defense of civil liberties
Charles Evans Hughes	■ Republican ■ Governor of New York (1907–1910) ■ Appointed by Taft to the Supreme Court (1910–1916) ■ Resigned to run for president against Woodrow Wilson in 1916 ■ Secretary of state (1921–1925) ■ Appointed by Hoover to be chief justice of the United States (1930–1941) ■ Started his career as a progressive reformer but later gained a more conservative reputation ■ Guided the Supreme Court through the Court-packing challenge and wrote key decisions upholding the New Deal
William Brennan	■ Democrat ■ New Jersey Supreme Court (1951–1956) ■ Appointed by Eisenhower to U.S. Supreme Court (1956–1990) ■ Chosen by Eisenhower as part of a reelection bid to appeal to Catholic Democrats, Brennan became one of the most significant justices of the twentieth century ■ Wrote many of the landmark decisions of the Warren Court and continued to be a major influence in the Burger Court; known for his strong advocacy of active judicial review and expansive liberal interpretation of constitutional rights

hostile terrain. Law professors who came of age during the 1960s, by comparison, taught their students that progressive courts were the norm and that the federal judiciary was the institution most likely to be sympathetic to liberal constitutional claims. One central question to think about throughout this chapter is whether the judiciary in the mid-twentieth century became a relatively enduring bastion of constitutional liberalism, or whether, as Scot Powe insists, the tribunal led by Earl Warren was "a historically unique Court operating in an historically unique era."[10]

10. Lucas A. Powe, *The Warren Court and American Politics* (Cambridge, MA: Harvard University Press, 2000), 486.

II. Foundations

MAJOR DEVELOPMENTS

- Special emphasis on democratic processes and the rights of discrete and insular minorities
- Incorporation of most provisions in the Bill of Rights
- Increased tendency to find state action in cases alleging unconstitutional racial discrimination

New Deal and Great Society liberals expanded the scope of constitutional rights and liberties. When Richard Nixon became president in 1969 state officials had to respect most provisions of the Bill of Rights. Governing officials abroad and in the military had to respect due process rights when punishing other Americans. Private individuals were considered state actors for constitutional purposes when they were performing a public function or were significantly involved with the government. Americans in the mid-twentieth century, however, rejected claims that international human rights agreements provided legal limitations on state officials or federal officials acting on foreign soil.

A. Sources

Prohibition repeal was the first constitutional achievement of the New Deal. The Association Against the Prohibition Amendment, a group of prominent industrialists, helped finance the Democratic Party during the 1928 and 1932 campaigns. The Democratic Party platform in 1932 called for the repeal of the Eighteenth Amendment. Immediately after Franklin Roosevelt was elected, Congress approved and a constitutional majority of states ratified the Twenty-First Amendment. Looking backward, the Twenty-First Amendment might be understood as returning to states their traditional power to regulate the health, safety, morals, and welfare of the citizenry. Many participants in state constitutional conventions who voted to repeal the Eighteenth Amendment relied heavily on Republican Era conceptions of the police power and individual rights. Looking forward, the repeal of Prohibition anticipated later constitutional resistance to morals legislation.

Bruce Ackerman claims that Americans from 1933 to 1968 ratified de facto amendments to the Constitution. They first constitutionalized the basic principles underlying the New Deal, including national power to regulate all economic activities and the abandonment of the freedom of contract. "New Dealers," Ackerman writes, "us[ed] a series of national electoral victories as mandates that ultimately induced all three branches of the national government to recognize that the People had endorsed activist national government."[11] Ackerman views the civil rights revolution as a second constitutional moment. He writes, "Johnson's landslide victory [in 1964], accompanied by decisive Democratic majorities in Congress, established a new institutional pattern. All three branches were now mutually supporting one another in asserting that the People of the United States had made a considered judgment about human rights."[12] Popular support for the Civil Rights Act of 1964 and the Voting Rights Act of 1965 entrenched *Brown* as a constitutional decision, having the same status as a constitutional amendment passed consistently with Article V.

Ackerman's views are controversial, but his writings accurately capture an important dimension of liberal constitutionalism. Liberals (and many conservatives) during the second half of the twentieth century did not ground their constitutional understandings in the original constitutional text or constitutional practices at the time those texts were ratified. Supreme Court decisions in the 1950s and 1960s pointed to judicial decisions in the 1930s as constitutional authorities justifying national power over the economy. Constitutional debate over racial equality during the twentieth century focused on the meaning of *Brown* and the civil rights acts of the 1960s.

B. Principles

New Dealers emphasized rights to democratic processes rather than freedoms from government regulation. Free speech and, later, voting rights became "preferred freedoms" because those liberties provided citizens with the means for adequately protecting more substantive rights and interests. The freedom of speech, Justice Cardozo declared in *Palko v. Connecticut* (1937), was "the matrix, the indispensable condition, of

11. Bruce Ackerman, *We the People: Transformations* (Cambridge, MA: Harvard University Press, 1998), 268.

12. Ibid., 110.

Table 8-2 Tiers of Scrutiny of Legislative Classifications

Level of Judicial Scrutiny	Trigger	Doctrinal Test to Uphold Classification
Strict scrutiny	Suspect classifications, such as race and nationality, or infringement on fundamental rights	Serves a compelling government interest and is the least restrictive test necessary to serve that interest
Intermediate scrutiny	Quasi-suspect classifications, such as gender	Serves an important government interest and is substantially related to serving that interest
Rational basis test	All other classifications, economic classifications in particular	Serves a legitimate government interest and is rationally related to serving that interest

nearly every other form of freedom." Citizens able to articulate their policy preferences and freely cast ballots could determine for themselves what individual rights they thought fundamental.

The focus of constitutional equality turned from general prohibitions against so-called class legislation to prohibitions against laws that targeted "discrete and insular minorities." The principles underlying class legislation made little sense in a society increasingly committed to interest group liberalism. New Dealers thought private efforts to secure favorable legislation were legitimate. They doubted whether any public interest existed independent of the interest of particular social groups. Virtually all legislation, the "pluralist" political science of the 1940s and 1950s maintained, provides special benefits to particular groups. In a constitutional regime characterized by bargaining over public policy, New Dealers concluded, constitutional equality rights turned on whether particular groups, most notably African Americans, were participating as equals in electoral and legislative bargaining processes.

These New Deal/Great Society conceptions of liberty and equality inspired a new two-tiered scheme of constitutional protection for rights. Constitutional decision makers before the 1930s relied on a "one-size-fits-all" approach to constitutional guarantees. Legislation limiting the exercise of a right or distinguishing between people was constitutional if the law plainly served a legitimate public purpose and if any distinction was based on real differences between people. Liberals distinguished among rights. Most legislative restrictions or classifications satisfied constitutional standards if they met a very undemanding rationality standard. Legislation that restricted such preferred freedoms as the freedom of speech or burdened such "discrete and insular minorities" as persons of color, however, required what became known as "strict scrutiny." Such laws were ordinarily unconstitutional unless the measure was a necessary or narrowly tailored means for achieving a compelling government end.

United States v. Carolene Products Co., 144 U.S. 304 (1938)

The Carolene Products Company shipped "Milnut" across state lines in violation of the Filled Milk Act of 1923. That law forbade companies from shipping in interstate commerce "skimmed milk compounded with any fat or oil other than milk fat, so as to resemble milk or cream." The Carolene Products Company insisted that the bill was an unconstitutional effort to protect dairy farmers, not a legitimate exercise of the federal power to regulate interstate commerce. The federal district court agreed and declared the Filled Milk Act unconstitutional. The United States appealed that ruling to the Supreme Court.

The Supreme Court by a 6–1 vote had little difficulty finding constitutional grounds for sustaining the federal law. Justice Stone's majority opinion declared that federal officials could prohibit the interstate shipment of any good that they believed was in some way harmful. "Congress," he declared, "is free to exclude from interstate commerce articles whose use in the states for which they are destined it may reasonably conceive to be injurious to the public health, morals, or welfare." Moreover, Stone continued, federal justices should not second-guess congressional judgments that certain milk products were unhealthy. His majority opinion emphasized that legislative fact-findings must normally be presumed correct unless they are utterly irrational. "The existence of facts supporting the legislative judgment is to be presumed," Stone declared, "for regulatory legislation affecting ordinary commercial transactions is not to be pronounced unconstitutional unless in the light of the facts made known or generally assumed it is of such a character as to preclude the assumption that it rests upon some rational basis within the knowledge and experience of the legislators." The justices relied on this very weak rational basis test when determining the constitutionality of most legislative restrictions or classifications. Stone appended a footnote to this assertion that indicated that the justices might not always be so deferential to legislatures. Stricter scrutiny was warranted, he suggested, when legislation was inconsistent with explicit constitutional text, interfered with democratic processes, or violated the rights of "discrete and insular minorities."

Footnote Four of United States v. Carolene Products Co. *is the most famous footnote in Supreme Court history. What is the underlying logic of the footnote? Is the logic of the first paragraph, which was added after a suggestion by Chief Justice Hughes, consistent with the logic of the more famous second and third paragraphs? Was Justice Stone suggesting that some constitutional rights or principles are more important than other constitutional rights or principles? Was he suggesting that the judiciary is institutionally better suited than the elected branches of government to protect rights to political processes and prevent discrimination against "discrete and insular minorities"? Does the fundamental logic of the* Carolene Products *footnote reflect developments in the political system? For many decades the Court nurtured a reputation for happily second-guessing the wisdom of economic regulation. In light of the Court's capitulation to the New Deal a year earlier, might the justices have been looking for a new job description?*

JUSTICE STONE delivered the opinion of the Court.

. . .

[Footnote 4:] There may be narrower scope for operation of the presumption of constitutionality when legislation appears on its face to be within a specific prohibition of the Constitution, such as those of the first ten Amendments, which are deemed equally specific when held to be embraced within the Fourteenth. . . . It is unnecessary to consider now whether legislation which restricts those political processes which can ordinarily be expected to bring about repeal of undesirable legislation, is to be subjected to more exacting judicial scrutiny under the general prohibitions of the Fourteenth Amendment than are most other types of legislation. [These include] restrictions upon the right to vote, . . . on restraints upon the dissemination of information, . . . on interferences with political organizations, [and] prohibition of peaceable assembly. Nor need we enquire whether similar considerations enter into the review of statutes directed at particular religious, . . . or national . . . or racial minorities; whether prejudice against discrete and insular minorities may be a special condition, which tends seriously to curtail the operation of those political processes ordinarily to be relied upon to protect minorities, and which may call for a correspondingly more searching judicial inquiry.

C. Scope

Americans broadened the scope of constitutional rights protections during the New Deal and Great Society Era. By 1968 far more persons in more circumstances had to respect more constitutional provisions than was the case in 1933. State officials could no longer violate most provisions in the Bill of Rights. Federal officials could no longer violate the constitutional rights of American citizens residing in foreign countries. Private persons were far more likely to be considered state actors when they engaged in what had previously been thought to be private race discrimination.

Most provisions in the Bill of Rights were incorporated during the New Deal and Great Society years. When that era began the due process clause of the Fourteenth Amendment was understood as obligating states to respect only the free speech/free press clause of the First Amendment, the takings clause of the Fifth Amendment, and the right to counsel clause of the Sixth Amendment. Thirty-five years later states were bound by almost every provision in the Bill of Rights. The Supreme Court held both state and federal criminal trials to the same constitutional standards. The only provisions in the Bill of Rights not clearly incorporated when Earl Warren left the bench were the Second Amendment, the Third Amendment, the grand jury requirement of the Sixth Amendment, the Seventh Amendment, and, perhaps, the excessive bail clause of the Eight Amendment.

"Selective incorporation" was the process by which most provisions in the Bill of Rights were incorporated by the due process clause of the Fourteenth Amendment. As described in *Duncan v. Louisiana* (1968), selective incorporation required the justices to determine whether a particular constitutional provision was central to "ordered liberty" or "fundamental fairness." If the provision was deemed an element of ordered liberty, then the entire provision was incorporated. If a comment by a federal prosecutor on a criminal defendant's failure to testify violates the Fifth Amendment, then the same comment by a state prosecutor violates the Fourteenth Amendment. The same is true of state police, state prosecutorial, and state judicial decisions that violate any other incorporated provision of the Bill of Rights.

The Supreme Court during the New Deal and Great Society Era proved (nearly) as willing to impose Bill of Rights restrictions on the federal government acting overseas as it did to impose restrictions on state governments acting domestically. The increased and more permanent American presence in foreign countries after World War II led some liberals to rethink the rule in *Ross v. McIntyre* (1891) that constitutional practices do not travel outside of territories in which the United States is sovereign. In *Reid v. Covert* (1957) the justices declared that an American woman charged with murdering her husband was entitled to a jury trial, even though the crime and trial took place in England. Justice Black's plurality opinion for four justices asserted, "When the Government reaches out to punish a citizen who is abroad, the shield which the Bill of Rights and other parts of the Constitution provide to protect his life and liberty should not be stripped away just because he happens to be in another land." The Supreme Court later required civilian trials for active service members whose domestic crimes were not related to their military service. "We have concluded that the crime to be under military jurisdiction must be service connected," Justice Douglas concluded in *O'Callahan v. Parker* (1969), "lest 'cases arising in the land or naval forces, or in the Militia, when in actual service in time of War or public danger' . . . be expanded to deprive every member of the armed services of the benefits of an indictment by a grand jury and a trial by a jury of his peers."

New Deal and Great Society liberals often found government complicity with what justices in the Republican Era regarded as private race discrimination. The *Civil Rights Cases* (1883) held that the Fourteenth Amendment limited only state actors. Supreme Court majorities did not overrule that decision, but they often found state action behind what had previously been considered private behavior. Judicial decisions held:

- Private parties performing a public function had to respect constitutional norms. Company towns, shopping centers, and, most important, political parties and organizations participating in primary elections performed public functions.
- Private parties had to respect constitutional norms whenever the state was significantly involved in their activities. Significant state involvement included enforcing restrictive racial covenants and leasing property to a restaurant that refused to serve persons of color.
- State action was often present when southern businesses called on law enforcement officials to oust persons of color protesting segregation.
- State action was not necessary when private parties in the housing market discriminated against persons of color, because denying contract or property rights on the basis of race was a badge or incident of slavery outlawed by the Thirteenth Amendment.

Federal court decisions on state action provided crucial support for civil rights protestors. In *Lombard v. Louisiana* (1963) Chief Justice Earl Warren found state action when the proprietor of a segregated lunch counter claimed to have been influenced by a police announcement that protests against segregation would not be tolerated. Justice Black in *Robinson v. Florida* (1964) ruled that a state law requiring separate toilets in restaurants that hired persons of color provided sufficient grounds to find state involvement with Shell City Restaurant's refusal to serve persons of color. All told, for state action or other reasons, the justices overturned state court decisions convicting sit-in demonstrators in more than twenty cases. No conviction of a civil rights protestor was sustained before passage of the Civil Rights Act of 1964. In *Hamm v. Rock City* (1965) that act was interpreted as voiding all remaining state convictions not yet appealed to the Supreme Court.

Duncan v. Louisiana, 391 U.S. 145 (1968)

Gary Duncan, a nineteen-year-old African American, was arrested for battery after he allegedly slapped Herman Landry, a white boy. At trial Duncan's request for a jury trial was denied. The trial judge, accepting the account of the incident offered by the white witnesses who testified, sentenced Duncan to sixty days in prison and ordered him to pay a $150 fine. Federal law at that time required a jury trial in all criminal cases other than petty crimes with a maximum punishment of less than six months. The maximum punishment for simple battery in Louisiana was two years. Duncan appealed his conviction to the Supreme Court of the United States. He claimed that states were obligated by the due process clause of the Fourteenth Amendment to provide jury trials whenever a federal court would be obligated to provide a jury trial under the Sixth Amendment.

The Supreme Court by a 7–2 vote declared that Duncan had been unconstitutionally convicted. Justice White's majority opinion ruled that the due process clause of the Fourteenth Amendment required states to respect the rights protected by the jury clause of the Sixth Amendment. Instead of determining whether Duncan's trial was fundamentally fair, White considered whether the jury trial provision of the Sixth Amendment was necessary for fundamental fairness. After concluding that a jury trial was a necessary element of a fair trial, he ruled that any trial that violated the Sixth Amendment guarantee also violated the due process clause of the Fourteenth Amendment. Consider whether this reasoning is sound. In his concurring opinion Justice Black defended his longstanding commitment to the "total incorporation" of the Bill of Rights. Must Black's argument depend on the historical record, or may total incorporation rest on American traditions and that position's capacity to reduce judicial discretion? Justice Harlan's dissent asserts that many particulars of the

Table 8-3 U.S. Supreme Court Cases Applying the Federal Bill of Rights to the States

Amendment	Right	Case
First Amendment	Establishment of religion	*Everson v. Board of Education Free* (1947)
	Exercise of religion	*Cantwell v. Connecticut* (1940)
	Freedom of speech	*Gitlow v. New York* (1925)
	Freedom of the press	*Near v. Minnesota* (1931)
	Freedom of assembly	*DeJonge v. Oregon* (1937)
Second Amendment	Right to keep and bear arms	*McDonald v. Chicago* (2010)
Fourth Amendment	Unreasonable searches	*Wolf v. Colorado* (1949)
	Exclusionary rule	*Mapp v. Ohio* (1961)
Fifth Amendment	Double jeopardy	*Benton v. Maryland* (1969)
	Self-incrimination	*Malloy v. Hogan* (1964)
	Taking without just compensation	*Chicago, B & Q. R. Co. v. Chicago* (1897)
Sixth Amendment	Speedy trial	*Klopfer v. North Carolina* (1967)
	Public trial	*In re Oliver* (1948)
	Jury trial	*Duncan v. Louisiana* (1968)
	Impartial jury	*Irvin v. Dowd* (1961)
	Notice of charges	*Cole v. Arkansas* (1948)
	Confrontation of witnesses	*Pointer v. Texas* (1965)
	Right to subpoena witnesses	*Washington v. Texas* (1967)
	Right to counsel	*Gideon v. Wainwright* (1963)
Eighth Amendment	Cruel and unusual punishment	*Robinson v. California* (1962)

Sixth Amendment are not necessary for fundamental fairness; for example, a trial by a jury of ten persons would not be unfair even though the Sixth Amendment requires a twelve-person jury. Is he correct? Harlan claimed that total incorporation, which insists that every provision of the Bill of Rights is fully incorporated, and fundamental fairness, which insists that due process is limited to basic fairness, are the only two intellectually coherent positions. Is this correct?

JUSTICE WHITE delivered the opinion of the Court.

. . .

The test for determining whether a right extended by the Fifth and Sixth Amendments with respect to federal criminal proceedings is also protected against state action by the Fourteenth Amendment has been phrased in a variety of ways in the opinions of this Court. The question has been asked whether a right is among those "fundamental principles of liberty and justice which lie at the base of all our civil and political institutions," . . . whether it is "'basic in our system of jurisprudence,'" . . . and whether it is "a fundamental right, essential to a fair trial. . . . " Because we believe that trial by jury in criminal cases is fundamental to the American scheme of justice, we hold that the Fourteenth Amendment guarantees a right of jury trial in all criminal cases which—were they to be tried in a federal court—would come within the Sixth Amendment's guarantee.[13]

. . .

The guarantees of jury trial in the Federal and State Constitutions reflect a profound judgment about the way in which law should be enforced and justice administered. A right to jury trial is granted to criminal defendants in order to prevent oppression by the Government. Those who wrote our constitutions knew from history and experience that it was necessary to protect against unfounded criminal charges brought to eliminate enemies and against judges too responsive to the voice of higher authority. . . . Providing an accused with the right to be tried by a jury of his peers gave him an inestimable safeguard against the corrupt or overzealous prosecutor and against the compliant, biased, or eccentric judge. If the defendant preferred the common-sense judgment of a jury to the more tutored but perhaps less sympathetic reaction of the single judge, he was to have it. Beyond this, the jury trial provisions in the Federal and State Constitutions reflect a fundamental decision about the exercise of official power—a reluctance to entrust plenary powers over the life and liberty of the citizen to one judge or to a group of judges. Fear of unchecked power, so typical of our State and Federal Governments in other respects, found expression in the criminal law in this insistence upon community participation in the determination of guilt or innocence. The deep commitment of the Nation to the right of jury trial in serious criminal cases as a defense against arbitrary law enforcement qualifies for protection under the Due Process Clause of the Fourteenth Amendment, and must therefore be respected by the States.

. . .

JUSTICE BLACK, with whom JUSTICE DOUGLAS joins, concurring.

. . . In [my *Adamson v. California* (1947)] dissent, . . . I took the position . . . that the Fourteenth Amendment made all of the provisions of the Bill of Rights applicable to the States. . . . I am very happy to support

13. [Footnote by Justice White] In one sense recent cases applying provisions of the first eight Amendments to the States represent a new approach to the "incorporation" debate. Earlier the Court can be seen as having asked, when inquiring into whether some particular procedural safeguard was required of a State, if a civilized system could be imagined that would not accord the particular protection. . . . The recent cases, on the other hand, have proceeded upon the valid assumption that state criminal processes are not imaginary and theoretical schemes but actual systems bearing virtually every characteristic of the common-law system that has been developing contemporaneously in England and in this country. The question thus is whether given this kind of system a particular procedure is fundamental—whether, that is, a procedure is necessary to an Anglo-American regime of ordered liberty. . . . Of each of these determinations that a constitutional provision originally written to bind the Federal Government should bind the States as well it might be said that the limitation in question is not necessarily fundamental to fairness in every criminal system that might be imagined but is fundamental in the context of the criminal processes maintained by the American States. . . . A criminal process which was fair and equitable but used no juries is easy to imagine. . . . Yet no American State has undertaken to construct such a system. Instead, every American State, including Louisiana, uses the jury extensively, and imposes very serious punishments only after a trial at which the defendant has a right to a jury's verdict. In every State, including Louisiana, the structure and style of the criminal process—the supporting framework and the subsidiary procedures—are of the sort that naturally complement jury trial, and have developed in connection with and in reliance upon jury trial.

this selective process through which our Court has since the *Adamson* case held most of the specific Bill of Rights' protections applicable to the States to the same extent they are applicable to the Federal Government. Among these are the right to trial by jury decided today, the right against compelled self-incrimination, the right to counsel, the right to compulsory process for witnesses, the right to confront witnesses, the right to a speedy and public trial, and the right to be free from unreasonable searches and seizures.

. . . What I wrote [in *Adamson*] was the product of years of study and research. . . . My legislative experience has convinced me . . . to rely on what *was* said . . . by the men who actually sponsored the Amendment in the Congress. I know from my years in the United States Senate that it is to men like Congressman Bingham, who steered the Amendment through the House, and Senator Howard, who introduced it in the Senate, that members of Congress look when they seek the real meaning of what is being offered. And they vote for or against a bill based on what the sponsors of that bill and those who oppose it tell them it means. The historical appendix to my *Adamson* dissent leaves no doubt in my mind that both its sponsors and those who opposed it believed the Fourteenth Amendment made the first eight Amendments of the Constitution (the Bill of Rights) applicable to the States.

. . . [T]he dissent states that "the great words of the four clauses of the first section of the Fourteenth Amendment would have been an exceedingly peculiar way to say that 'The rights heretofore guaranteed against federal intrusion by the first eight Amendments are henceforth guaranteed against state intrusion as well.'" . . . In response to this I can say only that the words "No State shall make or enforce any law which shall abridge the privileges or immunities of citizens of the United States" seem to me an eminently reasonable way of expressing the idea that henceforth the Bill of Rights shall apply to the States. . . . What more precious "privilege" of American citizenship could there be than that privilege to claim the protections of our great Bill of Rights? I suggest that any reading of "privileges or immunities of citizens of the United States" which excludes the Bill of Rights' safeguards renders the words of this section of the Fourteenth Amendment meaningless. . . .

. . .

. . . I do want to point out what appears to me to be the basic difference between [Justice Harlan and me]. His view . . . is that "due process is an evolving concept" and therefore that it entails a "gradual process of judicial inclusion and exclusion" to ascertain those "immutable principles . . . of free government which no member of the Union may disregard." Thus the Due Process Clause is treated as prescribing no specific and clearly ascertainable constitutional command that judges must obey in interpreting the Constitution, but rather as leaving judges free to decide at any particular time whether a particular rule or judicial formulation embodies an "immutable principl[e] of free government" or is "implicit in the concept of ordered liberty," or whether certain conduct "shocks the judge's conscience" or runs counter to some other similar, undefined and undefinable standard. Thus due process, according to my Brother HARLAN, is to be a phrase with no permanent meaning, but one which is found to shift from time to time in accordance with judges' predilections and understandings of what is best for the country. If due process means this, the Fourteenth Amendment, in my opinion, might as well have been written that "no person shall be deprived of life, liberty or property except by laws that the judges of the United States Supreme Court shall find to be consistent with the immutable principles of free government." It is impossible for me to believe that such unconfined power is given to judges in our Constitution that is a written one in order to limit governmental power.

. . . [M]y Brother HARLAN [states] that "due process of law requires only fundamental fairness." But the "fundamental fairness" test is one on a par with that of shocking the conscience of the Court. Each of such tests depends entirely on the particular judge's idea of ethics and morals instead of requiring him to depend on the boundaries fixed by the written words of the Constitution. Nothing in the history of the phrase "due process of law" suggests that constitutional controls are to depend on any particular judge's sense of values. . . .

Finally I want to add that I am not bothered by the argument that applying the Bill of Rights to the States, "according to the same standards that protect those personal rights against federal encroachment," interferes with our concept of federalism in that it may prevent States from trying novel social and economic experiments. I have never believed that under the guise of federalism the States should be able to experiment with the protections afforded our citizens through the Bill of Rights. . . .

JUSTICE FORTAS, concurring. . . .

JUSTICE HARLAN, whom JUSTICE STEWART joins, dissenting.

. . .

The States have always borne primary responsibility for operating the machinery of criminal justice within their borders, and adapting it to their particular circumstances. In exercising this responsibility, each State is compelled to conform its procedures to the requirements of the Federal Constitution. The Due Process Clause of the Fourteenth Amendment requires that those procedures be fundamentally fair in all respects. It does not, in my view, impose or encourage nationwide uniformity for its own sake; it does not command adherence to forms that happen to be old; and it does not impose on the States the rules that may be in force in the federal courts except where such rules are also found to be essential to basic fairness.

. . .

I believe I am correct in saying that every member of the Court for at least the last 135 years has agreed that our Founders did not consider the requirements of the Bill of Rights so fundamental that they should operate directly against the States. . . . They were wont to believe rather that the security of liberty in America rested primarily upon the dispersion of governmental power across a federal system. . . . The Bill of Rights was considered unnecessary by some . . . but insisted upon by others in order to curb the possibility of abuse of power by the strong central government they were creating. . . .

A few members of the Court have taken the position that the intention of those who drafted the first section of the Fourteenth Amendment was simply, and exclusively, to make the provisions of the first eight Amendments applicable to state action. . . . This view has never been accepted by this Court. In my view, . . . the first section of the Fourteenth Amendment was meant neither to incorporate, nor to be limited to, the specific guarantees of the first eight Amendments. The overwhelming historical evidence marshalled by Professor Fairman[14] demonstrates, to me conclusively, that the Congressmen and state legislators who wrote, debated, and ratified the Fourteenth Amendment did not think they were "incorporating" the Bill of Rights and the very breadth and generality of the Amendment's provisions suggest that its authors did not suppose that the Nation would always be limited to mid-19th century conceptions of "liberty" and "due process of law" but that the increasing experience and evolving conscience of the American people would add new "intermediate premises." In short, neither history, nor sense, supports using the Fourteenth Amendment to put the States in a constitutional straitjacket with respect to their own development in the administration of criminal or civil law.

. . . Apart from the approach taken by the absolute incorporationists, I can see only one method of analysis that has any internal logic. That is to start with the words "liberty" and "due process of law" and attempt to define them in a way that accords with American traditions and our system of government. This approach, involving a much more discriminating process of adjudication than does "incorporation," is, albeit difficult, the one that was followed throughout the 19th and most of the present century. It entails a "gradual process of judicial inclusion and exclusion," . . . seeking, with due recognition of constitutional tolerance for state experimentation and disparity, to ascertain those "immutable principles . . . of free government which no member of the Union may disregard." . . . Due process was not restricted to rules fixed in the past, for that "would be to deny every quality of the law but its age, and to render it incapable of progress or improvement." . . . Nor did it impose nationwide uniformity in details. . . .

. . .

The relationship of the Bill of Rights to this "gradual process" seems to me to be twofold. In the first place it has long been clear that the Due Process Clause imposes some restrictions on state action that parallel Bill of Rights restrictions on federal action. Second, and more important than this accidental overlap, is the fact that the Bill of Rights is evidence, at various points, of the content Americans find in the term "liberty" and of American standards of fundamental fairness. . . . The logically critical thing, however, was not that the rights had been found in the Bill of Rights, but that they were deemed, in the context of American legal history, to be fundamental. . . .

. . . In sum, there is a wide range of views on the desirability of trial by jury, and on the ways to make it

14. Charles Fairman, "Does the Fourteenth Amendment Incorporate the Bill of Rights? The Original Understanding," *Stanford Law Review* 2 (1949): 5–139.

most effective when it is used; there is also considerable variation from State to State in local conditions such as the size of the criminal caseload, the ease or difficulty of summoning jurors, and other trial conditions bearing on fairness. . . .

This Court, other courts, and the political process are available to correct any experiments in criminal procedure that prove fundamentally unfair to defendants. That is not what is being done today: instead, and quite without reason, the Court has chosen to impose upon every State one means of trying criminal cases; it is a good means, but it is not the only fair means, and it is not demonstrably better than the alternatives States might devise.

Shelley v. Kraemer, 334 U.S. 1 (1948)

J. D. Shelley and his spouse, who were both persons of color, on August 11 purchased from Josephine Fitzgerald a house on Labadie Avenue in St. Louis, Missouri. Thirty-four years prior, most homeowners on that block had signed a restrictive covenant. The crucial provision of that agreement prohibited each owner from selling or renting his or her plot to "people of the Negro or Mongolian Race." Louis Kraemer, a party to that agreement, brought a lawsuit asking that the Shelley family be required to leave the house and be divested of their title to the property. The state trial court rejected this lawsuit on the ground that the original restrictive covenant had not been validly made. That decision was reversed by the Supreme Court of Missouri, which concluded that the restrictive covenant was valid and did not violate the constitutional rights of the Shelleys. The Shelleys appealed that verdict to the Supreme Court of the United States, claiming that judicial enforcement of the restrictive covenant violated the Fourteenth Amendment. For the first time in American history, the United States submitted an amicus brief on behalf of the party claiming unconstitutional racial discrimination.

Restrictive covenants were a popular means for fostering residential segregation after the Supreme Court in Buchanan v. Warley *(1917) ruled that elected officials could not mandate racial segregation in the housing market. If people in an entire neighborhood agreed not to sell or rent their homes to persons of color, however, such covenants could keep neighborhoods segregated in perpetuity. The Supreme Court in* Buckley v. Corrigan *(1926) declared such private agreements did not violate the Fourteenth Amendment.*

The Supreme Court unanimously ruled that courts could not enforce restrictive covenants. Chief Justice Vinson's majority opinion declared that state action occurred when courts enforced a restrictive covenant. He did not declare restrictive covenants illegal. Had Fitzgerald in 1948 refused to sell to persons of color, the Vinson Court would not have found a constitutional wrong. This meant that the impact of Shelley *was quite limited. Persons of color would gain constitutional rights only when persons who had signed a restrictive racial covenant either changed their mind or sold the property to someone who was later willing to sell to a person of color. Did the justices rule that states cannot prevent a willing seller from conveying property to a willing buyer of a different race? This was Chief Justice Vinson's understanding of* Shelley. *Five years later he insisted that persons who violated a restrictive racial covenant could be sued for damages by other parties to that agreement. His opinion in* Barrows v. Jackson *(1953) declared, "No non-Caucasian has been injured or could be injured if damages are assessed against respondent for breaching the promise which she willingly and voluntarily made to petitioners, a promise which neither the federal law nor the Constitution proscribes." That opinion was a lone dissent. Justice Minton's majority opinion declared that courts could not order any remedy when persons violated restrictive racial covenants. "This Court," he wrote, "will not permit or require California to coerce respondent to respond in damages for failure to observe a restrictive covenant that this Court would deny California the right to enforce in equity." This suggests that* Shelley *is based on the common law principle that contracts against public policy are not judicially enforceable. What is left of the requirement of "state action" after* Shelley? *Does* Shelley *permit police to enforce a restaurant's decision to not serve African Americans or your decision to invite only members of your ethnic group to a party? Was* Shelley *rooted more in politics than in law? The justices abhorred restrictive racial covenants. The United States government and prominent interest groups wanted restrictive covenants declared judicially unenforceable. Under these circumstances, the Vinson Court might not have needed much of a legal excuse to rule against the Kraemers.*

Brief for the United States as Amicus Curiae

The Federal Government has a special responsibility for the protection of the fundamental civil rights guaranteed to the people by the Constitution and laws of the United States. . . . The Government is of the view that judicial enforcement of racial restrictive covenants on real property is incompatible with the spirit and letter of the Constitution and laws of the United States. It is fundamental that no agency of government should participate in any action which will result in depriving any person of essential rights because of race or color or creed. This Court has held that such discriminations are prohibited by the organic law of the land, and that no legislative body has power to create them. It must follow, therefore, that the Constitutional rights guaranteed to every person cannot be denied by private contracts enforced by the judicial branch of government—especially where the discrimination created by private contracts have grown to such proportions as to become detrimental to the public welfare and against public policy.

...

Racial restrictive covenants ... are responsible for the creation of isolated areas in which over-crowded racial minorities are confined, and in which living conditions are steadily worsened. The avenues of escape are being narrowed and reduced. As to the people so trapped, there is no life in the accepted sense of the word; liberty is a mockery, and the right to pursue happiness a phrase without meaning, empty of hope and reality. This situation cannot be reconciled with the spirit of mutual tolerance and respect for the dignity and rights of the individual which give vitality to our democratic way of life. The time has come to destroy these evils which threaten the safety of our free institutions.

The fact that racial restrictive covenants are being enforced by instrumentalities of government has become a source of serious embarrassment to agencies of the Federal Government in the performance of many essential functions, including the programs relating to housing and home finance, to public health, to the protection of dependent native racial minorities in the United States and its territories, to the conduct of foreign affairs, and to the protection of civil rights.

CHIEF JUSTICE VINSON delivered the opinion of the Court.

...

It cannot be doubted that among the civil rights intended to be protected from discriminatory state action by the Fourteenth Amendment are the rights to acquire, enjoy, own and dispose of property. Equality in the enjoyment of property rights was regarded by the framers of that Amendment as an essential pre-condition to the realization of other basic civil rights and liberties which the Amendment was intended to guarantee. . . .

It is likewise clear that restrictions on the right of occupancy of the sort sought to be created by the private agreements in these cases could not be squared with the requirements of the Fourteenth Amendment if imposed by state statute or local ordinance. . . .

. . . Here the particular patterns of discrimination and the areas in which the restrictions are to operate, are determined, in the first instance, by the terms of agreements among private individuals. Participation of the State consists in the enforcement of the restrictions so defined. . . .

Since the decision of this Court in the *Civil Rights Cases* (1883), . . . the principle has become firmly embedded in our constitutional law that the action inhibited by the first section of the Fourteenth Amendment is only such action as may fairly be said to be that of the States. That Amendment erects no shield against merely private conduct, however discriminatory or wrongful.

We conclude, therefore, that the restrictive agreements standing alone cannot be regarded as a violation of any rights guaranteed to petitioners by the Fourteenth Amendment. So long as the purposes of those agreements are effectuated by voluntary adherence to their terms, it would appear clear that there has been no action by the State and the provisions of the Amendment have not been violated. . . .

But here there was more. These are cases in which the purposes of the agreements were secured only by judicial enforcement by state courts of the restrictive terms of the agreements. . . .

That the action of state courts and of judicial officers in their official capacities is to be regarded as action of the State within the meaning of the Fourteenth Amendment, is a proposition which has long been established by decisions of this Court. . . .

...

. . . We have no doubt that there has been state action in these cases in the full and complete sense of the phrase. The undisputed facts disclose that petitioners were willing purchasers of properties upon which they desired to establish homes. The owners of the properties were willing sellers; and contracts of sale were accordingly consummated. It is clear that but for the active intervention of the state courts, supported by the full panoply of state power, petitioners would have been free to occupy the properties in question without restraint.

These are not cases, as has been suggested, in which the States have merely abstained from action, leaving private individuals free to impose such discriminations as they see fit. Rather, these are cases in which the States have made available to such individuals the full coercive power of government to deny to petitioners, on the grounds of race or color, the enjoyment of property rights in premises which petitioners are willing and financially able to acquire and which the grantors are willing to sell. . . .

. . .

We hold that in granting judicial enforcement of the restrictive agreements in these cases, the States have denied petitioners the equal protection of the laws and that, therefore, the action of the state courts cannot stand. We have noted that freedom from discrimination by the States in the enjoyment of property rights was among the basic objectives sought to be effectuated by the framers of the Fourteenth Amendment. That such discrimination has occurred in these cases is clear. Because of the race or color of these petitioners they have been denied rights of ownership or occupancy enjoyed as a matter of course by other citizens of different race or color. . . . Only recently this Court has had occasion to declare that a state law which denied equal enjoyment of property rights to a designated class of citizens of specified race and ancestry, was not a legitimate exercise of the state's police power but violated the guaranty of the equal protection of the laws. . . .

. . .

JUSTICE REED, JUSTICE JACKSON, and JUSTICE RUTLEDGE took no part in the consideration or decision of these cases.

III. Judicial Power and Constitutional Authority

MAJOR DEVELOPMENTS

- The struggle over judicial supremacy in constitutional interpretation
- The struggle over how courts should use the power of judicial review
- The lowering of procedural barriers to bringing disputes into courts

Constitutional struggles over judicial power during the New Deal and Great Society Era reflected constitutional struggles over national power. During the early years of the New Deal, New Deal liberals tried to wrest control over the federal judiciary from both conservatives and older-style progressives. The four most conservative members of the Supreme Court during this period were known as the "Four Horsemen." Justices Butler, McReynolds, Sutherland, and Van Devanter strongly opposed the economic regulations that state and federal governments adopted in the early 1930s. Old-style progressives like Justice Brandeis and Cardozo were much more sympathetic to government intervention in the economy, but they were often skeptical about the centralized political power that they saw in the New Deal. Chief Justice Hughes and Justice Roberts occupied more centrist roles on the Court.

From 1933 to 1936 the four conservatives often won over at least one of the moderates on the Court and sometimes carried additional votes as well. The key victory for the New Deal came when Justice Roberts and Chief Justice Hughes swung decisively away from the conservatives in 1937. The constitutionality of the New Deal was then no longer an open question on the Court. Those who doubted the New Deal soon left the bench and were replaced by Roosevelt appointees.

From 1937 to 1968 the central questions over judicial power concerned debates within the New Deal/Great Society coalition. Some argued that the New Deal was committed to legislative supremacy in most areas of public policy and that judges should generally defer to both federal and state elected officials. Justice Felix Frankfurter, a former Harvard law professor who served on the Supreme Court from 1939 until 1962, is the person most associated with this view of judicial power. Others insisted that the New Deal was committed to national supremacy and that state officials should not receive the same deference from judges that federal officials did. Advocates of this position often argued that judges should make democracy work better and protect those who were not adequately protected in the democratic process. Justice Hugo Black, a former U.S. senator from Alabama who served on the Supreme Court from 1937 until 1971, is the person most associated with this view of judicial power. Frankfurter found important support for his views on the Court and played a key role in restraining that body until his retirement in 1962. After President John F. Kennedy chose famed labor

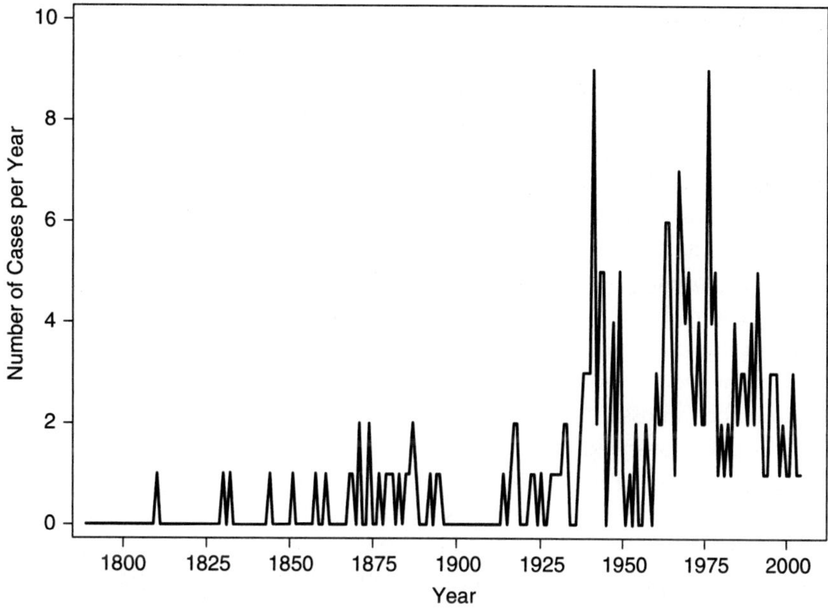

Figure 8-3 Precedents Overruled by the U.S. Supreme Court, 1790–2004

Source: Congressional Research Service, *The Constitution of the United States of America, Analysis and Interpretation* (Washington, DC: Government Printing Office, 2004).

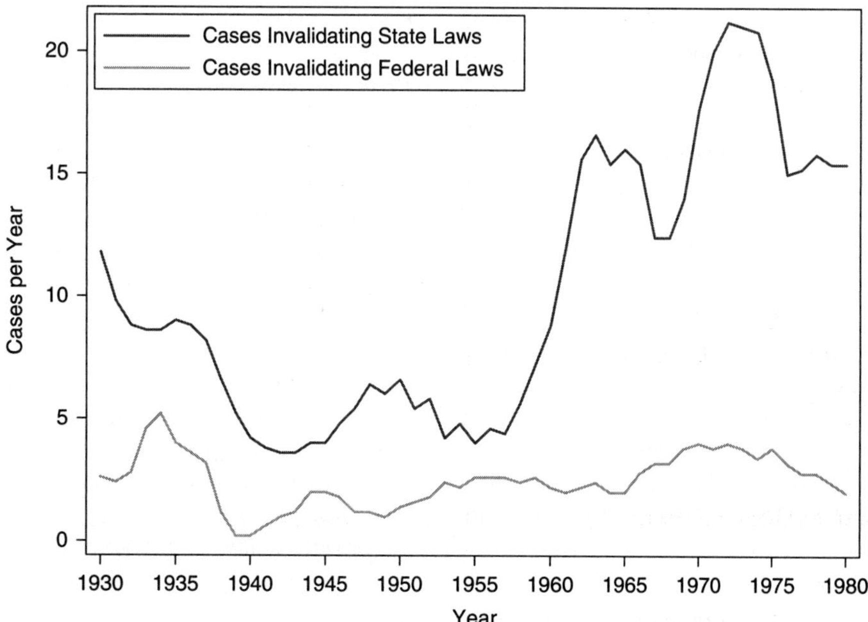

Figure 8-4 U.S. Supreme Court Invalidation of State and Federal Laws, 1930–1980

Sources: Congressional Research Service, *The Constitution of the United States of America, Analysis and Interpretation* (Washington, DC: Government Printing Office, 2004); Keith E. Whittington, The Judicial Review of Congress dataset.

Note: Centered, five-year moving averages.

lawyer Arthur Goldberg to replace Frankfurter, the core of the liberal wing of the Warren Court was in place. The Warren Court embarked on a new activist phase that lasted through Chief Justice Earl Warren's retirement in 1969.

A renewed constitutional commitment to judicial supremacy was perhaps the most surprising legacy of the New Deal and Great Society Era. As was the case with most presidents who rose to power challenging the fundamental constitutional commitments of an earlier regime, Franklin Roosevelt aggressively challenged the authority of the federal judiciary. He was privately prepared to ignore a possible judicial decision striking down his policy suspending gold payments, and he did little to keep this resolve a secret. After achieving a landslide victory during the 1936 presidential election, Roosevelt proposed a Court-packing plan that would have guaranteed a friendly, pro–New Deal Court. The effort to pack the Court with different justices rather than limit their jurisdiction or weaken their powers highlights the commitment of New Dealers to changing the direction of judicial decision making rather than challenging judicial authority per se. When a court "packed" with justices appointed to replace older justices who had died or retired began sustaining New Deal measures, liberal talk of judicial reform ceased.

Although New Dealers and Great Society liberals disagreed about how the Court should use its power, by the 1950s a broad consensus existed that the Supreme Court had the final authority to determine what the Constitution meant. All nine justices signed the opinion in *Cooper v. Aaron* (1958) that asserted that all elected officials are obligated to obey the Constitution as interpreted by the Supreme Court. President Eisenhower had already endorsed this idea before the Court heard the case. By the 1960s leaders of both political parties accepted the idea that courts should determine constitutional meaning. Political battles over the courts increasingly took the form of struggles over who would control judicial power and when it ought to be used.

Proponents of the New Deal and Great Society promoted litigation as an appropriate means for resolving contested constitutional questions. In the 1960s, the Warren Court sought to lower the barriers to constitutional litigation and judicial resolution of constitutional issues. *Baker v. Carr* (1962) and *Powell v. McCormack* (1969) demonstrated that the justices took a narrow view of the "political questions" doctrine. *Flast v. Cohen* (1968) indicated that the justices might find standing for nontraditional injuries when doing so enabled them to address constitutional wrongs. National elected officials during the Great Society promoted courts as constitutional decision makers by expanding the size of the federal judiciary, appointing sympathetic justices, creating financial incentives for litigation, and supporting public interest groups that litigated constitutional claims.

Franklin D. Roosevelt, **Undelivered Speech on the Gold Clause Cases** (1935)[15]

In the economic crisis of the 1930s, the supply of goods outstripped the demand for them. The causes for this situation are various and debatable, but the results were devastating—deflation (declining prices, or the declining value of goods relative to the currency), unemployment, bankruptcies, and debt repudiations. Among his first acts as president, Roosevelt halted trading in gold and soon thereafter took the United States off the gold standard, opening the door to various inflationary policies. In June 1933 a congressional joint resolution declared that any contract "which purports to give the obligee a right to require payment in gold" or a gold equivalent in U.S. currency was "declared to be against public policy" and void. Public and private debts were to be repaid only in current dollars, gold clauses notwithstanding. Progressive Republican senator William Borah, a supporter of the measure, argued that bondholders may "suffer, and suffer extremely [but] . . . it devolves upon the Government of the United States to find an escape from the present condition of affairs in some way or other. . . . We must cease to pay tribute to the gold standard at the expense of the average citizen of the United States."[16]

Several constitutional challenges to the suspension of the gold clauses made their way to the Supreme Court. These lawsuits were the first major challenges to Roosevelt's policies. Both Washington and the financial markets were aflame with speculation about what the Court would do. The attorney general, who argued the case personally before the

15. Excerpt taken from Franklin D. Roosevelt, "Proposed Gold Clause Statement, June 27, 1935," President's Personal File Speeches, Franklin D. Roosevelt Library, Hyde Park, New York.

16. *Congressional Record*, 73rd Cong., 1st Sess., June 3, 1933, 4905–06.

Supreme Court, emphasized the economic consequences of an adverse ruling as much as the legal supports for the government's actions. As the justices met to discuss the case, congressmen and administration officials publicly discussed what would happen if the government lost. Common suggestions included a constitutional convention, the immediate addition of new justices to the Court and a rehearing of the case, and the declaration of martial law.[17]

When the Court finally handed down its decision in the Gold Clause Cases *(1935), the government had won on a technicality. The justices were clearly uncomfortable with and critical of the suspension, but they concluded that the bondholders had no legal remedy and dismissed the suits. President Roosevelt had prepared a draft for a speech to be delivered in case the government lost. That speech would have announced that the president's higher obligation was "to protect the people of the United States," even from the Supreme Court. The draft does not specify the precise actions that the administration would have taken to negate the effects of the Court's decision, though several options were under active consideration, perhaps depending on the substance of the Court's decision. The existence of the speech was leaked to the press just after the Court issued its ruling. Might the justices have been influenced by this charged political environment? Would the president have been justified in taking extreme actions to prevent enforcement of the Court's decision in this case? Roosevelt quotes Lincoln's inaugural address in his speech (see Chapter Six, Section V). Were Lincoln's arguments appropriate to the situation facing FDR?*

Two years ago the welfare of all our citizens in every section of the United States was endangered by increasing bankruptcies and bank failures. In the short space of the previous three and one half years the purchasing power of the dollar had increased about sixty percent. This meant that debtors of all kinds . . . were being called on to pay their creditors in currency worth sixty percent more in purchasing power than the money which had been loaned to them.

. . .

But on the day of my inauguration, any attempt to collect in substance one hundred and sixty cents for every dollar owed would have brought universal bankruptcy.

17. See David Glick, "Conditional Strategic Retreat: The Court's Concession in the 1935 Gold Clause Cases," *Journal of Politics* 71 (2009): 800.

During the past twenty-three months we have moved rapidly toward establishing and maintaining a dollar of stable purchasing power. . . . All of our legislation of the past two years has been aimed at creating a currency of sound and standard purchasing power and then maintaining it.

In working toward our broad objective, the American currency was first taken off what is commonly known as the Gold Standard. . . .

The decisions of the Supreme Court are, of course, based on the legal proposition that the exact terms of a contract must be literally enforced.

Let me for a moment analyze the effect of the present decision by giving a few simple illustrations:

. . .

Consider the plight of the individual who is buying a home for himself and his family and paying each month a specified sum representing interest and reduction of the mortgage. If there is a gold clause in his mortgage—and most mortgages contain this clause—this decision would compel him to increase his payments 69% each month from now on, and perhaps to pay 69% more on some payments already made. Home owners, whether city workers or farmers, could not meet such a demand.

Consider now the other two decisions relating to government obligations on gold notes, gold certificates and gold clause bonds. An old lady came to see me the other day. She is dependent heavily on the income from government bonds which she owns; and her total income is about $800 a year. She owns $10,000 of government gold clause bonds. Under this new decision she would be entitled to ask the Treasury for $16,900. Being the right type of citizen, she volunteered to tell me that she does not consider herself entitled to more than the $10,000 which she had saved and invested.

The actual enforcement of the gold clause against the Government of the United States will not bankrupt the Government. It will increase our national debt by approximately nine billions of dollars. It means that this additional sum must eventually be raised by additional taxation. In our present major effort to get out of the depression, to put people to work, to restore industry and agriculture, the literal enforcement of this opinion would not only retard our efforts, but would put the Government and 125,000,000 people into an infinitely more serious economic plight than we have yet experienced.

. . .

I do not seek to enter into any controversy with the distinguished members of the Supreme Court of the United States who have participated in this (majority) decision. They have decided these cases in accordance with the letter of the law as they read it. But it is appropriate to quote a sentence from the First Inaugural Address of President Lincoln:

> At the same time, the candid citizen must confess that if the policy of the government, upon vital questions affecting the whole people, is to be irrevocably fixed by decisions of the Supreme Court, the instant they are made, in ordinary litigation between parties in personal actions, the people will have ceased to be their own rulers, having to that extent practically resigned their government into the hands of that eminent tribunal.

It is the duty of the Congress and the President to protect the People of the United States to the best of their ability. It is necessary to protect them from the unintended construction of voluntary acts, as well as from intolerable burdens involuntarily imposed. To stand idly by and to permit the decision of the Supreme Court to be carried through to its logical, inescapable conclusion would so imperil the economic and political security of this nation that the legislative and executive officers of the Government must look beyond the narrow letter of contractual obligations, so that they may sustain the substance of the promise originally made in accord with the actual intention of the parties.

For the value received the same value should be repaid. That is the spirit of the contract and of the law. . . . That would seem to be a decision in accordance with the Golden Rule, with the precepts of the Scriptures, and the dictates of common sense.

In order to attain this reasonable end, I shall immediately take such steps as may be necessary, by proclamation and by message to the Congress of the United States.

In the meantime, I ask every individual, every trustee, every corporation and every bank to proceed on the usual course of their honorable and legitimate business. They can rest assured that we shall carry on the business of the country tomorrow just as we did last week or last month, on the same financial basis, on the same currency basis, and in the same relationship of debtor and creditor as before.

Franklin D. Roosevelt, Fireside Chat on Court-Packing Plan (1937)[18]

During the first Roosevelt administration, intense conflict took place between the judicial and executive branches of government. Roosevelt believed the Depression created the need for substantial national regulation of the economy. By 5–4 and 6–3 majorities, the Supreme Court declared many of these policies unconstitutional. Judicial casualties included the Agricultural Adjustment Act and the National Industrial Recovery Act. Concerned that such measures as the National Labor Relations Act and the Social Security Act might not pass constitutional muster, the Roosevelt administration decided to take preemptive measures. Although some administration officials were inclined to seek a constitutional amendment to give the government more power, Roosevelt rejected that choice. An amendment was likely to be difficult to draft and ratify, might be seen as an admission that the justices were correctly interpreting the existing Constitution, and would ultimately leave the fate of the New Deal in the hands of the same judges as before. Instead, Roosevelt proposed the Court-packing plan.

Disingenuously claiming that the central problem was that the justices on the bench were too old and getting behind in their work, Roosevelt proposed allowing the president to appoint an additional justice for each sitting justice who reached the age of seventy, so long as the sitting justice had served at least ten years. The maximum size of the Court was set at fifteen under this scheme. The plan would have given FDR an immediate and large pro–New Deal majority on the Court. In this fireside chat, Roosevelt more honestly addressed the real political conflicts that were responsible for the Court-packing plan.

Despite the overwhelming Democratic majorities in Congress and the president's landslide reelection, the Court-packing plan was defeated in Congress partly for reasons laid out by the Senate Judiciary Committee. But, beginning in 1937, key swing justices began consistently supporting New Deal measures. The combination of that "switch in time" and a series of judicial appointments made through the normal process of retirements and

18. Excerpt taken from Franklin D. Roosevelt, "Fireside Chat on the Reorganization of the Judiciary, March 9, 1937," President's Personal File Speeches, Franklin D. Roosevelt Library, Hyde Park, New York.

Illustration 8-2 "Three's a Crowd!"

Cartoon critical of President Franklin Roosevelt's Court-packing plan.

Source: Cincinnati Times Star (February 16, 1937). © 2003 New Deal Network.

death made the Court-packing plan irrelevant. Whether the Court-packing plan had any influence on the New Deal turnaround is controversial. Several scholars claim that it had no impact. The 1937 decisions, they insist, were consistent with previous decisions striking down federal laws, and, besides, Justice Roberts had actually made the crucial switch before the Court-packing plan was announced. Others believe that some combination of the elections of 1936 and the numerous Court-curbing proposals that were introduced in Congress and discussed in the press played crucial roles in the decision Justice Roberts and Chief Justice Hughes made to become consistent supporters of New Deal policies.[19]

MY FRIENDS, last Thursday I described in detail certain economic problems which everyone admits now face the nation. . . .

I am reminded of that evening in March, four years ago, when I made my first radio report to you. We were then in the midst of the great banking crisis.

Soon after, with the authority of the Congress, we asked the nation to turn over all of its privately held gold, dollar for dollar, to the government of the United States.

Today's recovery proves how right that policy was.

But when, almost two years later, it came before the Supreme Court its constitutionality was upheld only by a five-to-four vote. The change of one vote would have thrown all the affairs of this great nation back into hopeless chaos. In effect, four justices ruled that the right under a private contract to exact a pound of flesh was more sacred than the main objectives of the Constitution to establish an enduring nation.

. . .

The American people have learned from the depression. For in the last three national elections an overwhelming majority of them voted a mandate that the Congress and the president begin the task of providing that protection—not after long years of debate, but now.

The courts, however, have cast doubts on the ability of the elected Congress to protect us against catastrophe by meeting squarely our modern social and economic conditions.

. . .

Last Thursday I described the American form of government as a three-horse team provided by the Constitution to the American people so that their field might be plowed. The three horses are, of course, the three branches of government—the Congress, the executive, and the courts. Two of the horses, the Congress and the executive, are pulling in unison today; the third is not. Those who have intimated that the president of the United States is trying to drive that team, overlook the simple fact that the president, as chief executive, is himself one of the three horses.

It is the American people themselves who are in the driver's seat. It is the American people themselves who want the furrow plowed. It is the American people themselves who expect the third horse to fall in unison with the other two.

I hope that you have re-read the Constitution of the United States in these past few weeks. Like the Bible, it ought to be read again and again.

. . . In its Preamble, the Constitution states that it was intended to form a more perfect union and promote the general welfare; and the powers given to the Congress to carry out those purposes can best be described by saying that they were all the powers needed to meet each and every problem which then had a national character and which could not be met by merely local action.

But the framers of the Constitution went further. Having in mind that in succeeding generations many other problems then undreamed of would become national problems, they gave to the Congress the ample broad powers "to levy taxes . . . and provide for the common defense and general welfare of the United States."

. . .

For nearly twenty years there was no conflict between the Congress and the Court. Then in 1803 Congress passed a statute which the Court said violated an express provision of the Constitution. The Court claimed the power to declare it unconstitutional and did so declare it. But a little later the Court itself admitted that it was an extraordinary power to exercise and through Mr. Justice Washington laid down this limitation upon it: he said, "It is but a decent respect due to the wisdom, the integrity and the patriotism of the legislative body, by which any law is passed, to presume in favor of its validity until its violation of the Constitution is proved beyond all reasonable doubt."

But since the rise of the modern movement for social and economic progress through legislation, the Court has more and more often and more and more boldly asserted a power to veto laws passed by the Congress and by state legislatures in complete disregard of this original limitation which I have just read.

19. On the significance of the Court-packing plan, see William E. Leuchtenburg, *The Supreme Court Reborn* (New York: Oxford University Press, 1995); Barry Cushman, *Rethinking the New Deal Court* (New York: Oxford University Press, 1998); Bruce Ackerman, *We the People: Transformations* (Cambridge, MA: Harvard University Press, 1998); Barry Friedman, *The Will of the People* (New York: Oxford University Press, 2009); Daniel E. Ho and Kevin M. Quinn, "Did a Switch in Time Save Nine?," *Journal of Legal Analysis* 2 (Spring 2010): 69.

In the last four years the sound rule of giving statutes the benefit of all reasonable doubt has been cast aside. The Court has been acting not as a judicial body, but as a policymaking body.

When the Congress has sought to stabilize national agriculture, to improve the conditions of labor, to safeguard business against unfair competition, to protect our national resources, and in many other ways, to serve our clearly national needs, the majority of the Court has been assuming the power to pass on the wisdom of these acts of the Congress—and to approve or disapprove the public policy written into these laws.

That is not only my accusation. It is the accusation of most distinguished justices of the present Supreme Court. . . .

. . .

In the face of these dissenting opinions, there is no basis for the claim made by some members of the Court that something in the Constitution has compelled them regretfully to thwart the will of the people.

In the face of such dissenting opinions, it is perfectly clear that, as Chief Justice Hughes has said, "We are under a Constitution, but the Constitution is what the judges say it is."

The Court in addition to the proper use of its judicial functions has improperly set itself up as a third house of the Congress—a super-legislature, as one of the justices has called it—reading into the Constitution words and implications which are not there, and which were never intended to be there.

We have, therefore, reached the point as a nation where we must take action to save the Constitution from the Court and the Court from itself. . . .

I want—as all Americans want—an independent judiciary as proposed by the framers of the Constitution. That means a Supreme Court that will enforce the Constitution as written, that will refuse to amend the Constitution by the arbitrary exercise of judicial power—in other words by judicial say-so. It does not mean a judiciary so independent that it can deny the existence of facts which are universally recognized.

. . .

When I commenced to review the situation with the problem squarely before me, I came by a process of elimination to the conclusion that, short of amendments, the only method which was clearly constitutional, and would at the same time carry out other much needed reforms, was to infuse new blood into all our courts. We must have men worthy and equipped to carry out impartial justice. But, at the same time, we must have judges who will bring to the courts a present-day sense of the Constitution—judges who will retain in the courts the judicial functions of a court, and reject the legislative powers which the courts have today assumed.

It is well for us to remember that in forty-five out of the forty-eight states of the Union, judges are chosen not for life but for a period of years. In many states judges must retire at the age of seventy. . . .

. . .

[My] plan has two chief purposes. By bringing into the judicial system a steady and continuing stream of new and younger blood, I hope, first, to make the administration of all federal justice, from the bottom to the top, speedier and, therefore, less costly; secondly, to bring to the decision of social and economic problems younger men who have had personal experience and contact with modern facts and circumstances under which average men have to live and work. This plan will save our national Constitution from hardening of the judicial arteries.

. . .

Those opposing this plan have sought to arouse prejudice and fear by crying that I am seeking to "pack" the Supreme Court and that a baneful precedent will be established.

. . .

If by that phrase "packing the Court" it is charged that I wish to place on the bench spineless puppets who would disregard the law and would decide specific cases as I wished them to be decided, I make this answer: that no president fit for his office would appoint, and no Senate of honorable men fit for their office would confirm, that kind of appointees to the Supreme Court.

But if by that phrase the charge is made that I would appoint and the Senate would confirm justices worthy to sit beside present members of the Court, who understand modern conditions, that I will appoint justices who will not undertake to override the judgment of the Congress on legislative policy, that I will appoint justices who will act as justices and not as legislators—if the appointment of such justices can be called "packing the Courts," then I say that I and with me the vast majority of the American people favor doing just that thing—now.

Is it a dangerous precedent for the Congress to change the number of the justices? The Congress has always had, and will have, that power. The number of justices has been changed several times before, in the administrations of John Adams and Thomas Jefferson—both of them signers of the Declaration of Independence—in the administrations of Andrew Jackson, Abraham Lincoln, and Ulysses S. Grant.

I suggest only the addition of justices to the bench in accordance with a clearly defined principle relating to a clearly defined age limit. Fundamentally, if in the future, America cannot trust the Congress it elects to refrain from abuse of our constitutional usages, democracy will have failed far beyond the importance to democracy of any kind of precedent concerning the judiciary.

. . .

During the past half-century the balance of power between the three great branches of the federal government has been tipped out of balance by the courts in direct contradiction of the high purposes of the framers of the Constitution. It is my purpose to restore that balance. You who know me will accept my solemn assurance that in a world in which democracy is under attack, I seek to make American democracy succeed. You and I will do our part.

Senate Judiciary Committee Report on President Roosevelt's Court-Packing Plan (1937)[20]

The president's bill to "reorganize" the federal judiciary was sent to the Senate Judiciary Committee on a fast track for consideration. That committee, like the Senate itself, had a solid Democratic majority. Nevertheless, some high-profile liberals who had been strong supporters of the New Deal and critics of the Court joined more conservative Democrats and opposed Court-packing. Republicans generally kept their silence and allowed Democrats to argue among themselves. The Senate Judiciary Committee came out with a strongly worded negative report on the bill. Pro–New Deal Washington Post *columnist Ray Clapper wrote in his diary that the committee report read "almost like a bill of impeachment."[21] Senate majority leader Joseph Robinson struggled to save the bill on the floor of the Senate but suffered a fatal heart attack before the bill was finally laid to rest in the summer of 1937.*

The Committee on the Judiciary, to whom was referred the bill (S. 1392) to reorganize the judicial branch of the Government, after full consideration, having unanimously amended the measure, hereby reports the bill adversely with the recommendation that it does not pass. . . .

The committee recommends that the measure be rejected for the following primary reasons:

The bill does not accomplish any one of the objectives for which it was originally offered.

It applies force to the judiciary and in its initial and ultimate effect would undermine the independence of the courts.

It violates all precedents in the history of our Government and would in itself be a dangerous precedent for the future.

The theory of the bill is in direct violation of the spirit of the American Constitution and its employment would permit alteration of the Constitution without the people's consent or approval; it undermines the protection our constitutional system gives to minorities and is subversive of the rights of individuals.

. . .

Shall we now, after 150 years of loyalty to the constitutional ideal of an untrammeled judiciary, duty bound to protect the constitutional rights of the humblest citizen even against the Government itself, create the vicious precedent which must necessarily undermine our system? The only argument for the increase which survives analysis is that Congress should enlarge the Court so as to make the policies of this administration effective.

We are told that a reactionary oligarchy defies the will of the majority, that this is a bill to "unpack" the Court and give effect to the desires of the majority; that is to say, a bill to increase the number of Justices for the express purpose of neutralizing the views of some of the present members. In justification we are told, but without authority, by those who would rationalize this program, that Congress was given the power to determine the size of the Court so that the legislative branch would be able to impose its will upon the judiciary. This amounts to nothing more than the declaration that when the Court stands in the way of a legislative enactment, the Congress may

20. Excerpt taken from U.S. Senate, Committee on the Judiciary, Report No. 711, 75th Cong., 1st Sess., 1937.

21. Quoted in Leuchtenburg, *Supreme Court Reborn*, 146.

reverse the ruling by enlarging the Court. When such a principle is adopted, our constitutional system is overthrown!

This, then is the dangerous precedent we are asked to establish. When proponents of the bill assert, as they have done, that Congress in the past has altered the number of Justices upon the Supreme Court and that this is reason enough for our doing it now, they show how important precedents are and prove that we should now refrain from any action that would seem to establish one which could be followed hereafter whenever a Congress and an executive should become dissatisfied with the decisions of the Supreme Court.

This is the first time in the history of our country that a proposal to alter the decisions of the court by enlarging its personnel has been so boldly made. Let us meet it. Let us now set a salutary precedent that will never be violated. Let us, of the Seventy-fifth Congress, in words that will never be disregarded by any succeeding Congress, declare that we would rather have an independent Court, a fearless Court, a Court that will dare to announce its honest opinions in what it believes to be the defense of the liberties of the people, than a Court that, out of fear or sense of obligation to the appointing power, or factional passion, approves any measure we may enact. We are not the judges of the judges. We are not above the Constitution.

Even if every charge brought against the so-called "reactionary" members of this Court be true, it is far better that we await orderly but inevitable change of personnel than that we impatiently overwhelm them with new members. Exhibiting this restraint, thus demonstrating our faith in the American system, we shall set an example that will protect the independent American judiciary from attack as long as this Government stands. . . .

The Southern Manifesto (1956)[22]

The Supreme Court in Brown v. Board of Education I (1954) *declared racially segregated public schools to be unconstitutional. In* Brown v. Board of Education II (1955) *the justices ordered all communities to desegregate their public schools with "all deliberate speed." Massive resistance followed. Many states in the South responded by passing ordinances declaring* Brown *to be null and void. Most southern representatives in Congress signed the Southern Manifesto, which urged resistance to the Supreme Court's decision ordering desegregation. Lyndon Johnson, the Senate majority leader at the time, was not asked to sign. The Manifesto was designed in part to pressure moderates into joining a united front and declaring their support for segregation in the face of the Supreme Court's decision. Especially in the Deep South, the Manifesto lent support to governors, state legislators, school administrators, and judges seeking to delay or obstruct the implementation of desegregation in schools and elsewhere.*

We regard the decisions of the Supreme Court in the school cases as a clear abuse of judicial power. It climaxes a trend in the Federal Judiciary undertaking to legislate, in derogation of the authority of Congress, and to encroach upon the reserved rights of the States and the people.

The original Constitution does not mention education. Neither does the 14th Amendment nor any other amendment. The debates preceding the submission of the 14th Amendment clearly show that there was no intent that it should affect the system of education maintained by the States.

In the case of *Plessy v. Ferguson* in 1896 the Supreme Court expressly declared that under the 14th Amendment no person was denied any of his rights if the States provided separate but equal facilities. . . .

This interpretation, restated time and again, became a part of the life of the people of many of the States and confirmed their habits, traditions, and way of life. It is founded on elemental humanity and commonsense, for parents should not be deprived by Government of the right to direct the lives and education of their own children.

Though there has been no constitutional amendment or act of Congress changing this established legal principle almost a century old, the Supreme Court of the United States, with no legal basis for such action, undertook to exercise their naked judicial power and substituted their personal political and social ideas for the established law of the land.

. . . Without regard to the consent of the governed, outside mediators are threatening immediate and revolutionary changes in our public schools systems. If done, this is certain to destroy the system of public education in some of the States.

22. Excerpt taken from *Congressional Record*, 84th Cong., 2nd Sess., 1956, 4515.

We reaffirm our reliance on the Constitution as the fundamental law of the land.

We decry the Supreme Court's encroachment on the rights reserved to the States and to the people, contrary to established law, and to the Constitution.

We commend the motives of those States which have declared the intention to resist forced integration by any lawful means.

We appeal to the States and people who are not directly affected by these decisions to consider the constitutional principles involved against the time when they too, on issues vital to them may be the victims of judicial encroachment.

Even though we constitute a minority in the present Congress, we have full faith that a majority of the American people believe in the dual system of government which has enabled us to achieve our greatness and will in time demand that the reserved rights of the States and of the people be made secure against judicial usurpation.

We pledge ourselves to use all lawful means to bring about a reversal of this decision which is contrary to the Constitution and to prevent the use of force in its implementation.

Dwight Eisenhower, Address to the Nation on the Introduction of Troops in Little Rock (1957)[23]

President Eisenhower was ambivalent about Brown v. Board of Education. *He signed the amicus brief urging the Supreme Court to declare segregated schools unconstitutional, supported northern liberals in his Justice Department, and appointed justices to the Supreme Court who were committed to the* Brown *precedent. But he refrained from praising the substantive result in* Brown *or claiming credit for the outcome. Eisenhower had made some significant electoral gains in the South, and he was convinced that incrementalism and quiet diplomacy with moderates in the South would be more effective in achieving desegregation than confrontation.*

His public statements on Brown *emphasized that the judicial decision was the law of the land, that judicial orders had to be obeyed, and that the president had no choice but to enforce them. When Governor Orval Faubus defied a federal judicial order and blocked the desegregation of Central High School in Little Rock, Arkansas, Eisenhower sent federal troops to enforce the judicial order. In contrast to the Southern Manifesto, Eisenhower emphasized judicial supremacy in interpreting the Constitution. The duty of citizens and officials was to obey, regardless of their "personal opinions" about what the Court had done. Was this a reasonable strategy to take in the wake of a controversial decision, or should Eisenhower have come out squarely in favor of the Court's decision?*

Good Evening, My Fellow Citizens: For a few minutes this evening I want to speak to you about the serious situation that has arisen in Little Rock. To make this talk I have come to the President's office in the White House. I could have spoken from Rhode Island, where I have been staying recently, but I felt that, in speaking from the house of Lincoln, of Jackson and of Wilson, my words would better convey both the sadness I feel in the action I was compelled today to take and the firmness with which I intend to pursue this course until the orders of the Federal Court at Little Rock can be executed without unlawful interference. In that city, under the leadership of demagogic extremists, disorderly mobs have deliberately prevented the carrying out of proper orders from a Federal Court. Local authorities have not eliminated that violent opposition and, under the law, I yesterday issued a Proclamation calling upon the mob to disperse.... It is important that the reasons for my action be understood by all our citizens. As you know, the Supreme Court of the United States has decided that separate public educational facilities for the races are inherently unequal and therefore compulsory school segregation laws are unconstitutional. Our personal opinions about the decision have no bearing on the matter of enforcement; the responsibility and authority of the Supreme Court to interpret the Constitution are very clear. Local Federal Courts were instructed by the Supreme Court to issue such orders and decrees as might be necessary to achieve admission to public schools without regard to race—and with all deliberate speed.... The very basis of our individual rights and freedoms rests upon the certainty that the President and the Executive Branch of Government will support and insure the carrying out of the decisions of the Federal Courts, even, when necessary, with all the means at the President's command. Unless the President did so, anarchy would result. There would be no security for

23. Excerpt taken from Dwight D. Eisenhower, *Public Papers of the Presidents of the United States, 1957* (Washington, DC: Government Printing Office, 1958), 689.

any except that which each one of us could provide for himself. The interest of the nation in the proper fulfillment of the law's requirements cannot yield to opposition and demonstrations by some few persons. Mob rule cannot be allowed to override the decisions of our courts. . . . A foundation of our American way of life is our national respect for law. In the South, as elsewhere, citizens are keenly aware of the tremendous disservice that has been done to the people of Arkansas in the eyes of the nation, and that has been done to the nation in the eyes of the world. At a time when we face grave situations abroad because of the hatred that Communism bears toward a system of government based on human rights, it would be difficult to exaggerate the harm that is being done to the prestige and influence, and indeed to the safety, of our nation and the world. Our enemies are gloating over this incident and using it everywhere to misrepresent our whole nation. We are portrayed as a violator of those standards of conduct which the peoples of the world united to proclaim in the Charter of the United Nations. There they affirmed "faith in fundamental human rights" and "in dignity and worth of the human person" and they did so "without distinction as to race, sex, language or religion." And so, with deep confidence, I call upon the citizens of the State of Arkansas to assist in bringing to an immediate end all interference with the law and its processes. If resistance to the Federal Court orders ceases at once, the further presence of Federal troops will be unnecessary and the City of Little Rock will return to its normal habits of peace and order and a blot upon the fair name and high honor of our nation in the world will be removed. Thus will be restored the image of America and of all its parts as one nation, indivisible, with liberty and justice for all. Good night, and thank you very much.

Cooper v. Aaron, 358 U.S. 1 (1958)

In Little Rock, Arkansas, federal troops were needed to protect the few children of color attending a formerly all-white high school. The school board had moved promptly after Brown I *to adopt a desegregation plan, but a state constitutional amendment was subsequently ratified instructing state officials to use all legal means to oppose the "unconstitutional"* Brown *decision. The governor called out the National Guard to block desegregation, but federal troops eventually allowed the school year to continue on a desegregated basis.*

Before the start of the next school year, the school board petitioned the federal district court to allow it to suspend the desegregation plan. Fearing more violence and chaos, the judge ordered the local desegregation plan to be suspended for two and a half years. That order was reversed by a federal circuit court. An appeal was taken to the Supreme Court. As the case was pending before the Supreme Court, President Eisenhower announced that he still believed that the Court had the responsibility to interpret the meaning of the Constitution and that he was prepared to send troops back to Little Rock to support the courts if needed.

A unanimous Supreme Court agreed that the desegregation plan had to be reinstated immediately. In an unprecedented opinion, signed individually by every member of the Court, the justices declared that Brown v. Board of Education *was the law of the land and that all elected officials were obligated to obey the Constitution as interpreted by the Supreme Court.* Cooper *was the first case to clearly cite* Marbury v. Madison *(1803) as establishing judicial supremacy as well as judicial review. Judicial decisions, the justices explicitly declared, bind all elected officials, even those who were not parties to the case before the Court, because the Supreme Court is specially authorized to determine what the Constitution means.*

CHIEF JUSTICE WARREN delivered the opinion of the Court.

As this case reaches us it raises questions of the highest importance to the maintenance of our federal system of government. It necessarily involves a claim by the Governor and Legislature of a State that there is no duty on state officials to obey federal court orders resting on this Court's considered interpretation of the United States Constitution. Specifically it involves actions by the Governor and Legislature of Arkansas upon the premise that they are not bound by our holding in *Brown v. Board of Education*. . . .

. . .

The constitutional rights of respondents are not to be sacrificed or yielded to the violence and disorder which have followed upon the actions of the Governor and Legislature. . . . The record before us clearly establishes that the growth of the Board's difficulties to a magnitude beyond its unaided power to control is the product of state action. Those difficulties, as counsel for the Board forthrightly conceded on the oral argument in this Court, can also be brought under control by state action.

The controlling legal principles are plain. The command of the Fourteenth Amendment is that no "State" shall deny to any person within its jurisdiction the equal protection of the laws. "A State acts by its legislative, its executive, or its judicial authorities. It can act in no other way. The constitutional provision, therefore, must mean that no agency of the State, or of the officers or agents by whom its powers are exerted, shall deny to any person within its jurisdiction the equal protection of the laws. Whoever, by virtue of public position under a State government, . . . denies or takes away the equal protection of the laws, violates the constitutional inhibition; and as he acts in the name and for the State, and is clothed with the State's power, his act is that of the State. This must be so, or the constitutional prohibition has no meaning." . . .

What has been said, in the light of the facts developed, is enough to dispose of the case. However, we should answer the premise of the actions of the Governor and Legislature that they are not bound by our holding in the *Brown* case. It is necessary only to recall some basic constitutional propositions which are settled doctrine.

Article VI of the Constitution makes the Constitution the "supreme Law of the Land." In 1803, Chief Justice Marshall, speaking for a unanimous Court, referring to the Constitution as "the fundamental and paramount law of the nation," declared in the notable case of *Marbury v. Madison*, . . . that "It is emphatically the province and duty of the judicial department to say what the law is." This decision declared the basic principle that the federal judiciary is supreme in the exposition of the law of the Constitution, and that principle has ever since been respected by this Court and the Country as a permanent and indispensable feature of our constitutional system. It follows that the interpretation of the Fourteenth Amendment enunciated by this Court in the *Brown* case is the supreme law of the land, and Art. VI of the Constitution makes it of binding effect on the States "any Thing in the Constitution or Laws of any State to the Contrary notwithstanding." Every state legislator and executive and judicial officer is solemnly committed by oath taken pursuant to Art. VI, cl. 3, "to support this Constitution." Chief Justice Taney, speaking for a unanimous Court in 1859, said that this requirement reflected the framers' "anxiety to preserve it [the Constitution] in full force, in all its powers, and to guard against resistance to or evasion of its authority, on the part of a State. . . . "

No state legislator or executive or judicial officer can war against the Constitution without violating his undertaking to support it. Chief Justice Marshall spoke for a unanimous Court in saying that: "If the legislatures of the several states may, at will, annul the judgments of the courts of the United States, and destroy the rights acquired under those judgments, the constitution itself becomes a solemn mockery. . . . " A Governor who asserts a power to nullify a federal court order is similarly restrained. If he had such power, said Chief Justice Hughes, in 1932, also for a unanimous Court, "it is manifest that the fiat of a state Governor, and not the Constitution of the United States, would be the supreme law of the land; that the restrictions of the Federal Constitution upon the exercise of state power would be but impotent phrases. . . . "

. . . The basic decision in *Brown* was unanimously reached by this Court only after the case had been briefed and twice argued and the issues had been given the most serious consideration. Since the first *Brown* opinion three new Justices have come to the Court. They are at one with the Justices still on the Court who participated in that basic decision as to its correctness, and that decision is now unanimously reaffirmed. The principles announced in that decision and the obedience of the States to them, according to the command of the Constitution, are indispensable for the protection of the freedoms guaranteed by our fundamental charter for all of us. Our constitutional ideal of equal justice under law is thus made a living truth.

JUSTICE FRANKFURTER, concurring.

While unreservedly participating with my brethren in our joint opinion, I deem it appropriate also to deal individually with the great issue here at stake.

. . .

. . . Every act of government may be challenged by an appeal to law, as finally pronounced by this Court. Even this Court has the last say only for a time. Being composed of fallible men, it may err. But revision of its errors must be by orderly process of law. The Court may be asked to reconsider its decisions, and this has been done successfully again and again throughout our history. Or, what this Court has deemed its duty to decide may be changed by legislation, as it often has been, and, on occasion, by constitutional amendment.

. . .

The duty to abstain from resistance to "the supreme Law of the Land," U.S. Const., Art. VI 2, as declared by the organ of our Government for ascertaining it, does not require immediate approval of it nor does it deny the right of dissent. Criticism need not be stilled. Active obstruction or defiance is barred. Our kind of society cannot endure if the controlling authority of the Law as derived from the Constitution is not to be the tribunal specially charged with the duty of ascertaining and declaring what is "the supreme Law of the Land." . . . Particularly is this so where the declaration of what "the supreme Law" commands on an underlying moral issue is not the dubious pronouncement of a gravely divided Court but is the unanimous conclusion of a long-matured deliberative process. The Constitution is not the formulation of the merely personal views of the members of this Court, nor can its authority be reduced to the claim that state officials are its controlling interpreters. Local customs, however hardened by time, are not decreed in heaven. . . .

. . .

. . . Compliance with decisions of this Court, as the constitutional organ of the supreme Law of the Land, has often, throughout our history, depended on active support by state and local authorities. It presupposes such support. To withhold it, and indeed to use political power to try to paralyze the supreme Law, precludes the maintenance of our federal system as we have known and cherished it for one hundred and seventy years.

. . .

Baker v. Carr, 369 U.S. 186 (1962)

New Deal and Great Society liberals waged a long campaign against malapportioned state and federal legislative districts. Through a combination of legislative gerrymandering and inertia, the population in most legislative districts by the end of World War II varied dramatically. Quite frequently, the population of one district would be ten times larger than the population of another district with the same power to elect one representative. Liberals opposed these malapportionments for two reasons. First, malapportioned districts were inconsistent with the general democratic principles and commitment to equality underlying mid-twentieth-century liberalism. Second, malapportionment often favored conservative rural voters at the expense of more liberal urban voters. This gave an electoral and legislative edge to Republicans and conservative Democrats. Political efforts to reapportion legislatures faced stiff resistance from many incumbent politicians and interests.

Federal litigation initially proved unsuccessful. A 4–3 majority in Colegrove v. Green *(1946) refused to determine whether malapportioned congressional districts in Illinois violated the "guarantee of republican government" clause in the Constitution. Justice Frankfurter's opinion for the shorthanded Court was joined by only two other justices:*

> *The short of it is that the Constitution has conferred upon Congress exclusive authority to secure fair representation by the States in the popular House and left to that House determination whether States have fulfilled their responsibility. If Congress failed in exercising its powers, whereby standards of fairness are offended, the remedy ultimately lies with the people. Whether Congress faithfully discharges its duty or not, the subject has been committed to the exclusive control of Congress. An aspect of government from which the judiciary, in view of what is involved, has been excluded by the clear intention of the Constitution cannot be entered by the federal courts because Congress may have been in default in exacting from States obedience to its mandate.*

"Courts ought not to enter this political thicket," Frankfurter concluded. Justice Rutledge's concurring opinion declared that the justices might be able to adjudicate this dispute in some circumstances but that those circumstances were not present in the case before the Court.

A decade later, proponents of reapportionment made another effort, one that focused on Tennessee. Although the Tennessee Constitution provided that seats in the state legislature be apportioned by population every ten years, the state legislature had not attempted a reapportionment in half a century. One consequence of this failure was that one state legislator represented two thousand voters in some rural counties, while one state legislator represented almost fifty thousand voters in some urban counties. Backed various interest groups, Charles Baker and other voters filed suit in federal district court against Tennessee secretary of state Joe Carr. They sought a declaration that the existing state statutes apportioning the legislative districts violated the equal protection clause of the Fourteenth Amendment and an injunction blocking the state from holding any future elections under that apportionment scheme. A three-judge district court panel dismissed the suit as a political question. An appeal was made to the U.S. Supreme Court. The Kennedy administration supported behind the interest groups seeking to reapportion the Tennessee state legislature.

In a 6–2 decision, the Court struck down the state apportionment law. Justice Brennan's majority opinion set out the modern formulation of the political question doctrine, even as it narrowed the scope of that doctrine by accepting the reapportionment cases as appropriate for judicial resolution. What was the significance of this change in the constitutional foundation of the claim against malapportioned legislative districts? You might also note that Justice Clark's concurring opinion in the case began as a dissent. Clark changed his mind when writing, concluding that judicial intervention was the only remedy available.

JUSTICE BRENNAN delivered the opinion of the Court.

...

We hold that the District Court has jurisdiction of the subject matter of the federal constitutional claim asserted in the complaint.

... We hold that the appellants do have standing to maintain this suit. ...

These appellants seek relief in order to protect or vindicate an interest of their own, and of those similarly situated. Their constitutional claim is, in substance, that the 1901 statute constitutes arbitrary and capricious state action, offensive to the Fourteenth Amendment in its irrational disregard of the standard of apportionment prescribed by the State's Constitution or of any standard, effecting a gross disproportion of representation to voting population. The injury which appellants assert is that this classification disfavors the voters in the counties in which they reside, placing them in a position of constitutionally unjustifiable inequality *vis-à-vis* voters in irrationally favored counties. A citizen's right to a vote free of arbitrary impairment by state action has been judicially recognized as a right secured by the Constitution, when such impairment resulted from dilution by a false tally, cf. *United States v. Classic* (1941). ...

...

In holding that the subject matter of this suit was not justiciable, the District Court relied on *Colegrove v. Green,* and subsequent *per curiam* cases. ... We understand the District Court to have read the cited cases as compelling the conclusion that since the appellants sought to have a legislative apportionment held unconstitutional, their suit presented a "political question" and was therefore nonjusticiable. We hold that this challenge to an apportionment presents no nonjusticiable "political question." The cited cases do not hold the contrary.

Of course the mere fact that the suit seeks protection of a political right does not mean it presents a political question. Such an objection "is little more than a play upon words." ...

We hold that the claim pleaded here neither rests upon nor implicates the Guaranty Clause and that its justiciability is therefore not foreclosed by our decisions of cases involving that clause. The District Court misinterpreted *Colegrove v. Green* and other decisions of this Court on which it relied. Appellants' claim that they are being denied equal protection is justiciable, and if "discrimination is sufficiently shown, the right to relief under the equal protection clause is not diminished by the fact that the discrimination relates to political rights."

... [I]n the Guaranty Clause cases and in the other "political question" cases, it is the relationship between the judiciary and the coordinate branches of the Federal Government, and not the federal judiciary's relationship to the States, which gives rise to the "political question."

We have said that "In determining whether a question falls within [the political question] category, the appropriateness under our system of government of attributing finality to the action of the political departments and also the lack of satisfactory criteria for a judicial determination are dominant considerations." *Coleman v. Miller* (1939). ... The nonjusticiability of a political question is primarily a function of the separation of powers. Much confusion results from the capacity of the "political question" label to obscure the need for case-by-case inquiry. Deciding whether a matter has in any measure been committed by the Constitution to another branch of government, or whether the action of that branch exceeds whatever authority has been committed, is itself a delicate exercise in constitutional interpretation, and is a responsibility of this Court as ultimate interpreter of the Constitution. ...

Foreign relations: There are sweeping statements to the effect that all questions touching foreign relations are political questions. Not only does resolution of such issues frequently turn on standards that defy judicial application, or involve the exercise of a discretion demonstrably committed to the executive or legislature; but many such questions uniquely demand single-voiced statement of the Government's views. Yet it is error to suppose that every case or controversy which touches foreign relations lies beyond judicial cognizance. ... For example, though a court will not ordinarily inquire whether a treaty has been terminated, since on that question "governmental action . . . must be regarded as of controlling importance," if there has been no conclusive "governmental action" then a court can construe a treaty and may find it provides the answer.

Dates of duration of hostilities: Though it has been stated broadly that "the power which declared the necessity is the power to declare its cessation, and what the cessation requires," . . . here too analysis reveals isolable reasons for the presence of political questions, underlying this Court's refusal to review the political departments' determination of when or whether a war has ended. Dominant is the need for finality in the political determination, for emergency's nature demands "A prompt and unhesitating obedience." . . . But deference rests on reason, not habit. The question in a particular case may not seriously implicate considerations of finality —*e.g.*, a public program of importance (rent control) yet not central to the emergency effort. . . .

Validity of enactments: In *Coleman v. Miller* (1939), this Court held that the questions of how long a proposed amendment to the Federal Constitution remained open to ratification, and what effect a prior rejection had on a subsequent ratification, were committed to congressional resolution and involved criteria of decision that necessarily escaped the judicial grasp. . . .

The status of Indian tribes: This Court's deference to the political departments in determining whether Indians are recognized as a tribe, while it reflects familiar attributes of political questions, . . . also has a unique element in that "the relation of the Indians to the United States is marked by peculiar and cardinal distinctions which exist nowhere else. . . . [The Indians are] domestic dependent nations . . . in a state of pupilage. Their relation to the United States resembles that of a ward to his guardian." *The Cherokee Nation v. Georgia* (1831). . . . Yet, here too, there is no blanket rule. While "'It is for [Congress] . . . , and not for the courts, to determine when the true interests of the Indian require his release from [the] condition of tutelage' . . . , it is not meant by this that Congress may bring a community or body of people within the range of this power by arbitrarily calling them an Indian tribe. . . . " Able to discern what is "distinctly Indian," . . . the courts will strike down any heedless extension of that label. They will not stand impotent before an obvious instance of a manifestly unauthorized exercise of power.

It is apparent that several formulations which vary slightly according to the settings in which the questions arise may describe a political question, although each has one or more elements which identify it as essentially a function of the separation of powers. Prominent on the surface of any case held to involve a political question is found a textually demonstrable constitutional commitment of the issue to a coordinate political department; or a lack of judicially discoverable and manageable standards for resolving it; or the impossibility of deciding without an initial policy determination of a kind clearly for nonjudicial discretion; or the impossibility of a court's undertaking independent resolution without expressing lack of the respect due coordinate branches of government; or an unusual need for unquestioning adherence to a political decision already made; or the potentiality of embarrassment from multifarious pronouncements by various departments on one question.

But it is argued that this case shares the characteristics of decisions that constitute a category not yet considered, cases concerning the Constitution's guaranty, in Art. IV, §4, of a republican form of government. A conclusion as to whether the case at bar does present a political question cannot be confidently reached until we have considered those cases with special care. We shall discover that Guaranty Clause claims involve those elements which define a "political question," and for that reason and no other, they are nonjusticiable. In particular, we shall discover that the nonjusticiability of such claims has nothing to do with their touching upon matters of state governmental organization.

. . .

. . . [S]everal factors were thought by the Court in *Luther v. Borden* (1849) to make the question there "political": the commitment to the other branches of the decision as to which is the lawful state government; the unambiguous action by the President, in recognizing the charter government as the lawful authority; the need for finality in the executive's decision; and the lack of criteria by which a court could determine which form of government was republican.

But the only significance that *Luther* could have for our immediate purposes is in its holding that the Guaranty Clause is not a repository of judicially manageable standards which a court could utilize independently in order to identify a State's lawful government. . . .

. . .

We come, finally, to the ultimate inquiry whether our precedents as to what constitutes a nonjusticiable "political question" bring the case before us under the umbrella of that doctrine. A natural beginning is to note whether any of the common characteristics which we have been able to identify and label descriptively are present. We find none: The question here is the consistency of state action with the Federal Constitution. We have no question decided, or to be decided, by a political branch of government coequal with this Court. Nor do we risk embarrassment of our government abroad, or grave disturbance at home if we take issue with Tennessee as to the constitutionality of her action here challenged. Nor need the appellants, in order to succeed in this action, ask the Court to enter upon policy determinations for which judicially manageable standards are lacking. Judicial standards under the Equal Protection Clause are well developed and familiar, and it has been open to courts since the enactment of the Fourteenth Amendment to determine, if on the particular facts they must, that a discrimination reflects *no* policy, but simply arbitrary and capricious action.

This case does, in one sense, involve the allocation of political power within a State, and the appellants might conceivably have added a claim under the Guaranty Clause. Of course, as we have seen, any reliance on that clause would be futile. But because any reliance on the Guaranty Clause could not have succeeded it does not follow that appellants may not be heard on the equal protection claim which in fact they tender. True, it must be clear that the Fourteenth Amendment claim is not so enmeshed with those political question elements which render Guaranty Clause claims nonjusticiable as actually to present a political question itself. But we have found that not to be the case here.

. . .

We conclude that the complaint's allegations of a denial of equal protection present a justiciable constitutional cause of action upon which appellants are entitled to a trial and a decision. The right asserted is within the reach of judicial protection under the Fourteenth Amendment.

JUSTICE CLARK, concurring.

. . . I would not consider intervention by this Court into so delicate a field if there were any other relief available to the people of Tennessee. But the majority of the people of Tennessee have no "practical opportunities for exerting their political weight at the polls" to correct the existing "invidious discrimination." Tennessee has no initiative and referendum. I have searched diligently for other "practical opportunities" present under the law. I find none other than through the federal courts. The majority of the voters have been caught up in a legislative strait jacket. Tennessee has an "informed, civically militant electorate" and "an aroused popular conscience," but it does not sear "the conscience of the people's representatives." This is because the legislative policy has riveted the present seats in the Assembly to their respective constituencies, and by the votes of their incumbents a reapportionment of any kind is prevented. The people have been rebuffed at the hands of the Assembly; they have tried the constitutional convention route, but since the call must originate in the Assembly it, too, has been fruitless. They have tried Tennessee courts with the same result, and Governors have fought the tide only to flounder. It is said that there is recourse in Congress and perhaps that may be, but from a practical standpoint this is without substance. To date Congress has never undertaken such a task in any State. We therefore must conclude that the people of Tennessee are stymied and without judicial intervention will be saddled with the present discrimination in the affairs of their state government.

. . .

. . . It is well for this Court to practice self-restraint and discipline in constitutional adjudication, but never in its history have those principles received sanction where the national rights of so many have been so clearly infringed for so long a time. National respect for the courts is more enhanced through the forthright enforcement of those rights rather than by rendering them nugatory through the interposition of subterfuges. In my view the ultimate decision today is in the greatest tradition of this Court.

JUSTICE DOUGLAS, concurring.

. . .

JUSTICE STEWART, concurring.

. . .

JUSTICE FRANKFURTER, with whom JUSTICE HARLAN joins, dissenting.

The Court today reverses a uniform course of decision established by a dozen cases, including one by which the very claim now sustained was unanimously rejected only five years ago. The impressive body of rulings thus cast aside reflected the equally uniform course of our political history regarding the relationship between population and legislative representation—a wholly different matter from denial of the franchise to individuals because of race, color, religion or sex. Such a massive repudiation of the experience of our whole past in asserting destructively novel judicial power demands a detailed analysis of the role of this Court in our constitutional scheme. Disregard of inherent limits in the effective exercise of the Court's "judicial Power" not only presages the futility of judicial intervention in the essentially political conflict of forces by which the relation between population and representation has time out of mind been and now is determined. It may well impair the Court's position as the ultimate organ of "the supreme Law of the Land" in that vast range of legal problems, often strongly entangled in popular feeling, on which this Court must pronounce. The Court's authority—possessed of neither the purse nor the sword—ultimately rests on sustained public confidence in its moral sanction. Such feeling must be nourished by the Court's complete detachment, in fact and in appearance, from political entanglements and by abstention from injecting itself into the clash of political forces in political settlements.

A hypothetical claim resting on abstract assumptions is now for the first time made the basis for affording illusory relief for a particular evil even though it foreshadows deeper and more pervasive difficulties in consequence. The claim is hypothetical and the assumptions are abstract because the Court does not vouchsafe the lower courts—state and federal—guidelines for formulating specific, definite, wholly unprecedented remedies for the inevitable litigations that today's umbrageous disposition is bound to stimulate in connection with politically motivated reapportionments in so many States. In such a setting, to promulgate jurisdiction in the abstract is meaningless. It is as devoid of reality as "a brooding omnipresence in the sky," for it conveys no intimation what relief, if any, a District Court is capable of affording that would not invite legislatures to play ducks and drakes with the judiciary. For this Court to direct the District Court to enforce a claim to which the Court has over the years consistently found itself required to deny legal enforcement and at the same time to find it necessary to withhold any guidance to the lower court how to enforce this turnabout, new legal claim, manifests an odd—indeed an esoteric—conception of judicial propriety. . . . Even assuming the indispensable intellectual disinterestedness on the part of judges in such matters, they do not have accepted legal standards or criteria or even reliable analogies to draw upon for making judicial judgments. To charge courts with the task of accommodating the incommensurable factors of policy that underlie these mathematical puzzles is to attribute, however flatteringly, omnicompetence to judges. The Framers of the Constitution persistently rejected a proposal that embodied this assumption and Thomas Jefferson never entertained it.

. . . In effect, today's decision empowers the courts of the country to devise what should constitute the proper composition of the legislatures of the fifty States. If state courts should for one reason or another find themselves unable to discharge this task, the duty of doing so is put on the federal courts or on this Court, if State views do not satisfy this Court's notion of what is proper districting.

We were soothingly told at the bar of this Court that we need not worry about the kind of remedy a court could effectively fashion once the abstract constitutional right to have courts pass on a state-wide system of electoral districting is recognized as a matter of judicial rhetoric, because legislatures would heed the Court's admonition. This is not only a euphoric hope. It implies a sorry confession of judicial impotence in place of a frank acknowledgment that there is not under our Constitution a judicial remedy for every political mischief, for every undesirable exercise of legislative power. The Framers carefully and with deliberate forethought refused so to enthrone the judiciary. In this situation, as in others of like nature, appeal for relief does not belong here. Appeal must be to an informed, civically militant electorate. In a democratic society like ours, relief must come through an aroused popular conscience that sears the conscience of the people's representatives. In any event there is nothing judicially more unseemly nor more self-defeating than for this Court to make *in terrorem* pronouncements, to indulge in merely empty rhetoric, sounding a word of promise to the ear, sure to be disappointing to the hope.

. . .

The *Colegrove* doctrine, in the form in which repeated decisions have settled it, was not an innovation. It represents long judicial thought and experience. From its earliest opinions this Court has consistently recognized a class of controversies which do not lend themselves to judicial standards and judicial remedies. To classify the various instances as "political questions" is rather a form of stating this conclusion than revealing of analysis. Some of the cases so labeled have no relevance here. But from others emerge unifying considerations that are compelling.

1. The cases concerning war or foreign affairs, for example, are usually explained by the necessity of the country's speaking with one voice in such matters. While this concern alone undoubtedly accounts for many of the decisions, others do not fit the pattern. It would hardly embarrass the conduct of war were this Court to determine, in connection with private transactions between litigants, the date upon which war is to be deemed terminated. . . . A controlling factor in such cases is that, decision respecting these kinds of complex matters of policy being traditionally committed not to courts but to the political agencies of government for determination by criteria of political expediency, there exists no standard ascertainable by settled judicial experience or process by reference to which a political decision affecting the question at issue between the parties can be judged. . . .

This may be, like so many questions of law, a matter of degree. Questions have arisen under the Constitution to which adjudication gives answer although the criteria for decision are less than unwavering bright lines. Often in these cases illumination was found in the federal structures established by, or the underlying presuppositions of, the Constitution. With respect to such questions, the Court has recognized that, concerning a particular power of Congress put in issue, " . . . effective restraints on its exercise must proceed from political rather than from judicial processes." *Wickard v. Filburn* (1942). . . . But this is merely to acknowledge that particular circumstances may differ so greatly in degree as to differ thereby in kind, and that, although within a certain range of cases on a continuum, no standard of distinction can be found to tell between them, other cases will fall above or below the range. The doctrine of political questions, like any other, is not to be applied beyond the limits of its own logic, with all the quiddities and abstract disharmonies it may manifest. . . .

2. The Court has been particularly unwilling to intervene in matters concerning the structure and organization of the political institutions of the States. The abstention from judicial entry into such areas has been greater even than that which marks the Court's ordinary approach to issues of state power challenged under broad federal guarantees. "We should be very reluctant to decide that we had jurisdiction in such a case, and thus in an action of this nature to supervise and review the political administration of a state government by its own officials and through its own courts. The jurisdiction of this court would only exist in case there had been . . . such a plain and substantial departure from the fundamental principles upon which our government is based that it could with truth and propriety be said that if the judgment were suffered to remain, the party aggrieved would be deprived of his life, liberty or property in violation of the provisions of the Federal Constitution."

3. The cases involving Negro disfranchisement are no exception to the principle of avoiding federal judicial intervention into matters of state government in the absence of an explicit and clear constitutional imperative. For here the controlling command of Supreme Law is plain and unequivocal. An end of discrimination against the Negro was the compelling motive of the Civil War Amendments. The Fifteenth expresses this in terms, and it is no less true of the Equal Protection Clause of the Fourteenth. . . .

4. The Court has refused to exercise its jurisdiction to pass on "abstract questions of political power, of sovereignty, of government." . . . The "political question" doctrine, in this aspect, reflects the policies underlying the requirement of "standing": that the litigant who would challenge official action must claim infringement of an interest particular and personal to himself, as distinguished from a cause of dissatisfaction with the general frame and functioning of government—a complaint that the political institutions are awry. . . . The crux of the matter is that courts are not fit instruments of decision where what is essentially at stake is the composition of those large contests of policy traditionally fought out in non-judicial forums, by which governments and the actions of governments are made and unmade. . . .

. . .

5. The influence of these converging considerations—the caution not to undertake decision where standards meet for judicial judgment are lacking, the reluctance to interfere with matters of state government in the absence of an unquestionable and effectively enforceable mandate, the unwillingness to make courts arbiters of the broad issues of political organization historically committed to other institutions and for whose adjustment the judicial process is ill-adapted—has

been decisive of the settled line of cases, reaching back more than a century, which holds that Art. IV, §4, of the Constitution, guaranteeing to the States "a Republican Form of Government," is not enforceable through the courts.

...

The present case involves all of the elements that have made the Guarantee Clause cases non-justiciable. It is, in effect, a Guarantee Clause claim masquerading under a different label. But it cannot make the case more fit for judicial action that appellants invoke the Fourteenth Amendment rather than Art. IV, §4, where, in fact, the gist of their complaint is the same—unless it can be found that the Fourteenth Amendment speaks with greater particularity to their situation. . . .

...

What, then, is this question of legislative apportionment? Appellants invoke the right to vote and to have their votes counted. But they are permitted to vote and their votes are counted. They go to the polls, they cast their ballots, they send their representatives to the state councils. Their complaint is simply that the representatives are not sufficiently numerous or powerful—in short, that Tennessee has adopted a basis of representation with which they are dissatisfied. Talk of "debasement" or "dilution" is circular talk. One cannot speak of "debasement" or "dilution" of the value of a vote until there is first defined a standard of reference as to what a vote should be worth. What is actually asked of the Court in this case is to choose among competing bases of representation—ultimately, really, among competing theories of political philosophy—in order to establish an appropriate frame of government for the State of Tennessee and thereby for all the States of the Union.

In such a matter, abstract analogies which ignore the facts of history deal in unrealities; they betray reason. This is not a case in which a State has, through a device however oblique and sophisticated, denied Negroes or Jews or redheaded persons a vote, or given them only a third or a sixth of a vote. That was *Gomillion v. Lightfoot* (1960). What Tennessee illustrates is an old and still widespread method of representation—representation by local geographical division, only in part respective of population—in preference to others, others, forsooth, more appealing. Appellants contest this choice and seek to make this Court the arbiter of the disagreement. They would make the Equal Protection Clause the charter of adjudication, asserting that the equality which it guarantees comports, if not the assurance of equal weight to every voter's vote, at least the basic conception that representation ought to be proportionate to population, a standard by reference to which the reasonableness of apportionment plans may be judged.

To find such a political conception legally enforceable in the broad and unspecific guarantee of equal protection is to rewrite the Constitution. . . . Certainly "equal protection" is no more secure a foundation for judicial judgment of the permissibility of varying forms of representative government than is "Republican Form." . . .

...

Manifestly, the Equal Protection Clause supplies no clearer guide for judicial examination of apportionment methods than would the Guarantee Clause itself. Apportionment, by its character, is a subject of extraordinary complexity, involving—even after the fundamental theoretical issues concerning what is to be represented in a representative legislature have been fought out or compromised—considerations of geography, demography, electoral convenience, economic and social cohesions or divergencies among particular local groups, communications, the practical effects of political institutions like the lobby and the city machine, ancient traditions and ties of settled usage, respect for proven incumbents of long experience and senior status, mathematical mechanics, censuses compiling relevant data, and a host of others. Legislative responses throughout the country to the reapportionment demands of the 1960 Census have glaringly confirmed that these are not factors that lend themselves to evaluations of a nature that are the staple of judicial determinations or for which judges are equipped to adjudicate by legal training or experience or native wit. And this is the more so true because in every strand of this complicated, intricate web of values meet the contending forces of partisan politics. The practical significance of apportionment is that the next election results may differ because of it. Apportionment battles are overwhelmingly party or intra-party contests. It will add a virulent source of friction and tension in federal-state relations to embroil the federal judiciary in them.

Although the District Court had jurisdiction in the very restricted sense of power to determine whether it could adjudicate the claim, the case is of that class of political controversy which, by the nature of its subject, is unfit for federal judicial action. The judgment of the District Court, in dismissing the complaint for failure to state a claim on which relief can be granted, should therefore be affirmed.

JUSTICE HARLAN, with whom JUSTICE FRANKFURTER joins, dissenting.

. . .

I can find nothing in the Equal Protection Clause or elsewhere in the Federal Constitution which expressly or impliedly supports the view that state legislatures must be so structured as to reflect with approximate equality the voice of every voter. Not only is that proposition refuted by history, as shown by my Brother FRANKFURTER, but it strikes deep into the heart of our federal system. Its acceptance would require us to turn our backs on the regard which this Court has always shown for the judgment of state legislatures and courts on matters of basically local concern.

. . .

IV. Powers of the National Government

MAJOR DEVELOPMENTS

- The expansion of national regulatory powers under the commerce clause
- Clarification and expansion of federal powers to enforce civil rights
- Acceptance of broad use of the tax-and-spend power to advance national policies

Proponents of the New Deal and Great Society believed that the Constitution vested the national government with the powers necessary to resolve all national problems. In their view, the Constitution implicitly incorporated the provision of the proposed Virginia Plan that gave power to Congress "to legislate in all cases for the general interests of the union, and also in those to which the states are separately incompetent, or in which the harmony of the United States may be interrupted by the exercise of individual legislation."[24] As Franklin Roosevelt informed Congress in 1934, "Our Constitution tells us [that] our Federal Government was established among other things 'to promote the general welfare.'"[25]

Franklin Roosevelt and his allies during the New Deal drew inspiration from the language of Article I of the Constitution when insisting that the Constitution granted ample authority to the federal government to regulate the national economy. Lyndon Johnson and his allies during the Great Society drew inspiration from the language of the post–Civil War Amendments when insisting that the Constitution granted ample authority to the federal government to eradicate racial discrimination and poverty. Liberals during this period disagreed over whether and how individual rights provisions of the Constitution limited the exercise of federal power, but they agreed that the Tenth Amendment and the principles of enumerated powers did not impose significant limits on federal power. If Congress thought a statute addressed a national problem, then that was sufficient for the judiciary.

Constitutional debate during the New Deal focused on what laws were necessary and proper regulations of interstate commerce. Immediately upon taking office in 1933, Franklin Roosevelt called for a more aggressive use of federal power than had been wielded by any other previous administration. Congress from 1933 to 1936 generally complied with administration requests, passing legislation that dramatically expanded federal oversight of prices, wages, industrial production, agriculture, and employer–employee relationships. The federal judiciary proved less obliging. Lower federal courts issued hundreds of injunctions against New Deal programs. Important programs were declared unconstitutional by the Supreme Court. While some Roosevelt programs were struck down by bare 5–4 majorities, progressive justices such as Louis Brandeis and Benjamin Cardozo in several cases also insisted that Congress was attempting to exercise powers not delegated to the national government. The Supreme Court struck down federal laws in more cases during Roosevelt's first term of office than in any other four-year period up to that point. The most important of those decisions came in 1935 and 1936, when the Court struck down key provisions of the National Industrial Recovery Act, the Agricultural Adjustment Act, and the Bituminous Coal Act in cases such as *Panama Refining Co. v. Ryan* (1935), *Schechter Poultry v. United States* (1935), *United States v. Butler* (1936), and *Carter v. Carter Coal* (1936).

Judicial resistance finally melted after Roosevelt's reelection in 1936. At first, the justices claimed to be

24. Robert L. Stern, "The Commerce Clause and the National Economy, 1933–1946: Part Two," *Harvard Law Review* 59 (1946): 947.

25. Samuel I. Rosenman, ed., *Public Papers and Addresses of Franklin D. Roosevelt* (New York: Random House, 1950), 3:291.

following precedents. When Chief Justice Hughes upheld the National Labor Relations Act in *Jones & Laughlin Steel* (1937), he maintained that the statute respected the traditional distinction between commerce and production and was properly limited in scope to interstate economic activity. Despite this conventional rhetoric, many liberal and conservative commentators insisted that a "constitutional revolution" had taken place, that the justices were now committed to sustaining New Deal measures regardless of whether they satisfied past constitutional standards.[26] By the early 1940s, a new constitutional regime was unquestionably in place. Roosevelt's judicial appointees felt no need to invoke constitutional rules announced before 1936 when justifying the administration's policies. Most of those justices had been appointed since 1936 and had previously been involved in drafting or defending New Deal policies. *United States v. Darby* (1941) and *Wickard v. Filburn* (1942) established federal power to regulate all activity that, standing alone or in combination with similar activity, affected interstate commerce in some way. Relying on this standard, the courts for decades rejected every claim that Congress was exceeding its enumerated powers.

The course of the federal power to tax and spend during the New Deal was identical to the course of the commerce clause. In *United States v. Butler* (1936), the majority of the justices found a Tenth Amendment limit on the federal power to tax and spend. As part of the 1937 revolution, however, the Court upheld the unemployment provisions of the Social Security Act in *Steward Machine Co. v. Davis* (1937) and the old-age pension provisions of the Social Security Act in *Helvering v. Davis* (1937). While the justices argued that there were differences between these cases and *Butler*, that case was practically overruled. The Supreme Court did not impose another tax-and-spend clause limit on the federal government until *NFIB. v. Sebelius* (2013).

The Great Society built upon the constitutional legacy of the New Deal. Following New Deal liberals, Great Society liberals insisted that the commerce clause gave the federal government broad power to regulate interstate commerce, even when the national government was more concerned with regulating social ills than economic ills. The Civil Rights Act of 1964, which barred racial discrimination in places of public accommodation, was passed as a regulation of interstate commerce. Congress took an equally broad view of federal powers under the post–Civil War Amendments. The Voting Rights Act of 1965 prohibited discrimination in voting and required states with past histories of discrimination to preclear any changes in voting laws with either the Department of Justice or the federal courts in Washington, DC.

The Warren Court upheld everything that Congress did in the name of civil rights in the 1960s. The justification for upholding federal law shifted between the commerce clause and the Reconstruction Amendments depending on whom Congress was attempting to regulate. When Congress wanted to regulate private actors, it used the commerce clause. When Congress wanted to regulate government officials, it used the Fourteenth and Fifteenth Amendments. In *Heart of Atlanta Motel, Inc. v. United States* (1964) and *Katzenbach v. McClung* (1964), the Supreme Court upheld the Civil Rights Act of 1964 under the commerce clause. In *South Carolina v. Katzenbach* (1966), the Court turned the Fifteenth Amendment to justify the Voting Rights Act. The justices insisted that this provision be interpreted as broadly as the New Deal Court had interpreted the commerce clause and other Article I powers.

The same year, the Court handed down *Katzenbach v. Morgan* (1966), which concluded that Congress could bar states from employing a voting rule that discriminated against Spanish speakers, even though the Court had never ruled that such discrimination was a constitutional violation. Section 5 of the Fourteenth Amendment was a "positive grant of legislative power" to Congress that allowed Congress "to enforce" but never "to restrict, abrogate, or dilute" the guarantees of the Fourteenth Amendment. By 1968 there were few apparent limits to congressional power to enforce civil rights under the Reconstruction Amendments.[27]

---

26. Edward S. Corwin, *Constitutional Revolution, Ltd.* (Claremont, CA: Claremont College, 1941).

27. Congress would encounter such a limit two years later when it passed a 1970 amendment to the Voting Rights Act granting eighteen-year-olds the right to vote in state and federal elections. The Court struck down this extension of voting rights to state elections in *Oregon v. Mitchell* (1970). Congress responded by passing the Twenty-Sixth Amendment to the Constitution.

Schechter Poultry Corp. v. United States, 295 U.S. 495 (1935)

Many liberals believed that the Great Depression required the national government to take a larger role in regulating the economy. One popular proposal was championed by Senator Hugo Black, who would later be Roosevelt's first appointment to the Supreme Court. This mandated a thirty-hour week as a means for reducing unemployment by spreading out available work. Although the measure passed the Senate, many thought the bill was unconstitutional. Surprisingly, President Roosevelt shared this assessment. As an alternative to the Black bill, the administration proposed the National Industrial Recovery Act (NIRA). The NIRA allowed industries to establish wage and hours regulations. Once an agreement was reached on wages, hours, and other working conditions, that agreement would be enforced by the national government. This greater flexibility, administration officials believed, would enable the NIRA to pass constitutional muster. They were wrong.

Schechter *was a poor case for the government to test the constitutionality of the NIRA. The Schechter brothers owned slaughterhouses in New York City. They acquired many of their live chickens from out of state, but sold only to local stores. They had been convicted in federal district court of violating the fair competition standards set by the National Recovery Administration, and their conviction had been affirmed by the appeals court. In* Schechter, *a unanimous Supreme Court ruled that the commerce clause did not allow the national government to determine the wages and hours of local butchers. Chief Justice Charles Evan Hughes concluded that the activities of local butchers did not directly affect interstate commerce and could not be controlled by Congress.*

One reason for the unanimity may have been poor government presentation. The government brief never explained the effect local slaughtering practices had on interstate commerce. As important, the more progressive justices on the Hughes Court were not as enamored as Roosevelt with central planning. The progressive Justice Louis Brandeis was so offended by NIRA provisions that he called the government lawyers into his office for a tongue-lashing immediately after the decision was announced, declaring, "This is the end of this business of centralization, and I want you to go back and tell the President that we're not going to let this government centralize everything. It's come to an end. As for your young men, you call them together and tell them to get out of Washington—tell them to go home, back to the states. That is where they must do their work."[28]

Schechter *was one of several early losses for the New Deal in the Supreme Court. As you read Hughes's opinion, consider how large of a defeat this might have seemed. How accommodating is this opinion for national economic regulation?*

CHIEF JUSTICE HUGHES delivered the opinion of the Court.

. . . We are told that the provision of the statute authorizing the adoption of codes must be viewed in the light of the grave national crisis with which Congress was confronted. Undoubtedly, the conditions to which power is addressed are always to be considered when the exercise of power is challenged. Extraordinary conditions may call for extraordinary remedies. But the argument necessarily stops short of an attempt to justify action which lies outside the sphere of constitutional authority. Extraordinary conditions do not create or enlarge constitutional power. The Constitution established a national government with powers deemed to be adequate, as they have proved to be both in war and peace, but these powers of the national government are limited by the constitutional grants. Those who act under these grants are not at liberty to transcend the imposed limits because they believe that more or different power is necessary. Such assertions of extra-constitutional authority were anticipated and precluded by the explicit terms of the Tenth Amendment,—"The powers not delegated to the United States by the Constitution, nor prohibited by it to the States, are reserved to the States respectively, or to the people."

. . .

(1) Were these transactions *"in"* interstate commerce? Much is made of the fact that almost all the poultry coming to New York is sent there from other States. But the code provisions, as here applied, do not concern the transportation of the poultry from other States to New York, or the transactions of the commission men or others to whom it is consigned, or the sales made by such consignees to defendants. When defendants had made their purchases, whether at the West Washington Market in New York City or at

28. Philippa Strum, *Louis D. Brandeis* (New York: Schocken Books, 1984), 352.

the railroad terminals serving the City, or elsewhere, the poultry was trucked to their slaughterhouses in Brooklyn for local disposition. The interstate transactions in relation to that poultry then ended. Defendants held the poultry at their slaughterhouse markets for slaughter and local sale to retail dealers and butchers who in turn sold directly to consumers. Neither the slaughtering nor the sales by defendants were transactions in interstate commerce. . . .

The undisputed facts thus afford no warrant for the argument that the poultry handled by defendants at their slaughterhouse markets was in a *"current"* or *"flow"* of interstate commerce and was thus subject to congressional regulation. The mere fact that there may be a constant flow of commodities into a State does not mean that the flow continues after the property has arrived and has become commingled with the mass of property within the State and is there held solely for local disposition and use. So far as the poultry here in question is concerned, the flow in interstate commerce had ceased. The poultry had come to a permanent rest within the State. . . .

(2) Did the defendants' transactions directly *"affect"* interstate commerce so as to be subject to federal regulation? The power of Congress extends not only to the regulation of transactions which are part of interstate commerce, but to the protection of that commerce from injury. It matters not that the injury may be due to the conduct of those engaged in intrastate operations. Thus, Congress may protect the safety of those employed in interstate transportation "no matter what may be the source of the dangers which threaten it." . . .

. . .

. . . This is not a prosecution for a conspiracy to restrain or monopolize interstate commerce in violation of the Anti-Trust Act. Defendants have been convicted, not upon direct charges of injury to interstate commerce or of interference with persons engaged in that commerce, but of violations of certain provisions of the Live Poultry Code and of conspiracy to commit these violations. Interstate commerce is brought in only upon the charge that violations of these provisions—as to hours and wages of employees and local sales—"affected" interstate commerce.

In determining how far the federal government may go in controlling intrastate transactions upon the ground that they "affect" interstate commerce, there is a necessary and well-established distinction between direct and indirect effects. The precise line can be drawn only as individual cases arise, but the distinction is clear in principle. Direct effects are illustrated by the railroad cases we have cited, as *e.g.*, the effect of failure to use prescribed safety appliances on railroads which are the highways of both interstate and intrastate commerce, injury to an employee engaged in interstate transportation by the negligence of an employee engaged in an intrastate movement, the fixing of rates for intrastate transportation which unjustly discriminate against interstate commerce. But where the effect of intrastate transactions upon interstate commerce is merely indirect, such transactions remain within the domain of state power. If the commerce clause were construed to reach all enterprises and transactions which could be said to have an indirect effect upon interstate commerce, the federal authority would embrace practically all the activities of the people and the authority of the State over its domestic concerns would exist only by sufferance of the federal government. Indeed, on such a theory, even the development of the State's commercial facilities would be subject to federal control. . . .

. . .

The question of chief importance relates to the provisions of the Code as to the hours and wages of those employed in defendants' slaughterhouse markets. It is plain that these requirements are imposed in order to govern the details of defendants' management of their local business. The persons employed in slaughtering and selling in local trade are not employed in interstate commerce. Their hours and wages have no direct relation to interstate commerce. The question of how many hours these employees should work and what they should be paid differs in no essential respect from similar questions in other local businesses which handle commodities brought into a State and there dealt in as a part of its internal commerce. . . . If the federal government may determine the wages and hours of employees in the internal commerce of a State, because of their relation to cost and prices and their indirect effect upon interstate commerce, it would seem that a similar control might be exerted over other elements of cost, also affecting prices, such as the number of employees, rents, advertising, methods of doing business, etc. All the processes of production and distribution that enter into cost could likewise be controlled. If the cost of doing an intrastate business is in itself the permitted object of federal control, the extent of the regulation of cost would be a question of discretion and not of power.

The Government also makes the point that efforts to enact state legislation establishing high labor standards have been impeded by the belief that unless similar action is taken generally, commerce will be diverted from the States adopting such standards, and that this fear of diversion has led to demands for federal legislation on the subject of wages and hours. The apparent implication is that the federal authority under the commerce clause should be deemed to extend to the establishment of rules to govern wages and hours in intrastate trade and industry generally throughout the country, thus overriding the authority of the States to deal with domestic problems arising from labor conditions in their internal commerce.

It is not the province of the Court to consider the economic advantages or disadvantages of such a centralized system. It is sufficient to say that the Federal Constitution does not provide for it. Our growth and development have called for wide use of the commerce power of the federal government in its control over the expanded activities of interstate commerce, and in protecting that commerce from burdens, interferences, and conspiracies to restrain and monopolize it. But the authority of the federal government may not be pushed to such an extreme as to destroy the distinction, which the commerce clause itself establishes, between commerce "among the several States" and the internal concerns of a State. The same answer must be made to the contention that is based upon the serious economic situation which led to the passage of the Recovery Act,—the fall in prices, the decline in wages and employment, and the curtailment of the market for commodities. Stress is laid upon the great importance of maintaining wage distributions which would provide the necessary stimulus in starting "the cumulative forces making for expanding commercial activity." Without in any way disparaging this motive, it is enough to say that the recuperative efforts of the federal government must be made in a manner consistent with the authority granted by the Constitution.

We are of the opinion that the attempt through the provisions of the Code to fix the hours and wages of employees of defendants in their intrastate business was not a valid exercise of federal power.

JUSTICE CARDOZO, with JUSTICE STONE, concurring.

. . .

National Labor Relations Board v. Jones & Laughlin Steel Corp., 301 U.S. 1 (1937)

The Court's half-century-long effort to shield production and manufacturing from federal authority continued through 1936. In Carter v. Carter Coal Company *a majority of the justices struck down the Bituminous Coal Conservation Act of 1935, which authorized the creation of fair competition standards and labor regulations in the coal industry. Even though compliance was voluntary (with tax refunds being used as incentives to follow the regulations) Justice Sutherland declared that Congress was impermissibly trying to control "local evils over which the federal government has no legislative control," since federal commerce power "does not attach until interstate commercial intercourse begins."*

Two events took place between the Carter Coal *decision and the next Supreme Court decision interpreting the commerce clause. The first was Roosevelt's landslide victory in the 1936 national election, an election that gave Democrats over three-quarters of the seats in Congress. The second was the announcement and controversy over Roosevelt's Court-packing plan. Justices making decisions in this political environment were aware that political retaliation might (but might not) take place should the justices continue opposing the New Deal.*

The first issue on the judicial agenda after the elections of 1936 was the constitutionality of the Wagner Act. The Wagner Act required that businesses recognize unions and pay minimum wages. Unlike some previous New Deal statutes, the Wagner Act was specifically limited to businesses engaged in interstate commerce. The act established the National Labor Relations Board (NLRB) to monitor and penalize unfair labor practices. A better-organized Justice Department prosecuted five test cases, carefully selected to represent a range of important interstate industries. The cases were heard and decided together.

Jones & Laughlin Steel Corp. *provided an ideal test case for the government. The corporation was based in Pennsylvania, but it was one of the largest producers of steel in the United States. Through the ownership and management of various subsidiaries, it ran a fully integrated operation, from mining to transportation by rail and barge to smelting and manufacturing and finally to distribution, storage, and sales throughout the United States and Canada. The NLRB had charged Jones & Laughlin Steel with interfering with unionization efforts at its plant in Aliquippa, Pennsylvania, which processed raw materials gathered from other states to manufacture steel for sale nationally. In each of the cases decided and argued with* Jones & Laughlin Steel, *the government and the majority emphasized the tight relationship between the particular plant being regulated by the NLRB and the stream of national commerce. The result was a major victory for the Roosevelt administration. Hughes and Roberts switched sides to join the dissenters from* Carter Coal *to give a 5–4 victory to the government. In* Washington, Virginia & Maryland Coach Co. v. NLRB *(1937), involving an interstate bus service, the justices were unanimous in upholding congressional authority to regulate the labor and wages of company employees.* NLRB v. Jones & Laughlin Steel Corp. *and the companion cases were the first decisions to sustain a major New Deal program under the commerce clause. Hughes insisted that the majority was just following earlier precedents in upholding the Wagner Act. The dissenters strongly disagreed. Who had the stronger argument?*

CHIEF JUSTICE HUGHES delivered the opinion of the Court.

. . . The authority of the federal government may not be pushed to such an extreme as to destroy the distinction, which the commerce clause itself establishes, between commerce "among the several States" and the internal concerns of a State. That distinction between what is national and what is local in the activities of commerce is vital to the maintenance of our federal system.

. . .

We think it clear that the National Labor Relations Act may be construed so as to operate within the sphere of constitutional authority. The jurisdiction conferred upon the Board, and invoked in this instance, is found in §10 (a), which provides:

> SEC. 10 (a). The Board is empowered, as hereinafter provided, to prevent any person from engaging in any unfair labor practice (listed in section 8) affecting commerce.

The Act specifically defines the "commerce" to which it refers (§2(6)):

> The term "commerce" means trade, traffic, commerce, transportation, or communication among the several States, or between the District of Columbia or any Territory of the United States and any State or other Territory, or between any foreign country and any State, Territory, or the District of Columbia, or within the District of Columbia or any Territory, or between points in the same State but through any other State or any Territory or the District of Columbia or any foreign country.

There can be no question that the commerce thus contemplated by the Act (aside from that within a Territory or the District of Columbia) is interstate and foreign commerce in the constitutional sense.

. . .

. . . The grant of authority to the Board does not purport to extend to the relationship between all industrial employees and employers. Its terms do not impose collective bargaining upon all industry regardless of effects upon interstate or foreign commerce. It purports to reach only what may be deemed to burden or obstruct that commerce and, thus qualified, it must be construed as contemplating the exercise of control within constitutional bounds. It is a familiar principle that acts which directly burden or obstruct interstate or foreign commerce, or its free flow, are within the reach of the congressional power. Acts having that effect are not rendered immune because they grow out of labor disputes. . . . It is the effect upon commerce, not the source of the injury, which is the criterion. . . . We are thus to inquire whether in the instant case the constitutional boundary has been passed.

. . . [I]n its present application, the statute goes no further than to safeguard the right of employees to self-organization and to select representatives of their own choosing for collective bargaining or other mutual protection without restraint or coercion by their employer.

That is a fundamental right. Employees have as clear a right to organize and select their representatives for lawful purposes as the respondent has to organize its business and select its own officers and agents. Discrimination and coercion to prevent the free exercise of the right of employees to self-organization and representation is a proper subject for condemnation by competent legislative authority. . . .

Respondent says that whatever may be said of employees engaged in interstate commerce, the industrial relations and activities in the manufacturing department of respondent's enterprise are not subject to federal regulation. The argument rests upon the proposition that manufacturing in itself is not commerce. . . .

. . .

We do not find it necessary to determine whether these features of defendant's business dispose of the asserted analogy to the "stream of commerce" cases. The instances in which that metaphor has been used are but particular, and not exclusive, illustrations of the protective power which the Government invokes in support of the present Act. The congressional authority to protect interstate commerce from burdens and obstructions is not limited to transactions which can be deemed to be an essential part of a "flow" of interstate or foreign commerce. Burdens and obstructions may be due to injurious action springing from other sources. The fundamental principle is that the power to regulate commerce is the power to enact "all appropriate legislation" for "its protection and advancement." . . . That power is plenary and may be exerted to protect interstate commerce "no matter what the source of the dangers which threaten it." . . . Although activities may be intrastate in character when separately considered, if they have such a close and substantial relation to interstate commerce that their control is essential or appropriate to protect that commerce from burdens and obstructions, Congress cannot be denied the power to exercise that control. . . . Undoubtedly the scope of this power must be considered in the light of our dual system of government and may not be extended so as to embrace effects upon interstate commerce so indirect and remote that to embrace them, in view of our complex society, would effectually obliterate the distinction between what is national and what is local and create a completely centralized government. . . . The question is necessarily one of degree. . . .

. . . [I]n the first *Coronado* case (1922) the Court . . . said that "if Congress deems certain recurring practices, though not really part of interstate commerce, likely to obstruct, restrain or burden it, it has the power to subject them to national supervision and restraint." . . .

It is thus apparent that the fact that the employees here concerned were engaged in production is not determinative. The question remains as to the effect upon interstate commerce of the labor practice involved. In the *Schechter* case (1935), we found that the effect there was so remote as to be beyond the federal power. To find "immediacy or directness" there was to find it "almost everywhere," a result inconsistent with the maintenance of our federal system. In the *Carter* case (1936), the Court was of the opinion that the provisions of the statute relating to production were invalid upon several grounds. . . . These cases are not controlling here.

. . . [T]he stoppage of [the respondent steel company's] operations by industrial strife would have a most serious effect upon interstate commerce. In view of respondent's far-flung activities, it is idle to say that the effect would be indirect or remote. It is obvious that it would be immediate and might be catastrophic. We are asked to shut our eyes to the plainest facts of our national life and to deal with the question of direct and indirect effects in an intellectual vacuum. Because there may be but indirect and remote effects upon interstate commerce in connection with a host of local enterprises throughout the country, it does not follow that other industrial activities do not have such a close and intimate relation to interstate commerce as to make the presence of industrial strife a matter of the most urgent national concern. When industries organize themselves on a national scale, making their relation to interstate commerce the dominant factor in their activities, how can it be maintained that their industrial labor relations constitute a forbidden field into which Congress may not enter when it is necessary to protect interstate commerce from the paralyzing consequences of industrial war? We have often said that interstate commerce itself is a practical conception. It is equally true that interferences with that commerce must be appraised by a judgment that does not ignore actual experience.

Experience has abundantly demonstrated that the recognition of the right of employees to self-organization and to have representatives of their own choosing for the purpose of collective bargaining is often an essential condition of industrial peace. Refusal to confer and negotiate has been one of the most prolific causes of strife. This is such an outstanding fact in the history of labor disturbances that it is a proper subject of judicial notice and requires no citation of instances. . . . But with respect to the appropriateness of the recognition of self-organization and representation in the promotion of peace, the question is not essentially different in the case of employees in industries of such a character that interstate commerce is put in jeopardy from the case of employees of transportation companies. And of what avail is it to protect the facility of transportation, if interstate commerce is throttled with respect to the commodities to be transported!

. . . Instead of being beyond the pale, we think that it presents in a most striking way the close and intimate relation which a manufacturing industry may have to interstate commerce and we have no doubt that Congress had constitutional authority to safeguard the right of respondent's employees to self-organization and freedom in the choice of representatives for collective bargaining.

[The next part of the opinion concluded that the National Labor Relations Act of 1935 did not violate property rights protected by the Fifth Amendment.]

JUSTICE McREYNOLDS, dissenting.[29]

JUSTICE VAN DEVANTER, JUSTICE SUTHERLAND, JUSTICE BUTLER and I are unable to agree with the decisions just announced.

. . .

The Court, as we think, departs from well-established principles followed in *Schechter Corp. v. United States* . . . and *Carter v. Carter Coal Co.* Upon the authority of those decisions, the Circuit Courts of Appeals of the Fifth, Sixth and Second Circuits in the causes now before us have held the power of Congress under the commerce clause does not extend to relations between employers and their employees engaged in manufacture, and therefore the Act conferred upon the National Labor Relations Board no authority in respect of matters covered by the questioned orders. Every consideration brought forward to uphold the Act before us was applicable to support the Acts held unconstitutional in causes decided within two years. And the lower courts rightly deemed them controlling.

. . .

Any effect on interstate commerce by the discharge of employees shown here, would be indirect and remote in the highest degree, as consideration of the facts will show. In [*Jones & Laughlin*] ten men out of ten thousand were discharged; in the other cases only a few. The immediate effect in the factory may be to create discontent among all those employed and a strike may follow, which, in turn, may result in reducing production, which ultimately may reduce the volume of goods moving in interstate commerce. By this chain of indirect and progressively remote events we finally reach the evil with which it is said the legislation under consideration undertakes to deal. A more remote and indirect interference with interstate commerce or a more definite invasion of the powers reserved to the states is difficult, if not impossible, to imagine.

The Constitution still recognizes the existence of states with indestructible powers; the Tenth Amendment was supposed to put them beyond controversy.

We are told that Congress may protect the "stream of commerce" and that one who buys raw material without the state, manufactures it therein, and ships the output to another state is in that stream. Therefore it is said he may be prevented from doing anything which may interfere with its flow.

This, too, goes beyond the constitutional limitations heretofore enforced. If a man raises cattle and regularly delivers them to a carrier for interstate shipment, may Congress prescribe the conditions under which he may employ or discharge helpers on the ranch? The products of a mine pass daily into interstate commerce; many things are brought to it from other states. Are the owners and the miners within the power of Congress in respect of the miners' tenure and discharge? . . .

And if this theory of a continuous "stream of commerce" as now defined is correct, will it become the duty of the Federal Government hereafter to suppress every strike which by possibility may cause a blockade in that stream? . . .

There is no ground on which reasonably to hold that refusal by a manufacturer, whose raw materials come from states other than that of his factory and whose products are regularly carried to other states, to bargain collectively with employees in his manufacturing plant, directly affects interstate commerce. In such business, there is not one but two distinct movements or streams in interstate transportation. The first brings in raw material and there ends. Then follows manufacture, a separate and local activity. Upon completion of this, and not before, the second distinct movement or stream in interstate commerce begins and the products go to other states. Such is the common course for small as well as large industries. It is unreasonable and unprecedented to say the commerce clause confers upon Congress power to govern relations between employers and employees in these local activities. . . .

---

29. As noted in the introduction to this excerpt, *Jones & Laughlin Steel* was one of five National Labor Relations Board cases decided by the Supreme Court on April 12, 1937. Justices McReynolds, Van Devanter, Sutherland, and Butler dissented in all cases. Their actual dissenting opinion was appended to *NLRB v. Friedman–Harry Marks Clothing Co.*, 301 U.S. 58 (1937).

It is gravely stated that experience teaches that if an employer discourages membership in "any organization of any kind" "in which employees participate, and which exists for the purpose in whole or in part of dealing with employers concerning grievances, labor disputes, wages, rates of pay, hours of employment or conditions of work," discontent may follow and this in turn may lead to a strike, and as the outcome of the strike there may be a block in the stream of interstate commerce. Therefore Congress may inhibit the discharge! Whatever effect any cause of discontent may ultimately have upon commerce is far too indirect to justify Congressional regulation. Almost anything—marriage, birth, death—may in some fashion affect commerce.

. . .

That Congress has power by appropriate means, not prohibited by the Constitution, to prevent direct and material interference with the conduct of interstate commerce is settled doctrine. But the interference struck at must be direct and material, not some mere possibility contingent on wholly uncertain events; and there must be no impairment of rights guaranteed. . . .

. . .

Illustration 8-3 Justice Robert H. Jackson

Source: Library of Congress Prints and Photographs Division, LC-USZ62-38828.

Wickard v. Filburn, 317 U.S. 111 (1942)

Wickard v. Filburn *demonstrated how far the Supreme Court was willing to go after 1937 to find a sufficient relationship to interstate commerce when considering the constitutionality of federal regulations of economic activity. The Agricultural Adjustment Act (AAA) of 1938 penalized farmers who harvested more than a specified quota of acres for wheat. Roscoe Filburn exceeded his quota but did not sell the excess wheat he grew in either local or national markets. Instead, the wheat was used solely to feed his family and their livestock on his small farm in Ohio. The case was not one that the government would have preferred to bring to the Court, but Filburn filed for an injunction in federal district court to block Secretary of Agriculture Claude Wickard and others from enforcing the AAA quotas against him and for a declaration that the act was unconstitutional. A divided district court panel ruled in favor of Filburn. A unanimous Supreme Court reversed the lower court and found that his activities could be federally regulated. Justice Jackson relied on a pragmatic approach when evaluating the scope of federal power. His opinion set down a new doctrinal standard, asking whether an activity considered in the aggregate exerts a substantial economic effect on interstate commerce.*

In the spring of 1942, Jackson confessed to Chief Justice Stone that he remained "baffled" as to how to resolve the case without leaving the Court with "no function but to stamp this Act O.K." and in the process render the "federal compact . . . pretty meaningless if Congress is to be the sole judge of the extent of its own commerce power." In the summer, Jackson began the process of drafting an opinion with a memo to his law clerk. The memo offers a more frank and political explanation for the Court's actions in the case than does the opinion that was eventually issued by the Court. Jackson wrote, "If we sustain the present Act, I don't see how we can ever sustain states' rights again as against a Congressional exercise of the commerce power." He summed up the case to Justice Sherman Minton after the opinion was handed down, "When we admit that it is an economic matter, we pretty nearly admit that it is not a matter which courts may judge."[30]

30. Quoted in Barry Cushman, *Rethinking the New Deal Court* (New York: Oxford University Press, 1998), 215, 221.

Wickard was the last landmark New Deal commerce clause case, and it laid down the doctrinal formulations that guided Congress and the judiciary through the remainder of the twentieth century. As you read the opinion, consider the following: Can the federal government limit people to five at-home dinners a week in order to increase commerce in restaurants? Can the federal government limit the extent to which people make their own clothes? Can the federal government mandate that individuals buy health insurance?

JUSTICE JACKSON delivered the opinion of the Court.

...

It is urged that under the Commerce Clause of the Constitution, Article I, §8, clause 3, Congress does not possess the power it has in this instance sought to exercise. The question would merit little consideration since our decision in *United States v. Darby* (1941), ... sustaining the federal power to regulate production of goods for commerce, except for the fact that this Act extends federal regulation to production not intended in any part for commerce but wholly for consumption on the farm. ... [M]arketing quotas not only embrace all that may be sold without penalty but also what may be consumed on the premises. ... Penalties do not depend upon whether any part of the wheat, either within or without the quota, is sold or intended to be sold. ...

...

... We believe that a review of the course of decision under the Commerce Clause will make plain ... that questions of the power of Congress are not to be decided by reference to any formula which would give controlling force to nomenclature such as "production" and "indirect" and foreclose consideration of the actual effects of the activity in question upon interstate commerce.

At the beginning Chief Justice Marshall described the federal commerce power with a breadth never yet exceeded. *Gibbons v. Ogden* (1824). ... He made emphatic the embracing and penetrating nature of this power by warning that effective restraints on its exercise must proceed from political rather than from judicial processes. ...

...

Not long after the decision of *United States v. Knight Co.* (1895), ... Mr. Justice Holmes, in sustaining the exercise of national power over intrastate activity, stated for the Court that "commerce among the States is not a technical legal conception, but a practical one, drawn from the course of business." *Swift & Co. v. United States* (1905). ... It was soon demonstrated that the effects of many kinds of intrastate activity upon interstate commerce were such as to make them a proper subject of federal regulation. In some cases sustaining the exercise of federal power over intrastate matters the term "direct" was used for the purpose of stating, rather than of reaching, a result; in others it was treated as synonymous with "substantial" or "material"; and in others it was not used at all. Of late its use has been abandoned in cases dealing with questions of federal power under the Commerce Clause.

In the *Shreveport Rate Cases* (1914), ... the Court held that railroad rates of an admittedly intrastate character and fixed by authority of the state might, nevertheless, be revised by the Federal Government because of the economic effects which they had upon interstate commerce. The opinion of Mr. Justice Hughes found federal intervention constitutionally authorized because of "matters having such a close and substantial relation to interstate traffic that the control is essential or appropriate to the security of that traffic, to the efficiency of the interstate service, and to the maintenance of conditions under which interstate commerce may be conducted upon fair terms and without molestation or hindrance." ...

The Court's recognition of the relevance of the economic effects in the application of the Commerce Clause, exemplified by this statement, has made the mechanical application of legal formulas no longer feasible. Once an economic measure of the reach of the power granted to Congress in the Commerce Clause is accepted, questions of federal power cannot be decided simply by finding the activity in question to be "production," nor can consideration of its economic effects be foreclosed by calling them "indirect." ...

Whether the subject of the regulation in question was "production," "consumption," or "marketing" is, therefore, not material for purposes of deciding the question of federal power before us. That an activity is of local character may help in a doubtful case to determine whether Congress intended to reach it. The same consideration might help in determining whether in the absence of Congressional action it would be permissible for the state to exert its power on the subject matter, even though in so doing it to some degree affected interstate commerce. But even if appellee's activity be local and though it may not be regarded as commerce, it may still, whatever its nature, be reached by Congress if it exerts a substantial economic effect on interstate commerce, and this irrespective of whether such effect is what might at some earlier time have been defined as "direct" or "indirect."

. . .

The maintenance by government regulation of a price for wheat undoubtedly can be accomplished as effectively by sustaining or increasing the demand as by limiting the supply. The effect of the statute before us is to restrict the amount which may be produced for market and the extent as well to which one may forestall resort to the market by producing to meet his own needs. That appellee's own contribution to the demand for wheat may be trivial by itself is not enough to remove him from the scope of federal regulation where, as here, his contribution, taken together with that of many others similarly situated, is far from trivial. . . .

It is well established by decisions of this Court that the power to regulate commerce includes the power to regulate the prices at which commodities in that commerce are dealt in and practices affecting such prices. One of the primary purposes of the Act in question was to increase the market price of wheat, and to that end to limit the volume thereof that could affect the market. It can hardly be denied that a factor of such volume and variability as home-consumed wheat would have a substantial influence on price and market conditions. This may arise because being in marketable condition such wheat overhangs the market and, if induced by rising prices, tends to flow into the market and check price increases. But if we assume that it is never marketed, it supplies a need of the man who grew it which would otherwise be reflected by purchases in the open market. Home-grown wheat in this sense competes with wheat in commerce. The stimulation of commerce is a use of the regulatory function quite as definitely as prohibitions or restrictions thereon. This record leaves us in no doubt that Congress may properly have considered that wheat consumed on the farm where grown, if wholly outside the scheme of regulation, would have a substantial effect in defeating and obstructing its purpose to stimulate trade therein at increased prices.

. . .

Reversed.

Congressional Debate over the Civil Rights Act of 1964[31]

Liberals in both the Democratic and the Republican parties relied primarily on the commerce power when passing the Civil Rights Act of 1964. Several years later Congress passed and President Johnson signed a new bill forbidding discrimination in the housing market. The Supreme Court sustained all of these measures, as well as the Voting Rights Act of 1965 under either the commerce power or the post-Civil War Amendments. Only a later amendment to the Voting Rights Act that lowered the voting age in state elections to eighteen met with defeat in the Supreme Court. That decision was reversed by the Twenty-Sixth Amendment to the Constitution.

The congressional debate over the Civil Rights Act was the longest in American history up to that time. Support for civil rights was bipartisan, with only southern Democrats and more libertarian Republicans raising objections. The measure passed easily in the House, with almost four-fifths of all Republicans joining northern Democrats in support of the bill. Senate passage was more difficult, given the usual filibuster by southern Democrats. Senator Everett Dirksen of Illinois, the Republican minority leader, proved crucial. Although a political conservative, Dirksen was personally disturbed by the brutal southern reaction to civil rights protests and aware of the strong civil rights vote in the north. After agreeing to a few compromises, he worked to provide the Republican support necessary to break the southern filibuster. The filibuster was broken on June 10, 1964. Within two weeks, the Senate voted to pass the Civil Rights Act of 1964. Shortly thereafter, the House agreed to the Senate's revisions. The measure became law on July 2, 1964. Title II of the Civil Rights Act prohibited racial discrimination in places of public accommodation, the key provision of the Civil Rights Act of 1875.

SENATOR HUBERT HUMPHREY (Democrat, Minnesota)

. . .

It is difficult for most of us to fully comprehend the monstrous humiliations and inconveniences that racial discrimination imposes on our Negro fellow citizens. If a white man is thirsty on a hot day, he goes to the nearest soda fountain. If he is hungry, he goes to the

31. Excerpt taken from *Congressional Record*, 88th Cong., 2nd Sess., March 30, 24, 1964, 6531, 6080.

nearest restaurant. If he needs a restroom, he can go to the nearest gas station. If it is night and he is tired, he takes his pick of the available motels and hotels.

But for a Negro the picture is different. Trying to get a glass of iced tea at a lunch counter may result in insult and abuse, unless he is willing to go out of his way, perhaps to walk across town. He can never count on using a restroom, on getting a decent place to stay, on buying a good meal. These are trivial matters in the life of a white person, but for some 20 million American Negroes, they are important considerations that must be planned for in detail. They must draw up travel plans much as a general advancing across hostile territory would establish his logistical support.

. . .

The American Negro does not seek to be set apart from the community of American life. He seeks participation in it. He does not seek separation. Instead, he seeks participation and inclusion. These Americans want to be full citizens, to enjoy all the rights and privileges, and to assume the duties and burdens. Surely Congress can do nothing less than to permit them to do their job, to be parts of the total community, and to be parts of the life of this Nation. America has become great because Americans are a united people. The American Negroes seek to be part of that society; and they are asking that it be made a legal reality. . . .

. . .

There has been considerable discussion as to whether the constitutional bases of the public accommodations provisions of H.R. 7152 should be the commerce clause or the 14th amendment. The contention will even be made that no constitutional authority whatsoever supports the legislation. I think there is little doubt that, with the careful changes that have been made during the course of its development, this bill finds firm support in both the commerce clause and the 14th amendment, and is not prohibited by any other provision of the Constitution.

. . . [T]hat title II does embody a moral judgment should not be a reason for failing to rely on our power to regulate commerce.

In fact, the Constitution of the United States is the Constitution of a Nation. All its provisions are properly available to effectuate the moral judgments of that Nation. That is why it is wholly appropriate to use any relevant constitutional authority with respect to a national problem. If more than one provision of the Constitution provides that authority, so much the better.

In fact, we have not hesitated to use the power to tax as an instrument against gambling and the narcotic traffic. We have not hesitated to use the power to regulate commerce to fight the white slavery trade.

. . .

Moreover, reliance on the commerce clause is not merely a legal device. The evil of racial discrimination with which title II is concerned has clear economic consequences. . . .

Among other things, that clause gives Congress authority to deal with conditions adversely affecting the allocation of resources. Discrimination and segregation on racial grounds have a substantial adverse effect on the interstate flow of goods, capital, and of persons. Skilled or educated men who are apt to be victims of discrimination in an area are reluctant to settle there even if opportunities are available. For this and other reasons, capital is reluctant to invest in such a region and, therefore the flow of goods to, and their sale within, such an area is similarly reduced. . . .

. . .

One hundred and ninety years have passed since the Declaration of Independence, and 100 years since the Emancipation Proclamation. Surely the goals of this bill are not too much to ask of the Senate of the United States.

SENATOR EDWIN WILLIS (Democrat, Louisiana)

. . . [T]he commerce clause does not say that Congress has the right to regulate habits, customs, human behavior, morals, or attitudes; it can only regulate interstate commerce.

You will hear about court cases concerning the manufacture of goods and farming operations, and so on. There is no doubt that the courts have gone far in this field. But you can at least see and feel corn and wheat; you can measure and buy these grains by the ton, and you can put them in a truck or a boxcar and ship them across State lines. But that is a far cry from what the proponents of this bill would twist the commerce clause to mean. And so even to those of you who are not lawyers, I ask you to remember the simple provision of the powers of Congress under the commerce clause, that is to regulate commerce among the several States.

In respect of "commerce" title II indulges the presumption that transients generate "commerce" and that offers to serve travelers affect "commerce." In the area of the 14th Amendment and the concomitant requirement of some sort of "State action," it equates "custom and usage" to affirmative action by a State. In both respects, title II constitutes a novel and dangerous experiment in political theory. Its adoption could work a revolutionary change in the existing balance of Federal–State relationships.

In my opinion, however, the attempted utilization of the 14th amendment and the commerce clause to support title II cannot be defended on constitutional grounds. You are well aware of the decision of the Supreme Court in the *Civil Rights* cases which held squarely and unequivocally that the act of Congress of 1875, entitled "An act to protect all citizens in their civil and legal rights" and proposed to do exactly what is proposed to be done by title II, was unconstitutional and could not be supported under the 14th amendment.

Since my guess is as good as anyone's, I venture to say that the reason no effort was made to base the 1875 Statute on, or to justify it under, the commerce clause was because of the feeling that there was far less chance to support its constitutionality on the commerce clause than there was to have its constitutionality upheld under the 14th amendment.

Heart of Atlanta Motel, Inc. v. United States, 379 U.S. 241 (1964)

Proponents and opponents of the Civil Rights Act of 1964 were eager for an immediate court test of the legislation, and they found no shortage of possible litigants. The Heart of Atlanta Motel was a large motel located near downtown Atlanta, Georgia. Three-quarters of its guests were from out of state. The motel did not rent rooms to blacks. Given that policy, the owners of the motel sought a declaratory judgment that the Civil Rights Act of 1964 unconstitutionally prohibited private discrimination in places of public accommodation, including motels. The motel owners argued that Congress had exceeded its authority under the interstate commerce clause in trying to reach a business such as the motel, violated the due process and takings clauses of the Fifth Amendment by attempting to direct them how to operate their business, and violated the Thirteenth Amendment by forcing them against their will to rent their rooms to African Americans. A three-judge district court panel upheld the statute against the constitutional challenge, and the motel owners appealed to the Supreme Court. The justices focused only on the commerce clause issue and unanimously upheld the law.

Heart of Atlanta *was heard with* Katzenbach v. McClung *(1964), which involved Ollie's Barbecue, a local restaurant in Birmingham, Alabama, that did not serve African Americans. The federal district court found that Ollie's Barbecue primarily served local patrons and would lose much of its business if forced to integrate. The federal government appealed, arguing that a significant quantity of the food and supplies used in the restaurant had crossed state boundaries at some point. That was sufficient, the appeal continued, to subject the restaurant's service policies to federal regulation under the interstate commerce clause. The Supreme Court held that no direct evidence was needed that a particular restaurant interfered with the flow of interstate commerce. It was enough that Congress had concluded that the existence of segregated accommodations discouraged travel and economic development. A few years later, in* Daniel v. Paul *(1969), the Court ruled that even a snack bar at a private park had enough of a connection to interstate commerce to trigger the Civil Rights Act and desegregate the park, prompting Justice Black to dissent.*

JUSTICE CLARK delivered the opinion of the Court.

. . .

The sole question posed is, therefore, the constitutionality of the Civil Rights Act of 1964 as applied to these facts. The legislative history of the Act indicates that Congress based the Act on §5 and the Equal Protection Clause of the Fourteenth Amendment as well as its power to regulate interstate commerce under Art. I, §8, cl. 3, of the Constitution.

The Senate Commerce Committee made it quite clear that the fundamental object of Title II was to vindicate "the deprivation of personal dignity that surely accompanies denials of equal access to public establishments." At the same time, however, it noted that such an objective has been and could be readily achieved "by congressional action based on the commerce power of the Constitution." . . . Our study of the legislative record, made in the light of prior cases, has brought us to the conclusion that Congress possessed ample power in this regard, and we have therefore not considered the other grounds relied upon. This is not to say that the remaining authority upon which it acted was not adequate, a question upon which we do not pass, but merely that since the commerce power is sufficient for our decision here we have considered it alone.

. . .

In light of our ground for decision, it might be well at the outset to discuss the *Civil Rights Cases* (1883), which declared provisions of the Civil Rights Act of 1875 unconstitutional. We think that decision inapposite, and without precedential value in determining the constitutionality of the present Act. Unlike Title II of the present legislation, the 1875 Act broadly proscribed discrimination in "inns, public conveyances on land or water, theaters, and other places of public amusement," without limiting the categories of affected businesses to those impinging upon interstate commerce. In contrast, the applicability of Title II is carefully limited to enterprises having a direct and substantial relation to the interstate flow of goods and people, except where state action is involved. Further, the fact that certain kinds of businesses may not in 1875 have been sufficiently involved in interstate commerce to warrant bringing them within the ambit of the commerce power is not necessarily dispositive of the same question today. Our populace had not reached its present mobility, nor were facilities, goods and services circulating as readily in interstate commerce as they are today. Although the principles which we apply today are those first formulated by Chief Justice Marshall in *Gibbons* v. *Ogden* (1824), the conditions of transportation and commerce have changed dramatically, and we must apply those principles to the present state of commerce. The sheer increase in volume of interstate traffic alone would give discriminatory practices which inhibit travel a far larger impact upon the Nation's commerce than such practices had on the economy of another day. Finally, there is language in the *Civil Rights Cases* which indicates that the Court did not fully consider whether the 1875 Act could be sustained as an exercise of the commerce power. Though the Court observed that "no one will contend that the power to pass it was contained in the Constitution before the adoption of the last three amendments [Thirteenth, Fourteenth, and Fifteenth]," the Court went on specifically to note that the Act was not "conceived" in terms of the commerce power and expressly pointed out:

> Of course, these remarks [as to lack of congressional power] do not apply to those cases in which Congress is clothed with direct and plenary powers of legislation over the whole subject, accompanied with an express or implied denial of such power to the States, as in the regulation of commerce with foreign nations, among the several States, and with the Indian tribes. . . . In these cases Congress has power to pass laws for regulating the subjects specified in every detail, and the conduct and transactions of individuals in respect thereof.

Since the commerce power was not relied on by the Government and was without support in the record it is understandable that the Court narrowed its inquiry and excluded the Commerce Clause as a possible source of power. In any event, it is clear that such a limitation renders the opinion devoid of authority for the proposition that the Commerce Clause gives no power to Congress to regulate discriminatory practices now found substantially to affect interstate commerce.

We, therefore, conclude that the *Civil Rights Cases* have no relevance to the basis of decision here where the Act explicitly relies upon the commerce power, and where the record is filled with testimony of obstructions and restraints resulting from the discriminations found to be existing. We now pass to that phase of the case.

. . .

While the Act as adopted carried no congressional findings the record of its passage through each house is replete with evidence of the burdens that discrimination by race or color places upon interstate commerce. . . . This testimony included the fact that our people have become increasingly mobile with millions of people of all races traveling from State to State; that Negroes in particular have been the subject of discrimination in transient accommodations, having to travel great distances to secure the same; that often they have been unable to obtain accommodations and have had to call upon friends to put them up overnight. . . . These exclusionary practices were found to be nationwide, the Under Secretary of Commerce testifying that there is "no question that this discrimination in the North still exists to a large degree" and in the West and Midwest as well. . . .

. . .

. . . [T]he determinative test of the exercise of power by the Congress under the Commerce Clause is simply whether the activity sought to be regulated is "commerce which concerns more States than one" and has a real and substantial relation to the national interest. Let us now turn to this facet of the problem.

That the "intercourse" of which the Chief Justice spoke included the movement of persons through more States than one was settled as early as 1849, in the *Passenger Cases*. . . . Again in 1913 Mr. Justice McKenna, speaking for the Court, said: "Commerce among the States, we have said, consists of intercourse and traffic between their citizens, and includes the transportation of persons and property." *Hoke v. United States* (1913). . . . Nor does it make any difference whether the transportation is commercial in character.

. . .

That Congress was legislating against moral wrongs in many of these areas rendered its enactments no less valid. In framing Title II of this Act Congress was also dealing with what it considered a moral problem. But that fact does not detract from the overwhelming evidence of the disruptive effect that racial discrimination has had on commercial intercourse. It was this burden which empowered Congress to enact appropriate legislation, and, given this basis for the exercise of its power, Congress was not restricted by the fact that the particular obstruction to interstate commerce with which it was dealing was also deemed a moral and social wrong.

It is said that the operation of the motel here is of a purely local character. But, assuming this to be true, "if it is interstate commerce that feels the pinch, it does not matter how local the operation which applies the squeeze." *United States v. Women's Sportswear Mfrs. Assn.* (1949). . . . As Chief Justice Stone put it in *United States v. Darby*:

> The power of Congress over interstate commerce is not confined to the regulation of commerce among the states. It extends to those activities intrastate which so affect interstate commerce or the exercise of the power of Congress over it as to make regulation of them appropriate means to the attainment of a legitimate end, the exercise of the granted power of Congress to regulate interstate commerce. See *McCulloch* v. *Maryland* (1819).

. . .

We find no merit in the remainder of appellant's contentions, including that of "involuntary servitude." . . .

JUSTICE DOUGLAS, concurring.

Though I join the Court's opinions, I am somewhat reluctant here, as I was in *Edwards v. California* (1941) to rest solely on the Commerce Clause. My reluctance is not due to any conviction that Congress lacks power to regulate commerce in the interests of human rights. It is rather my belief that the right of people to be free of state action that discriminates against them because of race, like the "right of persons to move freely from State to State" . . . "occupies a more protected position in our constitutional system than does the movement of cattle, fruit, steel and coal across state lines." . . .

Hence I would prefer to rest on the assertion of legislative power contained in §5 of the Fourteenth Amendment which states: "The Congress shall have power to enforce, by appropriate legislation, the provisions of this article"—a power which the Court concedes was exercised at least in part in this Act.

A decision based on the Fourteenth Amendment would have a more settling effect, making unnecessary litigation over whether a particular restaurant or inn is within the commerce definitions of the Act or whether a particular customer is an interstate traveler. Under my construction, the Act would apply to all customers in all the enumerated places of public accommodation. And that construction would put an end to all obstructionist strategies and finally close one door on a bitter chapter in American history.

. . .

JUSTICE GOLDBERG, concurring.

I join in the opinions and judgments of the Court, since I agree "that the action of the Congress in the adoption of the Act as applied here . . . is within the power granted it by the Commerce Clause of the Constitution, as interpreted by this Court for 140 years."

The primary purpose of the Civil Rights Act of 1964, however, as the Court recognizes, and as I would underscore, is the vindication of human dignity and not mere economics. The Senate Commerce Committee made this quite clear:

> The primary purpose of . . . [the Civil Rights Act], then, is to solve this problem, the deprivation of personal dignity that surely accompanies denials of equal access to public establishments. Discrimination is not simply dollars and cents, hamburgers and movies; it is the humiliation, frustration, and embarrassment that a person must surely feel when he is told that he is unacceptable as a member of the public because of his race or color. . . .

Moreover, that this is the primary purpose of the Act is emphasized by the fact that while §201 (c) speaks only in terms of establishments which "affect commerce," it is clear that Congress based this section not only on its power under the Commerce Clause but also on §5 of the Fourteenth Amendment. . . .

V. Federalism

MAJOR DEVELOPMENTS

- The decline of the Tenth Amendment
- The rise of federal judicial review of states outside of economic regulation
- The rise of cooperative federalism

When the Supreme Court abandoned dual federalism after 1936, the justices abandoned the notion that the Constitution vested states with control over specifically delineated social policies. Up through the early twentieth century, many lawyers and politicians argued that the states and national government occupied separate spheres and were each limited to their own area of responsibility. This was the vision of dual federalism that the Court often tried to enforce. New Deal nationalists insisted that the federal government was constitutionally authorized to act on any matter on which states were deemed incompetent. Equally important, Congress was the branch of government that determined when federal action was necessary. Chief Justice Harlan Fiske Stone stated basic New Deal constitutional commitments when, in *United States v. Darby* (1941), he described the Tenth Amendment as "but a truism that all is retained which has not been surrendered." In this new understanding, the Tenth Amendment was not an independent barrier to congressional action; nor did it indicate principles that might affect how the Court evaluated congressional power.

Table 8-4 Selection of U.S. Supreme Court Cases Reviewing State Laws Under the Interstate Commerce Clause

Case	Vote	Outcome	Decision
Gibbons v. Ogden, 22 U.S. 1 (1824)	6–0	Struck down	State law regulating navigation of interstate waterways trumped by federal statute
Brown v. Maryland, 25 U.S. 419 (1827)	6–0	Struck down	State license on importers trumped by federal statute
Mayor of New York v. Miln, 36 U.S. 102 (1837)	5–1	Upheld	State law requiring captains of out-of-state ships to indemnify state for passengers who go on poverty relief is an internal police regulation
Passenger Cases, 48 U.S. 283 (1849)	5–4	Struck down	State laws imposing a tax on every out-of-state passenger brought into port are unconstitutional
Cooley v. Board of Wardens, 53 U.S. 299 (1851)	8–1	Upheld	State law requiring large ships to pay for a local pilot to guide them into port does not interfere with interstate commerce since no uniform national policy is necessary
Wabash, St. Louis & Pacific Railroad Company v. Illinois, 118 U.S. 557 (1886)	6–3	Struck down	Because the regulation of goods traveling across state lines requires a uniform national policy, a state law regulating railroad rates for such goods unconstitutionally interferes with interstate commerce even in the absence of a federal law
Kidd v. Pearson, 128 U.S. 1 (1888)	8–0	Upheld	State law prohibiting the manufacture of liquor, even if intended for out-of-state sale, is within the internal police power of the state
Seaboard Air Line Railway v. Blackwell, 244 U.S. 310 (1917)	6–3	Struck down	State law regulating the stops and speeds of trains places a direct burden on interstate commerce and is unconstitutional
Bradley v. Public Utilities Commission of Ohio, 289 U.S. 92 (1933)	9–0	Upheld	State law regulating the licensing of common carrier motor vehicles in order to promote public safety and reduce traffic congestion is a valid exercise of police power

(*Continued*)

Table 8-4 *(Continued)*

Case	Vote	Outcome	Decision
Baldwin v. G. A. F. Seelig, Inc., 294 U.S. 511 (1935)	9–0	Struck down	State law regulating the sale of out-of-state purchased milk, with the effect of excluding it, is an act of economic isolation and unconstitutionally discriminatory
South Carolina State Highway Department v. Barnwell Brothers, Inc., 303 U.S. 177 (1938)	7–0	Upheld	State law regulating weight and width of trucks on highways is not an undue burden on interstate commerce
Parker v. Brown, 317 U.S. 341 (1942)	9–0	Upheld	California raisin program designed to prop up prices only has indirect effect on interstate commerce and is not inconsistent with congressional policy
Dean Milk Co. v. City of Madison, Wisconsin, 340 U.S. 349 (1951)	6–3	Struck down	Local ordinance restricting the sale of nonlocal milk, even in the interest of promoting public safety, unconstitutionally discriminates against interstate commerce when less restrictive alternatives are available
City of Philadelphia v. New Jersey, 430 U.S. 141 (1977)	7–2	Struck down	State law prohibiting the importation of most out-of-state solid or liquid waste without legitimate reason is discriminatorily protectionist
Hunt v. Washington State Apple Advertising Commission, 432 U.S. 333 (1977)	8–0	Struck down	State law prohibiting the display of any state apple inspection grades unconstitutionally discriminates against commerce from states with more rigorous standards and burdens interstate commerce
Exxon Corp. v. Governor of Maryland, 437 U.S. 117 (1978)	7–1	Upheld	State law prohibiting oil producers and refiners from operating gasoline stations is not discriminatory or impermissibly burdensome to interstate commerce
White v. Mass. Council of Construction Employers, 460 U.S. 204 (1983)	7–2	Upheld	Mayoral order requiring city-funded construction projects to employ a minimum number of city residents is valid because city is acting as a market participant rather than as a regulator
Maine v. Taylor, 477 U.S. 131 (1986)	8–1	Upheld	State law prohibiting the importation of live baitfish serves a legitimate local concern that cannot be reasonably served by nondiscriminatory alternatives
Oregon Waste Systems, Inc. v. Department of Environmental Quality of Oregon, 511 U.S. 93 (1994)	7–2	Struck down	State law imposing a surcharge on solid waste generated out of state and disposed of within the state is discriminatory on its face, and, without evidence that no less discriminatory means are available to forward some legitimate local interest, is unconstitutional
Granholm v. Heald, 544 U.S. 460 (2005)	5–4	Struck down	State laws restricting the ability of out-of-state wineries to directly ship alcohol to consumers discriminate against interstate commerce
United Haulers Association v. Oneida-Herkimer Solid Waste Management Authority, 550 U.S. 330 (2007)	6–3	Upheld	County ordinances requiring locally produced garbage to be delivered to local publicly owned processing facilities does not interfere with interstate commerce

VI. Separation of Powers

MAJOR DEVELOPMENTS

- Limits on presidential power to remove independent commissioners
- The decline of the nondelegation doctrine
- The expansion of presidential war powers and executive privilege

Presidential power during the New Deal and Great Society Era was fueled by the administrative state, foreign affairs, and electoral politics. As the federal government played a more active role in national life, Congress increasingly passed legislation aimed more at empowering administrative agencies than at establishing precise legal rules. One consequence of this practice was an increase in executive policy making, with the president frequently giving direction to the many administrative agencies.

Lawmaking in the modern administrative state differed from nineteenth-century practice. Congressional regulation before and immediately after the Civil War was usually quite specific. Congress during the Jacksonian Era determined the exact price at which public lands were sold and devised detailed schedules for duties on common goods. Regulation at the turn of the century was much less specific. The Sherman Anti-Trust Act of 1890 prohibited "contracts in restraint of trade," leaving courts with the burden of determining when contracts restrained trade. Crucial New Deal measures added a new dimension of imprecision. Congress often simply declared a vague goal, such as establishing fair competition, and then authorized the president or a department of the executive branch to make specific rules for achieving that end. The size of the executive branch was greatly expanded in order to implement these new directives.

Control over independent regulatory commissions was one point of tension in the New Deal Era. Progressive reformers of the late nineteenth and early twentieth centuries favored these commissions. Ideally, they were structured to be free of the everyday influence of political parties and the elected branches of government. The commissions, such as the Interstate Commerce Commission and the Federal Trade Commission, both made regulatory policy and enforced it in individual cases. These commissions posed a problem for Roosevelt, who preferred to create executive agencies inside cabinet departments to manage new programs, particularly those that were staffed primarily by Republican appointees. Roosevelt tried to force the issue by removing a Republican member of the Federal Trade Commission before his term was complete. In *Humphrey's Executor v. United States* (1935), the Supreme Court rebuffed the president, upholding the independence of the commissioners. When limiting presidential removals to purely executive officer officials, Justice Sutherland's majority opinion asserted that the removals in this case "threaten[] the independence of a commission, which is not only wholly disconnected from the executive department, but which, as already fully appears, was created by Congress as a means of carrying into operation legislative and judicial powers, and as an agency of the legislative and judicial departments."

Presidents benefited from the increased American presence in world affairs. Presidents had historically been granted more leeway in foreign policy than in domestic policy. As international affairs became more important to American life in the twentieth century, the presidency became a more important institution. From 1932 until 1968, congressional majorities supported most important executive policy initiatives and most increases in presidential power. When presidents acted unilaterally, they usually could rely on their legislative supporters to prevent a constitutional crisis. Presidents did not always get their way, but the normal expectation was that Congress and the White House would generally be united by party, ideology, and policy goals.

By 1940, the justices had effectively abandoned any effort to limit congressional decisions to increase executive authority. Separation of powers debates for the next thirty years were largely hypothetical. Presidents and members of Congress frequently disputed the precise scope of their authority, but Congress did not directly challenge most executive initiatives. President Roosevelt, for example, asserted that Congress had no constitutional right to include a legislative veto in legislation granting the president power to make arms deals with allied powers, but Congress never exercised that veto. The one exception to this practice was when President Truman seized steel mines during the Korean War. When the Supreme Court rejected this exercise of executive power in the *Steel Seizure Case* (1952), Truman backed down, thus avoiding a potential constitutional crisis.

Youngstown Sheet & Tube Co. v. Sawyer, 343 U.S. 579 (1952) (Steel Seizure Case)

The New Deal increased American involvement in world affairs, and the nature of twentieth-century military struggles raised basic questions about the viability of eighteenth-century notions of separation of powers in a twentieth-century world. These issues were at the heart of Youngstown Sheet & Tube, *a decision that has acquired canonical status as the leading modern expression of contemporary constitutional understandings of executive capacity to act unilaterally. One school of thought, exemplified by Justice Black, insists that the Constitution of 1789 clearly spells out the division of powers between the president and Congress. The other school of thought, exemplified by Justices Frankfurter and Jackson, insists that the constitutional text has very little to say about modern problems; constitutional standards must therefore be worked out through analysis of historical developments and pragmatic accommodations. The latter view has become increasingly dominant in American constitutionalism. Jackson's three-part categorization of separation of powers situations set the standard for judicial thinking about conflicts between Congress and the president.*

In December 1951, during the Korean War, the United Steelworkers of America gave notice of their intention to strike when the collective bargaining agreement between the steel mills and their employees expired at the end of that year. Federal mediation failed to resolve the impasse. In April 1952 the union called for a nationwide strike. President Harry Truman responded with an executive order directing Secretary of Commerce Charles Sawyer to take control of the steel mills and keep them operational. He argued that the continued production of steel was essential to the war effort and that the president had intrinsic constitutional authority under Article II to take such an action to secure the national interest. The commerce secretary took possession of the steel mills and directed their management to keep them running in accord with his directives. The president reported his orders to Congress, but Congress took no immediate action. The steel companies complied with the order but sought an injunction restraining the enforcement of the order. In an expedited process, the district court for the District of Columbia issued the injunction, which was stayed by the Court of Appeals. The Supreme Court heard arguments in the case less than two weeks later.

At the time of the Steel Seizure Case, *the Court included four Truman appointees, individuals who had also been political intimates of the president. The Truman justices split evenly, with two joining the majority (Burton and Clark) against the president and two in dissent (Vinson and Minton). In 1952 the justices also had a significant amount of personal experience with the challenges of presidential policy and administration. Jackson and Clark were former attorneys general, who had grappled with these kinds of legal issues from the perspective of the executive branch, and Vinson was a former secretary of treasury. Two others, Black and Burton, had come from the other end of Pennsylvania Avenue, both having served in the U.S. Senate. Clark had prepared a memo as Truman's attorney general defending inherent presidential power and advocating presidential seizures of key industrial plants during labor disputes as a good policy during wartime. Vinson had directly advised President Truman that a seizure of the steel mills would be constitutional. He might well have expected his dissenting opinion to have commanded the votes of the majority of the justices.*

JUSTICE BLACK delivered the opinion of the Court.

. . .

The President's power, if any, to issue the order must stem either from an act of Congress or from the Constitution itself. There is no statute that expressly authorizes the President to take possession of property as he did here. Nor is there any act of Congress to which our attention has been directed from which such a power can fairly be implied. Indeed, we do not understand the Government to rely on statutory authorization for this seizure. There are two statutes which do authorize the President to take both personal and real property under certain conditions. However, the Government admits that these conditions were not met and that the President's order was not rooted in either of the statutes. The Government refers to the seizure provisions of one of these statutes . . . as "much too cumbersome, involved, and time-consuming for the crisis which was at hand."

Moreover, the use of the seizure technique to solve labor disputes in order to prevent work stoppages was not only unauthorized by any congressional enactment; prior to this controversy, Congress had refused to adopt that method of settling labor disputes. . . .

It is clear that if the President had authority to issue the order he did, it must be found in some provisions of the Constitution. And it is not claimed that express constitutional language grants this power to the President. The contention is that presidential power should be implied from the aggregate of his powers under the Constitution. Particular reliance is placed on provisions in Article II which say that "the executive Power shall be vested in a President . . . "; that "he shall take Care that the Laws be faithfully executed"; and that he "shall be Commander in Chief of the Army and Navy of the United States."

The order cannot properly be sustained as an exercise of the President's military power as Commander in Chief of the Armed Forces. The Government attempts to do so by citing a number of cases upholding broad powers in military commanders engaged in day-to-day fighting in a theater of war. Such cases need not concern us here. Even though "theater of war" be an expanding concept, we cannot with faithfulness to our constitutional system hold that the Commander in Chief of the Armed Forces has the ultimate power as such to take possession of private property in order to keep labor disputes from stopping production. This is a job for the Nation's lawmakers, not for its military authorities.

Nor can the seizure order be sustained because of the several constitutional provisions that grant executive power to the President. In the framework of our Constitution, the President's power to see that the laws are faithfully executed refutes the idea that he is to be a lawmaker. The Constitution limits his functions in the lawmaking process to the recommending of laws he thinks wise and the vetoing of laws he thinks bad. And the Constitution is neither silent nor equivocal about who shall make laws which the President is to execute. . . .

The President's order does not direct that a congressional policy be executed in a manner prescribed by Congress—it directs that a presidential policy be executed in a manner prescribed by the President. . . . The power of Congress to adopt such public policies as those proclaimed by the order is beyond question. . . . The Constitution did not subject this lawmaking power of Congress to presidential or military supervision or control.

. . .

The Founders of this Nation entrusted the lawmaking power to the Congress alone in both good and bad times. It would do no good to recall the historical events, the fears of power and the hopes for freedom that lay behind their choice. Such a review would but confirm our holding that this seizure order cannot stand.

JUSTICE JACKSON, concurring.

That comprehensive and undefined presidential powers hold both practical advantages and grave dangers for the country will impress anyone who has served as legal adviser to a President in time of transition and public anxiety. While an interval of detached reflection may temper teachings of that experience, they probably are a more realistic influence on my views than the conventional materials of judicial decision which seem unduly to accentuate doctrine and legal fiction. . . . The tendency is strong to emphasize transient results upon policies—such as wages or stabilization—and lose sight of enduring consequences upon the balanced power structure of our Republic.

A judge, like an executive adviser, may be surprised at the poverty of really useful and unambiguous authority applicable to concrete problems of executive power as they actually present themselves. Just what our forefathers did envision, or would have envisioned had they foreseen modern conditions, must be divined from materials almost as enigmatic as the dreams Joseph was called upon to interpret for Pharaoh. A century and a half of partisan debate and scholarly speculation yields no net result but only supplies more or less apt quotations from respected sources on each side of any question. They largely cancel each other. . . .

The actual art of governing under our Constitution does not and cannot conform to judicial definitions of the power of any of its branches based on isolated clauses or even single Articles torn from context. While the Constitution diffuses power the better to secure liberty, it also contemplates that practice will integrate the dispersed powers into a workable government. It enjoins upon its branches separateness but interdependence, autonomy but reciprocity. Presidential powers are not fixed but fluctuate, depending upon their disjunction or conjunction with those of Congress. We may well begin by a somewhat over-simplified grouping of practical situations in which a President may doubt, or others may challenge, his powers, and by distinguishing roughly the legal consequences of this factor of relativity.

1. When the President acts pursuant to an express or implied authorization of Congress, his authority is at its maximum, for it includes all that he possesses in his own right plus all that Congress can delegate. In these circumstances, and in these only, may he be said (for what it may be worth), to personify the federal

sovereignty. If his act is held unconstitutional under these circumstances, it usually means that the Federal Government as an undivided whole lacks power. A seizure executed by the President pursuant to an Act of Congress would be supported by the strongest of presumptions and the widest latitude of judicial interpretation, and the burden of persuasion would rest heavily upon any who might attack it.

2. When the President acts in absence of either a congressional grant or denial of authority, he can only rely upon his own independent powers, but there is a zone of twilight in which he and Congress may have concurrent authority, or in which its distribution is uncertain. Therefore, congressional inertia, indifference or quiescence may sometimes, at least as a practical matter, enable, if not invite, measures on independent presidential responsibility. In this area, any actual test of power is likely to depend on the imperatives of events and contemporary imponderables rather than on abstract theories of law.[32]

3. When the President takes measures incompatible with the expressed or implied will of Congress, his power is at its lowest ebb, for then he can rely only upon his own constitutional powers minus any constitutional powers of Congress over the matter. Courts can sustain exclusive Presidential control in such a case only by disabling the Congress from acting upon the subject.[33] Presidential claim to a power at once so conclusive and preclusive must be scrutinized with caution, for what is at stake is the equilibrium established by our constitutional system.

Into which of these classifications does this executive seizure of the steel industry fit? It is eliminated from the first by admission, for it is conceded that no congressional authorization exists for this seizure. . . .

Can it then be defended under flexible tests available to the second category? It seems clearly eliminated from that class because Congress has not left seizure of private property an open field but has covered it by three statutory policies inconsistent with this seizure. . . . None of these were invoked. In choosing a different and inconsistent way of his own, the President cannot claim that it is necessitated or invited by failure of Congress to legislate upon the occasions, grounds and methods for seizure of industrial properties.

This leaves the current seizure to be justified only by the severe tests under the third grouping, where it can be supported only by any remainder of executive power after subtraction of such powers as Congress may have over the subject. In short, we can sustain the President only by holding that seizure of such strike-bound industries is within his domain and beyond control by Congress. . . .

I did not suppose, and I am not persuaded, that history leaves it open to question, at least in the courts, that the executive branch, like the Federal Government as a whole, possesses only delegated powers. The purpose of the Constitution was not only to grant power, but to keep it from getting out of hand. However, because the President does not enjoy unmentioned powers does not mean that the mentioned ones should be narrowed by a niggardly construction. Some clauses could be made almost unworkable, as well as immutable, by refusal to indulge some latitude of interpretation for changing times. I have heretofore, and do now, give to the enumerated powers the scope and elasticity afforded by what seem to be reasonable practical implications instead of the rigidity dictated by a doctrinaire textualism.

The Solicitor General seeks the power of seizure in three clauses of the Executive Article, the first reading, "The executive Power shall be vested in a President of the United States of America." Lest I be thought to exaggerate, I quote the interpretation which his brief puts upon it: "In our view, this clause constitutes a grant of all the executive powers of which the Government is capable." If that be true, it is difficult to see why the forefathers bothered to add several specific items, including some trifling ones.

. . . I cannot accept the view that this clause is a grant in bulk of all conceivable executive power but regard it as an allocation to the presidential office of the generic powers thereafter stated.

32. [Justice Jackson's footnote] Since the Constitution implies that the writ of habeas corpus may be suspended in certain circumstances but does not say by whom, President Lincoln asserted and maintained it as an executive function in the face of judicial challenge and doubt. *Ex parte Merryman*. . . . Congress eventually ratified his action. . . .

33. [Justice Jackson's footnote] President Roosevelt's effort to remove a Federal Trade Commissioner was found to be contrary to the policy of Congress and impinging upon an area of congressional control, and so his removal power was cut down accordingly. *Humphrey's Executor v. United States*. . . . However, his exclusive power of removal in executive agencies, affirmed in *Myers v. United States* . . . continued to be asserted and maintained.

The clause on which the Government next relies is that "The President shall be Commander in Chief of the Army and Navy of the United States. . . . " These cryptic words have given rise to some of the most persistent controversies in our constitutional history. . . . Hence, this loose appellation is sometimes advanced as support for any Presidential action, internal or external, involving use of force, the idea being that it vests power to do anything, anywhere, that can be done with an army or navy.

. . .

I cannot foresee all that it might entail if the Court should indorse this argument. Nothing in our Constitution is plainer than that declaration of a war is entrusted only to Congress. Of course, a state of war may in fact exist without a formal declaration. But no doctrine that the Court could promulgate would seem to me more sinister and alarming than that a President whose conduct of foreign affairs is so largely uncontrolled, and often even is unknown, can vastly enlarge his mastery over the internal affairs of the country by his own commitment of the Nation's armed forces to some foreign venture. I do not, however, find it necessary or appropriate to consider the legal status of the Korean enterprise to discountenance argument based on it.

Assuming that we are in a war *de facto*, whether it is or is not a war *de jure*, does that empower the Commander-in-Chief to seize industries he thinks necessary to supply our army? The Constitution expressly places in Congress power "to raise and *support* Armies" and "to *provide* and *maintain* a Navy." (Emphasis supplied.) This certainly lays upon Congress primary responsibility for supplying the armed forces. . . .

There are indications that the Constitution did not contemplate that the title Commander-in-Chief of the Army and Navy will constitute him also Commander-in-Chief of the country, its industries and its inhabitants. He has no monopoly of "war powers," whatever they are. While Congress cannot deprive the President of the command of the army and navy, only Congress can provide him an army or navy to command.

. . .

We should not use this occasion to circumscribe, much less to contract, the lawful role of the President as Commander-in-Chief. I should indulge the widest latitude of interpretation to sustain his exclusive function to command the instruments of national force, at least when turned against the outside world for the security of our society. But, when it is turned inward, not because of rebellion but because of a lawful economic struggle between industry and labor, it should have no such indulgence. . . .

. . .

The Solicitor General lastly grounds support of the seizure upon nebulous, inherent powers never expressly granted but said to have accrued to the office from the customs and claims of preceding administrations. The plea is for a resulting power to deal with a crisis or an emergency according to the necessities of the case, the unarticulated assumption being that necessity knows no law.

. . .

The appeal, however, that we declare the existence of inherent powers ex necessitate to meet an emergency asks us to do what many think would be wise, although it is something the forefathers omitted. They knew what emergencies were, knew the pressures they engender for authoritative action, knew, too, how they afford a ready pretext for usurpation. We may also suspect that they suspected that emergency powers would tend to kindle emergencies. Aside from suspension of the privilege of the writ of habeas corpus in time of rebellion or invasion, when the public safety may require it, they made no express provision for exercise of extraordinary authority because of a crisis. I do not think we rightfully may so amend their work, and, if we could, I am not convinced it would be wise to do so, although many modern nations have forthrightly recognized that war and economic crises may upset the normal balance between liberty and authority. Their experience with emergency powers may not be irrelevant to the argument here that we should say that the Executive, of his own volition, can invest himself with undefined emergency powers.

. . .

[The] contemporary foreign experience may be inconclusive as to the wisdom of lodging emergency powers somewhere in a modern government. But it suggests that emergency powers are consistent with free government only when their control is lodged elsewhere than in the Executive who exercises them. That is the safeguard that would be nullified by our adoption of the "inherent powers" formula. Nothing in my experience convinces me that such risks are warranted by any real necessity, although such powers would, of course, be an executive convenience.

In the practical working of our Government we already have evolved a technique within the framework of the Constitution by which normal executive powers may be considerably expanded to meet an emergency. Congress may and has granted extraordinary authorities which lie dormant in normal times but may be called into play by the Executive in war or upon proclamation of a national emergency. In 1939, upon congressional request, the Attorney General listed ninety-nine such separate statutory grants by Congress of emergency or war-time executive powers. They were invoked from time to time as need appeared. Under this procedure we retain Government by law—special, temporary law, perhaps, but law nonetheless. . . .

In view of the ease, expedition and safety with which Congress can grant and has granted large emergency powers, certainly ample to embrace this crisis, I am quite unimpressed with the argument that we should affirm possession of them without statute. Such power either has no beginning or it has no end. If it exists, it need submit to no legal restraint. I am not alarmed that it would plunge us straightway into dictatorship, but it is at least a step in that wrong direction.

. . .

But I have no illusion that any decision by this Court can keep power in the hands of Congress if it is not wise and timely in meeting its problems. A crisis that challenges the President equally, or perhaps primarily, challenges Congress. If not good law, there was worldly wisdom in the maxim attributed to Napoleon that "The tools belong to the man who can use them." We may say that power to legislate for emergencies belongs in the hands of Congress, but only Congress itself can prevent power from slipping through its fingers.

. . .

JUSTICE BURTON, concurring.

. . .

JUSTICE CLARK, concurring.

. . .

The limits of presidential power are obscure. However, Article II, no less than Article I, is part of "a constitution intended to endure for ages to come, and, consequently, to be adapted to the various crises of human affairs." Some of our Presidents, such as Lincoln, "felt that measures otherwise unconstitutional might become lawful by becoming indispensable to the preservation of the Constitution through the preservation of the nation." Others, such as Theodore Roosevelt, thought the President to be capable, as a "steward" of the people, of exerting all power save that which is specifically prohibited by the Constitution or the Congress. In my view—taught me not only by the decision of Chief Justice Marshall in *Little v. Barreme* (1804) . . . but also by a score of other pronouncements of distinguished members of this bench—the Constitution does grant to the President extensive authority in times of grave and imperative national emergency. In fact, to my thinking, such a grant may well be necessary to the very existence of the Constitution itself. As Lincoln aptly said, "(is) it possible to lose the nation and yet preserve the Constitution?" In describing this authority I care not whether one calls it "residual," "inherent," "moral," "implied," "aggregate," "emergency," or otherwise. I am of the conviction that those who have had the gratifying experience of being the President's lawyer have used one or more of these adjectives only with the utmost of sincerity and the highest of purpose.

I conclude that where Congress has laid down specific procedures to deal with the type of crisis confronting the President, he must follow those procedures in meeting the crisis; but that in the absence of such action by Congress, the President's independent power to act depends upon the gravity of the situation confronting the nation. I cannot sustain the seizure in question because . . . Congress had prescribed methods to be followed by the President in meeting the emergency at hand.

. . .

JUSTICE DOUGLAS, concurring.

There can be no doubt that the emergency which caused the President to seize these steel plants was one that bore heavily on the country. But the emergency did not create power; it merely marked an occasion when power should be exercised. And the fact that it was necessary that measures be taken to keep steel in production does not mean that the President, rather than the Congress, had the constitutional authority to act. The Congress, as well as the President, is trustee of the national welfare. The President can act more quickly than the Congress. The President with the armed services at his disposal can move with force as well as with speed. All executive power—from the reign of ancient kings to the rule of modern dictators—has the outward appearance of efficiency.

Legislative power, by contrast, is slower to exercise. There must be delay while the ponderous machinery of committees, hearings, and debates is put into motion. That takes time; and while the Congress slowly moves into action, the emergency may take its toll in wages, consumer goods, war production, the standard of living of the people, and perhaps even lives. Legislative action may indeed often be cumbersome, time-consuming, and apparently inefficient. But as Mr. Justice Brandeis stated in his dissent in *Myers v. United States* (1926) . . . "The doctrine of the separation of powers was adopted by the Convention of 1787 not to promote efficiency but to preclude the exercise of arbitrary power. . . . "

. . .

The legislative nature of the action taken by the President seems to me to be clear. When the United States takes over an industrial plant to settle a labor controversy, it is condemning property. The seizure of the plant is a taking in the constitutional sense. . . .

. . .

. . . Some future generation may . . . deem it so urgent that the President have legislative authority that the Constitution will be amended. We could not sanction the seizures and condemnations of the steel plants in this case without reading Article II as giving the President not only the power to execute the laws but to make some. Such a step would most assuredly alter the pattern of the Constitution.

We pay a price for our system of checks and balances, for the distribution of power among the three branches of government. It is a price that today may seem exorbitant to many. Today a kindly President uses the seizure power to effect a wage increase and to keep the steel furnaces in production. Yet tomorrow another President might use the same power to prevent a wage increase, to curb trade unionists, to regiment labor as oppressively as industry thinks it has been regimented by this seizure.

JUSTICE FRANKFURTER, concurring.

. . .

A constitutional democracy like ours is perhaps the most difficult of man's social arrangements to manage successfully. Our scheme of society is more dependent than any other form of government on knowledge and wisdom and self-discipline for the achievement of its aims. . . . [History] sheds a good deal of light not merely on the need for effective power, if a society is to be at once cohesive and civilized, but also on the need for limitations on the power of governors over the governed.

To that end they rested the structure of our central government on the system of checks and balances. For them the doctrine of separation of powers was not mere theory; it was a felt necessity. Not so long ago it was fashionable to find our system of checks and balances obstructive to effective government. It was easy to ridicule that system as outmoded—too easy. The experience through which the world has passed in our own day has made vivid the realization that the Framers of our Constitution were not inexperienced doctrinaires. These long-headed statesmen had no illusion that our people enjoyed biological or psychological or sociological immunities from the hazards of concentrated power. It is absurd to see a dictator in a representative product of the sturdy democratic traditions of the Mississippi Valley. The accretion of dangerous power does not come in a day. It does come, however slowly, from the generative force of unchecked disregard of the restrictions that fence in even the most disinterested assertion of authority.

. . .

The issue before us can be met, and therefore should be, without attempting to define the President's powers comprehensively. . . .

The question before the Court comes in this setting. Congress has frequently—at least 16 times since 1916—specifically provided for executive seizure of production, transportation, communications, or storage facilities. In every case it has qualified this grant of power with limitations and safeguards. This body of enactments . . . demonstrates that Congress deemed seizure so drastic a power as to require that it be carefully circumscribed whenever the President was vested with this extraordinary authority. . . .

. . .

. . . The utmost that the Korean conflict may imply is that it may have been desirable to have given the President further authority, a freer hand in these matters. Absence of authority in the President to deal with a crisis does not imply want of power in the Government. Conversely the fact that power exists in the Government does not vest it in the President. The need for new legislation does not enact it. Nor does it repeal or amend existing law.

. . .

It is not a pleasant judicial duty to find that the President has exceeded his powers and still less so when his purposes were dictated by concern for the Nation's wellbeing, in the assured conviction that he acted to avert danger. But it would stultify one's faith in our people to entertain even a momentary fear that the patriotism and the wisdom of the President and the Congress, as well as the long view of the immediate parties in interest, will not find ready accommodation for differences on matters which, however close to their concern and however intrinsically important, are overshadowed by the awesome issues which confront the world.

. . .

CHIEF JUSTICE VINSON, with whom JUSTICE REED and JUSTICE MINTON join, dissenting.

. . .

In passing upon the question of Presidential powers in this case, we must first consider the context in which those powers were exercised.

Those who suggest that this is a case involving extraordinary powers should be mindful that these are extraordinary times. A world not yet recovered from the devastation of World War II has been forced to face the threat of another and more terrifying global conflict.

Accepting in full measure its responsibility in the world community, the United States was instrumental in securing adoption of the United Nations Charter, approved by the Senate by a vote of 89 to 2. The first purpose of the United Nations is to "maintain international peace and security, and to that end: to take effective collective measures for the prevention and removal of threats to the peace, and for the suppression of acts of aggression or other breaches of the peace. . . . " In 1950, when the United Nations called upon member nations "to render every assistance" to repel aggression in Korea, the United States furnished its vigorous support. For almost two full years, our armed forces have been fighting in Korea, suffering casualties of over 108,000 men. Hostilities have not abated. The "determination of the United Nations to continue its action in Korea to meet the aggression" has been reaffirmed. Congressional support of the action in Korea has been manifested by provisions for increased military manpower and equipment and for economic stabilization. . . .

. . . The need for mutual security is shown by the very size of the armed forces outside the free world. Defendant's brief informs us that the Soviet Union maintains the largest air force in the world and maintains ground forces much larger than those presently available to the United States and the countries joined with us in mutual security arrangements. Constant international tensions are cited to demonstrate how precarious is the peace.

Even this brief review of our responsibilities in the world community discloses the enormity of our undertaking. Success of these measures may, as has often been observed, dramatically influence the lives of many generations of the world's peoples yet unborn. Alert to our responsibilities, which coincide with our own self preservation through mutual security, Congress has enacted a large body of implementing legislation. . . .

. . .

Congress recognized the impact of these defense programs upon the economy. Following the attack in Korea, the President asked for authority to requisition property and to allocate and fix priorities for scarce goods. In the Defense Production Act of 1950, Congress granted the powers requested and, in addition, granted power to stabilize prices and wages and to provide for settlement of labor disputes arising in the defense program. . . . [A Senate] Committee emphasized that the shortage of steel, even with the mills operating at full capacity, coupled with increased civilian purchasing power, presented grave danger of disastrous inflation.

The President has the duty to execute the foregoing legislative programs. Their successful execution depends upon continued production of steel and stabilized prices for steel. Accordingly, when . . . a strike shutting down the entire basic steel industry was threatened, the President acted to avert a complete shutdown of steel production. . . .

Twelve days passed [after the initial executive order] without action by Congress. On April 21, 1952, the President sent a letter to the President of the Senate in which he again described the purpose and need for his action and again stated his position that "The Congress can, if it wishes, reject the course of action I have followed in this matter." Congress has not so acted to this date.

. . .

One is not here called upon even to consider the possibility of executive seizure of a farm, a corner grocery store or even a single industrial plant. Such considerations arise only when one ignores the central fact of this case—that the Nation's entire basic steel production would have shut down completely if there had been no Government seizure. Even ignoring for the moment whatever confidential information the President may possess as "the Nation's organ for foreign affairs," the uncontroverted affidavits in this record amply support the finding that "a work stoppage would immediately jeopardize and imperil our national defense."

. . .

This comprehensive grant of the executive power [in Article II] to a single person was bestowed soon after the country had thrown the yoke of monarchy. Only by instilling initiative and vigor in all of the three departments of Government, declared Madison, could tyranny in any form be avoided. Hamilton added: "Energy in the Executive is a leading character in the definition of good government." . . . It is thus apparent that the Presidency was deliberately fashioned as an office of power and independence. Of course, the Framers created no autocrat capable of arrogating any power unto himself at any time. But neither did they create an automaton impotent to exercise the powers of Government at a time when the survival of the Republic itself may be at stake.

In passing upon the grave constitutional question presented in this case, we must never forget, as Chief Justice Marshall admonished, that the Constitution is "intended to endure for ages to come, and consequently, to be adapted to the various crises of human affairs," and that "(i)ts means are adequate to its ends." Cases do arise presenting questions which could not have been foreseen by the Framers. In such cases, the Constitution has been treated as a living document adaptable to new situations. But we are not called upon today to expand the Constitution to meet a new situation. For, in this case, we need only look to history and time-honored principles of constitutional law—principles that have been applied consistently by all branches of the Government throughout our history. It is those who assert the invalidity of the Executive Order who seek to amend the Constitution in this case.

. . .

A review of executive action demonstrates that our Presidents have on many occasions exhibited the leadership contemplated by the Framers when they made the President Commander in Chief, and imposed upon him the trust to "take Care that the Laws be faithfully executed." With or without explicit statutory authorization, Presidents have at such times dealt with national emergencies by acting promptly and resolutely to enforce legislative programs, at least to save those programs until Congress could act. Congress and the courts have responded to such executive initiative with consistent approval.

. . .

In an action furnishing a most apt precedent for this case, President Lincoln without statutory authority directed the seizure of rail and telegraph lines leading to Washington. Many months later, Congress recognized and confirmed the power of the President to seize railroads and telegraph lines and provided criminal penalties for interference with Government operation. This Act did not confer on the President any additional powers of seizure. Congress plainly rejected the view that the President's acts had been without legal sanction until ratified by the legislature. Sponsors of the bill declared that its purpose was only to confirm the power which the President already possessed. Opponents insisted a statute authorizing seizure was unnecessary and might even be construed as limiting existing Presidential powers.

. . .

. . .

Some six months before Pearl Harbor, a dispute at a single aviation plant at Inglewood, California, interrupted a segment of the production of military aircraft. In spite of the comparative insignificance of this work stoppage to total defense production as contrasted with the complete paralysis now threatened by a shutdown of the entire basic steel industry, and even though our armed forces were not then engaged in combat, President Roosevelt ordered the seizure of the plant "pursuant to the powers vested in (him) by the Constitution and laws of the United States, as President of the United States of America and Commander in Chief of the Army and Navy of the United States." The Attorney General [Robert Jackson] vigorously proclaimed that the President had the moral duty to keep this Nation's defense effort a "going concern." His ringing moral justification was coupled with a legal justification equally well stated:

> The Presidential proclamation rests upon the aggregate of the Presidential powers derived from the Constitution itself and from statutes enacted by the Congress.

The Constitution lays upon the President the duty "to take care that the laws be faithfully executed." Among the laws which he is required to find means to execute are those which direct him to equip an enlarged army, to provide for a strengthened navy, to protect Government property, to protect those who are engaged in carrying out the business of the Government. . . . For the faithful execution of such laws the President has back of him not only each general law-enforcement power conferred by the various acts of Congress but the aggregate of all such laws plus that wide discretion as to method vested in him by the Constitution for the purpose of executing the laws.

The Constitution also places on the President the responsibility and vests in him the powers of Commander in Chief of the Army and of the Navy. These weapons for the protection of the continued existence of the Nation are placed in his sole command and the implication is clear that he should not allow them to become paralyzed by failure to obtain supplies for which Congress has appropriated the money and which it has directed the President to obtain.

. . .

This is but a cursory summary of executive leadership. But it amply demonstrates that Presidents have taken prompt action to enforce the laws and protect the country whether or not Congress happened to provide in advance for the particular method of execution. . . . [T]he fact that Congress and the courts have consistently recognized and given their support to such executive action indicates that such a power of seizure has been accepted throughout our history.

History bears out the genius of the Founding Fathers, who created a Government subject to law but not left subject to inertia when vigor and initiative are required.

. . .

The absence of a specific statute authorizing seizure of the steel mills as a mode of executing the laws—both the military procurement program and the anti-inflation program—has not until today been thought to prevent the President from executing the laws. Unlike an administrative commission confined to the enforcement of the statute under which it was created, or the head to a department when administering a particular statute, the President is a constitutional officer charged with taking care that a "mass of legislation" be executed. Flexibility as to mode of execution to meet critical situations is a matter of practical necessity. . . .

There is no statute prohibiting seizure as a method of enforcing legislative programs. . . .

Whatever the extent of Presidential power on more tranquil occasions, and whatever the right of the President to execute legislative programs as he sees fit without reporting the mode of execution to Congress, the single Presidential purpose disclosed on this record is to faithfully execute the laws by acting in an emergency to maintain the status quo, thereby preventing collapse of the legislative programs until Congress could act. The President's action served the same purposes as a judicial stay entered to maintain the status quo in order to preserve the jurisdiction of a court. . . . [T]here is no evidence whatever of any Presidential purpose to defy Congress or act in any way inconsistent with the legislative will.

. . . The Framers knew, as we should know in these times of peril, that there is real danger in Executive weakness. There is no cause to fear Executive tyranny so long as the laws of Congress are being faithfully executed. Certainly there is no basis for fear of dictatorship when the Executive acts, as he did in this case, only to save the situation until Congress could act.

. . .

The diversity of views expressed in the six opinions of the majority, the lack of reference to authoritative precedent, the repeated reliance upon prior dissenting opinions, the complete disregard of the uncontroverted facts showing the gravity of the emergency and the temporary nature of the taking all serve to demonstrate how far afield one must go to affirm the order of the District Court.

The broad executive power granted by Article II to an officer on duty 365 days a year cannot, it is said, be invoked to avert disaster. Instead, the President must confine himself to sending a message to Congress recommending action. Under this messenger-boy concept of the Office, the President cannot even act to preserve legislative programs from destruction so that Congress will have something left to act upon. There is no judicial finding that the executive action was unwarranted because there was in fact no basis for the President's finding of the existence of an emergency; under this view, the gravity of the emergency and the immediacy of the threatened disaster are considered irrelevant as a matter of law.

. . .

As the District Judge stated, this is no time for "timorous" judicial action. But neither is this a time for timorous executive action. Faced with the duty of executing the defense programs which Congress had enacted and the disastrous effects that any stoppage in steel production would have on those programs, the President acted to preserve those programs by seizing the steel mills. There is no question that the possession was other than temporary in character and subject to congressional direction—either approving, disapproving or regulating the manner in which the mills were to be administered and returned to the owners. The President immediately informed Congress of his action and clearly stated his intention to abide by the legislative will. No basis for claims of arbitrary action, unlimited powers or dictatorial usurpation of congressional power appears from the facts of this case. On the contrary, judicial, legislative and executive precedents throughout our history demonstrate that in this case the President acted in full conformity with his duties under the Constitution. Accordingly, we would reverse the order of the District Court.

United States v. Curtiss-Wright Export Corporation, 299 U.S. 304 (1936)

The delegation of power over foreign affairs to the president was less controversial during the early New Deal than the delegation of power over domestic policy. Many nineteenth-century conservatives worried that an increased American presence in international affairs would unconstitutionally increase national powers and aggrandize the executive branch. In contrast, many twentieth-century conservatives insisted on a sharp difference between constitutional authority in domestic affairs and constitutional authority in foreign affairs. During World War I, the conservative Republican senator George Sutherland wrote an important book detailing why the federal government and the president had more authority in foreign policy than in domestic policy.[34] *He was soon given an opportunity to write those views into constitutional law when he was appointed to the U.S. Supreme Court in 1922. Sutherland's opinion in the* Curtiss-Wright *case became the source of the "sole organ" doctrine, which contends that the president is the "sole organ of the federal government in the field of international relations." Proponents of presidential power have subsequently cited Sutherland's argument as a reason to oppose any significant congressional intervention in foreign policy. Sutherland likewise emphasized in* United States v. Belmont *(1933) the unilateral power of the president to make international executive agreements that could trump state law.*

Curtiss-Wright *began with a 1934 congressional resolution authorizing the president, at his discretion, to prohibit or regulate arms sales to Bolivia and Paraguay, which were engaged in a border war. President Roosevelt immediately issued a proclamation barring the arms sales. Curtiss-Wright Export Corporation and others were indicted in federal district court for violating the arms embargo during the several months that it was in effect. They challenged the indictment on several grounds, including the constitutional objection that Congress had delegated excessive lawmaking authority to the president. The district court agreed, leading the government to appeal to the Supreme Court.*

The Supreme Court quickly disposed of those constitutional objections. Justice McReynolds aside, no other justice had difficulty finding a constitutional basis for legislation granting the president broad discretion in foreign affairs. As you read this opinion, consider whether Justice Sutherland made a convincing distinction between constitutional authority over domestic affairs and constitutional authority over foreign affairs.

JUSTICE SUTHERLAND delivered the opinion of the Court.

. . .

Whether, if the Joint Resolution had related solely to internal affairs, it would be open to the challenge that it constituted an unlawful delegation of legislative power to the Executive, we find it unnecessary to determine. The whole aim of the resolution is to affect a situation entirely external to the United States, and falling within the category of foreign affairs. The determination which we are called to make, therefore, is whether the Joint Resolution, as applied to that situation, is vulnerable to attack under the rule that forbids a delegation of the law-making power. In other words, assuming (but not deciding) that the challenged delegation, if it were confined to internal affairs, would be invalid, may it nevertheless be sustained on the ground that its exclusive aim is to afford a remedy for a hurtful condition within foreign territory?

34. George Sutherland, *Constitutional Power and World Affairs* (New York: Columbia University Press, 1919).

. . .

The two classes of powers are different, both in respect of their origin and their nature. The broad statement that the federal government can exercise no powers except those specifically enumerated in the Constitution, and such implied powers as are necessary and proper to carry into effect the enumerated powers, is categorically true only in respect of our internal affairs. In that field, the primary purpose of the Constitution was to carve from the general mass of legislative powers then possessed by the states such portions as it was thought desirable to vest in the federal government, leaving those not included in the enumeration still in the states. . . . That this doctrine applies only to powers which the states had is self-evident. And since the states severally never possessed international powers, such powers could not have been carved from the mass of state powers but obviously were transmitted to the United States from some other source. . . .

. . .

Not only . . . is the federal power over external affairs in origin and essential character different from that over internal affairs, but participation in the exercise of the power is significantly limited. In this vast external realm, with its important, complicated, delicate and manifold problems, the President alone has the power to speak or listen as a representative of the nation. He makes treaties with the advice and consent of the Senate; but he alone negotiates. Into the field of negotiation the Senate cannot intrude; and Congress itself is powerless to invade it. As Marshall said in his great argument of March 7, 1800, in the House of Representatives, "The President is the sole organ of the nation in its external relations, and its sole representative with foreign nations." *Annals*, 6th Cong. . . .

It is important to bear in mind that we are here dealing not alone with an authority vested in the President by an exertion of legislative power, but with such an authority plus the very delicate, plenary and exclusive power of the President as the sole organ of the federal government in the field of international relations—a power which does not require as a basis for its exercise an act of Congress, but which, of course, like every other governmental power, must be exercised in subordination to the applicable provisions of the Constitution. It is quite apparent that if, in the maintenance of our international relations, embarrassment—perhaps serious embarrassment—is to be avoided and success for our aims achieved, congressional legislation which is to be made effective through negotiation and inquiry within the international field must often accord to the President a degree of discretion and freedom from statutory restriction which would not be admissible were domestic affairs alone involved. Moreover, he, not Congress, has the better opportunity of knowing the conditions which prevail in foreign countries, and especially is this true in time of war. He has his confidential sources of information. He has his agents in the form of diplomatic, consular and other officials. Secrecy in respect of information gathered by them may be highly necessary, and the premature disclosure of it productive of harmful results. . . .

In the light of the foregoing observations, it is evident that this court should not be in haste to apply a general rule which will have the effect of condemning legislation like that under review as constituting an unlawful delegation of legislative power. The principles which justify such legislation find overwhelming support in the unbroken legislative practice which has prevailed almost from the inception of the national government to the present day.

. . .

The result of holding that the joint resolution here under attack is void and unenforceable as constituting an unlawful delegation of legislative power would be to stamp [a] multitude of comparable acts and resolutions as likewise invalid. And while this court may not, and should not, hesitate to declare acts of Congress, however many times repeated, to be unconstitutional if beyond all rational doubt it finds them to be so, an impressive array of legislation . . . , enacted by nearly every Congress from the beginning of our national existence to the present day, must be given unusual weight in the process of reaching a correct determination of the problem. A legislative practice such as we have here, evidenced not by only occasional instances, but marked by the movement of a steady stream for a century and a half of time, goes a long way in the direction of proving the presence of unassailable ground for the constitutionality of the practice, to be found in the origin and history of the power involved, or in its nature, or in both combined.

. . .

JUSTICE McREYNOLDS does not agree. He is of opinion that the court below reached the right conclusion and its judgment ought to be affirmed.

JUSTICE STONE took no part in the decision of this case.

VII. Individual Rights

MAJOR DEVELOPMENTS

- The Court abandons protection for the freedom of contract
- Public school prayer declared unconstitutional
- The Court protects the right of individuals to procreate, marry, and use birth control if married

Proponents of the New Deal and Great Society agreed on a hierarchy of individual constitutional rights. Religious freedom enjoyed constitutional protection from the very beginning of the New Deal, and that protection increased during the 1960s. Constitutional liberals during the 1960s began protecting constitutional rights to marriage and procreation within marriage. New Dealers insisted that economic matters were policy questions entrusted to elected officials. No prominent political party, political movement, or justice from 1933 until 1968 paid any significant attention to the Second Amendment. The Supreme Court's docket reflected these priorities, devoting increasing attention to civil liberties and exhibiting a declining interest in cases raising traditional property rights.

A. Property

New Deal and Great Society liberals had a very narrow conception of constitutional property rights. Commercial and economic matters raised policy questions that were constitutionally entrusted to the elected branches of government. When making public policy, those institutions considered the public interest, broadly understood. Economic life was left free only when elected officials believed not regulating promoted the general good. The Constitution was understood as neither constraining action thought to be in the public interest nor mandating in advance what constituted the public interest.

The contracts clause ceased to be of any constitutional significance. In *Home Building and Loan Association v. Blaisdell* (1934) a divided Supreme Court ruled that state legislatures could adjust existing contract obligations when doing so was perceived to be necessary to limit the impact of an economic depression. For the next forty years the notion that government could impair the obligations of contract when doing so was in the public interest reduced the contracts clause to a legal nullity, at least in federal courtrooms. Few litigants raised contracts clause claims, and those who did lost.

The freedom of contract was another early casualty of the New Deal. A 5–4 judicial majority in *Nebbia v. New York* (1934) abandoned the crucial public/private distinction when sustaining a state law regulating the price at which milk could be bought or sold. Such previous cases as *Munn v. Illinois* (1877) had held that government could regulate only "businesses affected with a public interest." This implied a class of private businesses beyond the scope of state regulation. Justice Roberts's majority opinion rejected that distinction when asserting, "There is no closed class or category of businesses affected with a public interest, and . . . [t]he phrase 'affected with a public interest' can, in the nature of things, mean no more than that an industry, for adequate reason, is subject to control for the public good." Libertarians detected a heartbeat in *Morehead v. People of State of New York ex rel. Tipaldo* (1936) when Justices Roberts joined the four most conservative justices in a decision declaring unconstitutional a New York law requiring employers to pay their female employees a wage determined to provide a "reasonable value" for their service. Roberts was willing to strike down the law, however, only because the lawyers for the state of New York did not ask the justices to overrule *Adkins v. Children's Hospital* (1923), a previous decision striking down minimum wage laws for women. When the same issue arose the next year in *West Coast Hotel v. Parrish* (1937), Roberts voted with the more liberal justices to sustain the law under constitutional attack. Chief Justice Hughes, writing for the majority, challenged the very existence of the freedom of contract. Four years later, in *Wickard v. Filburn* (1941), a unanimous Supreme Court ruled that farmers did not have a constitutional right to grow more than their allotted acreage of wheat, even when their entire crop was consumed on their farm. Justice Robert Jackson's unanimous opinion for the Court did not even consider whether the Constitution protected the right to grow food on a farm for home consumption.

Home Building & Loan Association v. Blaisdell, 290 U.S. 398 (1934)

John Blaisdell was one of many Minnesota homeowners who fell behind in their payments during the Depression. Fearful that the Home Building and Loan Association would foreclose, he applied to the Minnesota courts for relief under the Minnesota Moratorium Law of 1932. That statute extended the time period for overdue mortgages. Most properties covered by the law could not be foreclosed and sold by the lender until May 1, 1935, provided the owner continued to pay the lender the fair rental value of the home. The trial court agreed to extend the period in which Blaisdell could redeem his mortgage. That decision was upheld by the Supreme Court of Minnesota. The Home Building and Loan Association appealed to the Supreme Court of the United States.

The Supreme Court sustained the Minnesota law by a 5–4 vote. Chief Justice Hughes insisted that the contracts clause did not prevent states from passing laws for the public welfare, provided those laws did not destroy the value of a contract. As you read the opinions, consider what each justice believed to be fundamental constitutional purposes and what theories of constitutional interpretation follow from their logic. What did Chief Justice Hughes mean when he declared, "While emergency does not create power, emergency may furnish the occasion for the exercise of power"? How did Justice Sutherland respond to this claim? If Chief Justice Hughes's notion of the police power were applied to other rights, would courts protect any right? Does any good reason exist for thinking that the contracts clause ought to receive a more narrow interpretation than the First Amendment?

CHIEF JUSTICE HUGHES delivered the opinion of the Court.

. . .

Emergency does not create power. Emergency does not increase granted power or remove or diminish the restrictions imposed upon power granted or reserved. The Constitution was adopted in a period of grave emergency. Its grants of power to the federal government and its limitations of the power of the States were determined in the light of emergency, and they are not altered by emergency. . . .

While emergency does not create power, emergency may furnish the occasion for the exercise of power. . . . The constitutional question presented in the light of an emergency is whether the power possessed embraces the particular exercise of it in response to particular conditions. Thus, the war power of the federal government is not created by the emergency of war, but it is a power given to meet that emergency. It is a power to wage war successfully, and thus it permits the harnessing of the entire energies of the people in a supreme co-operative effort to preserve the nation. But even the war power does not remove constitutional limitations safeguarding essential liberties. When the provisions of the Constitution, in grant or restriction, are specific, so particularized as not to admit of construction, no question is presented. Thus, emergency would not permit a state to have more than two Senators in the Congress, or permit the election of President by a general popular vote without regard to the number of electors to which the States are respectively entitled, or permit the States to "coin money" or to "make anything but gold and silver coin a tender in payment of debts." But, where constitutional grants and limitations of power are set forth in general clauses, which afford a broad outline, the process of construction is essential to fill in the details. That is true of the contract clause. . . .

. . .

The obligation of a contract is the law which binds the parties to perform their agreement. . . . But this broad language cannot be taken without qualification. Chief Justice Marshall pointed out the distinction between obligation and remedy. . . . Said he: "The distinction between the obligation of a contract, and the remedy given by the legislature to enforce that obligation, has been taken at the bar, and exists in the nature of things. Without impairing the obligation of the contract, the remedy may certainly be modified as the wisdom of the nation shall direct."

. . .

Not only is the constitutional provision qualified by the measure of control which the state retains over remedial processes, but the state also continues to possess authority to safeguard the vital interests of its people. It does not matter that legislation appropriate to that end "has the result of modifying or abrogating contracts already in effect." . . . Not only are existing laws read into contracts in order to fix obligations as between the parties, but the reservation of essential attributes of sovereign power is also read into contracts as a postulate of the legal order. The policy of protecting contracts against impairment presupposes the maintenance of a government by virtue of which contractual relations are worthwhile,—a government which retains adequate authority to secure the peace and good order of society. This principle of harmonizing the constitutional prohibition with the necessary residuum of state power has had progressive recognition in the decisions of this Court.

. . . The Legislature cannot "bargain away the public health or the public morals." . . .

. . .

Undoubtedly, whatever is reserved of state power must be consistent with the fair intent of the constitutional limitation of that power. The reserved power cannot be construed so as to destroy the limitation, nor is the limitation to be construed to destroy the reserved power in its essential aspects. They must be construed in harmony with each other. This principle precludes a construction which would permit the state to adopt as its policy the repudiation of debts or the destruction of contracts or the denial of means to enforce them. But it does not follow that conditions may not arise in which a temporary restraint of enforcement may be consistent with the spirit and purpose of the constitutional provision and thus be found to be within the range of the reserved power of the state to protect the vital interests of the community. . . . It cannot be maintained that the constitutional prohibition should be so construed as to prevent limited and temporary interpositions with respect to the enforcement of contracts if made necessary by a great public calamity such as fire, flood, or earthquake. . . . The reservation of state power appropriate to such extraordinary conditions may be deemed to be as much a part of all contracts as is the reservation of state power to protect the public interest in the other situations to which we have referred. And, if state power exists to give temporary relief from the enforcement of contracts in the presence of disasters due to physical causes such as fire, flood, or earthquake, that power cannot be said to be nonexistent when the urgent public need demanding such relief is produced by other and economic causes.

. . .

In these cases of leases, it will be observed that the relief afforded was temporary and conditional; that it was sustained because of the emergency due to scarcity of housing; and that provision was made for reasonable compensation to the landlord during the period he was prevented from regaining possession. . . .

. . .

It is no answer to say that this public need was not apprehended a century ago, or to insist that what the provision of the Constitution meant to the vision of that day it must mean to the vision of our time. If by the statement that what the Constitution meant at the time of its adoption it means to-day, it is intended to say that the great clauses of the Constitution must be confined to the interpretation which the framers, with the conditions and outlook of their time, would have placed upon them, the statement carries its own refutation. It was to guard against such a narrow conception that Chief Justice Marshall uttered the memorable warning: "We must never forget, that it is a constitution we are expounding," . . . "a constitution intended to endure for ages to come, and, consequently, to be adapted to the various crises of human affairs. . . . The case before us must be considered in the light of our whole experience and not merely in that of what was said a hundred years ago."

Nor is it helpful to attempt to draw a fine distinction between the intended meaning of the words of the Constitution and their intended application. When we consider the contract clause and the decisions which have expounded it in harmony with the essential reserved power of the states to protect the security of their peoples, we find no warrant for the conclusion that the clause has been warped by these decisions from its proper significance or that the founders of our government would have interpreted the clause differently had they had occasion to assume that responsibility in the conditions of the later day. The vast body of law which has been developed was unknown to the fathers, but it is believed to have preserved the essential content and the spirit of the Constitution. With a growing recognition of public needs and the relation of individual right to public security, the court has sought to prevent the perversion of the clause through its use as an instrument to throttle the capacity of the states to protect their fundamental interests. . . .

An emergency existed in Minnesota which furnished a proper occasion for the exercise of the reserved power of the state to protect the vital interests of the community. . . .

The legislation was addressed to a legitimate end; that is, the legislation was not for the mere advantage of particular individuals but for the protection of a basic interest of society.

. . .

The conditions upon which the period of redemption is extended do not appear to be unreasonable. . . . [T]he integrity of the mortgage indebtedness is not impaired; interest continues to run; the validity of the sale and the right of a mortgagee-purchaser to title or to obtain a deficiency judgment, if the mortgagor fails to redeem within the extended period, are maintained; and the conditions of redemption, if redemption there be, stand as they were under the prior law. The mortgagor during the extended period is not ousted from possession, but he must pay the rental value of the premises as ascertained in judicial proceedings and this amount is applied to the carrying of the property and to interest upon the indebtedness. . . .

. . .

JUSTICE SUTHERLAND, with whom JUSTICE VAN DEVANTER, JUSTICE McREYNOLDS, and JUSTICE BUTLER join, dissenting.

. . .

A provision of the Constitution, it is hardly necessary to say, does not admit of two distinctly opposite interpretations. It does not mean one thing at one time and an entirely different thing at another time. If the contract impairment clause, when framed and adopted, meant that the terms of a contract for the payment of money could not be altered . . . by a state statute enacted for the relief of hardly pressed debtors to the end and with the effect of postponing payment or enforcement during and because of an economic or financial emergency, it is but to state the obvious to say that it means the same now. . . .

. . .

The provisions of the Federal Constitution, undoubtedly, are pliable in the sense that in appropriate cases they have the capacity of bringing within their grasp every new condition which falls within their meaning. . . . But, their meaning is changeless; it is only their application which is extensible. . . .

The whole aim of construction, as applied to a provision of the Constitution, is to discover the meaning, to ascertain and give effect to the intent of its framers and the people who adopted it. . . . The necessities which gave rise to the provision, the controversies which preceded, as well as the conflicts of opinion which were settled by its adoption, are matters to be considered to enable us to arrive at a correct result. . . . As nearly as possible we should place ourselves in the condition of those who framed and adopted it. . . . And, if the meaning be at all doubtful, the doubt should be resolved, wherever reasonably possible to do so, in a way to forward the evident purpose with which the provision was adopted. . . .

An application of these principles to the question under review removes any doubt, if otherwise there would be any, that the contract impairment clause denies to the several states the power to mitigate hard consequences resulting to debtors from financial or economic exigencies by an impairment of the obligation of contracts of indebtedness. A candid consideration of the history and circumstances which led up to and accompanied the framing and adoption of this clause will demonstrate conclusively that it was framed and adopted with the specific and studied purpose of preventing legislation designed to relieve debtors especially in time of financial distress. . . .

. . .

The present exigency is nothing new. From the beginning of our existence as a nation, periods of depression, of industrial failure, of financial distress, of unpaid and unpayable indebtedness, have alternated with years of plenty. The vital lesson that expenditure beyond income begets poverty, that public or private extravagance, financed by promises to pay, either must end in complete or partial repudiation or the promises be fulfilled by self-denial and painful effort, though constantly taught by bitter experience, seems never to be learned; and the attempt by legislative devices to shift the misfortune of the debtor to the shoulders of the creditor without coming into conflict with the contract impairment clause has been persistent and oft-repeated.

. . .

A statute which materially delays enforcement of the mortgagee's contractual right of ownership and possession does not modify the remedy merely; it destroys, for the period of delay, all remedy so far as the enforcement of that right is concerned. The phrase "obligation of a contract" in the constitutional sense imports a legal duty to perform the specified obligation of that contract, not to substitute and perform, against the will of one of the parties, a different, albeit equally valuable, obligation. And a state, under the contract impairment clause, has no more power to accomplish such a substitution than has one of the parties to the contract against the will of the other. It cannot do so either by acting directly upon the contract or by bringing about the result under the guise of a statute in form acting only upon the remedy. If it could, the efficacy of the constitutional restriction would, in large measure, be made to disappear. . . .

West Coast Hotel Co. v. Parrish, 300 U.S. 379 (1937)

Elise Parrish was employed as a chambermaid by the Cascadian Hotel in Wenatchee, Washington. After being discharged for unknown reasons, she sued the hotel for back pay. A Washington state law passed in 1913 declared that the weekly minimum wage for chambermaids was $14.50. Parrish, who had been paid 22 cents an hour, believed that she was owed $216.19. The local trial court disagreed, insisting that the Washington minimum wage law had been ruled unconstitutional in Adkins v. Children's Hospital *(1923). The Supreme Court of Washington reversed that finding. The West Coast Hotel immediately appealed to the Supreme Court of the United States.*[35]

Two months after the state court decision in Parrish, *the Supreme Court seemingly dealt a fatal blow to any effort to revive minimum wage laws for women. In* Morehead v. People of State of New York ex rel. Tipaldo *(1936), a 5–4 judicial majority declared unconstitutional a New York law requiring employers to pay their female employees a minimum wage. Convinced that the justices would not overrule* Adkins, *the lawyers for the state of New York emphasized what they believed was an important distinction between the law at issue in* Morehead *and measures previously declared unconstitutional. Congress had required employers in the District of Columbia to pay a "living wage." New York required employers to pay what a state board determined was the "reasonable value" of services. Justice Pierce Butler's majority opinion in* Morehead *rejected this distinction. The due process clause of the Fourteenth Amendment, in his view, prohibited almost all laws regulating wages. He declared,*

> *The right to make contracts about one's affairs is a part of the liberty protected by the due process clause. Within this liberty are provisions of contracts between employer and employee fixing the wages to be paid. In making contracts of employment, generally speaking, the parties have equal right to obtain from each other the best terms they can by private bargaining. Legislative abridgement of that freedom can only be justified by the existence of exceptional circumstances. Freedom of contract is the general rule and restraint the exception. . . .*
>
> *. . . [T]he state is without power by any form of legislation to prohibit, change or nullify contracts between employers and adult women workers as to the amount of wages to be paid.*

The Supreme Court in Parrish *sustained by a 5–4 vote the state law mandating minimum wage laws. Chief Justice Hughes's majority opinion overruled* Adkins. *Did any vestige of the freedom of contract survive* Parrish? *Hughes treated state assistance to the poor as a "subsidy for unconscionable employers." Is this correct? Is the dissent correct that minimum wage laws require employers to provide welfare that should be provided by the public? The justices in* Parrish *disputed the significance of gender differences. The more radical feminists of the 1930s, led by Alice Paul, abhorred* Parrish *for permitting legislators to make gender classifications. Professor Julie Novkov makes the intriguing suggestion that the Court opened the door for regulating the wages of men and women only by implicitly treating all workers as having the diminished capacities that women were thought to have during the early twentieth century.*[36]

Justice Roberts was the only justice who voted differently in Parrish *than he did in* Morehead. *Observers initially believed that Roberts had switched in response to Roosevelt's Court-packing plan (discussed in Section III of this chapter). Subsequent evidence proved this wrong. Roberts voted to overrule* Adkins *during a judicial conference held in December 1936, before Roosevelt sought to increase the number of justices on the Supreme Court. Roberts claimed that he voted to declare the New York statute unconstitutional only because state lawyers had not argued that* Adkins *should be overruled. An ongoing debate exists over whether this justification can be taken at face value.*[37] *Given the political circumstances of 1936 and 1937, do you believe that a justice who sustained a law he believed unconstitutional because counsel had not advanced proper arguments was acting in the best traditions of the adversary system or was stubbornly refusing to acknowledge the constitutional environment?*

---

35. For a detailed case study of the *Parrish* litigation, see Leuchtenburg, *Supreme Court Reborn*, 163–79.

36. See Julie Novkov, *Constituting Workers, Protecting Women: Gender, Law, and Labor in the Progressive Era and New Deal Years* (Ann Arbor: University of Michigan Press, 2001).

37. For an excellent summary of this controversy, see Alan Brinkley, Laura Kalman, William W. Leuchtenburg, and G. Edward White, "The Debate over the Constitutional Revolution of 1937," *American Historical Review* 110 (2005): 1046–115.

CHIEF JUSTICE HUGHES delivered the opinion of the Court.

. . .

. . . The Constitution does not speak of freedom of contract. It speaks of liberty and prohibits the deprivation of liberty without due process of law. In prohibiting that deprivation, the Constitution does not recognize an absolute and uncontrollable liberty. Liberty in each of its phases has its history and connotation. But the liberty safeguarded is liberty in a social organization which requires the protection of law against the evils which menace the health, safety, morals, and welfare of the people. Liberty under the Constitution is thus necessarily subject to the restraints of due process, and regulation which is reasonable in relation to its subject and is adopted in the interests of the community is due process.

. . .

It is manifest that this established principle is peculiarly applicable in relation to the employment of women in whose protection the state has a special interest. That phase of the subject received elaborate consideration in *Muller v. Oregon* (1908) . . . where the constitutional authority of the state to limit the working hours of women was sustained. We emphasized the consideration that "woman's physical structure and the performance of maternal functions place her at a disadvantage in the struggle for subsistence" and that her physical well being "becomes an object of public interest and care in order to preserve the strength and vigor of the race." . . .

With full recognition of the earnestness and vigor which characterize the prevailing opinion in [*Adkins v. Children's Hospital* (1923)], we find it impossible to reconcile that ruling with these well-considered declarations. What can be closer to the public interest than the health of women and their protection from unscrupulous and overreaching employers? And if the protection of women is a legitimate end of the exercise of state power, how can it be said that the requirement of the payment of a minimum wage fairly fixed in order to meet the very necessities of existence is not an admissible means to that end? The Legislature of the state was clearly entitled to consider the situation of women in employment, the fact that they are in the class receiving the least pay, that their bargaining power is relatively weak, and that they are the ready victims of those who would take advantage of their necessitous circumstances. The Legislature was entitled to adopt measures to reduce the evils of the "sweating system," the exploiting of workers at wages so low as to be insufficient to meet the bare cost of living, thus making their very helplessness the occasion of a most injurious competition. The Legislature had the right to consider that its minimum wage requirements would be an important aid in carrying out its policy of protection. The adoption of similar requirements by many states evidences a deep seated conviction both as to the presence of the evil and as to the means adapted to check it. Legislative response to that conviction cannot be regarded as arbitrary or capricious and that is all we have to decide. Even if the wisdom of the policy be regarded as debatable and its effects uncertain, still the Legislature is entitled to its judgment.

There is an additional and compelling consideration which recent economic experience has brought into a strong light. The exploitation of a class of workers who are in an unequal position with respect to bargaining power and are thus relatively defenseless against the denial of a living wage is not only detrimental to their health and well being, but casts a direct burden for their support upon the community. What these workers lose in wages the taxpayers are called upon to pay. The bare cost of living must be met. We may take judicial notice of the unparalleled demands for relief which arose during the recent period of depression and still continue to an alarming extent despite the degree of economic recovery which has been achieved. . . . The community is not bound to provide what is in effect a subsidy for unconscionable employers. The community may direct its law-making power to correct the abuse which springs from their selfish disregard of the public interest. . . .

JUSTICE SUTHERLAND, joined by JUSTICE VAN DEVANTER, JUSTICE McREYNOLDS, and JUSTICE BUTLER, dissenting.

. . .

In the *Adkins Case* we . . . said that while there was no such thing as absolute freedom of contract, but that it was subject to a great variety of restraints, nevertheless, freedom of contract was the general rule and restraint the exception; and that the power to abridge that freedom could only be justified by the existence of exceptional circumstances. . . .

We further pointed out four distinct classes of cases in which this court from time to time had upheld statutory interferences with the liberty of contract. They were, in brief, (1) statutes fixing rates and charges to be exacted by businesses impressed with a public interest; (2) statutes relating to contracts for the performance of public work; (3) statutes prescribing the character, methods, and time for payment of wages; and (4) statutes fixing hours of labor. It is the last class that has been most relied upon as affording support for minimum-wage legislation; and much of the opinion in the *Adkins Case* . . . is devoted to pointing out the essential distinction between fixing hours of labor and fixing wages. What is there said need not be repeated. It is enough for present purposes to say that statutes of the former class deal with an incident of the employment, having no necessary effect upon wages. The parties are left free to contract about wages, and thereby equalize such additional burdens as may be imposed upon the employer as a result of the restrictions as to hours by an adjustment in respect of the amount of wages. This court, wherever the question is adverted to, has been careful to disclaim any purpose to uphold such legislation as fixing wages, and has recognized an essential difference between the two.

. . .

. . . The common-law rules restricting the power of women to make contracts have, under our system, long since practically disappeared. Women today stand upon a legal and political equality with men. There is no longer any reason why they should be put in different classes in respect of their legal right to make contracts; nor should they be denied, in effect, the right to compete with men for work paying lower wages which men may be willing to accept. And it is an arbitrary exercise of the legislative power to do so. . . .

. . .

Since the contractual rights of men and women are the same, does the legislation here involved, by restricting only the rights of women to make contracts as to wages, create an arbitrary discrimination? We think it does. Difference of sex affords no reasonable ground for making a restriction applicable to the wage contracts of all working women from which like contracts of all working men are left free. Certainly a suggestion that the bargaining ability of the average woman is not equal to that of the average man would lack substance. The ability to make a fair bargain, as every one knows, does not depend upon sex.

Williamson v. Lee Optical, Inc., 348 U.S. 483 (1955)

The Lee Optical Company prepared lenses and frames for persons who needed glasses. In 1953 Oklahoma passed a law that prohibited opticians from providing lenses and frames without a prescription from a licensed ophthalmologist or optometrist. Opticians were required to obtain or have on hand these prescriptions, even when replacing lost glasses or repairing broken frames. The Lee Optical Company asked for an injunction against Mac Williamson, the attorney general of Oklahoma, claiming that the law was an unreasonable violation of the due process clause of the Fourteenth Amendment. Oklahoma insisted that the law was a reasonable means to ensure that persons had regular checkups. The local federal district court declared part of the law unconstitutional. Oklahoma appealed to the Supreme Court of the United States.

A unanimous Court had no difficulty finding this law constitutional. Justice Douglas's majority opinion ruled that economic regulations would have to satisfy a very toothless rational basis standard. Do you believe Justice Douglas's explanation for the law's purpose? What do you believe was the actual purpose of the measure? Should that matter? After Williamson, *can you imagine an economic regulation that a legislature might actually pass that New Deal/Great Society justices would find an unreasonable violation of due process?*

JUSTICE DOUGLAS delivered the opinion of the Court.

. . .

The Oklahoma law may exact a needless, wasteful requirement in many cases. But it is for the legislature, not the courts, to balance the advantages and disadvantages of the new requirement. It appears that, in many cases, the optician can easily supply the new frames or new lenses without reference to the old written prescription. It also appears that many written prescriptions contain no directive data in regard to fitting spectacles to the face. But in some cases the directions contained in the prescription are essential if the glasses are to be fitted so as to correct the particular defects of vision or alleviate the eye condition. The legislature might have concluded that the frequency of occasions when a prescription is necessary was sufficient to justify this regulation of the fitting of eyeglasses. Likewise, when it is necessary to duplicate a lens, a written prescription may or may not be necessary. But the legislature might have concluded that one was needed often enough to require one in every case. Or the legislature may have concluded that eye examinations were so critical, not only for correction of vision but also for detection of latent ailments or diseases, that every change in frames and every duplication of a lens should be accompanied by a prescription from a medical expert. To be sure, the present law does not require a new examination of the eyes every time the frames are changed or the lenses duplicated. For if the old prescription is on file with the optician, he can go ahead and make the new fitting or duplicate the lenses. But the law need not be in every respect logically consistent with its aims to be constitutional. It is enough that there is an evil at hand for correction, and that it might be thought that the particular legislative measure was a rational way to correct it.

The day is gone when this Court uses the Due Process Clause of the Fourteenth Amendment to strike down state laws, regulatory of business and industrial conditions because they may be unwise, improvident, or out of harmony with a particular school of thought. . . . "For protection against abuses by legislatures, the people must resort to the polls, not to the courts."

[In evaluating equal protection claims the] problem of legislative classification is a perennial one, admitting of no doctrinaire definition. Evils in the same field may be of different dimensions and proportions, requiring different remedies. Or so the legislature may think. . . . Or the reform may take one step at a time, addressing itself to the phase of the problem which seems most acute to the legislative mind. . . . The legislature may select one phase of one field and apply a remedy there, neglecting the others. . . . The prohibition of the Equal Protection Clause goes no further than the invidious discrimination. We cannot say that that point has been reached here. For all this record shows, the ready-to-wear branch of this business may not loom large in Oklahoma or may present problems of regulation distinct from the other branch.

Third, the District Court held unconstitutional, as violative of the Due Process Clause of the Fourteenth Amendment, that portion of §3 which makes it unlawful "to solicit the sale of . . . frames, mountings . . . or any other optical appliances." . . .

An eyeglass frame, considered in isolation, is only a piece of merchandise. But an eyeglass frame is not used in isolation . . . ; it is used with lenses; and lenses, pertaining as they do to the human eye, enter the field of health. Therefore, the legislature might conclude that to regulate one effectively it would have to regulate the other. Or it might conclude that both the sellers of frames and the sellers of lenses were in a business where advertising should be limited, or even abolished, in the public interest. . . . The advertiser of frames may be using his ads to bring in customers who will buy lenses. If the advertisement of lenses is to be abolished or controlled, the advertising of frames must come under the same restraints—or so the legislature might think. We see no constitutional reason why a State may not treat all who deal with the human eye as members of a profession who should use no merchandising methods for obtaining customers. . . .

B. Religion

Increasing religious diversity fostered greater religious freedom. During the Republican Era many conflicts over religion were between traditional Protestants, who favored what they believed were nonsectarian religious activities in public schools while opposing state aid to private religious schools, and Catholics, who favored state aid to private religious schools while opposing what they believed were quite sectarian religious activities in public schools. Members of less mainstream religious sects, most notably Mormons, enjoyed little political or judicial support when they claimed that their religious rights were being violated. The constitutional politics of religion became more fragmented during the twentieth century. Three new groups joined the fray—liberal Protestants, Jews, and secularists. All three opposed state programs that aided or accommodated religious education and voluntary prayer in public schools. On issues of religious exemptions from general laws, the alliance fractured. Liberal Protestant and Jewish organizations favored exemptions. Secularists opposed them.

Most justices agreed that voluntary religious exercises in public schools unconstitutionally breached the wall between church and state. Justice Black spoke for a 6–1 judicial majority in *Engel v. Vitale* (1962) when declaring a state prayer exercise unconstitutional. The justices immediately made clear that the constitutional problem in *Engel* was the state-sponsored religious exercise, not the state-written prayer. Pennsylvania law required that the school day begin with a reading of ten Biblical verses. Maryland law required that the school day begin with a recitation of the Lord's Prayer. Both were declared unconstitutional in *Abington School Dist. v. Schempp* (1963). Justice Clark's majority opinion declared, "[These] are religious exercises, required by the States in violation of the command of the First Amendment that the Government maintain strict neutrality, neither aiding nor opposing religion." Such rulings proved hard to implement, not least because many teachers and school boards remained committed to prayer in public schools.

New Deal/Great Society liberals concluded that strict scrutiny was the appropriate standard when states refused to grant persons exemptions from laws that significantly burdened their religious practice. "Any incidental burden on the free exercise of appellant's religion," Justice Brennan wrote in *Sherbert v. Verner* (1963), "may be justified by a 'compelling state interest in the regulation of a subject within the State's constitutional power to regulate.'" Applying this test, the judicial majority ruled that South Carolina could not deny unemployment benefits to persons who refused to work on their Sabbath. Justice Brennan declared,

> Here not only is it apparent that appellant's declared ineligibility for benefits derives solely from the practice of her religion, but the pressure upon her to forego that practice is unmistakable. The ruling forces her to choose between following the precepts of her religion and forfeiting benefits, on the one hand, and abandoning one of the precepts of her religion in order to accept work, on the other hand. Governmental imposition of such a choice puts the same kind of burden upon the free exercise of religion as would a fine imposed against appellant for her Saturday worship.

Engel v. Vitale, 370 U.S. 421 (1962)

Steven Engel was a parent of a Jewish public school student in New Hyde Park, New York. At that time public school days in New York began with the following prayer, written by the New York Board of Regents: "Almighty God, we acknowledge our dependence upon Thee, and we beg Thy blessings upon us, our parents, our teachers and our Country." Students were not required to say these words if their parents objected. Engel and other parents insisted that state-mandated religious exercises in public schools violated the establishment clause of the First Amendment as incorporated by the Fourteenth Amendment, even if those exercises were voluntary. New York insisted that nonsectarian prayers were an American tradition and were consistent with religious freedom (and a vital bulwark against communist influence). A lower state court rejected the parents'

Table 8-5 Public School Teacher Attitudes on Prayer in the Classroom, 1965

	Percent of Teachers Agreeing with Statement				
Statement	**South**	**New England**	**Midwest**	**Mid-Atlantic**	**Mountain West**
Prayer and Bible-reading decisions interfere with teacher freedom	69	73	54	58	53
Devotional services have no place in the public school	11	25	48	41	60
Should not stop prayers and Bible readings because of a few dissenters	94	89	71	70	65
Bible readings and prayers are beneficial to students	94	91	86	75	80
Public school is not the proper place to develop religious values	34	43	62	58	72

Source: H. Frank Way, Jr., "Survey Research on Judicial Decisions: The Prayer and Bible Reading Cases," *Western Political Quarterly* 21 (1968): 199.

claim, as did the New York Court of Appeals. Engel appealed to the Supreme Court of the United States.

The Supreme Court by a 6–1 vote declared unconstitutional the New York regents' prayer. Justice Black's majority opinion asserted that states could not sponsor religious exercises in public schools. To what extent did the justices in the majority object to state officials writing prayers? To what extent did the justices in the majority object to the state sponsoring a religious exercise? New York claimed that the prayer was nonsectarian. Do you agree? Given the diversity of religion in the United States, is nonsectarian prayer possible? Was Justice Stewart nevertheless correct when he insisted that, as a historical matter, Americans have endorsed the concept of nonsectarian prayer?

Engle v. Vitale *is one of the most politically controversial decisions in the history of the Supreme Court. President Kennedy at a press conference declared that the American people should "support the Constitution and the responsibility of the Supreme Court in interpreting it." The* Christian Century, *a liberal Protestant publication, stated that the court had "protect[ed] the integrity of the religious conscience and the proper function of religious and government institutions." Conservatives sharply disagreed. Cardinal Francis Spelling accused the Supreme Court of "strik[ing] at the heart of the Godly tradition in which America's children have for so long been raised." The* Wall Street Journal *described the outcome as a "violent wrecking of the Constitution's language."*[38] *Many rural school districts ignored the* Engel *decision. Regional resistance to this opinion continues to this day, especially in communities dominated by a Southern Baptist tradition.*

JUSTICE BLACK delivered the opinion of the Court.

. . .

We think that by using its public school system to encourage recitation of the Regents' prayer, the State of New York has adopted a practice wholly inconsistent with the Establishment Clause. There can, of course, be no doubt that New York's program of daily classroom invocation of God's blessings as prescribed in the Regents' prayer is a religious activity. . . . [T]he constitutional prohibition against laws respecting an establishment of religion must at least mean that in this country it is no part of the business of government to compose official prayers for any group of the American people to recite as a part of a religious program carried on by government.

. . .

By the time of the adoption of the Constitution, our history shows that there was a widespread awareness among many Americans of the dangers of a union of Church and State. . . . The First Amendment was added to the Constitution to stand as a guarantee that neither the power nor the prestige of the Federal Government would be used to control, support or influence the kinds of prayer the American people can say—that the people's religions must not be subjected to the pressures of government for change each time a new political administration is elected to office. Under that Amendment's prohibition against governmental establishment of religion, as reinforced by the provisions of the Fourteenth Amendment, government in this country, be it state or federal, is without power to prescribe by law any particular form of prayer which is to be used as an official prayer in carrying on any program of governmentally sponsored religious activity.

. . . Neither the fact that the [New York] prayer may be denominationally neutral nor the fact that its observance on the part of the students is voluntary can serve to free it from the limitations of the Establishment Clause. . . . The Establishment Clause, unlike the Free Exercise Clause, does not depend upon any showing of direct governmental compulsion and is violated by the enactment of laws which establish an official religion whether those laws operate directly to coerce nonobserving individuals or not. . . . When the power, prestige and financial support of government is placed behind a particular religious belief, the indirect coercive pressure upon religious minorities to conform to the prevailing officially approved religion is plain. But the purposes underlying the Establishment Clause go much further than that. Its first and most immediate purpose rested on the belief that a union of government and religion tends to destroy government and to degrade religion. The history of governmentally established religion, both in England and in this country, showed that whenever government had allied itself with one particular form of religion, the inevitable result had been that it had incurred the hatred, disrespect and even contempt of those who held contrary beliefs. . . . The Establishment Clause thus stands as an expression of principle on the part of the Founders

38. For these and other responses, see Powe, *Warren Court,* 187–88.

of our Constitution that religion is too personal, too sacred, too holy, to permit its "unhallowed perversion" by a civil magistrate. Another purpose of the Establishment Clause rested upon an awareness of the historical fact that governmentally established religions and religious persecutions go hand in hand. The Founders knew that . . . persecutions had received the sanction of law in several of the colonies in this country soon after the establishment of official religions in those colonies. It was in large part to get completely away from this sort of systematic religious persecution that the Founders brought into being our Nation, our Constitution, and our Bill of Rights with its prohibition against any governmental establishment of religion. The New York laws officially prescribing the Regents' prayer are inconsistent both with the purposes of the Establishment Clause and with the Establishment Clause itself.

. . . [T]he First Amendment, which tried to put an end to governmental control of religion and of prayer, was not written to destroy either. . . . [I]t was written to quiet well-justified fears . . . arising out of an awareness that governments of the past had shackled men's tongues to make them speak only the religious thoughts that government wanted them to speak and to pray only to the God that government wanted them to pray to. It is neither sacrilegious nor antireligious to say that each separate government in this country should stay out of the business of writing or sanctioning official prayers and leave that purely religious function to the people themselves and to those the people choose to look to for religious guidance.

. . .

JUSTICE DOUGLAS, concurring. . . .

JUSTICE STEWART, dissenting.

. . .

. . . I cannot see how an "official religion" is established by letting those who want to say a prayer say it. On the contrary, I think that to deny the wish of these school children to join in reciting this prayer is to deny

Table 8-6 Selection of State and Lower Federal Court Applications of *Engel v. Vitale*

Case	Decision
DeSpain v. DeKalb County Community School District, 384 F. 2d 836 (7th Cir., 1967)	Kindergarten "thank you" verse constitutes a prayer, even when stripped of explicit references to God, and is therefore unconstitutional
Lincoln v. Page, 109 N.H. 30 (NH 1968)	Prayer before town meeting is constitutional
Aronow v. United States, 432 F.2d 242 (9th Cir., 1970)	Use of "In God We Trust" is ceremonial, not religious
Mangold v. Albert Gallatin Area School District, 438 F.2d 1194 (3rd Cir., 1971)	Administration-initiated "voluntary" student Bible reading and mass prayer are unconstitutional
Fox v. Los Angeles, 22 Cal. 3d 792 (CA 1978)	Display of lighted cross at Christmas at city hall is unconstitutional
Collins v. Chandler Unified School District, 470 F. Supp. 959 (D. AZ, 1979)	Student council–initiated prayer before school assemblies is unconstitutional
Malnak v. Yogi, 592 F.2d 197 (3rd Cir., 1979)	Public school class in transcendental meditation is unconstitutional
Brandon v. Board of Education, 487 F. Supp. 1219 (D. NY, 1980)	Use of school facilities by student prayer group is unconstitutional
Breen v. Runkel, 614 F. Supp. 355 (D. MI, 1985)	Bible reading and classroom prayer by individual teachers without direction from school administrators is still unconstitutional state action
Jager v. Douglas County School District, 862 F.2d 824 (11th Cir., 1989)	Religious invocation before school football games is unconstitutional

them the opportunity of sharing in the spiritual heritage of our Nation.

. . .

At the opening of each day's Session of this Court we stand, while one of our officials invokes the protection of God. Since the days of John Marshall our Crier has said, "God save the United States and this Honorable Court." Both the Senate and the House of Representatives open their daily Sessions with prayer. Each of our Presidents, from George Washington to John F. Kennedy, has upon assuming his Office asked the protection and help of God.

. . .

I do not believe that this Court, or the Congress, or the President has by the actions and practices I have mentioned established an "official religion" in violation of the Constitution. And I do not believe the State of New York has done so in this case. What each has done has been to recognize and to follow the deeply entrenched and highly cherished spiritual traditions of our Nation—traditions which come down to us from those who almost two hundred years ago avowed their "firm Reliance on the Protection of divine Providence" when they proclaimed the freedom and independence of this brave new world.

C. Guns

Gun rights were ignored during the New Deal/Great Society period. Democrats and Republicans did not mention gun rights or gun control in their national party platforms. No prominent interest group championed either gun rights or gun control. Legislation requiring gun registration, prohibiting concealed weapons, and forbidding convicted felons from owning weapons was constitutionally uncontroversial. Most persons assumed that constitutional provisions did not bar such regulations, either because gun rights were restricted to the militia or because legislative restrictions that reasonably promoted the public interest were consistent with constitutional rights to bear arms. The Senate Report on the Omnibus Crime Control and Safe Streets Act of 1968 bluntly declared, "The [Second] amendment presents no obstacle to the enactment and enforcement of" gun control legislation.[39]

A general consensus formed by the middle of the twentieth century that the Second Amendment had no bearing on a private right to bear arms independent of a state militia. Justice McReynolds repeated this conventional wisdom in *United States v. Miller* (1939). An occasional dissent aside, every lower federal and state court that discussed gun rights reached the same or similar conclusions.[40]

D. Personal Freedom and Public Morality

The New Deal/Great Society Era was marked by an apparent abandonment of and then a slow but steady increase in constitutional privacy rights. During the 1930s and early 1940s, businesses lost what had previously been some immunity to government investigations of private records. Beginning in the 1940s, a series of judicial decisions provided protection for different forms of privacy, procreation rights, the right of married couples to use birth control, and the right to marry.

Most states outside of the South repealed bans on interracial marriage. The Supreme Court of California in *Perez v. Sharpe* (CA 1948) declared that state's prohibition of interracial marriage unconstitutional.

The three most important Supreme Court decisions on privacy handed down from 1933 to 1968—*Skinner v. Oklahoma* (1942) (the right not to be sterilized), *Griswold v. Connecticut* (1965) (the right of married people to use birth control), and *Loving v. Virginia* (1966) (the right to marry a person of a different race)—protected discrete and insular minorities or rejected positions identified with the Catholic Church. *Skinner,* decided just fifteen years after the Court in *Buck v. Bell* (1927) declared there would be no judicial protections against enforced sterilizations, was handed down during World War II, when the United States was fighting totalitarian regimes that routinely implemented racialized eugenic and sterilization policies. In explaining the reasons for greater judicial protection Justice Douglas asserted, "We are dealing here with legislation which involves one of the basic civil rights of man. Marriage and procreation are fundamental to the very existence and survival of the race. [In] evil or reckless hands [the power to sterilize]

39. U.S. Senate, Senate Report 90–1097, Omnibus Crime Control and Safe Streets Act of 1968, 90th Cong., 2nd Sess., 1968, 52.

40. See Adam Winkler, "Scrutinizing the Second Amendment," *Michigan Law Review* 105 (2007): 683–733.

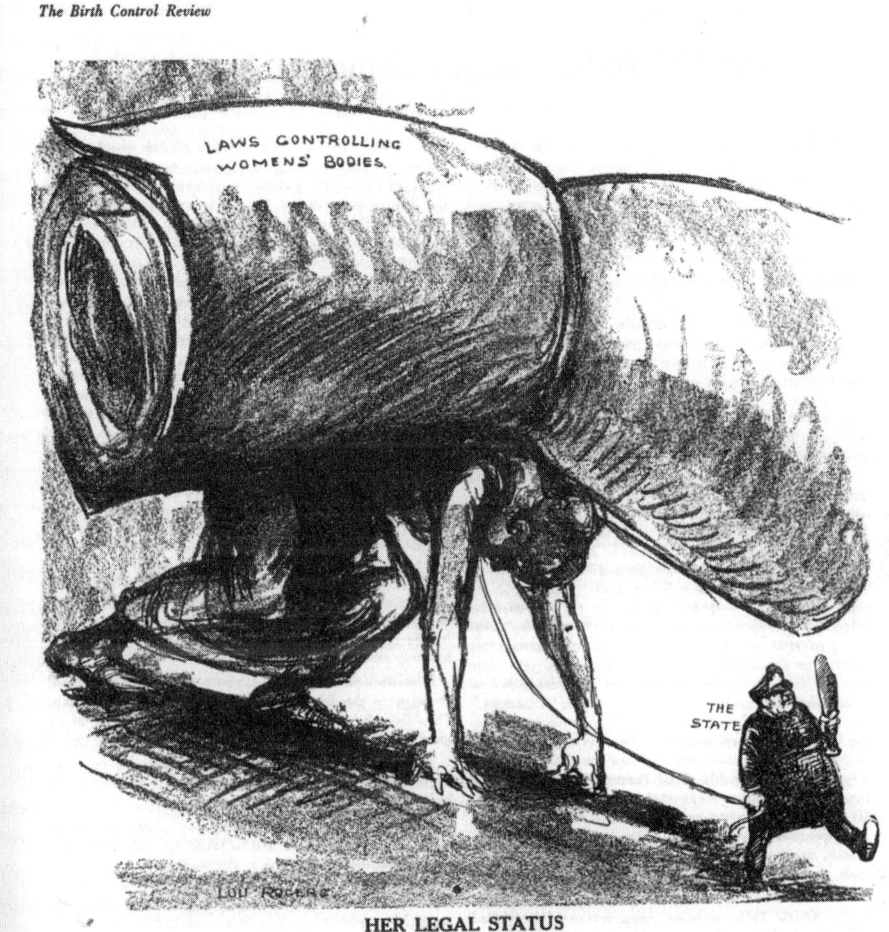

Illustration 8-4 Her Legal Status

Source: Cartoon in The Birth Control Review, May 1919. Margaret Sanger Papers. Photographer/creator: unknown. Copyright: unknown.

can cause races or types which are inimical to the dominant group to wither and disappear. . . . [S]trict scrutiny of the classification which a State makes in a sterilization law is essential." In subsequent decisions the offending restrictions on family and procreation had been abandoned by the vast majority of states, reflecting a general tendency toward liberalization in American political culture on matters relating to personal freedom and public morality. Judicial opinions, most notably those written by Justice Douglas, contained language that could be wielded in a broader judicial crusade against conservative family policies, but the justices did not elaborate on the meaning of those decisions before the Nixon presidency.

Griswold v. Connecticut, 381 U.S. 479 (1965)

Estelle Griswold, the executive director of Planned Parenthood in Connecticut, was arrested on November 10, 1961, for running a birth control clinic in New Haven. Connecticut law at that time forbade persons from "us[ing] any drug, medicinal article or instrument for the purpose of preventing conception." Griswold was charged with aiding and abetting that offense after she prescribed birth control for married couples. The trial court found her guilty and fined her $100. Griswold appealed, claiming that the Connecticut law unconstitutionally violated privacy rights protected by the Ninth and Fourteenth Amendments. Attorneys for the state of Connecticut insisted that the total ban on birth control helped *discourage illicit sexual relations and promoted the view that procreation was the primary justification for sex. The Supreme Court of Connecticut rejected Griswold's claims. She appealed to the Supreme Court of the United States.*

Griswold *culminated a long effort to have the Supreme Court make a decision on the constitutionality of birth control. Proponents of family planning targeted Connecticut because Connecticut and Massachusetts were the only states that banned all uses of birth control. The first effort failed when the Supreme Court in* Tileston v. Ullman *(1943) ruled that a doctor did not have standing to litigate the constitutional rights of his patients. The second effort failed when the Supreme Court in* Poe v. Ullman *(1961) ruled that litigants could not bring a case until after Connecticut had enforced the statutory ban on birth control. Justices Harlan and Douglas issued dissents in that case, urging the justices to declare the Connecticut law unconstitutional (Justice Harlan's dissent is noted in the following excerpt). Finally, in 1965, Planned Parenthood designed a case that ensured standing. Because Ms. Griswold had been arrested and fined, she had standing to challenge the constitutionality of the Connecticut law. By the time* Griswold *reached the Supreme Court more than one million women were using the pill, which had been approved by the Federal Drug Administration in 1960.*

The Supreme Court by a 7–2 vote reversed the Supreme Court of Connecticut. Justice Douglas's opinion for the court ruled that Connecticut could not constitutionally forbid married persons from using birth control. What is the constitutional foundation of this right? To what extent is that foundation sound? The justices in Griswold *emphasized that the right they were protecting was a right of married couples to not be interrogated about their private use of contraception. Suppose you were asked to write a statute that would limit birth control as much as possible in light of* Griswold. *How much conduct could you restrict? Could you shut down Planned Parenthood of Connecticut by banning doctors from prescribing birth control for their patients?*

JUSTICE DOUGLAS delivered the opinion of the Court.

. . .

. . . Overtones of some arguments suggest that *Lochner v. New York* (1905) should be our guide. But we decline that invitation. . . . We do not sit as a super-legislature to determine the wisdom, need, and propriety of laws that touch economic problems, business affairs, or social conditions. This law, however, operates directly on an intimate relation of husband and wife and their physician's role in one aspect of that relation.

The association of people is not mentioned in the Constitution nor in the Bill of Rights. The right to educate a child in a school of the parents' choice—whether public or private or parochial—is also not mentioned. Nor is the right to study any particular subject or any foreign language. Yet the First Amendment has been construed to include certain of those rights.

. . .

. . . [S]pecific guarantees in the Bill of Rights have penumbras, formed by emanations from those guarantees that help give them life and substance. . . . Various guarantees create zones of privacy. The right of association contained in the penumbra of the First Amendment is one. . . . The Third Amendment in its prohibition against the quartering of soldiers "in any house" in time of peace without the consent of the owner is another facet of that privacy. The Fourth Amendment explicitly affirms the "right of the people to be secure in their persons, houses, papers, and effects, against unreasonable searches and seizures." The Fifth Amendment in its Self-Incrimination Clause enables the citizen to create a zone of privacy which government may not force him to surrender to his detriment. The Ninth Amendment provides: "The enumeration in the Constitution, of certain rights, shall not be construed to deny or disparage others retained by the people."

. . .

The present case concerns a relationship lying within the zone of privacy created by several fundamental constitutional guarantees. And it concerns a law which, in forbidding the use of contraceptives rather than regulating their manufacture or sale, seeks to achieve its goals by means having a maximum destructive impact upon that relationship. Such a law cannot stand in light of the familiar principle, so often applied by this Court, that a "governmental purpose to control or prevent activities constitutionally subject to state regulation may not be achieved by means which sweep unnecessarily broadly and thereby invade the area of protected freedoms." Would we allow the police to search the sacred precincts of marital bedrooms for telltale signs of the use of contraceptives? The very idea is repulsive to the notions of privacy surrounding the marriage relationship.

We deal with a right of privacy older than the Bill of Rights—older than our political parties, older than our school system. Marriage is a coming together for better or for worse, hopefully enduring, and intimate to the degree of being sacred. It is an association that promotes a way of life, not causes; a harmony in living, not political faiths; a bilateral loyalty, not commercial or social projects. Yet it is an association for as noble a purpose as any involved in our prior decisions.

JUSTICE GOLDBERG, whom THE CHIEF JUSTICE and JUSTICE BRENNAN join, concurring.

. . .

. . . This Court, in a series of decisions, has held that the Fourteenth Amendment absorbs and applies to the States those specifics of the first eight amendments which express fundamental personal rights. The language and history of the Ninth Amendment reveal that the Framers of the Constitution believed that there are additional fundamental rights, protected from governmental infringement, which exist alongside those fundamental rights specifically mentioned in the first eight constitutional amendments.

. . .

. . . To hold that a right so basic and fundamental and so deep-rooted in our society as the right of privacy in marriage may be infringed because that right is not guaranteed in so many words by the first eight amendments to the Constitution is to ignore the Ninth Amendment and to give it no effect whatsoever. . . .

. . . The Ninth Amendment simply shows the intent of the Constitution's authors that other fundamental personal rights should not be denied such protection or disparaged in any other way simply because they are not specifically listed in the first eight constitutional amendments. I do not see how this broadens the authority of the Court; rather it serves to support what this Court has been doing in protecting fundamental rights.

In determining which rights are fundamental, judges are not left at large to decide cases in light of their personal and private notions. Rather, they must look to the "traditions and [collective] conscience of our people" to determine whether a principle is "so rooted [there] . . . as to be ranked as fundamental." . . .

. . .

The entire fabric of the Constitution and the purposes that clearly underlie its specific guarantees demonstrate that the rights to marital privacy and to marry and raise a family are of similar order and magnitude as the fundamental rights specifically protected. Although the Constitution does not speak in so many words of the right of privacy in marriage, I cannot believe that it offers these fundamental rights no protection. The fact that no particular provision of the Constitution explicitly forbids the State from disrupting the traditional relation of the family—a relation as old and as fundamental as our entire civilization—surely does not show that the Government was meant to have the power to do so. Rather, as the Ninth Amendment expressly recognizes, there are fundamental personal rights such as this one, which are protected from abridgment by the Government though not specifically mentioned in the Constitution.

. . .

JUSTICE HARLAN, concurring in the judgment

[Justice Harlan concurred on the basis of his dissent in Poe v. Ullman *(1961). The crucial passages of that dissent are included here.]*

. . .

In my view, the proper constitutional inquiry in this case is whether this Connecticut statute infringes the Due Process Clause of the Fourteenth Amendment because the enactment violates basic values "implicit in the concept of ordered liberty." . . .

. . . [A] statute making it a criminal offense for married couples to use contraceptives is an intolerable and unjustifiable invasion of privacy in the conduct of the most intimate concerns of an individual's personal life. . . .

. . .

Due process has not been reduced to any formula; its content cannot be determined by reference to any code. The best that can be said is that through the course of this Court's decisions it has represented the balance which our Nation, built upon postulates of respect for the liberty of the individual, has struck between that liberty and the demands of organized society. If the supplying of content to this Constitutional concept has of necessity been a rational process, it certainly has not been one where judges have felt free to roam where unguided speculation might take them. The balance of which I speak is the balance struck by this country, having regard to what history teaches are the traditions from which it developed as well as the traditions from which it broke. That tradition is a living thing. A decision of this Court which radically departs from it could not long survive, while a decision which builds on what has survived is likely to be sound. No formula could serve as a substitute, in this area, for judgment and restraint.

. . .

. . . [T]he very inclusion of the category of morality among state concerns indicates that society is not limited in its objects only to the physical well-being of the community, but has traditionally concerned itself with the moral soundness of its people as well. . . . The laws regarding marriage which provide both when the sexual powers may be used and the legal and societal context in which children are born and brought up, as well as laws forbidding adultery, fornication and homosexual practices which express the negative of the proposition, confining sexuality to lawful marriage, form a pattern so deeply pressed into the substance of our social life that any Constitutional doctrine in this area must build upon that basis. . . .

. . .

Precisely what is involved here is this: the State is asserting the right to enforce its moral judgment by intruding upon the most intimate details of the marital relation with the full power of the criminal law. . . . In sum, the statute allows the State to enquire into, prove and punish married people for the private use of their marital intimacy.

. . . This enactment involves what, by common understanding throughout the English-speaking world, must be granted to be a most fundamental aspect of "liberty," the privacy of the home in its most basic sense, and it is this which requires that the statute be subjected to "strict scrutiny." . . .

. . .

It is clear, of course, that this Connecticut statute does not invade the privacy of the home in the usual sense, since the invasion involved here may, and doubtless usually would, be accomplished without any physical intrusion whatever into the home. What the statute undertakes to do, however, is to create a crime which is grossly offensive to this privacy. . . .

. . .

. . . [I]f the physical curtilage of the home is protected, it is surely as a result of solicitude to protect the privacies of the life within. Certainly the safeguarding of the home does not follow merely from the sanctity of property rights. The home derives its pre-eminence as the seat of family life. . . .

Of this whole "private realm of family life" it is difficult to imagine what is more private or more intimate than a husband and wife's marital relations. . . .

. . .

Adultery, homosexuality and the like are sexual intimacies which the State forbids altogether, but the intimacy of husband and wife is necessarily an essential and accepted feature of the institution of marriage, an institution which the State not only must allow, but which always and in every age it has fostered and protected. It is one thing when the State exerts its power either to forbid extra-marital sexuality altogether, or to say who may marry, but it is quite another when, having acknowledged a marriage and the intimacies inherent in it, it undertakes to regulate by means of the criminal law the details of that intimacy.

. . .

JUSTICE WHITE, concurring in the judgment.

. . .

. . . I wholly fail to see how the ban on the use of contraceptives by married couples in any way reinforces the State's ban on illicit sexual relationships. . . .

. . . A statute limiting its prohibition on use to persons engaging in the prohibited relationship would serve the end posited by Connecticut in the same way, and with the same effectiveness, or ineffectiveness, as the broad anti-use statute under attack in this case. I find nothing in this record justifying the sweeping scope of this statute, with its telling effect on the freedoms of married persons, and therefore conclude that it deprives such persons of liberty without due process of law.

JUSTICE BLACK, with whom JUSTICE STEWART joins, dissenting.

. . .

The Court talks about a constitutional "right of privacy" as though there is some constitutional provision or provisions forbidding any law ever to be passed which might abridge the "privacy" of individuals. But there is not. There are, of course, guarantees in certain specific constitutional provisions which are designed in part to protect privacy at certain times and places with respect to certain activities. Such, for example, is the Fourth Amendment's guarantee against "unreasonable searches and seizures." But I think it belittles that Amendment to talk about it as though it protects nothing but "privacy." . . . [A] person can be just as much, if not more, irritated, annoyed and injured by an unceremonious public arrest by a policeman as he is by a seizure in the privacy of his office or home.

. . . For these reasons I get nowhere in this case by talk about a constitutional "right of privacy" as an emanation from one or more constitutional provisions. I like my privacy as well as the next one, but I am nevertheless compelled to admit that government has a right to invade it unless prohibited by some specific constitutional provision. . . .

. . .

The due process argument which my Brothers HARLAN and WHITE adopt here is based, as their opinions indicate, on the premise that this Court is vested with power to invalidate all state laws that it considers to be arbitrary, capricious, unreasonable, or oppressive, or on this Court's belief that a particular state law under scrutiny has no "rational or justifying" purpose, or is offensive to a "sense of fairness and justice." If these formulas based on "natural justice," or others which mean the same thing, are to prevail, they require judges to determine what is or is not constitutional on the basis of their own appraisal of what laws are unwise or unnecessary. The power to make such decisions is of course that of a legislative body. . . .

My Brother GOLDBERG has adopted the recent discovery that the Ninth Amendment as well as the Due Process Clause can be used by this Court as authority to strike down all state legislation which this Court thinks violates "fundamental principles of liberty and justice," or is contrary to the "traditions and [collective] conscience of our people." He also states, without proof satisfactory to me, that in making decisions on this basis judges will not consider "their personal and private notions." One may ask how they can avoid considering them. . . . That Amendment was passed, not to broaden the powers of this Court or any other department of "the General Government," but, as every student of history knows, to assure the people that the Constitution in all its provisions was intended to limit the Federal Government to the powers granted expressly or by necessary implication. . . . This fact is perhaps responsible for the peculiar phenomenon that for a period of a century and a half no serious suggestion was ever made that the Ninth Amendment, enacted to protect state powers against federal invasion, could be used as a weapon of federal power to prevent state legislatures from passing laws they consider appropriate to govern local affairs. . . .

. . .

I realize that many good and able men have eloquently spoken and written, sometimes in rhapsodical strains, about the duty of this Court to keep the Constitution in tune with the times. The idea is that the Constitution must be changed from time to time and that this Court is charged with a duty to make those changes. For myself, I must with all deference reject that philosophy. The Constitution makers knew the need for change and provided for it. Amendments suggested by the people's elected representatives can be submitted to the people or their selected agents for ratification. That method of change was good for our Fathers, and being somewhat old-fashioned I must add it is good enough for me. . . .

. . .

JUSTICE STEWART, whom JUSTICE BLACK joins, dissenting.

. . . I think this is an uncommonly silly law. . . . But we are not asked in this case to say whether we think this law is unwise, or even asinine. We are asked to hold that it violates the United States Constitution. And that I cannot do.

. . .

What provision of the Constitution, then, does make this state law invalid? The Court says it is the right of privacy "created by several fundamental constitutional guarantees." With all deference, I can find no such general right of privacy in the Bill of Rights, in any other part of the Constitution, or in any case ever before decided by this Court. . . .

VIII. Democratic Rights

MAJOR DEVELOPMENTS

- Increased commitment to the United States as a constitutional democracy
- Free speech protected in numerous circumstances
- Voting considered a fundamental right

The "freedom of speech and expression" was the first "essential human freedom" that Roosevelt sought to ensure "everywhere in the world." *Thomas v. Collins*

(1945) spoke of "the preferred place given in our scheme to the great, indispensable democratic freedoms secured by the First Amendment." By the time Richard Nixon took office, liberals in the national government and federal judiciary had established constitutional rights to speak in public forums, to advocate (but not incite) illegal activity, and to criticize public officials, as long as the criticisms were not reckless or intentionally false.

Voting rights became fundamental during the Great Society. Congressional majorities during the New Deal sought to make voting a fundamental constitutional right but were defeated by consistent filibusters in the Senate. The Supreme Court in *Breedlove v. Suttles* (1937) sustained poll taxes with little difficulty. The next generation of constitutional liberals was more successful. The Voting Rights Act of 1965 provided strong remedies to ensure that persons of color were able to exercise what Congress maintained was their constitutional right to vote. Chief Justice Warren in 1964 declared, "The right to vote freely for the candidate of one's choice is of the essence of a democratic society." The democratic right to vote was considered a right to an equal vote. Justice Black in *Wesberry v. Sanders* (1964) asserted, "To say that a vote is worth more in one district than another would . . . run counter to our fundamental ideas of democratic government."

A. Free Speech

The First Amendment occupied the center of the constitutional stage during the New Deal/Great Society Era. Justice Benjamin Cardozo, in *Palko v. Connecticut* (1937), described the freedom of speech as "the matrix, the indispensable condition, of nearly every other form of freedom." Labor unions, Jehovah's Witnesses, Nazis, African Americans, and political radicals enjoyed far more constitutional protection than had previously been the case. Powerful forces remained committed to restricting speech, and anti-Communists exercised considerable influence during the 1950s. Nevertheless, free speech enjoyed far more constitutional protection by the end of the New Deal/Great Society Era than it had at the beginning. By 1969 the Supreme Court had handed down decisions striking down mandatory flag salutes in schools; limiting the scope of obscenity statutes; giving protestors access to public streets and parks; permitting those protestors to freely condemn existing laws, unless they incited others to imminent violence; and forbidding libel suits by public officials, unless they could prove the publication was reckless or intentionally false.

No account of free speech during the New Deal/Great Society Era can omit the exploits of Senator Joe McCarthy, the House Un-American Affairs Committee, Roosevelt administration efforts to prosecute neo-Nazis during World War II, southern efforts to suppress the civil rights movement, and various efforts to suppress political dissent during the Vietnam War. Nevertheless, those who sought to restrict speech confronted far greater opposition than had previously been the case. During World War I and the Red Scare elected officials who sought to restrict free speech were opposed by only a few isolated politicians and fledgling political movements. McCarthy and other proponents of limited speech rights confronted powerful progressive congressmen in leadership positions, unsympathetic executive branch officials, well-funded interest groups, and liberals on the bench. The result was often pitched battles over free speech rights in which neither side fully realized its constitutional goals. By the end of the New Deal/Great Society Era these battles had become a free speech rout.

During the 1960s, the federal judiciary with the full support of the national executive championed the free speech rights of civil rights protestors. This unprecedented protection included decisions striking down laws requiring the NAACP to reveal its membership to the general public, laws prohibiting certain protests, laws prohibiting NAACP attorneys from soliciting lawsuits against Jim Crow practices, and libel decisions that threatened to bankrupt the civil rights movement. The justices in *Brandenburg v. Ohio* (1969) announced that Justice Brandeis's libertarian concurrence in *Whitney v. California* (1927), which declared that government could restrict only incitement to imminent violence, was the constitutional law of the land.

Politics and law strengthened constitutional speech rights during the mid-twentieth century. The ACLU by the 1940s was a powerful, respectable organization. Many prominent New Dealers and proponents of the Great Society either were members of the ACLU or sympathized with mainstream ACLU positions. Several Roosevelt judicial appointees, most notably Wiley Rutledge and Robert Jackson, were selected in part because of their perceived commitment to free speech rights.

West Virginia State Board of Education v. Barnette, 319 U.S. 624 (1943)

Walter Barnette was a Jehovah's Witness and the father of several children attending public schools in Charleston, West Virginia. On January 9, 1942, West Virginia mandated that all public children salute the flag of the United States during the school day. Barnette maintained that this decree violated his and his children's free speech and free exercise rights. Their faith regarded saluting the flag of any country as akin to worshiping false gods or idols. A federal district court agreed and ordered the West Virginia State Board of Education not to enforce the mandatory flag salute. The Board of Education appealed to the Supreme Court of the United States.

By an 8–1 vote in Minersville School District v. Gobitis *(1940) the Supreme Court had previously sustained a local policy mandating that public school students salute the flag. Justice Frankfurter's majority opinion in that case declared,*

> *We are dealing with an interest inferior to none in the hierarchy of legal values. National unity is the basis of national security. To deny the legislature the right to select appropriate means for its attainment presents a totally different order of problem from that of the propriety of subordinating the possible ugliness of littered streets to the free expression of opinion through distribution of handbills.*

Justice Stone was the lone dissenter.

Gobitis *provoked two intense reactions. The first was a mass assault on Jehovah's Witnesses. Members of that sect who refused to salute the flag found their children expelled from school, their property vandalized, and themselves victims of mob violence. The second was an elite assault on the Supreme Court. Prominent jurists and journalists excoriated the justices for failing to declare a constitutional right to refrain from saluting the flag. Two years after* Gobitis *was decided Justices Hugo Black, William O. Douglas, and Frank Murphy publicly confessed error in* Jones v. Opelika *(1942), writing, "We think this is an appropriate occasion to state that we now believe [*Gobitis*] was wrong decided" and "our democratic form of government . . . has a high responsibility to accommodate itself to the religious views of minorities." The two justices appointed to the Supreme Court between 1940 and 1943, Robert Jackson and Wiley Rutledge, were chosen for the bench in part because they supported the civil rights and liberties of Jehovah's Witnesses.*

Federal officials may have implicitly overruled Gobitis *legislatively or by executive degree before the justices decided* Barnette. *Disturbed that the existing pledge of allegiance ceremony bore too close a resemblance to the Nazi salute, Congress in 1942 passed a new law regulating public displays of loyalty. One provision in the bill stated, "Citizens will always show full respect to the flag when the pledge is given merely by standing at attention." The executive branch interpreted this law as preempting all state and local decrees requiring students to salute the flag and recite the Pledge of Allegiance. "State and local regulations demanding a different standard of performance," Justice Department lawyers declared, "must give way entirely, or at least be made to conform." After 1942 Roosevelt administration officials mandated that "a school board order respecting flag salute exercises should not now be permitted to exact more of the pupil with religious scruples against the flag salute than that he should stand at attention while the exercise is being conducted."*[41]

The Supreme Court in Barnette *formally overruled* Gobitis *by a 6–3 vote. Justice Jackson's majority opinion held that persons could not be constitutionally compelled to salute the flag. What explains this support for free speech rights? Jehovah's Witnesses were not a politically powerful group. Did the Jewish and Catholic members of the New Deal coalition believe that strong protections for the speech and religious rights of other religious minorities would establish precedents that would protect them in the future? Did New Dealers value free speech and religious freedom even though they believed it unlikely that their religious freedom or speech rights would be threatened in the future? Justice Jackson's opinion in* Barnette *famously declares, "One's right to life, liberty, and property, to free speech, a free press, freedom of worship and assembly, and other fundamental rights may not be submitted to vote; they depend on the outcome of no elections." Is this correct? Suppose that Woodrow Wilson (or Abraham Lincoln) had been president in 1940 and had previously appointed a majority of the sitting Supreme Court justices. Would the Court have produced the same result? Is Justice Frankfurter right that judicial officials in a democracy should not second-guess decisions made by elected officials? Is Justice Jackson correct when he maintains that justices in a democracy must prevent political coercion by elected officials?*

41. This introduction relies heavily on Shawn Francis Peters, *Judging Jehovah's Witnesses: Religious Persecution and the Dawn of the Rights Revolution* (Lawrence: University Press of Kansas, 2000).

Illustration 8-5 Elementary School Children Saluting the Flag, March 1943

Elementary school children starting the day by saluting the flag, March 1943, Rochester, New York. The hand-over-heart pledge style in the United States was not standardized until after World War II.

Source: Library of Congress Prints and Photographs Division Washington, D.C. 20540.

JUSTICE JACKSON delivered the opinion of the Court.

. . .

. . . [C]ensorship or suppression of expression of opinion is tolerated by our Constitution only when the expression presents a clear and present danger of action of a kind the State is empowered to prevent and punish. It would seem that involuntary affirmation could be commanded only on even more immediate and urgent grounds than silence. But here the power of compulsion is invoked without any allegation that remaining passive during a flag salute ritual creates a clear and present danger that would justify an effort even to muffle expression. To sustain the compulsory flag salute we are required to say that a Bill of Rights which guards the individual's right to speak his own mind, left it open to public authorities to compel him to utter what is not in his mind.

. . .

The very purpose of a Bill of Rights was to withdraw certain subjects from the vicissitudes of political controversy, to place them beyond the reach of majorities and officials and to establish them as legal principles to be applied by the courts. One's right to life, liberty, and property, to free speech, a free press, freedom of worship and assembly, and other fundamental rights may not be submitted to vote; they depend on the outcome of no elections. . . . The right of a State to regulate, for example, a public utility may well include, so far as the due process test is concerned, power to impose all of the restrictions which a legislature may have a "rational basis" for adopting. But freedoms of speech and of press, of assembly, and of worship may not be infringed on such slender grounds. They are susceptible of restriction only to prevent grave and immediate danger to interests which the state may lawfully protect. . . .

. . .

Struggles to coerce uniformity of sentiment in support of some end thought essential to their time and country have been waged by many good as well as by evil men. Nationalism is a relatively recent phenomenon but at other times and places the ends have been racial or territorial security, support of a dynasty or regime, and particular plans for saving souls. As first and moderate methods to attain unity have failed, those bent on its accomplishment must resort to an ever-increasing severity. As governmental pressure toward unity becomes greater, so strife becomes more bitter as to whose unity it shall be. Probably no deeper division of our people could proceed from any provocation than from finding it necessary to choose what doctrine and whose program public educational officials shall compel youth to unite in embracing. Ultimate futility of such attempts to compel coherence is the lesson of every such effort from the Roman drive to stamp out Christianity as a disturber of its pagan unity, the Inquisition, as a means to religious and dynastic unity, the Siberian exiles as a means to Russian unity, down to the fast failing efforts of our present totalitarian enemies. Those who begin coercive elimination of dissent soon find themselves exterminating dissenters. Compulsory unification of opinion achieves only the unanimity of the graveyard.

. . .

The case is made difficult not because the principles of its decision are obscure but because the flag involved is our own. Nevertheless, we apply the limitations of the Constitution with no fear that freedom to be intellectually and spiritually diverse or even contrary will disintegrate the social organization. To believe that patriotism will not flourish if patriotic ceremonies are voluntary and spontaneous instead of a compulsory routine is to make an unflattering estimate of the appeal of our institutions to free minds. We can have intellectual individualism and the rich cultural diversities that we owe to exceptional minds only at the price of occasional eccentricity and abnormal attitudes. When they are so harmless to others or to the State as those we deal with here, the price is not too great. But freedom to differ is not limited to things that do not matter much. That would be a mere shadow of freedom. The test of its substance is the right to differ as to things that touch the heart of the existing order.

If there is any fixed star in our constitutional constellation, it is that no official, high or petty, can prescribe what shall be orthodox in politics, nationalism, religion, or other matters of opinion or force citizens to confess by word or act their faith therein. If there are any circumstances which permit an exception, they do not now occur to us.

. . .

The decision of this Court in *Minersville School District v. Gobitis* (1940) [is] overruled.

JUSTICE ROBERTS and JUSTICE REED adhere to the views expressed by the Court in *Minersville School District v. Gobitis*. . . .

JUSTICE BLACK and JUSTICE DOUGLAS, concurring. . . .

JUSTICE MURPHY, concurring. . . .

JUSTICE FRANKFURTER, dissenting.

One who belongs to the most vilified and persecuted minority in history[42] is not likely to be insensible to the freedoms guaranteed by our Constitution. Were my purely personal attitude relevant I should wholeheartedly associate myself with the general libertarian views in the Court's opinion, representing as they do the thought and action of a lifetime. But as judges we are neither Jew nor Gentile, neither Catholic nor agnostic. We owe equal attachment to the Constitution and are equally bound by our judicial obligations whether we derive our citizenship from the earliest or the latest immigrants to these shores. As a member of this Court I am not justified in writing my private notions of policy into the Constitution, no matter how deeply I may cherish them or how mischievous I may deem their disregard. The duty of a judge who must decide which of two claims before the Court shall prevail, that of a State to enact and enforce laws within its general competence or that of an individual to refuse obedience because of the demands of his conscience, is not that of the ordinary person. It can never be emphasized too much that one's own opinion about the wisdom or evil of a law should be excluded altogether when one is doing one's duty on the bench. The only

42. Justice Frankfurter was Jewish.

opinion of our own even looking in that direction that is material is our opinion whether legislators could in reason have enacted such a law. In the light of all the circumstances, including the history of this question in this Court, it would require more daring than I possess to deny that reasonable legislators could have taken the action which is before us for review. . . . I cannot bring my mind to believe that the "liberty" secured by the Due Process Clause gives this Court authority to deny to the State of West Virginia the attainment of that which we all recognize as a legitimate legislative end, namely, the promotion of good citizenship, by employment of the means here chosen.

. . .

. . . The Constitution does not give us greater veto power when dealing with one phase of "liberty" than with another. . . . Our power does not vary according to the particular provision of the Bill of Rights which is invoked. The right not to have property taken without just compensation has, so far as the scope of judicial power is concerned, the same constitutional dignity as the right to be protected against unreasonable searches and seizures, and the latter has no less claim than freedom of the press or freedom of speech or religious freedom. . . .

. . .

We are told that a flag salute is a doubtful substitute for adequate understanding of our institutions. The states that require such a school exercise do not have to justify it as the only means for promoting good citizenship in children, but merely as one of diverse means for accomplishing a worthy end. We may deem it a foolish measure, but the point is that this Court is not the organ of government to resolve doubts as to whether it will fulfill its purpose. Only if there be no doubt that any reasonable mind could entertain can we deny to the states the right to resolve doubts their way and not ours.

. . .

One's conception of the Constitution cannot be severed from one's conception of a judge's function in applying it. The Court has no reason for existence if it merely reflects the pressures of the day. Our system is built on the faith that men set apart for this special function, freed from the influences of immediacy and from the deflections of worldly ambition, will become able to take a view of longer range than the period of responsibility entrusted to Congress and legislatures. We are dealing with matters as to which legislators and voters have conflicting views. Are we as judges to impose our strong convictions on where wisdom lies? That which three years ago had seemed to five successive Courts to lie within permissible areas of legislation is now outlawed by the deciding shift of opinion of two Justices. What reason is there to believe that they or their successors may not have another view a few years hence? . . . Of course, judicial opinions, even as to questions of constitutionality, are not immutable. As has been true in the past, the Court will from time to time reverse its position. But I believe that never before these Jehovah's Witnesses cases (except for minor deviations subsequently retraced) has this Court overruled decisions so as to restrict the powers of democratic government. Always heretofore, it has withdrawn narrow views of legislative authority so as to authorize what formerly it had denied.

. . .

Of course patriotism cannot be enforced by the flag salute. But neither can the liberal spirit be enforced by judicial invalidation of illiberal legislation. Our constant preoccupation with the constitutionality of legislation rather than with its wisdom tends to preoccupation of the American mind with a false value. The tendency of focusing attention on constitutionality is to make constitutionality synonymous with wisdom, to regard a law as all right if it is constitutional. Such an attitude is a great enemy of liberalism. Particularly in legislation affecting freedom of thought and freedom of speech much which should offend a free-spirited society is constitutional. Reliance for the most precious interests of civilization, therefore, must be found outside of their vindication in courts of law. Only a persistent positive translation of the faith of a free society into the convictions and habits and actions of a community is the ultimate reliance against unabated temptations to fetter the human spirit.

Dennis v. United States, 341 U.S. 494 (1951)

Eugene Dennis was the general secretary of the American Communist Party. In 1948 he and ten other party leaders were indicted for violating the Smith Act of 1940. They were charged with a conspiracy to "organize as the Communist Party of the United States, a society, group, and assembly of persons who teach and advocate the overthrow and destruction of the Government of the United States by force and violence, and knowingly and willfully to advocate and teach the duty and necessity of overthrowing and destroying the Government of the United States." After a trial marked by dubious behavior on the part of counsel for both sides and of the trial judge, Dennis and nine of his peers were sentenced to five years in prison. (Every lawyer on the defense team was cited for contempt.) After Dennis's appeal was denied by the Court of Appeals for the District of Columbia Circuit he appealed to the Supreme Court of the United States.

The Supreme Court ruled by a 7–2 vote that Dennis had been constitutionally convicted. Chief Justice Vinson's plurality opinion claimed that Dennis's activities presented a "clear and present danger." How do the various judicial opinions in Dennis *interpret the clear and present danger test? Which interpretation of the test do you believe is correct? Was Justice Jackson correct to note that the clear and present danger test is best applied to isolated speakers and that Communist Party leaders are best understood as criminal conspirators? Was Justice Douglas correct that the only conspiracy that had occurred was an effort to persuade Americans to believe something? What evidence would you require before convicting the defendants in this case?*

CHIEF JUSTICE VINSON announced the judgment of the Court and an opinion in which JUSTICE REED, JUSTICE BURTON and JUSTICE MINTON join.

. . .

That it is within the power of the Congress to protect the Government of the United States from armed rebellion is a proposition which requires little discussion. Whatever theoretical merit there may be to the argument that there is a "right" to rebellion against dictatorial governments is without force where the existing structure of the government provides for peaceful and orderly change. We reject any principle of governmental helplessness in the face of preparation for revolution, which principle, carried to its logical conclusion, must lead to anarchy. No one could conceive that it is not within the power of Congress to prohibit acts intended to overthrow the Government by force and violence. The question with which we are concerned here is not whether Congress has such power, but whether the means which it has employed conflict with the First . . . Amendment . . . to the Constitution.

. . .

The . . . Smith Act . . . is directed at advocacy, not discussion. Thus, the trial judge properly charged the jury that they could not convict if they found that petitioners did "no more than pursue peaceful studies and discussions or teaching and advocacy in the realm of ideas." . . . Congress did not intend to eradicate the free discussion of political theories, to destroy the traditional rights of Americans to discuss and evaluate ideas without fear of governmental sanction. Rather Congress was concerned with the very kind of activity in which the evidence showed these petitioners engaged.

. . .

Although no case subsequent to *Whitney* [*v. California* (1927)] and *Gitlow* [*v. New York* (1925)] has expressly overruled the majority opinions in those cases, there is little doubt that subsequent opinions have inclined toward the Holmes-Brandeis rationale. . . . But . . . neither Justice Holmes nor Justice Brandeis ever envisioned that a shorthand phrase ["clear and present danger"] should be crystallized into a rigid rule to be applied inflexibly without regard to the circumstances of each case. Speech is not an absolute, above and beyond control by the legislature when its judgment, subject to review here, is that certain kinds of speech are so undesirable as to warrant criminal sanction. Nothing is more certain in modern society than the principle that there are no absolutes, that a name, a phrase, a standard has meaning only when associated with the considerations which gave birth to the nomenclature. . . . To those who would paralyze our Government in the face of impending threat by encasing it in a semantic straitjacket we must reply that all concepts are relative.

. . .

Obviously, the words cannot mean that before the Government may act, it must wait until the putsch is about to be executed, the plans have been laid and the signal is awaited. If Government is aware that a group aiming at its overthrow is attempting to indoctrinate its members and to commit them to a course whereby they will strike when the leaders feel the circumstances permit, action by the Government is required. The argument that there is no need for Government to concern itself, for Government is strong, it possesses ample powers to put down a rebellion, it may defeat the revolution with ease needs no answer. . . . Certainly an attempt to overthrow the Government by force, even though doomed from the outset because of inadequate numbers of power of the revolutionists, is a sufficient evil for Congress to prevent. The damage which such attempts create both physically and politically to a nation makes it impossible to measure the validity in terms of the probability of success, or the immediacy of a successful attempt. . . .

The situation with which Justices Holmes and Brandeis were concerned in *Gitlow* was a comparatively isolated event, bearing little relation in their minds to any substantial threat to the safety of the community. . . They were not confronted with any situation comparable to the instant one—the development of an apparatus designed and dedicated to the overthrow of the Government, in the context of world crisis after crisis.

Chief Judge Learned Hand, writing for the majority below, interpreted the phrase as follows: "In each case [courts] must ask whether the gravity of the 'evil,' discounted by its improbability, justifies such invasion of free speech as is necessary to avoid the danger." . . . We adopt this statement of the rule. As articulated by Chief Judge Hand, it is as succinct and inclusive as any other we might devise at this time. It takes into consideration those factors which we deem relevant, and relates their significances. More we cannot expect from words.

. . .

. . . Petitioners intended to overthrow the Government of the United States as speedily as the circumstances would permit. Their conspiracy to organize the Communist Party and to teach and advocate the overthrow of the Government of the United States by force and violence created a "clear and present danger" of an attempt to overthrow the Government by force and violence. They were properly and constitutionally convicted for violation of the Smith Act. . . .

JUSTICE CLARK took no part in the consideration or decision of this case.

JUSTICE FRANKFURTER, concurring in affirmance of the judgment.

. . .

. . . The demands of free speech in a democratic society as well as the interest in national security are better served by candid and informed weighing of the competing interests, within the confines of the judicial process, than by announcing dogmas too inflexible for the non-Euclidian problems to be solved.

But how are competing interests to be assessed? Since they are not subject to quantitative ascertainment, the issue necessarily resolves itself into asking, who is to make the adjustment?—who is to balance the relevant factors and ascertain which interest is in the circumstances to prevail? Full responsibility for the choice cannot be given to the courts. Courts are not representative bodies. They are not designed to be a good reflex of a democratic society. Their judgment is best informed, and therefore most dependable, within narrow limits. Their essential quality is detachment, founded on independence. History teaches that the independence of the judiciary is jeopardized when courts become embroiled in the passions of the day and assume primary responsibility in choosing between competing political, economic and social pressures.

Primary responsibility for adjusting the interests which compete in the situation before us of necessity belongs to the Congress. . . . We are to set aside the judgment of those whose duty it is to legislate only if there is no reasonable basis for it.

. . .

On the one hand is the interest in security. The Communist Party was not designed by these defendants as an ordinary political party. . . . The jury found that the Party rejects the basic premise of our political system—that change is to be brought about by nonviolent constitutional process. The jury found that the Party advocates the theory that there is a duty and necessity to overthrow the Government by force and violence. It found that the Party entertains and promotes this view, not as a prophetic insight or as a bit of unworldly speculation, but as a program for winning adherents and as a policy to be translated into action.

. . . [I]n determining whether application of the statute to the defendants is within the constitutional powers of Congress, we are not limited to the facts found by the jury. . . . We may take judicial notice that the Communist doctrines which these defendants have conspired to advocate are in the ascendency in powerful nations who cannot be acquitted of unfriendliness to the institutions of this country. . . . In sum, it would amply justify a legislature in concluding that recruitment of additional members for the Party would create a substantial danger to national security.

On the other hand is the interest in free speech. The right to exert all governmental powers in aid of maintaining our institutions and resisting their physical overthrow does not include intolerance of opinions and speech that cannot do harm although opposed and perhaps alien to dominant, traditional opinion. . . .

. . . No matter how clear we may be that the defendants now before us are preparing to overthrow our Government at the propitious moment, it is self-delusion to think that we can punish them for their advocacy without adding to the risks run by loyal citizens who honestly believe in some of the reforms these defendants advance. It is a sobering fact that in sustaining the convictions before us we can hardly escape restriction on the interchange of ideas.

. . .

It is not for us to decide how we would adjust the clash of interests which this case presents were the primary responsibility for reconciling it ours. Congress has determined that the danger created by advocacy of overthrow justifies the ensuing restriction on freedom of speech. The determination was made after due deliberation, and the seriousness of the congressional purpose is attested by the volume of legislation passed to effectuate the same ends.

Civil liberties draw at best only limited strength from legal guaranties. Preoccupation by our people with the constitutionality, instead of with the wisdom, of legislation or of executive action is preoccupation with a false value. . . Focusing attention on constitutionality tends to make constitutionality synonymous with wisdom. When legislation touches freedom of thought and freedom of speech, such a tendency is a formidable enemy of the free spirit. Much that should be rejected as illiberal, because repressive and envenoming, may well be not unconstitutional. The ultimate reliance for the deepest needs of civilization must be found outside their vindication in courts of law; apart from all else, judges, howsoever they may conscientiously seek to discipline themselves against it, unconsciously are too apt to be moved by the deep undercurrents of public feeling. A persistent, positive translation of the liberating faith into the feelings and thoughts and actions of men and women is the real protection against attempts to strait-jacket the human mind. Such temptations will have their way, if fear and hatred are not exorcized. The mark of a truly civilized man is confidence in the strength and security derived from the inquiring mind. We may be grateful for such honest comforts as it supports, but we must be unafraid of its incertitudes. Without open minds there can be no open society. And if society be not open the spirit of man is mutilated and becomes enslaved.

JUSTICE JACKSON, concurring.

. . .

I would save ["clear and present danger"], unmodified, for application as a "rule of reason" in the kind of case for which it was devised. When the issue is criminality of a hot-headed speech on a street corner, or circulation of a few incendiary pamphlets, or parading by some zealots behind a red flag, or refusal of a handful of school children to salute our flag, it is not beyond the capacity of the judicial process to gather, comprehend, and weigh the necessary materials for decision whether it is a clear and present danger of substantive evil or a harmless letting off of steam. It is not a prophecy, for the danger in such cases has matured by the time of trial or it was never present. . . . The formula in such cases favors freedoms that are vital to our society, and, even if sometimes applied too generously, the consequences cannot be grave. But its recent expansion has extended, in particular to Communists, unprecedented immunities. Unless we are to hold our Government captive in a judge-made verbal trap, we must approach the problem of a well-organized, nation-wide conspiracy, such as I have described, as realistically as our predecessors faced the trivialities that were being prosecuted until they were checked with a rule of reason.

. . .

The authors of the clear and present danger test never applied it to a case like this, nor would I. If applied as it is proposed here, it means that the Communist plotting is protected during its period of incubation; its preliminary stages of organization and preparation are immune from the law; the Government can move only after imminent action is manifest, when it would, of course, be too late.

. . .

JUSTICE BLACK, dissenting.

. . .

. . . [T]he only way to affirm these convictions is to repudiate directly or indirectly the established "clear and present danger" rule. . . . The opinions for affirmance indicate that the chief reason for jettisoning the rule is the expressed fear that advocacy of Communist doctrine endangers the safety of the Republic. Undoubtedly, a governmental policy of unfettered communication of ideas does entail dangers. To the Founders of this Nation, however, the benefits derived from free expression were worth the risk. . . . I have always believed that the First Amendment is the keystone of our Government, that the freedoms it guarantees provide the best insurance against destruction of all freedom. At least as to speech in the realm of public matters, I believe that the "clear and present danger" test does not "mark the furthermost constitutional boundaries of protected expression" but does "no more than recognize a minimum compulsion of the Bill of Rights."

So long as this Court exercises the power of judicial review of legislation, I cannot agree that the First Amendment permits us to sustain laws suppressing freedom of speech and press on the basis of Congress' or our own notions of mere "reasonableness." Such a doctrine waters down the First Amendment so that it amounts to little more than an admonition to Congress. The Amendment as so construed is not likely to protect any but those "safe" or orthodox views which rarely need its protection. . . .

. . .

JUSTICE DOUGLAS, dissenting.

. . .

. . . Free speech has occupied an exalted position because of the high service it has given our society. Its protection is essential to the very existence of a democracy. The airing of ideas releases pressures which otherwise might become destructive. When ideas compete in the market for acceptance, full and free discussion exposes the false and they gain few adherents. Full and free discussion even of ideas we hate encourages the testing of our own prejudices and preconceptions. Full and free discussion keeps a society from becoming stagnant and unprepared for the stresses and strains that work to tear all civilizations apart.

. . .

There comes a time when even speech loses its constitutional immunity. Speech innocuous one year may at another time fan such destructive flames that it must be halted in the interests of the safety of the Republic. That is the meaning of the clear and present danger test. When conditions are so critical that there will be no time to avoid the evil that the speech threatens, it is time to call a halt. Otherwise, free speech which is the strength of the Nation will be the cause of its destruction.

Yet free speech is the rule, not the exception. The restraint to be constitutional must be based on more than fear, on more than passionate opposition against the speech, on more than a revolted dislike for its contents. There must be some immediate injury to society that is likely if speech is allowed.

. . .

. . . If we are to take judicial notice of the threat of Communists within the nation, it should not be difficult to conclude that as a political party they are of little consequence. Communists in this country have never made a respectable or serious showing in any election. I would doubt that there is a village, let alone a city or county or state, which the Communists could carry. Communism in the world scene is no bogeyman; but Communism as a political faction or party in this country plainly is. Communism has been so thoroughly exposed in this country that it has been crippled as a political force. Free speech has destroyed it as an effective political party. . . .

How it can be said that there is a clear and present danger that this advocacy will succeed is, therefore, a mystery. . . . [I]n America they are miserable merchants of unwanted ideas; their wares remain unsold. The fact that their ideas are abhorrent does not make them powerful.

New York Times Co. v. Sullivan, 376 U.S. 254 (1964)

The New York Times *on March 29, 1960, published a full-page advertisement sponsored by the Committee to Defend Martin Luther King and the Struggle for Freedom in the South. Under the heading "Heed Their Rising Voices," the advertisement described the nonviolent struggle of civil rights activists and the often-violent responses of southern police officers to their protests. Harry Belafonte, Nat King Cole, Sammy Davis, Jr., Mahalia Jackson, John Lewis, Sidney Poitier, A. Philip Randolph, Jackie Robinson, and Eleanor Roosevelt were among the notables who signed the call for financial help. L. B. Sullivan, a city commissioner of Montgomery, Alabama, accurately claimed that the advertisement made several false statements about his conduct during several civil rights protests—for example, contrary to the claim made in the* Times, *Sullivan did not padlock the dining hall at Alabama State College in order to starve students into abandoning civil rights protests. Sullivan wrote a letter to the* Times *demanding that the false statements be retracted. When the* Times *refused Sullivan sued the newspaper and four Alabama ministers for libel. Other Alabama officials similarly sued the* Times, *the four ministers, and Martin Luther King, Jr., for libel on the basis of the statements made in the advertisement. The total damages asked for were $3 million, more than enough to bankrupt crucial civil rights organizations and seriously curtail newspaper coverage of the civil rights movement. An Alabama trial court awarded Sullivan $500,000 in damages, the highest libel award in the history of the state. The Supreme Court of Alabama sustained that appeal, and the New York Times appealed to the Supreme Court of the United States.*[43]

The Supreme Court unanimously overturned the Alabama decision. Justice Brennan's majority opinion declared that public officials could receive damages for libel only if the jury found actual malice. In law, "actual malice" means that the speech was false and that the speaker either knew the speech was false or recklessly disregarded the truth. Consider whether New York Times v. Sullivan *was a free speech case or a civil rights case. Suppose that Martin Luther King, Jr., had won a $500,000 verdict in a New York court against an Alabama newspaper. Would the Supreme Court have issued the same ruling?* New York Times v. Sullivan *has been hailed as a great victory for freedom of the press and condemned as a license for sloppy reporting. Which assessment do you believe is correct? Does the actual malice standard chill a good deal of reporting, given that many small entrepreneurs cannot afford to fight an expensive lawsuit? Does the same standard give too much immunity to press magnates with large pockets? Is there any viable way to protect against vexatious lawsuits while promoting ethical journalism? Does the First Amendment have anything in particular to say about that subject?*

JUSTICE BRENNAN delivered the opinion of the Court.

. . .

. . . [W]e consider this case against the background of a profound national commitment to the principle that debate on public issues should be uninhibited, robust, and wide-open, and that it may well include vehement, caustic, and sometimes unpleasantly sharp attacks on government and public officials. . . . The present advertisement, as an expression of grievance and protest on one of the major public issues of our time, would seem clearly to qualify for the constitutional protection. The question is whether it forfeits that protection by the falsity of some of its factual statements and by its alleged defamation of respondent.

Authoritative interpretations of the First Amendment guarantees have consistently refused to recognize an exception for any test of truth—whether administered by judges, juries, or administrative officials—and especially one that puts the burden of proving truth on the speaker. . . . As Madison said, "Some degree of abuse is inseparable from the proper use of every thing; and in no instance is this more true than in that of the press." . . .

. . . [E]rroneous statement is inevitable in free debate, and . . . must be protected if the freedoms of expression are to have the "breathing space" that they "need . . . to survive." . . .

Injury to official reputation affords no more warrant for repressing speech that would otherwise be free than does factual error. . . . Criticism of their official conduct does not lose its constitutional protection merely because it is effective criticism and hence diminishes their official reputations.

If neither factual error nor defamatory content suffices to remove the constitutional shield from criticism of official conduct, the combination of the two elements is no less inadequate. This is the lesson to be drawn from the great controversy over the Sedition Act of 1798, . . . which first crystallized a national awareness of the central meaning of the First Amendment. . . . The Act allowed the defendant the defense of truth, and provided that the jury were to be judges both of the law and the facts. Despite these qualifications, the Act was vigorously condemned as unconstitutional in an attack joined in by Jefferson and Madison. . . . [Madison's] premise was that the Constitution created a form of government under which "The people, not the government, possess the absolute sovereignty." The structure of the government dispersed power in reflection of the people's distrust of concentrated power, and of power itself at all levels. This form of government was "altogether different" from the British form, under which the Crown was sovereign and the people were subjects. "Is it not natural and necessary, under such different circumstances," he asked, "that a different degree of freedom in the use of the press should be contemplated?" . . .

Although the Sedition Act was never tested in this Court, the attack upon its validity has carried the day in the court of history. Fines levied in its prosecution were repaid by Act of Congress on the ground that it

43. For a complete history, see Anthony Lewis, *Make No Law: The* Sullivan *Case and the First Amendment* (New York: Vintage, 1992).

was unconstitutional. . . . Calhoun, reporting to the Senate on February 4, 1836, assumed that its invalidity was a matter "which no one now doubts." . . . Jefferson, as President, pardoned those who had been convicted and sentenced under the Act and remitted their fines. . . .

. . .

A rule compelling the critic of official conduct to guarantee the truth of all his factual assertions—and to do so on pain of libel judgments virtually unlimited in amount—leads to . . . "self-censorship." Allowance of the defense of truth, with the burden of proving it on the defendant, does not mean that only false speech will be deterred. . . . Under such a rule, would-be critics of official conduct may be deterred from voicing their criticism, even though it is believed to be true and even though it is in fact true, because of doubt whether it can be proved in court or fear of the expense of having to do so. . . .

The constitutional guarantees require, we think, a federal rule that prohibits a public official from recovering damages for a defamatory falsehood relating to his official conduct unless he proves that the statement was made with "actual malice"—that is, with knowledge that it was false or with reckless disregard of whether it was false or not.

. . .

JUSTICE BLACK, with whom JUSTICE DOUGLAS joins, concurring.

. . . I base my vote to reverse on the belief that the First and Fourteenth Amendments not merely "delimit" a State's power to award damages to "public officials against critics of their official conduct" but completely prohibit a State from exercising such a power. The Court goes on to hold that a State can subject such critics to damages if "actual malice" can be proved against them. "Malice," even as defined by the Court, is an elusive, abstract concept, hard to prove and hard to disprove. The requirement that malice be proved provides at best an evanescent protection for the right critically to discuss public affairs and certainly does not measure up to the sturdy safeguard embodied in the First Amendment. . . .

. . .

. . . To punish the exercise of this right to discuss public affairs or to penalize it through libel judgments is to abridge or shut off discussion of the very kind most needed. This Nation, I suspect, can live in peace without libel suits based on public discussions of public affairs and public officials. But I doubt that a country can live in freedom where its people can be made to suffer physically or financially for criticizing their government, its actions, or its officials. . . . An unconditional right to say what one pleases about public affairs is what I consider to be the minimum guarantee of the First Amendment.

. . .

JUSTICE GOLDBERG, with whom JUSTICE DOUGLAS joins, concurring in the result.

. . .

In my view, the First and Fourteenth Amendments to the Constitution afford to the citizen and to the press an absolute, unconditional privilege to criticize official conduct despite the harm which may flow from excesses and abuses. . . . The right should not depend upon a probing by the jury of the motivation of the citizen or press. The theory of our Constitution is that every citizen may speak his mind and every newspaper express its view on matters of public concern and may not be barred from speaking or publishing because those in control of government think that what is said or written is unwise, unfair, false, or malicious. In a democratic society, one who assumes to act for the citizens in an executive, legislative, or judicial capacity must expect that his official acts will be commented upon and criticized. Such criticism cannot, in my opinion, be muzzled or deterred by the courts at the instance of public officials under the label of libel.

. . .

The conclusion that the Constitution affords the citizen and the press an absolute privilege for criticism of official conduct does not leave the public official without defenses against unsubstantiated opinions or deliberate misstatements. . . . The public official certainly has equal if not greater access than most private citizens to media of communication. In any event, despite the possibility that some excesses and abuses may go unremedied, we must recognize that "the people of this nation have ordained in the light of history, that, in spite of the probability of excesses and abuses, [certain] liberties are, in the long view, essential to enlightened opinion and right conduct on the part of the citizens of a democracy." . . .

Brandenburg v. Ohio, 395 U.S. 444 (1969)

Clarence Brandenburg was a leader of a local Ku Klux Klan affiliate in Ohio. During a speech at a rally Brandenburg asserted,

> *The Klan has more members in the State of Ohio than does any other organization. We're not a revengent organization, but if our President, our Congress, our Supreme Court, continues to suppress the white, Caucasian race, it's possible that there might have to be some revengeance taken.*

For these and similar comments Brandenburg was convicted under an Ohio law that forbade "advocat[ing] . . . the duty, necessity, or propriety of crime, sabotage, violence, or unlawful methods of terrorism as a means of accomplishing industrial or political reform." The Supreme Court of Ohio sustained his conviction. Brandenburg appealed to the Supreme Court of the United States.

A unanimous Supreme Court reversed. The per curiam decision insisted that speakers may be convicted only if their words incited imminent illegal conduct. No justice made a distinction between advocacy of racial or ethnic hatred and advocacy of communist revolution. Does this demonstrate a principled commitment to the freedom of speech or a failure to make constitutionally relevant distinctions? The justices claimed that the decision in Whitney v. California *(1927) had been discredited in* Dennis v. United States *(1951). Is this accurate? Is the constitutional standard used in* Dennis *more consistent with* Whitney *than the constitutional standard used in* Brandenberg*? Justice Brandeis in his* Whitney *concurrence insisted that only serious evils justified restricting free speech. Does* Brandenbug *adopt this element of the Brandeis concurrence?*

PER CURIAM.

. . .

The Ohio Criminal Syndicalism Statute was enacted in 1919. From 1917 to 1920, identical or quite similar laws were adopted by 20 States and two territories. . . . In 1927, this Court sustained the constitutionality of California's Criminal Syndicalism Act, . . . the text of which is quite similar to that of the laws of Ohio. *Whitney v. California* (1927). . . . The Court upheld the statute on the ground that, without more, "advocating" violent means to effect political and economic change involves such danger to the security of the State that the State may outlaw it. But *Whitney* has been thoroughly discredited by later decisions. See *Dennis v. United States* (1951). . . . These later decisions have fashioned the principle that the constitutional guarantees of free speech and free press do not permit a State to forbid or proscribe advocacy of the use of force or of law violation except where such advocacy is directed to inciting or producing imminent lawless action and is likely to incite or produce such action. . . . A statute which fails to draw this distinction impermissibly intrudes upon the freedoms guaranteed by the First and Fourteenth Amendments. It sweeps within its condemnation speech which our Constitution has immunized from governmental control. . . .

Measured by this test, Ohio's Criminal Syndicalism Act cannot be sustained. The Act punishes persons who "advocate or teach the duty, necessity, or propriety" of violence "as a means of accomplishing industrial or political reform"; or who publish or circulate or display any book or paper containing such advocacy; or who "justify" the commission of violent acts "with intent to exemplify, spread or advocate the propriety of the doctrines of criminal syndicalism"; or who "voluntarily assemble" with a group formed "to teach or advocate the doctrines of criminal syndicalism." Neither the indictment nor the trial judge's instructions to the jury in any way refined the statute's bald definition of the crime in terms of mere advocacy not distinguished from incitement to imminent lawless action.

. . . The contrary teaching of *Whitney v. California* . . . cannot be supported, and that decision is therefore overruled.

JUSTICE BLACK, concurring. . . .

JUSTICE DOUGLAS, concurring.

. . .

. . . I see no place in the regime of the First Amendment for any "clear and present danger" test, whether strict and tight as some would make it, or free-wheeling as the Court in *Dennis* rephrased it.

The line between what is permissible and not subject to control and what may be made impermissible and subject to regulation is the line between ideas and overt acts.

The example usually given by those who would punish speech is the case of one who falsely shouts fire in a crowded theatre.

This is, however, a classic case where speech is brigaded with action. . . . They are indeed inseparable and a prosecution can be launched for the overt acts actually caused. Apart from rare instances of that kind, speech is, I think, immune from prosecution. . . . The quality of advocacy turns on the depth of the conviction; and government has no power to invade that sanctuary of belief and conscience.

B. Voting

Voting became a fundamental constitutional right during the New Deal/Great Society Era. By 1969 general agreement existed in all three branches of the national government that neither the national nor a state government could deny a person a right to vote in a general election unless there was a compelling reason to do so. The justices in *Reynolds v. Sims* (1964) determined that all state and legislative districts were constitutionally required to be apportioned on the principle of one person, one vote. *Harper v. Virginia Board of Elections* (1966) declared poll taxes unconstitutional. Justice Douglas's majority opinion asserted, "Wealth, like race, creed, or color, is not germane to one's ability to participate intelligently in the electoral process. Lines drawn on the basis of wealth or property, like those of race . . . are traditionally disfavored." Equally as important, Congress passed and the federal government actively enforced legislation ensuring that persons of color, the most common targets of laws denying the ballot, could exercise their constitutional right to vote. For the first time in American history, Americans enjoyed near-universal adult suffrage.

The civil rights movement provided the impetus for the voting rights gains of the 1960s. Overwhelming majorities in both parties supported the Voting Rights Act of 1965. That measure outlawed all voting tests in districts in which less than half the adult population had voted in the 1964 presidential election. Congress required those districts to gain approval or preclearance from either a federal court in the District of Columbia or the attorney general before making any changes to their voting laws. Before 1965, when the NAACP or national government secured a judicial ruling declaring a state literacy test unconstitutional (after a decade or so of litigation), the offending state usually responded by either adopting a different literacy test or switching to an "understanding" test—thus setting off another round of litigation. After 1965 offending states could adopt new tests only with permission of the federal government. The Supreme

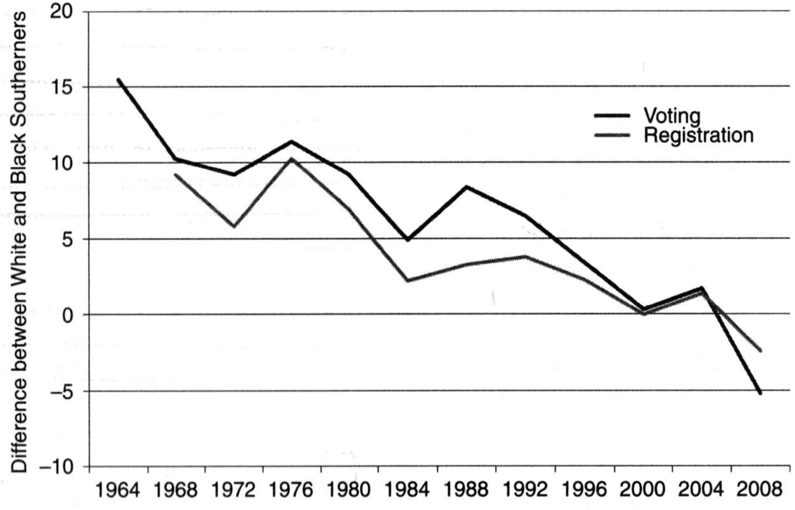

Figure 8-5 Difference between White and Black Southern Registration and Voting Rates, 1964–2008

Source: U.S. Census Bureau, Historical Current Population Survey Time Series Tables A-9 and A-10.

Note: Voting registration and voter turnout numbers based on self-reports from surveys administered by the U.S. Census for presidential elections.

Court in *South Carolina v. Katzenbach* (1966) had little difficulty finding all these provisions constitutional. "As against the reserved powers of the States," Chief Justice Warren stated, "Congress may use any rational means to effectuate the constitutional prohibition of racial discrimination in voting." The Supreme Court in *Katzenbach v. Morgan* (1966) ruled that Congress could also prohibit otherwise constitutional state laws when doing so might prevent or deter unconstitutional practices. Results were immediate. A sharp increase in African American voting and African American elected officials occurred almost immediately after the Voting Rights Act of 1965 became law and withstood judicial scrutiny.

Congressional Reports on the Voting Rights Act of 1965[44]

President Lyndon Johnson was determined to pass an effective voting rights bill. His State of the Union message on January 4, 1965, proposed that the nation "eliminate every remaining obstacle to the right and the opportunity to vote." Governor George Wallace of Alabama perversely contributed to national support for African American voting when his state troopers attacked a civil rights march in Selma on March 7. Buttressed by increased popular support, Justice Department officials drafted a bill with three crucial features. First, all literacy and other voting tests were suspended in all jurisdictions where less than 50 percent of the adult population had voted in the 1964 election. Second, federal officials were sent to those jurisdictions and given the power to register qualified voters. Third, those "covered" jurisdictions were permitted to make changes in the voting laws only if those changes were approved (precleared) by the Justice Department or the Court of Appeals for the District of Columbia.

The resulting congressional debate focused on poll taxes and the preclearance provision. Liberals attempted to add a ban on state and local poll taxes but settled for a provision that authorized the attorney general to challenge the constitutionality of such measures in court. Conservatives sought to limit the preclearance provisions. They were unsuccessful. In early August the House approved the Voting Rights Act by a 328–74 vote, and the Senate approved by a 79–18 vote. President Johnson signed the measure into law on August 6, 1965.

44. U.S. Senate, Senate Report 162, "Voting Rights Legislation," 89th Cong., 1st Sess., 1965, 2–26.

Majority Report

The bill as introduced and reported is primarily intended to enforce the 15th amendment to the Constitution of the United States. . . .

. . .

We all recognize the necessity to eradicate once and for all the chronic system of racial discrimination which has for so long excluded so many citizens from the electorate because of the color of their skins, contrary to the explicit command of the 15th amendment. . . .

. . .

Experience has shown that the case-by case litigation approach [adopted in the Civil Rights Acts of 1957, 1960, and 1964] will not solve the voting discrimination problem. The statistics alone are conclusive. In Alabama in 1964 only 19.4 percent of voting age Negroes were registered to vote, an increase of only 9.2 percent since 1958. In Mississippi approximately 6.4 percent of voting age Negroes were registered in 1964, compared to 4.4 percent 10 years earlier. And in Louisiana Negro registration appears to have increased only one-tenth of 1 percent between 1958 and 1965.

The inadequacy of existing laws is attributable to both the intransigence of local officials and dilatory tactics, two factors which have largely neutralized years of litigating effort by the Department of Justice. . . .

Dallas County, [Alabama,] with Selma as the county seat, has a voting-age population of approximately 29,500, of whom 14,500 are white persons and 15,000 are Negroes. In 1961, 9,195 of the whites—64 percent of the voting-age total—and 156 Negroes—1 percent of the total—were registered to vote in Dallas County.

On April 13, 1961, the Government filed a lawsuit against the county board of registrars under the Civil Rights Acts of 1957 and 1960. The district court and the court of appeals found that the registrars in office when the suit was filed had been engaging in a pattern and practice of discrimination against Negroes. But when the case came to trial 13 months later, those registrars had resigned and new ones had been appointed. Although there was proof of discrimination by prior registrars, including the misuse of the application form as a test, the court found that the present registrars were not discriminating and it declined to issue an injunction. . . .

. . .

Another example of the difference in treatment accorded whites and Negroes occurred in George County, Miss., where Negro college graduates were rejected while a white applicant [was accepted] who gave the following interpretation of a State constitutional provision that "there shall be no imprisonment for debt": "I think that a Neorger should have 2 years in college be fore voting be cause he don't understand." He also explained to the registrar's evident satisfaction that the duties and obligations of citizenship were "under Standing of pepper & Government ship blessing."

Often whites are not made to take the tests at all. . . .

. . .

. . . History has shown that the suspension of the tests and devices alone would not assure access of all persons to voting and registration without regard to race or color. The maladministration of tests and devices has been the major problem. Other tactics of discrimination, however, have been used and could readily be resorted to by State or local election officials where tests and devices have been suspended.

That this is so is demonstrated by two recent actions in Louisiana and Alabama. The registrars in East and West Feliciana Parishes were enjoined by the three-judge district court in *United States v. Louisiana* (1965) . . . from using various State literacy tests. Their response was to close the registration office thus freezing the unlawful registration disparity in those parishes. In Dallas County, Ala., the registrars . . . slowed down the pace of registration so as to prevent any appreciable number of Negroes, qualified or not, from completing the registration process. . . .

. . .

The proposed statute implements the explicit command of the 15th amendment that "the right . . . to vote shall not be denied or abridged . . . by any State on account of race [or] color."

. . .

The factual background is always relevant in assessing the constitutional "appropriateness" of legislation. . . .

There can be no doubt about the present need for Federal legislation to correct widespread violations of the 15th amendment. The prevailing conditions in those areas where the bill will operate offer ample justification for congressional action because there is little basis for supposing that [without] action, the States and subdivisions affected will themselves remedy the present situation in view of the history of the adoption and administration of the several tests and devices reached by the bill.

The choice of the means to solve a problem within the legitimate concern of the Congress is largely a legislative question. What the Supreme Court said in sustaining the constitutionality of the Civil Rights Act of 1964 is fully applicable:

> . . . where we find that the legislators, in light of the facts and testimony before them, have a rational basis for finding a chosen regulatory scheme necessary to the protection of commerce, our investigation is at an end. . . .

In enforcing the 15th amendment Congress may forbid the use of voter qualification laws where necessary to meet the risk of continued or renewed violations of constitutional rights even though, in the absence of the course of illegal conduct predicated upon the use of such tests, the same State laws might be unobjectionable.

Minority Report[45]

Statement of CHARLES J. BLOCH

. . .

The sole power given to Congress by [the 15th] amendment . . . is to *prevent* the United States or any State from denying certain people the right to vote on account of their race or color.

That amendment does not confer the right upon Congress to confer upon anyone the right to vote.

. . .

The theory of this bill and of the Attorney General is that if in the opinion of Congress a State imposes standards which are discriminatory, or applies legal standards (test and devices) discriminatorily, Congress may by statute divest that State of its constitutional powers of determining the conditions upon which the right of suffrage may be exercised; may substitute its own conditions, and may do all of that retroactively.

45. Rather than write a separate minority report, Senators Eastland, McClellan, and Ervin adopted statements made by the witnesses, attorneys Charles J. Bloch and Thomas H. Watkins, during the Senate hearings on the Voting Rights Act.

This Constitution gives the Congress no such power over any State of this Union, North or South, East or West, Republican or Democrat.

. . .

. . . [T]he United States of America would be divided into two groups—the good and the bad—if you please.

The "good" the 41 States and a portion of 2 others, could go on exercising their rights and freedoms, and enforcing their statutes.

The "bad"—seven and a portion of those two others—could not.

[*Bloch then discussed the conditions for becoming a "covered jurisdiction."*]

The dates are purely arbitrary.

The percentage used is equally arbitrary.

The events are purely arbitrary.

The supposed result from the facts determined is purely arbitrary.

. . .

The *New York Times* of March 18 editorially said of the "drafters" of this bill in the Justice Department:

> . . . In the six Southern States where less than half the voting population participated in the last presidential election, *presumption of past discrimination will be automatic, and no literacy or other qualifying test will be allowed to bar anyone from the ballot box in Federal, State, or local elections.*

That same Constitution which is held to guarantee freedom to the owners of the *New York Times* to make money by printing what they please, guarantees to every State of this Union, the people of every State of this Union,—including the "six Southern States"—the right to be free from this tyrannical provision sought to be imposed on the basis of "presumptions."

. . .

. . . [T]here are 416 counties or political subdivisions as to which the Attorney General says "voting discrimination has unquestionably been widespread."

In how many of these counties has the Department of Justice instituted suits in the last 8 years? In how many of these suits has the Court found a "pattern and practice" of discrimination authorizing the appointment of federal referees?

One of two states of facts is unquestionably true. There is no widespread discrimination forbidden by the 15th amendment, or the Department of Justice has, purposefully or neglectfully, been lax in the exercise of the processes at its disposal which would remedy such widespread discrimination if it in fact existed.

. . .

Statement of THOMAS WATKINS

. . .

In destroying the constitutional rights of Mississippi and other States to use literacy tests as a qualification of the privilege of voting, S. 1564 constitutes an undisguised frontal assault on the Constitution, as interpreted by the Supreme Court of the United States for more than 100 years. This bill flies squarely in the face of the same Constitution that every U.S. Senator has taken an oath to uphold.

The very first article of that Constitution authorizes the individual States to decide the qualifications of voters in both Federal and State elections, subject only to the proviso that whoever is deemed qualified to vote for "the most numerous branch of the State legislature" is automatically qualified to vote in Federal elections.

. . .

The 15th amendment did not give Congress the power to prohibit discrimination on grounds of education. This bill, in seeking to abolish literacy tests, does just that. . . .

It is clear that Congress and the States intended the 15th amendment to mean exactly what it said. The color of a man cannot be a reason to grant or deny him the right to vote. But all other qualifications are left entirely to the wisdom of the States.

. . .

The Attorney General states that the bill will deny the use of "onerous, vague, unfair tests and devices enacted for the purpose of disenfranchising Negroes." The bill, however, does not use this language. It prohibits the use of any literacy tests. If the bill prohibited onerous, vague, and unfair tests which tended to disenfranchise Negroes, it would be very much closer to the power granted Congress by the 15th amendment.

. . .

This act does not apply to all States or political subdivisions but is applicable only to a special class of States or political subdivisions. This classification violates the fifth amendment to the Constitution. The prohibition against denial of due process of law is, under this amendment, applicable to the United States. . . .

. . .

It is thoroughly established that any classification must rest always upon some difference, and *this difference must bear a reasonable and just relation to the purpose of the act in respect to which classification is proposed.*

The members of the class are determined by the Attorney General, based on findings of the Director of the Census, either: (1) That less than 50 percent of the persons of voting age residing therein were registered on November 1, 1964; *or* (2) that less than 50 percent of such persons voted in the presidential election of November 1964.

This classification is unrealistic, arbitrary, and unreasonable, as well as discriminatory. It does not pretend to prevent discriminatory use of tests except in approximately six States. Other States can have and use the tests as much as they please and yet not be within the class. . . .

. . .

. . . There is no such thing as a second-class State. Every State in this Union is equal to every other State and is guaranteed the rights and privileges enjoyed by every other State. . . .

. . .

The present emotionalism does not justify taking constitutional shortcuts. A desirable goal does not justify an unconstitutional means. If the accomplishments of this bill are desirable, let them be forthcoming in the only legal way—by constitutional amendment.

Katzenbach v. Morgan, 384 U.S. 641 (1966)

John P. Morgan and Christine Morgan were voters in New York who objected to a provision in the Voting Rights Act of 1965 that prohibited states from denying the vote to any person who had completed the sixth grade in Puerto Rico merely because that person could not read English. They filed a lawsuit in federal court asking for an injunction prohibiting the attorney general of the United States, Nicholas Katzenbach, from enforcing that provision. The local federal district court ruled that the provision was unconstitutional. The United States appealed to the Supreme Court.

A 7–2 judicial majority declared that Congress had acted constitutionally. Justice Brennan's majority opinion clearly held that Congress could prohibit otherwise constitutional laws when doing so might prevent unconstitutional action. Permitting Spanish speakers to vote, he observed, deter state officials from violating their equal protection rights. More controversially, Brennan's opinion suggested that Congress could interpret as well as enforce the post–Civil War Amendments—in other words, that Congress had the authority under Section 5 of the Fourteenth Amendment to determine whether the Constitution prohibited discrimination against non-English speakers. Did Justice Brennan make that claim? If so, is that claim correct?

Section 5 of the Fourteenth Amendment might permit Congress to exercise the following powers:

- *Provide remedies for judicially ascertained constitutional violations; for example, provide that victims of unconstitutional discrimination should receive $1,000 in damages*
- *Find the factual predicates of constitutional violations; for example, if the Supreme Court has said that literacy tests do not necessarily discriminate against persons of color, Congress may conclude after an investigation that such tests are in fact consistently applied in ways that intentionally discriminate against persons of color, and on that basis ban literacy tests*
- *Forbid otherwise constitutional actions in order to prevent or deter unconstitutional behavior; for example, require state police officers to receive training in multiculturalism*
- *Independently interpret the rights protected by the Fourteenth Amendment; for example, find that the equal protection clause forbids discrimination against the physically handicapped unless a compelling reason exists for the discrimination*

Which of these powers did Justice Brennan endorse? Which did Justice Harlan endorse? Which do you believe the Constitution sanctions?

JUSTICE BRENNAN delivered the opinion of the Court.

. . .

. . . A construction of §5 that would require a judicial determination that the enforcement of the state law precluded by Congress violated the Amendment, as a condition of sustaining the congressional enactment, would depreciate both congressional resourcefulness and congressional responsibility for implementing the Amendment. It would confine the legislative power in this context to the insignificant role of abrogating only those state laws that the judicial branch was prepared to adjudge unconstitutional, or of merely informing the judgment of the judiciary by particularizing the "majestic generalities" of §1 of the Amendment.

. . .

By including §5 the draftsmen sought to grant to Congress, by a specific provision applicable to the Fourteenth Amendment, the same broad powers expressed in the Necessary and Proper Clause, Art. I, §8, cl. 18. The classic formulation of the reach of those powers was established by Chief Justice Marshall in *McCulloch v. Maryland* (1819). . . .

> Let the end be legitimate, let it be within the scope of the constitution, and all means which are appropriate, which are plainly adapted to that end, which are not prohibited, but consistent with the letter and spirit of the constitution, are constitutional.

. . . There can be no doubt that §4 (e) may be regarded as an enactment to enforce the Equal Protection Clause. Congress explicitly declared that it enacted §4 (e) "to secure the rights under the fourteenth amendment of persons educated in American-flag schools in which the predominant classroom language was other than English." The persons referred to include those who have migrated from the Commonwealth of Puerto Rico to New York and who have been denied the right to vote because of their inability to read and write English, and the Fourteenth Amendment rights referred to include those emanating from the Equal Protection Clause. More specifically, §4 (e) may be viewed as a measure to secure for the Puerto Rican community residing in New York nondiscriminatory treatment by government—both in the imposition of voting qualifications and the provision or administration of governmental services, such as public schools, public housing and law enforcement.

Section 4 (e) may be readily seen as "plainly adapted" to furthering these aims of the Equal Protection Clause. The practical effect of §4 (e) is to prohibit New York from denying the right to vote to large segments of its Puerto Rican community. Congress has thus prohibited the State from denying to that community the right that is "preservative of all rights." . . . This enhanced political power will be helpful in gaining nondiscriminatory treatment in public services for the entire Puerto Rican community. Section 4 (e) thereby enables the Puerto Rican minority better to obtain "perfect equality of civil rights and the equal protection of the laws." It was well within congressional authority to say that this need of the Puerto Rican minority for the vote warranted federal intrusion upon any state interests served by the English literacy requirement. It was for Congress, as the branch that made this judgment, to assess and weigh the various conflicting considerations—the risk or pervasiveness of the discrimination in governmental services, the effectiveness of eliminating the state restriction on the right to vote as a means of dealing with the evil, the adequacy or availability of alternative remedies, and the nature and significance of the state interests that would be affected by the nullification of the English literacy requirement as applied to residents who have successfully completed the sixth grade in a Puerto Rican school. It is not for us to review the congressional resolution of these factors. It is enough that we be able to perceive a basis upon which the Congress might resolve the conflict as it did. There plainly was such a basis to support §4 (e) in the application in question in this case. Any contrary conclusion would require us to be blind to the realities familiar to the legislators.

The result is no different if we confine our inquiry to the question whether §4 (e) was merely legislation aimed at the elimination of an invidious discrimination in establishing voter qualifications. We are told that New York's English literacy requirement originated in the desire to provide an incentive for non-English speaking immigrants to learn the English language and in order to assure the intelligent exercise of the franchise. Yet Congress might well have questioned, in light of the many exemptions provided, and some evidence suggesting that prejudice played a prominent role in the enactment of the requirement, whether these were actually the interests being served. Congress might have also questioned whether denial of a right deemed so precious and fundamental in our society was a necessary or appropriate means of encouraging persons to learn English, or of furthering the goal of an intelligent exercise of the franchise. Finally, Congress might well have concluded that as a means of furthering the intelligent exercise of the franchise, an ability to read or understand Spanish is as effective as ability to read English for those to whom Spanish-language newspapers and Spanish-language radio and television programs are available to inform them of election issues and governmental affairs. Since Congress undertook to legislate so as to preclude the enforcement of the state law, and did so in the context of a general appraisal of literacy requirements for voting, . . . to which it brought a specially informed legislative competence, it was Congress' prerogative to weigh these competing considerations. Here again, it is enough that we perceive a basis upon which Congress might predicate a judgment that the application of New York's English literacy requirement to deny the right to vote to a person with a sixth grade education in Puerto Rican schools in which the language of instruction was other than English constituted an invidious discrimination in violation of the Equal Protection Clause.

JUSTICE HARLAN, whom JUSTICE STEWART joins, dissenting.

Worthy as its purposes may be thought by many, I do not see how §4 (e) of the Voting Rights Act of 1965 can be sustained except at the sacrifice of fundamentals in the American constitutional system—the separation between the legislative and judicial function and the boundaries between federal and state political authority. . . .

. . .

When recognized state violations of federal constitutional standards have occurred, Congress is of course empowered by §5 to take appropriate remedial measures to redress and prevent the wrongs. . . . But it is a judicial question whether the condition with which Congress has thus sought to deal is in truth an infringement of the Constitution, something that is the necessary prerequisite to bringing the §5 power into play at all. . . .

A more recent Fifteenth Amendment case serves to illustrate this distinction. In *South Carolina v. Katzenbach* (1966), . . . decided earlier this Term, we held certain remedial sections of this Voting Rights Act of 1965 constitutional under the Fifteenth Amendment, which is directed against deprivations of the right to vote on account of race. In enacting those sections of the Voting Rights Act the Congress made a detailed investigation of various state practices that had been used to deprive Negroes of the franchise. . . . In passing upon the remedial provisions, we reviewed first the "voluminous legislative history" as well as judicial precedents supporting the basic congressional finding that the clear commands of the Fifteenth Amendment had been infringed by various state subterfuges. . . . Given the existence of the evil, we held the remedial steps taken by the legislature under the Enforcement Clause of the Fifteenth Amendment to be a justifiable exercise of congressional initiative.

Section 4 (e), however, presents a significantly different type of congressional enactment. The question here is not whether the statute is appropriate remedial legislation to cure an established violation of a constitutional command, but whether there has in fact been an infringement of that constitutional command, that is, whether a particular state practice or, as here, a statute is so arbitrary or irrational as to offend the command of the Equal Protection Clause of the Fourteenth Amendment. That question is one for the judicial branch ultimately to determine. Were the rule otherwise, Congress would be able to qualify this Court's constitutional decisions under the Fourteenth and Fifteenth Amendments, let alone those under other provisions of the Constitution, by resorting to congressional power under the Necessary and Proper Clause. . . . In effect the Court reads §5 of the Fourteenth Amendment as giving Congress the power to define the *substantive* scope of the Amendment. If that indeed be the true reach of §5, then I do not see why Congress should not be able as well to exercise its §5 "discretion" by enacting statutes so as in effect to dilute equal protection and due process decisions of this Court. In all such cases there is room for reasonable men to differ as to whether or not a denial of equal protection or due process has occurred, and the final decision is one of judgment. Until today this judgment has always been one for the judiciary to resolve.

. . .

. . . [No] factual data provide a legislative record supporting §4 (e) by way of showing that Spanish-speaking citizens are fully as capable of making informed decisions in a New York election as are English-speaking citizens. Nor was there any showing whatever to support the Court's alternative argument that §4 (e) should be viewed as but a remedial measure designed to cure or assure against unconstitutional discrimination of other varieties, *e.g.*, in "public schools, public housing and law enforcement," . . . to which Puerto Rican minorities might be subject in such communities as New York.

Thus, we have here not a matter of giving deference to a congressional estimate, based on its determination of legislative facts, bearing upon the validity *vel non* of a statute, but rather what can at most be called a legislative announcement that Congress believes a state law to entail an unconstitutional deprivation of equal protection. Although this kind of declaration is of course entitled to the most respectful consideration, coming as it does from a concurrent branch and one that is knowledgeable in matters of popular political participation, I do not believe it lessens our responsibility to decide the fundamental issue of whether in fact the state enactment violates federal constitutional rights. . . .

Reynolds v. Sims, 377 U.S. 533 (1964)

M. O. Sims and other members of a Birmingham business association sued the Alabama state officials responsible for conducting elections, claiming that the state legislative failure to apportion violated their Fourteenth Amendment rights. One of the officials sued was B. A. Reynolds, a judge of a county probate court. Sims based his claim in part on a provision in the constitution of Alabama requiring that the state legislature be reapportioned every ten years to reflect population changes and shifts. The Alabama legislature had failed to redistrict after 1900. The result by 1960 was significant inequalities in representation. Counties with more than half a million people were entitled to the same one senator as counties with barely over 10,000 persons. A three-judge panel on the federal district court declared unconstitutional the Alabama plan, as well as two similar substitutes that had just passed the Alabama state legislature. Alabama appealed to the Supreme Court of the United States.

The Supreme Court affirmed the lower court decision by an 8–1 vote. Chief Justice Earl Warren's majority opinion insisted that the Constitution required state legislatures to be apportioned in a manner consistent with the one person, one vote principle. Reynolds *and* Baker v. Carr *(1961), which held that courts could adjudicate conflicts over apportionment, are among the most important and controversial opinions handed down by the Supreme Court of the United States. Earl Warren, who also wrote* Brown, *believed that these decisions were his most important contributions to constitutional law. What is the constitutional foundation of one person, one vote? Is that foundation sound? Given that only one house in the national government is apportioned by population, on what basis did Warren determine that both houses in state legislatures must be apportioned by population? Was his analysis correct? Did Warren insist that the populations of all legislative districts must be equal or merely that states must make population equality their primary concern in apportioning legislative districts? Under what conditions does* Reynolds *suggest that states may deviate from the principle of population equality? How much deviation is constitutionally acceptable?*

The Supreme Court's decisions in the reapportionment cases caused an intense but short-lived political firestorm. One month after Reynolds *was handed down the Republican Party called for a constitutional amendment that would partly reverse the result of that decision. Members of Congress proposed numerous bills that would either prevent federal courts from adjudicating apportionment controversies or mandate different decisions. A proposed constitutional amendment barely missed Senate passage in 1965.*

Efforts to reverse Reynolds *nevertheless failed and failed quickly. Most Democrats supported the decision. The principle one person, one vote was reasonably popular among the general public. Finally, and perhaps most important, within a few years all national and state legislators were elected in districts apportioned in a manner consistent with the principles announced in* Reynolds. *The winners of these elections had little incentive to denounce the electoral system under which they had been elected.*

Substantial debate exists over the impact of the reapportionment decisions. General agreement exists that the Supreme Court changed electoral practice. The dramatic malapportionments that once dotted the political landscape no longer exist. Differences between congressional districts within states are now minimal, and differences between state legislative districts are much smaller than was the case before Reynolds *was decided. How these electoral changes changed American politics is more controversial. Most political actors at the time believed that reapportionment would shift power from conservative rural districts to more liberal urban districts. A survey by Gerald Rosenberg concludes that this hypothesis was not proved true. He writes, "While there are studies both finding and not finding effects, an overall reading seems to be that any [policy] effects that can be traced to reapportionment are small."[46] One recent study found that reapportionment benefited Democrats and incumbents. Democrats benefited in part because previous districts had often resulted from Republican gerrymanders, in part because the Democratic landslide in 1964 increased the number of state legislators committed to Democratic gerrymanders after* Reynolds, *and in part because the majority of the justices who reapportioned districts after* Reynolds *were Democrats. Incumbents benefited because* Reynolds

46. Gerald N. Rosenberg, *The Hollow Hope: Can Courts Bring About Social Change?* (Chicago: University of Chicago Press, 1991), 297.

Table 8-7 Selection of U.S. Supreme Court Cases Reviewing State Apportionment of Legislative Districts

Case	Vote	Outcome	Decision
McPherson v. Blacker, 146 U.S. 1 (1892)	9–0	Upheld	At-large election of presidential electors does not violate federal Constitution
Richardson v. McChesney, 218 U.S. 487 (1910)	9–0	Dismissed	A case is moot when election results have already been certified
State of Ohio on Relation of Davis v. Hildebrant, 241 U.S. 565 (1916)	6–0	Upheld	States may reapportion by referendum
Smiley v. Holm, 285 U.S. 355 (1932)	8–0	Struck down	State legislatures exercise a regular lawmaking function when drawing congressional districts, which are potentially subject to gubernatorial veto
Colegrove v. Green, 328 U.S. 549 (1946)	4–3	Dismissed	Evaluation of whether congressional districts meet federal statutory requirements is a political question for Congress to assess
Baker v. Carr, 369 U.S. 186 (1962)	6–2	Remanded	Legislative districting is subject to equal protection scrutiny by courts
Gray v. Sanders, 372 U.S. 368 (1963)	8–1	Struck down	County-based voting system for primaries for statewide offices violates one person, one vote requirement
Wesberry v. Sanders, 376 U.S. 1 (1964)	6–3	Struck down	Congressional districts must be drawn so as to give equal representation to equal numbers of people
Reynolds v. Sims, 377 U.S. 533 (1964)	8–1	Struck down	Both chambers of a state legislature must be apportioned on the basis of population and equally sized districts
Gaffney v. Cummings, 412 U.S. 735 (1973)	6–3	Upheld	Minor variations in state legislative district size are acceptable, and districting plans may take into account partisanship of voters
White v. Regester, 412 U.S. 755 (1973)	6–3	Struck down	Minor variations in state legislative district size are acceptable, but multimember districts are unconstitutional when they negatively impact the electoral chances of historically disadvantaged groups
United Jewish Organizations of Williamsburgh v. Carey, 430 U.S. 144 (1977)	7–1	Upheld	Districting plans may take into account the race of voters in order to positively impact the electoral changes of historically disadvantaged groups
Connor v. Finch, 431 U.S. 407 (1977)	7–1	Struck down	Preserving county boundaries is not an adequate justification for creating variations in district size
Karcher v. Daggett, 462 U.S. 725 (1983)	5–4	Struck down	Even trivial variations in congressional district size are unacceptable unless justified by a legitimate state interest
Thornburg v. Gingles, 478 U.S. 30 (1986)	9–0	Struck down	Districting plans that move a cohesive minority group into an electoral district such that its favored candidate will be consistently defeated are illegal

(*Continued*)

Table 8-7 (*Continued*)

Case	Vote	Outcome	Decision
Shaw v. Reno, 509 U.S. 630 (1993)	5–4	Remanded	Bizarrely drawn legislative districts that separate voters based on race may be unconstitutional
Bush v. Vera, 517 U.S. 952 (1996)	5–4	Struck down	Highly irregular legislative districts that separate voters based on race are unconstitutional
League of Latin American Citizens v. Perry, 548 U.S. 399 (2006)	5–4	Upheld	States may redraw legislative boundaries as often as they want and may draw "partisan gerrymanders"

increased opportunities for redistricting, and incumbents were in a position to ensure that they would benefit from the new apportionments.[47] *Many observers think the lasting legacy of* Reynolds *is the increased use of gerrymanders in state legislatures as each party seeks to maximize its seats in Congress and state legislatures.*

CHIEF JUSTICE WARREN delivered the opinion of the Court.

. . .

Undeniably the Constitution of the United States protects the right of all qualified citizens to vote, in state as well as in federal elections. A consistent line of decisions by this Court in cases involving attempts to deny or restrict the right of suffrage has made this indelibly clear. . . . The right to vote freely for the candidate of one's choice is of the essence of a democratic society, and any restrictions on that right strike at the heart of representative government. And the right of suffrage can be denied by a debasement or dilution of the weight of a citizen's vote just as effectively as by wholly prohibiting the free exercise of the franchise. . . .

. . .

. . . [T]he fundamental principle of representative government in this country is one of equal representation for equal numbers of people, without regard to race, sex, economic status, or place of residence within a State. Our problem, then, is to ascertain, in the instant cases, whether there are any constitutionally cognizable principles which would justify departures from the basic standard of equality among voters in the apportionment of seats in state legislatures.

. . .

Legislators represent people, not trees or acres. Legislators are elected by voters, not farms or cities or economic interests. As long as ours is a representative form of government, and our legislatures are those instruments of government elected directly by and directly representative of the people, the right to elect legislators in a free and unimpaired fashion is a bedrock of our political system. . . . If a State should provide that the votes of citizens in one part of the State should be given two times, or five times, or 10 times the weight of votes of citizens in another part of the State, it could hardly be contended that the right to vote of those residing in the disfavored areas had not been effectively diluted. It would appear extraordinary to suggest that a State could be constitutionally permitted to enact a law providing that certain of the State's voters could vote two, five, or 10 times for their legislative representatives, while voters living elsewhere could vote only once. And it is inconceivable that a state law to the effect that, in counting votes for legislators, the votes of citizens in one part of the State would be multiplied by two, five, or 10, while the votes of persons in another area would be counted only at face value, could be constitutionally sustainable. Of course, the effect of state legislative districting schemes which give the same number of representatives to unequal numbers of constituents is identical. . . . Weighting the votes of citizens differently, by any method or means, merely because of where they happen to reside, hardly seems justifiable. . . .

. . .

Logically, in a society ostensibly grounded on representative government, it would seem reasonable

47. See Gary W. Cox and Jonathan N. Katz, *The Electoral Consequences of the Reapportionment Revolution* (New York: Cambridge University Press, 2002).

that a majority of the people of a State could elect a majority of that State's legislators. To conclude differently, and to sanction minority control of state legislative bodies, would appear to deny majority rights in a way that far surpasses any possible denial of minority rights that might otherwise be thought to result. Since legislatures are responsible for enacting laws by which all citizens are to be governed, they should be bodies which are collectively responsive to the popular will. And the concept of equal protection has been traditionally viewed as requiring the uniform treatment of persons standing in the same relation to the governmental action questioned or challenged. With respect to the allocation of legislative representation, all voters, as citizens of a State, stand in the same relation regardless of where they live. Any suggested criteria for the differentiation of citizens are insufficient to justify any discrimination, as to the weight of their votes, unless relevant to the permissible purposes of legislative apportionment. Since the achieving of fair and effective representation for all citizens is concededly the basic aim of legislative apportionment, we conclude that the Equal Protection Clause guarantees the opportunity for equal participation by all voters in the election of state legislators. Diluting the weight of votes because of place of residence impairs basic constitutional rights under the Fourteenth Amendment just as much as invidious discriminations based upon factors such as race, *Brown v. Board of Education* (1954), or economic status, *Griffin v. Illinois* (1956). . . . Our constitutional system amply provides for the protection of minorities by means other than giving them majority control of state legislatures. And the democratic ideals of equality and majority rule, which have served this Nation so well in the past, are hardly of any less significance for the present and the future.

. . .

To the extent that a citizen's right to vote is debased, he is that much less a citizen. The fact that an individual lives here or there is not a legitimate reason for overweighting or diluting the efficacy of his vote. . . . The weight of a citizen's vote cannot be made to depend on where he lives. Population is, of necessity, the starting point for consideration and the controlling criterion for judgment in legislative apportionment controversies. A citizen, a qualified voter, is no more nor no less so because he lives in the city or on the farm. This is the clear and strong command of our Constitution's Equal Protection Clause. This is an essential part of the concept of a government of laws and not men. This is at the heart of Lincoln's vision of "government of the people, by the people, [and] for the people." The Equal Protection Clause demands no less than substantially equal state legislative representation for all citizens, of all places as well as of all races.

We hold that, as a basic constitutional standard, the Equal Protection Clause requires that the seats in both houses of a bicameral state legislature must be apportioned on a population basis. Simply stated, an individual's right to vote for state legislators is unconstitutionally impaired when its weight is in a substantial fashion diluted when compared with votes of citizens living in other parts of the State. Since, under neither the existing apportionment provisions nor either of the proposed plans was either of the houses of the Alabama Legislature apportioned on a population basis, the District Court correctly held that all three of these schemes were constitutionally invalid. . . .

. . .

The system of representation in the two Houses of the Federal Congress is one ingrained in our Constitution, as part of the law of the land. It is one conceived out of compromise and concession indispensable to the establishment of our federal republic. Arising from unique historical circumstances, it is based on the consideration that in establishing our type of federalism a group of formerly independent States bound themselves together under one national government. Admittedly, the original 13 States surrendered some of their sovereignty in agreeing to join together "to form a more perfect Union." But at the heart of our constitutional system remains the concept of separate and distinct governmental entities which have delegated some, but not all, of their formerly held powers to the single national government. . . . Political subdivisions of States—counties, cities, or whatever—never were and never have been considered as sovereign entities. Rather, they have been traditionally regarded as subordinate governmental instrumentalities created by the State to assist in the carrying out of state governmental functions. . . . The relationship of the States to the Federal Government could hardly be less analogous.

. . .

. . . So long as the divergences from a strict population standard are based on legitimate considerations incident to the effectuation of a rational state policy, some deviations from the equal-population principle are constitutionally permissible with respect to the apportionment of seats in either or both of the two houses of a bicameral state legislature. But neither history alone, nor economic or other sorts of group interests, are permissible factors in attempting to justify disparities from population-based representation. Citizens, not history or economic interests, cast votes. Considerations of area alone provide an insufficient justification for deviations from the equal-population principle. Again, people, not land or trees or pastures, vote. . . .

A consideration that appears to be of more substance in justifying some deviations from population-based representation in state legislatures is that of insuring some voice to political subdivisions, as political subdivisions. . . . Local governmental entities are frequently charged with various responsibilities incident to the operation of state government. . . . And a State may legitimately desire to construct districts along political subdivision lines to deter the possibilities of gerrymandering. However, permitting deviations from population-based representation does not mean that each local governmental unit or political subdivision can be given separate representation, regardless of population. . . . But if, even as a result of a clearly rational state policy of according some legislative representation to political subdivisions, population is submerged as the controlling consideration in the apportionment of seats in the particular legislative body, then the right of all of the State's citizens to cast an effective and adequately weighted vote would be unconstitutionally impaired.

. . .

JUSTICE CLARK, concurring in the affirmance.

It seems to me that all that the Court need say in this case is that each plan considered by the trial court is "a crazy quilt," clearly revealing invidious discrimination in each house of the Legislature and therefore violative of the Equal Protection Clause. . . .

. . .

JUSTICE STEWART. . . .

JUSTICE HARLAN, dissenting.

. . .

. . . [T]e Equal Protection Clause was never intended to inhibit the States in choosing any democratic method they pleased for the apportionment of their legislatures. This is shown by the language of the Fourteenth Amendment taken as a whole, by the understanding of those who proposed and ratified it, and by the political practices of the States at the time the Amendment was adopted. It is confirmed by numerous state and congressional actions since the adoption of the Fourteenth Amendment, and by the common understanding of the Amendment as evidenced by subsequent constitutional amendments and decisions of this Court before *Baker v. Carr* (1961). . . .

. . .

. . . Of the 23 loyal States which ratified the Amendment before 1870, five had constitutional provisions for apportionment of at least one house of their respective legislatures which wholly disregarded the spread of population. Ten more had constitutional provisions which gave primary emphasis to population, but which applied also other principles, such as partial ratios and recognition of political subdivisions, which were intended to favor sparsely settled areas. Can it be seriously contended that the legislatures of these States, almost two-thirds of those concerned, would have ratified an amendment which might render their own States' constitutions unconstitutional?

. . .

. . . As of 1961, the Constitutions of all but 11 States, roughly 20% of the total, recognized bases of apportionment other than geographic spread of population. . . . [I]t is evident that the actual practice of the States is even more uniformly than their theory opposed to the Court's view of what is constitutionally permissible.

. . .

Generalities cannot obscure the cold truth that cases of this type are not amenable to the development of judicial standards. No set of standards can guide a court which has to decide how many legislative districts a State shall have, or what the shape of the districts shall be, or where to draw a particular district line. No judicially manageable standard can determine whether a State should have single-member districts or multimember districts or some combination of both. No such standard can control the balance between keeping up with population shifts and having stable districts. In all these respects, the courts will be called upon to make particular decisions with respect to which a principle of equally populated districts will be of no assistance whatsoever. Quite obviously, there are limitless possibilities for districting consistent with such a principle. Nor can these problems be avoided by judicial reliance on legislative judgments so far as possible. Reshaping or combining one or two districts, or modifying just a few district lines, is no less a matter of choosing among many possible solutions, with varying political consequences, than reapportionment broadside.

. . .

. . . [P]eople are not ciphers and . . . legislators can represent their electors only by speaking for their interests—economic, social, political—many of which do reflect the place where the electors live. The Court does not establish, or indeed even attempt to make a case for the proposition that conflicting interests within a State can only be adjusted by disregarding them when voters are grouped for purposes of representation.

. . .

These decisions also cut deeply into the fabric of our federalism. What must follow from them may eventually appear to be the product of state legislatures. Nevertheless, no thinking person can fail to recognize that the aftermath of these cases, however desirable it may be thought in itself, will have been achieved at the cost of a radical alteration in the relationship between the States and the Federal Government, more particularly the Federal Judiciary. Only one who has an overbearing impatience with the federal system and its political processes will believe that that cost was not too high or was inevitable.

Finally, these decisions give support to a current mistaken view of the Constitution and the constitutional function of this Court. This view, in a nutshell, is that every major social ill in this country can find its cure in some constitutional "principle," and that this Court should "take the lead" in promoting reform when other branches of government fail to act. The Constitution is not a panacea for every blot upon the public welfare, nor should this Court, ordained as a judicial body, be thought of as a general haven for reform movements. The Constitution is an instrument of government, fundamental to which is the premise that in a diffusion of governmental authority lies the greatest promise that this Nation will realize liberty for all its citizens. This Court, limited in function in accordance with that premise, does not serve its high purpose when it exceeds its authority, even to satisfy justified impatience with the slow workings of the political process. For when, in the name of constitutional interpretation, the Court adds something to the Constitution that was deliberately excluded from it, the Court in reality substitutes its view of what should be so for the amending process.

IX. Equality

MAJOR DEVELOPMENTS

- Race-conscious measures required to meet strict scrutiny standard
- School segregation declared unconstitutional

The modern understanding of equal protection took shape during the New Deal/Great Society Era. Constitutional decision makers before the 1930s believed that legislation could distinguish among groups of people when doing so advanced the public good and was related to a real difference between the groups. In theory all groups were judged by the same standard. By the late 1960s, constitutional equality was bifurcated. In most circumstances government was free to make any distinction between most groups of people as long as the distinction satisfied a very weak rational basis test. When government discriminated on the basis of race or ethnicity or against other "discrete and insular minorities," elected officials had to demonstrate that their actions were necessary means to achieve compelling ends.

Strict scrutiny was limited to distinctions of race and ethnicity. Some proponents of women's rights claimed that arguments for racial equality supported greater gender equality. These arguments did not gain official sanction until the late 1970s. Warren Court opinions on gender equality resembled Waite Court opinions delivered in the late nineteenth century.

A. Equality Under Law

The Supreme Court abandoned inherited concerns with class legislation. Judicial opinions held that unless race or a related classification was at issue, elected officials could make any distinction between people or classes of people that might be thought rational. *Railway Express Agency v. People of State of New York* (1949) is a typical case. A New York City ordinance forbade any person from operating an "advertising vehicle" unless the vehicle was "engaged in the usual business or regular work of the owner."

Table 8-8 Selection of U.S. Supreme Court Cases Reviewing State Laws Under Equal Protection Clause

Case	Vote	Result	Outcome
Slaughter-House Cases, 83 U.S. 36 (1873)	5–4	Upheld	Equal protection clause has no application to laws not aimed at creating hardships for blacks as a class; state law restricting the ability of some butchers to practice their profession is constitutional
Strauder v. West Virginia, 100 U.S. 303 (1880)	7–2	Struck down	States may not categorically exclude blacks from juries
Yick Wo v. Hopkins, 118 U.S. 356 (1886)	9–0	Struck down	States may not systematically deny permits to operate wooden laundries to Chinese laundry owners
Plessy v. Ferguson, 163 U.S. 537 (1896)	7–1	Upheld	States may require separate accommodations on railway cars for blacks and whites
Connolly v. Union Sewer Pipe Co., 184 U.S. 540 (1902)	7–1	Struck down	Anti-trust statute that exempts only farmers and ranchers unconstitutionally makes arbitrary distinctions among otherwise similar acts and vocations
Lindsley v. Natural Carbonic Gas Co., 220 U.S. 61 (1911)	9–0	Upheld	Legislative classifications are consistent with the equal protection clause so long as they are not wholly arbitrary and have some reasonable basis, and the courts should assume a reasonable factual situation that could support the classification; consequently, states may prohibit some methods of extracting natural gas while allowing others
Buck v. Bell, 274 U.S. 200 (1927)	8–1	Upheld	States may require the forced sterilization of patients at state institutions who are considered "feeble-minded"
Stewart Dry Goods Co. v. Lewis, 294 U.S. 550 (1935)	6–3	Struck down	A graduated tax on a business' sales that increases with the amount of total sales is arbitrary and unconstitutional
Brown v. Board of Education, 347 U.S. 483 (1954)	9–0	Struck down	Segregation of children in public schools on the basis of race is unconstitutional
Williamson v. Lee Optical Co., 348 U.S. 483 (1955)	9–0	Upheld	Law that limits persons who are not optometrists or ophthalmologists from fitting lenses to faces has a rational basis and does not represent the kind of invidious discrimination that requires more careful judicial scrutiny
Baker v. Carr, 369 U.S. 186 (1962)	6–2	Struck down	Malapportioned legislative districts raise equal protection concerns that may be addressed by courts
Peterson v. City of Greenville, 373 U.S. 244 (1963)	8–1	Struck down	Trespass convictions of black sit-in protesters violate the equal protection clause when state law exists requiring segregated lunch counters
Reed v. Reed, 404 U.S. 71 (1971)	9–0	Struck down	Mandatory preference for men over women as probate administrators is an arbitrary distinction and violates equal protection clause

(*Continued*)

Table 8-8 (*Continued*)

Case	Vote	Result	Outcome
San Antonio Independent School District v. Rodriguez, 411 U.S. 1 (1973)	5–4	Upheld	Equal protection clause does not require equal resources or advantages, and unequal funding of school districts is constitutional
Milliken v. Bradley, 418 U.S. 717 (1974)	5–4	Upheld	De facto racial segregation across school districts does not violate the equal protection clause
Craig v. Boren, 429 U.S. 190 (1976)	7–2	Struck down	Statute that prohibits the sale of beer to men under twenty-one but allows women over eighteen to purchase is unconstitutional; gender classifications should be reviewed on the basis of an "intermediate" level of scrutiny
Regents of the University of California v. Bakke, 438 U.S. 265 (1978)	5–4	Struck down	Universities may consider race in admissions in order to achieve a diverse student body but may not establish a quota system
Plyler v. Doe, 457 U.S. 202 (1982)	5–4	Struck down	States may not deny public services such as education to illegal aliens
McCleskey v. Kemp, 481 U.S. 279 (1987)	5–4	Upheld	Racially disparate results from death penalty sentencing do not prove violation of the equal protection clause without a demonstration of racially discriminatory purpose
City of Richmond v. J. A. Croson Co., 488 U.S. 469 (1989)	6–3	Struck down	States may not use racial set-asides for public contracts on the basis of generalized assertions of past discrimination
Romer v. Evans, 517 U.S. 620 (1996)	6–3	Struck down	Colorado's "Amendment 2," preventing government offices throughout the state from prohibiting all forms of discrimination against gays and lesbians, is inexplicable by anything but animus toward the affected class and lacks a rational relationship to a legitimate state interest
United States v. Virginia, 518 U.S. 515 (1996)	7–1	Struck down	Virginia Military Institute's male-only admission policy denies women "full citizenship stature"
Grutter v. Bollinger, 539 U.S. 306 (2003)	5–4	Upheld	Universities may consider race in admissions in order to achieve a "critical mass" of minority students

A unanimous Supreme Court quickly dismissed claims that the law violated the equal protection clause. Justice Douglas's opinion for the Court asserted,

> We cannot say that that judgment is not an allowable one. Yet if it is, the classification has relation to the purpose for which it is made and does not contain the kind of discrimination against which the Equal Protection Clause affords protection. It is by such practical considerations based on experience rather than by theoretical inconsistencies that the question of equal protection is to be answered. . . . And the fact that New York City sees fit to eliminate from traffic this kind of distraction but does not touch what may be even greater ones in a different category, such as the vivid displays on Times Square, is immaterial. It is no requirement of equal protection that all evils of the same genus be eradicated or none at all.

B. Race

The New Deal/Great Society Era witnessed dramatic changes in the constitutional status of African Americans. Jim Crow reigned supreme when Franklin Roosevelt took office in 1933. By the time Lyndon Johnson left office in 1969 Americans were living in a new constitutional universe. *Plessy v. Ferguson* (1896) had been overruled by a series of decisions beginning with *Brown v. Board of Education* (1954) and *Bolling v. Sharpe* (1954). *Brown* was considered as central to the constitutional order as *Marbury v. Madison* (1803). Congress had passed such powerful antidiscrimination laws as the Civil Rights Act of 1964 and the Voting Rights Act of 1965. Racial equality had by no means been achieved, but a general consensus existed that Jim Crow was moribund.

All three branches of the national government participated in this assault on racial segregation. Beginning in 1957, Congress passed ever-tougher antidiscrimination laws. Members of the executive branch sought pro–civil rights jurists for the federal bench, submitted amicus briefs urging justices to declare Jim Crow practices unconstitutional, and, during the 1960s, proposed bold civil rights initiatives.[48] The Supreme Court repeatedly sided with African Americans, in cases concerned with equal protection and on other constitutional matters. Thurgood Marshall by 1965 had become the most successful Supreme Court advocate in American history.

An increasingly powerful civil rights movement successfully prodded elected officials to promote racial equality. Charles Houston, Thurgood Marshall, and other lawyers from the NAACP Legal Defense Fund developed the litigation strategy responsible for first undermining and then overruling *Plessy v. Ferguson.* A. Philip Randolph and Martin Luther King, Jr., organized protest movements that induced governing officials to adopt antidiscrimination policies and increased support for such policies in the North. Violent southern responses to the peaceful civil rights protests organized by Martin Luther King, Jr., outraged many racial moderates in the North and led to the Civil Rights Act of 1964 and the Voting Rights Act of 1965. The Supreme Court dramatically challenged Jim Crow segregation in *Brown v. Board of Education* (1954) and *Bolling v. Sharpe* (1954). *Brown* held that school segregation in the states violated the equal protection clause of the Fourteenth Amendment. *Bolling* held that school segregation in the nation's capitol violated the due process clause of the Fifth Amendment. Chief Justice Warren's unanimous opinion in that latter case declared, "Segregation in public education is not reasonably related to any proper governmental objective, and thus it imposes on Negro children of the District of Columbia a burden that constitutes an arbitrary deprivation of their liberty in violation of the Due Process Clause." The justices then temporized in *Brown v. Board of Education II* (1955), rejecting claims that schools be desegregated immediately in favor of a policy of "all deliberate speed."

During the late 1950s and early 1960s Americans experienced deliberation but no speed in desegregating public schools, except in the border states. A few federal district court justices aggressively sought to abolish dual school systems. Judge J. Skelley Wright in 1960 issued an injunction against the entire Louisiana legislature, threatening them with prison should they interfere with school desegregation in New Orleans. More federal judges were satisfied with school plans that enabled a few children of color to attend formerly all-white schools. Judge Frank Hooper of the federal district court in Georgia informed the school board in Atlanta that he would accept any plan that allowed for "token integration." He proved a person of his word when Atlanta adopted a program permitting high school seniors to request transfers to different high schools, with a commitment to extending the program by one grade every year. Some judges engaged in outright resistance. Judge T. Whitfield Davison of Dallas rejected a plan that would desegregate the first grade and then increase the number of desegregated grades by one every year thereafter. Mixing six-year-olds, he claimed, "would lead, in the opinion and the light of history and unquestionable sources to an amalgamation of the races."[49]

The Civil Rights Act of 1964 dramatically changed the constitutional politics of school desegregation. That measure contained two provisions that spurred

48. Kevin J. McMahon, *Reconsidering Roosevelt on Race: How the Presidency Paved the Road to* Brown (Chicago: University of Chicago Press, 2003).

49. This paragraph relies on J. W. Peltason, *58 Lonely Men: Southern Justices and School Desegregation* (Urbana: University of Illinois Press, 1971), 221–43, 130–31, 121.

desegregation. First, Congress cut off all federal funds to school districts not in compliance with *Brown*, and compliance was determined by the executive branch of the federal government. Second, Congress authorized the Justice Department to bring lawsuits that would desegregate public schools, thus extending the constitutional attack beyond the limited budgets and staffs of civil rights organizations. Two results were immediate. First, the number of African American children in desegregated schools increased dramatically after 1965. Second, the Warren Court became markedly more aggressive when ruling on school desegregation cases. In *Green v. County School Board of New Kent County* (1968), Justice Brennan's unanimous opinion declared that school districts in violation of *Brown* had an "affirmative duty to take whatever steps might be necessary to convert to a unitary system in which racial discrimination would be eliminated root and branch" and that "the burden on a school board today is to come forward with a plan that promises realistically to work, and promises realistically to work now."

Contemporary scholars debate the extent to which litigation campaigns deserve the credit for abolishing Jim Crow. Conventional accounts maintain that it was judicial decisions that destroyed segregation in the South. "It was the Warren Court," a prominent Yale law professor writes, "that spurred the great changes to follow, and inspired and protected those who sought to implement them."[50] Gerald Rosenberg's *The Hollow Hope* insists that the litigation campaign achieved little and that Americans moved toward racial equality only when the mass African American protests organized by Randolph and King pushed the national government to pass and enforce civil rights legislation. In his view,

> The courts were ineffective in producing significant social reform in civil rights in the first decade after *Brown* [because] . . . political leadership at the national, state, and local levels was arrayed against civil rights, making implementation of judicial decisions nearly impossible, . . . the culture of the South was segregationist, leaving the courts with few public supporters . . . , [and] the American court system was itself designed to lack implementation powers, to move slowly, and to be strongly tied to local concerns.[51]

Michael Klarman suggests a fascinating third view. His "backlash" thesis asserts that *Brown* initially empowered the worst racists in the South, but their violent efforts to suppress the civil rights movement turned northern public opinion in favor of greater constitutional equality.[52]

Constitutional liberals insisted that racial classifications satisfy higher constitutional standards. By the end of the New Deal/Great Society Era federal courts had determined that racial discriminations and distinctions were constitutional only if they satisfied a "strict scrutiny" test. This test required that the law be a necessary means (or narrowly tailored) to achieve a compelling government end. With one exception, no racial classification litigated during the New Deal/Great Society Era satisfied that standard. The one exception, *Korematsu v. United States* (1944), sustained President Roosevelt's decision to require Japanese Americans on the West Coast to be removed to relocation camps during World War II. Remarkably, *Korematsu*, a case presently regarded as one of the most racist decisions in American history, was also the first case in which the Supreme Court used the strict scrutiny test.

Korematsu v. United States, 323 U.S. 214 (1944)

Fred Toyosaburo Korematsu was a Japanese American citizen who lived and worked as a welder in San Leandro, California. On February 19, 1942, President Roosevelt issued an executive order authorizing military commanders to define "military areas" and exclude any or all persons from them. On May 3, 1942, Lieutenant General John DeWitt, the military commander of the Western Defense Command, issued Exclusion Order No. 34, which declared that "from and after 12 o'clock noon, P. W. T., of Saturday, May 9, 1942, all persons of Japanese ancestry, both alien and

---

50. Owen Fiss, "A Life Twice Lived," *Yale Law Journal* 100 (1991): 1117, 1118.

51. Gerald N. Rosenberg, *The Hollow Hope: Can Courts Bring About Social Change?* (Chicago: University of Chicago Press, 1991), 93.

52. Michael J. Klarman, *From Jim Crow to Civil Rights: The Supreme Court and the Struggle for Racial Equality* (New York: Oxford University Press, 2006).

non-alien, be excluded" from Alameda County, California. Overall, more than 100,000 Japanese Americans were forced to leave their homes, often with no more than a week's notice, and become essentially prisoners of war for three years in relocation camps. Families were typically given one room with no private baths or kitchens. Korematsu, who lived in Alameda County, refused to leave his home and job. He was arrested for violating the ordinance, found guilty, and sentenced to five years on probation. After the Court of Appeals for the Ninth Circuit affirmed the conviction, Korematsu appealed to the Supreme Court of the United States.

The relocation orders sharply divided the Roosevelt War Department, which favored removing the Japanese, from prominent civil libertarians in the Roosevelt Justice Department. Justice Department lawyers were particularly concerned when they learned that General DeWitt's report justifying the relocation order contained many false or unproven facts. After noting that claims made in that report were "in conflict with information in the possession of the Department of Justice," an early draft of the federal government's brief in Korematsu *asserted, "In view of the contrariety of the reports on the matter we do not ask the Court to take judicial notice of the recital of those facts contained in the Report." War Department lawyers edited that passage to read that the report was based on "tendencies and probabilities as evidenced by attitudes, opinions, and slight experience, rather than a conclusion based upon objectively ascertainable facts."*

The Supreme Court in Korematsu *sustained the relocation order by a 6–3 vote. Justice Black's majority opinion, while insisting that racial classifications are "immediately suspect," nevertheless found that military necessities justified removing Japanese Americans from the West Coast. Why did Justice Black reach that decision? Did he share the popular sentiment that Japanese Americans threatened the West Coast? Did he believe that the justices should defer to the president in wartime? What do you make of the view expressed by Justice (and former attorney general) Jackson that the Court should have stayed out of the dispute and not have given judicial sanction to the use of race? Support for* Korematsu *vanished the day that World War II ended. Almost all constitutional scholars presently believe that the* Korematsu *case was a judicial "disaster."[53] Mark Tushnet has an interesting take on this consensus. He writes, "*Korematsu *was part of a process of social learning that . . . diminishes contemporary threats to civil liberties in our present situation."[54] In his view, having made the wrong decision in* Korematsu *and learned from that experience, Americans are less likely to engage in such acts as racial profiling in the future. Is this correct? To what extent do you believe that the general consensus that the Japanese internment was wrong has influenced public policy during the War on Terror?*

The U.S. government in 1988 formally apologized to those Japanese Americans who were forced to leave their homes during World War II. Ten years later Fred Korematsu received the Presidential Medal of Freedom.

JUSTICE BLACK delivered the opinion of the Court.

. . .

It should be noted, to begin with, that all legal restrictions which curtail the civil rights of a single racial group are immediately suspect. That is not to say that all such restrictions are unconstitutional. It is to say that courts must subject them to the most rigid scrutiny. Pressing public necessity may sometimes justify the existence of such restrictions; racial antagonism never can.

. . .

. . . [W]e are unable to conclude that it was beyond the war power of Congress and the Executive to exclude those of Japanese ancestry from the West Coast war area at the time they did. True, exclusion from the area in which one's home is located is a far greater deprivation than constant confinement to the home from 8 p.m. to 6 a.m. Nothing short of apprehension by the proper military authorities of the gravest imminent danger to the public safety can constitutionally justify either. But exclusion from a threatened area, no less than curfew, has a definite and close relationship to the prevention of espionage and sabotage. The military authorities, charged with the primary responsibility of defending our shores, concluded that curfew provided inadequate protection and ordered exclusion. They did so . . . in accordance with Congressional authority to the military to say who should, and who should not, remain in the threatened areas.

. . .

Like curfew, exclusion of those of Japanese origin was deemed necessary because of the presence of an

53. The classic citation is Eugene Rostow, "The Japanese American Cases—A Disaster," *Yale Law Journal* 54 (1945): 489–533.

54. Mark Tushnet, "Defending *Korematsu*? Reflections on Civil Liberties in Wartime," *Wisconsin Law Review 2003* (2003): 274.

unascertained number of disloyal members of the group, most of whom we have no doubt were loyal to this country. It was because we could not reject the finding of the military authorities that it was impossible to bring about an immediate segregation of the disloyal from the loyal that we sustained the validity of the curfew order as applying to the whole group. In the instant case, temporary exclusion of the entire group was rested by the military on the same ground. The judgment that exclusion of the whole group was for the same reason a military imperative answers the contention that the exclusion was in the nature of group punishment based on antagonism to those of Japanese origin. That there were members of the group who retained loyalties to Japan has been confirmed by investigations made subsequent to the exclusion. . . .

. . .

It is said that we are dealing here with the case of imprisonment of a citizen in a concentration camp solely because of his ancestry, without evidence or inquiry concerning his loyalty and good disposition towards the United States. Our task would be simple, our duty clear, were this a case involving the imprisonment of a loyal citizen in a concentration camp because of racial prejudice. Regardless of the true nature of the assembly and relocation centers—and we deem it unjustifiable to call them concentration camps with all the ugly connotations that term implies—we are dealing specifically with nothing but an exclusion order. To cast this case into outlines of racial prejudice, without reference to the real military dangers which were presented, merely confuses the issue. Korematsu was not excluded from the Military Area because of hostility to him or his race. He was excluded because we are at war with the Japanese Empire, because the properly constituted military authorities feared an invasion of our West Coast and felt constrained to take proper security measures, because they decided that the military urgency of the situation demanded that all citizens of Japanese ancestry be segregated from the West Coast temporarily, and finally, because Congress, reposing its confidence in this time of war in our military leaders—as inevitably it must—determined that they should have the power to do just this. There was evidence of disloyalty on the part of some, the military authorities considered that the need for action was great, and time was short. We cannot—by availing ourselves of the calm perspective of hindsight—now say that at that time these actions were unjustified.

JUSTICE FRANKFURTER, concurring.

. . .

The provisions of the Constitution which confer on the Congress and the President powers to enable this country to wage war are as much part of the Constitution as provisions looking to a nation at peace. . . . To find that the Constitution does not forbid the military measures now complained of does not carry with it approval of that which Congress and the Executive did. That is their business, not ours.

JUSTICE ROBERTS, dissenting.

. . . The liberty of every American citizen freely to come and to go must frequently, in the face of sudden danger, be temporarily limited or suspended. The civil authorities must often resort to the expedient of excluding citizens temporarily from a locality. The drawing of fire lines in the case of a conflagration, the removal of persons from the area where a pestilence has broken out, are familiar examples. . . . [But] the exclusion was but a part of an over-all plan for forceable detention. This case cannot, therefore, be decided on any such narrow ground as the possible validity of a Temporary Exclusion Order under which the residents of an area are given an opportunity to leave and go elsewhere in their native land outside the boundaries of a military area. To make the case turn on any such assumption is to shut our eyes to reality.

. . .

JUSTICE MURPHY, dissenting.

This exclusion of all persons of Japanese ancestry, both alien and non-alien, from the Pacific Coast area on a plea of military necessity in the absence of martial law ought not to be approved. Such exclusion goes over "the very brink of constitutional power" and falls into the ugly abyss of racism.

. . .

. . . The judicial test of whether the Government, on a plea of military necessity, can validly deprive an individual of any of his constitutional rights is whether the deprivation is reasonably related to a public danger that is so "immediate, imminent, and impending" as not to admit of delay and not to permit the intervention of ordinary constitutional processes to alleviate the danger. . . . Civilian Exclusion Order No. 34, banishing from a prescribed area of the Pacific Coast "all persons of Japanese ancestry, both alien and non-alien," clearly does not meet that test. Being an obvious racial discrimination, the order deprives all those within its scope of the equal protection of the laws as guaranteed by the Fifth Amendment. It further deprives these individuals of their constitutional rights to live and work where they will, to establish a home where they choose and to move about freely. In excommunicating them without benefit of hearings, this order also deprives them of all their constitutional rights to procedural due process. Yet no reasonable relation to an "immediate, imminent, and impending" public danger is evident to support this racial restriction which is one of the most sweeping and complete deprivations of constitutional rights in the history of this nation in the absence of martial law.

It must be conceded that the military and naval situation in the spring of 1942 was such as to generate a very real fear of invasion of the Pacific Coast, accompanied by fears of sabotage and espionage in that area. The military command was therefore justified in adopting all reasonable means necessary to combat these dangers. In adjudging the military action taken in light of the then apparent dangers, we must not erect too high or too meticulous standards; it is necessary only that the action have some reasonable relation to the removal of the dangers of invasion, sabotage and espionage. But the exclusion, either temporarily or permanently, of all persons with Japanese blood in their veins has no such reasonable relation. And that relation is lacking because the exclusion order necessarily must rely for its reasonableness upon the assumption that all persons of Japanese ancestry may have a dangerous tendency to commit sabotage and espionage and to aid our Japanese enemy in other ways. It is difficult to believe that reason, logic or experience could be marshaled in support of such an assumption.

. . .

. . . The reasons appear, instead, to be largely an accumulation of much of the misinformation, half-truths and insinuations that for years have been directed against Japanese Americans by people with racial and economic prejudices—the same people who have been among the foremost advocates of the evacuation. A military judgment based upon such racial and sociological considerations is not entitled to the great weight ordinarily given the judgments based upon strictly military considerations. . . .

. . . [T]o infer that examples of individual disloyalty prove group disloyalty and justify discriminatory action against the entire group is to deny that under our system of law individual guilt is the sole basis for deprivation of rights. Moreover, this inference, which is at the very heart of the evacuation orders, has been used in support of the abhorrent and despicable treatment of minority groups by the dictatorial tyrannies which this nation is now pledged to destroy. To give constitutional sanction to that inference in this case, however well-intentioned may have been the military command on the Pacific Coast, is to adopt one of the cruelest of the rationales used by our enemies to destroy the dignity of the individual and to encourage and open the door to discriminatory actions against other minority groups in the passions of tomorrow.

No adequate reason is given for the failure to treat these Japanese Americans on an individual basis by holding investigations and hearings to separate the loyal from the disloyal, as was done in the case of persons of German and Italian ancestry. . . .

. . .

I dissent, therefore, from this legalization of racism. Racial discrimination in any form and in any degree has no justifiable part whatever in our democratic way of life. It is unattractive in any setting but it is utterly revolting among a free people who have embraced the principles set forth in the Constitution of the United States. All residents of this nation are kin in some way by blood or culture to a foreign land. Yet they are primarily and necessarily a part of the new and distinct civilization of the United States. They must accordingly be treated at all times as the heirs of the American experiment and as entitled to all the rights and freedoms guaranteed by the Constitution.

JUSTICE JACKSON, dissenting.

. . .

. . . [I]f any fundamental assumption underlies our system, it is that guilt is personal and not inheritable. Even if all of one's antecedents had been convicted of treason, the Constitution forbids its penalties to be visited upon him, for it provides that "no Attainder of Treason shall work Corruption of Blood, or Forfeiture except during the Life of the Person attained." But here is an attempt to make an otherwise innocent act a crime merely because this prisoner is the son of parents as to whom he had no choice, and belongs to a race from which there is no way to resign. If Congress in peace-time legislation should enact such a criminal law, I should suppose this Court would refuse to enforce it.

. . .

It would be impracticable and dangerous idealism to expect or insist that each specific military command in an area of probable operations will conform to conventional tests of constitutionality. When an area is so beset that it must be put under military control at all, the paramount consideration is that its measures be successful, rather than legal. The armed services must protect a society, not merely its Constitution. The very essence of the military job is to marshal physical force, to remove every obstacle to its effectiveness, to give it every strategic advantage. . . . No court can require such a commander in such circumstances to act as a reasonable man; he may be unreasonably cautious and exacting. Perhaps he should be. But a commander in temporarily focusing the life of a community on defense is carrying out a military program; he is not making law in the sense the courts know the term. He issues orders, and they may have a certain authority as military commands, although they may be very bad as constitutional law.

But if we cannot confine military expedients by the Constitution, neither would I distort the Constitution to approve all that the military may deem expedient. This is what the Court appears to be doing, whether consciously or not. I cannot say, from any evidence before me, that the orders of General DeWitt were not reasonably expedient military precautions, nor could I say that they were. But even if they were permissible military procedures, I deny that it follows that they are constitutional. If, as the Court holds, it does follow, then we may as well say that any military order will be constitutional and have done with it.

. . .

In the very nature of things military decisions are not susceptible of intelligent judicial appraisal. . . .

Much is said of the danger to liberty from the Army program for deporting and detaining these citizens of Japanese extraction. But a judicial construction of the due process clause that will sustain this order is a far more subtle blow to liberty than the promulgation of the order itself. A military order, however unconstitutional, is not apt to last longer than the military emergency. Even during that period a succeeding commander may revoke it all. But once a judicial opinion rationalizes such an order to show that it conforms to the Constitution, or rather rationalizes the Constitution to show that the Constitution sanctions such an order, the Court for all time has validated the principle of racial discrimination in criminal procedure and of transplanting American citizens. The principle then lies about like a loaded weapon ready for the hand of any authority that can bring forward a plausible claim of an urgent need. Every repetition imbeds that principle more deeply in our law and thinking and expands it to new purposes. All who observe the work of courts are familiar with what Judge Cardozo described as "the tendency of a principle to expand itself to the limit of its logic." A military commander may overstep the bounds of constitutionality, and it is an incident. But if we review and approve, that passing incident becomes the doctrine of the Constitution. There it has a generative power of its own, and all that it creates will be in its own image. Nothing better illustrates this danger than does the Court's opinion in this case.

. . . I should hold that a civil court cannot be made to enforce an order which violates constitutional limitations even if it is a reasonable exercise of military authority. The courts can exercise only the judicial power, can apply only law, and must abide by the Constitution, or they cease to be civil courts and become instruments of military policy.

Civil Rights Advocates Debate Strategy (1935)

The Journal of Negro Education *in 1935 ran a special edition on "The Courts and the Separate Negro School." Many prominent African American intellectuals contributed essays analyzing and critiquing efforts to eradicate by litigation the Jim Crow system of education. The most famous and controversial article was written by W. E. B. Du Bois, the leading African American scholar of the first third of the twentieth century and a founding member of the NAACP. Vigorously opposed to the litigation campaign implemented by Charles Houston, Du Bois resigned from the NAACP in the 1930s.*

The Du Bois and Thompson essays highlight significant disagreements within the African American community over how to best achieve racial equality in the United States. Suppose that the NAACP had adopted Du Bois's arguments. What would have been the probable consequences for the constitutional status of race relationships in the United States?

W. E. B. Du Bois, Does the Negro Need Separate Schools? (1935)[55]

...

... I know that race prejudice in the United States today is such that most Negroes cannot receive proper education in white institutions. If the public schools of Atlanta, Nashville, New Orleans and Jacksonville were thrown open to all races tomorrow, the education that colored children would get in them would be worse than pitiable. It would not be education. And in the same way, there are many public school systems in the North where Negroes are admitted and tolerated, but they are not educated; they are crucified. There are certain Northern universities where Negro students, no matter what their ability, desert, or accomplishment, cannot get fair recognition, either in classroom or on the campus, in dining halls and student activities, or in common human courtesy. . . .

Under such circumstances, there is no room for argument as to whether the Negro needs separate schools or not. The plain fact faces us, that either he will have separate schools or he will not be educated.

...

... There are times when one must stand up for principle at the cost of discomfort, harm, and death. But in the case of the education of the young, you must consider not simply yourself but the children and the relation of children to life. It is difficult to think of anything more important for the development of a people than proper training for their children; and yet I have repeatedly seen wise and loving colored parents take infinite pains to force their little children into schools where the white children, white teachers, and white parents despised and resented the dark child, made a mock of it, neglected or bullied it, and literally rendered its life a living hell. . . . Therefore, in evaluating the advantage and disadvantage of accepting race hatred as a brutal but real fact, or of using a little child as a battering ram upon which its nastiness can be thrust, we must give greater value and greater emphasis to the rights of the child's own soul. We shall get a finer, better balance of spirit; an infinitely more capable and rounded personality by putting children in schools where they are wanted, and where they are happy and inspired, than in thrusting them into halls where they are ridiculed and hated.

...

... Negroes must know the history of the Negro race in America, and this they will seldom get in white institutions. . . . Negroes who celebrate the birthdays of Washington and Lincoln and the worthy, but colorless and relatively unimportant "founders" of various Negro colleges, ought not to forget the 5th of March—that first national holiday of this country, which commemorates the martyrdom of Crispus Attucks. They ought to celebrate Negro Health Week and Negro History Week. They ought to study intelligently and from their own point of view, the slave trade, slavery, emancipation, Reconstruction, and present economic development.

...

To sum up this; theoretically, the Negro needs neither segregated schools nor mixed schools. What he needs is Education. What he must remember is that there is no magic, either in mixed schools or in segregated schools. A mixed school with poor and unsympathetic teachers, with hostile public opinion, and no teaching of truth concerning black folk, is bad. A segregated school with ignorant placeholders, inadequate equipment, poor salaries, and wretched housing, is equally bad. Other things being equal, the mixed school is the broader, more natural basis for the education of all youth. It gives wider contacts; it suppresses the inferiority complex. But other things seldom are equal, and in that case, Sympathy, Knowledge, and the Truth, outweigh all that the mixed school can offer.

Chas. H. Thompson, Court Action the Only Reasonable Alternative to Remedy Immediate Abuses of the Negro Separate School (1935)[56]

...

In the first instance, I think most of us would agree that to *segregate* is to *stigmatize*, however much we may try to rationalize it. We segregate the criminal, the insane, pupils with low I.Q.'s, Negroes, and other undesirables. To argue that Negroes are no more stigmatized than white people who are also segregated is, and should be recognized, as sheer sophistry. For we

55. Excerpt taken from W. E. B. Du Bois, "Does the Negro Need Separate Schools?" *Journal of Negro Education* 4 (1935): 328–35.

56. Excerpt taken from Chas H. Thompson, "Court Action the Only Reasonable Alternative to Remedy Immediate Abuses of the Negro Separate School," *Journal of Negro Education* 4 (1935): 419–34.

all know that segregation is practically always initiated on the basis that Negroes are inferior and undesirable. Thus, when Negroes allow themselves to be cajoled into accepting the status defined by the separate school, they do something to their personalities which is infinitely worse than any of the discomforts *some* of them *may* experience in a mixed school.

In the second instance, the separate school is generally uneconomical, and frequently financially burdensome. Except in very large cities where the Negro population is fairly dense, separate schools mean costly duplication of facilities and an unreasonable increase in school expenditures. Consequently, where sufficient funds are not available to support decent schools for both whites and Negroes, and even in many cases where they are sufficient, it is the Negro school that suffers, and there is very little that is done about it. . . .

In the third instance, and finally, not only is the separate school uneconomical and undemocratic but it results in the *mis*-education of both races. Separation of the two racial groups, at an early age, when they should be learning to know and respect each other, develops anti-racial and provincial attitudes in both, and necessitates, in adulthood, re-education against tremendous odds. The net results of such an educational policy are that the Negro develops an almost ineradicable inferiority complex and evolves a set of

Illustration 8-6 Thurgood Marshall and Spottswood W. Robinson III

Thurgood Marshall (right) and Spottswood W. Robinson III, lead attorneys for the NAACP in *Brown v. Board of Education* (1954). Robinson became the first African-American to serve on the U.S. Court of Appeals for the District of Columbia when he was appointed by President Lyndon Johnson in 1964. Marshall became the first African-American to serve on the U.S. Supreme Court when Johnson appointed him to that office in 1967.

Source: Library of Congress Prints and Photographs Division Washington, D.C. 20540.

Jim Crow standards and values; the white child develops an unwarranted sense of superiority—if not an actual contempt for or indifference towards the Negro. And both races develop a misunderstanding of each other that necessitates all of the expensive and ineffective race-relations machinery that we have in this country at the present time. . . .

Brown v. Board of Education of Topeka (Brown I), 347 U.S. 483 (1954)

Linda Brown was a young girl who attended the Monroe School, an all-black school in Topeka, Kansas. When she was seven her father attempted to enroll her in the Summer School, which by local ordinance was restricted to white children. The Summer School was attractive to the Brown family because it had better facilities and was closer to their house than the Monroe School. When the Summer School refused to enroll Linda Brown, her father, assisted by the local NAACP, filed a lawsuit claiming that the segregation law violated the equal protection clause of the Fourteenth Amendment. The federal district court in Kansas rejected the lawsuit, and the Brown family appealed to the Supreme Court of the United States. In 1952 the Supreme Court announced that the justices would adjudicate that appeal, along with similar suits filed in South Carolina, Virginia, Delaware, and the District of Columbia. The Truman administration submitted a legal brief supporting the NAACP that included a long passage inserted by the State Department emphasizing the difficulties that segregation posed for America's diplomatic efforts to win the hearts and minds of the "Third World" in the Cold War. The Court was unable to reach an agreement after the initial arguments and scheduled a second hearing, asking the parties to focus particularly on the original meaning of the Fourteenth Amendment in regard to racially segregated public schools. By then Dwight Eisenhower had been inaugurated and his nomination of California's former Republican governor Earl Warren as chief justice had been confirmed. The Eisenhower Justice Department reaffirmed the federal government's support for judicial action against segregation.

Brown v. Board of Education *was the culmination of a long litigation campaign aimed at overturning the ruling in* Plessy v. Ferguson *(1896) that the Fourteenth Amendment did not prohibit "separate but equal" facilities for blacks and whites. By the early 1950s the NAACP had won a string of victories that chipped away at the concept of "separate but equal" in the context of segregated schools. In* State of Missouri ex rel. Gaines v. Canada *(1938) the Supreme Court ruled that states had to provide legal education to persons of color within the state.* Sipuel v. Board of Regents of University of Oklahoma *(1948) held that qualified persons of color were entitled to immediate admission into a formerly all-white law school and did not have to wait for the state to establish a separate institution for students of color.* McLaurin v. Oklahoma State Regents *(1950) added that African American students attending formerly all-white graduate programs could not be segregated from white students when doing so might interfere with their ability to obtain an equal education.* Sweatt v. Painter *(1950) established that a separate school for students of color had to be equal in all respects to a school restricted to white students. A crucial passage in the* Sweatt *opinion raised questions about whether, in a society in which white persons held all the positions of influence, a separate institution for students of color could ever be the equal of a white institution. Chief Justice Vinson observed,*

> *The University of Texas Law School possesses to a far greater degree those qualities which are incapable of objective measurement but which make for greatness in a law school. Such qualities, to name but a few, include reputation of the faculty, experience of the administration, position and influence of the alumni, standing in the community, traditions and prestige. It is difficult to believe that one who had a free choice between these law schools would consider the question close.*

Public primary and secondary education posed a tougher challenge. Because those schools affected far more people and involved young children, they were much more politically sensitive. Case-by-case litigation was a prohibitively expensive and time-consuming proposition. Hopes that southern states would abolish separate schools rather than fund them adequately proven futile. Such states as South Carolina were willing to commit the substantial funds perceived as necessary to salvage the separate schools. Many black parents and teachers were far more interested in increasing the resources flowing into black schools than in eliminating these schools in favor of integrated facilities. Persons who challenged segregated schools ran exceptional personal risks. Consider the fate of Joseph DeLaine, the person responsible for the South Carolina lawsuit against segregated schools:

> *Before it was over, they fired him from the little schoolhouse at the church he had taught devotedly for ten*

years. And they fired his wife and two of his sisters and a niece. And they threatened him with bodily harm. And they sued him on trumped-up charges and convicted him in a kangaroo court and left him with a judgment that denied him credit from any bank. And they burned his house to the ground while the fire department stood around watching the flames consume the night. And they stoned the church at which he pastored. And fired shotguns at him out of the dark.[57]

The Supreme Court in Brown *unanimously declared public school segregation unconstitutional. Chief Justice Earl Warren's opinion maintained that Jim Crow education deprived children of color of an equal education. No prominent (or even not-so-prominent) commentator at present would overrule the decision, but disagreement exists on the proper basis for declaring school segregation unconstitutional. On what basis did the Justice Department and Chief Justice Warren believe segregated schools to be unconstitutional? Do you believe that either justification is correct? Are the arguments in the* Brown *opinion even legally credible, or are they better explained by Warren's determination to rally a unanimous Court and not offend southern sensibilities any more than necessary? What is the best constitutional justification for* Brown?

Brief for the United States, Amicus Curiae, *Brown v. Board of Education*

. . .

[These cases raise] questions of the first importance in our society. For racial discriminations imposed by law, or having the sanction or support of government, inevitably tend to undermine the foundations of a society dedicated to freedom, justice, and equality. The proposition that all men are created equal is not mere rhetoric. It implies a rule of law—an indispensable condition to a civilized society—under which all men stand equal and alike in the rights and opportunities secured to them by their government. Under the Constitution every agency of government, national and local, legislative, executive, and judicial, must treat each of our people as an *American,* and not as a member of a particular group classified on the basis of race or some other constitutional irrelevancy. The color of a man's skin—like his religious beliefs, or his political attachments, or the country from which he or his ancestors came to the United States—does not diminish or alter his legal status or constitutional rights. "Our Constitution is color-blind, and neither knows nor tolerates classes among citizens."

. . .

It is in the context of the present world struggle between freedom and tyranny that the problem of racial discrimination must be viewed. The United States is trying to prove to the people of the world, of every nationality, race, and color, that a free democracy is the most civilized and most secure form of government yet devised by man. We must set an example for others by showing firm determination to remove existing flaws in our democracy.

The existence of discrimination against minority groups in the United States has an adverse effect upon our relations with other countries. Racial discrimination furnishes grist for the Communist propaganda mills, and it raises doubts even among friendly nations as to the intensity of our devotion to the democratic faith. . . .

The Government submits that compulsory racial segregation is itself, without more, an unconstitutional discrimination. "Separate but equal" is a contradiction in terms. Schools or other public facilities where persons are segregated by law, solely on the basis of race or color, cannot in any circumstances be regarded as equal. The constitutional requirement is that of equality, not merely in one sense of the word but in every sense. Nothing in the language or history of the Fourteenth Amendment supports the notion that facilities need be equal only in a physical sense.

People who are compelled by law to live in a ghetto do not enjoy equality, even though their houses are as good as, or better than, those on the outside. . . . The same is true of children who know that because of their color the law sets them apart from others, and requires them to attend separate schools specially established for members of their race. The facts of everyday life confirm the finding of the district court in the Kansas case that segregation has a "detrimental effect" on colored children; that it affects their motivation to learn; and that it has a tendency to retard their educational and mental development and to deprive them of benefits they would receive in an integrated school system. . . .

57. Richard Kluger, *Simple Justice: The History of* Brown v. Board of Education *and Black America's Struggle for Equality* (New York: Knopf, 1984), 3.

. . .

In these days, when the free world must conserve and fortify the moral as well as the material sources of its strength, it is especially important to affirm that the Constitution of the United States places no limitation, express or implied, on the principle of the equality of all men before the law. Mr. Justice Harlan said in his dissent in the *Plessy* case,

> We boast of the freedom enjoyed by our people above all other peoples. But it is difficult to reconcile that boast with a state of the law which, practically, puts the brand of servitude and degradation upon a large class of our fellow-citizens, our equals before the law.

The Government and people of the United States must prove by their actions that the ideals expressed in the Bill of Rights are living realities, not literary abstractions. As the President has stated:

> If we wish to inspire the people of the world whose freedom is in jeopardy, if we wish to restore hope to those who have already lost their civil liberties, if we wish to fulfill the promise that is ours, we must correct the remaining imperfections in our practice of democracy.

We know the way. We need only the Will.

CHIEF JUSTICE WARREN delivered the opinion of the Court.

. . .

The plaintiffs contend that segregated public schools are not "equal" and cannot be made "equal," and that hence they are deprived of the equal protection of the laws. . . .

Reargument was largely devoted to the circumstances surrounding the adoption of the Fourteenth Amendment in 1868. . . . This discussion and our own investigation convince us that, although these sources cast some light, it is not enough to resolve the problem with which we are faced. At best, they are inconclusive. The most avid proponents of the post-War Amendments undoubtedly intended them to remove all legal distinctions among "all persons born or naturalized in the United States." Their opponents, just as certainly, were antagonistic to both the letter and the spirit of the Amendments and wished them to have the most limited effect. What others in Congress and the state legislatures had in mind cannot be determined with any degree of certainty.

An additional reason for the inconclusive nature of the Amendment's history, with respect to segregated schools, is the status of public education at that time. In the South, the movement toward free common schools, supported by general taxation, had not yet taken hold. Education of white children was largely in the hands of private groups. Education of Negroes was almost nonexistent, and practically all of the race were illiterate. In fact, any education of Negroes was forbidden by law in some states. Today, in contrast, many Negroes have achieved outstanding success in the arts and sciences as well as in the business and professional world. It is true that public school education at the time of the Amendment had advanced further in the North, but the effect of the Amendment on Northern States was generally ignored in the congressional debates. . . . As a consequence, it is not surprising that there should be so little in the history of the Fourteenth Amendment relating to its intended effect on public education.

. . .

. . . [T]here are findings below that the Negro and white schools involved have been equalized, or are being equalized, with respect to buildings, curricula, qualifications and salaries of teachers, and other "tangible" factors. Our decision, therefore, cannot turn on merely a comparison of these tangible factors in the Negro and white schools involved in each of the cases. We must look instead to the effect of segregation itself on public education.

In approaching this problem, we cannot turn the clock back to 1868 when the Amendment was adopted, or even to 1896 when *Plessy v. Ferguson* was written. We must consider public education in the light of its full development and its present place in American life throughout the Nation. Only in this way can it be determined if segregation in public schools deprives these plaintiffs of the equal protection of the laws.

Today, education is perhaps the most important function of state and local governments. Compulsory school attendance laws and the great expenditures for education both demonstrate our recognition of the importance of education to our democratic society. It is required in the performance of our most basic public responsibilities, even service in the armed forces. It is the very foundation of good citizenship. Today it is a principal instrument in awakening the child to cultural values, in preparing him for later professional training, and in helping him to adjust normally to his environment. In these days, it is doubtful that any child may reasonably be expected to succeed in life if he is denied the opportunity of an education. Such an opportunity, where the state has undertaken to provide it, is a right which must be made available to all on equal terms.

We come then to the question presented: Does segregation of children in public schools solely on the basis of race, even though the physical facilities and other "tangible" factors may be equal, deprive the children of the minority group of equal educational opportunities? We believe that it does.

In *Sweatt v. Painter* (1950), in finding that a segregated law school for Negroes could not provide them equal educational opportunities, this Court relied in large part on "those qualities which are incapable of objective measurement but which make for greatness in a law school." In *McLaurin v. Oklahoma State Regents* (1950), the Court, in requiring that a Negro admitted to a white graduate school be treated like all other students, again resorted to intangible considerations: " . . . his ability to study, to engage in discussions and exchange views with other students, and, in general, to learn his profession." Such considerations apply with added force to children in grade and high schools. To separate them from others of similar age and qualifications solely because of their race generates a feeling of inferiority as to their status in the community that may affect their hearts and minds in a way unlikely ever to be undone. . . . Whatever may have been the extent of psychological knowledge at the time of *Plessy v. Ferguson*, this finding is amply supported by modern authority.[58] Any language in *Plessy v. Ferguson* contrary to this finding is rejected.

58. [Footnote by the Court] K. B. Clark, *Effect of Prejudice and Discrimination on Personality Development* (Midcentury White House Conference on Children and Youth, 1950); Witmer and Kotinsky, *Personality in the Making* (1952), c. VI; Deutscher and Chein, The Psychological Effects of Enforced Segregation: A Survey of Social Science Opinion, 26 *J. Psychol.* 259 (1948); Chein, What are the Psychological Effects of Segregation Under Conditions of Equal Facilities?, 3 *Int. J. Opinion and Attitude Res.* 229 (1949); Brameld, Educational Costs, in *Discrimination and National Welfare* (MacIver, ed., 1949), 44–48; Frazier, *The Negro in the United States* (1949), 674–681. And see generally Myrdal, *An American Dilemma* (1944).

We conclude that in the field of public education the doctrine of "separate but equal" has no place. Separate educational facilities are inherently unequal. Therefore, we hold that the plaintiffs and others similarly situated for whom the actions have been brought are, by reason of the segregation complained of, deprived of the equal protection of the laws guaranteed by the Fourteenth Amendment. This disposition makes unnecessary any discussion whether such segregation also violates the Due Process Clause of the Fourteenth Amendment.

Because these are class actions, because of the wide applicability of this decision, and because of the great variety of local conditions, the formulation of decrees in these cases presents problems of considerable complexity. On reargument, the consideration of appropriate relief was necessarily subordinated to the primary question—the constitutionality of segregation in public education. We have now announced that such segregation is a denial of the equal protection of the laws. In order that we may have the full assistance of the parties in formulating decrees, the cases will be restored to the docket, and the parties are requested to present further argument. . . .

Green v. County School Board of New Kent County, 391 U.S. 430 (1968)

Charles Green was an African American child who attended public school in New Kent County, Virginia. When Green first entered the public school system New Kent County law required children to attend whatever school had previously been reserved for students of their race, unless their parents asked for a transfer. As of 1964 no student of either race had requested a transfer. In 1965 Green and other African American families sued the school board, claiming that the assignment system perpetuated the racial policies declared unconstitutional in Brown v. Board of Education *(1954). The school board responded by adopting a freedom of choice plan. Under this scheme for assigning pupils, parents could choose which school their children attended. All white children chose the school previously reserved for all-white children. Eighty-five percent of the African American parents chose the school previously reserved for children of color. The Greens renewed their lawsuit, insisting that New Kent County had still not complied with* Brown. *Their lawsuit was rejected by the federal district court and the Court of Appeals for the Fourth Circuit. The Greens appealed to the Supreme Court of the United States.*

Illustration 8-7 Elementary School Desegregation Protest in New Orleans, November 1960

Source: Times-Picayune.

The Supreme Court unanimously declared the freedom of choice plan unconstitutional. Justice Brennan's opinion for the Court insisted that school districts must immediately desegregate. Green *marks the end of "all deliberate speed" and the shift toward integration rather than desegregation as the remedy for* Brown *violations. How did Justice Brennan explain this decision? Do you think his explanation is correct? Is* Green *merely an application or an extension of* Brown?

JUSTICE BRENNAN delivered the opinion of the Court.

. . .

The pattern of separate "white" and "Negro" schools in the New Kent County school system established under compulsion of state laws is precisely the pattern of segregation to which *Brown I* and *Brown II* were particularly addressed, and which *Brown I* declared unconstitutionally denied Negro school children equal protection of the laws. Racial identification of the system's schools was complete, extending not just to the composition of student bodies at the two schools, but to every facet of school operations—faculty, staff, transportation, extracurricular activities and facilities. . . .

It was such dual systems that, 14 years ago, *Brown I* held unconstitutional. . . . It is, of course, true that, for the time immediately after *Brown II*, the concern was with making an initial break in a long-established pattern of excluding Negro children from schools attended by white children. . . . Under *Brown II*, that immediate goal was only the first step, however. The transition to a unitary, nonracial system of public education was and is the ultimate end to be brought about. . . .

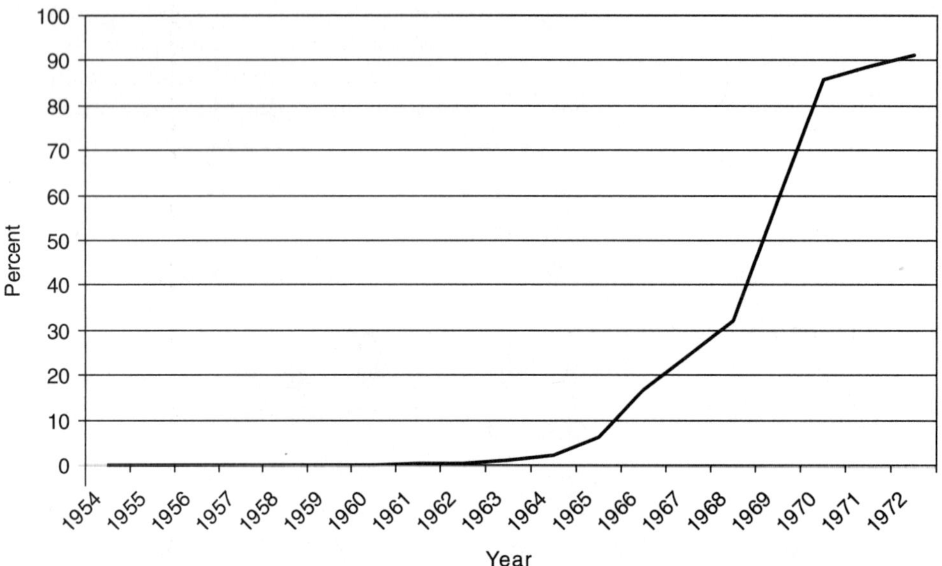

Figure 8-6 Percentage of All Black Southern Schoolchildren Attending School with Whites

Source: Gerald N. Rosenberg, *The Hollow Hope*, rev. ed. (Chicago: University of Chicago Press, 2008), 50. Missing data interpolated in figure.

It is against this background that 13 years after *Brown II* commanded the abolition of dual systems we must measure the effectiveness of respondent School Board's "freedom of choice" plan to achieve that end. The School Board contends that it has fully discharged its obligation by adopting a plan by which every student, regardless of race, may "freely" choose the school he will attend. The Board attempts to cast the issue in its broadest form by arguing that its "freedom of choice" plan may be faulted only by reading the Fourteenth Amendment as universally requiring "compulsory integration," a reading it insists the wording of the Amendment will not support. But that argument ignores the thrust of *Brown II.* In the light of the command of that case, what is involved here is the question whether the Board has achieved the "racially nondiscriminatory school system" *Brown II* held must be effectuated in order to remedy the established unconstitutional deficiencies of its segregated system. In the context of the state-imposed segregated pattern of long standing, the fact that, in 1965, the Board opened the doors of the former "white" school to Negro children and of the "Negro" school to white children merely begins, not ends, our inquiry whether the Board has taken steps adequate to abolish its dual, segregated system. *Brown II* was a call for the dismantling of well entrenched dual systems tempered by an awareness that complex and multifaceted problems would arise which would require time and flexibility for a successful resolution. School boards such as the respondent then operating state-compelled dual systems were nevertheless clearly charged with the affirmative duty to take whatever steps might be necessary to convert to a unitary system in which racial discrimination would be eliminated root and branch. . . .

In determining whether respondent School Board met that command by adopting its "freedom of choice" plan, it is relevant that this first step did not come until some 11 years after *Brown I* was decided and 10 years after *Brown II* directed the making of a "prompt and reasonable start." This deliberate perpetuation of the unconstitutional dual system can only have compounded the harm of such a system. Such delays are no longer tolerable. . . . Moreover, a plan that, at this late date, fails to provide meaningful assurance of prompt and effective disestablishment of a dual system is also intolerable. "The time for mere deliberate speed has run out." . . . The burden on a school board today is to come forward with a plan that promises realistically to work, and promises realistically to work now. . . .

C. Gender

American women from 1933 to 1968 gained many legal rights but no additional constitutional rights. Traditional restrictions on women's economic and social liberties were repealed or not enforced. A small but steadily increasing number of women became lawyers, doctors, members of other professions, and elected officials. Still, although many barriers collapsed, constitutional law remained largely the same. States less often passed laws that made gender distinctions or otherwise discriminated on the basis of gender, but most constitutional decision makers thought that those laws that were passed or remained on the books were consistent with the Fourteenth Amendment. In several decisions, most notably *Goesaert v. Cleary* (1948) and *Hoyt v. Florida* (1961), the Supreme Court insisted that gender distinctions and classifications merited no special protection.

X. Criminal Justice

MAJOR DEVELOPMENTS

- The Supreme Court begins to impose national standards on the criminal justice system in what has become known as the "Due Process Revolution"
- The Supreme Court excludes unconstitutionally obtained evidence from state criminal trials
- The Supreme Court requires police officers to read *Miranda* warnings to suspects in custody before beginning interrogations

The New Deal/Great Society Era witnessed the Due Process Revolution. Federal and state courts dramatically expanded the constitutional rights of criminal suspects. During the 1930s and 1940s the Supreme Court aggressively protected victims of particularly egregious police practices, most notably persons of color in the Jim Crow South. During the 1950s and 1960s the justices nationalized almost every constitutional protection for criminal suspects in the Bill of Rights. The Warren Court handed down decisions that significantly expanded the constitutional protections offered by the Fourth, Fifth, Sixth, and Eighth Amendments. By the time Richard Nixon took office persons accused of crimes enjoyed unprecedented constitutional protections from the moment that the police first suspected they had broken the law until all the collateral consequences of their criminal sentences were removed. As Figure 8-7 suggests, the liberal justices of the post–New Deal period were not united on these developments. Liberal New Deal justices were often more supportive of other civil liberties claims than they were of the claims made by criminal defendants and criminal suspects. The replacement of New Dealers such as Justice Reed with a new generation of Great Society liberals such as Justice Brennan proved crucial to the Due Process Revolution.

The Due Process and civil rights revolutions were closely connected. Prominent elites expressed concern with local practices that discriminated against poor persons and persons of color. The Wickersham Commission of 1931 was the first of many blue-ribbon panels that found "much evidence that despite this constitutional declaration and because of the obstacles thus presented, confessions of guilt frequently are unlawfully extorted by the police from prisoners by means of cruel treatment, colloquially known as the third degree."[59] Many prominent Warren Court decisions protecting the rights of criminal suspects concerned persons of color who were victims of racist practices. Quite frequently the Supreme Court insisted that southern law enforcement officials adopt practices already implemented by federal law enforcement officials. Decisions such as *Miranda v. Arizona* (1965), Lucas Powe suggests, were intended "to force state systems to behave like [the justices] assumed the Federal Bureau of Investigation (FBI), United States attorneys, and the federal courts behaved."[60]

A. Due Process and Habeas Corpus

Due process and habeas corpus rights were expanded during the New Deal/Great Society Era. The Supreme Court declared that the due process clause of the Fourteenth Amendment required states to respect virtually every provision in the Bill of Rights that regulated criminal procedure. The justices ruled that the due process clause required giving indigent defendants access to state transcripts (*Griffin v. Illinois* [1956]) and lawyers (*Douglas v. California* [1963]) during their first appeal of a criminal conviction, as well as requiring states to take steps to make sure adverse pretrial publicity did not

59. Wickersham Commission Reports, *No. 11 Report on Lawlessness in Law Enforcement* (Montclair, NJ: Patterson Smith, 1968), 153.

60. Powe, *Warren Court*, 492.

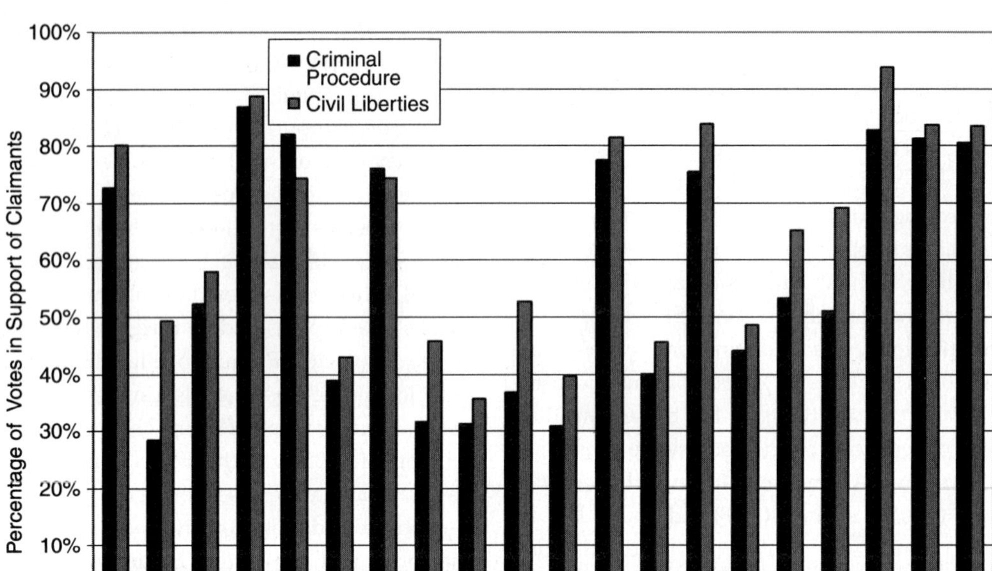

Figure 8-7 Individual Justice Support for Claimants in Criminal Procedure and Civil Liberties Cases on the Vinson and Warren Courts

Source: Supreme Court Database, www.scdb.wustl.edu.

Notes: Justices listed in order of appointment. Category of civil liberties cases excludes criminal justice cases.

interfere with the defendant's right to a fair trial (*Estes v. Texas* [1965]; *Sheppard v. Maxwell* [1966]). The Warren Court dramatically expanded access to federal habeas corpus. In a series of decisions, the most important of which was *Brown v. Allen* (1953), the justices opened the federal courthouse doors to any state prisoner who believed that his constitutional rights had been violated at trial. *Fay v. Noia* (1963) ruled that federal courts could sometimes hear constitutional claims that had not first been raised in state courts. *Townsend v. Sain* (1963) permitted federal courts to hold factual hearings on those claims, and, as every civil rights lawyer knew, federal courts in the 1960s were far more likely than state courts to find facts favorable to the defendant. Congress codified these decisions when passing the Federal Habeas Corpus Act of 1966.

B. Search and Seizure

New Deal liberals were initially inclined to limit constitutional protections against official searches. In *Oklahoma Press Publishing Company v. Walling* (1946) the Supreme Court unanimously brushed aside a claim that federal officials had no right to search corporate books to see whether a corporation was acting in a manner consistent with the Federal Labor Standards Act. Justice Wiley Rutledge's majority opinion bluntly asserted, "The Fifth Amendment affords no protection by virtue of the self-incrimination provision, whether for the corporation or for its officers; and the Fourth, if applicable, at the most guards against abuse only by way of too much indefiniteness or breadth in the things required to be 'particularly described.'" The judicial majority in *Wolf v. People of the State of Colorado* (1949) held that states were not required to adhere to the federal exclusionary rule established in *Weeks v. United States* (1914).

Great Society liberals had a more expansive interpretation of constitutional rights against search and seizure. In 1961 the Supreme Court ruled that the due process clause of the Fourteenth Amendment forbade states from introducing unconstitutionally obtained evidence during criminal trials. When nationalizing the exclusionary rule in *Mapp v. Ohio* (1961), Justice Clark's majority opinion stated, "Having once recognized that the right to privacy embodied in the Fourth Amendment is enforceable against the States, and that the right to be secure against rude invasions of privacy by state officers is, therefore, constitutional in origin, we can no longer permit that right to remain an empty promise." Six years later the Supreme Court overruled *Olmstead v. United States* (1928). *Katz v. United States* (1967) determined that police must normally obtain a warrant before wiretapping. Justice Stewart's majority opinion declared that the Fourth and Fourteenth Amendments protect areas and matters in which people have "a reasonable expectation of privacy" and that warrantless searches, no matter how reasonable, are presumptively unconstitutional.

Mapp v. Ohio, 367 U.S. 643 (1961)

Several Cleveland police officers forcibly entered the home of Dollree Mapp on May 23, 1957. Despite having no search warrant, the officers searched the house and found obscene material. On the basis of that evidence, Ms. Mapp was tried, convicted, and sentenced to an indeterminate prison term. The Supreme Court of Ohio sustained the conviction on the ground that the evidence was not unconstitutionally obtained and, even if unconstitutionally obtained, was admissible at trial under Ohio constitutional law. Mapp appealed that decision to the Supreme Court of the United States primarily on the ground that her conviction for obscenity violated the First Amendment.

The Supreme Court by a 6–3 vote ruled that Mapp's Fourth and Fourteenth Amendment rights had been violated when unconstitutionally obtained evidence was introduced at her trial. Justice Clark's Mapp *opinion overruled* Wolf v. People of the State of Colorado *(1949), which held that evidence seized in violation of the Fourth Amendment could be introduced in a state criminal trial. Clark stated that the "factual considerations" underlying* Wolf *had changed. What were those factual considerations? How had they changed? Did those changes make a constitutional difference? How did Justice Clark justify the exclusionary rule? Did he claim that the exclusionary rule deters unconstitutional searches? Did he insist that the government should not profit by its own wrongdoing? Does either justification explain satisfactorily why courts must exclude reliable evidence of guilt from a criminal trial?*

JUSTICE CLARK delivered the opinion of the Court.

. . .

The Court in *Wolf v. Colorado* (1949) first stated that "[t]he contrariety of views of the States" on the adoption of the exclusionary rule of *Weeks v. United States* (1914) was "particularly impressive." . . . While in 1949, prior to the *Wolf* case, almost two-thirds of the States were opposed to the use of the exclusionary rule, now, despite the *Wolf* case, more than half of those since passing upon it, by their own legislative or judicial decision, have wholly or partly adopted or adhered to the *Weeks* rule. . . . Significantly, among those now following the rule is California, which, according to its highest court, was "compelled to reach that conclusion because other remedies have completely failed to secure compliance with the constitutional provisions. . . ." In connection with this California case, we note that the second basis elaborated in *Wolf* in support of its failure to enforce the exclusionary doctrine against the States was that "other means of protection" have been afforded "the right to privacy." The experience of California that such other remedies have been worthless and futile is buttressed by the experience of other States. The obvious futility of relegating the Fourth Amendment to the protection of other remedies has, moreover, been recognized by this Court since *Wolf*. . . .

. . .

It, therefore, plainly appears that the factual considerations supporting the failure of the *Wolf* Court to include the *Weeks* exclusionary rule when it recognized the enforceability of the right to privacy against the States in 1949, while not basically relevant to the constitutional consideration, could not, in any analysis, now be deemed controlling.

. . .

Since the Fourth Amendment's right of privacy has been declared enforceable against the States through the Due Process Clause of the Fourteenth, it is enforceable against them by the same sanction of exclusion as is used against the Federal Government. Were it otherwise, then just as without the *Weeks* rule the assurance against unreasonable federal searches and seizures would be "a form of words," valueless and undeserving of mention in a perpetual charter of inestimable human liberties, so too, without that rule the freedom from state invasions of privacy would be so ephemeral and so neatly severed from its conceptual nexus with the freedom from all brutish means of coercing evidence as not to merit this Court's high regard as a freedom "implicit in the concept of ordered liberty." At the time that the Court held in *Wolf* that the Amendment was applicable to the States through the Due Process

Clause, the cases of this Court, as we have seen, had steadfastly held that as to federal officers the Fourth Amendment included the exclusion of the evidence seized in violation of its provisions. Even *Wolf* "stoutly adhered" to that proposition. . . . Therefore, in extending the substantive protections of due process to all constitutionally unreasonable searches—state or federal—it was logically and constitutionally necessary that the exclusion doctrine—an essential part of the right to privacy—be also insisted upon as an essential ingredient of the right newly recognized by the *Wolf* case. In short, the admission of the new constitutional right by *Wolf* could not consistently tolerate denial of its most important constitutional privilege, namely, the exclusion of the evidence which an accused had been forced to give by reason of the unlawful seizure. To hold otherwise is to grant the right but in reality to withhold its privilege and enjoyment. . . .

. . .

. . . [O]ur holding that the exclusionary rule is an essential part of both the Fourth and Fourteenth Amendments is not only the logical dictate of prior cases, but it also makes very good sense. There is no war between the Constitution and common sense. Presently, a federal prosecutor may make no use of evidence illegally seized, but a State's attorney across the street may, although he supposedly is operating under the enforceable prohibitions of the same Amendment. Thus the State, by admitting evidence unlawfully seized, serves to encourage disobedience to the Federal Constitution which it is bound to uphold.

. . .

There are those who say, as did Justice (then Judge) Cardozo, that under our constitutional exclusionary doctrine "[t]he criminal is to go free because the constable has blundered." *People v. Defore* (1926). . . . In some cases this will undoubtedly be the result. But . . . "there is another consideration—the imperative of judicial integrity." . . . The criminal goes free, if he must, but it is the law that sets him free. Nothing can destroy a government more quickly than its failure to observe its own laws, or worse, its disregard of the charter of its own existence. . . . Nor can it lightly be assumed that, as a practical matter, adoption of the exclusionary rule fetters law enforcement. Only last year this Court expressly considered that contention and found that "pragmatic evidence of a sort" to the contrary was not wanting. *Elkins v. United States* (1960). . . . The Court noted that

The federal courts themselves have operated under the exclusionary rule of *Weeks* for almost half a century; yet it has not been suggested either that the Federal Bureau of Investigation has thereby been rendered ineffective, or that the administration of criminal justice in the federal courts has thereby been disrupted. . . .

The ignoble shortcut to conviction left open to the State tends to destroy the entire system of constitutional restraints on which the liberties of the people rest. Having once recognized that the right to privacy embodied in the Fourth Amendment is enforceable against the States, and that the right to be secure against rude invasions of privacy by state officers is, therefore, constitutional in origin, we can no longer permit that right to remain an empty promise. Because it is enforceable in the same manner and to like effect as other basic rights secured by the Due Process Clause, we can no longer permit it to be revocable at the whim of any police officer who, in the name of law enforcement itself, chooses to suspend its enjoyment. Our decision, founded on reason and truth, gives to the individual no more than that which the Constitution guarantees him, to the police officer no less than that to which honest law enforcement is entitled, and, to the courts, that judicial integrity so necessary in the true administration of justice.

JUSTICE BLACK, concurring.

. . .

. . . [W]hen the Fourth Amendment's ban against unreasonable searches and seizures is considered together with the Fifth Amendment's ban against compelled self-incrimination, a constitutional basis emerges which not only justifies but actually requires the exclusionary rule.

The close interrelationship between the Fourth and Fifth Amendments, as they apply to this problem, has long been recognized and, indeed, was expressly made the ground for this Court's holding in *Boyd v. United States* (1886). There the Court fully discussed this relationship and declared itself "unable to perceive that the seizure of a man's private books and papers to be used in evidence against him is substantially different from compelling him to be a witness against himself." . . . [I]t seems to me that the *Boyd* doctrine, though perhaps not required by the express language of the Constitution strictly construed, is amply justified from an historical standpoint, soundly based in reason, and entirely consistent with what I regard to be the proper approach to interpretation of our Bill of Rights. . . .

. . .

JUSTICE DOUGLAS, concurring.

. . .

When we allowed States to give constitutional sanction to the "shabby business" of unlawful entry into a home, . . . we did indeed rob the Fourth Amendment of much meaningful force. There are, of course, other theoretical remedies. One is disciplinary action within the hierarchy of the police system, including prosecution of the police officer for a crime. Yet . . . , "Self-scrutiny is a lofty ideal, but its exaltation reaches new heights if we expect a District Attorney to prosecute himself or his associates for well-meaning violations of the search and seizure clause during a raid the District Attorney or his associates have ordered."

The only remaining remedy, if exclusion of the evidence is not required, is an action of trespass by the homeowner against the offending officer. . . . The truth is that trespass actions against officers who make unlawful searches and seizures are mainly illusory remedies.

. . .

Memorandum of JUSTICE STEWART.

[*Justice Stewart insisted that Ms. Mapp's conviction violated the First Amendment and did not discuss the Fourth Amendment issue.*]

JUSTICE HARLAN, whom JUSTICE FRANKFURTER and JUSTICE WHITTAKER join, dissenting.

. . .

I would not impose upon the States this federal exclusionary remedy. The reasons given by the majority for now suddenly turning its back on *Wolf* seem to me notably unconvincing.

. . . [I]t is said that "the factual grounds upon which *Wolf* was based" have since changed, in that more States now follow the *Weeks* exclusionary rule than was so at the time *Wolf* was decided. While that is true, a recent survey indicates that at present one-half of the States still adhere to the common-law non-exclusionary rule, and one, Maryland, retains the rule as to felonies. . . . But in any case surely all this is beside the point, as the majority itself indeed seems to recognize. Our concern here, as it was in *Wolf*, is not with the desirability of that rule but only with the question whether the States are constitutionally free to follow it or not as they may themselves determine, and the relevance of the disparity of views among the States on this point lies simply in the fact that the judgment involved is a debatable one. Moreover, the very fact on which the majority relies, instead of lending support to what is now being done, points away from the need of replacing voluntary state action with federal compulsion.

. . .

An approach which regards the issue as one of achieving procedural symmetry or of serving administrative convenience surely disfigures the boundaries of this Court's functions in relation to the state and federal courts. Our role in promulgating the *Weeks* rule . . . was quite a different one than it is here. There, in implementing the Fourth Amendment, we occupied the position of a tribunal having the ultimate responsibility for developing the standards and procedures of judicial administration within the judicial system over which it presides. Here we review state procedures whose measure is to be taken not against the specific substantive commands of the Fourth Amendment but under the flexible contours of the Due Process Clause. I do not believe that the Fourteenth Amendment empowers this Court to mould state remedies effectuating the right to freedom from "arbitrary intrusion by the police" to suit its own notions of how things should be done. . . .

I regret that I find so unwise in principle and so inexpedient in policy a decision motivated by the high purpose of increasing respect for Constitutional rights. But in the last analysis I think this Court can increase respect for the Constitution only if it rigidly respects the limitations which the Constitution places upon it, and respects as well the principles inherent in its own processes. In the present case I think we exceed both, and that our voice becomes only a voice of power, not of reason.

C. Interrogations

Three decisions handed down between 1964 and 1966 moved American constitutional law from concerns with whether a confession in a particular case was reliable to a concern with taking the prophylactic steps necessary to ensure that defendants were aware of their right to not confess. In *Massiah v. United States* (1964) the justices ruled that federal agents could not interrogate a criminal suspect in the absence of counsel after the suspect had been indicted. *Esobedo v. State of Illinois* (1964) held that criminal suspects could not be interrogated by police after they had requested to speak with an attorney. *Miranda v. Arizona* (1966) required that police provide criminal suspects in custody with four pieces of information before beginning an interrogation.

- They had the right to remain silent.
- If they did not remain silent, the information they provided could be used in a court of law.
- They had a right to an attorney.
- If they could not afford an attorney, one would be provided for them.

Should an accused wish to exercise those rights, interrogation had to stop.

Miranda v. Arizona, 384 U.S. 436 (1966)

On March 13, 1963, Ernesto Miranda was arrested for kidnapping and raping an eighteen-year-old woman. At the time of his arrest Miranda was a twenty-three-year-old junior high school dropout. At the station house Miranda was questioned for two hours until he confessed. All parties agreed that he had not been informed of his right to have a lawyer present, but there was no evidence that Miranda was beaten or threatened in any way during the interrogation. That confession was admitted into evidence at a jury trial over defense counsel's objections. Miranda was found guilty and sentenced to twenty to thirty years in prison. The Supreme Court of Arizona affirmed the conviction. Miranda appealed to the Supreme Court of the United States.

The Supreme Court by a 5–4 vote declared that Miranda's confession was unconstitutionally obtained. Chief Justice Warren's majority opinion held that confessions may not normally be introduced at criminal trials unless suspects had been advised that they had a right to remain silent, that any confession could be used against them, that they had a right to an attorney, and that, if indigent, the court would appoint an attorney to represent them. Should the Supreme Court have made prophylactic rules aimed at reducing the number of coerced confessions or simply determined whether a confession in a particular case was voluntary? If constitutionality had to be determined on a case-by-case basis, would the Supreme Court have to review the specific circumstances of every challenged confession? Assuming that the Court was justified in making prophylactic rules, does Miranda *establish the correct rules? Chief Justice Warren's opinion maintains that pursuit of confessions distracts police from actually investigating crimes. Does this comment express the American commitment to an adversarial (as opposed to an inquisitorial) criminal process, or does the* Miranda *opinion seriously underestimate the role of interrogations and confessions?*

Whether and how Miranda *has influenced police practices remains controversial. One dispute concerns the Warren Court's degree of interference with law enforcement. Paul Cassell in 1996 claimed to have demonstrated statistically that "*Miranda *has significantly harmed law enforcement efforts in this country." He estimated that the* Miranda *decision has prevented a confession in one out of every six criminal cases, freeing about 28,000 "serious violent offenders" and 79,000 "property offenders."*[61] *Other scholars, most notably Stephen Schulhofer, question Cassell's data. Schulhofer insists that the statistical impact of* Miranda *is closer to zero.*[62] *A related controversy is over the extent to which* Miranda *warnings actually reduce confessions. Summarizing many studies on the subject, Gerald Rosenberg concludes that "warnings are given because . . . they don't affect police work very much." He notes that "while the police may give the warnings, they do so in a way calculated to diminish or disparage their impact," and that most criminal suspects, even after being warned, do "not appreciate the reasons for remaining silent."*[63]

Miranda *had a clearer influence on constitutional politics. For much of the New Deal/Great Society Era, constitutional criminal procedure was often part of a civil rights or antipoverty agenda.* Miranda *was decided at a time when crime rates were increasing substantially and riots were taking place in many inner cities, including south-central Los Angeles (Watts), Newark, Cleveland, Chicago, Atlanta, and Detroit. President Johnson responded by creating a commission to study the underlying causes. The most famous passage of the resultant Kerner Commission report warned that the United States was "moving toward two societies, one black, one white—separate and unequal."*[64] *Rather than focus on underlying causes, many Americans,*

61. Paul G. Cassell, "Miranda's Social Costs: An Empirical Reassessment," *Northwestern Law Review* 90 (1996): 387.

62. Stephen J. Schulhofer, "Miranda's Practical Effect: Substantial Benefits and Vanishingly Small Social Costs," *Northwestern Law Review* 90 (1996): 500–63.

63. Rosenberg, *Hollow Hope*, 327–29.

64. Kerner Commission, *Report of the National Advisory Commission on Civil Disorders* (Washington, DC: U.S. Government Printing Office, 1968), 1.

with encouragement from more conservative political entrepreneurs, made connections between these events and liberal Supreme Court decisions on constitutional criminal procedure. A strong backlash developed against justices who were perceived as caring more about the rights of criminals than their victims. Richard Nixon rode this backlash to power in 1968.

CHIEF JUSTICE WARREN delivered the opinion of the Court.

. . .

. . . [T]he modern practice of in-custody interrogation is psychologically rather than physically oriented. As we have stated before, "Since *Chambers v. Florida* (1940) . . . , this Court has recognized that coercion can be mental as well as physical, and that the blood of the accused is not the only hallmark of an unconstitutional inquisition." . . . Interrogation still takes place in privacy. Privacy results in secrecy and this in turn results in a gap in our knowledge as to what in fact goes on in the interrogation rooms.

. . .

. . . [T]he setting prescribed by [police] manuals and observed in practice [is] clear. In essence, it is this: To be alone with the subject is essential to prevent distraction and to deprive him of any outside support. The aura of confidence in his guilt undermines his will to resist. He merely confirms the preconceived story the police seek to have him describe. Patience and persistence, at times relentless questioning, are employed. To obtain a confession, the interrogator must "patiently maneuver himself or his quarry into a position from which the desired objective may be attained." When normal procedures fail to produce the needed result, the police may resort to deceptive stratagems such as giving false legal advice. It is important to keep the subject off balance, for example, by trading on his insecurity about himself or his surroundings. The police then persuade, trick, or cajole him out of exercising his constitutional rights.

. . .

It is obvious that such an interrogation environment is created for no purpose other than to subjugate the individual to the will of his examiner. This atmosphere carries its own badge of intimidation. To be sure, this is not physical intimidation, but it is equally destructive of human dignity. The current practice of incommunicado interrogation is at odds with one of our Nation's most cherished principles—that the individual may not be compelled to incriminate himself. Unless adequate protective devices are employed to dispel the compulsion inherent in custodial surroundings, no statement obtained from the defendant can truly be the product of his free choice.

. . .

. . . [T]he constitutional foundation underlying the privilege is the respect a government—state or federal—must accord to the dignity and integrity of its citizens. To maintain a "fair state-individual balance," to require the government "to shoulder the entire load," . . . to respect the inviolability of the human personality, our accusatory system of criminal justice demands that the government seeking to punish an individual produce the evidence against him by its own independent labors, rather than by the cruel, simple expedient of compelling it from his own mouth. . . . In sum, the privilege is fulfilled only when the person is guaranteed the right "to remain silent unless he chooses to speak in the unfettered exercise of his own will." . . .

. . .

It is impossible for us to foresee the potential alternatives for protecting the privilege which might be devised by Congress or the States in the exercise of their creative rule-making capacities. Therefore we cannot say that the Constitution necessarily requires adherence to any particular solution for the inherent compulsions of the interrogation process as it is presently conducted. . . . We encourage Congress and the States to continue their laudable search for increasingly effective ways of protecting the rights of the individual while promoting efficient enforcement of our criminal laws. However, unless we are shown other procedures which are at least as effective in apprising accused persons of their right of silence and in assuring a continuous opportunity to exercise it, the following safeguards must be observed.

At the outset, if a person in custody is to be subjected to interrogation, he must first be informed in clear and unequivocal terms that he has the right to remain silent. For those unaware of the privilege, the warning is needed simply to make them aware of it—the threshold requirement for an intelligent decision as to its exercise. More important, such a warning is an absolute prerequisite in overcoming the inherent pressures of the interrogation atmosphere.

It is not just the subnormal or woefully ignorant who succumb to an interrogator's imprecations, whether implied or expressly stated, that the interrogation will continue until a confession is obtained or that silence in the face of accusation is itself damning and will bode ill when presented to a jury. Further, the warning will show the individual that his interrogators are prepared to recognize his privilege should he choose to exercise it.

. . .

The warning of the right to remain silent must be accompanied by the explanation that anything said can and will be used against the individual in court. This warning is needed in order to make him aware not only of the privilege, but also of the consequences of forgoing it. It is only through an awareness of these consequences that there can be any assurance of real understanding and intelligent exercise of the privilege. Moreover, this warning may serve to make the individual more acutely aware that he is faced with a phase of the adversary system—that he is not in the presence of persons acting solely in his interest.

The circumstances surrounding in-custody interrogation can operate very quickly to overbear the will of one merely made aware of his privilege by his interrogators. Therefore, the right to have counsel present at the interrogation is indispensable to the protection of the Fifth Amendment privilege under the system we delineate today. Our aim is to assure that the individual's right to choose between silence and speech remains unfettered throughout the interrogation process. . . . Thus, the need for counsel to protect the Fifth Amendment privilege comprehends not merely a right to consult with counsel prior to questioning, but also to have counsel present during any questioning if the defendant so desires.

. . .

. . . No effective waiver of the right to counsel during interrogation can be recognized unless specifically made after the warnings we here delineate have been given. . . .

. . .

Once warnings have been given, the subsequent procedure is clear. If the individual indicates in any manner, at any time prior to or during questioning, that he wishes to remain silent, the interrogation must cease. . . . If the individual states that he wants an attorney, the interrogation must cease until an attorney is present. . . .

. . .

In announcing these principles, we are not unmindful of the burdens which law enforcement officials must bear, often under trying circumstances. We also fully recognize the obligation of all citizens to aid in enforcing the criminal laws. This Court, while protecting individual rights, has always given ample latitude to law enforcement agencies in the legitimate exercise of their duties. The limits we have placed on the interrogation process should not constitute an undue interference with a proper system of law enforcement. As we have noted, our decision does not in any way preclude police from carrying out their traditional investigatory functions. Although confessions may play an important role in some convictions, the cases before us present graphic examples of the overstatement of the "need" for confessions. In each case authorities conducted interrogations ranging up to five days in duration despite the presence, through standard investigating practices, of considerable evidence against each defendant. . . .

. . .

Over the years the Federal Bureau of Investigation has compiled an exemplary record of effective law enforcement while advising any suspect or arrested person, at the outset of an interview, that he is not required to make a statement, that any statement may be used against him in court, that the individual may obtain the services of an attorney of his own choice and, more recently, that he has a right to free counsel if he is unable to pay.

. . .

The practice of the FBI can readily be emulated by state and local enforcement agencies. The argument that the FBI deals with different crimes than are dealt with by state authorities does not mitigate the significance of the FBI experience.

. . .

JUSTICE CLARK, dissenting

. . .

Custodial interrogation has long been recognized as "undoubtedly an essential tool in effective law enforcement." . . . Recognition of this fact should put us on guard against the promulgation of doctrinaire rules.

Under the "totality of circumstances" rule . . . , I would consider in each case whether the police officer prior to custodial interrogation added the warning that the suspect might have counsel present at the interrogation and, further, that a court would appoint one at his request if he was too poor to employ counsel. In the absence of warnings, the burden would be on the State to prove that counsel was knowingly and intelligently waived or that in the totality of the circumstances, including the failure to give the necessary warnings, the confession was clearly voluntary.

...

JUSTICE HARLAN, whom JUSTICE STEWART and JUSTICE WHITE join, dissenting.

...

... The Fifth Amendment has never been thought to forbid all pressure to incriminate one's self in the situations covered by it....

...

Without at all subscribing to the generally black picture of police conduct painted by the Court, I think it must be frankly recognized at the outset that police questioning allowable under due process precedents may inherently entail some pressure on the suspect and may seek advantage in his ignorance or weaknesses. The atmosphere and questioning techniques, proper and fair though they be, can in themselves exert a tug on the suspect to confess, and in this light "[t]o speak of any confessions of crime made after arrest as being 'voluntary' or 'uncoerced' is somewhat inaccurate, although traditional. A confession is wholly and incontestably voluntary only if a guilty person gives himself up to the law and becomes his own accuser." ... Until today, the role of the Constitution has been only to sift out undue pressure, not to assure spontaneous confessions.

What the Court largely ignores is that its rules impair, if they will not eventually serve wholly to frustrate, an instrument of law enforcement that has long and quite reasonably been thought worth the price paid for it. There can be little doubt that the Court's new code would markedly decrease the number of confessions....

...

JUSTICE WHITE, with whom JUSTICE HARLAN and JUSTICE STEWART join, dissenting.

The proposition that the privilege against self-incrimination forbids in-custody interrogation without the warnings specified in the majority opinion and without a clear waiver of counsel has no significant support in the history of the privilege or in the language of the Fifth Amendment. As for the English authorities and the common-law history, the privilege, firmly established in the second half of the seventeenth century, was never applied except to prohibit compelled judicial interrogations. The rule excluding coerced confessions matured about one hundred years later, "[b]ut there is nothing in the reports to suggest that the theory has its roots in the privilege against self-incrimination. And so far as the cases reveal, the privilege, as such, seems to have been given effect only in judicial proceedings, including the preliminary examinations by authorized magistrates." ...

...

The obvious underpinning of the Court's decision is a deep-seated distrust of all confessions. As the Court declares that the accused may not be interrogated without counsel present, absent a waiver of the right to counsel, and as the Court all but admonishes the lawyer to advise the accused to remain silent, the result adds up to a judicial judgment that evidence from the accused should not be used against him in any way, whether compelled or not.... I see nothing wrong or immoral, and certainly nothing unconstitutional, in the police's asking a suspect whom they have reasonable cause to arrest whether or not he killed his wife or in confronting him with the evidence on which the arrest was based, at least where he has been plainly advised that he may remain completely silent.... Until today, "the admissions or confessions of the prisoner, when voluntarily and freely made, have always ranked high in the scale of incriminating evidence." ... Particularly when corroborated, as where the police have confirmed the accused's disclosure of the hiding place of implements or fruits of the crime, such confessions have the highest reliability and significantly contribute to the certitude with which we may believe the accused is guilty. Moreover, it is by no means certain that the process of confessing is injurious to the accused. To the contrary it may provide psychological relief and enhance the prospects for rehabilitation.

This is not to say that the value of respect for the inviolability of the accused's individual personality should be accorded no weight or that all confessions should be indiscriminately admitted. This Court has long read the Constitution to proscribe compelled confessions, a salutary rule from which there should be no retreat. But I see no sound basis, factual or otherwise, and the Court gives none, for concluding that the present rule against the receipt of coerced confessions is inadequate for the task of sorting out inadmissible evidence and must be replaced by the per se rule which is now imposed. . . .

. . .

The rule announced today will measurably weaken the ability of the criminal law to perform these tasks. It is a deliberate calculus to prevent interrogations, to reduce the incidence of confessions and pleas of guilty and to increase the number of trials. . . . There is, in my view, every reason to believe that a good many criminal defendants who otherwise would have been convicted on what this Court has previously thought to be the most satisfactory kind of evidence will now under this new version of the Fifth Amendment, either not be tried at all or will be acquitted if the State's evidence, minus the confession, is put to the test of litigation. . . .

D. Juries and Lawyers

Twentieth-century liberals regarded the right to an attorney, rather than the right to trial by jury, as the most important constitutional protection for persons accused of crime. *Gideon v. Wainwright* (1963), the decision that held that persons accused of felonies have a right to a state-appointed attorney, is the rare judicial decision favoring the rights of criminal defendants that is presently celebrated by most Americans. By comparison, federal courts during the mid-twentieth century did not hand down any major decisions on the right to a jury that are either celebrated or vilified. Indeed, liberal justices moved less aggressively against racial discrimination in jury selection than they did against racial discrimination in other facets of the criminal process. In *Swain v. Alabama* (1965) a divided Warren Court ruled that an African American convicted of raping a white woman was not entitled to a new trial merely because the prosecutor had peremptorily challenged every prospective African American juror. Judge White's opinion stated,

> We cannot hold that the Constitution requires an examination of the prosecutor's reasons for the exercise of his challenges in any given case. The presumption in any particular case must be that the prosecutor is using the State's challenges to obtain a fair and impartial jury to try the case before the court. The presumption is not overcome, and the prosecutor therefore subjected to examination, by allegations that, in the case at hand, all Negroes were removed from the jury, or that they were removed because they were Negroes.

Gideon v. Wainwright, 372 U.S. 335 (1963)

Clarence Gideon was arrested and charged with the burglary of a pool hall in Panama City, Florida. Gideon could not afford a lawyer. The trial judge rejected his request that a lawyer be appointed for him on the ground that defense counsel was constitutionally required only in capital cases. After being convicted and sentenced to five years in prison, Gideon brought a habeas corpus proceeding against the director of the Florida Division of Corrections, Louis Wainwright. The trial court and the Supreme Court of Florida rejected this contention on the basis of the Supreme Court's decision in Betts v. Brady *(1942). Justice Roberts's majority opinion in that case held that the constitutional right to counsel depended on the particular circumstances before the court. He wrote,*

> *The Fourteenth Amendment prohibits the conviction and incarceration of one whose trial is offensive to the common and fundamental ideas of fairness and right, and while want of counsel in a particular case may result in a conviction lacking in such fundamental fairness, we cannot say that the amendment embodies an inexorable command that no trial for any offense, or in any court, can be fairly conducted and justice accorded a defendant who is not represented by counsel.*

Gideon appealed the Florida decisions to the Supreme Court of the United States.

The Supreme Court unanimously overruled Betts v. Brady. *Justice Black's opinion for the Court declared that the right to counsel is fundamental and may not ordinarily be denied. On what basis did Justice Black reach that conclusion? Does* Gideon *give persons accused of any crime a right to government-appointed counsel? After* Gideon, *do you have a right to counsel when contesting a parking ticket? Does* Gideon *indicate when counsel must be appointed? Does* Gideon *require that counsel be appointed immediately after arrest, or is counsel required only when the actual trial begins?* Gideon *was decided at a time when Democrats were announcing a war on poverty. Might the justices have seen the right to a government-appointed counsel as the judicial contribution to that national effort?*

JUSTICE BLACK delivered the opinion of the Court.

... [R]eason and reflection require us to recognize that in our adversary system of criminal justice, any person haled into court, who is too poor to hire a lawyer, cannot be assured a fair trial unless counsel is provided for him. This seems to us to be an obvious truth. Governments, both state and federal, quite properly spend vast sums of money to establish machinery to try defendants accused of crime. Lawyers to prosecute are everywhere deemed essential to protect the public's interest in an orderly society. Similarly, there are few defendants charged with crime, few indeed, who fail to hire the best lawyers they can get to prepare and present their defenses. That government hires lawyers to prosecute and defendants who have the money hire lawyers to defend are the strongest indications of the wide-spread belief that lawyers in criminal courts are necessities, not luxuries. The right of one charged with crime to counsel may not be deemed fundamental and essential to fair trials in some countries, but it is in ours. From the very beginning, our state and national constitutions and laws have laid great emphasis on procedural and substantive safeguards designed to assure fair trials before impartial tribunals in which every defendant stands equal before the law. This noble ideal cannot be realized if the poor man charged with crime has to face his accusers without a lawyer to assist him. . . .

... Florida, supported by two other States, has asked that *Betts v. Brady* (1942) be left intact. Twenty-two States, as friends of the Court, argue that *Betts* was "an anachronism when handed down" and that it should now be overruled. We agree.

...

JUSTICE DOUGLAS. . . .

JUSTICE CLARK, concurring in the result. . . .

JUSTICE HARLAN, concurring.

...

I cannot subscribe to the view that *Betts v. Brady* represented "an abrupt break with its own well-considered precedents." ... In 1932, in *Powell v. Alabama*, a capital case, this Court declared that under the particular facts there presented—"the ignorance and illiteracy of the defendants, their youth, the circumstances of public hostility ... and above all that they stood in deadly peril of their lives" ...—the state court had a duty to assign counsel for the trial as a necessary requisite of due process of law. . . .

Thus when this Court, a decade later, decided *Betts v. Brady*, it did no more than to admit of the possible existence of special circumstances in noncapital as well as capital trials, while at the same time insisting that such circumstances be shown in order to establish a denial of due process. . . .

The principles declared in *Powell* and in *Betts*, however, have had a troubled journey throughout the years that have followed first the one case and then the other. . . .

In noncapital cases, the "special circumstances" rule has continued to exist in form while its substance has been substantially and steadily eroded. In the first decade after *Betts*, there were cases in which the Court found special circumstances to be lacking, but usually by a sharply divided vote. However, no such decision has been cited to us, and I have found none, after . . . 1950. At the same time, there have been not a few cases in which special circumstances were found in little or nothing more than the "complexity" of the legal questions presented, although those questions were often of only routine difficulty. The Court has come to recognize, in other words, that the mere existence of a serious criminal charge constituted in itself special circumstances requiring the services of counsel at trial. In truth the *Betts v. Brady* rule is no longer a reality. . . .

E. Punishments

Rudolph v. Alabama (1963) dramatically changed the constitutional politics of capital punishment. Dissenting from the Supreme Court's decision not to hear that case, Justices Goldberg, Douglas, and Brennan suggested that lawyers might make Eighth Amendment attacks on the death penalty per se, rather than point to constitutional violations peculiar to the particular defendant before the Court. "I would grant certiorari in the case," Goldberg wrote, "to consider whether the Eighth and Fourteen Amendments to the United States Constitution permit the imposition of the death penalty on a convicted rapist who has neither taken nor endangered human life." Such groups as the NAACP Legal Defense Fund immediately took up and expanded this challenge. Rather than simply attack the constitutionality of executing persons for rape, civil rights lawyers began claiming that capital punishment was an unconstitutional sanction for any crime.

The Supreme Court's commitment to a living Constitution fueled attacks on capital punishment. In *Trop v. Dulles* (1958) a 5–4 judicial majority held that a federal law stripping soldiers of citizenship as a punishment for desertion violated the Eighth Amendment. Chief Justice Warren's majority opinion asserted that the "[Eighth] Amendment must draw its meaning from the evolving standards of decency that mark the progress of a maturing society." If, as *Trop* indicated, common punishments at the time that the Bill of Rights was ratified could become cruel and unusual over time, then, opponents of capital punishment by 1968 were convinced, the time had come to declare capital punishment cruel and unusual.

Suggested Readings

Ackerman, Bruce A. 1998. *We the People, Vol. 2: Transformations.* Cambridge, MA: Harvard University Press.

Brown-Nagin, Tomiko. 2011. *Courage to Dissent: Atlanta and the Long History of the Civil Rights Movement.* New York: Oxford University Press.

Cortner, Richard C. 1981. *The Supreme Court and the Second Bill of Rights: The Fourteenth Amendment and the Nationalization of Civil Liberties.* Madison: University of Wisconsin Press.

Cray, Ed. 1997. *Chief Justice: A Biography of Earl Warren.* New York: Simon & Schuster.

Cushman, Barry. 1998. *Rethinking the New Deal Court: The Structure of a Constitutional Revolution.* New York: Oxford University Press.

Dudziak, Mary L. 2002. *Cold War Civil Rights: Race and the Image of American Democracy.* Princeton, NJ: Princeton University Press.

Emerson, Thomas Irwin. 1970. *The System of Freedom of Expression.* New York: Random House.

Feldman, Noah. 2010. *Scorpions: The Battles and Triumphs of FDR's Great Supreme Court Justices.* New York: Hachette.

Fisher, Louis. 1991. *Presidential Conflicts Between Congress and the President*, 3rd ed. Lawrence: University Press of Kansas.

———. 2004. *Presidential War Powers*, 2nd ed. Lawrence: University Press of Kansas.

Gillman, Howard. 1993. *The Constitution Besieged: The Rise and Demise of Lochner Era Police Power Jurisprudence.* Durham, NC: Duke University Press.

Goluboff, Risa Lauren. 2007. *The Lost Promise of Civil Rights.* Cambridge, MA: Harvard University Press.

Graham, Hugh Davis. 1990. *The Civil Rights Era: Origins and Development of National Policy.* New York: Oxford University Press.

Hirsch, H. N. 1981. *The Enigma of Felix Frankfurter.* New York: Basic.

Horwitz, Morton J. 1998. *The Warren Court and the Pursuit of Justice.* New York: Hill and Wang.

Irons, Peter H. 1983. *Justice at War.* New York: Oxford University Press.

Kalman, Laura. 1990. *Abe Fortas: A Biography.* New Haven, CT: Yale University Press.

Keck, Thomas M. 2004. *The Most Activist Supreme Court in History: The Road to Modern Judicial Conservatism.* Chicago: University of Chicago Press.

Klarman, Michael J. 2004. *From Jim Crow to Civil Rights: The Supreme Court and the Struggle for Civil Rights.* New York: Oxford University Press.

Kluger, Richard. 1984. *Simple Justice: The History of* Brown v. Board of Education *and Black America's Struggle for Equality.* New York: Knopf.

Lawrence, Susan E. 1990. *The Poor in Court: The Legal Services Program and Supreme Court Decision Making.* Princeton, NJ: Princeton University Press.

Leuchtenburg, William Edward. 1995. *The Supreme Court Reborn: The Constitutional Revolution in the Age of Roosevelt.* New York: Oxford University Press.

Lewis, Anthony. 1964. *Gideon's Trumpet.* New York: Random House.

Lovell, George. 2012. *This Is Not Civil Rights: Discovering Rights Talk in 1939 America.* Chicago: University of Chicago Press.

Mason, Alpheus Thomas. 1956. *Harlan Fiske Stone: Pillar of the Law.* New York: Viking Press.

McMahon, Kevin J. 2003. *Reconsidering Roosevelt on Race: How the Presidency Paved the Road to* Brown. Chicago: University of Chicago Press.

Meiklejohn, Alexander. 1965. *Political Freedom: The Constitutional Powers of the People.* New York: Oxford University Press.

Murphy, Bruce Allen. 2003. *Wild Bill: The Legend and Life of William O. Douglas.* New York: Random House.

Murphy, Walter F. 1962. *Congress and the Court: A Case Study in the American Political Process.* Chicago: University of Chicago Press.

Newman, Roger K. 1994. *Hugo Black: A Biography.* New York: Pantheon.

Novkov, Julie. 2001. *Constituting Workers, Protecting Women: Gender, Law and Labor in the Progressive Era and New Deal Years.* Ann Arbor: University of Michigan Press.

Peters, Shawn Francis. 2000. *Judging Jehovah's Witnesses: Religious Persecution and the Dawn of the Rights Revolution.* Lawrence: University Press of Kansas.

Powe, Lucas A. 2000. *The Warren Court and American Politics.* Cambridge, MA: Harvard University Press.

Silverstein, Gordon. 1997. *Imbalance of Powers: Constitutional Interpretation and the Making of American Foreign Policy.* New York: Oxford University Press.

Sundquist, James L. 1981. *Decline and Resurgence of Congress.* Washington, DC: Brookings Institution.

Tushnet, Mark V. 1994. *Making Civil Rights Law: Thurgood Marshall and the Supreme Court, 1936–61.* New York: Oxford University Press.

———. 1997. *Making Constitutional Law: Thurgood Marshall and the Supreme Court, 1961–1991.* New York: Oxford University Press.

———. 1999. *The Warren Court in Historical and Political Perspective.* Charlottesville: University of Virginia Press.

Vose, Clement E. 1959. *Caucasians Only: The Supreme Court, the NAACP, and the Restrictive Covenant Cases.* Berkeley: University of California Press.

Whittington, Keith E. 1999. *Constitutional Construction: Divided Powers and Constitutional Meaning.* Cambridge, MA: Harvard University Press.

———. 2007. *Political Foundations of Judicial Supremacy: The President, the Supreme Court, and Constitutional Leadership in U.S. History.* Princeton, NJ: Princeton University Press.

Wiecek, William M. 2006. *The Birth of the Modern Constitution: The United States Supreme Court, 1941–1953.* New York: Cambridge University Press.

Chapter 9

Liberalism Divided: 1969–1980

I. Introduction

The period from 1968 to 1980 marked the beginning of the end of the Democratic Party's New Deal coalition as well as the unquestioned dominance of its related constitutional vision. Since the formation of the Democratic Party during the Jacksonian Era, the "Solid South" had been an important part of the Democratic electoral and policy calculations. However, as Figure 9-1 illustrates, during this period voters in the South became far more willing to support the Republican Party.

This change reflected a process by which the political parties began sorting themselves out into more ideologically homogeneous but polarized groups, with liberals moving into the Democratic Party and conservatives moving into the Republican Party. The civil rights movement and the Voting Rights Act brought new liberal black voters into the Democratic fold, but many conservative white voters left. The Vietnam War and a variety of "social issues," including crime and abortion, shuffled allegiances that much more.[1]

This sorting process led, in the 1970s, to divided government and internal divisions within both major parties. Voters elected both Democrats and Republicans (including conservative Democrats and liberal Republicans) in sufficient numbers to give no clear message to governing officials. Presidents Richard Nixon and Jimmy Carter reflected this ambivalence. Nixon vigorously opposed busing while expanding affirmative action. Carter pushed for women's rights while opposing federal funding for abortion.

Developments. The development of constitutional law matched the erratic development of constitutional politics. Major Warren Court initiatives on crime and race stalled as judges and politicians wrestled over difficult details of implementation and remedies. The rights of persons suspected of crimes were narrowed, and the Supreme Court permitted states to impose capital punishment (*Gregg v. Georgia*). Debates over affirmative action divided traditional allies on issues of racial justice. In *San Antonio Independent School District v. Rodriguez* (1973) the justices ruled that education was not a fundamental constitutional right. However, women gained rights during the 1970s. A bipartisan coalition of justices in 1973 held that the right to choose abortion was protected by the Constitution (*Roe v. Wade*) and in 1976 announced a stricter constitutional standard for gender distinctions (*Craig v. Boren*). More generally, constitutional developments during the late 1960s and 1970s did not reflect any jurisprudential theory, the platform of any political party, or the positions championed by any particular interest group.

During this era there were also heated debates over questions of constitutional structure. Richard Nixon was the first president since 1848 whose party did not control at least one chamber of Congress. While Nixon often worked with Congress to expand federal protection for workers, consumers, and the environment, he also found himself entangled in persistent conflicts over how he was using presidential power—right up until his resignation during the Watergate scandal. Liberal disillusionment with Vietnam and unhappiness with the Johnson and Nixon administrations led to a reevaluation of the scope of presidential power. Barry Goldwater's presidential campaign in 1964 also reignited debates over "big government" and helped

1. See Donald Green, Bradley Palmquist, and Eric Shickler, *Partisan Hearts and Minds* (New Haven, CT: Yale University Press, 2002); Edward G. Carmines and James A. Stimson, *Issue Evolution* (Princeton, NJ: Princeton University Press, 1989).

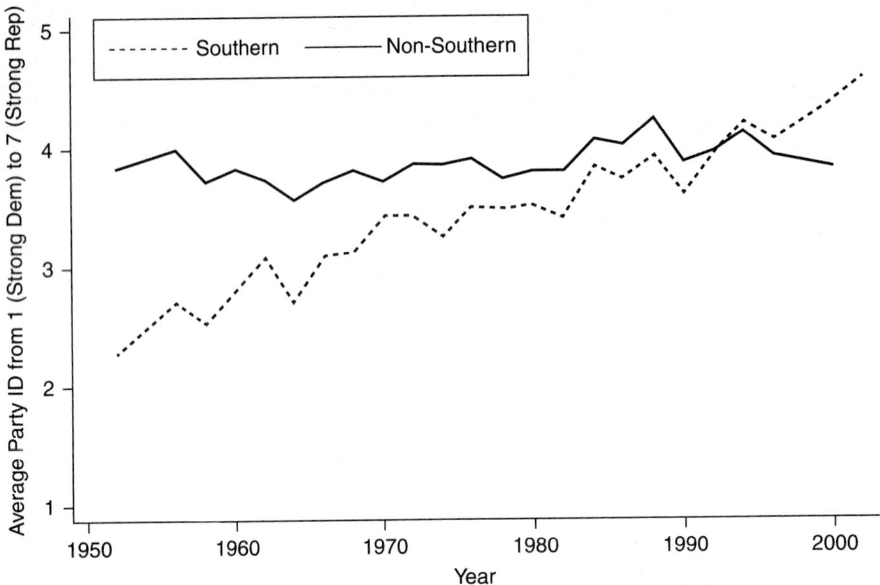

Figure 9-1 Partisan Identification of Southerners and Non-Southerners Since 1950

Source: National Election Studies.

put arguments about federalism and states' rights on the Republican political and legal agenda.

Parties. The Republicans decisively won the presidency in the midst of the Vietnam War in 1968, and Nixon cruised to reelection in 1972. GOP operatives talked hopefully of a new Republican majority that would leave the Democrats to wander in the political wilderness, suffering the same fate that the Republicans had after the Great Depression. But Nixon's coattails were not long enough. Nixon won electoral votes in the South, but few Republicans were able to defeat incumbent congressmen there.

From 1968 to 1980 the Democrats had little difficulty retaining control of both houses of Congress. They regained the White House in the first opportunity after Watergate, the 1976 elections, and for a short period of time had the benefit of a unified government. The Democrats elected to Congress after Watergate were strongly liberal and reform-minded, but they found themselves confronting increasingly vocal conservative elements within the party. These internal divisions undermined their advantage of unified government during Jimmy Carter's single term of office. Instead, conflicts within and between the political parties and between the executive and the legislative branches characterized the period.

Democrats were, on average, more liberal than Republicans, but neither party presented a united front to voters. Southern Democrats such as Senator Sam Ervin of North Carolina and Senator James Eastland of Mississippi remained the leading opponents of the Great Society. Such Republican liberals as Senator Jacob Javits of New York and Attorney General Eliot Richardson remained leading enthusiasts for an expanded Great Society. The formerly solid Democratic South became a political battleground as Richard Nixon's "southern strategy" sought to make the Republican Party competitive in the South by taking advantage of southern conservative opposition to Great Society programs and liberal judicial decisions on constitutional criminal procedure, school prayer, abortion, obscenity, and women's rights.

Interest Groups. Interest group activity was divided during this time. The ACLU lost many members after it supported the right of Nazis to march in Skokie, Illinois. The African American/Jewish alliance that was a pillar of the civil rights movement during the 1960s frayed when concerns over affirmative action replaced concerns over desegregation. Free exercise and establishment clause controversies broke out between liberal and conservative members of the same religion rather than along the traditional Protestant/Catholic/Jewish divides. Interest groups also became more specialized. During the New Deal/Great Society Era the ACLU was the leading liberal voice across a wide spectrum of constitutional issues. By 1980 every group and every right seemed to have an organization dedicated to lobbying and litigating on its behalf.

Conservative interest groups mobilized during the 1970s. Evangelicals entered politics in order to restore what they believed were traditional American social values. Libertarian activists launched litigation campaigns to restore what they believed were traditional property rights. These conservative interest groups often augmented and sometimes replaced the state governments, businesses, and churches that had opposed liberal interest group lobbying and litigation during the New Deal/Great Society Era. No conservative interest group in 1980 rivaled the ACLU or NAACP in influence, but both evangelical and libertarian associations had an increasing influence on American constitutional politics.

Courts. Importantly, Democrats had no opportunity to appoint new members to the Supreme Court during this period, since there were no vacancies during Carter's term. By contrast, Nixon was able to make four appointments to the Court, and his successor Gerald Ford was able to make a fifth. Carter had to content himself with making appointments to an expanded lower federal court system. As a result, despite the Democratic Party's control over Congress, the U.S. Supreme Court was transformed during this period into a more conservative institution, while the lower federal courts continued to be predominantly liberal.

In making his appointments Richard Nixon tried to score political points by looking either to the South or to Republican judges who were "tough on crime." He was able to make his first two appointments to the Supreme Court soon after his inauguration as president. First he replaced Chief Justice Earl Warren with Warren Burger, a conservative federal circuit court judge and a vocal critic of the Supreme Court under Warren's leadership. After a couple of false starts (with the Senate defeating initial choices who were very conservative) the president also managed to replace Justice Abe Fortas with circuit court judge Harry Blackmun. Whereas Fortas was one of the leading liberals on the Court, Blackmun had a reputation as a much more cautious figure. Nixon next chose Virginia lawyer Lewis Powell to replace New Dealer Hugo Black, who had become a crucial swing vote on the Court. Arch-conservative Justice Department official William Rehnquist replaced the Eisenhower Republican John Marshall Harlan II. After Watergate, Gerald Ford chose a political moderate, John Paul Stevens, to replace the idiosyncratic New Dealer William O. Douglas.

These appointments fractured the newly formed Burger Court. While the Court had shifted decisively to the right, its majority was now in the hands of the Kennedy and Eisenhower moderates rather than the Nixon conservatives. Liberals such as William Brennan and Thurgood Marshall enthusiastically endorsed new and expanded protections for rights and liberties, but they could no longer call the shots the way they had on the Warren Court. Conservatives such as William Rehnquist and, to a lesser extent, Warren Burger fought to reverse many constitutional decisions made during the Great Society but did not yet have the votes to make big changes in the law. That left Byron White, Potter Stewart, and Harry Blackmun as critical swing votes. The Court was still capable of issuing important liberal decisions—the decision in *Roe v. Wade*, striking down bans on abortion in forty-six states, was stunningly activist even by Warren Court standards—but more conservative majorities rejected constitutional welfare rights in *Dandridge v. Williams* (1970) and curtailed access to federal habeas corpus in *Wainwright v. Sykes* (1977). Frequently the centrist justices on the Burger Court split the difference, handing down decisions in gender discrimination, capital punishment, and affirmation action cases that were less liberal than the Warren Court would have made but not as conservative as Nixon and many of his supporters would have liked. Justices frequently wrote multiple opinions and had difficulty forming clear majorities.[2] The Burger Court was far more conservative than the Warren Court of the late 1960s, but the large bloc of centrist justices kept the Court generally in line with the Democratic Congress through the 1970s and 1980s.

---

2. Andrew D. Martin, Kevin M. Quinn, and Lee Epstein, "The Median Justice on the United States Supreme Court," *North Carolina Law Review* 83 (2005): 1275; Keith E. Whittington, "The Burger Court: Once More in Transition," in *The Supreme Court of the United States*, ed. Christopher Tomlins (New York: Houghton Mifflin, 2005).

Constitutional Thought. The political divisions that most influenced constitutional thought during this period were largely over the extent to which the work of the Great Society was unfinished, the particular aspects of the Great Society that were unfinished, and which governing institutions were primarily responsible for finishing the work of the Great Society. Most mainstream Democrats and Republicans were horrified when George Wallace and a growing number of conservative intellectuals called for overturning landmark constitutional decisions of the 1960s as well as the Civil Rights Act of 1964. Richard Nixon, by comparison, limited his complaints about an activist judiciary to the constitutional criminal procedure decisions of the 1960s and the school busing decisions of the 1970s.[3] Nixon celebrated *Brown v. Board of Education* (1954) and endorsed legislative efforts to expand the Voting Rights Act of 1965. He was more concerned with the future direction of constitutional rights and liberties than with returning the United States to the constitutional status quo of the 1950s.

In debating that future direction many progressives advanced constitutional arguments that were more rooted in philosophical claims about fundamental rights than in democratic theory. The New Deal/Great Society commitments to democracy and fundamental rights were mutually reinforcing. Liberals from 1933 until 1968 could justify commitments to racial equality, freedom of religion, the nationalization of the Bill of Rights, and broad rights for political and cultural dissenters as making the United States more democratic or as goals consistent with universal human rights. Differences between a democratic rights foundation for judicial activism and a fundamental rights foundation for judicial activism became more acute during the 1970s. The democratic theory underlying Footnote Four in *Carolene Products* (1938) emphasized history and political practice when determining whose rights needed special solicitude. Persons of color merited special constitutional protection because they were politically powerless and had historically been victims of discrimination. By the 1970s many progressives were more inspired by such works as John Rawls's *A Theory of Justice* (1971), which looked to moral philosophy as the proper source of rights and liberties. Persons of color and women merited special constitutional protection because race and gender were arbitrary bases for distinguishing people. American progressives placed greater emphasis on autonomy rights, such as the right to a legal abortion, than on the democratic theory rights that liberals had championed during the New Deal and Great Society Era.

More conservative thinkers challenged the liberal consensus of the 1960s. Robert Bork in 1971 published "Neutral Principles and Some First Amendment Problems," an influential essay that criticized numerous Warren Court decisions as inconsistent with the original meaning of constitutional provisions. Alexander Bickel's *The Morality of Consent* (1975) urged justices to pay greater heed to the eighteenth-century English conservative Edmund Burke than the more liberal John Locke. Richard Posner and other libertarian scholars published works in law and economics that called for greater judicial protection for property rights.[4] By 1980 conservative constitutional thought was far more respectable than it had been for a generation, even if that school of thought had not yet exerted substantial influence on the federal judiciary.

Under pressure from both the left and the right, the recently developed "preferred freedoms/compelling interest" structure of constitutional doctrine began to break down. New Deal liberals insisted that government needed a compelling interest to restrict such rights as free speech and the right to racial equality but needed only a rational basis to limit most property rights. The Burger Court provided greater doctrinal flexibility to handle such controversies by introducing a new intermediate standard of review. *Craig v. Boren* (1976) ruled that government could make gender distinctions when those distinctions were an important means to the achievement of a substantial government

3. See Kevin J. McMahon, *Nixon's Court: His Challenges to Judicial Liberalism and Its Political Consequences* (Chicago: University of Chicago Press, 2011).

4. See Robert H. Bork, "Neutral Principles and Some First Amendment Problems," *Indiana Law Review* 47 (1971): 29: Alexander Bickel, *The Morality of Consent* (New Haven, CT: Yale University Press, 1975); and Richard A. Posner, *Economic Analysis of Law* (Boston: Little, Brown and Company, 1973).

Table 9-1 Major Issues and Decisions of the Era of Liberalism Divided

Major Political Issues	Major Constitutional Issues	Major Court Decisions
Vietnam War	Judicial review	*Dandridge v. Williams* (1970)
Watergate	Presidential war powers	*New York Times v. Sullivan* (1971)
Extending or contracting the Great Society	Executive privilege	*Swann v. Charlotte-Meckleburg Board of Education* (1971)
Crime control	Tenth Amendment	*Wisconsin v. Yoder* (1972)
Aftermath of civil rights movement	Welfare rights	*United States v. United States District Court* (1972)
Minority rights revolution	Busing	*United States v. Nixon* (1973)
Women's movement	Affirmative action	*Roe v. Wade* (1973)
Sexual revolution	Free exercise of religion	*San Antonio Independent School District v. Rodriguez* (1973)
Environmental movement	Level of judicial scrutiny for gender classifications	*National League of Cities v. Usery* (1974)
Moral majority	Scope of *Mapp* and *Miranda*	*Buckley v. Valeo* (1976)
Money in elections	Abortion	*Gregg v. Georgia* (1976)
Iranian Hostage Crisis	Free speech and press freedoms	*Craig v. Boren* (1976)
		Wainwright v. Sykes (1977)
		Regents of the University of California v. Bakke (1978)

interest. Several justices suggested that the Court replace this two- or three-tiered scrutiny with a sliding scale that considered the importance of the right, the offensiveness of the classification, and the value of the state interest.

Legacies. The constitutional politics of the 1970s entrenched the constitutional liberalism of the New Deal/Great Society Era while simultaneously creating the conditions for future challenges. When Richard Nixon was first elected president many Americans realistically hoped or feared that the constitutional developments of the previous decades would be abandoned or reversed. That did not happen. Parochial schools obtained a few more state resources, and persons suspected of crimes enjoyed fewer procedural protections than might have been expected from the Warren Court. Nevertheless, most major Warren Court precedents and Great Society measures were less controversial in 1980 than they were in 1968. On the eve of the Reagan presidency no prominent party or political movement in the United States challenged claims that the Fourteenth Amendment incorporated most provisions in the Bill of Rights, that adults had the right to marry and use birth control, that government could not restrict speech that did not present an imminent danger of harm, and that state legislative apportionments had to approximate one person, one vote. *Brown v. Board of Education* (1954) was celebrated as the best judicial decision in American history. The Civil Rights Act of 1964 and the Voting Rights Act of 1965 were near-sacred texts, no more subject to revision than the principle of state equality in the Senate. Americans were also committed to some degree of gender equality by the start of the Reagan years. Americans might debate whether the Equal Rights Amendment was necessary, but a broad consensus existed that most traditional gender distinctions were unconstitutional.

The 1970s introduced many constitutional questions that continue to excite and divide Americans. Abortion, affirmative action, and campaign finance reform first enjoyed substantial national prominence during the Nixon presidency. Constitutional decision

Box 9-1 A Partial Cast of Characters of the Era of Liberalism Divided

Harry Blackmun	■ Republican ■ Minnesota lawyer ■ Appointed by Dwight Eisenhower to the federal circuit court (1959–1970) ■ Appointed by Richard Nixon to the Supreme Court (1970–1994) ■ Known as one of the "Minnesota Twins" for his close support of Warren Burger early in his tenure on the Court but later became closely allied with William Brennan ■ Best known for authoring majority opinion in *Roe v. Wade* (1973)
Warren Burger	■ Republican ■ Minnesota lawyer ■ Appointed by Dwight Eisenhower to the federal circuit court (1956–1969) ■ Appointed by Richard Nixon as chief justice of the United States (1969–1986) ■ Public critic of the Warren Court while serving as circuit court judge ■ Conservative on social issues and emphasized checks and balances on separation of powers issues; developed a reputation as a weak chief justice
William Fulbright	■ Democrat ■ Rhodes Scholar and lawyer from Arkansas ■ President of the University of Arkansas (1939–1941) ■ U.S. representative (1943–1945) ■ U.S. senator (1945–1974); long-serving chair of the Senate Foreign Relations Committee ■ Critic of conservative anti-Communists and a sponsor of the Gulf of Tonkin Resolution; he became a leading critic of the Vietnam War and of presidential war powers ■ Defeated for reelection in the Democratic primary in 1974
Lewis F. Powell	■ Democrat ■ Virginia lawyer ■ Presided over desegregation of public schools as chair of Richmond school board (1952–1961) ■ Facilitated the creation of the Legal Services Program as president of the American Bar Association (1964–1965) but also encouraged more active efforts by business to build public and political support for the "free enterprise system" ■ Appointed by Richard Nixon to the Supreme Court (1972–1987), where he became an important swing vote on the Burger Court and developed a reputation as a moderate
Byron White	■ Democrat ■ Rhodes Scholar and star football player from Colorado before World War II ■ Attended law school after serving in naval intelligence; clerked for Chief Justice Fred Vinson ■ Deputy attorney general (1961–1962) ■ Appointed by John F. Kennedy to the Supreme Court (1962–1993) ■ Known as a pragmatic jurist and a swing vote on the Warren and Burger Courts

makers did not resolve these problems, but they provided the constitutional ground rules for future debates. The next generation of campaign finance cases, following *Buckley v. Valeo* (1976), focused on the government interest to prevent corruption rather than political equality. Affirmative action debates after *Bakke v. Regents of the University of California* (1978) focused on diversity rather than national obligations to alleviate harms for past societal discrimination.

Liberals became increasingly wedded to judicial power. Liberals during the New Deal/Great Society Era celebrated the achievements of Franklin Roosevelt, Lyndon Johnson, and Martin Luther King, Jr., as well as Earl Warren and William Douglas. During the 1970s Thurgood Marshall and William Brennan stood alone as progressive constitutional heroes. At a time when Richard Nixon won two consecutive elections and conservatives gained power in many congressional elections, courts that protected abortion rights, outlawed much gender discrimination, curtailed capital punishment, and permitted the *New York Times* to publish the Pentagon Papers seemed the best institutional site for progressive constitutional politics to move forward. Frank Michelman spoke for many liberals when he observed that justices have a unique capacity to "listen . . . for voices from the margins."[5] Liberal commitments to judicial activism influenced progressive electoral politics. Congressional liberals did not aggressively oppose bans on federal funding for medically necessary abortions because they were confident that the Hyde Amendment would be declared unconstitutional by federal justices. Such legislators were bitterly disappointed when the Supreme Court in *Harris v. McRae* (1980) sustained that measure. Even with this and other disappointments, many liberals remained judicial supremacists long after federal courts ceased to be bastions of liberalism.

Many of the most prominent constitutional issues of the period revolved around separation of powers. Many postwar liberals had wanted a president who could exercise decisive "leadership," respond to crises, and cut through conservative obstructions and compromises in Congress. By the Nixon administration, however, liberals began to worry about an "imperial presidency" that was becoming so powerful that it could short-circuit important checks and balances in the constitutional system. The debate over presidential power reverberated long after the Nixon administration. Not only did Ford and Carter continue to grapple with legislative and administrative reforms in the wake of Vietnam and Watergate, but former Nixon administration officials such as Antonin Scalia and Richard Cheney carried forward their own concerns about the need to protect strong presidential authority. The scope of presidential war powers remained controversial as the United States continued to stand as a global superpower even while the Cold War consensus was collapsing.

5. Frank Michelman, "Law's Republic," *Yale Law Journal* 97 (1988): 1537.

II. Foundations

MAJOR DEVELOPMENTS

- Continued expansion of federal regulatory authority
- Resurgent debates over presidential power and federalism
- Failure to ratify the Equal Rights Amendment (ERA)
- More emphasis on substantive rights than democratic rights
- State action doctrine narrowed

Americans did not significantly alter the constitutional text or the scope of constitutional rights and liberties during the 1970s, but they did renew dormant debates about interbranch and federal-state relations. Vietnam and Watergate ignited arguments about the scope of presidential power at the same time that Nixon and the Democratic Congress expanded federal authority over welfare, health care, civil rights, and energy and environmental policy. Political divisions doomed the ERA. Persons who agreed on the general principle of gender equality could not agree sufficiently on the actual impact of the ERA to generate the supermajority needed under Article V. The Supreme Court did not tinker with Warren Court precedents that incorporated almost every provision of the Bill of Rights, applying them to the states, and insisted that American governing officials abroad respect the basic due process rights of American citizens. The Supreme Court did significantly narrow the state action doctrine, particularly when the rights of African Americans were not at issue.

Constitutional decision makers acted more often on socially liberal than on economically liberal principles. The Supreme Court declared that the due process clause protected the right to an abortion and required heightened, but not strict, scrutiny when government officials made gender discriminations. Proponents of economic liberalism did not enjoy the same success. The Supreme Court decisively rejected claims that poor persons have a right to basic necessities.

A. Sources

The sources of constitutional debate did not change significantly during this time. The Twenty-Sixth Amendment forbade federal and state officials from denying the ballot to citizens "eighteen years of age or older . . . on account of age." Divided liberals could not, however, produce a constitutional majority to pass the ERA, even though both major parties endorsed the amendment and most Americans rejected nineteenth-century rulings on the constitutional status of women. Constitutional understandings of rights and liberties that were first articulated during the New Deal and Great Society became further entrenched during the 1970s as Republicans in the executive branch pledged fidelity to New Deal understandings of property rights, the gains made by the civil rights movement in the 1960s, and other (but not all) aspects of Great Society constitutionalism.

Scholars still debate why the ERA failed,[6] but several reasons seem important. Liberals were internally divided over what policies the ERA forbade. More progressive liberals insisted that the ERA supported women serving in military units and, perhaps, constitutional rights to abortion. An article in the 1971 *Yale Law Journal* declared, "The principle of the Amendment must be applied comprehensively and without exception." After noting that "all combat is dangerous, degrading and dehumanizing," the authors insisted that there "is little to choose . . . between brutalizing our young men and brutalizing our young women."[7] Moderates responded that the ERA would not produce these controversial consequences. Professor William Van Alstyne stated, "It is extraordinarily implausible . . . to suppose that if the Congress and the President were mutually of the view that the insertion of women into combat infantry was not appropriate . . . that the Supreme Court would nonetheless presume to 'overrule' their combined judgment."[8] By the mid-1970s legislative and judicial reforms had achieved most of the goals sought by moderate proponents of the ERA. The federal government and most states had passed laws prohibiting many gender classifications. In a series of opinions culminating in *Craig v. Boren* (1976), the Supreme Court ruled that ordinary gender distinctions violated the equal protection clause of the Fourteenth Amendment. When more progressive and more moderate proponents of the ERA were unable to agree on language establishing that the constitutional amendment did not make more dramatic changes in gender relationships than most people wanted, enough moderates in crucial states joined with social conservatives to prevent the ERA from being ratified.[9]

The failure of the ERA did not leave American constitutionalism unchanged. By the time that Ronald Reagan was elected president no substantial opposition existed to Supreme Court decisions that heightened the level of scrutiny that gender distinctions received. A strong political consensus had formed that the equal protection clause required states to scrutinize gender classifications more carefully than ordinary legislative classifications but less carefully than racial classifications. Reagan, while opposed to the ERA, kept a campaign promise when he nominated Sandra Day O'Connor as the first female justice on the Supreme Court. More specifics about gender discrimination were unclear. As frequently occurred during the 1970s, Americans could neither agree wholeheartedly with champions of constitutional liberalism nor completely reject their norms.

B. Principles

Constitutional liberalism subtly changed during the period between the Great Society and Reagan Eras. The constitutional liberalism of the New Deal/Great Society Era emphasized democratic principles.

6. A particularly good account, on which we rely heavily here, is Jane J. Mansbridge, *Why We Lost the ERA* (Chicago: University of Chicago Press, 1986).

7. Barbara A. Brown, Thomas I. Emerson, Gail Falk, and Ann E. Freedman, "The Equal Rights Amendment: A Constitutional Basis for Equal Rights of Women," *Yale Law Journal* 80 (1971): 890, 977.

8. William W. Van Alstyne, "The Proposed Twenty-Seventh Amendment: A Brief Supportive Comment," *Washington University Law Quarterly* 65, no. 8 (1979): 189, 194–95, n.10.

9. See Mansbridge, *Why We Lost the ERA*, 78.

Free speech and voting rights merited special constitutional protection because both were necessary conditions of a democracy. Persons of color merited special constitutional protection because they were a "discrete and insular minority" that lacked a fair share of democratic political power. Progressives during the 1970s placed greater emphasis on liberal principles that imposed substantive limits on government. In a series of lectures revealingly entitled "The Unfinished Business of the Warren Court," Professor Charles Black of the Yale Law School insisted that the promise of the Great Society would be fulfilled only when the Supreme Court developed "a *corpus juris* of human rights." According to Black, the central principles underlying the Warren Court and the Great Society were "the positive content and worth of American citizenship" and the right to enjoy citizenship "in all its parts without respect to race." Some elements of citizenship were procedural. "Citizenship," Black wrote, "is the right to be heard and counted on public affairs, the right to vote on equal terms, to speak, and to hold office when legitimately chosen," as well as "the right to be treated fairly when one is the object of action by . . . government." Black also insisted that citizenship had a substantive component, conferring "the broad right to lead a *private* life—for without this all dignity and happiness are impossible."[10]

Liberals during the 1970s turned to Harvard philosopher John Rawls when elaborating what they believed were the appropriate governmental principles and fundamental rights for a constitutional democracy. Rawls's most influential work, *A Theory of Justice* (1971), claimed that constitutional government should be committed to the following norms:

> First: each person is to have an equal right to the most extensive basic liberty compatible with a similar liberty for others.
>
> Second: social and economic inequalities are to be arranged so that they are both (a) reasonably expected to be to everyone's advantages, and (b) attached to positions and offices open to all.[11]

Several liberal law professors called for the Supreme Court to integrate Rawlsian logic into constitutional law. Professor Frank Michelman of Harvard Law School urged constitutional decision makers to "take [their] cue from Professor Rawls' idea of 'justice as fairness.'"[12] Ronald Dworkin, when calling for "a fusion of constitutional law and moral theory," described *A Theory of Justice* as "an abstract and complex book about justice which no constitutional lawyer will be able to ignore."[13]

The precise influence of this liberal turn is unclear. If influence is measured by citation, Rawls had no influence on Supreme Court decision making. Many commentators continued insisting that democratic principles justified rights to abortion, basic necessities, and other progressive constitutional goals. Still, a reasonable argument can be made that Justices Brennan and Marshall, the two most prominent liberals on the Supreme Court, over time voted in a manner more consistent with the principles articulated in *A Theory of Justice* than with the principles underlying the *Carolene Products* footnote.

Persons who favored the democratic principles underlying Great Society constitutionalism criticized the new generation of liberal thinkers for belittling the constitutional commitment to majoritarianism. "Our society does not . . . accept the notion of a discoverable and objectively valid set of morals," John Hart Ely declared—"at least not a set that could plausibly serve to overturn the decisions of our elected representatives."[14] Justice William Rehnquist declared that living constitutionalism "misconceives the nature of the Constitution, which was designed to enable the popularly elected branches of government, not the judicial branch, to keep the country abreast of the times." Sharply rejecting a central premise of Rawlsian liberalism, both the conservative Rehnquist and the more politically liberal Ely challenged claims that persons could prove the existence of particular liberal values. "There is no conceivable way," Rehnquist

10. Charles L. Black, Jr., "The Unfinished Business of the Warren Court," *Washington Law Review* 46 (1970): 44, 8, 9.

11. John Rawls, *A Theory of Justice* (Cambridge, MA: Harvard University Press, 1971), 60.

12. Frank I. Michelman, "Foreword: On Protecting the Poor Through the Fourteenth Amendment," *Harvard Law Review* 83 (1969): 7, 14–15.

13. Ronald M. Dworkin, *Taking Rights Seriously* (Cambridge, MA: Harvard University Press, 1977), 149.

14. John Hart Ely, *Democracy and Distrust: A Theory of Judicial Review* (Cambridge, MA: Harvard University Press, 1980), 54.

wrote, "in which I can logically demonstrate to you that the judgments of my conscience are superior to the judgments of your conscience and vice versa."[15] Noting that the more libertarian Harvard philosopher Robert Nozick's *Anarchy, State and Utopia* (1974) reached very different conclusions than did Rawls, Ely stated, "There simply does not exist *a* method of moral philosophy." He imagined a Supreme Court opinion that read, "We like Rawls, you like Nozick. We win, 6–3."[16]

C. Scope

Constitutional decision makers during the Nixon and Carter years accepted inherited conceptions of incorporation and the extraterritorial force of the Constitution. The constitutional politics of state action and the direction of judicial decision making, however, changed after Richard Nixon was elected to the presidency. Fewer cases involved claims that the state should be held responsible for private race discrimination. Judicial majorities in non–racially based cases modified existing precedents in ways that made state action more difficult to prove.[17]

By 1969 the most important state action decisions of the previous generation were irrelevant. The Civil Rights Act of 1964 barred racial discrimination in restaurants, hotels, and other places of public accommodation. The Civil Rights Act of 1968 barred racial discrimination in the housing market. These measures relied on the commerce clause. This use of the commerce power meant that victims of race discrimination in the 1970s did not have to prove the state action required by the Fourteenth Amendment. All they had to demonstrate was that the individual behavior being regulated affected interstate commerce. This proved easy to demonstrate, particularly because the prevailing doctrine at the time required justices to give extraordinary deference to legislative claims that a regulation of individual behavior promoted interstate commerce.

Burger Court justices in non–racially based cases usually distinguished rather than overruled past precedents finding state action. Warren Court justices found state action whenever they determined that a nominally private entity played a "public function" or found "significant state involvement." By 1980 "public function" has been transformed into "exclusive public function," and "significant state involvement" had become "significant state encouragement." In *Moose Lodge No. 107 v. Irvis* (1972) the Supreme Court considered whether a private club with a state liquor license could refuse to serve African Americans. Justice Rehnquist's majority opinion looked for active state support. He found none. "However detailed this type of regulation may be in some particulars," his majority decision affirming a right to discriminate declared, "it cannot be said to in any way foster or encourage racial discrimination."

15. William H. Rehnquist, "The Notion of a Living Constitution," *Texas Law Review* 54 (1976): 699, 704.

16. John Hart Ely, *Democracy and Distrust* (Cambridge: Harvard University Press, 1980), 58.

17. See Terri Peretti, "Constructing the State Action Doctrine, 1940–1990," *Law and Social Inquiry* 35 (2010): 273.

Moose Lodge No. 107 v. Irvis, 407 U.S. 163 (1972)

K. Leroy Irvis, an African American man, was denied dining room service by Moose Lodge No. 107, the Harrisburg, Pennsylvania, affiliate of a national fraternal organization. Moose Lodge did not admit persons of color as members and did not serve food to persons of color who, like Irvis, were guests of white members. Irvis sued Moose Lodge, claiming that the organization's discriminatory policies violated the equal protection clause of the Fourteenth Amendment. His petition for relief asked Pennsylvania to withdraw the state's liquor license until Moose Lodge abandoned its racial practices. Moose Lodge responded that, as a private club, they were free to discriminate and that their state liquor license was an insufficient basis to find state action. The district court found for Irvis and invalidated Moose Lodge's liquor license. Moose Lodge appealed to the Supreme Court of the United States.

The Supreme Court by a 6–3 vote found no state action. Justice Rehnquist's majority opinion maintained that Pennsylvania did not encourage or participate in racial discrimination merely by giving the Moose Lodge a liquor license. Justice Rehnquist regarded the license as analogous to police protection, a state service available to (almost) all citizens. Justices Douglas and Brennan regarded the license as a scarce commodity. Which characterization do you believe is most appropriate? How does the proper characterization influence your understanding of the decision? What sort of state involvement did Justice Rehnquist demand for state action? Under what conditions would

Justice Douglas permit a private club to discriminate against persons of color?

JUSTICE REHNQUIST delivered the opinion of the Court.

. . .

The Court has never held . . . that discrimination by an otherwise private entity would be violative of the Equal Protection Clause if the private entity receives any sort of benefit or service at all from the State, or if it is subject to state regulation in any degree whatever. Since state-furnished services include such necessities of life as electricity, water, and police and fire protection, such a holding would utterly emasculate the distinction between private, as distinguished from state, conduct. . . .

. . .

Here, there is nothing approaching the symbiotic relationship between lessor and lessee that was present in *Burton v. Wilmington Parking Authority* (1961), where the private lessee obtained the benefit of locating in a building owned by the state-created parking authority, and the parking authority was enabled to carry out its primarily public purpose of furnishing parking space by advantageously leasing portions of the building constructed for that purpose to commercial lessees such as the owner of the Eagle Restaurant. Unlike *Burton*, the Moose Lodge building is located on land owned by it, not by any public authority. Far from apparently holding itself out as a place of public accommodation, Moose Lodge quite ostentatiously proclaims the fact that it is not open to the public at large. . . . In short, while Eagle was a public restaurant in a public building, Moose Lodge is a private social club in a private building.

. . . [T]he Pennsylvania Liquor Control Board plays absolutely no part in establishing or enforcing the membership or guest policies of the club that it licenses to serve liquor. There is no suggestion in this record that Pennsylvania law, either as written or as applied, discriminates against minority groups either in their right to apply for club licenses themselves or in their right to purchase and be served liquor in places of public accommodation. . . .

The District Court was at pains to point out in its opinion what it considered to be the "pervasive" nature of the regulation of private clubs by the Pennsylvania Liquor Control Board. As that court noted, an applicant for a club license must make such physical alterations in its premises as the board may require, must file a list of the names and addresses of its members and employees, and must keep extensive financial records. The board is granted the right to inspect the licensed premises at any time when patrons, guests, or members are present.

However detailed this type of regulation may be in some particulars, it cannot be said to in any way foster or encourage racial discrimination. Nor can it be said to make the State in any realistic sense a partner or even a joint venturer in the club's enterprise. . . . We therefore hold that . . . the operation of the regulatory scheme enforced by the Pennsylvania Liquor Control Board does not sufficiently implicate the State in the discriminatory guest policies of Moose Lodge to make the latter "state action" within the ambit of the Equal Protection Clause of the Fourteenth Amendment.

. . .

JUSTICE DOUGLAS, with whom JUSTICE MARSHALL joins, dissenting.

. . .

. . . Liquor licenses in Pennsylvania, unlike driver's licenses, or marriage licenses, are not freely available to those who meet racially neutral qualifications. There is a complex quota system. . . . What the majority neglects to say is that the quota for Harrisburg, where Moose Lodge No. 107 is located, has been full for many years. No more club licenses may be issued in that city.

This state-enforced scarcity of licenses restricts the ability of blacks to obtain liquor, for liquor is commercially available only at private clubs for a significant portion of each week. Access by blacks to places that serve liquor is further limited by the fact that the state quota is filled. A group desiring to form a nondiscriminatory club which would serve blacks must purchase a license held by an existing club, which can exact a monopoly price for the transfer. . . .

Thus, the State of Pennsylvania is putting the weight of its liquor license, concededly a valued and important adjunct to a private club, behind racial discrimination.

. . .

JUSTICE BRENNAN, with whom JUSTICE MARSHALL joins, dissenting.

When Moose Lodge obtained its liquor license, the State of Pennsylvania became an active participant in the operation of the Lodge bar. . . . Very few, if any, other licensed businesses experience such complete state involvement. Yet the Court holds that such involvement does not constitute "state action" making the Lodge's refusal to serve a guest liquor solely because of his race a violation of the Fourteenth Amendment. The vital flaw in the Court's reasoning is its complete disregard of the fundamental value underlying the "state action" concept. . . .

The state action doctrine reflects the profound judgment that denials of equal treatment, and particularly denials on account of race or color, are singularly grave when government has or shares responsibility for them. Government is the social organ to which all in our society look for the promotion of liberty, justice, fair and equal treatment, and the setting of worthy norms and goals for social conduct. Therefore something is uniquely amiss in a society where the government, the authoritative oracle of community values, involves itself in racial discrimination. . . .

. . .

However it may deal with its licensees in exercising its great and untrammeled power over liquor traffic, the state may not discriminate against others or disregard the operation of the Equal Protection Clause of the Fourteenth Amendment as it affects personal rights. Here, the state has used its great power to license the liquor traffic in a manner which has no relation to the traffic in liquor itself, but instead permits it to be exploited in the pursuit of a discriminatory practice. . . .

III. Judicial Power and Constitutional Authority

MAJOR DEVELOPMENTS

- Supreme Court vacancies filled with five Republicans and no Democratic appointments, resulting in more conservative decision making
- Active Supreme Court participation in politically charged cases despite increasing criticism of "judicial activism"
- Maintenance of broad ability of parties to bring constitutional cases to federal courts

Under the leadership of Chief Justice Warren Burger, the Supreme Court quickly moved in a more conservative direction. One indication of the transition can be seen in Figure 9-2.

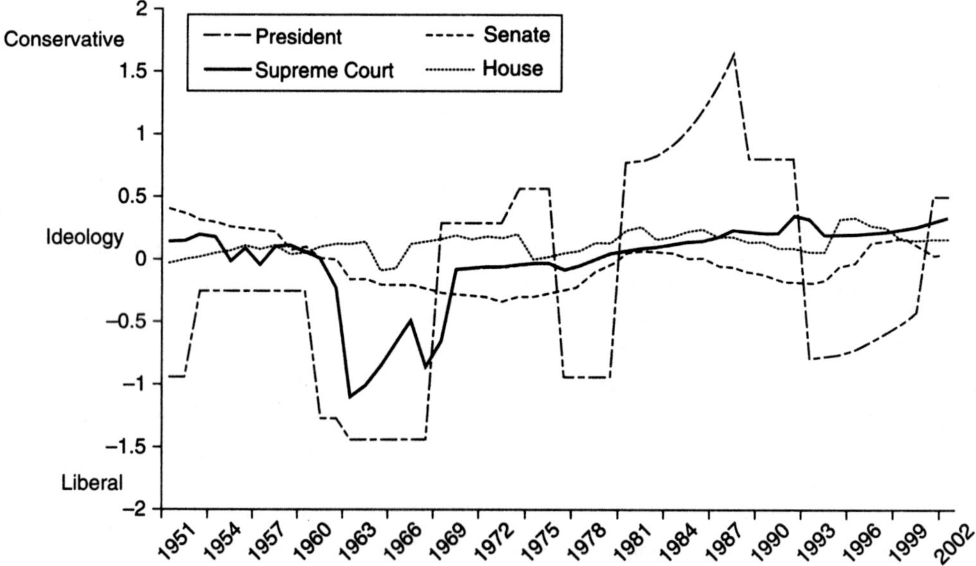

Figure 9-2 Left-Right Location of Supreme Court Relative to Other Branches, 1950–2002

Source: Michael Bailey, "Comparable Preference Estimates across Time and Institutions for the Court, Congress and Presidency," http://www9.georgetown.edu/faculty/baileyma/Data.htm.

Note: Median member of each institution placed on common ideological scale based on actual individual votes on cases (Court), bills (Congress), or individual statements about the actions taken by other institutions.

This figure tracks how conservative or liberal the median members of the various institutions of the federal government have been over the second half of the twentieth century, using one common measure of ideology. The 1960s stands out as an unusually liberal period in the Court's postwar history. By this measure, looking across all the Court's cases, the Court immediately shifted back into a relatively more conservative pattern with the start of the Burger Court and since then has continued to drift slightly more to the right. Of course, Figure 9-2 also suggests that the Burger Court was only about as conservative as the House of Representatives, which had a Democratic majority, and so it is no surprise that the Burger Court could produce new decisions like *Roe v. Wade* (1973) at the same time that it began to limit the implications of some Warren era decisions.

Despite Nixon's assault on "judicial activism" the Burger Court showed no hesitation about using the power of judicial review. Both Republicans and Democrats, conservatives and liberals, were committed to the notion that the judiciary should define and enforce constitutional limits. They disagreed, however, about what those limits were and about how far courts should go in trying to remedy constitutional and policy problems. As a result, the Burger Court in the 1970s struck down state and federal laws in even more cases than did the Warren Court in the 1960s. There may have been fewer landmark cases that laid out new areas of constitutional law in the 1970s, but the Burger Court proved just as willing to nullify the actions of elected officials.

At the same time, conservatives on and off the Court pressed the justices to pare down the broadened standards of justiciability that the Warren Court had set. Tightening those rules would keep constitutional cases out of the Supreme Court. More importantly, it would keep constitutional issues out of the predominantly liberal lower federal courts. These efforts to shut the courthouse doors were only partly successful. Burger Court majorities did rule that various parties lacked standing to raise challenges to the constitutionality of the Vietnam War, and some of the broader implications of *Flast v. Cohen* (1968), which allowed constitutional challenges to government policies based on an individual's standing as a taxpayer, were not realized. Nevertheless, as Ronald Reagan entered office, there were still far fewer barriers to constitutional litigation than when Franklin Roosevelt entered office.

Powell v. McCormack (1969) illustrates the Court's ongoing willingness to assert its authority even in areas that previously might have been governed by the political questions doctrine. The case arose after the House of Representatives improperly refused to seat Harlem's important black congressman Adam Clayton Powell, Jr., in the wake of allegations that he had misused funds and falsified reports. Setting aside the claim that Art. I, §5, assigns the resolution of these disputes exclusively to each house of Congress (under the power to judge the elections and qualifications of its own members and to punish its members for disorderly behavior), the Court held that the House did not have the constitutional authority to exclude a duly elected member who met the minimum qualifications laid out in the text of the Constitution. Even in judging the qualifications of the members of the legislature, the Court claimed that it, not Congress, was "the ultimate interpreter of the Constitution."

IV. Powers of the National Government

MAJOR DEVELOPMENTS

- Continued expansion of national activity in economic and social regulation

The justices had been clear since the 1940s that they were not interested in enforcing boundaries on national power. The Tenth Amendment was a mere "truism." Such "sweeping" clauses as the necessary and proper clause and the spending clause gave Congress ample authority and discretion for creative policy making. The scope of the commerce clause seemed fairly boundless.

After 1968 Congress launched bold new initiatives, further expanding the scope and size of the federal government. There were few mainstream debates about the constitutional limits of federal authority. An exception was *Oregon v. Mitchell* (1970), which held that Congress could not change the voting age in state and local elections. The result was not unexpected, and Congress quickly responded by passing the Twenty-Sixth Amendment to the Constitution, lowering the voting age to eighteen. But the federal government was expanding its role in a variety of other areas while giving somewhat less deference to state and local governments. In 1974 Congress passed the Emergency Highway Energy Conservation Act, which used the threat of a reduction of federal highway funds to force states to adopt a national speed limit of fifty-five miles per hour. In keeping with the "law and order" themes of the Nixon campaign, the federal government continued to expand its role in criminal justice with bills such as the Organized Crime Control Act of 1970 and the Omnibus Crime Control Act of 1970. Regulatory policy making took on new goals and approaches with the rise of such "social" regulation as the Clean Air Act of 1970 and the Water Pollution Control Act of 1972.

V. Federalism

MAJOR DEVELOPMENTS

- Expanded use of federal block grants and revenue sharing to fund state and local governments
- Supreme Court experiments with state immunity from federal regulations

Conservatives were more skeptical of liberal claims that judicial review of federalism was unnecessary because national officeholders adequately represented the interests of state and local governments. This skepticism was expressed in *National League of Cities v. Usery* (1976), the first case in forty years in which the Supreme Court declared a federal law unconstitutional on Tenth Amendment grounds. In 1974 Congress amended the Fair Labor Standards Act to apply to all state and local employees. A number of cities and states sued the secretary of labor to enjoin the enforcement of the new provisions and to have them declared unconstitutional. In a 5–4 decision the Court declared the 1974 amendments unconstitutional. Justice Rehnquist's majority opinion held that it violated "state sovereignty" for the federal government to regulate the salaries and hours of state employees, even when Congress was exercising otherwise-straightforward Article I powers to tax and regulate commerce: "One undoubted attribute of state sovereignty is the State's power to determine the wages which shall be paid to those whom they employ in order to carry out their government functions, what hours those persons will work, and what compensation will be provided where these employees may be called upon to work overtime." Justice Brennan's dissent insisted that states did not need judicial protection, because members of Congress sufficiently protected state interest.

Illustration 9-1 President Richard Nixon Presents William Rehnquist with His Commission to Be Associate Justice

Source: Richard Nixon Presidential Library and Museum.

While this revival of Tenth Amendment considerations was a notable achievement for conservative constitutionalists, Rehnquist's victory proved to be limited. The Burger Court declared no other federal law unconstitutional under the Tenth Amendment, and the case was eventually overturned in *Garcia v. San Antonio Metropolitan Transit Authority* (1985).

VI. Separation of Powers

MAJOR DEVELOPMENTS

- Congress challenges presidential war powers
- Supreme Court asserts the authority to override executive privilege
- Congress and the president struggle over control of executive branch and administrative policy making

Separation of powers issues became more central to American constitutional politics after 1968. Richard Nixon's election began a period of divided government when increasingly conservative Republican presidents faced increasingly liberal Democratic Congresses. Nixon maintained that the president had broad powers to act unilaterally when making both foreign and domestic policy. His decisions to expand the military conflict in Southeast Asia and impound funds appropriated by Congress were aggressively challenged by both national legislators and litigants.

The most high-profile assertion of executive privilege came during the Watergate investigation when Nixon sought to protect tapes of White House conversations from being used in a criminal prosecution. *United States v. Nixon* (1974) is unusual not only because of its extraordinarily dramatic circumstances, but also because it involved a claim of executive privilege in a criminal case in a judicial proceeding. The Supreme Court proved to be particularly unsympathetic to the administration's efforts to completely withhold potential evidence from a criminal investigation in the courts and willing to trust the judgment of a trial court judge to review presidential documents and determine which should remain confidential and which should not. Claims of executive privilege are usually more mundane, and they are more often aimed at the legislature than the courts. Presidents have often argued that their conversations and notes should be confidential if the White House is to function effectively and that ultimately it is the president's judgment of what can be safely revealed that preserves the autonomy and effectiveness of the executive branch. The decision to breach executive privilege is most often a matter of negotiation, rather than mandate. The *Nixon* case posed the question of when the courts might be able to trump the executive's claim of privilege.

The results of the political crisis that led to Watergate were ambiguous. On the one hand, President Nixon was forced to resign, the Supreme Court rejected his broad claims of executive privilege in *United States v. Nixon* (1974) and his efforts to impound federal funds in *Train v. City of New York* (1975), and the War Powers Act of 1973 limited presidential power to engage in military hostilities abroad. On the other hand, the War Powers Act also recognized an executive authority to initiate military combat that many liberals thought unconstitutional, and the Supreme Court, when it rejected President Nixon's more extreme claims, did give constitutional sanction to both executive privilege and executive immunity. Most important, the Nixon impeachment did not end the era of the imperial presidency. Both Republicans and Democrats who followed would seek to build on the constitutional foundations of the New Deal and Great Society presidency.

The Vietnam War shattered the New Deal consensus about the purposes of American foreign policy and the relative free hand the president should have in achieving those purposes. There was less agreement in Washington about geostrategic goals and strategy and less faith that the White House would make the right calls. Policy disputes triggered constitutional disputes. Congressional reformers challenged presidential authority to initiate and conduct military offenses. Presidential advocates looked to defend established executive prerogatives to exercise discretion to do what was necessary to advance American national interests. The War Powers Act of 1973 was one effort to redefine the relationship between Congress and the president over how military force could be used, recognizing that military forces would continue to be used without prior congressional authorization but seeking to prevent long-term or substantial engagements without explicit legislative involvement. From a different angle, after high-profile congressional hearings investigating the Central Intelligence Agency (CIA) and the FBI, the Foreign Intelligence Surveillance Act of 1978 tried to regulate the process by which the executive branch gathered intelligence.

Leonard C. Meeker, **Memorandum on the Legality of the United States Participation in the Defense of Vietnam** (1966)[18]

In 1966, State Department Legal Advisor Leonard Meeker produced a memorandum for submission to the Senate Committee on Foreign Relations explicating the legal basis for the Vietnam War. The memo was wide-ranging, primarily focusing on international law, American treaty obligations to Vietnam, and the 1964 Gulf of Tonkin Resolutions authorizing the use of military force in Vietnam. It included, however, a constitutional analysis of presidential war powers that later became influential as Congress became disillusioned with the war and began to debate its own proper role in authorizing or ending the use of military force by the United States. The Meeker memo became the starting point for defenders of the presidential direction of the war in Vietnam, not only in the Johnson administration but also in the Nixon administration and in Congress itself.

. . .

Under the Constitution, the President, in addition to being Chief Executive, is Commander in Chief of the Army and Navy. He holds the prime responsibility for the conduct of United States foreign relations. These duties carry very broad powers, including the power to deploy American forces abroad and commit them to military operations when the President deems such action necessary to maintain the security and defense of the United States.

At the Federal Constitutional Convention in 1787, it was originally proposed that Congress have the power "to make war." There were objections that legislative proceedings were too slow for this power to be vested in Congress; it was suggested that the Senate might be a better repository. Madison and Gerry then moved to substitute "to declare war" for "to make war," "leaving to the Executive the power to repel sudden attacks." It was objected that this might make it too easy for the Executive to involve the nation in war, but the motion carried with but one dissenting vote.

In 1787 the world was a far larger place, and the framers probably had in mind attacks upon the United States. In the 20th century, the world has grown much smaller. An attack on a country far from our shores can impinge directly on the nation's security. . . .

Since the Constitution was adopted there have been at least 125 instances in which the President has ordered the armed forces to take action or maintain positions abroad without obtaining prior congressional authorization, starting with the "undeclared war" with France (1798–1800). For example, President Truman ordered 250,000 troops to Korea during the Korean war of the early 1950's. President Eisenhower dispatched 14,000 troops to Lebanon in 1958.

The Constitution leaves to the President the judgment to determine whether the circumstances of a particular armed attack are so urgent and the potential consequences so threatening to the security of the United States that he should act without formally consulting Congress.

. . .

Over a very long period of our history, practice and precedent have confirmed the constitutional authority to engage United States forces in hostilities without a declaration of war . . .

James Madison, one of the leading framers of the Constitution, and Presidents John Adams and Jefferson all construed the Constitution, in their official actions during the early years of the Republic, as authorizing the United States to employ its armed forces abroad in hostilities in the absence of any congressional declaration of war. Their views and actions constitute persuasive evidence as to the meaning and effect of the Constitution. History has accepted the interpretation that was placed on the Constitution by the early Presidents and Congresses in regard to the lawfulness of hostilities without a declaration of war. The instances of such actions in our history are numerous.

. . .

It may be suggested that a declaration of war is the only available constitutional process by which congressional support can be made effective for the use of United States armed forces in combat abroad. But the Constitution does not insist on any rigid formalism. It gives Congress a choice of ways in which to exercise its powers. In the case of Viet-Nam the Congress has supported the determination of the President by the Senate's approval of the SEATO treaty, the adoption of the joint resolution of August 10, 1964, and the enactment of the necessary authorization and appropriations.

. . .

18. Excerpt taken from *Congressional Record,* 91st Cong., 2nd Sess., 1970, 20, 972–77.

J. William Fulbright, **Congress and Foreign Policy** (1967)[19]

J. William Fulbright, chairman of the Senate Foreign Relations Committee from 1959 through 1974, had ushered through the Senate the 1964 Gulf of Tonkin Resolution, which formally launched the Vietnam War. Within a few years, however, Fulbright was pressing for a more active congressional role in the making of foreign policy. The Foreign Relations Committee held numerous hearings and issued several reports highlighting what Fulbright viewed as an abdication by Congress of its constitutional role in foreign policy generally and the war powers specifically. Even as he raised those concerns, however, Fulbright and others in Congress struggled with what the practical congressional response could be to the perceived imbalance of power given the nature of American involvement in the world in the latter half of the twentieth century. Those efforts eventually led to the passage of the War Powers Resolution in 1973, but in the late 1960s Fulbright pressed for the National Commitments Resolution, which argued that presidents should not promise or commit American resources and support to foreign countries without active congressional approval.

. . .

The authority of Congress in foreign policy has been eroding since 1940, the year of America's emergence as a major and permanent participant in world affairs, and the erosion has created a significant constitutional imbalance. Many if not most of the major decisions of American foreign policy in this era have been executive decisions. . . . Since World War II the United States has fought two wars without benefit of Congressional declaration and has engaged in numerous small-scale military activities—in the Middle East, for example, in 1958, and in the Congo on several occasions—without meaningful consultation with the Congress.

New devices have been invented which have the appearance but not the reality of Congressional participation in the making of foreign policy. . . . One is the joint resolution; another is the congressional briefing session. Neither is a satisfactory occasion for deliberation or the rendering of advice; both are designed to win consent without advice. Their principal purpose is to put the Congress on record in support of some emergency action at a moment when it would be most difficult to withhold support and, therefore, to spare the executive subsequent controversy or embarrassment.

The cause of the constitutional imbalance is crisis. I do not believe that the executive has willfully usurped the constitutional authority of Congress; nor do I believe that the Congress has knowingly given away its traditional authority, although some of its members—I among them, I regret to say—have sometimes shown excessive regard for the executive freedom of action. In the main, however, it has been circumstance rather than design which has given the executive its great predominance in foreign policy. The circumstance has been crisis, an entire era of crisis in which urgent decisions have been required again and again, decisions of a kind that the Congress is ill-equipped to make with what has been thought to be the requisite speed. The President has the means at his disposal for prompt action; the Congress does not. . . . (I might add that I think there have been many occasions when the need for immediate action has been exaggerated, resulting in mistakes which might have been avoided by greater deliberation.)

The question before us is whether and how the constitutional balance can be restored. . . .

. . .

Prior to redefining our responsibilities, it is important for us to distinguish clearly between two kinds of power, that pertaining to the shaping of foreign policy, to its direction and purpose and philosophy, and that pertaining to the day-to-day conduct of foreign policy. The former is the power which the Congress has the duty to discharge, diligently, vigorously and continuously; the latter, by and large calling for specialized skills, is best left to the executive and its administrative arms. . . .

Our performance in recent years has, unfortunately, been closer to the reverse. We have tended to snoop and pry in matters of detail, interfering in the handling of specific problems in specific places which we happen to chance upon, and, worse still, harassing individuals in the executive departments, thereby undermining their morale and discouraging the creative initiative which is so essential to a successful foreign policy. At the same time we have resigned from our responsibility in the shaping of policy and the defining of its purposes, submitting too easily to the pressures of crisis,

19. Excerpt taken from *Congressional Record*, 90th Cong., 1st Sess., 1967, 20, 702–06.

giving away things that are not ours to give: the war power of Congress, the treaty power of the Senate and the broader advice and consent power.

. . .

Permit me to recall some recent crises and the extremely limited role of the Senate in dealing with them. . . . At the time of the Cuban missile crisis in October 1962, many of us were in our home states campaigning for re-election. . . . [N]one of us, so far as I know, were given official information until after the Administration had made its policy decisions. President Kennedy called the congressional leadership for a meeting at the White House on Monday, October 22, 1962. The meeting lasted from about 5 p.m. to about 6 p.m.; at 7 p.m. President Kennedy went on national television to announce to the country the decisions which had of course been made before the Congressional leadership were called in. The meeting was not a consultation but a briefing, a kind of courtesy or ceremonial occasion for the leadership of the Congress. At that meeting, the senior Senator from Georgia and I made specific suggestions as to how the crisis might be met; we did so in the belief that we had a responsibility to give the President our best advice on the basis of the limited facts then at our command. With apparent reference to our temerity in expressing our views, Theodore Sorensen in his book on President Kennedy described this occasion as "the only sour note" in an otherwise flawless process of decision making. It is not exaggeration to say that on the one occasion when the world has gone to the very brink of nuclear war . . . the Congress took no part whatever in the shaping of American policy.

. . .

On the Senate floor as well as in the Foreign Relations Committee, vigorous and responsible discussion of our foreign relations is essential both to the shaping of wise foreign policy and to the sustenance of our constitutional system. The criteria of responsible and constructive debate are restraint in matters of detail and the day-to-day conduct of foreign policy, combined with diligence and energy in discussing the values, direction and purposes of American foreign policy. Just as it is an excess of democracy when Congress is overly aggressive in attempting to supervise the conduct of foreign policy, it is a failure of democracy when it fails to participate actively in determining policy objectives and in the making of significant decisions.

. . .

The War Powers Act of 1973

In 1973 Congress passed the War Powers Resolution over President Richard Nixon's veto. For several years, Congress had been debating whether and by what means the legislature should take a more active role in setting foreign policy and initiating military conflict. The continuation and expansion of the Vietnam War, even after congressional sentiment had turned against it, and the weakness of the Nixon administration in the midst of the Watergate scandal and during the final days before his resignation from office spurred Congress to pass the resolution. The War Powers Resolution was a compromise between those who favored congressional supremacy in this area and those who simply favored greater and more effective congressional participation in the policy-making process. The resolution called for presidential "consultation" with Congress "in every possible instance" when American troops would be placed in harm's way, a requirement for reporting to Congress on the necessity and authority for presidential action when hostilities did occur, and a requirement that the president disengage American forces if Congress either passed a joint resolution calling for such disengagement or failed to authorize the continued use of military force.

Although presidents have formally complied with the terms of the resolution, they have also consistently maintained that they are not constitutionally required to do so. Congress has provided resolutions authorizing major military operations such as the Iraq War, but other, smaller-scale military actions such as the invasions of Grenada, Haiti, and Panama did not have prior congressional authorization. Such actions did not, in the words of President Clinton's assistant attorney general Walter Dellinger, rise to the level of "'war' in the constitutional sense," given their "anticipated nature, scope and duration."[20]

. . .

SEC. 2. (a) It is the purpose of this joint resolution to fulfill the intent of the framers of the Constitution of the United States and insure that the collective judgment of both the Congress and the President will apply to the introduction of United States Armed Forces into hostilities, or into situations where imminent involvement in hostilities is

20. Walter Dellinger, "Deployment of United States Armed Forces Into Haiti, September 27, 1994," 18 Op. O.L.C. 173 (1994).

clearly indicated by the circumstances, and to the continued use of such forces in hostilities or in such situations.

SEC. 2. (b) Under article I, section 8, of the Constitution, it is specifically provided that the Congress shall have the power to make all laws necessary and proper for carrying into execution, not only its own powers but also all other powers vested by the Constitution in the Government of the United States, or in any department or officer thereof.

SEC. 2. (c) The constitutional powers of the President as Commander-in-Chief to introduce United States Armed Forces into hostilities, or into situations where imminent involvement in hostilities is clearly indicated by the circumstances, are exercised only pursuant to (1) a declaration of war, (2) specific statutory authorization, or (3) a national emergency created by attack upon the United States, its territories or possessions, or its armed forces.

SEC. 3. The President in every possible instance shall consult with Congress before introducing United States Armed Forces into hostilities or into situations where imminent involvement in hostilities is clearly indicated by the circumstances, and after every such introduction shall consult regularly with the Congress until United States Armed Forces are no longer engaged in hostilities or have been removed from such situations.

SEC. 4. (a) In the absence of a declaration of war, in any case in which United States Armed Forces are introduced—

(1) into hostilities or into situations where imminent involvement in hostilities is clearly indicated by the circumstances;

(2) into the territory, airspace or waters of a foreign nation, while equipped for combat, except for deployments which relate solely to supply, replacement, repair, or training of such forces; or

(3) (A) the circumstances necessitating the introduction of United States Armed Forces;

(B) the constitutional and legislative authority under which such introduction took place; and

(C) the estimated scope and duration of the hostilities or involvement.

SEC. 4. (b) The President shall provide such other information as the Congress may request in the fulfillment of its constitutional responsibilities with respect to committing the Nation to war and to the use of United States Armed Forces abroad.

Sec. 4. (c) Whenever United States Armed Forces are introduced into hostilities or into any situation described in subsection (a) of this section, the President shall, so long as such armed forces continue to be engaged in such hostilities or situation, report to the Congress periodically on the status of such hostilities or situation as well as on the scope and duration of such hostilities or situation, but in no event shall he report to the Congress less often than once every six months.

. . .

SEC. 5. (b) Within sixty calendar days after a report is submitted or is required to be submitted pursuant to section 4(a)(1), whichever is earlier, the President shall terminate any use of United States Armed Forces with respect to which such report was submitted (or required to be submitted), unless the Congress (1) has declared war or has enacted a specific authorization for such use of United States Armed Forces, (2) has extended by law such sixty-day period, or (3) is physically unable to meet as a result of an armed attack upon the United States. Such sixty-day period shall be extended for not more than an additional thirty days if the President determines and certifies to the Congress in writing that unavoidable military necessity respecting the safety of United States Armed Forces requires the continued use of such armed forces in the course of bringing about a prompt removal of such forces.

SEC. 5. (c) Notwithstanding subsection (b), at any time that United States Armed Forces are engaged in hostilities outside the territory of the United States, its possessions and territories without a declaration of war or specific statutory authorization, such forces shall be removed by the President if the Congress so directs by concurrent resolution.

. . .

SEC. 8. (a) Authority to introduce United States Armed Forces into hostilities or into situations wherein involvement in hostilities is clearly indicated by the circumstances shall not be inferred—(1) from any provision of law (whether or not in effect before the date of the enactment of this joint resolution), including any provision contained in any appropriation Act, unless such provision specifically authorizes the introduction of United States Armed Forces into hostilities or into such situations and stating that it is intended to constitute specific statutory authorization within the meaning of this joint resolution;

or (2) from any treaty heretofore or hereafter ratified unless such treaty is implemented by legislation specifically authorizing the introduction of United States Armed Forces into hostilities or into such situations and stating that it is intended to constitute specific statutory authorization within the meaning of this joint resolution.

. . .

SEC. 8. (d) Nothing in this joint resolution—

(1) is intended to alter the constitutional authority of the Congress or of the President, or the provision of existing treaties; or

(2) shall be construed as granting any authority to the President with respect to the introduction of United States Armed Forces into hostilities or into situations wherein involvement in hostilities is clearly indicated by the circumstances which authority he would not have had in the absence of this joint resolution.

Richard Nixon, Veto of the War Powers Resolution (1973)[21]

President Nixon had threatened to veto the War Powers Resolution, but by the time it was passed he was mired in the Watergate scandal and the Vietnam War was regarded as a costly failure exacerbated by an unresponsive executive branch. Nixon was faced with Democratic majorities in both the House and the Senate throughout his time as president, but Congress, with bipartisan support for the bill, overrode his veto of the War Powers Resolution.

To the House of Representatives:

I hereby return without my approval House Joint Resolution 542—the War Powers Resolution. While I am in accord with the desire of the Congress to assert its proper role in the conduct of our foreign affairs, the restrictions which this resolution would impose upon the authority of the President are both unconstitutional and dangerous to the interests of our Nation.

The proper roles of the Congress and the Executive in the conduct of foreign affairs have been debated since the founding of our country. Only recently, however, has there been a serious challenge to the wisdom of the Founding Fathers in choosing not to draw a precise and detailed line of demarcation between the foreign policy powers of the two branches.

. . .

Clearly Unconstitutional

House Joint Resolution 542 would attempt to take away, by a mere legislative act, authorities which the President has properly exercised under the Constitution for almost 200 years. One of its provisions would automatically cut off certain authorities after sixty days unless the Congress extended them. Another would allow the Congress to eliminate certain authorities merely by the passage of a concurrent resolution—an action which does not normally have the force of law, since it denies the President his constitutional role in approving legislation.

I believe that both these provisions are unconstitutional. The only way in which the constitutional powers of a branch of the Government can be altered is by amending the Constitution—and any attempt to make such alterations by legislation alone is clearly without force.

Undermining Our Foreign Policy

. . . I am also deeply disturbed by the practical consequences of this resolution. For it would seriously undermine this Nation's ability to act decisively and convincingly in times of international crisis. . . .

. . .

Failure to Require Positive Congressional Action

I am particularly disturbed by the fact that certain of the President's constitutional powers as Commander in Chief of the Armed Forces would terminate automatically under this resolution 60 days after they were invoked. . . . In effect, the Congress is here attempting to increase its policymaking role through a provision that requires it to take absolutely no action at all.

In my view, the proper way for the Congress to make known its will on such foreign policy questions is through a positive action, with full debate on the merits of the issue and with each member taking the responsibility of casting a yes or no vote after considering those merits. The authorization and appropriations process represents one of the ways in which such

21. Excerpt taken from *Public Papers of the Presidents of the United States: Richard Nixon, 1973* (Washington, DC: Government Printing Office, 1975), 893–95.

influence can be exercised. . . . [The joint resolution] would give every future Congress the ability to handcuff every future President merely by doing nothing and sitting still. In my view, one cannot become a responsible partner unless one is prepared to take responsible action.

United States v. United States District Court, 407 U.S. 297 (1972) (the "Keith Case")

Robert Plamondon and two co-defendants were charged with the dynamite bombing of a CIA office in Ann Arbor, Michigan. During pretrial motions it was revealed that the government had wiretapped the defendants without first obtaining a search warrant. Plamondon's lawyers argued that this warrantless surveillance violated the Fourth Amendment and that any other evidence obtained as a result of this illegal search should be excluded from the trial. In response, the Justice Department—headed by Attorney General John Mitchell—claimed that the surveillance was lawful as a reasonable exercise of the president's independent Article II power to protect the national security and that any information so obtained did not have to be disclosed to the defendants. The Nixon administration also relied, in part, on Title III of the Omnibus Crime Control and Safe Streets Act of 1968. This act contained a provision that nothing in that law limits the president's constitutional power to protect against the overthrow of the government or against "any other clear and present danger to the structure or existence of the government."

District Court Judge Damon Keith disagreed and ordered the government to disclose the information. The government appealed Judge Keith's ruling (hence the "Keith case"), but its position was unanimously rejected by the Sixth Circuit Court of Appeals. The government fared no better before the Supreme Court. In an 8–0 opinion (with newly appointed Justice Rehnquist not participating owing to his prior association with the case in the Justice Department) the justices found that the government's internal security concerns did not justify a departure from the customary requirement of judicial approval prior to initiation of a search or surveillance. The justices did not address the question of whether similar requirements were necessary for "foreign surveillance." Is judicial oversight of intelligence gathering consistent with presidential responsibilities for national security? Would the constitutional implications be different if the case involved foreign groups?

JUSTICE POWELL delivered the opinion of the Court.

The issue before us is an important one for the people of our country and their Government. It involves the delicate question of the President's power, acting through the Attorney General, to authorize electronic surveillance in internal security matters without prior judicial approval. Successive Presidents for more than one-quarter of a century have authorized such surveillance in varying degrees, without guidance from the Congress or a definitive decision of this Court. This case brings the issue here for the first time. Its resolution is a matter of national concern, requiring sensitivity both to the Government's right to protect itself from unlawful subversion and attack and to the citizen's right to be secure in his privacy against unreasonable Government intrusion. . . .

During pretrial proceedings, the defendants moved to compel the United States to disclose certain electronic surveillance information and to conduct a hearing to determine whether this information "tainted" the evidence on which the indictment was based or which the Government intended to offer at trial. In response, the Government filed an affidavit of the Attorney General, acknowledging that its agents had overheard conversations in which Plamondon had participated. . . .

. . .

Together with the elaborate surveillance requirements in Title III, there is the following proviso, *18 U. S. C. §2511* (3):

> Nothing contained in this chapter or in section 605 of the Communications Act of 1934 (48 Stat. 1143; *47 U. S. C. 605*) shall limit the constitutional power of the President to take such measures as he deems necessary to protect the Nation against actual or potential attack or other hostile acts of a foreign power, to obtain foreign intelligence information deemed essential to the security of the United States, or to protect national security information against foreign intelligence activities. *Nor shall anything contained in this chapter be deemed to limit the constitutional power of the President to take such measures as he deems necessary to protect the United States against the overthrow of the Government by force or other unlawful means, or against any other clear and present danger to the structure or existence of the Government.* . . . (Emphasis supplied.)

The Government relies on §2511 (3). It argues that "in excepting national security surveillances from the Act's warrant requirement Congress recognized the President's authority to conduct such surveillances without prior judicial approval." The section thus is viewed as a recognition or affirmance of a constitutional authority in the President to conduct warrantless domestic security surveillance such as that involved in this case.

We think the language of §2511 (3), as well as the legislative history of the statute, refutes this interpretation. . . .

Section 2511 (3) . . . merely provides that the Act shall not be interpreted to limit or disturb such power as the President may have under the Constitution. In short, Congress simply left presidential powers where it found them. . . .

It is important at the outset to emphasize the limited nature of the question before the Court. This case raises no constitutional challenge to electronic surveillance as specifically authorized by Title III of the Omnibus Crime Control and Safe Streets Act of 1968. Nor is there any question or doubt as to the necessity of obtaining a warrant in the surveillance of crimes unrelated to the national security interest. Further, the instant case requires no judgment on the scope of the President's surveillance power with respect to the activities of foreign powers, within or without this country. . . .

We begin the inquiry by noting that the President of the United States has the fundamental duty, under Art. II, §1, of the Constitution, to "preserve, protect and defend the Constitution of the United States." Implicit in that duty is the power to protect our Government against those who would subvert or overthrow it by unlawful means. In the discharge of this duty, the President—through the Attorney General—may find it necessary to employ electronic surveillance to obtain intelligence information on the plans of those who plot unlawful acts against the Government. . . .

But a recognition of these elementary truths does not make the employment by Government of electronic surveillance a welcome development—even when employed with restraint and under judicial supervision. There is, understandably, a deep-seated uneasiness and apprehension that this capability will be used to intrude upon cherished privacy of law-abiding citizens. We look to the Bill of Rights to safeguard this privacy. Though physical entry of the home is the chief evil against which the wording of the Fourth Amendment is directed, its broader spirit now shields private speech from unreasonable surveillance. Our decision in *Katz v. United States* (1967) refused to lock the Fourth Amendment into instances of actual physical trespass. Rather, the Amendment governs "not only the seizure of tangible items, but extends as well to the recording of oral statements . . . without any 'technical trespass under . . . local property law.'" That decision implicitly recognized that the broad and unsuspected governmental incursions into conversational privacy which electronic surveillance entails necessitate the application of Fourth Amendment safeguards.

. . .

These Fourth Amendment freedoms cannot properly be guaranteed if domestic security surveillances may be conducted solely within the discretion of the Executive Branch. The Fourth Amendment does not contemplate the executive officers of Government as neutral and disinterested magistrates. . . . The historical judgment, which the Fourth Amendment accepts, is that unreviewed executive discretion may yield too readily to pressures to obtain incriminating evidence and overlook potential invasions of privacy and protected speech. . . .

. . .

We cannot accept the Government's argument that internal security matters are too subtle and complex for judicial evaluation. Courts regularly deal with the most difficult issues of our society. There is no reason to believe that federal judges will be insensitive to or uncomprehending of the issues involved in domestic security cases. . . .

Nor do we believe prior judicial approval will fracture the secrecy essential to official intelligence gathering. The investigation of criminal activity has long involved imparting sensitive information to judicial officers who have respected the confidentialities involved. Judges may be counted upon to be especially conscious of security requirements in national security cases. . . .

Thus, we conclude that the Government's concerns do not justify departure in this case from the customary Fourth Amendment requirement of judicial approval prior to initiation of a search or surveillance. Although some added burden will be imposed upon the Attorney General, this inconvenience is justified in a free society to protect constitutional values. . . .

The judgment of the Court of Appeals is hereby *Affirmed*

JUSTICE DOUGLAS, concurring.

While I join in the opinion of the Court, I add these words in support of it.

. . .

Here, federal agents wish to rummage for months on end through every conversation, no matter how intimate or personal, carried over selected telephone lines, simply to seize those few utterances which may add to their sense of the pulse of a domestic underground.

. . .

That "domestic security" is said to be involved here does not draw this case outside the mainstream of Fourth Amendment law. Rather, the recurring desire of reigning officials to employ dragnet techniques to intimidate their critics lies at the core of that prohibition. For it was such excesses as the use of general warrants and the writs of assistance that led to the ratification of the Fourth Amendment. . . .

. . . [W]e are currently in the throes of another national seizure of paranoia, resembling the hysteria which surrounded the Alien and Sedition Acts, the Palmer Raids, and the McCarthy era. Those who register dissent or who petition their governments for redress are subjected to scrutiny by grand juries, by the FBI, or even by the military. Their associates are interrogated. Their homes are bugged and their telephones are wiretapped. They are befriended by secret government informers. Their patriotism and loyalty are questioned. Senator Sam Ervin, who has chaired hearings on military surveillance of civilian dissidents, warns that "it is not an exaggeration to talk in terms of hundreds of thousands of . . . dossiers." . . . More than our privacy is implicated. Also at stake is the reach of the Government's power to intimidate its critics.

When the Executive attempts to excuse these tactics as essential to its defense against internal subversion, we are obliged to remind it, without apology, of this Court's long commitment to the preservation of the Bill of Rights from the corrosive environment of precisely such expedients. . . .

. . . We have as much or more to fear from the erosion of our sense of privacy and independence by the omnipresent electronic ear of the Government as we do from the likelihood that fomenters of domestic upheaval will modify our form of governing.

JUSTICE WHITE, concurring.

. . . I would affirm the Court of Appeals but on the statutory ground urged by defendant-respondents without reaching or intimating any views with respect to the constitutional issue decided by both the District Court and the Court of Appeals. . . .

. . . Because I conclude that on the record before us the surveillance undertaken by the Government in this case was illegal under the statute itself, I find it unnecessary, and therefore improper, to consider or decide the constitutional questions which the courts below improvidently reached. . . .

United States v. Nixon, 418 U.S. 683 (1974)

The crisis known as Watergate arose as a result of an investigation into potential White House involvement in the burglary and attempted bugging of the Democratic Party's headquarters at the Watergate Hotel on June 17, 1972. This investigation led to inquiries into an alleged secret White House "Special Investigations Unit" known as the "Plumbers." This group was made up of members and former members of America's intelligence community and was created in response to the release of the Pentagon Papers. These members' initial job (as plumbers) was to plug leaks. However, before long members of the Plumbers were recruited to engage in a variety of off-the-books campaign activities. These included the sabotaging of Ed Muskie's presidential campaign by such "dirty tricks" as creating fake banners designed to anger other Democrats, harassing people considered to be White House "enemies," mugging demonstrators at Republican events, and conspiring to obstruct justice. The Plumbers were funded by millions of dollars of secret contributions to Nixon's reelection campaign, known as CREEP (the Committee to Reelect the President).

It wasn't long before some of Nixon's top aides were implicated in the burglary and the subsequent pre-election cover-up of White House involvement. As District Judge John Sirica was busy presiding over the trial of the Watergate burglars, the Senate established a select committee, chaired by Sam Ervin, to investigate the Watergate affair. In testimony before this committee it was revealed that Nixon secretly taped all Oval Office conversations. This revelation prompted the special Watergate prosecutor, Archibald Cox, to begin legal proceedings to obtain from the president those tapes that were thought likely to contain evidence important for the prosecution of the suspected Watergate conspirators.

In October 1973 Nixon demanded that Cox drop his quest for the White House tapes. When he refused, Attorney General Richardson was ordered to fire Cox. Both Richardson and his deputy refused, citing promises made during Senate

"He says he's from the phone company . . ."

Illustration 9-2 "He Says He's From the Phone Company"

Source: Paul Conrad, *Los Angeles Times*, June 1972. Used by permission of the Paul Conrad estate.

confirmation hearings to respect Cox's independence, and so they too were fired by the third-ranking official in the Justice Department, Solicitor General Robert Bork, in what became known as the Saturday Night Massacre. In response to the political firestorm that followed the "massacre," Nixon informed Sirica that nine tapes would be forthcoming. Unfortunately, the tape of the first conversation between Nixon and chief of staff H.R. Haldeman after the Watergate break-in contained an eighteen-and-a-half-minute gap. Although the White House blamed the gap on an innocent mistake made by Nixon's secretary, it was later established that the erasure had been deliberate. One week after Nixon agreed to release these nine (edited) tapes, the House Judiciary Committee began its impeachment inquiry.

In a further attempt to mollify the opposition, Nixon agreed to hire a new special prosecutor, Leon Jaworski. Jaworski continued to push for the tapes. Specifically, he wanted an additional sixty-four tapes to use in his prosecution of former attorney general John Mitchell, Haldeman, and presidential aide John Ehrlichman. Nixon refused to turn over the tapes, claiming that they were protected by executive privilege. Jaworski sought a subpoena from the federal courts compelling the president to turn over the tapes.

United States v. Nixon *raised a classic separation of powers question: How should the president's interest in maintaining the confidentiality of White House conversations be balanced against the judiciary's interest in providing due process in a criminal proceeding? Does this issue represent a zero-sum game for these two branches, in the sense that supporting the president's position would make it impossible for the judiciary to carry out its constitutional responsibilities, while (conversely) supporting the judiciary's position would undermine the president's ability to carry out his or her responsibilities?*

As you read the opinion, consider the issues that the Court left unanswered. Apparently the need for relevant evidence in a criminal proceeding outweighed the general executive interest in confidential advice. What other competing interests might outweigh a general claim of privilege? Is executive confidentiality less weighty than the judiciary's interest in the operation of the criminal justice system but more weighty than a general congressional interest in administrative oversight? Does the judiciary's interest in relevant information extend to all judicial proceedings or simply those that involve high government officials charged with serious criminal offenses? Does an invocation of executive privilege on the grounds of national security always outweigh the competing interests of the other branches? Who decides whether a president's assertion of executive privilege on grounds of national security is legitimate? The president? The Congress? The courts?

When the tapes were finally released they revealed that from the very beginning the president and his top advisors had conspired to obstruct justice by arranging for millions of dollars in hush money for the Watergate burglars. They also showed that Haldeman had intended to use the CIA for political espionage; that Mitchell had initiated the break-in at the Watergate hotel, and that Nixon and his advisors had discussed contriving a "national security" justification for the break-in. Four days later, as senators of his own political party urged him to leave office, Nixon resigned.

Richard Nixon's claims of executive privilege went 1–3 in the Supreme Court, with two more important cases being heard after he left office. In Nixon v. Administrator of General Services *(1977), the Supreme Court by a 7–2 vote ruled that Congress could pass rules governing the disposal of Nixon's presidential papers and that a former president could not assert an absolute privilege to keep all presidential papers private. Nixon was more successful when defending against a civil lawsuit by a military analyst who claimed that he had been illegally fired by the former president in retaliation for his congressional testimony. The Supreme Court by a 5–4 vote in* Nixon v. Fitzgerald *(1982) asserted that the Constitution vested the president with absolute immunity for "acts in performance of particular functions of his office." "Because of the singular importance of the President's duties," Justice Powell's majority opinion declared, "diversion of his energies by concern with private lawsuits would raise unique risks to the effective functioning of government."*

CHIEF JUSTICE BURGER delivered the opinion of the Court.

. . .

In the performance of assigned constitutional duties each branch of the Government must initially interpret the Constitution, and the interpretation of its powers by any branch is due great respect from the others. The President's counsel, as we have noted, reads the Constitution as providing an absolute privilege of confidentiality for all Presidential communications. Many decisions of this Court, however, have unequivocally reaffirmed the holding of *Marbury v. Madison* (1803), that "[it] is emphatically the province and duty of the judicial department to say what the law is."...

. . .

In support of his claim of absolute privilege, the President's counsel urges two grounds, one of which is common to all governments and one of which is peculiar to our system of separation of powers. The first ground is the valid need for protection of communications between high Government officials and those who advise and assist them in the performance of their manifold duties; the importance of this confidentiality is too plain to require further discussion. Human experience teaches that those who expect public dissemination of their remarks may well temper candor with a concern for appearances and for their own interests to the detriment of the decisionmaking process. Whatever the nature of the privilege of confidentiality of Presidential communications in the exercise of Art. II powers, the privilege can be said to derive from the supremacy of each branch within its own assigned area of constitutional duties. Certain powers and privileges flow from the nature of enumerated powers; the protection of the confidentiality of Presidential communications has similar constitutional underpinnings.

The second ground asserted by the President's counsel in support of the claim of absolute privilege rests on the doctrine of separation of powers. Here it is argued that the independence of the Executive Branch within its own sphere insulates a President from a judicial subpoena in an ongoing criminal prosecution, and thereby protects confidential Presidential communications.

However, neither the doctrine of separation of powers, nor the need for confidentiality of high-level communications, without more, can sustain an absolute, unqualified Presidential privilege of immunity from judicial process under all circumstances. The President's need for complete candor and objectivity from advisers calls for great deference from the courts. However, when the privilege depends solely on the broad, undifferentiated claim of public interest in the confidentiality of such conversations, a confrontation with other values arises. Absent a claim of need to protect military, diplomatic, or sensitive national security secrets, we find it difficult to accept the argument that even the very important interest in confidentiality of Presidential communications is significantly diminished by production of such material for *in camera* inspection with all the protection that a district court will be obliged to provide.

The impediment that an absolute, unqualified privilege would place in the way of the primary constitutional duty of the Judicial Branch to do justice in criminal prosecutions would plainly conflict with the function of the courts under Art. III. In designing the structure of our Government and dividing and allocating the sovereign power among three co-equal branches, the Framers of the Constitution sought to provide a comprehensive system, but the separate powers were not intended to operate with absolute independence.

> While the Constitution diffuses power the better to secure liberty, it also contemplates that practice will integrate the dispersed powers into a workable government. It enjoins upon its branches separateness but interdependence, autonomy but reciprocity. *Youngstown Sheet & Tube Co.* v. *Sawyer* (1952) (Jackson, J., concurring).

To read the Art. II powers of the President as providing an absolute privilege as against a subpoena essential to enforcement of criminal statutes on no more than a generalized claim of the public interest in confidentiality of nonmilitary and nondiplomatic discussions would upset the constitutional balance of "a workable government" and gravely impair the role of the courts under Art. III.

. . .

We conclude that when the ground for asserting privilege as to subpoenaed materials sought for use in a criminal trial is based only on the generalized interest in confidentiality, it cannot prevail over the fundamental demands of due process of law in the fair administration of criminal justice. The generalized assertion of privilege must yield to the demonstrated, specific need for evidence in a pending criminal trial. . . .

. . . We now turn to the important question of the District Court's responsibilities in conducting the *in camera* examination of Presidential materials or communications delivered under the compulsion of the subpoena *duces tecum*.

. . . It is elementary that *in camera* inspection of evidence is always a procedure calling for scrupulous protection against any release or publication of material not found by the court, at that stage, probably admissible in evidence and relevant to the issues of the trial for which it is sought. That being true of an ordinary situation, it is obvious that the District Court has a very heavy responsibility to see to it that Presidential conversations, which are either not relevant or not admissible, are accorded that high degree of respect due the President of the United States. Chief Justice Marshall, sitting as a trial judge in the *Burr* case (25 Fed. Cas. 30 [C.C.D. Va. 1807]) was extraordinarily careful to point out that

> [in] no case of this kind would a court be required to proceed against the president as against an ordinary individual.

Marshall's statement cannot be read to mean in any sense that a President is above the law, but relates to the singularly unique role under Art. II of a President's communications and activities, related to the performance of duties under that Article. Moreover, a President's communications and activities encompass a vastly wider range of sensitive material than would be true of any "ordinary individual." It is therefore necessary in the public interest to afford Presidential confidentiality the greatest protection consistent with the fair administration of justice. The need for confidentiality even as to idle conversations with associates in which casual reference might be made concerning political leaders within the country or foreign statesmen is too obvious to call for further treatment. We have no doubt that the District Judge will at all times accord to Presidential records that high degree of deference suggested in *United States* v. *Burr*, and will discharge his responsibility to see to it that until released to the Special Prosecutor no *in camera* material is revealed to anyone. This burden applies with even greater force to excised material; once the decision is made to excise, the material is restored to its privileged status and should be returned under seal to its lawful custodian.

Since this matter came before the Court during the pendency of a criminal prosecution, and on representations that time is of the essence, the mandate shall issue forthwith.

JUSTICE REHNQUIST took no part in the decision of these cases.

VII. Individual Rights

MAJOR DEVELOPMENTS

- Supreme Court protects abortion rights
- Struggles between more liberal and more conservative religious groups replace traditional struggles between Protestants and Catholics
- Little or no protection for property or gun rights

Americans modified only slightly the constitutional priorities respecting individual rights of the New Deal and Great Society. *Roe v. Wade* (1973) vaulted family rights and rights to procreate to the top of the constitutional food chain, but liberal justices during the 1970s also maintained a fairly high wall between church and state. The justices in the late 1970s demonstrated that the contracts clause was not entirely moribund as a source of constitutional rights, but no constitutional decision maker made any effort to even partly restore pre–New Deal constitutional protections for property rights. Constitutional decision makers during the Nixon and Carter presidencies continued to ignore the Second Amendment.

A. Property

Political activists from 1969 to 1980 raised two very different challenges to the New Deal consensus that economic and social questions raised policy questions constitutionally entrusted exclusively to elected officials. Progressive advocacy groups claimed that the due process and equal protection clauses of the Fourteenth Amendment obligated states to provide certain welfare services for poorer citizens. Conservative advocacy groups claimed that environmental and other government regulations took property without compensation. Neither more progressive nor more conservative activists had much success changing the constitutional status quo during the 1970s. The Supreme Court refused to find a constitutional right to basic necessities. The freedom of contract remained moribund. The contracts clause was revived only as a marginal limit on state power. Takings clause law continued to be highly favorable to government regulation.

Divided liberals in the elected branches of government from 1969 to 1980 were more concerned with economic policy than economic rights. A broad consensus existed among most Democrats and Republicans that government was constitutionally entitled to pursue almost every regulatory policy that a reasonable person might think advanced the public good. Democrats and Republicans during these years competed over which party offered the mix of government regulations and redistributive policies that would best promote economic prosperity and alleviate poverty. No party championed measures or litigation that sought to revive the freedom of contract, the contracts clause, or substantial takings clause restrictions on government power.

During the 1960s and 1970s some liberal scholars and activists asserted that persons had constitutional rights to certain basic necessities. Charles Reich's "The New Property" argued that government was constitutionally obligated to provide the services that impecunious citizens needed to survive.[22] Frank Michelman claimed that persons have a constitutional right to "minimum protection against economic hazard." This "minimum protection" entails "constitutional rights to provision for certain basic ingredients of individual welfare, such as food, shelter, health care, and education."[23] Assisted significantly by federal funding, such public interest groups as the Legal Services Organization and the Center on Social Welfare Policy were

22. Charles Reich, "The New Property," *Yale Law Journal* 73 (1964): 733.

23. Frank I. Michelman, "Foreword: On Protecting the Poor Through the Fourteenth Amendment," *Harvard Law Review* 83 (1969): 7; Frank I. Michelman, "Welfare Rights in a Constitutional Democracy," *Washington University Law Quarterly* 1979 (1979): 659.

able to place the rights of poor people on the agenda of the Supreme Court and win several important victories that were initially thought to put a right to basic necessities within reach.[24]

Social welfare activists who hoped that the 1970s would witness a judicial declaration that welfare was a constitutional right were disappointed. The Supreme Court ruled that poor persons had no federal constitutional right to housing, no right to welfare, and no right to anything more than a minimal education. Social welfare policy, Justice Stewart's majority opinion in *Dandridge v. Williams* (1970) claimed, was as much a matter of legislative discretion as any other social or economic policy. Justice White's majority opinion in *Lindsey v. Normet* (1972) asserted that "the assurance of adequate housing . . . is a legislative not a judicial function." The next year Justice Powell denied that education was a fundamental right. Summarizing five years of judicial decisions rejecting claims that the Constitution guaranteed basic necessities, his majority opinion in *San Antonio Independent School District v. Rodriguez* (1973) asserted, "It is not the province of this Court to create substantive constitutional rights in the name of guaranteeing equal protection of the laws."

B. Religion

The constitutional politics of religious freedom took contemporary shape during the Nixon administration. Political debates over religious exercises in the public sphere and state assistance to religious organizations became struggles between more liberal and more conservative religious groups. Public debates over funding for parochial schools that once pitted Protestants against Catholics now pitted more liberal Protestants, Catholics, and Jews against more conservative Protestants, Catholics, and Jews. The very names of the leading parties in these fights reflect the changing cleavages in the constitutional politics of religion. "Protestants United for Separation of Church and State" became "Americans United for Separation of Church and State." The "Moral Majority" became a leading voice for school prayer and state assistance to church-supported schools. These fights became increasingly politicized as the Nixon administration sought judicial rulings that would enable more public moneys to support religious activities.

While controversies over the relationship between church and state intensified, constitutional law in this area in 1980 remained similar to constitutional law in 1969. States could burden the free exercise of religion only if they demonstrated a compelling interest. The judicial ban on nonsectarian school prayer remained the law of the land. The establishment clause forbade most, but not all, state assistance to religious schools and organizations. Newly appointed Justice William Rehnquist and, to a lesser extent, Chief Justice Warren Burger favored weakening the wall of separation between church and state, but Ford appointee John Stevens was, if anything, more committed to preventing funds from going to religious organizations than were traditional New Dealers. Liberals won most of the constitutional battles, but these wins produced a backlash that promised increased political support for conservative politicians in the future.

In its application of the establishment clause the Burger Court during the 1970s rejected state and local efforts to provide financial assistance to religious schools. In *Lemon v. Kurtzman* (1971) the Supreme Court announced an important three-part test for determining when state programs that assisted religious institutions were constitutional. Chief Justice Burger's majority opinion asserted, "First, the statute must have a secular legislative purpose; second, its principal or primary effect must be one that neither advances nor inhibits religion, . . . finally, the statute must not foster 'an excessive government entanglement with religion.'" Few state laws survived this test before Ronald Reagan became president.

When evaluating claims under the free exercise clause the Supreme Court continued to insist that states provide exemptions for religious believers from neutral state laws that burdened religious practice, unless a compelling interest justified the failure to provide an exemption. *Wisconsin v. Yoder* (1972) held that the Amish should enjoy an exemption from mandatory schooling laws. Justice Douglas dissented in part, but only because he thought that the justices had not adequately considered the free exercise rights of Amish teenagers who might want to attend public schools.

24. See Susan E. Lawrence, *The Poor in Court* (Princeton, NJ: Princeton University Press, 1990); Martha F. Davis, *Brutal Need: Lawyers and the Welfare Rights Movement, 1960–1973* (New Haven, CT: Yale University Press, 1993).

Wisconsin v. Yoder, 406 U.S. 205 (1972)

Jonas Yoder and his Old Order Amish neighbors refused to enroll their children in either a public or a private high school. Enrollment, Yoder and others insisted, would threaten their children's salvation and the integrity of the Amish community. Wisconsin law at this time required children to attend public or approved private schools until they were sixteen years old. Yoder was found guilty of violating this statute and fined $5. On appeal, the Supreme Court of Wisconsin ruled that the mandatory schooling statute violated the free exercise rights of religious believers. Wisconsin appealed that decision to the Supreme Court of the United States.

The Supreme Court by a 6–1 vote ruled that Yoder had a constitutional right to have his children exempted from the state mandatory education law. Chief Justice Burger's majority opinion places great weight on evidence that the Amish are a successful, law-abiding community that "rejects public welfare in any of its usual modern forms." Was Justice Douglas correct that such considerations should have no bearing on the case? Is the key issue whether the religious group has praiseworthy qualities or the extent of the harm to the community imposed by the state mandate? Was Justice Douglas correct that the children in this case had constitutional rights also in need of protection? Did you have a constitutional right to not attend the Sunday school of your parents' designation? Notice the interesting judicial alignment in Yoder. *Chief Justice Burger, generally thought of as conservative, was very supportive of the Amish claim. Justice Douglas, the most liberal member of the Court, had significant reservations. What might explain the alignment in* Yoder? *Does support for* Yoder *make one a liberal, a conservative, or something else?*

CHIEF JUSTICE BURGER delivered the opinion of the Court.

. . .

Amish objection to formal education beyond the eighth grade is firmly grounded in the[ir] central religious concepts. They object to the high school, and higher education generally, because the values they teach are in marked variance with Amish values and the Amish way of life; they view secondary school education as an impermissible exposure of their children to a "worldly" influence in conflict with their beliefs. The high school tends to emphasize intellectual and scientific accomplishments, self-distinction, competitiveness, worldly success, and social life with other students. Amish society emphasizes informal learning-through-doing; a life of "goodness," rather than a life of intellect; wisdom, rather than technical knowledge; community welfare, rather than competition; and separation from, rather than integration with, contemporary worldly society.

. . .

. . . [I]n order for Wisconsin to compel school attendance beyond the eighth grade against a claim that such attendance interferes with the practice of a legitimate religious belief, it must appear either that the State does not deny the free exercise of religious belief by its requirement, or that there is a state interest of sufficient magnitude to override the interest claiming protection under the Free Exercise Clause. . . .

. . . [O]nly those interests of the highest order and those not otherwise served can overbalance legitimate claims to the free exercise of religion. We can accept it as settled, therefore, that, however strong the State's interest in universal compulsory education, it is by no means absolute to the exclusion or subordination of all other interests. E.g., *Sherbert v. Verner* (1963). . . .

. . .

. . . [W]e see that the record in this case abundantly supports the claim that the traditional way of life of the Amish is not merely a matter of personal preference, but one of deep religious conviction, shared by an organized group, and intimately related to daily living. That the Old Order Amish daily life and religious practice stem from their faith is shown by the fact that it is in response to their literal interpretation of the Biblical injunction from the Epistle of Paul to the Romans, "be not conformed to this world." . . .

. . .

. . . The conclusion is inescapable that secondary schooling, by exposing Amish children to worldly influences in terms of attitudes, goals, and values contrary to beliefs, and by substantially interfering with the religious development of the Amish child and his integration into the way of life of the Amish faith community at the crucial adolescent stage of development, contravenes the basic religious tenets and practice of the Amish faith, both as to the parent and the child.

. . .

. . . [T]his case cannot be disposed of on the grounds that Wisconsin's requirement for school attendance to age 16 applies uniformly to all citizens of the State and does not, on its face, discriminate against religions or a particular religion, or that it is motivated by legitimate secular concerns. A regulation neutral on its face may, in its application, nonetheless offend the constitutional requirement for governmental neutrality if it unduly burdens the free exercise of religion. *Sherbert*. . . .

. . .

The State advances two primary arguments in support of its system of compulsory education. It notes . . . that some degree of education is necessary to prepare citizens to participate effectively and intelligently in our open political system if we are to preserve freedom and independence. Further, education prepares individuals to be self-reliant and self-sufficient participants in society. We accept these propositions.

However, the evidence adduced by the Amish in this case is persuasively to the effect that an additional one or two years of formal high school for Amish children in place of their long-established program of informal vocational education would do little to serve those interests. . . .

. . . Whatever their idiosyncrasies as seen by the majority, this record strongly shows that the Amish community has been a highly successful social unit within our society, even if apart from the conventional "mainstream." Its members are productive and very law-abiding members of society; they reject public welfare in any of its usual modern forms. . . .

. . .

Insofar as the State's claim rests on the view that a brief additional period of formal education is imperative to enable the Amish to participate effectively and intelligently in our democratic process, it must fall. The Amish alternative to formal secondary school education has enabled them to function effectively in their day-to-day life under self-imposed limitations on relations with the world, and to survive and prosper in contemporary society as a separate, sharply identifiable and highly self-sufficient community for more than 200 years in this country. In itself this is strong evidence that they are capable of fulfilling the social and political responsibilities of citizenship without compelled attendance beyond the eighth grade at the price of jeopardizing their free exercise of religious belief. . . .

. . .

Indeed it seems clear that if the State is empowered, as *parens patriae*, to "save" a child from himself or his Amish parents by requiring an additional two years of compulsory formal high school education, the State will in large measure influence, if not determine, the religious future of the child. . . . The history and culture of Western civilization reflect a strong tradition of parental concern for the nurture and upbringing of their children. This primary role of the parents in the upbringing of their children is now established beyond debate as an enduring American tradition. . . .

. . . Aided by a history of three centuries as an identifiable religious sect and a long history as a successful and self-sufficient segment of American society, the Amish in this case have convincingly demonstrated the sincerity of their religious beliefs, the interrelationship of belief with their mode of life, the vital role that belief and daily conduct play in the continued survival of Old Order Amish communities and their religious organization, and the hazards presented by the State's enforcement of a statute generally valid as to others. Beyond this, they have carried the even more difficult burden of demonstrating the adequacy of their alternative mode of continuing informal vocational education in terms of precisely those overall interests that the State advances in support of its program of compulsory high school education. In light of this convincing showing, one that probably few other religious groups or sects could make, and weighing the minimal difference between what the State would require and what the Amish already accept, it was incumbent on the State to show with more particularity how its admittedly strong interest in compulsory education would be adversely affected by granting an exemption to the Amish. *Sherbert*. . . .

. . .

JUSTICE POWELL and JUSTICE REHNQUIST took no part in the consideration or decision of this case.

JUSTICE STEWART, with whom JUSTICE BRENNAN joins, concurring. . . .

JUSTICE WHITE, with whom JUSTICE BRENNAN and JUSTICE STEWART join, concurring.

. . .

In the present case, the State is not concerned with the maintenance of an educational system as an end in itself, it is rather attempting to nurture and develop the human potential of its children, whether Amish or non-Amish: to expand their knowledge, broaden their sensibilities, kindle their imagination, foster a spirit of free inquiry, and increase their human understanding and tolerance. It is possible that most Amish children will wish to continue living the rural life of their parents, in which case their training at home will adequately equip them for their future role. Others, however, may wish to become nuclear physicists, ballet dancers, computer programmers, or historians, and for these occupations, formal training will be necessary. There is evidence in the record that many children desert the Amish faith when they come of age. A State has a legitimate interest not only in seeking to develop the latent talents of its children but also in seeking to prepare them for the life style that they may later choose, or at least to provide them with an option other than the life they have led in the past. In the circumstances of this case, although the question is close, I am unable to say that the State has demonstrated that Amish children who leave school in the eighth grade will be intellectually stultified or unable to acquire new academic skills later. The statutory minimum school attendance age set by the State is, after all, only 16.

. . .

JUSTICE DOUGLAS, dissenting in part

It is the future of the student, not the future of the parents, that is imperiled by today's decision. If a parent keeps his child out of school beyond the grade school, then the child will be forever barred from entry into the new and amazing world of diversity that we have today. The child may decide that that is the preferred course, or he may rebel. It is the student's judgment, not his parents', that is essential if we are to give full meaning to what we have said about the Bill of Rights and of the right of students to be masters of their own destiny. If he is harnessed to the Amish way of life by those in authority over him and if his education is truncated, his entire life may be stunted and deformed. The child, therefore, should be given an opportunity to be heard before the State gives the exemption which we honor today.

. . .

I think the emphasis of the Court on the "law and order" record of this Amish group of people is quite irrelevant. A religion is a religion irrespective of what the misdemeanor or felony records of its members might be. I am not at all sure how the Catholics, Episcopalians, the Baptists, Jehovah's Witnesses, the Unitarians, and my own Presbyterians would make out if subjected to such a test. . . . [T]he Amish, whether with a high or low criminal record, certainly qualify by all historic standards as a religion within the meaning of the First Amendment.

C. Guns

The constitutional politics of the right to bear arms changed more than the constitutional law of the Second Amendment during this period. The same legal principles that governed federal and state rights to bear arms during the New Deal/Great Society Era remained in force. Constitutional decision makers maintained that the right to bear arms either referred to the militia or was subject to reasonable regulation. This consensus, however, began to fray. As demands for gun control increased, opponents of regulation began articulating possible constitutional limits on state and federal crime control legislation.

In the wake of several political assassinations and inner-city riots, gun control gained a larger place on the national agenda during the Nixon and Carter presidencies. Initially both major political parties supported regulation. Democrats in 1968 boasted that "Democratic leadership [had] secured the enactment of a new gun control law as a step toward putting the weapons of wanton violence beyond the reach of criminal and irresponsible hands." Republicans called for "enactment of legislation to control indiscriminate availability of firearms, safeguarding the right of responsible citizens to collect, own and use firearms for legitimate purposes, retaining primary responsibility at the state level, with such federal laws as necessary to better enable the states to meet their responsibilities." After the Black Panthers staged a protest by carrying shotguns into the California state capitol, Governor Ronald Reagan signed a state law banning individuals from carrying loaded weapons in a city. Reagan emphasized that he was against any "restrictive gun law" but that this weapons ban would be welcomed by any "true sportsman or gun lover."[25]

Eight years later, both parties were more supportive of gun rights. Republicans in 1976 asserted, "We support the right of citizens to keep and bear arms. We oppose federal registration of firearms. Mandatory sentences for crimes committed with a lethal weapon

25. "Reagan Signs Curb on Loaded Weapons," *New York Times*, July 29, 1967, 16.

are the only effective solution to this problem." Democrats adopted a platform combining commitments to regulation and rights:

> Handguns simplify and intensify violent crime. Ways must be found to curtail the availability of these weapons. The Democratic Party must provide the leadership for a coordinated federal and state effort to strengthen the presently inadequate controls over the manufacture, assembly, distribution and possession of handguns and to ban Saturday night specials.
>
> The Democratic Party, however, affirms the right of sportsmen to possess guns for purely hunting and target-shooting purposes.

Both parties were responding to important changes in the broader political environment. Public opinion polls taken during the 1970s showed increased support for tougher sentences for criminals who used guns and less support for gun control. Powerful interests began aggressively promoting the constitutional right to bear arms. Political activists committed to fighting for broad Second Amendment rights seized control of the National Rifle Association (NRA) from moderates who had historically been willing to accept some gun control measures. This new generation of NRA leadership saw their role as championing "the political, civil and inalienable rights of the American people to keep and bear arms as a common law and Constitutional right both of the individual citizen and of the collective militia."[26]

This increased political support for Second Amendment rights did not immediately increase legal support for Second Amendment rights. The Supreme Court had no occasion from 1969 until 1980 to revisit past precedents. The overwhelming number of lower federal and state court decisions held that constitutional gun rights were restricted to the militia or subject to reasonable state regulation.

D. Personal Freedom and Public Morality

The 1970s witnessed the intensification and partial restructuring of the culture wars in American constitutional politics. Nineteenth-century culture wars were often fought between Catholics and Protestants and centered on such issues as prohibition and Protestant religious practices in public schools. During the twentieth century, some cultural issues, most notably temperance, were largely resolved, while new cultural divides emerged. *Roe v. Wade* (1973), the decision striking down bans on abortion in forty-six states, accelerated political struggles over gender roles, the sexual revolution, and morals legislation. Over time, Republicans became committed to a pro-life policy, stating in their 1976 platform, "The Republican Party favors a continuance of the public dialogue on abortion and supports the efforts of those who seek enactment of a constitutional amendment to restore protection of the right to life for unborn children." Democrats became the party committed to pro-choice policies, declaring in 1976, "We fully recognize the religious and ethical nature of the concerns which many Americans have on the subject of abortion. We feel, however, that it is undesirable to attempt to amend the U.S. Constitution to overturn the Supreme Court decision in this area." Intense debates over abortion and related policies took place in both the national and state legislatures. New interest groups emerged that reshaped constitutional understandings about the place of abortion and the role of courts in the American constitutional order.

As Figure 9-3 indicates, general public opinion has been consistently supportive of abortion rights with some restrictions, but partisan polarization on this issue has increased since the *Roe* decision.

The Supreme Court ignited a constitutional firestorm when ruling in *Roe* that the "right of privacy" first announced in *Griswold v. Connecticut* (1965) "is broad enough to encompass a woman's decision whether or not to terminate her pregnancy." The judicial majority in *Roe* divided pregnancy into three trimesters. States could not restrict abortion at all in the first trimester. Second-trimester restrictions were constitutional only if they promoted maternal health. During the third trimester a state could ban abortion, as long as such bans included a maternal health exception.

During the following years the justices considered various restrictions on abortion and birth control on an almost-annual basis. Every funding restriction was sustained. "The financial constraints that restrict an indigent woman's ability to enjoy the full range of constitutionally protected freedom of choice," Justice Stewart wrote in *Harris v. McRae* (1980), "are the product not of governmental restrictions on access to

---

26. Reva B. Siegel, "Dead or Alive: Originalism as Popular Constitutionalism in *Heller*," *Harvard Law Review* 122 (2008): 211. This paragraph relies heavily on Siegel's essay.

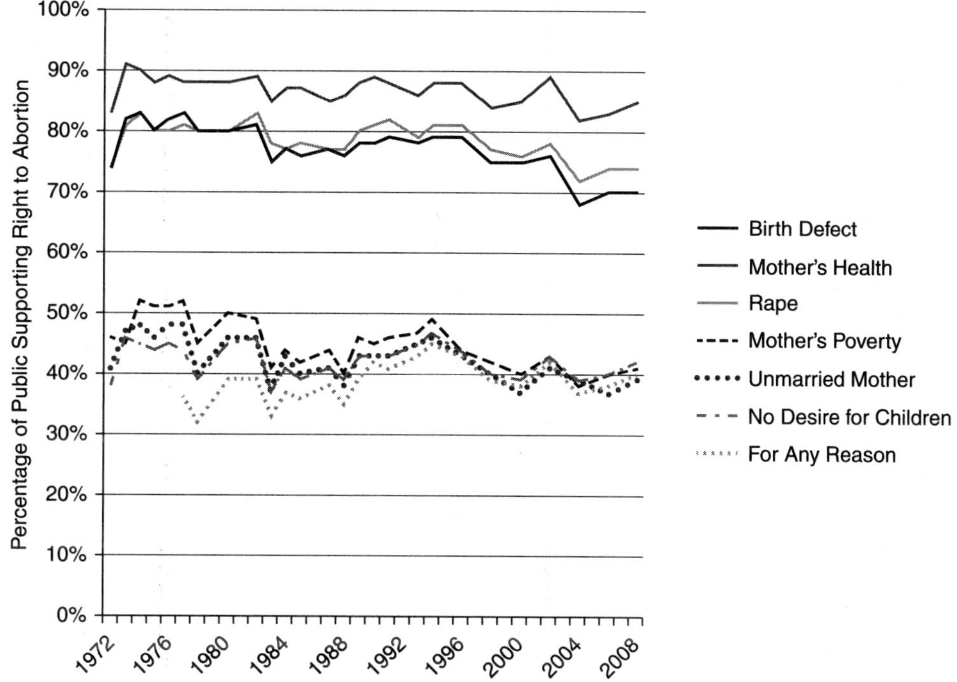

Figure 9-3 Public Support for Abortion Rights, 1972–2008

Source: General Social Survey.

abortions, but rather of her indigency." Almost every other restriction on abortion and birth control was declared unconstitutional. "'Compelling' is . . . the key word," Justice Brennan declared in *Carey v. Population Services International* (1975) when declaring unconstitutional a law prohibiting persons from giving contraception to teenagers. In his view, which was adopted by the judicial majority in the years immediately after *Roe*, "where a decision as fundamental as that of whether to bear or beget a child is involved, regulations imposing a burden on it may be justified only by compelling state interests, and must be narrowly drawn to express only those interests."

The Burger Court also defended rights to rear children. A 5–2 majority in *Stanley v. Illinois* (1972) struck down a state law that prohibited an unmarried father from obtaining custody of his natural children. Justice White's majority opinion insisted, "The private interest here, that of a man in the children he has sired and raised, undeniably warrants deference and, absent a powerful countervailing interest, protection." In *Moore v. City of East Cleveland, Ohio* (1977) a 5–4 majority declared that a woman had a right to rear her biological grandchildren in a single-family household, even if they had different parents. "The tradition of uncles, aunts, cousins, and especially grandparents sharing a household along with parents and children," Justice Powell wrote, "has roots equally venerable and equally deserving of constitutional recognition" as the nuclear family.

This judicial solicitude for marriage and child rearing did not extend to other forms of intimacy. The justices in *Hollenbaugh v. Carnegie Free Library* (1978) let stand a lower court opinion permitting local officials to discharge a librarian and a janitor who were having an adulterous affair. The proverbial "ménage à trois" enjoyed no constitutional protection. "Once a married couple admits strangers as onlookers," the Court of Appeals for the Fourth Circuit in *Lovisi v. Slayton* (1976) stated, "federal protection of privacy dissolves."[27] Gay rights barely registered on the judicial docket. Several lower federal court decisions sustained state bans on homosexual activities. A federal district judge in *Doe v. Commonwealth's Attorney for City of Richmond* (1975) dismissed a claim that homosexual intimacy

27. *Lovisi v. Slayton*, 535 F.2d 349 (1976).

enjoyed constitutional protection, noting that privacy rights were prohibitions against "trespasses upon the privacy of the incidents of marriage, upon the sanctity of the home, or upon the nurture of family life."[28] State courts routinely dismissed claims about same-sex marriage. "Marriage," the Ohio Supreme Court declared in *Irwin v. Lupardus* (OH 1980), "is by definition a heterosexual relationship which cannot exist between persons of the same sex."[29]

Roe v. Wade, 410 U.S. 113 (1973)

Norma McCorvey was a young unmarried woman who claimed that she became pregnant after being raped. McCorvey sought an abortion, but Texas law at the time permitted pregnancies to be terminated only for the "purpose of saving the life of the mother." Using the pseudonym Jane Roe, McCorvey sought an injunction against Henry Wade, the state attorney for Dallas County, Texas, that would forbid him from enforcing the state laws against abortion on the ground that they were unconstitutional. A three-judge panel declared the Texas law void for vagueness. Texas appealed to the Supreme Court of the United States.

The Supreme Court by a 7–2 vote ruled the Texas ban on abortion unconstitutional. Justice Blackmun's majority opinion maintained that the right of privacy discussed in Griswold v. Connecticut *(1965) encompassed the right to terminate a pregnancy. The majority opinions in* Roe *assume that the crucial question is whether the fetus is a person. Is this correct? States may ban animal sacrifices, even though no one thinks dogs are protected by the Fourteenth Amendment. Conversely, no state requires people to donate kidneys to needy persons. Is either of these analogies helpful in thinking about abortion? What is the source of the constitutional right in the opinions that follow? Does* Roe *follow from* Griswold *as easily as Justice Stewart suggested it did? Might* Griswold *be right and* Roe *wrong? On what logic? Justice Blackmun, who in the 1950s served as resident counsel for the Mayo Clinic in Rochester, Minnesota, divided pregnancy into trimesters. What is the significance of the trimester system? Does this system have sound constitutional roots, or is the trimester system further proof that* Roe *is illegitimate judicial legislation?*

In Doe v. Bolton *(1973), a companion case to* Roe v. Wade, *the Supreme Court considered Georgia laws that limited abortion to circumstances involving a serious health threat to the mother, required the woman seeking an abortion to be a Georgia resident, mandated that three doctors certify that the reason for the abortion was legitimate, and required that the abortion be performed in a hospital. These provisions were typical of abortion reform laws passed during the 1960s. All were declared unconstitutional by the same 7–2 majority. Justice Blackmun's majority opinion declared, "The woman's right to receive medical care in accordance with her licensed physician's best judgment and the physician's right to administer it are substantially limited by this statutorily imposed overview."*

JUSTICE BLACKMUN delivered the opinion of the Court.

. . .

Three reasons have been advanced to explain historically the enactment of criminal abortion laws in the 19th century and to justify their continued existence.

It has been argued occasionally that these laws were the product of a Victorian social concern to discourage illicit sexual conduct. Texas, however, does not advance this justification in the present case, and it appears that no court or commentator has taken the argument seriously. . . .

A second reason is concerned with abortion as a medical procedure. When most criminal abortion laws were first enacted, the procedure was a hazardous one for the woman. . . . Thus, it has been argued that a State's real concern in enacting a criminal abortion law was to protect the pregnant woman, that is, to restrain her from submitting to a procedure that placed her life in serious jeopardy.

Modern medical techniques have altered this situation. . . . Mortality rates for women undergoing early abortions, where the procedure is legal, appear to be as low as or lower than the rates for normal childbirth. Consequently, any interest of the State in protecting the woman from an inherently hazardous procedure, except when it would be equally dangerous for her to forgo it, has largely disappeared. . . .

The third reason is the State's interest—some phrase it in terms of duty—in protecting prenatal life. Some of the argument for this justification rests on the theory that a new human life is present from the moment of conception. The State's interest and general obligation to protect life then extends, it is argued,

28. *Doe v. Commonwealth's Attorney for City of Richmond*, 403 F. Supp. 1199 (E.D. Va. 1975).

29. *Irwin v. Lupardus*, 1980 WL 355015 (Ohio App., 8 Dist., 1980).

Illustration 9-3 "Alternative to *Roe v. Wade*"

Source: Paul Conrad, "Alternative to *Roe v. Wade*," *Los Angeles Times*, November 21, 1988, II5. © Copyright, Paul Conrad Estate.

to prenatal life. Only when the life of the pregnant mother herself is at stake, balanced against the life she carries within her, should the interest of the embryo or fetus not prevail. Logically, of course, a legitimate state interest in this area need not stand or fall on acceptance of the belief that life begins at conception or at some other point prior to life birth. In assessing the State's interest, recognition may be given to the less rigid claim that as long as at least potential life is involved, the State may assert interests beyond the protection of the pregnant woman alone.

...

The Constitution does not explicitly mention any right of privacy. In a line of decisions, however, ... the Court has recognized that a right of personal privacy, or a guarantee of certain areas or zones of privacy, does exist under the Constitution.... These decisions make it clear that only personal rights that can be deemed "fundamental" or "implicit in the concept of ordered liberty," *Palko v. Connecticut* (1937), are included in this guarantee of personal privacy. They also make it clear that the right has some extension to activities relating to marriage, procreation, contraception, family relationships, and child rearing and education. This right of privacy, whether it be founded in the Fourteenth Amendment's concept of personal liberty and restrictions upon state action, as we feel it is, or in the Ninth Amendment's reservation of rights to the people, is broad enough to encompass a woman's decision whether or not to terminate her pregnancy. The detriment that the State would impose upon the pregnant woman by denying this choice altogether is apparent. Specific and direct harm medically diagnosable even in early pregnancy may be involved. Maternity, or additional offspring, may force upon the woman a distressful life and future. Psychological harm may be imminent. Mental and physical health may be taxed by child care. There is also the distress, for all concerned, associated with the unwanted child, and there is the problem of bringing a child into a family already unable, psychologically and otherwise, to care for it. In other cases, as in this one, the additional difficulties and continuing stigma of unwed motherhood may be involved. All these are factors the woman and her responsible physician necessarily will consider in consultation.

On the basis of elements such as these, appellant and some amici argue that the woman's right is absolute and that she is entitled to terminate her pregnancy at whatever time, in whatever way, and for whatever reason she alone chooses. With this we do not agree. . . . [A] State may properly assert important interests in safeguarding health, in maintaining medical standards, and in protecting potential life. At some point in pregnancy, these respective interests become sufficiently compelling to sustain regulation of the factors that govern the abortion decision. . . .

. . .

Where certain "fundamental rights" are involved, the Court has held that regulation limiting these rights may be justified only by a "compelling state interest," . . . and that legislative enactments must be narrowly drawn to express only the legitimate state interests at stake. . . .

. . .

The appellee and certain amici argue that the fetus is a "person" within the language and meaning of the Fourteenth Amendment. . . . If this suggestion of personhood is established, the appellant's case, of course, collapses, for the fetus' right to life would then be guaranteed specifically by the Amendment. . . .

The Constitution does not define "person" in so many words. . . . But in nearly all [constitutional references to "person" in] these instances, the use of the word is such that it has application only postnatally. None indicates, with any assurance, that it has any possible prenatal application.

All this, together with our observation that throughout the major portion of the 19th century prevailing legal abortion practices were far freer than they are today, persuades us that the word "person," as used in the Fourteenth Amendment, does not include the unborn.

. . .

Texas urges that, apart from the Fourteenth Amendment, life begins at conception and is present throughout pregnancy, and that, therefore, the State has a compelling interest in protecting that life from and after conception. We need not resolve the difficult question of when life begins. When those trained in the respective disciplines of medicine, philosophy, and theology are unable to arrive at any consensus, the judiciary, at this point in the development of man's knowledge, is not in a position to speculate as to the answer.

. . .

With respect to the State's important and legitimate interest in the health of the mother, the "compelling" point, in the light of present medical knowledge, is at approximately the end of the first trimester. This is so because of the now-established medical fact . . . that until the end of the first trimester mortality in abortion may be less than mortality in normal childbirth. It follows that, from and after this point, a State may regulate the abortion procedure to the extent that the regulation reasonably relates to the preservation and protection of maternal health. . . .

With respect to the State's important and legitimate interest in potential life, the "compelling" point is at viability. This is so because the fetus then presumably has the capability of meaningful life outside the mother's womb. State regulation protective of fetal life after viability thus has both logical and biological justifications. If the State is interested in protecting fetal life after viability, it may go so far as to proscribe abortion during that period, except when it is necessary to preserve the life or health of the mother.

. . .

JUSTICE STEWART, concurring.

. . . *Griswold* stands as one in a long line of . . . cases decided under the doctrine of substantive due process, and I now accept it as such.

. . .

Several decisions of this Court make clear that freedom of personal choice in matters of marriage and family life is one of the liberties protected by the

Due Process Clause of the Fourteenth Amendment. *Loving v. Virginia* (1967) . . . ; *Griswold v. Connecticut* (1965) . . . ; *Pierce v. Society of Sister* (1925) . . . ; *Meyer v. Nebraska* (1923). . . . As recently as last Term, in *Eisenstadt v. Baird* (1972), we recognized "the right of the individual, married or single, to be free from unwarranted governmental intrusion into matters so fundamentally affecting a person as the decision whether to bear or beget a child." That right necessarily includes the right of a woman to decide whether or not to terminate her pregnancy. . . .

. . .

JUSTICE DOUGLAS, concurring

. . .

The Ninth Amendment obviously does not create federally enforceable rights. It merely says, "The enumeration in the Constitution, of certain rights, shall not be construed to deny or disparage others retained by the people." But a catalogue of these rights includes customary, traditional, and time-honored rights, amenities, privileges, and immunities that come within the sweep of "the Blessings of Liberty" mentioned in the preamble to the Constitution. Many of them, in my view, come within the meaning of the term "liberty" as used in the Fourteenth Amendment.

First is the autonomous control over the development and expression of one's intellect, interests, tastes, and personality.

. . .

Second is freedom of choice in the basic decisions of one's life respecting marriage, divorce, procreation, contraception, and the education and upbringing of children.

. . .

Third is the freedom to care for one's health and person, freedom from bodily restraint or compulsion, freedom to walk, stroll, or loaf.

. . .

. . . The "liberty" of the mother, though rooted as it is in the Constitution, may be qualified by the State. . . . But where fundamental personal rights and liberties are involved, the corrective legislation must be "narrowly drawn to prevent the supposed evil." . . .

. . .

The right to seek advice on one's health and the right to place reliance on the physician of one's choice are basic to Fourteenth Amendment values. We deal with fundamental rights and liberties, which, as already noted, can be contained or controlled only by discretely drawn legislation that preserves the "liberty" and regulates only those phases of the problem of compelling legislative concern. The imposition by the State of group controls over the physician-patient relationship is not made on any medical procedure apart from abortion, no matter how dangerous the medical step may be. The oversight imposed on the physician and patient in abortion cases denies them their "liberty," viz., their right of privacy, without any compelling, discernible state interest.

. . .

CHIEF JUSTICE BURGER, concurring.

. . .

I do not read the Court's holdings today as having the sweeping consequences attributed to them by the dissenting Justices; the dissenting views discount the reality that the vast majority of physicians observe the standards of their profession, and act only on the basis of carefully deliberated medical judgments relating to life and health. Plainly, the Court today rejects any claim that the Constitution requires abortions on demand.

JUSTICE WHITE, with whom JUSTICE REHNQUIST joins, dissenting.

. . .

With all due respect, I dissent. I find nothing in the language or history of the Constitution to support the Court's judgments. The Court simply fashions and announces a new constitutional right for pregnant women and, with scarcely any reason or authority for its action, invests that right with sufficient substance to override most existing state abortion statutes. The upshot is that the people and the legislatures of the 50 States are constitutionally disentitled to weigh the relative importance of the continued existence and development of the fetus, on the one hand, against a spectrum of possible impacts on the mother, on the other hand. As an exercise of raw judicial power, the Court perhaps has authority to do what it does today; but in my view its judgment is an improvident and extravagant exercise of the power of judicial review that the Constitution extends to this Court.

The Court apparently values the convenience of the pregnant woman more than the continued existence and development of the life or potential life that she carries. Whether or not I might agree with that marshaling of values, I can in no event join the Court's judgment because I find no constitutional warrant for imposing such an order of priorities on the people and legislatures of the States. In a sensitive area such as this, involving as it does issues over which reasonable men may easily and heatedly differ, I cannot accept the Court's exercise of its clear power of choice by interposing a constitutional barrier to state efforts to protect human life and by investing women and doctors with the constitutionally protected right to exterminate it. This issue, for the most part, should be left with the people and to the political processes the people have devised to govern their affairs.

. . .

JUSTICE REHNQUIST, dissenting.

. . .

If the Court means by the term "privacy" no more than that the claim of a person to be free from unwanted state regulation of consensual transactions may be a form of "liberty" protected by the Fourteenth Amendment, there is no doubt that similar claims have been upheld in our earlier decisions on the basis of that liberty. . . . The test traditionally applied in the area of social and economic legislation is whether or not a law such as that challenged has a rational relation to a valid state objective. *Williamson v. Lee Optical Co.* (1955). . . . The Due Process Clause of the Fourteenth Amendment undoubtedly does place a limit, albeit a broad one, on legislative power to enact laws such as this. If the Texas statute were to prohibit an abortion even where the mother's life is in jeopardy, I have little doubt that such a statute would lack a rational relation to a valid state objective. . . . But the Court's sweeping invalidation of any restrictions on abortion during the first trimester is impossible to justify under that standard, and the conscious weighing of competing factors that the Court's opinion apparently substitutes for the established test is far more appropriate to a legislative judgment than to a judicial one.

. . .

The decision here to break pregnancy into three distinct terms and to outline the permissible restrictions the State may impose in each one, for example, partakes more of judicial legislation than it does of a determination of the intent of the drafters of the Fourteenth Amendment.

The fact that a majority of the States reflecting, after all the majority sentiment in those States, have had restrictions on abortions for at least a century is

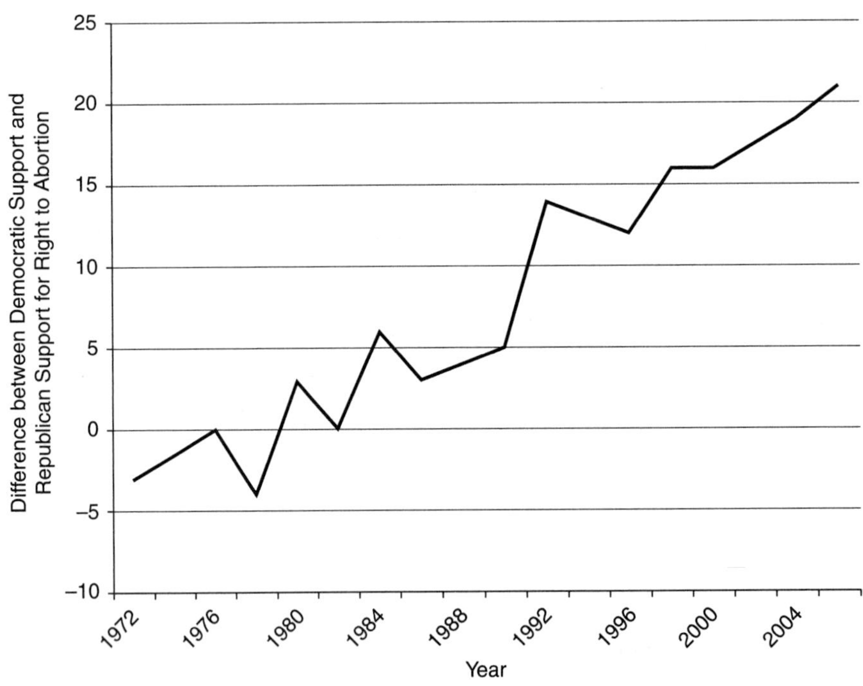

Figure 9-4 Partisan Divergence in Public Support for Abortion Rights, 1972–2008

Source: American National Election Studies.

a strong indication, it seems to me, that the asserted right to an abortion is not "so rooted in the traditions and conscience of our people as to be ranked as fundamental." . . .

To reach its result, the Court necessarily has had to find within the scope of the Fourteenth Amendment a right that was apparently completely unknown to the drafters of the Amendment. As early as 1821, the first state law dealing directly with abortion was enacted by the Connecticut Legislature. . . . By the time of the adoption of the Fourteenth Amendment in 1868, there were at least 36 laws enacted by state or territorial legislatures limiting abortion. . . .

There apparently was no question concerning the validity of this provision or of any of the other state statutes when the Fourteenth Amendment was adopted. The only conclusion possible from this history is that the drafters did not intend to have the Fourteenth Amendment withdraw from the States the power to legislate with respect to this matter.

Debate over the Human Life Amendment (1976)[30]

Opponents of legal abortion immediately sought constitutional amendments that would overturn Roe v. Wade *(1973). The Human Life Amendment was the most popular effort. That proposal asserted that genetic humans had a right to life from conception, fertilization, or implantation. Given that the Supreme Court in* Roe *emphasized that the unborn were not constitutional persons under the Fourteenth Amendment, such an amendment would undercut an important foundation of the decision declaring abortion a fundamental right.*[31] *Senator Jesse Helms of North Carolina in 1976 proposed the most popular version of the Human Life Amendment:*

> *SECTION 1. With respect to the right of life guaranteed in this Constitution, every human being subject to the jurisdiction of the United States, or of any State, shall be deemed, from the moment of fertilization, to be a person and entitled to the right of life.*
>
> *SECTION 2. Congress and the several States shall have concurrent power to enforce this article by appropriate legislation.*

The Senate Subcommittee on Constitutional Amendments rejected this proposal by a 5–2 vote. The Senate rejected by a 47–40 vote Senator Helms's motion to have a full debate on the Human Life Amendment.

Consider the pro-life strategy when reading the excerpts from that Senate debate. Would you have advised Senator Helms to propose the amendment that he did? Why not propose a constitutional amendment allowing states to choose whether to ban abortions? To what extent were the senators trying to make abortion policy, and to what extent were they trying to foist responsibility for making abortion policy onto the states or the federal judiciary?

SENATOR JESSE HELMS (Republican, North Carolina)

. . .

Mr. President, there is no more appropriate time than now for the Senate to take the initiative, and to exercise moral leadership in restoring the right to life of the unborn. The people of this Nation are looking to us for leadership because they recognize the simple fact that only Congress—not the President, not the several States, and certainly not the Federal judiciary—can put an end to this wholesale destruction of human life.

The main thrust of any human life amendment must be to insure that all human beings enjoy the protection of the right to life. This can be done by insuring that all human beings are considered "persons" under the protection of the fifth and fourth[32] amendments. . . .

. . .

It is most important . . . that the beginning of life, and therefore, the beginning of the constitutional protection of that life, be defined with precision and clarity. Our scientific knowledge today is sufficient to provide such a definition; and the language must not be so loose or general that the way is opened for arguments that the period of protected life should be shortened for the sake of convenience. On the other hand, it is not necessary to encumber the unborn child with

30. *Congressional Record*, 94th Cong., 2nd Sess., 1976, 11, 555–61.

31. Several prominent pro-choice arguments insist that women have the right to terminate pregnancies even if the fetus has a right to life. See Judith Jarvis Thomson, "A Defense of Abortion," *Philosophy and Public Affairs* 1 (1971): 47–66.

32. We suspect that Senator Helms misspoke, or else this is a mistranscription. No doubt he meant to say "Fifth and Fourteenth Amendments."

all the constitutional rights of an adult; our concern can be limited to the right to life.

. . .

Although the right to life can be made a constitutional right, the Federal Government should not preempt the rights of the States to prohibit abortion, prescribe penalties, and regulate the implementation of abortion. This is especially important, because there is some doubt whether restraints on Federal and State action can reach private action under the 14th amendment. Such a doctrine has been put forward in certain cases before the Supreme Court, but I think that it is wise and prudent, from the standpoint of the Constitution and the problems of enforcement, to leave room for the States to legislate prohibitions against abortion in the field of private action.

. . .

As already indicated, this amendment allows the States to act in the fields of State interest, without the Federal Government preempting all action. Both Federal and State governments can act concurrently to prohibit abortions. Any Federal action promoting abortions, including funding of actual abortions, use of Federal [facilities or equipment] intended [for abortion procedures], particularly research that involves clinical testing, would be clearly a violation of the constitutional rights of the unborn. The Federal Government could act to outlaw interstate commerce in abortions, and in drugs, instruments, and equipment intended to [be used in abortion procedures]. The States would have similar powers within their jurisdictions. The States, particularly, could delineate the spheres of culpability with respect to participating in abortions, prescribe penalties, and enforcement powers of local jurisdictions. . . .

. . .

The real evil of abortion is the distorted mentality in the living that is created when social convenience, pleasure, or utility is preferred to human life; or when the quality of life as a value supplants life itself as a value. We cannot allow our society to cross the line which allows the ultimate abrogation of the rights of an individual. We can debate the proper social measures that must be taken to alleviate the problems of human life; but there should be no debate about life itself.

SENATOR HUGH SCOTT (Republican, Pennsylvania)

. . . I believe a question of abortion should be decided by the State government under its police power. . . .

We live in a very diverse and large Nation, where people of various sections of the country have different points of view on a matter of this nature.

. . .

I shall read my amendment in the nature of a substitute to the joint resolution. . . .

. . .

> Except as otherwise provided in this Constitution the power to regulate the circumstances under which pregnancy may or may not be terminated is reserved to the States, except within the District of Columbia, Federal territory, or other area of exclusive Federal jurisdiction.

. . . My proposal places the responsibility where I believe it belongs and permits each State to decide for itself whether or not it wants any laws on abortion; and if a State wants a law on abortion, what type of law it favors.

. . .

SENATOR BIRCH BAYH (Democrat, Indiana)

. . .

I point out, as the chairman of the subcommittee, never before in my experience in the Senate, nor my 8 years in the Indiana State Legislature, have I been involved in an issue which involved this unique combination of moral and philosophical and religious beliefs commingled with political-legal-medical questions. It is an issue that has caused the Senator from Indiana a great deal of anguish regarding the position I should assume personally, on the other hand, and what position I should assume as a Senator, on the other. After a great deal of thought—and, indeed, some prayer—the Senator from Indiana came to the conclusion, personally, that abortion is wrong.

. . . I did not feel it would be right for me to take the personal moral decision that I was prepared to make and to impose that standard, on every other citizen of this country.

. . .

It is easy enough for me to say that I am opposed to abortion and that I think it is wrong. It is also wrong for me to impose my moral conviction on others who may well be faced with an entirely different set of circumstances from that of the Senator from Indiana.

. . .

I fear greatly that adoption of any of the proposed amendments regarding abortion would be far more in line with the unfortunate experience encountered with the 18th amendment [Prohibition] than with the rest of the Constitution. Without arguing the merits, can anyone seriously doubt that adoption of any of the proposed amendments would result in tens of thousands of women seeking abortion through illicit channels? Can there be doubt that if any of the proposed amendments were adopted that there would immediately be unleashed active political forces designed to repeal the amendment?

. . .

The means by which the Supreme Court decision in *Roe* . . . would be overturned under three of the proposed constitutional amendments, those introduced by Senators HELMS and BUCKLEY[,] is by establishing as part of the Constitution legal protection for a fetus at all stages of biological development. In other words, the language of the amendment nullifies the Court's distinction of viability, and establishes "life" as beginning at the moment of fertilization. No matter what one's personal views are as to when life begins, there can be no disagreement as to the clear fact that we have been unable to establish to everyone's satisfaction exactly when this mysterious transformation takes place. Is it at the time of conception? Or fertilization? Is it only after "quickening" or viability? By amending the Constitution to establish one view as to when life begins at a time when there is no clear agreement among people in general, appears to me a serious misreading of the nature of the Constitution itself. The very term Constitution implies a document of a permanent and abiding nature. As one who has great faith in this durable document, I feel that we cannot and must not use the Constitution as an instrument for moral preference. We cannot and should not presume to provide for the people of this country, people with widely varying opinions on such fundamental issues, a definitive answer to a question that is clearly not open to certitude.

. . .

While I am deeply disturbed by the concept of abortion for convenience sake, I find that I cannot support an amendment which would not allow a woman who has been brutalized by the crime of rape the option of terminating a pregnancy that resulted against her will. . . .

Similarly, I feel that I cannot support an amendment which is so absolute as to prevent a woman who is carrying a fetus with a detectable and deadly genetic disease—[such] as Tay-Sachs or [D]own's syndrome—the option of terminating her pregnancy. . . .

. . . [O]ne of the possible effects of the proposed amendments would be to prohibit the use of certain forms of contraceptive devices in use by millions of Americans. Because the amendments define life as beginning at fertilization, the use of many contraceptive devices, such as the intrauterine device used by almost 9 million women, would no longer be permitted since medical testimony indicated there is evidence that such devices may work by preventing implantation after fertilization. . . .

. . . The question is whether we, as elected representatives, feel that amending the Constitution to impose one conception of life on all our citizens, is indeed the most responsible course of action. I have concluded it is not a responsible course of action. Each of us must make that important choice for himself or herself.

VIII. Democratic Rights

MAJOR DEVELOPMENTS

- Voting Rights Act extended and expanded
- Judicial protection extended for the publication of the top-secret *Pentagon Papers*
- Supreme Court declares unconstitutional some constitutional limits on campaign finance

The democratic revolution that took place during the New Deal/Great Society Era became entrenched during the 1970s. No significant political or legal challenges were posed to the most important constitutional decisions on speech or voting rights. More often than not national institutions expanded democratic rights. *New York Times Co. v. United States* (1971) announced a strong constitutional barrier against government censorship of what many thought was the publication of top-secret government information. The Voting Rights Acts of 1970 and 1975 prohibited all literacy and understanding tests and banned residency requirements for presidential elections.

Unlike the Warren Court, which tended to declare only state laws unconstitutional, Burger Court majorities were often willing to impose constitutional limits on federal action. The Supreme Court in *New York Times Co. v. United States* (1971) declared that President Nixon had no constitutional right to obtain an injunction preventing the *New York Times* from publishing the Pentagon Papers. *Buckley v. Valeo* (1976) declared unconstitutional major sections of the Federal Election Campaign Act of 1974. In neither instance did the justices act against the dominant national coalition. By 1971 the Democratic majority in Congress had clearly turned against the Vietnam War. A badly divided Congress in 1974 enacted campaign finance reform only by including measures promising expedited judicial review of constitutionally controversial provisions.

A. Free Speech

A general consensus developed by the mid-1970s that many traditional restrictions on free speech were unconstitutional. No serious challenges were raised to either the holding in *Brandenburg v. Ohio* (1969) that government could punish speech criminally only if the speaker incited imminent criminal violence or the rule in *New York Times Co. v. Sullivan* (1964) that persons who criticized public officials could be sued for libel only if they spoke with reckless disregard for the truth or intentionally lied. The holding in *New York Times Co. v. United States* (1971) that speech could be censored only if the harm threatened was the equivalent of imperiling a ship at sea during wartime also enjoyed wide support. By the late 1970s most governing officials had abandoned traditional prosecutions for sedition or related offenses.

The constitutional politics of free speech shifted during the late 1960s and 1970s. Throughout most of the New Deal/Great Society Era free speech issues pitted liberal proponents of expression rights against conservative advocates of restriction. The new free speech issues of the 1970s cross-cut existing political cleavages. Campaign finance produced a bewildering series of political alignments. The plaintiffs in *Buckley v. Valeo* (1976) included James Buckley, one of the most conservative members of the U.S. Senate, and Eugene McCarthy, whose 1968 campaign for the presidency attacked President Lyndon Johnson from the political left. Many observers described campaign finance as a war between the ACLU, which by the 1970s was clearly aligned with the Democratic left, and Common Cause, a progressive interest group dedicated to regulating the political process. The Supreme Court split the difference. *Buckley* held that Congress could regulate campaign contributions in order to prevent corruption or the appearance of corruption but could not regulate campaign expenditures or independent expenditures. Most significant, the judicial majority determined that the political use of money was constitutionally protected speech and that government had no constitutional business leveling the political playing field.

Obscenity became a greater public concern. In 1970 the bipartisan Presidential Commission on Obscenity and Pornography reached the politically surprising conclusion that obscenity and pornography were not major social problems. "Empirical research designed to clarify the question," the Commission's report concluded, "has found no evidence to date that exposure to explicit sexual materials plays a significant role in the causation of delinquent or criminal behavior among youths or adults."[33] Rather than ban most erotic literature, the commission recommended more sex education and more frank talk about sex. Both President Nixon and the Senate (by a 60–5 vote) condemned the Commission's report. Nixon "categorically reject[ed] [the Commission's] morally bankrupt conclusions and major recommendations."[34] The Supreme Court in the 1970s sided more often with politicians than with social scientists. Chief Justice Burger, when sustaining a ban on obscenity in *Miller v. California* (1973), asserted,

> The First Amendment protects works which, taken as a whole, have serious literary, artistic, political, or scientific value, regardless of whether the government or a majority of the people approve of the ideas these works represent. . . . But the public portrayal of hard-core sexual conduct for its own sake, and for the ensuing commercial gain, is a different matter.

New York Times Co. v. United States, 403 U.S. 713 (1971)

In the winter of 1971 Daniel Ellsberg delivered to the New York Times *a forty-seven-volume secret study that former defense secretary Robert McNamara had commissioned on*

33. *The Report of the Commission on Obscenity and Pornography* (New York: Random House, 1971), 32.

34. Richard Nixon, "Statement about the Report of the Commission on Obscenity and Pornography," *Public Papers of the President* (Washington, D.C.: Government Printing Office, 1971), 940.

Illustration 9-4a Chief Justice Warren Burger **Illustration 9-4b** Associate Justice William Brennan

Chief Justice Burger led the effort in the 1970s and early 1980s to modify many of the liberal precedents written by Justice Brennan during the Warren Court years of the late 1950s and 1960s.

Source: Library of Congress, Prints and Photographs Division, Washington, DC 20540, USA.

the history of the Vietnam War.[35] *Ellsberg, a former employee of the Defense Department, had become convinced that publication of this study might turn American public opinion decisively against the war effort. The* Times, *after deliberating for three months, decided to publish selections from the papers in a ten-part series beginning on Sunday, June 13, 1971. Three days after the first installment was published, the Nixon administration obtained a temporary restraining order forbidding the* Times *from further publication. An evidentiary hearing was held on Friday, June 18. The injunction was removed the next day. Meanwhile, the* Washington Post *had obtained a copy of the Pentagon Papers and begun publication. On Monday, June 21, a federal district judge refused a Nixon administration request to enjoin publication of the* Post. *Two days later the Court of Appeals for the Second Circuit ordered the federal district court in New York to hold additional hearings on the* **Times** *publication, while the Court of Appeals for the District of Columbia Circuit affirmed the judicial order refusing to enjoin the* Washington Post. *The ink was hardly dry on these orders when the Supreme Court on June 25 declared that both cases would be reviewed and informed the parties that briefs were due and oral argument would take place the next day. Four days later the justices handed down their decision in* New York Times Co. v. United States.

As you read these opinions, compare the standards the individual justices used when determining whether a prior restraint was constitutional to the standards those justices used when determining whether speech might be sanctioned after publication. What reason did the justices give for imposing higher standards for prior restraints? Is the historical bias against prior restraints sufficient? Do other good constitutional reasons exist for permitting publication of materials that threaten the sort of harms that government may constitutionally regulate after publication? Consider

35. For a more detailed history of the *Pentagon Papers* case, see David Rudenstein, *The Day the Presses Stopped: A History of the* Pentagon Papers *Case* (Berkeley: University of California Press, 1996).

the speed at which the case was decided. Was Justice Black right when he indicated that immediate resolution was necessary, because every passing day aggravates the evil of censorship? Was Justice Harlan right to suggest that free speech cases should be resolved in the same orderly manner as other constitutional issues? Under what conditions, if any, should the Court expedite rulings on constitutional issues?

Determined to prevent further leaks of classified information, President Nixon formed a special surveillance unit in the White House. That group, which became known as the Plumbers, was initially formed to stop leaks but soon began to conduct espionage against Nixon's political opponents. Their burglary of the Democratic Party headquarters at the Watergate Hotel and the subsequent efforts by the White House to obstruct investigations of that crime eventually led to Nixon's resignation.

PER CURIAM.

...

Any system of prior restraints of expression comes to this Court bearing a heavy presumption against its constitutional validity. . . . The Government "thus carries a heavy burden of showing justification for the imposition of such a restraint." . . . The District Court for the Southern District of New York in the *New York Times* case, . . . and the District Court for the District of Columbia and the Court of Appeals for the District of Columbia Circuit, . . . in the *Washington Post* case held that the Government had not met that burden. We agree.

...

JUSTICE BLACK, with whom JUSTICE DOUGLAS joins, concurring.

. . . [T]he Government's case against the *Washington Post* should have been dismissed and . . . the injunction against the *New York Times* should have been vacated without oral argument when the cases were first presented to this Court. I believe that every moment's continuance of the injunctions against these newspapers amounts to a flagrant, indefensible, and continuing violation of the First Amendment. . . . In my view it is unfortunate that some of my Brethren are apparently willing to hold that the publication of news may sometimes be enjoined. Such a holding would make a shambles of the First Amendment.

. . . [F]or the first time in the 182 years since the founding of the Republic, the federal courts are asked to hold that the First Amendment does not mean what it says, but rather means that the Government can halt the publication of current news of vital importance to the people of this country.

. . . [T]he Executive Branch seems to have forgotten the essential purpose and history of the First Amendment. . . . Both the history and language of the First Amendment support the view that the press must be left free to publish news, whatever the source, without censorship, injunctions, or prior restraints.

In the First Amendment, the Founding Fathers gave the free press the protection it must have to fulfill its essential role in our democracy. The press was to serve the governed, not the governors. The Government's power to censor the press was abolished so that the press would remain forever free to censure the Government. The press was protected so that it could bare the secrets of government and inform the people. Only a free and unrestrained press can effectively expose deception in government. And paramount among the responsibilities of a free press is the duty to prevent any part of the government from deceiving the people and sending them off to distant lands to die of foreign fevers and foreign shot and shell. In my view, far from deserving condemnation for their courageous reporting, the *New York Times*, the *Washington Post*, and other newspapers should be commended for serving the purpose that the Founding Fathers saw so clearly. In revealing the workings of government that led to the Vietnam war, the newspapers nobly did precisely that which the Founders hoped and trusted they would do.

...

JUSTICE DOUGLAS, with whom JUSTICE BLACK joins, concurring.

...

The dominant purpose of the First Amendment was to prohibit the widespread practice of governmental suppression of embarrassing information. It is common knowledge that the First Amendment was adopted against the widespread use of the common law of seditious libel to punish the dissemination of material that is embarrassing to the powers-that-be. . . . The present cases will, I think, go down in history as the most dramatic illustration of that principle. A debate of large proportions goes on in the Nation over our posture in Vietnam. That debate antedated the disclosure of the contents of the present documents. The latter are highly relevant to the debate in progress.

Secrecy in government is fundamentally anti-democratic, perpetuating bureaucratic errors. Open debate and discussion of public issues are vital to our national health. On public questions there should be "uninhibited, robust, and wide-open" debate. . . .

JUSTICE BRENNAN, concurring.

. . .

. . . [T]he First Amendment tolerates absolutely no prior judicial restraints of the press predicated upon surmise or conjecture that untoward consequences may result. Our cases, it is true, have indicated that there is a single, extremely narrow class of cases in which the First Amendment's ban on prior judicial restraint may be overridden. . . . [O]nly governmental allegation and proof that publication must inevitably, directly, and immediately cause the occurrence of an event kindred to imperiling the safety of a transport already at sea can support even the issuance of an interim restraining order. . . .

. . .

JUSTICE STEWART, with whom JUSTICE WHITE joins, concurring.

. . .

. . . [I]n the cases before us we are asked neither to construe specific regulations nor to apply specific laws. We are asked, instead, to perform a function that the Constitution gave to the Executive, not the Judiciary. We are asked, quite simply, to prevent the publication by two newspapers of material that the Executive Branch insists should not, in the national interest, be published. I am convinced that the Executive is correct with respect to some of the documents involved. But I cannot say that disclosure of any of them will surely result in direct, immediate, and irreparable damage to our Nation or its people. That being so, there can under the First Amendment be but one judicial resolution of the issues before us. I join the judgments of the Court.

JUSTICE WHITE, with whom JUSTICE STEWART joins, concurring.

I concur in today's judgments, but only because of the concededly extraordinary protection against prior restraints enjoyed by the press under our constitutional system. I do not say that in no circumstances would the First Amendment permit an injunction against publishing information about government plans or operations. Nor, after examining the materials the Government characterizes as the most sensitive and destructive, can I deny that revelation of these documents will do substantial damage to public interests. Indeed, I am confident that their disclosure will have that result. But I nevertheless agree that the United States has not satisfied the very heavy burden that it must meet to warrant an injunction against publication in these cases, at least in the absence of express and appropriately limited congressional authorization for prior restraints in circumstances such as these.

. . .

The Criminal Code contains numerous provisions potentially relevant to these cases. . . . Section 798 . . . proscribes knowing and willful publication of any classified information concerning the cryptographic systems or communication intelligence activities of the United States as well as any information obtained from communication intelligence operations. If any of the material here at issue is of this nature, the newspapers are presumably now on full notice of the position of the United States and must face the consequences if they publish. I would have no difficulty in sustaining convictions under these sections on facts that would not justify the intervention of equity and the imposition of a prior restraint.

It is thus clear that Congress has addressed itself to the problems of protecting the security of the country and the national defense from unauthorized disclosure of potentially damaging information. . . . It has not, however, authorized the injunctive remedy against threatened publication. . . .

JUSTICE MARSHALL, concurring.

. . .

In these cases we are not faced with a situation where Congress has failed to provide the Executive with broad power to protect the Nation from disclosure of damaging state secrets. Congress has on several occasions given extensive consideration to the problem of protecting the military and strategic secrets of the United States. This consideration has resulted in the enactment of statutes making it a crime to receive, disclose, communicate, withhold, and publish certain documents, photographs, instruments, appliances, and information. . . .

. . .

Either the Government has the power under statutory grant to use traditional criminal law to protect the country or, if there is no basis for arguing that

Congress has made the activity a crime, it is plain that Congress has specifically refused to grant the authority the Government seeks from this Court. In either case this Court does not have authority to grant the requested relief. It is not for this Court to fling itself into every breach perceived by some Government official nor is it for this Court to take on itself the burden of enacting law, especially a law that Congress has refused to pass.

. . .

CHIEF JUSTICE BURGER, dissenting.

. . . In these cases, the imperative of a free and unfettered press comes into collision with another imperative, the effective functioning of a complex modern government and specifically the effective exercise of certain constitutional powers of the Executive. Only those who view the First Amendment as an absolute in all circumstances—a view I respect, but reject—can find such cases as these to be simple or easy.

These cases are not simple for another and more immediate reason. We do not know the facts of the cases. No District Judge knew all the facts. No Court of Appeals Judge knew all the facts. No member of this Court knows all the facts.

Why are we in this posture, in which only those judges to whom the First Amendment is absolute and permits of no restraint in any circumstances or for any reason, are really in a position to act?

I suggest we are in this posture because these cases have been conducted in unseemly haste. . . .

. . .

. . . An issue of this importance should be tried and heard in a judicial atmosphere conducive to thoughtful, reflective deliberation, especially when haste, in terms of hours, is unwarranted in light of the long period the *Times*, by its own choice, deferred publication.

. . .

The consequence of all this melancholy series of events is that we literally do not know what we are acting on. As I see it, we have been forced to deal with litigation concerning rights of great magnitude without an adequate record, and surely without time for adequate treatment either in the prior proceedings or in this Court. . . . I agree generally with Mr. Justice HARLAN and Mr. Justice BLACKMUN but I am not prepared to reach the merits.

. . .

JUSTICE HARLAN, with whom THE CHIEF JUSTICE and JUSTICE BLACKMUN join, dissenting.

. . .

. . . It is plain to me that the scope of the judicial function in passing upon the activities of the Executive Branch of the Government in the field of foreign affairs is very narrowly restricted. This view is, I think, dictated by the concept of separation of powers upon which our constitutional system rests.

In a speech on the floor of the House of Representatives, Chief Justice John Marshall, then a member of that body, stated: "The President is the sole organ of the nation in its external relations, and its sole representative with foreign nations." . . . From that time, shortly after the founding of the Nation, to this, there has been no substantial challenge to this description of the scope of executive power. . . .

. . .

The power to evaluate the "pernicious influence" of premature disclosure is not, however, lodged in the Executive alone. I agree that, in performance of its duty to protect the values of the First Amendment against political pressures, the judiciary must review the initial Executive determination to the point of satisfying itself that the subject matter of the dispute does lie within the proper compass of the President's foreign relations power. Constitutional considerations forbid "a complete abandonment of judicial control." . . . Moreover the judiciary may properly insist that the determination that disclosure of the subject matter would irreparably impair the national security be made by the head of the Executive Department concerned—here the Secretary of State or the Secretary of Defense—after actual personal consideration by that officer. . . .

But in my judgment the judiciary may not properly go beyond these two inquiries and redetermine for itself the probable impact of disclosure on the national security.

. . .

JUSTICE BLACKMUN, dissenting.

. . .

The First Amendment . . . is only one part of an entire Constitution. Article II of the great document vests in the Executive Branch primary power over the conduct of foreign affairs and places in that branch the responsibility for the Nation's safety. Each provision of the Constitution is important, and I cannot subscribe to a doctrine of unlimited absolutism for the First Amendment at the cost of downgrading other provisions. . . . What is needed here is a weighing, upon properly developed standards, of the broad right of the press to print and of the very narrow right of the Government to prevent. Such standards are not yet developed. . . .

I therefore would remand these cases to be developed expeditiously, of course, but on a schedule permitting the orderly presentation of evidence from both sides, with the use of discovery, if necessary, as authorized by the rules, and with the preparation of briefs, oral argument, and court opinions of a quality better than has been seen to this point. . . .

Buckley v. Valeo, 424 U.S. 1 (1976)

Americans of all political persuasions complained about campaign finance during the 1960s and 1970s. In their national platform, Democrats in 1968 were "alarmed at the growing costs of political participation in our country and the consequent reliance of political parties and candidates on large contributors." Republicans that year "favor[ed] a new Election Reform Act that will apply clear, reasonable restraints to political spending and fund-raising, whether by business, labor or individuals." The Watergate scandals intensified public demand for reform. "Shocked" by the fundraising techniques of CREEP, which included pressure on corporations to provide millions of dollars in secret campaign donations in exchange for government benefits (such as milk price supports), Congress was determined to bring under control the country's campaign financing system. The crucial provisions of the Federal Election Campaign Act of 1974 (FECA):

- *Prohibited persons from contributing more than $1,000 to a particular candidate and more than $25,000 to candidates in any particular election*
- *Limited independent expenditures on behalf of a candidate to $1,000*[36]
- *Limited the amount that candidates could contribute to their own campaigns*
- *Limited the amount that candidates could spend on their own campaigns*
- *Established a system of public financing for campaigns that distinguished between major parties that had received more than 25 percent of the vote in the most recent presidential election, minor parties that had received between 5 and 25 percent of the vote in that election, and other parties that had received less than 5 percent of the vote in that election*

Numerous national officials raised constitutional objections to these provisions. President Ford, when signing the FECA, stated, "I had some strong reservations about one version or one provision or another of the legislation and I suspect some of the people here on both sides of the aisle have the same." Many national officials allayed their constitutional doubts by placing a provision in the FECA that guaranteed swift judicial review of the bill's most important provisions.

A remarkably diverse group of plaintiffs challenged the constitutionality of these provisions. The named plaintiff, James L. Buckley, was the junior senator from New York, elected on the Conservative Party ticket. Other plaintiffs included Eugene McCarthy, the former Democratic senator from Minnesota; Stewart Mott, a multimillionaire who had spent a fortune financing opposition to the Vietnam War; and William Steiger, who was seeking a Republican congressional nomination in Wisconsin. Organizational plaintiffs included the New York Civil Liberties Union, the Mississippi Republican Party, the American Conservative Party, and the Libertarian Party. The named defendant, Francis Valeo, was the secretary of the Senate and a member of the Federal Elections Commission created by the FECA. After some complex jurisdictional maneuvering, the lower federal courts declared virtually every provision of the FECA constitutional. Plaintiffs appealed to the Supreme Court of the United States.

The Supreme Court by a 5–3 vote sustained most contribution limits but by a 7–1 vote struck down all the expenditure limits. The limit on how much candidates could contribute to their own campaigns was declared unconstitutional by a 6–2 vote. The per curiam opinion insisted that campaign contributions and expenditures were considered speech for constitutional purposes and that contributions could be regulated to prevent corruption, but that elected officials could not regulate expenditures to ensure a level political playing field. The per curiam opinion insisted that political contributions are as much constitutionally protected speech as a public address by a political candidate. Why did the justices equate political contributions with speech? Were they correct? What justifies restricting campaign finance? Are these justifications sound, or should courts also permit

36. An independent expenditure occurs when a person spends money on behalf of a candidate without consulting the candidate. Unsurprisingly, the line between independent expenditures and contributions is often easily skirted.

laws that "level the playing field"? Was Justice White correct that the per curiam opinion demonstrates little knowledge of the actual workings of political campaigns, or might he have underestimated the extent to which campaign finance laws are likely to be incumbent protection acts? On what basis did the justices distinguish contributions and expenditures? Are these distinctions constitutionally sound? The FECA was based on a series of compromises and complex assumptions about the way that campaign financing works. Even if striking down some provisions while retaining others made constitutional sense, a good argument might be made that the totality was unworkable.[37]

PER CURIAM.

. . .

The Act's contribution and expenditure limitations operate in an area of the most fundamental First Amendment activities. Discussion of public issues and debate on the qualifications of candidates are integral to the operation of the system of government established by our Constitution. . . .

. . .

A restriction on the amount of money a person or group can spend on political communication during a campaign necessarily reduces the quantity of expression by restricting the number of issues discussed, the depth of their exploration, and the size of the audience reached. This is because virtually every means of communicating ideas in today's mass society requires the expenditure of money. The distribution of the humblest handbill or leaflet entails printing, paper, and circulation costs. Speeches and rallies generally necessitate hiring a hall and publicizing the event. The electorate's increasing dependence on television, radio, and other mass media for news and information has made these expensive modes of communication indispensable instruments of effective political speech.

The expenditure limitations contained in the Act represent substantial rather than merely theoretical restraints on the quantity and diversity of political speech. The $1,000 ceiling on spending "relative to a clearly identified candidate" . . . would appear to exclude all citizens and groups except candidates, political parties, and the institutional press from any significant use of the most effective modes of communication. . . .

By contrast with a limitation upon expenditures for political expression, a limitation upon the amount that any one person or group may contribute to a candidate or political committee entails only a marginal restriction upon the contributor's ability to engage in free communication. A contribution serves as a general expression of support for the candidate and his views, but does not communicate the underlying basis for the support. . . . At most, the size of the contribution provides a very rough index of the intensity of the contributor's support for the candidate. A limitation on the amount of money a person may give to a candidate or campaign organization thus involves little direct restraint on his political communication, for it permits the symbolic expression of support evidenced by a contribution but does not in any way infringe the contributor's freedom to discuss candidates and issues. . . .

. . .

It is unnecessary to look beyond the Act's primary purpose—to limit the actuality and appearance of corruption resulting from large individual financial contributions—in order to find a constitutionally sufficient justification for the $1,000 contribution limitation. Under a system of private financing of elections, a candidate lacking immense personal or family wealth must depend on financial contributions from others to provide the resources necessary to conduct a successful campaign. The increasing importance of the communications media and sophisticated mass-mailing and polling operations to effective campaigning make the raising of large sums of money an ever more essential ingredient of an effective candidacy. To the extent that large contributions are given to secure a political quid pro quo from current and potential office holders, the integrity of our system of representative democracy is undermined. Although the scope of such pernicious practices can never be reliably ascertained, the deeply disturbing examples surfacing after the 1972 election demonstrate that the problem is not an illusory one.

Of almost equal concern as the danger of actual quid pro quo arrangements is the impact of the appearance of corruption stemming from public awareness of the opportunities for abuse inherent in a regime of large individual financial contributions. . . .

. . .

37. For an argument to that effect, see Gordon Silverstein, *Law's Allure: How Law Shapes, Constrains, Saves, and Kills Politics* (New York: Cambridge University Press, 2009), 152–74.

The Act's expenditure ceilings impose direct and substantial restraints on the quantity of political speech.... It is clear that a primary effect of these expenditure limitations is to restrict the quantity of campaign speech by individuals, groups, and candidates....

...

..[T]he independent advocacy restricted by the provision does not presently appear to pose dangers of real or apparent corruption comparable to those identified with large campaign contributions.... Unlike contributions, such independent expenditures may well provide little assistance to the candidate's campaign and indeed may prove counterproductive. The absence of prearrangement and coordination of an expenditure with the candidate or his agent not only undermines the value of the expenditure to the candidate, but also alleviates the danger that expenditures will be given as a quid pro quo for improper commitments from the candidate...

...

It is argued, however, that the ancillary governmental interest in equalizing the relative ability of individuals and groups to influence the outcome of elections serves to justify the limitation on express advocacy of the election or defeat of candidates imposed by 608 (e) (1)'s expenditure ceiling. But the concept that government may restrict the speech of some elements of our society in order to enhance the relative voice of others is wholly foreign to the First Amendment.... The First Amendment's protection against governmental abridgment of free expression cannot properly be made to depend on a person's financial ability to engage in public discussion....

...

The ceiling on personal expenditures by candidates on their own behalf... imposes a substantial restraint on the ability of persons to engage in protected First Amendment expression. The candidate, no less than any other person, has a First Amendment right to engage in the discussion of public issues and vigorously and tirelessly to advocate his own election and the election of other candidates. Indeed, it is of particular importance that candidates have the unfettered opportunity to make their views known so that the electorate may intelligently evaluate the candidates' personal qualities and their positions on vital public issues before choosing among them on election day....

The primary governmental interest served by the Act—the prevention of actual and apparent corruption of the political process—does not support the limitation on the candidate's expenditure of his own personal funds....

...

No governmental interest that has been suggested is sufficient to justify the restriction on the quantity of political expression imposed by... campaign expenditure limitations. The major evil associated with rapidly increasing campaign expenditures is the danger of candidate dependence on large contributions. The interest in alleviating the corrupting influence of large contributions is served by the Act's contribution limitations and disclosure provisions....

The interest in equalizing the financial resources of candidates competing for federal office is no more convincing a justification for restricting the scope of federal election campaigns. Given the limitation on the size of outside contributions, the financial resources available to a candidate's campaign, like the number of volunteers recruited, will normally vary with the size and intensity of the candidate's support. There is nothing invidious, improper, or unhealthy in permitting such funds to be spent to carry the candidate's message to the electorate. Moreover, the equalization of permissible campaign expenditures might serve not to equalize the opportunities of all candidates, but to handicap a candidate who lacked substantial name recognition or exposure of his views before the start of the campaign.

...

JUSTICE STEVENS took no part in the consideration or decision of these cases.

CHIEF JUSTICE BURGER, concurring in part and dissenting in part.

...

Congress intended to regulate all aspects of federal campaign finances, but what remains after today's holding leaves no more than a shadow of what Congress contemplated. I question whether the residue leaves a workable program.

...

...For me contributions and expenditures are two sides of the same First Amendment coin.

... By limiting campaign contributions, the Act restricts the amount of money that will be spent on political activity—and does so directly. . . . Limiting contributions, as a practical matter, will limit expenditures and will put an effective ceiling on the amount of political activity and debate that the Government will permit to take place. The argument that the ceiling is not, after all, very low as matters now stand gives little comfort for the future, since the Court elsewhere notes the rapid inflation in the cost of political campaigning . . .

. . .

. . . In my view Congress can no more ration political expression than it can ration religious expression; and limits on political or religious contributions and expenditures effectively curb expression in both areas. There are many prices we pay for the freedoms secured by the First Amendment; the risk of undue influence is one of them, confirming what we have long known: Freedom is hazardous, but some restraints are worse.

JUSTICE WHITE, concurring in part and dissenting in part.

. . .

. . . I dissent from the Court's view that the expenditure limitations . . . violate the First Amendment.

. . .

. . . Congress was plainly of the view that [independent] expenditures . . . have corruptive potential; but the Court strikes down the provision, strangely enough claiming more insight as to what may improperly influence candidates than is possessed by the majority of Congress that passed this bill and the President who signed it. Those supporting the bill undeniably included many seasoned professionals who have been deeply involved in elective processes and who have viewed them at close range over many years.

. . .

As an initial matter, the argument that money is speech and that limiting the flow of money to the speaker violates the First Amendment proves entirely too much. . . . Federal and state taxation directly removes from company coffers large amounts of money that might be spent on larger and better newspapers. . . . But it has not been suggested, nor could it be successfully, that these laws, and many others, are invalid because they siphon off or prevent the accumulation of large sums that would otherwise be available for communicative activities.

. . . [M]oney is not always equivalent to or used for speech, even in the context of political campaigns. I accept the reality that communicating with potential voters is the heart of an election campaign and that widespread communication has become very expensive. There are, however, many expensive campaign activities that are not themselves communicative or remotely related to speech. . . . The record before us no more supports the conclusion that the communicative efforts of congressional and Presidential candidates will be crippled by the expenditure limitations than it supports the contrary. . . .

. . . [E]xpenditure ceilings reinforce the contribution limits and help eradicate the hazard of corruption. . . . Without limits on total expenditures, campaign costs will inevitably and endlessly escalate. Pressure to raise funds will constantly build and with it the temptation to resort in "emergencies" to those sources of large sums, who, history shows, are sufficiently confident of not being caught to risk flouting contribution limits. Congress would save the candidate from this predicament by establishing a reasonable ceiling on all candidates. . . . It should be added that many successful candidates will also be saved from large, overhanging campaign debts which must be paid off with money raised while holding public office and at a time when they are already preparing or thinking about the next campaign. The danger to the public interest in such situations is self-evident.

. . .

It is also important to restore and maintain public confidence in federal elections. It is critical to obviate or dispel the impression that federal elections are purely and simply a function of money, that federal offices are bought and sold or that political races are reserved for those who have the facility—and the stomach—for doing whatever it takes to bring together those interests, groups, and individuals that can raise or contribute large fortunes in order to prevail at the polls.

. . .

I also disagree with the Court's judgment that [the provision] which limits the amount of money that a candidate or his family may spend on his campaign, violates the Constitution. Although it is true that this provision does not promote any interest in preventing the corruption of candidates, the provision does, nevertheless, serve salutary purposes related to the integrity of federal campaigns. By limiting the importance of personal wealth [the Federal Election

Campaign Act] helps to assure that only individuals with a modicum of support from others will be viable candidates. This in turn would tend to discourage any notion that the outcome of elections is primarily a function of money. Similarly, the statute tends to equalize access to the political arena, encouraging the less wealthy, unable to bankroll their own campaigns, to run for political office.

. . .

JUSTICE MARSHALL, concurring in part and dissenting in part.

I join in all of the Court's opinion except [the decision to declare unconstitutional limitations on how much candidates may personally contribute to their campaigns].

. . .

. . . In my view the interest is more precisely the interest in promoting the reality and appearance of equal access to the political arena. . . .

One of the points on which all Members of the Court agree is that money is essential for effective communication in a political campaign. It would appear to follow that the candidate with a substantial personal fortune at his disposal is off to a significant "headstart." Of course, the less wealthy candidate can potentially overcome the disparity in resources through contributions from others. But ability to generate contributions may itself depend upon a showing of a financial base for the campaign or some demonstration of pre-existing support, which in turn is facilitated by expenditures of substantial personal sums. . . . And even if the advantage can be overcome, the perception that personal wealth wins elections may not only discourage potential candidates without significant personal wealth from entering the political arena, but also undermine public confidence in the integrity of the electoral process.

The concern that candidacy for public office not become, or appear to become, the exclusive province of the wealthy assumes heightened significance when one considers the impact of [the contribution limits] which the Court today upholds. . . . While the limitations on contributions are neutral in the sense that all candidates are foreclosed from accepting large contributions, there can be no question that large contributions generally mean more to the candidate without a substantial personal fortune to spend on his campaign. Large contributions are the less wealthy candidate's only hope of countering the wealthy candidate's immediate access to substantial sums of money. With that option removed, the less wealthy candidate is without the means to match the large initial expenditures of money of which the wealthy candidate is capable. In short, the limitations on contributions put a premium on a candidate's personal wealth.

JUSTICE BLACKMUN, concurring in part and dissenting in part. . . .

JUSTICE REHNQUIST, concurring in part and dissenting in part. . . .

B. Voting

Americans during the late 1960s and 1970s could not decide whether to continue, maintain, or modify the crucial principles underlying the voting rights revolution of the previous decades. A broad consensus existed that the Voting Rights Act of 1965 was constitutionally sacred, that voting was a fundamental right protected by the Fourteenth Amendment, and that this protection included the principle of one person, one vote. Nevertheless, controversies arose over the application of these principles as progressives committed to universal adult suffrage sought to have more and more federal and state voting restrictions declared unconstitutional. The Supreme Court required congressional electoral districts to be as mathematically equal as possible, but states were permitted greater deviations from one person, one vote when apportioning state legislative districts. Residency requirements were held to unconstitutionally abridge the right to vote, but states were permitted to disenfranchise felons.

Voting rights initially enjoyed broad bipartisan support outside of the South. Democratic majorities in both houses of Congress passed and Republican presidents enthusiastically signed the Voting Rights Acts of 1970 and 1975. Those measures outlawed literacy tests throughout the nation, prohibited state residency requirements for presidential elections, provided additional protections for non-English-speaking voters, and gave eighteen-year-olds the right to cast a ballot in federal and state elections. The Supreme Court sustained all of these measures, with the exception of the provision in the Voting Rights Act of 1970 that extended the right to vote in state elections to eighteen-year-olds, which the Court declared unconstitutional in *Oregon v. Mitchell* (1970). Congress immediately proposed and the states quickly ratified a constitutional amendment granting eighteen-year-olds this right.

The main difference between the constitutional politics of voting rights during the New Deal/Great Society Era and these politics during the 1970s was institutional. Elected officials made the most important decisions on voting rights from 1940 until 1965. Federal justices assumed the burden of decision making on voting rights during the 1970s. The increasing importance of litigation stemmed from two sources. First, many cases arose in which the crucial question was the proper interpretation of voting rights provisions passed by Congress. Second, judicial decisions during the Great Society nationalized voting issues that had previously been resolved by state constitutional decision makers. The Burger Court was increasingly occupied with concerns about how to implement the one person, one vote principle announced in *Reynolds v. Sims* (1964), how far to extend the right to vote recognized in *Harper v. State Board of Elections* (1966), and the constitutionality of various state laws that entrenched two-party politics.

The Supreme Court, with one notable exception, expanded the holding of *Harper v. Virginia State Board of Elections* (1966) that the right to vote was fundamental under the equal protection clause of the Fourteenth Amendment. *Dunn v. Blumstein* (1972) held that states may not forbid bona fide residents who have only resided in the state for a short period of time from voting in state elections. Justice Marshall's majority opinion stated, "There is simply nothing in the record to support the conclusive presumption that residents who have lived in the State for less than a year and their county for less than three months are uninformed about elections." *Richardson v. Ramirez* (1974), which sustained state laws forbidding convicted felons from voting, was the only prominent Burger Court decision that upheld a state decision to limit access to the ballot.

In 1973 the Court once again weighed in on the constitutional restrictions associated with the drawing of legislative districts. *White v. Weiser* held that states must strive to obtain perfect equality when apportioning congressional districts. By contrast, in *Gaffney v. Cummings*, the justices by a 6–3 vote held that states have more latitude to deviate from strict equality when drawing state legislative districts. Justice White's majority opinion declared that deviations of less than 10 percent would not be considered prima facie evidence of constitutional wrong. In justifying the greater degree of latitude in these cases Justice White referenced the specific requirement in Article I, Section 2 that representatives to the federal Congress be chosen "by the People of the several States," which he said mandates that "one man's vote in a congressional election is to be worth as much as another's." By contrast, state legislative apportionments that were governed by the Fourteenth Amendment need only be "as nearly of equal population as practicable," with the understanding that "there are other relevant factors to be taken into account and other important interests that States may legitimately be mindful of."

During the late 1970s constitutional decision makers first confronted the majority-minority districts that would become constitutionally explosive in the Reagan Era. These districts, drawn in response to *Reynolds v. Sims* or the Voting Rights Acts, were structured to ensure that the majority of voters were persons of color who would likely elect persons of color to office. The Supreme Court first confronted the constitutional issues that majority-minority districts raised in *United Jewish Organizations v. Carey* (1977) after the New York legislature split a traditional Jewish community in order to create a predominantly African American legislative district. Justice White's majority opinion contended that under certain conditions, state officials could use race as a criterion when apportioning legislative seats. He wrote, "The Constitution does not prevent a State subject to the Voting Rights Act from deliberately creating or preserving black majorities in particular districts in order to ensure that its reapportionment plan complies with §5" of that act. Chief Justice Burger disagreed, asserting that the "drawing of political boundary lines with the sole, explicit objective of reaching a predetermined racial result cannot ordinarily be squared with the Constitution."

Congressional Debate on the Voting Rights Act of 1970[38]

In 1970 and 1975 Congress passed important amendments to the Voting Rights Act of 1965. While many provisions in each measure were aimed at eliminating ongoing discrimination against persons of color, both included provisions

38. *Congressional Record*, 91st Cong., 2nd Sess., 1970, 5517–23, 5542–48.

directed at other forms of discrimination. Both were rooted in congressional recognition that voting was a fundamental constitutional right. Both measures enjoyed substantial bipartisan support, with opposition based almost exclusively in the South. When signing the Voting Rights Act of 1970, President Nixon declared that the measure was of "great importance" and was "dramatic evidence that the American system works." President Ford, when mustering Republican support for the Voting Rights Act of 1975, declared that "the right to vote is the foundation of freedom, and . . . this right must be protected."

Title I of the Voting Rights Act of 1970 declared that the provisions of the 1965 Voting Rights Act would be maintained until 1975 and that districts where less than 50 percent of the voting-age population had voted in the 1968 presidential election would be required to obtain preclearance for any change in voting laws. For the first time, the legislation covered some northern electoral districts. Title II outlawed literacy or understanding tests for five years throughout the nation, abolished residency requirements for presidential elections, and mandated that states establish procedures for absentee voting in presidential elections. Title III prohibited states from denying persons ages eighteen or older a right to vote if they were otherwise qualified.

The Voting Rights Act of 1975 extended all the provisions of the Voting Rights Act of 1965 until 1982 and required political subdivisions where less than half the eligible population had voted in the 1972 presidential election to seek preclearance from the Justice Department or a panel of three federal district court judges on the District of Columbia Circuit before changing their voting rules. Title II of that measure placed a permanent ban on literacy and understanding tests. Title III provided language minorities with greater access to the ballot, with Section 203 declaring, "Where State and local officials conduct elections only in English, language minority citizens are excluded from participation in the electoral process."

The following excerpts are from the debates over the Voting Rights Act of 1970. To what extent did these debates repeat themes from the debate over the Voting Rights Act of 1965? Do you detect important new developments that took place in the intervening five years? What changes might you have made to the Voting Rights Act of 1965 in light of the experiences of the late 1960s and 1970s?

The Supreme Court in Oregon v. Mitchell *(1970) unanimously sustained every provision in the Voting Rights Act of 1970 except the provision granting eighteen-year-olds the right to vote in federal and state elections. A 5–4 majority sustained congressional power to grant younger Americans the right to vote in federal elections. A 5–4 majority rejected congressional power to grant younger Americans the right to vote in state elections.* Oregon v. Mitchell *exhibits a common pattern in Burger Court opinions. Eight justices believed that no good constitutional distinction existed between federal laws regulating the right to vote in state elections and federal laws regulating the right to vote in federal elections. Justice Douglas, speaking for four justices, maintained that Congress could lower the voting age in all elections, arguing, "Congress might well conclude that a reduction in the voting age from 21 to 18 was needed in the interest of equal protection. The Act itself brands the denial of the franchise to 18-year-olds as 'a particularly unfair treatment of such citizens in view of the national defense responsibilities imposed' on them." Justice Harlan, speaking for four justices, maintained that Congress could not lower the voting age in any election, writing, "I am of the opinion that the Fourteenth Amendment was never intended to restrict the authority of the States to allocate their political power as they see fit, and therefore that it does not authorize Congress to set voter qualifications, in either state or federal elections." Justice Black split the difference. He maintained that the provision lowering the age limit in national elections was constitutional because "Congress has ultimate supervisory power over congressional elections." He voted to strike the legislative attempt to lower the age limit in state elections because Congress was invading an area that he believed the Constitution of 1789 had reserved to the states and that this action was not warranted by congressional power to enforce the post–Civil War Amendments' ban on racial discrimination. Justice Black's view that Congress could lower the voting age to eighteen for federal but not state elections temporarily became the law of the land (until Americans ratified the Twenty-Sixth Amendment), even though Black was the only justice who believed that a constitutional distinction existed between federal power to regulate state elections and federal power to regulate federal elections.*

THE JOINT VIEWS OF THE MEMBERS OF THE SENATE JUDICIARY COMMITTEE

. . .

During the hearings on the Voting Rights Act before the Senate Judiciary Committee . . . extensive facts were presented which compel the conclusion that the Voting Rights Act of 1965 must be extended for an additional five years. The Voting Rights Act of 1965 has been the most effective civil rights legislation ever enacted by the Congress. It is the only federal legislation that has proven effective in implementing the

15th Amendment and making real the rights to register and vote which that Amendment secures on paper. The success of the 1965 Act is directly traceable to its distinguishing feature in comparison to prior civil rights legislation; its immediate and automatic application, without the need for lengthy and repeated litigation in jurisdictions which fall within the formula provided in section 4 of the Act. . . . Negroes have registered and voted in record numbers in areas where before 1965 they had been systemically denied the franchise. Discriminatory devices to deny the franchise have been struck down or deferred.

. . .

In Alabama, the nonwhite population registered to vote increased from 19.3 in 1964 to 56.7 percent in the late summer of 1968; in Georgia, from 27.4 to 56.1 percent; in Louisiana, from 31.6 to 59.3 percent; in Mississippi, from 6.7 to 59.9 percent; in South Carolina, from 37.3 to 50.8 percent.

In addition to the large numbers of black citizens registering and voting, many are now running for office in Southern states to help assure adequate representation of all interests.

While progress has been significant, it should not obscure the pressing needs which remain. Negro registration is still well below that of whites in [m]any areas covered by the Act—and less than one-half in many counties. The continuing resistance to equal voting rights and risk of back-sliding should the protections of the Act be weakened are amply demonstrated in the instances in which the Attorney General has found it necessary to send in observers to assure that all persons were able to vote and have their votes counted regardless of race and to initiate legal actions to set aside elections and voting changes infected by racial discrimination.

If the 1965 Act is not extended, states and counties presently covered by the Act will be able to petition the court for their removal in August 1970—five years after the statute's enactment. . . . That means that sections 4 and 5, which have made the Voting Rights Act of 1965 so successful, will cease to be effective this year and we will again be relegated to piecemeal judicial remedies which proved so unsuccessful in the past in keeping up with a rapid succession of ingenious roadblocks.

. . . The last five years has provided ample evidence that if these key provisions of the Act are permitted to expire, the procedural protections for voter registration will stop, thereby freeing—indeed, inviting—the resurgence of the discriminatory forces which operated so effectively prior to enactment of the law. . . .

. . .

While a great many citizens in the South have shown a commendable effort to comply with and help implement the Voting Rights Act of 1965, the intent and desire shown by others to circumvent the Act indicates that the dangers which necessitated the statute in the first place have not been eliminated. A wide range of obstructionist weapons have been experienced. Decided court cases demonstrate that boundary lines have been gerrymandered, elections have been switched to an at-large basis, elective offices have been abolished where Negroes had a chance of winning, the appointments process has been substituted for the elective process, election officials have withheld the necessary information for voting and running for office, and both physical and economic intimidation have been employed.

. . .

Even though other areas have no recent history of discriminatory abuses like that which prompted enactment of the 1965 Act, this extension is justified for two reasons; (1) because of the discriminatory impact which the requirement of literacy as a precondition to voting may have on minority groups and the poor; and (2) because there is insufficient relationship between literacy and responsible, interested voting to justify such a broad restriction of the franchise.

. . .

Professed state interests which are advanced to support restrictions on the franchise require close scrutiny. And as Father Hesburgh, Chairman of the Civil Rights Commission, stated in his letter of March 28, 1969, to the President: "the lives and fortunes of illiterates are no less affected by the actions of local, State and Federal governments than those of their more fortunate brethren. . . . Today, with television so widely available," he continued, "it is possible for one with little formal education to be a well-informed and intelligent member of the electorate." Thus, literacy tests not only abridge the right to suffrage on account of race and color, but also constitute an unreasonable classification against educationally disadvantaged persons in violation of the equal protection clause of the 14th Amendment.

Second, we propose to limit residency requirements in presidential elections. . . .

The main rationale for a residency requirement in statewide or local elections—to ensure that the new resident has sufficient time to familiarize himself with state or local issues—has little relevance to presidential elections because the issues tend to be nationwide in scope and receive nationwide dissemination by the communications media.

SENATOR SAM ERVIN (Democrat, North Carolina)

...

I have searched in vain for the constitutional justification for the 1965 act. Any person who can read and understand the English language can see that the Federal Constitution grants to the States the power to prescribe voter qualifications.... Until very recently neither the Congress nor the Federal courts has had difficulty understanding this plain language in the Constitution.

...

Regretfully, the Supreme Court in *South Carolina v. Katzenbach* (1966) departed from this old and wise view of the 15th amendment. According to this expansive view of congressional power under the 15th amendment, Congress can and has nullified state power to set voter qualifications without any judicial or reasonable determination that such qualifications violate the 15th amendment. If literacy tests, constitutional on their face and as applied, can be prohibited by Congress as in the 1965 act, then what is left of State power over voter qualifications?

...

The Supreme Court in *Katzenbach v. Morgan* (1966) ... asserted that section 5 of the 14th amendment in effect grants Congress the power to define the equal protection clause. This new theory of congressional power to "enact appropriate legislation" to secure equal protection of the law is a theory which can be employed to eliminate all State legislative and judicial power over any matter. The constitutional theory set forth in *Katzenbach v. Morgan* could quite literally establish the basis for dismantling completely the federal system provided for in the Constitution.

...

Mr. President, the Constitution was written to put restraints on government. The Founders rejected the theory that the liberty of a free people should depend on the self-restraint of the Governors. Yet, under Justice Brennan's theory, Congress can legislate on all matters from before the cradle to after the grave. And the only protection we now have for the preservation of our liberties is the hope that Congress will exercise self-restraint.

...

The formula used to bring six Southern States and 39 counties of North Carolina under the provisions of the act contains no reference whatever to a denial or abridgment of the right to vote on account of race, color, or previous condition of servitude. It arbitrarily and illogically assumes a violation of the 15th amendment whenever but only when States and counties with literacy tests had less than 50 percent of their voting age population registered or actually voting in the 1964 presidential election.

...

One of the particularly onerous forms of discriminatory treatment is incorporated in section 5 of the 1965 act. Under that section a State or political subdivision condemned under the trigger device of the act must submit any changes to the Attorney General or the three-judge district court for the District of Columbia. The State of North Carolina, which, in this century, has never been proven guilty of denying a single person the right to vote on account of race, must, hat-in-hand, take every change in its election laws to Washington for approval by persons who have no constitutional authority whatsoever over voter qualifications.

...

The legislative condemnation of the 1965 act of Southern States and election officials constitutes a bill of attainder expressly forbidden by the U.S. Constitution. The people of seven States and parts of other States, and more particularly the State election officials in those areas, are convicted under the formula of the 1965 act of violating the 15th amendment without any semblance of judicial trial....

The 1965 act violates another one of the most fundamental doctrines of our federal system of government, the equality of the States. The act operates to deny to certain Southern States the constitutional authority given all States to prescribe voting qualifications. While I believe that in the absence of proof of racial discrimination, any restriction by Congress on the States' power to set voting qualifications violates the Constitution, certainly a restriction on the power of only certain States constitutes an even greater disregard of constitutional principles....

Richardson v. Ramirez, 418 U.S. 24 (1974)

In 1952 Abran Ramirez was convicted of robbery by assault, a felony in the state of Texas. He served three months in prison and successfully completed parole in 1962. Ten years later Viola Richardson, a California election official, refused to allow Ramirez to register to vote on the ground that California law declared that "no . . . person convicted of an infamous crime . . . shall exercise the privileges of an elector in this state." Ramirez sued Richardson, claiming that the California ban on felons voting was unconstitutional. The Supreme Court of California declared unconstitutional the state law denying convicted felons the right to vote. Richardson appealed that decision to the Supreme Court of the United States.

The Supreme Court by a 6–3 vote declared that states could prohibit convicted felons from voting. Justice Rehnquist's majority opinion relies heavily on the language of the Fourteenth Amendment and the widespread nineteenth-century practice of disenfranchising felons. Justice Marshall in dissent pointed out that numerous Supreme Court decisions on voting rights during the 1960s and 1970s struck down practices that were widespread when the Fourteenth Amendment was ratified. Did either justice really engage the central contentions of the other, or is this a case in which historical arguments conflict with doctrinal arguments? On what basis would you resolve that conflict? Note that by the 1970s most former felons, who were disproportionately poor and persons of color, were likely to cast ballots for Democrats. How, if at all, has that influenced the constitutional politics of felon disenfranchisement?

JUSTICE REHNQUIST delivered the opinion of the Court.

. . .

. . . [R]espondents' claim implicates not merely the language of the Equal Protection Clause of Section 1 of the Fourteenth Amendment, but also the provisions of the less familiar [Section] 2 of the Amendment:

> . . . [W]hen the right to vote at any [federal or state] election is denied to any of the male inhabitants of such State, being twenty-one years of age, and citizens of the United States, or in any way abridged, except for participation in rebellion, or other crime, the basis of representation therein shall be reduced in the proportion which the number of such male citizens shall bear to the whole number of male citizens twenty-one years of age in such State. . . .

Petitioner contends that . . . [Section] 2 expressly exempts from the sanction of that section disenfranchisement grounded on prior conviction of a felony. She goes on to argue that those who framed and adopted the Fourteenth Amendment could not have intended to prohibit outright in [Section] 1 of that Amendment that which was expressly exempted from the lesser sanction of reduced representation imposed by [Section] 2 of the Amendment. This argument seems to us a persuasive one unless it can be shown that the language of [Section] 2, "except for participation in rebellion, or other crime," was intended to have a different meaning than would appear from its face.

. . .

. . . [A]t the time of the adoption of the Amendment, 29 States had provisions in their constitutions which prohibited, or authorized the legislature to prohibit, exercise of the franchise by persons convicted of felonies or infamous crimes.

. . .

As we have seen, . . . the exclusion of felons from the vote has an affirmative sanction in [Section] 2 of the Fourteenth Amendment, a sanction which was not present in the case of the other restrictions on the franchise which were invalidated in the cases on which respondents rely. We hold that the understanding of those who adopted the Fourteenth Amendment, as reflected in the express language of [Section] 2 and in the historical and judicial interpretation of the Amendment's applicability to state laws disenfranchising felons, is of controlling significance in distinguishing such laws from those other state limitations on the franchise which have been held invalid under the Equal Protection Clause by this Court. . . .

Pressed upon us by the respondents, and by amici curia, are contentions that these notions are outmoded, and that the more modern view is that it is essential to the process of rehabilitating the exfelon that he be returned to his role in society as a fully participating citizen when he has completed the serving of his term. We would by no means discount these arguments if addressed to the legislative forum which may properly weigh and balance them against those advanced in support of California's present constitutional provisions. But it is not for us to choose one set of values over the other. If respondents are correct, and the view which they advocate is indeed the more enlightened and sensible one, presumably the people of the State of California will ultimately come around to that view. And if they do not do so, their failure is some evidence, at least, of the fact that there are two sides to the argument.

. . .

JUSTICE MARSHALL, with whom JUSTICE BRENNAN joins, dissenting.

. . .

The Court's references to congressional enactments contemporaneous to the adoption of the Fourteenth Amendment . . . are inapposite. They do not explain the purpose for the adoption of [Section] 2 of the Fourteenth Amendment. They merely indicate that disenfranchisement for participation in crime was not uncommon in the States at the time of the adoption of the Amendment. . . . But "constitutional concepts of equal protection are not immutably frozen like insects trapped in Devonian amber." . . . We have repeatedly observed:

> "[T]he Equal Protection Clause is not shackled to the political theory of a particular era. In determining what lines are unconstitutionally discriminatory, we have never been confined to historic notions of equality, any more than we have restricted due process to a fixed catalogue of what was at a given time deemed to be the limits of fundamental rights." *Harper v. Virginia Board of Elections* (1966). . . .

Accordingly, neither the fact that several States had ex-felon disenfranchisement laws at the time of the adoption of the Fourteenth Amendment, nor that such disenfranchisement was specifically excepted from the special remedy of [Section] 2, can serve to insulate such disenfranchisement from equal protection scrutiny.

In my view, the disenfranchisement of ex-felons must be measured against the requirements of the Equal Protection Clause of [Section] 1 of the Fourteenth Amendment. That analysis properly begins with the observation that because the right to vote "is of the essence of a democratic society, and any restrictions on that right strike at the heart of representative government." . . .

. . .

The disenfranchisement of ex-felons had "its origin in the fogs and fictions of feudal jurisprudence and doubtless has been brought forward into modern statutes without fully realizing either the effect of its literal significance or the extent of its infringement upon the spirit of our system of government." I think it clear that measured against the standards of this Court's modern equal protection jurisprudence, the blanket disenfranchisement of ex-felons cannot stand.

I respectfully dissent.

JUSTICE DOUGLAS, dissenting. . . .

IX. Equality

MAJOR DEVELOPMENTS

- Fights over busing and affirmative action
- Gender discrimination subject to heightened judicial scrutiny
- Supreme Court declines to treat education as a fundamental right for equal protection purposes

The movement for racial equality during the New Deal/Great Society Era inspired numerous other constitutional demands for equality. Constitutional decision makers were asked to consider whether legislation discriminating against women, aliens, illegitimate children, the poor, and various other persons was presumptively unconstitutional. The lawyers and political activists involved in these campaigns borrowed heavily from the NAACP's campaign against Jim Crow. Proponents of women's rights asserted that gender and race classifications were equally suspect because gender and race are immutable characteristics, African Americans and women were relatively powerless politically, and both had experienced a long history of discrimination. Organizations following the path blazed by the NAACP Legal Defense Fund even adopted such names as the National Organization for Women Legal Defense Fund or the Mexican American Legal Defense Fund. Many of these movements were successful. John Skrentny speaks of a "minority rights revolution" that included, often as a matter of claimed constitutional right, "bilingual education for Latinos, equal rights for women in education, and equal rights for the disabled," as well as the expansion of affirmative action programs to non–African Americans.[39]

39. John D. Skrentny, *The Minority Rights Revolution* (Cambridge, MA: Harvard University Press, 2002), 2.

The new constitutional politics of equal rights splintered both liberals and equal protection clause doctrine. Progressives in Congress and on the Supreme Court maintained that state and federal laws discriminated against numerous groups and that such discriminations warranted the highest or at least a high degree of constitutional scrutiny. Proponents of gender equality urged that the ERA be ratified and that, regardless of its ratification, the Fourteenth Amendment be interpreted as requiring strict scrutiny of gender classifications. Other constitutional decision makers agreed that members of many groups had characteristics or a history that justified some degree of heightened judicial protection. Moderates worried that the ERA might unsettle traditional practices, such as all-male combat forces, and thought the Fourteenth Amendment should be interpreted as requiring intermediate scrutiny for gender classifications. More conservative Americans rejected the central premises of both progressive and moderate understandings of constitutional equality. History, in their view, sanctioned heightened judicial scrutiny only for racial classifications. Real differences between men and women justified many traditional gender classifications.

Affirmative action furthered muddied the waters. Liberals divided over whether classifications ostensibly designed to benefit members of historically disadvantaged groups merited the same constitutional scrutiny as classifications clearly designed to harm members of those groups. A very tenuous compromise was reached in *Bakke v. Regents of the University of California* (1978). Justice Powell's crucial fifth vote in this decision created a majority in favor of the principle that affirmative action was a constitutional means for seeking diversity but not for ameliorating social disadvantage.

A. Equality Under Law

Constitutional decision makers confronted an extraordinary variety of demands for equality. Initially the Supreme Court of the United States seemed sympathetic. When striking down a Louisiana law that declared that only legitimate children could be compensated under workmen's compensation for the death of a parent, Justice Powell's majority opinion in *Weber v. Aetna Casualty & Surety Co.* (1972) justified heightened judicial scrutiny for laws that discriminated against the children of unmarried parents by arguing that imposing the stigma of "illegitimacy" on "the head of an infant is illogical and unjust" and "contrary to the basic concept of our system that legal burdens should bear some relationship to individual responsibility or wrongdoing." *U.S. Department of Agriculture v. Moreno* (1973) ruled unconstitutional a federal law prohibiting households composed of unrelated persons from using food stamps. While purporting to use rational scrutiny, Justice Brennan's majority opinion maintained that the law "was intended to prevent so-called 'hippies' and 'hippie communes' from participating in the food stamp program." Brennan concluded, "A bare congressional desire to harm a politically unpopular group cannot constitute a legitimate government interest."

The Supreme Court became less solicitous of equality claims as the decade wore on. *San Antonio Independent School District v. Rodriguez* (1973) ruled that using local property taxes to fund public education neither discriminated against the class of persons who lived in property-poor school districts nor denied a fundamental right to the children who resided in those districts. That decision put a practical halt, for the most part, to efforts to expand both the suspect class and fundamental rights strands of equal protection analysis. In *United States Railroad Retirement Board v. Fritz* (1980) the justices reemphasized that a very deferential rationality standard was appropriate for virtually all equal protection claims. Justice Rehnquist's majority opinion asserted, "Where, as here, there are plausible reasons for Congress' action, our inquiry is at an end. It is, of course, constitutionally irrelevant whether this reasoning in fact underlay the legislative decision, . . . because this Court has never insisted that a legislative body articulate its reasons for enacting a statute."

San Antonio Independent School District v. Rodriguez, 411 U.S. 1 (1973)

Demetrio Rodriguez was a child who lived in the Edgewood Independent School District. Edgewood was an urban, residential, and relatively poor area in San Antonio, Texas, with a student population that was 90 percent Mexican American and 6 percent African American. Per-pupil spending in Edgewood in the 1967–1968 academic year was $356, of which $26 was raised locally. Children in the Alamo Heights School District were more fortunate. Alamo Heights, whose *students were mostly white, spent $594 per pupil. The disparity was largely explained by differences in revenue from local property taxes. Although Edgewood assessed property at a higher rate than did Alamo Heights, the more affluent Alamo Heights District raised substantially more school funds from a lesser tax rate. In 1968 Rodriguez was among the children and parents living in the Edgewood Independent School District who filed suit against state and county government officials, arguing that public school funding in Texas violated the equal protection clause of the Fourteenth Amendment. A three-judge panel in the local federal district court found the public school system in Texas in violation of the Fourteenth Amendment. Texas appealed to the Supreme Court of the United States.*

While Rodriguez *was being litigated, the Supreme Court of California in* Serrano v. Priest *(CA 1971) declared that a similar scheme for funding public education violated the state constitution. Justice Sullivan's majority opinion concluded that a school district financing system that "makes the quality of a child's education depend upon the resources of his school district and . . . the pocketbook of his parents . . . is not necessary to the attainment of any compelling state interest" and "does not withstand the requisite 'strict scrutiny.'"*[40] *The plaintiffs in* Rodriguez *hoped that the Supreme Court of the United States would similarly conclude that under the equal protection clause, wealth was a suspect classification, education was a fundamental interest, and the Texas scheme for financing public education was unconstitutional.*

The Supreme Court reversed the district court by a 5–4 vote. Justice Powell's majority opinion insisted that school finance decisions raise the economic and social policy questions that require, in the post–New Deal world, substantial judicial deference. Was Powell as deferential as the justices in the Williamson v. Lee Optical *line of cases, or does* Rodriguez *suggest circumstances in which wealth and education might trigger greater judicial scrutiny? Justice Marshall's dissent rejects the claim that justices should either strictly scrutinize legislation or passively defer to the legislature. Instead, his opinion insists that justices should use a sliding scale when evaluating equal protection claims. Does Marshall's account correctly identify what the Burger Court was doing? Does this account correctly identify what the justices should do? How do the various opinions identify suspect classes and fundamental interests? What is the best understanding of suspect classes and fundamental interests under the equal protection clause?*

40. *Serrano v. Priest*, 5 Cal. 3rd 584 (1971).

JUSTICE POWELL delivered the opinion of the Court.

. . .

. . . [L]ack of personal resources has not occasioned an absolute deprivation of the desired benefit. The argument here is not that the children in districts having relatively low assessable property values are receiving no public education; rather, it is that they are receiving a poorer quality education than that available to children in districts having more assessable wealth. Apart from the unsettled and disputed question whether the quality of education may be determined by the amount of money expended for it, a sufficient answer to appellees' argument is that, at least where wealth is involved, the Equal Protection Clause does not require absolute equality or precisely equal advantages. Nor, indeed, in view of the infinite variables affecting the educational process, can any system assure equal quality of education except in the most relative sense. . . .

. . .

However described, it is clear that appellees' suit asks this Court to extend its most exacting scrutiny to review a system that allegedly discriminates against a large, diverse, and amorphous class, unified only by the common factor of residence in districts that happen to have less taxable wealth than other districts. The system of alleged discrimination and the class it defines have none of the traditional indicia of suspectness: the class is not saddled with such disabilities, or subjected to such a history of purposeful unequal treatment, or relegated to such a position of political powerlessness as to command extraordinary protection from the majoritarian political process.

. . .

. . . It is not the province of this Court to create substantive constitutional rights in the name of guaranteeing equal protection of the laws. Thus, the key to discovering whether education is "fundamental" is not to be found in comparisons of the relative societal significance of education as opposed to subsistence or housing. Nor is it to be found by weighing whether education is as important as the right to travel. Rather, the answer lies in assessing whether there is a right to education explicitly or implicitly guaranteed by the Constitution.

Education, of course, is not among the rights afforded explicit protection under our Federal Constitution. Nor do we find any basis for saying it is implicitly so protected. As we have said, the undisputed importance of education will not alone cause this Court to depart from the usual standard for reviewing a State's social and economic legislation. . . .

. . .

. . . [W]e stand on familiar ground when we continue to acknowledge that the Justices of this Court lack both the expertise and the familiarity with local problems so necessary to the making of wise decisions with respect to the raising and disposition of public revenues. Yet, we are urged to direct the States either to alter drastically the present system or to throw out the property tax altogether in favor of some other form of taxation. No scheme of taxation, whether the tax is imposed on property, income, or purchases of goods and services, has yet been devised which is free of all discriminatory impact. In such a complex arena in which no perfect alternatives exist, the Court does well not to impose too rigorous a standard of scrutiny lest all local fiscal schemes become subjects of criticism under the Equal Protection Clause.

. . .

. . . We are unwilling to assume for ourselves a level of wisdom superior to that of legislators, scholars, and educational authorities in 50 States, especially where the alternatives proposed are only recently conceived and nowhere yet tested. The constitutional standard under the Equal Protection Clause is whether the challenged state action rationally furthers a legitimate state purpose or interest. We hold that the Texas plan abundantly satisfies this standard.

. . .

JUSTICE STEWART, concurring. . . .

JUSTICE BRENNAN, dissenting. . . .

JUSTICE WHITE, with whom JUSTICE DOUGLAS and JUSTICE BRENNAN join, dissenting.

. . .

The Equal Protection Clause permits discriminations between classes but requires that the classification bear some rational relationship to a permissible object sought to be attained by the statute. It is not enough that the Texas system before us seeks to achieve the valid, rational purpose of maximizing local initiative; the means chosen by the State must also be rationally related to the end sought to be achieved. . . .

Neither Texas nor the majority heeds this rule. If the State aims at maximizing local initiative and local choice, by permitting school districts to resort to the real property tax if they choose to do so, it utterly fails in achieving its purpose in districts with property tax bases so low that there is little if any opportunity for interested parents, rich or poor, to augment school district revenues. . . .

. . .

JUSTICE MARSHALL, with whom JUSTICE DOUGLAS concurs, dissenting.

. . .

I must once more voice my disagreement with the Court's rigidified approach to equal protection analysis. The Court apparently seeks to establish today that equal protection cases fall into one of two neat categories which dictate the appropriate standard of review—strict scrutiny or mere rationality. But this Court's decisions in the field of equal protection defy such easy categorization. A principled reading of what this Court has done reveals that it has applied a spectrum of standards in reviewing discrimination allegedly violative of the Equal Protection Clause. This spectrum clearly comprehends variations in the degree of care with which the Court will scrutinize particular classifications, depending, I believe, on the constitutional and societal importance of the interest adversely affected and the recognized invidiousness of the basis upon which the particular classification is drawn. . . .

. . .

. . . In the context of economic interests, we find that discriminatory state action is almost always sustained, for such interests are generally far removed from constitutional guarantees. . . . But the situation differs markedly when discrimination against important individual interests with constitutional implications and against particularly disadvantaged or powerless classes is involved. The majority suggests, however, that a variable standard of review would give this Court the appearance of a "superlegislature." I cannot agree. Such an approach seems to me a part of the guarantees of our Constitution and of the historic experiences with oppression of and discrimination against discrete, powerless minorities which underlie that document. In truth, the Court itself will be open to the criticism raised by the majority so long as it continues on its present course of effectively selecting in private which cases will be afforded special consideration without acknowledging the true basis of its action. . . .

. . .

. . . The opportunity for formal education may not necessarily be the essential determinant of an individual's ability to enjoy throughout his life the rights of free speech and association guaranteed to him by the First Amendment. But such an opportunity may enhance the individual's enjoyment of those rights, not only during but also following school attendance. . . . Education serves the essential function of instilling in our young an understanding of and appreciation for the principles and operation of our governmental processes. Education may instill the interest and provide the tools necessary for political discourse and debate. Indeed, it has frequently been suggested that education is the dominant factor affecting political consciousness and participation. . . .

. . .

The Court seeks solace for its action today in the possibility of legislative reform. The Court's suggestions of legislative redress and experimentation will doubtless be of great comfort to the schoolchildren of Texas' disadvantaged districts, but considering the vested interests of wealthy school districts in the preservation of the status quo, they are worth little more. The possibility of legislative action is, in all events, no answer to this Court's duty under the Constitution to eliminate unjustified state discrimination. . . .

B. Race

The political coalitions responsible for *Brown v. Board of Education* (1954) and the Civil Rights Act of 1964 splintered during the 1970s. General agreement existed that the liberal decisions striking down Jim Crow were constitutionally correct. By the middle of the 1970s attacks on *Brown* and the Civil Rights Act had disappeared from both public and private discourse. In practice both were treated as being as sacred constitutionally as the commerce clause. Constitutional fights now took place over the meaning of *Brown*. More moderate liberals insisted that Great Society measures had largely cured racial problems in the United States. As long as Americans remained committed to the antidiscrimination principles set out in *Brown* and the Civil Rights Act of 1964, racial equality would soon be achieved. More progressive liberals insisted that *Brown* and the Civil Rights Act of 1964 merely began the process by which the United States might become a more egalitarian society. Aggressive, often-race-conscious measures were necessary to eradicate the legacy of Jim Crow.

These racial issues slowly began to realign American politics. Progressive Democrats insisted that racial matters were getting worse, not better. Hubert Humphrey in 1975 informed the Senate that "segregation is spreading out over more and more central cities and even some inner suburbs are being absorbed into growing ghettos."[41] The Nixon administration maintained that the civil rights decisions of the 1960s had largely ended the reign of Jim Crow and that only a few mopping-up operations were necessary to complete that process. Nixon in 1972 declared that "dismantling the old dual school system . . . has now been substantially completed."[42]

The gradual hardening of party positions influenced the composition of each political coalition. By 1980 African Americans had become the most loyal Democratic Party members in the country. The once solidly Democratic South was now starkly divided between African American Democrats and an increasing number of white Republicans. Many working-class white Democrats in the North frequently crossed party lines to support Republicans who attacked affirmative action or welfare programs whose primary beneficiaries were perceived, usually incorrectly, as being persons of color.

The constitutional politics of race became national and partisan when NAACP lawyers attempted to integrate northern schools and federal judges attempted to implement *Brown* by busing students across metropolitan areas. Bitter controversies broke out, particularly when district judges ordered busing when implementing the Supreme Court's directive in *Green v. County School Board of New Kent County* (1968) to actively integrate schools. Busing plans were particularly common in and around cities. Patterns of residential segregation in urban America usually reinforced school segregation, even after the legal supports for school segregation had been removed. Some white Americans objected to busing because they objected to racially integrated schools. Others expressed concerns about the integrity of the local neighborhood school. Many complained that courts drew plans that

41. *Congressional Record*, 94th Cong., 1st Sess. (September 26, 1973), 30543.

42. Richard Nixon, *Public Papers of the Presidents of the United States* (Washington, D.C.: Government Printing Office, 1973), 425.

wreaked havoc on lower-middle-class white communities while largely immunizing more affluent communities from the costs of desegregation. President Nixon, in a special message to Congress on March 17, 1972, spoke for many Americans when he asserted, "A remedy for the historic evil of racial discrimination has often created a new evil of disrupting communities and imposing hardship on children—both black and white—who are themselves wholly innocent of the wrongs that the plan seeks to set right."[43]

The Supreme Court in the 1970s made a series of decisions that both sanctioned and limited busing as a tool for integrating school districts. The initial judicial decisions suggested that courts were prepared to make aggressive use of busing to secure racial equality. *Swann v. Charlotte-Mecklenburg Board of Education* (1971) ruled that federal courts could remedy *Brown* violations by busing children to any school within the offending school district. *Keyes v. School District No. 1, Denver, Colorado* (1973), the first northern school desegregation case the justices considered, held that courts could order busing throughout a large metropolitan school district after finding evidence of intentional segregation in one part of that district. The more moderate justices on the Burger Court, however, almost immediately began restraining lower federal court justices. *Milliken v. Bradley* (1974) ruled that courts could not order an interdistrict remedy for *Brown* violations unless those violations took place in both school districts. *Pasadena City Board of Education v. Spangler* (1976) held that remedies for school segregation need not be adjusted for demographic changes that recreated racial imbalances as long as these demographic changes were not caused by *Brown* violations. As many northern white families fled the cities for the suburbs, the combination of *Milliken* and *Pasadena* meant that federal judges could order busing only between inner-city public schools, an increasing number of which had very few white students.

Busing decisions reflected the distinction that the justices drew between de jure and de facto discrimination. De jure discrimination occurs when government officials pass laws or make decisions that explicitly separate children by race. Burger Court majorities ruled that federal courts could impose a variety of intrusive and creative remedies within any school district that had engaged in de jure segregation. De facto segregation occurs when private citizens choose not to associate with members of other races. Burger Court majorities ruled that federal courts had no authority to interfere with the consequences of de facto segregation. While the theoretical difference between de jure and de facto discrimination may be clear, distinguishing between them in practice is difficult. Most school cases in the 1970s required lengthy and expensive hearings in which lower court justices attempted to figure out whether the unbalanced racial composition of a school was the result of state practices or private prejudices.

Great Society liberals combined strong antidiscrimination rhetoric with the belief that various forms of affirmative action should be taken to promote increased representation of persons of color in education, employment, and politics. During the 1970s this concern for affirmative action hardened into various policies that specifically required school admissions officers and employers to take race into account when making decisions. The Nixon administration often aggressively insisted that employers hire targeted numbers of minorities. In part this reflected the continued commitment among many Republicans to a strong version of racial equality. Cynics pointed out that the Nixon administration was using affirmative action to divide traditional white, ethnic, Democratic voters from persons of color. White ethnic groups and trade groups became key opponents of affirmative action in the 1970s but were later replaced by more ideologically motivated organizations.

Four years later the Supreme Court by a series of 5–4 votes in *Regents of the University of California v. Bakke* (1978) attempted to split the difference on affirmative action. That case held:

- State affirmative action plans had to satisfy the same strict scrutiny standard as discrimination against persons of color
- Educational diversity was a compelling government interest that justified affirmative action, but affirmative action was not justified as a remedy for general societal discrimination
- Affirmative action plans could give applicants of color a "plus" but could not establish strict quotas

The justices in *Fullilove v. Klutznick* (1980) further muddied the affirmative action waters by suggesting that federal affirmative action plans might have to satisfy a lesser and not well-defined constitutional standard.

43. *Congressional Record*, 92nd Cong., 2nd Sess. (March 17, 1972), 8844.

In evaluating whether a person had been the victim of racial discrimination, constitutional decision makers in the 1970s rejected the notion that a "disparate impact" across racial groups was enough to establish a constitutional violation. Instead, they found race discrimination only when states either explicitly made nonremedial race-based classifications or when an ostensibly neutral state law had both a racial purpose and a racially disparate effect. *Palmer v. Thompson* (1971) ruled that a racial purpose was not sufficient to find discrimination in the absence of a racially disparate effect. This case arose after Jackson, Mississippi, closed all public pools rather than obey a court order requiring integration. Justice Black's majority opinion asserted, "[This is] not a case where a city is maintaining different sets of facilities for blacks and whites and forcing the races to remain separate in recreational or educational activities." *Washington v. Davis* (1976) ruled that a racially disparate effect was not sufficient to find discrimination in the absence of a racial purpose. Justice White maintained that "discriminatory impact" could be used to prove discriminatory purpose, but only when the state could not provide a race-neutral justification for the disparate result. This requirement is difficult to meet. In *Village of Arlington Heights v. Metropolitan Housing Development Corp.* (1977) a Burger Court majority indicated that persons of color would have trouble proving that longstanding single-family zoning regulations violated the equal protection clause. After noting that "official action will not be held unconstitutional solely because it results in a racially disproportionate impact," Justice Powell's majority opinion concluded that "the Village originally adopted its buffer policy long before [plaintiffs] entered the picture and has applied the policy too consistently for us to infer discriminatory purpose from its application in this case."

Swann v. Charlotte-Mecklenburg Board of Education, 402 U.S. 1 (1971)

The Charlotte-Mecklenburg school system was segregated by race prior to Brown. *The system remained largely racially segregated during the first decade after* Brown, *despite various court orders. The majority of the district's black students attended nearly all-black schools. Most of the black student population and the all-black schools were located inside the city of Charlotte. Most of the white population and the all-white schools were located in the outlying suburbs. Dissatisfied with the pace of desegregation, James E. Swann and other African American parents in 1965 brought a lawsuit against the Charlotte-Mecklenburg Board of Education. While the litigation was pending in the federal courts, the Supreme Court decided* Green v. County School Board of New Kent County *(1968). In light of that case's ruling that formally segregated schools districts must "convert to a unitary system in which racial discrimination [is] eliminated root and branch," U.S. District Judge James McMillan adopted a plan that redrew the attendance zones for each school, reassigned teachers to achieve a racial balance across schools, and bused students to achieve more equal racial balances in individual schools. Most controversially, Judge McMillan paired schools in all-white neighborhoods with schools in virtually all-black neighborhoods, with the result being that many children had to undergo lengthy bus rides before reaching their assigned school. The Court of Appeals for the Fourth Circuit sustained Judge McMillan's plan to desegregate high schools but rejected his plan to desegregate elementary schools. Both Swann and the Charlotte-Mecklenburg Board of Education appealed to the Supreme Court.*

The Supreme Court unanimously sustained Judge's McMillan's plan to desegregate schools in Charlotte-Mecklenburg. Chief Justice Burger's unanimous opinion cautiously approved the busing of children and the use of race in determining school assignments as a means for integrating schools that had been unconstitutionally segregated. The deliberations within the Court revealed important latent divisions that soon became public. Chief Justice Burger thought that Swann *limited busing. Other justices endorsed the* Swann *opinion because they approved of busing and race classifications as a remedy for past segregation. What limits, if any, do you believe that* Swann *places on remedies designed to desegregate schools? What limits do you believe the Constitution places on that process?*

The Court in Swann *was willing to bus schoolchildren between cities and suburbs only because all were part of one large school district. Three years later, the Supreme Court rejected a similar remedy because the city of Detroit and the Detroit suburbs had separate school districts. Chief Justice Burger declared, "The constitutional right of the Negro respondents residing in Detroit is to attend a unitary school system in that district. Unless petitioners drew the district lines in a discriminatory fashion, or arranged for white students residing in the Detroit District to attend schools in Oakland and Macomb Counties, they were under no constitutional duty to make provisions for Negro students to do so."*

CHIEF JUSTICE BURGER delivered the opinion of the Court.

. . .

The objective today remains to eliminate from the public schools all vestiges of state-imposed segregation. Segregation was the evil struck down by *Brown I* (1954) as contrary to the equal protection guarantees of the Constitution. That was the violation sought to be corrected by the remedial measures of *Brown II* (1955). That was the basis for the holding in *Green* (1968) that school authorities are "clearly charged with the affirmative duty to take whatever steps might be necessary to convert to a unitary system in which racial discrimination would be eliminated root and branch."

. . .

. . . In addition to the classic pattern of building schools specifically intended for Negro or white students, school authorities have sometimes, since *Brown*, closed schools which appeared likely to become racially mixed through changes in neighborhood residential patterns. This was sometimes accompanied by building new schools in the areas of white suburban expansion farthest from Negro population centers in order to maintain the separation of the races with a minimum departure from the formal principles of "neighborhood zoning." Such a policy does more than simply influence the short-run composition of the student body of a new school. It may well promote segregated residential patterns which, when combined with "neighborhood zoning," further lock the school system into the mold of separation of the races. Upon a proper showing a district court may consider this in fashioning a remedy.

In ascertaining the existence of legally imposed school segregation, the existence of a pattern of school construction and abandonment is thus a factor of great weight. In devising remedies where legally imposed segregation has been established, it is the responsibility of local authorities and district courts to see to it that future school construction and abandonment are not used and do not serve to perpetuate or re-establish the dual system. When necessary, district courts should retain jurisdiction to assure that these responsibilities are carried out.

. . .

Our objective in dealing with the issues presented by these cases is to see that school authorities exclude no pupil of a racial minority from any school, directly or indirectly, on account of race; it does not and cannot embrace all the problems of racial prejudice, even when those problems contribute to disproportionate racial concentrations in some schools.

. . .

. . . If we were to read the holding of the District Court to require, as a matter of substantive constitutional right, any particular degree of racial balance or mixing, that approach would be disapproved and we would be obliged to reverse. The constitutional command to desegregate schools does not mean that every school in every community must always reflect the racial composition of the school system as a whole.

. . .

As we said in *Green*, a school authority's remedial plan or a district court's remedial decree is to be judged by its effectiveness. Awareness of the racial composition of the whole school system is likely to be a useful starting point in shaping a remedy to correct past constitutional violations. In sum, the very limited use made of mathematical ratios [for assignments of students to individual schools] was within the equitable remedial discretion of the District Court.

. . .

The record in this case reveals the familiar phenomenon that in metropolitan areas minority groups are often found concentrated in one part of the city. In some circumstances certain schools may remain all or largely of one race until new schools can be provided or neighborhood patterns change. Schools all or predominately of one race in a district of mixed population will require close scrutiny to determine that school assignments are not part of state-enforced segregation.

In light of the above, it should be clear that the existence of some small number of one-race, or virtually one-race, schools within a district is not in and of itself the mark of a system that still practices segregation by law. . . .

An optional majority-to-minority transfer provision has long been recognized as a useful part of every desegregation plan. Provision for optional transfer of those in the majority racial group of a particular school to other schools where they will be in the minority is an indispensable remedy for those students willing to transfer to other schools in order to lessen the impact on them of the state-imposed stigma of segregation. . . .

. . .

Absent a constitutional violation there would be no basis for judicially ordering assignment of students on a racial basis. All things being equal, with no history of discrimination, it might well be desirable to assign pupils to schools nearest their homes. But all things are not equal in a system that has been deliberately constructed and maintained to enforce racial segregation. The remedy for such segregation may be administratively awkward, inconvenient, and even bizarre in some situations and may impose burdens on some; but all awkwardness and inconvenience cannot be avoided in the interim period when remedial adjustments are being made to eliminate the dual school systems.

No fixed or even substantially fixed guidelines can be established as to how far a court can go, but it must be recognized that there are limits. The objective is to dismantle the dual school system. "Racially neutral" assignment plans proposed by school authorities to a district court may be inadequate; such plans may fail to counteract the continuing effects of past school segregation resulting from discriminatory location of school sites or distortion of school size in order to achieve or maintain an artificial racial separation. . . .

. . .

The decree provided that the buses used to implement the plan would operate on direct routes. Students would be picked up at schools near their homes and transported to the schools they were to attend. The trips for elementary school pupils average about seven miles and the District Court found that they would take "not over 35 minutes at the most." This system compares favorably with the transportation plan previously operated in Charlotte under which each day 23,600 students on all grade levels were transported an average of 15 miles one way for an average trip requiring over an hour. In these circumstances, we find no basis for holding that the local school authorities may not be required to employ bus transportation as one tool of school desegregation. Desegregation plans cannot be limited to the walk-in school.

. . .

It does not follow that the communities served by such systems will remain demographically stable, for in a growing, mobile society, few will do so. Neither school authorities nor district courts are constitutionally required to make year-by-year adjustments of the racial composition of student bodies once the affirmative duty to desegregate has been accomplished and racial discrimination through official action is eliminated from the system. This does not mean that federal courts are without power to deal with future problems; but in the absence of a showing that either the school authorities or some other agency of the State has deliberately attempted to fix or alter demographic patterns to affect the racial composition of the schools, further intervention by a district court should not be necessary. . . .

Executive and Legislative Attacks on Busing

Judicial decisions mandating busing as a remedy for desegregation were unpopular. Working-class whites, upset by both the prospect of desegregation and the class bias of many busing orders, fought court orders by rioting, removing their children from public schools, and supporting conservative politicians who promised to stand up to liberal justices. Massive resistance occurred on a national scale. Some of the most violent protests over busing took place in Boston, the capital of the only state to vote for George McGovern in 1972.[44] *President Nixon proposed that Congress prohibit courts from ordering busing as a remedy for segregation except under extraordinary circumstances. Congressional liberals, concerned with the establishment of precedents that would limit judicial power, defeated these measures. Instead, elected officials concerned with existing remedies for desegregation frequently united on such measures as the Eagleton-Biden Amendment, which forbade the Department of Health, Education, and Welfare from using federal funds to facilitate busing.* Brown v. Califano *(1980) sustained that measure.*

President Nixon and Senator Humphrey of Minnesota had very different beliefs about race relations in the United States. Nixon insisted that Jim Crow had largely been abolished. Humphrey claimed that segregation was on the rise. Do these differences explain their different perspectives on busing and congressional power, or did each have a fundamentally different constitutional understanding of race?

44. See J. Harvie Wilkinson III, *From* Brown *to* Bakke: *The Supreme Court and School Integration: 1954–1978* (New York: Oxford University Press, 1979), 131–249.

Richard Nixon, Special Message to the Congress on Equal Educational Opportunities and School Busing (March 17, 1972)[45]

. . .

There is no escaping the fact that some people oppose busing because of racial prejudice. But to go on from this to conclude that "anti-busing" is simply a code word for prejudice is an exercise in arrant unreason. There are right reasons for opposing busing, and there are wrong reasons—and most people, including large and increasing numbers of blacks and other minorities, oppose it for reasons that have little or nothing to do with race. It would compound an injustice to persist in massive busing simply because some people oppose it for the wrong reasons.

. . .

. . . [I]n the past 3 years, progress toward eliminating the vestiges of the dual system has been phenomenal—and so too has been the shift in public attitudes in those areas where dual systems were formerly operated. In State after State and community after community, local civic, business and educational leaders of all races have come forward to help make the transition peacefully and successfully. Few voices are now raised urging a return to the old patterns of enforced segregation.

. . .

At the same time, there has been a marked shift in the focus of concerns by blacks and members of other minorities. Minority parents have long had a deep and special concern with improving the quality of their children's education. For a number of years, the principal emphasis of this concern—and of the Nation's attention—was on desegregating the schools. Now that the dismantling of the old dual system has been substantially completed there is once again a far greater balance of emphasis on improving schools, on convenience, on the chance for parental involvement—in short, on the same concerns that motivate white parents—and, in many communities, on securing a greater measure of control over schools that serve primarily minority-group communities. Moving forward on desegregation is still important but the principal concern is with preserving the principle, and with ensuring that the great gains made since *Brown,* and particularly in recent years, are not rolled back in a reaction against excessive busing. Many black leaders now express private concern, moreover, that a reckless extension of busing requirements could bring about precisely the results they fear most: a reaction that would undo those gains, and that would begin the unraveling of advances in other areas that also are based on newly expanded interpretations of basic Constitutional rights.

Also, it has not escaped their notice that those who insist on system-wide racial balance insist on a condition in which, in most communities, every school would be run by whites and dominated by whites, with blacks in a permanent minority—and without escape from that minority status. The result would be to deny blacks the right to have schools in which they are the majority.

. . .

As we cut through the clouds of emotionalism that surround the busing question, we can begin to identify the legitimate issues.

Concern for the quality of education a child gets is legitimate.

Concern that there be no retreat from the principle of ending racial discrimination is legitimate.

Concern for the distance a child has to travel to get to school is legitimate.

Hubert Humphrey, Senate Retreats from Equal Opportunity (1975)[46]

Mr. President, the U.S. Senate has dealt a severe blow to the hopes of millions of fellow Americans by its action to limit and curtail the use of Federal funds for the transportation of students by reason of race.

. . .

. . . Congress is saying that the only available way to integrate most urban schools is wrong and illegitimate. The action can only encourage supporters of segregation and increase the already immense pressures on the Federal courts.

Instead of providing aid to help make a difficult transition work better, Congress is taking the posture of State legislatures in the 1950s, striking out in every possible way to remove financial and administrative resources to support the process. This will not stop the courts from implementing constitutional

45. *Congressional Record,* 92nd Cong., 2nd Sess. (March 17, 1972), 8844.

46. *Congressional Record,* 94th Cong., 1st Sess., 1975, 30, 542–43.

requirements, but will intensify the atmosphere of racial polarization surrounding the change and minimize the chances of carefully planned desegregation.

. . .

While Congress rails against school desegregation, no one gives much notice to the fact that the grim predictions of the "[Kerner] Commission" about 7 years ago[47] are coming true, perhaps even faster than the Commission foresaw in some of the largest metropolitan areas. Segregation is spreading out over more and more central cities and even some inner suburbs are being absorbed into growing ghettos. . . . In the face of these powerful segregating trends and the growing evidence that State action played a major role in setting them in motion, a decision to prohibit administrative enforcement of desegregation is a decision for intensifying segregation. Our cities are moving steadily toward a level of segregation and inequality that can only have terrifying consequences for American Society. . . .

Regents of the University of California v. Bakke, 438 U.S. 265 (1978)

Alan Bakke was a Marine captain in Vietnam and an engineer. His lifelong ambition was to be a doctor. In 1973 he was rejected by all twelve medical schools to which he applied. One of those institutions was the University of California, Davis. Davis had just instituted a program in which sixteen of the one hundred seats in the entering class were committed to students of color. Bakke, whose grades and board scores were considerably higher than the average of those persons admitted under the special program, sued the university, claiming that the special program violated the Fourteenth Amendment. The trial court rejected his contentions, but that decision was reversed by the Supreme Court of California. The university appealed to the Supreme Court of the United States.

The Supreme Court by a 5–4 vote declared that Davis had unconstitutionally discriminated against Bakke. Justice Powell's crucial opinion for the Court insisted that all racial classifications must satisfy a strict scrutiny standard, that diversity was the only government interest in Bakke *that met that standard, and that diversity could justify only racial preferences as opposed to racial quotas. No other justice on the court drew these fine distinctions. Four justices insisted that "benign" racial classifications that were designed to assist previously disadvantaged groups rather than harm discrete and insular minorities need meet only a lesser judicial standard. The other four justices limited their analysis to a statutory question. Powell's opinion nevertheless became the official law of the land because he was the median justice on all issues. Powell maintained that all race-conscious laws must meet strict scrutiny. Why did he make that claim? Why did other justices disagree? Who was correct? Powell also maintained that diversity is the best and only justification for affirmative action. Is that correct? Given the pervasiveness of racial discrimination in the United States, could any public institution make a good case that past practices had skewed their admissions or hiring processes, leaving them with some obligation to compensate for past practices? Do all or the overwhelming majority of white persons in the United States benefit from these processes because they are white? Does affirmative action ignore the numerous ways in which many persons are disadvantaged? Why did Powell differentiate between quotas and the "plus" system? Is that distinction sound in theory? Is that distinction sound in practice, or will schools adjust pluses to obtain a fairly fixed number of students of color?*

JUSTICE POWELL announced the judgment of the Court.

. . .

The guarantees of the Fourteenth Amendment extend to all persons. Its language is explicit: "No State shall . . . deny to any person within its jurisdiction the equal protection of the laws." It is settled beyond question that the rights created by the first section of the Fourteenth Amendment are, by its terms, guaranteed to the individual. . . . The guarantee of equal protection cannot mean one thing when applied to one individual and something else when applied to a person of another color. If both are not accorded the same protection, then it is not equal.

Nevertheless, petitioner argues that the court below erred in applying strict scrutiny to the special admissions program because white males, such as respondent, are not a "discrete and insular minority" requiring extraordinary protection from the majoritarian political process. . . . This rationale, however,

47. This report warned that the nation was "moving toward two societies, one black, one white—separate and unequal." National Advisory Commission on Civil Disorders, *Report of the Advisory Commission on Civil Disorders* (Washington, DC: Government Printing Office, 1968).

has never been invoked in our decisions as a prerequisite to subjecting racial or ethnic distinctions to strict scrutiny. . . . Racial and ethnic classifications . . . are subject to stringent examination without regard to these additional characteristics. . . .

. . .

Although many of the Framers of the Fourteenth Amendment conceived of its primary function as bridging the vast distance between members of the Negro race and the white "majority," . . . the Amendment itself was framed in universal terms, without reference to color, ethnic origin, or condition of prior servitude. . . . [T]he 39th Congress was intent upon establishing in the federal law a broader principle than would have been necessary simply to meet the particular and immediate plight of the newly freed Negro slaves. . . .

. . .

. . . [T]he difficulties entailed in varying the level of judicial review according to a perceived "preferred" status of a particular racial or ethnic minority are intractable. The concepts of "majority" and "minority" necessarily reflect temporary arrangements and political judgments. . . . [T]he white "majority" itself is composed of various minority groups, most of which can lay claim to a history of prior discrimination at the hands of the State and private individuals. . . . There is no principled basis for deciding which groups would merit "heightened judicial solicitude" and which would not. . . .

. . . [T]here are serious problems of justice connected with the idea of preference itself. First, it may not always be clear that a so-called preference is, in fact, benign. . . . Nothing in the Constitution supports the notion that individuals may be asked to suffer otherwise impermissible burdens in order to enhance the societal standing of their ethnic groups. Second, preferential programs may only reinforce common stereotypes holding that certain groups are unable to achieve success without special protection based on a factor having no relationship to individual worth. . . . Third, there is a measure of inequity in forcing innocent persons in respondent's position to bear the burdens of redressing grievances not of their making.

. . .

We have held that, in order to justify the use of a suspect classification, a State must show that its purpose or interest is both constitutionally permissible and substantial and that its use of the classification is "necessary . . . to the accomplishment" of its purpose or the safeguarding of its interest. . . . The special admissions program purports to serve the purposes of: (i) "reducing the historic deficit of traditionally disfavored minorities in medical schools and in the medical profession" . . . ; (ii) countering the effects of societal discrimination; (iii) increasing the number of physicians who will practice in communities currently underserved; and (iv) obtaining the educational benefits that flow from an ethnically diverse student body. It is necessary to decide which, if any, of these purposes is substantial enough to support the use of a suspect classification.

If petitioner's purpose is to assure within its student body some specified percentage of a particular group merely because of its race or ethnic origin, such a preferential purpose must be rejected not as insubstantial, but as facially invalid. Preferring members of any one group for no reason other than race or ethnic origin is discrimination for its own sake. This the Constitution forbids. . . .

. . .

We have never approved a classification that aids persons perceived as members of relatively victimized groups at the expense of other innocent individuals in the absence of judicial, legislative, or administrative findings of constitutional or statutory violations. . . . After such findings have been made, the governmental interest in preferring members of the injured groups at the expense of others is substantial, since the legal rights of the victims must be vindicated. . . . Without such findings of constitutional or statutory violations, it cannot be said that the government has any greater interest in helping one individual than in refraining from harming another. Thus, the government has no compelling justification for inflicting such harm.

. . .

Petitioner identifies, as another purpose of its program, improving the delivery of health care services to communities currently underserved. It may be assumed that, in some situations, a State's interest in facilitating the health care of its citizens is sufficiently compelling to support the use of a suspect classification. But there is virtually no evidence in the record indicating that petitioner's special admissions program is either needed or geared to promote that goal. . . .

. . .

The fourth goal asserted by petitioner is the attainment of a diverse student body. This clearly is a constitutionally permissible goal for an institution of higher education. Academic freedom, though not a specifically enumerated constitutional right, long has been viewed as a special concern of the First Amendment. . . .

The atmosphere of "speculation, experiment and creation"—so essential to the quality of higher education—is widely believed to be promoted by a diverse student body. . . . [I]t is not too much to say that the "nation's future depends upon leaders trained through wide exposure" to the ideas and mores of students as diverse as this Nation of many peoples.

. . .

Physicians serve a heterogeneous population. An otherwise qualified medical student with a particular background—whether it be ethnic, geographic, culturally advantaged or disadvantaged—may bring to a professional school of medicine experiences, outlooks, and ideas that enrich the training of its student body and better equip its graduates to render with understanding their vital service to humanity.

. . .

It may be assumed that the reservation of a specified number of seats in each class for individuals from the preferred ethnic groups would contribute to the attainment of considerable ethnic diversity in the student body. But petitioner's argument that this is the only effective means of serving the interest of diversity is seriously flawed. . . . The diversity that furthers a compelling state interest encompasses a far broader array of qualifications and characteristics, of which racial or ethnic origin is but a single, though important, element. Petitioner's special admissions program, focused solely on ethnic diversity, would hinder, rather than further, attainment of genuine diversity.

. . . The experience of other university admissions programs, which take race into account in achieving the educational diversity valued by the First Amendment, demonstrates that the assignment of a fixed number of places to a minority group is not a necessary means toward that end. . . . In such an admissions program, race or ethnic background may be deemed a "plus" in a particular applicant's file, yet it does not insulate the individual from comparison with all other candidates for the available seats. The file of a particular black applicant may be examined for his potential contribution to diversity without the factor of race being decisive when compared, for example, with that of an applicant identified as an Italian-American if the latter is thought to exhibit qualities more likely to promote beneficial educational pluralism. Such qualities could include exceptional personal talents, unique work or service experience, leadership potential, maturity, demonstrated compassion, a history of overcoming disadvantage, ability to communicate with the poor, or other qualifications deemed important. In short, an admissions program operated in this way is flexible enough to consider all pertinent elements of diversity in light of the particular qualifications of each applicant, and to place them on the same footing for consideration, although not necessarily according them the same weight. . . .

This kind of program treats each applicant as an individual in the admissions process. The applicant who loses out on the last available seat to another candidate receiving a "plus" on the basis of ethnic background will not have been foreclosed from all consideration for that seat simply because he was not the right color or had the wrong surname. It would mean only that his combined qualifications, which may have included similar nonobjective factors, did not outweigh those of the other applicant. . . .

. . .

JUSTICE BRENNAN, JUSTICE WHITE, JUSTICE MARSHALL, and JUSTICE BLACKMUN, concurring in the judgment in part and dissenting in part.

. . . Government may take race into account when it acts not to demean or insult any racial group, but to remedy disadvantages cast on minorities by past racial prejudice, at least when appropriate findings have been made by judicial, legislative, or administrative bodies with competence to act in this area.

. . .

The Fourteenth Amendment, the embodiment in the Constitution of our abiding belief in human equality, has been the law of our land for only slightly more than half its 200 years. And for half of that half, the Equal Protection Clause of the Amendment was largely moribund. . . . Worse than desuetude, the Clause was early turned against those whom it was intended to set free, condemning them to a "separate but equal" status before the law, a status always separate but seldom equal. Not until 1954—only 24 years ago—was this odious doctrine interred by our decision in *Brown v. Board of Education* (1954). . . . Even then, inequality was not eliminated with "all deliberate speed." . . . Against this background, claims that law must be "colorblind" or that the datum of race is no longer relevant to public policy must be seen as aspiration, rather than as description of reality. This is not to denigrate aspiration; for reality rebukes us that race has too often been used by those who would stigmatize and oppress minorities. Yet we cannot—and, as we shall demonstrate, need not under our Constitution . . . let color blindness become myopia which masks the reality that many "created equal" have been treated within our lifetimes as inferior both by the law and by their fellow citizens.

. . .

Unquestionably we have held that a government practice or statute which restricts "fundamental rights" or which contains "suspect classifications" is to be subjected to "strict scrutiny," and can be justified only if it furthers a compelling government purpose and, even then, only if no less restrictive alternative is available. . . . But no fundamental right is involved here. . . . Nor do whites, as a class, have any of the traditional indicia of suspectness: the class is not saddled with such disabilities, or subjected to such a history of purposeful unequal treatment, or relegated to such a position of political powerlessness as to command extraordinary protection from the majoritarian political process. . . . Nor has anyone suggested that the University's purposes contravene the cardinal principle that racial classifications that stigmatize—because they are drawn on the presumption that one race is inferior to another or because they put the weight of government behind racial hatred and separatism—are invalid without more. . . .

. . .

. . . [A] number of considerations . . . lead us to conclude that racial classifications designed to further remedial purposes "'must serve important governmental objectives, and must be substantially related to achievement of those objectives.'" . . . First, race, like, "gender-based classifications, too often [has] been inexcusably utilized to stereotype and stigmatize politically powerless segments of society." While a carefully tailored statute designed to remedy past discrimination could avoid these vices, . . . we nonetheless have recognized that the line between honest and thoughtful appraisal of the effects of past discrimination and paternalistic stereotyping is not so clear, and that a statute based on the latter is patently capable of stigmatizing all women with a badge of inferiority. . . . State programs designed ostensibly to ameliorate the effects of past racial discrimination obviously create the same hazard of stigma, since they may promote racial separatism and reinforce the views of those who believe that members of racial minorities are inherently incapable of succeeding on their own. . . .

Second, race, like gender and illegitimacy . . . is an immutable characteristic which its possessors are powerless to escape or set aside. . . . [S]uch divisions are contrary to our deep belief that "legal burdens should bear some relationship to individual responsibility or wrongdoing," . . . and that advancement sanctioned, sponsored, or approved by the State should ideally be based on individual merit or achievement, or at the least on factors within the control of an individual. . . .

. . .

Davis' articulated purpose of remedying the effects of past societal discrimination is, under our cases, sufficiently important to justify the use of race-conscious admissions programs where there is a sound basis for concluding that minority underrepresentation is substantial and chronic, and that the handicap of past discrimination is impeding access of minorities to the Medical School.

. . .

Certainly, on the basis of the undisputed factual submissions before this Court, Davis had a sound basis for believing that the problem of underrepresentation of minorities was substantial and chronic, and that the problem was attributable to handicaps imposed on minority applicants by past and present racial discrimination. Until at least 1973, the practice of medicine in this country was, in fact, if not in law, largely the prerogative of whites. In 1950, for example, while Negroes constituted 10% of the total population, Negro physicians constituted only 2.2% of the total number of physicians. The overwhelming majority of these, moreover, were educated in two predominantly Negro medical schools, Howard and Meharry. By 1970, the gap between the proportion of Negroes in medicine and their proportion in the population had widened: the number of Negroes employed in medicine remained frozen at 2.2%, while the Negro population had increased to 11.1%. The number of Negro admittees to predominantly white medical schools, moreover, had declined in absolute numbers during the years 1955 to 1964.

. . .

Davis clearly could conclude that the serious and persistent underrepresentation of minorities in medicine depicted by these statistics is the result of handicaps under which minority applicants labor as a consequence of a background of deliberate, purposeful discrimination against minorities in education and in society generally, as well as in the medical profession. From the inception of our national life, Negroes have been subjected to unique legal disabilities impairing access to equal educational opportunity. Under slavery, penal sanctions were imposed upon anyone attempting to educate Negroes. After enactment of the Fourteenth Amendment the States continued to deny Negroes equal educational opportunity, enforcing a strict policy of segregation that itself stamped Negroes as inferior, ... that relegated minorities to inferior educational institutions, and that denied them intercourse in the mainstream of professional life necessary to advancement. ... [M]assive official and private resistance [to *Brown* and related decisions] prevented, and to a lesser extent still prevents, attainment of equal opportunity in education at all levels and in the professions. The generation of minority students applying to Davis Medical School since it opened in 1968—most of whom were born before or about the time *Brown I* was decided—clearly have been victims of this discrimination. ... [T]he conclusion is inescapable that applicants to medical school must be few indeed who endured the effects of *de jure* segregation, the resistance to *Brown I*, or the equally debilitating pervasive private discrimination fostered by our long history of official discrimination, ... and yet come to the starting line with an education equal to whites.

...

JUSTICE WHITE, concurring. ...

JUSTICE MARSHALL, concurring.

... [I]t must be remembered that, during most of the past 200 years, the Constitution, as interpreted by this Court, did not prohibit the most ingenious and pervasive forms of discrimination against the Negro. Now, when a State acts to remedy the effects of that legacy of discrimination, I cannot believe that this same Constitution stands as a barrier.

...

... It is plain that the Fourteenth Amendment was not intended to prohibit measures designed to remedy the effects of the Nation's past treatment of Negroes. The Congress that passed the Fourteenth Amendment is the same Congress that passed the 1866 Freedmen's Bureau Act, an Act that provided many of its benefits only to Negroes. ...

...

While I applaud the judgment of the Court that a university may consider race in its admissions process, it is more than a little ironic that, after several hundred years of class-based discrimination against Negroes, the Court is unwilling to hold that a class-based remedy for that discrimination is permissible. In declining to so hold, today's judgment ignores the fact that, for several hundred years, Negroes have been discriminated against not as individuals, but rather solely because of the color of their skins. It is unnecessary in 20th-century America to have individual Negroes demonstrate that they have been victims of racial discrimination; the racism of our society has been so pervasive that none, regardless of wealth or position, has managed to escape its impact. The experience of Negroes in America has been different in kind, not just in degree, from that of other ethnic groups. It is not merely the history of slavery alone, but also that a whole people were marked as inferior by the law. And that mark has endured. The dream of America as the great melting pot has not been realized for the Negro; because of his skin color, he never even made it into the pot.

... It is because of a legacy of unequal treatment that we now must permit the institutions of this society to give consideration to race in making decisions about who will hold the positions of influence, affluence, and prestige in America. For far too long, the doors to those positions have been shut to Negroes. If we are ever to become a fully integrated society, one in which the color of a person's skin will not determine the opportunities available to him or her, we must be willing to take steps to open those doors. ...

...

JUSTICE BLACKMUN, concurring. ...

JUSTICE STEVENS, with whom THE CHIEF JUSTICE, JUSTICE STEWART, and JUSTICE REHNQUIST join, concurring in the judgment in part and dissenting in part.

[*Justice Stevens concluded that the affirmative action program violated Title VI of the Civil Rights Act. He did not discuss the constitutional issue.*]

Washington v. Davis, 426 U.S. 229 (1976)

George Harley and John Dugan Sellers were African American men who were not hired as police officers in the District of Columbia because they failed a civil service examination known as Test 21. Harley and Sellers, along with Alfred E. Davis, an African American police officer who had been denied promotion on the basis of the exam, sued Mayor Walter Washington and the Metropolitan Police Department (MPD). They claimed that the test discriminated against persons of color because persons of color were far more likely to fail the examination than white persons and that the test had not been demonstrated to correlate with job performance. The federal district court ruled that the MPD's hiring and promotion policies did not violate the equal protection clause. The Circuit Court of Appeals for the District of Columbia Circuit, however, found that the use of Test 21 in the hiring process was unconstitutional. Mayor Washington and the MPD appealed to the Supreme Court of the United States.

The Supreme Court by a 7–2 vote ruled that the test was constitutional. Justice White's opinion for the Court in Washington *holds that persons who make equal protection claims must prove discriminatory intent as well as discriminatory impact. What reason did Justice White give for this conclusion? Should plaintiffs have to prove either discriminatory intent or discriminatory impact, but not both? One, but not the other? Why did Justice White fail to find discriminatory intent in this case? Consider two possible reasons. First, White concluded that the test was fair. Second, White concluded that the MPD's overall hiring process was fair. Both of these reasons are noted in the opinion. Do you agree with both or either? Suppose that someone wanted to sue a public university that used the LSAT. Does* Washington v. Davis *foreclose that possibility, or can you think of a way to distinguish that claim?*

JUSTICE WHITE delivered the opinion of the Court.

. . .

The central purpose of the Equal Protection Clause of the Fourteenth Amendment is the prevention of official conduct discriminating on the basis of race. . . . But our cases have not embraced the proposition that a law or other official act, without regard to whether it reflects a racially discriminatory purpose, is unconstitutional solely because it has a racially disproportionate impact.

. . .

The school desegregation cases have also adhered to the basic equal protection principle that the invidious quality of a law claimed to be racially discriminatory must ultimately be traced to a racially discriminatory purpose. That there are both predominantly black and predominantly white schools in a community is not alone violative of the Equal Protection Clause. The essential element of de jure segregation is "a current condition of segregation resulting from intentional state action." . . .

This is not to say that the necessary discriminatory racial purpose must be express or appear on the face of the statute, or that a law's disproportionate impact is irrelevant in cases involving Constitution-based claims of racial discrimination. A statute, otherwise neutral on its face, must not be applied so as invidiously to discriminate on the basis of race. . . . It is also clear from the cases dealing with racial discrimination in the selection of juries that the systematic exclusion of Negroes is itself such an "unequal application of the law . . . as to show intentional discrimination." . . . A prima facie case of discriminatory purpose may be proved as well by the absence of Negroes on a particular jury combined with the failure of the jury commissioners to be informed of eligible Negro jurors in a community . . . or with racially non-neutral selection procedures. . . . With a prima facie case made out, "the burden of proof shifts to the State to rebut the presumption of unconstitutional action by showing that permissible racially neutral selection criteria and procedures have produced the monochromatic result." . . .

Necessarily, an invidious discriminatory purpose may often be inferred from the totality of the relevant facts, including the fact, if it is true, that the law bears more heavily on one race than another. . . . Nevertheless, we have not held that a law, neutral on its face and serving ends otherwise within the power of government to pursue, is invalid under the Equal Protection Clause simply because it may affect a greater proportion of one race than of another. Disproportionate impact is not irrelevant, but it is not the sole touchstone of an invidious racial discrimination forbidden by the Constitution. . . .

. . .

As an initial matter, we have difficulty understanding how a law establishing a racially neutral qualification for employment is nevertheless racially discriminatory and denies "any person . . . equal protection of the laws" simply because a greater proportion of Negroes fail to qualify than members of other racial or ethnic groups. . . . Test 21, which is administered generally to prospective Government employees, concededly seeks to ascertain whether those who take it have acquired a particular level of verbal skill; and it is untenable that the Constitution prevents the Government from seeking modestly to upgrade the communicative abilities of its employees rather than to be satisfied with some lower level of competence, particularly where the job requires special ability to communicate orally and in writing. . . .

Nor on the facts of the case before us would the disproportionate impact of Test 21 warrant the conclusion that it is a purposeful device to discriminate against Negroes and hence an infringement of the constitutional rights of respondents as well as other black applicants. As we have said, the test is neutral on its face and rationally may be said to serve a purpose the Government is constitutionally empowered to pursue. Even agreeing with the District Court that the differential racial effect of Test 21 called for further inquiry, we think the District Court correctly held that the affirmative efforts of the Metropolitan Police Department to recruit black officers, the changing racial composition of the recruit classes and of the force in general, and the relationship of the test to the training program negated any inference that the Department discriminated on the basis of race or that "a police officer qualifies on the color of his skin rather than ability." . . .

. . . A rule that a statute designed to serve neutral ends is nevertheless invalid, absent compelling justification, if in practice it benefits or burdens one race more than another would be far reaching and would raise serious questions about, and perhaps invalidate, a whole range of tax, welfare, public service, regulatory, and licensing statutes that may be more burdensome to the poor and to the average black than to the more affluent white. . . .

. . .

JUSTICE STEVENS, concurring.

. . .

. . . [T]he line between discriminatory purpose and discriminatory impact is not nearly as bright, and perhaps not quite as critical, as the reader of the Court's opinion might assume. I agree, of course, that a constitutional issue does not arise every time some disproportionate impact is shown. On the other hand, when the disproportion is as dramatic as in . . . *Yick Wo v. Hopkins* (1886), it really does not matter whether the standard is phrased in terms of purpose or effect. . . .

There are two reasons why I am convinced that the challenge to Test 21 is insufficient. First, the test serves the neutral and legitimate purpose of requiring all applicants to meet a uniform minimum standard of literacy. Reading ability is manifestly relevant to the police function, there is no evidence that the required passing grade was set at an arbitrarily high level, and there is sufficient disparity among high schools and high school graduates to justify the use of a separate uniform test. Second, the same test is used throughout the federal service. The applicants for employment in the District of Columbia Police Department represent such a small fraction of the total number of persons who have taken the test that their experience is of minimal probative value in assessing the neutrality of the test itself. That evidence, without more, is not sufficient to overcome the presumption that a test which is this widely used by the Federal Government is in fact neutral in its effect as well as its "purpose" as that term is used in constitutional adjudication.

. . .

JUSTICE BRENNAN, with whom JUSTICE MARSHALL joins, dissenting.

[*Justices Brennan and Marshall claimed that Test 21 violated federal statutory law. The dissent did not discuss the constitutional issues, although it did express the view that "petitioners should have been required to prove that the police training examinations either measure job-related skills or predict job performance."*]

C. Gender

No consensus formed behind any clear constitutional vision of gender equality. Governing officials failed to ratify the ERA, but they also repealed or failed to enforce many laws that reinforced traditional gender roles. The Supreme Court, at first implicitly and then explicitly, held government officials to higher constitutional standards when making gender classifications than when making ordinary classifications, but not as high a standard as was required for racial classifications. Congress, but not the Supreme Court, forbade discrimination on the basis of pregnancy. The Court of Appeals for the Third Circuit in *Vorchheimer v. School*

District of Philadelphia (1976) divided evenly when adjudicating the constitutionality of all-male and all-female public high schools.[48]

Americans across the political spectrum endorsed some vision of gender equality but did not agree on how a general principle of gender equality should be implemented. After legislative and judicial decisions removed the most offensive gender classifications from public life, public attention focused on such serious matters as women in combat and such less serious concerns as unisex bathrooms. Consensus on abstract norms collapsed as these specifics took center stage. The more the ERA was perceived as mandating substantive changes in gender roles, the greater the public opposition became. Thirty-five states eventually ratified the amendment, three short of the constitutionally mandated three-fifths.

The constitutional politics of gender equality from 1968 to 1980 was marked by greater public interest group participation. The most important of these groups, the National Organization for Women (NOW), was committed "to bring[ing] women into full participation in the mainstream of American society now, exercising all the privileges and responsibilities thereof in truly equal partnership with men."[49] The newly formed Women's Rights Project of the ACLU, headed by future Supreme Court justice Ruth Bader Ginsburg, lobbied for the passage of the ERA and sponsored litigation aimed at having courts declare gender a suspect classification, a ruling that would require all laws distinguishing between men and women to be necessary means to compelling government interests. These groups were not strong enough to achieve their ultimate goals, but NOW and the Women's Rights Project did help bring about laws and judicial decisions that substantially changed the status of women in the United States.

Divisions over gender rights during the 1970s were exacerbated by the increased visibility of two additional perspectives on the constitutional rights of men and women. Many religious men and women insisted that traditionally legal distinctions between the sexes were more natural and appropriate than even more conservative liberals were willing to acknowledge. Led by Phyllis Schlafly, cultural conservatives claimed that laws based on longstanding gender roles were constitutionally sound. More radical feminists insisted that liberal conceptions of equality rooted in the civil rights movement could not achieve equality for women. Led by Catharine MacKinnon, these feminists asserted that the constitutional requirement that women be judged by the same standards used to judge men devalued distinctively female perspectives by treating inherently male norms as universal.

Judicial majorities debated the proper standard for laws that made gender distinctions before settling on a standard of intermediate scrutiny. The justices in *Reed v. Reed* (1971) for the first time in Supreme Court history ruled that a state law unconstitutionally discriminated against women. Chief Justice Burger ostensibly used a rational scrutiny standard when striking down a state law preferring men to women when determining the administrator of a will. His opinion asserted, "To give a mandatory preference to members of either sex over members of the other, merely to accomplish the elimination of hearings on the merits, is to make the very kind of arbitrary legislative choice forbidden by the Equal Protection Clause of the Fourteenth Amendment." Given that administrative convenience had historically been considered a legitimate government purpose, many commentators believed that the justices were moving toward a higher standard for judging the constitutionality of gender discriminations and distinctions. Four justices in *Frontiero v. Richardson* (1973) proposed that gender discrimination be as strictly scrutinized as race discrimination. Unable to obtain a fifth vote for strict scrutiny, the justices compromised in *Craig v. Boren* (1976) on an intermediate scrutiny standard. Justice Brennan's majority opinion asserted, "To withstand constitutional challenge, previous cases establish that classifications by gender must serve important governmental objectives and must be substantially related to achievement of those objectives."

Despite these developments, Americans during this period maintained traditional restrictions against women in the military. Responding to the Soviet Union's invasion of Afghanistan in 1980, the Carter administration urged that both men and women be required to register for the draft. President Carter's proposal to Congress declared, "Equity is achieved when both men and women are asked

48. *Vorchheimer v. School District of Philadelphia*, 532 F.2d 880 (1976).

49. National Organization for Women, "Statement of Purpose," in *From Many, One: Readings in American Political and Social Thought*, ed. Richard C. Sinopoli (Washington, DC: Georgetown University Press, 1997), 150.

to serve in proportion to the ability of the Armed Forces to use them effectively."[50] Congress chose to require only men to register for the draft. The Senate report claimed, "The arguments for treating men and women equally—so compelling in many areas of our national life—simply cannot overcome the judgment of our military leaders and of the congress itself that a male-only system best serves our national security."[51] The Supreme Court in *Rostker v. Goldberg* (1981) sustained the congressional decision to register only men. Justice Rehnquist's majority opinion asserted, "That Congress and the Executive have decided that women should not serve in combat fully justifies Congress in not authorizing their registration, since the purpose of registration is to develop a pool of potential combat troops."

Debate over the Equal Rights Amendment

The ERA proved surprisingly contentious. After sailing through both houses of Congress by overwhelming majorities and being ratified immediately by more than half the states, the process stalled. Several issues bedeviled the amendment's sponsors. First, in light of legislative decisions providing for a greater degree of gender equality and Supreme Court decisions striking down gender classifications, many Americans wondered what difference the ERA made in practice. Second, many Americans feared that while the ERA might no longer be necessary to remove offensive gender classifications from American life, more liberal justices might use that text to promote gender practices popular majorities thought undesirable.

The following two readings are from two leading participants in the debate over the ERA. Ruth Bader Ginsburg in 1977 was a professor at Columbia Law School and the head of the Women's Rights Project of the ACLU. Phyllis Schlafly was a prominent conservative activist and head of the Eagle Forum. To what extent did Ginsburg and Schlafly dispute the probable impact of the ERA? To what extent did they dispute whether those consequences would be desirable? Suppose you agreed with Schlafly's account of the ERA. Would that make you more or less likely to support ratification?

50. *Congressional Record*, 96th Cong., 2nd Sess., 1980, E1602.
51. *Congressional Record*, 96th Cong., 2nd Sess., 1980, 13,881.

Ruth Bader Ginsburg and Brenda Feigen Fasteau, Sex Bias in the U.S. Code (1977)[52]

. . .

Equalization of the treatment of women and men under Federal law is an overdue task which should command priority attention of the President and Congress. . . . [A] myriad of unwarranted differentials clutter the U.S. Code. While many are obsolete or of minor importance when viewed in isolation, the cumulative effect is reflective of a society that assigns to women, solely on the basis of their sex, a subordinate or dependent role.

. . .

Underlying the recommendations made in this report is the fundamental point that allocation of responsibilities within the family is a matter properly determined solely by the individuals involved. Government should not steer individual decisions concerning household or breadwinning roles by casting the law's weight on the side of (or against) a particular method of ordering private relationships. Rather, a policy of strict neutrality should be pursued. That policy would accommodate both traditional and innovative patterns. At the same time, it should assure removal of artificial constraints so that women and men willing to explore their full potential as human beings may create new traditions by their actions.

. . .

The main rule the Commission proposes . . . calls for sex-neutral terminology except in the rare instance where no suitable sex-neutral substitute term exists, or the reference is to a physical characteristic unique to some or all members of one sex, or the constitutional right to privacy necessitates a sex-specific reference.

. . .

Provision of payments for wives and widows, but not for similarly situated husbands and widowers, has been characteristic of Federal social and employment benefit legislation. Increased female participation in the paid labor force has impelled reassessment of the quality of this differential. . . . A scheme built upon the breadwinning husband–dependent homemaking wife concept inevitably treats the woman's efforts or

52. Excerpt taken from Ruth Bader Ginsburg and Brenda Feigen Fasteau, *Sex Bias in the U.S. Code: A Report of the U.S. Commission on Civil Rights* (Washington, DC: Government Printing Office, 1977), 204–20.

Illustration 9-5 Equal Rights Amendment Rally with Eleanor Smeall, Betty Ford, and Lady Bird Johnson

NOW President Eleanor Smeall (L) and former first ladies Betty Ford (C), and Lady Bird Johnson (R) kick off a rally for equal rights on October 12, 1981, at the Lincoln Memorial in Washington.

Source: UPI Photo/Files.

aspirations in the economic sector as less important than the man's.

. . .

. . . Women temporarily unable to work due to childbirth or pregnancy-related physical disability should not be treated as labor force outcasts. Job security, income protection, and health insurance coverage during such physical disability is essential if equal opportunity in the job market is to become a reality for women. . . . [T]he increasingly common two-earner family pattern should impel development of a comprehensive program of government-supported child care.

. . .

. . . [A] spouse's or former marriage partner's alimony should be based on financial ability.

. . .

Current provisions dealing with statutory rape, rape, and prostitution are discriminatory on their face. With respect to prostitution, enforcement practices compound the discrimination. . . . There is a growing national movement recommending unqualified decriminalization as sound policy, implementing equal rights and individual privacy principles. . . .

. . .

Supporters of the equal rights principle firmly reject draft or combat exemption for women, as Congress did when it refused to qualify the equal rights amendment by incorporating any military service exemption. The equal rights principle implies that women must be subject to the draft if men are, that military assignments must be made on the basis of individual capacity rather than sex, and that a woman must have the same opportunity as a man to qualify for any position to which she aspires in the uniformed services.

. . .

Phyllis Schlafly, A Short History of E.R.A. (1986)[53]

The Equal Rights Amendment was presented to the American public as something that would benefit women, "put women in the U.S. Constitution," and lift women out of their so-called "second-class citizenship." However, in thousands of debates, the ERA advocates were unable to show any way that ERA would benefit women or end any discrimination against them. The fact is that women already enjoy every constitutional right that men enjoy and have enjoyed equal employment opportunity since 1964.

. . .

The opponents of ERA were able to show many harms that ERA would cause.

1. ERA would take away legal rights that women possessed—*not* confer any new rights on women.
   A. ERA would take away women's traditional exemption from military conscription and also from military combat duty. . . .
   B. . . . ERA would make unconstitutional the laws, which then existed in every state, that impose on a husband the obligation to support his wife.
2. ERA would take away important rights and powers of the states and confer these on other branches of government which are farther removed from the people.
   A. ERA would give enormous power to the Federal courts to decide the definitions of the words in ERA, "sex" and "equality of rights." . . .
3. Section II of ERA would give enormous new powers to the Federal Government that now belong to the states. . . .
4. ERA's impact on education would take away rights from women students, upset many customs and practices, and bring government intrusion into private schools.
   A. ERA would make unconstitutional all the current exceptions in Title IX which allow for single-sex schools and colleges and for separate treatment of the sexes for certain activities. ERA would mean the end of single-sex colleges. ERA would force the sex integration of fraternities, sororities, Boy Scouts, Girl Scouts, YMCA, YWCA, Boys State and Girls State conducted by the American Legion, and mother-daughter and father-son school events.
5. ERA would put abortion rights into the U.S. Constitution, and make abortion funding a new constitutional right.
6. ERA would put "gay rights" into the U.S. Constitution, because the word in the Amendment is "sex" not women.

53. Excerpt taken from Phyllis Schlafly, "A Short History of E.R.A.," *Phyllis Schlafly Report* 20 (1986).

Frontiero v. Richardson, 411 U.S. 677 (1973)

Lieutenant Sharron Frontiero of the U.S. Air Force was turned down when she applied to obtain housing and medical benefits for her husband, Joseph Frontiero, because she did not provide half the support for the family. Male officers could obtain benefits for their spouses without having to prove any dependency. Frontiero brought a lawsuit against Elliott Richardson, the secretary of defense, claiming that this military policy violated the equal protection component of the due process clause of the Fifth Amendment. A federal district court denied relief. Frontiero appealed to the Supreme Court of the United States.

The Supreme Court by an 8–1 vote ruled that Frontiero had a right to the same benefits that were available to similarly situated male officers. Justice Brennan and three other members of the Court applied the strict scrutiny test, which required that laws making gender classifications be necessary means to compelling government ends. On what basis did they apply that standard? Do you think their analysis is compelling? Four other justices insisted that the law in this case did not even satisfy the rational scrutiny test. Do you think that this assertion is correct, or were the justices smuggling in a higher standard? Was Justice Powell correct in thinking that justices should not have changed the law at this point in time in light of what most persons thought was the impending ratification of the ERA? Might a justice thinking strategically deny Frontiero's claim, thus strengthening the case for the ERA? Notice that Justice Brennan analogized sex discrimination to racial discrimination. What are the merits and demerits of that analogy?

JUSTICE BRENNAN announced the judgment of the Court and an opinion in which JUSTICE DOUGLAS, JUSTICE WHITE, and JUSTICE MARSHALL join.

. . .

There can be no doubt that our Nation has had a long and unfortunate history of sex discrimination.

Traditionally, such discrimination was rationalized by an attitude of "romantic paternalism" which, in practical effect, put women, not on a pedestal, but in a cage. . . . As a result of [such] notions . . ., our statute books gradually became laden with gross, stereotyped distinctions between the sexes and, indeed, throughout much of the 19th century the position of women in our society was, in many respects, comparable to that of blacks under the pre–Civil War slave codes. Neither slaves nor women could hold office, serve on juries, or bring suit in their own names, and married women traditionally were denied the legal capacity to hold or convey property or to serve as legal guardians of their own children. . . . And although blacks were guaranteed the right to vote in 1870, women were denied even that right—which is itself "preservative of other basic civil and political rights"—until adoption of the Nineteenth Amendment half a century later.

It is true, of course, that the position of women in America has improved markedly in recent decades. Nevertheless, it can hardly be doubted that, in part because of the high visibility of the sex characteristic, women still face pervasive, although at times more subtle, discrimination in our educational institutions, in the job market and, perhaps most conspicuously, in the political arena.

Moreover, since sex, like race and national origin, is an immutable characteristic determined solely by the accident of birth, the imposition of special disabilities upon the members of a particular sex because of their sex would seem to violate "the basic concept of our system that legal burdens should bear some relationship to individual responsibility. . . ." . . . And what differentiates sex from such nonsuspect statuses as intelligence or physical disability, and aligns it with the recognized suspect criteria, is that the sex characteristic frequently bears no relation to ability to perform or contribute to society. As a result, statutory distinctions between the sexes often have the effect of invidiously relegating the entire class of females to inferior legal status without regard to the actual capabilities of its individual members.

. . .

With these considerations in mind, we can only conclude that classifications based upon sex, like classifications based upon race, alienage, or national origin, are inherently suspect, and must therefore be subjected to strict judicial scrutiny. . . .

. . .

. . . [A]ny statutory scheme which draws a sharp line between the sexes, solely for the purpose of achieving administrative convenience, necessarily commands "dissimilar treatment for men and women who are . . . similarly situated," and therefore involves the "very kind of arbitrary legislative choice forbidden by the [Constitution]. . . ." We therefore conclude that, by according differential treatment to male and female members of the uniformed services for the sole purpose of achieving administrative convenience, the challenged statutes violate the Due Process Clause of the Fifth Amendment insofar as they require a female member to prove the dependency of her husband.

JUSTICE STEWART concurs in the judgment, agreeing that the statutes before us work an invidious discrimination in violation of the Constitution. *Reed v. Reed* (1971). . . .

JUSTICE POWELL, with whom THE CHIEF JUSTICE and JUSTICE BLACKMUN join, concurring in the judgment.

I agree that the challenged statutes constitute an unconstitutional discrimination against servicewomen in violation of the Due Process Clause of the Fifth Amendment, but I cannot join the opinion of MR. JUSTICE BRENNAN, which would hold that all classifications based upon sex, "like classifications based upon race, alienage, and national origin," are "inherently suspect and must therefore be subjected to close judicial scrutiny." . . . It is unnecessary for the Court in this case to characterize sex as a suspect classification, with all of the far-reaching implications of such a holding. . . . In my view, we can and should decide this case on the authority of *Reed v. Reed* (1971) and reserve for the future any expansion of its rationale.

There is another, and I find compelling, reason for deferring a general categorizing of sex classifications as invoking the strictest test of judicial scrutiny. The Equal Rights Amendment, which if adopted will resolve the substance of this precise question, has been approved by the Congress and submitted for ratification by the States. If this Amendment is duly adopted, it will represent the will of the people accomplished in the manner prescribed by the Constitution. By acting prematurely and unnecessarily, as I view it, the Court has assumed a decisional responsibility at the very time when state legislatures, functioning within the traditional democratic process, are debating the proposed Amendment. It seems to me that this reaching out to pre-empt by judicial action a major political decision which is currently in process of resolution does not reflect appropriate respect for duly prescribed legislative processes.

. . .

JUSTICE REHNQUIST, dissenting.

[*Justice Rehnquist adopted the opinion of the lower federal court. The crucial section of that opinion is excerpted here.*]

. . .

Congress apparently reached the conclusion that it would be more economical to require married female members claiming husbands to prove actual dependency than to extend the presumption of dependency to such members. Such a presumption made to facilitate administration of the law does not violate the equal protection guarantee of the Constitution if it does not unduly burden or oppress one of the classes upon which it operates. Nothing in the instant statutory classification jeopardizes the ability of a female member to obtain the benefits intended to be bestowed upon her by the statutes. The classification is burdensome for a female member who is not actually providing over one-half the support for her claimed husband only to the extent that were she a man she could receive dependency benefits in spite of the fact that her spouse might not be actually dependent, as that term has been defined by Congress. In other words, the alleged injustice of the distinction lies in the possibility that some married service men are getting "windfall" payments, while married service women are denied them. Sharron Frontiero is one of the service women thus denied a windfall.

All dependency benefits are unquestionably valuable, windfalls are not, but we are of the opinion that the incidental bestowal of some undeserved benefits on male members of the uniformed services does not so unreasonably burden female members that the administrative classification should be ruled unconstitutional.

X. Criminal Justice

MAJOR DEVELOPMENTS

- Crime becomes a national political issue
- *Mapp* and *Miranda* are narrowed but remain the law of the land
- All capital punishment statutes declared unconstitutional in 1972, but states subsequently adopt revised statutes that are sustained by the Supreme Court in 1976

Crime became a national issue during the late 1960s. Many liberals insisted that increases in violent offenses demonstrated the importance of expanding Great Society programs to eliminate the economic causes of criminal activity. More Americans were convinced that the crime wave was rooted in permissive politicians and judges. Critics charged the Warren Court with handcuffing the police and permitting hardened criminals to escape justice on petty technicalities. In one influential essay, Judge Henry Friendly asked, "Is Innocence Irrelevant?" This article complained that convicted criminals often raised numerous constitutional issues in habeas corpus petitions that had no bearing on their guilt. The end result was "abuse by prisoners, a waste of the precious and limited resources available for the criminal process, and public disrespect for the judgment of criminal courts."[54]

Richard Nixon repeatedly emphasized his opposition to Warren Court decisions protecting the rights of persons suspected and convicted of crime. Warren Burger, the judge who Nixon chose to replace Earl Warren, gained public attention for his vocal criticisms of Supreme Court decisions expanding Fourth, Fifth, and Sixth Amendment rights. When nominating Justices Lewis Powell and William Rehnquist to the Supreme Court, Nixon asserted, "I believe some court decisions have gone too far in the past in weakening the peace forces as against the criminal forces in our society. I believe the peace forces must not be denied the legal tools they need to protect the innocent from criminal elements."[55]

Nixon achieved some of his goals, but neither he nor his judicial appointments reversed the Due Process Revolution. Compared to the 1960s, criminal defendants won fewer cases in the Supreme Court after Nixon's election, as illustrated in Figure 9-4. The Burger Court narrowly interpreted such decisions as *Mapp v. Ohio* (1961) and *Miranda v. Arizona* (1966). *United States v. Calandra* (1974) held that prosecutors could use unconstitutionally obtained evidence in grand jury proceedings. *Harris v. New York* (1971) ruled that statements obtained in violation of *Miranda* could be used to impeach witnesses. *Stone v. Powell* (1976) declared that federal courts in habeas corpus cases would

54. Henry J. Friendly, "Is Innocent Irrelevant? Collateral Attack on Criminal Judgments," *University of Chicago Law Review* 38 (1970): 172.

55. Richard Nixon, *Public Papers of the Presidents of the United States* (Washington, D.C.: Government Printing Office, 1972), 1053.

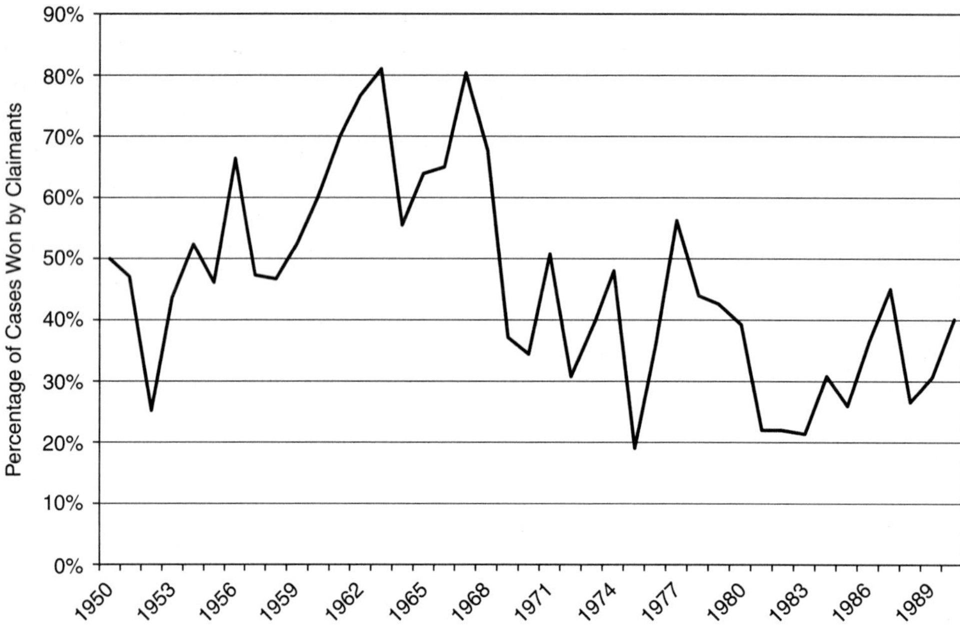

Figure 9-5 Percentage of Victories in U.S. Supreme Court by Claimants in Criminal Justice Cases, 1950–1990

not normally consider Fourth Amendment claims. Nevertheless, the basic landmarks of the Due Process Revolution remained standing. *Miranda* and *Mapp* did not survive the 1970s unscathed, but when President Reagan assumed office, they "appear[ed] more secure [than] they ha[d] been for a number of years."[56] Burger Court decisions built on the liberalism of the Warren Court on such matters as the right to counsel, juries, and capital punishment. In 1972 a 5–4 judicial majority declared unconstitutional all state procedures used to impose the death penalty. Although the justices in *Gregg v. Georgia* (1976) found a new set of procedures constitutional, the end result was that capital punishment by 1980 was subject to far more constitutional restraints than it was when Richard Nixon took office in 1969.

A. Due Process and Habeas Corpus

The Burger Court exhibited what many thought was a surprising concern with due process rights before and during trials. A judicial majority in *In re Winship* (1970) asserted that due process required the prosecution to prove all elements of a crime beyond a reasonable doubt, even in proceedings for juvenile delinquency. The justices in another series of decisions aggressively policed the plea bargaining process. Chief Justice Burger's majority opinion in *Santobello v. New York* (1971) asserted that "'plea bargaining,' is an essential component of the administration of justice," but that judges must ensure that (a) the defendant has adequate counsel; (b) the plea is "voluntary and knowing"; (c) "if it [is] induced by promises, the essence of those promises must in some ways be known"; and (d) the plea bargain must be kept. The Supreme Court in *Bordenkircher v. Hayes* (1978), however, found no due process problem when a prosecutor threatened a criminal suspect with a more severe offense if that person refused to accept a plea bargain.

The justices were less accommodating to constitutional claims regarding habeas corpus matters. Two decisions sharply limited access to that writ. *Stone v. Powell* (1976) held that federal courts would not hear habeas corpus claims based on the exclusionary rule whenever the state court had held a full and fair hearing on the matter, even if the state court had reached an erroneous legal conclusion. After noting that "[a]pplication of the [exclusionary] rule deflects the truthfinding

56. Yale Kamisar, "The Warren Court (Was It Really So Defense-Minded?), the Burger Court (Is It Really So Prosecution-Minded?), and Police Investigatory Practices," in *The Burger Court: The Counter-Revolution That Wasn't*, ed. Vincent Blasi (New Haven, CT: Yale University Press, 1983), 90.

process and often frees the guilty," Justice Powell's majority opinion stated that "there is no reason to believe that the overall educative effect of the exclusionary rule would be appreciably diminished if search-and-seizure claims could not be raised in federal habeas corpus review of state convictions." *Wainwright v. Sykes* (1977) declared that federal habeas corpus petitioners could ordinarily raise only those constitutional claims that they had first raised at trial. Overruling *Fay v. Noia* (1963), the Burger Court adopted a presumption that defense lawyers—even overworked and inexperienced public defenders—had strategic reasons for failing to make constitutional objections to the trial judge. This was a conservative application of adequate and state grounds. The constitutional state law that requires a criminal defendant to make a timely objection to some alleged constitutional wrong may prevent federal courts from considering whether the conviction was, in fact, unconstitutional. State judges did not necessarily believe that their increased autonomy and responsibility would alter their behavior in such cases, but they did recognize the Burger Court's greater willingness to trust the state courts.

In re Winship, 397 U.S. 358 (1970)

A family court judge in New York found that Samuel Winship, a twelve-year-old boy, had stolen $112 from a pocketbook. The judge admitted that the evidence did not support a finding that Winship was guilty beyond a reasonable doubt but chose to rely on New York law that required delinquency determinations to be made on "a preponderance of the evidence." Winship was placed in a training school for a period between eighteen months and six years. Winship appealed this verdict, claiming that he could be constitutionally adjudged a delinquent only if there was no reasonable doubt that he had committed a criminal offense. Several New York appellate courts rejected this claim. Winship appealed to the Supreme Court of the United States.

The Supreme Court by a 6–3 vote ruled that Winship had been unconstitutionally convicted. Justice Brennan's majority opinion held that due process required that both adults and juveniles be found guilty of a crime only if all elements were proven beyond a reasonable doubt. On what constitutional foundation does the "beyond reasonable doubt" rule rest? What reasons did the justices give for insisting that the "beyond reasonable doubt" requirement is one of the "essentials of due process" that must structure a juvenile court proceeding? Does the case shed any light on the earlier incorporation debate? Justice Black, a liberal on incorporation, dissented in Winship *because the federal Bill of Rights does not include a provision requiring proof beyond a reasonable doubt. Justice Harlan, who opposed incorporation, was in the majority, because the requirement of reasonable doubt, in his view, was an element of fundamental fairness. Is reasonable doubt an element of fundamental fairness in the juvenile system? Does the Bill of Rights not require reasonable doubt?*

JUSTICE BRENNAN delivered the opinion of the Court.

. . .

The requirement that guilt of a criminal charge be established by proof beyond a reasonable doubt dates at least from our early years as a Nation. . . . Although virtually unanimous adherence to the reasonable-doubt standard in common-law jurisdictions may not conclusively establish it as a requirement of due process, such adherence does "reflect a profound judgment about the way in which law should be enforced and justice administered." . . .

Expressions in many opinions of this Court indicate that it has long been assumed that proof of a criminal charge beyond a reasonable doubt is constitutionally required. . . . Mr. Justice Frankfurter stated that "[i]t [is] the duty of the Government to establish . . . guilt beyond a reasonable doubt. This notion—basic in our law and rightly one of the boasts of a free society—is a requirement and a safeguard of due process of law in the historic, procedural content of due process." . . .

The reasonable-doubt standard plays a vital role in the American scheme of criminal procedure. It is a prime instrument for reducing the risk of convictions resting on factual error. The standard provides concrete substance for the presumption of innocence—that bedrock "axiomatic and elementary" principle whose "enforcement lies at the foundation of the administration of our criminal law." . . .

The requirement of proof beyond a reasonable doubt has this vital role in our criminal procedure for cogent reasons. The accused during a criminal prosecution has at stake interest of immense importance, both because of the possibility that he may lose his liberty upon conviction and because of the certainty that he would be stigmatized by the conviction. Accordingly, a society that values the good name and freedom of every individual should not condemn a man for commission of a crime when there is reasonable doubt about his guilt. . . .

Moreover, use of the reasonable-doubt standard is indispensable to command the respect and confidence of the community in applications of the criminal law. It is critical that the moral force of the criminal law not be diluted by a standard of proof that leaves people in doubt whether innocent men are being condemned. It is also important in our free society that every individual going about his ordinary affairs have confidence that his government cannot adjudge him guilty of a criminal offense without convincing a proper factfinder of his guilt with utmost certainty.

Lest there remain any doubt about the constitutional stature of the reasonable-doubt standard, we explicitly hold that the Due Process Clause protects the accused against conviction except upon proof beyond a reasonable doubt of every fact necessary to constitute the crime with which he is charged.

. . . The same considerations that demand extreme caution in factfinding to protect the innocent adult apply as well to the innocent child. . . . [C]ivil labels and good intentions do not themselves obviate the need for criminal due process safeguards in juvenile courts, for "[a] proceeding where the issue is whether the child will be found to be 'delinquent' and subjected to the loss of his liberty for years is comparable in seriousness to a felony prosecution." . . .

. . .

. . . It is true, of course, that the juvenile may be engaging in a general course of conduct inimical to his welfare that calls for judicial intervention. But that intervention cannot take the form of subjecting the child to the stigma of a finding that he violated a criminal law and to the possibility of institutional confinement on proof insufficient to convict him were he an adult.

. . .

JUSTICE HARLAN, concurring.

. . .

. . . I view the requirement of proof beyond a reasonable doubt in a criminal case as bottomed on a fundamental value determination of our society that it is far worse to convict an innocent man than to let a guilty man go free. It is only because of the nearly complete and long-standing acceptance of the reasonable-doubt standard by the States in criminal trials that the Court has not before today had to hold explicitly that due process, as an expression of fundamental procedural fairness, requires a more stringent standard for criminal trials than for ordinary civil litigation.

. . . Although there are no doubt costs to society (and possibly even to the youth himself) in letting a guilty youth go free, I think here, as in a criminal case, it is far worse to declare an innocent youth a delinquent. I therefore agree that a juvenile court judge should be no less convinced of the factual conclusion that the accused committed the criminal act with which he is charged than would be required in a criminal trial.

. . .

CHIEF JUSTICE BURGER, with whom JUSTICE STEWART joins, dissenting.

. . .

My hope is that today's decision will not spell the end of a generously conceived program of compassionate treatment intended to mitigate the rigors and trauma of exposing youthful offenders to a traditional criminal court; each step we take turns the clock back to the pre-juvenile-court era. I cannot regard it as a manifestation of progress to transform juvenile courts into criminal courts, which is what we are well on the way to accomplishing. We can only hope the legislative response will not reflect our own by having these courts abolished.

JUSTICE BLACK, dissenting.

. . . The Bill of Rights . . . does by express language provide for, among other things, a right to counsel in criminal trials, a right to indictment, and the right of a defendant to be informed of the nature of the charges against him. And in two places the Constitution provides for trial by jury, but nowhere in that document is there any statement that conviction of crime requires proof of guilt beyond a reasonable doubt. The Constitution thus goes into some detail to spell out what kind of trial a defendant charged with crime should have, and I believe the Court has no power to add to or subtract from the procedures set forth by the Founders. I realize that it is far easier to substitute individual judges' ideas of "fairness" for the fairness prescribed by the Constitution, but I shall not at any time surrender my belief that that document itself should be our guide, not our own concept of what is fair, decent, and right. . . . As I have said time and time again, I prefer to put my faith in the words of the written Constitution itself rather than to rely on the shifting, day-to-day standards of fairness of individual judges.

. . .

I admit a strong, persuasive argument can be made for a standard of proof beyond a reasonable doubt in criminal cases—and the majority has made that argument well—but it is not for me as a judge to say for that reason that Congress or the States are without constitutional power to establish another standard that the Constitution does not otherwise forbid. It is quite true that proof beyond a reasonable doubt has long been required in federal criminal trials. It is also true that this requirement is almost universally found in the governing laws of the States. And as long as a particular jurisdiction requires proof beyond a reasonable doubt, then the Due Process Clause commands that every trial in that jurisdiction must adhere to that standard. . . . But when, as here, a State through its duly constituted legislative branch decides to apply a different standard, then that standard, unless it is otherwise unconstitutional, must be applied to insure that persons are treated according to the "law of the land." The State of New York has made such a decision, and in my view nothing in the Due Process Clause invalidates it.

B. Search and Seizure

The exclusionary rule announced in *Mapp v. Ohio* (1961) remained the law of the land, but the Nixon appointees to the Supreme Court, often joined by Justice White, carved out numerous exceptions or limitations to the principle that prosecutors may not rely on unconstitutionally obtained evidence to secure criminal convictions:

- Unconstitutionally obtained evidence may be used in a criminal trial when the defendant was not the victim of the unconstitutional search (*Alderman v. United States* [1969])
- Unconstitutionally obtained evidence may be introduced in a grand jury proceeding (*United States v. Calandra* [1974])
- Claims that persons were convicted of a crime on the basis of unconstitutionally obtained evidence may not be heard in habeas corpus procedures if the state court held a full and fair hearing on the underlying Fourth Amendment issue (*Stone v. Powell* [1976])
- Unconstitutionally obtained evidence may be introduced in civil tax proceedings (*United States v. Janis* [1976])
- Unconstitutionally obtained evidence may be used at trial to impeach a criminal defendant's testimony (*United States v. Havens* [1980])

Proponents of these exceptions insisted that the sole purpose of the exclusionary rule was to deter unconstitutional behavior and that the deterrent effect in the particular situation before the court was minimal. In this view the exclusionary rule reflected the principle that state actors should not benefit from state wrongs. As was often the case with Burger Court decisions, the power of decision rested with centrist judges who often made fine distinctions that appeared obscure to both such conservatives as Justice Rehnquist, who preferred to overrule *Mapp*, and such progressives as Justices Brennan and Marshall, who thought that *Mapp* should be extended.

The Supreme Court was more liberal in determining when a search violated the Fourth and Fourteenth Amendments. *United States v. United States District Court* (1972) rejected claims that the president had the power to order wiretaps without a warrant. Justice Powell's opinion for the Court asserted,

> The Government's concerns do not justify departure in this case from the customary Fourth Amendment requirement of judicial approval prior to initiation of a search or surveillance. . . . A prior warrant establishes presumptive validity of the surveillance and will minimize the burden of justification in post-surveillance judicial review. By no means of least importance will be the reassurance of the public generally that indiscriminate wiretapping and bugging of law-abiding citizens cannot occur.

Payton v. New York (1980) held that warrantless home arrests are normally unconstitutional. The "basic principle of Fourth Amendment law that searches and seizures inside a home without a warrant are presumptively unreasonable," Justice Stevens stated, "has equal force when the seizure of a person is involved."

C. Interrogations

The temptation exists to repeat verbatim the first paragraph of the introduction to the previous section, substituting only *Miranda v. Arizona* (1966) for *Mapp v. Ohio* (1961). As was the case with *Mapp*, *Miranda* bent during this period but did not break. Nixon appointees were willing to make exceptions to the rule that prosecutors could not introduce confessions at trial unless the persons arrested had been given *Miranda* warnings. *Harris v. New York* (1971) permitted prosecutors to use such confessions when cross-examining the defendant, and many state courts embraced that greater leniency toward prosecutors. Nevertheless, the centrist judges on the Burger Court were unwilling to overrule *Miranda*.

The Burger Court had a more mixed record when determining what constituted a custodial confession. Many cases turned on slight changes in the fact pattern. Both *Brewer v. Williams* (1977) and *Rhode Island v. Innis* (1980) concerned confessions obtained in squad cars after the suspect had invoked the right to remain silent. In *Brewer* the police officers struck up a conversation with the defendant in which they commented that the victim's family really wanted to find the body in order to have a proper Christian burial. In *Innis* the police officers struck up a conversation with themselves in which they expressed concern that children might find and use the loaded gun used in the murder. *Brewer*, by a 5–4 vote, tossed out the subsequent confession. *Innis*, by a 6–3 vote, declared the confession constitutionally obtained. Few persons other than Justices Stewart and Powell perceived any significant differences in the cases.

Harris v. New York, 401 U.S. 222 (1971)

Viven Harris was arrested for selling heroin to an undercover police officer. During an interrogation that day Harris made several incriminating statements. The state prosecutor, aware that Harris was not given proper Miranda *warnings, did not introduce those statements during the direct examination of the arresting officer. When cross-examining Harris, the prosecutor introduced the incriminating statements into evidence after Harris declared that he could not remember what he had said after being arrested. The trial judge instructed members of the jury that they could use the incriminating statements when considering whether Harris's testimony was credible, but not when considering whether he had committed the crime. The jury found Harris guilty of selling narcotics. He was sentenced to prison for six to eight years. The Supreme Court, Appellate Division of New York, and the New York Court of Appeals affirmed the trial court's ruling that the incriminating statements were admissible. Harris appealed to the Supreme Court of the United States.*

The Supreme Court by a 5–4 vote ruled the confessions admissible. Chief Justice Burger's majority opinion declared that confessions obtained in violation of Miranda *could be used to impeach a criminal defendant. Why did the chief justice claim that a prosecutor could introduce evidence of a confession secured without* Miranda *warnings on cross-examination, even though such evidence could not be admitted on direct examination? Do you believe that* Harris *exploits a legal ambiguity in* Miranda, *or was this case a first step toward overruling that decision? If you were a defense attorney after* Harris, *would you ever allow your client to take the stand if the client had made a confession without proper* Miranda *warnings?*

Some state supreme courts decided not to follow the U.S. Supreme Court's lead on this issue. In People v. Disbrow *(CA 1976) the California Supreme Court held that the self-incrimination provision of the California Constitution barred any use of confessions obtained without proper warning. In his opinion for the court Justice Stanley Mosk wrote,*

> *We pause finally to reaffirm the independent nature of the California Constitution and our responsibility to separately define and protect the rights of California citizens despite conflicting decisions of the United States Supreme Court interpreting the federal Constitution. . . . [I]n light of recent erosion of* Miranda *standards as a matter of federal constitutional law, it is appropriate to observe that no State is precluded by the decision from adhering to higher standards under state law. Each State has power to impose higher standards governing police practices under state law than is required by the Federal Constitution. . . .*[57]

CHIEF JUSTICE BURGER delivered the opinion of the Court.

. . .

Some comments in the *Miranda* opinion can indeed be read as indicating a bar to use of an uncounseled statement for any purpose, but discussion of that issue was not at all necessary to the Court's holding and cannot be regarded as controlling. *Miranda* barred the prosecution from making its case with statements of

57. *People v. Disbrow*, 16 Cal.3rd 101 (1976).

an accused made while in custody prior to having or effectively waiving counsel. It does not follow from *Miranda* that evidence inadmissible against an accused in the prosecution's case in chief is barred for all purposes, provided of course that the trustworthiness of the evidence satisfies legal standards.

. . .

. . . Petitioner's testimony in his own behalf . . . contrasted sharply with what he told the police shortly after his arrest. The impeachment process here undoubtedly provided valuable aid to the jury in assessing petitioner's credibility, and the benefits of this process should not be lost, in our view, because of the speculative possibility that impermissible police conduct will be encouraged thereby. Assuming that the exclusionary rule has a deterrent effect on proscribed police conduct, sufficient deterrence flows when the evidence in question is made unavailable to the prosecution in its case in chief.

Every criminal defendant is privileged to testify in his own defense, or to refuse to do so. But that privilege cannot be construed to include the right to commit perjury. . . . Having voluntarily taken the stand, petitioner was under an obligation to speak truthfully and accurately, and the prosecution here did no more than utilize the traditional truth-testing devices of the adversary process. . . .

The shield provided by *Miranda* cannot be perverted into a license to use perjury by way of a defense, free from the risk of confrontation with prior inconsistent utterances. We hold, therefore, that petitioner's credibility was appropriately impeached by use of his earlier conflicting statements.

JUSTICE BLACK dissents.

JUSTICE BRENNAN, with whom JUSTICE DOUGLAS and JUSTICE MARSHALL join, dissenting.

[The privilege against self-incrimination] is fulfilled only when an accused is guaranteed the right "to remain silent unless he chooses to speak in the unfettered exercise of his own will." . . . The choice of whether to testify in one's own defense must therefore be "unfettered," since that choice is an exercise of the constitutional privilege. . . . [T]he accused is denied an "unfettered" choice when the decision whether to take the stand is burdened by the risk that an illegally obtained prior statement may be introduced to impeach his direct testimony denying complicity in the crime charged against him. We settled this proposition in *Miranda* where we said:

> The privilege against self-incrimination protects the individual from being compelled to incriminate himself in any manner. . . . [S]tatements merely intended to be exculpatory by the defendant are often used to impeach his testimony at trial. . . . These statements are incriminating in any meaningful sense of the word and may not be used without the full warnings and effective waiver required for any other statement.

. . .

The objective of deterring improper police conduct is only part of the larger objective of safeguarding the integrity of our adversary system. The "essential mainstay" of that system . . . is the privilege against self-incrimination, which for that reason has occupied a central place in our jurisprudence since before the Nation's birth. Moreover, "we may view the historical development of the privilege as one which groped for the proper scope of governmental power over the citizen. . . . All these policies point to one overriding thought: the constitutional foundation underlying the privilege is the respect a government . . . must accord to the dignity and integrity of its citizens." . . . These values are plainly jeopardized if an exception against admission of tainted statements is made for those used for impeachment purposes. . . . The Court today tells the police that they may freely interrogate an accused incommunicado and without counsel and know that although any statement they obtain in violation of *Miranda* cannot be used on the State's direct case, it may be introduced if the defendant has the temerity to testify in his own defense. This goes far toward undoing much of the progress made in conforming police methods to the Constitution. I dissent.

D. Juries and Lawyers

Judicial decisions emphasized the right to a jury that represented a fair cross-section of the community. *Peters v. Kiff* (1972) held that white defendants had a right to a jury from which persons of color were not unconstitutionally excluded. *Duren v. Missouri* (1979) held that men had a right to a jury from which women were not unconstitutionally excluded.

Judicial decisions on the right to an attorney broke very little ground. *Argensinger v. Hamlin* (1972) ruled that the right to counsel in *Gideon v. Wainwright* (1963) entailed that "no imprisonment may be imposed . . . unless the accused is represented by counsel." Justice Douglas wrote:

> The requirement of counsel may well be necessary for a fair trial even in a petty-offense prosecution. We are by no means convinced that legal and constitutional questions involved in a case that actually leads to imprisonment even for a brief period are any less complex than when a person can be sent off for six months or more.

In 1979 the justices limited *Gideon* and *Argensinger* to cases in which a prison sentence was actually imposed. A 5–4 judicial majority in *Scott v. Illinois* determined that criminal defendants who were merely fined had no right to counsel, even if they could have been sentenced to prison for the offense they were found guilty of committing. Justice Rehnquist's majority opinion asserted, "Actual imprisonment is a penalty different in kind from fines or the mere threat of imprisonment."

E. Punishments

No executions took place in the United States in the years between 1968 and 1976. Governors refused to issue death warrants. Winthrop Rockefeller, the governor of Arkansas, commuted the sentence of every person on death row, asserting that the death penalty was "cruel and unusual punishment" and maintaining that "the exercise of executive clemency has provided a form of moral leadership that has brought about substantive changes in the law."[58] The Supreme Court by a 5–4 vote in *Furman v. Georgia* (1972) put what many thought was a permanent halt to executions by declaring unconstitutional every state statute authorizing capital punishment. Justices Brennan and Marshall insisted that capital punishment in any circumstance was cruel and unusual. Justice Douglas leaned toward a similar conclusion, although his opinion was unclear. Justices White and Stewart, while maintaining that the death penalty in the abstract might be constitutional, insisted that capital punishment in the United States was too arbitrarily imposed to withstand constitutional scrutiny. Justice Stewart's opinion asserted,

> These death sentences are cruel and unusual in the same way that being struck by lightning is cruel and unusual. For, of all the people convicted of rapes and murders in 1967 and 1968, many just as reprehensible as these, the petitioners are among a capriciously selected random handful upon whom the sentence of death has in fact been imposed. My concurring Brothers have demonstrated that, if any basis can be discerned for the selection of these few to be sentenced to die, it is the constitutionally impermissible basis of race. . . . But racial discrimination has not been proved, and I put it to one side. I simply conclude that the Eighth and Fourteenth Amendments cannot tolerate the infliction of a sentence of death under legal systems that permit this unique penalty to be so wantonly and so freakishly imposed.

The reaction to *Furman* was swift. Thirty-five states and the federal government immediately passed new capital punishment statutes. Most were based on recommendations made by the authors of the Model Penal Code (MPC). The MPC urged states to adopt a bifurcated process: a trial on guilt followed by a trial on punishment. The jury during the penalty phase would be guided by a series of statutory aggravating and mitigating factors. Aggravating factors included previous convictions, the murder of a police officer, and whether a murder was particularly heinous. Mitigating factors included the lack of previous convictions, any mental incapacity, and evidence of remorse. Persons could be sentenced to death only if the jury found beyond a reasonable doubt at least one aggravating factor and determined that the aggravating factors outweighed the mitigating factors. A few states responded to *Furman* by passing mandatory death statutes. Under such measures, anyone convicted of a particular crime—for example, murder of a police officer—would automatically be sentenced to death.

The Burger Court in *Gregg v. Georgia* (1976) and *Woodson v. North Carolina* (1976) split the difference. Justices Brennan and Marshall repeated their claim in *Furman* that the death penalty was always unconstitutional. Chief Justice Burger and Justices Rehnquist, White, and Blackmun insisted that the new statutes cured whatever defects had doomed pre-*Furman* measures. Justices Stevens, Powell, and Stewart cast

58. Winthrop Rockefeller, "Executive Clemency and the Death Penalty," *Catholic University Law Review* 21 (1971): 94, 99, 100.

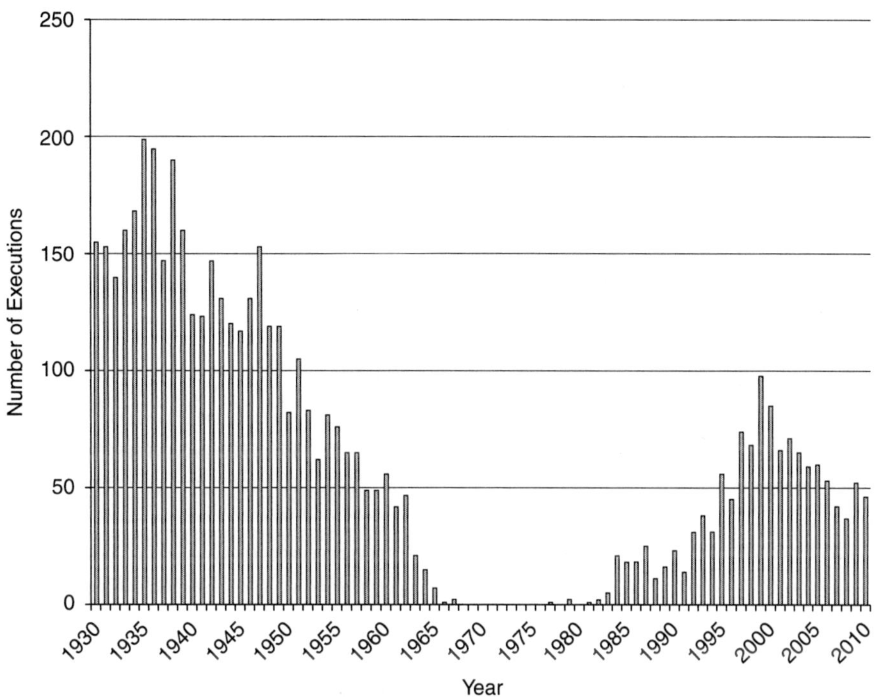

Figure 9-6 Executions in the United States, 1930–2010

Source: Hugo Adam Bedau, ed., *The Death Penalty in America*, 3rd ed. (New York: Oxford University Press, 1982), 25. The Death Penalty Information Center (http://www.deathpenaltyinfo.org).

the crucial votes declaring constitutional in *Gregg* the statutes based on the MPC but declaring unconstitutional in *Woodson* the mandatory death penalty statutes. Remarkably, these centrist judges concluded that mandatory death penalties resulted in more arbitrary death sentences than did a regime of guided jury discretion. In their view, juries faced with a mandatory death scheme tended for idiosyncratic reasons to find some defendants guilty of only second-degree murder. For this reason, the plurality concluded, guided discretion would actually result in less variation in death sentences than laws that only superficially gave juries no discretion at all.

Most constitutional decision makers cheered the restoration of capital punishment. After *Gregg*, state executions rose to levels not seen since the 1950s. A few state judges dissented from the pro–capital punishment consensus. The Supreme Judicial Court of Massachusetts repeatedly found that state legislative attempts to reintroduce the death penalty violated the state constitution. One opinion declared,

> [A]rt. 26 of the Declaration of Rights "No magistrate or court of law, shall . . . inflict cruel or unusual punishments" forbids the imposition of a death penalty in this Commonwealth in the absence of a showing on the part of the Commonwealth that the availability of that penalty contributes more to the achievement of a legitimate State purpose—for example, the purpose of deterring criminal conduct—than the availability in like cases of the penalty of life imprisonment. Existing studies of the entire subject have provided no such demonstration regarding any of the situations of murder that would be covered by the proposed legislation, nor has the Legislature made findings resulting from investigation that might furnish the demonstration.[59]

This strategy proved politically risky. California Chief Justice Rose Bird was defeated for reelection in 1986 after consistently blocking the implementation of the death penalty in that state.

59. *Opinion of the Justices*, 372 Mass. 912 (1977). See also *District Attorney for Suffolk District v. Watson*, 381 Mass. 648 (1980).

Gregg v. Georgia, 428 U.S. 153 (1976)

Troy Gregg and Floyd Allen were hitchhiking in northern Florida when they were picked up by Fred Simmons and Bob Moore. At a rest stop just outside of Atlanta, Georgia, Gregg and Allen robbed and murdered their benefactors. A jury rejected Gregg's claim of self-defense. He was convicted of two counts of armed robbery and two counts of murder. Consistent with Georgia law, the trial judge convened a penalty hearing to determine whether Gregg would be sentenced to death. At that hearing the jury found two aggravating factors sufficient to justify capital punishment: the murder was committed while Gregg was engaged in armed robbery, another capital felony, and the murder was committed for pecuniary gain. The Supreme Court of Georgia affirmed the death sentence. Although the justices rejected the first aggravating factor on the ground that defendants in Georgia were not being sentenced to death for armed robbery, the judges found the other factor sufficient to impose capital punishment. Gregg appealed to the Supreme Court of the United States.

The Supreme Court by a 7–2 vote sustained the death sentence. Justice Stewart's plurality opinion declared that the Georgia procedure for imposing capital punishment would reduce the arbitrary infliction of the sentence that offended the justices in Furman v. Georgia *(1972). On what basis did the justices claim that bifurcated trials are more likely to reduce arbitrariness than are mandatory death sentences? Note that only three of the nine justices on the Court believed that mandatory death schemes were constitutionally different from guided jury discretion. Do you believe that distinction sound? What is the constitutional significance of the response to* Furman*? Do you believe that any justice changed his mind on the constitutionality of capital punishment between 1972 and 1976? Do you believe that the outpouring of support for capital punishment had constitutional significance, or do you agree with Justice Marshall that the evidence still demonstrated that the death penalty was inconsistent with informed public opinion? Did the* Furman *precedent influence any justice? Why did Justice White, a member of the* Furman *majority, vote to sustain both mandatory and discretionary death penalties, while Justice Stewart, a dissenter in* Furman*, voted to strike down mandatory death penalty laws?*

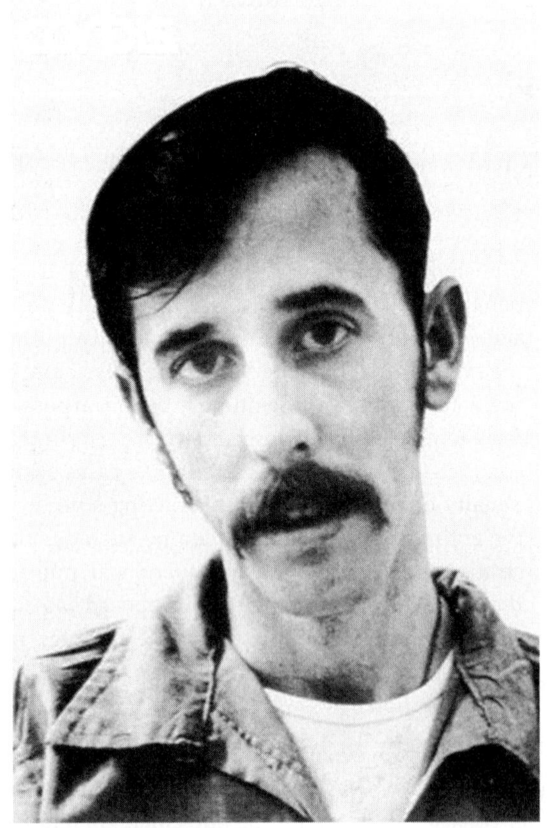

Illustration 9-6 Troy Leon Gregg

Troy Leon Gregg on Georgia death row, July 2, 1976. He died in a bar fight in North Carolina on the night of his escape from the Georgia State Prison in Reidsville in 1980.

Source: © Bettmann/CORBIS.

Judgment of the Court, and opinion of JUSTICE STEWART, JUSTICE POWELL, and JUSTICE STEVENS, announced by JUSTICE STEWART.

. . .

. . . We . . . hold that the punishment of death does not invariably violate the Constitution.

. . .

. . . [I]n assessing a punishment selected by a democratically elected legislature against the constitutional measure, we presume its validity. We may not require the legislature to select the least severe penalty possible so long as the penalty selected is not cruelly inhumane or disproportionate to the crime involved. And a heavy burden rests on those who would attack the judgment of the representatives of the people.

. . .

The imposition of the death penalty for the crime of murder has a long history of acceptance both in the United States and in England. The common-law rule imposed a mandatory death sentence on all convicted murderers. . . . And the penalty continued to be used into the 20th century by most American States, although the breadth of the common-law rule was diminished, initially by narrowing the class of murders to be punished by death and subsequently by widespread adoption of laws expressly granting juries the discretion to recommend mercy. . . .

It is apparent from the text of the Constitution itself that the existence of capital punishment was accepted by the Framers. At the time the Eighth Amendment was ratified, capital punishment was a common sanction in every State. Indeed, the First Congress of the United States enacted legislation providing death as the penalty for specified crimes. . . . The Fifth Amendment, adopted at the same time as the Eighth, contemplated the continued existence of the capital sanction by imposing certain limits on the prosecution of capital cases. . . . [T]he Fourteenth Amendment, adopted over three-quarters of a century later, similarly contemplates the existence of the capital sanction in providing that no State shall deprive any person of "life, liberty, or property" without due process of law.

. . .

The most marked indication of society's [continued] endorsement of the death penalty for murder is the legislative response to *Furman v. Georgia* (1972). The legislatures of at least 35 States have enacted new statutes that provide for the death penalty for at least some crimes that result in the death of another person. And the Congress of the United States, in 1974, enacted a statute providing the death penalty for aircraft piracy that results in death. . . . [A]ll of the post-*Furman* statutes make clear that capital punishment itself has not been rejected by the elected representatives of the people.

. . .

The death penalty is said to serve two principal social purposes: retribution and deterrence of capital crimes by prospective offenders.

In part, capital punishment is an expression of society's moral outrage at particularly offensive conduct. This function may be unappealing to many, but it is essential in an ordered society that asks its citizens to rely on legal processes rather than self-help to vindicate their wrongs.

. . . [T]he decision that capital punishment may be the appropriate sanction in extreme cases is an expression of the community's belief that certain crimes are themselves so grievous an affront to humanity that the only adequate response may be the penalty of death.

Statistical attempts to evaluate the worth of the death penalty as a deterrent to crimes by potential offenders have occasioned a great deal of debate. The results simply have been inconclusive. . . . We may nevertheless assume safely that there are murderers, such as those who act in passion, for whom the threat of death has little or no deterrent effect. But for many others, the death penalty undoubtedly is a significant deterrent. . . .

The value of capital punishment as a deterrent of crime is a complex factual issue the resolution of which properly rests with the legislatures, which can evaluate the results of statistical studies in terms of their own local conditions and with a flexibility of approach that is not available to the courts. . . .

. . .

Finally, we must consider whether the punishment of death is disproportionate in relation to the crime for which it is imposed. There is no question that death as a punishment is unique in its severity and irrevocability. . . . But we are concerned here only with the imposition of capital punishment for the crime of murder, and when a life has been taken deliberately by the offender, we cannot say that the punishment is invariably disproportionate to the crime. It is an extreme sanction, suitable to the most extreme of crimes.

. . . [T]he penalty of death is different in kind from any other punishment imposed under our system of criminal justice. Because of the uniqueness of the death penalty, *Furman* held that it could not be imposed under sentencing procedures that created a substantial risk that it would be inflicted in an arbitrary and capricious manner. . . .

. . . [W]here discretion is afforded a sentencing body on a matter so grave as the determination of whether a human life should be taken or spared, that discretion must be suitably directed and limited so as to minimize the risk of wholly arbitrary and capricious action.

. . .

The . . . [Georgia] procedures require the jury to consider the circumstances of the crime and the criminal before it recommends sentence. No longer can a Georgia jury do as *Furman*'s jury did: reach a finding of the defendant's guilt and then, without guidance or direction, decide whether he should live or die. Instead, the jury's attention is directed to the specific circumstances of the crime: Was it committed in the course of another capital felony? Was it committed for money? Was it committed upon a peace officer or judicial officer? Was it committed in a particularly heinous way or in a manner that endangered the lives of many persons? In addition, the jury's attention is focused on the characteristics of the person who committed the crime: Does he have a record of prior convictions for capital offenses? Are there any special facts about this defendant that mitigate against imposing capital punishment (e. g., his youth, the extent of his cooperation with the police, his emotional state at the time of the crime). As a result, while some jury discretion still exists, "the discretion to be exercised is controlled by clear and objective standards so as to produce nondiscriminatory application." . . .

As an important additional safeguard against arbitrariness and caprice, the Georgia statutory scheme provides for automatic appeal of all death sentences to the State's Supreme Court. That court is required by statute to review each sentence of death and determine whether it was imposed under the influence of passion or prejudice, whether the evidence supports the jury's finding of a statutory aggravating circumstance, and whether the sentence is disproportionate compared to those sentences imposed in similar cases. . . .

. . .

The basic concern of *Furman* centered on those defendants who were being condemned to death capriciously and arbitrarily. . . . The new Georgia sentencing procedures . . . focus the jury's attention on the particularized nature of the crime and the particularized characteristics of the individual defendant. While the jury is permitted to consider any aggravating or mitigating circumstances, it must find and identify at least one statutory aggravating factor before it may impose a penalty of death. In this way the jury's discretion is channeled. No longer can a jury wantonly and freakishly impose the death sentence; it is always circumscribed by the legislative guidelines. In addition, the review function of the Supreme Court of Georgia affords additional assurance that the concerns that prompted our decision in *Furman* are not present to any significant degree in the Georgia procedure applied here.

. . .

JUSTICE WHITE, with whom THE CHIEF JUSTICE and JUSTICE REHNQUIST join, concurring in the judgment.

. . .

. . . Petitioner has argued in effect that no matter how effective the death penalty may be as a punishment, government, created and run as it must be by humans, is inevitably incompetent to administer it. This cannot be accepted as a proposition of constitutional law. Imposition of the death penalty is surely an awesome responsibility for any system of justice and those who participate in it. Mistakes will be made and discriminations will occur which will be difficult to explain. However, one of society's most basic tasks is that of protecting the lives of its citizens and one of the most basic ways in which it achieves the task is through criminal laws against murder. I decline to interfere with the manner in which Georgia has chosen to enforce such laws on what is simply an assertion of lack of faith in the ability of the system of justice to operate in a fundamentally fair manner.

. . .

Statement of THE CHIEF JUSTICE and JUSTICE REHNQUIST. . . .

JUSTICE BLACKMUN, concurring in the judgment. . . .

JUSTICE BRENNAN, dissenting.

. . .

The fatal constitutional infirmity in the punishment of death is that it treats "members of the human race as nonhumans, as objects to be toyed with and discarded. [It is] thus inconsistent with the fundamental premise of the Clause that even the vilest criminal remains a human being possessed of common human dignity." . . . As such it is a penalty that "subjects the individual to a fate forbidden by the principle of civilized treatment guaranteed by the [Clause]." I therefore would hold, on that ground alone, that death is today a cruel and unusual punishment prohibited by the Clause. . . .

. . .

JUSTICE MARSHALL, dissenting.

. . .

Since the decision in *Furman*, the legislatures of 35 States have enacted new statutes authorizing the imposition of the death sentence for certain crimes, and Congress has enacted a law providing the death penalty for air piracy resulting in death. . . . I would be less than candid if I did not acknowledge that these developments have a significant bearing on a realistic assessment of the moral acceptability of the death penalty to the American people. But if the constitutionality of the death penalty turns, as I have urged, on the opinion of an informed citizenry, then even the enactment of new death statutes cannot be viewed as conclusive. In *Furman*, I observed that the American people are largely unaware of the information critical to a judgment on the morality of the death penalty, and concluded that if they were better informed they would consider it shocking, unjust, and unacceptable. . . . A recent study, conducted after the enactment of the post-*Furman* statutes, has confirmed that the American people know little about the death penalty, and that the opinions of an informed public would differ significantly from those of a public unaware of the consequences and effects of the death penalty.

Even assuming, however, that the post-*Furman* enactment of statutes authorizing the death penalty renders the prediction of the views of an informed citizenry an uncertain basis for a constitutional decision, the enactment of those statutes has no bearing whatsoever on the conclusion that the death penalty is unconstitutional because it is excessive. . . .

. . .

The death penalty, unnecessary to promote the goal of deterrence or to further any legitimate notion of retribution, is an excessive penalty forbidden by the Eighth and Fourteenth Amendments. I respectfully dissent from the Court's judgment upholding the sentences of death imposed upon the petitioners in these cases.

Suggested Readings

Baer, Judith A. 1983. *Equality Under the Constitution: Reclaiming the Fourteenth Amendment.* Ithaca, NY: Cornell University Press.

Belz, Herman. 1991. *Equality Transformed: A Quarter-Century of Affirmative Action.* New Brunswick, NJ: Transaction.

Blasi, Vincent, ed. 1983. *The Burger Court: The Counter-Revolution That Wasn't.* New Haven, CT: Yale University Press.

Burgess, Susan A. 1992. *Contest for Constitutional Authority.* Lawrence: University Press of Kansas.

Bussiere, Elizabeth. 1997. *Disentitling the Poor: The Warren Court, Welfare Rights, and the American Political Tradition.* University Park: Pennsylvania State University Press.

Carmines, Edward G., and James A. Stimson. 1989. *Issue Evolution: Race and the Transformation of American Politics.* Princeton, NJ: Princeton University Press.

Craig, Barbara Hinkson, and David M. O'Brien. 1993. *Abortion and American Politics.* Chatham, NJ: Chatham House.

Devins, Neal. 1996. *Shaping Constitutional Values: Elected Government, the Supreme Court, and the Abortion Debate.* Baltimore, MD: Johns Hopkins University Press.

Ely, John Hart. 1993. *War and Responsibility: Constitutional Lessons of Vietnam and Its Aftermath.* Princeton, NJ: Princeton University Press.

Epp, Charles R. 2010. *Making Rights Right: Activists, Bureaucrats, and the Creation of the Legalistic State.* Chicago: University of Chicago Press.

Epstein, Lee, and Joseph Fiske Kobylka. 1992. *The Supreme Court and Legal Change: Abortion and the Death Penalty.* Chapel Hill: University of North Carolina Press.

Fisher, Louis. 1991. *Presidential Conflicts Between Congress and the President*, 3rd ed. Lawrence: University Press of Kansas.

———. 2004. *Presidential War Powers*, 2nd ed. Lawrence: University Press of Kansas.

Frymer, Paul. 2008. *Black and Blue: African Americans, the Labor Movement, and the Decline of the Democratic Party.* Princeton, NJ: Princeton University Press.

Garrow, David J. 1994. *Liberty and Sexuality: The Right to Privacy and the Making of* Roe v. Wade. Berkeley: University of California Press.

Jeffries, John Calvin. 1994. *Justice Lewis F. Powell, Jr.* New York: C. Scribner's Sons.

Keck, Thomas M. 2004. *The Most Activist Supreme Court in History: The Road to Modern Judicial Conservatism.* Chicago: University of Chicago Press.

Kutler, Stanley I. 1990. *The Wars of Watergate: The Last Crisis of Richard Nixon.* New York: Norton.

Ladd, Everett Carll, Jr., with Charles D. Hadley. 1975. *Transformations of the American Party System: Political Coalitions from the New Deal to the 1970s.* New York: Norton.

Luker, Kristin. 1984. *Abortion and the Politics of Motherhood.* Berkeley: University of California Press.

Mansbridge, Jane J. 1986. *Why We Lost the ERA.* Chicago: University of Chicago Press.

Mayeri, Serena. 2011. *Reasoning from Race: Feminism, Law, and the Civil Rights Revolution.* Cambridge, MA: Harvard University Press.

McGirr, Lisa. 2001. *Suburban Warriors: The Origins of the New American Right.* Princeton, NJ: Princeton University Press.

McMahon, Kevin J. 2011. *Nixon's Court: His Challenge to Judicial Liberalism and Its Political Consequences.* Chicago: University of Chicago Press.

Michelman, Frank I. 1999. *Brennan and Democracy.* Princeton, NJ: Princeton University Press.

O'Neill, Timothy J. 1985. Bakke *and the Politics of Equality: Friends and Foes in the Classroom of Litigation.* Middleton, CT: Wesleyan University Press.

Perlstein, Rick. 2008. *Nixonland: The Rise of a President and the Fracturing of America.* New York: Scribner.

Rudenstine, David. 1996. *The Day the Presses Stopped: A History of the* Pentagon Papers *Case.* Berkeley: University of California Press.

Schlesinger, Arthur M., Jr. 1973. *The Imperial Presidency.* Boston: Houghton Mifflin.

Schwartz, Bernard. 1990. *The Ascent of Pragmatism: The Burger Court in Action.* Reading, MA: Addison Wesley.

———, ed. 1998. *The Burger Court: Counter-Revolution or Confirmation?* New York: Oxford University Press.

Silverstein, Gordon. 1996. *Imbalance of Powers: Constitutional Interpretation and the Making of American Foreign Policy.* New York: Oxford University Press.

Silverstein, Mark. 1994. *Judicious Choices: The New Politics of Supreme Court Confirmations.* New York: W. W. Norton & Co.

Strentny, John D. 2004. *The Minority Rights Revolution.* Cambridge, MA: Harvard University Press.

Sundquist, James L. 1981. *Decline and Resurgence of Congress.* Washington, DC: Brookings Institution.

Wermiel, Stephen. 2010. *Justice Brennan: Liberal Champion.* New York: Houghton Mifflin Harcourt.

Whittington, Keith E. 1999. *Constitutional Construction: Divided Powers and Constitutional Meaning.* Cambridge, MA: Harvard University Press.

———. 2007. *Political Foundations of Judicial Supremacy: The President, the Supreme Court, and Constitutional Leadership in U.S. History.* Princeton, NJ: Princeton University Press.

Woodward, Bob, and Scott Armstrong. 1979. *The Brethren: Inside the Supreme Court.* New York: Simon and Schuster.

Yalof, David. 1999. *Pursuit of Justices: Presidential Politics and the Pursuit of Supreme Court Nominees.* Chicago: University of Chicago Press.

Part 3 **Contemporary Issues**

Chapter 10

The Reagan Era: 1981–1993

I. Introduction

The 1980 national election shocked liberals. Ronald Reagan, a former actor, won a landslide victory in the presidential election, Republicans gained control of the Senate, and the Democratic margin in the House of Representatives was substantially reduced. Reagan, the new Republicans in the Senate, the working majority in the House of Representatives established after 1980, and the eventual Republican judicial majority on the federal courts were more conservative on economic and social matters than any other governing coalition of the past generation. The Republican establishment in the early 1970s often questioned the perceived excesses of the Great Society but not its foundations. By contrast, Republican Party platforms in 1980, 1984, 1988, and 1992 championed policies that would reverse many core tenets of Great Society constitutionalism.

Liberal Democrats fought back. The 1982 midterm election eroded the gains that Republicans had made in Congress during the 1980 election. In 1986 the control of the Senate slipped back into Democratic hands, despite Reagan's overwhelming reelection in 1984. Nevertheless, liberals during the 1980s more often sought to slow conservative inroads into American constitutionalism than to blaze new progressive trails.

Developments. Reagan Era constitutional debates were distinctly post–New Deal, both in the sense that they were guided by different political commitments and in the sense that they still took for granted most accomplishments of the New Deal.[1] Members of the Reagan coalition opposed many political and social developments that occurred in the 1960s and 1970s. They sought to overturn such liberal constitutional decisions as *Roe v. Wade* (1973) (abortion rights), *Engel v. Vitale* (1962) (school prayer), and *Mapp v. Ohio* (1961) (exclusionary rule). Few challenged earlier liberal decisions such as *West Coast Hotel v. Parrish* (1937) (no constitutional protection for the freedom of contract) or *Brown v. Board of Education* (1954) (desegregation of schools). Conservatives made strong efforts to bolster presidential power, which was considered to have been weakened by Vietnam and Watergate. Some conservative politicians, lawyers, and judges raised questions about the scope and legitimacy of government powers that had been regarded as settled for fifty years. Nevertheless, more radical challenges to the New Deal constitutional order were usually on the intellectual margins. The constitutional order that conservatives wished to preserve looked more like the United States in 1955 than the United States in 1925.

Parties. The Republican Party of Ronald Reagan was far more conservative on constitutional matters than the Republican Party of Dwight Eisenhower. The conservative coalition assembled by Reagan drew upon Barry Goldwater's original movement, as well as Richard Nixon's successful electoral coalition, Reagan's own experiences in California, and those who had become disaffected with the Democratic Party during the 1970s. To the base of "establishment" and "Main Street" Republicans Reagan and his allies added economic libertarians (who emphasized small government, free markets, and individual liberty), social and religious conservatives, states' rights "federalists," tax cutters, and Cold War hard-liners. In the process, Reagan accelerated the shift in the

1. For one description of "the new constitutional order," see Mark V. Tushnet, *The New Constitutional Order* (Princeton, NJ: Princeton University Press, 2004).

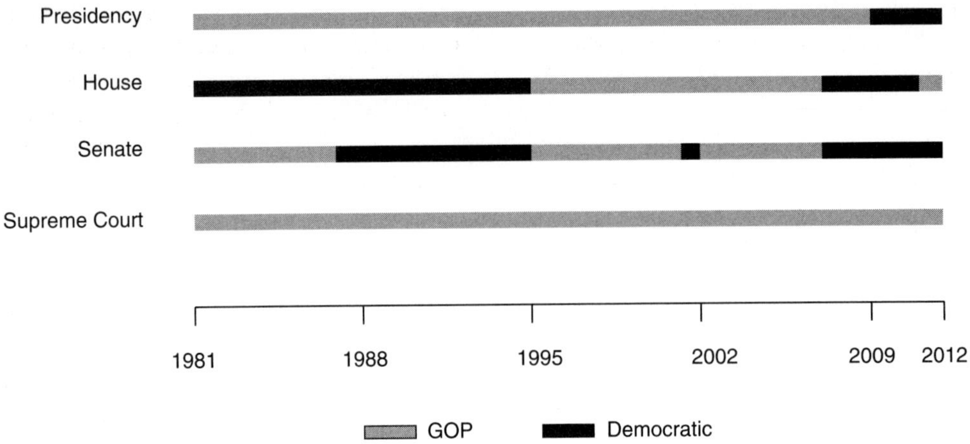

Figure 10-1 Partisan Control of the U.S. Government, 1981–2012

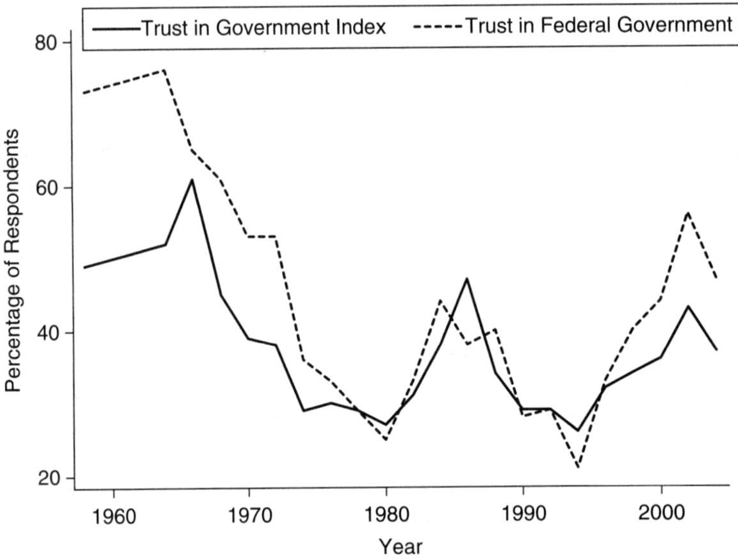

Figure 10-2 Trust in Government Index, 1958–2004

Source: American National Election Studies.

Note: Respondents answering that they trust "most of the time" or "just about always" to a generic trust in government question and a specific trust in the federal government question.

regional center of the GOP from its birthplace in New England to the South and the West.

At the heart of the Reagan Era Republican constitutional philosophy was a distrust of the government, and particularly distrust of the federal government. Goldwater's campaign against big government was particularly ill timed in coming at the high-water mark of public trust in government, but Reagan capitalized on a decade of steady decline in popular faith in government.

As Figure 10-2 indicates, the public was ready to listen to Reagan's constitutional philosophy by the late 1970s. Tax cuts, spending cuts, deregulation of the economy, and decentralization of power to state and local governments were cornerstones of Reagan's first-term agenda.

Reagan repeatedly condemned liberals and liberal justices for constructing what he considered unjustifiable constitutional barriers to the passage of conservative social policies. Appointing judges who would practice "judicial restraint" would restore more traditional constitutional understandings and enable conservatives to restore voluntary prayer in school, ban abortion, and prevent criminals from going free on constitutional technicalities. Individual Republicans had previously championed many of these constitutional positions. What was new in 1980 was the central place that these positions occupied in the official constitutional vision of the Republican Party.

Democrats became more conservative on economic matters during the 1980s but held the liberal line on most constitutional rights. The party excoriated the measures that Republicans thought necessary for restoring fundamental constitutional commitments as an abandonment of constitutional rights. Debates over the future of abortion rights were among the most bitterly contentious issues dividing the parties and the country. The two parties also offered sharply divergent understandings of constitutional equality. Democrats saw the United States as a society still wracked by structural disadvantages for vulnerable groups. By contrast, Republicans called for a public policy that was color-blind and sex-blind. While Democrats became increasingly committed to feminist perspectives on public policy, Republicans in 1980 dropped from the party platform their coalition's longstanding commitment to ratifying the ERA. As a candidate, however, Reagan promised to make a woman his first appointment to the Supreme Court of the United States.

All elected branches of the national government moved to the right during the Reagan Era. The new Republicans elected to the Senate were far more conservative than previous Republicans had been. The small Democratic margins in the House of Representatives often left practical power in the hands of senior southern Democrats, who, while more liberal than southern Republicans, had never accepted the Great Society rights and liberties agenda. The Voting Rights Act brought to power a new generation of southern Democrats who were far more liberal than the more veteran Democrats from Dixie. Nevertheless, liberal successes in the 1980s were largely limited to defeating conservative civil rights proposals and refusing to confirm some of Reagan's more conservative judicial nominees. With rare exceptions, liberals could not pass new federal legislation, object to conservative executive actions, or force Republican presidents to appoint liberals to the federal bench.

Interest Groups. Powerful interest groups supported the strong rightward turn in American politics. By the 1980s prominent interest groups were lobbying and litigating on every constitutional issue of interest to the political right. The National Rifle Association became a political thorn in the side of any elected official who voted for gun control. Such newly created organizations as the Washington Legal Foundation and the Pacific Legal Foundation provided legal assistance to property holders who believed that government regulations violated their constitutional rights and white applicants who believed that an affirmative action program explained why they had not been promoted or accepted to some higher education program. No umbrella organization analogous to the ACLU formed that championed conservative constitutional positions on all questions of rights and liberties. The conservative movement in the Reagan Era was instead an often-uneasy alliance between religious conservatives who opposed the secularist bent of Great Society liberalism, libertarians who opposed the redistributive bent of Great Society liberalism, and foreign policy hawks who opposed the internationalist trends of Great Society liberalism.

Two associations played particularly important roles in conservative constitutional politics. The first was the Moral Majority and the evangelical movement. Such preachers as Jerry Falwell and Pat Robertson helped organize conservative Christians into politically active coalitions. Evangelicals by the late 1980s were solid Republican voters. They wielded powerful influence, particularly in the South and the Midwest, supporting candidates who proposed banning abortion, permitting voluntary school prayer, and allowing state funding for church-affiliated parochial schools. The second was the Federalist Society, an association formed by law students, lawyers, and law professors who opposed the dominant New Deal liberalism of the legal academy and legal profession. Federalist Society members did not agree on a common conservative agenda. Many were libertarians far more committed to

Table 10-1 Major Issues and Decisions of the Reagan Era

Major Political Issues	**Major Constitutional Issues**	**Major Court Decisions**
Political polarization	Legitimacy of controversial Warren Court precedents	*Haig v. Agee* (1981)
Partisan transformation of federal judiciary	Judicial review	*Plyler v. Doe* (1982)
Christian conservatism	Original meaning	*Immigration and Naturalization Service v. Chadha* (1983)
Rise of conservative Public interest groups	Presidential war powers	*United States v. Leon* (1984)
Deficit reduction	Independent counsel	*Garcia v. SAMTA* (1985)
Tax reform	Balanced budget amendment	*Bowers v. Hardwick* (1986)
Immigration reform	Legislative delegation	*Batson v. Kentucky* (1986)
Iran-Contra scandal	Property rights	*South Dakota v. Dole* (1987)
Cold War	Abortion	*Johnson v. Transportation Agency, Santa Clara County* (1987)
Gay rights movement	Public funds and parochial schools	*McCleskey v. Kemp* (1987)
Second-wave feminism	School prayer	*Morrison v. Olson* (1988)
Campus speech codes and hate speech	Exemptions for religious believers	*City of Richmond v. J. A. Croson* (1989)
Fairness doctrine	Flag burning	*Doe v. University of Michigan* (1989)
Voting rights	Second Amendment	*Skinner v. Railway Labor Executives Association* (1989)
Crime control	Criminalization of homosexual sodomy	*Employment Division v. Smith* (1990)
	Affirmative action	*Lee v. Weisman* (1992)
	Gender discrimination	*Planned Parenthood of Southeastern Pennsylvania v. Casey* (1992)
	Majority-minority districts	*Lucas v. South Carolina Coastal Council* (1992)
	Limits on speech considered harmful to discrete and insular minorities	*Shaw v. Reno* (1993)
	Good-faith exceptions to Fourth Amendment	
	Interrogations	
	Jury selection	
	Death penalty	
	Exclusionary rule	

limiting government regulation than to banning abortion. Others were social conservatives more concerned with eradicating pornography than cutting taxes. Nevertheless, the Federalist Society soon became a clearinghouse for conservative constitutional ideas and activism. Numerous conservative justices and members of the Justice Department from 1981 until 1993 were either Federalist Society members or regular participants in Federalist Society meetings.

Courts. The federal judiciary moved to the right in large part because Republican presidents appointed ten consecutive Supreme Court justices from 1969 to 1993. Democrat Jimmy Carter was the only president in the twentieth century who did not a fill Supreme Court vacancy. By contrast, Richard Nixon filled four seats, Gerald Ford filled one seat, Ronald Reagan filled three seats, and George Bush in his one term in office filled two seats. The vast majority of lower federal court justices by 1992 had been appointed by Republican presidents. Many justices appointed by Presidents Reagan and Bush, most notably Antonin Scalia and Clarence Thomas, were far more conservative on rights and liberties issues than was any justice other than William Rehnquist appointed between 1933 and 1980. In 1985 President Reagan elevated Rehnquist to the chief justiceship. By 1993 the median justices on the Rehnquist Court were Reagan appointees Anthony Kennedy and Sandra Day O'Connor. The two most liberal justices, Harry Blackmun and John Paul Stevens, were pre-Reagan Republican judicial appointees.

The new conservative majority pushed constitutional law rightward. While neither the Burger nor the early Rehnquist Court overruled such decisions as *Mapp v. Ohio* (1961), *Miranda v. Arizona* (1965), or other landmark liberal decisions, judicial majorities carved out numerous exceptions to the exclusionary rule, *Miranda* warnings, and other cherished liberal rulings. Other judicial decisions eased constitutional restrictions on the flow of government money to parochial schools. Economic rights returned to the judicial agenda. Supreme Court decisions interpreting the takings clause of the Fifth Amendment enabled landowners to challenge government restrictions that rendered their property or parts of their property economically useless.

Conservative Republicans had more difficulty reversing Great Society rights policies. Liberals in Congress retained the votes necessary to defeat constitutional amendments permitting elected officials to regulate abortion, sanction prayer in public schools, and ban flag burning. Conservatives could not cobble together a legislative majority willing to limit the federal judicial power to integrate schools by busing schoolchildren. Conservative efforts to place more conservatives on the federal bench were limited by the infrequency with which openings occurred on the Supreme Court, as well as by vigorous liberal opposition to particularly conservative appointees. After Democrats regained control of the Senate in 1986 liberals successfully defeated the proposed Supreme Court nomination of Robert Bork, a lower federal court judge who was on record as opposing almost all important liberal Warren Court decisions. (The more moderate Justice Anthony Kennedy was eventually confirmed to fill that vacancy.) The result was a judiciary far more conservative than the Warren Court but not nearly as conservative as the Reagan and Bush administrations.

After a decade of steady movement to the right the Reagan Revolution hit surprising roadblocks in 1992. The Supreme Court decisions in *Lee v. Weisman* (1992) and *Planned Parenthood of Southeastern Pennsylvania v. Casey* (1992) refused to overrule previous decisions outlawing school prayer and legalizing abortion, respectively. Both *Lee* and *Casey* suggested that the more moderate Republican justices Sandra Day O'Connor and Anthony Kennedy thought that the Reagan Revolution had gone far enough. While these justices would not expand the liberal precedents of the past, they were not willing to abandon the central constitutional precedents of the New Deal and Great Society. That November Democrats won their first presidential election in sixteen years, making it unlikely that a liberal constitutional vision would be substantially weakened for the foreseeable future.

Constitutional Thought. Most conservatives during the 1980s championed some version of originalism. Such originalists as Robert Bork and Antonin Scalia insisted that justices should interpret constitutional provisions in light of what those provisions meant at the time they were ratified. In this view, the phrase "cruel and unusual punishment" in the Eighth Amendment meant exactly what "cruel and unusual punishment" meant in 1791. Originalists during the 1970s and early 1980s generally employed originalist

Box 10-1 A Partial Cast of Characters of the Reagan Era

Ronald Reagan	▪ Republican ▪ California conservative ▪ Actor who made his political debut in Barry Goldwater's 1964 presidential campaign ▪ Governor of California (1967–1975) ▪ President of the United States (1981–1989) ▪ United social conservatives, economic conservatives, and foreign policy hawks into a single coalition ▪ Emphasized a constitutional philosophy that combined traditional morality, law and order, small government, and judicial restraint
Sandra Day O'Connor	▪ Republican ▪ Arizona moderate conservative ▪ Arizona state senator (1969–1974) ▪ Arizona state judge (1975–1981) ▪ First female justice on the U.S. Supreme Court, appointed by Ronald Reagan (1981–2006) ▪ Became a swing vote on the Burger and Rehnquist Courts, often joining the conservatives on federalism and separation of powers issues, but with liberals on abortion
Edwin Meese	▪ Republican ▪ Conservative lawyer and businessman ▪ A long-time advisor and chief of staff to Ronald Reagan from his days as California governor ▪ Counselor to the president (1981–1985) ▪ U.S. attorney general (1985–1988) ▪ A key organizer of legal conservatives in the federal government in the 1980s and a leading spokesman for originalism
Robert Bork	▪ Republican ▪ Conservative Yale law professor ▪ Solicitor general (1973–1977) ▪ Judge on the D.C. circuit court (1982–1988), appointed by Ronald Reagan ▪ Nominated for U.S. Supreme Court by Ronald Reagan and defeated for confirmation in a deeply contested vote in 1987 ▪ A leading organizer and spokesman for the conservative legal movement in the 1970s and 1980s and a chief proponent of originalism
John Paul Stevens	▪ Republican ▪ Chicago anti-trust lawyer ▪ Judge on the federal circuit court (1970–1975), appointed by Richard Nixon ▪ Associate justice of the U.S. Supreme Court (1975–2010), appointed by Gerald Ford ▪ A consensus, nonpolitical choice for the Court after Watergate, Stevens was not known for a distinctive judicial philosophy but became a vocal member of the liberal wing as the Court became more conservative over time

arguments when criticizing liberal judicial activism. *Roe v. Wade* (1973) wrongly held that the due process clause of the Fourteenth Amendment protected abortion, originalists asserted, because Americans did not believe "due process" entailed the right to terminate a pregnancy when the Fourteenth Amendment was ratified in 1868. Voluntary prayer in public school was constitutional because a long tradition supported that practice. As conservatives gained more control over the federal courts, some originalists championed greater judicial activism on behalf of conservative causes. Such originalists as Richard Epstein insisted that the Constitution limited federal and state power to redistribute property. Other conservatives looked to the past when constructing arguments against affirmative action and in favor of exempting religious believers from various secular policies.

Constitutional doctrine became more complex. Supreme Court justices, Justice O'Connor in particular, employed the very deferential rational basis test or the very strict compelling interest test in fewer rights and liberties cases. New tests emerged that seemed hybrids of the old tests. When determining whether state regulations on abortion were constitutional, the plurality opinion in *Planned Parenthood of Southeastern Pennsylvania v. Casey* (1992) substituted an "undue burden" test for the compelling interest test employed after *Roe v. Wade*. The majority opinion in *Dolan v. City of Tigard* (1994) preferred a "rough proportionality" standard to the rational basis test that many state courts used when determining the constitutionality of land use restrictions. Multipart tests for constitutional violations multiplied, particularly in First Amendment cases. *Clark v. Community for Creative Non-Violence* (1984) held that time, place, and manner restrictions on speech in public parks and other public fora were constitutional if the restrictions were "justified without reference to the content of the regulated speech," "narrowly tailored to serve a significant state interest," and left "open ample alternative channels for communication of the information." By the end of the Reagan Era there seemed to be more exceptions to than applications of the requirement that police give *Miranda* warnings.

Legacies. Ronald Reagan and his political allies accomplished a great deal from 1981 until 1993, even if they did not entirely transform the American constitutional regime. Reagan took consistent steps to reenergize presidential power in the wake of Watergate and Vietnam. Conservatives in the 1980s complained about the "fettered presidency," and they advocated for a vision of a president able to control the executive branch and solve national problems without burdensome interference by Congress or the courts.[2] Military actions were ordered in Grenada (where a "rescue mission" of American medical students led to the overthrow of the "revolutionary government" that had taken control of the Caribbean island nation in a military coup), Beirut (where a peacekeeping force was eventually removed after the truck bombing of a Marine barracks killed 241 American servicemen), and Libya (where an air strike was carried out in response to the bombing of a Berlin discotheque by Libyan agents). In none of these cases did the president's unilateral decision lead to any serious conflicts with Congress. Reagan's long-term policies in Latin America were more controversial on Capitol Hill. The administration circumvented congressional attempts to limit its ability to aid the "Contra" rebels who were trying to overthrow the left-wing government of Nicaragua by allowing the National Security Council to secretly find alternative sources of funding for the rebels. When Congress discovered that this off-the-books operation was partially funded by an "arms for hostages" sale of weapons to the Iranian government, it held a series of hearings that led to resignations and criminal convictions but not impeachment. President George H. W. Bush's decision to lead a United Nations coalition against Saddam Hussein in response to the Iraqi dictator's invasion of Kuwait in 1990 was debated by Congress for two days and was eventually supported by both chambers, but the White House insisted that the president had the authority to proceed even without prior congressional approval. Indeed, Bush did not seek congressional approval before invading Panama and overthrowing General Manuel Noriega in 1989.

For most of the twentieth century constitutional debate was over whether Americans should retain the status quo or move constitutional politics to the left. After 1981 constitutional debate focused just as often on the merits of adopting more conservative constitutional commitments. Liberal constitutional campaigns were abandoned or at least modified. Litigants

2. L. Gordon Crovitz and Jeremy A. Rabkin, eds., *The Fettered Presidency* (Washington, DC: American Enterprise Institute, 1989).

stopped asking the Supreme Court to declare that capital punishment violated the Eighth and Fourteenth Amendments. Instead, liberals argued that the execution of a particular individual or small class of persons violated constitutional standards. Conservatives did not win every constitutional struggle during the Reagan years or after, but they have played major roles in every constitutional controversy that has roiled the public since 1980. Constitutional debates would never again be contests between different liberals. Rather, from 1980 until the present, liberals and conservatives have debated on relatively equal terms the constitutional meanings of free speech, cruel and unusual punishment, and the due process clause.

II. Foundations

MAJOR DEVELOPMENTS

- Increased emphasis on limiting federal power and restoring state sovereignty
- Increased emphasis on the original meaning of constitutional provisions
- Defeat of amendments overturning Supreme Court decisions on school prayer, flag burning, and abortion
- Bill of Rights held to not limit searches of foreign citizens residing outside the United States

Reagan Republicans believed that the Great Society had perverted the American constitutional regime. The continued dominance of federal authority was a special target, as were "activist" judges. Leading Reagan conservatives often complained that unelected justices were seizing power from elected officials. They condemned courts for hamstringing legislative efforts to fight crime, improve education, secure public morality, and assert American power abroad. The campaign to return constitutional authority to elected officials included the proposal of a series of constitutional amendments that would overturn liberal judicial decisions; self-conscious efforts to staff federal courts with conservatives committed to overruling liberal precedents; and a public constitutional philosophy, originalism, which clearly explained why past liberal decisions were illegitimate. Robert Bork, the most visible proponent of Reagan constitutional conservatism, condemned such judicial decisions as *Roe v. Wade* (1973) as inconsistent with the original intentions of the persons responsible for the Bill of Rights and the Fourteenth Amendment. Most originalists in the 1980s emphasized the need for greater judicial restraint. Bork's writings immediately before and during the Reagan Era rarely discussed instances in which justices who applied the original intentions of the framers would need to strike down laws passed by popular majorities.

Conservatives enjoyed mixed success in their efforts to reshape constitutional foundations. The Reagan administration found reasons to compromise its federalist commitments once it became apparent that a significant rearrangement of federal and state responsibilities was not politically feasible. Despite originally pledging to dismantle the U.S. Department of Education, the administration eventually embraced the department as a platform from which to advocate for public school reform. Originalism gained respectability and prominence as a method of constitutional interpretation. Conservative judicial majorities narrowed the conditions in which private parties were considered state actors and the circumstances in which federal officials were bound by the Bill of Rights when acting outside the United States. Nevertheless, almost all pillars of constitutional liberalism remained standing. Conservative efforts to secure constitutional amendments overruling decisions that struck down abortion bans and voluntary school prayer failed. No Supreme Court justice accepted Reagan administration invitations to reconsider the incorporation of the Bill of Rights.

A. Sources

The textual and extratextual sources of constitutional rights and liberties remained the same. Conservatives proposed, but Congress did not approve, constitutional amendments that would reverse liberal judicial rights decisions. Federal judges maintained the traditional practice of treating customary international law, including the customary international law of human rights, as part of the law of the United States. A lower federal court, however, ruled that courts were bound to respect the customary international law of human rights only in the absence of a federal statute or executive decree.

Conservative Republicans proposed several constitutional amendments to overturn Supreme Court decisions protecting civil liberties. Shortly after winning the 1980 presidential election President Reagan proposed a constitutional amendment to permit voluntary prayer in public schools. Prominent congressmen at the same time proposed a constitutional amendment permitting states and Congress to ban abortion. Shortly after the Supreme Court in *Texas v. Johnson* (1989) declared that the First Amendment protected the right to burn the American flag, President George Bush proposed a constitutional amendment to overturn that decision.

These amendments enjoyed broad support, but all were defeated. The Senate in 1982 rejected a proposed constitutional amendment that would overturn *Roe v. Wade* (1973). The proposed amendment restoring voluntary prayer died the same year in the Senate. The proposed amendment permitting Congress and the states to prohibit flag burning came closer to passage. Congressional Democrats first stalled a constitutional amendment by passing a new federal law prohibiting flag burning. When the Supreme Court declared that law unconstitutional in *United States v. Eichman* (1990), the "flag protection" amendment was reintroduced. The resulting 58–42 vote in the Senate and 254–177 vote in the House fell just short of the required two-thirds majority.

The debates over these constitutional amendments were similar. Republicans and some conservative Democrats insisted that the amendments were necessary to correct Supreme Court decisions that had misinterpreted the Constitution. Democrats and some liberal Republicans maintained that the Supreme Court should retain the final word over the meaning of constitutional provisions protecting civil liberties and that elected officials ought not challenge those decisions, even by constitutional amendment. This liberal commitment to a particularly powerful form of judicial supremacy stemmed from the ideological belief that courts had special capacities to protect rights and powerless minorities; the pragmatic assessment that the Supreme Court, even augmented by Reagan appointees, was likely to be more liberal on rights issues than the Reagan administration; and the political calculation that foisting responsibility for such issues as abortion on the courts was a good political tactic in a badly divided polity.

Americans agreed that customary international law was a source of individual rights, but the precise constitutional status of the law of nations remained unclear. The Court of Appeals for the Second Circuit in *Filártiga v. Peña-Irala* (1980) adopted a broad interpretation of federal judicial power to enforce international human rights law when ruling that federal courts could adjudicate a lawsuit brought by a Paraguayan citizen charging members of the Paraguayan government with torturing his son. Judge Kaufmann's unanimous opinion held that Article III gave Congress the power to authorize federal courts to hear a lawsuit between Paraguayan citizens over human rights violations that occurred in Paraguay because "the Laws of the United States" included customary international law. "The law of nations forms an integral part of the common law," Kaufmann declared, "and a review of the history surrounding the adoption of the Constitution demonstrates that it became a part of the common law of the United States upon the adoption of the Constitution."[3]

President Reagan and his political allies did not question assertions that international law was part of the law of the United States. Administration officials claimed that international law permitted the United States to mine Nicaraguan harbors in response to charges that such actions violated the law of nations. Nevertheless, conservatives insisted that American constitutional authorities were the only persons authorized to determine whether American policy was consistent with the law of nations and that, for constitutional purposes, international law was merely a default rule or a rule of statutory interpretation. No administration accepted the authority of the International Court of Justice (ICJ) or any ICJ ruling on whether American actions violated international law. The Court of Appeals for the Eleventh Circuit in *Garcia-Mir v. Meese* (1986) articulated the Reagan administration position that an executive decree was a higher source of legal authority than customary international law. The issue in that case concerned the conditions under which the United States could detain Cuban refugees who had not legally entered the country. The Cuban refugees asserted that their continued detention violated international law. Judge Johnson agreed that "courts must construe American law so as to avoid violating principles of public international law." Nevertheless, he maintained that the Constitution required courts to follow international law only when no other conflicting legal authority existed. Noting that Attorney General Meese had approved the detention, Judge Johnson rejected the petition because "public international law is controlling only

3. *Filártiga v. Peña-Irala*, 630 F.2d 876 (2d. Cir. 1980).

where there is no treaty and no controlling executive or legislative act or judicial decision."[4]

B. Principles

Great Society liberals had a principled commitment to expanding the role of the federal government, weakening the notions of state sovereignty that for so long had undermined black civil rights, expanding the authority of courts to extend new rights protections, and encouraging notions of the "living Constitution" so that constitutional law could adapt to evolving historical contexts. Reagan conservatives challenged these liberal orthodoxies. A fiscal agenda that included tax cuts, deregulation, and decentralization of political authority was linked to constitutional arguments about the proper scope of federal power.

Reagan conservatives heralded originalism as the only legitimate means for interpreting constitutional provisions protecting civil liberties. Robert Bork declared, "Only by limiting themselves to the historic intentions underlying each clause of the Constitution can judges avoid becoming legislators, avoid enforcing their own moral predilections, and ensure the Constitution is law."[5] Reagan administration officials in the Justice Department enthusiastically adopted this jurisprudential principle. Richard Viguerie, a prominent New Right activist, identified core conservative commitments as "a moral order, based on God" and "the Constitution of the United States, as originally conceived by the Founding Fathers."[6]

Office of Legal Policy, **Guidelines on Constitutional Litigation** (1988)[7]

The Reagan administration aggressively advanced a conservative constitutional vision. Led by Attorney General Edwin Meese, conservatives carefully scrutinized all potential Justice Department appointees and candidates for federal judicial nominations to ensure a commitment to originalism and opposition to such liberal judicial precedents as Roe v. Wade *(1973). Justice Department officials made numerous speeches and produced many position papers detailing and justifying their conservative commitments.* The Constitution in the Year 2000: Choices Ahead in Constitutional Interpretation *(1988) and* Guidelines on Constitutional Litigation *(1988) were two particularly influential expositions of the constitutional philosophy of the Reagan administration.* Guidelines on Constitutional Litigation *was designed "to guide the government's litigating attorneys." That manual sets forth a particular theory of constitutional interpretation, originalism, and the constitutional positions that Reagan administration officials believed followed from originalism.*

When reading the following excerpts from the Guidelines on Constitutional Litigation, *consider the following questions. Many critics of the Reagan administration believed that conservatives had politicized the Justice Department. On what basis was that claim made? Was that claim correct? What was the difference between the Reagan administration Justice Department and past Justice Departments that had actively promoted such decisions as* Brown v. Board of Education *(1954)? Was the Reagan administration more ideological, more thorough, or simply more conservative? To what extent did the Reagan administration correctly capture the original meaning of constitutional provisions? To what extent was originalism merely a pretext for justifying politically conservative stances?*

As Robert Bork reminds us, "constitutional adjudication starts from the proposition that the Constitution is law" and thus "constrain[s] judgment." . . . Consequently, constitutional language should be construed as it was publicly understood at the time of its drafting and ratification and government attorneys should advance constitutional arguments based solely on this "original meaning." To do this, government attorneys should attempt to construct arguments based solely on the ordinary use of the words at the time the provision at issue was ratified. . . .

. . .

Decisions Inconsistent with These Principles of Interpretation

The so-called "right of privacy" cases provide examples of judicial creation of rights not reasonably found in the Constitution. The Supreme Court first articulated a

---

4. *Garcia-Mir v. Meese,* 788 F.2d 1446 (11th Cir. 1986).

5. Judge Robert H. Bork, "The Constitution, Original Intent, and Economic Rights," *University of San Diego Law Review* 23 (1986): 823.

6. Richard A. Viguerie, *The New Right: We're Ready to Lead* (Falls Church, VA: Viguerie Co., 1980), 11.

7. Excerpt taken from U.S. Department of Justice, Office of Legal Policy, *Guidelines for Constitutional Litigation* (Washington, DC: Government Printing Office, 1988).

Bork was defeated in the Senate in 1987, Reagan eventually settled for Anthony Kennedy, who proved to be a crucial swing vote on the Supreme Court along with Justice O'Connor. President George H. W. Bush succeeded in dividing Senate Democrats to win confirmation for conservative Clarence Thomas but failed to satisfy conservatives when appointing the relatively unknown "stealth candidate" David Souter, who later aligned with the liberals on the Court. The result was a distinctly more conservative Court, but not a Court that was completely satisfying to either conservatives or liberals.

Conservatives had a particular interest in challenging the notion that the U.S. Supreme Court was the ultimate interpreter of the U.S. Constitution and that the justices had the final say on the meaning of the Constitution. Attorney General Edwin Meese delivered a speech at Tulane Law School in 1987 that called into question the Supreme Court's assertion in *Cooper v. Aaron* (1958) that the Constitution and the constitutional law of the Supreme Court were of equal authority.[9] The Court's decision upholding the right to abortion in *Roe v. Wade* (1973) was the flashpoint for Meese and many conservatives in the 1970s and 1980s to argue that the requirements of judge-made constitutional law should be distinguished from the requirements of the Constitution itself. Although they admitted that government officials might be legally bound by specific judicial rulings, they thought that officials should ultimately be guided by the Constitution itself. For citizens, this view might justify civil disobedience and protest, as well as political mobilization and voting decisions. For legislators and executives, it might underwrite efforts to read judicial decisions as narrowly as possible, to look for ways to circumvent them or mitigate their effect, to look for opportunities to challenge and chip away at existing precedents, and ultimately to appoint judges committed to overturning those precedents.

The newly organized conservative legal movement of the 1980s found an institutional home in the Republican White House and the Department of Justice of the Reagan and Bush administrations. A central goal of the movement was to change how judicial review was exercised. Conservative lawyers in and around the Nixon administration made similar efforts in the late 1960s and early 1970s, but the lawyers surrounding the Reagan administration took a more detailed approach. Attorney General Edwin Meese gave public speeches questioning how the courts were exercising the power of judicial review, the Department of Justice prepared detailed litigation guidelines in an effort to identify areas of law that could be pushed in a more conservative direction, and the administration took greater care to identify judicial candidates who shared its constitutional philosophy. The effort to secure Robert Bork's appointment to the Supreme Court to fill the seat vacated by swing justice Lewis Powell triggered an intense mobilization of political resources by conservatives and liberals alike.

William H. Rehnquist, The Notion of a Living Constitution (1976)[10]

William Rehnquist operated in the background before appointed to the U.S. Supreme Court by President Nixon in 1972. A former clerk for Supreme Court Justice Robert Jackson, Rehnquist was a private lawyer who has involved in Republican politics in Phoenix, Arizona, including Barry Goldwater's presidential campaign. When Nixon captured the White House in 1968, some of those Arizona lawyers, including Rehnquist, were pulled into the Justice Department. Rehnquist worked closely with the White House in the Office of Legal Counsel, where he distinguished himself as a brilliant and highly conservative constitutional lawyer. As an associate justice, he displayed those same traits. He was the most conservative of the Nixon appointees and a frequent lone dissenter on the Burger Court.

His speech on the "notion of the living constitution" was one of his first major statements off the bench and articulated the constitutional and judicial philosophy that influenced the growing conservative legal movement and the future Reagan administration. For Rehnquist, both constitutional design and historical experience cautioned judges to exercise judicial restraint and defer to elected officials in developing solutions to public problems. As you read this excerpt, notice how Rehnquist invoked arguments

9. Edwin A. Meese III, "The Law of the Constitution," *Tulane Law Review* 61 (1987): 979–90.

10. Excerpt taken from William H. Rehnquist, "The Notion of a Living Constitution," *Texas Law Review* 54 (1976): 693–706. Reprinted with the permission of the Texas Law Review Association.

generally associated with the New Deal, such as the rejection of Lochner v. New York *(1905). How much weight did Rehnquist put on original meaning specifically as an alternative to "a living Constitution"?*

. . . At first blush it seems certain that a living Constitution is better than what must be its counterpart, a dead Constitution. . . . If we could get one of the major public opinion research firms in the country to sample public opinion concerning whether the United States Constitution should be living or dead, the overwhelming majority of the responses doubtless would favor a living Constitution.

If the question is worth asking a Supreme Court nominee during his confirmation hearings, however, it surely deserves to be analyzed in more than just the public relations context. . . .

. . . The phrase is really a shorthand expression that is susceptible of at least two quite different meanings.

. . .

The framers of the Constitution wisely spoke in general language and left to succeeding generations the task of applying that language to the unceasingly changing environment in which they would live. Those who framed, adopted, and ratified the Civil War amendments to the Constitution likewise used what have been aptly described as "majestic generalities" in composing the fourteenth amendment. Merely because a particular activity may not have existed when the Constitution was adopted, or because the framers could not have conceived of a particular method of transacting affairs, cannot mean that general language in the Constitution may not be applied to such a course of conduct. Where the framers of the Constitution have used general language, they have given latitude to those who would later interpret the instrument to make that language applicable to cases that the framers might not have foreseen.

In my reading and travels I have sensed a second connotation of the phrase "living Constitution.". . . Embodied in its most naked form, it recently came to my attention in some language from a brief that had been filed in a United States District Court on behalf of state prisoners asserting that the conditions of their confinement offended the United States Constitution. The brief argued:

> We are asking a great deal of the Court because other branches of government have abdicated their responsibility. . . . Prisoners are like other "discrete and insular" minorities for whom the Court must spread its protective umbrella because no other branch of government will do so. . . . This Court, as the voice and conscience of contemporary society, as the measure of modern conception of human dignity, must declare that the [named prison] and all it represents offends the Constitution of the United States and will not be tolerated.

Here we have a living Constitution with a vengeance. Although the substitution of some other set of values for those which may be derived from the language and intent of the framers is not urged in so many words, that is surely the thrust of the message. Under this brief writer's version of the living Constitution, nonelected members of the federal judiciary may address themselves to a social problem simply because other branches have failed or refused to do so. The same judges, responsible to no constituency whatever, are nonetheless acclaimed as "the voice and conscience of contemporary society."

. . .

John Marshall's justification for judicial review [in *Marbury v. Madison*] makes the provision for an independent federal judiciary not only understandable but also thoroughly desirable. Since the judges will be merely interpreting an instrument framed by the people, they should be detached and objective. A mere change in public opinion since the adoption of the Constitution, unaccompanied by a constitutional amendment, should not change the meaning of the Constitution. A mere temporary majoritarian groundswell should not abrogate some individual liberty truly protected by the Constitution.

. . . The Constitution is in many of its parts obviously not a specifically worded document but one couched in general phraseology. There is obviously wide room for honest difference of opinion over the meaning of general phrases in the Constitution; any particular Justice's decision when a decision arises under one of these general phrases will depend to some extent on his own philosophy of constitutional law. One may nevertheless concede all of these problems that inhere in Marshall's justification of judicial review, yet feel that his justification for nonelected judges exercising the power of judicial review is the only one consistent with democratic philosophy of representative government.

. . .

The brief writer's version [of the living Constitution] seems instead to be based upon the proposition that federal judges, perhaps judges as a whole, have a role of their own, quite independent of the popular will, to play in solving society's problems. Once we have abandoned the idea that the authority of the courts to declare laws unconstitutional is somehow tied to the language of the Constitution that the people adopted, a judiciary exercising the power of judicial review appears in a quite different light. Judges then are no longer the keepers of the covenant; instead they are a small group of fortunately situated people with a roving commission to second-guess Congress, state legislatures, and state and federal administrative officers concerning what is best for the country. Surely there is no justification for a third legislative branch in the federal branch in the federal government, and there is even less justification for a federal legislative branch's reviewing on a policy basis the laws enacted by the legislatures of the fifty states. . . .

. . .

The second difficulty with the brief writer's version of the living Constitution lies in its inattention to or rejection of the Supreme Court's historical experience gleaned from similar forays into problem solving.

. . .

One reads the history of these episodes in the Supreme Court to little purpose if he does not conclude that prior experimentation with the brief writer's expansive notion of a living Constitution has done the Court little credit. There remains today those . . . who appear to cleave nonetheless to the view that the experiments of the Taney Court before the Civil War, and of the Fuller and Taft Courts in the first part of this century, ended in failure not because they sought to bring into the Constitution a principle that the great majority of objective scholars would have to conclude was not there but because they sought to bring into the Constitution the *wrong* extraconstitutional principle. . . . To the extent that one must, however, go beyond even a generously fair reading of the language and intent of that document in order to subsume these principles, it seems to me that they are not really distinguishable from those espoused in *Dred Scott* and *Lochner*.

The third difficulty with the brief writer's notion of the living Constitution is that it seems to ignore totally the nature of political value judgments in a democratic society. If such a society adopts a constitution and incorporates in that constitution safeguards for individual liberty, these safeguards indeed do take on a generalized moral rightness or goodness. . . . It is the fact of their enactment that gives them whatever moral claim they have upon us as a society, however, and not any independent virtue they may have in any particular citizen's own scale of values.

Beyond the Constitution and the laws in our society, there simply is no basis other than the individual conscience of the citizen that may serve as a platform for the launching of moral judgments. . . . Many of us necessarily feel strongly and deeply about our own moral judgments, but they remain only personal moral judgments until in some way given the sanction of law. . . .

. . .

. . . It is always time consuming, frequently difficult, and not infrequently impossible to run successfully the legislative gauntlet and have enacted some facet of one's own deeply felt value judgments. It is even more difficult for either a single individual or indeed for a large group of individuals to succeed in having such a value judgment embodied in the Constitution. All of these burdens and difficulties are entirely consistent with the notion of a democratic society. It should not be easy for any one individual or group of individuals to impose by law their value judgments upon fellow citizens who may disagree with those judgments. Indeed, it should not be easier just because the individual in question is a judge. . . .

. . .

William J. Brennan, The Constitution of the United States: Contemporary Ratification (1985)[11]

William Brennan was a Democratic judge on the New Jersey Supreme Court when he was nominated to the U.S. Supreme Court by President Dwight Eisenhower on the eve of the 1956 elections, in part to shore up Eisenhower's support among Catholic Democrats. He soon emerged as

11. Excerpt taken from William J. Brennan, "The Constitution of the United States: Contemporary Ratification," in *The Great Debate: Interpreting Our Written Constitution* (Washington, DC: Federalist Society, 1986). © The Federalist Society. Reprinted with permission.

the intellectual and political leader of the liberal wing of the Warren Court, and he authored many of the Court's landmark decisions on voting rights, religious liberty, free speech, criminal procedure, and civil rights. He remained a potent force on the Court until his retirement in 1990, but his influence waned with the addition of more conservative justices over time.

Brennan and Rehnquist were frequent sparring partners on the bench, offering sharply divergent views across a range of constitutional issues. Brennan took the rise of the Reagan administration and its vocal defense of originalism and judicial restraint as a fundamental challenge to his constitutional vision and jurisprudential legacy. In this speech, delivered shortly after Attorney General Edwin Meese's well-publicized address to the American Bar Association on originalism, Brennan offered an alternative vision of the Constitution that frankly embraced judicial activism and an ever-evolving "aspiration to social justice."[12] *Was Brennan right that the Court's role is to "adapt" the terms of the Constitution to present values and social needs? Is this role different from the "brief writer's notion" that Rehnquist criticized in the previous excerpt?*

. . . [T]he Constitution embodies the aspiration to social justice, brotherhood, and human dignity that brought this nation into being. The Declaration of Independence, the Constitution and the Bill of Rights solemnly committed the United States to be a country where the dignity and rights of all persons were equal before all authority. In all candor we must concede that part of this egalitarianism in America has been more pretension than realized fact. But we are an aspiring people, a people with faith in progress. Our amended Constitution is the lodestar for our aspirations. Like every text worth reading, it is not crystalline. The phrasing is broad and the limitations of its provisions are not clearly marked. Its majestic generalities and ennobling pronouncements are both luminous and obscure. This ambiguity of course calls forth interpretation, the interaction of reader and text. . . .

. . .

There are those who find legitimacy in fidelity to what they call "the intentions of the Framers." In its most doctrinaire incarnation, this view demands that Justices discern exactly what the Framers thought about the question under consideration and simply follow that intention in resolving the case before them. It is a view that feigns self-effacing deference to the specific judgments of those who forged our original social compact. But in truth it is little more than arrogance cloaked as humility. It is arrogant to pretend that from our vantage we can gauge accurately the intent for the Framers on application of principle to specific, contemporary questions. All too often, sources of potential enlightenment such as records of the ratification debates provide sparse or ambiguous evidence of the original intentions. Typically, all that can be gleaned is that the Framers themselves did not agree about the application or meaning of particular constitutional provisions, and hid their differences in cloaks of generality. . . . And apart from the problematic nature of the sources, our distance of two centuries cannot but work as a prism refracting all we perceive. . . .

Perhaps most importantly, while proponents of this facile historicism justify it as a depoliticization of the judiciary, the political underpinnings of such a choice should not escape notice. A position that upholds constitutional claims only if they were within the specific contemplation of the Framers in effect establishes a presumption of resolving textual ambiguities against the claim of constitutional right. It is far from clear what justifies such a presumption against claims of right. Nothing intrinsic in the nature of interpretation—if there is such a thing as the "nature" of interpretation—commands such a passive approach to ambiguity. This is a choice no less political than any other; it expresses antipathy to claims of the minority rights against the majority. Those who would restrict claims of right to the values of 1789 specifically articulated in the Constitution turn a blind eye to social progress and eschew adaptation of overarching principles to changes of social circumstances.

. . .

The view that all matters of substantive policy should be resolved through the majoritarian process has appeal under some circumstances, but I think it ultimately will not do. Unabashed enshrinement of majority would permit the imposition of a social caste system or wholesale confiscation of property so long as a majority of the authorized legislative body, fairly elected, approved. Our Constitution could not abide such a situation. It is the very purpose of a Constitution—and particularly of the Bill of Rights—to declare certain values transcendent, beyond the

12. See also Frank I. Michelman, *Brennan and Democracy* (Princeton, NJ: Princeton University Press, 1999).

reach of temporary political majorities. The majoritarian process cannot be expected to rectify claims of minority right that arise as a response to the outcomes of that very majoritarian process. . . .

To remain faithful to the content of the Constitution, therefore, an approach to interpreting the text must account for the existence of these substantive value choices, and must accept the ambiguity inherent in the effort to apply them to modern circumstances. The Framers discerned fundamental principles through struggles against particular malefactions of the Crown; the struggle shapes the particular contours of the articulated principles. But our acceptance of the fundamental principles has not and should not bind us to those precise, at times anachronistic, contours. Successive generations of Americans have continued to respect these fundamental choices and adopt them as their own guide to evaluating quite different historical practices. Each generation has a choice to overrule or add to the fundamental principles enunciated by the Framers; the Constitution can be amended or it can be ignored. Yet with respect to its fundamental principles, the text has suffered neither fate. . . .

We current Justices read the Constitution in the only way that we can: as Twentieth Century Americans. We look to the history of the time of the framing and to the intervening history of interpretation. But the ultimate question must be, what do the words of the text mean in our time. For the genius of the Constitution rests not in any static meaning it might have had in a world that is dead and gone, but in the adaptability of its great principles to cope with the current problems and current needs. . . .

Interpretation must account for the transformative purpose of the text. Our Constitution was not intended to preserve a preexisting society but to make a new one, to put in place new principles that the prior political community had not sufficiently recognized. . . .

. . . [T]he Constitution is a sublime oration on the dignity of man, a bold commitment by a people to the ideal of libertarian dignity protected through law. . . .

. . .

If we are to be as a shining city upon a hill, it will be because of our ceaseless pursuit of the constitutional ideal of human dignity. . . . As we adapt our institutions to the ever-changing conditions of national and international life, those ideals of human dignity—liberty and justice for all individuals—will continue to inspire and guide us because they are entrenched in our Constitution. The Constitution with its Bill of Rights thus has a bright future, as well as a glorious past, for its spirit is inherent in the aspirations of our people.

The Nomination of Robert H. Bork to the U.S. Supreme Court (1987)

When nominated to the Supreme Court by Ronald Reagan in 1987, Robert Bork was a judge on the influential Court of Appeals for the District of Columbia, having been easily confirmed early in Reagan's presidency. Within political and legal circles, Bork a leading conservative intellectual. A well-respected litigator, U.S. solicitor general during the Nixon administration, and a former Yale law professor, Bork had long been a forceful advocate for conservative constitutional and legal causes. As a vocal critic of many of the decisions of the Warren and early Burger Courts, he was particularly known for supporting judicial restraint and championing originalism. Both supporters and opponents of the Reagan administration saw his nomination as a symbol of conservative ambitions to remake the judiciary and advance a distinct constitutional philosophy through judicial appointments.

Bork's nomination took on added significance not only because he was thought to have the intellectual skills and beliefs to influence the direction of the Court, but also because the vacancy was created by the departure of the moderate Lewis Powell, a swing vote on many issues including abortion and affirmative action. Bork's nomination also came after the midterm elections of 1986, when the Republicans lost their majority in the Senate. Conservative Associate Justice William Rehnquist had been elevated to chief justice and conservative Antonin Scalia had also joined the Court the year before, when the Republicans still held the majority.

Given Bork's strong qualifications and the absence of scandal or doubts about his character, Republicans hoped Bork would be easily confirmed by a bipartisan vote, as Scalia had been and as other nominees had been in similar circumstances. Instead, and surprisingly, the confirmation debate focused explicitly on Bork's conservative judicial philosophy, with organized lobbying campaigns on both sides and a special presidential address. The battle was particularly bitter, with conservatives complaining that the judge's record had been badly misrepresented, a charge remembered afterwards as having been "Borked." His nomination was ultimately defeated in a largely party-line vote on the Senate floor. The Court vacancy was eventually filled by Anthony Kennedy, a lower-profile and more moderate figure who has often been a swing vote on the Rehnquist and Roberts Courts.

Illustration 10-1 "You Were Expecting Maybe Edward M. Kennedy?"

Source: Herblock, *Washington Post*, July 2, 1987. Copyright by *The Herb Block Foundation.*

Ronald Reagan, Address to the Nation (October 14, 1987)

. . .

In the last 6½ years I have spoken with you and asked for your help many times. When special interests and power brokers here in Washington balked at cutting your taxes, I asked for your help. You went to your Congressmen and Senators, and the tax cuts passed. And by the way, as a result, at the end of this month we will mark the longest peacetime economic expansion on record.

. . . Yes, all that America has achieved in the last 6½ years—our record economic expansion, the new pride we have at home, the new strength that may soon bring us history's first agreement to eliminate an entire class of U.S. and Soviet nuclear missiles—all of this has happened because, when the chips were down, you and I worked together.

As you know, I have selected one of the finest judges in America's history, Robert Bork, for the Supreme Court. You've heard that this nomination is a lost cause. You've also heard that I am determined to fight right down to the final ballot on the Senate floor. I'm doing this because what's now at stake in this battle must never in our land of freedom become a lost cause. And whether lost or not, we Americans must never give up this particular battle: the independence of our judiciary.

Back in July when I nominated Judge Bork, I thought the confirmation process would go forward with a calm and sensible exchange of views. Unfortunately, the confirmation process became an ugly spectacle, marred by distortions and innuendos, and casting aside the normal rules of decency and honesty. As Judge Bork said last Friday, and I quote: "The process of confirming Justices for our nation's highest court has been transformed in a way that should not and, indeed, must not be permitted to occur again. The tactics and techniques of national political campaigns have been unleashed on the process of confirming judges. That is not simply disturbing; it is dangerous. Federal judges are not appointed to decide cases according to the latest opinion polls; they are appointed to decide cases impartially, according to law. But when judicial nominees are assessed and treated like political candidates, the effect will be to chill the climate in which judicial deliberations take place, to erode public confidence in the impartiality of courts, and to endanger the independence of the judiciary."

. . .

During the hearings, one of Judge Bork's critics said that among the functions of the Court was reinterpreting the Constitution so that it would not remain, in his words, "frozen into ancient error because it is so hard to amend." Well, that to my mind is the issue, plain and simple. Too many theorists believe that the courts should save the country from the Constitution. Well, I believe it's time to save the Constitution from them. The principal errors in recent years have had nothing to do with the intent of the framers who finished their work 200 years ago last month. They've had to do with those who have looked upon the courts as their own special province to impose by judicial fiat what they could not accomplish at the polls. They've had to do with judges who too often have made law enforcement a game where clever lawyers try to find ways to trip up the police on the rules.

. . .

So, my agenda is your agenda, and it's quite simple: to appoint judges like Judge Bork who don't confuse the criminals with the victims; judges who don't invent new or fanciful constitutional rights for those criminals; judges who believe the courts should interpret the law, not make it; judges, in short, who understand the principle of judicial restraint. That starts with the Supreme Court. It takes leadership from the Supreme Court to help shape the attitudes of the courts in our land and to make sure that principles of law are based on the Constitution. That is the standard to judge those who seek to serve on the courts: qualifications, not distortions; judicial temperament, not campaign disinformation.

In the next several days, your Senators will cast a vote on the Bork nomination. It is more than just one vote on one man: It's a decision on the future of our judicial system. The purpose of the Senate debate is to allow all sides to be heard. Honorable men and women should not be afraid to change their minds based on that debate.

I hope that in the days and weeks ahead you will let them know that the confirmation process must never again be compromised with high-pressure politics. Tell them that America stands for better than that and that you expect them to stand for America. . . .

Thank you, and God bless you all.

Senate Judiciary Committee Hearings on the Nomination of Robert Bork (1987)[13]

Chairman JOSEPH BIDEN (Democrat, Delaware)

. . .

Judge, each generation in some sense has had as much to do to author our Constitution as the 39 men who affixed their signatures to it 200 years ago. Indeed, two years after its signing, following a bitter national debate over its ratification, at the insistence of the people, the Constitution was profoundly ennobled by the addition of what has come to be known as the Bill of Rights.

. . .

America is the promised land because each generation bequeathed to their children a promise, a promise that they might not come to enjoy but which they fully expected their offspring to fulfill. So the words "all men are created equal" took a life of their own, ultimately destined to end slavery and enfranchise women. And the words, "equal protection and due process" inevitably led to the end of the words,

13. Excerpt taken from "Hearings Before the Committee on the Judiciary, United States Senate, One Hundredth Congress, First Session on the Nomination of Robert H. Bork to Be Associate Justice on the Supreme Court of the United States," September 15–19, 21–23, 25, 28–30, 1987, Serial No. J-100-64 (Washington, DC: Government Printing Office, 1989).

"separate but equal," ensuring that the walls of segregation would crumble, whether at the lunch counter or in the voting booth.

. . .

So let's make no mistake about it, the unique importance of this nomination is in part because of the moment in history in which it comes, for I believe that a greater question transcends the issue of this nomination. And that question is, will we retreat from our tradition of progress or will we move forward, continuing to expand and envelope the rights of individuals in a changing world which is bound to have an impact upon the individuals' sense of who they are and what they can do, will these ennobling human rights and human dignity, which is a legacy of the past two centuries, continue to mark the journey of our people?

. . .

. . . In passing on this nomination to the Supreme Court, we must also pass judgment on whether or not your particular philosophy is an appropriate one at this time in our history.

. . .

You have been a man of significant standing in the academic community and thus in a special way, a vote to confirm you requires, in my view, an endorsement of your basic philosophic views as they relate to the Constitution. And thus the Senate, in exercising its constitutional role of advice and consent, has not only the right in my opinion but the duty to weigh the philosophy of the nominee as it reaches its own independent decision. . . .

. . .

I believe all Americans are born with certain inalienable rights. As a child of God, I believe my rights are not derived from the Constitution. My rights are not derived from any Government. My rights are not derived from any majority. My rights are because I exist I have certain rights. They were given to me and each of my fellow citizens by our creator and they represent the essence of human dignity.

I agree with Justice Harlan, the most conservative jurist and Justice of our era, who stated that the Constitution is, quote, "a living thing" and that "its protections are enshrined in majestic phrases like 'equal protection under the law' and 'due process' and thus cannot be," as he said, and I quote, "reduced to any formula."

It is, as the great Chief Justice John Marshall said, intended, and I quote, "intended to endure for ages to come and consequently to be adapted to the various crises of human affairs, only its great outlines marked." . . .

. . .

Judge ROBERT BORK

. . . As you have said, quite correctly, Mr. Chairman, and as others have said here today, this is in large measure a discussion of judicial philosophy, and I want to make a few remarks at the outset on that subject of central interest.

That is, my understanding of how a judge should go about his or her work. That may also be described as my philosophy of the role of a judge in a constitutional democracy.

The judge's authority derives entirely from the fact that he is applying the law and not his personal values. That is why the American public accepts the decisions of its courts, accepts even decisions that nullify the laws a majority of the electorate or of their representatives voted for.

The judge, to deserve that trust and that authority, must be every bit as governed by law as is the Congress, the President, the state governors and legislatures, and the American people. No one, including a judge, can be above the law. Only in that way will justice be done and the freedom of Americans assured.

How should a judge go about finding the law? The only legitimate way, in my opinion, is by attempting to discern what those who made the law intended. The intentions of the lawmakers govern whether the lawmakers are the Congress of the United States enacting a statute or whether they are those who ratified our Constitution and its various amendments.

Where the words are precise and the facts simple, that is a relatively easy task. Where the words are general, as is the case with some of the most profound protections of our liberties—in the Bill of Rights and in the Civil War Amendments—the task is far more complex. It is to find the principle or value that was intended to be protected and to see that it is protected.

As I wrote in an opinion for our court, the judge's responsibility "is to discern how the Framers' values, defined in the context of the world they knew, apply in the world we know."

If a judge abandons intention as his guide, there is no law available to him and he begins to legislate a social agenda for the American people. That goes well beyond his legitimate power.

. . .

Times come, of course, when even a venerable precedent can and should be overruled. The primary example of a proper overruling is Brown against Board of Education, the case which outlawed racial segregation accomplished by Government action. *Brown* overturned the rule of separate but equal laid down 58 years before in Plessy against Ferguson. Yet *Brown*, delivered with the authority of a unanimous Court, was clearly correct and represents perhaps the greatest moral achievement of our constitutional law.

. . .

I can put the matter no better than I did in an opinion on my present court. Speaking of the judge's duty, I wrote: "The important thing, the ultimate consideration, is the constitutional freedom that is given into our keeping. A judge who refuses to see new threats to an established constitutional value and hence provides a crabbed interpretation that robs a provision of its full, fair and reasonable meaning, fails in his judicial duty. That duty, I repeat, is to ensure that the powers and freedoms the Framers specified are made effective in today's circumstances."

But I should add to that passage that when a judge goes beyond this and reads entirely new values into the Constitution, values the Framers and the ratifiers did not put there, he deprives the people of their liberty. That liberty, which the Constitution clearly envisions, is the liberty of the people to set their own social agenda through the processes of democracy.

Conservative judges frustrated that process in the mid-1930's by using the concept they had invented, the Fourteenth Amendment's supposed guarantee of a liberty of contract to strike down laws designed to protect workers and labor unions. That was wrong then and it would be wrong now.

My philosophy of judging, Mr. Chairman, as you pointed out, is neither liberal nor conservative. It is simply a philosophy of judging which gives the Constitution a full and fair interpretation but, where the constitution is silent, leaves the policy struggles to the Congress, the President, the legislatures and executives of the 50 states, and to the American people.

. . .

Senator ORRIN HATCH (Republican, Utah)

. . .

The great danger I see in the impending ideological inquisition is injury to the independence and integrity of the Supreme Court and the whole Federal judiciary. When we undertake to judge a judge according to political rather than legal criteria, we have stripped the judicial office of all that makes it a distinct separated power. . . .

Now, recognizing precisely this danger, the Senate has refused to employ political litmus tests while confirming 53 justices over this past century. Senate precedent does not support subjecting judicial nominees to ideological inquisitions.

Moreover, the Constitution itself does not support that practice. Based on the common sense observation that a diverse congressional body would have difficulty overcoming jealousies and politics to select the best candidate, the Framers . . . unanimously voted to vest the nomination power in the President. The Senate, however, was given a checking function. In the words of Alexander Hamilton, the advice and consent function was to prevent "nepotism" and "unfit characters." The advice and consent function is a checking function, not a license to exert political influence on another branch, not a license to control the outcome of future cases by overriding the President's prerogatives.

. . .

This is the reason that politics are injected into this proceeding, because many politicians are hoping to win from unelected judges what they cannot win in the Congress or with the people of the United States of America. My fear, however, is that the price of a politicized judiciary is too high to pay in exchange for a short-term policy set of gains. If judges fear to uphold the Constitution due to political pressures or sense that their judicial careers might be advanced by reading that document in the smokey back rooms of political intrigue, then the Constitution will no longer be the solid anchor holding our nation in place during the times of storm and crisis. Instead, the Constitution will just become part of that political storm, blowing hot and cold whenever the wind changes. That is a price that we in this country cannot afford to pay, and I think it is important that the American people understand that here.

. . .

Senator EDWARD KENNEDY (Democrat, Massachusetts)

. . .

From the beginning, America has set the highest standards for our highest Court. We insist that a nominee should have outstanding ability and integrity. But we also insist on even more: that those who sit on the Supreme Court must deserve the special title we reserve for only nine Federal judges in the entire country, the title that sums up in one word the awesome responsibility on their shoulders—the title of "Justice."

Historically, America has set this high standard because the Justices of the Supreme Court have a unique obligation: to serve as the ultimate guardians of the Constitution, the rule of law, and the liberty and the equality of every citizen. To fulfill these responsibilities, to earn the title of "Justice," a person must have special qualities:

A commitment to individual liberty as the cornerstone of American democracy.

A dedication to equality for all Americans, especially those who have been denied their full measure of freedom, such as women and minorities.

A respect for justice for all whose rights are too readily abused by powerful institutions, whether by the power of government or by giant concentrations of power in the private sector.

. . .

These are the standards by which the Senate must evaluate any judicial nominee. And by these standards, Robert Bork falls short of what Americans demand of a man or woman as a Justice on the Supreme Court. Time and again, in his public record over more than a quarter of a century, Robert Bork has shown that he is hostile to the rule of law and the role of the courts in protecting individual liberty.

He has harshly opposed—and is publicly itching to overrule—many of the great decisions of the Supreme Court that seek to fulfill the promise of justice for all Americans.

He is instinctively biased against the claims of the average citizen and in favor of concentrations of power, whether that is governmental or private.

And in conflicts between the legislative and executive branches of Government, he has repeatedly expressed a clear contempt for Congress and an unbridled trust in the power of the President.

. . .

In Robert Bork's America, there is no room at the inn for blacks and no place in the Constitution for women, and in our America there should be no seat on the Supreme Court for Robert Bork.

Mr. Bork has been equally extreme in his opposition to the right to privacy. In an article in 1971, he said, in effect, that a husband and wife have no greater right to privacy under the Constitution than a smokestack has to pollute the air.

President Reagan has said that this controversy is pure politics, but that is not the case. I and others who oppose Mr. Bork have often supported nominees to the Supreme Court by Republican Presidents, including many with whose philosophy we disagree. I voted for the confirmation of Chief Justice Burger and also Justices Blackmun, Powell, Stevens, O'Connor and Scalia. But Mr. Bork is a nominee of a different stripe. President Reagan has every right to take Mr. Bork's reactionary ideology into account in making the nomination, and the Senate has every right to take that ideology into account in acting on the nomination.

. . .

. . . All Americans should realize that the confrontation over this nomination is the result of a deliberate decision by the Reagan Administration. Rather than selecting a real judicial conservative to fill Justice Powell's vacancy, the President has sought to appoint an activist of the right whose agenda would turn us back to the battles of a bitterly divided America, reopening issues long thought to be settled and wounds long thought to be healed.

I for one am proud of the accomplishments of America in moving towards the constitutional ideas of liberty and equality and justice under law. I am also proud of the role of the Senate in ensuring that Supreme Court nominees adhere to the tradition of fairness, impartiality, and the freedom from bias.

I believe the American people strongly reject the Administration's invitation to roll back the clock and relive the more troubled times of the past. I urge the Committee and the Senate to reject the nomination of Mr. Bork.

IV. Powers of the National Government

MAJOR DEVELOPMENTS

- Growing conservative rhetoric aimed at criticizing the expansion of federal power since the New Deal
- Supreme Court upholds the use of federal spending power as a tool to influence state policy making

Reagan committed the Republican Party to a conservative constitutional philosophy that emphasized the constitutional limits on the powers of the national government. A conservative legal movement organized both inside the administration and outside of it through the formation of new organizations such as the Federalist Society and legal advocacy groups such as the Institute for Justice and the Pacific Legal Foundation. These conservative lawyers sought a rethinking of the powers of the national government.[14] Although the Reagan administration initially emphasized a strategy of legislation and public education to advance its constitutional philosophy on federalism, it eventually turned to judicial nominations and litigation as an alternative strategy. The strategy seemed to yield its most substantial results once Reagan and George H. W. Bush were able, by the early 1990s, to place five justices on the bench who shared important elements of this constitutional philosophy. The resulting "federalism revolution" of the late 1990s was one of the most distinctive features of the Rehnquist Court. The Reagan and Bush years laid the groundwork for those later judicial innovations.

During the 1980s, however, the Supreme Court was still quite supportive of federal power. In *South Dakota v. Dole* (1987), the Court upheld Congress' authority to impose restrictions on how state and local governments may spend federal funds. Congress often uses federal funds as political leverage to convince states to cooperate with federal policy goals. The less controversial type of restrictions on federal funds is when Congress specifies, for example, where a highway should be built, what quality of road materials ought to be used in its construction, or even the ethnic diversity and union membership of the workers who will build the highway. The more controversial restriction on federal funds is when Congress threatens to withhold part of a state's annual highway appropriation unless the state adopts a set of policies that the federal government favors. When is the federal government "buying a favor" from a state, and when is it "holding the state hostage"?

South Dakota v. Dole, 483 U.S. 203 (1987)

In 1984 Congress passed the National Minimum Drinking Age Amendment to the Federal Aid Highway Act. The measure directed Secretary of Transportation Elizabeth Dole to withhold 10 percent of a state's allotted federal highway funds if it refused to adopt a minimum legal drinking age of twenty-one years. At the time of passage, thirty-one states had a legal drinking age below twenty-one. In response to the law, every state eventually shifted to the national drinking age set by Congress. Threats to reduce or cut off federal funds to states had been successfully used on other occasions to induce the states to adopt policies that the federal government wanted. Threats to highway funds had been used in the 1970s to induce states to set a national maximum speed limit and were used in the 1990s to encourage states to adopt mandatory seat belt and motorcycle helmet laws. Threats to federal assistance to public schools were used to encourage desegregation in the 1960s. This federal leverage over state policy making was a side effect of the "fiscal federalism" or "cooperative federalism" that had grown since the New Deal, and had shown itself to be quite powerful in driving states to conform to national political preferences.

The drinking age proposal was a favorite of the recently formed and highly successful activist group Mothers Against Drunk Driving (MADD). Democrats in the House and Senate pressed the issue hard as a basic safety issue in the 1984 election year. Although President Reagan and Republicans in the Senate were initially opposed to the measure, after House passage Reagan announced that he would not veto the bill. South Dakota sought a declaratory judgment in federal district court that the measure was an invalid exercise of the congressional spending power and a violation of the Twenty-First Amendment (which repealed Prohibition and reserved control over the sale of alcohol to the states). The district court rejected the state's arguments, and a federal circuit court affirmed the ruling of the trial judge. The U.S. Supreme Court heard the case on certiorari.

In a 7–2 decision, the Court affirmed the lower court and upheld Congress's power to use the spending power in this way. Justices Brennan and O'Connor were the lone justices in dissent. This alignment of justices was particularly notable in pitting Chief Justice Rehnquist and Justice O'Connor, normally two strong voices on behalf of states' rights and frequent allies in federalism cases, against one another. It was equally unusual for the liberal Brennan and the more conservative O'Connor dissent together. As you read these opinions, consider how willing Rehnquist and O'Connor were to revisit and unsettle the New Deal precedents relating to the congressional spending power. For Rehnquist, might this case have been an example of the occasional tension between a commitment to "original intent" and a commitment to "judicial restraint"? If the Court had overturned the drinking age law, could the precedent have been easily limited, or would it have necessarily had implications for a wide range of

14. Steven M. Teles, *The Rise of the Conservative Legal Movement* (Princeton, NJ: Princeton University Press, 2008).

other conditions that Congress might put on receipt of federal grants? Also, if the federal government is given broad authority to use the spending power to influence state behavior, then how meaningful are other limits on federal power over states?

CHIEF JUSTICE REHNQUIST delivered the opinion of the Court.

. . .

. . . [W]e need not decide in this case whether [the Twenty-First] Amendment would prohibit an attempt by Congress to legislate directly a national minimum drinking age. Here, Congress has acted indirectly under its spending power to encourage uniformity in the States' drinking ages. As we explain below, we find this legislative effort within constitutional bounds even if Congress may not regulate drinking ages directly.

The Constitution empowers Congress to "lay and collect Taxes, Duties, Imposts, and Excises, to pay the Debts and provide for the common Defense and general Welfare of the United States." Incident to this power, Congress may attach conditions on the receipt of federal funds, and has repeatedly employed the power "to further broad policy objectives by conditioning receipt of federal moneys upon compliance by the recipient with federal statutory and administrative directives." *Fullilove* v. *Klutznick* (1980) (opinion of Burger, C. J.). . . . The breadth of this power was made clear in *United States* v. *Butler* (1936), where the Court, resolving a longstanding debate over the scope of the Spending Clause, determined that "the power of Congress to authorize expenditure of public moneys for public purposes is not limited by the direct grants of legislative power found in the Constitution." Thus, objectives not thought to be within Article I's "enumerated legislative fields," may nevertheless be attained through the use of the spending power and the conditional grant of federal funds.

The spending power is of course not unlimited. . . . The first of these limitations is derived from the language of the Constitution itself: the exercise of the spending power must be in pursuit of "the general welfare." . . In considering whether a particular expenditure is intended to serve general public purposes, courts should defer substantially to the judgment of Congress. . . . Second, we have required that if Congress desires to condition the States' receipt of federal funds, it "must do so unambiguously . . . enabl[ing] the States to exercise their choice knowingly, cognizant of the consequences of their participation." . . Third, our cases have suggested (without significant elaboration) that conditions on federal grants might be illegitimate if they are unrelated "to the federal interest in particular national projects or programs." . . Finally, we have noted that other constitutional provisions may provide an independent bar to the conditional grant of federal funds. . . .

. . . Congress found that the differing drinking ages in the States created particular incentives for young persons to combine their desire to drink with their ability to drive, and that this interstate problem required a national solution. The means it chose to address this dangerous situation were reasonably calculated to advance the general welfare. The conditions upon which States receive the funds, moreover, could not be more clearly stated by Congress. . . . [T]he condition imposed by Congress is directly related to one of the main purposes for which highway funds are expended—safe interstate travel. . . . This goal of the interstate highway system had been frustrated by varying drinking ages among the States.

. . .

. . . [W]e think that the language in our earlier opinions stands for the unexceptionable proposition that the [spending] power may not be used to induce the States to engage in activities that would themselves be unconstitutional. Thus, for example, a grant of federal funds conditioned on invidiously discriminatory state action or the infliction of cruel and unusual punishment would be an illegitimate exercise of the Congress' broad spending power. But no such claim can be or is made here. . . .

. . .

Here Congress has offered relatively mild encouragement to the States to enact higher minimum drinking ages than they would otherwise choose. But the enactment of such laws remains the prerogative of the States not merely in theory but in fact. Even if Congress might lack the power to impose a national minimum drinking age directly, we conclude that encouragement to state action found in §158 is a valid use of the spending power. Accordingly, the judgment of the Court of Appeals is

Affirmed.

JUSTICE BRENNAN, dissenting.

I agree with Justice O'CONNOR. . . .

JUSTICE O'CONNOR, dissenting.

The Court today upholds the National Minimum Drinking Age Amendment as a valid exercise of the spending power conferred by Article I, §8. But §158 is not a condition on spending reasonably related to the expenditure of federal funds and cannot be justified on that ground. Rather, it is an attempt to regulate the sale of liquor, an attempt that lies outside Congress' power to regulate commerce because it falls within the ambit of §2 of the Twenty-First Amendment.

. . . We have repeatedly said that Congress may condition grants under the spending power only in ways reasonably related to the purpose of the federal program. . . . In my view, establishment of a minimum drinking age of 21 is not sufficiently related to interstate highway construction to justify so conditioning funds appropriated for that purpose.

. . .

When Congress appropriates money to build a highway, it is entitled to insist that the highway be a safe one. But it is not entitled to insist as a condition of the use of highway funds that the State impose or change regulations in other areas of the State's social and economic life because of an attenuated or tangential relationship to highway use or safety. Indeed, if the rule were otherwise, the Congress could effectively regulate almost any area of a State's social, political, or economic life on the theory that use of the interstate transportation system is somehow enhanced. . . .

There is a clear place at which the Court can draw the line between permissible and impermissible conditions on federal grants. It is the line identified in the Brief for the National Conference of State Legislatures et al. as *Amici Curiae*:

> Congress has the power to *spend* for the general welfare, it has the power to *legislate* only for delegated purposes. . . .
>
> The appropriate inquiry, then, is whether the spending requirement or prohibition is a condition on a grant or whether it is regulation. The difference turns on whether the requirement specifies in some way how the money should be spent, so that Congress' intent in making the grant will be effectuated. Congress has no power under the Spending Clause to impose requirements on a grant that go beyond specifying how the money should be spent. A requirement that is not such a specification is not a condition, but a regulation, which is valid only if it falls within one of Congress' delegated regulatory powers.

. . .

Of the other possible sources of congressional authority for regulating the sale of liquor only the commerce power comes to mind. But in my view, the regulation of the age of the purchasers of liquor, just as the regulation of the price at which liquor may be sold, falls squarely within the scope of those powers reserved to the States by the Twenty-First Amendment. . . .

The immense size and power of the Government of the United States ought not obscure its fundamental character. It remains a Government of enumerated powers. Because 23 U. S. C. §158 cannot be justified as an exercise of any power delegated to the Congress, it is not authorized by the Constitution. The Court errs in holding it to be the law of the land, and I respectfully dissent.

V. Federalism

MAJOR DEVELOPMENTS

- States lose exemptions from congressional regulatory authority under the commerce clause

The U.S. Supreme Court in the latetwentieth century considered federalism limits on congressional power. Justice Rehnquist wrote the majority opinion in *National League of Cities v. Usery* (1976), which held that there were limits on congressional authority to regulate the "states qua states." Under that decision, state and local governments were entitled to constitutional exemptions from some national regulations, such as employment regulations. The Tenth Amendment, according to this line of argument, implicitly recognized a special constitutional status for the states, and the national government was restricted from adopting policies that undermined the independence and functioning of the state governments. If the federal government could not tax state officials (*Collector v. Day* [1871]) or designate where the state capital would be (*Coyle v. Smith* [1911]), then the federal government could not determine what minimum wage state and local governments paid their employees.

With President Reagan appointing the pro-federalism Sandra Day O'Connor to replace the retiring Justice Potter Stewart (a member of the original *National League of Cities* majority) in 1981, *National League of Cities* was seemingly secure when the Court heard *Garcia v. San Antonio Metropolitan Transit Authority* in

1985, since the other eight members of the Court were the same ones who had voted in *National League of Cities*. In *Garcia*, however, Justice Blackmun switched his vote. He wrote a 5–4 majority opinion overruling *National League of Cities*, leaving Justice Rehnquist to write a dissent hoping that his views would once again "command the support of a majority of this Court." To do so, he needed reinforcements. President Reagan soon elevated Rehnquist to the chief justiceship, in part because of his views about federalism, and added Justices Scalia and Kennedy to the Court, although the latter two appointments filled vacancies created by *Garcia* dissenters (Burger and Powell). It was not until the first Bush presidency that any members of the *Garcia* majority left the bench and were replaced (Brennan was replaced by Souter, and then, most importantly, Marshall was replaced by Thomas). The Court has not reconsidered *Garcia*, but a decade after *Garcia* the justices reconsidered judicial enforcement of constitutional limits on federal power.

Garcia v. San Antonio Metropolitan Transit Authority et al., 469 U.S. 528 (1985)

In 1974 Congress removed the last longstanding exemption of state and local government employees from the minimum wage and overtime provisions of the Fair Labor Standards Act (FLSA). After the 1976 National League of Cities *decision, the San Antonio Metropolitan Transit Authority (SAMTA) refused to comply with the act's overtime provisions. In 1979 the Department of Labor determined that the FLSA did apply to SAMTA. SAMTA filed suit in federal district court against the Department of Labor seeking a declaratory judgment that it was immune from the application of the overtime provisions of the FLSA The Department of Labor and a number of SAMTA employees, including Joe Garcia, countersued, seeking enforcement of the FLSA. The district court granted summary judgment to SAMTA, a decision that was appealed directly to the Supreme Court and remanded for further consideration in light of a recent decision involving a commuter rail service. The district court again ruled in favor of SAMTA, and the ruling was again appealed to the U.S. Supreme Court. This time the Court heard arguments and ruled on the merits, reversing the district court.*

When should the Supreme Court be willing to overturn precedent, according to Justice Blackmun? Is this a persuasive case for doing so? Is the constitutional status of states adequately protected through the political process, or should the judiciary take an interest in protecting states from federal actions?

JUSTICE BLACKMUN delivered the opinion of the Court.

We revisit in these cases an issue raised in *National League of Cities v. Usery*. In that litigation, this Court, by a sharply divided vote, ruled that the Commerce Clause does not empower Congress to enforce the minimum-wage and overtime provisions of the Fair Labor Standards Act (FLSA) against the States "in areas of traditional governmental functions." Although *National League of Cities* supplied some examples of "traditional governmental functions," it did not offer a general explanation of how a "traditional" function is to be distinguished from a "nontraditional" one. Since then, federal and state courts have struggled with the task, thus imposed, of identifying a traditional function for purposes of state immunity under the Commerce Clause.

. . .

Our examination of this "function" standard applied in these and other cases over the last eight years now persuades us that the attempt to draw the boundaries of state regulatory immunity in terms of "traditional governmental function" is not only unworkable but is also inconsistent with established principles of federalism and, indeed, with those very federalism principles on which *National League of Cities* purported to rest. That case, accordingly, is overruled.

The history of public transportation in San Antonio, Tex., is characteristic of the history of local mass transit in the United States generally. Passenger transportation for hire within San Antonio originally was provided on a private basis by a local transportation company. In 1913, the Texas Legislature authorized the State's municipalities to regulate vehicles providing carriage for hire. . . . The city continued to rely on such publicly regulated private mass transit until 1959, when it purchased the privately owned San Antonio Transit Company and replaced it with a public authority. . . .

As did other localities, San Antonio reached the point where it came to look to the Federal Government for financial assistance in maintaining its public mass transit. [The San Antonio Transit System (SATS)] managed to meet its operating expenses and bond obligations for the first decade of its existence without federal or local financial aid. By 1970, however, its financial position had deteriorated to the point where federal subsidies were vital for its continued operation. . . .

. . .

Appellees have not argued that SAMTA is immune from regulation under the FLSA on the ground that it is a local transit system engaged in intrastate commercial activity. In a practical sense, SAMTA's operations might well be characterized as "local." Nonetheless, it long has been settled that Congress' authority under the Commerce Clause extends to intrastate economic activities that affect interstate commerce. See, e.g., *Heart of Atlanta Hotel, Inc. v. United States* (1964); *Wickard v. Filburn* (1942). Were SAMTA a privately owned and operated enterprise, it could not credibly argue that Congress exceeded the bounds of its Commerce Clause powers in prescribing minimum wages and overtime rates for SAMTA's employees. Any constitutional exemption from the requirements of the FLSA therefore must rest on SAMTA's status as a governmental entity rather than on the "local" nature of its operations.

. . .

The controversy in the present cases has focused on the . . . requirement . . . that the challenged federal statute trench on "traditional governmental functions." The District Court voiced a common concern: "Despite the abundance of adjectives, identifying which particular state functions are immune remains difficult." Just how troublesome the task has been is revealed by the results reached in other federal cases. Thus, courts have held that regulating ambulance services, . . . licensing automobile drivers, . . . operating a municipal airport, . . . performing solid waste disposal . . . and operating a highway authority . . . are functions *protected* under *National League of Cities.* At the same time, courts have held that issuance of industrial development bonds, . . . regulation of traffic on public roads, . . . regulation of air transportation, . . . operation of a telephone system, . . . operation of a mental health facility, . . . are *not* entitled to immunity. We find it difficult, if not impossible, to identify an organizing principle that places each of the cases in the first group on one side of a line and each of the cases in the second group on the other side. The constitutional distinction between licensing drivers and regulating traffic, for example, or between operating a highway authority and operating a mental health facility, is elusive at best.

. . .

. . . The problem is that neither the governmental/proprietary distinction nor another that purports to separate out important governmental functions can be faithful to the role of federalism in a democratic society. The essence of our federal system is that within the realm of authority left open to them under the Constitution, the States must be equally free to engage in any activity that their citizens choose for the common weal, no matter how unorthodox or unnecessary anyone else—including the judiciary—deems state involvement to be. Any rule of state immunity that looks to the "traditional," "integral," or "necessary" nature of governmental functions inevitably invites an unelected federal judiciary to make decisions about which state policies it favors and which ones it dislikes. . . .

We therefore now reject, as unsound in principle and unworkable in practice, a rule of state immunity from federal regulation that turns on a judicial appraisal of whether a particular governmental function is "integral" or "traditional." Any such rule leads to inconsistent results at the same time that it disserves principles of democratic self-governance, and it breeds inconsistency precisely because it is divorced from those principles. . . . If there are to be limits on the Federal Government's power to interfere with state functions—as undoubtedly there are—we must look elsewhere to find them. . . .

. . .

When we look for the States' "residuary and inviolable sovereignty," The Federalist No. 39 . . . (J. Madison), in the shape of the constitutional scheme rather than in predetermined notions of sovereign power, a different measure of state sovereignty emerges. Apart from the limitation on federal authority inherent in the delegated nature of Congress' Article I powers, the principal means chosen by the Framers to ensure the role of the States in the federal system lies in the structure of the Federal Government itself. It is no novelty to observe that the composition of the Federal Government was designed in large part to protect the States from overreaching by Congress. The Framers thus gave the States a role in the selection both of the Executive and the Legislative Branches of the Federal Government. The States were vested with indirect influence over the House of Representatives and the Presidency by their control of electoral qualifications and their role in Presidential elections. They were given more direct influence in the Senate, where each State received equal representation and each Senator was to be selected by the legislature of his State. The significance attached to the States' equal representation in the Senate is underscored by the prohibition of any constitutional amendment divesting a State of equal representation without the State's consent.

. . . In short, the Framers chose to rely on a federal system in which special restraints on federal power over the States inhered principally in the workings of the National Government itself, rather than in discrete limitations on the objects of federal authority. State sovereign interests, then, are more properly protected by procedural safeguards inherent in the structure of the federal system than by judicially created limitations on federal power.

The effectiveness of the federal political process in preserving the States' interests is apparent even today in the course of federal legislation. On the one hand, the States have been able to direct a substantial proportion of federal revenues into their own treasuries in the form of general and program-specific grants in aid. . . . Moreover, at the same time that the States have exercised their influence to obtain federal support, they have been able to exempt themselves from a wide variety of obligations imposed by Congress under the Commerce Clause. For example, the Federal Power Act, the National Labor Relations Act, the Labor-Management Reporting and Disclosure Act, the Occupational Safety and Health Act, the Employee Retirement Income Security Act, and the Sherman Act all contain express or implied exemptions for States and their subdivisions. The fact that some federal statutes such as the FLSA extend general obligations to the States cannot obscure the extent to which the political position of the States in the federal system has served to minimize the burdens that the States bear under the Commerce Clause.

We realize that changes in the structure of the Federal Government have taken place since 1789, not the least of which has been the substitution of popular election of Senators by the adoption of the Seventeenth Amendment in 1913, and that these changes may work to alter the influence of the States in the federal political process. Nonetheless, against this background, we are convinced that the fundamental limitation that the constitutional scheme imposes on the Commerce Clause to protect the "States as States" is one of process rather than one of result. . . .

. . .

We do not lightly overrule recent precedent. We have not hesitated, however, when it has become apparent that a prior decision has departed from a proper understanding of congressional power under the Commerce Clause. . . . Due respect for the reach of congressional power within the federal system mandates that we do so now.

National League of Cities . . . is overruled. The judgment of the District Court is reversed, and these cases are remanded to that court for further proceedings consistent with this opinion.

It is so ordered.

JUSTICE POWELL, with whom CHIEF JUSTICE BURGER, JUSTICE REHNQUIST, and JUSTICE O'CONNOR join, dissenting.

. . .

There are . . . numerous examples over the history of this Court in which prior decisions have been reconsidered and overruled. There have been few cases, however, in which the principle of *stare decisis* and the rationale of recent decisions were ignored as abruptly as we now witness. The reasoning of the Court in *National League of Cities*, and the principle applied there, have been reiterated consistently over the past eight years. Since its decision in 1976, *National League of Cities* has been cited and quoted in opinions joined by every Member of the present Court. . . . [T]he five Justices who compose the majority today participated in *National League of Cities* and the cases reaffirming it. The stability of judicial decision, and with it respect for the authority of this Court, are not served by the precipitate overruling of multiple precedents that we witness in these cases.

Whatever effect the Court's decision may have in weakening the application of *stare decisis*, it is likely to be less important than what the Court has done to the Constitution itself. . . . A unique feature of the United States is the *federal* system of government guaranteed by the Constitution and implicit in the very name of our country. Despite some genuflecting in the Court's opinion to the concept of federalism, today's decision effectively reduces the Tenth Amendment to meaningless rhetoric when Congress acts pursuant to the Commerce Clause. . . .

To leave no doubt about its intention, the Court renounces its decision in *National League of Cities* because it "inevitably invites an unelected federal judiciary to make decisions about which state policies its favors and which ones it dislikes." In other words, the extent to which the States may exercise their authority, when Congress purports to act under the Commerce

Clause, henceforth is to be determined from time to time by political decisions made by members of the Federal Government, decisions the Court says will not be subject to judicial review. I note that it does not seem to have occurred to the Court that *it*—an unelected majority of five Justices—today rejects almost 200 years of the understanding of the constitutional status of federalism. In doing so, there is only a single passing reference to the Tenth Amendment. Nor is so much as a dictum of any court cited in support of the view that the role of the States in the federal system may depend upon the grace of elected federal officials, rather than on the Constitution as interpreted by this Court.

. . .

Much of the Court's opinion is devoted to arguing that it is difficult to define *a priori* "traditional governmental functions." *National League of Cities* neither engaged in, nor required, such a task. . . . [N]owhere does it mention that *National League of Cities* adopted a familiar type of balancing test for determining whether Commerce Clause enactments transgress constitutional limitations imposed by the federal nature of our system of government. This omission is noteworthy, since the author of today's opinion joined *National League of Cities* and concurred separately to point out that the Court's opinion in that case "[adopts] a balancing approach [that] does not outlaw federal power in areas . . . where the federal interest is demonstrably greater and where state . . . compliance with imposed federal standards would be essential."

. . .

Today's opinion does not explain how the States' role in the electoral process guarantees that particular exercises of the Commerce Clause power will not infringe on residual state sovereignty. Members of Congress are elected from the various States, but once in office they are Members of the Federal Government. Although the States participate in the Electoral College, this is hardly a reason to view the President as a representative of the States' interest against federal encroachment. We noted recently "[the] hydraulic pressure inherent within each of the separate Branches to exceed the outer limits of its power. . . ." The Court offers no reason to think that this pressure will not operate when Congress seeks to invoke its powers under the Commerce Clause, notwithstanding the electoral role of the States.

The Court apparently thinks that the States' success at obtaining federal funds for various projects and exemptions from the obligations of some federal statutes is indicative of the "effectiveness of the federal political process in preserving the States' interests. . . ." But such political success is not relevant to the question whether the political *processes* are the proper means of enforcing constitutional limitations. The fact that Congress generally does not transgress constitutional limits on its power to reach state activities does not make judicial review any less necessary to rectify the cases in which it does do so. The States' role in our system of government is a matter of constitutional law, not of legislative grace. "The powers not delegated to the United States by the Constitution, nor prohibited by it to the States, are reserved to the States, respectively, or to the people." U.S. Const., Amdt. 10.

. . .

As I view the Court's decision today as rejecting the basic precepts of our federal system and limiting the constitutional role of judicial review, I dissent.

JUSTICE REHNQUIST, dissenting.

I join both Justice POWELL's and Justice O'CONNOR's thoughtful dissents. . . . [But] I do not think it incumbent on those of us in dissent to spell out further the fine points of a principle that will, I am confident, in time again command the support of a majority of this Court.

JUSTICE O'CONNOR, with whom JUSTICE POWELL and JUSTICE REHNQUIST join, dissenting.

The Court today surveys the battle scene of federalism and sounds a retreat. Like JUSTICE POWELL, I would prefer to hold the field and, at the very least, render a little aid to the wounded. I join JUSTICE POWELL's opinion. I also write separately to note my fundamental disagreement with the majority's views of federalism and the duty of this Court.

. . .

. . . The true "essence" of federalism is that the States *as States* have legitimate interests which the National Government is bound to respect even though its laws are supreme. . . . If federalism so conceived and so carefully cultivated by the Framers of our Constitution is to remain meaningful, this Court cannot abdicate its constitutional responsibility to oversee the Federal Government's compliance with its duty to respect the legitimate interests of the States.

. . .

. . . The Court based the expansion on the authority of Congress [in the twentieth century], through the Necessary and Proper Clause, "to resort to all means for the exercise of a granted power which are appropriate and plainly adapted to the permitted end." *United States v. Darby* (1941). . . . It is worth recalling the cited passage in *McCulloch v. Maryland* (1819) that lies at the source of the recent expansion of the commerce power. "Let the end be legitimate, let it be within the scope of the constitution," Chief Justice Marshall said, "and all means which are appropriate, which are plainly adapted to that end, which are not prohibited, but consist with the letter *and spirit* of the constitution, are constitutional" (emphasis added). The *spirit* of the Tenth Amendment, of course, is that the States will retain their integrity in a system in which the laws of the United States are nevertheless supreme. . . .

It is not enough that the "end be legitimate"; the means to that end chosen by Congress must not contravene the spirit of the Constitution. Thus many of this Court's decisions acknowledge that the means by which national power is exercised must take into account concerns for state autonomy. See, e.g., *NLRB v. Jones & Laughlin Steel Corp.* (1937) ("Undoubtedly, the scope of this [commerce] power must be considered in light of our dual system of government and may not be extended so as to embrace effects upon interstate commerce so indirect and remote that to embrace them, in view of our complex society, would effectually obliterate the distinction between what is national and what is local and create a completely centralized government"). . . .

This principle requires the Court to enforce affirmative limits on federal regulation of the States to complement the judicially crafted expansion of the interstate commerce power. *National League of Cities v. Usery* represented an attempt to define such limits. The Court today rejects *National League of Cities* and washes its hands of all efforts to protect the States. . . .

. . .

. . . It is insufficient, in assessing the validity of congressional regulation of a State pursuant to the commerce power, to ask only whether the same regulation would be valid if enforced against a private party. That reasoning, embodied in the majority opinion, is inconsistent with the spirit of our Constitution. It remains relevant that a *State* is being regulated, as *National League of Cities* and every recent case have recognized. . . .

It has been difficult for this Court to craft bright lines defining the scope of the state autonomy protected by *National League of Cities*. Such difficulty is to be expected whenever constitutional concerns as important as federalism and the effectiveness of the commerce power come into conflict. Regardless of the difficulty, it is and will remain the duty of this Court to reconcile these concerns in the final instance. That the Court shuns the task today by appealing to the "essence of federalism" can provide scant comfort to those who believe our federal system requires something more than a unitary, centralized government. I would not shirk the duty acknowledged by *National League of Cities* and its progeny, and I share JUSTICE REHNQUIST's belief that this Court will in time again assume its constitutional responsibility.

I respectfully dissent.

VI. Separation of Powers

MAJOR DEVELOPMENTS

- The Court strikes down legislative vetoes
- Continued recognition of the legislature's broad authority to delegate policy-making discretion
- Court moves closer to the view that officials performing executive duties are ultimately accountable within the executive branch

The Reagan administration hoped that the Republicans would build a new conservative majority. From 1981 to 1993 the GOP controlled the White House, but the Democrats controlled one if not both chambers of Congress. Some observers suggested that the Republicans had an effective electoral lock on the presidency, while the Democrats could not be dislodged from the legislature, where "politics is local." The Republicans dug into the institution under their control, building up the executive branch. The Democrats did the same with the legislative branch. For the Reagan administration, this included elaborating such arguments as the theory of the "unitary executive" (arguing that the "take care" clause required that all lower-level executive branch members be accountable to the president) and expanding the use of "signing statements" (whereby presidents, while signing a bill, articulate their own views on the meaning and scope of the new law). For Congress, this included the use of legislative hearings and statutory checks to monitor and limit executive branch activities and embed Democratic preferences into law.

The Iran-Contra scandal was perhaps the most serious constitutional and political confrontation between the executive and legislative branches during the 1980s. The Reagan White House was deeply committed to providing aid to anti-Communist governments and groups in Latin America as part of its global Cold War strategy. The Democratic House of Representatives was skeptical of many of these ventures. A particular flashpoint was American funding for the "Contra" rebels in Nicaragua. Massachusetts Democrat Edward Boland sponsored a series of amendments to defense appropriations bills designed to limit American funding for the Contras. National Security Advisor John Poindexter and his aide, Oliver North, sought ways to continue to funnel money to the Contras. The most problematic of these efforts was the diversion of funds from a separate project—the secret sale of missiles to Iran. When the arms sales were exposed in the press in the fall of 1986, the money trail and larger covert operation eventually came to light as well.

With the Democrats in control of both houses of Congress after the 1986 elections and Reagan entering the final phase of his second term of office, the Iran-Contra scandal was a major blow to Reagan's presidency. The administration immediately moved to cooperate with the congressional investigations, to undertake its internal investigations, and to seek an appointment of an independent counsel. Key members of Congress quickly resolved not to pursue the impeachment of the president. Nonetheless, the scandal severely weakened the administration when it sought, for example, to push forward the Robert Bork nomination. The investigations revealed the extent to which the legislature and the executive had played cat-and-mouse with the power of the purse, with executive officials constantly looking for loopholes and discretionary funds to continue to pursue their favored policies as Congress squeezed their ability to do so. At the extreme, some White House staff had tried to run foreign policy operations completely off the books of government financing and eventually had used the sale of government assets (the missiles) to fund their enterprise when congressional appropriations were not forthcoming. Like all scandals, Iran-Contra revealed individuals behaving badly, but the episode also showed how difficult it is for one branch of government to control the actions of another.[15]

Congress during the New Deal and Great Society sought to maintain some measure of control over powers that were being increasingly delegated to the executive branch of the national government. The "legislative veto," first suggested by President Herbert Hoover to facilitate a reorganization of the executive branch, proved a popular device. The national legislature granted authority to an executive official or an administrative agency to promulgate particular regulations or make certain decisions but reserved the right to reject those regulations or decisions if they were thought wrong. Sometimes the veto power was lodged in a single chamber of Congress, but other vetoes merely required a majority vote of a legislative committee. By the 1970s legislative vetoes had become a standard device by which Congress exercised oversight over executive officials and administrative agencies. Several congressmen routinely attached legislative vetoes to all legislation delegating power to any nonlegislative official. With the increased popularity and use of legislative vetoes came controversy. Many public interest groups condemned legislative vetoes as a means that enabled Congress to reject environmental and consumer protection regulations adopted by administrative agencies. Presidents signed bills containing legislative vetoes in order to get the broad delegations of authority associated with the device, but they also insisted that, once power had been delegated, Congress could change lawful executive branch decisions only by passing new legislation consistent with Article I's requirement of bicameralism (passage by both houses of Congress) and presentment (transmission of legislation to the president for his signature or veto). By the time *Immigration and Naturalization Service v. Chadha* (1983) was decided, legislative vetoes could be found in more than two hundred laws.

Alongside questions about the legitimacy of "sharing" the legislative power were renewed assertions of

15. See also Harold Hongju Koh, "Why the President (Almost) Always Wins in Foreign Affairs: Lessons of the Iran-Contra Affair," *Yale Law Journal* 97 (1988): 1255–1342; Louis Fisher, "How Tightly Can Congress Draw the Purse Strings?," *American Journal of International Law* 83 (1989): 758–766.

the importance of exclusive presidential control over the executive branch. The "unitary executive" theory holds that *all* the executive power of the federal government is vested in the president of the United States. The president is fully the chief executive, and the constitutional responsibility that the president "take care that the laws be faithfully executed" requires that the president have supervisory control over all lower-level executive officials. The unitary executive theory envisions the structure of the executive branch as a pyramid, with the president at the top. In particular, the president must have the authority—directly or indirectly—to select, supervise, and remove executive branch officers if he is to retain and perform his own constitutional functions.

The idea of the unitary executive found a new set of aggressive advocates in the modern legal conservative movement that gained influence in the Reagan administration. During the Reagan years, the theory was developed and expounded in memos and briefs prepared by the Department of Justice, speeches, and publications by think tanks and interest groups and in academic journals. At the same time, the Reagan administration expanded centralized oversight of the regulatory and other decisions being made throughout the executive branch. Litigation decisions involving the federal government were vetted by top officials in the Justice Department. Regulatory decisions with important economic consequences followed presidentially specified procedures and were vetted by the Office of Management and Budget, part of the Executive Office of the President.[16]

The argument gained less traction among the justices on the Supreme Court. Justice Antonin Scalia, who had worked on related arguments as a Justice Department lawyer in the aftermath of Watergate, proved most receptive to such views. The Court as a whole generally favored a balancing test that focused on the extent to which congressional action interfered with executive responsibilities. The unitary executive theory is part of a class of arguments about the separation of powers that are classified as "formalist." These arguments emphasize the forms and definitions of the parts of government and look for bright-line rules to guide the constitutional division of power among offices and levels of government. By contrast, "functionalist" arguments emphasize pragmatic, fluid, less clear-cut, but "workable" approaches to thinking about the structures of government. They focus less on trying to derive logical implications from an overarching theory of a given constitutional office than on trying to maintain a set of relationships that more or less preserve essential constitutional goals. In *Bowsher v. Synar* (1986) the Court by a 7–2 vote struck down the Gramm-Rudman-Hollings Deficit Control Act of 1985 on the grounds that the law gave enforcement authority to the Comptroller General, an official who was subservient to the legislative branch rather than to the executive branch; in effect, the Court found that Congress may not control how its laws were executed. However, the justices (over Justice Scalia's dissent) were less protective of presidential prerogatives in *Morrison v. Olson* (1988), which upheld the provision of the Ethics in Government Act that authorized the appointment of an "independent counsel" or "special prosecutor" who was insulated from direct executive branch control, despite the fact that the prosecutorial function was a core responsibility of the executive branch.

16. See Steven G. Calabresi and Christopher S. Yoo, *The Unitary Executive* (New Haven, CT: Yale University Press, 2008); Lawrence Lessig and Cass R. Sunstein, "The President and the Administration," *Columbia Law Review* 94 (1994): 1–119; Robert D. Sloane, "The Scope of Executive Power in the Twenty-First Century: An Introduction," *Boston University Law Review* 88 (2008): 341–351.

Immigration and Naturalization Service v. Chadha, 462 U.S. 919 (1983)

Jaglish Chadha provided an opportunity for opponents of the legislative veto to litigate its constitutionality. Chadha, born in Kenya and holding a British passport, came to the United States as a student. Neither Kenya nor the United Kingdom permitted him to return when his American student visa expired. Chadha sought permanent residency in the United States. For more than 150 years, this problem had been dealt with by private legislation. Congress voted on whether someone like Chadha should be given permanent residency, and, if the vote was favorable, the resulting bill was signed by the president. Overwhelmed with the number of requests, Congress delegated that authority to the attorney general and the Immigration and Naturalization Service (INS), but reserved the right to veto any decision giving residence. Chadha suffered this fate. His application was initially approved by the INS but then "vetoed" by the House of Representatives.

The resulting litigation illustrated how constitutional politics made strange bedfellows. Chadha was represented by Alan Morrison, who was the main attorney for Ralph Nader's consumer protection organization. Nader's group was supported by the Reagan administration, which sought to free the executive branch from the burden of legislative vetoes. The law professor (and later Supreme Court justice) Antonin Scalia filed a brief for the American Bar Association as an amicus curiae arguing that the legislative veto was unconstitutional. Because the INS did not defend the statute, the Supreme Court asked Congress to intervene. Prominent congressmen wrote the brief in Chadha *and were responsible for oral argument.*

Neither an immigration judge nor the Board of Immigration was willing to address the constitutional issue. Chadha appealed to the federal circuit court, which struck down the legislative veto in the immigration statute as unconstitutional. The INS appealed to the U.S. Supreme Court. A 6–3 Court struck down the legislative veto in Chadha. *Nonetheless, Congress has continued to include legislative vetoes in statutes despite the Court's ruling. Congress has not tried to formally veto executive actions. Instead, it has used the threat of a veto combined with informal pressure to win accommodations from the executive. As a result, these vetoes remain on the books and unchallenged in court. Should the Court be deferential to how Congress and the president work together, or are there larger values and concerns at stake? Is the Court likely to be effective when it interferes with cooperative relationships between the other two branches of government? If this decision were fully enforced, would the effect be to protect congressional authority or expand executive power?*

CHIEF JUSTICE BURGER delivered the opinion of the Court.

. . .

. . . [T]he fact that a given law or procedure is efficient, convenient, and useful in facilitating functions of government, standing alone, will not save it if it is contrary to the Constitution. Convenience and efficiency are not the primary objectives—or the hallmarks—of democratic government and our inquiry is sharpened rather than blunted by the fact that congressional veto provisions are appearing with increasing frequency in statutes which delegate authority to executive and independent agencies. . . .

. . .

Explicit and unambiguous provisions of the Constitution prescribe and define the respective functions of the Congress and of the Executive in the legislative process. Since the precise terms of those familiar provisions are critical to the resolution of these cases, we set them out verbatim. Article I provides:

> All legislative Powers herein granted shall be vested in a Congress of the United States, which shall consist of a Senate *and* House of Representatives. Art. I, §1. (Emphasis added.)
>
> Every Bill which shall have passed the House of Representatives *and* the Senate, *shall,* before it becomes a law, be presented to the President of the United States. . . . Art. I, §7, cl. 2. (Emphasis added.)
>
> *Every* Order, Resolution, or Vote to which the Concurrence of the Senate and House of Representatives may be necessary (except on a question of Adjournment) *shall be* presented to the President of the United States; and before the Same shall take Effect, *shall be* approved by him, or being disapproved by him, *shall be* repassed by two thirds of the Senate and House of Representatives, according to the Rules and Limitations prescribed in the Case of a Bill. Art. I, §7, cl. 3. (Emphasis added.)

. . .

The decision to provide the President with a limited and qualified power to nullify proposed legislation by veto was based on the profound conviction of the Framers that the powers conferred on Congress were the powers to be most carefully circumscribed. It is beyond doubt that lawmaking was a power to be shared by both Houses and the President. . . .

. . .

The President's role in the lawmaking process also reflects the Framers' careful efforts to check whatever propensity a particular Congress might have to enact oppressive, improvident, or ill-considered measures. . . .

. . .

. . . The Court also has observed that the Presentment Clauses serve the important purpose of assuring that a "national" perspective is grafted on the legislative process:

> The President is a representative of the people just as the members of the Senate and of the House are, and it may be, at some times, on some subjects, that the President elected by all the people is rather more representative of them all than are the members of either body of the Legislature whose constituencies are local and not countrywide. . . .

The bicameral requirement of Art. I, §§1, 7, was of scarcely less concern to the Framers than was the Presidential veto and indeed the two concepts are interdependent. By providing that no law could take effect without the concurrence of the prescribed majority of the Members of both Houses, the Framers reemphasized their belief, already remarked upon in connection with the Presentment Clauses, that legislation should not be enacted unless it has been carefully and fully considered by the Nation's elected officials. . . .

. . .

. . . [T]he Framers were acutely conscious that the bicameral requirement and the Presentment Clauses would serve essential constitutional functions. The President's participation in the legislative process was to protect the Executive Branch from Congress and to protect the whole people from improvident laws. The division of the Congress into two distinctive bodies assures that the legislative power would be exercised only after opportunity for full study and debate in separate settings. . . .

. . .

Examination of the action taken here by one House pursuant to §244(c)(2) reveals that it was essentially legislative in purpose and effect. . . . [T]he House took action that had the purpose and effect of altering the legal rights, duties, and relations of persons, including the Attorney General, Executive Branch officials and Chadha, all outside the Legislative Branch. Section 244(c)(2) purports to authorize one House of Congress to require the Attorney General to deport an individual alien whose deportation otherwise would be canceled under §244.

. . .

. . . Disagreement with the Attorney General's decision on Chadha's deportation—that is, Congress' decision to deport Chadha—no less than Congress' original choice to delegate to the Attorney General the authority to make that decision, involves determinations of policy that Congress can implement in only one way; bicameral passage followed by presentment to the President. Congress must abide by its delegation of authority until that delegation is legislatively altered or revoked.

. . .

The veto authorized by §244(c)(2) doubtless has been in many respects a convenient shortcut; the "sharing" with the Executive by Congress of its authority over aliens in this manner is, on its face, an appealing compromise. In purely practical terms, it is obviously easier for action to be taken by one House without submission to the President; but it is crystal clear from the records of the Convention, contemporaneous writings and debates, that the Framers ranked other values higher than efficiency. The records of the Convention and debates in the States preceding ratification underscore the common desire to define and limit the exercise of the newly created federal powers affecting the states and the people. There is unmistakable expression of a determination that legislation by the national Congress be a step-by-step, deliberate and deliberative process.

The choices we discern as having been made in the Constitutional Convention impose burdens on governmental processes that often seem clumsy, inefficient, even unworkable, but those hard choices were consciously made by men who had lived under a form of government that permitted arbitrary governmental acts to go unchecked. There is no support in the Constitution or decisions of this Court for the proposition that the cumbersomeness and delays often encountered in complying with explicit constitutional standards may be avoided, either by the Congress or by the President. . . . With all the obvious flaws of delay, untidiness, and potential for abuse, we have not yet found a better way to preserve freedom than by making the exercise of power subject to the carefully crafted restraints spelled out in the Constitution.

JUSTICE POWELL, concurring.

The Court's decision, based on the Presentment Clauses, . . . apparently will invalidate every use of the legislative veto. The breadth of this holding gives one pause. Congress has included the veto in literally hundreds of statutes, dating back to the 1930's. Congress clearly views this procedure as essential to controlling the delegation of power to administrative agencies. One reasonably may disagree with Congress' assessment of the veto's utility, but the respect due its judgment as a coordinate branch of Government cautions that our holding should be no more extensive than necessary to decide these cases. In my view, the cases may be decided on a narrower ground. When Congress finds that a particular person does not satisfy the statutory criteria for permanent residence in this country it has assumed a judicial function in violation of the principle of separation of powers. Accordingly, I concur only in the judgment.

. . .

Illustration 10-2 Jagdish Rai Chadha, the respondent in *Immigration and Naturalization Service v. Chadha*
Source: © Roger Ressmeyer/CORBIS.

JUSTICE WHITE, dissenting.

Today the Court not only invalidates §244(c)(2) of the Immigration and Nationality Act, but also sounds the death knell for nearly 200 other statutory provisions in which Congress has reserved a "legislative veto." For this reason, the Court's decision is of surpassing importance. And it is for this reason that the Court would have been well advised to decide the cases, if possible, on the narrower grounds of separation of powers, leaving for full consideration the constitutionality of other congressional review statutes operating on such varied matters as war powers and agency rulemaking, some of which concern the independent regulatory agencies.

The prominence of the legislative veto mechanism in our contemporary political system and its importance to Congress can hardly be overstated. It has become a central means by which Congress secures the accountability of executive and independent agencies. Without the legislative veto, Congress is faced with a Hobson's choice: either to refrain from delegating the necessary authority, leaving itself with a hopeless task of writing laws with the requisite specificity to cover endless special circumstances across the entire policy landscape, or in the alternative, to abdicate its law-making function to the Executive Branch and independent agencies. To choose the former leaves major national problems unresolved; to opt for the latter risks unaccountable policymaking by those not elected to fill that role. Accordingly, over the past five decades, the legislative veto has been placed in nearly 200 statutes. The device is known in every field of governmental concern: reorganization, budgets, foreign affairs, war powers, and regulation of trade, safety, energy, the environment, and the economy.

. . .

. . . [T]he legislative veto is more than "efficient, convenient, and useful." . . . It is an important if not indispensable political invention that allows the President and Congress to resolve major constitutional and policy differences, assures the accountability of independent regulatory agencies, and preserves Congress' control over lawmaking. Perhaps there are other means of accommodation and accountability, but the increasing reliance of Congress upon the legislative veto suggests that the alternatives to which Congress must now turn are not entirely satisfactory.

The history of the legislative veto also makes clear that it has not been a sword with which Congress has struck out to aggrandize itself at the expense of the other branches—the concerns of Madison and Hamilton. Rather, the veto has been a means of defense, a reservation of ultimate authority necessary if Congress is to fulfill its designated role under Art. I as the Nation's lawmaker. While the President has often objected to particular legislative vetoes, generally those left in the hands of congressional Committees, the Executive has more often agreed to legislative review as the price for a broad delegation of authority. To be sure, the President may have preferred unrestricted power, but that could be precisely why Congress thought it essential to retain a check on the exercise of delegated authority.

For all these reasons, the apparent sweep of the Court's decision today is regrettable. The Court's Art. I analysis appears to invalidate all legislative vetoes irrespective of form or subject. Because the legislative veto is commonly found as a check upon rulemaking by administrative agencies and upon broad-based policy decisions of the Executive Branch, it is particularly unfortunate that the Court reaches its decision in cases involving the exercise of a veto over deportation decisions regarding particular individuals. Courts should always be wary of striking statutes as unconstitutional; to strike an entire class of statutes based on consideration of a somewhat atypical and more readily indictable exemplar of the class is irresponsible.

. . .

The reality of the situation is that the constitutional question posed today is one of immense difficulty over which the Executive and Legislative Branches—as well as scholars and judges—have understandably disagreed. That disagreement stems from the silence of the Constitution on the precise question: The Constitution does not directly authorize or prohibit the legislative veto. Thus, our task should be to determine whether the legislative veto is consistent with the purposes of Art. I and the principles of separation of powers which are reflected in that Article and throughout the Constitution. . . . From the summer of 1787 to the present the Government of the United States has become an endeavor far beyond the contemplation of the Framers. Only within the last half century has the complexity and size of the Federal Government's responsibilities grown so greatly that the Congress must rely on the legislative veto as the most effective if not the only means to insure its role as the Nation's lawmaker. But the wisdom of the Framers was to anticipate that the Nation would grow and new problems of governance would require different solutions. Accordingly, our Federal Government was intentionally chartered with the flexibility to respond to contemporary needs without losing sight of fundamental democratic principles. . . .

. . .

. . . Absent the veto, the agencies receiving delegations of legislative or quasi-legislative power may issue regulations having the force of law without bicameral approval and without the President's signature. It is thus not apparent why the reservation of a veto over the exercise of that legislative power must be subject to a more exacting test. In both cases, it is enough that the initial statutory authorizations comply with the Art. I requirements.

. . .

. . . Under the Court's analysis, the Executive Branch and the independent agencies may make rules with the effect of law while Congress, in whom the Framers confided the legislative power, Art. I, §1, may not exercise a veto which precludes such rules from having operative force. If the effective functioning of a complex modern government requires the delegation of vast authority which, by virtue of its breadth, is legislative or "quasi-legislative" in character, I cannot accept that Art. I—which is, after all, the source of the nondelegation doctrine—should forbid Congress to qualify that grant with a legislative veto.

The Court also takes no account of perhaps the most relevant consideration: However resolutions of disapproval under §244(c)(2) are formally characterized, in reality, a departure from the status quo occurs only upon the concurrence of opinion among the House, Senate, and President. Reservations of legislative authority to be exercised by Congress should be upheld if the exercise of such reserved authority is consistent with the distribution of and limits upon legislative power that Art. I provides.

. . .

The central concern of the presentment and bicameralism requirements of Art. I is that when a departure from the legal status quo is undertaken, it is done with the approval of the President and both Houses of Congress—or, in the event of a Presidential veto, a two-thirds majority in both Houses. This interest is fully satisfied by the operation of §244(c)(2). The President's approval is found in the Attorney General's action in recommending to Congress that the deportation order for a given alien be suspended. The House and the Senate indicate their approval of the Executive's action by not passing a resolution of disapproval within the statutory period. Thus, a change in the legal status quo—the deportability of the alien—is consummated only with the approval of each of the three relevant actors. The disagreement of any one of the three maintains the alien's pre-existing status: the Executive may choose not to recommend suspension; the House and Senate may each veto the recommendation. The effect on the rights and obligations of the affected individuals and upon the legislative system is precisely the same as if a private bill were introduced but failed to receive the necessary approval. . . .

. . .

. . . [T]the history of the separation-of-powers doctrine is also a history of accommodation and practicality. Apprehensions of an overly powerful branch have not led to undue prophylactic measures that handicap the effective working of the National Government as a whole. The Constitution does not contemplate total separation of the three branches of Government. "[A] hermetic sealing off of the three branches of Government from one another would preclude the establishment of a Nation capable of governing itself effectively."

. . .

I regret that I am in disagreement with my colleagues on the fundamental questions that these cases present. But even more I regret the destructive scope of the Court's holding. It reflects a profoundly different conception of the Constitution than that held by the courts which sanctioned the modern administrative state. Today's decision strikes down in one fell swoop provisions in more laws enacted by Congress than the Court has cumulatively invalidated in its history. I fear it will now be more difficult to "[insure] that the fundamental policy decisions in our society will be made not by an appointed official but by the body immediately responsible to the people." . . . I must dissent.

JUSTICE REHNQUIST, with whom JUSTICE WHITE joins, dissenting.

. . . Over the years, Congress consistently rejected requests from the Executive for complete discretion in this area. Congress always insisted on retaining ultimate control, whether by concurrent resolution, as in the 1948 Act, or by one-House veto, as in the present Act. Congress has never indicated that it would be willing to permit suspensions of deportation unless it could retain some sort of veto.

. . .

Because I do not believe that [the Court can sever the original grant of power to the executive from the provision of the one-House veto], I would reverse the judgment of the Court of Appeals.

Morrison v. Olson, 487 U.S. 654 (1988)

Scandal rocked American politics during the last third of the twentieth century. Both presidents and executive officials seemed under constant investigation for criminal misdeeds. These investigations significantly influenced relationships between the two branches of government and national policy. One president, Richard Nixon, was forced to resign. Others suffered significant drops in public opinion that weakened their ability to influence Congress. Many investigations responded to substantial allegations of wrongdoing. As the Watergate, Iran-Contra, and Whitewater affairs indicated, members of the executive branch were not above violating the law. Nevertheless, a good case can be made that no more executive wrongdoing occurred from 1970 to the present than did at any other time in American history. What differed were the political incentives for emphasizing alleged scandals. In a time of divided government and close partisan divisions among the electorate, many political actors believed they could gain power more effectively by exposing their rivals as corrupt than by proposing new policy initiatives.

Independent counsels were one consequence of the new focus on executive scandals. Concerned that an increasingly politicized Department of Justice would not aggressively pursue allegations of wrongdoing and corruption against executive department officials, Congress passed and President Carter signed the Ethics in Government Act. Title VI of that measure created a special court that was authorized to appoint a special counsel on application from the attorney general. Once appointed, the independent counsel would investigate the particular allegation of wrongdoing largely free from executive interference and could only be removed by a showing of good cause. During the 1980s and 1990s this device was frequently used and highly controversial. Republicans claimed that independent counsel Lawrence Walsh was overly aggressive in prosecuting members of the Reagan administration during the Iran-Contra scandal. Democrats cried foul when Kenneth Starr investigated President Clinton's behavior during the Whitewater scandal. Congress let the independent counsel statute lapse late in the Clinton presidency. Presidents have now returned to the earlier practice of using the Department of Justice or appointing a special prosecutor under the attorney general to investigate wrongdoing by government officials.

The constitutionality of the independent counsel statute was tested during a more low-level investigation. After a long dispute between the president and Congress, the Reagan administration agreed to provide Congress with some documents concerning the administration's environmental policies. When Assistant Attorney General Theodore Olson testified before Congress about the role of the Department of Justice during this controversy, many Democrats believed he made false and misleading statements. The chair of the Judiciary Committee repeated these allegations in a public report and passed that information on to the attorney general of the United States. After a short investigation, the allegations were found sufficiently credible to request the appointment of an independent counsel. The special court appointed James McKay to further investigate the incident, and when McKay resigned, Alexina

Morrison was appointed in his place. Morrison sought to obtain a subpoena that would require Olson and two other Justice Department officials to testify before a grand jury. Olson responded by asserting that the independent counsel statute violated the "appointments clause" (which outlines the process by which these kinds of officers must be appointed) and the principle of separation of powers, which under Article II vests "the executive power" in an executive branch controlled by the president. A federal district court upheld the statute and eventually charged Olson with contempt for refusing to comply with the subpoena. On appeal, the court of appeals reversed the trial court and struck down the independent counsel law as a violation of the separation of powers. In an 8–1 decision, the U.S. Supreme Court reversed the court of appeals and upheld the statute.

After the Whitewater investigations, many liberals came to praise Justice Scalia's dissent as far-sighted. How much of his argument is about the "constitutionality" of the independent counsel, and how much is about the "policy" of having an independent counsel? How did Scalia differ from Rehnquist in his conception of the separation of powers? Is one approach more helpful to modern conservatives or the presidency than the others?

CHIEF JUSTICE REHNQUIST delivered the opinion of the Court.

This case presents us with a challenge to the independent counsel provisions of the Ethics in Government Act of 1978. . . . We hold today that these provisions of the Act do not violate the Appointments Clause of the Constitution, Art. II, §2, cl. 2, or the limitations of Article III, nor do they impermissibly interfere with the President's authority under Article II in violation of the constitutional principle of separation of powers.

. . .

The Appointments Clause of Article II reads as follows:

> [The President] shall nominate, and by and with the Advice and Consent of the Senate, shall appoint Ambassadors, other public Ministers and Consuls, Judges of the supreme Court, and all other Officers of the United States, whose Appointments are not herein otherwise provided for, and which shall be established by Law: but the Congress may by Law vest the Appointment of such inferior Officers, as they think proper, in the President alone, in the Courts of Law, or in the Heads of Departments. . . .

. . . The initial question is, accordingly, whether appellant is an "inferior" or a "principal" officer. If she is the latter, as the Court of Appeals concluded, then the Act is in violation of the Appointments Clause.

The line between "inferior" and "principal" officers is one that is far from clear, and the Framers provided little guidance into where it should be drawn. . . . We need not attempt here to decide exactly where the line falls between the two types of officers, because in our view appellant clearly falls on the "inferior officer" side of that line. . . .

First, appellant is subject to removal by a higher Executive Branch official. Although appellant may not be "subordinate" to the Attorney General (and the President) insofar as she possesses a degree of independent discretion to exercise the powers delegated to her under the Act, the fact that she can be removed by the Attorney General indicates that she is to some degree "inferior" in rank and authority. Second, appellant is empowered by the Act to perform only certain, limited duties. An independent counsel's role is restricted primarily to investigation and, if appropriate, prosecution for certain federal crimes. . . .

Third, appellant's office is limited in jurisdiction. Not only is the Act itself restricted in applicability to certain federal officials suspected of certain serious federal crimes, but an independent counsel can only act within the scope of the jurisdiction that has been granted by the Special Division pursuant to a request by the Attorney General. Finally, appellant's office is limited in tenure. There is concededly no time limit on the appointment of a particular counsel. Nonetheless, the office of independent counsel is "temporary" in the sense that an independent counsel is appointed essentially to accomplish a single task, and when that task is over the office is terminated. . . . In our view, these factors relating to the "ideas of tenure, duration . . . and duties" of the independent counsel . . . are sufficient to establish that appellant is an "inferior" officer in the constitutional sense.

. . .

. . . Appellees argue that even if appellant is an "inferior" officer, the Clause does not empower Congress to place the power to appoint such an officer outside the Executive Branch. They contend that the Clause does not contemplate congressional authorization of "interbranch appointments," in which an officer of one branch is appointed by officers of another branch. The relevant language of the Appointments Clause is worth repeating. It reads: " . . . but the Congress may by Law vest the Appointment of such inferior Officers, as they think proper, in the President alone, in the courts of Law, or in the Heads of Departments." On its face, the language of this "excepting clause" admits of no limitation on interbranch appointments. Indeed, the inclusion of "as they think proper" seems clearly to give Congress significant discretion to determine whether it is "proper" to vest the appointment of, for example, executive officials in the "courts of Law.". . .

. . .

We do not mean to say that Congress' power to provide for interbranch appointments of "inferior officers" is unlimited. . . . In this case, however, we do not think it impermissible for Congress to vest the power to appoint independent counsel in a specially created federal court. We thus disagree with the Court of Appeals' conclusion that there is an inherent incongruity about a court having the power to appoint prosecutorial officers. . . .

. . .

. . . Clearly, once it is accepted that the Appointments Clause gives Congress the power to vest the appointment of officials such as the independent counsel in the "courts of Law," there can be no Article III objection to the Special Division's exercise of that power, as the power itself derives from the Appointments Clause, a source of authority for judicial action that is independent of Article III. Appellees contend, however, that the Division's Appointments Clause powers do not encompass the power to define the independent counsel's jurisdiction. We disagree. In our view, Congress' power under the Clause to vest the "Appointment" of inferior officers in the courts may, in certain circumstances, allow Congress to give the courts some discretion in defining the nature and scope of the appointed official's authority. Particularly when, as here, Congress creates a temporary "office" the nature and duties of which will by necessity vary with the factual circumstances giving rise to the need for an appointment in the first place, it may vest the power to define the scope of the office in the court as an incident to the appointment of the officer pursuant to the Appointments Clause. . . .

. . .

. . . [O]ne purpose of the broad prohibition upon the courts' exercise of "executive or administrative duties of a nonjudicial nature," is to maintain the separation between the Judiciary and the other branches of the Federal Government by ensuring that judges do not encroach upon executive or legislative authority or undertake tasks that are more properly accomplished by those branches. . . . The Act simply does not give the Division the power to "supervise" the independent counsel in the exercise of his or her investigative or prosecutorial authority. And, the functions that the Special Division is empowered to perform are not inherently "Executive"; indeed, they are directly analogous to functions that federal judges perform in other contexts, such as deciding whether to allow disclosure of matters occurring before a grand jury.

. . .

We now turn to consider whether the Act is invalid under the constitutional principle of separation of powers. Two related issues must be addressed: The first is whether the provision of the Act restricting the Attorney General's power to remove the independent counsel to only those instances in which he can show "good cause," taken by itself, impermissibly interferes with the President's exercise of his constitutionally appointed functions. The second is whether, taken as a whole, the Act violates the separation of powers by reducing the President's ability to control the prosecutorial powers wielded by the independent counsel.

. . .

. . . [T]his case does not involve an attempt by Congress itself to gain a role in the removal of executive officials other than its established powers of impeachment and conviction. The Act instead puts the removal power squarely in the hands of the Executive Branch; an independent counsel may be removed from office, "only by the personal action of the Attorney General, and only for good cause.". . .

. . .

. . . [W]hether the Constitution allows Congress to impose a "good cause"-type restriction on the President's power to remove an official cannot be made to turn on whether or not that official is classified as "purely executive." The analysis contained in our removal cases is designed not to define rigid categories of those officials who may or may not be removed at will by the President, but to ensure that Congress does not interfere with the President's exercise of the "executive power" and his constitutionally appointed duty to "take care that the laws be faithfully executed" under Article II. . . .

. . . [T]he real question is whether the removal restrictions are of such a nature that they impede the

President's ability to perform his constitutional duty, and the functions of the officials in question must be analyzed in that light.

. . .

Nor do we think that the "good cause" removal provision at issue here impermissibly burdens the President's power to control or supervise the independent counsel, as an executive official, in the execution of his or her duties under the Act. This is not a case in which the power to remove an executive official has been completely stripped from the President, thus providing no means for the President to ensure the "faithful execution" of the laws. Rather, because the independent counsel may be terminated for "good cause," the Executive, through the Attorney General, retains ample authority to assure that the counsel is competently performing his or her statutory responsibilities in a manner that comports with the provisions of the Act.

. . .

The final question to be addressed is whether the Act, taken as a whole, violates the principle of separation of powers by unduly interfering with the role of the Executive Branch. . . .

We observe first that this case does not involve an attempt by Congress to increase its own powers at the expense of the Executive Branch. . . . Indeed, with the exception of the power of impeachment—which applies to all officers of the United States—Congress retained for itself no powers of control or supervision over an independent counsel. The Act does empower certain Members of Congress to request the Attorney General to apply for the appointment of an independent counsel, but the Attorney General has no duty to comply with the request, although he must respond within a certain time limit. . . .

. . .

. . . [W]e do not think that the Act "impermissibly undermine[s]" the powers of the Executive Branch . . . or "disrupts the proper balance between the coordinate branches [by] prevent[ing] the Executive Branch from accomplishing its constitutionally assigned functions." . . . It is undeniable that the Act reduces the amount of control or supervision that the Attorney General and, through him, the President exercises over the investigation and prosecution of a certain class of alleged criminal activity. The Attorney General is not allowed to appoint the individual of his choice; he does not determine the counsel's jurisdiction; and his power to remove a counsel is limited. Nonetheless, the Act does give the Attorney General several means of supervising or controlling the prosecutorial powers that may be wielded by an independent counsel. Most importantly, the Attorney General retains the power to remove the counsel for "good cause," a power that we have already concluded provides the Executive with substantial ability to ensure that the laws are "faithfully executed" by an independent counsel. No independent counsel may be appointed without a specific request by the Attorney General, and the Attorney General's decision not to request appointment if he finds "no reasonable grounds to believe that further investigation is warranted" is committed to his unreviewable discretion. The Act thus gives the Executive a degree of control over the power to initiate an investigation by the independent counsel. . . . Notwithstanding the fact that the counsel is to some degree "independent" and free from executive supervision to a greater extent than other federal prosecutors, in our view these features of the Act give the Executive Branch sufficient control over the independent counsel to ensure that the President is able to perform his constitutionally assigned duties.

JUSTICE SCALIA, dissenting.

. . .

. . . [T]he Founders conspicuously and very consciously declined to sap the Executive's strength in the same way they had weakened the Legislature: by dividing the executive power. Proposals to have multiple executives, or a council of advisers with separate authority were rejected.

That is what this suit is about. Power. The allocation of power among Congress, the President, and the courts in such fashion as to preserve the equilibrium the Constitution sought to establish—so that "a gradual concentration of the several powers in the same department" . . . can effectively be resisted. Frequently an issue of this sort will come before the Court clad, so to speak, in sheep's clothing: the potential of the asserted principle to effect important change in the equilibrium of power is not immediately evident, and must be discerned by a careful and perceptive analysis. But this wolf comes as a wolf. . . .

As a general matter, the Act before us here requires the Attorney General to apply for the appointment of an independent counsel within 90 days after receiving a request to do so, unless he determines within that period that "there are no reasonable grounds to believe that further investigation or prosecution is warranted." As a practical matter, it would be surprising if the Attorney General had any choice (assuming this statute is constitutional) but to seek appointment of an independent counsel to pursue the charges against the principal object of the congressional request, Mr. Olson. Merely the political consequences (to him and the President) of seeming to break the law by refusing to do so would have been substantial. How could it not be, the public would ask, that a 3,000-page indictment drawn by our representatives over 2½ years does not even establish "reasonable grounds to believe" that further investigation or prosecution is warranted with respect to at least the principal alleged culprit? But the Act establishes more than just practical compulsion. Although the Court's opinion asserts that the Attorney General had "no duty to comply with the [congressional] request" that is not entirely accurate. He *had* a duty to comply unless he could conclude that there were *"no reasonable grounds to believe,"* not that prosecution was warranted, but merely that *"further investigation"* was warranted. . . . The Court also makes much of the fact that "the courts are specifically prevented from reviewing the Attorney General's decision not to seek appointment, §592(f)." Yes, but *Congress* is not prevented from reviewing it. The context of this statute is acrid with the smell of threatened impeachment. Where, as here, a request for appointment of an independent counsel has come from the Judiciary Committee of either House of Congress, the Attorney General must, if he decides not to seek appointment, explain to that Committee why.

Thus, by the application of this statute in the present case, Congress has effectively compelled a criminal investigation of a high-level appointee of the President in connection with his actions arising out of a bitter power dispute between the President and the Legislative Branch. Mr. Olson may or may not be guilty of a crime; we do not know. But we do know that the investigation of him has been commenced, not necessarily because the President or his authorized subordinates believe it is in the interest of the United States, in the sense that it warrants the diversion of resources from other efforts, and is worth the cost in money and in possible damage to other governmental interests; and not even, leaving aside those normally considered factors, because the President or his authorized subordinates necessarily believe that an investigation is likely to unearth a violation worth prosecuting; but only because the Attorney General cannot affirm, as Congress demands, that there are *no reasonable grounds to believe* that further investigation is warranted. The decisions regarding the scope of that further investigation, its duration, and, finally, whether or not prosecution should ensue, are likewise beyond the control of the President and his subordinates.

If to describe this case is not to decide it, the concept of a government of separate and coordinate powers no longer has meaning. . . .

. . . Article II, §1, cl. 1, of the Constitution provides:

> "The executive Power shall be vested in a President of the United States."

. . . [T]his does not mean *some of* the executive power, but *all of* the executive power. It seems to me, therefore, that the decision of the Court of Appeals invalidating the present statute must be upheld on fundamental separation-of-powers principles if the following two questions are answered affirmatively: (1) Is the conduct of a criminal prosecution (and of an investigation to decide whether to prosecute) the exercise of purely executive power? (2) Does the statute deprive the President of the United States of exclusive control over the exercise of that power? Surprising to say, the Court appears to concede an affirmative answer to both questions, but seeks to avoid the inevitable conclusion that since the statute vests some purely executive power in a person who is not the President of the United States it is void.

The Court concedes that "[t]here is no real dispute that the functions performed by the independent counsel are 'executive,'" though it qualifies that concession by adding "in the sense that they are law enforcement functions that typically have been undertaken by officials within the Executive Branch." . . . There is no possible doubt that the independent counsel's functions fit this description. She is vested with the "full power and independent authority to exercise all *investigative and prosecutorial* functions and powers of the Department of Justice [and] the Attorney General." . . . Governmental investigation and prosecution of crimes is a quintessentially executive function.

As for the second question, whether the statute before us deprives the President of exclusive control over that quintessentially executive activity: The Court does not, and could not possibly, assert that it does not. That is indeed the whole object of the statute. Instead, the Court points out that the President, through his

Attorney General, has at least *some* control. That concession is alone enough to invalidate the statute, but I cannot refrain from pointing out that the Court greatly exaggerates the extent of that "some" Presidential control. . . . [L]imiting removal power to "good cause" is an impediment to, not an effective grant of, Presidential control. . . . What we in *Humphrey's Executor* (1935) found to be a means of eliminating Presidential control, the Court today considers the "most importan[t]" means of assuring Presidential control. Congress, of course, operated under no such illusion when it enacted this statute, describing the "good cause" limitation as "protecting the independent counsel's ability to act independently of the President's direct control" since it permits removal only for "misconduct."

. . . Almost all investigative and prosecutorial decisions—including the ultimate decision whether, after a technical violation of the law has been found, prosecution is warranted—involve the balancing of innumerable legal and practical considerations. Indeed, even political considerations (in the nonpartisan sense) must be considered, as exemplified by the recent decision of an independent counsel to subpoena the former Ambassador of Canada, producing considerable tension in our relations with that country. Another preeminently political decision is whether getting a conviction in a particular case is worth the disclosure of national security information that would be necessary. The Justice Department and our intelligence agencies are often in disagreement on this point, and the Justice Department does not always win. . . . In sum, the balancing of various legal, practical, and political considerations, none of which is absolute, is the very essence of prosecutorial discretion. To take this away is to remove the core of the prosecutorial function, and not merely "some" Presidential control.

As I have said, however, it is ultimately irrelevant *how much* the statute reduces Presidential control. . . . It is not for us to determine, and we have never presumed to determine, how much of the purely executive powers of government must be within the full control of the President. The Constitution prescribes that they *all* are.

. . .

Is it unthinkable that the President should have such exclusive power, even when alleged crimes by him or his close associates are at issue? No more so than that Congress should have the exclusive power of legislation, even when what is at issue is its own exemption from the burdens of certain laws. . . . No more so than that this Court should have the exclusive power to pronounce the final decision on justiciable cases and controversies, even those pertaining to the constitutionality of a statute reducing the salaries of the Justices. . . . A system of separate and coordinate powers necessarily involves an acceptance of exclusive power that can theoretically be abused. . . . While the separation of powers may prevent us from righting every wrong, it does so in order to ensure that we do not lose liberty. The checks against any branch's abuse of its exclusive powers are twofold: First, retaliation by one of the other branch's use of *its* exclusive powers: Congress, for example, can impeach the executive who willfully fails to enforce the laws; the executive can decline to prosecute under unconstitutional statutes. . . . Second, and ultimately, there is the political check that the people will replace those in the political branches . . . who are guilty of abuse. Political pressures produced special prosecutors—for Teapot Dome and for Watergate, for example—long before this statute created the independent counsel.

. . .

. . . [T]he independent counsel is not an inferior officer because she is not *subordinate* to any officer in the Executive Branch (indeed, not even to the President). Dictionaries in use at the time of the Constitutional Convention gave the word "inferiour" two meanings which it still bears today: (1) "[l]ower in place, . . . station, . . . rank of life, . . . value or excellency," and (2) "[s]ubordinate." . . . In a document dealing with the structure (the constitution) of a government, one would naturally expect the word to bear the latter meaning—indeed, in such a context it would be unpardonably careless to use the word *unless* a relationship of subordination was intended. If what was meant was merely "lower in station or rank," one would use instead a term such as "lesser officers." At the only other point in the Constitution at which the word "inferior" appears, it plainly connotes a relationship of subordination. Article III vests the judicial power of the United States in "one supreme Court, and in such *inferior* Courts as the Congress may from time to time ordain and establish."

. . .

Because appellant is not subordinate to another officer, she is not an "inferior" officer and her appointment other than by the President with the advice and consent of the Senate is unconstitutional. . . .

Since our 1935 decision in *Humphrey's Executor v. United States* . . . it has been established that the line of permissible restriction upon removal of principal officers lies at the point at which the powers exercised by those officers are no longer purely executive. Thus, removal restrictions have been generally regarded as lawful for so-called "independent regulatory agencies." . . . It has often been observed, correctly in my view, that the line between "purely executive" functions and "quasi-legislative" or "quasi-judicial" functions is not a clear one or even a rational one. . . . But at least it permitted the identification of certain officers, and certain agencies, whose functions were entirely within the control of the President. Congress had to be aware of that restriction in its legislation. Today, however, *Humphrey's Executor* is swept into the dustbin of repudiated constitutional principles. . . .

. . . There are now no lines. If the removal of a prosecutor, the virtual embodiment of the power to "take care that the laws be faithfully executed," can be restricted, what officer's removal cannot? This is an open invitation for Congress to experiment. What about a special Assistant Secretary of State, with responsibility for one very narrow area of foreign policy, who would not only have to be confirmed by the Senate but could also be removed only pursuant to certain carefully designed restrictions? Could this possibly render the President "[un]able to accomplish his constitutional role"? . . . The Court essentially says to the President: "Trust us. We will make sure that you are able to accomplish your constitutional role." I think the Constitution gives the President—and the people—more protection than that.

The purpose of the separation and equilibration of powers in general, and of the unitary Executive in particular, was not merely to assure effective government but to preserve individual freedom. . . .

Under our system of government, the primary check against prosecutorial abuse is a political one. The prosecutors who exercise this awesome discretion are selected and can be removed by a President, whom the people have trusted enough to elect. Moreover, when crimes are not investigated and prosecuted fairly, nonselectively, with a reasonable sense of proportion, the President pays the cost in political damage to his administration. If federal prosecutors "pick people that [they] thin[k] [they] should get, rather than cases that need to be prosecuted," if they amass many more resources against a particular prominent individual, or against a particular class of political protesters, or against members of a particular political party, than the gravity of the alleged offenses or the record of successful prosecutions seems to warrant, the unfairness will come home to roost in the Oval Office. I leave it to the reader to recall the examples of this in recent years. . . .

That is the system of justice the rest of us are entitled to, but what of that select class consisting of present or former high-level Executive Branch officials? . . . Can one imagine a less equitable manner of fulfilling the executive responsibility to investigate and prosecute? What would be the reaction if, in an area not covered by this statute, the Justice Department posted a public notice inviting applicants to assist in an investigation and possible prosecution of a certain prominent person? Does this not invite what Justice Jackson described as "picking the man and then searching the law books, or putting investigators to work, to pin some offense on him"? To be sure, the investigation must relate to the area of criminal offense specified by the life-tenured judges. But that has often been (and nothing prevents it from being) very broad—and should the independent counsel or his or her staff come up with something beyond that scope, nothing prevents him or her from asking the judges to expand his or her authority or, if that does not work, referring it to the Attorney General, whereupon the whole process would recommence and, if there was "reasonable basis to believe" that further investigation was warranted, that new offense would be referred to the Special Division, which would in all likelihood assign it to the same independent counsel. It seems to me not conducive to fairness. But even if it were entirely evident that unfairness was in fact the result—the judges hostile to the administration, the independent counsel an old foe of the President, the staff refugees from the recently defeated administration—*there would be no one accountable to the public to whom the blame could be assigned.*

. . .

The notion that every violation of law should be prosecuted, including—indeed, *especially*—every violation by those in high places, is an attractive one, and it would be risky to argue in an election campaign that that is not an absolutely overriding value. *Fiat justitia, ruat coelum.* Let justice be done, though the heavens may fall. The reality is, however, that it is not an absolutely overriding value, and it was with the hope that we would be able to acknowledge and apply such realities that the Constitution spared us, by life tenure, the necessity of election campaigns. I cannot imagine that there are not many thoughtful men and women in Congress who realize that the benefits of this legislation are far outweighed by its harmful effect upon our system of government, and even upon the nature of justice received by those men and women who agree to serve in the Executive Branch. But it is difficult to vote not to enact, and even more difficult to vote to repeal, a statute called, appropriately enough, the Ethics in Government Act. If Congress is controlled by the party other than the one to which the President belongs, it has little incentive to repeal it; if it is controlled by the same party, it dare not. By its shortsighted action today, I fear the Court has permanently encumbered the Republic with an institution that will do it great harm.

VII. Individual Rights

MAJOR DEVELOPMENTS

- Some judicial protection for property rights under the takings clause
- Courts reaffirm the constitutional right to an abortion and the prohibition on state-sponsored prayer exercises in public schools
- Greater judicial solicitude for state assistance to religious organizations
- No right to homosexual conduct

The constitutional politics of individual rights was subtly transformed during the Reagan Era. At the dawn of the 1980s most conservatives championed judicial restraint on almost all individual rights issues, from the right to bear arms to the right to terminate a pregnancy. As Reagan conservatism matured and conservatives established a foothold in the judiciary, many political actors on the right demanded constitutional protections for a different set of individual rights. This conservative rights agenda included judicial protection for property rights, the rights of evangelical Christians, and the rights of gun holders. By the mid-1990s constitutional politics had become a struggle between liberal and conservative conceptions of constitutional rights rather than a contest between liberal proponents of judicial activism and conservative proponents of judicial restraint.

When reading the materials in this section, consider two different explanations for increased conservative calls for judicial activism (and corresponding liberal calls for judicial restraint). The first is political. By 1990 the majority of the justices on the Supreme Court and federal bench were conservatives appointed by Republican presidents. These justices were often sympathetic to property rights and the right to bear arms. The second is jurisprudential. Warren Court activism helped fashion a constitutional culture committed to judicial protection for fundamental rights. Conservatives socialized in this culture were more inclined to change the ideological direction of activist decisions than to abandon judicial rights protection.

A. Property

Reagan Republicans had an ambivalent attitude toward due process protections for property rights. Conservatives celebrated economic liberty. Ronald Reagan consistently spoke of "economic freedom." Nevertheless, the Reagan years saw few efforts to revive the constitutional protection for the freedom of contract asserted in *Lochner v. New York* (1905). Most prominent conservative constitutional thinkers scorned *Lochner*. In a speech criticizing conservatives who favored reviving *Lochner*, Robert Bork declared, "Judicial review of economic regulations . . . works a massive shift away from democracy and toward judicial role."[17] The Reagan Justice Department worked up some enthusiasm for broader interpretations of the contracts clause and the takings clause. *The Constitution in the Year 2000* called for constitutional decision makers to use those provisions to "shield . . . the liberty of private property from governmental interference much the same way as the First Amendment shields the liberty of speech."[18] The *Guidelines on Constitutional Litigation* said nothing about property rights.

Conservative intellectuals, public interest groups, and justices enjoyed increasing success in their campaign to impose takings clause limitations on various environment laws and land use regulations. Professor Richard Epstein of the University of Chicago led the

17. Bork, "Constitution, Original Intent, and Economic Rights," 829.

18. U.S. Department of Justice, Office of Legal Policy, *Constitution in the Year 2000*, 117.

fight for property rights in the academy. His influential book *Takings* asserted that the Fifth and Fourteenth Amendments were violated any time that state regulations lowered the value of property. That work concluded, "First, the eminent domain logic allows forced exchanges only for the public use, which excludes naked transfers from one person to another. Second, it requires compensation, so everyone receives something of greater value in exchange for the *rights* surrendered."[19] Such libertarian public interest groups as the Rocky Mountain Legal Foundation, the Washington Legal Foundation, and the Institute for Justice supported hundreds of lawsuits claiming takings violations, some of which found their way to the Supreme Court. Justices divided on ideological lines, with the more conservative justices voting to declare that the state regulation in question violated constitutional property rights and the more liberal justices voting to sustain the government decision. More frequently than in the recent past, the Supreme Court found takings clause violations.

A 5–4 judicial majority in *Lucas v. South Carolina Coastal Council* (1992) ruled that a regulation could take property even when the government did not physically invade the land in question. Speaking for the five most conservative justices on the Rehnquist Court, Justice Scalia declared that a compensable taking occurred whenever a regulation deprived persons of "all economically beneficial use" of their holdings. In both *Nollan v. California Coastal Commission* (1987) and *Dolan v. City of Tigard* (1994) 5–4 conservative judicial majorities ruled that legislative conditions on development had to satisfy Fifth and Fourteenth Amendment standards. Chief Justice Rehnquist's majority opinion in *Dolan* announced a two-part test for determining when conditions on development were constitutional. He declared that courts "must first determine whether the 'essential nexus' exists between the legitimate state interest and the permit condition exacted by the city" and then determine "the required degree of connection between the exactions and the projected impact of the proposed development." "Rough proportionality," Rehnquist insisted, was required. He maintained that governing officials "must make some sort of individualized determination that the required dedication is related both in nature and extent to the impact of the proposed development." The city of Tigard failed this test. City officials sought to condition a permit to double the size of an electrical supply store on the petitioner's willingness to dedicate part of her property for flood drainage and part of her property for a bicycle path. The judicial majority in *Dolan* concluded that the city's interest in flood control could be as well secured by a private as a public greenway and that local officials had not sufficiently demonstrated that the increased traffic that might result if the store were expanded justified creating an easement for a public bicycle path.

The Supreme Court was more deferential to elected officials when interpreting the constitutional requirement that private property "be taken for public use." *Hawaii Housing Authority v. Midkiff* (1984) sustained a law that required major landowners in Hawaii to sell parcels to their tenants. Justice O'Connor's unanimous opinion employed a traditional rational basis test when permitting Hawaii to exercise the power of eminent domain to transfer title from large property holders to smaller property holders.

After a brief reemergence, the contracts clause returned to oblivion. *Allied Structural Steel Co. v. Spannaus* (1978) and *United Trust Co. of New York v. New Jersey* (1977) suggested that conservative justices might impose significant contracts clause limits on state power to impair existing contractual relationships without sufficient justification. The justices did not, however, expand those precedents. The Supreme Court decided very few contracts clause cases and almost always upheld the state regulation being constitutionally challenged. *Energy Reserves Group, Inc., v. Kansas Power and Light Co.* (1983) sustained a Kansas law that altered the price at which suppliers could purchase natural gas. Justice Blackmun's majority opinion claimed that the parties should have expected legal changes because the natural gas industry was "heavily regulated" and that the Kansas law rested on a "significant and legitimate state interest" in "protect[ing] consumers from the escalation of natural gas prices caused by deregulation." *General Motors Corp. v. Romein* (1992) declared that the Michigan legislature could give retroactive effect to a law overturning a state judicial decision that permitted companies to withhold disability payments. Justice O'Connor's unanimous opinion declared, "Petitioners' suggestion

19. Richard A. Epstein, *Takings: Private Property and the Power of Eminent Domain* (Cambridge, MA: Harvard University Press, 1985), 332.

that we should read every workplace regulation into the private contractual arrangements of employers and employees would expand the definition of contract so far that the constitutional provision would lose its anchoring purpose, *i.e.*, 'enabl[ing] individuals to order their personal and business affairs according to their particular needs and interests.'"

Lucas v. South Carolina Coastal Council, 505 U.S. 1003 (1992)

David Lucas was a real estate developer. In 1986 he paid nearly $1 million for two residential lots on the Isle of Palms, a barrier island near Charleston, South Carolina. Lucas intended to build single-family houses on his newly acquired property. His plans were thwarted when the South Carolina legislature in 1988 passed the Beachfront Management Act, which prohibited all construction (other than small decks and wooden walkways) within designated areas near beaches, including the lots owned by Lucas. Lucas challenged the constitutionality of the government's action in state court. The trial court agreed that Lucas's land had been rendered "valueless" by the government's action and that he was entitled to compensation. The Supreme Court of South Carolina reversed that decision, arguing that the construction would cause a public harm that could be prohibited under the state's police powers. Lucas appealed to the Supreme Court of the United States.

The Supreme Court by a 5–4 vote ruled that a compensable taking had occurred. Justice Scalia's majority opinion maintained that the takings clause required states to provide compensation when a regulation made private property worthless, unless the owner had no preexisting right to use the property in the prohibited way. What is the constitutional foundation of that rule? Did Scalia refer to history, precedent, or general constitutional principles? What differences do you perceive between judicial activism on behalf of property rights and such cases as Roe v. Wade *(1973)? Justice Scalia noted that no compensation is required if the new restriction is consistent with previously existing property law or the common law of nuisance. South Carolina can forbid people from mining on their property if such an action is likely to cause poison gas to rise to the surface. What is the constitutional foundation of that rule? Under what conditions did the dissenting judges believe that South Carolina could pass regulations that would destroy the entire value of Lucas's property? What is the correct constitutional rule?*

JUSTICE SCALIA delivered the opinion of the Court.

. . .

. . . We have described at least two discrete categories of regulatory action as compensable without case-specific inquiry into the public interest advanced in support of the restraint. The first encompasses regulations that compel the property owner to suffer a physical "invasion" of his property. In general (at least with regard to permanent invasions), no matter how minute the intrusion, and no matter how weighty the public purpose behind it, we have required compensation. . . . The second situation in which we have found categorical treatment appropriate is where regulation denies all economically beneficial or productive use of land. . . . As we have said on numerous occasions, the Fifth Amendment is violated when land-use regulation "does not substantially advance legitimate state interests *or denies an owner economically viable use of his land.*"

. . .

. . . [T]he *functional* basis for permitting the government, by regulation, to affect property values without compensation—that "Government hardly could go on if to some extent values incident to property could not be diminished without paying for every such change in the general law,"—does not apply to the relatively rare situations where the government has deprived a landowner of all economically beneficial uses. . . . [R]egulations that leave the owner of land without economically beneficial or productive options for its use—typically, as here, by requiring land to be left substantially in its natural state—carry with them a heightened risk that private property is being pressed into some form of public service under the guise of mitigating serious public harm. . . .

. . .

Where the State seeks to sustain regulation that deprives land of all economically beneficial use, we think it may resist compensation only if the logically antecedent inquiry into the nature of the owner's estate shows that the proscribed use interests were not part of his title to begin with. This accords, we think, with our "takings" jurisprudence, which has traditionally been guided by the understandings of our citizens regarding the content of, and the State's power over, the "bundle of rights" that they acquire when they obtain title to property. It seems to us that the property owner necessarily expects the uses of his property to be restricted, from time to time, by various measures newly enacted by the State in legitimate exercise of its police powers; "as long recognized, some values are enjoyed under an implied limitation and must yield to the police power." And in the case of personal property, by reason of the State's traditionally high degree of control over commercial dealings, he ought to be aware of the possibility that new regulation might even render his property economically worthless (at least if the property's only economically productive use is sale or manufacture for sale). In the case of land, however, we think the notion pressed by the Council that title is somehow held subject to the "implied limitation" that the State may subsequently eliminate all economically valuable use is inconsistent with the historical compact recorded in the Takings Clause that has become part of our constitutional culture.

Where "permanent physical occupation" of land is concerned, we have refused to allow the government to decree it anew (without compensation), no matter how weighty the asserted "public interests" involved, though we assuredly *would* permit the government to assert a permanent easement that was a pre-existing limitation upon the land owner's title. We believe similar treatment must be accorded confiscatory regulations, *i.e.*, regulations that prohibit all economically beneficial use of land: Any limitation so severe cannot be newly legislated or decreed (without compensation), but must inhere in the title itself, in the restrictions that background principles of the State's law of property and nuisance already place upon land ownership. A law or decree with such an effect must, in other words, do no more than duplicate the result that could have been achieved in the courts—by adjacent landowners (or other uniquely affected persons) under the State's law of private nuisance, or by the State under its complementary power to abate nuisances that affect the public generally, or otherwise.

. . .

It seems unlikely that common-law principles would have prevented the erection of any habitable or productive improvements on petitioner's land; they rarely support prohibition of the "essential use" of land. The question, however, is one of state law to be dealt with on remand. . . .

JUSTICE KENNEDY, concurring in the judgment.

. . .

. . . Where a taking is alleged from regulations which deprive the property of all value, the test must be whether the deprivation is contrary to reasonable, investment-backed expectations. . . .

In my view, reasonable expectations must be understood in light of the whole of our legal tradition. The common law of nuisance is too narrow a confine for the exercise of regulatory power in a complex and interdependent society. The State should not be prevented from enacting new regulatory initiatives in response to changing conditions, and courts must consider all reasonable expectations whatever their source. The Takings Clause does not require a static body of state property law; it protects private expectations to ensure private investment. I agree with the Court that nuisance prevention accords with the most common expectations of property owners who face regulation, but I do not believe this can be the sole source of state authority to impose severe restrictions. Coastal property may present such unique concerns for a fragile land system that the State can go further in regulating its development and use than the common law of nuisance might otherwise permit.

. . . The promotion of tourism [however] ought not to suffice to deprive specific property of all value without a corresponding duty to compensate. . . .

JUSTICE BLACKMUN, dissenting.

. . .

The Court creates its new takings jurisprudence based on the trial court's finding that the property had lost all economic value. This finding is almost certainly erroneous. Petitioner still can enjoy other attributes of ownership, such as the right to exclude others, "one of the most essential sticks in the bundle of rights that are commonly characterized as property." Petitioner can picnic, swim, camp in a tent, or live on the property in a movable trailer. State courts frequently have recognized that land has economic value where the only residual economic uses are recreation or camping. Petitioner also retains the right to alienate the land, which would have value for neighbors and for those prepared to enjoy proximity to the ocean without a house.

. . .

. . . [T]he State has full power to prohibit an owner's use of property if it is harmful to the public. "Since no individual has a right to use his property so as to create a nuisance or otherwise harm others, the State has not 'taken' anything when it asserts its power to enjoin the nuisance-like activity." It would make no sense under this theory to suggest that an owner has a constitutionally protected right to harm others, if only he makes the proper showing of economic loss.

. . .

Until today, the Court explicitly had rejected the contention that the government's power to act without paying compensation turns on whether the prohibited activity is a common-law nuisance. The brewery closed in *Mugler v. Kansas* (1887) itself was not a common-law nuisance, and the Court specifically stated that it was the role of the legislature to determine what measures would be appropriate for the protection of public health and safety. . . .

. . .

Even more perplexing, however, is the Court's reliance on common-law principles of nuisance in its quest for a value-free takings jurisprudence. In determining what is a nuisance at common law, state courts make exactly the decision that the Court finds so troubling when made by the South Carolina General Assembly today: They determine whether the use is harmful. Common-law public and private nuisance law is simply a determination whether a particular use causes harm. . . .

. . .

JUSTICE STEVENS, dissenting.

. . .

In addition to lacking support in past decisions, the Court's new rule is wholly arbitrary. A landowner whose property is diminished in value 95% recovers nothing, while an owner whose property is diminished 100% recovers the land's full value. The case at hand illustrates this arbitrariness well. The Beachfront Management Act not only prohibited the building of new dwellings in certain areas, it also prohibited the rebuilding of houses that were "destroyed beyond repair by natural causes or by fire." . . . Thus, if the homes adjacent to Lucas' lot were destroyed by a hurricane one day after the Act took effect, the owners would not be able to rebuild, nor would they be assured recovery. Under the Court's categorical approach, Lucas (who has lost the opportunity to build) recovers, while his neighbors (who have lost *both* the opportunity to build *and* their homes) do not recover. The arbitrariness of such a rule is palpable.

. . .

Viewed more broadly, the Court's new rule and exception conflict with the very character of our takings jurisprudence. We have frequently and consistently recognized that the definition of a taking cannot be reduced to a "set formula" and that determining whether a regulation is a taking is "essentially [an] ad hoc, factual inquiry." *Penn Central Transportation Co. v. New York City* (1978). The rigid rules fixed by the Court today clash with this enterprise: "fairness and justice" are often disserved by categorical rules. . . .

B. Religion

Ronald Reagan helped solidify the new constitutional politics of religion. The traditional constitutional politics of religion pitted Protestants, who favored public expressions of religion but opposed providing state funds for sectarian institutions, against Catholics, who took the opposite position on both matters. Richard Nixon created a new alliance of conservative Protestants and Catholics (as well as orthodox Jews) who favored public expressions of religion and the provision of state aid to sectarian institutions. Ronald Reagan and the Republican Party appealed to that coalition. The Republican Party promised to adopt policies and appoint judges that would permit some public funding for private religious schools and restore voluntary prayer in public schools. Republicans enjoyed substantial political and some constitutional success. By the end of the 1980s most evangelical Christians were reliable Republican voters. The party made substantial inroads into the Catholic vote. Government provided more aid to private schools. The late Burger and Rehnquist Courts usually sustained the provision of such aid. Conservatives failed, however, to obtain their highest public priority—reintroducing prayer into public schools.

Private religious schools and religious institutions gained more access to public funds during the Reagan years. Supreme Court doctrine focused on whether the government aid discriminated between religious and nonreligious institutions and individuals, rather than on whether government money was financing religious activities or organizations. In *Mueller v. Allen* (1983) the Supreme Court sustained a Minnesota law that permitted taxpayers to deduct school expenses from their taxes, including expenses incurred sending children to private, paraochial schools. *Bowen v. Kendrick* (1988) permitted the federal government to give grants to religious organizations that urged teenagers to abstain from sexual relationships. These laws provided benefits for both secular and religious choices. Chief Justice Rehnquist's majority opinion in *Bowen* declared, "Nothing in our previous cases prevents Congress from . . . recognizing the important part religion or religious organizations may play in resolving certain secular problems," most notably those problems associated with "adolescent sexual activity and adolescent pregnancy." The justices drew a line, however, when the state of New York drew a school district boundary for the purpose of creating a special program for Satmar Hasidic children with special educational needs. Justice Souter's opinion in *Board of Education of Kiryas Joel Village School v. Grumet* (1984) stated that the legislature's act was "substantially equivalent to defining a political subdivision and hence the qualification for its franchise by a religious test, resulting in a purposeful and forbidden fusion of governmental and religious functions."

Reagan administration failed to convince federal courts to overrule o *Engle v. Vitale* (1962), the decision holding that public schools could not sponsor voluntary prayer exercises. The Supreme Court in *Wallace v. Jaffree* (1985) declared unconstitutional an Alabama statute requiring a moment of silence for prayer or meditation. Justice Stevens's majority opinion maintained that state law could not privilege prayer over other activities, declaring, "The addition of 'or voluntary prayer' indicates that the State intended to characterize prayer as a favored practice. Such an endorsement is not consistent with the established principle that the government must pursue a course of complete neutrality toward religion." Social conservatives were particularly disappointed when in *Lee v. Weisman* (1992) two of Ronald Reagan's judicial appointees, Justices Kennedy and O'Connor, joined with four other justices to form a majority supporting the ruling that public officials could not constitutionally authorize a nonsectarian prayer at a middle school graduation ceremony. Kennedy's majority opinion maintained that the establishment clause forbids both direct and subtle coercion and that middle school–aged children were subtly coerced into participating in prayer exercises at their graduation. Although doctrinally ambiguous, *Lee v. Weisman* practically ended the conservative quest to restore voluntary prayer to public schools. The early Rehnquist Court consistently rejected perceived attempts to bring religion more directly into the public school classroom. *Edwards v. Aguillard* (1987) declared unconstitutional a Louisiana law that required public schools to teach the theory of creation science along with the theory of evolution or refrain from teaching anything about human origins.

The main conflicts over free exercise rights were waged between elected officials and judges. Congress passed legislation reversing two important Supreme Court decisions. After the Supreme Court in *Goldman v. Weinberger* (1986) ruled that an Air Force chaplain had no constitutional right to wear a yarmulke, bipartisan majorities in Congress passed legislation permitting military chaplains to dress as their religion commanded. After the Supreme Court in *Employment Division v. Smith* (1990) ruled that the free exercise clause did not grant religious believers exemptions from generally applicable laws that burdened their religious practices, bipartisan majorities in Congress passed the Religious Freedom Restoration Act. That measure required states and the federal government to grant religious believers exemptions unless there was a compelling interest not to do so. Liberals in Congress and the courts both tended to support free exercise rights. Many conservatives in Congress, however, supported the compelling state interest test to determine free exercise rights that the most conservative justices on the Supreme Court rejected.

The Rehnquist Court was more supportive of free exercise claims when they perceived that state laws were directed against a religion or a religious practice. The justices in *Church of the Babalu Aye v. Hialeah* (1993) unanimously agreed that the city of Hialeah could not pass ordinances prohibiting animal sacrifice when the rules in question were clearly gerrymandered to outlaw only the religious practices of the local Santerian sect. Justice Kennedy's opinion for the Court maintained that government could not discriminate "against some or all religious beliefs or regulate . . . or prohibit . . . conduct because it is undertaken for religious reasons."

Lee v. Weisman, 505 U.S. 577 (1992)

Deborah Weisman was a student at Nathan Bishop Middle School in Providence, Rhode Island. The principal at Nathan Bishop regularly asked a member of the Providence clergy to offer an invocation and benediction at graduation. The Weisman family insisted that the practice was unconstitutional, but to no avail. In June 1989 the principal, Robert Lee, asked a local rabbi to offer prayers, and that offer was accepted. The Weismans filed a lawsuit against Lee, claiming that prayer at graduation violated the First and Fourteenth Amendments. The local district court refused to issue a temporary injunction barring the prayer exercise but later issued an injunction prohibiting similar prayer exercises during future graduations. The United States Court of Appeals for the First Circuit affirmed that decision. Lee appealed to the Supreme Court of the United States.

The Supreme Court by a 5–4 vote ruled that prayer exercises during middle school graduation ceremonies violated the establishment clause. Justice Kennedy's majority opinion maintained that the constitutional violation occurred because middle school students were "indirectly" coerced by the state into participating in a religious exercise. What was that coercion? Why did Justice Scalia claim that no coercion took place? Does the establishment clause require coercion, or is state sponsorship of a religious exercise sufficient? What might explain why Justices O'Connor and Kennedy, Reagan judicial appointees, were more willing to support funding for religious institutions than voluntary school prayer?

JUSTICE KENNEDY delivered the opinion of the Court.

. . .

These dominant facts mark and control the confines of our decision: State officials direct the performance of a formal religious exercise at promotional and graduation ceremonies for secondary schools. Even for those students who object to the religious exercise, their attendance and participation in the state-sponsored religious activity are, in a fair and real sense, obligatory, though the school district does not require attendance as a condition for receipt of the diploma.

. . .

. . . It is beyond dispute that, at a minimum, the Constitution guarantees that government may not coerce anyone to support or participate in religion or its exercise, or otherwise act in a way which "establishes a [state] religion or religious faith, or tends to do so." . . . The State's involvement in the school prayers challenged today violates these central principles.

That involvement is as troubling as it is undenied. A school official, the principal, decided that an invocation and a benediction should be given; this is a choice attributable to the State, and, from a constitutional perspective, it is as if a state statute decreed that the prayers must occur. The principal chose the religious participant, here a rabbi, and that choice is also attributable to the State. The reason for the choice of a rabbi is not disclosed by the record, but the potential for divisiveness over the choice of a particular member of the clergy to conduct the ceremony is apparent.

. . .

The State's role did not end with the decision to include a prayer and with the choice of clergyman. Principal Lee provided Rabbi Gutterman with a copy of the "Guidelines for Civic Occasions" and advised him that his prayers should be nonsectarian. Through these means, the principal directed and controlled the content of the prayers. . . . It is a cornerstone principle of our Establishment Clause jurisprudence that it is no part of the business of government to compose official prayers for any group of the American people to recite as a part of a religious program carried on by government, *Engel v. Vitale* (1962), and that is what the school officials attempted to do.

. . .

Our decision . . . in *Engel v. Vitale* . . . recognize[d], among other things, that prayer exercises in public schools carry a particular risk of indirect coercion. . . . What to most believers may seem nothing more than a reasonable request that the nonbeliever respect their religious practices, in a school context may appear to the nonbeliever or dissenter to be an attempt to employ the machinery of the State to enforce a religious orthodoxy.

We need not look beyond the circumstances of this case to see the phenomenon at work. The undeniable fact is that the school district's supervision and control of a high school graduation ceremony places public pressure, as well as peer pressure, on attending students to stand as a group or, at least, maintain respectful silence during the invocation and benediction. This pressure, though subtle and indirect, can be as real as any overt compulsion. . . . [F]or the dissenter of high school age, who has a reasonable perception that she is being forced by the State to pray in a manner her conscience will not allow, the injury is no less real. There can be no doubt that for many, if not most, of the students at the graduation, the act of standing or remaining silent was an expression of participation in the rabbi's prayer. That was the very point of the religious exercise. It is of little comfort to a dissenter, then, to be told that, for her, the act of standing or remaining in silence signifies mere respect, rather than participation. What matters is that, given our social conventions, a reasonable dissenter in this milieu could believe that the group exercise signified her own participation or approval of it.

Finding no violation under these circumstances would place objectors in the dilemma of participating, with all that implies, or protesting. We do not address whether that choice is acceptable if the affected citizens are mature adults, but we think the State may not, consistent with the Establishment Clause, place primary and secondary school children in this position. Research in psychology supports the common assumption that adolescents are often susceptible to pressure from their peers towards conformity, and that the influence is strongest in matters of social convention. . . .

. . .

. . . Law reaches past formalism. And to say a teenage student has a real choice not to attend her high school graduation is formalistic in the extreme. True, Deborah could elect not to attend commencement without renouncing her diploma; but we shall not allow the case to turn on this point. Everyone knows that, in our society and in our culture, high school graduation is one of life's most significant occasions. . . . Graduation is a time for family and those closest to the student to celebrate success and express mutual wishes of gratitude and respect, all to the end of impressing upon the young person the role that it is his or her right and duty to assume in the community and all of its diverse parts.

. . .

JUSTICE BLACKMUN, with whom JUSTICE STEVENS and JUSTICE O'CONNOR join, concurring.

. . .

The mixing of government and religion can be a threat to free government, even if no one is forced to participate. When the government puts its imprimatur on a particular religion, it conveys a message of exclusion to all those who do not adhere to the favored beliefs. A government cannot be premised on the belief that all persons are created equal when it asserts that God prefers some. . . .

. . .

JUSTICE SOUTER, with whom JUSTICE STEVENS and JUSTICE O'CONNOR join, concurring.

. . .

. . . [T]he Establishment Clause forbids state-sponsored prayers in public school settings no matter how nondenominational the prayers may be. In barring the State from sponsoring generically theistic prayers where it could not sponsor sectarian ones, we hold true to a line of precedent from which there is no adequate historical case to depart.

Since *Everson v. Board of Education* (1947), we have consistently held the Clause applicable no less to governmental acts favoring religion generally than to acts favoring one religion over others. . . .

. . .

. . . [T]he Framers meant the Establishment Clause's prohibition to encompass nonpreferential aid to religion. . . . The House . . . persuad[ed] the Senate to accept this as the final text of the Religion Clauses: "Congress shall make no law respecting an establishment of religion, or prohibiting the free exercise thereof." What is remarkable is that, unlike the earliest House drafts or the final Senate proposal, the prevailing language is not limited to laws respecting an establishment of "a religion," "a national religion," "one religious sect," or specific "articles of faith." The Framers repeatedly considered and deliberately rejected such narrow language, and instead extended their prohibition to state support for "religion" in general.

Implicit in their choice is the distinction between preferential and nonpreferential establishments, which the weight of evidence suggests the Framers appreciated. . . .

While these considerations are, for me, sufficient to reject the nonpreferentialist position, one further concern animates my judgment. In many contexts, including this one, nonpreferentialism requires some distinction between "sectarian" religious practices and those that would be, by some measure, ecumenical enough to pass Establishment Clause muster. Simply by requiring the enquiry, nonpreferentialists invite the courts to engage in comparative theology. I can hardly imagine a subject less amenable to the competence of the federal judiciary, or more deliberately to be avoided where possible.

. . .

Petitioners contend that, because the early Presidents included religious messages in their inaugural and Thanksgiving Day addresses, the Framers could not have meant the Establishment Clause to forbid noncoercive state endorsement of religion. The argument ignores the fact, however, that Americans today find such proclamations less controversial than did the founding generation, whose published thoughts on the matter belie petitioners' claim. President Jefferson, for example, steadfastly refused to issue Thanksgiving proclamations of any kind, in part because he thought they violated the Religion Clauses. . . .

During his first three years in office, James Madison also refused to call for days of thanksgiving and prayer, though later, amid the political turmoil of the War of 1812, he did so on four separate occasions. . . .

To be sure, the leaders of the young Republic engaged in some of the practices that separationists like Jefferson and Madison criticized. The First Congress did hire institutional chaplains, . . . and Presidents Washington and Adams unapologetically marked days of "'public thanksgiving and prayer.'" Yet in the face of the separationist dissent, those practices prove, at best, that the Framers simply did not share a common understanding of the Establishment Clause, and, at worst, that they, like other politicians, could raise constitutional ideals one day and turn their backs on them the next. . . .

. . .

JUSTICE SCALIA, with whom THE CHIEF JUSTICE, JUSTICE WHITE, and JUSTICE THOMAS join, dissenting.

. . .

. . . The history and tradition of our Nation are replete with public ceremonies featuring prayers of thanksgiving and petition. . . .

. . . The Declaration of Independence, the document marking our birth as a separate people, "appeal[ed] to the Supreme Judge of the world for the rectitude of our intentions" and avowed "a firm reliance on the protection of divine Providence." In his first inaugural address, after swearing his oath of office on a Bible, George Washington deliberately made a prayer a part of his first official act as President. . . .

. . .

The other two branches of the Federal Government also have a long-established practice of prayer at public events. . . . Congressional sessions have opened with a chaplain's prayer ever since the First Congress. . . .

In addition to this general tradition of prayer at public ceremonies, there exists a more specific tradition of invocations and benedictions at public school graduation exercises. By one account, the first public high school graduation ceremony took place in Connecticut in July, 1868—the very month, as it happens, that the Fourteenth Amendment (the vehicle by which the Establishment Clause has been applied against the States) was ratified—when "15 seniors from the Norwich Free Academy marched in their best Sunday suits and dresses into a church hall and waited through majestic music and long prayers." . . .

. . .

. . . [T]he Court's notion that a student who simply sits in "respectful silence" during the invocation and benediction (when all others are standing) has somehow joined—or would somehow be perceived as having joined—in the prayers is nothing short of ludicrous. . . . [S]urely "our social conventions" have not coarsened to the point that anyone who does not stand on his chair and shout obscenities can reasonably be deemed to have assented to everything said in his presence. . . .

. . . [I]f it is a permissible inference that one who is standing is doing so simply out of respect for the prayers of others that are in progress, then how can it possibly be said that a "reasonable dissenter . . . could believe that the group exercise signified her own participation or approval"? Quite obviously, it cannot. I may add, moreover, that maintaining respect for the religious observances of others is a fundamental civic virtue that government (including the public schools) can and should cultivate—so that, even if it were the case that the displaying of such respect might be mistaken for taking part in the prayer, I would deny that the dissenter's interest in avoiding even the false appearance of participation constitutionally trumps the government's interest in fostering respect for religion generally.

. . .

The other "dominant fac[t]" identified by the Court is that "[s]tate officials direct the performance of a formal religious exercise" at school graduation ceremonies. . . All the record shows is that principals of the Providence public schools, acting within their delegated authority, have invited clergy to deliver invocations and benedictions at graduations; and that Principal Lee invited Rabbi Gutterman, provided him a two-page pamphlet, prepared by the National Conference of Christians and Jews, giving general advice on inclusive prayer for civic occasions, and advised him that his prayers at graduation should be nonsectarian. How these facts can fairly be transformed into the charges that Principal Lee "directed and controlled the content of [Rabbi Gutterman's] prayer," . . . that school officials "monitor prayer," . . . and attempted to

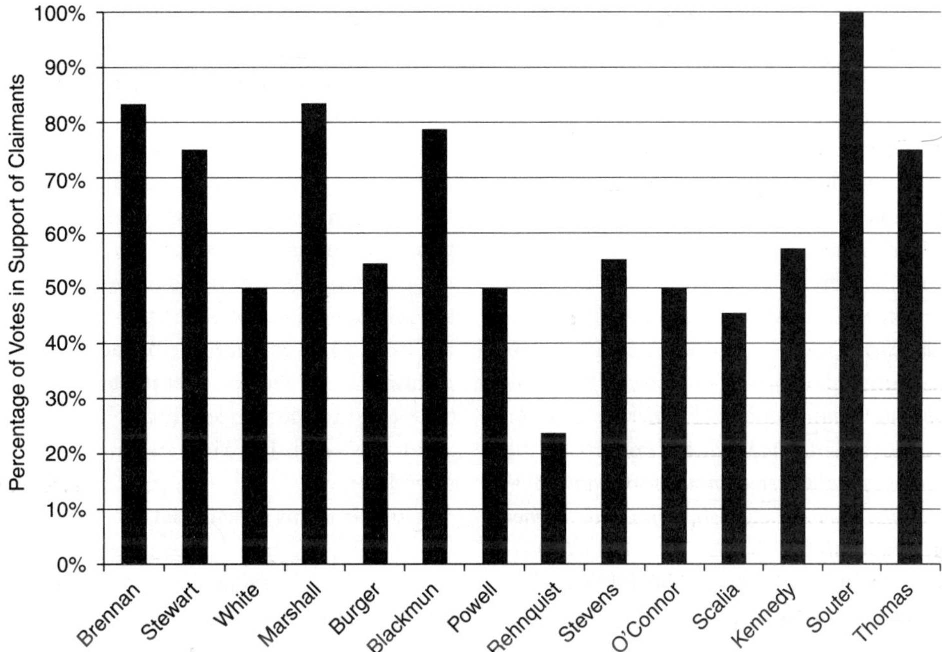

Figure 10-3 Individual Justice Support for Claimants in Religious Liberty Cases on Burger and Rehnquist Courts

Notes: Justices listed in order of appointment. Minimum of three votes in religious free exercise cases during chief justice tenure of Warren Burger and William Rehnquist.

"'compose official prayers,'" . . . and that the "government involvement with religious activity in this case is pervasive," . . . is difficult to fathom. . . .

. . .

The coercion that was a hallmark of historical establishments of religion was coercion of religious orthodoxy and of financial support by force of law and threat of penalty. Typically, attendance at the state church was required; only clergy of the official church could lawfully perform sacraments; and dissenters, if tolerated, faced an array of civil disabilities. . . .

. . .

I must add one final observation: the Founders of our Republic knew the fearsome potential of sectarian religious belief to generate civil dissension and civil strife. And they also knew that nothing, absolutely nothing, is so inclined to foster among religious believers of various faiths a toleration—no, an affection—for one another than voluntarily joining in prayer together, to the God whom they all worship and seek. Needless to say, no one should be compelled to do that, but it is a shame to deprive our public culture of the opportunity, and indeed the encouragement, for people to do it voluntarily. The Baptist or Catholic who heard and joined in the simple and inspiring prayers of Rabbi Gutterman on this official and patriotic occasion was inoculated from religious bigotry and prejudice in a manner that cannot be replicated. To deprive our society of that important unifying mechanism in order to spare the nonbeliever what seems to me the minimal inconvenience of standing, or even sitting in respectful nonparticipation, is as senseless in policy as it is unsupported in law.

Employment Division v. Smith, 494 U.S. 872 (1990)

Alfred Smith and Galen Black were fired from their jobs as drug counselors after they used peyote for sacramental purposes during a Native American religious ceremony. Their firing was consistent with Oregon law, which forbade the knowing or intentional possession of a "controlled substance," classified peyote as a controlled substance, and denied benefits to persons discharged for work-related reasons. Smith and Black sued Oregon, claiming that their firing and subsequent denial of unemployment benefits violated their free exercise rights. Both the Oregon Court of Appeals and the Oregon Supreme Court ruled that Smith and Black had a constitutional right to an exemption from the state ban on peyote. Oregon appealed to the Supreme Court of the United States.

The Supreme Court by a 6–3 vote ruled that Oregon had not violated Smith and Black's constitutional rights. Justice Scalia and four other justices maintained that religious believers had no free exercise right to exemptions from generally applicable state laws. Justice O'Connor insisted that religious believers ordinarily had rights to exemptions, but that Oregon had a compelling reason not to exempt Smith and Black from state drug laws. All justices in Smith *claimed to be following precedent, but each opinion interprets precedent differently. On what grounds did Justice Scalia distinguish* Sherbert v. Verner *(1963) and* Wisconsin v. Yoder *(1972) from* Smith*? Is his distinction convincing? Did Justice O'Connor offer a convincing interpretation of the line of cases between* Yoder *and* Smith *in which the Court almost always rejected free exercise claims? Was Justice O'Connor correct when she insisted that Oregon has a compelling interest in not exempting religious believers from drug laws? Justices Scalia and O'Connor disputed the extent to which minority religions are capable of politically defending their rights and interests. Based on what you have read and your experience, who had the better argument?*

JUSTICE SCALIA delivered the opinion of the Court.

. . .

. . . The free exercise of religion means, first and foremost, the right to believe and profess whatever religious doctrine one desires. . . . The government may not compel affirmation of religious belief, . . . punish the expression of religious doctrines it believes to be false, . . . impose special disabilities on the basis of religious views or religious status, . . . or lend its power to one or the other side in controversies over religious authority or dogma. . . .

. . .

Respondents in the present case, however, seek to carry the meaning of "prohibiting the free exercise [of religion]" one large step further. . . . They assert . . . that "prohibiting the free exercise [of religion]" includes requiring any individual to observe a generally applicable law that requires (or forbids) the performance of an act that his religious belief forbids (or requires). As a textual matter, we do not think the words must be given that meaning. It is no more necessary to regard the collection of a general tax, for example, as "prohibiting the free exercise [of religion]" by those citizens who believe support of organized government to be sinful than it is to regard the same tax as "abridging the freedom . . . of the press" of those publishing companies that must pay the tax as a condition of staying in business. It is a permissible reading of the text, in the one case as in the other, to say that, if prohibiting the exercise of religion (or burdening the activity of printing) is not the object of the tax, but merely the incidental effect of a generally applicable and otherwise valid provision, the First Amendment has not been offended. . . .

Our decisions reveal that the latter reading is the correct one. We have never held that an individual's religious beliefs excuse him from compliance with an otherwise valid law prohibiting conduct that the State is free to regulate. On the contrary, the record of more than a century of our free exercise jurisprudence contradicts that proposition. . . . We first had occasion to assert that principle in *Reynolds v. United States* (1878), . . . where we rejected the claim that criminal laws against polygamy could not be constitutionally applied to those whose religion commanded the practice. . . .

The only decisions in which we have held that the First Amendment bars application of a neutral, generally applicable law to religiously motivated action have involved not the Free Exercise Clause alone, but the Free Exercise Clause in conjunction with other constitutional protections, such as . . . the right of parents . . . to direct the education of their children, see *Wisconsin v. Yoder* (1972). . . .

. . .

Respondents argue that, even though exemption from generally applicable criminal laws need not automatically be extended to religiously motivated actors, at least the claim for a religious exemption must be evaluated under the balancing test set forth in *Sherbert v. Verner* (1963). . . . Under the *Sherbert* test, governmental actions that substantially burden a religious practice must be justified by a compelling governmental interest. . . . We have never invalidated any governmental action on the basis of the *Sherbert* test except the denial of unemployment compensation. Although we have sometimes purported to apply the *Sherbert* test in contexts other than that, we have always found the test satisfied. . . . In recent years we have abstained from applying the *Sherbert* test (outside the unemployment compensation field) at all. . . .

. . .

. . . To make an individual's obligation to obey such a law contingent upon the law's coincidence with his religious beliefs, except where the State's interest is "compelling"—permitting him, by virtue of his beliefs, "to become a law unto himself," . . . contradicts both constitutional tradition and common sense.

. . .

If the "compelling interest" test is to be applied at all, then, it must be applied across the board, to all actions thought to be religiously commanded. . . . Any society adopting such a system would be courting anarchy, but that danger increases in direct proportion to the society's diversity of religious beliefs, and its determination to coerce or suppress none of them. Precisely because "we are a cosmopolitan nation made up of people of almost every conceivable religious preference," . . . and precisely because we value and protect that religious divergence, we cannot afford the luxury of deeming presumptively invalid, as applied to the religious objector, every regulation of conduct that does not protect an interest of the highest order. . . .

Values that are protected against government interference through enshrinement in the Bill of Rights are not thereby banished from the political process. Just as a society that believes in the negative protection accorded to the press by the First Amendment is likely to enact laws that affirmatively foster the dissemination of the printed word, so also a society that believes in the negative protection accorded to religious belief can be expected to be solicitous of that value in its legislation as well. It is therefore not surprising that a number of States have made an exception to their drug laws for sacramental peyote use. . . But to say that a nondiscriminatory religious practice exemption is permitted, or even that it is desirable, is not to say that it is constitutionally required, and that the appropriate occasions for its creation can be discerned by the courts. It may fairly be said that leaving accommodation to the political process will place at a relative disadvantage those religious practices that are not widely engaged in; but that unavoidable consequence of democratic government must be preferred to a system in which each conscience is a law unto itself or in which judges weigh the social importance of all laws against the centrality of all religious beliefs.

. . .

JUSTICE O'CONNOR . . . concurring.

. . .

. . . [A] law that prohibits certain conduct—conduct that happens to be an act of worship for someone—manifestly does prohibit that person's free exercise of his religion. A person who is barred from engaging in religiously motivated conduct is barred from freely exercising his religion. Moreover, that person is barred from freely exercising his religion regardless of whether the law prohibits the conduct only when engaged in for religious reasons, only by members of that religion, or by all persons. It is difficult to deny that a law that prohibits religiously motivated conduct, even if the law is generally applicable, does not at least implicate First Amendment concerns.

The Court responds that generally applicable laws are "one large step" removed from laws aimed at specific religious practices. The First Amendment, however, does not distinguish between laws that are generally applicable and laws that target particular religious practices. Indeed, few States would be so naive as to enact a law directly prohibiting or burdening a religious practice as such. Our free exercise cases have all concerned generally applicable laws that had the effect of significantly burdening a religious practice. If the First Amendment is to have any vitality, it ought not be construed to cover only the extreme and hypothetical situation in which a State directly targets a religious practice. . . .

To say that a person's right to free exercise has been burdened, of course, does not mean that he has an absolute right to engage in the conduct. Under our established First Amendment jurisprudence, we have recognized that the freedom to act, unlike the freedom to believe, cannot be absolute. . . . Instead, we have respected both the First Amendment's express textual mandate and the governmental interest in regulation of conduct by requiring the Government to justify any substantial burden on religiously motivated conduct by a compelling state interest and by means narrowly tailored to achieve that interest. . . .

. . .

The Court endeavors to escape from our decision . . . in *Yoder* by labeling [it a] "hybrid" decision . . . but there is no denying that [*Yoder*] expressly relied on the Free Exercise Clause. . . . [W]e have never distinguished between cases in which a State conditions receipt of a benefit on conduct prohibited by religious beliefs and cases in which a State affirmatively prohibits such conduct. The *Sherbert* compelling interest test applies in both kinds of cases. . . .

. . .

. . . [T]he Court today suggests that the disfavoring of minority religions is an "unavoidable consequence" under our system of government, and that accommodation of such religions must be left to the political process. . . . In my view, however, the First Amendment was enacted precisely to protect the rights of those whose religious practices are not shared by the majority and may be viewed with hostility. The history of our free exercise doctrine amply demonstrates the harsh impact majoritarian rule has had on unpopular or emerging religious groups such as the Jehovah's Witnesses and the Amish. . . .

The Court's holding today not only misreads settled First Amendment precedent; it appears to be unnecessary to this case. I would reach the same result applying our established free exercise jurisprudence.

There is no dispute that Oregon's criminal prohibition of peyote places a severe burden on the ability of respondents to freely exercise their religion. Peyote is a sacrament of the Native American Church, and is regarded as vital to respondents' ability to practice their religion. . . .

There is also no dispute that Oregon has a significant interest in enforcing laws that control the possession and use of controlled substances by its citizens. . . . As we recently noted, drug abuse is "one of the greatest problems affecting the health and welfare of our population" and thus "one of the most serious problems confronting our society today." . . . In light of our recent decisions holding that the governmental interests in the collection of income tax, . . . a comprehensive social security system, . . . and military conscription, . . . are compelling, respondents do not seriously dispute that Oregon has a compelling interest in prohibiting the possession of peyote by its citizens.

. . . Although the question is close, I would conclude that uniform application of Oregon's criminal prohibition is "essential to accomplish" . . . its overriding interest in preventing the physical harm caused by the use of a Schedule I controlled substance. Oregon's criminal prohibition represents that State's judgment that the possession and use of controlled substances, even by only one person, is inherently harmful and dangerous. Because the health effects caused by the use of controlled substances exist regardless of the motivation of the user, the use of such substances, even for religious purposes, violates the very purpose of the laws that prohibit them. . . . Moreover, in view of the societal interest in preventing trafficking in controlled substances, uniform application of the criminal prohibition at issue is essential to the effectiveness of Oregon's stated interest in preventing any possession of peyote. . . .

. . .

JUSTICE BLACKMUN, with whom JUSTICE BRENNAN and JUSTICE MARSHALL join, dissenting.

. . .

In weighing respondents' clear interest in the free exercise of their religion against Oregon's asserted interest in enforcing its drug laws, it is important to articulate in precise terms the state interest involved. It is not the State's broad interest in fighting the critical "war on drugs" that must be weighed against respondents' claim, but the State's narrow interest in refusing to make an exception for the religious, ceremonial use of peyote. . . .

The State's interest in enforcing its prohibition, in order to be sufficiently compelling to outweigh a free exercise claim, cannot be merely abstract or symbolic. The State cannot plausibly assert that unbending application of a criminal prohibition is essential to fulfill any compelling interest if it does not, in fact, attempt to enforce that prohibition. In this case, the State actually has not evinced any concrete interest in enforcing its drug laws against religious users of peyote. Oregon has never sought to prosecute respondents, and does not claim that it has made significant enforcement efforts against other religious users of peyote. The State's asserted interest thus amounts only to the symbolic preservation of an unenforced prohibition. . . .

. . .

The State also seeks to support its refusal to make an exception for religious use of peyote by invoking its interest in abolishing drug trafficking. There is, however, practically no illegal traffic in peyote. . . . Peyote simply is not a popular drug; its distribution for use in religious rituals has nothing to do with the vast and violent traffic in illegal narcotics that plagues this country. . . .

House Committee on the Judiciary, Report on the Religious Freedom Restoration Act (1993)[20]

The Religious Freedom Restoration Act (RFRA) was passed by a bipartisan coalition outraged by the Supreme Court's decision in Employment Division v. Smith *(1990). Great Society liberals historically favored granting exemptions to religious believers. Many conservatives touted the virtues of exemptions as evangelical Christians faced challenges to the practice of their faith in more liberal communities. Such traditional rivals as the ACLU and the Christian Legal Society joined forces in lobbying Congress to reverse* Smith. *Congress needed little prodding. The RFRA passed the House by a unanimous vote and the Senate with only three dissenting votes.*

Compare the House report on the RFRA to the dissents in Smith. *Did the legislative sponsors of the RFRA enshrine Justice O'Connor's opinion? Why did national legislators believe that they were authorized to overturn a Supreme Court decision? Does the near-unanimous vote suggest that Justice Scalia was right to think that religious minorities do not need special judicial protection? While attempting to overturn a Supreme Court decision, Congress also provided federal courts with a powerful tool to strike down state laws. To what extent does the RFRA empower or disempower justices? Four years later, the Supreme Court declared the RFRA unconstitutional in* Boerne v. Flores *(1997).*

H.R. 1308, the Religious Freedom Restoration Act of 1993, responds to the Supreme Court's decision in *Employment Division, Department of Human Resources of Oregon v. Smith* (1990) by creating a statutory right requiring that the compelling governmental interest test be applied in cases in which the free exercise of religion has been burdened by a law of general applicability.

. . .

The Free Exercise Clause of the First Amendment states in relevant part that "Congress shall make no law . . . prohibiting the free exercise (of religion)." However, the clarity of the Constitution has not prevented government from burdening religiously inspired action. Though laws directly targeting religious practices have become increasingly rare, facially neutral laws of general applicability have nefariously burdened the free exercise of religion in the United States throughout American history. Such laws, often upheld by the courts, undermined the exercise of religion by various groups.

. . .

The effect of the *Smith* decision has been to subject religious practices forbidden by laws of general applicability to the lowest level of scrutiny employed by the courts. Because the "rational relationship test" only requires that a law must be rationally related to a legitimate state interest, the *Smith* decision has created a climate in which the free exercise of religion is continually in jeopardy; facially neutral and generally applicable laws have and will, unless the Religious Freedom Restoration Act is passed, continue to burden religion. After *Smith*, claimants will be forced to convince courts that an inappropriate legislative motive created statutes and regulations. However, legislative motive often cannot be determined and courts have been reluctant to impute bad motives to legislators.

It is not feasible to combat the burdens of generally applicable laws on religion by relying upon the political process for the enactment of separate religious exemptions in every Federal, State, and local statute. As the Supreme Court itself said:

> The very purpose of a Bill of Rights was to withdraw certain subjects from the vicissitudes of political controversy, to place them beyond the reach of majorities and officials and to establish them as legal principles to be applied by the courts. One's right to life, liberty, and property, to free speech, a free press, freedom of worship and assembly, and other fundamental rights may not be submitted to vote; they depend on the outcome of no elections.

The Committee believes that the compelling governmental interest test must be restored. As Justice O'Connor stated in *Smith*, "[t]he compelling interest test reflects the First Amendment's mandate of preserving religious liberty to the fullest extent possible in a pluralistic society. For the Court to deem this command a luxury, is to denigrate the very purpose of a Bill of Rights."

. . .

. . . [T]he Committee believes that Congress has the constitutional authority to enact H.R. 1308. Pursuant to Section 5 of the Fourteenth Amendment and the Necessary and Proper Clause embodied in Article I,

20. Excerpt taken from House Committee on the Judiciary, *Religious Freedom Restoration Act of 1993*, 103rd Cong., 1st Sess., 1993, H. Rep. 103–88.

Section 8 of the Constitution, the legislative branch has been given the authority to provide statutory protection for a constitutional value when the Supreme Court has been unwilling to assert its authority. The Supreme Court has repeatedly upheld such congressional action after declining to find a constitutional protection itself. However, limits to congressional authority do exist. Congress may not (1) create a statutory right prohibited by some other provision of the Constitution, (2) remove rights granted by the Constitution, or (3) create a right inconsistent with an objective of a constitutional provision. Because H.R. 1308 is well within these limits, the Committee believes that in passing the Religious Freedom Restoration Act, Congress appropriately creates a statutory right within the perimeter of its power.

Additional Views of Hon. Henry J. Hyde, Hon. F. James Sensenbrenner, Hon. Bill McCollum, Hon. Howard Coble, Hon. Charles T. Canady, Hon. Bob Inglis, Hon. Robert W. Goodlatte

. . .

When this legislation was considered by the Subcommittee on Civil and Constitutional Rights and the full Judiciary Committee in the 102nd Congress, Congressman Henry J. Hyde (Ill.) offered several amendments. These amendments were designed to alleviate concerns that had been raised with respect to (1) abortion-related claims, (2) third-party challenges to government-funded social service programs run by religious institutions and (3) third-party challenges to the tax-exempt status of religious institutions. Since that time, each of these concerns has been resolved either through explicit statutory language or has been addressed in the Committee report.

In justification of the need for this legislation, proponents have provided the Committee with long lists of cases in which free exercise claims have failed since *Smith* was decided. Unfortunately, however, even prior to *Smith*, it is well known that the "compelling state interest" test had proven an unsatisfactory means of providing protection for individuals trying to exercise their religion in the face of government regulations. Restoration of the pre-*Smith* standard, although politically practical, will likely prove, over time, to be an insufficient remedy. It would have been preferable, given the unique opportunity presented by this legislation, to find a solution that would give solid protection to religious claimants against unnecessary government intrusion.

An attempt was made to cure these deficiencies through an amendment offered in the Subcommittee markup in the 102nd Congress. The amendment would have focused the attention of courts on those interests which are truly "compelling." The amendment defined the term "compelling state interest" as, "an interest in the nondiscriminatory enforcement of generally applicable and otherwise valid civil or criminal law directed to: (a) the protection of an individual from death or serious bodily harm, (b) the protection of the public health from identifiable risks of infection or other public health hazards, (c) the protection of private or public property, (d) the protection of individuals from abuse or neglect, or discrimination on the basis of race or national origin, or (e) the protection of national security, including the maintenance of discipline in the Armed Forces of the United States."

. . . The amendment was not adopted by the Subcommittee.

In reality, the Act will not guarantee that religious claimants bringing free exercise challenges will win, but only that they have a chance to fight. It will perpetuate, by statute, both the benefits and frustrations faced by religious claimants prior to the Supreme Court's decision in *Smith*. Although we have this remaining concern, we support enactment of the legislation.

C. Guns

Guns were a late-developing but important battleground for the culture wars that wracked American politics in the second half of the century.[21] For most of the twentieth century the NRA played little role in constitutional politics. During the late 1970s a new generation of NRA leaders began aggressively challenging gun control legislation as inconsistent with the Second Amendment. Ronald Reagan and his political allies supported this new movement for the right to bear arms. Prominent scholars provided substantial support for the individual rights interpretation of the Second Amendment. In a particularly influential article entitled "The Embarrassing Second Amendment," Professor Sanford Levinson questioned how liberals such as himself could interpret most provisions of the

21. For a good account of these constitutional politics, see Reva Siegel, "Dead or Alive: Originalism as Popular Constitutionalism in *Heller*," *Harvard Law Review* 122 (2008): 191–245.

Bill of Rights broadly while adopting the most cribbed interpretation of constitutional gun rights possible. He chided "most members of the legal academy [for] treat[ing] the Second Amendment as the equivalent of an embarrassing relative, whose mention brings a quick change of subject to other, more respectable family members."[22]

The imbroglio over the Clinton administration's attempt to ban assault weapons highlighted the new ferocity of constitutional debates over gun rights.

Few were prepared for the vigorous attack of the NRA and other proponents of gun rights on Clinton's effort to prohibit semi-automatic weapons. The Federal Assault Weapons Ban became law, but many of its proponents were defeated in the 1994 national elections.

D. Personal Freedom and Public Morality

Reagan conservatives made reversing *Roe v. Wade* (1973) their highest public priority. Republican Party platforms in 1980, 1984, 1988, and 1992 adopted strong pro-life positions. President Reagan repeatedly made speeches condemning abortion. Members of the Justice Department strategized on the best means for obtaining a judicial decision that would overrule *Roe.* Solicitor generals in the Reagan and Bush administrations wrote Supreme Court briefs urging the justices to rethink constitutional protections for abortion. All federal judicial nominees were scrutinized to ensure that they supported the administration position on reproductive choice. The five justices appointed from 1980 to 1992—Sandra Day O'Connor, Antonin Scalia, Anthony Kennedy, David Souter, and Clarence Thomas—wereless supportive of abortion rights than the justices they replaced.

Administration efforts to overrule *Roe v. Wade* made steady progress. Justice O'Connor, who joined the Court in 1981, voted to sustain every abortion regulation brought before the Court during the 1980s. Justices Scalia and Kennedy, who joined the Court in the mid-1980s, voted similarly. By 1989 the judicial majority seemed poised to abandon judicial protection for reproductive choice. Chief Justice William Rehnquist's majority opinion in *Webster v. Reproductive Health Services* (1989) found no constitutional problem with a Missouri law that declared "the life of each human being begins at conception" and banned any public funds from being used to support abortion. He asserted, "The key elements of the *Roe* framework—trimesters and viability—are not found in the text of the Constitution or in any place else one would expect to find a constitutional principle. Since the bounds of the inquiry are essentially indeterminate, the result has been a web of legal rules that have become increasingly intricate, resembling a code of regulations rather than a body of constitutional doctrine." Rehnquist concluded that reproductive choice was better described as "a liberty interest protected by the Due Process Clause" than as a "fundamental right." Liberals on and off the Court despaired. Justice Blackmun's dissent moaned, "Not with a bang, but a whimper, the plurality discards a landmark case of the last generation, and casts into darkness the hopes and visions of every woman in this country who had come to believe that the Constitution guaranteed her the right to exercise some control over her unique ability to bear children."

The Supreme Court by 1990 seemed prepared to abandon or at least sharply curtail all judicial activism on behalf of substantive rights under the due process clause. Conservative majorities maintained that the due process clause of the Fourteenth Amendment did not protect gays and lesbians. Justice White's opinion in *Bowers v. Hardwick* (1986) asserted that history clearly foreclosed a "fundamental right . . . to engage in acts of consensual sodomy." *Cruzan v. Director, Missouri Dept. of Health* (1990) sustained a Missouri judicial decision requiring clear and convincing evidence that a person in a vegetative state would not wish to be administered life-sustaining treating. Chief Justice Rehnquist emphasized the state "interest in the protection and preservation of human life" as justifying the Missouri decision to "place an increased risk of an erroneous decision on those seeking to terminate an incompetent individual's life-sustaining treatment." Conservatives on the court announced a method for interpreting the due process clause that cabined judicial activism. In *Michael H. v. Gerald D.* (1989) Justice Scalia declared, "We refer to the most specific level at which a relevant tradition protecting, or denying protection to, the asserted right can be identified." Scalia's opinion for the Court concluded that an adulterous father had no rights with respect to children conceived and born when the mother was

---

22. Sanford Levinson, "The Embarrassing Second Amendment," *Yale Law Journal* 99 (1989): 658.

married to another man. Justice Brennan's dissent in *Michael H.* sharply disputed Justice Scalia's approach to interpreting the due process clause. He wrote,

> In construing the Fourteenth Amendment to offer shelter only to those interests specifically protected by historical practice, moreover, the plurality ignores the kind of society in which our Constitution exists. We are not an assimilative, homogeneous society, but a facilitative, pluralistic one, in which we must be willing to abide someone else's unfamiliar or even repellent practice because the same tolerant impulse protects our own idiosyncrasies.

Closer inspection suggested that liberals were holding their own in the culture wars, even as they were losing particular skirmishes. Justice O'Connor gave conservatives particular concern. During her first years on the Court, although she consistently voted to sustain regulations on abortion, her opinions provided far narrower grounds for rejecting pro-choice arguments than did those penned by Chief Justice Rehnquist or Justice Scalia. Her separate opinion in *Webster* pointedly refused to overrule *Roe*. In other cases Justice O'Connor expressed some support for using the due process clause to protect substantive freedoms. In *Turner v. Safley* (1987) O'Connor spoke for a unanimous Court when ruling that inmates had a constitutional right to marry. Her concurring opinion in *Cruzan* interpreted the due process clause as granting persons the right to refuse life-sustaining treatment under certain conditions. O'Connor's one-paragraph concurrence in *Michael H.* declared that Scalia's "mode of historical analysis" was "somewhat inconsistent with our past decisions" and that she "would not foreclose the unanticipated by the prior imposition of a single mode of historical analysis."

Conservative fears were realized when the Supreme Court decided *Planned Parenthood of Southeastern Pennsylvania v. Casey* (1992). Justices O'Connor, Kennedy, and Souter formed a three-judge plurality that, while narrowing the scope of *Roe*, reaffirmed its basic principle. Justice Blackmun celebrated the plurality decision to keep abortion legal even as he disputed the decision to sustain various laws regulating abortion. Justice Scalia was apoplectic. When the Democrats returned to the White House after the 1992 national election and President Clinton appointed two new members of the Supreme Court, the conservative goal of overturning *Roe* seemed more distant than ever.

Planned Parenthood of Southeastern Pennsylvania v. Casey, 505 U.S. 833 (1992)

Planned Parenthood of Southeastern Pennsylvania, other abortion clinics, and a physician sought an injunction prohibiting Governor Robert Casey from enforcing the Pennsylvania Abortion Control Act of 1982. That measure required that a woman seeking an abortion (1) give informed consent prior to the procedure after being provided certain information about abortion and alternatives to abortion; (2) wait at least twenty-four hours after receiving that information before having the abortion; (3) obtain informed consent from one parent if the woman seeking the abortion was a minor (although the statute provided for a judicial bypass); and (4) if married, sign a statement indicating that she had notified her husband of her decision to obtain an abortion. The district court granted the plaintiffs' request, holding that the provisions violated their constitutional rights. The Court of Appeals for the Third Circuit struck down the spousal notification provision but reversed the district court's rulings as to the rest of the provisions. All parties appealed to the Supreme Court

The Supreme Court by a 7–2 vote sustained every provision in the Pennsylvania Abortion Control Act except the spousal notification requirement. Justices O'Connor, Kennedy, and Souter issued a crucial plurality opinion that abandoned the trimester system adopted in Roe v. Wade *(1973) but reaffirmed* Roe's *holding that the due process clause protected the right to terminate a pregnancy. Henceforth, the plurality declared, all restrictions on abortion would have to satisfy an "undue burden" standard, not a compelling interest test. The plurality opinion in* Casey *has been hailed as an example of judicial statesmanship and condemned for judicial arrogance. Which characterization do you think is best? To what extent did Justices O'Connor, Kennedy, and Souter maintain* Roe *because they believed the case correctly decided, and to what extent do you believe that their opinion rested on the judicial duty to act in a manner consistent with precedent? Does the plurality opinion give too much deference to precedent by following* Roe *or too little by abandoning the trimester system detailed in* Roe*? Are the concurrences and dissenting opinions correct when they insist that strict scrutiny and the trimester system are central to the abortion right protected in* Roe*? The plurality emphasized fundamental differences between the judicial decision to overrule* Lochner v. New York *(1905) and the judicial decision to overrule* Plessy v. Ferguson *(1896). What are* *those differences? Do you agree with the plurality? Justice Scalia's dissent ridiculed many assertions made by the plurality. Do you find his ridicule merited or inappropriate? Can justices settle controversies in the manner suggested by the plurality opinion? Did* Casey *settle the constitutional controversy over abortion?*

Kathryn Kolbert, the lawyer for Planned Parenthood, vigorously challenged any effort to find a middle position that would weaken, but not overrule, constitutional protections for abortion. She refused to suggest any standard other than strict scrutiny for evaluating the Pennsylvania statute. "To abandon strict scrutiny for a less protective standard," Kolbert bluntly declared, "would be the same as overruling Roe.*"*[23] *What strategy would you have adopted had you been asked to defend your preferred position before the Supreme Court? If you are strongly pro-life or pro-choice, would you defend that position to the hilt, or would you offer the Court a middle ground somewhat more favorable to your preferred position than the status quo when* Casey *was being litigated?*

JUSTICE O'CONNOR, JUSTICE KENNEDY, and JUSTICE SOUTER announced the judgment of the Court.

Liberty finds no refuge in a jurisprudence of doubt. Yet 19 years after our holding that the Constitution protects a woman's right to terminate her pregnancy in its early stages, *Roe v. Wade* (1973), . . . that definition of liberty is still questioned. . . .

. . .

After considering the fundamental constitutional questions resolved by *Roe*, principles of institutional integrity, and the rule of *stare decisis*, we are led to conclude this: the essential holding of *Roe v. Wade* should be retained and once again reaffirmed.

. . .

Constitutional protection of the woman's decision to terminate her pregnancy derives from the Due Process Clause of the Fourteenth Amendment. It declares that no State shall "deprive any person of life, liberty, or property, without due process of law." The controlling word in the cases before us is "liberty." Although a literal reading of the Clause might suggest that it governs only the procedures by which a State may deprive persons of liberty, for at least 105 years, since *Mugler v. Kansas* (1887), the Clause has been understood to contain a substantive component as well, one "barring certain government actions regardless of the fairness of the procedures used to implement them."

. . .

Our law affords constitutional protection to personal decisions relating to marriage, procreation, contraception, family relationships, child rearing, and education. . . . Our cases recognize "the right of the *individual*, married or single, to be free from unwarranted governmental intrusion into matters so fundamentally affecting a person as the decision whether to bear or beget a child." *Eisenstadt v. Baird* (1972). . . . Our precedents "have respected the private realm of family life which the state cannot enter.". . . These matters, involving the most intimate and personal choices a person may make in a lifetime, choices central to personal dignity and autonomy, are central to the liberty protected by the Fourteenth Amendment. At the heart of liberty is the right to define one's own concept of existence, of meaning, of the universe, and of the mystery of human life. Beliefs about these matters could not define the attributes of personhood were they formed under compulsion of the State.

. . . Though abortion is conduct, it does not follow that the State is entitled to proscribe it in all instances. That is because the liberty of the woman is at stake in a sense unique to the human condition and so unique to the law. The mother who carries a child to full term is subject to anxieties, to physical constraints, to pain that only she must bear. That these sacrifices have from the beginning of the human race been endured by woman with a pride that ennobles her in the eyes of others and gives to the infant a bond of love cannot alone be grounds for the State to insist she make the sacrifice. Her suffering is too intimate and personal for the State to insist, without more, upon its own vision of the woman's role, however dominant that vision has been in the course of our history and our culture. The destiny of the woman must be shaped to a large extent on her own conception of her spiritual imperatives and her place in society.

. . .

. . . [W]hen this Court reexamines a prior holding, its judgment is customarily informed by a series of prudential and pragmatic considerations designed to test the consistency of overruling a prior decision with the ideal of the rule of law, and to gauge the respective costs of reaffirming and overruling a prior case.

23. Linda Greenhouse, "Abortion and the Law: Court Gets Stark Argument on Abortion," *New York Times*, April 23, 1992, A1, A17.

Thus, for example, we may ask whether the rule has proven to be intolerable simply in defying practical workability . . . ; whether the rule is subject to a kind of reliance that would lend a special hardship to the consequences of overruling and add inequity to the cost of repudiation . . . ; whether related principles of law have so far developed as to have left the old rule no more than a remnant of abandoned doctrine . . . ; or whether facts have so changed, or come to be seen so differently, as to have robbed the old rule of significant application or justification. . . .

Although *Roe* has engendered opposition, it has in no sense proven "unworkable," . . . representing as it does a simple limitation beyond which a state law is unenforceable. . . .

. . .

. . . [F]or two decades of economic and social developments, people have organized intimate relationships and made choices that define their views of themselves and their places in society, in reliance on the availability of abortion in the event that contraception should fail. The ability of women to participate equally in the economic and social life of the Nation has been facilitated by their ability to control their reproductive lives. . . . The Constitution serves human values, and while the effect of reliance on *Roe* cannot be exactly measured, neither can the certain cost of overruling *Roe* for people who have ordered their thinking and living around that case be dismissed.

No evolution of legal principle has left *Roe*'s doctrinal footings weaker than they were in 1973. No development of constitutional law since the case was decided has implicitly or explicitly left *Roe* behind as a mere survivor of obsolete constitutional thinking.

. . .

In a less significant case, *stare decisis* analysis could, and would, stop at the point we have reached. But the sustained and widespread debate *Roe* has provoked calls for some comparison between that case and others of comparable dimension that have responded to national controversies and taken on the impress of the controversies addressed. . . .

The first example is that line of cases identified with *Lochner v. New York* (1905), which imposed substantive limitations on legislation limiting economic autonomy in favor of health and welfare regulation, adopting, in Justice Holmes's view, the theory of laissez-faire. . . . *West Coast Hotel Co. v. Parrish* (1937), signaled the demise of *Lochner*. . . . In the meantime, the Depression had come and, with it, the lesson that seemed unmistakable to most people by 1937, that the interpretation of contractual freedom protected in [*Lochner* and related cases] rested on fundamentally false factual assumptions about the capacity of a relatively unregulated market to satisfy minimal levels of human welfare. . . .

The second comparison that 20th century history invites is with the cases employing the separate-but-equal rule for applying the Fourteenth Amendment's equal protection guarantee. They began with *Plessy v. Ferguson* (1896). . . .

The Court in *Brown v. Board of Education* (1954) . . . observ[ed] that whatever may have been the understanding in *Plessy*'s time of the power of segregation to stigmatize those who were segregated with a "badge of inferiority," it was clear by 1954 that legally sanctioned segregation had just such an effect, to the point that racially separate public educational facilities were deemed inherently unequal. . . . Society's understanding of the facts upon which a constitutional ruling was sought in 1954 was thus fundamentally different from the basis claimed for the decision in 1896. . . .

. . .

. . . Because neither the factual underpinnings of *Roe*'s central holding nor our understanding of it has changed (and because no other indication of weakened precedent has been shown), the Court could not pretend to be reexamining the prior law with any justification beyond a present doctrinal disposition to come out differently from the Court of 1973. To overrule prior law for no other reason than that would run counter to the view repeated in our cases, that a decision to overrule should rest on some special reason over and above the belief that a prior case was wrongly decided. . . .

. . .

. . . [T]he Court's legitimacy depends on making legally principled decisions under circumstances in which their principled character is sufficiently plausible to be accepted by the Nation.

. . .

Where, in the performance of its judicial duties, the Court decides a case in such a way as to resolve the sort of intensely divisive controversy reflected in *Roe* and those rare, comparable cases, its decision has a dimension that the resolution of the normal case does not carry. It is the dimension present whenever the Court's interpretation of the Constitution calls the contending sides of a national controversy to end their national division by accepting a common mandate rooted in the Constitution.

The Court is not asked to do this very often, having thus addressed the Nation only twice in our lifetime, in the decisions of *Brown* and *Roe*. But when the Court does act in this way, its decision requires an equally rare precedential force to counter the inevitable efforts to overturn it and to thwart its implementation. . . . But whatever the premises of opposition may be, only the most convincing justification under accepted standards of precedent could suffice to demonstrate that a later decision overruling the first was anything but a surrender to political pressure, and an unjustified repudiation of the principle on which the Court staked its authority in the first instance. So to overrule under fire in the absence of the most compelling reason to reexamine a watershed decision would subvert the Court's legitimacy beyond any serious question. . . .

. . .

. . . A decision to overrule *Roe's* essential holding under the existing circumstances would address error, if error there was, at the cost of both profound and unnecessary damage to the Court's legitimacy, and to the Nation's commitment to the rule of law. It is therefore imperative to adhere to the essence of *Roe's* original decision, and we do so today.

. . . [T]he basic decision in *Roe* was based on a constitutional analysis which we cannot now repudiate. The woman's liberty is not so unlimited, however, that from the outset the State cannot show its concern for the life of the unborn, and at a later point in fetal development the State's interest in life has sufficient force so that the right of the woman to terminate the pregnancy can be restricted.

. . .

We conclude the line should be drawn at viability, so that before that time the woman has a right to choose to terminate her pregnancy. We adhere to this principle for two reasons. First, as we have said, is the doctrine of *stare decisis*. . . .

The second reason is that the concept of viability, as we noted in *Roe*, is the time at which there is a realistic possibility of maintaining and nourishing a life outside the womb, so that the independent existence of the second life can in reason and all fairness be the object of state protection that now overrides the rights of the woman. . . .

. . .

We reject the trimester framework, which we do not consider to be part of the essential holding of *Roe*. . . . Measures aimed at ensuring that a woman's choice contemplates the consequences for the fetus do not necessarily interfere with the right recognized in *Roe*, although those measures have been found to be inconsistent with the rigid trimester framework announced in that case. A logical reading of the central holding in *Roe* itself, and a necessary reconciliation of the liberty of the woman and the interest of the State in promoting prenatal life, require, in our view, that we abandon the trimester framework as a rigid prohibition on all previability regulation aimed at the protection of fetal life. The trimester framework suffers from these basic flaws: in its formulation it misconceives the nature of the pregnant woman's interest; and in practice it undervalues the State's interest in potential life, as recognized in *Roe*.

. . .

. . . Only where state regulation imposes an undue burden on a woman's ability to make this decision does the power of the State reach into the heart of the liberty protected by the Due Process Clause.

. . .

A finding of an undue burden is a shorthand for the conclusion that a state regulation has the purpose or effect of placing a substantial obstacle in the path of a woman seeking an abortion of a nonviable fetus. A statute with this purpose is invalid because the means chosen by the State to further the interest in potential life must be calculated to inform the woman's free choice, not hinder it. And a statute which, while furthering the interest in potential life or some other valid state interest, has the effect of placing a substantial obstacle in the path of a woman's choice cannot be considered a permissible means of serving its legitimate ends. . . .

. . .

[*Informed Consent*.] To the extent [past precedents] find a constitutional violation when the government requires, as it does here, the giving of truthful, nonmisleading information about the nature of the procedure, the attendant health risks and those of childbirth, and the "probable gestational age" of the fetus, those cases go too far, are inconsistent with *Roe's* acknowledgment of an important interest in potential life, and are overruled. . . .

. . .

[*Twenty-Four-Hour Waiting Law.*] . . . The idea that important decisions will be more informed and deliberate if they follow some period of reflection does not strike us as unreasonable, particularly where the statute directs that important information become part of the background of the decision. . . .

. . .

[*Spousal Notification.*] In well-functioning marriages, spouses discuss important intimate decisions such as whether to bear a child. But there are millions of women in this country who are the victims of regular physical and psychological abuse at the hands of their husbands. Should these women become pregnant, they may have very good reasons for not wishing to inform their husbands of their decision to obtain an abortion. . . .

The spousal notification requirement is thus likely to prevent a significant number of women from obtaining an abortion. It does not merely make abortions a little more difficult or expensive to obtain; for many women, it will impose a substantial obstacle. We must not blind ourselves to the fact that the significant number of women who fear for their safety and the safety of their children are likely to be deterred from procuring an abortion as surely as if the Commonwealth had outlawed abortion in all cases.

. . .

[*Parental Consent.*] Our cases establish, and we reaffirm today, that a State may require a minor seeking an abortion to obtain the consent of a parent or guardian, provided that there is an adequate judicial bypass procedure. . . .

. . .

Our Constitution is a covenant running from the first generation of Americans to us and then to future generations. It is a coherent succession. Each generation must learn anew that the Constitution's written terms embody ideas and aspirations that must survive more ages than one. We accept our responsibility not to retreat from interpreting the full meaning of the covenant in light of all of our precedents. We invoke it once again to define the freedom guaranteed by the Constitution's own promise, the promise of liberty.

JUSTICE STEVENS, concurring in part and dissenting in part.

. . .

. . . A state-imposed burden on the exercise of a constitutional right is measured both by its effects and by its character: A burden may be "undue" either because the burden is too severe or because it lacks a legitimate, rational justification.

The 24-hour delay requirement fails both parts of this test. The findings of the District Court establish the severity of the burden that the 24-hour delay imposes on many pregnant women. Yet even in those cases in which the delay is not especially onerous, it is, in my opinion, "undue" because there is no evidence that such a delay serves a useful and legitimate purpose. . . .

The counseling provisions are similarly infirm. Whenever government commands private citizens to speak or to listen, careful review of the justification for that command is particularly appropriate. . . . The statute requires that this information be given to *all* women seeking abortions, including those for whom such information is clearly useless, such as those who are married, those who have undergone the procedure in the past and are fully aware of the options, and those who are fully convinced that abortion is their only reasonable option. Moreover, the statute requires physicians to inform all of their patients of "[t]he probable gestational age of the unborn child." . . . This information is of little decisional value in most cases, because 90% of all abortions are performed during the first trimester when fetal age has less relevance than when the fetus nears viability. Nor can the information required by the statute be justified as relevant to any "philosophic" or "social" argument, . . . either favoring or disfavoring the abortion decision in a particular case. In light of all of these facts, I conclude that the information requirements . . . do not serve a useful purpose and thus constitute an unnecessary—and therefore undue—burden on the woman's constitutional liberty to decide to terminate her pregnancy.

JUSTICE BLACKMUN, concurring in part, concurring in the judgment in part, and dissenting in part.

. . .

State restrictions on abortion violate a woman's right of privacy in two ways. First, compelled continuation of a pregnancy infringes upon a woman's right to bodily integrity by imposing substantial physical intrusions and significant risks of physical harm. . . .

Further, when the State restricts a woman's right to terminate her pregnancy, it deprives a woman of the right to make her own decision about reproduction and family planning—critical life choices that this Court long has deemed central to the right to privacy. . . . Because motherhood has a dramatic impact on a woman's educational prospects, employment opportunities, and self-determination, restrictive abortion laws deprive her of basic control over her life. . . .

A State's restrictions on a woman's right to terminate her pregnancy also implicate constitutional guarantees of gender equality. State restrictions on abortion compel women to continue pregnancies they otherwise might terminate. By restricting the right to terminate pregnancies, the State conscripts women's bodies into its service, forcing women to continue their pregnancies, suffer the pains of childbirth, and in most instances, provide years of maternal care. The State does not compensate women for their services; instead, it assumes that they owe this duty as a matter of course. This assumption—that women can simply be forced to accept the "natural" status and incidents of motherhood—appears to rest upon a conception of women's role that has triggered the protection of the Equal Protection Clause. . . .

. . .

Roe's requirement of strict scrutiny as implemented through a trimester framework should not be disturbed. No other approach has gained a majority, and no other is more protective of the woman's fundamental right. Lastly, no other approach properly accommodates the woman's constitutional right with the State's legitimate interests.

Application of the strict scrutiny standard results in the invalidation of all the challenged provisions. Indeed, as this Court has invalidated virtually identical provisions in prior cases, *stare decisis* requires that we again strike them down.

. . .

CHIEF JUSTICE REHNQUIST, with whom JUSTICE WHITE, JUSTICE SCALIA, and JUSTICE THOMAS join, concurring in the judgment in part and dissenting in part.

We believe that *Roe* was wrongly decided, and that it can and should be overruled consistently with our traditional approach to *stare decisis* in constitutional cases.

. . .

In *Roe v. Wade,* the Court recognized a "guarantee of personal privacy" which "is broad enough to encompass a woman's decision whether or not to terminate her pregnancy." . . . We are now of the view that, in terming this right fundamental, the Court in *Roe* read the earlier opinions upon which it based its decision much too broadly. Unlike marriage, procreation, and contraception, abortion "involves the purposeful termination of a potential life." . . . The abortion decision must therefore "be recognized as *sui generis*, different in kind from the others that the Court has protected under the rubric of personal or family privacy and autonomy."

Nor do the historical traditions of the American people support the view that the right to terminate one's pregnancy is "fundamental." The common law which we inherited from England made abortion after "quickening" an offense. At the time of the adoption of the Fourteenth Amendment, statutory prohibitions or restrictions on abortion were commonplace; in 1868, at least 28 of the then-37 States and 8 Territories had statutes banning or limiting abortion. . . . By the turn of the century virtually every State had a law prohibiting or restricting abortion on its books. By the middle of the present century, a liberalization trend had set in. But 21 of the restrictive abortion laws in effect in 1868 were still in effect in 1973 when *Roe* was decided, and an overwhelming majority of the States prohibited abortion unless necessary to preserve the life or health of the mother.

. . .

. . . [T]he opinion asserts that the Court could justifiably overrule its decision in *Lochner* only because the Depression had convinced "most people" that constitutional protection of contractual freedom contributed to an economy that failed to protect the welfare of all. . . . Surely the joint opinion does not mean to suggest that people saw this Court's failure to uphold minimum wage statutes as the cause of the Great Depression! In any event, the *Lochner* Court did not base its rule upon the policy judgment that an unregulated market was fundamental to a stable economy; it simply believed, erroneously, that "liberty" under the Due Process Clause protected the "right to make a contract." . . .

. . .

The joint opinion also agrees that the Court acted properly in rejecting the doctrine of "separate but equal" in *Brown*. . . . This is strange, in that under the opinion's "legitimacy" principle the Court would seemingly have been forced to adhere to its erroneous decision in *Plessy* because of its "intensely divisive" character. . . . Fortunately, the Court did not choose that option in *Brown*, and instead frankly repudiated *Plessy*. . . . The rule of *Brown* is not tied to popular opinion about the evils of segregation; it is a judgment that the Equal Protection Clause does not permit racial segregation, no matter whether the public might come to believe that it is beneficial. On that ground it stands, and on that ground alone the Court was justified in properly concluding that the *Plessy* Court had erred.

. . .

. . . The joint opinion asserts that, in order to protect its legitimacy, the Court must refrain from overruling a controversial decision lest it be viewed as favoring those who oppose the decision. But a decision to *adhere* to prior precedent is subject to the same criticism, for in such a case one can easily argue that the Court is responding to those who have demonstrated in favor of the original decision. . . .

The end result of the joint opinion's paeans of praise for legitimacy is the enunciation of a brand new standard for evaluating state regulation of a woman's right to abortion—the "undue burden" standard. . . . *Roe v. Wade* adopted a "fundamental right" standard under which state regulations could survive only if they met the requirement of "strict scrutiny." While we disagree with that standard, it at least had a recognized basis in constitutional law at the time *Roe* was decided. The same cannot be said for the "undue burden" standard, which is created largely out of whole cloth by the authors of the joint opinion. . . .

In evaluating abortion regulations under that standard, judges will have to decide whether they place a "substantial obstacle" in the path of a woman seeking an abortion. . . . In that this standard is based even more on a judge's subjective determinations than was the trimester framework. . . .

. . .

We have stated above our belief that the Constitution does not subject state abortion regulations to heightened scrutiny. . . . A woman's interest in having an abortion is a form of liberty protected by the Due Process Clause, but States may regulate abortion procedures in ways rationally related to a legitimate state interest.

. . .

[*Informed Consent.*] . . . [T]his required presentation of "balanced information" is rationally related to the State's legitimate interest in ensuring that the woman's consent is truly informed, . . . and in addition furthers the State's interest in preserving unborn life. . . .

[*Waiting Periods.*] . . . We are of the view that, in providing time for reflection and reconsideration, the waiting period helps ensure that a woman's decision to abort is a well-considered one, and reasonably furthers the State's legitimate interest in maternal health and in the unborn life of the fetus.

. . .

[*Parental Consent.*] We think it beyond dispute that a State "has a strong and legitimate interest in the welfare of its young citizens, whose immaturity, inexperience, and lack of judgment may sometimes impair their ability to exercise their rights wisely." A requirement of parental consent to abortion, like myriad other restrictions placed upon minors in other contexts, is reasonably designed to further this important and legitimate state interest. . . .

. . .

[*Spousal Notification.*] . . . In our view, the spousal notice requirement is a rational attempt by the State to improve truthful communication between spouses and encourage collaborative decisionmaking, and thereby fosters marital integrity. . . . The spousal notice provision will admittedly be unnecessary in some circumstances, and possibly harmful in others, but "the existence of particular cases in which a feature of a statute performs no function (or is even counterproductive) ordinarily does not render the statute unconstitutional or even constitutionally suspect." . . . The Pennsylvania Legislature was in a position to weigh the likely benefits of the provision against its likely adverse effects, and presumably concluded, on balance, that the provision would be beneficial. Whether this was a wise decision or not, we cannot say that it was irrational. . . .

. . .

JUSTICE SCALIA, with whom THE CHIEF JUSTICE, JUSTICE WHITE, and JUSTICE THOMAS join, concurring in the judgment in part and dissenting in part.

. . . The States may, if they wish, permit abortion on demand, but the Constitution does not *require* them to do so. The permissibility of abortion, and the limitations upon it, are to be resolved like most important questions in our democracy: by citizens trying to persuade one another and then voting. . . .

. . . I reach that conclusion not because of anything so exalted as my views concerning the "concept of existence, of meaning, of the universe, and of the mystery of human life." . . . Rather, I reach it for the same reason I reach the conclusion that bigamy is not constitutionally protected—because of two simple facts: (1) the Constitution says absolutely nothing about it, and (2) the longstanding traditions of American society have permitted it to be legally proscribed. . . .

. . .

. . . I must, however, respond to a few of the more outrageous arguments in today's opinion, which it is beyond human nature to leave unanswered. . . .

. . .

> *While we appreciate the weight of the arguments . . . that* Roe *should be overruled, the reservations any of us may have in reaffirming the central holding of* Roe *are outweighed by the explication of individual liberty we have given combined with the force of* stare decisis.

. . .

The Court's reliance upon *stare decisis* can best be described as contrived. It insists upon the necessity of adhering not to all of *Roe*, but only to what it calls the "central holding." It seems to me that *stare decisis* ought to be applied even to the doctrine of *stare decisis*, and I confess never to have heard of this new, keep-what-you-want-and-throw-away-the-rest version. . . .

. . . I must confess . . . that I have always thought . . . the arbitrary trimester framework, which the Court today discards, was quite as central to *Roe* as the arbitrary viability test, which the Court today retains. . . .

. . .

> *Where, in the performance of its judicial duties, the Court decides a case in such a way as to resolve the sort of intensely divisive controversy reflected in* Roe *. . . , its decision has a dimension that the resolution of the normal case does not carry. It is the dimension present whenever the Court's interpretation of the Constitution calls the contending sides of a national controversy to end their national division by accepting a common mandate rooted in the Constitution.*

The Court's description of the place of *Roe* in the social history of the United States is unrecognizable. Not only did *Roe* not, as the Court suggests, *resolve* the deeply divisive issue of abortion; it did more than anything else to nourish it, by elevating it to the national level where it is infinitely more difficult to resolve. National politics were not plagued by abortion protests, national abortion lobbying, or abortion marches on Congress before *Roe v. Wade* was decided. Profound disagreement existed among our citizens over the issue—as it does over other issues, such as the death penalty—but that disagreement was being worked out at the state level. . . .

. . .

> . . . *"[T]o overrule under fire . . . would subvert the Court's legitimacy. . . ."*

. . .

The Imperial Judiciary lives. . . .

. . .

. . . [T]he American people love democracy and the American people are not fools. As long as this Court thought (and the people thought) that we Justices were doing essentially lawyers' work up here—reading text and discerning our society's traditional understanding of that text—the public pretty much left us alone. Texts and traditions are facts to study, not convictions to demonstrate about. But if in reality our process of constitutional adjudication consists primarily of making *value judgments*; if we can ignore a long and clear tradition clarifying an ambiguous text, . . . if, as I say, our pronouncement of constitutional law rests primarily on value judgments, then a free and intelligent people's attitude towards us can be expected to be (*ought* to be) quite different. The people know that their value judgments are quite as good as those taught in any law school—maybe better. If, indeed, the "liberties" protected by the Constitution are, as the Court says, undefined and unbounded, then the people *should* demonstrate, to protest that we do not implement *their* values instead of *ours*. Not only that, but confirmation hearings for new Justices *should* deteriorate into question-and-answer sessions in which Senators go through a list of their constituents' most favored and most disfavored alleged constitutional rights, and seek the nominee's commitment to support or oppose them. Value judgments, after all, should be voted on, not dictated; and if our Constitution has somehow accidently committed them to the Supreme Court, at least we can have a sort of plebiscite each time a new nominee to that body is put forward.

. . .

We should get out of this area, where we have no right to be, and where we do neither ourselves nor the country any good by remaining.

Bowers v. Hardwick, 478 U.S. 186 (1986)

An Atlanta police officer on August 3, 1982, sought to arrest Michael Hardwick for failing to appear in court after Hardwick was given a summons for public drinking. The officer entered Hardwick's bedroom and observed him engaging in oral sex with another man. The officer arrested Hardwick for violating a Georgia law that declared, "A person commits the offense of sodomy when he performs or submits to any sexual act involving the sex organs of one person and the mouth or anus of another." Although the local district attorney elected not to press charges, Hardwick brought a lawsuit in federal court against Michael Bowers, the attorney general of Georgia, claiming that he was in imminent danger of being arrested under an unconstitutional statute. Bowers responded that no one had a constitutional right to practice sodomy. The district court dismissed Hardwick's complaint, but that decision was reversed by the Court of Appeals for the Eleventh Circuit. Bowers appealed to the Supreme Court.

The Supreme Court by a 5–4 vote declared that states could regulate homosexual sodomy. Justice White's majority opinion emphasized that states had historically regulated same-sex intimacy and that the right to sodomy bore no resemblance to the privacy rights the court had previously protected. Why did White reject the analogy between homosexuality and abortion? Why did Justice Blackmun disagree? Who has the better argument? Was the method of finding fundamental rights in Bowers *consistent with* Roe v. Wade? *If not, what explains the difference?*

In 1990, after his retirement, Justice Powell told students at New York University Law School, "I think I probably made a mistake in [Bowers]*."*[24]

JUSTICE WHITE delivered the opinion of the Court.

. . .

. . . [N]one of the rights announced in [previous substantive due process] cases bears any resemblance to the claimed constitutional right of homosexuals to engage in acts of sodomy that is asserted in this case. No connection between family, marriage, or procreation on the one hand and homosexual activity on the other has been demonstrated, either by the Court of Appeals or by respondent. Moreover, any claim that these cases nevertheless stand for the proposition that any kind of private sexual conduct between consenting adults is constitutionally insulated from state proscription is unsupportable. . . .

. . .

Striving to assure itself and the public that announcing rights not readily identifiable in the Constitution's text involves much more than the imposition of the Justices' own choice of values on the States and the Federal Government, the Court has sought to identify the nature of the rights qualifying for heightened judicial protection. In *Palko v. Connecticut (1937)*, it was said that this category includes those fundamental liberties that are "implicit in the concept of ordered liberty," such that "neither liberty nor justice would exist if [they] were sacrificed." A different description of fundamental liberties appeared in *Moore v. East Cleveland (1977)* where they are characterized as those liberties that are "deeply rooted in this Nation's history and tradition."

It is obvious to us that neither of these formulations would extend a fundamental right to homosexuals to engage in acts of consensual sodomy. Proscriptions against that conduct have ancient roots. . . . Sodomy was a criminal offense at common law and was forbidden by the laws of the original thirteen States when they ratified the Bill of Rights. In 1868, when the Fourteenth Amendment was ratified, all but 5 of the 37 States in the Union had criminal sodomy laws. In fact, until 1961, all 50 States outlawed sodomy, and today, 24 States and the District of Columbia continue to provide criminal penalties for sodomy performed in private and between consenting adults. Against this background, to claim that a right to engage in such conduct is "deeply rooted in this Nation's history and tradition" or "implicit in the concept of ordered liberty" is, at best, facetious.

Nor are we inclined to take a more expansive view of our authority to discover new fundamental rights imbedded in the Due Process Clause. The Court is most vulnerable and comes nearest to illegitimacy when it deals with judge-made constitutional law having little or no cognizable roots in the language or design of the Constitution. . . .

. . .

. . . [I]llegal conduct is not always immunized whenever it occurs in the home. Victimless crimes, such as the possession and use of illegal drugs, do not escape the law where they are committed at

24. John C. Jeffries Jr., *Justice Lewis F. Powell, Jr.* (New York: Charles Scribner's Sons, 1994), 528.

home. . . . And if respondent's submission is limited to the voluntary sexual conduct between consenting adults, it would be difficult, except by fiat, to limit the claimed right to homosexual conduct while leaving exposed to prosecution adultery, incest, and other sexual crimes even though they are committed in the home. We are unwilling to start down that road.

. . . The law is constantly based on notions of morality, and if all laws representing essentially moral choices are to be invalidated under the Due Process Clause, the courts will be very busy indeed. . . .

CHIEF JUSTICE BURGER, concurring.

. . .

. . . [T]the proscriptions against sodomy have very "ancient roots." Decisions of individuals relating to homosexual conduct have been subject to state intervention throughout the history of Western civilization. Condemnation of those practices is firmly rooted in Judeao-Christian moral and ethical standards. . . . Blackstone described "the infamous crime against nature" as an offense of "deeper malignity" than rape, a heinous act "the very mention of which is a disgrace to human nature," and "a crime not fit to be named." The common law of England, including its prohibition of sodomy, became the received law of Georgia and the other Colonies. In 1816 the Georgia Legislature passed the statute at issue here, and that statute has been continuously in force in one form or another since that time. To hold that the act of homosexual sodomy is somehow protected as a fundamental right would be to cast aside millennia of moral teaching.

. . .

JUSTICE POWELL, concurring.

. . . I agree with the Court that there is no fundamental right. . . . This is not to suggest, however, that respondent may not be protected by the Eighth Amendment of the Constitution. The Georgia statute at issue in this case, authorizes a court to imprison a person for up to 20 years for a single private, consensual act of sodomy. In my view, a prison sentence for such conduct—certainly a sentence of long duration—would create a serious Eighth Amendment issue. . . .

. . .

JUSTICE BLACKMUN, with whom JUSTICE BRENNAN, JUSTICE MARSHALL, and JUSTICE STEVENS join, dissenting.

This case is no more about "a fundamental right to engage in homosexual sodomy" than *Stanley v. Georgia* (1969) was about a fundamental right to watch obscene movies or *Katz v. United States* (1967) was about a fundamental right to place interstate bets from a telephone booth. Rather, this case is about "the most comprehensive of rights and the right most valued by civilized men," namely, "the right to be let alone."

. . . I believe we must analyze Hardwick's claim in the light of the values that underlie the constitutional right to privacy. If that right means anything, it means that, before Georgia can prosecute its citizens for making choices about the most intimate aspects of their lives, it must do more than assert that the choice they have made is an "'abominable crime not fit to be named among Christians.'"

. . .

"Our cases long have recognized that the Constitution embodies a promise that a certain private sphere of individual liberty will be kept largely beyond the reach of government." In construing the right to privacy, the Court has proceeded along two somewhat distinct, albeit complementary, lines. First, it has recognized a privacy interest with reference to certain decisions that are properly for the individual to make. . . . Second, it has recognized a privacy interest with reference to certain places without regard for the particular activities in which the individuals who occupy them are engaged. . . . The case before us implicates both the decisional and the spatial aspects of the right to privacy.

. . .

Only the most willful blindness could obscure the fact that sexual intimacy is "a sensitive, key relationship of human existence, central to family life, community welfare, and the development of human personality." . . . The fact that individuals define themselves in a significant way through their intimate sexual relationships with others suggests, in a Nation as diverse as ours, that there may be many "right" ways of conducting those relationships, and that much of the richness of a relationship will come from the freedom an individual has to choose the form and nature of these intensely personal bonds. . . .

. . . The Court claims that its decision today merely refuses to recognize a fundamental right to engage in homosexual sodomy; what the Court really has refused to recognize is the fundamental interest all individuals have in controlling the nature of their intimate associations with others.

The behavior for which Hardwick faces prosecution occurred in his own home, a place to which the Fourth Amendment attaches special significance. The Court's treatment of this aspect of the case is symptomatic of its overall refusal to consider the broad principles that have informed our treatment of privacy in specific cases. Just as the right to privacy is more than the mere aggregation of a number of entitlements to engage in specific behavior, so too, protecting the physical integrity of the home is more than merely a means of protecting specific activities that often take place there. . . .

. . .

The assertion that "traditional Judeo-Christian values proscribe" the conduct involved cannot provide an adequate justification. That certain, but by no means all, religious groups condemn the behavior at issue gives the State no license to impose their judgments on the entire citizenry. The legitimacy of secular legislation depends instead on whether the State can advance some justification for its law beyond its conformity to religious doctrine.

This case involves no real interference with the rights of others, for the mere knowledge that other individuals do not adhere to one's value system cannot be a legally cognizable interest, let alone an interest that can justify invading the houses, hearts, and minds of citizens who choose to live their lives differently.

. . . I can only hope that . . . the Court soon will reconsider its analysis and conclude that depriving individuals of the right to choose for themselves how to conduct their intimate relationships poses a far greater threat to the values most deeply rooted in our Nation's history than tolerance of nonconformity could ever do. . . .

JUSTICE STEVENS, with whom JUSTICE BRENNAN and JUSTICE MARSHALL join, dissenting.

. . .

Our prior cases make two propositions abundantly clear. First, the fact that the governing majority in a State has traditionally viewed a particular practice as immoral is not a sufficient reason for upholding a law prohibiting the practice; neither history nor tradition could save a law prohibiting miscegenation from constitutional attack. Second, individual decisions by married persons, concerning the intimacies of their physical relationship, even when not intended to produce offspring, are a form of "liberty" protected by the Due Process Clause of the Fourteenth Amendment. Moreover, this protection extends to intimate choices by unmarried as well as married persons. . . .

. . .

Although the meaning of the principle that "all men are created equal" is not always clear, it surely must mean that every free citizen has the same interest in "liberty" that the members of the majority share. From the standpoint of the individual, the homosexual and the heterosexual have the same interest in deciding how he will live his own life, and, more narrowly, how he will conduct himself in his personal and voluntary associations with his companions. State intrusion into the private conduct of either is equally burdensome. . . .

VIII. Democratic Rights

MAJOR DEVELOPMENTS

- Supreme Court protects the constitutional right to burn the flag
- Supreme Court rejects some federal and state efforts to create black-majority legislative districts

Reagan conservatives transformed the constitutional politics of democracy. For most of the twentieth century constitutional struggles over political processes pitted liberals, who favored judicial activism on behalf of expanded free speech and voting rights, against conservatives, who supported restricting expression and the franchise. The constitutional politics of democracy during the 1980s and early 1990s often pitted conservative champions of judicial activism against liberal proponents of legislation regulating expression and voting. Conservatives raised constitutional objections to campus hate speech restrictions, broadcast regulations, campaign finance laws, and efforts to create election districts where a majority of voters were persons of color. Most liberals defended these measures as consistent with the constitutional commitment to democracy.

The Supreme Court neither fully endorsed nor rejected conservative claims that government officials were unconstitutionally regulating the democratic process. The laws and practices that the Court declared unconstitutional included prohibitions on burning the flag, state restrictions on campaign finance, the drawing of bizarrely shaped black-majority districts, and a state law that permitted Jerry Falwell to sue *Hustler* magazine for intentional infliction of emotional distress. The justices permitted Democrats and Republicans to engage in partisan gerrymanders but forbade the use of race in the legislative districting process. The latter decisions relied on conservative antipathy to race-conscious measures but may have benefited Democrats politically.

A. Free Speech

The partisan structure of free speech debates shifted during this period. Political liberals by the 1980s were as inclined to regulate the marketplace of ideas as political conservatives. The controversy over whether the Constitution protected flag burning pitted conservative proponents of restriction against liberal proponents of free speech. Proposals to prohibit hate speech on college campuses pitted liberal proponents of restriction against conservative proponents of free speech. An unusual alliance of radical feminists and conservative Christians championed bans on pornography. More traditional liberals and more conservative libertarians often joined forces to fight these proposed limits on free speech. The Supreme Court typically sided with more traditional liberals and more libertarian conservatives when defeating efforts from both the left and the right to prohibit various forms of expression.

A general consensus existed during the 1980s that the main Warren Court precedents on free speech had been correctly decided. Americans accepted the principle stated in *Brandenburg v. Ohio* (1969) that "the constitutional guarantees of free speech and free press do not permit a State to forbid or proscribe advocacy of the use of force or of law violation except where such advocacy is directed to inciting or producing imminent lawless action and is likely to incite or produce such action." Constitutional decision makers abided by *New York Times Co. v. Sullivan* (1964), which prohibited "a public official from recovering damages for a defamatory falsehood relating to his official conduct unless he proves that the statement was made with 'actual malice'—that is, with knowledge that it was false or with reckless disregard of whether it was false or not." When finding that public figures could not normally collect damages for intentional infliction of emotional distress, Chief Justice Rehnquist's unanimous opinion in *Hustler Magazine v. Falwell* (1988) stated, "The First Amendment recognizes no such thing as a 'false' idea." The Reagan Justice Department's *Guidelines on Constitutional Litigation* celebrated Justice Holmes's dissent in *Abrams v. United States* (1919) and informed federal attorneys that *Brandenburg v. Ohio* had been rightly decided.[25]

Both liberals and conservatives tested the boundaries of these libertarian principles. President George Bush, Republicans in Congress, and many Democrats insisted that elected officials could prohibit flag burning, even as they contended that Americans were free to express hatred for the United States. Prominent liberals who sought to prohibit hate speech on college campuses and in the workplace claimed that insults were not constitutionally protected speech. Many conservatives maintained that obscenity did not advance any ideas. Radical feminists insisted that pornography subordinated women in violation of the constitutional commitment to equality.

Proponents of these restrictions enjoyed more success in nonjudicial arenas than in the courts. Congress enthusiastically banned flag burning. Many colleges prohibited hate speech. Indianapolis passed an ordinance based on the feminist critique of pornography. Judges proved more committed to libertarian understandings of free speech. The Supreme Court in *Texas v. Johnson* (1989) and *United States v. Eichman* (1990) declared unconstitutional prohibitions on flag burning. Federal judges declared unconstitutional several university attempts to ban hate speech. A federal appeals court in *American Booksellers Association, Inc. v. Hudnut* (1985) declared unconstitutional the Indianapolis ordinance prohibiting pornography.

The Supreme Court of the United States weighed in on controversies over hate speech when declaring unconstitutional in *R.A.V. v. St. Paul* (1992) a Minneapolis statute that prohibited placing "on public or private property a symbol . . . which one knows . . . arouses anger, alarm or resentment in others on the basis of race, color, creed, religion or gender." The justices agreed that the states could constitutionally prohibit "fighting words" that threatened a breach of the peace, but that the Minneapolis statute prohibited constitutionally protected speech. They disputed whether

25. U.S. Department of Justice, Office of Legal Policy, *Guidelines in Constitutional Litigation*, 76.

a better-drafted measure might pass constitutional muster. The main controversy was over whether the Minneapolis statute was content neutral. Content neutrality forbids government when passing otherwise-constitutional regulations from discriminating against people who hold certain ideas or speak on certain subjects. Government may ban murder, but public officials may not ban murder by proponents of progressive taxation or scholars who have published articles discussing the income tax. Justice Scalia's opinion in *R.A.V.* maintained that hate speech laws violate this constitutional commitment to content neutrality. He wrote:

> [T]he ordinance applies only to "fighting words" that insult, or provoke violence, "on the basis of race, color, creed, religion or gender." Displays containing abusive invective, no matter how vicious or severe, are permissible unless they are addressed to one of the specified disfavored topics. Those who wish to use "fighting words" in connection with other ideas—to express hostility, for example, on the basis of political affiliation, union membership, or homosexuality—are not covered. The First Amendment does not permit St. Paul to impose special prohibitions on those speakers who express views on disfavored subjects.

Justice Blackmun's concurrence insisted that hate speech laws prohibited the most dangerous fighting words and did not unconstitutionally discriminate against speech on disfavored topics. He declared,

> Just as Congress may determine that threats against the President entail more severe consequences than other threats, so St. Paul's City Council may determine that threats based on the target's race, religion, or gender cause more severe harm to both the target and to society than other threats. This latter judgment—that harms caused by racial, religious, and gender-based invective are qualitatively different from that caused by other fighting words—seems to me eminently reasonable and realistic.

The American welfare state generated new free speech controversies. Most previous free speech controversies had involved private persons speaking on private property or a public thoroughfare or using private resources to communicate some message. By the 1980s many free speech controversies involved persons who wished to speak on public property, beneficiaries of government funds, or public employees. With the decline of the traditional town green as a site for speech, speakers aiming to reach the public sought access to various public properties. Such government programs as the National Endowment for the Arts provided millions of dollars to subsidize speech. Far more Americans than ever before were employed by the federal, state, and local governments. These changes in the broader environment forced constitutional decision makers to consider more often and more deeply the constitutional rules for speech on public property, speech subsidized by public money, and speech by public employees.

The Supreme Court gave elected officials broad power to regulate speech on public property, subsidized speech, the speech of public employees, and speech in public schools. When sustaining a state law banning solicitations in airport terminals, the Court in *International Society for Krishna Consciousness v. Lee* (1992) largely confined "public forums" to parks and public streets. This is significant, because restrictions on speech in public fora, defined as "government property that has traditionally been available for public expression," are "subject to the highest scrutiny." Chief Justice Rehnquist, by placing particular emphasis on the words "traditionally been available," concluded that most new forms or uses of government property do not constitute public fora. "Given the lateness with which the modern air terminal has made its appearance," he wrote, "it hardly qualifies for the description of having immemorially . . . [,] time out of mind[,] been held in the public trust and used for purposes of expressive activity." *Clark v. Community for Creative Non-Violence* (1984) showed great deference to official decisions regulating speech in public fora, as long as the regulation was viewpoint and subject-matter neutral. Past precedents required state officials to demonstrate that state regulations on the time, manner, and place of speech were narrowly tailored to restrict only as much speech as was necessary to serve a legitimate state purpose. Justice White, when permitting the National Park Service to forbid persons protesting homelessness to sleep in Lafayette Park, insisted that courts accept any reasonable assertion that state regulations meet that standard. "We do not believe," he wrote, that past First Amendment cases "assign to the judiciary the authority to replace the Park Service as the manager of the Nation's parks or endow the judiciary with the competence to judge how much protection of park lands is wise and how that level of conservation is to be attained." The justices were as accommodating when public authorities restricted the expression rights of schoolchildren. *Bethel School District No. 403 v. Fraser* (1986) deferred to a principal's judgment about appropriate speech in public schools. When sustaining the suspension of a student who used sexual innuendo when making a speech during an assembly, Chief Justice Burger declared, "The undoubted freedom to advocate unpopular and controversial views in schools and classrooms must be balanced against the society's countervailing interest in teaching students the boundaries of socially appropriate behavior."

Texas v. Johnson, 491 U.S. 397 (1989)

Gregory Johnson burned an American flag during a protest outside the Republican Party's 1984 national convention in Dallas, Texas. He was arrested and charged with violating a Texas law forbidding "desecrating . . . a state or national flag." Johnson was found guilty by the trial court, sentenced to a year in prison, and fined $2,000. That conviction was reversed by the Texas Court of Criminal Appeals. Texas appealed to the Supreme Court of the United States.

The Supreme Court by a 5–4 vote ruled that Johnson had been unconstitutionally convicted. Justice Brennan's majority opinion asserts that burning the flag is an expressive activity protected by the First Amendment. Consider the unusual line-up of the justices in this case. Justices Scalia and Kennedy provided crucial votes for the majority, while Justice Stevens dissented. What might explain that judicial voting pattern? The majority and dissenting opinions dispute whether the flag has partisan content. Why did Brennan believe that laws banning flag burning prohibit the expression of ideas? Why did Chief Justice Rehnquist disagree? What did Kennedy mean when he declared, "Sometimes we must make decisions we do not like"? Did Kennedy believe that a better Constitution would permit elected officials to burn flags?

Congress responded to Texas v. Johnson *by passing the Flag Protection Act of 1989. The crucial provision of that legislation declared, "Whoever knowingly mutilates, defaces, physically defiles, burns, maintains on the floor or ground, or tramples upon any flag of the United States shall be fined under this title or imprisoned for not more than one year, or both." No justice altered his or her position when deciding the constitutionality of that measure. Justice Brennan's majority opinion in* United States v. Eichman *(1990) declared, "Government may create national symbols, promote them, and encourage their respectful treatment. But the Flag Protection Act of 1989 goes well beyond this by criminally proscribing expressive conduct because of its likely communicative impact."*

JUSTICE BRENNAN delivered the opinion of the Court.

. . .

Johnson was convicted of flag desecration for burning the flag rather than for uttering insulting words. This fact somewhat complicates our consideration of his conviction under the First Amendment. We must first determine whether Johnson's burning of the flag constituted expressive conduct, permitting him to invoke the First Amendment in challenging his conviction. . . .

. . .

In deciding whether particular conduct possesses sufficient communicative elements to bring the First Amendment into play, we have asked whether "[a]n intent to convey a particularized message was present, and [whether] the likelihood was great that the message would be understood by those who viewed it." . . .

. . .

Johnson burned an American flag as part—indeed, as the culmination—of a political demonstration that coincided with the convening of the Republican Party and its renomination of Ronald Reagan for President. The expressive, overtly political nature of this conduct was both intentional and overwhelmingly apparent. . . . In these circumstances, Johnson's burning of the flag was conduct "sufficiently imbued with elements of communication" . . . to implicate the First Amendment.

. . .

. . The State offers two separate interests to justify this conviction: preventing breaches of the peace and preserving the flag as a symbol of nationhood and national unity. We hold that the first interest is not implicated on this record and that the second is related to the suppression of expression.

Texas claims that its interest in preventing breaches of the peace justifies Johnson's conviction for flag desecration. However, no disturbance of the peace actually occurred or threatened to occur because of Johnson's burning of the flag. . . .

The State's position, therefore, amounts to a claim that an audience that takes serious offense at particular expression is necessarily likely to disturb the peace and that the expression may be prohibited on this basis. Our precedents do not countenance such a presumption. On the contrary, they recognize that a principal "function of free speech under our system of government is to invite dispute. It may indeed best serve its high purpose when it induces a condition of unrest, creates dissatisfaction with conditions as they are, or even stirs people to anger." . . .

. . .

Nor does Johnson's expressive conduct fall within that small class of "fighting words" that are "likely to provoke the average person to retaliation, and thereby cause a breach of the peace." . . . No reasonable onlooker would have regarded Johnson's generalized expression of dissatisfaction with the policies of the Federal Government as a direct personal insult or an invitation to exchange fisticuffs. . . .

. . .

The State also asserts an interest in preserving the flag as a symbol of nationhood and national unity. . . . The State, apparently, is concerned that such conduct will lead people to believe either that the flag does not stand for nationhood and national unity, but instead reflects other, less positive concepts, or that the concepts reflected in the flag do not in fact exist, that is, that we do not enjoy unity as a Nation. These concerns blossom only when a person's treatment of the flag communicates some message, and thus are related "to the suppression of free expression." . . .

. . .

If there is a bedrock principle underlying the First Amendment, it is that the government may not prohibit the expression of an idea simply because society finds the idea itself offensive or disagreeable. . . .

. . .

Texas' focus on the precise nature of Johnson's expression . . . misses the point of our prior decisions: their enduring lesson, that the government may not prohibit expression simply because it disagrees with its message, is not dependent on the particular mode in which one chooses to express an idea. If we were to hold that a State may forbid flag burning wherever it is likely to endanger the flag's symbolic role, but allow it wherever burning a flag promotes that role—as where, for example, a person ceremoniously burns a dirty flag—we would be saying that when it comes to impairing the flag's physical integrity, the flag itself may be used as a symbol—as a substitute for the written or spoken word or a "short cut from mind to mind"—only in one direction. We would be permitting a State to "prescribe what shall be orthodox" by saying that one may burn the flag to convey one's attitude toward it and its referents only if one does not endanger the flag's representation of nationhood and national unity.

. . .

We are tempted to say, in fact, that the flag's deservedly cherished place in our community will be strengthened, not weakened, by our holding today. Our decision is a reaffirmation of the principles of freedom and inclusiveness that the flag best reflects, and of the conviction that our toleration of criticism such as Johnson's is a sign and source of our strength. Indeed, one of the proudest images of our flag, the one immortalized in our own national anthem, is of the bombardment it survived at Fort McHenry. It is the Nation's resilience, not its rigidity, that Texas sees reflected in the flag—and it is that resilience that we reassert today.

. . .

JUSTICE KENNEDY, concurring.

. . .

The hard fact is that sometimes we must make decisions we do not like. We make them because they are right, right . . . in the sense that the law and the Constitution, as we see them, compel the result. And so great is our commitment to the process that, except in the rare case, we do not pause to express distaste for the result, perhaps for fear of undermining a valued principle that dictates the decision. This is one of those rare cases.

. . .

CHIEF JUSTICE REHNQUIST, with whom JUSTICE WHITE and JUSTICE O'CONNOR join, dissenting.

. . .

The American flag throughout more than 200 years of our history, has come to be the visible symbol embodying our Nation. It does not represent the views of any particular political party, and it does not represent any particular political philosophy. The flag is not simply another "idea" or "point of view" competing for recognition in the marketplace of ideas. Millions and millions of Americans regard it with an almost mystical reverence regardless of what sort of social, political, or philosophical beliefs they may have. I cannot agree that the First Amendment invalidates the Act of Congress, and the laws of 48 of the 50 States, which make criminal the public burning of the flag.

. . .

But the Court insists that the Texas statute prohibiting the public burning of the American flag infringes on respondent Johnson's freedom of expression. Such freedom, of course, is not absolute. . . .

. . . [T]he public burning of the American flag by Johnson was no essential part of any exposition of ideas, and at the same time it had a tendency to incite a breach of the peace. Johnson was free to make any verbal denunciation of the flag that he wished; indeed, he was free to burn the flag in private. He could publicly burn other symbols of the Government or effigies of political leaders. He did lead a march through the streets of Dallas, and conducted a rally in front of the Dallas City Hall. He engaged in a "die-in" to protest nuclear weapons. He shouted out various slogans during the march, including: "Reagan, Mondale which will it be? Either one means World War III"; "Ronald Reagan, killer of the hour, Perfect example of U.S. power"; and "red, white and blue, we spit on you, you stand for plunder, you will go under." . . . For none of these acts was he arrested or prosecuted; it was only when he proceeded to burn publicly an American flag stolen from its rightful owner that he violated the Texas statute.

. . . [Johnson's] act . . . conveyed nothing that could not have been conveyed and was not conveyed just as forcefully in a dozen different ways. As with "fighting words," so with flag burning, for purposes of the First Amendment: It is "no essential part of any exposition of ideas, and [is] of such slight social value as a step to truth that any benefit that may be derived from [it] is clearly outweighed" by the public interest in avoiding a probable breach of the peace. . . .

. . . The Texas statute deprived Johnson of only one rather inarticulate symbolic form of protest—a form of protest that was profoundly offensive to many—and left him with a full panoply of other symbols and every conceivable form of verbal expression to express his deep disapproval of national policy. Thus, in no way can it be said that Texas is punishing him because his hearers—or any other group of people—were profoundly opposed to the message that he sought to convey. Such opposition is no proper basis for restricting speech or expression under the First Amendment. It was Johnson's use of this particular symbol, and not the idea that he sought to convey by it or by his many other expressions, for which he was punished.

. . .

JUSTICE STEVENS, dissenting.

. . .

A country's flag is a symbol of more than "nationhood and national unity." . . . It also signifies the ideas that characterize the society that has chosen that emblem as well as the special history that has animated the growth and power of those ideas. . . .

. . .

The value of the flag as a symbol cannot be measured. Even so, I have no doubt that the interest in preserving that value for the future is both significant and legitimate. Conceivably that value will be enhanced by the Court's conclusion that our national commitment to free expression is so strong that even the United States as ultimate guarantor of that freedom is without power to prohibit the desecration of its unique symbol. But I am unpersuaded. The creation of a federal right to post bulletin boards and graffiti on the Washington Monument might enlarge the market for free expression, but at a cost I would not pay. Similarly, in my considered judgment, sanctioning the public desecration of the flag will tarnish its value—both for those who cherish the ideas for which it waves and for those who desire to don the robes of martyrdom by burning it. That tarnish is not justified by the trivial burden on free expression occasioned by requiring that an available, alternative mode of expression—including uttering words critical of the flag . . . be employed.

. . .

. . . The content of respondent's message has no relevance whatsoever to the case. The concept of "desecration" does not turn on the substance of the message the actor intends to convey, but rather on whether those who view the act will take serious offense. Accordingly, one intending to convey a message of respect for the flag by burning it in a public square might nonetheless be guilty of desecration if he knows that others—perhaps simply because they misperceive the intended message—will be seriously offended. Indeed, even if the actor knows that all possible witnesses will understand that he intends to send a message of respect, he might still be guilty of desecration if he also knows that this understanding does not lessen the offense taken by some of those witnesses. . . .

Doe v. University of Michigan, 721 F. Supp. 852 (E.D. Mich., 1989)

John Doe was the pseudonym of a University of Michigan graduate student who wished to discuss controversial biological theories suggesting significant racial and gender differences. Doe claimed that he did not raise these issues in class because he feared that such assertions as "biological differences explain why more men than women are engineers" violated the University of Michigan's Policy on Discrimination and Discriminatory Harassment. With the assistance of several public interest groups, Doe asked a federal district court to declare the offending university policy unconstitutional.

The federal district court in Doe v. University of Michigan *issued a permanent injunction barring enforcement of the speech provisions in the university's Policy on Discrimination and Discriminatory Harassment. Judge Cohn ruled that the prohibitions were overbroad and vague. The Michigan policy, he maintained, could be interpreted as banning constitutionally protected speech, and reasonable persons could not determine what was prohibited. Suppose you were asked to rewrite the Michigan policy. What regulations do you believe Judge Cohn would find constitutional? What regulations do you believe are constitutional? Under what conditions, if any, should members of a university community be able to assert the following:*

1. *There is only one true religion, and nonadherents will go to hell.*
2. *Specific gender roles or sexual practices are unnatural (or disgusting).*
3. *Members of one sex, race, ethnic group, or religion have certain capacities that members of other races, ethnic groups, religions, or the other sex lack.*

JUDGE COHN delivered the following opinion.

. . .

. . . It is clear that so-called "fighting words" are not entitled to First Amendment protection. *Chaplinsky v. New Hampshire* (1942). These would include "the lewd and obscene, the profane, the libelous, and the insulting or 'fighting words'—those which by their very utterance inflict injury or tend to incite an immediate breach of the peace." Under certain circumstances racial and ethnic epithets, slurs, and insults might fall within this description and could constitutionally be prohibited by the University. In addition, such speech may also be sufficient to state a claim for common law intentional infliction of emotional distress. Credible threats of violence or property damage made with the specific intent to harass or intimidate the victim because of his race, sex, religion, or national origin is punishable both criminally and civilly under state law. Similarly, speech which has the effect of inciting imminent lawless action and which is likely to incite such action may also be lawfully punished. Civil damages are available for speech which creates a hostile or abusive working environment on the basis of race or sex. . . . If the Policy had the effect of only regulating in these areas, it is unlikely that any constitutional problem would have arisen.

What the University could not do, however, was establish an anti-discrimination policy which had the effect of prohibiting certain speech because it disagreed with ideas or messages sought to be conveyed. As the Supreme Court stated in *West Virginia State Board of Education v. Barnette* (1943): "If there is any star fixed in our constitutional constellation, it is that no official, high or petty, can prescribe what shall be orthodox in politics, nationalism, religion, or other matters of opinion or force citizens to confess by word or act their faith therein." Nor could the University proscribe speech simply because it was found to be offensive, even gravely so, by large numbers of people. . . .

These principles acquire a special significance in the university setting, where the free and unfettered interplay of competing views is essential to the institution's educational mission.

. . .

. . . [T]he state may not prohibit broad classes of speech, some of which may indeed be legitimately regulable, if in so doing a substantial amount of constitutionally protected conduct is also prohibited. This was the fundamental infirmity of the Policy.

The University repeatedly argued that the Policy did not apply to speech that is protected by the First Amendment. . . . However, as applied by the University over the past year, the Policy was consistently applied to reach protected speech.

On December 7, 1988, a complaint was filed against a graduate student in the School of Social Work alleging that he harassed students based on sexual orientation and sex. The basis for the sexual orientation charge was apparently that in a research class, the student openly stated his belief that homosexuality was a disease and that he intended to develop a counseling plan for changing gay clients to straight. . . . A formal hearing on the charges was held on January 28, 1989. The hearing panel unanimously found that the student was guilty of sexual harassment but refused to convict him of harassment on the basis of sexual orientation.

. . . Although the student was not sanctioned over the allegations of sexual orientation harassment, the fact remains that the Policy Administrator—the authoritative voice of the University on these matters—saw no First Amendment problem in forcing the student to a hearing to answer for allegedly harassing statements made in the course of academic discussion and research. . . .

. . .

Doe also urges that the policy be struck down on the grounds that it is impermissibly vague. A statute is unconstitutionally vague when "men of common intelligence must necessarily guess at its meaning." A statute must give adequate warning of the conduct which is to be prohibited and must set out explicit standards for those who apply it. . . . These considerations apply with particular force where the challenged statute acts to inhibit freedoms affirmatively protected by the constitution. However, the chilling effect caused by an overly vague statute must be both real and substantial and a narrowing construction must be unavailable before a court will set it aside.

Looking at the plain language of the Policy, it was simply impossible to discern any limitation on its scope or any conceptual distinction between protected and unprotected conduct. . . . The operative words in the cause section required that language must "stigmatize" or "victimize" an individual. However, both of these terms are general and elude precise definition. Moreover, it is clear that the fact that a statement may victimize or stigmatize an individual does not, in and of itself, strip it of protection under the accepted First Amendment tests.

The first of the "effects clauses" stated that in order to be sanctionable, the stigmatizing and victimizing statements had to "involve an express or implied threat to an individual's academic efforts, employment, participation in University sponsored extra-curricular activities or personal safety." It is not clear what kind of conduct would constitute a "threat" to an individual's academic efforts. It might refer to an unspecified threat of future retaliation by the speaker. Or it might equally plausibly refer to the threat to a victim's academic success because the stigmatizing and victimizing speech is so inherently distracting. Certainly the former would be unprotected speech. However, it is not clear whether the latter would.

Moving to the second "effect clause," a stigmatizing or victimizing comment is sanctionable if it has the purpose or reasonably foreseeable effect of interfering with an individual's academic efforts, etc. Again, the question is what conduct will be held to "interfere" with an individual's academic efforts. The language of the policy alone gives no inherent guidance. . . .

. . .

While the Court is sympathetic to the University's obligation to ensure equal educational opportunities for all of its students, such efforts must not be at the expense of free speech. Unfortunately, this was precisely what the University did. . . . [T]here is no evidence in the record that any officials at the University ever seriously attempted to reconcile their efforts to combat discrimination with the requirements of the First Amendment. . . .

B. Voting

The constitutional politics of voting rights during the Great Society was better for conservatives than Republicans. Many conservatives had principled objections to the provisions in the Voting Rights Acts that interfered with state prerogatives, to Warren Court decisions that announced an unenumerated fundamental right to vote, and to the increased use of racial classifications when apportioning legislative districts. Many Republicans welcomed the large number of white southerners who had abandoned the Democratic Party once persons of color gained access to the ballot and the high probability that majority-minority districts would increase the number of both African American and Republican elected officials. Republicans, who gained control of more state legislatures during the 1980s, learned that they could gerrymander with the best of the Democrats.

These differences in constitutional politics and constitutional law explain why partisan divisions during the voting rights debates of the 1980s and early 1990s often diverged from judicial divisions. Judicial decisions were structured by ideology. Conservative justices interpreted the Voting Rights Act narrowly, insisted that race could not be the predominant factor when apportioning legislative districts, and rejected judicial power to correct gerrymanders. Many Republican elected officials supported legislation broadening the Voting Rights Act, endorsed efforts to increase the number of majority-minority legislative districts, and gerrymandered whenever they were the majority party in the state legislature. Democrats in both the judiciary and the legislature supported broad readings of the Voting Rights Act, but liberal justices supported the majority-minority legislative districts that Democratic elected officials often opposed. The result of the sometimes-strange alliances between judges identified with one party and elected officials identified with the other was that by the mid-1990s the Voting Rights Act had been slightly strengthened, the federal judiciary had declared unconstitutional several efforts to increase the number of majority-minority legislative districts, and the constitutional status of legislative gerrymanders was unclear.

The Supreme Court initially sent mixed signals on the Voting Rights Acts of 1965, 1970, and 1975. *City of Rome v. United States* (1980) ruled that the attorney general had power under the Voting Rights Acts to reject a proposed change in local voting practices that would have a discriminatory effect on persons of color, even if those changes did not have a discriminatory purpose. Justice Marshall's majority opinion declared, "The Act's ban on electoral changes that are discriminatory in effect is an appropriate method of promoting the purposes of the Fifteenth Amendment, even if it is assumed that §1 of the Amendment prohibits only intentional discrimination in voting," because "Congress could rationally have concluded that, because electoral changes by jurisdictions with a demonstrable history of intentional racial discrimination in voting create the risk of purposeful discrimination, it was proper to prohibit changes that have a discriminatory impact." *City of Mobile v. Bolden* (1980) reached a more conservative result, ruling that Mobile, Alabama, violated neither the Fifteenth Amendment nor the Voting Rights Act by maintaining an at-large system for voting for city commissions, even though no member of the city's African American population had ever been elected to office. Justice Stewart's plurality opinion declared, "Our decisions have made clear that action by a State that is racially neutral on its face violates the Fifteenth Amendment only if motivated by a discriminatory purpose." *Rome* and *Mobile* reached different conclusions solely because Rome adopted an election procedure that had a discriminatory effect while Mobile maintained a procedure that had a discriminatory effect.

Over strong opposition from the Reagan administration, a coalition of Democrats and moderate Republicans amended the Voting Rights Act to empower federal courts to prohibit all election and voting laws that had discriminatory effects. The Voting Rights Act Amendments of 1982 declared,

> (a) No voting qualification or prerequisite to voting or standard, practice, or procedure shall be imposed or applied by any State or political subdivision in a manner which results in a denial or abridgement of the right of any citizen of the United States to vote on account of race or color. . . .
>
> (b) A violation of subsection (a) is established if, based on the totality of circumstances, it is shown that the political processes leading to nomination or election in the State or political subdivision are not equally open to participation by members of a class of citizens protected by subsection (a) in that its members have less opportunity than other members of the electorate to participate in the political process and to elect representatives of their choice. The extent to which members of a protected class have been elected to office in the State or political subdivision is one circumstance which may be considered: *Provided*, That nothing in this section establishes a right to have members of a protected class elected in numbers equal to their proportion in the population.

The Supreme Court incorporated this statutory change into its voting rights jurisprudence. In *Gingles v. Thornburg* (1986) all nine justices on the Burger Court acknowledged that persons of color could demonstrate a rights violation if the "totality of circumstances" demonstrated that they could not elect the candidates of their choice. The justices did not agree on precisely what encompassed that "totality of circumstances," but they agreed that the focus of litigation under the Voting Rights Act would be on how voting systems actually affected the political power of persons of color, and not on whether local voting laws had a discriminatory purpose.

During the Reagan Era the Court began addressing issues relating to so-called "majority-minority districts." Majority-minority districts are legislative districts apportioned to ensure that members of a racial minority, typically either African Americans or Hispanic Americans, constitute a majority of voters. Such districts increased dramatically during the 1980s for legal and partisan reasons. The Supreme Court in *Thornburg v. Gingles* (1986) ruled that the necessary elements of a vote dilution claim under the Voting Rights Act of 1982 included whether "the minority group . . . is politically cohesive" and whether "the white majority votes sufficiently as a bloc to . . . usually defeat the minority's preferred candidate." Many state legislatures interpreted this language as requiring them to create legislative districts in which the majority of voters were either African American or Hispanic American. Republican Party leaders and at least some Republicans in the Department of Justice interpreted this language as an opportunity to disrupt relationships between white Democratic incumbents and voters of color. During the late 1980s, one commentator observes, "the Republican National Committee undertook a campaign of guerilla warfare, working with black Democrats against white Democrats in legislatures throughout the South."[26] By 1992 state legislatures had created at least twenty-five majority-minority congressional districts.

Legislative efforts to create majority-minority districts were controversial. The constitutional controversy concerned the use of race in the legislative districting process. The Supreme Court in *Shaw v. Reno* (1993) declared that racial gerrymanders were constitutional only if they were narrowly tailored to serve compelling ends, such as compliance with the Voting Rights Act. The political controversy erupted when President Clinton nominated Professor Lani Guinier to be assistant attorney general for civil rights. Guinier, who as a scholar proposed various electoral schemes designed in part to increase representatives of color, eventually withdrew after a bitter debate that included charges that she was a "Quota Queen." An ongoing scholarly controversy concerns the electoral consequences of majority-minority districts. Most studies conclude that the existence of majority-minority districts in a state increases the number of Republicans elected statewide, but no agreement exists on whether that increase is substantial or slight.[27]

The Supreme Court showed far more deference to partisan gerrymanders than racial gerrymanders. A badly divided Court in *Davis v. Bandemer* (1986) suggested that federal courts would rarely interfere when state legislators drew electoral districts in ways that enabled the majority party to gain more representatives than were merited by their statewide percentage of the vote. Four justices demanded that plaintiffs challenging a partisan gerrymander demonstrate longstanding problems with the operation of state elections. Justice White wrote,

> An equal protection violation may be found only where the electoral system substantially disadvantages certain voters in their opportunity to influence the political process effectively. In this context, such a finding of unconstitutionality must be supported by evidence of continued frustration of the will of a majority of the voters or effective denial to a minority of voters of a fair chance to influence the political process.

Three justices maintained that partisan gerrymanders raised no justiciable issues. Justice O'Connor declared, "The Equal Protection Clause does not supply judicially manageable standards for resolving purely political gerrymandering claims, and no group right to an equal share of political power was ever intended by the Framers of the Fourteenth Amendment." Justice Powell and Justice Stevens were more open to striking down partisan gerrymanders. They maintained that an examination of such factors as "the shapes of voting districts" and "established political subdivision boundaries" could demonstrate that "a districting plan purposefully discriminates against political opponents."

26. David T. Canon, *Race, Redistricting, and Representation: The Unintended Consequences of Black Majority Districts* (Chicago, IL: University of Chicago Press, 1999), 77.

27. For a summary, see Canon, *Race*, 73–74.

Senate Committee on the Judiciary, Senate Report on the Voting Rights Act Amendments of 1982 (1982)[28]

The Voting Rights Act Amendments of 1982 extended the temporary preclearance provisions of the Voting Rights Act of 1965 for twenty-five years, modified the legal conditions for "bailing out" of the preclearance procedures, and reversed the ruling in City of Mobile v. Bolden *(1980) that plaintiffs must prove purposeful discrimination to demonstrate a voting rights violation. The amendments substituted an effects test for a motives test. Plaintiffs had to prove only that they had "less opportunity than other members of the electorate to participate in the political process and to elect representatives of their choice."*

The debate over the amendments was largely limited to the "effects" provision. The Democratic majority in the House of Representatives passed a bill explicitly reversing the decision in City of Mobile. *A very conservative Senate subcommittee issued a report defending the purposeful discrimination requirement. The Reagan administration strongly supported the Senate subcommittee's version of the Voting Rights Act. Senator Bob Dole brokered a compromise when he proposed adding the following disclaimer to the House proposal: "That nothing in this section establishes a right to have members of a protected class elected in numbers equal to their proportion in the population." So amended, the Voting Rights Act Amendments passed the House and Senate with overwhelming majorities. President Reagan signed the bill on June 29, 1982.*

Consider the following questions when reading the excerpts from the Senate report. Why do you believe that a bipartisan consensus formed on the need to jettison the purpose test? Was this a matter of principle? What was the role of partisan advantage? What are the strengths and weaknesses of the results test? What test would you require that plaintiffs in voting rights cases meet? The Judiciary Committee claimed that it was not reversing a Supreme Court decision, but merely amending a federal statute. Is that what the Senate was doing? Was the decision to reverse City of Mobile *constitutional?*

28. Excerpt taken from Senate Committee on the Judiciary, *Senate Report on the Voting Rights Act Amendments of 1982*, 97th Cong., 2nd Sess., 1982, S. Rep. 97–417.

. . .

Although we have come a long way since 1965, the nation's task in securing voting rights is not finished. Continued progress toward equal opportunity in the electoral process will be halted if we abandon the act's crucial safeguards now.

The committee is equally concerned about the risk of losing what progress has already been won. The gains are fragile. Without the preclearance of new laws, many of the advances of the past decade could be wiped out overnight with new schemes and devices.

. . .

A review of the kinds of proposed changes that have been objected to by the Attorney General in recent years reveals the types of impediments that still face minority voters in the covered jurisdictions. Among the types of changes that have been objected to most frequently in the period from 1975–1980 are annexations; the use of at-large elections, majority vote requirements, or numbered posts; and the redistricting of boundary lines. This reflects the fact that, since the adoption of the voting rights act, covered jurisdictions have substantially moved from the direct impediments to the right to vote to more sophisticated devices that dilute minority voting.

. . . In January 1980, the De Kalb County Georgia board of registration adopted a policy that it would no longer approve community groups' requests to conduct voter registration drives, even though only 24 percent of black eligible voters were registered, compared to 81 percent of whites. A lawsuit was required to make the county submit the change, and the attorney general objected.

. . .

In the three years following passage of the voting rights act, the city of Indianola, Mississippi reduced the proportion of its black population by more than 30 percent through annexation of outlying white areas while refusing contemporaneous request to annex 11 adjoining predominantly black subdivisions. These predominantly black subdivisions receive city services but are excluded from voting for city officials. Not one of the annexations was ever submitted for preclearance.

. . .

The amendment to the language of section 2 is designed to make clear that plaintiffs need not prove a discriminatory purpose in the adoption or maintenance of the challenged system of practice in order to establish a violation. Plaintiffs must either prove such intent, or, alternatively, must show that the challenged system or practice, in the context of all the circumstances in the jurisdiction in question, results in minorities being denied equal access to the political process.

. . .

. . . To establish a violation, plaintiffs could show a variety of factors, depending upon the kind of rule, practice, or procedure called into question.

Typical factors include:

1. The extent of any history of official discrimination in the state or political subdivision that touched the right of the members of the minority group to register, to vote, or otherwise to participate in the democratic process;
2. The extent to which voting in the elections of the state or political subdivision is racially polarized;
3. The extent to which the state or political subdivision has used unusually large election districts, majority vote requirements, anti-single shot provisions, or other voting practices or procedures that may enhance the opportunity for discrimination against the minority group;
4. If there is a candidate slating process, whether the members of the minority group have been denied access to that process;
5. The extent to which members of the minority group in the state or political subdivision bear the effects of discrimination in such areas as education, employment and health, which hinder their ability to participate effectively in the political process;
6. Whether political campaigns have been characterized by overt or subtle racial appeals;
7. The extent to which members of the minority group have been elected to public office in the jurisdiction.

Additional factors that in some cases have had probative value as part of plaintiffs' evidence to establish a violation are:

Whether there is a significant lack of responsiveness on the part of elected officials to the particularized needs of the members of the minority group.

Whether the policy underlying the state or political subdivision's use of such voting qualification, prerequisite to voting, or standard, practice or procedure is tenuous.

While these enumerated factors will often be the most relevant ones, in some cases other factors will be indicative of the alleged dilution.

. . .

When a federal judge is called upon to determine the validity of a practice challenged under section 2, as amended, he or she is required to act in full accordance with the disclaimer in section 2 which reads as follows:

> The extent to which members of a protected class have been elected to office in the state or political subdivision is one "circumstance" which may be considered, provided that nothing in this section establishes a right to have members of a protected class elected in numbers equal to their proportion in the population.

. . . [T]his provision is both clear and straightforward. . . . It puts to rest any concerns that have been voiced about racial quotas.

. . . The intent test is inappropriate as the exclusive standard for establishing a violation of section 2. . . . The main reason is that, simply put, the test asks the wrong question. . . . [I]f an electoral system operates today to exclude blacks or hispanics from a fair chance to participate, then the matter of what motives were in an official's mind 100 years ago is of the most limited relevance. The standard under the committee amendment is whether minorities have equal access to the process of electing their representatives. If they are denied a fair opportunity to participate, the committee believes that the system should be changed, regardless of what may or may not be provable about events which took place decades ago.

Second, the committee has heard persuasive testimony that the intent test is unnecessarily divisive because it involves charges of racism on the part of individual officials or entire communities. . . .

. . .

Third, the intent test will be an inordinately difficult burden for plaintiffs in most cases. In the case of laws enacted many decades ago, the legislators cannot be subpoenaed from their graves for testimony about the motives behind their actions. . . .

. . .

The proposed amendment modifying a results test to section 2 is a clearly constitutional exercise of congressional power under article 1 and the Fourteenth and Fifteenth amendments. By now the breadth of congressional power to enforce these provisions is hornbook law.

. . .

Congress may enact measures going beyond the direct requirements of the Fifteenth Amendment, if such measures are appropriate and reasonably adapted to protect citizens against the risk that the right to vote will be denied in violation of the fifteenth amendment. That point, clearly established in [*South Carolina v. Katzenbach* (1966)], has not been seriously challenged in subsequent years.

. . .

The committee has concluded that to enforce fully the Fourteenth and Fifteenth Amendments, it is necessary that section 2 ban election procedures and practices that result in a denial or abridgment of the right to vote. In reaching this conclusion, we find (1) that the difficulties faced by plaintiffs forced to prove discriminatory intent through case-by-case adjudication create a substantial risk that intentional discrimination barred by the Fourteenth and Fifteenth Amendments will go undetected, uncorrected and undeterred unless the results test proposed for section 2 is adopted; and (2) that voting practices and procedures that have discriminatory results perpetuate the effects of past purposeful discrimination.

. . .

Congress cannot alter the judicial interpretations in [*City of Mobile v. Bolden* (1980)] of the Fourteenth and Fifteenth Amendments by simple statute. But the proposed amendment to Section 2 does not seek to reverse the court's constitutional interpretation. Rather, the proposal is a proper statutory exercise of congress' enforcement power described above and it is not a redefinition of the scope of the constitutional provisions. . . .

. . .

Additional Views of SENATOR ORRIN G. HATCH (Republican, Utah)

. . .

The objectives of these amendments are vastly different than those of the original Act. In place of the traditional focus upon equal access to registration and the ballot, the amendments would focus upon equal outcome in the electoral process. Instead of aiming ultimately at the nonconsideration of race in the electoral process as did the original act, the amendments would make race the over-riding factor in public decisions in this area. Instead of directing its protections toward the individual citizen as did the original act—and as does the constitution—the amendments would make racial and ethnic groups the basic unit of protection. Instead of reinforcing the great constitutional principle of equal protection as did the original act, the amendments would substitute a totally alien principle of equal results.

. . .

There is no core value under the results test other than election results. There is no core value that can lead anywhere other than toward proportional representation by race and ethnic group. There is no ultimate or threshold question that a court must ask under the results test that will lead in any other direction. . . .

. . .

. . . [T]he concept of a process "equally open to participation" brings to the fore what is perhaps the major defect to the results test. To the extent that it leads anywhere other than to pure proportional representation (and I do not believe that it does), the test provides absolutely no intelligible guidance to courts in determining whether or not a section 2 violation has been established or to communities in determining whether or not their electoral structures and policies are in conformity with the law. What is an "equally open" political process? How can it be identified in terms other than statistical or results-oriented analysis? Under what circumstances is an "objective factor of discrimination," such as an at-large system, a barrier to such an "open" political process and when is it not? What would a totally "open" political process look like? How would a community effectively overcome evidence that their elected representative bodies lacked proportional representation?

. . .

Perhaps most importantly, the proposed "compromise" suffers from the defects of the House provision in that it attempts statutorily to overturn the Supreme Court's decision in *City of Mobile* interpreting the Fifteenth Amendment. . . . [T]he Congress simply cannot overturn a constitutional decision of the Supreme Court through a mere statute. The Court has held that the Fifteenth Amendment requires a demonstration of intentional or purposeful discrimination. To the extent that the voting rights act generally and Section 2 specifically are predicated upon this amendment—and they are—there is no authority with congress to reinterpret its requirements and to impose greater restrictions upon the states in the conduct of their own affairs. There is no power within congress to act outside the boundaries of the Fifteenth Amendment, as interpreted by the court, at least so long as the federal government remains a government of delegated powers.

. . .

The new voting rights act will also enhance enormously the role of the federal judiciary in the state and municipal governmental process. Race-neutral or ethnic-neutral decisions affecting countless aspects of this process will suddenly be subject to new scrutiny by the courts on the basis of whether such aspects are "tenuous," whether they contribute to an "equal opportunity to participate," whether they permit protected minorities to "elect representatives of their choice," and so forth. As the committee report accurately states, the new section 2 requires, above all, the application of "the court's overall judgment." There is, in fact, little more to the test than this.

Above all, the present measure plays havoc with traditional notions of civil rights and discrimination, and distorts these concepts beyond all recognition. In the process, it can only contribute toward undermining the virtually-realized consensus in this nation in behalf of equality and civil rights in their traditional form—equality of opportunity and equality of access, not equality of result and equality of outcome. The historical evolution of this nation away from the consideration of race in public policy decisions will be halted. The present amendments in the voting rights act represent nothing less than a full retreat from the color-blind principles of law fostered by *Brown v. Board of Education* (1954), the Civil Rights Act of 1964, and the original Voting Rights Act itself. . . .

Shaw v. Reno, 509 U.S. 630 (1993)

Ruth Shaw was a white resident of North Carolina. After the 1990 census North Carolina gained a twelfth seat in the House of Representatives. With strong support from

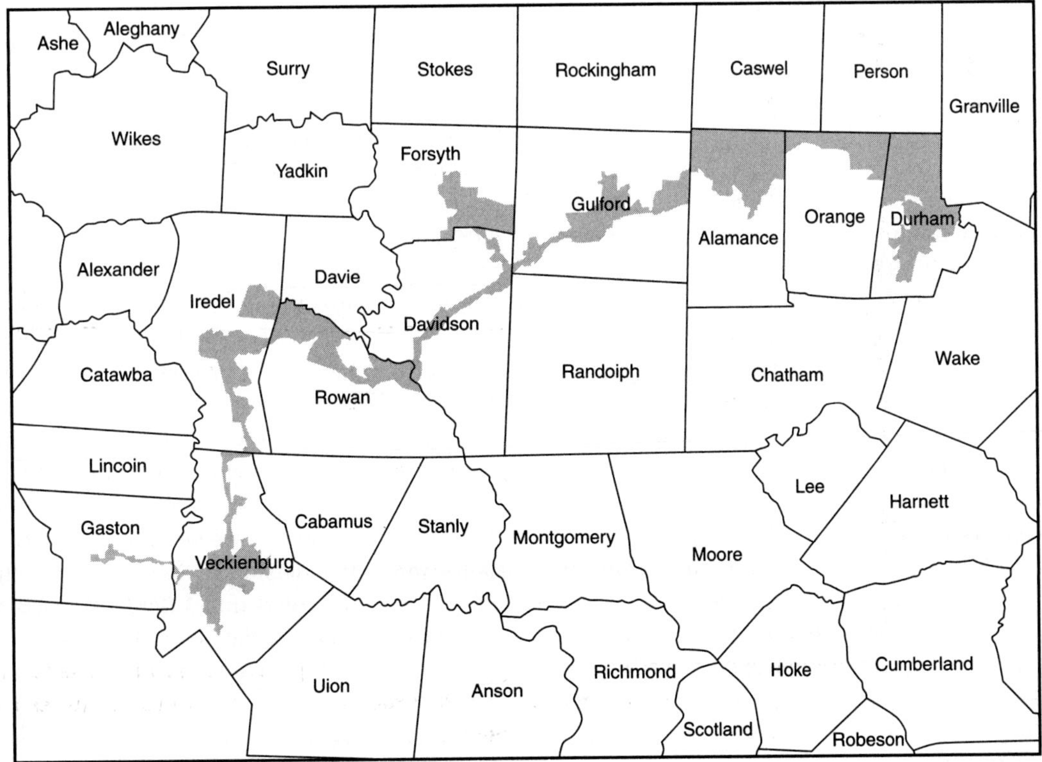

Figure 10-4 North Carolina Congressional District 12, 1992

the Bush administration, the state legislature used that opportunity to carve a second black-majority district. The resulting legislative district was irregularly shaped. One state legislator quoted in the majority opinion observed, "If you drove down the interstate with both car doors open, you'd kill most of the people in the district." Shaw objected to being moved from the Second Congressional District to the newly formed majority-minority Twelfth Congressional District. She filed a lawsuit against the attorney general of the United States, who by the time the case reached the Supreme Court was Janet Reno. The local district court rejected the lawsuit. Shaw appealed to the Supreme Court of the United States.

The Supreme Court by a 5–4 vote ruled that the United States and North Carolina had engaged in an unconstitutional racial gerrymander. Justice O'Connor's majority opinion insisted that race-conscious electoral districting had to meet the same strict scrutiny standard as other race-conscious programs. Why did Justice O'Connor reach that conclusion? Why did the dissenting judges disagree? Who had the better argument? The 5–4 split in Shaw *pitted the more conservative justices on the early Rehnquist Court against the more liberal justices. Republican elected officials, by comparison, were at least as supportive of the Twelfth District as Democrats. How do you explain the differences between elected officials and judges on racial gerrymanders?*

JUSTICE O'CONNOR delivered the opinion of the Court.

. . .

Classifications of citizens solely on the basis of race "are by their very nature odious to a free people whose institutions are founded upon the doctrine of equality." They threaten to stigmatize individuals by reason of their membership in a racial group and to incite racial hostility. Accordingly, we have held that the Fourteenth Amendment requires state legislation that expressly distinguishes among citizens because of their race to be narrowly tailored to further a compelling governmental interest.

. . .

Appellants contend that redistricting legislation that is so bizarre on its face that it is "unexplainable on grounds other than race," demands the same close scrutiny that we give other state laws that classify citizens by race. Our voting rights precedents support that conclusion.

. . .

The difficulty of proof . . . does not mean that a racial gerrymander, once established, should receive less scrutiny under the Equal Protection Clause than other state legislation classifying citizens by race. Moreover, it seems clear to us that proof sometimes will not be difficult at all. In some exceptional cases, a reapportionment plan may be so highly irregular that, on its face, it rationally cannot be understood as anything other than an effort to "segregat[e] . . . voters" on the basis of race. *Gomillion v. Lightfoot (1960)*, in which a tortured municipal boundary line was drawn to exclude black voters, was such a case. . . .

Put differently, we believe that reapportionment is one area in which appearances do matter. A reapportionment plan that includes in one district individuals who belong to the same race, but who are otherwise widely separated by geographical and political boundaries, and who may have little in common with one another but the color of their skin, bears an uncomfortable resemblance to political apartheid. It reinforces the perception that members of the same racial group—regardless of their age, education, economic status, or the community in which they live—think alike, share the same political interests, and will prefer the same candidates at the polls. We have rejected such perceptions elsewhere as impermissible racial stereotypes. . . . By perpetuating such notions, a racial gerrymander may exacerbate the very patterns of racial bloc voting that majority-minority districting is sometimes said to counteract.

The message that such districting sends to elected representatives is equally pernicious. When a district obviously is created solely to effectuate the perceived common interests of one racial group, elected officials are more likely to believe that their primary obligation is to represent only the members of that group, rather than their constituency as a whole. This is altogether antithetical to our system of representative democracy. . . .

For these reasons, we conclude that a plaintiff challenging a reapportionment statute under the Equal Protection Clause may state a claim by alleging that the legislation, though race-neutral on its face, rationally cannot be understood as anything other than an effort to separate voters into different districts on the basis of race, and that the separation lacks sufficient justification. . . .

The state appellees suggest that a covered jurisdiction may have a compelling interest in creating majority-minority districts in order to comply with the Voting Rights Act. The States certainly have a very strong interest in complying with federal antidiscrimination laws that are constitutionally valid as interpreted and as applied. But in the context of a Fourteenth Amendment challenge, courts must bear in mind the difference between what the law permits and what it requires.

For example, on remand North Carolina might claim that it adopted the revised plan in order to comply with the §5 "nonretrogression" principle. Under that principle, a proposed voting change cannot be precleared if it will lead to "a retrogression in the position of racial minorities with respect to their effective exercise of the electoral franchise." . . .

. . . [W]e do not read . . . any of our . . . §5 cases to give covered jurisdictions carte blanche to engage in racial gerrymandering in the name of nonretrogression. A reapportionment plan would not be narrowly tailored to the goal of avoiding retrogression if the State went beyond what was reasonably necessary to avoid retrogression. . . .

. . .

Racial classifications of any sort pose the risk of lasting harm to our society. They reinforce the belief, held by too many for too much of our history, that individuals should be judged by the color of their skin. Racial classifications with respect to voting carry particular dangers. Racial gerrymandering, even for remedial purposes, may balkanize us into competing racial factions; it threatens to carry us further from the goal of a political system in which race no longer matters—a goal that the Fourteenth and Fifteenth Amendments embody, and to which the Nation continues to aspire. It is for these reasons that race-based districting by our state legislatures demands close judicial scrutiny.

. . .

JUSTICE WHITE, with whom JUSTICE BLACKMUN and JUSTICE STEVENS join, dissenting.

. . .

The grounds for my disagreement with the majority are simply stated: Appellants have not presented a cognizable claim, because they have not alleged a cognizable injury. To date, we have held that only two types of state voting practices could give rise to a constitutional claim. The first involves direct and outright deprivation of the right to vote, for example by means of a poll tax or literacy test. . . . Plainly, this variety is not implicated by appellants' allegations and need not detain us further. The second type of unconstitutional practice is that which "affects the political strength of various groups" in violation of the Equal Protection Clause. As for this latter category, we have insisted that members of the political or racial group demonstrate that the challenged action have the intent and effect of unduly diminishing their influence on the political process.

. . .

. . . [W]e have limited such claims by insisting upon a showing that "the political processes . . . were not equally open to participation by the group in question—that its members had less opportunity than did other residents in the district to participate in the political processes and to elect legislators of their choice." . . .

. . .

. . . [I]t strains credulity to suggest that North Carolina's purpose in creating a second majority-minority district was to discriminate against members of the majority group by "impair[ing] or burden[ing their] opportunity . . . to participate in the political process." . . . Whites constitute roughly 76% of the total population and 79% of the voting age population in North Carolina. Yet, under the State's plan, they still constitute a voting majority in 10 (or 83%) of the 12 congressional districts. Though they might be dissatisfied at the prospect of casting a vote for a losing candidate—a lot shared by many, including a disproportionate number of minority voters—surely they cannot complain of discriminatory treatment.

. . .

The other part of the majority's explanation of its holding is related to its simultaneous discomfort and fascination with irregularly shaped districts. Lack of compactness or contiguity, like uncouth district lines, certainly is a helpful indicator that some form of gerrymandering (racial or other) might have taken place and that "something may be amiss." . . .

But while district irregularities may provide strong indicia of a potential gerrymander, they do no more than that. In particular, they have no bearing on whether the plan ultimately is found to violate the Constitution. Given two districts drawn on similar, race-based grounds, the one does not become more injurious than the other simply by virtue of being snakelike, at least so far as the Constitution is concerned and absent any evidence of differential racial impact. . . . It is shortsighted as well, for a regularly shaped district can just as effectively effectuate racially discriminatory gerrymandering as an odd-shaped one. By focusing on looks rather than impact, the majority "immediately casts attention in the wrong direction—toward superficialities of shape and size, rather than toward the political realities of district composition." . . .

. . .

JUSTICE BLACKMUN, dissenting . . .

JUSTICE STEVENS, dissenting.

. . .

I believe that the Equal Protection Clause is violated when the State creates . . . uncouth district boundaries . . . for the sole purpose of making it more difficult for members of a minority group to win an election. The duty to govern impartially is abused when a group with power over the electoral process defines electoral boundaries solely to enhance its own political strength at the expense of any weaker group. That duty, however, is not violated when the majority acts to facilitate the election of a member of a group that lacks such power because it remains underrepresented in the state legislature—whether that group is defined by political affiliation, by common economic interests, or by religious, ethnic, or racial characteristics. The difference between constitutional and unconstitutional gerrymanders has nothing to do with whether they are based on assumptions about the groups they affect, but whether their purpose is to enhance the power of the group in control of the districting process at the expense of any minority group, and thereby to strengthen the unequal distribution of electoral power.

. . . If it is permissible to draw boundaries to provide adequate representation for rural voters, for union members, for Hasidic Jews, for Polish Americans, or for Republicans, it necessarily follows that it is permissible to do the same thing for members of the very minority group whose history in the United States gave birth to the Equal Protection Clause.

JUSTICE SOUTER, dissenting.

. . .

. . . Unlike other contexts in which we have addressed the State's conscious use of race, electoral districting calls for decisions that nearly always require some consideration of race for legitimate reasons where there is a racially mixed population. As long as members of racial groups have the commonality of interest implicit in our ability to talk about concepts like "minority voting strength," and "dilution of minority votes," and as long as racial bloc voting takes place, legislators will have to take race into account in order to avoid dilution of minority voting strength in the districting plans they adopt. One need look no further than the Voting Rights Act to understand that this may be required. . . .

In districting, . . . the mere placement of an individual in one district instead of another denies no one a right or benefit provided to others. All citizens may register, vote, and be represented in whatever district, the individual voter has a right to vote in each election, and the election will result in the voter's representation. . . . It is true, of course, that one's vote may be more or less effective depending on the interests of the other individuals who are in one's district, and our cases recognize the reality that members of the same race often have shared interests. "Dilution" thus refers to the effects of districting decisions not on an individual's political power viewed in isolation, but on the political power of a group. . . .

. . . [B]ecause there frequently will be a constitutionally permissible use of race in electoral districting, as exemplified by the consideration of race to comply with the Voting Rights Act . . . , it has seemed more appropriate for the Court to identify impermissible uses by describing particular effects sufficiently serious to justify recognition under the Fourteenth Amendment. Under our cases there is in general a requirement that in order to obtain relief under the Fourteenth Amendment, the purpose and effect of the districting must be to devalue the effectiveness of a voter compared to what, as a group member, he would otherwise be able to enjoy. . . .

IX. Equality

MAJOR DEVELOPMENTS

- Fierce battles in states over funding for public schools
- Strict curbs on affirmative action
- Emergence of strong gender gaps in American constitutional politics

Reagan conservatives sought to preserve what they believed was the constitutional status quo on equality issues before the late 1960s. Reagan and his allies celebrated *Brown v. Board of Education* (1954). Conservatives endorsed the bans on racial and gender discrimination decreed by the Civil Rights Act of 1964. Many, however, thought that success had spoiled the civil rights movement. Civil rights activists, Reagan and others complained, were now seeking special privileges rather than equal treatment. More generally, conservatives insisted that new demands for equality by persons of color, women, and others often ignored real differences between people, imposed racial and gender classifications that repeated the odious policies of the past, and called on judges to substitute their elite perspectives for those of democratically elected officials.

Many liberals claimed that this conservative willingness to endorse the constitutional status quo was based less on sincere commitments to racial and gender equality than on a pragmatic concession that the constitutional clock could not be turned further back than 1964. Noting the strong appeals that Republicans made to southern whites, civil rights activists insisted that opposition to such policies as affirmative action and comparative worth were the most recent manifestations of the same prejudices that had underpinned Jim Crow. Liberals in the 1980s maintained that *Brown* was based on anti-subordination, not anti-classification principles, and that the decision was certainly not limited to racial classifications. Achieving the promise of *Brown* required a broad-scale attack on numerous status-based inequalities, abandoning "neutral" policies that in practice favored white men, and creating strong affirmative action programs that would bring members of historically disadvantaged groups into positions of political, economic, and educational influence.

A. Equality Under Law

Reagan conservatives maintained that the equal protection clause forbade only intentional race discrimination and some intentional gender discrimination. The 1988 *Guidelines on Constitutional Litigation* informed federal attorneys that, "with exception of racial equality, which under the Fourteenth Amendment is entitled to special scrutiny," they "should avoid making arguments, and should attack arguments advanced by opposing counsel, for creating new suspect classes not found in the Constitution." Reagan and his political allies also sought to narrow the fundamental rights strand of equal protection jurisprudence. Federal attorneys were informed that they "should avoid making arguments, and should attack arguments advanced by opposing counsel, for creating new fundamental rights not found in the Constitution."[29]

This effort to cabin the equal protection clause was mostly successful. No new suspect classifications were created. The late Burger and early Rehnquist Courts did not find any new fundamental rights that warranted heightened scrutiny. Nevertheless, in *City of Cleburne, Texas v. Cleburne Living Center* (1985), the Supreme Court ignored an amicus brief from the Reagan administration and unanimously declared unconstitutional a city ordinance banning a group home for the mentally retarded. Justice White's majority opinion claimed to use rational scrutiny. He asserted that the ban on the group home "appears to us to rest on an irrational prejudice against the mentally retarded." Justice Marshall was skeptical. Insisting that laws discriminating against the mentally handicapped be subject to heightened scrutiny, he wrote, "Cleburne's ordinance surely would be valid under the traditional rational-basis test applicable to economic and commercial regulation."

State courts more aggressively used state equal protection clauses to create new suspect classes and fundamental rights, particularly when adjudicating attacks on public school funding. "The reluctance of the U.S. Supreme Court to declare school finance equity a constitutional right," Douglas Reed notes, "created a decentralized, state-by state litigation effort."[30] Some state courts rejected such claims, interpreting state equality clauses as protecting no more rights than the federal equal protection clauses protected. Many state courts insisted that their state constitution demanded far more egalitarian school funding policies than the federal Constitution did. The Supreme Court of Kentucky in *Rose, et al. v. Council for Better Education* (KY 1989), when ordering the state legislature to provide more funds for schools and allocate those funds

---

29. U.S. Department of Justice, Office of Legal Policy, *Guidelines on Constitutional Litigation*, 77, 78.

30. Douglas S. Reed, *On Equal Terms: The Constitutional Politics of Educational Opportunity* (Princeton, NJ: Princeton University Press, 2001), xix. For another excellent study of the constitutional politics of public school financing, see Michael Paris, *Framing Equal Opportunity: Law and the Politics of School Reform* (Stanford, CA: Stanford University Press, 2010).

more equitably, asserted, "The children of the poor and the children of the rich, the children who live in the poor districts and the children who live in the rich districts must be given the same opportunity and access to an adequate education."[31] By the mid-1990s many state judiciaries were engaged in protracted battles with state legislatures over the constitutionally appropriate means for financing public education.

The status of illegal aliens in the United States raised questions about who was equal under law, as well as questions about rights to equal education. National parties were slow to take strong positions. The Reagan administration was more proactive, maintaining that "withholding benefits from illegal aliens" would "reduce the incentive for illegal immigration" and "reduce the tax burden on Americans."[32] States took the lead in passing statutes denying government services to illegal aliens. The Burger Court did not look kindly on those laws. In *Plyler v. Doe* (1982) a 5–4 judicial majority declared unconstitutional a Texas law permitting local school boards to exclude from public schools children who were illegally in the United States.

Plyler v. Doe, 457 U.S. 202 (1982)

The Texas legislature authorized local officials to exclude from public schools all children who had not legally been admitted into the United States. In 1977 numerous children who could not prove their legal status filed a class action against James Plyler, the superintendent of the Tyler Independent School District in Texas. They claimed that the Texas law violated the due process and equal protection clauses of the Fourteenth Amendment. The local federal court issued an injunction forbidding Plyler from excluding the children from public schools. That decision was sustained by the Court of Appeals for the Fifth Circuit. Texas appealed to the Supreme Court of the United States.

The Supreme Court by a 5–4 vote declared unconstitutional the Texas law banning undocumented children from public schools. Justice Brennan's majority opinion held that no good reason existed to deprive these children of an education. Brennan insisted that laws discriminating against the children of illegal aliens merited heightened constitutional scrutiny. Why did he make this claim? Why did the dissenters disagree? Who had the better argument? Chief Justice Burger's dissent concludes, "The solution to this seemingly intractable problem is to defer to the political processes, unpalatable as that may be to some." Was he correct? Which governing institution should be responsible for determining the status of illegal aliens and their children?

JUSTICE BRENNAN delivered the opinion of the Court.

. . .

"The Fourteenth Amendment to the Constitution is not confined to the protection of citizens. It says: 'Nor shall any state deprive any person of life, liberty, or property without due process of law; nor deny to any person within its jurisdiction the equal protection of the laws.' These provisions are universal in their application, to all persons within the territorial jurisdiction, without regard to any differences of race, of color, or of nationality; and the protection of the laws is a pledge of the protection of equal laws."

. . .

Use of the phrase "within its jurisdiction" thus does not detract from, but rather confirms, the understanding that the protection of the Fourteenth Amendment extends to anyone, citizen or stranger, who is subject to the laws of a State, and reaches into every corner of a State's territory. That a person's initial entry into a State, or into the United States, was unlawful, and that he may for that reason be expelled, cannot negate the simple fact of his presence within the State's territorial perimeter. Given such presence, he is subject to the full range of obligations imposed by the State's civil and criminal laws. And until he leaves the jurisdiction—either voluntarily, or involuntarily in accordance with the Constitution and laws of the United States—he is entitled to the equal protection of the laws that a State may choose to establish.

. . .

Persuasive arguments support the view that a State may withhold its beneficence from those whose very presence within the United States is the product of their own unlawful conduct. These arguments do not apply with the same force to classifications imposing disabilities on the minor children of such illegal entrants. At the least, those who elect to enter our territory by stealth and in violation of our law should be prepared to bear the consequences, including, but not limited to, deportation. But the children of those

31. *Rose, et al. v. Council for Better Education*, 790 Ky. 55 (1989).

32. U.S. Department of Justice, Office of Legal Policy, *Constitution in the Year 2000*, 166.

illegal entrants are not comparably situated. Their "parents have the ability to conform their conduct to societal norms," and presumably the ability to remove themselves from the State's jurisdiction; but the children who are plaintiffs in these cases "can affect neither their parents' conduct nor their own status." . . .

Of course, undocumented status is not irrelevant to any proper legislative goal. Nor is undocumented status an absolutely immutable characteristic since it is the product of conscious, indeed unlawful, action. But [the Texas law] is directed against children, and imposes its discriminatory burden on the basis of a legal characteristic over which children can have little control. It is thus difficult to conceive of a rational justification for penalizing these children for their presence within the United States. . . .

Public education is not a "right" granted to individuals by the Constitution. But neither is it merely some governmental "benefit" indistinguishable from other forms of social welfare legislation. Both the importance of education in maintaining our basic institutions, and the lasting impact of its deprivation on the life of the child, mark the distinction. . . . We have recognized "the public schools as a most vital civic institution for the preservation of a democratic system of government." . . . In addition, education provides the basic tools by which individuals might lead economically productive lives to the benefit of us all. In sum, education has a fundamental role in maintaining the fabric of our society. We cannot ignore the significant social costs borne by our Nation when select groups are denied the means to absorb the values and skills upon which our social order rests.

. . .

These well-settled principles allow us to determine the proper level of deference. . . . Undocumented aliens cannot be treated as a suspect class because their presence in this country in violation of federal law is not a "constitutional irrelevancy." Nor is education a fundamental right; a State need not justify by compelling necessity every variation in the manner in which education is provided to its population. But more is involved in these cases than the abstract question whether §21.031 discriminates against a suspect class, or whether education is a fundamental right. Section 21.031 imposes a lifetime hardship on a discrete class of children not accountable for their disabling status. The stigma of illiteracy will mark them for the rest of their lives. By denying these children a basic education, we deny them the ability to live within the structure of our civic institutions, and foreclose any realistic possibility that they will contribute in even the smallest way to the progress of our Nation. In determining the rationality of §21.031, we may appropriately take into account its costs to the Nation and to the innocent children who are its victims. In light of these countervailing costs, the discrimination contained in §21.031 can hardly be considered rational unless it furthers some substantial goal of the State.

. . .

. . . [A]ppellants appear to suggest that the State may seek to protect itself from an influx of illegal immigrants. While a State might have an interest in mitigating the potentially harsh economic effects of sudden shifts in population, §21.031 hardly offers an effective method of dealing with an urgent demographic or economic problem. There is no evidence in the record suggesting that illegal entrants impose any significant burden on the State's economy. To the contrary, the available evidence suggests that illegal aliens underutilize public services, while contributing their labor to the local economy and tax money to the state fisc. . . .

. . . [W]hile it is apparent that a State may "not . . . reduce expenditures for education by barring [some arbitrarily chosen class of] children from its schools," appellants suggest that undocumented children are appropriately singled out for exclusion because of the special burdens they impose on the State's ability to provide high-quality public education. But the record in no way supports the claim that exclusion of undocumented children is likely to improve the overall quality of education in the State. . . .

. . . The State has no assurance that any child, citizen or not, will employ the education provided by the State within the confines of the State's borders. In any event, the record is clear that many of the undocumented children disabled by this classification will remain in this country indefinitely, and that some will become lawful residents or citizens of the United States. It is difficult to understand precisely what the State hopes to achieve by promoting the creation and perpetuation of a subclass of illiterates within our boundaries, surely adding to the problems and costs of unemployment, welfare, and crime. It is thus clear that whatever savings might be achieved by denying these children an education, they are wholly insubstantial in light of the costs involved to these children, the State, and the Nation.

If the State is to deny a discrete group of innocent children the free public education that it offers to other children residing within its borders, that denial must be justified by a showing that it furthers some substantial state interest. . . .

JUSTICE MARSHALL, concurring.

. . . It continues to be my view that a class-based denial of public education is utterly incompatible with the Equal Protection Clause of the Fourteenth Amendment.

JUSTICE BLACKMUN, concurring.

. . .

. . . [W]hen the State provides an education to some and denies it to others, it immediately and inevitably creates class distinctions of a type fundamentally inconsistent with . . . the Equal Protection Clause. . . . [C]lassifications involving the complete denial of education are in a sense unique, for they strike at the heart of equal protection values by involving the State in the creation of permanent class distinctions. In a sense, then, denial of an education is the analogue of denial of the right to vote: the former relegates the individual to second-class social status; the latter places him at a permanent political disadvantage.

This conclusion is fully consistent with [*San Antonio Independent School District v. Rodriguez* (1973)]. The Court there reserved judgment on the constitutionality of a state system that "occasioned an absolute denial of educational opportunities to any of its children," noting that "no charge fairly could be made that the system [at issue in *Rodriguez*] fails to provide each child with an opportunity to acquire . . . basic minimal skills." . . . Here, however, the State has undertaken to provide an education to most of the children residing within its borders. And, in contrast to the situation in *Rodriguez*, it does not take an advanced degree to predict the effects of a complete denial of education upon those children targeted by the State's classification. In such circumstances, the voting decisions suggest that the State must offer something more than a rational basis for its classification.

JUSTICE POWELL, concurring.

. . .

Our review in a case such as these is properly heightened. . . . The classification at issue deprives a group of children of the opportunity for education afforded all other children simply because they have been assigned a legal status due to a violation of law by their parents. These children thus have been singled out for a lifelong penalty and stigma. A legislative classification that threatens the creation of an underclass of future citizens and residents cannot be reconciled with one of the fundamental purposes of the Fourteenth Amendment. In these unique circumstances, the Court properly may require that the State's interests be substantial and that the means bear a "fair and substantial relation" to these interests.

. . .

CHIEF JUSTICE BURGER, with whom JUSTICE WHITE, JUSTICE REHNQUIST, and JUSTICE O'CONNOR join, dissenting.

The dispositive issue in these cases, simply put, is whether, for purposes of allocating its finite resources, a state has a legitimate reason to differentiate between persons who are lawfully within the state and those who are unlawfully there. The distinction the State of Texas has drawn—based not only upon its own legitimate interests but on classifications established by the Federal Government in its immigration laws and policies—is not unconstitutional.

. . .

The Court first suggests that these illegal alien children, although not a suspect class, are entitled to special solicitude under the Equal Protection Clause because they lack "control" over or "responsibility" for their unlawful entry into this country. . . . However, the Equal Protection Clause does not preclude legislators from classifying among persons on the basis of factors and characteristics over which individuals may be said to lack "control." Indeed, in some circumstances persons generally, and children in particular, may have little control over or responsibility for such things as their ill health, need for public assistance, or place of residence. Yet a state legislature is not barred from considering, for example, relevant differences between the mentally healthy and the mentally ill, or between the residents of different counties, simply because these may be factors unrelated to individual choice or to any "wrongdoing." The Equal Protection Clause protects against arbitrary and irrational classifications, and against invidious discrimination stemming from prejudice and hostility; it is not an all-encompassing "equalizer" designed to eradicate every distinction for which persons are not "responsible."

. . .

The importance of education is beyond dispute. Yet we have held repeatedly that the importance of a governmental service does not elevate it to the status of a "fundamental right" for purposes of equal protection analysis. . . . Moreover, the Court points to no meaningful way to distinguish between education and other governmental benefits in this context. Is the Court suggesting that education is more "fundamental" than food, shelter, or medical care?

. . .

Once it is conceded—as the Court does—that illegal aliens are not a suspect class, and that education is not a fundamental right, our inquiry should focus on and be limited to whether the legislative classification at issue bears a rational relationship to a legitimate state purpose.

The State contends primarily that §21.031 serves to prevent undue depletion of its limited revenues available for education, and to preserve the fiscal integrity of the State's school-financing system against an ever-increasing flood of illegal aliens—aliens over whose entry or continued presence it has no control. Of course such fiscal concerns alone could not justify discrimination against a suspect class or an arbitrary and irrational denial of benefits to a particular group of persons. Yet I assume no Member of this Court would argue that prudent conservation of finite state revenues is per se an illegitimate goal. . . .

Without laboring what will undoubtedly seem obvious to many, it simply is not "irrational" for a state to conclude that it does not have the same responsibility to provide benefits for persons whose very presence in the state and this country is illegal as it does to provide for persons lawfully present. By definition, illegal aliens have no right whatever to be here, and the state may reasonably, and constitutionally, elect not to provide them with governmental services at the expense of those who are lawfully in the state.

. . .

The Constitution does not provide a cure for every social ill, nor does it vest judges with a mandate to try to remedy every social problem. Moreover, when this Court rushes in to remedy what it perceives to be the failings of the political processes, it deprives those processes of an opportunity to function. When the political institutions are not forced to exercise constitutionally allocated powers and responsibilities, those powers, like muscles not used, tend to atrophy. Today's cases, I regret to say, present yet another example of unwarranted judicial action which in the long run tends to contribute to the weakening of our political processes.

. . .

The solution to this seemingly intractable problem is to defer to the political processes, unpalatable as that may be to some.

B. Race

The constitutional politics of racial equality witnessed struggles over the legacy of *Brown v. Board of Education* (1954). All prominent political actors celebrated *Brown* as a landmark statement of fundamental American values. Constitutional arguments about equality often referred to *Brown* instead of the text or history of the Fourteenth Amendment. Nevertheless, this celebratory consensus masked bitter disputes over what *Brown* meant and what *Brown* had achieved.

Reagan conservatives regarded *Brown* as resting on the principle that racial and related classifications were constitutionally odious. Racial classifications were wrong because no real differences existed between persons of different races. This anti-classification logic explains why Reagan conservatives vigorously opposed state- and federally mandated affirmative action programs, or at least those that explicitly relied on race when making admissions or employment decisions. "Discrimination on the basis of race," Justice Scalia wrote in *City of Richmond v. J. A. Croson Co.* (1989), "is illegal, immoral, unconstitutional, inherently wrong, and destructive of democratic society." Anti-classification arguments frequently maintained that the promise of *Brown* had largely been achieved. They observed that Americans by 1980 had abandoned laws that explicitly granted rights to persons of one race but not another. While government needed to be vigilant to prevent backsliding, proponents of this view argued, policies such as continued federal court efforts to integrate schools and affirmative action were both unnecessary and destructive, unless they were efforts to remedy the particular victims of racial discrimination or specific acts of past racial discrimination. Conservatives remained committed to eradicating de jure segregation, or segregation clearly rooted in state decisions. They opposed efforts to combat de facto segregation, or segregation rooted in private decisions by individuals to associate with members of their race.

Many progressive liberals regarded *Brown* as resting on the principle that no group of persons should have a subordinate status in the United States. So understood, *Brown* was a precedent that supported the rights of woman, aliens, homosexuals, and other historically disadvantaged groups. Anti-subordinationists insisted that Jim Crow and affirmative action policies were fundamentally different. The former were intended to create a subordinate class. The latter were aimed at achieving greater social equality. Persons committed to the anti-subordination interpretation of *Brown* maintained that the promise of that decision was largely unfulfilled. Too many African Americans, women, and members of historically disadvantaged groups were poorly educated, remained in poverty, and were outside the corridors of power. Justice Marshall's dissent in *Croson* spoke of "the tragic and indelible fact that discrimination against blacks and other racial minorities in this Nation has pervaded our Nation's history and continues to scar our society." Affirmative action and continued judicial efforts to integrate public schools, in this view, were among the many policies necessary for the United States to become a truly racially egalitarian society. Progressive liberals did not sharply distinguish between de jure and de facto discrimination. What conservatives claimed were private decisions to associate with members of one's race, progressives insisted were another baneful consequence of past state-mandated racial discrimination.

The constitutional law of racial equality was often at odds with actual practice. Local race-conscious policies often flourished, even as the Supreme Court in *Croson* insisted that such policies satisfy the same strict scrutiny standard as laws discriminating against persons of color. Cities interested in establishing minority set-asides (programs that required that a certain percentage of public contracts be given to persons of color) simply commissioned an expensive disparity study that demonstrated that past racial prejudice in their community explained the lack of minority contractors or subcontractors.[33] Many American public schools and school systems exhibited considerable segregation, even as Supreme Court opinions proclaimed that the last vestiges of state-mandated segregation had disappeared. Gary Orfield's study of public schooling in the early 1990s concluded, "More than forty years after *Brown*, racial separation both between and within school districts is an ordinary, unnoticed fixture in K–12 education."[34]

Federal judges began relinquishing control over school districts previously found in violation of the principles announced in *Brown v. Board of Education* (1954). The early Rehnquist Court established standards that encouraged lower federal courts to end their oversight over the desegregation process. *Board of Education of Oklahoma City Public Schools v. Dowell* (1991) declared, "Dissolving a desegregation decree after the local authorities have operated in compliance with it for a reasonable period of time properly recognizes that necessary concern for the important values of local control of public school systems dictates that a federal court's regulatory control of such systems not extend beyond the time required to remedy the effects of past intentional discrimination." *Freeman v. Pitts* (1992) permitted the justices to return control to the local school district even if public schools remained highly segregated as long as the trial judge concluded that present segregation was de facto and better explained by recent demographic trends than by past de jure official discrimination.

Affirmative action replaced busing as the most contentious racial issue dividing Americans. Reagan Republicans insisted that race-conscious employment and university admissions policies were unconstitutional unless they were narrowly tailored to remedy identifiable victims of discrimination. Liberal Democrats as vigorously defended affirmative action policies. The Supreme Court consistently sided with conservatives when adjudicating state and local affirmative action programs. *Wygant v. Jackson Board of Education* (1986) struck down a contract that gave teachers of color special protections against layoffs during recessions. *City of Richmond v. J. A. Croson* (1989) declared unconstitutional a set-aside program that required contractors doing business with the city to give at least 30 percent of their subcontracts to minority-owned businesses. The opinions for the Court in both cases insisted that

33. See Martin J. Sweet, *Merely Judgment: Ignoring, Evading, and Trumping the Supreme Court* (Charlottesville: University of Virginia Press, 2010).

34. Gary Orfield, Susan E. Eaton, and the Harvard Project on School Desegregation, *Dismantling Desegregation: The Quiet Reversal of* Brown v. Board of Education (New York: New Press, 1996), xiv.

affirmative action programs were subject to the same constitutional standards as Jim Crow segregation. After noting that the justices had "consistently repudiated distinctions between citizens solely because of their ancestry as being odious to a free people whose institutions are founded upon the doctrine of equality," Justice Powell's plurality opinion in *Wygant* asserted, "The level of scrutiny does not change merely because the challenged classification operates against a group that historically has not been subject to government discrimination." *Croson* more clearly stated that strict scrutiny was the appropriate standard for reviewing state and local affirmative action programs.

Liberals fared better when the Supreme Court examined a federal affirmative action policy. By a 5–4 vote the Supreme Court in *Metro Broadcasting, Inc. v. FCC* (1990) sustained an administrative decision to consider race when awarding broadcast licenses. Justice Brennan's majority opinion insisted that intermediate scrutiny was the appropriate standard of review in light of the special congressional responsibility to enforce the equal protection clause. He stated, "Benign race-conscious measures mandated by Congress . . . are constitutionally permissible to the extent that they serve important governmental objectives within the power of Congress and are substantially related to achievement of those objectives." The Federal Communications Commission's minority enhancement policy, Brennan concluded, was a constitutional means to "promote programming diversity."

City of Richmond v. J. A. Croson Co., 488 U.S. 469 (1989)

The Richmond City Council in 1983 passed an ordinance requiring contractors who did business with the city to give at least 30 percent of their subcontracts to minority-owned businesses. This policy was partly based on evidence that although the community was 50 percent African American, less than 1 percent of all city contracts went to persons of color. That fall the J. A. Croson Company was denied a contract to install plumbing fixtures at a city jail because the company failed to abide by the set-aside policy. Croson sued the city of Richmond, claiming that the minority set-aside program was unconstitutional. After a series of decisions, appeals, and remands the Court of Appeals for the Fourth Circuit declared the Richmond ordinance unconstitutional. Richmond appealed to the Supreme Court of the United States.

The Supreme Court by a 6–3 vote agreed that the minority set-aside was unconstitutional. Justice O'Connor's opinion for the Court insisted that Richmond's race-conscious policy did not satisfy the strict scrutiny standard. Why did Justice O'Connor insist that the policy meet this standard? Why did Justice Marshall disagree? In Fullilove v. Klutznick *(1980) the Supreme Court sustained a similar federal minority set-aside program. How did O'Connor distinguish* Croson *from* Fullilove*? Was that distinction sound? Was that distinction sincere? How do you explain increasing judicial hostility to race-conscious programs?*

JUSTICE O'CONNOR announced the judgment of the Court.

. . .

. . . Congress, unlike any State or political subdivision, has a specific constitutional mandate to enforce the dictates of the Fourteenth Amendment. The power to "enforce" may at times also include the power to define situations which *Congress* determines threaten principles of equality and to adopt prophylactic rules to deal with those situations. . . .

That Congress may identify and redress the effects of society-wide discrimination does not mean that, *a fortiori*, the States and their political subdivisions are free to decide that such remedies are appropriate. Section 1 of the Fourteenth Amendment is an explicit *constraint* on state power, and the States must undertake any remedial efforts in accordance with that provision. To hold otherwise would be to cede control over the content of the Equal Protection Clause to the 50 state legislatures and their myriad political subdivisions. The mere recitation of a benign or compensatory purpose for the use of a racial classification would essentially entitle the States to exercise the full power of Congress under §5 of the Fourteenth Amendment and insulate any racial classification from judicial scrutiny under §1. We believe that such a result would be contrary to the intentions of the Framers of the Fourteenth Amendment, who desired to place clear limits on the States' use of race as a criterion for legislative action, and to have the federal courts enforce those limitations. . . .

It would seem equally clear, however, that a state or local subdivision (if delegated the authority from the State) has the authority to eradicate the effects of private discrimination within its own legislative jurisdiction. This authority must, of course, be exercised within the constraints of §1 of the Fourteenth

Amendment. . . . As a matter of state law, the city of Richmond has legislative authority over its procurement policies, and can use its spending powers to remedy private discrimination, if it identifies that discrimination with the particularity required by the Fourteenth Amendment.

Thus, if the city could show that it had essentially become a "passive participant" in a system of racial exclusion practiced by elements of the local construction industry, we think it clear that the city could take affirmative steps to dismantle such a system. It is beyond dispute that any public entity, state or federal, has a compelling interest in assuring that public dollars, drawn from the tax contributions of all citizens, do not serve to finance the evil of private prejudice.

. . . The Richmond Plan denies certain citizens the opportunity to compete for a fixed percentage of public contracts based solely upon their race. To whatever racial group these citizens belong, their "personal rights" to be treated with equal dignity and respect are implicated by a rigid rule erecting race as the sole criterion in an aspect of public decisionmaking.

Absent searching judicial inquiry into the justification for such race-based measures, there is simply no way of determining what classifications are "benign" or "remedial" and what classifications are in fact motivated by illegitimate notions of racial inferiority or simple racial politics. Indeed, the purpose of strict scrutiny is to "smoke out" illegitimate uses of race by assuring that the legislative body is pursuing a goal important enough to warrant use of a highly suspect tool. The test also ensures that the means chosen "fit" this compelling goal so closely that there is little or no possibility that the motive for the classification was illegitimate racial prejudice or stereotype.

Classifications based on race carry a danger of stigmatic harm. Unless they are strictly reserved for remedial settings, they may in fact promote notions of racial inferiority and lead to a politics of racial hostility. We thus reaffirm the view . . . that the standard of review under the Equal Protection Clause is not dependent on the race of those burdened or benefited by a particular classification.

. . .

In this case, blacks constitute approximately 50% of the population of the city of Richmond. Five of the nine seats on the city council are held by blacks. The concern that a political majority will more easily act to the disadvantage of a minority based on unwarranted assumptions or incomplete facts would seem to militate for, not against, the application of heightened judicial scrutiny in this case. . . .

. . .

. . . [A] generalized assertion that there has been past discrimination in an entire industry provides no guidance for a legislative body to determine the precise scope of the injury it seeks to remedy. It "has no logical stopping point." "Relief" for such an ill-defined wrong could extend until the percentage of public contracts awarded to MBE's [minority business enterprises] in Richmond mirrored the percentage of minorities in the population as a whole.

. . .

. . . The 30% quota cannot in any realistic sense be tied to any injury suffered by anyone. . . .

. . .

Reliance on the disparity between the number of prime contracts awarded to minority firms and the minority population of the city of Richmond is similarly misplaced. There is no doubt that "[w]here gross statistical disparities can be shown, they alone in a proper case may constitute prima facie proof of a pattern or practice of discrimination" under Title VII. But it is equally clear that "[w]hen special qualifications are required to fill particular jobs, comparisons to the general population (rather than to the smaller group of individuals who possess the necessary qualifications) may have little probative value."

In this case, the city does not even know how many MBE's in the relevant market are qualified to undertake prime or subcontracting work in public construction projects. . . .

Without any information on minority participation in subcontracting, it is quite simply impossible to evaluate overall minority representation in the city's construction expenditures.

. . .

. . . To accept Richmond's claim that past societal discrimination alone can serve as the basis for rigid racial preferences would be to open the door to competing claims for "remedial relief" for every disadvantaged group. The dream of a Nation of equal citizens in a society where race is irrelevant to personal opportunity and achievement would be lost in a mosaic of shifting preferences based on inherently unmeasurable claims of past wrongs. "Courts would be asked to evaluate the extent of the prejudice and consequent harm suffered by various minority groups. Those whose societal injury is thought to exceed some arbitrary level of tolerability then would be entitled to preferential classifications. . . ." We think such a result would be contrary to both the letter and spirit of a constitutional provision whose central command is equality.

The foregoing analysis applies only to the inclusion of blacks within the Richmond set-aside program. There is *absolutely no evidence* of past discrimination against Spanish-speaking, Oriental, Indian, Eskimo, or Aleut persons in any aspect of the Richmond construction industry. The District Court took judicial notice of the fact that the vast majority of "minority" persons in Richmond were black. It may well be that Richmond has never had an Aleut or Eskimo citizen. The random inclusion of racial groups that, as a practical matter, may never have suffered from discrimination in the construction industry in Richmond suggests that perhaps the city's purpose was not in fact to remedy past discrimination.

. . .

JUSTICE STEVENS, concurring in part and concurring in the judgment.

. . .

. . . [T]his litigation involves an attempt by a legislative body, rather than a court, to fashion a remedy for a past wrong. Legislatures are primarily policy-making bodies that promulgate rules to govern future conduct. . . . It is the judicial system, rather than the legislative process, that is best equipped to identify past wrongdoers and to fashion remedies that will create the conditions that presumably would have existed had no wrong been committed. Thus, in cases involving the review of judicial remedies imposed against persons who have been proved guilty of violations of law, I would allow the courts in racial discrimination cases the same broad discretion that chancellors enjoy in other areas of the law.

. . .

The justification for the ordinance is the fact that in the past white contractors—and presumably other white citizens in Richmond—have discriminated against black contractors. The class of persons benefited by the ordinance is not, however, limited to victims of such discrimination—it encompasses persons who have never been in business in Richmond as well as minority contractors who may have been guilty of discriminating against members of other minority groups. . . .

. . . [T]he composition of the disadvantaged class of white contractors presumably includes some who have been guilty of unlawful discrimination, some who practiced discrimination before it was forbidden by law, and some who have never discriminated against anyone on the basis of race. Imposing a common burden on such a disparate class merely because each member of the class is of the same race stems from reliance on a stereotype rather than fact or reason.

JUSTICE KENNEDY, concurring in part and concurring in the judgment. . . .

JUSTICE SCALIA, concurring in the judgment.

. . . The benign purpose of compensating for social disadvantages, whether they have been acquired by reason of prior discrimination or otherwise, can no more be pursued by the illegitimate means of racial discrimination than can other assertedly benign purposes we have repeatedly rejected. The difficulty of overcoming the effects of past discrimination is as nothing compared with the difficulty of eradicating from our society the source of those effects, which is the tendency—fatal to a Nation such as ours—to classify and judge men and women on the basis of their country of origin or the color of their skin. . . . [D]iscrimination on the basis of race is illegal, immoral, unconstitutional, inherently wrong, and destructive of democratic society.

. . .

A sound distinction between federal and state (or local) action based on race rests not only upon the substance of the Civil War Amendments, but upon social reality and governmental theory. It is a simple fact that . . . "the dispassionate objectivity [and] the flexibility that are needed to mold a race-conscious remedy around the single objective of eliminating the effects of past or present discrimination"—political qualities already to be doubted in a national legislature,—are substantially less likely to exist at the state or local level. The struggle for racial justice has historically been a struggle by the national society against oppression in the individual States. . . .

In my view there is only one circumstance in which the States may act *by race* to "undo the effects of past discrimination": where that is necessary to eliminate their own maintenance of a system of unlawful racial classification. . . .

. . .

It is plainly true that in our society blacks have suffered discrimination immeasurably greater than any directed at other racial groups. But those who believe that racial preferences can help to "even the score" display, and reinforce, a manner of thinking by race that was the source of the injustice and that will, if it endures within our society, be the source of more injustice still. The relevant proposition is not that it was blacks, or Jews, or Irish who were discriminated against, but that it was individual men and women, "created equal," who were discriminated against. And the relevant resolve is that that should never happen again. Racial preferences appear to "even the score" (in some small degree) only if one embraces the proposition that our society is appropriately viewed as divided into races, making it right that an injustice rendered in the past to a black man should be compensated for by discriminating against a white. Nothing is worth that embrace. Since blacks have been disproportionately disadvantaged by racial discrimination, any race-neutral remedial program aimed at the disadvantaged *as such* will have a disproportionately beneficial impact on blacks. Only such a program, and not one that operates on the basis of race, is in accord with the letter and the spirit of our Constitution.

. . .

JUSTICE MARSHALL, with whom JUSTICE BRENNAN and JUSTICE BLACKMUN join, dissenting.

. . .

. . . As much as any municipality in the United States, Richmond knows what racial discrimination is; a century of decisions by this and other federal courts has richly documented the city's disgraceful history of public and private racial discrimination. In any event, the Richmond City Council *has* supported its determination that minorities have been wrongly excluded from local construction contracting. Its proof includes statistics showing that minority-owned businesses have received virtually no city contracting dollars and rarely if ever belonged to area trade associations; testimony by municipal officials that discrimination has been widespread in the local construction industry; and exhaustive and widely publicized federal studies . . . which showed that pervasive discrimination in the Nation's tight-knit construction industry had operated to exclude minorities from public contracting. These are precisely the types of statistical and testimonial evidence which, until today, this Court had credited in cases approving of race-conscious measures designed to remedy past discrimination.

. . .

. . . My view has long been that race-conscious classifications designed to further remedial goals "must serve important governmental objectives and must be substantially related to achievement of those objectives" in order to withstand constitutional scrutiny. Analyzed in terms of this two-pronged standard, Richmond's set-aside, like the federal program on which it was modeled, is "plainly constitutional."

Richmond has two powerful interests in setting aside a portion of public contracting funds for minority-owned enterprises. The first is the city's interest in eradicating the effects of past racial discrimination. It is far too late in the day to doubt that remedying such discrimination is a compelling, let alone an important, interest. . . . Richmond has a second compelling interest in setting aside, where possible, a portion of its contracting dollars. That interest is the prospective one of preventing the city's own spending decisions from reinforcing and perpetuating the exclusionary effects of past discrimination.

. . .

. . . When government channels all its contracting funds to a white-dominated community of established contractors whose racial homogeneity is the product of private discrimination, it does more than place its *imprimatur* on the practices which forged and which continue to define that community. It also provides a measurable boost to those economic entities that have thrived within it, while denying important economic benefits to those entities which, but for prior discrimination, might well be better qualified to receive valuable government contracts. In my view, the interest in ensuring that the government does not reflect and reinforce prior private discrimination in dispensing public contracts is every bit as strong as the interest in eliminating private discrimination—an interest which this Court has repeatedly deemed compelling. . . .

. . .

. . . [W]here the issue is not present discrimination but rather whether *past* discrimination has resulted in the *continuing exclusion* of minorities from a historically tight-knit industry, a contrast between population and work force is entirely appropriate to help gauge the degree of the exclusion. . . . This contrast is especially illuminating in cases like this, where a main avenue of introduction into the work force—here, membership in the trade associations whose members presumably train apprentices and help them procure subcontracting assignments—is itself grossly dominated by nonminorities. The majority's assertion that the city "does not even know how many MBE's in the relevant market are qualified" is thus entirely beside the point. If Richmond indeed has a monochromatic contracting community, this most likely reflects the lingering power of past exclusionary practices. . . .

. . .

In my judgment, Richmond's set-aside plan also comports with the second prong of the equal protection inquiry, for it is substantially related to the interests it seeks to serve in remedying past discrimination and in ensuring that municipal contract procurement does not perpetuate that discrimination. . . . Like the federal provision [at issue in *Fullilove v. Klutznick* (1980)], Richmond's is limited to five years in duration, and was not renewed when it came up for reconsideration in 1988. Like the federal provision, Richmond's contains a waiver provision freeing from its subcontracting requirements those nonminority firms that demonstrate that they cannot comply with its provisions. Like the federal provision, Richmond's has a minimal impact on innocent third parties. While the measure affects 30% of *public* contracting dollars, that translates to only 3% of overall Richmond area contracting.

. . .

Today, for the first time, a majority of this Court has adopted strict scrutiny as its standard of Equal Protection Clause review of race-conscious remedial measures. This is an unwelcome development. A profound difference separates governmental actions that themselves are racist and governmental actions that seek to remedy the effects of prior racism or to prevent neutral governmental activity from perpetuating the effects of such racism.

Racial classifications "drawn on the presumption that one race is inferior to another or because they put the weight of government behind racial hatred and separatism" warrant the strictest judicial scrutiny because of the very irrelevance of these rationales. By contrast, racial classifications drawn for the purpose of remedying the effects of discrimination that itself was race based have a highly pertinent basis: the tragic and indelible fact that discrimination against blacks and other racial minorities in this Nation has pervaded our Nation's history and continues to scar our society. . . .

In concluding that remedial classifications warrant no different standard of review under the Constitution than the most brutal and repugnant forms of state-sponsored racism, a majority of this Court signals that it regards racial discrimination as largely a phenomenon of the past, and that government bodies need no longer preoccupy themselves with rectifying racial injustice. I, however, do not believe this Nation is anywhere close to eradicating racial discrimination or its vestiges. In constitutionalizing its wishful thinking, the majority today does a grave disservice not only to those victims of past and present racial discrimination in this Nation whom government has sought to assist, but also to this Court's long tradition of approaching issues of race with the utmost sensitivity.

. . .

Congress' concern in passing the Reconstruction Amendments, and particularly their congressional authorization provisions, was that States would *not* adequately respond to racial violence or discrimination against newly freed slaves. To interpret any aspect of these Amendments as proscribing state remedial responses to these very problems turns the Amendments on their heads. The Amendments specifically empowered the Federal Government to combat discrimination at a time when the breadth of federal power under the Constitution was less apparent than it is today. But nothing in the Amendments themselves, or in our long history of interpreting or applying those momentous charters, suggests that States, exercising their police power, are in any way constitutionally inhibited from working alongside the Federal Government in the fight against discrimination and its effects.

. . .

JUSTICE BLACKMUN, with whom JUSTICE BRENNAN joins, dissenting. . . .

C. Gender

The Reagan Era witnessed the rise of several gender gaps in American constitutional politics. Democratic and Republican Party platforms adopted different positions on women's rights. Democrats strongly favored the ERA and legal abortion. Republicans abandoned previous support for the ERA and opposed legal abortion. Such feminist groups as NOW became influential partners in the Democratic Party coalition.

Such conservative groups as Concerned Women of American cast their lot with the Republican Party. In every national election held during the 1980s and afterward, women were more inclined than men to vote for candidates nominated by the Democratic Party. Remarkably, this gender gap in voting has not been strongly related to the different positions that the major parties take on women's rights. Public opinion suggests that support for the ERA and legal abortion more often divide better- and lesser-educated Americans than they divide men from women. Other surveys suggest that women vote more Democratic than men because women are more likely than men to favor Democratic Party positions on such issues as health care and foreign military interventions.[35]

Neither Reagan conservatives nor social liberals were pleased with the trend of constitutional decisions on gender equality in the 1980s and early 1990s. By the end of Ronald Reagan's first term the ERA was dead, but a fair degree of gender equality had been incorporated into American constitutional law. Many states ratified state equal rights amendments containing language identical or nearly identical to the language of the failed federal ERA. The Supreme Court in *Mississippi University for Women v. Hogan* (1982) reaffirmed and sharpened previous decisions holding all official gender distinctions to a higher constitutional standard. When declaring unconstitutional a state law maintaining an all-women school of nursing, Justice O'Connor wrote,

> A statute that classifies individuals on the basis of their gender must carry the burden of showing an "exceedingly persuasive justification" for the classification. The burden is met only by showing at least that the classification serves "important governmental objectives and that the discriminatory means employed" are "substantially related to the achievement of those objectives."

The Supreme Court in *Johnson v. Transportation Agency* (1987) ruled that affirmative action programs for woman did not violate either Title VII or the Civil Rights Act of 1964 (and, implicitly, did not violate the equal protection clause). Claims based on more radical understandings of gender equality failed. State and federal judges consistently rejected "comparable worth" arguments that asserted that employers violated equality rights by paying workers in traditionally male jobs a higher salary than workers in traditionally female jobs.

Johnson v. Transportation Agency, Santa Clara County, 480 U.S. 616 (1987)

Paul Johnson and Diane Joyce were employees of the Transportation Agency of Santa Clara County, California. Both applied for a promotion to road dispatcher. Agency supervisors concluded that both were qualified for the position but recommended Johnson for promotion. The agency's affirmative action coordinator disagreed, contending that promoting Joyce was more consistent with the agency's affirmative action program. James Graebner, the director of the agency, promoted Joyce. Johnson filed a lawsuit, claiming that this decision violated his rights under Title VII of the Civil Rights Act of 1964. The crucial provision of that statute declares that employers may not "discriminate against any individual with respect to his compensation, terms, conditions, or privileges of employment, because of such individual's race, color, religion, sex or national origin." The local federal district court ruled that unlawful discrimination had taken place. The Court of Appeals for the Ninth Circuit reversed that ruling. Johnson appealed to the Supreme Court of the United States.[36]

The Supreme Court by a 6–3 vote declared that Paul Johnson was not legally entitled to the promotion. Justice Brennan's majority opinion declared that employers could legally adopt affirmative action plans to correct "manifest" racial and gender "imbalances" in the workplace. What reasons did he give for reaching that conclusion? Why did Justice Scalia disagree? Who had the better argument? The majority opinion does not discuss whether the Transportation Agency violated the equal protection clause of the Constitution (a claim that Johnson did not make). If that was their concern, what standard should the justices have used? During the Reagan Era courts maintained that discrimination against persons of color had to satisfy a stricter standard than discrimination against women. Does this mean

35. Carole Kennedy Chaney, R. Michael Alvarez, and Jonathan Nagler, "Explaining the Gender Gap in U.S. Presidential Elections, 1980–1992," *Political Research Quarterly* 51 (1998): 311–339.

36. For a good account of the case, see Melvin I. Urofsky, *Affirmative Action on Trial: Sex Discrimination in Johnson v. Santa Clara* (Lawrence: University Press of Kansas, 1997).

that affirmative action programs for women had to satisfy a lesser constitutional standard than affirmative action programs for persons of color?

JUSTICE BRENNAN delivered the opinion of the Court.

. . .

The first issue is whether consideration of the sex of applicants for Skilled Craft jobs was justified by the existence of a "manifest imbalance" that reflected underrepresentation of women in "traditionally segregated job categories." . . . The requirement that the "manifest imbalance" relate to a "traditionally segregated job category" provides assurance both that sex or race will be taken into account in a manner consistent with Title VII's purpose of eliminating the effects of employment discrimination, and that the interests of those employees not benefiting from the plan will not be unduly infringed.

. . .

It is clear that the decision to hire Joyce was made pursuant to an Agency plan that directed that sex or race be taken into account for the purpose of remedying underrepresentation. The Agency Plan acknowledged the "limited opportunities that have existed in the past" for women to find employment in certain job classifications "where women have not been traditionally employed in significant numbers." As a result, observed the Plan, women were concentrated in traditionally female jobs in the Agency, and represented a lower percentage in other job classifications than would be expected if such traditional segregation had not occurred. Specifically, 9 of the 10 Para-Professionals and 110 of the 145 Office and Clerical Workers were women. By contrast, women were only 2 of the 28 Officials and Administrators, 5 of the 58 Professionals, 12 of the 124 Technicians, none of the Skilled Craft Workers, and 1—who was Joyce—of the 110 Road Maintenance Workers. The Plan sought to remedy these imbalances through "hiring, training and promotion of . . . women throughout the Agency in all major job classifications where they are underrepresented."

. . .

The Agency's Plan emphatically did not authorize blind hiring. It expressly directed that numerous factors be taken into account in making hiring decisions, including specifically the qualifications of female applicants for particular jobs. . . .

. . . Given the obvious imbalance in the Skilled Craft category, and given the Agency's commitment to eliminating such imbalances, it was plainly not unreasonable for the Agency to determine that it was appropriate to consider as one factor the sex of Ms. Joyce in making its decision. The promotion of Joyce thus satisfies the first requirement . . . , since it was undertaken to further an affirmative action plan designed to eliminate Agency work force imbalances in traditionally segregated job categories.

We next consider whether the Agency Plan unnecessarily trammeled the rights of male employees or created an absolute bar to their advancement. . . . [T]he Plan sets aside no positions for women. . . . As the Agency Director testified, the sex of Joyce was but one of numerous factors he took into account in arriving at his decision. The Plan thus resembles the "Harvard Plan" approvingly noted by Justice POWELL in *Regents of University of California v. Bakke* (1978), which considers race along with other criteria in determining admission to the college. . . . No persons are automatically excluded from consideration; all are able to have their qualifications weighed against those of other applicants.

. . .

. . . The Agency has identified a conspicuous imbalance in job categories traditionally segregated by race and sex. It has made clear from the outset, however, that employment decisions may not be justified solely by reference to this imbalance, but must rest on a multitude of practical, realistic factors. It has therefore committed itself to annual adjustment of goals so as to provide a reasonable guide for actual hiring and promotion decisions. The Agency earmarks no positions for anyone; sex is but one of several factors that may be taken into account in evaluating qualified applicants for a position. As both the Plan's language and its manner of operation attest, the Agency has no intention of establishing a work force whose permanent composition is dictated by rigid numerical standards.

. . .

JUSTICE STEVENS, concurring.

. . .

. . . I see no reason why the employer has any duty, prior to granting a preference to a qualified minority employee, to determine whether his past conduct might constitute an arguable violation of Title VII. Indeed, in some instances the employer may find it more helpful to focus on the future. Instead of retroactively scrutinizing his own or society's possible exclusions of minorities in the past to determine the outer limits of a valid affirmative-action program—or indeed, any particular affirmative-action decision—in many cases the employer will find it more appropriate to consider other legitimate reasons to give preferences to members of under-represented groups. Statutes enacted for the benefit of minority groups should not block these forward-looking considerations.

. . .

JUSTICE O'CONNOR, concurring in the judgment.

. . .

In my view, the proper initial inquiry in evaluating the legality of an affirmative action plan by a public employer under Title VII is no different from that required by the Equal Protection Clause. In either case, consistent with the congressional intent to provide some measure of protection to the interests of the employer's nonminority employees, the employer must have had a firm basis for believing that remedial action was required. An employer would have such a firm basis if it can point to a statistical disparity sufficient to support a prima facie claim under Title VII by the employee beneficiaries of the affirmative action plan of a pattern or practice claim of discrimination.

. . .

In this case, I am also satisfied that respondents had a firm basis for adopting an affirmative action program. Although the District Court found no discrimination against women in fact, at the time the affirmative action plan was adopted, there were no women in its skilled craft positions. Petitioner concedes that women constituted approximately 5% of the local labor pool of skilled craft workers in 1970. Thus, when compared to the percentage of women in the qualified work force, the statistical disparity would have been sufficient for a prima facie Title VII case brought by unsuccessful women job applicants. . . .

JUSTICE WHITE, dissenting. . . .

JUSTICE SCALIA, with whom THE CHIEF JUSTICE joins, and with whom JUSTICE WHITE joins in part, dissenting.

. . . The Court today completes the process of converting [Title VII of the Civil Rights Act of 1964] from a guarantee that race or sex will not be the basis for employment determinations, to a guarantee that it often will. Ever so subtly, . . . we effectively replace the goal of a discrimination-free society with the quite incompatible goal of proportionate representation by race and by sex in the workplace. . . .

. . .

. . . [T]he plan's purpose was assuredly not to remedy prior sex discrimination by the Agency. It could not have been, because there was no prior sex discrimination to remedy. The majority, in cataloging the Agency's alleged misdeeds, neglects to mention the District Court's finding that the Agency "has not discriminated in the past, and does not discriminate in the present against women in regard to employment opportunities in general and promotions in particular." . . .

Not only was the plan not directed at the results of past sex discrimination by the Agency, but its objective was not to achieve the state of affairs that this Court has dubiously assumed would result from an absence of discrimination—an overall work force "more or less representative of the racial and ethnic composition of the population in the community." Rather, the oft-stated goal was to mirror the racial and sexual composition of the entire county labor force, not merely in the Agency work force as a whole, but in each and every individual job category at the Agency. In a discrimination-free world, it would obviously be a statistical oddity for every job category to match the racial and sexual composition of even that portion of the county work force qualified for that job; it would be utterly miraculous for each of them to match, as the plan expected, the composition of the entire work force. Quite obviously, the plan did not seek to replicate what a lack of discrimination would produce, but rather imposed racial and sexual tailoring that would, in defiance of normal expectations and laws of probability, give each protected racial and sexual group a governmentally determined "proper" proportion of each job category.

. . .

The most significant proposition of law established by today's decision is that racial or sexual discrimination is permitted under Title VII when it is intended to overcome the effect, not of the employer's own discrimination, but of societal attitudes that have limited the entry of certain races, or of a particular sex, into certain jobs. Even if the societal attitudes in question consisted exclusively of conscious discrimination by other employers, this holding would contradict a decision of this Court rendered only last Term. *Wygant v. Jackson Board of Education (1986)*, held that the objective of remedying societal discrimination cannot prevent remedial affirmative action from violating the Equal Protection Clause. . . .

. . .

. . . It is absurd to think that the nationwide failure of road maintenance crews, for example, to achieve the Agency's ambition of 36.4% female representation is attributable primarily, if even substantially, to systematic exclusion of women eager to shoulder pick and shovel. It is a "traditionally segregated job category" . . . in the sense that, because of longstanding social attitudes, it has not been regarded by women themselves as desirable work. . . . There are, of course, those who believe that the social attitudes which cause women themselves to avoid certain jobs and to favor others are as nefarious as conscious, exclusionary discrimination. Whether or not that is so (and there is assuredly no consensus on the point equivalent to our national consensus against intentional discrimination), the two phenomena are certainly distinct. And it is the alteration of social attitudes, rather than the elimination of discrimination, which today's decision approves as justification for state-enforced discrimination. This is an enormous expansion, undertaken without the slightest justification or analysis.

. . .

. . . [W]hat the Court means by "taking distinctions in qualifications into account" consists of no more than eliminating from the applicant pool those who are not even minimally qualified for the job. Once that has been done, once the promoting officer assures himself that all the candidates before him are "M.Q.'s" (minimally qualifieds), he can then ignore, as the Agency Director did here, how much better than minimally qualified some of the candidates may be, and can proceed to appoint from the pool solely on the basis of race or sex, until the affirmative-action "goals" have been reached. The requirement that the employer "take distinctions in qualifications into account" thus turns out to be an assurance, not that candidates' comparative merits will always be considered, but only that none of the successful candidates selected over the others solely on the basis of their race or sex will be utterly unqualified. That may be of great comfort to those concerned with American productivity; and it is undoubtedly effective in reducing the effect of affirmative-action discrimination upon those in the upper strata of society, who (unlike road maintenance workers, for example) compete for employment in professional and semiprofessional fields where, for many reasons, including most notably the effects of past discrimination, the numbers of "M.Q." applicants from the favored groups are substantially less. But I fail to see how it has any relevance to whether selecting among final candidates solely on the basis of race or sex is permissible under Title VII, which prohibits discrimination on the basis of race or sex.

X. Criminal Justice

MAJOR DEVELOPMENTS

- Increased limits on federal habeas corpus petitions
- Good-faith exception to the exclusionary rule
- Increased use of capital punishment

Reagan conservatives inherited from Richard Nixon a commitment to reversing liberal decisions that they believed hampered police efforts to fight crime. The Reagan Justice Department bluntly declared, "Neither the search and seizure exclusionary rule nor the procedural rules for custodial interrogations established by *Miranda v. Arizona* (1966) are required by the Constitution."[37] Democrats were decidedly more ambivalent about constitutional criminal procedure and the death penalty. Democratic Party platforms said little or nothing about the constitutional rights of persons accused or convicted of criminal offenses.

The Reagan Revolution in criminal justice enjoyed far more success in the courts than in Congress. Liberals in Congress consistently blocked proposed laws that would curb the rights of criminal suspects and persons convicted of crimes. The Supreme Court was more receptive than Congress to many proposals. Reagan's four judicial appointees often formed a judicial majority with Nixon's judicial appointees (and Justice Byron White) on questions of constitutional criminal procedure. By 1994 the Supreme Court had declared that unconstitutionally seized evidence could be admitted at a criminal trial if the police had acted on a "good faith" belief

37. U.S. Department of Justice, Office of Legal Policy, *Guidelines on Constitutional Litigation*, 86.

that the search was constitutional (*United States v. Leon* [1984]); established important exceptions to the rule that confessions could be admitted only if preceded by *Miranda* warnings (*New York v. Quarles* [1984]); sharply narrowed access to habeas corpus (*McCleskey v. Zant* [1991]), even when capitally sentenced prisoners made claims of actual innocence (*Herrera v. Collins* [1993]); and rejected challenges to capital punishment based on statistical evidence that murderers whose victims were white were far more likely to be executed than those who murdered persons of color (*McCleskey v. Kemp* [1987]).

Despondent liberals experienced a few rays of light. The Supreme Court did not actually overrule such liberal pillars as *Mapp v. Ohio* (1961) (exclusionary rule) and *Miranda v. Arizona* (1966). Some death sentences were reversed. The judicial majority in *Batson v. Kentucky* (1986) ruled that prosecutors could not use peremptory challenges to remove persons of color from juries. Finally, Justice Blackmun and Justice Stevens, Republican appointees in the 1970s, took more liberal positions in cases concerned with constitutional criminal procedure. By the end of the Reagan Era Stevens, Blackmun, and Justice Sandra Day O'Connor had forming a nascent majority committed to preventing further erosion of the liberal constitutional decisions handed down during the 1960s and 1970s.

A. Due Process and Habeas Corpus

Reagan conservatives were committed to a crime-control model of constitutional criminal procedure. Proponents of this model insist that constitutional provisions protecting the rights of persons suspected of crime be interpreted to enable law enforcement officials to identify, arrest, and punish criminals. Conservatives in the 1980s combined this appeal to crime control with concerns for federalism and finality. They maintained that the federal government should not routinely intervene in state criminal proceedings. Chief Justice Rehnquist combined appeals to federalism and finality in *Herrera v. Collins* (1993) when denying a person under a sentence of death the right to a new trial on the basis of newly discovered exculpatory evidence. His opinion declared, "But because of the very disruptive effect that entertaining claims of actual innocence would have on the need for finality in capital cases, and the enormous burden that having to retry cases based on often stale evidence would place on the States, the threshold showing for such an assumed right would necessarily be extraordinarily high."

President Reagan and his political allies enjoyed mixed success when promoting greater solicitude for federalism in constitutional criminal procedure. No Supreme Court justice displayed any interest in overruling or even narrowing past decisions holding that the due process clause of the Fourteenth Amendment required states to respect the protections set out in the Bill of Rights for persons suspected and convicted of crime. The Burger and Rehnquist Courts, however, were more sympathetic to claims that expansive federal habeas corpus rights interfered with the sovereign power of states to punish crimes. Several decisions placed sharp limits on federal habeas corpus rights in the name of federalism (and finality). *Teague v. Lane* (1989) held that persons convicted in state courts could not base federal habeas corpus petitions on judicial decisions handed down after their initial round of appeals, even if a judicial majority might think those rules were mandated by the Constitution. If the Supreme Court in 1990 expanded the scope of *Miranda* rights, a person whose conviction became final in 1989 could not base a habeas corpus claim on that decision. In *McCleskey v. Zant* (1991) the justices placed sharp curbs on second or successive habeas corpus petitions. The judicial majority, invoking federalism and finality, ruled that federal courts shouldhear a second habeas corpus petition only if the convicted prisoner could demonstrate that the constitutional claim could not possibly have been known when the first petition was filed.

Herrera v. Collins, 506 U.S. 390 (1993)

Lionel Torres Herrera in 1982 was convicted by a Texas jury of murdering police officers David Rucker and Enrique Carrisalez. He was subsequently sentenced to death. The Texas Court of Criminal Appeals affirmed the sentence, and the Supreme Court of Texas denied certiorari. Herrera's first habeas corpus petition was unsuccessful. In 1990 Herrera filed a second habeas corpus petition in state court, claiming that newly discovered evidence proved that he was not the murderer. That evidence consisted of affidavits from the lawyer who represented his brother, Raul Herrera, Sr., and Raul Herrera's former cellmate. Both claimed that Raul had confessed to the murders before dying in 1984. After the

Texas courts denied relief, Herrera filed a federal habeas corpus claim in federal court. Herrera's petition included additional affidavits from persons who swore that Raul had confessed to them and an affidavit from Raul Herrera, Jr., who claimed that he saw his father commit the murders. Both the federal district court and the Court of Appeals for the Fifth Circuit rejected Herrera's claim on the ground that "actual innocence" does not state a claim for relief in federal habeas corpus. Herrera appealed to the Supreme Court of the United States.

The Supreme Court by a 6–3 vote rejected Herrera's claim. Chief Justice Rehnquist's majority opinion ruled that the due process clause does not give persons the right to a new trial based on newly discovered evidence of actual innocence. He also maintained that Herrera did not make an adequate showing of innocence even if such a right existed. On what basis did the Chief Justice deny that persons have a due process right to a new trial? Why did Justice Blackmun disagree? Under what conditions, if any, do you think that a new trial is constitutionally required? Are the standards different in death penalty cases? The Chief Justice insisted that executive clemency is the appropriate vehicle when prisoners raise claims of actual innocence. What institution do you believe is best suited for making the judgment that a person constitutionally convicted at trial may actually be innocent? Suppose you agreed with Justice Rehnquist that black-letter law provided no remedy, but you were convinced that the petitioner before you was innocent. As a justice of the Supreme Court, what would you do?

CHIEF JUSTICE REHNQUIST delivered the opinion of the Court.

. . .

Once a defendant has been afforded a fair trial and convicted of the offense for which he was charged, the presumption of innocence disappears. . . . Here, it is not disputed that the State met its burden of proving at trial that petitioner was guilty of the capital murder of Officer Carrisalez beyond a reasonable doubt. Thus, in the eyes of the law, petitioner does not come before the Court as one who is "innocent," but, on the contrary, as one who has been convicted by due process of law of two brutal murders.

. . .

Claims of actual innocence based on newly discovered evidence have never been held to state a ground for federal habeas relief absent an independent constitutional violation occurring in the underlying state criminal proceeding. . . . This rule is grounded in the principle that federal habeas courts sit to ensure that individuals are not imprisoned in violation of the Constitution—not to correct errors of fact.

. . .

This is not to say that our habeas jurisprudence casts a blind eye toward innocence. . . . [W]e have held that a petitioner otherwise subject to defenses of abusive or successive use of the writ may have his federal constitutional claim considered on the merits if he makes a proper showing of actual innocence. . . . But this body of our habeas jurisprudence makes clear that a claim of "actual innocence" is not itself a constitutional claim, but instead a gateway through which a habeas petitioner must pass to have his otherwise barred constitutional claim considered on the merits.

Petitioner in this case is simply not entitled to habeas relief based on the reasoning of this line of cases. For he does not seek excusal of a procedural error so that he may bring an independent constitutional claim challenging his conviction or sentence, but rather argues that he is entitled to habeas relief because newly discovered evidence shows that his conviction is factually incorrect. . . .

Petitioner asserts that this case is different because he has been sentenced to death. But we have "refused to hold that the fact that a death sentence has been imposed requires a different standard of review on federal habeas corpus." . . .

. . .

. . . [W]e cannot say that Texas' refusal to entertain petitioner's newly discovered evidence eight years after his conviction transgresses a principle of fundamental fairness "rooted in the traditions and conscience of our people." This is not to say, however, that petitioner is left without a forum to raise his actual innocence claim. For under Texas law, petitioner may file a request for executive clemency. Clemency is deeply rooted in our Anglo-American tradition of law, and is the historic remedy for preventing miscarriages of justice where judicial process has been exhausted.

. . .

Executive clemency has provided the "fail safe" in our criminal justice system. It is an unalterable fact that our judicial system, like the human beings who administer it, is fallible. But history is replete with examples of wrongfully convicted persons who have been pardoned in the wake of after-discovered evidence establishing their innocence. . . . Recent authority confirms that over the past century clemency has been exercised frequently in capital cases in which demonstrations of "actual innocence" have been made.

. . .

We may assume, for the sake of argument in deciding this case, that in a capital case a truly persuasive demonstration of "actual innocence" made after trial would render the execution of a defendant unconstitutional, and warrant federal habeas relief if there were no state avenue open to process such a claim. But because of the very disruptive effect that entertaining claims of actual innocence would have on the need for finality in capital cases, and the enormous burden that having to retry cases based on often stale evidence would place on the States, the threshold showing for such an assumed right would necessarily be extraordinarily high. The showing made by petitioner in this case falls far short of any such threshold.

Petitioner's newly discovered evidence consists of affidavits. In the new trial context, motions based solely upon affidavits are disfavored because the affiants' statements are obtained without the benefit of cross-examination and an opportunity to make credibility determinations. Petitioner's affidavits are particularly suspect in this regard because, with the exception of Raul Herrera, Jr.'s affidavit, they consist of hearsay. . . .

The affidavits filed in this habeas proceeding were given over eight years after petitioner's trial. No satisfactory explanation has been given as to why the affiants waited until the 11th hour—and, indeed, until after the alleged perpetrator of the murders himself was dead—to make their statements. . . .

. . . Finally, the affidavits must be considered in light of the proof of petitioner's guilt at trial—proof which included two eyewitness identifications, numerous pieces of circumstantial evidence, and a handwritten letter in which petitioner apologized for killing the officers and offered to turn himself in under certain conditions. . . .

. . .

JUSTICE O'CONNOR, with whom JUSTICE KENNEDY joins, concurring.

. . .

Ultimately, two things about this case are clear. First is what the Court does not hold. Nowhere does the Court state that the Constitution permits the execution of an actually innocent person. Instead, the Court assumes for the sake of argument that a truly persuasive demonstration of actual innocence would render any such execution unconstitutional and that federal habeas relief would be warranted if no state avenue were open to process the claim. Second is what petitioner has not demonstrated. Petitioner has failed to make a persuasive showing of actual innocence. . . . Accordingly, the Court has no reason to pass on, and appropriately reserves, the question whether federal courts may entertain convincing claims of actual innocence. That difficult question remains open. If the Constitution's guarantees of fair procedure and the safeguards of clemency and pardon fulfill their historical mission, it may never require resolution at all.

JUSTICE SCALIA, with whom JUSTICE THOMAS joins, concurring.

. . . There is no basis in text, tradition, or even in contemporary practice (if that were enough) for finding in the Constitution a right to demand judicial consideration of newly discovered evidence of innocence brought forward after conviction. In saying that such a right exists, the dissenters apply nothing but their personal opinions to invalidate the rules of more than two-thirds of the States, and a Federal Rule of Criminal Procedure for which this Court itself is responsible. If the system that has been in place for 200 years (and remains widely approved) "shock[s]" the dissenters' consciences, perhaps they should doubt the calibration of their consciences, or, better still, the usefulness of "conscience shocking" as a legal test.

. . .

JUSTICE WHITE, concurring in the judgment.

In voting to affirm, I assume that a persuasive showing of "actual innocence" made after trial, even though made after the expiration of the time provided by law for the presentation of newly discovered evidence, would render unconstitutional the execution of petitioner in this case. To be entitled to relief, however, petitioner would at the very least be required to show that based on proffered newly discovered evidence and the entire record before the jury that convicted him, "no rational trier of fact could [find] proof of guilt beyond a reasonable doubt." For the reasons stated in the Court's opinion, petitioner's showing falls far short of satisfying even that standard, and I therefore concur in the judgment.

JUSTICE BLACKMUN, with whom JUSTICE STEVENS and JUSTICE SOUTER join, dissenting.

Nothing could be more contrary to contemporary standards of decency or more shocking to the conscience than to execute a person who is actually innocent.

. . .

This Court has ruled that punishment is excessive and unconstitutional if it is "nothing more than the purposeless and needless imposition of pain and suffering," or if it is "grossly out of proportion to the severity of the crime." If it is violative of the Eighth Amendment to execute someone who is guilty of those crimes, then it plainly is violative of the Eighth Amendment to execute a person who is actually innocent. Executing an innocent person epitomizes "the purposeless and needless imposition of pain and suffering."

. . .

The Court also suggests that allowing petitioner to raise his claim of innocence would not serve society's interest in the reliable imposition of the death penalty because it might require a new trial that would be less accurate than the first. This suggestion misses the point entirely. The question is not whether a second trial would be more reliable than the first but whether, in light of new evidence, the result of the first trial is sufficiently reliable for the State to carry out a death sentence. Furthermore, it is far from clear that a State will seek to retry the rare prisoner who prevails on a claim of actual innocence. . . .

. . .

Execution of the innocent is equally offensive to the Due Process Clause of the Fourteenth Amendment. . . .

. . . Execution of an innocent person is the ultimate "'arbitrary impositio[n].'" It is an imposition from which one never recovers and for which one can never be compensated. Thus, I also believe that petitioner may raise a substantive due process challenge to his punishment on the ground that he is actually innocent.

. . .

The majority's discussion of petitioner's constitutional claims is even more perverse when viewed in the light of this Court's recent habeas jurisprudence. Beginning with a trio of decisions in 1986, this Court shifted the focus of federal habeas review of successive, abusive, or defaulted claims away from the preservation of constitutional rights to a fact-based inquiry into the habeas petitioner's guilt or innocence. The Court sought to strike a balance between the State's interest in the finality of its criminal judgments and the prisoner's interest in access to a forum to test the basic justice of his sentence. In striking this balance, the Court adopted the view . . . that there should be an exception to the concept of finality when a prisoner can make a colorable claim of actual innocence. . . .

Having adopted an "actual-innocence" requirement for review of abusive, successive, or defaulted claims, however, the majority would now take the position that "a claim of 'actual innocence' is not itself a constitutional claim, but instead a gateway through which a habeas petitioner must pass to have his otherwise barred constitutional claim considered on the merits." In other words, having held that a prisoner who is incarcerated in violation of the Constitution must show he is actually innocent to obtain relief, the majority would now hold that a prisoner who is actually innocent must show a constitutional violation to obtain relief. The only principle that would appear to reconcile these two positions is the principle that habeas relief should be denied whenever possible.

. . .

. . . The possibility of executive clemency is not sufficient to satisfy the requirements of the Eighth and Fourteenth Amendments. . . . The vindication of rights guaranteed by the Constitution has never been made to turn on the unreviewable discretion of an executive official or administrative tribunal. . . .

. . .

. . . I would hold that, to obtain relief on a claim of actual innocence, the petitioner must show that he probably is innocent. This standard is supported by several considerations. First, new evidence of innocence may be discovered long after the defendant's conviction. Given the passage of time, it may be difficult for the State to retry a defendant who obtains relief from his conviction or sentence on an actual-innocence claim. The actual-innocence proceeding thus may constitute the final word on whether the defendant may be punished. In light of this fact, an otherwise constitutionally valid conviction or sentence should not be set aside lightly. Second, conviction after a constitutionally adequate trial strips the defendant of the presumption of innocence. . . . When a defendant seeks to challenge the determination of guilt after he has been validly convicted and sentenced, it is fair to place on him the burden of proving his innocence, not just raising doubt about his guilt. . . .

I do not understand why the majority so severely faults petitioner for relying only on affidavits. It is common to rely on affidavits at the preliminary-consideration stage of a habeas proceeding. The opportunity for cross-examination and credibility determinations comes at the hearing, assuming that the petitioner is entitled to one. It makes no sense for this Court to impugn the reliability of petitioner's evidence on the ground that its credibility has not been tested when the reason its credibility has not been tested is that petitioner's habeas proceeding has been truncated by the Court of Appeals and now by this Court. In its haste to deny petitioner relief, the majority seems to confuse the question whether the petition may be dismissed summarily with the question whether petitioner is entitled to relief on the merits of his claim.

B. Search and Seizure

Conservatives enjoyed two important successes during the Reagan Era. *United States v. Leon* (1984) adopted what many conservatives believed was the second-best position on the exclusionary rule. While not overruling *Mapp v. Ohio* (1961), as Reagan administration officials wished, the justices ruled that unconstitutionally obtained evidence could be admitted at trial when the police had acted on a good-faith belief that their actions were consistent with constitutional norms. Justice White's majority opinion claimed that *Mapp* should not apply, because the exclusionary rule would not deter police officers who were unknowingly violating the Constitution. Conservatives (and liberals committed to the war on drugs) also cheered Supreme Court decisions in *Skinner v. Railway Labor Executives Association* (1989) and *National Treasury Employees Union v. Von Raab* (1989) sustaining government power to test railway employees and customs officials for drug and alcohol use, even if no reason existed for suspecting them of any wrongdoing. Justice Kennedy's majority opinion in *Skinner* asserted that suspicionless searches were constitutional when conditions "present . . . special needs beyond normal law enforcement that may justify departures from the usual warrant and probable-cause requirements."

The Supreme Court was not implacably hostile to claims that government officials had violated Fourth and Fourteenth Amendment rights. *Arizona v. Hicks* (1987) held that police officers lawfully in a house to investigate a shooting could not conduct a search to discover evidence of other crimes unless they had a warrant or probable cause to justify that search. Justice Scalia's majority opinion asserted, "Taking action, unrelated to the objectives of the authorized intrusion, which exposed to view concealed portions of the apartment or its contents, did produce a new invasion of respondent's privacy unjustified by the exigent circumstance that validated the entry." Still, liberals lost far more ground than they gained with respect to the percentage of cases rejecting claims of constitutional right and the breadth of judicial opinions in those cases. *United States v. Sokolow* (1989) was a more typical early Rehnquist Court case. Federal agents stopped Andrew Sokolow at the Honolulu airport because his behavior matched the profile of a drug courier. Chief Justice Rehnquist's majority opinion found that the search was reasonable under the circumstances. "A court sitting to determine the existence of reasonable suspicion must require the agent to articulate the factors leading to that conclusion," he wrote, "but the fact that these factors may be set forth in a 'profile' does not somehow detract from their evidentiary significance as seen by a trained agent."

United States v. Leon, 468 U.S. 897 (1984)

Officer Cyril Rombach of the Burbank Police Department obtained a tip from an informant that Alberto Leon had illegal drugs in his house and car. Based on this information, Rombach obtained a search warrant from a California judge. The search was successful. Leon was arrested and charged by federal prosecutors with conspiracy to possess and distribute cocaine. At trial Leon claimed that the search had been unconstitutional. The judge lacked probable cause to issue the warrant, Leon claimed, because Rombach's informant was not reliable. The federal district court agreed with Leon. The evidence obtained by Officer Rombach's search was suppressed. The United States appealed, claiming that probable cause had existed for the search warrant and that the Fourth Amendment did not require that evidence be suppressed when police officers had a good-faith belief that they were acting on the basis of a constitutional search warrant. The Court of Appeals for the Ninth Circuit rejected both claims. The United States appealed to the Supreme Court.

The Supreme Court by a 6–3 vote ruled that admitting the seized drugs into trial had been constitutional. Justice White's majority opinion held that prosecutors may introduce unconstitutionally obtained evidence at trial when the police officers had acted on a good-faith belief that their search was constitutional. Why did White claim that the exclusionary rule is not essential to the Fourth Amendment? Does the dissent effectively criticize this position? What do you believe are the likely consequences of the good-faith exception? Will fewer criminals go free, as Justice White believed, because police officers made good-faith mistakes? Or, as the dissents maintain, will Leon *encourage ignorance of the law?*

JUSTICE WHITE delivered the opinion of the Court.

. . .

The Fourth Amendment contains no provision expressly precluding the use of evidence obtained in violation of its commands, and an examination of its origin and purposes makes clear that the use of fruits of a past unlawful search or seizure "work[s] no new Fourth Amendment wrong." . . . The rule . . . operates as "a judicially created remedy designed to safeguard Fourth Amendment rights generally through its deterrent effect, rather than a personal constitutional right of the party aggrieved." . . .

. . .

The substantial social costs exacted by the exclusionary rule for the vindication of Fourth Amendment rights have long been a source of concern. . . . An objectionable collateral consequence of this interference with the criminal justice system's truth-finding function is that some guilty defendants may go free or receive reduced sentences as a result of favorable plea bargains. Particularly when law enforcement officers have acted in objective good faith or their transgressions have been minor, the magnitude of the benefit conferred on such guilty defendants offends basic concepts of the criminal justice system. . . . Indiscriminate application of the exclusionary rule, therefore, may well "generat[e] disrespect for the law and administration of justice." . . . Accordingly, "[a]s with any remedial device, the application of the rule has been restricted to those areas where its remedial objectives are thought most efficaciously served." . . .

. . .

As yet, we have not recognized any form of good-faith exception to the Fourth Amendment exclusionary rule. But the balancing approach that has evolved during the years of experience with the rule provides strong support for the modification currently urged upon us. As we discuss below, our evaluation of the costs and benefits of suppressing reliable physical evidence seized by officers reasonably relying on a warrant issued by a detached and neutral magistrate leads to the conclusion that such evidence should be admissible in the prosecution's case in chief.

. . .

To the extent that proponents of exclusion rely on its behavioral effects on judges and magistrates . . . , their reliance is misplaced. First, the exclusionary rule is designed to deter police misconduct rather than to punish the errors of judges and magistrates. Second, there exists no evidence suggesting that judges and magistrates are inclined to ignore or subvert the Fourth Amendment or that lawlessness among these actors requires application of the extreme sanction of exclusion.

. . . [W]e discern no basis, and are offered none, for believing that exclusion of evidence seized pursuant to a warrant will have a significant deterrent effect on the issuing judge or magistrate. Many of the factors that indicate that the exclusionary rule cannot provide an effective "special" or "general" deterrent for individual offending law enforcement officers apply as well to judges or magistrates. And, to the extent that the rule is thought to operate as a "systemic" deterrent on a wider audience, it clearly can have no such effect on individuals empowered to issue search warrants. Judges and magistrates are not adjuncts to the law enforcement team; as neutral judicial officers, they have no stake in the outcome of particular criminal prosecutions. The threat of exclusion thus cannot be expected significantly to deter them. Imposition of the exclusionary sanction is not necessary meaningfully to inform judicial officers of their errors, and we cannot conclude that admitting evidence obtained pursuant to a warrant while at the same time declaring that the warrant was somehow defective will in any way reduce judicial officers' professional incentives to comply with the Fourth Amendment, encourage them to repeat their mistakes, or lead to the granting of all colorable warrant requests.

. . .

We have frequently questioned whether the exclusionary rule can have any deterrent effect when the offending officers acted in the objectively reasonable belief that their conduct did not violate the Fourth Amendment. "No empirical researcher, proponent or opponent of the rule, has yet been able to establish with any assurance whether the rule has a deterrent effect. . . ." . . . But even assuming that the rule effectively deters some police misconduct and provides incentives for the law enforcement profession as a whole to conduct itself in accord with the Fourth Amendment, it cannot be expected, and should not be applied, to deter objectively reasonable law enforcement activity.

. . .

This is particularly true, we believe, when an officer acting with objective good faith has obtained a search warrant from a judge or magistrate and acted within its scope. In most such cases, there is no police illegality and thus nothing to deter. It is the magistrate's responsibility to determine whether the officer's allegations establish probable cause and, if so, to issue a warrant comporting in form with the requirements of the Fourth Amendment. In the ordinary case, an officer cannot be expected to question the magistrate's probable-cause determination or his judgment that the form of the warrant is technically sufficient. . . . Penalizing the officer for the magistrate's error, rather than his own, cannot logically contribute to the deterrence of Fourth Amendment violations.

. . .

JUSTICE BLACKMUN, concurring. . . .

JUSTICE BRENNAN, with whom JUSTICE MARSHALL joins, dissenting.

. . . That today's decisions represent the pièce de résistance of the Court's past efforts cannot be doubted, for today the Court sanctions the use in the prosecution's case in chief of illegally obtained evidence against the individual whose rights have been violated—a result that had previously been thought to be foreclosed.

. . .

The majority ignores the fundamental constitutional importance of what is at stake here. While the machinery of law enforcement and indeed the nature of crime itself have changed dramatically since the Fourth Amendment became part of the Nation's fundamental law in 1791, what the Framers understood then remains true today—that the task of combating crime and convicting the guilty will in every era seem of such critical and pressing concern that we may be lured by the temptations of expediency into forsaking our commitment to protecting individual liberty and privacy. It was for that very reason that the Framers of the Bill of Rights insisted that law enforcement efforts be permanently and unambiguously restricted in order to preserve personal freedoms. In the constitutional scheme they ordained, the sometimes unpopular task of ensuring that the government's enforcement efforts remain within the strict boundaries fixed by the Fourth Amendment was entrusted to the courts. . . .

. . .

At bottom, the Court's decision turns on the proposition that the exclusionary rule is merely a "'judicially created remedy designed to safeguard Fourth Amendment rights generally through its deterrent effect, rather than a personal constitutional right.'" . . . This view of the scope of the Amendment relegates the judiciary to the periphery. Because the only constitutionally cognizable injury has already been "fully accomplished" by the police by the time a case comes before the courts, the Constitution is not itself violated if the judge decides to admit the tainted evidence. . . .

. . .

Because seizures are executed principally to secure evidence, and because such evidence generally has utility in our legal system only in the context of a trial supervised by a judge, it is apparent that the admission of illegally obtained evidence implicates the same constitutional concerns as the initial seizure of that evidence. Indeed, by admitting unlawfully seized evidence, the judiciary becomes a part of what is in fact a single governmental action prohibited by the terms of the Amendment. Once that connection between the evidence-gathering role of the police and the evidence-admitting function of the courts is acknowledged, the plausibility of the Court's interpretation becomes more suspect. Certainly nothing in the language or history of the Fourth Amendment suggests that a recognition of this evidentiary link between the police and the courts was meant to be foreclosed. . . . The Amendment therefore must be read to condemn not only the initial unconstitutional invasion of privacy—which is done, after all, for the purpose of securing evidence—but also the subsequent use of any evidence so obtained.

. . .

. . . [S]eizures are generally executed for the purpose of bringing "proof to the aid of the Government," . . . that the utility of such evidence in a criminal prosecution arises ultimately in the context of the courts, and that the courts therefore cannot be absolved of responsibility for the means by which evidence is obtained. . . . [T]he obligations cast upon government by the Fourth Amendment are not confined merely to the police. In the words of Justice Holmes: "If the search and seizure are unlawful as invading personal rights secured by the Constitution those rights would be infringed yet further if the evidence were allowed to be used."

. . .

. . . [T]he deterrence theory is both misguided and unworkable. First, the Court has frequently bewailed the "cost" of excluding reliable evidence. In large part, this criticism rests upon a refusal to acknowledge the function of the Fourth Amendment itself. If nothing else, the Amendment plainly operates to disable the government from gathering information and securing evidence in certain ways. In practical terms, of course, this restriction of official power means that some incriminating evidence inevitably will go undetected if the government obeys these constitutional restraints. It is the loss of that evidence that is the "price" our society pays for enjoying the freedom and privacy safeguarded by the Fourth Amendment. Thus, some criminals will go free not, in Justice (then Judge) Cardozo's misleading epigram, "because the constable has blundered," . . . but rather because official compliance with Fourth Amendment requirements makes it more difficult to catch criminals. Understood in this way, the Amendment directly contemplates that some reliable and incriminating evidence will be lost to the government; therefore, it is not the exclusionary rule, but the Amendment itself that has imposed this cost.

In addition, the Court's decisions over the past decade have made plain that the entire enterprise of attempting to assess the benefits and costs of the exclusionary rule in various contexts is a virtually impossible task for the judiciary to perform honestly or accurately. . . .

. . .

To be sure, the [exclusionary] rule operates to some extent to deter future misconduct by individual officers who have had evidence suppressed in their own cases. But what the Court overlooks is that the deterrence rationale for the rule is not designed to be, nor should it be thought of as, a form of "punishment" of individual police officers for their failures to obey the restraints imposed by the Fourth Amendment. . . . Instead, the chief deterrent function of the rule is its tendency to promote institutional compliance with Fourth Amendment requirements on the part of law enforcement agencies generally. Thus, as the Court has previously recognized, "over the long term, [the] demonstration [provided by the exclusionary rule] that our society attaches serious consequences to violation of constitutional rights is thought to encourage those who formulate law enforcement policies, and the officers who implement them, to incorporate Fourth Amendment ideals into their value system." . . . It is only through such an institution wide mechanism that information concerning Fourth Amendment standards can be effectively communicated to rank-and-file officers.

. . .

. . . A chief consequence of today's decisions will be to convey a clear and unambiguous message to magistrates that their decisions to issue warrants are now insulated from subsequent judicial review. Creation of this new exception for good-faith reliance upon a warrant implicitly tells magistrates that they need not take much care in reviewing warrant applications, since their mistakes will from now on have virtually no consequence: If their decision to issue a warrant was correct, the evidence will be admitted; if their decision was incorrect but the police relied in good faith on the warrant, the evidence will also be admitted. Inevitably, the care and attention devoted to such an inconsequential chore will dwindle. Although the Court is correct to note that magistrates do not share the same stake in the outcome of a criminal case as the police, they nevertheless need to appreciate that their role is of some moment in order to continue performing the important task of carefully reviewing warrant applications. Today's decisions effectively remove that incentive.

. . . Moreover, the good-faith exception will encourage police to provide only the bare minimum of information in future warrant applications. The police will now know that if they can secure a warrant, so long as the circumstances of its issuance are not "entirely unreasonable," . . . all police conduct pursuant to that warrant will be protected from further judicial review. The clear incentive that operated in the past to establish probable cause adequately because reviewing courts would examine the magistrate's judgment carefully, . . . has now been so completely vitiated that the police need only show that it was not "entirely unreasonable" under the circumstances of a particular case for them to believe that the warrant they were issued was valid. . . . The long-run effect unquestionably will be to undermine the integrity of the warrant process.

. . .

When the public, as it quite properly has done in the past as well as in the present, demands that those in government increase their efforts to combat crime, it is all too easy for those government officials to seek expedient solutions. In contrast to such costly and difficult measures as building more prisons, improving law enforcement methods, or hiring more prosecutors and judges to relieve the overburdened court systems in the country's metropolitan areas, the relaxation of Fourth Amendment standards seems a tempting, costless means of meeting the public's demand for better law enforcement. In the long run, however, we as a society pay a heavy price for such expediency, because as Justice Jackson observed, the rights guaranteed in the Fourth Amendment "are not mere second-class rights but belong in the catalog of indispensable freedoms." . . . Once lost, such rights are difficult to recover. There is hope, however, that in time this or some later Court will restore these precious freedoms to their rightful place as a primary protection for our citizens against overreaching officialdom.

JUSTICE STEVENS . . . dissenting.

. . .

. . . Today, for the first time, this Court holds that although the Constitution has been violated, no court should do anything about it at any time and in any proceeding. In my judgment, the Constitution requires more. Courts simply cannot escape their responsibility for redressing constitutional violations if they admit evidence obtained through unreasonable searches and seizures, since the entire point of police conduct that violates the Fourth Amendment is to obtain evidence for use at trial. If such evidence is admitted, then the courts become not merely the final and necessary link in an unconstitutional chain of events, but its actual motivating force. . . . Nor should we so easily concede the existence of a constitutional violation for which there is no remedy. To do so is to convert a Bill of Rights into an unenforced honor code that the police may follow in their discretion. The Constitution requires more; it requires a remedy. If the Court's new rule is to be followed, the Bill of Rights should be renamed.

C. Interrogations

Miranda v. Arizona (1966) barely survived the Reagan Era. The Reagan and Bush administrations were determined to reverse the Supreme Court's ruling that confessions could normally not be admitted into evidence unless the persons in custody had been informed that they had a right to remain silent, that their comments could be used against them in a court of law, that they had a right to an attorney, and that an attorney would be appointed for them if they could not afford counsel. "Because there is no constitutional or statutory basis for these rules, and because they have a detrimental effect on the search for truth in criminal investigations and adjudication," the 1988 *Guidelines on Constitutional Litigation* declared, "government lawyers should seek to convince the courts to construe these rules narrowly and, where possible, to limit further their scope or abandon them entirely."[38] Conservatives enjoyed considerable success employing this litigation strategy. *Miranda* was not overruled, but the Supreme Court carved out numerous exceptions to the constitutional rule that confessions may not be admitted into evidence unless *Miranda* warnings had been given.

New York v. Quarles (1984) exemplifies how the Supreme Court narrowed *Miranda*. In response to questions asked after his arrest before *Miranda* warnings were given, Benjamin Quarles informed police officers where he had stashed a gun in a supermarket. The justices found the confession admissible. Justice Rehnquist's majority opinion treated *Miranda* warnings as a means to a constitutional end rather than as a constitutional right. "The prophylactic *Miranda* warnings," he wrote, "are not themselves rights protected by the Constitution but [are] instead measures to insure that the right against compulsory self-incrimination [is] protected." Rehnquist concluded, "There is a 'public safety' exception to the requirement that *Miranda* warnings be given before a suspect's answers may be admitted into evidence." The more liberal Justice Marshall was appalled. "Without establishing that interrogations concerning the public's safety are less likely to be coercive than other interrogations," his dissent declared, "the majority cannot endorse the 'public-safety' exception and remain faithful to the logic of *Miranda v. Arizona*."

---

38. U.S. Department of Justice, Office of Legal Policy, *Guidelines on Constitutional Litigation*, 87.

Other Supreme Court decisions further narrowed *Miranda*:

- *Davis v. United States* (1994) held that police officers may question a suspect after *Miranda* warnings unless the suspect clearly asserts a right to remain silent.
- *Illinois v. Perkins* (1990) held that undercover police agents posing as cellmates to persons in prison are not required to give *Miranda* warnings.
- *Michigan v. Harvey* (1990) held that statements otherwise inadmissible under *Miranda* may be admitted to impeach a witness.
- *Pennsylvania v. Bruder* (1988) held that an ordinary traffic stop is not an arrest for *Miranda* purposes.
- *Arizona v. Mauro* (1987) held that *Miranda* warnings are not necessary when a defendant speaks with his spouse and is tape-recorded by a police officer.
- *Colorado v. Spring* (1987) held that suspects may knowingly waive their right to remain silent even if they are unaware of the crimes of which they are suspected.
- *Colorado v. Connelly* (1986) held that statements made to police officers by persons not in custody are admissible at trial, even if no *Miranda* warnings were given.
- *Morn v. Burbine* (1986) held that *Miranda* does not require police to inform a suspect that an attorney hired by a family member is trying to reach him.
- *Oregon v. Elstad* (1985) held that police need not inform a suspect that a custodial confession given before *Miranda* warnings is not admissible in court before asking the suspect to repeat the confession after giving *Miranda* warnings.
- *Nix v. Williams* (1984) held that evidence obtained by a confession made before *Miranda* warnings is admissible if the evidence would have inevitably been discovered by the police.

Miranda nevertheless retained some bite. *Michigan v. Jackson* (1986) held that once a suspect asserted the right to remain silent, any confession gained by subsequent police questioning was inadmissible. Nevertheless, most persons by the early 1990s predicted that *Miranda* would not survive the appointment of one or two additional judicial conservatives.

D. Juries and Lawyers

The right to a jury and an attorney bucked the conservative trend of constitutional criminal justice. Republican Party platforms and Reagan Justice Department manifestos were indifferent to the constitutional status of *Gideon v. Wainwright* (1963), the decision that interpreted the Sixth Amendment as requiring states to provide counsel for indigent criminal defendants. Conservatives raised few strong objections to past judicial decisions expanding the constitutional right to a jury trial. Ideological divisions on the Supreme Court were less rigid when litigants claimed that Sixth Amendment rights had been violated. The resulting decisions were more liberal than those in other areas of constitutional justice. *Batson v. Kentucky* (1986), which limited the use of race-based peremptory challenges to prospective jurors, was the only instance during the 1980s when the Supreme Court overruled a Warren Court decision that had *rejected* a rights claim made by a defendant in a criminal trial.

Batson v. Kentucky was the most important case on jury trials decided during the Reagan Era. That case overruled *Swain v. Alabama* (1965) and held that defendants could prove that prosecutors were using their peremptory challenges to exclude persons of a particular race from a jury solely by examining prosecutorial behavior at their trial. The Rehnquist Court almost immediately expanded *Batson* to cover civil trials and other uses of peremptory challenges to exclude members of suspect or quasi-suspect classes from juries. *Edmonson v. Leesville Concrete Co. Inc.* (1991) held that civil litigants could not use peremptory challenges to strike members of a particular race from a jury. *Georgia v. McCollum* (1992) ruled that the *Batson* rule prohibited both prosecutors and defense lawyers from using peremptory challenges to exclude members of a particular race from a jury. "Be it at the hands of the State or the defense," Justice Blackmun declared, if a court allows jurors to be excluded because of group bias, "[it] is [a] willing participant in a scheme that could only undermine the very foundation of our system of justice—our citizens' confidence in it." *J. E. B. v. Alabama ex. rel. T. B.* (1994) ruled that *Batson* prohibited peremptory challenges that excluded jurors solely on the basis of gender. Justice Blackmun's majority opinion asserted, "When state actors exercise peremptory challenges in reliance on gender stereotypes, they ratify and reinforce prejudicial views of the relative abilities of men and women."

The Supreme Court made two important decisions on the rights of indigent criminal defendants. *Strickland v. Washington* (1984) established tough standards for determining when counsel's poor performance at trial

Illustration 10-3 Race and Jury Selection
Source: Illustration by Harry Campbell.

violated the Sixth and Fourteenth Amendments. Justice O'Connor's majority opinion declared, "The defendant must show that there is a reasonable probability that, but for counsel's unprofessional errors, the result of the proceeding would have been different." Rarely did judges find counsel's performance to be below that standard. *Ake v. Oklahoma* (1985) ruled that indigent defendants sometimes had a right to psychiatric services, in addition to a right to counsel. Justice Marshall's majority opinion stated, "When a defendant demonstrates to the trial judge that his sanity at the time of the offense is to be a significant factor at trial, the State must, at a minimum, assure the defendant access to a competent psychiatrist who will conduct an appropriate examination and assist in evaluation, preparation, and presentation of the defense."

Both *Strickland* and *Ake* were decided by 8–1 votes. Justice Marshall was the only dissenter in *Strickland*. Justice Rehnquist was the only dissenter in *Ake*. This was a far higher degree of consensus than occurred in the other constitutional criminal procedure decisions handed down during the Reagan Era. What explains that consensus? What explains the more liberal (or less conservative) direction of decisions on the right to a jury and the right to counsel?

Batson v. Kentucky, 476 U.S. 79 (1986)

James Kirkland Batson, an African American man, was arrested for second-degree burglary and receipt of stolen goods. At his trial the prosecutor used peremptory challenges to strike all four members of the jury venire who were black. Traditionally both sides at trial have a certain number of peremptory challenges that may be used for any reason. For example, defendants may challenge a prospective juror when they have a hunch that the juror does not like them based on the juror's body language. Batson's defense counsel unsuccessfully objected to the prosecutor's actions. The all-white jury convicted Batson on all charges. Batson appealed, claiming that allowing the prosecutor to strike all African Americans from the jury violated his right to a fair jury trial. The Supreme Court of Kentucky rejected that plea. Batson appealed to the Supreme Court of the United States.

The Supreme Court by a 7–2 vote declared that Batson had been deprived of a fair jury trial. Justice Powell's majority opinion ruled that defendants in a criminal trial had a right to prove racial discrimination solely based on evidence concerning how the prosecutor exercised peremptory challenges in their cases. Batson *overruled* Swain v. Alabama *(1965), which required defendants to demonstrate that a prosecutor or prosecutors from the same office consistently struck all African Americans from trial juries. Why did Justice Powell believe that* Swain *should be overruled? Why did Justice Rehnquist disagree? Who had the better argument? What explains why the Supreme Court in the conservative Reagan Era reversed a conservative precedent from the liberal New Deal/Great Society Era?*

JUSTICE POWELL delivered the opinion of the Court.

. . .

More than a century ago, the Court decided that the State denies a black defendant equal protection of the laws when it puts him on trial before a jury from which members of his race have been purposefully excluded. *Strauder v. West Virginia* (1880). . . .

In holding that racial discrimination in jury selection offends the Equal Protection Clause, the Court in *Strauder* recognized, however, that a defendant has no right to a "petit jury composed in whole or in part of persons of his own race." . . .

Purposeful racial discrimination in selection of the venire violates a defendant's right to equal protection because it denies him the protection that a trial by jury is intended to secure. . . . Those on the venire must be "indifferently chosen," to secure the defendant's right under the Fourteenth Amendment to "protection of life and liberty against race or color prejudice."

Racial discrimination in selection of jurors harms not only the accused whose life or liberty they are summoned to try. Competence to serve as a juror ultimately depends on an assessment of individual qualifications and ability impartially to consider evidence presented at a trial. . . . A person's race simply "is unrelated to his fitness as a juror." . . .

The harm from discriminatory jury selection extends beyond that inflicted on the defendant and the excluded juror to touch the entire community. Selection procedures that purposefully exclude black persons from juries undermine public confidence in the fairness of our system of justice. . . .

. . .

. . . [T]he State's privilege to strike individual jurors through peremptory challenges is subject to the commands of the Equal Protection Clause. Although a prosecutor ordinarily is entitled to exercise permitted peremptory challenges "for any reason at all, as long as that reason is related to his view concerning the outcome" of the case to be tried, . . . the Equal Protection Clause forbids the prosecutor to challenge potential jurors solely on account of their race or on the assumption that black jurors as a group will be unable impartially to consider the State's case against a black defendant.

. . .

The standards for assessing a prima facie case in the context of discriminatory selection of the venire have been fully articulated since *Swain v. Alabama* (1965). . . . These principles support our conclusion that a defendant may establish a prima facie case of purposeful discrimination in selection of the petit jury solely on evidence concerning the prosecutor's exercise of peremptory challenges at the defendant's trial. To establish such a case, the defendant first must show that he is a member of a cognizable racial group, . . . and that the prosecutor has exercised peremptory challenges to remove from the venire members of the defendant's race. Second, the defendant is entitled to rely on the fact, as to which there can be no dispute, that peremptory challenges constitute a jury selection practice that permits "those to discriminate who are of a mind to discriminate." . . . Finally, the defendant must show that these facts and any other relevant circumstances raise an inference that the prosecutor used that practice to exclude the veniremen from the petit jury on account of their race. This combination of factors in the empaneling of the petit jury, as in the selection of the venire, raises the necessary inference of purposeful discrimination.

. . .

Once the defendant makes a prima facie showing, the burden shifts to the State to come forward with a neutral explanation for challenging black jurors. Though this requirement imposes a limitation in some cases on the full peremptory character of the historic challenge, we emphasize that the prosecutor's explanation need not rise to the level justifying exercise of a challenge for cause. . . . But the prosecutor may not rebut the defendant's prima facie case of discrimination by stating merely that he challenged jurors of the defendant's race on the assumption—or his intuitive judgment—that they would be partial to the defendant because of their shared race. . . . Just as the Equal Protection Clause forbids the States to exclude black persons from the venire on the assumption that blacks as a group are unqualified to serve as jurors . . . , so it forbids the States to strike black veniremen on the assumption that they will be biased in a particular case simply because the defendant is black. The core guarantee of equal protection, ensuring citizens that their State will not discriminate on account of race, would be meaningless were we to approve the exclusion of jurors on the basis of such assumptions, which arise solely from the jurors' race. Nor may the prosecutor rebut the defendant's case merely by denying that he had a discriminatory motive or "affirm[ing] [his] good faith in making individual selections." . . . The prosecutor therefore must articulate a neutral explanation related to the particular case to be tried. The trial court then will have the duty to determine if the defendant has established purposeful discrimination.

. . .

While we recognize, of course, that the peremptory challenge occupies an important position in our trial procedures, we do not agree that our decision today will undermine the contribution the challenge generally makes to the administration of justice. The reality of practice, amply reflected in many state—and federal—court opinions, shows that the challenge may be, and unfortunately at times has been, used to discriminate against black jurors. By requiring trial courts to be sensitive to the racially discriminatory use of peremptory challenges, our decision enforces the mandate of equal protection and furthers the ends of justice. In view of the heterogeneous population of our Nation, public respect for our criminal justice system and the rule of law will be strengthened if we ensure that no citizen is disqualified from jury service because of his race.

. . .

JUSTICE WHITE, concurring. . . .

JUSTICE MARSHALL, concurring.

. . .

Misuse of the peremptory challenge to exclude black jurors has become both common and flagrant. Black defendants rarely have been able to compile statistics showing the extent of that practice, but the few cases setting out such figures are instructive. . . . An instruction book used by the prosecutor's office in Dallas County, Texas, explicitly advised prosecutors that they conduct jury selection so as to eliminate "'any member of a minority group.'" In 100 felony trials in Dallas County in 1983–1984, prosecutors peremptorily struck 405 out of 467 eligible black jurors; the chance of a qualified black sitting on a jury was 1 in 10, compared to 1 in 2 for a white.

. . .

I wholeheartedly concur in the Court's conclusion that use of the peremptory challenge to remove blacks from juries, on the basis of their race, violates the Equal Protection Clause. I would go further, however, in fashioning a remedy adequate to eliminate that discrimination. Merely allowing defendants the opportunity to challenge the racially discriminatory use of peremptory challenges in individual cases will not end the illegitimate use of the peremptory challenge.

Evidentiary analysis similar to that set out by the Court . . . has been adopted as a matter of state law in States including Massachusetts and California. Cases from those jurisdictions illustrate the limitations of the approach. First, defendants cannot attack the discriminatory use of peremptory challenges at all unless the challenges are so flagrant as to establish a prima facie case. This means, in those States, that where only one or two black jurors survive the challenges for cause, the prosecutor need have no compunction about striking them from the jury because of their race. . . .

Second, when a defendant can establish a prima facie case, trial courts face the difficult burden of assessing prosecutors' motives. . . . Any prosecutor can easily assert facially neutral reasons for striking a juror, and trial courts are ill equipped to second-guess those reasons. How is the court to treat a prosecutor's statement that he struck a juror because the juror had a son about the same age as defendant, . . . or seemed "uncommunicative," . . . or "never cracked a smile" and, therefore "did not possess the sensitivities necessary to realistically look at the issues and decide the facts in this case?" If such easily generated explanations are sufficient to discharge the prosecutor's obligation to justify his strikes on nonracial grounds, then the protection erected by the Court today may be illusory.

Nor is outright prevarication by prosecutors the only danger here. . . . A prosecutor's own conscious or unconscious racism may lead him easily to the conclusion that a prospective black juror is "sullen," or "distant," a characterization that would not have come to his mind if a white juror had acted identically. . . .

The inherent potential of peremptory challenges to distort the jury process by permitting the exclusion of jurors on racial grounds should ideally lead the Court to ban them entirely from the criminal justice system. . . .

. . .

JUSTICE STEVENS, with whom JUSTICE BRENNAN joins, concurring. . . .

JUSTICE O'CONNOR, concurring. . . .

CHIEF JUSTICE BURGER, joined by JUSTICE REHNQUIST, dissenting.

. . .

Today the Court sets aside the peremptory challenge, a procedure which has been part of the common law for many centuries and part of our jury system for nearly 200 years. It does so on the basis of a constitutional argument that was rejected, without a single dissent, in *Swain v. Alabama*. . . .

. . .

A moment's reflection quickly reveals the vast differences between the racial exclusions involved in *Strauder* and the allegations before us today:

> Exclusion from the venire summons process implies that the government (usually the legislative or judicial branch) . . . has made the general determination that those excluded are unfit to try *any* case. Exercise of the peremptory challenge, by contrast, represents the discrete decision, made by one of two or more opposed *litigants* in the trial phase of our adversary system of justice, that the challenged venireperson will likely be more unfavorable to that litigant in that *particular case* than others on the same venire.

. . .

Unwilling to rest solely on jury venire cases such as *Strauder*, the Court also invokes general equal protection principles in support of its holding. But peremptory challenges are often lodged, of necessity, for reasons "normally thought irrelevant to legal proceedings or official action, namely, the race, religion, nationality, occupation or affiliations of people summoned for jury duty." . . . Moreover, in making peremptory challenges, both the prosecutor and defense attorney necessarily act on only limited information or hunch. The process cannot be indicted on the sole basis that such decisions are made on the basis of "assumption" or "intuitive judgment." . . . As a result, unadulterated equal protection analysis is simply inapplicable to peremptory challenges exercised in any particular case. . . .

. . .

. . . Our system permits two types of challenges: challenges for cause and peremptory challenges. Challenges for cause obviously have to be explained; by definition, peremptory challenges do not. "It is called a peremptory challenge, because the prisoner may challenge peremptorily, on his own dislike, *without showing of any cause*." . . . Analytically, there is no middle ground: A challenge either has to be explained or it does not. It is readily apparent, then, that to permit inquiry into the basis for a peremptory challenge would force "the peremptory challenge [to] collapse into the challenge for cause." . . .

. . .

JUSTICE REHNQUIST, with whom THE CHIEF JUSTICE joins, dissenting.

. . .

I cannot subscribe to the Court's unprecedented use of the Equal Protection Clause to restrict the historic scope of the peremptory challenge, which has been described as "a necessary part of trial by jury." . . . In my view, there is simply nothing "unequal" about the State's using its peremptory challenges to strike blacks from the jury in cases involving black defendants, so long as such challenges are also used to exclude whites in cases involving white defendants, Hispanics in cases involving Hispanic defendants, Asians in cases involving Asian defendants, and so on. This case-specific use of peremptory challenges by the State does not single out blacks, or members of any other race for that matter, for discriminatory treatment. Such use of peremptories is at best based upon seat-of-the-pants instincts, which are undoubtedly crudely stereotypical and may in many cases be hopelessly mistaken.

But as long as they are applied across-the-board to jurors of all races and nationalities, I do not see—and the Court most certainly has not explained—how their use violates the Equal Protection Clause.

. . .

The use of group affiliations, such as age, race, or occupation, as a "proxy" for potential juror partiality, based on the assumption or belief that members of one group are more likely to favor defendants who belong to the same group, has long been accepted as a legitimate basis for the State's exercise of peremptory challenges. . . . Indeed, given the need for reasonable limitations on the time devoted to *voir dire*, the use of such "proxies" by both the State and the defendant may be extremely useful in eliminating from the jury persons who might be biased in one way or another. The Court today holds that the State may not use its peremptory challenges to strike black prospective jurors on this basis without violating the Constitution. But I do not believe there is anything in the Equal Protection Clause, or any other constitutional provision, that justifies such a departure from the substantive holding . . . of *Swain*. Petitioner in the instant case failed to make a sufficient showing to overcome the presumption announced in *Swain* that the State's use of peremptory challenges was related to the context of the case. I would therefore affirm the judgment of the court below. . . .

E. Punishments

Ronald Reagan and his political allies sought to restore capital punishment.

Many moderate and conservative Democrats supported these pro–capital punishment initiatives, particularly after Democratic presidential candidate Michael Dukakis's anti–capital punishment response to a question in the 1988 presidential debates was seen as detrimental to his campaign. Public support for the death penalty had ebbed in the 1960s but had surged back in the 1970s and 1980s. When campaigning for the presidency in 1992, Governor Bill Clinton of Arkansas recognized this change in public opinion when he very publically demonstrated his commitment to capital punishment by returning to his home state to oversee the execution of Ricky Ray Rector.

The Supreme Court of the United States was in step with the rest of constitutional politics on the death penalty. *McCleskey v. Kemp* (1987) rejected a broad challenge to capital punishment statutes as administered. McCleskey's lawyers relied on statistics demonstrating that persons who murdered white victims were far more likely to be sentenced to death than murderers whose victims were persons of color. Justice Powell's majority opinion rejected this use of statistics because McCleskey had not demonstrated that racial prejudice specifically influenced the jury decision to sentence him to death. Many important decisions curtailed access to federal habeas corpus, the process that during the 1970s and early 1980s had enabled many capitally sentenced persons to avoid execution. *McCleskey v. Zant* (1991) sharply restricted the use of successive habeas corpus petitions in death cases. *Herrera v. Collins* (1993) ruled that federal habeas corpus proceedings could rarely consider new evidence that a capitally sentenced prison was innocent. In *Butler v. McKellar* (1990) and *Penry v. Lynaugh* (1989) a 5–4 judicial majority extended *Teague v. Lane* (1989) to death cases. Persons sentenced to death could not normally have their conviction or sentence reversed in habeas corpus proceedings, even when a judicial majority believed that the trial court had made a constitutional mistake, unless the judicial majority maintained that previous precedents so clearly dictated the right constitutional rule that the trial court decision was an unreasonable interpretation of the constitutional law.

Justices Blackmun and Stevens rethought their original support for capital punishment in light of the Supreme Court's increased willingness to sustain death sentences. Before retiring, Blackmun recanted completely. His dissent from the denial of certiorari in *Callins v. Collins* (1994) stated, "Experience has taught us that the constitutional goal of eliminating arbitrariness and discrimination from the administration of death can never be achieved without compromising an equally essential component of fundamental fairness—individualized sentencing." Justice Scalia blasted this attack on the capital sentencing process. His opinion in *Callins* called on the Supreme Court to reverse the past precedents imposing significant limits on state capacity to execute vicious criminals. In his view, if popular majorities "merely conclude that justice requires such brutal deaths to be avenged by capital punishment[,] the creation of false, untextual, and unhistorical contradictions within the Court's Eighth Amendment jurisprudence should not prevent them."

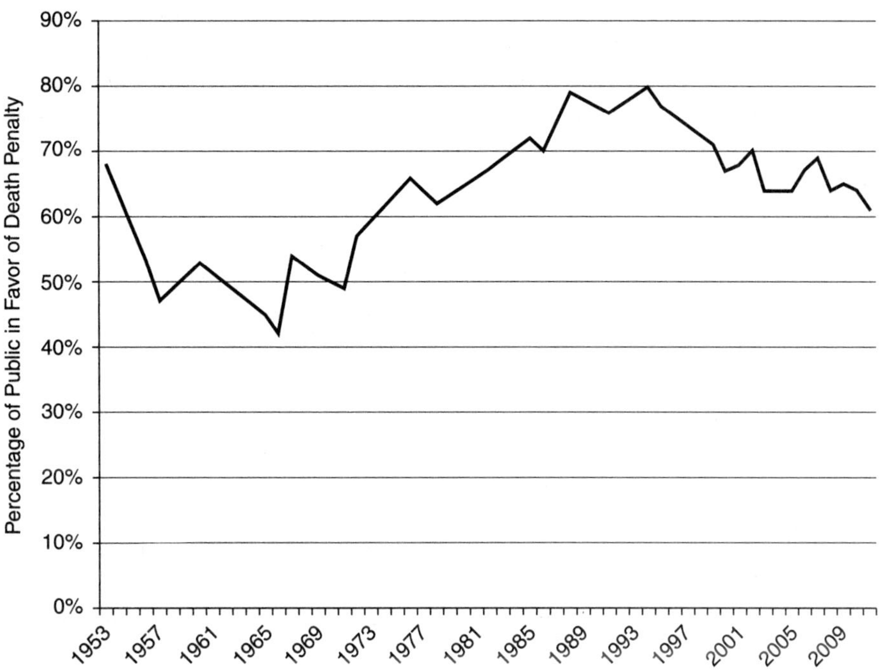

Figure 10-5 Public Support for the Death Penalty, 1953–2011

Source: Copyright © Gallup, Inc. All rights reserved. The content is used with permission; however, Gallup retains all rights of republication.

McCleskey v. Kemp, 481 U.S. 279 (1987)

Warren McCleskey shot and killed a white police officer during a robbery. He was convicted of murder and sentenced to death after a Georgia jury found two aggravating circumstances beyond a reasonable doubt: first, that McCleskey had murdered a police officer, and second, that the murder was committed during an armed robbery. The Supreme Court of Georgia affirmed the sentence, and the Supreme Court of the United States rejected McCleskey's request for a writ of certiorari. McCleskey instituted an action for habeas corpus, insisting that Georgia's procedures for imposing capital punishment discriminated against persons of color. McCleskey, an African American man, claimed that Georgia disproportionately sentenced to death persons who murdered white victims, even when the aggravating and mitigating circumstances were identical.[39] *After the Georgia state courts and lower federal courts rejected this claim, McCleskey appealed to the Supreme Court of the United States.*

The Supreme Court rejected McCleskey's petition by a 5–4 vote. Justice Powell's majority opinion held that McCleskey had failed to demonstrate that he was a victim of racial discrimination. Justice Powell worried that if the Court accepted McCleskey's claim, the justices would soon face claims that race and other forms of discrimination influenced other aspects of the criminal justice system. Is this a legitimate prudential argument? Is there a basis for distinguishing between racial discrimination in the capital sentencing process and racial discrimination in the criminal justice system more generally? The evidence that McCleskey presented to the Supreme Court of the United States differed from the evidence that opponents of capital punishment had presented to the Supreme Court in Furman v. Georgia *(1972). Before 1970 persons of color were far more likely to be sentenced to death than white persons, even when the circumstances of their crimes were similar. McCleskey's claim focused on the race of murder victims. The studies he presented indicated that criminal defendants who murdered whites had a far greater chance of being sentenced to death*

39. See David C. Balbus, Charles Pulaski, and George Woodworth, "Comparative Review of Death Sentences: An Empirical Study of the Georgia Experience," *Journal of Criminal Law and Criminology* 74 (1983): 661–753.

than criminal defendants who murdered persons of color. Do you believe that a constitutional difference exists between discrimination on the basis of the race of the defendant and discrimination on the basis of the race of the victim?[40] *Did any of the justices see a distinction? How did the justices treat the evidence that McCleskey presented?*

McCleskey *was the last major effort that opponents of capital punishment made to strike a serious blow against the practice. Lawyers still attacked the constitutionality of individual death sentences or small categories of death-sentenced persons, but in no subsequent case was the constitutionality of most death sentences in the United States seriously questioned. While proponents of capital punishment cheered this development and the increase in executions that took place during the 1980s and 1990s, Justice Powell did not. Shortly after retiring from the bench, Powell recanted his* McCleskey *opinion.*[41]

JUSTICE POWELL delivered the opinion of the Court.

. . .

Our analysis begins with the basic principle that a defendant who alleges an equal protection violation has the burden of proving "the existence of purposeful discrimination." . . . A corollary to this principle is that a criminal defendant must prove that the purposeful discrimination "had a discriminatory effect" on him. . . . Thus, to prevail under the Equal Protection Clause, McCleskey must prove that the decisionmakers in *his* case acted with discriminatory purpose. He offers no evidence specific to his own case that would support an inference that racial considerations played a part in his sentence. Instead, he relies solely on the Baldus study. McCleskey argues that the Baldus study compels an inference that his sentence rests on purposeful discrimination. McCleskey's claim that these statistics are sufficient proof of discrimination, without regard to the facts of a particular case, would extend to all capital cases in Georgia, at least where the victim was white and the defendant is black.

The Court has accepted statistics as proof of intent to discriminate in certain limited contexts. First, this Court has accepted statistical disparities as proof of an equal protection violation in the selection of the jury venire in a particular district. . . . Second, this Court has accepted statistics in the form of multiple-regression analysis to prove statutory violations under Title VII of the Civil Rights Act of 1964. . . .

But the nature of the capital sentencing decision, and the relationship of the statistics to that decision, are fundamentally different from the corresponding elements in the venire-selection or Title VII cases. Most importantly, each particular decision to impose the death penalty is made by a petit jury selected from a properly constituted venire. Each jury is unique in its composition, and the Constitution requires that its decision rest on consideration of innumerable factors that vary according to the characteristics of the individual defendant and the facts of the particular capital offense. . . . Thus, the application of an inference drawn from the general statistics to a specific decision in a trial and sentencing simply is not comparable to the application of an inference drawn from general statistics to a specific venire-selection or Title VII case. In those cases, the statistics relate to fewer entities, and fewer variables are relevant to the challenged decisions.

Another important difference between the cases in which we have accepted statistics as proof of discriminatory intent and this case is that, in the venire-selection and Title VII contexts, the decisionmaker has an opportunity to explain the statistical disparity. . . . Here, the State has no practical opportunity to rebut the Baldus study. "[C]ontrolling considerations of . . . public policy," . . . dictate that jurors "cannot be called . . . to testify to the motives and influences that led to their verdict." . . . Similarly, the policy considerations behind a prosecutor's traditionally "wide discretion" suggest the impropriety of our requiring prosecutors to defend their decisions to seek death penalties, "often years after they were made." . . . Moreover, absent far stronger proof, it is unnecessary to seek such a rebuttal, because a legitimate and unchallenged explanation for the decision is apparent from the record: McCleskey committed an act for which the United States Constitution and Georgia laws permit imposition of the death penalty.

. . .

. . . Even Professor Baldus does not contend that his statistics *prove* that race enters into any capital sentencing decisions or that race was a factor in McCleskey's particular case. Statistics at most may show only a likelihood that a particular factor entered into some

40. For a good discussion of these issues, see Randall L. Kennedy, "*McCleskey v. Kemp*: Race, Capital Punishment, and the Supreme Court," *Harvard Law Review* 101 (1988): 1388–1443.

41. See Mark Graber, "Judicial Recantations: Two Thoughts About Second Thoughts," *Syracuse Law Review* 45 (1995): 807–814.

decisions. There is, of course, some risk of racial prejudice influencing a jury's decision in a criminal case. There are similar risks that other kinds of prejudice will influence other criminal trials. . . . The question "is at what point that risk becomes constitutionally unacceptable." . . .

. . .

At most, the Baldus study indicates a discrepancy that appears to correlate with race. Apparent disparities in sentencing are an inevitable part of our criminal justice system. The discrepancy indicated by the Baldus study is "a far cry from the major systemic defects identified in *Furman*." . . . "[T]here can be 'no perfect procedure for deciding in which cases governmental authority should be used to impose death.'" . . . Despite these imperfections, our consistent rule has been that constitutional guarantees are met when "the mode [for determining guilt or punishment] itself has been surrounded with safeguards to make it as fair as possible." . . . Where the discretion that is fundamental to our criminal process is involved, we decline to assume that what is unexplained is invidious. In light of the safeguards designed to minimize racial bias in the process, the fundamental value of jury trial in our criminal justice system, and the benefits that discretion provides to criminal defendants, we hold that the Baldus study does not demonstrate a constitutionally significant risk of racial bias affecting the Georgia capital sentencing process.

. . .

. . . McCleskey's claim, taken to its logical conclusion, throws into serious question the principles that underlie our entire criminal justice system. The Eighth Amendment is not limited in application to capital punishment, but applies to all penalties. . . . Thus, if we accepted McCleskey's claim that racial bias has impermissibly tainted the capital sentencing decision, we could soon be faced with similar claims as to other types of penalty. Moreover, the claim that his sentence rests on the irrelevant factor of race easily could be extended to apply to claims based on unexplained discrepancies that correlate to membership in other minority groups, and even to gender. . . . If arbitrary and capricious punishment is the touchstone under the Eighth Amendment, such a claim could—at least in theory—be based upon any arbitrary variable, such as the defendant's facial characteristics, or the physical attractiveness of the defendant or the victim. . . . The Constitution does not require that a State eliminate any demonstrable disparity that correlates with a potentially irrelevant factor in order to operate a criminal justice system that includes capital punishment. As we have stated specifically in the context of capital punishment, the Constitution does not "plac[e] totally unrealistic conditions on its use."

McCleskey's arguments are best presented to the legislative bodies. It is not the responsibility—or indeed even the right—of this Court to determine the appropriate punishment for particular crimes. It is the legislatures, the elected representatives of the people, that are "constituted to respond to the will and consequently the moral values of the people." Legislatures also are better qualified to weigh and "evaluate the results of statistical studies in terms of their own local conditions and with a flexibility of approach that is not available to the courts."

JUSTICE BRENNAN, with whom JUSTICE MARSHALL joins, and with whom JUSTICE BLACKMUN and JUSTICE STEVENS join . . . dissenting.

. . .

At some point in this case, Warren McCleskey doubtless asked his lawyer whether a jury was likely to sentence him to die. A candid reply to this question would have been disturbing. First, counsel would have to tell McCleskey that few of the details of the crime or of McCleskey's past criminal conduct were more important than the fact that his victim was white. . . . Furthermore, counsel would feel bound to tell McCleskey that defendants charged with killing white victims in Georgia are 4.3 times as likely to be sentenced to death as defendants charged with killing blacks. . . . In addition, frankness would compel the disclosure that it was more likely than not that the race of McCleskey's victim would determine whether he received a death sentence: 6 of every 11 defendants convicted of killing a white person would not have received the death penalty if their victims had been black, . . . while, among defendants with aggravating and mitigating factors comparable to McCleskey's, 20 of every 34 would not have been sentenced to die if their victims had been black. . . .

. . .

It is important to emphasize at the outset that the Court's observation that McCleskey cannot prove the influence of race on any particular sentencing decision is irrelevant in evaluating his Eighth Amendment claim. Since *Furman v. Georgia* (1972), . . . the Court has been concerned with the *risk* of the imposition of an arbitrary sentence, rather than the proven fact of one. *Furman* held that the death penalty "may not be imposed under sentencing procedures that create a substantial risk that the punishment will be inflicted in an arbitrary and capricious manner." . . . This emphasis on risk acknowledges the difficulty of divining the jury's motivation in an individual case. In addition, it reflects the fact that concern for arbitrariness focuses on the rationality of the system as a whole, and that a system that features a significant probability that sentencing decisions are influenced by impermissible considerations cannot be regarded as rational. . . .

. . .

The Baldus study indicates that, after taking into account some 230 nonracial factors that might legitimately influence a sentencer, the jury *more likely than not* would have spared McCleskey's life had his victim been black. The study distinguishes between those cases in which (1) the jury exercises virtually no discretion because the strength or weakness of aggravating factors usually suggests that only one outcome is appropriate; and (2) cases reflecting an "intermediate" level of aggravation, in which the jury has considerable discretion in choosing a sentence. McCleskey's case falls into the intermediate range. In such cases, death is imposed in 34% of white-victim crimes and 14% of black-victim crimes, a difference of 139% in the rate of imposition of the death penalty. . . . In other words, just under 59%—almost 6 in 10—defendants comparable to McCleskey would not have received the death penalty if their victims had been black.

. . .

. . . Furthermore, blacks who kill whites are sentenced to death at nearly *22 times* the rate of blacks who kill blacks, and more than *7 times* the rate of whites who kill blacks. . . . In addition, prosecutors seek the death penalty for 70% of black defendants with white victims, but for only 15% of black defendants with black victims, and only 19% of white defendants with black victims. . . . Since our decision upholding the Georgia capital sentencing system in *Gregg*, the State has executed seven persons. All of the seven were convicted of killing whites, and six of the seven executed were black. . . . Such execution figures are especially striking in light of the fact that, during the period encompassed by the Baldus study, only 9.2% of Georgia homicides involved black defendants and white victims, while 60.7% involved black victims.

. . . Georgia's legacy of a race-conscious criminal justice system . . . indicates that McCleskey's claim is not a fanciful product of mere statistical artifice.

For many years, Georgia operated openly and formally precisely the type of dual system the evidence shows is still effectively in place. The criminal law expressly differentiated between crimes committed by and against blacks and whites, distinctions whose lineage traced back to the time of slavery.

. . .

The discretion afforded prosecutors and jurors in the Georgia capital sentencing system creates . . . opportunities [for continued discrimination]. No guidelines govern prosecutorial decisions to seek the death penalty, and Georgia provides juries with no list of aggravating and mitigating factors, nor any standard for balancing them against one another. . . . The Georgia sentencing system therefore provides considerable opportunity for racial considerations, however subtle and unconscious, to influence charging and sentencing decisions.

. . .

In fairness, the Court's fear that McCleskey's claim is an invitation to descend a slippery slope also rests on the realization that any humanly imposed system of penalties will exhibit some imperfection. Yet to reject McCleskey's powerful evidence on this basis is to ignore both the qualitatively different character of the death penalty and the particular repugnance of racial discrimination, considerations which may properly be taken into account in determining whether various punishments are "cruel and unusual."

. . .

JUSTICE BLACKMUN, with whom JUSTICE MARSHALL and JUSTICE STEVENS join, and with whom JUSTICE BRENNAN joins in part, dissenting.

. . .

Under *Batson v. Kentucky* (1986) . . . , McCleskey must meet a three-factor standard. First, he must establish that he is a member of a group "that is a recognizable, distinct class, singled out for different treatment." Second, he must make a showing of a substantial degree of differential treatment. Third, he must establish that the allegedly discriminatory procedure is susceptible to abuse or is not racially neutral. . . .

. . . The Baldus study demonstrates that black persons are a distinct group that are singled out for different treatment in the Georgia capital sentencing system. . . .

. . .

McCleskey demonstrated the degree to which his death sentence was affected by racial factors by introducing multiple-regression analyses that explain how much of the statistical distribution of the cases analyzed is attributable to the racial factors. . . . The most persuasive evidence of the constitutionally significant effect of racial factors in the Georgia capital sentencing system is McCleskey's proof that the race of the victim is more important in explaining the imposition of a death sentence than is the factor whether the defendant was a prime mover in the homicide. Similarly, the race-of-victim factor is nearly as crucial as the statutory aggravating circumstance whether the defendant had a prior record of a conviction for a capital crime. . . .

McCleskey produced evidence concerning the role of racial factors at the various steps in the decision-making process, focusing on the prosecutor's decision as to which cases merit the death sentence. McCleskey established that the race of the victim is an especially significant factor at the point where the defendant has been convicted of murder and the prosecutor must choose whether to proceed to the penalty phase of the trial and create the possibility that a death sentence may be imposed or to accept the imposition of a sentence of life imprisonment. McCleskey demonstrated this effect at both the statewide level . . . and in Fulton County where he was tried and sentenced. . . .

. . .

. . . The issue in this case is the extent to which the constitutional guarantee of equal protection limits the discretion in the Georgia capital sentencing system. As the Court concedes, discretionary authority can be discriminatory authority. . . . Prosecutorial decisions may not be "'deliberately based upon an unjustifiable standard such as race, religion, or other arbitrary classification.'" . . .

. . .

JUSTICE STEVENS, with whom JUSTICE BLACKMUN joins, dissenting.

. . .

The Court's decision appears to be based on a fear that the acceptance of McCleskey's claim would sound the death knell for capital punishment in Georgia. If society were indeed forced to choose between a racially discriminatory death penalty (one that provides heightened protection against murder "for whites only") and no death penalty at all, the choice mandated by the Constitution would be plain. . . . But the Court's fear is unfounded. One of the lessons of the Baldus study is that there exist certain categories of extremely serious crimes for which prosecutors consistently seek, and juries consistently impose, the death penalty without regard to the race of the victim or the race of the offender. If Georgia were to narrow the class of death-eligible defendants to those categories, the danger of arbitrary and discriminatory imposition of the death penalty would be significantly decreased, if not eradicated. As Justice BRENNAN has demonstrated in his dissenting opinion, such a restructuring of the sentencing scheme is surely not too high a price to pay.

Suggested Readings

Bell, Derrick. 1987. *And We Are Not Saved: The Elusive Quest for Racial Justice.* New York: Basic.

Bork, Robert H. 1990. *The Tempting of America: The Political Seduction of the Law.* New York: Free Press.

Brisbin, Richard A., Jr. 1997. *Justice Antonin Scalia and the Conservative Revival.* Baltimore, MD: Johns Hopkins University Press.

Choper, Jesse H. 1995. *Securing Religious Liberty: Principles for Judicial Interpretation of the Religion Clauses.* Chicago: University of Chicago Press.

Conlan, Timothy J. 1998. *The New Federalism: Twenty-Five Years of Intergovernmental Reform.* Washington, DC: Brookings Institution.

Craig, Barbara. 1988. Chadha: *The Story of an Epic Constitutional Struggle.* New York: Oxford University Press.

Crovitz, L. Gordon, and Jeremy A. Rabkin, eds. 1989. *The Fettered Presidency: Legal Constraints on the Presidency.* Washington, DC: American Enterprise Institute.

Davis, Sue. 1989. *Justice Rehnquist and the Constitution.* Princeton, NJ: Princeton University Press.

Downs, Donald Alexander. 1989. *The New Politics of Pornography.* Chicago: University of Chicago Press.

Ely, John Hart. 1993. *War and Responsibility: Constitutional Lessons of Vietnam and Its Aftermath.* Cambridge, MA: Harvard University Press.

Epps, Garrett. 2001. *To an Unknown God: Religious Freedom on Trial.* New York: St. Martin's.

Epstein, Richard. 1985. *Takings: Private Property and the Power of Eminent Domain.* Cambridge, MA: Harvard University Press.

Fisher, Louis. 1995. *Presidential War Power.* Lawrence: University Press of Kansas.

———. 1997. *Constitutional Conflicts Between Congress and the President.* Lawrence: University Press of Kansas.

Gerhardt, Michael. 2000. *The Federal Appointments Process: A Constitutional and Historical Analysis.* Durham, NC: Duke University Press.

Graber, Mark A. 1996. *Rethinking Abortion: Equal Choice, the Constitution, and Reproductive Politics.* Princeton, NJ: Princeton University Press.

Guinier, Lani. 1994. *The Tyranny of the Majority: Fundamental Fairness in Representative Democracy.* New York: Free Press.

Jones, Charles O. 1994. *The Presidency in a Separated System.* Washington, DC: Brookings Institution.

Kahn, Ronald. 1994. *The Supreme Court and Constitutional Theory, 1953–1993.* Lawrence: University Press of Kansas.

Karst, Kenneth L. 1989. *Belonging to America: Equal Citizenship and the Constitution.* New Haven, CT: Yale University Press.

Keck, Tom. 2004. *The Most Activist Supreme Court in History: The Road to Modern Judicial Conservatism.* Chicago: University of Chicago Press.

Koh, Harold H. 1990. *The National Security Constitution: Sharing Powers After the Iran-Contra Affair.* New Haven, CT: Yale University Press.

Korn, Jessica. 1996. *The Power of Separating: American Constitutionalism and the Myth of the Legislative Veto.* Princeton, NJ: Princeton University Press.

Lazarus, Edward. 1998. *Closed Chambers: The First Eyewitness Account of the Epic Struggles Inside the Supreme Court.* New York: Times.

Licht, Robert A., and Robert A. Goldwein, eds. 1990. *Foreign Policy and the Constitution.* Washington, DC: American Enterprise Institute.

MacKinnon, Catherine A. 1987. *Feminism Unmodified: Discourses on Life and Law.* Cambridge, MA: Harvard University Press.

Maltz, Earl M. 2003. *Rehnquist Justice: Understanding the Court Dynamic.* Lawrence: University Press of Kansas.

Matsuda, Mari J., Charles R. Lawrence III, Richard Delgado, and Kimberle Williams Crenshaw. 1993. *Words that Wound: Critical Race Theory, Assaultive Speech, and the First Amendment.* Boulder, CO: Westview.

Maveety, Nancy. 1996. *Justice Sandra Day O'Connor: Strategist on the Supreme Court.* Lanham, MD: Rowman & Littlefield.

McCann, Michael W. 1994. *Rights at Work: Pay Equity Reform and the Politics of Legal Mobilization.* Chicago: University of Chicago Press.

Minow, Martha. 1990. *Making All the Difference: Inclusion, Exclusion, and American Law.* Ithaca, NY: Cornell University Press.

O'Neill, Johnathan G. 2005. *Originalism in American Law and Politics: A Constitutional History.* Baltimore, MD: Johns Hopkins University Press.

Perry, Michael J. 1982. *The Constitution, the Courts, and Human Rights: An Inquiry into the Legitimacy of Constitutional Policymaking by the Judiciary.* New Haven, CT: Yale University Press.

Savage, David G. 1992. *Turning Right: The Making of the Rehnquist Court.* New York: Wiley.

Teles, Steven M. 2008. *The Rise of the Conservative Legal Movement: The Battle for the Control of the Law.* Princeton, NJ: Princeton University Press.

Thernstrom, Abigail M. 1987. *Whose Votes Count? Affirmative Action and Minority Voting Rights.* Cambridge, MA: Harvard University Press.

Tribe, Laurence H. 1985. *Constitutional Choices.* Cambridge, MA: Harvard University Press.

Walker, David B. 1995. *The Rebirth of Federalism: Slouching Toward Washington.* Chatham, NJ: Chatham House.

Yarbrough, Tinsley E. 2000. *The Rehnquist Court and the Constitution.* New York: Oxford University Press.

Chapter 11

The Contemporary Era: 1994–Present

I. Introduction

Conservatism seemed ascendant in the Reagan Era, but victory proved elusive. Republicans could not dislodge the Democrats from the House of Representatives or hold the Senate after 1986. Despite high poll numbers early in his term, after the fall of the Berlin Wall and the first Iraq War, President George H. W. Bush proved vulnerable. Bill Clinton seized the White House for the Democrats in 1992 as the economy entered a downturn, with businessman H. Ross Perot emerging as an independent candidate. Clinton won, however, by the smallest popular vote margin since Woodrow Wilson's victory in the splintered campaign of 1912. Eight years later, Texas governor George W. Bush wrested the White House from Vice President Al Gore after a bruising election dispute that ended in the U.S. Supreme Court. In 2008 the White House again changed hands, as Barack Obama handily won election in the midst of an economic recession.

Neither political party gained the political control over national institutions necessary to make either distinctively conservative or distinctively liberal constitutional visions the official law of the land. Today, politics remains fractured and uncertain. Divided government and slim, unstable congressional majorities have become common. Liberal Democrats briefly appeared to have established national domination after the elections of 1992, when they gained control of the White House, Senate, and House of Representatives, but a far more conservative Republican party captured both houses of Congress in 1994. President George W. Bush hoped to build on earlier GOP success and national security crises, but his second term was mired in war and recession, and Democrats regained control of the House and Senate in the 2006 midterm elections. In 2008 Democrat Barack Obama won a decisive victory, but those gains, too, quickly eroded. In 2010 Republicans gained 63 seats in the House of Representatives, recapturing the majority with the largest seat change since 1948. Divided government persisted after the 2012 elections, with the president facing an increasingly oppositional House of Representatives and a Senate bogged down with an unprecedented number of filibusters.

Developments. Contemporary constitutional politics is frequently structured by polarized national parties and surprisingly centrist judicial decisions.

Republican and Democratic elites take sharply different positions on such issues as federalism, abortion, capital punishment, and the role of religion in public life. When such matters are adjudicated by the Supreme Court, the justices by increasingly narrow margins often adopt moderate positions that fail to satisfy the most important constituencies on both the political left and the political right. Conservative justices issued a series of federalism decisions in the late 1990s and assembled majorities on other issues as well, but the liberal wing of the Court was able to peel off swing justices, especially in rights and liberties cases. This period of polarized parties and more centrist courts has led to the following series of constitutional decisions and practices. Abortion may be heavily regulated but not completely prohibited. Campaign contributions may be limited, but campaign expenditures may not. States may constitutionally impose capital punishment, but not for crimes committed by persons who are mentally retarded or younger than eighteen years old. The Supreme Court declared that

Table 11-1 Major Issues and Decisions of the Contemporary Era

Major Political Issues	Major Constitutional Issues	Major Court Decisions
Partisan polarization and divided government	Judicial supremacy	*United States v. Lopez* (1995)
Terrorism	War powers and domestic surveillance	*Romer v. Evans* (1996)
Iraq War	Independent counsel	*City of Boerne v. Flores* (1997)
Deficit reduction	Impeachment power	*Alden v. Maine* (1999)
Health care reform	Interstate commerce clause	*United States v. Morrison* (2000)
Money in elections	Congress's authority to enforce rights	*Bush v. Gore* (2000)
Immigration reform	State sovereign immunity	*Kyllo v. United States* (2001)
Crime control	Executive privilege	*Lawrence v. Texas* (2003)
Gun control	Second Amendment	*Grutter v. Bollinger* (2003)
Culture wars	Takings clause	*Hamdi v. Rumsfeld* (2004)
Disputed presidential election	Regulation of abortion	*Gonzales v. Raich* (2005)
Voting rights	Homosexual rights and same-sex marriage	*Kelo v. City of New London* (2005)
	Campaign finance reform	*Boumediene v. Bush* (2008)
	Religious liberty	*District of Columbia v. Heller* (2008)
	Equal protection	*Citizens United v. Federal Election Commission* (2010)
	Fourth Amendment and new technologies	*Shelby County v. Holder* (2013)
	Due process and habeas corpus	*United States v. Windsor* (2013)

the University of Michigan had adopted constitutional race-conscious policies for law school admissions but unconstitutional race-conscious policies for undergraduate admissions. Frequently, liberals and conservatives bitterly condemn the same judicial ruling as abandoning vital constitutional principles.

The course of contemporary constitutional politics has been erratic. A list of contemporary constitutional winners might include gays and lesbians, parents who send their children to religious schools, persons subject to the death penalty (the execution rate has been cut in half since 2000), proponents of an individual right to bear arms, and multimillionaires who wish to make very large independent campaign expenditures. What these groups have in common is for the reader to determine. Some Supreme Court decisions have had substantial impacts on the course of constitutional politics. *Bush v. Gore* (2000) played a major role in deciding the 2000 presidential election. Other Supreme Court decisions, despite the overheated rhetoric from both sides of the political spectrum, were of far less consequence. American policy on the War on Terror barely changed after the Supreme Court in three cases—*Hamdi v. Rumsfeld* (2004), *Hamdan v. Rumsfeld* (2006), and *Boumediene v. Bush* (2008)—declared unconstitutional various Bush administration policies on detaining suspected terrorists.

Parties. Every president since George H. W. Bush has called himself "post-partisan," yet all of them have done so in a time of deep partisan division. Voters have become more reliable supporters of one party or the other; political combat has extended to criminal investigations, public hearings, and impeachment threats. The two parties have become more disciplined, staking out divergent positions on constitutional issues from abortion to federalism.[1]

An overriding theme has been "responsible" or "accountable" government. The conservative vision of smaller government, decentralization, and individual responsibility remains influential. The Republican "Contract with America" of 1994, championed by future House Speaker Newt Gingrich, included such populist policies as congressional term limits and balanced budgets. Democratic president Bill Clinton declared that the "era of big government is over." After Barack Obama's election Tea Party Republicans again raised concerns about the cost and growth of government. Still, Republicans and Democrats continue to look to the federal government for solutions to a variety of social and economic problems, from education to health care. Even "welfare reform" and anticrime measures were put forward as ways of making government work better. Neither George W. Bush nor Barack Obama made reducing the size of government a goal, and the growth of the national security state has been a constant of the modern era.

The constitutional politics of civil liberties is more polarized than at any previous time in American history. The Republican Party is presently the home for persons committed to the constitutional rights of gun holders, property owners, religious conservatives, and white Americans aggrieved by affirmative action. The Democratic Party is presently the home for persons committed to the rights associated with nontraditional lifestyles, reproductive choice, and persons of color. The Democratic Party is also home to the decreasing number of persons committed to the rights of persons suspected of crimes, although President Clinton, President Obama, and many Democrats in Congress frequently reject positions on constitutional criminal procedure taken by such groups as the ACLU.

Interest Groups. Interest groups remain active in constitutional politics. More than one hundred interest groups participated when Congress considered revising campaign finance laws or contributed amicus briefs when courts considered the constitutional status of same-sex marriage. Many interest groups pour substantial resources into political and constitutional contests. Whether liberal and conservative associations cancel each other out or bias American constitutional politics in particular directions is controversial.

Many contemporary rights-oriented interest groups are closely identified with and sometimes connected to a particular political party. One recent study observed, "Electoral competition among interest groups . . . appears polarized along partisan lines."[2] The NRA usually supports Republicans. Americans United for the Separation of Church and State is composed largely of Democrats. The Tea Party is presently seeking to push the Republican Party to the right. MoveOn.org continually seeks to push Democrats to the left. The relative power of interest groups is also changing. Pro-choice and gay rights organizations have gained influence in the Democratic Party at the expense of organized labor. The 2012 Republican primary witnessed intense struggles between Christian conservatives, businesspersons, and libertarians for the soul of the party.

Courts. Political polarization helps explain the increasingly bitter tone of debates over the staffing of the federal judiciary and executive offices charged with the responsibility for making constitutional decisions. Ideological voting in judicial confirmations began to rise in the late 1960s, but most senators from one party did not routinely vote against every person nominated to the Supreme Court by a president from the other party. By comparison, almost half of all Democratic senators voted against confirming Bush nominee John Roberts as chief justice, and more than two-thirds voted against confirming Samuel Alito. Similarly, more than two-thirds of Senate Republicans voted against Obama's two judicial nominees, Sonya Sotomayor and Elena Kagan. Contests over the appointments of lower federal court justices, once unheard of, are becoming routine. Democrats threatened

1. Larry M. Bartels, "Partisanship and Voting Behavior, 1952–1996," *American Journal of Political Science* 44 (2000): 35–50; Benjamin Ginsberg and Martin Shefter, *Politics by Other Means* (New York: W. W. Norton, 2002); Geoffrey C. Layman and Thomas M. Carsey, "Party Polarization and 'Conflict Extension' in the American Electorate," *American Journal of Political Science* 46 (2002): 786–802; H. W. Perry, Jr., and L. A. Powe, Jr., "The Political Battle for the Constitution," *Constitutional Commentary* 21 (2004): 641–696.

2. Matt Grossmann and Casey B. K. Dominguez, "Party Coalitions and Interest Group Networks," *American Politics Research* 37 (2009): 794.

to filibuster President Bush's court of appeals nominees. Republicans responded by threatening to invoke a rare Senate procedure that would eliminate filibusters for judicial nominees. Republican members of the Senate similarly delayed votes on Barack Obama's judicial nominees for the lower federal courts. Debates over the qualifications of any official entrusted with legal responsibilities are common. Both Republicans and Democrats routinely scrutinize the qualifications and ideology of the attorney general and members of the Justice Department and the Office of Legal Counsel. The staffing of state courts is equally as controversial. The overlap between constitutional disputes and policy debates explain why state judicial elections, which once drew less attention in the United States than the average program on a local cable channel, now often become heated contests over gay marriage, capital punishment, and campaign spending.

The division among Supreme Court justices on numerous constitutional issues reflects the polarization of the polity at large, with one very important institutional exception. Justices Ginsburg and Breyer consistently adopt the more liberal position, as did former Justices Souter and Stevens. Justice Scalia and Justice Thomas consistently take the more conservative position, as did the late Chief Justice Rehnquist. Chief Justice John Roberts and Justice Samuel Alito, who replaced Rehnquist and O'Connor, respectively, are reliable conservative voters. Justices Sonya Sotomayor and Elena Kagan, who replaced Justices Souter and Stevens, are reliable liberals. This has left the outcome of almost all politically salient cases in the hands of Justices O'Connor and Kennedy, and after Justice O'Connor left the bench in 2005, solely in the hands of Justice Kennedy. Significantly, because justices on the Supreme Court cannot prevent decisions by filibusters or hold up decisions in committee, the two centrist justices on the late Rehnquist and early Roberts Courts probably exercise more power than does the median senator or representative. At the very least, Kennedy and O'Connor's votes have determined which party wins a case. O'Connor in particular often wrote crucial concurring opinions that reached constitutional middle grounds on the basis of distinctions that seven, and sometimes eight, members of the Court maintained were constitutionally indefensible.

These divisions among the liberal, conservative, and centrist judges help explain why, for the first time in history, Americans are experiencing judicial activism in both conservative and liberal directions. As one law professor notes,

> We have a Supreme Court that engages in unparalleled activism—from the left and the right simultaneously! When Justices O'Connor and Kennedy are in their conservative mode, affirmative action, minority voting districts, hate speech regulations, and environmental land use restrictions are all constitutionally suspect, notwithstanding the absence of convincing originalist arguments against them. When these pivotal Justices are in their liberal mode, abortion restrictions, school prayer, restrictions on gay rights, exclusion of women from VMI, and limitations on the right to die fall victim to the Court's constitutional axe.[3]

Most commentators have difficulty discerning any reason to this pattern, other than a general commitment to judicial activism on the part of all members of the federal bench, with the justices striking down laws at an unusually rapid pace. Thomas Keck points out, "Supreme Court Justices appointed by Republican presidents have been no more restrained than those appointed by Democrats. They exercise judicial review just as frequently, and they are no more reluctant to enter political thickets."[4]

Constitutional Thought. Neither conservative Republicans nor liberal Democrats bring new ideological weapons to bear on this constitutional trench warfare. Republicans retain constitutional commitments from the Reagan Era. Conservative constitutional commentators insist more strongly than in any previous post–New Deal period that the Constitution be interpreted in light of the original meaning of constitutional provisions. Originalists at the turn of the twenty-first century, however, are more inclined to wield originalism in service of an activist agenda than the previous generation of originalists, who were more committed to judicial deference to elected officials.[5] Democrats retain their

---

3. Michael J. Klarman, "Majoritarian Judicial Review: The Entrenchment Problem," *Georgetown Law Journal* 85 (1997): 548.

4. Thomas M. Keck, *The Most Activist Supreme Court in History: The Road to Modern Judicial Conservatism* (Chicago: University of Chicago Press, 2004), 286.

5. See Keith E. Whittington, "The New Originalism," *Georgetown Journal of Law and Policy* 2 (2004): 599–614.

Box 11-1 A Partial Cast of Characters of the Contemporary Era

Ruth Bader Ginsburg	■ Democrat ■ Moderate liberal ■ Co-founded the *Women's Rights Law Reporter*, the first law journal in the United States to focus on women's rights (1970), and co-authored the first law school casebook on sex discrimination ■ First woman to receive tenure at the Columbia University Law School (1972) ■ Co-founded the Women's Rights Project at the ACLU (1972); ACLU's general counsel (1973) ■ Argued several landmark Supreme Court cases, including *Reed v. Reed* (1971) and *Frontiero v. Richardson* (1973) ■ Appointed by Jimmy Carter to federal circuit court (1980–1993) ■ Appointed by Bill Clinton to U.S. Supreme Court (1993–present) ■ A reliable member of the Court's liberal wing, demonstrating consistent support for abortion rights, sexual equality, and affirmative action
Anthony Kennedy	■ Republican ■ Moderate conservative ■ California lawyer and lobbyist ■ Appointed by Gerald Ford to federal circuit court (1975–1988) ■ Appointed by Ronald Reagan to U.S. Supreme Court (1988–present) after Robert Bork's nomination failed ■ Became a pivotal swing vote on the late Rehnquist and Roberts Courts; often votes with conservatives on governmental powers issues and liberals on rights and liberties issues
Theodore Olson	■ Republican ■ Lawyer ■ Assistant attorney general in the Reagan administration (1981–1984) ■ Was a party to the Supreme Court case *Morrison v. Olson*, which upheld the constitutionality of the law authorizing creation of so-called "independent counsels" ■ Successfully represented presidential candidate George W. Bush before the Supreme Court during the disputed election of 2000 ■ Solicitor general of the United States in the George W. Bush administration (2001–2004) ■ Joined with David Boies, his opposing counsel in *Bush v. Gore*, to bring a federal lawsuit challenging California's state constitutional amendment banning same-sex marriage (2009–2013)
Antonin Scalia	■ Republican ■ Conservative law professor ■ Assistant attorney general and head of the Office of Legal Counsel in the Nixon and Ford administrations (1974–1977) ■ Appointed to the D.C. Circuit Court by Ronald Reagan (1982–1986) and to the U.S. Supreme Court (1986–present) ■ First Italian American appointed to the Court ■ An influential leader of the conservative legal movement since the 1970s; since joining the Court a vocal advocate for "originalism" and "textualism" and a proponent of formalistic approaches to the separation of powers

(*Continued*)

Box 11-1 *(Continued)*

David Souter	■ Republican ■ Moderate New Hampshire prosecutor and judge ■ New Hampshire attorney general (1976–1978) and justice on state supreme court (1983–1990) ■ Appointed by George H. W. Bush to the federal circuit court (1990) and to the U.S. Supreme Court (1990–2009) ■ Known as a "stealth nominee" with little public record on national or constitutional issues, he was easily confirmed by a Democratic Senate to replace liberal icon William Brennan; emphasizing caution and respect for precedent in his opinions, he soon joined the liberal wing of the Court
Clarence Thomas	■ Republican ■ Conservative lawyer, assistant secretary of education (1981), and director of the Equal Employment Opportunity Commission (1981–1990) during the Reagan and Bush administrations ■ Appointed by George H. W. Bush to the D.C. Circuit Court (1990–1991) and to the U.S. Supreme Court (1991–present) ■ After a bruising battle in the Senate ended in one of the closest successful confirmation votes in history, Thomas became the second African American to serve on the Court ■ Emerged as one of the most conservative members of the Court and as a strong advocate for a less deferential brand of originalism than that favored by some of the other conservative justices
John Yoo	■ Republican ■ Berkeley law professor ■ General counsel to the U.S. Senate Judiciary Committee (1995–1996), deputy assistant attorney general in the Office of Legal Counsel (2001–2003) ■ Authored a number of memos defending presidential power in foreign policy during the George W. Bush administration, including memos supporting so-called "enhanced interrogation" techniques (aka, the "Torture Memos")

constitutional commitments from the New Deal/Great Society Era. Liberal constitutional commentators either insist on a living Constitution or devise an originalism that requires constitutional interpreters to understand the original meaning of constitutional language in terms of contemporary understandings of the principles laid down in 1791 or 1868.[6] Some liberals advance a popular constitutionalism rooted in a greater constitutional role for elected officials.[7] Whether popular constitutionalism is a good-faith position or a reaction to increased conservative control of the federal courts is a fair question. "A broad generalization, inaccurate only at the margins," one skeptic maintains, "is that nearly every constitutional theorist urges minimal judicial review and vigorous democratic dialogue on issues on which the theorist believes her preferred position is likely to prevail in the democratic dialogue and more-than-minimal review on issues on which the theorist believes her preferred position is unlikely to prevail there."[8]

6. See Jack M. Balkin, *Living Originalism* (Cambridge, MA: Harvard University Press, 2011).

7. See Larry D. Kramer, *The People Themselves: Popular Constitutionalism and Judicial Review* (Oxford: Oxford University Press, 2005).

8. Mark Tushnet, "Policy Distortion and Democratic Debilitation: Comparative Illumination of the Countermajoritarian Difficulty," *Michigan Law Review* 94 (1995): 245–4.

Legacies. Determining the legacy of constitutional politics over the last twenty years is impossible. We cannot even determine whether Americans are locked in an enduring era of polarized politics or whether a new constitutional regime is dawning. Many liberals hope that the elections of 2006 and 2008 marked a new constitutional era, one that will be characterized by far more progressive constitutional commitments than has recently been the case. Republicans hope that 2010 marked either a return to power of the previous Republican coalition or, perhaps, a new and more conservative constitutional regime. It will not be known for some time whether recent elections were the beginning of a new progressive era, mark no change from the increased polarization of American politics that began in the late 1960s, or are merely a short-term deviation from the period of conservative Republican hegemony that began with the election of George W. Bush in 2000.

II. Foundations

MAJOR DEVELOPMENTS

- Sharp partisan disagreement on the meaning of almost all constitutional protections for civil liberties
- Judicial protection for detainees at Guantanamo Bay in Cuba
- Incorporation of the Second Amendment

Contemporary constitutional struggles are structured by unprecedented agreements that a strong judiciary should protect constitutional rights and unprecedented partisan disagreements over the sources, underlying principles, and scope of the constitutional rights the judiciary should protect. Almost all Americans presently support aggressive use of the judicial power to declare laws unconstitutional while just as aggressively disputing how justices should wield that authority. Liberal Democrats want courts to protect abortion rights and strike down laws that permit government money to flow to private religious schools. Conservative Republicans want courts to protect property rights and declare gun control laws unconstitutional. Neither the Democratic nor Republican Party, nor any justice on the Supreme Court, champions judicial restraint across a wide range of issues. The voting blocs on the Supreme Court and in Congress on such matters of high political salience as abortion, gun control, and capital punishment are frequently the same.

Never before in American history have both political parties and the Supreme Court been so divided on such a wide variety of rights and liberties issues. Should either Republicans or Democrats gain more permanent control of the national government, or should either liberals or conservatives gain decisive control over the federal judiciary, the consequences for the sources, underlying principles, and scope and substance of constitutional rights are likely to be significant.

A. Sources

Struggles over the sources of constitutional rights moved to different arenas. Disputes over constitutional amendments moved from the national government to the states. Social conservatives responded to liberal state court decisions declaring a constitutional right to same-sex marriage by proposing and, in many states, ratifying state constitutional amendments that restricted marriage to heterosexual couples. New disputes broke out over the constitutional status of constitutional decisions in other countries. Conservatives concerned with Supreme Court opinions in gay rights and capital punishment cases that cited foreign sources demanded that constitutional rights be based exclusively on distinctively American sources. International law provided another site for conservative and liberal disagreements over the proper sources for rights and liberties, as liberals advocated various legal doctrines that required judicial protection for certain rights set out in several international human rights agreements.

Political activists promoting constitutional amendments turned to the states after the Supreme Judicial Court of Massachusetts in *Goodridge v. Department of Public Health* (MA 2004) declared that bans on same-sex marriage violated the state constitution. Their efforts were often successful, in part because all state constitutions are easier to amend than the federal Constitution. More than half the states ratified constitutional amendments limiting marriage to one man and one woman. Many of these amendments were ratified by overwhelming majorities. Utah voters in 2004 passed a constitutional amendment declaring, "Marriage consists only of the legal union between a man and a woman. No other domestic union, however denominated, may be recognized as a marriage or given the same or substantially equivalent legal effect." Florida in 2008 adopted a constitutional amendment declaring, "Inasmuch as marriage is the legal union of one man and one woman as husband and wife, no other legal union that is treated as marriage or the substantial equivalent thereof shall be valid or recognized." Some observers believe that by increasing conservative turnout in the 2004 national elections, proposed constitutional amendments banning same-sex marriage explain why George Bush defeated John Kerry in crucial states.

The constitutional status of customary international law is also contested. Many prominent conservatives maintain that giving the law of nations any independent legal status violates popular sovereignty. Curtis Bradley and Jack Goldsmith declare, "The modern position that CIL [customary international law] is federal common law is in tension with basic notions of American representative democracy." This tension exists because "when a federal court applies CIL as federal common law, it is not applying law generated by U.S. lawmaking processes. Rather, it is applying law derived from the views and practices of the international community."[9] Prominent liberals who defend the independent legal status of customary international law emphasize American participation and leadership in the international human rights regime. "The capacity of federal courts to incorporate customary international law into federal law," Harold Koh insists, "is absolutely critical to maintaining the coherence of federal law in areas of international concern." Otherwise, state governments would have "no domestic legal obligation to obey customary norms against genocide" in the absence of a treaty explicitly declaring those norms to be binding law.[10]

B. Principles

Contemporary Americans are governed by three constitutions: the constitution of liberal Democrats, the constitution of conservative Republicans, and the muddled set of constitutional rules that result in most cases when neither political faction has the power necessary to make its constitutional vision the official law of the land.[11] The only major change that has occurred during this era is that, inspired by a more conservative judiciary, conservative Republicans have become more enamored and liberal Democrats less enamored of judicial activism.

Two organizations, the Federalist Society and the American Constitutional Society, are crucial players in the contemporary battle over constitutional principle. The Federalist Society caters to conservatives and libertarians. Its mission statement declares that the society "is founded on the principles that the state exists to preserve freedom, that the separation of governmental powers is central to our Constitution, and that it is emphatically the province and duty of the judiciary to say what the law is, not what it should be. . . . This entails reordering priorities within the legal system to place a premium on individual liberty, traditional values, and the rule of law."[12] Most prominent conservative law professors either belong to the Federalist Society or frequently speak at its meetings. Numerous Bush administration officials and judicial appointees have Federalist Society backgrounds.

The less effective American Constitutional Society is the organization of choice for liberal constitutional thinkers, particularly those with judicial ambitions. While less established and prominent than the Federalist Society, many members of the Obama Justice Department and Obama judicial appointees have American Constitutional Society connections. The mission statement of that organization declares that "law should be a force to improve the lives of all people" and to accomplish this the society "brings together many of the country's best legal minds to articulate a progressive vision of our Constitution and laws" and to "debunk[] conservative buzzwords such as 'originalism' and 'strict construction' that use neutral-sounding language but all too often lead to conservative policy outcomes."[13]

C. Scope

Contemporary Americans experience polarization with a slight twist when they consider the scope of constitutional protection for civil liberties. The same sharp liberal and conservative divides that occur on other

9. Curtis A. Bradley and Jack L. Goldsmith, "Customary International Law and the Federal Common Law: A Critique of the Modern Position," *Harvard Law Review* 110 (1997): 857.

10. Harold Hongju Koh, "Is International Law Really State Law?" *Harvard Law Review* 111 (1998): 1840.

11. See Perry and Powe, "Political Battle for the Constitution," 688–89.

12. Federalist Society, "About Us," http://www.fed-soc.org/aboutus.

13. American Constitution Society, "About ACS," http://www.acslaw.org/about.

constitutional issues appear during debates over incorporation, state action, and the extraterritorial scope of the constitutional provisions protecting civil liberties. Justices O'Connor and Kennedy cast swing votes when these issues came before the Supreme Court. Unsurprisingly, liberals are more inclined than conservatives to find state action and insist that federal officials respect constitutional norms when acting outside the United States. In sharp contrast to the debates over incorporation that took place during the twentieth century, however, twenty-first-century conservatives are far more enthusiastic than twenty-first-century liberals when requiring state officials to respect the provisions of the Bill of Rights.

Liberals won the most important state action case decided in recent years. In *Brentwood Academy v. Tennessee Secondary School Athletic Association* (2001) a 5–4 majority found a high school athletic board to be a state actor when the overwhelming majority of participants were public school employees. Justice Souter's majority opinion declared, "The nominally private character of the Association is overborne by the pervasive entwinement of public institutions and public officials in its composition and workings." Liberals successfully convinced the Supreme Court to require federal officials acting outside the territory of the United States to respect constitutional norms when their actions took place in a location where the United States was exercising de facto sovereignty. In *Boumediene v. Bush* (2008) a 5–4 Supreme Court majority ruled that persons detained in Guantanamo Bay could petition federal courts for habeas corpus. Justice Kennedy's majority opinion emphasized that the United States was the de facto sovereign over the territory, even if not the de jure sovereign. He observed, "By surrendering formal sovereignty over any unincorporated territory to a third party, while at the same time entering into a lease that grants total control over the territory back to the United States, it would be possible for the political branches to govern without legal constraint."

McDonald v. City of Chicago (2010) was the most interesting and consequential recent case on the scope of constitutional protections for civil liberties. The 5–4 majority in that case ruled that the due process clause of the Fourteenth Amendment incorporated the Second Amendment. State officials, *McDonald* held, had to respect the same gun rights as federal officials did. Political actors on and off the court abandoned their previous attitudes toward incorporation when considering the incorporation of the Second Amendment. Conservatives, who had once regarded incorporation as an assault against federalism, championed *McDonald*'s sharp restrictions on states. Justice Alito's majority opinion declared, "Incorporated Bill of Rights protections are all to be enforced against the States under the Fourteenth Amendment according to the same standards that protect those personal rights against federal encroachment." Liberals in *McDonald* harkened back to doctrines previously championed by conservative opponents of incorporation. Justice Stevens in dissent stated, "The rights protected against state infringement by the Fourteenth Amendment's Due Process Clause need not be identical in shape or scope to the rights protected against Federal Government infringement by the various provisions of the Bill of Rights."

Boumediene v. Bush, 553 U.S. 723 (2008)

Lakhdar Boumediene was born in Algeria and acquired Bosnian citizenship during the 1990s. In 2001 he and five other persons were arrested by the Bosnian police, who suspected them of international terrorism. On January 17 the Supreme Court of Bosnia and Herzegovina ordered them released on the ground that no evidence supported that accusation. That night Bosnian police transferred custody of Boumediene and his alleged confederates to the United States. They were immediately shipped to the detention center in Guantanamo Bay, Cuba. According to their brief, from 2002 to 2008 the six men were subject to the following conditions:

> *They are confined to individual 8′ × 6′ cells consisting of concrete walls and steel mesh. Above each man's steel bunk, a fluorescent light remains on 24 hours a day. Petitioners have been subject to, among other things, up to 15 consecutive months of solitary confinement, sleep deprivation, and extreme temperature conditions. In 2004, for example, rogue soldiers crushed Mr. Ait Idir's face into a gravel courtyard and broke one of his fingers, even though he was restrained and posed no threat. Each Petitioner suffers from serious medical ailments caused or exacerbated by the conditions of his detention.*

Sometime during 2004 each man appeared before a Combatant Status Review Tribunal (CSRT). Each was determined to be an enemy combatant. Each asked for a writ of habeas corpus. Two separate proceedings were held. One federal district judge determined that aliens had no constitutional right to the writ. The other federal district judge determined that aliens had a constitutional right to the writ. Before the appeals could be heard by the federal circuit court, Congress passed the Detainee Treatment Act (DTA), which declared that "no court, justice, or judge shall have jurisdiction to hear or consider . . . an application for a writ of habeas corpus filed by or on behalf of an alien detained by the Department of Defense at Guantanamo Bay, Cuba." The Court of Appeals for the District of Columbia consolidated all cases and determined that the DTA was constitutional. Boumediene and others appealed to the Supreme Court of the United States.

The Supreme Court by a 5–4 vote determined that Congress could not deprive Guantanamo Bay detainees of their right to habeas corpus. Justice Kennedy's majority opinion ruled that aliens being held in areas where Americans had de facto sovereignty had a right to habeas corpus and that Congress had not provided an adequate substitute. Kennedy claimed that the majority opinion was supported both by past precedents and by basic constitutional principles. How did the majority and the dissent characterize those precedents and principles? Which side had the better argument? When Boumediene *was decided in 2008, support for President Bush and the Iraq War had fallen to new lows. Do you think that the political environment influenced the justices? Would the case have been decided similarly had President Bush enjoyed a 70 percent approval rating?*

JUSTICE KENNEDY delivered the opinion of the Court.

. . .

. . . [T]he parties in these cases have examined historical sources to construct a view of the common-law writ as it existed in 1789. . . . Diligent search by all parties reveals no certain conclusions. In none of the cases cited do we find that a common-law court would or would not have granted, or refused to hear for lack of jurisdiction, a petition for a writ of habeas corpus brought by a prisoner deemed an enemy combatant, under a standard like the one the Department of Defense has used in these cases, and when held in a territory, like Guantanamo, over which the Government has total military and civil control.

. . .

The Government argues . . . that Guantanamo is more closely analogous to Scotland and Hanover, territories that were not part of England but nonetheless controlled by the English monarch (in his separate capacities as King of Scotland and Elector of Hanover). . . . Lord Mansfield can be cited for the proposition that, at the time of the founding, English courts lacked the "power" to issue the writ to Scotland and Hanover, territories Lord Mansfield referred to as "foreign." But what matters for our purposes is why common-law courts lacked this power. Given the English Crown's delicate and complicated relationships with Scotland and Hanover in the 1700's, we cannot disregard the possibility that the common-law courts' refusal to issue the writ to these places was motivated not by formal legal constructs but by what we would think of as prudential concerns. This appears to have been the case with regard to other British territories where the writ did not run. . . .

. . .

We do not question the Government's position that Cuba, not the United States, maintains sovereignty, in the legal and technical sense of the term, over Guantanamo Bay. But this does not end the analysis. Our cases do not hold it is improper for us to inquire into the objective degree of control the Nation asserts over foreign territory. . . . Cuba, and not the United States, retains de jure sovereignty over Guantanamo Bay. . . . [T]he United States, by virtue of its complete jurisdiction and control over the base, maintains de facto sovereignty over this territory. . . .

. . .

True, the Court in [*Johnson v.*] *Eisentrager* (1950) denied access to the writ, and it noted the prisoners "at no relevant time were within any territory over which the United States is sovereign, and [that] the scenes of their offense, their capture, their trial and their punishment were all beyond the territorial jurisdiction of any court of the United States." . . . The Government seizes upon this language as proof positive that the *Eisentrager* Court adopted a formalistic, sovereignty-based test for determining the reach of the Suspension Clause. . . . We reject this reading. . . .

. . .

. . . Nothing in *Eisentrager* says that de jure sovereignty is or has ever been the only relevant consideration in determining the geographic reach of the Constitution or of habeas corpus. Were that the case, there would be considerable tension between *Eisentrager,* on the one hand, and the *Insular Cases* (1901–04) and *Reid [v. Covert] (1957),* on the other. . . .

The Government's formal sovereignty-based test raises troubling separation-of-powers concerns as well. . . . [A]lthough it recognized, by entering into the 1903 Lease Agreement, that Cuba retained "ultimate sovereignty" over Guantanamo, the United States continued to maintain the same plenary control it had enjoyed since 1898. Yet the Government's view is that the Constitution had no effect there, at least as to noncitizens, because the United States disclaimed sovereignty in the formal sense of the term. The necessary implication of the argument is that by surrendering formal sovereignty over any unincorporated territory to a third party, while at the same time entering into a lease that grants total control over the territory back to the United States, it would be possible for the political branches to govern without legal constraint.

Our basic charter cannot be contracted away like this. The Constitution grants Congress and the President the power to acquire, dispose of, and govern territory, not the power to decide when and where its terms apply. Even when the United States acts outside its borders, its powers are not "absolute and unlimited" but are subject "to such restrictions as are expressed in the Constitution." . . . Abstaining from questions involving formal sovereignty and territorial governance is one thing. To hold the political branches have the power to switch the Constitution on or off at will is quite another. The former position reflects this Court's recognition that certain matters requiring political judgments are best left to the political branches. The latter would permit a striking anomaly in our tripartite system of government, leading to a regime in which Congress and the President, not this Court, say "what the law is." *Marbury v. Madison* (1803).

. . .

Based on . . . *Eisentrager,* and the reasoning in our other extraterritoriality opinions, we conclude that at least three factors are relevant in determining the reach of the Suspension Clause: (1) the citizenship and status of the detainee and the adequacy of the process through which that status determination was made; (2) the nature of the sites where apprehension and then detention took place; and (3) the practical obstacles inherent in resolving the prisoner's entitlement to the writ.

Applying this framework, we note at the onset that the status of these detainees is a matter of dispute. . . .

As to the second factor relevant to this analysis, the detainees here are similarly situated to the *Eisentrager* petitioners in that the sites of their apprehension and detention are technically outside the sovereign territory of the United States. As noted earlier, this is a factor that weighs against finding they have rights under the Suspension Clause. But there are critical differences between Landsberg Prison, circa 1950, and the United States Naval Station at Guantanamo Bay in 2008. Unlike its present control over the naval station, the United States' control over the prison in Germany was neither absolute nor indefinite. Like all parts of occupied Germany, the prison was under the jurisdiction of the combined Allied Forces. . . .

As to the third factor, . . . [t]he Government presents no credible arguments that the military mission at Guantanamo would be compromised if habeas corpus courts had jurisdiction to hear the detainees' claims. And in light of the plenary control the United States asserts over the base, none are apparent to us.

. . .

We hold that Art. I, §9, cl. 2, of the Constitution has full effect at Guantanamo Bay. If the privilege of habeas corpus is to be denied to the detainees now before us, Congress must act in accordance with the requirements of the Suspension Clause. . . .

In light of this holding the question becomes whether the statute stripping jurisdiction to issue the writ avoids the Suspension Clause mandate because Congress has provided adequate substitute procedures for habeas corpus. . . .

. . .

. . . [T]he privilege of habeas corpus entitles the prisoner to a meaningful opportunity to demonstrate that he is being held pursuant to "the erroneous application or interpretation" of relevant law. . . . And the habeas court must have the power to order the conditional release of an individual unlawfully detained—though release need not be the exclusive remedy and is not the appropriate one in every case in which the writ is granted. . . .

. . .

Petitioners identify what they see as myriad deficiencies in the CSRTs. The most relevant for our purposes are the constraints upon the detainee's ability to rebut the factual basis for the Government's assertion that he is an enemy combatant. . . . He does not have the assistance of counsel and may not be aware of the most critical allegations that the Government relied upon to order his detention. . . . The detainee can confront witnesses that testify during the

CSRT proceedings. But given that there are in effect no limits on the admission of hearsay evidence—the only requirement is that the tribunal deem the evidence "relevant and helpful," . . .—the detainee's opportunity to question witnesses is likely to be more theoretical than real.

. . .

Although we make no judgment as to whether the CSRTs, as currently constituted, satisfy due process standards, we agree with petitioners that, even when all the parties involved in this process act with diligence and in good faith, there is considerable risk of error in the tribunal's findings of fact. . . . And given that the consequence of error may be detention of persons for the duration of hostilities that may last a generation or more, this is a risk too significant to ignore.

. . .

Although we hold that the DTA is not an adequate and effective substitute for habeas corpus, it does not follow that a habeas corpus court may disregard the dangers the detention in these cases was intended to prevent. . . . [T]he Suspension Clause does not resist innovation in the field of habeas corpus. Certain accommodations can be made to reduce the burden habeas corpus proceedings will place on the military without impermissibly diluting the protections of the writ.

. . .

Our opinion does not undermine the Executive's powers as Commander in Chief. On the contrary, the exercise of those powers is vindicated, not eroded, when confirmed by the Judicial Branch. Within the Constitution's separation-of-powers structure, few exercises of judicial power are as legitimate or as necessary as the responsibility to hear challenges to the authority of the Executive to imprison a person. Some of these petitioners have been in custody for six years with no definitive judicial determination as to the legality of their detention. Their access to the writ is a necessity to determine the lawfulness of their status, even if, in the end, they do not obtain the relief they seek.

. . .

It bears repeating that our opinion does not address the content of the law that governs petitioners' detention. That is a matter yet to be determined. We hold that petitioners may invoke the fundamental procedural protections of habeas corpus. The laws and Constitution are designed to survive, and remain in force, in extraordinary times. Liberty and security can be reconciled; and in our system they are reconciled within the framework of the law. The Framers decided that habeas corpus, a right of first importance, must be a part of that framework, a part of that law.

. . .

JUSTICE SOUTER, with whom JUSTICE GINSBURG and JUSTICE BREYER join, concurring.

. . .

A . . . fact insufficiently appreciated by the dissents is the length of the disputed imprisonments, some of the prisoners represented here today having been locked up for six years. . . . Hence the hollow ring when the dissenters suggest that the Court is somehow precipitating the judiciary into reviewing claims that the military (subject to appeal to the Court of Appeals for the District of Columbia Circuit) could handle within some reasonable period of time. . . .

. . .

CHIEF JUSTICE ROBERTS, with whom JUSTICE SCALIA, JUSTICE THOMAS, and JUSTICE ALITO join, dissenting.

. . .

I believe the system the political branches constructed adequately protects any constitutional rights aliens captured abroad and detained as enemy combatants may enjoy. I therefore would dismiss these cases on that ground. With all respect for the contrary views of the majority, I must dissent.

. . .

. . . Step back and consider what, in the real world, Congress and the Executive have actually granted aliens captured by our Armed Forces overseas and found to be enemy combatants:

- The right to hear the bases of the charges against them, including a summary of any classified evidence.
- The ability to challenge the bases of their detention before military tribunals modeled after Geneva Convention procedures. Some 38 detainees have been released as a result of this process. . . .
- The right, before the CSRT, to testify, introduce evidence, call witnesses, question those the Government calls, and secure release, if and when appropriate.
- The right to the aid of a personal representative in arranging and presenting their cases before a CSRT.

- Before the D.C. Circuit, the right to employ counsel, challenge the factual record, contest the lower tribunal's legal determinations, ensure compliance with the Constitution and laws, and secure release, if any errors below establish their entitlement to such relief.

In sum, the DTA satisfies the majority's own criteria for assessing adequacy. This statutory scheme provides the combatants held at Guantanamo greater procedural protections than have ever been afforded alleged enemy detainees—whether citizens or aliens—in our national history.

. . .

JUSTICE SCALIA, with whom THE CHIEF JUSTICE, JUSTICE THOMAS, and JUSTICE ALITO join, dissenting.

. . . The writ of habeas corpus does not, and never has, run in favor of aliens abroad; the Suspension Clause thus has no application, and the Court's intervention in this military matter is entirely ultra vires.

. . .

. . . A mere two Terms ago in *Hamdan v. Rumsfeld* (2006) . . . when the Court held (quite amazingly) that the Detainee Treatment Act of 2005 had not stripped habeas jurisdiction over Guantanamo petitioners' claims, four Members of today's five-Justice majority joined an opinion saying the following: "Nothing prevents the President from returning to Congress to seek the authority [for trial by military commission] he believes necessary. . . ." Turns out they were just kidding. For in response, Congress, at the President's request, quickly enacted the Military Commissions Act, emphatically reasserting that it did not want these prisoners filing habeas petitions. It is therefore clear that Congress and the Executive—both political branches—have determined that limiting the role of civilian courts in adjudicating whether prisoners captured abroad are properly detained is important to success in the war that some 190,000 of our men and women are now fighting. . . .

But it does not matter. The Court today decrees that no good reason to accept the judgment of the other two branches is "apparent." . . . "The Government," it declares, "presents no credible arguments that the military mission at Guantanamo would be compromised if habeas corpus courts had jurisdiction to hear the detainees' claims." . . . What competence does the Court have to second-guess the judgment of Congress and the President on such a point? None whatever. But the Court blunders in nonetheless. Henceforth, as today's opinion makes unnervingly clear, how to handle enemy prisoners in this war will ultimately lie with the branch that knows least about the national security concerns that the subject entails.

. . .

The Court would have us believe that *Eisentrager* rested on "[p]ractical considerations," such as the "difficulties of ordering the Government to produce the prisoners in a habeas corpus proceeding." . . . Formal sovereignty, says the Court, is merely one consideration "that bears upon which constitutional guarantees apply" in a given location. . . . This is a sheer rewriting of the case. *Eisentrager* mentioned practical concerns, to be sure—but not for the purpose of determining under what circumstances American courts could issue writs of habeas corpus for aliens abroad. It cited them to support its holding that the Constitution does not empower courts to issue writs of habeas corpus to aliens abroad in any circumstances.

. . .

The category of prisoner comparable to these detainees are not the *Eisentrager* criminal defendants, but the more than 400,000 prisoners of war detained in the United States alone during World War II. Not a single one was accorded the right to have his detention validated by a habeas corpus action in federal court—and that despite the fact that they were present on U.S. soil. . . . The Court's analysis produces a crazy result: Whereas those convicted and sentenced to death for war crimes are without judicial remedy, all enemy combatants detained during a war, at least insofar as they are confined in an area away from the battlefield over which the United States exercises "absolute and indefinite" control, may seek a writ of habeas corpus in federal court. And, as an even more bizarre implication from the Court's reasoning, those prisoners whom the military plans to try by full-dress Commission at a future date may file habeas petitions and secure release before their trials take place.

. . .

What drives today's decision is neither the meaning of the Suspension Clause, nor the principles of our precedents, but rather an inflated notion of judicial supremacy. The Court says that if the extraterritorial applicability of the Suspension Clause turned on formal notions of sovereignty, "it would be possible for the political branches to govern without legal constraint" in areas beyond the sovereign territory of the United States. . . . That cannot be, the Court says, because it is the duty of this Court to say what the law is. . . . It would be difficult to imagine a more question-begging analysis. "The very foundation of the power of the federal courts to declare Acts of Congress unconstitutional lies in the power and duty of those courts to decide cases and controversies properly before them." . . . Our power "to say what the law is" is circumscribed by the limits of our statutorily and constitutionally conferred jurisdiction. . . . And that is precisely the question in these cases: whether the Constitution confers habeas jurisdiction on federal courts to decide petitioners' claims. It is both irrational and arrogant to say that the answer must be yes, because otherwise we would not be supreme.

. . .

It is entirely clear that, at English common law, the writ of habeas corpus did not extend beyond the sovereign territory of the Crown. To be sure, the writ had an "extraordinary territorial ambit," because it was a so-called "prerogative writ," which, unlike other writs, could extend beyond the realm of England to other places where the Crown was sovereign. . . .

But prerogative writs could not issue to foreign countries, even for British subjects; they were confined to the King's dominions—those areas over which the Crown was sovereign. . . . Thus, the writ has never extended to Scotland, which, although united to England when James I succeeded to the English throne in 1603, was considered a foreign dominion under a different Crown—that of the King of Scotland. . . .

. . .

The Court dismisses the example of Scotland on the grounds that Scotland had its own judicial system and that the writ could not, as a practical matter, have been enforced there. . . . Those explanations are totally unpersuasive. The existence of a separate court system was never a basis for denying the power of a court to issue the writ. . . . And as for logistical problems, the same difficulties were present for places like the Channel Islands, where the writ did run. . . .

. . .

Today the Court warps our Constitution in a way that goes beyond the narrow issue of the reach of the Suspension Clause, invoking judicially brainstormed separation-of-powers principles to establish a manipulable "functional" test for the extraterritorial reach of habeas corpus (and, no doubt, for the extraterritorial reach of other constitutional protections as well). It blatantly misdescribes important precedents, most conspicuously Justice Jackson's opinion for the Court in *Johnson v. Eisentrager.* It breaks a chain of precedent as old as the common law that prohibits judicial inquiry into detentions of aliens abroad absent statutory authorization. And, most tragically, it sets our military commanders the impossible task of proving to a civilian court, under whatever standards this Court devises in the future, that evidence supports the confinement of each and every enemy prisoner.

III. Judicial Power and Constitutional Authority

MAJOR DEVELOPMENTS

- Increasing use of judicial review against federal and state legislation
- Intensifying controversy over judiciary's assertion of supremacy on matters of constitutional meaning
- Enhanced politicization of judicial elections and appointments

Republicans dominated the nomination of Supreme Court justices from the presidency of Richard Nixon in 1969 to the end of the presidency of George H. W. Bush in 1993. Nixon put the Court on a more conservative path with his appointments in the early 1970s, but it was not until the end of the George H. W. Bush administration that conservatives seemed to have an occasionally reliable working majority on the Supreme Court (along with supportive judges in the lower courts). Rehnquist, Thomas, and Scalia formed a clear conservative coalition on the late Rehnquist Court. Stevens, Blackmun, and Souter (whose shift disappointed conservatives) quickly emerged as a liberal wing. White, O'Connor, and Kennedy were swing votes, often joining the conservatives. Subsequent appointments largely maintained this balance. Clinton appointed Breyer and Ginsburg to replace White and Blackmun. George W. Bush appointed Roberts and Alito to replace Rehnquist and O'Connor. Obama appointed Sotomayor and Kagan to replace Souter and Stevens. Since the beginning of the Clinton administration, the Court has become more polarized, but

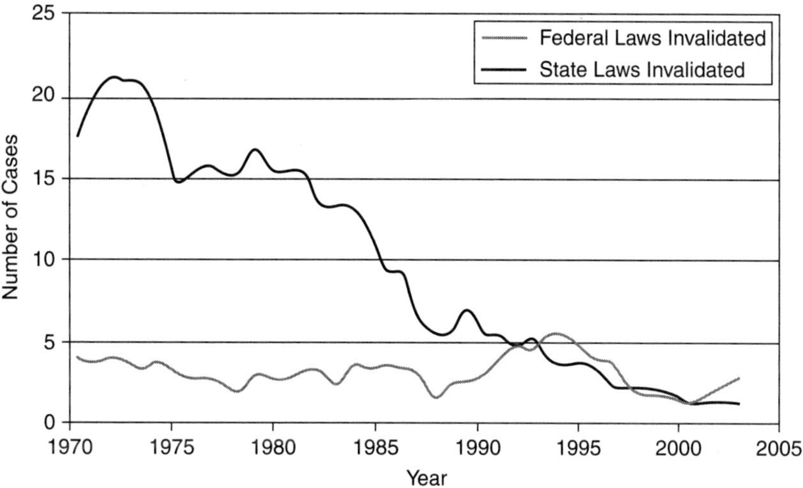

Figure 11-1 Supreme Court Invalidation of State and Federal Laws, 1970–2012

it remains divided between liberal and conservative wings, and Kennedy is now alone in playing the pivotal role of swing vote.

Figure 11-1 tracks the number of U.S. Supreme Court cases that have invalidated the application of state and federal laws on constitutional grounds since 1970. It continues the story of judicial review by the Court where Figure 8-4 left off. As Figure 8-4 indicated, the Warren and early Burger Courts reached new levels of activity in striking down state laws in the 1960s and 1970s, resulting in a strong political backlash in Congress and elsewhere. Once conservatives won a majority on the Court, the Court decreased the number of state laws that it struck down. That decrease was especially dramatic with the appointment of the Reagan justices in the 1980s. Meanwhile, the Rehnquist Court in the late 1990s briefly turned its attention to Congress. It struck down more federal statutory provisions than had been struck down during any other five-year period since the New Deal. For a short time, the Court even found itself in the historically unusual circumstance of deciding more cases in which it struck down federal laws than cases in which it struck down state laws.

In the late 1990s the trend that attracted the most attention was the increase in the number of cases in which the Court struck down acts of Congress. A large number of those decisions—though certainly not all of them—were decided on federalism or separation of powers grounds, and conservative justices led the way in many of those cases. For the first time since the New Deal, the Supreme Court enforced limitations on the federal government with regard to the interstate commerce clause, state sovereign immunity, and Section 5 of the Fourteenth Amendment. Liberals began to debate whether it was the conservatives who were engaged in judicial activism. Perhaps judicial restraint—or even the elimination of judicial review—might not be a bad thing after all.[14] The eagerness of the Court's conservative majority to enter the 2000 presidential election dispute intensified concerns among liberals that a philosophy of judicial supremacy was undermining appropriate institutional boundaries. However, in the 2000s the pace of invalidations of federal laws began to fall off. Moreover, even during that period, the Court's review of Congress never had the same kind of huge impact on public policy that it had had during, say, the 1930s.

Still, the Contemporary Era is characterized by the increased exercise of judicial power, and this in part flows from the justices' willingness to strike down

14. Cass R. Sunstein, *Radicals in Robes* (New York: Basic Books, 2005); Larry D. Kramer, "Popular Constitutionalism, Circa 2004," *California Law Review* 92 (2004): 959–1011.

Illustration 11-1 Judicial Nominations

Source: Clay Bennett, *Chattanooga Times Free Press,* May 11, 2010. Used with the permission of Clay Bennett, the Washington Post Writers Group and the Cartoonist Group. All rights reserved.

laws from both the left and the right. Swing justices join liberal coalitions to strike down statutes that the conservatives think should be upheld, but they also join conservative coalitions to strike down statutes that the liberals think should be upheld. Some of the most controversial decisions of the Rehnquist and Roberts Courts have favored the left, such as those striking down homosexual sodomy laws (*Lawrence v. Texas* [2003]), military detentions of suspected terrorists (*Boumediene v. Bush* [2008]), and flag-burning laws (*Texas v. Johnson* [1989]). Still others have favored the right, such as those striking down parts of campaign finance reform (*Citizens United v. FEC* [2010]), the District of Columbia's ban on handguns (*District of Columbia v. Heller* [2008]), and parts of the Americans with Disabilities Act (*Board of Trustees of Alabama v. Garrett* [2001]). The Court has drawn criticism from both sides of the political aisle, while making particularly strong claims for its own authority to define constitutional meaning in cases such as *City of Boerne v. Flores* (1997).

The more active exercise of judicial power, combined with a closely divided political system, has led to intensified battles over judicial appointments, both in the Supreme Court and in the lower courts. Over the course of American history there have been twenty-seven failed Supreme Court nominations. In total, 18 percent of the presidential nominations submitted to the Senate for vacancies on the Supreme Court have been withdrawn, voted down, or permanently postponed.[15] Most of those failures occurred in the nineteenth century, and they often occurred when the same party at least nominally held both the White House and the Senate. After a long period of unequaled presidential success, failed nominations have become somewhat more common again in recent decades. Lyndon Johnson, Richard Nixon, Ronald Reagan, and George W. Bush all lost Supreme Court nominees, with Robert Bork's rejection by a Democratic Senate in 1987 being perhaps the most notable.

15. Keith E. Whittington, "Presidents, Senators, and Failed Supreme Court Nominations," *Supreme Court Review* 2006 (2007): 401.

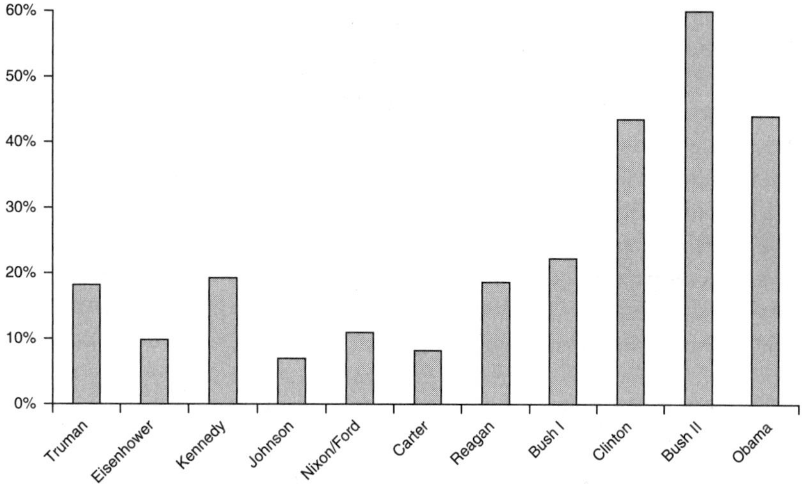

Figure 11-2 Percentage of Federal Circuit Court Nominations Not Confirmed, 1945–2012

Perhaps as significant as the reemergence of failed Supreme Court nominations has been the new level of contestation surrounding each vacancy on the Court. Interest groups now routinely mobilize their supporters in the general public and on Capitol Hill whenever a vacancy occurs. The media closely cover the process, and senators are expected to be visible. Potential nominees are carefully scrutinized by the White House to ensure both that they are aligned with the beliefs of the president and that they do not have any "skeletons in the closet" or an unflattering "paper trail" that might create controversy during the confirmation hearings. Since the 1960s it has become common for even successful Supreme Court nominees to receive a significant number of no votes at their confirmations.[16]

Lower court nominees, especially nominees to the U.S. circuit courts, now get something like the same treatment as Supreme Court nominees. They are carefully vetted by the White House and the Senate. Interest groups mobilize to support or block their nominations. It is now recognized that many important legal decisions are made in the circuit courts and that the nominees for the circuit courts are both important intellectual and legal figures in their own right and potential future Supreme Court nominees. There are many more ways to block circuit court nominations than Supreme Court nominations, however. Supreme Court nominations are high profile, and there is a great deal of pressure on senators to move those nominations toward a vote by the full Senate in a timely way. The political battle over lower court nominations mostly takes place well away from the Senate floor and the public spotlight.

The most effective way to kill a lower court nomination is to delay it. For most low-profile executive and judicial nominations, opponents of the nomination prefer to obstruct the process and avoid a final vote on confirmation for as long as possible. This might involve a filibuster by a minority of senators to prevent a floor vote on the confirmation. But long before such tactics are necessary this obstruction might involve delaying committee hearings through a variety of formal or informal means or simply delaying the scheduling of a floor vote by the majority party in the Senate. As a result, the time between nomination and successful confirmation of a circuit court judge approached a year during the second half of the Clinton administration and the George W. Bush administration. But, as Figure 11-2 illustrates, successful nominations were hard to come by.

16. See Lee Epstein and Jeffrey A. Segal, *Advice and Consent* (New York: Oxford University Press, 2005); Michael J. Gerhardt, *The Federal Appointments Process* (Durham, NC: Duke University Press, 2003).

Democrats filibustered President George W. Bush's 2001 nomination of Miguel Estrada to the United States Court of Appeals for the District of Columbia, and the nomination was withdrawn in 2003. Minority Republicans filibustered President Barack Obama's 2010 nomination of Goodwin Liu to the United States Court of Appeals for the Ninth Circuit before it was withdrawn in 2011. Both nominees were considered likely future Supreme Court appointments. In the ongoing battle over the future of constitutional law, parties and interest groups find themselves battling on more fronts.[17]

City of Boerne v. Flores, 521 U.S. 507 (1997)

In Sherbert v. Verner *(1963) the Warren Court altered the Court's longstanding understanding of the requirements of the free exercise clause of the First Amendment. Under* Sherbert, *individuals could claim a constitutional exemption from laws that substantially burdened religious practices unless those burdens were justified by a compelling government interest. In 1990 a divided Court led by Justice Scalia returned to the earlier standard in* Employment Division v. Smith. *By that standard, it is not constitutionally required that individuals be exempted from neutral, generally applicable laws that only incidentally burden religious practices.*

The Smith *decision sparked an immediate outcry from civil libertarians and religious organizations. An unusual bipartisan and cross-ideological coalition passed the Religious Freedom Restoration Act of 1993 (RFRA), which imposed the* Sherbert *standard by statute. The controversy was over whether Congress could use Section 5 of the Fourteenth Amendment to impose that rule on the states. When the Catholic archbishop of San Antonio filed suit under the RFRA to block the application of the city of Boerne's zoning laws, the district court ruled that Congress had exceeded its constitutional authority by extending the RFRA to the states. On appeal, the circuit court reversed. In a 6–3 decision, the Supreme Court reversed the circuit court and struck down the RFRA as it applied to the states.*

For members of Congress and the Court, as well as outside observers, the RFRA was an effort to reverse a constitutional doctrine by statute. The speed and decisiveness with which Congress responded to the Smith *decision suggested to some that the justices should defer to that legislative judgment as to how best to understand the principles and requirements of the free exercise clause. Even the justices who disagreed with the* Smith *standard were reluctant to accept a rebuke from Congress on a matter of constitutional interpretation, however. The RFRA instead led the justices to assert once again that the judiciary, not the legislature, was the ultimate interpreter of the Constitution.*[18]

The RFRA and Boerne *were only the first round of responses to the* Smith *decision. Many state legislatures passed their own "mini-RFRAs" that were enforceable in state courts. Congress has explored more targeted legislative options for extending the scope of federal protections in this area, such as the Religious Land Use and Institutionalized Persons Act of 2000. At the same time, there has been a more sustained discussion in Congress and elsewhere about the substantive merits of across-the-board religious exemptions to generally applicable laws and government policies in circumstances ranging from land use to prison administration.*

Kennedy's opinion for the Court leaned on John Marshall's language from Marbury v. Madison *(1803) to emphasize the primacy of the Court's role in interpreting the Constitution. Did* Marbury *determine the result here? To what extent did O'Connor disagree with the majority in* Boerne?

JUSTICE KENNEDY delivered the opinion of the Court.

A decision by local zoning authorities to deny a church a building permit was challenged under the Religious Freedom Restoration Act of 1993 (RFRA).... The case calls into question the authority of Congress to enact RFRA. We conclude the statute exceeds Congress' power.

. . .

Congress enacted RFRA in direct response to the Court's decision in *Employment Div., Dept. of Human Resources of Ore.* v. *Smith* (1990)....

. . .

Smith held that neutral, generally applicable laws may be applied to religious practices even when not supported by a compelling governmental interest.

17. See Nancy Scherer, *Scoring Points* (Stanford, CA: Stanford University Press, 2005); Sarah A. Binder and Forrest Maltzman, *Advice and Dissent* (Washington, DC: Brookings Institution Press, 2009); Roger E. Hartley and Lisa M. Holmes, "The Increasing Senate Scrutiny of Lower Federal Court Nominees," *Political Science Quarterly* 117 (2002): 259–278.

18. See "Symposium: Reflections on City of Boerne v. Flores," *William and Mary Law Review* 39 (1998): 601–960.

Four Members of the Court disagreed. They argued the law placed a substantial burden on the Native American Church members so that it could be upheld only if the law served a compelling state interest and was narrowly tailored to achieve that end. . . . JUSTICE O'CONNOR concluded Oregon had satisfied the test, while Justice Blackmun, joined by Justice Brennan and Justice Marshall, could see no compelling interest justifying the law's application to the members.

These points of constitutional interpretation were debated by Members of Congress in hearings and floor debates. Many criticized the Court's reasoning, and this disagreement resulted in the passage of RFRA. Congress announced:

> (1) The framers of the Constitution, recognizing free exercise of religion as an unalienable right, secured its protection in the First Amendment to the Constitution;
>
> (2) laws "neutral" toward religion may burden religious exercise as surely as laws intended to interfere with religious exercise;
>
> (3) governments should not substantially burden religious exercise without compelling justification;
>
> (4) in *Employment Division v. Smith*, the Supreme Court virtually eliminated the requirement that the government justify burdens on religious exercise imposed by laws neutral toward religion; and
>
> (5) the compelling interest test as set forth in prior Federal court rulings is a workable test for striking sensible balances between religious liberty and competing prior governmental interests.

The Act's stated purposes are: "(1) to restore the compelling interest test as set forth in *Sherbert v. Verner* (1963). . . . "

. . .

Under our Constitution, the Federal Government is one of enumerated powers. . . . The judicial authority to determine the constitutionality of laws, in cases and controversies, is based on the premise that the "powers of the legislature are defined and limited; and that those limits may not be mistaken, or forgotten, the constitution is written." *Marbury v. Madison* (1803).

Congress relied on its Fourteenth Amendment enforcement power in enacting the most far reaching and substantial of RFRA's provisions, those which impose its requirements on the States. . . .

. . .

In defense of the Act respondent contends . . . that RFRA is permissible enforcement legislation. Congress, it is said, is only protecting by legislation one of the liberties guaranteed by the Fourteenth Amendment's Due Process Clause, the free exercise of religion, beyond what is necessary under *Smith*. It is said the congressional decision to dispense with proof of deliberate or overt discrimination and instead concentrate on a law's effects accords with the settled understanding that Section Five includes the power to enact legislation designed to prevent as well as remedy constitutional violations. It is further contended that Congress' Section Five power is not limited to remedial or preventive legislation.

All must acknowledge that Section Five is "a positive grant of legislative power" to Congress. . . .

Legislation which deters or remedies constitutional violations can fall within the sweep of Congress' enforcement power even if in the process it prohibits conduct which is not itself unconstitutional and intrudes into "legislative spheres of autonomy previously reserved to the States." . . . For example, the Court upheld a suspension of literacy tests and similar voting requirements under Congress' parallel power to enforce the provisions of the Fifteenth Amendment . . . as a measure to combat racial discrimination in voting . . . despite the facial constitutionality of the tests. . . .

It is also true, however, that "as broad as the congressional enforcement power is, it is not unlimited." . . . In assessing the breadth of Section Five's enforcement power, we begin with its text. Congress has been given the power "to enforce" the "provisions of this article." . . .

Congress' power under Section Five, however, extends only to "enforcing" the provisions of the Fourteenth Amendment. . . . The design of the Amendment and the text of Section Five are inconsistent with the suggestion that Congress has the power to decree the substance of the Fourteenth Amendment's restrictions on the States. Legislation which alters the meaning of the Free Exercise Clause cannot be said to be enforcing the Clause. Congress does not enforce a constitutional right by changing what the right is. It has been given the power "to enforce," not the power to determine what constitutes a constitutional violation. Were it not so, what Congress would be enforcing would no longer be, in any meaningful sense, the "provisions of [the Fourteenth Amendment]."

. . .

If Congress could define its own powers by altering the Fourteenth Amendment's meaning, no longer would the Constitution be "superior paramount law, unchangeable by ordinary means." It would be "on a level with ordinary legislative acts, and, like other acts, . . . alterable when the legislature shall please to alter it." *Marbury v. Madison* (1803). . . . Under this approach, it is difficult to conceive of a principle that would limit congressional power. . . . Shifting legislative majorities could change the Constitution and effectively circumvent the difficult and detailed amendment process contained in Article V.

. . .

Our national experience teaches that the Constitution is preserved best when each part of the government respects both the Constitution and the proper actions and determinations of the other branches. When the Court has interpreted the Constitution, it has acted within the province of the Judicial Branch, which embraces the duty to say what the law is. . . . When the political branches of the Government act against the background of a judicial interpretation of the Constitution already issued, it must be understood that in later cases and controversies the Court will treat its precedents with the respect due them under settled principles, including *stare decisis*, and contrary expectations must be disappointed. RFRA was designed to control cases and controversies, such as the one before us; but as the provisions of the federal statute here invoked are beyond congressional authority, it is this Court's precedent, not RFRA, which must control.

JUSTICE STEVENS, concurring.

It is my opinion, the Religious Freedom Restoration Act of 1993 (RFRA) is a "law respecting an establishment of religion" that violates the First Amendment to the Constitution.

. . .

JUSTICE SCALIA, with whom JUSTICE STEVENS joins, concurring in part.

I write to respond briefly to the claim of Justice O'Connor's dissent . . . that historical materials support a result contrary to the one reached in *Employment Division, Department of Human Resources of Oregon v. Smith* (1990). We held in *Smith* that the Constitution's Free Exercise Clause "does not relieve an individual of the obligation to comply with a 'valid and neutral law of general applicability on the ground that the law proscribes (or prescribes) conduct that his religion prescribes (or proscribes).'" . . . The material that the dissent claims is at odds with *Smith* either has little to say about the issue or is in fact more consistent with *Smith* than with the dissent's interpretation of the Free Exercise Clause. . . .

. . .

JUSTICE O'CONNOR, with whom JUSTICE BREYER joins, dissenting.

I dissent from the Court's disposition of this case. I agree with the Court that the issue before us is whether the Religious Freedom Restoration Act (RFRA) is a proper exercise of Congress' power to enforce Section Five of the Fourteenth Amendment. But as a yardstick for measuring the constitutionality of RFRA, the Court uses its holding in *Employment Division, Department of Human Resources of Oregon v. Smith* (1990), the decision that prompted Congress to enact RFRA as a means of more rigorously enforcing the Free Exercise Clause. I remain of the view that *Smith* was wrongly decided, and I would use this case to reexamine the Court's holding there. . . .

I agree with much of the reasoning set forth in . . . the Court's opinion. Indeed, if I agreed with the Court's standard in *Smith*, I would join the opinion. As the Court's careful and thorough historical analysis shows, Congress lacks the "power to decree the substance of the Fourteenth Amendment's restrictions on the States." Rather, its power under Section Five of the Fourteenth Amendment extends only to enforcing the Amendment's provisions. In short, Congress lacks the ability independently to define or expand the scope of constitutional rights by statute. . . .

Stare decisis concerns should not prevent us from revisiting our holding in *Smith*. "[S]tare decisis is a principle of policy and not a mechanical formula of adherence to the latest decision, however recent and questionable, when such adherence involves collision with a prior doctrine more embracing in its scope, intrinsically sounder, and verified by experience." *Adarand Constructors, Inc. v. Pena*, 515 U.S. 200, 213 (1995). . . . This principle is particularly true in constitutional cases where—as this case plainly illustrates—"correction through legislative action is practically impossible." . . . I believe that, in light of both our precedent and our Nation's tradition of religious liberty,

Smith is demonstrably wrong. Moreover, it is a recent decision. As such, it has not engendered the kind of reliance on its continued application that would militate against overruling it. Cf. *Planned Parenthood of Southeastern Pennsylvania v. Casey* (1992).

. . .

I respectfully dissent from the Court's disposition of this case.

JUSTICE SOUTER, dissenting. . . .

JUSTICE BREYER, dissenting. . . .

The Nomination of Samuel Alito to the U.S. Supreme Court (2006)[19]

Judge Samuel Alito was known as a respected but low-key conservative who had made a career as a prosecutor and a judge. He had served in the Reagan administration and been appointed to the Third Circuit Court of Appeals by President George W. Bush. In 2005 he was nominated to fill the vacancy of the retiring Justice Sandra Day O'Connor, and his confirmation hearings were scheduled to follow those of John Roberts, who had been nominated to replace the deceased Chief Justice William Rehnquist.

O'Connor's departure had particular significance because she had cast a critical vote to uphold abortion rights in the 1992 Casey v. Planned Parenthood *decision, which had emphasized the importance of* stare decisis, *or following precedent, in such cases. Alito's confirmation hearings thus became an opportunity for the senators and the nominee to articulate their varying views on the importance of following established precedent in future cases and the conditions under which precedent should be followed or might be set aside. Recent confirmation hearings have also become an opportunity for senators to attempt to influence Supreme Court nominees, as well as showcase their own views for their political supporters and constituents in a very public event. The members of the Senate Judiciary Committee tend to be drawn from the ideological extremes, since they have the most interest in the issues that come before the committee. Committee Chairman Arlen Specter was an exception in being a relative moderate from a swing state. At the time of the Alito nomination, Specter was a Republican; he later switched parties after Obama's presidential victory in 2008. By contrast, Republican Sam Brownback was preparing to run a presidential campaign as a social conservative, and Democrat Charles Schumer was organizing the national Democratic campaign for the 2006 midterm Senate elections.*

SENATOR SPECTER (REPUBLICAN, PENNSYLVANIA): Let me move directly into *Casey v. Planned Parenthood* (1992). . . . How would you weigh that consideration [*stare decisis*] on the woman's right to choose?

JUDGE ALITO: Well, I think the doctrine of stare decisis is a very important doctrine. It's a fundamental part of our legal system.

And it's the principle that courts in general should follow their past precedents. And it's important for a variety of reasons. It's important because it limits the power of the judiciary. It's important because it protects reliance interests. And it's important because it reflects the view that courts should respect the judgments and the wisdom that are embodied in prior judicial decisions.

It's not an exorable command, but it is a general presumption that courts are going to follow prior precedents. . . .

SPECTER: Let me move on to another important quotation out of *Casey*.

QUOTE: "A terrible price would be paid for overruling *Casey*—or overruling *Roe*. It would seriously weaken the court's capacity to exercise the judicial power and to function as the Supreme Court of a nation dedicated to the rule of law. And to overrule *Roe v. Wade* (1973) under fire would subvert the court's legitimacy."

Do you see the legitimacy of the court being involved in the precedent of *Casey*?

ALITO: Well, I think that the court and all the courts—the Supreme Court, my court, all of the federal courts—should be insulated from public opinion. They should do what the law requires in all instances.

That's why the members of the judiciary are not elected. We have a basically democratic form of government, but the judiciary is not elected. And that's the reason: so that they don't do anything under fire. They do what the law requires. . . .

19. Excerpt taken from U.S. Senate Judiciary Committee, *Confirmation Hearing on the Nomination of Samuel A. Alito, Jr., to Be Associate Justice of the Supreme Court of the United States*, 109th Cong., 2nd Sess., January 10–11, 2006.

SPECTER: Judge Alito, let me move to the dissenting opinion by Justice Harlan in *Poe v. Ullman* (1961) where he discusses the constitutional concept of liberty and says, quote, "The traditions from which liberty developed, that tradition is a living thing."

Would you agree with Justice Harlan that the Constitution embodies the concept of a living thing?

ALITO: I think the Constitution is a living thing in the sense that matters . . .—it sets up a framework of government and a protection of fundamental rights that we have lived under very successfully for 200 years. And the genius of it is that it is not terribly specific on certain things. It sets out—some things are very specific, but it sets out some general principles and then leaves it for each generation to apply those to the particular factual situations that come up.

. . .

SPECTER: Judge Alito, the commentators have characterized *Casey* as a super-precedent.

. . .

Do you agree that *Casey* is a super-precedent . . . ?

ALITO: Well, I personally would not get into categorizing precedents as super-precedents or super-duper precedents or any . . .

SPECTER: Did you say super-duper?

ALITO: Right.
(laughter)

SPECTER: Good. I like that.

ALITO: Any sort of categorization like that sort of reminds me of the size of the laundry detergent in the supermarket.

I agree with the underlying thought that when a precedent is reaffirmed . . . each time it's reaffirmed that is a factor that should be taken into account in making the judgment about stare decisis. And when a precedent is reaffirmed on the ground that stare decisis precludes or counsels against reexamination of the merits of the precedent, then I agree that that is a precedent on precedent.

. . .

SENATOR SCHUMER (DEMOCRAT, NEW YORK): Now you've tried to reassure us that stare decisis means a great deal to you. You point out that prior Supreme Court precedents, like *Roe*, will stand because of the principle.

. . .

I just want to ask you this. Stare decisis is not an immutable principle, right?

ALITO: It is a strong principle. And in general courts follow precedents. The Supreme Court needs a special justification for overruling a prior case.

SCHUMER: But they have found them. . . .

In recent years the court has overruled various cases in a rather short amount of time. You mentioned I think it was *National League of Cities* (1976) about fair labor standards, and it was overruled just nine years later by *Garcia* (1985). . . . *Bowers v. Hardwick* (1986) was overruled by *Lawrence v. Texas* (2003). And of course . . . *Plessy* (1896) was overruled by *Brown* (1954). . . .

So the only point I'm making is that despite stare decisis, it doesn't mean a Supreme Court justice who strongly believes in stare decisis won't ever overrule a case. Is that correct? You can give me a yes or no.

ALITO: Yes.

. . .

SCHUMER: OK. . . . And remember what [Justice Thomas] said when he was sitting in the same chair you're sitting in. He pledged fealty to stare decisis.

Justice Scalia said Justice Thomas, "doesn't believe in stare decisis, period. If a constitutional line of authority is wrong, he would say, 'Let's get it right.'"

Then Justice Scalia said, "I wouldn't"—speaking of himself—"I wouldn't do that."

. . .

And I'm not saying Justice Thomas was disingenuous with the committee when he was here. I'm just saying that stare decisis is something of an elastic concept that different judges apply in different ways.

. . .

SENATOR BROWNBACK (REPUBLICAN, KANSAS): Judge Alito, the Supreme Court has gotten a number of things wrong at times, too. That would be correct. And the answer when the court gets things wrong is to overturn the case.— . . . [T]hat's the way it works, isn't that correct?

ALITO: Well, when the court gets something wrong and there's a prior precedent, then you have to analyze the doctrine of stare decisis. It is an important doctrine, and I've said a lot about it—

BROWNBACK: Wait. Let me just ask you. Was *Plessy* wrong, *Plessy v. Ferguson*?

ALITO: *Plessy* was certainly wrong.

BROWNBACK: OK, I mean, and you've gone through this. *Brown v. Board of Education*, which is in my hometown of Topeka, Kansas. . . . Fifty years ago, that overturned *Plessy*. *Plessy* had stood on the books since 1896. I don't know if you knew the number. And I've got a chart up here. It was depended upon by a number of people for a long period of time. You've got it sitting on the books for 60 years, twice the length of time of *Roe v. Wade*. You've got these number of cases that considered *Plessy* and uphold *Plessy* to the dependency. And yet *Brown* comes along. . . . And the court looks at this and they say unanimously, that's just not right.

Now, stare decisis would say in the *Brown* case you should uphold *Plessy*. Is that correct?

ALITO: . . . [C]ertainly it would be a factor that you would consider in determining whether to overrule it. It's a doctrine that you would consider.

BROWNBACK: But obviously—obviously, *Brown* overturned it. And thank goodness it did, correct?

ALITO: Certainly.

BROWNBACK: That it overturned all these super-duper precedents that had been depended upon in this case because the court got it wrong in *Plessy*. Is that correct?

ALITO: The court certainly got it wrong in *Plessy*, and it got it spectacularly wrong in *Plessy*, and it took a long time for that erroneous decision to be overruled.

. . .

BROWNBACK: I want to give you another number. And that is that in over 200 other cases, the court has revisited and revised earlier judgments. In other words, in some portion or in all the cases, the court got it wrong in some 200 cases. And thank goodness the court's willing to review various cases.

. . .

Settled law? Super-duper precedents? I think there's places where the court gets it wrong, and hopefully they will continue to be willing to revisit it.

. . .

. . .

IV. Powers of the National Government

MAJOR DEVELOPMENTS

- Assertion of new limits to the scope of Congress's power under the commerce clause
- Heightened restrictions on congressional power to enforce rights

Conservatives in the Reagan Era sought to reopen previous debates over federalism and the constitutional powers of the national government. Borrowing themes from Barry Goldwater's 1964 presidential campaign, among other places, conservatives in the 1980s often linked libertarian criticisms of "big government" with a call for greater respect for the limits on national power and for decentralization of power to states and localities. As Figure 11-3 indicates, Democratic and Republican party platforms diverged in this period.

Republicans began to talk more and more about federalism. They often focused on constitutional limitations on national power rather than, for example, the system of federal grants to states and cities. While Republicans talked about constitutional limits on national power, Democrats called for more effective government and pragmatic solutions to state and local problems. At the extreme, these Republican arguments might mean calling into question the legitimacy of the New Deal itself. There were plenty of more immediate targets, however, such as the creation of the Department of Education during the Carter administration, which conservatives denounced as illegitimate.

Conservatives expected the courts to be a critical battleground over the limits of national power. Starting in the 1980s, lawyers in the Justice Department, in conservative interest groups, and in state governments began to map out strategies for testing those constitutional limits in court. These efforts bore some fruit. A wide-ranging burst of decisions by the U.S. Supreme Court in the late 1990s struck down a variety of provisions of federal statutes and developed several

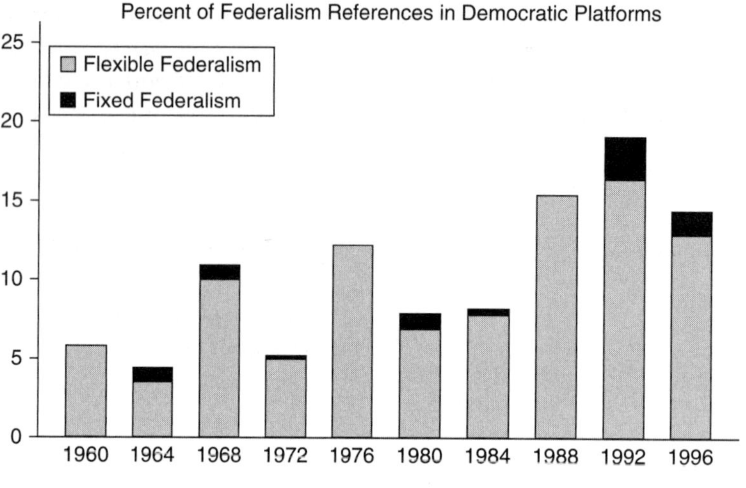

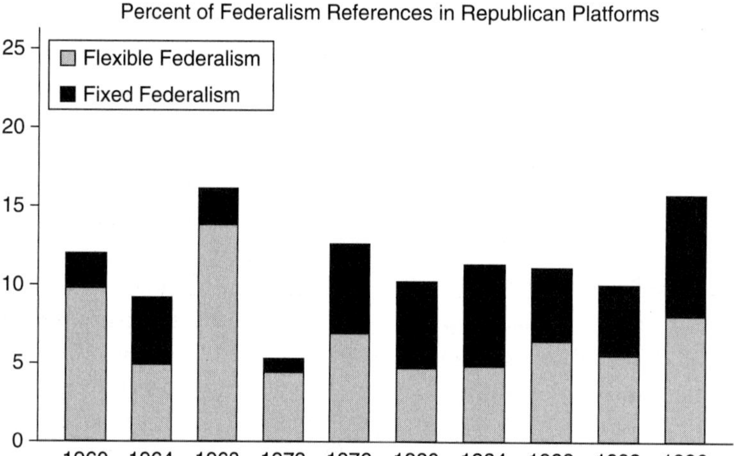

Figure 11-3 Federalism References in Party Platforms, 1960–1996

Source: Cornell W. Clayton and J. Mitchell Pickerill, "Guess What Happened on the Way to Revolution? Precursors to the Supreme Court's Federalism Revolution," *Publius* 34:3 (2004):85. Copyright © 2004, Oxford University Press.

new doctrines limiting congressional power. In *United States v. Lopez* (1995) the Rehnquist Court, for the first time since the New Deal, ruled that a federal statute had exceeded Congress's power under the commerce clause. By a 5–4 margin the conservative majority struck down the federal Gun-Free School Zones Act, emphasizing that Congress could not criminalize mere possession of a firearm that did not have any connection to a commercial transaction or economic activity that in the aggregate could substantially affect interstate commerce.

In subsequent cases the Supreme Court developed new doctrine on state sovereign immunity, the power of the federal government to "commandeer" state government officials, and congressional authority under Section 5 of the Fourteenth Amendment to define the rights of individuals vis-à-vis the state governments. Still, the federal government was not always on the losing end of these cases. National power survived a different challenge in *Gonzales v. Raich* (2005), in which the Court concluded that Congress could criminalize mere possession of marijuana within state lines on the grounds that this was necessary as part of a successful national regulatory framework. In that case Justices Kennedy and Scalia switched sides to make a 6–3 majority in favor of federal power, emphasizing (in Scalia's words) that it is "immaterial" that "simple possession" of marijuana is "a noneconomic activity," since "marijuana that is grown at home and possessed for personal use is never more than an instant from the interstate market." More generally, compared to the late 1990s, the pace of decisions in the 2000s challenging federal authority dramatically slowed. However, after Barack Obama's election, Republican Party activists revived calls for a more limited federal government. In 2009 a conservative journalist asked Democratic House Speaker Nancy Pelosi where the Constitution authorized Congress to pass the Affordable Care Act, a significant reform of the health care system that included an "individual mandate" that required most persons to either purchase health insurance by 2014 or pay a "penalty" based on their income and the cost of insurance. She replied, "Are you serious?" Her press secretary followed up by emphasizing, "That is not a serious question."[20] After Republicans retook control of the House of Representatives in the midterm elections of 2010, however, constitutional attacks on the Affordable Care Act intensified. The Court's eventual decision, in *National Federation of Independent Business v. Sebelius* (2012), illustrated once again how deeply divided the Court and the political system have been on the scope of national power, with the four more liberal associate justices arguing that the act was a valid exercise of the commerce power and the taxing power; the four most conservative associate justices concluding that the act exceeded Congress's commerce and taxing power; and the chief justice, John Roberts, deciding that it exceeded the commerce power but could be sustained under the taxing power.

The Contemporary Era also saw developments with respect to Congress's power under Section 5 of the Fourteenth Amendment "to enforce by appropriate legislation" the other provisions of that amendment. At the end of the 1960s the Court was primarily interested in freeing Congress to pass expansive new civil rights laws. At the turn of the twenty-first century the range of issues that might fall within Section 5 was more diverse, and the Court was more concerned with reemphasizing its role as the primary interpreter of the Constitution and defining some boundaries on the congressional authority to regulate the states. The Rehnquist Court heard a number of cases raising Section 5 concerns after *Boerne*. Initially, many of the challenged federal statutory provisions failed to pass constitutional muster under this test. The Court restricted an age discrimination statute in *Kimel v. Florida Board of Regents* (2000) and the Americans with Disabilities Act in *Board of Trustees of the University of Alabama v. Garrett* (2001). In *United States v. Morrison* (2000) a 5–4 majority struck down the Violence Against Women Act, which attempted to provide a federal civil remedy for victims of "violence motivated by gender." Chief Justice Rehnquist concluded that the act was not a legitimate enforcement of Fourteenth Amendment guarantees because "it is directed not at any State or state actor, but at individuals who have committed criminal acts motivated by gender bias." The dissenters decided not to focus on the Section 5 argument, preferring instead to make the point that the act could be upheld as a valid exercise of the commerce power, on the theory that Congress had amassed a "mountain of data . . . showing the effects of violence against women on interstate commerce."

Other statutes fared better. The Court upheld portions of the Family and Medical Leave Act and other elements of the Americans with Disabilities Act against Section 5 challenges in *Nevada Department of Human Resources v. Hibbs* (2003) and *Tennessee v. Lane* (2004). However, as we discuss later in this chapter, in 2013 the justices renewed these battles by calling into question the scope of Congress's power to enforce the voting rights provisions of the Fifteenth Amendment's in *Shelby County v. Holder.*

United States v. Lopez, 514 U.S. 549 (1995)

From 1937 until 1995 the Supreme Court announced no limits on the federal power to regulate interstate commerce. Every claimed exercise of the national commerce power was sustained. This sixty-year trend was broken in 1995 when the justices in United States v. Lopez *declared that Congress had no power to pass the Gun-Free School Zones Act (GFSZA) of 1990. The crucial question is whether* Lopez *(and* United States v. Morrison*) signaled a serious effort to declare sharp limitations on federal power or merely represented an effort to prune largely symbolic statutes.*

---

20. Matt Cover, "When Asked Where the Constitution Authorizes Congress to Order Americans to Buy Health Insurance, Pelosi Says: 'Are You Serious?'," *CNS News*, October 22, 2009, http://www.cnsnews.com/node/55971.

The GFSZA was passed as part of a broader crime bill in 1990, when the Democrats controlled Congress and Republican George H. W. Bush was in the White House. For the Democrats in Congress, the GFSZA was seen as a modest gun control measure that simply modified the already-popular idea of "drug-free school zones." For federal politicians, it allowed them to claim credit for "doing something" about school violence, even though state and local laws already covered much of the same ground as the GFSZA, without the controversy that normally accompanied gun control legislation. No objections—constitutional or otherwise—were raised to the bill in Congress.

When twelfth-grader Alfonso Lopez faced federal charges under the GFSZA for carrying a handgun to his San Antonio, Texas, high school, his lawyers argued that Congress did not have the constitutional authority to pass the statute. The district court upheld the law under the commerce clause, and Lopez was convicted and sentenced to six months in prison and two years' supervised release. In a unanimous holding, however, a Fifth Circuit Court opinion written by a Reagan appointee and joined by two Carter appointees struck down the GFSZA as exceeding Congress's power under the commerce clause and marking with no explanation a federal encroachment into the traditional state arena of education. The majority of the justices on the Supreme Court agreed. Lopez *had no effect on state and local laws regulating guns in schools. Congress responded to the lower court decision by passing the Gun Free Schools Act of 1994, which required schools receiving federal funds to adopt a variety of policies to penalize those found with a gun on school grounds. Congress responded to the Supreme Court decision by passing the Gun Free School Zones Act of 1996, which added a requirement that federal charges could be filed only when the gun had previously moved through interstate commerce.* Lopez *was notable not only for its powerful symbolism of striking down a federal law on interstate commerce clause grounds but also for locking into place the five-justice majority of Rehnquist, O'Connor, Scalia, Kennedy, and Thomas that would become familiar in numerous federalism cases over the next several years of the Rehnquist Court (most of which did not involve the commerce clause).*

As you read the case, consider the differences between the majority opinion by Chief Justice Rehnquist and the concurring opinion by Justice Thomas. Did Rehnquist work within or significantly challenge the New Deal settlement? In what ways might the Gun-Free School Zones Act be understood as working at the margins of the New Deal settlement? In what ways might it be understood as being well within the bounds of that settlement?

CHIEF JUSTICE REHNQUIST delivered the opinion of the Court.

In the Gun-Free School Zones Act of 1990, Congress made it a federal offense "for any individual knowingly to possess a firearm at a place that the individual knows, or has reasonable cause to believe, is a school zone." . . . The Act neither regulates a commercial activity nor contains a requirement that the possession be connected in any way to interstate commerce. We hold that the Act exceeds the authority of Congress "to regulate Commerce . . . among the several States. . . . "

. . .

We start with first principles. The Constitution creates a Federal Government of enumerated powers. . . . As James Madison wrote, "the powers delegated by the proposed Constitution to the federal government are few and defined. Those which are to remain in the State governments are numerous and indefinite." . . .

The Constitution delegates to Congress the power "to regulate Commerce with foreign Nations, and among the several States, and with the Indian Tribes." . . . The Court, through Chief Justice Marshall, first defined the nature of Congress' commerce power in *Gibbons* v. *Ogden* (1824):

> Commerce, undoubtedly, is traffic, but it is something more: it is intercourse. It describes the commercial intercourse between nations, and parts of nations, in all its branches, and is regulated by prescribing rules for carrying on that intercourse.

The *Gibbons* Court, however, acknowledged that limitations on the commerce power are inherent in the very language of the Commerce Clause.

> It is not intended to say that these words comprehend that commerce, which is completely internal, which is carried on between man and man in a State, or between different parts of the same State, and which does not extend to or affect other States. Such a power would be inconvenient, and is certainly unnecessary.
>
> Comprehensive as the word "among" is, it may very properly be restricted to that commerce which concerns more States than one. . . . The enumeration presupposes something not enumerated; and that something, if we regard the language, or the subject of the sentence, must be the exclusively internal commerce of a State. . . .

For nearly a century thereafter, the Court's Commerce Clause decisions dealt but rarely with the extent of Congress' power, and almost entirely with the Commerce Clause as a limit on state legislation that discriminated against interstate commerce. . . . Under this line of precedent, the Court held that certain categories of activity such as "production," "manufacturing," and "mining" were within the province of state governments, and thus were beyond the power of Congress under the Commerce Clause. . . .

. . .

Jones & Laughlin Steel (1937), *Darby* (1941), and *Wickard* (1942) ushered in an era of Commerce Clause jurisprudence that greatly expanded the previously defined authority of Congress under that Clause. In part, this was a recognition of the great changes that had occurred in the way business was carried on in this country. Enterprises that had once been local or at most regional in nature had become national in scope. But the doctrinal change also reflected a view that earlier Commerce Clause cases artificially had constrained the authority of Congress to regulate interstate commerce.

But even these modern-era precedents which have expanded congressional power under the Commerce Clause confirm that this power is subject to outer limits. In *Jones & Laughlin Steel*, the Court warned that the scope of the interstate commerce power "must be considered in the light of our dual system of government and may not be extended so as to embrace effects upon interstate commerce so indirect and remote that to embrace them, in view of our complex society, would effectually obliterate the distinction between what is national and what is local and create a completely centralized government." . . . Since that time, the Court has heeded that warning and undertaken to decide whether a rational basis existed for concluding that a regulated activity sufficiently affected interstate commerce. . . .

. . .

Consistent with this structure, we have identified three broad categories of activity that Congress may regulate under its commerce power. . . . First, Congress may regulate the use of the channels of interstate commerce. . . . Second, Congress is empowered to regulate and protect the instrumentalities of interstate commerce, or persons or things in interstate commerce, even though the threat may come only from intrastate activities. . . . Finally, Congress' commerce authority includes the power to regulate those activities having a substantial relation to interstate commerce . . . *i.e.*, those activities that substantially affect interstate commerce. . . .

. . .

First, we have upheld a wide variety of congressional Acts regulating intrastate economic activity where we have concluded that the activity substantially affected interstate commerce. . . .

Even *Wickard*, which is perhaps the most far reaching example of Commerce Clause authority over intrastate activity, involved economic activity in a way that the possession of a gun in a school zone does not. . . . The Court said, in an opinion sustaining the application of the Act to Filburn's activity:

> One of the primary purposes of the Act in question was to increase the market price of wheat and to that end to limit the volume thereof that could affect the market. It can hardly be denied that a factor of such volume and variability as home-consumed wheat would have a substantial influence on price and market conditions. This may arise because being in marketable condition such wheat overhangs the market and, if induced by rising prices, tends to flow into the market and check price increases. But if we assume that it is never marketed, it supplies a need of the man who grew it which would otherwise be reflected by purchases in the open market. Home-grown wheat in this sense competes with wheat in commerce. . . .

Section 922(q) [of the GFSZA] is a criminal statute that by its terms has nothing to do with "commerce" or any sort of economic enterprise, however broadly one might define those terms. Section 922(q) is not an essential part of a larger regulation of economic activity, in which the regulatory scheme could be undercut unless the intrastate activity were regulated. It cannot, therefore, be sustained under our cases upholding regulations of activities that arise out of or are connected with a commercial transaction, which viewed in the aggregate, substantially affects interstate commerce.

Second, §922(q) contains no jurisdictional element which would ensure, through case-by-case inquiry, that the firearm possession in question affects interstate commerce. . . . §922(q) has no express jurisdictional element which might limit its reach to a discrete set of firearm possessions that additionally have an explicit connection with or effect on interstate commerce.

. . .

The Government's essential contention . . . is that we may determine here that §922(q) is valid because possession of a firearm in a local school zone does indeed substantially affect interstate commerce. . . . The Government argues that possession of a firearm in a school zone may result in violent crime and that violent crime can be expected to affect the functioning of the national economy in two ways. First, the costs of violent crime are substantial, and, through the mechanism of insurance, those costs are spread throughout the population. . . . Second, violent crime reduces the willingness of individuals to travel to areas within the country that are perceived to be unsafe. . . . The Government also argues that the presence of guns in schools poses a substantial threat to the educational process by threatening the learning environment. A handicapped educational process, in turn, will result in a less productive citizenry. That, in turn, would have an adverse effect on the Nation's economic well-being. As a result, the Government argues that Congress could rationally have concluded that §922(q) substantially affects interstate commerce.

We pause to consider the implications of the Government's arguments. The Government admits, under its "costs of crime" reasoning, that Congress could regulate not only all violent crime, but all activities that might lead to violent crime, regardless of how tenuously they relate to interstate commerce. . . . Similarly, under the Government's "national productivity" reasoning, Congress could regulate any activity that it found was related to the economic productivity of individual citizens: family law (including marriage, divorce, and child custody), for example. Under the theories that the Government presents in support of §922(q), it is difficult to perceive any limitation on federal power, even in areas such as criminal law enforcement or education where States historically have been sovereign. Thus, if we were to accept the Government's arguments, we are hard pressed to posit any activity by an individual that Congress is without power to regulate.

Although JUSTICE BREYER argues that acceptance of the Government's rationales would not authorize a general federal police power, he is unable to identify any activity that the States may regulate but Congress may not. . . .

. . .

. . . [I]f Congress can, pursuant to its Commerce Clause power, regulate activities that adversely affect the learning environment, then . . . it also can regulate the educational process directly. Congress could determine that a school's curriculum has a "significant" effect on the extent of classroom learning. As a result, Congress could mandate a federal curriculum for local elementary and secondary schools because what is taught in local schools has a significant "effect on classroom learning," . . . and that, in turn, has a substantial effect on interstate commerce.

. . . [A] determination whether an intrastate activity is commercial or noncommercial may in some cases result in legal uncertainty. But, so long as Congress' authority is limited to those powers enumerated in the Constitution, and so long as those enumerated powers are interpreted as having judicially enforceable outer limits, congressional legislation under the Commerce Clause always will engender "legal uncertainty." . . . The Constitution mandates this uncertainty by withholding from Congress a plenary police power that would authorize enactment of every type of legislation. . . . Any possible benefit from eliminating this "legal uncertainty" would be at the expense of the Constitution's system of enumerated powers.

. . .

. . . The possession of a gun in a local school zone is in no sense an economic activity that might, through repetition elsewhere, substantially affect any sort of interstate commerce. Respondent was a local student at a local school; there is no indication that he had recently moved in interstate commerce, and there is no requirement that his possession of the firearm have any concrete tie to interstate commerce.

To uphold the Government's contentions here, we would have to pile inference upon inference in a manner that would bid fair to convert congressional authority under the Commerce Clause to a general police power of the sort retained by the States. Admittedly, some of our prior cases have taken long steps down that road, giving great deference to congressional action. The broad language in these opinions has suggested the possibility of additional expansion, but we decline here to proceed any further. To do so would require us to conclude that the Constitution's enumeration of powers does not presuppose something not enumerated, . . . and that there never will be a distinction between what is truly national and what is truly local. This we are unwilling to do.

JUSTICE KENNEDY, with whom JUSTICE O'CONNOR joins, concurring.

The history of the judicial struggle to interpret the Commerce Clause during the transition from the economic system the Founders knew to the single, national market still emergent in our own era counsels great restraint before the Court determines that the Clause is insufficient to support an exercise of the national power. That history gives me some pause about today's decision, but I join the Court's opinion with these observations on what I conceive to be its necessary though limited holding.

. . .

The history of our Commerce Clause decisions contains at least two lessons of relevance to this case. The first, as stated at the outset, is the imprecision of content-based boundaries used without more to define the limits of the Commerce Clause. The second, related to the first but of even greater consequence, is that the Court as an institution and the legal system as a whole have an immense stake in the stability of our Commerce Clause jurisprudence as it has evolved to this point. *Stare decisis* operates with great force in counseling us not to call in question the essential principles now in place respecting the congressional power to regulate transactions of a commercial nature. That fundamental restraint on our power forecloses us from reverting to an understanding of commerce that would serve only an 18th-century economy, dependent then upon production and trading practices that had changed but little over the preceding centuries; it also mandates against returning to the time when congressional authority to regulate undoubted commercial activities was limited by a judicial determination that those matters had an insufficient connection to an interstate system. Congress can regulate in the commercial sphere on the assumption that we have a single market and a unified purpose to build a stable national economy.

. . .

The statute before us upsets the federal balance to a degree that renders it an unconstitutional assertion of the commerce power, and our intervention is required. . . .

. . .

The statute now before us forecloses the States from experimenting and exercising their own judgment in an area to which States lay claim by right of history and expertise, and it does so by regulating an activity beyond the realm of commerce in the ordinary and usual sense of that term. The tendency of this statute to displace state regulation in areas of traditional state concern is evident from its territorial operation. There are over 100,000 elementary and secondary schools in the United States. . . . Each of these now has an invisible federal zone extending 1,000 feet beyond the (often irregular) boundaries of the school property. In some communities no doubt it would be difficult to navigate without infringing on those zones. Yet throughout these areas, school officials would find their own programs for the prohibition of guns in danger of displacement by the federal authority unless the State chooses to enact a parallel rule.

JUSTICE THOMAS, concurring.

The Court today properly concludes that the Commerce Clause does not grant Congress the authority to prohibit gun possession within 1,000 feet of a school. . . . Although I join the majority, I write separately to observe that our case law has drifted far from the original understanding of the Commerce Clause. In a future case, we ought to temper our Commerce Clause jurisprudence in a manner that both makes sense of our more recent case law and is more faithful to the original understanding of that Clause.

We have said that Congress may regulate not only "Commerce . . . among the several States," . . . but also anything that has a "substantial effect" on such commerce. This test, if taken to its logical extreme, would give Congress a "police power" over all aspects of American life. Unfortunately, we have never come to grips with this implication of our substantial effects formula. Although we have supposedly applied the substantial effects test for the past 60 years, we *always* have rejected readings of the Commerce Clause and the scope of federal power that would permit Congress to exercise a police power; our cases are quite clear that there are real limits to federal power. *New York v. United States* (1992); *Maryland v. Wirtz* (1968). . . .

While the principal dissent concedes that there are limits to federal power, the sweeping nature of our current test enables the dissent to argue that Congress can regulate gun possession. But it seems to me that the power to regulate "commerce" can by no means encompass authority over mere gun possession, any more than it empowers the Federal Government to regulate marriage, littering, or cruelty to animals, throughout the 50 States. Our Constitution quite properly leaves such matters to the individual

States, notwithstanding these activities' effects on interstate commerce. Any interpretation of the Commerce Clause that even suggests that Congress could regulate such matters is in need of reexamination.

. . .

At the time the original Constitution was ratified, "commerce" consisted of selling, buying, and bartering, as well as transporting for these purposes. . . .

As one would expect, the term "commerce" was used in contradistinction to productive activities such as manufacturing and agriculture. Alexander Hamilton, for example, repeatedly treated commerce, agriculture, and manufacturing as three separate endeavors. . . .

Moreover, interjecting a modern sense of commerce into the Constitution generates significant textual and structural problems. For example, one cannot replace "commerce" with a different type of enterprise, such as manufacturing. When a manufacturer produces a car, assembly cannot take place "with a foreign nation" or "with the Indian Tribes." Parts may come from different States or other nations and hence may have been in the flow of commerce at one time, but manufacturing takes place at a discrete site. Agriculture and manufacturing involve the production of goods; commerce encompasses traffic in such articles.

. . .

In addition to its powers under the Commerce Clause, Congress has the authority to enact such laws as are "necessary and proper" to carry into execution its power to regulate commerce among the several States. . . . But on this Court's understanding of congressional power under these two Clauses, many of Congress' other enumerated powers under Art. I, §8, are wholly superfluous. After all, if Congress may regulate all matters that substantially affect commerce, there is no need for the Constitution to specify that Congress may enact bankruptcy laws, . . . or coin money and fix the standard of weights and measures, . . . or punish counterfeiters of United States coin and securities, clause 6. . . .

. . . [I]f a "substantial effects" test can be appended to the Commerce Clause, why not to every other power of the Federal Government? There is no reason for singling out the Commerce Clause for special treatment. Accordingly, Congress could regulate all matters that "substantially affect" the Army and Navy, bankruptcies, tax collection, expenditures, and so on. In that case, the Clauses of §8 all mutually overlap, something we can assume the Founding Fathers never intended.

Our construction of the scope of congressional authority has the additional problem of coming close to turning the Tenth Amendment on its head. Our case law could be read to reserve to the United States all powers not expressly *prohibited* by the Constitution. Taken together, these fundamental textual problems should, at the very least, convince us that the "substantial effects" test should be reexamined.

. . .

From the time of the ratification of the Constitution to the mid-1930's, it was widely understood that the Constitution granted Congress only limited powers, notwithstanding the Commerce Clause. . . . Moreover, there was no question that activities wholly separated from business, such as gun possession, were beyond the reach of the commerce power. If anything, the "wrong turn" was the Court's dramatic departure in the 1930's from a century and a half of precedent.

. . .

This extended discussion of the original understanding and our first century and a half of case law does not necessarily require a wholesale abandonment of our more recent opinions. It simply reveals that our substantial effects test is far removed from both the Constitution and from our early case law and that the Court's opinion should not be viewed as "radical" or another "wrong turn" that must be corrected in the future. The analysis also suggests that we ought to temper our Commerce Clause jurisprudence.

JUSTICE STEVENS, dissenting.

. . .

Guns are both articles of commerce and articles that can be used to restrain commerce. Their possession is the consequence, either directly or indirectly, of commercial activity. In my judgment, Congress' power to regulate commerce in firearms includes the power to prohibit possession of guns at any location because of their potentially harmful use; it necessarily follows that Congress may also prohibit their possession in particular markets. The market for the possession of handguns by school-age children is, distressingly, substantial. Whether or not the national interest in eliminating that market would have justified federal legislation in 1789, it surely does today.

JUSTICE SOUTER, dissenting.

In reviewing congressional legislation under the Commerce Clause, we defer to what is often a merely implicit congressional judgment that its regulation addresses a subject substantially affecting interstate commerce "if there is any rational basis for such a finding." . . .

The practice of deferring to rationally based legislative judgments "is a paradigm of judicial restraint." . . . In judicial review under the Commerce Clause, it reflects our respect for the institutional competence of the Congress on a subject expressly assigned to it by the Constitution and our appreciation of the legitimacy that comes from Congress's political accountability in dealing with matters open to a wide range of possible choices.

. . .

There is today, however, a backward glance at . . . the old pitfalls, as the Court treats deference under the rationality rule as subject to gradation according to the commercial or noncommercial nature of the immediate subject of the challenged regulation. . . . The distinction between what is patently commercial and what is not looks much like the old distinction between what directly affects commerce and what touches it only indirectly. . . . Thus, it seems fair to ask whether the step taken by the Court today does anything but portend a return to the untenable jurisprudence from which the Court extricated itself almost 60 years ago. The answer is not reassuring. To be sure, the occasion for today's decision reflects the century's end, not its beginning. But if it seems anomalous that the Congress of the United States has taken to regulating school yards, the Act in question is still probably no more remarkable than state regulation of bake shops 90 years ago. In any event, there is no reason to hope that the Court's qualification of rational basis review will be any more successful than the efforts at substantive economic review made by our predecessors as the century began . . .

. . .

JUSTICE BREYER, with whom JUSTICE STEVENS, JUSTICE SOUTER, and JUSTICE GINSBURG join, dissenting.

. . . In my view, the statute falls well within the scope of the commerce power as this Court has understood that power over the last half century.

In reaching this conclusion, I apply three basic principles of Commerce Clause interpretation. First, the power to "regulate Commerce . . . among the several States" . . . "encompasses the power to regulate local activities insofar as they significantly affect interstate commerce. . . . "

Second, in determining whether a local activity will likely have a significant effect upon interstate commerce, a court must consider, not the effect of an individual act (a single instance of gun possession), but rather the cumulative effect of all similar instances (*i.e.*, the effect of all guns possessed in or near schools). . . .

Third, the Constitution requires us to judge the connection between a regulated activity and interstate commerce, not directly, but at one remove. Courts must give Congress a degree of leeway in determining the existence of a significant factual connection between the regulated activity and interstate commerce—both because the Constitution delegates the commerce power directly to Congress and because the determination requires an empirical judgment of a kind that a legislature is more likely than a court to make with accuracy. The traditional words "rational basis" capture this leeway.

. . .

Applying these principles to the case at hand, we must ask whether Congress could have had a *rational basis* for finding a significant (or substantial) connection between gun-related school violence and interstate commerce. . . . As long as one views the commerce connection, not as a "technical legal conception," but as "a practical one," the answer to this question must be yes. Numerous reports and studies—generated both inside and outside government—make clear that Congress could reasonably have found the empirical connection that its law, implicitly or explicitly, asserts. . . .

To hold this statute constitutional is not to "obliterate" the "distinction between what is national and what is local," . . . nor is it to hold that the Commerce Clause permits the Federal Government to "regulate any activity that it found was related to the economic productivity of individual citizens," to regulate "marriage, divorce, and child custody," or to regulate any and all aspects of education. . . . First, this statute is aimed at curbing a particularly acute threat to the educational process—the possession (and use) of life-threatening firearms in, or near, the classroom. . . . Second, the immediacy of the connection between education and the national economic well-being is documented by scholars and accepted by society at large in a way and to a degree that may not hold true for other social institutions. . . .

In sum, a holding that the particular statute before us falls within the commerce power would not expand the scope of that Clause. Rather, it simply would apply pre-existing law to changing economic circumstances.

The majority's holding . . . creates three serious legal problems. First, the majority's holding runs contrary to modern Supreme Court cases that have upheld congressional actions despite connections to interstate or foreign commerce that are less significant than the effect of school violence.

In *Katzenbach* v. *McClung* (1964) . . . this Court upheld, as within the commerce power, a statute prohibiting racial discrimination at local restaurants, in part because that discrimination discouraged travel by African Americans and in part because that discrimination affected purchases of food and restaurant supplies from other States. . . . It is difficult to distinguish the case before us, for the same critical elements are present. Businesses are less likely to locate in communities where violence plagues the classroom. Families will hesitate to move to neighborhoods where students carry guns instead of books. . . . And (to look at the matter in the most narrowly commercial manner), interstate publishers therefore will sell fewer books and other firms will sell fewer school supplies where the threat of violence disrupts learning. Most importantly . . . the local instances here, taken together and considered as a whole, create a problem that causes serious human and social harm, but also has nationally significant economic dimensions.

The second legal problem the Court creates comes from its apparent belief that it can reconcile its holding with earlier cases by making a critical distinction between "commercial" and noncommercial "transaction[s]." . . .

. . . Although the majority today attempts to categorize . . . *McClung* and *Wickard* as involving intrastate "economic activity," . . . the Courts that decided each of those cases did *not* focus upon the economic nature of the activity regulated. Rather, they focused upon whether that activity *affected* interstate or foreign commerce.

. . . The third legal problem created by the Court's holding is that it threatens legal uncertainty in an area of law that, until this case, seemed reasonably well settled. . . .

In sum, to find this legislation within the scope of the Commerce Clause would permit "Congress . . . to act in terms of economic . . . realities." . . . Upholding this legislation would do no more than simply recognize that Congress had a "rational basis" for finding a significant connection between guns in or near schools and (through their effect on education) the interstate and foreign commerce they threaten.

National Federation of Independent Business v. Sebelius, 567 U.S. ___ (2012)

The passage of the Patient Protection and Affordable Care Act of 2010 (ACA) sparked the most heated partisan controversy in recent American constitutional politics. President Obama during his presidential campaign and immediately upon taking office declared that, after addressing the inherited financial crisis, the most important domestic priority was national health care legislation that would cut spiraling health care costs and guarantee all Americans adequate health care. Efforts to pass a bipartisan bill failed, with members of each party blaming the other for intransigence. The final version of the act was passed by a straight-line party vote in the Senate and a near-straight-line party vote in the House.

The National Federation of Independent Business (NFIB) is an advocacy group that opposes laws and regulations that members believe harm small businesses. That organization vigorously opposed the ACA. NFIB members were particularly critical of what became known as "the individual mandate." That provision, §5000A, required most persons to either purchase health insurance by 2014 or pay a "penalty" based on their income and the cost of health insurance. The ACA also encouraged (threatened?) states to expand Medicaid eligibility to all persons whose income was less than 133 percent above the poverty line by providing cooperating states with additional federal funds but also cutting off all federal Medicaid funds to states that refused to expand Medicaid coverage.

The NFIB, twenty-six states, and numerous individuals filed a series of lawsuits in federal courts claiming that the individual mandate and expansion of Medicaid were unconstitutional. They argued that (a) the commerce clause did not permit the federal government to require persons to participate in interstate commerce; (b) the individual mandate was not an exercise of the federal taxing power because Congress had explicitly labeled the mandate a "penalty," not a "tax"; and (c) the expanded Medicaid provisions exceeded Congress's spending powers by improperly coercing states to comply with federal policies. Democrats and some conservative opponents of judicial activism insisted that the ACA was consistent with longstanding precedents from McCulloch v. Maryland *(1819) and the New Deal and that opponents had jerry-rigged novel arguments solely for political purposes.*

ACA opponents enjoyed some initial successes in both electoral and judicial settings. Republicans in 2010 regained control of the House of Representatives and narrowed Democratic margins in the Senate. Several, but not all, federal courts declared the individual mandate unconstitutional. With rare exceptions, lower federal court judges divided on partisan lines when adjudicating lawsuits challenging the constitutionality of requiring persons to purchase health insurance. Judges appointed by Republican presidents tended to strike down the individual mandate. Judges appointed by Democrats tended to think the individual mandate constitutional. Partisanship had less influence when lower federal courts considered whether the expanded Medicaid provision violated the spending clause. That provision was uniformly sustained.

By the time the constitutional challenge came before the Supreme Court the 2012 presidential election cycle was in full swing. The incumbent president had made the ACA a top priority of his first term, while his opponent, Mitt Romney, insisted that one of his top priorities was to "abolish . . . root and branch" what Republicans dubbed "ObamaCare."[21] *(Democrats considered Romney's opposition to be tinged with irony, since, when he was governor of Massachusetts, he had advocated for a version of the individual mandate that became a model for the ACA; in response, Romney maintained that policies appropriate for one state were not necessarily appropriate for the entire country as part of a federal mandate.) During oral arguments the five conservative justices expressed grave doubts about whether the federal government had the power to require individuals to enter the marketplace for health insurance against their will, even as part of a comprehensive program to regulate the health care industry. As the Court's term was ending the country braced for a decision that would demonstrate whether the same ideological-partisan divide existing in Congress and in presidential election politics would be reproduced on the Supreme Court. Pundits debated how a 5–4 decision to strike down the act would impact the presidential election and the Court's reputation.*

On the last day of the term, the Supreme Court, by a surprising 5–4 vote, sustained the individual mandate. Joining the four more liberal justices on the Court (Breyer, Ginsburg, Sotomayor, and Kagan), Chief Justice Roberts held that the individual mandate could be interpreted as a tax that Congress had a right to impose under Article I, Section 8, Paragraph 1. The surprise was partly that the justices voted to sustain the mandate, but mostly that Chief Justice Roberts, rather than Justice Kennedy, was the swing vote. It was the first time that this particular line-up of votes had occurred since Roberts joined the Court. Speculation immediately began over whether Roberts had a more moderate streak than had previously been recognized, whether he felt an institutional obligation as chief justice to remove the Supreme Court as an issue in the 2012 presidential election, whether his opinion was a strategic effort to give the Obama administration a victory on a policy of immediate interest while providing conservatives with a stronger foundation to narrow future exercises of federal power, or whether (as he explained) he believed he had a constitutional obligation to adopt a "saving construction" of an act of Congress when one was available. Within days of the decision reporters were publishing stories, based on sources with direct knowledge of the deliberations and the drafting process (e.g., either justices or law clerks), about Roberts's original vote to strike down the mandate, the timing of the chief justice's vote switch, the drafting of the various opinions, and (unsuccessful) efforts by Justice Kennedy to bring Roberts back to his original position.

Chief Justice Roberts's opinion began by articulating a narrow conception of federal power; denying that the individual mandate was a legitimate exercise of the commerce clause; and, for the first time in post–New Deal history, imposing spending clause limits on the national government. His opinion also described the individual mandate as a tax increase—a characterization Republicans unsurprisingly endorsed almost immediately as a way of further criticizing President Obama. Thus, analogous to Marbury v. Madison *(1803), while the outcome favored the incumbent administration, the reasoning in the opinion provided foundations for precedents that might further chip away if not do serious damage to New Deal constitutional liberalism.*

Chief Justice Roberts's majority opinion rejected claims that Congress had the power under the commerce clause to require people to buy health insurance, but he concluded that Congress could constitutionally tax persons who did not buy health insurance. Consider first whether the individual mandate was a constitutional exercise of the commerce power. What were the major arguments for each position? Who had the better argument? Does the interstate market for health insurance provide sufficient constitutional grounds for the ACA? Are the opinions' various treatments of the necessary and proper clause consistent with the discussion in McCulloch v. Maryland*? Then consider whether the*

21. Mitt Romney, "Why I'd Repeal ObamaCare," *USA Today* (March 22, 2012).

individual mandate was a tax or a penalty. What reasons do the different opinions give for their conclusion? Which conclusion is correct? Congress explicitly labeled the mandate a penalty. Why did five justices nevertheless insist the mandate was a tax?

The Supreme Court by a 7–2 vote ruled that Congress could not withdraw all Medicaid funds from states that refused to comply with the new ACA mandates. Chief Justice Roberts insisted that the threat to take away federal funds that constituted 10 percent of state budgets unconstitutionally coerced states into expanding Medicaid coverage. Suppose, as Justice Ginsburg suggested, Congress had repealed Medicaid and passed an entirely new statute combining ACA and Medicaid functions. Would that have been constitutional? Was Sebelius *an effort to limit the enormous power the national government can exercise using the conditional spending power or an unrealistic failure to recognize that, given that most state programs are funded with federal dollars, the federal government has the right to determine how those dollars are spent?*

The three major opinions in Sebelius *begin by stating fundamental regime principles. What are those different principles? How do various judicial conclusions flow from them? How does each understand the Founding and New Deal Eras? The opinions make very little reference to the Reconstruction or post–Civil War Amendments. Why did no justice think these amendments were relevant? How might those principles influence debates over the constitutional status of the individual mandate and health care?*

CHIEF JUSTICE ROBERTS announced the judgment of the Court and delivered the opinion of the Court, in which JUSTICE BREYER and JUSTICE KAGAN join in part.

. . . .

In our federal system, the National Government possesses only limited powers; the States and the people retain the remainder. . . . The Federal Government "is acknowledged by all to be one of enumerated powers." That is, rather than granting general authority to perform all the conceivable functions of government, the Constitution lists, or enumerates, the Federal Government's powers. . . . The enumeration of powers is also a limitation of powers, because "[t]he enumeration presupposes something not enumerated." *Gibbons v. Ogden* (1824). The Constitution's express conferral of some powers makes clear that it does not grant others. And the Federal Government "can exercise only the powers granted to it."

Today, the restrictions on government power foremost in many Americans' minds are likely to be affirmative prohibitions, such as contained in the Bill of Rights. These affirmative prohibitions come into play, however, only where the Government possesses authority to act in the first place. If no enumerated power authorizes Congress to pass a certain law, that law may not be enacted, even if it would not violate any of the express prohibitions in the Bill of Rights or elsewhere in the Constitution.

The same does not apply to the States, because the Constitution is not the source of their power. . . . The States thus can and do perform many of the vital functions of modern government—punishing street crime, running public schools, and zoning property for development, to name but a few—even though the Constitution's text does not authorize any government to do so. Our cases refer to this general power of governing, possessed by the States but not by the Federal Government, as the "police power."

"State sovereignty is not just an end in itself: Rather, federalism secures to citizens the liberties that derive from the diffusion of sovereign power." Because the police power is controlled by 50 different States instead of one national sovereign, the facets of governing that touch on citizens' daily lives are normally administered by smaller governments closer to the governed. The Framers thus ensured that powers which "in the ordinary course of affairs, concern the lives, liberties, and properties of the people" were held by governments more local and more accountable than a distant federal bureaucracy. The independent power of the States also serves as a check on the power of the Federal Government: "By denying any one government complete jurisdiction over all the concerns of public life, federalism protects the liberty of the individual from arbitrary power."

. . .

. . .

The Constitution grants Congress the power to "regulate Commerce." The power to regulate commerce presupposes the existence of commercial activity to be regulated. If the power to "regulate" something included the power to create it, many of the provisions in the Constitution would be superfluous. For example, the Constitution gives Congress the power to "coin Money," in addition to the power to "regulate the Value thereof." And it gives Congress the power to "raise and support Armies" and to "provide and maintain a Navy," in addition to the power to "make Rules for the Government and Regulation of the land and naval Forces." If the power to regulate the armed forces or the value of money included the power to bring the subject of the regulation into existence, the specific grant of such powers would have been unnecessary. The language of the Constitution reflects the natural understanding that the power to regulate assumes there is already something to be regulated.

Our precedent also reflects this understanding. As expansive as our cases construing the scope of the commerce power have been, they all have one thing in common: They uniformly describe the power as reaching "activity." . . . The individual mandate, however, does not regulate existing commercial activity. It instead compels individuals to become active in commerce by purchasing a product, on the ground that their failure to do so affects interstate commerce. Construing the Commerce Clause to permit Congress to regulate individuals precisely because they are doing nothing would open a new and potentially vast domain to congressional authority. Every day individuals do not do an infinite number of things. In some cases they decide not to do something; in others they simply fail to do it. Allowing Congress to justify federal regulation by pointing to the effect of inaction on commerce would bring countless decisions an individual could potentially make within the scope of federal regulation, and—under the Government's theory—empower Congress to make those decisions for him.

. . . *Wickard v. Filburn* (1941) has long been regarded as "perhaps the most far reaching example of Commerce Clause authority over intrastate activity," but the Government's theory in this case would go much further. . . . The farmer in *Wickard* was at least actively engaged in the production of wheat, and the Government could regulate that activity because of its effect on commerce. The Government's theory here would effectively override that limitation, by establishing that individuals may be regulated under the Commerce Clause whenever enough of them are not doing something the Government would have them do.

Indeed, the Government's logic would justify a mandatory purchase to solve almost any problem. To consider a different example in the health care market, many Americans do not eat a balanced diet. . . . Under the Government's theory, Congress could address the diet problem by ordering everyone to buy vegetables.

People, for reasons of their own, often fail to do things that would be good for them or good for society. Those failures—joined with the similar failures of others—can readily have a substantial effect on interstate commerce. Under the Government's logic, that authorizes Congress to use its commerce power to compel citizens to act as the Government would have them act.

. . .

. . .

The Government repeats the phrase "active in the market for health care" throughout its brief, but that concept has no constitutional significance. An individual who bought a car two years ago and may buy another in the future is not "active in the car market" in any pertinent sense. The phrase "active in the market" cannot obscure the fact that most of those regulated by the individual mandate are not currently engaged in any commercial activity involving health care, and that fact is fatal to the Government's effort to "regulate the uninsured as a class." . . .

. . .

Everyone will likely participate in the markets for food, clothing, transportation, shelter, or energy; that does not authorize Congress to direct them to purchase particular products in those or other markets today. The Commerce Clause is not a general license to regulate an individual from cradle to grave, simply because he will predictably engage in particular transactions. Any police power to regulate individuals as such, as opposed to their activities, remains vested in the States.

. . .

As our jurisprudence under the Necessary and Proper Clause has developed, we have been very deferential to Congress's determination that a regulation is "necessary." We have thus upheld laws that are "'convenient, or useful' or 'conducive' to the authority's 'beneficial exercise.'" But we have also carried out our responsibility to declare unconstitutional those laws that undermine the structure of government established by the Constitution. Such laws, which are not "consist[ent] with the letter and spirit of the constitution," *McCulloch*, are not "proper [means] for carrying into Execution" Congress's enumerated powers. Rather, they are, "in the words of *The Federalist*, 'merely acts of usurpation' which 'deserve to be treated as such.'"

Applying these principles, the individual mandate cannot be sustained under the Necessary and

Proper Clause as an essential component of the insurance reforms. Each of our prior cases upholding laws under that Clause involved exercises of authority derivative of, and in service to, a granted power. . . . The individual mandate, by contrast, vests Congress with the extraordinary ability to create the necessary predicate to the exercise of an enumerated power.

. . .

That is not the end of the matter. Because the Commerce Clause does not support the individual mandate, it is necessary to turn to the Government's second argument: that the mandate may be upheld as within Congress's enumerated power to "lay and collect Taxes."

. . . It is of course true that the Act describes the payment as a "penalty," not a "tax." . . . That choice does not, however, control whether an exaction is within Congress's constitutional power to tax.

. . .

We have held that exactions not labeled taxes nonetheless were authorized by Congress's power to tax. In the *License Tax Cases* (1866), for example, we held that federal licenses to sell liquor and lottery tickets—for which the licensee had to pay a fee—could be sustained as exercises of the taxing power. . . . And in *New York v. United States* (1992) we upheld as a tax a "surcharge" on out-of-state nuclear waste shipments, a portion of which was paid to the Federal Treasury.

. . .

In distinguishing penalties from taxes, this Court has explained that "if the concept of penalty means anything, it means punishment for an unlawful act or omission." While the individual mandate clearly aims to induce the purchase of health insurance, it need not be read to declare that failing to do so is unlawful. Neither the Act nor any other law attaches negative legal consequences to not buying health insurance, beyond requiring a payment to the IRS. The Government agrees with that reading, confirming that if someone chooses to pay rather than obtain health insurance, they have fully complied with the law.

Indeed, it is estimated that four million people each year will choose to pay the IRS rather than buy insurance. We would expect Congress to be troubled by that prospect if such conduct were unlawful. That Congress apparently regards such extensive failure to comply with the mandate as tolerable suggests that Congress did not think it was creating four million outlaws. It suggests instead that the shared responsibility payment merely imposes a tax citizens may lawfully choose to pay in lieu of buying health insurance.

. . .

. . . An example may help illustrate why labels should not control here. Suppose Congress enacted a statute providing that every taxpayer who owns a house without energy efficient windows must pay $50 to the IRS. The amount due is adjusted based on factors such as taxable income and joint filing status, and is paid along with the taxpayer's income tax return. Those whose income is below the filing threshold need not pay. The required payment is not called a "tax," a "penalty," or anything else. No one would doubt that this law imposed a tax, and was within Congress's power to tax. That conclusion should not change simply because Congress used the word "penalty" to describe the payment. . . .

Our precedent demonstrates that Congress had the power to impose the exaction in §5000A under the taxing power, and that §5000A need not be read to do more than impose a tax. That is sufficient to sustain it. The "question of the constitutionality of action taken by Congress does not depend on recitals of the power which it undertakes to exercise."

. . .

. . .

. . . [I]t is abundantly clear the Constitution does not guarantee that individuals may avoid taxation through inactivity. A capitation, after all, is a tax that everyone must pay simply for existing, and capitations are expressly contemplated by the Constitution. The Court today holds that our Constitution protects us from federal regulation under the Commerce Clause so long as we abstain from the regulated activity. But from its creation, the Constitution has made no such promise with respect to taxes.

. . .

. . . Congress's authority under the taxing power is limited to requiring an individual to pay money into the Federal Treasury, no more. If a tax is properly paid, the Government has no power to compel or punish individuals subject to it. We do not make light of the severe burden that taxation—especially taxation motivated by a regulatory purpose—can impose. But imposition of a tax nonetheless leaves an individual with a lawful choice to do or not do a certain act, so long as he is willing to pay a tax levied on that choice.

. . .

Justice Ginsburg questions the necessity of rejecting the Government's commerce power argument, given that §5000A can be upheld under the taxing power. But the statute reads more naturally as a command to buy insurance than as a tax, and I would uphold it as a command if the Constitution allowed it. It is only because the Commerce Clause does not authorize such a command that it is necessary to reach the taxing power question. And it is only because we have a duty to construe a statute to save it, if fairly possible, that §5000A can be interpreted as a tax. Without deciding the Commerce Clause question, I would find no basis to adopt such a saving construction.

The Federal Government does not have the power to order people to buy health insurance. Section §5000A would therefore be unconstitutional if read as a command. The Federal Government does have the power to impose a tax on those without health insurance. Section 5000A is therefore constitutional, because it can reasonably be read as a tax.

. . .

The Spending Clause grants Congress the power "to pay the Debts and provide for the . . . general Welfare of the United States." We have long recognized that Congress may use this power to grant federal funds to the States, and may condition such a grant upon the States' "taking certain actions that Congress could not require them to take." . . .

At the same time, our cases have recognized limits on Congress's power under the Spending Clause to secure state compliance with federal objectives. "We have repeatedly characterized . . . Spending Clause legislation as 'much in the nature of a *contract*.'" The legitimacy of Congress's exercise of the spending power "thus rests on whether the State voluntarily and knowingly accepts the terms of the 'contract.'"

. . .

. . . Congress may use its spending power to create incentives for States to act in accordance with federal policies. But when "pressure turns into compulsion," the legislation runs contrary to our system of federalism. "[T]he Constitution simply does not give Congress the authority to require the States to regulate." That is true whether Congress directly commands a State to regulate or indirectly coerces a State to adopt a federal regulatory system as its own.

Permitting the Federal Government to force the States to implement a federal program would threaten the political accountability key to our federal system. "[W]here the Federal Government directs the States to regulate, it may be state officials who will bear the brunt of public disapproval, while the federal officials who devised the regulatory program may remain insulated from the electoral ramifications of their decision." Spending Clause programs do not pose this danger when a State has a legitimate choice whether to accept the federal conditions in exchange for federal funds. In such a situation, state officials can fairly be held politically accountable for choosing to accept or refuse the federal offer. But when the State has no choice, the Federal Government can achieve its objectives without accountability. . . .

. . .

In this case, the financial "inducement" Congress has chosen is much more than "relatively mild encouragement"—it is a gun to the head. A State that opts out of the Affordable Care Act's expansion in health care coverage thus stands to lose not merely "a relatively small percentage" of its existing Medicaid funding, but all of it. Medicaid spending accounts for over 20 percent of the average State's total budget, with federal funds covering 50 to 83 percent of those costs. . . . The threatened loss of over 10 percent of a State's overall budget is economic dragooning that leaves the States with no real option but to acquiesce in the Medicaid expansion.

. . .

The Medicaid expansion . . . accomplishes a shift in kind, not merely degree. The original program was designed to cover medical services for four particular categories of the needy: the disabled, the blind, the elderly, and needy families with dependent children. Previous amendments to Medicaid eligibility merely altered and expanded the boundaries of these categories. Under the Affordable Care Act, Medicaid is transformed into a program to meet the health care needs of the entire nonelderly population with income below 133 percent of the poverty level. It is no longer a program to care for the neediest among us, but rather an element of a comprehensive national plan to provide universal health insurance coverage.

. . .

As we have explained, "[t]hough Congress' power to legislate under the spending power is broad, it does not include surprising participating States with post-acceptance or 'retroactive' conditions." A State could hardly anticipate that Congress's reservation of the right to "alter" or "amend" the Medicaid program included the power to transform it so dramatically.

. . .

Nothing in our opinion precludes Congress from offering funds under the Affordable Care Act to expand the availability of health care, and requiring that States accepting such funds comply with the conditions on their use. What Congress is not free to do is to penalize States that choose not to participate in that new program by taking away their existing Medicaid funding.

. . .

JUSTICE GINSBURG, with whom JUSTICE SOTOMAYOR joins, and with whom JUSTICE BREYER and JUSTICE KAGAN join [in part]. . . .

. . .

Since 1937, our precedent has recognized Congress' large authority to set the Nation's course in the economic and social welfare realm. The Chief Justice's crabbed reading of the Commerce Clause harks back to the era in which the Court routinely thwarted Congress' efforts to regulate the national economy in the interest of those who labor to sustain it. It is a reading that should not have staying power.

. . .

States cannot resolve the problem of the uninsured on their own. Like Social Security benefits, a universal health-care system, if adopted by an individual State, would be "bait to the needy and dependent elsewhere, encouraging them to migrate and seek a haven of repose." An influx of unhealthy individuals into a State with universal health care would result in increased spending on medical services. To cover the increased costs, a State would have to raise taxes, and private health-insurance companies would have to increase premiums. Higher taxes and increased insurance costs would, in turn, encourage businesses and healthy individuals to leave the State.

. . .

The Commerce Clause, it is widely acknowledged, "was the Framers' response to the central problem that gave rise to the Constitution itself." Under the Articles of Confederation, the Constitution's precursor, the regulation of commerce was left to the States. This scheme proved unworkable, because the individual States, understandably focused on their own economic interests, often failed to take actions critical to the success of the Nation as a whole. What was needed was a "national Government . . . armed with a positive & compleat authority in all cases where uniform measures are necessary." The Framers' solution was the Commerce Clause, which, as they perceived it, granted Congress the authority to enact economic legislation "in all Cases for the general Interests of the Union, and also in those Cases to which the States are separately incompetent."

The Framers understood that the "general Interests of the Union" would change over time, in ways they could not anticipate. Accordingly, they recognized that the Constitution was of necessity a "great outlin[e]," not a detailed blueprint, see *McCulloch v. Maryland*, and that its provisions included broad concepts, to be "explained by the context or by the facts of the case." "Nothing . . . can be more fallacious," Alexander Hamilton emphasized, "than to infer the extent of any power, proper to be lodged in the national government, from . . . its immediate necessities. There ought to be a capacity to provide for future contingencies[,] as they may happen; and as these are illimitable in their nature, it is impossible safely to limit that capacity." *The Federalist* No. 34.

. . .

Until today, this Court's pragmatic approach to judging whether Congress validly exercised its commerce power was guided by two familiar principles. First, Congress has the power to regulate economic activities "that substantially affect interstate commerce." This capacious power extends even to local activities that, viewed in the aggregate, have a substantial impact on interstate commerce. Second, we owe a large measure of respect to Congress when it frames and enacts economic and social legislation. When appraising such legislation, we ask only (1) whether Congress had a "rational basis" for concluding that the regulated activity substantially affects interstate commerce, and (2) whether there is a "reasonable connection between the regulatory means selected and the asserted ends." In answering these questions, we presume the statute under review is constitutional and may strike it down only on a "plain showing" that Congress acted irrationally.

Straightforward application of these principles would require the Court to hold that the minimum coverage provision is proper Commerce Clause legislation. Beyond dispute, Congress had a rational basis for concluding that the uninsured, as a class, substantially affect interstate commerce. Those without insurance consume billions of dollars of health-care products and services each year. Those goods are produced, sold, and delivered largely by national and regional companies who routinely transact business across state lines. The uninsured also cross state lines to receive care. Some have medical emergencies while away from home. Others, when sick, go to a neighboring State that provides better care for those who have not prepaid for care.

Not only do those without insurance consume a large amount of health care each year; critically, as earlier explained, their inability to pay for a significant portion of that consumption drives up market prices, foists costs on other consumers, and reduces market efficiency and stability. Given these far-reaching effects on interstate commerce, the decision to forgo insurance is hardly inconsequential or equivalent to "doing nothing," it is, instead, an economic decision Congress has the authority to address under the Commerce Clause.

The minimum coverage provision, furthermore, bears a "reasonable connection" to Congress' goal of protecting the health-care market from the disruption caused by individuals who fail to obtain insurance. By requiring those who do not carry insurance to pay a toll, the minimum coverage provision gives individuals a strong incentive to insure. This incentive, Congress had good reason to believe, would reduce the number of uninsured and, correspondingly, mitigate the adverse impact the uninsured have on the national health-care market.

. . .

. . . [M]ore than 60% of those without insurance visit a hospital or doctor's office each year. Nearly 90% will within five years. An uninsured's consumption of health care is thus quite proximate: It is virtually certain to occur in the next five years and more likely than not to occur this year.

. . .

. . . [I]t is Congress' role, not the Court's, to delineate the boundaries of the market the Legislature seeks to regulate. The Chief Justice defines the health-care market as including only those transactions that will occur either in the next instant or within some (unspecified) proximity to the next instant. But Congress could reasonably have viewed the market from a long-term perspective, encompassing all transactions virtually certain to occur over the next decade, not just those occurring here and now.

. . .

. . . The inevitable yet unpredictable need for medical care and the guarantee that emergency care will be provided when required are conditions nonexistent in other markets. That is so of the market for cars, and of the market for broccoli as well. Although an individual might buy a car or a crown of broccoli one day, there is no certainty she will ever do so. And if she eventually wants a car or has a craving for broccoli, she will be obliged to pay at the counter before receiving the vehicle or nourishment. She will get no free ride or food, at the expense of another consumer forced to pay an inflated price. Upholding the minimum coverage provision on the ground that all are participants or will be participants in the health-care market would therefore carry no implication that Congress may justify under the Commerce Clause a mandate to buy other products and services.

. . .

. . . Requiring individuals to obtain insurance unquestionably regulates the interstate health-insurance and health-care markets, both of them in existence well before the enactment of the ACA. Thus, the "something to be regulated" was surely there when Congress created the minimum coverage provision.

. . .

The Chief Justice could certainly uphold the individual mandate without giving Congress carte blanche to enact any and all purchase mandates. As several times noted, the unique attributes of the health-care market render everyone active in that market and give rise to a significant free-riding problem that does not occur in other markets.

. . .

Consider the chain of inferences the Court would have to accept to conclude that a vegetable-purchase mandate was likely to have a substantial effect on the health-care costs borne by lithe Americans. The Court would have to believe that individuals forced to buy vegetables would then eat them (instead of throwing or giving them away), would prepare the vegetables in a healthy way (steamed or raw, not deep-fried), would cut back on unhealthy foods, and would not allow other factors (such as lack of exercise or little sleep) to trump the improved diet. Such "pil[ing of] inference upon inference" is just what the Court refused to do in *United States v. Lopez* (1995) and *United States v. Morrison* (2000).

. . .

Supplementing these legal restraints is a formidable check on congressional power: the democratic process. As the controversy surrounding the passage of the Affordable Care Act attests, purchase mandates are likely to engender political resistance. This prospect is borne out by the behavior of state legislators. Despite their possession of unquestioned authority to impose mandates, state governments have rarely done so.

. . .

The Necessary and Proper Clause "empowers Congress to enact laws in effectuation of its [commerce] powe[r] that are not within its authority to enact in isolation." Hence, "[a] complex regulatory program . . . can survive a Commerce Clause challenge without a showing that every single facet of the program is independently and directly related to a valid congressional goal." "It is enough that the challenged provisions are an integral part of the regulatory program and that the regulatory scheme when considered as a whole satisfies this test." . . .

Recall that one of Congress' goals in enacting the Affordable Care Act was to eliminate the insurance industry's practice of charging higher prices or denying coverage to individuals with preexisting medical conditions. . . . Congress knew, however, that simply barring insurance companies from relying on an applicant's medical history would not work in practice. Without the individual mandate, Congress learned, guaranteed-issue and community-rating requirements would trigger an adverse-selection death-spiral in the health-insurance market: Insurance premiums would skyrocket, the number of uninsured would increase, and insurance companies would exit the market. When complemented by an insurance mandate, on the other hand, guaranteed issue and community rating would work as intended, increasing access to insurance and reducing uncompensated care. The minimum coverage provision is thus an "essential par[t] of a larger regulation of economic activity"; without the provision, "the regulatory scheme [w]ould be undercut." . . .

. . .

. . . The Chief Justice cites only two cases in which this Court concluded that a federal statute impermissibly transgressed the Constitution's boundary between state and federal authority: *Printz v. United States* (1997) . . . and *New York v. United States* (1992). . . . The statutes at issue in both cases, however, compelled *state officials* to act on the Federal Government's behalf. . . . The minimum coverage provision, in contrast, acts "directly upon individuals, without employing the States as intermediaries." The provision is thus entirely consistent with the Constitution's design. . . .

. . .

Ultimately, the Court upholds the individual mandate as a proper exercise of Congress' power to tax and spend "for the . . . general Welfare of the United States." . . . I concur in that determination, which makes the Chief Justice's Commerce Clause essay all the more puzzling. Why should the Chief Justice strive so mightily to hem in Congress' capacity to meet the new problems arising constantly in our ever-developing modern economy? I find no satisfying response to that question in his opinion.

. . .

. . . The spending power conferred by the Constitution, the Court has never doubted, permits Congress to define the contours of programs financed with federal funds. And to expand coverage, Congress could have recalled the existing legislation, and replaced it with a new law making Medicaid as embracive of the poor as Congress chose.

The question posed by the 2010 Medicaid expansion, then, is essentially this: To cover a notably larger population, must Congress take the repeal/reenact route, or may it achieve the same result by amending existing law? The answer should be that Congress may expand by amendment the classes of needy persons entitled to Medicaid benefits. A ritualistic requirement that Congress repeal and reenact spending legislation in order to enlarge the population served by a federally funded program would advance no constitutional principle and would scarcely serve the interests of federalism. . . .

. . .

Medicaid, as amended by the ACA is not two spending programs; it is a single program with a constant aim—to enable poor persons to receive basic health care when they need it. Given past expansions, plus express statutory warning that Congress may change the requirements participating States must meet, there can be no tenable claim that the ACA fails for lack of notice. Moreover, States have no entitlement to receive any Medicaid funds; they enjoy only the opportunity to accept funds on Congress' terms. Future Congresses are not bound by their predecessors' dispositions; they have authority to spend federal revenue as they see fit. The Federal Government, therefore, is not, as The Chief Justice charges, threatening States with the loss of "existing" funds from one spending program in order to induce them to opt into another program. Congress is simply requiring States to do what States have long been required to do to receive Medicaid funding: comply with the conditions Congress prescribes for participation.

A majority of the Court, however, buys the argument that prospective withholding of funds formerly available exceeds Congress' spending power. Given that holding, I entirely agree with The Chief Justice as to the appropriate remedy. It is to bar the withholding found impermissible—not, as the joint dissenters would have it, to scrap the expansion altogether.

. . .

JUSTICE SCALIA, JUSTICE KENNEDY, JUSTICE THOMAS, and JUSTICE ALITO, dissenting.

. . .

. . . What is absolutely clear, affirmed by the text of the 1789 Constitution, by the Tenth Amendment ratified in 1791, and by innumerable cases of ours in the 220 years since, is that there are structural limits upon federal power—upon what it can prescribe with respect to private conduct, and upon what it can impose upon the sovereign States. Whatever may be the conceptual limits upon the Commerce Clause and upon the power to tax and spend, they cannot be such as will enable the Federal Government to regulate all private conduct and to compel the States to function as administrators of federal programs.

That clear principle carries the day here. The striking case of *Wickard v. Filburn* (1942), which held that the economic activity of growing wheat, even for one's own consumption, affected commerce sufficiently that it could be regulated, always has been regarded as the ne plus ultra of expansive Commerce Clause jurisprudence. To go beyond that, and to say the failure to grow wheat (which is not an economic activity, or any activity at all) nonetheless affects commerce and therefore can be federally regulated, is to make mere breathing in and out the basis for federal prescription and to extend federal power to virtually all human activity.

As for the constitutional power to tax and spend for the general welfare: The Court has long since expanded that beyond (what Madison thought it meant) taxing and spending for those aspects of the general welfare that were within the Federal Government's enumerated powers, see *United States v. Butler* (1936). Thus, we now have sizable federal Departments devoted to subjects not mentioned among Congress' enumerated powers, and only marginally related to commerce: the Department of Education, the Department of Health and Human Services, the Department of Housing and Urban Development. The principal practical obstacle that prevents Congress from using the tax-and-spend power to assume all the general-welfare responsibilities traditionally exercised by the States is the sheer impossibility of managing a Federal Government large enough to administer such a system. That obstacle can be overcome by granting funds to the States, allowing them to administer the program. That is fair and constitutional enough when the States freely agree to have their powers employed and their employees enlisted in the federal scheme. But it is a blatant violation of the constitutional structure when the States have no choice.

. . .

In *Gibbons v. Ogden* (1824), Chief Justice Marshall wrote that the power to regulate commerce is the power "to prescribe the rule by which commerce is to be governed." That understanding is consistent with the original meaning of "regulate" at the time of the Constitution's ratification, when "to regulate" meant "[t]o adjust by rule, method or established mode." It can mean to direct the manner of something but not to direct that something come into being. There is no instance in which this Court or Congress (or anyone else, to our knowledge) has used "regulate" in that peculiar fashion. If the word bore that meaning, Congress' authority "[t]o make Rules for the Government and Regulation of the land and naval Forces," would have made superfluous the later provision for authority "[t]o raise and support Armies," and "[t]o provide and maintain a Navy."

. . .

Congress has impressed into service third parties, healthy individuals who could be but are not customers of the relevant industry, to offset the undesirable consequences of the regulation. Congress' desire to force these individuals to purchase insurance is motivated by the fact that they are further removed from the market than unhealthy individuals with pre-existing conditions, because they are less likely to need extensive care in the near future. If Congress can reach out and command even those furthest removed from an interstate market to participate in the market, then the Commerce Clause becomes a font of unlimited power. . . .

. . .

. . . §5000A does not apply only to persons who purchase all, or most, or even any, of the health care services or goods that the mandated insurance covers. Indeed, the main objection many have to the Mandate is that they have no intention of purchasing most or even any of such goods or services and thus no need to buy insurance for those purchases. The Government responds that the health-care market involves "essentially universal participation." The principal difficulty with this response is that it is, in the only relevant sense, not true. It is true enough that everyone consumes "health care," if the term is taken to include the purchase of a bottle of aspirin. But the health care "market" that is the object of the Individual Mandate not only includes but principally consists of goods and services that the young people primarily affected by the Mandate do not purchase. They are quite simply not participants in that market, and cannot be made so (and thereby subjected to regulation) by the simple device of defining participants to include all those who will, later in their lifetime, probably purchase the goods or services covered by the mandated insurance.

. . .

Wickard v. Filburn has been regarded as the most expansive assertion of the commerce power in our history. A close second is *Perez v. United States* (1971), which upheld a statute criminalizing the eminently local activity of loan-sharking. Both of those cases, however, involved commercial activity. To go beyond that, and to say that the failure to grow wheat or the refusal to make loans affects commerce, so that growing and lending can be federally compelled, is to extend federal power to virtually everything. All of us consume food, and when we do so the Federal Government can prescribe what its quality must be and even how much we must pay. But the mere fact that we all consume food and are thus, sooner or later, participants in the "market" for food, does not empower the Government to say when and what we will buy. That is essentially what this Act seeks to do with respect to the purchase of health care. It exceeds federal power.

. . .

As far as §5000A is concerned, we would stop there. Congress has attempted to regulate beyond the scope of its Commerce Clause authority, and §5000A is therefore invalid. The Government contends, however, that "The Minimum Coverage Provision Is Independently Authorized By Congress's Taxing Power." The phrase "independently authorized" suggests the existence of a creature never hitherto seen in the United States Reports: A penalty for constitutional purposes that is also a tax for constitutional purposes. In all our cases the two are mutually exclusive. The provision challenged under the Constitution is either a penalty or else a tax. Of course in many cases what was a regulatory mandate enforced by a penalty could have been imposed as a tax upon permissible action; or what was imposed as a tax upon permissible action could have been a regulatory mandate enforced by a penalty. But we know of no case, and the Government cites none, in which the imposition was, for constitutional purposes, both. . . . The issue is not whether Congress had the power to frame the minimum-coverage provision as a tax, but whether it did so.

. . .

Our cases establish a clear line between a tax and a penalty: "'[A] tax is an enforced contribution to provide for the support of government; a penalty . . . is an exaction imposed by statute as punishment for an unlawful act.'" . . . So the question is, quite simply, whether the exaction here is imposed for violation of the law. It unquestionably is. The minimum-coverage provision is found in 26 U.S.C. §5000A, entitled "*Requirement* to maintain minimum essential coverage." (Emphasis added.) It commands that every "applicable individual shall . . . ensure that the individual . . . is covered under minimum essential coverage." . . .

. . .

Quite separately, the fact that Congress (in its own words) "imposed . . . a penalty," for failure to buy insurance is alone sufficient to render that failure unlawful. It is one of the canons of interpretation that a statute that penalizes an act makes it unlawful: "[W]here the statute inflicts a penalty for doing an act, although the act itself is not expressly prohibited, yet to do the act is unlawful, because it cannot be supposed that the Legislature intended that a penalty should be inflicted for a lawful act."

. . .

. . . [T]o say that the Individual Mandate merely imposes a tax is not to interpret the statute but to rewrite it. Judicial tax-writing is particularly troubling. Taxes have never been popular, and in part for that reason, the Constitution requires tax increases to originate in the House of Representatives. That is to say, they must originate in the legislative body most accountable to the people, where legislators must weigh the need for the tax against the terrible price they might pay at their next election, which is never more than two years off. . . . Imposing a tax through judicial legislation inverts the constitutional scheme, and places the power to tax in the branch of government least accountable to the citizenry.

. . .

Th[e] practice of attaching conditions to federal funds greatly increases federal power. "[O]bjectives not thought to be within Article I's enumerated legislative fields, may nevertheless be attained through the use of the spending power and the conditional grant of federal funds." This formidable power, if not checked in any way, would present a grave threat to the system of federalism created by our Constitution. If Congress' "Spending Clause power to pursue objectives outside of Article I's enumerated legislative fields" is "limited only by Congress' notion of the general welfare, the reality, given the vast financial resources of the Federal Government, is that the Spending Clause gives 'power to the Congress to tear down the barriers, to invade the states' jurisdiction, and to become a parliament of the whole people, subject to no restrictions save such as are self-imposed.'"

. . . Coercing States to accept conditions risks the destruction of the "unique role of the States in our system." . . . When Congress compels the States to do its bidding, it blurs the lines of political accountability. If the Federal Government makes a controversial decision while acting on its own, "it is the Federal Government that makes the decision in full view of the public, and it will be federal officials that suffer the consequences if the decision turns out to be detrimental or unpopular." But when the Federal Government compels the States to take unpopular actions, "it may be state officials who will bear the brunt of public disapproval, while the federal officials who devised the regulatory program may remain insulated from the electoral ramifications of their decision." . . .

. . .

. . . When a heavy federal tax is levied to support a federal program that offers large grants to the States, States may, as a practical matter, be unable to refuse to participate in the federal program and to substitute a state alternative. Even if a State believes that the federal program is ineffective and inefficient, withdrawal would likely force the State to impose a huge tax increase on its residents, and this new state tax would come on top of the federal taxes already paid by residents to support subsidies to participating States.

. . .

Acceptance of the Federal Government's interpretation of the anticoercion rule would permit Congress to dictate policy in areas traditionally governed primarily at the state or local level. Suppose, for example, that Congress enacted legislation offering each State a grant equal to the State's entire annual expenditures for primary and secondary education. Suppose also that this funding came with conditions governing such things as school curriculum, the hiring and tenure of teachers, the drawing of school districts, the length and hours of the school day, the school calendar, a dress code for students, and rules for student discipline. As a matter of law, a State could turn down that offer, but if it did so, its residents would not only be required to pay the federal taxes needed to support this expensive new program, but they would also be forced to pay an equivalent amount in state taxes. And if the State gave in to the federal law, the State and its subdivisions would surrender their traditional authority in the field of education. . . .

. . .

. . . [T]he offer that the ACA makes to the States—go along with a dramatic expansion of Medicaid or potentially lose all federal Medicaid funding—is quite unlike anything that we have seen in a prior spending-power case. In *South Dakota v. Dole (1987)*, the total amount that the States would have lost if every single State had refused to comply with the 21-year-old drinking age was approximately $614.7 million—or about 0.19% of all state expenditures combined. South Dakota stood to lose, at most, funding that amounted to less than 1% of its annual state expenditures. Under the ACA, by contrast, the Federal Government has threatened to withhold 42.3% of all federal outlays to the states, or approximately $233 billion. South Dakota stands to lose federal funding equaling 28.9% of its annual state expenditures. . . .

What the statistics suggest is confirmed by the goal and structure of the ACA. In crafting the ACA, Congress clearly expressed its informed view that no State could possibly refuse the offer that the ACA extends.

The stated goal of the ACA is near-universal health care coverage. . . . If any State—not to mention all of the 26 States that brought this suit—chose to decline the federal offer, there would be a gaping hole in the ACA's coverage. . . . If Congress had thought that States might actually refuse to go along with the expansion of Medicaid, Congress would surely have devised a backup scheme so that the most vulnerable groups in our society, those previously eligible for Medicaid, would not be left out in the cold. But nowhere in the over 900-page Act is such a scheme to be found. . . .

. . .

The Federal Government does not dispute the inference that Congress anticipated 100% state participation, but it argues that this assumption was based on the fact that ACA's offer was an "exceedingly generous" gift. . . . This characterization of the ACA's offer raises obvious questions. If that offer is "exceedingly generous," as the Federal Government maintains, why have more than half the States brought this lawsuit, contending that the offer is coercive? And why did Congress find it necessary to threaten that any State refusing to accept this "exceedingly generous" gift would risk losing all Medicaid funds?

. . .

In sum, it is perfectly clear from the goal and structure of the ACA that the offer of the Medicaid Expansion was one that Congress understood no State could refuse. The Medicaid Expansion therefore exceeds Congress' spending power and cannot be implemented.

Seven Members of the Court agree that the Medicaid Expansion, as enacted by Congress, is unconstitutional. Because the Medicaid Expansion is unconstitutional, the question of remedy arises. The most natural remedy would be to invalidate the Medicaid Expansion. However, the Government proposes—in two cursory sentences at the very end of its brief—preserving the Expansion. Under its proposal, States would receive the additional Medicaid funds if they expand eligibility, but States would keep their pre-existing Medicaid funds if they do not expand eligibility. We cannot accept the Government's suggestion.

The reality that States were given no real choice but to expand Medicaid was not an accident. Congress assumed States would have no choice, and the ACA depends on States' having no choice, because its Mandate requires low-income individuals to obtain insurance many of them can afford only through the Medicaid Expansion. . . . Worse, the Government's proposed remedy introduces a new dynamic: States must choose between expanding Medicaid or paying huge tax sums to the federal fisc for the sole benefit of expanding Medicaid in other States. If this divisive dynamic between and among States can be introduced at all, it should be by conscious congressional choice, not by Court-invented interpretation. We do not doubt that States are capable of making decisions when put in a tight spot. We do doubt the authority of this Court to put them there.

. . .

The Constitution, though it dates from the founding of the Republic, has powerful meaning and vital relevance to our own times. The constitutional protections that this case involves are protections of structure. Structural protections—notably, the restraints imposed by federalism and separation of powers—are less romantic and have less obvious a connection to personal freedom than the provisions of the Bill of Rights or the Civil War Amendments. Hence they tend to be undervalued or even forgotten by our citizens. It should be the responsibility of the Court to teach otherwise, to remind our people that the Framers considered structural protections of freedom the most important ones, for which reason they alone were embodied in the original Constitution and not left to later amendment. The fragmentation of power produced by the structure of our Government is central to liberty, and when we destroy it, we place liberty at peril. Today's decision should have vindicated, should have taught, this truth; instead, our judgment today has disregarded it.

JUSTICE THOMAS, dissenting.

. . . I adhere to my view that "the very notion of a 'substantial effects' test under the Commerce Clause is inconsistent with the original understanding of Congress' powers and with this Court's early Commerce Clause cases." As I have explained, the Court's continued use of that test "has encouraged the Federal Government to persist in its view that the Commerce Clause has virtually no limits." The Government's unprecedented claim in this suit that it may regulate not only economic activity but also inactivity that substantially affects interstate commerce is a case in point.

V. Federalism

MAJOR DEVELOPMENTS

- Restrictions on federal ability to control state officers
- Enhanced protection of state and local governments from civil lawsuits
- Restrictions on state ability to control federal officers and elections

While many supporters of the Reagan Revolution praised federalism, some of their moves to empower states raised no interesting constitutional issues. For example, welfare reform reduced federal involvement and shifted power to states, but it violated no New Deal constitutional principle. Moreover, as we have seen time and time again, one's views on federalism often depend on the underlying substantive policy issue at stake. Pro-slavery advocates declared their commitment to states' rights when they attempted to prevent federal meddling with pro-slavery policies in the southern states, but they quickly turned into strong advocates of national power when debating the scope of federal power to return fugitive slaves from uncooperative northern states. In the previous section we saw that some conservatives articulated a cramped conception of federal power when debating national laws against gun possession near schools but a more generous conception when defending federal power to regulate narcotics. Gay rights advocates became proponents of federalism when some states passed laws allowing for same-sex marriage. Conservatives who decried federal meddling with traditional state prerogatives were often silent when it came to passage of the national Defense of Marriage Act.

Among the most important principles developed by Court conservatives during the Contemporary Era was the notion of "non-commandeering," or the protection of state officials against being controlled (or "commandeered") by the federal government. States are often integral to the implementation of federal statutes, and states often have their own reasons for wanting to be involved in how federal policies are administered and enforced. In *Gregory v. Ashcroft* (1991) the Supreme Court issued a 7–2 ruling authored by Justice O'Connor holding that the application of the federal Age Discrimination in Employment Act to state judges would raise constitutional problems under the Tenth Amendment by interfering with how states organized their basic political offices. In 1992 the Court decided *New York v. United States* in a 6–3 decision authored by Justice O'Connor holding that Congress could not "commandeer" the states' legislative process by requiring them to adopt a particular regulatory scheme for disposing of low-level radioactive waste. Justice Souter, appointed to the Court by the first President Bush in 1990, joined those early decisions but subsequently became a dissenter from the conservative federalism decisions of the Rehnquist Court.

The anti-commandeering principle seemed potentially idiosyncratic in *New York v. United States*, but it was tested again in *Printz v. United States* (1997). A 5–4 Court in *Printz* held that Congress could not require that local law enforcement officers perform a federal background check before handgun purchases were finalized. Justice Scalia argued that the Tenth Amendment imposed an independent check on how the federal government could design and implement its laws. The supremacy clause of the Constitution meant that federal laws could preempt conflicting state laws and that state courts were required to recognize and apply federal law in appropriate cases. But it was not the responsibility of state officials to enforce federal laws.

A similar debate was rehearsed in *Arizona v. United States* (2012), in which another five-justice majority held that the state of Arizona could not interfere with a comprehensive federal scheme of immigration regulation by making it a state crime for a person to fail to comply with federal alien registration requirements or for an unauthorized alien to seek or engage in work in the state. The state law also authorized state and local officials to arrest without a warrant any person the officer had probable cause to believe was an unauthorized alien and required police officers who conducted a stop, detention, or arrest to make efforts to verify the person's immigration status. Justice Kennedy's majority opinion emphasized that the federal immigration statutes preempted and rendered invalid those provisions of the Arizona law that imposed new penalties or requirements relating to registration and employment. It was not acceptable that "the State would have the power to bring criminal charges against individuals for violating a federal law even in circumstances where federal officials in charge of the comprehensive scheme determine that prosecution would frustrate federal policies." Moreover, the federal government decided that it should not be a crime for a removable alien to remain present in the United States, and that the state's alternative policy could result in "the unnecessary harassment of some aliens (for instance, a veteran, college student, or someone assisting a federal investigation) whom federal officials determine should not be removed." Kennedy did uphold the provision requiring police officers to make efforts to verify a person's immigration status. In his dissenting opinion Justice Scalia accused the majority of "depriving States of what most would consider the defining characteristic of sovereignty: the power to exclude from the sovereign's territory people who have no right to be there. . . . The most important point is that . . . Arizona is entitled to have 'its own immigration policy'—including a more rigorous enforcement policy—so long as that does not conflict with federal law."

In the late twentieth century, responding in part to a suggestion of the Warren Court, Congress increasingly allowed private lawsuits against state governments as a means of enforcing regulatory policies against the states. The possibility of recovering monetary damages and penalties created incentives for lawyers to take such cases and push them through the courts. Although not posing the same level of threat to the state treasuries as the outstanding Revolutionary War debts that led to the passage of the Eleventh Amendment, the "unfunded mandates" and "coercive federalism" of the late twentieth century were a frequent source of complaint and financial concern to state governments.

In 1996 the Supreme Court unexpectedly intervened in *Seminole Tribe of Florida v. Florida*, holding that Congress could not through statute use its Article I powers to waive state sovereign immunity in federal courts. *Alden v. Maine* (1999) extended *Seminole Tribe*'s logic to state courts while producing more elaborate opinions explaining the original arguments surrounding *Seminole Tribe*. The case involved a federal lawsuit by nearly one hundred state probation officers against their employer, the state of Maine, seeking compensation and monetary damages for violations of the overtime provisions of the federal Fair Labor Standards Act. Justice Kennedy acknowledged that in *Chisholm v. Georgia*, decided just five years after the Constitution was adopted, the Supreme Court upheld a lawsuit by a private citizen against a state and that the Eleventh Amendment only subsequently immunized the states from lawsuits commenced by citizens of a different state or subjects of a foreign state. Still, he concluded that *Chisholm* had been wrongly decided and that "the sovereign immunity of the States neither derives from nor is limited by the terms of the Eleventh Amendment." Rather, it "is a fundamental aspect of the sovereignty which the States enjoyed before the ratification of the Constitution."

The inverse of the question of whether the Tenth and Eleventh Amendments protected state governments from federal intrusion was the question of whether the Supreme Court would recognize protections of federal processes against state interference. At issue in *U.S. Term Limits v. Thornton* (1995) was whether states could impose "term limits" on members of Congress. The Court had previously decided in *Powell v. McCormack* (1969) that Congress could not impose additional "qualifications" for federal officeholding beyond the ones listed in the Constitution itself and remove duly elected members from office. Were selective ballot access restrictions a "qualification" for office? Could states regulate who could run for federal office within their borders? A narrowly divided U.S. Supreme Court held that they could not. In his majority opinion Justice Stevens held that state-imposed ballot restrictions on federal officeholders are "contrary to the 'fundamental principle of our representative democracy' embodied in the Constitution, that 'the people should choose whom they please to govern them,'" and that these restrictions are "inconsistent with the Framers' vision of a uniform National Legislature representing the people of the United States." In response to the argument that the Tenth Amendment reserved to the states and the people all powers not delegated to the national government, the majority responded that "the power to add qualifications is not part of the original powers of sovereignty that the Tenth Amendment reserved to the States" since "that Amendment could only 'reserve' that which existed before," and by definition the power to impose restrictions on the qualifications of federal legislators never existed in the states prior to the creation of the federal government. Justice Thomas's dissenting opinion, joined by O'Connor, Scalia, and Chief Justice Rehnquist, emphasized that "the Constitution is simply silent on this question" and that "where the Constitution is silent, it raises no bar to action by the States or the people."

Printz v. United States, 521 U.S. 898 (1997)

After James Brady, Ronald Reagan's press secretary, was permanently disabled in the assassination attempt on the president in 1981, his wife, Sarah Brady, helped found Handgun Control, Inc., to lobby for restrictions on guns, including waiting periods on gun purchases and mandatory background checks on those seeking to purchase guns. The Brady Bill languished until the early 1990s, when Democrats made a major push for it. They faced a lobbying campaign by the NRA, a veto threat from President Bush, and a filibuster in the Senate that defeated the bill. After Bill Clinton won the presidency in 1992, the Democrats pressed the issue again. A bipartisan compromise avoided another filibuster. The NRA and its supporters had previously proposed a system of "instant background checks." These could keep guns "out of the wrong hands" with no mandatory waiting periods, but the computer database for such a system did not yet exist. The compromise reduced the mandatory waiting period. It also required local law enforcement officers to perform background checks as a temporary measure until the national database for the instant background check came online. Thus, the federal mandate to local officials came from conservative legislators seeking to minimize federal intrusion.

Sheriff Jay Printz of Ravalli County, Montana, objected to Congress adding to the duties of his officers. He filed suit in federal district court challenging the constitutionality of the background check. The trial court agreed, but a divided circuit court reversed. In a 5–4 decision the Supreme Court reversed the circuit court, striking down the provision of the Brady Act as inconsistent with the anti-commandeering principle of the federal system. The local background check provisions of the Brady Act had been set to be replaced by the instant background check system in 1998, and so Congress did not respond to the Court's ruling in Printz. *Many local law enforcement officials continued to perform background checks on gun purchasers until the federal computer database came online. Is such a principle a necessary part of a two-tiered system of government? What arguments did Scalia use in his majority opinion?*

JUSTICE SCALIA delivered the opinion of the Court.

. . .

. . . [T]he Brady Act purports to direct state law enforcement officers to participate, albeit only temporarily, in the administration of a federally enacted regulatory scheme. Regulated firearms dealers are required to forward Brady Forms not to a federal officer or employee, but to the CLEOs [chief law enforcement officers of the local community], whose obligation to accept those forms is implicit in the duty imposed upon them to make "reasonable efforts" within five days to determine whether the sales reflected in the forms are lawful. While the CLEOs are subjected to no federal requirement that they prevent the sales determined to be unlawful (it is perhaps assumed that their state-law duties will require prevention or apprehension), they are empowered to grant, in effect, waivers of the federally prescribed 5-day waiting period for handgun purchases by notifying the gun dealers that they have no reason to believe the transactions would be illegal.

The petitioners here object to being pressed into federal service, and contend that congressional action compelling state officers to execute federal laws is unconstitutional.

Because there is no constitutional text speaking to this precise question, the answer to the CLEOs' challenge must be sought in historical understanding and practice, in the structure of the Constitution, and in the jurisprudence of this Court. . . .

. . .

The Government observes that statutes enacted by the first Congresses required state courts to record applications for citizenship, . . . to transmit abstracts of citizenship applications and other naturalization records to the Secretary of State, . . . and to register aliens seeking naturalization and issue certificates of registry. . . . Other statutes of that era apparently or at least arguably required state courts to perform functions unrelated to naturalization, such as resolving controversies between a captain and the crew of his ship concerning the seaworthiness of the vessel, . . . hearing the claims of slave owners who had apprehended fugitive slaves and issuing certificates authorizing the slave's forced removal to the State from which he had fled, . . . taking proof of the claims of Canadian refugees who had assisted the United States during the Revolutionary War, . . . and ordering the deportation of alien enemies in times of war. . . .

These early laws establish, at most, that the Constitution was originally understood to permit imposition of an obligation on state *judges* to enforce federal prescriptions, insofar as those prescriptions related to matters appropriate for the judicial power. That assumption was perhaps implicit in one of the provisions of the Constitution, and was explicit in another. In accord with the so-called Madisonian Compromise, Article III, §1, established only a Supreme Court, and made the creation of lower federal courts optional with the Congress—even though it was obvious that the Supreme Court alone could not hear all federal cases throughout the United States. . . .

For these reasons, we do not think the early statutes imposing obligations on state courts imply a power of Congress to impress the state executive into its service. Indeed, it can be argued that the numerousness of these statutes, contrasted with the utter lack of statutes imposing obligations on the States' executive (notwithstanding the attractiveness of that course to Congress), suggests an assumed *absence* of such power. . . .

Not only do the enactments of the early Congresses, as far as we are aware, contain no evidence of an assumption that the Federal Government may command the States' executive power in the absence of a particularized constitutional authorization, they contain some indication of precisely the opposite assumption. On September 23, 1789—the day before its proposal of the Bill of Rights . . . —the First Congress enacted a law aimed at obtaining state assistance of the most rudimentary and necessary sort for the enforcement of the new Government's laws: the holding of federal prisoners in state jails at federal expense. Significantly, the law issued not a command to the States' executive, but a recommendation to their legislatures. . . .

. . . The Government also invokes the Federalist's . . . observations that the Constitution would "enable the [national] government to employ the ordinary magistracy of each [State] in the execution of its laws" . . . and that it was "extremely probable that in other instances, particularly in the organization of the judicial power, the officers of the States will be clothed in the correspondent authority of the Union" . . . But none of these statements necessarily implies—what is the critical point here—that Congress could impose these responsibilities *without the consent of the States*. They appear to rest on the natural assumption that the States would consent to allowing their officials to assist the Federal Government. . . .

To complete the historical record, we must note that there is not only an absence of executive-commandeering statutes in the early Congresses, but there is an absence of them in our later history as well, at least until very recent years. The Government points to the Act of August 3, 1882, . . . which enlisted state officials "to take charge of the local affairs of immigration in the ports within such State, and to provide for the support and relief of such immigrants therein landing as may fall into distress or need of public aid"; to inspect arriving immigrants and exclude any person found to be a "convict, lunatic, idiot," or indigent; and to send convicts back to their country of origin "without compensation." The statute did not, however, *mandate* those duties, but merely empowered the Secretary of the Treasury "to *enter into contracts* with such State . . . officers as *may be designated* for that purpose *by the governor* of any State." (Emphasis added.)

. . .

The constitutional practice we have examined above tends to negate the existence of the congressional power asserted here, but is not conclusive. We turn next to consideration of the structure of the Constitution, to see if we can discern among its "essential postulates," . . . a principle that controls the present cases.

It is incontestible that the Constitution established a system of "dual sovereignty." Although the States surrendered many of their powers to the new Federal Government, they retained "a residuary and inviolable sovereignty." . . . Residual state sovereignty was also implicit, of course, in the Constitution's conferral upon Congress of not all governmental powers, but only discrete, enumerated ones, which implication was rendered express by the Tenth Amendment's assertion that "the powers not delegated to the United States by the Constitution, nor prohibited by it to the States, are reserved to the States respectively, or to the people."

The Framers' experience under the Articles of Confederation had persuaded them that using the States as the instruments of federal governance was both ineffectual and provocative of federal–state conflict. . . . As Madison expressed it: "The local or municipal authorities form distinct and independent portions of the supremacy, no more subject, within their respective spheres, to the general authority than the general authority is subject to them, within its own sphere."

We have thus far discussed the effect that federal control of state officers would have upon the first element of the "double security" alluded to by Madison: the division of power between State and Federal Governments. It would also have an effect upon the second element: the separation and equilibration of powers between the three branches of the Federal Government itself. The Constitution does not leave to speculation who is to administer the laws enacted by Congress; the President, it says, "shall take Care that the Laws be faithfully executed," . . . personally and through officers whom he appoints. . . . The Brady Act effectively transfers this responsibility to thousands of CLEOs in the 50 States, who are left to implement the program without meaningful Presidential control (if indeed meaningful Presidential control is possible without the power to appoint and remove). The insistence of the Framers upon unity in the Federal Executive—to insure both vigor and accountability—is well known. . . . That unity would be shattered, and the power of the President would be subject to reduction, if Congress could act as effectively without the President as with him, by simply requiring state officers to execute its laws.

The dissent of course resorts to the last, best hope of those who defend *ultra vires* congressional action, the Necessary and Proper Clause. . . . What destroys the dissent's Necessary and Proper Clause argument, however, is not the Tenth Amendment but the Necessary and Proper Clause itself. When a "Law . . . for carrying into Execution" the Commerce Clause violates the principle of state sovereignty reflected in the various constitutional provisions we mentioned earlier, it is not a "Law . . . *proper* for carrying into Execution the Commerce Clause," and is thus, in the words of The Federalist, "merely [an] act of usurpation" which "deserves to be treated as such."

. . .

The Government . . . maintains that requiring state officers to perform discrete, ministerial tasks specified by Congress does not violate the principle of *New York* because it does not diminish the accountability of state or federal officials. This argument fails even on its own terms. By forcing state governments to absorb the financial burden of implementing a federal regulatory program, Members of Congress can take credit for "solving" problems without having to ask their constituents to pay for the solutions with higher federal taxes. And even when the States are not forced to absorb the costs of implementing a federal program, they are still put in the position of taking the blame for its burdensomeness and for its defects. . . .

. . .

We held in *New York* that Congress cannot compel the States to enact or enforce a federal regulatory program. Today we hold that Congress cannot circumvent that prohibition by conscripting the State's officers directly. The Federal Government may neither issue directives requiring the States to address particular problems, nor command the States' officers, or those of their political subdivisions, to administer or enforce a federal regulatory program. It matters not whether policymaking is involved, and no case-by-case weighing of the burdens or benefits is necessary; such commands are fundamentally incompatible with our constitutional system of dual sovereignty. . . .

JUSTICE O'CONNOR, concurring.

. . .

JUSTICE THOMAS, concurring.

The Court today properly holds that the Brady Act violates the Tenth Amendment in that it compels state law enforcement officers to "administer or enforce a federal regulatory program." . . . Although I join the Court's opinion in full, I write separately to emphasize that the Tenth Amendment affirms the undeniable notion that under our Constitution, the Federal Government is one of enumerated, hence limited, powers. . . .

In my "revisionist" view, . . . the Federal Government's authority under the Commerce Clause, which merely allocates to Congress the power "to regulate Commerce . . . among the several states," does not extend to the regulation of wholly *intra* state, point-of-sale transactions. . . . Absent the underlying authority to regulate the intrastate transfer of firearms, Congress surely lacks the corollary power to impress state law enforcement officers into administering and enforcing such regulations. . . .

JUSTICE STEVENS, with whom JUSTICE SOUTER, JUSTICE GINSBURG, and JUSTICE BREYER join, dissenting.

When Congress exercises the powers delegated to it by the Constitution, it may impose affirmative obligations on executive and judicial officers of state and local governments as well as ordinary citizens. This conclusion is firmly supported by the text of the Constitution, the early history of the Nation, decisions of this Court, and a correct understanding of the basic structure of the Federal Government.

. . .

Indeed, since the ultimate issue is one of power, we must consider its implications in times of national emergency. Matters such as the enlistment of air raid wardens, the administration of a military draft, the mass inoculation of children to forestall an epidemic, or perhaps the threat of an international terrorist, may require a national response before federal personnel can be made available to respond. If the Constitution empowers Congress and the President to make an appropriate response, is there anything in the Tenth Amendment, "in historical understanding and practice, in the structure of the Constitution, [or] in the jurisprudence of this Court," . . . that forbids the enlistment of state officers to make that response effective? More narrowly, what basis is there in any of those sources for concluding that it is the Members of this Court, rather than the elected representatives of the people, who should determine whether the Constitution contains the unwritten rule that the Court announces today?

. . .

The text of the Constitution provides a sufficient basis for a correct disposition of this case.

Article I, §8, grants the Congress the power to regulate commerce among the States. . . . [T]here can be no question that that provision adequately supports the regulation of commerce in handguns effected by the Brady Act. Moreover, the additional grant of authority in that section of the Constitution "to make all Laws which shall be necessary and proper for carrying into Execution the foregoing Powers" is surely adequate to support the temporary enlistment of local police officers in the process of identifying persons who should not be entrusted with the possession of handguns. In short, the affirmative delegation of power in Article I provides ample authority for the congressional enactment.

Unlike the First Amendment, which prohibits the enactment of a category of laws that would otherwise be authorized by Article I, the Tenth Amendment imposes no restriction on the exercise of delegated powers. . . .

There is not a clause, sentence, or paragraph in the entire text of the Constitution of the United States that supports the proposition that a local police officer can ignore a command contained in a statute enacted by Congress pursuant to an express delegation of power enumerated in Article I.

. . .

. . . [I]ndeed, the historical materials strongly suggest that the Founders intended to enhance the capacity of the federal government by empowering it—as a part of the new authority to make demands directly on individual citizens—to act through local officials. Hamilton made clear that the new Constitution, "by extending the authority of the federal head to the individual citizens of the several States, will enable the government to employ the ordinary magistracy of each, in the execution of its laws." Hamilton's meaning was unambiguous; the federal government was to have the power to demand that local officials implement national policy programs. . . .

More specifically, during the debates concerning the ratification of the Constitution, it was assumed that state agents would act as tax collectors for the federal government. Opponents of the Constitution had repeatedly expressed fears that the new federal government's ability to impose taxes directly on the citizenry would result in an overbearing presence of federal tax collectors in the States. Federalists rejoined that this problem would not arise because, as Hamilton explained, "the United States . . . will make use of the State officers and State regulations for collecting" certain taxes. . . . Similarly, Madison made clear that the new central government's power to raise taxes directly from the citizenry would "not be resorted to, except for supplemental purposes of revenue . . . and that the eventual collection, under the immediate authority of the Union, will generally be made by the officers . . . appointed by the several States." . . .

The Court's response to this powerful historical evidence is weak. The majority suggests that "none of these statements necessarily implies . . . Congress could impose these responsibilities without the consent of the States." . . . No fair reading of these materials can justify such an interpretation. As Hamilton explained, the power of the government to act on "individual citizens"—including "employing the ordinary magistracy" of the States—was an answer to the problems faced by a central government that could act only directly "upon the States in their political or collective capacities." . . .

This point is made especially clear in Hamilton's statement that "the legislatures, courts, and magistrates, of the respective members, will be incorporated into the operations of the national government as far as its just and constitutional authority extends; and *will be rendered auxiliary to the enforcement of its laws*." . . . It is hard to imagine a more unequivocal statement that state judicial and executive branch officials may be required to implement federal law where the National Government acts within the scope of its affirmative powers.

...

Bereft of support in the history of the founding, the Court rests its conclusion on the claim that there is little evidence the National Government actually exercised such a power in the early years of the Republic. . . . This reasoning is misguided in principle and in fact. While we have indicated that the express consideration and resolution of difficult constitutional issues by the First Congress in particular "provides 'contemporaneous and weighty evidence' of the Constitution's meaning since many of [its] Members . . . 'had taken part in framing that instrument,'" . . . we have never suggested that the failure of the early Congresses to address the scope of federal power in a particular area or to exercise a particular authority was an argument against its existence. . . .

More importantly, the fact that Congress did elect to rely on state judges and the clerks of state courts to perform a variety of executive functions . . . is surely evidence of a contemporary understanding that their status as state officials did not immunize them from federal service. . . .

...

The Court's evaluation of the historical evidence, furthermore, fails to acknowledge the important difference between policy decisions that may have been influenced by respect for state sovereignty concerns, and decisions that are compelled by the Constitution. Thus, for example, the decision by Congress to give President Wilson the authority to utilize the services of state officers in implementing the World War I draft . . . surely indicates that the national legislature saw no constitutional impediment to the enlistment of state assistance during a federal emergency. The fact that the President was able to implement the program by respectfully "requesting" state action, rather than bluntly commanding it, is evidence that he was an effective statesman, but surely does not indicate that he doubted either his or Congress' power to use mandatory language if necessary. If there were merit to the Court's appraisal of this incident, one would assume that there would have been some contemporary comment on the supposed constitutional concern that hypothetically might have motivated the President's choice of language.

...

Perversely, the majority's rule seems more likely to damage than to preserve the safeguards against tyranny provided by the existence of vital state governments. By limiting the ability of the Federal Government to enlist state officials in the implementation of its programs, the Court creates incentives for the National Government to aggrandize itself. In the name of State's rights, the majority would have the Federal Government create vast national bureaucracies to implement its policies. This is exactly the sort of thing that the early Federalists promised would not occur, in part as a result of the National Government's ability to rely on the magistracy of the states. . . .

...

Far more important than the concerns that the Court musters in support of its new rule is the fact that the Framers entrusted Congress with the task of creating a working structure of intergovernmental relationships around the framework that the Constitution authorized. Neither explicitly nor implicitly did the Framers issue any command that forbids Congress from imposing federal duties on private citizens or on local officials. As a general matter, Congress has followed the sound policy of authorizing federal agencies and federal agents to administer federal programs. That general practice, however, does not negate the existence of power to rely on state officials in occasional situations in which such reliance is in the national interest. Rather, the occasional exceptions confirm the wisdom of Justice Holmes' reminder that "the machinery of government would not work if it were not allowed a little play in its joints." . . .

...

JUSTICE SOUTER, dissenting.

...

In deciding these cases, which I have found closer than I had anticipated, it is The Federalist that finally determines my position. I believe that the most straightforward reading of No. 27 is authority for the Government's position here, and that this reading is both supported by No. 44 and consistent with Nos. 36 and 45.

Hamilton in No. 27 first notes that because the new Constitution would authorize the National Government to bind individuals directly through national law, it could "employ the ordinary magistracy of each [State] in the execution of its laws." . . . Were he to stop here, he would not necessarily be speaking of anything beyond the possibility of cooperative arrangements by agreement. But he then addresses the combined effect of the proposed Supremacy Clause . . . and state officers' oath requirement, . . . and he states that "the Legislatures, Courts and Magistrates of the respective members will be incorporated into the operations of the national government, *as far as its just and constitutional authority extends*; and will be rendered auxiliary to the enforcement of its laws." . . . The natural reading of this language is not merely that the officers of the various branches of state governments may be employed in the performance of national functions; Hamilton says that the state governmental machinery "will be incorporated" into the Nation's operation, and because the "auxiliary" status of the state officials will occur because they are "bound by the sanctity of an oath" . . . I take him to mean that their auxiliary functions will be the products of their obligations thus undertaken to support federal law, not of their own, or the States', unfettered choices.

. . .

In the light of all these passages, I cannot persuade myself that the statements from No. 27 speak of anything less than the authority of the National Government, when exercising an otherwise legitimate power (the commerce power, say), to require state "auxiliaries" to take appropriate action.

. . .

JUSTICE BREYER, with whom JUSTICE STEVENS joins, dissenting.

I would add to the reasons JUSTICE STEVENS sets forth the fact that the United States is not the only nation that seeks to reconcile the practical need for a central authority with the democratic virtues of more local control. At least some other countries, facing the same basic problem, have found that local control is better maintained through application of a principle that is the direct opposite of the principle the majority derives from the silence of our Constitution. The federal systems of Switzerland, Germany, and the European Union, for example, all provide that constituent states, not federal bureaucracies, will themselves implement many of the laws, rules, regulations, or decrees enacted by the central "federal" body. . . .

Of course, we are interpreting our own Constitution, not those of other nations, and there may be relevant political and structural differences between their systems and our own. . . . But their experience may nonetheless cast an empirical light on the consequences of different solutions to a common legal problem—in this case the problem of reconciling central authority with the need to preserve the liberty-enhancing autonomy of a smaller constituent governmental entity. . . . And that experience here offers empirical confirmation of the implied answer to a question JUSTICE STEVENS asks: Why, or how, would what the majority sees as a constitutional alternative—the creation of a new federal gun-law bureaucracy, or the expansion of an existing federal bureaucracy—better promote either state sovereignty or individual liberty? . . .

VI. Separation of Powers

MAJOR DEVELOPMENTS

- Rejection of the line-item veto by the Supreme Court
- Debate over presidential power to refuse to enforce statutes
- Controversy over unilateral presidential actions justified on grounds of national security
- Recognition of some executive immunity from judicial proceedings

The intensity of debates over the separation of powers during the Contemporary Era should not be a surprise. First, the two political parties have become increasingly polarized. Conservative Democrats and liberal Republicans were once common, but they are now increasingly rare in the halls of Congress. Political activists in both parties are not merely political professionals; they tend to be ideologically committed. They emphasize issues and principles, and they hold candidates and politicians accountable to them.[22] Second, divided government has become commonplace. For long periods in American history, unified government—when both the legislature and the executive are controlled by the same political party—has been the norm. The majority party was expected to govern with little assistance from the minority party. In modern politics, divided politics has often been the norm, with no expectation that unified government is just around the corner. Both Congress and the White House have viewed the other branch of government with suspicion, if not outright hostility.

22. Nolan McCarty, Keith T. Poole, and Howard Rosenthal, *Polarized America* (Cambridge, MA: MIT Press, 2007); Geoffrey C. Layman, Thomas M. Carsey, and Julianna Menasce Horowitz, "Party Polarization in American Politics: Characteristics, Causes, and Consequences," *Annual Review of Political Science* 9 (2006): 83–110.

Illustration 11-2 The National Security State

Source: Tom Toles, *Washington Post*, May 18, 2006. © 2006 The Washington Post. Reprinted with permission of UNIVERSAL UCLICK. All rights reserved.

They have often looked for ways to work around the other branch or to constrain it.[23]

The sharing of the legislative power has been at the center of many of these struggles. During the Reagan Era, the Court in *Immigration and Naturalization Service v. Chadha* (1983) and *Bowsher v. Synar* (1986) took a dim view of some of the creative ways that the legislative and executive branches had tried to manipulate the separation of powers in order to manage the complexities of modern government. Congress and the president nevertheless have continued to seek out creative ways to address the administrative and political challenges of modern politics. Each legislative innovation raises its own set of constitutional questions about how well it fits within the constitutional scheme of separation of powers. In *Clinton v. New York* (1998), the Court confronted a statutory "line-item veto." The Line Item Veto Act allowed the president to mark out any specific items of which he disapproved in an enacted spending law. In an expedited procedure, Congress would then vote on a separate "bill of disapproval" containing all the items that the president had lined out. That bill of disapproval would then be subject to the regular presidential veto and possible override. Unless the bill of disapproval passed, the funds for those items from the original appropriations bill would not be spent. The complicated scheme was designed to comply with the Court's earlier decision in *Chadha* while providing something comparable to what could be achieved through a constitutional amendment. Nevertheless, by a 6–3 vote the Court struck down the act. Justice Stevens explained that the president's "return" of the bill under the act violated Article I, §7 in that the "constitutional return takes place before the bill becomes law" rather than after, and that the "constitutional return is of the entire bill" rather than just a part. The major defect of this act was that it "gives the President the unilateral power to change the text of duly enacted statutes."

While in the context of the line-item veto Congress was willing to give the president some additional authority vis-à-vis the legislature, it has been more frequently the case during the Contemporary Era that

23. Morris P. Fiorina, "An Era of Divided Government," *Political Science Quarterly* 107 (1992): 387–410; David R. Mayhew, *Divided We Govern* (New Haven, CT: Yale University Press, 2005).

controversies have arisen over the scope of the president's discretion in executing the law. When President George W. Bush signed legislation into law, he often issued public statements ("signing statements") at the same time. While signing statements have been used throughout American history, the Bush administration made them routine and used them more aggressively to challenge congressional views on constitutional powers. Over the course of his first term of office President Bush issued dozens of signing statements that noted hundreds of possible constitutional objections to new federal laws that the president was signing.

These signing statements aroused little controversy at first but became the subject of public and political debate in 2006. The issue first attracted attention when the president signed a hotly contested supplemental appropriations bill on December 30, 2005. The appropriations bill included essential funds for continuing operations by the Department of Defense (including those involved in the war in Iraq) and aid to the areas recently affected by Hurricane Katrina (which had flooded New Orleans). Because the administration regarded the immediate passage of the appropriations bill as essential, it was a perfect vehicle for Congress to attach amendments that the administration opposed. Most notably, Republican senator John McCain had included an amendment prohibiting cruel and degrading treatment of military detainees, regardless of where they might be held, by United States personnel. The McCain amendment added legislative pressure to ongoing disputes over the American treatment of detainees in the American military base at Guantanamo Bay in Cuba, as well as in detention facilities in Iraq and other countries. The president responded by stating, "The executive branch shall construe [the McCain amendment] in a manner consistent with the constitutional authority of the President to supervise the unitary executive branch and as Commander in Chief and consistent with the constitutional limitations on the judicial power, which will assist in achieving the shared objective of the Congress and the President . . . of protecting the American people from further terrorist attacks."[24]

Republican Senate Judiciary Committee chairman Arlen Specter held hearings that were critical of presidential signing statements in the summer of that year. At the same time, the American Bar Association (ABA) appointed a task force to examine the practice of presidential signing statements and "how they comport with the Constitution." The ABA task force recommended that presidents in the future strive to communicate their constitutional concerns to Congress earlier in the legislative process and that Congress be informed promptly of any signing statements that the president might issue regarding a law. More controversial was the conclusion that such signing statements were contrary to "our constitutional system of separation of powers." The president's only constitutional options, the hearings claimed, are to exercise the veto power or to enforce the law as written. The president should not "usurp [the] judicial authority as the final interpreter of the constitutionality of congressional acts" or preempt its right to issue "definitive constitutional interpretations."[25] A number of law professors, many formerly associated with the Office of Legal Counsel in the George H. W. Bush or William Clinton presidencies, objected to the ABA task force report. They argued that the veto-or-enforce-it choice on which the task force insisted ignored longstanding practice, the president's primary obligation to uphold the Constitution itself, and the realities of modern government.

While battles over the legislative process have been persistent, no issues have been more weighty during the Contemporary Era than those relating to presidential war and foreign affairs powers. Most of the controversies have revolved around the scope of presidential authority to take action on his own initiative to defend American national security interests. The highest profile and most far-reaching disputes have involved the president's authority to launch military offensives and engage in military operations abroad without prior congressional authorization. As commander in chief, the president has operational control of troop movements and both constitutional and statutory responsibilities to protect American lives and property. Only Congress, however, has the

24. George W. Bush, "Statement on Signing H.R. 2863, the Department of Defense, Emergency Supplemental Appropriation to Address Hurricanes in the Gulf of Mexico, and Pandemic Influenza Act, 2006, December 30, 2005," *Weekly Compilation of Presidential Documents* 41 (January 2, 2006): 1918.

25. American Bar Association, *Report of the Task Force on Presidential Signing Statements and the Separation of Powers Doctrine*, July 24, 2006, 4.

constitutional power to "declare war," and the recurring conflict between the legislative and executive branches is whether the congressional power to declare war is enough to prevent presidents from launching de facto wars on their own, as well as whether the exclusive congressional power to declare war limits the ability of the president to respond militarily to national security crises as they arise. The situation has been further complicated in the modern era by the rise of overseas military bases (which put American troops at greater risk of attack than if they remained based in the United States), networks of defense treaties and commitments, changing military technology, and the diversity of military options at the president's command. President George W. Bush received broad congressional authorization for the use of military force in the Persian Gulf, though the vote over the Iraq War was far more controversial than the vote over the war in Afghanistan. But other military offensives, both large and small, have not received explicit prior congressional approval, including the extended bombing campaigns by the Clinton administration in Yugoslavia and the Obama administration in Libya.

A related set of debates concerns *how* presidents exercise the war powers. The decision to initiate military action is one important decision that presidents might make in the name of national security, but the executive routinely makes myriad other decisions in exercising the war powers. How constrained is the president in exercising the war powers, and how far can Congress go in instructing or limiting the president in how he acts as commander in chief? Is the constitutional responsibility and power of the president to do what it takes to win the war, once it has been declared? Or can Congress force the president to fight a limited war? Are there intelligence-gathering techniques that presidents can be prohibited from employing? Are there battlefield tactics that presidents can be barred from ordering? Such issues gained renewed attention during the George W. Bush administration, when it was revealed that the government was engaging in a wide range of covert activities as part of the War on Terror, from electronic eavesdropping to "enhanced interrogation," that were difficult to justify under current statutes. In 2013 new revelations about the scope of the National Security Agency's surveillance program (discussed more fully at the end of this chapter in the section on Criminal Justice) intensified debates about how much power the government should have to collect information about Americans' phone records, email, and Internet activity.

Walter Dellinger, Presidential Authority to Decline to Execute Unconstitutional Statutes (1994)[26]

Early in President Bill Clinton's first term of office, law professor Walter Dellinger was named assistant attorney general and head of the Office of Legal Counsel (OLC), the primary legal advisor to the attorney general and the president. The OLC helps formulate many of the basic constitutional positions of the administration, especially as regards the powers of the presidency itself.

This memo by Dellinger laid out broad principles for presidential nonenforcement of unconstitutional laws. Dellinger aligned the Clinton administration with previous administrations in supporting the view that presidents did in fact have the authority to refuse to enforce laws that the president regarded as unconstitutional. But Dellinger's memo was centrally concerned with distinguishing the Clinton OLC on this issue from its Republican predecessors. An OLC opinion during the George H. W. Bush administration argued, for example, that "unconstitutional statutes are not laws the President must faithfully execute" and that the president was under no obligation to await a judicial determination of a law's constitutionality.[27] *One of Dellinger's colleagues (who was unsuccessfully nominated to head Obama's OLC) characterized this approach as one of "routine" nonenforcement.*[28]

Are presidents obliged to identify constitutional violations in statutes? Lawyers in and around the Reagan and Bush administrations had argued strongly for just that. By the responsibilities of their office, these lawyers claimed, presidents must avoid enforcing laws in a way that would violate constitutional requirements. Liberal critics, in turn, charged that such arguments subverted the special role of the courts.

26. Excerpt taken from Office of Legal Counsel, "Presidential Authority to Decline to Enforce Unconstitutional Statutes, November 2, 1994," 18 Op. Off. Legal Counsel 199 (1994).

27. William P. Barr, "Issues Raised by Foreign Relations Authorization Bill," 14 Op. Off. Legal Counsel 37, 50 (1990).

28. Dawn E. Johnsen, "Presidential Non-Enforcement of Constitutionally Objectionable Statutes," *Law and Contemporary Problems* 63 (2000): 16.

The Constitution, they argued, does not set the president up as a dictator who can "defy" the laws of Congress. Dellinger's approach suggested a more flexible response to constitutional doubts about a law and left open the possibility of judicial resolution of such doubts. As you read the memo, consider whether Dellinger's approach tended to replace constitutional limitations on Congress with judicial limitations on Congress. Did Dellinger still allow for too much executive noncompliance with congressional statutes?[29]

I have reflected further on the difficult questions surrounding a President's decision to decline to execute statutory provisions that the President believes are unconstitutional, and I have a few thoughts to share with you. Let me start with a general proposition that I believe to be uncontroversial: there are circumstances in which the President may appropriately decline to enforce a statute that he views as unconstitutional.

First, there is significant judicial approval of this proposition. Most notable is the Court's decision in *Myers v. United States* (1926). There the Court sustained the President's view that the statute at issue was unconstitutional without any member of the Court suggesting that the President had acted improperly in refusing to abide by the statute. . . .

Second, consistent and substantial executive practice also confirms this general proposition. Opinions dating to at least 1860 assert the President's authority to decline to effectuate enactments that the President views as unconstitutional. See, e.g., Memorial of Captain Meigs, 9 Op. Att'y Gen. 462, 469–70 (1860) (asserting that the President need not enforce a statute purporting to appoint an officer). . . . Moreover, numerous Presidents have provided advance notice of their intention not to enforce specific statutory requirements that they have viewed as unconstitutional, and the Supreme Court has implicitly endorsed this practice. See *INS v. Chadha*, 462 U.S. 919, 942 n.13 (1983) (noting that Presidents often sign legislation containing constitutionally objectionable provisions and indicate that they will not comply with those provisions).

While the general proposition that in some situations the President may decline to enforce unconstitutional statutes is unassailable, it does not offer sufficient guidance as to the appropriate course in specific circumstances. To continue our conversation about these complex issues, I offer the following propositions for your consideration.

1. The President's office and authority are created and bounded by the Constitution; he is required to act within its terms. Put somewhat differently, in serving as the executive created by the Constitution, the President is required to act in accordance with the laws—including the Constitution, which takes precedence over other forms of law. This obligation is reflected in the Take Care Clause and in the President's oath of office.

2. When bills are under consideration by Congress, the executive branch should promptly identify unconstitutional provisions and communicate its concerns to Congress so that the provisions can be corrected. Although this may seem elementary, in practice there have been occasions in which the President has been presented with enrolled bills containing constitutional flaws that should have been corrected in the legislative process.

3. The President should presume that enactments are constitutional. There will be some occasions, however, when a statute appears to conflict with the Constitution. In such cases, the President can and should exercise his independent judgment to determine whether the statute is constitutional. In reaching a conclusion, the President should give great deference to the fact that Congress passed the statute and that Congress believed it was upholding its obligation to enact constitutional legislation. Where possible, the President should construe provisions to avoid constitutional problems.

4. The Supreme Court plays a special role in resolving disputes about the constitutionality of enactments. As a general matter, if the President believes that the Court would sustain a particular provision as constitutional, the President should execute the statute, notwithstanding his own beliefs about the constitutional issue. If, however, the President, exercising his independent judgment, determines both that a provision would violate the Constitution and that it is probable that the Court would agree with him, the President has the authority to decline to execute the statute.

5. Where the President's independent constitutional judgment and his determination of the Court's probable decision converge on a conclusion of unconstitutionality, the President must make a decision about whether or not to comply with the provision.

29. See also David Barron, "Constitutionalism in the Shadow of Doctrine: The President's Non-Enforcement Power," *Law and Contemporary Problems* 63 (2000): 61–106.

That decision is necessarily specific to context, and it should be reached after careful weighing of the effect of compliance with the provision on the constitutional rights of affected individuals and on the executive branch's constitutional authority. Also relevant is the likelihood that compliance or non-compliance will permit judicial resolution of the issue. That is, the President may base his decision to comply (or decline to comply) in part on a desire to afford the Supreme Court an opportunity to review the constitutional judgment of the legislative branch.

6. The President has enhanced responsibility to resist unconstitutional provisions that encroach upon the constitutional powers of the Presidency. Where the President believes that an enactment unconstitutionally limits his powers, he has the authority to defend his office and decline to abide by it, unless he is convinced that the Court would disagree with his assessment. If the President does not challenge such provisions (*i.e.*, by refusing to execute them), there often will be no occasion for judicial consideration of their constitutionality; a policy of consistent Presidential enforcement of statutes limiting his power thus would deny the Supreme Court the opportunity to review the limitations and thereby would allow for unconstitutional restrictions on the President's authority.

Some legislative encroachments on executive authority, however, will not be justiciable or are for other reasons unlikely to be resolved in court. If resolution in the courts is unlikely and the President cannot look to a judicial determination, he must shoulder the responsibility of protecting the constitutional role of the presidency. This is usually true, for example, of provisions limiting the President's authority as Commander in Chief. Where it is not possible to construe such provisions constitutionally, the President has the authority to act on his understanding of the Constitution.

. . .

In accordance with these propositions, we do not believe that a President is limited to choosing between vetoing . . . and executing an unconstitutional provision in it. In our view, the President has the authority to sign legislation containing desirable elements while refusing to execute a constitutionally defective provision.

. . .

Illustration 11-3 War Powers

Source: Nick Anderson, *Houston Chronicle*, June 18, 2011. Used with the permission of Nick Anderson, the Washington Post Writers Group and the Cartoonist Group.

John Yoo, The President's Constitutional Authority to Conduct Military Operations (2001)[30]

Shortly after the attacks on the World Trade Center and the Pentagon on September 11, 2001, Deputy Assistant Attorney General John Yoo, in the Office of Legal Counsel, produced a memorandum opinion for the deputy counsel to the president, Tim Flanigan. Yoo's memo laid out the president's authority to respond militarily to the attacks. By the time the memo was produced, two weeks after the attacks, Congress had passed a joint resolution authorizing the use of military force. The language of the joint resolution itself was the product of discussions with the White House and Office of Legal Counsel, and it gave the president a relatively free hand in responding to the attacks. Although the memo drew on the joint resolution, it primarily relied on inherent presidential power under Article II to launch military operations in the nation's defense. This extended to preemptive military action and military action against governments that were not directly involved in the events of September 11. The memo thus sketched out the second Bush administration's constitutional supports for the developing War on Terror.

The memo was not designed for public release, but it did eventually become public. Its bold claims on behalf of presidential war powers made it one of the most famous OLC memos ever produced—along with a series of memos relating to Bush administration war policies. Although the invasion of Iraq in 2003 received separate congressional authorization, the memo had more immediate relevance for American military activity in a range of locales, including the Philippines and Yemen in early 2002.[31] *Was Yoo persuasive that the president has his own constitutional authority to deploy troops into combat in order to protect national security? What are the limits of such an authority? How can President Obama's bombing of Libya without congressional authorization best be justified?*

30. Excerpt taken from Office of Legal Counsel, "The President's Constitutional Authority to Conduct Military Operations Against Terrorists and Nations Supporting Them," September 25, 2001.

31. Yoo has subsequently expanded on this argument; see John Yoo, *The Powers of War and Peace* (Chicago: University of Chicago Press, 2006). A critical account of presidential power can be found in Louis Fisher, *Presidential War Powers* (Lawrence: University Press of Kansas, 2004).

You have asked for our opinion of the scope of the President's authority to take military action in response to terrorist attacks on the United States on September 11, 2001. We conclude that the President has broad constitutional powers to use military force. Congress has acknowledged this inherent executive power in both the War Powers Resolution . . . and in the Joint Resolution passed by Congress on September 14, 2001. . . . Further, the President has the constitutional power not only to retaliate against any person, organization, or State suspected of involvement in terrorist attacks on the United States, but also against foreign States suspected of harboring or supporting such organizations. Finally, the President may deploy military force preemptively against terrorist organizations or the States that harbor or support them, whether or not they can be linked to the specific terrorist incidents of September 11.

. . .

The President's constitutional power to defend the United States and the lives of its people must be understood in light of the Founders' express intention to create a federal government "clothed with all the powers requisite to [the] complete execution of its trust." *The Federalist* No. 23. . . . Within the limits that the Constitution itself imposes, the scope and distribution of powers to protect national security must be construed to authorize the most efficacious defense of the Nation and its interests in accordance "with the realistic purposes of the entire instrument." *Lichter v. United States* (1948). Nor is the authority to protect the national security limited to actions necessary for "victories in the field." *Application of Yamashita* (1946). The authority over national security "carries with it the inherent power to guard against the immediate renewal of the conflict." *Id.*

. . .

Constitutional Text. The text, structure and history of the Constitution establish that the Founders entrusted the President with the primary responsibility, and therefore the power, to use military force in situations of emergency. Article II, Section 2 states that the "President shall be Commander in Chief of the Army and Navy of the United States. . . . " He is further vested with all of "the executive Power" and the duty to execute the laws. . . . These powers give the President broad constitutional authority to use military force in response to threats to the national security and foreign policy of the United States. During the period leading up to the Constitution's ratification, the power to initiate hostilities and to control the escalation of conflict had been long understood to rest in the hands of the executive branch.

By their own terms, these provisions vest full control of the military forces of the United States in the President. The power of the President is at its zenith under the Constitution when the President is directing military operations of the armed forces, because the power of Commander-in-Chief is assigned solely to the President. It has long been the view of this Office that the Commander-in-Chief clause is a substantive grant of authority to the President and that the scope of the President's authority to commit the armed forces to combat is very broad. *See, e.g.*, Memorandum for Honorable Charles W. Colson, Special Counsel to the President, from William H. Rehnquist, Assistant Attorney General, Office of Legal Counsel, *Re: The President and the War Power: South Vietnam and the Cambodian Sanctuaries* (May 22, 1970).... The President's complete discretion in exercising the Commander-in-Chief power has also been recognized by the courts. In the *Prize Cases* (1862), for example, the Court explained that, whether the President "in fulfilling his duties as Commander in Chief" had met with a situation justifying treating the southern States as belligerents and instituting a blockade, was a question "to be *decided by him*" and which the Court could not question, but must leave to "the political department of the Government to which this power was entrusted."

Some commentators have read the constitutional text differently. They argue that the vesting of the power to declare war gives Congress the sole authority to decide whether to make war. This view misreads the constitutional text and misunderstands the nature of a declaration of war. Declaring war is not tantamount to making war—indeed, the Constitutional Convention specifically amended the working draft of the Constitution that had given Congress the power to make war. . . . A State constitution at the time of the ratification included provisions that prohibited the governor from "making" war without legislative approval. . . . If the Framers had wanted to require congressional consent before the initiation of military hostilities, they knew how to write such provisions.

. . .

Constitutional Structure. Our reading of the text is reinforced by analysis of the constitutional structure. First, it is clear that the Constitution secures all federal executive power in the President to ensure a unity of purpose and energy in action. "Decision, activity, secrecy, and dispatch will generally characterize the proceedings of one man in a much more eminent degree than any proceedings of any greater number." *The Federalist* No. 70. . . . The centralization of authority in the president alone is particularly crucial in matters of national defense, war, and foreign policy. . . .

Second, the Constitution makes clear that the process used for conducting military hostilities is different from other government decisionmaking. In the area of domestic legislation, the Constitution creates a detailed, finely wrought procedure in which Congress plays the central role. In foreign affairs, however, the Constitution does not establish a mandatory, detailed, Congress-driven procedure for taking action. Rather, the Constitution vests the two branches with different powers—the President as Commander in Chief, Congress with control over funding and declaring war—without requiring that they follow a specific process in making war. By establishing this framework, the Framers expected that the process for warmaking would be far more flexible, and capable of quicker, more decisive action, than the legislative process. Thus, the President may use his Commander-in-Chief and executive powers to use military force to protect the Nation, subject to congressional appropriations and control over domestic legislation.

Third, the constitutional structure requires that any ambiguities in the allocation of a power that is executive in nature—such as the power to conduct military hostilities—must be resolved in favor of the executive branch. . . . [T]he enumeration in Article II marks the points at which several traditional executive powers were diluted or reallocated. Any *other*, unenumerated executive powers, however, were conveyed to the President by the Vesting Clause.

There can be little doubt that the decision to deploy military force is "executive" in nature, and was traditionally so regarded. It calls for action and energy in execution, rather than the deliberate formulation of rules to govern the conduct of private individuals. . . .

. . .

Conducting military hostilities is a central tool for the exercise of the President's plenary control over the conduct of foreign policy. There can be no doubt that the use of force protects the Nation's security and helps it achieve its foreign policy goals. Construing the Constitution to grant such power to another branch could prevent the President from exercising his core constitutional responsibilities in foreign affairs. . . .

Executive Branch Construction and Practice. The position we take here has long represented the view of the executive branch and the Department of Justice. Attorney General (later Justice) Robert Jackson formulated the classic statement of the executive branch's understanding of the President's military powers in 1941:

> Article II, section 2, of the Constitution provides that the President "shall be Commander in Chief of the Army and Navy of the United States." By virtue of this constitutional office he has supreme command over the land and naval forces of the country and may order them to perform such military duties as, in his opinion, are necessary or appropriate for the defense of the United States. These powers exist in time of peace as well as in time of war.

. . .

The historical practice of all three branches confirms the lessons of the constitutional text and structure. The normative role of historical practice in constitutional law, and especially with regard to separation of powers, is well settled. . . .

. . .

The historical record demonstrates that the power to initiate military hostilities, particularly in response to the threat of an armed attack, rests exclusively with the President. As the Supreme Court has observed, "[t]he United States frequently employs Armed Forces outside the country—over 200 times in our history—for the protection of American citizens or national security." *United States v. Verdugo-Urquidez* (1990). On at least 125 such occasions, the President has acted without prior express authorization from Congress. *See* Bosnia Opinion, 19 Op. O.L.C. at 331. Such deployments, based on the President's constitutional authority alone, have occurred since the Administration of George Washington. . . . Perhaps the most significant deployment without specific statutory authorization took place at the time of the Korean War, when President Truman, without prior authorization from Congress, deployed United States troops in a war that lasted for over three years and caused over 142,000 American casualties.

Recent deployments ordered solely on the basis of the President's constitutional authority have also been extremely large, representing a substantial commitment of the Nation's military personnel, diplomatic prestige, and financial resources. On at least one occasion, such unilateral deployment has constituted full-scale war. On March 24, 1999, without any prior statutory authorization and in the absence of an attack on the United States, President Clinton ordered hostilities to be initiated against the Republic of Yugoslavia. . . . In recent decades, no President has unilaterally deployed so much force abroad.

. . .

The terrorist incidents of September 11, 2001, were surely far graver a threat to the national security of the United States than the 1998 attacks on our embassies (however appalling those events were). The President's power to respond militarily to the later attacks must be correspondingly broader. Nonetheless, President Clinton's action in 1998 illustrates some of the breadth of the President's power to act in the present circumstances.

First, President Clinton justified the targeting of specific groups on the basis of what he characterized as "convincing" evidence of their involvement in the embassy attacks. While that is not a standard of proof appropriate for a criminal trial, it is entirely appropriate for military and political decisionmaking. Second, the President targeted not merely one particular group or leader, but a network of affiliated groups. Moreover, he ordered the action, not only because of particular attacks on United States embassies, but because of a pattern of terrorist activity, aimed at both Americans and non-Americans, that had unfolded over several years. Third, the President explained that the military action was designed to deter *future* terrorist incidents, not only to punish for past ones. Fourth, the President specifically justified military action on the territory of two foreign states because their governments had "harbor[ed]" and "support[ed]" terrorist groups for years, despite warnings from the United States.

. . .

. . . [T]he President can be said to be acting at the apogee of his powers if he deploys military force in the present situation, for he is operating both under his own Article II authority and with the legislative support of Congress. Under the analysis outlined by Justice Jackson in *Youngstown Sheet & Tube Co. v. Sawyer* (1952), the President's power in this case would be "at its maximum." . . .

The executive branch consistently "has taken the position from the very beginning that section 2(c) of the [War Powers Resolution] does not constitute a legally binding definition of Presidential authority to deploy our armed forces."[32] Moreover, as our Office has noted, "even the defenders of the WPR [War Powers Resolution] concede that this declaration [in section 2(c)]—found in the 'Purpose and Policy' section of the WPR—either is incomplete or is not meant to be binding." . . .

. . .

The Joint Resolution of September 14, 2001. Whatever view one may take of the meaning of section 2(c)(3) of the WPR, we think it clear that Congress, in enacting the "Joint Resolution [t]o authorize the use of United States Armed Forces against those responsible for the recent attacks launched against the United States," . . . has confirmed that the President has broad constitutional authority to respond, by military means or otherwise, to the incidents of September 11.

First, the findings of the Joint Resolution include an express statement that "the President has authority under the Constitution to take action to deter and prevent acts of international terrorism against the United States." This authority is in addition to the President's authority to respond to *past* acts of terrorism. In including this statement, Congress has provided its explicit agreement with the executive branch's consistent position, as articulated in Parts I–III of this memorandum, that the President has the plenary power to use force even before an attack upon the United States actually occurs, against targets and using methods of his own choosing.

. . .

Memoranda on Standards of Conduct of Interrogation ("Torture Memos")

In the months after the attacks of September 11, 2001, advisors to President George W. Bush asked the OLC to provide legal guidance on a variety of questions relating to the rapidly expanding War on Terror. Among the questions asked were the legal limits on interrogation methods that the United States might use on suspected terrorists and those captured on the battlefields of Afghanistan. The OLC produced two memos for the then–White House legal counsel Alberto Gonzales. One, by Assistant Attorney General Jay Bybee, examined the interpretation and limits of treaty and statutory prohibitions on torture. Another, by Deputy Assistant Attorney General John Yoo, further examined the treaty obligations of the United States and the jurisdiction of the International Criminal Court over the interrogation of al-Qaeda operatives. Both memos offered a relatively narrow interpretation of the treaty and statutory provisions and an additional constitutional analysis that limited the extent to which Congress could direct how the president conducted the military campaign.

The legal interpretation of the political appointees within the OLC was met with some consternation by the career legal staff within the Department of Justice and the Pentagon, as well as by some other political appointees. In the summer of 2004, after revelations of the abuse of prisoners in military custody in Iraq became public, these so-called "torture memos" were leaked to the press. By then, Bybee had left the OLC for a seat on a federal circuit court, Yoo had returned to academia, and the White House was in the midst of a reelection campaign. Under international and domestic pressure, President Bush quickly emphasized that the administration was against torture. Gonzales distanced himself and the White House from the memos. He announced that the memos had been withdrawn, and he directed the OLC to produce a new opinion on legal standards affecting interrogations. In December 2004 Acting Assistant Attorney General Daniel Levin produced a new opinion, which was made public. Its broadened definition of torture was intended to guide administration policy relating to interrogations. After Levin's departure in 2005, the OLC produced new opinions, which were not publicly released, that once again shrank the definition of torture under existing statutes and treaties. These opinions indicated that a wider range of interrogation techniques were legally acceptable.[33] *Did the Levin memo disavow the constitutional analysis in the Bybee and Yoo memos?*

The Bybee memo cited the Supreme Court in Johnson v. Eisentrager *(1950) as recognizing implied presidential*

32. [Editors' note] Section 2(c) of the War Powers Resolution states: "The constitutional powers of the President as Commander-in-Chief to introduce United States Armed Forces into hostilities, or into situations where imminent involvement in hostilities is clearly indicated by circumstances, are exercised only pursuant to (1) a declaration of war, (2) specific statutory authorization, or (3) a national emergency created by attack upon the United States, its territories or possessions, or its armed forces."

33. On the interrogation memos, see also Jack Goldsmith, *The Terror Presidency* (New York: W. W. Norton, 2008); Jane Mayer, *The Dark Side* (Boston: Anchor Books, 2008); John Yoo, *War by Other Means* (Washington, DC: Atlantic Monthly Press, 2006); Karen J. Greenberg and Joshua L. Dratel, eds., *The Torture Papers* (New York: Cambridge University Press, 2005).

powers that are "necessary and proper" to carrying out the "enumerated powers" in Article II of the U.S. Constitution. The language and structure also mirrored the constitutional text in Article I. Consider how the Supreme Court has understood the scope of the necessary and proper clause of Article I after the New Deal. What are the implications of that characterization of presidential powers? Are implied powers more confined in the context of separation of powers than they are in the context of federalism?

The constitutional authority of Congress to limit how the president may use the military forces that Congress supplies to him has been a recurrent issue. During World War I, former president William Howard Taft argued that "Congress could not order battles to be fought on a certain plan, and could not direct parts of the army to be moved from one part of the country to another."[34] *After World War II, Cold War liberals beat back conservative proposals to curtail the president's authority to station troops abroad. During the waning days of the Vietnam War, Congress sought to prevent the use of American air and ground forces in neighboring Cambodia. During the Reagan administration, proposals to prohibit the president from making first use of nuclear weapons were made and defeated. Having appropriated funds to build weapon systems or create an army, can Congress direct how the president can use those instruments of war? Or do those decisions fall within the discretion of the president as commander in chief?*

Jay S. Bybee, Memo to Alberto R. Gonzales, Counsel to the President (2002)[35]

You have asked for our Office's views regarding the standards of conduct under the Convention Against Torture and Other Cruel, Inhuman and Degrading Treatment or Punishment as implemented by Sections 2340–2340A of Title 18 of the United States Code. As we understand it, this question has arisen in the context of the conduct of interrogations outside the United States. We conclude below that Section 2340A proscribes acts inflicting, and that are specifically intended to inflict, severe pain or suffering, whether mental or physical. Those acts must be of an extreme nature to rise to the level of torture within the meaning of Section 2340A and the Convention. . . .

. . .

Even if an interrogation method arguably were to violate Section 2340A, the statute would be unconstitutional if it impermissibly encroached on the President's constitutional power to conduct a military campaign. As Commander-in-Chief, the President has the constitutional authority to order interrogations of enemy combatants to gain intelligence information concerning military plans of the enemy. The demands of the Commander-in-Chief power are especially pronounced in the middle of a war in which the nation has already suffered a direct attack. In such a case, the information gained from interrogations may prevent future attacks by foreign enemies. Any effort to apply Section 2340A in a manner that interferes with the President's direction of such core war matters as the detention and interrogation of enemy combatants thus would be unconstitutional.

. . .

. . . [T]he President enjoys complete discretion in the exercise of his Commander-in-Chief authority and in conducting operations against hostile forces. Because both "[t]he executive power and the command of the military and naval forces is vested in the President," the Supreme Court has unanimously stated that it is *"the President alone* who is constitutionally invested with the *entire charge of hostile operations." Hamilton v. Dillin*, 88 U.S. 73, 87 (1874) (emphasis added). That authority is at its height in the middle of a war.

In light of the President's complete authority over the conduct of war, without a clear statement otherwise, we will not read a criminal statute as infringing on the President's ultimate authority in these areas. We have long recognized, and the Supreme Court has established a canon of statutory construction that statutes are to be construed in a manner that avoids constitutional difficulties so long as a reasonable alternative construction is available. . . .

In order to respect the President's inherent constitutional authority to manage a military campaign against al Qaeda and its allies, Section 2340A must be construed as not applying to interrogations undertaken pursuant to his Commander-in-Chief authority. As our Office has consistently held during this Administration and previous Administrations, Congress lacks authority under Article I to set the terms and

---

34. William Howard Taft, "The Boundaries Between the Executive, the Legislative, and the Judicial Branches of Government," *Yale Law Journal* 25 (1915): 610.

35. Excerpt taken from Office of Legal Counsel, *Re: Standards for Conduct of Interrogation Under 18 U.S.C. §§2340–2340A*, August 1, 2002.

conditions under which the President may exercise his authority as Commander in Chief to control the conduct of operations during a war. . . .

. . .

It could be argued that Congress enacted 18 U.S.C. §2340A with full knowledge and consideration of the President's Commander-in-Chief power, and that Congress intended to restrict his discretion in the interrogation of enemy combatants. Even were we to accept this argument, however, we conclude that the Department of Justice could not . . . enforce Section 2340A against federal officials acting pursuant to the President's constitutional authority to wage a military campaign.

Indeed, in a different context, we have concluded that both courts and prosecutors should reject prosecutions that apply federal criminal laws to activity that is authorized pursuant to one of the President's constitutional powers. This Office, for example, has previously concluded that Congress could not constitutionally extend the congressional contempt statute to executive branch officials who refuse to comply with congressional subpoenas because of an assertion of executive privilege. . . . Although Congress may define federal crimes that the President, through the Take Care Clause, should prosecute, Congress cannot compel the President to prosecute outcomes taken pursuant to the President's own constitutional authority. If Congress could do so, it could control the President's authority through the manipulation of federal criminal law.

. . . The President's constitutional power to protect the security of the United States and the lives and safety of its people must be understood in light of the Founders' intention to create a federal government "clothed with all the powers requisite to the complete execution of its trust." *The Federalist* No. 23. . . . Foremost among the objectives committed to that trust by the Constitution is the security of the nation. As Hamilton explained in arguing for the Constitution's adoption, because "the circumstances which may affect the public safety" are not "reducible within certain determinate limits,"

> it must be admitted, as a necessary consequence, that there can be no limitation of that authority, which is to provide for the defense and protection of the community, in any matter essential to its efficacy.

. . .

The text, structure and history of the Constitution establish that the Founders entrusted the President with the primary responsibility, and therefore the power, to ensure the security of the United States in situations of grave and unforeseen emergencies. . . . This Office has long understood the Commander-in-Chief Clause in particular as an affirmative grant of authority to the President. *See, e.g.*, Memorandum for Charles W. Colson, Special Counsel to the President, from William H. Rehnquist, Assistant Attorney General, Office of Legal Counsel, *Re: The President and the War Power: South Vietnam and the Cambodian Sanctuaries* (May 22, 1970). . . . The implication of constitutional text and structure are confirmed by the practical consideration that national security decisions require the unity in purpose and energy in action that characterize the Presidency rather than Congress.

As the Supreme Court has recognized, the Commander-in-Chief power and the President's obligation to protect the nation imply the ancillary powers necessary to their successful exercise. "The first of the enumerated powers of the President is that he shall be Commander-in-Chief of the Army and Navy of the United States. And, of course, the grant of war power includes all that is necessary and proper for carrying those powers into execution." *Johnson v. Eisentrager*, 339 U.S. 763, 788 (1950). In wartime, it is for the President alone to decide what methods to use to best prevail against the enemy. . . . The President's complete discretion in exercising the Commander-in-Chief power has been recognized by the courts. [See] the *Prize Cases* (1863). . . .

One of the core functions of the Commander-in-Chief is that of capturing, detaining, and interrogating members of the enemy. . . .

Any effort of Congress to regulate the interrogation of battlefield combatants would violate the Constitution's sole vesting of the Commander-in-Chief authority in the President. There can be little doubt that intelligence operations, such as the detention and interrogation of enemy combatants and leaders, are both necessary and proper for the effective conduct of a military campaign. . . . Congress can no more interfere with the President's conduct of the interrogation of enemy combatants than it can dictate strategic or tactical decisions on the battlefield. Just as statutes that order the President to conduct warfare in a certain manner or for specific goals would be unconstitutional, so too are laws that seek to prevent the President from gaining the intelligence he believes necessary to prevent attacks upon the United States.

. . .

John Yoo, Memo to William Haynes II, General Counsel of the Department of Defense (2003)[36]

You have asked our Office to examine the legal standards governing military interrogations of alien unlawful combatants held outside the United States. You have requested that we examine both domestic and international law that might be applicable to the conduct of those interrogations.

. . . [C]riminal statutes, if they were misconstrued to apply to the interrogation of enemy combatants, would conflict with the Constitution's grant of the Commander in Chief power solely to the President.

. . .

. . . The September 11, 2001 terrorist attacks marked a state of international armed conflict between the United States and the al Qaeda terrorist organization. Pursuant to his Commander-in-Chief power, as supported by an act of Congress, the President has ordered the Armed Forces to carry out military operations against al Qaeda, which includes the power both to kill and to capture members of the enemy. Interrogation arises as a necessary and legitimate element of the detention of al Qaeda and Taliban members during an armed conflict.

. . .

. . . [T]he text, structure and history of the Constitution establish that the Founders entrusted the President with the primary responsibility, and therefore the power, to protect the security of the United States. The decision to deploy military force in the defense of U.S. interests is expressly placed under Presidential authority by the Vesting Clause . . . and by the Commander-in-Chief Clause. . . . The framers understood the Commander-in-Chief Clause to grant the President the fullest range of power recognized at the time of the ratification as belonging to the military commander. In addition, the structure of the Constitution demonstrates that any power traditionally understood as pertaining to the executive—which includes the conduct of warfare and the defense of the nation—unless expressly assigned to Congress, is vested in the President. Article II, Section 1 makes this clear by stating that the "executive Power shall be vested in a President of the United States of America." This sweeping grant vests in the President the "executive power" and contrasts with the specific enumeration of the powers—those "herein"—granted to Congress in Article I. Our reading of the constitutional text and structure are confirmed by historical practice, in which Presidents have ordered the use of military force more than 100 times without congressional authorization, and by the functional consideration that national security decisions require a unity in purpose and energy that characterizes the Presidency alone.

As the Supreme Court has recognized, the Commander-in-Chief power and the President's obligation to protect the nation imply the ancillary powers necessary to their successful exercise. . . . In wartime, it is for the President alone to decide what methods to use to best prevail against the enemy. . . . The President's complete discretion in exercising the Commander-in-Chief power has been recognized by the courts. In the *Prize Cases* (1863) . . . the Court explained that whether the President "in fulfilling his duties as Commander in Chief" had appropriately responded to the rebellion of the southern states was a question "to be decided *by him*" and which the Court could not question, but must leave to "the political department of the Government to which this power was entrusted." . . .

One of the core functions of the Commander in Chief is that of capturing, detaining, and interrogating members of the enemy. . . . It is well settled that the President may seize and detain enemy combatants, at least for the duration of the conflict, and the laws of war make clear that prisoners may be interrogated for information concerning the enemy, its strength, and its plans. . . . Recognizing this authority, Congress has never attempted to restrict or interfere with the President's authority on this score.

. . .

. . . [T]he Fifth Amendment was not designed to restrict the unique war powers of the President as Commander in Chief. As long ago as 1865, Attorney General Speed explained the unquestioned rule that,

36. Excerpt taken from Office of Legal Counsel, *Re: Military Interrogation of Alien Unlawful Combatants Held Outside the United States*, March 14, 2003.

as Commander in Chief, the President waging a war may authorize soldiers to engage in combat that could not be authorized as a part of the President's role in enforcing the laws. . . . As Attorney General Speed concluded, the Due Process Clause has no application to the conduct of a military campaign:

> That portion of the Constitution which declares that "no person shall be deprived of his life, liberty, or property without due process of law," has such direct reference to, and connection with, trials for crime or criminal prosecutions that comment upon it would seem to be unnecessary. Trials for offences against the laws of war are not embraced or intended to be embraced in those provisions. . . . The argument that flings around offenders against the laws of war these guarantees of the Constitution would convict all the soldiers of our army of murder; no prisoners could be taken and held; the army could not move. The absurd consequences that would of necessity flow from such an argument show that it cannot be the true construction—it cannot be what was intended by the framers of the instrument. One of the prime motives for the Union and a federal government was to confer the powers of war. If any provisions of the Constitution are so in conflict with the power to carry on war as to destroy and make it valueless, then the instrument, instead of being a great and wise one, is a miserable failure, a felo de se.

. . .

. . . If each time the President captured and detained enemy aliens outside the United States, those aliens could bring suit challenging the deprivation of their liberty, such a result would interfere with and undermine the President's capacity to protect the Nation and to respond to the exigencies of war.

The Supreme Court has repeatedly refused to apply the Due Process Clause or even the Just Compensation Clause to executive and congressional actions taken in the direct prosecution of a war effort against enemies of the Nation. . . .

. . .

. . . [E]ven if the Fifth Amendment applied to enemy combatants in wartime, it is clear that . . . the Fifth Amendment does not operate outside the United States to regulate the executive's conduct toward aliens. . . . As the Supreme Court explained in [*Johnson v.*] *Eisentrager* (1950), construing the Fifth Amendment to apply to aliens who are outside the United States and have no connection to the United States:

> would mean that during military occupation irreconcilable enemy elements, guerrilla fighters, and "werewolves" could require the American Judiciary to assure them freedom of speech, press, and assembly as in the First Amendment, right to bear arms as in the Second, security against "unreasonable" searches and seizures as in the Fourth, as well as rights to jury trial as in the Fifth and Sixth Amendments. Such extraterritorial application of organic law would have been so significant an innovation in the practice of governments that, if intended or apprehended, it could scarcely have failed to excite contemporary comment. Not one word can be cited. No decision of this Court supports such a view.

. . .

As the Supreme Court has recognized, . . . the President enjoys complete discretion in the exercise of his Commander-in-Chief authority in conducting operations against hostile forces. Because both "[t]he executive power and the command of the military and naval forces is vested in the President," the Supreme Court has unanimously stated that it is "*the President alone* [] who is constitutionally invested with the *entire charge of hostile operations*." *Hamilton v. Dillin* (1874).

. . .

In the area of foreign affairs and war powers in particular, the avoidance canon has special force. In contrast to the domestic realm, foreign affairs and war clearly place the President in the dominant constitutional position due to his authority as Commander in Chief and Chief Executive and his plenary control over diplomatic relations. There can be little doubt that the conduct of war is a matter that is fundamentally executive in nature, the power over which the Framers vested in a unitary executive. . . . Correspondingly, during war Congress plays a reduced role in the war effort and the courts generally defer to executive decisions concerning the conduct of hostilities.

. . .

In order to respect the President's inherent constitutional authority to direct a military campaign against al Qaeda and its allies, general criminal laws must be construed as not applying to interrogations undertaken pursuant to his Commander-in-Chief authority. Congress cannot interfere with the President's exercise of his authority as Commander in Chief to control the conduct of operations during a war. . . . As we have discussed above, the President's power to detain and interrogate enemy combatants arises out of his constitutional authority as Commander in Chief. Any construction of criminal laws that regulated the President's authority as Commander in Chief to determine the interrogation and treatment of enemy combatants would raise serious constitutional questions whether Congress had intruded on the President's constitutional authority. Moreover, we do not believe that Congress enacted general criminal provisions such as the prohibitions against assault, maiming, interstate stalking, and torture pursuant to any express authority that would allow it to infringe on the President's constitutional control over the operation of the Armed Forces in wartime. In our view, Congress may no more regulate the President's ability to detain and interrogate enemy combatants than it may regulate his ability to direct troop movements on the battlefield. In fact, the general applicability of these statutes belies any argument that these statutes apply to persons under the direction of the President in the conduct of war.

. . .

Even if these statutes were misconstrued to apply to persons acting at the direction of the President during the conduct of war, the Department of Justice could not enforce this law or any of the other criminal statutes applicable to the special maritime and territorial jurisdiction against federal officials acting pursuant to the President's constitutional authority to direct a war. Even if an interrogation method arguably were to violate a criminal statute, the Justice Department could not bring a prosecution because the statute would be unconstitutional as applied in this context. . . .

. . . Any effort by Congress to regulate the interrogation of enemy combatants would violate the Constitution's sole vesting of the Commander-in-Chief authority in the President. There can be little doubt that intelligence operations, such as the detention and interrogation of enemy combatants and leaders, are both necessary and proper for the effective conduct of a military campaign. Indeed, such operations may be of more importance in a war with an international terrorist organization than one with the conventional armed forces of a nation-state, due to the former's emphasis on covert operations and surprise attacks against civilians. It may be the case that only successful interrogations can provide the information necessary to prevent future attacks upon the United States and its citizens. Congress can no more interfere with the President's conduct of the interrogation of enemy combatants than it can dictate strategic or tactical decisions on the battlefield. Just as statutes that order the President to conduct warfare in a certain manner or for specific goals would be unconstitutional, so too are laws that would prevent the President from gaining the intelligence he believes necessary to prevent attacks upon the United States.

. . .

Daniel Levin, Memo to James B. Comey, Deputy Attorney General (2004)[37]

Torture is abhorrent both to American law and values and to international norms. This universal repudiation of torture is reflected in our criminal law, for example, 18 U.S.C. §§2340–2340A; international agreements, exemplified by the United Nations Convention Against Torture (the "CAT"); customary international law; centuries of Anglo-American law; and the longstanding policy of the United States, repeatedly and recently reaffirmed by the President.

This Office interpreted the federal criminal prohibition against torture—codified at 18 U.S.C. §§2340–2340A. . . . The August 2002 Memorandum [the Bybee memo] also addressed a number of issues beyond the interpretation of those statutory provisions, including the President's Commander-in-Chief power, and various defenses that might be asserted to avoid potential liability under sections 2340–2340A. . . .

Questions have since been raised, both by this Office and by others, about the appropriateness and relevance of the non-statutory discussion in the August 2002 Memorandum, and also about various aspects of the statutory analysis, in particular the statement that "severe" pain under the statute was limited to pain "equivalent in intensity to the pain accompanying serious physical injury, such as organ failure, impairment of bodily function, or even death." . . . We decided to withdraw the August 2002 Memorandum, a decision you announced in June 2004. At that time,

37. Excerpt from Office of Legal Counsel, *Re: Legal Standards Applicable Under 18 U.S.C. §§2340–2340A*, December 30, 2004.

you directed this Office to prepare a replacement memorandum. Because of the importance of—and public interest in—these issues, you asked that this memorandum be prepared in a form that could be released to the public so that interested parties could understand our analysis of the statute.

This memorandum supersedes the August 2002 Memorandum in its entirety. Because the discussion in that memorandum concerning the President's Commander-in-Chief power and the potential defenses to liability was—and remains—unnecessary, it has been eliminated from the analysis that follows. Consideration of the bounds of any such authority would be inconsistent with the President's unequivocal directive that United States personnel not engage in torture.

. . .

The Criminal Division of the Department of Justice has reviewed this memorandum and concurs in the analysis set forth below.

. . .

Caroline D. Krass, Memorandum Opinion on the Authority to Use Military Force in Libya (2011)[38]

In February 2011 widespread popular protests against the military government broke out in Libya, as they had in other Middle Eastern and North African countries in the previous months. Libyan leader Muammar Qadhafi responded with aggressive military force, and the country soon collapsed into civil war. As government forces prepared to retake the city of Benghazi on March 17, the United Nations Security Council adopted a resolution imposing a no-fly zone in Libya and authorizing military force to protect civilians. The next day President Barack Obama announced that Qadhafi would need to implement an immediate ceasefire and withdraw from rebel-controlled areas in order to comply with the UN resolution. On March 19 the United States began air strikes against the Libyan military and government. Congressional leaders were consulted prior to the launch of the American military campaign, and a report indicating that foreign military operations were under way was filed with Congress consistent with the War Powers Act. But the administration denied that the actions in Libya were constrained by the sixty-day limit on "hostilities" without congressional authorization laid out in the War Powers Act. After military operations had begun Republican senator Rand Paul of Kentucky introduced resolutions requiring that the president cease his efforts until Congress provided the necessary authorization, claiming, "The Congress has become not just a rubber stamp for an unlimited Presidency, but, worse, Congress has become a doormat to be stepped upon, to be ignored, and basically to be treated as irrelevant. . . . There is no excuse for the Senate not to vote on going to war before we go to war."[39]

Before the air strikes began, Principal Deputy Assistant Attorney General Caroline Krass in the OLC provided an informal opinion on the constitutionality of the president launching such an offensive in Libya. Her conclusions were subsequently incorporated into a formal opinion justifying the presidential power to use military force in Libya. The administration offered a variety of documents supporting the legality of those actions, but the Krass opinion provided the key arguments in the most detail. Krass was serving as the acting head of the OLC in the spring of 2011 and had been a long-serving national security lawyer in the Bush, Clinton, and Obama administrations.

What type of constitutional arguments did Krass use to build support for her position? Did she adopt a formalist or a functionalist approach to determining when a "war" has begun?

. . .

The President explained in his March 21, 2011 report to Congress that the use of military force in Libya serves important U.S. interests in preventing instability in the Middle East and preserving the credibility and effectiveness of the United Nations Security Council. The President also stated that he intended the anticipated United States military operations in Libya to be limited in nature, scope, and duration. The goal of action by the United States was to "set the stage" for further action by coalition partners in implementing UNSC Resolution 1973, particularly through destruction of Libyan military assets that could either threaten coalition aircraft policing the UNSC-declared no-fly zone or engage in attacks on civilians and civilian-populated areas. In addition, no U.S. ground forces would be deployed, except

38. Memorandum Opinion for the Attorney General, April 1, 2011 (www.fas.org/irp/agency/doj/olc/libya.pdf).

39. *Congressional Record,* 112nd Cong., 1st Sess., April 5, 2011, S2110.

possibly for any search and rescue missions, and the risk of substantial casualties for U.S. forces would be low. As we advised you prior to the commencement of military operations, we believe that, under these circumstances, the President had constitutional authority, as Commander in Chief and Chief Executive and pursuant to his foreign affairs powers, to direct such limited military operations abroad, even without prior specific congressional approval.

Earlier opinions of this Office and other historical precedents establish the framework for our analysis. As we explained in 1992, Attorneys General and this Office "have concluded that the President has the power to commit United States troops abroad," as well as to "take military action," "for the purpose of protecting important national interests," even without specific prior authorization from Congress. *Authority to Use United States Military Forces in Somalia*, 16 Op. O.L.C. 6, 9 (1992) ("Military Forces in Somalia"). This independent authority of the President, which exists at least insofar as Congress has not specifically restricted it, see *Deployment of United States Armed Forces into Haiti*, 18 Op. O.L.C. 173, 176 n.4, 178 (1994) ("Haiti Deployment"), derives from the President's "unique responsibility," as Commander in Chief and Chief Executive, for "foreign and military affairs," as well as national security. *Sale v. Haitian Centers Council, Inc.*, 509 U.S. 155, 188 (1993); U.S. Const. art. II, §1, cl. 1, §2, cl. 2.

The Constitution, to be sure, divides authority over the military between the President and Congress, assigning to Congress the authority to "declare War," "raise and support Armies," and "provide and maintain a Navy," as well as general authority over the appropriations on which any military operation necessarily depends. U.S. Const. art. I, §8, cl. 1, 11–14. Yet, under "the historical gloss on the 'executive Power' vested in Article II of the Constitution," the President bears the "'vast share of responsibility for the conduct of our foreign relations,'" *Am. Ins. Ass'n v. Garamendi*, 539 U.S. 396, 414 (2003) (quoting *Youngstown Sheet & Tube Co. v. Sawyer*, 343 U.S. 579, 610–11 (1952) (Frankfurter, J., concurring)), and accordingly holds "independent authority 'in the areas of foreign policy and national security.'" Id. at 429 (quoting *Haig v. Agee*, 453 U.S. 280, 291 (1981)); see also, e.g., *Youngstown Sheet & Tube Co.*, 343 U.S. at 635–36 n.2 (Jackson, J., concurring) (noting President's constitutional power to "act in external affairs without congressional authority"). . . .

This understanding of the President's constitutional authority reflects not only the express assignment of powers and responsibilities to the President and Congress in the Constitution, but also, as noted, the "historical gloss" placed on the Constitution by two centuries of practice. *Garamendi*, 539 U.S. at 414. "Our history," this Office observed in 1980, "is replete with instances of presidential uses of military force abroad in the absence of prior congressional approval." *Presidential Power*, 4A Op. O.L.C. at 187; see generally Richard F. Grimmett, Cong. Research Serv., *Instances of Use of United States Armed Forces Abroad, 1798–2010* (2011). Since then, instances of such presidential initiative have only multiplied, with Presidents ordering, to give just a few examples, bombing in Libya (1986), an intervention in Panama (1989), troop deployments to Somalia (1992), Bosnia (1995), and Haiti (twice, 1994 and 2004), air patrols and airstrikes in Bosnia (1993–1995), and a bombing campaign in Yugoslavia (1999), without specific prior authorizing legislation. This historical practice is an important indication of constitutional meaning, because it reflects the two political branches' practical understanding, developed since the founding of the Republic, of their respective roles and responsibilities with respect to national defense, and because "[m]atters intimately related to foreign policy and national security are rarely proper subjects for judicial intervention." *Haig*, 453 U.S. at 292. In this context, the "pattern of executive conduct, made under claim of right, extended over many decades and engaged in by Presidents of both parties, 'evidences the existence of broad constitutional power.'" *Haiti Deployment*, 18 Op. O.L.C. at 178 (quoting *Presidential Power*, 4A Op. O.L.C. at 187). . . .

. . .

We have acknowledged one possible constitutionally-based limit on this presidential authority to employ military force in defense of important national interests—a planned military engagement that constitutes a "war" within the meaning of the Declaration of War Clause may require prior congressional authorization. . . . In our view, determining whether a particular planned engagement constitutes a "war" for constitutional purposes instead requires a fact-specific assessment of the "anticipated nature, scope, and duration" of the planned military operations. *Haiti Deployment*, 18 Op. O.L.C. at 179. This standard generally will be satisfied only by prolonged and substantial military engagements, typically involving exposure of U.S. military personnel to significant risk over a substantial period. Again, Congress's own key enactment on the subject reflects this understanding. [See, the War Powers Resolution.] . . .

Applying this fact-specific analysis, we concluded in 1994 that a planned deployment of up to 20,000 United States troops to Haiti to oust military leaders and reinstall Haiti's legitimate government was not a "war" requiring advance congressional approval. . . . Similarly, a year later we concluded that a proposed deployment of approximately 20,000 ground troops to enforce a peace agreement in Bosnia and Herzegovina also was not a "war," even though this deployment involved some "risk that the United States [would] incur (and inflict) casualties." . . .

Under the framework of these precedents, the President's legal authority to direct military force in Libya turns on two questions: first, whether United States operations in Libya would serve sufficiently important national interests to permit the President's action as Commander in Chief and Chief Executive and pursuant to his authority to conduct U.S. foreign relations; and second, whether the military operations that the President anticipated ordering would be sufficiently extensive in "nature, scope, and duration" to constitute a "war" requiring prior specific congressional approval under the Declaration of War Clause.

. . .

In our view, the combination of at least two national interests that the President reasonably determined were at stake here—preserving regional stability and supporting the UNSC's credibility and effectiveness—provided a sufficient basis for the President's exercise of his constitutional authority to order the use of military force. . . .

. . .

. . . At the same time, turning to the second element of the analysis, we do not believe that anticipated United States operations in Libya amounted to a "war" in the constitutional sense necessitating congressional approval under the Declaration of War Clause. This inquiry, as noted, is highly fact-specific and turns on no single factor. See *Proposed Bosnia Deployment*, 19 Op. O.L.C. at 334 (reaching conclusion based on specific "circumstances"); *Haiti Deployment*, 18 Op. O.L.C. at 178 (same). Here, considering all the relevant circumstances, we believe applicable historical precedents demonstrate that the limited military operations the President anticipated directing were not a "war" for constitutional purposes.

. . . The planned operations thus avoided the difficulties of withdrawal and risks of escalation that may attend commitment of ground forces—two factors that this Office has identified as "arguably" indicating "a greater need for approval [from Congress] at the outset," to avoid creating a situation in which "Congress may be confronted with circumstances in which the exercise of its power to declare war is effectively foreclosed." *Proposed Bosnia Deployment*, 19 Op. O.L.C. at 333. Furthermore, also as in prior operations conducted without a declaration of war or other specific authorizing legislation, the anticipated operations here served a "limited mission" and did not "aim at the conquest or occupation of territory." Id. at 332. President Obama directed United States forces to "conduct[] a limited and well-defined mission in support of international efforts to protect civilians and prevent a humanitarian disaster"; American airstrikes accordingly were to be "limited in their nature, duration, and scope." Obama March 21, 2011 Report to Congress. . . .

Accordingly, we conclude that President Obama could rely on his constitutional power to safeguard the national interest by directing the anticipated military operations in Libya—which were limited in their nature, scope, and duration—without prior congressional authorization.

VII. Individual Rights

MAJOR DEVELOPMENTS

- Supreme Court recognizes an individual right to bear arms
- Several states recognize a constitutional right to same-sex marriage
- States permitted to adopt school-choice programs that subsidize tuition at private religious schools

The contemporary constitutional politics of individual rights is structured by unprecedented range, polarization, and the influence of one or two centrist justices. With the exception of the contracts clause, controversies swirl around virtually every constitutional right. Americans fight over takings, punitive damages, vouchers for religious schools, creationism, abortion, same-sex marriage, the right to die, and gun control. Most controversies pit Republicans against Democrats and more conservative justices against more liberal justices. Democrats and liberals favor abortion rights, same-sex marriage, the right to die, and bans on government support for religious activities. Republicans and conservatives favor property rights, granting religious groups access on equal terms to public benefits, and the right to bear arms. Justices dispute the proper occasions for judicial activism. The Supreme Court decides numerous rights cases by 5–4 margins, with Justice Kennedy (and formerly Justices Kennedy and O'Connor) almost always casting the deciding vote. No member of the Rehnquist or Roberts Court champions judicial restraint on all or most issues of individual rights.

A. Property

Conservatives, libertarians, and Republicans are seeking to revive some but not all the traditional constitutional protections for property rights. The contracts clause remains moribund. Efforts to resurrect the freedom of contract are largely limited to the legal academy.[40] Both Republicans and conservatives, however, promote the takings clause as a bulwark against what they believe is overreaching government regulation. When the Republican Party platform in 2008 asserted, "At the center of a free economy is the right of citizens to be secure in their property," the emphasis was on what party members believed were unjust takings. The party's platforms in 2008 and 2012 condemned the Supreme Court's decision in *Kelo v. City of New London* (2005) for "allowing local governments to seize a person's home or land, not for vital public use, but for transfer to private developers." Republicans "call[ed] on state legislatures to moot the *Kelo* decision by appropriate legislation or constitutional amendments" and "pledge[d] on the federal level to pass legislation to protect against unjust federal takings."

The takings clause is the main front in contemporary battles over constitutional protection for property rights. Supported by conservative politicians and libertarian public interest groups, homeowners and small businesses are challenging environmental laws and land use regulations that they believe impair or destroy property rights. Many challenges have been successful, particularly in the states. Often, local officials who are fearful of lawsuits either alter land use regulations or make exceptions when faced with a potential takings claim.

Liberals have held the line in national constitutional politics. The Supreme Court in the two most important recent takings clause cases sustained state policies under constitutional attack. In *Kelo v. City of New London* (2005) a 5–4 judicial majority ruled that promoting economic development satisfied the "public use" prong of the takings clause when government used the power of eminent domain to transfer property from one private owner to another private owner who promised to create more jobs for the community. *Stop the Beach Renourishment, Inc. v. Florida Dept. of Environmental Protection* (2010) unanimously rejected a takings clause attack on Florida's effort to restore beaches eroded by hurricanes. The justices divided ideologically on whether a judicial decision could violate the takings clause. The more conservative justices on the Roberts Court insisted that judicial decisions could take property but that the Florida Supreme Court had not taken property in this instance. Justice Kennedy and the four more liberal justices on the Roberts Court insisted that no need existed to resolve that question.

Proponents of property rights in the states are enjoying more success.[41] In the wake of *Kelo* forty-two states passed laws limiting the circumstances in which elected officials could exercise the power of eminent domain. While many laws are vague, some clearly limit legislative discretion. The Kansas legislature in 2007 declared, "The taking of private property by eminent domain for the purpose of selling, leasing or otherwise transferring such property to any private entity is prohibited except [in certain narrowly defined circumstances]."[42] Several state courts have interpreted the takings clause of the state constitution as providing greater restrictions on state officials than does the takings clause of the national Constitution. The Supreme Court of Oklahoma in *Board of County Commissioners of Muskogee County v. Lowery* (OK 2006) stated, "As a matter of Oklahoma constitutional and

40. See David Bernstein, *Rehabilitating* Lochner: *Defending Individual Rights Against Progressive Reform* (Chicago: University of Chicago Press, 2011). Very few liberals in the academy defend constitutional protections for welfare rights.

41. See Ilya Somin, "The Judicial Reaction to *Kelo*," *Albany Government Law Review* 4 (2011): 1–37; R. Benjamin Lingle, "Post-*Kelo* Eminent Domain Reform: A Double-Edged Sword for Historic Preservation," *Florida Law Review* 63 (2011): 985–1012.

42. Kan. Stat. Ann. § 26–501b (2009).

Illustration 11-4 Life, Liberty, and the Pursuit of Tax Revenue
Source: Cox & Forkum Editorial Cartoons.

statutory law, economic development alone is not a public purpose to justify the exercise of county's power of eminent domain."[43] State decisions to provide additional constitutional rights are legitimate and common in other areas of state constitutional law. While a state court may not interpret a state constitution as permitting behavior forbidden by the national Constitution, state officials are free to interpret or amend a state constitution to forbid behavior permitted by the national Constitution.

Kelo v. City of New London, 545 U.S. 469 (2005)

Susette Kelo owned a home in the Fort Trumbull area of New London, Connecticut. In 1990 a state agency declared New London to be a "distressed municipality" in light of decades of job and population losses. In order to revitalize the city New London officials authorized an economic redevelopment plan that gave a significant parcel of land to the Pfizer Corporation. Pfizer in return promised to build a pharmaceutical research facility, which was expected to substantially increase the number of jobs in the area. The land targeted for redevelopment included privates homes occupied by Susette Kelo and others. New London offered a fair market price for those homes, but Kelo and some other longtime residents did not want to leave communities in which they had lived for most of their lives. When New London began condemnation proceedings against these residents' properties, Kelo filed a lawsuit in state court, claiming that the condemnation violated the takings clause of the Fifth and Fourteenth Amendments because government action transferring property from one private owner to another is not a "public use" for constitutional purposes. The trial court ruled that Connecticut could condemn some properties, but not others. On appeal the Supreme Court of Connecticut upheld all the proposed takings as a valid public use. Kelo appealed to the Supreme Court of the United States.

43. *Board of County Commissioners of Muskogee County v. Lowery*, 136 P.3d 639 (Okla. 2006).

The Supreme Court by a 5–4 vote sustained New London's use of eminent domain. Justice Stevens's majority opinion declared that the public use requirement of the Fifth Amendment was satisfied any time a taking had a public benefit. Why did he reach that conclusion? Did Justice O'Connor successfully reconcile cases in which she thought that the eminent domain power was illegitimate with cases in which she thought that the power was legitimate? Alternatively, were both Justice Stevens and Justice Thomas correct in thinking that either government is free to give condemned land to a private owner whenever doing so might advance a public interest or else government can never give condemned land to a private owner? Property rights activists protesting the Kelo *decision urged New Hampshire to condemn Justice Souter's farmhouse and convert the property into the Lost Liberty Inn, which might provide greater tax revenues for the state. If New Hampshire decided that the Lost Liberty Inn would provide an economic boon to the community, could they constitutionally condemn Justice Souter's property?*

In 2010 Pfizer announced it was closing down operations in New London.

JUSTICE STEVENS delivered the opinion of the Court.

. . .

Two polar propositions are perfectly clear. On the one hand, it has long been accepted that the sovereign may not take the property of *A* for the sole purpose of transferring it to another private party *B*, even though *A* is paid just compensation. On the other hand, it is equally clear that a State may transfer property from one private party to another if future "use by the public" is the purpose of the taking; the condemnation of land for a railroad with common-carrier duties is a familiar example. . . .

. . .

The disposition of this case turns on the question whether the City's development plan serves a "public purpose." Without exception, our cases have defined that concept broadly, reflecting our longstanding policy of deference to legislative judgments in this field.

In *Berman v. Parker* (1954), this Court upheld a redevelopment plan targeting a blighted area of Washington, D.C., in which most of the housing for the area's 5,000 inhabitants was beyond repair. Under the plan, the area would be condemned and part of it utilized for the construction of streets, schools, and other public facilities. The remainder of the land would be leased or sold to private parties for the purpose of redevelopment, including the construction of low-cost housing. . . . Writing for a unanimous Court, Justice Douglas refused to evaluate this claim in isolation, deferring instead to the legislative and agency judgment that the area "must be planned as a whole" for the plan to be successful. . . .

In *Hawaii Housing Authority v. Midkiff* (1984), the Court considered a Hawaii statute whereby fee title was taken from lessors and transferred to lessees (for just compensation) in order to reduce the concentration of land ownership. We unanimously upheld the statute and rejected the Ninth Circuit's view that it was "a naked attempt on the part of the state of Hawaii to take the property of A and transfer it to B solely for B's private use and benefit." Reaffirming *Berman*'s deferential approach to legislative judgments in this field, we concluded that the State's purpose of eliminating the "social and economic evils of a land oligopoly" qualified as a valid public use. . . .

. . .

Those who govern the City were not confronted with the need to remove blight in the Fort Trumbull area, but their determination that the area was sufficiently distressed to justify a program of economic rejuvenation is entitled to our deference. The City has carefully formulated an economic development plan that it believes will provide appreciable benefits to the community, including—but by no means limited to—new jobs and increased tax revenue. As with other exercises in urban planning and development, the City is endeavoring to coordinate a variety of commercial, residential, and recreational uses of land, with the hope that they will form a whole greater than the sum of its parts. To effectuate this plan, the City has invoked a state statute that specifically authorizes the use of eminent domain to promote economic development. Given the comprehensive character of the plan, the thorough deliberation that preceded its adoption, and the limited scope of our review, it is appropriate for us, as it was in *Berman*, to resolve the challenges of the individual owners, not on a piecemeal basis, but rather in light of the entire plan. Because that plan unquestionably serves a public purpose, the takings challenged here satisfy the public use requirement of the Fifth Amendment.

. . .

. . . In affirming the City's authority to take petitioners' properties, we do not minimize the hardship that condemnations may entail, notwithstanding the payment of just compensation. We emphasize that nothing in our opinion precludes any State from placing further restrictions on its exercise of the takings power. Indeed, many States already impose "public use" requirements that are stricter than the federal baseline. Some of these requirements have been established as a matter of state constitutional law, while others are expressed in state eminent domain statutes that carefully limit the grounds upon which takings may be exercised. As the submissions of the parties and their *amici* make clear, the necessity and wisdom of using eminent domain to promote economic development are certainly matters of legitimate public debate. This Court's authority, however, extends only to determining whether the City's proposed condemnations are for a "public use" within the meaning of the Fifth Amendment to the Federal Constitution. Because over a century of our case law interpreting that provision dictates an affirmative answer to that question, we may not grant petitioners the relief that they seek.

JUSTICE KENNEDY, concurring.

. . .

This Court has declared that a taking should be upheld as consistent with the Public Use Clause as long as it is "rationally related to a conceivable public purpose." This deferential standard of review echoes the rational-basis test used to review economic regulation under the Due Process and Equal Protection Clauses. The determination that a rational-basis standard of review is appropriate does not, however, alter the fact that transfers intended to confer benefits on particular, favored private entities, and with only incidental or pretextual public benefits, are forbidden by the Public Use Clause.

A court applying rational-basis review under the Public Use Clause should strike down a taking that, by a clear showing, is intended to favor a particular private party, with only incidental or pretextual public benefits, just as a court applying rational-basis review under the Equal Protection Clause must strike down a government classification that is clearly intended to injure a particular class of private parties, with only incidental or pretextual public justifications.

. . .

JUSTICE O'CONNOR, with whom THE CHIEF JUSTICE, JUSTICE SCALIA, and JUSTICE THOMAS join, dissenting.

. . .

While the Takings Clause presupposes that government can take private property without the owner's consent, the just compensation requirement spreads the cost of condemnations and thus "prevents the public from loading upon one individual more than his just share of the burdens of government." . . . The public use requirement, in turn, imposes a more basic limitation, circumscribing the very scope of the eminent domain power: Government may compel an individual to forfeit her property for the *public's* use, but not for the benefit of another private person. This requirement promotes fairness as well as security. . . .

. . .

Our cases have generally identified three categories of takings that comply with the public use requirement, though it is in the nature of things that the boundaries between these categories are not always firm. Two are relatively straightforward and uncontroversial. First, the sovereign may transfer private property to public ownership—such as for a road, a hospital, or a military base. . . . Second, the sovereign may transfer private property to private parties, often common carriers, who make the property available for the public's use—such as with a railroad, a public utility, or a stadium. . . . But "public ownership" and "use-by-the-public" are sometimes too constricting and impractical ways to define the scope of the Public Use Clause. Thus we have allowed that, in certain circumstances and to meet certain exigencies, takings that serve a public purpose also satisfy the Constitution even if the property is destined for subsequent private use. See, *e.g., Berman* v. *Parker* (1954); *Hawaii Housing Authority* v. *Midkiff* (1984).

. . .

The Court's holdings in *Berman* and *Midkiff* were true to the principle underlying the Public Use Clause. In both those cases, the extraordinary, precondemnation use of the targeted property inflicted affirmative harm on society—in *Berman* through blight resulting from extreme poverty and in *Midkiff* through oligopoly resulting from extreme wealth. And in both cases, the relevant legislative body had found that eliminating the existing property use was necessary to remedy the harm. . . . Thus a public purpose was realized when the harmful use was eliminated. Because each taking *directly* achieved a public benefit, it did not matter that the property was turned over to private use. Here, in contrast, New London does not claim that Susette

Kelo's and Wilhelmina Dery's well-maintained homes are the source of any social harm. Indeed, it could not so claim without adopting the absurd argument that any single-family home that might be razed to make way for an apartment building, or any church that might be replaced with a retail store, or any small business that might be more lucrative if it were instead part of a national franchise, is inherently harmful to society and thus within the government's power to condemn.

In moving away from our decisions sanctioning the condemnation of harmful property use, the Court today significantly expands the meaning of public use. It holds that the sovereign may take private property currently put to ordinary private use, and give it over for new, ordinary private use, so long as the new use is predicted to generate some secondary benefit for the public—such as increased tax revenue, more jobs, maybe even aesthetic pleasure. But nearly any lawful use of real private property can be said to generate some incidental benefit to the public. Thus, if predicted (or even guaranteed) positive side-effects are enough to render transfer from one private party to another constitutional, then the words "for public use" do not realistically exclude *any* takings, and thus do not exert any constraint on the eminent domain power.

. . .

JUSTICE THOMAS, dissenting.

. . .

The most natural reading of the Clause is that it allows the government to take property only if the government owns, or the public has a legal right to use, the property, as opposed to taking it for any public purpose or necessity whatsoever. At the time of the founding, dictionaries primarily defined the noun "use" as "the act of employing any thing to any purpose." The term "use," moreover, "is from the Latin *utor,* which means 'to use, make use of, avail one's self of, employ, apply, enjoy, etc.'" . . . When the government takes property and gives it to a private individual, and the public has no right to use the property, it strains language to say that the public is "employing" the property, regardless of the incidental benefits that might accrue to the public from the private use. . . .

. . .

Tellingly, the phrase "public use" contrasts with the very different phrase "general Welfare" used elsewhere in the Constitution. . . . The Framers would have used some such broader term if they had meant the Public Use Clause to have a similarly sweeping scope. Other founding-era documents made the contrast between these two usages still more explicit. . . .

. . .

The public purpose interpretation of the Public Use Clause also unnecessarily duplicates a similar inquiry required by the Necessary and Proper Clause. The Takings Clause is a prohibition, not a grant of power: The Constitution does not expressly grant the Federal Government the power to take property for any public purpose whatsoever. Instead, the Government may take property only when necessary and proper to the exercise of an expressly enumerated power. . . . In other words, a taking is permissible under the Necessary and Proper Clause only if it serves a valid public purpose. Interpreting the Public Use Clause likewise to limit the government to take property only for sufficiently public purposes replicates this inquiry. If this is all the Clause means, it is, once again, surplusage. . . .

. . .

The "public purpose" test applied by *Berman* and *Midkiff* also cannot be applied in principled manner. "When we depart from the natural import of the term 'public use,' and substitute for the simple idea of a public possession and occupation, that of public utility, public interest, common benefit, general advantage or convenience . . . we are afloat without any certain principle to guide us." Once one permits takings for public purposes in addition to public uses, no coherent principle limits what could constitute a valid public use—at least, none beyond JUSTICE O'CONNOR's (entirely proper) appeal to the text of the Constitution itself. I share the Court's skepticism about a public use standard that requires courts to second-guess the policy wisdom of public works projects. The "public purpose" standard this Court has adopted, however, demands the use of such judgment, for the Court concedes that the Public Use Clause would forbid a purely private taking. It is difficult to imagine how a court could find that a taking was purely private except by determining that the taking did not, in fact, rationally advance the public interest. . . .

. . .

The consequences of today's decision are not difficult to predict, and promise to be harmful. So-called "urban renewal" programs provide some compensation for the properties they take, but no compensation is possible for the subjective value of these lands to the individuals displaced and the indignity inflicted by uprooting them from their homes. Allowing the government to take property solely for public purposes is bad enough, but extending the concept of public purpose to encompass any economically beneficial goal guarantees that these losses will fall disproportionately on poor communities. Those communities are not only systematically less likely to put their lands to the highest and best social use, but are also the least politically powerful. If ever there were justification for intrusive judicial review of constitutional provisions that protect "discrete and insular minorities," *United States v. Carolene Products Co.* (1938), surely that principle would apply with great force to the powerless groups and individuals the Public Use Clause protects. The deferential standard this Court has adopted for the Public Use Clause is therefore deeply perverse. . . .

B. Religion

Religious freedom in the United States is presently structured by a series of complex relationships among interest groups, parties, elected officials, and judges. The constitutional politics of establishment is different than the constitutional politics of free exercise. The differences between most Democrats and most Republicans on religious freedom issues are not the same as the differences between the more liberal and more conservative justices on the Supreme Court.

Religious groups divide on establishment issues but are united on free exercise issues. Conservative religious groups favor government policies that accommodate religious belief. Liberal religious groups and more secular Americans support a greater separation between church and state. Virtually all religious groups favor granting religious groups exemptions from neutral state laws that burden religious practice, unless a strong state reason exists for not granting the exemption. When conversations turn to specifics, such as whether religious apartment owners must be required to rent to gay couples or whether Catholic organizations must offer employees health plans that pay for contraceptive services, the divide between conservative and liberal religious groups reemerges.

In establishment clause debates conservatives retained the initiative gained in the Reagan years. While liberals are merely trying to hold on to New Deal and Great Society precedents sharply separating church and state, conservatives continue to press for more accommodations for religion. Depending on your perspective Republicans and conservative religious groups have made considerable progress in either reducing discrimination against religious institutions in public aid programs or funneling more money to religious institutions. The Supreme Court has also shown greater tolerance for the placement of religious symbols in public places. Liberals have, however, held the line on school prayer. *Engle v. Vitale* (1962), which declared state-mandated prayer exercises unconstitutional, remains the law of the land, even as prayer continues in public school districts throughout rural America.[44] In the Contemporary Era judicial opinions in establishment cases have relieved more heavily on the "endorsement" test, a test formulated by Justice O'Connor and the more liberal justices on the Rehnquist and Roberts Courts. The test of constitutionality of government practices under the establishment clause, O'Connor claimed in numerous cases, was whether "the reasonable observer would view a government practice as endorsing religion."[45]

The Supreme Court in four important contemporary cases found that public moneys were being directed to religious schools only as a result of private choices. In *Zobrest v. Catalina Foothills School District* (1993) a 5–4 judicial majority ruled that Congress under the Individuals with Disabilities Education Act could provide a sign interpreter for a deaf child who was attending a Catholic school. After noting that the federal law entitled any disabled child to take advantage of the same benefit, Chief Justice Rehnquist declared, "Government programs that neutrally provide benefits to a broad class of citizens defined without reference to religion are not readily subject to an Establishment Clause challenge just because sectarian institutions may also receive an attenuated financial benefit." Four years later, in *Agostini v. Felton* (1997), a 5–4 judicial majority permitted public schoolteachers to provide remedial educational services to disadvantaged children on the grounds of a religious school. Citing *Zobrest*, Justice O'Connor's majority opinion announced that the justices had "abandoned the presumption . . . that the placement of public employees on parochial school grounds inevitably results in the

---

44. See Kevin T. McGuire, "Public Schools, Religious Establishments, and the U.S. Supreme Court: An Examination of Policy Compliance," *American Politics Research* 37 (2009): 50–74.

45. *Capitol Square Review and Advisory Board v. Pinette*, 515 U.S. 753 (1995).

impermissible effect of state-sponsored indoctrination or constitutes a symbolic union between government and religion." *Mitchell v. Helms* (2002) loosened the conditions under which the federal government and states could provide instructional materials to religious schools as part of a general program of aid to education. Justice Thomas's opinion for the judicial plurality insisted, "If the religious, irreligious, and areligious are all alike eligible for governmental aid, no one would conclude that any indoctrination that any particular recipient conducts has been done at the behest of the government."

Finally, in *Zelman v. Simmons-Harris* (2003) the Supreme Court by a 5–4 vote sustained an Ohio law that provided financial assistance to parents who sent their children to private schools, the vast majority of which are religious. Chief Justice Rehnquist's opinion for the Court asserted that the establishment clause requirement that programs be neutral between religion and nonreligion was met because money flowed to religious schools only as a consequence of private choices made by parents. The dissenting opinions in *Zelman* objected that, under such programs, public officials were using funding as a way to influence religious indoctrination. Each side remained divided on what facts were most relevant to the constitutional analysis: was the issue that religious schools were not singled out as special beneficiaries, or that because of the extensive preexisting network of religious schools in Cleveland, religious schools were the primary financial beneficiaries of this government program?

Americans and the Supreme Court have continued to have difficulty determining the place of religion, and religious monuments in particular, in the public sphere. Two cases decided in 2005 illustrate the fine line between monuments that the judicial majority believed reflect the nation's heritage and monuments that unconstitutionally establish religion. *McCreary County v. ACLU of Kentucky* by a 5–4 vote declared unconstitutional several efforts by a local government to display the Ten Commandments in the local courthouse. Justice Souter's majority opinion stated, "The display's unstinting focus was on religious passages, showing that the Counties were posting the Commandments precisely because of their sectarian content." That same day the justices by a 5–4 vote in *Van Orden v. Perry* decided that Texas could include a monument displaying the Ten Commandments in a collection of other monuments displaying facets of state history. Chief Justice Rehnquist declared, "Texas has treated its Capitol grounds monuments as representing the several strands in the State's political and legal history. The inclusion of the Ten Commandments monument in this group has a dual significance, partaking of both religion and government." Eight justices could find no difference between the two cases. Justice Breyer, who could, cast the deciding votes.

Neither the Supreme Court nor the lower federal courts have showed any inclination to revisit previous decisions forbidding public schools from conducting prayer exercises (*Lee v. Weisman* [1993]) or teaching religious alternatives to evolution (*Edwards v. Aguillard* [1987]). *Santa Fe Independent School District v. Doe* (2000) declared unconstitutional a policy that allowed students to determine by election whether prayers would be said before football games. Justice Stevens's majority opinion declared, "An objective Santa Fe High School student will unquestionably perceive the inevitable pregame prayer as stamped with her school's seal of approval." Federal courts rebuffed efforts to have public schools teach "intelligent design," the view that the universe was created by an intelligent entity. A federal district court in *Kitzmiller v. Dover Area School District* (2005) maintained that intelligent design was no different than the creationist theories that the Supreme Court in *Edwards* declared violated the establishment clause when taught in public schools.

Recent years suggest a sharp shift in the constitutional politics of the free exercise clause. The most politically salient constitutional claims are presently made by evangelical Christians and other religious conservatives. Many maintain that they have a constitutional right to exemptions from mandatory school requirements, particular reading assignments in public schools, laws mandating that personnel in public hospitals provide reproductive services such as abortion, and laws that require that individuals not discriminate against gays and lesbians. In 2012 the U.S. Conference of Catholic Bishops denounced the Obama administration for requiring all nonchurch employers to provide their employees with health plans that included benefits for contraception. Although some states have passed statutes recognizing religious exemptions from these and similar decrees, most judges refuse to give those claims constitutional sanction.[46] In *Parker v. Hurley* (2008) the Court of Appeals for the First Circuit rejected a claim that parents had a free exercise right to prevent teachers from reading certain books to their children. Judge Lynch's unanimous opinion asserted, "While parents can choose between public and private schools, they do not have a constitutional right to direct how a public school teaches their child."[47]

Same-sex marriage has raised particularly heated free exercise controversies. As an increasing number of states recognize same-sex marriage, religious conservatives increasingly insist that they have a constitutional right to treat such persons as not married. Many state laws authorizing same-sex marriage contain provisions that provide exemptions to persons who think such unions sinful.[48] Some proponents of same-sex marriage think this is a good compromise. They regard religious exemptions as an acceptable price to pay for achieving gay marriage or maintain that religious believers are entitled to exemptions as a matter of principle. Robin Fretwell Wilson maintains, "Forcing a public employee with a religious objection to facilitate a same-sex marriage would be intolerant in the extreme when little is to be gained by such rigid demands."[49] Others find offensive the notion that religious believers are entitled to exemptions from laws they believe protect basic human rights. Laura Underkuffler writes, "Why should religiously grounded discrimination be tolerated against gay and lesbian citizens when, regarding racial, religious, gender, national-origin, and other groups, it is not?"[50]

With one very important exception the Supreme Court permits elected officials to choose whether to include religious groups in various benefit programs. A 7–2 majority in *Locke v. Davey* (2004) sustained a Washington law that excluded students studying devotional theology from a state scholarship program. Chief Justice Rehnquist's opinion emphasized the "play in the joints" between the free exercise and establishment clauses. While he declared that a state could "permit Promise Scholars to pursue a degree in devotional theology," consistent with the establishment clause, Rehnquist added that a state's law that "deal[s] differently with religious education for the ministry than with education for other callings is . . . not evidence of hostility toward religion" that would violate the free exercise clause. The exceptional case when state officials have no choice about religious inclusion is when states create a limited public forum, a forum for speech on certain subjects. In such circumstances judicial majorities, inspired by such interest groups as the Center for Individual Rights, have ruled that the free speech clause of the First Amendment forbids discrimination against religious perspectives. In *Rosenberger v. Rector and Visitors of University of Virginia* (1995) a 5–4 judicial majority ruled that the University of Virginia had to pay the printing costs for a student-run religious newspaper when the university paid the printing costs for all other student newspapers. Justice Kennedy's majority opinion asserted that state officials had "select[ed] for disfavored treatment those student journalistic efforts with religious editorial viewpoints." For a public university to grant access to its facilities "on a religion-neutral basis to a wide spectrum of student groups," he continued, "does not violate the Establishment Clause." A 6–3 majority in *Good News Club v. Milford Central School* (2001) applied these principles when ruling that public schools could not forbid Christian groups from meeting in public schools when secular groups were routinely granted access to those facilities. Justice Thomas's majority opinion stated, "When Milford denied the Good News Club access to the school's limited public forum on the ground that the Club was religious in nature, it discriminated against the Club because of its religious viewpoint in violation of the Free Speech Clause of the First Amendment."

C. Guns

The trend toward increased support for an individual right to bear arms, which began in the Reagan Era, is accelerating. The Republican Party has adopted an ever-stronger stance on Second Amendment rights,

46. For a good summary, see Laura Underkuffler, "Odious Discrimination and the Religious Exemption Quest," *Cardozo Law Review* 32 (2011): 2087–2092.

47. *Parker v. Hurley*, 514 F. 3d 87 (1st Cir. 2008).

48. See, for example, *McKinney's Consolidated Laws of New York*, §10-b (2011).

49. Robin Fretwell Wilson, "Insubstantial Burdens: The Case for Government Exemptions to Same-Sex Marriage," *Northwestern Journal of Law & Social Policy* 5 (2010): 360.

50. Underkuffler, "Odious Discrimination," 2087.

declaring in its 2012 platform that "Gun ownership is responsible citizenship, enabling Americans to defend their homes and communities" and opposing "legislation that is intended to restrict our Second Amendment rights by limiting the capacity of clips or magazines or otherwise restoring the ill considered Clinton gun ban." Democrats, who previously never discussed Second Amendment rights, now combine support for an individual right to bear arms with calls for gun control. The national party platform in 2012 declared that the party would "preserve Americans' Second Amendment right to own and use firearms" but that "the right to own firearms is subject to reasonable regulation," such as background checks, assault weapons bans, and closing the gun-shop loophole.

The Supreme Court in two path-breaking cases supported constitutional gun rights. The justices in *District of Columbia v. Heller* (2008) by a 5–4 vote held that the Second Amendment protected an individual right to bear arms. *McDonald v. City of Chicago* (2010) by the same 5–4 vote held that the due process clause of the Fourteenth Amendment incorporated this individual right to bear arms.

Contemporary constitutional debates over the Second Amendment revolve around the relationship between the prefatory clause, "a well regulated Militia, being necessary to a free state," and the declaration that "the right of the people to keep and bear arms, shall not be infringed." Proponents of the standard, or collective, interpretation insist that Americans have no rights independent of the militia. Individuals may have a right to belong to existing state militias, but they have no right to bear arms for individual protection or hunting. Given that militias no longer exist or do not exist in their original form, the Second Amendment in this view has almost no practical implications for contemporary constitutional politics.[51] Proponents of the individual rights model assert that the preface declares one reason for the right to bear arms but does not exhaust the scope of the right. As championed by such scholars as Eugene Volokh and Randy Barnett, this constitutional understanding insists that citizens have a constitutional right to bear arms for their protection and recreational use, even when their actions are not affiliated with a state militia.[52]

The lower federal courts are in the process of assessing the proper application of *Heller* to other assertions of an individual right to bear arms. The Court of Appeals for the District of Columbia in *Heller v. District of Columbia* II (2011) sustained most aspects of the registration requirements and the ban on assault weapons that the District of Columbia passed in the wake of the Supreme Court's *Heller* decision. The judges upheld "the requirement of mere registration" because that requirement was "longstanding." Judge Douglas Ginsburg asserted, "A regulation that is 'longstanding' . . . has long been accepted by the public" and "is not likely to burden a constitutional right." Applying intermediate scrutiny, Ginsburg then sustained the ban on semi-automatic rifles and similar weapons. That ban, he asserted, serves "important interests in protecting police officers and controlling crime" and does not "prevent a person from keeping a suitable and commonly used weapon in the home or for hunting."[53] A federal district court in Maryland was more solicitous of gun rights when declaring unconstitutional a state law requiring persons to demonstrate "good and substantial reason" to receive a permit to carry a handgun. Judge Legg's opinion in *Wollard v. Sheridan* (2012), after declaring that intermediate scrutiny was an appropriate standard of review, asserted, "Maryland's goal of 'minimizing the proliferation of handguns among those who do not have a demonstrated need for them,' is not a permissible method of preventing crime or ensuring public safety; it burdens the right too broadly."[54]

District of Columbia v. Heller, 554 U.S. 570 (2008)

Dick Heller, a special police officer in Washington, DC, applied for a license to keep a handgun in his home. The District of Columbia at the time banned all handguns but permitted

51. See H. Richard Uviller and William G. Merkel, *The Militia and the Right to Bear Arms, or, How the Second Amendment Fell Silent* (Durham, NC: Duke University Press, 2002).

52. See Eugene Volokh, "The Commonplace Second Amendment," *New York University Law Review* 73 (1998): 793–821; Randy E. Barnett and Don B. Kates, "Under Fire: The New Consensus on the Second Amendment," *Emory Law Journal* 45 (1996): 1139–1260.

53. *Heller v. District of Columbia*, 670 F.3d 1244 (C.A. D.C. 2011).

54. *Woollard v. Sheridan*, 2012 U.S. Dist. LEXIS 28498, *33 (D. Md. 2012).

the chief of police to issue individuals a license for one year. When Heller was denied a permit he and several other citizens of the District challenged the constitutionality of the prohibition in federal court. The local district court dismissed their appeal, but that dismissal was reversed by the Court of Appeals for the District of Columbia. The appellate court decision found that Heller had an individual right to carry a gun for self-defense and that the total ban on handguns violated the Second Amendment. The District of Columbia appealed to the Supreme Court of the United States.

The Supreme Court by a 5–4 vote affirmed the Court of Appeals' decision that Heller had a Second Amendment right to have a handgun in his home. Justice Scalia's majority opinion maintained that both the text and the history of the Second Amendment support an individual right to bear arms. Both Justice Scalia and Justice Stevens relied heavily on the original meaning of constitutional provisions. Are they the same kind of originalists who simply interpret the same materials differently, or are they different kinds of originalists who place different emphasis on different materials? To what extent do you believe that historical materials, rather than policy preferences, drove each analysis? Consider also the implications of Heller. *What gun regulations would you predict would be unconstitutional after* Heller? *To what extent are you basing those predictions on your beliefs about judicial policy preferences or the language in the judicial opinions?*

JUSTICE SCALIA delivered the opinion of the Court.

. . .

The Second Amendment is naturally divided into two parts: its prefatory clause and its operative clause. The former does not limit the latter grammatically, but rather announces a purpose. The Amendment could be rephrased, "Because a well regulated Militia is necessary to the security of a free State, the right of the people to keep and bear Arms shall not be infringed." . . .

Logic demands that there be a link between the stated purpose and the command. . . . But apart from [a] clarifying function, a prefatory clause does not limit or expand the scope of the operative clause. . . .

. . .

The first salient feature of the operative clause is that it codifies a "right of the people." The unamended Constitution and the Bill of Rights use the phrase "right of the people" two other times, in the First Amendment's Assembly-and-Petition Clause and in the Fourth Amendment's Search-and-Seizure Clause. The Ninth Amendment uses very similar terminology ("The enumeration in the Constitution, of certain rights, shall not be construed to deny or disparage others retained by the people"). All three of these instances unambiguously refer to individual rights, not "collective" rights, or rights that may be exercised only through participation in some corporate body.

. . .

This contrasts markedly with the phrase "the militia" in the prefatory clause. As we will describe below, the "militia" in colonial America consisted of a subset of "the people"—those who were male, able bodied, and within a certain age range. Reading the Second Amendment as protecting only the right to "keep and bear Arms" in an organized militia therefore fits poorly with the operative clause's description of the holder of that right as "the people."

. . .

At the time of the founding, as now, to "bear" meant to "carry." . . . When used with "arms," however, the term has a meaning that refers to carrying for a particular purpose—confrontation. . . . Although the phrase implies that the carrying of the weapon is for the purpose of "offensive or defensive action," it in no way connotes participation in a structured military organization.

From our review of founding-era sources, we conclude that this natural meaning was also the meaning that "bear arms" had in the 18th century. In numerous instances, "bear arms" was unambiguously used to refer to the carrying of weapons outside of an organized militia. The most prominent examples are those most relevant to the Second Amendment: Nine state constitutional provisions written in the 18th century or the first two decades of the 19th, which enshrined a right of citizens to "bear arms in defense of themselves and the state" or "bear arms in defense of himself and the state." It is clear from those formulations that "bear arms" did not refer only to carrying a weapon in an organized military unit. . . .

. . .

Putting all of these textual elements together, we find that they guarantee the individual right to possess and carry weapons in case of confrontation.

. . .

It is therefore entirely sensible that the Second Amendment's prefatory clause announces the purpose for which the right was codified: to prevent elimination of the militia. The prefatory clause does not suggest that preserving the militia was the only reason Americans valued the ancient right; most undoubtedly thought it even more important for self-defense and hunting. But the threat that the new Federal Government would destroy the citizens' militia by taking away their arms was the reason that right—unlike some other English rights—was codified in a written Constitution. . . .

. . .

Our interpretation is confirmed by analogous arms-bearing rights in state constitutions that preceded and immediately followed adoption of the Second Amendment. Four States adopted analogues to the Federal Second Amendment in the period between independence and the ratification of the Bill of Rights. Two of them—Pennsylvania and Vermont—clearly adopted individual rights unconnected to militia service. Pennsylvania's Declaration of Rights of 1776 said: "That the people have a right to bear arms *for the defence of themselves*, and the state. . . . " . . . In 1777, Vermont adopted the identical provision, except for inconsequential differences in punctuation and capitalization. . . .

. . .

That . . . of the nine state constitutional protections for the right to bear arms enacted immediately after 1789 at least seven unequivocally protected an individual citizen's right to self-defense is strong evidence that that is how the founding generation conceived of the right. . . .

. . .

. . . [V]irtually all interpreters of the Second Amendment in the century after its enactment interpreted the amendment as we do.

. . .

St. George Tucker's version of *Blackstone's Commentaries* . . . conceived of the Blackstonian arms right as necessary for self-defense. . . . Tucker elaborated on the Second Amendment: "This may be considered as the true palladium of liberty. . . . The right to self-defence is the first law of nature: in most governments it has been the study of rulers to confine the right within the narrowest limits possible. Wherever standing armies are kept up, and the right of the people to keep and bear arms is, under any colour or pretext whatsoever, prohibited, liberty, if not already annihilated, is on the brink of destruction." . . . He believed that the English game laws had abridged the right by prohibiting "keeping a gun or other engine for the destruction of game."

. . .

Antislavery advocates routinely invoked the right to bear arms for self-defense. Joel Tiffany, for example, citing Blackstone's description of the right, wrote that "the right to keep and bear arms, also implies the right to use them if necessary in self defence; without this right to use the guaranty would have hardly been worth the paper it consumed." . . .

. . .

Like most rights, the right secured by the Second Amendment is not unlimited. From Blackstone through the 19th-century cases, commentators and courts routinely explained that the right was not a right to keep and carry any weapon whatsoever in any manner whatsoever and for whatever purpose. . . . For example, the majority of the 19th-century courts to consider the question held that prohibitions on carrying concealed weapons were lawful under the Second Amendment or state analogues. . . . [N]othing in our opinion should be taken to cast doubt on longstanding prohibitions on the possession of firearms by felons and the mentally ill, or laws forbidding the carrying of firearms in sensitive places such as schools and government buildings, or laws imposing conditions and qualifications on the commercial sale of arms.

. . .

. . . [T]he inherent right of self-defense has been central to the Second Amendment right. The handgun ban amounts to a prohibition of an entire class of "arms" that is overwhelmingly chosen by American society for that lawful purpose. The prohibition extends, moreover, to the home, where the need for defense of self, family, and property is most acute. Under any of the standards of scrutiny that we have applied to enumerated constitutional rights, banning from the home "the most preferred firearm in the nation to 'keep' and use for protection of one's home and family," . . . would fail constitutional muster.

. . .

We know of no other enumerated constitutional right whose core protection has been subjected to a freestanding "interest-balancing" approach. The very enumeration of the right takes out of the hands of government—even the Third Branch of Government—the power to decide on a case-by-case basis whether the right is *really worth* insisting upon. A constitutional guarantee subject to future judges' assessments of its usefulness is no constitutional guarantee at all. Constitutional rights are enshrined with the scope they were understood to have when the people adopted them, whether or not future legislatures or (yes) even future judges think that scope too broad. . . .

In sum, we hold that the District's ban on handgun possession in the home violates the Second Amendment, as does its prohibition against rendering any lawful firearm in the home operable for the purpose of immediate self-defense. Assuming that Heller is not disqualified from the exercise of Second Amendment rights, the District must permit him to register his handgun and must issue him a license to carry it in the home.

. . .

JUSTICE STEVENS, with whom JUSTICE SOUTER, JUSTICE GINSBURG, and JUSTICE BREYER join, dissenting.

. . .

The Second Amendment was adopted to protect the right of the people of each of the several States to maintain a well-regulated militia. It was a response to concerns raised during the ratification of the Constitution that the power of Congress to disarm the state militias and create a national standing army posed an intolerable threat to the sovereignty of the several States. Neither the text of the Amendment nor the arguments advanced by its proponents evidenced the slightest interest in limiting any legislature's authority to regulate private civilian uses of firearms. Specifically, there is no indication that the Framers of the Amendment intended to enshrine the common-law right of self-defense in the Constitution.

. . .

The preamble to the Second Amendment makes three important points. It identifies the preservation of the militia as the Amendment's purpose; it explains that the militia is necessary to the security of a free State; and it recognizes that the militia must be "well regulated." In all three respects it is comparable to provisions in several State Declarations of Rights that were adopted roughly contemporaneously with the Declaration of Independence. Those state provisions highlight the importance members of the founding generation attached to the maintenance of state militias; they also underscore the profound fear shared by many in that era of the dangers posed by standing armies. While the need for state militias has not been a matter of significant public interest for almost two centuries, that fact should not obscure the contemporary concerns that animated the Framers.

. . .

The parallels between the Second Amendment and these state declarations, and the Second Amendment's omission of any statement of purpose related to the right to use firearms for hunting or personal self-defense, is especially striking in light of the fact that the Declarations of Rights of Pennsylvania and Vermont *did* expressly protect such civilian uses at the time. . . . The contrast between those two declarations and the Second Amendment reinforces the clear statement of purpose announced in the Amendment's preamble. It confirms that the Framers' single-minded focus in crafting the constitutional guarantee "to keep and bear arms" was on military uses of firearms, which they viewed in the context of service in state militias.

. . .

The Court . . . overlooks the significance of the way the Framers used the phrase "the people." . . . In the First Amendment, no words define the class of individuals entitled to speak, to publish, or to worship; in that Amendment it is only the right peaceably to assemble, and to petition the Government for a redress of grievances, that is described as a right of "the people." These rights contemplate collective action. . . . Likewise, although the act of petitioning the Government is a right that can be exercised by individuals, it is primarily collective in nature. For if they are to be effective, petitions must involve groups of individuals acting in concert.

Similarly, the words "the people" in the Second Amendment refer back to the object announced in the Amendment's preamble. They remind us that it is the collective action of individuals having a duty to serve in the militia that the text directly protects and, perhaps more importantly, that the ultimate purpose of the Amendment was to protect the States' share of the divided sovereignty created by the Constitution.

. . .

The term "bear arms" is a familiar idiom; when used unadorned by any additional words, its meaning is "to serve as a soldier, do military service, fight." . . . Had the Framers wished to expand the meaning of the phrase "bear arms" to encompass civilian possession and use, they could have done so by the addition of phrases such as "for the defense of themselves," as was done in the Pennsylvania and Vermont Declarations of Rights. The *unmodified* use of "bear arms," by contrast, refers most naturally to a military purpose, as evidenced by its use in literally dozens of contemporary texts. The absence of any reference to civilian uses of weapons tailors the text of the Amendment to the purpose identified in its preamble.

. . .

Until today, it has been understood that legislatures may regulate the civilian use and misuse of firearms so long as they do not interfere with the preservation of a well-regulated militia. The Court's announcement of a new constitutional right to own and use firearms for private purposes upsets that settled understanding, but leaves for future cases the formidable task of defining the scope of permissible regulations. Today judicial craftsmen have confidently asserted that a policy choice that denies a "law-abiding, responsible citize[n]" the right to keep and use weapons in the home for self-defense is "off the table." . . . Given the presumption that most citizens are law abiding, and the reality that the need to defend oneself may suddenly arise in a host of locations outside the home, I fear that the District's policy choice may well be just the first of an unknown number of dominoes to be knocked off the table.

. . .

JUSTICE BREYER, with whom JUSTICE STEVENS, JUSTICE SOUTER, and JUSTICE GINSBURG join, dissenting.

. . .

. . . [T]he protection the Amendment provides is not absolute. The Amendment permits government to regulate the interests that it serves. Thus, irrespective of what those interests are—whether they do or do not include an independent interest in self-defense—the majority's view cannot be correct unless it can show that the District's regulation is unreasonable or inappropriate in Second Amendment terms. This the majority cannot do.

. . .

. . . [A] legislature could reasonably conclude that the law will advance goals of great public importance, namely, saving lives, preventing injury, and reducing crime. The law is tailored to the urban crime problem in that it is local in scope and thus affects only a geographic area both limited in size and entirely urban; the law concerns handguns, which are specially linked to urban gun deaths and injuries, and which are the overwhelmingly favorite weapon of armed criminals; and at the same time, the law imposes a burden upon gun owners that seems proportionately no greater than restrictions in existence at the time the Second Amendment was adopted. In these circumstances, the District's law falls within the zone that the Second Amendment leaves open to regulation by legislatures.

. . .

. . . The majority is wrong when it says that the District's law is unconstitutional "[u]nder any of the standards of scrutiny that we have applied to enumerated constitutional rights." . . . How could that be? It certainly would not be unconstitutional under, for example, a "rational basis" standard, which requires a court to uphold regulation so long as it bears a "rational relationship" to a "legitimate governmental purpose."

. . .

I would simply adopt an interest-balancing inquiry explicitly. The fact that important interests lie on both sides of the constitutional equation suggests that review of gun-control regulation is not a context in which a court should effectively presume either constitutionality (as in rational-basis review) or unconstitutionality (as in strict scrutiny). Rather, "where a law significantly implicates competing constitutionally protected interests in complex ways," the Court generally asks whether the statute burdens a protected interest in a way or to an extent that is out of proportion to the statute's salutary effects upon other important governmental interests. . . . Any answer would take account both of the statute's effects upon the competing interests and the existence of any clearly superior less restrictive alternative. . . .

In applying this kind of standard the Court normally defers to a legislature's empirical judgment in matters where a legislature is likely to have greater expertise and greater institutional factfinding capacity. . . .

. . .

No one doubts the constitutional importance of the statute's basic objective, saving lives. . . .

[*Justice Breyer then discussed the evidence on which the District relied when imposing the handgun ban and the evidence indicating whether such bans are effective in practice. On the basis of this evidence, he concluded the following.*]

. . .

The upshot is a set of studies and counterstudies that, at most, could leave a judge uncertain about the proper policy conclusion. But from respondent's perspective any such uncertainty is not good enough. That is because legislators, not judges, have primary responsibility for drawing policy conclusions from empirical fact. And, given that constitutional allocation of decisionmaking responsibility, the empirical evidence presented here is sufficient to allow a judge to reach a firm *legal* conclusion.

. . .

In weighing needs and burdens, we must take account of the possibility that there are reasonable, but less restrictive alternatives. . . . Here I see none.

The reason there is no clearly superior, less restrictive alternative to the District's handgun ban is that the ban's very objective is to reduce significantly the number of handguns in the District, say, for example, by allowing a law enforcement officer immediately to assume that *any* handgun he sees is an *illegal* handgun. And there is no plausible way to achieve that objective other than to ban the guns.

. . .

. . . [A]ny measure less restrictive in respect to the use of handguns for self-defense will, to that same extent, prove less effective in preventing the use of handguns for illicit purposes. If a resident has a handgun in the home that he can use for self-defense, then he has a handgun in the home that he can use to commit suicide or engage in acts of domestic violence. . . . If it is indeed the case, as the District believes, that the number of guns contributes to the number of gun-related crimes, accidents, and deaths, then, although there may be less restrictive, *less effective* substitutes for an outright ban, there is no less restrictive *equivalent* of an outright ban.

. . .

. . . [T]he District law is tailored to the life-threatening problems it attempts to address. The law concerns one class of weapons, handguns, leaving residents free to possess shotguns and rifles, along with ammunition. The area that falls within its scope is totally urban. . . . That urban area suffers from a serious handgun-fatality problem. The District's law directly aims at that compelling problem. And there is no less restrictive way to achieve the problem-related benefits that it seeks.

. . .

. . . [T]he majority's decision threatens severely to limit the ability of more knowledgeable, democratically elected officials to deal with gun-related problems. The majority says that it leaves the District "a variety of tools for combating" such problems. It fails to list even one seemingly adequate replacement for the law it strikes down. I can understand how reasonable individuals can disagree about the merits of strict gun control as a crime-control measure, even in a totally urbanized area. But I cannot understand how one can take from the elected branches of government the right to decide whether to insist upon a handgun-free urban populace in a city now facing a serious crime problem and which, in the future, could well face environmental or other emergencies that threaten the breakdown of law and order. . . .

D. Personal Freedom and Public Morality

The main front of the constitutional culture wars began to change at the turn of the twenty-first century. The constitutional politics and law of abortion were relatively static from *Planned Parenthood v. Casey* (1992) to the 2010 midterm elections. Public attention turned to gay rights—in particular, federal and state constitutional protections for same-sex marriage. Important skirmishes are also currently taking place over the constitutional right to die. After the 2010 election, however, many state legislatures made renewed attempts to ban most if not all abortions. During the 2012 Republican primary prominent conservatives even challenged the constitutional right to birth control many thought was firmly established by *Griswold v. Connecticut* (1965) and *Eisenstadt v. Baird* (1972).

Until recently fundamental rights analysis seemed entrenched in contemporary American constitutionalism. Constitutional debates were more often over the precise contours of rights to reproductive choice, same-sex intimacy, and a dignified death. Neither political liberals nor political conservatives gained the political power necessary to fashion a firm majority in both electoral institutions and the judiciary in favor of either a robust set of rights or the abandonment of modern protections for certain individual choices. Whether more recent attacks on abortion and birth control are largely symbolic gestures or the beginning of a new round in the culture wars will only become clear after the completion of a few more election cycles.

The abortion wars cooled during the late 1990s and the first decade of the twenty-first century. Neither liberal Democrats nor conservative Republicans have had the opportunity in the past twenty years to appoint a justice who would either cast a fifth vote for striking down most restrictions on abortion or overrule *Roe v. Wade* (1973). The rule of *Planned Parenthood v. Casey* (1992) that abortion be legal and, if states wish, heavily regulated seems likely to endure for the foreseeable future. Public opinion polls suggest that most Americans prefer the present middle-ground position of the Supreme Court to either the strongly pro-choice Democratic Party platform or the strongly pro-life Republican platform.

The most important constitutional struggle over reproductive choice during most of the Contemporary Era has been over partial-birth abortions. Consistent with the general pro-choice commitment of most Democrats, President Clinton opposed legislation that did not contain what he believed was the constitutionally mandated health exception. President Bush reversed this practice upon taking office. When signing the Partial Birth Act of 2003, he declared, "The bill I am about to sign protecting innocent new life from this practice reflects the compassion and humanity of America."

The Supreme Court also reversed course on the constitutionality of laws banning partial-birth abortions. In *Sternberg v. Carhart* (2000) the Supreme Court declared a state ban on partial-birth abortion unconstitutional. Quoting *Casey*, Justice Breyer's majority opinion declared, "First, the law lacks any exception 'for the preservation of the . . . health of the mother.' Second, it 'imposes an undue burden on a woman's ability' to choose a D & E [dilation and evacuation] abortion, thereby unduly burdening the right to choose abortion itself." In *Gonzales v. Carhart* (2007) the Supreme Court sustained a nearly identical federal ban. Justice Kennedy's majority opinion asserted, "A premise central to [*Casey*'s] conclusion—that the government has a legitimate and substantial interest in preserving and promoting fetal life—would be repudiated" should the justices strike down bans on partial-birth abortion. The major difference between the two cases was that Justice O'Connor, who cast the fifth vote in *Sternberg*, had retired and been replaced by the more pro-life Chief Justice Roberts.

The 2010 midterm elections, which resulted in substantial gains for Republicans in Congress and state legislatures, has revived, at least temporarily, the abortion wars. Popular pro-life proposals include laws requiring women to have ultrasounds before being allowed to have an abortion, sharp limits on insurance coverage for abortion, further restrictions on abortion clinics, and bans on abortion after twenty weeks. Texas in 2011 passed a law requiring that before performing an abortion a physician inform the pregnant women of "the possibility of increased risk of breast cancer following an induced abortion"[55]; perform a sonogram; and, unless the women declares she is uninterested, provide her with "a verbal explanation of the results of the sonogram images" as well as "make . . . audible the heart auscultation for the pregnant women to hear." The Court of Appeals for the Fifth Circuit sustained that law in *Texas Medical Providers Performing Abortion Services v. Lakey* (2012). Judge Jones stated, "The required disclosures of a sonogram, the fetal heartbeat, and their medical descriptions are the epitome of truthful, non-misleading information. They are not different in kind, although more graphic and scientifically up-to-date, than the disclosures discussed in *Casey*—probable gestational age of the fetus and printed material showing a baby's general prenatal development stages."[56] Not all justices have reached the same conclusion. A local court in Oklahoma struck down a state law requiring women seeking abortions to be exposed to a sonogram of their fetus before the doctor could perform the procedure. Judge Bryan Dixon asserted that the Oklahoma measure was an "unconstitutional special law" that "improperly is addressed only to patients, physicians and sonographers concerning abortions and does not address all patients, physicians and sonographers concerning other medical care where a general law could clearly be made applicable."[57] In the summer of 2012 a Mississippi judge issued an injunction prohibiting state officials from enforcing a law that required all persons performing abortions to have admitting privileges at the local hospital. "The threatened injury," a state judge noted, "the closure of the state's only clinic, create[s] a substantial obstacle to the right to choose." Governor Phil Bryant, when signing that bill, had declared that the legislation was designed to make Mississippi "abortion-free."[58]

---

55. The National Cancer Institute at the National Institutes of Health reports that the most recent studies "consistently show . . . no association between induced and spontaneous abortions and breast cancer risk." National Cancer Institute, "Abortion, Miscarriage, and Breast Cancer Risk," http://www.cancer.gov/cancer-topics/factsheet/Risk/abortion-miscarriage.

56. *Texas Medical Providers Performing Abortion Services v. Lakey*, 667 F.3d 570 (5th Cir. 2012).

57. *Nova Health Sys. v. Pruitt*, No. CV-2010–533 (Okla. Dist. Ct. 2012).

58. *Jackson Women's Health Org. v. Currier*, No. 3:12cv436-DPJ-FKB, 2012 U.S. Dist. LEXIS 97272 (S.D. Miss. 2012); Phil Bryant, "State of the State" speech, Jackson, Mississippi, January 24, 2012, http://www.governorbryant.com/governor-phil-bryant-gives-his-first-state-of-the-state-address/.

Illustration 11-5 Massachusetts Chief Justice Margaret Marshall
Source: AP Photo/George Rizer, Pool.

Abortion rights dominated debates about personal freedom and public morality for many decades, but since 2000 the rights of gays, lesbians, and same-sex couples have become the main front in contemporary constitutional culture wars. The Supreme Court intensified constitutional struggles when in *Lawrence v. Texas* (2003) the justices ruled that consenting adults had the right to engage in homosexual (and heterosexual) sodomy. Gay rights activists almost immediately saw *Lawrence* as a precedential vehicle for a constitutional right to same-sex marriage. Opponents of gay rights immediately mobilized to place constitutional and statutory barriers in the way of same-sex marriage.

Recently proponents of same-sex marriage appear to have accelerated momentum. Polls suggest that a slim majority of Americans believe that government officials should permit same-sex couples to marry. Increasing numbers of states have decided to legalize same-sex marriage. In 2003, the same year that *Lawrence* was decided by the U.S. Supreme Court, the Supreme Judicial Court of Massachusetts in *Goodridge v. Department of Public Health* decided by a 4–3 vote that the state's ban on same-sex marriage did not even satisfy a rational basis test. Chief Justice Margaret Marshall noted that procreation was not a precondition for eligibility to marry and concluded that there was no other rational justification for preventing a person from choosing a same-sex marriage partner.[59]

In May 2012 President Obama on ABC News declared that he personally favored extending marriage rights to same-sex couples.[60] The Democratic Party platform in 2012 followed Obama's lead, "support[ing] marriage equality" and calling for the "full repeal of the so-called Defense of Marriage Act." Red America did not react passively to these developments. Most states still refuse to recognize same-sex marriage. On May 8, 2012, North Carolina became the thirtieth state to pass a constitutional amendment limiting marriage

59. *Goodrich v. Department of Public Health*, 440 Mass. 309 (2003).
60. "Transcript: Robin Roberts ABC News Interview with President Obama," May 9, 2012, http://abcnews.go.com/Politics/transcript-robin-roberts-abc-news-interview-president-obama/story?id=16316043#.UBQoOEQ1bgE.

to a man and a woman. A small majority of the state courts that have considered the issue have ruled that neither the federal nor the state constitution give same-sex couples the right to marry. The Republican Party in 2012 called for "a [federal] Constitutional amendment defining marriage as the union of one man and one woman" and described same-sex marriage as "an assault on the foundations of our society, challenging the institution which, for thousands of years . . . has been entrusted with the rearing of children and transmission of cultural values."

The Supreme Court caught up with these developments in *U.S. v. Windsor* (2013). By a vote of 5–4 the justices ruled that Section 3 of the Defense of Marriage Act, which limited the definition of marriage in federal law to "a legal union between one man and one woman as husband and wife," was an illegitimate means of demeaning same-sex couples. After noting that the state of New York in this case had extended marital status to same-sex couples, Justice Kennedy's majority opinion declared that "DOMA seeks to injure the very class New York seeks to protect," and by doing so "it violates basic due process and equal protection principles applicable to the Federal Government. . . . The federal statute is invalid, for no legitimate purpose overcomes the purpose and effect to disparage and to injure those whom the State, by its marriage laws, sought to protect in personhood and dignity." Writing in dissent Justice Scalia argued that "the Constitution neither requires nor forbids our society to approve of same-sex marriage, much as it neither requires nor forbids us to approve of no-fault divorce, polygamy, or the consumption of alcohol." The Court limited its holding to the question of whether the federal government could disapprove of one definition of marriage that some states were embracing, stopping short of declaring that same-sex couples had a constitutional right to marry. This left in place, for the time being, the evolving patchwork of state policies.

The cause of gay rights has advanced over the past twenty years, but the constitutional politics responsible for that advance remain controversial. Many commentators believe that the courts have played a vital role in promoting rights to same-sex intimacy. Dan Pinello asserts that such cases as *Goodridge v. Board of Health* (MA 2004) "brought about enormous social change. . . . With nearly all other state and national policy makers at odds with its goal, the Massachusetts [high court] nonetheless achieved singular success in expanding the ambit of who receives the benefits of getting married in America, in inspiring political elites elsewhere in the country to follow suit, and in mobilizing grass-roots supporters to entrench their legal victory politically."[61] Other commentators insist that judicial victories are responsible for the conservative countermobilization and backlash that has had more costs than benefits for proponents of same-sex intimacy. "The most significant short-term consequence of *Goodridge*," Michael Klarman wrote, "may have been the political backlash that it inspired. By outpacing public opinion on issues of social reform, such rulings mobilize opponents, undercut moderates, and retard the cause they purport to advance."[62]

Lawrence v. Texas, 539 U.S. 558 (2003)

Houston police entered John Lawrence's apartment in response to a complaint about gunfire. While in the apartment one police officer reported seeing Lawrence and Tyron Garner engaging in anal sex, a second reported seeing them engaging in oral sex, and the other two officers did not report seeing the pair engaging in any sexual activity. A leading scholarly account maintains that Lawrence and Garner were clothed and in separate rooms when the police entered Lawrence's apartment.[63] *Whatever the actual facts, both men were arrested, convicted, and fined $200 under a Texas law that prohibited persons from "engag[ing] in deviate sexual intercourse with another individual of the same sex." After the Texas appellate courts denied their appeals, Lawrence and Garner appealed to the Supreme Court of the United States.*

The Supreme Court by a 6–3 vote declared the Texas law unconstitutional. Justice Kennedy's opinion held that states could not criminalize intimate relationships between consenting adults. What is the source of this constitutional

61. Daniel Pinello, *America's Struggle for Same-Sex Marriage* (New York: Cambridge University Press, 2006), 192–93. See also Thomas M. Keck, "Beyond Backlash: Assessing the Impact of Judicial Decisions on LGBT Rights," *Law and Society Review* 43 (2009): 151–186.

62. Michael Klarman, "*Brown* and *Lawrence* (and *Goodridge*)," *Michigan Law Review* 104 (2005): 482. See also Gerald N. Rosenberg, *The Hollow Hope: Can Courts Bring About Social Change?*, rev. ed. (Chicago: University of Chicago Press, 2008).

63. Dale Carpenter, *Flagrant Conduct: The Story of* Lawrence v. Texas (New York: Norton, 2012).

right? What is the scope of this constitutional right? Does Lawrence *commit the Court to recognizing same-sex marriages? What is the difference between the Kennedy opinion and the O'Connor concurrence? The* Lawrence *decision did not inspire nearly the backlash that occurred after* Roe v. Wade *(1973). Why might that have been the case?* Lawrence *overruled* Bowers v. Hardwick *(1986). Why did Justice Kennedy think overruling appropriate in this case, but not in* Planned Parenthood v. Casey *(1993)? Is there a principled difference between the two cases?*

JUSTICE KENNEDY delivered the opinion of the Court.

. . .

Liberty protects the person from unwarranted government intrusions into a dwelling or other private places. In our tradition the State is not omnipresent in the home. And there are other spheres of our lives and existence, outside the home, where the State should not be a dominant presence. Freedom extends beyond spatial bounds. Liberty presumes an autonomy of self that includes freedom of thought, belief, expression, and certain intimate conduct. The instant case involves liberty of the person both in its spatial and in its more transcendent dimensions.

. . .

The Court began its substantive discussion in *Bowers v. Hardwick* (1986) as follows: "The issue presented is whether the Federal Constitution confers a fundamental right upon homosexuals to engage in sodomy and hence invalidates the laws of the many States that still make such conduct illegal and have done so for a very long time." . . . That statement, we now conclude, discloses the Court's own failure to appreciate the extent of the liberty at stake. To say that the issue in *Bowers* was simply the right to engage in certain sexual conduct demeans the claim the individual put forward, just as it would demean a married couple were it to be said marriage is simply about the right to have sexual intercourse. The laws involved in *Bowers* and here are, to be sure, statutes that purport to do no more than prohibit a particular sexual act. Their penalties and purposes, though, have more far-reaching consequences, touching upon the most private human conduct, sexual behavior, and in the most private of places, the home. The statutes do seek to control a personal relationship that, whether or not entitled to formal recognition in the law, is within the liberty of persons to choose without being punished as criminals.

This, as a general rule, should counsel against attempts by the State, or a court, to define the meaning of the relationship or to set its boundaries absent injury to a person or abuse of an institution the law protects. It suffices for us to acknowledge that adults may choose to enter upon this relationship in the confines of their homes and their own private lives and still retain their dignity as free persons. When sexuality finds overt expression in intimate conduct with another person, the conduct can be but one element in a personal bond that is more enduring. The liberty protected by the Constitution allows homosexual persons the right to make this choice.

. . .

. . . [F]ar from possessing "ancient roots," . . . American laws targeting same-sex couples did not develop until the last third of the 20th century. . . .

It was not until the 1970's that any State singled out same-sex relations for criminal prosecution, and only nine States have done so. . . . Post-*Bowers* even some of these States did not adhere to the policy of suppressing homosexual conduct. Over the course of the last decades, States with same-sex prohibitions have moved toward abolishing them. . . . In summary, the historical grounds relied upon in *Bowers* are more complex than the majority opinion and the concurring opinion by Chief Justice Burger indicate. Their historical premises are not without doubt and, at the very least, are overstated.

. . .

. . . [W]e think that our laws and traditions in the past half century are of most relevance here. These references show an emerging awareness that liberty gives substantial protection to adult persons in deciding how to conduct their private lives in matters pertaining to sex. . . .

. . .

. . . [A]lmost five years before *Bowers* was decided the European Court of Human Rights considered a case with parallels to *Bowers* and to today's case. An adult male resident in Northern Ireland alleged he was a practicing homosexual who desired to engage in consensual homosexual conduct. The laws of Northern Ireland forbade him that right. He alleged that he had been questioned, his home had been searched, and he feared criminal prosecution. The court held that the laws proscribing the conduct were invalid under the European Convention on Human Rights. . . . Authoritative in all countries that are members of the Council of Europe . . . the decision is at odds with the premise in *Bowers* that the claim put forward was insubstantial in our Western civilization.

In our own constitutional system the deficiencies in *Bowers* became even more apparent in the years following its announcement. The 25 States with laws prohibiting the relevant conduct referenced in the *Bowers* decision are reduced now to 13, of which 4 enforce their laws only against homosexual conduct. In those States where sodomy is still proscribed, whether for same-sex or heterosexual conduct, there is a pattern of nonenforcement with respect to consenting adults acting in private. The State of Texas admitted in 1994 that as of that date it had not prosecuted anyone under those circumstances.

Two principal cases decided after *Bowers* cast its holding into even more doubt. In *Planned Parenthood of Southeastern Pa. v. Casey* (1992), the Court . . . confirmed that our laws and tradition afford constitutional protection to personal decisions relating to marriage, procreation, contraception, family relationships, child rearing, and education. . . . The second post-*Bowers* case of principal relevance is *Romer v. Evans* (1996). There the Court struck down class-based legislation directed at homosexuals as a violation of the Equal Protection Clause. . . .

. . .

When homosexual conduct is made criminal by the law of the State, that declaration in and of itself is an invitation to subject homosexual persons to discrimination both in the public and in the private spheres. The central holding of *Bowers* has been brought in question by [*Romer*], and it should be addressed. Its continuance as precedent demeans the lives of homosexual persons.

. . .

To the extent *Bowers* relied on values we share with a wider civilization, it should be noted that the reasoning and holding in *Bowers* have been rejected elsewhere. The European Court of Human Rights has followed not *Bowers* but its own decision in *Dudgeon v. United Kingdom* (1981). . . . The right the petitioners seek in this case has been accepted as an integral part of human freedom in many other countries. There has been no showing that in this country the governmental interest in circumscribing personal choice is somehow more legitimate or urgent.

The doctrine of *stare decisis* is essential to the respect accorded to the judgments of the Court and to the stability of the law. It is not, however, an inexorable command. . . . The holding in *Bowers* . . . has not induced detrimental reliance comparable to some instances where recognized individual rights are involved.

. . .

Bowers was not correct when it was decided, and it is not correct today. It ought not to remain binding precedent. *Bowers v. Hardwick* should be and now is overruled.

The present case does not involve minors. It does not involve persons who might be injured or coerced or who are situated in relationships where consent might not easily be refused. It does not involve public conduct or prostitution. It does not involve whether the government must give formal recognition to any relationship that homosexual persons seek to enter. The case does involve two adults who, with full and mutual consent from each other, engaged in sexual practices common to a homosexual lifestyle. The petitioners are entitled to respect for their private lives. The State cannot demean their existence or control their destiny by making their private sexual conduct a crime. Their right to liberty under the Due Process Clause gives them the full right to engage in their conduct without intervention of the government. . . . The Texas statute furthers no legitimate state interest which can justify its intrusion into the personal and private life of the individual.

. . .

JUSTICE O'CONNOR, concurring in the judgment.

The Court today overrules *Bowers v. Hardwick* (1986). I joined *Bowers*, and do not join the Court in overruling it. Nevertheless, I agree with the Court that Texas' statute banning same-sex sodomy is unconstitutional. . . . Rather than relying on the substantive component of the Fourteenth Amendment's Due Process Clause, as the Court does, I base my conclusion on the Fourteenth Amendment's Equal Protection Clause.

. . .

This case raises a different issue than *Bowers*: whether, under the Equal Protection Clause, moral disapproval is a legitimate state interest to justify by itself a statute that bans homosexual sodomy, but not heterosexual sodomy. It is not. Moral disapproval of this group, like a bare desire to harm the group, is an interest that is insufficient to satisfy rational basis review under the Equal Protection Clause. . . . Indeed, we have never held that moral disapproval, without any other asserted state interest, is a sufficient rationale under the Equal Protection Clause to justify a law that discriminates among groups of persons.

. . .

Whether a sodomy law that is neutral both in effect and application, . . . would violate the substantive component of the Due Process Clause is an issue that need not be decided today. I am confident, however, that so long as the Equal Protection Clause requires a sodomy law to apply equally to the private consensual conduct of homosexuals and heterosexuals alike, such a law would not long stand in our democratic society. . . .

JUSTICE SCALIA, with whom THE CHIEF JUSTICE and JUSTICE THOMAS join, dissenting.

"Liberty finds no refuge in a jurisprudence of doubt." *Planned Parenthood of Southeastern Pa. v. Casey* . . . (1992). That was the Court's sententious response, barely more than a decade ago, to those seeking to overrule *Roe v. Wade* . . . (1973). The Court's response today, to those who have engaged in a 17-year crusade to overrule *Bowers v. Hardwick* (1986), is very different. The need for stability and certainty presents no barrier.

. . .

It seems to me that the "societal reliance" on the principles confirmed in *Bowers* and discarded today has been overwhelming. Countless judicial decisions and legislative enactments have relied on the ancient proposition that a governing majority's belief that certain sexual behavior is "immoral and unacceptable" constitutes a rational basis for regulation. . . . State laws against bigamy, same-sex marriage, adult incest, prostitution, masturbation, adultery, fornication, bestiality, and obscenity are likewise sustainable only in light of *Bowers'* validation of laws based on moral choices. Every single one of these laws is called into question by today's decision; the Court makes no effort to cabin the scope of its decision to exclude them from its holding. . . .

. . .

The Court today does not . . . describe homosexual sodomy as a "fundamental right" or a "fundamental liberty interest," nor does it subject the Texas statute to strict scrutiny. Instead, having failed to establish that the right to homosexual sodomy is "'deeply rooted in this Nation's history and tradition,'" the Court concludes that the application of Texas's statute to petitioners' conduct fails the rational-basis test, and overrules *Bowers'* holding to the contrary. . . .

It is (as *Bowers* recognized) entirely irrelevant whether the laws in our long national tradition criminalizing homosexual sodomy were "directed at homosexual conduct as a distinct matter." . . . Whether homosexual sodomy was prohibited by a law targeted at same-sex sexual relations or by a more general law prohibiting both homosexual and heterosexual sodomy, the only relevant point is that it *was* criminalized—which suffices to establish that homosexual sodomy is not a right "deeply rooted in our Nation's history and tradition." The Court today agrees that homosexual sodomy was criminalized and thus does not dispute the facts on which *Bowers actually* relied.

. . .

. . . [T]he Court says: "[W]e think that our laws and traditions in the past half century are of most relevance here. These references show *an emerging awareness* that liberty gives substantial protection to adult persons in deciding how to conduct their private lives *in matters pertaining to sex*." . . . Apart from the fact that such an "emerging awareness" does not establish a "fundamental right," the statement is factually false. States continue to prosecute all sorts of crimes by adults "in matters pertaining to sex": prostitution, adult incest, adultery, obscenity, and child pornography. Sodomy laws, too, have been enforced "in the past half century," in which there have been 134 reported cases involving prosecutions for consensual, adult, homosexual sodomy. . . .

In any event, an "emerging awareness" is by definition not "deeply rooted in this Nation's history and tradition[s]," as we have said "fundamental right" status requires. Constitutional entitlements do not spring into existence because some States choose to lessen or eliminate criminal sanctions on certain behavior. Much less do they spring into existence, as the Court seems to believe, because *foreign nations* decriminalize conduct. . . .

. . .

Today's opinion is the product of a Court, which is the product of a law-profession culture, that has largely signed on to the so-called homosexual agenda, by which I mean the agenda promoted by some homosexual activists directed at eliminating the moral opprobrium that has traditionally attached to homosexual conduct. . . .

. . . It is clear . . . that the Court has taken sides in the culture war, departing from its role of assuring, as neutral observer, that the democratic rules of engagement are observed. Many Americans do not want persons who openly engage in homosexual conduct as partners in their business, as scoutmasters for their children, as teachers in their children's schools, or as boarders in their home. They view this as protecting themselves and their families from a lifestyle that they believe to be immoral and destructive. The Court views it as "discrimination" which it is the function of our judgments to deter. So imbued is the Court with the law profession's anti-anti-homosexual culture, that it is seemingly unaware that the attitudes of that culture are not obviously "mainstream"; that in most States what the Court calls "discrimination" against those who engage in homosexual acts is perfectly legal; that proposals to ban such "discrimination" under Title VII have repeatedly been rejected by Congress, . . . that in some cases such "discrimination" is *mandated* by federal statute . . . ; and that in some cases such "discrimination" is a constitutional right, see *Boy Scouts of America v. Dale* . . . (2000).

Let me be clear that I have nothing against homosexuals, or any other group, promoting their agenda through normal democratic means. . . . I would no more *require* a State to criminalize homosexual acts—or, for that matter, display *any* moral disapprobation of them—than I would *forbid* it to do so. What Texas has chosen to do is well within the range of traditional democratic action, and its hand should not be stayed through the invention of a brand-new "constitutional right" by a Court that is impatient of democratic change. . . . [I]t is the premise of our system that those judgments are to be made by the people, and not imposed by a governing caste that knows best.

. . .

JUSTICE THOMAS, dissenting. . . .

The Defense of Marriage Act

The Defense of Marriage Act of 1996 (DOMA) was passed after the Supreme Court of Hawaii in Baehr v. Lewin *(HI 1993) declared unconstitutional a state law limiting marriage to a man and a woman. DOMA declared that no state was required to recognize an out-of-state marriage between two persons of the same sex and stated that federal law would not recognize same-sex marriages. The crucial Section 3 of DOMA declared, "In determining the meaning of any Act of Congress, or of any ruling, regulation, or interpretation of the various administrative bureaus and agencies of the United States, the word 'marriage' means only a legal union between one man and one woman as husband and wife, and the word 'spouse' refers only to a person of the opposite sex who is a husband or a wife."*

We have excerpted the majority and minority congressional reports on DOMA, as well as the Obama administration's claim that Section 3 is unconstitutional. Why did the congressional majority believe DOMA necessary? What reasons did they give for thinking DOMA constitutional? Why did the minority and the Obama administration disagree? Seventeen years after the act was passed the Supreme Court, in U.S. v. Windsor *(2013), declared DOMA unconstitutional by a 5–4 vote.*

House Committee on the Judiciary, Report on the Defense of Marriage Act (1996)[64]

. . . [T]he Defense of Marriage Act, has two primary purposes. The first is to defend the institution of traditional heterosexual marriage. The second is to protect the right of the States to formulate their own public policy regarding the legal recognition of same-sex unions, free from any federal constitutional implications that might attend the recognition by one State of the right for homosexual couples to acquire marriage licenses.

. . .

Simply stated, the gay rights organizations and lawyers driving the Hawaiian lawsuit have made plain that they consider Hawaii to be only the first step in a national effort to win by judicial fiat the right to same-sex "marriage." And the primary mechanism for nationalizing their break-through in Hawaii will be the Full Faith and Credit Clause of the U.S. Constitution.

. . .

The general rule for determining the validity of a marriage is "lex celebrationis," that is, a marriage is valid if it is valid according to the law of the place where it was celebrated. States observing that rule would, of course, presumptively recognize as valid a same-sex "marriage" license from Hawaii. There is, however, an important exception to the general rule. . . .

"A marriage which satisfies the requirements of the state where the marriage was contracted will everywhere be recognized as valid unless it violates the

64. House Committee on the Judiciary, *Report on the Defense of Marriage Act*, 104th Cong., 2nd Sess., 1996, H.R. Rep. 104–664.

strong public policy of another state which had the most significant relationship to the spouses and the marriage at the time of the marriage."

. . .

Because no State in the United States has ever recognized same-sex "marriages," it would seem that courts in other States would be justified in invoking this exception. The matter is somewhat more complicated, however, as the U.S. Constitution speaks to this issue. The first sentence of the Full Faith and Credit Clause provides: "Full Faith and Credit shall be given in each State to the public Acts, Records, and judicial Proceedings of every other State."

Notwithstanding the seemingly mandatory terms of the Full Faith and Credit Clause, the U.S. Supreme Court has recognized a public policy exception that, in certain circumstances, would permit a State to decline to give effect to another State's laws. Indeed, despite the presumption created by lex celebrationis and reinforced by the Full Faith and Credit Clause, the Committee believes that a court conscientiously applying the relevant legal principles would be amply justified in refusing to give effect to a same-sex "marriage" license from another State.

But even as the Committee believes that States currently possess the ability to avoid recognizing a same-sex "marriage" license from another State, it recognizes that that conclusion is far from certain. For example, there is a burgeoning body of legal scholarship—some of it inspired directly by the Hawaiian lawsuit—to the effect that the Full Faith and Credit Clause does mandate extraterritorial recognition of "marriage" licenses given to homosexual couples. . . .

. . .

Recognition of same-sex "marriages" in Hawaii could also have profound implications for federal law as well. The word "marriage" appears in more than 800 sections of federal statutes and regulations, and the word "spouse" appears more than 3,100 times. With very limited exceptions, these terms are not defined in federal law.

. . . [T]o the extent that federal law has simply accepted state law determinations of who is married, a redefinition of marriage in Hawaii to include homosexual couples could make such couples eligible for a whole range of federal rights and benefits. . . .

. . .

We are, each of us, born a man or a woman. The committee needs no testimony from an expert witness to decode this point: Our engendered existence, as men and women, offers the most unmistakable, natural signs of the meaning and purpose of sexuality. And that is the function and purpose of begetting. At its core, it is hard to detach marriage from what may be called the "natural teleology of the body": namely, the inescapable fact that only two people, not three, only a man and a woman, can beget a child.

At bottom, civil society has an interest in maintaining and protecting the institution of heterosexual marriage because it has a deep and abiding interest in encouraging responsible procreation and child-rearing. Simply put, government has an interest in marriage because it has an interest in children.

. . .

Closely related to this interest in protecting traditional marriage is a corresponding interest in promoting heterosexuality. While there is controversy concerning how sexual "orientation" is determined, "there is good reason to think that a very substantial number of people are born with the potential to live either gay or straight lives." . . . "Maintaining a preferred societal status of heterosexual marriage thus will also serve to encourage heterosexuality."

. . .

Dissenting Views on H.R. 3396

. . .

The legal history of the full faith and credit clause which is central to this dispute is a sparse one, and no one can speak with absolute certainly about all aspects of this matter. But one thing is quite clear: whatever powers states have to reject a decision by another state to legalize same sex marriage, and to refuse to recognize such marriages within its own borders, derives directly from the Constitution and nothing Congress can do by statute either adds to or detracts from that power.

. . .

Section three of the bill, ironically for legislation which has been hailed as a defender of states rights, represents for the first time in our history a Congressional effort, if successful, to deny states full discretion over their own marriage laws. Section three of this bill says that no matter what an individual state says, and no matter by what procedure it does it, Congress will refuse to recognize same sex marriages. In debating against an amendment by Congresswoman

Schroeder, one of the Senior Republicans on the Committee said that her amendment would make certain marriages "second class marriages" by denying them federal recognition. This acknowledgment that denying a marriage federal recognition substantially diminishes its legal force applies to this bill. If Hawaii or any other state were to allow people of the same sex who were deeply and emotionally attached to each other to regularize that relationship in a marriage, this bill says that the federal government would refuse to recognize it. Note that this is the case whether such decision is made by a State Supreme Court, a referendum of the state's population, a vote of the state's legislature, or some combination thereof. Thus, the bill is exactly the opposite of a states rights measure: the only real force it will have will be to deny a state and the people of that state the right to make decisions on the question of same sex marriage.

Our final ground for opposing this bill is our vehement disagreement with the notion that same sex marriages are a threat to marriage. By far the weakest part of this bill logically is its title, but its title is not simply accidental, but rather reflects the calculated political judgment that went into introducing this bill at this time, months before a national election, and rushing it through with inadequate analysis of its impact. . . .

The notion that allowing two people who are in love to become legally responsible to and for each other threatens heterosexual marriage is without factual basis. Indeed, when pressed during Subcommittee and Committee debate, majority Members could give no specific content to this assertion. The attraction that a man and a woman feel for each other, which leads them to wish to commit emotionally and legally to each other for life, obviously could not be threatened in any way, shape or form by the love that two other people feel for each other, whether they be people of the same sex or opposite sexes. There are of course problems which men and women who seek to marry, or seek to maintain a marriage, confront in our society. No one anywhere has produced any evidence, or even argued logically, that the existence of same sex couples is one of those difficulties. And to prove that this is simply an effort to capitalize on the public dislike of the notion of same sex marriages, as noted below, when Congresswoman Schroeder attempted to offer amendments that deal more directly with threats to existing heterosexual marriages, the majority unanimously and vehemently objected. . . .

Eric Holder, Letter from the Attorney General to Congress on Litigation Involving the Defense of Marriage Act (February 23, 2011)[65]

Dear Mr. Speaker:

. . .

. . . [T]he President and I have concluded that classifications based on sexual orientation warrant heightened scrutiny and that, as applied to same-sex couples legally married under state law, Section 3 of DOMA is unconstitutional.

The Supreme Court has yet to rule on the appropriate level of scrutiny for classifications based on sexual orientation. It has, however, rendered a number of decisions that set forth the criteria that should inform this and any other judgment as to whether heightened scrutiny applies: (1) whether the group in question has suffered a history of discrimination; (2) whether individuals "exhibit obvious, immutable, or distinguishing characteristics that define them as a discrete group"; (3) whether the group is a minority or is politically powerless; and (4) whether the characteristics distinguishing the group have little relation to legitimate policy objectives or to an individual's "ability to perform or contribute to society."

Each of these factors counsels in favor of being suspicious of classifications based on sexual orientation. First and most importantly, there is, regrettably, a significant history of purposeful discrimination against gay and lesbian people, by governmental as well as private entities, based on prejudice and stereotypes that continue to have ramifications today. . . .

Second, while sexual orientation carries no visible badge, a growing scientific consensus accepts that sexual orientation is a characteristic that is immutable; it is undoubtedly unfair to require sexual orientation to be hidden from view to avoid discrimination. . . .

Third, the adoption of laws like those at issue in *Romer v. Evans* (1996), and *Lawrence* [*v. Texas* (2003)], the longstanding ban on gays and lesbians in the military, and the absence of federal protection for employment discrimination on the basis of sexual orientation show the group to have limited political power and "ability

---

65. Excerpt taken from U.S. Department of Justice, Office of Public Affairs, "Letter from the Attorney General to Congress on Litigation Involving the Defense of Marriage Act," http://www.justice.gov/opa/pr/2011/February/11-ag-223.html.

to attract the [favorable] attention of the lawmakers." And while the enactment of the Matthew Shepard Act and pending repeal of Don't Ask, Don't Tell indicate that the political process is not closed *entirely* to gay and lesbian people, that is not the standard by which the Court has judged "political powerlessness." Indeed, when the Court ruled that gender-based classifications were subject to heightened scrutiny, women already had won major political victories such as the Nineteenth Amendment (right to vote) and protection under Title VII (employment discrimination).

Finally, there is a growing acknowledgment that sexual orientation "bears no relation to ability to perform or contribute to society." Recent evolutions in legislation (including the pending repeal of Don't Ask, Don't Tell), in community practices and attitudes, in case law . . . , and in social science regarding sexual orientation all make clear that sexual orientation is not a characteristic that generally bears on legitimate policy objectives.

. . .

In reviewing a legislative classification under heightened scrutiny, the government must establish that the classification is "substantially related to an important government objective." Under heightened scrutiny, "a tenable justification must describe actual state purposes, not rationalizations for actions in fact differently grounded." "The justification must be genuine, not hypothesized or invented post hoc in response to litigation."

. . . [T]he legislative record underlying DOMA's passage contains discussion and debate that undermines any defense under heightened scrutiny. The record contains numerous expressions reflecting moral disapproval of gays and lesbians and their intimate and family relationships—precisely the kind of stereotype-based thinking and animus the Equal Protection Clause is designed to guard against.

After careful consideration, including a review of my recommendation, the President has concluded that given a number of factors, including a documented history of discrimination, classifications based on sexual orientation should be subject to a heightened standard of scrutiny. The President has also concluded that Section 3 of DOMA, as applied to legally married same-sex couples, fails to meet that standard and is therefore unconstitutional. Given that conclusion, the President has instructed the Department not to defend the statute.

Notwithstanding this determination, the President has informed me that Section 3 will continue to be enforced by the Executive Branch. To that end, the President has instructed Executive agencies to continue to comply with Section 3 of DOMA, consistent with the Executive's obligation to take care that the laws be faithfully executed, unless and until Congress repeals Section 3 or the judicial branch renders a definitive verdict against the law's constitutionality. This course of action respects the actions of the prior Congress that enacted DOMA, and it recognizes the judiciary as the final arbiter of the constitutional claims raised.

VIII. Democratic Rights

MAJOR DEVELOPMENTS

- Supreme Court declares corporations have rights to make independent expenditures
- *Bush v. Gore* (2000) resolves presidential election
- Debates over continued vitality of the Voting Rights Act of 1965

The contemporary politics of constitutional democracy is about the application of New Deal/Great Society principles rather than a struggle over whether those principles should be superseded by a different constitutional conception of democracy. The Brandeis/Holmes dissents in the World War I free speech cases and the Voting Rights Act of 1965 today have canonical status. When the Supreme Court debated the Florida recount in *Bush v. Gore* (2000), the issue was whether the means for counting ballots was consistent with the one person, one vote standard announced in *Reynolds v. Sims* (1964). When the Supreme Court considers constitutional attacks on campaign finance regulation, all parties to the debate agree that speech can be regulated only when government demonstrates a compelling interest.

While liberals and conservatives agree that free speech and voting rights are fundamental to our form of government, they dispute the circumstances under which government regulation might improve the marketplace of ideas, promote democracy, or protect citizenship. Political liberals are inclined to favor campaign finance reform, restrictions on hate speech (although many liberals oppose such regulations as well), regulations on commercial speech, greater access to public property for speech, granting students free speech rights, fewer restrictions on federal funding for speech, majority-minority election districts, judicial oversight of partisan gerrymanders, and policies granting illegal aliens basic rights. Political conservatives are far more inclined to think unconstitutional laws regulating hate speech, laws regulating commercial advertising, campaign finance reform, and laws creating majority-minority districts. They do not believe that judges should interfere when elected officials limit the use of public property for speech, selectively fund different speakers, engage in partisan gerrymanders, or restrict the rights of illegal aliens. With important exceptions, the Supreme Court in the Contemporary Era generally supports more conservative notions of constitutional democracy.

Whether these diverse issue positions cohere into a principled whole is controversial. All parties claim that their preferred policies are rooted in principle and that their opponents seek only political advantage. Liberals insist that they are committed to diversity and the principle that all persons should have an equal influence on the official decisions that affect their lives. Conservatives note that this commitment to diversity often excludes evangelical Christians and speakers who sharply challenge perceived liberal orthodoxies on race and gender. Conservatives claim to be committed to the original understanding of the Constitution and government neutrality, but liberals note that the persons responsible for crucial constitutional provisions said nothing about campaign finance and the legitimacy of majority-minority districts. Stephen Feldman suggests that struggles over constitutional democracy are between liberal proponents of pluralist democracy, who insist that Americans must incorporate diverse perspectives on the public good, and proponents of republican democracy, who insist on respect for traditional virtues.[66] Another possible distinction between contemporary liberals and contemporary conservatives is that liberals are more inclined to consider historical and social context when evaluating regulations of constitutional democracy, while conservatives distrust government capacity to distinguish between better and worse speech or better and worse democratic behaviors.

66. Stephen M. Feldman, *Free Expression and Democracy in America: A History* (Chicago: University of Chicago Press, 2008).

A. Free Speech

Champions of unpopular or dangerous ideas enjoy more freedom than at any previous point in American history. Recent Supreme Court decisions have protected the rights of persons who wish to sell violent video games to children (*Brown v. Entertainment Merchants Association*), make videos portraying cruelty to animals (*United States v. Stevens* [2010]), lie about their military service (*United States v. Alvarez*), and disrupt military funerals (*Snyder v. Phelps*). Rejecting claims that "depictions of animal cruelty . . . are categorically unprotected by the First Amendment," Chief Justice Roberts's majority opinion in *Stevens* asserted, "The First Amendment itself reflects a judgment by the American people that the benefits of its restrictions on the Government outweigh the costs. Our Constitution forecloses any attempt to revise that judgment simply on the basis that some speech is not worth it." When declaring the Stolen Valor Act unconstitutional in *United States v. Alvarez*, Justice Kennedy asserted, "Our constitutional tradition stands against the idea that we need Oceania's Ministry of Truth." This case declared that persons had a right to claim falsely that they had won military honors, because "absent any evidence that the speech was used to gain a material advantage," permitting regulation "would give government a broad censorial power unprecedented in this Court's cases or in our constitutional tradition." The justices are also sensitive to the possibility of compelled speech. A 7–2 majority in *Knox v. Service Employees International Union, Local 1000* (2012) held that the First Amendment requires public service unions to permit persons to "opt out" whenever any change takes place in the percentage or amount of union dues that are used to fund political activities. Justice Alito's majority opinion asserted that "nonmembers should not be required to fund a union's political and ideological projects unless they choose to do so after having 'a fair opportunity' to assess the impact of paying for nonchargeable union activities."

Contemporary legislators ban advocacy only in specific contexts that suggest particular dangers. In *Holder v. Humanitarian Law Project* (2010) several advocacy organizations were charged with providing material support to terrorist groups. Chief Justice Roberts's majority opinion, while sustaining a statute forbidding groups from providing any training to terrorist groups, even training limited to securing demands peaceably, emphasized that "plaintiffs may say anything they wish on any topic." "Foreign organizations that engage in terrorist activity," Roberts insisted, "are so tainted by their criminal conduct that any contribution to such an organization facilitates that conduct."

In *Virginia v. Black* (2003) the justices declared unconstitutional a Virginia law that permitted juries to presume from evidence that persons had burned a cross that they intended to threaten local persons of color. All nine justices agreed that "true threats" were not constitutionally protected. Only Justice Thomas was willing to categorically ban cross-burning. The issue dividing the other justices was the connection between cross-burning and threats. Justice O'Connor's crucial plurality opinion insisted that the state had to demonstrate something more than the fact of a cross-burning to demonstrate that a true threat had been made. She observed that the Virginia statute "does not distinguish between a cross burning done with the purpose of creating anger or resentment and a cross burning done with the purpose of threatening or intimidating a victim."

When speakers claim rights to speak on public property, in public schools, or with public moneys the Supreme Court permits substantial regulation. Cases frequently turn on the extent to which speech is seen as purely private or entwined with some public largess. While the Court in *Boy Scouts of America v. Dale* (2000) ruled that states could not require a private expressive organization to accept members whose beliefs or habits were inconsistent with the message the organization wished to communicate, the justices in *Christian Legal Society Chapter of the University of California, Hastings College of Law v. Martinez* (2010) sustained a university rule that required official law school groups, including the Christian Legal Society (CLS), to not "discriminate unlawfully on the basis of race, color, religion, national origin, ancestry, disability, age, sex, or sexual orientation." Justice Ginsburg's plurality opinion stated, "CLS may exclude any person for any reason if it forgoes the benefits of official recognition. The expressive-association precedents on which CLS relies, in contrast, involved regulations that *compelled* a group to include unwanted members, with no choice to opt out."

The late Rehnquist and Roberts Courts continue to narrowly define what constitute public fora, or places that are traditionally held open for speech. *United States v. American Library Association* (2003) reaffirmed previous decisions rejecting claims that libraries were public fora. When sustaining a federal law requiring libraries receiving federal money to block Internet access to obscenity and indecent material, Chief Justice Rehnquist declared, "A public library does not acquire Internet terminals in order to create a public forum for Web publishers to express themselves." *Arkansas Educational Television Commission v. Forbes* (1998) rejected claims that political debates sponsored by public television were obligated to include all candidates listed on the ballot. Justice Kennedy's majority opinion maintained that "the debate was a nonpublic forum, for which [the television station] could exclude Forbes in the reasonable, viewpoint-neutral exercise of its journalistic discretion."

The justices in three cases—*Madsen v. Women's Health Center, Inc.* (1994), *Schenck v. Pro-Choice Network of Western New York* (1997), and *Hill v. Colorado* (2000)—sustained most provisions in injunctions limiting pro-life protests outside of abortion clinics. Chief Justice Rehnquist's majority opinion in *Madsen* rejected claims that the ban on pro-life protests violated content neutrality, the principle that time, place, and manner restrictions on speech must not discriminate on the basis of particular viewpoints or subject matters. He wrote,

> The fact that the injunction in the present case did not prohibit activities of those demonstrating in favor of abortion is justly attributable to the lack of any similar demonstrations by those in favor of abortion, and of any consequent request that their demonstrations be regulated by injunction. There is no suggestion in this record that Florida law would not equally restrain similar conduct directed at a target having nothing to do with abortion; none of the restrictions imposed by the court were directed at the contents of petitioner's message.

Watchtower Bible and Tract Society of New York v. Village of Stratton (2002) is a rare example of a contemporary case in which the Supreme Court declared unconstitutional a law restricting speech on public property. Stratton required that persons engaged in door-to-door advocacy obtain a permit. Justice Stevens declared this requirement "offensive—not only to the values protected by the First Amendment, but to the very notion of a free society—that in the context of everyday public discourse a citizen must first inform

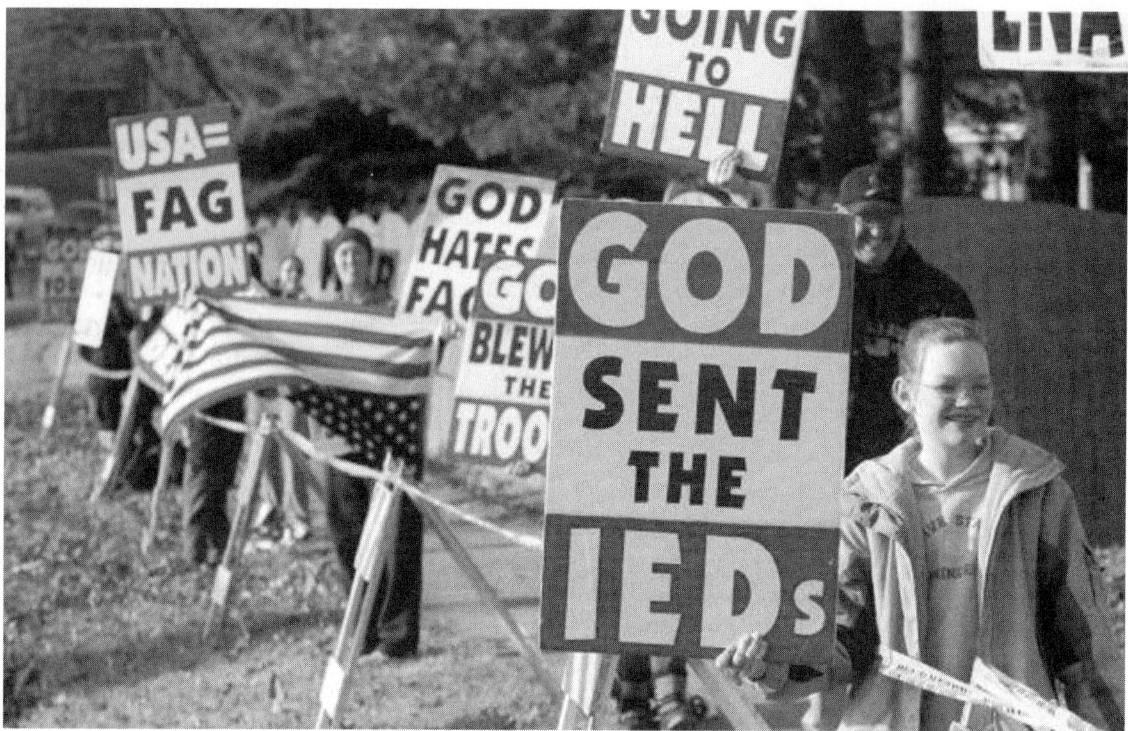

Illustration 11-6 Westboro Baptist Church Demonstration at Military Funeral, December 2005

Members of the Westboro Baptist Church demonstrating outside church services for the funeral of U.S. Army Private Peter Navarro, who was killed by an improvised explosive device in Iraq. The Westboro Church primarily consists of Fred Phelps and his family. This demonstration was held in Missouri on December 23, 2005. In 2010 the Missouri county where the funeral was held passed an ordinance banning protests near funerals.

Source: UPI/Bill Greenblatt.

the government of her desire to speak to her neighbors and then obtain a permit to do so."

The justices have been more conflicted when considering free speech rights in cases concerned with public subsidies. *National Endowment for the Arts v. Finley* (1998) ruled that Congress could require federal officials to consider "general standards of decency and respect for the diverse beliefs and values of the American public" when awarding grants to artists. Justice O'Connor's majority opinion stated,

> Although the First Amendment certainly has application in the subsidy context, we note that the Government may allocate competitive funding according to criteria that would be impermissible were direct regulation of speech or a criminal penalty at stake. So long as legislation does not infringe on other constitutionally protected rights, Congress has wide latitude to set spending priorities. And as we held in *Rust v. Sullivan* (1991), Congress may "selectively fund a program to encourage certain activities it believes to be in the public interest, without at the same time funding an alternative program which seeks to deal with the problem in another way."

The justices distinguished *Rust v. Sullivan*, the decision that permitted the federal government to forbid doctors accepting federal funds to discuss abortion with their patients, in *Legal Services Corporation v. Velazquez* (2001), a case concerned with the free speech rights of federally funded lawyers. A 5–4 judicial majority declared unconstitutional a federal law that forbade the Legal Services Corporation from funding litigation aimed at changing welfare laws. Justice Kennedy's majority opinion asserted, "The advice from the attorney to the client and the advocacy by the attorney to the courts cannot be classified as governmental speech even under a generous understanding of that concept." Readers may wonder whether a court composed of doctors would similarly conclude that the lawyer-client relationship is constitutionally different from and merits more constitutional protection than the doctor-patient relationship.

If there is a new central battleground for the contemporary constitutional politics of free speech it is campaign finance reform. The contemporary struggle over campaign finance began in 1995 when Arizona Republican senator John McCain and Wisconsin Democratic senator Russell Feingold introduced what became known as the Bipartisan Campaign Reform Act (BCRA). The BCRA forbade corporations and unions from using their general treasury funds to make independent expenditures for "electioneering communication," defined as "any broadcast, cable, or satellite communication" that "refers to a clearly identified candidate for Federal office" and is made within thirty days of a primary election. Another provision placed sharp limits on soft money, contributions that nominally go toward party-building activities but are in fact used to support particular candidates. After a long debate both houses of Congress passed the BCRA in 2002. President Bush signed the bill, although he expressed significant constitutional reservations. His signing statement praised the provisions in the bill "prevent[ing] unions and corporations from making unregulated, 'soft' money contributions" and "creat[ing] new disclosure requirements." Bush nevertheless criticized those provisions in the BCRA "preventing all individuals, not just unions and corporations, from making donations to political parties in connection with Federal elections" and questioned "the constitutionality of the broad ban on issue advertising, which restrains the speech of a wide variety of groups on issues of public import in the months closest to an election."

A 5–4 Supreme Court majority in *McConnell v. Federal Election Commission* (2003) sustained most of the constitutionally controversial provisions in the BCRA, applying the "less rigorous scrutiny" the justices believed applicable to legislation imposing limits on campaign contributions. The soft money prohibitions, Justices Stevens and O'Connor concluded, were constitutional means for combating "the danger that officeholders will decide issues not on the merits or the desires of their constituencies, but according to the wishes of those who have made large, financial contributions valued by the officeholder." Congress, the majority opinion continued, had the right "to prohibit corporations and unions from using funds in their treasuries to finance advertisements expressly advocating the election or defeat of candidates in federal elections." Besides, Justices O'Connor and Stevens reasoned, corporations and unions interested in express advocacy could simply create a separate, segregated fund for that purpose.

The Supreme Court began scrutinizing campaign finance laws more strictly when Justice O'Connor left the bench. Numerous decisions exhibited increased judicial hostility to federal laws restricting or regulating the use of money in political campaigns.

- *Randall v. Sorrell* (2006) declared unconstitutional a Vermont law limiting campaign contributions in state elections to $200 or $400 per candidate.
- *Federal Election Commission v. Wisconsin Right to Life* (2007) ruled that political advertisements violate the BCRA ban on electoral communications only "if the ad is susceptible of no reasonable interpretation other than as an appeal to vote for or against a specific candidate."
- *Citizens United v. Federal Election Commission* (2008) partly overruled *McConnell* and overruled completely *Austin v. Michigan Chamber of Commerce* (1990) when holding that corporations had the right to make independent expenditures on behalf of named candidates.
- *Arizona Free Enterprise Club's Freedom Club PAC v. Bennett* (2011) declared unconstitutional a state law that provided public funds to candidates when their electoral rival exceeded certain spending limits.
- *American Tradition Partnership, Inc. v. Bullock* (2012) summarily reversed a Montana Supreme Court decision that held that, because of the unique influence of corporate wealth on Montana politics, the Montana legislature could restrict independent corporate expenditures during political campaigns.

When deciding these cases, Chief Justice Roberts declared in *Arizona Free Enterprise*, the justices "repeatedly rejected the argument that the government has a compelling state interest in leveling the playing field that can justify undue burdens on political speech." He concluded, "The First Amendment embodies our choice as a Nation that, when it comes to [campaigning for office], the guiding principle is freedom—the 'unfettered interchange of ideas'—not whatever the State may view as fair."

Contemporary Americans apply First Amendment principles to an array of media and technologies that would have been as bewildering to the framers as they often are to many parents.

- Print journalism enjoys the same high degree of constitutional protection as ordinary speakers.
- Broadcasters enjoy a lesser degree of constitutional protection, because government owns the airwaves, facilities are scarce, and broadcast media can be intrusive (*Red Lion Broadcasting Co. v. FCC* [1969]; *FCC v. Pacifica Foundation* [1978]).
- Dial-up telephone services enjoy the same high degree of constitutional protection as newspapers and ordinary speakers (*Sable Communications of California v. FCC* [1989]).
- Cable television operators enjoy more protection than broadcast media (*Turner Broadcasting System v. FCC* [1994]), but not the same protections as ordinary speakers, newspapers, and dial-up telephone services (*Denver Area Educational Telecommunications Consortium v. FCC* [1996]).
- Internet services enjoy the same high degree of constitutional protection as ordinary speakers, print journalists, and dial-up telephone services (*Reno v. ACLU* [1997]).

Two factors complicate this fairly neat summary. First, elected officials sometimes disagree with Supreme Court doctrine. The Reagan administration abandoned the "Fairness Doctrine" because officials believed that broadcasters had the same constitutional rights as print journalists. Second, substantial disagreement exists in the present federal judiciary over the precise First Amendment standards that ought to govern particular media. Consider the judicial line-up in *Turner Broadcasting Systems, Inc: v. FCC* (1994):

> KENNEDY, J., announced the judgment of the Court and delivered the opinion for a unanimous Court with respect to Part I, the opinion of the Court with respect to Parts II-A and II-B, in which REHNQUIST, C. J., and BLACKMUN, O'CONNOR, SCALIA, SOUTER, THOMAS, and GINSBURG, JJ., joined, the opinion of the Court with respect to Parts II-C, II-D, and III-A, in which REHNQUIST, C. J., and BLACKMUN, STEVENS, and SOUTER, J., joined, and an opinion with respect to Part III-B, in which REHNQUIST, C. J., and BLACKMUN and SOUTER, JJ., joined. BLACKMUN, J., filed a concurring opinion. STEVENS, J., filed an opinion concurring in part and concurring in the judgment. O'CONNOR, J., filed an opinion concurring in part and dissenting in part, in which SCALIA and GINSBURG, JJ., joined, and in Parts I and III of which THOMAS, J., joined. GINSBURG, J., filed an opinion concurring in part and dissenting in part.

Whether justices who reach maturity in the age of the Internet, cable television, and iPhones will reach greater consensus is for the future to determine.

During the Contemporary Era First Amendment rights of expressive association have tended to focus on arguments over the right of associations to exclude nonbelievers. *Hurley v. Irish-American Gay, Lesbian and Bisexual Group of Boston* (1995) held that the organizers of the St. Patrick's Day parade in Boston had a right to exclude gay and lesbian groups. Justice Souter's unanimous opinion stated that "when dissemination of a view contrary to one's own is forced upon a speaker intimately connected with the communication advanced, the speaker's right to autonomy over the message is compromised." The justices were more divided when considering whether states could require the Boy Scouts to maintain an openly gay troop leader. Chief Justice Rehnquist, speaking for the five most conservative justices in *Boy Scouts of America v. Dale* (2000), insisted that such rules violated expressive association rights. In *Rumsfeld v. Forum for Academic and Institutional Rights, Inc.* (2006), however, the justices unanimously held that Congress did not violate the rights of expressive association when requiring universities that accepted federal funds to allow the military to recruit on campus. "Unlike a parade organizer's choice of parade contingents," Chief Justice Roberts wrote, "a law school's decision to allow recruiters on campus is not inherently expressive." In *Agency for International Development v. Alliance for Open Society International* (2013) the Court by a 6–2 vote declared that Congress could not require organizations receiving federal funds for particular projects to support specific policies when those organizations were engaged in activities outside the scope of their federal funding. In this case an organization supporting the global fight against HIV/AIDS objected to federal law that made ineligible for funding any organization that failed to have an explicit policy opposing prostitution and sex trafficking.

Citizens United v. Federal Election Commission, 558 U.S. 310 (2010)

The nonprofit corporation Citizens United in January 2008 released a documentary entitled Hillary. *The movie was critical of then-senator Hillary Clinton, a candidate for the Democratic Party's presidential nomination. Citizens United wanted to make the movie available on cable television through video-on-demand in the hope that they could influence the primary elections. The Federal Election Commission prohibited the airing of* Hillary *on the ground that the BCRA forbade corporations from broadcasting within thirty days of a primary election any advertisement that advocated the election or defeat of a specific candidate. That decision was supported by a federal district court. Citizens United appealed to the Supreme Court of the United States.*

The Supreme Court by a 5–4 vote reversed. In an opinion that overruled Austin v. Michigan Chamber of Commerce *(1990) and partially overruled* McConnell v. Federal Election Commission *(2003) Justice Kennedy ruled that corporations had the same right as individuals to make independent expenditures during political campaigns. Why did Justice Kennedy conclude that corporations have the same rights as individuals to make independent expenditures? Why did the dissents disagree? Who had the better argument? Compare the judicial line-up in* Citizens United *to the judicial line-up in* Buckley v. Valeo *(1976). Why has judicial voting in campaign finance cases become more ideological over the past thirty years?*

In his second State of the Union address President Barack Obama declared, "Last week, the Supreme Court reversed a century of law to open the floodgates for special interests—including foreign corporations—to spend without limit in our elections. Well, I don't think American elections should be bankrolled by America's most powerful interests, or worse, by foreign entities." Television coverage of the address caught Justice Alito wincing at the accusation and muttering, "Not true." What was true and what was not true about President Obama's assertions? Were these assertions appropriate presidential comments on constitutional issues or inappropriate efforts to interfere with judicial decisions? What steps could President Obama constitutionally take to limit or reverse the impact of Citizens United?

JUSTICE KENNEDY delivered the opinion of the Court.

The law before us is an outright ban, backed by criminal sanctions. Section 441b makes it a felony for all corporations—including nonprofit advocacy corporations—either to expressly advocate the election or defeat of candidates or to broadcast electioneering communications within 30 days of a primary election and 60 days of a general election. Thus, the following acts would all be felonies under §441b: The Sierra Club runs an ad, within the crucial phase of 60 days before the general election, that exhorts the public to disapprove of a Congressman who favors logging in national forests; the National Rifle Association publishes a book urging the public to vote for the challenger because the incumbent U.S. Senator supports a handgun ban; and the American Civil Liberties Union creates a Web site telling the public to vote for a Presidential candidate in light of that candidate's defense of free speech. These prohibitions are classic examples of censorship.

. . .

Section 441b's prohibition on corporate independent expenditures is thus a ban on speech. As a "restriction on the amount of money a person or group can spend on political communication during a campaign," that statute "necessarily reduces the quantity of expression by restricting the number of issues discussed, the depth of their exploration, and the size of the audience reached." *Buckley v. Valeo* (1976). Were the Court to uphold these restrictions, the Government could repress speech by silencing certain voices at any of the various points in the speech process. . . .

. . .

Premised on mistrust of governmental power, the First Amendment stands against attempts to disfavor certain subjects or viewpoints. . . . [I]t is inherent in the nature of the political process that voters must be free to obtain information from diverse sources in order to determine how to cast their votes. . . . We find no basis for the proposition that, in the context of political speech, the Government may impose restrictions on certain disfavored speakers. Both history and logic lead us to this conclusion.

. . .

Austin v. Michigan Chamber of Commerce (1990) "uph[eld] a direct restriction on the independent expenditure of funds for political speech for the first time in [this Court's] history." . . . [T]he *Austin* Court identified a new governmental interest in limiting political speech: an antidistortion interest. *Austin* found a compelling governmental interest in preventing "the corrosive and distorting effects of immense aggregations of wealth that are accumulated with the help of the corporate form and that have little or no correlation to the public's support for the corporation's political ideas."

. . .

If the First Amendment has any force, it prohibits Congress from fining or jailing citizens, or associations of citizens, for simply engaging in political speech. If the antidistortion rationale were to be accepted, however, it would permit Government to ban political speech simply because the speaker is an association that has taken on the corporate form. . . . If *Austin* were correct, the Government could prohibit a corporation from expressing political views in media beyond those presented here, such as by printing books. . . .

. . . The rule that political speech cannot be limited based on a speaker's wealth is a necessary consequence of the premise that the First Amendment generally prohibits the suppression of political speech based on the speaker's identity.

. . . All speakers, including individuals and the media, use money amassed from the economic marketplace to fund their speech. The First Amendment protects the resulting speech, even if it was enabled by economic transactions with persons or entities who disagree with the speaker's ideas.

Austin's antidistortion rationale would produce the dangerous, and unacceptable, consequence that Congress could ban political speech of media corporations. Media corporations are now exempt from §441b's ban on corporate expenditures. Yet media corporations accumulate wealth with the help of the corporate form, the largest media corporations have "immense aggregations of wealth," and the views expressed by media corporations often "have little or no correlation to the public's support" for those views. Thus, under the Government's reasoning, wealthy media corporations could have their voices diminished to put them on par with other media entities. There is no precedent for permitting this under the First Amendment.

. . .

The Government contends further that corporate independent expenditures can be limited because of its interest in protecting dissenting shareholders from being compelled to fund corporate political speech. This asserted interest . . . would allow the Government to ban the political speech even of media corporations. Assume, for example, that a shareholder of a corporation that owns a newspaper disagrees with the political views the newspaper expresses. Under the Government's view, that potential disagreement could give the Government the authority to restrict the media corporation's political speech. The First Amendment does not allow that power. There is, furthermore, little evidence of abuse that cannot be corrected by shareholders "through the procedures of corporate democracy."

. . .

Due consideration leads to this conclusion: *Austin* should be and now is overruled. We return to the principle established in *Buckley* and *First National Bank of Boston v. Bellotti* (1978) that the Government may not suppress political speech on the basis of the speaker's corporate identity. No sufficient governmental interest justifies limits on the political speech of nonprofit or for-profit corporations.

. . .

CHIEF JUSTICE ROBERTS, with whom JUSTICE ALITO joins, concurring.

The Government urges us in this case to uphold a direct prohibition on political speech. It asks us to embrace a theory of the First Amendment that would allow censorship not only of television and radio broadcasts, but of pamphlets, posters, the Internet, and virtually any other medium that corporations and unions might find useful in expressing their views on matters of public concern. Its theory, if accepted, would empower the Government to prohibit newspapers from running editorials or opinion pieces supporting or opposing candidates for office, so long as the newspapers were owned by corporations—as the major ones are. First Amendment rights could be confined to individuals, subverting the vibrant public discourse that is at the foundation of our democracy.

The Court properly rejects that theory, and I join its opinion in full. The First Amendment protects more than just the individual on a soapbox and the lonely pamphleteer. . . .

. . .

JUSTICE SCALIA, with whom JUSTICE ALITO joins, and with whom JUSTICE THOMAS joins in part, concurring.

. . .

The dissent says that when the Framers "constitutionalized the right to free speech in the First Amendment, it was the free speech of individual Americans that they had in mind." That is no doubt true. All the provisions of the Bill of Rights set forth the rights of individual men and women—not, for example, of trees or polar bears. But the individual person's right to speak includes the right to speak *in association with other individual persons*. Surely the dissent does not believe that speech by the Republican Party or the Democratic Party can be censored because it is not the speech of "an individual American." It is the speech of many individual Americans, who have associated in a common cause, giving the leadership of the party the right to speak on their behalf. The association of individuals in a business corporation is no different—or at least it cannot be denied the right to speak on the simplistic ground that it is not "an individual American."

But to return to, and summarize, my principal point, which is the conformity of today's opinion with the original meaning of the First Amendment. The Amendment is written in terms of "speech," not speakers. Its text offers no foothold for excluding any category of speaker, from single individuals to partnerships of individuals, to unincorporated associations of individuals, to incorporated associations of individuals—and the dissent offers no evidence about the original meaning of the text to support any such exclusion. We are therefore simply left with the question whether the speech at issue in this case is "speech" covered by the First Amendment. No one says otherwise. A documentary film critical of a potential Presidential candidate is core political speech, and its nature as such does not change simply because it was funded by a corporation. Nor does the character of that funding produce any reduction whatever in the "inherent worth of the speech" and "its capacity for informing the public." Indeed, to exclude or impede corporate speech is to muzzle the principal agents of the modern free economy. We should celebrate rather than condemn the addition of this speech to the public debate.

JUSTICE STEVENS, with whom JUSTICE GINSBURG, JUSTICE BREYER, and JUSTICE SOTOMAYOR join, concurring in part and dissenting in part.

... Neither Citizens United's nor any other corporation's speech has been "banned." All that the parties dispute is whether Citizens United had a right to use the funds in its general treasury to pay for broadcasts during the 30-day period. The notion that the First Amendment dictates an affirmative answer to that question is, in my judgment, profoundly misguided. ...

...

In the context of election to public office, the distinction between corporate and human speakers is significant. Although they make enormous contributions to our society, corporations are not actually members of it. They cannot vote or run for office. Because they may be managed and controlled by nonresidents, their interests may conflict in fundamental respects with the interests of eligible voters. The financial resources, legal structure, and instrumental orientation of corporations raise legitimate concerns about their role in the electoral process. Our lawmakers have a compelling constitutional basis, if not also a democratic duty, to take measures designed to guard against the potentially deleterious effects of corporate spending in local and national races.

...

The election context is distinctive in many ways, and the Court, of course, is right that the First Amendment closely guards political speech. But in this context the authority of legislatures to enact viewpoint-neutral regulations based on content and identity is well settled. We have, for example, allowed state-run broadcasters to exclude independent candidates from televised debates. We have upheld statutes that prohibit the distribution or display of campaign materials near a polling place. Although we have not reviewed them directly, we have never cast doubt on laws that place special restrictions on campaign spending by foreign nationals. And we have consistently approved laws that bar Government employees, but not others, from contributing to or participating in political activities. These statutes burden the political expression of one class of speakers, namely, civil servants. Yet we have sustained them on the basis of longstanding practice and Congress' reasoned judgment that certain regulations which leave "untouched full participation . . . in political decisions at the ballot box," help ensure that public officials are "sufficiently free from improper influences," and that "confidence in the system of representative Government is not . . . eroded to a disastrous extent."

The same logic applies to this case with additional force because it is the identity of corporations, rather than individuals, that the Legislature has taken into account. . . . Campaign finance distinctions based on corporate identity tend to be less worrisome . . . because the "speakers" are not natural persons, much less members of our political community, and the governmental interests are of the highest order. Furthermore, when corporations, as a class, are distinguished from noncorporations, as a class, there is a lesser risk that regulatory distinctions will reflect invidious discrimination or political favoritism.

. . .

The Framers took it as a given that corporations could be comprehensively regulated in the service of the public welfare. Unlike our colleagues, they had little trouble distinguishing corporations from human beings, and when they constitutionalized the right to free speech in the First Amendment, it was the free speech of individual Americans that they had in mind. While individuals might join together to exercise their speech rights, business corporations, at least, were plainly not seen as facilitating such associational or expressive ends. Even "the notion that business corporations could invoke the First Amendment would probably have been quite a novelty," given that "at the time, the legitimacy of every corporate activity was thought to rest entirely in a concession of the sovereign." . . . In light of these background practices and understandings, it seems to me implausible that the Framers believed "the freedom of speech" would extend equally to all corporate speakers, much less that it would preclude legislatures from taking limited measures to guard against corporate capture of elections.

. . .

. . . [I]n *Austin*, we considered whether corporations . . . could be barred from using general treasury funds to make independent expenditures in support of, or in opposition to, candidates. We held they could be. Once again recognizing the importance of "the integrity of the marketplace of political ideas" in candidate elections, we noted that corporations have "special advantages—such as limited liability, perpetual life, and favorable treatment of the accumulation and distribution of assets"—that allow them to spend prodigious general treasury sums on campaign messages that have "little or no correlation" with the beliefs held by actual persons. In light of the corrupting effects such spending might have on the political process, we permitted the State of Michigan to limit corporate expenditures on candidate elections to corporations' PACs, which rely on voluntary contributions and thus "reflect actual public support for the political ideals espoused by corporations." . . .

. . .

On numerous occasions we have recognized Congress' legitimate interest in preventing the money that is spent on elections from exerting an "'undue influence on an officeholder's judgment'" and from creating "'the appearance of such influence,'" beyond the sphere of *quid pro quo* relationships. . . . Corruption operates along a spectrum, and the majority's apparent belief that *quid pro quo* arrangements can be neatly demarcated from other improper influences does not accord with the theory or reality of politics. It certainly does not accord with the record Congress developed in passing BCRA, a record that stands as a remarkable testament to the energy and ingenuity with which corporations, unions, lobbyists, and politicians may go about scratching each other's backs—and which amply supported Congress' determination to target a limited set of especially destructive practices.

. . .

. . . The legislative and judicial proceedings relating to BCRA generated a substantial body of evidence suggesting that, as corporations grew more and more adept at crafting "issue ads" to help or harm a particular candidate, these nominally independent expenditures began to corrupt the political process in a very direct sense. The sponsors of these ads were routinely granted special access after the campaign was over. . . . Many corporate independent expenditures, it seemed, had become essentially interchangeable with direct contributions in their capacity to generate *quid pro quo* arrangements. In an age in which money and television ads are the coin of the campaign realm, it is hardly surprising that corporations deployed these ads to curry favor with, and to gain influence over, public officials.

. . .

The fact that corporations are different from human beings might seem to need no elaboration, except that the majority opinion almost completely elides it. *Austin* set forth some of the basic differences. Unlike natural persons, corporations have "limited liability" for their owners and managers, "perpetual life," separation of ownership and control, "and favorable treatment of the accumulation and distribution of assets . . . that enhance their ability to attract capital and to deploy their resources in ways that maximize the return on their shareholders' investments." Unlike voters in U.S. elections, corporations may be foreign controlled. Unlike other interest groups, business corporations have been "effectively delegated responsibility for ensuring society's economic welfare"; they inescapably structure the life of every citizen. "'[T]he resources in the treasury of a business corporation,'" furthermore, "'are not an indication of popular support for the corporation's political ideas.'" . . .

It might also be added that corporations have no consciences, no beliefs, no feelings, no thoughts, no desires. Corporations help structure and facilitate the activities of human beings, to be sure, and their "personhood" often serves as a useful legal fiction. But they are not themselves members of "We the People" by whom and for whom our Constitution was established.

. . .

In a democratic society, the longstanding consensus on the need to limit corporate campaign spending should outweigh the wooden application of judge-made rules. The majority's rejection of this principle "elevate[s] corporations to a level of deference which has not been seen at least since the days when substantive due process was regularly used to invalidate regulatory legislation thought to unfairly impinge upon established economic interests." At bottom, the Court's opinion is thus a rejection of the common sense of the American people, who have recognized a need to prevent corporations from undermining self-government since the founding, and who have fought against the distinctive corrupting potential of corporate electioneering since the days of Theodore Roosevelt. It is a strange time to repudiate that common sense. While American democracy is imperfect, few outside the majority of this Court would have thought its flaws included a dearth of corporate money in politics.

JUSTICE THOMAS, concurring in part and dissenting in part. . . .

B. Voting

The contemporary constitutional politics of voting is polarized on two different dimensions: constitutional principle and political advantage. Some divisions between conservatives and liberals are best explained in terms of different constitutional principles. The more conservative Supreme Court justices vote to strike down and the more liberal Supreme Court justices vote to sustain majority-minority legislative districts that most scholars believe advance Republican Party interests in the long run. *Bush v. Gore* (2000) is generally regarded as an instance in which political advantage better explained the difference between conservatives and liberals, as well as between Republicans and Democrats. In that case, the five most conservative justices on the Supreme Court, supported by Republicans in elected office, declared unconstitutional efforts to recount presidential ballots in Florida. This decision in effect gave the White House to the Republican candidate, Texas governor George W. Bush. Although both the majority and dissenting opinions declared that enduring constitutional principles supported their voting decisions, few observers can detect in other cases substantial commitment to the principles announced in that decision.

The constitutional politics of voting encompasses numerous issues, including whether ex-felons have a right to vote, whether the Supreme Court should review partisan gerrymanders, the constitutionality of various state voter registration laws, whether states may regulate the primary process, and the continued vitality of the Voting Rights Act. The stakes are high. Given the sharp divisions between Democrats and Republicans, as well as increasingly tight struggles for control of national and state institutions, slight changes in voting laws may alter partisan and ideological control of governing institutions.

The Supreme Court's decision in *Reynolds v. Sims* (1964) requiring legislative districting to adhere to the one person, one vote principle touched off intense partisan struggles that remain vibrant today. *Bush v. Gore* (2000) was decided in part on the principle that different procedures for recounting ballots create the possibility that one citizen's ballot might be counted differently than another person's ballot. Gerrymandering is the more frequent consequence of *Reynolds*, as Democrats and Republicans struggle to draw congressional and state legislative district lines in ways that maximize partisan advantage. The Supreme Court has so far insisted that these struggles are not justiciable. Justice Scalia and three other justices in *Vieth v. Jubelirer* (2004) maintained that courts should not adjudicate claims that partisan gerrymanders are unconstitutional, because no judicially manageable standards exist for evaluating such claims. Scalia noted, "The fact that partisan districting is a lawful and common practice means that there is almost always room for an election-impeding lawsuit contending that partisan advantage was the predominant motivation." Justice Kennedy's concurring opinion suggested that some standards might exist but that he had not yet discovered them. *League of United Latin American Citizens v. Perry* (2006) similarly held nonjusticiable a mid-decennial political gerrymander by the Republican Party–dominated Texas legislature that was not necessitated by either demographic shifts or changes in the number of state congressional seats. Justice Kennedy wrote, "The text and structure of the Constitution and our case law indicate there is nothing inherently suspect about a legislature's decision to replace mid-decade a court-ordered plan with one of its own."

The contemporary constitutional politics of the Voting Rights Act threatens to pit elected officials against judges, rather than liberal Democrats against conservative Republicans. A bipartisan congressional majority in 2006 voted to reauthorize crucial provisions of past Voting Rights Acts, most notably those provisions that required covered districts to preclear all changes in voting laws with the Department of Justice or the Court of Appeals for the District of Columbia. The House Committee report supporting reauthorization stated, "Forty years has been an insufficient amount of time to address the century during which racial minorities were denied the full rights of citizenship. While substantial strides have been made toward racial equality, the attitudes and actions of some States and political subdivisions continue to fall short."[67] President George W. Bush, when signing the Fannie Lou Hamer, Rosa Parks, and Coretta Scott King Voting Rights Act Reauthorization and Amendments Act of 2006 declared, "Today we renew a bill that helped bring a community on the margins into the life of American democracy."

The continued constitutional vitality of the Voting Rights Act is unclear. In *Shelby County v. Holder* (2013) the justices, by a 5–4 vote, declared unconstitutional the specific preclearance formula that was used in Section 4 of the Voting Rights Act on the grounds that the formula was based on outdated evidence. While in principle the Congress had the authority to pass a new formula based on evidence that would be more acceptable to the Court majority, as a matter of practice in an era of divided government the Court's decision had the effect of freeing all previously covered jurisdictions from the longstanding preclearance requirements. In September 2013 the NAACP's Legal Defense Fund warned that a growing list of states and local jurisdictions were "implement[ing] new discriminatory voting changes in the wake of the decision," including voter ID laws, shifts to at-large elections for council seats, and limits to early voting.[68]

Constitutional controversies over majority-minority districts have temporarily abated. The Supreme Court in *Shaw v. Reno* (1993) declared unconstitutional a highly irregularly shaped congressional district in North Carolina that was structured to create an African American majority. In *Miller v. Johnson* (1995) the five most conservative justices made it clear that racial motivation was the problem in *Shaw*, not the shape of the district. "Parties alleging that a State has assigned voters on the basis of race are neither confined in their proof to evidence regarding the district's geometry and makeup nor required to make a threshold showing of bizarreness," Justice Kennedy wrote. He continued,

> The plaintiff's burden is to show, either through circumstantial evidence of a district's shape and demographics or more direct evidence going to legislative purpose, that race was the predominant factor motivating the legislature's decision to place a significant number of voters within or without a particular district. To make this showing, a plaintiff must prove that the legislature subordinated traditional race-neutral districting principles, including but not limited to compactness, contiguity, and respect for political subdivisions or communities defined by actual shared interests, to racial considerations.

The force of both *Shaw* and *Miller* was substantially blunted by *Easley v. Cromartie* (2001), in which the justices by a 5–4 vote ruled that the district court made a clear error when concluding that North Carolina, in redrawing a district, was motivated by racial considerations rather than a desire to create a safe Democratic district. Legislatures were interested in race, Justice Breyer claimed, only because African American Democrats in North Carolina voted more reliably Democrat

---

67. House Committee on the Judiciary, "Fannie Lou Hamer, Rose Parks and Coretta Scott King Voting Rights Act Reauthorization and Amendments Act of 2006," 109th Cong., 2nd Sess., 2006, H.R. Rep. 109–478, 56.

68. NAACP Legal Defense Fund, "How States and Localities Are Responding to the Supreme Court's Voting Rights Act Decision," September 11, 2013, http://www.naacpldf.org/files/case_issue/States' Responses to Shelby Decision (as of 9.11.13).pdf.

than did white Democrats. He wrote, "A legislature may, by placing reliable Democratic precincts within a district without regard to race, end up with a district containing more heavily African-American precincts, but the reasons would be political rather than racial." After *Easley v. Cromartie* may any good lawyer mask the use of race in the districting process by insisting that the legislature was seeking only to group reliable Democrats?

The Supreme Court sometimes divides on partisan or ideological lines when adjudicating laws regulating voting. The five most conservative justices on the Roberts Court, joined by Justice Stevens, in *Crawford v. Marion County Election Board* (2008) sustained an Indiana law requiring persons to present a government-issued photo identification in order to cast a ballot. Partisanship played a lesser role in *California Democratic Party v. Jones* (2000), in which the Supreme Court considered the constitutionality of the blanket primary. Both the Democratic and Republican parties urged the justices to declare unconstitutional a California law that mandated one primary election with all candidates running on a single ballot. The Supreme Court complied with these partisan wishes in a 7–2 decision that celebrated the constitutional significance of parties. Justice Scalia's opinion stated, "Our cases vigorously affirm the special place the First Amendment reserves for, and the special protection it accords, the process by which a political party select[s] a standard bearer who best represents the party's ideologies and preferences."

Bush v. Gore, 531 U.S. 98 (2000)

The 2000 national presidential election between Democratic vice president Albert Gore and Republican governor George Bush was extraordinarily close. Democrats celebrated prematurely when networks called Florida, a crucial swing state for Gore, in their favor. Several hours later many networks reversed their original projection and indicated that Bush was likely to win Florida's crucial electoral votes. By early morning all that was clear was that Governor Bush had a razor-thin margin, pending recounts. After an initial machine recount found that Governor Bush retained a 327-vote lead, Vice President Gore asked for a manual recount of the vote in four Florida counties: Broward, Miami-Dade, Volusia, and Palm Beach. Under Florida law all such recounts were subject to the reasonable discretion of the Florida secretary of state. That office in 2000 was held by Katherine Harris, a strong Bush supporter. She refused to order a recount, but her decision was unanimously overruled by the Supreme Court of Florida. When that recount found that Governor Bush had won by 537 votes Vice President Gore brought another lawsuit, claiming that the canvassing boards of a few heavily Democratic counties had failed to count a number of ballots for which the intent of the voter could be clearly discerned. The crucial counties used punch-card ballots, which required the voter to dislodge a "chad" in order to cast a legal vote. Gore insisted that many ballots demonstrated that the voter had attempted to vote for him, even though the voter had not fully dislodged the "chad" from the punch-card ballot. A divided Florida Supreme Court agreed that longstanding precedents in state law required that "every citizen's vote be counted whenever possible"; however, rather than order a selective recount of a small number of Democratic counties, the state justices ordered a statewide recount as a way of ensuring equal treatment of all ballots. Bush appealed to the Supreme Court of the United States.

The Supreme Court first ordered that the recount be stayed and then issued a 7–2 decision declaring unconstitutional the Florida court decision ordering the recount. The five most conservative members of the Rehnquist Court ruled that the recount ordered by the Florida Supreme Court might allow for variations in the way that ballots were counted in different counties. The possibility that a ballot in one county might be counted and an identical ballot in other county discarded, the judicial majority concluded, violated the principle of one person, one vote. This concern, combined with the disputed view that no time existed for organizing a better recount, led a bare majority of the most conservative justices to rule that no recount was possible. The decision effectively decided the presidential election.

Bush v. Gore *raises important questions about the relationship between law and politics. Consider whether the justices were relying on neutral principles of law or voting in favor of the candidate they preferred to occupy the presidency. Were the majority opinions inconsistent with the way the conservative majority normally adjudicated federalism, voting rights, and equal protection issues, as some of the dissenters charged? Was the dissenting claim that the Supreme Court should not have adjudicated this issue consistent with liberal understandings of judicial power in other areas of the law? If we treat the majority's equal protection concerns as a serious point of law, then how might these principles apply in other cases in which states allow counties to use different methods for counting votes? Why would the majority (famously) write, "Our consideration is limited to the present circumstances, for the problem of equal protection in election processes generally presents many complexities"? Is it significant that, in the decade following the decision, no serious changes have been made to an election system based on counties using different methods of counting votes? While the Supreme Court of the United States divided on seemingly ideological grounds in* Bush v. Gore, *state and lower federal court decisions during the 2000 election crisis demonstrated a less partisan pattern. Democratic appointees on lower federal courts rejected some legal claims made by the Gore campaign, while Republican appointees supported some of these claims. How might you explain this difference?*[69]

PER CURIAM

. . .

The individual citizen has no federal constitutional right to vote for electors for the President of the United States unless and until the state legislature chooses a statewide election as the means to implement its power to appoint members of the electoral college. . . . When the state legislature vests the right to vote for President in its people, the right to vote as the legislature has prescribed is fundamental; and one source of its fundamental nature lies in the equal weight accorded to each vote and the equal dignity owed to each voter. . . .

The right to vote is protected in more than the initial allocation of the franchise. Equal protection applies as well to the manner of its exercise. Having once granted the right to vote on equal terms, the State may not, by later arbitrary and disparate treatment, value one person's vote over that of another. See, e.g., *Harper v. Virginia Bd. of Elections* (1966). . . .

. . .

The recount mechanisms implemented in response to the decisions of the Florida Supreme Court do not satisfy the minimum requirement for nonarbitrary treatment of voters necessary to secure the fundamental right. Florida's basic command for the count of legally cast votes is to consider the "intent of the voter." . . . This is unobjectionable as an abstract proposition and a starting principle. The problem inheres in the absence of specific standards to ensure its equal application. The formulation of uniform rules to determine intent based on these recurring circumstances is practicable and, we conclude, necessary.

The want of those rules here has led to unequal evaluation of ballots in various respects. . . . As seems to have been acknowledged at oral argument, the standards for accepting or rejecting contested ballots might vary not only from county to county but indeed within a single county from one recount team to another.

. . .

The question before the Court is not whether local entities, in the exercise of their expertise, may develop different systems for implementing elections. Instead, we are presented with a situation where a state court with the power to assure uniformity has ordered a statewide recount with minimal procedural safeguards. When a court orders a statewide remedy, there must be at least some assurance that the rudimentary requirements of equal treatment and fundamental fairness are satisfied.

. . .

Upon due consideration of the difficulties identified to this point, it is obvious that the recount cannot be conducted in compliance with the requirements of equal protection and due process without substantial additional work. It would require not only the adoption (after opportunity for argument) of adequate statewide standards for determining what is a legal vote, and practicable procedures to implement them, but also orderly judicial review of any disputed matters that might arise. In addition, the Secretary has advised that the recount of only a portion of the ballots requires that the vote tabulation equipment be used to screen out undervotes, a function for which the machines were not designed. If a recount of overvotes were also required, perhaps even a second screening would be necessary. Use of the equipment for this purpose, and any new software developed for it, would have to be evaluated for accuracy by the Secretary, as required by [Florida law].

The Supreme Court of Florida has said that the legislature intended the State's electors to "participat[e] fully in the federal electoral process," as provided by [federal law]. [Federal law], in turn, requires that any controversy or contest that is designed to lead to a conclusive selection of electors be completed by December 12. That date is upon us, and there is no recount procedure in place under the State Supreme

69. See Howard Gillman, *The Votes that Counted: How the Supreme Court Decided the 2000 Presidential Election* (Chicago: University of Chicago Press, 2001).

Court's order that comports with minimal constitutional standards. Because it is evident that any recount seeking to meet the December 12 date will be unconstitutional for the reasons we have discussed, we reverse the judgment of the Supreme Court of Florida ordering a recount to proceed.

. . .

CHIEF JUSTICE REHNQUIST, with whom JUSTICE SCALIA and JUSTICE THOMAS join, concurring.

. . .

In most cases, comity and respect for federalism compel us to defer to the decisions of state courts on issues of state law. That practice reflects our understanding that the decisions of state courts are definitive pronouncements of the will of the States as sovereigns. . . . Of course, in ordinary cases, the distribution of powers among the branches of a State's government raises no questions of federal constitutional law, subject to the requirement that the government be republican in character. . . . But there are a few exceptional cases in which the Constitution imposes a duty or confers a power on a particular branch of a State's government. This is one of them. Article II, §1, cl. 2, provides that "[e]ach State shall appoint, in such Manner as the *Legislature* thereof may direct," electors for President and Vice President. (Emphasis added.) Thus, the text of the election law itself, and not just its interpretation by the courts of the States, takes on independent significance.

In *McPherson v. Blacker* (1892), . . . we explained that Art. II, §1, cl. 2, "convey[s] the broadest power of determination" and "leaves it to the legislature exclusively to define the method" of appointment. . . . A significant departure from the legislative scheme for appointing Presidential electors presents a federal constitutional question.

. . .

In Florida, the legislature has chosen to hold statewide elections to appoint the State's 25 electors. Importantly, the legislature has delegated the authority to run the elections and to oversee election disputes to the Secretary of State (Secretary). . . . Isolated sections of the code may well admit of more than one interpretation, but the general coherence of the legislative scheme may not be altered by judicial interpretation so as to wholly change the statutorily provided apportionment of responsibility among these various bodies. In any election but a Presidential election, the Florida Supreme Court can give as little or as much deference to Florida's executives as it chooses, so far as Article II is concerned, and this Court will have no cause to question the court's actions. But, with respect to a Presidential election, the court must be both mindful of the legislature's role under Article II in choosing the manner of appointing electors and deferential to those bodies expressly empowered by the legislature to carry out its constitutional mandate.

Acting pursuant to its constitutional grant of authority, the Florida Legislature has created a detailed, if not perfectly crafted, statutory scheme that provides for appointment of Presidential electors by direct election. . . . Under the statute, "[v]otes cast for the actual candidates for President and Vice President shall be counted as votes cast for the presidential electors supporting such candidates." The legislature has designated the Secretary as the "chief election officer," with the responsibility to "[o]btain and maintain uniformity in the application, operation, and interpretation of the election laws." . . . The state legislature has delegated to county canvassing boards the duties of administering elections. . . . Those boards are responsible for providing results to the state Elections Canvassing Commission, comprising the Governor, the Secretary of State, and the Director of the Division of Elections. . . .

. . .

The [Supreme Court of Florida] determined that canvassing boards' decisions regarding whether to recount ballots past the certification deadline . . . are to be reviewed *de novo*, although the Election Code clearly vests discretion whether to recount in the boards, and sets strict deadlines subject to the Secretary's rejection of late tallies and monetary fines for tardiness. . . . Moreover, the Florida court held that all late vote tallies arriving during the contest period should be automatically included in the certification regardless of the certification deadline . . . thus virtually eliminating both the deadline and the Secretary's discretion to disregard recounts that violate it.

. . .

Given all these factors, and in light of the legislative intent identified by the Florida Supreme Court to bring Florida within the "safe harbor" provision of 3 U.S.C. §5, the remedy prescribed by the Supreme Court of Florida cannot be deemed an "appropriate" one as of December 8. It significantly departed from the statutory framework in place on November 7, and authorized open-ended further proceedings which could not be completed by December 12, thereby preventing a final determination by that date.

. . .

JUSTICE STEVENS, with whom JUSTICE GINSBURG and JUSTICE BREYER join, dissenting.

The Constitution assigns to the States the primary responsibility for determining the manner of selecting the Presidential electors. . . . When questions arise about the meaning of state laws, including election laws, it is our settled practice to accept the opinions of the highest courts of the States as providing the final answers. On rare occasions, however, either federal statutes or the Federal Constitution may require federal judicial intervention in state elections. This is not such an occasion.

. . .

. . . The legislative power in Florida is subject to judicial review pursuant to Article V of the Florida Constitution, and nothing in Article II of the Federal Constitution frees the state legislature from the constraints in the State Constitution that created it. Moreover, the Florida Legislature's own decision to employ a unitary code for all elections indicates that it intended the Florida Supreme Court to play the same role in Presidential elections that it has historically played in resolving electoral disputes. The Florida Supreme Court's exercise of appellate jurisdiction therefore was wholly consistent with, and indeed contemplated by, the grant of authority in Article II.

. . .

Admittedly, the use of differing substandards for determining voter intent in different counties employing similar voting systems may raise serious concerns. Those concerns are alleviated—if not eliminated—by the fact that a single impartial magistrate will ultimately adjudicate all objections arising from the recount process. Of course, as a general matter, "[t]he interpretation of constitutional principles must not be too literal. We must remember that the machinery of government would not work if it were not allowed a little play in its joints." . . . If it were otherwise, Florida's decision to leave to each county the determination of what balloting system to employ—despite enormous differences in accuracy—might run afoul of equal protection. So, too, might the similar decisions of the vast majority of state legislatures to delegate to local authorities certain decisions with respect to voting systems and ballot design.

. . .

In the interest of finality, . . . the majority effectively orders the disenfranchisement of an unknown number of voters whose ballots reveal their intent—and are therefore legal votes under state law—but were for some reason rejected by ballot-counting machines. It does so on the basis of the deadlines set forth in Title 3 of the United States Code. . . . But, as I have already noted, those provisions merely provide rules of decision for Congress to follow when selecting among conflicting slates of electors. . . . They do not prohibit a State from counting what the majority concedes to be legal votes until a bona fide winner is determined. . . .

. . .

What must underlie petitioners' entire federal assault on the Florida election procedures is an unstated lack of confidence in the impartiality and capacity of the state judges who would make the critical decisions if the vote count were to proceed. Otherwise, their position is wholly without merit. The endorsement of that position by the majority of this Court can only lend credence to the most cynical appraisal of the work of judges throughout the land. It is confidence in the men and women who administer the judicial system that is the true backbone of the rule of law. Time will one day heal the wound to that confidence that will be inflicted by today's decision. One thing, however, is certain. Although we may never know with complete certainty the identity of the winner of this year's Presidential election, the identity of the loser is perfectly clear. It is the Nation's confidence in the judge as an impartial guardian of the rule of law.

JUSTICE SOUTER, with whom JUSTICE BREYER joins, and with whom JUSTICE STEVENS and JUSTICE GINSBURG join in part, dissenting.

. . .

Petitioners have raised an equal protection claim (or, alternatively, a due process claim . . .) in the charge that unjustifiably disparate standards are applied in different electoral jurisdictions to otherwise identical facts. It is true that the Equal Protection Clause does not forbid the use of a variety of voting mechanisms within a jurisdiction, even though different mechanisms will have different levels of effectiveness in recording voters' intentions; local variety can be justified by concerns about cost, the potential value of innovation, and so on. But evidence in the record here suggests that a different order of disparity obtains under rules for determining a voter's intent that have been applied. . . . I can conceive of no legitimate state interest served by these differing treatments of the expressions of voters' fundamental rights. The differences appear wholly arbitrary.

In deciding what to do about this, we should take account of the fact that electoral votes are due to be cast in six days. I would therefore remand the case to the courts of Florida with instructions to establish uniform standards for evaluating the several types of ballots that have prompted differing treatments, to be applied within and among counties when passing on such identical ballots in any further recounting (or successive recounting) that the courts might order.

Unlike the majority, I see no warrant for this Court to assume that Florida could not possibly comply with this requirement before the date set for the meeting of electors, December 18. . . . There is no justification for denying the State the opportunity to try to count all disputed ballots now.

I respectfully dissent.

JUSTICE GINSBURG, dissenting. . . .

JUSTICE BREYER, with whom JUSTICE STEVENS, JUSTICE GINSBURG, and JUSTICE SOUTER join in part, dissenting.

. . .

. . . Those who caution judicial restraint in resolving political disputes have described the quintessential case for that restraint as a case marked, among other things, by the "strangeness of the issue," its "intractability to principled resolution," its "sheer momentousness, . . . which tends to unbalance judicial judgment," and "the inner vulnerability, the self-doubt of an institution which is electorally irresponsible and has no earth to draw strength from." Those characteristics mark this case.

At the same time, . . . the Court is not acting to vindicate a fundamental constitutional principle, such as the need to protect a basic human liberty. No other strong reason to act is present. Congressional statutes tend to obviate the need. And, above all, in this highly politicized matter, the appearance of a split decision runs the risk of undermining the public's confidence in the Court itself. That confidence is a public treasure. It has been built slowly over many years, some of which were marked by a Civil War and the tragedy of segregation. It is a vitally necessary ingredient of any successful effort to protect basic liberty and, indeed, the rule of law itself. We run no risk of returning to the days when a President (responding to this Court's efforts to protect the Cherokee Indians) might have said, "John Marshall has made his decision; now let him enforce it!" But we do risk a self- inflicted wound—a wound that may harm not just the Court, but the Nation. . . .

Shelby County v. Holder, 570 U.S. ___ (2013)

Shelby County, Alabama, was a covered jurisdiction under the Voting Rights Act of 1965, as amended in 2006. As such, all voting changes in the county had to be precleared by either the attorney general of the United States or federal judges on the Court of Appeals for the District of Columbia. In 2010 county officials filed a lawsuit against Attorney General Eric Holder, claiming that the preclearance formula (Section 4) and requirements (Section 5) of the Voting Rights Act were unconstitutional. A federal district court rejected that claim, as did the Court of Appeals for the District of Columbia. Shelby County appealed to the Supreme Court of the United States.

The Supreme Court by a 5–4 vote declared unconstitutional the preclearance formula in Section 4 of the Voting Rights Act. Chief Justice Roberts's majority opinion asserted that the formula was based on outdated evidence inconsistent with contemporary voting rights practices. Why did he reach that conclusion? Why did Justice Ginsburg disagree? Under the Fifteenth Amendment, what are the respective roles of the Congress and the judiciary when determining whether a sufficient factual basis supports the ongoing need for the Section 4 formula? The chief justice paid much attention to federalism principles, most notably the principle of "equal sovereignty." Justice Ginsburg, by comparison, discussed standards under the Civil War Amendments. What explains the different constitutional focus of each opinion? How would you integrate federalism and the post–Civil War Amendments? Both opinions commented on the status of voting discrimination in the contemporary United States. Who painted the more accurate picture? How do these pictures influence your attitude toward the case? Does Shelby County *in practice sound the death knell for preclearance? Is preclearance as well as the specific formula Congress used a relic of the past or a vital means for preventing racial discrimination in voting and elections?*

CHIEF JUSTICE ROBERTS delivered the opinion of the Court.

. . .

. . . The Federal Government does not have a general right to review and veto state enactments before they go into effect. A proposal to grant such authority to "negative" state laws was considered at the Constitutional Convention, but rejected in favor of allowing state laws to take effect, subject to later challenge under the Supremacy Clause.

Outside the strictures of the Supremacy Clause, States retain broad autonomy in structuring their governments and pursuing legislative objectives. Indeed, the Constitution provides that all powers not specifically granted to the Federal Government are reserved to the States or citizens. This "allocation of powers in our federal system preserves the integrity, dignity, and residual sovereignty of the States." But the federal balance "is not just an end in itself: Rather, federalism secures to citizens the liberties that derive from the diffusion of sovereign power."

. . .

Not only do States retain sovereignty under the Constitution, there is also a "fundamental principle of equal sovereignty" among the States. Over a hundred years ago, this Court explained that our Nation "was and is a union of States, equal in power, dignity and authority." *Coyle v. Smith* (1911). Indeed, "the constitutional equality of the States is essential to the harmonious operation of the scheme upon which the Republic was organized." . . .

The Voting Rights Act sharply departs from these basic principles. It suspends "all changes to state election law—however innocuous—until they have been precleared by federal authorities in Washington, D.C." States must beseech the Federal Government for permission to implement laws that they would otherwise have the right to enact and execute on their own, subject of course to any injunction in a §2 action. . . . And despite the tradition of equal sovereignty, the Act applies to only nine States (and several additional counties). While one State waits months or years and expends funds to implement a validly enacted law, its neighbor can typically put the same law into effect immediately, through the normal legislative process. . . .

. . .

In 1966, we found these departures from the basic features of our system of government justified. The "blight of racial discrimination in voting" had "infected the electoral process in parts of our country for nearly a century." Several States had enacted a variety of requirements and tests "specifically designed to prevent" African-Americans from voting. Case-by-case litigation had proved inadequate to prevent such racial discrimination in voting, in part because States "merely switched to discriminatory devices not covered by the federal decrees," "enacted difficult new tests," or simply "defied and evaded court orders." Shortly before enactment of the Voting Rights Act, only 19.4 percent of African-Americans of voting age were registered to vote in Alabama, only 31.8 percent in Louisiana, and only 6.4 percent in Mississippi. Those figures were roughly 50 percentage points or more below the figures for whites.

. . .

At the time, the coverage formula—the means of linking the exercise of the unprecedented authority with the problem that warranted it—made sense. We found that "Congress chose to limit its attention to the geographic areas where immediate action seemed necessary." The areas where Congress found "evidence of actual voting discrimination" shared two characteristics: "the use of tests and devices for voter registration, and a voting rate in the 1964 presidential election at least 12 points below the national average." . . . The formula ensured that the "stringent remedies [were] aimed at areas where voting discrimination ha[d] been most flagrant."

Nearly 50 years later, things have changed dramatically. . . . In the covered jurisdictions, "[v]oter turnout and registration rates now approach parity. Blatantly discriminatory evasions of federal decrees are rare. And minority candidates hold office at unprecedented levels." The tests and devices that blocked access to the ballot have been forbidden nationwide for over 40 years.

Those conclusions are not ours alone. Congress said the same when it reauthorized the Act in 2006, writing that "[s]ignificant progress has been made in eliminating first generation barriers experienced by minority voters, including increased numbers of registered minority voters, minority voter turnout, and minority representation in Congress, State legislatures, and local elected offices." The House Report elaborated that "the number of African-Americans who are registered and who turn out to cast ballots has increased significantly over the last 40 years, particularly since 1982," and noted that "[i]n some circumstances, minorities register to vote and cast ballots at levels that surpass those of white voters." That Report also explained that there have been "significant increases in the number of African-Americans serving in elected offices"; more specifically, there has been approximately a 1,000 percent increase since 1965 in the number of African-American elected officials in the six States originally covered by the Voting Rights Act.

. . .

There is no doubt that these improvements are in large part because of the Voting Rights Act. . . . Problems remain . . . , but there is no denying that, due to the Voting Rights Act, our Nation has made great strides.

Yet the Act has not eased the restrictions in §5 or narrowed the scope of the coverage formula in §4(b) along the way. Those extraordinary and unprecedented features were reauthorized—as if nothing had changed. In fact, the Act's unusual remedies have grown even stronger. When Congress reauthorized the Act in 2006, it did so for another 25 years on top of the previous 40—a far cry from the initial five-year period. Congress also expanded the prohibitions in §5. We had previously interpreted §5 to prohibit only those redistricting plans that would have the purpose or effect of worsening the position of minority groups. In 2006, Congress amended §5 to prohibit laws that could have favored such groups but did not do so because of a discriminatory purpose, even though we had stated that such broadening of §5 coverage would "exacerbate the substantial federalism costs that the preclearance procedure already exacts, perhaps to the extent of raising concerns about §5's constitutionality." . . .

Respondents do not deny that there have been improvements on the ground, but argue that much of this can be attributed to the deterrent effect of §5, which dissuades covered jurisdictions from engaging in discrimination that they would resume should §5 be struck down. Under this theory, however, §5 would be effectively immune from scrutiny; no matter how "clean" the record of covered jurisdictions, the argument could always be made that it was deterrence that accounted for the good behavior.

. . .

Coverage today is based on decades-old data and eradicated practices. . . . In 1965, the States could be divided into two groups: those with a recent history of voting tests and low voter registration and turnout, and those without those characteristics. Congress based its coverage formula on that distinction. Today the Nation is no longer divided along those lines, yet the Voting Rights Act continues to treat it as if it were.

. . .

. . . [H]istory did not end in 1965. By the time the Act was reauthorized in 2006, there had been 40 more years of it. In assessing the "current need[ ]" for a preclearance system that treats States differently from one another today, that history cannot be ignored. During that time, largely because of the Voting Rights Act, voting tests were abolished, disparities in voter registration and turnout due to race were erased, and African-Americans attained political office in record numbers. And yet the coverage formula that Congress reauthorized in 2006 ignores these developments, keeping the focus on decades-old data relevant to decades-old problems, rather than current data reflecting current needs.

. . .

In defending the coverage formula, the Government, the intervenors, and the dissent also rely heavily on data from the record that they claim justify disparate coverage. Congress compiled thousands of pages of evidence before reauthorizing the Voting Rights Act. . . . Regardless of how to look at the record, however, no one can fairly say that it shows anything approaching the "pervasive," "flagrant," "widespread," and "rampant" discrimination that faced Congress in 1965, and that clearly distinguished the covered jurisdictions from the rest of the Nation at that time.

But a more fundamental problem remains: Congress did not use the record it compiled to shape a coverage formula grounded in current conditions. It instead reenacted a formula based on 40-year-old facts having no logical relation to the present day. The dissent relies on "second-generation barriers," which are not impediments to the casting of ballots, but rather electoral arrangements that affect the weight of minority votes. That does not cure the problem. Viewing the preclearance requirements as targeting such efforts simply highlights the irrationality of continued reliance on the §4 coverage formula, which is based on voting tests and access to the ballot, not vote dilution. We cannot pretend that we are reviewing an updated statute, or try our hand at updating the statute ourselves, based on the new record compiled by Congress. Contrary to the dissent's contention, we are not ignoring the record; we are simply recognizing that it played no role in shaping the statutory formula before us today.

. . .

The dissent treats the Act as if it were just like any other piece of legislation, but this Court has made clear from the beginning that the Voting Rights Act is far from ordinary. At the risk of repetition, *South Carolina v. Katzenbach* (1966) indicated that the Act was "uncommon" and "not otherwise appropriate," but was justified by "exceptional" and "unique" conditions. Yet the dissent goes so far as to suggest instead that the preclearance requirement and disparate treatment of the States should be upheld into the future "unless there [is] no or almost no evidence of unconstitutional action by States."

. . .

Our decision in no way affects the permanent, nationwide ban on racial discrimination in voting found in §2. We issue no holding on §5 itself, only on the coverage formula. Congress may draft another formula based on current conditions. Such a formula is an initial prerequisite to a determination that exceptional conditions still exist justifying such an "extraordinary departure from the traditional course of relations between the States and the Federal Government." Our country has changed, and while any racial discrimination in voting is too much, Congress must ensure that the legislation it passes to remedy that problem speaks to current conditions.

JUSTICE THOMAS, concurring.

. . .

While the Court claims to "issue no holding on §5 itself," its own opinion compellingly demonstrates that Congress has failed to justify "'current burdens'" with a record demonstrating "'current needs.'" By leaving the inevitable conclusion unstated, the Court needlessly prolongs the demise of that provision. For the reasons stated in the Court's opinion, I would find §5 unconstitutional.

JUSTICE GINSBURG, with whom JUSTICE BREYER, JUSTICE SOTOMAYOR, and JUSTICE KAGAN join, dissenting.

. . .

Although the Voting Rights Act (VRA) wrought dramatic changes in the realization of minority voting rights, the Act, to date, surely has not eliminated all vestiges of discrimination against the exercise of the franchise by minority citizens. Jurisdictions covered by the preclearance requirement continued to submit, in large numbers, proposed changes to voting laws that the Attorney General declined to approve, auguring that barriers to minority voting would quickly resurface were the preclearance remedy eliminated. Congress also found that as "registration and voting of minority citizens increas[ed], other measures may be resorted to which would dilute increasing minority voting strength." Efforts to reduce the impact of minority votes, in contrast to direct attempts to block access to the ballot, are aptly described as "second-generation barriers" to minority voting.

Second-generation barriers come in various forms. One of the blockages is racial gerrymandering, the redrawing of legislative districts in an "effort to segregate the races for purposes of voting." Another is adoption of a system of at-large voting in lieu of district-by-district voting in a city with a sizable black minority. By switching to at-large voting, the overall majority could control the election of each city council member, effectively eliminating the potency of the minority's votes. A similar effect could be achieved if the city engaged in discriminatory annexation by incorporating majority-white areas into city limits, thereby decreasing the effect of VRA-occasioned increases in black voting.

. . .

After considering the full legislative record, Congress made the following findings: The VRA has directly caused significant progress in eliminating first-generation barriers to ballot access, leading to a marked increase in minority voter registration and turnout and the number of minority elected officials. But despite this progress, "second generation barriers constructed to prevent minority voters from fully participating in the electoral process" continued to exist, as well as racially polarized voting in the covered jurisdictions, which increased the political vulnerability of racial and language minorities in those jurisdictions. Extensive "[e]vidence of continued discrimination," Congress concluded, "clearly show[ed] the continued need for Federal oversight" in covered jurisdictions. . . .

. . .

In answering this question, the Court does not write on a clean slate. It is well established that Congress' judgment regarding exercise of its power to enforce the Fourteenth and Fifteenth Amendments warrants substantial deference. . . . Notably, "the Founders' first successful amendment told Congress that it could 'make no law' over a certain domain"; in contrast, the Civil War Amendments used "language [that] authorized transformative new federal statutes to uproot all vestiges of unfreedom and inequality" and provided "sweeping enforcement powers . . . to enact 'appropriate' legislation targeting state abuses."

The stated purpose of the Civil War Amendments was to arm Congress with the power and authority to protect all persons within the Nation from violations of their rights by the States. In exercising that power, then, Congress may use "all means which are appropriate, which are plainly adapted" to the constitutional ends declared by these Amendments. So when Congress acts to enforce the right to vote free from racial discrimination, we ask not whether Congress has chosen the means most wise, but whether Congress has rationally selected means appropriate to a legitimate end. "It is not for us to review the congressional resolution of [the need for its chosen remedy]. It is enough that we be able to perceive a basis upon which the Congress might resolve the conflict as it did." *Katzenbach v. Morgan* (1966).

. . .

True, conditions in the South have impressively improved since passage of the Voting Rights Act. Congress noted this improvement and found that the VRA was the driving force behind it. But Congress also found that voting discrimination had evolved into subtler second-generation barriers, and that eliminating preclearance would risk loss of the gains that had been made. . . .

. . .

There is no question, moreover, that the covered jurisdictions have a unique history of problems with racial discrimination in voting. . . .

. . .

Although covered jurisdictions account for less than 25 percent of the country's population, [a] study revealed that they accounted for 56 percent of successful §2 litigation since 1982. Controlling for population, there were nearly four times as many successful §2 cases in covered jurisdictions as there were in noncovered jurisdictions. The study further found that §2 lawsuits are more likely to succeed when they are filed in covered jurisdictions than in noncovered jurisdictions. From these findings—ignored by the Court—Congress reasonably concluded that the coverage formula continues to identify the jurisdictions of greatest concern.

. . .

The sad irony of today's decision lies in its utter failure to grasp why the VRA has proven effective. The Court appears to believe that the VRA's success in eliminating the specific devices extant in 1965 means that preclearance is no longer needed. With that belief, and the argument derived from it, history repeats itself. The same assumption—that the problem could be solved when particular methods of voting discrimination are identified and eliminated—was indulged and proved wrong repeatedly prior to the VRA's enactment. Unlike prior statutes, which singled out particular tests or devices, the VRA is grounded in Congress' recognition of the "variety and persistence" of measures designed to impair minority voting rights. In truth, the evolution of voting discrimination into more subtle second-generation barriers is powerful evidence that a remedy as effective as preclearance remains vital to protect minority voting rights and prevent backsliding.

. . .

IX. Equality

MAJOR DEVELOPMENTS

- Ongoing controversies over affirmative action
- Increased constitutional protection against gender discrimination
- Congress and the Court dispute the proper standard of constitutional protection for people with disabilities

Americans are both committed to and conflicted about constitutional equality. No prominent political movement champions the status inequalities of the past. Neither Democrats nor Republicans maintain that persons are entitled to special privileges or ought to shoulder particular burdens because of their race, gender, ethnicity, religion, or social class. Native Americans who choose to live on reservations aside, no political movement champions the notion that nominal equals may nevertheless have very different legal rights and obligations. Nevertheless, controversies rage over the legacy of the civil rights movement. Liberals and conservatives dispute whether persons of color and women have achieved actual equality, what other groups continue to be victims of inegalitarian social policies, what social policies best rectify past inequalities, and when real differences between different classes of persons justify laws that provide special benefits and burdens to only some people or groups. New disputes over whether communities may adopt zoning and other regulations designed to prevent superstores from taking business away from local shops have emerged while ongoing disputes over affirmative action continue to rage.

Democrats and Republicans dispute what equality means. Prominent Democrats insist that the concerns that animated the civil rights revolution remain vibrant. Liberal Democrats support affirmative action programs for persons of color and women; believe that other Americans suffer from status inequalities; and champion anti-subordination conceptions of equality that focus on the actual condition of persons of different races, genders, and groups. The Democratic Party platform of 2008 asserted:

> Democrats will fight to end discrimination based on race, sex, ethnicity, national origin, language, religion, sexual orientation, gender identity, age, and disability in every corner of our country, because that's the America we believe in.
>
> . . .
>
> We are committed to ensuring full equality for women: we reaffirm our support for the Equal Rights Amendment. . . . We will restore and support the White House Initiative on Asian-American and Pacific Islanders, including enforcement on disaggregation of Census data. We will make the Census more culturally sensitive, including outreach, language assistance, and increased confidentiality protections to ensure accurate counting of the growing Latino and Asian American, and Pacific Islander populations, and continue working on efforts to be more inclusive. We will sign the U.N. Convention on the Rights of Persons with Disabilities and restore the original intent of the Americans with Disabilities Act.
>
> We support the full inclusion of all families, including same-sex couples, in the life of our nation, and support equal responsibility, benefits, and protections. . . .
>
> . . . We support affirmative action, including in federal contracting and higher education, to make sure that those locked out of the doors of opportunity will be able to walk through those doors in the future.

Republicans are more inclined to think that the civil rights revolution has strayed from proper egalitarian paths. Conservatives oppose affirmative action policies, are more inclined than liberals to limit the beneficiaries of antidiscrimination policies, and champion anti-classification conceptions of equality that emphasize the value of formal legal equality. The Republican Party platform of 2008 stated,

> Our commitment to equal opportunity extends from landmark school-choice legislation for the students of Washington D.C. to historic appointments at the highest levels of government. We consider discrimination based on sex, race, age, religion, creed, disability, or national origin to be immoral, and we will strongly enforce anti-discrimination statutes. We ask all to join us in rejecting the forces of hatred and bigotry and in denouncing all who practice or promote racism, anti-Semitism, ethnic prejudice, or religious intolerance. As a matter of principle, Republicans oppose any attempts to create race-based governments within the United States, as well as any domestic governments not bound by the Constitution or the Bill of Rights.
>
> Precisely because we oppose discrimination, we reject preferences, quotas, and set-asides, whether in education or in corporate boardrooms. The government should not make contracts on this basis, and neither should corporations. We support efforts to help low-income individuals get a fair shot based on their potential and merit, and we affirm the commonsense approach of the Chief Justice of the United States: that the way to stop discriminating on the basis of race is to stop discriminating.

The Supreme Court has reflected these partisan divisions. The more liberal justices on the Rehnquist and early Roberts Courts supported affirmative action, stricter scrutiny for gender discrimination, and more aggressive policing of other status inequalities. The more conservative justices opposed affirmative action, urged lesser scrutiny for gender discriminations, and opposed the creation of heightened scrutiny for new classes. Justices Kennedy and O'Connor, who held the balance of power, tended to favor the liberal position on women and the conservative position on heightened scrutiny for new classes, and split the difference on affirmative action. Interestingly, the standard partisan divisions on the Court did not occur in the few cases in which the justices considered the constitutional rights of Native Americans, which were generally decided in favor of tribal sovereignty.

A. Equality Under Law

A remarkable array of contemporary citizens maintain that they are not being treated as constitutional equals. Americans with disabilities, Wal-Mart stores, children in poorer school districts, gay rights activists, and numerous others have lobbied and litigated for policies that they believe promote equality under the law. Federal courts have been unsympathetic to these claims. No new suspect class has been announced in the past three decades. With the exception of rights associated with civil and criminal trials, the Supreme Court has not announced a new fundamental interest that requires heightened scrutiny. Indeed, the Supreme Court declared unconstitutional several congressional efforts to use Section 5 of the Fourteenth Amendment to expand equal protection rights outside of race and gender. *Board of Trustees of the University of Alabama v. Garrett* (2001) declared unconstitutional Title I of the Americans with Disabilities Act. The judicial majority insisted that Congress could protect handicapped Americans only from state discrimination that did not satisfy the rational basis test. Chief Justice Rehnquist's majority opinion asserted that "Congress had failed to identify a history and pattern of unconstitutional employment discrimination by the States against the disabled adequate to show that the states had engaged in irrational discrimination." The justices were more supportive of Congress and the disabled in *Tennessee v. Lane* (2004). In that case the justices ruled that Congress could require states to ensure that the handicapped had adequate access to courthouses as a means of implementing the constitutional "right to be present at all stages of a [criminal] trial."

Romer v. Evans (1996) was the important exception to the judicial tendency to restrict equal protection to race and gender. That case arose after Colorado voters passed an amendment to the state constitution forbidding localities from passing laws prohibiting discrimination against gays and lesbians. The justices by a 6–3 vote declared the amendment unconstitutional, with Justice Kennedy explaining on behalf of the majority that the equal protection clause prohibits the state and its people from "withdraw[ing] from homosexuals, but no others, specific legal protection from the injuries caused by discrimination" and from "forbid[ding] reinstatement of these laws and policies." In his dissenting opinion, Justice Scalia asserted that "the amendment prohibits *special treatment* of homosexuals, and nothing more." By assuming invidious discrimination, Scalia declared, "the Court has mistaken a Kulturkampf [culture war or culture struggle] for a fit of spite"; furthermore, he asserted, "This Court has no business imposing upon all Americans the resolution favored by an elite class from which the Members of this institution are selected, pronouncing that 'animosity' toward homosexuality . . . is evil."

State courts have been more sympathetic to various claims of constitutional equality under the state constitution. One commentary notes,

> Many states have seen fit in cases involving equality to reconstitute the multi-tier system of review developed in the federal courts. In some instances, this has been done by expanding the scope of strict or intermediate scrutiny to encompass classifications or rights; which in the federal courts are assigned to lower regions. State courts have upgraded gender classifications from intermediate to strict scrutiny and have ruled that classifications based on sexual orientation are subject to heightened scrutiny. State courts have taken the position that education is a fundamental right; therefore, public school financing schemes are to be reviewed with strict scrutiny. And state courts have held that strict scrutiny should be applied to determine the constitutionality of laws that deny funding for abortions. In other instances, the tiers of review have been reconstituted by intensifying rationality review to give it an edge lacking under the federal approach. State courts may sharpen rationality review to assess the constitutionality of economic legislation that denies benefits for no apparent reason, interferes with fair competition, or grants special entitlements to a favored few. On occasion, state courts may enhance rationality review to examine the constitutionality of criminal laws that provide differential penalties or treatment for similar offenses. One state court even used a sharpened version of rationality review to invalidate a statute that discriminated against adopted persons.[70]

---

70. Jeffrey M. Shaman, "The Evolution of Equality in State Constitutional Law," *Rutgers Law Journal* 34 (2003): 1013.

B. Race

Many commentators claim that the United States has entered a "postracial era." The president is an African American. Mass civil rights demonstrations are no longer a regular occurrence on city streets and college campuses. Neither the Democratic nor Republican parties have specific sections in their platforms detailing their positions on race issues. Major Supreme Court decisions on race issues now occur only once every five years or so.

Americans dispute the significance of the reduced salience of racial issues in constitutional politics. Many believe that the United States has successfully become a color-blind nation. With the unfortunate exception of affirmative action and isolated instances of racial discrimination, they claim, official policies reflect a national commitment to formal racial equality. Others insist that the low salience of race is better interpreted as an abandonment of the quest for racial equality. While official policies no longer explicitly discriminate against persons of color, these individuals point out that the life chances of the average person of color remain substantially less than the life chances of the average white person.

The conditions under which government may consider race are vigorously disputed. Many progressives insist that government should consider race in order to achieve diversity and compensate for past injustices. Others think that race is sometimes a legitimate consideration when police are seeking to apprehend criminals and terrorists. These issues are fought in almost every setting, from state referenda on affirmative action to the law school admissions process to executive decisions about the conditions under which racial profiling is legitimate.

Affirmative action remains the main lightning rod for racial issues in the contemporary United States. Republicans condemn the use of race in school assignments, college admissions, and employment decisions. The amicus brief filed by the second Bush administration in *Parents Involved in Community Schools v. Seattle School District No. 1* (2007) asserted that "race-conscious measures . . . are not only at odds with *Brown*'s ultimate objective of 'achiev[ing] a system of determining admission to the public schools on a nonracial basis,' but contravene the fundamental liberties guaranteed to each citizen by the Equal Protection Clause."[71] Democrats, sometimes with less enthusiasm, insist that affirmative action policies are legitimate means for achieving greater racial equality. The amicus brief submitted by the Obama administration in *Fisher v. University of Texas at Austin* (2012) declared,

> The educational benefits of diversity . . . are of critical importance to the United States. Careers in a range of fields that are vital to the national interest—such as the military officer corps, science, law, medicine, finance, education, and other professions . . . must be open to all segments of American society, regardless of race and ethnicity. That is not simply a matter of civic responsibility; it is a pressing necessity in an era of intense competition in the global economy and ever-evolving worldwide national-security threats.

For this reason, the Obama Justice Department concluded, "a university may institute a narrowly tailed policy that considers race as part of a holistic, individualized admissions process, when doing so is necessary to achieve the educational benefits of diversity."

The U.S. Supreme Court in *Adarand Constructors, Inc. v. Peña* (1995) sent confusing signals on the constitutionality of affirmative action. Justice Scalia's opinion clearly stated that race-conscious measures were never or hardly ever constitutional unless designed to remedy specific victims of past discrimination. He wrote, "Under our Constitution there can be no such thing as either a creditor or a debtor race." The four more liberal justices on the Rehnquist Court insisted that Congress had broad powers to use race-conscious measures. Justice Ginsburg stated, "Congress [has] authority to act affirmatively, not only to end discrimination, but also to counter discrimination's lingering effects." Justice O'Connor's crucial plurality opinion split the difference. She insisted that affirmative action programs must meet three tough constitutional conditions:

- "Skepticism: Any preference based on racial or ethnic criteria must necessarily receive a most searching examination."

71. Brief for the United States as Amicus Curiae Supporting Petitioner, *Parents Involved in Community Schools v. Seattle School District No. 1*, 551 U.S. 701 (2007), 7.

- "Consistency: The standard of review under the Equal Protection clause is not dependent on the race of those burdened or benefitted by a particular classification."
- "Congruence: Equal protection analysis in the Fifth Amendment area is the same as that under the Fourteenth Amendment."

"Taken together," O'Connor stated, "these three presumptions lead to the conclusion that any person, of whatever race, has the right to demand that any government actor subject to the Constitution justify any racial classification subjecting that person to unequal treatment under the strictest judicial scrutiny." Justice O'Connor concluded her opinion, however, by mitigating the apparent force of the skepticism, consistency, and congruence conditions. "We wish to dispel the notion that strict scrutiny is 'strict in theory, but fatal in fact,'" she wrote. "The unhappy persistence of both the practice and the lingering effects of racial discrimination against minority groups in this country is an unfortunate reality, and government is not disqualified from acting in response to it."

O'Connor again took an intermediate position eight years later when litigants challenged admissions policies at the University of Michigan. She provided the crucial fifth vote in *Grutter v. Bollinger* (2003), which sustained the use of race in the admissions criteria policy at Michigan Law School, while voting in *Gratz v. Bollinger* (2003) with the *Grutter* dissenters and Justice Breyer to strike down the use of race in determining undergraduate admissions at the University of Michigan. The policies were different. The law school required students to write an essay detailing their contributions to diversity, thus making all students in theory eligible for diversity consideration. The undergraduate admissions process gave a fixed number of points to persons of color. Nevertheless, only Justices Breyer and O'Connor believed that this difference made a constitutional difference. Significantly, this 1–1 "tie" strongly favored proponents of affirmative action. Universities committed to affirmative action programs simply adopted the Michigan Law School policy that the court sustained in *Grutter.*

Illustration 11-7 Diversity and College Admissions

Source: Signe Wilkinson Editorial Cartoon used with the permission of Signe Wilkinson, the Washington Post Writers Group and the Cartoonist Group. All rights reserved.

Justice O'Connor's retirement has cast doubt on the future of affirmative action. Since then, the Roberts Court by 5–4 votes has declared unconstitutional or illegal two race-conscious policies. *Parents Involved in Community Schools v. Seattle School District No. 1* (2007) held that school boards could not use race when assigning students to public schools unless they were complying with a court order to remedy the effects of past legal segregation. *Ricci v. DeStefano* (2009) ruled that New Haven violated the Civil Rights Act of 1964 when the city refused to promote firefighters on the basis of an exam on which white applicants scored substantially higher than applicants of color. When given the opportunity to revisit the question of affirmative action in university admissions in *Fisher v. University of Texas at Austin* (2013), the justices by a 7–1 vote decided to send the case back to the lower federal courts. Justice Kennedy explained that the lower court upheld the university's program after concluding that the university made a "good faith" decision to use race as a factor, when instead the lower court should have applied strict scrutiny and asked whether the university's compelling interest in diversity could have been accomplished with a race-neutral alternative.

Grutter v. Bollinger, 539 U.S. 306 (2003)

In 1996 Barbara Grutter was denied admission to the University of Michigan School of Law. The admissions policy of the law school at the time sought to "achieve that diversity which has the potential to enrich everyone's education and thus make a law school class stronger than the sum of its parts." The law school sought to achieve this objective partly through personal examination of all applications and partly by requiring each applicant to submit an essay on how he or she would diversify the institution. While the admissions policy recognized "many possible bases for diversity admissions," the law school explicitly emphasized "one particular type of diversity"—"racial and ethnic diversity with special reference to the inclusion of students from groups which have been historically discriminated against, like African Americans, Hispanics and Native Americans, who without this commitment might not be represented in our student body in meaningful numbers." Michigan claimed not to have fixed quotas, but the law school did seek to enroll a "critical mass" of African American and other students of color. Grutter claimed that this policy discriminated against her in violation of the equal protection clause of the Fourteenth Amendment. A federal district court declared that the law school's policy was unconstitutional, but that decision was reversed by the Court of Appeals for the Sixth Circuit. Grutter appealed to the Supreme Court of the United States.

Justice O'Connor's majority opinion sustained the Michigan race/diversity policy. Her majority opinion declared that diversity was a compelling state interest and that the Michigan policy was narrowly tailored to achieve that goal. Why did Justice O'Connor declare that the policy was narrowly tailored? Why did the dissents disagree? Was her scrutiny as strict as that used in strict scrutiny cases in which laws had discriminated against persons of color? Notice the emphasis the majority opinion places on the amicus briefs submitted by retired military officers and major corporations in favor of affirmative action. The military and major corporations are normally thought to be conservative organizations. Why did they support affirmative action? Do you think that these briefs influenced the result in Grutter?

On the same day that Grutter *was decided the Supreme Court by a 6–3 vote declared unconstitutional in* Gratz v. Bollinger *the use of race in undergraduate admissions at the University of Michigan. Michigan evaluated candidates on a 150-point scale. Up to 110 points could be gained through grades and test scores. Michigan awarded students twenty points for being a member of a historically underrepresented group. Persons might also receive twenty points for athletic skills or sociological disadvantage, but such characteristics as leadership skills or demonstrated artistic talent were given far fewer points. Justice O'Connor's crucial concurring opinion in* Gratz *asserted,*

> *[This] selection index, by setting up automatic, predetermined point allocations for the soft variables, ensures that the diversity contributions of applicants cannot be individually assessed. This policy stands in sharp contrast to the law school's admissions plan, which enables admissions officers to make nuanced judgments with respect to the contributions each applicant is likely to make to the diversity of the incoming class.*

Did Justice O'Connor provide a persuasive distinction between constitutional and unconstitutional affirmative action plans? Were the two Michigan plans likely to operate very differently in practice? What affirmative action plans do you believe will pass constitutional muster after Grutter *and* Gratz*? What affirmative action plans do you believe should pass constitutional muster?*

JUSTICE O'CONNOR delivered the opinion of the Court.

. . .

The Equal Protection Clause provides that no State shall "deny to any person within its jurisdiction the equal protection of the laws." Because the Fourteenth Amendment "protects *persons*, not *groups*," all "governmental action based on race—a *group* classification long recognized as in most circumstances irrelevant and therefore prohibited—should be subjected to detailed judicial inquiry to ensure that the *personal* right to equal protection of the laws has not been infringed." *Adarand Constructors, Inc. v. Peña* (1995). . . .

We have held that all racial classifications imposed by government "must be analyzed by a reviewing court under strict scrutiny." This means that such classifications are constitutional only if they are narrowly tailored to further compelling governmental interests. "Absent searching judicial inquiry into the justification for such race-based measures," we have no way to determine what "classifications are 'benign' or 'remedial' and what classifications are in fact motivated by illegitimate notions of racial inferiority or simple racial politics." *Richmond v. J. A. Croson Co.* (1989). We apply strict scrutiny to all racial classifications to "'smoke out' illegitimate uses of race by assuring that [government] is pursuing a goal important enough to warrant use of a highly suspect tool."

Strict scrutiny is not "strict in theory, but fatal in fact." *Adarand Constructors.* Although all governmental uses of race are subject to strict scrutiny, not all are invalidated by it. . . .

. . .

We have long recognized that, given the important purpose of public education and the expansive freedoms of speech and thought associated with the university environment, universities occupy a special niche in our constitutional tradition. . . . Our conclusion that the Law School has a compelling interest in a diverse student body is informed by our view that attaining a diverse student body is at the heart of the Law School's proper institutional mission, and that "good faith" on the part of a university is "presumed" absent "a showing to the contrary."

. . .

These benefits are substantial. As the District Court emphasized, the Law School's admissions policy promotes "cross-racial understanding," helps to break down racial stereotypes, and "enables [students] to better understand persons of different races." These benefits are "important and laudable," because "classroom discussion is livelier, more spirited, and simply more enlightening and interesting" when the students have "the greatest possible variety of backgrounds."

. . . These benefits are not theoretical but real, as major American businesses have made clear that the skills needed in today's increasingly global marketplace can only be developed through exposure to widely diverse people, cultures, ideas, and viewpoints. What is more, high-ranking retired officers and civilian leaders of the United States military assert that, "based on [their] decades of experience," a "highly qualified, racially diverse officer corps . . . is essential to the military's ability to fulfill its principle mission to provide national security." . . . At present, "the military cannot achieve an officer corps that is *both* highly qualified *and* racially diverse unless the service academies and the ROTC used limited race-conscious recruiting and admissions policies." . . .

. . .

In order to cultivate a set of leaders with legitimacy in the eyes of the citizenry, it is necessary that the path to leadership be visibly open to talented and qualified individuals of every race and ethnicity. All members of our heterogeneous society must have confidence in the openness and integrity of the educational institutions that provide this training. As we have recognized, law schools "cannot be effective in isolation from the individuals and institutions with which the law interacts." Access to legal education (and thus the legal profession) must be inclusive of talented and qualified individuals of every race and ethnicity, so that all members of our heterogeneous society may participate in the educational institutions that provide the training and education necessary to succeed in America.

. . .

To be narrowly tailored, a race-conscious admissions program cannot use a quota system—it cannot "insulate each category of applicants with certain desired qualifications from competition with all other applicants." Instead, a university may consider race or ethnicity only as a "'plus' in a particular applicant's file," without "insulating the individual from comparison with all other candidates for the available seats." In other words, an admissions program must be "flexible enough to consider all pertinent elements of diversity in light of the particular qualifications of each applicant, and to place them on the same footing for consideration, although not necessarily according them the same weight."

We find that the Law School's admissions program bears the hallmarks of a narrowly tailored plan. As Justice Powell made clear in *Regents of the University of California v. Bakke* (1978), truly individualized consideration demands that race be used in a flexible, nonmechanical way. It follows from this mandate that universities cannot establish quotas for members of certain racial groups or put members of those groups on separate admissions tracks. Nor can universities insulate applicants who belong to certain racial or ethnic groups from the competition for admission. Universities can, however, consider race or ethnicity more flexibly as a "plus" factor in the context of individualized consideration of each and every applicant.

. . .

Here, the Law School engages in a highly individualized, holistic review of each applicant's file, giving serious consideration to all the ways an applicant might contribute to a diverse educational environment. The Law School affords this individualized consideration to applicants of all races. There is no policy, either *de jure* or *de facto*, of automatic acceptance or rejection based on any single "soft" variable. Unlike the program at issue in *Gratz v. Bollinger* (2003), the Law School awards no mechanical, predetermined diversity "bonuses" based on race or ethnicity. . . .

. . .

. . . All applicants have the opportunity to highlight their own potential diversity contributions through the submission of a personal statement, letters of recommendation, and an essay describing the ways in which the applicant will contribute to the life and diversity of the Law School. What is more, the Law School actually gives substantial weight to diversity factors besides race. The Law School frequently accepts nonminority applicants with grades and test scores lower than underrepresented minority applicants (and other nonminority applicants) who are rejected. . . .

. . .

We take the Law School at its word that it would "like nothing better than to find a race-neutral admissions formula" and will terminate its race-conscious admissions program as soon as practicable. It has been 25 years since Justice Powell first approved the use of race to further an interest in student body diversity in the context of public higher education. Since that time, the number of minority applicants with high grades and test scores has indeed increased. We expect that 25 years from now, the use of racial preferences will no longer be necessary to further the interest approved today.

JUSTICE GINSBURG, with whom JUSTICE BREYER joins, concurring.

. . .

. . . [I]t remains the current reality that many minority students encounter markedly inadequate and unequal educational opportunities. Despite these inequalities, some minority students are able to meet the high threshold requirements set for admission to the country's finest undergraduate and graduate educational institutions. As lower school education in minority communities improves, an increase in the number of such students may be anticipated. From today's vantage point, one may hope, but not firmly forecast, that over the next generation's span, progress toward nondiscrimination and genuinely equal opportunity will make it safe to sunset affirmative action.

CHIEF JUSTICE REHNQUIST, with whom JUSTICE SCALIA, JUSTICE KENNEDY, and JUSTICE THOMAS join, dissenting.

. . .

In practice, the Law School's program bears little or no relation to its asserted goal of achieving "critical mass." Respondents explain that the Law School seeks to accumulate a "critical mass" of *each* underrepresented minority group. But the record demonstrates that the Law School's admissions practices with respect to these groups differ dramatically and cannot be defended under any consistent use of the term "critical mass."

From 1995 through 2000, the Law School admitted between 1,130 and 1,310 students. Of those, between 13 and 19 were Native American, between 91 and 108 were African-Americans, and between 47 and 56 were Hispanic. If the Law School is admitting between 91 and 108 African-Americans in order to achieve "critical mass," thereby preventing African-American students from feeling "isolated or like spokespersons for their race," one would think that a number of the same order of magnitude would be necessary to accomplish the same purpose for Hispanics and Native Americans. Similarly, even if all of the Native American applicants admitted in a given year matriculate, which the record demonstrates is not at all the case, how can this possibly constitute a "critical mass" of Native Americans in a class of over 350 students? In order for this pattern of admission to be consistent with the Law School's explanation of "critical mass," one would have to believe that the objectives of "critical mass" offered by respondents are achieved with only half the number of Hispanics and one-sixth the number of Native Americans as compared to African-Americans. But respondents offer no race-specific reasons for such disparities. Instead, they simply emphasize the importance of achieving "critical mass," without any explanation of why that concept is applied differently among the three underrepresented minority groups.

...

But the correlation between the percentage of the Law School's pool of applicants who are members of the three minority groups and the percentage of the admitted applicants who are members of these same groups is far too precise to be dismissed as merely the result of the school paying "some attention to [the] numbers." ... [F]rom 1995 through 2000 the percentage of admitted applicants who were members of these minority groups closely tracked the percentage of individuals in the school's applicant pool who were from the same groups. ...

...

JUSTICE KENNEDY, dissenting. ...

JUSTICE SCALIA, with whom JUSTICE THOMAS joins, concurring in part and dissenting in part. ...

JUSTICE THOMAS, with whom JUSTICE SCALIA joins [in part], concurring in part and dissenting in part.

Frederick Douglass, speaking to a group of abolitionists almost 140 years ago, delivered a message lost on today's majority:

> In regard to the colored people, there is always more that is benevolent, I perceive, than just, manifested towards us. What I ask for the negro is not benevolence, not pity, not sympathy, but simply *justice.* The American people have always been anxious to know what they shall do with us. ... I have had but one answer from the beginning. Do nothing with us! Your doing with us has already played the mischief with us. Do nothing with us! If the apples will not remain on the tree of their own strength, if they are worm-eaten at the core, if they are early ripe and disposed to fall, let them fall! ... And if the negro cannot stand on his own legs, let him fall also. All I ask is, give him a chance to stand on his own legs! Let him alone! ...

Like Douglass, I believe blacks can achieve in every avenue of American life without the meddling of university administrators. Because I wish to see all students succeed whatever their color, I share, in some respect, the sympathies of those who sponsor the type of discrimination advanced by the University of Michigan Law School. The Constitution does not, however, tolerate institutional devotion to the status quo in admissions policies when such devotion ripens into racial discrimination. Nor does the Constitution countenance the unprecedented deference the Court gives to the Law School, an approach inconsistent with the very concept of "strict scrutiny."

...

The Constitution abhors classifications based on race, not only because those classifications can harm favored races or are based on illegitimate motives, but also because every time the government places citizens on racial registers and makes race relevant to the provision of burdens or benefits, it demeans us all.

...

The interest in remaining elite and exclusive that the majority thinks so obviously critical requires the use of admissions "standards" that, in turn, create the Law School's "need" to discriminate on the basis of race. The Court validates these admissions standards by concluding that alternatives ... would require "a dramatic sacrifice of ... the academic quality of all admitted students." ... The majority errs, however, because race-neutral alternatives must only be "workable," and do "about as well" *in vindicating the compelling state interest.* The Court never explicitly holds that the Law School's desire to retain the status quo in "academic selectivity" is itself a compelling state interest, and ... it is not. Therefore, the Law School should be forced to choose between its classroom aesthetic and its exclusionary admissions system—it cannot have it both ways.

...

Putting aside the absence of any legal support for the majority's reflexive deference, there is much to be said for the view that the use of tests and other measures to "predict" academic performance is a poor substitute for a system that gives every applicant a chance to prove he can succeed in the study of law. The rallying cry that in the absence of racial discrimination in admissions there would be a true meritocracy ignores the fact that the entire process is poisoned by numerous exceptions to "merit." For example, in the national debate on racial discrimination in higher education admissions, much has been made of the fact that elite institutions utilize a so-called "legacy" preference to give the children of alumni an advantage in admissions. This, and other, exceptions to a "true" meritocracy give the lie to protestations that merit admissions are in fact the order of the day at the Nation's universities. The Equal Protection Clause does not, however, prohibit the use of unseemly legacy preferences or many other kinds of arbitrary admissions procedures. What the Equal Protection Clause does prohibit are classifications made on the basis of race. So while legacy preferences can stand under the Constitution, racial discrimination cannot. I will not twist the Constitution to invalidate legacy preferences or otherwise impose my vision of higher education admissions on the Nation. The majority should similarly stay its impulse to validate faddish racial discrimination the Constitution clearly forbids.

. . .

It is uncontested that each year, the Law School admits a handful of blacks who would be admitted in the absence of racial discrimination. Who can differentiate between those who belong and those who do not? The majority of blacks are admitted to the Law School because of discrimination, and because of this policy all are tarred as undeserving. This problem of stigma does not depend on determinacy as to whether those stigmatized are actually the "beneficiaries" of racial discrimination. When blacks take positions in the highest places of government, industry, or academia, it is an open question today whether their skin color played a part in their advancement. The question itself is the stigma—because either racial discrimination did play a role, in which case the person may be deemed "otherwise unqualified," or it did not, in which case asking the question itself unfairly marks those blacks who would succeed without discrimination. Is this what the Court means by "visibly open"?

. . .

For the immediate future, however, the majority has placed its *imprimatur* on a practice that can only weaken the principle of equality embodied in the Declaration of Independence and the Equal Protection Clause. "Our Constitution is color-blind, and neither knows nor tolerates classes among citizens." *Plessy v. Ferguson* (1896) (Harlan, J., dissenting). It has been nearly 140 years since Frederick Douglass asked the intellectual ancestors of the Law School to "[d]o nothing with us!" and the Nation adopted the Fourteenth Amendment. Now we must wait another 25 years to see this principle of equality vindicated. I therefore respectfully dissent from the remainder of the Court's opinion and the judgment.

C. Gender

Most Americans are committed to some form of gender equality. The Democratic Party platform in 2008 and 2012 included specific provisions endorsing women's rights. After declaring, "We believe that our daughters should have the same opportunities as our sons," Democrats in 2008 declared, "We will pass the 'Lilly Ledbetter' Act, which will make it easier to combat pay discrimination; we will pass the Fair Pay Act; and we will modernize the Equal Pay Act." Contemporary Republican Party platforms announce a commitment to equality under law that includes women. The party platform in 2008 declared, "We consider discrimination based on sex, race, age, religion, creed, disability, or national origin to be immoral, and we will strongly enforce anti-discrimination statutes."

United States v. Virginia (1996) is the most important decision on gender rights handed down in the Contemporary Era. In this case a 7–1 majority declared that women had a constitutional right to be admitted to the Virginia Military Institute. Justice Ginsburg's majority opinion insisted that laws providing different treatment on the basis of gender required "an exceedingly persuasive justification" to pass constitutional muster, a standard some thought tougher than the previous requirement that such laws be a substantial means to an important government end. The Supreme Court has sustained some gender classifications. *Tuan Anh Nguyen v. I.N.S.* (2001) upheld federal laws that provide more onerous requirements for fathers to establish paternity than are required for mothers to establish maternity when a child is born out of wedlock and the other parent is not a citizen of the United States. Justice Kennedy's majority opinion asserted, "The critical importance of the Government's interest in ensuring some opportunity for a tie between citizen father and foreign born child . . . is a reasonable substitute for the opportunity manifest between mother and child at the time of birth."

State courts in the Contemporary Era confront a wider variety of constitutional issues, particularly issues applying state equal rights amendments. The vast majority of state constitutions contain recently adopted provisions prohibiting gender discrimination. Most, but not all, state courts interpret these amendments as requiring strict scrutiny for laws that distinguish between men and women. Nevertheless, important differences between states exist. Several state courts interpret state equal rights amendments as requiring that states fund medically necessary abortions. The Supreme Court of New Mexico in *New Mexico Right to Choose/NARAL v. Johnson* (NM 1998) held that a state law restricting funding for abortion "undoubtedly singles out for less favorable treatment a gender-linked condition that is unique to women" and for that reason was "presumptively unconstitutional."[72] Other state courts insist that abortion funding restrictions do not violate state constitutional bans on gender discrimination. The Supreme Court of Texas in *Bell v. Low Income Women of Texas* (TX 2002) stated, "To say that the State's funding restriction discriminates on the basis of pregnancy, which in turn is gender based, misses the mark. The classification here is not so much directed at women as a class as it is abortion as a medical treatment, which, because it involves a potential life, has no parallel as a treatment method."[73]

United States v. Virginia, 518 U.S 515 (1996)

The United States in 1990 brought a lawsuit against Virginia on behalf of several women who wished to attend Virginia Military Institute (VMI), a public, all-male university. The local federal district court sided with Virginia, concluding that single-sex education benefited both sexes and that women could not be admitted to VMI without severely disrupting the educational mission of that institution. After a federal circuit court reversed that decision on the ground that diversity was not promoted by restricting military education to men, Virginia established a parallel all-female program, Virginia Women's Institute for Leadership (VWIL), at Mary Baldwin College. The education provided by the all-female program was similar in some respects to the education offered at VMI but did not include the military environment. Nor, as all parties agreed, did VWIL enjoy the same reputation and alumni network as VMI. Despite these differences, the federal district court again sided with Virginia. This time, a divided Court of Appeals for the Fourth Circuit declared that Virginia had adequately provided diverse educational choices for state men and women. The United States appealed to the Supreme Court.

The Supreme Court by a 7–1 vote declared that VMI was constitutionally required to admit women. Justice Ginsburg's majority opinion insisted that all-male education at VMI was not intended to promote diverse educational choices, that co-education would not disrupt educational practices at VMI, and that VWIL was not an adequate substitute for the educational experience offered at the all-male military academy. Justice Ginsburg claimed that gender distinctions required "an exceedingly persuasive justification" to pass constitutional muster. Is this standard identical to intermediate scrutiny, more like strict scrutiny, or somewhere in between? The majority opinion places great emphasis on historical practices that barred women from higher education, often on the basis of pseudoscientific claims that higher education would damage female reproductive organs. Both the concurring and dissenting opinions insist that only contemporary history should be considered when evaluating the purpose of all-male universities. Which opinions have the better argument? A fairly high probability exists that more women would prefer the program at VWIL to the program at VMI. If this is correct, why did Justice Ginsburg, a champion of women's rights and gender equality, insist that women be admitted to VMI? Was Justice Scalia correct that the principles she advanced, if followed consistently, would require abandoning all public single-sex schools and probably prohibit under present federal law any federal financial aid to private single-sex colleges? Would that prohibition be a constitutional good or wrong?

JUSTICE GINSBURG delivered the opinion of the Court.

. . .

Parties who seek to defend gender-based government action must demonstrate an "exceedingly

72. *New Mexico Right to Choose/NARAL v. Johnson*, 986 P.2d 450 (NM 1998).

73. *Bell v. Low Income Women of Texas*, 95 S.W.3d 253 (TX 2002). For good surveys of the status of gender rights in contemporary federal and state constitutional law, see Martha F. Davis, "The Equal Rights Amendment: Then and Now," *Columbia Journal of Gender and Law* 17 (2008): 419; and Lisa Baldez, Lee Epstein, and Andrew D. Martin, "Does the U.S. Constitution Need an Equal Rights Amendment?," *Journal of Legal Studies* 35 (2006): 243–283.

persuasive justification" for that action. Without equating gender classifications, for all purposes, to classifications based on race or national origin, the Court . . . has carefully inspected official action that closes a door or denies opportunity to women (or to men). . . . To summarize the Court's current directions for cases of official classification based on gender: Focusing on the differential treatment or denial of opportunity for which relief is sought, the reviewing court must determine whether the proffered justification is "exceedingly persuasive." The burden of justification is demanding and it rests entirely on the State. . . . The State must show "at least that the [challenged] classification serves 'important governmental objectives and that the discriminatory means employed' are 'substantially related to the achievement of those objectives.'" . . . The justification must be genuine, not hypothesized or invented *post hoc* in response to litigation. And it must not rely on overbroad generalizations about the different talents, capacities, or preferences of males and females. . . .

. . .

"Inherent differences" between men and women, we have come to appreciate, remain cause for celebration, but not for denigration of the members of either sex or for artificial constraints on an individual's opportunity. Sex classifications may be used to compensate women "for particular economic disabilities [they have] suffered," . . . to advance full development of the talent and capacities of our Nation's people. But such classifications may not be used, as they once were . . . to create or perpetuate the legal, social, and economic inferiority of women.

. . .

. . . Virginia . . . asserts two justifications in defense of VMI's exclusion of women. First, the Commonwealth contends, "single-sex education provides important educational benefits," . . . and the option of single-sex education contributes to "diversity in educational approaches." . . . Second, the Commonwealth argues, "the unique VMI method of character development and leadership training," the school's adversative approach, would have to be modified were VMI to admit women. . . .

. . .

Neither recent nor distant history bears out Virginia's alleged pursuit of diversity through single-sex educational options. In 1839, when the Commonwealth established VMI, a range of educational opportunities for men and women was scarcely contemplated. . . . In admitting no women, VMI followed the lead of the Commonwealth's flagship school, the University of Virginia, founded in 1819.

. . .

Virginia describes the current absence of public single-sex higher education for women as "an historical anomaly." . . . But the historical record indicates action more deliberate than anomalous: First, protection of women against higher education; next, schools for women far from equal in resources and stature to schools for men; finally, conversion of the separate schools to coeducation.

. . .

The District Court forecast from expert witness testimony, and the Court of Appeals accepted, that coeducation would materially affect "at least these three aspects of VMI's program—physical training, the absence of privacy, and the adversative approach." . . . And it is uncontested that women's admission would require accommodations, primarily in arranging housing assignments and physical training programs for female cadets. . . . It is also undisputed, however, that "the VMI methodology could be used to educate women." . . . [S]ome women may prefer it to the methodology a women's college might pursue. . . . In sum, . . . "neither the goal of producing citizen soldiers," VMI's *raison d'être*, "nor VMI's implementing methodology is inherently unsuitable to women."

. . .

It may be assumed, for purposes of this decision, that most women would not choose VMI's adversative method. . . . The issue, however, is not whether "women—or men—should be forced to attend VMI"; rather, the question is whether the Commonwealth can constitutionally deny to women who have the will and capacity, the training and attendant opportunities that VMI uniquely affords.

The notion that admission of women would downgrade VMI's stature, destroy the adversative system and, with it, even the school, is a judgment hardly proved, a prediction hardly different from other "self-fulfilling prophec[ies]," . . . once routinely used to deny rights or opportunities. When women first sought admission to the bar and access to legal education, concerns of the same order were expressed. . . .

Women's successful entry into the federal military academies, and their participation in the Nation's military forces, indicate that Virginia's fears for the future of VMI may not be solidly grounded. The Commonwealth's justification for excluding all women from "citizen-soldier" training for which some are qualified, in any event, cannot rank as "exceedingly persuasive," as we have explained and applied that standard.

. . .

Virginia proposed a separate program, different in kind from VMI and unequal in tangible and intangible facilities. . . .

. . .

Virginia Women's Institution for Leadership (VWIL) students participate in ROTC and a "largely ceremonial" Virginia Corps of Cadets, . . . but Virginia deliberately did not make VWIL a military institute. The VWIL House is not a military-style residence and VWIL students need not live together throughout the 4-year program, eat meals together, or wear uniforms during the schoolday. . . . VWIL students thus do not experience the "barracks" life "crucial to the VMI experience," the spartan living arrangements designed to foster an "egalitarian ethic." . . .

VWIL students receive their "leadership training" in seminars, externships, and speaker series, . . . episodes and encounters lacking the "[p]hysical rigor, mental stress, . . . minute regulation of behavior, and indoctrination in desirable values" made hallmarks of VMI's citizen-soldier training. . . . Kept away from the pressures, hazards, and psychological bonding characteristic of VMI's adversative training, . . . VWIL students will not know the "feeling of tremendous accomplishment" commonly experienced by VMI's successful cadets. . . .

Virginia maintains that these methodological differences are "justified pedagogically," based on "important differences between men and women in learning and developmental needs," "psychological and sociological differences" Virginia describes as "real" and "not stereotypes." . . .

. . .

In myriad respects other than military training, VWIL does not qualify as VMI's equal. VWIL's student body, faculty, course offerings, and facilities hardly match VMI's. Nor can the VWIL graduate anticipate the benefits associated with VMI's 157-year history, the school's prestige, and its influential alumni network.

. . .

A prime part of the history of our Constitution, is the story of the extension of constitutional rights and protections to people once ignored or excluded. VMI's story continued as our comprehension of "We the People" expanded. . . . There is no reason to believe that the admission of women capable of all the activities required of VMI cadets would destroy the Institute rather than enhance its capacity to serve the "more perfect Union."

JUSTICE THOMAS took no part in the consideration or decision of these cases.

CHIEF JUSTICE REHNQUIST, concurring in the judgment.

. . .

While terms like "important governmental objective" and "substantially related" are hardly models of precision, they have more content and specificity than does the phrase "exceedingly persuasive justification." That phrase is best confined, as it was first used, as an observation on the difficulty of meeting the applicable test, not as a formulation of the test itself. . . .

. . .

Before this Court, Virginia has sought to justify VMI's single-sex admissions policy primarily on the basis that diversity in education is desirable, and that while most of the public institutions of higher learning in the Commonwealth are coeducational, there should also be room for single-sex institutions. I agree with the Court that there is scant evidence in the record that this was the real reason that Virginia decided to maintain VMI as men only. But, unlike the majority, I would consider only evidence that postdates our [contemporary decisions on gender classifications] and would draw no negative inferences from the Commonwealth's actions before that time. . . .

Even if diversity in educational opportunity were the Commonwealth's actual objective, the Commonwealth's position would still be problematic. The difficulty with its position is that the diversity benefited only one sex; there was single-sex public education available for men at VMI, but no corresponding single-sex public education available for women. . . .

. . .

Accordingly, the remedy should not necessarily require either the admission of women to VMI or the creation of a VMI clone for women. An adequate remedy in my opinion might be a demonstration by Virginia that its interest in educating men in a single-sex environment is matched by its interest in educating women in a single-sex institution. To demonstrate such, the Commonwealth does not need to create two institutions with the same number of faculty Ph.D.'s, similar SAT scores, or comparable athletic fields. . . . Nor would it necessarily require that the women's institution offer the same curriculum as the men's; one could be strong in computer science, the other could be strong in liberal arts. It would be a sufficient remedy, I think, if the two institutions offered the same quality of education and were of the same overall caliber.

. . .

In the end, the women's institution Virginia proposes, VWIL, fails as a remedy, because it is distinctly inferior to the existing men's institution and will continue to be for the foreseeable future. VWIL simply is not, in any sense, the institution that VMI is. In particular, VWIL is a program appended to a private college, not a self-standing institution; and VWIL is substantially underfunded as compared to VMI. I therefore ultimately agree with the Court that Virginia has not provided an adequate remedy.

JUSTICE SCALIA, dissenting.

Today the Court shuts down an institution that has served the people of the Commonwealth of Virginia with pride and distinction for over a century and a half. To achieve that desired result, it rejects (contrary to our established practice) the factual findings of two courts below, sweeps aside the precedents of this Court, and ignores the history of our people. As to facts: It explicitly rejects the finding that there exist "gender-based developmental differences" supporting Virginia's restriction of the "adversative" method to only a men's institution, and the finding that the all-male composition of the Virginia Military Institute (VMI) is essential to that institution's character. As to precedent: It drastically revises our established standards for reviewing sex-based classifications. And as to history: It counts for nothing the long tradition, enduring down to the present, of men's military colleges supported by both States and the Federal Government.

. . .

. . . [I]n my view the function of this Court is to *preserve* our society's values regarding (among other things) equal protection, not to *revise* them; to prevent backsliding from the degree of restriction the Constitution imposed upon democratic government, not to prescribe, on our own authority, progressively higher degrees. For that reason it is my view that, whatever abstract tests we may choose to devise, they cannot supersede—and indeed ought to be crafted *so as to reflect*—those constant and unbroken national traditions that embody the people's understanding of ambiguous constitutional texts. More specifically, it is my view that "when a practice not expressly prohibited by the text of the Bill of Rights bears the endorsement of a long tradition of open, widespread, and unchallenged use that dates back to the beginning of the Republic, we have no proper basis for striking it down."

The all-male constitution of VMI comes squarely within such a governing tradition. Founded by the Commonwealth of Virginia in 1839 and continuously maintained by it since, VMI has always admitted only men. And in that regard it has not been unusual. For almost all of VMI's more than a century and a half of existence, its single-sex status reflected the uniform practice for government-supported military colleges. . . . [T]he tradition of having government-funded military schools for men is as well rooted in the traditions of this country as the tradition of sending only men into military combat. The people may decide to change the one tradition, like the other, through democratic processes; but the assertion that either tradition has been unconstitutional through the centuries is not law, but politics-smuggled-into-law.

. . .

Only the amorphous "exceedingly persuasive justification" phrase, and not the standard elaboration of intermediate scrutiny, can be made to yield this conclusion that VMI's single-sex composition is unconstitutional because there exist several women (or, one would have to conclude under the Court's reasoning, a single woman) willing and able to undertake VMI's program. Intermediate scrutiny has never required a least-restrictive-means analysis, but only a "substantial relation" between the classification and the state interests that it serves. . . . There is simply no support in our cases for the notion that a sex-based classification is invalid unless it relates to characteristics that hold true in every instance.

. . .

. . . [I]f the question of the applicable standard of review for sex-based classifications were to be regarded as an appropriate subject for reconsideration, the stronger argument would be not for elevating the standard to strict scrutiny, but for reducing it to rational-basis review. The latter certainly has a firmer foundation in our past jurisprudence: Whereas no majority of the Court has ever applied strict scrutiny in a case involving sex-based classifications, we routinely applied rational-basis review until the 1970's. . . . It is hard to consider women a "discrete and insular minorit[y]" unable to employ the "political processes ordinarily to be relied upon," when they constitute a majority of the electorate. And the suggestion that they are incapable of exerting that political power smacks of the same paternalism that the Court so roundly condemns. . . .

. . . As an initial matter, Virginia demonstrated at trial that "[a] substantial body of contemporary scholarship and research supports the proposition that, although males and females have significant areas of developmental overlap, they also have differing developmental needs that are deep-seated. . . . " This finding alone, which even this Court cannot dispute, should be sufficient to demonstrate the constitutionality of VMI's all-male composition.

. . .

The Court's analysis at least has the benefit of producing foreseeable results. Applied generally, it means that whenever a State's ultimate objective is "great enough to accommodate women" (as it always will be), then the State will be held to have violated the Equal Protection Clause if it restricts to men even one means by which it pursues that objective—no matter how few women are interested in pursuing the objective by that means, no matter how much the single-sex program will have to be changed if both sexes are admitted, and no matter how beneficial that program has theretofore been to its participants.

The Court argues that VMI would not have to change very much if it were to admit women. . . . The principal response to that argument is that it is irrelevant: If VMI's single-sex status is substantially related to the government's important educational objectives, as I have demonstrated above and as the Court refuses to discuss, that concludes the inquiry. There should be no debate in the federal judiciary over "how much" VMI would be required to change if it admitted women and whether that would constitute "too much" change.

But if such a debate were relevant, the Court would certainly be on the losing side. The District Court found as follows: "[T]he evidence establishes that key elements of the adversative VMI educational system, with its focus on barracks life, would be fundamentally altered, and the distinctive ends of the system would be thwarted, if VMI were forced to admit females and to make changes necessary to accommodate their needs and interests." . . . Changes that the District Court's detailed analysis found would be required include new allowances for personal privacy in the barracks, such as locked doors and coverings on windows, which would detract from VMI's approach of regulating minute details of student behavior, "contradict the principle that everyone is constantly subject to scrutiny by everyone else," and impair VMI's "total egalitarian approach" under which every student must be "treated alike"; changes in the physical training program, which would reduce "[t]he intensity and aggressiveness of the current program"; and various modifications in other respects of the adversative training program that permeates student life. . . .

. . .

VWIL was carefully designed by professional educators who have long experience in educating young women. The program *rejects* the proposition that there is a "difference in the respective spheres and destinies of man and woman" . . . and is designed to "provide an all-female program that will achieve substantially similar outcomes [to VMI's] in an all-female environment." . . .

. . .

Under the constitutional principles announced and applied today, single-sex public education is unconstitutional.

. . . This is especially regrettable because, as the District Court here determined, educational experts in recent years have increasingly come to "suppor[t] [the] view that substantial educational benefits flow from a single-gender environment, be it male or female, *that cannot be replicated in a coeducational setting.*" . . .

X. Criminal Justice

MAJOR DEVELOPMENTS

- Supreme Court protects rights of suspected terrorists detained by the United States
- Exclusionary rule and *Miranda* warnings remain the law of the land
- Narrow judicial majorities cut back on capital punishment and life sentences without parole for juveniles

Contemporary liberals and conservatives are engaged in trench warfare over domestic constitutional criminal procedure. Neither liberal proponents of due process models of constitutional criminal procedure, which emphasize protecting rights, nor conservative proponents of crime-control models of constitutional criminal procedure, which emphasize reducing crime, have moved the constitutional status quo more than a few legal feet. Capital punishment remains constitutional, even as narrow judicial majorities rule that the mentally retarded and minors may not be executed. The exclusionary rule and *Miranda* warnings remain the law of the land, although the Supreme Court often narrows the precise circumstances in which either is required. The Anti-Terrorism and Effective Death Penalty Act of 1996, which severely limited postconviction appeals, is the only major decision that arguably significantly altered constitutional understandings about criminal procedure inherited from the Reagan Era.

Several factors explain the relative stasis of contemporary constitutional criminal procedure. Neither liberal Democrats nor conservative Republicans have gained the control over national institutions necessary to make a due process or crime-control model the official law of the land. As Figure 11-4 indicates, the contemporary justices differ dramatically in their willingness to support claimants in criminal justice cases. Justices Kennedy and O'Connor, the swing votes on the Rehnquist and Roberts Courts, vote as if they believe the conservative Reagan Revolution has gone far enough but are rarely willing to make liberal decisions that have far-reaching consequences. The legal profession and perhaps American constitutional culture accept the landmark cases decided during the Great Society. Many judges take *Mapp v. Ohio* (1961) and *Miranda v. Arizona* (1966) for granted. Constitutional debate is limited to more narrow questions about the precise circumstances in which the exclusionary rule and *Miranda* warnings should apply. The War on Drugs, however, sometimes moves more moderate justices to narrow constitutional protections. In *Board of Education of Independent School District No. 92 of Pottawatomie County v. Earls* (2002) a 5–4 majority ruled that the Fourth Amendment did not bar random drug testing of all students participating in extracurricular activities. Other decisions cast doubt on the scope of any "drug exception" to the rights of persons suspected of crime. *Kyllo v. United States* (2001) ruled that prosecutors could not introduce drugs found after a thermal imager revealed the probable use of heat lamps used to grow marijuana.

The War on Terror is the leading story in the annals of contemporary constitutional criminal procedure. Both the Bush and Obama administrations have insisted that federal authorities have broad powers to investigate, detain, and punish suspected terrorists. Congress generally supports executive claims that constitutional rights provisions should be interpreted narrowly when the federal government is seeking to prevent terrorist activity. The USA Patriot Act of 2001 limited rights and expanded federal power to investigate terrorist activities. The Detainee Treatment Act of 2005 sharply curtailed habeas corpus rights for persons detained in the War on Terror. The Supreme Court was less supportive of Bush administration policies. The justices in *Hamdi v. Rumsfeld* (2004), *Hamdan v. Rumsfeld* (2006), and *Boumediene v. Bush* (2008) placed limits on national capacity to detain persons suspected of terrorism or try them before military tribunals. These decisions were hailed by civil libertarians but did little to change American policy. Justices played almost no role in other debates, most notably those over enhanced interrogation techniques and targeted assassinations, whose constitutionality continues to be debated solely in the elected branches of government and the general media.

A. Due Process and Habeas Corpus

The domestic constitutional politics and law of due process and habeas corpus has not changed substantially since the end of the Reagan Era. State laws and constitutional decisions giving defendants rights to DNA testing under certain circumstances aside, persons accused of crime have neither gained nor lost significant due process rights. Much to the annoyance of conservatives and many state officials, federal courts continue to correct numerous constitutional errors in habeas corpus proceedings. Much to the annoyance of liberals, habeas petitioners must typically have objected to the alleged constitutional error at trial (*Wainwright v. Sykes* [1977]), must have included all their habeas claims in their first habeas corpus petition (*McCleskey v. Zant* [1991]), and cannot allege new rules of law (*Teague v. Lane* [1989]).

Congress did significantly restrict habeas corpus rights when passing the Antiterrorism and Effective Death Penalty Act of 1996 (AEDPA). That measure, originally designed to counter domestic terrorism, focused far more on habeas corpus procedures in capital

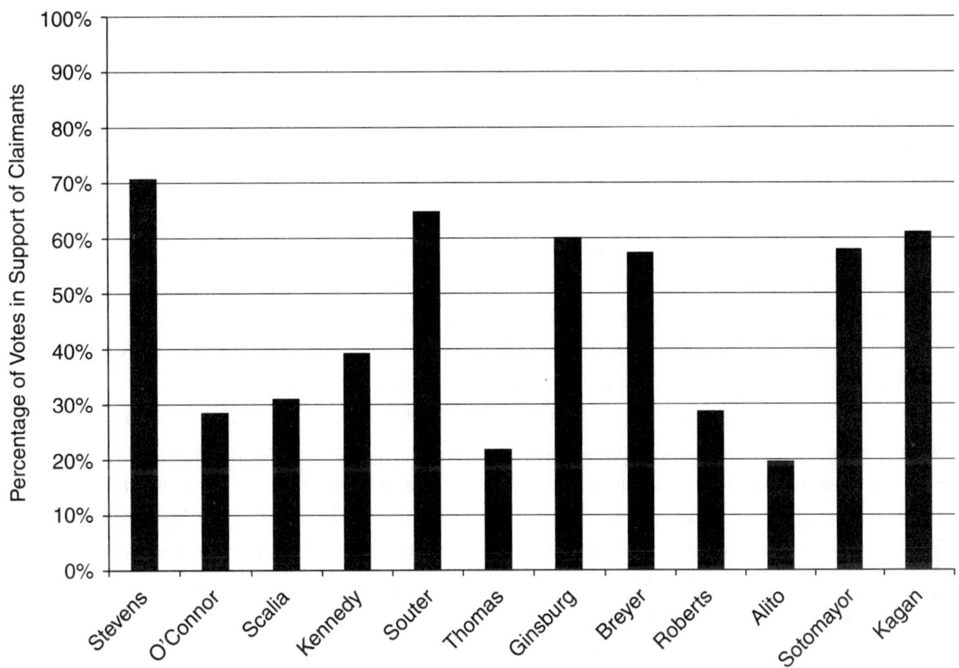

Figure 11-4 Individual Justice Support for Claimants in Criminal Procedure Cases Before the Roberts Court

Note: Justices listed in order of appointment.

cases. Congress, with the blessing of President Clinton, placed time limits on when persons could file habeas corpus petitions; limited relief to cases in which the state court decision "was contrary to, or involved an unreasonable application of, clearly established Federal law" or "an unreasonable determination of the facts in light of the evidence"; sharply limited the circumstances under which persons in prison could present second or successive habeas corpus petitions; and provided special procedures designed to streamline the death penalty process. The Supreme Court in *Felker v. Turpin* (1996) sustained the AEDPA.

B. Search and Seizure

Constitutional decision makers face difficult challenges when attempting to apply constitutional rules for search and seizure written during the late eighteenth century to twenty-first-century technologies. *Kyllo v. United States* (2001) considered the constitutionality of thermal imagers that can be used to detect different levels of heat in a house. *United States v. Jones* (2012) discussed the constitutionality of using a GPS device to track a suspect's movements. Trying to think of a late-eighteenth-century analogy to a GPS device, Justice Alito imaged "a constable secret[ing] himself in a coach . . . [and] remain[ing] there for a period of time in order to monitor the movements of the coach's owner," which he observed "would have required either a gigantic coach, a very tiny constable, or both, not to mention a constable with incredible fortitude and patience."

More often than not, the justices have not allowed police to use new technologies to conduct searches that would have been unconstitutional had they attempted to procure the same information by more traditional means. *Kyllo* declared unconstitutional the warrantless use of a thermal imaging device to determine whether a suspect was growing marijuana in his garage (which requires heat lamps). *Jones* declared unconstitutional the warrantless installation of a GPS device in a car. Justice Scalia's majority opinion asserted, "The Government physically occupied private property for the purpose of obtaining information. We have no doubt that such a physical intrusion would have been considered a 'search' within the meaning of the Fourth Amendment when it was adopted." In *Florida v. Jardines* (2013) the justices, by a 5–4 vote, declared that in the absence of a warrant, police may not walk a trained drug-sniffing dog to the front porch of a house in order to detect illegal substances. Writing for the majority, Justice Scalia declared that the "very core" of the Fourth Amendment stands in "the right of a man to retreat into his own home and there be free from unreasonable governmental intrusion" and that "this right would be of little practical value if the State's agents could stand in a home's porch or side garden and trawl for evidence with impunity." Writing on behalf of the dissenters, Justice Alito asserted, "It is clear that the occupant of a house has no reasonable expectation of privacy with respect to odors that can be smelled by human beings who are standing in such places. And I would not draw a line between odors that can be smelled by humans and those that are detectible only by dogs."

The constitutional law of more traditional searches and seizures remains hotly contested, with the justices handing down both more liberal and more conservative decisions that frequently depend on particular facts. A 5–4 judicial majority in *Florence v. Board of Chosen Freeholders of County of Burlington* (2012) ruled that persons arrested for minor criminal offenses could be strip-searched if they were in a general jail population but left open whether a different result might be constitutionally required for persons arrested for really minor offenses who were not being detained in a jail with more serious offenders. Other important Fourth Amendment cases include:

- *Herring v. United States* (2009), which held that the exclusionary rule applies only when the police recklessly or intentionally violate the Fourth Amendment.
- *Knowles v. Iowa* (1998), which held that police may not rely on the "search incident to arrest" exception to the warrant requirement to justify searches of persons given traffic citations.
- *Atwater v. City of Lago Vista* (2001), which held that police may arrest a person without a warrant for such minor offenses as a failure to use seatbelts.
- *Arizona v. Gant* (2009), which held that police may only search a car after arresting the occupant when the person arrested can reach the passenger compartment or the police believe the car contains evidence of the crime for which the occupant was arrested.
- *Bond v. United States* (2001), which held that bus passengers have a reasonable privacy expectation that their luggage will not be squeezed by police officers without a warrant.
- *Board of Education of Independent School District No. 92 of Pottawatomie County v. Earls* (2002), which held that schools could require suspicionless drug tests for all students who participate in extracurricular activities.
- *Safford Unified School District No. 1 v. Redding* (2009), which held that schools could not ordinarily strip-search teenage students.
- *Missouri v. McNeeley* (2013), which rejected the claim that warrants were never needed when police gave blood tests to suspected drunk drivers.
- *Maryland v. King* (2013), which held that taking buccal swabs to the inside of an arrestee's cheek during the booking process for the purposes of obtaining a DNA sample was a constitutionally reasonable means for ensuring the identity of the persons arrested by police officers.

One pattern in these cases might be a judicial tendency to slightly expand the substance of Fourth Amendment rights while expanding the application of both the good-faith exception in *United States v. Leon* (1984) and cases that restrict access to federal habeas corpus. The end result is that Americans have more Fourth Amendment rights but fewer opportunities to vindicate those rights.

C. Interrogations

The law of confessions remains a site for constitutional trench warfare. Conservatives are unable to form the majorities in politics or on the Supreme Court to reverse the Supreme Court's decision in *Miranda v. Arizona* (1966). Liberals are unable to form the majorities in politics or on the Supreme Court to overturn past decisions carving out numerous exceptions to the rule that a confession may not be admitted into evidence unless the person under arrest was given *Miranda* warnings. Much legal talent has been employed in a series of cases that have done little more than move the status quo a few legal feet to the left or right.

Dickerson v. United States (2000) was the most significant conservative challenge to *Miranda*. After a thirty-year hiatus, the Court of Appeals for the Fourth Circuit revived the provision in the Omnibus Crime

Control and Safe Streets Act of 1968 that permitted federal courts to admit all voluntary confessions, whether given after warnings or not. Supported by the Clinton administration, a 7–2 judicial majority quickly reversed the circuit court's decision. Chief Justice Rehnquist declared, "*Miranda* announced a constitutional rule that Congress may not supersede legislatively." Rehnquist's newfound support for *Miranda* may have been influenced by a long period of incremental conservative adjustment to the basic doctrine and the increasing number of police officers who accepted *Miranda*.

The next decade witnessed skirmishes over precisely what interrogation practices are consistent with *Miranda*. The more liberal justices almost always found constitutional violations. The more conservative justices almost always found the police behavior constitutional. Justice Kennedy usually cast the deciding vote. In *Missouri v. Siebert* (2004) Kennedy declared that police could not withhold *Miranda* warnings, obtain a confession, give *Miranda* warnings, and then ask the suspect to repeat the confession. "The interrogation technique used in this case," he declared, "is designed to circumvent *Miranda v. Arizona*." In *Berghuis v. Thompkins* (2010) Kennedy found no constitutional violation when a suspect, after not responding to police questions for nearly three hours, made one incriminating statement. In his view, "If an accused makes a statement concerning the right to counsel that is ambiguous or equivocal or makes no statement, the police are not required to end the interrogation." Justice Kennedy found principled differences between these cases. His fellow justices and many commentators did not perceive that principle.

Dickerson v. United States, 530 U.S. 428 (2000)

Before he was given Miranda *warnings Charles Thomas Dickerson made incriminating statements to the FBI about his participation in a bank robbery. His lawyer moved to suppress those statements on the ground that they were unconstitutionally obtained. The federal district court agreed, but that decision was reversed by the Court of Appeals for the Fourth Circuit. The Fourth Circuit majority insisted that Dickerson's case was governed by the Omnibus Crime Control and Safe Streets Act of 1968, which had not been enforced for thirty years. Section 3501 of that federal law declared, "If the trial judge determines that the confession was voluntarily made it shall be admitted in evidence." When justifying the decision to follow Congress rather than the Supreme Court's decision in* Miranda, *Judge Williams wrote,*

> *Congress has the power to overrule judicially created rules of evidence and procedure that are not required by the Constitution. Thus, whether Congress has the authority to enact §3501 turns on whether the rule set forth by the Supreme Court in* Miranda *is required by the Constitution. Clearly it is not. At no point did the Supreme Court in* Miranda *refer to the warnings as constitutional rights. Indeed, the Court acknowledged that the Constitution did not require the warnings, disclaimed any intent to create a "constitutional straightjacket," referred to the warnings as "procedural safeguards," and invited Congress and the States "to develop their own safeguards for [protecting] the privilege." Since deciding* Miranda, *the Supreme Court has consistently referred to the Miranda warnings as "prophylactic,"* New York v. Quarles *(1984), and "not themselves rights protected by the Constitution." We have little difficulty concluding, therefore, that §3501, enacted at the invitation of the Supreme Court and pursuant to Congress's unquestioned power to establish the rules of procedure and evidence in the federal courts, is constitutional. As a consequence, we hold that the admissibility of confessions in federal court is governed by §3501, rather than the judicially created rule of* Miranda.

Dickerson appealed to the Supreme Court of the United States.

The Supreme Court by a 7–2 vote declared that Dickerson's confession could not be constitutionally admitted as evidence at his trial. Chief Justice Rehnquist's majority opinion insisted that Miranda *was a constitutional decision that could not be overruled by Congress. How do you explain Rehnquist's decision to uphold* Miranda*? Did Rehnquist think* Miranda *correctly decided? Was he convinced that past precedent compelled the Court to sustain* Miranda*? Did crucial justices on the Rehnquist Court regard the assertion of judicial supremacy as more important than making what they might have thought were more desirable rules for constitutional criminal procedure? Suppose if instead of reinstituting "the totality of circumstances" test, Congress had mandated a different verbal formula for giving warnings or required that attorneys be present whenever a confession was made. Would the result in* Dickerson *have been different?*

CHIEF JUSTICE REHNQUIST delivered the opinion of the Court.

. . .

Congress may not legislatively supersede our decisions interpreting and applying the Constitution. This case therefore turns on whether the *Miranda* Court announced a constitutional rule or merely exercised its supervisory authority to regulate evidence in the absence of congressional direction.

. . .

. . . [F]irst and foremost of the factors on the . . . side that *Miranda v. Arizona* (1966) is a constitutional decision is that both *Miranda* and two of its companion cases applied the rule to proceedings in state courts—to wit, Arizona, California, and New York. . . . It is beyond dispute that we do not hold a supervisory power over the courts of the several states. With respect to proceedings in state courts, our "authority is limited to enforcing the commands of the United States Constitution."

The *Miranda* opinion itself begins by stating that the Court granted certiorari "to explore some facets of the problems . . . of applying the privilege against self-incrimination to in-custody interrogation, *and to give concrete constitutional guidelines for law enforcement agencies and courts to follow.*" In fact, the majority opinion is replete with statements indicating that the majority thought it was announcing a constitutional rule. Indeed, the Court's ultimate conclusion was that the unwarned confessions obtained in the four cases before the Court in *Miranda* "were obtained from the defendant under circumstances that did not meet constitutional standards for protection of the privilege."

Additional support for our conclusion that *Miranda* is constitutionally based is found in the *Miranda* Court's invitation for legislative action to protect the constitutional right against coerced self-incrimination. . . . [T]he Court emphasized that it could not foresee "the potential alternatives for protecting the privilege which might be devised by Congress or the States," and it accordingly opined that the Constitution would not preclude legislative solutions that differed from the prescribed *Miranda* warnings but which were "at least as effective in apprising accused persons of their right of silence and in assuring a continuous opportunity to exercise it."

The Court of Appeals relied on the fact that we have, after our *Miranda* decision, made exceptions from its rule in cases such as . . . *Harris v. New York* (1971). These decisions illustrate the principle—not that *Miranda* is not a constitutional rule—but that no constitutional rule is immutable. No court laying down a general rule can possibly foresee the various circumstances in which counsel will seek to apply it, and the sort of modifications represented by these cases are as much a normal part of constitutional law as the original decision.

. . .

. . . In *Miranda*, the Court noted that reliance on the traditional totality-of-the-circumstances test raised a risk of overlooking an involuntary custodial confession, a risk that the Court found unacceptably great when the confession is offered in the case in chief to prove guilt. The Court therefore concluded that something more than the totality test was necessary. §3501 reinstates the totality test as sufficient. Section 3501 therefore cannot be sustained if *Miranda* is to remain the law.

Whether or not we would agree with *Miranda*'s reasoning and its resulting rule, were we addressing the issue in the first instance, the principles of *stare decisis* weigh heavily against overruling it now. . . .

We do not think there is such justification for overruling *Miranda*. *Miranda* has become embedded in routine police practice to the point where the warnings have become part of our national culture. . . . If anything, our subsequent cases have reduced the impact of the *Miranda* rule on legitimate law enforcement while reaffirming the decision's core ruling that unwarned statements may not be used as evidence in the prosecution's case in chief.

The disadvantage of the *Miranda* rule is that statements which may be by no means involuntary, made by a defendant who is aware of his "rights," may nonetheless be excluded and a guilty defendant go free as a result. But experience suggests that the totality-of-the-circumstances test which §3501 seeks to revive is more difficult than *Miranda* for law enforcement officers to conform to, and for courts to apply in a consistent manner. . . .

In sum, we conclude that *Miranda* announced a constitutional rule that Congress may not supersede legislatively. Following the rule of *stare decisis*, we decline to overrule *Miranda* ourselves. . . .

JUSTICE SCALIA, with whom JUSTICE THOMAS joins, dissenting.

. . .

It takes only a small step to bring today's opinion out of the realm of power-judging and into the mainstream of legal reasoning: The Court need only go beyond its carefully couched iterations that "*Miranda* is a constitutional decision," that "*Miranda* is constitutionally based," that *Miranda* has "constitutional underpinnings," and come out and say quite clearly: "We reaffirm today that custodial interrogation that is not preceded by *Miranda* warnings or their equivalent violates the Constitution of the United States." It cannot say that, because a majority of the Court does not believe it. The Court therefore acts in plain violation of the Constitution when it denies effect to this Act of Congress.

. . .

Miranda was objectionable for innumerable reasons, not least the fact that cases spanning more than 70 years had rejected its core premise that, absent the warnings and an effective waiver of the right to remain silent and of the (thitherto unknown) right to have an attorney present, a statement obtained pursuant to custodial interrogation was necessarily the product of compulsion. Moreover, history and precedent aside, the decision in *Miranda*, if read as an explication of what the Constitution *requires*, is preposterous. There is, for example, simply no basis in reason for concluding that a response to the very first question asked, by a suspect who already *knows* all of the rights described in the *Miranda* warning, is anything other than a volitional act. And even if one assumes that the elimination of compulsion absolutely requires informing even the most knowledgeable suspect of his right to remain silent, it cannot conceivably require the right to have *counsel* present. There is a world of difference, which the Court recognized under the traditional voluntariness test but ignored in *Miranda*, between compelling a suspect to incriminate himself and preventing him from foolishly doing so of his own accord. . . .

. . . Thus, what is most remarkable about the *Miranda* decision—and what made it unacceptable as a matter of straightforward constitutional interpretation in the *Marbury* [*v. Madison*] (1803) tradition—is its palpable hostility toward the act of confession *per se*, rather than toward what the Constitution abhors, *compelled* confession. The Constitution is not, unlike the *Miranda* majority, offended by a criminal's commendable qualm of conscience or fortunate fit of stupidity.

. . .

The Court has squarely concluded that it is possible—indeed not uncommon—for the police to violate *Miranda* without also violating the Constitution. *Michigan v. Tucker* (1974), an opinion for the Court written by then-Justice REHNQUIST, rejected the true-to-*Marbury*, failure-to-warn-as-constitutional-violation interpretation of *Miranda*. It held that exclusion of the "fruits" of a *Miranda* violation—the statement of a witness whose identity the defendant had revealed while in custody—was not required. The opinion explained that the question whether the "police conduct complained of directly infringed upon respondent's right against compulsory self-incrimination" was a "separate question" from "whether it instead violated only the prophylactic rules developed to protect that right." The "procedural safeguards" adopted in *Miranda*, the Court said, "were not themselves rights protected by the Constitution but were instead measures to insure that the right against compulsory self-incrimination was protected," and to "provide practical reinforcement for the right." . . .

. . .

. . . [I]t is simply no longer possible for the Court to conclude, even if it wanted to, that a violation of *Miranda*'s rules is a violation of the Constitution. But as I explained at the outset, that is what is required before the Court may disregard a law of Congress governing the admissibility of evidence in federal court. . . . [W]hat makes a decision "constitutional" in the only sense relevant here—in the sense that renders it impervious to supersession by congressional legislation such as §3501—is the determination that the Constitution *requires* the result that the decision announces and the statute ignores. By disregarding congressional action that concededly does not violate the Constitution, the Court flagrantly offends fundamental principles of separation of powers, and arrogates to itself prerogatives reserved to the representatives of the people.

. . .

Thus, while I agree with the Court that §3501 cannot be upheld without also concluding that *Miranda* represents an illegitimate exercise of our authority to review state-court judgments, I do not share the Court's hesitation in reaching that conclusion. . . . Despite the Court's Orwellian assertion to the contrary, it is undeniable that later cases have "undermined [*Miranda*'s] doctrinal underpinnings," denying constitutional violation and thus stripping the holding of its only constitutionally legitimate support. . . .

. . .

I am not convinced by petitioner's argument that *Miranda* should be preserved because the decision occupies a special place in the "public's consciousness." As far as I am aware, the public is not under the illusion that we are infallible. I see little harm in admitting that we made a mistake in taking away from the people the ability to decide for themselves what protections (beyond those required by the Constitution) are reasonably affordable in the criminal investigatory process. . . .

D. Juries and Lawyers

The right to a jury and an attorney are among the most litigated but least politically explosive issues in contemporary constitutional criminal procedure. Intense political debates exist over whether *Mapp* and *Miranda* will be overruled and over who can constitutionally be executed. By comparison, a broad consensus exists that indigent criminal defendants have a right to have a defense lawyer and that jury selection should not be infected by racial prejudice. Contemporary federal and state cases raising Sixth Amendment questions typically feature long factual battles over whether counsel was adequate or whether racial prejudice actually infected the jury selection process.

Miller-El v. Dretke (2005) and *Burdine v. Johnson* (2001)[74] illustrate the nature of much contemporary constitutional debate over jury trials and assistance of counsel. The majority and dissenting opinions in both cases agreed on certain basic principles. In *Miller-El* Justice Souter (majority) and Justice Thomas (dissent) agreed that prosecutors could not base peremptory challenges on the race of prospective jurors. Judge Benavides (majority) and Judge Barksdale (dissent) in *Burdine* agreed that persons claiming ineffective assistance of counsel must demonstrate prejudice. The dispute in both cases was over facts or inferences from the facts. Were the prosecutorial decisions at issue in *Miller-El* motivated by an unconstitutional desire to reduce the number of African Americans on the jury or a constitutional desire to secure a pro–capital punishment jury? Was Burdine's lawyer unconscious for major portions of the capital trial or merely dozing while unimportant testimony was elicited? Both cases demonstrate the difficulties that defendants have proving racial prejudice and ineffective assistance of counsel. Strong presumptions exist that prosecutors have race-neutral motivations for challenging African American jurors and that counsel's decisions are strategic rather than the result of incompetence or inattention.

Miller-El and *Burdine* are atypical in one important respect: the defendant won in each. The Supreme Court in *Miller-El* concluded that prosecutorial decisions to exercise peremptory challenges for ten of the eleven African Americans eligible to sit on the jury were motivated by racial prejudice. Justice Souter's majority opinions stated, "The State's attempts to explain the prosecutors' questioning of particular witnesses on nonracial grounds fit the evidence less well than the racially discriminatory hypothesis." More often, lower federal court justices credit prosecutorial claims that they had race-neutral reasons for challenging prospective African American jurors. The Fifth Circuit in *Burdine* concluded that defendants had a constitutional right to an attorney who was awake during the trial. In other cases, state and federal courts have failed to find prejudice when defense council was drunk or impaired by drugs during trial. In some cases, sleeping counsel has been deemed to provide a constitutionally acceptable level of representation.

E. Punishments

The constitutional law of punishment is moving in a slightly liberal direction. The number of persons executed each year in the United States is steadily decreasing. The Supreme Court has ruled that the Eighth and Fourteenth Amendments forbid executing the mentally retarded (*Atkins v. Virginia* [2002]), teenagers aged seventeen or younger at the time of their offense (*Roper v. Simmons* [2005]), and criminals who commit offenses other than murder (*Kennedy v. Louisiana* [2008]).

The justices have held that juvenile offenders may not be sentenced to life in prison without parole (*Miller v. Alabama* [2012]) and that juveniles guilty of crimes other than homicide may not constitutionally be sentenced to life in prison (*Graham v. Florida* [2010]). In *Brown v. Plata* (2011) a 5–4 judicial majority ordered California to release 46,000 prisoners on the ground that the health conditions in overcrowded state prisons violated the Eighth and Fourteenth Amendments. Justice Kennedy's majority opinion asserted, "A prison that deprives prisoners of basic sustenance, including adequate medical care, is incompatible with the concept of human dignity and has no place in civilized society."

---

74. *Burdine v. Johnson*, 262 F.3d 336 (5th Cir. 2001).

Illustration 11-8 Juveniles and the Death Penalty

Source: Jeff Parker, Florida Today, 2005, http://www.cagle.com/news/deathpenaltyjuveniles/main.asp. © Copyright 2005 Parker–All Rights Reserved.

Brown v. Plata aside, liberal Supreme Court decisions have influenced punitive practices at the margins. The present judicial majority seems willing to declare particular criminal sanctions unconstitutional only when the federal government and most states (and perhaps most Western nations) do not impose that punishment for that crime or for that offender. The justices have left standing such precedents as *McCleskey v. Kemp* (1987), which has sharply limited claims that racial discrimination is affecting the capital sentencing process. *Ewing v. California* (2003) sustained California's controversial three-strikes law. That law mandated life in prison for any person convicted of three felonies. Justice O'Connor's majority opinion asserted,

> When the California Legislature enacted the three strikes law, it made a judgment that protecting the public safety requires incapacitating criminals who have already been convicted of at least one serious or violent crime. Nothing in the Eighth Amendment prohibits California from making that choice. To the contrary, our cases establish that States have a valid interest in deterring and segregating habitual criminals.

Party platforms suggest that the constitutional politics of punishment is moving slightly rightwards. Republicans endorse capital punishment and stricter sentences for criminal offenders. The 2008 Republican Party platform asserted,

> We support mandatory sentencing provisions for gang conspiracy crimes, violent or sexual offenses against children, rape, and assaults resulting in serious bodily injury.
>
> Gang rape, child rape, and rape committed in the course of another felony deserve, at the least, mandatory life imprisonment.

We oppose the granting of parole to dangerous or repeat felons.

Courts must have the option of imposing the death penalty in capital murder cases and other instances of heinous crime, while federal review of those sentences should be streamlined to focus on claims of innocence and to prevent delaying tactics by defense attorneys.

Democrats now endorse capital punishment while insisting that the capital sentencing process include numerous safeguards. The 2008 Democratic Party platform stated, "We believe that the death penalty must not be arbitrary. DNA testing should be used in all appropriate circumstances, defendants should have effective assistance of counsel in all death row cases, and thorough post-conviction reviews should be available."

F. Infamous Crimes and Criminals

The War on Terror

The Bush administration and Congress responded sharply to the September 11, 2001, terrorist attacks on the United States. Numerous suspected terrorists were detained at an American military base in Guantanamo Bay, Cuba, and at undisclosed sites in Europe. Some suspected terrorists were subjected to "enhanced interrogation," the precise nature of which is not known to any degree of certainty but which certainly included the use of sleep deprivation, controlled fear (muzzled dogs), stress positions, hypothermia, and waterboarding. The Bush administration insisted that these detainees, a few of whom were American citizens, had no right to any hearings on their status and no right to habeas corpus, and could be tried by military commissions as unlawful combatants. Administrative officials, supported by the USA Patriot Act of 2001, engaged in extensive wiretapping in order to gain knowledge about terrorist activity. Many persons suspected that the Bush administration also engaged in racial profiling. Federal officials made use of a federal law that permitted the government to detain for an indefinite period of time persons suspected of having material information about possible terrorist attacks. The Obama administration has engaged in some of these activities, abandoned others, and proposed new constitutionally controversial means for fighting the War on Terror.[75] Most notably, the Obama administration in 2011 ordered a drone attack in Yemen that killed Anwar al-Awlaki, an American citizen suspected of being an al-Qaeda leader. Harold Koh, the legal advisor to the State Department, justified that policy by maintaining that "individuals who are part of such an armed group are belligerent and, therefore, lawful targets under international law."[76]

Bush and Obama administration policies raise many constitutional questions. The first is the proper constitutional categories to use when thinking about the rights of suspected terrorists and suspected terrorist organizations.

- They might be common criminals, to be treated in the same manner as persons suspected of murder and other particularly despicable crimes.
- They might be enemy combatants, to be treated in the same manner as German and Japanese soldiers during World War II.
- They might be unlawful combatants, to be treated in the same manner as the German saboteurs tried in *Ex parte Quirin* (1942).
- They might merit an entirely new classification.

The second series of questions concerns how to apply existing rules of constitutional criminal procedure to the War on Terror. Preventing terrorism is a compelling interest. Whether that compelling interest justifies such actions as indefinite detention of material witnesses, extensive wiretapping, "enhanced methods of interrogation," or targeting persons for assassination is a more difficult question. A third series of questions concerns constitutional authority for resolving these controversies.

- Congress may have the power as part of the congressional power to punish crimes against the United States and determine the laws of war.
- The president may have the power as part of the president's authority as commander in chief.

75. Jack Goldsmith, *Power and Constraint: The Accountable Presidency After 9/11* (New York: Norton, 2012), 3–22.

76. Harold Hongju Koh, "The Obama Administration and International Law," speech at the Annual Meeting of the American Society of International Law, Washington, DC, March 25, 2010, http://www.state.gov/s/1/releases/remarks/139119.htm.

- The Supreme Court may have the power as part of the judicial authority to interpret the Constitution (and existing federal laws).

A fair bipartisan consensus supports many actions taken against terrorists. Most Americans support giving government extensive powers to investigate suspected terrorists. The Obama administration supported legislation extending the Patriot Act's authorization of "roving wiretaps" and other related intrusions on privacy. The Obama administration also insisted on military trials for some suspected terrorists and, as of the publication of this book, has not shut down the detainee center at Guantanamo Bay. Both the Bush and Obama administrations have ordered and defended targeted assassinations of al-Qaeda leaders.

The sharpest partisan divisions exist on the treatment of persons being detained as suspected terrorists. Most Democrats believe that Bush administration policies violated numerous constitutional rights. The Democratic Party platform in 2008 stated,

> To build a freer and safer world, we will lead in ways that reflect the decency and aspirations of the American people. We will not ship away prisoners in the dead of night to be tortured in far-off countries, or detain without trial or charge prisoners who can and should be brought to justice for their crimes, or maintain a network of secret prisons to jail people beyond the reach of the law. We will respect the time-honored principle of habeas corpus, the seven century-old right of individuals to challenge the terms of their own detention that was recently reaffirmed by our Supreme Court. We will close the detention camp in Guantanamo Bay, the location of so many of the worst constitutional abuses in recent years. With these necessary changes, the attention of the world will be directed where it belongs: on what terrorists have done to us, not on how we treat suspects.

Republicans are more divided. Most oppose giving suspected terrorists habeas corpus rights. Most defended the provisions in the Detainee Treatment Act denying habeas corpus rights to persons detained in Guantanamo Bay. Republican presidential candidates sharply disputed the circumstances in which enhanced methods of interrogation are warranted. Led by Senator John McCain of Arizona, many Republicans in Congress supported placing restrictions on intelligence methods. Section 102 of a defense spending measure proposed in 2007 stated, "No person in the custody or under the effective control of the United States Government shall be subject to any treatment or technique of interrogation not authorized by and listed in the United States Army Field Manual."[77] President Bush indicated that enhanced methods of interrogation might nevertheless be legally employed in some circumstances. His letter to Congress objecting to that provision asserted,

> This bill would jeopardize the safety of the American people by undermining the CIA's enhanced interrogation program, which has helped the United States capture senior al Qaeda leaders and disrupt multiple attacks against the homeland, thus saving American lives. Section 102 has no place in an emergency wartime appropriations bill that should be focused on ensuring that the men and women of our Armed Forces have the funding they need to complete their mission.[78]

The Supreme Court ruled in favor of detainee rights in three important cases. *Hamdi v. Rumsfeld* (2004) held that American citizens could not be held as unlawful combatants unless they were given a hearing to contest that status. *Hamdan v. Rumsfeld* (2006) held that Congress had not authorized military trials for suspected terrorists. *Boumediene v. Bush* (2008) ruled that detainees in Guantanamo Bay had the right to petition for a writ of habeas corpus. While civil libertarians hailed each decision as a triumph for fundamental rights, these decisions' effect on policy has been minimal. Guantanamo Bay remains open. While many detainees have been released, the releases seem to have been for reasons other than Supreme Court decisions.

In 2013 Edward Snowden, an employee of a private contractor working at the National Security Agency (NSA), leaked information to a British newspaper, which published a series of stories on the NSA's access to data on electronic communications held by a variety of telecommunications and Internet companies.

---

77. 153 *Congressional Record*, 110th Cong., 2nd Sess. (2007), 24561. H.R. 4165 did not pass.

78. Statement of Administration Policy, November 16, 2007 (http://www.whitehouse.gov/sites/default/files/omb/legislative/sap/110-1/hr4156sap-s.pdf)

President Obama defended the NSA as striking the "right balance" between privacy and security. Congressional reactions were mixed, with some members wondering whether more restrictions and oversight were needed to control extensive government surveillance and data collection on the phone calls, emails, and social networking interactions of Americans. By July 2013 a poll released by Pew Research found that a majority of Americans (56%) believe that federal courts fail to provide adequate limits on the government's collection of telephone and Internet data. The poll also revealed persistent splits in public opinion, with 47 percent saying that they are more concerned that the government has gone too far in restricting the average person's civil liberties, and 35 percent saying that they are more concerned that the government has not gone far enough.[79]

The USA Patriot Act

The USA Patriot Act of 2001 was the main congressional response to the terrorist attacks of September 11, 2001. Within days of that attack the Bush administration proposed that law enforcement agencies be given new powers to conduct searches, share information, detain and deport immigrants suspected of terrorist involvement, and freeze financial assets of suspected terrorists. Many Democrats insisted that Bush administration proposals violated the Constitution. After intense negotiations among the House, Senate, and White House, a modified bill passed both houses of Congress by overwhelming majorities. President Bush signed the bill into law on October 26, 2001.

The most constitutionally controversial provisions in the USA Patriot Act permit the government to not inform persons for a period of time that their houses have been searched (so-called sneak-and-peek warrants), permit various intelligence agencies to share information, and permit intelligence agencies to get wiretaps for reasons that would not justify a wiretap in a criminal investigation. Why did Senator Feingold criticize these practices? How did Senator Hatch and President Bush respond to those criticisms? Senator Leahy noted the many compromises that occurred during the debate over the Patriot Act. Were these compromises reasonable accommodations, or did one party give away the store (and, if so, which party and why)? Notice the emphasis placed on the four-year sunset provision. Was that provision wise? Could a court place a four-year sunset provision on a constitutionally borderline practice?

Senate Debate over the Patriot Act (October 25, 2001)[80]

SENATOR PATRICK LEAHY (Democrat, Vermont)

The bill we are passing today makes potentially sweeping changes in the relationships between the law enforcement and intelligence agencies. In the current crisis, there is justification for expanding authority specifically for counterintelligence to detect and prevent international terrorism. I support the FBI request for broader authority under FISA [Foreign Intelligence Surveillance Act] for pen registers and access to records without having to meet the statutory "agent of a foreign power" standard, because the Fourth Amendment does not normally apply to such techniques and the FBI has comparable authority in its criminal investigations. However, I have insisted that this authority to investigate U.S. persons be limited to counterintelligence investigations conducted to protect against international terrorism and spying activities and that such investigations may not be based solely on activities protected by the First Amendment. . . .

The gravest departure from that framework, and the one with most potential for abuses, is the new and unprecedented statutory authority for sharing of "foreign intelligence" from criminal investigations with "any other Federal law enforcement, intelligence, protective, immigration, national defense, or national security official."

. . .

The new authority to disseminate "foreign intelligence" from criminal investigations, including grand juries and law enforcement wiretaps, is an invitation to abuse without special safeguards. Fortunately, the final bill includes a provision, which was not in the Administration's original proposal, to maintain some degree of judicial oversight of the dissemination of grand jury information. Within a "reasonable time"

79. Pew Research Center for the People and the Press, "Few See Adequate Limits on NSA Surveillance Program, But More Approve Than Disapprove," July 26, 2013, http://www.people-press.org/2013/07/26/few-see-adequate-limits-on-nsa-surveillance-program.

80. Excerpt taken from *Congressional Record,* 107th Cong., 1st Sess., 2001, 20673–705.

after the disclosure of grand jury information, a government attorney "shall file under seal a notice with the court stating the fact that such information was disclosed and the departments, agencies, or entities to which the disclosure was made." No such judicial role is provided for the disclosure of information from wiretaps and other criminal investigative techniques including the infiltration of organizations with informants. However, that authority to disclose without judicial review is subject to the sunset in four years.

...

Another issue that has caused serious concern relates to the Administration's proposal for so-called "sneak and peek" search warrants. . . . Normally, when law enforcement officers execute a search warrant, they must leave a copy of the warrant and a receipt for all property seized at the premises searched. Thus, even if the search occurs when the owner of the premises is not present, the owner will receive notice that the premises have been lawfully searched pursuant to a warrant rather than, for example, burglarized.

...

I was able to make significant improvements in the Administration's original proposal that will help to ensure that the government's authority to obtain sneak and peek warrants is not abused. First, the provision that is now in section 213 of the bill prohibits the government from seizing any tangible property or any wire or electronic communication or stored electronic information unless it makes a showing of reasonable necessity for the seizure. . . . Second, the provision now requires that notice be given within a reasonable time of the execution of the warrant rather than giving a blanket authorization for up to a 90-day delay. What constitutes a reasonable time, of course, will depend upon the circumstances of the particular case. But I would expect courts to be guided by the teachings of the Second and the Ninth Circuits that, in the ordinary case, a reasonable time is no more than seven days.

...

Among the more controversial changes in FISA requested by the Administration was the proposal to allow surveillance and search when "a purpose" is to obtain foreign intelligence information. Current law requires that the secret procedures and different probable cause standards under FISA be used only if a high-level executive official certifies that "the purpose" is to obtain foreign intelligence information. The Administration's aim was to allow FISA surveillance and search for law enforcement purposes, so long as there was at least some element of a foreign intelligence purpose. This proposal raised constitutional concerns. . . .

...

Section 218 of the bill adopts "significant purpose," and it will be up to the courts to determine how far law enforcement agencies may use FISA for criminal investigation and prosecution beyond the scope of the statutory definition of "foreign intelligence information."

...

We have done our utmost to protect Americans against abuse of these new law enforcement tools, and there are new law enforcement tools involved. In granting these new powers, the American people but also we, their representatives in Congress, grant the administration our trust that they are not going to be misused. It is a two way street. We are giving powers to the administration; we will have to extend some trust that they are not going to be misused.

The way we guarantee that is congressional oversight. . . .

Interestingly enough, the 4-year sunset provision included in this final agreement will be an enforcement mechanism for adequate oversight. We did not have a sunset provision in the Senate bill. The House included a 5-year provision. The administration wanted even 10 years. We compromised on 4. It makes sense. It makes sense because with everybody knowing there is that sunset provision, everybody knows they are going to have to use these powers carefully and in the best way. If they do that, then they can have extensions. If they don't, they won't. It also enhances our power for oversight.

SENATOR ORRIN HATCH (Republican, Utah)

Another troublesome change concerns the 4-year sunset provision. . . . In my opinion, a sunset will undermine the effectiveness of the tools we are creating here and send the wrong message to the American public that somehow these tools are extraordinary.

One hardly understands the need to sunset legislation that both provides critically necessary tools and protects our civil liberties. Furthermore, as the Attorney General stated, how can we sunset these tools when we know full well that the terrorists will not sunset their evil intentions? I sincerely hope we undertake a thorough review and further extend the legislation once the 4-year period expires. At least, we will have 4 years of effective law enforcement against terrorism that we currently do not have.

SENATOR RUSSELL FEINGOLD (Democrat, Wisconsin)

As it seeks to combat terrorism, the Justice Department is making extraordinary use of its power to arrest and detain individuals, jailing hundreds of people on immigration violations and arresting more than a dozen "material witnesses" not charged with any crime. Although the Government has used these authorities before, it has not done so on such a broad scale. Judging from Government announcements, the Government has not brought any criminal charges related to the attacks with regard to the overwhelming majority of these detainees.

. . .

Of course, there is no doubt that if we lived in a police state, it would be easier to catch terrorists. If we lived in a country that allowed the police to search your home at any time for any reason; if we lived in a country that allowed the government to open your mail, eavesdrop on your phone conversations, or intercept your email communications; if we lived in a country that allowed the government to hold people in jail indefinitely based on what they write or think, or based on mere suspicion that they are up to no good, then the government would no doubt discover and arrest more terrorists.

But that probably would not be a country in which we would want to live. And that would not be a country for which we could, in good conscience, ask our young people to fight and die. In short, that would not be America.

Preserving our freedom is one of the main reasons we are now engaged in this new war on terrorism. We will lose that war without firing a shot if we sacrifice the liberties of the American people.

. . .

SENATOR HATCH

. . . [T]o respond to the suggestion that the legislation is not properly mindful of our constitutional liberties—my friend from Wisconsin talks theoretically about maybe the loss of some civil liberties—I would like to talk concretely about the loss of liberty of almost 6,000 people because of the terrorist acts on September 11. I am a little bit more concerned right now about their loss of life. I am even more concerned now that they have lost their lives that thousands of other Americans don't lose their lives because we fail to act and fail to give law enforcement the tools that are essential.

It is a nice thing to talk about theory. But we have to talk about reality. We have written this bill so the constitutional realities are that the Constitution is not infringed upon and civil liberties are not infringed upon except to the extent that the Constitution permits law enforcement to correct difficulties.

. . .

The tools we are promoting in this legislation have been carefully crafted to protect civil liberties. In addition to protecting civil liberties, give law enforcement the tools they need so we, to the extent we possibly can, will be able to protect our citizens from events and actions such as happened on September 11 of this year.

. . .

I think most people in this country would be outraged to know that various agencies of Government, the intelligence community, and law enforcement community, under current law—until this bill is passed—cannot exchange information that might help interdict and stop terrorism. People are outraged when they hear this. And they ought to be.

. . .

I think most people are shocked to find out that you can't electronically surveil the terrorists. You have to go after the phone, and then you have to get a warrant in every jurisdiction where that phone shows up. Terrorists don't pay any attention to those antiquated laws. They just buy 10 cell phones, talk for a while, and throw it out the window. We have to be able to track terrorists. Under current law, we cannot do that with the efficiency that needs to be used here. I don't see any civil liberties violated there, but I see some of them protected. I think of the civil liberties of those approximately 6,000 people who lost their lives, and potentially many others if we don't give law enforcement the tools they need to do the job. . . .

George W. Bush, Remarks on Signing the USA Patriot Act of 2001 (October 26, 2001)[81]

Good morning and welcome to the White House. Today we take an essential step in defeating terrorism, while protecting the constitutional rights of all Americans.

81. Excerpt taken from *Public Papers of the Presidents of the United States* (Washington, D.C.: Government Printing Office, 2001), 1306.

With my signature, this law will give intelligence and law enforcement officials important new tools to fight a present danger.

...

Surveillance of communications is another essential tool to pursue and stop terrorists. The existing law was written in the era of rotary telephones. This new law that I sign today will allow surveillance of all communications used by terrorists, including e-mails, the Internet, and cell phones. As of today, we'll be able to better meet the technological challenges posed by this proliferation of communications technology.

Investigations are often slowed by limit[s] on the reach of Federal search warrants. Law enforcement agencies have to get a new warrant for each new district they investigate, even when they're after the same suspect. Under this new law, warrants are valid across all districts and across all States.

And finally, the new legislation greatly enhances the penalties that will fall on terrorists or anyone who helps them. Current statutes deal more severely with drug traffickers than with terrorists. That changes today. We are enacting new and harsh penalties for possession of biological weapons. We're making it easier to seize the assets of groups and individuals involved in terrorism. The Government will have wider latitude in deporting known terrorists and their supporters. The statute of limitations on terrorist acts will be lengthened, as will prison sentences for terrorists.

This bill was carefully drafted and considered. Led by the Members of Congress on this stage and those seated in the audience, it was crafted with skill and care, determination and a spirit of bipartisanship for which the entire Nation is grateful. This bill met with an overwhelming—overwhelming—agreement in Congress because it upholds and respects the civil liberties guaranteed by our Constitution. . . .

Hamdi v. Rumsfeld, 542 U.S. 507 (2004)

Yaser Esam Hamdi was an American citizen who was born in Louisiana but raised in Saudi Arabia. In 2001 he was captured by Northern Alliance forces in Afghanistan and turned over to the American military. The military transferred Hamdi to a detention facility in Guantanamo Bay, Cuba. Once governing officials determined that Hamdi was an American citizen, he was transferred to a naval brig in Norfolk, Virginia, and later to Charleston, South Carolina. The U.S. government designated Hamdi as an "enemy combatant" to be held indefinitely and without trial. The government based this classification on a report submitted by Defense Department official Michael Mobbs that stated that Hamdi had received military training from the Taliban, had carried a rifle, and was captured with his unit on the battlefield. Hamdi's father petitioned for a writ of habeas corpus on his son's behalf. He contended that Hamdi was a relief worker in Afghanistan, not a combatant for the Taliban or al-Qaeda. Equally as important, Hamdi's father insisted that the due process clause of the Constitution entitled American citizens to a full evidentiary hearing before they could be detained as enemy combatants. The federal district court ordered the government to produce more evidence that Hamdi was an enemy combatant, but that order was reversed by the Court of Appeals for the Fourth Circuit. Hamdi appealed to the Supreme Court of the United States.

The Supreme Court by an 8–1 vote declared Hamdi's detention illegal. Justice O'Connor, Justice Souter, and four other justices insisted that Hamdi's detention was inconsistent with federal law. Justices Stevens and Scalia insisted that Hamdi's detention was inconsistent with the Constitution. Justice Thomas maintained that the president had the power to detain American citizens as enemy combatants. As you read these opinions, consider the extent to which they depend on federal law or constitutional provisions. What did the various justices think were the constitutional rules for detaining American citizens as enemy combatants? What do you believe are the constitutional rules? Many observers were surprised when the Rehnquist Court declared that Hamdi was being illegally detained. What do you think explains the 8–1 decision rejecting Bush administration policy?

JUSTICE O'CONNOR announced the judgment of the Court and delivered an opinion, in which the CHIEF JUSTICE, JUSTICE KENNEDY, and JUSTICE BREYER join.

...

The [Authorization to Use Military Force] AUMF authorizes the President to use "all necessary and appropriate force" against "nations, organizations, or persons" associated with the September 11, 2001, terrorist attacks. There can be no doubt that individuals who fought against the United States in Afghanistan as part of the Taliban, an organization known to have supported the al Qaeda terrorist network responsible for those attacks, are individuals Congress sought to target in passing the AUMF. We conclude that detention of individuals falling into the limited category we are considering, for the duration of the particular conflict in which they were captured, is so fundamental and accepted an incident to war as to be an exercise of the "necessary and appropriate force" Congress has authorized the President to use.

The capture and detention of lawful combatants and the capture, detention, and trial of unlawful combatants, by "universal agreement and practice," are "important incident[s] of war." *Ex parte Quirin* (1942). The purpose of detention is to prevent captured individuals from returning to the field of battle and taking up arms once again. . . .

There is no bar to this Nation's holding one of its own citizens as an enemy combatant. In *Quirin*, one of the detainees, Haupt, alleged that he was a naturalized United States citizen. We held that "[c]itizens who associate themselves with the military arm of the enemy government, and with its aid, guidance and direction enter this country bent on hostile acts, are enemy belligerents within the meaning of . . . the law of war." . . . A citizen, no less than an alien, can be "part of or supporting forces hostile to the United States or coalition partners" and "engaged in an armed conflict against the United States" . . . ; such a citizen, if released, would pose the same threat of returning to the front during the ongoing conflict.

. . .

Ex parte Milligan (1866) . . . does not undermine our holding about the Government's authority to seize enemy combatants, as we define that term today. In that case, the Court made repeated reference to the fact that its inquiry into whether the military tribunal had jurisdiction to try and punish Milligan turned in large part on the fact that Milligan was not a prisoner of war, but a resident of Indiana arrested while at home there. That fact was central to its conclusion. Had Milligan been captured while he was assisting Confederate soldiers by carrying a rifle against Union troops on a Confederate battlefield, the holding of the Court might well have been different. . . .

. . .

Even in cases in which the detention of enemy combatants is legally authorized, there remains the question of what process is constitutionally due to a citizen who disputes his enemy-combatant status. Hamdi argues that he is owed a meaningful and timely hearing and that "extra-judicial detention [that] begins and ends with the submission of an affidavit based on third-hand hearsay" does not comport with the Fifth and Fourteenth Amendments. The Government counters that any more process than was provided below would be both unworkable and "constitutionally intolerable." . . .

. . .

. . . The ordinary mechanism that we use for balancing such serious competing interests, and for determining the procedures that are necessary to ensure that a citizen is not "deprived of life, liberty, or property, without due process of law" is the test that we articulated in *Mathews* v. *Eldridge* (1976). . . . *Mathews* dictates that the process due in any given instance is determined by weighing "the private interest that will be affected by the official action" against the Government's asserted interest, "including the function involved" and the burdens the Government would face in providing greater process. . . .

It is beyond question that substantial interests lie on both sides of the scale in this case. Hamdi's "private interest . . . affected by the official action," is the most elemental of liberty interests—the interest in being free from physical detention by one's own government. . . . Moreover, as critical as the Government's interest may be in detaining those who actually pose an immediate threat to the national security of the United States during ongoing international conflict, history and common sense teach us that an unchecked system of detention carries the potential to become a means for oppression and abuse of others who do not present that sort of threat. . . . We reaffirm today the fundamental nature of a citizen's right to be free from involuntary confinement by his own government without due process of law, and we weigh the opposing governmental interests against the curtailment of liberty that such confinement entails.

. . .

We hold that a citizen-detainee seeking to challenge his classification as an enemy combatant must receive notice of the factual basis for his classification, and a fair opportunity to rebut the Government's factual assertions before a neutral decisionmaker.

At the same time, the exigencies of the circumstances may demand that, aside from these core elements, enemy combatant proceedings may be tailored to alleviate their uncommon potential to burden the Executive at a time of ongoing military conflict. Hearsay, for example, may need to be accepted as the most reliable available evidence from the Government in such a proceeding. Likewise, the Constitution would not be offended by a presumption in favor of the Government's evidence, so long as that presumption remained a rebuttable one and fair opportunity for rebuttal were provided. . . .

We think it unlikely that this basic process will have the dire impact on the central functions of warmaking that the Government forecasts. The parties agree that initial captures on the battlefield need not receive the process we have discussed here; that process is due only when the determination is made to *continue* to hold those who have been seized. . . . While we accord the greatest respect and consideration to the judgments of military authorities in matters relating to the actual prosecution of a war, and recognize that the scope of that discretion necessarily is wide, it does not infringe on the core role of the military for the courts to exercise their own time-honored and constitutionally mandated roles of reviewing and resolving claims like those presented here. . . .

. . .

In so holding, we necessarily reject the Government's assertion that separation of powers principles mandate a heavily circumscribed role for the courts in such circumstances. Indeed, the position that the courts must forgo any examination of the individual case and focus exclusively on the legality of the broader detention scheme cannot be mandated by any reasonable view of separation of powers, as this approach serves only to *condense* power into a single branch of government. We have long since made clear that a state of war is not a blank check for the President when it comes to the rights of the Nation's citizens. *Youngstown Sheet & Tube* (1951). Whatever power the United States Constitution envisions for the Executive in its exchanges with other nations or with enemy organizations in times of conflict, it most assuredly envisions a role for all three branches when individual liberties are at stake. . . .

. . .

JUSTICE SCALIA, with whom JUSTICE STEVENS joins, dissenting.

. . .

Where the Government accuses a citizen of waging war against it, our constitutional tradition has been to prosecute him in federal court for treason or some other crime. Where the exigencies of war prevent that, the Constitution's Suspension Clause allows Congress to relax the usual protections temporarily. Absent suspension, however, the Executive's assertion of military exigency has not been thought sufficient to permit detention without charge. No one contends that the congressional Authorization for Use of Military Force, on which the Government relies to justify its actions here, is an implementation of the Suspension Clause. Accordingly, I would reverse the decision below. . . .

JUSTICE O'CONNOR, writing for a plurality of this Court, asserts that captured enemy combatants (other than those suspected of war crimes) have traditionally been detained until the cessation of hostilities and then released. That is probably an accurate description of wartime practice with respect to enemy *aliens*. The tradition with respect to American citizens, however, has been quite different. Citizens aiding the enemy have been treated as traitors subject to the criminal process.

. . .

There are times when military exigency renders resort to the traditional criminal process impracticable. English law accommodated such exigencies by allowing legislative suspension of the writ of habeas corpus for brief periods. . . .

. . .

President Lincoln, when he purported to suspend habeas corpus without congressional authorization during the Civil War, apparently did not doubt that suspension was required if the prisoner was to be held without criminal trial. In his famous message to Congress on July 4, 1861, he argued only that he could suspend the writ, not that even without suspension, his imprisonment of citizens without criminal trial was permitted.

. . .

. . . In *Ex parte Quirin* (1942) it was uncontested that the petitioners were members of enemy forces. They were "*admitted* enemy invaders," (emphasis added), and it was "undisputed" that they had landed in the United States in service of German forces. . . . But where those jurisdictional facts are *not* conceded—where the petitioner insists that he is *not* a belligerent—*Quirin* left the pre-existing law in place: Absent suspension of the writ, a citizen held where the courts are open is entitled either to criminal trial or to a judicial decree requiring his release.

It follows from what I have said that Hamdi is entitled to a habeas decree requiring his release unless

(1) criminal proceedings are promptly brought, or (2) Congress has suspended the writ of habeas corpus. . . .

. . .

JUSTICE THOMAS, dissenting.

. . .

The Founders intended that the President have primary responsibility—along with the necessary power—to protect the national security and to conduct the Nation's foreign relations. They did so principally because the structural advantages of a unitary Executive are essential in these domains. "Energy in the executive is a leading character in the definition of good government. It is essential to the protection of the community against foreign attacks." *The Federalist* No. 70. . . .

Congress, to be sure, has a substantial and essential role in both foreign affairs and national security. But it is crucial to recognize that *judicial* interference in these domains destroys the purpose of vesting primary responsibility in a unitary Executive. . . .

For these institutional reasons and because "Congress cannot anticipate and legislate with regard to every possible action the President may find it necessary to take or every possible situation in which he might act," it should come as no surprise that "[s]uch failure of Congress . . . does not, 'especially . . . in the areas of foreign policy and national security,' imply 'congressional disapproval' of action taken by the Executive." Rather, in these domains, the fact that Congress has provided the President with broad authorities does not imply—and the Judicial Branch should not infer—that Congress intended to deprive him of particular powers not specifically enumerated. . . .

. . .

I acknowledge that the question whether Hamdi's executive detention is lawful is a question properly resolved by the Judicial Branch, though the question comes to the Court with the strongest presumptions in favor of the Government. The plurality agrees that Hamdi's detention is lawful if he is an enemy combatant. But the question whether Hamdi is actually an enemy combatant is "of a kind for which the Judiciary has neither aptitude, facilities nor responsibility and which has long been held to belong in the domain of political power not subject to judicial intrusion or inquiry." That is, although it is appropriate for the Court to determine the judicial question whether the President has the asserted authority, we lack the information and expertise to question whether Hamdi is actually an enemy combatant, a question the resolution of which is committed to other branches. . . .

. . .

The Government's asserted authority to detain an individual that the President has determined to be an enemy combatant, at least while hostilities continue, comports with the Due Process Clause. As these cases also show, the Executive's decision that a detention is necessary to protect the public need not and should not be subjected to judicial second-guessing. Indeed, at least in the context of enemy-combatant determinations, this would defeat the unity, secrecy, and dispatch that the Founders believed to be so important to the warmaking function. . . .

. . .

JUSTICE SOUTER, with whom JUSTICE GINSBURG joins, concurring in part, dissenting in part, and concurring in the judgment.

. . .

The defining character of American constitutional government is its constant tension between security and liberty, serving both by partial helpings of each. In a government of separated powers, deciding finally on what is a reasonable degree of guaranteed liberty whether in peace or war (or some condition in between) is not well entrusted to the Executive Branch of Government, whose particular responsibility is to maintain security. For reasons of inescapable human nature, the branch of the Government asked to counter a serious threat is not the branch on which to rest the Nation's entire reliance in striking the balance between the will to win and the cost in liberty on the way to victory; the responsibility for security will naturally amplify the claim that security legitimately raises. A reasonable balance is more likely to be reached on the judgment of a different branch, just as Madison said in remarking that "the constant aim is to divide and arrange the several offices in such a manner as that each may be a check on the other—that the private interest of every individual may be a sentinel over the public rights." *The Federalist* No. 51. Hence the need for an assessment by Congress before citizens are subject to lockup, and likewise the need for a clearly expressed congressional resolution of the competing claims.

Under this principle of reading [the AUMF] robustly to require a clear statement of authorization to detain, none of the Government's arguments suffices to justify Hamdi's detention.

. . .

. . . [T]he need to give practical effect to the conclusions of eight members of the Court rejecting the Government's position calls for me to join with the plurality in ordering remand on terms closest to those I would impose.

House Hearings on Disclosure of NSA Intelligence Gathering (2013)[82]

On May 20, 2013, Edward Snowden, an employee of the private contractor Booz Allen Hamilton working at the NSA, flew to Hong Kong with four laptop computers loaded with classified information describing the structure and operation of the NSA's electronic intelligence-gathering activities. He soon leaked that information to a British newspaper, which published a series of stories on the NSA's access to data on electronic communications held by a variety of American telecommunications and Internet companies. The Obama administration claimed this surveillance was constitutional and legal. The Patriot Act and the Foreign Intelligence Surveillance Act (FISA) provided statutory authority for the collection of information about phone calls and other electronic communications ("metadata") and for accessing the content of phone calls and emails of foreigners located outside the United States. Section 702 of the FISA allowed the government to obtain the content of phone calls and emails of persons outside the United States. Section 215 of the Patriot Act allowed the government to obtain access to electronic metadata. As a senator Obama had been critical of the Patriot Act and the Bush administration's intelligence activities. In the aftermath of the leaks, President Obama defended the NSA as striking the "right balance" between privacy and security. He emphasized that the intelligence agency was receiving proper oversight from the executive, legislative, and judicial branches.

Congressional reaction to the leaks was mixed. Members of Congress took to the floor to denounce both the leaks and the NSA. Texas Republican representative Ted Poe asked rhetorically, "Do you think the government spooks are drunk on power, and it's time for Congress to intervene to prevent the invasion of privacy by government against the citizens?" Democratic Florida representative Alan Grayson argued, "I don't understand why anyone would think that it's somehow okay for the Department of Defense to get every single one of our call records regardless of who we are, regardless of whether we are innocent or guilty of anything. . . . We are not North Koreans. We don't live in Nazi Germany."[83] Congressional committees held public hearings that aired explanations of the programs and offered opportunities to administration officials to defend the programs against charges that they had unduly infringed on the privacy rights of Americans.

Is there a reasonable expectation of privacy for the list of phone numbers from which you received calls? Is there a difference between the government creating a database of the records of all phone calls received in the United States and accessing the specific list of phone calls received by an individual person? If the government could demonstrate that assembling and using such a database has been useful in preventing terrorist attacks within the United States, would that justify this intelligence gathering? Should there be restrictions on surveillance of non-U.S. citizens or residents who are located outside the United States? Is executive reporting to select congressional committees whose members have security clearance sufficient to provide legislative oversight of intelligence-gathering activities? Should the general public be made aware of what databases the NSA is assembling and how electronic searches of records are conducted?

REPRESENTATIVE MIKE ROGERS (Republican, Michigan)

. . .

The committee has been extensively briefed on these efforts over a regular basis as a part of our ongoing oversight responsibility over the 16 elements of the intelligence community and the national intelligence program.

In order to fully understand the intelligence collection programs most of these briefings and hearings have taken place in classified settings. Nonetheless, the collection efforts under the business records provision in Section 702 of the Foreign Intelligence Surveillance Act are legal, court-approved and subject to an extensive oversight regime.

82. U.S. House of Representatives, *Disclosure of NSA Programs: Hearings Before the House Select Intelligence Committee*, 113th Cong., 1st Sess., 2013.

83. *Congressional Record*, 113th Cong., 1st Sess., June 11, 2013, H3261; *Congressional Record*, 113th Cong., 1st Sess., June 14, 2013, H3640.

. . .

The public trusts the government to protect the country from another 9/11-type attack, but that trust can start to wane when they are faced with inaccuracies, half-truths, and outright lies about the way the intelligence programs are being run.

One of the more damaging aspects of selectively leaking incomplete information is that it paints an inaccurate picture and fosters distrust in our government.

. . .

It is critically important to protect sources and methods so we aren't giving the enemy our play book.

It is also important, however, to be able to talk about how these programs help protect us so they can continue to be reauthorized. And then we highlight the protections and oversight of which these programs operate under.

. . .

REPRESENTATIVE C. A. RUPPERSBERGER (Democrat, Maryland)

. . .

. . . NSA is in my district. I have an occasion to communicate, and a lot of the people who go to work to protect our country, who work hard every day, are concerned that the public think they're doing something wrong. And that's not the case at all.

. . .

We're here today because of the brazen disclosure of critical classified information that keeps our country safe. . . . The terrorists now know many of our sources and methods.

. . .

To be clear, the National Security Agency is prohibited from listening in on phone calls of Americans without proper, court-approved legal authorities.

We live in a country of laws. These laws are strictly followed and layered with oversight from three branches of government. . . .

. . .

. . . In fact, these [laws] have been instrumental in helping to prevent dozens of terrorist attacks, many on U.S. soil.

. . .

We need to change our systems and practices, and employ the latest in technology that would alert superiors when a worker tries to download and remove this type of information. We need to seal this crack in the system.

. . .

GENERAL KEITH ALEXANDER, Director of the National Security Agency

. . .

The events of September 11, 2001 occurred, in part, because of a failure on the part of our government to connect [the] dots. . . .

Section 215 of [the Patriot Act] . . . helps the government close [the] gap by enabling the detection of telephone contact between terrorists overseas and operatives within the United States. . . . [I]f we had had Section 215 in place prior to 9/11, we may have known that the 9/11 hijacker Mihdhar was located in San Diego and communicating with a known Al Qaida safe house in Yemen.

. . .

I believe we have achieved the security and relative safety in a way that does not compromise the privacy and civil liberties of our citizens. We would like to make three fundamental points. First, these programs are critical to the intelligence community's ability to protect our nation and our allies' security. . . .

Second, these programs are limited, focused, and subject to rigorous oversight. . . .

Third, the disciplined operation of these programs protects the privacy and civil liberties of the American people. . . .

DEPUTY ATTORNEY GENERAL JAMES M. COLE, U.S. Department of Justice

. . .

. . . This is not a program that's off the books, that's been hidden away. This is part of what government puts together and discusses. Statutes are passed. It is overseen by three branches of our government. . . . The process of oversight occurs before, during, and after the process that we're talking about today.

. . .

. . . First of all, it's metadata. These are phone records. . . . We do not get the identity of any of the parties to this phone call. . . . We don't get any cell site or location information. . . . And, most importantly . . . , we don't get any content under this.

. . . [T]he way it works is, there is an application that is made by the FBI under the statute to the FISA court. We call it the FISC. They ask for and receive permission under the FISC . . . to get records that are relevant to a national security investigation. And they must demonstrate to the FISC that it will be operated under the guidelines that are set forth by the attorney general. . . .

. . . [I]t is quite explicitly limited to things that you could get with a grand jury subpoena, those kinds of records. Now, it's important to know that prosecutors issue grand jury subpoenas all the time and do not need any involvement of a court or anybody else to do so.

Under this program, we need to get permission from the court to issue this ahead of time. . . .

. . . [W]e have to re-up and renew these orders every 90 days in order to do this. Now, there are strict controls over what we can do under the order. . . . There're restrictions on who can access it. . . .

In order to access [the collected records], there needs to be a finding that there is a responsible suspicion . . . that the person whose phone records you want to query is involved with some sort of terrorist organizations. . . . So there has to be independent evidence . . . that the person you're targeting is involved. . . .

If that person is a United States citizen, or a lawful permanent resident, you have to have something more than just their own speeches. . . .

Now, one of the things to keep in mind is under the law, the Fourth Amendment does not apply to these records . . . because people don't have a reasonable expectation of privacy in who they called and when they called. . . . [*Smith v. Maryland* (1979)]

. . .

We also provide the Intelligence and Judiciary Committees with any significant interpretations that the court makes of the [statute]. If they make a ruling that is significant or issue an order that is significant in its interpretation, we provide those, as well as the applications made for those orders, to the Intelligence and to the Judiciary Committee.

And every 30 days, we are filing with the FISC a report that describes how we implement this program. . . .

At least once every 90 days and sometimes more frequently, the Department of Justice, the Office of the Director of National Intelligence, and the NSA meet to assess NSA's compliance with all of these requirements that are contained in the court order. Separately, the Department of Justice meets with the inspector general for the National Security Agency and assesses the NSA's compliance on a regular basis.

Finally, there is by statute reporting of certain information to Congress in semiannual reports that we make on top of the periodic reports we make if there's a compliance incident. . . .

Now, the 702 statute under the FISA Amendments Act is different. Under this, we do get content, but there's a big difference. You are only allowed . . . to target for this purpose non-U.S. persons who are located outside of the United States. So if you have a U.S. permanent resident who's in Madrid, Spain, we can't target them under 702. Or if you have a non-U.S. person who's in Cleveland, Ohio, we cannot target them under 702. . . .

. . . The FISC gives a certificate that allows this targeting to be done for a year period. It then has to be renewed. . . . [and similar reporting and oversight processes are followed for FISA].

. . .

[A report recently found that] the U.S. is more transparent about its [intelligence-gathering] procedures, requires more due process protections in its investigations that involve national security, terrorism and foreign intelligence [than our partner countries, including those in the European Union].

. . .

REPRESENTATIVE JANICE SCHAKOWSKY (Democrat, Illinois)

. . . [W]ill you release these [FISA] court opinions with the necessary redactions, of course? And if not, why?

ROBERT LITT, General Counsel, National Security Agency

As you may know, we have been working for some time on trying to declassify opinions of the FISA court. It's been a very difficult task, because like most legal opinions, you have facts intermingled with legal discussion. And the facts frequently involve classified information, sensitive sources and methods. And what we've been discovering is that when you remove all of the information that needs to be classified, you're left with something that looks like Swiss cheese, and is not really very comprehensible. . . .

REPRESENTATIVE JAMES HIMES (Democrat, Connecticut)

. . . [The programs that Snowden revealed] trouble me because of the breadth and the scope of the information collected. They trouble me because I think this is historically unprecedented in the extent of the data that is being collected on potentially all American citizens. . . . We know that when a capability exists, there's potential for abuse. . . .

. . . And one of the things that I'm concerned about is that [Snowden] . . . had access to some of the most sensitive information that we have. . . . Could have accessed phone numbers and—though we spent a lot of time on the fact that you don't get names, we all know that with a phone number and Google, you can get a name pretty quickly.

He could have chosen to make a point about Congressman Himes making 2:00 am phone calls out of a bar in Washington. . . . Or anything really. Information that we hold to be private.

. . .

DEPUTY ATTORNEY GENERAL JAMES M. COLE, U.S. Department of Justice

I think some of it is a matter for the United States Congress to decide as policy matters. . . . Certainly the courts have looked at this and determined that under the statutes we have, there is a relevance requirement, and they're not just saying out of whole cloth you're allowed to gather these things. . . . And they're only saying that you can gather this volume under these circumstances, under these restrictions, with these controls. . . . [T]he acquisition comes together with the restriction on access.

. . .

GENERAL KEITH ALEXANDER, Director of the National Security Agency

. . . So your question is, could somebody get your phone number and see that you were at a bar last night? The answer is no. Because first in our system, somebody would have had to approve, and there's only 22 people that can approve, a reasonable articulable suspicion on a phone number. . . . Only those phone numbers that are approved could then be queried. And so you have to have one of those 22 break a law [to approve access to a congressman's phone number]. Then you have to have somebody go in and break the law [by actually accessing the phone number]. And the system is 100 percent auditable, so it will be caught.

. . . And then that person would be found by the [FISA] court to be in violation of a court order, and that's much more serious. We have never had that happen.

. . .

REPRESENTATIVE MICHELE BACHMANN (Republican, Minnesota)

[D]oes the federal government have a database with video data in it tracking the whereabouts of the American people?

DEPUTY DIRECTOR SEAN JOYCE, Federal Bureau of Investigation

The FBI does not have such a database, nor am I aware of one.

REPRESENTATIVE MICHELE BACHMANN (Republican, Minnesota)

[D]oes the American government have a database that has the GPS location whereabouts of Americans . . . ?

DEPUTY DIRECTOR CHRIS INGLIS, National Security Agency

NSA does not hold such a database.

REPRESENTATIVE MICHELE BACHMANN (Republican, Minnesota)

Does the NSA have a database that you maintain that holds the content of Americans' phone calls? . . .

GENERAL KEITH ALEXANDER, Director of the National Security Agency

We're not allowed to do that, nor do we do that, unless we have a court order to do that. And it would be only in specific cases and almost always that would be an FBI lead, not ours.

. . .

DEPUTY ATTORNEY GENERAL JAMES M. COLE, U.S. Department of Justice

. . . [I]f you're looking for a needle in the haystack, you have to get the haystack first. And that's why we have the ability under the court order to acquire—and the key word here is acquire—all that data.

We don't get to use all of that data necessarily. That is the next step, which is to have to be able to determine that there is reasonable, articulable suspicion to use that data.

So if we want to find that there is a phone number that we believe is connected with terrorist organizations and terrorist activity, we need to have the rest of the haystack, all the other numbers, to find out which ones it was in contact with.

. . .

Suggested Readings

Baer, Judith A. 1999. *Our Lives Before the Law: Constructing a Feminist Jurisprudence.* Princeton, NJ: Princeton University Press.

Balkin, Jack M., and Sanford A. Levinson. 2001. "Understanding the Constitutional Revolution." *Virginia Law Review* 87:1045–1109.

Balkin, Jack M., and Reva B. Siegel. 2009. *The Constitution in 2020.* New York: Oxford University Press.

Brisbin, Richard A., Jr. 1997. *Justice Antonin Scalia and the Conservative Revival.* Baltimore, MD: Johns Hopkins University Press.

Carpenter, Dale. 2012. *Flagrant Conduct: The Story of* Lawrence v. Texas. New York: Norton.

Colucci, Frank J. 2009. *Justice Kennedy's Jurisprudence: The Full and Necessary Meaning of Liberty.* Lawrence: University Press of Kansas.

Fisher, Louis. 1997. *Constitutional Conflicts Between Congress and the President.* Lawrence: University Press of Kansas.

Gerber, Scott Douglas. 1999. *First Principles: The Jurisprudence of Clarence Thomas.* New York: New York University Press.

Gerhardt, Michael. 2000. *The Federal Appointments Process: A Constitutional and Historical Analysis.* Durham, NC: Duke University Press.

Gillman, Howard. 2000. *The Votes that Counted: How the Court Decided the 2000 Presidential Election.* Chicago: University of Chicago Press.

Hamilton, Marci A. 2005. *God vs. the Gavel: Religion and the Rule of Law.* New York: Cambridge University Press.

Keck, Thomas M. 2004. *The Most Activist Court in History: The Road to Modern Judicial Conservatism.* Chicago: University of Chicago Press.

King, Desmond S., and Rogers M. Smith. 2011. *Still a House Divided: Race and Politics in Obama's America.* Princeton, NJ: Princeton University Press.

Knowles, Helen J. 2009. *The Tie Goes to Freedom: Justice Anthony M. Kennedy on Liberty.* Lanham, MD: Rowman & Littlefield.

Koppelman, Andrew. 2002. *The Gay Rights Question in Contemporary American Law.* Chicago: University of Chicago Press.

Maltz, Earl M. 2003. *Rehnquist Justice: Understanding the Court Dynamic.* Lawrence: University Press of Kansas.

Maveety, Nancy. 2008. *Queen's Court: Judicial Power in the Rehnquist Era.* Lawrence: University Press of Kansas.

Pinello, Daniel R. 2003. *Gay Rights and American Law.* New York: Cambridge University Press.

Posner, Eric A., and Adrian Vermeule. 2011. *The Executive Unbound: After the Madisonian Republic.* New York: Oxford University Press.

Siegel, Reva B. 2008. "Dead or Alive: Originalism as Popular Constitutionalism in *Heller.*" *Harvard Law Review* 122:191–245.

Sweet, Martin J. 2010. *Merely Judgment: Ignoring, Evading, and Trumping the Supreme Court.* Charlottesville: University of Virginia Press.

Teles, Steven M. 2008. *The Rise of the Conservative Legal Movement: The Battle for the Control of the Law.* Princeton, NJ: Princeton University Press.

Tushnet, Mark. 2003. *The New Constitutional Order.* Princeton, NJ: Princeton University Press.

———, ed. 2005a. *The Constitution in Wartime: Beyond Alarmism and Complacency.* Durham, NC: Duke University Press.

Tushnet, Mark. 2005b. *A Court Divided.* New York: Norton.

Winkler, Adam. 2011. *Gunfight: The Battle over the Right to Bear Arms in America.* New York: Norton.

Yarbrough, Tinsley E. 2000. *The Rehnquist Court and the Constitution.* New York: Oxford University Press.

———. 2005. *David Hackett Souter: Traditional Republican on the Supreme Court.* New York: Oxford University Press.

Appendix 1

Constitution of the United States of America

We the People of the United States, in Order to form a more perfect Union, establish Justice, insure domestic Tranquility, provide for the common defense, promote the general Welfare, and secure the Blessings of Liberty to ourselves and our Posterity, do ordain and establish this Constitution for the United States of America.

Article. I.

Section. 1. All legislative Powers herein granted shall be vested in a Congress of the United States, which shall consist of a Senate and House of Representatives.

Section. 2. The House of Representatives shall be composed of Members chosen every second Year by the People of the several States, and the Electors in each State shall have the Qualifications requisite for Electors of the most numerous Branch of the State Legislature.

No Person shall be a Representative who shall not have attained to the Age of twenty five Years, and been seven Years a Citizen of the United States, and who shall not, when elected, be an Inhabitant of that State in which he shall be chosen.

[Representatives and direct Taxes shall be apportioned among the several States which may be included within this Union, according to their respective Numbers, which shall be determined by adding to the whole Number of free Persons, including those bound to Service for a Term of Years, and excluding Indians not taxed, three fifths of all other Persons.][1] The actual Enumeration shall be made within three Years after the first Meeting of the Congress of the United States, and within every subsequent Term of ten Years, in such Manner as they shall by Law direct. The number of Representatives shall not exceed one for every thirty Thousand, but each State shall have at Least one Representative; and until such enumeration shall be made, the State of New Hampshire shall be entitled to choose three, Massachusetts eight, Rhode-Island and Providence Plantations one, Connecticut five, New-York six, New Jersey four, Pennsylvania eight, Delaware one, Maryland six, Virginia ten, North Carolina five, South Carolina five, and Georgia three.

When vacancies happen in the Representation from any State, the Executive Authority thereof shall issue Writs of Election to fill such Vacancies.

The House of Representatives shall choose their Speaker and other Officers; and shall have the sole Power of Impeachment.

Section. 3. The Senate of the United States shall be composed of two Senators from each State, [chosen by the Legislature thereof,][2] for six Years; and each Senator shall have one Vote.

Immediately after they shall be assembled in Consequence of the first Election, they shall be divided as equally as may be into three Classes. The Seats of the Senators of the first Class shall be vacated at the Expiration of the second Year, of the second Class at the Expiration of the fourth Year, and of the third Class at the Expiration of the sixth Year, so that one third may be chosen every second Year; [and if Vacancies happen by Resignation, or otherwise, during the Recess of the Legislature of any State, the Executive thereof may make temporary Appointments until the next Meeting of the Legislature, which shall then fill such Vacancies.][3]

1. Changed by Section 2 of the Fourteenth Amendment.

2. Changed by the Seventeenth Amendment.

3. Changed by the Seventeenth Amendment.

No Person shall be a Senator who shall not have attained to the Age of thirty Years, and been nine Years a Citizen of the United States, and who shall not, when elected, be an Inhabitant of that State for which he shall be chosen.

The Vice President of the United States shall be President of the Senate, but shall have no Vote, unless they be equally divided.

The Senate shall choose their other Officers, and also a President pro tempore, in the Absence of the Vice President, or when he shall exercise the Office of President of the United States.

The Senate shall have the sole Power to try all Impeachments. When sitting for that Purpose, they shall be on Oath or Affirmation. When the President of the United States is tried, the Chief Justice shall preside: And no Person shall be convicted without the Concurrence of two thirds of the Members present.

Judgment in Cases of Impeachment shall not extend further than to removal from Office, and disqualification to hold and enjoy any Office of honor, Trust or Profit under the United States: but the Party convicted shall nevertheless be liable and subject to Indictment, Trial, Judgment and Punishment, according to Law.

Section. 4. The Times, Places and Manner of holding Elections for Senators and Representatives, shall be prescribed in each State by the Legislature thereof; but the Congress may at any time by Law make or alter such Regulations, except as to the Places of choosing Senators.

The Congress shall assemble at least once in every Year, and such Meeting shall be [on the first Monday in December,][4] unless they shall by Law appoint a different Day.

Section. 5. Each House shall be the Judge of the Elections, Returns and Qualifications of its own Members, and a Majority of each shall constitute a Quorum to do Business; but a smaller Number may adjourn from day to day, and may be authorized to compel the Attendance of absent Members, in such Manner, and under such Penalties as each House may provide.

Each House may determine the Rules of its Proceedings, punish its Members for disorderly Behavior, and, with the Concurrence of two thirds, expel a Member.

Each House shall keep a Journal of its Proceedings, and from time to time publish the same, excepting such Parts as may in their Judgment require Secrecy; and the Yeas and Nays of the Members of either House on any question shall, at the Desire of one fifth of those Present, be entered on the Journal.

Neither House, during the Session of Congress, shall, without the Consent of the other, adjourn for more than three days, nor to any other Place than that in which the two Houses shall be sitting.

Section. 6. The Senators and Representatives shall receive a Compensation for their Services, to be ascertained by Law, and paid out of the Treasury of the United States. They shall in all Cases, except Treason, Felony and Breach of the Peace, be privileged from Arrest during their Attendance at the Session of their respective Houses, and in going to and returning from the same; and for any Speech or Debate in either House, they shall not be questioned in any other Place.

No Senator or Representative shall, during the Time for which he was elected, be appointed to any civil Office under the Authority of the United States, which shall have been created, or the Emoluments whereof shall have been increased during such time; and no Person holding any Office under the United States, shall be a Member of either House during his Continuance in Office.

Section. 7. All Bills for raising Revenue shall originate in the House of Representatives; but the Senate may propose or concur with Amendments as on other Bills.

Every Bill which shall have passed the House of Representatives and the Senate, shall, before it becomes a Law, be presented to the President of the United States; If he approve he shall sign it, but if not he shall return it, with his Objections to that House in which it shall have originated, who shall enter the Objections at large on their Journal, and proceed to reconsider it. If after such Reconsideration two thirds of that House shall agree to pass the Bill, it shall be sent, together with the Objections, to the other House, by which it shall likewise be reconsidered, and if approved by two thirds of that House, it shall become a Law. But in all such Cases the Votes of both Houses shall be determined by yeas and Nays, and the Names of the Persons voting for and against the Bill shall be entered on the Journal of each House respectively. If any Bill shall not be returned by

4. Changed by the Twentieth Amendment.

the President within ten Days (Sundays excepted) after it shall have been presented to him, the Same shall be a Law, in like Manner as if he had signed it, unless the Congress by their Adjournment prevent its Return, in which Case it shall not be a Law.

Every Order, Resolution, or Vote to which the Concurrence of the Senate and House of Representatives may be necessary (except on a question of Adjournment) shall be presented to the President of the United States; and before the Same shall take Effect, shall be approved by him, or being disapproved by him, shall be repassed by two thirds of the Senate and House of Representatives, according to the Rules and Limitations prescribed in the Case of a Bill.

Section. 8. The Congress shall have Power To lay and collect Taxes, Duties, Imposts and Excises, to pay the Debts and provide for the common Defense and general Welfare of the United States; but all Duties, Imposts and Excises shall be uniform throughout the United States;

To borrow Money on the credit of the United States;

To regulate Commerce with foreign Nations, and among the several States, and with the Indian Tribes;

To establish an uniform Rule of Naturalization, and uniform Laws on the subject of Bankruptcies throughout the United States;

To coin Money, regulate the Value thereof, and of foreign Coin, and fix the Standard of Weights and Measures;

To provide for the Punishment of counterfeiting the Securities and current Coin of the United States;

To establish Post Offices and post Roads;

To promote the Progress of Science and useful Arts, by securing for limited Times to Authors and Inventors the exclusive Right to their respective Writings and Discoveries;

To constitute Tribunals inferior to the Supreme Court;

To define and punish Piracies and Felonies committed on the high Seas, and Offenses against the Law of Nations;

To declare War, grant Letters of Marque and Reprisal, and make Rules concerning Captures on Land and Water;

To raise and support Armies, but no Appropriation of Money to that Use shall be for a longer Term than two Years;

To provide and maintain a Navy;

To make Rules for the Government and Regulation of the land and naval Forces;

To provide for calling forth the Militia to execute the Laws of the Union, suppress Insurrections and repel Invasions;

To provide for organizing, arming, and disciplining, the Militia, and for governing such Part of them as may be employed in the Service of the United States, reserving to the States respectively, the Appointment of the Officers, and the Authority of training the Militia according to the discipline prescribed by Congress;

To exercise exclusive Legislation in all Cases whatsoever, over such District (not exceeding ten Miles square) as may, by Cession of particular States, and the Acceptance of Congress, become the Seat of the Government of the United States, and to exercise like Authority over all Places purchased by the Consent of the Legislature of the State in which the Same shall be, for the Erection of Forts, Magazines, Arsenals, dock-Yards and other needful Buildings;—And

To make all Laws which shall be necessary and proper for carrying into Execution the foregoing Powers, and all other Powers vested by this Constitution in the Government of the United States or in any Department or Officer thereof.

Section. 9. The Migration or Importation of such Persons as any of the States now existing shall think proper to admit, shall not be prohibited by the Congress prior to the Year one thousand eight hundred and eight, but a Tax or duty may be imposed on such Importation, not exceeding ten dollars for each Person.

The Privilege of the Writ of Habeas Corpus shall not be suspended, unless when in Cases of Rebellion or Invasion the public Safety may require it.

No Bill of Attainder or ex post facto Law shall be passed.

No Capitation, or other direct, Tax shall be laid, [unless in Proportion to the Census or Enumeration herein before directed to be taken.][5]

No Tax or Duty shall be laid on Articles exported from any State.

No Preference shall be given by any Regulation of Commerce or Revenue to the Ports of one State over

5. Changed by Sixteenth Amendment.

those of another: nor shall Vessels bound to, or from, one State, be obliged to enter, clear, or pay Duties in another.

No Money shall be drawn from the Treasury, but in Consequence of Appropriations made by Law; and a regular Statement and Account of the Receipts and Expenditures of all public Money shall be published from time to time.

No Title of Nobility shall be granted by the United States: And no Person holding any Office of Profit or Trust under them, shall, without the Consent of the Congress, accept of any present, Emolument, Office, or Title, of any kind whatever, from any King, Prince, or foreign State.

Section. 10. No State shall enter into any Treaty, Alliance, or Confederation; grant Letters of Marque and Reprisal; coin Money; emit Bills of Credit; make any Thing but gold and silver Coin a Tender in Payment of Debts; pass any Bill of Attainder, ex post facto Law, or Law impairing the Obligation of Contracts, or grant any Title of Nobility.

No State shall, without the Consent of the Congress, lay any Imposts or Duties on Imports or Exports, except what may be absolutely necessary for executing it's inspection Laws: and the net Produce of all Duties and Imposts, laid by any State on Imports or Exports, shall be for the Use of the Treasury of the United States; and all such Laws shall be subject to the Revision and Control of the Congress.

No State shall, without the Consent of Congress, lay any Duty of Tonnage, keep Troops, or Ships of War in time of Peace, enter into any Agreement or Compact with another State, or with a foreign Power, or engage in War, unless actually invaded, or in such imminent Danger as will not admit of delay.

Article. II.

Section. 1. The executive Power shall be vested in a President of the United States of America. He shall hold his Office during the Term of four Years, and, together with the Vice President, chosen for the same Term, be elected, as follows.

Each State shall appoint, in such Manner as the Legislature thereof may direct, a Number of Electors, equal to the whole Number of Senators and Representatives to which the State may be entitled in the Congress: but no Senator or Representative, or Person holding an Office of Trust or Profit under the United States, shall be appointed an Elector.

[The Electors shall meet in their respective States, and vote by Ballot for two Persons, of whom one at least shall not be an Inhabitant of the same State with themselves. And they shall make a List of all the Persons voted for, and of the Number of Votes for each; which List they shall sign and certify, and transmit sealed to the Seat of the Government of the United States, directed to the President of the Senate. The President of the Senate shall, in the Presence of the Senate and House of Representatives, open all the Certificates, and the Votes shall then be counted. The Person having the greatest Number of Votes shall be the President, if such Number be a Majority of the whole Number of Electors appointed; and if there be more than one who have such Majority, and have an equal Number of Votes, then the House of Representatives shall immediately choose by Ballot one of them for President; and if no Person have a Majority, then from the five highest on the List the said House shall in like Manner choose the President. But in choosing the President, the Votes shall be taken by States, the Representation from each State having one Vote; A quorum for this Purpose shall consist of a Member or Members from two thirds of the States, and a Majority of all the States shall be necessary to a Choice. In every Case, after the Choice of the President, the Person having the greatest Number of Votes of the Electors shall be the Vice President. But if there should remain two or more who have equal Votes, the Senate shall choose from them by Ballot the Vice President.][6]

The Congress may determine the Time of choosing the Electors, and the Day on which they shall give their Votes; which Day shall be the same throughout the United States.

No Person except a natural born Citizen, or a Citizen of the United States, at the time of the Adoption of this Constitution, shall be eligible to the Office of President; neither shall any person be eligible to that Office who shall not have attained to the Age of thirty five Years, and been fourteen Years a Resident within the United States.

[In Case of the Removal of the President from Office, or of his Death, Resignation, or Inability to

6. Changed by Twelfth Amendment.

discharge the Powers and Duties of the said Office, the Same shall devolve on the Vice President, and the Congress may by Law provide for the Case of Removal, Death, Resignation or Inability, both of the President and Vice President, declaring what Officer shall then act as President, and such Officer shall act accordingly, until the Disability be removed, or a President shall be elected.][7]

The President shall, at stated Times, receive for his Services, a Compensation, which shall neither be increased nor diminished during the Period for which he shall have been elected, and he shall not receive within that Period any other Emolument from the United States, or any of them.

Before he enter on the Execution of his Office, he shall take the following Oath or Affirmation:—"I do solemnly swear (or affirm) that I will faithfully execute the Office of President of the United States, and will to the best of my Ability, preserve, protect and defend the Constitution of the United States."

Section. 2. The President shall be Commander in Chief of the Army and Navy of the United States, and of the Militia of the several States, when called into the actual Service of the United States; he may require the Opinion, in writing, of the principal Officer in each of the executive Departments, upon any Subject relating to the Duties of their respective Offices, and he shall have Power to grant Reprieves and Pardons for Offenses against the United States, except in Cases of Impeachment.

He shall have Power, by and with the Advice and Consent of the Senate, to make Treaties, provided two thirds of the Senators present concur; and he shall nominate, and by and with the Advice and Consent of the Senate, shall appoint Ambassadors, other public Ministers and Consuls, Judges of the supreme Court, and all other Officers of the United States, whose Appointments are not herein otherwise provided for, and which shall be established by Law: but the Congress may by Law vest the Appointment of such inferior Officers, as they think proper, in the President alone, in the Courts of Law, or in the Heads of Departments.

The President shall have Power to fill up all Vacancies that may happen during the Recess of the Senate, by granting Commissions which shall expire at the End of their next Session.

7. Changed by Twenty-Fifth Amendment.

Section. 3. He shall from time to time give to the Congress Information of the State of the Union, and recommend to their Consideration such Measures as he shall judge necessary and expedient; he may, on extraordinary Occasions, convene both Houses, or either of them, and in Case of Disagreement between them, with Respect to the Time of Adjournment, he may adjourn them to such Time as he shall think proper; he shall receive Ambassadors and other public Ministers; he shall take Care that the Laws be faithfully executed, and shall Commission all the Officers of the United States.

Section. 4. The President, Vice President and all civil Officers of the United States, shall be removed from Office on Impeachment for, and Conviction of, Treason, Bribery, or other high Crimes and Misdemeanors.

Article. III.

Section. 1. The judicial Power of the United States shall be vested in one supreme Court, and in such inferior Courts as the Congress may from time to time ordain and establish. The Judges, both of the supreme and inferior Courts, shall hold their Offices during good Behavior, and shall, at stated Times, receive for their Services, a Compensation, which shall not be diminished during their Continuance in Office.

Section. 2. The judicial Power shall extend to all Cases, in Law and Equity, arising under this Constitution, the Laws of the United States, and Treaties made, or which shall be made, under their Authority;—to all Cases affecting Ambassadors, other public Ministers and Consuls;—to all Cases of admiralty and maritime Jurisdiction;—to Controversies to which the United States shall be a Party;—to Controversies between two or more States;—[between a State and Citizens of another State;—][8] between Citizens of different States,—between Citizens of the same State claiming Lands under Grants of different States, and between a State, or the Citizens thereof, and foreign States, Citizens or Subjects.

In all Cases affecting Ambassadors, other public Ministers and Consuls, and those in which a State shall be Party, the supreme Court shall have original

8. Changed by Eleventh Amendment.

Jurisdiction. In all the other Cases before mentioned, the supreme Court shall have appellate Jurisdiction, both as to Law and Fact, with such Exceptions, and under such Regulations as the Congress shall make.

The Trial of all Crimes, except in Cases of Impeachment; shall be by Jury; and such Trial shall be held in the State where the said Crimes shall have been committed; but when not committed within any State, the Trial shall be at such Place or Places as the Congress may by Law have directed.

Section. 3. Treason against the United States, shall consist only in levying War against them, or in adhering to their Enemies, giving them Aid and Comfort. No Person shall be convicted of Treason unless on the Testimony of two Witnesses to the same overt Act, or on Confession in open Court.

The Congress shall have Power to declare the Punishment of Treason, but no Attainder of Treason shall work Corruption of Blood, or Forfeiture except during the Life of the Person attainted.

Article. IV.

Section. 1. Full Faith and Credit shall be given in each State to the public Acts, Records, and judicial Proceedings of every other State; And the Congress may by general Laws prescribe the Manner in which such Acts, Records and Proceedings shall be proved, and the Effect thereof.

Section. 2. The Citizens of each State shall be entitled to all Privileges and Immunities of Citizens in the several States.

A Person charged in any State with Treason, Felony, or other Crime, who shall flee from Justice, and be found in another State, shall on Demand of the executive Authority of the State from which he fled, be delivered up, to be removed to the State having Jurisdiction of the Crime.

[No Person held to Service or Labor in one State, under the Laws thereof, escaping into another, shall, in Consequence of any Law or Regulation therein, be discharged from such Service or Labor, but shall be delivered up on Claim of the Party to whom such Service or Labor may be due.][9]

9. Changed by Thirteenth Amendment.

Section. 3. New States may be admitted by the Congress into this Union; but no new State shall be formed or erected within the Jurisdiction of any other State; nor any State be formed by the Junction of two or more States, or Parts of States, without the Consent of the Legislatures of the States concerned as well as of the Congress.

The Congress shall have Power to dispose of and make all needful Rules and Regulations respecting the Territory or other Property belonging to the United States; and nothing in this Constitution shall be so construed as to Prejudice any Claims of the United States, or of any particular State.

Section. 4. The United States shall guarantee to every State in this Union a Republican Form of Government, and shall protect each of them against Invasion; and on Application of the Legislature, or of the Executive (when the Legislature cannot be convened) against domestic Violence.

Article. V.

The Congress, whenever two thirds of both Houses shall deem it necessary, shall propose Amendments to this Constitution, or, on the Application of the Legislatures of two thirds of the several States, shall call a Convention for proposing Amendments, which, in either Case, shall be valid to all Intents and Purposes, as Part of this Constitution, when ratified by the Legislatures of three fourths of the several States, or by Conventions in three fourths thereof, as the one or the other Mode of Ratification may be proposed by the Congress; Provided that no Amendment which may be made prior to the Year One thousand eight hundred and eight shall in any Manner affect the first and fourth Clauses in the Ninth Section of the first Article; and that no State, without its Consent, shall be deprived of it's equal Suffrage in the Senate.

Article. VI.

All Debts contracted and Engagements entered into, before the Adoption of this Constitution, shall be as valid against the United States under this Constitution, as under the Confederation.

This Constitution, and the Laws of the United States which shall be made in Pursuance thereof; and all Treaties made, or which shall be made, under the Authority of the United States, shall be the supreme Law of the Land; and the Judges in every State shall be bound thereby, any Thing in the Constitution or Laws of any State to the Contrary notwithstanding.

The Senators and Representatives before mentioned, and the Members of the several State Legislatures, and all executive and judicial Officers, both of the United States and of the several States, shall be bound by Oath or Affirmation, to support this Constitution; but no religious Test shall ever be required as a Qualification to any Office or public Trust under the United States.

Article. VII.

The Ratification of the Conventions of nine States, shall be sufficient for the Establishment of this Constitution between the States so ratifying the Same.

Done in Convention by the Unanimous Consent of the States present the Seventeenth Day of September in the Year of our Lord one thousand seven hundred and Eighty seven and of the Independence of the United States of America the Twelfth In Witness whereof We have hereunto subscribed our Names,

George Washington—President and deputy from Virginia

New Hampshire	John Langdon Nicholas Gilman
Massachusetts	Nathaniel Gorham Rufus King
Connecticut	William Samuel Johnson Roger Sherman
New York	Alexander Hamilton
New Jersey	William Livingston David Brearley William Paterson Jonathan Dayton
Pennsylvania	Benjamin Franklin Thomas Mifflin Robert Morris George Clymer Thomas FitzSimons Jared Ingersoll James Wilson Gouverneur Morris
Delaware	George Read Gunning Bedford, Jr. John Dickinson Richard Bassett Jacob Broom
Maryland	James McHenry Daniel of St. Thomas Jenifer Daniel Carroll
Virginia	John Blair James Madison, Jr.
North Carolina	William Blount Richard Dobbs Spaight Hugh Williamson
South Carolina	John Rutledge Charles Cotesworth Pinckney Charles Pinckney Pierce Butler
Georgia	William Few Abraham Baldwin

Attest William Jackson, Secretary

In Convention Monday
September 17th 1787.

Present
The States of

New Hampshire, Massachusetts, Connecticut, Mr. Hamilton from New York, New Jersey, Pennsylvania, Delaware, Maryland, Virginia, North Carolina, South Carolina and Georgia.

Resolved,

That the preceding Constitution be laid before the United States in Congress assembled, and that it is the Opinion of this Convention, that it should afterwards be submitted to a Convention of Delegates, chosen in each State by the People thereof, under the Recommendation of its Legislature, for their Assent and Ratification; and that each Convention assenting to, and ratifying the Same, should give Notice thereof to the United States in Congress assembled. Resolved, That it is the Opinion of this Convention, that as soon as the Conventions of nine States shall have ratified this Constitution, the United States in Congress assembled should fix a Day on which Electors should be appointed by the States which shall have ratified the same, and a Day on which the Electors should assemble to vote for the President, and the Time and Place for commencing Proceedings under this Constitution.

That after such Publication the Electors should be appointed, and the Senators and Representatives elected: That the Electors should meet on the Day fixed for the Election of the President, and should transmit their Votes certified, signed, sealed and directed, as the Constitution requires, to the Secretary of the United States in Congress assembled, that the Senators and Representatives should convene at the Time and Place assigned; that the Senators should appoint a President of the Senate, for the sole Purpose of receiving, opening and counting the Votes for President; and, that after he shall be chosen, the Congress, together with the President, should, without Delay, proceed to execute this Constitution.

By the unanimous Order of the Convention
George WASHINGTON—President

William JACKSON Secretary.

[Adding the Bill of Rights][10]

Congress of the United States begun and held at the City of New-York, on Wednesday the fourth of March, one thousand seven hundred and eighty nine:

THE Conventions of a number of the States, having at the time of their adopting the Constitution, expressed a desire, in order to prevent misconstruction or abuse of its powers, that further declaratory and restrictive clauses should be added: And as extending the ground of public confidence in the Government, will best ensure the beneficent ends of its institution:

10. On September 25, 1789, Congress transmitted to the state legislatures twelve proposed amendments, the first two of which, having to do with Congressional representation and congressional pay, were not adopted. The remaining ten amendments became the Bill of Rights. The amendment regarding congressional pay was later ratified and became the Twenty-Seventh Amendment.

RESOLVED by the Senate and House of Representatives of the United States of America, in Congress assembled, two thirds of both Houses concurring, that the following Articles be proposed to the Legislatures of the several States, as Amendments to the Constitution of the United States, all or any of which Articles, when ratified by three fourths of the said Legislatures, to be valid to all intents and purposes, as part of the said Constitution; viz.

ARTICLES in addition to, and Amendment of the Constitution of the United States of America, proposed by Congress, and ratified by the Legislatures of the several States, pursuant to the fifth Article of the original Constitution....

FREDERICK AUGUSTUS MUHLENBERG
Speaker of the House of Representatives.

JOHN ADAMS, Vice-President of the United States and President of the Senate.

ATTEST,

JOHN BECKLEY, Clerk of the House of Representatives.

SAMUEL A. OTIS, Secretary of the Senate.

AMENDMENTS
TO THE CONSTITUTION
OF THE
UNITED STATES OF AMERICA

Amendment I.[11]

Congress shall make no law respecting an establishment of religion, or prohibiting the free exercise thereof; or abridging the freedom of speech, or of the press, or the right of the people peaceably to assemble, and to petition the Government for a redress of grievances.

Amendment II.

A well regulated Militia, being necessary to the security of a free State, the right of the people to keep and bear Arms, shall not be infringed.

11. The first ten Amendments (Bill of Rights) were ratified effective December 15, 1791.

Amendment III.

No Soldier shall, in time of peace be quartered in any house, without the consent of the Owner, nor in time of war, but in a manner to be prescribed by law.

Amendment IV.

The right of the people to be secure in their persons, houses, papers, and effects, against unreasonable searches and seizures, shall not be violated, and no Warrants shall issue, but upon probable cause, supported by Oath or affirmation, and particularly describing the place to be searched, and the persons or things to be seized.

Amendment V.

No person shall be held to answer for a capital, or otherwise infamous crime, unless on a presentment or indictment of a Grand Jury, except in cases arising in the land or naval forces, or in the Militia, when in actual service in time of War or public danger; nor shall any person be subject for the same offence to be twice put in jeopardy of life or limb, nor shall be compelled in any criminal case to be a witness against himself, nor be deprived of life, liberty, or property, without due process of law; nor shall private property be taken for public use without just compensation.

Amendment VI.

In all criminal prosecutions, the accused shall enjoy the right to a speedy and public trial, by an impartial jury of the State and district wherein the crime shall have been committed; which district shall have been previously ascertained by law, and to be informed of the nature and cause of the accusation; to be confronted with the witnesses against him; to have compulsory process for obtaining witnesses in his favor, and to have the assistance of counsel for his defense.

Amendment VII.

In Suits at common law, where the value in controversy shall exceed twenty dollars, the right of trial by jury shall be preserved, and no fact tried by a jury shall be otherwise re-examined in any Court of the United States, than according to the rules of the common law.

Amendment VIII.

Excessive bail shall not be required, nor excessive fines imposed, nor cruel and unusual punishments inflicted.

Amendment IX.

The enumeration in the Constitution of certain rights shall not be construed to deny or disparage others retained by the people.

Amendment X.

The powers not delegated to the United States by the Constitution, nor prohibited by it to the States, are reserved to the States respectively, or to the people.

Amendment XI.[12]

The Judicial power of the United States shall not be construed to extend to any suit in law or equity, commenced or prosecuted against one of the United States by Citizens of another State, or by Citizens or Subjects of any Foreign State.

Amendment XII.[13]

The Electors shall meet in their respective states, and vote by ballot for President and Vice President, one of whom, at least, shall not be an inhabitant of the same state with themselves; they shall name in their ballots the person voted for as President, and in distinct ballots the person voted for as Vice-President, and they shall make distinct lists of all persons voted for as President, and of all persons voted for as Vice-President, and of the number of votes for each, which lists they shall sign and certify, and transmit sealed to the seat of the government of the United States, directed to the President of the Senate;—The President of the Senate shall, in the presence of the Senate and House of Representatives, open all the certificates and the votes shall then be counted;—The person having the greatest number of votes for President, shall be the

12. The Eleventh Amendment was ratified February 7, 1795.
13. The Twelfth Amendment was ratified June 15, 1804.

President, if such number be a majority of the whole number of Electors appointed; and if no person have such majority, then from the persons having the highest numbers not exceeding three on the list of those voted for as President, the House of Representatives shall choose immediately, by ballot, the President. But in choosing the President, the votes shall be taken by states, the representation from each state having one vote; a quorum for this purpose shall consist of a member or members from two-thirds of the states, and a majority of all the states shall be necessary to a choice. [And if the House of Representatives shall not choose a President whenever the right of choice shall devolve upon them, before the fourth day of March next following, then the Vice President shall act as President, as in the case of the death or other constitutional disability of the President—].[14] The person having the greatest number of votes as Vice-President, shall be the Vice-President, if such number be a majority of the whole number of Electors appointed, and if no person have a majority, then from the two highest numbers on the list, the Senate shall choose the Vice-President; a quorum for the purpose shall consist of two-thirds of the whole number of Senators, and a majority of the whole number shall be necessary to a choice. But no person constitutionally ineligible to the office of President shall be eligible to that of Vice President of the United States.

Amendment XIII.[15]

Section 1. Neither slavery nor involuntary servitude, except as a punishment for crime whereof the party shall have been duly convicted, shall exist within the United States, or any place subject to their jurisdiction.

Section 2. Congress shall have power to enforce this article by appropriate legislation.

Amendment XIV.[16]

Section 1. All persons born or naturalized in the United States and subject to the jurisdiction thereof, are citizens of the United States and of the State wherein they reside. No State shall make or enforce any law which shall abridge the privileges or immunities of citizens of the United States; nor shall any State deprive any person of life, liberty, or property, without due process of law; nor deny to any person within its jurisdiction the equal protection of the laws.

Section 2. Representatives shall be apportioned among the several States according to their respective numbers, counting the whole number of persons in each State, excluding Indians not taxed. But when the right to vote at any election for the choice of electors for President and Vice President of the United States, Representatives in Congress, the Executive and Judicial officers of a State, or the members of the Legislature thereof, is denied to any of the male inhabitants of such State, being twenty-one years of age, and citizens of the United States, or in any way abridged, except for participation in rebellion, or other crime, the basis of representation therein shall be reduced in the proportion which the number of such male citizens shall bear to the whole number of male citizens twenty-one years of age in such State.

Section 3. No person shall be a Senator or Representative in Congress, or elector of President and Vice President, or hold any office, civil or military, under the United States, or under any State, who, having previously taken an oath, as a member of Congress, or as an officer of the United States, or as a member of any State legislature, or as an executive or judicial officer of any State, to support the Constitution of the United States, shall have engaged in insurrection or rebellion against the same, or given aid or comfort to the enemies thereof. But Congress may by a vote of two-thirds of each House, remove such disability.

Section 4. The validity of the public debt of the United States, authorized by law, including debts incurred for payment of pensions and bounties for services in suppressing insurrection or rebellion, shall not be questioned. But neither the United States nor any State shall assume or pay any debt or obligation incurred in aid of insurrection or rebellion against the United States, or any claim for the loss or emancipation of any slave; but all such debts, obligations and claims shall be held illegal and void.

Section 5. The Congress shall have power to enforce, by appropriate legislation, the provisions of this article.

14. Changed by the Twentieth Amendment.

15. The Thirteenth Amendment was ratified December 6, 1865.

16. The Fourteenth Amendment was ratified July 9, 1868.

Amendment XV.[17]

Section 1. The right of citizens of the United States to vote shall not be denied or abridged by the United States or by any State on account of race, color, or previous condition of servitude.

Section 2. The Congress shall have power to enforce this article by appropriate legislation.

Amendment XVI.[18]

The Congress shall have power to lay and collect taxes on incomes, from whatever source derived, without apportionment among the several States, and without regard to any census or enumeration.

Amendment XVII.[19]

The Senate of the United States shall be composed of two Senators from each State, elected by the people thereof, for six years; and each Senator shall have one vote. The electors in each State shall have the qualifications requisite for electors of the most numerous branch of the State legislatures.

When vacancies happen in the representation of any State in the Senate, the executive authority of such State shall issue writs of election to fill such vacancies: Provided, That the legislature of any State may empower the executive thereof to make temporary appointments until the people fill the vacancies by election as the legislature may direct.

This amendment shall not be so construed as to affect the election or term of any Senator chosen before it becomes valid as part of the Constitution.

Amendment XVIII.[20]

[Section 1. After one year from the ratification of this article the manufacture, sale, or transportation of intoxicating liquors within, the importation thereof into, or the exportation thereof from the United States and all territory subject to the jurisdiction thereof for beverage purposes is hereby prohibited.

Section 2. The Congress and the several States shall have concurrent power to enforce this article by appropriate legislation.

Section 3. This article shall be inoperative unless it shall have been ratified as an amendment to the Constitution by the legislatures of the several States, as provided in the Constitution, within seven years from the date of the submission hereof to the States by the Congress.]

Amendment XIX.[21]

The right of citizens of the United States to vote shall not be denied or abridged by the United States or by any State on account of sex.

Congress shall have power to enforce this article by appropriate legislation.

Amendment XX.[22]

Section 1. The terms of the President and Vice President shall end at noon on the 20th day of January, and the terms of Senators and Representatives at noon on the 3rd day of January, of the years in which such terms would have ended if this article had not been ratified; and the terms of their successors shall then begin.

Section 2. The Congress shall assemble at least once in every year, and such meeting shall begin at noon on the 3rd day of January, unless they shall by law appoint a different day.

Section 3. If, at the time fixed for the beginning of the term of the President, the President elect shall have died, the Vice President elect shall become President. If a President shall not have been chosen before the time fixed for the beginning of his term, or if the President elect shall have failed to qualify, then the Vice President elect shall act as President until a President shall have qualified; and the Congress may by law provide for the case wherein neither a President elect nor a Vice President elect shall have qualified, declaring who shall then act as President, or the manner in which one

17. The Fifteenth Amendment was ratified February 3, 1870.

18. The Sixteenth Amendment was ratified February 3, 1913.

19. The Seventeenth Amendment was ratified April 8, 1913.

20. The Eighteenth Amendment was ratified January 16, 1919. Repealed by the Twenty-First Amendment, December 5, 1933.

21. The Nineteenth Amendment was ratified August 18, 1920.

22. The Twentieth Amendment was ratified January 23, 1933.

who is to act shall be selected, and such person shall act accordingly until a President or Vice President shall have qualified.

Section 4. The Congress may by law provide for the case of the death of any of the persons from whom the House of Representatives may choose a President whenever the right of choice shall have devolved upon them, and for the case of the death of any of the persons from whom the Senate may choose a Vice President whenever the right of choice shall have devolved upon them.

Section 5. Sections 1 and 2 shall take effect on the 15th day of October following the ratification of this article.

Section 6. This article shall be inoperative unless it shall have been ratified as an amendment to the Constitution by the legislatures of three-fourths of the several States within seven years from the date of its submission.

Amendment XXI.[23]

Section 1. The eighteenth article of amendment to the Constitution of the United States is hereby repealed.

Section 2. The transportation or importation into any State, Territory, or possession of the United States for delivery or use therein of intoxicating liquors, in violation of the laws thereof, is hereby prohibited.

Section 3. This article shall be inoperative unless it shall have been ratified as an amendment to the Constitution by conventions in the several States, as provided in the Constitution, within seven years from the date of the submission hereof to the States by the Congress.

Amendment XXII.[24]

Section 1. No person who has held the office of President, or acted as President, for more than two years of a term to which some other person was elected President shall be elected to the office of the President more than once. But this Article shall not apply to any person holding the office of President when this Article was proposed by the Congress, and shall not prevent any person who may be holding the office of President, or acting as President, during the term within which this Article becomes operative from holding the office of President or acting as President during the remainder of such term.

Section 2. This article shall be inoperative unless it shall have been ratified as an amendment to the Constitution by the legislatures of three-fourths of the several States within seven years from the date of its submission to the States by the Congress.

Amendment XXIII.[25]

Section 1. The District constituting the seat of Government of the United States shall appoint in such manner as the Congress may direct:

A number of electors of President and Vice President equal to the whole number of Senators and Representatives in Congress to which the District would be entitled if it were a State, but in no event more than the least populous State; they shall be in addition to those appointed by the States, but they shall be considered, for the purposes of the election of President and Vice President, to be electors appointed by a State; and they shall meet in the District and perform such duties as provided by the twelfth article of amendment.

Section 2. The Congress shall have power to enforce this article by appropriate legislation.

Amendment XXIV.[26]

Section 1. The right of citizens of the United States to vote in any primary or other election for President or Vice President, for electors for President or Vice President, or for Senator or Representative in Congress, shall not be denied or abridged by the United States or any State by reason of failure to pay any poll tax or other tax.

Section 2. The Congress shall have power to enforce this article by appropriate legislation.

23. The Twenty-First Amendment was ratified December 5, 1933.

24. The Twenty-Second Amendment was ratified February 27, 1951.

25. The Twenty-Third Amendment was ratified March 29, 1961.

26. The Twenty-Fourth Amendment was ratified January 23, 1964.

Amendment XXV.[27]

Section 1. In case of the removal of the President from office or of his death or resignation, the Vice President shall become President.

Section 2. Whenever there is a vacancy in the office of the Vice President, the President shall nominate a Vice President who shall take office upon confirmation by a majority vote of both Houses of Congress.

Section 3. Whenever the President transmits to the President pro tempore of the Senate and the Speaker of the House of Representatives his written declaration that he is unable to discharge the powers and duties of his office, and until he transmits to them a written declaration to the contrary, such powers and duties shall be discharged by the Vice President as Acting President.

Section 4. Whenever the Vice President and a majority of either the principal officers of the executive departments or of such other body as Congress may by law provide, transmit to the President pro tempore of the Senate and the Speaker of the House of Representatives their written declaration that the President is unable to discharge the powers and duties of his office, the Vice President shall immediately assume the powers and duties of the office as Acting President.

Thereafter, when the President transmits to the President pro tempore of the Senate and the Speaker of the House of Representatives his written declaration that no inability exists, he shall resume the powers and duties of his office unless the Vice President and a majority of either the principal officers of the executive department or of such other body as Congress may by law provide, transmit within four days to the President pro tempore of the Senate and the Speaker of the House of Representatives their written declaration that the President is unable to discharge the powers and duties of his office. Thereupon Congress shall decide the issue, assembling within forty-eight hours for that purpose if not in session. If the Congress, within twenty-one days after receipt of the latter written declaration, or, if Congress is not in session, within twenty-one days after Congress is required to assemble, determines by two-thirds vote of both Houses that the President is unable to discharge the powers and duties of his office, the Vice President shall continue to discharge the same as Acting President; otherwise, the President shall resume the powers and duties of his office.

Amendment XXVI.[28]

Section 1. The right of citizens of the United States, who are eighteen years of age or older, to vote shall not be denied or abridged by the United States or by any State on account of age.

Section 2. The Congress shall have power to enforce this article by appropriate legislation.

Amendment XXVII.[29]

No law, varying the compensation for the services of the Senators and Representatives, shall take effect, until an election of Representatives shall have intervened.

---

27. The Twenty-Fifth Amendment was ratified February 10, 1967.

28. The Twenty-Sixth Amendment was ratified July 1, 1971.

29. Congress submitted the text of the Twenty-Seventh Amendment to the States as part of the proposed Bill of Rights on September 25, 1789. The Amendment was not ratified together with the first ten Amendments, which became effective on December 15, 1791. The Twenty-Seventh Amendment was ratified May 7, 1992, by the vote of Michigan.

Appendix 2

Researching and Reading Government Documents

This volume contains a variety of government documents, as well as other types of materials such as political speeches and newspaper articles. Each type of document has its own peculiarities of form and serves its own purposes. Here we provide a brief guide to these sources.

U.S. Supreme Court Opinions

Although the relative importance of the U.S. Supreme Court as an interpreter of the U.S. Constitution has varied over the course of American history, the opinions of the Court are one of the primary sources for understanding how the Constitution has been read and applied over time. Judicial opinions are not always easy to read, even for those who are familiar with their particular style and the technical issues that they discuss. They are unlike any other text that you are likely to encounter in school or in life. You should expect to read and reread them carefully, but the reading becomes easier as you become practiced at it.

The U.S. Supreme Court is primarily an appellate court. It rarely exercises its "original jurisdiction" and serves as the trial court in which the issues of a case are first raised and the facts evaluated (and when it does hear such cases, it usually assigns them to a special master to hear the evidence and make a report to the justices). Instead, the Supreme Court generally hears cases after a trial has already been conducted and most of the issues in the case have already been resolved. The Supreme Court, like other appellate courts, exists to hear disagreements about the meaning and application of the law. The concern with the justices is with setting and clarifying the legal rules that courts will be applying in future cases, not necessarily with doing justice to the parties immediately in front of them.

After accepting a case for its consideration, the Supreme Court issues a decision that specifies how the legal question at issue in the case has been answered and an order that disposes of the case. The opinion in the case supplements these basic elements of the decision, explaining the reasoning of the justices in reaching that outcome. The Supreme Court decides many cases without an opinion, usually because the issues raised in those cases are relatively easy and do not have broader significance beyond that individual case. The Court provides opinions for all of its important decisions, and these opinions both provide a justification for what the Court has done and provides further guidance to lawyers and judges as to how they should understand what the Court has done and what they should do in similar cases in the future.

The decisions and opinions of the U.S. Supreme Court are available from a variety of sources. Initially, Supreme Court opinions were collected and published by private reporters. Because these early private efforts were not always profitable, Congress eventually stepped in to arrange that the official reports of the Court be published at government expense. Opinions in cases are first printed individually as "slip opinions" and later published in bound volumes of the *United States Reports*. The ninety volumes issued before 1875 were often cited by the name of the reporter who produced them (Dallas, Cranch, Wheaton, Peters, Howard, Black, Wallace, and Otto). Since then, they have been known simply as the *U.S. Reports*. Cases are cited by the volume of the *U.S. Reports* in which they appear, the page on which the case starts, and the year in which the case was decided. Thus, the case of *Marbury v. Madison* is cited as *Marbury v. Madison*, 5 U.S.

137 (1803), indicating that the case was decided in 1803 and can be found at page 137 of volume 5 of the *U.S. Reports*. Since the cases reported in the first 90 volumes of the *U.S. Reports* are also known by the individual reporter, *Marbury* can also be cited as 1 Cr. 137 (1803), indicating that the case can be found in the first volume of Cranch's reports (which is the same as volume 5 of the *U.S. Reports*). Both numbering systems can be cited together as 5 U.S. (1 Cr.) 137 (1803).

Besides the official *U.S. Reports*, Supreme Court decisions can also be found in other sources. The *Lawyers' Edition* of the *U.S. Reports* is published by the Lawyers' Cooperative Publishing Company and includes additional notes about the case. These versions are also cited by volume and page number with the abbreviation "L.Ed." indicating the *Lawyers' Edition* ("L.Ed. 2d" for the second series of the *Lawyers' Edition*, which began in 1957). Thus, *Marbury* can be found at 2 L.Ed. 60 (1803). For modern cases, the West Publishing Company also produces the *Supreme Court Reporter*, which is known by the initials "S.Ct.," which appears in print before the slip opinions are collected into the *U.S. Reports* (e.g., *City of Boerne v. Flores*, 117 S.Ct. 2157 [1997]). Three commercial, electronic services also reproduce these Supreme Court cases: Lexis-Nexis, Westlaw, and HeinOnline (the last provides electronic images of the *U.S. Reports* pages). Less complete sets of Supreme Court opinions can also be found on the Internet. The Supreme Court itself provides an electronic version of recent cases at http://www.supremecourtus.gov. Cases are also collected at FindLaw at http://www.findlaw.com/casecode/supreme.html and at Cornell Law School's Legal Information Institute at http://lii.law.cornell.edu. *Shepard's United States Citations* is a reference source that tracks the citation of Supreme Court cases in other opinions written by the Supreme Court and other courts. "Shepardizing" a case by tracking how a decision has been used by subsequent courts provides both a history of the use of that decision and an indication of the current state of the law. A similar service is provided by Westlaw's "KeyCite" system.

When the Supreme Court schedules a case for decision, it will typically accept written briefs from the parties in the case and will often schedule oral arguments as well. The oral arguments were once free-wheeling affairs that could last for days for a single case. They are now tightly regulated by the Court. At oral argument, lawyers are typically allowed thirty minutes to present their side of the case, with the chief justice immediately cutting off the argument when the time has expired. The justices typically ask questions at oral argument, and so the arguments often take the form of an exchange among the justices and the presenting lawyer rather than a monologue by the attorney. The justices also allow some interested parties who are not directly involved in a case to submit amicus curia ("friend of the court") briefs in order to supplement the record and highlight additional features of the case. On occasion, the justices will also allow an amicus to participate in oral arguments (often the U.S. government when the interpretation of a federal law or the Constitution is at issue but the United States is not an official party to the case). Some arguments and attorney briefs can be found in published sources, including Lexis-Nexis and *Landmark Briefs and Arguments of the Supreme Court of the United States*. Early volumes of the *U.S. Reports* often included summaries of the arguments of the attorneys in the case, and they are sometimes excerpted in this volume before the beginning of the Court's opinion. Audio files of some Supreme Court oral arguments can be found at Northwestern University's OYEZ website at http://www.oyez.org.

There are several elements in a typical appellate court decision. It usually begins with a *statement of the facts* in the case and an outline of the *prior history* of the case and how and why it reached the Supreme Court (in this volume, this information is frequently provided in the introductory headnote to the case). It then describes the *legal issue* raised by the case and the question to be resolved by the Court. It then explains the law that is relevant to deciding the case. It is here that the Court will provide its interpretation of the Constitution or other relevant laws that are necessary for deciding the case at hand. It is also here where the Court will describe or articulate the *doctrine* that encapsulates the Court's understanding of the law and that is to guide its application to individual cases. The opinion will then *apply the law* so understood to the particular facts of the case to resolve the questions raised by the case. Finally, the Court will conclude with an *order* disposing of the case.

The form of the order depends on how the case has reached the Court and what the justices have done. Earlier in its history, the judges on a lower court that found themselves divided on some legal question relevant to a case could "certify" those questions for Supreme Court review before a judgment was rendered. In those cases, the Court would answer the questions and send them back to the lower court for it to complete its work and issue a final judgment in the case. More typically, cases reach the Supreme Court after a final judgment has already been rendered in the lower courts, and the appellant in the case wants the Supreme Court to review and revise that judgment. The current route by which cases typically reach the Supreme Court is outlined in Figure A-1. Most cases reach the U.S. Supreme Court from the federal courts, but a significant number come from the state supreme courts. The appellate jurisdiction of the U.S. Supreme Court has been expanded by federal statute over time. Cases may be appealed from the state courts if they raise a "federal question," a question of the interpretation of federal law, treaties, or the U.S. Constitution, or if the parties are from different jurisdictions. The Court will typically "affirm" what the lower court has done or "reverse" it. In some cases, the order might "remand," or send back, the case to the court in which it originated for a final judgment that takes into account what the Supreme Court has done. If the Court finds that it does not have proper jurisdiction to hear and decide the case, it will dismiss the case. The consequence of a dismissal is that the judgment of the lower court will continue to stand. When cases come to the Supreme Court through a petition (e.g., a prisoner's petition for a writ of habeas corpus) or original jurisdiction (e.g., one state bringing suit against another state in a dispute over the location of the state boundary), rather than through an appeal, then the Court will rule directly on the case (e.g., granting or denying the petition) and not simply review the record of the lower court. Since the early twentieth century, the Court's docket has primarily been discretionary. The Court now receives thousands of requests each year that it issue a writ of certiorari (or "cert") scheduling a case to be heard on appeal. As Figure A-2 shows, the Court reached a peak of hearing nearly 300 cases per year in the late nineteenth century, before Congress began to reduce the number of cases that the Court had to hear on mandatory appeal. In recent years, the Court has granted cert in around a hundred cases per year. Thus, not only does the Court review only a tiny fraction of the total number of cases decided each year by the lower federal appellate courts and the state supreme courts, but it agrees to hear only a very small percentage of the cases that it is actively asked to review by the parties involved. Only four justices are needed to grant cert, a practice known as the Rule of Four. When the Court refuses to grant cert, then the justices are not making a decision on the merits of the case and the denial sets no new law for later cases.

In deciding cases on the merits, the Supreme Court operates on the basis of majority rule. The justices vote on what the judgment of the Court should be in each case, and a majority determines the Court's action. If the Court is equally divided (if, for example, one of the justices does not participate in the case due to illness or

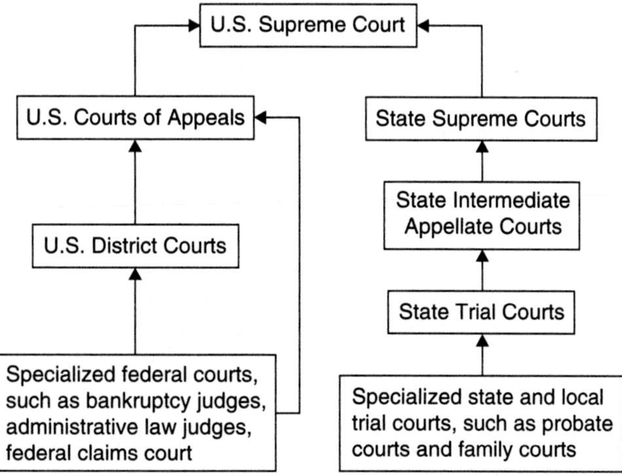

Figure A-1 Getting to the U.S. Supreme Court

Note: In some less common circumstances, cases can reach the U.S. Supreme Court by other routes.

a conflict of interest), then the judgment of the lower court stands. The justices discuss each case and vote in private conference after the case has been briefed and argued. By tradition, if the chief justice is a member of the majority, he may assign which of the members of the majority will write the official opinion of the Court. If the chief justice is a dissenter in the case, then the justice voting with the majority having the most seniority on the Court makes the assignment. After the opinions are drafted, they are circulated to the other justices for comments and revisions. Justices may, and sometimes do, change their votes after the opinions are drafted, and it is possible for enough justices to change their positions to change the outcome in the case. Once the opinions and votes are finalized, then the decision is publicly announced and the slip opinions are published. The decisions are typically announced by the justices orally from the bench, and occasionally the opinions will be read aloud by the justices from the bench (this was once the routine practice, but it is now very rare).

Judicial decisions may be announced in several ways. A unanimous opinion is one in which all the judges agree with the decision and reasoning. A majority opinion is one in which at least five justices agree with the decision and reasoning (or less than five if fewer than eight justices voted). An opinion might announce the judgment of the court but gives reasons that only a minority of justices support. A per curiam opinion ("by the court") is an unsigned opinion. These sometimes reflect a judicial consensus, but are sometimes used when there is significant disagreement among the justices (for example in Bush v. Gore [2000]).

Justices write concurring opinions when they agree with the result in the opinion announcing the judgment of the court, but not the reasoning. Justices write dissenting opinions when they disagree with the result in the opinion announcing the judgment of the court. When a case involves more than one issue (was the petitioner at trial denied the right to jury and/or the right to counsel), a justice may write an opinion that concurs in part and dissents in part. Justices may also sign part of another justice's opinion, but write a concurrence or dissent that only covers some aspect of the judicial reasoning. In cases with no majority opinions, the holding consists of any proposition that at least five justices seem to support. Lawyers are paid a good deal of money to identify and argue for the interpretation of such decisions that best help their client or cause. At earlier points in the Court's history, justices frequently refrained from writing separate opinions and often refrained from announcing their disagreement with the majority. Since the early twentieth century, however, the justices have proven very willing to voice their individual opinions in the Court's cases. Figure A-2 shows the number of cases with separate opinions produced by the justices on the Supreme Court over time. Until

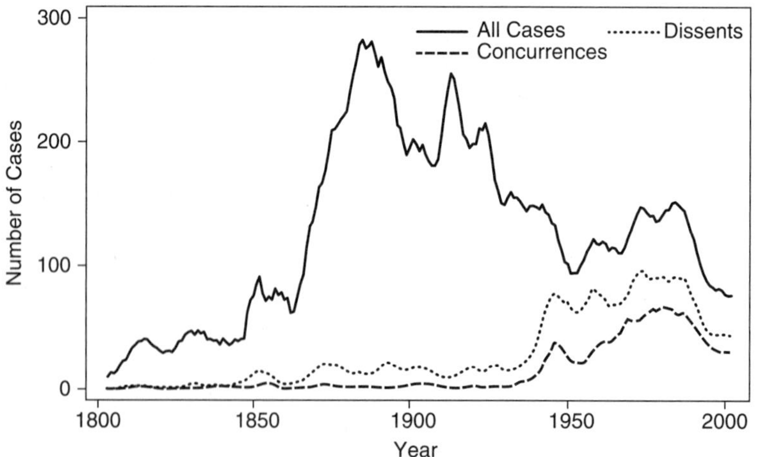

Figure A-2 Number of Supreme Court Cases with Separate Opinions

Source: Lee Epstein, Jeffrey A. Segal, Harold J. Spaeth, Thomas G. Walker, *The Supreme Court Compendium*, 4th ed. (Washington, DC: CQ Press, 2007), Tables 3.2, 3.3.

Note: Centered five-year moving averages.

the late 1930s, a steady 10 percent of the Court cases included a separately authored opinion. Since then, however, the justices have routinely produced dissenting and concurring opinions to supplement the majority opinion. Well over half of all cases decided since World War II include at least one dissenting opinion, and nearly half the cases decided since the mid-1960s include a concurring opinion. Concurring and dissenting opinions have no official standing, and the practice of producing such opinions has been criticized for weakening the authority of the Court and for muddying the state of the law. But separate opinions can be influential either by their own persuasive power or by signaling the possible future trajectory of the Court's majority.

Briefing a Case

Students often find it helpful to "brief" the cases that they read. This is not writing a lawyer's brief, such as those submitted to the Supreme Court. Briefing a case for study is a process of note-taking that identifies and summarizes the key elements in a judicial decision. Some basic elements of a brief are provided next, along with an explanation and an example (in italics) from *United States v. E.C. Knight Company* (1895).

Name of the case—This identifies the parties in the case (some cases also become known by their subject matter, such as *The Legal Tender Cases*). The first party listed is usually the appellant, the party that lost in the lower court and brought the case to the Supreme Court for review. The second party listed is usually the appellee, the party that won in the lower court and is responding to the appeal to the Supreme Court.

U.S. v. E. C. Knight Company

Citation of the case—The citation provides the specific location where the opinion can be found, preferably in the *U.S. Reports*.

156 U.S. 1

Year of the case—The year the case was decided provides important information about the context in which the decision was made.

1895

Vote in the case—The public vote in the case can be determined by identifying the justices who sign on to any dissenting opinions and subtracting them from the total number of justices who participated in the case (giving you the number of justices who must have voted with the majority). Remember that the publicly revealed vote is not necessarily the same as the vote of the justices in their private conference, and note that the decision will usually indicate if any of the sitting justices did not participate in the case.

8–1

Factual circumstances of the case—What are the key factual details that identify what the dispute is and what triggered the litigation? Note that the Court's opinions often provide more information than is essential for understanding the case. One challenge for the student is learning to identify which facts are critical to the case and help explain the legal and political significance of the case.

The American Sugar Refining Company of New Jersey tried to acquire E. C. Knight Company of Pennsylvania, which would have given the combined company control of 98 percent of the national market in refined sugar. The United States Department of Justice intervened under the authority of the Sherman Anti-Trust Act, petitioning the Court of Appeals for the Third Circuit to void the sale as an illegal restraint of trade.

Legal issue or question raised by the case—What are the legal questions being addressed by the Court in the case? (Note that there may be more than one.) What statutory or constitutional provisions are at issue?

Does Congress have authority under the interstate commerce clause of the U.S. Constitution to prohibit monopolies in the manufacturing of goods?

Outcome of the case—How did the Court dispose of the case, and who won? It is often useful also to know what subsequently happened to the parties and the issue in the case, though this will not of course appear in the Court's own decision.

Affirmed the circuit court. The appellee, E. C. Knight, won.

Legal holding of the case—How did the Court answer the legal question raised in the case?

Congress cannot directly regulate manufacturing.

Doctrine announced or applied in the case—What is the rule for decision that the Court used to resolve the case? This may be a doctrine that the Court invented in this same case, or it may be a doctrine that had been previously announced by the Court and is being used in the case. When the Court is using a previously announced doctrine, you will want to be aware of whether the justices are subtly altering or elaborating that rule as they are deciding this case.

The interstate commerce clause only authorizes Congress to regulate actions that directly affect interstate commerce, not actions that indirectly affect interstate commerce.

Author and legal reasoning of the majority opinion—Even though the majority opinion is formally the opinion of the Court and reflects the input of all the justices in the majority, the core reasoning of the decision will still reflect the particular ideas, commitments and style of the individual justice who wrote the opinion. The legal reasoning used in the majority opinion is frequently the most important aspect of a case, for it will guide future judges seeking to understand what the Court has done and how future cases should be decided. You will want to be able to provide a concise summary of the explanation that the Court offered for its decision and the interpretation of the relevant law that the Court provided.

Fuller. Sherman Anti-Trust Act must be interpreted in light of the constitutional limits on the power of Congress, and therefore cannot be understood to encroach on the police powers of the states. The states have the exclusive authority to regulate manufacturing and prohibit monopolies. Manufacturing affects interstate commerce only "incidentally and indirectly." Federal power extends only to the actual "articles of interstate commerce," and not to goods that are merely intended for interstate commerce. Commerce is the buying, selling and transportation of goods. Manufacturing is the production of goods, and the sale of one sugar refining company to another is a contract relating to manufacturing of sugar, not the interstate sale of sugar.

Author and legal reasoning of any concurring opinions—Concurring opinions are more individual efforts of the justices who write them than are majority opinions, and they provide an alternative legal explanation of how the case was decided. Note that a concurring opinion may attract as many or more justices than the official opinion of the court, meaning that more members of the Court agree with the legal reasoning of the concurring opinion than agree with the legal reasoning of the "court" opinion even though it is the majority opinion that has official status and announces the outcome of the case. Concurring opinions influence the holding of a case when there is no majority opinion. In such cases, the holding is any proposition that five justices arguably agree upon.

None.

Author and legal reasoning of any dissenting opinions—Like concurring opinions, dissenting opinions tend to be much more individualistic than the majority opinion. Justices often write dissenting opinions "for the future," in the hopes that a majority of the Court will eventually change its mind and in some future case adopt the reasoning of the dissent as its own. But dissenting opinions can also be written with a more immediate goal in mind, of attempting to persuade wavering members of the majority to change their votes before the decision is announced. Since the published dissents remain mere dissents, those particular efforts at persuasion were obviously unsuccessful.

Harlan. As decided in Gibbons v. Ogden *(1824) and other decisions, Congress has the authority to regulate "intercourse and traffic" among the states and things that are "incidental" to the interstate buying, selling and transportation of goods. Manufacturing, like transportation, is "incidental" to the buying and selling of goods, and is therefore covered by the interstate commerce clause. Any combination that "disturbs or unreasonably obstructs" interstate commerce directly affects the nation as a whole and can be prohibited by Congress. Prohibiting monopolies in manufacturing is an "appropriate" means for preventing the obstruction of interstate commerce (see* McCulloch v. Maryland *[1819]). Matters that "directly and injuriously affects" national commerce and "cannot be adequately controlled by any one State" can be regulated by Congress.*

Significance of case for American constitutional development—Unlike the other elements of the brief, this will not be obvious within the decision itself; but when reading the case, students should be thinking about why the case was included in the volume and is being taught in this course. Answering this question will often require thinking beyond the case itself and considering the context in which it was decided and its implications for subsequent politics. How did the case clarify or change the meaning of the law? What new issues or ideas were reflected in the case? What disputes or forces does the case reflect? How did the dispute and the outcome in the case fit into the political and social context of the time? How might the case have affected the politics, economy and society of the time? How might it have affected subsequent developments in those fields?

The case significantly limited one of the first and most important efforts of the federal government to regulate the national economy and imposed significant limits on the ability of the federal government to make future economic policy. The case bolstered conservatives in the Democratic and Republican parties and the emerging interstate corporations, but frustrated populists and their constituencies among farmers, workers, and small businesses. The decision reflected bipartisan conservative commitments (only one dissenter, and opinion author was a Democratic appointee), but came on the eve of the populist takeover of the Democratic Party in the elections of 1896, which also ended Democratic competitiveness in national elections until the 1930s.

Other Court Opinions

This volume contains decisions by a number of other courts besides the U.S. Supreme Court, and other courts are certainly relevant to American constitutionalism and to legal research. Decisions from other courts excerpted here come from elsewhere in the federal judicial system or from the state judicial systems.

The decisions of federal courts below the U.S. Supreme Court are not reported in the *U.S. Reports*, and as a consequence have a different citation system. Most significant decisions from the federal district courts (trial courts at the lowest level of the modern federal judicial system) are reported in the *Federal Supplement.* Those decisions are cited by the volume and page number in which they appear in the *Federal Supplement*, abbreviated as "F.Supp." Early district court cases were reported in *Federal Cases*, abbreviated as "F.Cas." Before the year in which the case was decided in the parenthesis after the page cite, the specific court is identified by "D," meaning district court, and an abbreviation for the state in which the court sits. If there is more than one federal district court in a state, the specific court will be identified by geography; e.g., "E.D. Mass." refers to the federal district court in the eastern district of Massachusetts. Thus the citation for *United States v. The William*, an early district court case from Massachusetts, is *United States v. The William*, 28 F. Cas. 614 (D. Mass. 1808). Although there is more than one judge assigned to each federal district, usually only one sits on any given case (and therefore, there can be no concurring or dissenting opinions). In certain important cases, Congress may require a three-judge panel to hear the case initially. One of those judges is expected to be from the circuit court, and appeals from such panels go directly to the U.S. Supreme Court. Since district courts are trial courts where cases start, cases decided there generally have no prior history in the judiciary. District court opinions are binding only in the district in which they are issued, and are good law until they are reversed by the same district court, by the circuit court that oversees that district, or by the U.S. Supreme Court.

Significant decisions from the federal circuit courts (the intermediate courts between the district courts and the U.S. Supreme Court, which now operate only as appellate courts but once also operated as trial courts) are reported in the *Federal Reporter*. The *Federal Reporter* is abbreviated as "Fed." or "F.," followed by "2d" or "3d" in the case of the second or third series of that reporter. Instead of "D." and a state, circuit courts are now identified by their circuit number (e.g., 3d Cir.). Early circuit court cases were also reported in *Federal Cases* and were known by the district of the state in which the circuit court was sitting rather than by number (e.g., Cir. Ct. Dist. So. Car., or CCDSC). Thus, *Elkison v. Deliesseline*, an early circuit court case from South Carolina, is *Elkison v. Deliesseline*, 8 F. Cas. 493 (Cir. Ct. Dist. So. Car. 1823). Circuit courts sit in panels of more than one judge, and thus there is a potential for dissenting and concurring opinions (though individual opinions are far more rare in these courts than in the Supreme Court). Circuit court cases are binding law only within the circuits in which they are handed down, and they are good law until overturned by that same circuit court or by the U.S. Supreme Court. Both types of federal cases, district and circuit, can also be found in Lexis-Nexis and Westlaw.

Biographical information about those who have served as federal judges, as well as other information about the federal courts, has been made available on the Internet by the Federal Judicial Center at http://www.fjc.gov.

State judicial systems have a similar structure to the federal judicial system, with trial courts and multi-member appellate courts capped by a highest appellate court for that type of case (some states create separate tracks, and separate supreme courts, for different kinds of cases, such as criminal and civil cases). State court decisions are published in reports maintained within each individual state, and those state reporting systems have sometimes changed over time. Thus, the Pennsylvania Supreme Court case of *Sharpless v. Mayor of Philadelphia*, published in the *Pennsylvania State Reports*, is cited as *Sharpless v. Mayor of Philadelphia*, 21 Pa. 147 (1853). Modern state cases are also collected and published in several regional reporters, such as the *Atlantic Reporter* and the *North Western Reporter*. State court decisions can also be found in Lexis-Nexis and Westlaw. State supreme court decisions are binding only within the state in which they are issued. State supreme courts are the highest authority on the laws and constitutions of their own states, just as the U.S. Supreme Court is the highest authority on federal laws and the U.S. Constitution. Federal laws and the U.S. Constitution are binding within each state and must also be interpreted and applied by state courts when they are relevant to deciding cases that arise within the state judicial systems. When interpreting federal laws or the U.S. Constitution, the state supreme courts can be reviewed and corrected by the U.S. Supreme Court (or any federal court, in the case of habeas petitions).

Congressional Documents

The most important documents produced by Congress are federal laws. Private laws are legislation intended to benefit particular individuals, such as laws waiving any financial claims that the government might have against an individual or excepting an individual from the usual application of immigration laws. Public laws are legislation that affect the general public. Once a bill becomes a law, it is assigned a public law number reflecting the Congress that passed it and its place in the sequence of laws passed by that Congress (e.g., PL 104–1 was the first law passed by the 104th Congress). Public laws and private laws and resolutions (pronouncements of one or both chambers of Congress that do not have the force of law) are collected and published in the *U.S. Statutes at Large*, which is cited by volume and page number, and year; e.g., PL 104-1 is printed at 109 U.S. Stat. 109 (1995). As laws are revised and amended over time, the still valid laws have been consolidated and codified, first in two editions of the *Revised Statutes* in the 1870s and since in several editions of the *United States Code*. The code is cited by subject-matter "title" number, section, and edition (e.g., PL 104–1 was incorporated into 2 USC 1301 [2000]).

Congress also produces a variety of other documents besides statutes and resolutions. The official actions of each chamber of Congress are recorded in constitutionally mandated journals. The debates on the floor of the House of Representatives and the Senate are reported in the *Congressional Record* and its predecessors (*Annals of Congress*, *Register of Debates*, and the *Congressional Globe*). Congressional committees, where most of the work of Congress is done, produce Documents (a wide range of materials that Congress has ordered published, including executive-branch reports and records), Reports (official reports by House and Senate committees to their parent chambers, usually explaining bills being recommended by the committee), and Transcripts of Hearings (transcripts of public testimony and discussion that committees gather on topics of interest). These are published separately by the committees. Early Documents and Reports were bound together in the *American State Papers*. Since 1817, Documents and Reports have been collected and published in the *United States Serial Set*. Committee Reports may include reports from both the majority and the minority (from the committee members who disagree with the majority report or the legislative action being recommended). All of these documents are commonly cited by the body that produced it, the title, the type of document, the number of the Congress that produced it, the session number, and the date; e.g., House Committee on the Judiciary, Apportionment Bill, 27th Cong., 2nd Sess. (1842), H.R. Rep. 27–909. Bill sponsors and the chairmen of the committees reporting legislation are understood to have a privileged voice in explaining the meaning and purpose of a bill, but Congress votes only on the text of the legislation itself, and the body as a whole does not have to approve or agree to anything that is said during legislative debate, written in committee reports, or contained in similar documents created during the legislative process.

Many of these documents are available in the CongressionalUniverse service of Lexis-Nexis and on HeinOnline. Many congressional documents produced through Reconstruction have been placed on the Internet by the Library of Congress at http://lcweb2.loc.gov/ammem/amlaw/lawhome.html. Very recent materials are available at the THOMAS website at http://thomas.loc.gov. Useful biographical information on individuals who have served in Congress can be found in the *Biographical Directory of the U.S. Congress*, available on the Internet at http://bioguide.congress.gov.

Executive Branch Documents

The various components of the federal executive branch produce a vast number and variety of documents.

The president himself produces a variety of documents, all of which have political significance but only some of which have immediate legal effect. The Constitution recognizes only two types of presidential documents. The first are general purpose presidential messages to Congress, the most famous of which is the annual message, or "State of the Union address." The second is the veto message to Congress, explaining the president's reasons for vetoing a proposed law.

These two constitutionally mandated forms of communication have been supplemented by other formal messages, most notably the inaugural address and the signing statement (remarking on a law being signed by the president, sometimes simply to commemorate the occasion, sometimes to note interpretations of, qualifications to, or concerns about the legislation being signed). Of course, the president also delivers a large number of informal speeches and public statements. Formal messages to Congress have routinely been published in the *Congressional Record*. The messages and speeches of the presidents through the early twentieth century were collected and published in *A Compilation of the Messages and Papers of the Presidents*. Franklin Roosevelt's speeches were published privately in *The Public Papers and Addresses of Franklin Delano Roosevelt*. Those of subsequent presidents have been published by the government in *Public Papers of the Presidents of the United States* and more frequently in *The Weekly Compilation of Presidential Documents*.

The president also produces documents with more immediate legal effect. Executive orders are directives from the president to members of the executive branch (military orders are their counterpart directed to the armed forces). So long as they do not contradict a constitutionally valid statute, these instructions are understood to be binding on subordinate executive officers, directing how they will implement laws and perform executive functions. Presidential proclamations are directed to the general public. Proclamations are often innocuous, declaring days of celebration and the like, but they are sometimes momentous, such as Abraham Lincoln's proclamation calling forth the state militias to put down secession and his Emancipation Proclamation. Executive orders through the early twentieth century were compiled in *Presidential Executive Orders*. They have subsequently been published in the *Federal Register* and compiled in the *Codification of Presidential Executive Orders and Proclamations*. Much of this material is available in HeinOnline. Some of it (along with press conference transcripts, party platforms, and other materials) has been made available on the Internet by the University of California at Santa Barbara's The American Presidency Project at http://www.presidency.ucsb.edu and through the National Archives at http://www.archives.gov/federal-register/index.html.

More routine are regulations and orders produced by executive branch agencies, primarily in the course of interpreting and implementing statutes. These regulations have the immediate force of law and receive substantial deference from the courts. They are published in the *Federal Register* and compiled in the *Code of Federal Regulations*.

Of particular significance to American constitutionalism are the legal opinions of the attorney general. These opinions derive from the constitutional authority of the president to command the written opinion of principal officers of the executive departments upon subjects relating to their office and from the statute originally creating the office of attorney general. The attorney general now routinely provides advisory opinions on legal issues, including constitutional issues. Attorney general opinions have more recently been supplemented by the legal opinions of the Office of Legal Counsel (OLC), which advises the attorney general. Attorney general opinions are compiled in *The Official Opinions of the Attorneys General of the United States*, which is cited by volume, the abbreviation "Op. Att'y Gen.," the page, and the date. A selection of the OLC opinions are published in *Opinions of the Office of Legal Counsel*, which is cited in the same fashion with the abbreviation "Op. O.L.C." These formal opinions guide the executive branch in its interpretation and application of the law, including constitutional law, and frequently guide private actors and other government officials, including judges, in their understandings of the law.

State-level executive branch officials perform many of these same functions in the state government. Such state documents are often compiled in equivalent state publications, but they are not always readily accessible and have not generally been collected in the same comprehensive fashion as the federal documents.

Legal Literature

Commentaries on the law produced by private citizens such as law professors or government officials writing in a private capacity have no official status, but they can reflect the currents of legal thinking at the time and exert substantial persuasive power on their own and future generations. As such, they can influence and be cited as authority by government actors who do have formal power, such as judges. Before the twentieth century, scholarly legal treatises that seek to critically synthesize the state of the law have had the greatest influence. Relevant examples of these include St. George Tucker's American edition of William Blackstone's *Commentaries on the*

Laws of England (1803), Joseph Story's *Commentaries on the Constitution of the United States* (1833), John Alexander Jameson's *A Treatise on Constitutional Conventions* (1866), Thomas Cooley's *Constitutional Limitations* (1868), and, more recently, Laurence H. Tribe's *American Constitutional Law* (1978). More diverse is the law review literature, scholarly articles in legal periodicals. An important guide to legal journals is the *Index to Legal Periodicals*. This venerable guide has recently been supplemented by various less comprehensive guides, including LegalTrac. The content of many law reviews is available through services such as Lexis-Nexis, Westlaw, and (with greater historical depth but somewhat less breadth) HeinOnline.

Citation guides for government and legal documents include *The Chicago Manual of Style* (most commonly used in the humanities and social sciences) and *The Bluebook: A Uniform System of Citation* (the most commonly used citation guide in the law schools). A generally helpful resource is the Law Library of Congress's Guide to Law Online, available at http://www.loc.gov/law/public/law-guide.html.

Appendix 3

Chronological Table of Presidents, Congress, and the Supreme Court

Years	President	House of Representatives	U.S. Senate	Supreme Court[1]
1789–1791	G. Washington (F)	Federalist	Federalist	Federalist
1791–1793	G. Washington (F)	Federalist	Federalist	Federalist
1793–1795	G. Washington (F)	Republican[2]	Federalist	Federalist
1795–1797	G. Washington (F)	Federalist	Federalist	Federalist
1797–1799	J. Adams (F)	Federalist	Federalist	Federalist
1799–1801	J. Adams (F)	Federalist	Federalist	Federalist
1801–1803	T. Jefferson (R)	Republican	Republican	Federalist
1803–1805	T. Jefferson (R)	Republican	Republican	Federalist
1805–1807	T. Jefferson (R)	Republican	Republican	Federalist
1807–1809	T. Jefferson (R)	Republican	Republican	Federalist
1809–1811	J. Madison (R)	Republican	Republican	Federalist
1811–1813	J. Madison (R)	Republican	Republican	Federalist
1813–1815	J. Madison (R)	Republican	Republican	Republican
1815–1817	J. Madison (R)	Republican	Republican	Republican
1817–1819	J. Monroe (R)	Republican	Republican	Republican
1819–1821	J. Monroe (R)	Republican	Republican	Republican
1821–1823	J. Monroe (R)	Republican	Republican	Republican
1823–1825	J. Monroe (R)	Republican	Republican[3]	Republican
1825–1827	J. Q. Adams (R)	Republican	Democrat	Republican
1827–1829	J. Q. Adams (R)	Democrat	Democrat	Republican
1829–1831	A. Jackson (D)	Democrat	Democrat	Republican
1831–1833	A. Jackson (D)	Democrat	Democrat	Republican
1833–1835	A. Jackson (D)	Democrat	Whig	Republican

(Continued)

1. Party control of Supreme Court represented by party affiliation of median member.
2. An "Anti-administration" majority that predates the formation of an organized political party.
3. Majority formed from coalition of states' rights Republicans and supporters of Andrew Jackson.

Years	President	House of Representatives	U.S. Senate	Supreme Court
1835–1837	A. Jackson (D)	Democrat	Democrat	Republican
1837–1839	M. Van Buren (D)	Democrat	Democrat	Democrat
1839–1841	M. Van Buren (D)	Democrat	Democrat	Democrat
1841–1843	W. H. Harrison/J. Tyler (W)	Whig	Whig	Democrat
1843–1845	J. Tyler (W)	Democrat	Whig	Democrat
1845–1847	J. Polk (D)	Democrat	Democrat	Democrat
1847–1849	J. Polk (D)	Whig	Democrat	Democrat
1849–1851	Z. Taylor/M. Fillmore (W)	Democrat	Democrat	Democrat
1851–1853	M. Fillmore (W)	Democrat	Democrat	Democrat
1853–1855	F. Pierce (D)	Democrat	Democrat	Democrat
1855–1857	F. Pierce (D)	Republican[4]	Democrat	Democrat
1857–1859	J. Buchanan (D)	Democrat	Democrat	Democrat
1859–1861	J. Buchanan (D)	Democrat	Democrat	Democrat
1861–1863	A. Lincoln (R)	Republican	Republican	Democrat
1863–1865	A. Lincoln (R)	Republican	Republican	Republican
1865–1867	A. Lincoln/A. Johnson (R)	Republican	Republican	Republican
1867–1869	A. Johnson (R)	Republican	Republican	Republican
1869–1871	U. S. Grant (R)	Republican	Republican	Republican
1871–1873	U. S. Grant (R)	Republican	Republican	Republican
1873–1875	U. S. Grant (R)	Republican	Republican	Republican
1875–1877	U. S. Grant (R)	Democrat	Republican	Republican
1877–1879	R. Hayes (R)	Democrat	Republican	Republican
1879–1881	R. Hayes (R)	Democrat	Republican	Republican
1881–1883	J. Garfield/C. Arthur (R)	Republican	Republican	Republican
1883–1885	C. Arthur (R)	Democrat	Republican	Republican
1885–1887	G. Cleveland (D)	Democrat	Republican	Republican
1887–1889	G. Cleveland (D)	Democrat	Republican	Republican
1889–1891	B. Harrison (R)	Republican	Republican	Republican
1891–1893	B. Harrison (R)	Democrat	Republican	Republican
1893–1895	G. Cleveland (D)	Democrat	Democrat	Republican
1895–1897	G. Cleveland (D)	Republican	Republican	Republican
1897–1899	W. McKinley (R)	Republican	Republican	Republican
1899–1901	W. McKinley (R)	Republican	Republican	Republican
1901–1903	W. McKinley/T. Roosevelt (R)	Republican	Republican	Republican
1903–1905	T. Roosevelt (R)	Republican	Republican	Republican
1905–1907	T. Roosevelt (R)	Republican	Republican	Republican
1907–1909	T. Roosevelt (R)	Republican	Republican	Republican

(*Continued*)

4. Majority formed from coalition of Republican and American (or "Know Nothing") Party members.

Years	President	House of Representatives	U.S. Senate	Supreme Court
1909–1911	W. H. Taft (R)	Republican	Republican	Republican
1911–1913	W. H. Taft (R)	Democrat	Republican	Republican
1913–1915	W. Wilson (D)	Democrat	Democrat	Republican
1915–1917	W. Wilson (D)	Democrat	Democrat	Republican
1917–1919	W. Wilson (D)	Democrat	Democrat	Republican
1919–1921	W. Wilson (D)	Republican	Republican	Republican
1921–1923	W. Harding/C. Coolidge (R)	Republican	Republican	Republican
1923–1925	C. Coolidge (R)	Republican	Republican	Republican
1925–1927	C. Coolidge (R)	Republican	Republican	Republican
1927–1929	C. Coolidge (R)	Republican	Republican	Republican
1929–1931	H. Hoover (R)	Republican	Republican	Republican
1931–1933	H. Hoover (R)	Democrat	Republican	Republican
1933–1935	F. D. Roosevelt (D)	Democrat	Democrat	Republican
1935–1937	F. D. Roosevelt (D)	Democrat	Democrat	Republican
1937–1939	F. D. Roosevelt (D)	Democrat	Democrat	Republican
1939–1941	F. D. Roosevelt (D)	Democrat	Democrat	Democrat
1941–1943	F. D. Roosevelt (D)	Democrat	Democrat	Democrat
1943–1945	F. D. Roosevelt/H. Truman (D)	Democrat	Democrat	Democrat
1945–1947	H. Truman (D)	Democrat	Democrat	Democrat
1947–1949	H. Truman (D)	Republican	Republican	Democrat
1949–1951	H. Truman (D)	Democrat	Democrat	Democrat
1951–1953	H. Truman (D)	Democrat	Democrat	Democrat
1953–1955	D. Eisenhower (R)	Republican	Republican	Democrat
1955–1957	D. Eisenhower (R)	Democrat	Democrat	Democrat
1957–1959	D. Eisenhower (R)	Democrat	Democrat	Democrat
1959–1961	D. Eisenhower (R)	Democrat	Democrat	Democrat
1961–1963	J. Kennedy (D)	Democrat	Democrat	Democrat
1963–1965	J. Kennedy/L. B. Johnson (D)	Democrat	Democrat	Democrat
1965–1967	L. B. Johnson (D)	Democrat	Democrat	Democrat
1967–1969	L. B. Johnson (D)	Democrat	Democrat	Democrat
1969–1971	R. Nixon (R)	Democrat	Democrat	Democrat
1971–1973	R. Nixon (R)	Democrat	Democrat	Democrat
1973–1975	R. Nixon/G. Ford (R)	Democrat	Democrat	Democrat
1975–1977	G. Ford (R)	Democrat	Democrat	Republican
1977–1979	J. Carter (D)	Democrat	Democrat	Republican
1979–1981	J. Carter (D)	Democrat	Democrat	Republican
1981–1983	R. Reagan (R)	Democrat	Republican	Republican
1983–1985	R. Reagan (R)	Democrat	Republican	Republican
1985–1987	R. Reagan (R)	Democrat	Republican	Republican

(*Continued*)

Years	President	House of Representatives	U.S. Senate	Supreme Court
1987–1989	R. Reagan (R)	Democrat	Democrat	Republican
1989–1991	G. Bush (R)	Democrat	Democrat	Republican
1991–1993	G. Bush (R)	Democrat	Democrat	Republican
1993–1995	W. Clinton (D)	Democrat	Democrat	Republican
1995–1997	W. Clinton (D)	Republican	Republican	Republican
1997–1999	W. Clinton (D)	Republican	Republican	Republican
1999–2001	W. Clinton (D)	Republican	Republican	Republican
2001–2003	G. W. Bush (R)	Republican	Democrat[5]	Republican
2003–2005	G. W. Bush (R)	Republican	Republican	Republican
2005–2007	G. W. Bush (R)	Republican	Republican	Republican
2007–2009	G. W. Bush (R)	Democrat	Democrat	Republican
2009–2011	B. Obama (D)	Democrat	Democrat	Republican
2011–2013	B. Obama (D)	Republican	Democrat	Republican

5. Majority control of the Senate changed three times during the 107th Congress, with the Democrats holding the majority most of the term.

Glossary

acquittal a legal declaration that the accused is not guilty.

adjudicate to preside over, as in a court presiding over a case.

advisory opinion a court statement on the constitutionality of a matter, such as a law or government action, outside the context of a civil or criminal trial. Not accepted in most court systems in the United States.

affidavit a written, sworn statement of fact.

affirm to uphold, as in the decision of a lower court.

affirmative action giving preference to members of historically oppressed groups in hiring or school admittance policies.

amicus (or amici) curiae literally "friend of the court"; a person or entity who is not a party to the case but provides information to the court, whether in a brief or testimony.

annul to declare void, to eliminate.

anti-Federalists those who opposed the ratification of the U.S. Constitution in the late eighteenth century.

appeal to contest the decision of a court before a higher authority, such as a higher court or an executive official.

appellant the party who contests a court's decisions after losing a case by bringing an appeal. Also called the petitioner.

appellate jurisdiction a court's authority to hear and decide challenges to the decisions of lower courts; the range of issues and cases that a court can hear on appeal.

appellee the party who responds to the appeal of a court decision that was in his or her favor. Also called the respondent.

arraignment a hearing in which the court reads the charges against a criminal defendant from the indictment, and the defendant enters a formal plea (i.e., guilty or not guilty).

Articles of Confederation the supreme law that governed the union of the original thirteen states of the United States from 1781 to 1789, predating the Constitution.

attitudinal model the theory that one can describe and predict a judge's legal decisions based on one's knowledge of the judge's policy preferences.

balancing test a tool used by courts to decide cases by weighing the benefit regulation offers to society against the cost to individual rights.

bicameral two-chambered, as in the U.S. Congress, which is divided between the House of Representatives and the Senate.

bill a piece of proposed legislation.

brief a written statement presented to the court that lays out the argument for one party.

briefing a case a summary and analysis of a case or judicial opinion.

case a dispute brought before a court.

case law the body of cases that make up legal precedent.

case or controversy rule the requirement in Article III that the business of courts be limited to resolving active disputes between parties, prohibiting, for example, court involvement in speculative questions of legal interpretation.

certiorari (writ of) an appellate court's order to an inferior court to send it the records from a case that the appellate court has agreed to review. Appellants generally ask the U.S. Supreme Court to take a case by asking it to grant this writ.

checks and balances the legal structures that limit the power of government by granting each branch enough power to prevent the tyranny of other branches.

chilling effect a person's or entity's reluctance to act within its constitutional rights and powers because of a law or court ruling punishing similar (but not identical) behavior.

civil law law pertaining to the relationships among individuals or organizations.

civil right behavior and government action to which people are legally entitled, such as free speech and equal protection.

class-action lawsuit a dispute brought before a court on behalf of a group, members of whom have sustained a common injury or harm.

comity respect for the decisions of other political entities, especially respect by federal courts for the decisions of state courts.

common law laws and procedures that are not formally codified in written constitutions or statutes but are instead built through judicial precedent.

compensatory damages reparations granted to a winning plaintiff in a civil suit that cover the monetary value of losses or injuries caused by the defendant.

concurrent powers jurisdiction shared by national and state governments.

concurring opinion a judge's (or several judges') written statement(s) agreeing with the outcome arrived at by the majority of the court in a case but disagreeing with or adding to the majority's reasoning.

confrontation a defendant's right to hear testimony from and cross-examine the prosecution's witnesses in court.

constitutional law the body of legal decisions pertaining to matters arising under a constitution.

constitutionalism constitutional interpretation and practice concerning the structure of and limitations on government.

contempt disrespect to or failure to comply with the authority of a court.

contract a legally binding agreement between parties.

criminal law law pertaining to the regulation of the interaction between individuals and the community or state, and the punishment of infractions thereof.

de facto literally, "in point of fact." As a situation or condition appears in reality, irrespective of legal conditions.

de jure literally, "as a matter of law." As a situation or condition is codified in law.

decree a legal order.

defamation slander or libel, injury to a person's or an entity's reputation.

defendant the person accused in a criminal suit or sued in a civil suit.

delegation the act of one entity granting its powers to another.

deposition a witness' sworn statement taken out of court.

dicta; obiter dicta language in a judge's opinion that goes beyond what is necessary to reach the judgment and is therefore not considered a part of legal precedent.

direct effects in pre–New Deal commerce clause jurisprudence, the idea that local actions are subject to federal regulation only if they directly affect interstate commerce.

dissenting opinion a judge's (or several judges') written statement(s) disagreeing with the outcome arrived at by the majority of the court in a case.

diversity jurisdiction cases that the federal courts can hear because the parties involved are from two different jurisdictions, even though the case may not raise issues of federal law.

docket the list of cases to be heard by a court.

dormant commerce power the implicit prohibition on state government regulation of interstate commerce, even in the absence of conflicting federal regulations.

double jeopardy trying a party more than once in the same jurisdiction for the same offense. Unconstitutional in the United States.

due process the legal rights and procedures to which individuals are constitutionally entitled before being subjected to legal constraints or disabilities.

eminent domain the power of the government to confiscate private property without the owner's consent, provided just compensation is paid.

enjoin to prohibit or demand the performance of certain acts.

enumerated powers those powers of the government that are specifically listed in the Constitution.

equity principles developed by courts based on fairness and equality that go beyond positive law.

ex post facto law a law that applies retroactively, subjecting parties to criminal sanctions for actions that were not illegal at the time they were committed. Unconstitutional in the United States.

exclusionary rule the prohibition against illegally obtained evidence being used at trial.

exclusive powers jurisdiction retained by national or state governments and not shared with the other.

federal question jurisdiction power of federal courts to hear cases that raise issues under federal law, regardless of who the parties to the case are.

federalism the principle that governing authority is divided between independent national and state governments.

felony a serious crime (in contrast to a misdemeanor), usually punishable by incarceration for at least a year.

gerrymander to design political boundaries in order to intentionally favor a certain political party or interest.

grand jury a body of citizens who decide whether to issue an indictment based on evidence presented to them by a prosecutor.

habeas corpus (writ of) literally, "you have the body." An order brought by or on behalf of a prisoner commanding a review of the lawfulness of the prisoner's detention.

hearsay an out-of-court statement by someone other than the witness, introduced to determine the truth of the matter.

immunity protection from prosecution for a party's criminal activity, often in exchange for his or her cooperation with prosecutors.

In re in regard to.

incorporation the process of defining the scope of the due process clause of the Fourteenth Amendment. The debate over incorporation specifically addresses which parts of the federal Bill of Rights are to be applied against the states.

indictment the formal, written charges against a criminal defendant presented by a grand jury.

indirect effects in pre–New Deal commerce clause jurisprudence, the idea that local actions are not subject to federal regulation if they only indirectly affect interstate commerce.

injunction a court order prohibiting or commanding the performance of certain acts.

intermediate scrutiny the amount of suspicion with which a court examines a regulation that impinges on some constitutional rights. To pass intermediate scrutiny, a regulation must further a substantial government interest and the restriction on constitutional rights must be no greater than necessary to the pursuit of that interest. Most notably applied to laws that make sex-based distinctions.

judgment of the court the official decision reached by a court specifying the legal outcome in a case.

judicial activism the philosophy that judges should frequently review and, when necessary, use constitutional grounds to strike down decisions by elected officials or other political figures.

judicial restraint the philosophy that judges should show deference to the decisions of political figures, particularly those of elected officials.

judicial review the power of courts to find acts of executive and legislative officials unconstitutional and declare them void.

judicial supremacy the theory that the judiciary can determine how all governing officials must interpret the Constitution.

jurisdiction a government, branch of government, legal body, or person's authority over a certain territory or type of matter or dispute.

jurisprudential concerning the court system.

justiciable able to be reviewed and resolved by a court, as in a dispute.

legislative veto the power of the legislature, or portion of the legislature, to nullify an executive or administrative action.

libel published defamation of a party's character or reputation.

line-item veto the power of a chief executive to reject part of a bill while approving the larger piece of legislation.

litigant a party to a lawsuit.

majority opinion the written statement detailing the official decision and reasoning of a court in a case.

***mandamus* (writ of)** a court order demanding the performance of a duty by a public official or government body.

Miranda warning the rights of the accused with which police must acquaint suspects at the time of their arrest.

misdemeanor a minor crime (in contrast to a felony), usually punishable by fine, penalty, or confiscation, but little or no jail time.

mistrial a trial that the presiding judge declares void before its completion because of miscarriages of justice.

moot already resolved or irrelevant, as in a dispute. Courts will not hear cases in which the controversy between the parties has already been resolved or in which the parties involved no longer have a direct stake.

motion a request made to the court on behalf of one party in a suit.

natural law the rights of humans that are presumed to exist independent of government.

nonjusticiable unable to be decided in court.

opinion of the court a written statement detailing the court's decision in a case and its reasoning.

oral argument the hearing before an appellate court during which lawyers for each side in a case present their spoken legal arguments before the judges and the judges ask questions.

original jurisdiction a government, branch of government, legal body, or person's authority to be the first to decide a matter, as opposed to hearing an appeal.

partisan pertaining to a political party.

penumbra rights and powers that are not enumerated in a constitution but are implied by enumerated rights and powers.

per curiam opinion literally, "by the court." An opinion by the court acting as a whole, as opposed to an opinion written by individual judges.

petitioner a party who appeals to a court to resolve a dispute. In the appeals process, the party filing the appeal is called the petitioner; the party against whom the appeal is filed is called the respondent.

plaintiff the party who brings suit in a civil case.

plenary whole or complete, leaving no residuum; as in plenary power.

plurality opinion a written statement detailing the decision supported by the greatest number of judges in a case in which no judicial majority exists.

police power a government's power to regulate the health, safety, and morality of people within its territory.

political questions doctrine the legal view that certain matters are the exclusive domain of the legislative and executive branches of government and should therefore not be adjudicated by the judiciary.

popular sovereignty the principle that the ultimate authority in a system of government rests with the people.

precedent a previous court decision on an issue.

preemption the principle that an otherwise constitutional state law may be declared void by a court if a federal law is intended to be the sole regulation of the subject matter or if the state law is inconsistent with a federal law.

prima facie literally, "on the face of it." Assumed to be true unless effectively disproven.

prior restraint censorship of speech before publication.

public forum a place that, according to the Supreme Court, "by long tradition or by government fiat ha[s] been devoted to assembly and debate."

punitive damages reparations granted to a winning plaintiff in a civil dispute that cover no specific costs or losses but are instead intended to punish the respondent and deter similar actions.

rational basis test the lowest level of scrutiny a court will give to a challenged regulation; the test presumes the constitutionality of government action. To pass a rational basis test, a regulation must be rationally related to a legitimate public purpose. Generally applied when the law does not infringe any fundamental rights or make use of any suspect classifications.

remand to send back, as when sending a case back to a lower court for review or sending a defendant back to jail pending sentencing.

respondent a party against whom legal action is taken. In the appeals process, the party against whom the appeal is filed is called the respondent; the party filing the appeal is called the petitioner.

reverse to overturn, as in the decision of a lower court.

ripe ready to be decided by a court. A dispute's "ripeness" is determined by the court based on a number of criteria, including the predicted ability of a legal remedy to resolve the dispute.

selective incorporation the application of individual clauses of the Bill of Rights against the states through the Fourteenth Amendment on a case-by-case basis.

separation of powers the functional division of government powers among independent branches of government in order to prevent any one government official from accumulating too much power and to take advantage of specialization.

solicitor general the Justice Department official who argues cases on behalf of the U.S. government before the Supreme Court.

sovereign immunity protection from civil liability for sovereign governments.

standing to sue the right of a party to bring a dispute before a court. In order to have standing, parties must demonstrate that that they have suffered harm as a result of actions that may be remedied by the court.

stare decisis literally, "to stand by things decided." The judicial principle that courts should respect precedent.

state action conduct by a state government or official; conduct performed under state law or state authorization, or by a private party with a sufficient connection to the state.

state courts courts established under state authority that hear disputes and controversies.

statute of limitations a law limiting the period of time that some action may form the basis of a lawsuit.

stay a temporary suspension of a court order, for example, a stay of execution.

strategic model the theory that one can describe and predict a judge's legal decisions based on one's knowledge of the judge's policy preferences and the institutional circumstances that constrain the ability of a judge to act on those preferences.

strict construction the narrow reading of constitutional and statutory law.

strict scrutiny the greatest amount of suspicion with which a court examines a regulation that restricts a constitutional right, which presumes that a government action is unconstitutional. To pass strict scrutiny, a regulation must be a narrowly tailored or least restrictive means to achieving a compelling governmental interest. Generally applied when a government action interferes with fundamental rights or employs a suspect classification (such as race).

subpoena an order to give information to a court.

substantive due process rights that are so fundamental that they cannot be infringed without violating the constitutional protection against wrongful and arbitrary government coercion. Often applied to "unenumerated" rights to property or sexual liberty.

test a set of criteria used by courts to determine if actions are legal.

tort a civil wrong.

vacate to annul or eliminate; for example, the decision by a higher court to void the decision of a lower court.

warrant a legal authorization for law enforcement officials to perform a search or make an arrest.

writ a legal order.

Index

Note: *t* refers to table, *f* refers to figure, and *b* refers to box.

AAA. *See* Agricultural Adjustment Act
Abolitionists
 anti-slavery speech of, 266–71
 gun rights and, 264
 incendiary publications mailed by, 266–71
 increase in, 272
Abortion rights
 Blackmun on, 769–70, 774–75
 Commentaries on the Laws of England and, 52
 in Contemporary Era, 915–17
 Democratic Party on, 915–16
 due process protecting, 623, 717
 foundations for, 438
 funding restrictions on, 955
 Human Life Amendment and, 655–57
 Kennedy, Anthony, on, 769–71
 in Liberalism Divided Era, 648–57, 649*f*, 654*f*
 O'Connor on, 769–71
 originalism and, 10, 717
 partial-birth, 916
 Planned Parenthood of Southeastern Pennsylvania v. Casey and, 714*t*, 715, 717, 770–77, 853–54, 915–16, 920–21
 protests against, 927
 public opinion on, 648, 649*f*, 654*f*
 Rehnquist on, 769–70, 775–76
 Republican Party against, 648, 769, 915–16
 restrictions on, 648–49
 Roe v. Wade and, 3, 423*t*, 617, 619, 621*t*, 643, 648, 650–55, 711, 717–19, 721, 769–77, 921
 Scalia on, 769–70, 775–77
 Souter on, 769–71
 Thomas on, 769, 775–76
 trimester system and, 648, 650, 652, 654, 770
 White, Byron, on, 775–76
Abrams, Jacob, 443
ACA. *See* Affordable Care Act
Ackerman, Bruce, 23, 483, 486
ACLU. *See* American Civil Liberties Union
Act for Establishing Religious Freedom, 112–16
Actual malice, 571–72
Adams, Abigail, 126–27, 151–52, 283
Adams, John, 43, 51–52, 118, 145, 180
 gender equality and, 126–27
 overview of, 32*b*
 on Second Continental Congress, 3
 Sedition Act and, 199
 on universal male suffrage, 119–21
 vetoes and, 187
 on war, 632
Adams, John Quincy, 135, 193, 217, 255–57
Adams, Samuel, 31, 41, 43, 126
 Massachusetts Circular Letter of February 11, 1768, by, 37
 overview of, 32*b*
"Address to the Alabama Constitutional Convention" (Knox), 459–61
"Address to the Nation on the Introduction of Troops in Little Rock" (Eisenhower), 506–7
Administrative discretion, 454
AEDPA. *See* Anti-Terrorism and Effective Death Penalty Act of 1996
Affirmative action, 456, 617–18, 623, 674
 City of Richmond v. J. A. Croson Co. and, 588*t*, 714*t*, 801–7
 in Contemporary Era, 948–50
 gender equality and, 808–11
 Grutter v. Bollinger and, 588*t*, 834*t*, 949–54
 Regents of the University of California v. Bakke and, 588*t*, 621*t*, 678, 683–87, 809, 952
Affordable Care Act (ACA)
 birth control covered by, 908
 individual mandate in, 857, 864–68, 871–72, 874–76
 National Federation of Independent Business v. Sebelius and, 517, 857, 864–76
 Obama and, 864–65
 Pelosi on, 857
 taxation and, 864–76
Afghanistan, 887
AFL. *See* American Federation of Labor
Agricultural Adjustment Act (AAA), 516, 524
Alabama, state income tax in, 406n18
Alabama Constitutional Convention, 454, 459–61
Alcohol prohibition. *See* Prohibition
Alexander, James, 55
Alexander, Keith, 978, 980
Alien and Sedition Laws, 180, 198–201, 268, 441. *See also* Sedition Act of 1798
Alito, Samuel, 931, 961*f*
 on *Florida v. Jardines*, 962
 on *McDonald v. City of Chicago*, 841
 nomination of, 835, 853–55
 on polarized Supreme Court, 836, 846
 on *United States v. Jones*, 961
Allen, Floyd, 704
All-male and all-female schools, 690
Amar, Akhil, 22
Amendments. *See* Constitutional amendments
American Anti-Slavery Society, 219, 222, 266
American Bar Association, 372, 410, 722, 726, 886
American Civil Liberties Union (ACLU), 370, 481, 618–19, 713
 formation of, 372
 free speech and, 562
 in *McCreary County v. ACLU of Kentucky*, 908
 signature victories, 432*t*
 Women's Rights Project, 690–91

American Communist Party, 471, 566–68
American constitutionalism. *See* Constitutionalism
American Constitutional Society, 840
American Federation of Labor (AFL), 372
American imperialism, 370
American Jewish Congress, 432*t*
American Revolution, 31, 44, 52
  gender equality and, 125–26
  voting and, 119
American Sugar Refining Company, 397
Americans United for Separation of Church and State, 432*t*
Americans with Disabilities Act, 857, 947
American System, 218
American Temperance Society, 265
American Woman Suffrage Association, 372
Amish, 644–47
Anarchy, State and Utopia (Nozick), 626
Ancient constitutionalism, 4–5
Animal cruelty, 926
Anthony, Susan B., 354
Anti-Federalists, 73–74, 76–78, 102, 133
  "Centinel," Letter No. 1 and, 108–9
  contracts clause and, 111
  gun rights and, 117
Anti-Saloon League, 373, 377
Anti-slavery speech, 266–71
Anti-Terrorism and Effective Death Penalty Act of 1996 (AEDPA), 960–61
Anti-Trust Act. *See* Sherman Anti-Trust Act
Appointments clause, 748–49
Appropriation, 178
Aristocracy, 58–59
Aristotle, 4–5
Arizona statehood, vetoed, 388–90
Article I of Constitution, 78, 178, 629
  powers of national government in, 155–56, 414, 516–17, 630, 734, 743–46, 882, 894, 896, 900
  Section 2, 122, 668, 983
  Section 4, 119, 984
  Section 7, 885, 984–85
  Section 8, 98–99, 156, 313, 403, 768, 865, 985
  Section 9, 121, 127, 843, 985–86
  Section 10, 110, 986
  taxation and, 392
Article II of Constitution, 76, 360, 416, 986–87
  interpretation of, 185, 641
  separation of powers in, 535, 538–39, 748–49, 751, 890, 896
Article III of Constitution, 76, 642, 752, 987–88
  on citizenship, 273
  Judiciary Act of 1789 and, 142–43
  Section 2, 127, 180
Article IV of Constitution, 230, 326, 511, 988
  Section 2, 122, 232
  Section 3, 207
Article V of Constitution, 22–23, 486, 623, 988
Article VI of Constitution, 111, 988–89
  judicial review and, 143
  supremacy clause, 8, 88, 99–100, 877, 883, 942
Article VII of Constitution, 22, 989–90
Articles of Confederation
  origin of, 71–73
  powers of national government and, 93–98, 179
Ashley, James, 349
Aspirationalism, 13
Association Against the Prohibition Amendment, 486
Attitudinal model, 14–15, 14*f*
Australian ballot, 369, 453
An Autobiography (Roosevelt, T.), 418–19

Babcock, John Martin Luther, 453
Bachmann, Michele, 980
Backus, Isaac, 126
Bad tendency test, 443
Baker, Charles, 509
Bakeshop Act, 428–32
Bakke, Alan, 683–87
Baldwin, Henry, 226*t*
Balkin, Jack, 10
Ballots, 369, 453, 937
Balzac, Jesus, 380–82
Bank of the United States
  chartering of, 134
  debate on, 159–64
  deposits removed from, 250–54
  Hamilton, Alexander, for, 159–60, 163–64
  Jackson, Andrew, against, 221, 233–36, 250–54, 271
  Jefferson and, 159–60, 162–63, 169
  Madison and, 156, 159–61, 169
  McCulloch v. Maryland and, 164–72, 232–35
  Second, 159–60, 221, 233–36
Bankruptcy, 190
Bargaining process, 421
Barlow, Joel, 296
Barnett, Randy, 10, 910
Barnette, Walter, 563–66
Barron, John, 224
Bates, Edward, 359–61
Bates, Ruby, 471
Batson, James Kirkland, 822–26
Bayh, Birch, 656–57
BCRA. *See* Bipartisan Campaign Reform Act
Beard, Charles, 76
Beck, James, 415
Bedford, Gunning, 101, 104
Benson, Egbert, 112, 116
Bible reading, in schools, 264
Bickel, Alexander, 12, 19, 481, 620
Biddle, Nicholas, 250
Biden, Joseph, 729–30
Bill of Rights, 990–95. *See also* Constitutional amendments; English Bill of Rights; Extraterritoriality; Incorporation, of Bill of Rights; State bills of rights
  Barron v. Baltimore and, 223–25
  Fourteenth Amendment and, 621
  Jefferson and, 74, 78, 82–83
  nationalized, 479
  origin of, 73–74
  Pennsylvania ratification debates over, 78–80
  ratification and, 77–83, 614
  scope of, 87, 142, 223–25, 293, 305–9, 379–81, 486, 488–96, 490*t*, 697, 718, 722, 841
  Supreme Court applying to states, 490*t*
Bingham, John, 302–3, 305
Bipartisan Campaign Reform Act (BCRA), 929, 931–35
Bird, Rose, 703
Birth control, 438
  Griswold v. Connecticut and, 423*t*, 432*t*, 480*t*, 556–61, 648, 650, 652–53, 721, 915
  health insurance plans covering, 908
Bishop, Nathan, 759
Bituminous Coal Act, 516, 520
Black, Charles, 12, 625
Black, Galen, 763–66
Black, Hugo, 11, 518, 528, 573, 604*f*, 619
  on *Chambers v. Florida*, 481
  on *Dennis v. United States*, 569–70
  on *Duncan v. Louisiana*, 490–92
  on *Engle v. Vitale*, 552, 554–55
  on *Gideon v. Wainwright*, 612–13
  on *Griswold v. Connecticut*, 560–61
  on *Harris v. New York*, 701
  on *Jones v. Opelika*, 563
  judicial power and, 496
  on *Korematsu v. United States*, 591–92
  on *Mapp v. Ohio*, 606–7
  on *New York Times Co. v. Sullivan*, 572
  on *New York Times Co. v. United States*, 660
  on *Oregon v. Mitchell*, 669
  overview of, 485*b*
  on *Palmer v. Thompson*, 679
  on *Reid v. Covert*, 489
  on *In re Winship*, 698–99
  on *Robinson v. Florida*, 489
  on *Youngstown Sheet & Tube Co. v. Sawyer*, 534–35

Black, Jeremiah, 326–27
Black Codes, 300, 320
Blackmun, Harry, 715, 763*f*, 812
on abortion rights, 769–70, 774–75
attitudinal model and, 14–15, 14*f*
on *Bowers v. Hardwick*, 779–80
on *Buckley v. Valeo*, 667
on capital punishment, 702, 706, 826, 830–31
on *Employment Division v. Smith*, 766, 851
on *Energy Reserves Group, Inc., v. Kansas Power and Light Co.*, 755
on *Frontiero v. Richardson*, 694
on *Garcia v. San Antonio Metropolitan Transit Authority*, 736
on *Herrera v. Collins*, 815–16
on jury trials, 821
on *Lee v. Weisman*, 761
in liberal coalition, 846
on *Lucas v. South Carolina Coastal Council*, 757–58
on *McCleskey v. Kemp*, 830–31
on *New York Times Co. v. United States*, 662–63
overview of, 622*b*
on *R.A.V. v. St. Paul*, 782
on *Regents of the University of California v. Bakke*, 685–87
on *Roe v. Wade*, 650–52
as swing vote, 619
Blackstone, William, 33, 39*f*, 71, 118, 779. *See also Commentaries on the Laws of England*
on freedom of press, 449, 451
on libel, 53–55
on liberty, 384
Of Offences Against God and Religion by, 46–48
on voting rights, 57
Blair, Montgomery, 296
Blaisdell, John, 545–48
Blake, George, 204
Blanket Amendment, 461–63
The Blast, 445
Bloch, Charles J., 576–77
Blood libel, 464
The Bloudy Tenent (Williams), 50–51
Boland, Edward, 741
Booth, Sherman, 283–84
Borah, William, 498
Bork, Robert, 620, 640, 718, 720
on judicial review, 754
overview of, 716*b*
Supreme Court nomination of, 715, 723, 727–32, 741, 848
Boudinot, Elias, 116
Boumediene, Lakhdar, 841–46
Bowers v. Hardwick, 12
Bradley, Curtis, 840
Bradley, Joseph, 313, 319, 354
on *Boyd v. United States*, 464–65
on *Civil Rights Cases*, 382–84, 390, 394
on *Munn v. Illinois*, 409
on *Wabash, St. Louis & Pacific Railroad v. Illinois*, 408–9
Brady, James, 879
Brandeis, Louis, 376, 402, 496, 516, 567–68
on *Abrams v. United States*, 443
on constitutional democracy, 441
on federalism, 405
on *Muller v. Oregon*, 433
on *Myers v. United States*, 417–18
on *Olmstead v. United States*, 467–70
overview of, 375*b*
on *Pennsylvania Coal Co. v. Mahon*, 425–26
on *Whitney v. California*, 444, 447–49, 573
Brandenburg, Clarence, 573–74
Brennan, William, 559, 603, 604*f*, 619, 623, 763*f*
aspirational approach of, 13
attitudinal model and, 14, 14*f*
Burger and, 659
on capital punishment, 613, 702, 706, 829–30
on *Carey v. Population Services International*, 649
compromises by, 15
"The Constitution of the United States: Contemporary Ratification" by, 725–27
on *Craig v. Boren*, 690
Eisenhower nominating, 725
on *Frontiero v. Richardson*, 693–94
on *Green v. County School Board of New Kent County*, 590, 601–2
on *Harris v. New York*, 701
on *Johnson v. Transportation Agency, Santa Clara County*, 808–9
on *Katzenbach v. Morgan*, 578–80
on *McCleskey v. Kemp*, 829–30
on *Michael H. v. Gerald D.*, 770
on *Moose Lodge No. 107 v. Irvis*, 626–28
on *National League of Cities v. Usery*, 630
on *New York Times Co. v. Sullivan*, 571–72
on *New York Times Co. v. United States*, 661
overview of, 485*b*
on *Plyler v. Doe*, 798–800
on *Regents of the University of California v. Bakke*, 685–87
Rehnquist and, 726
on *In re Winship*, 697–98
on *Richardson v. Ramirez*, 673
on *South Dakota v. Dole*, 733–34
on *Texas v. Johnson*, 783–84
on *United States v. Leon*, 818–20
on *U.S. Department of Agriculture v. Moreno*, 674
on *Washington v. Davis*, 689
Brewer, David J.
on *Muller v. Oregon*, 432–34
overview of, 375*b*
Breyer, Stephen, 836, 949, 961*f*
on *Bush v. Gore*, 941
on *District of Columbia v. Heller*, 914–15
on *Easley v. Cromartie*, 936–37
on *Printz v. United States*, 884
on *Sternberg v. Carhart*, 916
on *United States v. Lopez*, 863–64
Briefing, of cases, 1001
British Constitution, 31, 35–37, 42–43
British Parliament
in Colonial Era, 31–35, 37–45, 51, 53, 58–59, 64
in Founding Era, 71, 77, 119
Brown, Henry B., 456–58
Brown, Linda, 597–600
Brownback, Sam, 853–55
Brownell, Herbert, 479
"Brutus" essays (Yates), 88–90
Bryan, William Jennings, 372, 392
Bryant, Phil, 916
Buchanan, James, 284, 326–27, 387
Buck, Carrie, 440–41
Buckley, James, 658, 663
Bull, Caleb, 139
Burger, Warren, 619, 695, 763*f*, 783
attitudinal model and, 14, 14*f*
on *Batson v. Kentucky*, 825
on *Bowers v. Hardwick*, 779, 919
Brennan and, 659
on *Buckley v. Valeo*, 665–66
on capital punishment, 702, 706
conservative transition under, 628–29, 628*f*
on *Harris v. New York*, 700–701
on *Immigration and Naturalization Service v. Chadha*, 743–44
on *Lemon v. Kurtzman*, 644
on *Miller v. California*, 658
on *New York Times Co. v. United States*, 662
overview of, 622*b*
on *Plyler v. Doe*, 800–801
on *Reed v. Reed*, 690
on *In re Winship*, 698
on *Roe v. Wade*, 653
on *Santobello v. New York*, 696
on separation of church and state, 644
on *Swann v. Charlotte-Mecklenburg Board of Education*, 679–81
on *United States v. Nixon*, 641–43
Warren and, 659
on *Wisconsin v. Yoder*, 645–46

Burger Court, 619–20, 626, 668, 678, 812
on capital punishment, 696, 702–7
on confessions, 700
divided, 722
on establishment clause, 644
judicial review by, 629, 631
on *Oregon v. Mitchell*, 669
religious rights supported by, 763*f*
state courts trusted by, 697
Burke, Edmund, 620
Burnside, Ambrose, 342–44
Burton, Harold H., 534, 538, 567, 604*f*
Bush, George H. W., 715, 717, 719, 723, 733, 833
Bush, George W., 13, 835, 846, 848, 850, 936
BCRA signed by, 929
Bush v. Gore and, 13, 834, 834*t*, 925, 935, 937–41, 1000
election of, 833, 840
on partial-birth abortion, 916
Patriot Act signed by, 970, 972–73
signing statements by, 886
"Torture Memos" and, 893
in War on Terror, 968–70
war powers and, 887
Bush v. Gore, 13
Busing, school, 677–83
Butler, Pierce, 103, 523, 548, 550
in Four Horsemen, 496
on *Near v. Minnesota*, 450–51
on *Olmstead v. United States*, 470
on *Powell v. Alabama*, 473
Bybee, Jay, 893–96

Calhoun, John C., 137, 159, 176, 245, 325
against deposit removal, 251–54
"Fort Hill Address" by, 248–49
incendiary publications in mail supported by, 267–69
on nullification, 246, 248–49
overview of, 220*b*
Callender, James, 213
Campaign finance
BCRA on, 929, 931–35
cases, 621, 623, 658, 663–67, 929, 931–35
FECA on, 658, 663–67
Campbell, John, 226*t*
on *Dred Scott v. Sandford*, 241, 277
on *Slaughter-House Cases*, 306, 341
Capital punishment
Anti-Terrorism and Effective Death Penalty Act of 1996 on, 960–61
Blackmun on, 702, 706, 826, 830–31
Brennan on, 613, 702, 706, 829–30
Burger Court on, 696, 702–7
in Civil War and Reconstruction Era, 367
common law and, 129
in Contemporary Era, 960–61, 966–68
cruel and unusual punishment and, 4, 473–74, 614, 702, 715
Douglas, William, on, 613, 702
Eighth Amendment and, 10, 613–14, 707, 966
executions, 703*f*
Fourteenth Amendment and, 613, 702, 705, 707, 966
Gregg v. Georgia and, 617, 621*t*, 696, 702–7
in Jacksonian Era, 288
in Liberalism Divided Era, 617, 696, 702–6, 703*f*
Lincoln and, 367
Marshall, Thurgood, on, 702, 706–7
McCleskey v. Kemp and, 588*t*, 714*t*, 826, 827–31, 967
in New Deal and Great Society Era, 613–14
Powell, Lewis, on, 703–4, 826–29
public support for, 827*f*
On Punishing Murder by Death on, 129–30
in Reagan Era, 718, 826–31, 827*f*
Rehnquist on, 702, 706
in Republican Era, 474
Scalia on, 826
Stevens, John Paul, on, 703–4, 826, 831
Stewart, Potter, on, 702, 704–6
White, Byron, on, 702, 706
Cardozo, Benjamin, 20, 496, 516, 520
on *Palko v. Connecticut*, 486–87, 562
on *People v. Defore*, 466–67
Carpet bagging, 306
Carr, Joe, 509
Carter, Jimmy, 617–18, 623, 715, 747
gun rights and, 647
on military draft, 690–91
Casey, Robert, 770–77
Cassell, Paul, 608
CAT. *See* Convention Against Torture
Catholics, 264, 552, 556
Catron, John, 226*t*, 277
Center for Individual Rights, 432*t*
"Centinel," Letter No. 1, 108–9
Central Intelligence Agency (CIA), 631
Chadha, Jaglish, 741–47
"A Charter of Democracy" (Roosevelt, T.), 387–88
Charter of Rhode Island and Providence Plantations, 35, 51
Charters, 35
Chase, Salmon, 293, 320
on *Ex parte McCardle*, 312–13
on *Ex parte Milligan*, 362
on *Hepburn v. Griswold*, 313–17
overview of, 294*b*
on *Texas v. White*, 324, 330–32
Chase, Samuel, 23, 137
on *Calder v. Bull*, 139–40, 191
on *United States v. Callender*, 212–14
Checks and balances, 102, 106. *See also* Separation of powers
Cheney, Richard, 623
Child labor, 392–93, 400–403
Children, right to rear, 650
Chisholm, Alexander, 180
Church. *See* Separation of church and state
CIA. *See* Central Intelligence Agency
Cigar manufacturing, 426–28
Citation guides, 1006
Citizenship
Article III on, 273
Eighth Amendment and, 614
Fourteenth Amendment on, 279, 301–2, 304, 307
in Jacksonian Era, 264, 266, 272–74, 277, 279, 282
rights of, 384–86, 625
Civil rights. *See also* School segregation
in *Civil Rights Cases*, 374*t*, 380, 382–86, 390, 394, 489, 495, 528–29
FDR and, 481
modern movement of, 454–55
protesters, 489, 562, 590
in Republican Era, 454–55
strategy, debate over, 594–97
Civil Rights Act of 1866, 292, 305, 310, 314, 620
excerpt, 323
Senate debate over, 320–23
Civil Rights Act of 1870, 314, 390
Civil Rights Act of 1875, 292, 314, 382–86, 526, 528
Civil Rights Act of 1964, 479, 481, 489, 677, 793, 797
Congressional debate over, 526–28
Heart of Atlanta Motel, Inc. v. United States and, 517, 528–30
interstate commerce and, 517, 526–30, 626
popular support for, 486
as sacred text, 621
school segregation and, 589–90
Title VII, 808–11, 828
women's suffrage and, 354
Civil War and Reconstruction Era (1861–1876). *See also* Secession
cast of characters, 294*b*
constitutional authority in, 310–13
constitutional thought in, 293–94
courts in, 293
criminal justice in, 357–67
Democratic Party in, 291–93, 296, 300, 305–6, 310–11, 320, 333, 341–42
democratic rights in, 342–45
developments, 291–92
due process in, 357–66
equality in, 346–57
federalism in, 323–33
foundations, 295–309, 301*t*–302*t*

free speech in, 342–45
gender equality in, 354–57
gun rights in, 341
habeas corpus in, 291, 342–45, 357–66
individual rights in, 340–42
interest groups in, 293
interrogations in, 366–67
introduction to, 291–95, 294*b*
judicial power in, 310–13
juries in, 367
law of nations in, 337, 339–40
lawyers in, 367
legacies, 295
Lincoln in, 291–93, 295–96, 304–5, 310, 314, 324–29, 333–37, 342–45, 349, 357–62, 367
major issues and decisions in, 292*t*
martial law in, 291–93, 310–12, 357–58, 362, 364, 367
partisan alignments influenced by, 371
personal freedom in, 341–42
political parties in, 292–93
powers of national government in, 313–23
principles, 304–5
property rights in, 340–41
public morality in, 341–42
punishments in, 367
racial equality in, 293, 349–53, 483
religious rights in, 341
search and seizure in, 366
separation of powers in, 333–40, 338*t*
voting rights in, 300–304, 345, 354–57
Clapper, Ray, 504
Clark, Tom C., 568, 604*f*, 613
on *Baker v. Carr*, 512
on *Heart of Atlanta Motel, Inc. v. United States*, 528–30
on *Mapp v. Ohio*, 604–6
on *Miranda v. Arizona*, 610–11
on *Reynolds v. Sims*, 585
on *Youngstown Sheet & Tube Co. v. Sawyer*, 534, 538
Class legislation, 59, 271–72, 487, 586
Clay, Henry, 137, 158, 176, 248, 251–54
Clean Air Act of 1970, 630
Clear and present danger
Dennis as, 567–70
free speech and, 442*t*, 443–44, 446–48, 567–70, 573
Clifford, Nathan, 226*t*
Clinton, Bill, 747, 769–70, 789, 826, 835
election of, 833
on partial-birth abortion, 916
war powers and, 892
CLP. *See* Communist Labor Party
Cohn, Avern, 786–87
Coke, Edward, 36, 38, 40, 63, 67
Cole, James M., 978, 980–81
Colonial Era (before 1776)
British Parliament in, 31–35, 37–45, 51, 53, 58–59, 64
cast of characters, 32*b*
constitutional authority in, 37–42
constitutional thought in, 33–34
courts, 33
criminal justice in, 62–70
democratic rights in, 53–58
developments, 31–32
due process in, 62–65
equality in, 58–62
factions, 32–33
foundations, 34–37
free speech in, 53–57
gender equality in, 61–62
gun rights in, 51–52
habeas corpus in, 63–64
individual rights in, 44–53
interrogations in, 67–68
introduction to, 31–34, 32*b*, 34*t*
judicial power in, 37–42
jury trials in, 62, 69
lawyers in, 69
legacies, 34
major issues, 34*t*
personal freedom in, 52–53
powers of national government in, 43
principles, 36
property rights in, 44–45
public morality in, 52–53
punishments in, 69–70
racial equality in, 58–61
religious rights, 45–52
search and seizure rights in, 65–67
separation of powers in, 43–44
taxation in, 33, 36–37, 43
voting rights in, 57–58
Commentaries on the Laws of England (Blackstone), 44–45, 51, 64, 912
abortion rights and, 52
excerpt from, 38–41
on gender equality, 61–62
Commerce. *See also* Interstate commerce
clause, 245–46, 395–97, 406, 408, 481, 523, 525, 527–30, 738–39
manufacture and, 398–99
Commercial activities, category of, 390
Commitments, credible, 7–8
Committee of Citizens, 456
Committee to Reelect the President (CREEP), 639, 663
Common law, 11, 35, 41
capital punishment and, 129
right to counsel and, 471
Communist Labor Party (CLP), 446
Communists
American Communist Party, 471, 566–68
Communist Labor Party, 446
free speech rights of, 478–79, 566–70
Compact theory, 178–79, 245–46, 295
Compelling interest, 620
Compromise, constitution as, 9
Comstock, George M., 260–63
Concurring opinions, author and legal reasoning of, 1002
Confederate Constitution, 305
Confederate states, 324–27
Confederation Congress, 73
Confessions
Burger Court on, 700
in Jacksonian Era interrogations, 287–88
Miranda's, 608–12
Congress. *See also* House of Representatives; Senate; Separation of powers
chronological table of, 1007*t*–1010*t*
Civil Rights Act of 1964 debated in, 526–28
executive power and, 419–20
First, 138, 155, 186, 416, 883
foreign policy and, 633–37
Human Life Amendment and, 655–57
incendiary publications debated in, 266–71
"Letter from the Attorney General to Congress on Litigation Involving the Defense of Marriage Act" to, 924–25
lynching debated in, 393–95
powers of, 155–56, 207, 231, 277–78, 285, 365–66, 372, 392, 395, 399–402, 539
Prohibition debated in, 377–79
Second Freedmen's Bureau Act debated in, 350–53
Voting Rights Act of 1965 reports, 575–78
Voting Rights Act of 1970 debated in, 667–71
Congressional documents, researching and reading, 1004
Congressional Record, 1004
Connecticut Charter, 35
Connecticut Compromise, 96
Conscientious objectors, 116
Conservatism
conservative transition of Supreme Court and, 628–29, 628*f*
interest groups, 619
Constitution. *See also* Bill of Rights; British constitution; Confederate Constitution; Living Constitution; State constitutions
Article I, 78, 98–99, 110, 119, 121–22, 127, 155–56, 178, 313, 392, 403, 414, 516–17, 629–30, 668, 734, 743–46, 768, 843, 865, 882, 885, 894, 896, 900, 983–86

Constitution (*continued*)
  Article II, 76, 185, 360, 416, 535, 538–39, 641, 748–49, 751, 890, 896, 986–87
  Article III, 76, 127, 142–43, 180, 273, 642, 752, 987–88
  Article IV, 122, 207, 230, 232, 326, 511, 988
  Article V, 22–23, 486, 623, 988
  Article VI, 8, 88, 99–100, 111, 143, 877, 883, 942, 988–89
  Article VII, 22, 989–90
  basic questions of, 3–4
  changes in, 22–24
  compact theory of, 178–79, 245–46, 295
  as compromise, 9
  The Constitution, a Pro-Slavery Compact on, 223
  "The Constitution of the United States: Contemporary Ratification" on, 725–27
  creation of, 22
  defined, 4–5
  development of, 1002–3
  excerpt, 983–95
  "A Friend of the Constitution" on, 169, 171–72
  as fundamental law, 5–6
  Madison and, 8, 22–24, 71, 73–74, 82–83, 88, 95–96, 98–102, 104–5, 119, 122, 858
  New Deal and, 486
  purposes of, 6–9
  ratification of, 73, 74*t*, 77–83, 178–79
  scope of, 87, 142, 223–25, 293, 305–9, 316, 379–86, 486, 488–96, 490*t*, 626–28, 722–32, 840–46
  secession and, 324, 328–29
  success of, 133
  worldwide, 7, 25
The Constitution, a Pro-Slavery Compact (Phillips), 223
Constitutional amendments
  Blanket, 461–63
  Eighteenth Amendment, 377, 406, 486, 993
  Eighth Amendment, 10, 483, 489, 490*t*, 603, 613–14, 707, 779, 966, 991
  Eleventh Amendment, 178–79, 878, 991
  ERA, 461–63, 621, 623–24, 674, 689–90, 691–93, 692, 807–8
  Fifteenth Amendment, 292, 295, 301, 314, 345, 349, 379, 390, 517, 576, 580, 788, 993
  Fifth Amendment, 110, 128, 224–25, 279, 373, 410, 425, 464–69, 488–89, 490*t*, 491, 559, 589, 603–4, 606, 610–12, 643, 693–94, 705, 715, 755–58, 896–97, 902–7, 991
  First Amendment, 9, 11, 111, 118, 199, 380–81, 444, 446, 488, 490*t*, 553–55, 558, 562, 572–73, 658–66, 717, 719, 721, 759, 764–67, 781–85, 909, 913, 926–34, 990
  Fourteenth Amendment, 10, 17–18, 279, 292–93, 295, 299–309, 301*t*–302*t*, 314, 341–42, 349, 354, 373, 380, 382–83, 385–86, 390, 394–95, 406, 410, 413, 421, 427–29, 431–32, 438–40, 453, 457, 461, 468, 471–73, 483, 488–95, 505, 508–17, 530, 549–54, 557, 559–61, 572–73, 578–81, 584–85, 587*t*–588*t*, 597–600, 602–3, 605–7, 612–13, 621, 624, 626–28, 643, 651–54, 668, 672–76, 683–85, 688–89, 702, 705, 707, 717, 767, 769–73, 775–76, 778–80, 798–800, 803, 812, 823–26, 850–51, 856–57, 920–21, 947, 966, 992
  Fourth Amendment, 128, 373, 464, 466–69, 490*t*, 559–61, 603–7, 638–39, 699, 722, 780, 816–20, 961–62, 991
  Human Life Amendment, 655–57
  Nineteenth Amendment, 23, 372, 377, 406, 453, 993
  Ninth Amendment, 557, 559, 561, 651–53, 991
  Reagan Era proposals, 718–19
  against same-sex marriage, 839–40, 917–18
  Second Amendment, 117, 196, 264, 488, 490*t*, 545, 556, 643, 647–48, 768–69, 841, 909–14, 990
  Seventeenth Amendment, 377, 406, 993
  Seventh Amendment, 488, 991
  Sixteenth Amendment, 377, 392, 406, 993
  Sixth Amendment, 380, 488, 490–91, 490*t*, 603, 821, 991
  Tenth Amendment, 156, 325, 404, 481, 517–19, 523, 531, 629–31, 735, 878, 880–82, 991
  Third Amendment, 488, 559, 991
  Thirteenth Amendment, 292, 295–301, 305–9, 314, 321, 334, 341–42, 350–52, 380, 444, 457, 992
  Twelfth Amendment, 76, 991–92
  Twentieth Amendment, 993–94
  Twenty-Fifth Amendment, 995
  Twenty-First Amendment, 486, 733–35, 994
  Twenty-Fourth Amendment, 994–95
  Twenty-Second Amendment, 994
  Twenty-Seventh Amendment, 995
  Twenty-Sixth Amendment, 624, 629, 669, 995
  Twenty-Third Amendment, 994
  unconstitutional, 3
Constitutional authority
  in Civil War and Reconstruction Era, 310–13
  in Colonial Era, 37–42
  in Contemporary Era, 846–55, 847*f*, 849*f*
  countermajoritarian difficulty and, 19–21, 481
  departmentalism and, 18–19
  in Early National Era, 142–55, 144*t*
  in Founding Era, 88–93
  in Jacksonian Era, 225–31, 226*t*, 227*f*
  Jefferson's, 17–18
  judicial supremacy and, 18, 310, 629
  in Liberalism Divided Era, 628–29
  in New Deal and Great Society Era, 496–516, 497*f*
  politics of, 21
  "The President's Constitutional Authority to Conduct Military Operations" on, 890–93
  in Reagan Era, 722–32
  in Republican Era, 386–90
Constitutional Convention, 88, 93, 95–96, 119
  Alabama, 454, 459–61
  debate in, 99–106
  Kansas, 282
  Massachusetts, 195–96, 202–4
  Ohio, 226–29, 387
  slavery and, 122
Constitutional interpretation
  arguments, 10–17
  aspirationalism and, 13
  attitudinal model of, 14–15, 14*f*
  decision making and, 9–17
  departmentalist view of, 151–52
  doctrinalism and, 11–12
  historical institutionalism and, 16–17
  judicial supremacy of, 629
  legal model of, 16
  originalism and, 10, 715, 717–18
  prudentialism and, 12
  strategic model of, 15–16
  structuralism and, 12
  textualism and, 10–11
Constitutionalism
  ancient, 4–5
  commitment to, 3
  Declaration of Independence as foundation of, 341
  executive power and, 186–87
  as governance, 4
  introduction to, 3–25
  norms, 625
  politics influenced by, 9–10
  popular, 838
  Roosevelt, Theodore, believing in, 387
  rule of law and, 5–8

Constitutional litigation
barriers to, 498, 629
Fourteenth Amendment, 386
growth of, 386–87
guidelines on, 720–22, 754, 781, 797, 820
Constitutional politics
of constitutional argument, 13–17
of constitutional authority, 21
of free exercise clause, 908–9
of gay rights, 918
law and, 24–25
transformed, 780
Constitutional rights and liberties. *See also* Bill of Rights; Constitutional authority; Constitutional interpretation; Constitutional thought
categories of, 7
Civil War and Reconstruction Era major issues and decisions concerning, 292*t*
Colonial Era major issues concerning, 34*t*
Contemporary Era major issues and decisions concerning, 834*t*
disputes over, 141
Early National Era major issues and decisions concerning, 134*t*
Jacksonian Era major issues and decisions concerning, 218*t*
Liberalism Divided Era major issues and decisions concerning, 621*t*
New Deal and Great Society Era major issues and decisions concerning, 480*t*
polarized politics of, 835, 901
principles, 141–42
Reagan Era major issues and decisions concerning, 714*t*
Republican Era major issues and decisions concerning, 374*t*
sources of, 35–36, 77–83, 139–41, 222–23, 296–304, 377–79, 624, 718–20, 839–40
in wartime, 294–95, 335–36
Constitutional thought
in Civil War and Reconstruction Era, 293–94
in Colonial Era, 33–34
in Contemporary Era, 836–38
in Early National Era, 137–38
in Founding Era, 74–76
in Jacksonian Era, 221–22
in Liberalism Divided Era, 620, 621*t*
in New Deal and Great Society Era, 482–83
preferred freedoms/compelling interest, 620
in Reagan Era, 715–17
in Republican Era, 373
"The Constitution of the United States: Contemporary Ratification" (Brennan), 725–27
Constructionists, 186–87
Contemporary Era (1994–present)
abortion rights in, 915–17
affirmative action in, 948–50
cast of characters, 837*b*–838*b*
constitutional authority in, 846–55, 847*f*, 849*f*
constitutional thought in, 836–38
courts in, 835–36
criminal justice in, 959–81, 961*f*
Democratic Party in, 833–39, 855, 856*f*, 858, 865, 901–2, 915–17, 935–46, 954, 960, 968–69
democratic rights in, 925–45
developments, 833–34
due process in, 960–61
equality in, 945–59
executive power in, 885–901
extraterritoriality in, 841, 843, 845–46, 897
federalism in, 855, 856*f*, 877–84
foundations, 839–46
free speech in, 926–35
gay rights in, 839, 917–25
gender equality in, 954–59
gun rights in, 909–15
habeas corpus in, 841–46, 960–61, 969
individual rights in, 901–25
infamous crimes and criminals in, 968–81
interest groups, 835
interrogations in, 887, 893–99, 962–66, 969
introduction to, 833–39, 834*t*, 837*b*–838*b*
judicial power in, 846–55, 847*f*, 849*f*
juries in, 966
lawyers in, 966
legacies, 838
major issues and decisions, 834*t*
necessary and proper clause in, 867, 872, 881, 894, 906
personal freedom in, 915–25
political parties in, 834–35
powers of national government in, 855–76, 856*f*
principles, 840
property rights in, 902–7
public morality in, 915–25
punishments in, 960–61, 966–68
racial equality in, 948–54
religious rights in, 907–9
Republican Party in, 833–39, 855, 856*f*, 865, 901–2, 915–16, 918, 935–46, 954, 960, 967–69
search and seizure rights in, 961–62
separation of powers in, 884–901
voting rights in, 935–45
war powers in, 886–87, 889–902
Contract rights, 110, 190–91, 191*t*–192*t*
Anti-Federalists and, 111
freedom of contract, 428–31, 545, 549, 643, 755
in Liberalism Divided Era, 643
limits of, 756
in New Deal and Great Society Era, 545–48
scope of, 424
West Coast Hotel Co. v. Parrish and, 545, 549–50
yellow dog contracts and, 421
Contra rebels, 717
Convention Against Torture (CAT), 898
Cooley, Aaron, 246
Cooley, Thomas, 346–49, 367
Corporate allies, of Republican Party, 370–71
Counsel, right to
Gideon v. Wainwright and, 480*t*, 490*t*, 612–13, 702, 821
Powell v. Alabama and, 374*t*, 464, 471–73
in Reagan Era, 821–26
in Republican Era, 470–73
Strauder v. West Virginia and, 454, 587*t*
United States v. Callender and, 212–14
Countermajoritarian difficulty, 19–21, 481
"Court Action the Only Reasonable Alternative to Remedy Immediate Abuses of the Negro Separate School" (Thompson, C.), 594–97
Courts. *See also* Supreme Court
in "A Charter of Democracy," 387–88
in Civil War and Reconstruction Era, 293
in Colonial Era, 33
in Contemporary Era, 835–36
in Early National Era, 137
in Founding Era, 73–74
in Jacksonian Era, 221
jurisdiction of, 142–43, 180, 312–13, 387
in Liberalism Divided Era, 619
in New Deal and Great Society Era, 498, 500–505
opinions of, 1003–4
packing of, 498, 500–505, 520
in Reagan Era, 715
in Republican Era, 373, 481–82, 482*f*
route of, to Supreme Court, 999*f*
state, 221, 225, 697, 1003–4
Cowan, Edgar, 322–23, 354–55
Cox, Archibald, 21, 639–40
Crafts, Wilbur, 434
Craig, John, 224
CREEP. *See* Committee to Reelect the President

Crescent City Live-Stock Landing and Slaughtering Company, 306
Criminal justice. *See also* Due process; Habeas corpus; Infamous crimes and criminals; Interrogations; Jury trials; Lawyers; Punishments; Search and seizure rights
  in Civil War and Reconstruction Era, 357–67
  in Colonial Era, 62–70
  in Contemporary Era, 959–81, 961*f*
  in Early National Era, 209–14
  exclusionary rule in, 366, 376, 464–66, 604–7, 697, 699, 960
  in Founding Era, 127–30
  in Jacksonian Era, 283–88
  in Liberalism Divided Era, 630, 695–707, 696*f*
  in New Deal and Great Society Era, 603–14, 604*f*
  in Pennsylvania ratification debates, 79–80
  in Reagan Era, 811–31, 960
  in Republican Era, 464–74
  state constitutions and, 127
  Supreme Court support for claimants, 960, 961*f*
Criminal libel, 380–82
Cross-burning, 927
Cruel and unusual punishments, 4, 473–74, 614, 702, 715
Cuban refugees, 719
Cultural homogeneity, 439, 441
Curtis, Benjamin R., 226*t*, 242
  on *Cooley v. Board of Wardens* and, 246–48
  on *Dred Scott v. Sandford*, 273–74, 277–79, 334
  "Executive Power" by, 334–36
  overview of, 220*b*
Cushing, William, 118, 123, 182

Dahl, Robert, 19
Danbury Baptists, 196, 437
Dangerous speech laws, Supreme Court cases reviewing, 442*t*–443*t*
Daniel, Peter, 226*t*, 236, 239, 247
Darwin, Charles, 379
Daugherty, H. M., 394
Davis, Alfred E., 688–89
Davis, David, 293–94, 310, 362–65
Davis, Jefferson, 291, 294*b*
Davison, T. Whitfield, 589
Dawes Act, 453
Day, William R.
  on *Hammer v. Dagenhart*, 401–2
  on *Weeks v. United States*, 465–66
Death penalty. *See* Capital punishment
Debs, Eugene V., 443
Decision making
  constitutional interpretation and, 9–17
  intelligent, 8–9
Declaration of Independence (Jefferson), 31, 43, 113, 121, 182
  excerpt, 84–85
  as foundation of American constitutionalism, 341
  slavery and, 274–75, 299
Declaration of Sentiments, 281
De facto discrimination, 678, 801
Defense counsel, 128
Defense of Marriage Act (DOMA)
  House report on, 922–24
  "Letter from the Attorney General to Congress on Litigation Involving the Defense of Marriage Act" on, 924–25
  repeal of, 917–18
Defense Production Act of 1950, 540
Defore, John, 466–67
De jure discrimination, 678, 801
Delaine, Joseph, 597–98
Delancy, James, 55
Delaware Constitution, 111
Dellinger, Walter, 634, 887–89
Democracy
  Brandeis on, 441
  in "A Charter of Democracy," 387–88
  necessary conditions of, 624–25
  politics of, transformed, 780
  republic and, 83–84, 86–87
  revered, 265
  states as laboratories of, 405
Democratic Party
  on abortion rights, 915–16
  in Civil War and Reconstruction Era, 291–93, 296, 300, 305–6, 310–11, 320, 333, 341–42
  in Contemporary Era, 833–39, 855, 856*f*, 858, 865, 901–2, 915–17, 935–46, 954, 960, 968–69
  in Early National Era, 135*f*
  on gun rights, 910
  in Jacksonian Era, 217–19, 219*f*, 223, 225, 227–29, 231–32, 244–45, 250, 264, 271–72, 274, 418
  in Liberalism Divided Era, 617–19, 618*f*, 643, 647–48, 663, 677
  in New Deal and Great Society Era, 477–79, 477*f*, 486, 556, 581
  at Ohio Constitutional Convention, 227–29
  in Reagan Era, 711–13, 712*f*, 733, 740–41, 747, 787–88, 807–8
  in Republican Era, 370–71, 370*f*, 372*t*, 379, 387–88, 392, 441, 811, 826, 833
  on same-sex marriage, 917
  Southern Democrats, 232
  2008 platform, 946, 954
  2012 platform, 946, 954
Democratic Review, 265
Democratic rights. *See also* Free speech; Voting rights
  in Civil War and Reconstruction Era, 342–45
  in Colonial Era, 53–58
  in Contemporary Era, 925–45
  in Early National Era, 198–204
  in Founding Era, 117–21
  in Jacksonian Era, 265–71
  in Liberalism Divided Era, 657–73
  in New Deal and Great Society Era, 561–86, 574*f*, 582*t*–583*t*
  in Reagan Era, 780–96
  in Republican Era, 441–53, 442*t*–443*t*, 451*t*–452*t*
Dennis, Eugene, 566–70
Departmentalism, 18–19, 151–52
Deposit removal, from Bank of the United States, 250–54
Desegregation. *See* Segregation
Detainee Treatment Act (DTA), 841–46, 960, 969
Dewey, Thomas, 479
DeWitt, John, 590–91
Dickerson, Charles Thomas, 963–66
Dickinson, John, 42, 71, 93, 103
Direct legislation, 406
Dirksen, Everett, 526
Discrimination. *See also* Equality rights
  de jure and de facto, 678, 801
  equal protection and, 10, 453, 461, 515, 552
  against non-English speakers, 578
  against same-sex marriage, 909
Dissenting opinions, author and legal reasoning of, 1002
Dixon, Bryan, 916
Doctrinalism, 11–12
Doctrine, 998
"Does the Negro Need Separate Schools?" (DuBois), 594–95
Dole, Bob, 790
Dole, Elizabeth, 733–35
DOMA. *See* Defense of Marriage Act
Dormant commerce clause, 245–46, 406
Dorr, Thomas, 229
Douglas, Stephen A., 243, 310
Douglas, William O., 491, 512, 555, 572, 604*f*, 619
  on *Argensinger v. Hamlin*, 702
  attitudinal model and, 14–15, 14*f*
  on *Brandenburg v. Ohio*, 573–74
  on capital punishment, 613, 702
  on *Dennis v. United States*, 570
  on *Griswold v. Connecticut*, 558–59, 721
  on *Harper v. Virginia Board of Elections*, 574
  on *Harris v. New York*, 701
  on *Heart of Atlanta Motel, Inc. v. United States*, 530

on *Jones v. Opelika*, 563
on *Mapp v. Ohio*, 607
on *Moose Lodge No. 107 v. Irvis*, 626–27
on *New York Times Co. v. United States*, 660–61
on *O'Callahan v. Parker*, 489
on *Oregon v. Mitchell*, 669
on *Railway Express Agency v. People of State of New York*, 588
on *Roe v. Wade*, 653
on sterilization, 556–57
on *United States v. United States District Court*, 639
on *Williamson v. Lee Optical Co.*, 551–52
on *Wisconsin v. Yoder*, 644, 647
on *Youngstown Sheet & Tube Co. v. Sawyer*, 538–39
Douglass, Frederick, 223, 296, 305, 953
Dow, David, 23
Draft. *See* Military draft
Drinking age, minimum, 733
DTA. *See* Detainee Treatment Act
Dual federalism, 373
Duane, James, 77
Duane, William, 250
DuBois, W. E. B., 454, 594–95
Due process
abortion rights protected by, 623, 717
in Civil War and Reconstruction Era, 357–66
in Colonial Era, 62–65
in Contemporary Era, 960–61
in Early National Era, 190, 209–10
economic bargains and, 421
in Fifth Amendment, 373, 410, 468, 491, 589, 693–94, 896–97
in Founding Era, 128
in Fourteenth Amendment, 17, 373, 406, 410, 413, 421, 427–29, 431–32, 438, 468, 471–73, 488–93, 549–52, 559–61, 605–7, 643, 653–54, 717, 769–71, 773, 775–76, 778–80, 812, 920–21
Herrera v. Collins and, 812–16
in Jacksonian Era, 283–87
in Liberalism Divided Era, 696–99
minimum standards, 464
in New Deal and Great Society Era, 603–4
in Reagan Era, 812–16
in Republican Era, 464
revolution, 603, 695–96
In re Winship and, 696–99
Duncan, Gary, 490–94
Dutton, Warren, 204
Dworkin, Ronald, 13, 625
Dyer, Leonidas, 394

Earl, Robert, 426–28
Early National Era (1791–1828)
cast of characters, 136*b*
constitutional authority in, 142–55, 144*t*
constitutional thought in, 137–38
courts, 137
criminal justice in, 209–14
Democratic Party in, 135*f*
democratic rights in, 198–204
developments, 133–34
due process in, 190, 209–10
equality in, 204–8, 206*f*
federalism in, 178–85
Federalists in, 119, 133–35, 135*f*, 137–38, 145–51, 156, 158–60, 179, 198–200, 202–3
foundations, 138–42
free speech in, 198–202
gender equality in, 208–9
gun rights in, 196–98
habeas corpus in, 209–10
impeachment in, 134, 137, 152, 187–89
individual rights in, 190–98, 191*t*–192*t*, 258
interest groups, 137
interrogations in, 212
introduction to, 133–38, 134*t*, 135*f*, 136*b*
Jeffersonians in, 134–38, 135*f*, 143, 153, 178–80, 198–99, 203–5
judicial power in, 142–55, 144*t*, 179
juries in, 212–14
law of nations in, 138–39
lawyers in, 212–14
legacies, 138
major issues and decisions, 134*t*
personal freedom in, 198
political parties in, 133–37, 135*f*
powers of national government in, 155–78, 157*t*–158*t*
principles, 141–42
property rights in, 190–95, 258
public morality in, 198
punishments in, 214–15
racial equality in, 206–8, 206*f*
religious rights in, 135, 195–96, 201, 204
search and seizure in, 210–12
separation of powers in, 185–90
voting rights in, 202–4, 202*f*–203*f*
Eastland, James, 618
Economic bargains, 421
Economic equality, 349
Economic hazard, minimum protection against, 643
Edmunds, George, 395, 397
Ehrlichman, John, 640
Eighteenth Amendment, 993
Prohibition and, 377, 486
repealed, 486
state reforms and, 406
Eighth Amendment, 483, 779, 991
applied to states, 490*t*
capital punishment and, 10, 613–14, 707, 966
citizenship and, 614
excessive bail clause of, 489
expanded, 603
Eisenhower, Dwight, 477, 479, 498, 597, 711
"Address to the Nation on the Introduction of Troops in Little Rock" by, 506–7
Brennan nominated by, 725
Elected officials, recall of, 389
Election. *See also* Campaign finance; Voting rights
of Bush, George W., 833, 840
of Clinton, 833
of FDR, 477, 486, 498, 516, 520, 589
of Hayes, 409
of Johnson, Lyndon, 486
laws, Supreme Court reviewing, 451*t*–452*t*
of Lincoln, 272–93, 324, 326
of Nixon, 609, 618, 621, 623, 626, 711
of Obama, 833, 835, 857
of Reagan, 711, 718
regulation, 453
Senate, 376
of Wilson, Woodrow, 370, 387–88, 833
Electoral College, 9, 370
Electoral districts, 9
Eleventh Amendment, 178–79, 878, 991
Elkin, Steven, 5
Ellsberg, Daniel, 658–59
Ellsworth, Oliver, 122, 142
Ely, John Hart, 625–26, 721
Emancipation Proclamation (Lincoln), 291, 333–36
Embargo Act, 158
Emergency Highway Energy Conservation Act, 629–30
Emerson, John, 240, 273
Eminent domain, 902–6
Enactments, validity of, 511
Endorsement test, 907
Engel, Steven, 553–56
English Bill of Rights, 33–36, 44, 51–52, 81
Enlightenment, 4
Epstein, Lee, 16
Epstein, Richard, 717, 754–55
Equality rights. *See also* Gender equality; Racial equality
in Civil War and Reconstruction Era, 346–57
in Colonial Era, 58–62
in Contemporary Era, 945–59
defined, 7
in Early National Era, 204–8, 206*f*
in Founding Era, 121–27
in Jacksonian Era, 271–83
in Liberalism Divided Era, 617, 626–28, 673–95
in New Deal and Great Society Era, 586–603, 587*t*–588*t*, 602*f*

Equality rights (*continued*)
in Reagan Era, 796–811
in Republican Era, 453–63
Equality under law
in Civil War and Reconstruction Era, 346–47
in Colonial Era, 58–59
in Contemporary Era, 947
in Early National Era, 205–6
in Founding Era, 122
in Jacksonian Era, 271–72
in Liberalism Divided Era, 674–77
in New Deal and Great Society Era, 586–88, 587*t*–588*t*
Plyler v. Doe and, 588*t*, 714*t*, 798–801
in Reagan Era, 797–801
in Republican Era, 453–54
San Antonio Independent School District v. Rodriguez and, 674–77
in state constitutions, 947
Equal protection clause
discrimination and, 10, 453, 461, 515, 552
enforcement of, 579
in Fourteenth Amendment, 10, 453, 461, 508–16, 552, 579–81, 584–85, 587*t*–588*t*, 597, 603, 624, 626–28, 643, 668, 672–76, 683–85, 688–89, 772, 775, 789, 798–800, 823–26
gay rights and, 920–21
gerrymandering and, 789
state laws, Supreme Court reviewing, 587*t*–588*t*
Equal Rights Amendment (ERA), 621, 674
Blanket Amendment and, 461–63
debate over, 691–93, 807–8
failure of, 623–24, 689–90
rally, 692
Ertman, Martha, 436
Ervin, Sam, 618, 639, 671
Espionage Act of 1917, 441, 443–44
Establishment clause
Burger Court on, 644
Fourteenth Amendment and, 553–54
purpose of, 554–55
school prayer and, 759–63
Estrada, Miguel, 850
Ethics in Government Act, 742, 747, 754
Eugenic sterilization, 440–41, 556–57
Evangelicals, 619, 713
Evarts, William, 426
Evening Post, 271–72
Excessive bail clause, 489
Exclusionary rule
in criminal justice, 366, 376, 464–66, 604–7, 697, 699, 960
limitations, 699
Exclusion Order No. 34, 590–91
Executions, 703*f*
Executive branch. *See also* Political scandals
chronological table of, 1007*t*–1010*t*
debates over, 102–8
documents, researching and reading, 1004–5
energetic, 102, 107
federal judiciary vetted by, 478–79
officers, 187–90, 250–51, 414–18
in unitary executive theory, 740, 742
Executive power. *See also* Separation of powers; Vetoes; War powers
American constitutionalism and, 186–87
bank deposit removal and, 250–54
Black, Jeremiah, on, 326–27
bolstered, 711, 717, 740
Congress and, 419–20
in Contemporary Era, 885–901
Curtis on, 334–36
foreign policy and, 543–44
habeas corpus and, 358–61
Hamilton, Alexander, on, 185, 187, 541
Jackson, Robert, on, 541–42, 892
Jefferson on, 185–87
Marshall, John, on, 662
Morrison v. Olson and, 747–54
Myers v. United States and, 414–18
in New Deal and Great Society Era, 533
Nixon and, 617, 623, 631, 639–43, 657, 661
"Presidential Authority to Decline to Execute Unconstitutional Statutes" on, 887–89
Prize Cases and, 337–40
of removal, 187–90, 250–51, 414–18
Roosevelt, Theodore, on, 418–20
Supreme Court cases reviewing, 338*t*
Taft on, 419–20
"Executive Power" (Curtis), 334–36
Executive privilege, 133, 631, 641, 895
Ex post facto law, 194
Extraterritoriality
Boumediene v. Bush and, 841–46
in Contemporary Era, 841, 843, 845–46, 897
Ross v. McIntyre and, 379

"The Failure of Universal Suffrage" (Parkman), 453
Fair Labor Standards Act (FLSA), 630, 736–38
Falwell, Jerry, 713, 781
Fannie Lou Hamer, Rosa Parks, and Coretta Scott King Voting Rights Act Reauthorization and Amendments Act of 2006, 936
Fasteau, Brenda Feigen, 691–92
Faubus, Orval, 506
FBI. *See* Federal Bureau of Investigation
FDR. *See* Roosevelt, Franklin
FECA. *See* Federal Election Campaign Act of 1974
Federal Aid Highway Act, 733
Federal Bureau of Investigation (FBI), 603, 610, 631
Federal Election Campaign Act of 1974 (FECA), 658, 663–67
Federal Habeas Corpus Act of 1966, 604
Federal income tax
Sixteenth Amendment and, 376, 392
state income tax and, 406, 406n18
Federalism
in Civil War and Reconstruction Era, 323–33
in Contemporary Era, 855, 856*f*, 877–84
dual, 373
in Early National Era, 178–85
in Founding Era, 99–101
Garcia v. San Antonio Metropolitan Transit Authority and, 735–40
intelligent decision making promoted by, 8–9
in Jacksonian Era, 244–49, 267
in Liberalism Divided Era, 630–31
Munn v. Illinois and, 409–12
in New Deal and Great Society Era, 531, 531*t*–532*t*
populists and, 405–6
Printz v. United States and, 879–84
progressives and, 405–6
in Reagan Era, 735–40
religious freedom and, 111
in Republican Era, 405–13
revolution, 733
secession and, 323–26
Wabash, St. Louis & Pacific Railroad v. Illinois and, 406–9
The Federalist Papers
No. 10 (Madison), 85–87, 110, 117
No. 27 (Hamilton), 883–84
No. 34 (Hamilton), 870
No. 37 (Madison), 23
No. 40 (Madison), 22
No. 51 (Madison), 106–7, 186, 976
No. 57 (Madison), 122
No. 70 (Hamilton), 107, 891
No. 71 (Hamilton), 107–8
No. 76 (Hamilton), 73
No. 78 (Hamilton), 90–93
No. 84 (Hamilton), 78, 80–81
Federalists
in Early National Era, 119, 133–35, 135*f*, 137–38, 145–51, 156, 158–60, 179, 198–200, 202–3
in Founding Era, 73–75
on voting rights, 119, 202–3
Federalist Society, 713, 715, 733, 840
Federal judiciary
circuits, 225, 226*t*, 227*f*

civil rights protesters and, 562
executive branch vetting, 478–79
FDR and, 478–79, 498, 516
ideological transformation of, 481
Federal Labor Standards Act, 604
Federal laws
Supreme Court invalidating, 386*f*, 497*f*, 847*f*
Supreme Court review of, 372–73
"Federal questions" jurisdiction, 387, 999
Federal ratio, 9
Federal Reporter, 1003
Federal Supplement, 1003
Federal Trade Commission, 533
Feingold, Russell, 929, 972
Feldman, Stephen, 926
Felon disenfranchisement, 672–73
Field, Stephen, 293, 308–9, 314, 317, 320, 342
on *Munn v. Illinois*, 412–13
overview of, 347, 375*b*
Fifteenth Amendment, 345, 379, 390, 993
enforcement of, 301, 314, 576, 580
importance of, 295
ratified, 292, 349
Voting Rights Act and, 517, 788
Fifth Amendment, 464, 489, 705, 991
applied to states, 490*t*
due process clause, 373, 410, 468, 491, 589, 693–94, 896–97
expanded, 603
on interrogations, 128, 610–12, 896–97
property rights and, 110, 279, 425, 755, 903–5
scope of, 224–25, 373
on search and seizure, 465–69, 606
self-incrimination clause, 559, 604
takings clause of, 488, 643, 715, 756–58, 902–7
Filled Milk Act of 1923, 487–88
"Fireside Chat on Court-Packing Plan" (FDR), 500–504
First Amendment, 558, 913, 990
applied to states, 490*t*
free speech in, 118, 199, 380–81, 444, 446, 488, 562, 572–73, 658–66, 717, 719, 721, 781–85, 909, 926–34
as national aspiration, 9
religious rights in, 111, 553–55, 721, 759, 764–67
tests, 717
textualism and, 11
First Congress, 138, 155, 186, 416, 883
First Reconstruction Act, 357
FISA. *See* Foreign Intelligence Surveillance Act
Fitzgerald, Josephine, 494
Flag
burning, 719, 781, 783–86
saluting, 562–65
Flag Protection Act of 1989, 783
Fletcher, Robert, 193
FLSA. *See* Fair Labor Standards Act
Ford, Betty, 692
Ford, Gerald, 15, 619, 623, 663, 722
Foreign Intelligence Surveillance Act (FISA), 631, 977–79
Foreign policy
Congress and, 633–37
executive power and, 543–44
international law and, 377, 719, 839–40
political questions, 510–11, 514
Fortas, Abe, 604*f*, 619
"Fort Hill Address" (Calhoun), 248–49
Fort Sumter, 291, 328, 337
Forum, 461
Foster, Edmund, 203–4
Founding Era (1776–1791)
British Parliament in, 71, 77, 119
cast of characters, 72*b*
constitutional authority in, 88–93
constitutional thought in, 74–76
courts in, 73–74
criminal justice in, 127–30
democratic rights in, 117–21
developments, 71–73
due process in, 128
equality in, 121–27
factions, 73
federalism in, 99–101
Federalists in, 73–75
foundations, 77–87
free speech in, 118
gender equality in, 125–27, 125*f*
gun rights in, 80, 117
habeas corpus in, 127–28
impeachment in, 96–97, 105–6
individual rights in, 109–17, 112*t*
interrogations in, 128
introduction to, 71–76, 74*t*, 75*f*
judicial power in, 88–93
jury trials in, 127–29
law of nations in, 77, 82
lawyers in, 128–29
legacies, 76
personal freedom in, 117
powers of national government in, 93–99
principles, 83–87
property rights in, 110–11
public morality in, 117
punishments in, 129–30
racial equality in, 122–25
religious rights in, 79, 82, 111–16
search and seizure rights in, 128
separation of powers in, 101–9
voting rights in, 110, 119–21
Four Horsemen, 496
Fourteenth Amendment, 18, 293, 341, 349, 517, 992
Bill of Rights and, 621
capital punishment and, 613, 702, 705, 707, 966
on citizenship, 279, 301–2, 304, 307
Civil Rights Cases and, 380, 382–83, 385, 390, 489
debates over, 299–305
due process clause, 17, 373, 406, 410, 413, 421, 427–29, 431–32, 438, 468, 471–73, 488–93, 549–52, 559–61, 605–7, 643, 653–54, 717, 769–71, 773, 775–76, 778–80, 812, 920–21
enforcement of, 301, 314, 530
equal protection clause, 10, 453, 461, 508–16, 552, 579–81, 584–85, 587*t*–588*t*, 597, 603, 624, 626–28, 643, 668, 672–76, 683–85, 688–89, 772, 775, 789, 798–800, 823–26
establishment clause and, 553–54
free speech and, 17, 572–73
gay rights and, 769, 778
gender equality and, 674
importance of, 295, 386
jury trials and, 612
liberty in, 413, 432, 438–40, 651, 653–54, 705
litigation, 386
lynching debate and, 394–95
passage and ratification of, 292, 301*t*–302*t*
privacy rights, 557, 605, 651–52
privileges and immunities clause of, 342, 354
restrictive covenants and, 494–95
school segregation and, 597–600, 602
Section 1, 803
Section 2, 301
Section 3, 301
Section 5, 394, 517, 578, 767, 850–51, 856–57, 947
segregation and, 457, 483, 505, 597–600, 602
Slaughter-House Cases and, 306–9, 342
Thirteenth Amendment and, 299–300
women's suffrage and, 354
Fourth Amendment, 373, 722, 780, 991
applied to states, 490*t*
current understandings of, 464
expanded, 603
on search and seizure, 128, 464, 466–69, 559–61, 604–7, 638–39, 699, 816–20, 961–62
Frank, Leo, 464
Frankfurter, Felix, 16, 483, 496, 604*f*, 607, 697
on *Baker v. Carr*, 512–16
on *Colegrove v. Green*, 509
on *Cooper v. Aaron*, 508–9
on *Dennis v. United States*, 568–69
on *Korematsu v. United States*, 592

Frankfurter (*continued*)
on *Minersville School District v. Gobitis*, 563
overview of, 484*b*
on *West Virginia State Board of Education v. Barnette*, 565–66
on *Youngstown Sheet & Tube Co. v. Sawyer*, 539
Franklin, Benjamin, 31–32
Articles of Confederation and, 71
in Constitutional Convention debates, 103
on universal male suffrage, 119–21
Free blacks, 206, 272, 286
Freedmen's Bureau, 314, 350–53
Freedmen's Bureau Act of 1866, 314
Freedom of contract, 428–31, 545, 549, 643, 755
Free exercise clause
religious rights and, 721, 759, 764, 766–67, 908–9
shift in constitutional politics of, 908–9
Free Soil Party, 266, 279
Free speech
ACLU and, 562
Balzac v. Porto Rico and, 380–82
Brandenburg v. Ohio and, 443*t*, 480*t*, 562, 573–74, 658, 781
Buckley v. Valeo and, 452*t*, 621*t*, 623, 658, 663–67, 931–32
Citizens United v. Federal Election Commission and, 452*t*, 834*t*, 848, 929, 931–35
in Civil War and Reconstruction Era, 342–45
clear and present danger and, 442*t*, 443–44, 446–48, 567–70, 573
in Colonial Era, 53–57
of Communists, 478–79, 566–70
in Contemporary Era, 926–35
Dennis v. United States and, 442*t*, 480*t*, 566–70, 573
Doe v. University of Michigan and, 714*t*, 786–87
in Early National Era, 198–202
as essential, 561
in First Amendment, 118, 199, 380–81, 444, 446, 488, 562, 572–73, 658–66, 717, 719, 721, 781–85, 909, 926–34
in Founding Era, 118
Fourteenth Amendment and, 17, 572–73
in Jacksonian Era, 266–71
Jefferson and, 199
in Liberalism Divided Era, 657–67
Lincoln and, 342
NAACP and, 562
Near v. Minnesota and, 374*t*, 442*t*, 444, 449–51, 490*t*
in New Deal and Great Society Era, 561–74
in Reagan Era, 781–87
in Republican Era, 441–51, 442*t*–443*t*
Schenck v. United States and, 374*t*, 442*t*, 443, 444–47
Texas v. Johnson and, 719, 781, 783–86, 848
Truman and, 479
West Virginia State Board of Education v. Barnette and, 563–66, 786
Whitney v. California and, 374*t*, 442*t*, 444, 446–49, 562, 567, 573
World War I and, 441, 443–46, 562
Zenger trial and, 33, 54–57, 55*f*, 62, 69, 129, 212
Friendly, Henry, 695
"A Friend of the Constitution" (Marshall, J.), 169, 171–72
Frontiero, Sharron, 693–95
Fugitive Slave Act of 1793, 206, 236, 283
Fugitive Slave Act of 1850, 283–84
Fugitive slaves, 9, 122, 206, 222
Booth Cases and, 283–87
Prigg v. Pennsylvania and, 218*t*, 232, 236–40
Fulbright, William, 622*b*, 633–34
Fuller, Melville, 398–99, 421
Fuller, Timothy, 208
Fulton, Robert, 172
Fundamental rights, 6

Gallatin, Albert, 159–60
Garfield, James, 369
Garrison, William Lloyd, 222–23, 272
Gay rights. *See also* Same-sex marriage
Bowers v. Hardwick and, 12, 714*t*, 769, 778–80, 854, 919–21
constitutional politics of, 918
in Contemporary Era, 839, 917–25
equal protection and, 920–21
Fourteenth Amendment and, 769, 778
Lawrence v. Texas and, 12–13, 21, 423*t*, 432*t*, 834*t*, 848, 854, 917–22, 924
in Liberalism Divided Era, 649–50
Gender equality. *See also* Equal Rights Amendment; Women's suffrage
Adams, John and Abigail, on, 126–27
affirmative action and, 808–11
American Revolution and, 125–26
in Civil War and Reconstruction Era, 354–57
in Colonial Era, 61–62
Commentaries on the Laws of England on, 61–62
in Contemporary Era, 954–59
in Early National Era, 208–9
in Founding Era, 125–27, 125*f*
Fourteenth Amendment and, 674
Frontiero v. Richardson and, 690, 693–95
in Jacksonian Era, 281–83
Johnson v. Transportation Agency, Santa Clara County and, 714*t*, 808–11
in Liberalism Divided Era, 617, 689–95
in New Deal and Great Society Era, 586, 603
property rights and, 282
in Reagan Era, 807–11
in Republican Era, 432–34, 461–63
United States v. Virginia and, 588*t*, 954–59
Warren Court on, 586
General laws, 348
George, James, 395–97
German, teaching, 438–40
Gerry, Elbridge, 100, 105, 187–90
Gerrymandering
Shaw v. Reno and, 583*t*, 714*t*, 789, 793–96, 793*f*, 936
voting rights and, 509, 581, 583, 583*t*, 714*t*, 781, 787, 789, 793–96, 793*f*, 935–36
Gettysburg Address (Lincoln), 305
GFSZA. *See* Gun-Free School Zones Act
Gibson, William, 225
Gideon, Clarence, 612–13
Gilmer, Thomas W., 256
Gingrich, Newt, 835
Ginsburg, Douglas, 910
Ginsburg, Ruth Bader, 836, 961*f*
on *Adarand Constructors, Inc. v. Peña*, 948
on *Grutter v. Bollinger*, 952–53
on *National Federation of Independent Business v. Sebelius*, 870–73
overview of, 837*b*
Sex Bias in the U.S. Code by, 691–92
on *Shelby County v. Holder*, 944–45
on *United States v. Virginia*, 954–57
Women's Rights Project and, 690–91
Gitlow, Benjamin, 446
Glover, Joshua, 283–84
Goldberg, Arthur, 498, 604*f*, 613
on *Griswold v. Connecticut*, 559
on *Heart of Atlanta Motel, Inc. v. United States*, 530
on *New York Times Co. v. Sullivan*, 572
Gold clause, 498–500
Goldsmith, Jack, 840
Goldstein, Leslie, 10–11
Goldwater, Barry, 617, 711–12
Gonzales, Alberto, 893–96
Goold, Mary, 436
GOP. *See* Republican Party
Gordon, Nathaniel, 367
Gordon, Thomas, 54
Gore, Al, 833, 937–41
Gotcher, Mrs. E., 432
Governance, constitutionalism as, 4
Government. *See* National government

Government documents. *See* Researching and reading, of government documents
Graebner, James, 808
Gramm-Rudman-Hollings Deficit Control Act of 1985, 742
Grand jury, 69
Grand Laundry, 432
Grand Old Party. *See* Republican Party
The Grange, 409–10
Grant, Ulysses, 293, 311
Gray, Horace, 377
Grayson, Alan, 977
Great Depression, 518
Great Society, 678, 711, 715. *See also* New Deal and Great Society Era
  Johnson, Lyndon, and, 477, 516
  New Deal and, 517
  opposition to, 618–19, 713, 718
  unfinished work of, 620, 625
Greece, 4–5
Green, Charles, 600–602
Gregg, Troy, 704–7
Grenada, 717
Grier, Robert, 226*t*, 277, 313–14
  on *Prize Cases*, 337–39
  on *Texas v. White*, 332–33
Griswold, Estelle, 557–61
Griswold, Henry, 314
Grutter, Barbara, 949–54
Guantanamo Bay, 841–46, 968–69, 973
Guaranty Clause, 510–11, 515
Guidelines on Constitutional Litigation (Office of Legal Policy), 720–22, 754, 781, 797, 820
Guinier, Lani, 789
Gun-Free School Zones Act (GFSZA), 856–64
Gun rights
  abolitionists and, 264
  anti-Federalists and, 117
  Carter and, 647
  in Civil War and Reconstruction Era, 341
  in Colonial Era, 51–52
  in Contemporary Era, 909–15
  Democratic Party on, 910
  District of Columbia v. Heller and, 834*t*, 848, 910–15
  in Early National Era, 196–98
  in Founding Era, 80, 117
  in Jacksonian Era, 264–65
  in Liberalism Divided Era, 647–48
  in New Deal and Great Society Era, 556
  Nixon and, 647
  racial equality and, 264–65
  in Reagan Era, 647, 768–69
  in Republican Era, 438
  Republican Party on, 909–10
  in Second Amendment, 117, 196, 556, 647–48, 768–69, 841, 909–14

Habeas corpus
  in Civil War and Reconstruction Era, 291, 342–45, 357–66
  in Colonial Era, 63–64
  in Contemporary Era, 841–46, 960–61, 969
  in Early National Era, 209–10
  executive power and, 358–61
  Ex parte Merryman and, 292*t*, 357–60, 536n32
  Ex parte Milligan and, 361–66
  in Founding Era, 127–28
  Herrera v. Collins and, 812–16, 826
  in Jacksonian Era, 283–87
  in Liberalism Divided Era, 695–99
  Lincoln and, 291, 342–45, 357–61
  in New Deal and Great Society Era, 603–4, 612–13
  in Reagan Era, 812–16, 826
  in Republican Era, 464
Habeas Corpus Act of 1863, 357–58, 361–62
Habeas Corpus Act of 1867, 310–12
Habeas Corpus Act of 1966, 604
Hackney, Leonard, 473
Haldeman, H. R., 640
Hale, Matthew, 411–12
Hall, Hiland, 267
Hamdi, Yaser Esam, 973–77
Hamilton, Alexander, 77, 134, 156, 179, 882
  for Bank of the United States, 159–60, 163–64
  "Brutus" essays response by, 88, 90–93
  at Constitutional Convention, 102, 104–5
  on executive power, 185, 187, 541
  The Federalist Papers No. 27 by, 883–84
  The Federalist Papers No. 34 by, 870
  The Federalist Papers No. 70 by, 107, 891
  The Federalist Papers No. 71 by, 107–8
  The Federalist Papers No. 76 by, 73
  The Federalist Papers No. 78 by, 90–93
  The Federalist Papers No. 84 by, 78, 80–81
Hamilton, Alice, 461, 463
"Hampden essays" (Roane), 169–70
Hand, Learned, 481–82, 568
Harding, Warren, 394, 403
Hardwick, Michael, 778–80
Harlan, James, 297–98, 341–42
Harlan, John Marshall, I
  on *Berea College v. Commonwealth of Kentucky*, 456
  on *Civil Rights Cases*, 384–86
  on *Cumming v. Richmond County Board of Education*, 456
  on *Hawaii v. Mankichi*, 380–81
  on *Mugler v. Kansas*, 423
  overview of, 376*b*
  on *Plessy v. Ferguson*, 456–59
  on *United States v. E. C. Knight*, 397, 399–400
Harlan, John Marshall, II, 483, 604*f*, 619, 854
  on *Baker v. Carr*, 512, 516
  on *Duncan v. Louisiana*, 490–94
  on *Gideon v. Wainwright*, 613
  on *Griswold v. Connecticut*, 558–60
  on *Katzenbach v. Morgan*, 580–81
  on *Mapp v. Ohio*, 607
  on *Miranda v. Arizona*, 611
  on *New York Times Co. v. United States*, 662
  on *Oregon v. Mitchell*, 669
  on *In re Winship*, 698
  on *Reynolds v. Sims*, 585–86
Harley, George, 688
Harper, Robert, 193
Harrington, James, 33, 36
Harris, Katherine, 937
Harris, Viven, 700–701
Harrison, William Henry, 233, 255
Hatch, Orrin, 731, 792–93, 971–72
Hate speech, 781–82, 786–87
Hawaii, 379–80
Hawes, Harry, 394–95
Hayes, Rutherford B., 409
Hayne, Robert, 245, 267
Health care reform. *See* Affordable Care Act
Health insurance, birth control covered by, 908
Heart of Atlanta Motel, Inc., 517, 528–30
HeinOnline, 998, 1004–6
Heller, Dick, 910–15
Helms, Jesse, 655–56
Hendricks, Thomas, 351–52
Henry, Patrick, 31, 37, 53, 74, 112–13
Hepburn, Mrs., 314
Herrera, Lionel Torres, 812–16
Highway speed limit, 629–30
Himes, James, 979–80
Historical institutionalism, 16–17
Hitchcock, Reuben, 228
Hobbes, Thomas, 36
Holden, Moses, 205
Holder, Eric, 924–25, 941–45
Holmes, Oliver Wendell, Jr., 11, 376, 525, 567–68, 883
  on *Abrams v. United States*, 443–44
  on *Block v. Hirsh*, 423
  on *Buck v. Bell*, 440–41, 453
  on *Hammer v. Dagenhart*, 402–3
  on living Constitution, 404
  on *Lochner v. New York*, 428, 431–32
  on *Meyer v. Nebraska*, 440
  on *Missouri v. Holland*, 393, 404–5

Holmes (*continued*)
on *Moore v. Dempsey*, 464
on *Myers v. United States*, 417
on *Olmstead v. United States*, 470
overview of, 375*b*
on *Pennsylvania Coal Co. v. Mahon*, 424–25
on *Schenck v. United States*, 443–46
Holmes, Stephen, 6–7
Holt, John, 38
Home Building and Loan Association, 192*t*, 480*t*, 545–48
Hooper, Frank, 589
Hoover, Herbert, 372, 741
Hostilities, dates of duration, 511
House of Representatives
chronological table of, 1007*t*–1010*t*
conscientious objectors debated in, 116
DOMA report, 922–24
hearings on disclosure of NSA intelligence gathering, 977–81
internal improvements report, 176–77
removal of executive officers debated in, 187–90
RFRA report, 767–68
veto power debated in, 255–58
Houston, Charles, 589, 594
Howard, Jacob, 305
Hughes, Charles E., 481, 488, 496, 502, 508
on *Home Building & Loan Association v. Blaisdell*, 546–48
on *National Labor Relations Board v. Jones & Laughlin Steel Corp.*, 517, 521–23
on *Near v. Minnesota*, 444, 449–50
overview of, 485*b*
on *Schechter Poultry Corp. v. United States*, 518–20
on *West Coast Hotel Co. v. Parrish*, 545, 549–50
Human Life Amendment, 655–57
Humphrey, Hubert, 526–27, 677, 682–83
Hunting regulations, 392–93, 403–5
Hutchinson, Thomas, 41, 44
Hyde Amendment, 623

ICJ. *See* International Court of Justice
Illegal immigration, 798
Illinois Constitution, 411
Immigration, 451, 798
Impeachment, 695, 699–701, 741, 749–52
in Early National Era, 134, 137, 152, 187–89
in Founding Era, 96–97, 105–6
of Johnson, Andrew, 291–92, 311, 329, 333
of Nixon, 631, 640
of Tyler, John, 250, 255
Imperialism. *See* American imperialism
Implied powers, 98, 156, 160, 165–66, 319
Incendiary publications in mail, debate over, 266–71
Income tax. *See* Federal income tax; State income tax
Incorporation, of Bill of Rights
debate, 490–91, 491n13, 493
McDonald v. City of Chicago and, 841
selective, 489
Independent counsel, 747–54
Independent regulatory commissions, 533
Index to Legal Periodicals, 1006
Individual mandate, in ACA, 857, 864–68, 871–72, 874–76
Individual rights. *See also* Gun rights; Personal freedom; Property rights; Public morality; Religious rights
in Civil War and Reconstruction Era, 340–42
in Colonial Era, 44–53
in Contemporary Era, 901–25
defined, 7
in Early National Era, 190–98, 191*t*–192*t*, 258
in Founding Era, 109–17, 112*t*
hierarchy of, 545
in Jacksonian Era, 258–65, 261*t*
in Liberalism Divided Era, 643–57, 649*f*, 654*f*
in New Deal and Great Society Era, 438, 545–61, 553*t*, 555*t*
privacy, 557–61, 604–6, 638, 648–55, 720–21
in Reagan Era, 754–80, 763*f*
in Republican Era, 420–41
Individuals with Disabilities Education Act, 907
Industrialization, 395
Infamous crimes and criminals
in Contemporary Era, 968–81
Hamdi v. Rumsfeld and, 969, 973–77
House hearings on disclosure of NSA intelligence gathering and, 977–81
in War on Terror, 968–72
Inglis, Chris, 980
Initiative and referendum process, 406
Institute for Justice, 432*t*, 733
Institutes of the Laws of England (Coke), 63
Interest groups
in Civil War and Reconstruction Era, 293
in Contemporary Era, 835
in Early National Era, 137
in Jacksonian Era, 219
in Liberalism Divided Era, 618–19
in New Deal and Great Society Era, 479–81
in Reagan Era, 713–15
in Republican Era, 372–73, 432*t*
Intermediate scrutiny, 487*t*, 690
Internal improvements
debates over, 158–59
House report on, 176–77
Madison and, 159, 176
Monroe and, 159, 176–78
International Court of Justice (ICJ), 719
International law, 377, 719, 839–40
Interracial marriage, 556
Interrogations. *See also* "Torture Memos"
in Civil War and Reconstruction Era, 366–67
in Colonial Era, 67–68
in Contemporary Era, 887, 893–99, 962–66, 969
Dickerson v. United States and, 962–66
in Early National Era, 212
Fifth Amendment on, 128, 610–12, 896–97
in Founding Era, 128
Harris v. New York and, 695, 700–701, 964
in Jacksonian Era, 287–88
in Liberalism Divided Era, 699–701
Miranda v. Arizona and, 478, 603, 608–12
in New Deal and Great Society Era, 607–12
in Reagan Era, 820–21
in Republican Era, 470
Interstate commerce, 155–56, 177, 390
ACA and, 864–76
child labor and, 392–93, 400–403
Civil Rights Act of 1964 and, 517, 526–30, 626
Cooley v. Board of Wardens and, 218*t*, 245–48
Filled Milk Act of 1923 and, 487–88
in *Gibbons v. Ogden*, 172–75
Heart of Atlanta Motel, Inc. v. United States and, 517, 528–30
Jacksonian Era federalism and, 245–48
limitations on, 858–64
National Labor Relations Board v. Jones & Laughlin Steel Corp. and, 520–23
Schechter Poultry Corp. v. United States and, 518–20
Sherman Anti-Trust Act and, 395–400
state laws, Supreme Court reviewing, 531*t*–532*t*
United States v. E. C. Knight and, 397–400
Wickard v. Filburn and, 524–26
Interstate Commerce Act of 1887, 390

Interstate Commerce Commission, 390
Invalidation of laws, by Supreme Court, 386*f*, 497*f*, 847*f*
Iran-Contra scandal, 741, 747
Iraq War, 887
Iredell, James, 137–38, 140–41, 180–81, 212
Iron law of oligarchy, 8
Irvis, K. Leroy, 626–28
Isolationism, 403

Jackson, Andrew
- against anti-slavery literature in mail, 267
- against Bank of the United States, 221, 233–36, 250–54, 271
- censure of, 251, 254–55
- deposits removed by, 250–54
- inauguration of, 217
- against nullification, 246
- overview of, 220*b*
- vetoes by, 217, 232–36, 250

Jackson, Charles, 205–6
Jackson, James, 116
Jackson, Robert H., 8, 12, 562, 604*f*, 723, 820
- on *Dennis v. United States*, 567, 569
- on executive power, 541–42, 892
- on *Korematsu v. United States*, 593–94
- overview of, 485*b*
- on *West Virginia State Board of Education v. Barnette*, 563–65
- on *Wickard v. Filburn*, 524–26, 545
- on *Youngstown Sheet & Tube Co. v. Sawyer*, 535–38

Jacksonian Era (1829–1860)
- cast of characters, 220*b*–221*b*
- citizenship in, 264, 266, 272–74, 277, 279, 282
- constitutional authority in, 225–31, 226*t*, 227*f*
- constitutional thought in, 221–22
- courts in, 221
- criminal justice in, 283–88
- Democratic Party in, 217–19, 219*f*, 223, 225, 227–29, 231–32, 244–45, 250, 264, 271–72, 274, 418
- democratic rights in, 265–71
- developments, 218
- due process in, 283–87
- equality in, 271–83
- federalism in, 244–49, 267
- foundations, 222–25
- free speech in, 266–71
- gender equality in, 281–83
- gun rights in, 264–65
- habeas corpus in, 283–87
- individual rights in, 258–65, 261*t*
- interest groups, 219
- interrogations in, 287–88
- introduction to, 217–22, 218*t*, 219*f*, 220*b*–221*b*
- Jeffersonians in, 219, 219*f*, 222
- judicial power in, 225–31, 226*t*, 227*f*
- legacies, 222
- major issues and decisions, 218*t*
- necessary and proper clause in, 232, 234, 237, 240
- personal freedom in, 265
- political parties in, 218–19, 219*f*, 222
- powers of national government in, 231–44
- principles, 223
- Prohibition in, 260–65, 261*t*
- property rights in, 258–64, 261*t*
- public morality in, 265
- punishments in, 288
- racial equality in, 272–81
- religious rights in, 264
- Republican Party in, 219, 219*f*, 223, 266, 274
- search and seizure in, 287
- separation of powers in, 249–58
- slavery in, 219, 223, 225–26, 231–32, 236–44, 265–81, 283–84
- spoils system, 227, 414–15
- strict construction in, 219, 221, 232
- voting rights in, 271
- Whigs in, 218–19, 219*f*, 223, 225, 227–29, 231–33, 250, 255, 264, 271, 418

Jacobs, Peter, 426–28
James, Eleazer, 205
Japanese Americans, detained, 12, 590–94
Javits, Jacob, 618
Jaworski, Leon, 640–41
Jay, John, 90, 179, 182
Jefferson, Thomas, 6, 43, 52, 112, 122, 135, 632. *See also* Declaration of Independence
- Bank of the United States and, 159–60, 162–63, 169
- Bill of Rights and, 74, 78, 82–83
- constitutional authority of, 17–18
- constitutional change and, 24
- on departmentalism, 151–52
- Embargo Act and, 158
- on executive power, 185–87
- free speech and, 199
- inaugural address, 205
- on Kentucky Resolutions, 137, 141, 143, 151, 180, 184–85, 199–200, 246, 248
- "Letter to the Danbury Baptists" by, 196, 437
- *Marbury v. Madison* and, 143, 145
- *Notes on the State of Virginia* by, 123–25
- originalism and, 10
- overview of, 136*b*
- Sedition Act and, 198–99, 571–72
- on separation of church and state, 195, 762
- slavery and, 85n15, 123–25
- strict construction by, 186–87
- *A Summary View of the Rights of British America* by, 58–59
- vetoes and, 187

Jeffersonians
- in Early National Era, 134–38, 135*f*, 143, 153, 178–80, 198–99, 203–5
- in Jacksonian Era, 219, 219*f*, 222

Jehovah's Witnesses, 563, 927–28
Jews, 195, 552
- American Jewish Congress, 432*t*
- Frank's conviction and death sentence mobilizing, 464
- *Near v. Minnesota* and, 449–50
- *United Jewish Organizations of Williamsburgh v. Carey* and, 582*t*, 668

Jim Crow, 454–55
- abolished, 589–90, 677
- adoption of, 453

Johnson, Andrew
- *Ex parte Milligan* and, 362
- impeachment of, 291–92, 311, 329, 333
- overview of, 294*b*
- Reconstruction and, 292–93, 295, 305, 311, 320–21, 324, 333, 350, 414
- vetoes by, 305, 311, 350

Johnson, Gregory, 783–86
Johnson, Lady Bird, 692
Johnson, Lyndon, 483, 505, 589, 658, 848
- election of, 486
- Great Society of, 477, 516
- Kerner Commission of, 608
- Voting Rights Act of 1965 and, 575

Johnson, Paul, 808–11
Johnson, Reverdy, 356–57
Johnson, T. A., 263
Johnson, William, 10, 138–39, 172, 175, 177
Jones, Edith, 916
Journal of Negro Education, 594–97
Joyce, Diane, 808–11
Joyce, Sean, 980
Judicial activism, 718
- of Burger Court, 629
- of polarized Supreme Court, 836
- of Warren Court, 482, 498, 629, 754

Judicial circuits, 225, 226*t*, 227*f*
Judicial power
- Black, Hugo, and, 496
- in Civil War and Reconstruction Era, 310–13
- in Colonial Era, 37–42
- in Contemporary Era, 846–55, 847*f*, 849*f*
- in Early National Era, 142–55, 144*t*, 179
- electoral accountability and, 226–29
- in Founding Era, 88–93
- in Jacksonian Era, 225–31, 226*t*, 227*f*

Judicial power (*continued*)
in Liberalism Divided Era, 623, 628–29
in New Deal and Great Society Era, 496–516, 497*f*
in Reagan Era, 722–32
in Republican Era, 376, 386–90, 386*f*
Judicial recall, 387–88
Judicial restraint, 19, 138, 145–51, 713, 718, 754
Judicial review, 18–21, 38, 724
Article VI and, 143
Bork on, 754
by Burger Court, 629, 631
in Early National Era, 142–43
in Founding Era, 88–93
in Republican Era, 376, 387
Judicial scrutiny, tiers of, 487, 487*t*
Judicial supremacy
constitutional authority and, 18, 310, 629
defined, 310
struggle over, 18, 141, 143, 498, 506–7, 719, 845, 847, 963
Judiciary. *See* Federal judiciary
Judiciary Act of 1789, 137, 142–43, 144*t*, 145, 152–53
Judiciary Act of 1801, 134*t*, 143, 145, 311
Judiciary Act of 1837, 226
Judiciary Act of 1862, 310
Judiciary Act of 1875, 311
Judiciary and Removal Act of 1875, 387
Jurisdiction
of courts, 142–43, 180, 312–13, 387
"federal questions," 387, 999
removal, 387
Jury trials
Balzac v. Porto Rico and, 380–82
Batson v. Kentucky and, 714*t*, 812, 821–26, 830
in Civil War and Reconstruction Era, 367
in Colonial Era, 62, 69
in Contemporary Era, 966
Duncan v. Louisiana and, 480*t*, 489–94, 490*t*, 722
in Early National Era, 212–14
in Founding Era, 127–29
Fourteenth Amendment and, 612
in Liberalism Divided Era, 701–2
Milligan and, 361–63
in New Deal and Great Society Era, 612–13
in Reagan Era, 821–26
in Republican Era, 470–73

Kagan, Elena, 835–36, 846, 961*f*
Kansas Constitutional Convention, 282
Katzenbach, Nicholas, 578–81
Keating–Owen Act, 400–401
Keck, Thomas, 836
Keith, Damon, 637–39
Kelo, Susette, 903–7
Kendall, Amos, 266–67
Kennedy, Anthony, 18, 715, 763*f*, 836, 856, 935
on abortion rights, 769–71
on *Arizona v. United States*, 877–78
on *Arkansas Educational Television Commission v. Forbes*, 927
aspirationalism and, 13
on *Boumediene v. Bush*, 841–44
on *Brown v. Plata*, 966
on *Church of the Babalu Aye v. Hialeah*, 759
on *Citizens United v. Federal Election Commission*, 931–32
on *City of Boerne v. Flores*, 850–52
on *Fisher v. University of Texas at Austin*, 950
on *Gonzales v. Carhart*, 916
on *Lawrence v. Texas*, 918–20
on *League of Latin American Citizens v. Perry*, 936
on *Lee v. Weisman*, 759–61
on *Legal Services Corporation v. Velazquez*, 928–29
on *Lucas v. South Carolina Coastal Council*, 757
on *Miller v. Johnson*, 936
overview of, 837*b*
on *Romer v. Evans*, 947
on *Rosenberger v. Rector and Visitors of University of Virginia*, 909
support for claimants in criminal procedure cases, 960, 961*f*
as swing vote, 14, 723, 727, 836, 841, 846, 902, 946, 960
on *Texas v. Johnson*, 784
on *Tuan Anh Nguyen v. I.N.S.*, 954–55
on *United States v. Alvarez*, 926
on *United States v. Lopez*, 861
Kennedy, Edward, 731–32
Kennedy, John F., 496, 554
Kentucky
Constitution, 197
Resolutions, 137, 141, 143, 151, 180, 184–85, 199–200, 246, 248
Kenyon, William, 378
Kerner Commission, 608
King, Martin Luther, Jr., 481, 483, 570–71, 589–90
King, Rufus, 105
King, Samuel, 229
Klarman, Michael, 590, 918
Knight, Jack, 16
Knox, John B., 459–61
Koh, Harold, 840, 968
Kohler Act, 424
Kolbert, Kathryn, 770
Korean War, 533–34, 537, 539–40, 892
Korematsu, Fred Toyosaburo, 590–94
Krass, Caroline D., 899–901
Ku Klux Klan, 314
Brandenburg and, 573–74
in Reconstruction, 293

Labor and wage regulation. *See also* Unions
FLSA and, 630, 736–38
National Labor Relations Board v. Jones & Laughlin Steel Corp. and, 391*t*, 480*t*, 517, 520–24, 740, 859
Schechter Poultry Corp. v. United States and, 157*t*, 516, 518–20, 522–23
Laissez-faire economics, 135, 374
Lambda Legal, 432*t*
Landmark Briefs and Arguments of the Supreme Court of the United States, 998
Landry, Herman, 490
Latter-Day Saints. *See* Mormons
Law. *See also* Common law; Equality under law; Federal laws; Martial law; State laws
applied, 998
constitutional politics and, 24–25
fundamental, constitution as, 5–6
general, 348
international, 377, 719, 839–40
natural, 138–39, 191, 222
rule of, 5–8
Supreme Court invalidating, 386*f*, 497*f*, 847*f*
Law of nations, 13, 237
in Civil War and Reconstruction Era, 337, 339–40
in Early National Era, 138–39
in Founding Era, 77, 82
Lawrence, John, 918
Lawyers. *See also* Counsel, right to
American Bar Association for, 372, 410, 722, 726, 886
in Civil War and Reconstruction Era, 367
in Colonial Era, 69
in Contemporary Era, 966
in Early National Era, 212–14
in Founding Era, 128–29
in Liberalism Divided Era, 701–2
in New Deal and Great Society Era, 612–13
in Reagan Era, 821–26
in Republican Era, 470–73
Lawyers' Edition, United States Reports, 998
League of Nations, 403
Leahy, Patrick, 970–71
Lee, Mrs., 317
Lee, Richard Henry, 93
Lee, Robert, 759–60
Lee, Robert E., 291, 293
"The Left-Wing Manifesto" (Gitlow), 446

Legal issue, 998
Legal literature, researching and reading, 1005–6
Legal model, 16
Legal Services Corporation, 481
Legal Tender Act of 1862
controversies, 313, 341
Hepburn v. Griswold and, 311, 313–17, 319–20
Legal Tender Cases and, 157*t*, 292*t*, 313–14, 317–20
Legg, Benson, 910
Legislative classifications, tiers of scrutiny of, 487*t*
Legislative districts, apportioned by states, 509, 581, 582*t*–583*t*, 583–85. *See also* Gerrymandering
Leon, Alberto, 816–20
A Letter Concerning Toleration (Locke), 46, 48–53
"Letter from the Attorney General to Congress on Litigation Involving the Defense of Marriage Act" (Holder), 924–25
Letters from a Farmer in Pennsylvania (Dickinson), 42
"Letter to the Danbury Baptists" (Jefferson), 196, 437
"Letter to the Jews of Newport" (Washington), 195
Levin, Daniel, 893, 898–99
Levinson, Sanford, 24, 768–69
Lexis-Nexis, 998, 1003–4, 1006
Libel
blood, 464
criminal, 380–82
in *New York Times Co. v. Sullivan*, 480*t*, 570–72, 621*t*, 658, 781
seditious, 53–55
Liberalism, 33, 59
heyday of, 477–79, 481, 485
traditions, 76
Liberalism Divided Era (1969–1980)
abortion rights in, 648–57, 649*f*, 654*f*
cast of characters, 622*b*
constitutional authority in, 628–29
constitutional thought in, 620, 621*t*
contracts in, 643
courts in, 619
criminal justice in, 630, 695–707, 696*f*
Democratic Party in, 617–19, 618*f*, 643, 647–48, 663, 677
democratic rights in, 657–73
due process in, 696–99
equality in, 617, 626–28, 673–95
federalism in, 630–31
foundations, 623–29, 628*f*
free speech in, 657–67
gay rights in, 649–50
gender equality in, 617, 689–95
gun rights in, 647–48
habeas corpus in, 695–99
individual rights in, 643–57, 649*f*, 654*f*
interest groups in, 618–19
interrogations in, 699–701
introduction to, 617–23, 618*f*, 621*t*, 622*b*
judicial power in, 623, 628–29
juries in, 701–2
lawyers in, 701–2
legacies, 621, 623
major issues and decisions, 621*t*
personal freedom in, 648–57, 649*f*, 654*f*
political parties in, 617–18, 618*f*
powers of national government in, 629–30
principles, 624–26
property rights in, 643–44
public morality in, 648–57, 649*f*, 654*f*
punishments in, 617, 696, 702–6, 703*f*
racial equality in, 626–28, 677–89
religious rights in, 644–47
search and seizure in, 697, 699
separation of powers in, 631–43
voting rights in, 667–73
war powers in, 631–39
Liberal Protestants, 552
Libertarians, 198–99, 619, 713, 715
Liberty, 44, 348. *See also* Constitutional rights and liberties
Blackstone on, 384
blessings of, 109–10
in Fourteenth Amendment, 413, 432, 438–40, 651, 653–54, 705
meaning of, 413, 427, 432, 438, 493, 919
Webster on, 244
Libya, 717, 899–901
Lincoln, Abraham, 4, 16, 219, 222, 387, 541
capital punishment and, 367
in Civil War and Reconstruction Era, 291–93, 295–96, 304–5, 310, 314, 324–29, 333–37, 342–45, 349, 357–62, 367
Douglas, Stephen, debating, 310
Dred Scott v. Sandford and, 18–20, 310
election of, 272–93, 324, 326
Emancipation Proclamation by, 291, 333–36
first inaugural address of, 327–29, 388, 500
free speech and, 342
Gettysburg Address by, 305
habeas corpus and, 291, 342–45, 357–61
on Mexican War, 250
overview of, 294*b*
on slavery in the territories, 243–44
unilateral actions of, 333
Line-item veto, 885
Liquor license, 626–28
Litt, Robert, 979
Liu, Goodwin, 850
Living Constitution, 376, 379, 388, 421, 854
Holmes on, 404
in New Deal and Great Society Era, 483, 720
Rehnquist on, 625, 723–25
Warren on, 483
Livingston, Robert, 172
Local zoning ordinances, 423–24
Locke, John, 33, 36, 40, 45, 76, 620
Declaration of Independence and, 84
A Letter Concerning Toleration by, 46, 48–53
Louisiana Purchase, 17–18, 133, 142, 186
Lucas, David, 755–58
Lumpkin, Joseph Henry, 223
Lynch, Sandra, 909
Lynching, Congressional debate over, 393–95
Lyon, Matthew, 199

MacKinnon, Catharine, 690
MADD. *See* Mothers Against Drunk Driving
Madison, James, 135, 178, 217, 416, 632, 880
Bank of the United States and, 156, 159–61, 169
Constitution and, 8, 22–24, 71, 73–74, 82–83, 88, 95–96, 98–102, 104–5, 119, 122, 858
on departmentalism, 18
The Federalist Papers No. 10 by, 85–87, 110, 117
The Federalist Papers No. 37 by, 23
The Federalist Papers No. 40 by, 22
The Federalist Papers No. 51 by, 106–7, 186, 976
The Federalist Papers No. 57 by, 122
internal improvements and, 159, 176
overview of, 72*b*
religious rights and, 112–16, 195, 437, 762
on removal of executive officers, 187–88
Sedition Act and, 198–200, 268, 571
separation of powers and, 541, 976
vetoes by, 187–88
Virginia Plan and, 73, 93, 95–96, 98–99, 482
Virginia Report of 1799 by, 200–202
Virginia Resolutions and, 137, 143, 151, 180, 183–84, 199–200, 248
Magna Carta, 35–36, 62–63, 81
Magruder, Benjamin, 421
Mahon, H. J., 424–26
Majoritarian, 19–21, 625
Majority-minority districts, 668, 789, 935

Majority opinion, author and legal reasoning of, 1002
Malcolm, Joyce Lee, 52
Malice, 571–72
Mansfield, Lord, 59, 61
Manufacture, commerce and, 398–99
Mapp, Dollree, 605–7
Marbury, William, 145–51
Marriage. *See also* Same-sex marriage
  birth control in, 556–61
  defined, 650
  interracial, 556
  polygamous, 435–38
Marshall, John, 16, 143, 180, 388, 541
  on *Barron v. Baltimore*, 224–25
  on executive power, 662
  on *Fletcher v. Peck*, 191, 193–95
  "A Friend of the Constitution" by, 169, 171–72
  on *Gibbons v. Ogden*, 172–75, 245, 529, 873
  on *Little v. Barreme*, 538
  on *Marbury v. Madison*, 145–51, 508, 724
  on *McCulloch v. Maryland*, 156, 160, 164–72, 179, 232, 315–16, 468, 579
  on obligation and remedy, 546
  overview of, 136*b*
Marshall, Margaret, 917
Marshall, Thurgood, 17, 604*f*, 619, 623, 763*f*
  attitudinal model and, 14–15, 14*f*
  on *Batson v. Kentucky*, 824–25
  Brown v. Board of Education and, 596
  on *Buckley v. Valeo*, 667
  on capital punishment, 702, 706–7
  on *City of Cleburne, Texas v. Cleburne Living Center*, 797
  on *City of Richmond v. J. A. Croson Co.*, 802, 806–7
  on *City of Rome v. United States*, 788
  on *Dunn v. Blumstein*, 668
  on *Frontiero v. Richardson*, 693
  on *Harris v. New York*, 701
  on jury trials, 822, 824–25
  on *Miranda* warnings, 820
  Moose Lodge No. 107 v. Irvis and, 627–28
  on *New York Times Co. v. United States*, 661–62
  overview of, 484*b*
  on *Plyler v. Doe*, 800
  on *Regents of the University of California v. Bakke*, 685–87
  on *Richardson v. Ramirez*, 673
  on *San Antonio Independent School District v. Rodriguez*, 676–77
  success of, 589
  A Theory of Justice and, 625
  on *Washington v. Davis*, 689
Martial law
  in Civil War and Reconstruction Era, 291–93, 310–12, 357–58, 362, 364, 367
  Ex parte Milligan and, 292*t*, 293–94, 310, 338*t*, 357, 361–66, 974
Martin, Denny, 152
Martin, Luther, 111, 193
Maryland Toleration Act, 45
Mason, George, 72*b*, 74, 117
Mason, Priscilla, 209
Massachusetts, 37, 41–42
  Body of Liberties, 35, 70–71
  Constitution, 122, 195–96, 202–5, 280
  property qualifications debated in, 202–4
  slavery in, 123, 280
Massachusetts Circular Letter of February 11, 1768 (Adams, S.), 37
Mather, Cotton, 65
Matthews, Stanley, 454
McCain, John, 886, 929, 969
McCardle, William, 311
McCarthy, Eugene, 658, 663
McCarthy, Joe, 562
McCleskey, Warren, 827–31
McCloskey, Robert, 274
McCormick, Joseph, 229
McCorvey, Norma, 650–55
McCulloch, James, 164
McGovern, George, 681
McIlwain, Charles, 5
McKay, James, 747
McKenna, Joseph, 423
McKinley, John, 226*t*
McKinley, William, 441
McLean, John, 226*t*, 242, 247
  on *Dred Scott v. Sandford*, 274, 277
  on *Prigg v. Pennsylvania*, 237, 239
McMillan, James, 679
McNamara, Robert, 658
McReynolds, James, 7, 543–44, 548, 550
  in Four Horsemen, 496
  on *Meyer v. Nebraska*, 439–40
  on *Myers v. United States*, 417
  on *National Labor Relations Board v. Jones & Laughlin Steel Corp.*, 523–24
  on *United States v. Miller*, 556
Meeker, Leonard, 632
Meese, Edwin, 716*b*, 719–20, 722–23, 726
Memoranda on Standards of Conduct of Interrogation. *See* "Torture Memos"
Memorandum on the Legality of the United States Participation in the Defense of Vietnam (Meeker), 632
Memorandum Opinion on the Authority to Use Military Force in Libya (Krass), 899–901
Memo to Alberto R. Gonzales, Counsel to the President (Bybee), 894–96
Memo to James B. Comey, Deputy Attorney General (Levin), 898–99
Memo to William Haynes II, General Counsel of the Department of Defense (Yoo), 896–98
Mere evidence rule, 465
Merryman, John, 358
Mexican War, 250, 266, 272
Meyer, Robert T., 438–40
Michelman, Frank, 623, 625, 643
Michels, Robert, 8
Migratory Bird Treaty Act, 403
Military draft, 291, 690–91
Militias, 117, 196, 264, 556, 910–14
Miller, Samuel, 305–9, 407–8
Milligan, Lambdin, 361–64
Milnut, 487–88
Minimum drinking age, 733
Minimum wage, 374*t*, 423, 549–51
Minnesota Moratorium Law of 1932, 546
Minton, Sherman, 494, 524, 540, 567, 604*f*
Miranda, Ernesto, 608–12
Miranda warnings
  Dickerson v. United States and, 962–66
  Harris v. New York and, 695, 700–701, 964
  Miranda v. Arizona and, 478–79, 480*t*, 603, 608–12, 695–96, 699–701, 715, 717, 721, 811–12, 820–21, 960, 962–66
Missouri Compromise, 138, 206–8, 206*f*, 232, 273
Mitchell, John, 637, 640
Mitchell, M. H., 227–28
Mob violence, 395, 464
Model Penal Code (MPC), 702–3
Monopolies
  Sherman Anti-Trust Act and, 373, 390, 395–400, 519, 533
  Slaughter-House Cases on, 305–9
  steamboat, 172
Monroe, James
  internal improvements and, 159, 176–78
  overview of, 136*b*
Moose Lodge No. 107, 626–28
The Morality of Consent (Bickel), 620
Moral Majority, 644, 713
Morgan, Christine, 578–81
Morgan, John P., 578–81
Morgan, Margaret, 236
Mormons, 435–38, 552
Morris, Gouverneur, 122
Morrison, Alan, 743
Morrison, Alexina, 747–54
Morrison, Norman, 139
Morse, Samuel, 264
Morton, J., 473–74
Mothers Against Drunk Driving (MADD), 734

Mott, Lucretia, 282
MoveOn.org, 835
MPC. *See* Model Penal Code
Muller, Curt, 432–34
Murphy, Frank, 22, 563, 565, 592–93, 604*f*
Murphy, Walter, 22
Myers, Frank S., 414–18
Myers, Henry, 378–79

NAACP. *See* National Association for the Advancement of Colored People
Nader, Ralph, 743
Nash, Nathaniel, 434
National Association for the Advancement of Colored People (NAACP), 370, 372, 376, 393, 471, 597
  free speech of, 562
  influence of, 619
  Legal Defense Fund, 432*t*, 589, 613, 673, 936
  liberalism and, 481
  Niagara Movement and, 455
National Center for Law and Economic Justice, 432*t*
National Consumers' League, 432*t*, 433
National Federation of Independent Business (NFIB), 857, 864–76
National government. *See also* Powers of national government; Separation of powers
  branches, 102, 107
  compact theory and, 178–79
  limits on, 625
  partisan control of, 135*f*, 219*f*, 370*f*, 477*f*, 712*f*, 740–41, 833
  responsibilities of, 478
  trust in, 712*f*
National Industrial Recovery Act (NIRA), 516, 518
Nationalism, 244–45
National Labor Relations Act, 517, 520–24
National Labor Relations Board (NLRB), 391*t*, 480*t*, 520–24
National Organization for Women (NOW), 690
National Popular Government League, 464
National Republicans, 137, 156, 159–60, 179, 218
National Rifle Association (NRA), 648, 713, 768, 835, 879
National Security Agency (NSA), 887, 969–70, 977–81
National Woman's Party, 461–63
National Woman Suffrage Association (NWSA), 372
Native Americans, 945, 947
  The Cherokee Nation v. Georgia and, 511
  Dawes Act and, 453
  Employment Division v. Smith and, 714*t*, 759, 763–68, 850–52
  Seminole Tribe of Florida v. Florida and, 878
  status of, 511
Natural law, 138–39, 191, 222
Natural rights, 6, 278
Nazis, 562–653, 618
Near, Jay, 449–51
Necessary and proper clause, 579–80
  in Contemporary Era, 867, 872, 881, 894, 906
  in Jacksonian Era, 232, 234, 237, 240
Negative commerce clause. *See* Dormant commerce clause
Negative rights, 7, 482
Nelson, Samuel, 226*t*, 339–40
"Neutral Principles and Some First Amendment Problems" (Bork), 620
New Deal, 620, 711, 715, 855
  Constitution and, 486
  Great Society building on, 517
  independent regulatory commissions and, 533
  powers of national government and, 516
New Deal and Great Society Era (1933–1968)
  cast of characters, 484*b*–485*b*
  constitutional authority in, 496–516, 497*f*
  constitutional thought in, 482–83
  contracts in, 545–48
  courts in, 498, 500–505
  criminal justice in, 603–14, 604*f*
  Democratic Party in, 477–79, 477*f*, 486, 556, 581
  democratic rights in, 561–86, 574*f*, 582*t*–583*t*
  developments, 477–79
  due process in, 603–4
  equality in, 586–603, 587*t*–588*t*, 602*f*
  executive power in, 533
  federalism in, 531, 531*t*–532*t*
  foundations, 486–96, 487*t*, 490*t*
  free speech in, 561–74
  gender equality in, 586, 603
  gun rights in, 556
  habeas corpus in, 603–4, 612–13
  individual rights in, 438, 545–61, 553*t*, 555*t*
  interest groups, 479–81
  interrogations in, 607–12
  introduction to, 477–85, 477*f*, 480*t*, 482*f*, 484*b*–485*b*
  judicial power in, 496–516, 497*f*
  juries in, 612–13
  lawyers in, 612–13
  legacies, 483–85
  living Constitution in, 483, 720
  major issues and decisions, 480*t*
  personal freedom in, 556–61
  political parties in, 479
  powers of national government in, 481, 516–30
  principles, 486–88, 487*t*
  property rights in, 489, 545–52
  public morality in, 556–61
  punishments in, 613–14
  racial equality in, 479, 483, 486–96, 505–9, 514, 517, 526–30, 574–75, 574*f*, 586, 589–602, 602*f*
  religious rights in, 552–56, 553*t*, 555*t*
  Republican Party in, 477–79, 477*f*, 556, 581
  search and seizure in, 604–7
  segregation in, 589–602, 602*f*
  separation of powers in, 533–44
  Supreme Court's role in, 478–79, 481–82, 482*f*, 496–505, 497*f*, 516–17, 520–21
  voting rights in, 478–79, 517, 562, 574–86, 574*f*, 582*t*–583*t*
New Hampshire Constitution, 210
New Jersey Constitution, 128
New Jersey Plan, 93, 96–99
New Mexico Constitution, 389
"The New Property" (Reich), 643
New York Constitution, 112
NFIB. *See* National Federation of Independent Business
Niagara Movement, 454–55
Nicholas, George, 213
Nichols, Samuel, 382
Nineteenth Amendment, 23, 993
  state reforms and, 406
  women's suffrage and, 372, 377, 453
Ninth Amendment, 557, 559, 561, 651–53, 991
NIRA. *See* National Industrial Recovery Act
Nixon, Richard, 477, 486, 562, 603, 620, 811
  ambivalence of, 617
  election of, 609, 618, 621, 623, 626, 711
  executive power and, 617, 623, 631, 639–43, 657, 661
  gun rights and, 647
  impeachment and, 631, 640
  against judicial activism, 629
  Pentagon Papers and, 623, 657–63
  on Presidential Commission on Obscenity and Pornography, 658
  on racial equality, 677–78, 681–82
  religious rights and, 644, 758
  Southern strategy of, 618
  Supreme Court nominations of, 619, 630, 695, 715, 722, 846, 848
  in *United States v. Nixon*, 621*t*, 631, 639–43
  vetoes by, 634, 636–37
  Voting Rights Act of 1970 signed by, 669
  Watergate and, 631, 636, 639–43, 747

NLRB. *See* National Labor Relations Board
Nobel Peace Prize, 414
Non-commandeering, 877
Non-conformists, 47
Non-English speakers, discrimination against, 578
Nonmajoritarian, 19–21
Nonsectarian prayer, 552–54
Normative controversies, 9
North, Oliver, 741
Northwest Ordinance, 77, 232, 243
Notes on the State of Virginia (Jefferson), 123–25
"The Notion of a Living Constitution" (Rehnquist), 723–25
NOW. *See* National Organization for Women
Nozick, Robert, 626
NRA. *See* National Rifle Association
NSA. *See* National Security Agency
Nullification, 246, 248–49
NWSA. *See* National Woman Suffrage Association

Oath ex officio, 67
Obama, Barack, 840, 846, 850, 908, 931, 948
  ACA and, 864–65
  election of, 833, 835, 857
  Libya bombing by, 899–901
  on NSA, 970, 977
  same-sex marriage supported by, 917, 922, 924–25
  in War on Terror, 968–70
Obligation, remedy and, 546
Obscenity, 658, 781
O'Connor, Sandra Day, 763*f*, 808, 812, 822, 877, 916
  on abortion rights, 769–71
  on *Adarand Constructors, Inc. v. Peña*, 948–49
  on *Agostini v. Felton*, 907–8
  on *City of Boerne v. Flores*, 852–53
  on *City of Richmond v. J. A. Croson Co.*, 803–5
  on *Employment Division v. Smith*, 764–67, 851
  on *Ewing v. California*, 967
  on *Garcia v. San Antonio Metropolitan Transit Authority*, 739–40
  on *General Motors Corp. v. Romein*, 755–56
  on *Grutter v. Bollinger*, 949–52
  on *Hamdi v. Rumsfeld*, 973–75
  on *Herrera v. Collins*, 814
  on *Johnson v. Transportation Agency, Santa Clara County*, 810
  on *Lawrence v. Texas*, 920–21
  on *Lee v. Weisman*, 759, 761
  on *National Endowment for the Arts v. Finley*, 928
  overview of, 716*b*
  on polarized Supreme Court, 836
  Reagan nominating, 624, 715, 722, 735
  on *Shaw v. Reno*, 794–95
  on *South Dakota v. Dole*, 733–35
  support for claimants in criminal procedure cases, 960, 961*f*
  as swing vote, 723, 836, 841, 846, 902, 946, 960
  tests employed by, 717, 755, 907
  on *Virginia v. Black*, 927
Office of Legal Counsel (OLC), 887, 893, 899. *See also* "Torture Memos"
Office of Legal Policy, 720–22, 754, 781, 797, 820
Of Offences Against God and Religion (Blackstone), 46–48
Ogden, Aaron, 172
Ohio Constitutional Convention, 226–29, 387
OLC. *See* Office of Legal Counsel
Old Republicans, 134, 136, 159–60. *See also* Jeffersonians
Ollie's Barbecue, 528
Olmstead, Roy, 467–70
Olson, Theodore, 747–54, 837*b*
Omnibus Crime Control Act of 1970, 630
Omnibus Crime Control and Safe Streets Act of 1968, 637–38, 962–63
On Punishing Murder by Death (Rush), 129–30
"Opinion on the Power of the President in Executing the Laws" (Black, J.), 326–27
Opinion on the Suspension of the Privilege of the Writ of Habeas Corpus (Bates), 359–61
Oregon System, 406
Organized Crime Control Act of 1970, 630
Originalism, 10, 715, 717–18
O'Sullivan, John L., 265
Otis, Harrison, 199
Otis, James, 31, 32*b*, 35–36, 41
Our Chief Magistrate and His Powers (Taft), 419–20

Pacific Legal Foundation, 713, 733
"Paper on the Removal of the Deposits" (Jackson, A.), 251–52
Parker v. Hurley, 909
Parkman, Francis, 453
Parrish, Elise, 549–50
Partial-birth abortion, 916
Parties. *See* Political parties
Party ballot, 369
Paterson, William, 93, 96
Patriot Act, 960, 969–73, 977
Patrons of Husbandry, 409–10
Paul, Alice, 461
Paul, Rand, 899
Peace Democrats, 291
Peck, John, 193
Peckham, Rufus, 428–30, 434
Pelosi, Nancy, 857
Penn, William, 32*b*, 45–46, 69
Pennsylvania
  Bill of Rights, 912–13
  Constitution, 120–21, 128
  ratification debates, 78–80
Pennsylvania Abortion Control Act, 770–77
Penrose, Boies, 377–78
Pentagon Papers, 623, 657–63
Perot, H. Ross, 833
Personal freedom. *See also* Abortion rights; Free speech; Gay rights
  Buck v. Bell and, 438, 440–41, 453, 556, 587*t*
  in Civil War and Reconstruction Era, 341–42
  in Colonial Era, 52–53
  in Contemporary Era, 915–25
  in Early National Era, 198
  in Founding Era, 117
  Griswold v. Connecticut and, 423*t*, 432*t*, 480*t*, 556–61, 648, 650, 652–53, 721, 915
  in Jacksonian Era, 265
  in Liberalism Divided Era, 648–57, 649*f*, 654*f*
  in New Deal and Great Society Era, 556–61
  in Reagan Era, 769–80
  in Republican Era, 438–41
Petty, Maximilian, 36
Peyote, 763–66
Philippines, 377, 381
Phillips, Wendell, 223
Pinckney, Charles, 100, 105, 111
Pinello, Dan, 918
Pitney, Mahlon, 464
Plamondon, Robert, 637–39
Planned Parenthood, 557–58
Plea bargaining, 288, 470, 696
Plessy, Homer, 455–59
Pluralism, 441
Plural marriage. *See* Polygamy
Plyler, James, 798–801
Poe, Ted, 977
Poindexter, John, 741
Police power, 306–7, 373, 443, 456–57
Political parties. *See also specific parties*
  in Civil War and Reconstruction Era, 292–93
  in Contemporary Era, 834–35
  in Early National Era, 133–37, 135*f*
  formation of, 133
  in Jacksonian Era, 218–19, 219*f*, 222
  in Liberalism Divided Era, 617–18, 618*f*

national government controlled by, 135*f*, 219*f*, 370*f*, 477*f*, 712*f*, 740–41, 833
in New Deal and Great Society Era, 479
in Reagan Era, 711–13, 712*f*
in Republican Era, 370–71, 370*f*, 372*t*
in South, 617, 618*f*
Political questions, 229–30, 510–11, 514
Political rights, 7
Political scandals
independent counsel and, 747–54
Iran-Contra scandal, 741, 747
Watergate, 631, 636, 639–43
Whitewater, 747–48
Politics. *See also* Constitutional politics
constitutionalism influencing, 9–10
of democracy, transformed, 780
organizing of, 6–7
polarized, 835–36, 846, 884, 901
Politics (Aristotle), 4–5
Polk, James, 218, 221, 250, 266
Poll tax, 574
Polygamy, 435–38
Pomeroy, John Norton, 410
Pomeroy, Samuel, 341
Popular constitutionalism, 838
Populist Party, 371–72, 372*t*, 420–21
federalism and, 405–6
income tax and, 392
Pornography, 658, 781
Positive rights, 6–7, 482–83
Posner, Richard, 620
Postmaster, removal of, 414–18
Post office, incendiary publications and, 266–71
Post Office Act of 1836, 267
Powe, Scot, 485
Powell, Adam Clayton, Jr., 629
Powell, Lazarus, 299
Powell, Lewis, 723, 763*f*
appointment of, 619, 695
attitudinal model and, 14–15, 14*f*
on *Batson v. Kentucky*, 823–24
on *Bowers v. Hardwick*, 778–79
on capital punishment, 703–4, 826–29
on *Frontiero v. Richardson*, 694–95
on *Garcia v. San Antonio Metropolitan Transit Authority*, 738–39
on *Immigration and Naturalization Service v. Chadha*, 744
on *McCleskey v. Kemp*, 826–29
on *Moore v. City of East Cleveland, Ohio*, 649
on *Nixon v. Fitzgerald*, 641
overview of, 622*b*
on *Plyler v. Doe*, 800
on *Regents of the University of California v. Bakke*, 683–85
on *San Antonio Independent School District v. Rodriguez*, 644, 675–76
on *Stone v. Powell*, 696–97
on *United States v. United States District Court*, 637–39, 699
on *Village of Arlington Heights v. Metropolitan Housing Development Corp.*, 679
on *Weber v. Aetna Casualty & Surety Co.*, 674
on *Wygant v. Jackson Board of Education*, 803
Powell, Ozie, 471
Power, Lucas, 603
Powers. *See also* Executive power; Judicial power; Separation of powers; War powers
enumerated, 78
implied, 98, 156, 160, 165–66, 319
police, 306–7, 373, 443, 456–57
Powers of national government
in Article I, 155–56, 414, 516–17, 630, 734, 743–46, 882, 894, 896, 900
Articles of Confederation and, 93–98, 179
in Civil War and Reconstruction Era, 313–23
in Colonial Era, 43
Congress and, 155–56, 207, 231, 277–78, 285, 365–66, 372, 392, 395, 399–402, 539
in Contemporary Era, 855–76, 856*f*
in Early National Era, 155–78, 157*t*–158*t*
FDR and, 516–18, 520–21
in Founding Era, 93–99
Heart of Atlanta Motel, Inc. v. United States and, 517, 528–30, 737
in Jacksonian Era, 231–44
in Liberalism Divided Era, 629–30
National Federation of Independent Business v. Sebelius and, 517, 857, 864–76
National Labor Relations Board v. Jones & Laughlin Steel Corp. and, 391*t*, 480*t*, 517, 520–24, 740, 859
in New Deal and Great Society Era, 481, 516–30
in Reagan Era, 732–35
in Republican Era, 390–405, 391*t*–392*t*
Schechter Poultry Corp. v. United States and, 157*t*, 516, 518–20, 522–23
South Dakota v. Dole and, 733–35
taxation, 167–68, 174, 178
United States v. Lopez and, 392*t*, 834*t*, 856–64
Wickard v. Filburn and, 391*t*, 517, 524–26, 545, 721, 737, 859, 864, 867, 873–74
Pragmatists, 379
Prayer
nonsectarian, 552–54
in schools, 552–56, 553*t*, 555*t*, 759–63, 907
teacher attitudes on, 553*t*
Precedent, 138–39, 497*f*, 770–76, 854–55
Preferred freedoms, 486, 620
President. *See* Executive branch
"Presidential Authority to Decline to Execute Unconstitutional Statutes" (Dellinger), 887–89
Presidential Commission on Obscenity and Pornography, 658
Presidential power. *See* Executive power
"The President's Constitutional Authority to Conduct Military Operations" (Yoo), 890–93
Press, freedom of, 81
Blackstone on, 449, 451
Near v. Minnesota and, 374*t*, 442*t*, 444, 449–51, 490*t*
New York Times Co. v. Sullivan and, 480*t*, 570–72, 621*t*, 658, 781
New York Times Co. v. United States and, 657–63
Price, Victoria, 471
Prigg, Edward, 236
Printz, Jay, 879–84
Prior history, 998
Privacy
Griswold v. Connecticut and, 423*t*, 432*t*, 480*t*, 556–61, 648, 650, 652–53, 721, 915
Guidelines on Constitutional Litigation on, 720–21
rights, 557–61, 604–6, 638, 648–55, 720–21
Roe v. Wade and, 648, 650–55
Privileges and immunities clause, 342, 354
Privy Council, 38, 65, 88
Procedural rights, 7
Progressive Era. *See* Republican Era
Progressives, 371, 372*t*, 373, 387, 479, 623
administration and, 415
Blanket Amendment and, 461
for eugenic sterilization, 440–41
federalism and, 405–6
on free speech, 441, 444
government limits and, 625
independent regulatory commissions and, 533
individual rights and, 421, 428, 433, 438
Prohibition
Anti-Saloon League for, 373, 377
Congressional debate over, 377–79
Eighteenth Amendment and, 377, 486
in Jacksonian Era, 260–65, 261*t*
major state statutes, 261*t*
repeal, 486
World War I and, 377

Property qualifications, for voting, 202–4, 202*f*–203*f*
Property rights
 in Civil War and Reconstruction Era, 340–41
 in Colonial Era, 44–45
 in Contemporary Era, 902–7
 in Early National Era, 190–95, 258
 Fifth Amendment and, 110, 279, 425, 755, 903–5
 in Founding Era, 110–11
 gender equality and, 282
 Home Building & Loan Association v. Blaisdell and, 192*t*, 480*t*, 545–48
 in Jacksonian Era, 258–64, 261*t*
 Kelo v. City of New London and, 834*t*, 902–7
 in Liberalism Divided Era, 643–44
 Lochner v. New York and, 421, 428–32
 Lucas v. South Carolina Coastal Council and, 755–58
 Muller v. Oregon and, 432–34
 in New Deal and Great Society Era, 489, 545–52
 Pennsylvania Coal Co. v. Mahon and, 424–26
 Proprietors of the Charles River Bridge v. Proprietors of the Warren Bridge and, 191*t*, 218*t*, 258–60
 in Reagan Era, 754–58
 In re Jacobs and, 374*t*, 421, 426–28
 in Republican Era, 410–13, 421–34, 422*t*–423*t*, 432*t*
 slavery and, 276, 297–99
 state constitutions and, 110
 West Coast Hotel Co. v. Parrish and, 422*t*, 545, 549–50
 Williamson v. Lee Optical Co. and, 422*t*, 551–52
 World War I and, 423
 Wynehamer v. People and, 218*t*, 260–64
"Protection for Women Workers" (Hamilton, Alice), 463
Protestants, 264, 552
"Protest of the Censure Resolution" (Jackson, A.), 254–55
Prudentialism, 12
Public fora, 927
Public morality
 Buck v. Bell and, 438, 440–41
 in Colonial Era, 52–53
 in Contemporary Era, 915–25
 in Early National Era, 198
 in Founding Era, 117
 Griswold v. Connecticut and, 423*t*, 432*t*, 480*t*, 556–61, 648, 650, 652–53, 721, 915
 in Jacksonian Era, 265
 in Liberalism Divided Era, 648–57, 649*f*, 654*f*
 Meyer v. Nebraska and, 438–40
 in New Deal and Great Society Era, 556–61
 in Reagan Era, 769–80
 in Republican Era, 438–41
Public use clause, 902–7
Puerto Rico
 acquisition of, 377, 381
 Balzac v. Porto Rico and, 380–82
 voting rights and, 578–79
Pugh, George E., 344–45
Punishments. *See also* Capital punishment
 in Civil War and Reconstruction Era, 367
 in Colonial Era, 69–70
 in Contemporary Era, 960–61, 966–68
 cruel and unusual, 4, 473–74, 614, 702, 715
 in Early National Era, 214–15
 in Founding Era, 129–30
 in Jacksonian Era, 288
 in Liberalism Divided Era, 617, 696, 702–6, 703*f*
 in New Deal and Great Society Era, 613–14
 in Reagan Era, 718, 826–31, 827*f*
 in Republican Era, 473–74
Puritans, 45

Qadhafi, Muammar, 899
Quakers, 45–46, 59, 69
Quarles, Benjamin, 820
Quebec, 31
Quincy, Josiah, 204

Racial equality. *See also* Affirmative action; Segregation; Slavery
 civil rights strategy debate, 594–97
 in Civil War and Reconstruction Era, 293, 349–53, 483
 in Colonial Era, 58–61
 in Contemporary Era, 948–54
 in Early National Era, 206–8, 206*f*
 in Founding Era, 122–25
 gun rights and, 264–65
 in Jacksonian Era, 272–81
 Korematsu v. United States and, 12, 480*t*, 590–94
 in Liberalism Divided Era, 626–28, 677–89
 lynching and, 393–95
 in New Deal and Great Society Era, 479, 483, 486–96, 505–9, 514, 517, 526–30, 574–75, 574*f*, 586, 589–602, 602*f*
 Nixon on, 677–78, 681–82
 Plessy v. Ferguson and, 17, 374*t*, 454–59, 483, 587*t*, 589, 597, 599–600, 770, 772, 776, 854–55
 in Reagan Era, 801–7
 in Republican Era, 372, 379, 393–95, 454–61
 Roberts v. City of Boston and, 272, 279–81
 Second Freedmen's Bureau Act and, 350–53
 Washington v. Davis and, 679, 688–89
Railroad regulation, 405–9
Ramirez, Abram, 672
Randolph, A. Philip, 589–90
Randolph, Edmund, 93, 103, 105–6, 159, 180–81
Randolph, John, 136, 159
Ranger estate, 205
Rational basis test, 487*t*, 586, 717, 870, 917
Rawls, John, 620, 625
Reading. *See* Researching and reading, of government documents
Reagan, Ronald, 621, 629, 644, 696, 768, 797
 against abortion rights, 769
 Brady and, 879
 election of, 711, 718
 gun rights and, 647
 in Iran-Contra scandal, 741, 747
 overview of, 716*b*
 religious rights and, 758
 Supreme Court nominations by, 624, 715, 722–23, 727–33, 735, 741, 811, 848
 vetoes by, 741
Reagan Era (1981–1993)
 amendments proposed in, 718–19
 cast of characters, 716*b*
 constitutional authority in, 722–32
 constitutional thought in, 715–17
 courts in, 715
 criminal justice in, 811–31, 960
 Democratic Party in, 711–13, 712*f*, 733, 740–41, 747, 787–88, 807–8
 democratic rights in, 780–96
 developments, 711
 due process in, 812–16
 equality in, 796–811
 federalism in, 735–40
 foundations, 718–22
 free speech in, 781–87
 gender equality in, 807–11
 gun rights in, 647, 768–69
 habeas corpus in, 812–16, 826
 individual rights in, 754–80, 763*f*
 interest groups in, 713–15
 interrogations in, 820–21
 introduction to, 711–18, 712*f*, 714*t*, 716*b*
 judicial power in, 722–32
 juries in, 821–26
 lawyers in, 821–26
 legacies, 717–18
 major issues and decisions, 714*t*
 majority-minority districts in, 668

personal freedom in, 769–80
political parties in, 711–13, 712*f*
powers of national government in, 732–35
principles, 720–22
property rights in, 754–58
public morality in, 769–80
punishments in, 718, 826–31, 827*f*
racial equality in, 801–7
religious rights in, 758–68, 763*f*
Republican Party in, 711–13, 712*f*, 715, 718–19, 722–23, 727, 732–33, 740–41, 747, 754, 758, 787–88, 808, 811, 821, 826, 833
search and seizure in, 816–20
separation of powers in, 740–54, 885
voting rights in, 787–96, 793*f*

Recall
of elected officials, 389
judicial, 387–88

Reconstruction. *See also* Civil War and Reconstruction Era
First Reconstruction Act, 357
Johnson, Andrew, and, 292–93, 295, 305, 311, 320–21, 324, 333, 350, 414
racial equality in, 293, 483
retreat on, 454
Second Freedmen's Bureau Act and, 350–53
separation of powers in, 333
Texas v. White and, 292*t*, 324, 329–33

Redistricting, 509, 581, 583–85
Red Scare, 443, 562
Reed, Douglas, 797
Reed, Stanley, 565, 567, 603, 604*f*
Reemelin, Charles, 228
Regional reporters, 1003

Rehnquist, William, 619, 637, 763*f*
on abortion rights, 769–70, 775–76
appointment of, 695, 715, 722, 736
attitudinal model and, 14–15, 14*f*
on *Batson v. Kentucky*, 825–26
on *Blum v. Yaretsky*, 722
on *Board of Trustees of the University of Alabama v. Garrett*, 947
on *Bowen v. Kendrick*, 759
on *Boy Scouts of America v. Dale*, 930
Brennan and, 726
on *Buckley v. Valeo*, 667
on *Bush v. Gore*, 939–40
on capital punishment, 702, 706
in conservative coalition, 846
on *Cruzan v. Director, Missouri Dept. of Health*, 769
on *DeShaney v. Winnebago County Department of Social Services*, 722
on *Dickerson v. United States*, 963–64
on *Dolan v. City of Tigard*, 755
on *Frontiero v. Richardson*, 695
on *Garcia v. San Antonio Metropolitan Transit Authority*, 736, 738–39
on *Herrera v. Collins*, 812–14
on *Hustler Magazine v. Falwell*, 781
on *Immigration and Naturalization Service v. Chadha*, 747
on *International Society for Krishna Consciousness v. Lee*, 782
on jury trials, 822, 825–26
on living constitutionalism, 625, 723–25
on *Locke v. Davey*, 909
on *Madsen v. Women's Health Center, Inc.*, 927
on *Miranda* warnings, 820
on *Moose Lodge No. 107 v. Irvis*, 626–27
on *Morrison v. Olson*, 748–50
on *National League of Cities v. Usery*, 630–31, 735
on *Richardson v. Ramirez*, 672–73
on *Roe v. Wade*, 654–55
on *Rostker v. Goldberg*, 691
on *Scott v. Illinois*, 702
on separation of church and state, 644
on separation of powers, 891, 895
on *South Dakota v. Dole*, 733–34
on *Texas v. Johnson*, 784–85
on *United States Railroad Retirement Board v. Fritz*, 674
on *United States v. American Library Association*, 927
on *United States v. Lopez*, 858–60
on *United States v. Sokolow*, 816
on *United States v. Verdugo-Urquidez*, 722
on *United States v. Virginia*, 957–58
on *Van Orden v. Perry*, 908
on *Zobrest v. Catalina Foothills School District*, 907

Rehnquist Court, 733, 759, 812, 856, 902
Reich, Charles, 643
Religious actions, 436

Religious establishment. *See also* Establishment clause
in Early National Era, 135, 195, 201, 204
in Founding Era, 82, 111, 113

Religious Freedom Restoration Act (RFRA), 759, 767–68, 850–52
Religious monuments, 908

Religious rights. *See also* Prayer; Separation of church and state
in Civil War and Reconstruction Era, 341
in Colonial Era, 45–52
of conscientious objectors, 116
in Contemporary Era, 907–9
in Early National Era, 135, 195–96, 201, 204
Employment Division v. Smith and, 714*t*, 759, 763–68, 850–52
Engle v. Vitale and, 480*t*, 552–56, 555*t*, 711, 759–60, 907
federalism and, 111
in First Amendment, 111, 553–55, 721, 759, 764–67
in Founding Era, 79, 82, 111–16
free exercise clause, 721, 759, 764, 766–67, 908–9
individual justice support for, 763*f*
in Jacksonian Era, 264
Lee v. Weisman and, 714*t*, 715, 759–63, 908
in Liberalism Divided Era, 644–47
Madison and, 112–16, 195, 437, 762
in New Deal and Great Society Era, 552–56, 553*t*, 555*t*
Nixon and, 644, 758
in Pennsylvania ratification debates, 79
polygamy and, 435–38
in Reagan Era, 758–68, 763*f*
in Republican Era, 434–38
Reynolds v. United States and, 374*t*, 436–38, 764
RFRA for, 759, 767–68, 850–52
in state constitutions, 111–12, 112*t*
Virginia debate over, 113–16
West Virginia State Board of Education v. Barnette and, 563–66, 786
Wisconsin v. Yoder and, 621*t*, 644–47, 764–65

Religious schools, 438–40, 758, 907–8
Remedy, obligation and, 546
Removal jurisdiction, 387
Repealer Act, 311–12
"Report from the Select Committee on the Circulation of Incendiary Publications" (Calhoun), 268–69
"Report of a Select Committee on the Petitions Praying for a Repeal of the Alien and Sedition Laws," 200–201
"Report of the Minority of the Committee on Post Offices and Post Roads on the President's Message," 269–71

Republic
democracy and, 83–84, 86–87
Supreme Court opinions on, 441

Republican Era (1877–1932)
cast of characters, 375*b*–376*b*
civil rights in, 454–55
constitutional authority in, 386–90
constitutional thought in, 373
courts in, 373, 481–82, 482*f*
criminal justice in, 464–74
Democratic Party in, 370–71, 370*f*, 372*t*, 379, 387–88, 392, 441, 811, 826, 833
democratic rights in, 441–53, 442*t*–443*t*, 451*t*–452*t*

Republican Era (*continued*)
developments, 369–70
due process in, 464
equality in, 453–63
federalism in, 405–13
foundations, 376–86
free speech in, 441–51, 442*t*–443*t*
gender equality in, 432–34, 461–63
gun rights in, 438
habeas corpus in, 464
individual rights in, 420–41
interest groups, 372–73, 432*t*
interrogations in, 470
introduction to, 369–76, 370*f*–371*f*, 372*t*, 374*t*, 375*b*–376*b*
judicial power in, 376, 386–90, 386*f*
jury trials in, 470–73
lawyers in, 470–73
legacies, 374–76
major issues and decisions, 374*t*
personal freedom in, 438–41
political parties, 370–71, 370*f*, 372*t*
powers of national government in, 390–405, 391*t*–392*t*
principles, 379
property rights in, 410–13, 421–34, 422*t*–423*t*, 432*t*
public morality in, 438–41
punishments in, 473–74
racial equality in, 372, 379, 393–95, 454–61
religious rights in, 434–38
Republican Party in, 370–71, 370*f*–371*f*, 372*t*, 373, 379, 387–88, 393, 403, 435, 441
search and seizure in, 464–70
separation of powers in, 413–20
voting rights in, 369, 372, 451–53, 451*t*–452*t*
Republicanism, 33, 36, 76, 83–84, 96
Republican Party (GOP), 156, 160
against abortion rights, 648, 769, 915–16
in Civil War and Reconstruction Era, 291–93, 295–96, 300–301, 305–6, 310–11, 320, 324, 333, 341–42, 349, 677
in Contemporary Era, 833–39, 855, 856*f*, 865, 901–2, 915–16, 918, 935–46, 954, 960, 967–69
corporate allies of, 370–71
formation of, 134–37, 135*f*, 219
on gun rights, 909–10
in Jacksonian Era, 219, 219*f*, 223, 266, 274
in Liberalism Divided Era, 617–19, 618*f*, 643, 647–48, 663
in New Deal and Great Society Era, 477–79, 477*f*, 556, 581
in Reagan Era, 711–13, 712*f*, 715, 718–19, 722–23, 727, 732–33, 740–41, 747, 754, 758, 787–88, 808, 811, 821, 826, 833
in Republican Era, 370–71, 370*f*–371*f*, 372*t*, 373, 379, 387–88, 393, 403, 435, 441
against slavery, 219, 266, 274, 291
2008 platform, 946, 954, 967–68
Researching and reading, of government documents
congressional documents, 1004
executive branch documents, 1004–5
legal literature, 1005–6
Supreme Court opinions, 997–1003, 999*f*–1000*f*
Restrictive covenants, 494–95
Revolutionary War. *See* American Revolution
Reynolds, B. A., 581–86
Reynolds, George, 436–38
RFRA. *See* Religious Freedom Restoration Act
Rhode Island charter, 229
Richardson, Eliot, 618, 639, 693–95
Richardson, Viola, 672
Richardson, William M., 210–12
Rights. *See also* Bill of Rights; Civil rights; Constitutional rights and liberties; Contract rights; Criminal justice; Democratic rights; Equality rights; Individual rights
of citizenship, 384–86, 625
fundamental, 6
liberal constitutionalism and, 6
natural, 6, 278
negative, 7, 482
political, 7
positive, 6–7, 482–83
procedural, 7
revolution, 482
secured, 7
Ritchie, Thomas, 136
Roane, Spencer, 151–53, 156
"Hampden essays" by, 169–70
overview of, 136*b*
Roberts, Benjamin, 279
Roberts, John, 15, 835, 916, 961*f*
on *Arizona Free Enterprise Club's Freedom Club PAC v. Bennett*, 929–30
on *Citizens United v. Federal Election Commission*, 932
on *Holder v. Humanitarian Law Project*, 926–27
on *National Federation of Independent Business v. Sebelius*, 865–70
on polarized Supreme Court, 836, 846
on *Rumsfeld v. Forum for Academic and Institutional Rights, Inc.*, 930
on *Shelby County v. Holder*, 942–44
on *United States v. Stevens*, 926
Roberts, Owen J., 496, 501–2
on *Betts v. Brady*, 612
on *Korematsu v. United States*, 592
on *Minersville School District v. Gobitis*, 565
on *Morehead v. People of State of New York ex rel. Tipaldo*, 545, 549
on *Nebbia v. New York*, 545
on *West Coast Hotel Co. v. Parrish*, 545, 549
Roberts, Sarah, 279
Roberts Court, 14, 847, 902, 961*f*
Robertson, Daniel, 228
Robertson, Pat, 713
Robinson, Harriet, 273
Robinson, Joseph, 504
Robinson, Spottswood W., III, 596
Rockefeller, Nelson, 479
Rockefeller, Winthrop, 702
Rodriguez, Demetrio, 674–77
Rogers, Andrew J., 302–3
Rogers, Mike, 977–78
Rombach, Cyril, 816
Roosevelt, Franklin (FDR), 15, 23, 373, 455, 483, 629
civil rights and, 481
court-packing plan of, 498, 500–505, 520
election of, 477, 486, 498, 516, 520, 589
federal judiciary and, 478–79, 498, 516
Great Depression and, 478
Humphrey's Executor v. United States and, 533
Japanese Americans detained by, 12, 590–94
overview of, 484*b*
powers of national government and, 516–18, 520–21
separation of powers and, 541
"Undelivered Speech on the *Gold Clause Cases*" by, 498–500
Roosevelt, Theodore, 370, 392, 414
An Autobiography by, 418–19
"A Charter of Democracy" by, 387–88
on executive power, 418–20
overview of, 376*b*
Taft and, 387–88
Rosenberg, Gerald, 21, 581, 590, 608
Rousseau, Jean-Jacques, 36
Rule of law, 5–8
Ruppersberger, C. A., 978
Rush, Benjamin, 72*b*, 129–30, 196
Rutledge, Wiley, 509, 562–63, 604, 604*f*
Ryan, Michael, 382

Sabbath laws, 434
Same-sex marriage, 436, 909. *See also* Defense of Marriage Act
constitutional amendments against, 839–40, 917–18
legalization of, 917–18
Obama supporting, 917, 922, 924–25

San Antonio Metropolitan Transit Authority (SAMTA), 631, 714t, 735–40
Sanford, Edward, 446–47
Sanford, John, 240, 273
Sartori, Giovanni, 6
Saturday Press, 449
Sawyer, Charles, 534
Scalia, Antonin, 623, 715, 722, 743, 763*f*, 854, 961*f*
 on abortion rights, 769–70, 775–77
 on *Adarand Constructors, Inc. v. Peña*, 948
 on *Arizona v. Hicks*, 816
 on *Arizona v. United States*, 878
 on *Boumediene v. Bush*, 845–46
 on *California Democratic Party v. Jones*, 937
 on capital punishment, 826
 on *Citizens United v. Federal Election Commission*, 932–33
 on *City of Richmond v. J. A. Croson Co.*, 801, 805–6
 in conservative coalition, 846
 on *Dickerson v. United States*, 964–66
 on *District of Columbia v. Heller*, 911–13
 on DOMA, 918
 on *Employment Division v. Smith*, 764–65
 on *Florida v. Jardines*, 962
 on *Hamdi v. Rumsfeld*, 975–76
 on *Herrera v. Collins*, 814
 on *Johnson v. Transportation Agency, Santa Clara County*, 810–11
 on *Lee v. Weisman*, 762–63
 legal model and, 16
 on *Lucas v. South Carolina Coastal Council*, 755–57
 on *Michael H. v. Gerald D.*, 769–70
 on *Morrison v. Olson*, 748, 750–54
 on *National Federation of Independent Business v. Sebelius*, 873–76
 overview of, 837*b*
 on polarized Supreme Court, 836
 powers of national government and, 856–57
 on *Printz v. United States*, 879–81
 on *R.A.V. v. St. Paul*, 782
 on *Romer v. Evans*, 947
 structuralism and, 12
 unitary executive theory supported by, 742
 on *United States v. Jones*, 961
 on *United States v. Virginia*, 958–59
 on *Vieth v. Jubelirer*, 935
Scandals. *See* Political scandals
Schakowsky, Janice, 979
Schauer, Frederick, 5
Schenck, Charles, 443–46
Schlafly, Phyllis, 690, 693
Schnapper, Eric, 350
Schofield, Amelia Jane, 436
Schools
 all-male and all-female, 690
 Amish and, 644–47
 Bible reading in, 264
 financing systems of, 674–77
 GFSZA for, 856–64
 prayer in, 552–56, 553*t*, 555*t*, 759–63, 907
 religious, 438–40, 758, 907–8
School segregation
 "Address to the Nation on the Introduction of Troops in Little Rock" and, 506–7
 Berea College v. Commonwealth of Kentucky and, 456
 Bolling v. Sharpe and, 589
 Brown v. Board of Education and, 11, 18, 21, 23, 295, 432*t*, 478–79, 480*t*, 481, 483, 486, 505–8, 584, 587*t*, 589–90, 596–602, 620–21, 677, 679, 685, 711, 720, 772–73, 775–76, 793, 797, 801–2, 854–55
 busing and, 677–83
 Civil Rights Act of 1964 and, 589–90
 Cooper v. Aaron and, 507–9
 Cumming v. Richmond County Board of Education and, 456
 Fourteenth Amendment and, 457, 483, 597–600, 602
 Green v. County School Board of New Kent County and, 590, 600–602, 677, 679–80
 Roberts v. City of Boston and, 272, 279–81
 Southern Manifesto and, 505–6
 strategy debate, 594–97
 Swann v. Charlotte-Mecklenburg Board of Education and, 621*t*, 678–81
Schulhofer, Stephen, 608
Schumer, Charles, 853–54
Scott, Dred, 240, 273
Scott, Hugh, 656
Scott, Thomas, 116
Scottsboro Boys, 471
Scrutiny, tiers of, 487, 487*t*, 620
Search and seizure rights
 in Civil War and Reconstruction Era, 366
 in Colonial Era, 65–67
 in Contemporary Era, 961–62
 in Early National Era, 210–12
 Fifth Amendment and, 465–69, 606
 in Founding Era, 128
 Fourth Amendment and, 128, 464, 466–69, 559–61, 604–7, 638–39, 699, 816–20, 961–62
 in Jacksonian Era, 287
 in Liberalism Divided Era, 697, 699
 Mapp v. Ohio and, 432*t*, 480*t*, 490*t*, 604–7, 695–96, 699–700, 711, 715, 812, 816, 960, 966
 Mayo v. Wilson and, 210–12
 in New Deal and Great Society Era, 604–7
 Olmstead v. United States and, 374*t*, 467–70, 605
 People v. Defore and, 465–67, 606
 in Reagan Era, 816–20
 in Republican Era, 464–70
 United States v. Leon and, 714*t*, 812, 816–20, 962
 Weeks v. United States and, 374*t*, 376, 465–66, 604
Secession
 federalism and, 323–26
 legacy of, 295
 in Lincoln's first inaugural address, 327–29
 South Carolina Ordinance of, 324–26
 unconstitutionality of, 324, 328–29
Second Amendment, 488, 545, 643, 990
 applied to states, 490*t*
 gun rights in, 117, 196, 556, 647–48, 768–69, 841, 909–14
 Story on, 264
Second Bank of the United States, 159–60, 221, 233–36
Second Continental Congress, 3
Second Freedmen's Bureau Act, 350–53
Second Great Awakening, 258
Secret ballot. *See* Australian ballot
Sectionalism, 371
Secularists, 552
Sedgwick, Theodore, 161–62
Sedition Act of 1798, 180, 202, 212
 Jefferson and, 198–99, 571–72
 Madison and, 198–200, 268, 571
 "Report of a Select Committee on the Petitions Praying for a Repeal of the Alien and Sedition Laws," 200–201
Sedition Act of 1918, 441
Seditious libel, 53–55
Segal, Jeffrey, 14
Segregation. *See also* Jim Crow; School segregation
 constitutional change regarding, 23
 Fourteenth Amendment and, 457, 483, 505, 597–600, 602
 Heart of Atlanta Motel, Inc. v. United States and, 517, 528–30, 737
 in New Deal and Great Society Era, 589–602, 602*f*
 Plessy v. Ferguson and, 17, 374*t*, 454–59, 483, 587*t*, 589, 597, 599–600, 770, 772, 776, 854–55
 police power and, 456–57
 protests against, 489
 restrictive covenants and, 494–95

Selective incorporation, 489
Self-censorship, 572
Self-dealing, 8
Self-defense, 264
Self-incrimination clause, 559, 604
Sellers, John Dugan, 688
Senate, 218
busing attacked by, 681–83
chronological table of, 1007*t*–1010*t*
Civil Rights Act of 1866 debated in, 320–23
court-packing report, 504–5
Judiciary Committee hearings, on Bork's nomination, 729–32
Patriot Act debated in, 970–72
popular elections for, 376
Sherman Anti-Trust Act debated in, 395–97
Voting Rights Act Amendments of 1982 report, 790–93
women's suffrage debated in, 354–57
Seneca Falls Convention, 281–83
Separate spheres, 208
Separation of church and state, 15, 112, 644
Americans United for Separation of Church and State, 432*t*
Jefferson on, 195, 762
Locke on, 46, 48–53
Separation of powers
in Article II, 535, 538–39, 748–49, 751, 890, 896
in Civil War and Reconstruction Era, 333–40, 338*t*
in Colonial Era, 43–44
in Contemporary Era, 884–901
in Early National Era, 185–90
in Founding Era, 101–9
Immigration and Naturalization Service v. Chadha and, 741–47
in Jacksonian Era, 249–58
in Liberalism Divided Era, 631–43
Madison and, 541, 976
Morrison v. Olson and, 742, 747–54
Myers v. United States and, 414–18
in New Deal and Great Society Era, 533–44
in Reagan Era, 740–54, 885
Rehnquist on, 891, 895
in Republican Era, 413–20
United States v. Curtiss-Wright Export Corporation and, 543–44
United States v. Nixon and, 621*t*, 631, 639–43
United States v. United States District Court and, 637–39
Youngstown Sheet & Tube Co. v. Sawyer and, 12, 338*t*, 480*t*, 534–43, 892, 900, 975
September 11, 2001, 968, 970
Seriatim opinions, 180
Seventeenth Amendment, 377, 406, 993
Seventh Amendment, 488, 991
Sex Bias in the U.S. Code (Ginsburg, R., and Fasteau), 691–92
Shafer, Eliza, 283
Shaw, Lemuel, 271, 273, 279–81
Shaw, Ruth, 793–96
Shelley, J. D., 494–96
Shepard's United States Citations, 998
Sherman, John, 395–97
Sherman, Roger, 100, 103–4, 116
Sherman Anti-Trust Act
interstate commerce and, 395–400
monopolies and, 373, 390, 395–400, 519, 533
Senate debate on, 395–97
United States v. E. C. Knight and, 373, 391*t*, 392, 397–402, 525, 1001
A Short History of the E.R.A. (Schlafly), 693
Signing statements, 886
Sims, O., 581–86
Singleton, Samuel, 382
Sixteenth Amendment, 993
federal income tax and, 377, 392
passage and ratification of, 392
state reforms and, 406
Sixth Amendment, 380, 488, 490–91, 821, 991
applied to states, 490*t*
expanded, 603
Skrentny, John, 673
Slavery, 4, 9, 16, 59–61. *See also* Abolitionists; Civil War and Reconstruction Era; Fugitive slaves
auctions, 60*f*
Constitutional Convention and, 122
Declaration of Independence and, 274–75, 299
Dred Scott v. Sandford and, 18–21, 218*t*, 223, 232, 240–43, 264, 271–79, 310, 334, 382, 387, 725
Emancipation Proclamation ending, 291, 333–36
in Jacksonian Era, 219, 223, 225–26, 231–32, 236–44, 265–81, 283–84
Jefferson and, 85n15, 123–25
in Massachusetts, 123, 280
Missouri Compromise and, 138, 206–8, 206*f*, 232, 273
natural law and, 139
property rights and, 276, 297–99
Republican Party against, 219, 266, 274, 291
Second Freedmen's Bureau Act and, 350–53
in territories, Lincoln's speech on, 243–44
Slocum, Holder, 204
Smeall, Eleanor, 692
Smilie, John, 78–79
Smith, Abram, 284–86
Smith, Alfred, 763–66
Smith, Margaret Bayard, 217
Smyth, Alexander, 207–8
Snowden, Edward, 969–70, 977, 980
Social Darwinism, 379
Socialists, 372*t*, 444–46
Social reform movements, 219, 222
Social regulation, 630
Social Security Act, 517
Sole organ doctrine, 543
Sotomayor, Sonya, 835–36, 846, 961*f*
Souter, David, 15, 723, 763*f*, 836, 846, 961*f*
on abortion rights, 769–71
on *Board of Education of Kiryas Joel Village School v. Grumet*, 759
on *Boumediene v. Bush*, 844–45
on *Brentwood Academy v. Tennessee Secondary School Athletic Association*, 841
on *Bush v. Gore*, 940–41
on *Hamdi v. Rumsfeld*, 976–77
on *Hurley v. Irish-American Gay, Lesbian and Bisexual Group of Boston*, 930
on *Lee v. Weisman*, 761–62
on *McCreary County v. ACLU of Kentucky*, 908
on *Miller-El v. Dretke*, 966
overview of, 838*b*
on *Printz v. United States*, 883–84
on *Shaw v. Reno*, 796
on *United States v. Lopez*, 862–63
South, political parties in, 617, 618*f*
South Carolina Constitution, 111
South Carolina Ordinance of Secession, 324–26
South Dakota, 406
Southern Christian Leadership Conference, 481
Southern Democrats, 232
Southern Manifesto of 1956, 505–6
Southern strategy, 618
Sovereignty
sovereign immunity, 178–80, 856, 878
of states, 179, 244–45, 287, 630, 720, 737, 739, 866, 880–84
Spaeth, Harold, 14
Spanish-American War, 369, 377, 381
Specter, Arlen, 853–54, 886
"Speech on the Removal of the Deposits" (Clay), 252–54
Spelling, Francis, 554
Spending clause, 481
Spoils system, 227, 414–15
Stamp Act of 1765, 37
Stanbery, Henry, 228
Stanley, Murray, 382
Stanton, Benjamin, 229
Stanton, Elizabeth Cady, 354

overview of, 221*b*
Seneca Falls Convention keynote address by, 282–83
Star Chamber, 67–68
Starr, Kenneth, 747
State action, 380, 382–83, 390, 489
Barron v. Baltimore and, 224–25
Brentwood Academy v. Tennessee Secondary School Athletic Association and, 841
Moose Lodge No. 107 v. Irvis and, 626–28
narrowed, 623, 626, 722
Shelley v. Kraemer and, 494–96
Warren Court and, 626
State bills of rights, 139, 912–13
State constitutions. *See also specific constitutions*
criminal justice and, 127
equality under law in, 947
first, 71
property rights and, 110
religious rights in, 111–12, 112*t*
State courts, 221, 225, 697, 1003–4
State income tax, 406, 406n18
State laws
equal protection, Supreme Court reviewing, 587*t*–588*t*
interstate commerce, Supreme Court reviewing, 531*t*–532*t*
invalidated, 386*f*, 497*f*, 847*f*
prohibition statutes, 261*t*
Statement of the facts, 998
States. *See also* Incorporation, of Bill of Rights; Secession; Separation of church and state
Bill of Rights applied to, 490*t*
compact theory and, 178–79, 245–46, 295
Confederate, 324–27
interests of, 99, 244–45
as laboratories of democracy, 405
legislative districts apportioned by, 509, 581, 582*t*–583*t*, 583–85
militias of, 117, 196, 264, 556, 910–14
nullification by, 246, 248–49
reform in, 406
sovereignty of, 179, 244–45, 287, 630, 720, 737, 739, 866, 880–84
Tenth Amendment and, 518–19, 523, 531, 735, 878, 880–82
Statutory despotism, 436
Steamboat monopoly, 172
Stephens, Alexander, 305
Sterilization, eugenic, 440–41, 556–57
Stevens, Doris, 461–63
Stevens, John Paul, 15, 619, 699, 715, 763*f*, 812, 961*f*
on *Bowers v. Hardwick*, 780
on *Bush v. Gore*, 940
on capital punishment, 703–4, 826, 831
on *Citizens United v. Federal Election Commission*, 933–35
on *City of Boerne v. Flores*, 852
on *City of Richmond v. J. A. Croson Co.*, 805
on *District of Columbia v. Heller*, 913–14
on *Johnson v. Transportation Agency, Santa Clara County*, 809–10
on *Kelo v. City of New London*, 904–5
in liberal coalition, 846
on *Lucas v. South Carolina Coastal Council*, 757–58
on *McCleskey v. Kemp*, 831
on *McDonald v. City of Chicago*, 841
overview of, 716*b*
on *Planned Parenthood of Southeastern Pennsylvania v. Casey* and, 774
on polarized Supreme Court, 836
on *Printz v. United States*, 881–83
on *Regents of the University of California v. Bakke*, 687
on *Santa Fe Independent School District v. Doe*, 908
on separation of church and state, 644
on separation of powers, 885
on *Shaw v. Reno*, 795–96
on *Texas v. Johnson*, 785–86
on *United States v. Leon*, 820
on *United States v. Lopez*, 862
on *U.S. Term Limits v. Thornton*, 878
on *Wallace v. Jaffree*, 759
on *Washington v. Davis*, 689
on *Watchtower Bible and Tract Society of New York v. Village of Stratton*, 927–28
Stevens, Thaddeus, 300, 304, 349
Stewardship theory, 418
Stewart, Potter, 493, 512, 580, 604*f*, 611, 763*f*
attitudinal model and, 14–15, 14*f*
on capital punishment, 702, 704–6
on *City of Mobile v. Bolden*, 788
on *Dandridge v. Williams*, 644
on *Engle v. Vitale*, 555–56
on *Frontiero v. Richardson*, 694
on *Griswold v. Connecticut*, 560–61
on *Harris v. McRae*, 648–49
on *Mapp v. Ohio*, 607
on *New York Times Co. v. United States*, 661
on *In re Winship*, 698
on *Roe v. Wade*, 652–53
as swing vote, 619
Stone, Harlan Fiske, 19, 481, 520, 524, 544
on *Miller v. Schoene*, 424
on *Minersville School District v. Gobitis*, 563
on *United States v. Carolene Products Co.*, 487–88
on *United States v. Darby*, 530–31
Storey, Moorfield, 393
Story, Joseph, 10, 16, 138, 145, 190, 193, 226*t*
on inauguration of Jackson, Andrew, 217
on interstate commerce, 245
on *Martin v. Hunter's Lessee*, 152–55
overview of, 136*b*
on power of removal, 417
on *Prigg v. Pennsylvania*, 236–40
on Second Amendment, 264
on *United States v. Gooding*, 210
Strategic model, 15–16
Strict construction, 3, 159, 173, 178
debates over, 155–56
in Jacksonian Era, 219, 221, 232
by Jefferson, 186–87
Strict scrutiny, 487, 487*t*, 586, 590, 674–75, 690
Strong, William, 313, 317–19
Structuralism, 12
"Suffrage Does Not Give Equality" (Stevens, D.), 461–63
Sullivan, James, 120
Sullivan, Kathleen, 24
Sullivan, L. B., 570–72
A Summary View of the Rights of British America (Jefferson), 58–59
Sumner, Charles, 279–80, 300, 346, 349
Civil Rights Act of 1866 and, 320, 322
overview of, 294*b*
in Thirteenth Amendment debates, 296, 298–99
Supremacy clause, 8, 88, 99–100, 877, 883, 942
Supreme Court, 847, 849–50, 849*f*. *See also specific justices*
agenda change of, 482*f*
Alito nominated to, 835, 853–55
attitudinal model and, 14–15, 14*f*
Bill of Rights applied to states by, 490*t*
Bork nominated to, 715, 723, 727–32, 741, 848
Brennan nominated to, 725
chronological table of, 1007*t*–1010*t*
conservative coalition of, 846
court-packing plan and, 498, 500–505, 520
dangerous speech laws reviewed by, 442*t*–443*t*
election laws reviewed by, 451*t*–452*t*
elite assault on, 563
executive power cases reviewed by, 338*t*
federal laws reviewed by, 372–73
Four Horsemen, 496
left-right location of, 628*f*
liberal coalition of, 846
Nixon's nominations to, 619, 630, 695, 715, 722, 846, 848

Supreme Court (*continued*)
polarization of, 14, 14*f*, 836, 846, 937–38, 946–47
precedents overruled by, 497*f*
public opinion and, 20, 20*f*
Reagan's nominations to, 624, 715, 722–23, 727–33, 735, 741, 811, 848
on republic, 441
researching and reading opinions of, 997–1003, 999*f*–1000*f*
role of, in New Deal and Great Society Era, 478–79, 481–82, 482*f*, 496–505, 497*f*, 516–17, 520–21
route to, 999*f*
separate opinions of, 1000–1001, 1000*f*
state and federal laws invalidated by, 386*f*, 497*f*, 847*f*
state apportionment of legislative districts reviewed by, 581, 582*t*–583*t*, 583–85
state equal protection laws reviewed by, 587*t*–588*t*
state laws under interstate commerce clause reviewed by, 531*t*–532*t*
support for claimants in criminal procedure cases, 960, 961*f*
as ultimate Constitution interpreter, 629
Sutherland, George, 423–24, 523
on *Connally v. General Construction Co.*, 464
in Four Horsemen, 496
on *Home Building & Loan Association v. Blaisdell*, 548
on *Patton v. United States*, 470–71
on *Powell v. Alabama*, 471–73
on *United States v. Curtiss-Wright Export Corporation*, 543–44
on *West Coast Hotel Co. v. Parrish*, 550
Swayne, Noah, 333
Sweeping clauses, 98
Swift, Zephaniah, 212–13
Syndicalism, 446–48, 573

Taft, William Howard, 370, 894
Arizona statehood veto by, 388–90
on *Balzac v. Porto Rico*, 380–82
on executive power, 419–20
Myers v. United States and, 414–16
on *Olmstead v. United States*, 467–68
Our Chief Magistrate and His Powers by, 419–20
overview of, 375*b*
Roosevelt, Theodore, and, 387–88
Takings (Epstein, R.), 755
Takings clause
in Fifth Amendment, 488, 643, 715, 756–58, 902–7
public use and, 902–7
Tallmadge, James, 207
Taney, Roger, 218, 221, 226*t*, 245, 251
on *Ableman v. Booth*, 284, 286–87
on *Dred Scott v. Sandford*, 240–43, 264, 271–76, 382
on *Ex parte Merryman*, 357–59
on *License Cases*, 411
on *Luther v. Borden*, 229–31
overview of, 220*b*
on *Prigg v. Pennsylvania*, 236, 239
on *Proprietors of the Charles River Bridge v. Proprietors of the Warren Bridge*, 258–60
Tariff Act of 1894, 373
Taxation. *See also* Federal income tax
ACA and, 864–76
Article I and, 392
child labor and, 392–93
in Colonial Era, 33, 36–37, 43
McCulloch v. Maryland and, 167–68
poll, 574
power of, 167–68, 174, 178
representation linked to, 33, 36–37, 43, 59, 203–4, 355
state income tax, 406, 406n18
Tenth Amendment and, 517
Taylor, John, 136, 207
Teacher attitudes, on prayer, 553*t*
Tea Party, 835
Temperance laws, 265
Tennessee Constitution, 509
Tenth Amendment, 156, 325, 404, 481, 991
National League of Cities v. Usery and, 630–31
states and, 518–19, 523, 531, 735, 878, 880–82
taxation and, 517
as truism, 531, 629
Tenure of Office Act of 1867, 414–16
Terrorism, policy on, 834, 890, 892–99. *See also* War on Terror
Textualism, 10–11
Theocracy, 436
A Theory of Justice (Rawls), 620, 625
Third Amendment, 488, 559, 991
Third parties, 372, 833
Thirteenth Amendment, 334, 380, 444, 457, 992
debates over, 296–99, 305, 341–42
enforcement of, 301, 314, 321
Fourteenth Amendment and, 299–300
importance of, 295–96
ratified, 292
Section 2, 350–52
Slaughter-House Cases and, 306–9
Thomas, Clarence, 15, 715, 723, 854, 927, 961*f*
on abortion rights, 769, 775–76
in conservative coalition, 846
on *Good News Club v. Milford Central School*, 909
on *Grutter v. Bollinger*, 953–54
on *Hamdi v. Rumsfeld*, 976
on *Kelo v. City of New London*, 906–7
on *Mitchell v. Helms*, 908
on *National Federation of Independent Business v. Sebelius*, 876
overview of, 838*b*
on polarized Supreme Court, 836
on *Printz v. United States*, 881
religious rights supported by, 763*f*
on *Shelby County v. Holder*, 944
on *United States v. Lopez*, 861–62
on *U.S. Term Limits v. Thornton*, 878
Thompson, Charles H., 594–97
Thompson, Smith, 226*t*, 236, 239
Three-strikes law, 967
Tiffany, Joel, 912
Tories, 33
"Torture Memos"
leaked, 893
Memo to Alberto R. Gonzales, Counsel to the President, 894–96
Memo to James B. Comey, Deputy Attorney General, 898–99
Memo to William Haynes II, General Counsel of the Department of Defense, 896–98
Tourgee, Albion, 456
Townshend Act, 42–44
Toynbee, Thomas, 260
Transportation revolution, 258
Treason Act of 1695, 69
Treasury Department, 250–54
A Treatise on the Constitutional Limitations Which Rest upon the Legislative Power of the States of the American Union (Cooley, T.), 346–49
Treaty power, 392, 403–5
Trenchard, John, 54
Trimester system, 648, 650, 652, 654, 770
Trotter, William Monroe, 454
Truman, Harry, 12, 597
free speech and, 479
Korean War and, 533–34, 537, 539–40, 892
Youngstown Sheet & Tube Co. v. Sawyer and, 12, 338*t*, 480*t*, 534–43
Trumbull, Lyman, 314, 321–22, 342, 352–53
Tucker, St. George, 39, 77, 176, 196, 912
Tuddenham, Polly Ann, 436
Twelfth Amendment, 76, 991–92
Twentieth Amendment, 993–94
Twenty-Fifth Amendment, 995
Twenty-First Amendment, 486, 733–35, 994
Twenty-Fourth Amendment, 994–95
Twenty-Second Amendment, 994
Twenty-Seventh Amendment, 995

Twenty-Sixth Amendment, 624, 629, 669, 995
Twenty-Third Amendment, 994
Tyler, John, 221, 233–34, 250, 255

Unconstitutional constitutional amendments, 3
"Undelivered Speech on the *Gold Clause Cases*" (FDR), 498–500
Underkuffler, Laura, 909
Undue burden test, 717
"The Unfinished Business of the Warren Court" (Black, C.), 625
Unions
  AFL, 372
  United Steelworkers of America, 534
  yellow dog contracts and, 421
Unitary executive theory, 740, 742
United Nations, 540, 898
United States Reports. See U.S. Reports
United Steelworkers of America, 534
Universal adult suffrage, 574, 667
Universal male suffrage, 119–21, 202–3, 229
University of Michigan, 786–87, 949–54
Upshur, Abel P., 271
USA Patriot Act of 2001. *See* Patriot Act
U.S. Reports, 997–98, 1003

Valeo, Francis, 663
Vallandigham, Clement, 342–45
Van Alstyne, William, 624
Van Buren, Martin, 218, 245, 251
VanBurkleo, Sandra, 126
Van Devanter, Willis, 496, 523, 548, 550
Varnum, James, 77
Vermont Bill of Rights, 912–13
Vermont Constitution, 128
Vetoes
  Adams, John, and, 187
  Arizona statehood, 388–90
  Hoover and, 741
  House debate on, 255–58
  Immigration and Naturalization Service v. Chadha and, 741–47
  by Jackson, Andrew, 217, 232–36, 250
  Jefferson and, 187
  by Johnson, Andrew, 305, 311, 350
  line-item, 885
  by Madison, 187–88
  by Nixon, 634, 636–37
  by Reagan, 741
  by Taft, 388–90
  by Tyler, 250, 255
  by Washington, George, 187
Vietnam War, 617–18, 629, 631–32, 658
"Views of the President of the United States on the Subject of Internal Improvements" (Monroe), 177–78
Viguerie, Richard, 720
A Vindication of the Rights of Women (Wollstonecraft), 209
Vinson, Fred, 481, 604*f*
  on *Barrows v. Jackson*, 494
  on *Dennis v. United States*, 567–68
  on *Shelley v. Kraemer*, 494–96
  on *Sweatt v. Painter*, 597
  on *Youngstown Sheet & Tube Co. v. Sawyer*, 538, 540–43
Virginia
  debate over religious assessments, 113–16
  Declaration of Rights, 59, 121, 139
  Plan, 73, 93, 95–96, 98–99, 482
  Resolutions, 137, 143, 151, 180, 183–84, 199–200, 248
Virginia Military Institute (VMI), 954–59
Virginia Report of 1799 (Madison), 200–202
Virginia Women's Institute for Leadership (VWIL), 955–59
VMI. *See* Virginia Military Institute
Volstead, A. J., 394
Voting rights. *See also* Women's suffrage
  age and, 629, 667–68
  American Revolution and, 119
  Blackstone on, 57
  Bush v. Gore and, 935, 937–41
  in Civil War and Reconstruction Era, 300–304, 345, 354–57
  in Colonial Era, 57–58
  in Contemporary Era, 935–45
  in Early National Era, 202–4, 202*f*–203*f*
  Federalists on, 119, 202–3
  in Founding Era, 110, 119–21
  gerrymandering and, 509, 581, 583, 583*t*, 714*t*, 781, 787, 789, 793–96, 793*f*, 935–36
  immigration and, 451
  in Jacksonian Era, 271
  laws, Supreme Court reviewing, 451*t*–452*t*
  in Liberalism Divided Era, 667–73
  in New Deal and Great Society Era, 478–79, 517, 562, 574–86, 574*f*, 582*t*–583*t*
  property qualifications for, 202–4, 202*f*–203*f*
  Puerto Rico and, 578–79
  in Reagan Era, 787–96, 793*f*
  registration and, 574*f*, 575
  in Republican Era, 369, 372, 451–53, 451*t*–452*t*
  Reynolds v. Sims and, 480*t*, 574, 581–86, 582*t*, 668, 925, 935
  Richardson v. Ramirez and, 668, 672–73
  Shaw v. Reno and, 583*t*, 714*t*, 789, 793–96, 793*f*, 936
  Shelby County v. Holder and, 941–45
  universal adult suffrage, 574, 667
  universal male suffrage, 119–21, 202–3, 229
  Warren on, 562
Voting Rights Act of 1965, 478–79, 481, 562, 589, 620
  amendments, 668–71, 788, 790–93, 936, 941–45
  Congressional reports on, 575–78
  Fifteenth Amendment and, 517, 788
  Johnson, Lyndon, and, 575
  Katzenbach v. Morgan and, 452*t*, 480*t*, 517, 575, 578–81, 671, 721, 945
  popular support for, 486, 574
  as sacred text, 621, 667
Voting Rights Act of 1970, 667–71
Voting Rights Act of 1975, 667
VWIL. *See* Virginia Women's Institute for Leadership

Wade, Benjamin, 303–4, 355–56
Wages. *See* Labor and wage regulation
Wagner Act. *See* National Labor Relations Act
Wainwright, Louis, 612
Waite, Morrison, 293, 305, 314
  on *Munn v. Illinois*, 410–12, 421
  on *Reynolds v. United States*, 436–38
  on *Stone v. Mississippi*, 424
  on *United States v. Reese*, 390
Waldron, Jeremy, 19
Wallace, George, 575, 620
War Democrats, 293, 314
War hawks, 248
War of 1812, 134, 137, 156, 160, 198
War on Drugs, 960
War on Terror, 834, 887, 890, 893
  Bush, George W., in, 968–70
  infamous crimes and criminals in, 968–72
  Obama in, 968–70
  Patriot Act in, 960, 969–73, 977
War powers
  in Contemporary Era, 886–87, 889–902
  in Liberalism Divided Era, 631–39
War Powers Act of 1973, 631, 633–37
Warren, Earl, 18, 479, 488, 498, 604*f*
  on *Brown v. Board of Education*, 581, 597–600
  Burger and, 659
  on *Cooper v. Aaron*, 507–8
  on living Constitution, 483
  on *Lombard v. Louisiana*, 489
  on *Miranda v. Arizona*, 609–10
  overview of, 484*b*
  on *Reynolds v. Sims*, 581, 583–85
  on *South Carolina v. Katzenbach*, 575
  on *Trop v. Dulles*, 614
  on voting rights, 562

Warren (*continued*)
Warren Court, 17, 481, 485, 517, 604*f*, 623, 878
criticism of, 620, 695, 715
Due Process Revolution of, 603
on gender equality, 586
implementation and, 617
Jim Crow abolished by, 590
judicial activism of, 482, 498, 629, 754
state action and, 626
transformation of, 722
unfinished work of, 625
Wartime, constitutional rights and liberties in, 294–95, 335–36
Washington, George, 124, 133, 135, 159, 186, 272
"Letter to the Jews of Newport" by, 195
Sedition Act and, 199
vetoes by, 187
Washington, Walter, 688–89
Washington Legal Foundation, 713
Washington Post, 659–60
Watergate, 631, 636, 639–43
Water Pollution Control Act of 1972, 630
Watkins, Thomas, 577–78
Wayne, James, 226*t*, 238
WCTU. *See* Women's Christian Temperance Union
Webster, Daniel, 137, 164, 191, 217, 248
against deposit removal, 251
on liberty, 244
overview of, 220*b*
Weeks, Fremont, 465–66
Weeks, John, 379
Weisman, Deborah, 759–63
Westboro Baptist Church, 928
Westlaw, 998, 1003, 1006
Whatley, Thomas, 37
Whigs, 33, 310
in Jacksonian Era, 218–19, 219*f*, 223, 225, 227–29, 231–33, 250, 255, 264, 271, 418
at Ohio Constitutional Convention, 227–29
White, Byron, 604*f*, 763*f*, 782, 811
on abortion rights, 775–76
attitudinal model and, 14–15, 14*f*
on *Bowers v. Hardwick*, 769, 778–79
on *Buckley v. Valeo*, 666–67
on capital punishment, 702, 706
on *City of Cleburne, Texas v. Cleburne Living Center*, 797
on *Davis v. Bandemer*, 789
on *Frontiero v. Richardson*, 693
on *Gaffney v. Cummings*, 668
on *Griswold v. Connecticut*, 560
on *Herrera v. Collins*, 814
on *Immigration and Naturalization Service v. Chadha*, 745–47
on *Lindsey v. Normet*, 644
on *Miranda v. Arizona*, 611–12, 721
on *New York Times Co. v. United States*, 661
overview of, 622*b*
on *Regents of the University of California v. Bakke*, 685–87
on *Roe v. Wade*, 653–54
on *San Antonio Independent School District v. Rodriguez*, 676
on *Shaw v. Reno*, 795–96
on *Stanley v. Illinois*, 649
as swing vote, 619, 846
on *United Jewish Organizations of Williamsburgh v. Carey*, 668
on *United States v. Leon*, 816–18
on *United States v. United States District Court*, 639
on *Washington v. Davis*, 679, 688–89
on *Wisconsin v. Yoder*, 646–47
White, Edward D., 474
Whitewater, 747–48
Whitney, Charlotte Anita, 446–49
Whittaker, Charles, 604*f*, 607
Wickard, Claude, 524–26
Wickersham Commission of 1931, 603
Williams, Roger, 32*b*, 33, 45, 50–51, 195
Williamson, Hugh, 100
Williamson, Mac, 551–52
Willis, Edwin, 527–28
Wilson, Henry, 356
Wilson, James, 77–79, 98, 128, 139, 180
at Constitutional Convention, 100–101, 104
on free speech, 118
overview of, 72*b*
on separate spheres, 208
Wilson, Robin Fretwell, 909
Wilson, Woodrow, 369, 414–15, 441
election of, 370, 387, 389, 833
hunting regulations and, 393, 403
Keating–Owen Act and, 400–401
Wilson Tariff of 1894, 392
Winship, Samuel, 697
Winthrop, John, 61, 68, 68*f*
Wiretapping, 467–70, 699, 969
Wirt, William, 164
Wisconsin, state income tax in, 406
Witchcraft, 48
Wollstonecraft, Mary, 209
Women's Christian Temperance Union (WCTU), 377
Women's Rights Project, 690–91
Women's suffrage
Fourteenth Amendment and, 354
groups, 372
Nineteenth Amendment and, 372, 377, 453
Senate debates over, 354–57
state reforms, 406
Wood, Gordon, 36
Woodbury, Levi, 226*t*, 229
Woods, William, 438
World War I, 369, 894
free speech and, 441, 443–46, 562
Prohibition and, 377
property rights and, 423
World War II
Japanese Americans detained during, 12, 590–94
sterilization and, 556
Wright, J. Skelley, 589
Wynehamer, James, 260

Yates, Robert, 72*b*, 88–90
Yazoo affair, 193
Yellow dog contracts, 421
Yoder, Jonas, 644–47
Yoo, John
Memo to William Haynes II by, 896–98
overview of, 838*b*
"The President's Constitutional Authority to Conduct Military Operations" by, 890–93
Young, Brigham, 435–36

Zenger, John Peter, 54–57, 55*f*, 62, 69, 129, 212
Zion Parochial School, 438–40
Zoning ordinances, 423–24

Cases

Note: *t* refers to table, *f* refers to figure, and *b* refers to box.

Ableman v. Booth, 218*t*, 225, 284, **286–87**
Abrams v. United States, 442*t*, 443–44, 781
Adair v. United States, 421, 423
Adamson v. California, 491–92
Adarand Constructors, Inc. v. Peña, 852, 948–49, 951
Addyston Pipe & Steel Co. v. United States, 392
Adkins v. Children's Hospital, 374*t*, 423, 545, 549–51
Agency for International Development v. Alliance for Open Society International, 930
Agostini v. Felton, 907–8
Ake v. Oklahoma, 822
Alden v. Maine, 834*t*, 878
Alderman v. United States, 699
Allgeyer v. Louisiana, 423
Allied Structural Steel Co. v. Spannaus, 192*t*, 755
American Booksellers Association, Inc. v. Hudnut, 781
American Tradition Partnership, Inc. v. Bullock, 929
Argensinger v. Hamlin, 702
Arizona Free Enterprise Club's Freedom Club PAC v. Bennett, 929–30
Arizona v. Gant, 962
Arizona v. Hicks, 816
Arizona v. Mauro, 821
Arizona v. United States, 877–78
Arkansas Educational Television Commission v. Forbes, 927
Aronow v. United States, 555*t*
Atkins v. Virginia, 966
Atwater v. City of Lago Vista, 962
Austin v. Michigan Chamber of Commerce, 931–32, 934
Austin v. Tennessee, 422*t*

Baehr v. Lewin, 922
Bailey v. Alabama, 455
Bailey v. Drexel Furniture Co., 401
Baker v. Carr, 21, 480*t*, 498, **509–16**, 581, 582*t*, 587*t*
Bakke v. Regents of the University of California, 623, 674
Baldwin v. G. A. F. Seelig, Inc., 532*t*
Balzac v. Porto Rico, **380–82**
Barbier v. Connolly, 422*t*, 454
Barnette v. West Virginia State Board of Education, 480*t*
Barron v. Baltimore, 223, **224–25**, 295, 305, 380
Barrows v. Jackson, 494
Batson v. Kentucky, 714*t*, 812, 821, **822–26**, 830
Bayard v. Singleton, 111, 144*t*
Beer Company v. Massachusetts, 192*t*
Bell v. Low Income Women of Texas, 955
Bennis v. Michigan, 423*t*
Benton v. Maryland, 490*t*
Berea College v. Commonwealth of Kentucky, 456
Berman v. Parker, 904–6
Bethel School District No. 403 v. Fraser, 783
Betts v. Brady, 612–13
Bliss v. Commonwealth, **197–98**
Block v. Hirsh, 423
Blum v. Yaretsky, 722
Board of County Commissioners of Muskogee County v. Lowery, 902–3
Board of Education of Independent School District No. 92 of Pottawatomie County v. Earls, 960, 962
Board of Education of Kiryas Joel Village School v. Grumet, 759
Board of Education of Oklahoma City Public Schools v. Dowell, 802
Board of Trustees of the University of Alabama v. Garrett, 848, 857, 947
Bolling v. Sharpe, 589
Bond v. United States, 962
Booth Cases, 283, **284–87**
Bordenkircher v. Hayes, 696
Boumediene v. Bush, 834, 834*t*, **841–46**, 848, 960, 969
Bowen v. Kendrick, 758–59
Bowers v. Hardwick, 12, 714*t*, 769, **778–80**, 854, 919–21
Bowman v. Middleton, 111, 139, 144*t*
Bowsher v. Synar, 742, 885
Boyd v. United States, 464–65, 606
Boy Scouts of America v. Dale, 922, 927, 930
Bradfield v. Roberts, 434
Bradley v. Public Utilities Commission of Ohio, 531*t*
Bradwell v. State, 354
Brandenburg v. Ohio, 443*t*, 480*t*, 562, **573–74**, 658, 781
Brandon v. Board of Education, 555*t*
Breedlove v. Suttles, 451*t*
Breen v. Runkel, 555*t*
Brentwood Academy v. Tennessee Secondary School Athletic Association, 841
Brewer v. Williams, 700
Bronson v. Kinzie, et al., 191*t*
Brooks v. United States, 391*t*
Brown v. Allen, 604
Brown v. Board of Education of Topeka, 11, 18, 21, 23, 295, 432*t*, 478–79, 480*t*, 481, 483, 486, 505–8, 584, 587*t*, 589–90, 596, **597–600**, 601–2, 620–21, 677, 679, 685, 711, 720, 772–73, 775–76, 793, 797, 801–2, 854–55
Brown v. Califano, 681
Brown v. Entertainment Merchants Association, 926
Brown v. Hartlage, 452*t*
Brown v. Maryland, 245, 531*t*
Brown v. Plata, 966
Brown v. United States, 338*t*
Buchanan v. Warley, 374*t*, 455, 494
Buckley v. Valeo, 452*t*, 621*t*, 623, 658, **663–67**, 931–32
Buck v. Bell, 438, **440–41**, 453, 556, 587*t*
Bunting v. Oregon, 422*t*, 432*t*
Burdine v. Johnson, 966
Burson v. Freeman, 452*t*
Bushell's Case, 33, 69
Bush v. Gore, 13, 834, 834*t*, 925, 935, **937–41**, 1000
Bush v. Vera, 583*t*
Butler v. McKellar, 826

Cafeteria & Restaurant Workers Unions v. McElroy, 338*t*
Calder v. Bull, 134*t*, 137, **139–41**, 144*t*, 191
Califano v. Westcott, 432*t*
California Democratic Party v. Jones, 937
Callins v. Collins, 826
Calvin's Case, 36
Campbell v. State, 223
Cantwell v. Connecticut, 490*t*
Capen v. Foster, 271
Carey v. Population Services International, 649
Carroll v. United States, 465
Carter v. Carter Coal Co., 157*t*, 391*t*, 480*t*, 516, 520–21, 523
Cases of the Judges, 144*t*
Chambers v. Florida, 481
Champion v. Ames, 391*t*, 392, 403
Chaplinsky v. New Hampshire, 442*t*, 786
The Cherokee Nation v. Georgia, 511
Chicago, B. & Q. R. Co. v. Chicago, 490*t*
Chicago, Milwaukee, and St. Paul Railway Company v. Minnesota, 406, 410
Child Labor Tax Case, 392–93
Chisholm v. Georgia, 134*t*, 178–79, **180–83**, 878
Christian Legal Society Chapter of the University of California, Hastings College of Law v. Martinez, 927
Church of the Babalu Aye v. Hialeah, 759
Citizens United v. Federal Election Commission, 452*t*, 834*t*, 848, 929, **931–35**
City of Boerne v. Flores, 767, 834*t*, 848, **850–53**, 857
City of Cleburne, Texas v. Cleburne Living Center, 797
City of Cleveland v. Cleveland City Railway Company, 192*t*
City of Mobile v. Bolden, 788, 790, 792
City of Philadelphia v. New Jersey, 532*t*
City of Richmond v. J. A. Croson Co., 588*t*, 714*t*, 801–2, **803–7**
City of Rome v. United States, 788
Civil Rights Cases, 374*t*, 380, **382–86**, 390, 394, 489, 495, 528–29
Clark v. Community for Creative Non-Violence, 717, 782
Clinton v. New York, 885
Cohens v. Virginia, 134*t*
Colegrove v. Green, 509–10, 513, 582*t*
Coleman v. Miller, 510–11
Cole v. Arkansas, 490*t*
Collector v. Day, 735
Collins v. Chandler Unified School District, 555*t*
Colorado v. Connelly, 821
Colorado v. Spring, 821
Commonwealth v. Aves, 273
Commonwealth v. Campbell, 438
Commonwealth v. Dana, 287
Commonwealth v. Hutchings, 288
Commonwealth v. Jennison, **123**
Commonwealth v. Sharpless, 199
Commonwealth v. Wolf, 195
Commonwealth v. Wyatt, 214
Connally v. General Construction Co., 464
Connolly v. Union Sewer Pipe Co., 587*t*
Connor v. Finch, 582*t*
Cooley v. Board of Wardens of the Port of Philadelphia, 218*t*, 245, **246–48**, 406, 409, 531*t*
Cooper v. Aaron, 498, **507–9**
Cooper v. Telfair, 144*t*
Coppage v. Kansas, 423
Corfield v. Coryell, 308
Coronado Case, 522
Coyle v. Smith, 735, 942
Craig v. Boren, 15, 588*t*, 617, 620, 621*t*, 624, 690
Crawford v. Marion County Election Board, 937
Cross, Hobson & Co. v. Harrison, 338*t*
Cruzan v. Director, Missouri Dept. of Health, 769
Cummings v. Missouri, 341
Cumming v. Richmond County Board of Education, 456

Dandridge v. Williams, 619, 621*t*, 644
The Daniel Bell, 391*t*
Daniel v. Paul, 528
Darnel's Case, 64
Dartmouth College v. Woodward, 134*t*, 190–91, 191*t*
Davis v. Bandemer, 789
Davis v. Beason, 451*t*
Davis v. United States, 821
Dean Milk Co. v. City of Madison, Wisconsin, 532*t*
DeJonge v. Oregon, 442*t*, 490*t*
Dennis v. United States, 442*t*, 480*t*, **566–70**, 573
Denver Area Educational Telecommunications Consortium v. FCC, 930
Department of the Navy v. Egan, 338*t*
DeShaney v. Winnebago County Department of Social Services, 722
DeSpain v. DeKalb County Community School District, 555*t*
Dickerson v. United States, 962, **963–66**
District of Columbia v. Heller, 834*t*, 848, **910–15**
Dr. Bonham's Case, 33, 38, 41
Doe v. Bolton, 650
Doe v. Commonwealth's Attorney for City of Richmond, 649–50
Doe v. University of Michigan, 714*t*, **786–87**
Dolan v. City of Tigard, 717, 755
Dooley v. United States, 338*t*
Douglas v. California, 603
Downes v. Bidwell, 379, 381
Dred Scott v. Sandford, 18–21, 218*t*, 223, 232, **240–43**, 264, 271–72, **273–79**, 310, 334, 382, 387, 725
Dudgeon v. United Kingdom, 920
Duncan v. Louisiana, 480*t*, 489, **490–94**, 490*t*, 722
Dunn v. Blumstein, 668
Duren v. Missouri, 701
Durousseau v. The United States, 312

Eakin v. Raub, 225
Easley v. Cromartie, 936–37
Edmonson v. Leesville Concrete Co. Inc., 821
Edwards v. Aguillard, 759, 908
Edwards v. California, 530
Eisenstadt v. Baird, 653, 771, 915
Elkins v. United States, 606
Employment Division v. Smith, 714*t*, 759, **763–66**, 767–68, 850–52
Energy Reserves Group, Inc., v. Kansas Power and Light Co., 192*t*, 755
Engle v. Vitale, 480*t*, 552, **553–56**, 555*t*, 711, 759–60, 907
Entick v. Carrington, **65–67**, 69, 128, 464
Estes v. Texas, 604
Everson v. Board of Education of Ewing Tp., 490*t*, 761
Ewing v. California, 967
Ex parte Bollman, 209
Ex parte Bushell, 35
Ex parte McCardle, 292*t*, **311–13**
Ex parte Merryman, 292*t*, 357, **358–59**, 360, 536n32
Ex parte Milligan, 292*t*, 293–94, 310, 338*t*, 357, **361–66**, 974
Ex parte Quirin, 338*t*, 480*t*, 968, 974–75
Ex parte Virginia, 394
Ex parte Yarbrough, 157*t*, 451*t*
Ex parte Young, 374*t*
Exxon Corp. v. Eagerton, 192*t*
Exxon Corp. v. Governor of Maryland, 532*t*

Fay v. Noia, 604, 697
FCC v. Pacifica Foundation, 930
Federal Election Commission v. Conservative Political Action Committee, 452*t*
Federal Election Commission v. Wisconsin Right to Life, 929
Feiner v. New York, 442*t*
Felker v. Turpin, 961
Filártiga v. Peña-Irala, 719
First National Bank of Boston v. Bellotti, 932
Fisher v. McGirr, 287
Fisher v. University of Texas at Austin, 948, 950

Flast v. Cohen, 432*t*, 498, 629
Fletcher v. Peck, 134*t*, 138–39, 190–91, 191*t*, **193–95**, 260
Florence v. Board of Chosen Freeholders of County of Burlington, 962
Florida v. Jardines, 961–62
Fong Yue Ting v. United States, 374*t*
Fox v. Los Angeles, 555*t*
Fox v. Washington, 442*t*
Frank v. Mangum, 464
Freeman v. Pitts, 802
Frontiero v. Richardson, 690, **693–95**
Fry v. United States, 392*t*
Fullilove v. Klutznick, 678, 734, 803, 807
Furman v. Georgia, 16, 432*t*, 702, 704–7, 827, 829–30

Gaffney v. Cummings, 582*t*, 668
Garcia-Mir v. Meese, 719
Garcia v. San Antonio Metropolitan Transit Authority, 631, 714*t*, 735, **736–40**
Garcia v. Territory of New Mexico, 367
Geer v. Connecticut, 403–4
Gelpcke v. City of Dubuque, 192*t*
General Motors Corp. v. Romein, 755–66
Georgia v. McCollum, 821
Georgia v. Stanton, 311
Gibbons v. Ogden, 134*t*, 158, **172–75**, 245, 391*t*, 398, 400, 525, 529, 531*t*, 866, 873
Gideon v. Wainwright, 480*t*, 490*t*, **612–13**, 702, 821
Gilbert v. Minnesota, 442*t*
Giles v. Harris, 454
Gindrat v. People, 465
Gingles v. Thornburg, 788–89
Gitlow v. New York, 442*t*, 446, 490*t*, 567–68
Goesaert v. Cleary, 603
Goldberg v. Kelly, 432*t*
Gold Clause Cases, **498–500**
Goldman v. Weinberger, 759
Gomillion v. Lightfoot, 515, 794
Gonzales v. Carhart, 916
Gonzales v. Raich, 158*t*, 392*t*, 834*t*, 856
Good News Club v. Milford Central School, 909
Goodridge v. Department of Public Health, 839, 917–18
Gouled v. United States, 465
Graham v. Florida, 966
Granholm v. Heald, 432*t*, 532*t*
The Grapeshot, 338*t*
Gratz v. Bollinger, 432*t*, 949–50, 952
Gray v. Sanders, 582*t*
Green v. Biddle, 191*t*
Green v. County School Board of New Kent County, 590, **600–602**, 677, 679–80
Gregg v. Georgia, 617, 621*t*, 696, 702–3, **704–7**
Gregory v. Ashcroft, 877
Griffin v. Illinois, 584, 603
Griswold v. Connecticut, 423*t*, 432*t*, 480*t*, 556, **557–61**, 648, 650, 652–53, 721, 915
Groves v. Slaughter, 245
Grovey v. Townsend, 451*t*
Grutter v. Bollinger, 588*t*, 834*t*, 949, **950–54**
Guinn and Beal v. United States, 455

Haig v. Agee, 714*t*
Hamdan v. Rumsfeld, 338*t*, 834, 845, 960, 969
Hamdi v. Rumsfeld, 834, 834*t*, 960, 969, **973–77**
Hamilton v. Dillin, 897
Hammer v. Dagenhart, 374*t*, 391*t*, 392, **400–403**
Hamm v. Rock City, 489
Harper v. Virginia State Board of Elections, 480*t*, 574, 668, 673, 938
Harris v. McRae, 623, 648–49, 721
Harris v. New York, 695, **700–701**, 964
Hawaii Housing Authority v. Midkiff, 904–6
Hawaii v. Mankichi, 379–81
Hayburn's Case, 144*t*
Heart of Atlanta Motel, Inc. v. United States, 517, **528–30**, 737
Heller v. District of Columbia II, 910
Helvering v. Davis, 517
Hepburn v. Griswold, 311, 313, **314–17**, 319–20
Herndon v. Lowry, 442*t*
Herrera v. Collins, **812–16**, 826
Herring v. United States, 962
Hill v. Colorado, 927
Hobbs v. State, 473
Hoke v. United States, 530
Holden v. Hardy, 373
Holden v. James, **205–6**
Holder v. Humanitarian Law Project, 443*t*, 926–27
Hollenbaugh v. Carnegie Free Library, 649
Home Building & Loan Association v. Blaisdell, 192*t*, 480*t*, **545–48**
Hopkirk v. Bell, 405
Hoyt v. Florida, 603
Humphrey's Executor v. United States, 533, 536n33, 752–53
Hunt v. Washington State Apple Advertising Commission, 532*t*
Hurley v. Irish-American Gay, Lesbian and Bisexual Group of Boston, 930
Hurtado v. California, 379, 422*t*
Hustler Magazine v. Falwell, 781
Hylton v. United States, 134, 134*t*, 144*t*

Illinois v. Perkins, 821
Immigration and Naturalization Service v. Chadha, 714*t*, 741, **742–47**, 885, 888
Income Tax Cases, 347, 374*t*
In re Debs, 373
In re Jacobs, 374*t*, 421, **426–28**
In re Kemmler, 474
In re Oliver, 490*t*
In re Rahrer, 391*t*
In re Tarble, 292*t*
In re Turner, 349
In re Winship, 696, **697–99**
Insular Cases, 379, 842
International Society for Krishna Consciousness v. Lee, 782
Irvin v. Dowd, 490*t*
Irwin v. Lupardus, 650

Jager v. Douglas County School District, 555*t*
James v. Commonwealth, 214
J. E. B. v. Alabama ex. rel. T. B., 821
Johnson v. Eisentrager, 842–43, 845–46, 893, 897
Johnson v. Transportation Agency, Santa Clara County, 714*t*, **808–11**
Jones v. Opelika, 563
J. W. Hampton, Jr. & Co. v. United States, 414

Kadderly v. Portland, 406
Kamper v. Hawkins, 77, 144*t*
Karcher v. Daggett, 582*t*
Katzenbach v. McClung, 158*t*, 391*t*, 517, 528, 864
Katzenbach v. Morgan, 452*t*, 480*t*, 517, 575, **578–81**, 671, 721, 945
Katz v. United States, 480*t*, 605, 638, 779
Kelo v. City of New London, 834*t*, 902, **903–7**
Kennedy v. Louisiana, 966
Keyes v. School District No. 1, Denver, Colorado, 678
Keystone Bituminous Coal Association v. DeBenedictis, 192*t*
Kidd v. Pearson, 398, 531*t*
Kimel v. Florida Board of Regents, 857
Kitzmiller v. Dover Area School District, 908
Klopfer v. North Carolina, 490*t*
Knowles v. Iowa, 962
Knox v. Lee, 341
Knox v. Service Employees International Union, Local 1000, 926
Korematsu v. United States, 12, 480*t*, **590–94**
Kramer v. Union Free School District No. 15, 452*t*
Kyllo v. United States, 834*t*, 960–61

Lambert v. Yellowley, 157*t*
Lawrence v. Texas, 12–13, 21, 423*t*, 432*t*, 834*t*, 848, 854, 917, **918–22**, 924

League of Latin American Citizens v. Perry, 583*t*, 936
Lee v. Weisman, 714*t*, 715, **759–63**, 908
Legal Services Corporation v. Velazquez, 928–29
Legal Tender Cases, 157*t*, 292*t*, 313–14, **317–20**
Lemon v. Kurtzman, 432*t*, 644
Leser v. Garnett, 23
The License Cases, 245, 411
Lichter v. United States, 157*t*, 890
Lincoln v. Page, 555*t*
Lindsey v. Normet, 644
Lindsley v. Natural Carbonic Gas Co., 587*t*
Little v. Barreme, 538
Lochner v. New York, 373, 374*t*, 376, 421, 422*t*, **428–32**, 433, 438, 456, 558, 724–25, 754, 770, 772, 775
Locke v. Davey, 909
Lombard v. Louisiana, 489
Loving v. Virginia, 423*t*, 556, 653
Lovisi v. Slayton, 649
Lucas v. South Carolina Coastal Council, 714*t*, 755, **756–58**
Luther v. Borden, 218*t*, **229–31**, 511

Madsen v. Women's Health Center, Inc., 927
Maine v. Taylor, 532*t*
Malloy v. Hogan, 490*t*
Malnak v. Yogi, 555*t*
Mangold v. Albert Gallatin Area School District, 555*t*
Mapp v. Ohio, 432*t*, 480*t*, 490*t*, 604, **605–7**, 695–96, 699–700, 711, 715, 812, 816, 960, 966
Marbury v. Madison, 16, 134*t*, 138, 141, 143, 144*t*, **145–51**, 225, 374, 376, 507–8, 589, 641, 724, 843, 851–52, 865, 997–98
Martin v. Commonwealth, 208
Martin v. Hunter's Lessee, 134*t*, 145, **152–55**
Maryland v. King, 962
Maryland v. Wirtz, 861
Mason v. Haile, 191*t*
Mason v. Missouri, 451*t*
Massiah v. United States, 607–8
Mathews v. Eldridge, 974
Mayor and City Council of Baltimore v. Radecke, 454
Mayor of New York v. Miln, 218*t*, 531*t*
Mayo v. Wilson, **210–12**
McCabe v. Atchison, Topeka & Santa Fe Railway Company, 455
McCleskey v. Kemp, 588*t*, 714*t*, 812, 826, **827–31**, 967
McCleskey v. Zant, 812, 826, 960
McCollum v. Board of Education, 432*t*
McConnell v. Federal Election Commission, 452*t*, 929, 931
McCreary County v. ACLU of Kentucky, 908
McCulloch v. Maryland, 134*t*, 138, 151, 156, 157*t*, 159–60, **164–72**, 177, 179, 221, 232–35, 315–16, 318, 399, 468, 530, 579, 740, 864, 867
McDonald v. City of Chicago, 490*t*, 841, 910
McDonald v. Commonwealth, 473–74
McGlothlin v. State, 366–67
McLaurin v. Oklahoma State Regents, 597, 600
McPherson v. Blacker, 582*t*, 939
Metro Broadcasting, Inc. v. FCC, 803
Meyer v. Nebraska, 7, 374*t*, 422*t*, **438–40**, 653
Michael H. v. Gerald D., 423*t*, 769–70
Michigan v. Harvey, 821
Michigan v. Jackson, 821
Miller-El v. Dretke, 966
Miller v. Alabama, 966
Miller v. California, 658
Miller v. Johnson, 936
Miller v. Schoene, 424
Miller v. Texas, 438
Milliken v. Bradley, 588*t*, 678
Mills v. Alabama, 452*t*
Minersville School District v. Gobitis, 563, 565
Minnesota Rate Case, 406, 410
Minor v. Happersett, 345, 354, 451*t*
Miranda v. Arizona, 478–79, 480*t*, 603, **608–12**, 695–96, 699–701, 715, 717, 721, 811–12, 820–21, 960, 962–66
Mississippi University for Women v. Hogan, 808
Mississippi v. Johnson, 292*t*, 310
Missouri v. Holland, 393, **403–5**
Missouri v. McNeeley, 962
Mitchell v. Helms, 908
Moore v. City of East Cleveland, Ohio, 423*t*, 649, 778
Moore v. Dempsey, 464
Moose Lodge No. 107 v. Irvis, **626–28**
Morehead v. People of State of New York ex rel. Tipaldo, 545, 549
Morn v. Burbine, 821
Morrison v. Olson, 714*t*, 742, **747–54**
Mossman v. Higginson, 144*t*
Mueller v. Allen, 758
Mugler v. Kansas, 423, 425, 758
Muller v. Oregon, **432–34**, 432*t*, 550
Munn v. Illinois, 374*t*, 406–7, **409–12**, 421, 545
Murphy v. California, 422*t*
Myers v. United States, **414–18**, 536n33, 888

National Endowment for the Arts v. Finley, 928
National Federation of Independent Business v. Sebelius, 517, 857, **864–76**
National Labor Relations Board v. Jones & Laughlin Steel Corp., 391*t*, 480*t*, 517, **520–24**, 740, 859
National League of Cities v. Usery, 621*t*, 630–31, 735–40, 854
National Treasury Employees Union v. Von Raab, 816
Near v. Minnesota, 374*t*, 442*t*, 444, **449–51**, 490*t*
Nebbia v. New York, 422*t*, 545
Nevada Department of Human Resources v. Hibbs, 857
Newberry v. United States, 451*t*
New Jersey v. Wilson, 191*t*
New Mexico Right to Choose/NARAL v. Johnson, 955
New State Ice Co. v. Liebmann, 422*t*
New York Times Co. v. Sullivan, 480*t*, **570–72**, 621*t*, 658, 781
New York Times Co. v. United States, 657, **658–63**
New York v. Quarles, 812, 820, 963
New York v. United States, 861, 872, 877
Nixon v. Administrator of General Services, 641
Nixon v. Fitzgerald, 641
Nix v. Williams, 821
Nollan v. California Coastal Commission, 755
Northern Securities Company v. United States, 391*t*
Nunn v. State, 264

O'Callahan v. Parker, 489
Ogden v. Saunders, 190, 191*t*
Oklahoma Press Publishing Company v. Walling, 604
Olmstead v. United States, 374*t*, **467–70**, 605
Oregon v. Elstad, 821
Oregon v. Mitchell, 158*t*, 452*t*, 629, 668–69
Oregon Waste Systems, Inc. v. Department of Environmental Quality of Oregon, 532*t*
Orloff v. Willoughby, 338*t*

Pacific States Telephone and Telegraph Co. v. Oregon, 406
Palko v. Connecticut, 480*t*, 486–87, 562, 651, 778
Palmer v. Thompson, 679
Panama Refining Co. v. Ryan, 516
The Paquete Habana, 377
Parents Involved in Community Schools v. Seattle School District No. 1, 948, 950
Parker v. Brown, 532*t*
Pasadena City Board of Education v. Spangler, 678
The Passenger Cases, 245, 530, 531*t*
Patton v. United States, 470–71
Payton v. New York, 699

Penn Central Transportation Co. v. New York City, 758
Pennsylvania Coal Co. v. Mahon, **424–26**
Pennsylvania College Cases, 192*t*
Pennsylvania v. Bruder, 821
Penry v. Lynaugh, 826
People v. Croswell, 199
People v. Defore, 465, **466–67**, 606
People v. Disbrow, 700
People v. Gallagher, 265
People v. McMahon, 288
People v. Napthaly, 471
People v. Phillips, 195
People v. Pierson, 435
Perez v. Sharpe, 556
Perez v. United States, 391*t*, 874
Peterson v. City of Greenville, 587*t*
Peters v. Kiff, 701
Pierce v. Society of Sisters, 422*t*, 653
Planned Parenthood of Southeastern Pennsylvania v. Casey, 714*t*, 715, 717, **770–77**, 853–54, 915–16, 920–21
Plessy v. Ferguson, 17, 374*t*, 454, **455–59**, 483, 587*t*, 589, 597, 599–600, 770, 772, 776, 854–55
Plyler v. Doe, 588*t*, 714*t*, **798–801**
Poe v. Ullman, 558–59, 854
Pointer v. Texas, 490*t*
Pollock v. Farmers' Loan and Trust Company, 373, 392
Powell v. Alabama, 374*t*, 464, **471–73**
Powell v. McCormack, 498, 629, 878
Powell v. Pennsylvania, 422*t*
Presser v. Illinois, 438
Prigg v. Pennsylvania, 218*t*, 232, **236–40**
Printz v. United States, 12, 158*t*, 872, 877, **879–84**
Prize Cases, 292*t*, 293, **337–40**, 338*t*, 891, 896
Proprietors of the Charles River Bridge v. Proprietors of the Warren Bridge, 191*t*, 218*t*, **258–60**

Railway Express Agency v. People of State of New York, 586, 588
Randall v. Sorrell, 929
Ratcliffe v. Beale, 454
R.A.V. v. City of St. Paul, 443*t*, 781–82
Red Lion Broadcasting Co. v. FCC, 930
Reed v. Reed, 587*t*, 690, 694
Regents of the University of California v. Bakke, 588*t*, 621*t*, 678, **683–87**, 809, 952
Reid v. Covert, 489, 842
Republican Party of Minnesota v. White, 452*t*
Reynolds v. Sims, 480*t*, 574, **581–86**, 582*t*, 668, 925, 935
Reynolds v. United States, 374*t*, **436–38**, 764
Rhode Island v. Innis, 700
Ricci v. DeStefano, 950
Richardson v. McChesney, 582*t*
Richardson v. Ramirez, 668, **672–73**
Richmond v. J. A. Croson Co., 951
Ritchie v. People, 421
Roberts v. City of Boston, 272, **279–81**
Robinson v. California, 490*t*
Robinson v. Florida, 489
Roe v. Wade, 3, 423*t*, 617, 619, 621*t*, 643, 648, **650–55**, 711, 717–19, 721, 769–77, 921
Rohan v. Sawin, 287
Romer v. Evans, 432*t*, 588*t*, 834*t*, 920, 924, 947
Roper v. Simmons, 966
Rose, et al. v. Council for Better Education, 797–98
Rosenberger v. Rector and Visitors of University of Virginia, 432*t*, 909
Ross v. McIntyre, 379, 489
Rostker v. Goldberg, 691
Rudolph v. Alabama, 613
Rumsfeld v. Forum for Academic and Institutional Rights, Inc., 930
Rust v. Sullivan, 928
Rutgers v. Waddington, 77

Sable Communications of California v. FCC, 930
Safford Unified School District No. 1 v. Redding, 962
San Antonio Independent School District v. Rodriguez, 588*t*, 617, 621*t*, 644, **674–77**
Santa Fe Independent School District v. Doe, 908
Santiago v. Nogueras, 338*t*
Santobello v. New York, 696
Schechter Poultry Corp. v. United States, 157*t*, 516, **518–20**, 522–23
Schenck v. Pro-Choice Network of Western New York, 927
Schenck v. United States, 374*t*, 442*t*, 443, **444–46**, 447
Schneiderman v. United States, 22
Scott v. Illinois, 702
Seaboard Air Line Railway v. Blackwell, 531*t*
Selective Draft Law Cases, 157*t*
Seminole Tribe of Florida v. Florida, 878
Serrano v. Priest, 675
Shanks v. DuPont, 282
Shaw v. Reno, 583*t*, 714*t*, 789, **793–96**, 793*f*, 936
Shelby County v. Holder, 834*t*, 857, 936, **941–45**
Shelley v. Kraemer, 432*t*, 480*t*, **494–96**
Sheppard v. Maxwell, 604
Sherbert v. Verner, 480*t*, 645, 721, 764–65, 850
Shreveport Rate Cases, 525
Sipuel v. Board of Regents University of Oklahoma, 597
Skinner v. Oklahoma, 480*t*, 56, 721
Skinner v. Railway Labor Executives Association, 714*t*, 816
Slaughter-House Cases, 17, 92*t*, 293, 305, **306–9**, 341–42, [illegible], 409–10, 422*t*, 587*t*
Smiley v. Holm, 582*t*
Smith v. Allwright, 452*t*, 48*t*
Smith v. Maryland, 979
Smyth v. Ames, 422*t*
Snyder v. Phelps, 443*t*, 926
Somerset v. Stewart, 34*t*, 5859, **60–61**
South Carolina State Highway Department v. Barnwell Brothers, Inc., 532*t*
South Carolina v. Katzenbach, 517, 575, 580, 671, 792, 944
South Dakota v. Dole, 714*t*, **33–35**
Stafford v. Wallace, 391*t*
Standard Oil Company of New Jersey v. United States, 392
Stanley v. Illinois, 649
State of Missouri ex rel. Gaines v. Canada, 597
State of Ohio on Relation of Davis v. Hildebrant, 582*t*
State v. Buzzard, 264
State v. Guild, 212
State v. McCann, 366
State v. McCauley, 288
State v. Newsom, 265
State v. Worth, 266
Sternberg v. Carhart, 916
Steward Machine Co. v. Davis, 517
Stewart Dry Goods Co. v. Lewis, 587*t*
Stidger v. Rogers, 144*t*
Stone v. Mississippi, 192*t*, 424
Stone v. Powell, 695–97, 699
Stop the Beach Renourishment, Inc. v. Florida Dept. of Environmental Protection, 902
Strauder v. West Virginia, 454, 587*t*
Strickland v. Washington, 821–22
Stuart v. Laird, 134*t*, 143, 144*t*
Sturges v. Crowninshield, 190, 191*t*
Swaim v. United States, 338*t*
Swain v. Alabama, 821, 825
Swann v. Charlotte-Mecklenburg Board of Education, 621*t*, 678, **679–81**
Sweatt v. Painter, 597, 600
Sweezy v. New Hampshire, 443*t*
Swift v. United States, 392, 525

Teague v. Lane, 826, 960
Tennessee v. Davis, 292*t*
Tennessee v. Lane, 857, 947
Ten-Pound Act Cases, 144*t*
Terminiello v. City of Chicago, 12, 442*t*
Territory v. Ah Lim, 438

Texas MedicaProviders Performing Abortionervices v. Lakey, 916
Texas v. Johnn, 719, 781, **783–86**, 848
Texas v. Whit 292*t*, 324, **329–33**
Thomas v. Cons, 561–62
Thornburg v. ingles, 582*t*
Tileston v. Uhan, 558
Totten v. Unid States, 338*t*
Townsend v. in, 604
Train v. City New York, 631
Trevett v. Welen, 77
Trop v. Dulle 614
Tuan Anh Ngyen v. I.N.S., 954–55
Turner Broadasting System v. FCC, 930
Turner v. Safly, 770
Twining v. Nw Jersey, 379, 422*t*

United Haules Association v. Oneida-Herkimer Slid Waste Management Authority, 32*t*
United JewishOrganizations of Williamsurgh v. Carey, 582*t*, 668
United States x rel. Toth v. Quarles, 158*t*, 338
United States x rel. Turner v. Williams 442*t*
United StatesRailroad Retirement Board v. Fritz, 67
United StatesTrust Co. v. New Jersey, 192*t*
United States v. Alvarez, 926
United States v. American Library Associaton, 927
United States v. Belmont, 543
United States v. Burr, 642–43
United States v. Butler, 516, 517, 734, 873
United States v. Calandra, 695, 699
United States v. Callender, 212, **213–14**
United States v. Carolene Products Co., 480*t*, **487–88**, 620, 625, 906
United States v. Classic, 157*t*, 451*t*, 510
United States v. Comstock, 158*t*
United States v. Coombs, 157*t*
United States v. Cruikshank, 292*t*, 293, 305, 350, 390, 438
United States v. Curtiss-Wright Export Corporation, 480*t*, **543–44**
United States v. Darby, 517, 525, 530–31, 740, 859
United States v. E. C. Knight Company, 373, 391*t*, 392, **397–400**, 401–2, 525, 1001
United States v. Eichman, 719, 781, 783
United States v. Fisher, 157*t*
United States v. Fox, 157*t*
United States v. Gettysburg Electric Railroad Co., 157*t*
nited States v. Gooding, 209–10
United States v. Gooseley, 212
United States v. Havens, 699
United States v. Janis, 699
United States v. Jones, 961
United States v. La Vengeance, 144*t*
United States v. Leon, 714*t*, 812, **816–20**, 962
United States v. Lopez, 392*t*, 834*t*, 856, **857–64**
United States v. Miller, 556
United States v. Morrison, 834*t*, 857
United States v. Nixon, 621*t*, 631, **639–43**
United States v. Reese, 314, 390
United States v. Reynolds, 455
United States v. Sokolow, 816
United States v. Stevens, 926
United States v. Sullivan, 391*t*
United States v. United States District Court, 621*t*, **637–39**, 699
United States v. Verdugo-Urquidez, 722, 892
United States v. Virginia, 588*t*, 954, **955–59**
United States v. Windsor, 834*t*, 918, 922
United States v. Women's Sportswear Mfrs. Assn., 530
United Trust Co. of New York v. New Jersey, 755
U.S. Department of Agriculture v. Moreno, 674
U.S. Term Limits v. Thornton, 452*t*, 878

Vanhorne's Lessee v. Dorrance, 144*t*
Van Orden v. Perry, 908
Veazie v. Moor, 396
Vieth v. Jubelirer, 935–36
Village of Arlington Heights v. Metropolitan Housing Development Corp., 679
Village of Euclid v. Ambler Realty Co., 422*t*, 423
Virginia v. Black, 443*t*, 927
Von Hoffman v. City of Quincy, 192*t*
Vorchheimer v. School District of Philadelphia, 689–90

Wabash, St. Louis & Pacific Railroad v. Illinois, 374*t*, **406–9**, 531*t*
Wainwright v. Sykes, 619, 621*t*, 697, 960
Wallace v. Jaffree, 759
Wally's Heirs v. Kennedy, 271–72, 281
Ward v. Bernard, 205
Ware v. Hylton, 139, 405
Washington, Virginia & Maryland Coach Co. v. NLRB, 521
Washington v. Davis, 679, **688–89**
Washington v. Glucksberg, 423*t*
Washington v. Texas, 490*t*
Watchtower Bible and Tract Society of New York v. Village of Stratton, 927–28
W. B. Worthen Co. v. Thomas, 192*t*
Weber v. Aetna Casualty & Surety Co., 674
Webster v. Reid, 381
Webster v. Reproductive Health Services, 769–70
Weeks v. United States, 374*t*, 376, **465–66**, 604
Weems v. United States, 474
Wesberry v. Sanders, 562, 582*t*
West Coast Hotel Co. v. Parrish, 422*t*, 480*t*, 545, **549–50**, 711, 772
West Virginia State Board of Education v. Barnette, **563–66**, 786
White v. Mass. Council of Construction Employers, 532*t*
White v. Regester, 582*t*
White v. Weiser, 668
White v. White, 282
Whitney v. California, 374*t*, 442*t*, 444, **446–49**, 562, 567, 573
Wickard v. Filburn, 391*t*, 517, **524–26**, 545, 721, 737, 859, 864, 867, 873–74
Wilkerson v. Utah, 474
Wilkes v. Wood, 35, 69, 128
Wilkinson v. Leland, 190
Williamson v. Lee Optical Co., 422*t*, **551–52**, 587*t*, 654, 675
Williams v. Mississippi, 451*t*, 459
Williams v. Rhodes, 452*t*
Wisconsin v. Yoder, 621*t*, 644, **645–47**, 764–65
Wolf v. People of the State of Colorado, 490*t*, 604–7
Wollard v. Sheridan, 910
Woodson v. North Carolina, 702–3
Worcester v. Georgia, 218*t*
Wygant v. Jackson Board of Education, 802–3
Wynehamer v. People, 218*t*, **260–64**

Yates v. United States, 442*t*
Yick Wo v. Hopkins, 454, 587*t*
Youngstown Sheet & Tube Co. v. Sawyer, 12, 338*t*, 480*t*, **534–43**, 892, 900, 975

Zelman v. Simmons-Harris, 432*t*, 908
Zenger's Case, 33, **54–57**, 55*f*, 62, 69, 129, 212
Zobrest v. Catalina Foothills School District, 907
Zylstra v. Corporation of City of Charleston, 212